Mercer Dictionary of the Bible

Mercer Dictionary of the Bible

GENERAL EDITOR

Watson E. Mills

ASSOCIATE EDITORS

Roger A. Bullard
Joel F. Drinkard, Jr.
Walter Harrelson
Edgar V. McKnight

ASSISTANT EDITORS

Rollin S. Armour
Edd Rowell
Richard F. Wilson

WITH MEMBERS OF THE

National Association
of Baptist Professors of Religion

MERCER UNIVERSITY PRESS ■ MACON, GEORGIA

ISBN 0-86554-299-6 (casebound)
ISBN 0-86554-373-9 (paperback)

Mercer Dictionary of the Bible

Mercer University Press, Macon, Georgia 31207

Printed in the United States of America

The paper used in this publication meets
the minimum requirements of American National Standard
for Information Sciences—Permanence of Paper
for Printed Library Materials, ANSI Z39.48-1984.

Library of Congress Cataloging-in-Publication Data

Mercer dictionary of the Bible / general editor, Watson E. Mills ; associate editor, Roger Bullard . . . [et al.].

xxi + 987 + 64 (maps and photographs) pages 17.5 x 25 cm., 7x10″
ISBN 0-86554-299-6 (casebound) — ISBN 0-86554-373-9 (pbk.)
1. Bible—Dictionaries. I. Mills, Watson E. II. Bullard, Roger Aubrey.
BS440.M429 1990 89-13857
220.3—dc20 CIP

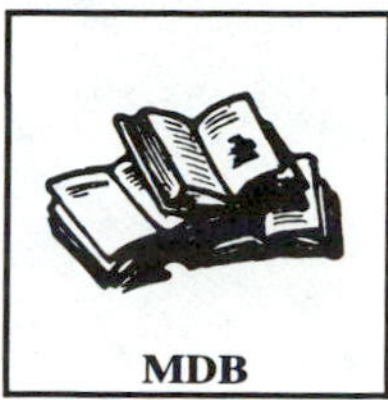

Foreword

For 2,000 years the Bible has exercised an unparalleled influence in the lives of individuals and nations, an imprint woven into the very fabric of civilization and, in large measure, determining its direction and quality. Mercer University's foundations can be traced to this very influence, where the search for truth has been fostered by reverence for God. For almost 160 years a major dimension of our educational endeavors at Mercer has been the search for *biblical* truth. Likewise, the National Association of Baptist Professors of Religion (NABPR), a fraternity of "teachers of religion" and/or "teachers of Bible," arose among persons who were committed to understand clearly, to interpret faithfully, and to teach effectively those truths that come to us through the Bible. In the *Mercer Dictionary of the Bible* (*MDB*) the teachers of NABPR have joined with Mercer University Press in bringing together a new and important resource for interpreting the Bible. Our hope and expectation is that *MDB* will serve as a critical and enlightening pedagogue for those who are seeking to enhance their understanding of that most significant body of literature we call the biblical literature.

In his classic study of ancient Israel's life and culture Johannes Pedersen described Canaan, the "land of the Bible," as a "narrow borderland dividing sea from coast" that quite naturally became the highway between the ancient Northern (Mesopotamian) and Southern (Egyptian/Arabian) centers of civilization. Through that narrow hinterland flowed a steady commerce in goods and culture, politics and religion. It is no wonder, Pedersen observed, that many people should meet there, some to pass through and some to stay. The books that have been written about and emerged from those peoples, and specifically, the heritage they have passed to us through the writings we call scripture would fill many libraries. Yet here, within the one-volume borders of *MDB*, one may discover a newly marked "highway" to biblical understanding.

The "land of the Bible" was populated by persons of diverse, variegated stock. The pages and the writings of *MDB* were composed by diverse people, diverse in background and viewpoint. More than 225 persons have contributed to this significant work. These contributors have been encouraged to express themselves freely, within the confines only of presenting facts fairly and clearly, and interpreting truth honestly and openly. Therefore, a wide range of biblical perspectives and theological views may be found in the *MDB*. Readers will search these pages in vain for evidence of any attempt to fit the contributions of these Bible teachers into the procrustean beds of any theological or even nontheological prescription. This plurality of perspectives is an entirely appropriate approach to the diversity of biblical literature itself and, in the end, we believe that *MDB* will become an exceedingly valuable tool in the effort to uncover the rich truth of the Bible.

Despite their diversity and individuality, the contributors and editors of *MDB* have diligently worked with common purpose. Each of them is a teacher or is directly involved in the support of teaching and scholarly research. The *Mercer Dictionary of the Bible* will serve as an enduring tribute to their commitment to the high purposes of learning and teaching and to the importance of understanding the Bible as a primary means for understanding truth itself.

R. Kirby Godsey
President
Mercer University

Editor's Preface

The *Mercer Dictionary of the Bible* (*MDB*) is the result of four years of research and writing on the part of more than 225 members of the National Association of Baptist Professors of Religion (NABPR). The *MDB* is the most ambitious scholarly endeavor ever undertaken by the NABPR. Since its inception in 1924, the NABPR has engaged in a number of publishing projects: *Perspectives in Religious Studies* (a quarterly journal), *Special Studies/Monograph Series, Bibliographic Series, Dissertation Series,* and the *Festschriften Series*. The present project is another natural expression of the NABPR's conscious decision to make specific contributions to the broad field of religious studies.

In a real sense, the *MDB* is a product of the professional, teaching, and research careers of each scholar who has contributed to its pages. Yet its 1.2 million words, 1,050+ pages, and 150 illustrations make no claim to tell readers all they need to know about the Bible—no one book or even library could do that. Rather our hope is that the *MDB* will provide accurate, relevant, and even interesting information regarding the history, traditions, and literature collected in what we know as "scripture." Since *MDB* is a product of a professional community of scholars, it reflects a broad range of opinions and approaches to the critical issues involved in the study of the Bible. There has been a studied attempt *not* to require contributors to follow any specific school of interpretation: every effort has been made to avoid "evangelizing" for a particular position on this or that issue.

Obviously, the *MDB* is no substitute for studying the scripture. To encourage such study, *MDB* provides thousands of specific references to the biblical materials, canonical and noncanonical. Nor does *MDB* pretend to supplant the more comprehensive standard Bible dictionaries or the many one-volume student handbook-type dictionaries. Rather *MDB* seeks to fill a real need for a one-volume dictionary intended for use by both beginning and advanced Bible students in college, university, and seminary. *MDB* begins with a classroom perspective: the editors of and contributors to *MDB* are all members of the National Association of Baptist Professors of Religion; all are either directly involved in teaching beginning and advanced Bible students or in the support of those who are teaching. The needs of the student have shaped the structure and content of the *MDB*.

Character

With so many Bible dictionaries on the market today, what distinguishes *MDB*?

(1) *MDB* has been conceived, designed, and written for use in the classroom as a supplement to or in the place of a traditional introductory textbook. To facilitate such use, several *MDB* contributors have prepared course syllabi that focus on *MDB*'s use in both OT and NT survey courses. These syllabi have been collected into a single volume and are available from the publisher without charge to any professor adopting *MDB*.

(2) All maps are original to this volume, having been created by Margaret Jordan Brown, designer at Mercer University Press. These four-color copyrighted maps are also available on 2x2 color slides for classroom use. You may write or call MUP for information on availability.

(3) Every canonical book contains an original outline written either by the author of the article in which it is found or by the area editor. These outlines have been highlighted in the text for easy identification.

(4) The *MDB* contains an article on virtually every noncanonical book found in the various collections such as the OT Apocrypha, NT Apocrypha, Nag Hammadi library, Dead Sea Scrolls, and so forth.

(5) Finally, we have attempted to give representation to still-emerging concerns such as liberation theology and feminist theology.

Range of Subjects

MDB includes articles on most of the proper names and distinctive terms in the Bible (including the Apocrypha). In addition, comprehensive articles on key persons (e.g., Jesus, Paul) and subjects (e.g., Text/Manuscripts/Versions; Biblical Theology) are included. The range of terms goes beyond the specifically biblical to include subjects that have a direct bearing on one's understanding of the Bible (e.g., Archaeology; Writing Systems) and includes categories regarding the interpretation of the Bible up to the present time (e.g., Textual Criticism; English Bible, History of).

By intent, *MDB* is based on the text itself and not on any particular English version. Yet the list of names and terms included herein was compiled from the Revised Standard Version and more significant variants in other English translations (King James Version, New English Bible, e.g., among others) have been noted.

Arrangement

Entries in *MDB* appear in alphabetical order. Indeed, series of articles on both testaments are arranged alphabetically rather than according to their interbiblical relationship—that is, Textual Criticism of the New Testament *precedes* Textual Criticism of the Old Testament.

A name or term is routinely entered only once in what is the main entry for that subject. However, common variants also are listed in alphabetical order and there the reader is referred to the main entry (Esaias, e.g., refers to Isaiah). Names occur in the form found in the RSV, while other subjects are listed according to the form we assume the reader will seek.

Closely related subjects are presented in comprehensive articles that organize the biblical terms ordinarily in the order in which they are encountered in the Bible so the relationship between the terms and their individual development may be treated as a unit (see, e.g., the article on Sheol that also treats or refers to Abyss, Gehenna, Hades, and Hell in order to demonstrate their relationship and historical development). Each such related term also will occur as a separate entry where it will refer to the main entry and may or may not be given brief treatment.

The reader should seek information under whatever name seems most logical. If treatment of a subject does not occur in its presumed order, the reader most likely will find a reference to a more comprehensive article where the subject sought will be treated along with its related subjects.

Organization

Following is a typical article in *MDB*. This particular example is complete with five distinctive parts: title, main treatment, reference to related entries, bibliography, and byline. Other articles occur in the same order. Shorter entries may have fewer parts (e.g., no bibliography). Longer articles may also include outlines (for books of the Bible), charts or tables, or relevant illustrative materials.

• **Anathoth.** [an'uh-thoth] One of the four towns in the territory of the tribe of Benjamin given to the Levites (Josh 21:18), best known as the hometown of JEREMIAH. It is located just north of JERUSALEM (PLATE 13) and is usually identified with Ras el-Kharrubeh near the modern village of Anata, which preserves the name of the ancient town. ABIATHAR, the high priest under DAVID, was banished to this town by SOLOMON (1 Kgs 2:26). Lesser-known biblical references to the town are: the home of two of David's "mighty men," Abiezer and Jehu (1 Chr 11:28; 12:3); a town mentioned by ISAIAH (10:30) in a doom oracle; the place where JEREMIAH purchased some property from his cousin Hanamel while the Babylonians were besieging Jerusalem (Jer 32); a town resettled by returning exiles (Ezra 2:23; Neh 7:27).

See also JEREMIAH.

Bibliography. M. Avi-Yonah, "Anathoth," *EncJud*; N. Rubingen, "Jeremiah's Epistle to the Exiles and the Field in Anathoth," *Jud* 26 (1977): 84-91.

—BRUCE C. CRESSON

The parts of this example are as follows:

1. The title of the entry appears in boldface type, caps and lowercase, with a small "bullet" preceding the title as an aid in locating the title on the page. Immediately following many biblical names is, as here, a suggested more-or-less standard pronunciation. These pronunciation guides use only regular English letters, with an italicized *i* to indicate a long-i sound (as in sky) and an italicized *oo* to indicate the long-u sound (as in shoot). Pronunciation stress is indicated by a single prime mark following the syllable to be stressed, and where necessary, double stress is indicated by a double prime mark: Adonijah is pronounced ad'uh-n*i*"juh.

2. The main text of the article immediately follows.

3. Following the main treatment of the subject will often be a "See also" listing that refers to related subjects with the title of the related article printed in small caps. In addition, in lengthy articles titles of related subjects occurring in the main text will be printed in small caps to call attention to their appearance in the dictionary.

4. For many entries there will be a selected bibliography of sources where more detailed information may be found.

5. Finally, the entry will be "signed" by the contributor.

As noted above, some subjects are treated under a comprehensive title and will occur in alphabetical order as a blind entry that merely lists the term being sought and refers the reader to the title of the article within which it is treated. For example:

• **Coming of Christ, Second.** *See* ESCHATOLOGY IN THE NEW TESTAMENT; MILLENNIUM; PAROUSIA/SECOND COMING

• **Second Coming of Christ.** *See* ESCHATOLOGY IN THE NEW TESTAMENT; MILLENNIUM; PAROUSIA/SECOND COMING

• **Typology.** *See* ADAM; INTERPRETATION, HISTORY OF

There are thus two blind entries for "Second Coming of Christ," one for students who may look for the term in its normal order (Second Coming) and one for those who may look for it in its "index" order (Coming, Second), both of which refer to general and specific treatments of the subject. Those seeking information regarding "Typology" will find general treatment in the article on the History of Interpretation and a specific example of the use of typology in the article on Adam.

Conventions on Style

Dictionary editors, so it seems, are destined to serve the god of consistency in unrelenting fashion. In setting out upon this impossible course, many of the finer (if not virtually irrelevant!) points of writing style were carefully formulated and articulated to writers and editors in an unending stream of memoranda, each the final word "supplanting all previous." The only small problem was that these were then promptly ignored, forgotten, or otherwise repressed by contributors and editors alike! And so the level of consistency we have been able to achieve may be, to a large extent, the result of luck as much as design.

Realistically, no style guide or set of conventions, however carefully conceived, can cover every question that arises in a community endeavor of this magnitude: the scope is too great, the degrees of specialization too narrow. Nonetheless, we set out to make the volume consistent and readable in matters of style and grammar. There have been cases where a contributor and area editor have been persuasive in arguments to modify or even in some cases to abandon certain agreed-upon conventions. So, in a few instances, the reader may notice some deviations from our stated stipulations aimed at consistency. Such is the nature of this kind of undertaking.

Aside from the obvious conventions, there follows a list of some of the more important in the pages of *MDB*.

Small caps within the text of specific articles signal references to other articles of specific or general interest (the only other instances in which small caps are used are C.E., B.C.E., abbreviations for translations such as RSV, TEV, etc., and in references to PLATES that occur in a separate section at the center of the volume). The "match" is exact except that alphabetical reference is not forced, i.e., the running text may refer to the GOSPEL OF MATTHEW when the actual entry is MATTHEW, GOSPEL OF. Of course, not *every* match within *every* article is placed in small caps; only those that, in the editors' view, relate immediately to the article under review are treated in this way.

We have followed the abbreviations for biblical books, apocrypha, and other extracanonical books as found in the widely used SBL list (except that intervening spaces have been omitted).

Bibliographies, where included, are necessarily brief. To save space, we give only the essential bibliographic information, i.e., the author's last name and initial(s) and the title of the work; periodical citations include sufficient information to locate the reference; encyclopedia references include only the author, title, and referenced work (so long as the work being cited arranges articles alphabetically—in cases where the reference work arranges articles in some other way, volume and/or page numbers are supplied).

The purpose of the triple running heads is to facilitate the location of specific articles. The left head is the article carried over from the previous page, or the first article on the present page if none is carried over; the centered head is the first article to begin on the page; the right head is the last article to begin on the page.

Acknowledgments

It has been personally gratifying and professionally stimulating to work with the four area editors of the *MDB*. It is they more than I who have shaped the contours of this volume; their diligence, leadership, and scholarship have contributed enormously to the quality and character of this work. It is with grateful appreciation that I acknowledge the years of work given to this project by Roger Bullard (Atlantic Christian College), Joel Drinkard (Southern Baptist Theological Seminary), Walter Harrelson (Vanderbilt University), and Edgar McKnight (Furman University).

The Mercer-based editorial staff has also contributed many long hours to the *MDB*. They have made a herculean effort toward bringing these hundreds of articles into a consistent pattern. I gratefully acknowledge the contribution of Rollin S. Armour, Edd Rowell, and Richard F. Wilson for their tireless contributions to the project. Their contributions to this volume are incalculable.

Special thanks are due to the staff of Mercer University Press. These individuals have given many hours to *MDB* while maintaining their regular work load. Especially should I acknowledge the work of Ms. Irene H. Palmer, who performed all the clerical tasks relating to receipting, routing, and processing the articles. She supervised the keying and correcting of the articles as well. The quality and quantity of her work throughout this project has been above and beyond what anyone could reasonably expect. Edd Rowell did the initial design of the page layouts and the various charts and tables. Both as a colleague and a coworker, his contribution is a major one, and I acknowledge it gladly. Ms. Margaret Jordan Brown has led the design team and she has personally created each of the four-color maps as well as many of the black-and-white drawings that are found throughout the text. Her contribution is of central importance because by her special talents she has been able to give visual expression to the ideas and concepts that make up the *MDB*. She has been ably assisted in her work by Ms. Alesa Jones, who not only processed the articles through the phototypesetter, but helped in the performance of much of the handwork necessary to prepare the final materials for the printer.

MDB acknowledges the editors and many of the contributors who provided personal slides and photos for inclusion.

Mr. Jimmy Gardner, president of Accurate Graphics (Atlanta, Georgia) graciously donated the color separations for the color photos found in this publication. Ron Williams and Warren Rowland of Williams-Rowland Printing (Macon, Georgia) kindly donated the separations for the color maps found in this publication.

Finally, I wish to acknowledge the continuing support and encouragement of the president of Mercer University, R. Kirby Godsey. His willingness to support this project over the years is acknowledged and appreciated. We are fortunate to be associated with an institution that respects and encourages this kind of scholarly endeavor. It is our hope that the *MDB* will be of real help in the larger world of biblical scholarship, and thus reflect well upon this great university.

Watson E. Mills
Mercer University
June 1990

Acknowledgments

The Scripture quotations contained herein are from the Revised Standard Version of the Bible, copyrighted 1946, 1952, 1971, 1973 by the Division of Christian Education of the National Council of Churches of Christ in the USA, and are used by permission. All rights reserved.

PLATE 28 is based upon original artwork that appeared in the *New Bible Atlas* published by InterVarsity, Lion Publishing, Tyndale House, 1985. Used by permission.

PLATE 33 and the endleaves of the casebound edition contain photographic materials furnished by and used with the permission of the National Aeronautics and Space Administration.

PLATE 57 is reproduced here courtesy of the Oriental Institute of the University of Chicago.

The black-and-white photographs that include the reference "Courtesy of the Eisenberg Museum of Biblical Archaeology, Southern Baptist Theological Seminary" were taken by the general editor in consultation with the Museum's Director, Joel Drinkard. The cooperation of the Seminary and the Museum is gratefully acknowledged.

The pronunciation aids that follow the main entry for most non-English terms are from *Harper's Bible Pronunciation Guide* edited by William O. Walker, Jr. Copyright © 1989 by the Society of Biblical Literature. Reprinted by permission of Harper & Row, Publishers, Inc.

Editorial Board

About the Editors

WATSON E. MILLS, general editor, is Professor of New Testament Studies at Mercer University, Macon, GA. He is a graduate of the University of Richmond (BA), the University of Louisville (MA), the Southern Baptist Theological Seminary (BD, ThM, ThD), and Baylor University (PhD). He has published widely, having written or edited a dozen books and scores of articles. He has contributed to numerous dictionaries and encyclopedias. He is editor of the quarterly *Perspectives in Religious Studies* and managing editor of *Religious Studies Review* and the *Bulletin of the Council of Societies for the Study of Religion*.

He served on the faculty at Averett College, Danville, VA from 1968-1979. He has been at Mercer University since 1979.

Mills serves as the executive officer of the Council of Societies for the Study of Religion and as executive secretary-treasurer of the National Association of Baptist Professors of Religion. He is a member of the Society of New Testament Studies, the Catholic Biblical Association, the American Academy of Religion, and the Society of Biblical Literature. He is a fellow in the International Institute for the Renewal of Gospel Studies.

ROGER A. BULLARD, associate editor of the extracanonical section, was educated at Union University (BA in English), the University of Kentucky (MA in Classics), Southeastern Baptist Theological Seminary (BD), and Vanderbilt University (PhD in Biblical Studies). Since 1965 he has been on the faculty of Atlantic Christian College in Wilson, NC, where he is Professor of Religion and Philosophy. He has served as Visiting Professor at Southeastern Seminary and Brite Divinity School.

He is an associate editor of *The Abingdon Dictionary of Living Religions* (now published as *The Perennial Dictionary of World Religions*). He served on the translation committee preparing the Old Testament and Apocrypha of Today's English Version of the Bible and is the author of *The Hypostasis of the Archons: The Coptic Text with English Translation and Commentary*, as well as numerous articles and reviews.

Bullard is a member of the National Association of Baptist Professors of Religion, the Society of Biblical Literature, the American Association of University Professors, and the North Carolina Teachers of Religion. He has served as Corresponding Member of the Institute for Antiquity and Christianity, working on the Coptic Gnostic Project. He has received awards from the Christian Research Foundation, the American Council of Learned Societies, and the National Endowment for the Humanities.

JOEL F. DRINKARD, JR., associate editor of the archaeology section, is Associate Professor of Old Testament Interpretation at the Southern Baptist Theological Seminary. He is a graduate of the University of North Carolina (BA), the Southeastern Baptist Theological Seminary (MDiv, ThM), and the Southern Baptist Theological Seminary (PhD). He has done additional study at Regent's Park College (Oxford) and Johns Hopkins University.

Drinkard is a member of the Society of Biblical Literature, American Schools of Oriental Research, Israel Exploration Society, and the National Association of Professors of Hebrew.

He has written numerous articles in a wide range of publications and is presently writing *Jeremiah 1–26* to appear in the *Word Biblical Commentary*.

WALTER HARRELSON, associate editor of the Old Testament section, is Distinguished Professor of Hebrew Bible at the Divinity School of Vanderbilt University. His undergraduate studies were completed at Mars Hill College and the University of North Carolina and his theological and graduate degrees are from Union Theological Seminary in NY. He taught at Andover Newton Theological School and at the Divinity School of the University of Chicago before coming in 1960 to Vanderbilt.

He is the author of five books and has published extensively in biblical and theological encyclopedias, dictionaries, and periodicals. His most recent book is *The Ten Commandments and Human Rights*. A forthcoming work, written with Rabbi Randall M. Falk, deals with the relations of Judaism and Christianity.

He was Vice Chair of the committee that produced the New Revised Standard Version of the Bible, has served as the Rector of the Ecumenical Institute for Theological Research in Jerusalem, and has been Dean of the Divinity Schools of the University of Chicago and Vanderbilt University.

EDGAR V. MCKNIGHT, associate editor for the New Testament section, is the William R. Kenan, Jr. Professor of Religion at Furman University. He received his undergraduate education in Charleston, graduating from the College of Charleston in 1953. After professional and graduate studies at the Southern Baptist Theological Seminary (MDiv, 1956; PhD, 1960) and a brief appointment as chaplain at Chowan College in Murfreesboro, NC, he joined the faculty of Furman University in 1963; he has taught in the departments of Classical Languages and Religion, chaired the Department of Classical Languages, served as Associate Dean of Academic Affairs, and, since 1982, as William R. Kenan, Jr. Professor of Religion. Early publications include a *History of Chowan College*; *Opening the Bible: A Guide to Understanding the Scriptures*; *What Is Form Criticism?*; and *Introduction to the New Testament*.

During his first sabbatical (1973–74), McKnight studied philosophical theology with John Macquarrie of Christ Church, Oxford. Early studies and writings in the biblical field were thereby supplemented by work in philosophical and theological hermeneutics. *Meaning in Texts: The Historical Shaping of a Narrative Hermeneutics* resulted from this work. A Senior Fulbright Professorship at the University of Tübingen (1981–82) provided opportunity for further study and writing in the relationship between biblical and literary studies. Two books grew out of this work: *The Bible and the Reader: An Introduction to Literary Criticism* and *Postmodern Use of the Bible*. McKnight is presently at work on a manuscript entitled "Theology and the Revolution in Biblical Studies."

ROLLIN S. ARMOUR, assistant editor, is Professor in the Roberts Department of Christianity, Mercer University. A graduate of Baylor University and the Southern Baptist Theological Seminary, he holds the STM and ThD degrees from Harvard University. His book, *Anabaptist Baptism: A Representative Study*, was designated the Franklin S. and Elizabeth D. Brewer Prize Essay of the American Society of Church History in 1966. He has taught in the Department of Religion of Stetson University, served as head of the Department of Religion at Auburn University, and was Dean of the College of Liberal Arts at Mercer before assuming his present full-time teaching position. He has served as president of the southeastern region of the American Academy of Religion and president of the Southern Baptist Historical Society. Although the history of Christianity has been his first interest, he has also worked in the area of world religions. The Society for Religion (now Values) in Higher Education awarded him a Fellowship for the Study of World Religions, which allowed a semester of study at the Center for the Study of World Religions at Harvard and six months of travel and study in North Africa, India, Southeast Asia, and Japan. Armour has written for *The Encyclopedia of Southern Baptists, Church History*, the *Journal of Modern History, Religious Studies Review*, and the *International Journal for Philosophy of Religion*. Since 1987, Armour has served as associate editor of *Perspectives in Religious Studies*. He is treasurer of the Council of Societies for the Study of Religion.

EDD ROWELL, assistant editor, is director of Mercer University Press. He earned his AB in religious studies and languages at Howard College (Samford University) and his BD/MDiv at the Southeastern Baptist Theological Seminary. From 1958 until 1980 he was pastor of Baptist churches in Alabama and Virginia. He has been at Mercer since August 1980. Rowell has written numerous curriculum materials for the Sunday School Board and has contributed articles and reviews to a variety of scholarly and popular journals. Recently his article on "Philippi of Macedonia: Beachhead in Europe" in the *Biblical Illustrator* (1978) was selected to be included in *The Best of the Illustrator* (1990). He also was author of the two-volume study of Acts in the Bible Book Study Commentary series (1979, 1980) and of *Apostles—Jesus' Special Helpers* in the BibLearn series for children (1979). He is a member of the Society of Biblical Literature and the American Academy of Religion, and an associate of the National Association of Baptist Professors of Religion and the International Institute for the Renewal of Gospel Studies.

RICHARD F. WILSON, assistant editor, is Associate Professor in the Roberts Department of Christianity of Mercer University. He earned the BA degree in Religion at Mississippi College (1975) and the MDiv and PhD degrees at the Southern Baptist Theological Seminary (1978; 1982). For two years he was Ecumenical Minister at Bellarmine College in Louisville, KY before accepting an appointment as Assistant Professor in the Department of Religious Studies and Philosophy at Gardner-Webb College in 1982, where he also served as Assistant Dean for Academic Affairs for one year. While at Gardner-Webb he received the Faculty Merit Award in recognition of teaching excellence. Since 1982 Professor Wilson has read papers at several professional meetings, has been guest lecturer on college campuses, has led studies in numerous churches in the Southeast, and has held interim pastorates in North and South Carolina. He is a member of the National Association of Baptist Professors of Religion and the American Academy of Religion.

Contributors

Dale C. Allison, Jr.
Research Scholar
St. Paul School of Theology
Kansas City MO 64127

Niels-Erik A. Andreasen
Professor of Old Testament; Associate Dean
School of Religion
Loma Linda University
Riverside CA 92515

Stephen J. Andrews
Pastor
Forest Park Baptist Church
Cincinnati OH 45240

J. William Angell
Easley Professor of Religion
Wake Forest University
Winston-Salem NC 27109

Rollin S. Armour
Professor
Roberts Department of Christianity
Mercer University
Macon GA 31207

Morris Ashcraft
Professor of Theology
Southeastern Baptist Theological Seminary
Wake Forest NC 27587

David E. Aune
Professor of Religious Studies
St. Xavier College
Chicago IL 60655

Lloyd R. Bailey
Associate Professor of Hebrew Bible
Duke University Divinity School
Durham NC 27706

Raymond Bailey
Professor of Preaching
Southern Baptist Theological Seminary
Louisville KY 40280

Wilma Ann Bailey
Assistant Professor of Old Testament
Messiah College
Granthame PA 17027

Douglas C. Bain, Jr.
Professor of Biblical and Associated Studies
Blue Mountain College
Blue Mountain MS 38610

Samuel E. Balentine
Associate Professor of Hebrew and Old Testament
Southeastern Baptist Theological Seminary
Wake Forest NC 27587

Robert B. Barnes
Professor of Religion and Philosophy
Wingate College
Wingate NC 28174

Joe E. Barnhart
Professor of Philosophy
University of North Texas
Denton TX 76201

Lloyd M. Barré
Escondido CA 92025

S. Scott Bartchy
Adjunct Associate Professor, Early Christian History
University of California, Los Angeles
Los Angeles CA 90024

Joe R. Baskin
Professor of Religion
Shorter College
Rome GA 30161

G. R. Beasley-Murray
Senior Professor of New Testament
Southern Baptist Theological Seminary
Louisville KY 40280

W. H. Bellinger, Jr.
Associate Professor of Religion
Department of Religion
Baylor University
Waco TX 76798

Mark E. Biddle
Assistant Professor of Religion
Carson-Newman College
Jefferson City TN 37760

Reidar B. Bjornard
Professor of Old Testament Interpretation, Emeritus
Northern Baptist Theological Seminary
Marietta GA 30064

David Alan Black
Professor of New Testament and Greek
Grace Theological Seminary, West Campus
Long Beach CA 90807

James L. Blevins
Professor of New Testament Interpretation
Southern Baptist Theological Seminary
Louisville KY 40280

Gerald L. Borchert
Professor of New Testament Interpretation
Southern Baptist Theological Seminary
Louisville KY 40280

Margaret Dee Bratcher
Assistant Professor
Roberts Department of Christianity
Mercer University
Macon GA 31207

Robert G. Bratcher
Translation Consultant
United Bible Societies
Chapel Hill NC 27514

Paul D. Brewer
Professor of Philosophy and Religion
Carson-Newman College
Jefferson City TN 37760

Edwin K. Broadhead
Assistant Professor
Furman University
Greenville SC 29613

William F. Bromley
Professor of Religion
Lees College
Jackson KY 41339

James A. Brooks
Professor of New Testament
Southwestern Baptist Theological Seminary
Ft. Worth TX 76122

Walter E. Brown
Associate Professor of Old Testament and Hebrew
New Orleans Baptist Theological Seminary
New Orleans LA 70126

Roger A. Bullard
Professor of Religion and Philosophy
Atlantic Christian College
Wilson NC 27893

Robert E. Burks
Chair, Department of Religion
Anderson College
Anderson SC 29621

Henry L. Carrigan, Jr.
Assistant Professor of Religion and Philosophy
Otterbein College
Westerville OH 43801

Tony W. Cartledge
Pastor
Woodhaven Baptist Church
Cary NC 27511

Robert L. Cate
Dean of Academic Affairs
Golden Gate Baptist Theological Seminary
Mill Valley CA 94941

J. Bradley Chance
Assistant Professor of Religion
William Jewell College
Liberty MO 64068

Duane L. Christensen
Professor of Old Testament Languages and Literature
American Baptist Seminary of the West
Berkeley CA 94704

Paul Ciholas
Professor of the History of Ideas
Kentucky State University
Danville KY 40422

Bernard H. Cochran
Professor
Department of Religion and Philosophy
Meredith College
Raleigh NC 27607

G. Byrns Coleman
Professor of Religion; Chair, Humanities Division
Wingate College
Wingate NC 28174

A. O. Collins
Chair, Department of Christianity and Philosophy
Houston Baptist University
Houston TX 77074

John J. Collins
Professor of Hebrew Bible and Judaica
University of Notre Dame
Notre Dame IN 46556

John Collins
Professor of Religion
Wake Forest University
Winston-Salem NC 27109

E. Luther Copeland
Missionary to Japan, Emeritus
Professor of Missions, Retired
Southeastern Baptist Theological Seminary
Raleigh NC 27601

Charles H. Cosgrove
Assistant Professor of New Testament
Northern Baptist Theological Seminary
Lombard IL 60148

Lorin L. Cranford
Associate Professor of New Testament
Southwestern Baptist Theological Seminary
Ft. Worth TX 76122

Robert W. Crapps
Pitts Professor of Religion, Emeritus
Furman University
Greenville SC 29613

Timothy G. Crawford
Instructor in Old Testament
Southern Baptist Theological Seminary
Louisville KY 40280

James L. Crenshaw
Professor of Old Testament
Duke University Divinity School
Durham NC 27706

Bruce C. Cresson
Professor of Old Testament
Baylor University
Waco TX 76798

Bennie R. Crockett, Jr.
Associate Professor of Religion; Chair
William Carey College
Hattiesburg MS 39401

Loren D. Crow
Graduate Department of Religion
Vanderbilt University
Nashville TN 37240

R. Alan Culpepper
Harrison Professor of New Testament Interpretation
Southern Baptist Theological Seminary
Louisville KY 40280

Bruce T. Dahlberg
Professor of Religion
Smith College
Northampton MA 01063

Frederick William Danker
Professor, Emeritus
Lutheran School of Theology at Chicago
St. Louis MO 63104

Contributors

John P. Dever
Professor of Church and Community
Southern Baptist Theological Seminary
Louisville KY 40280

William G. Dever
Professor of Near Eastern Archaeology and Anthropology
University of Arizona
Tucson AZ 85721

LaMoine DeVries
Campus Minister/Teacher
Southwest Missouri State University
Springfield MO 65804

Simon J. DeVries
Research Professor
Methodist Theological School in Ohio
Delaware OH 43015

Sharyn E. Dowd
Associate Professor of New Testament
Lexington Theological Seminary
Lexington KY 40508

Frederick L. Downing
Professor of Religion
Louisiana College
Pineville LA 71359

John R. Drayer
Executive Vice President; Academic Dean
Bethel College
McKenzie TN 38201

Joel F. Drinkard, Jr.
Associate Professor of Old Testament Interpretation
Southern Baptist Theological Seminary
Louisville KY 40280

David Nelson Duke
Associate Professor; Chair
Department of Religion
William Jewell College
Liberty MO 64068

Robert C. Dunston
Assistant Professor
Cumberland College
Williamsburg KY 40769

Frank E. Eakin, Jr.
Weinstein-Rosenthal Professor of Jewish and Christian Studies
University of Richmond
Richmond VA 23173

Herbert O. Edwards, Sr.
Professor
Morgan State University
Baltimore MD 21239

W. T. Edwards
Professor of Religion; Chair
Samford University
Birmingham AL 35229

Bob R. Ellis
Instructor of Old Testament
Southwestern Baptist Theological Seminary
Ft. Worth TX 76122

Judy Yates Ellis
Teaching Assistant
University of North Carolina
Chapel Hill NC 27599

Ron Farmer
Assistant Professor of Religious Studies
University of Missouri-Columbia
Columbia MO 65211

Danna Nolan Fewell
Assistant Professor of Old Testament
Perkins School of Theology
Dallas TX 75275

Michael Fink
Manager, Adult Life and Work Curriculum
Baptist Sunday School Board
Nashville TN 37234

Henry Jackson Flanders, Jr.
W. W. Melton Professor of Religion
Baylor University
Waco TX 76798

David M. Fleming
Instructor
Southern Baptist Theological Seminary
Louisville KY 40280

Virgil Fry
Pastor
First Baptist Church
Young America IN 46998

Reginald H. Fuller
Professor, Emeritus
Union Theological Seminary
Richmond VA 23227

David E. Garland
Professor of New Testament
Southern Baptist Theological Seminary
Louisville KY 40280

Donald W. Garner
Associate Professor of Religion
Carson-Newman College
Jefferson City TN 37760

Edwin S. Gaustad
Professor of History
University of California, Riverside
Riverside CA 92521

Timothy George
Dean, Beason Divinity School
Samford University
Birmingham AL 35229

William H. Geren
Professor of Religion
Mercer University Atlanta
Atlanta GA 30341

W. Hulitt Gloer
Associate Professor of New Testament
Midwestern Baptist Theological Seminary
Kansas City MO 64118

Mary Jane Gorman
Associate Professor of Economics
Furman University
Greenville SC 29613

Michael D. Greene
Chair, Department of Religion and Philosophy
Chowan College
Murfreesboro NC 27855

Mark W. Gregory
Pastor
Parkway Baptist Church
Tupelo MS 38801

Russell I. Gregory
Associate Professor of Philosophy and Religion
Radford University
Radford VA 24142

Carol Stuart Grizzard
Assistant Professor of Religion
Pikeville College
Pikeville KY 41501

Robert K. Gustafson
Professor of Philosophy and Religion
Pembroke State University
Pembroke NC 28372

G. Thomas Halbrooks
Professor of Church History
Southeastern Baptist Theological Seminary
Wake Forest NC 27587

Emmett W. Hamrick
Professor of Religion
Wake Forest University
Winston-Salem NC 27109

Omer J. Hancock, Jr.
Associate Professor of Applied Christianity
Hardin-Simmons University
Abilene TX 79698

Walter Harrelson
Distinguished Professor of Hebrew Bible
Vanderbilt Divinity School
Vanderbilt University
Nashville TN 37240

Clayton K. Harrop
Professor of New Testament Interpretation
Golden Gate Baptist Theological Seminary
Mill Valley CA 94941

David H. Hart
Doctoral Candidate, Hebrew Bible
Vanderbilt University
Nashville TN 37240

Philip R. Hart
Professor of Religion
University of Richmond
Richmond VA 23173

John H. Hayes
Professor of Old Testament
Candler School of Theology
Emory University
Atlanta GA 30322

Stephen Z. Hearne
Assistant Professor of Religion
North Greenville College
Tigerville SC 29688

Charles W. Hedrick
Professor of Religious Studies
Southwest Missouri State University
Springfield MO 65804

William L. Hendricks
Professor of Christian Theology
Southern Baptist Theological Seminary
Louisville KY 40280

Carl F. H. Henry
Visiting Professor of Biblical and Systematic Theology
Trinity Evangelical Divinity School
Deerfield IL 60015

William R. Herzog II
Professor of New Testament Interpretation; Dean
Central Baptist Theological Seminary
Kansas City MO 66102

T. Furman Hewitt
Professor of Christian Ethics
Southeastern Baptist Theological Seminary
Wake Forest NC 27587

E. Glenn Hinson
David T. Porter Professor of Church History
Southern Baptist Theological Seminary
Louisville KY 40280

Stephen M. Hooks
Professor of Biblical Studies
Atlantic Christian College
East Point GA 30344

David C. Hopkins
Associate Professor of Old Testament
Wesley Theological Seminary
Washington DC 20016

Denise Dombkowski Hopkins
Associate Professor of Old Testament
Wesley Theological Seminary
Washington DC 20016

Carol D. C. Howard
Doctoral Candidate
Harvard Divinity School
Harvard University
Cambridge MA 02138

F. B. Huey, Jr.
Professor of Old Testament
Southwestern Baptist Theological Seminary
Ft. Worth TX 76133

Frank Witt Hughes
Assistant Minister
St. Luke's Church, Germantown
Philadelphia PA 19144

Fisher Humphreys
Professor of Divinity
Beason Divinity School
Samford University
Birmingham AL 35229

W. Lee Humphreys
Professor of Religious Studies
Director, Learning Research Center
University of Tennessee/Knoxville
Knoxville TN 37996

Contributors

Harry B. Hunt, Jr.
Associate Professor of Old Testament
Southwestern Baptist Theological Seminary
Ft. Worth TX 76122

Clayton N. Jefford
Assistant Professor of Scripture
St. Meinrad School of Theology
St. Meinrad IN 47577

Richard L. Jeske
Pastor
Holy Trinity Lutheran Church
New York NY 10023

E. Earl Joiner
Professor of Religion
Stetson University
DeLand FL 32720

Karen Randolph Joines
Professor of Religion
Samford University
Birmingham AL 35229

Peter Rhea Jones
Senior Pastor
First Baptist Church
Decatur GA 30030

Naymond H. Keathley
Associate Professor of Religion
Baylor University
Waco TX 76798

Howard Clark Kee
William Goodwin Aurelio Professor of Biblical Studies
Boston University
Boston MA 02215

George L. Kelm
Professor of Biblical Backgrounds and Archaeology
Southwestern Baptist Theological Seminary
Ft. Worth TX 76122

Douglas A. Knight
Professor of Hebrew Bible
Vanderbilt University
Nashville TN 37240

George W. Knight
Cook-Derrick Professor of New Testament and Greek
Hardin Simmons University
Abilene TX 79698

Glenn A. Koch
Professor of New Testament Studies; Associate Dean
Eastern Baptist Theological Seminary
Philadelphia PA 19151

Joanne Kuemmerlin-McLean
Assistant Professor of Religious Studies
Montana State University
Bozeman MT 59717

Robert L. Lamb
Professor of Religious Education
Gardner-Webb College
Boiling Springs NC 28017

John C. H. Laughlin
Professor of Religion
Averett College
Danville VA 24541

H. Page Lee
Professor of Religion
Mars Hill College
Mars Hill NC 28754

Jerry Wallace Lee
Professor of Old Testament
Baptist Bible Institute
Graceville FL 32440

C. Earl Leininger
Dean of Faculty
Mars Hill College
Mars Hill NC 28754

Joe O. Lewis
Vice President for Academic Affairs
Georgetown College
Georgetown KY 40324

Lamontte M. Luker
Assistant Professor of Old Testament
Lutheran Theological Southern Seminary
Columbia SC 29203

Joe E. Lunceford
Associate Professor of Religion
Georgetown College
Georgetown KY 40324

Thomas F. McDaniel
Professor of Old Testament
Eastern Baptist Theological Seminary
Philadelphia PA 19151

Daniel B. McGee
Professor of Christian Ethics
Baylor University
Waco TX 76798

Edgar V. McKnight
William R. Kenan, Jr. Professor of Religion
Furman University
Greenville SC 29613

Richard C. McMillan
Professor of Ethics and Humanities
School of Medicine
Mercer University
Macon GA 31207

Phillip E. McMillion
Director, Biblical Studies Center
Boise ID 83706

Paula M. McNutt
Assistant Professor of Religious Studies
Canisius College
Buffalo NY 14208

Warren McWilliams
Auguie Henry Professor of Bible
Oklahoma Baptist University
Shawnee OK 74801

Vernon R. Mallow
Professor of Religion
Georgetown College
Georgetown KY 40324

David C. Maltsberger
Doctoral Candidate
Southwestern Baptist Theological Seminary
Ft. Worth TX 76115

Claude F. Mariottini
Associate Professor of Old Testament
Northern Baptist Theological Seminary
Lombard IL 60148

Molly Marshall-Green
Assistant Professor of Christian Theology
Southern Baptist Theological Seminary
Louisville KY 40280

D. C. Martin
Professor of Christian Studies; Chair
Grand Canyon College
Phoenix AZ 85061

Dean M. Martin
Associate Professor of Religion and Philosophy
Campbell University
Buies Creek NC 27506

Ralph P. Martin
Professor in Biblical Studies Department
University of Sheffield
Sheffield S10 2TN England

T. J. Mashburn III
Assistant Professor of Religion
Mobile College
Mobile AL 36613

M. Pierce Matheney
Professor of Old Testament and Hebrew
Midwestern Baptist Theological Seminary
Kansas City MO 64118

Victor H. Matthews
Associate Professor of Religious Studies
Southwest Missouri State University
Springfield MO 65804

Gerald L. Mattingly
Professor of Biblical Studies
Johnson Bible College
Knoxville TN 37998

Frank Louis Mauldin
Professor of Philosophy
University of Tennessee at Martin
Martin TN 38238

David M. May
Baptist Chair of Bible
Central Missouri State University
Warrensburg MO 64093

Loyd Melton
Associate Professor of Christian Missions
Erskine Theological Seminary
Due West SC 29639

Calvin Mercer
Assistant Professor of Religious Studies
East Carolina University
Greenville NC 27858

J. Ramsey Michaels
Professor of Religious Studies
Southwest Missouri State University
Springfield MO 65804

William R. Millar
Professor of Religious Studies
Linfield College
McMinnville OR 97128

J. Maxwell Miller
Director, Graduate Studies in Religion
Candler School of Theology
Emory University
Atlanta GA 30322

Watson E. Mills
Professor
Roberts Department of Christianity
Mercer University
Macon GA 31207

Dale Moody
Professor of Christian Theology, Emeritus
Southern Baptist Theological Seminary
Louisville KY 40280

Wilda W. (Wendy) Morris
Assistant Professor of Christian Education
Northern Baptist Theological Seminary
Lombard IL 60148

James C. Moyer
Professor of Old Testament; Chair
Southwest Missouri State University
Springfield MO 65804

David L. Mueller
Professor of Christian Theology
Southern Baptist Theological Seminary
Louisville KY 40280

Donald W. Musser
Associate Professor of Religion
Stetson University
DeLand FL 32720

Scott Nash
Religious and Philosophical Studies; Chair
Brewton-Parker College
Mt. Vernon GA 30445

Jimmie L. Nelson
Professor of Preaching; Associate Dean
Southwestern Baptist Theological Seminary
Ft. Worth TX 76122

John P. Newport
Vice President for Academic Affairs; Provost
Southwestern Baptist Theological Seminary
Ft. Worth TX 76122

J. Randall O'Brien
Assistant Professor of Religion
Ouachita Baptist University
Arkadelphia AR 71923

Don H. Olive
Professor of Philosophy
Carson-Newman College
Jefferson City TN 37760

Mark J. Olson
Faculty
Virginia Polytechnic Institute and State University
Blacksburg VA 24061

Roger L. Omanson
Translation Consultant
United Bible Societies
Jeffersonville IN 47130

John Joseph Owens
Southern Baptist Theological Seminary
Louisville KY 40280

Contributors

V. Steven Parrish
Assistant Professor of Old Testament
Memphis Theological Seminary
Memphis TN 38104

Heber F. Peacock
United Bible Societies, Retired
Asheville NC 28804

Malcolm L. Peel
Greater Cedar Rapids Foundation
Cedar Rapids IA 52401

Donald N. Penny
Associate Professor of Religion
Campbell University
Buies Creek NC 27506

Leo G. Perdue
Professor of Old Testament; Dean
Brite Divinity School
Ft. Worth TX 76129

Melvin K. H. Peters
Associate Professor of Religion
Duke University
Durham NC 27706

Ted Peters
Professor of Systematic Theology
Pacific Lutheran Seminary
Berkeley CA 94708

John B. Polhill
Professor of New Testament Interpretation
Southern Baptist Theological Seminary
Louisville KY 40280

William Bruce Prescott
Pastor
Easthaven Baptist Church
Houston TX 77075

Ronnie Prevost
Associate Professor of Christian Education
Southern Baptist Theological Seminary
Louisville KY 40280

Joseph L. Price
Associate Professor of Religion
Whittier College
Whittier CA 90608

Theron D. Price
Pitts Professor of Religion, Emeritus
Furman University
Greenville SC 29613

Kandy M. Queen-Sutherland
Assistant Professor of Old Testament
Baptist Theological Seminary
8803 Ruschlikon Switzerland

Robert Rainwater
Professor of Religion and Philosophy
Virginia Intermont College
Bristol VA 24201

Mitchell G. Reddish
Assistant Professor of Religion
Stetson University
DeLand FL 32720

Paul L. Redditt
Professor of Old Testament
Georgetown College
Georgetown KY 40324

G. Willard Reeves
Chair, Religion, Biblical Languages, and Philosophy
Cumberland College
Williamsburg KY 40769

John C. Reeves
Doctoral Candidate
Hebrew Union College-Jewish Institute of Religion
Cincinnati OH 45220

John S. Reist, Jr.
Professor of Christianity and Literature
Vice President for Academic Affairs
Hillsdale College
Hillsdale MI 49242

J. A. Reynolds
Chair, Department of Religion
University of Mary Hardin-Baylor
Belton TX 76513

Jeffrey S. Rogers
Dana Faculty Fellow in Old Testament Studies
Furman University
Greenville SC 29613

Edd Rowell
Director, Mercer University Press
Mercer University
Macon GA 31207

Eddie L. Ruddick
Chair, Department of Religion
Clarke College
Newton MS 39345

Eric C. Rust
Professor of Christian Philosophy, Emeritus
Southern Baptist Theological Seminary
Louisville KY 40280

David W. Rutledge
Associate Professor of Religion
Furman University
Greenville SC 29613

W. Thomas Sawyer
Professor of Religion
Mars Hill College
Mars Hill NC 28754

Pamela J. Scalise
Assistant Professor of Old Testament
Southern Baptist Theological Seminary
Louisville KY 40280

David M. Scholer
Distinguished Professor of New Testament
and Early Church History
North Park College and Theological Seminary
Chicago IL 60625

Betty Jean Seymour
Professor of Religious Studies
Randolph-Macon College
Ashland VA 23005

Steven Sheeley
Assistant Professor of Religion
Shorter College
Rome GA 30161

John C. Shelley
Associate Professor of Religion
Furman University
Greenville SC 29613

Gerald T. Sheppard
Associate Professor of Old Testament Literature
Emmanuel College, Victoria University
Toronto, Ontario Canada M5S 1K7

Robert M. Shurden
Professor of Religion
Carson-Newman College
Jefferson City TN 37760

Walter B. Shurden
Calloway Professor
Roberts Department of Christianity
Mercer University
Macon GA 31207

Paul D. Simmons
Professor of Christian Ethics;
Director, Clarence Jordan Center
Southern Baptist Theological Seminary
Louisville KY 40280

Steven Simpler
Associate Professor
Belmont College
Nashville TN 37212

Robert B. Sloan
Associate Professor of Religion
Baylor University
Waco TX 76798

David A. Smith
Professor of Religion
Furman University
Greenville SC 29613

T. C. Smith
Professor of Religion, Emeritus
Furman University
Simpsonville SC 29681

Thomas G. Smothers
Professor of Old Testament
Southern Baptist Theological Seminary
Louisville KY 40280

Klyne R. Snodgrass
Professor of Biblical Literature; Dean
North Park Theological Seminary
Chicago IL 60625

Graydon F. Snyder
Professor of New Testament; Dean
Chicago Theological Seminary
Chicago IL 60637

Marion L. Soards
Professor of New Testament
United Theological Seminary
Dayton OH 45406

Harold S. Songer
Professor of New Testament Interpretation
Vice President for Academic Affairs
Southern Baptist Theological Seminary
Louisville KY 40280

Richard A. Spencer
Professor of New Testament
Southeastern Baptist Theological Seminary
Wake Forest NC 27587

Stuart P. Sprague
Professor
Anderson College
Anderson SC 29621

Frank Stagg
Professor of New Testament Interpretation, Emeritus
Southern Baptist Theological Seminary
Louisville KY 40280

Cecil P. Staton, Jr.
Assistant Professor of Christianity
Brewton-Parker College
Mount Vernon GA 30410

James F. Strange
Professor of Religious Studies
University of South Florida
Tampa FL 33620

Robert A. Street, Jr.
Professor of Christian Studies
Campbellsville College
Campbellsville KY 42718

Ray Sutherland
Assistant Professor
Pembroke State University
Pembroke NC 28372

Charles H. Talbert
Wake Forest Professor of Religion
Wake Forest University
Winston-Salem NC 27109

Marvin B. Tate
Professor of Old Testament
Southern Baptist Theological Seminary
Louisville KY 40280

Raymond Hargus Taylor
Chaplain to the College
Chowan College
Murfreesboro NC 27855

Anthony M. Tetrow
Instructor
School of Discipleship
First Southern Baptist Church
Beaumont CA 92223

Malcolm O. Tolbert
Professor of New Testament Interpretation
Southeastern Baptist Theological Seminary
Wake Forest NC 27587

W. Sibley Towner
The Reverend Archibald McFadyen
Professor of Biblical Interpretation
Union Theological Seminary
Richmond VA 23227

CONTRIBUTORS

John T. Townsend
Professor of New Testament and Judaism
Episcopal Divinity School
Cambridge MA 02138

Joseph L. Trafton
Associate Professor of Religious Studies
Western Kentucky University
Bowling Green KY 42101

John H. Tullock
Professor of Biblical Studies
Belmont College
Nashville TN 37212

Richard B. Vinson
Associate Professor of Religion and Philosophy
Averett College
Danville VA 24541

Robert W. Wall
Professor of Biblical Studies
Seattle Pacific University
Seattle WA 98119

Wayne E. Ward
Professor of Christian Theology
Southern Baptist Theological Seminary
Louisville KY 40280

Jack Weir
Professor of Philosophy
Hardin-Simmons University
Abilene TX 79698

Roy D. Wells, Jr.
Professor of Religion
Birmingham Southern College
Birmingham AL 35254

John Keating Wiles
Assistant Professor of Old Testament
Southeastern Baptist Theological Seminary
Wake Forest NC 27587

Johnny L. Wilson
Adjunct Professor of Old Testament Interpretation
Golden Gate Baptist Theological Seminary
Mill Valley CA 94941

Richard F. Wilson
Associate Professor
Roberts Department of Christianity
Mercer University
Macon GA 31207

Forrest Wood, Jr.
Professor of Philosophy and Religion
University of Southern Mississippi
Hattiesburg MS 39406

John A. Wood
Associate Professor
Baylor University
Waco TX 76798

Ralph C. Wood
Professor of Religion
Wake Forest University
Winston-Salem NC 27109

Norm Yance
Associate Professor of Religious Studies
George Mason University
Fairfax VA 22030

Fred E. Young
Professor of Old Testament, Retired
Central Baptist Seminary
Kansas City KS 66102

Abbreviations

Periodicals

AASOR *Annual of the American Schools of Oriental Research*
ADAJ *Annual of the Department of Antiquities of Jordan*
AJA *American Journal of Archaeology*
Arch *Archaeology*
AS *Asiatische Studien*
ASORN *American Schools of Oriental Research Newsletter*
ATR *Anglican Theological Review*
AUSS *Andrews University Seminary Studies*
BA *Biblical Archaeologist*
BAR *Biblical Archaeology Review*
BASOR *Bulletin of the American Schools of Oriental Research*
BASOR Supp *Bulletin of the American Schools of Oriental Research, Supplement*
BETL *Bibliotheca ephemeridum theologicarum lovaniensium*
BHH *Baptist History and Heritage*
BI *Biblical Illustrator*
Bib *Biblica*
BiR *Biblical Research*
BJRL *Bulletin of the John Rylands University Library of Manchester*
BJS *British Journal of Sociology*
BL *Bibel und Leben*
BR *Biblical Research*
BS *Bibliotheca Sacra*
BT *Bible Today*
BTB *Biblical Theology Bulletin*
BTS *Bible et terre sainte*
BYUS *Brigham Young University Studies*
CBQ *Catholic Biblical Quarterly*
CJ *Concordia Journal*
Conc *Concilium*
CQR *Church Quarterly Review*
CSBSB *Canadian Society of Biblical Studies Bulletin*
CTQ *Concordia Theological Quarterly*
DA *Dissertation Abstracts International*
DTT *Dansk teologisk tidsskrift*
DR *Downside Review*
EB *Estudios biblicos*
ETL *Ephemerides théologicae lovanienses*
ETR *Etudes théologiques et religieuses*
EvQ *Evangelical Quarterly*
ExpTim *Expository Times*
GOTR *Greek Orthodox Theological Review*
HAR *Hebrew Annual Review*
HeyJ *Heythrop Journal*
HR *History of Religions*
HTR *Harvard Theological Review*
HUCA *Hebrew Union College Annual*
IEJ *Israel Exploration Journal*
Int *Interpretation*
IR *Iliff Review*
IrTQ *Irish Theological Quarterly*
JAAR *Journal of the American Academy of Religion*
JAOS *Journal of the American Oriental Society*
JBL *Journal of Biblical Literature*
JCS *Journal of Cuneiform Studies*
JCU *Judentum Christentum Urkirche*
JEA *Journal of Egyptian Archaeology*
JJS *Journal of Jewish Studies*
JLR *Journal of Law and Religion*
JNES *Journal of Near Eastern Studies*
JPH *Journal of Presbyterian History*
JQR *Jewish Quarterly Review*
JR *Journal of Religion*
JRH *Journal of Religious History*
JSJ *Journal for the Study of Judaism*
JSNT *Journal for the Study of the New Testament*
JSOT *Journal for the Study of the Old Testament*
JSS *Journal of Semitic Studies*
JSSR *Journal for the Scientific Study of Religion*
JTC *Journal for Theology and the Church*
JTS *Journal of Theological Studies*
Judm *Judaism*
KD *Kerygma und Dogma*
NKZ *Neue kirchliche Zeitschrift*
NovT *Novum Testamentum*
NovTSupp *Novum Testamentum Supplement*
NTS *New Testament Studies*
NTT *Nederlands Theologisch Tijdschrift*
OTS *Oudtestamentische Studiën*
PEQ *Palestine Exploration Quarterly*
Proof *Prooftexts*

PRS *Perspectives in Religious Studies*
PRZ *The Patristic and Byzantine Review*
PSB *Princeton Seminary Bulletin*
PTR *Princeton Theological Review*
QDAP *Quarterly of the Department of Antiquities of Palestine*
RB *Revue biblique*
RE *Review and Expositor*
RefR *Reformed Review*
RevQ *Revue de Qumran*
RHR *Revue de l'historie des religions*
RL *Religion in Life*
RQ *Reformation Quarterly*
RSR *Religious Studies Review*
Scr *Scripture*
SJT *Scottish Journal of Theology*
SLJ *Saint Luke Journal*
SMS *Syro-Mesopotamian Studies*
SR *Studies in Religion/Sciences religieuses*
ST *Studia theologica*
SVTQ *Saint Vladimir's Theological Quarterly*
SWJT *Southwestern Journal of Theology*
TJT *Taiwan Journal of Theology*
TLZ *Theologische Literaturzeitung*
Trad *Tradition*
TRu *Theologische Rundschau*
TS *Theological Studies*
TT *Theology Today*
TynBul *Tyndale Bulletin*
UF *Ugarit-Forschungen*
USQR *Union Seminary Quarterly Review*
VC *Vigiliae christianae*
VT *Vetus Testamentum*
VTSupp *Vetus Testamentum, Supplements*
WTJ *Westminster Theological Journal*
ZAW *Zeitschrift für die alttestamentliche Wissenschaft*
ZMR *Zeitschrift für Missionskunde und Religionswissenschaft*
ZNW *Zeitschrift für die neutestamentliche Wissenschaft*

Reference Works

Encyclopedias

AEHL *Archaeological Encyclopedia of the Holy Land*
CAH *Cambridge Ancient History*
EAEHL *Encyclopedia of Archaeological Excavations in the Holy Land,* ed. M. Avi-Yonah
EB *Encyclopedia Biblica*
EBL *Encyclopedia of Bible Life,* 3rd ed.
EncJud *Encyclopedia Judaica*
EncRel *The Encyclopedia of Religion*
ISBE *International Standard Bible Encyclopedia*
NCE *New Catholic Encyclopedia*
NIDNTT *New International Dictionary of New Testament Theology,* ed. Colin Brown
RGG *Die Religion in Geschichte und Gegenwart*
TRE *Theologische Realenzyklopädie*
UnivJewEnc *The Universal Jewish Encyclopedia*
WBE *Wycliff Bible Encyclopedia,* ed. Charles Franklin Pfeiffer et al.
ZPED *The Zondervan Pictorial Encyclopedia of the Bible*

Bible Dictionaries

DB *Dictionary of the Bible,* ed. James Hastings
DBA *Dictionary of Biblical Archeology*
DCB *Dictionary of Christian Biography*
DNT *Dictionary of the New Testament*
HBD *Harper's Bible Dictionary*
HDB *Hastings's Dictionary of the Bible*
HDBSupp *Hastings's Dictionary of the Bible Supplement*
IBD *Illustrated Bible Dictionary*
IDB *Interpreter's Dictionary of the Bible*
IDBSupp *Interpreter's Dictionary of the Bible, Supplement*
NBD *New Bible Dictionary,* 2nd ed., ed. Douglas Hillyer
TDNT *Theological Dictionary of the New Testament*
TDOT *Theological Dictionary of the Old Testament*
TWAT *Theologisches Wörterbuch zum Alten Testament*
WDCE *Westminster Dictionary of Christian Ethics*

Lexicons

BAGD Walter A. Bauer, *Greek-English Lexicon of the New Testament and Other Early Christian Literature,* translation and adaption of Bauer's 4th ed. by W. F. Arndt and F. W. Gingrich, 2nd ed., revised and augmented by F. W. Gingrich and F. Danker
BDB Brown, Francis, Samuel R. Driver, and Charles A. Briggs, *A Hebrew and English Lexicon of the Old Testament, with an Appendix Containing the Biblical Aramaic*
KB Koehler, Ludwig H., and Walter Baumgartner, eds., *Lexicon in Veteris Testamenti Libros: A Dictionary of the Hebrew Old Testament in German and English*
RdA *Reallexikon der Assyriologie*
TWBB *A Theological Wordbook of the Bible,* ed. Alan Richardson

Commentaries

AncB *Anchor Bible*
BBC *Broadman Bible Commentary,* ed. Clifton J. Allen
CB *Cambridge Bible*
ComB *A Companion to the Bible,* ed. J.-J. von Allmen
HBC *Harper's Bible Commentary*
IB *Interpreter's Bible,* ed. George Arthur Buttrick
ICC *International Critical Commentary*
JBC *Jerome Biblical Commentary,* ed. R. E. Brown et al.
NCB *New Century Bible*
NICNT *New International Commentary on the New Testament*
NICOT *New International Commentary on the Old Testament*
OTL *Old Testament Library*
WBC *Word Biblical Commentary*

Collections of Essays

BARead *Biblical Archaeology Reader*
BZAW *Beihefte zur Zeitschrift für die alttestamentliche Wissenschaft*

CHJ *Cambridge History of Judaism*
JSOTSup *Journal for the Study of the Old Testament, Supplement Series*
SBLASP *Society of Biblical Literature Abstracts and Seminar Papers*

Series

NHS *Nag Hammadi Studies*
SBLDS *Society of Biblical Literature Dissertation Series*

Pseudepigrapha

ApocBar *Apocalypse of Baruch*
ApocMos *Apocalypse of Moses*
ApocZeph *Apocalypse of Zephaniah*
AscIsa *Ascension of Isaiah*
AsMos *Assumption of Moses*
EpArist *Epistle of Aristeas*
Hom *Homilies*, Pseudo-Clement
JosAsen *Joseph and Asenath*
Jub *Jubilees*
Life *Life of Adam and Eve*
LivProph *Lives of the Prophets*
MartIsa *Martyrdom of Isaiah*
PssSol *Psalms of Solomon*
Recog *Recognitions*, Pseudo-Clement
SibOr *Sibylline Oracles*
SyrMen *Syriac Meander*
TAsher *Testament of Asher (Testaments of the Twelve Patriarchs)*
TBenj *Testament of Benjamin (Testaments of the Twelve Patriarchs)*
TDan *Testament of Dan (Testaments of the Twelve Patriarchs)*
TGad *Testament of Gad (Testaments of the Twelve Patriarchs)*
TIss *Testament of Issachar (Testaments of the Twelve Patriarchs)*
TJos *Testament of Joseph (Testaments of the Twelve Patriarchs)*
TJud *Testament of Judah (Testaments of the Twelve Patriarchs)*
TLevi *Testament of Levi (Testaments of the Twelve Patriarchs)*
TMos *Testament of Moses*
TNaph *Testament of Naphtali (Testaments of the Twelve Patriarchs)*
TReu *Testament of Reuben (Testaments of the Twelve Patriarchs)*
TSim *Testament of Simeon (Testaments of the Twelve Patriarchs)*
TSol *Testament of Solomon*
TZeb *Testament of Zebulun (Testaments of the Twelve Patriarchs)*

New Testament Apocrypha

ActPet *Act of Peter*, Berlin Codex 8502
ActsJn *Acts of John*
ActsPet *Acts of Peter*
DialSav *Dialogue of the Savior (NH)*
PistS *Pistis Sophia*
POxy *Oxyrhynchus Papyri*
ProtJames *Protoevangelium of James*
SMark *The Secret Gospel of Mark*

Dead Sea Scrolls, Related Texts

CD (Cairo) *Damascus Document (Zadokite Fragments)*
1QapGen *Genesis Apocryphon*
1QH *Thanksgiving Hymns*, Cave 1
1QM *War Scroll*
1QpHab *Pesher on Habakkuk*, Cave 1
1QS *Manual of Discipline*
1QSa Appendix A (*Rule of the Congregation*) to 1QS
4QAgesCreat *The Ages of Creation*
4QFlor *Florilegium*, Cave 4
4QPBless *Patriarchal Blessings*
4QPEzek *Pseudo-Ezekiel, Cave 4*
4QpNah *Pesher on Nahum*, Cave 4
4QPssJosh *Psalms of Joshua*, Cave 4
4QMess Aramaic "Messianic" Text, Cave 4
4QShirShabb *Song of the Sabbath Sacrifice*, Cave 4
4QTestim *Testimonia text*, Cave 4
4QTLevi *Testament of Levi*, Cave 4
11QMelch *Melchizedek*, Cave 11
11QTem *Temple Scroll*, Cave 11
11QtgJob *Targum of Job*, Cave 11

Nag Hammadi Codices

AcPet12 *Acts of Peter and the 12 Apostles*
ApJas *Apocryphon of James*
ApJohn *Apocryphon of John*
ApocAdam *Apocalypse of Adam*
Disc8–9 *Discourse on the Eighth and Ninth*
EpPetPhil *Epistle of Peter to Philip*
GosEg *Gospel of the Egyptians*
GosMary *Gospel of Mary*
GosPhil *Gospel of Philip*
GosThom *Gospel of Thomas*
GosTruth *Gospel of Truth*
HypArch *Hypostatis of the Archons*
NHC Nag Hammadi Codices
OrigWorld *On the Origin of the World*
ParaphShem *Paraphrase of Shem*
PrThanks *Prayer of Thanksgiving*
SentSextus *Sentences of Sextus*
SophJC *Sophia of Jesus Christ*
SteleSeth *Three Steles of Seth*
TeachSilv *Teachings of Silvanus*
ThomCont *Book of Thomas the Contender*
Thund *Thunder, Perfect Mind*
TreatSeth *The Treatise of Seth*
TrimProt *Trimorphic Protennoia*
TriTrac *Tripartite Tractate*

Tractates of the Mishnah and Talmud

BQam *Baba Qamma*
Ed *'Eduyyot*
Erub *'Erubin*
GenR *Genesis Rabbah*
Meg *Megilla*
Middot *Middot*
Ned *Nedarim*
Šab *Šabbat*
Sanh *Sanhedrin*
Taan *Ta'anit*
Yad *Yadayim*

Texts

ANEP *Ancient Near East in Pictures*, ed. J. B. Pritchard
ANET *Ancient Near Eastern Texts*, ed. J. B. Pritchard
InscrGr *Inscriptiones Graecae*
RST *Ras Shamra Texts*

Apostolic Fathers

Barn *Epistle of Barnabas*
1 Clem *1 Clement*
Did *Didache*
IgnEph *Epistle to the Ephesians*, Ignatius
Magn *Epistle to the Magnesians*, Ignatius
Philad *Epistle to the Philadelphians*, Ignatius
IgnRom *Epistle to the Romans*, Ignatius
Smyrn *Epistle to the Smyrnaeans*, Ignatius
Vis *Visions, Shepherd of Hermas*

Ancient Authors

AdFam *Ad familiares*, Cicero
AdvHaer *Adversus omnes haereses*, Irenaeus
AdvMarc *Adversus Marcionem*, Tertullian
AgPrax *Against Praxeas*, Tertullian
Anab *Anabasis*, Xenophon
Ann *Annals*, Tacitus
Ant *Aniquities*, Josephus
ApChOrd *Apostolic Church Order*
Apol *Apologia*, Aristides
Apol *Apologia*, Justin Martyr
Apol *Apologeticum*, Tertullian
AppWo *Apparel of Women*, Tertullian
BJ *Jewish Wars*, Josephus
CAp *Contra Apionem*, Josephus
CCel *Contra Celsum*, Origen
CEph *Commentary on Ephesians*, Jerome
CEzek *Commentary on Ezekiel*, Jerome
ChrDoc *On Christian Doctrine*, Augustine
CIsa *Commentary on Isaiah*, Jerome
CivDei *City of God*, Augustine
2 Clem *2 Clement*
CMatt *Commentary on Matthew*, Jerome
CMic *Commentary on Micah*, Jerome
Cohort15 *Cohortatio 15*, Pseudo-Justin
DePat *De patientia*, Tertullian
DeVir *De viris illustribus*, Jerome
DivInst *Divinae institutiones*, Lactantius
EccHist *Ecclesiastical History*, Eusebius
Ep *Epistles*, Augustine
EvGood *Every Good Man Is Free*, Philo
ExcTheod *Excerpts from Theodotus*
Frag *Fragment*, Heraclitus
Geog *Geography*, Strabo
Haer *Haereticarum fabularum compendium*, Theodoret
Haer *Adversus lxxx haereses*, Epiphanius
Hist *Historiae*, Tacitus
Hist *History*, Herodotus
HLuke *Homily on Luke*, Origen
HMatt *Homily on Matthew*, John Chrysostom
HJere *Homily on Jeremiah*, Origen
Hyp *Hypothetica*, Philo
CJohn *Commentary on John*, Origen
LAB *Liber Antiquitatum Biblicarum*, Pseudo-Philo
Lives *Lives of the Twelve Caesars*, Suetonius
MartPol *Martyrdom of Polycarp*
Mon2 *Monarchia 2*, Pseudo-Justin
NatHist *Naturalis historia*, Pliny the Elder
Od *Odyssey*, Homer
OnAnt *On Antichrist*, Hippolytus
OnFF *On Flight and Finding*, Philo
Onom *Onomasticon*, Eusebius
OnPrin *On First Principles*, Origen
OpHist *Opuscula Historica*, Nicephorus
Pan *Panarion*, Epiphanius
Phaed *Phaedrus*, Plato
Plot *Life of Plotinus*, Porphyry
PraepEv *Praeparatio Evangelica*, Eusebius
PraescHaer *De praescriptione haereticorum*, Tertullian
Protrept *Protrepticus*, Clement of Alexandria
Ref *Refutatio omnium haeresium*
RomHist *Roman History*, Dio Cassius
Scorp *Scorpiace*, Tertullian
SpecLeg *On Special Laws*, Philo
Strom *Stromata*, Clement of Alexandria
Trypho *Dialogue with Trypho*, Justin

Versions

ASV *American Standard Version*
KJV *King James Version*
LXX *Septuagint*
MT *Masoretic Text*
NASB *New American Standard Bible*
NASV *New American Standard Version*
RSV *Revised Standard Version*
TEV *Today's English Version*

Miscellaneous

b. born
ca. circa (approximately)
chap. chapter
chaps. chapters
cf. compare
d. died
esp. especially
fl. flourished
frag. fragment
ft. foot/feet
Gk. Greek
Heb. Hebrew
in. inch(es)
km. kilometer(s)
lit. literally
Log. Logion
m. meter(s)
ms. manuscript
mss. manuscripts
mg. marginal reading
mi. mile(s)
NCCJ National Council of Christians and Jews
oz. ounce
ozs. ounces
par. parallel(s)
Rab Rabbinic interpretation
v. verse
vs. versus
vv. verses

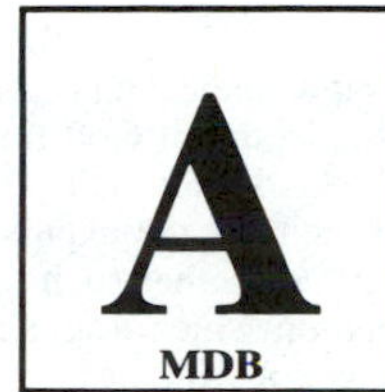

• **Aaron.** [air'uhn] *Aharôn,* a personal name, perhaps of Egyptian origin. In the OT Aaron is presented as a priest and elder brother of MOSES. They both are "sons of Levi," i.e., they are considered to belong to the tribe of LEVI.

It is therefore puzzling that in Exod 4:14 God mentions Aaron to Moses as his brother *and* a Levite. Why is this apparently redundant epithet used? A number of further questions present themselves as well. Is the designation "Levite" really referring to his trade as a priest rather than to his family origin? How is one to explain the clear division between Aaron and the Levites in numerous texts (Num 3:4; 16:40; 18:1-2) although by tradition Aaron is a Levite? In Exod 2:1f. Moses seems clearly to be the firstborn of that marriage. Why then is Aaron in Exod 7:7 presented as Moses' three years older brother? In Exod 4:2-5 Moses' rod is turned into a serpent, but in Exod 7:8-12 it is Aaron's rod that is changed into a reptile, and in addition it sprouts blossoms, making it a clearly superior rod. Why is it that Aaron is mentioned only once in the prophets (Mic 6:4) even though he has left an aura of importance great enough for later Israelite priesthoods to claim him as an ancestral father?

One cannot help but be puzzled by the general elevation of Aaron throughout the OT, and yet there is the grim story about his role connected with the golden calf in Exod 32. It is tempting to consider this a story told for the purpose of denigrating any priesthood tied to Aaron's name, just as the incident in Judg 17–18 is told for the purpose of devaluing the sanctuary and priesthood at Dan in northern Israel.

The figure of Aaron, then, clearly is an enigma in the OT story of the priesthood. His name is unique in the Bible (an honor he shares with Moses). His story is presented in conflicting ways in the ancient biblical sources. He appears to be little known and of minor importance in the older traditions (J and E); but in the later tradition (P) he is exalted as equal to or above Moses. This upward trend continues into the Apocrypha, where in Sir 45 Aaron is praised in more lofty terms than Moses.

It lies near at hand, then, to surmise that the Aaronitic priesthood originally was a northern institution, which served the bull-image in the north (1 Kgs 12:25-32). Then the priesthood was introduced into Judah by the Levites as they moved south after the fall of the northern kingdom, Israel, in 722 B.C.E. There it was opposed initially (cf. the bull story in Exod 32), but as time passed it came to be seen as presenting no threat. After the Exile, the Jerusalemitic priesthood, the Zadokites, claimed the venerable name of Aaron for themselves, just as they had done earlier with the name of Levi (Ezek 44:15-16).

See also CALF, GOLDEN; JEROBOAM I; MOSES; PRIESTS.

Bibliography. R.E. Clements, *God and Temple*; A. Cody, *A History of OT Priesthood*; R. de Vaux, *Ancient Israel: Its Life and Institutions*.

—REIDAR B. BJORNARD

• **Aaronites.** [air'uh-n*its*] "Of/belonging to Aaron," as such occurs only in KJV at 1 Chr 12:27 and 27:17 (RSV "house of Aaron," "Aaron"), but is equivalent to "son(s) of" (2 Chr 13:9), "house of" (Ps 115:10), and "order of Aaron" (Heb 7:11). It designates those whose descent is traced from AARON, the first "chief priest" (Ezra 7:5; cf. Exod 28; Lev 8). Aaronites were distinguished from LEVITES (Josh 21:4, 10, 13), and by postexilic times the priesthood had assumed its traditional pyramid configuration with Aaron at the apex, the Aaronites next, and the Levites as "assistant priests" below (cf. 1 Chr 6:48-49; 23:32). According to the tradition in 1 Chr 24:1-19, Aaronites were divided into twenty-four "divisions" or "courses" of priestly families, each division serving the temple for a week ("course"). JOHN THE BAPTIST was doubly an Aaronite: his father Zechariah was an Aaronite of the eighth division of Abijah (Luke 1:5; cf. 1 Chr 24:10) and his mother Elizabeth was a "daughter of Aaron" (Luke 1:5).

See also AARON; LEVI/LEVITES; PRIESTS.

—EDD ROWELL

• **Ab, Ninth of.** [ab] A significant fast day (*Tisha B'ab*) and a day of mourning for orthodox Jews. Though the Bible never mentions the name of the month, the events commemorated are recorded in 2 Kgs 25:8ff. and Jer 52:12ff. On that day the destruction of the Jerusalem TEMPLE was commemorated. Though the Bible describes only the destruction of the first Temple, the day commemorated both the destructions of 587/6 B.C.E. and 70 C.E. According to the Talmud, on the ninth of Ab "disasters recurred again and again to the Jewish people."

The record in the Kings indicates that Solomon's Temple was destroyed by the Babylonians on the seventh day of the fifth month. JEREMIAH dated the destruction on the tenth day of the fifth month. Doubtless both of these days are correct depending upon the viewpoint of the writer.

The second Temple was destroyed by the Romans under Titus on the tenth day of the fifth month, 70 C.E. The rebellion leading to that destruction continued in BAR KOCHBA's struggle against Rome. His last stronghold, Bethar, fell on the ninth of Ab (135 C.E.). It is felt by many that the Talmud's setting of the ninth of Ab for the fast commemorating the Temple's destructions was probably influenced by that event.

The Mishnah (*Ta'an* 4:6) includes a list of tragic events that happened on that day in Jewish history beginning with the decree of God forbidding the Israelites from entering the land after their failure to enter by faith (Num 14:22b). It includes the expulsion of the Jews from Spain in 1492 C.E. and other such events. Thus, the day was viewed as one on which tragic events occurred repeatedly. The day was not without hope, however; according to some traditions the Messiah was to be born on that day.

The Ninth of Ab (the fifth month) occurs in July of our calendar. The name Ab means father. It may be a reference to God as our Father.

The day is commemorated as is the Day of Atonement by a fast lasting a full twenty-four hours. The service calls for the reading of the Book of Lamentations and the recitation of dirges written to commemorate tragic occasions of Jewish history. These are read while sitting on the floor or on low benches as a gesture of mourning. Prayer shawls and phylacteries are worn in the afternoon service, but not in the morning service. In Jerusalem since 1967 orthodox Jews make a pilgrimage to the western wall of the Temple area. It is also a day to visit the graves of relatives.

See also JERUSALEM.

—JERRY WALLACE LEE

• **Abba.** [ab'buh] *Abba* (father) is an ARAMAIC word occurring in the NT in three places: Mark 14:36, Rom 8:15, and Gal 4:6. In other Greek literature of early Christianity it is found only in quotations of these passages.

In Aramaic *abba* is originally a word derived from baby-language, equivalent to "daddy," but even before the advent of the Christian era the word underwent extension of meaning. It came to replace the older form of address common to biblical Hebrew and Aramaic (*abi,* my father) as well as the Aramaic descriptive terms for "the father" and "my father." The word *abba* came to be used by adult sons and daughters. Thus, the word came to acquire the warm, familiar meaning of "dear father." Jeremias maintains that it was an everyday word, a homely, family-word, a secular word, the tender filial address to a father.

According to Jeremias there is no evidence in the literature of ancient Palestinian Judaism that *abba* was used as a personal address to God in prayer. Though this is an argument from silence and qualified by Jeremias, it is true that *abba* as a form of address to God is extremely uncommon in Jewish literature of the Greco-Roman period, doubtless because it would have appeared irreverent to address God with this familiar term. Evidence from the Gospels indicates that Jesus customarily addressed God as "Father" in all his prayers except the prayer from the cross which is a quotation of Ps 22:1 (Matt 27:46; Mark 15:34). Scholars usually assume that the Aramaic *abba* was the original form of address used in each of these prayers.

Jesus spoke with God as a son would his father, simply and intimately, indicating his unique relationship to the Father.

The early church took over the use of *abba* in prayer. This is evident from Rom 8:15 and Gal 4:6. Thus, those who come to the Father through childlike faith in Jesus Christ become spiritual children of God and address him as *abba,* Father. In fact Paul says that there is no surer sign or guarantee of the possession of the Holy Spirit and of the gift of sonship than this, that a person makes bold to repeat "Abba, Father" (Rom 8:15; Gal 4:6).

See also GOD; LORD'S PRAYER, THE.

Bibliography. J. Jeremias, *The Lord's Prayer*.

—J. A. REYNOLDS

• **Abel.** *See* CAIN AND ABEL

• **Abgar Legend.** [ab'gahr] The Abgar legend concerns a supposed exchange of letters between King Abgar V of Edessa (9–46 C.E.) and Jesus, and the subsequent evangelization of Edessa by the apostle Thaddeus, or Addai, said to be one of the Seventy (Luke 10:1). The legend first appears in Eusebius, *EccHist* 1.13, 2.1, from the early fourth century. Eusebius, writing in Greek, claims to have discovered the correspondence, in the Syriac language, in the royal archives of Edessa. Later, about 400, the legend appears in a much expanded form in a Syriac work, *The Doctrine of Addai*. From this time on it spread rapidly; it is found not only in Syriac and Greek, but also in Latin, Armenian, Coptic, Slavonic, and Persian.

As Eusebius quotes the material, King Abgar writes Jesus, asking him to visit and heal him of an affliction. He has heard of Jesus' miracles, and believes him to be the Son of God. Jesus replies in a letter, blessing the king in Johannine terms for believing in him without having seen him (John 20:29). Jesus says that he cannot visit Abgar, because of the mission he must fulfill where he is, but promises that after his ASCENSION, he will send a disciple to heal him and preach the gospel to his people. The legend goes on to describe the coming of Thaddeus, who heals the king as well as many others, and converts Edessa to Christianity by his preaching of Jesus. Eusebius's source dates this to 28/29 C.E.

The origin of the legend is disputed. There is no justification for assuming that Abgar V was in any way involved with the Christianization of Edessa; we have no record of orthodox Christianity in the city before 313 C.E.. Indeed, the legend appears to have been either unknown or discounted in Edessa itself during the fourth century, for the Syrian church father Ephraem (306?–373?) provides an account of the city's conversion, and while he mentions Thaddeus, he never refers to the alleged correspondence between Abgar V and Jesus. The major theologians of the ancient church never took it seriously. Both Augustine and Jerome state that Jesus left nothing in writing. The *Decretum Gelasianum* (date uncertain; perhaps late fifth century), a list "of books to be received and not to be received," specifically pronounces the Abgar–Jesus correspondence fictional. In spite of this, copies of the letters seem to have been made and used as protective amulets in late antiquity.

Walter Bauer argues that the legend originated in orthodox circles in Edessa, perhaps with the involvement of Bishop Kûnô, to whom the *Edessene Chronicle* (sixth century) ascribes the foundation of the orthodox church in the city. The "letters" could then have been deliberately placed in Eusebius' hands in the hope that their publication might legitimate the antiquity of orthodoxy in Edessa, a city long influenced by such heretical figures as MARCION, Bardesanes, and MANI.

See also SYRIA AND CILICIA.

Bibliography. W. Bauer, "The Abgar Legend," *New Testament Apocrypha,* ed. E. Hennecke and W. Schneemelcher and *Orthodoxy and Heresy in Earliest Christianity*; F. C. Burkitt, *Early Eastern Christianity*.

—ROGER A. BULLARD

• **Abi.** *See* ABIJAH

• **Abia.** *See* ABIJAH

• **Abiathar.** [uh-bi′uh-thar] Chief priest under DAVID in Jerusalem, along with ZADOK (2 Sam 8:17). Abiathar was a son of Ahimelech. His association with David began after Abiathar escaped as the only survivor of a massacre of the priestly family at Nob carried out by Doeg the Edomite at the command of SAUL (1 Sam 22:6-23). At the close of David's reign, Abiathar was among the supporters of the king's oldest living son, ADONIJAH, in the struggle over succession won by Solomon's party (1 Kgs 2). Abiathar may initially have retained his post under SOLOMON (1 Kgs 4:4), but he was shortly exiled to Anathoth (1 Kgs 2:26-27) in Solomon's purge of those associated with Adonijah's bid for the throne.

It was Abiathar's father Ahimelech who was the priest involved in the incident recounted in Mark 2:25-26 (cf. 1 Sam 21:1-6).

—JEFFREY S. ROGERS

• **Abigail.** [ab′uh-gayl] *1.* The wife of NABAL, Abigail saved her husband's life by intervening between him and DAVID. David himself had fled for his life from SAUL (1 Sam 20:42) and had gathered about him a band of four hundred (1 Sam 22:2-3) or six hundred (23:13) debtors and rebels and settled in the hill country of JUDAH, outside of territory that Saul actually ruled. Apparently, he survived by protecting various Judahites from raiders in exchange for gifts of goods and other essential materials. One man who especially benefited from David's protection was Nabal, who owned a substantial flock of sheep and goats (25:2). David sent ten messengers to collect Nabal's payment, but he refused. In anger David took four hundred of his men to slay Nabal and his family. Abigail heard of her husband's treatment of David's men, collected an appropriate present, and set out to intercept David. When they met she begged forgiveness, telling David to consider her husband's name (which meant "fool") and spare him and his family despite his foolishness (25:24-28). David granted her wish.

Upon returning home Abigail found her husband drunk at a lavish feast, so she waited until morning to tell him what she had done. Upon receiving the news, "his heart died within him, and he became as stone" (25:37). It is probably pointless to seek a medical diagnosis for his malady; the biblical writer ascribes his death to the action of God ten days later. David claimed that God had avenged the insult Nabal had inflicted on him (25:39). David at once offered marriage to Abigail, who accepted. After David was elected king in HEBRON, she bore him one son, named Chileab (2 Sam 3:3) or Daniel (2 Chr 3:2).

This marriage (along with one to Ahinoam of Jezreel) probably was at least partly political. Several of the cities that figure so prominently in 1 Sam 22–27 (e.g., Ziph, Maon, Carmel, and Jezreel) appear in the list of cities belonging to Judah in Josh 15:55-57. Nabal belonged to a subgroup within Judah called Calebites, whose eponymous ancestor had been named as Judah's representative among the twelve spies Moses sent to Canaan. The early history of the tribe of Judah is unclear, but the prominence of CALEB in Num 13 and Josh 15:13-19 suggests that the group was quite powerful. Thus David may have been attempting to curry favor with them by marrying such a prominent widow. Saul, meanwhile, gave his daughter Michal to another man, signifying yet one more way that he wanted David out of his life.

David had also ingratiated himself with the PHILISTINES, and one of their chiefs, a man named ACHISH, had commanded David and his men to join them for their final attack on Saul. David complied, leaving Abigail and Ahinoam in the city of Ziklag with the families of his other men. The Philistines never quite trusted David and sent him home before the battle with Saul. Upon returning, David found that the city had been destroyed by AMALEKITE raiders, whom David followed and defeated, thus rescuing Abigail (30:1-20).

2. A sister of David (1 Chr 2:16-17), also listed (2 Sam 17:25) as the daughter of Nahash, the sister of Zeruiah (cf. 1 Chr 2:16), the aunt of JOAB, David's general, and the mother of Amasa, with whom ABSALOM replaced Joab as the general of Israel's army during his revolt. Since both texts seem to refer to the same woman, several solutions have been offered to explain this difference in names of her father, for example that the phrase slipped into the text of 2 Sam 17:25 from verse 27 or that Nahash was another name for Jesse.

See also DAVID; NABAL.

Bibliography. H.W. Hertzberg, *I and II Samuel, OTL*; P.K. McCarter, *I Samuel, AncB* and *II Samuel, AncB*.

—PAUL L. REDDITT

• **Abihu.** [uh-bi′hyoo] One of the sons of Aaron, designated a priest (Exod 28:1), who died childless because of a ritual offense, the nature of which is uncertain (Lev 10:1; Num 3:2, 4).

See also NADAB.

—WALTER HARRELSON

• **Abijah.** [uh-bi′juh] Abijah, Abi(h), "my father (is) Yah(weh)." (1) The seventh son of Becher (1 Chr 7:8) the second son of BENJAMIN (1 Chr 7:6). (2) In KJV, the wife of Hezron (grandson of JUDAH) and the mother of Ashur, father of Tekoa. But RSV translates as "his father" (in apposition to Hezron) and further emends the corrupted text to give Hezron's (and Caleb's) wife's name as EPHRATHAH (1 Chr 2:24). (3) The second son of SAMUEL who served as judge in BEERSHEBA and whose wickedness and ineptitude as judge are given as part of the reason Israel demanded a king (1 Sam 8:2; 1 Chr 6:28). (4) An AARONITE and head of the eighth division of priests in the temple service (1 Chr 24:10; 26:20; KJV Abia, Luke 1:5). (5) A son of REHOBOAM who succeeded his father as king of Judah (1 Chr 3:10; 2 Chr 13:1–14:1; Matt 1:7; Abijam in 1 Kgs 14:31; 15:1ff.), and who continued his father's efforts to take the tribe of Benjamin (evidently with some temporary success). The simple notice of 1 Kgs 15:7 that there was "war between Abijam [Judah] and Jeroboam [Israel]" becomes a lengthy hyperbolic account in 2 Chr 13, probably a reflection of the Chronicler's anti-northern bias. (6) A son of JEROBOAM whose death in childhood was prophesied by AHIJAH as a sign of judgment on the house of Jeroboam (1 Kgs 14:1-18). (7) A daughter of ZECHARIAH and the mother of HEZEKIAH, king of Judah (2 Chr 29:1; KJV Abi in 2 Kgs 18:2). (8) One of several priests who accompanied ZERUBBABEL from Babylon to Jerusalem (Neh 12:4; cf. 12:17). (9) One of several priests (or priestly families) who sealed the covenant made by Nehemiah and the people to serve God (Neh 10:7).

—EDD ROWELL

• **Abijam.** *See* ABIJAH

• **Abimelech.** [uh-bim′uh-lek] A Canaanite personal name, perhaps meaning "Melek is father" or "Father of the king."

King of Gerar. Little is known about Abimelech, King

of Gerar, except that he appears in two Genesis narratives (Gen 20–21; 26) concerning ABRAHAM and ISAAC. In each passage there is a repeat of the motif established earlier in Gen 12:10-20 where Abraham pretends his wife is his sister. Since the king's name is the same, some have suggested that it is a royal title. It is more realistic to see the stories as doublets and only one King Abimelech.

The Gen 20:1-18 account is far more theologically oriented than the folklore account in 12:10-20. Abimelech plays a crucial role in the theological assertion that God has chosen Abraham, regardless of any weaknesses, to be the means of life and blessing to the nations. Abimelech, a non-Israelite, becomes a model of faith as he trusts God and emerges subservient and dependent upon Abraham because he perceives that God is with Abraham in all that he does.

It should be noted that Gen 21:34 "land of the Philistines" and Gen 26:1 "King of the Philistines" are anachronisms. The Philistines came into Canaan after 1200 B.C.E.

In Gen 26, Isaac and REBEKAH deceive Abimelech in the same manner, but in a milder and less objectionable way. The king is angry, but proceeds to protect them and eventually settles the argument over water rights with a covenant at Beersheba.

Son of Jerubbaal (GIDEON)*, Judg 8:31 and 9:1-57.* The story of Abimelech's attempt to establish a kingship in his mother's town of SHECHEM is one of the most instructive accounts of the struggle between the Israelites and Canaanites for supremacy. Gideon had refused to establish a monarchy, but Abimelech, his son by a Shechemite concubine, took advantage of his inherited position and sought to rule over Shechem and the surrounding area. After persuading the Canaanite residents to support him with money from the treasury of the house of Ba'al-berith, he hired "worthless and reckless fellows" to help him kill his brothers, the seventy sons of Gideon. Only Jotham escaped.

Jotham, from the safety of Mount Gerizim, cries out against Abimelech with a fable about the trees who once tried to anoint a king over them. The olive tree, the fig tree, and the grape vine refused the kingship because it was improper. Only the bramble bush, a useless shrub, would accept. Obviously this is a literary method of denouncing monarchial rule. The fable is followed by a curse against Abimelech and the Canaanites for the unscrupulous murder of Gideon's heirs and the grasping of the kingship. Future events proved the curse to be prophetic.

Abimelech ruled only three years and eventually brought ruin to the Shechemites and himself. Gaal, son of Ebed, a Canaanite, led a rebellion against Abimelech. The king countered by putting down the rebellion and destroying Shechem. (There is some archaeological evidence to substantiate the destruction of Shechem during this period.) Abimelech is later injured in battle at Thebez when a woman dropped an upper millstone upon his head from a fortified tower. He persuaded his armor-bearer to kill him with his sword so that he would not suffer the embarrassment of being killed by a woman. The writers see this as the moral retribution of God.

Mentioned in the Title of Ps 34. Generally agreed to be a copyist's error for Achish, King of Gath.

A Priest, Son of Abiathar (1 Chr 18:16). A copyist's error for Ahimelech. LXX, 1 Chr 24:6 and 2 Sam 8:17 read Ahimelech.

See also GERAR; GIDEON; KINGSHIP; SHECHEM.

Bibliography. W. Brueggemann, *Genesis*; G. Von Rad, *Genesis, OTL.*

—JOHN P. DEVER

• **Abiram.** [uh-bi'ruhm] Name meaning "father of height" or "my father is exalted," which occurs twice in the OT.

1. Abiram, the son of Eliab the Reubenite, conspired with his brother Dathan and the sons of KORAH to rebel against Moses' leadership in the wilderness (Num 16). Abiram and his fellow conspirators were swallowed by a crack in the earth. This event served as a warning to ancient Israel (Num 26:9-10; Deut 11:6) and was extolled as a mighty act of judgment (Ps 106).

2. Abiram, the eldest son of Hiel of Bethel, was killed when his father rebuilt JERICHO during Ahab's reign (1 Kgs 16:34). The death of Abiram and his brother Segub appears to have resulted from the ignorance or presumption of their father, who disregarded the curse pronounced by Joshua when he first destroyed Jericho (Josh 6:26).

See also KORAH.

—W. H. BELLINGER, JR.

• **Abner.** A renowned warrior and commander in chief of the army of SAUL (1 Sam 14:50). After Saul's death, Abner placed ISHBOSHETH, Saul's son, upon the throne and virtually ruled in Ishbosheth's name (2 Sam 2:8-10). Because the tribe of Judah had defected to DAVID, Abner sustained prolonged warfare with David's armies and their leader, JOAB (2 Sam 2:12-31). A conflict with Ishbosheth arose after Abner took one of Saul's concubines and Ishbosheth questioned the general. Abner then abandoned the house of Saul and allied himself with David (2 Sam 3:6-21). However, Joab killed Abner, who was buried at HEBRON and lamented by David (2 Sam 3:22-34). Although in the Deuteronomistic account in Samuel Abner fails to exhibit much religious fervor, the Chronicler notes the general's generosity in dedicating to the Tabernacle gifts from the spoils of war (1 Chr 26:28).

See also DAVID; ISHBOSHETH; JOAB; SAUL.

—W. H. BELLINGER, JR.

• **Abomination of Desolation.** The phrase "abomination of desolation" (RSV: "abomination that makes desolate") in DANIEL and the synoptic Gospels refers to something disgusting which pollutes the worship of God. In Dan 8:13, 9:27, 11:31, and 12:11 reference is to the detestable profanation of the Jerusalem Temple by Antiochus IV who set up an altar upon which sacrifices were offered to the Olympian Zeus (1 Macc 1:54-64; 2 Macc 6:1-6). The altar to Zeus may have included an image of Zeus bearing the features of Antiochus IV who was surnamed Epiphanes ("the manifest [God]") thus deepening the repugnance.

The purpose of the apocalyptic Book of Daniel was to give assurance that God's deliverance from persecution would occur within a short period from the time of the erection of the altar. Daniel was taken as prophecy by later readers who saw the "abomination of desolation" as a sign which must take place before the end. It is possible that Caligula's attempt to erect his statue in the Temple (40 C.E.) was taken as a fulfillment of this "prophecy."

Mark 13:1-37 (and par.) is an apocalyptic discourse containing the phrase: "when you see the desolating sacrilege standing where it ought not to be." The introductory words of the discourse discuss the destruction of the Temple, but the remainder deals with the end of the age and the PAROUSIA of the Son of man. "The desolating sacrilege" is a thinly veiled reference to the abomination wrought by

Antiochus when he offered a heathen sacrifice in the Temple. Matthew and Mark use "the desolating sacrilege" as a familiar symbol to refer to events which cannot be spoken of literally, but which are known to the reader—as seen in the admonition, "let the reader understand" (Matt 24:15; Mark 13:14). If the desolating sacrilege is the Roman power forcibly occupying Jerusalem and setting up its insignia in the Temple, the caution can be understood.

Even though the original saying probably referred to the destruction of Jerusalem by the Romans, the saying was clothed in the synoptic Gospels in phrases drawing out the theological and eschatological implications of the Roman destruction of Jerusalem. Matthew explicitly relates the desolation to Daniel and thereby to the Temple: "So when you see the desolating sacrilege spoken of by the prophet Daniel standing in the holy place . . ." (24:15). Luke 21:20 indicates that the appalling horror is the Roman Army: "but when you see Jerusalem surrounded by armies, then know that its desolation has come near."

See also APOCALYPTIC LITERATURE; DANIEL, BOOK OF; ESCHATOLOGY IN THE NEW TESTAMENT; ESCHATOLOGY IN THE OLD TESTAMENT; PAROUSIA/SECOND COMING; TEMPLE/TEMPLES.

Bibliography. F. W. Beare, *The Gospel According to Matthew*; G. R. Beasley-Murray, *A Commentary on Mark Thirteen*; C. H. Dodd, *More New Testament Studies*.

—FRANK LOUIS MAULDIN

• **Abortion.** Abortion is the expulsion of the fetus from the womb prior to full term pregnancy. A miscarriage or *spontaneous abortion* is a natural termination of a pregnancy often related to accident, illness, or fetal deformity. *Induced abortions* involve a deliberate termination for reasons which may be either *therapeutic* (threat to life or health of woman, rape or incest, or radical fetal deformity) or *elective* (fertility control, inconvenience, life plan, etc.).

Historically, abortion has generated various responses. Miscarriage belongs to nature and thus has been experienced from the beginnings of time. It poses the problem of natural evil but no special moral issue is involved. Certainly, it caused the grief of loss and was regarded as a curse by the Hebrews (Hos 9:14).

Elective abortion has been both tolerated and scorned. Documents dated ca. 2700 B.C.E. indicate that the Chinese used drugs to induce abortion without legal penalty. Semitic tribes harshly punished women for the practice. The Bible is silent on the subject. The biblical silence apparently means simply that the practice was not regulated by law nor the subject of public polemics. It is reasonable to assume that women occasionally aborted; certainly abortion was commonly practiced in the Greco-Roman world, yet Paul never forbade the practice.

The Bible certainly yields sufficient and authoritative guidance on the theological issues at stake in abortion. At issue are questions about the fetus as person, the status of woman in religion and law, God's relation to conception and natural processes, and human stewardship of sexual and procreative powers.

Biblical theology affirms the glory and power of God as creator. People rightly celebrate the gift of life and rejoice that God shares his powers with people. Those who experienced the joys of childbearing (1 Sam 2:1; Gen 21:6) after the frustration of childlessness (1 Sam 1:5-18) captured the essence of the worship due the creator for his unspeakable gift.

Not every pregnancy conveys God's grace or evidences his action, as evil may attend pregnancy by rape or incest or fetal deformity. The Bible stops short of declaring every pregnancy to be the will of God (cf. Gen 39:7-19). Jesus underscored the importance of distinguishing good from evil in speaking of God's actions (e.g. Matt 12:22-32).

A clear distinction is also made between the protection given the woman and that of the fetus under the law in Exod 21:22-25. An accident that resulted in a miscarriage involved a fine if there were injury to the fetus, while any injury to the woman was dealt with in terms of "eye for eye, limb for limb, life for life." The woman had full standing as a person under the Law; the fetus did not.

A theology of sexuality requires a responsible stewardship of procreative powers. People, bearing the image of God (Gen 1:27), are given the task to care for God's creation (Gen 1:28-31) which includes responsible parenting. Pregnancy will be sought as the joyful privilege of working with God to create new people (Ps 127:3). Life *in utero* will thus be protected, nourished, and respected. Problem pregnancies will require difficult decisions. Abortion is neither forbidden nor the option of first choice.

The Bible supports neither an absolutist legal or moral ban on abortion nor a calloused, casual attitude toward abortion. The fetus is not a person to the same degree or in the same sense as the woman, but neither is it a mass of cells or a mere "thing." Abortion is not murder; but it is of moral significance. It is a sinful act if justifiable reasons are not present. The decision should be made only after careful deliberation, prayer, and professional counsel.

See also FAMILY; MARRIAGE IN THE NEW TESTAMENT; MARRIAGE IN THE OLD TESTAMENT.

—PAUL D. SIMMONS

Designed by Margaret Jordan Brown ©Mercer University Press

• **Abraham.** [ay′bruh-ham] Israel's founding father, the son of TERAH, husband of SARAH, and father of ISHMAEL and ISAAC. His personal history is recorded in Gen 11:26–25:18 (cf. Acts 7:2-8 and Heb 11:8-12). Abraham plays a prominent role as an example of faith in three major world religions: Judaism, Christianity, and Islam.

Name. From Gen 11:26 through 17:4, the patriarch is known as Abram (Heb *'abrām*; LXX *Abram*). The etymology of Abram is by no means certain. It appears to be a typical variant of the west Semitic personal name Ab(i)ram attested from the time of the Mari texts down through the Neo-Assyrian period. It probably means "the father is exalted," although scholars disagree about its precise rendering.

Abram is given a new and distinctive name in the covenant ceremony of Gen 17. This name, Abraham (Heb. *'abrāhām*; Gk. *Abraam*), is generally considered a dialectical variant of Abram. According to Gen 17:5, the longer form was understood by popular etymology to mean "father of multitudes." Up to this point, however, a semitic root, *rhm* = "multitude," has only been attested in Arabic. Nevertheless, the text clearly regards Abraham as a God-given " 'dynastic' ancestral name" signifying that "God would make Abraham, then childless, ancestor of both his own people (12:2) and of many different groups (17:5-6)" (Wiseman, 159).

Career and Character. Prior to his seventy-fifth birthday, Abraham immigrated with his father Terah, his barren wife Sarah, and his nephew LOT to Haran (Gen 11:26-32). After the death of his father, and in response to God's call and promise, Abraham left Haran bound for Canaan (12:5). At SHECHEM, BETHEL (12:6-8) and MAMRE near HEBRON (13:18) Abraham set up altars to the Lord. Later he lived in BEERSHEBA (22:19). He settled for a while in EGYPT (12:10) and GERAR (20:1).

Abraham acted as the leader of a coalition that rescued his nephew Lot who had been forcibly taken from Sodom (14:12f.). Furthermore, he was well respected by the foreigners with whom he dealt in Egypt, Gerar and Hebron. The Hittites acknowledged his stature as "a mighty prince among us" (23:5f.). No doubt, Abraham and his house presented a formidable foe (14:14).

He was a wealthy man (13:2) and lived peacefully among the peoples of Palestine (12:6; 13:7-12; etc.). He entertained strangers with respect and hospitality (18:2ff.). Indeed, Abraham classified himself as a "resident-alien" (*gēr*) and a "sojourner" (*tôšāb*) in the land. Nevertheless, he made a covenant on equal terms with such an individual as Abimelech, King of Gerar (21:22ff.). This rank and dignity has prompted some scholars to suggest that Abraham as "prince" carried out the functions of a local or district governor. He died at age 175 and was buried alongside Sarah in the cave of Machpelah (25:7-10).

Abraham declared his faith in God Almighty (17:1), the righteous judge of nations (15:14) and all humankind (18:25). He walked before God and spoke with him in intimate fellowship (17:1; 18:1, 33; 22:11; 24:40). Abraham was always ready to obey God's call. By faith he left his father's house and land (12:1; cf. Acts 7:2-4). In a great test of faith he prepared to offer his son as a sacrifice to the Lord (22:2ff.; cf. Heb 11:17-19). By faith he accepted the promise of posterity and believed in the Lord, and it was counted to him for righteousness (Gen 15:5f.).

Abraham was offered land and posterity in his initial election and call (12:1-3). Later, the same promise is confirmed three times in covenant ceremonies that included animal sacrifice and a vision (15:7-17), a name change and the covenant sign of male CIRCUMCISION (17), and a theophany (with a play on "laughter") under the terebinths at Mamre (18:1-19).

The quest for the fulfillment of God's covenant promises functions as the major unifying theme in the patriarchal narratives. Tension and movement are provided by the complications that arise. Abraham's seed is to become a great nation (12:2). Sarah, however, is barren (11:30). The land of Canaan is promised to Abraham and his descendants (12:1, 7), but the Canaanites possess it (12:6). Abraham is to be a blessing (12:2f.), but his lapse in Egypt (12:10-20) and again at Gerar (20:1-18) bring plague and the threat of death to innocent people. Even at the death of Abraham, the reader is gently driven on through the rest of the patriarchal stories to seek a resolution. The complete fulfillment is not apparent until Israel occupies the land (cf. Exod 6:2-9).

The text does not offer a white-washed portrayal of Abraham's thoughts and actions. In fact, Abraham's limitations and flaws dramatically contribute to the narrative's realism. He is afraid that Sarah's beauty will cost him his life on two occasions (12:11-13; 20:2-11). Even though Sarah was Abraham's half-sister (20:12), the charade of passing Sarah off only as his sister reflected a lack of trust in God's promises in all situations.

Archaeology and the Date of Abraham. Today, some scholars regard Abraham essentially as a real figure who can be placed with reasonable accuracy in a historical period. Two distinct periods of the Middle Bronze Age, the twentieth-ninteenth and the fifteenth-fourteenth centuries B.C.E. appear to be the favorite choices. Recent archaeological and epigraphic discoveries from these periods are said to provide a clear reflection of the cultural background of Abraham's day as portrayed in the Bible.

While some social institutions, personal and place names, and general historical situations of the ancient Near East in the second millennium B.C.E. do illuminate the unique milieu of the personal history of Abraham, due caution must be maintained in recognizing the limits of this vast array of external evidence. However, much the same must be said about approaches that limit their investigation exclusively to the text of the Bible. In the end, a balanced approach would suggest that the patriarchal narratives reflect a social and historical setting prior to Israel's early monarchy. Given such comparative parallels, the historical existence of Abraham appears more likely.

Abraham in the NT. In the NT Abraham was considered to be the father of the Israelites (Acts 13:26) as well as of those who, following the Spirit, share his faith (Matt 3:9; Rom 4:16; Gal 3:29). His obedience in his call and in the offering of Isaac are listed as outstanding examples of faith (Heb 11:8-19; Jas 2:21). For PAUL, Abraham's faith was the type that led to justification (Rom 4:3-12).

See also PATRIARCH; SARAH.

Bibliography. W. F. Albright, *From the Stone Age to Christianity*; A. Alt, "The God of the Fathers," *Essays on Old Testament History and Religion*; J. J. Bimson, "Archaeological Data and the Dating of the Patriarchs," *Essays on the Patriarchal Narratives*, ed. A. R. Millard and D. J. Wiseman; J. Bright, *A History of Israel*, 3rd ed.; F. M. Cross, *Canaanite Myth and Hebrew Epic*; W. G. Dever and W. M. Clark, "The Patriarchal Traditions," *Israelite and Judean History*, ed. J. H. Hayes and J. M. Miller; R. K. Harrison, *Introduction to the Old Testament*; M. J. Selman, "Comparative Customs and the Patriarchal Age," *Essays on the Patriarchal Narratives*, ed. A. R. Millard and D. J. Wiseman; T. L. Thompson, *The Historicity of the Patriarchal Narratives*; J. Van Seters, *Abraham in History and Tradition*; J. Wellhausen, *Prolegomena to the History of Ancient Israel*; G. J. Wenham, "The Religion of the Patriarchs," *Essays on the Patriarchal Narratives,* ed. A. R. Millard and D. J. Wiseman; D. J. Wiseman, "Abraham Reassessed," *Essays on the Patriarchial Narratives*, ed. A. R. Millard and D. J. Wiseman.

—STEPHEN J. ANDREWS

• **Abraham, Apocalypse of.** The *Apocalypse of Abraham* is a pseudonymous expansion of the story of the call of ABRAHAM. Narrated in the first person, it falls into two parts. Abraham first describes how his work for his father TERAH, an idol maker, led him to reject idolatry. God then calls him to leave his father's house, and as he does so, Terah, his house, and everything in it, are burned to the ground. The second part of the book is an elaboration of God's call of Abraham, especially as found in Gen 15. After instructing Abraham to make a sacrifice, God sends the angel Iaoel to take Abraham up to heaven, where Iaoel leads Abraham in a song of worship. Abraham sees God's throne and heavenly court, then the firmaments below. God tells Abraham that his seed will outnumber the stars. God then shows Abraham the world and all of humanity divided into two halves: the heathen and Abraham's descendants. After showing Abraham the FALL and the wickedness of humanity, God reveals to him the future, including the destruction of the TEMPLE, ten PLAGUES, the coming of the chosen one, and the final judgment of the idolatrous heathen. The story ends with Abraham accepting the words of God in his heart.

The *Apocalypse of Abraham* is extant only in a Slavonic translation of a Greek version. The unity of the book is problematic. Some scholars have argued that the apocalyptic section (9–32) was originally independent of the narrative section (1–8), but in its present form there is a clear connection between the two sections. There also seem to be some interpolations, the most significant being Abraham's speech in chapter 7 and the description of the man coming from the heathen in 29:3-13. Behind the editing, however, probably lies a Hebrew or Aramaic original composed by a Jew near the end of the first century, or the beginning of the second century C.E.

The theology behind the *Apocalypse of Abraham* reflects an intriguing mixture of Jewish concepts. There is a concern for God's justice in the light of the destruction of the Second Temple (cf. *4 Ezra; 2 ApocBar*), a periodization of history into twelve ages (cf. *2 ApocBar*; *1 Enoch*), eschatological plagues (cf. *4 Ezra; 2 ApocBar*), Azazel as the chief of the fallen angels (cf. *1 Enoch*; 4Q *AgesCreat*), seven heavens (cf. *2 Enoch*; *AscIsa*), and a mystical visionary experience (cf. *3 Enoch*; the Merkabah books). In addition there is the strange description of the man in chapter 29. He comes (from the heathen? the Jews?) in the twelfth age and is worshiped not only by some from both the heathen and the Jewish sides, but also by (with?) Azazel. But he also offends many of the Jews, who insult him and beat him. This passage is usually seen as a Christian redaction, but it is an unusual depiction of Christ. In any event, the *Apocalypse of Abraham* is an important document for understanding developments in Judaism around 100 C.E.

See also ENOCH, FIRST.

Bibliography. A. Pennington, "The Apocalypse of Abraham," *The Apocryphal Old Testament,* ed. H. F. D. Sparks; R. Rubinkiewicz and H. G. Lunt, "The Apocalypse of Abraham," *The Old Testament Pseudepigrapha,* ed. J. H. Charlesworth; M. E. Stone, "Apocalyptic Literature," *Jewish Writings of the Second Temple Period,* ed. M. E. Stone.

—JOSEPH L. TRAFTON

• **Abraham, Testament of.** The *Testament of Abraham* is a legendary account of the events leading up to the death of ABRAHAM. It begins with a lengthy prelude in which God sends the archangel MICHAEL to prepare Abraham for his death. Michael comes in the guise of a stranger, to whom Abraham shows great hospitality. When Michael balks at informing Abraham directly of his impending death, God gives ISAAC a dream, which Michael interprets, identifying himself and his mission in the process. Abraham, however, refuses to give up his soul until he sees all of the inhabited world. Michael then takes Abraham up in a chariot and shows him the whole world. Incensed at the sin which he observes, Abraham begins to call down God's judgment on various sinners. Fearing that Abraham will thus destroy all of humanity, God abruptly ends the tour and directs Michael to take Abraham to a throne, upon which is seated ADAM and which stands before two gates: a narrow one leading to PARADISE and a broad one leading to eternal punishment. Entering the broad gate, Abraham sees the judgment throne, upon which is seated Abel. After observing the judgment process and interceding for one soul, Abraham repents of his rashness in condemning the other sinners. Michael then returns Abraham to his house. When Abraham still refuses to die, God sends Death, who, after a lengthy interchange with Abraham, ultimately tricks him, enabling Michael and the other angels to take his soul.

The *Testament of Abraham* was probably composed in Greek during the first or second century C.E. It is extant in two recensions: a longer one (A) supported by several Greek manuscripts and a Rumanian version, and a shorter one (B) supported by several Greek manuscripts, a Rumanian version, and the Coptic, Ethiopic, Arabic, and Slavonic versions. The precise relationship between A and B is unclear, but it seems likely that A retains more of the original contents while B is closer to the original wording. The author of the *Testament* was probably an Egyptian Jew. Attempts to link it to a particular sect, such as the Theraputae, have proved inconclusive. The *Testament of Abraham* served as a model for two later documents, the *Testament of Isaac* and the *Testament of Jacob*.

The *Testament of Abraham* is not really a testament, having little concern for any final exhortations by Abraham. It is an example of Merkabah mysticism, with a strong concern for the method of final judgment: people are judged by fire, which tests their works, and by balance, which weighs their righteous deeds against their sins. There is also an interest in the efficacy of repentance and of intercessory prayer. These concerns tie closely with the author's keen interest in death. Not only is death the driving force behind the plot, but Abraham's face-to-face encounter with personified death provides a striking climax. The juxtaposition of death in all of its horror with Abraham's own peaceful death suggests an author attempting to put death in its proper perspective.

See also TESTAMENTS, APOCRYPHAL.

Bibliography. G. W. E. Nicklesburg, Jr., *Studies on the Testament of Abraham;* E. P. Sanders, "Testament of Abraham," *The Old Testament Pseudepigrapha,* ed. J. H. Charlesworth; N. Turner, "The Testament of Abraham," *The Apocryphal Old Testament,* ed. H. F. D. Sparks.

—JOSEPH L.TRAFTON

• **Abram.** *See* ABRAHAM

• **Absalom.** [ab'suh-luhm] A personal name ("Absalom/

Abishalom") meaning "My father is peace," or "My father is Shalom." Absalom, whose life is treated in 2 Sam 13–19, was DAVID's third son, born in HEBRON from a political marriage to Maacah, the daughter of Talmai, the king of GESHUR (2 Sam 3:3).

The tragedy of Absalom lies in wisdom's bad counsel. AMNON, advised by JONADAB (2 Sam 13:3-5), attempts to seduce TAMAR, Absalom's sister. The seduction, turned to rape (2 Sam 13–14), prefaces the rebellion of Absalom described in chapters 15–20. The story about Tamar shows Absalom to be handsome and winning, vindictive and irreconcilable, as well as self-willed and reckless (14:25-33). The hair of kings accumulated on their heads. Absalom's hair grew profusely (14:26), as did a recurrent conviction that he would be king someday. Two years after Amnon's sacrilege, Absalom avenged his sister by luring Amnon to a feast and having him killed.

After his murder of Amnon, Absalom took refuge for three years with his grandfather in Geshur (in Transjordan). To get Absalom back into the land, JOAB used a wise woman from Tekoa. She procured from David an oath to spare the heir. After Absalom returned, David kept him under surveillance for two years. Unwelcomed at first to the court, Absalom established himself just outside the hall of justice. There, Absalom won a following among the dissatisfied. Absalom got a chariot and his personal elite corps. He built a base of support in the land, from Dan to Beersheba, by appeasing disgruntled citizens. Showing himself approachable and sympathetic, Absalom misled the thinking of the people of Israel, including some from Judah. After four years, the revolt began at Hebron; Absalom was crowned there; David, leaving JERUSALEM, did not take refuge in Judah. On the pretense of worshiping, Absalom had carried with him from Jerusalem 200 men, who knew nothing about the rebellion. However, they gave to David the distinct impression of Jerusalem's desertion.

The success or failure of Absalom's plot hinged upon wise counsel. Ahithophel urged haste; HUSHAI, sent back by David to confound the counsel of Ahithophel, urged caution and consolidation. Hushai's counsel allowed David to appraise the rebellion's strength, get provisions for his army, organize his forces, and select the location for the battle. When Absalom hesitated before attacking, Ahithophel anticipated defeat. Ahithophel committed suicide; David lost not only a valuable counselor, but a beloved son would die.

David divided his army into three forces, and his troops engaged the rebels near MAHANAIM in Transjordan. David was not present; Absalom, on poor advice, was. Caught in the branches of a tree, unseated from both his royal mule and his new throne, an escaping Absalom hung in midair. Joab, who was more brutal than wise, killed the suspended Absalom, against David's explicit orders.

David lamented Absalom and made overtures to the tribes, but Judah remained unwilling to make concessions to the northern tribes. In the aftermath of that tribe's indecision, David put down Sheba's counter-revolution, which resulted in further rebellion. The tragedy of Absalom disclosed an unstable kingdom, a land bankrupt of wisdom at the court and in the villages.

See also DAVID; JOAB; SUCCESSION NARRATIVE.

Bibliography. P. R. Ackroyd, "The History of Israel," *A Companion to the Bible*, 2nd ed., ed. H. H. Rowley; D. R. Ap-Thomas, "Absalom, Abishalom," *Dictionary of the Bible*, 2nd ed., ed. F. C. Grant and H. H. Rowley; H. S. Cazelles, "The History of Israel in the Pre-Exilic Period," *Tradition & Interpretation*, ed. G. W. Anderson; H. W. Hertzberg, *I & II Samuel*, trans. J. S. Bowden; P. K. McCarter, Jr., *II Samuel*; R. de Vaux, *Ancient Israel: Its Life and Institutions*, trans. J. McHugh.

—EDDIE L. RUDDICK

• **Acco.** [ak'oh] Acco is a coastal city in northwestern Palestine, situated on a small plain some eight miles north of Mount Carmel (PLATE 13). Most recently the neighboring city of Haifa has achieved greater commercial strength than Acco, but this should not obscure Acco's historic and strategic importance in ancient times. Because its adjacent waters were naturally suited for a harbor, Acco was a valued possession of many ancient rulers, including such figures as the Egyptians Thutmose III and Seti I, and the Assyrians Tiglath-pileser III, Sennacherib, and Ashurbanipal. In the third century B.C.E., following the death of Alexander the Great, Acco came for a while under the control of the Ptolemies, who changed its name to Ptolemais. Then again in the Middle Ages the name was changed to Acre, in honor of the crusader St. Jean d'Acre.

The single OT reference to Acco is Judg 1:31. Here it is stated that in the Israelite conquest of the promised land, the tribe of Asher was unable to drive out the inhabitants of Acco. The sole NT reference to the city is Acts 21:7 where we find that, in making his final journey to Jerusalem, Paul traveled southward from Tyre to Ptolemais (Acco), where he remained one day before moving on to Caesarea.

—MICHAEL D. GREENE

Designed by Margaret Jordan Brown ©Mercer University Press

• **Achaia.** [uh-kay'yuh] During the Late Bronze Age (ca. 1400–1200 B.C.E.), Achaia was a term used in Hittite and Egyptian texts to designate Greeks. Geographically, the term referred to the southern half of Greece, particularly southeast Thessaly and the northern half of the Peloponnesus (PLATE 1). In the NT, Achaia is paired with MACEDONIA to refer to Greece as a whole (cf. Acts 19:21; Rom 15:26; 1 Thess 1:7-8).

In antiquity, Achaia played a relatively unimportant role in Greek history, and like Crete, did not aid the Greeks during the Persian War. The Achaians did, however, help colonize certain cities in Italy such as Croton and Metapontum. When the northern half of the Peloponnesus was first inhabited is still unclear, but the rich soil and plentiful water would have insured early settlements.

Politically, the Achaians were organized into a league, the earliest of which lasted until the fourth century B.C.E. This league, composed of twelve towns, centered around the cult of Poseidon Helironius. But the most powerful and best known Achaian League existed during the third and second centuries B.C.E. This league lasted until Achaia became part of the Roman Empire in the second century B.C.E.

In 27 B.C.E. Achaia became a Roman senatorial province that included most of the Greek mainland as well as several islands. For most of Roman rule, the province was governed by a proconsul, such as GALLIO who administered the area during the time of Paul (Acts 18:12). However, from 15–44 C.E., both Achaia and Macedonia were under the control of the imperial legate of Moesia. Achaia was also granted a few years of political independence by Nero beginning in 67 C.E.

The territory of Achaia was divided among the cities of the province, the most important of which during the NT period was CORINTH. Other important cities established by the Romans were Patrae and Nicopolis.

While ATHENS, with its philosophical traditions, proved to be unresponsive to the message of Christianity, Paul had more success in Corinth and Achaia in general. The household of Stephanas is said to be the first Christian converts in Achaia (1 Cor 16:15), and one of Paul's letters to the church at Corinth is also addressed to the Achaian Christians (2 Cor 1:1). How large a Christian following there was in Achaia is unknown, but Paul found them cooperative in his efforts to aid the Jerusalem church (cf. 2 Cor 9:2).

See also ATHENS; CORINTH; GALLIO; MACEDONIA.

Bibliography. J. Keil, "The Greek Provinces: Achaea," *CAH*, 11:556-65.

—JOHN C. H. LAUGHLIN

• **Achish.** [ay'kish] King of GATH of the PHILISTINES during the period of united Israel. There are two stories about David's contact with this ruler. The first (1 Sam 21:10-15) relates how DAVID, fleeing from Saul, sought refuge with Achish. The king's servants informed him about David's exploits, and it was necessary for David to feign madness in order to escape alive. In the second account (1 Sam 27–29) David was on friendlier terms with Achish. He became the king's vassal, receiving a city in exchange for military service. David remained with Achish for more than a year until the other Philistine lords became suspicious of him. Whether these two accounts refer to the same incident is uncertain. Earlier source critics understood them in this way, but contemporary scholars tend to view them separately.

See also DAVID; PHILISTINES.

—DAVID H. HART

• **Acropolis.** *See* AREOPAGUS; ATHENS

• **Acrostic.** *See* LITERATURE, BIBLE AS

• **Acts of the Apostles.** *See* APOSTLES, ACTS OF THE

• **Adam.** The first man or the species of humankind are both understandings of the term Adam. He and his wife were driven from EDEN after disobeying God's commands. In later Jewish apocalyptic and pseudepigraphic works, Adam and his life become highly exaggerated. In the thought patterns evident in the NT, he is seen as representative of humankind in his rebellion against God's rule and is the antitype of the Christ.

OT usage of the term is varied—from the word's generic use for humankind to the rare usage of the word to represent one man as in a proper name. In Gen 1, the priestly tradition would seem to argue for the generic meaning as the climax of a series of divine creative acts. These other creations are generic as well (i.e., fish, birds, and beasts in general). Given the commonality of much within human nature, it would seem that such a representative understanding would be appropriate. Even in Gen 2–3, the presence of the article with the term, i.e., "the man" (Heb *hā'ādām*), would argue against the use of a proper name, though this usage changes in Gen 4–5. With the evident play on words for earth (*'ădāmâ*) and man (*'ādām*) as well as some similarities in other ancient texts (Sumerian and Akkadian), it might be proper to understand that God made an earthling from earth.

Interpretations of the GENESIS passages produce varied images of Adam in physical, mental, and spiritual ways. In the priestly tradition, as the climax of the series of divine creative acts, man (male and female) is given dominion over the earlier creations. According to Aggadah, in creation whatever was created later had dominion over prior creations.

In the J strand of Gen 2–3, God fashioned "the man" from dust, breathed life into him and made him a caretaker of all of creation. Man was in partnership with the remainder of the earth. This is evidenced when all of creation loses its perfection in the fall.

As theology and philosophy advanced, ideas about Adam diversified. Rabbinical literature reflected understandings that ranged from Adam as the prototype of humankind to the image of God representing perfect human intellect. PHILO of Alexandria saw the creation of two men—one in human form from the dust and one that is heavenly in the image of God, which was found in the mind of man. Others contended that Adam was perfect in body, but this perfection was lost in the fall. Maimonides argues that the "image of God" in Adam was the creation of a human intellect that resembled the divine intellect. Adam was intellectually perfect so as to contemplate metaphysics. Still others posit that the "image of God" reflects a spiritual capacity for communion with God and one's fellow human beings, which makes humankind the superior creation to animals.

In the NT and Christian tradition, Adam is viewed in two ways. First, as the progenitor of the human race, he is seen in connection with the order of the community and society. In 1 Tim 2 his creation sets the tone for a hierarchy between man and woman. Women are to be subordinate to men because at creation the man was given supremacy by being the first created (2:13) and because the woman was the first deceived (2:14). However, these arguments might be altered based on a generic reading of Gen 1 concerning the creation of the two together (humankind).

The second Christian tradition is to see an Adam/Christ typology. Adam is the antitype of Christ. The temptations faced and overcome by Jesus in the Gospels show how the new man, Jesus, has overcome and set right the defeated (fallen) order of the first man. Hence, Jesus makes the Paradise that was taken away from the first man available again.

PAUL is the main proponent of the Adam/Christ typology. In Rom 5:12-21, he seeks to show the universality of the grace lost by the first Adam but redeemed through the last Adam (Christ). Hence, Adam is the type of the Messiah because of the total effect his disobedience had on all humanity. The last Adam, Christ, will have the same effect in grace. One brought disobedience and death while Christ brings obedience and life to humankind.

Paul also uses the Adam/Christ typology to establish the certainty of the doctrine of resurrection (1 Cor 15:22). As all experience death through the first Adam, the head of the old humanity, so now all who are in Christ have life, for he is the head of the new humanity. Since in our earthly bodies we are like the first Adam, Christians are like the last Adam (Christ) in our resurrected bodies (1 Cor 15:45-49).

In the typology found in 1 Cor 15:22 ff. there is also a parallel in authority. The first Adam was given the position of having dominion over and being caretaker of the earthly creation. The last Adam has been given dominion over and is caretaker of not only the earthly but the heavenly realm of the universe through the authority of God.

See also CREATION; EDEN, GARDEN OF; EVE; FALL; HERMENEUTICS IN THE BIBLE.

Bibliography. G. Bornkamm, *Paul*; J. Carmody, D. L. Carmody, and R. L. Cohn, *Exploring the Hebrew Bible*; J. L. Crenshaw, *Story and Faith*; W. Eichrodt, *Theology of the Old Testament*; H. Gunkel, *Genesis*; J. Jeremias, " 'Αδάμ," *TDNT*; M. Pope, E. E. Halevy, D. Kadosh, and A. Wolfe, "Adam," *EncJud*; H. Ridderbos, *Paul: An Outline of His Theology*; E. A. Speiser, "Genesis," *AncB*.

—STEPHEN Z. HEARNE

• **Adam and Eve, Life of.** The *Life of Adam and Eve* is a narrative about the repentance of the first couple after their expulsion from EDEN, their dealings with their sons CAIN, ABEL, and Seth, and their final instructions, deaths, and burials. It is extant in a number of manuscripts; the two earliest versions are in Latin and Greek (the Greek version is traditionally known as the *Apocalypse of Moses,* although it is not an apocalypse and has nothing to do with Moses). The date is uncertain; the *Life* probably should not be dated earlier than 100 B.C.E. nor later than 200 C.E. It represents the thought-world of Hellenistic JUDAISM.

The GENESIS account of the rebellion of ADAM and EVE and its consequences raised a number of questions in the minds of the JEWS of later centuries. Some of their answers have made their way into these texts.

Why does the devil hate humanity so much? The Latin *Life* includes a speech by SATAN in which he explains that he and his angels were thrown out of heaven for refusing to obey God's command to worship Adam, the image of God. Jealous of the bliss of the pair in Eden, Satan then decided to arrange for their expulsion from the earthly PARADISE, blaming Adam for his own expulsion from the heavenly one.

Why do wild animals pose a threat to humans, to whom they were originally subjected by God? The Greek text (*ApocMos*) explains that the rebellion of the animals against humanity is a result of humanity's rebellion against God.

Why do humans suffer with so many illnesses? *ApocMos* answers that these are punishments for the sin of Adam and Eve.

Does evil have the final victory over humanity, then? Both texts insist on the RESURRECTION of the body and the restoration of humanity to the presence of God. Adam is promised the throne forfeited by Satan. Until the resurrection, Adam's soul ascends to the third heaven where it waits to be reunited with his body at the last day.

This reference to Paradise as "the third HEAVEN" is similar to Paul's vision report in 2 Cor 12:2-3, and Paul also shares with the *Life* the conviction that Satan can disguise himself as an angel of light (2 Cor 11:14). The *Life* has a number of motifs in common with the literature of apocalyptic Judaism, including a complex angelology. Cain and Abel are dispensed with in short order, but considerable attention is focused on Seth, who accompanies Eve back to Paradise in a vain attempt to secure a remedy for Adam's pains, and who witnesses the reception of Adam's soul into heaven. Interest in Seth is also typical of some of the Gnostic literature.

The influence of Greek mythology is not as pervasive in the *Life* as in some other Jewish literature of the same period. It is interesting to note, however, that in the *ApocMos,* before Adam's soul enters Paradise it is washed in the Lake of Acheron, an allusion to the underworld stream of Greek tradition.

Bibliography. M. D. Johnson, "Life of Adam and Eve," *The Old Testament Pseudepigrapha,* ed. J. H. Charlesworth.

—SHARYN E. DOWD

• **Adam, Apocalypse of.** The *Apocalypse of Adam* is a Jewish-gnostic writing discovered in Egypt in 1946 in the NAG HAMMADI library. It is not to be identified with any previously known ADAM text. Date and provenance of the document is not certain. It was written in Greek sometime after the appearance of the SEPTUAGINT (ca. 250-200 B.C.E.), and translated into Coptic (Sahidic dialect) before the middle of the fourth century C.E., when the books of the Nag Hammadi library were manufactured. In its present form it has been dated as early as the end of the first century C.E. It has been described as an original writing of the Gnostic sect of the Sethians.

The narrative is cast as a revelatory discourse delivered by Adam to his son Seth "in the 700th year"; that is, just prior to Adam's death (cf. Gen 5:3-5 LXX). Hence, the text is to be understood as the "last testament" of Adam and associated with other testamentary literature in antiquity.

Unlike other Gnostic texts, Adam describes his "creation" in a positive way. His "fall" is described as a lapse into ignorance when he and Eve were separated, rather than as an act of disobedience to God's command not to eat of the tree "of the knowledge of good and evil." Three unnamed heavenly figures then appear to Adam and their revelation to him becomes the subject of Adam's last testament to Seth.

Adam tells Seth about the origin of a special race of people and their struggle against God, the Almighty. Three attempts are made by the Almighty to destroy the special race. Two of these attempts by FLOOD and fire are well known in Jewish tradition (i.e., NOAH and SODOM/GOMORRAH, but in this text they are given new interpretations. For example, the biblical flood narrative is interpreted as an attempt of a wicked creator to destroy the special race rather than as in the biblical narrative the judgment of a righteous God upon the wickedness of humankind.

After these attempts to destroy the special race, Adam describes the descent of a heavenly figure, the illuminator of knowledge. His appearing shakes the foundation of the world. The illuminator comes to "redeem" the souls of Noah's seed from the day of death and leave for himself "fruit-bearing trees." He performs SIGNS AND WONDERS and as the "man on whom the holy spirit has come," he "suffers in his flesh." Perplexed by these events, the "powers" ask about the source of the disturbance, and thirteen "kingdoms" give erroneous answers, followed by the correct response of the "kingless generation." The narrative concludes with an apocalyptic scene reminiscent of Matt 25, in which those who oppose the illuminator fall under the condemnation of death, but those who receive his knowledge "will live forever." The document ends with a description of competing baptismal traditions.

The struggle between the Almighty and the special race is cast as a Gnostic midrash or commentary, on the biblical story in which four parts of the story are followed by four explanations that set out Sethian interpretations of the story. The thirteen erroneous explanations given by the kingdoms for the illuminator's origin are set out in highly structured prose with a recurring refrain: "And thus he came to the water."

It is generally agreed that these explanations constitute traditional material that was later incorporated into the present document. And it has also been argued that the document breaks down into two originally separate sources harmonized by an editor with editorial comments at the point of the literary seams. The two sources were brought together in a community that argued for a spiritualized understanding of baptism.

The text reflects a non-Christian type of Jewish GNOSTICISM. It is Jewish in its knowledge and use of Jewish traditions but in its intention the document is radically anti-Jewish. There are parallels to the Christian tradition but the text has no features that are necessarily Christian and it makes no use of NT texts. The redeemer-illuminator mythology in the document draws upon pre-Christian Jewish traditions of the persecution and subsequent exaltation of the righteous man as reflected in Wis 1–6 and Isa 52–53.

See also APOCALYPTIC LITERATURE; GNOSTICISM; NAG HAMMADI; TESTAMENTS, APOCRYPHAL.

Bibliography. C. W. Hedrick, *The Apocalypse of Adam: A Literary and Source Analysis*; G. MacRae, "The Apocalypse of Adam," *Nag Hammadi Codices V, 2-5 and VI with Papyrus Berolinensis 8502, 1 and 4,* ed. D. M. Parrott (*NHS* 11); G. MacRae and D. Parrott, "The Apocalypse of Adam," *The Nag Hammadi Library in English,* ed. J. M. Robinson; B. Pearson, "The Problem of 'Jewish Gnostic' Literature," *Nag Hammadi, Gnosticism, and Early Christianity,* ed. C. W. Hedrick and R. Hodgson, Jr.

—CHARLES W. HEDRICK

• **Adam, Testament of.** The *Testament of Adam* is a composite work combining Jewish and Christian traditions edited by a Christian redactor no earlier than the third century C.E. The original language seems to have been Syriac.

In its present form, the work has three parts, the first two of which purport to be information passed on by ADAM to his son Seth. In the first section, or Horarium, Adam describes how God, "the Lord of all," is praised each hour of the day and night by a different being or aspect of creation. The second section, or prophecy, consists of Adam's predictions of the flood, the birth, ministry, death, and resurrection of Christ, and the end of the world. The prophecy is clearly dependent on Christian traditions represented in the NT.

Adam explains that, although he was punished with death for listening to the serpent, God will have mercy on him; in fact, God is twice portrayed as promising Adam, "I will make you a god." Christ's birth, death, and resurrection are for the sake of Adam's deification.

The third section of the *Testament* is an explanation of the hierarchy of "the heavenly powers" and their functions. The angels watch over humans; the archangels direct the rest of creation. The weather is controlled by archons, the heavenly bodies by authorities, and the demons by powers. Earthly kingdoms and military conquests are governed by dominions. The thrones, seraphim, and cherubim serve in the heavenly throne chamber. This list seems to have influenced medieval angelologies.

See also TESTAMENTS, APOCRYPHAL.

Bibliography. S.E. Robinson, "Testament of Adam," *The Old Testament Pseudepigrapha,* ed. J. H. Charlesworth.

—SHARYN E. DOWD

• **Adonijah.** [ad'uh-ni″juh] Hebrew, "Yah is my lord," son of DAVID and Haggith, born at HEBRON. After the death of ABSALOM Adonijah was in line to succeed his father as king of Israel. With popular support and the backing of the military commander JOAB and the priest ABIATHAR, Adonijah set himself up as monarch in the latter days of David's reign (1 Kgs 1:5-10). David's favorite wife BATHSHEBA, however, intended that her son SOLOMON become king. Supported by the captain of the guard BENAIAH, the priest ZADOK, and the prophet NATHAN, she gained the blessing of David and installed her son as king. Solomon spared Adonijah's life until he requested Abishag, David's concubine, as wife (1 Kgs 2:13-25). Such action Solomon took as tantamount to treason and had Adonijah killed.

See also DAVID; SOLOMON; SUCCESSION NARRATIVE.

—DAVID H. HART

• **Adoption.** Adoption is the act of voluntarily taking a child of other parents as one's child. In a theological sense, it is the act of God's grace by which sinful people are made members of his redeemed FAMILY.

The term adoption does not appear in the OT. There were no provisions for adoption in Israelite law, and the examples which do occur came from outside Israelite culture (Eliezer, Gen 15:1-4; Moses, Exod 2:10; Genubath, 1 Kgs 11:20; Esth 2:7, 15). The Nuzi Tablets have thrown some light on a semitic form of adoption. At Nuzi it was the custom for a childless couple to adopt a son who should serve them while they lived and bury them when they died. The adopted son would receive in return the inheritance; however, a son born after the adoption became the chief heir.

The germ of the use of the term in a religious sense may be present in the OT description of Israel as a son of God (Exod 4:22), and the focus of this relationship in the king as representative of his people (2 Sam 7:14; 1 Chr 28:6; Ps 2:7). Paul speaks of his kinspeople the Israelites, "to them belongs the sonship" (Rom 9:4; KJV "adoption").

In the NT the term "adoption" is strictly a Pauline idea, occurring in Rom 8:15,23; 9:4; Gal 4:5; and Eph 1:5. Paul was able to use the Greek word for adoption because both word and practice were familiar in the Greco-Roman world. Adoption is one of the many analogies employed to portray SALVATION. It stresses the family relationship in salvation, the free grace by which one is adopted into God's family, and the fact that one is not a child of God by nature.

Israel was God's son by adoption (Rom 9:4), chosen on the basis of God's free grace alone. Eph 1:5 states that our adoption was planned from eternity and mediated through Christ.

Believers also have privileges belonging to salvation which grow out of the Father's grace. Believers are not slaves living in fear, but adopted children living in security

(Rom 8:15). They are "heirs of God and fellow heirs with Christ" (Rom 8:17; cf. Gal 4:6-7).

The four "moments" of adoption, then, can be seen as (1) determined by God before creation on the basis of His grace alone (Rom 8:29; Eph 1:4-5), (2) made possible by the sending of the Son (Gal 4:5), (3) actually received when by faith one is brought into a vital union with Christ (Gal 3: 26-29), and (4) completed in the redemption of the body (Rom 8:23).

See also ABBA; ELECTION; FAMILY; SALVATION IN THE NEW TESTAMENT; SALVATION IN THE OLD TESTAMENT; SLAVERY IN THE NEW TESTAMENT; SLAVERY IN THE OLD TESTAMENT.

Bibliography. F. Stagg, *New Testament Theology*.

—J. A. REYNOLDS

• **Adorn/Adornment.** *See* DRESS

• **Adramyttium.** [ad'ruh-mit''ee-uhm] Adramyttium was a port city in Mysia in the northwest part of the Roman province of ASIA (PLATE 20). Luke, in keeping with his keen interest in Paul's travels, tells us that the ship which was to take Paul from Caesarea on the way to Rome was a ship of the fleet of Adramyttium (Acts 27:2).

Adramyttium is recognized in Herodotus, Strabo, and Plutarch as the home of the orator Xenocles, with whom Cicero studied. Luke must have thought it noteworthy that Paul would set out for Rome in a ship of this distinguished city. The ship of Adramyttium was to take Paul and his company as far as Myra in Lycia, where they got aboard a ship of Alexandria "sailing for Italy" (Acts 27:6).

See also ASIA.

—WILLIAM H. GEREN

• **Adullam.** *See* DAVID

• **Adultery in the New Testament.** The primary meaning of "adultery" in the NT is a breach in MARRIAGE unity caused specifically by sexual intercourse with someone other than one's spouse or generally by sexual infidelity in thought, word, or deed. "Adultery" is used figuratively to refer to religious infidelity (Matt 12:39; 16:4; Mark 8:38; Rev 2:18-23).

The Gospel writers explicate four teachings of Jesus concerning adultery. First, Jesus modifies the male-centered view in the OT which equates adultery with sexual intercourse between a man and another man's wife or between a married woman and any man (hence, an emphasis on the infidelity of a married woman). In the teaching on DIVORCE (Matt 5:32; 19:9; Mark 10:11-12; Luke 16:18), Jesus specifies several instances which establish adultery as a sin by either spouse: marriage between a divorced man and a woman (Matt, Mark, Luke); marriage between a man and divorced woman (Matt, Luke); marriage between a woman who divorces her husband and a man (Mark); and a husband who divorces his wife thereby making her an adulteress, presumably because she will remarry (Matt). In Matthew only, divorce caused by unchastity does not involve adultery upon REMARRIAGE of the innocent party. Jesus thus revolutionizes the concept of adultery by binding husbands to wives as wives were bound to husbands by the OT. Mutuality, equality, and faithfulness define marriage. Adultery represents a breach of such, and is a sin against someone as well as with someone. Second, while not setting aside the commandment to abstain from the deed of adultery (Matt 19:16-21; Mark 10:17-22; Luke 18:18-24; John 8:1-11), Jesus deepens the meaning of adultery to include intentions. To lust is to commit adultery in the heart or will (Matt 5:28; cf. Mark 7:18-23 and Matt 15:19). To lust is neither to glance occasionally and appreciatively at the opposite sex nor to entertain a momentary desire. Lust refers to a state of inordinate desire, voluntarily chosen, which reduces persons to things. Third, Jesus taught (Mark 10:2-12; Matt 19:3-9) that Deut 24:1-4 was permissive legislation about divorce. Marriage has a real and moral basis in human nature and in the relation of sexuality to God's purpose of a life-long union: "What therefore God has joined together, let not man put asunder" (Mark 10:9). Any breach of marriage is a rejection of divine intention and marriage sanctity. Fourth, while not condoning adultery, Jesus offers forgiveness to an adulterous woman (John 8:1-11), and thereby rejects the OT death penalty for adultery (Lev 20:10; Deut 22:22).

Paul affirms that adultery merits God's judgment (1 Cor 5:9; Gal 5:19); holds that marriage after divorce is adultery, but after the death of a spouse is not (Rom 7:1-3; 1 Cor 7:39-40); and grounds the motivation to refrain from adultery in the positive command to love (Rom 13:9). He also counsels Christians not to withdraw from "the immoral of this world" but to deal decisively with sexual immorality within the Christian community (1 Cor 5:1-12). He relates the basis of adultery to a violation of marital unity and conjugal rights of the body as the temple of the Holy Spirit, and of participation "in Christ" (1 Cor 6:15-20; 7:3-4).

Other NT letters state God's judgment of adultery (Heb 13:4; Jas 2:11; 4:4; 2 Pet 2:9-15) and speak of his forgiveness (Jas 4:6-8).

See also ADULTERY IN THE OLD TESTAMENT; DIVORCE; FAMILY; FORNICATION; MARRIAGE IN THE NEW TESTAMENT; REMARRIAGE; WOMAN TAKEN IN ADULTERY.

Bibliography. O. Piper, *The Biblical View of Sex and Marriage*; H. Thielicke, *The Ethics of Sex*; G. J. Wehnam, "Gospel Definitions of Adultery and Women's Rights," *ExpTim* 95 (1984): 30-32.

—FRANK LOUIS MAULDIN

• **Adultery in the Old Testament.** The seventh commandment (Exod 20:14; Deut 5:18) prohibits adultery, a note often repeated in the OT (cf. Prov 2:16-19; Jer 5:9; 29:23; Hos 4:2). The term referred to sexual intercourse by a married person, male or female, with a person other than one's spouse. It is to be distinguished from FORNICATION, sexual activity outside of marriage often called "playing the HARLOT" (cf. Deut 22:21; Hos 4:13-14). Apparently neither polygamy nor concubinage was thought of as a violation of the proscription against adultery, though both seem largely confined to the patriarchal period and the monarchs.

Although adultery could be rationalized (Prov 30:20), it was regarded as a capital offense (cf. especially Lev 20:10-21), administered by stoning (Deut 22:23-24). In the event a woman was accused by her husband, who had no proof, she could be forced to undergo a trial by ordeal. She would drink a solution that was supposed to cause the stomach of an adulteress to bloat and her leg to rot (Num 5:11-31). Concern over adultery was prompted first because of the moral and personal dimensions involved (note the expression "to know" for intercourse). Perhaps another reason was that adultery struck at the economic basis of arranged marriages, which were often accompanied by exchanges of property benefiting the bride's family or the husband. This economic basis is very clear in the law of seduction. If a man seduced a VIRGIN and thereby reduced her chances of marrying, he was required to pay a price of fifty shekels of silver and marry her with no prospect of divorce (Deut 22:28-29).

Additionally, the term adultery could be used figuratively to designate IDOLATRY (cf. Jer 3:8-9; 5:7-8; 23:24). The use of the term adultery perhaps arose because the particular form idolatry took in ancient Israel often involved fertility worship.

See also FAMILY; FORNICATION; IDOLATRY; MARRIAGE.

Bibliography. F. Hauck, "μοιχεύω, κτλ.," *TDNT*.

—PAUL L. REDDITT

• **Adversary.** *See* SATAN IN THE NEW TESTAMENT

• **Advocate/Paraclete.** [pair'uh-kleet] JESUS or the HOLY SPIRIT is referred to several times in the Johannine writings (once in 1 John and four times in the Gospel of John), as "the paraclete," a Greek term meaning "advocate," "helper," or COUNSELOR. The term occurs in one of the fullest descriptions of the nature and function of the Holy Spirit and is therefore more important than its limited use would suggest.

If John was the last gospel written, as was suggested early by Clement of Alexandria (150–215 C.E.), then it is not surprising to find there a fuller expression of the nature of the spirit than was usually present in the OT or the synoptic Gospels (including Acts). In the Gospel and Letters of John, the spirit is described as being sent from the father to be in and with believers, teaching them, and reminding them of Jesus' words and deeds (John 14:15-26). The paraclete is identified with Christ (1 John 2:1) and with the spirit (John 14:26), is said to proceed from the father as "the spirit of truth," and will guide Christians to the truth (John 15:26; 16:13). Though the NT does not explicitly define the relations among the persons of the TRINITY, these passages directly imply the fundamental belief that after his death and resurrection, Christ's continuing presence in the community is through the Holy Spirit (John 14:25-26; 15:26-27).

Outside the NT, paraclete is used with the sense of a "mediator," a "counselor" or "comforter," or one who pleads for someone else as a helper. The idea expressed in the word is sometimes said to originate in Gnostic beliefs in heavenly messengers or "helpers," but the primary source of the NT idea is probably the frequent OT pattern of humans or angels acting as advocates for others before God (Abraham: Gen 18:23-33; Moses: Exod 32:11 et al.; Samuel: 1 Sam 7:8 et al.; Job 33:23; Zech 1:12 et al.). In intertestamental writings, this advocacy is extended to the Spirit of God, who acts before God's judgment seat to defend believers and condemn sinners.

While continuing these earlier patterns, the Johannine paraclete transforms them by relating this advocate to Jesus Christ. When Jesus is no longer physically present, the paraclete will bear witness to Christ and to the father, judging the world and declaring "the things that are to come" (John 15:26; 16:15). The paraclete thus combines functions of prophet, teacher, and judge with that of sustaining the community of faith by dwelling in its members as the spirit of God (John 14:16-20).

Many translations of the NT simply use "paraclete," the English form of the Greek word. "Helper," "supporter," or "counselor" are appropriate English translations, but "comforter," while a popular rendering in later Christian history, is a less accurate version of the NT Greek.

See also COUNSELOR; HOLY SPIRIT; JESUS; JOHN, GOSPEL AND LETTERS OF; TRINITY.

Bibliography. R. E. Brown, "The Paraclete in the Fourth Gospel," *NTS* 13 (1966/67): 113-32; G. Johnston, *The Spirit-Paraclete in the Gospel of John.*

—DAVID W. RUTLEDGE

• **Aelia Capitolina.** *See* JERUSALEM

• **Aeneas.** [i-nee'uhs] Aeneas was a resident of Lydda (some ten mi. southeast of Joppa), who was cured of his paralysis by PETER, as recorded in Acts 9:32-35. The unfortunate Aeneas was paralyzed and bedridden for eight years, until Peter came and said, "Aeneas, Jesus Christ heals you; rise and make your bed" (Acts 9:34). As a result of this divine work, the people of the region "turned to the Lord" (Acts 9:35).

—WILLIAM H. GEREN

• **Agabus.** [ag'uh-buhs] Agabus was a Christian prophet from Judea whose prophecies were fulfilled, but not in precise detail. Acts 11:27-28 indicates that he traveled from Jerusalem to Antioch and there predicted that a great famine would soon strike all the inhabited world. Luke and the Roman historian Suetonius confirm that a famine or a series of droughts occurred during Claudius' reign, and Josephus mentions a severe famine in Judea ca. 47 C.E. Yet there is no evidence of a worldwide famine.

Later, Agabus warned Paul that he would be bound by Jews and delivered to gentiles if he went to Jerusalem (Acts 21:10-11). Paul did go to Jerusalem and was seized by the Jews, but rather than being delivered to the gentiles he was rescued by Romans from the Jewish crowd.

See also PROPHECY.

—MARK J. OLSON

• **Agape.** *See* LOVE IN THE NEW TESTAMENT

• **Agora.** *See* MARKET/MARKETPLACE

• **Agrapha.** [ag'ruh-fuh] Agrapha is a technical term designating sayings of Jesus which are not found in the canonical Gospels. The term, a Greek word meaning "unwritten things," was applied in the eighteenth century when it was supposed there was an original gospel from which all the sayings of Jesus derived. The collection of these non-canonical sayings, it was thought, would help to "restore" the original. Such a view is no longer held, but the term agrapha has been retained.

The final verse of the GOSPEL OF JOHN says: "But there are also many other things which Jesus did; were every one of them to be written, I suppose the world itself could not contain the books that would be written" (John 21:25). The same apparently could apply to the things Jesus *said.* The study of the Gospels has demonstrated a period of oral tradition preceding the writing of these gospels. Other writings may have used oral traditions not included in the canonical gospels, particularly sayings of Jesus, which were viewed with special authority by the Christian communities.

An early attempt to collect the sayings of Jesus was made by Papias, who wrote a five volume work called *Expositions of the Oracles of the Lord* (ca. 130 C.E.). Unfortunately this work has not survived, but was known to Eusebius of Caesarea (*EccHist* 3.39.1).

The monumental task of collecting all the known noncanonical sayings of Jesus was accomplished in modern times by Alfred Resch in his *Agrapha: Aussercanonische Schriftfragmente* (1889, 2nd ed. 1906), where he lists 361 agrapha. Resch's work was critically refined by J. H. Ropes, *Die Sprüche Jesu* (1896), in which he established criteria for sifting Resch's materials, ending up with twenty-seven sayings which were "valuable." In more recent times Joachim Jeremias, in his *Unknown Sayings of Jesus* (English 1958), has provided a convenient summary of the investigation and an exposition of twenty-one sayings which Jeremias feels "has the same claim to historicity as the sayings in our four Gospels" (33). The historian is not limited by the CANON when seeking materials relating to Jesus; however, it is often discovered that the non-canonical sayings are derivative from the Gospel sayings, or prove to be modified sayings fostering particular theological positions. But not all are like this. Some accord well with what Jesus said, or might have said. The historian, or one working as such, needs to establish criteria for the authenticity of any of Jesus' sayings, whether in the canon or not. Such are not easily formulated.

The sources in which agrapha are found are: (1) the NT other than the four Gospels; (2) the Greek manuscript tradition, particularly the "Western" text type; (3) the church fathers, including their quotations of APOCRYPHAL GOSPELS; (4) the Talmud, the repository of Jewish oral traditions; (5) Greek and Coptic papyri; (6) Islamic traditions dating from the eighth century and later.

The NT contains the following non-gospel sayings of Jesus:

Acts 20.35—"It is more blessed to give than to receive."

Rom 14:14 (?)—"I know and am persuaded in the Lord Jesus that nothing is unclean in itself; but it is unclean for any one who thinks it unclean."

1 Cor 7:10—"To the married I give charge, not I but the Lord, that the wife should not separate from her husband."

1 Cor 9:14—"In the same way, the Lord commanded that those who proclaim the gospel should get their living by the gospel."

1 Cor 11:24-25—"This is my body which is for you. Do this in remembrance of me. . . . This cup is the new covenant in my blood. Do this, as often as you drink it, in remembrance of me."

1 Thess 4:15-16—"For this we declare to you by the word of the Lord, that we who are alive, who are left until the coming of the Lord, shall not precede those who have fallen asleep. . . . "

In the "Western" text type of the Greek manuscript tradition, particularly Codex Bezae (D), additional materials are often found, which textual critics usually value as later additions to the text. Consequently, these do not show up in translations of the Gospels. Agrapha are found in "Western" text manuscripts in three notable places: Luke 6:5—"On the same day he saw a man performing a work on the Sabbath. Then he said unto him: Man! If thou knowest what thou doest, thou art blessed. But if thou knowest not, thou art cursed and a transgressor of the Law" (Jeremias, 61); Luke 10:16—"He that heareth you heareth me; and he that rejecteth you rejecteth me; and he that rejecteth me rejecteth him that sent me; and he that heareth me heareth him that sent me" (Jeremias, pp. 5-6); Matt 20:28—"But ye, seek to increase from smallness and from the greater to become less" (Jeremias, p. 6).

From the church fathers come a variety of interesting agrapha, found in Justin Martyr, Theodotus, Tertullian, Clement of Alexandria, Origen, Jerome, and Augustine. These also include quotations from the apocryphal gospels and heretical sources.

The Talmudic agrapha are very few in number and tend to put Jesus and Christians in a bad light. However, an Aramaic form of Matt 5:17 is provided by *Šab* 116 a, b. The Islamic sources, while late, for the most part show that Jesus pointed the way to Muhammad, or was a great prophet.

The sayings in the Oxyrhynchus papyri, and the Coptic GOSPEL OF THOMAS are important sources for agrapha. The latter, a Greek document discovered in a Coptic version in 1946, is the largest single collection of sayings of Jesus—114 logia, many of which are variations on canonical Gospel sayings, perhaps supporting Gnostic understandings of Jesus. However, some of the sayings may be genuine; #82, for instance, "Whoever is near to me is near to the fire, and whoever is far from me is far from the Kingdom"; or #77, "Cleave a (piece of) wood, I am there; lift up the stone and you will find Me there" (Guillaumont, 45, 43).

See also GOSPEL FRAGMENTS, PAPYRI; THOMAS, GOSPEL OF.

Bibliography. F. F. Bruce, *Jesus and Christian Origins Outside the New Testament*; D. G. A. Calvert, "An Examination of the Criteria for Distinguishing the Authentic Words of Jesus," *NTS* 18 (1971): 209-10; A. Guillaumont et al., *The Gospel According to Thomas*; J. Jeremias, *Unknown Sayings of Jesus*; J. H. Ropes, "Agrapha," *HDBSupp*.

—GLENN A. KOCH

• **Agrarian.** *See* AGRICULTURE/FARMING

Depiction of Sennedjem plowing and his wife sowing seeds.

• **Agriculture/Farming.** Even from a cursory reading of the OT and NT, it becomes readily apparent that the world of agriculture was the preeminent way of life for the Israelite people. The Bible often directly mentions the agricultural process, and quite frequently draws from that realm in its use of metaphors to describe the people of God. Isa 5:1-7 describes a process of preparation of the land for the planting of a vineyard. The process in turn is used as a parable to reveal to the people that they are like the worthless grapes which resulted; "For the vineyard of the Lord of hosts is the house of Israel." From the NT, note that the words of Christ also demonstrate this use of agricultural metaphors: "the fields are already white unto harvest" (John 4:35).

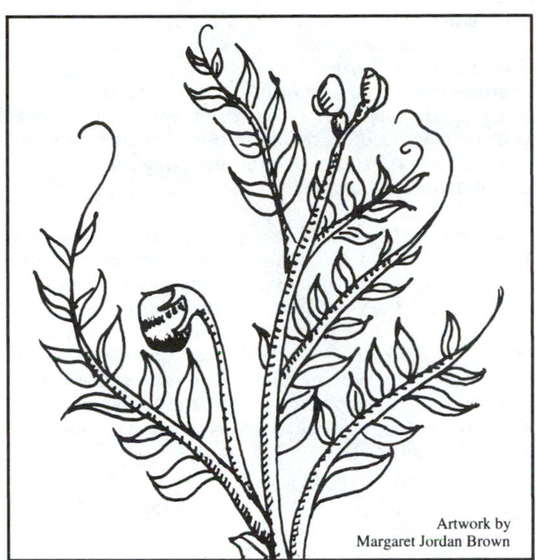

Lentil branch with seeds, a source of protein and carbohydrates.

It is known from early Canaanite times that agriculture and religion were closely associated. The Canaanite religion tended to be oriented around sympathetic magic in which the participants in worship acted out in a ritual what they desired the gods to do from the heavens. Thus they cried out to Baal, the lord of thunder and rain, and to Dagan, the lord of the grain, to accomplish the harvest. It is known from ancient texts that the worshipers would cut themselves in furrows with knives and allow the blood to drop on the ground in order to coerce the gods to bring forth the rain upon their crops. In stark contrast, the religion of Israel was ideologically far removed from this form of sympathetic magic. Yet, the people of God were very much aware that their God, Yahweh, was the giver of all good and abundant crops. Certainly, the land was the gift of God; it was a "land which the Lord your God cares for; the eyes of the Lord your God are always upon it, from the beginning of the year to the end of the year" (Deut 11:12). It was a land upon which God himself would provide the rain and the harvest (Deut 11:14). As such, many of the religious festivals such as the Feast of Weeks (commonly called Feast of First-fruits) were organized around the agricultural year to coincide with the harvests and other special events.

The land which spawned the nation of Israel is distinctly varied in agricultural soil and climate. Much of Israel is considerably littered with rock and stones; thus site preparation is toilsome. Indeed, there is actually very little farmland that would be considered worthy of cultivation. Nevertheless, farming was carried on with perseverance and ingenuity. In the hill country, where rapid erosion was a problem, terracing was adopted to maintain soil and moisture consistency. A system of crop rotation was developed: a fallow year was even stipulated by covenantal law (Lev 25:4). The plains and valleys were often the more fruitful of the lands, but even then there were problems to overcome. For example, in the plain of Sharon, the soil was of shifting red sand and was not capable of feasible agricultural work. Areas such as the valley of Jezreel, which was one portion of what is known as the "Great Plain," the area north of the Carmel mountain range, was a very productive agricultural area. This type of area, however, was limited. In the south, the Negeb desert was covered with a shallow top soil that could have produced crops, but this region was too arid. The farmer of ancient Israel would have to make use of what water was provided through natural rain and dew. The rains, however, mostly came in the winter months and were minimal in the summer months. Indeed, the summer months are particularly barren, thus water was collected and stored in cisterns, later to be used for irrigation. Therefore, when there was a winter with little rain, there was a much greater propensity for drought. The frequent heavy dew was utilized to its greatest extent as a necessity.

The primary growing season begins in October and continues until approximately the next April–May. It is with this cycle that the former and the latter rains are crucial. Planting would begin around the time of the first rains and would be staggered over an initial period of the growing season to increase the likelihood of crop preservation. Despite the unfortunate agricultural problems, the land of Israel is described as the land of milk and honey (Num 13:27), and today has regained some of that status with the Israeli land reclamation and utilization efforts.

In Deut 8:8 the biblical reader is given a partial indication of the crops of ancient Israel: "a land of wheat and barley, of vines and fig trees and pomegranates, a land of olive trees and honey." These words give an overview of what was grown in Israel. To this list certainly flax, lentils, coarse beans, peas, cucumbers, onions, and leeks would have to be added. From biblical texts it is apparent that GRAIN was the preeminent crop of ancient Israel. The designation of grain would include varieties of wheat, spelt, emmer, and barley. Corn as is known in modern times was not a part of the ancient agricultural scheme. References to the "vine" obviously indicate cultivation of grapes. Not only were grapes utilized in the making of wines, but apparently were dried into raisins as well. The olive tree was a hardy plant that could be cultivated and survive well in

Courtesy of the Eisenberg Museum of Biblical Archaeology, Southern Baptist Theological Seminary.

A grinding stone.

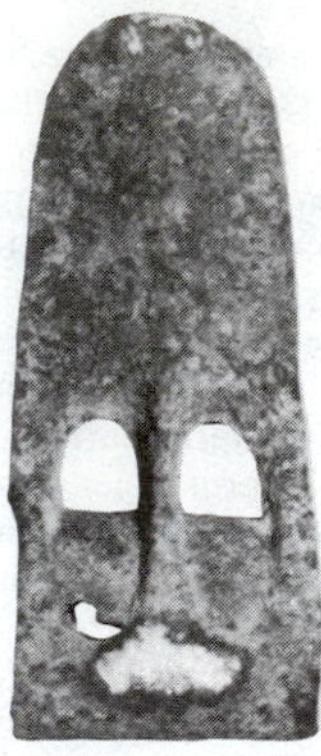

An axe head.

an environment such as Israel's. Olives were essential for oil as well as for practical food. Flax, though not completely natural to this environ, was nevertheless grown in parts of Israel and Syria. These crops represent the primary crops that were also commonly used for barter and trade. Israel was situated along important trade routes and thus was in an advantageous position even though resources were limited.

There was considerable development in the area of tools and farm implements. Even so, the implements were quite primitive. Initially, tools such as plows were comprised of soft metals that could hardly have been efficient. With the introduction of iron materials around 1000 B.C.E. the agricultural process was greatly enhanced. The plow was made of wood with a funneled iron point. The plow was pulled by oxen hooked to a yoke. At times donkeys were used to till the soil; however, Deut 22:10 stipulates that a donkey and an ox should not be yoked together. The yoke was typically made of wood and would be single or double poled depending upon the number of animals used to pull the plow. Once the soil was prepared, the seed was apparently sowed by hand. The long bladed sickle was the primary harvest tool; it was initially equipped with a flint blade which was later replaced by iron. The threshing floor, mentioned many times in the OT, was where the grain was separated from the stalk. The stalks would have been beaten by sticks or with some other instrument; in addition, livestock could have been driven across the threshing floor. The grain was winnowed by casting it into the air so that the loose grain could be separated from plant stalks. A shovel or pronged instrument was most likely used. The grain was then run through a sieve as a last effort to cull the ruffage. The grain would then have been stored in storage pits, silos, or in jars.

See also GRAIN.

—MARK W. GREGORY

• **Agrippa I and II.** [uh-grip'uh] The last members of the family of HEROD the Great to exercise significant Roman governmental authority.

Agrippa I, a grandson of Herod the Great, was born about 10 B.C.E. After his father's (ARISTOBULUS) death, his mother (Bernice) took him to Rome where he was educated, met important people, and developed a taste for luxury. Soon after Caligula became emperor (37 C.E.), Agrippa was given the title "king" and was assigned territory in Syria. Later the emperor added the area previously ruled by Herod Antipas.

Claudius (41 C.E.) succeeded Caligula, and Agrippa's favored position continued. To his holdings, the emperor added Judea and Samaria. Until his death (44 C.E.), Agrippa controlled lands equal to those held by his grandfather Herod the Great. He supported Judaism and took action against the church by executing JAMES and arresting Simon PETER (cf. Acts 12:1-4). Agrippa died an agonizing death after receiving divine acclamation (cf. Acts 12:20-23; Josephus, *Ant* 19.8.2).

Agrippa II (Marcus Julius Agrippa) was the only male child who survived Agrippa I. Because he was a minor, Claudius did not confirm him in his father's title. In 50 C.E. and again in 53 he was assigned small territories earlier governed by relatives. When Nero ascended to the throne (54 C.E.), Agrippa II also received part of the area previously overseen by Herod Antipas. He tried to create peace, but in the end he supported Rome in the Jewish rebellion of 66–70 C.E. His response to Paul's situation is a fair presentation of his position.

See also ARISTOBULUS; HEROD.

—ROBERT O. BYRD

• **Ahab.** [ay'hab] Son of OMRI and king of the Northern Kingdom, ca. 869–850 B.C.E. The biblical account of Ahab's reign is in 1 Kgs 16:29–22:40, a combination of stories woven into a narrative dominated by the struggle between Ahab's wife, Jezebel, and the prophet ELIJAH.

Ahab was married to the Phoenician princess JEZEBEL, a political arrangement that provided ISRAEL with considerable economic advantage by opening Phoenician ports for trade with all areas of the Mediterranean. However, the biblical narrative is focused upon the religious problems that Jezebel brought to the land. As an enthusiastic, even fanatical, missionary for her native religion, she vigorously promoted the worship of Baal-Melqart in overt violation of prophetic tradition represented by Elijah. And this occurs under Ahab's sponsorship! The narrative reaches a climax by describing a contest on Mount Carmel with Elijah pitted against 450 prophets of BAAL (1 Kgs 18:17-40). With high drama, and not a little humor, Jezebel's gods are shown to be no gods at all.

Jezebel is also the villain in an episode about NABOTH's vineyard (1 Kgs 21). Naboth refused to surrender a family vineyard the king wanted, a right protected by Israel's COVENANT tradition. Ahab pouted but understood that the king, like all Hebrews, was bound by covenant. Not so Jezebel. She, believing that the king's wish was above law, arranged Naboth's death and confiscated the vineyard for Ahab. For the biblical narrator, Ahab is no less guilty than Jezebel; from the historian's point of view Ahab is clearly among the worst of the Northern kings.

The negative slant of the biblical story hides the genuine ability of Ahab. His reign of two decades was marked by internal progress in spite of continuing military struggles. In 1 Kgs 22:39 reference is made to "all the cities that he built," but only specific constructions at JERICHO (1 Kgs 16:33-34), probably fortifications for military operations against MOAB, are mentioned. But archeology suggests construction projects at SAMARIA, MEGIDDO, and in TRANSJORDAN. Evidently prosperity typical of Omri's reign continued into his son's tenure, enhanced by favorable relations with PHOENICIA.

Also Ahab was a military leader of some stature. Biblical and other Eastern sources do not permit reconstructing the details, but clearly Ahab was able to hold his own in military engagements with Aram or Assyria and occasionally led in organizing sizeable coalitions in the struggle. During most of Ahab's reign, Israel and Aram under BEN-HADAD were at war. The materials in 1 Kgs 20 reflect these encounters and depict Israel as the stronger of the two kingdoms. Eventually, however, affairs in the East, marked by the increasing power of ASSYRIA, forced Israel and Aram, along with other smaller states, into a confederacy against Assyria. The significant encounter between Assyria and the coalition occurred at Karkar (Qarqar) on the Orontes River in 853 B.C.E. Although the biblical materials are silent on the battle, it is described in the Annals of SHALMANESER III of Assyria. The inscription notes the presence of "Ahab the Israelite" who contributed "two thousand chariots, ten thousand men," thus suggesting that Ahab was a leader in the coalition and indicating that the number of Israel's chariots was the largest among the confederates. The reference not only validates Ahab's military prowess among the western states, but also provides a significant date for calculating OT chronology.

Respite from struggles with Assyria again placed Israel and Aram at odds. The prize was Ramoth-Gilead, a border town between the two kingdoms. In spite of alliance with JEHOSHAPHAT of Judah and reassurance from court prophets, Ahab was killed in the battle, as MICAIAH the prophet had predicted, bringing to an end a period that the biblical materials view as one of Israel's darkest times.

Another Ahab was a false prophet during the Babylonian exile, condemned by Jeremiah (Jer 29:21-22).

See also BAAL; ELIJAH; JEZEBEL; KINGSHIP.

—ROBERT W. CRAPPS

• **Ahasuerus.** *See* ESTHER, BOOK OF

• **Ahaz.** [ay'haz] King of Judah and son of Jotham, Ahaz was twenty years old when he began to reign. He ruled sixteen years over Judah (2 Kgs 16:2; 2 Chr 18:1). The end of his reign is fixed by the accession of his son, HEZEKIAH, ca. 716 B.C.E. This would make his accession ca. 732 B.C.E. However, Assyrian inscriptions indicate that he was ruling ca. 734 B.C.E. He was also clearly on the throne by the Syro-Ephraimitic crisis in ca. 735 B.C.E. Thiele has suggested that he had a co-regency with his father, making all data correlate, and making his actual reign to be ca. 735 B.C.E. to ca. 716 B.C.E.

His name means "he has seized." It appears to have been a contraction of Jehoahaz, "Yahweh has seized." If that name expressed the faith or hope of his parents, it was sadly misplaced, for Ahaz was anything but securely in the hand of God (2 Kgs 16:10-18). His mother's name is not given, unusual for the identification formula of a king of Judah.

Politically, Ahaz was threatened by PEKAH of Israel in coalition with Syria (Aram) in the Syro-Ephraimitic crisis of 735 B.C.E. (Isa 7:3-12). They sought to force Ahaz to join with them in an attack against Assyria. If that failed, they planned to replace him on Judah's throne with one "son of Tabeel." Attempting to avoid this, Ahaz sent tribute to TIGLATH-PILESER III of Assyria, pleading for deliverance. ISAIAH advised against this, but Ahaz was already committed. This act brought his nation under the long-term suzerainty of Assyria.

Religiously, Ahaz imported the worship of foreign gods, especially the gods of ASSYRIA. He also practiced child-sacrifice. Thoroughly disapproved, he was apparently buried in the royal cemetery, but later exhumed and buried elsewhere (2 Kgs 16:20; 2 Chr 28:27).

See also ISAIAH.

—ROBERT L. CATE

• **Ahijah.** [uh-hi'juh] A prophet from Shiloh. Ahijah announced the imminent division of the United Kingdom and designated JEROBOAM the son of Nebat as Yahweh's choice to be king over the ten tribes of Israel (1 Kgs 11:29-39). Later, Ahijah announced that YHWH's judgment on Jeroboam would result in the end of his "house" (dynasty) (1 Kgs 14:7-16; cf. 1 Kgs 15:29-30).

Ahijah is also the name of a son of Ehud (1 Chr 8:7); a son of Jerahmeel (1 Chr 2:25); a priest from Shiloh associated with SAUL (1 Sam 14:18-19); one of DAVID's elite warriors (1 Chr 11:36); a Levite in charge of the temple treasuries under David (1 Chr 26:20); a scribe under SOLOMON (1 Kgs 4:3); the father of Baasha, king of Israel (1 Kgs 15:27); and one of the "chiefs of the people" in the time of Nehemiah (Neh 10:26).

—JEFFREY S. ROGERS

• **Ahinoam.** *See* ABIGAIL

• **Ahiqar.** [uh-hi'kahr] A wise and learned official in the court of the Assyrian kings SENNACHERIB and ESARHADDON, according to the surviving traditions preserved in many languages. Ahiqar is mentioned in the book of TOBIT (1:21-22), where he is identified as Tobit's nephew, and therefore from the tribe of Naphtali. But the narrative and sayings of Ahiqar may not be Jewish in origin. The narrative may have originated in the court of the Assyrian kings, while the sayings or proverbs may have their origin in northern Syria.

The Narrative. The story of Ahiqar in its basic form appears in an ARAMAIC papyrus manuscript found at Elephantine, an island in the Nile in upper EGYPT near the Aswan Dam, in the ruins of a Jewish settlement of the fifth century B.C.E. The story may be summarized as follows:

Ahiqar attained great fame in the court of Sennacherib as a wise and skillful counselor. He continued his service under Sennacherib's son Esarhaddon, arranging that his own nephew Nadan or Nadin, whom he had adopted as his son, should succeed him as counselor to the king. With the king's authorization, Nadan did succeed Ahiqar, but before long he had turned against his uncle, denounced him as a traitor to the state, leading Esarhaddon to order Ahiqar's execution.

Ahiqar, however, was spared by the official sent to kill him. A slave was executed in his place and Ahiqar was hidden away [the Aramaic text breaks off at this point, but the story surely continued, since it is known in many later versions. A portion of these later stories follows].

Some time later, Esarhaddon faced great danger. The king of Egypt demanded that he come to Egypt and arrange for the building of a palace between heaven and earth. The king recognized that the demand for him to accomplish this impossible task was only a ruse to create an occasion for the Egyptian king to go to war against him (cf. 2 Kgs 5:5-7). He lamented the loss of his great adviser Ahiqar. Then he was told that Ahiqar had not in fact been put to death, but was safe. Ahiqar was brought quickly before the king, restored to honor, and given the task of responding to the king of Egypt.

He trained eagles to fly in a circle carrying a large basket, trained young boys to ride in the basket, and gave them their instructions. Then, in Egypt, he sent the eagles and the young boys aloft. They circled over the crowds and the boys cried out to the workers below, "Send up the bricks!

We are ready to build!'' Ahiqar had saved the day for his king.

On Ahiqar's return he had his evil nephew arrested, put in chains, and beaten. Then he reproached him at great length, at the end of which Nadan swelled up and died.

The Sayings. There is a large collection of sayings preserved in the Aramaic manuscript from Elephantine, sayings that have similarities with other ancient Near Eastern collections, including those in the OT. They are not, however, a direct part of Israelite WISDOM LITERATURE, as can be seen from the references to the west semitic deities in the sayings.

Significance. The book of *Ahiqar* is the oldest surviving part of the literature associated with the OT APOCRYPHA and Pseudepigrapha, in all probability dating to the end of the seventh or the early sixth century B.C.E. It shows how ancient Israel was able to take over narratives, sayings, motifs, and traditions from the religious world within which it flourished, put them to the service of its own religious faith, and also share them with the surrounding nations and peoples in their new dress. Ahiqar's experiences with his nephew offer another fine example of how greed and ambition can tempt one to turn against one's faith and family teaching. Ahiqar's restoration also discloses that a righteous life eventually brings reward to the faithful, even though the reward may come only after great trials and perils. This theme is well illustrated in other late Jewish texts such as the books of ESTHER and DANIEL.

Bibliography. J. R. Harris, F. C. Conybeare and A. S. Lewis, *The Story of Ahikar;* J. M. Lindenberger, ''Ahiqar,'' *The Old Testament Pseudepigrapha,* ed. J. H. Charlesworth.

—WALTER HARRELSON

• **Ai.** [*i*] Ai, along with JERICHO and HAZOR, was one of three cities destroyed by the Hebrews during their conquest of Canaan. According to Josh 7:1–8:29, the victory over this town, which followed immediately Israel's destruction of Jericho, was won with trickery after some difficulty. The initial attack on Ai failed because Achan kept loot from Jericho, all of which had been devoted to the Lord. After Achan was executed, a second attack on Ai was made, the Hebrews ambushed its Canaanite defenders, the city was put to the torch, and the entire population of Ai was slaughtered.

In Josh 8:28, the Hebrew historian noted that JOSHUA burned Ai ''and made it for ever a heap of ruins, as it is to this day,'' i.e., it was in ruins when the Book of Joshua was written. Here, the result of the Hebrew invasion was the transformation of a prosperous Canaanite settlement into ''a heap of ruins forever'' (Hebrew *tel 'olam*). This last phrase is, for all practical purposes, a description of an archaeological site, and the attempt to harmonize the detailed biblical account of Ai's destruction with the available archaeological data is, at best, problematic or, according to some scholars, impossible. Though the identification of biblical Ai with the archaeological site of et-Tell (Arabic of ''heap'' or ''mound'') is still disputed by a few scholars, the connection was made by nearly everyone at the beginning of this century, and it remains the majority opinion to this day.

According to Josh 7:2, Ai is ''near Beth-aven, east of BETHEL'' (cf. Gen 12:8; 13:3); the physical proximity between Bethel and Ai is also reflected in texts from a later period (Ezra 2:28; Neh 7:32; 11:31). Since Bethel has been linked with confidence to the Arab village of Beitin in central Palestine, Ai has been identified with et-Tell, which is located about two mi. southeast of Beitin and ca. nine mi. north-northeast of Jerusalem (PLATE 3). While the topographical evidence in the Bible, according to the analysis of patristic and modern scholars, points to this identification, the archaeological evidence does not confirm this conclusion.

Archaeological investigations at et-Tell have been conducted by John Garstang (soundings in 1928), Judith Marquet-Krause (excavations from 1933–1935), S. Yeivin (excavations in 1936), and Joseph Callaway (major excavations from 1964–1972). By all standards, the excavations at et-Tell have been thorough. Callaway's work is highly respected and has led to several major publications; his fieldwork at et-Tell included excavations at several other sites in this same region, an effort to consider other candidates for identification with Ai. Unfortunately, the archaeological evidence from et-Tell is mainly negative, since the site does not appear to have been occupied during the Late Bronze Age (ca. 1500–1200 B.C.E.). More specifically, et-Tell was the location of a significant walled town (of some twenty-seven acres) from ca. 3000–2400 B.C.E., but it was not reoccupied again until ca. 1200 B.C.E. This Iron Age I settlement, which survived for about a century and a half, covered only ca. two and one-half acres and was unwalled.

Thus, there was no Canaanite occupation, and certainly no walled city, at et-Tell during the historical period in which most scholars place the Hebrew conquest. This serious conflict between the archaeological and textual evidence relating to Ai has been solved by scholars in one of four ways: (1) deny the historical credibility of Josh 7–8 and view the biblical text as a legend that explained the presence of a ''heap of ruins'' at et-Tell; (2) change the biblical account in some way so that the contradiction between text and archaeological data can be eliminated; (3) locate Ai at an archaeological site other than et-Tell; or (4) suspend judgment on this problem in the belief that more evidence is forthcoming.

—GERALD L. MATTINGLY

• **Akeldama.** [uh-kel'duh-muh] Akeldama is an Aramaic word meaning ''field of blood.'' According to Acts 1:18-19, JUDAS, after purchasing a plot with his reward for having betrayed Jesus, fell headlong on the plot, his bowels gushing out. The plot is alleged to have been called Field of Blood thereafter by the inhabitants of Jerusalem. The narrator of Acts sees the tragic end of Judas as exemplifying the curse of Pss 69:25 and 109:8. By contrast, Matt 27:3-10 claims that Judas not only returned the silver earned by betraying Jesus, but hanged himself. The chief priest then used the blood money to purchase potter's field, which came to be named Field of Blood. Matthew sees Judas's end as fulfillment of Jeremiah's prophecy. (But see Zech 11:12-13.) Because Matthew emphasizes Jesus' blood rather than Judas's he cannot present the field as the field of Judas's blood. Legend locates Akeldama south of Mount Zion at the Valley of Hinnom.

See also JUDAS.

—JOE E. BARNHART

• **Akhenaton.** [ahk'uh-nah"tuhn] Akhenaton was king of Egypt from 1377–1360 B.C.E. often named as history's first monotheist, he is best known for his exclusivistic worship of the Sun-disc (*Aton*) as the sole god. Not only did he limit his own piety to the worship of the Sun-disc as the only god, he enforced his exclusivistic faith on his subjects. Later

Egyptian tradition anathematized him and sought to erase every trace of his reign.

Succeeding his father Amenophis III (1416–1377 B.C.E.), Akhenaton took the throne of Egypt under the name of Amenophis IV. He ruled from the capital city of Thebes in Upper Egypt until the fifth year of his reign when he moved to a new capital in Middle Egypt which he built from scratch. His new capital, the famous Tell el-AMARNA, he called Akhetaton ("Horizon of the Sun-disc") (PLATE 8). At this time, he changed his name from Amenophis ("Amun is satisfied") to Akhenaton ("He who is useful to the Sun-disc"). This move also involved re-plastering his previous name in temple inscriptions and replacing it with his new name. It is probable that this was also the occasion for desecration of the name of Amun in all manner of inscriptions throughout Egypt.

Akhenaton's iconoclastic vandalism was requited. Horemheb (1347–1318 B.C.E.) returned the capital to Thebes, closed the temples of the Sun-disc, and dismantled his buildings, using the blocks as fill in new projects. Even before this, the exclusivistic worship of the Sun-disc had ceased in Egypt. Upon Akhenaton's death, his totalitarian cult continued for a time, but not as the only one in Egypt. The return to cultic toleration is most obvious in royal name changes: following the very brief reign by Smenkhare, Tutankh*aton* (1360–1350 B.C.E.) and his queen Ankhesen-pa*aton,* Akhenaton's daughter, changed their names to Tutankh*amun* and Ankhesenpa*amun*. Only time was needed before Akhenaton's monotheism fell by the wayside.

Prior to Akhenaton, the word *aton* had wide usage in Egyptian literature. It meant simply "disc"; it was quite natural to use the word to refer to that shining "disc" in the sky, the sun. Long before Akhenaton, the sun god Amun-Re had been called the one "who is in his disc." By the decades preceding Akhenaton, the icon of the sun-disc, although still a manifestation of the sun god, was becoming an independent title. Akhenaton's father, Amenophis III, was called "the Dazzling Sun-disc."

Akhenaton was heir to this tolerant Theban tradition. Apart from his initial throne name, the early iconography of Akhenaton's reign also evidences some cultic toleration. Akhenaton's god is portrayed as a falcon-headed man with a sun-disc on his head and a scepter in his hand. This links the Sun-disc with the traditional sun god Reharakhty. Soon this figure is replaced by the Sun-disc alone with straight lines ending in human hands, the only indication of anthropomorphism. Akhenaton's god must have been a sterile, passionless deity. Only Akhenaton himself, "the beautiful child of the Disc," could really claim any particular warmth for this god.

See also AMARNA; EGYPT; MONOTHEISM.

Bibliography. F. J. Giles, *Ikhnaton: Legend and History*; D. B. Redford, *Akhenaten, the Heretic King*.

—JOHN KEATING WILES

• **Alexander.** Alexander the Great, born in 356 B.C.E., the son of Philip of Macedon, came to the throne at age twenty when his father was assassinated in 336. After uniting the Greek city-states, Alexander began his conquest into the east in 334. Victories at Granicus (334) and Issus (333) brought him as far as Asia Minor. From there he moved into Syria and Palestine, conquered Egypt (331), defeated once and for all DARIUS III at Gaugamela (331), and advanced victoriously through Mesopotamia and the Persian Empire as far as the Indus River (326) in present day Pakistan.

When his troops refused to go farther, Alexander's dreams of the conquest of India were halted. He died from a fever in Babylon in 323 B.C.E. at age thirty-two after a prolonged drunken orgy marking the funeral feast in honor of a friend. After his death, a fierce squabble developed over who should rule, resulting in the rise of the Seleucids of Syria and the Ptolemies of Egypt. Palestine became a kind of political battleground between them.

References to Alexander are found in 1 Macc. 1:1-8 and 6:2. Some scholars also suggest veiled references in Dan 7; 8; and 11:3-4, with a possible allusion in Zech 9:1-8 to Alexander's conquest of Palestine.

Alexander's "one-world" concept perhaps reflected the influence of both his father Philip, who had envisioned Greek mastery of the Persian Empire, and his teacher Aristotle, who once said: "The Greeks might govern the world, could they but combine into one political system." His efforts gave a unity of language and culture to the world, which even the division of the kingdom at his death did not destroy, and became the foundation for the emergence of the ROMAN EMPIRE. This oneness of language led to the first translation of the OT into Greek (the LXX) and to the writing of the NT in the same language. During the first Christian century this common language and culture facilitated the spread of the gospel. Through his efforts, barriers between East and West were broken down. Although Alexander seems to have shown favor to the Jews (cf. Josephus, *Ant* 11.8.), attempts at further Hellenization after his death brought much heartbreak to the Jewish people.

A second Alexander was Alexander Balas (1 Macc 10:1–11:19; Josephus, *Ant* 13.3-4), king of Syria (150–146 B.C.E.). Although he is identified by both the writer of 1 Maccabees and JOSEPHUS as the son of Antiochus Epiphanes, this claim is now questioned by many scholars. Attempting to win the throne in opposition to Demetrius I, Alexander sought the favor of the Hasmoneans by nominating Jonathan, the brother of Judas Maccabeus, to be high priest in Jerusalem and honoring him in a special way. He was later defeated by Demetrius II.

Five others named Alexander are noted in the NT: the son of Simon of Cyrene (Mark 15:21) and brother of Rufus, who may have been known to the Christians in Rome (cf. Rom 16:13), a possible destination of Mark's Gospel; one of those who questioned PETER's preaching, possibly a member of the high-priestly family (Acts 4:6); a Jewish spokesman at EPHESUS (Acts 19:33); a man identified by PAUL as "delivered to Satan" along with Hymenaeus for their blasphemy (1 Tim 1:20); and a coppersmith mentioned as one who had done Paul "great harm" (2 Tim 4:14), believed by some to have been the Alexander of 1 Tim 1:20.

See also MACCABEES, FIRST.

Bibliography. "Alexander Balas," *EncJud*; W. F. Arndt and F. W. Gingrich, *A Greek-English Lexicon of the New Testament*; R. L. Fox, *Alexander the Great*; A. T. Olmstead, *History of the Persian Empire*; W. W. Tarn, *Alexander the Great*.

—G. BYRNS COLEMAN

• **Alexandria.** *See* EGYPT

• **Alien.** *See* SOJOURNER/RESIDENT ALIEN

• **Allegory.** Allegory strictly defined as an entire book of extended metaphor is not found in the OT. However, there are numerous cases of allegorical materials. The allegory of old age in Eccl 12:1-7 is the most noted.

The prophets' words contain numerous fragmentary allegories. HOSEA's story of his marriage and his wife's unfaithfulness is a familiar example. EZEKIEL is commanded (17:2) to "speak an allegory to the house of Israel"; eagles representing Babylonian kings follow. The "wood of the vine" (15:1-8) represents the inhabitants of Jerusalem, Yahweh's unfaithful wife (16:1-63) is Jerusalem. A lioness (19:1-9) and a vine (19:10-14) represent JUDAH; the caldron of 24:1-14 bespeaks JERUSALEM. Ezekiel's actions may be called allegorical: he uses a brick and an iron plate; he lies on his side, eats unclean and rationed food (Ezek 4), cuts his hair (5:1-17), digs through the city wall and escapes with "an exile's baggage" (12:7); he eats and drinks while trembling (12:18-19), all to signify aspects of the coming judgment. Ezekiel's famous story of the two harlots (23:1-49) is allegorical, as are the "eagles" and "cedar" (Messiah) of 17:2-24. Zechariah's metaphors of the shepherds (11:4-17; 13:7-9), like the book of Daniel's "statue" (chap. 2) and "beasts" (chaps. 7-8), seem allegorical.

Jotham's parable of trees and the bramble (Judg 9:7-15) is an allegory in historical narrative. The SONG OF SONGS has been read traditionally as an allegory of God's love for Israel (by rabbis), and of Christ's love for the soul (by early Christians) and for the church (by Protestants). Less frequently have interpreters seen JONAH as allegorical: Jonah ("dove") as symbolic of ISRAEL, and the fish of the EXILE.

See also PARABLES; PROPHET; SYMBOL.

—ROLLIN S. ARMOUR

• **Allogenes.** [a-loj'uh-neez] *Allogenes* is a non-Christian Gnostic work from the NAG HAMMADI library. Its title is a Greek word meaning "one from another race," "foreigner." In this text Allogenes is a Gnostic seer who receives a series of visions and then writes them down for his son (or disciple), Messos. The work can be classified as a revelation discourse, a genre of literature used often by Gnostics. It bears formal similarities to Jewish APOCALYPTIC LITERATURE.

The first part of the text contains revelations from a female deity, Youel, to Allogenes. These are complex descriptions of divine powers, all the more difficult to understand because of the damaged state of the text's first twelve pages. Part two narrates a journey in which Allogenes is guided by Luminaries through the three aeons that constitute the spiritual universe: Blessedness, Vitality, and Existence. Together they are called Triple Power or Triple Male and are self-contained within the Barbelo aeon. When Allogenes reaches the third and highest level, he sees the "First One," who is described by the Luminaries in a lengthy section of negative predicates, e.g. "He is neither divinity nor blessedness or perfection. . . . Rather he is another one better than the blessedness and the divinity and the perfect." Such negative theology expresses the gnostic belief in the radical transcendence and unknowability of God.

The threefold structure of the divine hierarchy through which Allogenes ascends in his heavenly tour corresponds to a three-stage process of mystical contemplation. The goal of both journeys—the outer one through the heavens and the inner one of the soul—is knowledge, knowledge of God and of oneself. Knowledge of self leads to knowledge of God because for the Gnostic the divine is within the self. Hence to know oneself is to know God and it is found by withdrawal to silence and rest. Allogenes says his revelation occurred after 100 years of meditation. Knowledge of self and God is not, however, a rational knowledge, but a personal acquaintance or recognition. Therefore, when Allogenes seeks rationally to comprehend the deity that has been revealed to him, he is told, "Do not know him, for it is impossible; but if by means of an enlightened thought you should know him, become ignorant of him."

The writing, *Allogenes,* exhibits strong similarities in content and terminology to several other Nag Hammadi tractates: *Marsanes, Zostrianos, Steles Seth,* and to a lesser extent, APOCRYPHON OF JOHN and TRIMORPHIC PROTENNOIA. These documents have been used, along with other evidence, to establish the existence of a branch of Gnosticism that revered the figure Seth. The name "Seth" does not occur in *Allogenes,* but it is reported that some Gnostics understood the epithet "Allogenes" to refer to Seth. In other Gnostic texts, Seth is described as being from another race, which fits with the meaning of the word *allogenes*.

The text also contains close parallels to the metaphysical world and language of Neoplatonism, especially the Mind, Life, Existence triad. Plotinus, a Neoplatonist, knew of and attacked a Gnostic book called *Allogenes.* This Nag Hammadi text thus testifies to the interaction of Gnosticism and Platonic philosophy in late antiquity. It is probably due to Neoplatonic influence that some forms of Gnosticism moved away from radical DUALISM to a more monistic understanding of reality as seen in Allogenes.

The place of composition of *Allogenes* is unknown. Its date must be before the late third century when Plotinus encountered it.

See also GNOSTICISM; NAG HAMMADI.

Bibliography. P. Perkins, *The Gnostic Dialogue: The Early Church and the Crisis of Gnosticism*; J. M. Robinson, "The Three Steles of Seth and the Gnostics of Plotinus," *Proceedings of the International Colloquium on Gnosticism,* ed. G. Widengren; J. Sieber, "The Barbelo Aeon as Sophia in Zostrianos and Related Tractates," *The Rediscovery of Gnosticism,* ed. B. Layton; A. C. Wire, J. D. Turner, and O. S. Wintermute, "Allogenes," *The Nag Hammadi Library in English,* ed. J. M. Robinson.

—CAROL D. C. HOWARD

• **Allusiveness.** *See* LITERATURE, BIBLE AS

• **Almond.** Heb. *šāqēd,* identified as the *Amygdalus communis,* the first tree to flower before the end of winter in Palestine. For that reason, the almond symbolized the onset or the hastening of certain events. Others know the almond as the wakeful tree, for its flowers were the first sign of spring. The almond's shape resembles the womb; accordingly in mythology and folklore of the world the almond frequently represents the feminine, and thus fertility.

In Eccl 12:5, the blossoms, mostly pink but sometimes white, become a metaphor alongside of others for the signs of old age. Gen 43:11 represents the almond as one of the choicest fruits one could present as a gift. Aaron's rod, described in Num 17:8 (Heb 17:23), budded, blossomed, and bore fruit overnight. This wonder accorded Aaron and his descendants the exclusive rights to the Hebrew priesthood. Aaron's staff and its special power became the magician's wand or divining rod of the Middle Ages.

The prophet Jeremiah, during his call, saw an almond rod or shoot and associated the name *šāqēd* with the designation *šōqēd,* "watcher": God was watching over Judah to bring judgment. Even so, it was *God* who watched over Judah, and thus the almond shoot could be understood in a positive way as well.

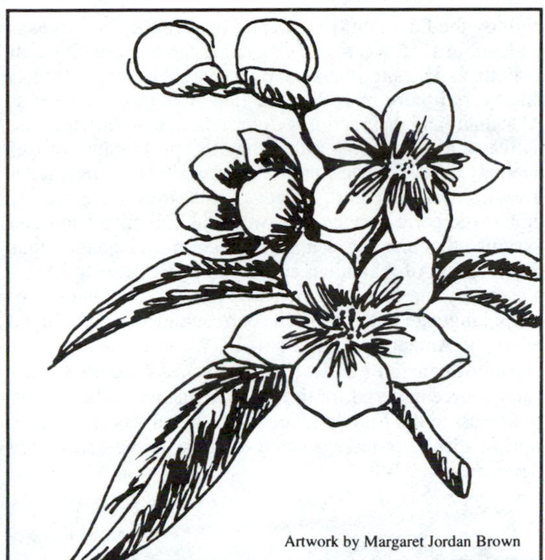
Artwork by Margaret Jordan Brown

A branch with almonds.

See also FOOD; SIGNS AND WONDERS; SYMBOL.

—RUSSELL I. GREGORY

• **Alms.** Voluntary acts of mercy or charity, designed to meet the needs of the poor. Although there is no specific term for alms in the OT, there are innumerable expressions of concern for those in need. There are numerous exhortations to respond liberally to the plight of the poor or dispossessed (Exod 23:10-11; Lev 19:9-10; Deut 24:19-22; Job 31:16-23; Ps 112:5, 9; Isa 58:6-12).

The apocryphal book of Tobit portrays Tobit as a model of piety and almsgiving (Tob 1).

In the NT the specific references to alms are translations of the term *eleēmosynē*. The giving of alms is emphasized in the SERMON ON THE MOUNT. There, as elsewhere, such giving is treated as synonymous with righteousness (Matt 6:1-4). Here and in Luke 11:41 the emphasis is upon sincerity in almsgiving. In other passages as well, the moral obligation to give alms is asserted (Luke 12:33; Acts 10:2, 4, 31; 24:17).

See also POOR.

—DANIEL B. MCGEE

• **Alpha and Omega.** *See* REVELATION, BOOK OF

• **Alphabet.** *See* WRITING SYSTEMS

• **Alphaeus.** *See* MATTHEW

• **Altar.** *See* BLOOD IN THE NEW TESTAMENT; HORN/HORNS OF THE ALTAR

• **Altar-Hearth.** *See* ARIEL

• **Altars.** *See* SACRIFICE

• **Amalek/Amalekites.** [am'uh-lek/uh-mal'uh-k*i*ts] Amalek appears in the genealogy of ESAU in Gen 36:12. This is probably based on the association of this tribal group with the steppe region of the Negeb and the area of Kadesh (Gen 14:7). As a people, the Amalekites are identified in the OT as a recurrent enemy of the Israelites. They first appear in the narrative of the journey to Mount Sinai following the Exodus. With stragglers and the weak falling prey to these fierce tribesmen (Deut 25:17-18), open violence erupted between the two tribal groups when the Israelites violated Amalekite territory near Kadesh (Exod 17:8-16). This conflict set the stage for the designation of Israel's God as a divine warrior, introducing into Israelite literature the language of HOLY WAR (Heb. *ḥerem*) found throughout the conquest narrative. In these passages Yahweh directly aided the Israelites in defeating their enemies in battle. Thus, in Exod 17:16, perpetual war is declared against the Amalekites by both the Israelites and by Yahweh (cf. Deut 25:19 and Num 24:20).

Continuing their role as perpetual enemies, the Amalekites are included in the list of peoples, compiled by MOSES' spies, who were dwelling in the promised land (Num 13:29; 14:25), and thus posed a hazard to the invading Israelites. During the anarchic period of the Judges, EHUD (Judg 3:13) and GIDEON (Judg 6:3, 33) both faced the invasion of their tribal territory by raiders, which included the allied forces of the Ammonites, Moabites, Midianites, and the Amalekites.

Once the Israelite monarchy had been established under SAUL, the Amalekites, living "from Havilah as far as Shur, which is east of Egypt," were targeted for extermination in a holy war (1 Sam 15:2-9). Saul's failure to carry out his instructions to completely destroy the Amalekites further weakened his relationship with SAMUEL and contributed to his downfall (1 Sam 15:10-35). It is particularly ironic that Saul, at least temporarily, spared the life of the Amalekite king Agag (1 Sam 15:9), and then was forced to ask an Amalekite to kill him (Saul) in order to prevent his capture by the PHILISTINES (2 Sam 1:8-10; cf. 1 Sam 31:1-6).

Perhaps in contrast to Saul's failure, DAVID is portrayed as constantly raiding the Amalekites. This began while he was serving the Philistine king ACHISH of Gath as a mercenary. Operating out of the village of Ziklag, David, unlike Saul, left no witnesses or enemies to trouble him after these raids (1 Sam 27:8-11). The Amalekites did make one major retaliatory attack on Ziklag while David was away at a war conference. They looted and burned the village and carried David's wives ABIGAIL and Ahinoam away as captives (1 Sam 30:1-5). After consulting Yahweh through the use of the EPHOD of ABIATHAR, David mounted a rescue expedition (cf. Gen 14:13-16), attacking them while the Amalekites were celebrating their victory. A general massacre ensued with only 400 men on camels escaping (1 Sam 30:7-20).

The general threat of raids by the Amalekites was apparently ended during the monarchy as David and later kings consolidated their control of the region south of BEERSHEBA. Tribute payments were exacted from them (2 Sam 8:11-12), signifying their submission to Israelite rule of the area. In Hezekiah's time (late eighth century), a group of Simeonites eliminated the remnant of the Amalekites near Mount Seir (1 Chr 4:42-43).

The final chapter in the history of these two peoples is found in ESTHER. Haman the Agagite (and thus an Amalekite—1 Sam 15:7-9) is portrayed as a deadly enemy of the Jews at the Persian court (Esth 3). It is only the courage and swift thinking of MORDECAI and Esther that prevented Haman's plan to exterminate the Jews from being carried out (Esth 4; 8:2).

See also HOLY WAR.

Bibliography. D. Edelman, "Saul's Battle Against Amaleq

(1 Sam 15),'' *JSOT* 35 (1986): 71-84; J. D. Levenson, ''Is There a Counterpart in the Hebrew Bible to New Testament Antisemitism,'' *JES* 22/2 (1985): 242-60; B. P. Robinson, ''Israel and Amalek, the Context of Exodus 17:8-16,'' *JSOT* 32 (1985): 15-22.

—VICTOR H. MATTHEWS

• **Amanuensis.** [uh-man'y*oo*-en"sis] The English word ''amanuensis'' is a transliteration of a Latin word meaning ''at/by hand.'' The term is used for one who writes for another, either from dictation or as copyist of something previously written. It was a craft which required specialized training, and a form of shorthand was often used by those taking dictation.

The use of a writer by the creator/originator of something to be placed in written form has been common across the ages. Illiteracy, poor penmanship, and desire for a professional quality are but a few reasons.

Although the term is not found in the Bible, the practice of writing for another or copying is observable throughout. Examples: 1 Kgs 21:8-9; 1 Chr 24:6; Ezra 4:7-23; Neh 9:38–10:27; Esth 3:12-14; 8:3-10; 9:29; Jer 36:4-6, 27-32; 45:1; Rom 16:22; 1 Pet 5:12.

It is probable that the term scribe in its earliest usage referred to a secretary or copyist, although later usage gave it a broader connotation.

See also SCRIBE IN THE NEW TESTAMENT; SCRIBE IN THE OLD TESTAMENT.

—HENRY JACKSON FLANDERS, JR.

• **Amariah.** [am'uh-r*i*"uh] Hebrew, ''Yah has promised''; name of several men in the OT. (1) A Levite, the son of Meraioth and the father of Ahitub (1 Chr 6:7, 52). EZRA was his descendant (Ezra 7:3). (2) Another Levite, the second son of Hebron (1 Chr 23:19; 24:23). (3) High priest in the time of King JEHOSHAPHAT (2 Chr 19:11). (4) A Levite during the reign of King HEZEKIAH (2 Chr 31:15). (5) One of the sons of Binnui forced by Ezra to divorce his foreign wife (Ezra 10:42). (6) A priest who returned from exile with ZERUBBABEL (Neh 10:3; 12:2). (7) A descendant of Perez (Neh 11:4). (8) Name of a priestly family in postexilic Jerusalem whose leader was Jehohanan (Neh 12:13). (9) Ancestor of Zephaniah the prophet and probably the son of King Hezekiah (Zeph 1:1).

—DAVID H. HART

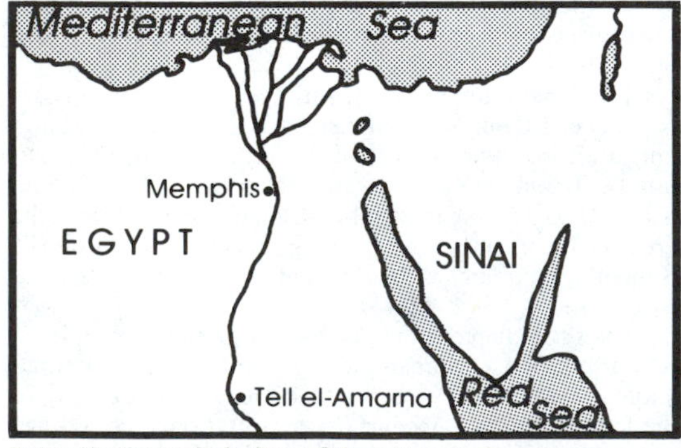

Designed by Margaret Jordan Brown ©Mercer University Press

• **Amarna.** [uh-mahr'nuh] Tell el-Amarna is the modern name for the site of the ancient city Akhetaton, capital city built by the Pharoah AKHENATON (PLATE 8). The city was built about 1365 B.C.E. and was then abandoned within half a century. The site is especially remarkable for the tablets discovered there in 1887. The language of the tablets is Akkadian, and their script is CUNEIFORM, both of which are native to Mesopotamia rather than Egypt. Because of this anomaly the tablets were at first dismissed as forgeries. Later investigation revealed, however, that they were mainly diplomatic correspondence between the Egyptian court and various other ancient Near Eastern courts. The anomalous preservation of Akkadian cuneiform in Egypt is to be explained by the fact that such was the international diplomatic language of the age. The correspondence dates to the reigns of Amenophis III (1414–1377 B.C.E.) and his successor Akhenaton (1377–1360 B.C.E.). As a body of primary source material for the political history of the ancient Near East in the fourteenth century, the tablets are of such significance as to have given their name to the period, the ''Amarna age.''

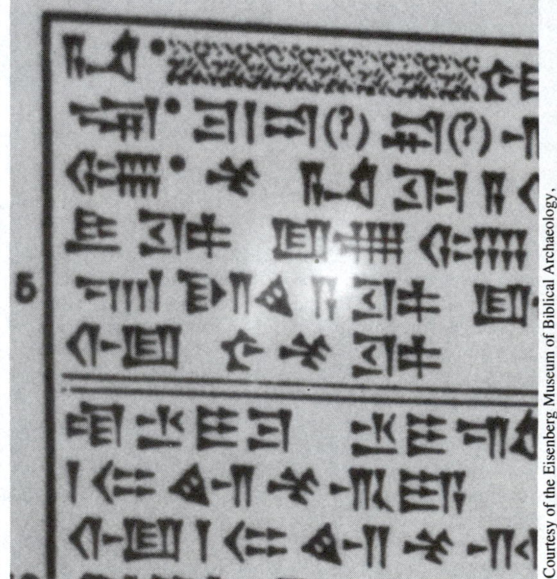

Courtesy of the Eisenberg Museum of Biblical Archaeology.

A section of an Amarna tablet written in Cuneiform.

By the time scholars recognized them as something other than a hoax, about 350 tablets were still preserved. Other pieces of correspondence to the Egyptian court have since been found in excavations elsewhere bringing the total number up to 378 pieces, of which 356 are letters. Forty-three are letters between Egypt and other major powers who had parity with Egypt (e.g., Tushratta of Mitanni, Kassite kings of Babylon, Asshur-uballit I of Assyria, Suppiluliumas of the Hittite kingdom, and the king of Alashia [=Cyprus]). Most of the letters are between the Egyptian court and vassal kings in Syria, Phoenicia, and Palestine (e.g., Qatna, Byblos, Beirut, Sidon, Tyre, Jerusalem, Hazor, Akko, Megiddo, Gezer, Ashkelon, Lachish). The letters reveal a situation of factionalism within the Egyptian sphere of influence in Syria-Palestine; local rulers accuse fellow vassals of treachery; requests of aid from the Egyptian overlord are frequent.

Mentioned in the tablets are the *Àpiru* (=*Habiru*

= *SA.GAZ*) who have been much discussed and studied by biblical scholars. Early in the study of the Amarna tablets, some scholars identified these figures with the Hebrews and thus with the Israelites, some even claiming that the *Àpiru* of the Amarna tablets were none other than the invading Israelites under Joshua. Such identifications proved to be hasty and finally unconvincing, for the *Àpiru* have since been found mentioned in sources all over the ancient Near East throughout the second millenium B.C.E. Rather than an ethnic group, they are better described as a social group. Wherever they are mentioned, they are characterized as "foreign" and in a relation of dependency upon the native population. Apart from very tenuous connections between the *Àpiru* and the Hebrews of biblical tradition, "further historical combinations between the two groups appear to be highly doubtful; they may serve now, as they have served in the past, only to obscure the distinctive features of each." (Greenberg, 96)

See also AKHENATON.

Bibliography. E. F. Campbell, Jr., "The Amarna Letters and the Amarna Period," *BA* 23 (1960): 2-22; M. Greenberg, *The Hab/piru*; J. A. Knudtzon, *Die El-Amarna Tafeln*, I-II; C. F. Pfeiffer, *Tell el Amarna and the Bible*.

—JOHN KEATING WILES

• **Amasa.** *See* ABIGAIL

• **Amaziah.** [am'uh-zi'uh] "Yahweh is Strong," the name of several persons in the Hebrew Bible, primarily two. One was king of Judah from ca. 800-783 B.C.E., the son of Joash. A young man when he took the throne, he spent some of his career engaged against EDOM, thus exhibiting in history the legendary JACOB-ESAU struggle as reflected in the legends of Genesis and such foreign nation oracles as OBADIAH. When his successful conquest of Edom went to his head, however, he foolishly challenged and was soundly defeated by his other brother-nation, Israel, which was ruled by another Joash. He had begun his career by executing his father's murderers, but in the end he himself was assassinated. A twenty-nine year reign (2 Kgs 14; 2 Chr 25) has been much debated by scholars and may have been ten years shorter.

But the most famous and significant reference to "Amaziah" in the Hebrew Bible is to Amaziah, the priest of BETHEL in Israel under the reign of Joash's son, JEROBOAM II (ca. 786-746) in Amos 7:10-17. This rare biographical sketch of a latter prophet demonstrates how the king and high priest were in league together such that the palace and temple functioned as royal residence and chapel. Amaziah ordered AMOS to leave Bethel and return home to Judah, because by his political criticism he was offending the religious establishment. Amos's defense, as well as the message of the prophet in general, makes clear the danger of identifying the affairs of state with the will of God, and simple identification of religion and politics.

See also AMOS; PROPHET.

—LAMONTTE M. LUKER

• **Amidah.** *See* BENEDICTIONS, EIGHTEEN

• **Ammon/Ammonites.** [am'uhn/am'uh-nits] A semitic people who lived in the highlands of Transjordan, in a tiny kingdom northeast of the DEAD SEA. The Ammonites, whose story centered around the fate of their capital city, RABBAH (modern Amman), played a major role in the ancient history of the Jordanian plateau. Though they were related by blood to Israel, the Ammonites were constantly at war with their neighbors west of the Jordan River, the accounts of which fill up most of the biblical references to Ammon. Unlike MOAB and EDOM, Ammonite territory was not demarcated from the surrounding nations too clearly, at least from our vantage point. In general, Ammon was wedged between Moab and GILEAD in the modern Belqa, between southeastern Gilead and the Syrian Desert to the east (PLATES 9, 10). Early in their history, the Ammonites settled in the territory of the Zamzummim (or Rephaim), which was located between the ARNON and the JABBOK (Deut 2:20-21, 37; 3:11). Later, the Amorites wrested part of this region from Ammonite control, and the latter were confined to the region east of where the Jabbok flows north out of Rabbah (Num 21:24; Deut 2:37; Josh 12:2; 13:10, 25). It has been correctly observed that the existence—and persistence—of such a tiny kingdom must be explained by Ammon's abundant water, the fertility of soil in the upper Jabbok, and the strength of Rabbah.

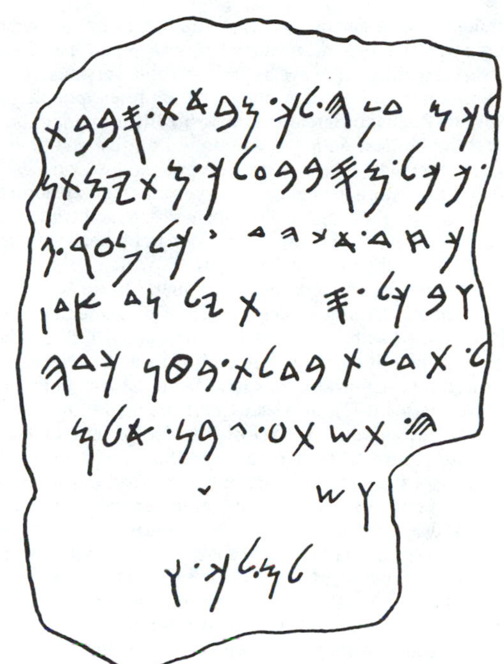

An inscription from the Amman Citadel.

Sources for reconstructing Ammonite history are limited. Aside from a number of OT references to this important people, the Ammonites are named in Neo-Assyrian documents. In addition to the information that can be gleaned from ostraca, seals, and seal impressions, a few precious texts have been recovered from Ammonite soil (e.g., Amman Citadel Inscription, Amman Theater Inscription, Siran Bottle Inscription). Mute archaeological evidence supplements our knowledge of Ammonite history and culture but, as might be expected, the Bible remains the single most important source.

According to Gen 19:30–38, the Ammonites were descended from Ben-'ammi, the son of LOT by his younger daughter. Thus, the ancestor who gave a name to all his descendants was a cousin to Moab, son of Lot by his older daughter. The ethnic designation, Bᵉnê ‘Ammon, has been translated in different ways by various Bible versions: sons of Ammon, children of Ammon, Ammonites, people of Ammon. Archaeological data help to fill in the gap between the biblical notice of Ammonite origins and references to them at the time of the Hebrew Exodus/Conquest. It seems that Ammon began to emerge as a kingdom during the early part of the thirteenth century B.C.E., and while we do not know when the Ammonite monarchy began, there was a king by the time of JEPHTHAH.

In the period of the Exodus/Conquest, Israel was told not to conquer Ammon, since the Lord was safeguarding this territory for the "sons of Lot" (Deut 2:19, 37; Judg 11:15). When opposed by SIHON, however, the Hebrews captured this Amorite king's land from the Arnon to the Jabbok (Judg 11:22), and later "half the land of the Ammonites" was given to GAD (Josh 13:25). Because of their opposition to Israel, perhaps in their alliance with Moab in the hiring of Balaam, the Ammonites were forbidden to enter the Israelite assembly "to the tenth generation" (Deut 23:3-4). From this same era comes the intriguing reference to the oversized iron bedstead of OG, which could be seen in Rabbah of the Ammonites (Deut 3:11). This allusion to the Rephaim inhabitants of the environs of Ammon is accompanied by the earliest biblical reference to the Ammonite capital, Rabbah (also known as Rabbath-ammon and, still later, as Philadelphia). Today the presence of the large, modern city of Amman, Jordan, at the same location testifies to the significance of this site, at the source of the Jabbok River.

In the days of the judges, the Ammonites took opportunity to oppress Israel (Judg 3:13; 10:6; 11:4-40). These hostile relations between Ammon and the Israelites continued into the period of Saul and David and beyond, with Ammon assuming the status of a vassal to Israel and Assyria most of the time. SAUL was victorious over Nahash and the Ammonites at JABESH-GILEAD (1 Sam 11:1-11; 12:12; 14:47). According to 2 Sam 10 and 1 Chr 14, JOAB and Abishai, two of David's generals, defeated the Ammonites and their Syrian mercenaries. A major blow to the Ammonites came a year later when King David—and Joab—captured Rabbah, "the city of waters," and took slaves and loot, including the crown of Ammon's king (2 Sam 12:26-31; 1 Chr 20:1-3). Interestingly enough, David found refuge among the Ammonites when he fled from ABSALOM (2 Sam 17:27-29; 23:37; 1 Chr 11:39). Though it was later defiled by Josiah (2 Kgs 23:13), Solomon built a high place near Jerusalem for the Ammonite deity Milkom/Molech, along with other foreign gods, since the king had Ammonite women in his harem (1 Kgs 11:1, 5, 6, 33).

The animosity between Ammon and Israel continued throughout the period of the divided monarchy (2 Chr 20:1–30; 24:26; 26:8; 27:5). During the ninth century B.C.E., the Ammonites joined with other small states in the region to oppose Neo-Assyrian expansion (Battle of QARQAR, 853 B.C.E.), but in the eighth and seventh centuries B.C.E. Ammon submitted to the Assyrian yoke and paid tribute. After NEBUCHADREZZAR captured Jerusalem in 587 B.C.E., the Ammonites, among others, made life even more difficult for the Judaeans (2 Kgs 25:25; Jer 40:11-14; cf. 2 Kgs 24:2). For this and other opposition, Ammon was indicted by the Hebrew prophets (Jer 49:1-6; Ezek 21:20; 25:1-7; Amos 1:13-15; Zeph 2:8-11; cf. Ps 83:7). Though exact details are unavailable, it is assumed that the Ammonites suffered defeat at the hands of the Babylonians during their invasion of Syria and Transjordan in 582 B.C.E..

Ammonite/Judaean conflicts continued in the post-exilic period, when Tobiah joined other enemies of the Jews in opposing NEHEMIAH's efforts to rebuild Jerusalem's walls (Neh 2:10, 19; 4:3, 7). Intermarriage between Jews and Ammonites was forbidden by Ezra (9:1-2) and Nehemiah (13:1, 23-31). The Ammonites, especially the Tobiad family, persisted until the second century B.C.E., as is demonstrated by archaeological and textual evidence from Transjordan and Egypt. First Macc 5:6 reports that Judas Maccabeus fought against the Ammonites. As remarkable as this long, albeit partially understood, history may be, even more remarkable is the fact that the biblical, Assyrian, and native Ammonite texts have provided a fairly complete list of Ammon's kings from the tenth century until the early years of the sixth century B.C.E. In chronological order, these kings were Nahash, Hanum, Basha, Shanip, Padoel, Amminadab I, Hissalel, Amminadab II, and Baalis.

Archaeological exploration of the Ammonite territory has recovered a wealth of data, but much more work remains. Recent excavations at Ain Ghazal, Sahab, Tell Hesban, Tell el-‘Umeiri, and at the Amman citadel, among other sites, have added to the understanding of Ammon's history and culture from prehistoric times until the Islamic period. Little is known about Ammonite religion, aside from the fact that Milkom was the national deity (e.g., 1 Kgs 11:5, 7, 33; Zeph 1:4-6), but a recent archaeological discovery has shed light on the centrality of this god. This new find, a seal impression from Tell el-‘Umeiri reads as follows: "Belonging to Milkom'ur, servant of Baalis." The inscription dates to ca. 600 B.C.E. and is, remarkably, the only known occurrence of the deity's name (i.e., Milkom) in a personal name. Furthermore, Milkom'ur, the owner of the seal, was a servant of Baalis (a personal name which includes the divine name or title, Baal), who is now thought to be the latest known king of Ammon.

—GERALD L. MATTINGLY

• **Amnon.** [am'non] The eldest son of DAVID, born to Ahinoam of Jezreel (2 Sam 3:2) in HEBRON. His name, spelled Aminon (2 Sam 13:20), means "faithful." Along with his cousin, Jonadab, he plotted and carried out the rape of his half-sister, Tamar. The rape was avenged by a murder carefully planned and executed by her blood brother, ABSALOM (2 Sam 13). This was the beginning of God's punishment of David for his sin against BATHSHEBA and URIAH the Hittite, as David saw his own lust and violence mirrored in the lives of his sons (2 Sam 12:10-11a). It is also a part of the involved plot of the succession history to the throne of David (2 Sam 9–20; 1 Kgs 1–2), whereby Amnon and Absalom were eliminated as threats to SOLOMON's succession.

Another Amnon was a Judahite son of Shimon (1 Chr 4:20).

—M. PIERCE MATHENEY

• **Amorites.** [am'uh-*r*its] Derived from the Akkadian, *Amurru,* the term Amorite is used frequently by the biblical writers to refer to the native population of CANAAN (Amos 9:2). Additionally, the pre-Israelite inhabitants are also indentified as Canaanites. Though Amorite and Canaanite are interchangeable in some biblical contexts, they also distinguish between different groups within the original populace (Num 13:29). This impreciseness presents a problem concerning the identity of the Amorites and the

Canaanites. The Canaanites and the Amorites should not be viewed as two distinct peoples, separated by origin, culture or time. Rather, the term Canaanite came to be used for peoples who had been called Amorites. However, the adoption of one term for another did not remove the prior word from the language. Both terms continued to be used. The situation is complicated further since the terms also identified geographic regions. The geographic terminology continued to be used even after the political forces which gave the areas their names were no longer in existence. This impreciseness is consistent with the historiography of the ancient world.

The pre-conquest inhabitants of Transjordan are called Amorites. The Hebrews conquered the Amorite kingdoms of HESHBON ruled by Sihon and BASHAN ruled by Og as they approached Canaan (Num 21:21-35; Josh 2:10; 9:10; 24:8; Deut 4:46). Areas west of the Jordan inhabited by the Amorites included the central highlands (Deut 1:7, 19-20), Hebron and Lachish (Josh 10:5), Jerusalem (Ezek 16:3), and Gibeon (2 Sam 21:2). The Amorites remained an identifiable group even until Solomon's reign (1 Kgs 9:20-23).

The term *Amurru* in Akkadian means "westerner" and referred to the diverse semitic inhabitants from an indefinite region west of Mesopotamia. The area likely included Syria and portions of Palestine. The Amurru were a political/tribal unit living at Jebel Bisri in Syria according to records of Shar-kali-sharri (ca. 2250 B.C.E.). Fortifications were built to protect Akkad and Sumer from Amorite attacks. King Shu-Sin of Ur (2037-2029 B.C.E.) built a wall 280 km. long for protection. The Amorite threat was also directed southward, and by 1750 B.C.E. they had become the dominant population in Syro-Palestine. By the second millennium, the Amorites dominated Mesopotamia. MARI (Tell Hariri) on the Upper Euphrates was a center of Amorite control under Zimri-lim. Much information has been recovered from the excavations at Mari, including the Mari Tablets. About 1759 B.C.E., another Amorite, HAMMURABI, conquered Mari, extended Amorite control over the Lower Euphrates, and established the first dynasty of Babylon. This dynasty ended when the Hittite monarch Mursilis I destroyed the city in 1595 B.C.E. Though Amorite control was gone, their presence in Mesopotamia continued. Inscriptions from Tiglath-pileser I and Ashur-nasir-pali II attest to a region near Mount Lebanon which paid Assyria tribute. Sennacherib refers to the rulers of Phoenicia, Philistia, Ammon, Moab, and Edom as kings of the Amurru. Sargon II cites Damascus as being in the land of the Amurru. The preciseness of the word Amurru was lost, even among the rulers of Mesopotamia.

See also CANAAN.

Bibliography. S. Moscati, *The Face of the Ancient Orient*; M. Liverani, "The Amorites" in *Peoples of Old Testament Times*, ed. D. J. Wiseman.

—ROBERT A. STREET, JR.

• **Amos.** The earliest of the so-called writing prophets, though he was not a prophet by profession. When challenged by AMAZIAH, priest of the royal sanctuary at BETHEL, and told never again to prophesy in that place, Amos responded: "I am no prophet, nor a prophet's son, but I am a herdsman, and a dresser of sycamore trees, and the Lord took me from following the flock, . . . and said to me, 'Go, prophesy to my people Israel' " (7:14, 15).

With his answer Amos intended to emphasize the genuineness of his call and the urgency of his proclamation. He had nothing at all in common with the popular but venal "prophets for profit" of his day. Court prophets were hired and fed by the king. Naturally their prophecies were biased, and even tailored to please the king.

Amos was as appalled at the religious situation in Israel (2:7, 8; 4:4,5; 5:21-24; 9:1-4), as he was stunned by the social ills. The false prophets and kept priests of his time were, to Amos, immoral persons whose teaching corresponded to their character. People and priest alike in Israel lacked a personal devotion to the Lord, and the test of morality proved it. On the other hand, those in a true covenant relationship with Yahweh, give evidence of it by their ethical living. Moreover, a true prophet condemns sin, calls for repentance, and inspires radical faith in Yahweh. Thus Amos gave testimony to the authenticity of his call.

Perhaps since his message had been so soundly rejected, Amos decided to commit it to writing, to seek vindication in time. Or perhaps, one who heard the message that day at Bethel recorded the prophecy for posterity. In any event, Amos is known today as the first canonical prophet, or the one who ushered in the age of the writing prophets.

Amos's name probably means "burdened" or "burden-bearer." That the prophet had been suddenly overwhelmed by God, burdened by his five visions, and called to prophesy to Israel is evident. Here is one who had not heard a gentle whisper, " a still small voice," but a Lord who roared (1:2) like a lion. Who could help but fear, and respond? (3:8).

Even though little is known of Amos directly (he is mentioned nowhere else in the Bible), much can be known about him indirectly. A prophet, according to Heschel, was one generally characterized as: sensitive to evil, luminous and explosive, one who seeks the highest good, but speaks "one octave too high," is an iconoclast, sounds a blast from heaven, and is often extremely lonely. Amos would appear to embody these characteristics.

While lacking professional training for his religious office, it is nonetheless clear that Amos was providentially suited for his prophetic task. Throughout the Book of Amos, awareness of pastoral life, as well as city life, is reflected in analogy, metaphor, and vivid imagery. It is evident that the prophet was a highly literate person, if not formally trained. His gifts as orator and thinker are of the highest order.

Amos's occupation, as it were, assumes an important place in his total call experience. As a pincher of sycamore-fig fruit (one who hastened the ripening stage of the fruit), Amos would have traveled extensively, or certainly enough to have witnessed various lifestyles. The sycamore fruit, in fact, grew only in lowlands and along coastal plains where it could escape the frost. Since Amos lived in Tekoa, only ten miles south of mountainous Jerusalem, his work would have taken him into Israel with frequency. So the country boy would have been able to witness city life firsthand. Furthermore, his duties as a shepherd might well have afforded similar opportunities, as well as time for reflection and meditation. It is also possible that he was a sheep breeder, connected with the Temple, as some scholars have surmised.

Israel, during the reign of JEROBOAM II (786-746 B.C.E.), and the time of Amos, attained a height of national power and prosperity unknown since DAVID and SOLOMON, and never again reached. The resurgence brought with it territorial expansion, thriving trade, and a popular but changing religion. Yahwism remained the official national religion, but it had, in reality, merged with the Canaanite fertility cult of BAAL. Although religious decay had reached an advanced stage, the people continued to interpret military successes and national prosperity as signs of divine blessing.

With commercial success came sharply distinguished privileged and peasant classes, and shady business practices and sundry legal tricks (8:5, 6) marked the society into which Amos stepped. Israel had become a nation that cared more for rites than rights. Religion was increasing but morality was decreasing.

Against this backdrop of eighth century B.C.E. Israelite history, Amos' time on center stage (sometime between 760-745 B.C.E.) was brief but brilliant. It is conceivable that his prophetic ministry may have lasted no longer than twenty to thirty minutes. For when the material dealing with his previous visions, and the confrontation with Amaziah is removed, the book is the length of a typical sermon.

Having been inspired by a series of five visions (chaps. 7–9) in which Amos saw the Lord's judgment poured out on Israel, the prophet's urgent cry became: "Repent or die." Israel was shocked. How dare one prophesy against Israel! How could doom come to God's people? What about their unique covenant relationship with God?

Although Amos never uses the word covenant, the essence of his message strikes clearly at Israel's disregard for covenant law. Simply put, Israel had broken the covenant.

Perhaps there is no more severe manner of pronouncing judgment than that employed by Amos when he wailed his "woe-cry" (5:18; 6:1, 4) over Israel. Whereas the curse is applied to living persons, the "woe-cry" often laments the dead. Israel's hour of grace was past.

For the prophet, the Israelite God is a God of justice and righteousness who demands the same from his people. Pious religiosity may never be substituted for right relations with others (5:21-24).

The Day of the Lord, therefore, will not be glorious, as Israel expected, but will instead be "darkness, and not light, gloom with no brightness in it" (5:20).

Was there any hope for Israel? To be sure, Amos was a prophet of doom. Yet, it seems best to say that he left the door open for Israel to repent (5:4, 6, 14, 15, 21-24), even though the prophet must not have expected Israel to do so (9:1-4, et al.).

See also AMOS, BOOK OF; PROPHECY; PROPHET.

Bibliography. J. Bright, *A History of Israel*; A. J. Heschel, *The Prophets*; J. L. Mays, *Amos: A Commentary*; T. H. Robinson, *Prophecy and the Prophets in Ancient Israel*; J. D. Smart, "Amos," *IDB*; R. L. Smith, "Amos," *BBC*; D. L. Williams, "The Theology of Amos," *RE* 63 (1966): 393-404; H. W. Wolff, *Amos the Prophet*.

—J. RANDALL O'BRIEN

• **Amos, Book of.** The earliest surviving collection of prophetic oracles in book form and very likely the first so recorded. Great prophets such as MOSES, SAMUEL, ELIJAH, ELISHA, NATHAN, and MICAIAH SON OF IMLAH predate AMOS. Their words and deeds are preserved in Israel's general history, however, not in separate books bearing their names. Thus Amos represents a turning point for Hebrew prophecy. In time, the essence of Israel's faith would be canonized in the collection of its prophetic books.

During the long, prosperous, and peaceful reign of JEROBOAM II (786-746 B.C.E.), Israel prospered in a fashion unknown since SOLOMON. Luxury flourished as wealth multiplied. Soon the nation consisted of two sharply divided classes: the upper class and the lower. Built upon the greed of the rich and the misery of the poor, Israel's was a society where the rich got richer and the poor got poorer. All the while, the official religious shrines attracted larger and larger crowds.

• OUTLINE OF AMOS •

The Book of Amos

I. Oracles against the Foreign Nations and against Israel (1:1–2:16)
   A. Superscription (1:1)
   B. Motto of entire book (1:2)
   C. Oracles against the foreign nations (1:3–2:3)
   D. Oracles against Judah and Israel (2:4-16)
II. Judgments against Various Groups (3:1–6:14)
   A. God's election of Israel (3:1-2)
   B. Prophets speak under divine compulsion (3:3-8)
   C. Threats of coming judgment (3:9-15)
   D. Judgment upon the unjust women (4:1-3)
   E. Past judgments were of no avail (4:4-13)
   F. Threats of coming judgment and summons to repentance (5:1-17)
   G. The Day of the Lord and condemnation of sacrifices (5:18-27)
   H. Additional judgments against Israel (6:1-14)
III. Prophetic Visions, Judgments, and Promises (7:1–9:15)
   A. Three visions (7:1-9)
   B. Encounter with the priest Amaziah (7:10-17)
   C. A fourth vision (8:1-3)
   D. Judgments and threats against evildoers (8:4-14)
   E. A fifth vision (9:1-6)
   F. Final judgment against Israel (9:7-8)
   G. Promises for Israel's future (9:9-15)

Onto this scene stepped Amos, sometime between 760 and 745 B.C.E. His words were first delivered orally at BETHEL, the official sanctuary of the northern kingdom of Israel, probably on the occasion of a crowded religious festival. Most scholars believe that the oracles were then recorded at a later date by the prophet himself. Another possibility is that the inspired utterances were preserved by a hearer.

The heart of Amos's message is that the just and righteous God of Israel moves among all nations, including Israel, to vindicate his universal moral laws. No people might violate these laws and escape retribution. "For three transgressions . . . and for four, I will not revoke the punishment," cries the prophet repeatedly, first to neighboring peoples (DAMASCUS, GAZA, TYRE, EDOM, AMMON, MOAB, and JUDAH), and then to ISRAEL. Israel's sins of greed, injustice, exploitation of the poor and oppression of the needy, false worship, self-righteousness, and pride would bring certain judgment. Divine election does not exclude divine rejection. Thus Israel's only hope is to "Seek the Lord and live" (5:6).

The Book of Amos consists of nine chapters that fall into two broad divisions. The first six chapters contain the words of Amos. Chaps. 7–9 record his visions. Within these sections lie several unique components. The first two chapters preserve the prophet's scathing denunciation of the crimes against humanity committed by neighboring nations. That Amos subscribed to the doctrine of the universality of Yahweh cannot be disputed.

In chaps. 3–6, Amos prophesies doom upon Israel. As the first to preach a message of judgment concerning the end of Israel, Amos would later have his words validated.

In the biographical section of the book (7:10-17), evidence of an editor's hand surfaces. Here Amos is mentioned in the third person, as he is in 1:1.

The visions of Amos are found in the last section of the book (7–9). No chronology for the visions is given, but it is likely that the shepherd-turned-prophet received his revelation in successive stages, and then delivered the message with cumulative force. First, he saw a locust plague (7:1-3) symbolizing the destruction of the land. Immediately Amos interceded on Israel's behalf and God relented. Next, he saw a judgment of fire (7:4-6) again symbolizing destruction. As before, Amos interceded for Israel and God relented. Third, Amos saw the Lord with a plumbline measuring Israel for destruction (7:7-9). The case appeared to be closed, so the prophet no longer interceded. His fourth vision was a basket of summer fruit (8:1-3). This vision included a play on words to depict the end of Israel (*qayiṣ* is Hebrew for summer fruit, while *qeṣ* is the word for end). Amos's fifth and final vision was of God destroying worshippers in the temple (9:1-4). The prophet saw no escape for Israel in this vision, only doom.

Finally, a lively debate among scholars remains concerning the authenticity of the words in 4:13; 5:8-9; 9:5-6; and 9:11-15. Some argue that the first three references are mere doxologies inserted at a later date, while the latter reference should be taken as an editorial note of hope. However, there is nothing within these verses incongruent with the theology of Amos.

During a time in Israel's history when religious rites were honored but human rights were violated, Amos spoke with an impassioned purpose. The key verse of the book (5:24) concludes a fiery burst that begins: "I hate, I despise your feasts, and I take no delight in your solemn assemblies. . . . Take away from me the noise of your songs; to the melody of your harps I will not listen. But let justice roll down like waters, and righteousness like an ever-flowing stream" (5:21, 23, 24).

So it is the book of Amos that has immortalized the unforgettable message of one whose words still echo through the ages, sounding a clarion call for justice and righteousness among all people everywhere, but among God's COVENANT people with special force.

See also AMOS; PROPHET; PROPHECY.

Bibliography. J. Bright, *A History of Israel*; A. J. Heschel, *The Prophets*; J. L. Mays, *Amos: A Commentary*; T. H. Robinson, *Prophecy and the Prophets in Ancient Israel*; J. D. Smart, "Amos," *IDB*; R. L. Smith, "Amos," *BBC*; D. L. Williams, "The Theology of Amos," *RE* 63 (1966): 393-404; H. W. Wolff, *Amos the Prophet*.

—J. RANDALL O'BRIEN

• **Amphictyony/Confederacy.** [am-fik'tee-uh-nee] Frequently used to refer to the tribal league of ancient Israel during the period of the judges—from JOSHUA to the Davidic monarchy. The term itself is Greek (*amphiktuonia*) and is probably erroneously applied to the OT. Nevertheless, the biblical materials indicate that some type of tribal organization or confederacy existed, and hence the term is still often used.

Drawing upon comparisons to ancient Greek and Italian (Etruscan) leagues of tribes that were united around a central religious shrine or temple, Martin Noth proposed that Israel's twelve tribes were also an amphictyony (*Das System der zwölf Stämme Israels* (1930) and *The History of Israel* (2d ed., 1960). The best Greek example for Noth's thesis was at Delphi, where tribes met at a shrine for autumn festivals, sent delegates to an assembly to conduct the business of the shrine, and pledged holy war against anyone who attacked the temple. Noth held that the Israelite amphictyony was originally six tribes (the "Leah group") organized at the SHECHEM shrine. Over time, other tribes migrated into the region, but not until the arrival of the "Joseph tribes" from Egypt did the amphictyony expand to include twelve tribes. Limiting the member tribes to the numbers six or twelve facilitated delegating sacred duties at the shrine according to a twelve month calendar year. When ABIMELECH destroyed Shechem, the tribal shrine was moved to SHILOH. After the death of SAUL, Judah seceded from the amphictyony and organized at MAMRE an Abrahamic amphictyony composed of six tribes (Judah, Simeon, Caleb, Othniel, Jerachmeel, and Cain). Under the Davidic monarchy, the old Israelite amphictyony was restored with the shrine located at JERUSALEM, a neutral site. Noth maintained that the tribes celebrated common religious festivals and rituals at the shrine, had a council of elders, possessed a law code (the Book of the Covenant), and waged amphictyonic holy wars (such as against GIBEAH of Benjamin, Judg 19–21).

Objections to Noth's thesis are overwhelming. The full Greek model at Delphi did not exist until three or four centuries after the Israelite tribal period, and Near Eastern roots are more probable. The most likely source is northern Mesopotamian nomadic tribes in the process of becoming sedentary. Flexible tribal and shrine patterns similar to Israel's have been found among the Arameans, Chaldeans, and Arabs. Moreover, in JUDGES and SAMUEL, neither a central shrine nor a central authority was ever present, and the individual tribes conquered their own territories. Only on rare occasions did a few tribes form coalitions against a common threat. The uniting of Israel under Saul proceeded without the ark, the so-called symbol of amphictyonic unity, which had been left twenty years at a private house (1 Sam 7:1-2) and which is mentioned only once in Judg (20:27). A council of delegates (elders) administering the shrine is never mentioned in the historical books of the OT.

Probably the Israelite tribes before the monarchy were somewhat ethnically and religiously diverse. Most were north Mesopotamian nomads, but a few came from Egypt. They worshiped various "gods," usually named EL or some semitic variant thereof. Not until the external pressures of the early monarchy were the tribes forced to unite religiously and politically under Yahweh and DAVID—a unity lasting only until the end of Solomon's reign.

See also JOSHUA, BOOK OF; JUDGES, BOOK OF; TRIBES.

Bibliography. M. C. Astour, "Amphictyony," *IDBSupp*; N. K. Gottwald, *The Tribes of Yahweh*.

—JACK WEIR

• **Amphipolis.** [am-fip'uh-lis] Amphipolis ("around city") was located on a terraced hill in a mountain pass above the Gulf of Strymon (PLATES 18, 20) and commanded the only easy communication northward into the Macedonian plains. It was originally named "Nine Roads" because of the great number of Thracian and Macedonian roads which converged there. In the fifth century B.C.E., Athenian colonists ousted the original Thracian inhabitants and established a new town. The name "Amphipolis" was derived from the fact that the town was surrounded on three sides by the river Strymon and was conspicuous from all sides since it could be seen from the sea.

When Philip of Macedon gained control in the north Aegean, Amphipolis became a part of MACEDONIA and later of the Roman province. In 167 B.C.E. Macedonia was declared free and was divided into four districts. Amphipolis, on the Egnatian Way, became the capital of the first district.

Apparently Paul and company made no attempt to win converts while enroute from Philippi to Thessalonica (Acts 17:1).

See also MACEDONIA.

—G. WILLARD REEVES

• **Amran/Amramites.** *See* MOSES

• **Anadipolis.** *See* INCLUSIO

• **Analogy.** *See* SYMBOL

• **Ananias.** [an'uh-ni''uhs] Ananias is the Greek form of the Hebrew name Hannaniah (Hanani or Hanan) which means "God is gracious." The name occurs frequently in the Apocrypha (cf. 1 Esdr 9:21, 43, 48; Jdt 8:1; and Tob 5:12) and is used of three different persons in the NT:

1. Ananias, the husband of Sapphira, was a member of the church in Jerusalem who conspired with his wife in giving part of the selling price of a parcel of land to the church while claiming they gave the entire amount (Acts 5:1-10). PETER confronted Ananias, accusing him of lying to God and reminding him that he was not forced to give. Upon being confronted with the deliberate sin, Ananias died suddenly and was immediately buried. The incident has attracted much discussion by commentators, and clearly marks the end of the complete communal sharing that was practiced earlier in the Jerusalem church and exemplified by Barnabas (Acts 4:34-37).

2. Ananias, a Christian of Damascus, was instructed in a vision to go to PAUL just after Paul's experience on the road to Damascus and prior to his baptism (Acts 9:10-19). Ananias was at first reluctant, knowing of Paul's fierce persecution of Christians (Acts 9:13-14); but upon being told the second time to go (9:15-16), Ananias went and laid his hands upon Paul who received the Holy Spirit, recovered his sight, and was baptized (9:17-18). Paul mentions Ananias, of whom nothing more is known, in the recounting of his conversion in Acts 22:12-16, but not in Acts 26:12-18.

3. Ananias, the twenty-first Jewish high priest in the Roman period of domination of Palestine, presided over the Jewish council when Paul appeared before Claudius Lysias in Jerusalem (Acts 22:30; 23:2) and was one of the leaders of the Jewish group when Paul was accused before FELIX (Acts 24:1). The priesthood of Ananias was marked with violence and greed, and he was so disliked that he was murdered by his own countrymen when war broke out in 66 C.E.

See also FELIX; PAUL; PETER.

—HAROLD S. SONGER

• **Ananus.** *See* ANNAS

• **Anathema.** [uh-nath'uh-muh] Anathema (Gk., "something set up or placed") signifies something which has been devoted or consecrated to God. The term can be used in a positive sense of an object dedicated to God, such as a votive offering (Luke 21:5), but its usual reference is to something which has been given over to God's wrath for destruction. Thus anathema denotes that which is accursed. Paul uses the word in this negative manner in 1 Cor 16:22, "If any one has no love for the Lord, let him be accursed" (cf. 1 Cor 12:3; Gal 1:8-9; Rom 9:3; Acts 23:14). The church later used the term when issuing declarations against heretics.

See also CURSE AND BLESSING.

—MITCHELL G. REDDISH

• **Anathoth.** [an'uh-thoth] One of the four towns in the territory of the tribe of Benjamin given to the Levites (Josh 21:18), best known as the hometown of JEREMIAH. It is located just north of JERUSALEM (PLATE 13) and is usually identified with Ras el-Kharrubeh near the modern village of Anata, which preserves the name of the ancient town. ABIATHAR, the high priest under King DAVID, was banished to this town by SOLOMON (1 Kgs 2:26). Lesser-known biblical references to the town are: the home of two of David's "mighty men," Abiezer and Jehu (1 Chr 11:28; 12:3); a town mentioned by ISAIAH (10:30) in a doom oracle; the place where JEREMIAH purchased some property from his cousin Hanamel while the Babylonians were besieging Jerusalem (Jer 32); a town resettled by returning exiles (Ezra 2:23; Neh 7:27).

See also JEREMIAH.

Bibliography. M. Avi-Yonah, "Anathoth," *EncJud*; N. Rubingen, "Jeremiah's Epistle to the Exiles and the Field in Anathoth," *Jud* 26 (1977): 84-91.

—BRUCE C. CRESSON

• **Ancestor.** One's progenitor, often understood in terms of biological descent but not necessarily so. In the patriarchal, patrilineal society of the OT the emphasis was naturally on male ancestors (*'abôt*). This term is thus most often appropriately rendered "forefathers," though there are some instances where the more general "ancestors" seems to be intended. In a society strongly organized along FAMILY lines great importance was attached to tracing one's lineage back to a particular ancestor. Individual identity was rooted in the extended family derived from a common progenitor. DEATH meant a return to one's ancestors. It is said of DAVID at his death that he "slept with his forefathers" (1 Kgs 2:10). A similar note describes the end of most of his successors. On a larger scale all Israel, though composed of disparate groups, liked to think it was descended from ABRAHAM and SARAH. All considered themselves participants in the EXODUS and the COVENANT. Such an understanding strengthened communal unity.

It seems likely that some form of ancestor worship was practiced in early ISRAEL and continued on the popular level even after Yahwism became the norm. If the biblical Rephaim (Josh 13:12, etc.) are related to the Ugaritic Rephaim, then they can be viewed on one level as the semideified spirits of dead ancestors. Such spirits could be summoned by mediums like the witch of Endor (1 Sam 28). The funeral festival as held in Ugarit and Israel seems to have sometimes involved dead ancestors. The biblical writers, however, obscured most such references since they were contrary to Yahwism.

See also GENEALOGY IN THE NEW TESTAMENT; GENEALOGY IN THE OLD TESTAMENT

—DAVID H. HART

• **Andrew.** Andrew was one of the TWELVE disciples, the brother of Simon PETER. "Andrew" is a Greek name meaning "manly." Simon and Andrew were fishermen from BETHSAIDA (John 1:44), from the family of Jonah (Matt 16:17) or John (John 1:42; 21:15-17).

According to John 1:35-42, Andrew was a disciple of JOHN THE BAPTIST, who pointed out Jesus as "the lamb of

God." Andrew and an unidentified disciple were the first to follow Jesus. Andrew then told his brother, Simon, that they had found the Messiah. According to Mark 1:16-18 and Matt 4:18 the two brothers were fishing when Jesus called them to follow him. Jesus later visited the home of Peter and Andrew in CAPERNAUM (Mark 1:29).

Andrew is mentioned in each of the lists of the twelve apostles, and his is always among the first four names (Matt 10:2; Mark 3:18; Luke 6:14; Acts 1:13). Although he is not included in the inner group of three disciples at the raising of Jairus's daughter (Mark 5:37), the transfiguration (Mark 9:2), or the Garden of Gethsemane (Mark 14:33), Andrew does appear with these three in Mark 13:3.

In the Gospel of John, Andrew appears in other scenes in the company of Philip. At the feeding of the five thousand, Andrew brings the boy with the fish and the loaves to Jesus (John 6:8-9). Later he brings the Greek pilgrims to Jesus (John 12:20-22). Indeed, each time Andrew appears in the Gospel of John he brings someone to Jesus.

Andrew is not mentioned elsewhere in the NT, but he figures prominently in the legends of the early church. According to tradition (Eusebius *EccHist* 3.1), Andrew worked in Scythia (north of the Black Sea). He later became the patron saint of Russia. The ACTS OF ANDREW describe his martyrdom in Achaia, where he was crucified at the order of the proconsul Eges. Other legends are contained in the *Acts of Peter and Andrew*, the *Acts of Andrew and Mathias*, and the *Acts of Andrew and Paul*.

See also APOSTLE/APOSTLESHIP; DISCIPLE/DISCIPLESHIP; JOHN THE BAPTIST; PETER; TWELVE, THE.

Bibliography. P. M. Peterson, *Andrew, Brother of Simon Peter: His History and His Legends*.

—R. A. CULPEPPER

• **Andrew, Acts of.** The *Acts of Andrew* is one of a group of NT apocryphal works written during the third century. While originally it may have been the longest volume of all the APOCRYPHAL ACTS, it is now the least preserved.

EUSEBIUS (fourth century) is the first to make reference to this work and lists it as a text highly regarded by heretical groups such as the Gnostics. The extant copies of the *Acts* reveal little of the original emphases which would have caused it to be labelled heretical. This is due to its reworking by editors who purged the text of undesirable elements. The monk Gregory of Tours (sixth century) in his work *Liber de Miraculis Beati Andreae Apostoli* used the *Acts of Andrew* as a basic narrative framework, but removed features he considered heretical. Some have suggested that the original philosophy undergirding this *Acts* is not necessarily Gnostic, but reflects a general perspective on life which is associated with Hellenistic thought.

The *Acts of Andrew* is composed of two major parts: a journey of ANDREW, and his eventual martyrdom which resulted from his ascetic beliefs and practices. A significant emphasis throughout this work is the disregard for the values and material possessions of this world. This lesson is illustrated by Andrew's message to shun the false images of the world and seek God. This teaching is summarized by one of Andrew's discourses to a crowd: "I always exhorted you to keep clear [of harmful delusions] and to press towards the things that are permanent and to take flight from all that is transient."

See also APOCRYPHAL ACTS; GNOSTICISM.

Bibliography. M. Hornschuh, "The Acts of Andrew," *New Testament Apocrypha*, ed. E. Hennecke and W. Schneemelcher.

—DAVID M. MAY

• **Angel.** An angel (ἄγγελος, "messenger") is a supernatural, spiritual being who serves as God's messenger or agent to do his will on earth. The term translates a Hebrew as well as a Greek word which literally means "messenger."

Angels appear throughout the OT but are especially prominent in Genesis, Judges, and Zechariah. With the exception of Zechariah, they are mentioned very infrequently in the prophetic writings. The most common function of angels is, as their name implies, to deliver God's message to his people. In Gen 22:11, an angel tells Abraham not to sacrifice his son Isaac. All of the people of Israel are addressed by an angel in Judg 2:1-4, where he reminds them that Yahweh was faithful and brought them out of Egypt but they have failed to obey his commands and thus have broken the covenant. Sometimes the message is a harbinger or foretelling of an important event, such as the birth of Samson (Judg 13:3-7). Angels also take a more active role as God's agents by either protecting his people or punishing and even destroying their enemies. As the Israelites fled Egypt, an angel protected them from the pursuing Egyptian army by placing a protective pillar of cloud between the two groups (Exod 14:19-20). According to 2 Kgs 19:35, an angel slaughtered 185,000 Assyrians who were beseiging Jerusalem. In every case, the angel is described as functioning only on behalf of Yahweh, never as an autonomous agent. The outward appearance of angels is clearly secondary in importance to their function. They are usually recognized immediately as divine beings, but in Gen 18:1–19:38, Abraham entertains three angels who look so much like humans that he does not at first recognize their true character.

Many angelic references in the OT speak of "the angel of the Lord" or "the angel of Yahweh." In some of these texts, such as Exod 3:2-4, this particular angel is virtually indistinguishable from Yahweh himself:

> And the angel of the Lord appeared to him [Moses] in a flame of fire out of the midst of a bush; and he looked, and lo, the bush was burning, yet it was not consumed. . . . When the Lord saw that he turned aside to see, God called to him out of the bush, "Moses, Moses!"

In this case and others (Gen 21:17-21; 22:11-14), the term "angel of the Lord" seems to be a reference to God as he is perceived by human beings.

In addition to angels, the OT also describes other superhuman creatures subordinate to GOD which are sometimes considered to be angels in a broader sense of the term. These include the winged SERAPHIM and cherubim (Isa 6:2; Ps 80:1) as well as the mysterious "sons of God" in Gen 6:1-4.

Jewish angelology developed greatly during the late B.C.E. period and most of the numerous Jewish apocalypses written then featured angels in prominent roles. Except within the Book of Daniel, angels were never named in the OT; but MICHAEL, Gabriel, and Uriel were named in *1 Enoch* 9:1 and Raphael appeared in Tob 3:17. These four are described as archangels, and a hierarchy of angels is elsewhere described (*1 Enoch* 90:21). The Qumran scrolls (*1QM* 15:14) also tell of a fearsome army of angels which will lead God's people to victory in the final battle against the forces of evil. All of this suggests a development in Jewish thought. Whereas in the OT angels had little significance apart from their role as God's messengers or agents, many late B.C.E. writers saw them as important figures in and of themselves. This development is usually attributed to Persian influence in the fifth and fourth centuries B.C.E., but the extent of Persian influence upon Jewish angelology has recently been challenged. Perhaps one fairly certain area of Persian influence is in the increased emphasis on evil or fallen angels, often in apocalyptic texts which elaborate the story of Gen 6:1-4 (*1 Enoch* 6–14).

Angels appear throughout the NT, but are most prominent in Matthew, Luke-Acts, Hebrews, and Revelation. They function in much the same fashion as their counterparts in the OT and late B.C.E. writings. The angel Gabriel appears to Zechariah promising the birth of a son, John the Baptist, to him and his wife Elizabeth in their old age (Luke 1:5-23). Gabriel also appears to Mary to announce the birth of Jesus with the words, "Hail, O favored one, the Lord is with you!" (Luke 1:28). According to Matthew, an unnamed angel speaks to Joseph three times in dreams, telling him to take Mary as his wife, and then telling him when to flee to Egypt and when to return (Matt 1:18-25; 2:13, 19). The shepherds see a multitude of angels who praise God in chorus in honor of Jesus' birth (Luke 2:13-14).

In Jesus' time the Jews were divided in their opinion of angels. The Sadducees denied the existence of angels while the Pharisees accepted them (Acts 23:6-10). Most Jews probably believed in angels along with the Pharisees and it is certain that Jesus did. According to his story of the rich man and Lazarus, an angel carried Lazarus to Abraham's bosom (Luke 16:22). Jesus also criticized the Sadducees for their denial of a resurrection by explaining that people will rise from the dead and when they do they will be like the angels—neither marrying nor being given in marriage (Mark 12:24-27).

Paul mentions angels only occasionally in his letters, but the casual comments that do occur demonstrate that both he and his readers simply assume the existence of angels. They watch over believers (1 Cor 4:9; 11:10) but eventually they will be judged by believers (1 Cor 6:3). Some angels are evil (Rom 8:38) and Satan disguises himself as an angel of light (2 Cor 11:14). While there are many good angels, even these should not be worshipped (Col 2:18).

This same theme, that angels are not to be worshipped, is further emphasized in Rev 19:10 and 22:8-9, suggesting that angel worship was not an uncommon problem in the early church. Like most apocalypses, Revelation highlights the role of angels in the end times.

See also APOCALYPTIC LITERATURE; CHERUB; DEMON IN THE NEW TESTAMENT; DEMON IN THE OLD TESTAMENT; GOD; SATAN IN THE NEW TESTAMENT; SATAN IN THE OLD TESTAMENT.

Bibliography. J. Barr, "The Question of Religious Influence: The Case of Zoroastrianism, Judaism, and Christianity," *JAAR* 53 (1985): 201-35; K. Barth, *Church Dogmatics*, III/3, 477-531; E. F. F. Bishop, "Angelology in Judaism, Islam, and Christianity," *ATR* 46 (1964): 142-54; R. Bauckham, "The Worship of Jesus in Apocalyptic Christianity," *ATR* 46 (1964): 142-54 and "The Worship of Jesus in Apocalyptic Christianity," *NTS* 27 (1981): 322-41; W. Grundmann et al., "ἄγγελος, κτλ.," *TDNT*; E. Langton, *The Angel Teaching of the New Testament, The Ministries of the Angelic Powers*; R. North, "Separated Spiritual Substances in the Old Testament," *CBQ* 29 (1967): 419-49; M. Takahashi, "An Oriental's Approach to the Problems of Angelology," *ZAW* 78 (1966): 343-50.

—MARK J. OLSON

• **Angel of the Lord.** *See* ANGEL

• **Angelic Liturgy.** The *Angelic Liturgy* (*4QShirShabb*), or *Songs of the Sabbath Sacrifice*, is a collection of thirteen liturgical songs, one for each SABBATH during the first quarter of the year. It is extant in nine fragmentary Hebrew manuscripts from Qumran—eight from Cave 4 and one from Cave 11, the earliest dating from 75-50 B.C.E.—and one from MASADA, dating to ca. 50 C.E. The songs seem to follow a certain progression over the thirteen week cycle. Songs 1–5 focus on the earthly worshipping community. Songs 6–8 shift the attention to the heavenly worship, highlighting the number seven, which is developed elaborately in Song 7 in seven calls to praise directed to the seven angelic priesthoods. Songs 9–13 center on the features of the heavenly sanctuary and the participants in the heavenly worship.

The presence of nine manuscripts of the *Angelic Liturgy* at Qumran attests to its centrality in the cultic practices of the community. The songs may have been intended to lead the worshipper into an experience of angelic worship and thereby reinforce the community's understanding of itself as God's faithful and legitimate priesthood. Such mystical participation in the heavenly worship (cf. *1QSa*) is paralleled in Revelation (cf. *AscIsa*) and may stand behind the problem addressed in Colossians. The discovery of the document at Masada suggests that after the destruction of the Qumran settlement by the Romans in 68 C.E. some of its members may have joined the ZEALOTS in their final and ill-fated stand.

See also DEAD SEA SCROLLS; ESSENES.

Bibliography. C. Newsom, "Merkabah Exegesis in the Qumran Sabbath Shirot," *JJS* 38 (1987): 11-30 and *Songs of the Sabbath Sacrifice*.

—JOSEPH L. TRAFTON

• **Animals.** In the Bible the category animals includes a broad spectrum of fauna often without clear identification or classification of species, or families. Gen 1:20-25 distinguishes birds and water creatures, created on the fifth day (1:20-23), from land creatures, created on the sixth day (1:24-25). This distinction, however, is neither scientific nor precise (insects, for example, are creatures of both air and land) and is not consistently followed elsewhere, as in the list of clean and unclean animals in Lev 11:1-47. Of the impressive number of animals known to biblical people only about forty percent can be identified with zoological certainty. Many are mentioned only a few times and then in contexts that do not clearly give characteristics, habits, or habitats. Therefore, the identity by name of most animals in translations of the Bible reflect more the translators' ideas about the supposed fauna of the ancient biblical world than actual zoological identities.

Useful for a basic understanding of animals in biblical life are distinctions the Bible does make, distinctions between wild and domestic animals, between clean and unclean animals including the ritual use of clean animals, and between real and mythological or symbolic animals.

Wild and Domestic Animals. Many wild animals lived in the ancient biblical world, much of the terrain being more suitable for them than for human habitation. Often domesticated areas when abandoned were overrun by wild beasts (Hos 2:12; Is 5:5; 2 Kgs 17:25-26; Lam 5:18). Some of these animals were wild forms of domesticated animals, asses, camels, cattle, and goats. Some wild animals were a threat to humans and to domestic livestock. Among these were lions, bears, wolves, jackals, leopards and venomous snakes (Amos 5:19; 2 Kgs 2:23-24; 17:25; Ps 63:10; Jer 5:6). Bears also damaged fruit trees. Other wild animals, like deer, antelopes, wild cattle and goats, mice and other rodents damaged other crops and stored foodstuffs. Such damage to humans, livestock, and crops was often interpreted as divine punishment (Lev 26:22; 2 Kgs 2:23-24; 17:25-26; Jer 5:6). Wild beasts are occasionally used as metaphors for Israel's enemies (Ps 74:19; Jer 12:9), and the prophets likened the behavior of disobedient Israel to that of wild beasts. (Jer 2:23-24; 12:7-9).

Wild game must have been hunted for food since the list of ritually clean animals permitted as food included "the hart, the gazelle, the roebuck, the wild goat, the ibex, the antelope, and the mountain sheep" (Deut 14:5). Solomon's festive tables included some of these as well as "fatted fowl" (1 Kgs 4:22-23).

Domestic animals included horses, camels, asses, cattle, sheep, goats, and dogs. Frequent mention is made of the use of the horse in war, either ridden (Exod 14:9; 15:1; 2 Sam 1:6; 1 Kgs 20:20; Jer 50:42; Ezek 38:4; Acts 23:23), or with chariots (Exod 14:9; Judg 5:22; 1 Kgs 20:1; Isa 5:28; Jer 4:13). Horses were also used in both these ways for transport (Gen 41:43; 2 Sam 15:1; 2 Kgs 14:20). One of Solomon's commercial enterprises was buying and selling horses (1 Kgs 10:26-29). Israel regarded war horses as a luxury and as a sign of dependence on physical power for defense (1 Sam 8:11; Isa 31:1). The horse even became a symbol of war. Even so Israel made extensive use of the war horse (2 Sam 8:4; 1 Kgs 4:26; 18:5; 22:4). Camels were also used in war (Judg 6:5; 1 Chr 12:40) and for transportation, especially long-distance trade (1 Kgs 10:2). Camels were also raised as livestock by nomadic Arabs and others who, unlike Israel for whom camels were unclean, used both their milk and meat for food. Asses were used for transport both by nomads and by settled people (1 Sam 16:20-21; Num 22). Cattle were kept more as work animals to pull plows, threshing sledges, and carts than for milk and meat. Goats and sheep supplied food as well as hair and wool for cloth. Keeping large flocks of sheep and goats was a major occupation and some shepherds ranged widely in search of pasturage for their animals.

Few families owned horses or camels, but most had an ass, some cattle, and small flocks of goats and/or sheep. As in all traditional cultures, biblical families felt a close relationship with their domestic animals, which represented their wealth and which almost were part of the family. The animals were stabled close by, in the ground floor of the house or in an attached shed: "The ox knows its owner, and the ass its master's crib" (Isa 1:3). The law of the Sabbath provided a day of rest for beasts from work (Exod 20:10; Deut 5:14), straying animals should be returned to their owners (Exod 23:4), fallen animals should be helped (Exod 23:5; Deut 22:4), and abuse of animals was seriously criticized (Prov 12:10). This almost intimate relationship between humans and domestic animals is illustrated by the fact that children were sometimes named for animals—Rachel/ewe, Jonah/dove, Leah/deer or antelope—by the story of Balaam and his ass (Num 22), by Nathan's parable of the poor man who had only one ewe lamb which he loved as he would a child (2 Sam 12:1-4), and by the proverbial concern shepherds had for their flocks (Ps 23; John 10:1-18; Luke 15:3-7). Dogs lived in villages and towns as scavengers (1 Kgs 21:23-24). They were not highly regarded and apparently were never kept as pets.

In the eschatological future distinction between domestic and wild animals would be broken down (Isa 11:6-9).

Clean and Unclean Animals. The Levitical laws concerning uncleanness (Lev 11–16) and concerning sacrifice (chaps. 1–7) clearly specify certain animals as unclean and thereby forbidden as food or as sacrificial offerings. Clovenhoofed, cud chewing land animals were clean and could be eaten and sacrificed. All other mammals were unclean (Lev 11:2-8). Only fishes that have fins and scales could be eaten; they were not, however, used for offerings (Lev 11:9-12). A long list of birds, some not scientifically identifiable, but all apparently considered by Israel to be birds of prey, were unclean (Lev 11:13-19). Flying insects were unclean, but hopping insects were clean and edible (Lev 11:20-23). No insects were used as offerings. Swarming animals, including mice, lizards, multilegged insects etc. were unclean. The Bible gives no reasons for some animals being considered clean and others unclean. Various explanations have been suggested, most of them inadequate. That distinctions between clean and unclean were arbitrary designations by God to be obeyed as tests of obedience does not really explain anything and represents a theologically narrow view of God. The suggestion that unclean animals were either those used in non-Israelite worship or were associated or identified with non-Israelite deities explains only a small part of the evidence and is contradicted by the rather widespread use throughout the ancient world of most of the clean animals for various ritual purposes. Hygiene, more a modern than an ancient concern, accounts only for some of the prohibitions. Some of the "clean" animals are more suspect on grounds of health than some unclean; and if hygiene was the grounds of uncleanness why would Jesus pronounce all foods clean (Mark 7:19; cf. Acts 10:9-16)? Symbolic interpretations like Aristeas's suggestions that chewing the cud made an animal clean because this reminded people to meditate on the law (*Letter of Aristeas*, 154ff.) are more ingenious and imaginative than satisfactory. The prohibitions against eating unclean animals and their use in ritual is best explained as the concern of a traditional culture, like that of ancient Israel, with normality and wholeness as characteristics of purity. This explanation is supported by the requirement that all sacrificial animals be "perfect" animals (Lev 1:3, 10). The clean animals were those that Israel thought of as standard. Sheep, goats, and cattle would have been the standard for pastoralists and they chew the cud and have cloven feet. Fish should have scales and fins; insects should have wings and two hopping legs. Birds of prey are not standard because they eat flesh and blood. Only what is normally pure and whole could be eaten or offered to God. In the NT the dietary distinction between clean and unclean was gradually abandoned at the instruction of Jesus (Mark 7:19) and through the experience of the early apostles (Acts 10:1-16; 1 Cor 8).

Any clean domestic animal was acceptable as a sacrifice. Preferably they should be young unblemished males from the herds and flocks (Lev 1:2-3), but turtle doves and pigeons were acceptable (Lev 1:14-17). Offering of these animals, representing as they did wealth and an almost family-like relationship to the worshiper, would have been a real "sacrifice" symbolizing the gift of the worshiper's own life to God (2 Sam 24:24). Although clean game could be eaten (Deut 14:5), it was not used in sacrifices, presumably because there was no close attachment to it and because it cost nothing (Mal 1:7, 13).

Real and Mythological or Symbolic Animals. So far the focus has been on actual animals. Now we turn to animals of theological and literary imagination. At an elementary level certain animals illustrated abstract concepts: ass/peace, horse/war, lion/danger, and lamb/meekness and sacrifice. Much more creative is the range of mythological and apocalyptic animals that play a prominent role in many biblical texts.

Mythological animals include the serpent of Gen 3:1-7, LEVIATHAN or RAHAB, the chaos monster, and cherubim and SERAPHIM, the guardians of God's holiness. In Gen 3 the serpent is an attractive, cunning, and deceiving actor in a theological story about primeval times. It is neither an actual snake nor a clear symbol of sex, evil, temptation, or SATAN. Later it is identified with all of these things, but in the Genesis story is an imaginative literary creation essential to the plot of the story and its theological meaning.

Leviathan and Rahab are names of the mythological chaos monster vanquished by God in primordial creative combat (Job 3:8; 9:13; 26:12-13; 41:1-34; Ps 74:13-14; 89:10; 104:26). This chaos monster, thus subdued, lingered on as a threat to humanity's ordered world. God's power over this monster, however, makes it a mere plaything (Job 41:5; Ps 104:26) to be ultimately defeated with all other forms of wickedness (Isa 26:20–27:1).

Cherubim and seraphim were artistic and literary creations that functioned as guardians of divine majesty. Cherubim were creatures of various forms, always with wings, but with a variety of human and animal faces. Their bodies were bipedal or quadrupedal. They represented the mobility of God as parts of his throne (Exod 25:10-22), his chariot, or as his steeds (2 Sam 22:11; Ps 18:10). Seraphim are winged, fiery, serpentine beings that guarded the divine throne (Isa 6:1-3) and were emissaries of divine judgment (Num 21:6-9; Deut 8:15).

Apocalyptic animal imagery represents a literarily vivid extension of chaos symbolism into ongoing history by imagining certain oppressive kingdoms and figures in terrible composite beastly forms. Classic examples are the beasts of the visions in DANIEL (chaps. 7 and 8) and those of the BOOK OF REVELATION (chaps. 12–17). Others appear in the pseudepigraphic books of Enoch and the APOCALYPSE OF ABRAHAM.

See also AGRICULTURE/FARMING; CLEAN/UNCLEAN.

Bibliography. G. Bare, *Plants and Animals of the Bible*; M. Douglas, *Purity and Danger*.

—DAVID A. SMITH

• **Anna.** [an'uh] A female prophet, described in Luke 2:36–38, who spoke of the infant Jesus in the Jerusalem Temple to all who were waiting for the "redemption of Jerusalem" (cf. Isa 52:9 and the similar phrase used on documents and coins in BAR-KOKHBA's 132–35 C.E. Jewish revolt against Rome). Anna (the equivalent of the Hebrew Hannah), the daughter of Phanuel of the tribe of Asher, was a widow who spent most of her time fasting and praying in the Temple (cf. Luke 24:53 for the clue that not all of her time was literally spent there). It is unclear whether she is 84 years old at the time or whether she has been a widow for 84 years (probably 14 at marriage + 7 years of marriage + 84 years as a widow = 105 years old, significant as the age reached by the widow Judith, a hero in Israel; Jdt 16:23). For Luke, Anna is one of the three pious women who witness to the importance of Jesus in the redemption of God's people (Luke 1–2; the other women are Elizabeth and Mary).

See also SIMEON.

—DAVID M. SCHOLER

• **Annals.** *See* KINGS, BOOKS OF FIRST AND SECOND

• **Annas.** [an'uhs] Annas was installed as HIGH PRIEST by QUIRINIUS, Roman governor of Syria, in 6 C.E. Under Roman rule, tradition was swept aside (cf. Num 35:25) and the high priest became a political appointee. From the time of Annas's appointment until 41 C.E., the Romans limited the power of the high priest by keeping the vestments of the office in the TOWER OF ANTONIA at the northwest end of the Temple. Despite these restrictions, only the PROCURATOR exerted more power than Annas in the regions of Idumea, Judea, and Samaria. After Valerius, Roman procurator of Judea, removed him from office in 15 C.E. Annas continued to exercise considerable influence over political and religious affairs as a kind of high priest *emeritus* until his death in 35 C.E.

Six members of his family served as high priest after him. His son-in-law CAIAPHAS ministered from 18-37 C.E. Annas's dominance during these years is underscored in Luke 3:2 and Acts 4:6, where Annas is listed together with Caiaphas as high priest, and in John 18:13ff., where Jesus' trial begins with an appearance before Annas. Additional indications of Annas's influence can be found in rabbinical writings recording that around 30 C.E. the SANHEDRIN transferred its meeting place from "the hall of hewn stones" to the "bazaars." These "bazaars of the sons of Annas" are probably to be associated with the Temple markets that incited the anger of Jesus. Other than his son-in-law, Annas had five sons who served as high priest between 16 C.E. and 62 C.E. The last, Annas II, was responsible for the death of James the brother of Jesus.

See also CAIAPHAS; HIGH PRIEST; QUIRINIUS; SANHEDRIN.

—WM. BRUCE PRESCOTT

• **Anoint.** To pour or smear a sacred oil on a person's body, usually the head, or on sacred objects associated with worship rituals. The practice of anointing for secular and religious purposes appears frequently in the biblical narratives as well as in ancient Near East cultures.

Cultures outside Israel performed anointing to symbolize the elevation in legal status of an individual. For example, one was anointed on the occasion of the transfer of property or on the betrothal of a bride.

The cultic significance of anointing is the major focus of the biblical accounts. In the OT, anointing was performed on those who had a special function in Israel's religion. The kings of Israel (1 Sam 10:1), prophets (1 Kgs 19:16), High Priests (Lev 21:10), and priests (Exod 28:41) were anointed. Likewise the Tabernacle, the altar, and sacred objects used in worship (Exod 40:9) were anointed.

The ceremony of anointing was viewed as symbolic of the coming of God's spirit on a person or an object. Oil poured on the head of a king represented God's leadership in the life of the monarch chosen by God. Sacred oil used in the ceremony was made by mixing aromatic spices with olive oil (Exod 30:22-24).

The word MESSIAH comes from the Hebrew term "anointed one." The Greek equivalent of this word is "christos" from which the word "Christ" is derived. In the NT, Jesus is anointed by God with the Holy Spirit and power (Luke 4:18; Acts 10:38).

See also MESSIAH/MESSIANISM; WORSHIP IN THE OLD TESTAMENT.

Bibliography. E. Jacob, *Theology of the Old Testament*; "Anoint," *EncJud*; J. B. Payne, *The Theology of the Old Testament*.

—STEVEN SIMPLER

• **Anointed One.** *See* MESSIAH/CHRIST

• **Anthropology in the Old Testament.** *See* SOCIOLOGY OF THE OLD TESTAMENT

• **Anthropomorphism.** Conceiving of God as having human form or characteristics, derived from a combination of Greek words for "humankind" and "form." Unlike Egyptian and other portrayals of GOD in animal form or combinations of animal and human form, and unlike abstract impersonal Greek philosophical concepts of God as First Cause, Israel's distinctive understanding of God was personal. Biblical language describes Yahweh as possessing human form (anthropomorphism) and human feelings (anthropopathism). Typical anthropomorphic expressions in the OT include: God *walked* "in the garden in the cool of the day" (Gen 3:8); God *shut* Noah and his family into the Ark (Gen 7:16); God "*came down to see* the city and the tower" of Babel (Gen 11:5) and *scattered* the people "over the face of all the earth" (Gen 11:8); God *smelled* "the pleasing odor" of Noah's sacrifice (Gen 8:21); and God *said* to Moses, "I will *cover* you with my *hand* . . . and you shall see my *back* but my *face* shall not be seen" (Exod 33:22-23). Though conceiving of God as human-like, ISRAEL never allowed God to be portrayed by graven images. Conceptions of God as "Father" are rooted in OT usage and were used by JESUS, especially in the imagery of the "Model" or LORD'S PRAYER. The ultimate anthropomorphic description of God is the NT assertion that God has been revealed supremely in a person, Jesus of Nazareth. The advantage of conceiving of God in personal categories is that it makes relationship to God understandable and close, as contrasted with impersonal categories such as the "Ground of Being." Much needs to be done, and is being done, to demonstrate the wide range of personal references to God found in the Bible: the many references to God as mother (Isa 42:14-15) or midwife (Ezek 16:6, 9), or other references that stress God as the friend and companion of Israel or of the early Christian community.

The obvious danger in using anthropomorphic language is the possibility that the analogy will be absolutized. God is not to be understood as male or female or as having the characteristics of any single human grouping or class. Clearly, the biblical portrayal of God as Spirit, reiterated vividly in the Gospel of John (4:24), documents this understanding.

See also GOD; GOD LANGUAGE, INCLUSIVE; GOD, NAMES OF.

—BERNARD H. COCHRAN

• **Anthropopathism.** *See* ANTHROPOMORPHISM

• **Anti-Judaism in the New Testament.** Christian anti-Judaism has its roots in the NT and continues with varying intensity to the present. These anti-Jewish roots have evolved into three charges which Christians have used against Jews at different times with varying emphases. The charges are (1) that Jews were stiff-necked, hypocritical legalists who were responsible for the death of Jesus; (2) that this murder was deicide since Jesus was God, and (3) that Judaism could have no continuing validity since God has replaced it with Christianity. All three of these charges, however, need qualification.

It is true that much of the NT teaches that Jews, especially the PHARISEES, opposed Jesus on hypocritical, legalistic grounds. Jesus' own teaching, however, as represented by the NT, appears quite similar to that of the Pharisees. Moreover, Jesus' condemnation of hypocrisy is not unlike what can be found in early rabbinic sources. It is also true that throughout the NT Jews are blamed for Jesus' CRUCIFIXION (Acts 2:22, 36; 3:13-15; 4:10; 7:52; John 19:12-16; Acts 2:23, 36; 3:13-15; 4:10; 7:52; etc.); but Jesus was in fact condemned under Roman jurisdiction for claiming kingship (Mark 15:2, 9, 18, 26, 32, and par.) The Jews involved were priestly leaders appointed by the Roman governor. Still, even groundless charges can sway public opinion. Pharisee has become synonymous with hypocrite; and the gospel portrayal of Jews framing Jesus before Pontius Pilate together with their crying out for Jesus' blood to be upon them and their children (Matt 27:25) still lives in pulpits, paintings, passion plays, and motion pictures.

The charge that the Jews had killed Jesus was heightened by NT interpretations that made Jesus the equal of God. Such interpretations also served to explain Jewish opposition to Jesus and his followers. To regard any human as equal to God was certainly incompatible with Jewish monotheism; however, one should not assume that the NT actually did exalt Jesus to full equality with God. No NT book does so unequivocally. In fact, the opposite appears to be so. Against those who would accuse Christians of making this claim (John 5:18), the Fourth Gospel stresses that Jesus only had the authority granted him by God (John 5:19, 30, 34-35; 8:54). Nor is this book exceptional. Paul also clearly states that Christ must be subject to God as one who is all in all (1 Cor 15:28). Even the rarely applied title "God" need not have exalted Christ to a point that would have forced his followers out of the Jewish community. Jews also could apply such language to humans. In the first century, Philo tended to use divine language of Moses, Josephus referred to Moses as a "divine man" (*Ant* 3.3.7), and in later times even a rabbinic text freely affirms that God shared the divine glory with Moses by calling him "God" (*Tanhuma*, Buber, *Behaàlotekha* 15). The same passage also speaks of God sharing divine glory with Elijah and the messianic king. Although some Jews in NT and later times may have been offended by the Christian glorification of Christ, it need not have represented so wide a gulf between church and synagogue as commonly assumed.

The belief that Christianity replaced Judaism also needs some qualification. Recent interpretations, including those of Gager and Van Buren, show that this simple replacement theory may not do justice to the writings of Paul (Rom 2:25; 11:1-32); nevertheless, it is quite clear that elsewhere within the NT (e.g., Hebrews) such a replacement theology is implicit. In fact some writers found historical justification for the theory by equating the divine replacement of Judaism with the physical destruction of Jerusalem by the Romans in 70 C.E. (cf. Mark 15:38 and par.)

The reasons for anti-Jewish invective in the NT are manifold. First, it is quite common for a breaking-away religious sect to express a hostility toward a parent religion similar to that shown by adolescents breaking away from parental control. Second, as the church became less Jewish, it became relatively easy for the later NT writers to treat Jews superficially as a hostile unity. Third, the fact that Jesus had been condemned in a Roman trial for claiming Jewish kingship (Mark 15:2, 9, 18, 26, 32, and par.) posed a problem for his followers. The same Romans who condemned Jesus would certainly condemn his followers. The Christian solution was to declare that Jesus had been falsely charged by the Jews and was innocent of any crime against Rome.

In the case of the Pharisees, what is said against them

may well reflect the bias of the Evangelists. After the fall of Jerusalem in 70 C.E. when most of the NT was written, the Pharisees had become the most powerful party in Judaism, the party with which the early church had to contend. Still some anti-Pharisaic teachings were so similar to what Jesus reportedly preached, it is not surprising some Pharisees came to hear him. Jesus, therefore, may well have directed remarks against the shortcomings of certain Pharisees simply because they were present.

Whatever the historical reasons for early Christian anti-Judaism, what Christians said at first had little effect on most Jews. There were many Jews and few Christians. But the situation changed as the Roman Empire became Christian. What had been written in one context for understandable historical and sociological reasons, now became the Christian justification for persecuting Jews. In time such anti-Jewish attitudes infected the world of Christian biblical scholarship, and many scholars (e.g., Paulus, Strauss, Renan, and G. Kittel) were quite open about their contempt for Jews. Indeed it is necessary to question the extent to which modern NT scholarship has been influenced by generations of an anti-Jewish climate in university circles.

Unfortunately, scholarly explanations of NT anti-Judaism in historical and sociological terms have little effect on popular attitudes. How can such attitudes be changed? One may certainly try to root out NT anti-Judaism where later translators and interpreters have read it into the text; but many aspects of our culture, such as passion plays, seem to be rather intensifying this secondary anti-Judaism. A more serious problem is that much anti-Judaism forms part of the NT text and is not merely the product of biased interpretation. Various solutions are being proposed. One comes from Norman Beck. He would simply rewrite the NT and remove what is anti-Jewish. A less radical suggestion is to avoid reading passages with anti-Jewish biases in public worship. In the case of readings like the passion narratives which could be hardly omitted entirely, one might use a nonbiblical, liturgical version like the liturgical passion narrative published by the NCCJ. There is a precedent for such usage in the liturgical versions of the Last Supper which occur in eucharistic liturgies. A third approach is that of Van Buren, who argues that Christian theology must recognize the continuation of the Jewish people as part of the divine plan.

See also CRUCIFIXION; PHARISEES; TRIAL OF JESUS.

Bibliography. N. A. Beck, *Mature Christianity: The Recognition and Repudiation of the Anti-Jewish Polemic of the New Testament*; A. T. Davies, ed., *Anti-Semitism and the Foundations of Christianity*; J. Gager, *The Origins of Anti-Semitism*; J. Isaac, *Jesus and Israel*; J. Koenig, *Jews and Christians in Dialogue: New Testament Foundations*; R. Ruether, *Faith and Fratricide*; S. Sandmel, *Anti-Semitism in the New Testament?*; J. T. Townsend, *A Liturgical Interpretation in Narrative Form of the Passion of Jesus Christ*, 2nd ed.; P. Van Buren, *A Theology of Jewish-Christian Reality*; C. M. Williamson, *Has God Rejected His People? Anti-Judaism in the Christian Church*.

—JOHN T. TOWNSEND

• **Antichrist.** The Antichrist is an evil individual of apocalyptic eschatology who is to arise in the last days as an opponent of Christ. Whereas the term "antichrist" appears only in four passages in the NT (1 John 2:18, 22; 4:3; 2 John 7), the concept of an antichrist is present in several NT texts. The Antichrist will appear prior to the return of Christ and will lead a campaign of persecution and deception against Christ's followers. His power will end when Christ returns to earth and defeats the Antichrist and his forces.

Jewish thought seems to provide the rudiments of the antichrist concept, for the idea of a great adversary of God and his people is present in several Jewish writings. The oracles in Ezek 38–39 describe in apocalyptic language the attack against the people of God by Gog of Magog "in the latter years" and the defeat of Gog and his forces by God. Dan 7–8 describe a "little horn," Antiochus IV, who will come as an oppressor of God's faithful. The evil of this wicked ruler will be great and he will be successful initially. In the end, however, God will prevail. Noncanonical Jewish writings mention similar opponents under the name of Beliar or Belial.

All of these ideas are reflected in various places in the NT. Gog and Magog from Ezekiel reappear in Rev 20:8. The visions of Daniel also influenced the writing of Revelation (esp. chap. 13). Paul mentions Belial/Beliar in 2 Cor 6:15. The final opponent of God has become in the NT the final opponent of Christ.

The belief in some kind of ultimate opponent who will arise in the last days before the return of Christ was apparently widespread in the first century C.E., as evidenced by the way in which various NT writers make use of the idea. The author of 2 Thessalonians gives no explanation about the enigmatic MAN OF LAWLESSNESS (2:3-12) who will arise in the last days, likely a variant of the antichrist concept. This individual "opposes and exalts himself against every so-called god or object of worship, so that he takes his seat in the temple of God proclaiming himself to be God" (2:4). This lawless one, an agent of SATAN, will deceive many people before he is destroyed by Christ when he returns. The author of the Johannine Letters has broadened the idea so that he speaks not only of one antichrist, but of many antichrists. Whoever denies the Father and the Son is an antichrist (1 John 2:22), as well as those who "will not acknowledge the coming of Jesus Christ in the flesh" (2 John 7).

The fullest development of the idea of the Antichrist is in Revelation. Even though the term "antichrist" never appears in the book, the dragon of chap. 12 and the two beasts of chap. 13 all are in some sense antichrist figures, although the first beast, the one from the sea, most fully deserves the title. This evil triumvirate is guilty of deceiving the people of the earth, of slaughtering faithful believers, and of leading a final struggle against God. The two beasts (or beast and false prophet) are defeated by Christ in chap. 19, whereas the dragon is finally destroyed in chap. 20.

See also APOCALYPTIC LITERATURE; JOHN, GOSPEL AND LETTERS OF; MAN OF LAWLESSNESS; REVELATION, BOOK OF; THESSALONIANS, LETTERS TO THE.

Bibliography. W. Boussett, *The Antichrist Legend*; R. Yates, "The Antichrist," *EvQ* 46 (1974): 42-50.

—MITCHELL G. REDDISH

• **Antioch.** [an'tee-ok] Two of the ancient cities which bore the name Antioch (named for Antiochus) are important for NT times (PLATES 26, 27).

Antioch of Syria. Antioch, the capital of the province of Syria, was the third largest city in the Roman Empire, surpassed only by Rome and Alexandria. It was founded by Seleucus Nicator in 301 B.C.E. and was the seat of the old Seleucid Empire. The city was situated on the banks of the Orontes river about sixteen mi. inland from the Mediterranean Sea. Its seaport was Seleucia which was at the mouth of the Orontes. In addition to having access to trade through the seaport of Seleucia, the city was also astride the best land route between Asia Minor, Syria, and Palestine.

Since Antioch was a free city, people of various cultures were attracted to the metropolis on the Orontes. In the first century C.E. the population was estimated to be about 500,000. The inhabitants were Macedonians, Greeks, and native Syrians plus a large Jewish group stemming from the time of Seleucus who gave land to Jewish veterans in his army as a reward for services rendered. The large Jewish population had a tremendous influence on the gentiles. Many of them accepted the Jewish way of life and became proselytes to Judaism. The relationship between Jews and non-Jews in the city of Antioch was very pleasant and peaceful. Josephus (*BJ* 7.3.3) said that the Jews were granted equal privileges with the Greek citizens.

When Rome occupied Syria in 64 B.C.E. Antioch became the capital of the East and the military headquarters for the Roman forces. Pompey made it the seat of the legate of Syria. The city owed much of its splendor in streets and porticos to Antiochus Epiphanes and Herod the Great. It was noted as a center of Greek life and culture. Under the domination of the Romans, Antioch was enlarged and beautified along Roman lines. The city was famous for its splendid public buildings, colonnaded streets, and the beauty of its suburbs. One of these suburbs was Daphne which housed the celebrated sanctuary of Apollo and Artemis.

Christians in Antioch played an important role in the spread of early Christianity. It was here that the first attempt was made to preach directly to the gentiles. This was accomplished by the Hellenistic Jewish Christians who fled to Antioch to escape persecution by the Jews after the stoning of Stephen (Acts 8:1). The followers of Jesus were called Christians for the first time in this city. PAUL and BARNABAS with the help of the church in Antioch launched the first missionary movement by going to Cyprus.

In the last half of the fourth century and the first half of the fifth century C.E. the Antiochene school of theology was firmly established and boasted of such names as Diodorus, Theodore, John Chrysostom, and Theodoret. Antioch is now called Antakya, and it is in Turkey rather than Syria. Once a city of splendor and famous for its large number of inhabitants, today the city is not very attractive, and the population is less than 50,000.

Pisidian Antioch was located on the border between the ancient districts of Phrygia and Pisidia. Today archaeologists identify the site of the ancient city with the ruins about two mi. east of modern Yalvac in Turkey. It was situated on a plateau and had full protection by its natural defenses. It served the Seleucids as a border fortress and as a first line of defense against the Pisidian mountaineers.

Originally the inhabitants of Antioch were Phrygian, an ethnical group known for emotional excess. The territory was a center for highly emotional religious cults. In his *Republic* Plato banned an exciting type of music known as the "Phrygian mode." The Phrygian cap was a necessary head gear in the rite of initiation for one of the mystery cults. In addition to the Phrygian element Antioch had Greek and Roman inhabitants and a large Jewish community that settled there during the time of Seleucus I.

After the defeat of Antiochus III at the battle of Magnesia in 189 B.C.E. the Romans declared Antioch a free city. This permitted the citizens to have their own elective form of self-government, popular assemblies, and education of their children along Hellenistic lines.

In 36 B.C.E. Mark Antony made Antioch a part of the rule of the Galatian king Amyntas. After the death of Amyntas in 25 B.C.E. the city and the whole domain were incorporated into the Roman province of GALATIA. The official name for Antioch became *Colonia Caesarea* in 11 B.C.E. when it was made a Roman colony. Roman veterans moved in as colonists among the native inhabitants, and the city was Romanized. During his lifetime Augustus established an emperor cult in Antioch which added to the indigenous expressions of religious experience. The chief god of the city was Men Askaenas whose temple was the Square of Augustus. The symbol of this god was a bull's head. Magna Mater, the mother goddess of a mystery cult, was duly venerated among the inhabitants.

After Paul and Barnabas had completed their mission on the island of Cyprus, they journeyed to Pisidian Antioch by way of Perga in Pamphylia. As was their custom, they went to the Jewish synagogue on the Sabbath day, and after the reading of the assigned portion of the Law and Prophets, the rulers of the synagogue asked them to speak. Paul delivered a sermon that was quite appropriate for the congregation which was made up of Jews and gentiles who had become proselytes or were attracted to Judaism without submitting to circumcision or proselyte baptism. Many members of the congregation were interested in what Paul said and invited him to remain in the city. The following Sabbath he preached in the synagogue, but the Jews stirred up a persecution against Paul and Barnabas and drove them out of the city.

During their mission in the province of Galatia Paul and Barnabas established churches in Antioch, Iconium, Lystra, and Derbe. Later Paul wrote a letter to the churches of Galatia defending his gospel of freedom against the Judaizers who were leading his converts astray.

See also BARNABAS; GALATIA; PAUL; SYRIA AND CILICIA.

Bibliography. C. R. Morey, *The Mosaics of Antioch*; J. Finegan, *Light from the Ancient Past*; G. E. Wright, *Biblical Archaeology*; B. M. Metzger, "Antioch-on-the-Orontes," *BA* 11/4 (1948): 69-88; W. M. Ramsey, *The Cities of St. Paul* and *St. Paul The Traveller and Roman Citizen*.

—T. C. SMITH

• **Antiochus.** *See* MACCABEES, THE

• **Antipas.** [an'tee-puhs] From the Greek ἀντίπας, a shortened form of ἀντίπατρος, "instead of [his] father."

1. Son of HEROD the Great by his Samaritan wife, Malthace (one of nine wives that Herod had simultaneously). Antipas is best known as the tetrarch of Galilee and Perea from 4 B.C.E. to 39 C.E. (Luke 3:1, 19). He ordered John the Baptist imprisoned and later beheaded (Matt 14:1-11). According to Luke 23:7-12 he mocked Jesus during his trial. Antipas was probably the most capable administrator among the sons of Herod though Luke describes him as "that fox" (13:32). He built several important cities including Tiberias.

2. A Christian martyr at Pergamum (Rev 2:12).

See also HEROD.

—WATSON E. MILLS

• **Antipatris.** *See* APHEK

• **Anti-Semiticism.** *See* ANTI-JUDAISM IN THE NEW TESTAMENT; ESTHER, BOOK OF

• **Antonia, Tower of.** [an'toh"nee-uh] A Hasmonean fortress located at the northwest end of the Temple court in Jerusalem (PLATE 22). It had been restored after the Exile by John Hyrcanus (135-105 B.C.E.). This palatial guard tower was luxuriously enlarged by HEROD the Great in the late first century B.C.E. and named after Herod's friend Mark Antony. The term Antonia does not occur in scripture; rather the structure is referred to as παρεμβολή (barracks) in Acts 21:34-37; 22:24; 23:10, 16, 32.

Josephus describes the spacious interior of the tower indicating that it included apartments, baths, and courtyards as well as the barracks themselves. There was a staircase leading into the Temple's Court of the Gentiles.

Beginning as early as the time of David, the fortress gave the defenders of Jerusalem an excellent view of their enemies to the north. But with the rise of power of the Roman Empire the tower functioned as a station from which the Romans occupying Jerusalem could watch over the Jews who lived there. Josephus indicates that more than 500 soldiers were quartered here where the highest tower overlooked the courtyards of the Temple.

According to Acts 21, Antonia was the scene of Paul's disagreement with some of the Jewish leaders. Paul sought to address the angry mob from the steps of the fortress but had to be taken inside for his own safety. There he was questioned by the commander CLAUDIUS LYSIAS who did not punish Paul once he learned Paul was a Roman citizen. But Claudius Lysias realized that Paul's continued presence in Jerusalem posed a threat and so he made plans to transfer him to Casearea.

The tower was finally destroyed during the Jewish-Roman War.

See also HEROD; HERODIAN FORTRESSES; LYSIAS, CLAUDIUS; TEMPLE/TEMPLES.

—WATSON E. MILLS

• **Antonius Felix.** *See* FELIX

• **Aphek.** [ay'fek] *1.* Ras el-Ain, located twenty-six mi. south of Caesarea, has been identified as Aphek of Sharon (PLATES 12, 23). Situated on the ancient Via Maris between Megiddo and Joppa, the town had strategic importance. According to 1 Sam 4, the PHILISTINES assembled at Aphek and the Hebrews at Ebenezer before the disastrous defeat in which the Philistines captured the Ark of the covenant. The position of Ras el-Ain on the frontier between Israel and Philistia corresponds well for the 1050 B.C.E. encounter. Whether this is the Aphek at which the Philistines camped prior to the battle with and defeat of Saul at Mount Gilboa (1 Sam 29:1) is uncertain. Saul's Aphek might have been located in the vicinity of Mount Gilboa at the southeastern end of the Jezreel valley. Herod the Great rebuilt the city in 35 B.C.E. and named it Antipatris after his father Antipater. Paul was taken through Antipatris on his way to Caesarea from Jerusalem (Acts 23:31).

Aphek of Sharon has been excavated by The Palestine Department of Antiquities (1934-36), by The Israel Department of Antiquities (1958, 1961) and by Tel Aviv University and the New Orleans Baptist Theological Seminary since 1972. These excavations have revealed that the site was occupied as early as the Early Bronze Age (first half of the third millennium B.C.E.). The site was deserted for over five hundred years, when it began to flourish again during the Middle and Late Bronze Age. The city, which covered about thirty acres, met with violent destruction at the end of the Late Bronze Age (roughly the thirteenth century B.C.E.) by the intrusion of the Sea Peoples. Archaeological evidence from the tombs in the area has yielded both Late Bronze and Iron Age materials. Fragments of trilingual tablets utilizing Sumerian, Babylonian, and Canaanite have been unearthed in the final Late Bronze town. These are postulated to have been part of a revolving prism which was used as a dictionary.

This site is probably the Aphek of the nineteenth century Egyptian Execration Texts, whose Prince Yanakilu, has a west semitic name. The Memphis Stela of Amenhotep II mentions Aphek as the first town conquered in his second Asiatic campaign (ca. 1440). Asshurbanipal of Assyria mentions a border town of Samaria located on the military road to Egypt. The name also appears in the Aramaic letter of Adon, a Palestinian king, to his Egyptian overlord. Adon's letter dates to about 600 B.C.E. and tells of the advancing Babylonian army.

2. A city named Aphek is associated with Israel's warring against Syria. 1 Kgs 20 relates that Ben-Hadad of Syria was defeated by Ahab of Israel on the plain near Aphek. The routed Syrian forces fled to the city for refuge but met with disaster when the city wall fell, killing 27,000 soldiers. 1 Kgs 13:14-19 gives Elisha's prediction that Joash of Israel would defeat the Syrians at Aphek. The situations presented in these passages indicate a city located east of the Jordan. The modern village of Fiq, about three miles east of the Sea of Galilee on the highway between Beth-Shan and Damascus, might be the site of these events.

3. Aphek, or Aphik, was designated as part of the inheritance of the tribe of Asher (Josh 19:24-30). However, the Phoenician coastal town was not conquered according to Judg 1:31-32. Commonly identified with Tell Kerdanah, it is located about six mi. southeast of Acco.

4. Josh 13:4 lists Aphek as a city on Israel's northern boundary. Modern Afqa is generally recognized as being the site. This site is fifteen mi. east of Jebeil and twenty-three mi. northeast of Beirut. Like the Aphek of Asher, this region was never conquered by the Israelites.

Bibliography. M. Kochavi, "The History and Archeology of Aphek-Antipatris," *BA* 44/2 (Spring 1981): 75-86; W. H. Morton, "Aphek," *IDB*; M. W. Prausnitz, "Aphek (in the Sharon)," *IDBSupp*; J. M. Miller and J. Hayes, *A History of Ancient Israel and Judah, Israelite and Judaean History*.

—ROBERT A. STREET, JR.

• **Apocalyptic Literature.** [uh-pok'uh-lip"tik] The adjective "apocalyptic" refers to a field of literature that includes a GENRE of literature called apocalypses (in the Bible the books of DANIEL and REVELATION qualify) as well as other types of literature (for example certain letters or the WAR SCROLL from Qumran) whose subject matter closely resembles that of the apocalypses. The noun "apocalypse" comes from the Greek word ἀποκάλυψις, which means "revelation." An apocalypse is thus a book that reveals hidden information. To describe the nature of that information is to describe the genre itself.

Description of an Apocalypse. Scholars have typically listed a number of characteristics belonging to apocalypses. In terms of literary characteristics, they mention the prevalence of visions and auditions, the revelation of secrets, and the activity of a celestial being to interpret the vision. Apocalypses are often pseudonymous, that is, they are written under the name of a worthy past figure. Often the name of the figure will give the reader an insight into the contents of the apocalypse. For example, 4 EZRA utilizes the Jewish tradition that EZRA copied the whole OT by having him receive numerous "secret" works for the last days. 2 BARUCH deals with the destruction of the second TEMPLE in 70 C.E. through the eyes of JEREMIAH's scribe, who witnessed the destruction of the First Temple in 586 B.C.E. Apocalypses employ coded speech, in which numbers, animals, and unusual natural occurrences take on special meanings. The images of the apocalyptic literature are reused by later writers, so that meanings are piled on top of one another. Also, apocalypses employ much hortatory or paranetic material, instructing persons how to live on the basis of the secrets revealed to them. Finally, apocalypses employ narration, which identifies the seer, his state of mind, his reactions, and any final instructions about preserving the revelation.

Themes characteristic of apocalypses are numerous. One such element is the periodization of history, in which the vicissitudes of national life are arranged according to a definite model (see the bright and dark waters of *2 Baruch*). However history is presented, the time of the actual author of the apocalypse is depicted as the last, bitter days of this age, with the age to come already casting its influence over those who have insight. Much of the "prediction" in an apocalypse is actually "prophecy after the fact," a review of the time between the alleged author and the time of the actual author. This practice gives apocalypses the appearance of determinism, but apocalypses presume that individuals have the full right to choose, and they hold people accountable for their choices. Apocalyptic ESCHATOLOGY tends toward DUALISM. It envisions two aeons, this age and the age to come. This age is speeding toward an imminent end, often including cosmic upheavals. The periodization of history allows those in the know to read the signs of the coming eschaton or end. That eschaton will be marked by the reversal of the sociological status quo, with the righteous triumphing. This reversal will be brought about by God's activity, either directly or through his MESSIAH. Judgment will properly compensate good and evil people. Often the seer will tour HEAVEN and/or HELL. God's rival, SATAN, will be defeated. The entire cosmos might be renewed. The righteous will enjoy an eschatological banquet. Often the nations, perhaps after being purged, will be allowed to join in. Finally, apocalypses develop systems of angelology, demonology, COSMOLOGY, ASTROLOGY, and even botany.

By no means are all of these characteristics unique to apocalypses. Nor does the listing of them adequately define an apocalypse. Some scholars, therefore, have attempted to reduce the list of characteristics to one essential characteristic. That one characteristic might be the apocalyptic view of history, or the failure of apocalyptic to translate its picture of the future into historical, political terms, or the emphasis on visions and wisdom. None of these suggestions has won widespread acceptance. A new definition for an apocalypse has emerged which defines the genre in terms of structure, content and function: " 'Apocalypse' is a genre of revelatory literature with a narrative framework, in which a revelation is mediated by an otherworldly being to a human recipient, disclosing a transient reality which is both temporal, insofar as it envisages eschatological salvation, and spatial insofar as it involves another, supernatural world" (J. J. Collins, 9), "intended to interpret present, earthly circumstances in light of the supernatural world and of the future, and to influence both the understanding and the behavior of the audience by means of divine authority" (A. Y. Collins, "Introduction," 7).

Types of Apocalypses. This definition lends itself to designing a typology of apocalypses. Apocalypses, both Jewish and Christian, can be distinguished on the basis of the presence or absence of an otherworldly journey (*Semeia* 14:30-44, 70-95). Type I apocalypses will be those lacking such a journey, while Type II apocalypses will describe an otherworldly tour. Each type manifests three subtypes: (a) apocalypses with a historical review, (b) apocalypses with a cosmic and/or political eschatology, and (c) apocalypses with only a personal eschatology. There are no Jewish examples of Type Ib and Ic, and no Christian example of Type IIa. A list of apocalypses written between the mid second century B.C.E. and the late third century C.E. follows, classified by type.

Type Ia. Apocalypses with a historical review and no otherworldly journey. Jewish: Daniel (7–12), the "Animal Apocalypse" of 1 ENOCH 87–90, the "Apocalypse of Weeks" (1 Enoch 93; 91:12-17), JUBILEES 23, *4 Ezra*, and *2 Baruch*. Christian: LADDER OF JACOB.

Type Ib. Apocalypses with a cosmic and/or political eschatology and no otherworldly journey. Jewish: none extant. Christian: Revelation, the APOCALYPSE OF PETER, the SHEPHERD OF HERMAS, the *Book of Elchasai,* the *Apocalypse of St. John the Theologian,* and the *Testament of the Lord* 1:1-14.

Type Ic. Apocalypses with only personal eschatology and no otherworldly journey. Jewish: none extant. Christian: *5 Ezra* (2 Esdr 1–2) 2:42-48, the TESTAMENT OF ISAAC 2–3a, the TESTAMENT OF JACOB 1–3a, the *Questions of Bartholomew,* and the *Book of the Resurrection of Jesus Christ* by Bartholomew the Apostle 8b–14a.

Type IIa. Apocalypses with a historical review and an otherworldly journey. Jewish: the APOCALYPSE OF ABRAHAM. Christian: none extant.

Type IIb. Apocalypses with cosmic and/or political eschatology and an otherworldly journey. Jewish: *1 Enoch* 1–36, the *Book of the Heavenly Luminaries* (*1 Enoch* 72–82), the *Similitudes of Enoch* (*1 Enoch* 37–71), 2 ENOCH (or Slavonic Enoch), and the *Testament of Levi* 2–5. Christian: the ASCENSION OF ISAIAH 6–11, the APOCALYPSE OF PAUL, *4 Ezra* and the *Apocalypse of the Virgin Mary*.

Type IIc. Apocalypses with only personal eschatology and an otherworldly journey. Jewish: 3 BARUCH, the *Testament of Abraham,* and the APOCALYPSE OF ZEPHANIAH. Christian: the *Testament of Isaiah* 5–6, the *Testament of Jacob* 5, the *Story of Zosimus,* the *Apocalypse of the Holy Mother of God concerning the Punishments*, the APOCALYPSE OF JAMES, the Brother of the Lord, the *Mysteries of St. John the Apostle and the Holy Virgin,* the *Book of the Resurrection of Jesus Christ* (by Bartholomew the Apostle) 17b–19b, and the APOCALYPSE OF SEDRACH.

Origin of Apocalyptic Thinking. Where did this genre arise? The subject of the origin of apocalyptic has drawn much attention from scholars, whose opinions can be reviewed under three main headings. Many, perhaps most, scholars (e.g., R. H. Charles, H. H. Rowley, D. S. Russell) have argued that apocalyptic literature is a child of prophecy. Postexilic, eschatological prophecy in the OT seems to provide a natural link between the classical, preexilic prophets and apocalypses (see below), so scholars point to texts like Ezek 38–39, Isa 24–27, 34–35, 56–66, Joel, and Zech 9–14 as the seedbed for apocalyptic thinking.

Not all scholars, however, agree with this view. An alternative was proposed by Gerhard von Rad, who argued that the essence of apocalyptic literature was its deterministic view of history, a view unaffected by the prophetic conception built on reciting the creeds about God's mighty deeds, and derived from WISDOM LITERATURE. Still others saw apocalyptic literature as the child of foreign influences. Usually characteristics like dualism caused scholars (e.g., Wilhelm Bousset) to point to Zoroastrianism as the most likely source of influence, but T. Francis Glasson and Franz Boll looked toward Greece and Rudolf Otto thought pre-Hindu Aryan thinking had made an impact.

All of these views build on a degree of evidence, so where did apocalyptic thinking originate? Recently, biblical scholars have looked to the disciplines of anthropology and sociology to help answer this question. Scholars in those disciplines indicate that apocalyptic thinking arises in societies or subcultures of a society which experience relative deprivation, i.e., when the reality of their lives becomes too far separated negatively from their hopes and aspirations. Hence, external attacks or persecutions, as well as internal disarray that threatens a group's internalized system of assumptions, values and commitments, threatens the group's self identity, and challenges its worldview and its perception of moral order, may cause some members of a society to break with its leaders and their program and formulate a new program. The Book of Daniel gives evidence of just such a break. The book contains stories about Jews living in foreign courts and remaining faithful to Judaism. Such stories would be told by people attempting to cope with life and work in a foreign court. Apocalyptic thought could develop among such people, however, if their expectations were not met. In the same way, priests out of power or prophets conscious of the discrepancy between prophetic expectations for the restoration and the realities of the post-exilic period began to think in an apocalyptic fashion. The time when the pressures reached a climax in ancient Israel seems to have been the period of persecution under Antiochus Epiphanes, and apocalyptic thought gave birth to the genre of apocalypses as the authors' vehicles for expressing their hopes.

The insight that apocalyptic literature arises from groups experiencing at least relative deprivation may explain why apocalyptic did not develop among some Jews. PHILO and the author of 4 MACCABEES were quite at home in the dominant Greek culture and needed only to defend their worldview and sense of moral order, which they did in Greek terms. Likewise, the SADDUCEES constituted a priestly collaborationist group, standing far from apocalypticism. By contrast, the impotent priests at Qumran became somewhat apocalyptic in their thought.

There were, of course, antecedents in the OT for apocalypses. The visions of Zech 1–6 anticipate the characteristic report of visions with an interpreting ANGEL. Further, texts like Ezek 38–39, Isa 24–27, 34–35, 56–66, Joel, and Zech 9–14 develop eschatological thinking, providing later apocalyptic literature with such themes as the imminent inbreak the KINGDOM OF GOD, judgment, the return of the exiles, protection of God's people, an eschatological banquet, the defeat and/or conversion of the nations, paradisical living conditions, natural disorders heralding the end, and salvation to the faithful.

Related Literature. Apocalyptic thinking also emerged in literature other than apocalypses. Scholars often cite the TESTAMENTS OF THE TWELVE PATRIARCHS (especially the *Testaments of Levi, Dan* and *Judah*) and the SIBYLLINE ORACLES as books containing apocalyptic thinking. Among the DEAD SEA SCROLLS a number of the sectarian works, especially the *War Scroll*, share a thought world very similar at least to that of the apocalypses. New Testament scholars speak of Mark 13 and its parallels as the synoptic apocalypse, though the material occurs within the genre of gospel and takes the *form* of a farewell discourse. The eschatology of Paul, particularly in 1 Thess 4, resembles apocalyptic eschatology in terms of its expectation of the imminent return of the Messiah and the end of this age. Further, Ernst Käsemann argued that behind the Gospel of Matthew stood, among others, an apocalyptic group that generated a type of legal saying of Jesus in which the protasis is conditional, but the apodosis is apodictic (for example, Matt 5:23-24), and a set of sayings by Jesus summarizing who he was in the form: "I am come . . . " (e.g., Matt 10:34-35). According to Käsemann the Gospel of Matthew preserves the compulsion of early, apocalyptic preachers to make known the secret things of the Lord.

Summary. Apocalyptic literature includes both apocalypses and other genres that exhibit a distinctive worldview and eschatology. This worldview involves a multi-storied universe, with earth, heaven and hell. It involves further a view of history that is divided into periods. That history is leading humankind nowhere, and must soon be brought to an end by God himself. The endtime will be characterized by cosmic disorders, social class reversal, warfare; in short, the *status quo* will be reversed and the apocalyptic group will receive its due recompense. The people by whom and for whom apocalyptic literature is written perceived themselves to be deprived of that recompense in this age. They designed the literary genre called an apocalypse to convey their message of eschatological reversal. Specifically, an apocalypse exhibits a narrative structure within which an otherworldly being conveys a revelation of eschatological salvation and a supernatural world.

See also DANIEL; REVELATION.

Bibliography. G. Allan, "A Theology of Millenarianism: The Irvingite Movement as an Illustration," *BJS* 25 (1974): 296-310; R. H. Charles, *A Critical History of the Doctrine of the Future Life*; A. Y. Collins, "The Early Christian Apocalypses," *Semeia* 14 (1979): 61-121 and "Introduction: Early Christian Apocalypticism," *Semeia* 36 (1986): 1-11; J. J. Collins, "Introduction: Towards the Morphology of a Genre" and "The Jewish Apocalypses," *Semeia* 14 (1979): 1- 59; T. F. Glasson, *Greek Influences in Eschatology*; P. D. Hanson, *The Dawn of Apocalyptic*; E. Käsemann, "The Beginnings of Christian Theology," *JTC* 6 (1969): 17-46; R. Otto, *The Kingdom of God and the Son of Man*; O. Plöger, *Theocracy and Eschatology*; G. von Rad, *Old Testament Theology*; H. H. Rowley, *The Relevance of Apocalyptic*; D. S. Russell, *The Method and Message of Apocalyptic*; W. Schmithals, *The Apocalyptic Movement*; P. Vielhauer, *New Testament Apocrypha*; R. D. Wilson, "From Prophecy to Apocalyptic; Reflections on the Shape of Israelite Religion," *Semeia* 21 (1981): 79-95; P. Worsley, *The Trumpet Shall Sound*.

—PAUL L. REDDITT

• **Apocalypticism.** *See* APOCALYPTIC LITERATURE; ESCHATOLOGY IN THE NEW TESTAMENT; ESCHATOLOGY IN THE OLD TESTAMENT

• **Apocrypha.** *See* APOCRYPHAL LITERATURE

• **Apocrypha, Modern.** [uh-pok'ruh-fuh] Refers to numerous writings, especially from the nineteenth and twentieth centuries C.E., that purport to be ancient, first-century accounts of various events in the life of Jesus and the early church. These fraudulent and often bizarre texts have no historical value for the biblical period. It is important to know of them in order to prevent unsuspecting persons from being misled by them.

One of the most widely circulated texts of these writings is the *Report of Pilate*, which purports to be a report on the trial and death of Jesus written by PILATE directly to the Roman Emperor Tiberius. Actually, this was published in 1879 by W. D. Mahan, a Presbyterian minister from Boonville, Missouri. Although details on Mahan's immediate sources are vague, the story was originally published in 1837 in French by Joseph Méry, a short story writer.

Two very helpful books have been published by Edgar J. Goodspeed and Per Beskow which provide extensive information on these curious texts known as "modern apocrypha."

Bibliography. P. Beskow, *Strange Tales about Jesus;* E. J. Goodspeed, *Modern Apocrypha*, also published as *Famous "Biblical" Hoaxes*.

—DAVID M. SCHOLER

• **Apocryphal Acts.** [uh-pok'ruh-fuhl] Apocryphal Acts is the general designation for a group of works written in the second and third centuries relating legends concerning the apostles. This group of works includes the ACTS OF ANDREW, JOHN, PAUL, PETER, and THOMAS. With the possible exception of *Thomas*, which may have been written in Syriac, it is assumed that the various Acts were composed in Greek. Subsequent manuscripts show that they were translated into numerous languages: Latin, Syriac, Coptic, Armenian, Slavonic, Arabic, and Ethiopic.

The extent to which the texts of the Acts have survived varies; none exists *in toto*. The *Acts of Andrew*, which originally may have been the longest, is now the most fragmentary. The *Acts of Thomas* is the most complete.

The question of authorship is perplexing and without any definite answer. When viewed collectively the Acts bear many stylistic similarities. The variations within each, however, betray the hands of different authors and locales. Tradition since the fifth century has ascribed the works to Leucius Charinus either as author or as collector and editor.

While each apocryphal Acts is distinct in the elements comprising its content and local color, some typical and recurring features are observable in all. Many of these traits have precedent in the genre of Hellenistic romances. This type of work appealed to the masses and has several well-defined features.

The journey motif is typical of the Hellenistic stories and is also characteristic of the Acts. This theme is illustrated by the apostles who, as the protagonists of the Acts, wander through many of the major cities as Asia Minor. The *Acts of Thomas* is the most distinctive of the Acts in this regard since the apostle's activities take place in India. The journey motif is a literary device which allows the apostles to encounter numerous situations in which to preach and demonstrate the supernatural power of God.

In whatever context each apostle might find himself in his travel, he is portrayed as having the ability to perform spectacular deeds. The apostles as bearers of God's authority are able to heal the sick, give sight to the blind, escape from life-threatening situations, and raise the dead. Besides these activities, which have precedents in the canonical literature, the apocryphal Acts also deal with less restrained manifestations of power, such as bringing a fish back to life, causing a flood, baptizing a lion, and destroying a pagan temple. The utilization of power is occasionally for the mundane, such as personal comfort in order to sleep. In the *Acts of John*, the apostle, unable to rest at night because of bedbugs, commands them to assemble in a group on one side of the room until he awakes in the morning. They obediently comply.

A third and closely related feature is the appearance of incredible wonders, or events contrary to nature. Numerous accounts are recorded of talking animals or reptiles, such as a dog, an ass's colt, and a serpent. The *Acts of Thomas* includes a personal description of HEAVEN by one raised from the dead, as well as a conducted tour of HELL.

A fourth feature is the use of speeches. The miraculous deeds of the apostles are usually either opportunities for the apostles to deliver their messages to the audiences, or incidents which punctuate the speeches with the exclamation point of God's power. These speeches have as their central theme to persuade the apostles' audiences (including the reader) to adopt a particular attitude or perspective on life.

The particular attitude emphasized in the speeches of the Acts comprise a fifth feature. This emphasis is usually one related to the proper attitude of a person to the world, particularly in regard to sexual practices. The basic premise of the apostles is that any sexual activity outside of or within marriage is considered wrong for a Christian. This emphasis upon holiness by sexual continence is illustrated by the beatitudes in the *Acts of Paul*: "Blessed are they who have kept the flesh pure, for they shall become a temple of God. Blessed are the continent, for to them will God speak. Blessed are they who have wives as if they had them not, for they shall inherit God."

A primary focus, therefore, is on the ascetic and encratic models, which demonstrate the highest level of holiness. The apostle himself is the one to emulate in relationship to sexual continence. An example of this attitude is John's gratitude to God for blinding him for two years and giving him an infirmity of the body in order that he might be "till this present hour pure for thyself and untouched by union with a woman."

The sexual continence theme often carries erotic overtones, a feature which would intrigue the coarser elements of the population. For example, the Acts record attempted rapes, a woman possessed by a demon of lust, and attempted intercourse with a corpse.

The overall purpose of the apocryphal Acts is not to discourse on specific doctrines. Far from being theological treatises, the Acts are primarily books of entertainment. The incredible and fantastic stories are told and arranged in such a fashion as to capture and maintain the reader's attention. Once the process of drawing the reader into the story is achieved through recounting the prodigious activities, the Acts function as a propaganda medium. They are able to promote a particular view in regard to the proper attitudes of a believer to the world in general and sexual relationships in particular.

Because of the romanticized and larger-than-life picture which the Acts described, they became popular with the general public. This popularity stemmed in part from the fact that they purported to detail further adventures and episodes in the lives of the apostles. While the canonical Gospels and the Acts of the Apostles leave open questions regarding the apostles' lives, the apocryphal Acts supplement their accounts with legendary information. The apocryphal Acts push the apostles' lives to their logical conclusion which is martyrdom. Only in the *Acts of John* does the apostle not suffer martyrdom.

The early church, however, never felt comfortable with the apocryphal Acts. Pope Leo the Great's comment is representative: "The apocryphal writings, however, which under the names of the Apostles contain a hotbed of manifold perversity, should not only be forbidden but altogether removed and burnt with fire." While an official sanction was made against the Acts by the Nicene Council of 787, it was not easy to suppress such popular works. Those groups which were inclined toward encratic and ascetic tendencies continued to use them. The Manichaeans and the Priscillianists particularly favored these Acts over the more conventional canonical Acts of the Apostles. The continued popularity of some of the apocryphal Acts is illustrated by the fact that the *Acts of John* was still being copied as late as the fourteenth century.

One reason for the invectives of the early church against the apocryphal Acts has to do with their Gnostic and docetic tendencies. The docetic trait is illustrated in an account of a vision of Jesus seen simultaneously by two individuals, one of whom described Jesus as a young man, while the other saw him as an old man. Also, in the Acts of John the apostle recounts that when he reclined on the breast of Jesus it was at times firm and solid while at other times it was soft and immaterial. The Gnostic tendencies are generally seen in the portrayal of Jesus as the REDEEMER who is a guide able to reveal heavenly mysteries. The *Acts of Thomas* has Jesus addressed as the one "who dost reveal hidden mysteries and make manifest words that are secret."

Those within the church who wanted to use the apocryphal Acts had to do so with extreme caution. Usually they would expunge any elements that were offensive to the theological sensibilities of their time.

The historical value of the apocryphal Acts is not found in the reconstruction of the apostles' lives, for the material in the Acts is much too legendary. Their value is in revealing the social environment of the second and third centuries. Theses books illustrate embryonic ideas and attitudes which would develop later in Christian thought and practice, such as asceticism. They also provide evidence for the development of the early practice of laying on of hands, anointing with oil, the administering of the LORD'S SUPPER, and ALMS for the poor.

See also ANDREW, ACTS OF; GNOSTICISM; JOHN, ACTS OF; PAUL, ACTS OF; PETER, ACTS OF; THOMAS, ACTS OF.

Bibliography. F. Bovon and E. Junod, "Reading the Apocryphal Acts of the Apostles," *Semeia* 38 (1986): 161-71; V. Burrus, "Chastity as Autonomy: Women in the Stories of the Apocryphal Acts," *Semeia* 38 (1986): 101-117; D. R. Cartlidge, "Transfiguration of Metamorphosis Tradition in the Acts of John, Thomas, and Peter," *Semeia* 38 (1986): 53-66; S. L. Davies, *The Revolt of the Widows: The Social World of the Apocryphal Acts*; E. Hennecke and W. Schneemelcher, *New Testament Apocrypha*; M. R. James, *The Apocryphal New Testament;* D. MacDonald, "The Role of Women in the Production of the Apocryphal Acts of the Apostles," *IR* 40 (1984): 21-38; H. Musurillo, *The Acts of the Christian Martyrs: Introduction, Texts and Translations*; W. Wright, *Apocryphal Acts of the Apostles.*

—DAVID M. MAY

• **Apocryphal Gospels.** The apocryphal gospels are documents outside the NT CANON which recount alleged words, deeds, or events of Jesus' life. Some of these materials in the form in which we find them are not part of connected gospels. These are the AGRAPHA. They are found as textual variants in some ancient manuscripts of the NT, as quotations in numerous early Christian authors, and among the Oxyrhynchus Papyri. Most of them come from some lost gospel. Modern study concludes that most of the agrapha are not historically authentic.

The earliest apocryphal gosples are known only in fragments. Among these are the GOSPEL OF THE HEBREWS, which contained such interesting traditions as that about Jesus' response to his family's request that he join them in being baptized by John the Baptist; that which translated the Lord's Prayer request for bread as "bread for the morrow, that is, the bread which thou wilt give us in thy kingdom, give us today"; and that which recounts the risen Jesus' appearance to James. Another fragmentary work is the GOSPEL OF THE EBIONITES whose vegetarian and adoptionistic author described John the Baptist's diet as wild honey with the taste of manna, and Jesus' baptism as accompanied by a voice from heaven that said, "Thou are my beloved Son, in thee I am well pleased: and again: This day have I begotten thee." Still another is the GOSPEL OF THE EGYPTIANS (not the same as the NAG HAMMADI piece of the same name) whose ascetic author has Jesus say, "I came to destroy the works of the female." There are also two early gospel fragments designated Papyrus Oxyrhynchus 840 and PAPYRUS EGERTON 2.

From the second and third centuries a number of apocryphal gospels with extensive remains are extant. From the following list some whose title includes "Gospel" are excluded: e.g., the GOSPEL OF TRUTH, a second-century Gnostic meditation on the theme of the gospel as "good news," because it does not treat the life or words of Jesus. Included are writings whose title does not include the term "Gospel" because they do treat the words and deeds of Jesus in some way. Such a list of apocryphal gospels would include the following.

The PROTEVANGELIUM OF JAMES is a second-century account of the birth, childhood, marriage, supernatural pregnancy, and marvelous delivery of MARY. Jesus enters the narrative only as an example of Mary's ascetic virtue. Origen (*On Matthew* 10.17) correctly discerned that this document's purpose was to exalt Mary as an ascetic ideal.

The INFANCY GOSPEL OF THOMAS is a second-century gospel that portrays Jesus as a god in a little boy's body, working miracles such as making birds out of clay and bringing them to life so that they fly away, or stretching out to its proper length a bed which Joseph had made too short.

The Coptic GOSPEL OF THOMAS is a second century gospel which begins, "The words of the living Jesus to Didymus Judas Thomas," and continues with one logion after another, usually introduced by, "Jesus said."

The GOSPEL OF PETER is a second-century gospel which, in its present form at least, is a passion gospel telling of Jesus' death and resurrection. According to EUSEBIUS (*EccHist* 6.12), Serapion claimed the writing was composed by docetists because while on the cross Jesus says, "My power, my power, why have you forsaken me?"

The EPISTLE OF THE APOSTLES is a second century letter purporting to be from the twelve apostles and giving a revelation which the risen Christ made to them. The revelation is theologically orthodox for the most part, unlike the bulk of revelations which follow in this list.

The APOCRYPHON OF JOHN is probably a second-century revelation delivered by the risen Christ to John the son of Zebedee which deals with two questions: What is the origin of evil? How can we escape from this evil world to our heavenly home?

The LETTER OF PETER TO PHILLIP dates perhaps from the late second or the third century. The letter reflected in the title comprises only the first part of the tractate. It is dominated by a dialogue of the resurrected Christ with his disciples about the fall of humanity; about how fullness and restoration can only be attained by hearkening to the call of the heavenly redeemer, Christ; and why Christ and his disciples suffer.

The SOPHIA OF JESUS CHRIST, from the late second or the third century, gives a revelation of the risen Christ to the twelve disciples and seven holy women in which he expounds mysteries and resolves problems that still perplex them.

The PISTIS SOPHIA, a third-century work, has the usual form of the Gnostic type of gospel. The risen Christ imparts esoteric teaching to his disciples in response to their questions in the form of a dialogue. In *Pistis Sophia* the resurrected Lord spends eleven years discoursing with the disciples.

The BOOK OF THOMAS THE CONTENDER is a dialogue between the resurrected Jesus and his brother Judas Thomas, allegedly recorded by a certain Mathaias who hears them speaking together, followed by a monologue delivered by the Savior. This tractate was probably produced in the first half of the third century.

The DIALOGUE OF THE SAVIOR, another early dialogue of the risen Christ with his disciples, focuses on ESCHATOLOGY. Realized eschatology is juxtaposed with futuristic eschatology. Although the elect have already passed from death to life, they still look to the future for the final place of life and light.

The SECOND TREATISE OF THE GREAT SETH is yet another early Gnostic revelation dialogue delivered by the risen Lord to an audience of perfect and incorruptible ones, that is, Gnostic believers. The first part describes the history of Jesus and emphasizes his docetic passion. The second part aims to refute orthodoxy's claim to be the true church.

The GOSPEL OF MARY, a third century text in two parts, is still another Gnostic revelation. In part one the risen Christ is in dialogue with his disciples who ask him questions. The second part consists of Mary Magdalene's relating a vision of the Lord and describes a revelation of the ascending soul being interrogated by the powers it encounters on its way upward.

Earlier generations regarded these apocryphal gospels as amplifications of and developments from the canonical Gospels in ways that distorted the normative four. Recently there has been an attempt to understand the apocryphal gospels as continuations of forms of Jesus materials that had roots in the first century.

One type of collection of Jesus matter in early Christianity was the miracle gospel. The *Infancy Gospel of Thomas* is a second-century example. It is likely a continuation of a form exemplified in the first century by the signs source used by the Fourth Gospel, namely, a collection of seven or eight miracles climaxed by the words: "Now Jesus did many other signs in a presence of the disciples, which are not written in this book; but these are written that you may believe that Jesus is the Christ, the Son of God" (John 20:30).

A second type of collection of Jesus material was that which grouped sayings of Jesus together; the Coptic *Gospel of Thomas* is an example. That such a collection should not be regarded as a deviation from the model of the canonical gospels is made clear by the existence of such collections of Jesus' sayings in the first century, e.g. Q, assuming the two source solution of the SYNOPTIC PROBLEM.

A third type of collection of Jesus material was one that portrayed Christ as a revealer, as one who makes a revelation to some disciple or disciples, usually after the resurrection. The *Apocryphon of John* and the following seven gospels in the above list fit into this category. In the first century, the REVELATION to John resembles this type of collection. There the risen Lord appears to the prophet John to give him a prophecy of the last days.

A fourth type of collection of Jesus materials was an account of the last days of Jesus' life, his death, and his resurrection. If the *Gospel of Peter* contained no more material than our present copy, then it, like the fourth-century ACTS OF PILATE, is an apocryphal representative of this form. The pre-Markan, pre-Johannine passion narrative was a first-century example of this type.

A fifth type of collection of Jesus material was a composite including miracles, sayings, revelation matter, and a passion narrative. The four canonical Gospels, of course, belong to this variety, as do at least some of the early apocryphal gospels known only in fragments. If this typology is accepted, then the various apocryphal gospels may be understood as literary developments of forms of gospels that were already circulating in the first century and not just as distorted developments from the canonical four.

Of what value are these apocryphal gospels? It seems safe to say that, with the possible exception of the Coptic *Gospel of Thomas,* they provide us with no authentic traditions of words or deeds of Jesus, except insofar as they reproduce the canonical tradition. Their value is rather in what they reveal about the people who wrote them, about their hopes, likes, and beliefs. They thereby provide the church historian with valuable information about popular Christianity that is often different from that espoused by the theologians of the mainstream church.

See also AGRAPHA; NAG HAMMADI.

Bibliography: E. Hennecke and W. Schneemelcher, eds., *New Testament Apocrypha*; J. Jeremias, *Unknown Sayings of Jesus*; H. Koester, "One Jesus and Four Primitive Gospels, *Trajectories Through Early Christianity,* ed. J. M. Robinson and H. Koester; J. M. Robinson, ed., *The Nag Hammadi Library*; C. H. Talbert, "The Gospel and the Gospels," *Interpreting the Gospels,* ed. J. L. Mays.

—CHARLES H. TALBERT

• **Apocryphal Literature.** A general term given to a vast number of ancient Jewish and Christian writings which have certain affinities with the various books in the OT and NT but which did not themselves become a part of the CANON. The word "apocrypha" comes from the Greek word *apokrypha,* which means "things which are hidden, or secret." Its earliest usage as a designation for books is by Clement of Alexandria, who said that the Gnostics used "apocryphal books"—i.e., books that contained secret teachings. The concept of secret books, especially those hidden away until the last days, was already present in JUDAISM (cf. Dan 12:4; 4 Ezra 14). The connection of "apocryphal" with Gnostic writings, however, gave the term a negative connotation in the eyes of "orthodox" Christians, who rejected the Gnostic books. Thus, "apocryphal" came to mean "rejected" or "false." As the process of the canonization of the Bible continued in the early church, "apocryphal" eventually acquired a third meaning: those books which do not belong to the canon but which may be read for edification.

Apocryphal literature can be divided roughly, according to current scholarly convention, into six somewhat artificial categories: the Apocrypha, the Pseudepigrapha, the DEAD SEA SCROLLS, the NT Apocrypha, the NAG HAMMADI documents, and the APOSTOLIC FATHERS. There are problems with this scheme of classification, as will be seen, but at present no alternate consensus is in sight.

The Apocrypha. The Apocrypha is a relatively fixed collection of Jewish books which are noteworthy for their presence in the OT canons of Roman Catholic and Eastern Orthodox Christianity and their absence from the Protestant and Jewish canons of the Bible. Roman Catholics call the books "Deuterocanonical": those added later to the canon. The Deuterocanonical books consist of TOBIT, JUDITH, the ADDITIONS TO ESTHER, the Additions to DANIEL (the PRAYER OF AZARIAH and the Three Young Men, SUSANNA, and BEL AND THE DRAGON), the WISDOM OF SOLOMON, SIRACH (Ecclesiasticus), BARUCH (1 Baruch), the LETTER OF JEREMIAH, 1 MACCABEES, and 2 MACCABEES. The Greek Orthodox Church adds to these 1 ESDRAS, Ps 151, the PRAYER OF MANASSEH, and 3 MACCABEES, with 4 MACCABEES in an appendix. The Russian Orthodox Church adds 1 Esdras, 2 Esdras (4 EZRA and 5 EZRA), Ps 151, and *3 Maccabees*. The Roman Catholic canon places the Prayer of Manasseh, 1 Esdras, and 2 Esdras in an appendix without implying canonicity.

The origins of this collection are somewhat obscure. All of the texts except 2 Esdras were written, at various times and in various places, prior to the Christian era. Although most of them were probably composed in HEBREW, they apparently never formed a part of the Hebrew canon. Rather, at an early date they were translated into GREEK; most, again with the exception of 2 Esdras, were preserved in manuscripts of the LXX, a pre-Christian Greek translation of the OT. Some scholars believe that these manuscripts serve as evidence for an "Alexandrian canon." They argue that this canon of the OT, written in Greek and used by Jews outside of Palestine, contained more texts (i.e., the Apocrypha) than did the Hebrew, or "Palestinian," canon. It was only natural that as early Christianity became increasingly gentile, it would adopt the expanded Greek canon.

Apart from the LXX manuscripts, however, evidence for an "Alexandrian canon" is wanting. PHILO of Alexandria, the greatest of the Hellenized Jews in Alexandria, never quotes any of these extra writings; his Bible seems to have been the Hebrew canon. In addition, the extant manuscripts of the LXX were copied by Christian, not Jewish, scribes. Finally, the manuscripts do not all contain the same extra-canonical writings. More probable therefore is that the presence of these documents in manuscripts containing the OT is the work not of Jews, but of Christians, who, in transmitting the Greek translations of OT writings, added other texts known to have been read by Jews. This process would have been facilitated by the introduction in the second century C.E. of the codex, which permitted the collection of writings into a single book, thereby replacing the older Jewish practice of using a separate scroll for each document.

Whatever the origins of the collection, Christians were using the various books of the Apocrypha by the end of the first century C.E. (1 CLEMENT cites the Wisdom of Solomon). Gentile Christians with little knowledge of Judaism and even less of Hebrew began to accept indiscriminately the Jewish writings which they found in their Greek codices, especially since the books of Apocrypha did not stand as a separate collection in the manuscripts but were found at various places among the OT books. When an Old Latin version was made from the LXX in the second century C.E., the now enlarged "canon" became entrenched in Latin-speaking, as well as Greek-speaking, Christianity. Church Fathers such as IRENAEUS, Clement of Alexandria, and Tertullian cited passages from the Apocrypha alongside those from the OT without distinction.

It was in the fourth century that Cyril of Jerusalem and Jerome first labeled the extra books in the Greek/Latin canon as "Apocrypha." They argued that the Hebrew canon was alone authoritative; the "Apocrypha" could, however, be read for edification. Yet when Jerome made his famous Latin translation of the Bible, the Vulgate, he was persuaded to include translations of a few of the Apocrypha. This opened the door for others to add the rest of the books of the Apocrypha as the Vulgate increased in popularity, even though Jerome's comments about the priority of the Hebrew canon circulated along with his Vulgate. Thus, despite Jerome's personal commitment to the Hebrew canon, the eventual acceptance of the Vulgate by the Council of Trent in 1546 resulted in the official canonization of the Apocrypha in the Roman Catholic Church.

In the tradition of Jerome and of various Roman Catholic scholars throughout the Middle Ages, the Protestant Reformers generally affirmed the unique authority of the Hebrew canon. Theological considerations also entered into this affirmation, since Roman Catholics used passages from the Apocrypha to support doctrines and practices to which the Reformers objected (e.g., purgatory, and prayers and masses for the dead; cf. 1 Macc 12:43-45). Yet most of the Reformers allowed that the books of the Apocrypha were useful for reading. Thus, Martin Luther, in his German translation of the Bible, placed the Apocrypha, with an appropriate preface, in an appendix at the end of the OT. This became the standard treatment of the Apocrypha in sixteenth and seventeenth century translations of the Bible by Protestants, making it easy, however, for them to ignore these books and, later, to omit them completely from their Bible translations. No Protestant church today accepts the Apocrypha as canonical; most have nothing to do with these books. The Anglican Church, however, affirms their importance "for example of life and instruction of manners" (Article VI of the Thirty-Nine Articles).

Apart from the issue of canonicity, the Apocrypha has had a pronounced and pervasive influence on Western culture. The stories, themes, and language of these books (especially Judith, Tobit, Susanna, the Maccabees, Sirach, and the Wisdom of Solomon) have been utilized by literary figures such as Shakespeare, Milton, and Longfellow, composers such as Charles Wesley, Handel, and Rubinstein, and artists such as Michaelangelo, Rembrandt, and van Dyck, to name only a few. The Apocrypha even played a role in the discovery of the New World: Christopher Columbus used 2 Esdr 6:42, a passage which was understood to imply that sixth-sevenths of the earth's surface is covered by land, to solicit support for his voyage, arguing that the distance from Europe westward to the Indies was less than it was believed to be.

The Pseudepigrapha. A second category of apocryphal literature is the pseudepigrapha. "Pseudepigrapha" comes from a Greek noun which denotes writings "with false superscription"—i.e., by a writer other than the one named. It was used by the second-century bishop Serapion as a designation for Christian writings which were falsely attributed to the apostles. In time, however, the term came to be applied to Jewish writings which were falsely attributed to OT figures. It is this latter usage of the term which underlies the current classification of certain books as "the pseudepigrapha." Some scholars prefer "the OT pseudepigrapha," to be distinguished from "the NT Pseudepigrapha," a title which, however, has not won widespread support. Others find the word "pseudepigrapha" of little value or even misleading and opt for "the Apocryphal OT," a title which, however, risks confusion with the Apocrypha. Canonical lists of the Middle Ages, such as the so-called Gelasian Decree (sixth century) and the Stichometry of Nicephorus (ninth century), often classified these writings as "apocryphal" in the sense of "rejected."

Formulating a precise definition of the pseudepigrapha as a collection of books is not an easy task. The writings are frequently attributed to OT figures (e.g., Enoch: 1 ENOCH, 2 ENOCH; Abraham: APOCALYPSE OF ABRAHAM; the twelve sons of Jacob: TESTAMENTS OF THE TWELVE PATRIARCHS; Moses: JUBILEES, TESTAMENT OF MOSES; Solomon: TESTAMENT OF SOLOMON; Isaiah: MARTYRDOM AND ASCENSION OF ISAIAH; Baruch: 2 BARUCH, 3 BARUCH; Ezra: *4 Ezra*, GREEK APOCALYPSE OF EZRA; Zephaniah: APOCALYPSE OF ZEPHANIAH), although some are attributed to other authors (e.g., SIBYLLINE ORACLES, SYRIAC MENANDER). They typically build upon OT stories (e.g., LIFE OF ADAM AND EVE, *Jubilees*, PSEUDO-PHILO, *1 Enoch*, JOSEPH AND ASENETH, JANNES AND JAMBRES, TESTAMENT OF JOB, 4 BARUCH, LIVES OF THE PROPHETS), although some do not (e.g., AHIQAR, LETTER OF ARISTEAS, *3 Maccabees*, *4 Maccabees*, PSALMS OF SOLOMON). Most were composed between 200 B.C.E. and 200 C.E., although some are later (e.g., 3 ENOCH, *Testament of Solomon*, REVELATION OF EZRA, VISION OF EZRA, APOCALYPSE OF DANIEL). Finally, most are of Jewish origin, although many have been reworked by Christians (e.g., *Testaments of the Twelve Patriarchs*, TESTAMENT OF ISAAC, TESTAMENT OF JACOB, APOCALYPSE OF ELIJAH, *Testament of Solomon*, *Martyrdom and Ascension of Isaiah*, APOCALYPSE OF SEDRACH, HISTORY OF THE RECHABITES), and some were probably composed by Christians (e.g., ODES OF SOLOMON, *Vision of Ezra*, *Apocalypse of Daniel*). The pseudepigrapha are sometimes classified by literary form into apocalyptic literature (e.g., *1 Enoch*, *4 Ezra*), testaments (e.g., *Testaments of the Twelve Patriarchs*, *Testament of Job*), expansions of the OT legends (e.g., *Joseph and Aseneth*, *Life of Adam and Eve*), wisdom and philosophical literature (e.g., *Ahikar*, *4 Maccabees*), and prayers, psalms, and odes (e.g., *Psalms of Solomon*, *Odes of Solomon*), but such a classification is not precise.

Clearly the books of the pseudepigrapha are not a unified collection. Yet as a group of Jewish writings (or Christian writings based upon Jewish traditions) which are not in the OT or in the Apocrypha (although *3* and *4 Maccabees*, the Prayer of Manasseh, and *4 Ezra* [as part of 2 Esdras] are sometimes included in the latter), which come from the same general time period (the later documents might be based upon an earlier Jewish core), most of which are concerned with OT figures, and many of which are pseudonymous, such documents may be conveniently grouped together, despite a current lack of consensus over whether certain texts (e.g., *Ahikar*, *Revelation of Ezra*, *Apocalypse of Daniel*) should be included. As research on these and other documents proceeds, the countours of the collection will undoubtedly change.

There is nothing to indicate that any of the pseudepigrapha were accepted as canonical by the larger Jewish populace in the second Temple period. On the other hand, *Jubilees* is cited as authoritative in a sectarian writing, the DAMASCUS RULE. Many of the pseudepigrapha (e.g., *Jubilees*, *1 Enoch*, *2 Enoch*, *Apocalypse of Abraham*, *2 Baruch*, *4 Ezra*) claim to record revelations from God. *4 Ezra* 14 explicitly claims for "seventy" books a divine inspiration equal to that of the canonical books. It is entirely likely, therefore, that certain groups of Jews, such as the Qumran community, placed some of the pseudepigrapha on the same level as the OT books. Today most Jews accept only the latter as canonical; the Falasha Jews of Ethiopia, however, have an expanded canon including *Jubilees* and *1 Enoch*.

In time, however, Christians came to appreciate the pseudepigrapha even more than Jews did. Already in the NT, writers exhibit familiarity with some of these documents: the author of JUDE cites *1 Enoch* and seems to know *Jubilees* and the *Testament of Moses*; the writer of 2 Timothy reflects a knowledge of *Jannes and Jambres*; the author of HEBREWS apparently knows the *Martyrdom of Isaiah*. Citations are found also in early Christian writings such as 1 Clement, the SHEPHERD OF HERMAS, and the EPISTLE OF BARNABAS, as well as in church Fathers such as Clement of Alexandria, Tertullian, Origen, and Epiphanius. Christians read the pseudepigrapha, added Christian sections to them, and even composed them, all the while translating them into their ethnic languages, such as Syriac, Coptic, Ethiopic, Slavonic, Armenian, and Arabic. Although these writings have rarely been viewed as having the same status as the OT or even the Apocrypha, they have been widely read throughout the history of the Church and, thus, have served in their own ways to influence the various cultures in which Christianity developed.

The Dead Sea Scrolls. Unlike the Apocrypha and the pseudepigrapha, which by definition, are apocryphal literature, the Dead Sea Scrolls, a vast collection of ancient Jewish manuscripts discovered beginning in 1947 in caves along the Dead Sea, only contain such writings. These scrolls are the remains of a library which belonged to a group of sectarian Jews, probably ESSENES, who lived by the Dead Sea at a site called Qumran from ca. 141 B.C.E. to 68 C.E. Some of the scrolls are merely copies of OT books. Others, however, should be classified with the pseudepigrapha. In fact, several known pseudepigrapha (i.e., *Jubilees*, parts of *1 Enoch*, and two Testaments which seem to be related to the *Testaments of the Twelve Patriarchs*), as well as several of the Apocrypha (i.e., Tobit, Sirach, and the Letter of Jeremiah), have been found among the scrolls. Previously unknown pseudepigrapha found at Qumran, many of which have not yet been published, include the GENESIS APOCRYPHON and related writings, such as the *Book of Giants* and the *Book of Noah*, the *Testament of Amram*, the *Words of Moses*, the *Samuel Apocryphon*, the *Prayer of Nabonidus*, and *Pseudo-Daniel*.

One might argue that the sectarian documents found among the Dead Sea Scrolls, such as the various rules (e.g., the MANUAL OF DISCIPLINE, the RULE OF THE CONGREGATION, the *Damascus Rule*, the War Rule, the TEMPLE SCROLL), the poetical/liturgical texts (the THANKSGIVING SCROLL, the ANGELIC LITURGY, the *Blessings*, the *Words of the Heavenly Lights*), the commentaries (PESHARIM), and the other examples of sectarian biblical interpretation (the FLORILEGIA/TESTIMONIA, MELCHIZEDEK 11Q) comprise a distinct group which should not be classified as apocryphal. The issue is complicated by two factors. First, the sectarian writings include several different literary genres. It may be true that the rules and the commentaries are unparalleled in Jewish literature of the period, but the same cannot be said for the *Thanksgiving Scroll* (cf. the *Psalms of Solomon*), for example, or for the *Temple Scroll* (cf. DEUTERONOMY). Second, distinctive perspectives are hardly unique to the scrolls; such viewpoints are characteristic of most of the Apocrypha and pseudepigrapha (cf., e.g., Sirach, *2 Enoch,* and especially *Jubilees*).

The Dead Sea Scrolls, therefore, comprise a diverse collection of writings which adds previously unknown texts to the pseudepigrapha. Some of the apocryphal writings preserved among the scrolls, such as *Jubilees,* might have been afforded canonical status by the Qumran community. Sectarian documents such as the rules certainly had an authoritative role within the sect. But when the members of the community hid their library just prior to the destruction of the community in 68 C.E., those books which were not being used by other Jews passed out of circulation and, hence, ceased to have any influence on either Judaism or Christianity.

With the exception of some of the pseudepigrapha, all of the writings in the first three categories were composed by Jews. The final three categories contain, for the most part, apocryphal texts authored by Christians.

The NT Apocrypha. The NT Apocrypha is a collection of writings most of which are about, or pseudonymously attributed to, NT figures. As in the case of the pseudepigrapha, the limits of this corpus are not definitively set. The books which make up this collection are generally modeled after the literary forms found in the NT: there are APOCRYPHAL GOSPELS (e.g., GOSPEL OF PETER, INFANCY GOSPEL OF THOMAS, PROTEVANGELIUM OF JAMES), APOCRYPHAL ACTS (e.g., ACTS OF PETER, ACTS OF PAUL, ACTS OF JOHN, ACTS OF ANDREW, ACTS OF THOMAS), apocryphal letters (e.g., *3 Corinthians, Letter to the Laodiceans,* PSEUDO-TITUS), and apocryphal revelations (e.g., APOCALYPSE OF PETER (ANT), APOCALYPSE OF PAUL (ANT), APOCALYPSE OF THOMAS). A few documents, such as Christian Sibylline Oracles and the *Book of Elchasai,* are neither about NT figures or patterned after NT books. Although imaginative tales about Jesus and the apostles continued to be composed for centuries, scholars usually restrict the title "NT Apocrypha" to books that are contemporaneous with the process of the canonization of the NT—i.e., through the fourth century C.E.

The texts which make up the NT Apocrypha were written at various times and in various places in the early centuries of Christianity. Like the pseudepigrapha, they did not circulate as a distinct collection, and they were generally classified as "apocryphal" (i.e., rejected) in medieval canonical lists. There were a few exceptions, however. According to the MURATORIAN CANON (ca. 200 C.E.) the *Apocalypse of Peter* was accepted, with some dissent, in Rome at the end of the second century. Codex Claromontanus (sixth century) lists both the *Apocalypse of Peter* and the *Acts of Paul* as part of the NT. *Third Corinthians* circulated as one of the Pauline letters in both the Syriac and the Armenian churches. By and large, however, the NT Apocrypha never really contended for a place in the NT canon.

It is quite likely, however, that certain Christian groups in the second and third centuries viewed some of the NT Apocrypha as authoritative: e.g., Jewish Christians (GOSPEL OF THE NAZARAEANS, GOSPEL OF THE EBIONITES, GOSPEL OF THE HEBREWS, the Pseudo-Clementine *Homilies* and *Recognitions*) and Docetists (ACTS OF JOHN). In addition, the translation of the various NT Apocrypha into the ethnic languages of the disparate churches attests to their widespread popularity among Christians throughout the Middle Ages. In addition to inspiring further legends concerning Jesus and the apostles, these writings provided the source for many enduring Christian traditions, including JOSEPH being a widower with children when he married MARY (*Protevangelium of James*), PETER being crucified upside down (*Acts of Peter*), PAUL's physical description (*Acts of Paul*), THOMAS founding the church in India (*Acts of Thomas*), and JOHN being spared a martyr's death (*Acts of John*). Also, books such as the *Apocalypse of Peter* and the *Apocalypse of Paul* had a major impact on the development of Christian perspectives on HELL (cf. Dante).

The Nag Hammadi Library. The Nag Hammadi documents consist of thirteen codices which were discovered in 1945 near Nag Hammadi, Egypt. These codices, which date from the fourth century C.E., are the remains of a library which apparently belonged to a Christian monastery at nearby Chenoboskion. The codices contain about fifty-two documents, forty of which were previously unknown. Especially significant is that most of the documents reflect the viewpoints of the early Christian movement known as GNOSTICISM. As in the case of the Dead Sea Scrolls, the collection is a mixed one which contains, but does not consist solely of, apocryphal literature. One writing, the APOCALYPSE OF ADAM, is Jewish and seems to fit logically into the pseudepigrapha. Others seem to be closely related to the literary forms of the NT Apocrypha (e.g., ACTS OF PETER AND THE TWELVE APOSTLES, LETTER OF PETER TO PHILIP, APOCALYPSE OF PETER (NH), APOCALYPSE OF PAUL (NH)). Others purport to record secret teachings which Jesus gave to his disciples (e.g., GOSPEL OF THOMAS, APOCRYPHON OF JAMES, APOCRYPHON OF JOHN, BOOK OF THOMAS THE CONTENDER, SOPHIA OF JESUS CHRIST). Still others are primarily essays on Gnostic themes: some are Christian (e.g., GOSPEL OF TRUTH, GOSPEL OF PHILIP, HYPOSTASIS OF THE ARCHONS, TREATISE ON THE RESURRECTION, EXEGESIS ON THE SOUL, TRIPARTITE TRACTATE, ON THE ORIGIN OF THE WORLD), some are not (e.g., DISCOURSE ON THE EIGHTH AND NINTH, THREE STELES OF SETH, ZOSTRIANOS, ALLOGENES). Finally, there are miscellaneous writings, such as the TEACHINGS OF SILVANUS, a Christian wisdom text, and even an excerpt from PLATO'S REPUBLIC. To classify all of these documents as apocryphal literature (especially Plato's *Republic*) would make the category so broad as to be virtually meaningless. Furthermore, some (e.g., *Discourse on the Eighth and Ninth*) are neither Jewish nor Christian at all; they were simply read by Christians. On the other hand, it was the existence of those which claimed to contain secret teachings which led to the original designation by Clement of Alexandria of certain books as "apocryphal" in the first place.

There is no indication that the Nag Hammadi writings were read to any extent after the suppression of Gnosticism by the Catholic Church in the fourth century. The *Gospel of Thomas,* which is attested outside of Nag Hammadi, is cited as apocryphal (i.e., rejected) in the *Stichometry* of Nicephorus, but most of the texts are never mentioned in medieval canonical lists. Instructive in this regard is the so-called Gelasian Decree, which, after listing a large number of books as apocryphal, including such general categories as the works of Tertullian and of Clement of Alexandria, names a host of "heretics and schismatics," with the directive that what they have taught or compiled "is to be not merely rejected but excluded from the whole Roman catholic and apostolic Church and with its authors and the adherents of its authors to be damned in the inextricable shackles of anathema for ever." It is clear that the Catholic Church did an effective job not only of suppressing the "heretical" books but of destroying them as well. The survival of the Nag Hammadi library is due to the fact that it was so well hidden from the "orthodox" authorities that it remained lost for another sixteen hundred years.

The situation before the fourth century was a different story, however. Gnosticism was such a widespread and multifaceted movement in the early centuries of Christianity that it drew the attention (and the opposition) of many of the early church Fathers, including Irenaeus, Clement of Alexandria, Hippolytus, and Origen. In their attacks on Gnosticism these writers mention numerous "heretical" documents which are no longer extant (e.g., *Gospel of Basilides, Gospel of Cerinthus, Gospel of Matthias*). Undoubtedly, many of these writings, as well as those found at Nag Hammadi, were viewed as authoritative scripture by those sects which read them. The Nag Hammadi library, along with smaller discoveries such as the Berlin Codex, provides an important, albeit limited, glimpse at the extensive world of "heretical" writings which were central to certain early Christian communities but which became effectively sealed off to subsequent generations by the "orthodox" Church.

The Apostolic Fathers. The Apostolic Fathers, the final category of apocryphal literature, is a collection of fifteen or sixteen Christian writings from the first two centuries of the Christian era: 1 CLEMENT, 2 CLEMENT, seven letters of IGNATIUS (to the Ephesians, Magnesians, Trallians, Romans, Philadelphians, Smyrneans, and to Polycarp), the letter of POLYCARP TO THE PHILIPPIANS, the DIDACHE, the *Epistle of Barnabas,* the *Shepherd of Hermas,* the MARTYRDOM OF POLYCARP, the EPISTLE TO DIOGNETUS, and, sometimes, the Fragments of PAPIAS. These documents differ from the NT Apocrypha in that they do not tell stories about Jesus or the apostles, nor do they, with the exception of the *Didache* and the *Epistle of Barnabas,* claim to be written by NT figures. On the other hand, Christian tradition connects most of the authors with the apostles in some way (e.g., Clement and Hermas with Paul; Polycarp, Ignatius, and Papias with John). The Apostolic Fathers did not form a distinct corpus in the early church; it was not until the seventeenth century that the letters of Clement, Ignatius, Barnabas, and Polycarp were brought together and called "Apostolic Fathers." Eventually the other five texts were added, the last being the *Didache,* which was discovered in 1873.

All of the Apostolic Fathers except the Letter to Diognetus circulated widely in the early centuries of Christianity. Several were apparently viewed at times as canonical. *First Clement* and the *Shepherd of Hermas* are quoted as authoritative, for example, by Irenaeus, Clement of Alexandria, and Origen; the *Epistle of Barnabas* by Clement and Origen. The Muratorian Canon praises the *Shepherd of Hermas* as a book which ought to be read, although not publicly. Eusebius (fourth century) counts it, along with the *Epistle of Barnabas* and the *Didache,* among the rejected books; yet he notes that some regard the *Shepherd* as very important and that it has been read publicly in the churches. Athanasius (fourth century) excludes the *Shepherd* from the canon but names it and the Didache among the books which may be read by those desiring to be instructed in piety. Several manuscripts of the NT contain some of these writings: e.g., Codex Sinaiticus (fourth century) and Codex Claromontanus include the *Shepherd* and *Barnabas,* Codex Alexandrinus (fifth century adds *1* and *2 Clement*). Medieval canonical lists designate these books as apocryphal: so the so-called Gelasian Decree for the *Shepherd;* the Stichometry of Nicephorus for the *Shepherd, 1* and *2 Clement,* the letters of Ignatius and Polycarp, and the *Didache* (*Barnabas* is classified as "disputed").

Apart from the issue of canonicity, several of the Apostolic Fathers had a significant impact upon Christianity. The *Didache,* a small manual of church discipline, was later incorporated into larger manuals, such as the *Apostolic Constitutions,* which in turn influenced the development of church order and worship. The *Martyrdom of Polycarp* marked the beginning of a new form of Christian literature, the martyr acts, which encouraged the development of martyrology in the church and have inspired persecuted Christians of subsequent ages. The *Epistle of Barnabas* is one of the earliest examples of Christian allegorical treatment of the OT, a method which came to dominate Christian OT interpretation for a long time afterwards. The Letters of Ignatius anticipated later theological developments concerning, for example, the INCARNATION, the TRINITY, the Eucharist, the nature of the CHURCH, the primacy of ROME, and church organization. Finally, the *Shepherd of Hermas* had a significant impact on the developing theology regarding repentance for sins committed after BAPTISM, a theology which ultimately led to the doctrine of penance and the practice of indulgences, the abuse of which sparked the Reformation. The *Shepherd* also influenced Dante.

These, then, are the six categories into which scholars currently classify apocryphal literature. Together, they combine, in a not entirely satisfactory way, all three meanings of "apocryphal": hidden, rejected, and noncanonical but edifying. This sixfold classification is not particularly logical; the current delineation of categories is based upon such diverse matters as an inner-Christian dispute over the OT canon (the Apocrypha), historical and/or literary features (the pseudepigrapha, the NT Apocrypha, the Apostolic Fathers), and chance archaeological discoveries (the Dead Sea Scrolls, the Nag Hammadi documents). As a result, some texts fit more than one catgory (e.g., *Jubilees*: the pseudepigrapha and the Dead Sea Scrolls; *Gospel of Thomas*: the Nag Hammadi documents and the NT Apocrypha), while other texts do not belong under the rubric of "apocryphal literature" at all (e.g., some of the Dead Sea Scrolls and the Nag Hammadi documents). What all of the texts have in common is that they did not become part of the Protestant or Jewish Bible. In addition, most of the apocryphal books are either anonymous or pseudonymous (but not, e.g., Sirach or the Letters of Ignatius), and most either deal with biblical figures (but not, e.g., 1 Maccabees or the *Treatise on the Resurrection*) or are related to biblical literary forms (but not, e.g., the *Manual of Discipline* or the *Gospel of Truth*).

The Jewish and Christian apocryphal writings are a part of an extensive literary effort on the part of Jews and Christians between ca. 200 B.C.E. and 400 C.E. It is important to note, however, that the apocryphal writings do not comprise the totality of extracanonical Jewish and Christian writings during this period. Omitted, for example, from the heading "apocryphal" are the writings of Jews such as PHILO and JOSEPHUS, not to mention the RABBINIC LITERATURE, and the vast literature of the early Christian Fathers, such as Irenaeus, Clement of Alexandria, Tertullian, and Origen. In addition, it is clear from church fathers and canonical lists that the extant apocryphal writings represent only a portion of a larger body of apocryphal texts which were composed. Presumably still lost are such documents as the *Apocryphon of Lamech* (List of Sixty Books) sixth-seventh century], the *Apocryphon of Habakkuk* (*Stichometry* of Nicephorus), and the Gospels of Barnabas, James, Bartholomew, and Andrew (so-called Gelasian Decree), just to list a few which are named in antiquity.

Yet the extant apocryphal literature is of immense historical, if not canonical, significance. A few of the books, such as 1 and 2 Maccabees, are important historical chronicles. In the same vein, although much more controversial, is the question of whether or not parts of the apocryphal gospels add to a knowledge of the historical Jesus. However, most of the narratives in the apocryphal books are legendary; furthermore, there is no reason to believe that any of them were written by OT or NT luminaries. The contribution which this literature makes to our historical knowledge of OT or NT persons and events is therefore minimal. What makes this literature important, in addition to its enduring impact upon culture, is the light which it sheds on literary and theological developments in second Temple Judaism and early Christianity. It attests to a rich diversity in both religions beyond those forms which came to become "normative" Judaism and "orthodox" Christianity. No attempt to understand Judaism at the time of Jesus, the NT in its Jewish context, or early Christianity through Constantine can ignore the apocryphal literature.

See also APOCRYPHAL ACTS; APOCRYPHAL GOSPELS; TESTAMENTS, APOCRYPHAL; APOSTOLIC FATHERS; CANON; DEAD SEA SCROLLS; GNOSTICISM; NAG HAMMADI.

Bibliography. J. H. Charlesworth (ed.), *The Old Testament Pseudepigrapha* and *The Old Testament Pseudepigrapha and the New Testament*; J. H. Charlesworth with J. R. Mueller, *The New Testament Apocrypha and Pseudepigrapha*; J. Dart, *The Jesus of Heresy and History: The Discovery and Meaning of the Gnostic Nag Hammadi Library*; F. X. Glimm, J. M. F. Marique, and G. G. Walsh (ed.), *The Apostolic Fathers*; E. J. Goodspeed, *A History of Early Christian Literature*, rev. R. M. Grant; R. M. Grant (ed.), *The Apostolic Fathers*; E. Hennecke and W. Schneemelcher (eds.), *New Testament Apocrypha*; M. R. James (ed.), *The Apocryphal New Testament*; J. Lawson, *A Theological and Historical Introduction to the Apostolic Fathers*; B. Layton, *The Gnostic Scriptures*; B. M. Metzger, *An Introduction to the Apocrypha* and (ed.), *The Oxford Annotated Apocrypha*; G. W. E. Nickelsburg, *Jewish Literature Between the Bible and the Mishnah*; R. H. Pfeiffer, *History of New Testament Times with an Introduction to the Apocrypha*; J. M. Robinson (ed.), *The Nag Hammadi Library*; E. Schürer, *The History of the Jewish People in the Age of Jesus Christ*, Vol. III, rev. and ed. G. Vermes, F. Millar, and M. Goodman; H. F. D. Sparks (ed.), *The Apocryphal Old Testament*; M. E. Stone (ed.), *Jewish Writings of the Second Temple Period*; G. Vermes, *The Dead Sea Scrolls in English*, 3rd ed.

—JOSEPH L. TRAFTON

• **Apollos.** [uh-pol'uhs] The NT refers to Apollos (an abbreviated form of Apollonius) in Acts 18:24-28 and 1 Cor 1:12; 3:1-9, 21-23). The Acts account describes Apollos as an Alexandrian Jew who was (1) "an eloquent man" (the Greek expression may mean "learned" or "eloquent," i.e., skilled in Greek rhetoric); (2) "well versed in the scriptures" (this has been taken to mean either knowledgeable in the Hebrew scriptures or gifted in their Christian interpretation); and (3) "fervent in spirit" (i.e., either full of enthusiasm or full of the Holy Spirit).

Apollos arrived in Ephesus after Paul's departure on his second missionary journey (Acts 18:18-21). Prior to his arrival at Ephesus, Apollos had been "instructed in the way of the Lord"; however, he knew "only the BAPTISM of John" (i.e., the Baptist; Acts 18:25). Numerous suggestions have been offered to explain this strange circumstance: (1) that he was a representative of an early Christian circle which celebrated a baptism of repentance with reference to the coming Messiah but without invocation of the name of Jesus; (2) that he represented a syncretistic half-Christian belief; (3) that he was a Christian teacher independent of apostolic authority; and (4) that his knowledge was not derived along the line of transmission traced in Acts but perhaps from a Galilean source.

Upon arriving at Ephesus, Apollos began "to speak boldly in the synagogue" (Acts 18:26). Upon hearing his teaching, Priscilla (Prisca) and Aquila, Christians who had recently arrived from Rome "took him and expounded to him the way of God more accurately" (Acts 18:26). When he desired to extend his teaching ministry to Achaia, "the brothers encouraged him, and wrote to the disciples to receive him" (18:27). In Achaia he "greatly helped those who through grace had believed, for he powerfully confuted the Jews in public, showing by the scriptures that the Christ was Jesus" (Acts 18:27-28).

According to 1 Corinthians, Apollos had a successful ministry in Corinth. When divisions later arose in that church, some members of the church identified themselves with Apollos while others identified with Cephas, PAUL, or Christ (1 Cor 1:12). In 1 Corinthians Paul wrote to remind the Corinthians that he and Apollos were "fellow workers" with God (3:9). Indeed he had "planted" and Apollos had "watered," but God alone brought the harvest (3:6). Therefore, they must not be "puffed up in favor of one against another" (4:6). Paul also indicates that while he had encouraged Apollos to return to engage in further ministry in Corinth, Apollos had resisted the suggestion perhaps fearing that his presence might encourage the factious spirit.

In Titus 3:13 Titus who was overseeing the church on the island of Crete (1:5) is instructed to do his best to speed Apollos and Zenas on their way. This suggests that Apollos was travelling through Crete on a mission for the sender of the letter. Perhaps he was the bearer of the letter to Titus. Jerome says that after his stay in Crete, Apollos returned to Corinth and became the bishop of the church there. Based on the NT's description of Apollos as an Alexandrian who was "eloquent" and "well-versed in scripture," Martin Luther suggested that he was the author of the Book of Hebrews.

See also BAPTISM; CORINTHIAN CORRESPONDENCE; JOHN THE BAPTIST; PAUL; PRISCILLA AND AQUILA.

Bibliography. E. Haenchen, *The Acts of the Apostles;* F. F. Bruce, *The Acts of the Apostles.*

—W. HULITT GLOER

• **Apophthegm.** [ap"uhf-them'] A terse, pointed saying usually contained in a brief context. When used in regard to NT material, it refers to a pointed saying of Jesus.

NT form critics adapted the term from Greek literature to refer to the sayings of Jesus. Rudolf Bultmann developed its use and designated it as one of the four basic forms of literary material in the Gospels (the others being miracle stories, legends, and sayings). Martin Dibelius preferred the term "paradigm" and Vincent Taylor the term "pronouncement story."

As Bultmann uses the term, apophthegm refers to a unit consisting of both a saying of Jesus and its context, with the context being clearly secondary. The saying is compact, given in as concise a form as possible, and comes at the end of the apophthegm. The interest is concentrated on the saying, with little interest in details of the story or in other persons involved; the persons exist in essence as "types." Although details such as place may be indicated, usually there is little interest in such matters. Thus the apophthegm, as a rule, is not tied to any particular time or place. The "occasion" is often something that happens to Jesus. In these instances, the apophthegm is said to reflect a secondary formation, i.e., it has been embellished. The Gospel apophthegms do not fit the Greek literary category precisely since those of the NT reflect varying degrees of embellishment while those from Greek literature tend to be more concise.

Bultmann designates three types of apophthegms: controversy dialogues, scholastic dialogues, and biographical apophthegms.

In the controversy dialogues, the starting point resides in some action or attitude seized on by an opponent of Jesus and used in an attack by accusation or question. The reply usually takes the form of a counter question or metaphor or both, or can consist of scripture, as can the attack. The primary element is, of course, the saying of Jesus. Such sayings were preserved in the early church that then tended to clothe them in the form of the controversy dialogue through its views and fundamental beliefs.

The scholastic dialogues are quite similar to the controversy dialogues, the major difference being the starting point. Someone simply questions Jesus seeking knowledge. Bultmann admits that such a dialogue could contain an historical reminiscence, and the less it expresses the specific interests of the church, the more likely that it contains an actual saying of Jesus.

The construction of biographical apophthegms is more varied than the other two types. They involve stories about some aspect of the life of Jesus in which the saying of Jesus comes at the end. Yet rather than being historical reports, they are symbolic because they embody a truth in a metaphorical situation that has a much wider reference than the story itself.

The settings for the first two types were likely apologetic and polemical situations in the early church, while biographical apophthegms were probably edifying paradigms for sermons.

See also FORM/GATTUNG.

Bibliography. R. Bultmann, *The History of the Synoptic Tradition,* trans. J. Marsh; M. Dibelius, *From Tradition to Gospel,* trans. B. L. Woolf; R. A. Spencer, "A Study of the Form and Function of the Biographical Apophthegms in the Synoptic Tradition in Light of Their Hellenistic Background," unpublished Ph.D. dissertation, Emory University, 1976; V. Taylor, *The Formation of the Gospel Tradition.*

—G. THOMAS HALBROOKS

• **Apostasy.** [uh-pos'tuh-see] From the Gk. noun (ἡ ἀποστασία) meaning abandonment or rebellion. The term is probably from a verb (ἀφίστημι) to put away, to separate. First used in a political sense to refer to a "rebel" (1 Esdr 2:23) the term was later used in a religious sense to refer to one who had rebelled or departed from obedience to the Law of God, worship in the Temple, or the abandonment of God in general. This usage may be seen in the LXX (2 Macc 5:8) and in the OT (Josh 22:23; 2 Chr 29:19; 33:19; Jer 2:19).

This second "religious" use of the term may be seen in two NT passages: (1) Acts 21:21. Here the term is used to describe Paul's alleged rejection of Moses, i.e., rejection of the Torah (because Paul neither demanded circumcision nor the observance of custom); (2) 1 Thess 2:3. This passage reflects the Jewish apocalyptic tradition that before the eschaton there will occur a rebellion (apostasy). The notion of a postponed eschaton is common in 2 Thessalonians and 1 Peter.

Though the Greek term is not used, the English term apostasy occurs in Heb 6:6 where it is used to translate παραπεσόντας (falling back) and probably refers to a denial of the Christian faith during the persecution.

See also FAITH AND FAITHLESSNESS.

—WATSON E. MILLS

• **Apostle/Apostleship.** The word "apostle" (a transliteration of the Gk. word ἀπόστολος) appears in the NT with a general meaning of "messenger" and a specific designation of the twelve disciples of JESUS. In historical usage, the specific identification of apostles and the Twelve has prevailed.

Jesus called twelve disciples who served as the nucleus of his missionary ministry. They were the primary witnesses of his life, teachings, death, and resurrection. The number twelve was so important that a replacement was sought when Judas killed himself. Matthias replaced Judas (Acts 1:26), but does not thereafter figure in Christian history. The apostles were, however, a very important group of leaders in the Jerusalem church as indicated in Acts 15.

A brief concordance review will reveal that the two NT writers who speak most of apostles are Luke and PAUL. One will also notice that in Paul's writings persons other than the twelve are called apostles. In one passage (1 Cor 15:5ff.) he spoke of the twelve and of "all of the apostles." Evidently, when he wrote that Epistle, the term had not become identified specifically with the Twelve. Paul appeared to have included Andronicus and Junias (Rom 16:7) among the apostles. He spoke of Epaphroditus as the apostle from Philippi (Phil 2:25), but the RSV correctly translates the term simply as "messenger."

Antecedents to NT Apostles. The apostle is "one sent" on a mission (the verb ἀποστέλλειν means "to send"). In Greek literature prior to the NT the word appeared often and meant messenger, delegate, envoy, and ambassador. The word even designated a fleet, an expedition, and an admiral. Itinerant teachers and proclaimers were called apostles, but the term did not designate religious teachers prior to the NT.

Numerous scholars have sought to interpret the apostles of the NT against the background of a certain type of Hebrew messenger or agent. Harnack, in particular, interpreted the NT apostolate in light of the Hebrew institution of agents representing persons of authority. Most of the Hebrew information on the Jewish "apostles" comes not from the pre-Christian but the post-Christian literature. These messengers may be related to the general use of apostle in the NT, but we must look to the NT itself for an understanding of apostleship.

The Apostle Paul. Paul's preferred identification of himself was the term apostle (see the beginning of his letters to Rome, Corinth, Galatia, Ephesus, Colossae, Timothy, and Titus). Paul could not have used the title for himself if the term had already been limited to the Twelve.

The challenge to Paul's authority came to focus on his claim of apostleship (1 Cor 9; Gal 1). Paul defended his apostleship in terms of his call and commission from God and the Lord Jesus Christ.

Paul's defense of his apostleship appears specifically in Galatians and rather clearly in Romans and 1-2 Corinthians. Paul's understanding of his apostleship reflects an almost total dependence on the Hebrew prophetic consciousness and very little dependence on those who had been apostles before him (Gal 1 and 2).

The Hebrew PROPHET was conscious of (1) a call from God, (2) a mission for God, and (3) a message to proclaim (Robinson). Paul's discussion of his own apostolic call, mission, and message is strikingly similar to that of the Hebrew prophet. He even states his own call by quoting Jeremiah (Gal 1:15; cf. Jer 1:4-5). In short, Paul contended that God had called him to his apostleship to the gentiles, and had given him this mission which focused on the proclamation of the gospel.

Paul's experience on the road to Damascus entitled him to list himself as one of the witnesses of the resurrection of Jesus (1 Cor 15:8). This is almost certainly the basis also of his claim that his gospel is genuine (Gal 1).

The other apostles certainly included the Twelve who were leaders in Jerusalem. Paul also recognized a larger, or more general, group of apostles (1 Cor 15:7) and specific individuals such as Andronicus and Junias and Epaphroditus who were not among the Twelve.

The Twelve Apostles. While the writers of the Gospels most often spoke of Jesus' closest disciples as the Twelve, or the disciples, or the twelve disciples, they also spoke of the twelve apostles and the apostles (Matt 10:2; Mark 3:14; Luke 6:13). It is probable that Paul's popularization of the term in his Letters, which were written and circulated earlier than the Gospels, lead to the identification of the Twelve as the apostles.

In his Gospel and Acts, Luke used the term thirty-four times. Paul used the term twenty-eight times omitting the Pastorals. It is obvious that these two writers are the primary witnesses for understanding the concept. Luke clearly identified the apostles as that special group of twelve who were Jesus' disciples from the time of Jesus' baptism and witnesses of the resurrection (Luke 6:13; Acts 1:22).

The apostles in the book of Acts held a special place in the early church because of their previous relationship with Jesus. They appear to be a council in the Jerusalem Conference (Acts 15), but, quite strangely, are not mentioned after 16:4.

The apostles of the NT were the primary witnesses of Jesus and gospel events. Their authority was related to that witness. The NT writings were later selected or canonized because they were apostolic, either written by an apostle or bearing apostolic authority because of the association of the writer with an apostle (Mark with Peter, Luke with Paul). Such apostolicity was the guarantee of the writings' reliability.

Apostleship. The traditional understanding of apostles is that they are the twelve disciples chosen by Jesus with Matthias replacing Judas, and somehow including Paul whose inclusion is never explained. Some speculate that Paul instead of Matthias was the choice of the Holy Spirit.

The role of the apostles was that of being the primary witnesses of Jesus' life, teaching, death, and resurrection—the gospel. They testify to its truthfulness. As such, they were important in the formation of the NT. As primary witnesses they were irreplaceable. Other terms designate later ministers. Contemporary attempts to re-establish the office do not enjoy great acceptance.

The authority of the apostles derives from their first-hand knowledge of Jesus, the true authority for Christian faith.

See also CHURCH; DISCIPLE/DISCIPLESHIP; JESUS; PAUL; PROPHET; TWELVE, THE.

Bibliography. H. F. Camperhausen, "Der Urchristliche Apostelbegriff," *ST* 1 (1947): 95-130; C. H. Dodd, *The Apostolic Preaching and Its Developments;* F. Gavin, "Shaliach and Apostolos," *ATR* 9 (1927): 250-59; A. Harnack, *The Mission and Expansion of Christianity in the First Three Centuries*; K. Kirk, ed., *The Apostolic Ministry*; H. Knight, *The Hebrew Prophetic Consciousness*; T. W. Manson, *The Church's Ministry*; H. Mosbech, "Apostolos in the New Testament," *ST* 2 (1948): 166-200; J. Munch, "Paul, the Apostles, and the Twelve," *ST* 3 (1949): 96-110; K.H. Rengstorf, "ἀποστέλλω, κτλ." *TDNT*; H. W. Robinson, *The Religious Ideas of the Old Testament*; H. Vogelstein, "The Development of the Apostolate in Judaism and Its Transformation in Christianity," *HUCA* 2 (1925): 99-123.

—MORRIS ASHCRAFT

• **Apostles, Acts of the.** The Book of Acts is related to a prior work which traced all the things which Jesus "began to do and teach" up to his ascension (1:1-2). The former work is certainly the Gospel of Luke. Ties between Luke and Acts go far beyond their prefaces (Luke 1:1-4; Acts 1:1-5). Their commonalities in perspective, purpose, and plan

• OUTLINE OF ACTS •

The Book of Acts

Preface. The Risen Jesus and the Promised Spirit (1:1-5)
Part I. The Early Jewish Church in Jerusalem (1:6–5:42)
- I. The Problem Posed: An Israelite Kingdom or Gospel Preached to the Whole World? (1:6-8)
- II. The Character and Vigor of Early Christian Judaism (1:9–5:42)

Part II. The Hellenistic Breakthrough of National-Religious Barriers (6:1–12:25)
- I. Stephen: Witness to God beyond National Boundaries and Martyr for It (6:1-8:1a)
- II. Saul of Tarsus and Pharisaic Persecution (8:1b-3)
- III. Philip: Unhindered Preaching to Samaritans and an Ethiopian Eunuch (8:4-40)
- IV. Saul's Conversion, Commission, and Reception (9:1-30)
- V. Summary: Peace and Growth in Judea, Galilee, and Samaria (9:31)
- VI. Conversion of Apostles to Inclusion of Uncircumcised Persons (9:32–11:18)
- VII. Further Breakthrough: Unnamed Men of Cyprus and Cyrene Preach to Greeks in Antioch (11:19-26)
- VIII. Disciples in Antioch Send Relief to Famine-threatened Brethren in Judea (11:27-30)
- IX. Herod the King Persecutes the Church (12:1-23)
- X. Summary: Power and Growth for Word of God (12:24-25)

Part III. The Gospel Penetrates the Gentile World (13:1–19:20)
- I. Jews and Gentiles Approached Chiefly through the Synagogues: Door of Faith Opened to Gentiles (13:1–16:5)
- II. Jews and Gentiles Approached Chiefly Apart from the Synagogues: Increasing Resistance of the Jews (16:6–19:20)

Part IV. A Peace Mission to Jerusalem and Its Results (19:21–28:16)
Part V. Conclusion: Jewish Self-exclusion and the Gospel Preached "Unhindered" (28:17-31)

are such that scholars now refer to them as Luke-Acts. They are two volumes on a continuing, developing theme.

Both books are anonymous, but an early and unrivaled tradition ascribes them to LUKE, otherwise little known (see Col 4:14; 2 Tim 4:11; Phlm 24). The question of authorship, itself indecisive, has little if any bearing on understanding Luke-Acts. As to date, Acts follows Luke, but how soon after cannot be determined.

Like the Gospels, Acts is a theological work whose message is contained in a setting of events and discourses. Acts ascribes to divine impulse developments which began within the piety of Judaism (cf. Luke 1-2; Acts 1-5) and struggled through religious and social barriers into the larger non-Jewish world.

The question of sources behind Acts has long been argued with little consensus. Some see a travel source behind the WE-SECTIONS of Acts (16:10-17; 20:5-15; 21:1-18; 27:1–28:16), where narration shifts from third person to first. Semitic sources, probably Aramaic, may lie behind the early chapters of Acts. Attempts to find even further sources remain inconclusive. The seventeen speeches in Acts receive special attention, with debate as to whether historical or the author's creations.

More important is the overriding purpose of Acts. That there are many prominent concerns is incontestible: the impulse given the Christian movement by the unshakable confidence that Jesus was alive; close-knit fellowship and also tensions within the Christian community; conflicts with various Jewish and pagan forces; the expansion of the movement from Jerusalem to the far reaches of the Roman Empire; key persons in the movement; the power of the HOLY SPIRIT in the life and work of the church; and others. No one of these factors is able to exhaust all of the data of the book. Nevertheless, it is proper to seek an overriding design or purpose. Such a design should be and can be demonstrated from the entirety of the book.

The early title, "The Acts of the Apostles," is not original and helps little as a clue to content or intention. Nine of the Twelve appear only in the listing of the disciples (1:13). John appears only briefly (3:1; 4:1-22; 8:14). His brother JAMES was soon beheaded (12:2). PETER is prominent through 15:11 and then drops out. Another James, presumably brother to Jesus, plays a major role among Christian Jews in Jerusalem (15:13-21; 21:17-26). PAUL is the dominant figure from 8:1 to the end of Acts. STEPHEN and PHILIP, not apostles, were catalysts in breaking out of the narrow limits of Christian Judaism, freely preaching to Samaritans and God-fearing gentiles. BARNABAS opened the way for Paul in Jerusalem and Syrian ANTIOCH and a subsequent missionary tour, yet he is abruptly dropped at 15:39. Unnamed Cypriotes and Cyrenians preached to "Greeks" as well as Jews in Syrian Antioch, thus laying a new foundation for world missions (11:20). Thus, persons are prominent in Acts, apostles and others; but the focus is on the movement itself, not upon individuals for their own sakes.

Although often claimed, Acts is not designed to trace the movement from Jerusalem to Rome. Geographical expansion belongs to the frame of Acts, but it is not the picture. In 1:8, the risen Christ commissions the preaching of the gospel in Jerusalem and in all Judea and Samaria and to the ends of the earth. Summary statements appear, marking stages in the expansion of the movement (6:7; 9:31; 12:24; 16:5; 19:20; 28:31; cf. 2:47; 11:21). Maps thus are important for studying Acts, but they are not primary. Acts shows how Paul reached Rome, but the movement was there already. Acts does not show when or how the gospel reached such cities as Damascus, Syrian Antioch, Ephesus, or Rome.

Channels for the geographical expansion of Christianity were cut already by the Jewish synagogues all over the Roman Empire. The struggle came in crossing religious and social lines separating Jews, Samaritans, and gentiles. That is the struggle traced in Acts, the struggle for an "unhindered" gospel (28:31). Luke-Acts shows how what began in the piety of Judaism, at home in synagogues and Temple, broke through to Samaritans, God-fearing "Greeks" (gentiles already attracted to Judaism), and finally to uncircumcised gentiles. With this triumph is shown the cost, the separation of Christianity and Judaism over the issue of including uncircumcised gentiles.

Acts 1:6 introduces the basic problem, the disciples' anticipating the restoration of the kingdom to Israel. This linkage of the kingdom with Israel persisted, some seeking to impose CIRCUMCISION and its cultic implications upon gentile converts (15:1). It was Stephen's stance that God has never limited himself to any nation or land that infuriated Saul of Tarsus until his own traumatic conversion (6:8–8:1). Peter required a special vision before his eyes were opened to the fallacy of viewing uncircumcised persons as "unclean" (10:15). The apostles in Jerusalem were slow to accept Peter's new stance (11:1). James validated the gentile mission without the requirement of circumcision (15:13-21), but he was not comfortable with Paul's gentile mission (21:17-26). Acts closes with Paul's arrest in Jerusalem on the charge of taking uncircumcised men into the Temple (21:27-36), his imprisonment and trials over his gentile involvement, and finally his arrival in Rome, where for two years under house arrest he preached to any who would hear, "unhindered."

See also BARNABAS; CIRCUMCISION; HOLY SPIRIT; JAMES; LUKE; LUKE, GOSPEL OF; PAUL; PETER; PHILIP; STEPHEN; THEOPHILUS; TONGUES; WE-SECTIONS.

Bibliography. J. Dupont, *The Sources of Acts*; F. J. Foakes-Jackson and K. Lake, eds., *The Beginnings of Christianity*; E. Haenchen, *The Acts of the Apostles, a Commentary*; J. Jervell, *Luke and the People of God*; L. E. Keck and J. L. Martyn, eds., *Studies in Luke-Acts*; I. H. Marshall, *Luke: Historian and Theologian*; J. C. O'Neill, *The Theology of Acts in Its Historical Setting*; F. Stagg, *The Book of Acts: The Early Struggle for an Unhindered Gospel*; C. H. Talbert, ed., *Perspectives on Luke-Acts*; S. G. Wilson, *The Gentiles and the Gentile Mission in Luke-Acts*.

—FRANK STAGG

• **Apostles, Epistle of the.** The *Epistle of the Apostles* is a mid-second century apocryphal work in the form of a letter from eleven APOSTLES (Peter and Cephas are not the same person). The letter contains dialogues between the eleven and Christ after his RESURRECTION. The revelations were given to counter the gnostics Simon and Cerinthus and the letter itself addressed to the churches of the north, south, east and west.

The document is never mentioned in early Christian literature. A mutilated Coptic manuscript was discovered by C. Schmidt in 1895; later a complete Ethiopic copy was uncovered, as well as a Latin fragment. These were published by Schmidt in 1919 and an English translation of the letter was made by M. R. James in 1924.

The *Epistle of the Apostles* represents a unique point in the history of early Christianity. Its author(s) represents a nascent orthodoxy in its struggle with GNOSTICISM. For the most part it utilizes traditional materials, but in such a way as to remind one of gnostic documents. Some special elements are: Jesus came to earth in the form of Gabriel and entered Mary's womb (14). Jesus' (resurrection) is firmly maintained and spoken of as "in the flesh" (rather than in the body or from the dead). Despite the strong emphasis on INCARNATION and physical resurrection the unity of Father and Son stands out prominently (17).

The strange form of this document with its unusual language and revelations points to a type of Christian apologetic which was ultimately not found useful, and eventually dropped, only to be discovered in the late nineteenth century.

See also GNOSTICISM.

Bibliography. H. Duensing, *New Testament Apocrypha,* ed. E. Hennecke and W. Schneemelcher; Quasten, *Patrology*.

—GRAYDON F. SNYDER

• **Apostolic Fathers.** [ap'uh-stah"lik] The rubric "Apostolic Fathers" refers to a certain collection of first and second century texts written for the edification of local churches. The title given the "corpus" refers to certain church leaders of the first and second centuries who supposedly had some contact with the apostles themselves Though most of the writings derive from the second century, their collection as a related group occurred in recent times. In the seventeenth century the writings of Barnabas, Clement, Hermas, Ignatius, and Polycarp were published as Apostolic Fathers. In the eighteenth century the *Epistle of Diognetus* and the fragments of Papias and Quadratus were added. Finally, following its discovery in 1883, the *Didache* completed the corpus as we know it.

Although at least two documents—*The Epistle to Diognetus* and the *Apology of Quadratus*—hardly belong in a collection of writings for local churches, the apostolic Fathers as generally accepted include:

The EPISTLE OF BARNABAS. A second century pseudepigraphical writing of unknown origin. It exhibits a strong Jewish connection and contains a section dealing with the Two Ways.

The epistle of 1 CLEMENT. A letter purporting to be from the Roman church, i.e., Clement its bishop, to the church at CORINTH. As such it would have been written during the last decade of the first century. It shows a strong connection to the scriptures, especially the Hebrew scriptures, yet is written with a clear Greek rhetorical style.

The Epistle of 2 CLEMENT. A sermon identified with Clement, but written near the middle of the second century by an unknown writer and at an unknown place.

DIDACHE. A document sometimes known as *The Teaching* (διδαχή in Greek) *of the Twelve Apostles*. Coming from a Jewish-Christian community in the early second century, it contains information about the practices of the early church and a well defined Two Way section.

The EPISTLE TO DIOGNETUS. A second century apology.

The SHEPHERD OF HERMAS. A composite work from second century Rome. Written in the form of an apocalypse, it contains also mandates, parables, visions and Two Way material. It was included in some manuscripts of the NT (Sinaiticus).

The Epistles of IGNATIUS. Letters written by Ignatius, bishop of Antioch, en route to his eventual martyrdom in Rome. The seven genuine letters, very valuable for their information about the life and faith of the eastern churches, were written about 114.

PAPIAS. An extant fragment (see EUSEBIUS) of the lost *Expositions of the Dominical Logia,* written about 110. Papias came from Hierapolis in Phrygia.

The EPISTLE OF POLYCARP TO THE PHILIPPIANS. A letter (or letters) to the Philippians by the bishop of Smyrna during the time of Trajan.

The MARTYRDOM OF POLYCARP. A letter from the church at Smyrna to the church at Philomelium (also in Phrygia) which describes the martyrdom of Polycarp in that city about 160.

The Apology of QUADRATUS. A defense of Christianity addressed to Hadrian. This fragment was preserved in Eusebius.

Bibliography. R. M. Grant, *The Apostolic Fathers*; J. Quasten, *Patrology,*; E. J. Goodspeed, *A History of Early Christian Literature*, rev. R. M. Grant.

—GRAYDON F. SNYDER

• **Apphia.** [af'ee-uh] Apphia (whose name expresses endearment) is addressed by Paul in Phlm 2 (along with PHILEMON and ARCHIPPUS). She was a member of the church at Colossae or Laodicea, known by the apostle Paul, and greeted as a beloved member of the family of God in her city.

See also ARCHIPPUS; PHILEMON; PHILEMON, LETTER TO.

—WILLIAM H. GEREN

• **Aquila and Priscilla.** *See* PRISCILLA AND AQUILA

• **Arabah.** [air'uh-buh] The depression of the Jordan Valley extending from the southern end of the Sea of Galilee to the Dead Sea and beyond to the Gulf of Aqaba (PLATE 8).

The Arabah consists of three distinct regions: the Jordan Valley, the DEAD SEA, and the area between it and the Gulf of Aqaba.

The Jordan Valley portion of the Arabah is approximately fifty miles long and ranges from about 696 feet to 1286 feet below sea level (north to south). The northern part of the valley is quite wide and fruitful, for it is amply watered by a number of streams (such as the Yarmuk, Arab, Taiyibeh, Ziqlab, and Yabis) which flows into it. However, just opposite Samaria, the valley narrows and begins to become progressively barren the farther south one goes.

The Dead Sea area is about fifty miles long and eleven miles wide. Most of this area is occupied by the sea itself. Because of its unusual mineral concentration, the only place where vegetation can live is where the streams flow into it. Unfortunately, there are not enough of these places to do much good.

The region South of the Dead Sea, which is known today as Wadi el-Arabah is about a hundred miles long. The area near the Dead Sea consists of a marshy area watered by the Wadi el-Jeib. However, the valley quickly begins to slope upward and to widen out until it reaches Jebel er-Rishe. Then, the valley narrows and begins descending again until it reaches the Gulf of Aqaba near Ezion-geber. The whole southern region is desert area, just occasionally marked by an oasis.

Despite its desert-like terrain, the Arabah seems to have always been a major point of contention. First, its southern-most city, Ezion-geber, served as the port of entry for trade coming from Arabia, India, and Africa that was destined to move up either the Via Maris or the Kings Highway. Second, the Arabah (particularly in its southern section) contained the richest mineral deposits in the whole area (Deut 8:9). Thus, Israel, like the other developing nations, needed and sought to control the Arabah.

This area played a significant part in the life of God's people on several occasions. First, during the patriarchal days, Lot chose to live in the Arabah (Gen 13:11, 14; 18:17-19:28). Second, the children of Israel wandered into the southern Arabah several times during their journey to Canaan (Deut 2:8). However, once they reached it, they not only claimed it (Josh 1-12), but also the eastern side of the Jordan (Deut 3:1-20). Third, during the early days of the Kingdom, the Arabah was used as a sanctuary for political refugees (2 Sam 4:7; 15:13-23). Later, Solomon exploited the minerals and trade routes of the southern Arabah and thus raised the concern of his neighbors (1 Kgs 10:1-13). Fourth, during the last days of the Southern Kingdom, Zedekiah and others tried to flee into the northern Arabah, but were quickly captured (2 Kgs 25:4-5; Jer 39:4-5). Finally, several of the latter prophets spoke of a future fruitfulness for the whole area (Ezek 47:1-12; Joel 3:18; Zech 14:8).

See also JORDAN RIVER/VALLEY OF THE JORDAN.

Bibliography. Y. Aharoni, *The Land of the Bible: A Historical Geography;* N. Glueck, "Transjordan," *Archaeology and Old Testament Study,* ed. D.W. Thomas.

—HARRY B. HUNT, JR.

• **Arabia.** [uh-ray'bee-uh] The large peninsula located just to the east of Egypt, between the Red Sea and the Persian Gulf (PLATE 1).

Since it encompasses more than one million square mi., Arabia is the largest peninsula in the world (1400 mi. long and 800 mi. wide). It is bounded by water on three sides (the Red Sea on the west, the Gulf of Aden and Arabian Sea on the south, the Gulf of Oman and the Persian Gulf on the east) and by the Syrian Desert and the Euphrates River on the north. However, since it is shaped like a large plateau (sloping west to east) most of the peninsula receives almost no rainfall at all, and is very barren. Thus, most of its inhabitants live along the coastal areas.

Although it is not yet possible to understand the history of ancient Arabia very well, it seems that by about 1200 B.C.E. the whole peninsula was inhabited by very highly civilized semitic people. By the eighth century B.C.E. the city of Saba had gained control of the central and southern part of the peninsula. However, it was quickly replaced by the kingdoms of the Qataban, the Hadramaut, and the Himyarites. The last of these survived until the Ethiopians conquered them in ca. 575 C.E. By the last of the fourth century B.C.E., the NABATEANS had taken firm control of the northern part of the peninsula. Their kingdom lasted until it was destroyed by the Romans in 106 C.E. During its last days, it was challenged by the Palmyrans who managed to survive until 272 C.E. Ultimately, the whole peninsula as well as most of the Middle East was taken over by the Islamic state.

Although the word Arabia is not often referred to in the biblical texts, there are some allusions to the land and its people.

Several Arabian groups are found in the Table of Nations (Gen 10) as well as among the descendants of Abraham (Gen 25:1-4, 12-15) and Esau (Gen 36). Moreover, Job and his friends seem to have had a strong yet friendly Arabian influence (Job 1:1; 2:11). During Solomon's day the QUEEN OF SHEBA journeyed to his court (1 Kgs 9:26-10:13). Soon after that Solomon began to collect tribute from some of the Arabian kings (2 Chr 9:14). After the division of the kingdom, Jehoshaphat continued this policy (2 Chr 17:11); however, his son Jehoram was attacked by Arabians and they defeated him. All of the major prophets include Arabia among the rival nations that God was about to judge (Isa 21:13-17; Jer 25:24; Ezek 27:20-22; 30:5). Even Nehemiah had to struggle with them during the restoration (Neh 2:19; 4:7-13; 6:1-7).

The Apocrypha contains only three references to Arabia (as Nabateans—1 Macc 11:16; as near Damascus—Jdt 2:25; and as "dragons"—2 Esdr 15:29). Thus, Arabia was able to exert some influence upon Palestine during the prechristian period.

Though Christ did not refer to Arabia directly, He did mention the "Queen of the South" (Matt 12:42; Luke 11:13). Later, Paul went into Arabia after his conversion, though the text does not say where nor why (Gal 1:17). He also mentions Arabia in association with Hagar's descendants (Gal 4:25) as well as the rule of Aretas the Nabatean (2 Cor 11:32).

Bibliography. Y. Aharoni, *The Land of the Bible: A Historical Geography*; P. Johnson, *Civilizations of the Holy Land;* W. S. LaSor, "Arabia," *ISBE*.

—HARRY B. HUNT, JR.

• **Arad.** [air'ad] Arad was an ancient city in the NEGEB (present-day Tell Arad, approximately seventeen mi. southeast of Hebron) (PLATE 9) which figured prominently in the OT account of the wilderness wanderings. It is first mentioned in Num 21:1-3 which reports that the Canaanite king of Arad resisted Israel's passage through his territory. Initially he defeated Israel and took captives, we are told, but Israel finally prevailed and "utterly destroyed them and their cities." The reference to "their cities" suggests that the king of Arad's domain extended well beyond the city of Arad itself. The scene of the massacre was renamed

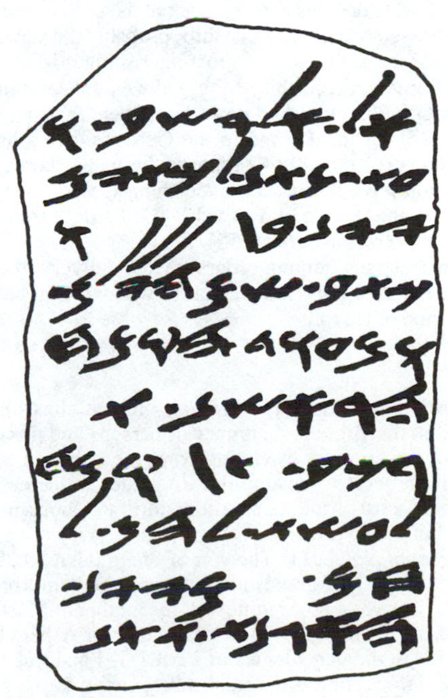

An Arad ostracon.

Hormah ("devoted to destruction") to commemorate this event (cf. Judg 1:17 and Josh 12:14). A brief reference to the encounter between Israel and the king of Arad appears also in Num 33:40.

Arad is mentioned again in a summary list of the kings whom Joshua conquered (Josh 12:14), although this is not mentioned in the preceding narrative account of Joshua's conquests. Finally, Judg 1:16 mentions the Negeb of Arad as the area where the sons of Judah and the KENITES went to live "among the people" (some manuscripts of the LXX read, "among the Amalekites," cf. 1 Sam 15:6). Outside the OT, Pharaoh Sheshonq's (SHISHAK) list of conquered cities (ca. 920 B.C.E.) mentions "Arad the great" and "Arad of Yrhm." Possibly "Yrhm" refers to the Jerahmeelites who are connected with the Kenites in the OT (1 Sam 27:10; 30:29).

Excavations at Tell Arad (beginning in 1962 under the direction of Y. Aharoni and R. Amiran) have revealed the extensive remains of an Early Bronze Age city as well as remains of an Iron Age fort. The latter was situated on the east side of the tell, apparently was established during the tenth century B.C.E., and continued in use through the sixth century. Thus it is to be regarded as a Judean fort which would have guarded Judah's southern frontiers in the direction of Edom. The fort showed evidence of six destructions and rebuildings during its approximately 500 years of existence.

Inside the walls near the northwest corner of the fortress stood a sanctuary which was almost certainly Israelite. Its design has affinities with the description of the Tabernacle in Exodus, and among the ostraca found in the sanctuary were two which bore the names of priestly families known from the OT, Meremoth and Pashhur (Ezra 8:33; 10:22). All told, over 200 ostraca were unearthed in various parts of the fortress. Written in Hebrew and Aramaic, these ostraca chiefly contain instructions concerning the distribution of stored goods such as wine, oil and grain. Many of these dockets date from about the sixth century and are addressed to a certain Eliashib, probably the steward of the royal stores. One of the most interesting reads,

"To my lord Eliashib. May Yahweh concern himself with your wellbeing. And now, give Shemaryahu a letek-measure(?) (of meal?) and to the Qerosite give a homer-measure(?) (of meal?). As regards the matter concerning which you gave me orders: everything is fine now: he is staying in the temple of Yahweh" (D. Pardee, *Handbook of Ancient Hebrew Letters,* 55).

Other ostraca contain orders for the delivery of goods to "the Kittim," Greek mercenaries who were probably in the service of Egypt.

—J. MAXWELL MILLER

• **Aram/Aramaeans.** [air'uhm/air'uh-mee"uhns] A term applied in the Bible to a number of persons and places located in the territory extending from the Lebanon Mountains in the west to beyond the Euphrates in the east and from the Taurus Mountains in the north to Damascus and beyond in the south.

Personal Name. (1) The son of Shem (Gen 10:22–23; 1 Chr 1:17); (2) the grandson of Nahor, Abraham's brother (Gen 22:21); (3) an "Aramitess," the mother of Machir by Manasseh (1 Chr 7:14); (4) a descendant of Asher (1 Chr 7:34); (5) in the genealogies of Matt 1:3–4 and Luke 3:33 KJV the name Aram is the misleading Greek form of Ram RSV and an entirely different name.

Place Name. (1) ARAM-NAHARAIM ("Aram of the two rivers"). Commonly associated with Paddan-aram (Gen 25:5; 24:10), this is the region along the upper Euphrates where the biblical patriarchs lived before they went to Canaan. Located here were the ancient cities of Haran and Nisibis and where later Edessa, the noted seat of Syrian culture arose. This is the Aram which the Israelites spoke of as "beyond the river" (2 Sam 10:16). (2) Aram-damascus—the city that was eventually to become the center of Aramaean influence west of the Euphrates and a periodic military nemesis of the Israelites (2 Sam 8:5; 1 Kgs 15:18). (3) Aram-zobah—a powerful Aramaean kingdom west of the Euphrates from Hamath to Damascus that flourished during the reigns of Saul, David, and Solomon (2 Sam 10:6; 1 Chr 18:3). (4) Aram-beth-rehob—also contemporary with Israel's united monarchy (2 Sam 10:6) the location of this kingdom is uncertain. If identical with the site mentioned in Num 13:21 and Judg 18:28, it was near both Maacah and Dan. (5) Aram-maacah—a site east of the Jordan within the contemplated bounds of Israel, near Mount Hermon (Josh 12:5; 13:11).

The Aramaeans. The term Aramaean is used to refer to a confederacy of tribes that spoke a north SEMITIC LANGUAGE and from the eleventh to the eighth centuries B.C.E. spread out from the fringes of the Syro-Arabian desert to occupy parts of the Fertile Crescent, from the Persian Gulf to the Amanus mountains, Lebanon, and the Transjordan. The earliest extra-biblical reference to the Aramaeans is from the time of Tiglath-pileser I (1116–1076 B.C.E.) where Aramaeans are already present in the Mount Bishri district of the upper Euphrates and the region east of the mountains of Lebanon. By the end of the eleventh century B.C.E., the Aramaeans had formed the state of Bit-Adini on both sides of the Euphrates below CARCHEMISH. They controlled the Khabur River Valley, areas of modern Turkish Kurdistan, and regions in northern Syria and Anti-Lebanon, including DAMASCUS. King David stopped an advance upon Israel by the southern Aramaeans under Hadadezer of Zobah, in league with Ammonites, Edomites, and the Aramaeans of Mesopotamia.

To the east, however, the Aramaean tribes spread into Babylonia, where an Aramaean usurper was crowned king of Babylon under the name of Adad-apal-iddin. By the ninth century the whole area from Babylon to the sea was in the hands of the Aramaean tribes known collectively as Kaldu (or Kashdu)—the biblical Chaldeans. Assyria, nearly encircled, took the offense and under Shalmaneser III (858–824 B.C.E.) overran the Aramaean states between Habur and the Euphrates. With the conquest of Bit-Adini in 855 B.C.E. and the Assyrian victory at Qarqar in 853 B.C.E. the rest of the Aramaean states were open to Assyrian conquest. This was completed by Tiglath-pileser III (744–727 B.C.E.) who reduced the Aramaean states in Syria to mere Assyrian provinces. The destruction of Hamath by Sargon II in 720 B.C.E. marked the end of the Aramaean kingdoms of the west.

Aramaeans of the lower Tigris maintained their independence longer. In 626 B.C.E., the Chaldean general, Nabopolassar, proclaimed himself king of Babylon and joined with the Medes and Scythians to overthrow Assyria. In the neo-Babylonian Empire Chaldeans, Aramaeans, and Babylonians became largely indistinguishable.

The Aramaic language is of the north Semitic family, closest to Hebrew and Phoenician and bearing some resemblance to Arabic. Though adopting the Phoenician alphabet, Aramaic developed its own specific form, and occasionally was even written in other scripts (cuneiform and demotic). Aramaic is attested as early as the ninth century B.C.E. and by the time of the Achaemenian Empire (539–332) "imperial" Aramaic was officially employed from Egypt to India. Although it was later displaced by Greek, Aramaic dialects survived into Roman times in such forms as Palmyrene, Nabataean, Samaritan, and Syriac.

The principal Aramaean deity in Syria was the ancient west-Semitic storm-god Hadad, or Ramman (OT Rimmon), equated with the Hurrian storm god Teshub. Their chief goddess was Atargatis, a fusion of two deities corresponding to the Phoenician Astarte and Anath. At Sam'al, the Aramaeans worshipped Hadad alongside the Dynastic gods Rakib-El, Ba'al Hamman, Ba'al Semed, and Ba'al Harran (whose cultic center was at Harran). Traces of Aramaean religion in the Hellenistic period appear at such places as Baalbeck and Hierapolis.

The Bible closely links the Hebrew patriarchs with the Aramaeans: not only is Abraham a brother of Nahor (grandfather of Aram, Gen 22:20–21), but Isaac and Jacob marry daughters of their cousins Bethuel "the Aramaean" and Laban "the Aramaean," respectively (Gen 25:20; 31:20). In one instance a patriarch himself (apparently Jacob) is designated "a wandering Aramaean" (Deut 26:5). This conforms with the Hebrew names for the ancestral habitat of the patriarchs: Paddan-aram and Aram-naharaim. The prophet Balaam of Pethor is said to have come from Aram or Aram-naharaim (Num 23:7; Deut 23:4) as is Cushan-Rishathaim, the first oppressor of Israel in the period of the Judges (Judg 3:8, 11).

From approximately 1000–700 B.C.E. Israel's relations with the Aramaean states were primarily hostile. Saul, David, and Solomon fought against Aram-zobah north of Damascus. In the second half of his reign David had a string of victories over Hadadezer son of Rehob and eventually annexed Damascus (2 Sam 8:3-12; 1 Chr 19). In the latter days of Solomon, Rezon removed Damascus from Israelite control and founded the kingdom of Aram-damascus (1 Kgs 11:23ff.). A new dynasty founded by Hezion fully exploited the division of the united kingdom of Israel (1 Kgs 15:18-19) tactfully playing sides and changing alliances. BEN-HADAD I, the grandson of Hezion, was a key player in the politics of this period. The Ben-hadad who later clashed with Ahab (1 Kgs 20) and was murdered by HAZAEL (ca. 843 B.C.E.) was probably (though not necessarily) a different king. The usurper Hazael attacked Israel under the reigns of Joram, Jehu, and Jehoahaz with only temporary relief through a "deliverer" sent by God (2 Kgs 13:5). As predicted by Elisha, Joash (798–782/1 B.C.E.) was able to recover from Hazael's son (another Ben-hadad) much of the Israelite territory previously lost to Hazael (2 Kgs 13:14-19, 22-25). Later, perhaps after the death of Jeroboam II of Israel in 753 B.C.E., a king Rezin appeared in Damascus and menaced Judah as Israel's ally, conquering the Transjordan. Ahaz of Judah then appealed to Tiglath-pileser III of Assyria, who then in 732 B.C.E. defeated and slew Rezin (2 Kgs 16:5-9), deporting the conquered Aramaeans to Qir as prophesied by Amos (1:4-5).

—STEPHEN M. HOOKS

• **Aram-Naharaim/Paddan-Aram.** [air'uhm-nay-huh-ray"im/pad'uhn-air"uhm] Aram-Naharaim and Paddan-Aram (KJV, Padan-Aram) are roughly synonymous terms. They are used in the Bible as geographical terms for a region of MESOPOTAMIA. Aram-Naharaim and Paddan-Aram, as geographical designations, refer to land in the northwest portion of the fertile crescent, in what is now the general area of Syria. Aram-Naharaim has been translated as "Aram of the two rivers." As such, the geographical term implies the vicinity of the upper Mesopotamian valley river system. Aram-Naharaim is a composite term with "ARAM" referring to the Aramean population, and "Naharaim" referring to the land of the rivers. Paddan-Aram is used in the patriarchal narratives to refer to the homeland of the patriarchal family, including HARAN. Paddan-Aram has been understood as "garden," "road," or "field" of Aram. In any case, like Aram-Naharaim, Paddan-Aram is a term for a geographical region in northwest Mesopotamia. Naharaim is attested to in Egyptian records (*Naharin*) and in the Amarna texts (*Naḫrima*) as a general geographic region north of Palestine. These contexts make associations for the terms with the system of rivers in upper Mesopotamia. Politically, some applied usage of the term Aram-Naharaim to the Mitanni Empire and Aramean city states is found in extrabiblical and biblical sources (e.g., Aram-Zobah; Aram-Maacah). The extent of the region is not definite, yet as a land unit, it encompasses the upper Mesopotamian valley. It reaches from the Orontes River in the west, to the east of the Euphrates, to the Habor, and possibly the Tigris (PLATE 2).

English versions normally translate Aram-Naharaim as Mesopotamia. A notable exception is the superscription to Ps 60, which places the psalm in the tradition of David's warfare with the Syrians. The Masoretic Text refers to Aram-Naharaim and Aram-Zobah (cf. the Ammonites of 1 Chr 19:6). The patriarchal narratives regularly refer to Aram-Naharaim and Paddan-Aram as the homeland of the patriarchs. Isaac's wife REBEKAH is located and brought from the house of Bethuel the Aramean in Paddan-Aram (Gen 24:10; 25:20). Jacob is sent to Paddan-Aram to find a wife and to flee from Esau (Gen 28). In Paddan-Aram, he marries the daughters of LABAN (Jacob's journeys to Paddan-Aram and Canaan are recorded in Gen 28–32). Deut 23:4 places the homeland of BALAAM son of Beor in Pethor of Aram-Naharaim. Judg 3:8, 10 provide an obscure reference to Aram-Naharaim. Judges identifies the first oppressor of Israel in the cycle of Judges as Cushan-rishathaim, king of Mesopotamia (MT Aram-Naharaim). Outside of Judges, nothing is known of this enigmatic figure. In the NT, Mesopotamia is referred to in Acts 2:9 and 7:2, which again refers to a geographical region. The texts in Acts include the broader Mesopotamian area rather than the upper northwest portion of the Fertile Crescent. The biblical sources generally use Aram-Naharaim, Paddan-Aram, and Mesopotamia to refer to the homeland of the patriarchs, and the region within the river system in the upper Mesopotamian valley.

See also MESOPOTAMIA.

Bibliography. C. H. Gordon, "Aram-Naharaim," *IDB* and "Paddan-Aram," *IDB*; A. Malamat, "Cushan Rishathaim and the Decline of the Near East Around 1200 B.C.," *JNES* 13 (1954): 231-42; B. Mazar, "The Aramean Empire and its Relations with Israel," *BA* 25 (1962): 98-120; R. T. O'Callaghan, *Aram-Naharaim, A Contribution to the History of Upper Mesopotamia in the Second Millennium B.C.*, Analecta Orientalia 26, 1948.

—DAVID M. FLEMING

• **Aramaic Language.** [air'uh-may"ik] Aramaic is an ancient Semitic language which predates OT Hebrew; when the Israelites invaded Palestine, they spoke a language far more Aramaic than Hebrew. Hebrew was the language of the Israelites, of course, and the OT was written for the most part in Hebrew. During the exilic and postexilic era (sixth century B.C.E.), however, Aramaic became the vernacular language of the Jews. This took place largely because Aramaic was the official tongue of the PERSIAN EMPIRE. Hebrew remained as the "religious" language and also the language of the schools. Although Greek generally triumphed during the Hellenistic era (330-30 B.C.E.), Aramaic became the common language in Palestine and Arabia—thus, the Dead Sea Scrolls of the Qumran community and Daniel were partly written in Aramaic.

Aramaic is a cognate of Hebrew (not a derivative), and as such it possesses the following elements: (1) an alphabet of twenty-two characters; (2) heavily consonantal and guttural qualities; (3) a trilateral word root for a basic vocabulary far smaller than English; (4) verbs of two main kinds of action (complete and incomplete); (5) expressive power—thundering, tender, explosive, poetic, vivid—through a directness and simplicity of expression.

Aramaic is important for an understanding of both OT and NT literature. Certain OT texts were written in Aramaic (Dan 2:4b–7:28; Ezra 4:8–6:18; 7:12-26; Gen 31:47; Jer 10:11), and it is difficult to interpret the sayings of Jesus accurately, unless we are aware that he spoke Aramaic (called Hebrew in such texts as John 5:2; 19:13,17). In addition, Paul spoke in Hebrew (Aramaic) to make his Jerusalem defense (Acts 21:40). Further, Revelation is written in a crude Greek with Semitic earthiness that must be acknowledged lest an abstract, metaphysical misinterpretation occur. The substratum of Aramaic in the sayings of Jesus and his followers has helped to prevent the misunderstanding that John's Gospel is a Hellenized, metaphysical second-century misreading of Jesus' person and ministry.

Future discoveries of papyri, ostraca, letters, scrolls, and other documents—religious or secular—will add to our understanding of the Bible by uncovering grammatical correspondences between Hebrew and Aramaic; by unveiling "Aramaisms" (idiomatic expressions) which will clarify Bible passages; by disclosing the Aramaic diction and thought of Jesus and helping to decide the authenticity of sayings attributed to him; and by sharpening our awareness of the intensely profound humanity of God's revelation. The "Aramaic question" (the study of cross–cultural language use in Hebrew, Greek, and Aramaic) was once thought to be confusing, unhelpful, and perhaps harmful to belief. Now it demonstrates the rich variety of God's revelation, and is a key element in the study of comparative religion as well as in biblical study.

See also ABBA; ARAMEANS; CALVARY; GREEK LANGUAGE; HEBREW LANGUAGE; MARANATHA; SEMITIC LANGUAGES.

Bibliography. M. Black, *An Aramaic Approach to the Gospels and Acts*; R. A. Bowman, "Arameans, Aramaic and the Bible," *JNES* 7/2 (1948): 65-90; J. A. Fitzmeyer, "The Aramaic Language and the Study of the New Testament," *JBL* 99/1 (1980): 5-21.

—JOHN S. REIST, JR.

• **Ararat.** [air'uh-rat] A country in the first millennium B.C.E. whose geographical center was in eastern Asia Minor (PLATE 1).

NOAH'S ark, reports the book of Gen (8:4), came to rest upon "the mountains of Ararat." The use of the plural ("mountains" rather than "mountain" or "Mount") suggests a geographical area of some extent and this is supported by other references in the Bible: "the land of Ararat" (2 Kgs 19:37; Isa 37:38) and the "kingdoms" of Ararat, Minni, and Ashkenaz (Jer 51:27). The term "Mount Ararat" does not occur in scripture.

With the aid of Assyrian records, the kingdom of Ararat (which the Assyrians called Urartu) may be located on the modern map as follows: mostly in eastern Turkey, centered around Lake Van, with slight extension into Russia, Iran, and Iraq. Beginning in the thirteenth century, references indicate that it reached its zenith in the ninth/eighth, was plundered by the Assyrians in the eighth, and was destroyed by the Medes in the sixth. By the fifth century, it had been settled by a new population from the southwest and thus the Persians refer to it as Armenia. However, they retained the older designation (Ararat) for one of its subdivisions, and this has produced a confusion about the location of "Mount Ararat" that persists to the present day. Thus, St. Jerome (fourth century, C.E.) remarks, "Ararat is a region in Armenia on the Araxis [River]" In this northerly sub-division there is a spectacular mountain, 16,000 ft. in elevation, which the local (Armenian) population called Masis and which they began to identify as the ark's landing place in the eleventh-twelfth centuries, C.E. Thus it has come to be called, by modern Christians, "Mount Ararat." It is known in Turkish as Büyük ("mount") Ağri Daği.

Since the ancient kingdom was much more extensive than the later subdivision ("Ararat"), early Jews and Christians sought the ark's landing place farther to the southeast where the mountains first rise from the plain of the River Tigris. The location of choice was an elevation now called (in Turkish) Cudi Daği, but known to the ancient Semitic peoples as Qardu(n). Hence the Aramaic and Syriac translations of the Bible rendered Gen 8:4 as "the mountains of Qardu," and Greek and Latin writers refer to the area as Gordyaea. The Nestorian Christians built several monasteries on this peak, including one on the summit known as the Cloister of the Ark. The Muslims, who conquered the area in the seventh century, then erected a mosque on the site and referred to the area as Jabal ("Mount") Judi. Even in recent times, representatives of various faiths (Christians, Jews, Muslims, Sabians, and Yezidis) gathered there annually to commemorate Noah's first sacrifice after the flood had ended.

A number of other sites were indentified in antiquity with the ark's landing place, among them: Jabal Judi in Arabia, Pira Magrun in the Zagros range, and peaks in the Caucasus range, Phrygia, and Ceylon.

See also ARK; NOAH

Bibliography. L. R. Bailey, *Where Is Noah's Ark?*; B. Piotrovsky, *The Ancient Civilization of Urartu.*

—LLOYD R. BAILEY

• **Archaeology.** From two Greek words (*archaios,* "ancient, old" and *logos,* "word, subject matter") archaeology deals with the study of ancient remains. More precisely, archaeology is concerned with the discovery, recovery and preservation of the material remains of ancient cultures. Archaeology in the modern sense developed after the Renaissance with the recovery of remains from the classic cultures of Greece and Rome. As such, archaeology was often aligned with those disciplines most closely related to the study of those cultures: classics, history, and philology. Not surprisingly, the emphasis of this archaeology focused on the recovery of texts and inscriptions, architectural units and complete artifacts such as pottery, sculpture and coins. This remained the emphasis of archaeology until the advent of prehistoric studies. Prehistoric archaeology possessed no texts and only few art forms. Even architectural remains were minimal. So other approaches were required

TABLE OF ARCHAEOLOGICAL PERIODS FOR SYRIA/PALESTINE

Cultural Period[1]	Dates[2]	Major Biblical Events
Paleolithic (Old Stone) Age	1,500,000–14,000 B.C.E.	
Epipaleolithic (Mesolithic, Middle Stone) Age	14,000–8000 B.C.E.	
Neolithic (New Stone) Age	8000–4500 B.C.E.	
Chalcolithic (Copper-Stone) Age	4500–3200 B.C.E.	
Early Bronze (EB) Age	3200–2200 B.C.E.	
Middle Bronze (MB) Age	2200–1550 B.C.E.	
MB I (formerly MB IIA)	2200–2000	
MB II (formerly MB IIA)	2000–1750	Patriarchal period
MB III (formerly MB IIC)	1750–1550	Israel in Egypt
Late Bronze (LB) Age	1550–1200 B.C.E.	
LB I	1550–1400	
LB II	1400–1200	Exodus and entry into Canaan
Iron Age	1200–586 B.C.E.	
Iron I	1200–1000	Judges
Iron IIA	1000–930	United monarchy
Iron IIB	930–721	Divided monarchy to fall of Samaria
Iron IIC	721–586	Judah to fall of Jerusalem
Babylonian Period	586–539 B.C.E.	Exile
Persian Period	539–332 B.C.E.	Postexilic period, Ezra, Nehemiah
Hellenistic Period	332–63 B.C.E.	
Early Hellenistic	332–198	Ptolemaic rule over Palestine
Late Hellenistic	198-63	Seleucid rule, Maccabees, Hasmoneans
Roman Period	63 B.C.E.–324 C.E.	
Early Roman	63 B.C.E.–135 C.E.	NT era through second Jewish revolt
Late Roman	135–324 C.E.	Early church era
Byzantine Period	324–640 C.E.	Expansion of Christianity

[1]Archaeologists use the convention of naming the early periods through the Iron Age for technological features, esp. for the materials used in tools and weapons. Beginning with the Babylonian Period, historical events are the basis for naming periods.
[2]All dates are approximate. Scholars often disagree over precise dates and terminology for certain periods.

to extract, as much information as possible from the remains, and an emphasis was placed on the reconstruction of the culture. Whereas archaeology of historic periods had tended to be diachronic and deductive, prehistoric archaeology was synchronic and inductive. The archaeology of the Near East, particularly Syria-Palestine with which this essay is concerned, has its roots in classical archaeology and has only in the last quarter century introduced elements of prehistoric archaeology. The discipline of Syro-Palestinian archaeology is still developing as newer sub-disciplines are incorporated and the synthesis between synchronic and diachronic approaches is formed. Even the name of the discipline is changing with many practitioners preferring the term Syro-Palestinian archaeology in place of the older name, biblical archaeology. And clearly archaeology has shifted from the major goal of recovering objects to that of recovering data, as much of the information the excavated portion of the site holds as may feasibly be recovered. Just one example shows how rich even small sites may be. Until recent years, it was assumed that little information concerning the flora of ancient Palestinian sites could be determined, little wood and few seeds remained. So reconstructions had to be made primarily on the basis of the current flora of the site. Now however, it has been discovered that the common mud bricks found at most sites preserve pollen remains from the site. Most mud bricks were made near the site where they were used, and they were most often made at the end of the rainy season, at the very time trees would be flowering. The sun dried bricks sealed the pollen remains inside preserving them to the present. Now a single mud brick can provide a pollen reading and, therefore, a picture of the flora of the site at the time when the brick was made.

Types of Archaeological Work. Until recently, one might assume there was only one method for archaeology, excavation. And to a certain extent that still is the primary method. However, many recent technological advances have opened new possibilities for the archaeologist. Even when excavation will be the end result, it is not necessarily the only important method of data collection to be used. Furthermore, different settings require quite different methods of excavation. Several different types of archaeological work can be mentioned.

(1) The excavation of tells: The most common technique used in twentieth century in Syria-Palestine has been the excavation of a TELL by large teams, generally using a professional staff, and many volunteers or paid laborers for most of the actual process of excavation. One thinks of the major excavations such as SAMARIA, MEGIDDO, LACHISH from the early 1900s until World War II as using this approach. Newer techniques were applied at HAZOR, SHECHEM, GEZER in the 1950s and 1960s. The technique was to expose a significant portion of a major tell with some areas going to the lowest levels of occupation in order to learn as much as possible about the history of the site. Major architectural features were usually the focus: walls and gates, water supplies, palaces and temples, public buildings, and homes of the wealthy. The primary excavation technique shifted its emphasis from the horizontal approach (sometimes called the Reisner-Fisher method) to the vertical approach (the Wheeler-Kenyon method). Both approaches were concerned with stratigraphy. The horizontal approach usually laid bare entire architectural units (and at times an entire strata) to find the relationship between buildings, roads, and walls at one time period. Unfortunately, the excavation technique did not always clearly differentiate the strata, and because it completely cleared an area, did not permit later excavators to check the stratigraphy. The vertical approach placed emphasis on a vertical balk left unexcavated in each square which clearly showed the strata. Ideally, every find was related to a specific strata. Also smaller areas of the tell were excavated, leaving future generations of archaeologists the possibility of applying newer techniques and rechecking the stratigraphy of a site. In the late 1960s and 1970s additional methods from "new archaeology" began to have an impact, primarily in

the addition of a multi-disciplinary approach bringing new members to the team and extracting additional data (see below).

(2) The excavation of low level sites: Along with tells, it has been recognized that many significant sites were occupied only during a limited number of phases, possibly, though not necessarily, during only one time period. Among low level sites would be classical sites such as ROME, CORINTH and EPHESUS, and Palestinian sites such as CAPERNAUM, CAESAREA, Jerash and PETRA. Very few such sites were occupied for only one occupational level; Tell el-AMARNA in Egypt is the best example. Caesarea, by contrast, was occupied over a period of about 1200 years, but never became a tell; instead it spread over an 8000 acre site. By their very nature, low level sites may have more horizontal than vertical expansion. Although stratigraphy is still crucial, larger squares may have to be opened to understand the site, and architectural units and their interrelation with nearby units play a necessary role in understanding low level sites.

(3) The excavation of tombs: TOMBS and burials present their own difficulties for excavation. Burials may be found in graves, pits, pyres, rock-cut tombs, caves, and monumental structures such as dolmens and mausoleums. In addition to a description of the actual burial site and the manner of burial (primary or secondary, individual or multiple, flexed or extended, etc.), undisturbed tombs often reveal much information about burial practices. What grave goods were buried with the person? Were only personal items such as jewelry buried with the person or was food and drink included? What religious practices or beliefs can be surmised from the evidence? What preparation was made of the body for burial? Was the burial site single or multiple? Was it a family burial site or part of a larger cemetery area used by a larger social unit?

Once a burial has been located, the entrance and interior is excavated using a stratigraphic method. The methods and tools used in construction of the tomb are studied. The bones can be analyzed to determine age, sex, and pathological matters. Finally the tomb goods can be analyzed as suggested above.

(4) Archaeological surveys: Not all archaeology involves excavation. The survey mentioned here and several additional methods mentioned below gain valuable archaeological data without excavation. The survey has long been used as a preliminary step to excavation, but has also proved its worth as a separate approach. In a survey surface remains such as houses, fortresses, dolmens, walls and cisterns are located and described. Potsherds and other material finds are collected from the surface of an individual site and studied to indicate the periods of occupation of the site. Where the survey covers a larger region rather than a single site, the finds from each site will be compared to note regional settlement patterns. Current flora and fauna, as well as geographical and geological features are also included. Many major excavations now include a regional survey as a part of the project methodology. The Lahav, Hesi, HESHBON and Yoqneam projects all made use of this methodology. Archaeological surveys have also been conducted as projects independently of excavation. Examples include Glueck's survey of the Negeb, Cohen's and Dever's work in the Central Negeb Highlands and Miller's Central Moab survey. Large regional surveys generally use a method chosen by the nature of the region and project to select the specific areas to be surveyed fully.

(5) Remote sensing: Remote sensing refers to a variety of methods of locating archaeological remains by remote means. Remote sensing can include such instruments as a proton magnetometer to measure deviations in the earth's magnetic field caused by subsurface objects. Soil resistivity can also be used to locate subterranean archaeological features. Both of these techniques require the presence of the technician and the instrument in the field in order to locate the remains. Other types of remote sensing can be accomplished at a distance from the site. Aerial photography has been used for many years as an adjunct to archaeology. It can reveal variations in contour and vegetation indicative of subsurface structures that are not visible from the ground. Recent technology has greatly increased the type and sensitivity of data available. Very sensitive cameras on high altitude airplanes and satellites have revealed previously unknown archaeological sites in desert and jungle settings. Radar and infra-red images have located ancient river beds and roadways. Further enhancement of these images through the use of computers can reveal even more detail, promising even more discoveries.

Excavation Technology. Excavation technique involves both a horizontal and a vertical dimension. After the site is selected, the permits secured, the team assembled, the tell (this paragraph assumes the site is a tell) must be thoroughly surveyed. A map is prepared showing contours every meter or two meters. A grid is superimposed over the map, usually set in five meter squares. Before excavation begins, extensive surveying of the site may have located walls, building remains, depressions that may indicate water systems and gate areas, and provided an indication of periods of occupation. These clues can aid the archaeologist in determining which squares should be excavated.

Once the squares have been chosen, permanent markers are placed at the intersection of the grid lines forming the square. The area to be excavated lies a half meter inside the grid line, thus assuring a balk remains on which stratigraphy can be read. Thus a four meter area can be excavated from a five meter square. The half meter remaining on each side of the square will leave a one meter balk if adjacent squares are excavated. The excavation begins with a test pit or trench no more than one meter wide dug downward from the surface, usually no more than a meter deep. All artifacts from this pit are kept separate because the stratigraphy is not certain. The purpose of the test trench is to provide a reading of stratigraphic layers in the vertical balk. When the test trench has been completed and the balk drawn, then the full square can be excavated by removing one layer at a time. All the artifacts are kept separate by layer. When walls are encountered, test pits should be dug perpendicular to the wall to compare strata on both sides of the wall. When each layer is removed, as the balk is reached, the layer is tagged on the balk. All features encountered in a layer must be cleaned, measured, drawn and photographed before being removed. Balks themselves are carefully drawn and photographed. The strata indicated in the balks are carefully coordinated for the entire site. Balks separating squares are removed when they obscure structures or interpretation, or when the balk reaches a depth of about four meters, making further excavation difficult. While most American excavators keep rather strict five meter balks, Israeli archaeologists tend to open larger squares when they encounter a structure, to expose as much of the structure as possible. The difference is that the latter approach places more emphasis on the uncovering of entire architectural units.

Problem Solving Excavation. With more archaeological teams in the field nearly every season and the rising cost of excavations, archaeologists are often resorting to problem solving excavations, small scale excavations intended to resolve particular problems. In these excavations very limited numbers of squares are opened on a site, usually to resolve specific strategraphic problems, or to locate specific features. Problem solving excavation has another distinct advantage in that it preserves the largest portion of a site for future excavation when new techniques are available. It can also be used effectively when only limited areas are available for excavation, perhaps due to present day structures or other factors.

Other small scale excavations may involve small sites such as villages or forts. These sites may be excavated thoroughly as a small scale excavation simply due to size. The choice of small sites may actually provide a better picture of the life of the common people or rural life than excavations of a large tell.

Dating Methods in Archaeology. One of the chief tasks of archaeology has been the dating of artifacts and structures recovered in excavations as well as the strata containing these structures. A number of methods, applicable to various situations, has been developed. All of the methods depend on the proper understanding of stratigraphy, and the careful excavation of artifacts by strata.

(1) Coins or datable inscriptions: From those strata that have coins or datable inscriptions, a fixed date can be ascertained before which the strata could not have been destroyed. For instance, if a coin or inscription is dated to the fifteenth year of Herod's reign, then the strata in which the coin or inscription is found must have been destroyed after that date. If a number of coins are found in a given strata, the latest coin is the one which provides the fixed date. The material gives no latest cutoff date for the destruction only the date after which the strata was destroyed. The strata above the given one usually provides the cutoff date before which the lower strata must have been destroyed.

Even if inscriptions provide no evidence for a precise date, they can be dated by means of epigraphy. The form of individual letters in inscriptions changes over time. By knowing how the letters develop, it is possible to fix the approximate time the inscription was written.

(2) Ceramic chronology: Unfortunately, few strata have such specific datable material. In that case the archaeologist must rely on other common artifacts that can provide a relative chronology. The most common means of dating strata for historic periods is POTTERY CHRONOLOGY. Sir Flinders Petrie was the first to recognize that changes in pottery could be used to give relative dating to strata. For Palestine, ceramic chronology was placed on a firm footing by Albright, Wright, Amiran and others. Certain parts of vessels such as rims, bases, handles and spouts are especially important for dating because they show changing styles. These sherds are called diagnostic sherds. While one or a few sherds can be important, for dating a strata the entire ceramic assemblage is most important. No pottery style appears or disappears at once. A style remains in use over a period of time, though the quantity of pottery exhibiting that style will begin, increase, and then wane over time. By providing a complete assemblage of diagnostic sherds, a good relative chronology for a strata can be determined.

(3) Radiocarbon and other dating methods from the sciences: All organic materials have amounts of carbon in them. Along with the common isotope of carbon, a small amount of radioactive carbon will be present. Once the organic material dies, no additional radioactive carbon is added, and the radioactive carbon begins to decay at a fixed rate. By comparing the percentage of radioactive carbon with the common isotope, the approximate age of the object can be determined. Radiocarbon dating can be especially useful for determining the age of wood, bone, food, and textile materials. Since the method is destructive and provides only an approximate date, it is used primarily when other dating methods are not available, or to provide additional support for other dating methods.

Dendrochronology has proved to be very useful for dating remains in the American Southwest. Since tree rings indicate growth patterns and are relatively constant regionwide, if wood remains have enough rings, usually twenty-five or so, it is possible to determine the time period in which the tree was alive. The more rings available, the more accurate dendrochronology is. A record for about 3,000 years has been compiled for the American Southwest. The record for Syria-Palestine is not so lengthy, but is being continually increased. One shortcoming of dendrochronology is that it provides only information about the time when the tree lived, but nothing about the age of the secondary use of the wood. For instance, if the wood is used in furniture or in a building, it may be found in a context a hundred or more years later than the date of the tree. Furthermore, if the wood is from a large tree that lived hundreds of years, the surviving piece of wood may only preserve a small segment of the rings and thus not fix the date of the furniture or building.

Several additional dating methods can be mentioned, but most of these are too specialized for general applicability at present. These methods include archaeomagnetic dating, obsidian hydration dating, potassium-argon dating, and thermoluminescence dating.

Multi-Disciplinary Approach. Until the 1960s the archaeological team consisted primarily the chief archaeologist and other field archaeologists, an architect/draftsman, a surveyor, a photographer, pottery specialist, a pottery restorer, and volunteers for most of the excavation and cataloging of finds. An epigrapher would be brought in if inscriptional finds were made. But with the shift to the "new archaeology" and the introduction of synchronic concerns of prehistoric archaeology, the amount of data extracted from an excavation, and the number of specialists added to the team both increased enormously. Now a team may have, in addition to the ones mentioned above, cultural anthropologists, biologists, paleoethnobotanists, palynologists, osteologists, geologists, zoologists, physical anthropologists, hydrologists, phytogeographers, agronomists, and metallurgists. Many additional specialists can be recruited as needed, and even more are available for specialized laboratory study of data. The advantages of such a multi-disciplinary approach include the possibility of extracting much additional information from the remains recovered in excavation. As an example, soil samples can be sieved, then put through a flotation device to recover seeds. These seeds can then be analyzed to indicate the flora of the area and also the diet of the people who lived at the site. Usually the project design will determine specialists to be included on the team. The particular goals of a given excavation project, that is, the questions being asked or the problems to be solved, will dictate the specialists needed on a team.

The New Archaeology. Already some of the innovations of "new archaeology" have been mentioned. The addition of new specialists and a multi-disciplinary staff is but one example. The development of problem solving excavations is another result of "new archaeology." But an even greater impact of "new archaeology" has been its introduction of cultural concerns alongside the historical and chronological concerns, and especially the impetus to develop excavation strategies, to formulate hypotheses and to test the hypotheses on the basis of the data excavated. From initial surveys and excavations, a series of hypotheses would be developed which might explain the data. Then additional excavation would be designed specifically to test the hypotheses and to confirm or modify them. "New archaeology" proposes to give a theoretical foundation to the excavation process. Interpretation of data would now be much more precise, and based on the scientific principles of hypothesis making and hypothesis testing. Traditionally, archaeology had stopped short of these interpretive steps.

On the basis of the hypotheses formulated and tested, the archaeologist then moves to a reconstruction of the culture that produced the data excavated. The cultural reconstruction has at least three levels: reconstruction of the culture of a particular time or strata (a synchronic approach), reconstruction of the cultural history (a diachronic approach), and an attempt to develop laws of cultural change (what processes led to the change from one stage to the next). Each of these reconstructions can be made on the basis of an individual site, but broader reconstructions require a region-wide application of the methodology.

The "new archaeology" is firmly entrenched in the discipline of Syro-Palestinian archaeology. But to date few final reports or projects have published results fully utilizing the methodology. "New archaeology" promises much in increasing knowledge of the cultures of Syria-Palestine. Previously unasked questions are now being examined. The next decade or so should produce exciting new insights from this approach.

The Bible and Archaeology. With all the new developments in archaeology, and even with the suggestion to eliminate the name "biblical" archaeology, what role does archaeology have in relating to the Bible? First, it must be said that the role between the Bible and archaeology has changed, at least on the basis of the common perception of that role. But more importantly, it can be affirmed that archaeology still has a critical and valid role in assisting in the interpretation of the Bible.

Among the pioneers in archaeology of the nineteenth century, a major concern was geography, topography and toponomy. Through a physical description of the land and the location of many biblical sites from modern Arabic place names, the places of the Bible began to come alive. Although a few of the identifications have proved incorrect, many more have been substantiated. Toponomy and historical geography continue as important disciplines in understanding the biblical text.

The work of Albright and Bright from the 1930s through the 1950s gave rise to a very positivistic interpretation of archaeological data relative to the biblical text. Archaeology was thought to have solved many of the critical historical issues of the text. One example was the evidence presented in support of a thirteenth century B.C.E. date for the CONQUEST OF CANAAN. The general historicity of the biblical account of the conquest was presumed. The finding of destruction layers dated to the middle of the thirteenth century B.C.E. which marked the end of Late Bronze Age cities of Canaan at sites such as Tell Beit Mirsim, BETHEL, EGLON, Lachish, and HAZOR seemed to confirm the historicity of the biblical record.

Challenges to this type of interpretation came from several directions, a major one being the negative evidence from other excavations. While the cities mentioned above did experience a destruction in the thirteenth century, several other cities prominent in the biblical account of the conquest did not provide such evidence. JERICHO lay abandoned during most of the Late Bronze Age. The fragmentary evidence of the Late Bronze Age includes only part of a floor and wall of one house, a few pieces of pottery and five tombs. There is no evidence of a walled town at the thirteenth century date proposed for the conquest. Evidence from AI was likewise negative. The site was abandoned from the Early Bronze Age until the beginning of the Iron Age. Not until about 1220 B.C.E. was Ai inhabited again, and then as an unwalled village.

Other questions were raised concerning the cities which did fall in the thirteenth century. Did the evidence of destruction necessarily mean the Hebrews were responsible? If the Bible alone is used as evidence, the Hebrews chiefly come to mind. Yet the Bible itself also notes that the Philistines entered the region at about the same time as the Hebrews. Furthermore, the Amarna letters indicate an unsettled condition in Palestine during the Late Bronze Age that could have resulted in the destruction of some cities. And if some city-states in Palestine were being disloyal to Egypt, as the Amarna letters imply, the Egyptians themselves may have undertaken military campaigns to reassert their control.

Along with the discussion of archaeological data, various models of the conquest period have emerged, all claiming to use archaeological data: a traditional conquest model, a peaceful settlement/gradual infiltration model, and a peasant revolt model. Using "new archaeology" one can readily see the need of constructing hypotheses for each model and conducting problem solving excavation to determine which hypotheses best explain the data.

This lengthy example shows the difficulties that the positivistic approach of Albright and Wright has faced. So what is the current relationship between archaeology and biblical studies? Even if archaeology does not today have the positivistic role envisioned by Albright and Wright, it still has a most important role in biblical studies, one future generations may recognize as even more helpful in interpreting the Bible.

Using "new archaeology" the biblical accounts would be considered as one historical reconstruction or one cultural reconstruction to be examined by hypothesis formulation and testing alongside other possible reconstructions. The biblical account would be given no more weight and no less weight than any other reconstruction. In most cases, the biblical data and archaeological data can be combined to provide a better interpretation than either alone can provide.

If archaeology hasn't confirmed any model of conquest/settlement period as yet, it has provided considerable data to inform biblical studies about the period. It is obvious that the period was a time of transition, from the Late Bronze Age to the Iron Age. It was also a time of disruption as many Late Bronze Canaanite cities were destroyed. Furthermore, it was a time when many small unwalled towns and villages appeared in the central hill country. These small villages probably signal the arrival of the Israelites. The villages indicate an agricultural basis of the settlements, suggesting the inhabitants were primarily from agricultural backgrounds rather than pastoral/semi-nomadic backgrounds. Some studies indicate these settlers came from the west rather than from the east on the basis of pottery and architectural parallels. Stager has provided a fascinating study of the family in Israel, using evidence from this period as well as data from the Bible. Not only is he able to enhance our understanding of the physical appearance of typical houses and settlements of this period, but he provides new insights into the family and kinship structure in Israel.

"New archaeology" provides much additional information on the culture of the biblical periods and how the people lived. It thus provides a backdrop against which the biblical accounts can be placed and interpreted. The historical element is still present, for archaeology shows changes and developments in culture over time. And archaeology can still impact directly on historical understandings when historical inscriptions and texts are recovered. Its just that now archaeology is providing a much broader interpretation than previously. Now archaeology and biblical studies can inform each other to improve and assist interpretations made by both disciplines.

See also ARCHITECTURE; CITY/CITIES; COINS AND MONEY; FORTS/FORTIFICATIONS; LETTERS/INSCRIPTIONS; TELL; WRITING SYSTEMS.

Bibliography. W. G. Dever, "Archaeology," *IDBSupp*; Drinkard, Mattingly, and Miller, eds., *Benchmarks in Time and Culture*; Perdue, Toombs, and Johnson, eds., *Archaeology and Biblical Interpretation*; L. E. Stager, "The Archaeology of the Family in Ancient Israel," *BASOR* 260 (1985): 1-35; G. W. Van Beek, "Archaeology," *IBD*.

—JOEL F. DRINKARD, JR.

• **Archangel.** *See* FALLEN ANGELS

• **Archelaus.** *See* HEROD

• **Archers.** The bow and arrow was used in ancient times in both the hunting of small game (such as birds), the shooting of larger animals for sport (such as lions), and in warfare. In the Assyrian military, as depicted on the Assyrian Panels in the British Museum, there were mounted bowmen as well as archers in the infantry, sometimes protected by heavy coats of mail. Others knelt or stood on the ground behind protective shields.

The OT does not indicate whether the Hebrew military had a specialized archery unit, but apparently it did. Hebrew archers are depicted atop the walls of Lachish, defending it from Sennacherib. Philistine archers seriously wounded King SAUL (1 Sam 31:3). Archers of the Ammonites killed URIAH the Hittite (2 Sam 11:24). Egyptian archers mortally wounded King JOSIAH (2 Chr 35:23). The Babylon military had archers covered with mail (Jer 51:3), as its enemies had archers (Jer 50:29). The glory of Kedar was predicted to fade as its number of archers diminished (Isa 21:16-17). The vigor of JOSEPH was portrayed in Jacob's blessing as one whose "bow remained unmoved" when "the archers fiercely attacked him, shot at him" (Gen 49:23-24). JOB accused God of having set him up as a practice target for his archers (16:12-13).

See also HUNTING, WEAPONS/WARFARE.

—KAREN RANDOLPH JOINES

• **Archippus.** [ahr-kip'uhs] Archippus was apparently an official of some importance in the church at COLOSSAE and was evidently quite intimate with PHILEMON. In Phlm 2, Paul describes him as "our fellow soldier" (cf. Phil 2:25; 2 Tim 2:3).

It is difficult to determine with any degree of confidence what position Archippus held. However, it is possible that it was of such importance that, perhaps indirectly, Paul was seeking the assistance of Archippus in his request to Philemon concerning Onesimus.

In Col 4:17, Paul asks the church at Colossae to say to Archippus: "See that you fulfill the ministry which you have received in the Lord." Paul may have been rebuking Archippus for some reported laxness on his part in regard to his ministry. It is also possible that the "good office" of Archippus was to be put to the service of Paul in the form of "pressure" on Philemon to accede to Paul's request regarding Onesimus.

See also APPHIA; COLOSSAE; ONESIMUS; PHILEMON, LETTER TO.

—HERBERT O. EDWARDS

• **Architecture.** Architecture is the art of designing and building structures for various human uses. In ancient Israel, with a few notable exceptions, the architectural remains are meager compared with those from Mesopotamia, Greece and Egypt. In many cases, only the foundations, or one or two courses above the foundations, of buildings and walls have survived. This paucity of remains is due to many reasons including destruction by natural causes as well as wars, rebuilding activities, and re-use of earlier material by subsequent inhabitants of sites. Other factors include wear due to time and weather.

Another characteristic of Palestinian architecture is its "homemade" quality. Most construction was done by unskilled labor using whatever material was readily at hand. This especially included stone (mainly limestone and basalt), and mudbrick. Wood products were also used, but little of this material has survived.

Only rarely in Palestine is there evidence of ambitious building programs carried out by professional craftsmen. Two such periods are those of SOLOMON (tenth century B.C.E.) and that of HEROD the Great (first century B.C.E.) whose architectural achievements reflect Phoenician and Greco-Roman influence respectively. While a thorough study of the architecture of ancient Palestine would include at least the Neolithic (7500–4000 B.C.E.) through the Early Arabic (640–1099 C.E.) periods, the discussion below will be restricted to the main Canaanite and Israelite occupations of the land (i.e., the Middle Bronze Age through the Iron Age).

The typical architectural remains on the ancient tells in Israel include those of walls, gates, official buildings (store houses, palaces, temples, etc.), domestic dwellings, tombs, and WATER SYSTEMS. Of course, only in rare instances has an individual site contained all of the above types.

During the Middle Bronze Age II period (2000–1550 B.C.E.), the defensive wall of almost every major city was constructed with a rampart, often with a glacis. The remains of these massive fortifications can still be seen at such sites as DAN, HAZOR, JERICHO, MEGIDDO, and GEZER. These walls were constructed of a solid core of stone or earth and stone against both sides of which was placed the rampart material. The gates of these cities are usually of the three-entryway type, fifty to sixty ft. long and about ten ft. wide. Often defensive towers flanked the passageway. One such tower at Gezer is over fifteen m. wide. This type of gate has also been found at Hazor, Shechem, and Megiddo as well as other sites. A unique Middle Bronze Age II gate has been found at Tel Dan. Made entirely of mudbrick, the gate consists of three arches and two defensive towers.

Other significant buildings from this period include palaces and temples. A palace at Megiddo, originally constructed in Middle Bronze II (ca. 1750–1550 B.C.E.), was enlarged to fifty meters in length during the Late Bronze Age. Temples during this time are thought to have been modeled on north Syrian types and have been found at Hazor, Megiddo, Shechem, Beth-shan and perhaps Lachish. Of special architectural note is the so-called "Fortress Temple" found at Megiddo and Shechem. The walls of these buildings are several meters thick indicating more than one story.

Israelite architectural achievement reached its peak during the time of Solomon (tenth century) and Omri (ninth century). The Bible credits Solomon with a major building program that included store-cities (1 Kgs 9:19), chariot cities (1 Kgs 9:19), palaces (1 Kgs 7:1, 9:24), special buildings (1 Kgs 7:2-7), fortifications (1 Kgs 9:15), and, of course, the Jerusalem TEMPLE. However, no material remains of Solomon's Temple have survived and it must be reconstructed from literary sources.

The most impressive Solomonic architectural remains that have survived are those of city fortifications, especially at Hazor, Megiddo, and Gezer. While some controversy still surrounds the stratigraphy at Megiddo, most scholars seem content to date the gate of Stratum V B–IV A to Solomon's time. Solomonic gates of these cities were well constructed of stone and contained six guard chambers and two guard towers each. Their width was sufficient to allow the passage of only one chariot at the time. Double walls with cross walls at intervals are associated with these gates and are called "casemate." During peace time, the rooms so created might be used for storage but would be filled with rubble in time of war. Other Israelite walls were solid and sometimes constructed with offsets and insets or salients and recesses.

Royal fortresses were also built during the Israelite period, the earliest so far known being at Tel el-Ful (Gibeah of Saul; 1 Sam 11:4), which is dated to the end of the eleventh century. During the Iron Age II (ca. 1000-586), several of these fortresses were built in the Negeb, the best example of which has been found at ARAD. Here the construction was of well-bossed ashlar masonry.

Remains from Solomon's palaces at Megiddo have been discovered, as well as those of Omri at Samaria. However, the sparsity of the remains of the latter make its reconstruction very difficult, though fine masonry technique is clearly evident. The Megiddo palaces consist of rectangular courts surrounded by rooms of various sizes. This architectural style has been called "Bit-Hilani" (lit. "house of pillared portico") and traced to northern Syrian prototypes of the second millennium B.C.E. These palaces offer direct evidence of the biblical assertion of Phoenician influence upon Solomon's building program. The largest Israelite "palace" yet found is at Lachish. Believed to have been constructed during the time of Rehoboam (late tenth century) and rebuilt several times, it was over 250 feet long and 116 feet wide. The building was destroyed by the Assyrians in the eighth century.

Other architectural remains from this period include pillared "store houses" found at such sites as Hazor, Megiddo, Beersheba, and Tell el-Hesi. The typical plan of these structures is a rectangular room divided by two rows of stone pillars with small chambers between them.

Few Israelite temples have been found. The earliest is at Arad, having been built in the middle of the tenth century. It consisted of one main room with the Holy of Holies to the west of it. This temple is quite small and simple compared to other temples of the Near East.

Many domestic dwellings have been found in Palestine from both the Bronze and Iron Ages. The typical construction is for several small rectangular rooms to be situated around or beside a small, open courtyard; all of which is enclosed by four walls. A single door in one of the walls provided access to the outside world. The roof would be made of reeds and mud or sod. In many cases, the city wall provided a common wall for the houses built against it as can be seen in the plans of several Judean towns: Beersheba, Tell Beit Mirsim, Beth-shemesh, and Mizpah.

Elaborate water supply systems have also been found from the Israelite periods. Often tunnels were dug from inside the city to a water source outside the walls. Such systems were built at Hazor, Megiddo, and Jerusalem as well as at Gibeon and Gezer. Hezekiah's tunnel in Jerusalem (PLATE 37) is over 1,500 feet long, while the one at Megiddo is only about 210 feet.

Following the destruction of Israel by Assyria at the end of the eighth century, a long decline in architectural construction occurred. But a new, ambitious building program began under Herod the Great. His temples, theaters, hippodromes, and baths are characterized by squared and paneled blocks of stone of enormous size. Remains at Caesarea, Jerusalem, Samaria, and Masada, among others, are witnesses to his architectural achievements.

See also AI; BEERSHEBA; DAN; HAZOR; JERICHO; JERUSALEM; LACHISH; MASADA; MEGIDDO.

Bibliography. Y. Aharoni, *The Archaeology of the Land of Israel;* M. Avi-Yonah and E. Stern, eds., *EAEHL;* H. J. Franken and C. A. Franken, *A Primer of Old Testament Archaeology;* H. Frankfort, *Art and Architecture of the Ancient Orient;* R. W. Hamilton, "Architecture," *IDB*.

—JOHN C. H. LAUGHLIN

• **Areopagus.** [air'ee-op"uh-guhs] The name "Areopagus" denotes both a low hill northwest of the Acropolis (PLATE 60) in Athens and the court of the Areopagus, which was an ancient Athenian council. The name itself is usually interpreted to mean "hill of Ares," though some have associated the name with the "Arai" or "Curses" (the godesses of destruction) whose shrine was located in a cave on the hill. Ares was the god of war, known as Mars in Roman mythology, thus the familiar designation, "Mars' Hill" in the KJV of Acts 17:22.

Tradition holds that Ares was the first to be tried on the hill for the murder of Halirrhothius. Orestes was also tried there for killing his mother, Clytemestra. The jurisdiction of the council of the Areopagus varied from time to time making it responsible for issues ranging from capital crimes to educational and religious concerns.

Attempts to locate material remains of the court of the Areopagus on the hill have proven unsuccessful. This is true also for other ancient sanctuaries associated with the area. The only known pre-Christian remains are a few house walls and cisterns that date to the Hellenistic and Roman periods.

There is now evidence that the hill was not the only place the council met. A stele found in 1952 locates the court of the Areopagus near the Bouleuterion. Other evidence locates the Areopagus, especially in later times, in the *Stoa Basileios* or "Royal Portico."

It may be the latter location before which PAUL appeared (cf. Acts 17:19, 22). Whether Paul was called officially before the council, or whether he met informally with Greek philosophers, is not clear from the text. The latter interpretation seems to be favored by most scholars.

—JOHN C. H. LAUGHLIN

• **Aretalogy.** [air'uh-tahl"uh-jee] Aretalogy is a term used to refer to a story (*logos*) of the virtuous (*areta*) deeds or MIRACLES of an outstanding person, whether human or divine. Tales of great deeds and lists of miraculous acts attributed to a hero or a god are a part of the literature of the Greco-Roman world. The intriguing question is whether or not these tales composed a form of literature that was adapted by the gospel writers to tell their story.

Some scholars, such as M. Hadas, M. Smith, H. Koester, and T. Weeden, have attempted to explain the literary form, GOSPEL, as an adaptation of the literary form, aretalogy. Others, such as H. C. Kee and D. L. Tiede, have argued that aretalogy is not a fixed literary form and is used in different situations. This issue is important because understanding the literary context of the Gospels aids in understanding the message they present. To resolve this issue it is necessary to examine the aretalogy of the ancient world.

Though the term aretalogy is relatively rare, it does occur in an inscription at Delos, in the Apocrypha in Sir 36:14, and as a translation in the LXX of a term in Ps 29:6. The inscription at Delos refers to an individual who reports virtuous acts and who interprets dreams. Other sources in the Greco-Roman world provide lists of miracles, lists of actions, and stories of great and wondrous men, but an examination of these lists and stories does not provide a clear type or form of literature. Despite some similarities, such as confronting authorities, miracles, wondrous acts, and admiration of the hero, no single fixed literary form emerges.

Tiede, however, says that aretalogy is a helpful descriptive term. He classifies aretalogies into three types: (1) aretalogy of self-praise, (2) aretalogy of divine wise men, and (3) aretalogy of the miracle worker. The last type is the most important for NT interpretation.

A possible collection of MIRACLE STORIES is found in Mark 4:35–6:56. It is possible that John is using a collection of miracle stories as a source when he refers to "the first of the signs" (2:11), "the second sign" (4:54), and when he ends his appeal to these signs, "that you may believe . . . " (20:31). John's ending is not unlike the ending of Sir 43:33 and 1 Macc 9:22. He is also clearly stating his purpose in referring to these signs (KJV, miracles).

The purpose of the aretalogies in Greek and Roman literature is an important issue. How are the miracles or great deeds of the aretalogies related to the concept of "divine man"? What does "divine man" mean in this literature? The concept of "divine man" is widely used in the Hellenistic world, but it is not a fixed concept. Interpreters must be careful in comparing references to a "divine man" in the Hellenistic literature with references to Jesus as a "divine man" or SON OF GOD.

The literary form gospel is composed of common elements such as miracles and fluid concepts (e. g., divine man) which existed in many stories from both Hellenistic and rabbinic literatures. But there are no close parallels of the form gospel. This literary form is not copied or adapted from a fixed literary structure used in the ancient world.

See also FORM/GATTUNG; GENRE, GOSPEL; MIRACLE STORY; MIRACLES.

Bibliography. M. Hadas and M. Smith, *Heroes and Gods: Spiritual Biographies in Antiquity*; H. C. Kee, "Aretalogy and Gospel," *JBL* 92 (1973): 402-44 and *Miracle in the Early Christian World*; H. Koester, "One Jesus and Four Gospels," *HTR* 61 (1968): 230-36; D. L. Tiede, *The Charismatic Figure As Miracle Worker*.

—FORREST WOOD, JR.

• **Aretas.** [air'uh-tuhs] Aretas was the name of a number of Nabatean kings. Aretas I (ca. 169 B.C.E.) is mentioned in 2 Macc 5:8 as the "ruler of the Arabs" before whom Jason was accused when he fled eastward across the Jordan after his failure to recover the high priesthood. Aretas IV (9 B.C.E.–40 C.E.) was the father-in-law of Herod Antipas. Under his reign Nabatean influence reached its peak, with Aretas even being a guest in Rome. When Antipas divorced his daughter, Aretas attacked Antipas' forces, bringing about the threat of Roman intervention in 37 C.E. Paul's life was endangered in Damascus (ca. 34-35 C.E.) under this Aretas (2 Cor 11:32-33; Acts 9:23-25).

See also NABATAEANS.

—HERBERT O. EDWARDS, SR.

• **Ariel.** [air'ee-uhl] The personal name *'ărî'ēl* means "lion of El [God]" and is the name of a chief man among Israel's returning exiles from Babylon (Ezra 8:16).

Elsewhere, the word appears five times in Isa 29:1-2, 7 as a cryptic reference to Jerusalem. Here the author's intended meaning is unclear. Is he calling Jerusalem the "lion of El [God]" or (another possibility) "the altar-hearth of God"? The slightly different *'ărî'êl* means "hearth" or "altar-hearth." The word appears, with some textual variations, in Ezek 43:15-16 of the Masoretic Text as *har'ēl* ("mountain of God") and as *'ărî'êl* ("hearth of God"), translated consistently in the RSV as "altar hearth." According to 2 Sam 23:20, "Benaiah the son of Jehoiada was a valiant man of Kabzeel, a doer of good deeds; he smote two ariels of Moab" (cf. 1 Chr 11:22). Mesha of Moab in line twelve of the Moabite Stone indicated that he "dragged" before his god Chemosh an *'ar'l*, obviously referring to a physical object.

It appears that the translation "hearth, altar-hearth" is best for *'ărî'ēl*. Isaiah's use of the term for Jerusalem connotes an air of cultic joy and festivity that the Lord will transform into "moaning and lamentation" (29:2). However, Ariel's enemies will not be allowed to distress her (29:7).

See also JERUSALEM.

—KAREN RANDOLPH JOINES

• **Arimathæa.** *See* ARIMATHEA

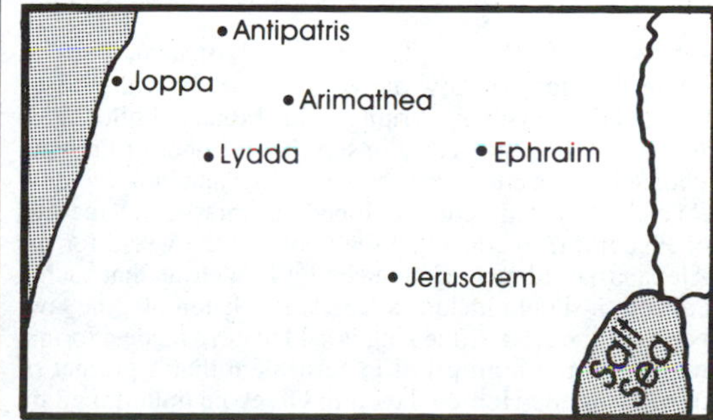

Designed by Margaret Jordan Brown ©Mercer University Press

• **Arimathea.** [air'uh-muh-thee"uh] Arimathea was the home of Joseph who buried Jesus (Matt 27:57; Mark 15:43; Luke 23:50; John 19:38). Luke identifies it as a Jewish town. The site is uncertain (PLATE 23) although it is generally considered to have been about twenty mi. east of Joppa (Jaffa). Eusebius identified Arimathea with Ramathaim-Zophim (Ramah) in Ephraim, which was the birthplace of Samuel (1 Macc 11:34 speaks of a Rathamin which may be identified with Ramathaim-Zophim). Eusebius was joined by Jerome in this identification which has the further support of the existence of a medieval monastery of Joseph of Arimathea.

Joseph of Arimathea's possession of a tomb in Jerusalem may be explained by the assumption that he had moved to Jerusalem. Mark supports this assumption in his statement of Joseph's membership in the council (15:43).

—JOHN R. DRAYER

• **Aristeas the Exegete.** [air'is-tee"uhs] Aristeas the Exegete was a Hellenistic Jewish author, probably not the same person as the author of the LETTER OF ARISTEAS. A fragment from a Greek work by Aristeas is preserved in the *PraepEv* (9.25.1-4) by Eusebius, who is quoting from the collection of Alexander Polyhistor. Thus, Aristeas wrote before Alexander (fl. ca. 50 B.C.E.); little more can be known about the date and provenance of his work.

The fragment is a summary of the story of JOB and depends heavily on the SEPTUAGINT translation, including the material in LXX Job 42:17b-e, which is not found in the Hebrew. Aristeas shares with this Greek epilogue to Job the view that Job is to be identified with Jobab (Gen 36:33), a descendant of Esau, and a king of Edom.

Aristeas's portrait of Job is that of the narrative framework of the biblical document rather than that of the central poetic sections; Job remains patient and pious in his afflictions. Although all four of Job's visitors are listed, there is no trace of their accusations against Job or of his angry self-defense.

The interpretation of Job's suffering provided by this fragment is that God brought misfortune on Job in order to test him. When Job proved faithful, God responded in admiration by restoring his health and possessions. Aristeas informs us that Job declared that even without the exhortation of his friends, he would have remained "steadfast in his piety even with his affliction." Job is being held up as a model of faithfulness in adversity.

See also ARISTEAS, LETTER OF; JOB.

Bibliography. R. Doran, "Aristeas the Exegete," *The Old Testament Pseudepigrapha*, ed. J. H. Charlesworth; C. R. Holladay, *Fragments from Hellenistic Jewish Authors*.

—SHARYN E. DOWD

• **Aristeas, Letter of.** The *Letter of Aristeas* purports to relate the story of how the Hebrew TORAH came to be translated into Greek. Writing to his brother, Philocrates, Aristeas, who represents himself as a member of Ptolemy Philadelphus's court, tells how the Egyptian king Ptolemy II (285-247 B.C.E.) commissioned his librarian, Demetrius of Phalerum, to collect all the books of the world for the Alexandrian library. Convinced by Demetrius that such a collection should include a Greek translation of "the law-books of the Jews," the king is said to have made a formal request to the high priest in Jerusalem that a project of translating the Hebrew law into Greek be undertaken by seventy-two Jewish elders, six from each tribe. The Greek translation of the Hebrew scriptures known as "the SEPTUAGINT" (literally "the seventy") derives its name from this story.

The origin of the translation project, together with the plans for carrying it out, is the subject of vv. 1-8. But no sooner is Aristeas into this introductory account than he digresses by relating how he succeeded in persuading the king to release the Jews who had been forcibly deported to Egypt by King Ptolemy, the father of Ptolemy II. Then, after describing in detail the arrangements for the translation project, Aristeas launches into an even more extended digression on Palestine, the Temple, and the Law in Judaism. He concludes this section by telling how the delegation elected for the project (vv. 46-51) was escorted to Alexandria and was received very graciously by the king, who arranged a seven-day banquet for them. Aristeas devotes almost a third of his work to the dinner conversation at this banquet (vv. 187-294), and then concludes his narrative by describing how the translation itself was carried out with great success.

It is universally agreed that "Aristeas" is the pseudonym of an author writing at a later time, probably between 250 B.C.E. and 100 C.E. Most scholars favor ca. 150-100 B.C.E. The author's fluency in Greek and detailed knowledge of Jewish practices suggest that he is a Hellenistic Jew, perhaps a native Alexandrian. The purpose of the writing is suggested by the various extended digressions in which the author presents few apologies for the Jewish faith. In vv. 128-71 Aristeas discusses the law in Judaism, giving special attention to the commandments governing the clean and the unclean, which are said to strike non-Jews as being incommensurate with the idea that creation is a unified whole. Aristeas interprets the dietary laws allegorically as applying to universal human virtues. In his account of the seven-day banquet Aristeas contrives an extended conversation between the king and the translators, in which the king poses questions to each of the scholars in turn. In this way Aristeas seeks to display the practical wisdom in affairs of both state and everyday life that the education of a Jewish scholar provided. As Aristeas had already explained in v. 121, the distinguished translators "had not only mastered the Jewish literature, but had made a serious study of that of the Greeks as well." Thus Aristeas's apology for Jewish faith is not exclusivistic or nationalistic. In fact, rather than depicting Judaism as a universal faith, our author represents Judaism as an authentic expression of a universalistic religion common to all who confess one God as "the overseer and creator of all" (v. 16).

See also SEPTUAGINT.

Bibliography. J. R. Bartlett, *Jews in the Hellenistic World*; H. G. Meecham, *The Letter of Aristeas*; M. Hadas, *Aristeas to Philocrates*; R. J. H. Shutt, "Letter of Aristeas," *Old Testament Pseudepigrapha*, ed. J. H. Charlesworth.

—CHARLES H. COSGROVE

• **Aristobulus.** [air'is-tob"yuh-luhs] Aristobulus is the earliest known Jewish philosopher. He wrote in Greek around the mid-second century B.C.E., probably in Alexandria. His work, extant only in fragments, appears to have been apologetic in character. Four fragments are quoted by EUSEBIUS in his *PraepEv* and one fragment appears in his *EccHist*, where he is citing Anatolius, *On The Passover*, which contains a citation from Aristobulus.

The first (*EccHist* 7.32.16-18) and fifth (*PræpEv* 13.12.9-16) fragments interpret the Jewish observances of PASSOVER and SABBATH in terms of the structure of reality; Passover occurs when both sun and moon are passing through equinoctial sectors, while the cosmic significance of the number seven and the holiness of the seventh day are attested by the Greek poets. Aristobulus's point seems to be that Jewish observances are not merely particularistic curiosities, but rather express universal insights into cosmic order.

The second (*PræpEv* 8.9.38–8.10.17) and fourth (*PræpEv* 13.12, 3-8) fragments explain the anthropomorphic language of the Pentateuch as metaphorical rather than literal. Aristobulus exhorts his reader "to grasp the fitting conception of God and not to fall into the mythical and human way of thinking about God."

Aristobulus asserts that the Greek philosophers borrowed their ideas from the Jewish scriptures. Both Plato and Pythagoras had read a Greek translation of the Bible, according to Aristobulus (*PræpEv* 13.12.1-2). In the fourth and fifth fragments Socrates, Orpheus, Homer and Hesiod are added to the list. This theme of Hellenistic Jewish apologetics is also found in Artapanus. Aristobulus's attempts to reconcile revelation with reason represent an important stage prior to the better-known efforts of PHILO.

See also PHILO.

Bibliography. A. Y. Collins, "Aristobulus," *The Old Testament Pseudepigrapha,* ed. J. H. Charlesworth.

—SHARYN E. DOWD

• **Ark.** A term used in the English Bible for a small basket into which the infant Moses was placed, for the immense ship by means of which the family of NOAH survived the universal deluge, and for a portable cultic object during Israel's early history. The word is derived from the Latin *arca,* "chest, box."

Moses' Ark. In order to save her child from persecution, the mother of Moses wove a small basket (KJV "ark") of bulrushes (papyrus), waterproofed it with bitumen, and hid him in it at the river's edge (Exod 2:3). Boats were made in this fashion in Egypt and Babylonia and are mentioned at Isa 18:2. The Hebrew word is apparently derived from Egyptian and is the same that is used for Noah's vessel.

Noah's Ark. A vessel by means of which Noah and his family escaped the waters of the universal deluge (Gen 6:5–9:19). At God's directions, it was to be constructed of "gopher wood" (identification unknown), caulked with bitumen, divided into three partitioned decks, provided with a door and window, and provisioned for Noah's family and for pairs of each land animal.

The dimensions of the craft suggest that it was a rectangular box and thus intended for floating rather than for sailing. Its size is given in "cubits" (300x50x30), and if the modern estimate of eighteen in. per cubit is correct, the craft would be 450 ft. long, seventy-five ft. wide, and forty-five ft. high. The dimensions are astonishing for an ancient vessel (the English ship Mayflower was only about ninety ft. long), and there is reason to suggest that they reflect an ideal based upon numerical preoccupation with the number sixty. Thus, the dimensions could be expresssed as (60x5) in length and (60 ÷ 2) in height. Its volume is 450,000 cubic cubits, or (60^3x2) + (60^2x5). Such numerological preoccupation with sixty characterizes the dimensions of the Babylonian flood-hero's ship as well.

The claim that the ark's landing-place was known and that parts of the vessel were yet visible was attested in the pre-Christian period and has continued to the present. Opinion varied, however, about where the remains were to be found: in Arabia, in eastern and northern Iraq, and in western or eastern Turkey. The claim for the last of these sites is no older than the eleventh–twelfth centuries C.E., and has been centered upon a spectacular mountain known as Masis (in Armenian) or as Ağri Daği (in Turkish). In the late nineteenth century, Christian ark-searchers became convinced that this was Mount ARARAT.

Within the last three decades, the claim that the ark has been found has appeared in newspapers, magazines, books, and in a movie that was shown on prime-time network television. Supporting evidence has included eyewitness testimony, photographs, and specimens of hewn wood that reportedly date from high antiquity. In actuality, however, the photographs and testimony do not withstand rigid scrutiny, and subsequent reliable tests of the wood date it to the seventh century C.E. There is not, then, any reason to believe that remains of Noah's ark are to be found anywhere in the world.

The Ark of the Covenant. An ancient, portable cultic object that served to remind Israel of the formal relationship ("covenant") between God and community. (The Bible uses a different term for it than for the previous two arks.)

The shape and function of the Ark are described in various ways during the long history of ancient Israel, and it may be that they evolved with the passage of time. In the early period, it seems to have been a simple wooden chest that was used to lead the army in battle or the community in procession and that was viewed as a symbol of the divine presence (Num 10:35–36; 1 Sam 4). Later, it was remembered as having contained stone tablets, perhaps engraved with the TEN COMMANDMENTS (Exod 25:16; 1 Kgs 8:21), and as having resided in an elaborate tent-like SHRINE called the "tabernacle" or "the tent of meeting" (Exod 25–27).

The biblical text contains a number of designations for this venerated object, among them: the Ark, the Ark of God, the Ark of the LORD, the Ark of the Covenant, the Ark of the Testimony, and the Holy Ark. These varying designations (as well as differing depictions of shape and function) reflect differing schools of thought in ancient Israel and have assisted modern interpreters in the complex task of distinguishing the schools and assigning a relative date to them.

The Ark is first mentioned in connection with Israel's wilderness journey after the Exodus from Egypt: elaborate instructions are given for fashioning it and the larger portable shrine (Exod 25–27). Thereafter, it headed the procession through the Sinai itinerary (Num 10:35-36) and across the Jordan into the land of Canaan (Josh 3–4). It then was carried into battle against opposing cities (e.g., Jericho, Josh 6–7), played a central role in worship at various shrines (Mount Ebal, Josh 8:30-35; Bethel, Judg 20:26-27), and finally resided at SHILOH (1 Sam 4:1-3).

How the Ark was removed from the ancient tribal sanctuary at Shiloh to the new monarchical capital at Jerusalem is chronicled in the account of the Philistine wars and their aftermath. Taken into battle because it was viewed as the near-embodiment of the deity's presence (1 Sam 4:1-9), the ark was lost to the enemy but then sent away toward the hill country because of a plague, which was attributed to its presence (4:10–7:2). There it remained (at Kiriath-jearim) until David brought it to Jerusalem (2 Sam 6:1-19) and his son Solomon placed it in the newly completed Temple (1 Kgs 6:14-19). Solomon's motivation was likely a mixture of piety (to provide a suitable place for the venerable relic) and desire for power (to remove it from the control of other sanctuaries and priestly lines).

It is likely that the Ark was destroyed when the Temple was burned by the Babylonians in the year 587/6 B.C.E. (2 Kgs 25:8-9). However, a late and pious tradition reports that the prophet Jeremiah saved the Ark by hiding it in a cave on Mount Nebo (2 Macc 2:1-8). There it was to remain hidden until "God gathers his people together again and shows his mercy" (v. 7). The Book of Revelation may be suggesting that such a moment has arrived when "God's temple in heaven was opened, and the ark of his covenant was seen within his temple" (11:19).

See also ARARAT; FLOOD; NOAH; TENT OF MEETING.

Bibliography. L. R. Bailey, *Noah, the Ark, and the Flood*; G. H. Davies, "Ark of the Covenant," *IDBSupp*.

—LLOYD R. BAILEY

• **Armageddon.** [ahr'muh-ged"uhn] Armageddon (occurring only in Rev 16:16) is the cryptic designation of the place of the final eschatological battle between the forces of good and evil. Because Armageddon is referred to in Rev 16:16 as a Hebrew term (which the author has evidently transliterated into Greek), it is generally supposed that the term in Hebrew should be *Har-Magedon,* meaning "Mount Megiddo." The manuscript evidence supports the English spelling Harmageddon, reflecting also the Septuagint spelling of MEGIDDO in Josh 12:21 and 17:11. The use of Megiddo as a symbol for a final battle between good and evil is an interesting literary problem.

The city of Megiddo rested on a tell or mound which, at a height of seventy feet, could hardly have been called a mountain. Moreover, Megiddo is never referred to as a place of eschatological conflict. As a city, however, it had a long history due to its strategic military location. It commanded the pass through the Carmel ridge and overlooked the plain of Esdraelon. Crucial battles have been waged there, from that of Thutmose III in the fifteenth century B.C.E. to that of General Allenby in 1917. In Israel's early history, Joshua defeated a king of Megiddo (Josh 12:21), and it was at the "waters of Megiddo" that Barak and Deborah met the Canaanites under Sisera and prevailed (Judg 5:19; cf. chaps. 4–5). Ahaziah, wounded in Jehu's revolt, fled to Megiddo and died there (2 Kgs 9:27), and the reformer—King Josiah—died near Megiddo at the hands of Pharoah Necho (2 Kgs 23:29; 2 Chr 35:22). Egyptian annals record Pharoah Sishak's conquest of Megiddo in 918 B.C.E. and its being named as a provincial capital under Tiglath Pileser III during the Assyrian conquest in northern Israel in 733-732 B.C.E. In sum, while Israel did experience some early critical triumphs there, Megiddo is more often the place where Israel's enemies actively sought Israel's downfall, the place of Israel's defeats, a place of mourning (Zech 12:11). It is a place of sinister historical memory, awaiting the avenging moment of God.

The lack of a direct connection of Megiddo with the place of eschatological triumph in the tradition does not limit the writer. John of Patmos uses his tradition in a creative way. He is able to make his own associations, as can be seen by his designation of the serpent in Gen 3 as the devil (Rev 20:2). Throughout his writings, moreover, it is the practice of John to forge word pictures by means of pastiches of OT imagery. The description of the risen one in Rev 1:13-16 and the description of the fall of "Babylon" (=Rome) in 18:2-24 are two examples among many.

Traditions available to John of Patmos spoke of the assault of the forces of evil against God's holy mountain (cf. Dan 11:45; *1 Enoch* 6:6). Isa 14:13 speaks of the future destruction of Babylon as planned and carried out from the "mount of assembly." Zechariah forsees the mourning on "that day" to be as intense as it was in the "plain of Megiddo" (12:11). And Ezek 38:3-21; 39:2 speaks of the great eschatological defeat of nations on the "mountains of Israel." By "Harmageddon" John of Patmos has combined the associations his readers would make with Megiddo from OT traditions with the mountain of the final eschatological triumph of God. It is one of the many symbols John uses for this triumph, a battle which is further defined in Rev 19 in which the "armies of heaven" do not participate in the conflict itself, but observe how the nations are overcome by the "sword which issues from its mouth," namely by the word of God alone.

See also ESCHATOLOGY IN THE NEW TESTAMENT; MEGIDDO; REVELATION, BOOK OF.

—RICHARD L. JESKE

• **Armlet.** *See* DRESS

• **Army.** *See* SOLDIER

• **Arnon.** [ahr'nuhn] A perennial stream, known today as Wadi Mojib, whose course of ca. thirty miles drains much of the Moabite plateau. From its source near Lejjun, ca. ten miles east-northeast of Kerak, the stream flows in a northerly direction first and then follows a westerly channel until it empties into the Dead Sea (PLATE 13). The Arnon's mouth is approximately halfway up the Dead Sea's eastern shore; its perennial flow, which is greatly increased by the merging water of Wadi Heidan, makes Wadi Mojib the major river on the sea's eastern side.

As one of the four major wadi systems that subdivide Transjordan into a number of topographical-political units, the Arnon canyon (up to three miles across and up to 2,300 feet deep) divided ancient MOAB into two parts. Political control of northern Moab, north of the Arnon, changed from time to time, but central and southern Moab—the undisputed Moabite heartland—stretched from the Arnon southward to the River Zered. In the Mesha Inscription (line 26), King Mesha mentioned his repair of the highway that crossed the Arnon gorge near Aroer, presumably the "King's Highway" (cf. Jer 48:20). The difficulties in negotiating the Arnon canyon enhanced the importance of the so-called "Desert Highway."

The Arnon is named in the Bible twenty-five times, mostly as a boundary between the Moabites and the Amorites (Num 21:13, 24, 26; 22:36) and the Israelites (Deut 2:24, 36; 3:8, 16; Josh 13:16; 2 Kgs 10:33; cf. 2 Sam 24:5). The numerous tributaries of the river are called "the valleys of the Arnon" in Num 21:14. In a poetic oracle against Moab, Isaiah (16:2) refers to "the fords of the Arnon."

—GERALD L. MATTINGLY

• **Artapanus.** [ahr'ta-pay"nuhs] Artapanus was an Egyptian Jew who wrote a Greek work probably entitled *Concerning the Jews,* now extant only in three fragments quoted from Alexander Polyhistor's collection by EUSEBIUS in his *PræpEv*. Precise dating of Artapanus is impossible; recent arguments focus on the late third or mid-second century B.C.E.

The three fragments deal with ABRAHAM (*PræpEv* 9.18.1), JOSEPH (*PræpEv* 9.23.1-4), and MOSES (*PræpEv* 9.27.1-37), with respect to their exploits in EGYPT. All three are depicted as cultural benefactors: Abraham taught ASTROLOGY to the Egyptians; Joseph discovered measurements and reformed agriculture; Moses invented "ships, machines for lifting stone, Egyptian weapons, devices for drawing water and fighting, and philosophy." Moses is identified with the god Hermes, and is credited with the establishment of the Egyptian cults, the interpretation of sacred writings, and the successful leadership of an Egyptian army against Ethiopian invaders. Artapanus says that the annual flooding of the Nile began when Moses struck the river with his rod. The account continues with a garbled version of the biblical PLAGUES and ends with the crossing of the Red Sea.

Artapanus's work belongs to the genre of the national historical romance. Babylonians, Egyptians, and Jews responded to the Greek conquest of their countries by writing romanticized versions of their own national histories that glorified their national heroes and deities as the originators of ideas and inventions that were subsequently of benefit to others. Artapanus's propaganda, written at a popular level, would have served a dual function; not only was it intended to defend Jews against their detractors, but also (and probably primarily), to enhance the self-esteem of the Jewish communities in Egypt.

See also CLEODEMUS MALCHUS; EUPOLEMUS, PSEUDO.

Bibliography. J. J. Collins, "Artapanus," *The Old Testament Pseudepigrapha,* ed. J. H. Charlesworth; C. R. Holladay, *Fragments from Hellenistic Jewish Authors.*

—SHARYN E. DOWD

• **Artaxerxes.** [ahr'tuh-zuhrk"seez] A proper name or an official title of three rulers of the Persian empire, meaning "strong king" or "great warrior." The name's origin may stem from the efforts of Xerxes to impress upon his son the "holy Arta," corresponding to "Righteousness" in Zoroastrian thought, by naming him Artakhshathra (Artaxerxes), "Arta's Kingdom."

Three persons bearing the name are important for the study of the Bible. Artaxerxes I (465-425 B.C.E.), son of Xerxes I, was called Macrocheir (Greek), or Longimanus (Latin), perhaps because of his deformed right hand. When his father was assassinated (465), the conspirator Artabanus accused the king's oldest son Darius of the crime. Seeking to avenge his father's death, Artaxerxes killed Darius and took the throne for himself. Revolts in Egypt and continuing attacks from the Greeks marked his reign. The Egyptian revolts, lasting from 460 to 454 B.C.E., were finally ended, but increasing internal problems and mounting Greek strength forced the king to assent to the "Peace of Callias" (449). Named for the negotiator and signed at Susa, the treaty ended the long, extended struggles with the Greeks, but marked one of Persia's greatest humiliations. Artaxerxes died in Susa (425) and was buried at Nagsh-i-Rustam, near his father and grandfather.

Artaxerxes I was benevolent toward Judah, probably because he needed this route into Egypt. Most scholars believe this Artaxerxes authorized the missions of both EZRA (458) and NEHEMIAH (445) to Jerusalem (Ezra 7:8, 11-26, 4:7-23; Neh 2:1ff.; 13:6).

Artaxerxes II (404-359 B.C.E.), known as Artakshatsu or Mnemon, was a son of Darius II and a grandson of Artaxerxes I. His reign was plagued by internal troubles and continued agitation from the Greeks. He crushed the rebellion of his brother Cyrus in the battle of Cunaxa (401) as related in Xenophon's *Anabasis.* Despite losing Egypt (401) and continuous rebellions throughout the kingdom during his reign, Artaxerxes II negotiated with the Athenians against the continuing threats of Sparta, and the "Peace of Antalcidas" signed at Sardis (386) succeeded in bringing Greece under Persian supremacy, something attempted in vain by both Darius and Xerxes.

Some scholars argue that the work of Ezra, and even perhaps that of Nehemiah, was during the reign of Artaxerxes II.

Artaxerxes III (359–338 B.C.E.), son of Artaxerxes II, known as Ochus, a brutal, bloodthirsty man, took the throne after killing all his relatives, including two brothers, as rivals. He crushed insurrections throughout the kingdom and brought Egypt under Persian rule after sixty years of independence (343 B.C.E.). Poisoned by his personal physician Bagoas, he was buried near his father's tomb at Persepolis (338).

This Artaxerxes is not mentioned in the Bible, but JOSEPHUS (*Ant* 11.7) records a revolt of the Jews during his reign that was ruthlessly squelched by the Persian general Bagoses (Bagoas). Tradition also tells of a number of Jews being carried into exile into Hyrcania and Babylonia during his reign.

See also PERSIAN EMPIRE.

Bibliography. J. Bright, *The History of Israel*; J. M. Myers, *The World of the Restoration*; W. O. E. Oesterley and T. H. Robinson, *A History of Israel,* vol. 2; A. T. Olmstead, *History of the Persian Empire.*

—G. BYRNS COLEMAN

Artemis of Ephesus, an ancient cultic goddess.

• **Artemis.** [ahr'tuh-mis] Sometimes identified with the Roman goddess Diana (KJV, Acts 19:24), Artemis was the goddess of wild nature usually accompanied in the mountains and forests by nymphs. She is only superficially identified with the Ephesian Artemis. The Greek goddess was worshipped very early on Crete as well as on the Greek mainland. In the myth she is the sister of Apollo and the daughter of Zeus and is known by the names Demeter and Athene as well. She came to be associated not only with hunting but also with childbirth. Certain wild animals were sacred to her: the stag, the wild boar, the hare, the wolf, the bear, and in some instances, birds and fish.

The origin of the Ephesian Artemis (Acts 19:23-41) is most likely related to the Greek goddess, although the understanding of the goddess as well as her worship was deeply influenced by the mother-goddess concepts found in the Near East, especially those related to Astarte, Ishtar, and other Near Eastern deities. The tradition placed her birth in the woods near Ephesus not far from the mouth of the Cayster River long before the settlement of EPHESUS (ca. 1100 B.C.E.). She was worshipped as a goddess of fertility in man, beast, and nature and from the second century B.C.E. was commonly depicted in sculpture as a female possessing numerous breasts.

Such a sculpture was not, however, the object of veneration in the temple; it was instead, "the sacred stone that fell from the sky" (Acts 19:35). The silver shrines which DEMETRIUS and other craftsmen produced (Acts 19:24) were not miniature replicas of the great temple in Ephesus (the Artemision) but either an image of the earlier shrine which was replaced by the Artemision or, less likely, an image of the goddess herself. These would be taken home by the pilgrims for use as household shrines between visits to the temple. According to Pliny the temple was completed in 120 years and then destroyed and rebuilt seven times, although this is disputed by modern scholars. The eighth rebuilding in the second century B.C.E. expanded the complex to a massive size (425 x 225 ft.) with 127 columns each 60 ft. high. An earlier burning of the temple had taken place on the night of Alexander the Great's birth in 356 B.C.E. when a deranged man named Erostratos set fire to the temple in order to achieve immortality in history.

The temple hierarchy was complex. The chief priest was a eunuch who assumed the Persian title Megabyzos. The leading priests may have comprised a group called the Megabyzoi; Strabo's description is unclear at this point. Additionally, young virgins served in the temple; most notable were those who had charge of the sacred adornment of the goddess. Also a celibate group called the Essenes served yearlong duties in the temple. Sacrifices were made primarily with food, libations, and incense, very rarely with animals. One month each year in Ephesus was devoted exclusively to the worship of Artemis. A sizeable bank existed in the temple and the temple offered asylum for fugitives, even for runaway slaves in certain cases.

See also DEMETRIUS; EPHESUS; PAUL; SYNCRETISM.

Bibliography. A. Bammer, "Forschungen im Artemision von Ephesus von 1976 bis 1981," *AS* 32 (1982): 61-87; Pliny, *Natural History* 35.40; 36.21; L. R. Taylor, "Artemis of Ephesus," *The Beginnings of Christianity*, ed. F. J. Foakes-Jackson and K. Lake.

—LORIN L. CRANFORD

• **Asaph.** [ay'saf] A son of Berechiah who was given charge, along with Heman and Ethan, of the service of song in the temple by DAVID (1 Chr 6:31-32, 39; 15:16-17). He is recognized as the ancestor of one of the three great families or guilds of temple musicians and singers, "the sons of Asaph" (e.g., 1 Chr 25:1-2; Ezra 3:10). In 2 Chr 29:30 he is identified as a cultic prophet, an indication of the prophetic function of music in temple worship (cf. 1 Chr 25:1-2; 2 Chr 20:13-19). Asaph's name occurs in the titles of twelve psalms (50, 73–83), probably an indication that these psalms came from an Asaphic collection or hymnal, or were performed according to an Asaphic style or tradition of psalm-singing.

Asaph is also the name of the father of Joah, a scribe under HEZEKIAH (2 Kgs 18:18, 37); and of an official under the Persian king ARTAXERXES (Neh 2:8).

See also WORSHIP IN THE OLD TESTAMENT.

—JEFFREY S. ROGERS

• **Ascension of Christ.** Luke is the only writer of the NT who gives a description of the ascension of Christ. However, there is a variation between the account that he gives in his Gospel and the record of the event in Acts. The difference has to do with both time and place of the occurrence. In Luke's Gospel the reader gets the impression that Jesus ascended on the same day as the resurrection (24:51). In Acts there is an interval of forty days between the resurrection and the ascension (1:3-11).

Luke in his Gospel locates the ascension at Bethany (24:50), a village about a mile-and-a-half from Jerusalem on the eastern slope of the MOUNT OF OLIVES. This was the home of Mary, Martha, and Lazarus, who were prominent persons in the Fourth Gospel. In Acts the place is not given, but it is assumed that it was the Mount of Olives because the author says that the apostles returned to Jerusalem from Olivet after the ascension (1:12). Olivet was a hill to the east of Jerusalem. It was here, on the eve of the crucifixion, that Jesus agonized in prayer.

In addition to the variations concerning time and place it is quite noticeable that there is a discrepancy about the content of Jesus' teaching in relation to this occasion. For the Gospel of Luke, the subject matter is the prophetic fulfillment of the Messiah's passion, death, and resurrection (24:44-47). On the contrary, in Acts Jesus speaks to the apostles about the Kingdom during the space of forty days (1:3). The two accounts do agree that Jesus promised his disciples that they would receive the power of the HOLY SPIRIT (Luke 24:49; Acts 1:8).

While Luke is the only NT author to refer to this event, the experience is referred to in other writings (1 Pet 3:22; Eph 4:10; Col 3:1; 1 Tim 3:16; Heb 4:14; 9:24).

See also HOLY SPIRIT; OLIVES, MOUNT OF; RESURRECTION IN THE NEW TESTAMENT.

Bibliography. F. F. Bruce, *The Acts of the Apostles*; T. C. Smith, "Acts," *BBC*; A. Harnack, *The Acts of the Apostles*.

—T. C. SMITH

• **Asceticism.** A word derived from the language of Greek athletics. The noun from which it originated had the meaning of "training" or "practice." It does not occur in the NT in the noun form. It does occur as a verb in Acts 24:16 where it has the sense of "strive." In this instance, Paul is presenting his defense before FELIX and depicts himself as one who always "takes pains" or "strives" to have a clear conscience.

Before the Christian era, the STOICS and others had already begun to apply the term to the practice of moral discipline. Asceticism is a system or regimen devoted to purifying or otherwise preparing individuals for the purpose of facing a specific spiritual challenge or attaining a spiritual goal. Christian asceticism has always included an element of renunciation, discipline, and often the care of others. Some of the assumptions on which early expressions of asceticism were built are to be found in the nature and teachings of Jesus.

Throughout the NT, Jesus is presented as the classic expression of self-abnegation and concern for others (cf. Phil 2:5-11). Very early, it became one of the goals of Jesus' followers to become like their Lord. The name "Christian" (Acts 11:26) may have emerged from this characteristic of the disciples. In addition, the teachings of Jesus promoted this ideal (cf. Mark 8:34-37; Matt 10:38-39; 16:24-25; Luke 9:23-25). The impact of Jesus' words to the rich young man ("Sell what you have and give it to the poor"; Mark 10:21) seemed applicable to all. The sharing of goods described in the early chapters of Acts was an attempt to carry out what those early Christians believed to be the intention of Jesus in this regard.

A little later, two other factors seem to have exercised

some impact on the development of Christian asceticism. One was the emergence of GNOSTICISM—a sect that held all matter to be evil. The result was not only a denial of value and meaning to flesh and human existence, but an active rejection of them. Consequently it was only a small step to conclude that one's physical life should be disciplined and denied in order to allow for greater impact by one's spiritual nature.

A second factor was the dichotomy that developed between ordinary Christians and those who had special spiritual interests. This became so prominent and common that by the time of Tertullian and Origen, distinctions were being made in the teachings of the church between "requirements" for each Christian and "suggestions" for those who sought the holier life. Many of those who desired a more spiritual existence discovered it in the ascetic way. As Christianity became more stable, asceticism became widely recognized as not only one way but the ideal way of holiness.

See also DISCIPLINE; ETHICS IN THE NEW TESTAMENT; GNOSTICISM; STOICS.

—ROBERT O. BYRD

• **Asclepius.** [as-klee'pee-uhs] The eighth tractate of Codex VI in the NAG HAMMADI library is attributed to "Asclepius," a disciple of the mythological Hermes Trismegistus ("Thrice greatest"), the Greek name of Thoth, Egyptian god of wisdom. Known previously from a Latin translation and two extant Greek fragments, the Coptic *Asclepius* contains only chaps. 21–29 of the original work and is stylistically closer to the Greek version. Both Coptic and Latin texts are translations and rhetorically embellished versions of a Greek original that was part of a larger body of HERMETIC LITERATURE written in Greco-Roman Egypt in the second or third century C.E.

Hermeticism was a syncretistic, religio-philosophical movement that attempted to reconcile some traditional Egyptian ideas with ASTROLOGY, Greek philosophy (notably, dualistic Platonism and pantheistic Stoicism), and Jewish thought. Representatives penned not only the *Asclepius,* but also early "vulgar" works of astrological and alchemical nature, and an extensive *Corpus Hermeticum* of seventeen tractates. No consistent mythic cycle or symbolic system unites these works, and no definite information exists about their parent sect. Uniting the philosophical works are such ideas as a basic distinction between spiritual and material, the need to apprehend the Ultimate (God) intellectually rather than empirically, and the importance of spiritual discipline to achieve mystical unity with God.

The literary form of Asclepius is an instructional dialogue between an initiate "Asclepius" (two others, Tat and Amon, are also named) and his "mystagogue" (guide into the mystery), Hermes Trismegistus. The teaching is not systematically developed but rather organized topically. First, in 65.15-37 the mystagogue likens mystical experience in ecstatic union with God to the act of sexual intercourse. It is characterized by mutual interaction of two parties and is too private to be fully understood by detached observers.

Second, in 65.37–68.19 a contrast is drawn between the impious many who are unbelieving, controlled by base passions, and bound for death and corruption, and the pious few who believe, control desires through learning and knowledge, and remain immortal.

Third, in 68.20–70.2 Hermes teaches that just as God has made the "inner man" in his own image, so "man on earth creates gods according to his likeness" (69.26-27). Such is not idolatry but represents man's "strength" (68.22-23).

Fourth, 70.3–74.6 offers an apocalyptic scenario of destruction God will bring upon formerly pious Egypt. This will be the prelude to a final restoration.

Fifth and finally, in 74.7–78.43 we read of the redemption of pious ones in an eternal city "in the west" through the will of the good God who established the universe and assigned lesser gods like Zeus and Kore to rule earth.

At death, souls separate from bodies, are judged by a great daimon in the air between earth and heaven, and receive reward or punishment.

Although its emphases on saving gnosis ("knowledge") and the dualistic nature of man give the tractate a somewhat Gnostic flavor, its evaluation of the world as good and its location in a Nag Hammadi codex whose works are principally non-Gnostic brings *Asclepius* more into the sphere of eclectic and mystical Middle Platonism.

See also HERMETIC LITERATURE; NAG HAMMADI.

Bibliography. J. Brashler, P. A. Dirkse, and D. M. Parrott, "Asclepius 21-29 (VI,8)," *The Nag Hammadi Library in English,* ed. J. M. Robinson; P. A. Dirkse and D. M. Parrott, "Asclepius 21-29; VI,8: 65.15–78.43," in *The Coptic Gnostic Library: Nag Hammadi Codices V,2-5 and VI with Papyrus Berolinensis 8502, 1 and 4,* ed. D. M. Parrott (*NHS* 11).

—MALCOLM L. PEEL

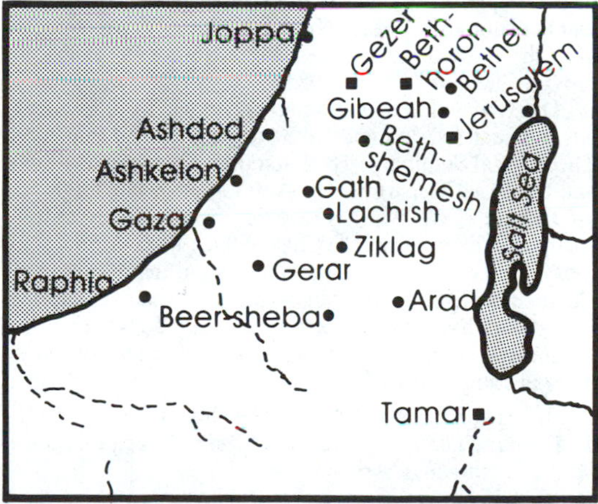

Designed by Margaret Jordan Brown ©Mercer University Press

• **Ashdod.** [ash'dod] Ancient Ashdod (NT "Azotus") was one of the cities of the famed PHILISTINE pentapolis (1 Sam 6:16-17—Ashdod, ASHKELON, EKRON, GATH, GAZA). The tell, or mound, of the Philistine city consists of two parts: the acropolis which grew to twenty acres and a lower city of seventy acres. The site is located about one-and-three-quarters mi. almost due south of the modern city, three mi. east of the Mediterranean Sea, and thirty mi. due west of Jerusalem (PLATES 12, 13). Tell Ashdod rises about fifty ft. above the surrounding land which is approximately 160 ft. above sea level.

The city of Ashdod, its language, or its inhabitants are mentioned in fourteen biblical passages. In Josh 22:11, some of the ancient race of giants, the Anakim, are said to still dwell there. It is grouped with the other Philistine cities in Josh 13:3 as land that yet remains to be conquered; and in Josh 15:46-47, it is listed with the territories allotted to the tribe of Judah. 1 Sam 5 and 6 recount the capture of the ARK of the Covenant by Philistine forces, its transportation in triumph to the temple of Dagon in Ashdod, and its return with the humiliating guilt offerings from the Philistine rulers. Ashdod is one of the cities Judean King Uzziah triumphed over (2 Chr 26:6). The people of Ashdod were members of the coalition that opposed Nehemiah's rebuilding program for Jerusalem (Neh 4:7); and women from Ashdod are listed among those with whom the returning Jewish captives intermarried (Neh 13:23-24). The capture of Ashdod by an Assyrian commander was used to date a prophetic message (Isa 20:1). Ashdod is part of a shortened list of the Philistine cities in Jer 25:20; Amos 1:6-8; Zeph 2:4; and Zech 9:6. Once Ashdod is referred to in the NT (Acts 8:40) by its Hellenistic and Roman name, Azotus.

Ashdod textile merchants are mentioned in Ugaritic documents from the fourteenth century B.C.E. The occupants of the city were Canaanite through the last quarter of the thirteenth century B.C.E. The attacks of the Sea Peoples brought the Philistines to power around 1200 B.C.E. Philistine culture flourished during the Iron Age I Period (1200–1000). The city experienced the same sort of domination by larger powers that Judah and Israel did: Assyria conquered it in 712 B.C.E.; Egypt took it after a long siege in the early seventh century; and it fell to Babylon when Judah did in the early sixth century.

Judah and Ashdod were apparently related through trade. Samples of eighth century B.C.E. writing from Ashdod are in the Hebrew script of the period. Ashdod might also have been conquered by King Josiah in the late seventh century and held until his death in 609 B.C.E. The city was occupied after the Babylonian conquest but never again reached its previous level.

D. N. Freedman, J. Swauger, and M. Dothan led excavations at Ashdod under the auspices of The Pittsburgh Theological Seminary, The Pittsburgh Carnegie Museum, and the Israel Department of Antiquities in the 1960s and 1970s. These excavations revealed twenty-three strata of occupation dating from the Chalcolithic (4000–3150 B.C.E.) to Byzantine (ca. 350 C.E.) periods. Significant finds at the site include distinctive pottery—red burnished vessels decorated with black bands—known as "Ashdod-ware," and an unusual statuette of a woman the lower half of whose body is combined with a throne.

Bibliography. M. Dothan, "Ashdod" in *EAEHL*; T. Dothan, *The Philistines and Their Material Culture*; D. N. Freedman, "Ashdod" in *IDBSupp*.

—TIMOTHY G. CRAWFORD

• **Asher.** [ash'uhr] A personal and tribal name (*'āšēr*, Heb. "blessed").

1. Son of JACOB by Zilpah (Gen 30:12-13), but named by LEAH, "for the daughters will call me blessed." The name "Ashar" is known as an Old Akkadian and Amorite name in ancient Mesopotamia, where it is the name of a god.

2. According to Josh 19:24-29, the tribal territory of Asher, named for the son of Jacob, extended east from Mount Carmel to the valley of Iphtahel (Wadi el-Malik), then turned north past Kabul to the border with Sidon, perhaps the river Litani. From there the border turned west to Tyre and the Sea. David's census followed this route (2 Sam 24:6-7). Asher included four levitical cities (Josh 21:30-31), but its most renowned city was Acco. The blessings of Jacob (Gen 49:20) and of Moses (Deut 33:24-25) speak of Asher's fertility, especially olive oil, still plentiful in the region (PLATE 12).

3. The tribe of Asher did not drive out the Canaanites (Judg 1:31), nor did it answer Deborah's call to fight SISERA (Judg 5:17), but it did aid GIDEON against the Midianites (Judg 6:35; 7:23).

4. SOLOMON's ninth administrative district (1 Kgs 4:16), which took its name from the tribe.

See also JACOB; LEAH; TRIBES.

—JAMES F. STRANGE

• **Asherah.** [uh-shihr'uh] A Hebrew word referring to a Canaanite goddess and the cult objects that represent her. The term was often translated as "grove" in the KJV; however, some texts clearly imply that the Asherah was a movable object rather than a stand of trees.

Asherah was the wife/consort of the chief god of the Canaanite and Phoenician pantheons. She is described as the mother of most of the "younger" gods, including BAAL and Anath. One of her titles was "Lady Asherah of the Sea," and some scholars believe that she was once worshiped as the one who defeated the sea monster. If that is true, then she was replaced as conqueror by Baal and his sister/consort, Anath. Judg 6:25 describes an altar to Baal that had an Asherah beside it, so apparently in some places, Asherah was Baal's consort rather than his mother.

The Canaanites also called her "Holiness," which is a name given to an Egyptian goddess who was depicted naked, with hair curling down like ram's horns, and standing on the back of a lion. If it is correct to connect the two deities, then perhaps the many small statues of naked women with curling hair found in Palestine were cult objects of Asherah; however, this remains uncertain. What is clear is that she was a fertility goddess whose worship involved sacred prostitution. A fifteenth-century text in Akkadian mentions a request for a "wizard of Asherah" to forecast the future, so apparently there were seers or oracles dedicated to the goddess.

The biblical texts are not interested in describing Asherah's cult objects or their use in worship. They merely tell the story of how a king sinned by using them or how another hero tore them down. One cult object was apparently made of wood (Judg 6:25-26; 1 Kgs 15:13) and stood beside an altar. There have been several theories as to what this object was. The most commonly held is that it was a carved pole resembling the goddess or her sacred tree. First Kgs 23:4 also mentions "vessels made for Baal and for Asherah," and v. 7 describes something woven, probably either a tapestry or a robe to drape over the Asherah.

According to the narrative of 1–2 Kgs, the cult of Asherah was very popular in Israel from the tenth through the sixth centuries B.C.E. Inscriptions at a Palestinian shrine dating from this period show that some Israelites thought Asherah was Yahweh's consort. JEZEBEL established shrines to Baal and Asherah at SAMARIA and employed 400 prophets of Asherah (1 Kgs 23:4). Asa removed and burned an Asherah that his mother had made (1 Kgs 15:13). Since Asa burned it in the Kidron Valley, scholars suppose it was in a shrine on the Mount of Olives, like those Solomon's wives constructed. MANASSEH rebuilt the Baal/Asherah shrines destroyed by HEZEKIAH, and as the worst of his crimes put an Asherah in the TEMPLE (2 Kgs 21:1-7). Interpreters suggest that he must have replaced God's altar with one for Baal and put an Asherah beside it; small wonder that the Deuteronomist blames the Babylonian Exile on the crimes of Manasseh. Later, JOSIAH cleaned all this out and burned all the things devoted to Asherah and Baal in JERUSALEM and in all the other places of Judah where the cult existed (2 Kgs 23).

See also BAAL; IDOLATRY; IMAGES/FIGURINES.

Bibliography. W. F. Albright, *Yahweh and the Gods of Canaan*; J. Day, "Asherah in the Hebrew Bible," *JBL* 105 (1986): 385-408; J. Pritchard, *The Ancient Near East*.

—RICHARD B. VINSON

• **Ashkelon.** [ash'kuh-lon] Ashkelon (KJV "Ascalon") was one of the cities of the PHILISTINE pentapolis (1 Sam 6:17—ASHDOD, Ashkelon, EKRON, GAZA, GATH). The tell, or mound, lies on the coast of the Mediterranean Sea about one-half mi. southwest of the modern city of Ashkelon and about forty-five mi. west-southwest of Jerusalem (PLATES 12, 13). The site is semi-circular in shape with the tell—known as "el Khadra"—rising in its midst. The tell—which is the location of the Bronze and Iron Age occupation levels—is approximately forty-two ft. high and occupies an area of about twelve acres. It was the only city on the southern coastal plain directly on the seaboard.

The city or its inhabitants are mentioned in ten OT passages. It is listed as land remaining to be conquered (Josh 13:1-3) and as among Judah's conquests (Judg 1:18—although the LXX text of this passage says the city was not taken and that does seem to have been the case). Samson went there to kill thirty of its inhabitants for their clothes in order to pay off a wager (Judg 14:19). First Sam 6 tells how the rulers of the five cities sent their unusual guilt offerings when they returned the captured ARK. In David's lament over Saul and Jonathan, he feared that their deaths would bring rejoicing in Ashkelon (2 Sam 1:20). Judgement was proclaimed against the city in Jer 25:20; 47:4-7; Amos 1:6-8; Zeph 2:4-7; and Zech 9:5-7.

Ancient Ashkelon was economically important for two reasons: its port and its strategic position on the Via Maris. As a Canaanite city, it was under Egyptian control and is mentioned in Egyptian texts of the nineteenth, fifteenth, and fourteenth centuries B.C.E. It tried unsuccessfully to revolt against the powerful Ramses II earlier in the thirteenth century. Its failed attempt against his successor is commemorated in the important Merneptah Stele (ca. 1220 B.C.E.).

A destruction level found in excavations marks the arrival of the Philistines about 1190 B.C.E. During the period of Philistine expansion (twelfth to eleventh centuries), each of the five cities was ruled by a *seren* (1 Sam 6:4) who was supported by a military aristocracy. The king of Ashkelon acknowledged the might of Assyrian King Tiglath-Pileser III when he invaded Palestine in 734 B.C.E., but revolted and was overthrown after the Assyrians defeated the Arameans of Damascus in 733 or 732 B.C.E. (cf. 2 Kgs 16:5ff). The city refused to take part in the various revolts against Assyria which took place between 732 and 705, and so was unharmed.

In 705, kings Ṣidqa of Ashkelon and Hezekiah of Judah led Palestine in revolt against Assyria when Sargon II died. Sennacherib stopped the revolt in 701. Ashkelon again revolted unsuccessfully in 671. It was captured by the Egyptians in 612, after the fall of Assyria, attacked and ransacked by the Scythians in 610, and laid waste by the Babylonians in 609. Nebuchadrezzar held captives from Ashkelon in his palace along with King Jehoiachin of Judah and his sons whom he took prisoner in 598 B.C.E. Ashkelon was inhabited during the Hellenistic, Roman, Byzantine, Muslim, and Crusader periods. It was destroyed by the Mamelukes in 1270 C.E. and not rebuilt.

Excavations at Ashkelon reveal occupation from the Neolithic (approximately 7000 B.C.E.) through the Crusader (1270 C.E.) periods. Ashkelon was the subject of a prescientific excavation, one of the earliest excavations in Palestine, in 1815, under the supervision of an English woman living in Syria, Lady Hester Stanhope. It was the subject of more scientific study 1920–1922 by J. Garstang and W. J. T. Phythian-Adams in behalf of the Palestine Exploration Fund, who excavated for Bronze and Iron Age artifacts. Work continued through the 1930s and 1940s, in 1955 (on Neolithic materials), and sporadically up to the present time. In the 1980s excavations have been under the supervision of Lawrence E. Stager of Harvard University.

Bibliography. M. Avi-Yonah and Y. Eph'al "Ashkelon," *EAEHL*; G. H. Davies, "British Archaeologists" in J. F. Drinkard, Jr., G. L. Mattingly, and J. M. Miller, eds., *Benchmarks in Time and Culture: An Introduction to the History and Methodology of Syro-Palestinian Archaeology*; T. Dothan, *The Philistines and Their Material Culture*; W. F. Stinespring, "Ashkelon," *IDB*.

—TIMOTHY G. CRAWFORD

• **Ashtoreth.** *See* QUEEN OF HEAVEN

• **Ashurbanipal.** [ash'uhr-ban"uh-puhl] Ashurbanipal (Assyr. *Ašur-bān-apli* "Ashur created a son") was confirmed crown prince of ASSYRIA by his father, ESARHADDON, in 672 B.C.E. At his father's death in 669 B.C.E., Ashurbanipal ascended the throne without incident.

He immediately set about reconquering Egypt, sending a strong Assyrian army there in 667 B.C.E. Memphis was taken, but Ashurbanipal was forced to come to the aid of its beleaguered garrison within a few years. In 663 B.C.E., Ashurbanipal's army captured and destroyed Thebes (Karnak). This destruction is referred to in Nah 3:8. No-Amon, "the city of (the god) Amon," is generally identified as Thebes.

About 645 B.C.E., Ashurbanipal sacked Susa, the capital of Elam. The deportation and resettlement of some men of Susa and Elam to Samaria by "the great and noble Osnapper" noted in Ezra 4:10 is usually regarded as a reference to Ashurbanipal and the Assyrian policy of forced exile.

Ashurbanipal is probably the king who freed MANASSEH from exile (2 Chr 33:13). Most likely, Manasseh was bound and carried to Babylon under Esarhaddon (2 Chr 33:11). At any rate, Ashurbanipal, in the course of his first campaign to Egypt, listed Manasseh of Judah among the kings from whom he received tribute (*ANET*, 294).

The end of Ashurbanipal's reign is obscure. He died ca. 627 B.C.E. The last of the great Assyrian kings, Ashurbanipal collected a massive library of cuneiform literature at Nineveh. Its value for understanding the history of the ancient Near East cannot be overestimated.

Bibliography. *ANET*, 294-301.

—STEPHEN J. ANDREWS

• **Asia.** The NT frequently refers to Asia, meaning the westernmost part of Asia Minor (modern Turkey). Originally the term described parts of the Seleucid Empire founded after the death of Alexander the Great, but after the kingdom of Pergamum became independent of the Seleucids in 262 B.C.E., the term was generally used to describe this northwestern corner of Asia Minor, bordering the Aegean Sea. With the rise of Rome and the death of the last king of Pergamum in 133 B.C.E., a new Roman province of Asia was established which included the traditional regions in eastern Asia Minor of Mysia, Lydia, Caria, Ionia, and most of Phrygia. This area remained intact as a unit of Roman governance for over 400 years, being represented in Rome by a senator and boasting, in the provincial capital of Ephesus, the fourth largest city of the empire. In Acts 13–16, 19, the evangelization of this province of Asia by early Christians is described, primarily through the activities of Paul and Barnabas. Paul's Letter to the Ephesians was sent to the community in the capital, in which he had labored for two years (Acts 19:10), and the Letter to the Colossians was addressed to a small community nearby. Brief references to Christians in Asia appear in 1 Peter, 2 Timothy, Romans, and the Corinthian correspondence, but the most-familiar passage may be Rev 1:4, 11 where John reports his vision "to the seven churches that are in Asia," these being in the cities of Ephesus, Smyrna, Pergamum, Thyatira, Sardis, Philadelphia, and Laodicea in the western part of the province.

See also ROMAN EMPIRE.

—DAVID W. RUTLEDGE

• **Ass.** One of the most common domestic ANIMALS mentioned in the Bible, used throughout the ancient Near East as an all-purpose animal. The ass or donkey was used for riding by both men and women (Num 22:22; Judg 1:14; Josh 15:18; 2 Sam 17:23), as a beast of burden (Gen 42:26; 1 Sam 16:20; 25:18), and in agricultural work (Isa 30:24). In addition, the ass was used widely by trade caravans as they crossed the deserts. People of prestige (Judg 10:3-4; 12:13-14), rich people (1 Sam 25:20), and kings (2 Sam 16:2) rode the ass.

The ass was often one of the most valuable household possessions of an individual (Exod 22:8-9) because it provided transportation and domestic help. Even the poorest person in Israel owned an ass (Job 24:3). In the postexilic community the ass continued to play an important role in the Israelite economy. Among the animals brought back to Jerusalem by those returning (Ezra 2:66-67), the ass was more numerous (6720) than the horse (736), the mule (245), or the camel (435).

The importance of the ass as a domestic animal in Israelite society is reflected in laws enacted to protect it. The Decalogue prohibits coveting the neighbor's ass (Exod 20:17; Deut 5:21); the Covenant Code deals with its treatment and its safety (Exod 21:33-34; 23:4-5, 12); the Deuteronomic Code forbids harnessing the ass and the ox together (Deut 22:10).

While the horse was often associated with war, the ass was considered a peaceful animal. In Zech 9:9 the messianic king comes riding on an ass (or colt of an ass in Matthew), an image used in the Gospels to describe the coming of Jesus to Jerusalem (Matt 21:1-11; John 12:12-15).

See also ANIMALS.

Bibliography. G. Cansdale, *All the Animals of the Bible Land,* 70-74; W. T. In der Smitten, חֲמוֹר *chᵃmôr, TDOT.*

—CLAUDE F. MARIOTTINI

• **Assembly.** The translation of several Hebrew terms, among which *ʿēdâ* and *qahal* are prominent. Throughout the history of Israel before the Exile, important political and cultic functions were carried out by various assemblies of Israelite citizens. Israelite assemblies of the premonarchic era seem to be solely local or tribal functions. There is little evidence for any national assemblies having any practical existence during this period, although a national assembly may have been an ideal (Judg 21:1-11). Judg 11:4-11 shows us that one of these premonarchic tribal assemblies was composed of a group known as the "elders," but status as an elder does not seem to be defined very narrowly since in Judg 8:22-23 a similar group has the more inclusive title "men of Israel." In 1 Sam 4:3-5, the terms "elders" and "the people" are used interchangeably in a situation where a gathering of influential males makes tactical military decisions on the battlefield. From this, it seems that the premonarchic assemblies were composed of the influential free Israelite males in military service. The duties of these assemblies were varied. In Judg 8:22-23 and 11:4-11, assemblies selected leaders for both war and peace. In Judg 6, the town assembly oversaw the town's shrine, and in Josh 9, the treaty with the Gibeonites was concluded by the "men of Israel," and in Josh 24, an idealized assembly reaffirmed Israel's covenant with God.

Although the national level assembly remained only an unattained ideal throughout the premonarchic era, a national assembly, or at least a multi-tribal regional assembly, became a reality simultaneously with the monarchy. Each of the accounts of SAUL's enthronement tells of some activity of some type of assembly of "all the elders of Israel" (1 Sam 8:4), or of "all the people" (1 Sam 10:24; 11:15). Later, DAVID's actual accession to the throne was made official by "the elders of Israel" (2 Sam 5). These references seem to apply to gatherings of the leaders of several tribes. Assemblies during the monarchic era had compositions similar to their predecessors, as is seen in the above references both to the "elders" and to the "people," and in 1 Kgs 16:15-16, where a king is chosen by "all Israel" at a battlefield encampment. Thus the free male militiamen are still the assembly members. This "national" assembly did not surrender its power to the king, however, particularly in the Northern Kingdom. Assemblies played major roles in selecting northern kings. In 1 Kgs 12, an assembly rejects Rehoboam as king and enthrones Jeroboam. In 1 Kgs 16:15-16, Omri is made king by a battlefield assembly, and in 1 Kgs 20:7-8, Israel's king confers with the "elders" and the "people" regarding a declaration of war with Aram. National assemblies are also seen as cultic entities as well as political bodies: in 1 Sam 6:2, 15 an assembly brings the Ark to Jerusalem, and in 1 Sam 25:1, "all Israel" performs funerary rites for SAMUEL.

In postexilic Judah, assemblies seem to have no role, having been replaced by a council of nobles known as "the princes of the congregation."

See also CONGREGATION; CONVOCATION; ELDER; GOVERNMENT; TRIBES.

Bibliography. B. Birch, *The Rise of the Israelite Monarchy*; T. N. D. Mettinger, *King and Messiah.*

—RAY SUTHERLAND

• **Assembly, Great.** According to Jewish tradition, a significant council having roots in the events described in Neh 8–10 and having Ezra as its head. The Mishnah tractates *Aboth* and *Baba Bathra* (compiled second century C.E.) are the earliest sources that speak of the great assembly. However, its membership and function have always been problematic.

The assertion of Elias Levita (d. 1549 C.E.) that the assembly, under Ezra's leadership, established the OT canon and divided it into its three parts, was widely accepted by both Jews and Christians. Serious reservations regarding this view emerged in the eighteenth century and culminated in the nineteenth century with A. Kuenen's position that the institution was purely legendary. The consensus of scholars at present is probably that the work of the assembly, if it existed at all, was much less extensive than tradition reveals.

Bibliography. D. Sperber, "Synagogue, the Great," *EncJud*.

—WALTER E. BROWN

• **Assumption of Moses.** *See* MOSES, TESTAMENT OF

• **Assurance.** On the side of human beings, assurance refers to confident and enduring faith in God, trust in the reality of divine faithfulness, expectant hope in the promises of God, and the state of security that results from unreserved commitment to God's will. In speaking of assurance, PAUL uses the example of God's promise to ABRAHAM that through the righteousness of faith he would be the father of a great nation and that his descendants would inherit the world. Although his own body was "as good as dead," the aged Abraham believed God and God's promises. In hope Abraham continued to have confidence in God's ability to actualize the divine promise, i.e., to make an old man the father of many nations (Rom 4:13-25). Assurance is a vital and energizing faith that puts into action what is believed (Isa 40:27-31). In Heb 11 Abraham responds to God's call, not knowing where he was to go. The confidence of Abraham and the other heroes of faith led them to act as though these promises were real and true. Hope is faith that does not yet see, but nevertheless still believes and acts on the basis of what is believed (Heb 11:1; Isa 8:17).

Finally, assurance results from a vital relation. God and the believing community participate in a living relationship characterized by mutual trust and commitment. Behind the word that is believed is the one who is to be trusted. This is as true of God's trust in the people as it is of their trust in God. In the OT this relationship is best expressed in terms of covenant. God has elected the people Israel and has actively entered in a relationship with them. As God's people, ISRAEL will receive divine oversight, blessings, and care. Israel enters into a relationship in which God is to be the ultimate object of their lives and their deepest commitment (cf. Deut 6:4-5). In the NT, the divine-human relationship is due to faith in God's eschatological act in Jesus Christ, through whom eternal salvation comes to the believers. The believers live in confident assurance that the promises of God made to them are realized once-and-for-all in the Christ event.

Assurance may be contrasted to a debilitating fear or the state of anxiety about life and the future. A lack of enduring confidence and hopeful trust in God leads to either passive despair or the attempt to place false confidence in human effort. Thus the psalmist condemns the generation who rebelled in the wilderness for not trusting in God's covenant and power to preserve (Ps 78:37). The wicked are often depicted as those whose arrogance and proud confidence in their own abilities eventually lead to their downfall (Ps 73).

See also FAITH.

—LEO G. PERDUE

• **Assyria.** An important Mesopotamian empire from about 1900 B.C.E. to about 612 B.C.E. The heartland of the empire was located in the alluvial plain west of the Tigris River along its upper region. Today it is located in northern Iraq. The major cities of Assyria were Asshur, NIMRUD/CALAH, Nineveh, and Dur-Sharrukin (PLATE 1). This heartland was rich agricultural land, and agriculture formed the basis of the Assyrian economy, although Assyria became a major trade center quite early.

Artwork by Margaret Jordan Brown

Artist's conception of the façade of an Assyrian temple.

In the earliest references to the area of Assyria from the twenty-fourth century B.C.E., it was under the domination of the empire of Agade and its Semitic rulers. Later, in the twenty-first century B.C.E., the area of Assyria was ruled by the Sumerian Third Dynasty of Ur.

The Old Assyrian period dates from about 1900–1650 B.C.E. Following the collapse of the Third Dynasty at Ur, a number of local rulers reigned from Asshur. In the king list, these rulers have Akkadian names and claim descent from Sargon of Akkad. A major ruler during this time was Shamshi-Adad I. He was an Amorite who originally came from the Habur valley. He conquered the area of Assyria and ruled an empire extending as far as Mari on the Euphrates. However, he never ruled from Asshur; his capital was Shubat-Enlil. His sons were defeated and the empire lost, part to Zimri-Lim of MARI and part to HAMMURABI of BABYLON.

Assyria was already quite active in trade during the Old Assyrian period. A major trading colony had been established at Kültepe in Cappadocia (modern Turkey). Assyria imported a great deal of tin from the region to be used in making bronze.

After a gap of nearly three centuries during which Assyria was ruled first by the Hurrian kingdom of Mittani and then by Babylon, Assyria again became independent. This period is called the Middle Assyrian period and dates to about 1360–1075 B.C.E. There were three important kings during the thirteenth century B.C.E., Adad-nirari I (1306–1274 B.C.E.), Shalmaneser I (1273–1244 B.C.E.) and Tukulti-Ninurta I (1243–1207 B.C.E.). Under this latter king, Assyria extended its control over neighboring, and rival, Babylon for the first time. However, this period of expansion was brief and soon followed by another period of decline. Tiglath-pileser I restored Assyria's military might for a short period about 1114–1076 B.C.E. But his reign was followed by over a century of decline marking the end of the Middle Assyrian period.

The neo-Assyrian period, 930–612 B.C.E., marks the period of Assyrian supremacy and the period during which Assyria had contact with Israel and Judah. For biblical studies, the neo-Assyrian period is therefore most important.

The first two rulers of this period were Asshur-dan II (934–912 B.C.E.) and Adad-nirari II (911–891 B.C.E.). These two rulers began the expansion of Assyria militarily toward the south and west. Adad-Nirari II reached the Euphrates and the Habur valley. Ashur-naṣir-apli II (883–859 B.C.E.) and SHALMANESER III (859–824 B.C.E.) extended this control over most of Babylon in the south, and as far as the coast of Syria, Phoenicia and Israel. Ashur-naṣir-apli II severely curtailed the expansion of the Aramean states in north Syria and the northern Euphrates region. He effectively disrupted all their trade routes into Mesopotamia. This is the reason for the Aramean-Phoenician-Israelite alliance against Assyria during the reign of Shalmaneser III. It was brought about by commercial concerns to regain trade routes to Mesopotamia. Whereas Ashur-naṣir-apli II had gone by a northern route through CARCHEMISH to reach the Syrian coast, Shalmaneser III used a southern approach through Hamath and Aleppo. Not only did this action indicate Assyrian intentions to control all of Syria-Palestine, it also led to the first direct contact between Israel and Assyria. The incursion of Shalmaneser led to the alliance mentioned above. The troops of the alliance met Shalmaneser's army at Qarqar in 853 B.C.E. In an inscription known as the Kurkh stela, Shalmaneser claims victory. He lists among the combatants 20,000 infantry of Hadadezer (of Damascus) and 2,000 chariots and 10,000 infantry of Ahab, the Israelite.

Another contact between Israel and Assyria during the reign of Shalmaneser is indicated on the Black Obelisk. In this stele dated to about 841 B.C.E. tribute of JEHU to Shalmaneser is reported and either Jehu or one of his emissaries is depicted prostrate before Shalmaneser bringing the tribute. A recently discovered stele records that Joash (Jehoash) of Israel paid tribute to Adad-Nirari III (810–783 B.C.E.). Shortly after this time during the early part of the eighth century B.C.E., Urartu to the north of Assyria began to expand and pressure Assyria. A brief period of Assyrian weakness followed.

The result of this weakness was a coup that brought a new ruler to the throne in 746 B.C.E., TIGLATH-PILESER III. He quickly began to reform administrative procedures including a reorganization of the governing of provinces. He also began expansion of the Assyrian empire. He quickly gained control over Babylon, then moved his attention westward. In his annals, Tiglath-pileser reports that MENAHEM of Israel paid tribute to him. Another reference in the annals speaks of the revolt of one Azriyau. Most scholars feel this reference is to a ruler and kingdom in north Syria, though others argue that Azariah (Uzziah) and Judah are intended. Only a few years later Syria and Israel entered into an alliance to oppose Tiglath-pileser. They tried to force Judah to join the alliance. AHAZ, then king of Judah, refused and sought assistance from Assyria. Tiglath-pileser responded, invaded Syria and Israel, removed PEKAH from the throne of Israel and replaced him with HOSHEA. By 732 B.C.E., Damascus had been captured and Syria was made a province of Assyria. In 734 B.C.E., a revolt occurred in Babylon. Tiglath-pileser put down the revolt and assumed the throne himself. For the first time since the reign of Tukulti-Ninurta I, 500 years previously, an Assyrian ruler took the title of king of Babylon.

Shalmaneser V succeeded Tiglath-pileser III as king and ruled for five years (727–722 B.C.E.). During his brief reign, Egypt and pro-Egyptian elements in Israel incited anti-Assyrian revolts. Shalmaneser invaded Israel, laid siege to Samaria and ultimately captured it in 722 B.C.E.

SARGON II (722–705 B.C.E.) founded the last royal dynasty of Assyria. He came to the throne after the death of Shalmaneser V. Sargon completed the destruction of the Northern Kingdom, by retaking Samaria and deporting many of the inhabitants. But most of Sargon's energies were spent in Mesopotamia. First he had to deal with Urartu to the north of Assyria. After that kingdom was defeated, Babylon was again in revolt. MERODACH-BALADAN, a former ally of Assyria, now claimed the throne of Babylon. Although Sargon drove him from Babylon, he was unable to capture Merodach-Baladan or fully quell the revolt.

SENNACHERIB (705–681 B.C.E.) was a major builder, able administrator and exceptional military leader. Much of his reign was occupied with war against Babylon. Merodach-Baladan again seized the throne of Babylon, this time with the support of Elam. Sennacherib undertook a major campaign against Merodach-Baladan. At about the same time, HEZEKIAH withheld tribute from Assyria, a renunciation of vassalage. Sennacherib came with his army against Judah and Egypt. He captured most of Judah including Lachish and besieged Jerusalem. Although Jerusalem was not captured, Sennacherib described the situation of Hezekiah as being like a bird in a cage. On his return to Assyria, Sennacherib had his throne room covered with reliefs depicting the siege and capture of Lachish. When he returned to Assyria, he resumed his battle against Babylon, ultimately capturing and sacking the city. He was murdered in 681 B.C.E.

ESHARHADDON (680–669 B.C.E.) succeeded Sennacherib. He rebuilt Babylon, and thereby gained the loyalty of its inhabitants. He also invaded Egypt because of continued revolts instigated in Palestine. Esarhaddon made vassal treaties with many of his subject nations. Copies of one such treaty have been recovered, treaties intended to assure his plans for succession to the throne would be successful. His plan was for one son ASHURBANIPAL to succeed him as king of Assyria. Another son would serve as a subordinate king/ruler of Babylon. This plan seems to have worked for about fourteen years. Esarhaddon's annals mention MANASSEH, king of Judah, among the vassals paying tribute.

Ashurbanipal (668-627 B.C.E.) did succeed his father. He is noted as a builder and scholar as well as military leader. He extended the empire to its greatest size. During his reign Egypt was brought under Assyrian control. Thebes, the capital of Egypt, was captured and sacked in 663 B.C.E. However, the Assyrian empire was rapidly weakening at this time. Much pressure was being exerted from northern invaders on Assyria. Furthermore, there was internal revolution as Ashurbanipal's brother, ruler of Babylon rebelled. Although Ashurbanipal defeated his brother and subdued Babylon by 648 B.C.E., Egypt was able to reassert independence at this time. War with Media continued another nine years. Little information is available on the last years of Ashurbanipal's reign. It is probable that the Assyrian empire was faced with continued turmoil and internal division.

After Ashurbanipal's death, the Assyrian empire collapsed rapidly. It was during this period of obvious Assyrian weakness that JOSIAH, king of Judah, enlarged his borders to include parts of Samaria, and perhaps parts of Gilead and Galilee. In 626 B.C.E., Nabopolassar took the throne of Babylon. After gaining Babylonian independence from Assyria, he then led a coalition of forces against Assyria. In 614 B.C.E., Asshur fell to forces of Babylon, Media, and the Scythians. This was followed in 612 B.C.E. by the fall of Nineveh. Although a remnant of the army survived and moved to Haran in north Mesopotamia, the Assyrian empire was at an end. This remaining army was defeated in 605 B.C.E. in the battle of Carchemish.

Assyrian kings also served as the chief priest of the cult of Asshur and as the god's vicegerent on earth. The king personally led the armies of Assyria. Assyrian expansion was understood as a command of the chief god, Asshur. Captives of war and booty were dedicated to the god Asshur.

A chain of command for the administration of the empire included the king, provincial governors and local officials. The eldest son and heir of the king usually served as administrator of the country. State policy entirely depended on the particular ruler at the time.

Assyrian religion was polytheistic. The chief god was Asshur; the old capital Asshur was named for the deity or vice-versa. Other gods included Ishtar the goddess of love, Nabu the god of learning and patron of scribes, and Ninurta the god of war.

Assyrian laws are known from the Middle Assyrian Law code. This compilation of case law has many similarities with Sumerian and Babylonian law, but at places has harsher penalties. The tablets date to Tiglath-pileser I though the code itself is probably older.

Assyrian art and architecture are known primarily from the excavation of the royal cities of Nimrud/Calah and Nineveh. Examples of monumental sculpture include the human-headed bulls or lions that guarded the throne rooms of the palaces. Numerous stone reliefs depicted battles, hunting scenes, and even domestic scenes. Superbly crafted ivory graced the royal palaces. This art shows both the skill of the artists and the artistic taste of the Assyrian kings.

The massive library of Ashurbanipal contained about 10,000 tablets and a total of 26,000 fragments. When he became king, Ashurbanipal had his scribes copy texts from various royal and temple archives. The texts include annalistic, legal, religious, and scientific documents as well as documents of court, treaties, business transactions and letters. It was largely the discovery of this library that provided the impetus for Assyriological studies in the latter part of the last century.

See also ASHURBANIPAL; BABYLONIAN EMPIRE; NIMRUD/CALAH; RELIGIONS OF THE ANCIENT NEAR EAST; SARGON; SENNACHERIB; SHALMANESER; TIGLATH-PILESER.

Bibliography. J. Laessøe, *People of Ancient Assyria*; A. L. Oppenheim, *Ancient Mesopotamia* and "Assyria and Babylonia," *IDB*; R. M. Talbert, "Assyria and Babylonia," *IDBSupp*; D. J. Wiseman, ed., *Peoples of Old Testament Times*.

—JOEL F. DRINKARD, JR.

• **Astarte.** *See* QUEEN OF HEAVEN

• **Astrologer.** Astrologers observe the position of the stars and planets, believing that they influence events on earth and that correct interpretation of their positions and relationships makes it possible to predict the future. Astrology was highly advanced in ASSYRIA and Babylonia and later spread to EGYPT and ROME under Greek influence.

Astrology was known in ancient Israel, although it is not known how widely it was practiced. The OT uses several terms to refer to astrologers: astrologer (Dan 2:27; 4:7; 5:7), one who gazes at or divides the heavens (Isa 47:13) and one who gazes at the stars (Isa 47:13).

The OT generally views astrologers negatively, often associating them with magicians and enchanters. Most OT references to the stars associate them with God's power or promises, not with astrology. The Magi (Matt 2:1-12) probably were astrologers, led to seek the Messiah by a study of the stars and planets.

See also MAGIC AND DIVINATION.

—JOANNE KUEMMERLIN-MCLEAN

• **Astrology.** Astrology is the study of the sun, moon, stars, and planets to determine their effect on nations and human beings as well as to predict the future. Modern scholars differentiate astrology from astronomy, which studies the heavenly bodies without assuming some mystical connection between their movements and humanity's fate. This distinction between astrology and astronomy was not strictly made in the ancient world—legitimate scientific observation was intermixed with fortune-telling.

Astrology probably originated in Mesopotamia during the third millennium B.C.E. The polytheistic people of that region identified the sun, moon, stars, and planets with various gods and goddesses and assumed that their movements carried great significance for nations and kings. The Assyrians, who conquered the northern kingdom of Israel in 722/1 B.C.E., and the Babylonians, who conquered the southern kingdom of Judah in 587/6 B.C.E., both followed astral movements closely. Their interest in astrology undoubtedly encouraged a corresponding interest among the conquered Israelites.

One of the earliest references to astrology in the OT is the prohibition of star worship in Deut 4:19. Frequent references in the prophetic writings to astral religion show that the prophets loyal to Yahweh fought a continuing battle to suppress astrology and the associated worship of heavenly bodies among the Israelites. Isa 47:13-14 ridicules Babylonian astrologers, declaring that they "are like stubble, the fire consumes them; they cannot deliver themselves from the power of the flame." Jeremiah also opposed astrology, exhorting his people not to be dismayed as other nations were when astrologers warned of negative "signs" in the heavens (10:2). He also condemned some Israelites for worshipping the Babylonian goddess Ishtar, who was called the "Queen of Heaven" and was associated with the planet Venus (44:15-19). These warnings would not have been issued unless many Israelites had become involved in astrology. Some knowledge of astronomical data was needed to construct and maintain Israel's solar-lunar calendar, but it proved impossible to completely exclude the religious aspects of astral observation from Israel.

Passages from late in the pre-Christian period—such as *1 Enoch* 8:3 and *Jub* 12:16-18—reveal a continuing battle against astrology. The *Sibylline Oracles* pictured the battle as already won, praising the Jews as "a race of most righteous men . . . for they do not worry about the cyclic course of the sun or the moon. . . . Neither do they practice the astrological predictions of the Chaldeans" (3:218-230).

The most famous NT passage relating to astrology is Matt 2:1-12, the story of the visit of the MAGI or wise men at the birth of Jesus. In the narrative, the magi had observed and followed a particular star and are probably being depicted as astrologers from Babylonia. Matthew does not report the story to encourage astrology, but to show how even the stars are under God's control, and to give witness to all men of the birth of Jesus Christ. Other NT passages, such as Acts 13:6-8, reveal early Christian opposition to astrology.

See also MAGI.

Bibliography. J. S. Holladay, Jr., "The Day(s) the *Moon*

Stood Still," *JBL* 87 (1968): 166-78; J. McKay, *Religion in Judah under the Assyrians*; P. I. H. Naylor, *Astrology: An Historical Examination*.

—MARK J. OLSON

• **Asylum.** *See* REFUGE, CITIES OF

• **Athens.** The Athens (PLATES 26, 27) which the apostle PAUL visited (Acts 17:15-18; 18:1; 1 Thess 3:1) was not the ancient city of Athens which was burned by the Persians in 480 B.C.E. The Athens of Paul's time (and the Athens of interest to students of the Bible) is the city which was rebuilt and reached its grandeur during the time of Pericles (443–428 B.C.E.). This classical Athens is important for politics, culture, philosophy, and religion.

Athens became a complete democracy and by its encouragement of the arts nurtured one of the greatest cultural periods in the history of mankind. The city was decorated with magnificent public buildings. The dramatists and historians recited its greatness. In the centuries before Christ, four great systems of philosophy flourished in Athens—Platonic, Peripatetic, Epicurean, and Stoic. The schools and teachers related to these systems attracted students from all over the ancient world.

It was during this period (fifth century B.C.E.) that the Parthenon, whose marble friezes are now displayed in the British Museum, was built in honor of the goddess Athena. This period also saw considerable building. In the agora (marketplace) and nearby were a prison, a council house, a building for semipublic meetings, and several colonnaded porches or stoa.

The sack of Athens by the Roman general Sulla in 86 B.C.E. did damage chiefly to private quarters, and the classical city was left intact. Moreover, in the reign of Augustus (27 B.C.E.–14 C.E.) new public buildings were added.

The city was under Roman rule when the apostle Paul came as a visitor (Acts 17:15). Paul's remark about the "superstitious" (religious) character of the Athenians (Acts 17:22) is confirmed by ancient writers. Pausanias and Philostratus, second century C.E. writers, record that they saw altars dedicated to "the unknown god" along the two-mile road from the port of Piraeus to the city and elsewhere in the city itself. Pausanias also states that Athenians surpassed all other states in the attention which they paid to the worship of the gods. Hence the city was crowded in every direction with temples, altars, and other sacred buildings. There are pagan temples still standing in Athens. These include the Hephaistion, which overlooks the marketplace or agora, the Temple of Zeus, and the architectural splendors of the Acropolis (PLATE 60). The buildings on the Acropolis include the Temple of the Wingless Victory, the Erechtheum, and the superb Parthenon.

Mars Hill, or the Areopagus, was at the west approach to the Acropolis. Here Paul preached the gospel of redemption. Dionysius, an Areopagite, and a few others were converted (Acts 17:34). The market where Paul argued (Acts 17:17) is north of the Areopagus. Despite Paul's preaching, he did not succeed in establishing a church at Athens, as he did at Corinth, Thessalonica, Philippi, Colossae, and Ephesus.

Doubtless while in Athens, Paul, the great missionary, saw many famous sites. These include the music hall or Odeion of Pericles (cf. 1 Cor 13:1), the stadium with its foot races (cf. 1 Cor 9:24) and wrestling contests (cf. Eph 6:12), and the great tower and waterclock of Andronicus (cf. Eph 5:16).

Despite its loss of military and economic significance, Athens remained supreme in philosophy and the arts. In fact, in Paul's time (Acts 17:15–18:1; 1 Thess 3:1) Athens was still the intellectual center of the world.

See also ACHAIA; PAUL.

—JOHN P. NEWPORT

• **Atonement, Day of.** The most solemn expression of faith and worship for ancient Israel, observed annually on the tenth day of the seventh month (Lev 16:29). As described in the priestly tradition, the Day of Atonement (from *Yom Ha Kippurim* "day of coverings" or "propitiations") with its elaborate ritual had a unique place among the religious festivals of the OT. The day was emphasized by "solemn rest," in which all work ceased, and by a strict fast that was enjoined on all the people. The principal details concerning the day are given in Leviticus 16 with supplementary material supplied in Lev 23:26-32, Num 29:7-11, and Exod 30:10.

The primary purpose of the observance was to "cover," to atone for the sins that had remained uncleansed in the course of the year (Lev 16:33-34). The dominant sacrificial action of the high priest, focusing on the MERCY SEAT, pointed to the urgent need of the people and to the gracious forgiveness and redeeming action of a holy God.

The pattern of ritual peculiar to the Day of Atonement involved several stages. In the preparatory stage (Lev 16:3-10), the high priest selected the appointed offerings for the purpose of cleansing himself and the priests. Laying aside the usual ornate vestments, he bathed and robed in a simple white tunic. He next selected two male goats and a ram for the people's offering. Of the two goats, one was selected for Yahweh and one as a scapegoat (for "Azazel" meaning "complete removal" or perhaps some proper name).

After the preparations were completed, the initial stage of the atonement itself (Lev 16:11-14) involved the high priest's offering a bullock as a sin offering for himself and for the priesthood. After filling his censer with live coals from the altar, the high priest entered the Holy of Holies with incense and the blood of the bull. The smoke of the incense created a cloud covering the mercy seat, while the blood of the bull was sprinkled on the mercy seat once and in front of the mercy seat seven times.

In the next stage, atonement was made for the people and ceremonial cleansing was offered for the instruments of the cult (Lev 16:15-19). The goat chosen by lot for Yahweh was slain as a purification offering for the people and its blood sprinkled successively on the Holy of Holies, the Holy Place, and the outer court.

The culminating stage of the ritual (Lev 16:20-22) involved the high priest's laying his hands on the head of the second goat and confessing over it the sins of ancient Israel. This goat, commonly called the scapegoat, was solemnly led into the wilderness, thus removing the guilt of the people. The day concluded as the high priest returned to the Holy Place to put off the holy garments, bathe, and return to his ordinary high priestly vestments (Lev 16:23-28).

The NT writer of the LETTER TO THE HEBREWS interprets the ritual of the Day of Atonement as a type of the atoning work of Christ (Heb 9–10).

See also FASTING.

Bibliography. R. E. Clements, "Leviticus," *BBC*; J. Milgrom, "Day of Atonement," *EncJud*; G. J. Wenham, *The Book of Leviticus, NICOT*.

—W. H. BELLINGER, JR.

• Atonement/Expiation in the New Testament. [ex′pee-ay″shun] Atonement refers to the work of Christ in dealing with SIN and in restoring human beings in their relationship with God. Atonement is an English word for which there is no Greek word in the NT. In the KJV the word "atonement" is found in the NT only in Rom 5:11. The underlying word (καταλλαγή) is better translated as "RECONCILIATION" as in the RSV (and elsewhere in the KJV). The English word "atonement" originally signified the result after two parties had been estranged. Secondarily, and now usually, it denotes the means through which harmony is restored. Although the word is not, the idea of atonement certainly is biblical.

The need for atonement was created by sin which separates human beings from God and which must be overcome. One's view of sin, then, largely determines the emphasis one places in understanding atonement. For example, if sin is interpreted primarily as transgression of law, then atonement is described as removing the penalty. On the other hand, if sin is understood as the manifestation of the forces of evil, then atonement is described as victory over such forces.

The variety of ideas and word pictures related to atonement in the NT convey a clear message. Whatever needed to be done to remove the sin that separates human beings from God was done in the life, death, and resurrection of Christ.

Atonement is the work of God and is an expression of divine love. "For God so loved the world that he gave his only Son" (John 3:16). "But God shows his love for us in that while we were yet sinners Christ died for us" (Rom 5:8; cf. Gal 4:4-5; Rom 3:25; 1 John 4:9-10; 2 Cor 5:18). The atoning work of Christ is also the work of the incarnate Son of God. The uniqueness of Christ's accomplishment is at least partially explained by the uniqueness of who he was. He was the Word that became flesh (John 1:14), the only Son (John 3:16; cf. Heb 1:1-4).

Atonement must never be stated so as to put the Father and the Son in opposition to each other. The NT does not allow a contrast between Father and Son. "God was in Christ reconciling the world to himself" (2 Cor 5:19, mg.). The Gospel of John says that the Father and Son are one (10:30). As Jesus contemplates his death, he commits himself to do the Father's will (Mark 14:36). The author of Hebrews says that Jesus' sacrifice represents the will of God (10:5-10). Just as the Father sent his Son in love, so the Son did his work in love (Gal 2:20; Rev 1:5). Divine love recognized the seriousness of sin, divine love acknowledged humanity's inability to cope with sin, and divine love provided the way to overcome sin.

The whole life of Christ, climaxed by his death and resurrection, is the work of atonement. The cross has a central, but not exclusive, place in the atoning work of Christ. From his baptism on, Jesus was overcoming the power of sin. At his baptism he was uniquely endowed with the Spirit (Mark 1:9-11; cf. Isa 11:1-2). In the power of the Spirit, Jesus went forth to minister to those who were oppressed by the devil (Acts 10:38). Empowered by the Spirit, Jesus cast out demons (Matt 12:28). As he neared the end of his public ministry Jesus said, "Now shall the ruler of this world be cast out" (John 12:31).

The climax of Jesus' warfare against evil was the cross. The thrust of the Gospels is toward the cross, and the cross was emphasized by Paul in his presentation of the gospel (e.g., 1 Cor 1:23; 2:2; 15:3). The cross is where the principalities and powers were disarmed and the victory was won (Col 2:15; cf. 2 Tim 1:10). The resurrection of Christ is the demonstration of his victory over sin and death (1 Cor 15). Christ's victory in death is also celebrated in Rev 5:9, 12.

The NT teaching on atonement may be treated appropriately by discussing the sacrificial, vicarious, and representative nature of the work of Christ (Taylor).

The NT writers often utilized ideas and terminology related to *sacrifice* when describing the death of Jesus. The idea of sacrifice lies behind many of the references to the cross (e.g., Phil 2:8; Col 2:14; Heb 12:2), blood (e.g., 1 Pet 1:18-19; Rom 5:9; Rev 1:5; Heb 9:14), and death (e.g., Rom 5:10; Phil 2:8; Col 1:22; Heb 2:9-17). Many scholars relate ideas of sacrifice to the servant in Isa 52:13–53:12 and to the NT passages which reflect the Servant (esp. Mark 10:45). Heb 9 describes the death of Christ in terms of the Day of Atonement, but most of the passages do not specify a particular Jewish sacrifice. The passages which refer to EXPIATION are also related to sacrifice (Rom 3:25; 1 John 2:2; 4:10). The shedding of blood as in the OT means especially the offering of life (Lev 17:11; cf. Gen 9:4; Heb 9:6-14).

The atoning work of Christ was also *vicarious*. He gave himself for us (Rom 5:8), he died for us (1 Thess 5:10), he died for all (2 Cor 5:14), and he died for our sins (1 Cor 15:3). In Galatians Paul wrote that Christ "loved me and gave himself for me" (2:20). According to Mark 10:45 Jesus said that he came to give his life as a ransom for many.

The atoning work of Christ was *representative*. In 1 Peter it is said that Christ bore our sins in his body (2:24), and that he died for sins once for all, the righteous for the unrighteous, that he might bring us to God (3:18). Paul wrote that Christ became a curse for us (Gal 3:13) and that for our sake God made Christ to be sin so that in him we might become the righteousness of God (2 Cor 5:21). Commenting on Paul's teaching, Taylor observed that Christ's death was substitutionary in the sense that he did for us that which we can never do for ourselves (*The Cross of Christ,* 31). The author of Hebrews spoke of the representative work of Christ as high priest (2:17; 9:11-14) and as mediator of a new COVENANT (9:15).

Other terms describe the atoning work of Christ and its effects. Jesus was the "Lamb" (John 1:29; Rev 5:8-12). Jesus was the "ransom for many" (Mark 10:45; cf. 1 Cor 6:20; 7:23). A similar thought is expressed in the words "redeem" and "redemption" (Rom 3:24-25; Gal 3:13; Titus 2:14; 1 Pet 1:18-19).

The death of Christ is the means of effecting the new covenant (Mark 14:24; 1 Cor 11:25; Heb 9:15) and its relationships.

The terms "once" and "once for all" testify to the uniqueness of the person of Christ and the sufficiency of his work (Heb 9–10; Rom 6:10; 1 Pet 3:18).

The atoning work of Christ is appropriated by faith (Rom 3:24-25; Gal 2:20). Faith completes the circle and results in reconciliation for the believer (Rom 5:6-11; 2 Cor 5:17-21).

See also ATONEMENT, DAY OF; BLOOD IN THE NEW TESTAMENT; BLOOD IN THE OLD TESTAMENT; COVENANT; EXPIATION; PRIESTS; RECONCILIATION; REDEMPTION IN THE NEW TESTAMENT; REDEMPTION IN THE OLD TESTAMENT; SACRIFICE; SALVATION IN THE NEW TESTAMENT; SALVATION IN THE OLD TESTAMENT; SIN.

Bibliography. M. Ashcraft, *The Forgiveness of Sins*; G. Aulen, *The Faith of the Christian Church*; F. W. Dillistone, *The Christian Understanding of Atonement*;

F. Humphreys, *The Death of Christ*; J. Macquarrie, *Principles of Christian Theology*; L. Morris, *The Atonement: Its Meaning and Significance*; V. Taylor, *The Atonement in New Testament Teaching* and *The Cross of Christ*.

—ROBERT E. BURKS

• **Atonement/Expiation in the Old Testament.** Generally, the restoration of a broken relationship between God and people.

The English word atonement originally meant "at-one-ment," that is being "at-one" with or in harmony with another. Two additional terms, propitiation and expiation, suggest ways whereby atonement can be achieved, either by propitiating or appeasing divine anger caused by human sin, or by expiating or making satisfaction for the offense that caused the broken relationship.

The OT word *kipper,* translated atone, reconcile, purge or the like, probably means "cover," though the meanings of "remove" and "purify" are also possible. The word appears in the name *kapporet,* the cover of the sacred Ark of the Covenant containing the tables with the Ten Commandments (Exod 25:17; 37:6). Some translations render the term "mercy seat" with special reference to the atonement (KJV, RSV). The expression *yôm kippurîm* ("day of atonement") refers to the tenth day of the seventh month in the OT and the Jewish calendar, a day of judgment and cleansing (Lev 23:27; Lev 16).

The word *kipper* occurred in a number of different contexts. It meant sometimes to appease the anger of an opponent such as Esau (Gen 32:20), or a king (Prov 16:14). Atonement could be achieved through a gift (Prov 21:14), or by divine pardon (Deut 21:8; 2 Chr 30:18; Ps 78:38; cf. Jer 18:23). Elsewhere, the idea of "cover" described the working of atonement (Exod 25:17; 37:6; cf. Isa 28:18). "Cleanse" or "purify" represented suitable translations in other instances (Num 35:33; Isa 6:7). Even punishment upon the guilty could bring atonement (2 Sam 21:3-9; Isa 27:9). But above all, atonement was associated with blood sacrifices in OT religion.

Atonement by sacrifice was made for the priest and the priest's family (Exod 29:36; Lev 10:17), for the Levites (Num 8:21), for the sanctuary and its furnishings (Exod 29:37; 30:10; Lev 16:16, 18, 33), for the people (Exod 30:15; Lev 4:20; 8:34; 16:30), for the individual sinner (Lev 1:4; Num 15:28), for the new ("impure") mother (Lev 12:7), for the leprous person just healed (Lev 14:18-20), for the unclean house (Lev 14:53), for the unclean person (Lev 15:15), over the sacrificial animal (Lev 16:10), for the souls of the people (Lev 17:11), and even for one's self (Num 31:50).

In every case atonement was achieved by sacrificial animals of various types and value, according to the requirement of the ritual and the wealth of the one instructed to bring the animal. According to Lev 17:11, the blood, symbolizing life, accomplished the atonement, with the result that priest and sanctuary once again become operational, and harmony was restored between God and people or between individuals. OT theologians have concluded that since God had ordained the means of the atonement for the purpose of restoring relationships (Lev 16:6-10; 2 Chr 30:18-20; Isa 6:7), the sacrifices themselves did not possess any inherent magical quality for removing sin, nor did they represent a payment to appease a displeased God. In other words, atonement in the OT was based less upon expiation and propitiation and more upon repentance, forgiveness, cleansing, and restoration. However, in a few places the idea of expiating past misdeeds seems to have assured atonement (2 Sam 21:3-7; Isa 27:9). Even the idea of propitiating or appeasing an angry person can be found (Gen 32:20). But propitiating or appeasing divine anger as a form of atonement did not play a role in the OT.

See also ATONEMENT, DAY OF; REDEMPTION IN THE OLD TESTAMENT; SIN.

—NIELS-ERIK A. ANDREASEN

• **Authoritative Teaching.** *Authoritative Teaching* is a tractate from the writings called the NAG HAMMADI library. It is a homily that sets forth the origin, condition, and fate of the soul. The story begins with the "invisible soul of righteousness" being cast from the heavens into a body. In this embodied state, she is related to a material soul and thus subject to the allurements of the material world. Numerous metaphors and images are used to describe the condition of the embodied soul. She is a prostitute who drinks the wine of debauchery. She is ill and feeble. She lives in a house of poverty, hungry and thirsty. She is a contender in the contest of life, a fighter against hostile forces. She is compared to wheat that when mixed with chaff is contaminated and worthless.

The soul's redemption is affected by her bridegroom (in other documents, the bridegroom or brother is the male counterpart of the soul to whom she was joined in her heavenly life; cf. EXEGESIS ON THE SOUL and GOSPEL OF PHILIP). He feeds her and applies the WORD (LOGOS/WORD) to her eyes as a medicine. This strengthens her and keeps her in contact with her heavenly roots. The soul triumphs over her adversaries because of her knowledge. "And as for those who contend with us . . . we are to be victorious over their ignorance through our knowledge, since we have already known the Inscrutable One from whom we have come forth." Renunciation of matter is also a necessary part of the salvation process. "But the soul . . . realized that sweet passions are transitory. . . . She went away from them (and) she entered into a new conduct."

The soul's final victory, like her struggle, is depicted with metaphors: receiving rest from labor, eating a heavenly banquet, and reclining in a bridal chamber. Most of the metaphors in *Authoritative Teaching* are common in Hellenistic literature, but two are somewhat distinctive: the extended metaphor of the soul as prey for evil fishermen (cf. Hab 1:13-17), and the "dealers in bodies" who cannot "do any business" with the soul because she has her own "invisible, spiritual body."

Near the end of the piece stands a vigorous polemic against "senseless ones" who do not seek after God nor inquire about worship, but persecute the pious. They are more wicked than the pagans, because the pagans give charity and know that God exists, even though they have not heard the word preached. This is one of the few clues to the document's historical setting, but the identity of these opponents is difficult to establish.

Authoritative Teaching is not a clearly Gnostic work. It does contain some typical Gnostic ideas, themes, and imagery: the divine soul imprisoned in an alien world; the created material world as evil and matter as the source of evil; the state of the soul in the world as intoxicated, forgetful, blind, and ignorant; and the necessity of knowledge and ascetic practice for salvation. But absent in *Authoritative Teaching* is a Gnostic myth explaining the origins of the evil world and of the human condition. Strikingly dissimilar to the transcendent gnostic God who stands opposed to the physical word is the statement in *Authoritative Teaching* that nothing came into being apart from the will of God. Even the great contest in this world between "things that come into being" and "the one that (always) exists" was designed by the Father to reveal his wealth and glory. This is distinctively non-Gnostic, but may reflect a transformation of classical Gnostic DUALISM in response to criticism.

Neither is *Authoritative Teaching* a clearly Christian or Jewish document. There is no mention of Christ nor any quotation of scripture. There are some expressions which recall NT language: the evangelists preaching the word, the wine of debauchery (Eph 5:18), principality or authority or the powers (1 Cor 15:24; Eph 1:21), the spiritual body (1 Cor 15:44), the true shepherd, children of the devil, and the secure storehouse. But whether these definitely establish Christian authorship is debatable.

Treatises on the soul are well-known in the second to fourth centuries C.E. from Christian authors (e.g., Clement of Alexandria, Tertullian, Augustine) and pagan philosophers (Porphyry, Iamblichus, Plotinus). Some of the terminology in *Authoritative Teaching* is found in Platonic discussions on the soul (e.g., the distinctions between and functions of the spiritual soul, material soul, and rational soul), but the document is non-philosophical in style. *Authoritative Teaching* bears special similarities with HERMETIC LITERATURE on the soul, especially in its clear doctrine of the soul's choice between the way of life and the way of death. "For death and life are set before everyone. Whichever of these two they wish, then, they will choose for themselves." Three hermetic compositions are included in codex VI of the Nag Hammadi library where *Authoritative Teaching* is located.

The word *logos* used in the title of the tractate can mean "teaching" or "doctrine." It occurs twice within the text itself in such a sense and is used thus in several contemporary treatises. But the Greek word *logos* is also used in the text to refer to a medicine that is applied to the soul's blind eyes. It may be this meaning to which the author refers in the title.

Authoritative Teaching bears similarities to other Nag Hammadi tractates. *Exegesis on the Soul* is a similar personified description of the female soul's plight in the world based on sexual metaphors. The TEACHING OF SILVANUS is an early Christian wisdom text containing moral instruction of ascetic flavor often addressed to the soul.

See also GNOSTICISM; NAG HAMMADI; SEXTUS, SENTENCES OF; THOMAS THE CONTENDER, BOOK OF.

Bibliography. R. van den Broek, "The Authentikos Logos: A New Document of Christian Platonism," *VC* 33 (1979): 260-86; G. W. MacRae, "A Nag Hammadi Tractate on the Soul," *Ex Orbe Religionum: Studia Geo Widengren (Studies in the History of Religions*; Supplements to *Numen* 21); G. W. MacRae and D. M. Parrott, "Authoritative Teaching," *The Nag Hammadi Library in English*, ed. J. M. Robinson; D. M. Parrott, ed. *Nag Hammadi Codices V.2-5 and VI with Papyrus Berolinensis 8502, 1 and 4* (*NHS* 11).

—CAROL D. C. HOWARD

• **Authority of the Bible.** *See* BIBLE, AUTHORITY OF

• **Avenger.** *See* LAMECH; VENGANCE/AVENGER

• **Azariah.** [az'uh-ri"uh] Azariah, "Yahweh helped," is the Hebrew name of no fewer than thirteen men in the Bible, most of whom are from Judea, from the eleventh to the third century B.C.E., unknown outside the Bible: (1) king of Judah, also called Uzziah (2 Kgs 14:21; 15:1, 7, 17, 23, 27; 1 Chr 3:12); (2) two sons of King JEHOSHAPHAT of Judea (2 Chr 21:2); (3) SOLOMON's official, the son of Zadok the Priest (1 Kgs 4:2); (4) Solomon's royal officer and governor, the son of Nathan (1 Kgs 4:5; 2 Chr 23:1); (5) a grandfather and grandson of the lineage of Levi (1 Chr 6:9-10; Ezra 7:3; 2 Chr 29:12; Neh 8:7; 1 Esdr 9:48); (6) a commander who emigrated to Egypt, son of Hoshaiah (Jer 42:1; 43:1-2); (7) four (or five) chiefs or officials: son of Ethan (1 Chr 2:8); son of Jehu (1 Chr 2:38-39); son of Maaseiah (Neh 3:23-24; 7:7?); a prince of Judah (Neh 12:33); (8) the Hebrew name of Abednego (Dan 1:6-7, 11, 19; 2:17; 1 Macc 2:59; PrAzar 1:65).

—JAMES F. STRANGE

• **Azariah, Prayer of.** The pair of psalms called the Prayer of Azariah and the Song of the Three Young Men appears in the Greek and Latin versions of the Book of DANIEL as an insertion between Dan 3:23 and 3:24. In it, the three young heroes of the Jewish faith demonstrate by their own words their extraordinary piety and faithfulness. That the text had a life of its own quite apart from Dan 3 is, however, suggested by the irrelevance of much of what is said to the situation of the lads as they strolled about in the fiery furnace. Furthermore, one of the earliest examples of the Hebrew/Aramaic text of the Book of Daniel, found among the DEAD SEA SCROLLS (*1QDb*), does not include the Prayer. Therefore, like the stories of SUSANNA and the Elders, BEL AND THE DRAGON, and the Qumran text, *The Prayer of Nabonidus* (*4QPrNab*), it has simply to be seen as part of a larger and, to Jews and most Protestants, extrabiblical Daniel cycle that existed in antiquity.

The Prayer opens with a stage setting. The three youths walk about in the flames of the fiery furnace "singing hymns and blessing God." Then one of the three, Azariah (i.e., Abednego; cf. Dan 1:7), offers a prayer (vv. 3-22) expressed in the form of a collective psalm of lament comparable to Pss 44, 74, 79, and 80. The prayer contains a benediction and ascription of truth and justice to God (vv. 3-5); a confession of national sin (vv. 6-10); and an appeal for mercy and deliverance (vv. 11-22). Recent commentators argue that the Prayer, like the rest of this addition to Dan, had a Hebrew original. Some also contend that the reference to the cessation of the TEMPLE cults in v. 15 suggests a date of composition coincidental with the canonical Dan itself, namely, during the period of the desecration of the Temple (167–164 B.C.E.) by the Syrian tyrant, Antiochus IV Epiphanes.

Following Azariah's prayer, a short prose account (vv. 23-27) details the destruction of the executioners by the heat of the fire and the arrival of the ANGEL of the Lord to drive the flames away from the three young men in the furnace. The question of how Azariah could have survived long enough to offer his prayer unless the angel had first done its work is answered by the hypothesis that the prose account was the introduction to the ensuing Song in the tradition of Dan 3 known to the Greek translators, and that the Prayer was rather clumsily inserted before the introduction at a later time.

In the Song (vv. 28-68), the three young Jews lift their voices together in a lovely hymn of praise reminiscent of Pss 103:19-22 and 148. The first portion of the psalm (vv. 28-34), built on the sentence "Blessed art thou, O Lord" (known in the western liturgical tradition as *Benedictus es Domine*), addresses Yahweh directly with a paean of praise for God's kingly power and glory. The second part (vv. 35-68), structured around the cry "Bless the Lord" (the beloved canticle *Benedicte* of Anglican morning prayer), calls upon all creatures from the heavens, angels, and celestial bodies right down to whales, birds, and people, to bless and praise God. Only at the end of the psalm do the singers come around to the subject of the surrounding narrative context. Even then, the poem reinterprets that context, for the singers celebrate God's power to deliver not simply from a fiery furnace, but from the flames of HELL itself: "Bless the Lord, Hananiah, Azariah, and Mishael, / sing praise to him and highly exalt him forever; / for he has rescued us from Hades and saved us from the hand of death, / and delivered us from the midst of the burning fiery furnace . . . " (v. 66).

See also APOCRYPHAL LITERATURE; DANIEL.

Bibliography. C. A. Moore, *Daniel, Esther, and Jeremiah: the Additions*.

—W. SIBLEY TOWNER

• **Azazel.** *See* ATONEMENT

Baal, the storm-god, wielding a club (right hand) and a thunder bolt.

• **Baal.** [bay'uhl, also bah-ahl'] A Canaanite fertility god. The word *baal* comes from a semitic stem that means "lord," "master," "owner," or "husband," and was used in reference both to people and to gods. The term especially denoted the ownership of a locality or territory. In reference to ancient Near Eastern gods, baal could be used in a variety of ways. The term was used both as a common noun and as a proper name, and, in many cases it is difficult to determine which function the writers intended. Used as a common noun, baal conveyed the idea of "owner" or "possessor" and referred to the territory over which the god was thought to have control. Its usage as a proper name is most clearly seen in the Canaanite god, Baal. Because baal was used in reference to other gods and because there were many localized baals or baal cults the task of interpretation is often difficult. The widespread usage of the word is reflected in such names as Baal-peor (Num 25:1-9), Baal-gad (Josh 11:17), Baal-berith (Judg 9:4), Baal-hamon (Cant 8:11), Baal-hazor (2 Sam 13:23), Baal-hermon (Judg 3:3), Baal-zebub (2 Kgs 1:2-16), and Baal-zephon (Exod 14:2).

The Canaanite god, Baal, is referred to in both the OT and the Ras Shamra/Ugaritic texts. The Ras Shamra tablets, which date to about the fifteenth century B.C.E., describe Baal as a weather or storm god. The storm god's role is reflected in the sculptured representations of Baal who is featured as a man equipped as a warrior, with a thunderbolt as a spear in his left hand, an uplifted mace in his right hand, a short kilt around his waist and thighs, and a helmet with horns. The horns were symbolic reminders of the bull, Baal's sacred animal and symbol of fertility, and of Baal's role as the god of fertility. Baal was one of a number of gods comprising the Canaanite pantheon. He is identified as the son of Dagon, the fertility god of the Philistines (Judg 16:23; 1 Sam 5:2); however, EL was generally recognized as the father of the gods of the pantheon. Baal is also referred to as Hadad or Baal-Hadad, though Hadad, a semitic storm god, and Baal are usually recognized as separate deities. As a storm god, Baal was described as "the rider of the clouds" reminiscent of a description of Yahweh (Ps 68:4). Baal was also called "the Prince." Baal was associated with Mount Zaphon. In the Ras Shamra texts, Anath, described as "the virgin Anath," was both sister and consort of Baal.

According to the Ugaritic texts two stories played an important role in shaping Canaanite thought about Baal and his role and achievements as a god. These were the stories of Baal and Yamm, the Sea, and Baal and Mot, Death. In these accounts Baal is featured as a god who faced extremely powerful destructive forces, confronted the challenge at hand, appeared to be near defeat at the heart of the confrontation, but in the end emerged victorious.

The story of Baal's encounter with the dragon, Yamm, highlights Baal's role as a god who confronted and defeated the monster who was the source of chaos. The theme of chaos, prevalent in many accounts from the ancient Near East, also appears in Gen 1:1-2 in which the Spirit of God, the ruaḥ Elohim, established order in the midst of chaos. In the Baal-Yamm account Baal emerged victorious and Yamm was confined to his realm, the Sea.

The story of Baal's encounter with Mot, Death, highlights Baal's role as a god of fertility. The story features the cycle the Canaanites believed Baal passed through each year. In the encounter Baal was defeated by Mot, sent to the underworld—the realm of the dead—and eventually reappeared victorious over Mot. The various features of the cycle corresponded to what happened annually in nature: Baal's descent to the underworld corresponded to that period in which rain did not fall and the land was not productive; Baal's reappearance corresponded to the coming of spring, that time of the year when the rains returned and the land became fertile and productive again. Accounts of this nature provided the focus for the celebrations of an annual New Year festival, a kind of festival apparently celebrated by many cultures in the ancient Near East.

Discussion about the installation of a window in Baal's palace further highlights Baal's role as the god of rain and fertility. The window or windows of his palace was the means by which Baal sent the rains. A large number of clay offering stands designed with windows have been found in excavations at OT sites in Palestine. Many of the stands were most likely designed as miniature localized palaces of the Canaanite god Baal.

While the Ras Shamra texts provide the most valuable information about Baal from the Canaanites themselves, the OT provides valuable information concerning the influence of Baal worship on Israel. The numerous references in the OT to Baal, the baals, the names of other gods associated with Baal, names compounded with Baal, or other features of Baalism suggest that Baal worship had a significant impact on the ancient Israelites. However, since the term baal meant "owner" or "master" and could be used in reference to any god, one cannot always determine if the name refers to the Canaanite Baal, some other god, or even Yahweh, the God of Israel.

According to the Book of Judges, Baal worship was prominent in Palestine during the period of the Israelite settlement. The Israelites were attracted to the baals (Judg 2:11, 13; 3:7), the Ashtaroth (Judg 2:13, the plural of the Canaanite goddess Astarte who was the goddess of fertility and war), and the Asheroth (Judg 3:7, the plural of the Canaanite fertility goddess ASHERAH). "The baals" most likely refer to the many localized baals, or localized expressions of Baal. Each community had its own baal or baal cult, such as the cult of "Baal of the Covenant" at SHECHEM (Judg 9:4). Since the Israelites and Canaanites lived side by side in many communities (Judg 1:27-35) the impact of the local baal cults was significant. The influence of Baal's associate Anath, goddess of war, is reflected in the account of the judgeship of Shamgar, who is identified as the "son of Anath" (Judg 3:31).

One of the greatest surges of Baal worship came during the reign of AHAB. Prompted by his wife JEZEBEL, Ahab initiated a cultural reform movement, the focal point of which was the Tyrian Baal, the god of Jezebel's homeland (1 Kgs 16:31). The cultural reform, which was in essence a missionary program, included the construction of a temple for Baal (1 Kgs 16:32), and the importing of Baal missionaries, that is, the prophets of Baal and Asherah (1 Kgs 18:19). The statement that the prophets of Baal and Asherah ate "at Jezebel's table" (v. 19c) probably indicates this was a government-funded program.

The worship of Baal was certainly present in the Southern Kingdom as well as the Northern Kingdom. A "house of Baal" was located in Jerusalem during the time of Athaliah (2 Kgs 11:18). AHAZ "made molten images for Baal" (2 Chr 28:2) and worshiped at the "high places" (2 Kgs 16:4; 2 Chr 28:4), Canaanite worship sites. While HEZEKIAH attempted to remove the Canaanite elements of worship (2 Kgs 18:4), his son MANASSEH reintroduced them (2 Kgs 21:3). Baalism was one of the major targets of JOSIAH's reform. The reform included the removal of the vessels used in worship rituals for Baal and ASHERAH (2 Kgs 23:4) as well as a purge of the high places and their personnel (2 Kgs 23:5, 8, 9, 13-15, 19-20).

More than anyone else, it was Israel's prophets who recognized and addressed the problem of Baal worship. ELIJAH, engaged in a confrontation with the prophets of Baal on Mount Carmel (1 Kgs 18), Hosea (Hos 2:16-17) and JEREMIAH (Jer 2:23) spoke out against the Canaanizing effect Baal worship had on the worship of Yahweh, the true God of Israel. The prophet Elisha sponsored the bloody revolution of Jehu, in which Baal worshipers were slaughtered wholesale.

Baal worship most likely included a variety of rituals such as a ritual dance in which the participants limped around the altar (1 Kgs 18:26); the custom of cutting oneself with swords and lances until blood gushed out (1 Kgs 18:28); the wearing of a special vestment or garb (2 Kgs 10:22); ritual prostitution in which the males of the families of Baal worshipers engaged in sexual intercourse with sacred prostitutes in order to insure the fertility of family, flocks, and fields (Amos 2:7b-8a); and the burning of incense (Jer 7:9; 11:13).

See also EL; IDOLATRY; UGARIT, RAS SHAMRA.

Bibliography. W. F. Albright, *Yahweh and the Gods of Canaan*; P. C. Craigie, *Ugarit and the Old Testament*; F. E. Eakin, Jr., *The Religion and Culture of Israel*; J. Gray, *The Canaanites*; H. Ringgren, *Israelite Religion* and *Religions of the Ancient Near East*; G. E. Wright, *Biblical Archaeology*.

—LAMOINE DEVRIES

• **Baal-zebub/Baal-zebul.** [bay'uhl-zee"buhb/bay'uhl-zee"buhl] Baal-zebub appears in 2 Kgs 1:1-4 as the name of the god of the Philistine city of EKRON. King Ahaziah of Israel used it as an oracle, asking it whether he would recover from a fall. The word means "Lord of the flies." Some scholars have taken this seriously, arguing that the god may have been represented by a fly, or that it might, like some Greek divinities, have controlled the flies that hang around animal sacrifices. However, most believe that this is a derogatory term used by the writer of 2 Kings to ridicule the foreign god. Some also think that the deity's true name was Baal-zebul, which means either "Baal the Mighty" or "Baal of the Exalted Abode."

According to Mark 3:22, Jesus was once accused of being possessed by Beelzebul, who is identified as "prince of the demons" (the parallels in Matt 12:24 and Luke 11:15 seem to suggest that Jesus uses Beelzebul to do his bidding). In what is an undoubtedly historical datum from Jesus' life, the scribes advanced the charge of demon possession as a means of explaining Jesus' reputation as a miracle worker. Jesus responded, according to all the Synoptics, that SATAN would not oppose himself, and so the scribes' explanation was illogical. The name "Beelzebul" appears here and nowhere else in extant literature. However, the DEAD SEA SCROLLS and other contemporary Jewish literature use names such as Beliar and Mastema for Satan and his chief demons; Beelzebul probably should be understood the same way.

—RICHARD B. VINSON

• **Baale-judah.** *See* BAB EDH-DHRA'

• **Bab edh-Dhra'.** [bahb-ehd'druh] An important archaeological site in the DEAD SEA valley, located halfway up the eastern side of the Lisan. Bab edh-Dhra', Arabic for "gate of the arm," is located ca. 550 feet above the level of the Dead Sea, on a terrace that is some thirteen miles west-northwest of Kerak, Jordan (PLATE 7). Its remains include a walled town from the third millennium B.C. and a huge cemetery whose tombs (shaft tombs, charnel houses, and tumuli) span the entire Early Bronze Age, from ca. 3300–

2050 B.C.E.

The site's history has been reconstructed as follows: EB IA (ca. 3250), use of location by pastoral nomads; EB IB (ca. 3100), beginning of permanent settlement; EB II–III (ca. 3000), development of the walled town, with its apogee in EB III (ca. 2750–2350); EB IV (ca. 2350), reoccupation by different settlers after the town's destruction at the end of EB III, followed by site abandonment ca. 2200. Thereafter, the site was unoccupied for a millennium, until its environs witnessed resettlement in the Iron Age and the Roman and Byzantine periods. In its heydey, the stone-and-mudbrick city wall of Bab edh-Dhra‘ was over twenty-two feet thick.

Bab edh-Dhra‘ was discovered by A. Mallon, W. F. Albright, and M. G. Kyle in 1924. P. Lapp led three seasons of excavation in the cemetery and town site from 1965 to 1967. Following their 1973 survey of the southeastern plain of the Dead Sea, in which four additional Early Bronze sites (Numeira, Safi, Feifa, and Khanazir) were discovered south of Bab edh-Dhra‘, W. Rast and T. Schaub directed four more seasons of excavation at the cemetery and walled town (1975, 1977, 1979, and 1981). Though speculative, the site of Bab edh-Dhra‘ has been linked, in one way or another, with SODOM.

—GERALD L. MATTINGLY

• **Babel, Tower of.** [bay′buhl] A tall structure built of brick and bitumen identified as a tower or fortress and situated in Shinar, a section of Babylon. According to Gen 11, the construction of this tower led to God's judgment: scattering the people and confusing their languages.

When humans first populated the earth, the biblical narrative relates, there was only one language. The people migrated to Shinar (the Tigris-Euphrates basin) and settled there.

Seeking both fame and community, the people decided to build a city with a tower ascending to the heavens. Displeased and convinced that plots even more disconcerting would be forthcoming, the Lord caused them to speak in many different languages and dispersed the people throughout the earth. "Therefore its name was called Babel, because there the LORD confused the language of all the earth" (Gen 11:9).

Babel is the Hebrew name for Babylon; in the Assyrian and Babylonian traditions it means "gate of god." It seems likely that the biblical author intended a taunt of Babylon, since the author makes a satirical play on words between babel and confusion (Heb. *bālal*).

Towers in Babylon, called *ziggurats,* were commonplace. *Ziggurat* is from the Akkadian word meaning "temple tower." A ziggurat was a stepped temple with a rectangular base. A sanctuary was located on its ground level and also on the top, where sacred images were kept and the god might appear.

Although ziggurats were common in Mesopotamian cities, the greatest and most famous was actually called "the tower of Babylon." *Etemenanki,* as it was known, means "house that is the foundation of heaven and earth." A seventh century B.C.E. reconstruction of an earlier ziggurat, this temple tower was rebuilt by King Nabopolassar of Babylon and dedicated to Babylon's chief deity, Marduk. There is much debate on the exact location of the tower of Babel, but most writers agree with the traditional view of the Jews and Arabs, who have identified the temple of Nabu (Nebo) in the city of Borsippa as the infamous tower.

As with the other stories found in Gen 1–11, the historical character of the Babel narrative is the subject of frequent debate. Many scholars believe the story is mythological. However, to dwell upon the historicity issue is to miss the point of the author. One should ask instead why the story is included in the Bible. What does the author want to say?

Beyond the mythology/literal history debate stands theology. The account presents a tragic picture of humanity's continued sin and rebellion against God, although the specific sin is unclear. Pride or self-exaltation perhaps, may have been the sin; that is, the desire to build a tower to the heavens may have been an Adamic lust to "be like God." Or perhaps humanity's sin was seeking fame, security, and community outside a concern for the one true God. Some have suggested that rebellion, or refusal to obey God's command to "fill the earth" was the transgression. Others suggest that exaggerated anxiety, fear and distrust rather than arrogance, may have been the problem.

In any event, God's judgment was provoked against sinful humanity with the consequence being linguistic and political confusion. With this event, history shifts. Brought on by repeated divine displeasure over the continual sin of humankind, even by the descendants of NOAH, God decides to deal with a chosen people of whom ABRAHAM (Gen 12) was to be the father.

Bibliography. T. Jacobsen, "Babel," *IDB*; D. F. Payne and T. G. Pinches, "Babel, Tower of," *ISBE*; "Babel," *HBD*.

—J. RANDALL O'BRIEN

• **Babylonian Captivity.** *See* EXILE

Babylonian tablet (ca. 1800 B.C.E.)

Courtesy of the Eisenberg Museum of Biblical Archaeology, Southern Baptist Theological Seminary.

• **Babylonian Empire.** [bab′uh-loh″nee-uhn] Ancient Babylonia takes its name from its capital city, Babylon. Though often used to refer in general to ancient Mesopotamian culture, "Babylonia" is actually a late name for this region. By the time the Old Babylonian empire reached its zenith under HAMMURABI (1792–1750 B.C.E.; the dates followed here are those given in *CAH*[3] unless otherwise noted), the empires of Sumer and Akkad had long since perished. Geographically, Babylonia occupied the southern portion of Mesopotamia in what is today modern Iraq. At its greatest, the empire stretched some 900 mi. from the Persian Gulf in the southeast to Assyria in the northwest. Its eastern boundary was Elam, and its southern and western boundaries, the Arabian Desert.

Beginning with the reign of Sumuabum (1894–1881 B.C.E.), the Babylonian Empire lasted, with major interruptions, nearly 2,000 years. It is customary for scholars to divide this period into three major subdivisions: Old Babylonian, Middle Babylonian, and Neo-Babylonian.

The Old Babylonian period began after the destruction

of Ur III (ca. 2113–2006) and reached its height under Hammurabi, the sixth king of the AMORITE dynasty, who was able to rule his kingdom from the capital city of Babylon. Remembered chiefly as the "great law giver" (though his laws are not the oldest known), his code consists of some 3,500 lines of cuneiform characters. This code and other literary finds make his the best attested period of the Babylonian Empire. But during his reign Hammurabi was beset with a long series of wars, and after his death political decline set in. By 1595 B.C.E., the Hittites had defeated the Babylonians and paved the way for control in the region by another group of people known as the Kassites, who came from the mountains east of Babylonia. The latter were able to establish a dynasty that lasted nearly 500 years (1595–1150 B.C.E.). This period in Babylonian history is something of a "Dark Age," due to the lack of written documents. It was finally brought to an end by the Elamites who destroyed the Kassite dynasty around 1156 B.C.E. In the struggle that followed the Kassite defeat, a new dynasty of Babylonian kings was established, of whom the most important was Nebuchadrezzar I (1124–1103 B.C.E.). Nebuchadrezzar was able to defeat the Elamites and hold at bay the Assyrians, who had formed an independent empire during the preceding "Dark Age." This "Middle Babylonian" period, however, lasted only until the end of the second millennium B.C.E., when a three-way struggle for control of the region began among the Assyrians, the Arameans, and the Chaldeans.

Ultimately, the Assyrians emerged victorious, and from the ninth century B.C.E. to the rise of Nabopolassar (626–602 B.C.E.), Babylonia was primarily under their control. During this period, Babylon was destroyed by Ashurbanipal around 650 B.C.E.. The son and successor of Nabopolassar was NEBUCHADREZZAR II (605–562B.C.E.), under whose rule the "Neo-Babylonian" empire reached its glory. He restored Babylon as a center of trade, built the famous "hanging gardens," and rebuilt many temples. The achievements of his rule are reflected in the thousands of administrative texts found at such cities as Sippar, Babylon, and Uruk. But perhaps he is remembered most for his defeat of Judah and Jerusalem in 587/86 B.C.E. The last Babylonian ruler was Nabonidus (555–39 B.C.E.) who spent most of his time away from Babylon where his son and coregent, Belshazzar, acted as king.

After 539 B.C.E., Babylonia was never again an independent state. Controlled first by the Persians then the Greeks, its last rulers, the Seleucids, abandoned Babylon sometime before the time of Christ.

The history of ancient Mesopotamia first began to come to light in the sixteenth century C.E. when travelers in the region began to make accidental discoveries. By the end of the nineteenth and first part of the twentieth centuries, major excavations had been conducted in Babylonia by French, British, American, and German teams. Such cities as Babylon, Nineveh, NIMRUD, Nippur, Uruk, UR and Senkereh had either been excavated or at least identified. While major architectural remains were found, such as temples and palaces, the most important discovery was tens of thousands of clay tablets. Dating from the oldest to the latest periods, these texts deal with every aspect of Mesopotamian culture and constitute the most important source available for reconstructing the history of that part of the world.

Written in CUNEIFORM (Latin for "wedge shape"), the history of the decipherment of these texts is a story in and of itself involving many scholars in a long and arduous task. Part of the difficulty lay in the fact that the texts are composed in three different systems of cuneiform writing: Old Persian, Elamite, and Babylonian. The Babylonian language itself is one of two main dialects of Akkadian (Assyrian is the other) which is one of the earliest known semitic languages. Akkadian was the common language of Babylonia until it was replaced by Aramaic in the third century B.C.E. The key that unlocked the mysteries of these languages is the trilingual inscription on the BEHISTUN Rock in what is known today as Iran. Dating to the time of Darius I (522–486 B.C.E.), the inscription is twenty-five feet high and fifty feet wide. Composed in all three of the cuneiform systems, it was copied by Sir Henry Rawlinson between 1835 and 1847.

One of the most difficult problems faced by all historians of Babylonian culture is chronology. Absolute chronology extends back only to the eighth century B.C.E. The issues are complex and filled with many uncertainties. The main sources available for trying to reconstruct dates are the many texts. These include astronomical observations such as the sixty-third tablet of the astrological series Enuma Anum Enlil. This tablet preserves observations of the planet Venus made during the reign of the tenth king of the Old Babylonian period, Ammisaduqa (1646–1626 B.C.E.). Unfortunately, the observations allow for three different dates during this general period. Thus, working backwards, scholars have arrived at three possibilities for the beginning of the reign of Hammurabi: 1856 (48), 1792, 1736 (28) B.C.E. Most scholars seem to favor the median date, but the issue has not been settled.

Other primary sources relevant to the chronology of the period are king lists covering most of the Babylonian period and date lists which contain year names based upon some significant event of the preceding year. But most of these texts are damaged, some exceedingly so, and the chronology of Babylonian kings depends in part on synchronisms with other king lists, particularly those of the Assyrians. In fact, during the second millennium B.C.E., it is Assyrian chronology that provides the basis for Babylonian dates.

Another important body of information comes from royal inscriptions that also date from the earliest to the latest periods. These inscriptions can vary from a few signs on votive offerings to prisms containing hundreds of lines. It can only be hoped that as more evidence becomes available, the murky chronological problem can be cleared up.

These tablets, which deal with a wide variety of subjects, are the best window through which to see and understand Babylonian culture. Among these are omen texts containing prognostications of many types; legal documents, both private and public; law codes; administrative texts listing transactions of palaces and temples; and many types of letters used for both commercial and international activities. Among the best known texts are those dealing with legendary heroes and religious themes. Included in the former is the famous story of Gilgamesh. Usually referred to as the *Gilgamesh Epic,* it is the story of a man's search for immortality. The parallels in this story to that of Noah in the Bible are well known. Other Babylonian epic texts include the story of Atrahasis, another hero of the flood, and the story of Etana, king of Kish who flew on an eagle to heaven to find a plant that would enable him to have a son.

Of the known religious texts, the most famous is the *Enuma Elish.* While the date of this myth is debated, most scholars place it in the Old Babylonian period. The story is contained on seven tablets, each containing between 115 and 170 lines. While the larger theme of the myth is Marduk's defeat of Tiamat and his ascendancy in the Babylonian pantheon, it contains a creation story with pronounced parallels to the biblical story in Gen 1.

In the realm of arts, the Babylonians excelled in only two mediums: monumental architecture and small-scale engravings on precious and semi-precious stones, particularly cylinder seals. The remains of palaces and temples at such sites as Babylon and Ur are clear evidence of their architectural achievements. Especially noteworthy are the ziggurats, which were stepped structures that reached heights of seventy feet or more. On the top of these buildings was the sanctuary of the god. Such structures form the background to the story of Babel in Genesis. The basic building material for these structures was mud brick, which was sometimes decorated with plaster or colored clay cone mosaics. Glazes were also used as evidenced by the famous Ishtar gate at Babylon from the time of Nebuchadrezzar II.

The cylinder seals, of which thousands have been found, are often engraved with intricate designs of monsters, animals, and ornaments as well as deities and worshippers. These seals were used to ''sign'' documents.

Economically, Babylonia depended primarily upon agriculture. This required the building of an intricate irrigation system which was tended by small freeholders or tenants who were held responsible for the day-to-day operations. However, most of the land was owned by the king and the temple priests. The major agricultural products included wheat and barley and a variety of vegetables. Animals such as goats and sheep were also kept as well as cattle and oxen. The horse seems to have been used primarily for military purposes.

While much of Babylonian society is still unknown, it was organized around three major institutions: kingship, the city, and the temple. While more is known about Assyrian kingship than its Babylonian counterpart, the latter was held to be of divine origin. The king ruled from Babylon where the god Marduk was worshipped. Babylonian kings surrounded themselves with a large number of officials, including the priests who were able to achieve positions of wealth and power.

The major cities of Babylonia known from both texts and/or archaeological discoveries include Eridu, Kish, Ur, Uruk, Larsa, Sippar, Nippur, Shuruppak, and of course, Babylon. The histories of the individual cities vary, with some surviving for longer periods of time than others. Ur, for example, has a two thousand year history as does Babylon. On the other hand, Eridu, Isin and Larsa disappeared before or during the Old Babylonian period. The survival of a particular city not only depended upon the politics of the day but the importance of its palace and temple as well as its water supply. Generally, the cities were divided into quarters each with its own gate, and were inhabited by such people as farmers and craftsmen. In certain cases, a city could obtain a special legal status from the king and be exempt from such things as taxes, military service and forced labor (corvée).

During the Old Babylonian period, the temple was a major institution organized as a redistributive system. In addition to cultic functions, the temple personnel also administered oaths, established standards for weights and measures, and even determined interest rates. In the name of the god(s), the temples exerted great influence in the empire and were centers of economic power. The building and funding of temples was a major part of every king's administration.

The thousands of clay tablets and impressive archaeological remains clearly show that the Babylonian empire was a rich and complex society. With roots extending back into ancient Sumer, the Babylonians made many contributions to the world. Among these are its astronomical and mathematical knowledge, the twenty-four hour day and the seven day week. With the achievements of such kings as Hammurabi in the Old period and Nebuchadrezzar II in the New, the Babylonian Empire can rightly lay claim to one of the world's truly great ancient civilizations.

See also RELIGIONS OF THE ANCIENT NEW EAST.

Bibliography. C. J. Gadd, ''The Cities of Babylonia,'' *CAH* I/2A (1971): 93-144, ''Babylonia c. 2120–1800 B.C.,'' *CAH* I/2B (1971): 595-643, ''Hammurabi And The End of His Dynasty,'' *CAH* II/1(1973): 176-227, and ''Assyria and Babylon c. 1370–1300,'' *CAH* II/2A (1975): 21-48; A. L. Oppenheim, ''Assyria And Babylonia,'' *IDB*; M. B. Rowtan, ''Ancient Western Asia,'' *CAH* I/1 (1970): 193-239; R. Cambell Thompson, ''The New Babylonian Empire,'' *CAH* III (1960): 206-25 and ''The Influence of Babylonia,'' *CAH* III (1960): 226-50; D. J. Wiseman, ''Assyria and Babylonia c. 1200-1000 B.C.,'' *CAH* II/2A (1975): 443-81.

—JOHN C. H. LAUGHLIN

• **Baker.** A person engaged in the baking of FOOD, especially bread. Usually, women performed this task (Lev 26:26; 1 Sam 8:13; 30:24), but men might do it as well (Gen 19:3; Gen 40). Baking was a daily household chore. Often servants would grind the flour. Jer 7:18 speaks of the typical division of labor in which children would gather wood, fathers would start the fire, and mothers would knead the dough and bake the bread. Jer 37:21 speaks of a baker's street, from which Jeremiah, while incarcerated, received a loaf of bread daily. It is not clear whether this verse proves the existence of a bakers' guild or was merely the location of the royal bakery. (cf. Gen 40, in which Joseph interprets dreams for Pharaoh's butler and baker.) In addition to households, the sacrificial cult also required bakers to make unleavened bread for PASSOVER (Exod 12:39) or for cereal offerings (Lev 2:4; 6:17, 19-23), though leavened bread was specified for the FESTIVAL OF WEEKS (Lev 23:17).

Baking could take any of three methods. (1) A person could build a fire and heat stones, which would be cleaned off and used as a surface for baking (1 Kgs 19:6). (2) A baker could use a griddle (Lev 2:5) or a pan (Lev 2:7; 2 Sam 13:8) to bake bread over a fire. Baked goods prepared by either method had to be turned over (Hos 7:8). (3) One could also use an oven (Lev 2:4), which would be superior to the other methods because one could provide more uniform heat. Hos 7:4–7 draws an analogy between the heat of an oven and the lust for ADULTERY and intrigue on the part of the people, while v. 8 speaks of the people's mixing with sinners (like mixing bread dough) and being baked in a pan on one side only (i.e., being worthless). The OT mentions wood (Isa 44:19) and dung (Ezek 4:12-15) as fuel.

See also FOOD.

Bibliography. A. Van Selms, ''Bread,'' *ISBE*.

—PAUL L. REDDITT

• **Balaam.** [bay'luhm] Balaam, son of Beor, is an enigmatic figure in the OT who is sometimes pictured as an authentic prophet and at other times as a devotee of the occult.

According to the account in Num 22, he was hired by Balak, king of Moab, to curse the Israelites and, hence, weaken their military strength. Appearing in a narrative strung together with ironic twists and turns, this mysterious figure seems to figure as both saint and sinner, hero and heathen. Even his cultural background has been subject to controversy. Once thought to have been a Hebrew prophet, he has been considered to have been (1) a north Syrian diviner from the land of *Amau,* (2) as identical to the king of Edom (Bela, son of Beor) who was mentioned in Gen 36:31–43, (3) as a Moabite prophet, and (4) most recently, as an Ammonite seer. Since the Samaritan Pentateuch reads Num 22:5 as stating that he was from the land of Ammon, and since recent archaeological evidence points to a Balaam tradition near the River Jabbok, it seems most reasonable to conclude that he was a seer from Ammon.

The archaeological evidence was uncovered in 1967 by a Dutch expedition at Tell DEIR ALLA. In excavating the area known as the sacred mound, they discovered some fragments of wall plaster covered with a text written in red and black ink. Earthquake activity has made the dating of the inscriptions difficult, but epigraphic evidence suggests a seventh century B.C.E. date. Even though this dating is much later than Balaam's pre-Conquest activity would have been, the discovery of texts mentioning Balaam alongside texts that use a curse vocabulary common with the scriptural account suggests an extra-biblical tradition concerning Balaam from which the biblical authors may have drawn.

In the scriptural narrative, then, it is best to deal with Balaam as a heathen diviner hired by the King of Moab to thwart God's plan for His people. Balaam's inability to change God's word demonstrates the sufficiency of God's revelation to Israel. The incident where Balaam's life is threatened may be taken as a warning not to treat God's word lightly. Causing the donkey to speak (Num 22:28), combined with Balaam's professed dependency on God's word (Num 22:38) serves to demonstrate the importance of being instruments of God's word to Israel.

Although Balaam serves a positive function in the Num 22–24 narrative, other scripture references are not as favorable. Num 31:16 and Josh 13:21-22 suggest that Balaam played an integral part in inciting the Israelites to infidelity at Baal Peor (Num 25). Balaam is also depicted as one who does the most despicable deeds for personal gain (Jude 11; 2 Pet 2:14-16; Rev 2:14). Also, Deut 23:5-6, Josh 24:9-10, and Neh 13:2 all speak as though Balaam either actually cursed or started to curse and Yahweh turned the curse into a blessing.

Bibliography. G. Coats, "Balaam: Sinner or Saint," *BiR* 18 (1973): 1-9; J. Hoftijzer and G. van der Kooj (eds.), *Aramaic Texts from Deir 'Alla.*

—JOHNNY L. WILSON

• **Ban.** Refers to persons or objects devoted to or claimed by God in a special way. Negatively speaking, it marked that which was cursed and given over to total exclusion or destruction. Positively speaking, it included what was holy and devoted to God for a religious purpose. Widespread throughout the Near East, the concept denoted matters barred from common use, such as the sacred precincts of Jerusalem and Mecca, or the harem, forbidden to all except husbands and eunuchs. In OT usage the concept appears to have fallen into three categories.

The Military Ban. Warfare provided the most common biblical setting for the ban, particularly in association with Israel's early history. Thus, the Canaanites, the original occupants of the promised land, were considered under the *ban.* Their cities were to be utterly destroyed (Num 21:2). The citizens of those cities (Deut 7:2), including men, women, and children (Deut 2:34; 3:6), and sometimes even the cattle (Deut 13:15; Josh 6:21; cf. Deut 2:35; 3:7) were to suffer the same fate, without mercy (Deut 7:2). The destruction of enemy kings receives special mention (Josh 2:10). The stories of the actual military engagements indicate that certain exceptions to the ban were, in fact, made at times. Virgins were spared (Judg 21:11-12), allies were exempted (Josh 6:17), cattle were taken as booty, and royal life was protected (1 Sam 15:17-21; 1 Kgs 20:42).

Following the establishment of monarchy, the religious motivation for the ban seems to have lessened in favor of a purely military one (2 Kgs 19:11; Isa 37:11; 2 Chr 20:23; 32:14; Jer 25:9; 50:21; 51:3). This may indicate that although the ban did occur in connection with warfare fought in the name of and at the command of God, it did not necessarily constitute a permanent element of holy warfare. Perhaps it was invoked primarily in crisis situations when God's help was particularly needed (Num 21:2f.; Judg 1:17-19).

The Judiciary Ban. At least one law invoked the ban as punishment (Exod 22:20), a punishment from which no exception seems to have been possible (Lev 27:29; cf. Exod 22:19-20). The story of Achan illustrates its implementation: the offender is killed and his possessions destroyed (Josh 7:10-26). Later, in postexilic times, the punishment of ban involved confiscation of property and excommunication for the offender (Ezra 10:8). However, the NT story of Ananias and Sapphira again describes a death penalty for withholding devoted property (Acts 5:1-11).

Even divine judgment is executed through ban (Isa 11:15; 34:2, 5; 43:28), a term which also describes the final destruction of the world (Zech 14:11; Mal 4:6; cf. Rev 22:3).

The Personal Ban. Property may be devoted to God or to individuals in such a way as to become an irrevocable gift. Lev 27:21 explains that a field illegally disposed of shall revert to divine ownership, as though it were under the ban—property confiscated during warfare. As such, it belonged to God alone (Deut 13:17) and could not be redeemed (Lev 27:28f.). It could also become the property of the priests, after having been dedicated by private individuals for religious purposes (Num 18:14; Ezek 44:29). The practice reported in Mark 7:9-13 of declaring property *corban* (given to God), thereby withdrawing it from parental use, may be related to the practice of ban.

See also HOLY WAR.

—NIELS-ERIK A. ANDREASEN

• **Banquet.** Held by Israelites on diverse celebrative occasions. As the Hebrew, *mišteh* (drinking), implies, ancient banquets involved heavy drinking and eating rich foods. Banquets were held for many reasons.

Sacrificial meals, associated with communion sacrifices (Lev 7), were one type of banquet. The PASSOVER meal should also be mentioned in this connection.

The *marzeah,* a pagan celebration associated with the cult of the dead, was also practiced in Israel. It was denounced by AMOS because of its excesses.

At the banquet of Ahasuerus in Esth 1, the king, "merry with wine," ordered Queen Vashti to appear before the guests to display her beauty, and she refused. The Book of Esther describes a series of banquets and culminates in the prescription of "days of feasting and gladness" for the festival of PURIM.

Dan 5 gives the account of Belshazzar's feast, at which the mysterious writing on the wall appears. The king is denounced for his arrogance in profaning the vessels of the Jerusalem temple.

Two other banquets are of greater theological significance. In Exod 24, MOSES, AARON, NADAB, ABIHU and seventy elders went up to the Lord on the mountain, "and they saw the God of Israel . . . and ate and drank." This meal is associated with the giving of the covenant. In the NT the cup at the LORD'S SUPPER is identified as "the new covenant in my blood" (1 Cor 11:25; cf. Mark 14:24).

In Isa 25:6 a promise of an eschatological banquet is found: "On this mountain the Lord of hosts will make for all peoples a feast of fat things, a feast of wine on the lees, of fat things full of marrow, of wine on the lees well refined." The prospect of this final banquet, where death will be swallowed up (25:8), is also relevant to the Christian understanding of the Eucharist.

In the DEAD SEA SCROLLS, a messianic banquet is described—a meal of the community at the end of days, at which the messiahs of Aaron and Israel would preside (*1QSa*).

The Book of Revelation describes an eschatological banquet of a different sort. In Rev 19:9 an angel declares: "Blessed are those who are invited to the marriage supper of the lamb." Shortly afterwards (v. 17) an angel summons all the birds of heaven to "Come, gather for the supper of God, to eat the flesh of kings, the flesh of captains . . . ." This grisly banquet has its prototype in Ezek 39:17-20, where birds and beasts are summoned to a sacrificial feast.

See also FEASTS AND FESTIVALS.

—JOHN J. COLLINS

• **Baptism.** The term "baptism" has come into English from a Greek word (βάπτισμα [occasionally βαπτισμός]) whose meaning is seen in its cognate verb (βαπτίζω). The verb denotes (a) to dip, (b) to destroy (e.g., a man by drowning, or a ship by sinking). In the Greek OT the verb appears four times only, the most significant occasion being in 2 Kgs 5:14, where it is used of Naaman's dipping in the river Jordan seven times. This well-known story almost certainly influenced the use of the term among Jews for taking a ritual bath.

Bathings for purification are often enjoined in the OT (e.g., Lev 14:8-9); the ceremonial washing of Aaron and his sons when they were set apart for the priesthood is particularly noteworthy (Lev 14:8-9). The Jews of the Qumran community, living beside the Dead Sea, attached great importance to such ritual ablutions. They were priests, but viewed the worship in the Jerusalem Temple as corrupt. Their refusal to participate in the Temple sacrifices was compensated for by immersing themselves daily in a communal bath, in a spirit of REPENTANCE for cleansing of sin (without repentance it was said to be of no avail). This conjunction of immersion and repentance may well have led JOHN THE BAPTIST to demand all Israel to submit to a radical, once-for-all baptism in preparation for the judgment of the Messiah (Matt 3:7-12). Mark describes his baptism as "a baptism of repentance for the FORGIVENESS of sins" (1:4); repentance signifies "turning to God," hence John's baptism was a "turning-to-God baptism," i.e., a conversion-baptism. This link of baptism with conversion remains constant throughout the NT.

That JESUS submitted to John's baptism must be viewed as a unique application of it. Whereas John's baptism prepared repentant sinners to meet the Messiah in his judgment, for Jesus it will have been an act of solidarity with sinners, that they might enter the Kingdom of which he was the agent.

According to the Gospel of John (3:26; 4:1-2) Jesus himself authorized the administration of baptism (through his disciples) during his ministry. This was probably during his early ministry in Judea. The significance of such a baptism was naturally different from that which the church later practiced, since the redeeming event to which Jesus' baptism pointed was not yet accomplished. It was a baptism in relation to the Messiah who was in the process of bringing the Kingdom of God to humankind.

In the missionary commission of the risen Lord (Matt 18:18-20) baptism is conjoined with the proclamation of the gospel and making of disciples. To be baptized "in the name of" the Father, Son, and Holy Spirit indicates the use of the name of God by the baptizer and by the baptized. The latter calls on the name of God in faith, acknowledges his sovereignty, and comes under his lordship.

The nature of baptism as a gospel ordinance is seen in the earliest proclamation of the good news of Jesus, the crucified and risen Christ, in Acts 2. Peter proclaims that God had made Jesus, whom his hearers had had put to death, both Lord and Christ (v. 36). In dismay they asked what they should do in their guilty situation. His reply was, "Repent, and be baptized in the name of Jesus Christ." They were to turn from the sin of repudiating Jesus as Messiah and confess him as God's true Messiah. Their baptism in his name embodied at once their repentance, faith, and confession of the lordship of Jesus, and to such faith forgiveness and the gift of the Spirit was assured (v. 38).

Christian baptism thus is distinguished by its reference to Jesus the crucified and risen Lord. It sets forth the faith union of the believer with him. Paul makes mention of this in Gal 3:27: "for as many of you as were baptized into Christ have put on Christ." The language reflects the symbolism of stripping off clothes at baptism, and with them the old life, and putting on new clothes, signifying the "new man," which is Christ (cf. Col 3:9-10). It is picture language for becoming one with the Savior.

Because the Lord is the crucified and risen Redeemer, to be baptized unto him is to be baptized with reference to his dying and rising for humankind. Observe that in Rom 6:3-4 the believer is not thought of as *imitating* Christ's burial and resurrection in the act of baptism, but as being *implicated* in the Lord's saving acts for us. We are one with him in *his* dying, in *his* burial, in *his* rising. Because of this fundamental reality baptism marks (or should do so!) the beginning of life by the grace of the Redeemer (a new life!), and the beginning of life in his way (a new kind of living!).

To begin life in the FELLOWSHIP of Christ entails entering into the fellowship of those who belong to him. That was made plain on the day of Pentecost, when Jewish believers owned Jesus as God's Christ; they stepped out of the ranks of the Christ-rejecters and joined the company of those who owned him as Lord and Messiah (Acts 2:41). The same point is made by Paul in 1 Cor 12:12-13 and Gal 3:27-28: to be baptized into Christ is to be baptized into his body, the church. These two passages further show that apostolic Christianity did not separate conversion-baptism (i.e., baptism in water) from baptism in the Spirit, as though they related to two different stages in the Christian life. Baptism sets forth alike God's turning to us in his saving action in Christ and the believer's turning to God in faith in Christ.

Accordingly Peter could affirm that the primary element in baptism is not water, but the "appeal (or confession) to God for a clear conscience" and "the resurrection of Jesus Christ" (1 Pet 3:21). Here baptism is the scene of a believer addressing God and Jesus present in risen power, a kind of trysting place of God and penitent man. This is powerful symbolism and both elements of it should be retained.

See also CLEAN/UNCLEAN; CRUCIFIXION; ESSENES; FELLOWSHIP; FORGIVENESS/PARDON; JESUS; JOHN THE BAPTIST; PROSELYTE; PURITY; REPENTANCE; RESURRECTION IN THE NEW TESTAMENT.

Bibliography. *Baptism, Eucharist and Ministry,* Faith and Order Paper no. 111, World Council of Churches; K. Barth, *Baptism as the Foundation of the Christian Life*; G. R. Beasley-Murray, *Baptism in the New Testament*; W. Carr, *Baptism: Conscience and Clue for the Church*; W. F. Flemington, *The New Testament Doctrine of Baptism*; D. Moody, *Baptism: Foundation of Christian Unity*; J. Ysebaert, *Greek Baptismal Terminology: Its Origins and Early Development*; R. E. O. White, *The Biblical Doctrine of Initiation*.

—G. R. BEASLEY-MURRAY

• **Baptism of Fire.** An expression attributed to JOHN THE BAPTIST as one of the characteristics that distinguished Jesus' BAPTISM from his own (Matt 3:11; Luke 3:16; 12:49). In the Gospels John is pictured as contrasting his own water baptism with a future baptism to be administered by one "mightier than I." "I baptize you with water for repentance, but he who is coming after me is mightier than I. . . ; he will baptize you with the Holy Spirit and with FIRE" (Matt 3:11).

Fire is used often as one of the elements in a theophany. It may also refer to purification. But judging from the context, John the Baptist used the term to refer to God's impending judgment of all people, though the term could definitely be understood as a signal of God's presence.

See also BAPTISM; FIRE; JOHN THE BAPTIST.

—WATSON E. MILLS

• **Baptist, The.** *See* JOHN THE BAPTIST

• **Bar-Kochba.** [bahr-kohk'buh] Simeon Bar-Kochba was the leader of the second Jewish revolt against Rome in 132–35 C.E. Recently discovered documents indicate that his name was actually Simeon Bar-Kosiba. Bar-Kochba ("Son of the Star") is a pun reflecting Jewish messianic interpretation of Num 24:17 ("A star will come out of Jacob . . . "; cf. *CD, 4QTestim, 1QM, 4QTLevi, TJud*). That Christian sources identified him as such is an indication that the Jews had hailed him as the MESSIAH. In Jewish tradition he came to be known by another play on words, Bar-Koziba ("Son of a Liar"), reflecting rabbinic judgment on the failed revolt.

Unlike the first revolt against Rome in 66–70 C.E., which is described in great detail by the first century Jewish historian JOSEPHUS, information about the Bar-Kochba revolt is scant. There are scattered traditions in Jewish (the Talmud and the Midrash), Christian (JUSTIN, EUSEBIUS, Jerome, and Epiphanius), and pagan sources (Dio Cassius and Spartianus). In addition, there is archaeological evidence, including coins proclaiming, for example, "year two of the freedom of Israel" or "year four of the freedom of Jerusalem." Especially important are letters, written both by and to Bar-Kochba, which were discovered in caves in the Judean desert at Wadi Murabba'at in 1951–52 and at Nahal Hever in 1960–61. In the latter area were found two caves containing the skeletons of men, women, and children who were trapped inside by the Romans.

Ancient sources attribute the outbreak of the Bar-Kochba revolt to one of two factors. First, the Emperor Hadrian decided to build in Jerusalem a new city which would include, on the site of the Jewish Temple, a temple dedicated to the Roman god Jupiter. Second, Hadrian issued a general order banning CIRCUMCISION. In the heightened tension between the Jews and the Romans which followed the first revolt, one or both of these factors was apparently enough to trigger a second revolt. The revolt swept the entire land, not in open warfare but with the Jews seizing and fortifying strategic places and making extensive use of underground caves and tunnels. Jerusalem was recaptured from the Romans. The Jews were so successful that Hadrian had to send to the area his best commanders who systematically besieged the various strongholds, capturing them one at a time but suffering heavy casualties along the way. Eventually, the Romans prevailed, and Aelia Capitolina was built on the site of Jerusalem, with the Jews prohibited under penalty of death from entering the new city. Over half a million Jews perished in the revolt.

The leader of the revolt was Bar-Kochba. He claimed the title "Prince of Israel" and was acclaimed the Messiah by the famous Rabbi Aqiba. He seems to have been an authoritarian leader who did not hesitate to threaten or punish his subordinates. Christian tradition viewed him as a murderous bandit who killed Christians when they refused to help him. Jewish tradition portrayed him as both courageous and ruthless. Bar-Kochba ruled for three years before he was finally slain at Bethar, the final fortress to fall to the Romans.

Bibliography. S. Abramsky, "Bar Kokhba," *EncJud*; E. Schürer, *The History of the Jewish People in the Age of Jesus Christ;* Y. Yadin, *Bar-Kokhba*.

—JOSEPH L. TRAFTON

• **Bar Kosiba.** *See* BAR-KOCHBA

• **Bar-Jesus.** *See* ELYMAS

• **Barabbas.** [buh-rab'uhs] Barabbas was a prisoner released by the Roman procurator Pontius Pilate during the trial of Jesus. He is described as a "notorious prisoner" (Matt 27:16) and as being "among the rebels in prison, who had committed murder in the insurrection" (Mark 15:7; Luke 23:19; Acts 3:14; John 18:40). According to the NT (Mark 15:6; cf. Matt 27:15; John 18:39) it was the custom to release one prisoner at the time of the Passover. While there is no extant extra-biblical evidence to support this custom, such a practice of releasing prisoners for various reasons was not unknown (cf. Josephus, *Ant* 20.9.3). When Pilate offered to release either Jesus or Barabbas, the crowd chose Barabbas.

The name Barabbas is probably an Aramaic patronym meaning "son of the father," though it might have meant "son of the teacher" (*bar-rabban*), suggesting that Barabbas's father may have been a leader among the Jews. Origen and some ancient manuscripts attribute to Barabbas the surname Jesus.

See also CROSS; TRIAL OF JESUS, THE.

—W. HULITT GLOER

• **Barak.** [bair'ak] An Israelite hero and judge.

According to Judg 4, Jabin, king of the Canaanite city

of Hazor, had an army commander named SISERA. Sisera "had nine hundred chariots of iron, and oppressed the people of Israel cruelly for twenty years" (v. 3), apparently because the people of Israel "did what was evil in the sight of the Lord" (v. 1). The iron chariots gave Sisera a significant advantage over Israel, as yet unfamiliar with iron-working procedures.

Advice was forthcoming from DEBORAH the prophetess and judge in territory north of JERUSALEM. She delivered an oracle to Barak, son of Abinoam, to gather at MOUNT TABOR ten thousand Hebrew warriors from the tribes of NAPHTALI and Zebulun. There the Lord promised to draw out Sisera's forces to meet Barak. Barak agreed to proceed provided Deborah accompany him. She did, and Sisera met them in full force at the river Kishon, a small stream flowing westward through the Esdraelon Valley north of Mount Carmel. Sisera's forces were routed, so that "not a man was left" (v. 16).

Sisera fled on foot to the tent of a certain Jael, wife of Heber the Kenite, a descendant of Moses' father-in-law. After the exhausted Sisera had fallen asleep, Jael drove through his head a tent peg. She then brought Barak to her tent to see the executed Canaanite commander. Thus began the fall of the northern Canaanites to the Hebrews.

The following chapter, Judg 5, contains "the Song of Deborah," probably the oldest extended extant segment of Hebrew literature. In reality the poem was composed not by Deborah (v. 7). She is rather the subject of it, though the content is placed not only in her mouth but also in that of Barak.

SAMUEL in his farewell speech included Barak among judges accredited with liberating Israel from the Canaanites (1 Sam 12:11). In addition, the author of the NT book of Hebrews listed Barak among OT characters exemplary in their faithfulness (11:32).

See also DEBORAH; JUDGES, BOOK OF.

—KAREN RANDOLPH JOINES

• **Barley.** *See* FOOD; GRAIN

• **Barnabas.** [bahr'nuh-buhs] "Barnabas" was the surname that the apostles gave to a man named Joseph (Acts 4:36). The name Barnabas literally means "son of encouragement" or "son of consolation," and Acts refers to Barnabas as a good man who was full of the Holy Spirit and faith (Acts 11:24). Barnabas was a Jewish native of CYPRUS and traced his ancestry to the priestly tribe of LEVI (Acts 4:36). In Acts, Barnabas was important in the spread of Christianity because of his role as an encourager.

Barnabas, like other Christians, sold property and gave the proceeds to the church (Acts 4:36-37). He presented and commended Saul, the persecutor of the church, to the apostles in Jerusalem after Saul saw the risen Lord and began to preach in the name of Jesus (Acts 9:27).

The Jerusalem church sent Barnabas to ANTIOCH of Syria to learn about the conversion of gentiles (Acts 11:22). Barnabas encouraged the gentiles in Antioch to remain steadfast in their faith. Barnabas went to Tarsus and found Saul; he brought Saul to Antioch, and they stayed there for one year teaching. The church at Antioch sent famine relief to the church at Jerusalem by the hands of Barnabas and Saul (Acts 11:30).

Barnabas and Saul conducted a mission tour of Cyprus and south Galatia (Acts 13–14). The church at Antioch rejoiced at the positive response that PAUL and Barnabas received from the gentiles. However, a group of men came from Judea, teaching that a person had to be circumcised before becoming Christian (Acts 15:1). Paul and Barnabas debated this point with the group, and the church at Antioch sent Paul and Barnabas to the apostles and elders in Jerusalem to discuss the issue of whether gentile Christians had to follow the Mosaic Law (Acts 15:2-5). The Jerusalem apostles and elders sent a letter with Paul and Barnabas to the Antioch church in which the apostles and elders outlined certain requirements for gentile believers (Acts 15:22-29).

As Paul and Barnabas set out to return to the areas of their first mission tour (Acts 15:36), they parted ways over the issue of taking John Mark with them because MARK had deserted them on the first mission tour (Acts 13:13). Barnabas took Mark (cf. Col 4:10) and went to Cyprus, while Paul took Silas and departed to south Galatia (Acts 15:36-41).

Interpreters debate whether Gal 2:1-14 concerns the same events recorded in Acts 15. The characterization of Barnabas is different; Paul, unlike the writer of Acts, was not intent on characterizing Barnabas as an encourager. According to Gal 2:1-10, Barnabas accompanied Paul on Paul's second visit to Jerusalem. Barnabas acted insincerely in refusing to eat with gentiles in Antioch when James sent a group of men to Antioch from Jerusalem (Gal 2:12-13). Despite Paul's condemnation of Barnabas (Gal 2:13), he referred to Barnabas positively in 1 Cor 9:3-7.

See also ANTIOCH; APOSTLE/APOSTLESHIP; CIRCUMCISION; CYPRUS; HEBREWS AND HELLENISTS; LEVI/LEVITES; MARK; PAUL; PETER; SYRIA AND CILICIA.

Bibliography. R. E. Brown and J. P. Meier, "The Antiochene Church of the First Christian Generation (A.D. 40–70—Galatians 2; Acts 11–15)," *Antioch and Rome: New Testament Cradles of Catholic Christianity*; F. F. Bruce, "Barnabas, the Levite from Cyprus," *The Pauline Circle*.

—BENNIE R. CROCKETT, JR.

• **Barnabas, Epistle of.** The *Epistle of Barnabas* is a second century pseudepigraphical work included in the collection known as the APOSTOLIC FATHERS. The author cannot be determined.

Barnabas purports to be a letter but its form belies that claim. Chap. 1 introduces the work and then chaps. 2–17 contain a long didactic statement about Christianity as the proper outcome of the message of the Hebrew scriptures. Chaps. 18–20 present a Two Way system not unlike the one found in the DIDACHE. Chap. 21 draws the letter to a close.

The document starts with language reminiscent of PAUL. In 1:4 it speaks of faith, love and hope in the life of the Lord. The same Pauline trilogy occurs in 1:6. The author defines his purpose in writing—to perfect the readers' *gnosis* (knowledge) along with their faith. The reader quickly discovers that the *gnosis* intended has no relationship with the spiritual *gnosis* known to Paul (1 Cor. 8:1-3). The author of *Barnabas* intends to reveal the inner depth of the Hebrew scriptures. His method is to recite a chain of scriptures which are interpreted for Christian purposes by means of allegory. There is practically no reference to the NT. The style reminds one somewhat of HEBREWS or parts of MATTHEW. In the didactic section (chaps. 2–17) the author writes of SACRIFICE (chap. 2); FASTING (chap. 3); CIRCUMCISION (chap. 9); dietary restrictions and sexual sins (chap. 10); the SABBATH (chap. 15) and the TEMPLE (chap. 16). In other sections the author deals with the end time, the nature of the COVENANT (4:6b-8; chaps. 13–14), the work and suffering of the Lord, as understood through the Hebrew scriptures (chaps. 5–8; 12), and BAPTISM (chap. 11).

The Two Way section (19:1-21:9) parallels the Two Way section of *Didache* 1:1-6:2. Two Way systems begin with the observation that there are two ways available. In Barnabas those ways are light and darkness; in the *Didache* (1:1) the ways are those of life and death. In the SHEPHERD OF HERMAS there are two angels (36:1). There are similar differences in the Two Way teaching found in the TESTAMENTS OF TWELVE PATRIARCHS or the DEAD SEA SCROLLS. The authors of *Barnabas* and the *Didache* took their Two Way material from an early, unknown common source.

The theology and the church organization reflected in *Barnabas* are not highly developed. For some that indicates an early date of composition (before 70 C.E.—taking 4:4 as a reference to Vespasian). For others it only indicates the local nature of a document similar to the *Didache* and *Hermas*. Barnabas was included in some early lists of the canon because the BARNABAS of Acts, the partner of Paul (Acts 11:19-26), was the presumed author. A second century date of composition precludes that possibility. A date comparable to *Hermas* and the *Didache* (early second century) is generally accepted. Likewise the provenance has been much disputed. Egypt seems most likely because of the style of interpreting the Hebrew scriptures.

Like the *Shepherd of Hermas* it was a part of some ancient manuscripts of the Bible. A complete Greek copy was found in the fourth century Codex Sinaiticus. Another complete copy was discovered in 1875 by Bryennios at Constantinople. This codex dates back to 1056.

Bibliography. H. Koester, *Introduction to the New Testament*; R. A. Kraft, *The Didache and Barnabas (The Apostolic Fathers,* 3); J. Quasten, *Patrology*.

—GRAYDON F. SNYDER

• **Barracks.** *See* ANTONIA, TOWER OF

• **Barsabbas.** [bahr-sab'uhs] Barsabbas, a patronym meaning "song of Sabba, Sabbath or Seba," is attributed to two men in the NT.

1. Joseph Barsabbas (Acts 1:23-26), who was surnamed Justus, was one of the two men who had accompanied Jesus and the apostles "from the baptism of John until the day when he was taken up from us" (Acts 1:21-22) and who were nominated to take the place of Judas Iscariot among THE TWELVE. According to tradition he was one of the seventy sent out by Jesus in Luke 10:1 (Eusebius, *EccHist* 1.12), he drank a cup of poison without harm (Papias), and was later imprisoned by Nero.

2. Judas Barsabbas (Acts 15:22-34) was one of the "leading men" and "prophets" of the Jerusalem church chosen to accompany Paul and Barnabas to Antioch to report and explain the council's decision with regard to the terms by which gentiles should be admitted to the church.

See also APOSTLE/APOSTLESHIP; JUDAS; PAUL; SILAS.

—W. HULITT GLOER

• **Bartholomew.** [bahr-thol'uh-my*oo*] Bartholomew is cited in four NT lists as one of THE TWELVE (Matt 10:3; Mark 3:18; Luke 6:14; Acts 1:13). Three of these texts agree in naming Bartholomew directly after the disciple PHILIP (Matthew, Mark, Luke). Outside of these lists no reference is made elsewhere in the NT to Bartholomew. It has been suggested that Bartholomew is identical with the disciple Nathanael mentioned only in the Gospel of John (1:45f.), but this is purely speculative. Later church traditions are of little assistance in trying to uncover the historical figure of Bartholomew, though the early church historian Eusebius (260-340 C.E.) does inform us that Bartholomew spread the gospel in India.

See also APOSTLE/APOSTLESHIP; DISCIPLE/DISCIPLESHIP; EUSEBIUS; PHILIP; TWELVE, THE.

—MICHAEL D. GREENE

• **Bartholomew, Gospel of.** The apocryphal *Gospel of Bartholomew* is represented by several manuscripts in Greek, Latin, Slavonic, and Coptic. The earliest of these is dated in the fifth century C.E. Knowledge of a gospel attributed to BARTHOLOMEW derives from fourth–sixth century patristic notices (Jerome, *Decretum Gelasianum,* pseudo-Dionysius Areopagita, and Epiphanius the monk) which mention it by name. The manuscript evidence suggests a possible origin for these materials in the third century C.E., probably in Greek.

The scope of the fragments does not suggest a full-formed gospel like the canonical Gospels. Rather, the materials attributed to Bartholomew (often referred to as the *Questions of Bartholomew*) attempt to describe the nature of the secret teaching given by Jesus to his disciples between his RESURRECTION and ASCENSION. Bartholomew is the singular disciple who has the courage to ask questions of Jesus which probe heavenly secrets. He is finally charged as the keeper of these secrets by Jesus himself. The veneration of Bartholomew by segments of early Christian communities is thus clearly visible.

The manuscript fragments show an interest in Christian liturgy, the primacy of MARY's prayer to God over those of the apostles, Mary's description of the conception of Jesus, Christ's DESCENT INTO HELL, the leading forth of ADAM and EVE into heaven, and Bartholomew's encounter with SATAN (Beliar), who informs him about the angelic realm. The manuscripts also venture the opinion that one or two marriages are permissible, but one who enters into a third marriage is not worthy of God. One of the best Coptic texts of the Bartholomew materials (London K^2) exhibits a *homoousios* theology.

See also APOCRYPHAL GOSPELS.

Bibliography. F. Scheidweiler and W. Schneemelcher, "The Gospel of Bartholomew," *New Testament Apocrypha,* ed. E. Hennecke and W. Schneemelcher.

—GLENN A. KOCH

• **Bartimaeus.** [bahr'tuh-mee"uhs] Bartimaeus was a blind beggar whose sight was restored by Jesus as he left Jericho on his final journey to Jerusalem (Mark 10:46-52; cf. Matt 20:29-34; Luke 18:35-42). The name is interpreted by Mark to mean "son of Timaeus." Upon hearing that Jesus was passing by, Bartimaeus called out to him addressing him with the messianic title "Son of David." Though rebuffed by those around him, he persisted in his appeal and was healed by Jesus. In terms echoing the response of the first disciples to Jesus' call, Mark says that he followed Jesus "in the way" (cf. Mark 1:18; 2:14). This has suggested to some that Bartimaeus is depicted by Mark as representing the insightful disciple who follows Jesus to Jerusalem and the cross that awaits him there.

See also BLINDNESS; DISEASE AND HEALING; MIRACLES; MIRACLE STORY.

—W. HULITT GLOER

• **Baruch.** [bair'uhk] The name of JEREMIAH's scribe and friend (Jer 36) and of two other biblical personalities, both of whom were associated with NEHEMIAH (Neh 3:20; 10:6; 11:5). Two events stand out in the record of Baruch's association with Jeremiah. The first, recorded in Jer 36, tells of Baruch's reading aloud a summary of Jeremiah's collected prophecies to groups within Jerusalem at a time when Jeremiah had been prohibited from speaking in public. The collection, written on a scroll (of papyrus, probably), eventually was taken to King JEHOIAKIM and read to him. The king burned the scroll, column by column, as the reading was completed, but the prophet Jeremiah simply dictated the contents once more to Baruch, adding other words—no doubt including words of condemnation of the king.

The other event is recorded in the brief chap. 45 of the book of Jeremiah. There Baruch speaks of his own inability to continue the fateful and unsuccessful ministry in which he and his master Jeremiah are engaged. God's word to Baruch on this occasion is that the doom promised by Jeremiah stands; that Baruch is not to seek great things for himself; and that even so, Baruch will receive his life as a prize of war, as booty, from the hands of God.

Baruch became the subject of speculation, stories, and legends in later times. Several documents bearing his name have survived. The apocryphal book of Baruch is the oldest of these, dating probably to the second century B.C.E., not long after the desecration of the TEMPLE by Antiochus IV Epiphanes (168). This document falls into three distinct parts, now woven together to comprise a loose unity. Part one contains an introduction (1:1-14) and a confession of sin (1:15–3:8) that shows similarities to Dan 9 and dependence on the thought of Deuteronomy. The confession is a moving acknowledgment of Israel's sin. Baruch grants that Israel is deserving of the promised curse on Israel (Deut 28), since Israel has not been faithful to the demands of the COVENANT. He also admits that Israel did not submit to the Babylonians as Jeremiah had called upon them to do (Jer 29). The confession is one of the great prayers of the Apocrypha and of the biblical tradition in general.

The second part of the book (3:8–4:4) is a poem on WISDOM. This poem stresses the theme of Job 28: only God knows the way to wisdom; mere human diligence or intelligence cannot search out the true character of wisdom, for wisdom is revealed by God alone. But the poem also relates this hidden wisdom to God's gift of the TORAH, an identification found as well in SIRACH 24. Wisdom (identified as feminine and almost personified here) appeared on earth in the form of God's book of commandments, given to Israel for Israel's enjoyment. If God's people will hold fast to wisdom, then they will be pleasing to God and will find enduring happiness on earth.

Part three of the book (4:5–5:9) is a series of promises of consolation and restoration in the spirit of ISAIAH 40–55. A voice urges Israel to take courage, despite the fact that the people sinned against God and brought divine judgment upon themselves. Mother ZION and this unidentified voice then take turns speaking, offering consolation in turn to the people and to Mother Zion herself. Some of the language is very close indeed to that found in Isa 40–55 (cf. 5:7 and Isa 40:4, for example). Even so, this composite work reads well, as one moves from section to section: Baruch in Babylonian EXILE reads words that had been entrusted to him as a prophet to the exiled King JEHOIACHIN and to those gathered around. He gives them the words of a confession of sin to place before God, following that with a splendid tribute to the mystery and splendor of divine Wisdom, securely planted within the words of the Torah, and closing with words of consolation to Mother Zion and from Mother Zion to her children.

Other Baruch literature includes an apocalypse of Baruch preserved in Syriac and entitled SECOND BARUCH, another apocalypse of Baruch preserved in Greek and entitled THIRD BARUCH, plus another document today titled FOURTH BARUCH but often identified by its Greek title "Paraleipomena Jeremiou," "The Things Omitted from Jeremiah."

This friend of Jeremiah, according to the book of Jeremiah, accompanied the prophet into Egypt (Jer 43:6). But Baruch was not to enter into oblivion; later tradition saw in him a prophet and visionary in his own right.

See also APOCRYPHAL LITERATURE; JEREMIAH.

Bibliography. G. W. E. Nickelsburg, *Jewish Literature between the Bible and the Mishnah*.

—WALTER HARRELSON

• **Baruch, Book of.** *See* BARUCH

• **Baruch, Second.** An apocalypse attributed to BARUCH and preserved as a whole only in Syriac. The original language was Hebrew, the date probably soon after 100 C.E., since the work shows dependence (according to most scholars) on 4 EZRA (2 Esdras), a work that dates to about 100 C.E. *Second Baruch* is believed to have been produced in Palestine, since it (unlike apocryphal Baruch) has its author in Israel giving encouragement to Jews in EXILE and since its contents seem to fit so well with a Jewish outlook like that of the Pharisaic or rabbinical community after the destruction of JERUSALEM in 70 C.E.

This long document opens with Baruch receiving an oracle from God about the imminent fate of Jerusalem and its people. Baruch pleads with God on behalf of Jerusalem and Israel, but to no avail. The enemy enters the city, and Baruch fasts and then laments to God about the fate of ZION and its people. There follow a series of questions to God and answers from God to Baruch. No interpreting angel is identified here, as in *4 Ezra* (2 Esdras), though some of the exchanges are clearly dependent on *4 Ezra* and may indeed be intended to "correct" the outlook of that document. Along with the exchanges between Baruch and God there also come (again, as in *4 Ezra*) visions in which the end of the age is laid out, the coming of the Anointed One (the MESSIAH), the RESURRECTION of the dead, and the final judgment (chaps. 29–30). The author is concerned in later chapters with the fate of the righteous at the judgment, with the question of free will and PREDESTINATION, the fate of the wicked nations, and God's final disposition of the cosmos.

This writing concludes with a long letter (chaps. 78–87) to the nine and one-half tribes of the Dispersion, calling on them to be faithful to God's TORAH. This part of the apocalypse circulated widely in the ancient church and has been preserved in many different manuscripts. It was clearly taken to be a message to the church in its exile in the world.

Second Baruch differs at a number of important points from the outlook of *4 Ezra*. Baruch does not seem to be as deeply involved in the question of the fate of the wicked as is *Ezra*. *Fourth Ezra* is dominated in chaps. 3–10 with this question, while *2 Baruch* puts the question to God but has Baruch quite well content, it seems, with the idea that all human affairs are in God's hands and control (cf. chap. 23).

At the same time, Baruch is convinced that ADAM's sin does not doom all to destruction, for all individuals become, through their own acts, their own Adam. This teaching (chap. 54) seems clearly to be refuting the view of *4 Ezra* (7:48 [118]) that Adam's sin has brought ruin upon all humankind and left only a very tiny righteous band whom God has spared as the lone survivors. *Second Baruch* believes in an overarching divine PROVIDENCE, but also believes in free will.

The most characteristic thing about this apocalypse is its orthodox Jewish outlook. The torment over EVIL and over how to make sense of life in face of Israel's tragic history (especially the fall of Jerusalem to the Romans in 66–70 C.E.) is not to be found in *2 Baruch,* though this document comes from the same period as does *4 Ezra*. But *2 Baruch* has equally powerful and beautiful prayers to those found in *4 Ezra*. It is, throughout, dotted with excellent poetic nuggets, revealing its author to be a person of literary gifts, imagination, and indomitable faith in God and in Israel's future.

Second Baruch sees the future of Israel to lie entirely in the hands of a loving God who has entrusted the Torah to Israel. Faithfulness to the Torah will enable Israel to survive without the benefit of Temple or independent control over the sacred land. With God and Torah, life is possible, and indeed can be thoroughly good, in whatever place or set of circumstances Israel may find itself.

See also APOCALPYTIC LITERATURE; EZRA, FOURTH.

Bibliography. A. F. J. Klijn, "2 (Syriac Apocalypse of) Baruch," *The Old Testament Pseudepigrapha,* ed. J. H. Charlesworth; G. W. E. Nickelsburg, *Jewish Literature between the Bible and the Mishnah*.

—WALTER HARRELSON

• **Baruch, Third.** *Third Baruch* belongs to that group of Jewish apocalypses that combine an otherworldly journey with cosmological speculation and are not especially concerned with historical development or the final outcome of history. As in many such works, the central character is a respected figure from the past (in this case the scribe BARUCH) who is escorted on a guided tour of the heavens by an angel. The text is extant in Slavonic and Greek; both are apparently derived from a Greek original, now lost. It was probably written in the first or second century C.E.

After a brief introduction, the text opens with Baruch weeping over the destruction of JERUSALEM by NEBUCHADREZZAR, "Lord, why have you set fire to your vineyard and laid it waste?" This suggests that the work is a response to the destruction of Jerusalem by Titus in 70 C.E. Although Baruch's question is never answered directly in the text, the insights he gains from his heavenly journey lead him at the end to praise and glorify God—no doubt the effect that the author hoped to produce in the readers.

In the first two heavens, Baruch observes the punishment of the tower builders who warred against God and of those who plotted to build the tower and forced others to work on it (Gen 11:1-9). The focus seems to be on the arrogance of those who set themselves up against God. The author may have had in mind the Romans, who are often the real villains behind "Babylonian" characters in literature of this period.

In the third heaven Baruch sees a great SERPENT who gobbles up the wicked. It is unclear whether the serpent guards Hades or is identified with Hades. Baruch also learns that the tree which led to ADAM's downfall was the vine, still the source of many evils, according to the interpreting angel. The fourth heaven is the peaceful dwelling place of the souls of the righteous dead.

The reward of the righteous and the punishment of the wicked take place during their lives as well as after their deaths. In the fifth heaven Baruch observes the angels assigned to individual humans bringing to the archangel MICHAEL the prayers and virtues of their human charges. Michael then offers the prayers and virtues to God in the heavenly throne room, from which he returns with rewards proportionate to the offerings. The especially righteous receive great rewards and the slightly righteous receive meager rewards. The angels assigned to wicked persons weep and beg to be transferred, but Michael sends them back to inflict punishment on their charges.

The classical mythological motives in *3 Baruch* include the portrayal of the sun and moon as being drawn through the heavens on chariots and the presence of the mysterious phoenix bird. There are a few Christian allusions: the Greek text quotes Matt 25:23, wine is called the "blood of God," entry into PARADISE is possible "through Jesus Christ Emmanuel," the wicked are said to despise churches and to insult priests. These are regarded by most scholars as later interpolations.

See also APOCALYPTIC LITERATURE; BARUCH.

Bibliography. J. J. Collins, *The Apocalyptic Imagination*; H. E. Gaylord, Jr., "3 (Greek Apocalypse of) Baruch," *The Old Testament Pseudepigrapha,* ed. J. H. Charlesworth; G. W. E. Nickelsburg, *Jewish Literature Between the Bible and the Mishnah*.

—SHARYN E. DOWD

• **Baruch, Fourth.** *Fourth Baruch* is one of the writings in the OT Pseudepigrapha. It is a narrative text that focuses on the prophet JEREMIAH, BARUCH the scribe, and Abimelech, the Ethiopian who befriended Jeremiah (cf. Jer 38:4-13, where this person is called Ebedmelech). The text purports to describe the activities of these three persons immediately before, during, and immediately after the EXILE.

The work has evidently undergone at least three redactions. The earliest Jewish narrative emphasized the importance of Jeremiah, a focus that may still be seen in chaps. 1–4, which recount a dialogue between Jeremiah and God about the fall of JERUSALEM. In chapts. 5–6, Abimelech is spared the sight of the destruction of Jerusalem by being sent out of the city on an errand and made to fall into a deep sleep, from which he awakens sixty-six years later.

The second redactional level is characterized by a reversal in importance of Jeremiah and Baruch. In chaps. 7–8, the messages from God come to Baruch, who communicates them to Jeremiah. It has been suggested that this shift from PROPHET to SCRIBE reflects Pharisaic influence. The final chapter has clearly been edited by a Christian. Here, Jeremiah falls into a trance from which he emerges "after three days" and predicts the coming of Christ. This enrages the bystanders, who stone Jeremiah to death. There are other evidences of Christian redaction throughout the text; many of them resemble Gnostic ideas.

The concern in *4 Baruch* about the destruction of the TEMPLE should probably be understood as a response to the Roman conquest in 70 C.E. The final Jewish redaction would have been designed to hold out hope for the restoration of Jewish worship and institutions, provided that the people follow the leadership of their scribes. This hope was crushed by the failure of the second revolt in 135 C.E. The work was Christianized, perhaps later in the second century, and preserved by the Eastern church.

The narrative of *4 Baruch* diverges from the biblical account in at least two significant ways. After the fall of Jerusalem, Baruch remains in Palestine, while Jeremiah goes into exile in Babylon with the people. By contrast, Jer 43:5-7 states that both Jeremiah and Baruch were taken to Egypt by the group who fled Judah after the murder of GEDELIAH. Against 2 Kgs 17:24-41, *4 Baruch* identifies the ancestors of the SAMARITANS as returning exiles who refused to give up their Babylonian wives, and so were denied participation in the restoration of Jerusalem.

A major emphasis of *4 Baruch,* at least in its present form, is the view that God is completely in control, even when God's people are defeated and oppressed. The Babylonians are not able to destroy Jerusalem until the heavenly host standing on the wall permits them to enter. Similarly, when it seems that Jeremiah will be stoned to death before he has finished telling his vision to Baruch and Abimelech, God commands a rock to take on Jeremiah's appearance. The crowd is fooled, and stones the rock until Jeremiah completes his speech. Only then does Jeremiah allow himself to be martyred.

Bibliography. R. A. Kraft and A. E. Purintun, *Paraleipomena Jeremiou*; G. W. E. Nickelsburg, *Jewish Literature Between the Bible and the Mishnah*; S. E. Robinson, "4 Baruch," *The Old Testament Pseudepigrapha,* ed. J. H. Charlesworth.

—SHARYN E. DOWD

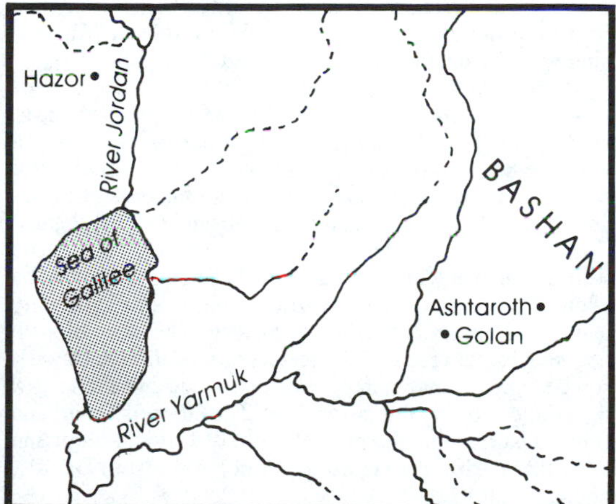

Designed by Margaret Jordan Brown ©Mercer University Press

• **Bashan.** [bay'shuhn] A fertile region on the Transjordanian plateau, north of ancient GILEAD, now mostly in modern Syria. The exact size and borders of ancient Bashan are not easily determined, though OT references allow for an approximate definition of its frontiers: north to Mount Hermon, south to just below the Yarmuk, east to Jebel Druze, and west to the Jordan-Arabah rift (PLATE 13). This basaltic tableland includes both plateau and mountains, and its rich soil and relatively high rainfall made Bashan famous for its agriculture, pasturage, and timberland. As a result, Bashan has been settled since prehistoric times. Bashan's fertility was so well known that the crops, livestock, and trees of the region were used in figurative language, sometimes symbolizing strength (e.g., Ps 22:12; Ezek 27:5-6), luxury (e.g., Amos 4:1), and pride (e.g., Isa 2:13; Nah 1:4; Zech 11:1-2).

Gen 14:5 associates the Rephaim with Bashan (cf. Deut 3:13), and the Bible makes many references to Israel's victory over Og, the Amorite king and last of the Rephaim whose capital was Ashtaroth (e.g., Num 21:33; Deut 3:1-3). The conquest of sixty fortified cities of Argob, a part of Bashan, is given special attention (cf. Deut 3:4-5; 1 Kgs 4:13). Most of this territory was assigned to MANASSEH (Deut 3:13), and it included a city of refuge, Golan (Josh 21:27). Its control was contested by Israel and Aram (2 Kgs 10:32-33; 14:25), and Bashan later fell into the hands of the Neo-Assyrians (2 Kgs 15:29). Bashan was within the region known as the Decapolis and included the towns of Hippos, Abila, GADARA, and Dion. The name Bashan was preserved in the Hellenistic and Roman periods in Batanea, whose rulers included Herod and Philip, the tetrarch.

—GERALD L. MATTINGLY

• **Basilides.** [bas'i-li″deez] Basilides, a major second century Gnostic teacher, was active in Alexandria during the reigns of Hadrian and Antoninus Pius (117–61 C.E.). He established a school, his "real son" Isidore succeeding him as its head. The school seems not to have spread outside of Egypt, and Epiphanius the Bishop of Salamis still knows of its activity there in the fourth century.

Basilides claimed to have received secret teaching from Glaucias, interpreter of PETER, and from Matthias. Some of this teaching may have been incorporated in Basilides's writings: a gospel, an exegetical commentary on this gospel, and hymns for worship. All that has survived are a few excerpts in Clement of Alexandria's *Strom.* These excerpts, primary source materials for Basilides's teachings, may be supplemented with care by descriptive information included in Irenaeus (*AdvHaer* 1.24.3-7). The account of Basilides's system found in Hippolytus (*Refutatio* 7.20-27) seems less reliable.

According to Irenaeus, Basilides taught that from an unbegotten Father there emanated five spiritual powers, the "pleroma." From the last pair were engendered 365 spheres in descending order, the world the lowest. Ruling in tyranny over earth was "Abrasax," God of the Jews. To release humanity from this evil rule, the Father sent his Christ-Mind in Jesus. A spiritual being incapable of suffering, Christ exchanged roles with Simon of Cyrene (cf. Mark 15:21), the latter crucified in his stead. Human souls are to be saved, reincarnated physical bodies being deficient.

Basilides's system incorporated a Stoically-influenced ethics, an Orphic or Pythagorean doctrine of reincarnation, and the view that providence (fate) is ultimately good and suffering is justly deserved.

See also GNOSTICISM.

Bibliography. R. Haardt, "Basilides," *Gnosis: Character and Testimony*; F. J. A. Hort, "Basilides," *DCB,* ed. W. Smith and H. Wace; B. Layton, "The Writings of Basilides," *The Gnostic Scriptures: A New Translation with Annotations and Introductions.*

—MALCOLM L. PEEL

• **Bastard.** The Heb. word (מַמְזֵר) translated "bastard" in the KJV appears in Deut 23:2 in a list of people who are banned from the cult of God. Commentators admit that the precise meaning of this term is unclear. The rabbis used the word to describe the offspring of a marriage which would be illegal under Jewish law. They reached this view by linking 23:2 with what follows, a section in which Ammonites and Moabites are also barred from the cult. Since these two nations arose, according to Gen 19, from the incestuous conduct of Lot and his daughters, the rabbis reasoned that the term must refer to the child of incestuous or illegal relationships.

Some modern interpreters, noting the stronger parallelism between 23:1 and 23:2, interpret the word in light of the prohibition against any male with incomplete or mutilated sex organs "entering the assembly." They believe that reference is to a man whose organs would function, though they were deformed.

The only other OT use of the word is in Zech 9:6, where it is used in a curse upon the city of Ashdod. The prophet either states that a half-breed people will live there, or predicted that Ashdod will suffer under a half-breed king.

The Gk. word for "bastard" (νόθος) appears in Heb 12:6. The Greek word was used in ancient times to mean the child of a marriage which was not recognized by the state, such as between a Greek and a foreigner. It was also used to mean a child born out of wedlock. Despite these differences, the word always meant "illegitimate," however that illegitimacy was defined, and that is the clear sense of its use in Hebrews. The author there argues that Christians may look upon hardships as signs that they are truly God's legitimate children, since God would not bother to discipline one who was not a real child of God.

Bibliography. R. Brown, *The Birth of the Messiah*; D. N. Freedman and M. P. O'Connor, "Bastard," *IDBSupp*.

—RICHARD B. VINSON

• **Bathing.** The act of washing the body for cleansing. References to bathing in the Bible fall into four categories: common washing for hygienic purposes, ritualistic washing, curative washing, and washing employed as a metaphor.

The dry, dusty climate of Palestine made frequent washing a necessity for good health. The Bible occasionally mentions bathing the whole body (Exod 2:5; Ruth 3:3; 2 Sam 11:2). More frequently it speaks of washing the face (Gen 43:31), hands (Deut 21:6; Ps 26:6), or feet (Gen 18:4; 2 Sam 11:8; Cant 5:3). Foot washing, normally a servant's task, was often a sign of humility and an essential for hospitality (Judg 19:21; 1 Sam 25:41; John 13:1-17; 1 Tim 5:10).

The most frequent references to bathing in the Bible appear in the context of ritualistic washing. Priests washed their bodies and clothes in preparation for ceremonial occasions (Lev 8:6; 16:4; Num 19:7-8). People and things that had become ceremonially unclean through disease or contact with other polluting elements were cleansed by ritualistic washing (Lev 14:8; 15:5; 17:15; Num 19:19). The entrails of sacrifical animals were also washed before being burned on the altar (Exod 29:17; Lev 1:9).

Occasionally bathing was related to the curative process, as with the healings of NAAMAN (2 Kgs 5:9-14) and the man born blind (John 9:11). The Bible sometimes employs the concept of bathing as a metaphor for such things as the removal of sin (Isa 1:16; Heb 10:22) or the declaration of innocence (Ps 73:13; Matt 27:24).

See also CLEAN/UNCLEAN.

Bibliography. R. de Vaux, *Ancient Israel, Its Life and Institutions;* J. Simons, *Jerusalem in the Old Testament*.

—BOB R. ELLIS

• **Bathsheba.** [bath-shee'buh] The daughter of Eliam (according to 1 Chr 3:5, the daughter of Bathshua and the mother of four of David's sons, the last being SOLOMON), the wife of Uriah the Hittite, and the mother of Solomon. Bathsheba is listed in the genealogy of JESUS along with RAHAB and Ruth (Matt 1:5-6) and ranks as another OT figure whose significance is matched only by her culpability.

The narrator in 2 Sam 11:1 relates that on an occasion when DAVID normally would have been in battle with his men, he remained in JERUSALEM. There he spied from his roof a very beautiful woman, Bathsheba, bathing in order to purify herself after her menstrual period. David, overcome by her beauty, invited her to his palace and had sexual intercourse with her. Subsequently, she became pregnant and David ordered her husband home to forestall a scandal. URIAH refused to circumvent the demands of holy warfare to which he had become committed, so David sent him back to battle with sealed instructions that called for Uriah's death. After his death and the appropriate time for mourning, Bathsheba became David's wife.

In a manner that recalled David's direction of this series of sins, which included adultery and murder (David "sends" again and again in 1 Sam 11), Yahweh directed ("sends") NATHAN, the prophet to condemn those actions. Nathan told a story about two men, one rich and one poor, and about the rich man's theft and slaughter of a lamb that "used to eat of his (his impoverished master's) morsel, and drink from his cup, and lie in his bosom" (1 Sam 12:3) to David who had attempted to get Uriah "to eat and to drink, and to lie with my wife (2 Sam 11:11)." The story kindled David's anger and he pronounced a harsh judgment on the rich man who pitied his own animals but killed the lamb (2 Sam 12:4, 6). The rich man who showed no pity must receive no pity. Nathan immediately revealed that David was the heartless man who had sinned against God in his adultery with Bathsheba and his murder of Uriah. From this point on, the reign of David took on a tragic cast, beginning with the death of the child the adultery generated.

Alongside this story should be set the earlier story of David and ABIGAIL and the story of AMNON and TAMAR. David took Abigail after the death of her husband, but in this case he acted honorably. She was a wise and beautiful woman who persuaded David to forego his passionate intention to kill NABAL, her churlish husband who had slighted David. She envisioned a marvelous future for someone who would keep Yahweh's will and law before him. Bathsheba excited his passion and he forgot his destiny, thereby choosing to unleash a different history. The story of Amnon and Tamar revealed the results of that choice; David's son became caught up in the same passions and exchanged the adultery of his father for rape. The story of David and Bathsheba remains the pivotal point of David's reign and after that period the sword never departed from David's house (2 Sam 12:10ff.)

At the end of David's reign as he lay shivering beside a young beautiful woman, Abishag, ADONIJAH, his son, began to insure his succession to David's throne. Nathan warned Bathsheba of Adonijah's plans and instructed her in the way to insure her son's succession. Bathsheba then went to David, reminded him of his oath promising the throne to Solomon, and informed him of Adonijah's plans (1 Kgs 1:15-21). After Nathan entered with a complementary message, David formalized Solomon's succession. Eventually, the defeated but scheming Adonijah asked Bathsheba to secure from Solomon the privilege of marrying Abishag. She faithfully delivered the request, but this request led to Adonijah's death.

See also DAVID; SOLOMON; URIAH; WOMEN IN THE OLD TESTAMENT.

—RUSSELL I. GREGORY

• **Beatitudes.** The term is used to designate the condition of individuals or groups who are faithful or righteous and who may therefore expect to enjoy the favor of God.

The concept is found in both the OT and NT as well as in the Apocrypha (cf. Sir 25:7-10). In the OT it is found most frequently in the Psalms. It supports the deuteronomic doctrine of two ways, promising material and spiritual well-being as rewards for those who love and obey Yahweh. Such blessings were expected to be realized in this life since apparently no concept of individual life after death was developed among the Hebrews until after the Babylonian Exile. Examples may be found in Pss 1:1, 2:12, 32:1-2, 40:4, 41:1, 65:4, 84:4-5, 106:3, 112:1, 128:1, Prov 8:32-36, Isa 32:20, 56:2, and Dan 12:12. It should be noted, however, that questions were raised concerning this teaching among the ancient Jews, as, for example, in Job, Habakkuk, and Ps 73. Occasionally pain and loss were interpreted as means to greater wisdom and blessedness (cf. Ps 94:12-15; Job 42).

The term and concept occur more prominently in the NT, especially in Matthew and Luke. However, the idea is expressed also in John 20:29, Rom 4:7, 8, 14:22, Rev 1:3, 14:13, 16:15, 19:9, 20:6, 2:7, and 14. The major distinction between the teaching about blessedness in the OT and NT is that the latter usually emphasizes the spiritual and eschatological character of the rewards. Hence the blessedness is paradoxical: it does not appear to be good, but its ultimate certainty rests upon the power and promise of God. The rewards to be received do not depend upon the worthiness of human beings but rather upon the victory of God in Christ over evil and death to be manifested in the appearance of the KINGDOM OF GOD and in the resurrection of the dead. The Apocalypse is a grand drama of hope depicting that blessed victory, accomplished by the slain and risen Lamb of God.

The most familiar beatitudes are those in Matt 5:3-12 where they serve as the introduction to the collection of Jesus' teaching known as the SERMON ON THE MOUNT. A similar group is given in Luke 6:20-26, a part of the sermon on the plain. Both probably were derived from the conjectured Q source, the material common to Matthew and Luke but not in Mark, a source largely composed of the teachings of Jesus. However, the two lists are as different as they are similar. Matthew has eight (or nine if the last one is divided), whereas Luke contains only four, each matched by a statement of woe. There is also a considerable difference in their form and content, reflecting the radical variation in the overall intentions and emphases of the two Gospels.

The central purpose of Matthew is to proclaim the advent of the new David, the Anointed One (Messiah), who has initiated the Kingdom of God. Appropriately, the beatitudes describe the characteristics of the ones who give allegiance to that Kingdom through faith and love. Luke, on the other hand, has a more universal concern for the outreach of the gospel. Hence his blessings are for the poor and lowly, and the woes are for the rich and powerful.

See also KINGDOM OF GOD; RIGHTEOUSNESS IN THE NEW TESTAMENT; RIGHTEOUSNESS IN THE OLD TESTAMENT; SERMON ON THE MOUNT.

Bibliography. I. W. Batdorf, *Interpreting the Beatitudes*; E. M. Ligon, *The Psychology of Christian Personality;* H. Windisch, *The Meaning of the Sermon on the Mount*.

—J. WILLIAM ANGELL

• **Beersheba.** [bee'uhr-shee"buh] A prominent location in the patriarchal narratives, located at the edge of the NEGEB (PLATES 8, 43), and often used to mark the geographical extremes of major population in Israel: " . . . from Dan to Beersheba" (Judg 20:1; 1 Sam 3:20; 1 Kgs 4:25).

Genesis contains two accounts of how the place received its name. (1) ABRAHAM concluded an agreement there with Abimelech (king of Gerar) concerning a well, utilizing seven (*sheba'*) lambs and swearing an OATH (expressed by the verb *sh-b-'*): "Therefore that place was called Beersheba" (21:25-31). (2) ISAAC and Abimelech concluded such an agreement and took an oath (*sh-b-'*). Therefore, Isaac called the place "Shibah" ("seven," although seven objects are not mentioned), and thus "the name of the city is Beersheba to this day" (26:26-33). In the first instance, the name is related to the swearing of an oath (with mention of the number seven); in the second instance, the name is related to the number (with no antecedent), with mention of an oath. Such word-play reflects not merely similarity of sound, but also the possibility that the verb "to swear" originally meant "to invoke the Seven (deities)." Thus, the true explanation of the name Beersheba may be: "the well (*be-'er*) where the Seven are worshipped" (so J. Lewy).

Wells and springs where a mysterious life-giving power was released, were not only the location of settlements but also of sanctuaries. It is not surprising, then, that the patriarchs had competition for wells or that a deity called El Olam ("the Everlasting God") was worshipped as the one under discussion and identified with "the Lord" (Gen 21:33). The elderly JACOB, on his way to Egypt, stopped there to offer sacrifice (46:1-5).

When the land of Canaan was divided among the tribes of Israel, the area of Beersheba was assigned to Simeon and later assimilated into Judah (Josh 19:1-2). Later, Samuel's sons served there as judges (1 Sam 8:2), Elijah passed by on his way to Mount Horeb (2 Kgs 19:3), the mother of king Jehoash was born there (2 Kgs 12:1), Josiah purged it as part of his reform (2 Kgs 23:8), the prophet Amos condemned activities there (5:5; 8:14), and it was resettled after the return from exile (Neh 11:27, 30).

The exact location of the patriarchal well and shrine have not been determined by modern geographers. Usually, it is identified with the modern city of Beersheba, which has archaeological remains from at least the monarchical period (ca. 1000 B.C.E. onward). However, three mi. to the east at a mound now called Tell es-Saba' (PLATE 3), a citadel was erected during the monarchical period. Scant remains from a much earlier time (the Chalcolithic Period) have been uncovered by excavations begun there by Tel Aviv University in 1969. It continued to be occupied until the Islamic Period (which began in the seventh century, C.E.), although there was a break in occupation which likely was caused by the invasion of the Assyrians in 701 B.C.E. (2 Kgs 18:13; Isa 1:7-8).

See also OATH.

Bibliography. Y. Aharoni, *EAEHL*, I: 160-68; J. Lewy and H. Lewy, "The Origin of the Week and the Oldest West Asiatic Calendar," *HUCA*, 17 (1942-43): 1-152.

—LLOYD R. BAILEY

• **Beggar.** The Bible has no term for the person who begs professionally, although such persons must have existed in ancient Israel. References to the POOR and the needy abound, and it seems likely that impoverished conditions would have led to the development of a professional class of those who earned their livelihood by begging. Such a situation is evident in John 9, which tells of a blind beggar regularly to be found by the pool of Siloam.

To be reduced to begging was considered a dreadful fate. Those from the privileged classes tended to see poverty as the result of laziness (Prov 10:4) or punishment for SIN (Job 4:8). In a curse against corrupt judges, Ps 109:10 linked the undesirable state of begging with the vulnerability of widows and orphans.

Those, however, who saw their poverty deriving from unjust oppression perceived Yahweh as a liberating deity coming to their aid (Exod 3:7-8; Amos 2:6-7; Isa 61:1-2). Liberation theologians have argued that there is evidence in the Bible that the gospel is a message of good news for the poor. It was BARTIMAEUS, a blind beggar at Jericho, who saw Jesus as the awaited Messiah, son of David. Others in the crowd, with sight, hastened to quiet the beggar but Jesus interceded and affirmed the man's faith, healing his blindness (cf. Peter's healing of the lame man begging at the temple, Acts 3:3). Similarly, Luke's version of the BEATITUDES affirms the privileged vantage point of the poor: "Blessed are the poor, for theirs is the kingdom of God" (Luke 6:20).

See also ETHICS IN THE NEW TESTAMENT; ETHICS IN THE OLD TESTAMENT; POOR; WEALTH.

—WILLIAM R. MILLAR

• **Behemoth.** *See* LEVIATHAN

• **Behistun.** [ba-hiss'toon] Village and high cliff (modern Bisitun in Iran) near Hamadan (PLATE 15), on the road from Ecbatana to Babylon. In the face of the cliff, 225 ft. above the plain, DARIUS the Great (521-486 B.C.E.) carved a relief and trilingual inscription. The relief depicts Darius, accompanied by two warriors with his foot upon a prostrate man, nine captives chained by the neck before him with a mythological figure above. Three CUNEIFORM inscriptions in Old Persian, Akkadian and Elamite set forth the monarch's genealogy, his victories over his enemies, the pacification of his empire and his thanks to the god Ahuramazda. According to the account Darius came to power in the following fashion: while Cambyses, son and successor of Cyrus the Great, was conquering Egypt, a usurper named Gaumata arose in Media, claiming to be Bardiya (Smerdis), Cambyses' brother, who had in fact been murdered by Cambyses. In July 522 B.C.E., Gaumata took the throne for himself, but on 29 September of that same year Darius led a conspiracy that overthrew Gaumata and laid claim to the throne. The inscription makes it clear, however, that Darius did not enjoy universal support in his rise to power. He spent the better part of his early reign putting down a series of rebellions. According to the inscription, the nine captives depicted in the bas relief were defeated rebel leaders.

The Behistun inscription provided an important key for the decipherment of cuneiform script. It was achieved by H. C. Rawlinson, a British army officer stationed in Persia. Between 1835 and 1847 Rawlinson copied the cuneiform columns and, with his knowledge of local dialects, was able to read the version recorded in Old Persian. Having virtually accomplished the task of deciphering the Old Persian cuneiform text, Rawlinson published his finding in 1849. He then turned his attention to the more difficult task of deciphering the Akkadian text. With the assistance of the Irish scholar Edward Hincks and the French scholar Felicien de Saulcy the task was finally completed in 1851.

The Behistun inscription was severely weathered and difficult to read. Early in the twentieth century efforts were made to achieve better copies and to clarify some of Rawlinson's readings. The first was done by the American A. V. Williams Jackson in 1903. The following year L. W. King and R. Campbell, working on behalf of the British Museum, made a copy that remained the standard text until 1948. In that year George Glenn Cameron of the University of Michigan produced a superior copy of the inscriptions through the use of photographs and latex squeezes. These copies led to an accurate rendering of the Elamite text.

According to the Elamite version, Darius made copies and translations of the inscription and had them sent to the various parts of his dominions. This claim has now been substantiated by discoveries of an Akkadian copy in Babylon and an Aramaic version among the papyri of Elephantine.

Bibliography. G. G. Cameron, "The Old Persian Text of the Bisitun Inscription," *JCS* 5 (1951); R. C. Thompson, *The Sculptures and Inscriptions of Darius the Great on the Rock of Behistun*.

—STEPHEN M. HOOKS

• **Bel.** *See* BAAL; MERODACH/MERODACH-BALADAN

• **Bel and the Dragon.** [bel] The story of Bel and the Dragon appears in the first century B.C.E. Greek version of the book of DANIEL which is attributed to Theodotion (the version which long ago supplanted the LXX in the Greek tradition) as an addition to Dan 12. In the Vulgate it appears after the story of SUSANNA and the Elders (Dan 13) as a fourteenth chapter of Daniel. Jews and Protestant Christians regard this story as apocryphal because it does not appear in the Hebrew/Aramaic text of Dan; other Christians whose canon is shaped by the LXX and Vulgate regard it as scripture.

The story has three parts, all of which celebrate the faith of the Jewish sage, Daniel, during his years of captivity in Babylon after its conquest by the Persian king, Cyrus. In the first section (vv. 1-22), Daniel challenges the priests of the god Bel (i.e., BAAL) to prove that their idol is, like Yahweh, a living god. They are asked to show the king that Bel in fact eats the immense meal of twelve bushels of flour, forty sheep, and fifty gallons of wine which the priests place before the idol each night. Daniel laughs when he assures the credulous king Cyrus that Bel "is but clay inside and brass outside, and it never ate or drank anything" (v. 7). But the stakes are high; if Daniel is wrong in his belief that the priests themselves are eating Bel's provisions, he will die.

On the night of the contest, servants are ordered to sift ashes on the floor of the temple of Bel before Daniel and the king alone lock the place. In the morning the footprints of the priests and their families are found and they confess to having entered the temple by a secret door in order to enjoy their nightly feast. After executing the imposters, Cyrus allows Daniel to destroy the idol of Bel and its temple.

In the second episode (vv. 23-27), Daniel follows up this triumph over pagan idolatry with another one. He brags that, without ever laying a hand on it, he can destroy a dragon which the ever-gullible Babylonians had been worshipping. With the king's permission, he feeds it cakes made of pitch, fat and hair, causing it to bloat and burst.

In the final episode (vv. 28-42), the king discovers that he has lost his credibility with the people in allowing the Jewish seer to deprive them of two of their non-gods. To save his own skin, he allows the people to throw Daniel into a lions' den. In a story that is clearly a doublet of the canonical Dan 6, the seven lions in the den are deprived of their usual daily two corpse ration in order that they might quickly dispose of Daniel. Wondrously, however, the lions decline the feast. For his part, Daniel is sustained through seven days of captivity by bread and boiled pottage which an angel of the Lord provides by bringing the prophet Habakkuk, lunch bowl and all, by the hair of his head from

Judea to the den in Babylon. The conclusion of the story of the vindication of faithful Daniel parallels that of the canonical story in Dan 6: the foreign king, worshipper of idols but also friend of Daniel, gladly affirms the superiority of the God of the Jews: "Thou are great, O Lord God of Daniel, and there is no other besides thee" (v. 41).

See also APOCRYPHAL LITERATURE; DANIEL.

Bibliography. C. A. Moore, *Daniel, Esther, and Jeremiah: the Additions.*

—W. SIBLEY TOWNER

• **Beloved Disciple, The.** The "beloved disciple" is mentioned in the fourth Gospel at the Last Supper (13:21-26) and at the foot of the cross (19:25-27)—he is also mentioned in two scenes alongside with Simon Peter in chap. 21. The "other disciple" in the dramatic scene of the race to the tomb with Simon Peter (20:2-10) has generally been identified as the beloved disciple.

Traditionally, this disciple—and the author of the fourth Gospel, the three Letters of John, and the Book of Revelation—has been identified as John, the son of Zebedee, one of THE TWELVE and one of the inner circle along with James and Peter, but this identity has been disputed. Some see no compelling reason to identify him as one of the Twelve. A few scholars have suggested that the beloved disciple was Lazarus, whom Jesus raised from the dead in John 11. The evidence is baffling enough to prevent any hypothesis from commanding a consensus in the scholarly world.

Since the fourth Gospel is organized around several events in the life of Jesus, referred to by the author as "signs," some see the beloved disciple as signifying what it means to be a believer or a disciple. Especially important in this regard is the empty tomb passage (20:2-10), where the beloved disciple comes to believe in the resurrection of Jesus on the basis of the empty tomb alone. In contrast, neither Mary Magdalene nor Peter believed until they had seen the risen Lord. The author directs his Gospel to those who could not have seen the risen Lord, and sees himself as an illustration of Jesus' statement, "Blessed are those who have not seen and have believed" (20:8, 29). The beloved disciple is the only disciple to remain with Jesus during the CRUCIFIXION, and Jesus places his mother into the care of this disciple. The beloved disciple epitomizes the one who is close to Jesus because of a faith commitment, who remains faithful to him, and who gives witness to his experience.

Paul Minear makes an interesting conjecture, building on the assumption that the audience of the fourth Gospel was primarily Jewish, that the author constructs a Moses-Benjamin typology, and that the beloved disciple corresponds to Benjamin, who was the best loved son of Jacob and the best loved brother of Joseph. Indeed, the whole tribe of Benjamin was referred to as the Lord's beloved (Deut 33:12). Minear sees many subtle correspondences between Moses' farewell address (Deut 29-33) and Jesus' farewell discourse (John 13-17). He also sees a wide complex of images as a result of the identification of the beloved disciple with a "second Benjamin": Jesus is a prophet like Moses; the twelve disciples are representatives of the separate tribes and of all Israel; and selected patriarchs and disciples are assigned special roles.

See also JOHN, GOSPEL AND LETTERS OF; JOHN THE APOSTLE.

Bibliography. R. Brown, *The Community of the Beloved Disciple*; P. Minear, "The Beloved Disciple in the Gospel of John," *NovT* 18 (1977): 105-23; J. P. O'Grady, "The Role of the Beloved Disciple," *BTB* 9 (1979): 58-65.

—JOHN A. WOOD

• **Belshazzar.** [bel-shaz′uhr] The story of Belshazzar is found in Dan 5. The name is from the Akkadian "Bêl-šar-uṣur" and means "Bel, protect the king." According to the story, Belshazzar, the son of NEBUCHADREZZAR (v. 2), held a great feast to which many of his subjects were invited. During the festivities, he and his guests drank from the sacred vessels that had been taken from the Jerusalem temple by Nebuchadrezzar. Belshazzar is thus portrayed as engaging in wanton acts of desecration in total disregard for the faith and the God of Israel.

The announcement of his punishment for such sacrilege took a very strange form. The king suddenly saw a man's hand writing on the plaster on the wall. The biblical description of his reaction is one of total terror: "Then the king's color changed, and his thoughts alarmed him; his limbs gave way, and his knees knocked together" (v. 6). Desperate for an interpretation of what this meant, Belshazzar promised the position of "third ruler" (v. 7) to whomever could interpret it.

When all the king's wise men failed at making sense of the writing, Daniel was summoned. After lecturing Belshazzar on the sins of his father, Nebuchadrezzar (vv. 17-23), Daniel then interpreted the words as God's judgment upon the blasphemous king. The sentence was immediately carried out: "That very night Belshazzar the Chaldean king was slain" (v. 30).

To appreciate fully this story one needs to be familiar with the history of the study of the book of Daniel in general. The story of Belshazzar has all of the markings of historical fiction and needs to be read in light of the Jewish persecution by Antiochus IV Epiphanes during the second century B.C.E. Thus, the primary concern of Dan 5 is not with the fall of the Babylonian empire, but the swift divine retribution visited upon an egotistical blasphemer.

There are two glaring non-historical references in the account that highlight the non-historical flavor of the story. First, there is the problem of Belshazzar himself. He was neither the son of Nebuchadrezzar, nor was he ever a "king" (cf. 5:1). Rather he was the son of NABONIDUS, who was a native of Haran and not a member of Nebuchadrezzar's family. The successor of Nebuchadrezzar was a son named Amel (Evil)-Merodach (cf. 2 Kgs 25:27) who ruled 561–560. He in turn was followed by a son-in-law of Nebuchadrezzar, Neriglissar, who was king from 560-556. His son, Labashi-Marduk, a grandson of Nebuchadrezzar, ruled for a few months in 556. Nabonidus then came to the throne and reigned until Babylon fell to the Persians under Cyrus in 539.

Furthermore, while Josephus and the Greek historian Xenophon claim that Belshazzar's feast took place on the eve of the city of Babylon's fall, the reliability of this reference is questionable. Nothing is known of Belshazzar's death from Assyriological sources, though the suggestion has been made that he died fighting the Persians in a battle that took place north of the city.

The second glaring historical error in the story is the reference to DARIUS the Mede (v. 31). Scholars have no knowledge of such a person, and the reference is almost certainly to Darius I the Great, the Persian king who recaptured Babylon from Nebuchadrezzar IV in 521 B.C.E. The actual conqueror of Babylon when Nabonidus was king was Cyrus.

The story of Belshazzar is a story of the sovereignty of God and of the triumph of faith over all evil forces. This kerygmatic message has made it gladly heard by all generations of the faithful who have witnessed the arrogance and abuse of human power.

See also DANIEL, BOOK OF; MENE, MENE, TEKEL PARSIN.

Bibliography. R. Dougherty, *Nabonidus and Belshazzar*.

—JOHN C. H. LAUGHLIN

• **Ben-Hadad.** [ben-hay′dad] The name means "son of Hadad" and is a common name for Syrian kings of DAMASCUS; Hadad is a storm god in Semitic mythology. The first mention of a Syrian king named Ben-hadad in the OT pertains to the early days of the divided monarchy when Asa, king of Judah, appealed to "Ben-hadad the son of Tabrimmon, the son of Hezion" for help against the military encroachments of Baasha, king of Israel (1 Kgs 15:16-22; 2 Chr 16:2-4). A Ben-hadad appears also in connection with the reign of Ahab (878–851 B.C.E.) when the Israelite king is reported to have fought three successive battles against the Syrian monarch (1 Kgs 20 and 22). Second Kgs 8:7-15 records the sickness and death (assassination?) of a Syrian king named Ben-hadad during Elisha's time. Finally, a Ben-hadad, son of Hazael, appears in 2 Kgs 13:3 and 24-25 as a foe of Israel in the days of Jehoahaz (818–800 B.C.E.) and his son Jehoash (Joash) (800–785 B.C.E.). Additionally, several extrabiblical texts either refer to a Ben-hadad (Melqart Stela, Zakir inscription) or provide information pertinent to Syrian politics during the time that the Ben-hadads of the biblical narratives would have lived (Assyrian Royal Inscriptions).

It is difficult to reconstruct the historical sequence of the Damascus kings for two reasons: (1) while it is clear that the biblical references mentioned above have to do with more than one king named Ben-hadad, it is less clear how many Ben-hadads were involved; (2) when the biblical texts are examined closely and compared to the extrabiblical materials, conflicts emerge (Assyrian records indicate that Hadadezer was followed on the throne by Hazael, for example, whereas in 2 Kgs 8:7-15 has Hazael following Ben-hadad). Many scholars believe that the narratives of the three battles with Ben-hadad (1 Kgs 20 and 22) are not in proper historical context, which would explain most of the conflicts. If this is the case, then two (possibly three) historical Ben-hadads emerge: Ben-hadad I, son of Tabbrimmon, contemporary of Asa and Baasha, who was succeeded by Hadadezer sometime toward the end of Ahab's reign; and Ben-hadad II, Son of Hazael, contemporary of Jehoahaz. The Ben-hadad in 2 Kgs 8:7 may be a third Ben-hadad who ruled briefly between Hadadezer and Hazael. More likely the reference is a mistaken inference on the part of an editor.

—J. MAXWELL MILLER

• **Benaiah.** [ben-nay′yuh] A son of Jehoiada, counted among the thirty champions of DAVID because of his reputation as a warrior (2 Sam 23:20-23). When David came to power, Benaiah was placed in charge of the Cherethites and Perethites (2 Sam 8:18, 20, 23), and over David's personal bodyguard (2 Sam 23:23). Such a position placed Benaiah in rivalry with JOAB, David's commander of the army. When David neared death, Benaiah chose to support SOLOMON as the king's successor, whereas Joab sided with ADONIJAH, a rival to Solomon. Solomon succeeded David and appointed Benaiah commander of his army. In time, Benaiah was ordered to kill Adonijah and Joab among others who were perceived as threats to Solomon's position and power.

There are other Benaiahs mentioned in the Bible: a son of Ephraim, from Pirathon, one of David's thirty champions (2 Sam 23:30); Benaiah listed among the clans of Simeon (1 Chr 4:36); a Levitical priest during David's reign (1 Chr 15:20), and another during Hezekiah's reign (2 Chr 31:13); four Benaiahs charged with marrying foreign women (Ezra 10: 25, 30, 35, 43); and Benaiah, the father of Pelatiah (Ezek 11:1, 13).

See also DAVID; SOLOMON.

—WILLIAM R. MILLAR

• **Benedictions, Eighteen.** The Eighteen Benedictions (*Shemoneh 'Esreh* or *Amidah*) is the name given to the fundamental prayer of JUDAISM. Every Jew is required to say it three times each day: in the morning, in the afternoon, and in the evening. So basic is the prayer that it is simply called "the Prayer" (*Tefillah*). In the prayer's oldest form there are eighteen petitions of varying length, each having a similar ending: "Blessed art thou, Lord. . . . " The prayer begins with three benedictions which praise the Lord as the shield of ABRAHAM, the one who raises the dead, and the holy God. There are thirteen petitions for knowledge; repentance; forgiveness; redemption from affliction; healing; blessing for the year; the gathering of dispersed Israelites; the restoration of just leaders; the destruction of apostates and heretics; mercy from proselytes and for those who please God; mercy for Jerusalem, the TEMPLE, and the kingship of the Davidic line; the hearing of prayer; and worship in Jerusalem. The prayer closes with thanksgiving to the Lord for his goodness and past mercies and with a general petition for peace and blessing upon Israel.

There are two primary recensions of the Benedictions: the Palestinian and the Babylonian. The Palestinian is probably the older, perhaps dating to the early second century C.E. The Babylonian is similar in structure, the main differences being that the benedictions number nineteen instead of eighteen (the fourteenth is divided into two with an elaboration of the Davidic MESSIAH), they are generally longer, and they reflect more clearly a post-70 C.E. perspective. According to Jewish tradition the Eighteen Benedictions were given their present order by Simeon the cotton merchant in the presence of Rabbi GAMALIEL II (ca. 80–110 C.E.). This step undoubtedly represents a certain fixation of a lengthy process, and it is probable that the Benedictions, in some form and number, were in use prior to 70 C.E. A Jewish tradition that the Eighteen Benedictions were drawn up by Jewish leaders at the beginning of the Second Temple period is, however, unlikely. According to Jewish tradition the proper use of the Eighteen Benedictions was debated by Gamaliel and his contemporaries. It was eventually agreed that all eighteen (nineteen) should be recited on weekdays, but on sabbaths and festival days only the first three and the last three should be recited, with the other thirteen replaced by a single prayer appropriate for the occasion.

Of special interest is the Twelfth Benediction, against the apostates and the heretics, which mentions the Nazarenes (Palestinian recension), presumably referring to the Christians. Tradition ascribes this petition to Samuel the Small when Gamaliel invited the sages to formulate a curse against heretics. The addition of this benediction may well reflect a decisive action on the part of the rabbis to force Jewish Christians, who would be expected to recite the Benedictions daily, to make a choice between their supposed allegiance to Judaism and their Christian faith. Some scholars have even attempted to view the Gospel of John in the light of the impact of this added benediction.

Bibliography. J. L. Martyn, *History and Theology in the Fourth Gospel*; G. F. Moore, *Judaism in the First Centuries of the Christian Era*; E. Schürer, *The History of the Jewish People in the Age of Jesus Chrsit*, ed. G. Vermes, F. Millar, and M. Black.

—JOSEPH L. TRAFTON

• **Benedictus.** [ben'uh-dik"toohs] Zechariah's song of praise in Luke 1:68-79, which opens with a blessing of the God of Israel, is called the Benedictus (Latin for "blessed"). According to this poetic passage of celebration, Zechariah's son, JOHN THE BAPTIST, will become the prophet who links the covenant of Abraham (Gen 12) with the new Kingdom of salvation about to be initiated. According to Zechariah, John's birth exemplifies the divine faithfulness that began with Abraham and continued through King David and the prophets. Even though of priestly descent, John will serve in the prophetic tradition to prepare the way for the Lord (Jesus) soon to appear in Israel. When seen in the context of both Luke's larger narrative about the infant Jesus and his entire Gospel, Zechariah's hymn of praise serves also to cast John in the role of a messenger of forgiveness, a theme emphasized by the Jesus of Luke's Gospel. Any conflict thought to have existed between the followers of Jesus and the followers of John is smoothed over by Luke's literary diplomacy. Whereas Jesus is the Son of the Most High (1:32), John is the prophet of the Most High (1:76). Their message is the same: forgiveness. John will preach it; Jesus will bring it into being in his Kingdom.

See also ELIZABETH; JOHN THE BAPTIST; ZECHARIAH.

—JOE E. BARNHART

• **Benjamin.** [ben'juh-muhn] The second son of RACHEL for whom Jacob labored for fourteen years. Rachel, who died as a result of his birth, named the child Benoni ("son of my sorrow"), but JACOB called him Benjamin ("son of the right hand" or "son of the south," Gen 35:18). Benjamin, like the other sons of Jacob, with the exception of JOSEPH, became the fountainhead of one of the twelve tribes of Israel.

Although Benjamin was never treasured in the same way as Joseph, the first-born of Rachel, he became precious when Jacob thought that Joseph had been slain by a wild animal. When the FAMINE forced Jacob to send his sons to EGYPT to obtain provisions, he held Benjamin back for fear that "harm might befall him (Gen 42:4)." In order to test the brothers who had treated him with such contempt years before and had sold him into slavery, Joseph, now governor of Egypt, accused them of spying and challenged them to produce this younger brother they spoke of in order to prove their reliability. They protested, but Joseph enjoyed the advantage. Keeping SIMEON as surety, he sent the other brothers back home with bulging sacks and anxious hearts. Their father, learning of the governor's demand, maintained that his youngest son would never go to Egypt with them. However, the famine continued and Jacob had to send all his sons, including Benjamin, to Egypt for additional provisions. On this trip, Joseph placed Benjamin at risk; he accused him of stealing, for he did indeed have Joseph's silver cup, which had been secretly placed in Benjamin's sack on Joseph's orders. When Judah, the brother who had suggested selling Joseph years ago, appealed for Benjamin's freedom, Joseph realized his brothers had changed and he revealed his true identity. Then Joseph embraced his brother Benjamin, and later all his brothers.

The tribe of Benjamin, which according to tradition sprang from Benjamin, was a small tribe; the area of its allotment included territory of less than 100 square miles north of JERUSALEM (PLATE 11) (Josh 18:21-18), yet it, along with the territories of Judah, Ephraim, and Manasseh, contained most of the significant locations of ancient Israel. Benjamin served as buffer between Judah and Ephraim, and was a frequent problem for the city of Jerusalem, which was somewhat vulnerable from that direction. Even so, the tribe boasted a fierce reputation. EHUD, a left-handed Benjaminite judge, murdered the obese EGLON and rescued Israel from the Moabites (Judg 3:15-30). At Taanach, under the leadership of DEBORAH and BARAK, Benjamin played a major role in the victory over SISERA's troops (Judg 5:14). This reputation was remembered in many of the blessings that are found throughout the Hebrew Bible in the mouths of notable persons (Jacob [Gen 49:27] and Moses [Deut 33:12]) and in historical records (1 Chr 8:40; 12:1-2; 2 Chr 14:7). No wonder that the first king of all Israel, SAUL, should come from this small tribe.

The story found in Judg 19-21 further illustrates the determination and fierceness of this tribe. When the other tribes came to avenge the hideous rape and murder of a Levite's concubine in GIBEAH, a city in the territory of Benjamin, the tribe of Benjamin would not hand over the guilty persons. There ensued a civil war in which the tribe of Benjamin turned back the other tribes twice, but was defeated so badly in the third encounter that only a few men survived at the Rock of Rimmon and the tribe's future was in jeopardy (Judg 20:46-48; 21:3). By means of two ingenious measures, taking 400 virgins from the ravaged city of JABESH-GILEAD (Judg 21:12) and allowing the remaining males of the tribe of Benjamin to kidnap women involved in a celebration (Judg 21:20-23), the other tribes took pity on the tribe of Benjamin. In this manner, the oath of the other tribes, i.e., that "no one of us shall give his daughter in marriage to Benjamin" (Judg 21:1), was kept and the future of the tribe of Benjamin was assured. One might witness the continuation of this tribe's contentiousness in the figures of Ishba'al (2 Sam 2:8-9; 3:17-21), SHIMEI (2 Sam 16:5; 19:16), and Sheba (2 Sam 20:1ff.) who opposed the Davidic dynasty.

See also JACOB; JOSEPH; RACHEL; TRIBES.

—RUSSELL I. GREGORY

• **Berea.** [bi-ree'uh] Berea was built in the fifth century B.C.E. on the eastern slope of Mount Bermius overlooking the Haliacmon and Axius Rivers in northern Greece. The city was located just south of the very important Via Egnatia, a little more than fifty mi. west of THESSALONICA, and twenty-two mi. south of Pella (PLATE 20). The city was mentioned by Strabo who described its location in the foothills of Mount Bermius. Cicero called Berea "an out of the way town." Berea always existed in the shadow of its sister cities PHILIPPI, Thessalonica, and Pella in the Greek province of MACEDONIA.

In the fourth century B.C.E., Berea and other cities in Macedonia were organized into a national kingdom. The earliest mention of Berea is found in a Greek inscription from that period. The monarchial Macedonian form of government stood in contrast to the democratic rule among the Greeks of the south. Philip II came to power in 356 B.C.E. and united the Macedonian cities into a powerful force in the Mediterranean world with Pella as his capital. He converted a poverty stricken pastoral people into a mighty armed camp. In 338 B.C.E., the Macedonians defeated the Greeks at Chaeronea, and by 337 B.C.E., Philip ruled over all of Greece.

Philip was assassinated in 336 B.C.E. and his son Alexander took over the rule—just a youth of twenty years. Berea played an important part in the wars of Alexander against the Persian empire. In 323 B.C.E., Alexander came down with malaria and died in Babylon. The Greek empire was divided among Alexander's generals. The successors of general Antigonus I ruled Macedonia along with Berea. Rome conquered Macedonia in 200–197 B.C.E. and finally took over full power in 168 B.C.E.. Berea was the first Macedonian city to surrender to the Romans. The Romans divided Macedonia into four districts and made Berea the capital of one of them.

In 146 B.C.E., Rome made all of Macedonia a province with Thessalonica as its capital. The Romans immediately started to build a major highway from Apollonia on the Adriatic coast to Philippi and Neapolis. Berea was one of the Macedonian cities by-passed by this major thoroughfare. The *Via Egnatia* channeled all the Roman-Greek commerce and traffic through nearby Pella instead of Berea. The transformation brought by the new road did not have much effect on Berea, situated in the shadow of Thessalonica, the new capital and Pella, the old.

Around 50–51 C.E., Paul and his traveling companions made their way along the famous *Via Egnatia* preaching the Gospel. Leaving Thessalonica, they came to Berea where Paul preached first of all in the Jewish synagogue. Many Jews had migrated to Berea, a populous trading center just south of the *Via Egnatia*. He found a better reception than he had in Thessalonica. Paul referred to the Jews there as "more noble" (Acts 17:11). However, the Jews from Thessalonica came over to Berea and stirred up trouble against the apostle. The believers at Berea then urged Paul to leave and journey on to Athens. Paul's companions Silas and Timothy remained behind to continue work.

The modern Greek city of Veria (Berea) has commemorated Paul's visit to their city with a white marble monument with a beautiful mosaic of St. Paul. According to church tradition, Sopater, son of Pyrrhus was Paul's first convert in Berea.

Bibliography. P. Meyers, *A History of Greece;* O. Meinardus, *St. Paul in Greece*; Strabo, *Geography* (7.330).

—JAMES L. BLEVINS

• **Beth-horon.** [beht-hor'uhn] Two towns, identified as Upper and Lower Beth-horon, dominated strategically-located promontories on the western slope of central hill country along the primary road between GIBEON and the Valley of Aijalon (PLATE 13). Located on a ridge between two deep ravines, the two towns controlled the easiest access from the coastal plain through the Aijalon to the watershed road linking Jerusalem and Shechem. This biblical "ascent of Beth-horon" and its towns are identified with the border between the tribal areas of EPHRAIM and BENJAMIN (Josh 16:3; 18:13-14).

Though the place names are identified with the Canaanite deity Horon (or Hauran) and mentioned in the Ugaritic tablets and other extra-biblical sources, the founding of the Israelite town(s) is attributed to Sheerah, daughter of Beriah, son of Ephraim (1 Chr 7:24). Archaeological evidence at the site of Lower Beth-horon (the modern Arab village, Beit 'Ur al-Tahta) (PLATE 3) indicates occupation at least since the Late Bronze Age, while at Upper Beth-horon ('Ur al-Fawqa) (PLATE 3) finds suggest a later establishment during the period of the Israelite monarchy. The identification of the towns with major historical events highlights the strategic and military importance of the region. During the Israelite conquest, the defeat of the Jerusalem coalition at Gibeon was followed by Joshua's pursuit of the Canaanite forces along this route to the Valley of Aijalon (Josh 10:10-11). The strategic location certainly was a factor in its assignment as a Levitical administrative center (Josh 21:22; 1 Chr 6:53). This pass was used by Philistine raiding parties in their confrontation with Saul at the battle of Michmash (1 Sam 13:18). The biblical references to Solomon's fortification of only Lower Beth-horon (1 Kgs 9:17) or both Upper and Lower Beth-horon (2 Chr 8:5) may suggest that Solomon established Upper Beth-horon as a second line of defense against possible attack from the coastal region dominated by the Philistines and Egyptians. In that connection it is interesting to note, that with the division of the kingdom at the end of Solomon's reign, Pharaoh Shishak's campaign, directed against Jerusalem, passed from Gezer through Aijalon and Beth-horon to Gibeon (2 Chr 12:1-9). Later Beth-horon is located within the kingdom of Judah (2 Chr 25:13), an identification that is maintained through the Persian and Hellenistic times. During the Maccabean revolt, the strategic location of the towns again is evident. Judah defeated Seron, the Seleucid general (1 Macc 3:16) and consequently Bacchides fortified both towns (1 Macc 9:50). During the First Jewish Revolt, Jewish Zealots defeated the Roman Governor Cestius Gallus in the region during his retreat from Jerusalem (Josephus, *BJ*, 2:538ff., 546ff.) According to Eusebius (*Onom* 46:21), Beth-horon is located twelve Roman mi. from Aelia Capitolina (Jerusalem).

—GEORGE L. KELM

• **Beth-shan.** [beth-shan'] The site of Beth-shan, also spelled Beth-shean, is a huge mound called Tell-el-Husn (mound of the fortress). It is located in the valley of JEZREEL about four mi. west of the Jordan River and fifteen mi. south of the Sea of Galilee (PLATES 3, 12). Beth-shan means "temple of Shan," but all identifications of the god Shan have been less than satisfactory. The University of Pennsylvania conducted excavations at Beth-shan from 1921–1933.

Beth-shan was first settled about 3500 B.C.E., but it did not enter the historical record until Pharaoh Thutmosis III of Egypt took possession of it about 1468 B.C.E.. He made it a military outpost to guard the grain-producing Plain of Esdraelon. According to the OT (Josh 17:11; Judg 1:27) and archaeology, Beth-shan was inhabited by Canaanites. A temple of the fifteenth or fourteenth century was dedicated to the Canaanite god "Mekal, the Lord (Baal) of Beth-shan." In a temple of the fourteenth century was a slab of stone depicting a fertility goddess. Two other temples dating from the eleventh and tenth centuries may have been the temple of Dagon in which Saul's head was fastened (1 Chr 10:10) and the temple of Ashtaroth in which his armor was displayed (1 Sam 31:10).

Evidently, the soldiers in the fortress at Beth-shan were mercenaries whom the Egyptians recruited from the SEA PEOPLES who had migrated to Palestine from islands in the Aegean Sea. When Egyptian authority broke down about 1167 B.C.E., the mercenaries took control of the city. Descendants of these mercenaries apparently were in alliance with other sea peoples known as PHILISTINES. This alliance helps explain why the Philistines, when they killed Saul and his sons in battle at Mount Gilboa nearby, were permitted to display his armor and his head in temples in Beth-shan and his body and the bodies of his sons on the city wall

(1 Sam 31:8-12; 1 Chr 10:10-12).

Although in the conquest of Canaan Beth-shan was in the region assigned to Issachar, it was allotted to MANASSEH (Josh 17:11). Manasseh, however, was unable to drive out the inhabitants of Beth-shan because "the Canaanites had chariots of iron" (Josh 17:12, 16; Judg 1:27). These chariots may not have belonged to the native Canaanites, but to the Egyptians and to the sea people who took control of Beth-shan from them.

The Israelites must have gained control of Beth-shan during the reign of David, for it appears in a list of cities in one of Solomon's administrative districts (1 Kgs 4:12). Beth-shan was completely destroyed by fire near the end of the tenth century. Although there is archaeological evidence of a small village on the site afterwards, Beth-shan was not mentioned again in history until the second century B.C.E. when it was known as Scythopolis. In Roman times Scythopolis belonged to the DECAPOLIS, a league of ten free cities with Greek culture (cf. Matt 4:25; Mark 5:20; 7:31).

The remains of a Roman temple, two synagogues, and a number of churches and monasteries during the Byzantine era (324–632 C.E.) demonstrate the continued presence of pagans, Jews, and Christians in Scythopolis. After the Arab conquest about 636 C.E., the name became Beisan, the Arabic for Beth-shan. The crusaders completely destroyed the city. Beth-shan survives today in the small Arab village of Beisan near the ancient site of the city.

Bibliography. G. M. Fitzgerald, "Beth-shean," *Archaeology and Old Testament Study,* ed. D. W. Thomas; R. W. Hamilton, "Beth-shan," *IDB;* A. Rowe, *Beth-shan: Four Temples;* H. O. Thompson, "Tell-el-Husn," *BA* 30/4 (1967): 110-135.

—VIRGIL FRY

• **Beth-shemesh.** [beth-shem'mish] A name, meaning "house of the sun (god)" or "house of Shemesh," probably given to several sites in recognition of the deity worshipped at the site.

1. An important town on the northern border of Judah (Josh 15:10), designated as one of the Levitical cities (Josh 21:16), and identified as one of the cities of Judah (2 Kgs 14:11). It was located about twenty mi. west of Jerusalem (PLATES 3, 12). Beth-shemesh has been identified with the present day site of Tell er-Rumeileh. The site was excavated from 1911 to 1913 by Duncan Mackenzie, and from 1928 to 1931 by C. S. Fisher and Elihu Grant.

Beth-shemesh was a strategically located fortified city in the Valley of Sorek near the upper part of the Shephelah. With its command of the valley, it guarded one of the major passes leading from the coastal plain inland to Jerusalem. It was a site to which the cows ventured as the Philistines returned the Ark of the Covenant to the Israelites (1 Sam 6:10–7:2). Excavations have revealed that during the time of David, Beth-shemesh, fortified with a substantial casemate wall, most likely served as a buffer between the Israelites and the Philistines. The city also had several industries including wine and olive presses for the production of wine and olive oil, as well as installations for a metalworking industry. Beth-shemesh was a part of Solomon's second administrative tax district (1 Kgs 4:9). Though not mentioned by name, Beth-shemesh was most likely among the fortified cities taken by Shishak, the king of Egypt (2 Chr 12:4). Excavations indicate that the occupation of the site came to an end during the latter part of the tenth century, a date which coincides with Shishak's invasion. The city was never again rebuilt as a fortified city, however, it was reoccupied during the latter part of the ninth century B.C.E. Beth-shemesh was the scene of a battle between Amaziah, king of Judah, and Jehoash, king of Israel (2 Kgs 14:11-14). The last reference to Beth-shemesh of Judah relates that the site was captured by the Philistines during the reign of Ahaz (2 Chr 28:18).

2. A city of the tribe of Issachar (Josh 19:22).

3. A city of the tribe of Naphtali (Josh 19:38).

4. A city in Egypt (Jer 43:13, "Beth-shemesh" in KJV; "Heliopolis" in the RSV), located about five mi. east of Cairo.

Bibliography. E. Grant and G. E. Wright, *Ain Shems Excavations,* 1-5.

—LAMOINE DEVRIES

• **Bethany.** [beth'uh-nee] The village of Bethany lies on the lower slope of an eastern ridge of the MOUNT OF OLIVES, about two mi. east of Jerusalem (PLATE 23). Its present Arabic name, el-Azariyeh, probably derives from the Latin *Lazarium,* a name traceable to the fourth century C.E. and used of both the village and an early church built on the traditional site of Lazarus's tomb.

The name Bethany may derive from the Hebrew *beth-ananiah,* "house of the poor/afflicted." Neh 11:32 refers to Ananiah as one of the Bejaminite villages around Jerusalem. Excavations uncovering Persian, Hellenistic, Roman, and Byzantine pottery indicate continuous occupation of Bethany since the sixth century B.C.E. Artifacts and tombs found in a nearby area attest to settlement as early as 1500 B.C.E.

The NT Bethany is noted as the home of MARY, MARTHA, and LAZARUS, close friends of Jesus with whom he apparently stayed during much of his last week. John (12:1-8) depicts Jesus visiting Bethany six days before the Passover and being anointed there by Mary. Simon the Leper also lived in Bethany, according to Matthew (26:6) and Mark (14:3). According to Luke (24:50), Jesus' ascension occurred there.

At least since the early fourth century C.E. pilgrims have visited the traditional crypt of Lazarus in Bethany. Franciscan excavations conducted in the early 1950s, prior to construction of the present church, uncovered evidence of four earlier churches on this site. Portions of mosaic floors from the first and second churches (late fourth and middle fifth centuries C.E. respectively) are visible today.

A Bethany beyond the Jordan is noted as the place where John the Baptist baptized (John 1:28). The location of this Bethany is unknown.

See also LAZARUS; MARTHA; MARY; OLIVES, MOUNT OF.

—SCOTT NASH

• **Bethel.** [beth'uhl] Bethel was located on the main water-parting route which ran north from Jerusalem. It was about twelve mi. north of Jerusalem (PLATE 13) on the territorial boundary between BENJAMIN and EPHRAIM (Josh 18:21-22). Bethel was one of the more important cities of the OT. Only Jerusalem is mentioned more frequently.

Identification and Excavation of the Site. The site of ancient Bethel was identified by Edward Robinson in the nineteenth century as being Tell Beitin. It was first excavated by a team led jointly by W. F. Albright and J. L. Kelso, and later by Kelso alone. The earliest levels of occupation go back to the Middle Bronze Age, ca. 2000 B.C.E. It was strongly fortified on the north by a major wall about eleven ft. thick near the end of the Middle Bronze Age. It was garrisoned and made into a Hyksos fortress ca. 1600 B.C.E.

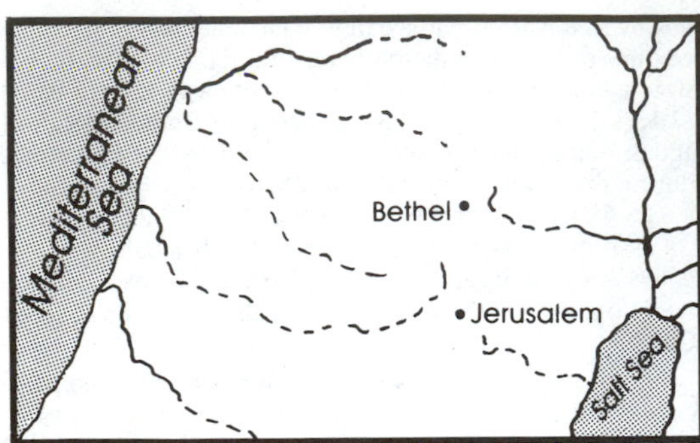

Designed by Margaret Jordan Brown ©Mercer University Press

The site was destroyed and thoroughly burned in the latter part of the thirteenth century B.C.E., leaving a layer of ash five ft. thick in places. This site reveals the most thorough burning found in Palestine to this time. The site was rebuilt shortly thereafter with a much less advanced style of construction, marking the beginning of the Iron Age I level at this site. Cultural evidence also confirms a more primitive society. The site was burned several more times immediately after this, apparently reflecting the chaotic conditions of the period of the judges.

Evidence from the early days of the Hebrew kingdom indicates a thriving city, serving as a center of its surrounding district. The calf-sanctuary of Jeroboam I has not been found. However, a few female figurines from the era of the divided monarchy have been found, probably reflecting the foreign influences of Jezebel, wife of Ahab.

No major destruction level has been found which can be dated to the Assyrians or to the Babylonians under Nebuchadrezzar. However, a major conflict leveled the city about the end of the Babylonian or the beginning of the Persian era. The city was reconstructed shortly thereafter. It was refortified during the time of the Maccabees, and was used as a Roman garrison during part of their occupation of Palestine. Its abundant water supply made it a choice site for ancient occupation.

History of the Site. Bethel was apparently already a sacred place in Canaan before Abraham built an altar there upon his entrance into Canaan (Gen 12:8; 13:3-4). However, it was Jacob's vision there which placed a special emphasis upon the meaning of its name, for Bethel means "House of God" (Gen 28:19; 35:1-7). Upon his subsequent return, Jacob's name was changed to Israel (Gen 35:10-15).

Although Bethel is not mentioned as one of Joshua's conquests, its destruction level at this time makes such an event likely. This issue is directly related to the problems involved at the excavations at AI. Destruction layers in the following era at Bethel most likely reflect Israel's growing problems with the Philistines during the time of the judges. Samuel used it as one of the worship centers on his circuit (1 Sam 7:16).

Following the division of the monarchy, Jeroboam I, the first king of Israel, established Bethel as one of his two official sanctuaries (1 Kgs 12:26-33). It was shortly thereafter conquered by Judah (2 Chr 13:19). Apparently it was fairly quickly reconquered by Israel, although no specific account is found. During the time of Elijah and Elisha, a school of the prophets was located there (2 Kgs 2:2-3).

It was to Bethel that Amos went for his ministry. His confrontation with Amaziah, high priest of Jeroboam II, took place there (Amos 7:12-13). Although Assyrian destruction of the northern kingdom apparently spared Bethel, Josiah of Judah attacked it during his reign in an attempt to purge his people's worship (2 Kgs 23:15-20).

After the Exile, the city was mentioned in the census lists of Ezra and Nehemiah, being relatively insignificant at that time (Ezra 2:28; Neh 7:32). It was refortified in the time of the Maccabees (1 Macc 9:50). The city is not mentioned in the NT.

Bibliography. Y. Aharoni, *The Land of the Bible*; R. K. Harrison, "Bethel," *DBA*; K. M. Kenyon, *Archaeology in the Holy Land*.

—ROBERT L. CATE

• **Bethlehem.** [beth'li-hem] Located about five mi. south of Jerusalem, Bethlehem was an important town during the early Israelite period (PLATE 23). The name itself is usually interpreted to mean "house of bread."

Archaeological surveys have shown that the area was occupied from prehistoric times, but what is believed to be the first historical reference to Bethlehem does not occur before the fourteenth century B.C.E., in one of the Tell el-ARMANA letters.

Bethlehem figures prominently in many OT stories. A popular tradition locates Rachel's tomb there (cf. Gen 35:19), though it may have actually been close to Ramah in BENJAMIN (cf. 1 Sam 10:2). Levitical priests are associated with the town (Judg 17–19), and Bethlehem is the setting for the story of Ruth (Ruth 1:1-2). The Philistines maintained a garrison there (2 Sam 23:14-16), and Asahel, the brother of Joab, was buried in the family tomb at Bethlehem (2 Sam 2:32).

The story best remembered about Bethlehem from the OT period has to do with DAVID. It was his homeplace (1 Sam 17:12, 15; 20:6, 28), and the site of his anointment as king by Samuel (1 Sam 16:1-13). The town was also the home of Elhanan (2 Sam 21:19), credited with killing the Philistine giant, Goliath. After the death of Solomon, REHOBOAM fortified the town (2 Chr 11:6), and in the eighth century B.C.E., the place is mentioned in an enigmatic oracle by the prophet Micah (5:2).

After this last reference, the site is not mentioned again until the time of the Exile (sixth century B.C.E.). According to Jeremiah (41:17) Judean refugees on their way to Egypt stayed near Bethlehem, and over a hundred Bethlehemites are said to have returned from Babylonian captivity with Ezra and Nehemiah (Ezra 2:21; Neh 7:26).

Bethlehem is best remembered, of course, as the birthplace of Jesus (Matt 2:1-16; Luke 2:4-15; John 7:42). No remains from the time of Christ have been found here, however, and the tradition that he was born in one of the local caves dates no earlier than the second century C.E.

In the fourth century C.E., Constantine built a church over the cave. After its destruction in the beginning of the sixth century, Justinian I (527–565) built the larger church which still exists. Excavations conducted in the church beginning in 1934 revealed the plan of the earlier church of Constantine, and discovered some of the earliest mosaics found to date in a Palestinian church. Curiously enough, the basic plan of Constantine's church is shown on a mosaic in the church of Santa Pudenziana in Rome. Since the time of Justinian, the church has been in continuous use as a Christian holy site.

Included among Bethlehem's more notable inhabitants

was Jerome who lived there from 386 until his death in 420. His tomb, as well as those of other Christians, is nearby.

There was also another town named Bethlehem that was located in the territory of Zebulun, near Nazareth (Josh 19:15). According to tradition, it was the home of Ibzan, one of the judges of Israel (Judg 12:8, 10).

See also BENJAMIN; DAVID; GIBEAH; JUDAH, KINGDOM OF; RACHEL; REHOBOAM.

Bibliography. J. Finegan, *Light From the Ancient Past*; V. Tzaferis, *The Wall Mosaics in the Church of the Nativity, Bethlehem.*

—JOHN C. H. LAUGHLIN

• **Bethsaida.** [beth-say'uh-duh] Bethsaida (house of the fisher) was a fishing village near the northern shore of the SEA OF GALILEE (PLATE 23). Nearby were a strong spring and a fertile plain where fruit was cultivated. An old village, about two-and-one-half mi. around the northern shore of the sea from Capernaum, Bethsaida was rebuilt by Herod Philip around 2 B.C.E. He designated the town a "city," and renamed it Bethsaida-Julias in honor of the daughter of Emperor Augustus. Philip died there in 34 C.E. and was buried nearby. The site, near modern et Tell, is today in ruins.

Frequently associated with Jesus' ministry, Bethsaida is mentioned seven times in the Gospels. Perhaps Jesus had visited, and failed, in Bethsaida, for he included it among cities he denounced for their failure to repent (Matt 11:21; Luke 10:13). Both Mark (6:45) and Luke (9:10) indicate that the feeding of the five thousand happened near Bethsaida. According to Mark (8:22), Jesus healed a blind man in the city. Finally, Bethsaida is said to have been the home town of PHILIP, ANDREW, and PETER (John 1:44; 12:21).

Some confusion exists about the exact location of Bethsaida. John's Gospel places it in Galilee (12:21), and Ptolemy, an ancient geographer, believed that it was part of Galilee. Josephus, however, declared that the Jordan was the border between the two territories, placing Bethsaida in the territory of Philip (*BJ* 3.3.1-3). Some have sought to clear away the confusion by listing two Bethsaidas, one in Galilee and one in Philip's territory of Gaulanitis. Perhaps some of the city extended across the Jordan into Galilee, or the writer of John did not intend to be exact in his description.

See also ANDREW; GALILEE, SEA OF; PETER; PHILIP.

—W. T. EDWARDS

• **Bethzatha.** [beth-zay'thuh] Bethzatha (Heb. "house of olives") is a name used in John 5:2 to refer to a pool by the Sheep Gate in Jerusalem which had five porticoes. Some manuscripts read Bethesda, "house of mercy," and others have Bethsaida, "house of the fisherman." The Copper Scroll from Qumran contains a similar name, *Beth Eshdatayin,* "house of the two pools," which seems to support the identification of the biblical site with the twin pools with five porticoes uncovered by Schick in 1888 in the grounds of St. Anne's churchyard in Jerusalem (near St. Stephen's Gate).

Bibliography. J. Jeremias, *The Rediscovery of Bethesda*; K. Schick et al., "Pool of Bethsda," *PEQ*.

—JERRY VARDAMAN

• **Betrothal.** *See* MARRIAGE IN THE NEW TESTAMENT; MARRIAGE IN THE OLD TESTAMENT

• **Bible.** Those ancient writings that the Christian church has acknowledged and passed on as authoritative and divinely inspired. The word "bible" is derived through French and Latin from the Greek *biblia,* meaning "little books," which in turn comes from *byblos,* "papyrus," a writing material that originated in the Nile region of Egypt.

The early Christian writing *2 Clement* (14:2) used this term to refer to the scriptures: "the books and the apostles declare that the church . . . has existed from the beginning." It had been used even earlier in the OT to refer to the body of prophetic writing (cf. Dan 9:2). More commonly, however, the sacred books were called simply *ta graphai,* "the writings," (cf. Matt 21:42) or *ta grammata,* "the scriptures," (cf. 2 Tim 3:15). As the biblical writings came to be seen and used as a single body of literature, the original Greek neuter plural was read as a Latin feminine singular, hence in French, *la Bible,* and in English, the Bible.

As it stands today, the Bible is a composite of sixty-six separate books, originally written in Hebrew, Aramaic, and Greek by scores of different authors over a period of more than 1,200 years. It contains an amazing variety of literary genres: narratives, poetry, oracles, hymns, epistles, parables, etc. The unifying theme of the Bible is the story of salvation conveyed through the history of a covenanted community in many stages of development. In the OT this theme is reflected in the mighty acts of God ("Remember the marvelous works that God has done," Ps 105:5), their rehearsal in the liturgy of Israel, and their (re)interpretation by the prophets. The same story is unfolded in the NT in the drama of the life, death, and resurrection of Jesus Christ and the creation of a new community that came to bear his name. The Christian church accepts the Bible, in both testaments, as the authoritative record of God's self-disclosure in history. From this perspective it may be studied as a definite body of literature with its own intrinsic unity.

The OT. The OT properly so-called is the corpus of writings accepted as scripture by Hebrew-speaking Jews in the first century C.E. Representing the central traditions of the religion of Israel, these sacred books were arranged in three divisions: the Law (*Tōrâ*), the Prophets (*Nĕbî'îm*) and the Writings (*Kĕtūbîm*). This threefold division is reflected in the words attributed to Jesus in Luke 24:44: "everything written about me in the law of Moses and the prophets and the psalms must be fulfilled." In the time of Christ the Law comprised the Pentateuch or Five Books of Moses. The Prophets were divided into the "former" (Joshua, Judges, Samuel, Kings) and the "latter" (Isaiah, Jeremiah, Ezekiel, and the twelve "minor" prophets). The Writings consisted of the remaining books found in the received canon of thirty-nine, although some such as Esther were not generally agreed upon. The primary position of the Pentateuch is reflected in the practice of its complete public reading according to a three-year lectionary cycle in the Jewish synagogue.

About the middle of the third century B.C.E. a Greek translation of the Hebrew Scriptures was made at Alexandria in Egypt. This version, known as the Septuagint (LXX), was compiled over a considerable period and eventually included many books not found in the Hebrew Bible. These are known as the "Apocrypha" and include 1 and 2 ESDRAS, TOBIT, JUDITH, SIRACH (Ecclesiasticus), and the WISDOM OF SOLOMON. The text of the LXX also differs significantly from its Hebrew counterpart at several points. The NT writers inherited the LXX and frequently, though not always, quoted OT citations from it. For example, Matthew's (1:23) quotation of Isa 7:14 conforms to the Septuagintal rendering of the Heb. word *'almâ* ("young woman") as *parthenos* ("virgin"). The early church fathers also regarded the LXX as the standard form of the OT. In the third century C.E. Origen compiled his *Hexapla* or six-column OT, which arranged the Hebrew text and various editions of the LXX in parallel columns. Jerome (d. 420) was the first scholar to attempt a complete translation from the Hebrew canon (cf. his Vulgate). He also argued for the exclusion of the apocryphal books from the Christian Bible, although his great contemporary Augustine (d. 430) believed in the verbal inspiration of both the LXX and the original Hebrew text. The Greek Orthodox Church is the one branch of the Christian family that has continued to use the LXX as its normative OT. At the Council of Trent (1546), the Roman Catholic Church, while adopting Jerome's Vulgate edition, also accepted the Apocrypha as fully canonical. Most Protestant churches have either denied any authority to the apocryphal books or, at best, have accorded them quasi-canonical status, worthy to be read "for example of life and instruction of manners," as the Thirty-Nine Articles of the Church of England puts it.

In the decades following the destruction of Jerusalem in 70 C.E., a group of Palestinian Jewish scholars collected and codified the Hebrew scriptures. They excluded the apocryphal writings and produced what became the standard edition of the consonantal text of the OT. This text in turn became the basis for the important editorial work of a later school of Jewish grammarians known as the Masoretes, from the Hebrew *masōrâ,* "tradition." Working between the sixth and tenth centuries C.E., these scholars produced an extended commentary on the OT text and also introduced a system of vowel points and accents to indicate how the Hebrew words were to be pronounced. The discovery of OT manuscripts among the DEAD SEA SCROLLS has confirmed the basic accuracy of the traditional "Masoretic Text" (MT).

The NT. The NT consists of five narratives, twenty-one letters, and one book of visions. The Christian church accepted the OT as holy scripture from the beginning of its existence; only gradually did it come to regard certain of its own writings as of equal authority and inspiration to those inherited from the Jewish tradition. At first the Gospels circulated as independent literary units among the communities for which they were written, but by the second century they had assumed their fourfold association. Irenaeus (d. 200) gave an extensive apology for the "quadrapartite" form of the gospel. Even earlier Tatian (d. 160) had produced his famous *Diatessaron,* a life of Christ based on a harmony of the four Gospels. Similarly, the letters of Paul were early on collected into a distinctive corpus. In 2 Pet 3:16 "all" the Pauline letters are included among "the other scriptures."

The formation of the NT canon was influenced by three developments in early church history. First, the settlement of the Hebrew canon and the promulgation of the Mishnah as an authoritative exegetical tradition called for a corresponding scriptural development in the Christian community. Justin Martyr (d. 165) described how the Christians placed the "memoirs of the apostles" on the same level with the writings of the prophets (*Apol* 1.67). Indeed, the NT functioned as a kind of "Christian Mishnah" in the polemical struggles between the church and the synagogue.

The second factor was the appearance of MARCION (d. 160), a brilliant heretic whose docetic leanings and disdain for the God of creation prompted him to construct his own canon. He eliminated the entire OT and, among Christian writings, accepted only a highly edited recension of the Gospel of Luke and some of Paul's epistles. The church could not endorse Marcion's radical disjunction of creation and redemption. Church fathers such as Irenaeus and Tertullian (d. 230) refuted his theology and defended the books Marcion had rejected or regarded as spurious.

A third factor also arose from within the church in the form of the Montanist movement. With their apocalyptic eschatology and emphasis on the immediacy of the Spirit, the Montanists produced many visions and sacred texts that bade for inclusion among the more established Christian documents. Whereas Marcion wanted to restrict severely the Christian canon, the Montanists tried to expand it promiscuously. Many Montanist documents are excluded in the MURATORIAN CANON, the oldest extant list of NT writings (ca. 180 C.E.).

The NT canon in its present form was basically settled by the early third century C.E., although some books such as Hebrews and Revelation were not universally accepted, while others such as the EPISTLE OF BARNABAS and the SHEPHERD OF HERMAS had not yet been definitely excluded. Athanasius (d. 373) gave the first extant inclusive listing of the twenty-seven books of our present NT canon in his Festal Letter in 367.

The Bible in the History of the Church. The Bible served along with the rule of faith (creed) and the organized ministry (bishop) as an organ of consolidation in the early church. Readings from both testaments became a standard part of the Sunday liturgy, and the continuous reading (*lectio continua*) of the Bible was incorporated into the daily office. The Bible also served as the basis of instruction for the catechumen who desired membership in the church. In addition, the Bible became increasingly appealed to as a primary source and standard for doctrine. For example, the bishops at the Council of Nicea (325) defended their decision on the nature of Christ by appealing to "what we have learned from the divine scriptures."

Several important traditions of biblical interpretation developed in the early Christian centuries. Origen and Clement of Alexandria were pioneers in allegorical exegesis. A rival school at Antioch emphasized the historical referent of the biblical text and made greater use of typology. Diodore of Tarsus and Theodore of Mopsuestia were outstanding teachers in this school. Augustine's famous treatise on biblical hermeneutics, *On Christian Doctrine,* set forth the ground rules for the study of the Bible in the Latin West. In the Middle Ages this tradition crystallized into the *quadriga,* the standard form of a fourfold sense of scripture—literal, allegorical, tropological (moral), and anagogical.

Medieval monasticism preserved the literary treasures of both classical and Christian antiquity, including the Bible. Monasteries under the Rule of St. Benedict made the copying of manuscripts an important part of their daily routine. Enormous labor was expended on the production of Bibles, Psalters, and Gospels. During the high Middle Ages, a revival of biblical exegesis flourished in the monastic and cathedral schools, such as the Abbey of St. Victor in Paris. Many of the medieval universities grew out of such centers. Scholars such as Thomas Aquinas (d. 1274) wrote commentaries on books of the Bible and incorporated their findings into their great scholastic *summae.* Perhaps the best-equipped biblical scholar of the Middle Ages was Nicholas of Lyra (d. 1340) who emphasized the literal sense of scripture over against the prevailing allegoristic interpretations.

In the late Middle Ages various dissenting groups such as the Waldensians produced vernacular translations from the Bible and distributed them to the common people. In England the followers of John Wycliffe (d. 1384), called Lollards, continued this practice until the time of the Reformation. The real pioneer in the translation of the Bible into English was William Tyndale (d. 1536) who died as a martyr to the cause. His work is reflected in the later officially sanctioned "Great Bible" (1539) and Authorized Version (1611).

During the Renaissance the advent of printing and the revival of learning gave a great impetus to the scholarly study of the Bible. In 1516 Erasmus of Rotterdam (d. 1536) published his *Novum Testamentum,* a critical edition of the Greek NT along with a new Latin translation. The humanist cry *ad fontes,* "back to the sources," was picked up by the Protestant reformers who based their program for the renewal of theology and church life on a fresh reading of the Bible. Martin Luther's (d. 1546) translation of the Bible into German had a marked influence on the development of his native tongue as well as on his reformation movement. Other reformers such as Ulrich Zwingli (d. 1531), Martin Bucer (d. 1551) and John Calvin (d. 1564) were expert scholars who produced commentaries on most of the books of the Bible. Without completely abandoning allegorical exegesis, they placed much more emphasis on the historical-grammatical approach to scripture.

In the centuries following the Reformation the Bible has played an important role in various awakenings throughout the church. The Pietists in Germany, the Methodists in England, and the Puritans in New England advanced a spirituality based on an intense devotional use of the Bible. At the same time, the refinement of the historical-critical method during the Enlightenment resulted in a closer scrutiny of the Bible than of any other set of documents in Western civilization. With the rise of the modern missionary movement and the formation of new Bible societies, the scriptures were translated into many languages and carried to the far corners of the earth. Despite its great importance in literature and culture, the Bible originated and remains the book of the church.

See also BIBLE AND WESTERN LITERATURE; CANON; LITERATURE, BIBLE AS; TEXTS, MANUSCRIPTS, AND VERSIONS.

Bibliography. J. Barr, *The Bible in the Modern World*; F. F. Bruce, *The Books and the Parchments*; H. von Campenhausen, *The Formation of the Christian Bible*; C. H. Dodd, *The Bible Today*; K. Froehlich, ed., *Biblical Interpretation in the Early Church*; T. George, *Theology of the Reformers*; F. C. Grant, *Translating the Bible*; R. M. Grant, *A Short History of the Interpretation of the Bible*; S. L. Greenslade, ed., *The Cambridge History of the Bible*; K. Hagen et al., *The Bible in the Churches*; W. J. Kooiman, *Luther and the Bible*; J. Rogers and D. McKim, *Authority and Interpretation of the Bible*; B. Smalley, *The Study of the Bible in the Middle Ages*; P. Stuhlmacher, *Historical Criticism and Theological Interpretation of Scripture*; B. Vawter, *Biblical Inspiration*; G. S. Vegener, *6,000 Years of the Bible.*

—TIMOTHY GEORGE

• Bible and Liberation Movements. Liberation movements have found the Bible both a profound source of inspiration, direction, support, and also a formidable barrier to be overcome. At times the Bible has appeared as an instrument sustaining a status quo in the hands of oppressive establishments, sometimes with support from established religious groups that wish to freeze and canonize inequalities of resources, position, power, and dignity. Yet the Bible has also provided the foundations for radical critiques of human power structures, issuing a call for the recognition of the fundamental dignity of each man and woman as created in the image of God. It has given to some a compelling vision of humanity as sons and daughters of God and thereby ideally brothers and sisters.

Is the Bible an oppressive residue of a patriarchal past, so rooted in certain male-dominated visions of human life and relationships that it is best jettisoned as we move to a new age informed by a richer vision of the human being as both male and female? Or are there vital, if neglected, resources in the Bible for this new vision, images of God as maternal as well as paternal, that call into question all structures supportive of inequalities and indignities rooted in race, gender, or any other dimension of the richness of being human?

The Bible has been perceived as all of the above by one group or another, and it has functioned in all of these ways. A vision of a heavenly existence in the bosom of a divine parent could be a comfort to those who have suffered persecution and martyrdom (2 Macc 7), and a tool in the hands of slave owners to stifle discontent and claims to justice in this life. At times oppressed people have found in the compassion of the God who would reach down into the slave quarters of Pharaoh's labor gangs to form his chosen people a vision that translated into political, social, economic, and cultural abolition of all forms of slavery. Martin Luther King's "I have a dream" address is laced with a rich matrix of themes from the Law and the Prophets. For some a reading of Gen 2–3 or segments of the Pauline tradition has shored up structures that subject women to the authority of men. Others have read Gen 2–3 as a remarkable vision of both the ideal and the real in the relations of men and women, with the present reality of inequality illustrative of the fallen state of humanity and not of God's design for the creation.

This diversity of perspectives illustrates what a complex process reading itself actually is when perceived as the active interplay of three forces: an author, a text, and a reader. All of the readings cited above are exercises in power, human power that can be creative or dangerous, especially when the complexities of reading are not recognized. Traditionally interpretation has centered on the text itself as the bearer, often on several levels, of spiritual insights and truths. Sometimes the Bible was mined for support of doctrines and morals already shaped. In time, critical historical and literary study of the Bible came to center on the message intended by an original author addressed to his or her particular sociohistorical context. More recently critical emphases have emerged that once more center on the text itself, independent of the author (and of course all authors at one point or another must set their work free), and on readers as more than passive vessels into which texts pour information. The experience of an encounter with a text is shaped significantly by the perceptions and perspectives of readers; it is an exercise in the making of meanings. Our readings reveal us, even as they reshape us. For some the experience of powerful texts calls forth what might otherwise remain unconscious values and perceptions, and this can be at once an experience of liberation and radical judgment.

Liberation readings generally center on what they discover to be two radical themes of the Bible. First, all of creation stands under the authority and judgment of the creator God, and no segment or structure of the created order is in itself sacrosanct. Second, almost paradoxically, the creator has invested a profound sanctity in creation as it is in relation to him; thus respect for the integrity of all human beings and for the created world of nature is a demonstration of allegiance to and reverence for God. The decalogue combines, for example, attention to fundamentals in human relations with each other and all of creation in its second segment. Relationships with God have a horizontal as well as vertical dimension:

> Thus says the Lord of hosts, "Render true judgments, show kindness and mercy each to his brother, do not oppress the widow, the fatherless, the sojourner or the poor; and let none of you devise evil against his brother in his heart." (Zech 7:9-10)

It is just these themes that emerge most sharply in liberation readings of the biblical tradition. Established structures of politics, economics, social orders, and culture that deny dignity and integrity in goods as well as in spirit are undercut by these readings. The sermons, letters, and diaries and other writings of many who fled oppression in an old world to come to the shores of this new promised land are informed by themes from the exodus traditions of the Hebrew Bible and from the judgments and promises of its prophets. The same is true of the rhetoric of both leaders and soldiers in the civil rights movement in the more recent history of this country. Priests and laity most in touch with the poor and powerless in parts of the so-called Third World today give compelling voice to these themes, sometimes in opposition to other segments of established churches that speak in cadences more attuned to the powerful and established. For some within the complex feminist movement the Bible is experienced as essentially the product of a patriarchal and oppressive past, and it has been read and interpreted within that context for two thousand years. As such it appears for some to be irredeemable, part of an oppressive order that is to be overturned. Others within the movement find strength in radically new readings of old texts like Gen 2–3 or the Song of Songs.

These readings that highlight such radical themes as shape the Song of Hannah, Isa 65:17-25, or the parables of Jesus among many other texts, stand as a challenge to more conventional readings of the Bible. They illustrate how powerful an activity reading can be. In the light they cast on all other readings they make clear that all readings are acts of power, a power that, under human control, can be either creative or destructive. Liberation movements accent often muted themes in the history of biblical readings, and they make clear our human responsibility for our readings even as they underscore the value and necessity of balancing our own readings with those of others.

See also HERMENEUTICS; LIBERTY.

Bibliography. J. S. Craato, *Exodus. A Hermeneutics of Freedom*; W. Harrelson, *The Ten Commandments and Human Rights*; J. P. Miranda, *Marx and the Bible. A Critique of the Philosophy of Oppression*; H.R. Niebuhr, *Christ and Culture*; P. Trible, *God and the Rhetoric of Sexuality* and *Texts of Terror*.

—W. LEE HUMPHREYS

• **Bible and Western Literature.** The Bible itself is literature. It is a collection of writings by many persons and in many genres, composed over a period of more than a thousand years. Like all literature, it reflects the cultural context out of which it arose, and it has continued to exert creative influences on the subsequent cultures that have known and used it.

The Bible is not only literature; it is by any measure the most significant body of literature in all human history. In its earliest form it provided continuity and cohesion to the diverse Hebrew tribes and kingdoms, beginning with the formation of Israel at the time of the Exodus from Egypt and the gradual settlement in the land of Canaan, and continuing until the fall of Judah in 587/6 B.C.E. Then, after the Babylonian and Roman dispersions, the Hebrew scriptures preserved the ancient charter and teachings of the Jews, giving them identity, unity, and guidance as the people of God in spite of their being increasingly scattered among the nations. Those scriptures have been the centripetal force in Jewish teaching, culture, and worship for more than two millennia, in spite of the threats of assimilation and annihilation that have arisen with demonic regularity.

Moreover, the influence of the Hebrew scriptures has reached far beyond its original confines within Judaism. Christianity, ultimately a separate and universal way of faith, arose precisely out of the teachings and piety of the Hebrew scriptures. Jesus, the center and founder of Christianity, was nurtured as a loyal Jew in the religion of Moses and the prophets. All that is known of him indicates that he maintained an unwavering loyalty to the faith of his ancestors, and he insisted that his purpose was not to destroy but to preserve and fulfill the law and the prophets (Matt 5:17-20). His earliest followers, the apostles, especially Paul, continued that purpose as they understood and interpreted it. Thus the Bible came to completion in the apostolic writings known as the NT. The earliest literary influence of the Bible was that of the first part, the Hebrew scriptures, on the creation of the second, the NT.

In broader scope, it may be seen that the influence of the Bible has continued to spread since its beginnings in the lands of the eastern Mediterranean, so that in modern times it has become the greatest single source of ideology and ethics in the whole world, especially in the West. The ancient culture of Greece and Rome, with its antecedents, was merged with biblical ideas in the early centuries of this era to form the basic principles of Western civilization. The missionary and educational efforts of the Christian churches, along with Western imperialism, modern travel and communication, and technological advancement, have led to the almost universally pervasive influence of Western civilization, with its biblical component, among the cultures and nations of the earth.

Since literature is a major factor in the creation, preservation, and transmission of culture, and since the Bible has been a primary source of Western civilization, it is no surprise to observe that the Bible has continued to be a dominant influence on the subsequent literature of that civilization. The purpose of this essay, then, is to demonstrate that influence. Obviously, that purpose is much too broad and demanding to be treated with anything approaching adequacy in so brief an essay. Rather, what follows is meant to be only a selective list, a sampling of some of the outstanding literary productions of the West that will indicate the depth and power of the Bible in Western literature.

Early Jewish Literature. Five major collections of ancient Jewish literature demonstrate the influence of the earlier Hebrew scriptures (sometimes in translation) in their composition: the APOCRYPHA, the pseudepigrapha, the works of PHILO, the works of JOSEPHUS, and the vast body of commentary and illustration known as the Talmud.

The Apocrypha (''hidden,'' of unknown origin) is a collection of approximately fourteen books, most of which were included in the ancient Greek texts of the Hebrew scriptures. Some of the books duplicate portions of the canonical writings (e.g., 1 Esdras). Others propose to supplement canonical books (e.g., additions to Esther and additions to Daniel, sometimes called the Song of the Three Children, Susanna, and Bel and the Dragon). Yet others supply the history of the Jews beyond that recorded in the ancient writings (e.g., 1 and 2 Maccabees). Pseudepigrapha is the name given to an indefinite collection of ancient Jewish writings of uneven value which nonetheless have been held in high esteem by both Jews and Christians. Most of these pseudonymous books reflect a direct dependence upon the canonical Hebrew scriptures (e.g., the *Book of Jubilees* and the *Testaments of the Twelve Patriarchs*). Philo was a scholarly and irenic Jew of Alexandria, an older contemporary of Jesus and Paul, who attempted to form a synthesis of Jewish piety and Greek idealistic philosophy. A large number of his writings have survived, among them such treatises as *Questions and Answers, The Allegory of the Torah,* and *The Exposition of the Torah.* He was thoroughly familiar with the Hebrew scriptures and most of his compositions are based upon them.

Josephus was another Jewish scholar, living during the last part of the first century C.E., whose well-known writings demonstrate a thorough knowledge of and dependence upon the Hebrew scriptures. His *Jewish Antiquities,* written for explanation and apologetic purposes on behalf of Judaism in a time of Roman persecution, retells the story of Israel from the creation to the rebellion against Rome. The scriptures were its main source, but Josephus often supplemented the account by reference to other histories. He also recorded many narratives and commentaries that would later appear in the traditions of the rabbis. That rabbinic literature is found primarily in the Talmud, a huge compilation (2.5 million words on 5,894 pages) of all the recognized traditions of the fathers. Actually, there were two Talmuds, the Palestinian and the Babylonian, but it was the latter that attained greater prominence. They were composed of Midrash, a collection of traditional commentary on the Torah, and the Mishnah, a more scholarly body of commentary. To these were later added the Gemara, intended to complete the theological development of ancient Judaism. Finally, the whole Talmud was divided into two types of literature, called Halachah and Haggadah. The former term means ''the Way,'' and signifies rules for living according to the Torah; the latter designates ''narrative'' and contains various stories, parables, and illustrations to make religious truth easier to understand and apply. Thus, all of this ancient Jewish literature was the direct outgrowth of the content and teachings of the Hebrew scriptures.

Early Christian Literature. During the three centuries following the death of Jesus, while Christianity was still an illegal and persecuted religion, a great mass of Christian literature was composed in addition to the New Testament itself. Many of those writings are known to have been lost or destroyed, but many others have survived either in copies, fragments, or lengthy quotations in other extant writings. Most of that literature reflects the direct undergirding of both the Hebrew scriptures and the apostolic writings that were concurrently being collected and canonized into the New Testament. At the same time, of course, many of the late classics of Greek and Latin literature were also in process of composition, but, due to the political and intellectual status of both Judaism and Christianity, the influence of the Bible on those writings was negligible at most. The extant Christian literature is in many genres: letters, gospels, acts, apocalypses, apologies, manuals, commentaries, and moral and theological treatises.

Space here permits only the barest mention of these pre-Constantinian Christian writings in order to demonstrate the early influence of the Bible on Western literature. Among the letters are the seven letters of Ignatius of Antioch (ca. 115) which reflect a thorough knowledge of both the OT and the gospel, and *1 Clement* (ca. 96), which quotes copiously from the LXX and is the earliest known post-NT document that expressly quotes one of Paul's letters (1 Corinthians). The *Shepherd of Hermas* (ca. 100), an apocalyptic treatise, was especially concerned with the NT book of Hebrews as well as with the genre of Jewish apocalypticism. There were many apologetic works composed in the second and third centuries, among them the *Apology* of Justin Martyr and the similar books by Tatian, Melito of Sardis, and Tertullian. They usually based their arguments in part on the fulfillment of OT prophecy found in the gospel, exhibiting thereby the strong influence of the scriptures. The most outstanding apologetic works of this early period are Irenaeus's *Against Heresies* (ca. 185) and Origen's *Against Celsus* (ca. 248), both of which preserve a great deal of otherwise unknown information about the sharp contest between Christianity and pagan, classical culture. They make constant reference to the scriptures of both the OT and NT. In fact, Irenaeus was the earliest Christian writer who seems to have been familiar with most of what was soon to become the NT, and he referred to those writings as ''scripture'' in the same way that he did to the OT. Origen was a thorough scholar of the Bible. It was the basis of all his theological writings, and his critical study of the text of the Hebrew scriptures, known as the *Hexapla,* is one of the earliest and greatest monuments of biblical criticism.

Following the acceptance and legal establishment of Christianity by Constantine and his successors in the early fourth century, the influence of the Bible on the literature of the whole Roman Empire, East and West, became dominant. Pagan and secular literature began to diminish and the interests of the church increasingly pervaded all of culture. That development is well illustrated by the famous letter of Pope Gregory the Great (d. 604) to the bishop of Vienne in Gaul, admonishing the bishop for studying secular literature. Gregory wrote that ''the praises of Christ do not belong in the same mouth with the praises of Jove.'' A large number of great scholars arose during the following centuries who produced a flood of Christian literature, much of it biblical commentary and nearly all of it suffused with scriptural assumptions, references, and teachings. These literary giants include such historic figures as Eusebius, the church historian; Jerome, the controversial biblical scholar and translator of the Vulgate; Lactantius, author of the *Divine Institutes* and many other religious and secular works, now lost; Boethius, whose *Consolation of Philosophy* is one of the masterpieces of antiquity; Ambrose of Milan, the spiritual father of Augustine, whose *On Offices* was based on a similar work by Cicero but now enlarged to encompass biblical teaching; and, the greatest of all, Augustine of Hippo himself.

Augustine lived at the close of antiquity and became the primary channel for the passing of classical learning into the dawning Middle Ages. He was a classical scholar of the highest rank before his conversion to orthodox Christianity and it is well known that the theology he bequeathed to future ages with such controlling power was a profound synthesis of Neoplatonism and apostolic Christianity. His voluminous writings are models of rhetorical grace and, in content, composed of both biblical and classical materials. The *Confessions* is one of the masterpieces of world literature; the *City of God* is at once a work of great apologetic power and a philosophy of history that has exercised incalculable influence; both are firmly based on the words and teachings of the Bible, as are all of his other 116 extant treatises.

Augustine died in 430 C.E. and the Western Roman Empire came to an end soon thereafter. The following four centuries, until the time of Charlemagne, are designated "the dark ages" because learning was at a low ebb while the barbarian peoples developed their own culture and absorbed that of the Greeks and Romans. Relatively little literature was produced during the period, as would be expected. Literacy itself was rare and the Bible that was known was transmitted for the most part through liturgy and catechism. It should be noted also that during the same time the original territory of Christendom was overrun by Islam, and the eastern churches began a long epoch of limited activity and bare survival. The fundamental scripture of Islam, the Qur'an, was reputedly written by the prophet Mohammed under the direction and instruction of the angels of Allah. That sacred book claims not only to provide the latest and final revelation to humankind; it also contains many references to the Jewish and Christian scriptures, frequently correcting the errors believed to be contained in them. Thus it is important to note that the Qur'an may be considered a major example of the Western literature that was greatly influenced by the Bible.

Medieval Literature. The massive literature of the Middle Ages was for the most part produced by Christian scholars. Much of it was theological in content and purpose, and it was usually written by monks and clerics. Nevertheless, a considerable amount of literature arose out of secular interests. Those interests may be generally identified as social courtesy (cultural structure and behavior) and courtly love (eroticism and the enjoyment of the natural). Most of the religious literature was derived ultimately from the Bible as well as more directly from the traditions of the church. However, the secular literature also frequently reflected the culture of the dominant Christian culture and therefore could not completely escape the influence of the Bible.

Most of the secular literature of the Middle Ages was in the form of poetry. It originated in folk ballads, epics, love songs, and the lyrics of the troubadours. Every language group and nation developed its repertoire and some of it has survived in later literature. Two of the best examples are the *Carmina Burana* and the songs of Provence, in the south of France. The *Carmina Burana* are various lyrics that were collected and preserved at the great Benediktbeuern Monastery in Bavaria, which served as a kind of archive of secular culture. *Carmina* means "songs" and *burana* is a Latin word derived from the name of the monastery. The lyrics often express both religious ideas and ordinary human interests. The Provençal lyrics apparently had their origin among the troubadours who traveled among the people, visiting the towns and courts to supply knowledge and joy to the hard lives of the people. It was a natural step to go from the singing of Christian hymns to Our Lady (Madonna) to the singing of love for "my lady" (*mia donna*), and there was a similar transition from the lyrical praise of battle heroes and chivalry to the development of social custom and civilizing law. In this manner, the superior culture of the Muslims in Spain crossed the Pyrenees to Provence and Aquitaine and on into northern Europe where it was synthesized with biblical, Christian culture to produce a civilization with components of Aristotelian methodology, love for the historical Jesus, and the ironic, comic vision of ambiguous existence.

The Greek philosophical tradition was the primary source of the methodology of rational dialectic that formed the basis of scholasticism. The idealistic vision of Plato and his successors, including the Neoplatonists, was compatible with the biblical desire for the perfect vision of the good, and the later Aristotelian logic provided the structures for empirical knowledge and technological development. The result can be seen in such literary masterpieces as Anselm's *Proslogion* and *Cur Deus homo?* as well as the *Summae* of Aquinas. The theme of erotic love was captured for the church and transformed into an intense love for the Jesus of history in place of the earlier intellectual concentration upon the christological dogmas. That transformation may be clearly seen in the writings of Bernard of Clairvaux whose mystical *Steps of Humility* and famous hymn, "Jesus the Very Thought of Thee," depict the new interest in Jesus and his ancient life in Palestine that fueled the crusades as attempts to recapture that land. It is a commonplace of history that the crusades, though politically and militarily failures, reopened the ancient East for the West and led ultimately to the rediscovery of much of Aristotle, then to the Renaissance, and thus to the later ages of discovery and science. Finally, the rediscovery of classical literature, especially Aristotle's rhetorical works, bore fruit in such medieval literature as Dante's *Divine Comedy*. That profound masterpiece reflects both the faith of the Middle Ages and the classical interests of the coming Renaissance. It uses allegory to show how Virgil symbolizes human reason's earthly attainments whereas the faith of Dante's beloved Beatrice leads to heavenly happiness.

Renaissance Literature. The word Renaissance itself points to the rebirth of the culture of antiquity at the end of the Middle Ages, which in turn laid the foundations for the modern age. The period of that rebirth, the fourteenth and fifteenth centuries, witnessed a remarkable creativity in every aspect of culture, especially in the productive fusion of biblical themes with classical forms of art and literature. It is sufficient here simply to note such literary giants of the time as Petrarch, Boccaccio, Chaucer, Pico della Mirandola, and Desiderius Erasmus.

These literary leaders of the Renaissance, along with most of their peers, were essentially humanists, of course, both in the sense that they drank deeply of classical learning and because they made humanity much more the center of their attention than had been the case with the medieval scholars. Their writings are filled with bawdy stories, illustrations of human weakness as well as grandeur, and devastating satire on religion. It is also true, however, that they were all serious sons of the church and students of the Bible. Petrarch, the first humanist, wrote passionate poems about his beloved Laura, admired the ruins of ancient Rome, and delighted in the magnificent view of nature from the peak of Mount Ventoux near Avignon; but he also immersed himself in the teachings of the Bible and the church. For example, his *De viris illustribus* is a study in biography in which he attempted to show the mutual idealism found in both the Bible and in classical antiquity; his *De vita solitaria* describes the life of solitude as an opportunity to enjoy nature and to practice prayer; and his *Secretum meum* is an autobiographical treatise consisting of imaginary dialogues between himself and Augustine in the presence of

Truth concerning the biblical themes of sin and grace.

Petrarch's friend and fellow Italian, Boccaccio, expressed many of the same themes: love of the classics, enjoyment of life, appreciation of nature, and constant seeking for true virtue. He composed many works on these and kindred subjects, but his most influential work was the *Decameron.* It has been called a "Human Comedy" that matches Dante's *Divine Comedy.* Brilliantly conceived, it recounts the events of a fortnight in the lives of ten young people who fled a plague in Florence by retiring to a pleasant rural setting. There they talked and danced, alternating between gaiety and solemnity, as they told one hundred stories during ten days. The stories are secular, as is the whole book, but the purpose seems to be the affirmation of moral values—values derived from both the classical tradition and from the Bible. After all, Boccaccio and Petrarch were both in minor orders and thus loyal devotees of the faith.

The great English poet, Geoffrey Chaucer, wrote a large number of major works, including *The Parliament of Fowls, Troilus and Criseyde,* and *The Canterbury Tales.* They all exhibit the same themes found in the writings of Petrarch and Boccaccio, and *The Canterbury Tales* especially contains material borrowed from both the *Decameron* and the Bible.

Pico della Mirandola was a typical Renaissance man, a member of the newly established Platonic Academy in Florence and best remembered for his treatise *On the Dignity of Man.* No work of the period better demonstrates the new appreciation for the possible dignity and glory of humanity in the creation. However, Pico also wrote a great commentary on Genesis, the *Heptaplus,* and in other writings as well took up the pen to defend the biblical teachings of the church against its enemies. He was especially opposed to the astrologers and other pagan proponents of belief in Fate, and his constant theme was the God-given freedom of human beings that allows them to choose their own destiny between "the lower natures which are brutes" and "the higher natures which are divine."

Desiderius Erasmus represents the crowning glory of the Renaissance in literature, being a truly universal man in both mind and spirit. A native of the Netherlands, he lived in several countries from England to Italy. He insisted on conversing and writing mainly in Latin because it was the international language, and he gave equal attention to classical learning and to Christian teaching. His *Praise of Folly* and *Enchiridion* demonstrate a thorough knowledge of the scriptures in the service of church reform and religious instruction; and one of his most significant accomplishments was the publication in 1516 of the Greek text of the NT, a landmark of textual criticism that opened the way for modern biblical study.

Reformation Literature. In the light of the Protestant principle of biblical authority, it is hardly necessary to go beyond a bare recognition of the formative influence of the Bible on the literature of Reformation times. Martin Luther, the prime mover of the Reformation, wrote numerous theological treatises, sermons, commentaries, letters, and catechetical manuals, enough to make him one of the most prolific authors in history, and they were all based directly on the scriptures. It should be remembered that it was Luther who helped to give shape and uniformity to the German language by his translation of Erasmus's Greek text into the vernacular. Ulrich Zwingli, the Swiss reformer who claimed to have arrived at his views independently of Luther, also demonstrated his dependence upon the scriptures, seen in the light of humanistic study, in his influential major work, *The Commentary on True and False Religion.*

The numerous followers of Luther and Zwingli during their time and in the next generation composed a vast literature in exposition and defense of the reformed understanding of the faith. John Calvin, for example, published his first book, *Commentary on Seneca's Two Books on Clemency,* at the age of twenty-two, and in it he praised Seneca's Stoic morality but attempted to show how it needs to be supplemented by the Christian ethics of the NT. As is well known, his chief work, the *Institutes of the Christian Religion,* is founded squarely on biblical principles and became the most significant early statement of Reformed theology.

Another major literary production of the age of the Reformation, written by a great humanist who, like his friend Erasmus, remained loyal to the Roman church, was *Utopia,* by Thomas More. In that powerful work, More argued for an ideal state in which religion and natural reason prevail. The *Utopia* is a splendid example of the use of biblical ideals in combination with classical culture to supply a vision of what humanity might achieve. There were many other authors in the countries of Western Europe during the sixteenth century, but the times were so completely occupied with religious controversy and wars that most of the great literature was theological.

Modern Literature. Modern Western literature—that written during the past four centuries—is so voluminous that it defies adequate description or analysis. The modern age has retained the cultural heritage it received from the revolutionary epochs of the Renaissance and the Reformation, working out the consequences of both their emphases on the freedom and value of humanity and their concern with the biblical messages of judgment and grace. The continuing cultural struggles that have thus characterized the modern age have been reflected and recorded in the plethora of literature of all types that has been produced in increasing volume. The place of the Bible as the great fundamental document of Western culture may be clearly seen in almost all of that literature, sometimes in a positive way but often in reaction and rejection.

Space here permits the mention of only a few of the outstanding examples, with major emphasis on English literature. At the beginning of the period, the Spanish novelist, playwright, and poet Cervantes composed *Don Quixote,* which has been called "the first and greatest of modern novels." Though apparently a thoroughly secular work, it nonetheless arose out of a Christian milieu and it reflects the special attitudes of religious dedication and acceptance of fate that have always characterized the Spanish soul. On the other hand, the great body of French literature during modern times has usually dealt with human society and personality—with social criticism, the use of reason, and romantic love as the major themes. One thinks immediately of such influential authors as the philosopher Descartes, the dramatists Molière and Racine, the satirist Voltaire, the social critics Rousseau, Hugo, and Zola, and the existentialists Camus and Sartre. But there have also been powerful voices of faith such as Fénelon, Pascal, and Chateaubriand.

Modern German literature has been represented by a long list of authors, but no one displays a clearer mixture of biblical faith and classical thought than Johann Wolfgang von Goethe, the greatest of them all. His *Faust* is undoubtedly one of the classics of world literature, containing in form a combination of literary types and themes while presenting in substance the essential human struggle for meaning and value. It has been well said that Goethe "remained a grateful heir to the Christian tradition—*bibelfest,* rooted in the Bible, as his language constantly proclaims." Two other major German authors that displayed a controlling biblical tutelage were Hegel and Lessing. Hegel's vast philosophical system, continuing the ancient synthesis of Platonic and biblical ideas, has borne incalculable fruit in modern science, philosophy, politics, and religion. In like manner, Lessing's works, especially his publication of the "Wolffenbüttel Fragments" of Reimarus and his own *The Education of the Human Race* and *Nathan the Wise,* have continued to produce lasting results in biblical study and Christian ecumenism. The works of Hamann, Herder, and Schiller were also suffused with biblical thought, and Thomas Mann's novels, *The Magic Mountain* and *Joseph and His Brothers,* both reveal a fascination with biblical concepts and materials.

No body of Western literature can serve as a better example of the influence of the Bible than that of the English-speaking peoples. The imported epic *Beowulf* aside, the earliest native literature of England is probably that from the monasteries of Northumberland, preserved in *The Ecclesiastical History of the English People* by the Venerable Bede (d. 735). That invaluable work recorded some paraphrases of portions of the Bible by the monastic poet Caedmon of Whitby. From the same location and time, another author, possibly the monk Cynewulf, wrote four poems that have survived, two of them containing legends of saints, another called the *Fates of the Apostles,* and a rhapsody called *Christ* which tells of his ascension and describes his future return. Since those early beginnings most of the greatest English writers have either drawn from the Bible as a source of their stories and ideas or have written on many subjects with the words and precepts of the scriptures often shining through.

Chaucer's use of the Bible has already been noted. Shakespeare, called the "star of poets" by his friend Ben Johnson, wrote mostly drama, of course, but also a large number of sonnets. He not only quoted and referred to the Bible frequently in his writings but his religious and moral allusions and assumptions were derived directly from that source. The same is demonstrably true of his fellow authors of the Elizabethan age: Spenser, Raleigh, Sidney, Bacon, and many others of equal renown.

The seventeenth century produced such major literary figures in England as John Donne, the preacher-poet; Robert Herrick, the lyricist; Jeremy Taylor, the eloquent author of *Holy Living and Holy Dying*; John Milton, the incomparable Puritan author of *Paradise Lost* and other writings that have achieved nearly canonical status; and John Bunyan, the Nonconformist author of *Grace Abounding* and *Pilgrim's Progress.* The central place of the scriptures in these writings is too obvious for comment. However, the eighteenth century, the age of the Enlightenment, saw a turn to the authority of reason and a concern with more mundane matters. In that period such major literary figures as Jonathan Swift, Addison and Steele, Alexander Pope, Samuel Johnson, and Oliver Goldsmith produced prose and poetry that revealed that they drank from the wells of a biblically informed conscience without frequent reference to the source. The same can be said of most of the giants of the Romantic age—Wordsworth, Coleridge, Byron, Shelley, Keats, and Scott. They reacted against the barren rationality of the previous century, but they found more solace in humanity and nature than in the Bible, though they usually took the scriptures and the Christian tradition for granted as assumed foundations for living. Their successors in literary dominance, the Victorians, often showed more direct concern with the stories and ideas of the Bible. That is especially true of the poetry of Tennyson and Browning, though the scriptural concepts of social righteousness and personal ethics reverberate also in the prose of Carlyle, Mill, Dickens, and Hardy. A similar development may be seen in the American authors of the century, among whom should be noted Hawthorne, Melville, Emerson, and Thoreau.

The twentieth century, properly understood to have begun with "the guns of August" in 1914, has seen a series of calamities that have caused the times to be characterized as "the age of anxiety." That condition, in turn, has led to a renewal of interest in the needed truth and direction to be discovered in the scriptures, as, for example, in the massive theological works of Karl Barth. Two outstanding illustrations of that development are the British-American poets T. S. Eliot and W. H. Auden. Eliot's *Waste Land, The Hollow Men,* and *Four Quartets* have convinced their readers that modern Western culture is spiritually bankrupt, causing the anxiety of meaninglessness. Auden's "For the Time Being, A Christmas Oratorio" points to the same danger and suggests the biblical antidote. In less overt ways, the novels of Steinbeck, Hemingway, Wolfe, Faulkner, and O'Connor suggest a nagging sense of moral and spiritual hunger caused by the nearly forgotten hope and security once found in the Bible. The conscience-raising writings of John Updike (*Rabbit Run*), James Baldwin (*The Fire Next Time*), and Ralph Ellison (*The Invisible Man*), among many others, could hardly have been written without the moral foundations supplied by the scriptures. The effects of biblical teaching continue to lie beneath the surface, erupting in active concerns for world peace, social justice, and human rights. There are those like C. S. Lewis who have sounded the call to biblical faith and living against the tides of earth-bound secularity.

In summary it may be said that the Bible has provided a major source and guide for Western civilization, not only through the religious study of it made available through the preaching and teaching of the churches but, perhaps with wider results, through the great literary creations that have channeled its formative archetypes and moral principles to culture and people during the past two millennia. The familiar stories, the moral precepts, and the indelible language of the Bible have helped, as nothing else has, to form and enrich Western civilization through its literature.

See also BIBLE IN AMERICA; LITERATURE, BIBLE AS.

Bibliography. R. Alter and F. Kermode, eds., *The Literary Guide to the Bible*; M. Arnold, *Literature and Dogma*; J. Barr, *The Bible in the Modern World*; A. S. Cook, *The Bible and English Prose Style*; E. Dobschütz, *The Influence of the Bible on Civilization*; D. C. Fowler, *The Bible in Early English Literature*; E. J. Goodspeed, *A History of Early Christian Literature*; G. Gunn, ed., *The Bible and American Arts and Letters*; R. G. Moulton, *The Literary Study of the Bible*; J. H. Randall, *The Making of the Modern Mind*; N. A. Scott, *Modern Literature and the Religious Frontier*; G. Sivan, *The Bible and Civilization*; V. L. Tollers and J. R. Maier, eds., *The Bible in its Literary Milieu*; A. N. Wilder, *Theology and Modern Literature* and *Modern Literature and the Religious Frontier*; D. Wilson, *The People and the Book.*

—J. WILLIAM ANGELL

• **Bible in America.** In American life, from the colonial period to the present, no book has occupied a more central place than the Bible. That centrality is evident whether one thinks in terms of the living room table, the village pulpit, the larger world of religious publishing, or the subtler world of influences and ideas. In their heritage from the past no less than in their aspirations for the future, Americans remain, to a remarkable degree, a "people of the book." This essay treats both its omnipresence as well as its persisting power.

The Bible as Import. In a literal no less than a figurative sense, American colonists brought their Bibles with them. This was true, of course, of seventeenth-century Puritans settling in Massachusetts, but likewise true of Anglicans then settling in Virginia, of Swedish Lutherans in Delaware, of Roman Catholics in Maryland, of Dutch Reformed in New York, and of Quakers in Pennsylvania. The eighteenth century saw no alteration in this pattern as German Protestants and Catholics migrated in great numbers to the Pennsylvania region, as Scottish Presbyterians settled chiefly in the Middle Colonies, as Lutherans fleeing from persecution found refuge in Georgia, as Moravians made their homes in North Carolina and interior Pennsylvania, as Jewish refugees settled in seacoast cities, as Methodists and Baptists moved far beyond early centers of strength to trans-Appalachian frontiers. And whether all carried Bibles in their hands, virtually all had both hearts and heads filled with biblical narratives, biblical injunctions, biblical models for corporate as well as private life. All of this "luggage" sustained the immigrants even as it enriched their posterity and helped to shape their adopted land.

The first truly popular (i.e., relatively inexpensive and eminently readable) English Bible was produced not in England but in Switzerland. There, under the watchful eye of John Calvin and with the critical assistance of Theodore Beza, English-speaking Protestant exiles in 1560 produced a translation enhanced by illustrations, chapter summaries, clear roman type, maps, marginal commentary, and useful chapter and verse divisions. Despite its unofficial status in England, the Geneva Bible found a wide audience, especially among the Puritans. Many of those emigrating to New England in the 1620s and 1630s brought with them their now well-worn, much-cherished Geneva Bibles. With such a Bible in hand (and in mind), Separatists and Puritans found laws for their society, rules for their churches, theology for their reflection, and inspiration for their lives.

Within a generation of the earliest North American permanent settlements, another and far more enduring translation gradually won a preeminent place near the hearth and on the pulpit. The King James Version (KJV), first issued in 1611, was indeed "authorized," the third English Bible to be so designated and the first to win wide currency (far more than its two predecessors had managed to do, the "Great Bible" of 1539 and the "Bishops' Bible" of 1568). The King James Bible, though issued at first in a large and expensive folio edition, soon imitated the Geneva Bible in utilizing less expensive paper and in producing smaller, more portable, more affordable volumes. Now, not just the Puritans of New England possessed and utilized this authorized Bible, but so did the Presbyterians of the Middle Colonies, the Anglicans of the South, and English-speaking Protestants of every stripe. England and Scotland, operating under exclusive Crown Copyright privileges, continued to be the major suppliers of the American market down to the very end of the colonial period. And the KJV continued long beyond that time to provide a common frame of discourse for much of the citizenry.

Continental Protestants, of whatever language, traced their biblical lineage to Martin Luther whose translation of scriptures into German in 1534 became both model and authority for making this vital body of literature available in the vernacular tongue. The humanist scholar, Erasmus, by providing a printed version of the Greek NT in 1516, also encouraged and facilitated translations into several European languages. So Scandinavian Lutherans, French Huguenots, Dutch Calvinists, no less than German Lutherans and German Reformed drew upon Luther's labors.

English Catholics early in the seventeenth century could benefit from the labors of Catholic exiles, just as English Protestants had been served by the exiles in Geneva. The Douay Bible (so called because the work was completed at Douay College in northern France) represented a translation from the official Latin Bible of the Roman Catholic Church, the Vulgate. Much revised in the eighteenth century by Bishop Richard Challoner of London, this Bible found its way into the homes of Catholics settling in Maryland and later in Pennsylvania. The nation's first Roman Catholic bishop, John Carroll, even succeeded in persuading the Philadelphia printer, Matthew Carey, to bring out an American edition in 1790. Other exceptions to the colonists' status as importers of Bibles will be noted below, but for the most part seventeenth and eighteenth century Americans depended upon Britain and the European continent to supply them with copies of the printed Word. This was likewise true of the tiny Jewish community, much too scattered and much too poor to consider any major publication venture on its own.

Ideas, of course, were easier than books to transport or import. And colonial Americans, however well or ill supplied they might be with copies of the Bible, suffered no deprivation so far as biblical imagery or ideology were concerned. No export taxes delayed or discouraged the free flow of these ideas; no theory of mercantilism could prevent the creation or distribution of biblical motifs and biblical perspectives. Slaves brought unwillingly to the New World found the slavery of the Israelites in Egypt comparable to their own captivity; likewise, they looked toward a Promised Land, here or hereafter, where every tear would be wiped away and every soul made free. Quakers compared themselves to the Bereans mentioned in the Book of Acts: namely, those who "received the word with all readiness of mind, and searched the Scriptures daily, whether these things are so." Pilgrims spoke of the "great hope and inward zeal" that propelled them toward America where they might be both more faithful to the Gospel and more effective in its propagation. Puritans, in their first code of laws, followed Leviticus scrupulously, determined to let the Bible be their guide in matters both civil and ecclesiastical. Lutherans fleeing the persecution of Salzburg upon sighting the coast of Georgia read Ps 66 with "great pleasure because it fitted our circumstances exceedingly well. At last we read from the 5th chapter of Joshua, with the admonition that those who needed it should use the last few days at sea to open their hearts."

And so it went with Presbyterians and Methodists, with Baptists and German Reformed, with Roman Catholics and Jews—all finding scriptural parallels to their exile and sufferings, scriptural promises to sustain them in an uncertain wilderness. No need for America to instruct these immigrants in the words of the prophets, the wisdom of the Psalms, the good news of the New Covenant: all this they brought with them, all this they planted more firmly in

American soil than the flags of the nations they had left behind. And their early plantings took root, finding much nurture in rich soil, much openness that would allow for luxuriant growth.

The Bible as Product. Special challenges in America early required the colonists to be producers as well as consumers of biblical publication. Missionary labors among the Indians demanded, first, a laborious learning of the tribal tongue and, second, some provision in that tongue of biblical or catechetical teaching. The earliest as well as the most ambitious effort of this kind was that of Puritan John Eliot; in 1663 he finished a translation of the entire Bible into the Algonkian tongue. His grand ambition was nearly matched by that of the Boston printers who, with limited resources and primitive equipment (but with some help from abroad), proceeded to set each piece of type by hand and then print a work nearly twelve hundred pages in length.

Philadelphia, made an important printing center because of German immigrants (notably Christopher Sauer) and New England migrants (notably Benjamin Franklin), managed in 1743 to publish the first American Bible in a European language, the language being German rather than English. A deeply pious immigrant to Germantown some two decades before, Sauer published his Bible (Martin Luther's translation) to serve the needs of the heavy German immigration into Pennsylvania in the first half of the eighteenth century. The reality of the need was demonstrated by the re-issuing of the Sauer Bible in 1763 and again in 1776.

By that latter year, importation of English Bibles was no longer possible as the colonies declared their independence and as the Mother Country suspended further commerce. A Philadelphia Scotsman, Robert Aitken, leaped into the breach with a NT produced in 1777, this followed by a New Jersey effort in 1779 (Isaac Collins) and a Massachusetts offering in 1780 (Thomas and John Fleet). But these were New Testaments only, obviously a much more manageable venture than a printing of the whole Bible. But in 1782 Robert Aitken managed to persuade the Continental Congress then sitting in Philadelphia to endorse his plan to produce the Bible in its entirety. With such official support, Aitken brought out his small and now quite rare Bible, his labors leading to no great economic success, no more than Matthew Carey's did a few years later. In the final decade of the eighteenth century, more impressive Bibles came from the press of Isaiah Thomas in Worcester, Massachusetts, his richly illustrated volumes testifying that American printing in general had reached a significantly higher level.

The nineteenth century ushered in a great new age of American Bible printing and distributing. The American Bible Society itself, created in 1816, set the pace for many local communities in which people organized for the purpose of purchasing and widely disseminating copies of the scriptures. Exclusively a Protestant effort at this early stage, the American Bible Society saw itself as rising above sectarianism and doctrinal quarrels in order to make available accurate and inexpensive Bibles not only all along the East Coast but far into the rapidly expanding American West. As the Society itself observed at the time of its founding, "the prodigious territory of the United States" and the rapidly increasing population made it necessary for Christians of good will to organize and cooperate, for only in this fashion could the frontier settlers maintain touch with those essential moral and religious influences derived from the Bible.

The Society did its work well, reaching across the Alleghenies, then across the Mississippi and the Missouri Rivers, then all the way to the Pacific Ocean. Within a generation of its founding, the American Bible Society had been responsible for the distribution of over five million copies of either the entire Bible or the NT. Such "products" reached not just the frontier, but into the prisons and orphanages, to men of the Army, Navy, and commercial fleets, to Sunday schools everywhere, and to newly arriving immigrants surprised to find copies of the Bible in their native tongues presented to them. By the middle of the nineteenth century—a century of enormous Anglo-American Protestant missionary effort, the American Bible Society had spanned the world. Printing, thanks to the invention of the stereotype plate, had become faster, cheaper, and more accurate. Even in the midst of the Civil War, the activities of the Society intensified rather than diminished, about one and one-half million Bibles being distributed to soldiers of the North, around three hundred thousand to soldiers of the South.

As the needs of the immigrants and of the missionaries to foreign lands increased, so the Society (as well as other entities) found itself engaged not simply in printing and distributing, but in translating as well. Translations were produced for such tribal groups in America as the Delaware, Mohawk, Seneca, Sioux, Dakota, and more. The insatiable demand, however, came from abroad: all the major languages of Europe, Asia, and Africa, along with many of the minor ones, required in whole or in part Bibles that were cheap, accurate, and readily available. But along with the demands of translation were those of an ever more reliable, ever more readable English text. And these demands, felt earliest among Protestants, pressed themselves also upon the nation's Roman Catholics and Jews.

An English Revised Version (ERV) in 1881–1885 led to an American Standard Version (ASV) in 1901, its major significance being that it started the excruciatingly slow process of weaning an American public from its centuries-old allegiance to the KJV (which had itself undergone many revisions since 1611). The Revised Standard Version (RSV) of 1946–1952 had far greater impact upon the Bible reading public and far wider adoption within the churches. While the way had been paved for the RSV to some extent by popular private translations (e.g., Edgar J. Goodspeed's NT in 1923 and J. M. Powis Smith and other's OT in 1927), the success of the 1952 Bible rested at least in part upon its corporate and cooperative character: Baptists, Congregationalists, Lutherans, Methodists, and Presbyterians joined in the revision process, along with Harry M. Orlinsky of the Jewish Institute of Religion. Not simply or even chiefly the changes in the English language dictated these twentieth-century revisions, but more significantly the important manuscript discoveries that offered translators a far more accurate text than was available in the early seventeenth century.

The American Bible Society returned to the contest with its issuance in 1966 (NT) and 1976 (entire Bible) of Today's English Version (Good News Bible), a translation designed to use language that was fresh and idioms that were current. In 1978 the evangelical community produced the New International Version, this achievement marking among other things the return of conservative scholarship (after the bruising battles of the 1920s) to the larger scholarly community. Although sectarian and confessional translations continued to appear (Jehovah's Witnesses provided their own in 1961, with revisions a decade later), something approaching a "common Bible" became a reality when Roman Catholics, Protestants, and Jews all agreed in the 1960s on the use of the RSV.

An American Catholic, Francis P. Kenrick (Bishop of Philadelphia, 1842–1851, and later Archbishop of Baltimore, 1851–1863) undertook the large task of offering a translation that moved beyond the Douay, now as "ancient" as the KJV. Though working primarily with the Latin Vulgate (as the Douay exiles had done), Kenrick often had occasion to refer to the original languages and to the writings of many other biblical scholars. By 1862, Kenrick issued the last of his six volumes, though never did his entire Bible appear in a single work, nor did his translation ever receive official sanction within the American Catholic Church.

A new era in Catholic biblical scholarship was inaugurated with the formation of the Catholic Biblical Association in 1938 and the launching of the *Catholic Biblical Quarterly* the following year. With papal encouragement to study carefully all early manuscripts and original languages, Catholic scholars moved to work now not from the Vulgate, itself a translation, but from the Greek and Hebrew. With further encouragement from Vatican Council II, the *New American Bible* at last appeared in 1970, the first translation in America under Roman Catholic auspices that did not maintain allegiance to St. Jerome's Vulgate as the prime loyalty or restraint. By that time, as indicated above, Catholics had already joined with Protestants in approving and utilizing the RSV.

Though the Hebrew text remains the only authoritative base for Judaism around the world, English translations have found wide currency among America's Jews as among America's Catholics and Protestants. Philadelphia's Isaac Leeser, concerned that Jews in the new land might lose their identity and their heritage, brought out the Torah in English in 1845, this to be followed by an English translation of the entire Bible in 1853. Somewhat to Leeser's surprise, his translation won acclaim in portions of the Christian as well as the Jewish community. He was praised for his fidelity to the Hebrew text, even though he understandably resisted the Christian interpretation of many OT passages.

By the end of the nineteenth century, the archaeological and manuscript discoveries suggested to all Americans interested in scriptural matters that newer and more reliable translations were required. The Jewish Publication Society, after many years of labor and some discouragements, brought out *The Holy Scriptures* in 1917, an impressive achievement of as well as tribute to American Jewish scholars. This translation represented major improvement over the Leeser Bible as well as emancipation from the inexpensive KJV on which English-speaking Jews had often depended. The translation also demonstrated that the Jewish community in America had come of age and was prepared to play a major scholarly role in Jewry around the world. But just as the ASV of 1901 yielded to a more competent and readable RSV in 1952, so the Jewish Publication Society version of 1917 required replacement a half-century or so later. Harry Orlinsky called for such a replacement in 1953, the ultimate result being the appearance of the New Jewish Version in 1982.

In the latter years of the twentieth century, Bible publishing no less than Bible translating showed no signs of levelling off. Indeed, the Bible remained the perennial best-seller in America. And if one added to Bible printing itself the enormous body of Bible helps, commentaries, dictionaries, encyclopedias, and the like, none could question that with respect to the "Bible as Product," the United States of America had taken an impressive lead.

The Bible as Cultural Force. If the early colonists brought with them a biblical worldview and a biblical storehouse of knowledge, later citizens only enlarged and deepened that which the seventeenth century had begun. In the American Revolution, for example, many Americans found the contest with England foreshadowed by Israel's conflicts with Assyria or Babylonia or Persia or even Rome. English taxes could be compared to curses or plagues visited upon a people by evil and alien hands. King George III was seen as like the new Pharaoh who "knew not Joseph." With respect to the tax on tea in the 1770s, a Presbyterian minister found in Col 2:21 a perfect text: "Touch not; taste not; handle not." In the Civil War, as Abraham Lincoln all too sadly and accurately noted, "both read the same Bible, and pray to the same God." And both sides found sanction and support in that Bible. Northerners (such as Theodore Parker) argued that the OT practice of slavery must be considered alongside its practice of polygamy, so why not "stock our houses with wives as well as with slaves?" At the same time, Southerners (such as Frederick Ross) argued that abolitionists applied "the rack to the Hebrew and the Greek" in order to turn the Bible into an antislavery tract; it is difficult, indeed impossible, "to persuade men that Moses and Paul were moved by the Holy Ghost to sanction the philosophy of Thomas Jefferson!"

In the Manifest Destiny policy of expansion, in the "splendid little war" of 1898, in the larger conflict of World War I, and well beyond, the Bible was enlisted in support of or in opposition to specific policies or programs. But beyond the moments of crisis, the Bible steadily exercised a powerful influence throughout the entire culture. It infused the grammar schools of an early day, and had not been bled from the public schools of a later day. Few decisions of the U.S. Supreme Court aroused as much ire as the *Abingdon* v. *Schempp* opinion of 1963 which declared the ritual reading of the Bible to be unconstitutional. In moral reforms, whether of race or of war, the Bible has been drafted by both sides, as it has in the contemporary struggles concerning abortion, homosexuality, feminism, and private or parochial education. One can never be sure on which side the Bible will be quoted, but one can be sure that neither side in any major confrontation will regard it as wholly irrelevant.

At another cultural level, the Bible also continues to permeate American art, music, and literature. From William Faulkner and Flannery O'Connor to Peter DeVries and John Updike, biblical motifs reveal themselves. "Godspell" became a musical hit, while a monologue presentation of the Gospel of Mark received favorable notice on Broadway. As one authority recently wrote, Americans, whatever their vaunted secularity might suggest, "have not been able to resist thinking in [the Bible's] images, speaking in its language, feeling in its forms." Both "folk" art and "high" art present biblical heroes and heroines, biblical episodes and apocalypses, in abundant and undiminishing supply.

In the realm of politics, it is easy to dismiss the frequent appearance of biblical language and even biblical theology as nothing more than the crassest sort of political utilitarianism or exploitation: one must offer to the crowd its scriptural bread and its spiritual circuses. Yet, careful scholars have noted that beneath this superficiality one sees a search for a thread of cultural unity to bind together all of the nation's noisy plurality. In the quest for coherence, it may be that biblical symbols, values, and assumptions hold more promise than any other accessible and recognizable alternative. Biblical covenants bound New Englanders together centuries ago, and perhaps such covenants (as Robert Bellah has suggested) hold the greatest hope of binding together Americans centuries later. So often in the national past, meaning and purpose have been found through an appeal to or reliance on biblical promises and norms. To lose that grounding may be to lose the best chance of mixing together the necessary social cement.

The Bible as Contest and Controversy. For all its potential as a unifier, the Bible in the last hundred years has also demonstrated its capacity to alienate and divide. Scientific, literary, philosophical, and historical developments in this time period have set clergy and laity against each other, have splintered churches, wrecked careers, weakened educational institutions, and turned much institutional religion in America into a scandal and offense. Such terms as "modernist" on the one hand and "fundamentalist" on the other offer a hint of the way in which religious armies divided, but even where these terms were not used, Catholics, Protestants, and Jews found themselves struggling with the mentalities and moods that those terms suggest.

In 1907 Pope Pius X listed some sixty-five "Errors of Modernists," then later that year in a long encyclical condemned the modernist movement wherever it might be found. The "errors" delineated and detailed related to attitudes toward science and history, psychology and politics, but also toward "Sacred Scripture." The modernists were wrong to believe and assert, stated the Pope, that the Church's understanding of the Bible needed "the more accurate judgment and correction of the exegetes." Modernists also erred in declaring that all of the Bible was not necessarily, in all parts, "free from every error." These and many similar judgments, authoritatively set down, put Catholic biblical scholarship "on hold" for more than a generation. Then, in 1943, another papal encyclical, this one issued by Pope Pius XII, gave its blessing and encouragement to a scholarly study of the Bible, noting that many questions regarding the scriptures remain unanswered and that it was a great mistake to suppose "that whatever is new should for that very reason be opposed or suspected." Let Catholic commentators, the pope added, exercise their skills and their learning freely "so that each may contribute his part to the advantage of all."

Within Judaism, the separation into Reform, Conservative, and Orthodox segments reflected varying attitudes toward the Law in particular (the Books of Moses) and the Hebrew Scriptures in general. Reform Judaism early accepted the results of literary and historical criticism, noting in 1885 that "modern discoveries" were not prejudicial to basic doctrines of Judaism, "the Bible reflecting the primitive ideas of its own age." Conservative Judaism came to this conclusion more slowly, Solomon Schechter early in the twentieth century finding biblical criticism to be ill-informed, damaging in its effect, and possibly anti-Semitic in its intent. But a half century or so later, Conservative scholar Nahum Sarna decried the wooden and literalist defense of the Bible as having the predictable effect of "de-sanctifying" that book in the eyes of an educated public.

In Protestantism, the confrontations were noisiest and the blood-letting fullest. Heresy trials, such as that of Presbyterian Charles A. Briggs in 1893, kept a large public informed and sometimes titillated. Baptists and Presbyterians of the North repeatedly suffered schism and recrimination. And even Episcopalians had their heresy trial, that of Algernon Crapsey in 1906. Most of the struggle had quieted by World War II, but it revived quite visibly in the 1970s with the Lutheran Church (Missouri Synod). With Concordia Seminary in St. Louis at the center of the dispute, this large branch of Lutheranism took a strong stand in favor of biblical infallibility, suspended the seminary president as well as several members of the faculty, and prompted the separation of about one hundred thousand members from the Missouri Synod. As its president at that time stated, "the overwhelming majority of the church . . . took the position that they did not want theological liberalism and the use of the historical-critical method in the Synod." And in the 1980s the Southern Baptist Convention found itself drawn toward opposing poles, one labelled fundamentalist and the other moderate. As in the Missouri Synod, so among Baptists in the South, many contended that the real issue was power and the lines of authority. But, again in both instances, the banner waved most insistently against liberal or moderate was that of biblical inerrancy. As Baptist leader James Draper argued, it was a case of reason versus revelation, human relativities against divine absolutes.

While much of the controverting and contending suggests that we learn from the past that we learn nothing from the past, religion in America does not always mindlessly repeat the same mistakes. Much of the "modernism" of an earlier era has repented of its overly optimistic view of human agency, has withdrawn from uncritical cultural endorsement and alliance. At the same time much of the "fundamentalism" of the past has moved toward an evangelicalism that is prepared to distance itself from rigid positions of the past. Conservatives, as Mark Noll has pointed out, have an obligation to abandon the close textual readings "based on arcane numerological tabulations, derived from word studies of allegorical fantasy . . . or teased by legerdemain from the apocalyptic visions of Ezekiel and Revelation." So while some segments of institutional religion continue to plunge toward dismaying schism, others rise toward new plateaus where the Bible may again bear witness to wholeness and reconciliation.

See also BIBLE AND WESTERN LITERATURE.

Bibliography. D. L. Barr and N. Piediscalzi, eds., *The Bible in American Education*; J. W. Brown, *The Rise of Biblical Criticism in America, 1800–1870*; E. S. Frerichs, ed., *The Bible and Bibles in America*; G. Gunn, ed., *The Bible and American Arts and Letters*; N. O. Hatch and M. A. Noll, eds., *The Bible in America*; J. T. Johnson, ed., *The Bible in American Law, Politics, and Political Rhetoric*; M. A. Noll, *Between Faith & Criticism: Evangelicals, Scholarship, and the Bible in America*; A. S. Phy, ed., *The Bible and Popular Culture in America*; J. B. Rogers and D. K. McKim, *The Authority and Interpretation of the Bible: An Historical Approach*; E. R. Sandeen, ed., *The Bible and Social Reform.*

—EDWIN S. GAUSTAD

• **Bible, Authority of.** The two key words in the title of this article require careful definition. What is meant by "authority" when used with reference to the BIBLE, and what are its essential characteristics? Also, exactly what is meant when one speaks of "the Bible," and how did it come to be so designated? After these two questions are examined, the historical development of the concept of the authority of scripture will be traced and the basis for the concept will be evaluated.

There is no exact term for "authority" in the Hebrew

scriptures. The nearest equivalent is a verb meaning "to rule, to have dominion over." However, there are numerous concrete references to the exercise of power or dominion by God (Ps 114:2; Eccl 8:8), by kings (Gen 41:35; 2 Chr 28:7; Esth 9:29), by human beings in general (Num 5:19; 27:20; Prov 29:2, 16; Neh 5:15), and even by heavenly bodies (Ps 136:8-9). The equivalent Greek term in the NT (ἐξουσία) is translated into Latin as *auctoritas* and into English as "authority" (cf. Matt 28:18; Mark 1:22; Luke 4:1-13; John 10:18; 17:2; Rom 13:1; Eph 1:21; 3 John 9). In all cases the references are to potential or active power or control, usually that of God or the agents of God.

When used in theology, the term "authority" has two primary meanings. First, it refers to power—original or ultimate force, as in Aristotle's efficient and final causes. Thus it is a synonym for God, in theistic terms. The second reference is to a standard of truth and right, a basis for judgment, that which provides instruction, guidance, and persuasion. The first is often called *causative* authority and the second *normative* authority. The latter is meant when the term is used with reference to the Bible.

Normative authority must possess three essential characteristics if it is to be acceptable, useful, and effective: immediate availability, intrinsic value, and ultimate claim. Immediate availability means that whatever is proposed as authority must be so objectively present and generally recognizable that there can be no confusion or difficulty in finding and using it. Authority must be public and open; it cannot be hidden or esoteric. Intrinsic value means that the worth of the authority will be self-evident and autonomous. Its truth must be axiomatic and its strength must be derived from its own coherence and integrity. And, third, ultimate claim means that the accepted authority must be the final arbiter, the highest court to which appeal can be made. Truth and right are determined in the light of this standard in such a way that subsequent debate is not about what they are but whether they are being followed. To find and follow it is to be led from error to truth, from sinfulness to righteousness, from alienation to reconciliation. The purpose of normative authority in religion is to lead to causative authority, to the knowledge and power of God.

The second term in the title of this article, Bible, raises the question of CANON—how the books of the OT and NT came to be composed, how they were transmitted, and, most of all, when, how, and why they were included. It is necessary here only to emphasize the significance and priority of the question of canon for the question of authority. Acceptance of biblical authority is uninformed credulity without some understanding of what the Bible is and how it came to be such.

The beginnings of the acceptance of certain documents as the written WORD OF GOD appear to be unrecorded and impossible to discover with certainty. This is true for nearly all of the major religions of the world, including biblical religion. There are many references in the Pentateuch to the recording of the revelations and commandments of Yahweh to Moses (Exod 17:14; 24:12; 32:15, 16, 19; 34:28; 40:20; Lev 27:34; Deut 28:58; 31:9). Similar references to the written Law may be found in the Former Prophets (cf. Josh 9:31, 32, 34; 23:6; 24:26; 1 Sam 10:25; 1 Kgs 14:29). Obviously the oracles of the prophets of the eighth, seventh, and sixth centuries were also preserved by the faithful until they were ultimately set in final form by their canonization no later than the second century B.C.E. One memorable example is the account of the recording of Jeremiah's oracles by Baruch the scribe, followed by the scroll's destruction by King Jehoiakim and its expanded rewriting by Baruch (Jer 36).

Nevertheless, it can be said with considerable confidence that the concept of an authoritative written Word of God, as opposed to the living Word formerly spoken by Moses and the prophets, had its beginning with the rediscovery of the "book of the law" in the Temple about 621 B.C.E. which resulted in the great reform under King Josiah (2 Kgs 22–23). That law is believed by most scholars to have been what is now most of the book of Deuteronomy (*deuteros nomos,* the second edition of the law). Jeremiah was beginning his work at about the same time, of course, and other prophets were to follow during the succeeding centuries. However, the voice of prophecy soon began to decline, and, following the Babylonian Exile, the people of Israel came to locate the Word of God in the written documents from the past rather than in the oral word of the present. Belief in the authority of scripture had begun. That belief led to the inclusion of some writings and the exclusion of others. The TORAH, which had its origins in the work of Moses, was fixed by the time of Ezra and Nehemiah (Neh 8:1-9). The Prophets, both Former and Latter, seem to have become recognized as complete by the second century B.C.E. (see the prologue of Sirach). The remainder of the Hebrew canon was not defined until the famous Council of Jamnia, about 90 C.E., after the fall of Jerusalem to the Romans and the permanent dispersion of the Jews from their homeland.

It is important to note that Jesus and the earliest Christians referred only to "the law and the prophets" (Matt 5:17; Luke 16:29), "the scriptures" (Mark 12:24; Gal 4:30; Rom 1:2; 3:21), or "the law of Moses and the prophets and the psalms" (Luke 24: 44; Acts 1:16). That is, the NT books themselves contain evidence that the Hebrew scriptures were not yet finally and fully defined; the Torah and the Prophets were canonized, but the Writings were still in process of being so until the end of the first century C.E. Apparently, one of the major factors in closing the canon by the rabbis at Jamnia was the beginning of the circulation of those Christian writings that were later to comprise the NT. Further, since the Jews of the dispersion spoke the languages of the Greco-Roman world, their scriptures had been translated after 250 B.C.E. into Greek. That version, known as the SEPTUAGINT (LXX), was the primary vehicle of Jewish piety, except among the scholars who could still read the no-longer-spoken Hebrew; it was also the version of the scriptures that the earliest Christian churches accepted as the authoritative, written Word of God. Thus Christianity began with the largest part of its Bible already in hand.

The books of the NT were composed during approximately the second half of the first century C.E., but of course they were not immediately available to the churches generally or accepted on the same level of authority as the LXX and its Hebrew original (cf. 2 Pet 3:15-16). Apparently the first Christian canon was that of MARCION, a misguided leader in Rome about 140 C.E., who rejected both the Jewish God and the Jewish scriptures. Later condemned as a heretic, Marcion collected ten letters of Paul and Luke-Acts, expurgated them to suit his anti-Jewish ideas, and thereby began the NT.

During the next three centuries numerous Christian writings were used and sanctioned as authoritative. The process of inclusion and exclusion was gradual. However, the canon began to take definite form as early as the time of IRENAEUS (ca. 185 C.E.), who, though a native of Asia Minor, was Bishop of Lugdunum (Lyons) in Gaul. He gave a central place to the four Gospels and recognized all of the books of the still developing NT except Hebrews, 2 Peter, 2 and 3 John, James, and Jude. He also accepted some books that were later excluded.

The first known list of NT books that included precisely the twenty-seven and no others was by Athanasius, the hero of Nicaea and several times Bishop of Alexandria in Egypt during the fourth century. The list is included in his famous Easter Letter of 367 C.E. He also explicitly rejected the OT Apocrypha, as did Origen before him, EUSEBIUS of Caesarea, his contemporary, and the great Jerome, translator of the Vulgate, in the next generation.

Several factors were involved in the gradual process of NT canonization, which meant its acceptance as authoritative. One was popular usage of certain revered books. Another was the belief that some books were peculiarly inspired whereas others, though respected, were not. But the evidence indicates that the major consideration was *apostolicity*. That is, a book was finally accepted in the Christian scriptures if it was believed to have been written by one of the apostles (including Paul) or by one of their companions (such as Mark or Luke). Apostolicity guaranteed dependable witness to the original gospel. The preservation of the original apostolic gospel was made urgent by the rise of many false teachings, especially that of the Gnostics.

With the limits thus determined for both the OT and NT, the canons of the two Testaments were complete. A dispute has remained, however, with respect to the authority of the Jewish Apocrypha. The rabbis at Jamnia rejected it from their canon, as did many early Christian scholars, some of whom are noted above. On the other hand the churches of both East and West have continued to recognize the canonicity and authority of certain parts of the Apocrypha. The Orthodox churches have not always been clear as to the limits of their canon, but there is general acceptance of it as defined by the Orthodox Synod of Jerusalem in 1672. The Roman Church since ancient times has also accepted parts of the Apocrypha, though with some variations from the Orthodox. The Roman canon was fixed by a decree of the Council of Trent in 1546. Protestants, however, have refused to accept the authority of any part of the Apocrypha and have agreed with the final Jewish definition of Jamnia with respect to the OT. It should be noted further that both the Orthodox and Roman churches have placed the authority of later tradition alongside that of the scriptures whereas Protestants, beginning with Luther, Zwingli, and Calvin, have insisted upon the sole authority of the scriptures for Christian faith and practice.

The authority of scripture has been seriously threatened in modern times by the development of the methods of literary and historical criticism. These methods did not begin entirely in the modern age, of course, but their application to biblical study and interpretation has become much more widespread since the Renaissance and especially since the Enlightenment. The results have frequently been devastating for traditional belief. Multiple questions have been raised regarding the reliability of the extant copies of the scriptures as well as with respect to sources, authorship, redaction, historical conditioning, and other such aspects of literary study. Nevertheless, the scriptures remain central in the faith, practice, and worship of most Christians, regardless of their denominational affiliation or critical opinions.

It is interesting and useful to investigate the basis for the belief in the authority of the scriptures. Aside from simple, unexamined credulity, there have always been two foundations for the belief, sometimes stated but more often merely implied. The first is the faith assumption that the books of the OT and NT are the written Word of God, sufficient and authoritative for all people in all ages, because they were written by persons chosen and inspired by God. According to this view, it was God's will that a saving knowledge of himself and his will should be provided in those particular records, and the HOLY SPIRIT, using human agents, caused it to be done. Hence no other standard of religious truth is necessary, no supplement is needed, and no contradiction can be accepted.

This doctrine of inspiration is the foundation most commonly used to support the conviction that the scriptures are the primary authority for questions of faith. Although expressed in various ways, the doctrine may be found, either implicitly or explicitly, in practically all creeds, statements of faith, and theological writings. It is frequently supported by reference to such texts as 2 Tim 3:16: "All scripture is inspired by God and profitable for teaching, for reproof, for correction, and for training in righteousness"; or 2 Pet 1:21: "No prophecy ever came by the impulse of man, but men moved by the Holy Spirit spoke from God."

Nevertheless, certain weaknesses have been noted that call into question the adequacy of the argument from inspiration alone as a basis for scriptural authority. First, is it not a faulty logic that attempts to prove the inspiration of scripture by quoting scripture? Do not such passages as those quoted above refer only to the then-existing Hebrew scriptures and not to the yet-to-be-completed NT? Second, does the doctrine of inspiration cover the canonizing process also? In the light of what is known about the writing, redaction, preservation, and canonization of the Bible, it is difficult to attribute infallibly divine guidance to the process. It is altogether possible, perhaps even probable, that equally inspired books were written, even by known biblical writers, that have not survived. We know that some books in the canon were reluctantly accepted.

Third, is it to be assumed that the doctrine of inspiration refers only to the autographs? If so, that leaves the Bible reader with disturbing problems concerning the text. No autographs exist. All that remain are copies of copies of copies, many times removed from the originals. Does not the process itself indicate a large degree of human frailty as well as human grandeur in the writing and transmission of the sacred text? Finally, it has been suggested that the doctrine of inspiration, especially when stated in terms of the concept of biblical inerrancy, may fall into the danger of doing with the scriptures what the ancient Gnostics did with Christ, denying the humanity and holding to the heresy of Docetism. If the Word was made flesh in Jesus (John 1:14), perhaps it is not too much to say that the Word was made flesh in the scriptures. In sum, it may be more biblical and accurate to believe in the inspiration of the writers of the Bible than in the inspiration of the product of their work. The Holy Spirit works in and through persons rather than through objects. Belief in spirit-filled objects has traditionally been called idolatry.

A second faith assumption that has supported belief in the authority of the scriptures is the view that they are the only available faithful and contemporary witnesses to the acts of God in those particular events and chosen persons by which he disclosed himself and his will in history for the redemption of a rebellious and alienated humanity. This view, along with the claim of inspiration, is intrinsic to the scriptures themselves. It was the view underlying the writings of the ancient Hebrews as they preserved and recorded their knowledge and understanding of the gracious acts of

God among the patriarchs, through Moses and the prophets, and in the history of Israel. The same view may be seen in the NT writings as they emphasize the life and works of Jesus and the story of the witness of the apostles and the mission of the faithful people of God during the first century.

This whole recorded witness to God's saving work in Moses and the prophets and in Jesus and the apostles is frequently and conveniently called *Heilsgeschichte* (holy history), pointing to the idea that the Bible is authoritative precisely because it is the only faithful and dependable record and channel of revelation. It is more than that, however, because the same Spirit of God who led the writers as they responded in faith to God's revelation also leads the multitudes of readers through subsequent ages as they respond with a similar faith to God's revelation and offer of forgiveness and reconciliation. Thus the revealed Word, found supremely in Jesus Christ, became the written Word in the Bible, both in human form; and the purposes of God are made complete when the revealed Word, constantly rediscovered in the written Word, is proclaimed, heard, and faithfully received by every believer in every generation.

This union of belief in the vitalizing inspiration of both biblical writers and biblical readers, and belief in the Bible as the inspiring witness to God's unique saving work on behalf of humanity, is the strong and sufficient foundation for appeal to the authority of the Bible.

See also APOCRYPHAL LITERATURE; BIBLE; CANON; EUSEBIUS; HOLY SPIRIT; INTERPRETATION, HISTORY OF; IRENAEUS; LAW IN THE NEW TESTAMENT; LITERARY CRITICISM; MARCION; OLD TESTAMENT; SCRIPTURE IN THE NEW TESTAMENT; SCRIPTURE IN THE OLD TESTAMENT; SEPTUAGINT; TORAH; WORD OF GOD.

Bibliography. K. Barth, *Church Dogmatics* 1/1; G. C. Berkouwer, *Holy Scripture*; E. Brunner, *The Divine-Human Encounter*; Y. Conger, *Tradition and the Traditions*; O. Cullmann, *The Early Church*; C. H. Dodd, *The Authority of the Bible*; L. Hodgson et al., *On the Authority of the Bible*; R. Johnson, *Authority in Protestant Theology*; D. H. Kelsey, *The Uses of Scripture in Recent Theology*; K. Rahner, *Inspiration in the Bible*; J. K. S. Reid, *The Authority of Scripture*; B. B. Warfield, *The Inspiration and Authority of the Bible*.

—J. WILLIAM ANGELL

• **Biblical Criticism.** *See* INTERPRETATION, HISTORY OF

• **Biblical Theology.** The term "biblical theology" may refer to comprehensive organization of the doctrinal content of a biblical book, a group of writings by a single biblical author, a literary group such as the synoptic Gospels, an entire Testament, or the entire BIBLE. No real distinction was made between dogmatic theology and biblical theology until the end of the eighteenth century. Then Johann Philip Gabler, in his inaugural address at the University of Altdorf, Germany, in 1787, emphasized the historical character of the biblical material as the controlling principle of organization for biblical theology, while the creeds and confessions of the churches were the controlling principle for dogmatic theology.

The historical orientation freed biblical theology from the necessity of conforming to a particular church dogma and permitted the researcher to develop the distinctive theology of Matthew, in contrast to Mark or Luke, or to emphasize the historical development of a theological concept in the setting of the biblical writer. It was a special contribution to the Reformation churches because of the possibility it provided to criticize and evaluate church doctrine or practice in the light of historical study of the primary biblical sources.

Biblical theology has enjoyed a great influence and popularity, especially during the middle of the twentieth century. Scores of formative theologians in the period between and following the two World Wars emphasized biblical theology and made contributions to it. Those whose primary orientation was systematic or dogmatic theology, such as Karl Barth or Emil Brunner, tended to emphasize great unifying themes, such as reconciliation, covenant, and Word of God; while biblical scholars, such as Rudolf Bultmann, tended to emphasize individual differences and diversity between biblical writers, such as Peter and Paul, or the Synoptics and John.

A very influential OT theology by Walther Eichrodt was written around the theme of the covenant, while an equally influential theology of the NT was written by Rudolf Bultmann with scant use of the Gospels and the building of his entire theology around the stackpole of Pauline theology as the foundational and controlling pattern of the NT, balanced and corrected at the end by the later developing Johannine theology. Such historical and topical study of biblical theology has declined toward the end of the twentieth century because of the perception that logical, topical, and historical categories have been imposed upon the biblical material to make it fit our doctrinal uses. Instead, recent writers are emphasizing "structuralism" (analysis of texts from the vantage-point of deep structures or themes which recur in all folk literature), the narrative (the form and power of the story to convey the truth which cannot be compressed into logical categories), or debate about the nature and philosophy of language itself as it creates its own context of new meaning. The great value of biblical theology is its capacity to correct, renew, and revitalize Christian life and thought by pulling it back to the primary documents of scripture.

See also BIBLE; HERMENEUTICS; THEOLOGY OF THE NEW TESTAMENT; THEOLOGY OF THE OLD TESTAMENT.

Bibliography. R. Bultmann, *New Testament Theology*; W. Eichrodt, *Theology of the Old Testament*; W. Harrington, *The Path of Biblical Theology*; R. Morgan, *The Nature of New Testament Theology*.

—WAYNE E. WARD

• **Bigamy.** *See* REMARRIAGE

• **Binding and Loosing.** In Matt 16:19 Jesus says to PETER, "I will give you the keys of the kingdom of heaven, and whatever you bind on earth shall be bound in heaven, and whatever you loose on earth shall be loosed in heaven." In Matt 18:18 a similar statement about binding and loosing is made to all the disciples and not just to Peter alone (cf. John 20:23). Most scholars understand these terms in light of their usage in rabbinic writings in which they normally mean either: (1) to declare which actions are prohibited and which are permitted according to Jewish law, or (2) to impose or remove a ban of excommunication against someone. Although this latter meaning is rare in rabbinic writings, the context of Matt 18:18, where instructions are given on how to deal with a recalcitrant church member, does support a disciplinary interpretation.

Others have suggested, on the basis of John 20:23, that to bind and loose means to forgive or not to forgive sins, and thus ultimately to have the power to exclude individuals from the Kingdom of God. This interpretation of Matthew's statements is unlikely, however, since in Matthew the disciples are commanded to be unlimited, not selective, in their forgiveness of others (Matt 18:21-35).

The best approach may be not to restrict binding and loosing to either doctrinal or disciplinary decisions alone. Rather, in Matthew, to have the power to bind and loose may be seen as having the power to make authoritative decisions for the welfare of the Christian community.

See also PETER.

—MITCHELL G. REDDISH

• **Birth from Above.** *See* NEW BIRTH

• **Birthright.** The right of the firstborn son to be the chief beneficiary in the father's estate. In Israel, a father verbally assigned his property to his sons just before his death. The eldest received twice the amount of the younger sons and became head of the family. The legal statute in Deut 21:15-17 prescribes this double portion as the eldest's INHERITANCE and prohibits the father's preferential treatment of another son, one of a favored wife. The most notable OT reference to birthright is ESAU's selling of his to JACOB to assuage his hunger (Gen 25:29-34). Examples are also to be found in the loss of the birthright because of a serious offense (REUBEN, Gen 35:22; 49:3-4) and because of the father's displacement of the eldest (MANASSEH, Gen 48:12-20). Israel's practice was typical of the ancient Near East, according to texts from Mari, Nuzi, Ugarit, and Assyria, for example. The law codes of Lipit-Ishtar and HAMMURABI, however, provide for equal distribution of a father's property.

See also INHERITANCE IN THE OLD TESTAMENT; LAW IN THE OLD TESTAMENT.

—MARGARET DEE BRATCHER

• **Bishop.** The English word ''bishop'' is derived from a Gk. word (ἐπίσκοπος, ''overseer'') which originally designated persons who provided protective care and which later denoted certain secular offices. Though it possessed no specifically religious meaning, the term was often applied to the gods in ancient Greece (Homer, *Iliad* 22.254-55) and occasionally to officials at cultic temples (*InscrGr* 12.1.731.8). The LXX uses the term sixteen times, employing it as a title for military commanders (Judg 9:28; 2 Kgs 11:15) and other overseers (Num 4:16; Isa 60:17), including two instances where the word characterizes God as the judge of human iniquity (Job 20:29 LXX) and the witness to truth (Wis 1:9).

The NT refers to bishops or overseers (ἐπίσκοποι) on five separate occasions. At 1 Pet 2:25 (KJV) the phrase ''shepherd and bishop'' of souls is used to describe the salvific role of Christ, who has the ultimate responsibility for his flock. Elsewhere, the term is applied to church functionaries. References to elders and presbyters as overseers (ἐπίσκοποι, Acts 20:17,28; *1 Clem* 42–44) and Paul's epistolary address to ''bishops'' in the plural (Phil 1:1), however, suggest that the term more commonly described a function within the first-century church rather than a formal, ecclesiastical office. First Tim 3:1-7 and Titus 1:7-9 list among the numerous qualifications for a bishop the traits of dignity, temperance, hospitality, sobriety, and holiness.

Bishops maintained responsibility for a variety of duties: instruction of the community (1 Tim 3:2; Titus 5:9; *Did* 15.1-2), administration of the liturgy (*1 Clem* 44.4; Ignatius *Smyrn* 8.2), and preservation of the true Christian faith (Hippolytus *Haer* 1 *proemium*). The bishop also assumed pastoral obligations, economic management, and social administration of the congregation, which included hospitality to strangers, care of orphans and the poor, management of church property, and community arbitration. Many such duties may have been modeled upon parallels found in early Judaism. The most obvious examples are the rulers of the synagogues, but the literature of Qumran also notes the importance of community ''superintendents,'' who were known to Josephus as the ''superiors'' of the Essenes (*BJ* 2.123-34).

The bishop's role and authority developed as early Christian communities matured. As early itinerant preachers disappeared and their authoritative influence dissipated, a vacuum remained within local churches. In order to fill that vacuum of authority, the office of bishop probably evolved from the ranks of the presbyters, who were religious officials associated with individual congregations. Bishops served as hedges against the challenges of heresy, whose divergent communities sought their own apostolic integrity. A complete and glorious picture of the bishop is outlined by Ignatius of Antioch (end of the first century), who advanced the view that the bishop was the supreme officer over the presbyters and deacons, thereby attaining to the authority of God the Father within the local church structure (Ignatius, *Magn* 6.1).

See also DEACON; ELDER.

Bibliography. H. W. Beyer, ''ἐπισκέπτομαι, κτλ.,'' *TDNT*; H. von Campenhausen, *Ecclesiastical Authority and Spiritual Power in the Church of the First Three Centuries*; H. Chadwick, ''The Role of the Christian Bishop in Ancient Society,'' *Protocol of the Colloquy of the Center for Hermeneutical Studies in Hellenistic and Modern Culture* 35 (1980): 1-14.

—CLAYTON N. JEFFORD

• **Bithynia.** [bi-thin'ee-uh] Bithynia was a mountainous, coastal province in northwest Asia Minor on the Propontis and the Black Sea (PLATES 26, 27). As it sloped toward the sea, the province formed a fertile plain watered by the Sangarius River. The first immigrants to the area were Thracians (Indo-Europeans). Once a part of the Lydian monarchy of Croesus, Bithynia came under Persian control in 546 B.C.E. When the Persian Empire fell to Alexander the Great, Bithynia became an independent kingdom. A dynasty established by Nicomedes I in 278 B.C.E. ruled the land until Nicomedes III, unable to withstand the threat of Mithradates of Pontus, bequeathed his kingdom to the Romans in 74 B.C.E.

The Romans often united Bithynia and neighboring Pontus for administrative purposes, governing them as a senatorial province by a proconsul. Social and cultural life revolved around the Greek cities of Nicea, Nicomedia, Chalcedon, Prusa, and Heraclea which governed the territories surrounding them as separate civic provinces. Diocletian made Nicomedia his capital city, and Bithynia remained a part of the Byzantine Empire until it was overrun by Turks in the 1320s.

Early legends attribute the evangelization of Bithynia to Peter or Andrew. First Peter is addressed to Christian congregations throughout the region. By the time Pliny the Younger was appointed special imperial legate by the emperor Trajan in 111 C.E., the success of the Christian mission was causing neglect of the pagan temples and social unrest. Christians were denounced as ''undesirables.'' From his correspondence with Trajan we learn that while Christianity was not a legal religion (*religio licita*) and Christians could be arrested and tried, they were not to be sought out as common criminals, and any charges must be made according to proper procedure by a private prosecutor. Upon recantation the Christian could be freed. This policy seems to have remained in effect until the time of Constantine. The First General Council of the church was held in Nicea in 325 C.E., and the Fourth Council, devoted to Christology, in Chalcedon in 451 C.E.

—W. HULITT GLOER

• **Blacks in the New Testament.** Dark-skinned peoples of Negroid features were well known to the classical world of Greece and Rome. Many writers of antiquity developed theories to account for the physical differences among peoples, but there is little evidence to suggest that they speculated about the racial superiority or inferiority of certain peoples. The Aristotelian school of "physiognomics" associated both extremely dark and extremely fair pigmentation with negative character dispositions, for example; but it produced no racial taxonomy of character types. In fact, the racial theorists of classical antiquity tended to advocate racial equality, although the very fact that the egalitarian position required defense testifies to the existence of racial prejudice in the classical world. This popular prejudice expressed itself toward both the extremely dark-skinned and the extremely light-skinned, hence egalitarians found it necessary to defend not only the Ethiopians but also the white, straight-haired, blue-eyed Scythians. Moreover, the Ethiopian and the Scythian were often named as an antithetical pair in order to express the extremes both of race (black/white) and of geography (north/south), which were typically linked in ancient environmental theories of racial difference. The Ethiopian could well have been mentioned in Col 3:11, where stereotypical cultural language is used for the differences that divide humanity. "Here there cannot be Greek and Jew, circumcised and uncircumcised, barbarian, Scythian, slave, freeman, but Christ is all, and in all."

The NT mentions at least two blacks explicitly: the finance minister to Queen Candace of ETHIOPIA, who is identified as an Ethiopian (Acts 8:26-40), and "SIMEON who was called Niger" (Acts 13:1). In the scheme of Luke-Acts the Ethiopian minister represents the inclusion of his own African race and at the same time the inclusion of all peoples beyond "Jerusalem, Judea, and Samaria" (see Acts 1:8; 8:1; 25–26) in the universal gospel of Christ, for he is the first full gentile convert, preceding even the Roman Cornelius (Acts 10) into the Kingdom. Simeon is mentioned among the prophets and teachers at Antioch. The fact that he is called "Niger" (Latin for "dark" or "black") indicates that his color distinguished him, although it did not hinder him from assuming a role of leadership in the first ethnically-mixed church.

It may be that other blacks appear in the NT. Simon of CYRENE (a city on the coast of northern Africa) is a possible candidate, together with his sons Alexander and Rufus (Mark 15:21; Luke 23:26; and Matt 27:32), but there were also Jews at Cyrene. (In fact, it is possible that the Isaiah-reading Ethiopian of Acts 8 is a Jew.) By the same token, some of the persons bearing Greek or Roman names in the NT may be blacks whose color did not seem to call for special mention. By and large, however, blacks do not figure significantly in the NT, which represents the northward and westward expansion of the early church. As Felder points out, the "world" of the NT is essentially that of the Roman Empire, hence the theme of blacks in the NT must be regarded as only one aspect of a larger history of blacks in early Christianity, a history only marginally reflected in the NT canon.

See also BLACKS IN THE OLD TESTAMENT; CYRENE; ETHIOPIA; ETHIOPIAN EUNUCH.

Bibliography. C. Felder, "Racial Ambiguities in the Biblical Narratives," *Conc* 15 (1982): 17-24; F. M. Snowden, Jr., *Before Color Prejudice: The Ancient View of Blacks* and *Blacks in Antiquity: Ethiopians in the Greco-Roman Experience*.

—CHARLES H. COSGROVE

• **Blacks in the Old Testament.** Who are blacks? In theory they are usually described as humans with dark skin, wooly hair, everted (turned outward) lips, original residents of Africa, and so on. In practice, however, it is not always easy to determine just where "blacks" end and "non-blacks" begin. About two-thirds of the world's population display some degree of color (melanin) in their skin but not all of these are considered blacks. If one uses only color to define a black person, one must establish how much or how little of it is required. If hair texture and lip configuration are the true markers of blackness, wooly hair and everted lips are found in light-skinned persons, while very dark-skinned persons sometimes have naturally straight hair and inverted lips. Which combination of criteria determines "blackness" accurately and who decides these questions?

If one defines blacks as the indigenous population of the African continent one must still ask: "Where does Africa end and Asia begin?" The OT story takes place on a land bridge between these continents, and important events occur in EGYPT. Is Egypt part of Africa? If it is, the story of the OT, which begins there, is a North African story, and to speak of blacks (defined in geographical terms) in the OT would be redundant.

The above issues make it clear that the people of the OT were not fair-skinned Europeans. The central OT characters had diverse origins even though they are portrayed as sharing a single ancestry, history, and tradition, and, as excluding from their inner circle, on ideological grounds, a wide range of persons. Tension in the OT is between Israelites and foreigners of all kinds. Among those excluded, Ethiopians, Cushites, Midianites, Libyans, and even Arabs, are mentioned occasionally. Discussion about blacks in the OT has centered around these references.

The terms often used to describe people that might today be considered blacks are Cushite (Hebrew), Ethiopian (Greek), or even Egyptian. Already in Gen 16, Abraham is given an Egyptian maid, Hagar. Her origin is noted by the editor in much the same way as is the Ethiopian/Cushite/Midianite origin of MOSES' wife and of his father-in-law—JETHRO/Reuel/Hobab (Exod 2:21; Num 12:1). In both portrayals, the alien character of the two women is highlighted. The dark-skinned female mentioned in the Song of Songs 1:5-6 shares the same characteristics—the object of anger of close relatives (v. 6) and sexual attractiveness to the main character. The narrative concerning SOLOMON and the Queen of Sheba in 1 Kgs 10/2 Chr 9 is not quite as clear, but is perhaps similar in intent.

The Ethiopian men in the OT also cut a distinctive profile. The most prominent two are an unnamed "Cushite" who brings news of Absalom's death to David (2 Sam 18), and Ebed-melech the Ethiopian who seeks and gets King

Zedekiah's permission to lift the prophet Jeremiah out of a cistern (Jer 38:7-13). Like the women, these men are close to prominent characters—kings and a prophet—and, while they both bear bad news to the king, they also show a gentleness of spirit, and a certain honesty; they are non-threatening. The "Cushite" tells DAVID "the whole truth" and is unconcerned about being upstaged by a faster messenger. Ebed-melech, a eunuch, is later (39:17) promised deliverance from the destruction of Jerusalem for his faithfulness.

Apart from these glimpses, there are but a few other allusions to Ethiopians as distant and/or dark peoples, occasionally in military conflict with Israelite kings. (Jer 13:23; Amos 9:7; Ps 68:31; Zeph 2:12; 2 Chr 14:8-12; 21:16). On balance, "Ethiopians" (blacks) in the OT are portrayed positively. Distinct from the majority of Israelites, they still figure prominently in the few narratives where they are specifically mentioned.

See also ETHIOPIA; EGYPT.

—MELVIN K. H. PETERS

• **Blasphemy against the Holy Spirit.** *See* UNPARDONABLE SIN

• **Blessing.** *See* BIRTHRIGHT; CURSE AND BLESSING; LAND; PRAYER/THANKSGIVING IN THE NEW TESTAMENT

• **Blessing, Cup of.** *See* LORD'S SUPPER

• **Blindness.** Refers either to a physical disability or to the inability to "see" or perceive the good. The word is used extensively throughout biblical literature. The numerous references suggest the widespread incidence of ocular disease among the ancient Hebrews. Its presence throughout the East is confirmed by comparable references in other Eastern literature, many pre-dating biblical records. Ancient Sumerian accounts prescribe treatment for eye diseases and the Code of HAMMURABI (ca. 1700 B.C.E.) lists these diseases as among those that could be treated by Babylonian physicians. In Egypt, treatments for blindness can be traced to about 5000 B.C.E.

In spite of the numerous references, the data are not sufficient to permit imposing modern diagnostic categories upon the ancient documents. Many of the ancient disorders may have come from climatic or health conditions typical of the East; others more certainly were associated with physical degeneration due to aging. The latter is the case in the Genesis narrative, which reports JACOB's deception of his father because ISAAC "was old and his eyes were dim" (Gen 27:1). On the contrary, the Deuteronomist attests Moses' greatness by the fact that "his eye was not dim" (Deut 34:7).

Those who were physically blind in ancient Israel, as in modern society, were severely disadvantaged and hence belonged to that general group of the socially deprived whose lot was a major concern to the religious community. The Mosaic code admonishes that stumbling blocks are not to be placed before the blind (Lev 19:14) and warns anyone who misleads the blind (Deut 27:18). The description of Jesus' mission to include "recovering of sight to the blind" (Luke 4:18) doubtless draws upon this tradition (Mark 8:22-26).

The biblical records also use this prevalent disease as an analogy to spiritual difficulties. In some references physical blindness is associated with impurity, consistent with the biblical view that illness itself represents a disruption of God's good creation. Blindness disqualifies the candidate for priesthood (Lev 21:18) and the animal for sacrifice (Lev 22:22). The disobedient risk being smitten "with madness and blindness and confusion of mind" (Deut 28:28). The most striking statement of this connection is in the Johannine story in which disciples asked Jesus, "Rabbi, who sinned, this man or his parents, that he was born blind?" (John 9:2). In other references the term blindness is used metaphorically, for example, Matthew's "blind guides" (Matt 23:16) and Luke's "blind man" leading a blind man (Luke 6:39).

The humane concern for the physically blind undoubtedly contributes to the metaphorical imagery. As the community must act compassionately toward the physically blind, so they must seek the welfare of the spiritually blind. Thus Deutero-Isaiah describes Israel's covenant mission as "to open the eyes that are blind" (Isa 42:7) and another Isaiah text envisions a glad day when "the eyes of the blind shall be opened" (Isa 35:5). Early believers found this imagery fitting for Jesus, who not only put clay on blind eyes (John 9:6), but also "came into this world that those who do not see may see" (John 9:39). In the Gospels, healings of physical blindness regularly convey the larger message of Jesus' mission to cure spiritual blindness.

The most impressive mention of blindness in non-Gospel NT materials is in the story of PAUL's conversion, told in Acts in three versions (9:1-9; 22:6-11; 26:12-18). Only Acts 9 describes Paul's difficulty as blindness, but Acts 26 clearly underscores the metaphorical meaning of the experience. Speculation about the psychodynamics of Paul's temporary blindness may be interesting, but Acts is undoubtedly concerned with the Apostle's spiritual transition from "blindness" to "sight." Paul, like Israel, is sent "to open their eyes, that they may turn from darkness to light" (Acts 26:18). And Paul "was not disobedient to the heavenly vision" (Acts 26:19).

See also DISEASE AND HEALING; MIRACLES.

—ROBERT W. CRAPPS

• **Blood in the New Testament.** Blood is the vital fluid circulating through the body by a system of arteries and veins connected to the heart. In biblical usage the word also designates the life force which comes from God, the life-giver.

In the NT, the word blood occurs ninety-seven times. It is used in four basic senses. First, blood can refer to the life principle in human and animal life; thus when blood is shed, life is destroyed (Rom 3:15; Heb 12:4). Used in this sense, blood can also denote the existence of man in God's sight. Hence Paul's statement, "Your blood be upon your heads" (Acts 18:6), means that his hearers were answerable to God for their life both temporal and eternal.

Second, blood is used as a symbol of human existence in its weakness and transitoriness. In this usage blood is coupled with "flesh," as in 1 Cor 15:50, "flesh and blood cannot inherit the kingdom of God." When Jesus said, "Flesh and blood has not revealed this to you, but my Father who is in heaven" (Matt 16:17), he was speaking of humankind's finite powers of revelation and knowledge. According to Paul, revelation must be based on divine disclosure, not on human authority (Gal 1:16). The NT also states emphatically that the Christian's struggle is not a human one, that is, "against flesh and blood" (Eph 6:12), but a war to the death against supernatural enemies. This menace can be defeated only through the armor that God provides (Eph 6:11).

Third, blood occurs frequently in reference to the shed blood of Christ, which symbolizes the atoning death of the Savior (1 Cor 10:16; Eph 2:13; Heb 9:14; 10:19; 1 Pet 1:2, 19; 1 John 1:7; Rev 7:14; 12:11). As the life is in the blood (Lev 17:11), and was forfeited by sin, life eternal can be secured only through the giving up of the sinless REDEEMER. Thus the death of Jesus is viewed as the fulfillment of the OT idea of a sacrifice of ATONEMENT. Christ's blood secures deliverance from the power of Satan and all wicked powers (Acts 20:28; Eph 1:7; 1 Pet 1:18-19; Rev 5:9), and justifies all who through faith accept his sacrifice (Rom 3:25). In the blood is the power for sanctification (Heb 13:12) and access to God (Heb 10:19). This redemption achieved by the blood of Christ is paralleled by the NT statements that speak of the sinner being reconciled to God by the "death" of Christ and saved "by his life" (e.g., Rom 5:10).

Finally, blood is sometimes used figuratively as an apocalyptic sign. This usage is especially common in the Book of Revelation with reference to the eschatological horrors on earth and in heaven in the last days. At that time the moon will become like blood (Rev 6:12), "hail and fire mixed with blood" will be thrown to the earth (Rev 8:7), a third of the sea will become blood (Rev 8:8), and blood will be poured from the wine press of the wrath of God (Rev 14:20). Here blood and its red color symbolically express the terror that will accompany God's final judgment upon evil and the consummation of God's Kingdom.

See also ATONEMENT; ATONEMENT, DAY OF; BLOOD IN THE OLD TESTAMENT; EXPIATION; EXPIATION IN THE NEW TESTAMENT; LIFE IN THE OLD TESTAMENT; LIFE IN THE NEW TESTAMENT; LORD'S SUPPER; PASSOVER; REDEEMER; SACRIFICE.

Bibliography. D. J. McCarthy, "The Symbolism of Blood and Sacrifice," *JBL* 88 (1969): 166-76; L. Morris, *The Apostolic Preaching of the Cross*; A. M. Stibbs, *The Meaning of the Word 'Blood' in Scripture*.

—DAVID A. BLACK

• **Blood in the Old Testament.** The blood of animals had a central role in Israelite SACRIFICES. The PRIESTS caught it in bowls as the sacrifices were killed and poured it out around the base of the altar upon which the animals were burned. This was true of all sacrifices, but there were additional directions to be followed for sacrifices that atoned for sin. If the sacrifice was for the SINS of the people or the HIGH PRIEST, some of the blood was to be put on the corners of the altar of INCENSE and some sprinkled on the curtain that separated the holy of holies from the rest of the sanctuary. On the DAY OF ATONEMENT, the high priest would take in the blood of the sacrifice and sprinkle it on God's MERCY SEAT inside the holy of holies. LEVITICUS explains that the blood works to atone for sins because it is the LIFE (the Hebrew word is *nepeš*, sometimes translated "soul") of the animal (Lev 17:11).

What the text means by this is the subject of much debate. Some believe that the worshiper's sins were transferred to the animal by the ceremonial laying on of hands. The sins that polluted the *nepeš* of the sinner were placed upon the *nepeš* of the animal, and then poured out at the altar, symbolizing repentance. Others believe that since life is God's possession, handling the life of the animal put the worshiper back into contact with the life of God, renewing the ties of the COVENANT. Solution of the problem is made harder by the fact that the PRIESTLY WRITERS of Leviticus were trying to regularize the cult and most likely smoothed over divergent explanations of why blood sacrifices worked. Another difficulty is that the Israelite use of blood to produce atonement is apparently without close parallels in the ancient Near East. Some ancient societies sacrificed animals, but made no use of the blood. Israel's neighbors used blood to propitiate the gods of death and the underworld, and did not connect it with forgiveness of sins. Some scholars think that the practice of putting the blood of the Passover on the outside of the house is connected somehow with this belief.

A flow of blood, like other emissions of bodily fluids, made an Israelite ritually unclean. Menstruation and the blood of childbirth made a woman unclean, and this state could be transferred to anything or anyone she touched. On the other hand, blood was necessary to remove the uncleanness of LEPROSY and to consecrate a high priest. Animals slaughtered for FOOD could not be consumed "with the blood," but had to be bled carefully before they could be eaten.

In noncultic contexts, blood was used sometimes as a symbol for a person, the part for the whole. It could be used as shorthand for "murder" (Deut 17:8) or for the guilt coming from murder (Exod 22:2) or for death in general (Ezek 3:18). Blood is often included in apocalyptic lists of cosmic disturbances ("blood and fire and columns of smoke"; Joel 2:30).

See also BLOOD IN THE NEW TESTAMENT; SACRIFICE.

Bibliography. D. J. McCarthy, "The Symbolism of Blood and Sacrifice," *JBL* 88 (June 1969): 166-76; J. Milgrom, "Sacrifices and Offerings, OT," *IDBSupp*; N. Zohar, "Repentance and Purification," *JBL* 107 (Dec 1988): 609-18.

—RICHARD B. VINSON

• **Boat.** *See* SHIP

• **Boaz.** [boh'az] Husband of Ruth. NAOMI belonged to a household in which all the males had died: her husband, Elimelech; and two sons, Mahlon and Chilion. The family holdings were in danger of being lost. Elimelech and a man named Boaz belonged to the same association of households (*mišpāḥâ*). They were Ephrathites from the town of Bethlehem. The association of households provided for the saving of a family inheritance if a man (*gō'ēl*) from the association were to marry the widow. If they should have a son, the inheritance would pass to the son, thereby rescuing the family name.

RUTH, a Moabite, had returned with Naomi to Bethlehem after her first husband, a son of Elimelech, had died. Ruth was, therefore, a member of Naomi's household. Ruth met Boaz after gleaning in his field. The closest in kinship (*gō'ēl*) to the household of Elimelech chose not to buy land from Naomi or marry Ruth because it put his own inheritance in jeopardy. He thus yielded his right to Boaz. Ruth and Boaz married. They had a son whom they named Obed, saving the family name. According to genealogical tradition, Obed became the father of JESSE, the father of DAVID. Both genealogies in Matthew and Luke, in tracing the lineage of JESUS through David, identify Boaz as the father of Obed, the father of Jesse, the father of David.

Boaz is also the name of the pillar standing to the left of the entrance of SOLOMON's temple (1 Kgs 7:21). There is debate over the meaning of the name. Some suggest it is the name of the donor or architect of the pillar; others, that it is a reference to the strength (*bĕ'oz*, "in strength") of Yahweh.

See also RUTH, BOOK OF.

—WILLIAM R. MILLAR

• **Body in the New Testament.** NT use of the term "body" may be divided into three categories: anthropological, ecclesiological, and christological.

Outside the writings of Paul, the term "body" is found fifty-one times. In most of these instances the word is used anthropologically and is consistent with the OT view of the person as a psychosomatic (soul-body) unity. The person is not divided into an evil body and an essential soul or spirit, as was done in many Greek systems of thought. Thus, body can refer to: (1) a corpse, as in Mark 15:43, Luke 17:37, and Jude 9; (2) a slave, as in Rev 18:13; (3) the physical body with its various functions and needs, as in Mark 5:29, 14:8, Luke 11:34, 12:22, Jas 2:16, and 3:6; (4) the body as an expression of personality, as in Matt 5:29, 6:22, 10:28; and (5) the body as a sacrifice. In this last regard Heb 10:5-13, 13:11, and 1 Pet 2:24 depict the body as the essence of life. Related to this use is the christological formula of the last supper, "This is my body" (Mark 14:22 and parallels), in which the emphasis is on the person of Jesus given sacrificially.

The Pauline literature provides the most frequent and significant NT use of body (ninety-one times). The majority of occurrences of the term in Paul's writings is associated with Corinth (fifty-six times in 1 and 2 Corinthians and thirteen times in Romans, which was probably written while at Corinth) and possibly reflects his reaction to aberrant views of the body held by certain Corinthian Christians.

Paul's anthropological use of body is generally aspective, not partitive: body describes the person from a certain perspective, not in terms of component parts. For Paul, human existence is necessarily somatic, or bodily, existence. It is always through the body that one relates to others and to God (Rom 6:12; 12:1-2; 1 Cor 6:12-20). The body is the person as that person lives and is known by other persons (Phil 1:20; 2 Cor 4:7, 10). There is no "essence" (in the Greek sense) apart from the body. Even the resurrected state will consist of a "spiritual body" (1 Cor 15:44). When Paul departs from this holistic perspective of the person as body, it appears to be in response to opponents' views. Thus, Paul can refer to being "out of the body" (2 Cor 12:1-3) or of longing to be "away from the body" to be at home with the Lord (2 Cor 5:6-10).

While Paul's anthropological perspective is basically consistent with the predominant biblical view, his ecclesiological and christological uses of "body" are novel. Paul refers to the CHURCH as the BODY OF CHRIST (Rom 12:5; 1 Cor 12:12-27). The imagery may reflect Stoicism or rabbinical speculation about the embryonic presence of every person in the body of Adam. For Paul, the imagery expresses the idea that the resurrected body of Jesus Christ constitutes the sphere in which the church exists. Through baptism into Christ (1 Cor 12:13) the members of the church become members of the one body of Christ (1 Cor 12:27).

In Colossians and Ephesians the imagery is developed to convey the idea of the church as the body of Christ growing out into all the world through the preaching of the gospel (Col 1:15-23; 2:19; Eph 2:11-22). Here Christ is the head of his body, the church, and also its savior (Eph 5:23). As Christ gave himself, his body, for the church (Eph 5:25), the church which now constitutes his body (Col 1:22; Eph 2:16) should give itself bodily in submission to its head and in service to the world (Col 1:24; Eph 4:1-6).

See also BODY IN THE OLD TESTAMENT; BODY OF CHRIST; FLESH AND SPIRIT; GNOSTICISM; INCARNATION; RELIGIONS, HELLENISTIC AND ROMAN; RESURRECTION; SOUL IN THE OLD TESTAMENT; STOICS.

Bibliography. R. Bultmann, *Theology of the New Testament*; J. A. T. Robinson, *The Body: A Study in Pauline Theology*; E. Schweizer, "σῶμα," *TDNT*.

—SCOTT NASH

• **Body in the Old Testament.** No single term in OT Hebrew is equivalent to "body" (LXX and NT Gk. *sōma*)—the structure and substance of a living or dead human being or animal. Nineteen different OT Hebrew words or phrases are translated sometimes, depending on context, by the RSV as "body" (eight of them but once); literally, each signifies some particular body part or aspect. The LXX renders a dozen different Hebrew expressions at times with *sōma*. Those most frequently thus rendered (RSV) are as follows: *bāśār*, "flesh" (Lev 14:9); *gĕwiyyâ*, "back," "torso" (1 Sam 31:10); *nĕbēlâ*, "carcass" (Jer 7:33); *peger*, "corpse" (Num 14:29); *nepeš*, "[deceased] life" (Num 9:10); *beṭen*, "belly," "abdomen," "womb" (Deut 7:13; *'eṣāmîm* (also *'eṣāmôt*), "bones" (Ps 32:3); *šĕ'ēr*, "[inner] flesh" (Prov 5:11); *mē'îm* (also *mē'ayim*), "bowels" (Isa 49:1); and [Aramaic] *gĕšēm*, "body," "bulk" (Dan 4:33).

To the foregoing may be added terms not usually translated as "body" but representing aspects belonging to it just as intimately and concretely as limbs or viscera: *gōlem*, "unformed substance" (or "embryo"; Ps 139:16); *nepeš*, "life," "soul" (Gen 2:7); *rûaḥ*, SPIRIT, "conscience," "consciousness" (Eccl 12:7); *nĕšāmâ*, "breath" (Prov 20:27); and the like.

Explicit belief in the RESURRECTION of the body is unattested in the OT until Dan 12:2 (taking Isa 26:19 and Ezek 37:1-14 figuratively), but the dead body was thought of as continuing to belong to the previously living person, whether as object of scorn (2 Kgs 9:37) or honored memory (Josh 24:32). Tradition remembers Enoch and Elijah, models of servanthood, as having been transported bodily to heaven without seeing death (Gen 5:24; 2 Kgs 2:11).

Extended celebration of the body's physical beauty and attraction, as in the Song of Solomon, is exceptional in the OT; descriptions elsewhere of physical attractiveness tend to be brief and stereotypical (Gen 24:16; 29:17; 1 Sam 9:2; 16:12). More often, the body's weakness and mortality receives extended consideration (Job 7:1–6), but the body is not thought of for that reason as an encumbrance burdening some purer self—a Greek view that does emerge in the Apocrypha (Wis 9:15). By contrast, Second Isaiah's use of body imagery approaches a theology of incarnation with his wordplay between "flesh" (*bāśār*; (Isa 40:5, 6-8) and "herald of good tidings" (*mĕbaśśeret*; Isa 40:9)—the roots are homonyms—and his focus on the physical appearance of the servant (Isa 42:19; 49:1; 52:13–53:12).

See also SPIRIT IN THE OT.

Bibliography. F. Baumgärtel and E. Schweizer, "σῶμα, κτλ., B. The Old Testament," *TDNT*; T. Boman, *Hebrew Thought Compared with Greek*; J. Pedersen, *Israel*; J. A. T. Robinson, *The Body*.

—BRUCE T. DAHLBERG

• **Body of Christ.** The phrase "body of Christ" describes the new community of believers created through Christ. The various parts of the body are united in Christ (Rom 12:5; 1 Cor 12:12-13; Eph 4:4), transcending the diversity of gifts among the members (1 Cor 12:12-31; Rom 12:4-8), as well as their social and ethnic diversity (1 Cor 12:13; Eph 2:16). This oneness is symbolized in the Lord's Supper by the one loaf which is shared by all believers (1 Cor 10:16-17; 11:23-32).

Conversely, the phrase "body of Christ" can also be used to emphasize the diversity that exists among believers. A variety of gifts of the Spirit are in evidence within the fellowship. No one is to think too highly of his or her own gift (Rom 12:3-8), nor to disparage the gifts of others (1 Cor 12:4-31). Rather, all gifts are to be used for the mutual benefit of the body of Christ (Eph 4:11-16).

In Romans and 1 Corinthians, Christ encompasses the whole body, composed of its several parts. In Ephesians and Colossians, on the other hand, Christ is described as the head, with believers constituting the remainder of his body, the CHURCH (Eph 1:22-23; 4:15-16; 5:23; Col 1:18; 2:19). As the head, Christ unites the body, guiding, nourishing, and loving it (Eph 4:16; 5:25-30; Col 2:19). Furthermore, in Ephesians and Colossians the body of Christ represents the church universal, whereas in Romans and 1 Corinthians the imagery is applied to local churches.

Even in passages in which the body of Christ has primary reference to the crucifixion of Jesus (Rom 7:4; Col 1:22), the idea of corporate fellowship is not totally absent. That believers "have died to the law through the body of Christ" (Rom 7:4) includes not only the idea that they benefit from his atoning death, but that they also benefit through participation in his new community, the church.

See also CHURCH.

—MITCHELL G. REDDISH

• **Bondservant.** *See* SERVANT; SLAVE IN THE OLD TESTAMENT

• **Book.** *See* SCROLL

• **Books, Lost.** *See* WARS OF THE LORD, BOOK OF THE

• **Booths, Feast of.** *See* TABERNACLES, FEAST OF, IN THE NEW TESTAMENT

• **Booths, Festival of.** *See* TABERNACLES, FESTIVAL OF

• **Borrowing and Lending.** Israelite laws regarding loans attempted to safeguard the poor as much as possible. In the Covenant Code (Exod 20:22–23:33), which many consider the oldest code in the Bible, the rules prohibit perpetual debt SLAVERY by requiring creditors to release Hebrew slaves after six years' service. Women, sold to cover their fathers' debts, were also given special protection (Exod 21:1-11). Creditors often took something from the borrower as a token promise of repayment, perhaps representing the creditor's power to enslave the borrower for nonpayment. If the token ("pledge") were something essential, such as the poor man's only cloak, it had to be returned before nightfall (Exod 22:25–27). In this code, Israelites were prohibited from charging interest on loans to the poor (Exod 22:25).

The laws of DEUTERONOMY repeated the provisions for debt slavery, and added a year of release for all debts as a means of keeping abject poverty to a minimum. Each seventh year (the text means a fixed cycle, so that all releases would happen simultaneously) every creditor was to forgive all debts between Israelites; the rule did not extend to foreigners. The law could not force a loan to a needy person, but creditors were warned against refusing a loan because the year of release was near, under threat of divine retribution (Deut 15:1-11). There is no evidence to show that this law was ever kept. Jeremiah complained that it was not kept in his time (Jer 34:14), and 2 Chr 36:21, speaking of the comparable SABBATICAL YEAR when farm lands were to lie fallow, explains the Exile as the fulfillment of all the unkept seventh years. Deuteronomy also prohibited interest on all loans between Israelites (20:19-20) and regulated even further what may not be accepted as a pledge on a loan.

The Priestly Code inaugurated the JUBILEE YEAR, which happened every forty-nine (some scholars say fifty) years. In this year all slaves were freed and all land returned to its ancestral owners (Lev 25). This law, if it ever was practiced, would have limited the numbers of landless poor created by debt slavery. The sabbatical release programs of Exodus and Deuteronomy released slaves but gave them no land of their own. Consequently, these codes allowed a slave to petition the owners to keep him/her forever, despite the sabbatical year. The jubilee, apparently, would have freed even these slaves and would have restored them to the land they sold when their fortunes turned sour. Again, there is no evidence that this was ever done. Leviticus also urges the wealthy to support the poor rather than buy them as slaves, and to treat them with kindness if they did become debt slaves.

The prophets often condemned the wealthy who ignored these regulations. AMOS attacked Israelites who kept the pledges of the poor rather than returning them (Amos 2:8). EZEKIEL lists keeping pledges and lending at interest among crimes God will punish (Ezek 18:12-13). Ps 15 describes the just person as one who does not lend at interest, and PROVERBS predicts that such ill-gotten gain will be redistributed to the charitable (28:8). NEHEMIAH found that in postexilic Palestine debt slavery had reappeared because of lending at interest (Neh 5). These passages show that the laws were not strictly obeyed. Other semitic cultures lent at rather high rates of interest, and so Israelites would have found it difficult not to do the same. Contracts found from a Jewish colony in Egypt show that often the interest was usurious and led to confiscation of property and imprisonment when the debt went unpaid.

After the Exile, the TEMPLE in Jerusalem became a sort of bank as well as a house of worship. Tithes and religious taxes collected were lent out at interest or invested in land. Thus the Temple leadership joined the ranks of the wealthiest families in Palestine, which helped to create "hostility and violent factionalism between high priests on one side, and the priests and leaders of the Jerusalem masses on the other" (so Josephus, *Ant* 10.180). Frequent droughts, warfare, and rebellions all contributed to the plight of the poor during this period, so that the demand for loans increased. During the reign of HEROD the Great, and in order to encourage the wealthy to lend to the poor, the rabbi Hillel is said to have instituted the use of the *Prosbul,* a clause in a loan in which the borrower gives up the right to the year of release. While this may have helped short-term poverty, it probably contributed to the long-term debt that engulfed the Palestinian poor.

This background helps to illuminate some of Jesus' teachings. His parable of the dishonest steward (Luke 16:1-9) has been explained as illustrating a business manager who lent out his master's assets at interest and then, when in danger of losing his position, revoked the illegal usury. Jesus commanded his own disciples to "lend, expecting nothing in return" and to give their surplus goods to the poor (Luke 6:27-38 and parallels).

In the Greco-Roman environment of early Christianity, loans were mostly made between friends or from an aristocrat to his clients. Cicero complained about a huge loan Brutus made to the city of Salamis at an interest rate of forty-eight percent. The parable of the unforgiving servant (Matt 18:23-35) illustrates the common practices of imprisoning debtors, sometimes torturing them as well to encourage their families to pay the price of their release, and of selling them into slavery if there was no hope of a ransom.

See also JUBILEE, YEAR OF; PROPHETS; SABBATICAL YEAR.

Bibliography. R. De Vaux, *Ancient Israel*; R. A. Horsley, *Bandits, Prophets, and Messiahs*; D. Patrick, *Old Testament Law*; A. Van Selms, "Jubilee," *IDBSupp*.

—RICHARD B. VINSON

A boundary stone recording a transfer of ownership.

• **Boundary Stones.** Boundary stones were used in the ancient Near East to delineate boundaries between property of individuals, districts, or nations. This practice is attested in many ancient texts. Moreover, archaeologists have uncovered examples of such stones in Mesopotamia dating as early as the Late Bronze Age (1550–1200 B.C.E.). Such stones were sometimes inscribed with information about the land about to be entered such as curses and warnings. The removal of boundary stones was considered a serious crime according to Babylonian, Egyptian, Greek, and Roman law (cf., for example, *The Instruction of Amen-em-Opet*, chap. 6).

Although archaeological and biblical evidence for the use of boundary stones in ancient Palestine is not prominent, biblical prohibitions against removing such stones indicate that they were certainly used in Israel. The earliest reference to their use is found in Gen 31 which reflects a boundary covenant between Abraham and Laban at Mizpah. Neither party was to pass beyond the boundary pillar (Heb. *maṣṣebah*) for purposes of harming their neighbor (vv. 51-52).

In the OT there are many more prohibitions against removing boundary stones set up by the "forefathers" than there are references to the use of such stones. Prohibitions are found in the laws of Deuteronomy (19:14; 27:17), as well as in wisdom literature (Prov 22:28; 23:10). The removal of boundary markers is given as an example of wickedness in Job 24:2 and Hos 5:10.

Bibliography. J. A. Wilson, "The Instruction of Amen-em-Opet," *ANET*.

—CECIL P. STATON, JR.

• **Bowing.** *See* OBEISANCE

• **Bowl.** *See* FOOD

• **Bread.** *See* BAKER

• **Breastplate, Priestly.** *See* DRESS; JEWELRY

• **Bride, Bridegroom.** *See* MARRIAGE IN THE NEW TESTAMENT

• **Bride-Price.** *See* MARRIAGE IN THE NEW TESTAMENT; MARRIAGE IN THE OLD TESTAMENT

• **Brass/Bronze.** Both brass (with zinc) and bronze (with tin) are alloys whose basic component is copper. Brass was not known in biblical times (unless the obscure "gleaming bronze"—KJV "amber"—of Ezek 1:4, 27; 8:2 refers to brass). In general, KJV "brass" and RSV "bronze" translate the OT נְחֹשֶׁת (Aramaic נְחָשׁ in Daniel) and NT χαλκός, which may designate COPPER (Ezra 8:27) a copper alloy (Gen 4:22 + ca. 116t.), or something fashioned therefrom (e.g., lavish appointments in Solomon's temple, 1 Kgs 7:13-47; 2 Chr 4:1ff.; armor, 1 Sam 17:5-6; "chains/fetters," Jer 39:7; and coins—KJV "brass," RSV "copper," Matt 10:9, i.e., "money," Mark 6:8; 12:41). Figuratively, hardness (and/or brightness), strength, or obstinacy (Job 40:18; Rev 1:15; Isa 48:4) is suggested. (Recent KJV "corrected" editions have "bronze"—not in original KJV, translated when "brass" designated various copper alloys; in four places KJV has "steel." "Brass" occurs in RSV only metaphorically—Lev 26:19; Deut 28:23; Isa 48:4; otherwise RSV has "bronze").

Bronze apparently was first discovered in Lower Mesopotamia, and the so-called Bronze Age began sometime between 4000 and 3000 B.C.E. (this indefinite transition period has been called the Aeneolithic, Chalcolithic, or Copper-Bronze Period). The biblical Bronze Age is dated ca. 3300–1200 B.C.E., roughly corresponding to the so-called "Canaanite" period (as the Iron Age, ca. 1200–300, roughly marks the "Israelite" period). "Bronze Age" designates that period characterized by the use of copper and its alloys, and is generally taken as marking the beginnings of urbanization. Copper and tin ores sometimes occur together, and it is not known exactly when some ancient metalworker distinguished the two or when it was learned that mixing copper and tin produced an alloy much harder than copper alone (it is assumed "bronze" objects assaying at more than two percent tin represent a deliberate attempt to produce bronze: two percent or less tin could have occurred naturally). But at some time it was learned that the addition of tin to copper produced a brighter ("yellow" as opposed to "red"), harder metal that could be cast with more precision, worked to a sharper edge, and burnished to a more durable sheen. Thus bronze was used not only for implements (armor and WEAPONS, tools of all kinds including various cutting tools, and even nails, mirrors, and musical instruments) but also for ornaments and veneer (jewelry and architectural ornamentation—even bronze-clad doors, Isa 45:2). The value of bronze is indicated by the fact it was included prominently among the spoils of war (2 Sam 8:8; 2 Kgs 25:13-17 = Jer 52:17-23).

Evidently bronze (and even iron) were in use in Palestine as early as 2300 B.C.E., and the Hebrews learned metalworking from (or alongside) the Canaanites. That

Solomon hired craftsmen from Tyre to provide metalwork for the temple (1 Kgs 7:13-14, 40-44) suggests that until that time Israel had no skilled metalworkers (yet the so-called "brazen serpent" episode—Num 21:8-9; 2 Kgs 18:4—suggests the Hebrews could have learned at least rudimentary metallurgy from the Egyptians or the Kenites).

See also COPPER.

—EDD ROWELL

• **Building Materials.** Various building materials were used throughout the periods of ancient times. Whether nomads, semi-nomads, or settled peoples, each would use what was readily available. These materials included: clay, wood, and stone. Of these materials stone was probably the most widely used throughout all periods. In the earliest periods in the Palestinian area the people would have been mostly migratory, and inhabitants resided in caves and natural shelters. As the Stone Age ended and technology progressed, land foragers became land managers and permanent settlements appeared. In the Neolithic Period, Jericho stands as an important site. By approximately 8000 B.C.E. this city had impressive buildings and fortifications. Homes and walls were made with clay bricks and stones as the primary building materials. From Chalcolithic times, the Ghassulian culture was known to have built homes of bricks on foundations of stone. In the Canaanite period, in the Palestinian area, fortifications such as Meggido and Ai arose as impressive fortresses. Megiddo's walls were made from bricks on stone foundations, while Ai's structure was of large stones. Homes of this period were stone or brick, rectangular in shape, with usually a wooden door. In the early Israelite period a typical house consisted of four rooms including a courtyard. Primary materials were again stone and brick. Stone pillars were used and there were certainly wooden roof beams and other wooden components. In addition, plastered cisterns became widely used at this time.

The type of stone most commonly used for building material was limestone; a softer chalkstone could also be found but was not adequate for building purposes. Sandstone from the Arabah was likewise not acceptable for building purposes. Wood in the ancient Palestinian area was more abundant than present-day surveys indicate. Wood was a primary building material for furniture, transportation vehicles such as wagons and ships, farm implements, musical instruments, and idols; it was also used extensively for fuel. Several types of wood are mentioned in the Bible: gopher, acacia, cedar, cypress, pine, olive wood. Cedar is mentioned as imported from Lebanon; acacia came from the Negeb and the Sinai area. Furniture items from acacia wood were largely associated with Tabernacle and Temple implements. The olive tree was a dominant fixture on the rocky landscape of the Palestinian area. It is a resilient tree

Two views of a brick from Untash-Gal (ca. 1250 B.C.E.)

Inscription on top of brick is Elamite.

Courtesy of the Eisenberg Museum of Biblical Archaeology, Southern Baptist Theological Seminary.

that requires little cultivation. Its usefulness was manifold. Its fruit was food; its branches were fuel; its oil was used for medicinal purposes; certainly it would have been used for carpentry. Another building material, the native clay, also served many purposes. It was used for pottery, bricks, for plastering walls, roofs, and cisterns.

—MARK W. GREGORY

• **Butler.** *See* CUPBEARER

• **Byblos/Gebal.** [bib′los/gee′buhl] *1.* An ancient port city of CANAAN and PHOENICIA located on the coast about twenty miles north of Beirut (PLATE 1). The ancient city of Gebal was given the name Byblos by the Greeks because papyrus scrolls played a role in the economy of the site.

The city, built on a slope along the Phoenician coast, had a harbor below. The harbor, along with the cedar, cypress, and spruce wood from the Lebanon mountains all played an important role in making Byblos a major center of trade. The city was famous for its shipbuilding industry, and the work of its skilled craftsmen such as carpenters and masons. References to the men of Gebal and its territory are found in the OT. During the period the Israelites settled in the land of Canaan, the territory of Gebal was recognized as land yet to be taken (Josh 13:5). Solomon's Temple was built with the assistance of craftsmen from Gebal (1 Kgs 5:18). Ezekiel mentions the work of Gebal's ship builders (Ezek 27:9).

The history of the site which reaches back to the Neolithic Age has been brought to light through excavations directed by Pierre Montet (1921–1924) and Maurice Dunand (beginning in 1925). During the Chalcolithic period Byblos was inhabited by a people, small in stature, who lived in small circular or rectangular huts, and who buried their dead in large pottery pots. Byblos became a great center of trade during the Bronze Age. Engaged in trade with Mesopotamia, Anatolia, and Egypt, Byblos exported not only supplies of lumber, but also leather, oil, wine, and spices.

Because Byblos had a limitless supply of wood, an essential for ship building, Egypt maintained control of the city whenever possible. During the Old Kingdom of Egyptian history, Byblos was virtually an Egyptian colony. The people of Byblos built a temple to the goddess Baalat, to which the Egyptians sent numerous votive offerings. Near the end of the third millennium B.C.E. Byblos was invaded and destroyed by the Amorites, and a new city was built. The Amorite era resulted in the development of a new culture at the site which included a cultural exchange with the Aegean islands. However, Byblos was dominated again by the Egyptians with the introduction of Egypt's Middle Kingdom. The name of the city appears in the cursing rituals of Egypt's Execration Texts from that era. During this period a temple was built for Resheph, the god of plagues and destruction. With the decline of the Middle Kingdom, the Egyptian delta and the cities of Palestine and Phoenicia came under the control of the HYKSOS. While the Egyptians attempted to reestablish their control of the Phoenician coast following the expulsion of the Hyksos, their control over cities like Byblos was apparently rather limited during the Amarna period. The AMARNA letters include correspondence from Rib-Addi, the city-state ruler of Byblos, requesting help against anti-Egyptian invaders. A revival of Egyptian domination of Byblos took place during the reign of Ramses II; howver, the city was destroyed shortly thereafter by the invading sea peoples, ca. 1195 B.C.E. During the period that followed, Egypt was extremely weak, and Phoenicia experienced a time of independence. Egypt's influence in the region is reflected in the rude reception the Egyptian, Wen-Amon, received as he attempted to buy lumber at Byblos.

One of the most important discoveries from Byblos dates to the time of King Ahiram, ca. 1000 B.C.E. Ahiram's sarcophagus bears an inscription written in the early Phoenician alphabetic characters, the same system of consonants of early Hebrew.

Eventually Byblos's role as a leading center of trade and commerce was surpassed by the city of TYRE. With the passing of time Byblos fell under the influence of those powers who gained control of the ancient Near Eastern world, including the Assyrians, Babylonians, Persians, Greeks, Romans, and Byzantines.

2. A territory located southeast of the Dead Sea mentioned in Ps 83:7.

Bibliography. K. Schoville, *Biblical Archaeology in Focus,* 247–52.

—LAMOINE DEVRIES

• **Caesarea.** [ses′uh-ree″uh] Caesarea is located on the Mediterranean Sea, approximately seven mi. to the northwest of Jerusalem (PLATES 21, 23). It was originally a small Phoenician anchorage called Strabo's Tower, the site being chosen because of some protective rocks offshore which provided safe anchorages for small ships.

In 63 B.C.E., the area was added to the Roman province of Syria; and Augustus gave the tower to HEROD the Great after winning the battle of Actium (30 B.C.E.). Herod built a new city on the old site and named it Caesarea Maritima in honor of Caesar Augustus. Among other constructions was a new port which was able to accommodate huge Alexandrian sailing vessels bearing grain to Rome. He called his new port Sebastos (the Gk. form of Augustus).

Excavations have uncovered construction from the Roman and Byzantine periods, including streets, palaces, public buildings, a temple, a hippodrome, and a theatre. It was in the theatre constructed by Herod that Herod AGRIPPA was smitten with his illness leading to death five days later (cf. Acts 12:21-23).

In the first century C.E., Caesarea was the home of the Roman procurators, such as Pilate, who normally ventured up to Jerusalem only during the Jewish festivals so that they could maintain order during those turbulent times. According to the Book of Acts, the gospel was preached in Caesarea by PHILIP (8:12) and PETER (10:1–11:18). Peter was responsible for the conversion of the Roman centurion CORNELIUS at Caesarea (Acts 10:23-48). Caesarea was the port used by PAUL for several of his journeys (Acts 9:30; 18:22; 21:8; 27:1-2), and he was brought from Jerusalem to Caesarea (Acts 23:23-35) to stand trial before Felix, Festus, and Agrippa II (Acts 24–26).

Origen moved to Caesarea from Alexandria; and EUSEBIUS, the first Christian geographer of the church, carried on his researches at Caesarea.

See also AGRIPPA I & II; CORNELIUS; EUSEBIUS; HEROD; PAUL; PETER; PHILIP.

—JERRY VARDAMAN

• **Caesarea Philippi.** [ses′uh-ree′uh-fil-ip″*i*] Caesarea Philippi was located in the southwestern foothills of Mount Hermon at one of the sources of the Jordan River (PLATE 23). It was important for military and religious reasons. The area serves as guard for the fertile plains to the west, and from antiquity the site contained a shrine to the nature god, Pan. The Greeks dedicated the spring to Pan and the nymphs and named the area Paneas.

Caesar Augustus visited Syria in 20 B.C.E. and gave the territory to Herod the Great who built a temple there and dedicated it to Augustus. When Herod's son Philip inherited this portion of his father's kingdom he enlarged the city and renamed it Caesarea Philippi in honor of Caesar and himself. A half-century later Agrippa II renamed it Neronias in honor of Nero, but it is the ancient Greek name (in the form Banyes) that has prevailed.

The population in NT times was largely pagan, though some Jews lived there. It was an important center of Greco-Roman civilization, and the town controlled the surrounding region.

Jesus journeyed from Bethsaida with his disciples to the outlying villages of Caesarea Philippi. Here for the first time Jesus was recognized (by Peter) as the Christ, the Son of the living God (Mark 8:27-29; Matt 16:13-20).

—JOE R. BASKIN

• **Caiaphas.** [kay′uh-fuhs] Caiaphas is the name of the Jewish high priest during Jesus' trial. If Josephus (*Ant* 18.2.2; 18.4.3) was correct, Valerius Gratus, the fourth Roman procurator over Judea and Samaria, deposed Ananus (taken to be the same as biblical ANNAS) as high priest when he became procurator, then appointed and deposed three others before he appointed Joseph Caiaphas (ca. 18 C.E.). Later during an unsettled situation Caiaphas as well as Pontius Pilate were deposed by Vitellius, governor of Syria (ca. 36 C.E.). Elsewhere Josephus (*Life* 38, 39) mentions an Ananus along with another as high priest in the 60s when war between the Jews and the Romans seemed imminent. This suggests that a former high priest might still retain the title of high priest.

Information about Caiaphas in the canonical Gospels and Acts (Matt 26:3, 57; Luke 3:2; John 11:49; 18:13, 14, 24, 28; Acts 4:6) is at first glance harder to interpret. In Luke 3:2 Annas and Caiaphas shared the high priestly title which could mean they were high priests concurrently or Caiaphas followed Annas in office immediately. Reasons for rejecting these possibilities follow.

In Acts 4:6 after "Annas the high priest," Caiaphas, John, and Alexander are included with "all who were of the high-priestly family." While in Matt 26 Caiaphas was the only high priest involved in the Jewish phase of Jesus' trial, in John 18 first Annas and then Caiaphas, Annas' son-in-law, had the lead in the Jewish phase; but Caiaphas was the high priest "that year" and said that it was fitting that "one man should die for the people." Also in John 18:35 PILATE told Jesus that it was the high priests who delivered Jesus to him for trial. Therefore, a general consistency is seen that the Gospel information indicated that Annas and Caiaphas had the high priestly title while Caiaphas was the one in office.

See also ANNAS; PILATE; PRIESTS; TRIAL OF JESUS, THE.

—G. WILLARD REEVES

• **Cain and Abel.** [kayn, ay'buhl] Recorded in Gen 4:1-16, the story of Cain and Abel reflects universal concerns characteristic of the narratives that comprise the primeval history—Gen 1–11. The story of the two brothers, addressing themes of temptation, rebellion, denial, and alienation, displays a crime-and-punishment motif similar to the drama of the man and woman of Genesis 3. Adam and Eve, followed by their firstborn son Cain, are presented canonically as parents and offspring; they also portray humanity's involvement in disobedience against a backdrop of the divine intentionality for creation. The name Cain seems to mean "metalworker"; cf. Gen 4:17-24, where Cain builds the first city and fathers Enoch, the ancestor of Tubal-cain, the first metalworker. The name is explained contextually in Gen 4:1 as meaning "created," or "acquired."

Since the end of the nineteenth century, the interpretation of the Cain and Abel story has divided along two basic lines. An individual explanation sees in the figure of Cain, as he takes his brother's life, a prototype of humanity at its worst. The murderer Cain addresses all human beings tempted to shed the blood of another. Such an act is the killing of one's brother, just as it was for Cain.

A collective approach treats Cain symbolically. Explanations range from a presumed conflict between two ways of life, the pastoral and the agricultural, to a portrayal of the life and culture of the KENITES, with Cain as their eponymous hero.

The main narrative, beginning and ending with genealogical material (vv. 1-2, 17-26), highlights the figure of Cain. Abel is a passive figure, his relevance to the story hinging on his being Cain's brother.

Cain is a tiller of the soil, while Abel is a keeper of sheep. Each presents an offering to Yahweh taken from their respective livelihoods. Abel's offering is accepted, while Cain's is not, with no explanation given as to why this was so. As Cain reacts with anger and a fallen countenance (v. 5), the voice of Yahweh is heard. The divine speech (v. 7) sets the stage for Cain's next act. Sin is indeed "couching at the door" of Cain's heart.

The scene shifts to the field, and the act of fratricide occurs. Abel passes from the story, just as his name suggests (in Hebrew, "Abel" means "breath," or "nothingness"). Contrast the NT references to Abel: in Matt 23:35, Luke 11:51, and Heb 12:24 Abel symbolizes innocent blood, while in Heb 11:4 he is an example of faith.

Confronted with his deed, Cain initially pleads ignorance, but then expresses concern over his future fate. A curse of alienation will separate him not only from the source of his livelihood, the ground, but also from Yahweh, the one to whom he brought the unacceptable offering. Destined by divine judgment to live a chaotic life of wandering, Cain sees death at the hands of others as the final consequence of his punishment, but is spared this fate. Even though the divine judgment stands, a conditional curse is uttered against anyone who would slay Cain, who now bears God's mark.

The occasion of the sacrifice, which arose naturally out of the context of the productive livelihoods of shepherd and farmer, turns ironic as the sacrificer who presents the acceptable sacrifice is himself slaughtered. Sacrifice in the Cain and Abel story, though intended to acknowledge the deity who makes offering possible and who assures future blessing, becomes paradoxically a context for murder and expulsion from God's presence.

Just as Abel's blood cannot be silenced but continues to cry from the ground, so Cain's crime will not be overlooked. The death of one brother results in the expulsion of the other (cf. Heb 11:4; 1 John 3:12; Jude 11). The story of Cain and Abel ends in a context of alienation, the same fate pictured for the parents in Gen 3. Like Adam and Eve, disobedient and therefore punished, yet clothed by Yahweh before their departure from the garden (Gen 3:21), Cain too departs protected by the mark of Yahweh.

See also KENITES; MURDER.

Bibliography. J. M. Miller, "The Descendants of Cain: Notes on Genesis 4," *ZAW* 86 (1974) 164-74; H. Thielicke, "The Story of Cain and Abel," *How the World Began;* C. Westermann, *Genesis 1–11.*

—KANDY M. QUEEN-SUTHERLAND

• **Calah.** *See* NIMRUD/CALAH

• **Caleb.** [kay'luhb] One of the twelve chosen to spy out the promised land, representing the tribe of Judah (Num 13:6). Supported only by JOSHUA, he brought the minority report that Israel was capable of taking the land (Num 13:30; 14:6). Because of their courage and faith, he and Joshua alone were spared from the plague that killed the spies (Num 14:38). Of all the wilderness generation only they were allowed to enter the promised LAND (Num 14:30; 26:65; 32:12; Deut 1:36). In the later apportionment of land, Caleb is given the hill country around HEBRON for an inheritance (Josh 14:6, 13). To his nephew OTHNIEL he gives his daughter Achsah in marriage for the successful conquest of Kiriath-sepher [Debir] (Josh 15:13-19).

The genealogical tables of Chronicles trace Caleb back to Judah, giving him as son of Hezron (1 Chr 2:18-19) and brother of Jerahmeel (1 Chr 2:25). The older traditions describe him as son of Jephunneh and as a Kenizzite (Num 32:12; Josh 14:6). Since the Kenizzites occupied southern Palestine in the patriarchal period (Gen 15:19), many scholars are of the opinion that the Calebites were among those older tribes that already occupied southern Judah at the time of the conquest and were gradually absorbed into Israel.

See also CONQUEST OF CANAAN; KENAZ/KENIZZITES; SPIES.

Bibliography. J. Bright, *A History of Israel*; R. F. Johnson, "Caleb," *IDB*.

—JOHN B. POLHILL

• **Calendar.** In the biblical period, there was no calendar such as is used today. The present Jewish calendar dates to the fourth century C.E. although it was under development for centuries before that time. Certainly the NT period was aware of the Greco-Roman calendars, the basis of modern calendars, as well as the dating known from the OT as indicated below.

The ancient Sumerians and Babylonians used a lunar calendar with an intercalary month periodically added. The Egyptians used a solar calendar based on the appearance of the star Sirius in their eastern sky shortly before sunrise after several months disappearance. Their calendar had a 365 day year. The best known Roman calendar is the Julian calendar, revised during the reign of Julius Caesar and set at 365 and one-fourth days length.

The OT knew three general systems of dating: that based on the regnal year of a king, the lunar system using a combination of Canaanite and Babylonian names, and the cul-

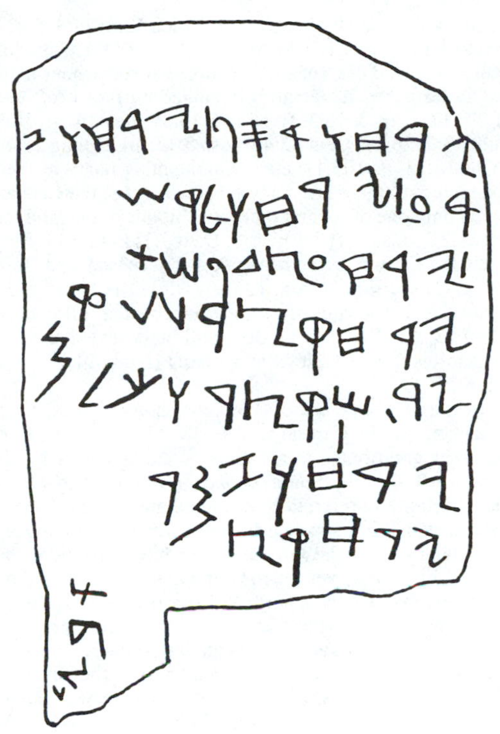

Gezer Calendar.

tic calendar based on holy seasons and festivals. Public records would be dated primarily in reference to the year of a given king's reign. Much of the chronology in the books of Kings and Chronicles is based on the regnal years of the Israelite and Judean kings. The Samaria ostraca likewise use this formula, though the name of the specific king or kings isn't given. However, since the ostraca were receipts for goods, the king's name would have been obvious at the time and probably unnecessary.

Hebrew had two words for month, *yērāḥ* and *ḥādāsh*. The former was the word for moon and shows the lunar basis for the Hebrew month. The latter was the word new, especially new moon, and likewise shows its lunar derivation. Apparently in the pre-exilic period, the Canaanite names for the months were used. After the Exile, the Babylonian names for the months replaced the Canaanite names. Like the Babylonian calendar, the Hebrew calendar had to add an intercalary month periodically.

The cultic calendar centered in the major pilgrim festivals of the Hebrew year. These are mentioned several times in the OT. In Exod 23, three festivals are mentioned, Unleavened Bread, First Fruits, and Ingathering. Exod 34 also mentions Passover along with the pilgrim festivals. An even fuller cultic calendar is given in Lev 23. To the festivals already mentioned are added Sabbath, New Year's, and Day of Atonement.

An early inscription, the Gezer calendar shows the agricultural year of ancient Israel. It lists the activities of each month or two month period, beginning with the fall harvest and ending with the summer fruit.

—JOEL F. DRINKARD, JR.

• **Calf, Golden.** An idol, bovine in shape and overlaid with gold, which was fashioned by Israel's leaders at two crucial moments in their history. Such animals were widely used in the ancient Near East, either to depict characteristics of a deity (e.g., the goddess Ishtar as lion-like and to whom lions were sacred), or to represent the mythological creatures by means of which a deity traveled. Thus, a golden calf might represent either (a) a deity which a part of Israel continued to worship along with Yahweh (possibly the moon-god of Mesopotamia who was represented by a golden bull, cf. Josh 24:14; or the Egyptian goddess Hathor who was depicted as a cow, cf. Ezek 20:7-8), or (b) a pedestal upon which the invisible Yahweh could ride, comparable to the bull upon which the Canaanite god BAAL was depicted as riding or to the sphinx-like cherubim which supported the divine throne (Ps 80:1) and upon which Yahweh flew (Ps 18:10).

1. When MOSES was atop Mt. Sinai, AARON fashioned a golden calf in response to the popular request to "make us gods" (Exod 32) and attributed the deliverance from Egypt to it.

2. When JEROBOAM became king of the northern tribes at the division of the Davidic state, he placed such images at sanctuaries in DAN and BETHEL (1 Kgs 12) and dedicated them with the same words that Aaron had used.

Some modern interpreters have proposed that the EXODUS account is without historical foundation: it was created by Judean leadership as a heinous precedent in order to discredit Jeroboam's alternative to the cherubim at Jerusalem (so Kaufmann). Others have proposed that the calf image represents an ancient prepatriarchal religion which survived in the northern kingdom. In any case, those who introduced the calf would be restoring an ancient inconographic custom (so Bailey).

See also BAAL; CHERUB; IDOLATRY; JEROBOAM I.

Bibliography. L. R. Bailey, "The Golden Calf," *HUCA* 42 (1971): 97-115; Y. Kaufmann, *The Religion of Israel*.

—LLOYD R. BAILEY

• **Call.** A word found frequently in the OT and NT with different meanings.

1. To name or call by name is the most frequent usage of the word in the Bible. To give a name implied authority or control over the person or object named (e.g., Gen 1:5; 2:19; Isa 7:14; Dan 10:1; Luke 1:13; 1 Pet 3:6).

2. To speak to God in PRAYER. This meaning also is found frequently in the Bible (e.g., Judg 16:28; 2 Sam 22:7; John 1:6; Acts 7:59; Rom 10:14; 1 Pet 1:17).

3. To speak or call to someone (e.g., Gen 3:9; Lev 1:1; Judg 9:54; Mark 10:49; Jonah 1:48; Acts 23:17).

4. To summon to oneself or assemble a group. A call with authority that demands a response (e.g., Gen 41:8; Deut 5:1; Esth 4:5; Matt 2:7; Mark 9:35; Acts 5:21).

5. To invite. A call that is less authoritative than a summons (e.g., Gen 31:54; 1 Kgs 1:9–10; Esth 5:12; Luke 14:13; 1 Cor 7:15; Gal 5:13).

6. To call one's own. A call that implies ELECTION or SALVATION (e.g., Gen 21:12; Deut 28:10; Isa 45:4; Rom 1:6; 8:30; Gal 1:6; 1 Pet 1:15).

7. A call to vocation or SERVICE (e.g., Exod 3:4; 1 Sam 3:10; Matt 4:21; Acts 16:10; Rom 1:1; 1 Cor 7:20).

See also ELECTION; NAMES.

—F. B. HUEY, JR.

• **Calvary.** Calvary is derived from the Vulgate's translation of the semitic word Golgotha, which means "skull"

(Luke 23:33). According to the Gospels (Mark 15:22; Matt 27:33; John 19:17), Jesus was crucified at Golgotha (PLATES 23, 24, 25). Although some make the claim that the site had the physical appearance of a skull, the name "skull" is probably rooted in the belief that Jesus was crucified at a site where many executions had been carried out. Calvary's precise location is disputed and surprisingly little is known about it. Jewish and Roman law would likely have required capital punishment to take place outside the city walls (John 19:20; Heb 13:12). Matt 27:39 suggests that perhaps Golgotha was near a road or field. Mark 15:40 states that the crucifixion could be seen at a distance, which suggests a hill or rise.

Given that the crucifixion of Jesus is central to the passion narrative of early Christianity, one would expect to find passages in the NT that clearly identify the location of Golgotha. In fact, the clues are not only sparse but nebulous. Commenting on Matt 27:33, Origen in the third century C.E. mentioned an early Christian belief that Adam's skull was buried under the CROSS. The fifth-century C.E. monk, Jerome, conjectured that skulls lay on the ground unburied at the crucifixion site, but this is unlikely since such a practice would have violated first-century C.E. custom in JERUSALEM. Official Roman interest in identifying the site of Golgotha emerged in the fourth century C.E., when the Roman emperor Constantine directed Bishop Macarius to ascertain the site. Since then, the site marked today by the Church of the Holy Sepulcher has been widely believed to be the place of Jesus' crucifixion and burial (a rival site is Gordon's Calvary, located northeast of the Damascus gate) (PLATE 39). No records remain to indicate what if any hard clues were available to the bishop. In the fifth century the legend had developed that the bishop was directed to the true site by a special vision from the Queen Mother Helena.

See also CROSS; JERUSALEM.

—JOE E. BARNHART

• **Canaan.** [kay'nuhn] Canaan first appears in the Bible as the son of Ham and the grandson of Noah (Gen 9:18; though in 9:24-25 he seems to be the son of Noah). In the table of nations in Gen 10, he is the brother of Put (Libya), Cush (Ethiopia), and Egypt (v. 6). He is also said to be the father of Sidon (Sidonians), Heth (Hittites), the Jebusites, the Amorites, the Girgashites, the Hivites, the Arkites, the Sinites, the Arvadites, the Zemarites, and the Hamathites (vv. 15-18). While the identity of some of these groups is not clear, taken as a whole, they represent the inhabitants of Syria-Palestine prior to the period of Israelite occupation. The first five peoples listed after Sidon occur frequently elsewhere in the OT as the inhabitants of Palestine (cf. Exod 3:5; 33:2; Deut 7:1); and the last five were important coastal or inland cities in Syria. Ultimately the term "Canaanite" would be used to describe all of the inhabitants of Cisjordan before Israel's arrival (Gen 12:6).

However, despite the frequent mention of "the land of Canaan," and "Canaanite(s)," in the Bible, the actual origin, meaning, and geographical limits of these terms are still very much a matter of dispute. Part of the problem has to do with the fact that the literary evidence for Canaanite culture comes indirectly from other sources, especially the Egyptians, the Hebrews, and various cuneiform inscriptions; and from archaeological data which are open to a variety of interpretations. Nevertheless, the term "Canaanite" is currently used by scholars in general to designate the pre-Israelite inhabitants of PALESTINE. Such usage is in conformity with many biblical texts (cf. Gen 12:6; 24:3; 50:11; Exod 13:11; Num 21:3; Josh 7:9; Judg 1:1ff.), and the formula, "the land of Canaan," occurs over sixty times in the OT to designate the territory inhabited by Israel (cf. Gen 11:31; 12:5; 13:2; 16:3; Exod 6:4; 16:35; Lev 14:34; 18:3; Num 13:2; 26:19; Deut 32:49; Josh 5:12; 14:1; Judg 21:21; 1 Chr 16:18; Ps 105:11; etc.). On the other hand, as mentioned above, there are many texts which list the Canaanites as only one of several other inhabitants of the land (cf. Exod 33:2; Josh 9:1; 3:10; 12:8; Deut 7:1; Ezra 9:1). Elsewhere the Canaanites are restricted to the coastal area (Josh: 5:1) and the Jordan (Num 13:29), while the Hittites, Jebusites, and Amorites are said to inhabit the hill country (Num 13:29; cf. Judg 1:34-36). Still other texts locate the Canaanites in the valleys and plains (Num 14:25; Josh 17:16).

This ambiguous, and often confusing usage of the terms "Canaan," and "Canaanite," by the biblical authors/editors, has contributed to a variety of explanations for the meaning of the term. Some scholars have argued that "Canaan" originally referred to a limited area on the Phoenician coast and only secondarily was extended to include all of the land west of the Jordan. Others have concluded that the Israelites took over the meaning that the name had before they inhabited the land. In such case, this would be the Egyptian Canaan of the fourteenth to thirteenth centuries B.C.E. The biblical traditions locate the southern, western, and eastern boundaries as the Dead Sea to the Brook of Egypt (the wadi el-'Arish), the Mediterranean Sea, and the Jordan River respectively (Num 24:2-12; Ezek 47:15-20; cf. Gen 10:19). It is the northern boundary of Canaan that is most difficult to fix. Some believe that it extended as far north as Latakia (just south of UGARIT) and inland to Hamath on the Orontes River. Others believe that the northern boundary never went any farther north than Qedes which is also on the Orontes but south of both Latakia and Hamath.

This uncertainty is created in part both by the fact that the biblical texts which mention Canaan or Canaanite all date much later than the settlement period, and also by the fact that the geographical connotations of the terms seem to have fluctuated in different periods. Furthermore, most texts, both biblical and nonbiblical, refer to Canaan with little or no geographical precision. In light of these considerations, perhaps the only safe conclusion is that the word "Canaan" is an old, perhaps native name, for parts of Syria-Palestine, whose precise boundaries in ancient times are no longer known.

Furthermore, the origin and etymology of the name "Canaan" are still unclear. Some scholars suggest it is a semitic word while others argue for a Hurrian background. The most popular interpretation is one that links Canaan with the Akkadian word, *kinahhu,* meaning "red dye," or "red purple." According to this theory, Canaan would have the meaning of "the land of purple." But the usage of *kinahhu* with this meaning has only been attested at Nuzi. Thus other suggestions have been put forth including "lowland," as opposed to the inhabitants of the hill country, "merchant," and "to bend" or "to incline," referring to the country in the west where the sun went down. Some of these arguments presuppose that the term Canaan originally had an ethnic or social class designation. However, if originally the term referred to a particular geographical region, its etymology may no longer be recoverable.

The ambiguity of the biblical texts is also found in nonbiblical literary sources where both geographical and social class or ethnic designations occur. One of the earliest nonbiblical references to Canaan is in the MARI texts of the eighteenth century B.C.E. The text consists of a letter written by an official to the king, Yasmah-Adad, the predecessor of Zimri-Lin. In the letter, the official states that he is planning to take action against "thieves and Canaanites," who are in Rahisum. While this reference does not aid in the quest for the origin or etymology of the word, it has been interpreted to indicate that Canaan, as a geopolitical entity, already existed in the Middle Bronze Age. However, the geographical boundaries of Canaan at this time are not specified at all.

Another Akkadian reference comes from the statue of Idrimi, king of Alalakh. Dated to the middle of the fifteenth century B.C.E., the text mentions the "land of Canaan," (*kin'ani*) as the place to which Idrimi fled. Specifically, he is said to have gone to the city of Ammia, which is on the Phoenician coast south of Tripoli. This clearly locates Canaan during this period to the south of Alalakh, but hardly delimits its geographical boundaries. Three other letters from Alalakh, of slightly later date, also use the same name for Canaan.

Also dating to the fifteenth century are the NUZI tablets, mentioned above, which contain the form, *kinahhu,* meaning "red purple." But whether this refers to a class of merchants or to a geographical locale is a moot point among scholars. Dating to approximately the same time as the Nuzi texts, are the thousands of clay tablets discovered at ancient Ugarit (modern Ras Shamra), beginning in 1929. Included in the tablets is a list of merchants from different countries, including Canaan. This reference implies that Ugarit did not consider itself as part of Canaan. Thus, whether or not Ugarit should properly be called "Canaanite" is a controversial issue among scholars.

In addition to the Hebrew and cuneiform references to Canaan, there are also several important Egyptian citations. The earliest known comes from the time of Amenhotep/Amenophis II (ca. 1447–1421 B.C.E.) and is included in a list of booty taken by the Pharaoh on an expedition reaching as far north as Qedes on the Orontes. The Pharaoh claims to have taken captive "640 Canaanites," who are listed right after the *maryannu* and their wives. Since the term "maryannu" is known to refer to a warrior class, it is believed by some that "Canaanites" in this list also refers to a social class, probably merchants. Certainly, Canaan came to have the meaning of "merchant" in later biblical literature (cf. Isa 23:8, 11; Ezek 16:29; 17:4 Hos 12:7; Zeph 1:11; Zech 11:7, 11 [reading LXX]; 14:21; Prov 31:24; Job 40:30 [41:6 Eng. trans.].

Among the most important Egyptian texts containing the word Canaan are the Tell el-AMARNA tablets. Dating to the first third of the fourteenth century B.C.E., many of these letters contain correspondence between local city rulers in Palestine and the Pharaohs of Egypt. In all, the name Canaan occurs eleven times. While the boundaries of Canaan are not specified, the cities mentioned include such places as Byblos in the north, and Gaza in the south. The meaning of Canaan described here may very well have been the Canaan experienced by the Israelites when the latter entered the land. Though the texts do not specify the geographical extent of Canaan, they do seem to exclude Ugarit as part of it. Other Egyptian texts which mention Canaan without specifying the territory included by the term, come from the time of Seti I (ca. 1318–1301 B.C.E.), from an inscription at Karnak; the Merneptah stelae (ca. 1230 B.C.E.); from the period of Ramses III (ca. 1195–1164 B.C.E.); and from a tenth century B.C.E. inscription which lists Canaan with the country determinative.

Thus in these extra-biblical references the word "Canaan" has a double geographical connotation, even as it does in the Bible. On the one hand, the term is used to designate the Egyptian province of Syria in general and the Phoenician coast in particular, while on the other, as in the Amarna letters, it is used to refer to cities in Palestine, PHOENICIA and Syria as a whole. In addition, it is also used as an ethnic appellation.

But even more difficult to define than the boundaries of Canaan, is "Canaanite culture." It is not even known when it actually began, though by the beginning of the third millennium B.C.E., if not earlier, a semitic population already existed in Syria-Palestine as attested to by ancient towns bearing semitic names. Among these are Beth-shan, Byblos, Jericho, Megiddo, and Ugarit. In addition, scholars usually equate Canaanite culture as a whole with that of the Bronze Age in Syria-Palestine (ca. 3100–1200 B.C.E.). While archaeologists have shed a great deal of light on this period, many issues are still hotly debated. One involves trying to fit the patriarchal stories of the OT to any known archaeological period. The most popular approach has been to locate the patriarchs within the Middle Bronze Age (ca. 2200–1550 B.C.E.), particularly Middle Bronze Age II (2000–1550). Despite uncertainties regarding the beginning, nature and ending of this period, much has been learned of this time from the excavations of such sites as Shechem, Hazor, Jericho, Tell Beit Mirsim, Aphek, Tel Dan, Akko, Yavne Yam, Tells Poleg, Zurekiyeh, Hefer and others. Many of these sites were protected by earthwork fortifications (ramparts) and in many cases the burial practices during this period have been recovered. This latter knowledge is extremely important since such practices are culturally determined, even as they are today.

Apart from the question of the Patriarchs, however, the archaeological evidence indicates that the Canaanites during this period never developed a homogeneous culture, creating instead local city-states, each with its own traditions. They seem to have been organized in a feudal system, controlled by a local "king." The same political picture can be drawn from the literary evidence, both biblical (cf. Judg 5:19; Ps 135:11; Num 21:1; Josh 16:10; 1 Sam 8:4-17), and nonbiblical (Ras Shamra, Amarna).

Another major issue has to do with the language of the Canaanites, which belongs to the northwest group of SEMITIC LANGUAGES which were spoken in a large area, with many local dialects. The discovery of the Ugaritic texts has opened many avenues of discussion in this regard. Among the thousands of tablets discovered are many containing various administrative and legal concerns. But of most importance to the biblical student, are the mythological and liturgical texts. While most scholars consider these texts to be primary source material for understanding Canaanite religion as it was practiced during the Middle and Late Bronze Ages, caution is in order. On the one hand, it is still not clear to what extent, if any, Ugarit was part of Canaan; and on the other, it is difficult to transfer religious concepts pertaining to one group of people to another.

But even if Ugarit and Canaan were separate political entities, most scholars would argue that the people of Ugarit still shared in a common Canaanite culture and language. The Ugaritic epics of EL and BAAL contain mythological conceptions which greatly influenced Hebrew thought, despite biblical injunctions that the Israelites were to have nothing to do with their Canaanite predecessors, particularly their religion (cf. Exod 34:13; Deut 20:16-18; and others). Furthermore, the language of the texts is closely related to Hebrew (cf. Isa 19:18 where for the first time in the Bible the Hebrew and Canaanite languages are equated), and many Hebrew literary conventions have Canaanite prototypes. Most students would agree with the conclusion reached by W. Beyerlin: "As the material (i.e., the Ugaritic texts) has been studied, more and more closely, it has become increasingly clear that Yahwistic religion assimilated far more Canaanite elements than had generally been supposed" (186).

While a detailed discussion of Canaanite religion and its influence upon Hebrew thought is beyond the scope of this discussion, study of the Ugaritic texts has shed considerable light on religious conceptions which were held and practiced in Canaan when the Israelites entered the land. In some instances, the Canaanite myths have been superficially applied to Yahweh, the God of Israel (cf. Ps 29). Certainly the Hebrews did not eradicate all of the Canaanites as some texts suggest (Josh 10:40; 11:16-20). Rather, the Canaanites were absorbed by Israel producing both positive as well as negative results. This positive influence upon Israelite religion needs to be appreciated fully if it is to be seen in its proper perspective.

See also CANAAN, INHABITANTS OF; RELIGIONS OF THE ANCIENT NEAR EAST.

Bibliography. W. Beyerlin, ed., *Near Eastern Texts Relating to the Old Testament*; A. R. Millard, "The Canaanites," *Peoples of the Old Testament,* ed. D. J. Wiseman; A. F. Rainey, "A Canaanite at Ugarit," *IEJ* 13 (1963): 158-61; W. H. Schmidt, "The Significance of the Canaanite Gods in the Old Testament," *The Faith of the Old Testament: A History*; R. de Vaux, "Canaan and the Canaanite Civilization," *The Early History of Israel.*

—JOHN C. H. LAUGHLIN

• **Canaan, Inhabitants of.** In the OT "inhabitants of Canaan" (Exod 15:15) are usually "Canaanites" (Gen 10:18, 19 + ca. 70 other occurrences), and sometimes AMORITES (e.g., Josh 24:8). Canaanites appear in "population lists" as one among many in the land (e.g., Gen 15:18-21; Josh 5:1; Judg 1:4, 5; Exod 3:8, 17; Deut 7:1). Occasionally "Canaanites" designates the inhabitants of a delimited area, notably PHOENICIA (Num 13:29; 14:25). In later texts Canaanite may equal Phoenician (Isa 23:11; Obad 20; cf. Matt 15:22 with Mark 7:26), or be an appellation for "trader/merchant" (cf. esp. Isa 23:8). As a rule, however, "Canaanites" designates the pre-Israelite inhabitants of "Canaan" *and* their descendants and cultural successors.

An isthmus between sea and desert, Canaan naturally became *the* main north-south highway connecting Mesopotamia and Egypt. Through the land flowed a steady commerce in goods and culture, politics and religion. One would expect many peoples would meet there, and it is no wonder the people called "Canaanites" were of diverse stock, still today frustrating ethnographic efforts to determine exactly who they were. From earliest times, Canaan was inhabited by groups of Hamites and/or Semites, Hurrians, Indo-Europeans, and many others. A conglomeration of ethnically diverse and nationally diffuse people, yet the "Canaanites" eventually held in common a language, culture, and religion, and at least by ca. 2000 a distinct if amalgamated culture appeared in the land that may be called "Canaanite."

Canaanite influence on the "Hebrews"—indeed on all successive peoples—cannot be gainsaid. Evidence (esp., e.g., at UGARIT) suggests a Canaanite family of languages that included Hebrew. The Canaanites invented—or developed—an alphabet that was the basis for subsequent alphabets, and their literature was precursory to many others (the so-called "Bible of the Canaanites," the temple library at Ugarit, has proved to be of inestimable value in OT studies).

When the Hebrews quit the desert (and/or the hills) and their generally pastoral and nomadic existence for a more agrarian and urban life in "the land," they learned from (or alongside) the Canaanites. They learned agriculture, e.g., and also to worship BAAL who, their Canaanite neighbors assured them, must be placated to insure a harvest. Patterns for the very structure of Hebrew society are to be found among the Canaanites—city-state, confederation, kingship. Language and literature, politics and religion, agriculture and artisanship—the Hebrews learned from/alongside the Canaanites. The eventual uniqueness of the OT Israelites is not to be denied, yet their life and faith may be best understood in comparison with or in stark contrast to that of the "Canaanites."

See also AMORITES; ARAMEANS; CONQUEST OF CANAAN; PHOENICIANS; UGARIT.

Bibliography. H. G. May, "The People of the OT World," *IOVC*; M. Noth, "Palestine as the Arena of Biblical History" and "Peoples," *The Old Testament World.*

—EDD ROWELL

• **Canon.** Canon denotes a list of authoritative writings usually recognized by use in public worship. Christianity inherited a "scripture" from Judaism. During the second century, MARCION's rejection of the OT pushed forward a process of collecting Christian "apostolic" writings into a Christian canon. By the end of the century the core of this collection was already universally recognized among the churches of the Roman empire. Some writings, however, remained in dispute until the end of the fourth century and were accepted largely on the authority of Augustine and Jerome in an African synod rather than in one of the universal councils. Churches outside the Roman Empire have adopted different lists, some containing as few as twenty-two and some as many as thirty-five books. The OT canon recognized by early Christianity came into dispute during the Protestant Reformation when Luther chose to base it on Hebrew originals and thus rejected several writings included in the Greek OT known as the SEPTUAGINT.

Meaning of the Term "Canon." The Greek word *kanon* is of semitic origin, originally meaning "reed." Since the reed was used as a carpenter's level or ruler, it gradually took on metaphorical nuances: written laws, the ideal person, the rules of philosophers and grammarians, ecclesiastical ordinance, an ordinance fixing amount of tribute to be paid, the canon of the mass, and a list. The basic nuance applied to scriptures was that of a "list." Whether a book was or was not read in public worship determined whether or not it was considered "canonical," that is, on the list. This formal designation was not used, however, until around 350 when Athanasius, Bishop of Alexandria, referred to it in a summary of the *Decrees of the Synod of Nicaea.*

Old Testament Canon. The Jewish community never used the word "canon," although they regarded certain writings as normative. The name generally applied to such documents was "scripture" or "scriptures." The Jewish canonization process took place in three phases.

The "Law," that is, the Pentateuch or TORAH, had authoritative status by around 400 B.C.E., judging by the age of the Samaritan Pentateuch. The breach between Manasseh and Ezra evidently occurred in 432 B.C.E. (Neh 13:28; Josephus, *Ant* 11.7.2, 8.2), but two other dates have also been suggested: (1) when a temple was built on Mount Gerizim during the reign of Alexander the Great (332 B.C.E.), and (2) when the Temple was destroyed and the break with the Jews completed in 128 B.C.E.

The "Prophets," including the historical writings (Joshua–2 Kings) as well as what are usually referred to as prophetic writings, were considered "scripture" by around 132 B.C.E. when the grandson of Jesus ben SIRACH composed a prologue to the Wisdom of Jesus ben Sirach. Later Jewish authors such as PHILO make quite clear, however, that the Prophets did not stand on the same level as the Law. So, too, did the custom of assigning texts from the Law while allowing readers to choose those from the Prophets (Luke 4:17).

The "writings," the remaining OT writings, never attained the normative status in Judaism they did in Christianity. At the so-called "Council of Jamnia," either 90 or 118 C.E., the rabbis made some decision concerning the limits of the canon. They pronounced a book "scripture" if they considered it "prophetic." This rule, however, led to dispute over certain books, for every book was attributed to a "prophet." Moses, for example, wrote Job; Samuel, Judges and Ruth; Jeremiah, the Books of Kings; Ezra, the Chronicles; David, the Psalms; Solomon, Proverbs, Canticles or Song of Songs, and Ecclesiastes. "Prophecy" meant inspiration by the Spirit. Works that came after the prophetic period such as the Wisdom of Jesus ben Sirach, therefore, were excluded. Ezekiel, Proverbs, Ecclesiastes, the Song of Solomon, and Esther occasioned debate, but there was no opposition to exclusion of the apocryphal writings found in the LXX. The term *Tanak* is often used in Judaism to designate the scripture. The word is an acronym, derived from the three major divisions of the Jewish canon: *Torah* (Law), *Nebi'im* (Prophets), and *Kethubim* (Writings).

The Greek Old Testament. The decision of the rabbis had little effect on the OT canon acknowledged by Christians, that is, the LXX. The name was derived from the LETTER OF ARISTEAS regarding the translation of the Hebrew Bible by Alexandrian Jewish scholars in the time of Ptolemy Philadelphus (285–247 B.C.E.). According to this legend, seventy scholars in separate cells came out with verbatim agreement on the entire Law. This translation met the needs of the Jews living outside Palestine who could no longer read Hebrew. Translation of other parts probably paralleled the canonization process in Palestine. The Greek Bible, however, came to include certain works for which there were no Hebrew originals: 1 and 2 Esdras, Tobit, Judith, Additions to Esther, the Wisdom of Solomon, Ecclesiasticus or Sirach, Baruch, Additions to Daniel (the Story of Susanna, the Song of the Three Young Men, and the Story of Bel and the Dragon), the Prayer of Manasseh, 1 and 2 Maccabees. Second Esdras is dated as late as 100 C.E. and Baruch 70 C.E. After the first century a Hebrew original was considered mandatory for canonical writings.

Jewish scholars took strong exception to the LXX in debates with Christians. As a consequence, both Jews and Christians produced new translations and revisions of the LXX. Aquila, a Jew of Pontus in Asia Minor (fl. 95–135 C.E.), produced a slavishly literal translation of the Hebrew. Theodotion, an Ebionite Christian (fl. 193-211), translated in good Greek style while remaining remarkably faithful to the Hebrew. His work influenced Jerome's Latin revision, the Vulgate. About 240 Origen, the most eminent Christian scholar of the third century, now at Caesarea, responded to Jewish objections to the LXX with the *Hexapla,* a six-column edition giving in parallel columns: the Hebrew text, a Greek transliteration, Aquila's translation, Symmachus's translation, the LXX with diacritical markings to indicate departures from the Hebrew, and Theodotion's translation.

In the early fourth century Pamphilus (d. 309) and Eusebius of Caesarea (d. 340) published Origen's fifth column. Lucian, a Christian of Samosata in Asia Minor and founder of the Antiochene "school" (d. 311), revised the LXX.

Until the Reformation, the LXX of Lucian supplied the authoritative text of the OT. Luther, judging all scriptures by their testimony to Christ, opted for the Jewish canon and questioned the propriety of including such a book as Esther in the canon, despite its Hebrew original. Other reformers followed suit, thus excluding the Apocrypha from the canon. In reaction against this, in 1546 the Council of Trent affirmed the LXX canon and established the Latin Vulgate as an authorized version.

Formation of a New Testament Canon. The early churches did not immediately relegate the OT to a position subordinate to Christian writings. Although they read in public worship letters or other writings composed by apostles, many still held fast to the scriptures inherited from Judaism. IGNATIUS of Antioch (d. 110–17) cited some persons saying, "Unless I find it in the charters (ἀρχεῖοι) I do not believe in the gospel" (*Philad* 8.2). When Ignatius responded that what he said was "in the scripture," that is, of the OT, they replied, "That is exactly the question."

Until as late as the fifth century, different churches within the Roman empire used different collections of scripture. Initially small collections were made. Churches exchanged writings they possessed with those used in other churches. Gradually churches all over the Roman empire developed a core of NT scriptures. Although synods in Carthage, capital of the Roman province of Africa, took formal action on the disputed books in 393 and 399, their decisions had authority chiefly in the Roman empire. Syrian churches never accepted the five "disputed" writings (2 Peter, 2 and 3 John, James, and Jude).

Marcion and His Canon. Marcion, a wealthy ship owner of Sinope in Pontus, was the first person to specify a NT canon. Excommunicated by the church in Pontus (which his father served as bishop) for "defiling a virgin," around 140 he came to Rome. He differed with the teaching of the Roman church on several critical matters, composing a work entitled the *Antitheses* in which he distinguished between the God of the OT and the God of the NT, insisted on interpreting the OT literally to point up its crudity, and denied the true humanity of Jesus. After the Roman Church excommunicated him, about 140, he founded a Marcionite Church. This church flourished during the second century, but, although it remained strong in the East, it declined thereafter in the West.

Marcion's NT canon consisted of the Gospel according to Luke and ten letters of PAUL, all edited by Marcion himself. He called Ephesians "Laodiceans." Although it is difficult to reconstruct Marcion's text, which is known only from quotations by anti-Marcionite polemicists, his anti-Jewish bias is quite clear. He exhibited a decided preference for Paul because he found in Paul's writings the basic arguments for his attack on Judaism.

How much influence Marcion's canon exerted on the

formation of a NT canon has been debated. Adolf Harnack and John Knox contended that Marcion's canon was the decisive reason for that development. Knox cited the following arguments: (1) The canon came into existence between 150 and 175, the period of Marcion's greatest influence. (2) The NT took shape in Rome. (3) The Old Roman Symbol, an early creed, also designed to refute Marcion, came into existence at this time. (4) Marcion was the most important of the so-called "Gnostics" of the mid-second century. (5) The prominence of Paul's letters in the canon argues for Marcionite influence. (6) The Marcionite Prologues to the letters of Paul attest the influence of Marcion on the makers of the NT. (7) The Catholic Church's canon adopted the pattern (Gospel/Apostle) of Marcion's. Other scholars have ascribed more limited influence to Marcion. Instead of supplying the *idea,* since some semblance of a canon antedated him, Marcion accelerated the process of formation.

The Muratorian Canon, Tatian, and Irenaeus. The oldest extant list of NT writings is one discovered in an eighth-century Ambrosiana manuscript and published in 1740 by Italian historian L. A. Muratori, and known as the MURATORIAN CANON. The list is usually dated between 170 and 200, although an attempt has recently been made to date it in the fourth century. It was evidently written to oppose the inclusion of the SHEPHERD OF HERMAS among canonical writings.

This list included the fourfold Gospel, Acts, thirteen letters ascribed to Paul (including the Pastorals), Jude, the Johannine Epistles, the Apocalypses of John and Peter, and the Wisdom of Solomon. Although the manuscript is fragmented at the beginning and omits Matthew and Mark, Luke is cited "third" and John "fourth." Like Marcion, the author designated Ephesians a letter to the "Laodiceans." He cited only two letters of John, but he may have intended 3 John as a part of 2 John. The *Apocalypse of Peter* and the Wisdom of Solomon were the only works not later recognized as canonical included in the list. *Hermas* was depicted as a work of "our own time." James, 1 and 2 Peter, and Hebrews were not mentioned, but 1 Peter may have been accidently omitted since it was cited frequently by IRENAEUS, a contemporary of the author.

Tatian, founder of the ascetic Encratite sect in Mesopotamia, confirms the essential place accorded the fourfold Gospel in the Muratorian Canon. Born in the East, probably Mesopotamia, he came to Rome and studied under JUSTIN MARTYR (ca. 100–163/5). Either just before or just after leaving Rome, perhaps around 170, he compiled his *Diatessaron,* a harmony of the four Gospels. The *Diatessaron* ("Between Four") became the standard Gospel in the Syriac-speaking church until Rabbula published the *Peshitto* in 411.

Irenaeus, Bishop of Lyons (177-202), confirms most elements listed in the Muratorian Canon. Against Gnostic claims to possess other "Gospels," Irenaeus insisted there can be neither more nor less than four. Four Gospels correspond to the four corners of the earth and the four principal winds. These possess one spirit under four aspects, like the cherubim. John is regal, like a lion; Luke is priestly, like a calf; Matthew is human, like a man; and Mark is prophetic, like an eagle (as Rev 4:7) (*AdvHaer* 3.11.8). (Later church tradition reversed Irenaeus's symbols for the evangelists, with the lion coming to represent Mark, and the eagle John.) The Bishop of Lyons attacked the *Alogoi,* a sect in Asia Minor, for their rejection of the Gospel according to John.

Irenaeus quoted from all NT writings except Jude, 2 Peter, James, Hebrews, 3 John, and Philemon. He may have known the last two, however, as a part of the canon but failed to cite them due to their brevity. A chiliast himself, Irenaeus took special interest in the Revelation, which he identified as a work written toward the end of Domitian's reign. He also cited the *Shepherd of Hermas,* another apocalyptic writing, as "scripture" (*AdvHaer* 4.20.2). As EUSEBIUS pointed out (*EccHist* 5.8), Irenaeus cited the Wisdom of Solomon, "the memoirs of a certain apostolic presbyter," Justin, and Ignatius with a degree of respect nearly as high as that accorded scriptures.

The First Collections. By the last quarter of the second century, then, the churches throughout the Roman empire were regarding the core of writings now in the NT as scripture with a few others given some recognition here and there. The bulk of canon consisted of the fourfold Gospel and the Pauline corpus. How did the collection occur?

Since Paul's letters were written first, it is natural to assume that they were collected first. Scholars have advanced two basic theories to explain this. According to one, the individual writings were read, their value recognized, and an exchange arranged by various churches almost immediately (Harnack and Gregory). Or, as a slight variation of this hypothesis, smaller collections appeared before the major corpus and were brought together to form the final collection. According to the other theory, the collection followed the publication of the book of Acts which stimulated widespread interest in Paul and his letters. In support of this view, several points are noted: (1) Shortly after Paul's death his writings dropped out of sight, for there is no mention of them before 90 C.E. (2) Immediately after the publication of Luke-Acts the letters began to be quoted. (3) These quotations are not of individual books but of the whole of the Pauline corpus, that is, the ten letters excluding the pastorals. (4) These data could be explained by assuming that someone collected the letters and wrote a kind of "cover letter" to head up the whole body of writings. Most likely, the editor was the author of Ephesians. (5) Hence, the body of writings which Marcion included in his canon was already a single collection before 150 C.E. (6) The Pastorals were added at a later date.

The deaths of the apostles probably served as a major stimulus to the composition of gospels. The earliest Christians, expecting the return of Jesus, relied on oral tradition. So long as they had apostles around to confirm their information, they did not have a compelling need for written accounts. When the Neronian persecution (64-68 C.E.) claimed the lives of the most illustrious of the apostles, written documents became urgent. Mark appeared in Rome between 67 and 70 C.E. A collection of sayings of Jesus usually designated by the letter Q (for the German *Quelle,* "source") came into existence at about the same time. About fifteen years later, Matthew, making use of both Mark and Q, furnished the Church of Antioch with a more comprehensive gospel addressing some of the needs there. Perhaps around 90 C.E. in Corinth or Rome, the locus being uncertain, Luke produced his two-volume Gospel/Acts. Meanwhile, the Johannine "school" at Ephesus busied itself with the final process of editing other traditions about Jesus.

For a time individual Gospels may have had restricted usage in their place of origin, but they soon attracted a larger audience. The DIDACHE, an early handbook of Syrian origin, quoted chiefly from Matthew, for instance, but cited Mark and Luke once and alluded to passages in Mark several times. The EPISTLE OF BARNABAS, probably of Alexandrian provenance, quoted only the Gospel of John. Ignatius of Antioch depended heavily on Matthew and John and to a lesser extent on Mark and Luke. FIRST CLEMENT cited only the OT as "scripture" and did not quote from any Gospel, although he cited Paul's letters and Hebrews. The *Shepherd of Hermas,* a Roman writing dated about 140 or after, alluded frequently to all four Gospels. Yet the Epistle of POLYCARP TO THE PHILIPPIANS cited only Luke and Acts. Justin, writing in Rome about 150, cited all four Gospels. Quite clearly, the early churches showed little interest in other "gospels," for instance, those turning up among Gnostics. For the period from 95 to 140 C.E. Theodore Zahn found only four citations from these—three in *1 Clement* and one in Ignatius. By 150 to 175, Marcion's selection of Luke notwithstanding, the fourfold Gospel was well established in the churches.

There was as yet no definite collection beyond the Gospel and the Apostle at this time, however. Acts was undoubtedly read in conjunction with Luke. First Peter and 1 John were accepted in the Roman province of Asia very early. The Revelation circulated in Asia Minor and seems to have had a secure position in the West, for it was read in Italy at an early date. Hebrews was cited extensively by *1 Clement,* though not as "scripture." The *Shepherd of Hermas* was read publicly in Rome and elsewhere at the close of the period.

Solidifying the Core of the Canon: The Third Century. Irenaeus essentially established the Catholic tradition of canon, creed, and authoritative teaching of apostolic churches by which the churches could determine where to stand. Tertullian, first as a Catholic and then as a Montanist, furthered Irenaeus's plan. A well-educated person, possibly trained in law, Tertullian converted to Christianity about 195 and immediately became in the West its most eloquent expositor and defender. Heretics must not be allowed to have any say about the canon, he insisted; ownership must be decided. Once that is decided, then believers must rely on doctrine taught by churches of apostolic foundation which have passed on what the apostles committed to them of the teaching of Christ. Quite clearly, heretics have no right to scriptures; therefore, they cannot claim to be Christians (*PræscHaer* 15, 17, 37).

Against Marcion, Tertullian argued, as did his mentor Irenaeus, in favor of retaining the OT as a Christian canon. The God of the OT is the God whom Jesus taught us about and whom he addressed as Father. Subtle in handling evidence for NT writings, Tertullian recognized that he could not claim apostolic authorship for all. Some were the work of "apostolic men," that is, successors of the apostles. John and Matthew were apostles, Luke and Mark apostolic men. In both instances, however, what they wrote went back to the Master. "Never mind if there does occur some variation in the order of their narratives, provided that there be agreement in essential matters of the faith, in which there is disagreement with Marcion" (*AdvMarc* 4.2). Tertullian scored Marcion for his mutilation of the ten letters of the Pauline corpus and quoted in other writings from all thirteen. He cited Hebrews as a work worthy of Paul but one probably written by BARNABAS. He failed to mention only 2 Peter, 2 and 3 John, and James among NT scriptures.

Clement of Alexandria, Tertullian's eastern contemporary, distinguished canonical from non-canonical gospels. He considered Matthew and Luke the earliest gospels because of their prologues. Mark, he believed, yielded to the entreaties of Christians in Rome to take down the teachings of Peter before he died (Eusebius, *EccHist* 2.15.2.). John wrote his "spiritual Gospel" last, "perceiving that the external facts had been made plain in the Gospel" (6.14.7). Reflecting still the fluidity of the canon in Alexandria in his day, Clement commented not only on the universally acknowledged writings but also, according to Eusebius (*EccHist* 6.14), on Jude and "the other Catholic epistles," *Barnabas,* and the APOCALYPSE OF PETER. He adjudged Hebrews a work written by Paul in Hebrew and translated into Greek by Luke. In other works he cited several writings not included in the canon: the Wisdom of Solomon and the Wisdom of Jesus ben Sirach for the OT, *Barnabas* and *1 Clement* for the NT. He apparently omitted commenting only on James, 2 Peter, and 3 John. One of the Beatty papyri, a manuscript of the letters of Paul dated as early as 150 to 200, included Hebrews among Paul's letters, but probably did not include the pastorals, although several pages are missing.

By the middle of the third century Origen could catalogue recognized canonical scriptures of both Testaments. For the OT he listed the Hebrew canon plus 1 Maccabees. For the NT he insisted with Irenaeus on four and only four "indisputable" Gospels: Matthew as the work of the apostle; Mark composed "according to the instructions of Peter"; Luke composed for gentile converts at Paul's recommendation; and John (Eusebius, *EccHist* 6.25.5-6). Among universally recognized works Origen also included Acts, thirteen letters of Paul, 1 Peter, 1 John, and the Revelation as the work of the apostles. He listed others as disputed writings. Second Peter, 2 and 3 John he thought to be of dubious authenticity. Hebrews, he observed, "is not rude like the language of the apostle" and yet it has admirable thoughts "not inferior to the acknowledged apostolic writings." Consequently Origen would commend any church which used it as an epistle of Paul, though God alone knows who wrote it (Eusebius, *EccHist* 6.25.12-14). Among other writings eventually included in the NT but still disputed Origen listed James and Jude. Among those recognized in some churches but never universally accepted he named the so-called *Epistle of Barnabas,* the *Shepherd of Hermas,* and the *Didache*. He cited the GOSPEL OF THE HEBREWS as universally disputed.

In the West at the same time Cyprian, Bishop of Carthage (248-258), and Novatian, the schismatic Roman presbyter, knew all writings included in the canon except the generally disputed catholic epistles (2 Peter, 2 and 3 John, James, and Jude). Novatian, like Tertullian, referred to Hebrews as the work of Barnabas. The Old Latin probably included all works cited by Tertullian as well as *Barnabas* and *Hermas*.

The Fixing of the Canon: The Fourth Century. By the mid-third century churches in the West, Italy and Africa, had nearly achieved a consensus on the canon. The churches of the East, divided into three or four sub-territories (Syria, Palestine, Asia Minor, and Egypt), reflected greater heterogeneity.

The earliest Syrian canon consisted of Tatian's *Diatessaron,* Acts, the thirteen letters of Paul, and Hebrews, viewed as a letter of Paul. When Lucian, Bishop of Antioch (d. 312), revised the NT, he excluded 2 Peter, 2 and 3 John, Jude, and the Revelation. Aphraates (fl. 336-345) commented only on these writings. Ephraem Syrus (ca. 378) omitted Philemon, apparently due to its brevity, and commented also on *3 Corinthians,* a pseudo-Pauline writing included in the ACTS OF PAUL, a late second-century writing. About 400 the Syrian churches added Hebrews to the list under Alexandrian influence. When Rabbula, Bishop of

Edessa, undertook the revision known as the *Peshitto* ("common"), the Syrian churches added James, 1 Peter, and 1 John, thus giving a canon of twenty-two books. In 509 Philoxenus revised the scriptures again and added the other five books. Although some Syrian churches accepted this as the authorized canon, most of them still retained the canon of twenty-two books named by Lucian.

Following his mentor Origen, Eusebius, Bishop of Caesarea (d. 340), classified writings in groups. Universally recognized writings included the fourfold Gospel, Acts, fourteen letters of Paul (including Hebrews), 1 John, 1 Peter, and the Revelation of John. Disputed were James, Jude, 2 Peter, 2 and 3 John. Disputed but rejected were the *Acts of Paul,* the *Shepherd of Hermas,* the *Apocalypse of Peter,* the *Epistle of Barnabas,* the *Didache,* and the *Gospel of the Hebrews.* To these three categories used by Origen, Eusebius added heretical writings: *Gospels of Peter, Thomas, Matthias,* and others; *Acts of Andrew, John,* and the rest of the apostles. These vary from apostolic writings, he insisted, not only in content but in style.

In Asia Minor Theodore, Bishop of Mopsuestia (ca. 340–428), rejected the Revelation and all catholic epistles on the grounds that they failed to meet the test of "prophecy," a test he also applied to the OT canon. His views, however, did not stand in the mainstream. Gregory of Nazianzus (d. ca. 389) accepted all writings in the present canon except the Revelation. Montanism, an early Pentecostal sect, caused many in Asia Minor to reject this book. The Synod of Laodicea, whose authenticity is sometimes questioned but which is traditionally dated 363, also omitted the Revelation. The other "great Cappadocians," Basil (d. 379) and Gregory of Nyssa (fl. 371-394), evidently agreed with Gregory of Nazianzus.

In Egypt the Sahidic version of the NT probably included the Revelation as well as other writings now in the canon. In 367 Athanasius, Bishop of Alexandria, laid down the principle that, in addition to the OT, the twenty-seven books of the present canon are alone canonical. As had become traditional by this time, he listed Hebrews as one of Paul's letters. "In these alone is proclaimed the doctrine of godliness," he declared. "Let no one add to them, neither let anyone subtract from them" (Easter Letter 39.6). Athanasius listed, too, some non-canonical writings of both Testaments which could be read with profit: the Wisdom of Solomon, the Wisdom of Jesus ben Sirach, Esther, Judith, Tobit, the *Didache,* and the *Shepherd of Hermas.*

In the West the churches differed still in their use of Hebrews, James, 2 Peter, 2 and 3 John, and Jude. Attitudes varied among individual writers, but a majority evidently favored Hebrews. The first person to cite James as scripture was Hilary of Poitiers (d. 366). Jerome and Augustine secured it a place in the canon. Second Peter was cited first by Ambrosiaster, a late fourth-century commentator on Paul's letters. Priscillian, a Spanish sect leader (ca. 370), Philaster, Bishop of Brescia (d. 397), Jerome (d. 420), and Augustine (d. 430) accepted it. Second and 3 John were cited as the writings of the apostle by Aurelius of Cillani in Numidia (North Africa) in 256. The African Canon (360), Jerome, and Augustine affirmed 3 John. Jude was acknowledged as scripture in Rome and Carthage early on and then fell into disuse. Later it appeared again in the writings of Lucifer, Bishop of Cagliari (d. 370 or 371), Priscillian, Philaster, the pseudo-Augustine *Speculum,* and Cassian, a monk of Marseilles (d. 435). The Revelation seems to have had consistent usage in the West, Montanism notwithstanding, but around 200 Gaius, a Roman presbyter, attributed it to the Gnostic Cerinthus.

Episcopal synods finally decided which of the disputed writings would be counted canonical. In 393 a synod of bishops meeting in Hippo affirmed both the LXX OT canon and all twenty-seven books in the present NT. In 397 a synod held at Carthage reiterated the conclusion at Hippo, appending a note about Hebrews after thirteen letters of Paul, "one by the same author to the Hebrews."

Reconsiderations in the Reformation. The emphasis placed on scriptures by the Protestant reformers evoked fresh discussion concerning the disputed writings of both testaments. Erasmus recognized Hebrews as non-Pauline and considered James unworthy of canonical status. Luther, insisting that all scriptures be tested by the rule of "justification by faith," relegated Hebrews, James, Jude, and the Revelation to the end of the NT. He labeled James "a right strawy epistle." He valued the letters of Paul, John, 1 John, and 1 Peter more than other NT books. Luther's one-time colleague and later opponent Karlstadt classified NT writings in three groups: the four Gospels and Acts; the thirteen undoubted letters of Paul, 1 Peter, and 1 John; and seven disputed works: James, 2 Peter, 2 and 3 John, Jude, Hebrews, and the Revelation. He doubted the value of the Revelation. Zwingli, Oecolampadius, and Calvin recognized the value of the entire canon, although they were sensitive to critical problems. Hugo Grotius, the noted Dutch Reformed jurist and theologian (1583-1645), however, was very critical of the disputed writings. In England Tyndale and Coverdale were more conservative, although Tyndale's NT of 1525 followed Luther in setting Hebrews, James, Jude, and Revelation off from the rest of the books.

Not unexpectedly, in its fourth session, 8 April 1546, the Council of Trent reacted against Protestant questioning of the canon by affirming the LXX canon for the OT and the twenty-seven books of the NT in the Vulgate edition. These were to be received with "an equal affection of piety and reverence" with ecclesiastical tradition. No person, moreover, should interpret privately "contrary to the sense which holy mother Church . . . has held or does hold."

Why the Canon? Scholars have put forward several theories concerning the selection of writings for the canon. According to the Council of Trent, the strict criterion was "apostolicity" in its restricted sense. Many church fathers and the Synods of Laodicea, Hippo, and Carthage can be invoked in support of this view also. In this theory the apostolic office alone satisfies the need for the proper *charisma.*

Some Roman Catholic scholars have qualified this view by citing doctrinal tradition plus apostolicity as the true criterion. Irenaeus and Tertullian first proposed some such solution in recognition of the obvious fact that some writings do not claim authorship by apostles.

C. R. Gregory pointed out that there never was a strict canon and disputed divine direction in the formation process. What Christians must seek is the truth contained in particular writings and not worry about the canon. In support of this viewpoint he cited the varied canons among the churches. The Ethiopic Church has a thirty-five member NT canon, the Syrian Church a twenty-two member canon, whereas the other churches have a twenty-seven member canon.

Other scholars have cited the evangelical character of writings as the more reliable criterion. In some cases the name of an apostle assured such authenticity; in other cases the content of a writing did so. Disputed writings obviously seemed to lack one or the other of these factors. Hebrews, for instance, did not bear the name of an apostle, but, as Origen noted, it was "worthy" of an apostle, though God alone could say who wrote it. James and Jude barely nudged out some other claimants because they lacked both apostolic author and apostolic content. Second Peter obviously appeared long after Paul wrote his letters (2 Peter 3:15-16) and could not have been the work of Peter, but it had just enough apostolic content to override that deficiency.

Ecumenical developments from the time of Pope John XXIII (1958-1963) on have caused all Christians to reopen discussion of the canon. Since the Second Vatican Council, some Protestant Bibles have been published with the Apocrypha, and some Protestant scholars have argued for its inclusion in the OT canon, although most Protestants still do not recognize and use it as they do other books of the OT. Recognizing the diversity of NT canons and the nature of their formation, some scholars have argued for an "open" canon. The core of the canon is quite secure, of course, but the borderline between disputed works which finally obtained acceptance and those which did not remains blurry. As a consequence, many students of early Christianity rely on the APOSTOLIC FATHERS to flesh out the picture of early Christian life and thought in much the same way they rely on late NT writings. This discussion feeds naturally into one concerning scripture and tradition.

See also APOCRYPHAL ACTS; APOCRYPHAL GOSPELS; APOCRYPHAL LITERATURE; SYNOPTIC PROBLEM; TEXTS, MANUSCRIPTS, VERSIONS.

Bibliography. G. W. Anderson, "The Old Testament: Canonical and Non-Canonical," *Cambridge History of the Bible*; E. C. Blackman, *Marcion and His Influence*; B. S. Childs, *Introduction to the Old Testament as Scripture* and *The New Testament as Canon: An Introduction*; C. H. Dodd, *The Apostolic Preaching and Its Developments*; W. R. Farmer and D. M. Farkasfalvy, *The Formation of the New Testament Canon: An Ecumenical Approach*; F. V. Filson, *Which Books Belong to the Bible?*; E. J. Goodspeed, "The Canon of the New Testament," *IB* 1:63-71, *The Key to Ephesians*, and *The Formation of the New Testament*; R. M. Grant, "The New Testament Canon," *Cambridge History of the Bible* 1:284-308; C. R. Gregory, *Canon and Text of the New Testament*; J. Knox, *Marcion and the New Testament: An Essay in the Early History of the Canon*; B. M. Metzger, *The Canon of the New Testament*; C. L. Mitton, *The Formation of the Pauline Corpus of Letters*; C. F. D. Moule, *The Birth of the New Testament*, 2nd ed.; A. Souter, *The Text and Canon of the New Testament*, 2nd ed.; C. S. C. Williams, "The History of the Text and Canon of the New Testament to Jerome," *Cambridge History of the Bible*, 2:27-53.

—E. GLENN HINSON

• **Canonical Criticism.** *See* NEW TESTAMENT USE OF THE OLD TESTAMENT

• **Capernaum.** [kuh-puhr'nay-uhm] Capernaum (Heb. "Village of Nahum") was the center of Jesus' Galilean ministry. Since 1856 Capernaum has been identified with Tell Hum on the northwest shore of the SEA OF GALILEE (PLATE 23) and has been irregularly excavated. Remains at Tell Hum include a fifth-century Christian church and a white limestone building which was identified as a SYNAGOGUE as early as 1838.

The church was a triple octagonal structure constructed over earlier structures. The Franciscans who purchased the site in 1894 claim that Peter's house was incorporated into a structure over which the fifth-century church was constructed. The synagogue remains date no earlier than the late second century C.E., but excavations in 1981 disclosed ruins of a basalt first-century synagogue beneath the limestone synagogue. Doubtless, the basalt synagogue was the one in which Jesus preached.

The main source of information concerning Capernaum are the Gospels. All four Gospels indicate that the city played a central role in the life of Jesus and his disciples during the Galilean ministry. They report that Jesus moved from Nazareth to Capernaum at the beginning of his public ministry, though the reason for the move is not clear. Matt 4:13-16 interprets the move, however, as fulfillment of the prophecy of Isa 9:1-2. In Isaiah, the region (not the city) is referred to. It is spoken of as the land of the gentiles, indicating that gentiles as well as Jews lived there.

The Gospels also tell that Jesus taught and healed in Capernaum (Mark 1:21; Luke 4:31). Notable examples of the healing miracles done there include the centurion's servant (Matt 8:5 and Luke 7:1f.) and Peter's mother-in-law (Mark 1:29-30). It was here that Jesus first attracted a wide reputation and a large following (Mark 1:28, 33). Jesus and his disciples often returned to Capernaum after the several trips they made around and beyond Galilee (Mark 2:1). Near the end of one of the last remaining trips and near the end of the Galilean ministry several important events occurred at Capernaum. One was a dialogue with the disciples after Jesus heard them arguing over who was the greatest. Jesus responded with a lesson in humility (Mark 9:33). Another was the dialogue with Peter over the poll tax collected by Jewish leaders for support of the Temple and allowed by the Romans (Matt 17:24).

John 6:59-66 reports a crisis among Jesus' disciples over his teachings, because some of them left, although THE TWELVE remained with Jesus. This reference in John's Gospel may provide a parallel to the strong condemnation of the residents of Capernaum in Matt 11:23 and Luke 10:15 because, despite all they saw and heard, they did not believe. Thus, Matthew and Luke are struck by the curious paradox that, despite the fact that the city of Capernaum became Jesus' adopted town and despite the great crowds that were attracted there, the end results seemed disappointing.

See also GALILEE, SEA OF; PETER; SYNAGOGUE.

—E. EARL JOINER

• **Caphtor.** *See* CRETE

• **Cappadocia.** [kap'uh-doh"shee-uh] A small, mountainous Roman province of eastern Asia Minor north of Cilicia and the Taurus Mountains, east of Lake Tatta and GALATIA, south of Pontus, and west of the Euphrates River and the kingdom of Armenia (PLATE 21). The Halys River flowed from east to west through Cappadocia for some 375 km. Cappadocia was famous for its wines, but also for horses, wheat, and cattle. Local minerals included lead, silver, red ocher, alabaster, and mica. Cappadocia occupied a strategic position across roads from Pontus to Cilicia and from Armenia to Galatia (Pliny *NatHist* 6.3; Strabo *Geog* 12.1).

Cappadocia was an important part of the Hittite Empire and earlier, as witness the great city of Kanish (Kültepe) near the center of Cappadocia, beside which stood a flourishing Assyrian trade colony as early as 1950 B.C.E. Some of the earliest known writings and finest art of Anatolia were found at Kültepe. During the Neo-Hittite period, or from about 1000 B.C.E., the Assyrians called Cappadocia the Kingdom of Tabal. TIGLATH-PILESER III (745–727 B.C.E.) added Cappadocia to his empire, but by the seventh century B.C.E. it belonged to the kingdom of the Medes. The Persians inherited Cappadocia as part of their empire from about 539 B.C.E. when Cyrus conquered Babylon. Cappadocia appears as the eighth satrapy of the Persian Empire after 538 B.C.E. (Herodotus, *Histories*).

Cappadocia appears in the Septuagint as a translation of the Hebrew "Kaphtor" at Deut 2:23 and Amos 9:7. This is surely a simple mistake of the translators.

Alexander the Great marched through western Cappadocia on his way through the Cilician Gates in the Taurus mountains to attack the forces of Darius of Persia. After Alexander's successes and untimely death, Cappadocia passed to the Seleucid generals, but developed independent, Hellenistic kingdoms after 255 B.C.E. Cappadocia could not hold out against aggressive Roman influence after Pergamum passed to Rome in 133 B.C.E. The emperor Tiberius finally took over Cappadocia in 17 C.E. at the death of the last client king, Archelaus. Tiberius made Cappadocia into a province under a procurator (Tacitus, *Ann* 11.42; Dio Cassius *RomHist* 57.17).

The most important urban centers of Roman Cappadocia were Mazca/Caesarea, Tyana, and Comana, where Jews of the Diaspora may have gathered. Possible evidence for this Cappadocian diaspora is the letter of Lucius (consul 140–139 B.C.E.) in 1 Macc 15:15-21, which purportedly was sent to Ariarathes V, king of Cappadocia (162–130 B.C.E.; v.22). Jews of Cappadocia were in Jerusalem at Pentecost in Acts 2:9, and 1 Pet 1:1 refers to its recipients in Cappadocia. By 211 C.E. Cappadocia was expanded to include Galatia.

The spread of Christianity into Cappadocia can be deduced from the NT and from Eusebius. Narcissus, bishop of Jerusalem from 180 C.E., originally was bishop in Cappadocia (*EccHist* 6.11). Eusebius also mentions Firmilian, bishop of Caesarea in Cappadocia at the time of Origen (*EccHist* 6.27; 7:28). He also mentions the "amazing martyrs" of Cappadocia during the reigns of Diocletian and Maximian (284–304 C.E.; *EccHist* 8.12). Finally, one must mention the Cappadocian theologians of the later fourth century, including Basil of Caesarea (later bishop of Caesarea), Gregory of Nazianzus, and Gregory of Nyssa.

Bibliography. E. Akurgal, *Ancient Civilizations and Ruins of Turkey*; R. J. A. Talbert, *Atlas of Classical History*.

—JAMES F. STRANGE

• **Captivity, The Babylonian.** *See* EXILE

• **Caravan.** A train of pack animals and their drivers, often including other travelers, going across land, and traveling together partly for protection. Caravans at times were organized for purposes of raiding or for resettlement (cf. Judg 6:3-5; 1 Sam 30:1-20). Caravans along certain routes had characteristic functions, as the spice and incense run from Southern Arabia (1 Kgs 10:1-2). Pliny indicates the trip from Southern Arabia to the Mediterranean required some sixty-five days. Major routes converged in Palestine-Syria, with African, Egyptian, Arabian, Babylonian, and Anatolian origin-destination points represented.

Intense donkey caravan activity existed as far back as the beginning of the second millennium B.C.E. Wagons, apparently pulled by oxen, were in use then (e.g., Gen 46:5; 45:16-27). Horses were used for swifter travel and chariots for military purposes. Elephants in Syria may have come in connection with the ebony trade from Ethiopia via the Sudan (1 Macc 6:30).

Toward the end of the second millennium B.C.E. camels were in use in Palestine, evidently in connection with war (cf. Judg 6:5; 1 Chr 12:38-40). The dominant camel-running peoples in Palestinian territory initially were Ishmaelites and Midianites (see Gen 37:25; Judg 6:5). From them the franchise passed to the Ammonites. Although the donkey remained in use for local freight traffic, after the twelfth or eleventh centuries B.C.E. the camel was typical for long hauls. Their capacity for carrying more cargo and for traveling longer distances without water made these "ships of the desert" more desirable and helped open previously inaccessible routes (for additional references see 1 Kgs 10:2; 2 Kgs 8:9; Job 6:18-19; Isa 60:6; for a reflection of Mediterranean commerce about the sixth century B.C.E. cf. Ezek 27 and Isa 23; cf. the sermons of AMOS for a picture of world affairs furnished by the communication network).

In the Christian era the Nabataean capital city of PETRA was the center of caravan trade in the area and was one of numerous caravan cities located along major routes. These wealthy centers provided caravansaries, extensive facilities for accommodating caravans.

More than a dozen OT references (depending on text and translation) reflect extensive caravan activity. One is thereby reminded that Israel was not isolated but was actively involved in semitic cross-cultural life and was at the center of a mercantile, communication, and industrial network.

See also ECONOMICS IN THE OLD TESTAMENT; SHIP.

—DOUGLAS C. BAIN, JR.

• **Carchemish.** [kahr'kuh-mish] Carchemish, an ancient city-state and later regional capital of the HITTITES, strategically located on the right bank of the Euphrates, a land "bridge" across which commerce passed and for which contending armies clashed. A major archaeological investigation at Carchemish, sponsored by the British Museum, was conducted by Sir Leonard Woolley and T. E. Lawrence. The site yielded significant information regarding the cultural, political, and military importance of this center which figures prominently in the late history of the southern kingdom of Judah.

The chief significance of Carchemish from a biblical perspective is that it was the site of the victory of the Babylonians under NEBUCHADREZZAR II against the Egyptians under Pharaoh NECHO II in 605 B.C.E. This event was the decisive battle which firmly established Babylonian mastery of the ancient Near East at that time.

Earlier, a coalition of Medes and Babylonians had conspired to end Assyria's domination of the region. Besieged for the three months, Nineveh fell in 612 B.C.E., marking the beginning of the end. The scattered Assyrian forces under Asshur-uballit II continued a futile resistance to Babylonian advance.

Meanwhile, Pharaoh Necho II marched northward from Egypt to effect a coalition with her former enemy Assyria, since it was clear that the unchecked power of Babylonia would thwart Egypt's designs for power in the region. JOSIAH (640–609 B.C.E.), Judah's able and ambitious king, acting perhaps independently (in order to curry favor) with the Babylonians, marched against the Egyptians in the hope of defeating Necho II or at least delaying his link with the remnants of the Assyrian forces near the Euphrates River. The encounter at the pass of Megiddo (609 B.C.E.) left Josiah dead and Judah a temporary vassal of Egypt. Only temporarily delayed, Necho continued to the Euphrates to do battle against the Babylonians.

The Battle of Carchemish (605 B.C.E.) resulted in a crushing defeat for the Egyptians, the victorious Babylonians pursuing them southward, inflicting further destruction on Necho's battered forces. The prophet Jeremiah described the fleeing Egyptian army as making "a sound like a serpent gliding away" (Jer 46:22). The victory at Carchemish consolidated Babylonia's claim to supremacy over the ancient Near East and marked the end of any further Egyptian attempts at international domination. The historian's description of the situation was: "And the king of Egypt did not come again out of his land, for the king of Babylon had taken all that belonged to the king of Egypt from the Brook of Egypt to the river Euphrates" (2 Kgs 24:7).

—BERNARD H. COCHRAN

• **Carmel, Mount.** [kahr'muhl] Mount Carmel, located near the shore of the Mediterranean and covered by the suburbs of the modern town of Haifa (PLATE 12), is the northern summit of the Carmel range. This fertile mountain range begins in the hills of Samaria and rises to 1,650 ft. above sea level. During Israel's history, this group of mountains formed the western boundary of the territory of ASHER (Josh 19:26). Mount Carmel itself rises a majestic 556 ft. above the plain. (Cant 7:6 refers to Carmel's stately presence in the description of the female lover). It forms the entrance of the JEZREEL Valley. The cliffs of this summit reveal hundreds of caves which have served as havens for prehistoric humans and refuges for hermits and fugitives throughout history. The river KISHON flows at the base of Mount Carmel.

Some believe that Mount Carmel is the site which Veni, a general of Phiops I, King of Egypt, described as the "gazelle's nose" on arriving at the coast of Palestine about 2300 B.C.E. As "Holy Head," it is listed in the records of Tuthmosis III (1549–1459 B.C.E.). Josephus, the Jewish historian, notes that the range of mountains was taken by the Hasmonean Alexander Jannaeus (*Ant.* 13.396) and was returned to Acco in 64 B.C.E. by Pompey (*BJ* 3.35).

Mount Carmel was the location at which ELIJAH and the 450 prophets of Baal vied for the loyalty of the people of Israel. The prophets of Baal were allowed to build their altar first and cry to their god. After an extended time with no response, Elijah built his altar, prayed to his God, and witnessed the fiery presence of Yahweh. By responding, Yahweh powerfully indicated his sovereignty over his people and this territory. Afterwards, the people of Israel slaughtered the prophets of Baal at the banks of the river Kishon. The site of this confrontation later became the site of the Carmelite monastery of St. Elijah (El Muhrakah) and a small mound in the valley below, next to the Kishon, marks the traditional spot for the slaughter. Elisha, the successor of Elijah, frequented this special mountain from time to time (2 Kgs 2:25; 4:25).

The story of Yahweh's triumph on Carmel coordinates with the larger tradition of the sacred mountain in the ancient Near East. In the ancient world, every high god had his mountain from which he ruled. Mount Zaphon was recognized as Baal's, just as Sinai/Horeb was identified as Yahweh's. Mount Carmel, with its position next to the Mediterranean, with its caves, with its fertile soil, and with its long identification with local and cosmic deities, served as an ideal location for this contest which would decide the true God for a divided Israel.

The writing prophets mention Carmel in the context of Yahweh's judgment. When Yahweh comes to punish his unrepentant people (Jer 46:18) who have defiled the land given to then (Jer 2:7), Carmel will languish (Amos 1:2; Isa 33:9; Nah 1:4) and people who try to hide there (in the caves) will be rooted out (Amos 9:3). Yet, when the people have been punished with unforgivable harshness by the nations which surrounded Israel, Carmel will return to its former beauty (Isa 35:2; Jer 50:19).

—RUSSELL I. GREGORY

• **Castration.** *See* EUNUCH

• **Catholic Epistles.** *See* GENERAL LETTERS

• **Cave.** The relatively soft limestone and sandstone strata of hills and deep ravines of Palestine have provided ideal geological formations for natural and artificial caves. Most of the natural caves, located within the rugged terrain of the hill country and penetrating the cliffs of the deep fissures that radiate from the Rift Valley, give evidence of human modification as places of temporary habitation and refuge or burial. Voluntary and involuntary settlement within the isolation of the Judean desert appears to have existed from earliest times. Political, religious and social environments occasionally prompted the withdrawal of individuals and groups to the seclusion of the natural shelters that caves provided. *Personae non grata,* for whatever reason, found welcome refuge in the inhospitable desolation of the nearby desert and left behind mute evidence of their periodic stays.

Cultural artifacts and skeletal remains preserved and recovered by archaeological excavation in caves in the Judean hill country, the Carmel range and the Galilee, have clarified the nature and lifestyle of Palestine's earliest settlers and their Stone Age cultures. These caves served as the repositories of cultural evidences that have long since been destroyed at contemporary open-air occupational sites. The excavation of caves such as Mugharet ez-Zuttiyeh ("the Galilee man"), northwest of the Sea of Galilee, Wadi el-Mugharah in the Carmel range south of Haifa, Wadi en-Natuf, northwest of Jerusalem, and Wadi Khareitun, east of Bethlehem, has greatly clarified the nature and culture of prehistoric man. The discovery and excavation of the artificial labyrinth of tunnels and caves that honeycombed the banks of Wadi Besor at Tell Abu Matar and Tell es-Safadi near Beersheba clarified the nature of cultural transition from cave to open site settlement in the Chalcolithic Period of the fifth-fourth millennia B.C. The Chalcolithic is one of the three major periods of occupation in the Judean desert caves. The "Cave of the Treasure," excavated by P. Bar-Adon, in the Mishmar Valley produced a cache of 429 copper, hematite, ivory and stone ritual articles that may represent the ceremonial treasure of a sanctuary located nearby. Other finds include plant remains and a unique form of emmer wheat related to the earliest periods of farming in the region.

The biblical record is replete with references to social and political alienation that prompted temporary or permanent use of caves for habitation. Lot and his daughters lived in a cave temporarily for fear of residing in Zoar (Gen 19:30). During periods of enemy oppression, the Israelite population generally was forced to seek refuge in caves (Judg 6:2; 1 Sam 13:6). David sought relief from Saul's wrath in an Adullam cave (1 Sam 22:1). The threats of Jezebel drove Elijah to a cave in Mount Horeb (1 Kgs 19:9), and Obadiah saved 100 prophets from the wrath of the same Jezebel in the caves of MOUNT CARMEL (1 Kgs 18:4-13).

Periods of political uncertainty and religious reform

stimulated desert settlement and cave occupation. The finds of the Judean desert are especially informative for the period of the First and Second Jewish revolts against the Romans. The entire Hellenistic-Roman period had fostered religious resentment toward and/or withdrawal from the established religious centers to the ascetic, monastic seclusion of separatist piety for which the caves of the Judean desert were ideally suited. There Jewish and later Christian communities were formed, removed from the defilement of their compromised origins in Jerusalem and other urban centers. Qumran, Wadi Murabba'at and Khirbet Mird provided the communal centers for the individual adherents or sympathizers who lived in and frequented the hundreds of caves in the Judean desert. There they prayed and meditated and studied, and their presence is documented by the recovery of their personal effects and their biblical and religious study scrolls and fragments. Most important among the many caves occupied in the immediate vicinity of Qumran is Cave Four where the religious archive or library of the community was hidden when the community was abandoned. The demise of the settlement is dated to the arrival of the Roman Tenth Legion under Vespasian in the spring of 68 C.E. when many Jewish communities in the vicinity of Jericho were destroyed. Because the Romans established a garrison at Qumran from 68 to 86 C.E., and Jewish religious life was so seriously disrupted by the Romans, recovery of the library from Cave Four and the religious collections of other ascetic communities and individuals awaited the mid-twentieth century when archaeological activity centered on the Judean desert and its cave treasures. Two major Israeli expeditions in 1960 and 1961 concentrated specifically on survey and excavation of four Judean desert caves ("Cave of the Pool," "Cave of Horror," "Cave of the Treasure," and "Cave of the Letters") with spectacular results and a general impression that the Judean desert experienced unusual activity as a refuge during the Chalcolithic period, the times of the First and Second Jewish Revolts against the Romans, and the period of the Islamic invasion in the seventh century C.E.

During all periods, natural or modified caves here served as repositories for the dead. Most notably the purchase of the Cave of MACHPELAH by Abraham specifically to bury Sarah but also to serve as the family tomb (Gen 23) is characteristic especially of cultures with a tradition of communal burial. "To sleep with the forefathers" implied the literal interment with the deceased family. Extensive catacombing to produce special necropolii are best illustrated by the Sanhedria cemetery on the northern outskirts of Jerusalem, at Beth She'arim near Nazareth in the Lower Galilee, and at Rome.

The caves of the early Edomites in their natural stronghold at Petra (Deut 2:12) were elaborately converted by the Nabataeans into the multi-storied dwellings and tombs with their Romanesque facades that still adorn the sandstone cliffs of their isolated center. Many Christian and Muslim shrines have been built above caves, identified as "holy places" because of significant events in the life of Jesus or some other religious notable.

Bibliography. N. Avigad, "Excavations at Beth She'arim," *IEJ* 4 (1954): 88-107; 5 (1955): 205-39; 7 (1957): 73-92, 239-55; 9 (1959): 205-20; 10 (1960): 264; N. Avigad et al., "The Expedition to the Judean Desert, 1960," *IEJ* 11 (1961): 1ff. and "The Expedition to the Judean Desert, 1961," *IEJ* 12 (1962): 169-83; P. Bar-Adon, *The Cave of the Treasure: The Finds from the Caves in Nahal Mishmar*; P. Benoit et al., *Discoveries in the Judaean Desert in Jordan*; G. L. Harding, "Khirbet Qumran and Wady Muraba'at," *PEQ* 84 (1952): 104-09; G. Horsfield and A. Horsfield, "Sela-Petra, the Rock, of Edom and Nabatene," *QDAP* 7 (1938): 1-42; B. (Maisler) Mazar, "The Catacombs I-IV" (with English summary), *Beth She'arim, Report on the Excavations during 1936–1940*, vol. 1; E. Oren, "The Caves of the Palestinian Shephelah," *Arch* 18 (1965): 218-24; J. Perrot, "The Excavations at Tell Abu Matar, Near Beersheba," *IEJ* 5 (1955): 17-40, 73-84, 167-89; Y. Yadin, *The Finds from the Bar-Kokhba Period in the Cave of Letters*.

—GEORGE L. KELM

• **Celibacy.** From a Latin word meaning "unmarried," celibacy is the state of not being married, but the word is normally used more specifically to describe the state of abstaining by vow from marriage for religious reasons. It is this sense of the word which will be assumed in this article. A third meaning occasionally found is abstention from sexual intercourse for religious reasons (whether one is married or single), though this is more properly termed "chastity." Celibacy seems almost unknown in OT life, but appears in very limited form after the post-Second Temple era. It is recommended in the NT for some persons as a way of achieving greater devotion to God, and by the end of the second century groups of virgins (male and female) were found within enough congregations to make their existence one of the first things noted by non-Christians. But it was not until the third and fourth centuries C.E. that celibacy became an institutionalized and widespread Christian practice.

The OT firmly places marriage and family in the center of life, and therefore does not recognize celibacy as having religious value. Though sexual abstinence was temporarily enjoined for ritual purposes (Exod 19:15; 1 Sam 21:5), or, according to the Midrashim, at times of national disaster, it was never suggested that this could be an acceptable permanent state. Indeed, marriage becomes a prominent symbol for the relation of God to his people (Isa 62:4-5; Jer 2:1-2; Ps 19:5). Though Nazirites and Rechabites follow somewhat ascetic practices, there is no suggestion that celibacy is one of these (Num 6:1-21; Jer 35).

After B.C.E. 200 a gradual change occurred in the entire Mediterranean world. Traditionally marriage was considered a duty in Greek and Roman culture as in Jewish, with legal penalties for those who did not marry. A greater variety of attitudes began to appear during the Hellenistic era as part of a general reassessment of traditional social roles of men and women. Thus, some philosophical schools, most notably the Epicureans, allowed women to abstain from their customary roles as wives and mothers to enter activities that had been reserved for males. In Judaism as well, though marriage is still strongly affirmed, a suspicion of sexuality and procreation does appear in some rabbinical writings. The Therapeutae sect of Egypt and the Essenes of Palestine are the chief examples of Jewish groups of the period who adopted some form of celibacy as part of their beliefs. It is unclear whether the celibacy was lifelong and whether it was only for certain members of the group, but this does reveal a new element in Jewish life.

The NT clearly belongs to the later stages of this development, for at least three of its major figures—Jesus, John the Baptist, and Paul—seem to have remained unmarried, and celibacy is accepted in the NT as a possible religious vocation, at least during the brief time while "the form of this world is passing away" (1 Cor 7:31). The NT affirms the centrality and importance of marriage in many places (Mark 10:6-9; 1 Cor 7:2-5; 9:5; Eph 5:31-33; Heb 13:4), and also continues the OT use of marriage as a metaphor for God and the faithful (Matt 9:14-15; 25:1-13; 2 Cor 11:2; Rev 19:7-9; 21:2, 9). In certain ways Jesus and Paul seemed to intensify the importance of monogamous marriage by rejecting certain patterns of divorce and remarriage (Matt 19:9; Luke 16:18; Mark 10:11; 1 Cor 7:10). And yet there was also a recognition that marriage must be qualified in certain ways, chiefly by the belief that the end or eschaton was imminent, requiring believers to devote their entire energies to the service of God and the bringing in of his kingdom (Luke 20:34-36; 1 Cor 7:8).

Passages of particular importance for an evaluation of celibacy in the NT are Matt 19:10-12, 1 Cor 7, and 1 Tim 2, 5. In the Matthean passage's reference to those "who have made themselves eunuchs for the sake of the kingdom of heaven," Jesus is often assumed to be speaking of those who have renounced sexual activity, but recent interpretations also have stressed the relation of the eunuch saying to Jesus' earlier words on marriage and remarriage, thus reading 19:10-12 as a prohibition of remarriage after divorce rather than as a recommendation of celibacy. The passage does seem to echo, however, places in the Gospels where Jesus expresses a somewhat ascetic perspective on family, possessions, and society (Luke 12:33; 14:26; 18:29; Mark 3:31-35; 10:29; Matt 10:34-39), though there are also places in which Jesus seems to recommend something other than a traditional life of renunciation (Mark 7:14-19; Luke 5:30-33; 7:31-35). A balanced summary sees Jesus insisting that believers give priority to their obligation to God, without suggesting that any particular ascetic practice (such as celibacy) is an essential ingredient of faith.

Paul's advice in 1 Corinthians is similar, though it seems to be conditioned more than the Gospels by his expectation of the imminent end. In the later deutero-Pauline correspondence there are passages accepting or approving marriage (Col 3:18; Eph 5:22; 1 Tim 4:3f.), but here Paul seems to exalt celibacy (7:1, 7a, 8, 32). It must be noted, however, that he qualifies his "opinion" in the chapter, and distinguishes it from a "command of the Lord" (7:12, 25). Because of the "impending distress" of the end times as well as the demands of the new creation, Paul stresses that everyone should "remain as he is," that is, in the state they were in when God called them, whether that be married or celibate (7:17, 20, 24, 26).

The Pastorals have been read increasingly in recent years as showing a reaction to a number of developments: the egalitarian tendencies of the earlier Pauline writings, the proliferation of ascetic Gnostic communities which often allowed women to have leadership roles, and the growth, especially in Asia Minor, of groups of so-called radical Pauline Christians who held to a number of antisocial practices including celibacy. Thus 1 Tim 2, 5 show great concern for the opinion of contemporary society, advocating that women marry and avoid the dangerous "gadding about" that was apparently practiced by many "widows." These women, who may have included virgins as well as "true widows," evidently constituted an independent group that the church elders felt was insufficiently obedient to the community.

Despite these signs that unmarried persons constituted an important minority in the NT community, it was only in the postbiblical period, especially the third and fourth centuries C.E., that celibacy replaced triumphant martyrdom as the ideal image of the Christian's victory over the world's evil and became a popular lifestyle, widely accepted by the church.

See also FAMILY; MARRIAGE IN THE NEW TESTAMENT; MARRIAGE IN THE OLD TESTAMENT.

Bibliography. J. M. Bassler, "The Widows' Tale: A Fresh Look at 1 Tim 5:3-16," *JBL* 103 (1984): 23-41; D. Cartlidge, "1 Cor 7 as a Foundation for a Christian Sex-Ethic," *JR* 55 (1975): 220-34; D. R. MacDonald, *The Legend and the Apostle*.

—DAVID W. RUTLEDGE

• **Cenchreae.** *See* CORINTH

• **Census/Enrollment.** The Bible records several enrollments of people in particular groups or areas (e.g., Exod 30; Num 1; 2 Sam 24; 1 Chr 21; 2 Chr 2; Ezra 2; Luke 2; Acts 5). The enrollment (or census) was usually for the purpose of taxation, but other ends were also served—such as forced labor.

The registration of Luke (2:1-3) is set in the reign of Herod the Great (who died in 4 B.C.E.) and during the time when QUIRINIUS was governor of Syria. The Gospel of Luke uses the census to stress the universal significance of the birth of Christ by stating that Caesar Augustus required that "all the world" should be registered for taxation. The Davidic ancestry of Jesus is stressed by Luke's statement that Joseph and Mary went from Galilee to BETHLEHEM because Joseph was of the "house and lineage of David." Jewish, rather than Roman, custom is reflected in the story, for under Roman law there would have been no reason for Joseph to go to Bethlehem in order to register. Ordinarily one would register where one was presently residing or in the nearest city.

From the perspective of Luke-Acts, the census mentioned in Acts (5:37) is different from that in the Gospel. The Acts census resulted in a revolt by Jews led by Judas of Galilee. Judas was killed and his followers were dispersed. Available evidence indicates that there was a regional census in Judea during the time when Quirinius was legate (governor) in 6 C.E. (Josephus, *BJ* 2.8.1; 7.8.1). But no external evidence confirms a census by Quirinius in the time of Herod. Two views emerge as to the relationship of the two enrollments of Luke-Acts: (1) that two different enrollments actually took place and (2) that one enrollment took place, with the enrollment of 6 C.E. (Acts 5) being used as the the basis for a theological statement in Luke 2.

It is argued by those who support the historicity of only the census of 6 C.E. that there is no evidence outside Luke's Gospel that there was more than one census during this period and therefore Luke has used literary license to add another census under Herod in connection with the birth of Christ for the theological purpose of combining Jewish heritage and expectations with a major Lucan theme of the universal significance of the Christ event. Those who defend Luke's historical accuracy (sometimes called "harmonizers") point to the fact that Augustus did conduct general enrollments in 28 and 8 B.C.E. and 14 C.E. Opponents point out that the word used in Luke 2:2 generally refers to a provincial census.

The dating of a census by Quirinius in the reign of Herod also presents a problem. It is known that Quirinius was governor in 6–7 C.E. He was ordered to take a census in Judea when Archelaus was deposed in 6 C.E. and to liquidate Archelaus's estate (Josephus, *Ant* 18.1.1). Not only is Josephus silent about any census other than the one in 6 C.E., there is no record of a governorship in Syria by Quirinius during the time of Herod. The harmonizers argue for an earlier governorship by Quirinius as a sort of "extraordinary command" when Saturnius was governor from 9–6 B.C.E. This would fit the period of military maneuvers in Cilicia led by Quirinius against the Homonadensian tribes. It would also fit the 8 B.C.E census of Augustus in Italy. Advocates of this view refer to Tertullian's statement that a census was taken in Judea under Saturnius (*AdvMarc* 4.19.10) and to a manuscript found in Tivoli, which mentions a governorship of Syria often assumed to refer to Quirinius even though part of the text is missing and the name of Quirinius is not mentioned.

It seems clear that Quirinius conducted a Judean census in 6 C.E. The external evidence supporting a census under Quirinius during the reign of Herod the Great, however, is weak. Matthew mentions no census despite his accent on the role of Herod. It seems likely that the census of 6 C.E. was used as the base for extension by Luke and that he added another census under Herod to serve the purpose of his narrative.

See also BETHLEHEM; MESSIAH/CHRIST; NAZARETH; QUIRINIUS.

Bibliography. J. A. Fitzmyer, *The Gospel According to Luke, I-IX*; J. G. Machen, *The Virgin Birth of Christ*.

—CARLTON T. MITCHELL

• **Census, David's.** The accounts of David's census appear in 2 Sam 24 and 1 Chr 21. At least two major factors complicate the reader's understanding of this incident. The first is the lack of any explanation of the nature of David's sin. Taking a census was not new and neither was it inherently wrong (cf. Num 1:2-3, 45-46; 26:2-4). However, these texts clearly indicate that David's action was sinful. The following are possible reasons: (1) David failed to collect the monetary offering required of each person counted (Exod 30:11-16). To do so would seem to be direct disobedience. However, the writer in Numbers mentions no offering in connection with a census, and the implication is that none was taken. (2) David was acting in simple pride. He wanted to gloat about the great numbers he had at his disposal. However, JOAB's response seems to indicate a more serious problem. (3) David was depending more upon himself than upon the Lord for direction and protection. For example, the census could have been a first step in organizing a military draft. It certainly had a military flavor. Such an act would, in turn, imply that David had personal ambitions to expand his kingdom and a tendency to feel falsely secure because of his great numbers of potential soldiers. The punishment that followed seems to confirm the legitimacy of this last explanation. Since David was tempted to overstep his bounds because of a potentially great army, its ranks were diminished significantly (cf. Gideon's experience in Judg 7).

The second factor that complicates the reader's understanding of this episode is the apparently contradictory accounts. Some examples are: (1) The Samuel text says that the Lord prompted David to take a census (24:1); the Chronicles text says SATAN did it (21:1). The first text probably reflects the people's strong view of the sovereignty of GOD. They believed that God was in complete control and that no power rivaled the divine power. Whatever happened, God was its author (cf. 1 Sam 16:14). The second text from a later period probably reflects a change in the people's theology. They had begun to believe that evil could be attributed to a personality opposing God, yet still assert that God was sovereign. (2) The Samuel text says that 800,000 warriors were counted in Israel and 500,000 in Judah; the Chronicles text records 1,100,000 in Israel and 470,000 in Judah. Explanations include scribal error in copying the manuscript; some numbers having been rounded off (500,000 for 470,000); figures being approximate, since the census was neither complete nor officially recorded (1 Chr 27:23-24). (3) The Samuel text says David paid Araunah fifty shekels of silver; the Chronicles text says 600 shekels of gold. Explanations include scribal error; intentional inflation of the price to reflect the importance of the site as the future location of the Temple; and the lower price for the threshing floor alone, the higher one for the floor plus the larger area where the temple would be built (cf. 1 Chr 21:25, "the site").

One last consideration: any explanation of these texts must include the recognition that the different writers used the record of David's census to stress differing ideas: in Sam, sin, judgment, and sacrifice; in Chronicles, preparation for building the Temple, a permanent place of sacrifice.

See also CENSUS/ENROLLMENT.

Bibliography. H. W. Hertzberg, *I & II Samuel, OTL*; C. F. Keil and F. Delitzsch, *Commentary on the Books of Samuel*; J. A. Sanders, "Census," *IDB*.

—WALTER E. BROWN

• **Centurion.** [sen-tyoor′ee-uhn] The centurion was probably the most important soldier in the Roman army. The office of centurion has no exact equivalent in the modern army. It could be called the highest ranking noncommissioned office, or the lowest ranking commissioned office, but neither description does the rank justice, for while centurions had no commission from the Roman Senate, they were appointed by the emperor.

The Roman army, excluding the auxiliaries and the praetorian guard, had as its basic tactical unit the legion, which was constituted theoretically of 6,000 men, though the number could in fact go up or down. A legion was to have ten cohorts, each consisting of 600 men, though the first cohort was normally made up of 1,000 (cf. Acts 21:31). Within each cohort were three divisions known as maniples, each having 200 men, or two centuries. The centurion, therefore, was one of two principal leaders for each maniple, and, in name at least, was in charge of 100 men. Each legion therefore would have sixty centurions.

A centurion at the time of Christ had to be of Italian birth and Roman citizenship. Though it was possible for a man from the equestrian order to lay aside voluntarily his higher class status in order to become a centurion (a job prized for its prestige, potential, and high pay), normally centurions came from the upper portions of the plebeian class and were career soldiers from the legions. Distinctions among centurions (theoretically there were sixty grades) were based primarily on seniority, with even greater distinction given those who belonged to the first cohort. The highest ranking centurion of the first cohort, and thus of the entire legion, was known as *primus pilus*.

The centurion was to be a model soldier, especially in matters of Roman discipline. To further that end, centurions were frequently moved from one legion to the next both as a means of promotion and as a way of avoiding local acculturation, thereby maintaining the distinctly Roman character and spirit of the centurion. The tasks of the centurion thus included not only drilling, training, and inspecting the troops, but especially the instilling of the Roman spirit into the soldiers. The centurion's symbol was a vine-staff which was unhesitatingly used for corporal prodding and punishment.

The centurion could also be called upon for special, detached service, as may be seen from the assignment of the Roman centurion Julius to the task of transferring Paul to Rome from Caesarea following the apostle's appeal to Caesar (Acts 27:1). Other centurions mentioned in the NT include Cornelius, whose conversion marked for Luke a significant stage in the progress of the gospel (Acts 10:1-11:18); the centurion at Capernaum, whose faith was greatly praised by Jesus (Matt 8:5-13; Luke 7:1-10); the centurion put in charge of Jesus' execution, who also later confessed his innocence and/or divine sonship (Matt 27:54; Mark 15:39, 45; Luke 23:47); and other unnamed centurions in Jerusalem at the time of Paul's arrest (Acts 22:25, 26; 23:17, 23). The unusual prestige accorded the centurion in NT times lent a special gravity and even thrilling appeal to Christian accounts of their faith and/or conversion.

Bibliography. M. P. Nilsson, *Imperial Rome*; G. R. Watson, *The Roman Soldier*; G. Webster, *The Roman Imperial Army of the First and Second Centuries*.

—ROBERT B. SLOAN

• **Chaldea.** [kal-dee'uh] (Heb. *kaśdîm*; Gk. *chaldaios*). The territory covering the southern marshes of ancient Iraq along the Persian Gulf. It was called "the land of the Chaldeans" after the seminomadic tribes (cf. Isa 23:13; Job 1:17) inhabiting the area. The earliest attestation of the name is found in ninth century B.C.E. Assyrian annals where it replaces the general term "Sea-land." The local name for the area prior to this time is unknown, and, therefore, it cannot be conclusively argued that the designation of Abraham's home as "UR of the Chaldeans" (Gen 11:28, 31; 15:7; cf. Neh 9:7; Acts 7:4) is a harmonizing gloss.

In 705 B.C.E., Merodach-baladan, chief of the Chaldean tribe of Bīt-Yakin, seized the throne of Babylon and sought to entice Hezekiah of Judah to revolt against the Assyrians (Isa 39). Isaiah denounced this relationship (Isa 23:13; 39:5-7; 43:14). He employed "Chaldean" several times as a synonym for Babylonian (Isa 13:19; 47:1, 5; 48:14, 20; but cf. Ezek 23:23).

The neo-Babylonian dynasty (627–539 B.C.E.) inaugurated by Nabopolassar, a native Chaldean governor, made the name Chaldea famous. Under NEBUCHADREZZAR, the Chaldean army destroyed Jerusalem, ransacked the Temple and carried away all but the poor in Exile to Babylon (2 Kgs 24-25).

In Dan, BELSHAZZAR, the king of the Chaldeans, is slain (Dan 5:30), and Darius the Mede is made king over the realm of the Chaldeans (Dan 9:1). The "tongue of the Chaldeans" (Dan 1:4), a Babylonian dialect, has been incorrectly identified with Aramaic. Finally, the famous "learning" of the Chaldeans always seemed to group them with the magicians, astrologers, and soothsayers (Dan 1:4; 2:2, 10; 4:7; 5:7, 11).

—STEPHEN J. ANDREWS

• **Chaos.** *See* TIAMAT

• **Chariot.** *See* WEAPONS/WARFARE

• **Charismata.** *See* GIFTS OF THE SPIRIT

• **Charismatic.** *See* GIFTS OF THE SPIRIT

• **Charity.** *See* ALMS

• **Chastity.** *See* CELIBACY

• **Chemosh.** [kee'mosh] The national god of MOAB. In Num 21:29, the Moabites are referred to as the "sons and daughters" of Chemosh. In his oracle against Moab, Jeremiah refers three times to their god Chemosh (Jer 48:7, 13, 46). As a part of his foreign-alliance policy, SOLOMON built an altar to Chemosh on the MOUNT OF OLIVES (1 Kgs 11:7, 33). Three hundred years later it was destroyed during JOSIAH's reforms (2 Kgs 23:13).

Chemosh is mentioned many times in the Moabite Stone, a stele discovered in 1868 at the Moabite capital in Dibon. It commemorates the military conquests of MESHA, a Moabite king of the mid-ninth century B.C.E., whose struggles with Israel are recounted also in 2 Kgs 3:4-27. The stele reflects many similarities between the worship of Chemosh and of Yahweh: the Israelite possession of Moabite territory is attributed to Chemosh's anger with the Moabite people, and Mesha's success in battle is attributed to the favor of the god. There are significant differences, however. The stele refers to Chemosh in one place as Ashtar-Chemosh, which may reflect an association of the god with the Venus star, and 2 Kgs 3:27 indicates that the WORSHIP of Chemosh may have involved human sacrifice.

Once (Judg 12:24), Chemosh is identified as the god of the Ammonites.

See also IDOLATRY; MESHA STELE; RELIGIONS OF THE ANCIENT NEAR EAST.

Bibliography. J. Finegan, *Light from the Ancient Past*; G. F. Moore, "Chemosh," *EB*.

—JOHN POLHILL

• **Cherub.** [cher'uhb] A suprahuman or celestial creature similar to an angel or seraphim. There is no definitive description of the appearance or function of the cherub in either the OT or the NT. The most common image is that of a being with an animal's body, wings, and a human head.

In some passages the cherubim are described as guardians. In Gen 3:24 they were placed by God at the east of the Garden of Eden "to guard the way to the tree of life" after ADAM and EVE were driven from the Garden. In Ezek 28:11-19 the fall of the king of Tyre is parallel to the fall in the Garden, and here the cherub (vv. 14, 16) was God's guardian. In another guardian image, the wings of the cherubim are spread above the mercy seat of the Ark of the Covenant (Exod 25:18-20; 37:7-9).

In other passages the wings of cherubim served as visible pedestals upon which God's presence rested (2 Sam 6:2; Ps 80:1; Ezek 9:3). This image is closely related to that of cherubim as transporters of God or the THRONE of God (2 Sam 22:11; Ezek 9:3; 10:1-22). God is pictured at other times as sitting between the cherubim (Exod 25:22; Num 7:8-9).

The cherub image was featured prominently as a decoration of holy objects and sites. Representations of cherubim adorned SOLOMON's Temple (1 Kgs 6:23-29; 2 Chr 3:10-14; 5:7-8). Cherubim also decorated the bronze basins used for ablutions (1 Kgs 7:29, 36) and the curtains and veils of the tabernacle (Exod 26:1, 31-34).

See also ARK; SERAPHIM; TEMPLE/TEMPLES; THEOPHANY.

—DANIEL B. MCGEE

• **Chiasm.** [kī″az'uhm] A chiasm (from the Gk. letter χ) is a form of repetition in the opposite order. In chiastic organization, the sentence or text is constructed around a center; and the size of the unit so organized is limited only by possibility of composition itself. At the level of the sentence, such repetition may be termed an *epanados*. Mark

2:27 is an example: "The sabbath was made for man, not man for the sabbath."

Isaiah 6:10 is a chiasm proper:

A Make the heart of this people fat,
B and their ears heavy,
C and shut their eyes;
C' lest they see with their eyes,
B' and hear with their ears,
A' and understand with their hearts,
and turn and be healed.

It has been argued that such texts as the Abraham story in Genesis, the travel section of Luke, and the whole of both Ruth and the Gospel of Matthew are organized in this way.

—EDGAR V. MCKNIGHT

• **Children of Israel.** *See* ISRAEL; ISRAELITE

• **Chinnereth.** *See* GALILEE, SEA OF

• **Chosen People, The.** *See* ELECTION

• **Christ.** *See* JESUS; MESSIAH/CHRIST

• **Christian.** Available evidence indicates that the name "Christian" ("partisan of Christ" or "one who owes allegiance to the person Christ") was first used by non-Christians to identify professed followers of Jesus of Nazareth. In its three occurrences in the NT (Acts 11:26; 26:28; 1 Pet 4:16), for example, it is clear that originally the term was not used by believers as a self-designation but by others of them. Nor would Jews who rejected the claim Jesus was the "Christ" (the expected MESSIAH of Israel) have been willing to so entitle his followers. Taking into consideration Luke's claim that it was "in ANTIOCH the disciples were for the first time called Christians" (Acts 11:26), as well as the probability that the name "Christianos" is derived from Latin, many scholars maintain Roman officials coined the name in Antioch perhaps as early as 40–44 C.E.

Initially, "Christian" seems not to have had a derisive meaning, but by the second century (and perhaps earlier) it was used by the Romans as a designation of illegality. The historian Tacitus (ca. 116 C.E.) notes that "Christians," who derived their name from "Christus," had been falsely accused and sorely persecuted by the Emperor Nero for setting the great fire of Rome in 64 C.E. (*Ann* 15.44). Later, during periods of persecution, confession or denial of the name could be serious. For example, Pliny the Younger, governor of the Roman province of Bithynia, wrote the Emperor Trajan (ca. 112 C.E.) to ask whether Christians should be "punished for the name" or only for specific crimes (*Letters* 97). It seems wide use of the name did not come into vogue in the empire, however, till the reign of Hadrian (117–138 C.E.) or Antoninus Pius (138–161 C.E.).

Pagans, unfamiliar with the confessional title "Christos" (Messiah), mistakenly understood it as a proper name. They sometimes confused it with a more familiar Greek word, *chrestus,* meaning "good" or "kind," and would speak of *Chrestiani* (cf. Suetonius's *Lives* 25). Christian Apologists retorted that although this was incorrect, Chrestiani accurately reflected the true character of the faithful and demonstrated they did not deserve persecution by the government (e.g., Tertullian, *Apol* 3).

By the late first and early second centuries the name "Christian," which early believers avoided using of themselves, was beginning to be accepted. So the author of 1 Pet 4:16 counsels, "if one suffers as a Christian, let him not be ashamed, but under that name let him glorify God." Ignatius, bishop of Antioch, affirms (ca. 115 C.E.): "Let me not merely be called 'Christian' but be found one" (*Rom* 3.2). Appropriation of the name continued among the Christian Apologists (120–220 C.E.), such as Justin Martyr, Athenagoras, Theophilus. With pride, Origen of Alexandria could write (ca. 225 C.E.): "I wish to be called by . . . the name which is blessed over the earth. I long to be and to be called 'Christian,' in spirit and deed" (*HLuke* 16). From the third century on, it was generally used throughout Christendom.

Bibliography. H. J. Cadbury, "Names for Christians and Christianity in Acts," in F. J. Foakes-Jackson and K. Lake, *Beginnings of Christianity*; A. Harnack, "The Names of Christian Believers," *The Mission and Expansion of Christianity in the First Three Centuries*; H. B. Mattingly, "The Origin of the Name Christian," *JTS* 9 (April 1958): 26-37.

—MALCOLM L. PEEL

• **Christmas.** Christmas is the commemoration of Christ's nativity. It is celebrated on 25 December among all Christian communions, with the exception of the Armenian churches. The latter continue to observe 6 January (Epiphany) as the anniversary of both the birth of JESUS and his manifestation as Son of God at the time of his baptism (Mark 1:11).

The NT provides no data regarding the month/day of Jesus' birth, and there is no evidence to suggest that the nativity of Jesus was celebrated during the apostolic and early postapostolic times. However, 6 January had been fixed upon as the date of Jesus' baptism, and was being celebrated as such ca. 200 C.E. by a Gnostic-Christian sect known as the Basilidians (after Basilides, a theologian who taught in Alexandria, Egypt). This date was gradually incorporated into the liturgical calendar as the Feast of the Epiphany (manifestation). Prior to the christological controversies of the fourth and fifth centuries, the date of 6 January prevailed in Eastern Christendom—at least—as a date for celebrating both the physical and spiritual birth of Christ.

Hippolytus of Rome (ca. 170–236 C.E.) appears to have been the first to settle upon 25 December as the correct anniversary of Jesus' birth. He reached this conclusion through calculations based upon the notion that the conception of Jesus occurred on 25 March, which he reckoned as the date of the spring equinox. Accordingly, Jesus' birth occurred exactly nine months later. The earliest record of 25 December as a church festival is found in the Philocalian Calendar (ca. 354 C.E.), representing Roman practice as early as 336 C.E. Gradually, churches in both the eastern and western portions of the empire (Armenia excepted) adopted 25 December as the Festival of the Nativity, with 6 January celebrated as the Festival of the Epiphany.

Various factors contributed to the acceptance of the December date as most appropriate for the celebration of Christmas. Theologically, the disassociation of Christmas and Epiphany served to negate any notion that Jesus "became" the Son of God at baptism—one facet of a rather naive Christology which was rejected as heretical during the course of the christological controversies of the fourth and fifth centuries. Moreover, the close chronological conjunction of 25 December with the popular Roman festivals of Saturnalia (17–24 December) and Brumalia (25 December) facilitated the Christianizing of pre-Christian pagan celebrations as the Christian religion gained more and more adherents among the populace. Later missionary expansion of the Christian faith throughout central and northern

Europe resulted in the assimilation of other native festive customs into the ecclesiastical Festival of the Nativity as the Christian faith became the religion of the masses.

Thus, while Christmas marks the anniversary of the birth of Jesus—who is confessed by Christians as the Christ of God—the date of the celebration and many of the customs associated therewith reflect both NT tradition and varied elements of the cultural heritage of its celebrants in any given time and place.

See also JESUS.

Bibliography. K. Lake, *The Christmas Festival: An Address Delivered at the Pierpont Morgan Library, 15 December, 1935.*

—R. HARGUS TAYLOR

• **Christology.** Christology is the confessional response of the believing community or the individual believer to the JESUS event. It answers the question, "Who do you say that I am?" (Mark 8:29). But this concern is always a concern about GOD: What is God doing in Jesus? NT Christology is in the last analysis *the*-ology. The christological response is made in terms of titles, images, and mythic patterns already current in the religious tradition of the communities or individuals making the response. During the NT period the respective environment in which these responses were made were Palestinian Jewish, Hellenistic Jewish, and Hellenistic Gentile.

The Jesus-Phenomenon. According to the critically assured evidence of the tradition behind the Gospels Jesus did not impose a christological understanding of his person. Rather, he saw his task to be that of fulfilling his God-given mission, which was to proclaim the advent of the KINGDOM OF GOD by his words and works. These words and works, however, *implied* a Christology. In his words and works the Kingdom of God was effectively breaking through in advance of its final coming. Jesus was the agent of the Kingdom's coming, the agent of God's Kingdom-bringing activity: "If it is by the finger of God that I cast out demons, then the kingdom of God has come upon you" (Luke 11:20 Q). Jesus spoke and acted with such authority as to raise the question of its source (Mark 11:27-33). Jesus often prefaced his sayings with the words, "Amen, I say to you" (e.g., Mark 11:23). "Amen" comes from the Hebrew word for truth, and denotes a claim to utter the very truth of God. Jesus can even go behind the word of God given on Sinai as in the antitheses of the Sermon on the Mount ("You have heard that it was said . . . but I say to you," Matt 5:21-48). Jesus characteristicly addressed God as ABBA, the intimate address of the child to its earthly father, normally avoided in addressing God. Jesus used the relationship between a father and his SON as a parable of his own relationship to God (Matt 11:27b; John 5:19-20a; the original parables, which spoke of "*a* father" and "*a* son" were christologized by the post-Easter community to read: "*the* Father" and "*the* Son"). Jesus invited his disciples to share in his Abba-relationship to God. But the Fatherhood of God was not a general religious truth: it was a relationship made possible only by becoming a disciple of Jesus.

Jesus also appeared as a speaker of wisdom. Many of his sayings took the form of wisdom sayings, e.g., the parable about the trees and their fruits (Matt 7:16-20 Q). More than that he explicitly formulated wisdom sayings (Luke 11:49 Q). Other sayings like the Savior's appeal (Matt 11:28-30 M; cf. John 6:35c; 7:37) were, to judge from their content, originally uttered by Jesus as wisdom sayings (cf. Sir 24:19; 51:23-24). In another saying (Luke 7:35 Q) Jesus speaks of the Baptist and himself as wisdom's envoys ("children"). Given his description of JOHN THE BAPTIST as the forerunner of the Kingdom in contrast to himself (Luke 16:16 Q) it follows that Jesus believed himself to be wisdom's *last* envoy.

Jesus did not normally speak of himself but rather of God, who had commissioned him. But on occasion he pointed to himself as the one through whom God was speaking and working: "Blessed is he who takes no offense at *me*" (Luke 7:23 Q); "If *I* by the finger of God . . . " (Luke 11:20 Q); "Blessed are the eyes . . . " (Matt 13:16-17 Q); "Follow *me*" (Mark 1:17, etc.). He forgave sins, speaking in the place of God (Mark 2:5; Luke 7:47 L). When he ate with the outcast he acted for God, seeking and saving the lost, as in the twin parables of the lost sheep and lost coin (Luke 15:4-7 Q; 8-10 L). To confess or deny Jesus now was to determine one's acceptance or rejection by God at the last judgment (Mark 8:38; Luke 12:8-9 Q). In sum, Jesus stood in God's place, speaking and acting as his agent.

Jesus claimed that God had "sent" him (Matt 10:40; Luke 10:16 Q?; John 13:20). He had "come" for a specific mission (Mark 2:17b; Matt 15:24 M). This points to a prophetic self-awareness (cf. Isa 61:1b) and indeed Jesus could indirectly place himself in the category of a PROPHET (Mark 6:4; Luke 13:33 L). There is much to be said for the view that his prophetic mission was conceived specifically in terms of the servant of Yahweh in Isa 40–61. Thus he describes his preaching and healing activity in language echoing Isa 61:1 (Matt 11:4-5 Q; Isa 35:5-6 is also reflected here). The beatitudes of the great sermon have a similar background (Luke 6:20-21 Q).

Although his use of Abba implied that he was a son and his prophetic self-consciousness implied that he had been anointed by God and therefore was in some sense a messianic figure, Jesus seems to have avoided any title that could be construed as messianic. When others proffered him the title MESSIAH he appears to have been reticent (Mark 8:30; Matt 26:64; Luke 22:67-68 *contra* Mark 14:62). The most we can say is that by his activity Jesus evoked messianic hopes from his friends and messianic fears from his enemies. This makes it intelligible that he should have been crucified as a messianic pretender (the inscription on the cross, Mark 15:26).

The one self-designation which all strands of the tradition agree was used by Jesus is SON OF MAN. The term is used in three types of context: (1) of Jesus in his present activity (Mark 2:10, 28; Matt 8:20 Q, etc.); (2) of Jesus in his impending suffering, death, and vindication (Mark 8:31; 9:31; 10:33); (3) of the one (whether himself or another) who will come as transcendent judge and savior at the end (Mark 13:26, etc.). Unfortunately the origin, meaning, and authenticity of the term Son of man as used by Jesus are highly disputed. In some scholarly circles the view is gaining ground that the present and suffering usages are basically authentic to Jesus, and that he intended the term to be a self-effacing self-designation, "a man," used in contexts in which he spoke of his calling, mission, and destiny. Its meaning is determined by the contexts in which it is used, not by any inherent meaning it may previously have had as a title.

The Easter Event. For Jesus' disciples their messianic hopes were radically called into question by the CRUCIFIXION (Luke 24:21). One who was hanged upon a tree had died under the curse of God and therefore could not be the agent of God's final salvation (Deut 21:23; cf. Gal 3:13; Acts 5:30). The RESURRECTION—EASTER event—however, revealed to the disciples that God had vindicated Jesus' words and works: Jesus was what he had implicitly claimed to be, the last emissary of God and the inaugurator of final salvation. Further this salvation would (shortly, they believed) be consummated with Jesus' return as the transcendent Son of man. The belief (as opposed to the hope) that Jesus was the Messiah thus has its origin in the Easter event, which was a revelatory occurrence (Gal 1:16). Thus the christological interpretation of the Jesus phenomenon originates in Easter, though it was prepared for by the quality of his historical career.

Designatory Christologies. The earliest Christians responded to the Jesus phenomenon, including the resurrection, by preaching it as God's act of salvation, by confessing it in worship, and by defending it against its critics. As Palestinian Jews who spoke Aramaic they availed themselves of titles, images, and myth patterns from their environment. Early on they adopted a two-stage pattern which spoke first of Jesus' earthly life (stage one) and then of his post-Easter status (stage two). It may be that at first they thought of him as having been designated (at his assumption into heaven) as the Messiah who would come again (Acts 3:20-21), a pattern which, it has been claimed, was the earliest of all Christologies. Soon however the community came to think of Jesus as one who has already been enthroned as Lord (*kyrios*) and Christ (Messiah) (Acts 2:36), as one who, born as son of David in his earthly life, had been designated or appointed SON OF GOD at his resurrection (Rom 1:4). This two-stage Christology is sometimes called "adoptionist," as though the man Jesus acquired divinity at his resurrection. Such an interpretation would be incorrect for two reasons. First, this early pattern portrays Jesus' earthly life already as christological: he was the servant of God (Acts 3:13) or son of David (Rom 1:3). God was already at work in Jesus' earthly ministry (Acts 2:22; cf. 10:38b). Second, the titles of majesty used at this stage had functional rather than metaphysical connotations: they denoted what Jesus was doing in heaven, not what his "nature" had become. It is especially important to note that Son of God at this stage (and for some time to come) meant not divinity—a Greek concept—but a role in salvation history. This is what it had meant when applied to Israel's king, who was similarly designated Son of God at his enthronement (Ps 2:7, a text applied to Jesus at his resurrection in Acts 13:33; cf. Heb 1:5; 5:5).

It is worth noting further that the high-priestly Christology of Hebrews is really a developed form of this designatory Christology, for it is at his death and exaltation that Jesus "becomes" high priest (Heb 2:17).

Retrojection of the Titles of Majesty. The titles of majesty, i.e., those which designated the function to which Jesus was promoted at his exaltation, came to be associated with earlier moments in his career, such as the transfiguration, baptism, birth, and conception. In Mark Jesus is designated Son (of God) already at his baptism (Mark 1:11). Again this type of Christology is not properly called adoptionist. Mark assumed that Jesus was a man, who at his baptism was called to a distinctive role, rather than made something he was not before. Nor does this mean the christologizing of an earthly life previously regarded as unchristological. Jesus had previously been regarded as servant of God already in his earthly life, and now the title, Son, takes over the function of servant. Indeed some hold that the voice from heaven earlier read "You are my servant in whom I am well pleased," thus making it a quotation exclusively from Isa 42:1.

Sending Christology. Associated with the projection of the title, Son of God, into the earthly life of Jesus is the development of the sending formula. Jesus, as we have already seen, had thought of himself as sent by or having come from God to fulfill a prophetic role. If the parable of the wicked husbandmen is authentic, Jesus even compared his mission to that of an owner of a vineyard sending his son to collect the rent (Mark 12:6). There was therefore an adequate basis in Jesus' history for the development of the sending Christology. The sending formula has the following pattern: (1) God as subject; (2) a verb of sending; (3) the Son as object of the verb; (4) a purpose clause denoting the saving intention behind the mission. An example occurs in what is probably a pre-Pauline formula (Gal 4:4-5). While Paul himself may have understood the sending in an incarnational sense (see below) the original formula would have intended to speak of a historical mission like that of the prophets. The moment of sending would have been either Jesus' call at his baptism or already at his birth (cf. "born of a woman," Gal 4:4).

Matthew and Luke both retroject Jesus' messiahship or sonship to the moment of conception (Matt 1:18-25; Luke 1:26-38). Both evangelists narrate this as a virginal conception through the Holy Spirit. This is not a historical statement but a christological affirmation in narrative form, indicating the divine initiative as does the sending formula. Nor does the virginal-Spirit conception imply a preexistence-incarnation Christology, although these two Christologies were later fused, as in the Nicene Creed. The son of David Christology is also a different Christology from the virginal-Spirit conception, although Matthew and Luke harmonize them by having Joseph, himself of Davidic descent, adopt the child Jesus.

The earlier tradition in the discourses of John's Gospel also contains a sending Christology (John 3:16-17 and many other references). Two different Greek verbs of sending are used in John, who also speaks of Jesus as coming and in 3:16, of God giving him. However the evangelist himself understood them (see below), such formulas were originally intended to express a historical mission.

Inspiration Christologies. We have seen that Jesus thought of himself as the speaker and emissary of wisdom, in fact, wisdom's final envoy. When the introduction "wisdom says" was dropped from the wisdom sayings the effect was to upgrade Jesus to be the actual *embodiment* of wisdom (cf. Matt 23:34 with Luke 11:49). Judging from the content of the saying this happened also to the Savior's appeal (Matt 11:28-30).

Paul identified Jesus as the embodiment of the wisdom of God (1 Cor 1:24, 30) and also of God's power, righteousness, sanctification, and redemption. Such expressions do not make Christ and wisdom the same divine person. They mean only that Jesus embodies or is fully inspired by wisdom. The same line of thinking underlies 2 Cor 4:4 where Christ is equated with the image of God. Also the phrase "God in Christ was . . . " (2 Cor 5:19) and the probably deutero-Pauline statement that "in him the whole fulness of God dwells bodily" (Col 2:9) express an inspiration rather than incarnation Christology.

The same is true of many passages in the discourses of John's Gospel. We have already noted that probably authentic wisdom sayings of Jesus in the Synoptics occur without their original introduction, "wisdom says." Such sayings also occur in John (6:37b). As the Johannine circle meditated on the sayings of Jesus it evolved further wisdom material, such as the great "I am" sayings (6:35b, etc.). Most of these can easily be understood as utterances of wisdom which Jesus embodies. For wisdom was regarded in Judaism as the bread from heaven, the light, etc. The saying, "Before Abraham was, I am" (8:58), would not originally have involved a personal claim to preexistence but was an utterance of wisdom embodied by Jesus.

Even statements in which Jesus speaks of his "coming down" from heaven were probably originally utterances of wisdom, as in 6:33, and did not imply his personal preexistence or incarnation. The same is true of passages which speak of Jesus being sent or coming into the world (3:17; 9:39 etc.).

Preexistence-Incarnation Christology. Prior to the later stages of the development of the discourses in the Gospel of John, the preexistence-incarnation Christology is found mainly in christological hymns. In these hymns preexistent wisdom and the man Jesus are identified personally through a relative pronoun embracing both. The earliest clear instance is in 1 Cor 8:6 where the relative pronoun ("through whom") qualifies "Jesus Christ," and the relative clause goes on to define him as the agent of creation, like wisdom (Prov 3:19). This makes Jesus not merely the embodiment of wisdom, but wisdom incarnate. The ego of Jesus is the same ego as the wisdom of God who was the agent of creation. The hymn in Phil 2:6-11 is usually interpreted in this way. Here the relative pronoun introduces statements which affirm that in Jesus Christ one who originally existed in the form of God (as wisdom) divested himself of his equality with God and was born in human fashion. Here again there is continuity of ego between the preexistent and the incarnate one.

The incarnation Christology has also influenced Paul's thinking outside the hymns. The early christological formula in Romans 8:3b states that God sent his Son "in the likeness of sinful flesh," again implying that the Son was already in existence before assuming flesh. Christ's preexistence before his historical life is also implied when Paul identifies the rock which followed the Israelites in the wilderness with Christ (1 Cor 10:4), an incident which was already interpreted in post-OT Judaism as referring to wisdom.

The Pauline corpus contains another hymn (Col 1:15-20) in which a relative pronoun brackets the creative, revelatory, and sustaining activity of the preexistent one and the redemptive activity of the incarnate one under a single grammatical subject. Here the preexistent one is discussed in wisdom terms: image of God, prior to creation and, principal of coherence in the universe. A similar hymn occurs in Heb 1:26-4, where the preexistent one is described in wisdom terms as the reflection of God's glory and the very stamp of his nature (cf. Wis 7:25-26) as well as the sustainer of the universe.

The climax in this development of preexistence-incarnation Christology however is to be found in the Johannine prologue (John 1:1-18), minus vv. 6-8 and 15, which are in prose. This is a hymn to the Word or LOGOS, which like wisdom (with which it is synonymous; cf. Wis 9:1-2) existed prior to creation, partook of God's deity, and was agent of creation and revelation. The Logos "became flesh," i.e., assumed humanity as Jesus Christ. The Logos Christology is deliberately fused with the earlier Father/Son Christology in v. 14c. This results in a reinterpretation of the Father/Son, the sending of the Son, and the wisdom Christologies. The sending of the Son, previously a historical commissioning, becomes the sending of the eternal Logos-Son from heaven. The Father/Son relationship, previously a historical one of call and obedience, becomes the revelation of an eternal relationship. The wisdom sayings become personal sayings of the Logos-made-flesh. It is not just wisdom that came down from heaven to inspire the man Jesus. The man Jesus is now himself the Logos come down from heaven. As the Logos incarnate he knows that he personally had come forth from God and is returning to God (13:3). He can pray to the Father to glorify him with the glory he had before the creation of the world (17:5). The Johannine Christ is now not merely the embodiment of wisdom who had descended from heaven as in John 6:33. He has personally descended from heaven to do the will of God who sent him (6:38; note here the combination of preexistence and sending Christology). All the sending formulas now express an incarnation Christology. The preexistent one had descended as Son of man (3:13). As always, the term, Son of man, derives its meaning from the context in which it is used. Similarly, the "coming" of Jesus into the world will mean his incarnation. The same type of Christology is expressed in the Johannine Epistles, though with more emphasis on the fact of the incarnation (1 John 4:2; 2 John 7) than upon the preexistence. It therefore cannot be argued that this high Christology is confined to the hymns or never made a matter for theological reflection. Nor is it to be interpreted merely in terms of the lower categories of inspiration and embodiment.

Jesus, God, and Man. The preexistence-incarnation Christologies raise the question of Christ's nature. Is he human or divine or both at once? Even those NT writers who accept the high Christology of preexistence and incarnation are very cautious about calling Christ "God." There are a few passages in the Epistles which could refer to Christ as God (e.g., Rom 9:5; Tit 2:13). But in such cases the punctuation or the textual tradition is uncertain. This leaves us with four passages in the Johannine literature. The first is John 1:1. Here the preexistent Logos, who later (v. 14) becomes incarnate as Jesus Christ, is called "God." But the definite article, usual in Greek when referring to God himself, is omitted. It is difficult to represent this omission in English, but it means that the preexistent Logos shared the deity of God without being all that God was. We may paraphrase it to say that the Logos was that aspect of the being of God which is God going out of himself in creative, revelatory, and redemptive action. The second passage comes later in the prologue (1:18), where the best texts read "God" rather than "Son" (RSV margin). Again the phrase is difficult to translate, since the adjective "only" goes more appropriately with "Son." The difficulty was evidently felt by the later copyists as well as by the translators of RSV and NEB. Hence it was corrected to "Son." The earlier reading "God" must mean that the earthly Jesus, the only Son, is God in the same sense in which the Logos is God, i.e., God in his self-expressive activity. The third passage is Thomas' confession, "My Lord and my God," addressed to the risen one (20:28). Here John's Gospel comes full circle with Thomas confessing the faith of the prologue. He has seen in Jesus the self-expressive activity of God in person. The fourth passage occurs at the end of 1 John: ". . . his Son Jesus Christ. This is the true God. . ." (5:20c). This passage probably has the same meaning as Thomas' confession.

It is remarkable that the three groups of NT writings with the highest Christology (the Pauline corpus, Hebrews, and the Johannine circle) also place the strongest emphasis on Jesus' humanity. The Philippian hymn (Phil 2:6-11) tells how one who was in the form of God and equal with God took human form and likeness, humbling himself and becoming obedient to death. The background of this emphasis on Jesus' obedience is the concept of Christ as the second or last Adam, perhaps Paul's major contribution to Christology (1 Cor 15:22, 45-49; Rom 5:12-21).

Alongside its portrayal of the preexistent one as the reflection of the divine glory and the bearer of the stamp of the divine nature (Heb 1:3), Hebrews also stresses that he shared the same nature of flesh and blood as "the children" (2:14). He was in every respect tempted as we are, yet without sin (2:18; 4:15). In the days of his flesh he offered up prayers and supplications, with loud cries and tears, and although he was a Son learned obedience through suffering (5:7-8). Though sonship implies divine nature, it does not give the Son an unfair advantage. He was completely human and subject to personal development.

John's Gospel has often been thought to lay a one-sided stress on Jesus' divinity and therefore to underestimate his humanity. John has been accused of a naive docetism. The Jesus of the Fourth Gospel, it has been said, walks on earth like a God an inch or two above the ground. But this is a superficial judgment. Quite apart from its formal stress on the flesh of Jesus (1:14; 6:51-58) and its recognition that Jesus could be thirsty or tired, the Johannine Jesus is always dependent upon and obedient to his Father (5:30; 8:26, 28; 12:49): "the Father is greater than I" (14:28). It is in the submission of the Son's will to the Father that the Father and the Son are one (10:30, a text which implies the humanity rather than the divinity of Jesus).

Conclusion. We have established three major types of Christology in the NT: designation Christology (including both the two-stage and the historical-sending type), inspiration Christology, and incarnation Christology. The first two types are functional in character. The third type is couched in terms of nature and being. The church's later Christology (Niçea and Chalcedon) was worked out almost exclusively on the basis of this third, the incarnation type. The dogma of Nicea and Chalcedon is often criticized today for a variety of reasons and proposals are made to revive one of the other types of NT Christology, e.g., the sending or the inspiration type. But it may be argued that, for all its problems, the incarnation type alone does justice to the Christian experience of the Jesus phenomenon and represents the most mature thinking of the NT theologians. For in him faith encounters one who in person is true man and true God. In his humanity he is not just the bearer of the Logos but in his person is God going out of himself toward us in self-expressive activity.

See also ABBA; COLOSSIANS, LETTER TO THE; CROSS; CRUCIFIXION; DIVINITY OF JESUS; EASTER; GOD; HEBREWS, LETTER TO THE; JESUS; JOHN, GOSPEL AND LETTERS OF; JOHN THE BAPTIST; KINGDOM OF GOD; LOGOS/WORD; LORD IN THE NEW TESTAMENT; LORD IN THE OLD TESTAMENT; MESSIAH/CHRIST; PAUL; PHILIPPIANS, LETTER TO THE; PRIESTS; PROPHET; RESURRECTION IN THE NEW TESTAMENT; RESURRECTION IN THE OLD TESTAMENT; SALVATION IN THE NEW TESTAMENT; SALVATION IN THE OLD TESTAMENT; SON; SON OF GOD; SON OF MAN; VIRGIN BIRTH; WISDOM IN THE NEW TESTAMENT; WISDOM IN THE OLD TESTAMENT.

Bibliography. R. E. Brown, *The Birth of the Messiah, The Community of the Beloved Disciple,* and *Jesus, God and Man*; G. Bornkamm, *Jesus of Nazareth;* O. Cullmann, *The Christology of the New Testament*; J. D. G. Dunn, *Christology in the Making;* R. H. Fuller, *The Foundations of New Testament Christology*; R. H. Fuller and P. Perkins, *Who Is This Christ?*; A. E. Harvey, *Jesus and the Constraints of History*; J. Jeremias, *New Testament Theology 1: The Proclamation of Jesus*; G. W. H. Lampe, *God as Spirit*; B. Lindars, *Jesus, Son of Man*; W. A. Meeks, *The Prophet King: Moses Traditions and the Johannine Christology;* C. F. D. Moule, *The Origin of Christology;* J. A. T. Robinson, *The Priority of John;* J. T. Sanders, *The New Testament Christological Hymns;* E. Schillebeeckx, *Christ: The Christian Existence in the Modern World* and *Jesus: An Experiment in Christology.*

—REGINALD H. FULLER

• OUTLINE OF CHRONICLES •

The Books of Chronicles

I. The Genealogy of Humankind from Adam to Israel's Return from Exile (1 Chr 1:1–9:34)
II. The Genealogy of Saul and Saul's Death (1 Chr 9:35–10:14)
III. The Reign of David (1 Chr 11–29)
IV. The Reign of Solomon (2 Chr 1–9)
V. The Reigns of Judah's Kings from Rehoboam to Zedekiah (2 Chr 10:1–36:21)
VI. The Edict of Cyrus (2 Chr 36:22-23)

• Chronicles, First and Second. Chronicles embraces essentially the time of the Hebrew monarchy. Initial parallels are found in the Pentateuch and extensive parallels in 2 Samuel and 1 and 2 Kings. Chronicles was not originally divided into two parts and apparently was combined with EZRA and NEHEMIAH material. This original single volume used the Judean history as a resource for its message, tracing genealogy back to ADAM and concluding with a reestablished "kingdom" under Ezra and Nehemiah.

The reading of Chronicles could be rather unproductive unless the reader has been alerted to the author's purpose. The study of Chronicles is for the careful student rather than the casual reader. An informed approach will avoid an extreme posture either of attacking the historical value of the material or of defending its accuracy in every detail. A forthright assessment of tendencies can be made while allowing the material its canonical integrity. Because the historical events are recounted more comprehensively by the DEUTERONOMIST in the books of Samuel and Kings, the present essay will focus more on the Chronicler's purpose in portraying the events.

That the author did not simply write history in the usual sense becomes evident from a close reading in light of parallels. As literature, Chronicles may be more akin to drama. It uses the past to paint a picture for a particular present occasion. It is crucial therefore to distinguish two levels of focus: the past events recounted and the present occasion for recounting those events.

The Chronicler wrote with a focus on certain aspects of the monarchy, but the focus was likewise on his own community, which was post-exilic. A specific date between 400 and 350 B.C.E. is the most likely although 300–250 has been suggested. The four components of the original volume reflect a unity of style and viewpoint that suggests a single author-editor. The unnamed Chronicler had strong Levitical leanings. He probably did not sing with the guild of Asaph in the Temple choir, but he was definitely interested in the musical function of the Levites (1 Chr 25:1-2; 2 Chr 5:11-12; 8:14).

Chronicles follows Ezra and Nehemiah in the Hebrew Bible and is in the canonical division entitled Writings. The present order in English Bibles derives from LXX. The title of Chronicles in Hebrew means "events of history." The Greek title in the LXX means "things left over." The English name derives from the Latin of Jerome, who entitles the volume a "*Chronicon* of the Whole of Sacred History."

The Chronicler's work has historical parallels in the deuteronomic prophetic history (Joshua–Kings) but in some ways is a sequel to the Pentateuchal priestly material. It could be suggested that the Chronicler has creatively combined deuteronomic with priestly perspectives, resulting in a unique emphasis. Contrasted with the apocalyptic perspective in Daniel, which contributed to Jewish survival by glorifying the future, Chronicles accentuates the past.

Approximately half the Chronicles material consists of clear references to existing sources now canonical. This material (esp. the Deuteronomic Samuel-Kings) was used faithfully, as evidence from Qumran studies indicates. Biblical sources are not cited in the text but references to some twenty-one others are. Although variously named, it is doubtful if all twenty-one are different documents. These nonextant sources, when grouped together, include official records, official genealogical lists, prophetic records, other official documents, and other references.

Recent study of Chronicles has concluded that the Chronicler's story is accurate wherever it can be checked and that the author used sources carefully. Still to be observed, however, are special features that have occasioned much discussion. (1) Omissions or suppressions from the record as it is known in Samuel and Kings. Examples include Exodus events, David's experience with Bathsheba, and Northern Kingdom history. (2) Additions, like those concerned with ritual and musical matters. Observe the repentance of Manasseh, which justified the lengthy reign of so evil a king. (3) Alterations, possibly to recast data potentially offensive to the postexilic age (cf. 2 Chr 14:15; 17:6 and Kings par.) (4) Anachronisms in which post-exilic phenomena (customs, ceremonies, names) apparently were projected to the earlier time (as in 1 Chr 26). (5) Exaggerated numbers (cf. par. for 1 Chr 18:4; 19:1-19; 2 Chr 13:3, 17). Recent attempts to clarify numerical inflation indicate that the Hebrew word often rendered "thousands" evidently means "units."

It is possible to discern an economic-political purpose in the Chronicler's efforts, but it is more likely that the aim is basically religious. Painfully aware of past failures, some disenchanted post-exilic Jews did need the encouragement of their former, God-given successes (cf. 2 Chr 13; 14; 20; 25). The Chronicler seemed to understand that the only hope for the returning refugees was in becoming a worshiping congregation centered upon the Temple and the praise of Yahweh. Rather than emphasize a royal messianism, the author emphasized the Temple and the worship aspect of Davidic tradition.

Understanding the author's redemptive agenda provides a clue in following his unfolding thought as observed in the outline below.

First Chr 1–9: Genealogies and Lists. Beginning Chronicles with a genealogy serves to legitimize and establish Judah as well as the Levites and to trace family descent and introduce the central figure of David. (1) Chap. 1. Adam to Israel and Esau. (2) Chaps. 2–8. The Sons of Israel. (3) Chap. 9. Exiles, Temple duties, and Saul.

First Chr 10–29: David. The founder of the City of David is also portrayed as founder of the Temple and its worship. (1) Chap. 10. Death of SAUL (transition to David). (2) Chaps. 11–21. David's rise to power and accomplishments. (3) Chaps. 22–29. Preparations for the Temple.

Second Chr 1–9: Solomon and the Temple. The working out of the Davidic vision of Temple worship is depicted in detail. A vision may also be seen of the ideal theocratic nation, worshiping and prosperous, under the wise ruler. (1) Chap. 1. Prosperity and wisdom of the early Solomon. (2) Chaps. 2–7. Building of the Temple. (3) Chaps. 8–9. The later reign of Solomon.

Second Chr 10–36: Judean Kings. The kings are seen to stand or fall as they are true to the Jerusalem Temple and the praise of Yahweh. Jehoshaphat, Hezekiah, and Josiah receive special attention, for each had a notable role in the Temple's history. (1) Chap. 10. Revolt of the northern tribes. (2) Chaps. 11–36:12. Kings of Judah. (3) Chaps. 36:13-21; Fall of Jerusalem; Epilogue: Chap. 36:22-23; Beginning of the New Era.

Even though the nation had its political origin under Moses, as a community of praise its real origin was under David, a second Moses. Hebrew history would begin with David and can be rendered in ecclesiastical terms. The Northern Kingdom falls; it has been separated from true worship. The Southern Kingdom falls; its lack of true worship is being judged. As Chronicles closes, Zedekiah, as paradigmatic for all Judah, receives harsh notice for rejecting JEREMIAH's message. Because the nation refused to engage gratefully in worship at Zion, judgment occurred. Yet, the epilogue sounds a note of optimism, showing Yahweh active in history to bring about his praise, which will reconstitute Israel.

Chronicles may be understood as proclamation from a stance of interpreted history. The dramatic presentation calls post-exilic Jews back to their destiny as a kingdom of priests and a holy nation (Exod 19:6). The Chronicler discerned the vitalities necessary for survival in his own day as well as in past monarchical times. Despite the particularities of both these eras, significant substructural truth is available for today also. Elevation of Yahweh to the status of monotheistic divinity and authentic worship of him brings a person to true identity and a people to true community. Praise of Yahweh is an act of ultimate value-centering that ushers one into the context of cosmic reality. By letting God be God, people move toward being fully human, as clarified in the new covenant literature.

See also DEUTERONOMIST/DEUTERONOMISTIC HISTORIAN; EZRA, BOOK OF; NEHEMIAH, BOOK OF.

Bibliography. P. R. Ackroyd, *Chronicles, I and II, IDB-Supp;* E. L. Curtis and A.A. Madsen, *Chronicles, ICC*; W. A. L. Elmslie, *The First and Second Books of Chronicles, IB*; C. T. Francisco, *1-2 Chronicles, BBC*; J. M. Myers, *I-II Chronicles, AncB;* R. H. Pfeiffer, *Chronicles, I and II, IDB*.

—DOUGLAS C. BAIN, JR.

• **Chronology.** The goal of chronology is to determine the correct order of events and, if possible, their absolute date. Given the conflicting historical data in the Bible and the disagreement between the Bible and other ancient Near Eastern and Greco-Roman sources, this goal is not easily achieved. In some cases an *absolute* chronology is possible, i.e., the events can be dated by some external CALENDAR and can be computed to either the exact date or to within a few years. On the other hand, one must often be content with a *relative* chronology in which events can be dated and arranged in reference to each other, but whose precise historical reckoning can only be approximated.

The canonical text of the Bible begins with an account of creation and the pre-Abrahamic ancestors, which includes elaborate genealogical records. From data, Bishop James Ussher (1581–1656) calculated that the world was created in 4004 B.C.E. Though few today would consider this an historical datum, we are beginning to understand, at least in part, the elaborate chronological system worked out by those who compiled the biblical tradition.Theirs was a theological agenda, not an historical one in the modern sense.

The chronological information about ABRAHAM, ISAAC, and JACOB in Genesis was arranged according to a mathematical scheme, which may be illustrated in terms of their respective ages at death.

	Age at Death	Sum of Digits
Abraham	$175 = 7 \times 5^2$	$[7+5+5 = 17]$
Isaac	$180 = 5 \times 6^2$	$[5+6+6 = 17]$
Jacob	$147 = 3 \times 7^2$	$[3+7+7 = 17]$

This rather simple scheme is in turn part of what appears to be an elaborate mathematical system worked out by ancient chronologers, which runs through the Hebrew Bible.

Particular numbers are associated with specific eras as one moves through the Pentateuch and beyond. The larger scheme seems to be oriented toward the manner in which ancient scribes thought about the future. In the modern period we face the future; people in the ancient Near East faced the past. To determine the future, they simply read the events of the past and projected them, as it were, behind themselves into the future, which then became a "rerun" of the past in reverse. The picture may be diagrammed as follows:

JOSHUA/JOSEPH ➧ NEW ISRAEL ➧ FATHERS ➧ NEW CREATION

Both JOSHUA and JOSEPH in this scheme are allotted 110 years, and together serve as a narrative frame to bracket the appearance of a new MOSES (perhaps originally understood in terms of the promulgation of the Torah as canonical scripture in ancient Israel, the historical moment in which the scheme was worked out). Since Israel consisted of twelve tribes, those ancient chronologers apparently chose the sum of the squares of the digits one through twelve, namely 650. The number associated with the Fathers is 140, the sum of the squares of the digits one through seven. Abraham was 140 years of age when Isaac married REBEKAH, a marriage which lasted 140 years. Rebekah was barren for twenty years before she gave birth to the twins Jacob and ESAU, who are identified before their birth as two nations (i.e., Israel and Edom). Since Isaac was sixty years old at the birth of Jacob and Esau (Gen 25:26), the twins were 120 when Jacob fled to Aram shortly before the death of Isaac at age 180. After serving LABAN for twenty years (Gen 31:38), Jacob returned following his wrestling match with the mysterious night visitor at the JABBOK. Jacob/Israel was thus 140 years old when he reentered the land of Canaan to encounter his brother Esau who, of course, was also 140. The 140 years allotted JOB (42:16) after his time of testing place him within this same scheme among the Fathers of Genesis.

Within the narrative tradition in Genesis, Abraham was 160 years old at the birth of his grandson Jacob/Israel. Isaac was sixty when Jacob was born; and Jacob lived with Isaac for sixty-three years and with Laban for twenty. At the time of Joseph's descent into Egypt at age seventeen, Isaac was thus 160 years old $(60+63+20+17)$. Moreover, the number of years between the birth of Shem and Terah in Gen 11 is 320, which is twice 160. Since the sum of the numbers 110 (Joshua/Joseph) + 650 (Israel) + 140 (the Fathers) is 900, it is interesting to note that 900 x 160 = 144,000. This curious number, which becomes the community of the elect within apocalyptic speculation (see Rev 14:1), apparently began in ancient Israel as simply the symbolic lapse of time in a chronological scheme from the promulgation of the Torah of Moses to the *eschaton*, conceived in terms of a grand reversal of past events in ancient Israel according to the formula:

JOSEPH ➧ NEW ISRAEL ➧ FATHERS ➧ NEW CREATION

$$(110 + 650 + 140) \times 160 = 144{,}000$$

It is not possible to construct an absolute chronology so far as the PATRIARCHS of Genesis are concerned, since none of the people or events of the narrative can be correlated to external events of their era. While it is true that these narratives reflect certain customs that can be documented in Amorite and Hurrian cultures of the early second millennium B.C.E., dating the Fathers remains problematic. In recent years the *Patriarchs* have been dated as early as the twenty-second century B.C.E., and their literary creation as late as the sixth century B.C.E. The majority of scholars, however, still prefer a relative chronology of ca. 2000–1850 for Abraham, ca. 1900–1750 for Isaac, and Jacob around 1800–1700. Joseph and the entrance into Egypt are dated around 1750–1650 B.C.E.

The date of the EXODUS is also uncertain. The scholarly consensus for a thirteenth century date has been challenged recently by those who would place it two centuries earlier. From 1 Kgs 6:1 we learn that the Exodus was established by ancient chronologers as having occurred 480 years before the founding of the Temple in King SOLOMON's fourth year. The Bible thus dates the Exodus to sometime in the fifteenth century, during the reign of Thutmose III (1490). J. Bimson has defended this traditional view on the basis that whereas there is no archaeological evidence for the destruction of such cities as JERICHO, AI, GIBEON, HEBRON, Hormah, ARAD, DEBIR, LACHISH, and HAZOR during the Late Bronze Age, when the thirteenth century option would necessitate the Conquest, there is evidence for this shortly before 1400 B.C.E. Thus Bimson dates the Exodus to ca. 1450 and the conquest to ca. 1410 B.C.E. This solution, however, creates as many problems as it solves, since the period of the Judges in Israel would then last 600 years. Moreover, Exod 1:11 states that the Hebrews were building the cities of Pithom and Ramses, which were largely built by RAMSES II (1290–24). Furthermore, if the conquest had occurred in 1410 B.C.E., then why does the book of Judges make no reference to the Asiatic campaigns of Seti I (1319–1301) and Ramses II (1301–1234)? From the Merneptah Stele (ca. 1220 B.C.E.) we learn that Israel was among the peoples in Palestine that Merneptah (ca. 1224–1214) defeated. The archaeological evidence for the destruction of a number of biblical sites in the thirteenth century suggests that this is the setting of the Conquest. Most scholars still date the Exodus to ca. 1290–1260 B.C.E. and the Conquest to about a half century later.

With the rise of the monarchy in ancient Israel historians have their first opportunity to establish an absolute chronology, but even here there are problems. The biblical data in the books of Kings can be cross-referenced with known Assyrian and Babylonian king lists, which have been precisely dated by means of calculating the exact dates of solar and lunar eclipses to which these lists (called *limmu* or eponym lists) refer. Two dates in the biblical text have consequently been established beyond reasonable doubt: the date for the battle of Qarqar in which King Ahab fought (853 B.C.E.) and Jehu's giving of tribute to the Assyrian king Shalmaneser III (841 B.C.E.). From these two fixed dates, the rest of the dates of the kings of Israel and Judah can be obtained by careful reckoning.

It must be noted, however, that the figures for the reigns of individual kings in Israel and Judah are not as clear as one would hope. There are numerous problems in matters of detail, which E. Thiele has resolved, though not to the satisfaction of all historians. Prior to Thiele, the two sets of figures given in the regnal summaries for the kings of Israel and Judah could not be made to agree without textual emendation. Thiele has demonstrated that the system of cross-referencing is in agreement, once one understands three complex factors. First, there are several implied co-regencies in the text, which would explain some of the excess years in these lists. Second, there were two systems for counting regnal years in the ancient Near East: the accession-year system, in which the rule of the kings was counted to have begun only with the beginning of the first new year; and the nonaccession-year system, which counted the year in which the coronation took place as a full year.

Kings of Israel & Judah	Thiele	Albright
[*indicates Judah]		
*Rehoboam	931/30–913	922–915
Jeroboam	931/30–910/09	922–901
*Abijah	913–911/10	915–913
*Asa	911/10–870/69	913–873
Nadab	910/09–909/8	901–900
Baasha	909/8–886/85	900–877
Elah	886/85–885/84	877–876
Zimri	885/84	876
Omri	885/84–874/73	876–869
*Jehoshaphat	873/73–848	873–849
Ahab	874/73–853	869–850
Ahaziah	853–852	850–849
*Jehoram	853–841	849–842
Jehoram	852–841	849–842
*Ahaziah	841	842
Jehu	841–814/13	842–815
*Athaliah	841–835	842–837
*Jehoash	835–796	837–800
Johoahaz	814/13–798	815–801
Joash	798–782/81	801–786
*Amaziah	796–767	800–783
Jeroboam II	793/92–753	786–746
*Azariah/Uzziah	792/1–740/39	783–742
Zechariah	753–752	746–745
Shallum	752	745
Menahem	752–742/41	745–738
*Jotham	750–732/31	750–735
Pekahiah	742/41–740/39	738–737
Pekah	752–732/31	737–732
*Jehoahaz [=Ahaz] I	735–716/15	735–715
Hoshea	732/31–723/22	732–724
*Hezekiah	716/15–687/86	715–687
*Manasseh	697/96–643/42	687–642
*Amon	643/42–641/40	642–640
*Josiah	641/40–609	640–609
*Jehoahaz II	609	609
*Jehoiakim	609–598	609–598
*Johoiachin	598–597	598
*Zedekiah	597–586	598–587

A year in which there was a royal transfer of power was counted twice by this latter method, which accounts for some of the problems in the biblical data, since both systems were used at different points in time. Finally, there were two different calendars in use in the ancient Near East. One began in the spring with the month of Nisan (Israel), while the other began in the fall with the month of Tishri (Judah). Complicating matters still further, Thiele argues that each of the kingdoms switched their methods of dating, and then switched back after a time. None of these factors, however, is explicitly cited by the text, and can only be deduced by careful reasoning and cross-checking with other ancient Near Eastern sources.

The positing of unmentioned co-regencies remains a problem to some historians, who see Thiele's method as overly subjective. While most current scholars side with Thiele, others hold to the older Albright chronology. Since there is still room for debate, both chronologies are given.

The fall of JERUSALEM and the Babylonian exile can be precisely dated by Babylonian documents. According to these texts, the fall of Jerusalem occurred on the second of Adar, i.e., 16/15 March of either 598 or 597 B.C.E. The ultimate destruction of Jerusalem and a second deportation occurred in the fall of 587 B.C.E. The third deportation recorded in Jer 52 is usually dated to 582/1 B.C.E. The Exile came to an end with the fall of Babylon under the Persian general Cyrus, who issued a decree allowing the exiles to return home in 539 B.C.E.

The events of the return of the Jews to Palestine and the restoration in Jerusalem are harder to date with absolute precision. While the work on the restoration of the Second Temple began in the second year of the return (Ezra 3:8), this work was suspended until the second year of Darius I in 520 (Ezra 4:24) and completed in 515 B.C.E. (Ezra 6:15).

If one correlates the traditional dates of EZRA and NEHEMIAH with Persian king lists, the respective dates for these two men would be 458 and 445 B.C.E. Because of inconsistencies in the biblical text, however, many scholars are convinced that the work of Ezra presupposes that of Nehemiah. Some who hold this view argue that Ezra returned in the seventh year of Artaxerxes II in 398 B.C.E., rather than Artaxerxes I. Others suggest that a mistake has slipped into the biblical record, and that Ezra 7:7 originally read the *thirty-seventh* year of Artaxerxes I, namely 428 B.C.E.

Any chronology of the NT must take into account the Roman hegemony over the Jewish people established on 10 Tishri in 63 B.C.E. under the Roman general Pompey. Though much is known about the subsequent history of Roman rule in Palestine, the data do not match up well with what is given in the NT.

The birth of JESUS is particularly difficult to ascertain with certainty. In Matt 2:1 we learn that he was born during the reign of Herod the Great, and Luke 2:2 speaks of a census at the time Quirinius was governor of Syria. It has been argued that the census mentioned here is to be associated with one that Augustus initiated in either 9 C.E. or 6 C.E., which would place the birth of Jesus in 8/7 or 5/4 C.E. Another possibility is that the star was connected with Halley's comet in 12 B.C.E. Others argue for an otherwise undocumented census in 4 B.C.E., to which Luke refers, or simply posit an error on Luke's part.

An equally difficult chronological problem lies in trying to ascertain the precise dates for the ministry of Jesus. Not only do we not know exactly when he began his public ministry; we do not know exactly how many years it lasted. Scholars have debated whether it lasted one year, in connection with the order of events connected with Jesus' trip to Jerusalem as presented in the Synoptics, or three years based on the three trips to Jerusalem recorded in the Gospel of John. Some have also argued that a two-year ministry is possible. The usual solution is to give the nod to John, and posit a three-year ministry, with the possibility of a two-year ministry based on the fact that some of the trips to Jerusalem recorded in John actually occurred in the same year. Luke 3:1-2 dates the baptism of Jesus to the precise date of the fifteenth year of TIBERIAS, whose rule can be interpreted to have begun in three different manners. In short, the majority of scholars date the beginning of Jesus' ministry to the years 27, 28 or 29 C.E. The crucifixion would then have occurred either one, two, or three years afterwards, depending on the length of his ministry. Thus Jesus died somewhere between 27 and 32 C.E.

The basic problem with establishing a Pauline chronology lies in the discrepancies that exist between Paul's own account of things, as portrayed in his letters, and the account of his life offered in Acts. PAUL mentions two trips to Jerusalem in Gal 1–2 whereas the record in Acts records five. Such discrepancies make it difficult to reconstruct the life of Paul with absolute confidence. Nonetheless, some dates can be given with certainty thanks to the Gallio inscription, which enables the historian to place the events of Acts 18:12 in the year 51 C.E. From this fixed point the biblical historian can work backward and forward. The two most recent treatments of this problem are those of P. Jewett and G. Luedemann, which may be summarized as follows:

Dates According to:		
Luedemann	**Jewett**	**Event**
27 (30)	Oct 34	Paul's conversion
33 (36)	Oct 37	First Jerusalem visit
34 (37)	40–45	In Syria/Cilicia
36 (39)ff.		Mission in Europe: Philippi, Thessalonica
	43–45	First missionary journey: Cyprus, Pamphylia, Galatia
	46–51	Second missionary journey: Galatia, Philippi, Thessalonica, Corinth
41	49	Claudius expelled Jews
41	50	Paul in Corinth
47 (50)	Aug–Oct 51	Second Jerusalem visit (Jerusalem Conference)
Summer 48 (51)	47	Paul in Galatia
	52–57	Third missionary journey
50 (53)	53–55	Paul in Ephesus
Winter 49/50	Winter 54/5	Ephesian imprisonment?
Spring 50 (53)		Journey to Macedonia
Summer 50 (53)		Corinthian correspondence
Winter 50/1 (53/4)		Paul in Macedonia
Spr/Sum 51 (54)		Journey to Corinth
Winter 51/2 (54/5)		Paul in Corinth (Romans)
Spring 52 (55)	April 57	Departure for Jerusalem
	June 57	Arrival in Jerusalem
	June 57–59	Imprisonment in Caesarea
	July 59	Paul before Festus
	Oct 59	Departure from Fair Havens
	Nov 59–Feb 60	Paul in Malta
	March 60	Arrival at Rome
	March 62	Paul's execution

It should be noted that these two studies depart from traditional reconstructions of Paul's life in several ways. The JERUSALEM COUNCIL is generally placed around 48–49 C.E., between the first and second missionary journeys. Many scholars posit a Roman imprisonment in 62–64 C.E., and others, a trip to Spain after this, based on the information in the pastoral epistles.

Though NT chronology ends with Paul in Rome, some books such as the Revelation probably came from the time of Domitian's persecution of the Christians in 95 C.E. Beyond 100 C.E. the era of the apostolic fathers begins.

See also CALENDAR; NUMBERS/NUMEROLOGY.

Bibliography. W. F. Albright, "The Chronology of the Divided Monarchy of Israel," *BASOR* 100 (Dec 1945): 16-22; W. Armstrong and J. Finegan, "Chronology of the NT," *ISBE*; J. Barr, "Why the World Was Created in 4004 B.C.: Archbishop Ussher and Biblical Chronology," *BJRL* 67 (1985): 575-605; J. J. Bimson, *Redating the Exodus and Conquest* and "Redating the Exodus," *BAR* 8/5 (Sep-Oct 1982): 40-68; G. Caird, "Chronology of the NT," *IDB*; D. L. Christensen, "Biblical Genealogies and Eschatological Speculation," *PRS* 14 (1987): 59-65; "Job and the Age of the Patriarchs," *PRS* 13 (1986): 225-28; S. J. De Vries, "Chronology of the OT," *IDB* and *IDBSupp*; J. Finegan, *Handbook of Biblical Chronology*; A. R. Green, "The Chronology of the Last Days of Judah: Two Apparent Discrepancies," *JBL* 101 (1982): 57-73; J. Hayes and P. Hooker, *A New Chronology for the Kings of Israel and Judah*; J. Hayes and J. Miller, eds., *Israelite and Judean History*: 678-83; D. Henige, "Comparative Chronology and the Ancient Near East: A Case for Symbiosis," *BASOR* 261 (1986): 57-68; S. H. Horn, "From Bishop Ussher to Edwin R. Thiele," *AUSS* 18 (1980): 37-49; R. Jewett, *A Chronology of Paul's Life*; M. Johnson, *The Purpose of Biblical Genealogies*; G. Luedemann, *Paul, Apostle to the Gentiles; Studies in Chronology*, vol. 1; J. Oswalt, "Chronology of the OT," *ISBE*; J. Shenkel, *Chronology and Recensional Development in the Greek Text of Kings*; E. Shulman, *The Sequence of Events in the Old Testament*; H. Tadmor, "The Chronology of the First Temple Period," *The World History of the Jewish People*; E. J. Thiele, *The Mysterious Numbers of the Hebrew Kings*, 3rd ed.; *A Chronology of the Hebrew Kings*.

—DUANE L. CHRISTENSEN

• **Church.** The word "church" is the English translation of a Gk. word (*ekklēsia*) which means "assembly" or "gathering." In the NT, the word *ekklēsia* is never used to refer to a building or to a denomination. It always refers to a group of people, either local congregations, all believers in a locality, or the whole people of God.

The significance of the NT word *ekklēsia* comes from its earlier use in the Greek translation of the OT (the LXX) to refer to the people of God. In the LXX, *ekklēsia* is used ordinarily to translate a Hebrew word (*qâhâl*) which itself meant "assembly." The Hebrew and Greek words were themselves of no religious significance. They became religiously significant when qualified by the words "God," "Lord," "Most High," etc. Thus, the "assembly of the Lord" (Deut 23:2ff.) and the "assembly of the faithful" (Ps 149:1). The actual character of the *ekklēsia* (as the people of God) is, therefore, not indicated by the word as such; it rather takes its character from the Lord who summons the people to himself, and by the quality of the interest and commitment of those who compose this "assembly" or "congregation."

In its most comprehensive meaning, the church is the whole company of those, in all times and places, who unite themselves, in loyalty and obedience, to God's activity in the world. The church is the people of God, the people who acknowledge God's rule as king and father, those whom he has made peculiarly his own through grace, who have trustingly responded to his judgment and goodness and made themselves free servants of his will. Various metaphors or images are more important for indicating the quality or character of the church than is the word *ekklēsia* itself. Just as ISRAEL, the church has been called "out of Egypt" and brought into full inheritance of the COVENANT promises. Its members function as one body (the instrument for Christ's continuing self-expression in the world); they are the vineyard God tends, the flock he shepherds, the temple he visits, the household of those who are brothers and sisters because they are made sons and daughters of their Father in heaven. They are a "colony of heaven," a fellowship of the divine spirit, a paradigm on earth of the heavenly Kingdom—an approximation in history to the eschatological summation of all things.

Three of these ideas have been treated as most potent both biblically and theologically in the Christian tradition. These are church as: (1) the congregation of the faithful; (2) the BODY OF CHRIST; and (3) the fellowship of the HOLY SPIRIT.

The Congregation of the Faithful. The people of God are gathered (from the world and unto God) either locally (Acts 8:1), or regionally (Acts 9:31; Gal 1:22). They also are regarded generally as the whole of those through whom God now manifests his many-sided wisdom (Eph 3:10). They are gathered in the name of Jesus Christ for the worship and service of God. Remembering its roots in Israel, this "congregation" of God in Christ (while not excluding Israel nor taking Israel's place: Moltmann) may claim the promises and blessings and calling which belong also to Israel as the covenant people (Heb 8:8-10). Thus, in the NT, descriptions of the church's life will make reference to the twelve tribes of Israel (Matt 19:28; Luke 22:30), or to the true CIRCUMCISION (Rom 2:29), or to the descent (even of faithful gentiles) from Abraham (Gal 3:29). Throughout the NT, the church is perceived, also, as a pilgrim and sojourning people—like Israel in Egypt (Heb 11:26; 1 Pet 1:17). This NT people's central rite of worship, the Eucharist, is a redefinition and renewal of the feast of Passover and possibly of the Jewish *Ḥaburah,* a more or less formal meal among devout companions (cf. 1 Cor 10; Mark 6:30-44; Luke 22:1-30). The fact of this community, as an organ through which God is ruling, evokes memories and sentiments associated with the throne of David (Isa 9:7; Luke 1:32-33; Acts 2:30; Col 1:13): Messiah shall reign, and the faithful shall gather at his great feast (Luke 16:23) and reign with him (2 Tim 2:12; Rev 11:15; 22:5).

These people are *one people* on the basis of their common faith in God through Christ. This oneness of faith is not the same as uniformity of doctrine. If the early Christians are one in their commitment to Christ, they certainly are diverse in their ways of understanding the reality and mystery that Christ was and is. All confess faith in Jesus Christ as Lord, but the christological perspectives which interpret this basic confession are varied indeed (cf. the christological understanding, e.g., of Luke with John, or of Colossians with Hebrews).

The church, then, is a renewed Israel brought to its fulfillment (as Christians saw the matter) in the great redemption of Jesus as the Christ. This is their identity: God's people in Christ, Messiah's people. They function in history as a priestly people (Exod 19:3-6; 1 Pet 2:5; Rev 5:10), representing God to the peoples and the peoples to God. They embody faith as trustful obedience, and are in one sense stewards of faith. They embody faith as faithfulness, loyalty, moral commitment—not faith as approved beliefs about God. They are stewards of faith, not as its custodian or *magister*, but as its servants, its witnesses, its interpreters. Their aim, essentially ethical in its sense and direction, is to have among themselves the mind that was also in Christ Jesus (Phil 2:5-8).

This perspective on church as the company of God's faithful people is supported by the whole NT. Jesus' earliest message of the Kingdom is a call to a trusting of life to God as king (Mark 1:15). The apostolic preaching in Jerusalem, in the earliest phase, treated faith as decisive at every point: faith was seen as the means (and, in that sense, as the condition) for entry into the heritage of God's children (Acts 3:16; 4:32; 16:31). John's Gospel even defines the *work* of God as "believing in Jesus whom God has sent" (John 6:29).

It is, however, in Paul that emphasis upon *faith,* as constitutive of the church and as the only proper corollary to revelation and redemption, is given strongest expression. This is the emphasis especially in Galatians and Romans. In Paul, faith is given precedence over law, as in connection with the covenant with Abraham. This giving of precedence to faith over law leads Paul into a full doctrine of the church as those justified by faith—that is, the whole of God's people who are put right with God on the basis of faithful obedience (loyal trust) towards God in terms of Jesus Christ. This justification (and clearly the apostle means justification *sola fide*) brings peace (the cessation of our resistance to God through satisfaction with our own righteousness); it gives access to grace and a joyful hope; and it builds firm character in the freedom and power of the Holy Spirit (Rom 5:1-5). In short, all the blessings of the "divine society" come to us through faith.

Looking at this side of the church's reality, it can be said that the "faithful people of God" are constituted solely on the basis of the divine calling, divine promise, and divine guidance as these are responded to in trustful obedience. In short, *the church is constituted by the Word of God as answered by faith.* (I take BAPTISM to be primarily a "visible *word* of God," and a "confession of *faith.*") This society of faith rests on the ancient promise, is nurtured on the continuing Presence, and moves with God through history towards a divine goal. An illustration of the importance of images for conveying the idea of church is the fact that, while the word "church" is absent from Rom 1–15 (appearing only in chap. 16, in the greetings and blessings), the whole letter is as much a statement on the church and her life in the world as it is on justification by faith.

The Body of Christ. This important Pauline image presents the church as those who have been incorporated into Christ. Commonly, the outward sign of this incorporation, its symbol, and (in one sense) its seal, is baptism. We are baptized *into Christ* (Rom 6:3). Beyond the suggestiveness intrinsic to this metaphor, another idea is especially important for the determination of its meaning: the Hebrew understanding of corporate personality. The individual (who, also in the NT, is never treated as an end in himself or herself) participates *as a member* in "the body of sin," "the old self," the self in "slavery to sin," and as captive to "the body of death" (Rom 6:6; 7:24; 8:10). We arrive in the world as members of a human race which knows guilt, shame, moral apathy, alienation, and "lawlessness." We are affected by this fact from our first breath until our last.

We participate, willy-nilly, in the losses and blessings of the human race. It is this race which Christ died to redeem. The race is redeemed! The continued existence of the race is its opportunity to learn what that redemption means and to realize it as a way of life in the world.

But just as we participate as members in the body's sin and loss, so do we live in Christ with all the redeemed. By God's grace we are made *members of his body*; we are "in Christ." Sin, and death which is its issue, no longer hold dominion over us (Rom 8). Christ's life is now given expression even in our mortal body (2 Cor 4:1-12).

One of the most potent of ethical motifs appears in this metaphor of the apostle. For, we are not only members of Christ and called to share in those virtues and values which God has put forward in him, we are also members one of another—a concrete social organism in which each member has his proper place and value (1 Cor 12:12-27), and upon whom has come an *agapē* equally liberating and compelling (1 Cor 13). Thus each is free; but all are interdependent or mutually obligated.

The life of the body is grounded in the transcendent, but it is exercised in the world. Paul sees the life of the body as a vital, mutual, continuing process whose proximate end is maturity in the graces (Phil 4:8-9), valor in the moral struggle (Eph 6:10-20), and whose final end is glorification and eternal life with him in whom we are given this great salvation (1 Cor 15:51-53), this cosmic freedom (Rom 8:18-21).

This is the vital, mutual, continuing process by which the church becomes what in the design of God it is. There are affinities here, especially for two other metaphors: (1) the vine, emphasizing the location of the church's root in Christ and the production of her fruits through continued association of the branches with the vine (John 15:1-11); and (2) the temple or building, in which we are being built into a "spiritual house," to function as a holy priesthood, to offer "spiritual sacrifices" acceptable to God in Christ—in short, the church as a place of organic life ("*living* stones"), of celebration ("spiritual sacrifices"), of proclamation ("declaring the mighty deeds"), and divine approval ("now you are God's people") (1 Pet 2:4-10).

Such metaphors—that of the body plus these used to extend its meaning—disclose a corporate life in which God's people, Christ's body, is held together in a common life "over which Christ rules, and through which a new creation emerges, a new humanity in Christ" (Minear). Paul coins a phrase with which to characterize this *koinōnia* or communion of life: being "in Christ" (Gal 2:20) and so built into one another through the receiving and sharing of *agapē*.

Here is the ground of the church's unity: Christ is not divided, and those who are "in Christ" are united in Christ—they form his body as *members*, they were baptized *in his name* (1 Cor 1:13). Party-spirit, faction, overconfidence in one's own understanding of the gospel, all divide and threaten Christ's body. The Eucharist (1 Cor 10, 11), as the sign of this unity, is a sharing in *one* loaf and *one* cup. Done in faith, in a state of *agapē* with one's neighbor, it is participation (*koinōnia*, Vulgate *participatio*) in the life and redemptive self-giving (the body and blood) of Christ.

The members of this body enter freely (voluntarily, i.e., out of an act of their own volition) into this corporate relationship. But this is an opting for membership in the body; it is not the creation of it. Faithful people volunteer, but the "body of Christ" is only in a secondary sense a "voluntary association of baptized believers." Primarily, it is a living organism whose existence does not depend on the vote of even baptized believers. We have a voice in whether we will be members of the body: we have no voice in whether there is such a body of Christ. For this body has its reality and takes its character not from its members but from its head. Jesus Christ alone is the source of the "sanctification" of this body (Eph 5:26), the truth on which it is built up (Eph 4:15), the moral power by which its members are brought to obedience (Col 2:10), are equipped for ministry and brought to maturity (Eph 4:12-14), and to a unified life in Christ and with each other (Eph 4).

The church as body, then, is the model of Christ's continuing self-expression in the world. This is why the church is sometimes described as "the continuation of the incarnation." I believe it might more helpfully be called (with T. W. Manson) the "extension of our Lord's Messianic ministry."

The Fellowship of the Holy Spirit. Lesslie Newbigin and Jürgen Moltmann have done well to stress this Spirit-dimension of the church's reality. Newbigin has seen the "giveness" of the reality of the church as body as its *organic* (Catholic) dimension; the "given" message, responded to in faith, as the *evangelical* (Protestant) principle, and the emphasis upon church as the community of the "given" Spirit he labels the *Pentecostal* principle. No doctrine of church can be fully a NT doctrine which ascribes small weight to this. The church as "community of the Spirit" exists, to be sure, as those who confess a *common* faith (Eph 4:4-6), it exists as those who know a *common* life in the body of Christ; and it should be noted that the word for "fellowship" (*koinōnia*) means life lived *in common*. But as a *common faith* does not mean unanimity in the understanding of faith, so does the common life of the body leave room for individual members (individual roles and functions). We are "saints," not clones. This *koinōnia* of the Spirit gives prominence to singular experiences, to the freedom of faith and life, to the unpredictable dimensions of faith acting in situations where no "preapproved" guidelines exist. As much as it is anything else at all, the church is "where the Holy Spirit [is] recognizably present with power" (Newbigin). It exists where lives are actually changed, are turned from their condition into their possibility. Little attention is given here to either order or creed. Emphasis falls on the presence, the power, the purpose of God the Spirit (Acts 2, 4, 10). It is this given Spirit who makes us belong to Christ (Rom 8:9); this Spirit is the power and sign of our obedience (Acts 5:32); and this Spirit is the title-deed of our final inheritance (Eph 1:14).

If, however, the Spirit works in members in ways unique to each, in the broadest and deepest sense the Holy Spirit is the *Spirit of the body* (in a quite exact sense, the *esprit de corps*). The NT makes room for spontaneity, for singularity, for the individual member—it is not an encouragement to individualism. The Spirit is given to us as members of the body, to us as those who confess authentic faith with our lives. "Winging it alone," "free-lance evangelism," and "untested private revelations" are very difficult to square with a biblically oriented faith. It is the reality and activity of the Holy Spirit which identify the church, and such things that violate the common life and the common faith of Christians also violate the church as the fellowship of God's Spirit.

At the same time, neither does confession, correct doctrine, rightly observing the sacraments, or maintaining membership in an organized church make one a Christian. This is the result alone of God's Holy Spirit bringing us into *living* relationship with Jesus as Savior and Lord. This makes for at least a "semi-sectarian" potential in the church in its fullness. This is dangerous but nothing is fatal to the church's life if exercised in *agapē*. The reality of the church, the mission of the church, and the hope of the church are guaranteed only in the giving, receiving, and sharing of *agapē*. All the potential one-sidedness of individual spiritual experience is contained within this wholeness.

To conclude: the church is a result of the divine calling (election), is sustained by the divine presence (grace), works with the divine purpose(s) in history (calling), and moves towards the far-off distant goal of creation and the new creation (consummation). The most decisive sign of its "churchliness" appears in terms of its mission in and to the world. "The Church exists by mission as fire exists by burning" (Brunner). It must not simply *have missionaries*; the church must *be mission*. For the church is the servant of God's Word in Christ (Barth); or witness to the New Being (Tillich); or the community whose purpose is the increase of love of God and Neighbor (H. R. Niebuhr); or the embodiment of what the Christian hopes is present as an unrecognized reality even outside of organized Christianity (Rahner); or it is that worshiping community which, through faith, receives God's act of justification of sinners as the truth about ourselves and also as hope for the whole world (Wainwright).

Christ loved this church and gave himself up for us all (Eph 5:25). We are related to each other in terms of our relationship to Christ and his church; failure of consideration and of kindness towards any one of us is, therefore, to "despise the church of God" (1 Cor 11:22).

See also BAPTISM; BODY OF CHRIST; CIRCUMCISION; COVENANT; FELLOWSHIP; HOLY SPIRIT; ISRAEL; KINGDOM OF GOD; LORD'S SUPPER.

Bibliography. M. Barth, *Israel and the Church;* R. N. Flew, *Jesus and His Church;* J. M. Gustafson, *The Church as Moral Decision Maker;* E. G. Hinson, *The Integrity of the Church;* F. J. A. Hort, *The Christian Ecclesia;* G. Johnston, *The Doctrine of the Church in the New Testament;* T. W. Manson, *The Church's Ministry;* P. Minear, *Images of the Church in the NT;* J. Moltmann, *The Church in the Power of the Spirit;* J. L. Newbigin, *The Household of God;* H. R. Niebuhr, *The Purpose of the Church and Its Ministry;* E. A. Payne, *The Fellowship of Believers;* K. L. Schmidt, *The Church;* L. S.Thornton, *The Common Life in the Body of Christ.*

—THERON D. PRICE

• **Church and Law.** From the earliest days of the church there were debates about the relevance of the OT law for Christians. Evidence of those debates is most obvious in Acts and the Letters of PAUL, but is present throughout much of the NT. The disagreements were serious enough that Titus was warned to avoid quarrels about the law because they are unprofitable and useless (Titus 3:9). Surprisingly, however, the NT documents do not discuss the subject of the OT law in the detail one might expect. There is no information about when the early church stopped performing sacrifices in the Temple. Apart from Hebrews there is little treatment of the subject of the Temple and its sacrifices at all. There is no discussion of laws about annual festivals or of various cleanliness and communal laws. Even the questions of Sabbath-keeping and unclean foods are treated only indirectly.

The Book of Acts. The first people to question the relevance of the law for Christians were the Hellenistic Jewish Christians, who were also the first to preach the gospel to gentiles (Acts 11:19-20). Numerous Jews had developed a Hellenistic mindset while living outside Palestine. On returning to Palestine they maintained their own communities and synagogues. Some of these Hellenistic Jews became Christians and were quicker than Palestinian Jewish Christians to draw conclusions about the effect of Christ's coming.

STEPHEN was a Hellenistic Jewish Christian, and Acts 6–7 narrates his confrontation with other Hellenistic Jews. Stephen was accused (falsely according to Luke) of speaking against the law and against the Temple (6:11-14). Stephen's defense in Acts 7 does not say anything negative about the law. In fact, he referred to the revelation to Moses on Mount Sinai as "living words" and accused the Jews of not obeying the law (7:38, 53). However, Stephen's insistance that God does not dwell in temples made by human hands diminished the importance of the Temple.

Another controversy about the law resulted from PETER's preaching the gospel to the household of CORNELIUS, a gentile (Acts 10–11). Two visions from God (one to Cornelius and one to Peter) were required before Peter would consider entering the house of a gentile. Peter had already begun to relax his Jewish scruples by living in the house of a tanner, but he still kept kosher food laws. In his dream unclean food was presented to him to eat. When he refused the food saying he had never eaten unclean foods, he was told, "What God has cleansed, you must not call common" (10:15). Rather than applying this statement to discussions about food, Acts applies it to relations with gentiles (10:28, 34-35). The Jewish laws requiring separation from gentiles were no longer valid. That the Holy Spirit came upon gentiles as well as on Jews validated the legitimacy of Peter's visiting and eating with gentiles (11:1-18).

The largest debate about the law is the account of the JERUSALEM COUNCIL in Acts 15. Jewish Christians with a Pharisaic tendency argued that gentile Christians had to be circumcised and keep the law in order to have salvation (15:5). The debate apparently began in Antioch, but Paul had to write to the Galatians about this same issue or one very nearly like it. A delegation was sent from Antioch to the apostles and elders in Jerusalem to settle the matter. Peter related his experience with Cornelius and referred to the law as a "yoke . . . which neither our fathers nor we have been able to bear" (15:10). This statement and the comment in 13:39 are the only derogatory statements made about the law in the Book of Acts. After Paul and Barnabas told of gentiles responding to the gospel, James gave a summary decision. Nothing from the law was to be placed as an obstacle to the conversion of gentiles, but a letter was sent to ask gentiles to avoid food sacrificed to idols, sexual immorality, meat from strangled animals, and blood. These items were all offensive to Jews because of the commands in Lev 17–18. Gentiles were asked to avoid them so that Jews could still be attracted to Christianity (Acts 15:19-21). (The avoidance of food sacrificed to idols continued to be debated in the church, as can be seen in Rom 14–15; 1 Cor 8–10; and Rev 2:14.)

The decision not to require gentiles to observe ritual aspects of the law was one of the most important decisions the early church made. A distinction was made between law and gospel, but there was no discussion about the relevance of the ethical aspects of the law. If the gentiles had been required to observe the ritual requirements of the law, Christianity probably would not have survived as an independent religion. While the early church seems to have distinguished between ritual and ethical aspects of the law, this is never explicitly stated. Many Jews would have viewed such a distinction as strange.

Acts relates other incidents that show the debates over the law in the first century. In 16:3 Paul is reported to have circumcised TIMOTHY because of the Jews in the area. Since Timothy's mother was a Jew, he would have been considered to be one as well. Omission of CIRCUMCISION in his case would have eliminated any chance of his being involved in a mission to the Jews. In 21:17-26 Paul is reported to have performed a Jewish purification vow to demonstrate to the Jews that, contrary to reports, he lived in obedience to the law. Many scholars doubt that Paul would have performed such a vow, but others appropriately argue that such action would agree with Paul's attempts to identify culturally with various groups insofar as possible (1 Cor 9:19-23). Paul, like Stephen, was arrested on the charge that he taught people against the law and the Temple (Acts 21:28). Paul denied this charge in several of the defense speeches recorded in the remaining chapters of Acts (24:14; 25:8; and 28:17).

There are many issues not discussed in Acts, but it is clear that Luke believed Paul and other Christians did not violate the law even though most did not keep ritual aspects of the law and no such observance was required of gentiles.

The Writings of Paul. The most heated debate about the law is reflected in Galatians. People usually referred to as "Judaizers" had persuaded the Galatian Christians that gentiles should be circumcised and follow the Mosaic Law. Earlier in Antioch even Peter and Barnabas stopped eating with gentiles because of their fear of Jews who insisted on the law (Gal 2:11-13). Paul resisted Peter to his face because he saw Peter's action as a violation of the gospel. Paul similarly saw the willingness of the Galatian Christians to follow the Jewish law as an attempt to follow another gospel. The only gospel he knew was the gospel of freedom in Christ. Paul's assumption is that a person is acquitted (justified) before God only on the basis of FAITH, not by "works of law" (Gal 2:16).

The rest of Galatians explains Paul's gospel of freedom and also explains how Paul viewed the law. The law was never intended to be a way to God. People always come to God by faith as the example of Abraham shows (3:6-18). The law is secondary to promise, but had the positive purpose of guarding people and bringing them to Christ (Gal 3:19-24). Paul saw any attempt to gain standing before God by ritual observance as a return to slavery and as a forfeit of relation to Christ (Gal 5:2-4). The gospel is a gospel of freedom, not law (5:1). The function of the law was temporary, yet at the same time Paul expected the love commands to be fulfilled by Christians (5:14). Paul's concern was to deny that regulations such as circumcision, food laws, and Sabbath-keeping had anything to do with standing before God. Such regulations were marks of separation between Jews and gentiles, but Paul asserted that racial, class, and gender distinctions were meaningless. "There is neither Jew nor Greek, there is neither slave nor free, there is neither male nor female" (Gal 3:28). To follow the law with its marks of distinction would destroy the unity that faith had achieved.

The discussion of the law in Romans parallels that of Galatians closely, but is more complete and does not reflect the heat of controversy. Romans demonstrates that the moral law too, not just the ritual aspects of the law, was viewed negatively by Paul. Even the good parts of the law, like the command not to covet, were tools that sin used to bring rebellion and cause death. The problem with law is its association with sin and the "flesh," by which Paul meant human effort that leaves God out of consideration (Rom 7:5, 13). Paul still viewed the law positively. The law distinguished right from wrong, and Paul expected that what the law taught morally would be lived by the person made alive by the Spirit. The problem was not with the law, but with sinful humans.

Paul's radical approach to the law is seen most easily in 1 Cor 7:19: "For neither circumcision counts for anything nor uncircumcision, but keeping the commandments of God" (cf. Gal 5:6; 6:15). Ritual observance, or the lack of it, is insignificant; obedience is what is important before God. The surprising fact is that circumcision had been one of the OT commands. Obviously Paul and other Christians made distinctions in the law, as Jews had before them. The prophets and Jesus called for mercy, not sacrifice (Mic 6:6-8; Matt 12:7). The authors of the Dead Sea Scrolls focused on spiritual rather than literal sacrifices (*1QS* 8.5-10). The problem is that none of these persons explains how distinctions were made in the law.

Paul's freedom in Christ allowed him to live like a Jew in conformity with the law or like a gentile without the law. Even so, he saw himself as loyal to God's law because he was obedient to the law of Christ (1 Cor 9:19-21).

Outside Romans and Galatians, references in Paul's writings to disputes over the law are infrequent. Phil 3:2-11 refers to the "dogs" who were advocating circumcision and a righteousness based on law. Col 2:16 warns against those who condemn others on the basis of food, times of the year, and Sabbaths. The Jewish opponents Paul faced in Corinth may have caused debate about the law (cf. 2 Cor 3), but this does not seem to have been the main point of contention.

Faith and Works. The discussion of faith and works is part of the discussion of the controversies over the law. When Paul rejected the view that salvation came from works, he was not rejecting the importance of obedience for Christians. The plural "works" is nearly always negative in Paul's writings, but the singular "work" is nearly always positive. Paul's use of the expression "works of law" refers to human activities designed to present people to God, and his primary reference is to those stipulations of the law like circumcision that separated Jews from gentiles. Paul would not accept that Jewish exclusivism brings salvation; only faith brings salvation.

Paul rejected works as a means of salvation, but he did not reject the *work* of faith. He repeated most of the Ten Commandments and urged his readers to the same kind of moral attitudes and actions the OT taught. He summarized his ministry as the attempt to call Gentiles to the *obedience* of faith (Rom 1:5). Paul expected the same productive life of faith that the rest of the Bible promotes.

James does not use words like "works" or "faith" in the same way Paul does. James is almost certainly reacting against a misunderstanding of Paul's teaching on faith and the law, a misunderstanding that Paul himself had to combat (Rom 3:8; 6:1). James rejected the possibility of an unproductive faith being useful for salvation. Although his language is different, Paul would have agreed (1 Cor 13:2). Both writers expected a life of obedience characterized by the love commands.

Other Indications of Controversy over the Law. Other NT writings point to controversies over the law as well. Although there is little discussion of the Temple and sacrifices outside Hebrews, there is emphasis on the replacement of the Temple by Jesus. Matt 12:6-7 points to Jesus as one greater than the Temple and emphasizes mercy rather than sacrifice. John 2:19-21 indicates that Jesus was referring to his body when he said, "Destroy this temple, and in three days I will raise it up." John 4:20-24 effectively nullifies the importance of the Temple by saying that worship is to be done in spirit and truth rather than on a Samaritan mountain or in Jerusalem.

Matthew especially reflects debates about the proper understanding of law between the religious authorities and Jesus and also between Matthew's community and its Jewish neighbors. The primary concerns of Matthew are to show the continuing validity of the law, the summation of the law in the love commands, and the rejection of hypocrisy and legalism.

Conclusion. The early church did not find a simple explanation to the question of the significance of the law. There was no sympathy for the external requirements of the law, but the church objected to more than externals. There were definite changes in the way the law was viewed. Certainly the coming of Jesus rendered the sacrificial system obsolete. Jesus and most of the church rejected the concern of the holiness code to separate righteous people from unclean food, unclean items, and unclean people. Instead of the holiness code, Jesus emphasized the aspects of the law that focused on mercy, love, and justice. The church likewise focused on these items as the will of God, and therefore held the law to be of permanent significance.

See also APOSTLES, ACTS OF THE; CIRCUMCISION; CORNELIUS; FAITH; GALATIANS, LETTER TO THE; JAMES, LETTER OF; JERUSALEM COUNCIL; LAW IN THE NEW TESTAMENT; LAW IN THE OLD TESTAMENT; PAUL; ROMANS, LETTER TO THE; STEPHEN.

Bibliography. R. Banks, *Jesus and the Law in the Synoptic Tradition*; C. L. Blomberg, "The Law in Luke-Acts," *JSNT* 22 (1984): 53-80; C. E. B. Cranfield, "St. Paul and the Law," *SJT* 17 (1964): 43-68; W. D. Davies, "Law in the New Testament," *Jewish and Pauline Studies*; M. Dibelius, *Studies in the Acts of the Apostles*; G. Ebeling, *The Truth of the Gospel*; D. P. Fuller, *Gospel and Law: Contrast or Continuum?*; H. Hübner, *Law in Paul's Thought*; J. Jervell, "Law in Luke-Acts," *HTR* 64 (1971): 21-36; R. S. McConnell, *Law and Prophecy in Matthew's Gospel*; H. Räisänen, *Paul and the Law*; E. P. Sanders, *Paul, the Law, and the Jewish People*; M. H. Scharlemann, *Stephen: A Singular Saint*; A. Schlatter, *The Church in the New Testament Period*; M. Simon, *St. Stephen and the Hellenists in the Primitive Church*; G. S. Sloyan, *Is Christ the End of the Law?*; S. G. Wilson, *Luke and the Law.*

—KLYNE R. SNODGRASS

• **Chuza.** *See* JOANNA

• **Cilicia.** *See* SYRIA AND CILICIA

• **Church of the Holy Sepulchre.** The Church of the Holy Sepulchre is a historic church building in Jerusalem erected over the traditional sites of the crucifixion, burial, and resurrection of Jesus. It is one of the most celebrated of all Christian churches. Constantine, the first Christian emperor to rule Palestine, initiated an effort in the fourth century to recover the holy places of Christianity. Following the Council of Nicea in 325 C.E., Constantine directed Macarius, the Bishop of Jerusalem, to identify the site of the "holy sepulchre," the Jerusalem cave where Joseph of Arimathea buried Jesus (Matt 27:59, 60). Eusebius, Constantine's ecclesiastical advisor and biographer, described the discovery of the tomb of Jesus which had been buried beneath a temple to Venus. After commanding the pagan temple demolished, Constantine commissioned the building of the Church of the Holy Sepulchre. Initially covering only the site of the burial and resurrection of Jesus, the church, during the period of the Crusades, was enlarged to include the place of the death of Jesus. According to John 19:41, the tomb and Calvary were located near each other.

Whether the Church of the Holy Sepulchre marks the authentic location of Jesus' death and resurrection has been vigorously debated by scholars. One objection, among others, to this claim is the fact that the present church is located within the walls of the old city of Jerusalem. The NT, however, implies that Jesus was crucified outside the city walls (John 19:20; Heb 13:12). Evidence exists that the site was outside the walls of first-century Jerusalem; no indisputable proof exists, however, to corroborate the long tradition surrounding the Church of the Holy Sepulchre.

See also CALVARY; TOMB OF JESUS.

—WALTER B. SHURDEN

• **Churches of Revelation.** Individual letters are addressed to seven churches of western Asia Minor in chaps. 2 and 3 of the BOOK OF REVELATION. The sevenfold pattern is found throughout the book, and some interpreters have thought that the seven churches represent the seven-branched menorah, or candlestick, which appears in the opening vision of the book. Some have even imposed the outline of a menorah upon the map of the seven cities and tried to pair the "good" churches and the "bad" churches in a symmetrical way. Others have speculated that the churches represent seven district capitals or postal zones that would have assured the wide distribution of this writing.

The first city is EPHESUS (Rev 2:1-7), magnificently excavated, revealing a beautiful Roman theater, the Temple of Diana (Aphrodite), a long marble street with temples and monuments, and traditional tombs of Mary the mother of Jesus and the apostle John. Site of a powerful early Christian bishopric, meeting place of ecumenical councils, the church exerted great influence in Christendom. SMYRNA (2:8-11) is the modern Turkish city of Izmir, with the ancient city fully excavated, confirming the influence of this early Christian church in a coastal city of Anatolia, seat of influential bishops, and recipient of letters from Polycarp and other patristic writers.

The third church is in PERGAMUM (2:12-17), the northernmost coastal city (modern Bergama), with Smyrna in the middle and Ephesus at the southernmost point. "Satan's throne" (v. 13) is thought to be the magnificent marble Temple of Zeus, which has been removed and rebuilt, stone by stone, in East Berlin. The faithful martyr, Antipas, was from this church (v. 13). The four remaining churches are all inland and complete a clockwise circle (begun with the northward sweep up the coast) southward from THYATIRA (where Jezebel, a self-styled prophetess leads the church into sexual immorality, 2:20); to SARDIS (3:1-6), where some pure and faithful people are commended for not "soiling their garments" with sinful practices; to PHILADELPHIA (3:7-13) which has "kept my word of patient endurance"; and, finally, to LAODICEA (3:14-22), which is not only the last, but the absolute nadir of spirituality, being "neither cold nor hot" and about to be spit out of the Lord's mouth (vv. 16).

Whatever specific references may apply historically to

each church, it is clear that as a complete group of seven churches they represent the main challenges to Christianity in Asia Minor near the end of the first century: corruption by immorality so prevalent in that day, "synagogue of Satan," perhaps a Jewish distortion and threat to faithful Christians in most of the churches; "Satan's throne," probably compulsory pagan or emperor-worship, enforced by the death penalty; and, most of all, lethargy and indifference of Christians. Such an analysis of the threats extends the relevance of these warnings throughout the history of the church: corruption by society; corruption by the state; and death by indifference!

See also EPHESUS; LAODICEA; PERGAMUM; PHILADELPHIA; REVELATION, BOOK OF; SARDIS; SMYRNA; THYATIRA.

Bibliography. J. W. Bowman, *The Drama of the Book of Revelation*; W. Ramsay, *Letters to the Seven Churches*; E. Akurgal, *Ancient Civilizations and Ruins of Turkey*.

—WAYNE E. WARD

• **Circumcision.** The act of excising the foreskin from the male genital. The provisions of the Pentateuch call for the circumcision of every Israelite male (Lev 12:2-3) as well as every slave (Exod 12:44) and even the resident alien who wishes to participate in the PASSOVER (Exod 12:48). Circumcision was not unique to the Israelites, but was widespread in the ancient Near East. It was practiced by other semitic tribes, the Egyptians, the Phoenicians, in fact by most of ISRAEL's neighbors excepting the Babylonians, Assyrians, and Philistines. Where the practice originated is unknown. The Greek historian Herodotus traced it to the Egyptians, and archaeological evidence does verify that it was practiced there as early as 3000 B.C.E. Jews and Muslims continue to circumcise as a religious rite, and circumcision is a common rite-of-passage for many African tribes as well as a widespread contemporary medical practice.

History of Circumcision in Israel. The original meaning of circumcision for Israel is uncertain and highly debated. Some scholars believe it originated as a puberty rite, connected with the onset of sexual potency. In ancient EGYPT, it was performed on boys of fourteen, and girls of the same age were subjected to an analogous operation. The circumcision of Ishmael took place when he was thirteen (Gen 17:25), and Israel's semitic neighbors likewise circumcised boys at puberty. A connection of circumcision with sexuality can perhaps be detected in Exod 4:24-26 where Zipporah's circumcising her *son* is said to have established MOSES as her "bridegroom of blood." Many scholars believe an original tradition of Moses' circumcision has been conformed here to the later practice of infant circumcision. There are indications that the practice was not always strictly maintained in Israel's early period. For example, an account in Josh 5:2-9 relates how all the sons of Israel who had been born in the wilderness period underwent a mass adult circumcision because they had not been circumcised as infants.

By the exilic period, circumcision of infants was the established practice. The priestly account of Gen 17:9-27 traces circumcision to ABRAHAM and interprets it as a mark of membership in God's covenant people (v. 10). The operation is to be performed on all males the eighth day from their birth (v. 12). Infant circumcision seems to have been a unique development among the Jews, and some scholars would see in this an indication that circumcision had come to take on associations of atonement and sacrifice. The later Mishnaic provisions for performance of the rite seem to bear this out with their insistence that blood must be shed (*Šabb* 19:2).

With the prophets one finds a non-cultic metaphorical interpretation of circumcision. JEREMIAH, for instance, spoke of Israel's uncircumcised ears that were dull of hearing (6:10) and of God's impending judgment on the people of Israel because of their uncircumcised hearts (9:25-26). This figurative usage would be taken up later by the apostle PAUL, but the dominant view of circumcision in postexilic Judaism was as a sign of membership in God's covenant people. Written during the Maccabean period, the book of *Jubilees* gives ample testimony to the high importance placed on circumcision as a sign of the covenant. It describes the rite as an eternal ordinance written on heavenly tablets (15:25), maintains that even the angels in heaven are all circumcised (15:27), and consigns all who do not bear the mark to eternal destruction (15:26). Without circumcision there is no salvation. Such an extreme view explains why many Jewish mothers were willing to die rather than leave their children uncircumcised when Antiochus Epiphanes forbade the practice (1 Macc 1:60-61). Such zeal for the rite also accounts for the mass circumcision of subject peoples such as the Idumeans by John Hyrcanus and the Itureans by Alexander Jannaeus (Josephus, *Ant* 8.257, 318).

Circumcision in the NT Era. Greeks and Romans seem never to have practiced circumcision and generally viewed it as crude and uncivilized. With the extension of their influence during the Hellenistic period, the practice was increasingly abandoned. For instance, Herodotus mentions that contact with Greeks led the Phoenicians to abandon the practice (*Hist* 2.104), and under Roman influence Egyptians seem to have curtailed the practice severely, limiting it solely to the priesthood. Roman satirists like Juvenal and Martial ridiculed the practice, viewing it as a sign of Jewish barbarity and superstition. In the early second century the Emperor Hadrian attempted to ban circumcision, and the Roman historian Spartian saw this as a major cause of the Jewish revolt under Bar Kochba (*Hadrianus* 14.2). Jewish apologists such as PHILO sought to defend the practice by appealing to its medical value or by resorting to the prophetic metaphorical interpretation of "heart circumcision," (*SpecLeg* 1.4-7), but such attempts did little to assuage the general Greco-Roman prejudice against the alien rite.

This conflict between Jewish and gentile views of circumcision is strongly reflected in the NT. The word is often used to distinguish between the two: the Jews are "the circumcised," the gentiles "the uncircumcised" (Rom 3:30; 4:9; 15:8; Gal 2:7-9; Eph 2:11; Titus 1:10). Indeed, there were those in early Jewish Christianity who insisted that there could be no membership in the new community of faith without the covenant mark of circumcision. Luke describes them as "those of the circumcision" (Acts 11:2). They represented the traditional Jewish understanding that all PROSELYTES to Judaism must be circumcised as a sign of membership in the covenant people. Since Christianity was a Jewish messianic sect, it followed logically for them that a gentile must first become a Jew in order to be a Christian, and conversion to Judaism entailed circumcision and observance of the Mosaic Law (Acts 15:2, 5). Paul did not see it that way. Whatever precedents or convictions about the messianic age may have led Paul in his decision not to circumcise gentile converts, the step was a key to the success of that mission. Given the gentile attitudes toward the rite, circumcision would have likely presented an insuperable barrier to the spread of the gospel outside Judaism. As it was, the Jerusalem leadership endorsed Paul's circumcision-free mission to the gentiles and maintained a separate witness to the Jews (Gal 2:1-10). The Jewish Christians continued to circumcise their infants and in general to abide by the Jewish law. There resulted in effect two types of Christians, the circumcised and the uncircumcised.

Paul continued to be troubled by the stricter Jewish Christian "Judaizers," who insisted that gentiles live by the whole law, including its ceremonial aspects. It is interesting to note that in Galatians, where the Judaizing threat was acute, Paul particularly centered on circumcision as the most offensive part of their agenda (5:12; 6:12-13). In his gentile mission, Paul ceased to believe the actual rite had any meaning: "neither circumcision nor uncircumcision means anything, but faith working through love . . . but a new creation" (Gal 5:6; 6:15). When he does speak positively of circumcision, it is in the language of the prophets, of that inward circumcision of the heart, wrought by the Spirit (Rom 2:29). At Colossae, Paul seems to have encountered a maverick practice of circumcision, where some of the gentiles were undergoing the rite as a sign of devotion through mortification of the flesh. To them he responds with another figurative reference, describing the believer's experience of dying with Christ as a complete "putting off of the flesh in the circumcision of Christ" (Col 2:11). The believer participates in Christ's death on the cross, and this comprises the complete mortification of the old self that renders any subsequent fleshly self-abnegation superfluous. For Paul, there simply remained no religious significance for the physical rite of circumcision under any interpretation, and so it has remained for gentile Christians to this day.

Bibliography. G. R. Beasley-Murray, *Baptism in the New Testament*; J. P. Hyatt, "Circumcision," *IDB*; J. M. Sasson, "Circumcision in the Ancient Near East," *JBL* 85 (1966): 473–76.

—JOHN B. POLHILL

• **Cistern.** *See* WATER SYSTEMS

• **City/Cities.** *Definition.* The city of premodern times can be described as a settled community of a numerous and dense population. Its inhabitants were largely engaged in specialized occupations, dependent upon food produced by others extracted through various forms of taxation, and stratified by class. Monumental architecture (e.g., a TEMPLE or FORTIFICATION system) represents an essential concrete manifestation of urban life, requiring a large, organized and directed labor force. The city is an integral element in a larger settlement region upon which it is dependent and over which it exercises some degree of control.

Perspectives on Urban Life. The prominent role played by cities in biblical history and tradition has long been obvious, but perspectives on the role of urban life in the Bible have changed markedly over the past two decades. The long-prevailing notion of a "nomadic ideal" which saw ancient Israel as fundamentally antagonistic to "city life" has been abandoned. The wholesale rejection of the sedentary life plays no part in the biblical view of the city. Instead, the dynamic of Israel's social history grows out of a fundamental conflict in the interdependent relationship of urban and rural life in which the socially stratified and powerful urban center presses its advantage to the detriment of the village-based sector. Alongside the recognition that biblical criticism of the city is rooted in this social and political opposition has grown a second fundamental realization. Biblical tradition itself has a decidedly urban orientation. Jerusalem-based groups preserved and transmitted the Hebrew Scriptures, and the Greco-Roman city was the dominant environment of the Christian movement. In both testaments, eschatological visions project the future life in a new city (Isa 65:17-25; Rev 21:1–22:5).

Characteristics of Cities. (1) Locations. The cities of ancient Palestine and the eastern Mediterranean share a set of factors which account for their locations and help explain their relative importance. This set consists of the availability of natural resources, the existence of economic networks (trade routes and lines of communication), the type of political organization, the defensibility of a particular site, and its religio-cultic traditions. Each city expresses its own balance of these factors, though in some cases one may stand out. CORINTH and MEGIDDO, for example, possess strategic locations with respect to trade. EPHESUS with its temple to ARTEMIS and JERUSALEM with its tenured importance to Judaism highlight the influence of religio-cultic traditions. The capital cities of ANTIOCH-on-the-Orontes and CAESAREA both owe their existence to political decisions which counted heavily upon strategic locations.

(2) Size. Estimates of the sizes of ancient cities are very rough. In keeping with modern parallels, an average density figure of between 160 to 200 tightly packed persons per urban acre can be used to arrive at a maximal site population. Palestine's small-sized cities had correspondingly small populations. Jerusalem at its largest reached a population of about 30,000. Antioch-on-the-Orontes achieved five times the size of Jerusalem but remained small by modern standards. The high density and small size of these cities work together to create low levels of privacy in which rumors and riots would spread quickly.

(3) Architectural features. The most important feature of the ancient city was the fortification system; the Roman goddess of the city, Fortuna, aptly wore a "wall crown." Archaeologists have concentrated a great deal of energy on elucidating the gates and walls and towers that constituted a city's basic defense. The gate was the centerpiece of the system and the hub of civic and commercial activity in the cities of ancient Israel. Most often, traffic climbed an incline parallel to the city wall and then turned sharply to enter through the gate. The path through the gate was dominated by two, three or four sets of piers which jutted out into it and created a series of chambers on either side. The chambers were lined with benches for guards or officials or elders who are said to administer justice "in the gate" (Deut 21:19; Josh 20:4; Ruth 4). A wooden door secured the outside entrance (Judg 16:3) whose width stretched to about four meters. Towers rose above the doorway on either side, providing added firepower around this weak point in the defense system. The Solomonic gates uncovered at Hazor, Megiddo and Gezer are the classic examples of the gate.

A variety of wall types led away from the gates to encompass the city. During Solomon's time a particular type of wall construction gained prominence. This wall—dubbed the "casemate wall"—consisted of solid outside and inside walls connected at intervals by perpendicular walls to create a series of "cases." These spaces were frequently filled with rubble so that a minimum of solid wall construction created a maximum thickness of wall, usually about five meters. The spaces could also be incorporated into the adjoining buildings as was the case in the later city wall of BEERSHEBA. After the period of the United Monarchy city perimeters were often protected by solid walls of stone designed with salients and recesses and usually mounted with mud brick superstructures. This "offset-inset" wall is well preserved at Megiddo, SAMARIA, HAZOR as well as LACHISH and the later Judean site of Ramat Rahel and may mirror the advent of Assyrian military campaigns in Palestine. City walls were often strengthened by a glacis, a sloping earth and stone structure which protected their foundations. Though only their foundations are generally preserved, the walls probably reached an average height of eight to ten m.

The strong and often indomitable fortification systems that protected cities produced the military strategy of the siege. To enable the city to withstand a protracted siege, considerable energy and engineering skill were marshaled to guarantee access to water. Waterworks are a conspicuous feature of the most important cities of Palestine. Hezekiah's tunnel (2 Kgs 20:20), built in anticipation of the Assyrian siege, stands as the most well-known example. It cut through over 500 m. of hard limestone to direct the waters of the spring at the foot of the city to a secure outlet within the walls. The outside entrance to the spring was sealed off. More frequently encountered are shaft systems which aim to tap a water-bearing layer of rock by tunneling a vertical shaft down to its level from within the city. Such systems have been found in the Israelite cities of Gibeon, Megiddo, Gezer, and Hazor. The Hazor installation included a wide rectangular shaft that reached down over forty meters and was bordered by a descending stairway. At its bottom a sloping path descended fifteen m. further, ending in a pool at the water table. A similar attempt to give access to the spring at Jerusalem's perimeter was a precursor to Hezekiah's tunnel. The vastness and ingenuity of these projects speaks eloquently about both the resources and fears of the ancient Israelite urbanites.

Within the city walls an acropolis or citadel was usually specially demarcated behind its own wall and elevated above the remainder of the city. This focal area was the site of the temple, palace and other buildings associated with governance. Hazor, Samaria, Arad, Ramat Rahel, and Lachish all witness this basic plan. Besides organizing essential administrative functions, the acropolis served as a place of last resort in battle time (Judg 9:50-52). Dominating the visual aspect of the city, these inner cities were potent symbols of the political power that the city wielded.

The area adjoining the gate on the inside of the city was also directed towards special purposes. At Beersheba, the gate empties out into a complex of administrative buildings on the west and a series of storehouses on the east. The proximity of gate and storehouse is also attested at Hazor and Megiddo, presumably in line with the cities' function as centers for tax collection or armories. In the minor cities careful town planning is evidenced throughout the monarchical period. Tell Beit Mirsim, Beth Shemesh, Tell en-Nasbeh and Beersheba all manifest a ring design with a casemate wall integrated into an outer belt of buildings which are separated from the core of the city by a circular road.

Town planning became a hallmark of the Hellenistic and Roman periods. The Greek city plan comprising a grid of perpendicular streets dividing the city into rectangular blocks (known as the Hippodamian plan) is preserved at Marisa on the western border of Judea. Among the innovative features of the Greek city was the *agora,* an open square which served as market and political meeting place and, thus, paralleled the gate of earlier times. Roman cities continue the grid design with an emphasis upon a main north-south street known as the *cardo* and a main east-west street known as the *decamus.* The late Byzantine Medeba map of Jerusalem dramatically portrays its *cardo,* portions of which have been uncovered in recent excavations. The characteristic monumental architecture of the Roman city usually included an amphitheater, a track, a sacred precinct (Capitolium), and a forum which succeeded the *agora* as the commercial and political center of the city. Concern for water supply is witnessed most dramatically by the aqueduct which directed water to Caesarea from springs over nine km away. Herod the Great is directly responsible for this grand construction as well as for many of the remains of Roman cities in Palestine. Strato's Tower (renamed Caesarea), Samaria (renamed Sebaste), and Jerusalem highlight his building activities which included public edifices at many other sites as well as a number of fortresses and palaces such as Masada and Herodium.

Urban Governance. With its emphasis on city autonomy and the rule of enfranchised citizens, the Greek tradition of city governance departed from the experience of city life in ancient Israelite times. At that time cities appear to have been governed by a body of "ELDERS" composed of the heads of the leading family or families of the city. This "city council" was related to the central authorities through the royal service of some of its members (Jer 26:16; Job 29:7-10). The capital cities, Samaria and Jerusalem, were administered by the "prince of the city" (1 Kgs 22:26; 2 Kgs 23:8) and other cities may have come under the command of the district officials (1 Kgs 4:7-19; 20:14ff). The centralizing policies of the monarchy were carried forward through the exercise of authority in the urban setting.

Greek and later Roman rulers of Palestine also administered their domains by means of the city through founding and re-founding cities organized along the lines of a Greek *polis* with an enrolled citizen body and ruling council. Veterans were a chief source of colonists for cities which served the dual purposes of economic and military extension. An alliance between city and empire was struck in which the city owed its charter as well as tangible benefits to its founder who in turn permitted the city's self-government. A client relationship extended as well to prominent urbanites who pursued imperial policy and their own ambition simultaneously. Herod's career is a model of this pathway and extended to his building of a temple to Augustus in the city, Sebaste, to which Herod gave the Greek form of Augustus's name. Rich finds of imported pottery, mosaic floors and superb frescoes in excavations in the Jewish quarter of Jerusalem reflect the economic and cultural success of Herod's rule. The friction in the relationship between the wealthy and powerful city and the dependent countryside plays a key role in the Maccabean revolt of the second century B.C.E. as well as in the career of the village-born Jesus and the later Jewish revolts.

See also ECONOMICS IN THE NEW TESTAMENT; ECONOMICS IN THE OLD TESTAMENT; WATER SYSTEMS.

Bibliography. F. Frick, *The City in Ancient Israel*; S. Paul and W. Dever, eds., *Biblical Archaeology*; Y. Shiloh, "Elements in the Development of Town Planning in the Israelite City," *IEJ* 28 (1978): 36-51; C. de Geus, "The Profile of an Israelite City," *BA* 49 (1986): 224-27; P. Hawkins, ed., *Civitas: Religious Interpretations of the City*; W. Meeks, *The First Urban Christians: The Social World of the Apostle Paul.*

—DAVID C. HOPKINS

• **Claudius Lysias.** *See* LYSIAS CLAUDIUS

• **Clean/Unclean.** Israelite ritual concerns have both religious and ultimately cosmic significance. The origins of the association of cleanness and uncleanness are often clouded in historical obscurity, but it was necessary to observe the proper rituals lest Israel be unholy and therefore offensive to the Holy God. These ritualistic concerns focused particularly around life—its extremities (birth and death), sexual intercourse, blood, food, and the disease that degenerated and repulsed life (leprosy). Generally, to be unclean was to be contaminated. Moreover, uncleanness was infectious and thus a threat to the community. Mechanisms were provided to remove impurities, ranging from sacrifices, to a waiting period, to the use of a cleansing agent (such as fire or water), or some combination of the three.

Women were considered unclean for seven days after giving birth to a male, and a lesser impure state continued for thirty-three days (cf. Lev 12), with a female birth doubling both time factors. The corpse was unclean as well as any individual coming into contact therewith (Num 19:11ff.). The infectious nature is evident in that soldiers returning from battle had to be purified (Num 31:19-24) if they had killed anyone or touched a dead body and in that cities of refuge were provided for murderers lest the murderer's presence defile their locale (Num 35; cities of refuge also were designed to prevent miscarriages of justice).

Sexual intercourse precipitated uncleanness, contaminating both parties until evening (Lev 15:16-18). Accidental seminal emission likewise contaminated the male until evening (Deut 23:10). When special cleanness was required, as when the soldiers went to war, total abstinence from women was mandated (Exod 19:15).

BLOOD was the source of life (Deut 12:23) and thus uniquely divine property (Gen 9:4). Menstrual blood was absolutely taboo, a highly contagious condition with which the male was not to come into contact (cf. Lev 15:2-15, 19-30 for details about purification).

The Noachian covenant forbade blood consumption (Gen 9:4). Lev 11 and Deut 14 give the specific dietary principles. Clean ANIMALS had to be cloven-footed and chew the cud, fishes had to have fins and scales. Birds were less clearly defined, although some unclean birds were enumerated. Also precluded for food was any animal that died either a natural or a violent death; swarming things and scavengers were also taboo. Even touching an unclean animal was thought to defile the individual. Around these restrictions Judaism developed the understanding of *Kashrut* (Kosher).

The only disease specifically classified as unclean was LEPROSY (Lev 13:43-45), one requiring purification rather than healing. The leper was excluded from the community (cf. 2 Kgs 7:3), but there were also procedures for the leper's return should the disease be declared healed (Lev 14).

Although Acts 15:29 retained some Jewish restrictions and whereas PAUL encouraged Christians not to cause others to stumble (Rom 14:13-23), nonetheless Paul's view that the Jewish ritual requirements were not mandated for Gentile Christians (Rom 14:14; 1 Cor 6:13 et al.) foreshadowed the Christian rejection of ritualistic cleanness and uncleanness (see also Acts 10, Peter at Joppa). Jesus' teachings, however, are more difficult to determine. His encounters with the Pharisees and his rejection of a rather staid view of Judaism are probably authentic (as Mark 7:1-5 et al.), but it is highly unlikely that this first-century Jew rejected the TORAH. He probably was aligned with the prophetic stance that proper motivation should precede external actions (cf. Mark 12:28-31).

See also BLOOD IN THE OLD TESTAMENT; FOOD; HOLINESS IN THE OLD TESTAMENT; LEPROSY; PURITY.

Bibliography. W. Eichrodt, *Theology of the Old Testament*; R. Otto, *The Idea of the Holy*; J. Pedersen, *Israel: Its Life and Culture*.

—FRANK E. EAKIN, JR.

• **Clement, First.** [klem'uhnt] *First Clement* is a letter written on behalf of the church of ROME to the church of CORINTH around 96 C.E. Although the author did not name himself, he was identified by Dionysius, Bishop of Corinth, around 170 (in EUSEBIUS, *EccHist* 4.23.11). Little is known about Clement. According to the list of Roman bishops cited by IRENAEUS (*AdvHaer* 3.3.3.), he followed Linus and Anacletus. Origen (*John* 6.54) and Eusebius (*EccHist* 3.15) thought he was the Clement mentioned by PAUL in Philippians 4:3, and evidently on similar grounds Tertullian (*PraescHaer* 32) supposed that PETER himself had appointed Clement. To reconcile conflicting theories, Epiphanius (*Haer* 27.6) suggested that Clement voluntarily relinquished the chair to Linus to preserve harmony. The CLEMENTINE LITERATURE erroneously identified Clement as the cousin of the Emperor Domitian, Titus Flavius Clemens, put to death in 96. The basilica of San Clemente in Rome allegedly stands on the site of Clement's house, but this too would be questionable. Since the letter itself names only two offices—presbyters or BISHOPS and DEACONS—in the church of Rome at the time, Clement would have been the leading presbyter-bishop and not a monarchical bishop. Nothing like the modern papacy existed at the time.

The letter can be dated with some precision in the last year or so of Domitian's reign (81-96). Clement mentioned a delay in the Romans' turning their attention to problems in Corinth "on account of the sudden and repeated misfortunes and calamities which have befallen us" (1.1). Although some scholars have wanted to associate the "misfortunes and calamities" with the Neronian persecution (64-68), Clement's later comment about being "in the same arena" and undergoing "the same struggle" precludes such a time gap.

First Clement has survived in two Greek manuscripts, in its entirety in the Codex Hierosolymitanus copied by Leo the Notary in 1056 and in a slightly mutilated form in the fifth century Codex Alexandrinus, which lacks 57.6–64.1. G. Morin discovered an eleventh-century manuscript of a Latin translation dating from the second or third centuries. The letter also is preserved in a twelfth century manuscript of a Syriac translation and in papyrus copies of two Coptic translations, both imperfect.

The letter consists of a brief introduction (1-3), two major sections (4-36, 37-61), and a summary (62-65). After explaining the reason for some tardiness in writing, Clement praised the Corinthians for their steadfastness of faith, gentleness of piety, magnificence of hospitality, security of knowledge, humbleness of mind, peacefulness, and compassion which put schism far from their minds (1-2). All of these qualities contrasted sharply with the schism which now rent the community (3).

In the first major section Clement took the Corinthians on a tour of the scriptures to show the folly and hurtfulness of their envy and strife (4-6) and to urge them to repentance (7-8), obedience (9-10), hospitality (11-12), humility and submissiveness (13-24), hope of RESURRECTION (25-27), and good deeds (28-36). In the second section he proceeded to deal more specifically with the problem at Corinth. Just as in an army, so also in the church must there be order (37). Members of the body of Christ must offer mutual help and encouragement (38-39) and observe order in religious services (40-41). Christ passed on to the apostles the message he received from God the Father; they preached and appointed some to be bishops and deacons (42). This has ancient precedent in "types" established by MOSES (43). The apostles, anticipating strife for the title of bishop, arranged for others to succeed those whom they appointed, so it is not just "to remove from their ministry those who were appointed by them, or later on by other eminent persons, with the consent of the whole church, and have ministered to the flock of Christ without blame, humbly, peaceably, and disinterestedly, and for many years have received a universally favorable testimony" (44.3). Scripture offers many exhortations to unity and against schism (44-46). The Apostle PAUL himself wrote to the Corinthians to urge unity, and it is shameful they now let one or two persons lead them to be disloyal to their presbyters (47). Not knowledge but rather love will bring them together (48-49). Thus they must pray for love (50) and forgiveness (51), confessing their sins (52) and receiving forgiveness (53). Whoever has love must be prepared to depart in order that the flock can have peace with the presbyters (54). Scriptures again offer testimony of God's forgiveness of the penitent. Those who laid the foundations for the schism, then, must submit to the presbyters and receive correction as scriptures enjoin (55-58). Clement concluded his appeals with a lengthy prayer which many scholars think may have belonged to the Roman liturgy (59.3-61.3). Of special interest here is the role assumed by the church of Rome. Although Clement did not invoke special prerogatives, he intervened in the Corinthian controversy with something more than mere courtesy or concern of a sister church. Does this indicate, as Roman Catholic scholars assume, a primacy of jurisdiction? Clement certainly came close to that assertion in his strong warning to the dissidents: "But if some are disobedient to what has been said by [Christ] through us, let them know that they will wrap themselves up in transgression and no little danger" (59.1). He was convinced that what he wrote was "written through the Holy Spirit" (63.2), so that the Corinthians owed obedience. Rudolph Sohm perceived in such claims the path that led from early Christian understanding of the church as a "purely spiritual entity" to the Catholic understanding of the church as a legal entity. Walter Bauer discerned in it some clues for the development of orthodoxy in earliest Christianity. Christianity began with diversity; Rome imposed orthodoxy.

First Clement provides important evidence for early Christian history in Rome. It confirms the martyrdoms of Peter and Paul in the ancient capital. Whether Peter died in or even visited Rome was long disputed by Protestants, but the fact is now generally accepted. It reports that the Apostle Paul traveled "as far as the limits of the West," that is, to Spain, a tradition still in dispute. Clement was also the first Christian author to cite the legend of the Phoenix as "proof" of resurrection (24-25). Subsequently it appeared often in early Christian literature and art.

See also APOSTOLIC FATHERS.

Bibliography. L. W. Barnard, *Studies in the Apostolic Fathers and Their Background*; R. M. Grant and H. H. Graham, *First and Second Clement*, in *The Apostolic Fathers*; J. Lawson, *A Theological and Historical Introduction to the Apostolic Fathers*; J. B. Lightfoot, *The Apostolic Fathers*; J. Quasten, *Patrology*.

—E. GLENN HINSON

• **Clement, Second.** *Second Clement* is not a letter, but a homily or appeal (17:3; 19:1) based on Isa 54:1 (cf. 2:1; 17:3; 19:1). As such it is the oldest Christian sermon known. The preacher interprets the text in terms of the Gentile church called into being by Jesus Christ (1-2). Christians are to respond to this deed with virtuous living and mercy to others (3-4). But life in this time is a warfare which calls for repentance while there is yet time.

The homily was associated with FIRST CLEMENT by the fourth century. Nothing is known of its provenance, date of writing or author. The homily is a rather ordinary composition which likely reflects the second century. Because of its association with *1 Clement* one should assume a Roman origin for the sermon.

A part of the Greek text of *2 Clement* is contained in Codex Alexandrinus (fifth century). The full text, found in an eleventh-century manuscript, was published in 1875 by Philotheos Byrennios.

Bibliography. R. M. Grant and H. H. Graham, *First and Second Clement*; J. Quasten, *Patrology*.

—GRAYDON F. SNYDER

• **Clementine Literature.** [klem'uhn-t*i*n] The Clementine literature is associated with the person of Clement of Rome, an "Apostolic Father" of the late first century (fl. 92–101). He has been variously identified as (a) a fellow worker with Paul as noted in Phil 4:3 (Origen *John* 6.36 and EUSEBIUS *EccHist* 3.4.10); (b) the third successor of PETER in Rome (Irenaeus, *AdvHaer* 3.3.3) who Tertullian believed was consecrated by Peter himself (*PraescHaer* 32); (c) a member of the Flavian family who became a Christian (Dio Cassius *Hist* 67.14), a view not regarded as reliable by most scholars.

His writings are divided into two groups: the genuine and the spurious. His first epistle to the church at CORINTH (FIRST CLEMENT) in the collection known as APOSTOLIC FATHERS, dated ca. 96, is the only writing considered genuine. He attempts in this letter to settle disputes which had arisen in the church at CORINTH during the last decade of the first century, and to establish ecclesiastical authority which had been seriously eroded in that community.

The spurious works consist of the following: (1) A second letter to the Corinthians (SECOND CLEMENT), which is a homily of a general character dated before 150. It has been described as "the oldest extant Christian sermon" (Altaner, 103). (2) Two pseudo-Clementine letters "To Virgins" written in the third century. These form one continuous circular letter written to ascetics opposing religious men and women living together outside of marriage. Only a few Greek fragments for these letters have been found, but a complete Syriac version and a Coptic version for the first letter exist. (3) The pseudo-Clementine *Homilies* and *Recognitions*, a "romance" which tells of the Palestinian journeys of Simon Peter, his confrontations with SIMON MAGUS, the conversion of Clement of Rome by Peter and his subsequent experiences as Peter's disciple. The *Homilies* consist of twenty sermons of Peter, which are prefaced by two letters of Peter and Clement to James the Less, bishop of Jerusalem. The *Recognitions* constitute ten books in which is narrated the story of Clement's scattered family, father, mother, and three sons, who are brought together by Peter. The *Homilies* and *Recognitions* are to be dated in the fourth century. (4) Two Greek excerpts from the *Homilies* and two Arabic excerpts from both *Homilies* and *Recognitions*.

Many complicated literary theories have been advanced to account for the relationship of the *Homilies* and *Recognitions* but none has commanded widespread assent. Hans Waitz recognized the parallel accounts in the two major pseudo-Clementines and postulated a "basic document" dated to the third century. It was Jewish-Christian in character, possibly Ebionite (Schoeps), or Elkasaite, but its positive identity with a known Jewish-Christian group has not been satisfactorily demonstrated. The "basic document" is found in sections of the *Homilies* and *Recognitions* which have a common narrative. Accompanying discourse varies widely.

In the *Homilies* and *Recognitions* Peter practices a daily "baptism" for ritual cleansing before eating and after touching the sick or the possessed. There is a strong rejection of animal sacrifice and an emphasis upon vegetarianism.

See also KERYGMATA PETROU.

Bibliography. B. Altaner, *Patrology;* J. Quasten, *Patrology*.

—GLENN A. KOCH

• **Cleodemus Malchus.** [klee-oh'duh-muhs-mal"kuhs] Cleodemus Malchus is a Hellenistic Jewish author of whose work only a few lines have been preserved. JOSEPHUS (*Ant* 1.239-41) quotes an account by "Cleodemus the prophet, also called Malchus," that had been preserved by Alexander Polyhistor. In his *Praeparatio Evangelica,* EUSEBIUS quotes Josephus (*PraepEv* 9.20.2-4). Otherwise unattested, Cleodemus Malchus must have written earlier than Alexander Polyhistor (fl. ca. 50 B.C.E.); he is usually dated sometime between 200–50 B.C.E.

The extant fragment concerns the descendants of ABRAHAM through Keturah (Gen 25:1-4). Cleodemus Malchus focuses on three of these and asserts that the countries of ASSYRIA and Africa and the city of Aphra (otherwise unknown) were named after children of Abraham and Keturah. He goes on to say that Heracles was assisted in his fight against the Libyan giant Antaeus by Apher (Africa) and Aphran (Aphra), and that Heracles subsequently married Aphran's daughter (Abraham's granddaughter). In the Greek traditions, of course, Heracles defeats Antaeus without any assistance.

Hellenistic Jewish apologists were fond of the device of linking Jewish patriarchs to the origins of respected nations and cultural achievements. On this motif, see 1 Macc 12:20-23, ARTAPANUS, and PSEUDO-EUPOLEMUS. Cleodemus Malchus does not hesitate to combine biblical and pagan traditions.

Some scholars consider Cleodemus Malchus a Samaritan; the Tyrian god Heracles-Melkart was worshiped by the SAMARITANS on MOUNT GERIZIM. Considering his emphasis on the descendants of Abraham as founders and benefactors of Africa, it is more likely that Cleodemus Malchus was a member of the Jewish diaspora in Africa, perhaps in Carthage.

See also ARTAPANUS; EUPOLEMUS, PSEUDO.

Bibliography. R. Doran, "Cleodemus Malchus," *The Old Testament Pseudepigrapha,* ed. J. H. Charlesworth; C. R. Holladay, *Fragments from Hellenistic Jewish Authors*.

—SHARYN E. DOWD

• **Cleopas.** [klee'oh-puhs] One of the two disciples Jesus encountered on the road to Emmaus after his resurrection (Luke 24:18). The Greek name Cleopas, a contracted form of Cleopatros, means "renowned father." Some have identified Cleopas with the Clopas of John 19:25, the husband of Mary who was present at the crucifixion. In any case, the mention of his name makes it likely that the person was known to Luke's readers. Failure to mention the name of Cleopas' fellow traveler has led to the speculation that it may have been his wife or son. One tradition identifies the other traveler as Simon and includes both in the group of seventy disciples sent out by Jesus according to Luke 10:1-24.

—W. HULITT GLOER

• **Cleophas.** *See* CLEOPAS

• **Close Reading.** *See* LITERATURE, BIBLE AS

• **Clothing.** *See* DRESS; SACKCLOTH

• **Cockcrowing.** Cockcrowing is the term for the third watch of the night (12:00–3:00 a.m.). The Romans divided the night into four watches (cf. Mark 13:35; cf. Strabo 7.35). Josephus (*BJ* 5.2.510) describes Titus's arrangements for three watches.

All four Gospels record Jesus' warning to Peter that Peter would deny him before the cockcrow (Matt 26:34; Luke 22:34; John 13:38). Mark alone states "before the cock crows twice" (14:30) and proceeds to report two crowings of the cock (14:72). This evidence is assessed variously. Some interpreters contend that Jesus spoke of the trumpet blast that marked the end of the third watch of the night. In this case, Mark's account is the result of a misunderstanding and legendary expansion of the story. Others argue that the two cockcrows in Mark are accurate. If the cock crowed twice, however, one wonders why Peter did not remember the words of Jesus after the first cockcrow.

The *Mishnah* (*Qam* 7.7) forbids the raising of fowl in Jerusalem, since they pick at dead things and could thereby bring uncleanness to houses. This regulation may not have been followed strictly by all Jews even if it was practiced by the Pharisees in Jerusalem before 70 C.E.

—R. ALAN CULPEPPER

• **Code.** *See* LAW IN THE OLD TESTAMENT

• **Codex.** The codex is the ancestor of the modern book, consisting of sheets of folded papyrus or parchment (leather) fastened at the spine and protected by covers. The English word derives from the Latin *codex* or *caudex*.

Prior to the first century C.E., the universal form of published literature among the Jews and pagans was the roll, popularly referred to as a scroll. These rolls of PAPYRUS or PARCHMENT were up to thirty feet in length and contained writing only on one side. The Greeks and Romans did use book-like writing tablets made up of a few wax-covered wooden blocks bound together with cords and also cheap parchment notebooks for non-literary work such as business accounts and school exercises. Yet, until the third and fourth centuries C.E., almost all pagan literary works were reproduced on rolls. In contrast, by the end of the first century C.E., Christians adopted the codex and copied all of their sacred writings in codex form instead of on the traditional roll. The codex was more practical than the roll: it was more compact, easier to use, and could hold several times more material. The increasing influence of Christian literature and obvious advantages of the codex eventually enabled it to completely replace the roll.

All of the earliest copies of Christian scriptures which have been found, including 𝔭52 (a fragment from the Gospel of John, dated ca. 125 C.E.), are in codex form. Perhaps the most important codex discovered to date is Codex Sinaiticus, a fourth-century Greek manuscript which contains the entire NT and part of the OT.

See also PARCHMENT; TEXTS/MANUSCRIPTS/VERSIONS; TEXTUAL CRITICISM OF THE NEW TESTAMENT.

—MARK J. OLSON

• **Coele-Syria** [see'lee-sihr"ee-uh] Coele-Syria is the modern Beqa' Valley in Lebanon, between the Lebanon and Antilebanon mountain ranges. This region of southwest Syria ("valley of Lebanon" in Josh 11:17) was named Coele-Syria (lit., "hollow" Syria) as a Seleucid province ca. 203 B.C.E.. The name occurs in the Apocrypha (RSV Coelesyria, 2 Macc 3:5; 4:4; 8:8).

• **Coins.** *See* MONEY

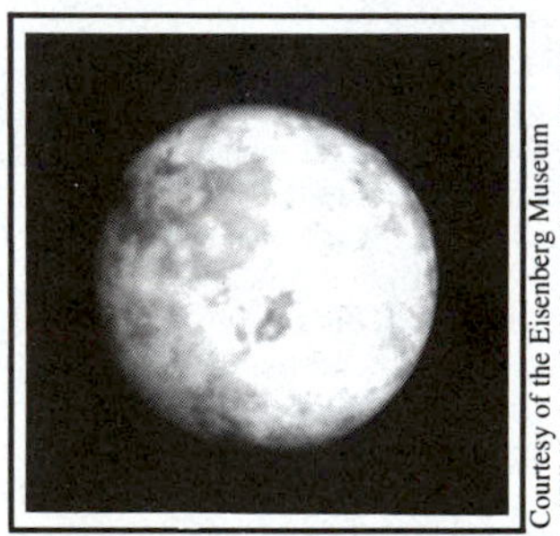

Courtesy of the Eisenberg Museum of Biblical Archaeology, Southern Baptist Theological Seminary.

An inscribed four-shekel stone weight.

• **Coins and Money.** The early economic exchanges in the OT involved barter in which commodities, such as animals or foodstuffs, were traded or used to pay for services or taxes (cf. 1 Kgs 5:11). Later, essential or precious metals (copper, silver, and gold) were exchanged by weight with approx. .37 ounces of silver constituting a shekel (cf. Gen 23:16).

Development of Minted Coins. Stamped uniform pieces of metal to be used in exchange first began to appear in the seventh century B.C.E. in Greece and Asia Minor. The minting of coins was a carefully controlled privilege of kingship (cf. 1 Macc 15:6) with the king's image often used on the coin to proclaim his sovereignty (Matt 22:20-21).

Coins in the OT Period. The earliest references to coinage in the OT are in Ezra and Nehemiah where Persian darics (approx. .27 oz. of gold) are mentioned (Ezra 2:69; 8:27; Neh 7:70-72). Archaeological discoveries make it clear that Greek and Persian silver coinage also circulated during the Persian Period (538–333 B.C.E.).

With the conquest of Alexander, unified coinage minted at various locations began to circulate. Archaeological discoveries verify that the Ptolemaic silver tetradrachma (approx. .466 oz. of silver) and bronze coins were in wide circulation during the third century B.C.E. During the second century B.C.E., Seleucid silver and bronze coins circulated; and when the Jews gained their freedom under the Maccabees, they began to mint bronze coins, probably beginning during the reign of John Hyrcanus (135–104 B.C.E.).

Coins in the NT Period. Bronze coins were minted by

Courtesy of the Eisenberg Museum of Biblical Archaeology.

A reconstruction of silver coins from NT era.

Herod (37–4 B.C.E.) as well as by his successors and by local Roman governors in areas outside Palestine, resulting in coins of many different origins commonly circulating in Palestine in the first century C.E. The smallest Greek bronze coin was a lepton (Mark 12:42; "mite," KJV), and the smallest of the Roman was a quadran (dilepton = two leptons), translated "penny" in the RSV (Mark 12:42). In addition to these, archaeological evidence reveals that many bronze coins of various sizes and weights with undesignated denominations were in circulation.

Silver coinage also circulated in first century Palestine with the most frequently mentioned in the NT being the denar or denarius (.112 to .1286 oz.) which was a laborer's daily wage (Matt 20:9), and two were used to pay the half-shekel or didrachma (two drachma) tax (Matt 17:24; 22:19) which roughly equalled two denars. The Tyrian tetradrachma (four drachmas) which was about one-half ounce of silver was also common, and thirty of them were probably used to pay Judas (Matt 26:15). A silver talent (Matt 25:14-30) contained 12,000 denars or approximately 1,344 to 1,543 ozs. of silver.

Value of Ancient Coins. The value of an ancient coin in current currency may be estimated in three ways. The weight of the metal in the ancient coin may be compared with the current value of the precious metal in it. Second, the amount of a commodity an ancient coin would purchase, such as oil or barley, may be assigned a value on the basis of current commodity prices; or third, the daily wage of a laborer in current society may be compared with that of the ancient worker. None of these three is precise, but the last one is the easiest to calculate and understand.

Bibliography. H. Hamburger, "Money, Coins," *IDB*; U. Rappaport, "Numismatics," *CHJ* 1:25-69.

—HAROLD S. SONGER

• **Collection.** *See* CONTRIBUTION FOR THE SAINTS

• **Colors.** *See* SCARLET

• **Colossae.** [kuh-los'ee] Colossae was the oldest of three neighboring cities in the valley of the Lycus River in Asia Minor (PLATES 26, 27); the other two were LAODICEA and Hierapolis. The religious situation of this area was complex. Large and influential Jewish communities were present in the first century C.E. Moreover, a variety of religious associations from both the East and West were established. During this time a slave named Epictetus began teaching his philosophy of Stoicism in his hometown, Hierapolis, some fifteen miles from Colossae. Christianity was likely introduced into this religiously and philosophically complex area by EPAPHRAS, a disciple of the apostle Paul. The city of EPHESUS, in which Paul ministered for a period of more than two years (Acts 19:10), was located roughly a hundred miles west of Colossae near the Aegean coast.

See also COLOSSIANS, LETTER TO THE; EPAPHRAS; EPHESUS; LAODICEA; STOICS.

—JOE E. BARNHART

• OUTLINE OF COLOSSIANS •

The Letter to the Colossians

I. Introduction to the Letter (1:1-14)
  A. Salutation (1:1-2)
  B. Thanksgiving and prayer (1:3-14)
II. The Person and Work of Christ (1:15-23)
  A. The preeminence of Christ (1:15-20)
  B. The reconciling work of Christ (1:21-23)
III. The Continuing Work of Christ through Paul (1:24–2:7)
  A. Paul's suffering for Christ and authority through him (1:21-29)
  B. Paul's concern and warning to the church (2:1-7)
IV. The Power of Christ and Freedom through Him in View of the Heresy (2:8-23)
  A. The fullness and power of Christ over empty deceit and legalism (2:8-15)
  B. The substantial nature of Christ over attempts to disqualify the Colossians (2:16-19)
  C. The adequacy of Christ over ascetic regulations (2:20-23)
V. True Christian Behavior (3:1–4:6)
  A. New life in Christ (3:1-17)
  B. Household ethics (3:18–4:1)
  C. Concluding ethical exhortations (4:2-6)
VI. Personal Matters (4:7-18)
  A. The role of Tychicus and Onesimus (4:7-9)
  B. Various greetings and the ministry of Epaphras (4:10-15)
  C. Instructions for Laodicea and Archippus (4:16-17)
  D. Final greeting and autograph (4:18)

• **Colossians, Letter to the.** [kuh-losh'uhns] The Letter to the Colossians is one of four so-called PRISON EPISTLES, along with Ephesians, Philippians, and Philemon, all of which are attributed to PAUL. In content and purpose, Colossians is very closely related to Philemon and Ephesians. The Epistle is known especially for its high CHRISTOLOGY and a sharp rebuke to a syncretistic heresy. Personal notes at the end of the Epistle have also evoked various theories as to its purpose.

Authorship. The Epistle appeared in canonical lists quite early and was accepted as being Pauline by Marcion (140 C.E.) and the Muratorian Canon (200 C.E.). Colossians remained undisputed as to authorship until the early nineteenth century when Meyerhoff considered it to be based on Ephesians. Later, Holtzmann (1872) and, more recently, Masson (1950) suggested that the author of Ephesians reworked Colossians from a shorter original form.

Objections to authenticity focus on two points: (1) the error promoted in COLOSSAE and the resulting view of Christ and the church are said to be from a later period than Paul, and (2) the literary relationship to Ephesians and other earlier letters of Paul presents a problem. Colossians also has thirty-four words not found elsewhere in the NT. The weight of evidence is toward Paul's authorship of the Epistle, however. There is no serious reason for doubting the existence of this kind of heresy in Paul's latter years. Also the peculiar vocabulary is to be attributed to the unusual nature of the religious movement or the use of liturgical material, esp. in 1:15-20. The literary connection with Ephesians is less harmful to the authenticity of Colossians than Ephesians. Most significant is the vital connection of Philemon, undoubtedly Pauline, to Colossians. There are so many links between these two Epistles in terms of people and purpose that the authenticity of Philemon carries Colossians along with it.

Time and Place. These go along with authorship, and one imprisonment must be decided upon from three possibilities: Rome, Caesarea, and Ephesus. Those who assume that ONESIMUS was a runaway slave postulate that he would have gone to nearby Ephesus or even Caesarea rather than faraway Rome. The proposed trips to and from the churches and Paul's prison have also been a problem for a Roman imprisonment (Col 1:7-8; 4:7-9; Phlm 22; Phil 2:25; 4:17-18). Problems arise with all three possibilities, but Rome seems most likely for several reasons. (1) Evidence for an Ephesian imprisonment is questionable. (2) Travel between Rome and other locations was relatively easy and would make the implied communications quite possible. (3) If Onesimus was a runaway, the city of Rome would give him the best sanctuary. (4) Sufficient time should be allowed for the heresy to develop, and Rome would be the latest imprisonment. (5) It seems incredible, if Paul developed such an advanced Christology at an earlier time (e.g., in Ephesus), that he would not have repeated this in later letters such as Romans. If written from Rome, Colossians and its companion Letter, Philemon, were written about 60 B.C.E. and were among the last letters of Paul.

Background and Occasion. In the time of Paul, Colossae was a declining city in Phrygia, situated about 100 miles west of Ephesus. The population was mainly Phrygian, but Greeks, Syrians, and Jews had also migrated to the area. The religious climate in Phrygia was quite diverse, with a host of elements coming together from the mystery religions, Iranian worship, Judaism, and Pauline Christianity. Against this background a syncretistic form of worship emerged which brought Christ within its scope but reduced his significance, according to Paul and his followers.

The Epistle is written in light of two problems which called for attention: (1) the theological and ethical issue of the encroaching heresy, which is called a "philosophy and empty deceit" (2:8); and (2) the personal issue of the circumstances of Onesimus and his owner, who apparently resides in Colossae. The former seems to be much more important in light of the direct way in which Paul attacks the movement in chaps. 1–2. However, the personal problem may have been just as significant to him, but much more difficult to deal with since it required a more subtle approach.

The identity of the Colossian heresy has been greatly debated. Without question, Judaism was involved, e.g., circumcision (2:11-13) and sabbath (2:16). Elements existing outside of Judaism were also present, e.g., "knowledge" (*gnōsis*) (2:3), "philosophy" (2:8), and "severe treatment of the body" (2:23). It seems to be a blending of some form of Jewish Christianity with incipient GNOSTICISM, influenced by elements of astrology and possibly the pagan mystery religions. The adherents focused on visions

(2:18), intermediaries between God and the earth (2:20), and food laws, and days (2:16). The result was a low Christology (cf. 1:15-20) and an extreme ascetic ethical stance (2:20-23).

The personal issue involves a request which focused on Onesimus, and one must take into consideration the companion Letter to Philemon to see the entire situation. Paul sent Onesimus back to his owner (Col 4:9) asking that he be forgiven and accepted as a brother, and probably requesting his release (Phlm 8-20).

Content of the Epistle. After the usual introductory words, a thanksgiving and a prayer (1:1-14), Paul presents the person and work of Christ in his preeminence (1:15-23). He sets forth a very high Christology even before warning the church about the heresy. The continuing work of Christ through Paul and the church follows in 1:24–2:7, in which he gives a warning to the congregation. The heart of the exposition of the errors is in 2:8-23. Paul depicts Christ as canceling legalistic demands and parading in triumph over principalities and powers. Extreme asceticism is shown as an inferior system by which to correct the tendencies toward the lower nature (2:23).

The second half of the Epistle deals with more general matters beginning with 3:1, where Paul expounds a more workable Christian ethic. The characteristic lists of vices and virtues appear in 3:5-15. Relationships within the household are discussed in 3:18–4:1. An unusually long section on slaves and masters appears in 3:22–4:1, doubtless because of Onesimus. Many personal notations appear in 4:7-17. The most discussed of these are 4:16 and 17, which concern the letter to Laodicea and the ministry of Archippus. The best known theory is that of J. Knox, who believes the Laodicean letter was our Philemon and Archippus was the owner of Onesimus. Paul is unusually attentive to the matter of slaves, and the connections between Colossians and Philemon certainly demonstrate that the fate of Onesimus was supremely important to him.

See also CHRISTOLOGY; COLOSSAE; GNOSTICISM; PAUL; PRISON EPISTLES.

Bibliography. M. Dibelius and H. Greeven, *An die Kolosser, Epheser, an Philemon*; J. L. Houlden, *Paul's Letters from Prison: Philippians, Colossians, Philemon, and Ephesians*; J. Knox, *Philemon among the Letters of Paul: A New View of Its Place and Importance*; J. B. Lightfoot, *Saint Paul's Epistles to the Colossians and to Philemon*; E. Lohse, *Colossians-Philemon: A Commentary on the Epistles to the Colossians and Philemon*; R. P. Martin, *Colossians and Philemon, NCB*; C. Masson, *L'épître de Saint Paul aux Colossiens*; C. F. D. Moule, *The Epistles of Paul the Apostle to the Colossians and to Philemon*; E. Schweizer, *The Letter to the Colossians: A Commentary.*

—W. THOMAS SAWYER

• **Comforter.** *See* ADVOCATE/PARACLETE; HOLY SPIRIT

• **Coming of Christ, Second.** *See* ESCHATOLOGY IN THE NEW TESTAMENT; MILLENNIUM; PAROUSIA/SECOND COMING

• **Commandment.** An authoritative mandate or order; also, the mandated deed or action itself. The OT Heb. word most often so translated is *miṣwâ* (1 Kgs 2:43; Ps 19:8[H9]), derived from the verb *ṣiwwâ,* "command," "commission," or "charge with responsibility" (Ps 91:11). In present Jewish tradition and practice it can also mean any worthy act, commanded or not. The Ten Commandments, however, are designated in Hebrew literally as the ten "words" (*dĕbārîm*; Deut 10:4) i.e., the "Decalogue" (derived from the Greek translation). As a metaphor, *peh,* "mouth," is occasionally translated by "commandment" (1 Sam 12:14–15).

The LXX renders *miṣwâ* usually with *èntolē,* which occasionally translates other law terms also. In the NT, *èntolē* typically stands for the individual commandment within the *nomos,* "law" (Matt 22:36, 40), though Paul seems to use "commandment" and "law" interchangeably (Rom 7:7-12).

A talmudic tradition that the commandments in the Torah total precisely 613—for which various explanations are given by differing systems of codification and enumeration—is significant chiefly for its attestation to faith in the ultimate unity and harmony of all the commandments.

The nuances of "commandment" or "commanding" in the Bible extend beyond simply the imposition of authority, whether divine or human. The verb *ṣiwwâ,* "command," often indicates explicitly the transmission or delegation of authority; that is, the recipient's freedom is enabled and empowered rather than restricted (Num 27:19; Ps 91:11). Jesus' "new commandment" (*èntolē kainē*; John 13:34) can be interpreted in this sense.

Bibliography. A. Altman and G. Scholem, "Commandments, Reasons for," *EncJud*; B. Levine, "*miṣwah*," *TWAT*; A. H. Rabinowitz, "613 Commandments, The," *EncJud.*

—BRUCE T. DAHLBERG

• **Commerce.** *See* CARAVAN; ECONOMICS IN THE NEW TESTAMENT; ECONOMICS IN THE OLD TESTAMENT

• **Common.** *See* CLEAN/UNCLEAN; HOLINESS IN THE OLD TESTAMENT

• **Concept of Our Great Power.** *Concept of Our Great Power* is a complex exposition of salvation history from the NAG HAMMADI library. It describes in apocalyptic form the creation of the physical world and the soul, the origin of EVIL, the life and work of a savior figure, the rise of an antichrist-type, and the final consummation. This historical survey is divided into three major ages or epochs, called eons. The "eon of the flesh" extends until Noah and is destroyed by the flood. The "psychic eon" is that in which the savior appears and is destroyed by fire. In the "unchangeable eon" or "eon of beauty" the pure souls find rest with God. "Then the souls will appear, who are holy through the light of the Power. . . . And they all have become as reflections in his light. They all have shone, and they have found rest in his rest."

The "great power" in the title (a title that appears both in the beginning and end of the text in slightly different form) seems to be the supreme God. The word "concept" (which could also be translated "thought" or "intellect") does not occur in the body of the work, but it is in keeping with one of its major themes: divine knowledge. Salvation occurs through knowledge of the great power. "He who would know our great Power will become invisible. And fire will not be able to consume him. . . . " Likewise, the savior figure who comes in the psychic eon is distinguished by his knowledge of the deity. The great power says of him, "He will receive me and he will know me."

The savior figure is not called Jesus Christ, but the description of him makes this identification clear. He speaks in parables, proclaims the eon that is to come, raises the dead, and many follow him. He is betrayed by one of his followers for nine bronze coins, he descends to Hades, and he triumphs over hostile archons. He is the LOGOS who abolishes the law of the eon. The text hints at a docetic Christology (one in which Christ's humanity is only apparent). When the savior figure is delivered to the ruler of Hades, the ruler "found that the nature of his flesh could not be seized," which probably reflects a belief that the flesh of Jesus was somehow different from human flesh. The document devalues the flesh in general, a constant feature in Gnosticism, which can lead either to asceticism or to libertinism. Entering into flesh is called "corruption" and "the sons of matter" perish in the final conflagration.

Concept of Our Great Power is a difficult work to understand. The text contains numerous grammatical, logical, and theological inconsistencies. The largely third person narration is broken at times with a first person speaker (whose identity is unclear but appears to be the same as "the great power") and at times with exhortations addressed in the second person plural. Some terms are introduced without explanation (e.g. "archons") and the meaning of some words changes (e.g., "eons"). The chronology of the text is also not straightforward (e.g., the conflagration is described at several points). These inconsistencies indicate a complicated literary history behind the text, probably with layers of composition.

These irregularities also cloud attempts at locating and classifying the document. In its present form, it is a Christian apocalypse with Gnostic tendencies. The Gnostic elements include the account of creation and the origin of the soul, the identification of the OT God as "the father of the flesh," the depiction of archons as the enemy, the ascetic characterization of the flesh as evil, and the call to awaken: "Yet you are sleeping, dreaming dreams. Wake up and return, taste and eat the true food."

The text contains few indications as to its date and provenance. A reference to *Anomoeans* (a Greek word meaning "unlike") probably refers to a fourth century C.E. heresy akin to Arianism that distinguished the Son as "unlike" the Father in essence. The statement that the Logos appeared first in the East suggests that the author lived west of Palestine. The linking of circumcision with the Antichrist may indicate a non-Jewish (anti-Jewish?) sect.

See also APOCALYPTIC LITERATURE; GNOSTICISM; NAG HAMMADI.

Bibliography. F. E. Williams, F. Wisse, and D. M. Parrott, "The Concept of Our Great Power," *The Nag Hammadi Library in English,* ed. J. M. Robinson.

—CAROL D. C. HOWARD

• **Confessions of Jeremiah.** *See* JEREMIAH, BOOK OF

• **Confidence.** *See* ASSURANCE

• **Confinement.** *See* PRISON

• **Conflict Story.** The form critics of the 1920s identified a literary form in the synoptic Gospels (*Streitgespräch*) which Vincent Taylor in 1933 called "conflict story." Rudolf Bultmann is the scholar primarily responsible for the understanding of the literary form; and in the English translation (1963) of his *History of the Synoptic Tradition,* the German term is translated "dialogue controversy."

The conflict story is a subdivision of the literary form APOPHTHEGM (which Taylor called "pronouncement story"). In the apophthegms of the synoptic Gospels important teachings of Jesus are embedded within short narrative settings. Distinctive settings can be detected: the "scholastic dialogue" in which an inquiry is raised by someone (friendly or hostile) seeking knowledge, the "conflict story" in which there is a hostile response to Jesus' healing or to the conduct of Jesus or his disciples, and the "biographical apophthegm" which is a brief idealized historical report designed primarily to characterize Jesus in heroic terms. The first two groupings are more closely related in style and form, and thus are sometimes treated in close connection with each other (e.g., Vincent Taylor). Bultmann viewed conflict stories as originating primarily in the struggles of the early church with issues over the OT law and synagogue opposition to the gospel. According to Bultmann some of the sayings themselves perhaps go back historically to the life and teaching of Jesus, but very little (if any) of the remainder. Other form critics (such as Taylor) argued for a connection with the historical Jesus through oral tradition. They suggest that the apparent collection of conflict stories in Mark 2:1–3:3 and in 11:15–12:40 was part of Mark's tradition, and they point to the admittedly Palestine tone of Bultmann's listing of conflict stories.

Conflict stories have two major parts: the initiation of dialogue by some hostile source and Jesus' reply. The hostile source is customarily the Jewish religious leaders who are upset at Jesus over such things as his association with undesirables (Mark 2:15-17), non-practice of Jewish regulations (Mark 2:18, 23, 25; 7:1-5), or his challenge of their authority (Mark 11:27-28). Jesus' reply typically takes the form of a counter question (Mark 2:25-26; 3:4; 11:29-30), a question or an assertion cast in metaphorical language (Mark 2:17, 19; 3:29-30), or a scripture citation (Mark 7:6-8; 10:5-8). These forms of reply are sometimes combined. The response of Jesus functions as the climactic central point of the narrative, but the exegesis of the conflict story must be sensitive both to the narrative context and to Jesus' statement.

Some recent scholars with literary-critical orientation have questioned the classification used by Bultmann. Klaus Berger argues that conflict stories fit in the overarching category of "chreia" (moral anecdote or saying). The different introductory rhetorical patterns of questions, assertions, and so on serve then as the basis for the subdivisions. However this may be viewed, the earlier work of the form critics has certainly made modern exegetes more sensitive to the literary patterns present in the Gospel texts.

See also APOPHTHEGM; FORM/GATTUNG; GOSPELS, CRITICAL STUDY OF; INTERPRETATION, HISTORY OF.

Bibliography. R. Bultmann, *The History of the Synoptic Tradition*; K. Berger, *Formgeschichte des Neuen Testament*; V. Taylor, *The Formation of the Gospel Tradition.*

—LORIN L. CRANFORD

• **Congregation.** The translation of at least seven Heb. words signifying a gathering. Most important are the two terms *'ēdâ* and *qāhāl*.

1. The term *'ēdâ* is a noun from *yā'ad* "to appoint," specifying a company assembled by appointment. Nevertheless, the noun itself does not imply the purpose of the gathering. The word may apply to a gathering of the righteous (Ps 22:16), the violent (Ps 86:14), or the godless (Job 15:34). The primary application of *'ēdâ,* however, is to the covenant community of Israel. The word occurs 147 times in the OT, mostly in the Pentateuch, but never in Genesis or Deuteronomy. It is used once in 2 Chr 5:6, ten times in the Psalms (e.g., 22:22), and three times in the Prophets (Jer 6:18; 30:20; Hos 7:12). In the majority of cases it describes the official socioreligious body during the period of the desert sojourn and the conquest.

2. The term *qāhāl* is a noun conjecturally derived from *qôl*, "to speak," designating "a summons to an ASSEMBLY and the act of assembling and is perhaps most accurately translated as mustering." It is used to designate various sorts of human gatherings, especially those of a religious nature. The gathering may be for evil counsel or deeds (Gen 49:6), civil affairs (1 Kgs 2:3), war (Num 22:4), or feasts, fasts, and worship (2 Chr 20:5). The word *qāhāl* appears less frequently in the Pentateuch than *'ēdâ*, and is preferred by later writers, the Chronicler, Ezra, Nehemiah, the psalmists, and Ezekiel. In the majority of occurrences the two words are used synonymously, designating the cult community of Israel.

See also ASSEMBLY; CHURCH; CONVOCATION; SYNAGOGUE.

Bibliography. L. Coenen, "Church, Synagogue," *NIDNTT*.

—ANTHONY M. TETROW, JR.

• **Coniah.** *See* JEHOIACHIN

• **Conquest of Canaan.** There are three distinct blocks of tradition which recount the conquest and settlement of Israel in Canaan: (1) Num 13–14 and 20–21; (2) Josh 1–12; and (3) Judg 1:1–2:5. In addition, the accounts in Gen 34; 49; Deut 2:26-37; 3:1-20, 33; and Judg 3–21 play a significant part in the scholarly discussion.

After the EXODUS from Egypt, the people of Israel arrived at Kadesh (Num 13–14). From there spies were sent into the land of the Canaanites. The conquest was postponed because of the negative report of these spies; and that entire generation of Israelites was judged and sentenced to die in the wilderness, except for CALEB and JOSHUA. To circumvent this decree, the people attempted a frontal attack from the south, resulting in a resounding defeat by the Amalekites and the Canaanites (Num 14:44-45). Some forty years later the Israelites passed around Edom and Moab in eastern Transjordan, seeking passage through Amorite territory. This resulted in conflict with OG and SIHON (Num 21), in which Israel defeated these two Amorite kings and took possession of their lands. At this time they established their camp in the plains of Moab across from Jericho (Num 22) and proceeded to give tribal allotments to Reuben, Gad, and half the tribe of Manasseh. After Moses' death, Joshua mobilized the Israelite tribes to conquer the central territory west of the Jordan. JERICHO was taken (Josh 2–6) from a base camp established at GILGAL. Soon afterwards they advanced westward into the central hill country, taking AI (Josh 7–8) and GIBEON (Josh 9–10). Next the Israelites turned their energies toward the south, which resulted in the conquests of Libnah, LACHISH, EGLON, HEBRON, and DEBIR. With southern Palestine under Israelite hegemony (Josh 10), Joshua then led an expedition against a coalition of five kings led by Jabin of HAZOR (Josh 11), resulting in the destruction of Hazor and the possession of northern Palestine. At this time Joshua divided the land among the remaining nine and one-half tribes (Josh 13–19; PLATE 10).

A rather different picture appears in Judg 1:1–2:5, where the Israelites are described as merely gaining a foothold in Canaan. The text lists scattered military operations by single tribes and presents what appears to be a peaceful settlement with the indigenous population of Canaan, including a list of twenty cities which Israel is said not to have conquered (cf. Deut 7:22 for a rationale for this). A number of tensions with the narrative in the book of Joshua are evident. In Josh 10, Hebron and Debir are said to have been conquered by Joshua, but in Judg 1:9-19 (and Josh 15:13-19) this is attributed to Caleb and OTHNIEL. Similarly, Num 32:39-41 attributes certain conquests in Transjordan to individual tribal groups like the Machirites, Jairites, and Nobahites, whereas Num 21:21-35 has the whole region (except for Edom, Moab, and Ammon) conquered as a result of a unified effort by all Israel. It should be noted that some scholars see a "pre-Exodus" conquest tradition in Gen 34. Thus it seems that the basic conquest story as related in Josh 1–12 is oversimplified.

The internal evidence for a more complex historical interpretation of events is compounded by conflicting archaeological data. A number of cities suffered violent destructions at the end of the Late Bronze Age (thirteenth and twelfth centuries B.C.E.) including MEGIDDO, BETH-SHAN, Hazor, Tell Abu Hawam, APHEK, BETHEL, GEZER, BETH-SHEMESH, Tell Beit Mirsim, Ashdod, etc. (PLATE 3). Following these destructions, numerous villages sprang up in the central hill country, the lower Galilee, the northern Negeb, and in central and southern Transjordan. Although at first sight this evidence seems to support the presentation of Josh 1–12, a close look reveals considerable tension with the biblical account. The archaeological evidence suggests that the cities of Hormah, Arad, HESHBON, Jericho, Ai, Gibeon, and Jarmuth were not occupied in the thirteeth century B.C.E. Most of these sites suffered either destruction or abandonment in the Middle Bronze Age or earlier. The major destruction of Ai took place hundreds of years before Joshua came on the scene. On the other hand, there are cities like Megiddo, Beth-shan, Gezer, and Bethel which did suffer destruction during the thirteenth century B.C.E.; but the biblical record states that the Israelites could not drive out the inhabitants of these cities (Judg 1). The historian is thus forced to reckon with more than one invading force at this time, perhaps the SEA PEOPLES, who also entered Palestine about the time of Israel's conquest. To complicate matters further, the Bible lists only five places which are said to have been destroyed: Hormah, Jericho, Ai, Lachish, and Hazor. Of these, only Hazor and Lachish are supported by archaeological evidence. In short, archaeological evidence points to far wider destruction at the end of the Late Bronze Age than is attributed to Joshua and his troops. The combination of internal tensions within the biblical text and the poor fit with the archaeological evidence has produced three different theories for the conquest and settlement of Israel.

The first school of thought is that of the conquest or forced entry model, in which the biblical picture as depicted in Josh 1–12 is taken as essentially historical and accurate. Those representing this point of view include G. Ernest Wright, J. Bright, P. Lapp, Y. Yadin, and A. Malamat. It was W. F. Albright who first adduced the evidence of the extensive destruction throughout Palestine during the Late Bronze Age as confirmation of the biblical account. In addition to the archaeological evidence already cited, the Merneptah stele (ca. B.C.E. 1224–1211) is taken as evidence for "Israel" being among the nations of Palestine at this time.

The poor fit of archaeological evidence with the biblical account in such instances as Jericho, Ai, and Bethel has caused some to abandon or revise the conquest model. D. Ussishkin has argued that Hazor and Lachish were destroyed nearly a century apart (end of thirteeth and twelfth centuries respectively). Thus, he concludes that the conquest was a much more drawn out affair than that described in Josh 1–12. A more radical solution to this archaeological problem is set forth by J. Bimson who notes that, whereas there is no archaeological evidence for the destruction of such cities as Jericho, Ai, Gibeon, Hebron, Hormah, Arad, Debir, Lachish, and Hazor during the Late Bronze Age, there is evidence for this shortly before 1400 B.C.E. Thus, Bimson redates the conquest and Exodus to a period 200 years earlier than the normal dating (as based on the references to Pithom and Ramses in Exod 1:1). This further entails a lowering of the end of the Middle Bronze Age from 1550 B.C.E. to shortly before 1400 B.C.E. It should be noted that Bimson does not cite sufficient evidence for lowering the date of the Middle Bronze Age. Moreover, his solution creates as many chronological problems as it solves (i.e., the period of the judges in Israel would now be nearly 600 years long).

A second model for interpreting the evidence was advanced by A. Alt and M. Noth, and more recently by M. Weippert, the so-called infiltration or peaceful settlement theory. Here the Genesis narratives are taken as the starting point, with Israel as nomadic or seminomadic tribes. Each year, in search of new pastures, they would enter the land, gradually becoming a sedentary people. At first their relationships with the urban population in Canaan were peaceful. It was only in the second stage, at the end of the Period of the Judges, that there would have been military conquests. The principle datum that Alt relied on was the fact that the Israelite tribes settled in the thinly populated mountainous regions which would have best enabled this process of gradual assimilation to Canaanite culture. Recently, this theory has been defended by Y. Aharoni, who argued that the biblical traditions associated with the Negeb battles are not to be associated with Moses and Joshua, but rather predate this period by almost three hundred years. A similar thesis has been offered by V. Fritz, who presents what he calls a "symbiosis model," developed from an anthropological perspective. Recent studies have shown that Alt was wrong in positing that nomads from the desert would invade the urban centers. Rather, the reverse is true. Studies have shown that pastoralists migrate from the urban center to the desert, not vice versa, and are sent out by the village in order to increase economic productivity during the nonproductive months of the agricultural year. Furthermore, archaeology has shown a dependence of Iron Age culture on that of the Late Bronze Age. Since the Iron Age settlements are not an offshoot of the Canaanite cities, this continuity is explained by Fritz as due to prolonged contact with Canaanite culture. Thus, there was no conquest as such, but rather a steady stream of independent migrations by separate tribal groups. The weakness of this theory is that it does not account for all of the archaeological data, and it too quickly dismisses the biblical stories as etiological in nature.

An interesting synthesis of the different proposals of these two schools of thought was offered by R. de Vaux, who proposed that there were four different regions each with a distinctive type of settlement. The southern region was characterized by a peaceful settlement by various tribes, as was the case in the central hill country. On the other hand, in Transjordan and the northern region there was more of a military operation as such.

A third alternative, the internal revolt model, has been proposed by G. Mendenhall and N. Gottwald, which proposes that Israel was the result of a social reorganization among the indigenous Canaanite population of the Late Bronze Age. This reorganization was the result of a social revolt within Canaanite society. Mendenhall drew attention to the social conditions reflected in the AMARNA letters, where the *'apiru* class of people appear as uprooted individuals of varied origins. They stood outside the societal structures. These *'apiru* are identified by Mendenhall as forerunners of the Hebrews. In this view, the ideological and religious structures had broken down in the Late Bronze Age, resulting in the withdrawal of the peasant class from urban society. Thus the Israelite conquest is a misnomer, having nothing to do with the massive destructions of the mid-thirteeth century, but rather with certain transitions within the Iron Age itself (1200–1175 B.C.E.).

Gottwald has defined the peasants' revolt along political and social lines rather than religious ones. He posits that there was conflict, not between pastoral and agricultural groups, but between urban and rural life. Israelite Yahwism is identified with rural life, which consciously rejected Canaanite centralization of power. The result of this conflict was a peasants' revolt which resulted in the formation of Israel. M. Chaney has advocated that the catalyst to this peasant revolt was the infusion via the Exodus group into an already unsettled Canaanite population.

The major weakness of this theory is three-fold: (1) the identification of *'apiru* elements with Hebrews is tenuous at best; (2) the peasant revolt model seems to be a modern Marxist construct superimposed on biblical traditions; and (3) the biblical tradition insists that Israel's ancestors came from Mesopotamia and not Canaan. This view, however, does promise greater control of the biblical traditions through the use of sociological categories. Its growing popularity is suggested by the third edition of J. Bright's *A History of Israel,* which states that the conquest must "to some degree" be an inside job.

In summary, the biblical picture of the conquest, as presented in Josh 1–12, has come under considerable scrutiny. The biblical and extra-biblical evidence gives rise to three different models: conquest, infiltration, and internal revolt. Given the variety of statements within the Bible itself, and the conflicting archaeological results, it may not be too much to say that the truth of the conquest probably lies somewhere in the synthesis of these three models. Such a synthesis must also be cognizant of the fact that memory of the conquest was transmitted within a worshipping community in ancient Israel, in which the Exodus-conquest was a celebrated ritual event in the current life of the people, as well as a memory of actual experiences in the more distant past.

See also CANAAN; CANAAN, INHABITANTS OF; EXODUS; ISRAEL; TRIBES.

Bibliography. Y. Aharoni, *The Land of the Bible,* and "The Israelite Occupation of Canaan," *BARead* (May/June 1982): 14-23; A. Alt, "The Settlement of the Israelites in Palestine," in *Essays on Old Testament History and Religion*; J. Bimson, *Redating the Exodus and Conquest, JSOTSupp* 5, "Redating the Exodus," *BARead* (Sep/Oct 1987): 40-68; J. Bright, *A History of Israel,* 3rd ed.; M. Chaney, "Ancient Palestinian Peasant Movements and the Formation of Premonarchic Israel," *Palestine in Transition*; F.M. Cross, Jr., "The Ritual Conquest," *Canaanite Myth and Hebrew Epic;* F. Frick, *The Formation of the State in Ancient Israel;* N. Gottwald, *The Tribes of Yahweh;* B. Halpern, *The Emergence of Israel in Canaan;* A. Malamat, "How Inferior Israelite Forces Conquered Fortified Canaanite Cities," *BARead* (Mar/Apr 1982): 24-35; G. Mendenhall, "The Hebrew Conquest of Palestine," *BA* 25

(1962): 66-87; J. Miller, "The Israelite Occupation of Canaan," *Israelite and Judean History;* D. Ussishkin, "Lachish: Key to the Israelite Conquest of Canaan?" *BARead* (Jan/Feb 1987): 18-39; R. de Vaux, *The Early History of Israel;* M. Weippert, *The Settlement of the Israelite Tribes in Palestine;* Y. Yadin, "Is the Biblical Account of the Israelite Conquest of Canaan Historically Reliable?" *BARead* (Mar/Apr 1982): 16-23; Z. Zevit, "The Problem of Ai," *BARead* (Mar/Apr 1985): 58-69.

—DUANE L. CHRISTENSEN

• **Conscience.** The Gk. term translated conscience occurs thirty times in the NT. The term is never used in the LXX, though the concept approaches the Hebrew notion of the HEART as the seat of moral feelings such as remorse, obligation, or innocence (cf. 1 Sam 24:5; 2 Sam 24:10; Job 27:6).

The origins of the term appear not to be in Stoic or Hellenistic philosophy as such but in popular or everyday ethical thought among the Greeks. It is one of a group of words used to express a certain kind of knowing, including a shared secret (whether of guilt or not), awareness or consciousness, and being convinced of a thing as truth.

The special realm of conscience is the moral life of the person and seems often to designate the human capacity for ethical discrimination in decisions and actions. It is an internal witness to moral obligation and is often regarded as a moral guide implanted by God. Conscience provides a private awareness of one's own actions or attitudes, but is never a source of knowledge of the actions or character of others. Further, the acts are past whether completed, and thus unchangeable, or begun but with alterable outcomes. Pain is often associated with conscience and connotes guilt from knowing one has done wrong.

These characteristics of the term are found in Rom 2:15 where Paul deals with gentiles whose "conscience bears witness" to the reality of God's work in their lives. Their thoughts may "accuse them" or "excuse them," he says, but conscience is at work in either case (cf. Acts 24:16; Rom 13:5; 2 Cor 1:12). The role of conscience as judge seems the primary use of the term in the writings of Paul. A "bad conscience" can cause pain (1 Tim 4:2; Titus 1:15; Heb 10:2, 22) or one can live free with a "clear conscience" (Acts 24:16; 1 Tim 3:9; 2 Tim 1:3; Heb 13:18; 1 Pet 3:16, 21), which establishes a strong incentive for moral living.

Conscience is neither the voice of God nor adequate as a moral guide, however. At one level, conscience represents the socialization of the person. It consists of the internalization of moral values taught by parents or other authority figures. Social customs, mores, and folkways establish expectations for acceptable behavior within particular groups or cultures. As one internalizes social values about what is right and wrong, a personal guide or belief system is established by which one makes decisions. What is believed to be right and wrong, good or bad, varies enormously from culture to culture and thus person to person.

As a moral guide, conscience reflects both cultural and individualistic relativism and thus could hardly be followed as an infallible voice. Paul makes this clear in 1 Cor 4:4 where he points out that troublemakers in the church claim a clear conscience even as he does, so that fact alone does not settle the issue. The inadequacy and unreliability of conscience as a moral guide was also apparent in the controversy over meat offered to idols. The "weak" felt condemned if they ate the meat, while others had no problem (1 Cor 8:7; 10:28ff.) A further problem is that of moral insensitivity. The Pastorals speak of the "seared" (1 Tim 4:2) or "corrupted" conscience (Titus 1:15), indicating that people do not always feel guilt for doing wrong.

Where conscience functions as a moral compass, however, the values at stake represent ground-of-meaning beliefs for the individual that are to be guarded and respected. Paul's sensitive and insightful treatment of the controversies at Corinth made two things clear: (1) there will be a variety of opinions on moral matters, and (2) conscientious beliefs are to be respected. He thus laid the foundations for the notions of freedom of conscience and religious liberty.

In American jurisprudence, conscience is the name given the governing principles of life to which a person is ultimately committed, which is both consistent with and a refinement of NT uses of the term. The truth upon which it builds is that the essence of the self and thus the integrity of personhood is involved in the moral dictates of conscience. The inner life of faith is the primary arena of the human spirit's struggle with the moral claims made by the will of God. Obeying one's conscience is tantamount to obeying God.

The violation of conscience is thus of ultimate significance on religious grounds. Willfully to disobey one's own conscience is to do violence to personal wholeness, as Paul made clear (1 Cor 8:11). Personality disorders and incapacitating guilt are predictable if not inevitable consequences of choices that betray one's own sense of right and wrong. The self is the first victim on the altar of moral compromise.

The corollary truth is that to coerce people to act contrary to their own beliefs or to punish those who act upon deeply held religious and moral opinion is also to violate God's will. The believer's direct access to God requires respect for different understandings of the demands of faith. This insight undergirds the notion of religious liberty as expressed in the First Amendment to the Constitution of the United States and in Article 18 of the Universal Declaration of Human Rights. Every person has an inalienable right to freedom of conscience and religion.

Obedience to God is the ultimate requirement of faith and relativizes all lesser loyalties, thus making a conflict between the claims of conscience and the demands of other authorities inevitable. First Pet 2:19 speaks of those who suffer unjustly because of "conscience of God." The RSV translation, "mindful of God," seems to miss the point. The AV and ASV seem closer with "for conscience toward God." Peter is depicting those who are willing to suffer because of conscientious convictions. As the history of those who have been persecuted because of religious beliefs has shown, not even the threats of death, torture, or imprisonment are sufficient to deter those whose conscience is captive to God and open to divine leadership.

See also ETHICS IN THE NEW TESTAMENT; FOOD OFFERED TO IDOLS; HEART.

Bibliography. C. A. Pierce, *Conscience in the New Testament.*

—PAUL D. SIMMONS

• **Contribution for the Saints.** The contribution for the saints was an offering PAUL gathered from churches he had founded in the gentile world for the relief of the poor Christians in Jerusalem. Although Jewish people took care of their orphans and widows, the Christians in Jerusalem had apparently been cut off from this aid. Early in its life the Jerusalem church "had all things in common" (Acts 2:44), and those who had property sold it and gave the money to the apostles for the welfare of the entire group. Later during a famine, the church at Antioch sent Paul and Barnabas with aid to Jerusalem (Acts 11:28-30).

Severe racial tensions, which sometimes invaded the church, existed between Jews and gentiles during the first century. Thus, when the gospel went to the gentiles, many Jewish Christians demanded that gentiles be circumcised and follow Jewish regulations. But at the Jerusalem conference (Acts 15) the church decided not to require circumcision. In his report of the conference (Gal 2:9-10), Paul wrote that the only stipulation was that he and the other missionaries remember the poor, which he said he was already doing.

Perhaps this requirement provided Paul's motivation for the collection. However, it took on added symbolic significance for him, providing a way to facilitate peace between Jewish and gentile Christians. Paul believed deeply that the offering provided both an opportunity for gentile churches to help the poor Christians in Jerusalem and to demonstrate their love for the Jewish Christians. While it would be normal for Jewish and proselyte converts to share with the Jerusalem church, it was different with gentiles who were never associated with Judaism. Paul did not order his churches to give, but appealed to their sense of obligation and to their generosity. Since the Jewish Christians had shared the spiritual blessings of the gospel with the gentiles, they should share their material blessings with the Jewish Christians (Rom 15:24-32).

Churches in Macedonia and Achaia participated in the offering (2 Cor 8:1ff.). The church at Philippi eagerly gave more than they could afford (2 Cor 8:6-11). Paul counseled them to set aside money each Sunday in order to have the funds on hand when he arrived (1 Cor 16:1-2). The Corinthians were slow to fulfill their pledge, and the apostle admonished them to complete the collection, declaring that giving to such a worthy cause was a grace equal to faith and love. By willingly, cheerfully, and proportionately giving they would have a ministry of fellowship to the Christians in Jerusalem (2 Cor 8-9).

Paul had each church send an envoy with him so that the churches would know how the funds were distributed. In spite of his enthusiasm for the offering, Paul dreaded the journey to Jerusalem. It delayed a planned trip to Rome, was dangerous, and he did not know how the Jerusalemites would respond to the offering (Rom 15:24-32). Acts records that Paul felt bound in the Spirit to go to Jerusalem, yet feared what might happen there (Acts 20:22-24). Nevertheless, Paul courageously delivered the collection. How the church in Jerusalem responded is not known, but Paul was arrested and imprisoned.

See also PAUL.

Bibliography. J. Knox, *Chapters in a Life of Paul*; W. L. Knox, *St. Paul and the Church of Jerusalem*.

—W. T. EDWARDS

• **Conversion.** The term conversion is seldom used in the English Bible (it appears in noun form only once in the NT [Acts 15:3]). Western medieval theology used the Latin term to signify entering monastic life and turning from the world. Luther preferred the word REPENTANCE or penitence and Calvin used resurrection imagery. Though the word is not used, the imagery is common to both the OT and NT and is clearly present in the dramatic experiences of Augustine and Luther.

The basic meaning of conversion in the Bible is that of "turning." The word can serve with no religious meaning as when Mary and Joseph return to Nazareth (Luke 2:39) or Peter turns to look at John (John 21:20). The outstanding examples of the religious concept of conversion (turning) in the NT are Paul (Acts 9:1-22), the jailer at Philippi (Acts 16:27-34), Zacchaeus (Luke 19:2-10), and the Ethiopian eunuch (Acts 8:26-40). The paradigm is the prodigal son who came to himself and returned to his father (Luke 15:11-32).

The Christian understanding of conversion has its roots in the OT. A unique use of the concept is that of God turning in relationship to his children whether favorably (Deut 13:17) or unfavorably (Josh 24:20). This action of God is his unchanging pursuit of his people for their salvation. It is also used to speak of the covenant people turning in relationship to God. They can turn to God (Jer 3:14), which is commitment to covenant loyalty (Ps 85:3), or from God (Jer 8:4-6; Ezek 33:18), which is rebellion (Josh 22:16).

The imagery conveyed by the use of the term in relation to the covenant people is that of rebelling subjects who come back to serve their rightful king, of a faithless wife returning to her husband, or of those seduced by Baal returning to the true God. Conversion is thus described as turning from evil (Jer 18:8) and to the Lord (Mal 3:7). God is the primary mover in this turning (Jer 31:18) but uses his prophets in the process of calling to conversion (Neh 9:26; Zech 1:4). The call to conversion is issued both to individuals (2 Kgs 23:15-16) and to nations (Jonah 3:10). Those who respond receive forgiveness (Isa 55:7) and fullness of life (Ezek 33:14).

The NT does not speak of God turning. Its most characteristic use is of a person turning to God (Acts 9:35; 15:19). It is also used to refer to turning from God (Gal 4:9). Conversion is often associated with words like repent (Acts 3:19; 26:20) or believe (Acts 11:21). It is often coupled with a word which indicates the nature of the turning such as from darkness to light (1 Pet 2:9; Acts 26:18), from death to life (John 5:24), from idols to the living God (1 Thess 1:9), or from vain things to the living God (Acts 14:15). It is this turning which issues in forgiveness (Acts 3:19; 26:18) and translates the forgiven into the Kingdom of God (Acts 26:18). This turning is not the result of outward deed but is a spiritual transformation effected by God (2 Cor 3:18).

Most contemporary psychological studies view conversion as a reunification of a divided self resulting in a sense of inward wholeness. The biblical emphasis is not on a psychological, subjective experience but on an objective change of lifestyle (Eph 5:2; Col 1:10; 2:10-12). Its imagery is that of two ways or options and the choice of the way of the Lord (Acts 9:2; 19:9; 22:4; Jas 5:19-20). The initial change is a first step in an ongoing process.

See also REPENTANCE.

—PAUL D. BREWER

• **Convocation.** "Holy convocation" (Heb. *miqrâ' qōdeš*), a technical term of the Pentateuch, always used in connection with the annual cultic festivals. Its literal meaning is "holy calling," and scholars are divided over whether this is to be seen as a calling of the CONGREGATION to WORSHIP or as a public proclamation of the FEAST days. The actual occurrences of the term favor the latter. It is found primarily in the discussion of the festivals in Num 28–29 and the parallel Holiness Code treatment in Lev 23. It occurs in priestly material and seems to reflect exilic or post-exilic usage.

Such public proclamations are specified for the first and seventh days of PASSOVER (Exod 12:16; Lev 23:7-8; Num

28:18, 25), for Pentecost (Lev 23:21; Num 28:26), for the NEW YEAR'S FESTIVAL (Lev 23:24; Num 29:1), for the DAY OF ATONEMENT (Lev 23:27; Num 29:7), and for the first and eighth days of the Festival of Booths (Lev 23:35-36; Num 29:12, 35). In every instance, along with the holy proclamation, there is the statement that no work is to be done on those days, which reflects a transferral of the old SABBATH provisions to these special holy days.

See also FEASTS AND FESTIVALS; PRIESTLY WRITERS; TABERNACLES, FESTIVAL OF; UNLEAVENED BREAD, FEAST OF; WEEKS, FESTIVAL OF; WORSHIP IN THE OLD TESTAMENT.

Bibliography. M. Noth, *Leviticus, OTL.*

—JOHN POLHILL

• **Copper.** A reddish chemical element. Pure or native copper is a relatively soft metal and can be found in its free metallic state in nature. Though rare, native copper can be worked into small objects, such as pins, rings, and necklaces, without smelting or casting by simply hammering. Larger objects were made by fusing and casting. Copper was often combined with tin to make bronze. Combining zinc with copper yielded brass. Greek uses the one word to refer to all three, as does Hebrew.

The earliest known fashioned copper object dates to about the eighth millennium B.C.E. at Çayönü Tepesi in southeast Anatolia, the only site with evidence of such an early metal use. Though small amounts of metal—basically copper with small amounts of lead—are known from a number of western Asiatic sites down to ca. 4000 B.C.E., metallurgy did not begin to have a real impact until in the fourth millennium B.C.E. A series of flat axes (fifty-five in the Louvre), large and small chisels, pins, and mirrors comes from Susa I (formerly known as Susa A), dating to the first half of the fourth millennium B.C.E. A spectacular Palestinian find from the period is the hoard of over 400 copper and arsenical copper artifacts from Nahal Mishmar on the west shore of the Dead Sea. These artifacts appear to be from a ritual or ceremonial context. Finds from related Late Chalcolithic (Ghassulian) sites indicate a regional metal industry, involving the smelting and casting of local copper.

Copper's malleability makes it unsatisfactory for tools used in everyday life. Since the cutting edges on copper implements would not last, flints continued to be of importance. With the introduction of alloys, it became possible to utilize copper in tools and weapons.

The third millennium (often designated as the Early Bronze Age), saw the full development of METALLURGY which included (1) the polymetallic technology in the use of smelted copper, copper alloyed with arsenic or tin, gold, silver, lead, and an occasional piece of iron (not necessarily meteoric); (2) the development of regional schools with distinctive methods and artifacts; and (3) the use of metal, especially bronze, for utilitarian articles such as hoes, saws, adzes, axes, and knives. Copper remained relatively scarce in Palestine during this period judging from archaeological finds.

The Middle Bronze Age saw an increased use of copper implements, but bronze began to replace copper. Pottery which seems to have metallic prototypes began to appear. Copper continued to be used into the Iron Age. Brass did not come into extensive use until late B.C.E.

Sources for copper included the Sinai Peninsula, Cyprus, Asia Minor, Syria, Lebanon, the Caucasus Mountains, Tarshish, Javan, Meshech and Tubal (Ezek 26:13).

The OT references to copper and copper-like implements are often associated with the Temple and its furnishings (Exod 26:37; 27:2-4; 1 Kgs 7:23-27; 14:27).

See also BRASS/BRONZE; METALLURGY.

—ROBERT A. STREET, JR.

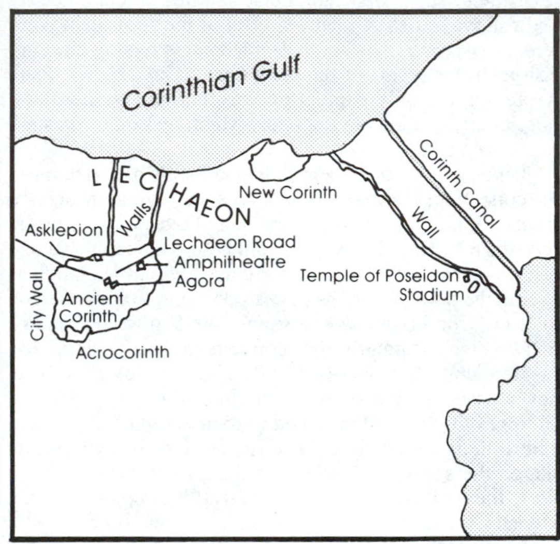

Designed by Margaret Jordan Brown ©Mercer University Press

• **Corinth.** [kor'inth] Corinth was an ancient city situated just across the narrow isthmus that connects the Greek mainland with the Peloponnesus (PLATES 26, 27). Founded by the Dorian Greeks in the tenth century B.C.E., it was located at the base of Acrocorinth, a rocky hill rising nearly two thousand ft. above sea level.

In the eighth century B.C.E., Corinth founded colonies at Corfu and Syracuse, and by the time of Periander (ca. 625–583 B.C.E.) had attained a position of power and wealth. A major factor in its prosperity was its location which enabled it to control the seaports at Lechaion on the Gulf of Corinth and at Cenchrea on the Saronic Gulf. In order to pull small ships from one gulf to the other, Periander constructed a five-ft. wide rock-cut track across the isthmus. But it was the emperor Nero who, in the first century C.E., first attempted to dig a canal connecting the two ports. However, his efforts were unsuccessful, and this ambitious project was not completed until 1881–93.

The city survived the Peloponnesian War (431–404) and the Corinthian War (395–87), but was totally destroyed by the Roman consul L. Mummius in 145 B.C.E. The devastation was so great that the city lay in ruins for a hundred years. Under a decree of Julius Caesar issued in 44 B.C.E., the city was rebuilt as a Roman colony. It is basically this city that PAUL knew in the middle of the first century C.E. By 27 B.C.E., Corinth was the capital of the province of ACHAIA.

The archaeological excavations at Corinth, which were begun in 1896 by the American School of Classical Studies in Athens, have shed considerable light on the city of Paul's time. These finds include the agora, with its many shops, and various temples such as that of Apollo, which dates originally to the sixth century B.C.E. Also discovered were the remains of the temple of Aphrodite which was built on top of Acrocorinth. The activities of the cult of Aphrodite have led some interpreters to paint Corinth as a city of unbridled sexual license.

A particularly noteworthy find from Paul's time is the *bema*, a public speaking platform built in 44 C.E. and located in the middle of the forum. This may be the place where Paul spoke when he was brought "before the tribunal" (Acts 18:12-17). Another important discovery that illuminates Paul's writings is the Lerna-Ascepeum, and other temples, which contained elaborate dining rooms for sacred meals (cf. 1 Cor 8, 10; note esp. 8:10).

Several important inscriptions have also been found. One, dated to the middle of the first century C.E., refers to a Roman official named Erastus. This is thought by some to be the same Erastus mentioned by Paul in Rom 16:23. Another inscription found near the agora contains the Latin word for shop or market, *macellum*, the Greek form of which Paul uses in 1 Cor 10:25. Also found is a Greek inscription on a broken lintel which has been translated "Synagogue of the Hebrews." Though thought to be from a time later than Paul, it may have come from the synagogue that succeeded the one in Paul's day (cf. Acts 18:4).

See also APOLLOS; CORINTHIAN CORRESPONDENCE; FOOD OFFERED TO IDOLS; GALLIO; PAUL; PRISCILLA AND AQUILA.

Bibliography. J. Murphy-O'Connor, *St. Paul's Corinth: Texts and Archaeology*.

—JOHN C. H. LAUGHLIN

• **Corinthian Correspondence.** [kuh-rin'thee-uhn] Alongside Romans and Galatians the Corinthian Letters stand in the heart of the Pauline corpus. These four canonical Letters encompass the breadth and depth of the mind of PAUL and provide the standards by which the shape of Pauline theology and ethics are measured. Among these "Pauline Pillars" the Corinthian Letters pose most intriguing issues, even for the casual reader. What sort of place was CORINTH? What was the relationship between Paul and the Corinthians? What kind of community of faith emerged at Corinth? How many letters did Paul write to Corinth? What themes are struck in them?

Corinth. By the time Paul arrived in Corinth, probably in the early 50s C.E., Corinth was a new city less than 100 years old built on an ancient site. Like all seaports Corinth was thoroughly cosmopolitan. Situated on a narrow isthmus linking lower and upper Achaia, Corinth had emerged as a key crossroads of the Roman world. Economic interests, military personnel, and philosophical and religious ideas freely flowed through the city. Corinth was also well known as a center for the WORSHIP of Aphrodite; throughout Roman provinces mention of Corinth was likely to elicit images of sexual license and excess.

Paul and the Corinthians. Acts 18 provides a synopsis of the initial missionary work Paul accomplished in Corinth. Over a period of eighteen months (v. 11) Paul, along with a number of co-workers, launched the gospel among Corinthians of Jewish and gentile heritage. Work in Corinth was conducted in the face of crisis and controversy. Soon after arriving Paul was forced out of the synagogue. At the end of the first Corinthian visit Paul was charged formally with violation of Jewish Law before the proconsul, Gallio (Acts 18:12-17). Perceiving the charge as internecine Jewish squabbling, Gallio refused to act. Paul's quick departure, however, suggests that the apostle may have been strongly encouraged to find other fields of labor. Acts is mute on further visits of Paul to Corinth, although there is mention of a three month sojourn in Greece near the end of the third missionary journey (Acts 20:1-6). Some would equate this brief visit with the "painful visit" of 2 Cor 2:1 or the "third visit" anticipated in 2 Cor 12:14 and 13:1.

The Corinthian Letters provide materials out of which a fuller picture of the relationship between Paul and the Corinthians may be constructed. One is struck by the extremes of feelings Paul had for the Corinthian community of faith and, by implication, the extreme attitudes they had about him. Paul was grateful for the Corinthians (1 Cor 1:4-9) but he considered them immature (1 Cor 3:1-3; 14:20; 2 Cor 6:11-13; passim). Paul expressed relief that he had baptized but a few of the Corinthians (1 Cor 14f.) lest they claim him as leader, and then boldly encouraged them to

• OUTLINE OF CORINTHIANS •

The Letters to the Corinthians

I. Introduction to 1 Cornithians
  A. Greetings (1:1-3)
  B. Thanksgivings (1:4-9)
II. Problems and Solutions
  A. Factions (1:10-12)
  B. The unity of Christ (1:13-17)
  C. The power of God at work in the cross (1:18-31)
  D. The wisdom of God; the mind of Christ (2:1-16)
  E. Cooperation: Paul and Apollos, a test case (3:1–4:21)
III. Ethics, Personal and Corporate
  A. A case of incest (5:1-13)
  B. Lawsuits in the fellowship (6:1-11)
  C. Sexual practice (6:12-20)
  D. The Corinthians' concerns for marriage (7:1-24)
  E. The Corinthians' concerns for the unmarried (7:25-40)
  F. The Corinthians' concerns for food (8:1-13; 10:14–11:1)
  G. A digression: Paul's rights as an apostle (9:1-27)
  H. A warning against idolatry (10:1-13)
  I. Worship practices (11:2–14:40)
IV. Resurrection, the Heart of the Gospel
  A. Reports of resurrection (15:1-11)
  B. The assurance of resurrection (15:12-34)
  C. The mystery of resurrection (15:35-58)
V. Personal Issues
  A. The Corinthians' concerns for the relief offering (1:1-4)
  B. Various requests (16:5-18)
  C. Closing remarks (16:19-24)
VI. The Stern Letter
  A. Paul defends his apostleship (2 Cor 10:1-18)
  B. Paul against the false apostles (2 Cor 11:1-15)
  C. Paul as an example of strength in weakness (2 Cor 11:1–12:10)
  D. Expressions of care (2 Cor 12:11-21)
  E. Warnings (2 Cor 13:1-10)
  F. Canonical closing of 2 Corinthians (2 Cor 13:11-15)
VII. The Mature Letter
  A. Canonical greetings of 2 Corinthians (2 Cor 1:1-2)
  B. A doxology (2 Cor 1:3-11)
  C. Paul's plans (2 Cor 1:12–2:4)
  D. The need for forgiveness (2 Cor 2:5-11)
  E. The new covenant (2 Cor 3:12-18)
  F. The humanity of God's ministers (2 Cor 4:1-18)
  G. Assurances in Christ (2 Cor 5:1-10)
  H. The shared ministry of reconciliation (2 Cor 5:11–6:2)
  I. Paul's difficulties (2 Cor 6:3-13)
  J. Caution toward unbelievers (2 Cor 6:14–7:1)
  K. Expressions of joy (2 Cor 7:2-16)
  L. Further encouragment for the relief offering (2 Cor 8:1-15)
  M. Concluding remarks (2 Cor 8:16–9:15)

imitate him (1 Cor 10:31–11:1). The Corinthians trusted Paul enough to ask for advice, as evidenced in the phrase, "Now concerning the matters about which you wrote" (1 Cor 7:1), which provides the framework for 1 Cor 7–16. The trust was challenged, however, by apparent doubts about Paul's authority as an apostle as seen, e.g., in 1 Cor 9 and 2 Cor 10.

In addition to letters which passed between Paul and the Corinthians there were also verbal reports, at least to Paul, which kept the relationship alive following Paul's initial visit. Over one-fourth of 1 Corinthians develops around a report from Chloe's people (1 Cor 1:11) regarding factions in the church at Corinth. Similar instances of second-hand reports to Paul as background to the Corinthian writings are certainly likely, even though explicit reference to those reports are lacking. In sum, the relationship between Paul and the Corinthians was variegated at best. Nonetheless, the Corinthian Letters bear witness to the desires of both parties to preserve and refine their common bonds of faith.

The Corinthian Community. Divisions within the Corinthian church cannot be disputed for the apostle himself spells out at least three, and possibly four, distinct groups vying for prominence (1 Cor 1:10ff.). Given the nature of the city of Corinth, and the unsettled nature of Paul's tenure during the initial visit, one should scarcely be surprised by the emergence of factions after Paul's departure. Paul identifies the factions according to each group's stated allegiances: some of the Corinthians claim Paul as founder; others Apollos; and others, Cephas. There is also the last-named group who claim Christ.

Taking clues from Gal 2, some readers have associated the Cephas party with the Judaizers who wanted gentile converts to the gospel to adhere to strict Jewish customs, rituals, and laws. While the possibility of a Judaizing faction may be the underlying reason for Paul's treatment of the issue of food offered to idols (1 Cor 8 and 10), it is unlikely Judaizers represented a full-blown sect within the Corinthian community.

The Paul and Apollos parties among the Corinthians may well have resulted from minor differences within broad agreement. Both Paul and Apollos had conducted missionary activity in Corinth (cf. Acts 18:24-28 for mention of the work of Apollos). Paul refers to Apollos as "our brother" in closing exhortations found at the end of 1 Corinthians. Throughout much of the section of 1 Corinthians addressing the factions issue, Paul consciously compares himself to Apollos in complementary fashion, encouraging the Corinthians to cooperate with one another even as he and Apollos had cooperated in the ministry of the gospel.

At least two opinions about the "Christ" party may be offered. One suggestion is that Paul names this fourth group in order to demonstrate the unity of Christ (1 Cor 1:13) and, thereby, encourage unity in the body of Christ, the church (cf. 1 Cor 12). Another suggestion takes the Christ party at face value, as a group which rather arrogantly lays claim to Christ, and links it with the "spiritual" members referred to in 1 Cor 12 and 14. If the Christ party is associated with the "spirituals" of 1 Corinthians, it may also be tied to the detractors of Paul's apostolic status—who apparently saw themselves as super-apostles (cf. 2 Cor 11:5 and 12:11)—which prompt the writing of the harsh words in 2 Cor 10–13.

Many readers of 1 and 2 Corinthians find evidence of nascent GNOSTICISM, that permutation of faith which blossomed late in the first century C.E. and became a formidable foe of orthodoxy in the second. Paul's major opponents, as reflected in the Corinthian Letters, may have been proponents of pre-Gnostic ideas.

A distinct picture of the Corinthian community is no more possible than is one of contemporary communities. The Corinthian church appears to have consisted of a broad middle eagerly seeking to discover mature faith, fringed with some who sought comfort in rigorous ritual and others who prided themselves on their own flamboyance and sophistication of thought.

Extent of Correspondence. Few issues in Pauline studies generate more scrutiny and speculation than that of counting, categorizing, and collating the Corinthian correspondence. Reasons for such critical activity are clear: the canonical shape of the NT acknowledges two Letters; internally, however, there are mentions of additional letters (1 Cor 5:9f.; 1 Cor 2:3f.; and 2 Cor 7:8) which may or may not refer to the canonical texts; and, finally, the content, style, and tone of the Letters themselves demonstrate multiple settings. Opinions as to the extent of the Corinthian correspondence range from a strict defence of only two letters, exactly as found in the NT, to as many as nine letters. One widely held position suggests four letters from Paul to Corinth, including one letter which has been lost and three found within the canonical texts.

(1) "Corinthians A": The Lost Letter. 1 Cor 5:9 alludes to a previous letter from Paul which encouraged the Corinthians "not to associate with immoral men." Little more may be said about this lost letter, except that the readers were confused about which immoral men the apostle had in mind. In part that confusion led to a second letter.

(2) "Corinthians B": 1 Corinthians. Canonical 1 Corinthians contains at least three explicit references to the reasons for its writing. The heart of the Letter addresses questions posed by the Corinthians in a letter they sent to Paul (1 Cor 7:1). Paul was in Ephesus when he wrote (1 Cor 16:8) and had apparently been actively continuing his ministry among the Corinthians through advice, oral and written.

A second reason for writing appears as a report "from Chloe's people" (1 Cor 1:11) that quarreling has erupted among the Corinthians. Chloe's people may have also brought the report of incest noted in 1 Cor 5:1f. Whether these reports were oral or written is not clear. If oral, Chloe's people may have been engaged in commerce between Corinth and Ephesus and, thereby, had contact with both Paul and the Corinthian church. If written, the report from Chloe's people may have come from a household which participated in the Corinthian fellowship. A third reason for writing was the Corinthian confusion about "immoral men." In 1 Cor 5:9–6:20 Paul emphasizes that immoral people may be found within the fellowship.

(3) "Corinthians C": The Stern Letter. Canonical 2 Corinthians contains two sharply defined sections, one quite harsh (2 Cor 10–13) and the other filled with words of RECONCILIATION (2 Cor 1–9). A difficulty arises because the harsh letter follows the more positive, reconciling letter. One would assume a reversed chronology. Furthermore, a reversed chronology gains support from 2 Cor 2:1-11 which explicitly notes a "painful visit" to Corinth which precipitated a stern letter. Accepting a four letter reconstruction of the Corinthian correspondence leads to the identification of 2 Cor 10–13 as the stern letter, at times identified as the "hurt letter" or the "tearful letter." Those who do not accept a four letter reconstruction suggest another lost letter, the "tearful letter," and read the final four chapters of 2 Corinthians as evidence of a new

flare-up in the relationship between Paul and the Corinthians.

(4) "Corinthians D": The Mature Letter. The first nine chapters of 2 Corinthians are congratulatory and congenial. Paul speaks of past conflicts as water under the bridge and encourages his friends to be as forgiving of former strife as he is (2 Cor 2:5-11). Paul further encourages the Corinthians to seize the mandate to ministry with maturity and to see themselves as bearers of the "message of reconciliation," participants in the "ministry of reconciliation," and "ambassadors for Christ" (2 Cor 5:16-21). The final encouragement of this mature letter is for the Corinthians to continue their support of the Jerusalem church, in whose name Paul was collecting a relief offering from the churches in Greece and Asia Minor (cf. Acts 11:29-30 for the initial decision).

Themes of the Corinthian Correspondence. The extent of the Corinthian Letters allows for treatment of a variety of themes: (1) Response to reports of strife. 1 Cor 1:10–4:21 addresses the factionalism in the Corinthian fellowship. After identifying three or four parties, including the Paul, Apollos, and Cephas groups, and, possibly, the Christ group, Paul develops the theme of the mysterious wisdom of God as revealed through the cross of Christ. The theme is forged powerfully, but subtly. Human perceptions of strength and wisdom are contrary to the activity of God through Christ. The wisdom of God transcends the wisdom of humanity and, therefore, calls for humanity to put aside ill-conceived notions of prestige and work together as good stewards of the wisdom of God. Paul punctuates this theme with illustrations of the cooperative spirit of ministry which allowed Apollos and Paul to work for the same goals in Corinth.

(2) Ethics, personal and corporate. In 1 Cor 5:1–6:20 Paul continues to respond to reports received concerning goings-on in the Corinthian church. The initial issue is a charge of incest which members of the church have either ignored or winked at. While Paul condemns the practice of immorality "of a kind not found even among pagans" he also chastises the Corinthians for their attitudes which allowed the immorality to continue. The point is clear: ethical behavior is neither exclusively personal nor corporate. Individuals contribute to the values of the community and the community, in turn, should encourage the adherence of commonly held values from individuals. The incest issue allows Paul to confront an apparent proclivity among the Corinthians to take one another to civil court and, also, the prideful sexual libertarian life-styles (no doubt influenced by the Aphrodite cult in Corinth) among some. In each instance Paul again asserts the interdependence of personal and corporate ethics: each person's attitudes and actions contribute to and are influenced by the values of the community.

(3) Issues raised by the Corinthians. The heart of 1 Cor 7:1–16:4 is devoted to five direct questions the Corinthians posed in a letter to Paul. The apostle also expands his response concerning spiritual gifts to include comments about women in worship, celebration of the Lord's Supper, and the place of resurrection in the faith of the community. (a) Questions of marriage (1 Cor 7:1-24). Paul announces his preference for celibacy but, nonetheless, affirms the institution of monogamous union. Continuing the line of logic throughout chaps. 5 and 6, Paul stresses the interdependence of marriage commitments, giving males and females equal status. Paul counsels for the ideal of permanent marriage but allows for the dissolution of marriages in the name of peace when an unbeliever so requests. (b) The unmarried (1 Cor 7:25-40). Convinced of the imminent return of Christ Paul discourages marriage in favor of a total investment of energies in the furtherance of the gospel. In those cases where temptation to sin is too great, Paul affirms marriage. (c) Meat offered to idols (1 Cor 8:1-13; 10:1-11:1). Once again demonstrating the interdependence of attitudes and actions within the community, Paul develops two principles to guide the Corinthians. The first principle favors the weaker member of the community: "If meat offends, I will not eat it." The second principle favors the exercise of personal freedom with integrity: "Whether I eat or drink I should do so for the glory of God." Between these two principles Paul defends his freedom as an apostle (1 Cor 9:1-27). (d) Worship practices (1 Cor 11:2–15:58). The Corinthians specifically inquired about spiritual gifts (1 Cor 12:1) but Paul's response locates that issue within the worshiping community. Paul commends the Corinthians for adopting the Jewish practice of having women veiled in worship as a sign of dignity and respect (without doubt providing a needed contrast to the Aphrodite worshiper) but chastises them for profligate practices surrounding the Lord's Supper. The thread of interdependent responsibility, which appeared at 5:1f., also is woven into Paul's response about spiritual gifts. The exhortation is clear: individuals should use their gifts for the common good. The Corinthians did not ask explicitly about resurrection but Paul chose to conclude his comments about worship with an extended treatment of the topic. Against those who would deny resurrection the apostle asserts that resurrection is the cornerstone of faith and, therefore, the cornerstone of the community of faith. While Paul readily confesses the mysteriousness of resurrection, he nonetheless identifies it as the mystery which defines authentic faith. Note how the theological underpinnings of 1 Corinthians have evolved: the wisdom of God revealed in the cross (1 Cor 1:18ff.) culminates in the mystery of God revealed through resurrection. Between cross and resurrection lie the responsibilities of the community of faith. (e) The Jerusalem collection (1 Cor 16:1-4). With quick dispatch Paul underscores his commitment to the relief offering. The collection is addressed further in 2 Cor 8:1–9:15, entrusting Titus with its administration and encouraging the Corinthians' participation.

(4) Paul's Apostolic Ministry. The theme of apostolic ministry dominates 2 Corinthians. The so-called stern letter is Paul's defence of his calling while the so-called mature letter is his celebration of that same calling. First Cor 9 contains similar defence and celebration.

Conclusion. The Corinthian correspondence provides a rare glimpse into the thoroughly human relationship forged by Paul and the Corinthians. These Letters also demonstrate the power of faith, found in the wisdom and mystery of God, to sift, encourage, and refine believing communities.

See also CORINTH; FOOD OFFERED TO IDOLS; GIFTS OF THE SPIRIT; GNOSTICISM; LOVE IN THE NEW TESTAMENT; MARRIAGE IN THE NEW TESTAMENT; PAUL; RECONCILIATION; RESURRECTION IN THE NEW TESTAMENT; TONGUES; WISDOM IN THE NEW TESTAMENT; WORSHIP IN THE NEW TESTAMENT.

Bibliography. C. K. Barrett, *The First Epistle to the Corinthians* and *The Second Epistle to the Corinthians*; F. F. Bruce, *1 & 2 Corinthians*; B. S. Childs, *The New Testament as Canon*; D. Gutherie, *New Testament Introduction*; J. C. Hurd, *The Origin of 1 Corinthians*; R. P. Martin,

2 Corinthians; M. Soards, *The Apostle Paul*.

—RICHARD F. WILSON

• **Cornelius.** [kor-neel'yuhs] A centurion of the Italian Cohort, stationed in CAESAREA (Acts 10:1). He was known as a "devout man who feared God with all his household, who gave alms liberally to the people [the Jews], and who prayed constantly to God" (v. 2). His conversion, attested by the coming of the Holy Spirit (v. 44), is described; but chief focus is upon tensions resulting in the church over the inclusion of gentiles, uncircumcised and thus seen as "unclean" by some elements within the church (10:28; 11:2). This was a problem to PETER and even more so to "the circumcision party" in Jerusalem (11:2; Gal 2:11-14).

Cornelius's eagerness to hear "the word" sharply contrasts with Peter's reluctance to preach it to him, seeing it as "unlawful" for himself as a "Jew" to enter the house of "anyone of another nation" (10:28-31). That Peter was required to defend his actions in Jerusalem (11:1ff.) is a part of a theme throughout Acts, where the divine impulse is traced which impelled followers of Jesus to move from their origins in Jewish piety into the larger world, with inclusion based on faith and not ethnic or cultic distinctions.

See also APOSTLES, ACTS OF THE; CAESAREA; GENTILE/GENTILES IN THE NEW TESTAMENT; HOLY SPIRIT; PETER.

—FRANK STAGG

• **Cornerstone.** The cornerstone is most often the large stone which is selected for its strength (Job 38:6) and placed at the foundation of a wall angle to bind the walls together. At times it is the capstone (the top or final stone) which completes the building. In either case it is a key stone in the building. Most biblical uses are figurative. A striking use of this imagery describes the covenant faith as being steadfast like the well-built Solomonic Temple (Isa 28:16).

The imagery of the rejected stone (Israel) becoming head of the corner (Ps 118:22) is quoted by Jesus as applicable to himself (Matt 21:42; Mark 12:10; Luke 20:17). Ephesians develops the metaphor further (2:20). First Peter makes it more explicit: the church is a spiritual house erected on Christ as chief cornerstone (2:5-7); and Christ is the stone that will make unbelievers stumble (2:8).

—PAUL D. BREWER

• **Cosmetics.** Cosmetics were used by men and women throughout the ancient Near East much as they are today. Numerous archaeological discoveries have revealed the importance of cosmetics for daily life in antiquity. Cosmetic receptacles, mirrors, paint sticks for kohl, ointment tubes and spoons, tweezers, and many other toiletry instruments have been unearthed.

Ointments, balms, and perfumes are the most common cosmetics in the Bible. These were manufactured, traded, and imported from other nations (Ezek 27:17). Ointments and perfumes were of particular importance given the hot, dry climate of the Middle East and were used to protect the skin and to neutralize body odors. In addition paints were made to decorate the eyes and to color nails. Eye painting, however, was apparently looked down upon in Israel and was not practiced by women of honor (cf. 2 Kgs 9:30; Jer 4:30; Ezek 23:40).

Henna may also have been used as a cosmetic in biblical times. The orange stain produced from this plant may have been used for dyeing hair and for painting nails. In Song of Solomon (4:13-14), it is listed with other plants from which perfume was derived. Though not mentioned

Courtesy of the Eisenberg Museum of Biblical Archaeology, Southern Baptist Theological Seminary.

A bronze or copper mirror.

Courtesy of the Eisenberg Museum of Biblical Archaeology, Southern Baptist Theological Seminary.

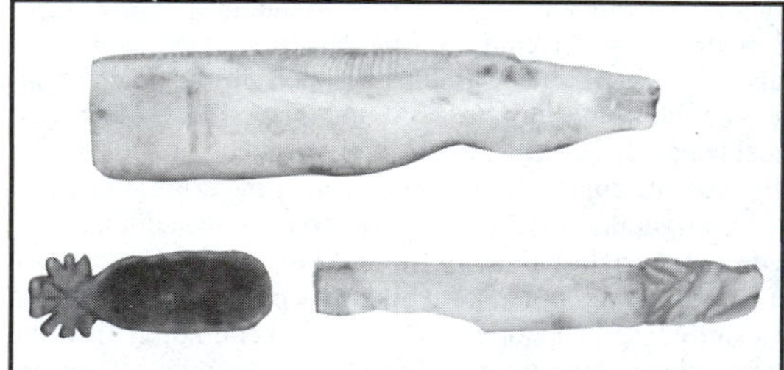

Instruments used to apply cosmetics.

Courtesy of the Eisenberg Museum of Biblical Archaeology, Southern Baptist Theological Seminary.

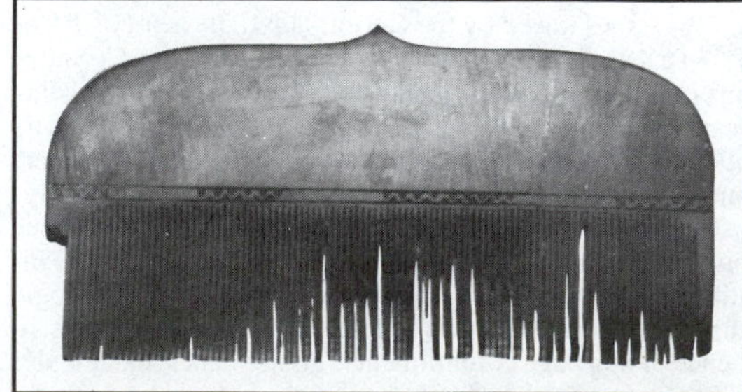

A Coptic comb.

in the Bible, rouge and powder were probably also used in biblical times. The Mishna forbids the use of rouge, eye painting, and hair dressing on the Sabbath.

See also OINTMENT/PERFUME.

—CECIL P. STATON, JR.

• **Cosmology.** A comprehensive view of all reality, attending both to the nature of the whole and also to the place of all parts within the whole. The origin, order, meaning, and destiny of all that exists are key issues in a cosmological system, as is also the question of what this "reality" in fact embraces.

The Bible does not develop a cosmology in the sense of a speculative philosophy, as in ancient Greece, or a scientific system, as in the modern world. Nonetheless, all-encompassing perspectives are present in both the Hebrew Bible and the NT, and from these and from ways in which the various components of reality are described it is possible to extrapolate a cosmology, or rather cosmologies, from the biblical literature.

Hebrew has no single word equivalent to cosmos, universe, or reality. Instead, various phrases are employed to express all-inclusiveness: "the heavens and the earth" (Gen 1:1; 2:4; more than seventy-five times in the Psalms), "the heavens and earth and sea" (Exod 20:11; Pss 69:34; 146:6—often with an addition such as "and all that is within them"), or "heaven above, earth beneath, and the waters under the earth" (Deut 5:8). The common word "all" or "everything" (*kōl,* sometimes with the definite article, "the entirety") can also occur in an attempt to embrace the whole of existence (Isa 44:24; Jer 10:16; Ps 103:19; Eccl 3:1; Sir 36:1).

The ancient Israelites' view of the physical world can be approximately reconstructed from such texts as Gen 1 and 7–8; Pss 33, 74, 104, 148; Job 38–41; and elsewhere. The universe, for them, is largely a closed entity consisting of three stories or levels. The earth is a flat disk surrounded by mountains or sea. Above is the firmament, a solid dome covering the entire world and resting on the mountains at the edges of the earth. Down in the heart of the earth is Sheol, the abode of the dead. The waters above and the waters below envelop the universe. The firmament overhead is transparent, allowing the blue color of the celestial water to be visible, and it has "windows" or sluices to let down water in the form of rain. The heavens, including the sun, moon, and stars, are under this vast canopy. The earth is supported from below by pillars sunk into the watery abyss. A variation of this conception is evident in Job 26:7, according to which the earth is hung over the void (see also Job 38:12-13). God, humans, and the dead each have their respective abode in the cosmos (Ps 115:16-17). However, God, who cannot be contained by the heavens (1 Kgs 8:27), is present on the earth and even in Sheol (Ps 139:8) as well.

This conception of the physical cosmos seems to have been widely held among the Israelites of the Hebrew Bible, although there were differences on certain specific details. Other ancient Near Eastern cultures shared similar perspectives also, as is evident from the creation myth of old Babylonia, the *Enuma Elish,* dating back to the first part of the second millennium B. C. E., and its Sumerian antecedent of one thousand years earlier. Cosmological parallels are also to be found in Ugaritic texts shortly before the ad-

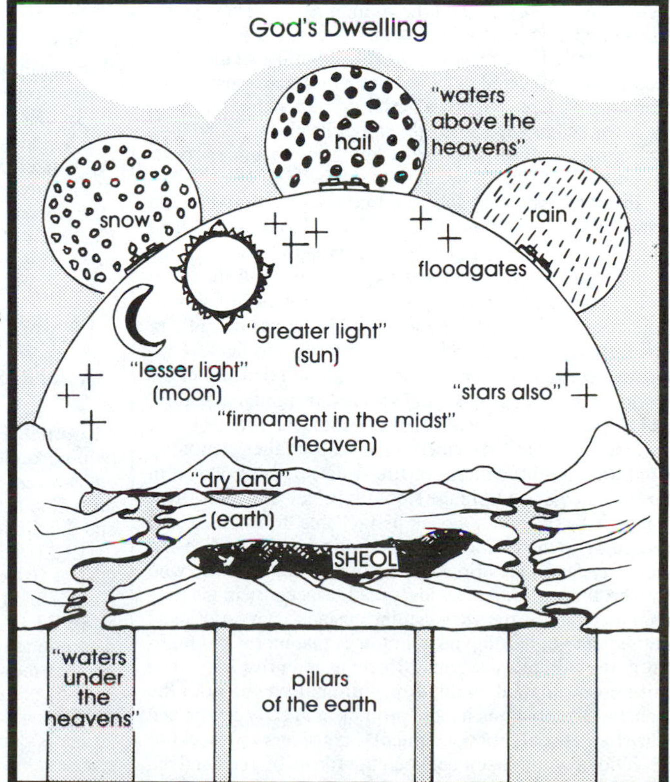

Ancient Hebrew conception of the cosmos (cf. Gen 1:1-19).

Artwork by Margaret Jordan Brown

vent of Israel's history. The Hebrew words used for the earth's surface (*tĕbēl*), the waters of the abyss (*tĕhôm*), and the underworld (*šĕ'ôl*) usually occur in the Hebrew Bible without a definite article—almost as if they were proper names—and this is thought by many to indicate a mythic background of the Israelite conceptions.

Of particular importance in understanding the biblical cosmology is the language used to express it, especially in poetic contexts. Without employing philosophical or scientific categories, the ancient Hebrews drew on images and concepts from their everyday life to articulate the nature and interrelationships among all that existed.

The awesome otherness of the world is often expressed through images of enormous features in nature: the mountains, a prominent place of God's revelation (Exod 19), can quake and smoke; the sea is fathomless and threatening; the sun, moon, and stars "rule over" the day and night (Gen 1:14-18) and seem to have some influence over humans (Judg 5:20; Ps 121:6; Job 38:33). Remarkable characteristics of animal life—bird migration, the undulating movement of a snake, the work of ants, the arrogant stride of lion and goat (e.g., Prov 30:18-19, 24-31; Jer 8:7)—underscore the mystery of all creation.

A series of human images also occurs cosmologically. The navel of the earth is Jerusalem (Ezek 38:12; referred to as the "center" of the earth in Ezek 5:5 and Ps 74:12). Breath is related to the wind and God's spirit. The underworld has a mouth and a ravenous appetite (Isa 5:14). Emotions are evident in nature: the heavens and mountains sing, the depths of the earth shout, nature groans in pain. Birth and death occur in consonance with the world (Ps 139:15; Gen 1:12, 20, 24; Job 1:21; 5:26; 14:7-19; Eccl 3:19-21). Domestic images—the father as provider, protector, and redeemer, and the mother as caretaker, seamstress, and source of compassion—are used especially of God's relation to life in this world. Familiar architectural features are projected to the structure of the cosmos: the firmament as a tent, windows in the sky, doors holding back the seas, beams supporting the upper level, the foundation and cornerstone of the earth, gates to the underworld, storehouses for the snow, hail, and wind.

From the political sphere come images of justice and order suggestive of the cooperative social structure of tribal life. Hierarchical notions of dominion and power in the cosmos parallel the people's experiences with the monarchy, just as also a vision of destructive cosmic oppositions (especially in apocalyptic thought) draws on military images. The religious categories of clean and unclean indicate a sense that there are anomalies and dangers in the world—among certain animal species, in human sexuality, and in sickness and death (Lev 11–15; Deut 14:3-21).

The universe, described with such images stemming from the familiar spheres of life in Israel, is evaluated in three main ways within the Hebrew Bible. Most broadly it is held to be ordered, rational, and reliable, functioning well according to the divinely ordained principles of justice and harmony, and deleterious consequences fall to those who subvert this order. Also widespread, especially in the wisdom literature, is the view that the cosmos is precarious and unpredictable, holding no guarantees that moral and faithful living will always bring blessings and prosperity. The third cosmological evaluation, minimally evident in the Hebrew Bible but much more prominent in early Jewish and Christian apocalyptic movements, considers the world to be divided within itself between the forces of good and the forces of evil, an antagonism which can only be overcome through radical intervention by God.

NT cosmology, drawing on these traditions as well as ancient Greek thought, views the world both as alienated from God yet also as the object of God's salvific plan. All-embracing terms are *kosmos* ("cosmos," the totality of all that exists) and *aiōn* ("aeon," temporally designating this world in contrast to the world to come).

Viewed negatively, the world is characterized fundamentally by the sinfulness of humanity, is severely judged by Jesus (John 16:8-11), is transient and should not be loved (1 John 2:15-17), and is incapable itself of attaining knowledge of God (1 Cor 1:20-25). Since it will soon pass away, Christians must "put off the old nature" (Eph 4:22) and "not be conformed to this world" (Rom 12:2).

More of a positive or hopeful conception is evident in the offer of God's salvation to the world, which was indeed divinely created (Acts 17:24) and continues to be sustained through God's providence (Matt 6:25-34). Paul gives a picture of "the whole creation groaning in travail together until now," awaiting the revelation of God (Rom 8:19-23). Jesus inaugurates the "kingdom of God" (or "of heaven," Matt 4:17 and elsewhere) on earth, bringing to fruition God's rule over all that exists. The world, the new creation, is thus reconciled to God through Christ (2 Cor 5:17-19), and his followers are charged with a mission to carry this message throughout the earth (Matt 28:18-20; Acts 1:8).

Biblical cosmology exists in neither the Hebrew Bible nor the NT as a doctrine or teaching in itself. To find it one must look to the many ways in which tangible and intangible realities are described. Theologically, these views of the universe are linked to beliefs in God as creator, lord, judge, and redeemer, and humans are consequently expected to act in moral harmony with God's intention for the world.

See also FIRMAMENT; HEAVEN; HELL; SHEOL; SKY.

Bibliography. H. D. Betz, "Cosmogony and Ethics in the Sermon on the Mount," in *Cosmogony and Ethical Order*; H. and H. A. Frankfort, J. A. Wilson, T. Jacobsen, and W. A. Irwin, *The Intellectual Adventure of Ancient Man*; W. Harrelson, "The Significance of Cosmology in the Ancient Near East," *Translating and Understanding the Old Testament,* ed. H. T. Frank and W. L. Reed; D. A. Knight, "Cosmogony and Order in the Hebrew Tradition," *Cosmogony and Ethical Order: New Studies in Comparative Ethics,* ed. R. W. Lovin and F. E. Reynolds.

—DOUGLAS A. KNIGHT

• **Council.** *See* COSMOLOGY

• **Council, Heavenly.** The assembly of servant deities who help make decisions about matters in heaven and on earth and who are sent from the council as messengers to accomplish God's purpose. The image is found throughout the OT and the literature of the ancient Near East. Micaiah (1 Kgs 22:19-23) was a witness to the actions of the council, as were ISAIAH (Isa 6:1-8) and the psalmist (Ps 82). MANASSEH (2 Kgs 21:3-5) built altars to the "host of Heaven." JEREMIAH 23:16-22 and Amos 3:7 indicate the true prophets' dependence on access to the council, but they also condemned the worship of it (Zeph 1:5; Jer 8:1-3; 19:13; 2 Kgs 23:4-5).

This widely held concept is not defined in the OT. The image is drawn by the use of several different words and phrases. In Jer 23:18, 22; Amos 3:7; Ps 89:7 (H 8) and Job 15:8, the word *sôd,* which refers to an intimate or secret council, is used. The term *'ēdâ* refers to a council assembled together by appointment; this term appears in Ps 82:1. Also widely used is the expression "host of heaven," referring to the council of angels and/or the council of the divine spirits that animated the sun, moon, and stars. The latter understanding of the council was the result of syncretism with the astrological cults of the ancient Near East. This term is found in Deut 4:19; 17:3; 1 Kgs 22:19; 2 Kgs 17:16; 21:3, 5; 23:4, 5; Isa 34:4; Jer 8:2; 19:13; 33:22; Zeph 1:5; Dan 8:10; Neh 9:16; 2 Chr 18:18; 33:3, 5. A similar phrase is found in Luke 2:13. The term "host on high" also refers to the "host of heaven" and is found in Isa 24:21. In this passage the "host of heaven" may refer to the patron angels found in Dan 10:13, 20, 21; 12:1.

Ps 89:5-8 (H 6-9) has four phrases that refer to the council and its members. In v. 5 is a reference to the "assembly of the holy ones." In v. 6 appear the "sons of the gods," rendered "heavenly beings" (cf. Job 1:6 and 2:1 for a similar phrase). The "council of the holy ones" is found in v. 7. In v. 8 appears the term "Lord God of hosts."

Ancient Near Eastern cultures picture the heavenly council and its decisions as a prototype of the earthly scene, but there was a difference in the way Israel used the familiar image. Whereas the other cultures pictured a polytheistic council with each of the members representing a force in nature, Israel reduced the gods to servant deities of Yahweh. The faith of Israel was focused on Yahweh's acts in history on behalf of the covenant people. The image of the heavenly council was used to show Yahweh planning in heaven to carry out events on earth. The importance of Yahweh's action in the events on earth points to another difference in Israel's use of the image of the council.

See also LORD OF HOSTS; MONOTHEISM.

Bibliography. J. I Durham, "Psalms," *BBC*; W. Harrelson, *Interpreting the Old Testament*; W. Zimmerli, *Ezekiel.*

—H. PAGE LEE

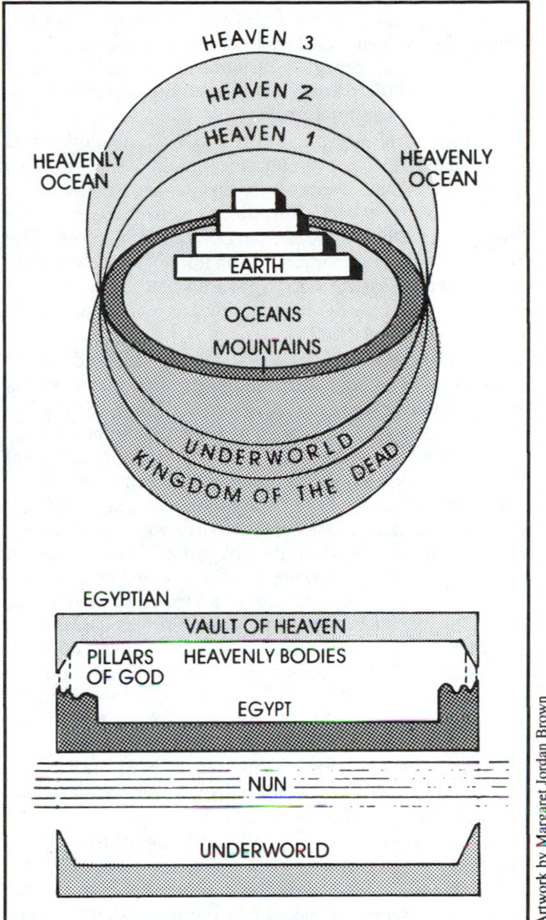

Ancient Babylonian and Egyptian conceptions of the cosmos.

• Counselor. One who gives advice or counsel, in particular to the leaders of the community. Kings in the OT period maintained official counselors for such guidance (2 Chr 25:16; Isa 1:26; Mic 4:9). Counselors to King DAVID included Ahithophel (2 Sam 16:23), Jehoiada and Abiathar (1 Chr 27:34), Zechariah (1 Chr 26:14), and Jonathan (1 Chr 27:32). King Rehoboam heeded the wrong counselors and contributed to the splitting of Israel from Judah (1 Kgs 12:6-20). Foreign kings also had their counselors (Isa 19:11; Ezra 7:14; Dan 3:2).

Counselors figure prominently in the wisdom books. Proverbs especially stresses the importance of parents (1:8) and other sources of counsel (11:14; 15:22; 24:6).

The ultimate source of guidance is God—a motif in several Psalms (16:7; 32:8; 33:11; 73:24; 106:13; 107:11). However, God does not need human counselors (Isa 40:13; 55:8-9; Rom 11:33-34). In the NT, the Holy Spirit is cast in the role (John 14:16).

See also ETHICS IN THE OLD TESTAMENT; KINGSHIP; WISDOM LITERATURE.

Bibliography. M. H. Cressey, "Counsellor," *IBD*; C. U. Wolf, "Counselor," *IDB*.

—DONALD W. GARNER

• Covenant. The Hebrew term בְּרִית (*bĕrît*), often, and traditionally the only term translated as "covenant" in the OT, has a wide semantic usage signifying in different contexts what could be and sometimes is rendered in English as "promise, pledge, obligation, agreement, contract, pact, or treaty." Although the OT speaks of many different covenants, the plural form of *bĕrît* never occurs.

In spite of various proposals and their defenses, the etymology of the word remains uncertain. The most widely advocated suggestions are: (1) from the verb *brh* "to eat, feed"; (2) from the verb *brh* "to see, decide"; (3) from a preposition *birit,* unattested in Hebrew but found in Akkadian, meaning "between"; and (4) from a noun parallel to the Akkadian and Talmudic *biritu*/*byryt* "clasp, fetter."

The most likely OT synonyms for *bĕrît* are *'ămānâ* (from *'mn* "to be firm, steadfast") in Neh 10:1, 11:23; *ḥōzeh*/*ḥāzût* (from *ḥzh* "to see"?) in Isa 28:15, 18; *šĕbû'â*/*'ālâ* ("oath") in some texts (see Gen 26:3); and *'ēd*/*'ēdût*/*'ēdôt* (from *'dh* "to witness"?) in Gen 31:44-52, Josh 24:27, Isa 32:14 (reading *bĕ'ad* as *kĕ'ēd*), and in expressions like the Ark of the *'ēdût*. The latter would parallel the terms *adū*/*adê* in Akkadian and *'dn*/*'dy* in Aramaic. Such synonyms occur very infrequently in the OT. Terms such as "peace" (*šālôm*), "good, friendship" (*ṭôb*), "law" (*tôrâ*), and "oath" (*'ālâ*), which may occur in covenantal contexts, are not to be viewed as interchangeable synonyms for *bĕrît* nor does their appearance in a text always presuppose that reference to a covenant stands as background to the text. Some terms, such as "peace," "friendship," and "brotherhood," were used however to refer to the conditions produced by covenant relationships.

In the OT, the term "covenant" (*bĕrît*) is employed with reference to three types of obligatory conditions. (1) In some cases, such as the covenant between God and NOAH and the Israelite patriarchs, the obligation is self-imposed by the deity. (2) In other contexts, the obligation is imposed by the divine or the superior party on an inferior or another party (cf. Jer 34 and Hos 2:18-23). (3) Elsewhere, as in the SINAI covenant, both parties are committed to reciprocal obligations (see Exod 34:10, 27).

The term "covenant" (*bĕrît*) could thus be used to refer to a variety of solemn, binding obligations or agreements involving two or more parties in a relationship. (1) The obligation might be self-assumed by the primary party for the benefit of the secondary party. In this case, the covenant was more like a pledge or a promise. The expected attitude of the primary party to the obligation was one of fidelity and the attitude of the secondary party was one of acceptance and trust. (2) When the obligation was imposed on the secondary party, it represented a demand or condition placed upon the obligated party and required obedience. Generally such a covenant relationship was assumed to benefit the party imposing the obligation although obedience to the obligation might be seen as beneficial to the obligated party as well. (3) Conditions and commitments accepted by both or all parties produced a situation of mutual obligation intended to benefit all parties concerned. In all three cases, the gravity and solemnity of the parties' commitment could be enhanced by verbal declaration, swearing, or the taking of an oath.

Diverse terminology is used with regard to making, maintaining, and fulfilling a covenant: cut, give, establish, enter, observe, break, transgress, remember, forget, and so on. This suggests a lack of any limited, specific vocabulary employed to speak about the operations and attitudes toward covenant conditions.

Ancient Near Eastern Evidence. As in the OT, the ancient Near Eastern evidence for covenants or treaties is diverse and reflects various conditions and relationships. Documentary evidence is known from the third through the first millennium (for a selection, cf. *ANET* 199-206, 531-41, 659-61). Although the majority of known texts are preserved in Akkadian cuneiform, Hittite, Aramaic, and Greek examples also exist.

In Akkadian documents, especially during the first millennium, treaties and their stipulations are referred to as *adê* (*'dn*/*'dy* in Aramaic), a term which, unlike *bĕrît*, always occurs in the plural. The most common use of *adê* is to refer to conditions in which a subordinate party is bound through loyalty oath to a superior party at the initiative of the latter. The inferior party may be either a foreign vassal or a domestic group. Several Assyrian texts bind the entire nation, including members of the royal family, the aristocracy, and the general populace, to observe particular conditions, in regard to succession to the throne and loyalty to the king. However, *adê* is also used to refer to divine promises made by a god to a ruler, to agreements between gods, to treaties between rulers of equal status, and to agreements sought by an inferior party.

The general structural pattern underlying ancient Near Eastern treaties can be seen in Hittite texts from the fourteenth and thirteenth centuries, although it should be noted that these and subsequent treaties vary in very significant ways, no two treaties are identical, and elements in the pattern may be omitted or expanded. The six main elements of the treaty pattern are: (1) a preamble identifying the parties, (2) a historical prologue noting past relationships between the parties (generally not present in first millennium texts), (3) the stipulations imposed on the inferior party or shared by the parties involved, (4) provisions for safely depositing and consultation/reading of the treaty document, (5) a list of gods and other witnesses to the treaty, and (6) curses and blessings. Many of the texts allude to various rites that accompanied the concluding of the treaty, in particular, actions used to illustrate the calamities and curses that would befall the disloyal and disobedient party for failure to live up to the imposed stipulations. Oaths of loyalty, undergirded with the threat of divine sanction and supervision, were sworn by the inferior party on whom the stipulations were imposed. Failure to live up to the stipulated arrangements and conditions was considered rebellion/sin against both the superior party and the deities called upon to sanction the treaty.

The parties to the treaty are referred to in various ways in the texts. The superior party might be referred to in the third person and the inferior party in the second person, both parties in the third person, or the superior party in the second or third person and the inferior party in the first person. In some texts, the parties are described in the third person and the stipulations imposed to insure the loyalty of the inferior party utilize second person address.

Covenants in Genesis–2 Kings. Numerous covenants/treaties are referred to in the OT and the term *bĕrît* occurs 286 times.

(1) Covenants between God and individuals: Although earlier commentators assumed that ADAM lived under a covenant (of works), the first reference to covenant and the first use of the word *bĕrît* appear in the Noah materials. Here the covenant seems to refer to the divine pledge made to Noah, to all creatures, and even to the earth as a whole (Gen 6:18; 9:9-16). In later interpretation the Noachic covenant was understood as involving the conditions and stipulations imposed on Noah (Gen 9:1-7) and thus all humankind (cf. Isa 24:5) and these stipulations were broadened to include a number of conditions not directly stated in the text (cf. Acts 15:19-21, 28-29; *GenR* 34.8).

The covenant with ABRAHAM, noted in Gen 15:18-19, appears to have been understood as a promise or pledge by the divine to give the land (of Canaan) to Abraham's offspring. Only the divine here is placed under any obligation and presumably the "smoking fire pot and flaming torch" (in v. 17) symbolize the deity and the divine commitment to the promise. This promise—to give the land to the patriarchs and their descendants—is spoken of throughout Genesis–Judges, sometimes using the word covenant (Exod 2:24; 6:4, 5; Lev 26:42-45; cf. 2 Kgs 13:23) and at other times merely referring to the sworn oath/promise to give the land (Gen 26:3; 50:24; Exod 13:5, 11; 32:13; 33:1; Num 11:12; 14:23; 32:11; Deut 1:8, 35; 6:10; 11:9, 21; 19:8; 26:3, 15; 28:11; 30:20; 31:7, 20-23; 34:4; Josh 1:6; 5:6; 21:43; Judg 2:1).

The covenant with Abraham described in Gen 17:1-14 is one of reciprocal obligations. Divine pledges include not only the promise of the land but also other commitments by the deity as well as the obligation of CIRCUMCISION imposed upon Abraham and his descendants. Circumcision is presented as both an obligation and a sign of the covenant (17:11; cf. 9:13).

Num 18:8-19 speaks of Yahweh's covenant with AARON, called a "covenant of salt" (v. 18; cf. Lev 2:13; 2 Chr 13:5), which grants the Aaronites the priestly perquisites (see Neh 13:29 [cf. Num 18:21-24]; cf. Deut 33:9; Jer 33:21-22; Mal 2:1-9). Although the covenant statement only refers to God's gift of the holy offerings to the Aaronites (v. 19), the preceding passage describing these in vv. 8-18 refers to incidental priestly obligations, in the form of cultic directives (vv. 10, 17b) and might be understood as priestly obligations.

A covenant/promise of perpetual priesthood is given to PHINEHAS in Num 25:10-13 as a reward for his zealous and atoning work on behalf of Yahweh and the community (see 25:6-9; cf. Gen 26:5).

A further example of a divine covenant with an individual (and his descendants) is the covenant with DAVID (2 Sam 23:5; Ps 89:3, 19-37; 132:11-18; cf. 2 Sam 7). Probably the earliest expression of the divine covenant with David was conceived as a promissory pledge made by Yahweh to the Davidic house authenticating and justifying the family's right to rule (cf. 2 Sam 23:5-7). The covenant could also be and was later understood as placing obligations on the rulers of the Davidic line (cf. Ps 89:30-34; 132:12).

(2) Covenants between human parties: Gen 14:13 refers to a covenant of Abraham apparently between the patriarch and his allies (called "*bĕʿālîm* of the covenant") in the war against northern invaders. Abraham and ABIMELECH made a covenant at Beersheba (Gen 21:22-34) as did ISAAC and Abimelech (Gen 26:23-33). LABAN and JACOB made a covenant in Transjordan (Gen 31:43-54) and set up a cairn called Galed (= "cairn of witness" or "covenant" if *ʿēd* = Akkadian *adê*), followed by a shared meal, a sign of mutual cooperation. The invading Hebrews made a covenant with inhabitants of the land, the Gibeonites (Josh 9:3-21), a practice discouraged in various passages in the Pentateuch (Exod 23:32; 34:11-16; Deut 7:2; see Judg 2:2). JOSHUA and the Israelites at SHECHEM covenanted to worship Yahweh (Josh 24:25). The people of JABESH-GILEAD sought to negotiate a covenant with Nahash the Ammonite (1 Sam 11:1). David and JONATHAN covenant together on more than one occasion with the covenants declared to be "of Yahweh" or "before Yahweh" (1 Sam 18:3; 20:8; 23:18). David entered a covenant with ABNER (2 Sam 3:12-13) and subsequently, "before Yahweh," with the elders of Israel (2 Sam 3:21; 5:3). SOLOMON and Hiram of Tyre concluded a covenant (1 Kgs 5:12) and both Kings Baasha of Israel and Asa of Judah did so with King BEN-HADAD I of Aram (1 Kgs 15:21) as did a later Israelite king with Ben-hadad II (1 Kgs 20:34). The priest JEHOIADA made a covenant with the military captains (which involved an oath in the temple precincts, 2Kgs 11:5), concerning a conspiracy against Queen Athaliah, and later presided over a covenant ceremony (involving the people, the new king, and Yahweh) to be Yahweh's people (2 Kgs 11:17—the reference at the end of the verse "and between the king and the people" is probably a scribal error). After the finding of the book of the law in the Temple (2 Kgs 22:8), King JOSIAH and the people covenanted "before Yahweh" to obey the stipulations of the book but nothing is said about with whom the covenant was made (2 Kgs 23:3). Jer 34:8-22 tells of a covenant made between King ZEDEKIAH and the owners of Hebrew slaves in Jerusalem (see v. 8). The covenant was made before Yahweh (v. 15) and could be spoken of as "Yahweh's covenant" (v. 18). Since breaking the covenant involved profaning the name of Yahweh (v. 16), an oath of loyalty to the covenant was probably sworn in the name of Yahweh. A particular feature of this account is the reference to passing through the severed parts of a calf (v. 18; cf. Gen 15:9-11, 17) probably as an act of self-imprecation.

Although the term "covenant" is not used with regard to Israel's and Judah's relationships to ASSYRIA and Babylonia in 2 Kings, it can be assumed that such covenants existed since such international relations with Mesopotamian powers, especially with vassal states, were based on treaties. The closest terminology to concluding a covenant appears in 2 Kgs 17:3 which speaks of King HOSHEA's becoming a servant to SHALMANESER V (726–722). That such covenants/treaties were concluded with Israelite and Judean kings is not only suggested by non-biblical evidence and international policy but also by Ezek 17:11-21 (cf. 16:59) which comments on the treaty between NEBUCHADREZZAR and Zedekiah. In speaking of this treaty, Ezekiel can describe the treaty and the associated loyalty oath as both Nebuchadrezzar's and Yahweh's treaty and oath (vv. 16 and 19). This indicates that such treaties were concluded and sworn in the name of Yahweh (cf. 2 Chr 36:13), thus making the Israelite deity a party to the arrangement. Thus disloyalty to the treaty was not only a sin against the sovereign overlord but also against Yahweh. Such treaties probably existed between Assyria and Israel from the time of JEHU's submission to Assyria in 841 (cf. *ANET* 281).

Treaties/covenants between human parties, national states, and a ruler with his people, if sworn in the name of God, created what might be called a triangular relationship. The basic bond was between the covenanting parties but, through the oath, the deity became involved as a tertiary participant, as custodian and guarantor of a party's or the parties' fidelity. Breaking the treaty meant breaking an oath, a pledge to the deity.

(3) The covenant between God and Israel: Without doubt, the most prominent portrayal of covenant in the OT is that between Yahweh and the Israelite people as a whole, which differs from the covenants with Noah, the patriarchs, Phinehas, and David. In the latter, the covenant was concluded with an individual although on behalf of subsequent descendants. It also differs from personal or national bilateral treaties in that the deity is a primary partner in the relationship.

Three sections of texts speak of the making of a covenant between Yahweh and Israel—Exod 19–24, 34 and Deut 28–31—but none of these is presented as the renewal of an already existing covenant (however, cf. Exod 34:1; Deut 29:1). The first of these is made after the arrival of the Hebrews at Sinai, the second after the golden calf episode, and the third in the plains of Moab. All three blocks of material presume and reflect elements of a covenant based on reciprocal obligations and refer to a collection of divine commandments to be obeyed by the people (Exod 20–23; 34:17-26; Deut 12–26), the writing down of these divine words (Exod 24:7, 12; 34:1, 27-28; Deut 31:9), the promise of blessings and the threat of curses (Exod 23:20-33; 34:10-16; Deut 28; cf. Lev 26), and the people's acceptance and pledge of obedience (Exod 19:8; 24:7; 34:31-32; Deut 26:17). Although the features reflected in these texts parallel elements in ancient Near Eastern treaty documents, it should be noted that such comparative features are drawn from both narratives and words of Yahweh or Moses, i.e., from both descriptions about the covenant making itself as well as the presumed contents of a covenant document.

Covenant Thought in the Prophets. The eighth-century prophets—HOSEA, AMOS, ISAIAH, and MICAH—were certainly acquainted with and their preaching was informed by covenant/treaty perspectives. Their preaching, however, does not reflect the idea or the existence of a covenant between Israel and Yahweh sealed by loyalty oaths but rather of covenants between two parties in which Yahweh was the guardian of the covenant, having become a party through oaths sworn in the divine name. From the time of David and Solomon, the Israelite monarchs had entered into treaty relationships with other rulers, as was noted above, and these, especially vassal treaties with Assyria, would have been concluded with loyalty oaths in the name of Yahweh. Breaking these treaties constituted sin and brought down upon the offender the wrath of both Assyria and Yahweh and profaned the name of Yahweh, requiring the offending party to offer restitution or suffer punishment. It is possible that the practice of swearing officers and troops to a covenant of loyalty may also have been a part of Israelite life at the time (cf. 2 Kgs 11:4).

The prophets certainly assumed that Yahweh was Israel's God and Israel was Yahweh's people (cf. Exod 6:7; Lev 26:12) but this is simply an expression of the nation-god relationship, not a relationship understood in the categories of covenant thought. While the two ideas are related, they are not identical and should not be confused.

Hosea uses the term covenant five times, in 2:18; 6:7; 8:1; 10:4; and 12:1. In 2:18, Yahweh presides over or imposes the making of a covenant between a female (probably Samaria since Israel as a people is always a male in the eighth-century prophets) and the beasts and birds and so forth. Here Yahweh imposes a covenant on two other parties. Agreements made either among the Israelites themselves or, less likely, with foreign states are referred to in 10:4. The other three references probably allude to Israel's covenant with Assyria. In 8:1, this treaty is referred to as Yahweh's treaty just as is the treaty between Nebuchadrezzar and Zedekiah in Ezek 17:19. "My law" or "my torah" would be a use of synonymous parallelism in which "my law" is equivalent to "my covenant." Whether the covenant referred to in 6:7 is Israel's covenant with Assyria or a loyalty covenant sworn by Pekah and broken when he rebelled against and attacked the Israelite monarch (cf. 2 Kgs 15:25) remains uncertain. Amos was certainly acquainted with the theological and legal considerations undergirding and embodied in international treaty thought and can refer to Tyre's failure to live up to treaty conditions (1:9). Behind much of Isaiah's and Micah's preaching lies the specter of the Assyrian treaty arrangements but their concern is somewhat different from that of Hosea since Isaiah and Micah preached in Judah where the covenant with Assyria remained generally intact. Only with the death of SARGON II in 705 and thus after the termination of a Judean-Assyrian treaty did Isaiah support rebellion against Assyria (Isa 24–27).

If the covenant perspectives of the eighth-century prophets were based on conceptions associated with international political treaties, the matter is radically different for the seventh-century prophets, Jeremiah and Ezekiel. Both prophets speak of a covenant between Yahweh and the people (cf. Jer 11:1-10; 14:21; 22:9; Ezek 16:8, 60-63). Ezekiel still utilized the perspective of international treaty conceptions as well. His allegory of the eagles in chap. 17 provides the clearest insight into the triangular treaty arrangement in the scriptures, especially in 17:11-21 in which the Nebuchadrezzar-Zedekiah treaty and oath are described as Yahweh's treaty and oath. It was the breaking of this treaty, not the Israel-Yahweh treaty, that the prophet proclaimed would bring judgment on Zedekiah (17:20-21).

The differences between the covenant preaching in the eighth-century prophets and the seventh-century prophets is to be explained as follows. In the three-quarters of a century separating the end of Isaiah's preaching (in 701–700) and the beginning (629–628) or early years of Jeremiah's preaching, Judean circles had given expression to the Israel-God relationship in terms of an Israel-God covenant. These circles are to be associated with what is called the deuteronomic-deuteronomistic movement which eventually gave final shape to the book of Deuteronomy and a major history of Israel extending, probably, from Genesis through 2 Kings. The parallels between the covenant material in Deuteronomy (especially in chaps. 1–11 and 28–31) and the treaties of ESARHADDON, especially his so-called vassal treaties dating from 672 to 671 (cf. *ANET* 534-41), suggest a connection between these two documents. Both Esarhaddon and his mother Zakutu swore their own people to fidelity and obedience. The form of this type of treaty, between sovereign and subjects, closely resembles that between Yahweh and Israel. In addition, Deut 28:68, with its reference to going to Egypt in ships, probably reflects ASHURBANIPAL's invasion of Egypt in 664–663 during which Judean troops, if not King MANASSEH himself, accompanied him, some being carried in ships (see *ANET* 294). The OT's particular theology of a covenant between Yahweh and Israel was thus probably formulated in the mid-seventh century.

Marriage as Covenant. Two OT texts, other indirect biblical evidence, and ancient Near Eastern materials suggest that MARRIAGE was understood in ancient Israel along the lines of a triangular covenantal arrangement in which the spouses were the primary partners and God was the custodian and guardian of the marriage relationship. Prov 2:17 describes the woman who forsakes the companion of her youth (her husband) as one who forgets the covenant (*bĕrît*) of her God, implying both that marriage was a covenant and that the covenant was under the sanction of God. Mal 3:14 speaks of God as witness to a marriage arrangement and the wife is referred to as the covenant woman. That marriage was so understood is also indicated by the fact that throughout the Near East, adultery was considered the "great" sin. Lev 19:20-22 also implies this triangular relation in marriage, here even in betrothal. An outside male who sexually interfered in a man-woman relationship was required to offer a reparation (guilt) offering (an *'āšām*) which was demanded when one transgressed against God by profaning the divine name or desecrating something holy to the deity. This would suggest that an oath in the name of Yahweh was sworn (or assumed to be implied) in marriage-betrothal arrangements. Unfortunately we possess no full descriptions of Israelite marriages nor marriage documents in the Bible, so it is uncertain whether or not marriage loyalty-oaths were made in the name of the deity.

The New Covenant. The prophets speak of a future covenant that God will make with the people (Isa 61:8; Jer 31:31-33; 32:40; Ezek 34:25; 37:26). Only Jeremiah uses the adjective "new" in speaking of this future covenant (31:31). Otherwise this future covenant is simply denoted as being "everlasting" (Isa 61:8; Jer 32:40) or "a covenant of peace" (or "friendship," Ezek 34:25; 37:26). The contexts of all these passages indicate that the prophets were addressing the issue of what conditions would need to prevail for the Israel of the future to be obedient to the divine will. The new or renewed covenant is to be part of a great transformation of both the people and the land. According to Jer 31:31-33, the new covenant will be inscribed upon the hearts of the house of Israel so that each person will instinctively and by nature know and heed the divine Torah.

Conclusions. A number of conclusions are in order regarding the nature and role of covenant in the OT. (1) The broad semantic range of the term *bĕrît* would indicate that "covenant" is not always the best translation of the term especially where "pledge/promise" or "obligation" better fits the context. The term *bĕrît* functioned in a broader fashion than is implied in the term "covenant." (2) There is a diversity of covenants in the OT and a single structural pattern does not encompass this diversity. (3) The OT contains no full covenant document per se. Hypothetical reconstructions of such are produced by combining narrative and "legal" material. (4) Comparisons between OT texts and Near Eastern treaty texts, for example the Hittite vassal treaties (first done by Karge), are informative but OT materials should not be pressed into a hypothetical stereotyped Near Eastern treaty pattern. (5) The role of treaty agreements between nation-states, with the theology and ethics implied by these, should not be overlooked. These treaties and their interpretation seem to have formed the basic background of the covenant theology of the eighth-century prophets. (6) The idea of a covenant between Israel and Yahweh was probably a literary/theological phenomenon rather than a sociological or institutional reality. There is no evidence in Joshua–2 Kings of a covenant festival or a covenant renewal celebration in which a covenant between Yahweh and the people was regularly reenacted. (7) The present canonical form of the Hexateuch is patterned around a series of covenants (Noah, Abraham, Sinai, after the golden calf episode, in the plains of Moab, and at Shechem). The canonical form of the text should be interpreted in light of this fact.

Covenant in the NT. The NT writers inherited from the Greek of the OT the use of the term *diathēkē* as a translation for *bĕrît* although the Greek term tended to denote a last will or testament (cf. Gal 3:15, 17; Heb 9:15-17). This terminology is the source of the designations "Old" and "New" Testaments.

The early church saw its relationship to God in terms of a new covenant, which it closely associated with the death of Jesus and the observance of the Lord's Supper (or Eucharist). Covenant terminology and its association with the blood (death) (cf. Exod 24:8; Zech 9:11) of JESUS are anchored in both the Gospels (Matt 26:28; Mark 14:24; Luke 22:20 [absent from many ancient MSS]; see John 6:52-58) and Epistles (1 Cor 11:23-32). Early Christians used the idea of the "new" covenant (Heb 8:6-10; Luke 22:20) inaugurated by Christ, contrasting it with the "old" covenant. The "old" covenant is sometimes associated with the law or the Pentateuch (2 Cor 3:6, 14; Gal 4:24) or what might be called non-Christian Jewish religion. Elsewhere, the "new" covenant is related positively to the Abrahamic covenant (Acts 3:25; cf. Gal 3:78; but see Acts 7:8). PAUL refers to the covenants of the Israelites (Rom 9:4) and associates the Christians with the divine promise to Abraham and God's fidelity to that promise (Rom 9:6-9; Gal 4:28-31). A central concern of the BOOK OF HEBREWS is to demonstrate the superiority of the Christian covenant (7:22; 8:7-13). The new covenant could also be spoken of in terms of the "spirit" as a "spiritual bond" (2 Cor 3:1-6).

See also TESTIMONY; THEOLOGY OF THE NEW TESTAMENT; THEOLOGY OF THE OLD TESTAMENT.

Bibliography. K. Baltzer, *The Covenant Formulary* (1971); J. Barr, "Some Semantic Notes on the Covenant," *Beiträge zur Alttestamentlichen Theologie: Festschrift für Walther Zimmerli*, ed. H. Donner et al.; R. T. Beckwith, "The Unity and Diversity of God's Covenants," *TynBul* 38 (1987): 93-118; R. Frankena, "The Vassal-Treaties of Esarhaddon and the Dating of Deuteronomy," *OTS* 14 (1965): 123-54; A. K. Grayson, "Akkadian Treaties of the Seventh Century B.C.," *JCS* 39 (1987): 127-60; E. Gerstenberger, "Covenant and Commandment," *JBL* 84 (1965): 38-51; D. R. Hillers, *Covenant: The History of a Biblical Idea*; P. Karge, *Geschichte des Bundesgedankens im Alten Testament*; D. J. McCarthy, *Treaty and Covenant*; G. E. Mendenhall, *Law and Covenant in Israel and the Ancient Near East*; E. W. Nicholson, *God and His People: Covenant and Theology in the Old Testament*; R. A. Oden, Jr., "The Place of Covenant in the Religion of Israel," *Ancient Israelite Religion: Essays in Honor of Frank Moore Cross*, ed. P. D. Miller et al.; S. Parpola, "Neo-Assyrian Treaties from the Royal Archives of Nineveh," *JCS* 39 (1987): 161-89; S. Parpola and K. Watanabe, *Neo-Assyrian Treaties and Loyalty Oaths*; L. Perlitt, *Bundestheologie im Alten Testament*; H. Tadmor, "Treaty and Oath in the Ancient Near East: A Historian's Approach," *Humanizing America's Iconic Book*, ed. G. M. Tucker and D. A. Knight; M. Tsevat, "The Neo-Assyrian and Neo-Babylonian Vassal Oaths and the Prophet Ezekiel," *JBL* 78 (1959): 199-204; M. Weber, *Ancient Judaism*; M. Weinfeld, "בְּרִית" *TDOT*; Z. Zevit, "A Phoenician Inscription and Biblical Covenant Theology," *IEJ* 27 (1977): 116-18.

—JOHN H. HAYES

• **Covenant with Noah.** The first of three covenants emphasized in the Pentateuchal priestly materials, the other two being the Abrahamic covenant (Gen 17) and the Mosaic covenant (Exod 19–24, 31). The Noah Covenant (Gen 9:1-17) climaxes the primeval themes of GENESIS—creation, rebellion, judgment (the tower of Babel and the flood), and COVENANT. The FLOOD marks the end of the old epoch, and God's word to the new era in the NOAH covenant is one of hope and blessing.

The word "covenant" (Heb. *bĕrît)* in its simplest sense means "relationship." It is a metaphorical or figurative term describing a relationship with God by analogy to some type of formal relationship among persons. Pacts and covenants were used extensively throughout the ancient world, ranging from international treaties and business contracts to marriage rules and religious practices. Scholars continue to debate the precise formal traditions behind the various OT covenants.

The Noah Covenant was a universal covenant since it included Noah, all Noah's descendants (not merely the Semites and Israelites), and all living creatures. It also was an everlasting covenant (Heb *bĕrît 'ôlām)*—an unconditional covenant—in which God promised never again to punish the earth by returning it to the primeval watery chaos. Because the covenant was unconditional, some scholars think it was fashioned after ancient suzerainty treaties in which a king made unilateral declarations that were not dependent upon the subject's responses.

The Noah Covenant included a new privilege: meat could now be eaten provided the animals were slaughtered in such a way that the blood was not consumed. Earlier in Genesis, diets were to be vegetarian; humanity's dominion over animals had not included meat-eating (Gen 1:28-30;

3:17-19). The principle of "reverence for life" (Gen 9:4) undergirds the stringent prohibition against the BLOOD: the life is the blood. Life (and hence the blood) was mysteriously and mystically sacred (cf. Gen 4:10-11). Strictly forbidden was the needless, wanton shedding of the lifeblood of any creature, but especially of human persons, for they were created in the image of God.

With the new promise and new privilege came a new sign. The universal covenant was signified by a symbol visible to all creatures, the RAINBOW. God and all creatures could now see and bear witness to the Almighty's promise and sovereignty. The rainbow was a particularly fitting symbol to the ancients, who imagined it as the divine weapon (bow) from which God shot lightning-arrows (Ps 7:12-13; Hab 3:9-11). By hanging up the bow, God showed that the divine wrath had indeed subsided.

Covenant is one of the dominant themes of the OT—indeed, of the entire Bible. After the time of the Mosaic Covenant, Israel both nationally and religiously understood itself as the people who had entered into covenant with Yahweh. David established a royal covenant with Yahweh, and the prophets charged in their "lawsuit" oracles that Israel had broken its covenant with God. Moreover, Jeremiah expressed the hope for the future in terms of renewing the covenant, and in the NT Jesus Christ was understood as the beginning of the new and final covenant.

See also COVENANT; NOAH; NOACHIC LAWS; RAINBOW.

Bibliography. G. E. Mendenhall, "Covenant," *IDB*; P. A. Riemann, "Mosaic Covenant," *IDBSupp*.

—JACK WEIR

• **Covenant Renewal.** *See* NEW YEAR'S FESTIVAL

• **Cover/Covering.** *See* MERCY SEAT

• **Coveting.** *See* TEN COMMANDMENTS

• **Creation.** The activity of God that results in the emergence of an ordered cosmos. Especially obvious in the Bible's opening chapters, creation motifs and themes are also found throughout the Bible (e.g., Exod 15:4-10; Job 38–41; Pss 8, 19, 24, 65, 74, 104; Prov 8:22-31; Isa 40–55; Jer 4:23-26; Amos 4:13; 5:8-9; 9:5-6; Sir 24; John 1:1-18; Col 1:15-20). Further, reflections on creation are not limited to biblical literature but are attested by a wide array of ancient Near Eastern texts. A review of the various texts reveals both shared and divergent ideas about creation.

Creation and Chaos. Fundamental to Babylonia, Egypt, and Canaan was the belief that chaos, a force hostile to existence, had been overcome by a victorious god. The Babylonian *Enuma eliš* opens with an account of the origin of the gods, or theogony. From primordial Apsu, the fresh underground waters, and the marine waters, Ti'amat, springs the society of the gods. Conflict within the divine society throws Ti'amat, who personifies chaos, into mortal combat with Marduk. Marduk is victorious and from the slain body of Ti'amat he establishes the heavens and the earth. Subsequently humans are created from the blood of the rebellious god Kingu, and a temple is constructed for Marduk in Babylon.

Egyptian creation accounts speak of a watery chaos called Nun. In one version of creation by the god Atum, a primal hill ascends from Nun. From there Atum creates the other gods in the divine society, the Ennead, by calling their names. The Egyptian cult center is understood to be located at the point where the hill arose from Nun. Another creation story affirms that Ptah is the creator. In "The Theology of Memphis," Ptah first intellectually conceives the thing to be fashioned and then speaks it into existence. The creation of humanity does not figure prominently in most Egyptian creation texts, although one of them tells that humanity is created from the tears of Re's angry eye. However, "The Instructions for King Meri-Ka-Re," a wisdom text, maintains that humans are created in the "images" of god and given plants and animals for food and rulers for leadership.

The Baal texts at Ugarit tell how BAAL becomes ruler by engaging in combat and defeating Yam, the sea. The creator god at Ugarit is El, but Baal is the deity who brings order to creation. Baal's palace is then built on Mount Zaphon with the aid of his wife and sister, Anat. The palace signals Baal's authority. Finally, Baal is challenged by El's son Mot (death). Baal descends into the underworld where he remains until Anat seizes Mot and effectively destroys him. Baal is then revived and reinstated as prince.

Texts from Babylonia, Egypt and Ugarit reveal the shared understanding that chaos is overcome by a victorious god who creates and/or establishes order. The battle with chaos (*Chaoskampf*) is most dramatic in Babylonia and Ugarit. Creation is not *ex nihilo,* from nothing, but results from an ordering of material that already exists. All three civilizations conceive of a plurality of gods who relate within the bounds of a society. Theogony is explicit in the Babylonian and Egyptian stories, implicit in the Ugaritic texts. Finally, creation has as much to do with establishing social and cosmic order as it does in accounting for origins, especially at Ugarit.

The Bible reveals shared and distinctive concerns. Like their neighbors, the Hebrews often speak of a watery chaos (Gen 1:2; Ps 104:6; however, Gen 2 envisions chaos as an arid wasteland). Because chaos is the material from which God creates, it is unlikely that the ancient Hebrews held any notion of *creatio ex nihilo.* The first clear expression of creation from nothing is found in 2 Macc 7:28 from the late second century B.C.E. Still, God's power over the deep is never questioned and is frequently expressed as a victory over surging waves and monstrous sea creatures: dragons, LEVIATHAN, RAHAB, or a SERPENT (Pss 74:13-14; 89:10; Job 26:12-13; Isa 51:9). Unlike other creation stories, however, the biblical accounts do not depict God in mortal combat with the forces of chaos. The raging waters and fearsome beasts that are so threatening in the *Enuma eliš* and in the Baal stories merely yield to the majestic power of God. It is most significant that the creation accounts in the Hebrew Bible know of no theogony. To be sure, certain texts give rise to speculation about a society of the gods (e.g., Gen 1:26; 3:22; 6:2; 11:7; Isa 6:8). However, such thoughts remain undeveloped and there is never any attempt to account for the origin of God.

Creation and Salvation History. The precise relationship between creation and salvation history is currently a matter of debate. Gerhard von Rad's opinion that the creation accounts in Gen 1–2 are merely the prologue to God's redemptive acts in history has been quite influential. In texts like Ps 136, Isa 42:5-9, and Isa 51:9-10 where creation and salvation are spoken of together, creation is ancillary, while the accent falls upon God's saving deeds. In von Rad's opinion, creation does not achieve the status of an independent theme. When one reads "But thus says the Lord, he who created you, O Jacob, he who formed you, O Israel: 'Fear not, for I have redeemed you; I have called you by name, you are mine' " (Isa 43:1), one sees that the prophet quickly leaves creation to talk about salvation. For von Rad and those persuaded by him, creation is merely the first of God's historical acts that paves the way for redemption.

Current scholarship is concerned to hear what the many biblical creation texts have to say without imposing von Rad's salvation-historical schema upon them. This, along with consideration of extrabiblical creation texts, has led many scholars to understand that creation says as much about *order* as origins. The priestly creation story in Gen 1 is clearly concerned with order. The waters above are separated from those below; light and darkness, seas and earth are distinguished from one another. One plant is distinct from another plant, and one animal unlike another animal. All boundaries are crisp and sharp. Within this divinely established order humans have their place. When humans act righteously and uphold the order of the cosmos, the world is at peace. When humans display unrighteousness, the order is usurped and, in Hosea's words, "the land mourns, and all who dwell in it languish . . . " (Hos 4:3). As the prophets see so clearly, cosmic and social order are intricately connected. The observation that a divinely established order inheres in the cosmos cautions against subordinating creation to salvation history and calls for a balanced estimation of their relationship.

Creation and the Cosmos. Numerous passages within the Bible reveal that the Hebrews, like their Near Eastern neighbors, conceive the world to be a three-storied structure. The Hebrew Bible presents a picture of the waters above the heavens (Gen 1:6-7; 7:11), the earth supported by pillars (1 Sam 2:8), and the waters below the earth (Gen 7:11; 49:25; Exod 20:4; Prov 8:28). The Bible affirms that it is God who has established this cosmos (Ps 24:1-2). Yet it also confesses that the world is dynamic and depends upon God for its continued existence. The flood story indicates that God, no longer able to endure human sin, opens the windows of the heavens and the fountains of the deep to inundate the earth (Gen 7:11). The account underscores both the total dependence of the earth upon God and the complete power of God who uses the chaotic waters for divine purposes. The appearance of God in 2 Sam 22:8-16 (cf. Ps 18:7-15) causes the earth to shake and tremble. Likewise, Ps 104:31-32 shows that the stability of the earth depends upon God's continued pleasure in the creation.

The role of humans within this cosmos is significantly different from that in the *Enuma eliš*. There humans are fashioned to serve the gods and deliver them from work. In Gen 1, humans share in the rule exercised by God. As God's creatures humans rule over other creatures and the earth. Given the precise care God pays to creation in Gen 1, it is inconceivable that human rule be anything other than careful and contributive to world order. There is no room for exploitation in God's cosmos. Gen 2 also assigns humans a significant role within the creation when God shares the divine prerogative and allows the first human to name the earth's creatures. Ps 8 sings of the special role of humans who exercise dominion over God's world and Ps 104:14-15 affirms God's desire that humans have the means to more than a miserable existence. Far more than mere servants of the gods as in the *Enuma eliš,* human beings are an important part of God's good creation, according to the Hebrew tradition.

God's care does not stop with humanity. Ps 104:16-26 proclaims that God has made the stately cedars of Lebanon solely for the storks' home. Mountain peaks exist for the goats to climb and rocky cliffs shelter the badgers. Day exists for human work, and night for lions that seek food under the cover of darkness. Even the sea, so fearsome in the *Enuma eliš* and the story of Baal and Yam, is a home for numberless creatures, including Leviathan, which sports in the waves. All of these creatures are constantly dependent upon God for their existence. Should God remove the divine presence, they are reduced to the dust whence they came.

The cosmos, then, is a dynamic world that stands constantly dependent upon its creator.

Creation, Wisdom and Torah. Israel's WISDOM LITERATURE (Job, Proverbs, Ecclesiastes [Qoheleth], Wisdom of Solomon, Sirach) presupposes a divinely ordered creation. The sages assert confidence in the human intellect to observe the world and draw the appropriate conclusions by which to order human life. For example, the teacher urges the student: "Go to the ant, O sluggard; consider her ways, and be wise" (Prov 6:6). To be sure, the sages know that there are limits to human reason and so they counsel: "A man's mind plans his way, but the Lord directs his steps" (Prov 16:9; cf. 14:12; 19:21; 20:24). Nonetheless, the person guided by wisdom and careful scrutiny of the created world gains insights for life. Even the vehement protests of Job, which question the reliability of appearances, and the skepticism of Qoheleth that questions whether or not wisdom is sufficient to discern the order of God's world, presuppose that there is a rational principle behind the world of experience. However, for Job and Qoheleth, human wisdom is simply too limited to be able to discern God's grand design in the world.

That such a design exists is affirmed in Prov 8:22-31. There personified Wisdom claims to be the first of God's creatures. Present from the beginning, Wisdom assumes the role of master builder while God establishes the heavens, restricts the chaotic waters, and shapes the mountains and fields. By the first century C.E. the Wisdom of Solomon extols Wisdom as "the fashioner of all things" (7:22), an emanation of God's glory that penetrates all things (7:24-25), an associate in God's works (8:4), present from the moment when God made the world (9:9).

Two centuries prior to the Wisdom of Solomon, Sirach (Ben Sira, Ecclesiasticus) achieved a remarkable synthesis of creation, wisdom and TORAH. As the creative mist that waters the face of the earth in Gen 2:6, wisdom covers the earth in search of a home (Sirach 24). At God's command wisdom takes up residence in Jerusalem. There she offers instruction on righteous living and finally reveals herself to be the "book of the covenant of the Most High God, the law which Moses commanded . . . " (Sir 24:23). Wisdom is effectively subsumed under Torah, which is now affirmed to have been present at the beginning of creation.

Creation and the Word. While the Jewish traditions came to equate Torah with personified Wisdom present with God from the beginning, Christian traditions made parallel claims about Jesus. The author of Colossians affirms that Jesus " . . . is the image of the invisible God, the first-born of all creation; for in him all things were created . . . " (1:15-16). The Fourth Gospel proclaims: "In the beginning was the WORD and the Word was with God, and the Word was God. He was in the beginning with God; all things were made through him, and without him was not anything made that was made" (John 1:1-3). No longer is Wisdom or Torah the preexistent agent of creation, but rather Jesus the Word. The christological claim made by this equation is that Jesus is the means by which to understand God's activity to bring order out of chaos. Just as God spoke the word that separated light from darkness in primeval moments, through the Word made flesh God the creator once again speaks to bring light from darkness.

See also COSMOLOGY; THEOLOGY OF THE OLD TESTAMENT; WORSHIP IN THE OLD TESTAMENT.

Bibliography. W. Harrelson, "The Significance of Cosmology in the Ancient Near East," *Translating and Understanding the Old Testament,* ed. H. Frank and W. Reed; D. A. Knight, "Cosmogony and Order in the Hebrew Tradition," *Cosmogony and Ethical Order,* ed. R. Lovin and F. Reynolds; J. B. Pritchard, *ANET*; H. H. Schmid, "Creation, Righteousness, and Salvation," *Creation in the Old Testament,* ed. B. W. Anderson; G. von Rad, *The Problem of the Hexateuch.*

—V. STEVEN PARRISH

• **Creeds.** *See* HYMNS/CREEDS

• **Creeping Things.** A phrase used in Gen 1, the translation of two Hebrew words. First, *šereṣ* from the root verb *šāraṣ* (to creep, to crawl, to swarm, to teem) is translated as "swarming thing," "creeping thing," or "living creatures" (Gen 1:20, 7:21). Elsewhere, *šereṣ* is employed with reference to unclean things (Lev 5:2; 11:21, 29, 41, 44; 22:5; Deut 14:19). Second, *remeś* from the verb *rāmaś* (to move, to creep, to swarm with) is also translated as "swarming creature" and "swarming things" (Gen 1:24, 25). *Remeś* appears in Gen 7:14; 9:3; 1 Kgs 4:33; Pss 104:25; 148:10. Both words are used in the OT as general terms to indicate water creatures, reptiles, insects, and small land creatures that appear in large numbers. Rather than any specific category of creature, the terms refer to a range of possibility, according to the context.

See also ANIMALS.

—W. H. BELLINGER, JR.

• **Crete.** [kreet] Located southeast of Greece, Crete is the fifth largest island in the Mediterranean (PLATE 18). It is approximately 155 mi. long and from 7.5 to 35 mi. wide. The island contains high rugged mountains, especially in the west where the White Mountains reach heights of over 8,000 ft. Due to this geographical feature the northern and eastern parts of Crete were inhabited first. The major environmental change that has occurred there since antiquity is the deforestation of its once heavily wooded areas.

Archaeological research conducted on the island since the last century has shown that the occupation of Crete began in the Neolithic Period (ca. 6000–5000 B.C.E.). The classical period in Crete (Middle and Late Bronze Ages) is sometimes called "Minoan" from the mythical story of Minos, the king of Crete and son of Zeus and Europa. During the Middle Minoan Age (ca. 2200–1600 B.C.E.), great palaces were built at such cities as Cnossos and Phaistos. In fact, from ca. 2000 to 1750 B.C.E., these two city-states seem to have ruled the island. Homer speaks of a hundred such cities, of which over forty are known. These independent cities were controlled by assemblies made up of local citizens. The Middle Minoan Period saw great advances in the material culture of the island and the appearance of a linear script (called "Linear B").

During the first part of the Late Minoan Period (ca. 1600–1400 B.C.E.), Crete experienced its most flourishing era until Roman times over a thousand years later. But this great civilization was brought to an end by a catastrophic earthquake ca. 1450 B.C.E. Political upheavals may also have contributed to its destruction. Many sites were abandoned and not reoccupied until the first century B.C.E.

While Crete lay outside the flow of major Greek history, its location on the trade routes made it important. To the Egyptians, the island was known as "Keftiu," and to the Akkadians as "Kaptara." The Hebrews knew it as "Caphtor" (cf. Deut 2:23; Amos 9:7), and the few OT references associate the place with the Philistines (Jer 47:4; Gen 10:14).

Only three references to Crete occur in the NT. It is listed in Acts 2:11 as one of the places from which Jews came to Jerusalem. Apparently a Jewish community was established there during the Hellenistic period but it does not seem to have had much importance. On his way to Rome, Paul sailed along the coast of Crete and experienced one of the dangers encountered in such travels, a sudden storm (Acts 27:7-22). Little is known of the spread of early Christianity to the island, but it seems to have spread quickly and easily, perhaps propagated by Jewish converts. Whatever the case, the Christian community was large enough for Titus to be left there to organize the island's first bishopric (Titus 1:5-14).

See also PHILISTINES.

Bibliography. J. L. Caskey, "Crete," *CAH* (3rd ed.) 1/2:799-804; Homer, *The Odyssey*; J. D. S. Pendlebury, *The Archaeology of Crete*; P. Romanelli, "Crete," *CAH* 11:660-67; R. F. Willetts, *The Civilization of Ancient Crete.*

—JOHN C. H. LAUGHLIN

• **Crimson.** *See* SCARLET

• **Cross.** Originally the cross was an upright stake, pole, or pale, often pointed at the top. In all four Gospels (Matt 27:40; Mark 15:30; Luke 23:26; John 19:25) and in twenty-four other places in the NT, the cross is identified as the instrument of Jesus' execution.

Death on the cross was regarded as a particularly tormenting and scornful means of execution. In the OT, stoning was the most frequently used form of capital punishment, and neither hanging nor crucifixion was acceptable. However, where there was a desire to show unusual contempt, the body would be hung in public view. After killing the King of Ai, whose forces had earlier dealt the people of Israel a bitter defeat, Joshua hung his body in open display so that all could witness the final humiliation of the once proud king (Josh 8:29). He did the same to five cowardly Amorite kings (Josh 10:26) who had fled from battle and hidden in a cave. In 2 Sam 4:11-12, David hung the bodies of the sons of Rimmon the Beerothite who had slain Ishbosheth, the son of Saul, in a public place because "they were wicked men who had killed a righteous man in his own house upon his own bed."

So abhorrent was the practice of public display to Israelite sensibilities that the law required that a body treated in this fashion be removed and disposed of before evening (Deut 21:22-23). Paul referred to this tradition in Gal 3:13 when he said that Christ by hanging on the cross has become a "curse" in our behalf and when he said in Gal 5:11 and 1 Cor 1:23 that the cross was a "scandal" or a "stumbling block" to the Jews. It would be very difficult indeed for a Jew to believe that "the chosen one of God" would ever be treated in this way.

In the ancient world the cross was used as an instrument of torture and death by the Persians, the Phoenicians, and the Carthaginians, but not by the Greeks, who considered themselves too civilized for such a barbaric practice (hence Paul's reference in 1 Cor 1:23 to the "foolishness" of the cross to the Greeks). Execution by crucifixion was used extensively by the Romans in Palestine from the time of Pompey's conquest in 63 B.C.E, but only for provincials, slaves, or the worst of criminals. It was not employed to execute Roman citizens. Thus the tradition which says that Peter was crucified but Paul was beheaded is in accord with known practice.

It is believed that three different kinds of crosses were used for Roman executions—the *crux commissa* which had the form of a T, the *crux decussata* whose shape was X and the *crux immissa* or *capitata* which is generally believed to be the type of cross on which Jesus died. This cross was constructed of a vertical beam, *stipes* or *staticula,* which was firmly planted in the ground and to which was attached a block or peg, *sedile,* which the victim straddled and by which most of the weight was supported. The horizontal beam, *patibulum* or *antenna,* was usually carried to the place of execution by the criminal, who might also carry or be preceded by a written statement, *titulus,* which described the crime for which the death sentence had been given. John 19:19 says that in Jesus' case this "title" read "Jesus of Nazareth, King of the Jews." The other Gospels report shorter versions (Matt 27:37; Mark 15:26; Luke 23:38). The victim who carried part of his cross also carried a "witness" which proclaimed the reason for the cross.

In many religious traditions a cross, in a variety of forms, is used to represent the coincidence of opposites because it has an obvious affinity with the intersection of heaven (the vertical) and earth (the horizontal), and because as it is planted in the ground and pointed toward the heavens it becomes symbolically the "great cosmic tree" which is the "center of the earth" and the place of divine revelation. In Christianity the cross is the supreme paradox of salvation, for out of the humiliating and agonizing death of Jesus on the cross have come glorification, RECONCILIATION, and SALVATION. The PASSION narratives in all four Gospels make it clear that Jesus suffered, and the disciples are told in a number of places that to follow Jesus in taking up the cross is to accept persecution, suffering, and even death of the body. But the cross, the most horrible instrument of death, was also the means to eternal life in the resurrected and glorified Christ. So Paul says that the glory of the Christian is in the cross alone (Gal 6:14); that the cross is the means of union between Jews and Greeks (Eph 2:16); and that in Christ's death on the cross God has made peace with all things in heaven and earth (Col 1:20). The cross also represents the whole of the gospel (1 Cor 1:17-18), and anyone who rejects the gospel or fails to conform to its demands has become an "enemy of the cross" (Phil 3:18; Heb 6:6).

See also CALVARY; CRUCIFIXION; DEATH; PASSION, THE.

—JOHN E. COLLINS

• **Crown of Thorns.** After Pilate had sentenced Jesus to death, the Roman soldiers took him aside and ridiculed him by placing upon him mock representations of kingship—a crown of thorns and a purple (or scarlet) robe (Matt 27:27-31; Mark 15:16-20; John 19:2-5). Matthew adds that they also placed a reed, symbolizing a royal scepter, in his hand. After exclaiming derisively, "Hail, King of the Jews!" the soldiers led Jesus out to be crucified.

The crown of thorns would have been a circle of thorns or briers woven together by the soldiers. Several types of thorny shrubs from which such a crown could be constructed were common in Palestine. The thorns may not have been intended to inflict pain, but rather possibly represented the spikes on the radiant crowns worn by some of the royalty of that period.

—MITCHELL G. REDDISH

• **Crown/Diadem/Tiara.** Distinctive headdress worn by kings, queens, and priests signifying honor and authority. "Crown" is also used metaphorically of honor, glory, and blessings. "Diadem," sometimes translated "crown," was originally the cloth headband, usually studded with jewels. "Tiara" translates several Hebrew words, usually as "turban" (Ezra 24:17, 23), but as "crown," "diadem," or "mitre" when it refers specifically to the headdress of the priest (Exod 28:4).

OT Usage. The term *qodqōd* designated the top ("crown") of the head (e.g., Gen 49:26; 2 Sam 14:25; Job 2:17), and *zēr,* found only in Exodus, depicted the ornamental features ("crown, molding, border") of the furnishing of the tabernacle (e.g., Exod 25:25; 30:4). Both *kether* and *nēzer* were crowns worn by royalty and priests. Perhaps a Persian loanword, *kether* is found only in Esther in the phrase "royal crown" (1:11; 2:17; 6:8). *Nēzer* ("consecration, crown") designated the crown of the king (2 Kgs 11:12; Esth 8:15; 2 Sam 1:10) and the headdress of the priest (Exod 29:6; 39:30) worn over his "turban" ("tiara"), which carried the golden plate inscribed, "Holy to the Lord" (Exod 28:36-37; Lev 8:9). The word *'ăṭārâ* ("crown, wreath") referred to the crown worn by the queen and king (Jer 13:18) and the crown or garland worn by the groom on his wedding day (Cant 3:11). Metaphorically, *'ăṭārâ* pictured a good wife as "the crown of her husband" (Prov 12:4), a hoary head as "a crown of glory" (Prov 16:31), and grandchildren as "the crown of the aged" (Prov 17:6).

NT Usage. Diadēma, found three times in the NT (Rev 12:3; 13:1; 19:12), was specifically the badge of royalty. The more common term, *stephanos,* was the crown of kings and queens, the crown of thorns used to mock Jesus (Matt 27:29; Mark 15:17; John 19:2, 5), and the garland given to the victor in the public games (1 Cor 9:25). The NT writers adapted the figure of the victor's prize to picture "a crown of righteousness" (2 Tim 4:8), "the crown of life" (Jas 1:12; Rev 2:10; 3:11), "the unfading crown of glory" (1 Pet 5:4). *Stephanos* described also that which brings joy and pride. Thus, Paul could call the Philippian Christians his "joy and crown" (Phil 4:1) and the Thessalonians became his "crown of boasting before the Lord Jesus" (1 Thess 2:19).

Bibliography. W. Grundmann, "στέφανος, στεφανόω," *TDNT*; J. M. Myers, "Turban," *IDB*.

—G. BYRNS COLEMAN

• **Crucifix.** *See* CROSS

• **Crucifixion.** Crucifixion was a form of punishment practiced in the ancient world in which a person was suspended on a vertical shaft by being bound and/or nailed to it. Sometimes a crossbar was affixed to the shaft. As practiced by the Romans it was the means of a slow, torturous, and degrading death.

The origin of crucifixion may be found in the practice of impaling "wrongdoers" and prisoners of war on an upright shaft. Evidence of this appears in the Code of Hammurabi which prescribed impalement as the punishment for a woman who brought about the death of her husband (cf. Ezra 6:11). A few OT texts refer to impalement as a Jewish punishment (Josh 8:29; 10:26; Num 25:4). Deut 21:23 ("a hanged man is accursed by God") makes the basic OT perspective clear. Hanging on a tree as a means of execution was a total disgrace.

Crucifixion, as distinct from impalement, was utilized by the Phoenicians, Persians and others, but was brought to its highest level of "refinement" and its greatest usage by the Romans. It was not usually the means of punishment for Roman citizens. At first, crucifixion was carried out only on slaves and people of captured areas. By the first century B.C.E., the Romans had forged it into a horrifying means of executing criminals, rebels, and unruly slaves.

During times of crisis the Roman authorities gave little heed to proper or legal procedure. Josephus says that during the attack on Jerusalem in 70 C.E., the Romans crucified so many that there was not space for the crosses nor enough crosses for the bodies. A common part of the pre-crucifixion punishment was a flogging that was so merciless that many died from its effects. Josephus recounts the capture by the Romans of a young Jew at the battle for Macharus. The sight of a cross and the flogging of the young man created such a sense of dread among the Jews in the garrison that they all surrendered.

Following the sentencing, the victim would be led to the place of crucifixion. On the way, he likely would have to carry the crossbar. He may already have been attached to it. In which case, he could be lifted up and the crossbar fixed on the top of or in a groove in the side of a previously-set vertical stake. If the victim were nailed to the cross, spikes would be driven through the base of the palm of the hand in the wrist area. Suspended in this fashion, death could occur relatively quickly as a result of asphyxiation because the body's weight produced increasing pressure on the chest cavity. The agony of the condemned might be prolonged by the use of a seat or foot support to partially and temporarily support the weight of the body. In such an instance he might live for days. If it became necessary to hasten death, the victim's legs were broken.

While the Gospels do not emphasize the physical details of Jesus' death, the accounts in Matt 27, Mark 16, Luke 23, and John 19 do reveal similarities to the typical pattern of crucifixion.

See also CROSS; JESUS.

Bibliography. P. Barbet, *A Doctor at Calvary: The Passion of Our Lord Jesus as Described by a Surgeon*; J. Blinzler, *The Trial of Jesus*; V. Tzaferis, "Crucifixion—The Archaeological Evidence," *BAR* (Jan/Feb 1985): 44-53.

—ROBERT O. BYRD

• **Cults.** A form of idolatry that threatened the vitality of ancient Israel's religion at various times. The Period of the Judges is noted for apostasy related to the Canaanite cults of BAAL and Ashtaroth. During the monarchy, SOLOMON's policy encouraged establishment of the cults of his foreign wives. From the accounts of the reforms of HEZEKIAH (2 Kgs 15:13) and JOSIAH (2 Kgs 23) and the prophetic literature, it is apparent that Canaanite cults, as well as cults from beyond the Jordan, had pervaded JERUSALEM and the temple. Among these were the cult of MOLECH, associated with child sacrifice, the Moabite cult of CHEMOSH, and the Ammonite cult of Milcom. Greek mystery cults were also part of the environment in NT times.

See also IDOLATRY.

—W. H. BELLINGER, JR.

• **Cuneiform.** [kyoo-nee'uh-form] The word cuneiform comes from the Latin *cuneus,* wedge, and is used to de-

A Cuneiform prism.

scribe objects resembling a wedge, or in the case of writing, characters composed of wedges. Cuneiform script was developed in southern Mesopotamia ca. 3000 B.C.E., apparently by the SUMERIANS. The utility and adaptability of cuneiform script resulted in its being adopted and developed to meet the distinctive requirements of several languages, including Akkadian, Hittite, Hurrian, Urartian, Elamite, and Eblaite. The people of the city of Ugarit and the Persians, peoples distinct from each other linguistically and culturally, used wedges to create their alphabetic scripts. A vast literature in cuneiform was produced. A partial listing of genres includes letters, economic texts, omens, epic texts, religious texts (rituals, prayers, hymns, myths), syllabaries, law codes, wisdom collections, historical annals, astronomical reports, treaties, and legal documents.

The earliest documents found in Mesopotamia are commercial/administrative clay tablets consisting of pictures (of objects, commodities, and personal names) and a system of numbers. This kind of writing is known as logography (one sign or picture representing one word). While such a system of writing could serve the simple needs of bookkeeping, it could not be used without further development to indicate grammatical elements or to meet the demands of sophisticated literary texts. This limitation of logographic representation soon led to phonetization, the practice of writing sounds by using signs indicating objects pronounced with the same or similar sounds.

The pictures, relatively difficult to draw, with their curved lines, were soon replaced by stylized pictures composed of wedges. The figures were then turned ninety degrees to the right and the direction of writing was reversed so that it ran left to right. The stylus was used to produce two kinds of wedges: the vertical, horizontal, or oblique wedge (*Keil*) made by using the entire tip of the stylus, and the head of the wedge (*Winkelhaken*) made by using the corner of the tip of the stylus.

A Cuneiform inscription of Shulgi.

Courtesy of the Eisenberg Museum of Biblical Archaeology, Southern Baptist Theological Seminary.

A Cuneiform tablet.

Courtesy of the Eisenberg Museum of Biblical Archaeology, Southern Baptist Theological Seminary.

While the Sumerians continued to use logograms, they began early to use their fund of signs to write syllables. Thus the sign for "mouth" (KA) could be used to write the syllable "ka," and the sign for "head" (SAG) could be used to write the syllable "sag" in multisyllable words. Signs were used also as determinatives (signs which precede or follow a word) in order to indicate classes of persons or objects, and as phonetic complements to clarify pronunciation. When the Akkadians took over the Sumerian system of cuneiform writing, therefore, they found available a highly developed and sophisticated system, which, with a number of adaptations, served the needs of the Akkadian language for almost three millennia. It was not until the Late Bronze Age that the scribes at Ugarit developed a cuneiform alphabetic script which made it possible to indicate in writing the voiced, voiceless, and emphatic consonants which characterize the Semitic languages.

Although cuneiform inscriptions stimulated much interest in Europe in the seventeenth and eighteenth centuries, it was not until the first half of the ninteenth century that real progress was made in the decipherment of cuneiform. Of greatest importance was the existence of trilingual inscriptions, such as those on the Behistun rock in Iran written in Old Persian, Elamite, and Akkadian. The significance of the trilinguals for the decipherment of cuneiform parallels that of the Rosetta Stone for the decipherment of Egyptian hieroglyphics. The scholars who made the greatest contributions to the decipherment of cuneiform were H. C. Rawlinson, Edward Hincks, and Jules Oppert. It was determined that one of the scripts was alphabetic and that it had been used to write Old Persian. Since Old Persian had already been studied successfully, it now became possible to read the alphabetic cuneiform, especially personal names, place names, and formulaic phrases. Once it was decided that the three different kinds of cuneiform script contained the same information in three languages, the way was opened to the decipherment of Elamite and Akkadian.

The excavations of several important sites in Mesopotamia, beginning with the work in 1842 at Nineveh, uncovered many thousands of inscriptions written on clay tablets, mud bricks, stone monuments, cylinder seals and metal objects. By 1857, it was generally acknowledged that the study of Akkadian had been put on a sound, scientific basis. The study of syllabaries (sign-lists and vocabularies) revealed the existence of the Sumerian language and made

PICTOGRAPH	SUMERIAN CUNEIFORM	SUMERIAN VALUES	OLD BABYLONIAN CUNEIFORM	NEO-ASSYRIAN CUNEIFORM	AKKADIAN SYLLABIS VALUES	AKKADIAN READINGS
*	*	DINGIR: God AN: Sky			an il	ilus god šamû: heavier
		SAG: head			sag riš	rešu: head

Development of Cuneiform from pictograph to later forms.

possible the study of that non-Semitic language. After more than a century of scholarly effort, the study of the languages which used the cuneiform script continues. The growing maturity of cuneiform studies is indicated by the appearance of comprehensive grammars for most of the languages and by the publication of dictionaries (several still in progress).

The picture of life and thought that emerges from the study of the cuneiform sources forms an important part of Israel's international context. A comparison of Akkadian myths such as *Enuma elish* and the Gilgamesh Epic with the Genesis accounts of creation and flood demonstrates important elements of a common literary heritage. Comparative study, however, highlights the distinctive theological qualities of the biblical accounts. Similarly, the myths and epics from Ugarit highlight and clarify OT texts, especially those of the Israelite poetic tradition. Law codes, such as the Code of HAMMURABI, the Laws of Eshnunna, and the Middle Assyrian Laws, are indispensable for the study of biblical law, often providing laws from early times which are identical with, or similar to, biblical laws. The great archives of EBLA, MARI, NUZI, and other sites have provided a clear look at the religious, legal, and economic environment out of which Israel eventually emerged. The archive of about 380 letters found at AMARNA in Egypt provides a valuable picture of life, politics, and language in Syria-Palestine during the first half of the fourteenth century, just prior to the emergence of Israel. The annals of the kings of Assyria and Babylonia fill out and often verify the history of the kingdoms of Israel and Judah. To understand the unique features of Israel's life and belief, it is necessary to view Israel in its cultural context. New and continuing excavations in the Near East will continue to provide a stream of data crucial for a better understanding of the Bible.

See also WRITING SYSTEMS.

Bibliography. G. Bergsträsser, *Introduction to the Semitic Languages: Text Specimens and Grammatical Sketches*; T. A. Caldwell, J. N. Oswalt, and J. F. X. Sheehan, *An Akkadian Grammar*; I. J. Gelb, *A Study of Writing*; S. N. Kramer, *The Sumerians: Their History, Culture and Character*; E. Posner, *Archives in the Ancient World*; C. B. F. Walker, *Cuneiform*.

—THOMAS SMOTHERS

• **Cupbearer.** In the ancient Near East, the cupbearer was an important official who poured the king's wine into his cup and then served it to him. Since poisoning was an ancient method for political assassinations, the cupbearer was among the most trusted servants and faithful bodyguards to enter the king's presence. Constant and close access to the king in such a sensitive role probably allowed the cupbearer to offer advice or counsel, sometimes even affecting official policy (note Neh 1:11–2:8).

Cupbearers are depicted in ancient Egyptian records as well as in the OT. The pharaoh's "butler" imprisoned with Joseph was literally his cupbearer (Gen 40:9-14, 21). SOLOMON's own impressive court included this role (1 Kgs 10:4–5). NEHEMIAH, though a Jewish foreigner in Persia, nevertheless received this trusted assignment (Neh 1:11).

See also COUNSELOR.

—DONALD W. GARNER

• **Curse and Blessing.** Curses and blessings are power-filled words pronounced in a cultic setting, usually by authoritative persons such as family heads, priests, kings, and prophets. They were often accompanied by symbolic actions that were believed to strengthen and effect the curse or blessing. As religious statements the power behind and in these words came from God whose purposes in cursing or blessing were initiated and focused through their public utterance by a power-filled person. Usually the statements of cursing and blessing directly attribute their power to God, and even when such attribution is not stated it is implied by the status of the one who pronounces curse or blessing and by the circumstances in which the pronouncement is made. God is the source and master of every blessing and curse.

Cursing. Curses express disapproval or displeasure along with appropriate judgment. The Hebrew words used of curses designate their power, contents, and effects. The words of the curse were believed to direct the destructive power of the deity toward the object of the curse as an act of punishment. Cursing, therefore, was always a serious act, never to be taken lightly.

In some cases God curses directly (the snake in Gen 3:14; the ground because of human sin in Gen 3:17-19; CAIN for the murder of ABEL in Gen 4:11; those who curse Abram, Gen 12:3) or threatens curses on his people if they do not keep the COVENANT (Deut 27–29). Other curses are cultic pronouncements made in connection with violations of covenant agreements (Deut 27:15-26), oaths (1 Sam 14:24), the putting of a city to a ban in HOLY WAR (Josh 6:26) and similar prohibitions or taboos (Judg 21:18). Many prophetic oracles are like curses though not specifically referred to as such. This is especially true of oracles against the nations as enemies of Israel and by association as enemies of God (Isa 13–23; Jer 25:15-38; and chaps. 46–51; Ezek 25–32; Amos 1:4–2:3). Judgment oracles against Israel (Amos 2:6-16) and Judah (Amos 2:4-5) also have the effect of curses especially when accompanied as in Jeremiah (19:1-13) and Ezekiel (4:1–5:17) by curse-form symbolic actions.

Personal maledictions in the form of appeal for or pronouncement of punishment on one's opponents are common in the PSALMS of lament (69:22-28; 109:28). In many psalms "the enemy" or "the wicked" seem to have used evil powers against the Israelite community or individual. The curses of these "workers of iniquity" (Pss 59:2, 5; 141:4) must be met with counter-curses of greater power, not just appropriate curse formulae, but appeals to the one whose cursing power is greater than those of the threatening chaotic demonic powers.

In their cultic setting such implicit curses are legitimate. Such cries of vindictiveness, however, while understandable, border on abuse when they become expressions of personal frustrations, revenge, and anger as in the case of the complaints of Jeremiah (11:20; 12:3; 15:15; 17:18; 18:21-22; 20:14-17) and Job (3:1-10). Indeed, cursing of God is explicitly forbidden (Exod 22:28; Lev 24:10-23; Job 2:9), as is cursing of rulers (Exod 22:28), parents (Exod 21:17), and the deaf (Lev 19:14). The Decalogue's prohibition against the vain use of the name of God clearly prohibits the use of its power in curses on one's enemies. Such prohibitions should indicate that cursing as a serious act is not a personal but a cultic matter, never casual but always religious. The cursing of enemies is legitimate only as the ritual expression of divine judgment upon them, never as reactions of anger or revenge. The most complete curse formula in the OT, "Cursed be the one who. . . . And all the people shall answer and say, 'Amen' " (Deut 27:15-26) suggests that curses are appropriately both cultic and corporate pronouncements. This means that the right to and the power of cursing rightly reside with God.

References to curses are infrequent in the NT. Jesus cursed the barren fig tree (Matt 21:18-19; Mark 11:12-14) and pronounced "woes" along with blessings (Luke 6:20-26), and the Revelation pronounces numerous woes on the wicked (8:13; 12:12; 18:2-8). Paul cursed those who did not love the Lord or who taught differently from the way he taught (1 Cor 16:22; Gal 1:8) and Peter's judgment words sent ANANIAS and Sapphira to abrupt deaths (Acts 5:1-11). Jesus, however, introduced an essential change in attitude by teaching his followers to love their enemies (Matt 5:44) and when cursed by them to respond with blessing (Luke 6:28). This revolutionary change was summed up by Paul, "Bless those who persecute you; bless and do not curse them" (Rom 12:14).

Blessings. The term "blessing" has two basic meanings in biblical contexts. In one meaning it is a form of prayer of adoration and praise of God, "Blessed be the Lord." Such prayers recognize God's power and his inclination to make his power available to his people in blessings. Blessing bestowed by or requested from God is the second meaning of the term. Blessing in this sense is an extension of sacred presence into the world through the transfer of God's beneficent power to enhance, "bless," the object or being that is the recipient of the blessing.

In the OT blessings are directly granted by God (all creatures, Gen 1:22; humankind, Gen 1:28; the seventh day, Gen 2:3; Abram, Gen 12:2; etc.). God's blessing of Abram included his descendants and is extended to all Israel in the cultic blessings of the covenant (Deut 28:1-6). By God's blessing, Israel is "chosen" or "elected" to be the servant people through whom God's blessing of salvation is mediated to all humanity. Israel's blessing, therefore, is a blessing of responsible servanthood.

Blessings were also requested by and given through power-filled mediators, family heads, priests, kings, and prophets. Patriarchs blessed their heirs by both the spoken word and the laying on of hands (Gen 27:1-45; 48:1-20). In this way the tribal leader pronounced upon his people the inclusive blessing of peace (*shalom*), which incorporated all the positive values that make life in community meaningful. The priestly benediction of Num 6:24-26 is a cultic extension of the patriarchal blessings and has the effect of ritually actualizing God's blessing presence among his people, a presence that assures divine benevolence, protection, and peace. In the Jerusalem cultus the priest and the king by virtue of both their office and their ritual actions were mediators of divine blessing. God, however, was always known to be the source of blessing, and ritual sought his favor and blessed him for the gracious deeds through which it was experienced as blessing (cf. the praise hymns in the Psalter).

Prophetic oracles of hope and promise, while not necessarily cultic, are the most comprehensive and moving expressions of God's blessings on his servant people, offering as they do a richness of covenantal life and responsibility to those who are faithful to God (Hos 2:14-23; Mic 4:1-4; Amos 9:11-15; Isa 9:2-7; 11:1-9; Jer 31:31-34). In effect, they offer life and peace as God's alternative to the curse of death that the prophets pronounce so forcefully on sin and disobedience. They affirm God's ultimate intention for humankind to be the blessing of "peace," which is the presence of God in every circumstance of life.

In the NT Jesus pronounces blessings on little children (Mark 10:16) and on his disciples (Luke 24:51) in the Gospel of John using the formula "Peace be with you" (20:19, 21). The blessing on his disciples should be understood in light of the more specific blessing of the beatitudes of the SERMON ON THE MOUNT (Matt 5:3-12). In these Beatitudes Jesus defines new dimensions of responsibility for his disciples as a covenant community and blesses them with promises of God's presence. For Jesus blessing is essentially based upon and experienced in acts of serving other persons.

Paul's letters open and close with blessings of "grace," God's favoring presence, and "peace," fullness of life (Rom 1:7; 1 Cor 1:3; 16:23; Gal 1:3; Eph 6:23-24). These blessings like those of OT patriarchs and priests would have been considered as extensions of God's presence through a power-filled person, in this case through an apostle. Finally the Revelation is filled with doxologies and benedictions (4:8; 5:9-10, 12; 11:17-18; 22:14) which praise God's saving acts and those who participate in them as the source of eternal blessing.

See also MAGIC AND DIVINATION; SYMBOL; WORSHIP IN THE OLD TESTAMENT.

Bibliography. H. C. Brichto, *The Problem of "Curse" in the Hebrew Bible*; L. K. Little, "Cursing," *EncRel*; J. Pedesen, *Israel: Its Life and Culture*; J. Ries, "Blessing," *EncRel*; C. Westermann, *Blessing in the Bible and the Life of the Church*.

—DAVID A. SMITH

• **Cynics.** A minor Socratic school of Greek philosophy traceable to the fifth century B.C.E. Antisthenes, a younger contemporary of Socrates, is the school's founder. Whether Cynics earn their name from the place Antisthenes taught, the *Kynosarges,* or the lifestyle he advocated, "live as a dog," is uncertain. Most likely both exerted some influence.

Antisthenes was absorbed by Socrates's quest for self-sufficiency and shaped a way of living around that ideal. For the Cynics, life was to be lived moment by moment with no concern for public opinion, the accumulation of possessions, or the cultivation of the arts. Virtue, claimed Antisthenes, was an end in itself and needed no supports. Technically, the idea of a philosophical "school" should not be applied to the Cynics. A true Cynic would not invest time in constructing metaphysical or moral systems to be followed. The true Cynic would merely live out his convictions.

The best known Cynic was Diogenes of Sinope (ca. 324 B.C.E.), the legendary wanderer of Athens in search of an honest man. Diogenes referred to himself as "the dog," causing some to credit him with the establishment of the Cynic school. Diogenes carried the Cynic lifestyle to its logical extremes, living under a tub, going naked, performing all bodily functions in public, and subsisting on what he could beg. Legend has it that Diogenes was once confronted by Alexander and the conqueror of worlds asked what he might do for the beggar. Diogenes asked Alexander to step aside so as not to block the light!

Without an appreciation for the development of systems of thought or action, it is not surprising that Cynicism never reached the institutional plateaus of Stoicism or Epicureanism in the Hellenistic world. Cynics appeared from time to time, known by their rough dress and coarse challenges to society, well into the Roman era. At best, the Cynics survived as a loose movement with occasional conversions of more established citizens of the realm. Apparently there was something of a Cynic literary tradition, in the form of pseudonymous letters, spanning nearly six centuries, ending during the third century C.E. Equally significant are the respectful anecdotes of the Cynics found in Stoic texts throughout the Roman period. The Cynics lived the kind of lives the Stoics could only imagine.

Bibliography. F. Copleston, *History of Philosophy*, vol. 1, *Greece and Rome*; F. Grant, *Hellenistic Religions*; W. Meeks, *The Moral World of the First Christians*.

—RICHARD F. WILSON

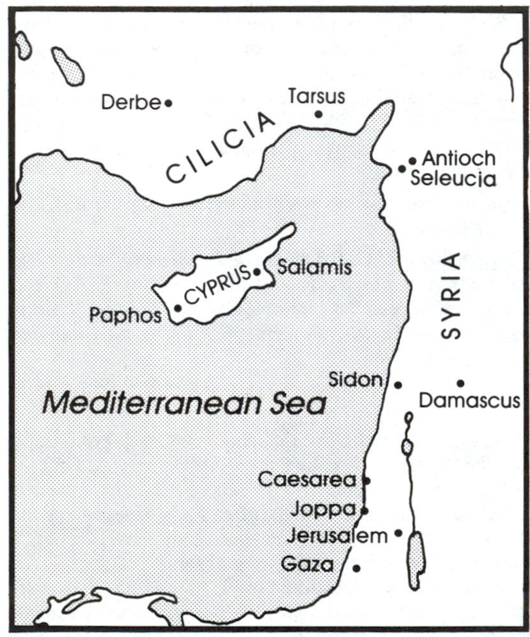

Designed by Margaret Jordan Brown ©Mercer University Press

• **Cyprus.** [*si*'pruhs] Approximately 140 by 60 mi. in size, the island of Cyprus lies roughly 60 mi. off the coasts of both Syria and Turkey (PLATES 26, 27).

Cyprus, known as *Alashia* in the cuneiform texts of Mari (eighteenth century B.C.E.) and as *A-ra-sa* in Egyptian sources, maintained an active trade with its neighbors on the mainland. Cypriot pottery from the Middle Bronze Age and Late Bronze Age has been discovered at Atchana, Lachish, Tell el-AMARNA, Troy, and Ugarit. From the tenth through the eighth centuries B.C.E. Cyprus was colonized by PHOENICIA, and became an important center for maritime shipping and commerce. The island was recognized in the OT by the names of Elishah (Gen 10:4; 1 Chr 1:7) and Kittim (Gen 10:4; 1 Chr 1:7; Isa 23:1, 12; Jer 2:10; Ezek 27:6; Dan 11:30). The latter name was probably derived from the city of Kition, which was located on the southeastern coast of the island. References to Elishah as the source of "blue and purple" (Ezek 27:7) and to Kittim as the country of Alexander (1 Macc 1:1; 8:5) suggest that both terms also may have been used by the Israelites to indicate the area of Greece in a broader sense.

Homer referred to the island of Cyprus (κύπρος, *Od* 4.83, etc.) in recognition of the famous copper mines which arose there under the influence of Crete and Mycenae in the fifteenth and fourteenth centuries B.C.E. (Pliny, *NatHist* 34.2-3). It is from this word that both the Latin term for "copper" (*cyprium*) and the modern name of Cyprus were derived. The LXX uses the term twice (1 Macc 15:23; 2 Macc 12:2) when mention is made of a Jewish population on the island during the reign of Ptolemy (late second century B.C.E.). Cyprus, which was incorporated with Cilicia by Rome in 58 B.C.E., was made an imperial province in 27 B.C.E. but came under the control of the Roman senate five years later.

The NT Book of Acts refers to Cyprus (as κύπρος or κύπριος) a total of eight times. Both Barnabas (4:36) and Mnason (21:16) are identified as former residents of the island, and it was to Phoenicia, Antioch, and Cyprus (11:19) that numerous Christians fled from Palestine after the persecution of Stephen. Barnabas returned to Cyprus during the first missionary journey of Paul (13:4), and took Mark there after the two friends separated from Paul during the second missionary journey (15:39). Paul later traveled past Cyprus twice, once on his way from Ephesus to Jerusalem (21:3) and again on his journey to Rome (27:4). The growth of the Cypriot Church is attested by missionaries whom it sent to Antioch in the first century (11:20) and later by the three bishops whom it sent to the Council of Nicaea in 325 C.E.

Bibliography. E. Gjerstad, *Swedish Cyprus Expedition I-IV*; G. F. Hill, *A History of Cyprus*; V. Karageorghis, *Cyprus from the Stone Age to the Romans*.

—CLAYTON N. JEFFORD

• **Cyrene.** [*si*-ree'nee] Cyrene is a city in Cyrenaica (modern Libya) on the northern coast of Africa (PLATE 20). Lying directly south of Greece across the Mediterranean Sea and west of Egypt and Jerusalem, Cyrene had a thriving Jewish community from the fourth century B.C.E. By confronting the Hellenistic culture in Cyrene, Judaism and Christianity were able to spread into the Greek-speaking world. In the process however, many Hellenistic practices, ideas, and images flowed back into Jewish and Christian life. Connections between Cyrene and Palestine were apparently strong (Acts 6:9). In the second century B.C.E. Jason of Cyrene had used bribery to become high priest in Jerusalem. His attempt to intensify the flow of Hellenistic ideas into Judaism earned him disfavor with the Jews and Jerusalem (2 Macc 4). Early Christians from Cyrene and the nearby island of CRETE traveled east to ANTIOCH to speak to the Greeks in the local church. The Greek-speaking Christians in Cyrene and Antioch were viewed somewhat as rivals by the church in Jerusalem (Acts 11:20; 13:1; Gal 1–2). Simon of Cyrene is alleged to have carried Jesus' cross (Mark 15:21), although the fourth Gospel (John 19:17) has Jesus carry it alone.

See also ANTIOCH; CRETE; HEBREWS AND HELLENISTS; HELLENISTIC WORLD.

—JOE E. BARNHART

• **Cyrus.** [*si*'ruhs] Cyrus II, the founder of a Persian empire that stretched from India to Greece, was the son of Cambyses I, king of Anshan (in present-day southern Iran), and his wife Mandane, the daughter of the king of the Median empire, Astyages. In 559 B.C.E., Cyrus succeeded his father as king of Anshan and vassal of Astyages. Forging an alliance of Persian tribes, he led a rebellion against his grandfather, and in 550 B.C.E. he captured the capital of Media, Ecbatana. From Ecbatana he set out to lay claim to all areas of the Median empire—MESOPOTAMIA, Syria, Armenia, and CAPPADOCIA. Defeating Croesus of Lydia in 547 B.C.E., he consolidated his hold on the Greek subjects of Lydia, most of Asia Minor, Upper Mesopotamia, and perhaps Syria as well. Cyrus then concentrated for several years on expanding the eastern frontier of his empire. In

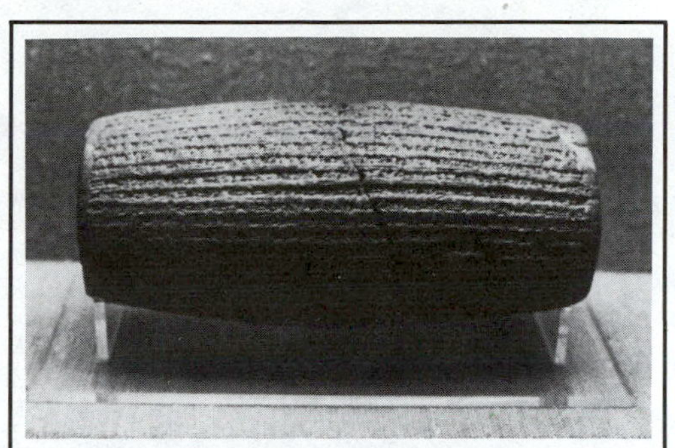

The Cyrus cylinder (ca. 539 B.C.E.)

540–539 B.C.E. he returned to Mesopotamia. After routing the Babylonian king NABONIDUS at Opis on the Tigris River, Cyrus took Babylon without a battle.

The rise of Cyrus and the threat he posed to Babylon were greeted with anticipation by some in the exiled community of Judeans. In Isa 45:1 Cyrus is proclaimed as Yahweh's messiah (the only non-Israelite so designated in the OT) who was to bring about freedom for the exiles (Isa 45:13) and the rebuilding of JERUSALEM and its TEMPLE (Isa 44:28). In fact, according to the Cyrus Cylinder, a building inscription unearthed in Babylon, part of Cyrus's imperial policy (with precedents among some Assyrian rulers) was the restoration of certain politically sensitive cities, their temples, and populations. Cyrus apparently pursued this policy with regard to Jerusalem. In 538 B.C.E., the Edict of Cyrus (preserved in Ezra 6:3-5) ordered the reconstruction of the Temple and the reinstitution of sacrifices there. According to this edict, the work on the Temple was to be funded from Cyrus's royal treasury. Another version of the edict, apparently in the form of an oral royal proclamation, is recorded in Ezra 1:2-4.

However, the rebuilding of the Temple was fraught with difficulties and delays and was not completed until 516/5 B.C.E., the seventh year of DARIUS. In addition to the local and regional problems faced by the returning exiles—e.g., crop failures (Hag 1:9-11; 2:15-17) and interference by neighboring populations (Ezra 4:4–6:13)—no doubt funding for the work was held up by affairs in the empire as a whole. Cyrus died campaigning on the eastern frontier in 530 B.C.E., and the expansionism of his son Cambyses II (e.g., adding Egypt to the empire) was hardly conducive to concern for projects such as the Jerusalem temple. When Cambyses died in 522 B.C.E., rebellions occurred in all parts of the empire. Darius, one of Cambyses' officers, claimed the throne and put down the revolts. It is not surprising then that by the second year of Darius the edict of Cyrus had been forgotten in Persian administrative circles, and only after an inquiry by the provincial governor and a search of the Persian archives was the edict recovered and reinstated by Darius (Ezra 5–6).

See also PERSIAN EMPIRE.

Bibliography. E. J. Bickerman, "The Edict of Cyrus in Ezra 1," *JBL* 65 (1946): 249-75; A. Kuhrt, "The Cyrus Cylinder and Achaemenid Imperial Policy," *JSOT* 25 (Feb 1983): 83-97; A. T. Olmstead, *History of the Persian Empire*.

—JEFFREY S. ROGERS

• **D.** *See* SOURCE CRITICISM

• **Damascus.** [duh-mas'kuhs] Damascus is located about sixty miles east of the Mediterranean city of Sidon. It is the capital of modern Syria and has a population exceeding two million. Damascus is a very ancient city; the name is nonsemitic and presumably predates the settlement of semitic Amorites in this territory around 2500 B.C.E.

Damascus is mentioned in numerous extrabiblical sources. The EBLA texts provide the earliest mention of the city. The Egyptian pharoah Thutmose III lists the city as under his control. The Assyrian king Adad-nirari II lists three campaigns against Damascus. The Assyrian king Shalmaneser III mentions Damascus in his description of the conflict he had with King Ahab of Israel at Qarqar. He says that Hadadezer of Damascus also opposed him.

Damascus figured in the biblical story long and often. It is mentioned in the account of Abraham's rescue of his kinsmen (Gen 14:15). David established control of Damascus when he defeated a coalition of Syrians. During the time of Solomon, Damascus was made the capital city by the first of a series of Aramean kings. Damascus continued to play a part in the story of Israel and Judah until the Assyrian conquest. Under Assyria, Damascus became an administrative zone, but it had no real power. The city fell to Alexander the Great during his struggles against Darius III (333 B.C.E.). When it was made a Nabatean capital in 85 B.C.E., a measure of power was regained. The conquest of ARETAS III by Pompey in 65 B.C.E. led to Roman rule through Nabatean governors. Aretas IV was the Nabatean governor in charge when Paul came to Damascus (Acts 9:2-30).

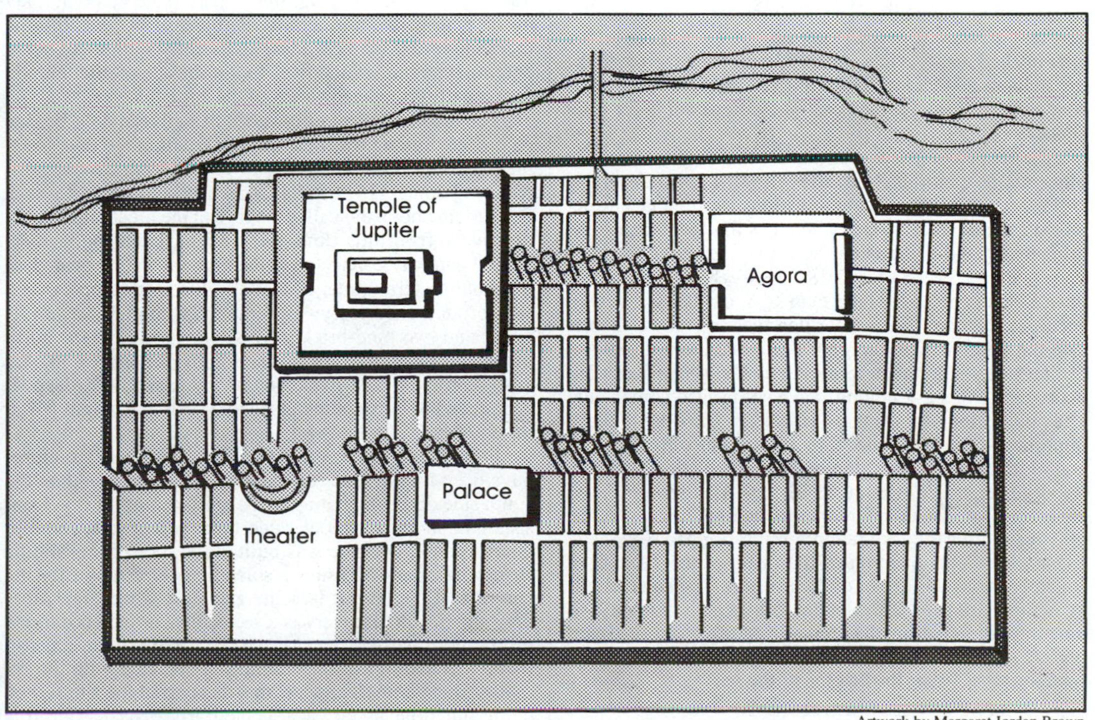

Layout of Damascus in the time of Paul.

Artwork by Margaret Jordan Brown

See also ARETAS; EBLA; SYRIA AND CILICIA.

—JERRY VARDAMAN

• **Damascus Rule.** The *Damascus Rule* (*CD*) is the only sectarian document among the DEAD SEA SCROLLS which was known before their discovery. Two Hebrew manuscripts of the document had been found in 1896 in the storeroom of an old synagogue in Cairo and published as "Fragments of a Zadokite Work." Manuscript A (tenth century C.E.) contains eight leaves inscribed on both sides. Manuscript B (twelfth century C.E.), consisting of a single leaf written on both sides, overlaps the end of manuscript A (with significant differences) and continues the document. The Qumran discoveries, also in Hebrew, consist of five small fragments (one of which has no parallel in the Cairo manuscripts) from Cave 6 of a manuscript dating from the first half of the first century C.E., one small fragment from Cave 5 of a manuscript from the second half of the first century B.C.E., and fragments of seven manuscripts from Cave 4, the earliest of which dates from 100 to 75 B.C.E. These latter manuscripts, which are still unpublished, apparently represent a different recension and contain material missing from the Cairo manuscripts.

As represented in the published manuscripts, the *Damascus Rule* consists of two parts. The first part is an exhortation to the members of the community. It begins with an historical prologue reviewing the origins of the community, praising the role of the Teacher of Righteousness and castigating that of the Man of Lies. There follows a sectarian interpretation of OT history culminating in the formation of the sect. Next comes a discussion of the three nets of Belial, followed by descriptions of the community and of the contrasting fates of the faithful and the apostates. The second part is the *Rule* proper. It contains legal statutes and organizational regulations for the community. The text breaks off at the beginning of a penal code. The unpublished manuscripts apparently prefix a section to the exhortation, add various prescriptions, and follow the penal code with a liturgy for the Feast of the Renewal of the Covenant.

The relationship between the *Damascus Rule*, and the other major Qumran Rule, the MANUAL OF DISCIPLINE (*1QS*) is problematic. There are strong ties in tone and detail; yet there are differences, such as the *Rule*'s openness to marriage and its apparent belief in one, not two, Messiahs (although cf. *CD* 6:7; 7:18). Most scholars believe that the *Rule* was composed later than *1QS*, ca. 100 B.C.E. Others argue that the *Rule* was written first and may even predate the settlement at Qumran. Elaborate literary analyses of the *Rule,* undertaken in an attempt to show that it has undergone extensive editing, have not proved convincing. The publication of the manuscripts from Cave 4 will prove important for a more adequate assessment of both its literary history and its function in the community at Qumran.

Other significant features of the *Damascus Rule* include the problematic references to the founding of the sect 390 years after the EXILE and a migration from Judea to "Damascus"; its mention of the death of the Teacher of Righteousness, and its use of the BOOK OF JUBILEES (cf. the TEMPLE SCROLL). All in all, the *Rule* is an important document for illuminating the regulations, organization, interpretive strategies, messianism, ESCHATOLOGY, and (along with the PESHARIM) the origins of the sect.

See also DEAD SEA SCROLLS; ESSENES.

Bibliography. P. R. Davies, *The Damascus Covenant*; D. Dimant, "Qumran Sectarian Literature," *Jewish Writings of the Second Temple Period,* ed. M. E. Stone; L. H. Schiffman, *The Halakhah at Qumran,* and *Sectarian Law in the Dead Sea Scrolls*; G. Vermes, "The Writings of the Qumran Community," in E. Schürer, *The History of the Jewish People in the Age of Jesus Christ,* rev. ed.

—JOSEPH L. TRAFTON

• **Dan, Tell.** Tell Dan is located at the foot of Mount Hermon, approximately twenty-five mi. north of the Sea of Galilee. A relatively large mound of around fifty acres, it is situated in a rich and fertile valley. During the time of the United Monarchy (ca. 1000–922 B.C.E.), Dan was the northernmost city of the empire, and the expression, "from Dan to Beersheba," was used to indicate the extent of the Hebrew kingdom (cf. Judg 20:1; 1 Sam 3:20; 2 Sam 3:19; 17:11; 24:2; etc.) (PLATES 3, 12, 13).

The excavation of the site, which began in 1966, has revealed a massive Canaanite mud-brick city gate and rampart defensive system dating to the Middle Bronze Age IIA-IIB (twentieth-nineteenth centuries B.C.E.); a large Mycenean tomb and Late Bronze settlement (fourteenth-thirteenth centuries B.C.E.); an extensive Iron Age II (tenth-seventh centuries B.C.E.) city; and Hellenistic and Roman remains. The site was apparently abandoned for good sometime during the fourth century C.E. A Greek and Aramaic inscription from the late third-early second century B.C.E. containing the word "Dan" almost assures the identification of the site.

What may be Pottery Neolithic (sixth millennium B.C.E.) remains have been found at the lowest levels reached on the site, and it has been estimated that during the Early Bronze Age (third millennium B.C.E.) a large city was built here with a population between 7,500 and 10,000 people. The attractiveness of the site was due in part to the fact that it lay in the path of the northern trade routes. But probably the most important factor leading to its early settlement is the perennial stream which rises to the surface on the tell and forms part of the headwaters of the Jordan River.

The archaeological discoveries from the Middle Bronze Age II are among the most impressive found to date in Israel. The Canaanite city was surrounded by a massive rampart wall some 175 ft. thick at its base and rising to sixty ft. or more above the valley floor. But the most remarkable discovery from this time is the magnificent mud-brick, arched gateway connected to the rampart wall. Located on the southeastern corner of the tell, this gate complex consists of an arched entryway some ten ft. high by seven ft. wide, and two mud-brick towers, one located to the north of the entryway, the other to the south. The entire complex is some forty-five ft. wide and nearly as many ft. deep. It is believed to be standing close to its original height (ca. 6 m. or 20 ft.).

From the Israelite period two very significant structures have been found. One is a major gate system found on the south side of the tell dating to the ninth century B.C.E. Consisting of an inner and outer threshold, two towers, and four guard rooms, the gate was built at the foot of the Middle Bronze rampart. Measuring some ninty-seven by fifty ft., it is one of the largest Israelite gates yet found. The other very significant discovery is a sacred area or temenos found on the northwestern part of the tell. While there are still many archaeological uncertainties associated with the remains found here, it appears that this part of the site served cultic functions as far back as the Early Bronze Age. It is the excavator's belief that the remains from the Israelite period belong to a *beth bamoth,* or "house of high-places" (cf. 1 Kgs 12:31; 13:32). Thus, though many questions still remain, the archaeological evidence clearly points to the importance of Dan as a major cult center during the period of the divided monarchy (ca. 922–722 B.C.E.).

Bibliography. A. Biran, "Tel Dan," *BA* 37 (1974): 26-51; "Tel Dan: Five Years Later," *BA* 43 (1980): 168-82 and "The Triple-Arched Gate of Laish at Tel Dan," *IEJ* 34/1 (1984): 1-19; J. C. H Laughlin, "The Remarkable Discoveries at Tel Dan," *BAR* 7/5 (Sep/Oct 1981): 20-37.

—JOHN C. H. LAUGHLIN

• **Dan/Danites.** Meaning "(God) judges," Dan originally was a proper name belonging to the fifth son of JACOB. His mother was Bilhah, RACHEL's handmaiden, and he became the eponymous ancestor of the Danites (Gen 30:6; 35:25). He was the full brother of NAPHTALI.

While we possess more detailed information about the movement of the tribe of Dan than any other tribe in the OT, that history, as well as the history of the Israelite tribal system in general, is extremely complex. According to the Book of Judges, the tribe was unable to secure a permanent place of settlement west of the territory of BENJAMIN because of pressure from the Amorites (Judg 1:34). Migrating north, the Danites appropriated the cultic paraphernalia of the Ephraimite, Micah, including the latter's private priest who was a Levite (Judg 17–18). They then destroyed the Canaanite city of Laish, which they rebuilt and inhabited, renaming it Dan, after their ancestor (Judg 18; cf. Josh 19:47 where "Laish" has been corrupted into "Leshem").

While these traditions give us important details about the movement of the tribe, caution is in order when they are evaluated historically. This is so not only because the story in its present form dates no earlier than 734–732 B.C.E. (Judg 18:30), but more importantly because the narrative, as it now stands, serves the polemical purpose of discrediting the Israelite sanctuary at Dan established by JEROBOAM I sometime after 926 or 922 B.C.E. (cf. 1 Kgs 12:26-31). Thus the narrative does not set out to give a tribal history of the Danites, but the sordid conditions under which the sanctuary came into existence.

Nevertheless, there is no good reason to doubt that the traditional material used by the redactors probably reflects tribal conditions at the time of the migration. The impression given in Judg 18:1 is that the tribe had never possessed any territory of its own, including any of the land on the coastal plain. In fact, the reference to Mahaneh Dan (the camp of Dan) in Judg 13:25 (cf. 18:12) indicates that they existed more as a semi-nomadic clan than as a settled tribe. This would mean that the list of cities allotted to them in Josh 19:40-46 has been highly idealized and contributes nothing to the history of the tribe. In actuality, these cities were controlled by the Amorites (cf. Judg 1:34) and/or PHILISTINES until the time of David.

The population of the tribe is also problematical, being given at over 60,000 in the census lists in Num 1:39; 26:42-43. Either the census figures are highly exaggerated or the population of the tribe had been drastically reduced by the time of the migration. A third possibility is that not all of the tribe participated in the movement. But the clear impression given in Judg 18 is that a mass departure of the tribe took place.

The date of the migration is also uncertain, and little help is given by the biblical traditions themselves. Further, the contribution of archaeology to this problem is ambiguous. The results of the recent excavations at TELL DAN have been interpreted to conclude that Laish was conquered in the late thirteenth century B.C.E. If it could be shown that this destruction was indeed caused by the Danites, then the date of the migration could be fixed. At the moment, however, any attempt to do so can only be speculative.

That Laish fell so easily to the Danites is no doubt related to the city's isolation and to the lack of military preparedness by its inhabitants (cf. Judg 18:7, though the text is difficult). How much territory around this northern city was ultimately controlled by the tribe is also unknown. What does seem clear is that the Danites might have passed from memory after the migration had it not been for the later interest in the sanctuary established there.

See also LEVI/LEVITES; MICAH; TRIBES.

Bibliography. N. Gottwald, *The Tribes of Yahweh*; H. H. Rowley, *From Joseph to Joshua*; J. A. Soggin, *Judges, OTL*; R. de Vaux, "Dan," *The Early History of Israel*.

—JOHN C. H. LAUGHLIN

• **Dancing.** In the ancient world, dancing is not only a physical activity and act of celebration, but also an act of WORSHIP. The Hebrew verbs *rāqad* and *pāzaz* refer to leaping and skipping, while the verbs *kārar* and *ḥûl* refer to whirling and circling. *Rāqad* is used both as an antithesis to mourning in Eccl 3:4 and as descriptive of DAVID's dancing around the ARK of the Covenant in 2 Sam 6:16, while *pāzaz* may only be found in a reference to dance in 2 Sam 6:16. The *kārar* root may only be found in 2 Sam 6. The *ḥûl* root is most typically used and reflects the cultic (religious) use of the dance in particular (Exod 15:20; Judg 21:21, 23; Pss 30:12; 149:3; 150:4, etc.).

The NT uses two basic words: *orcheomai* and *choros*. The former is the verb used for both Herodias's daughter's dance of death (Matt 14:6; Mark 6:22) and the dancing of children (Matt 11:17). The latter is a noun used to describe dancing in a band or chorus (Luke 15:25). The early church authorities also had traditions about dancing. They taught dancing as a circle, analogous to the Greek chorus used in the theatres. Chrysostom advised his parishioners to dance to the glory of God, using David's dances as an example and urging believers to avoid "unseemly motions" and keep the dances sacred.

See also WORSHIP IN THE NEW TESTAMENT; WORSHIP IN THE OLD TESTAMENT.

Bibliography. J. Martin, *Introduction to the Dance*.

—JOHNNY L. WILSON

• **Daniel.** [dan'yuhl] The hero of the Book of Daniel, and one of the Jewish exiles in Babylon in the sixth century B.C.E., where he is trained in "the letters and language of the Chaldeans" and becomes a member of the class of professional wise men at the Babylonian court. Daniel and his companions risk the displeasure of the king by refusing his food and observing the Jewish kosher laws, but nevertheless they excel among the wise men. When the lives of all the wise men are endangered by the king's impossible demand that they tell him his dream as well as the interpretation (chap. 2), it is Daniel who comes to their rescue. He learns the dream, not by the techniques of the wise men, but by revelation from his God. He is rewarded by promotion to become "ruler over all the province of Babylon."

His skill as an interpreter of dreams and mysteries is again in evidence in chaps. 4–5. In chap. 4 he interprets the king's dream about a great tree and foretells that the king will be driven from among people and will eat grass like an ox until he recognizes the Most High God. In chap. 5 he interprets the mysterious writing on the wall at BELSHAZZAR's feast. Even though his interpretation predicts the imminent fall of the kingdom, he is promoted to the rank of third in command. His religious fidelity is again highlighted in chap. 6. Because he persists in praying to his own God, Daniel is thrown into the lions' den. He emerges unscathed, however, and his enemies are devoured instead.

In the remainder of the book he recounts his visions and revelations. These are couched in mysterious language but refer to a great crisis in the future that will be followed by a definitive judgment of God.

It is unlikely that the Daniel described in the Book of Daniel ever existed. This judgment is based on the fact that he is not independently attested and on the genre of the stories told about him in the Book of Daniel itself. These stories are riddled with historical problems, the most famous of which concerns the introduction of DARIUS the Mede before CYRUS of Persia. Darius was the name of a later Persian monarch. He is introduced as a Mede here to fit a traditional schema of history in which Media preceded Persia. The story of NEBUCHADREZZAR's madness in Dan 4 is now known to be a variant of a tradition about NABONIDUS, the last king of Babylon. Another variant of this tradition is now known from the *Prayer of Nabonidus* at Qumran. Dan 5 identifies the last Babylonian king as Belshazzar, who was in fact regent of Babylon under Nabonidus. It appears then that the Book of Daniel preserves historical data only in a garbled fashion. The stories are not historical records but legends written to inspire wonder, stories that often conform to the patterns of folklore. The legendary character of the stories is most evident in the episode of the lions' den. A variant of this episode is found in the story of BEL AND THE DRAGON that is appended to the Greek translation of the Book of Daniel.

Daniel is not mentioned in any historical book prior to 1 Macc 2:60, where he is mentioned in a prayer. His absence is conspicuous in Ben Sira's "praise of the fathers" from the early second century B.C.E. The name Daniel occurs in Ezra 8:2 for a priest who returned from Babylonia to Jerusalem in the reign of ARTAXERXES, and again in Neh 10:6. The context of these references is approximately a century after the Exile, and so they cannot refer to the same individual. Two references in the Book of Ezekiel are of greater interest. Ezek 14:14 says that not even NOAH, Daniel and JOB could save a city by their righteousness and Ezek 28:3 taunts the king of Tyre: "Are you wiser than Daniel?" These references show that at the time of the Exile the name Daniel was associated with a legendary wise and righteous man like Noah and Job. This figure may be identical with the Daniel (Dnil) found in the epic of Aqhat at Ugarit 1,000 years earlier. The Ugaritic Daniel was, among other things, a judge who defended widows and orphans. The function of judge is suggested by the name Daniel ("God is my judge" or possibly "judge of God"). Daniel did not have this function in the Hebrew Bible, but he did in the story of SUSANNA. It is likely that the name of the biblical hero was chosen because of its traditional associations, but Daniel's identity is not defined by the older tradition. It is shaped by the stories in the Book of Daniel itself. In 1 Maccabees, Daniel is praised for his innocence and for enduring in time of trial. His primary identity in antiquity was as prophet (Matt 24:15; JOSEPHUS, *Ant* 10.11.7), although he is not included among the prophets in the Hebrew Bible (because of the late date of composition of the book). He was also venerated in antiquity as a holy man because of his abstention from delicacies (Dan 1:8; 10:3) and visionary powers.

See also APOCALYPTIC LITERATURE; DANIEL, BOOK OF; LIVES OF THE PROPHETS.

—JOHN J. COLLINS

• **Daniel, Apocalypse of.** The *Apocalypse of Daniel* is a Christian work of the Byzantine period. Heavily dependent on the REVELATION of John, it makes no reference to DANIEL, but its literary structure is similar to that of Dan 7–12, in that it begins with a historical summary (presented as prophecy) and then moves to predictions of the events of the last days.

The dating of the work depends upon how the historical allusions are understood. The writer describes a savior-king who defeats the invading Arabs. This is probably Constantine V (741–75). The next two rulers, regarded as evil by the writer, should be the Emperor Leo IV (775–80) and the Empress Irene (797–802), who is still in power when the kingdom is "taken up . . . and given to Rome." This should be understood as the coronation of Charlemagne by Pope Leo III, Christmas Day 800, and is the last identifiable historical reference. Presumably, then, the work should be dated between early 801 and the end of Irene's reign (31 Oct. 802).

The second half of the work consists of a description of the origin and reign of the ANTICHRIST, who, supported by the Jews, persecutes the Christians and is overthrown by the coming of Christ and the end of the world.

It has been suggested that the writer was a member of the iconoclastic party in Byzantium, who, despairing over the success of the "idolatrous" empress and viewing the coronation of Charlemagne as the transfer of God's favor to Rome, concluded that the end of the world must be at hand.

See also APOCALYPTIC LITERATURE.

Bibliography. G. T. Zervos, "Apocalypse of Daniel," *The Old Testament Pseudepigrapha*, ed. J. H. Charlesworth.

—SHARYN E. DOWD

• **Daniel, Book of.** The book is found among the Writings in the Hebrew Bible but appears as the fourth of the major Prophets in the Greek and Latin versions. The conventional explanation is that the Hebrew prophetic canon was

• OUTLINE OF DANIEL •

The Book of Daniel

I. Stories of Daniel in Babylonian Exile (1:1–6:28)
   A. Daniel and his colleagues in the court of Nebuchadrezzar (1:1-21)
   B. Nebuchadrezzar's dream of a great image and Daniel's interpretation (2:1-49)
   C. The companions of Daniel thrown into the furnace (3:1-30)
   D. Nebuchadrezzar's second dream: a great tree (4:1-37)
   E. Belshazzar's feast and the handwriting on the wall (5:1-31)
   F. Daniel thrown into the lions' den by Darius (6:1-28)
II. Visions of Daniel (7:1–12:13)
   A. The four beasts (7:1-28)
   B. The ram and the male goat (8:1-27)
   C. Daniel's prayer; the meaning of Jeremiah's prophecy of seventy years (9:1-27)
   D. The vision of the Last Days (10:1–12:4)
   E. Conclusion (12:5-13)

already closed when the book was written. The Greek version includes four substantial passages not found in the Hebrew Bible: the Song of the Three Young Men and the PRAYER OF AZARIAH in chap. 3 and the stories of SUSANNA and BEL AND THE DRAGON. These additional passages are accepted as canonical in Roman Catholicism, but are relegated to the Apocrypha by Protestants.

The book is already exceptional in the Hebrew Bible because of its bilingual character: chaps. 1:1–2:4a and 8:1–12:13 are in Hebrew; the remainder of chap. 2 and chaps. 3–7 are in ARAMAIC. There is also a clear difference in genre between chaps. 1–6, which are stories about Daniel and his companions in the Babylonian Exile, and chaps. 7–12, which are revelations given to Daniel about the future course of history. These divisions reflect a lengthy process of formation. The stories in chaps. 1–6 are traditional tales composed in Aramaic that evolved over a period of time. Scholars had long suspected that the story of NEBUCHADREZZAR's dream in Dan 4 was based on reminiscences about NABONIDUS, the last king of Babylon. This insight has now been confirmed by the discovery of *The Prayer of Nabonidus* at Qumran, obviously a variant of the same tradition. There are indications that these stories reached their present form in the Hellenistic period, probably in the third century B.C.E. (the famous schema of four kingdoms in chap. 2 implies that the fourth kingdom is the Greek). The revelations in chaps. 7–12 can be dated more precisely to the period of the Maccabean revolt (168–64 B.C.E.). The focus of each of the revelations is on the persecution of the Jews by Antiochus Epiphanes at that time. There is no apparent reason why Daniel in the Babylonian Exile should have been so preoccupied with events several centuries later. Moreover, Dan 11 contains a review of the history of the Hellenistic era that is exact down to the time of the persecution, but incorrectly predicts that the king would meet his death in the land of Israel. Already in antiquity, Porphyry inferred that the "correct" prophecies were written after the fact and that the real author wrote before the death of the king (late 164 B.C.E.). While the stories in chaps. 1–6 were relevant to the time of persecution, they do not show any knowledge of it and so are thought to be earlier. Chap. 7 was written in Aramaic, for continuity with the tales, but 8–12 were composed in Hebrew, possibly for reasons of nationalistic fervor. Chap. 1 was either composed in Hebrew as an introduction to the whole book, or most likely translated from Aramaic so that both the beginning and the end of the book would be in Hebrew.

The stories in Dan 1–6 have been aptly said to describe "a lifestyle for the Diaspora." The theme of these stories is that it is possible to serve gentile rulers and still be faithful to Jewish law—or even that fidelity to the law is precisely the key to success in the gentile world. Because Daniel and his friends refused to eat the king's food they fared better than did their gentile colleagues. Because Daniel prayed to his God he was able to interpret the dreams of the king and the writing on the wall, and he and his companions were rescued from mortal danger. These stories entertain the idea of the conversion and repentance of the gentile kings, a possibility no longer envisioned in chaps. 7–12.

In chap. 7 the gentile kings are portrayed as beasts rising from the sea. They were submitted to the judgment of an "ancient of days" who bestowed the kingdom on "one like a son of man." The imagery of this vision has old associations in Hebrew poetry and even in Canaanite myths of the second millennium. It suggests that the struggle in which the Jews were involved in the Maccabean era was like the primeval battle with the sea monster in Near Eastern mythology. The exaltation of the "one like a son of man" represents the victory of the Jewish people, although he should probably be identified as MICHAEL, the angelic patron of Israel, rather than as a collective symbol for the people.

A clue to the setting and purpose of the book can be found in 11:33-34. There it is said that in the time of persecution "those among the people who are wise shall make many understand, though they shall fall by sword and flame, by captivity and plunder for some days." The author probably belonged to the group of "the wise"; the revelations contained in the Book of Daniel are representative of the understanding they imparted. Crucial to that understanding was the belief that the archangel Michael was fighting for the faithful Jews against the angelic "prince of Greece" (10:20-21). In the end, "Michael will arise, the great prince who has charge of your people" (12:1). Then "many of those who sleep in the dust of the earth shall awake, some to everlasting life and some to shame and everlasting contempt, and the wise shall shine like the brightness of the firmament and those who turn many to righteousness like the stars for ever and ever" (12:2-3). This is the only passage in the Hebrew Bible that speaks clearly of the reward and punishment of individuals after death. The hope for resurrection is the underpinning of the stance of the "wise" who submit to martyrdom in the time of persecution. They can afford to lose their lives in this world because they hope to be elevated to the host of heaven hereafter.

The Book of Daniel was written for a very specific situation in the Maccabean era, but retained its significance long after that era had passed. The fourth kingdom of chaps. 2 and 7 was later identified as Rome, and continued to be reinterpreted down through the Middle Ages. The book acquired special importance for Christians because chap. 7 was read as a prophecy of the coming of Christ as "the son of man" on the clouds of heaven. Daniel also had a more general influence in shaping the apocalyptic expectations of early Christianity that found their most vivid expression in the Revelation of John.

See also APOCALYPTIC LITERATURE; DANIEL; MACCABEES.

Bibliography. J. J. Collins, *The Apocalyptic Vision of the Book of Daniel*; L. F. Hartman and A. DiLella, *The Book of Daniel*; A. Lacocque, *The Book of Daniel*.

—JOHN J. COLLINS

• **Darius.** [duh-r*i*'uhs] Darius occurs twenty-five times in the OT as the name of three Persian kings and of Darius the Mede.

Darius I, the Great (522–486 B.C.E.), born in 550, was the son of Hystaspes, a kinsman of CYRUS. His reign began in political turmoil when Gaumata usurped the throne of Cambyses, who had no children. Claiming to be Bardiya, the murdered brother of Cambyses, and promising tax remission and religious reforms, Gaumata won over almost all the empire. After slaying Gaumata, Darius took a full year to bring the rebels under control. His account of the struggle is in the famous BEHISTUN inscription written in three languages—Old Persian, Elamite, and Akkadian—on the cliff at Behistun in northern Mesopotamia (modern Iran). He organized the kingdom into twenty to twenty-three satrapies and ruled through governors or "satraps" directly responsible to the king and having no military under them. By eliminating vassal kings with armies trying to seize power and independence, Darius rendered powerless the vehicle for revolt. Darius extended his empire as far east as India, but failed in the west to conquer Greece. In his attempts, half his fleet was wrecked in a storm off Mount Athos (492 B.C.E.), and his army was defeated at Marathon (490). He died in 486 before he could resume the attack.

Continuing Cyrus's tolerant policy toward the Jews, Darius encouraged them in the completion of the Jerusalem Temple (Ezra 5:3ff.; 6:1-12, 15; Josephus, *Ant* 11.2-5). He was devoted to Ahuramazda, the only god mentioned in his inscriptions, but evidently believed that the Hebrew God could either help or harm his kingdom (Ezra 6:10). Darius I was contemporary with the Hebrew prophets Haggai (1:1; 2:1, 10) and Zechariah (1:1, 7; 7:1).

Darius II (423–404 B.C.E.), known as Nothus, was a son of ARTAXERXES I. He came to the throne after avenging the death of the rightful successor, Xerxes II. His weak reign resulted in uprisings throughout the kingdom, especially in the west. In the "Passover Papyrus" from Elephantine, dated in his fifth year, he authorized the Jews of Elephantine to observe the Passover. This may have been an attempt to bring about a renewed interest in religion to increase the collection of funds for the local temple of Yahu. The Elephantine temple was later destroyed (410). Some scholars identify the Darius of Neh 12:22 as Darius II.

Darius III (336–330 B.C.E.), known as Codomannus, became king with a difficult twofold task: to put down the constant revolts throughout the empire, and to resist the attacks of the advancing armies of ALEXANDER, whose move eastward had already begun. He was defeated by Alexander at Issus (333 B.C.E.) and at Gaugamela (331), mentioned in 1 Macc 1:1. Darius retreated, with Alexander's army following close behind. Alexander found him dead on the road to Bactria, murdered by conspirators.

Darius the Mede is mentioned only in the Book of Daniel (5:31; 6:1, 6, 9, 25, 28; 9:1; 11:1) as a king of Babylon. He is called the son of Ahasuerus (9:1), who followed BELSHAZZAR (5:31) and preceded Cyrus (6:28). He divided the kingdom into 120 satrapies and appointed Daniel as one of the three presidents over them (6:1ff.). Outside the book of Daniel, history knows no "Darius the Mede," and it becomes impossible to place such a character between Belshazzar, the son and co-regent of Nabonidus (556–539 B.C.E.) and Cyrus (539–522 B.C.E.). Many theories have been set forth in an attempt to solve the historical problems presented by this strange character. H. H. Rowley is right when he declares that the unsolvable historical problems of the Book of Daniel do not destroy, but strengthen, the religious value of the book.

Bibliography. A. T. Olmstead, *History of the Persian Empire*; N. W. Porteous, *Daniel*; H. H. Rowley, *Darius the Mede and the Four World Empires in the Book of Daniel.*

—G. BYRNS COLEMAN

• **Darkness.** Darkness is used in contrast to LIGHT throughout the Bible—as in other parts of the ancient Near East. Literally, physical darkness means the absence of light and the life it sustains. Darkness was present before creation (Gen 1:2) and for a portion of the crucifixion (Matt 27:45; Mark 15:33; Luke 23:44). Israel escaped from Egypt with the help of darkness (Exod 10:21-23; 14:19-20), and God sometimes is shrouded in it (Exod 20:21; Ps 18:11).

As a metaphor, darkness indicated many negative things: pain and misery (Job 18:18; Isa 9:1-2), defeat and captivity (Ezek 34:12; Isa 47:5; Ps 107:10), destruction and death (Mic 3:5-6; Ps 143:3). The judgment of God is a dark reality when the Day of the Lord arrives (Amos 5:18-20; Joel 2:1-2). Outer darkness means separation from God (Matt 8:12; 22:13).

In the moral sphere, sinful humans "love darkness rather than light" (John 3:19). Yet, in the face of dark human evil, God sent the Light, which darkness cannot overwhelm (John 1:5).

See also LIGHT/DARKNESS IN THE NEW TESTAMENT; LIGHT IN THE OLD TESTAMENT.

—DONALD W. GARNER

• **David.** The second king of ISRAEL and the first king of combined Israel and JUDAH. David ruled Judah from the city of HEBRON for about seven years, and the combined Israelite-Judean kingdom first from Hebron and then from JERUSALEM. He was the son of JESSE, a Bethlehemite (or Ephrathite; cf. 1 Sam 16:1, 18; 17:12).

The story of David's life, from his days as a young shepherd to his death, is told twice in the OT, once in 1 Sam 16–1 Kgs 2 and again in 1 Chr 10–29. The Chronicler's account was written some time after the Samuel–Kings account and is largely based upon it, although it makes very significant modifications to the earlier account in accordance with the Chronicler's theological and political purposes. One should keep in mind, moreover, that even the Samuel-Kings account was not written as a strict historical record, but as a carefully crafted narrative with certain theological and political perspectives. It is composed of a variety of traditional materials, primarily popular stories relating to events in David's life. Probably these stories had circulated independently before they were woven into the continuous account we now have. The basic compositional units of this account may be outlined as follows:

1. A collection of stories pertaining to David's rise to power, from his anointment by Samuel to the establishment of his rule in Jerusalem (1 Sam 16–2 Sam 5).

2. The continuation and conclusion of a narrative strand pertaining to the ARK of the covenant (2 Sam 6:1-23), the main part of which is to be found in 1 Sam 4:1–7:2.

3. A chapter emphasizing Yahweh's affirmation of David and his dynasty (2 Sam 7).

4. A summary of David's military accomplishments and administrative officials (2 Sam 8:1-15).

5. An essentially continuous narrative that describes various problems faced by David during his reign and explains how it happened that Solomon, rather than any of the older brothers, succeeded David to the throne (2 Sam 9–20; 1 Kgs 1–2).

6. Miscellaneous materials relevant to David's reign (2 Sam 21–24).

The first collection of stories tells of David's origins and rise to power. As an example of how originally independent stories have been woven together, one may note the three stories in 1 Sam 16–17 that recount how David's life took a decisively new direction. In the first story the prophet SAMUEL is sent by the Lord to anoint one of the sons of Jesse who turns out to be David, the youngest. In the second story the spirit of the Lord leaves SAUL, and an evil spirit torments him. David is summoned in order to play the lyre when Saul is tormented. Saul is very much impressed by David and makes him his armor bearer. In the third story the reader is introduced to David and his family as if for the first time (17:12-16), and we find David once again at home tending sheep. In this account David comes to Saul's attention by slaying the Philistine, GOLIATH. After inquiring about David's identity, Saul takes him into his service as a warrior (17:55–18:5). While it is difficult to discern the exact nature of the events from these three stories, it seems clear that David entered Saul's service as a young professional soldier and quickly distinguished himself in skirmishes against the Philistines.

As the story relates, David's prowess as a warrior and consequent popularity with the people brought him into conflict with Saul. Saul noted David's rising popularity and, reacting with suspicion and jealousy, attempted on several occasions to kill David. David was forced to flee to the territory in and around Judea where he hid from Saul and gathered around himself a small band of fighting men. Saul searched for David and sought to kill him. Eventually David turned to ACHISH, the Philistine king of GATH, for protection. David remained in the service of the Philistines until after Saul's death at MOUNT GILBOA.

Following the death of Saul, David moved with his band of soldiers to Hebron. There he was anointed king of Judah. Meanwhile, Saul's son, ISH-BOSHETH, attempted to rule Israel from the transjordanian stronghold of MAHANAIM. A war ensued between Ish-bosheth and David in which the power shifted increasingly to David (2 Sam 3:1). Eventually Ish-bosheth was assassinated and David became the king of Israel, thus uniting in his person the two kingdoms of Judah and Israel.

In order to strengthen his position as king over the combined kingdoms, David conquered the Jebusite city of Jerusalem and made it his capital. Jerusalem made an ideal administrative center since it lay between Judah and Israel while not being a part of either territory. David further centralized his power by transferring the Ark, the old and important religious symbol, to Jerusalem. Thus he made the city a center for the national cult.

David faced a number of challenges to his new position. The Philistines with whom he had been allied soon sensed that their former vassal was growing too strong. They attempted to check his power, and in two separate battles David's forces turned back the Philistines' attempt to assert their authority in the hill country.

The second major threat came from within David's kingdom in the form of two uprisings. The first was led by ABSALOM, one of David's sons, and the second by Sheba, a Benjaminite. Absalom actually replaced David on the throne for a short period of time, but because he was slow to pursue David and seize the advantage, David was able to regroup and defeat Absalom's forces. Absalom was killed in the fray. Sheba took advantage of the instability caused by Absalom's rebellion and attempted to lead Israel away from David. David moved quickly to quell Sheba's rebellion and was soon secure once again on the throne of his combined kingdom.

In his rise to power David received crucial support from his own private corps of warriors, the "mighty men" who had collected around him since his days of hiding from Saul (1 Sam 22:1-2; 2 Sam 23:8-39). Chief among these was JOAB, son of Zeruiah. Joab led the battle against Absalom and the pursuit of Sheba. He also served as David's field commander as the king began to expand his sphere of control into Ammonite, Moabite, and Edomite territories.

At its height David's kingdom included the area south from the Phoenician cities of TYRE and SIDON to northern Edom in the Negeb (not including Philistia along the coast), and Transjordan from the Aramean border south to the wadi Mujib canyon (biblical Arnon) (PLATE 12). He maintained close diplomatic ties with Phoenicia and may have exerted some control in Aramean territory.

A central event in the story of David is his affair with BATHSHEBA, the wife of URIAH the Hittite. Bathsheba became pregnant by David while Uriah was away fighting against Rabbah in Ammonite territory. David's misdeed was soon found out, and the prophet NATHAN condemned David publicly. Though David responded with exemplary repentance, the course of his life took a downward turn from that point on. As is the case in the stories of Saul and Solomon, David's life is structured on the scheme David under blessing . . . David under curse. The Bathsheba incident is the turning point in this scheme.

The story of David under curse is contained in 2 Sam 9–20 and 1 Kgs 1–2, an essentially continuous narrative often referred to as the throne succession story. The narrative appears to be designed to explain why Solomon and not any of his older brothers inherited David's throne. As the story goes, when David approached the end of his life and was no longer potent, his oldest son ADONIJAH proclaimed himself as king, presumably an appropriate move supported by Joab and the priest ABIATHAR. However, another group consisting of Nathan the prophet, Bathsheba, the priest ZADOK, and a military chief named BENAIAH moved quickly to put SOLOMON on the throne instead. Bathsheba reminded the ailing king of his promise to designate Solomon as the next king, and after obtaining David's word the group immediately had Solomon anointed king in a surprise ceremony.

David is remembered in tradition as a poet and musician. Indeed, seventy-three PSALMS bear the notation *lĕdāwîd*. Unfortunately, this designation is ambiguous and may mean "of David," "for David," "concerning David," or "dedicated to David." It is impossible to know how many, if any, of these Psalms actually come from David's hand. There are some indications that the image of David as a great poet and musician belongs to idealizations of a later age. In any case, it is very doubtful that all the *lĕdāwîd* psalms come from David. Rather it would appear that events in the story of David's life inspired psalmists of a later age or that later editors found it meaningful to ascribe preexisting psalms to David at certain crises in his life.

See also BATHSHEBA; JONATHAN; KINGSHIP; SAUL.

Bibliography. A. Alt, "The Formation of the Israelite State in Palestine," *Essays on Old Testament History and Religion*; R. A. Carlson, *David, the Chosen King: A Traditio-Historical Approach to the Second Book of Samuel*; E. H. Maly, *The World of David and Solomon*; J. M. Miller, and J. H. Hayes, *A History of Ancient Israel and Judah*; A. Soggin, "The Davidic-Solomonic Kingdom," *Israelite and Judean History*.

—J. MAXWELL MILLER

• **David, City of.** *See* JERUSALEM

• **Day of Atonement.** *See* ATONEMENT, DAY OF

• **Day of Judgment.** *See* JUDGMENT, DAY OF

• **Day of the Lord.** *See* ESCHATOLOGY IN THE NEW TESTAMENT; ESCHATOLOGY IN THE OLD TESTAMENT; JUDGMENT, DAY OF; TIME, BIBLICAL PERSPECTIVES ON; ZEPHANIAH, BOOK OF

• **Deacon.** [dee'kuhn] The title of deacon is derived from a Gk. word meaning SERVANT. The NT writers employed the word thirty times, and the most common meaning is that of servant. In John 2:5, 9, reference is to table waiters, while in Matt 22:13, reference is to a king's servants.

In the synoptic Gospels, the servanthood of the disciples of Jesus is emphasized. The hallmark of great disciples is servanthood (Mark 9:35; Matt 20:26; 23:11). The verb to serve appears on the lips of Jesus referring to his mission of service to the people of God (Mark 10:45). Because Jesus had apparently understood his role in terms of servanthood, the disciples likewise felt that they should be servants of one another.

Most references to servant in the NT occur in the letters of Paul. Paul referred to himself as a servant in multiple contexts (1 Cor 3:5; 2 Cor 3:6; Col 1:23, 25; Eph 3:7). Paul also referred to fellow workers as servants of Christ (1 Thess 3:2; Col 1:7; 4:7; Eph 6:21; 1 Tim 4:6). Furthermore, he referred to the authorities in the Roman state as servants of God (Rom 13:4), and on one occasion wrote that Christ was a servant for the Jews (Rom 15:8).

The word deacon in English translations comes from the use of the word servant as the title of an order of ministry. In Phil 1:1, Paul speaks of bishops and deacons, and in Rom 16:1 he refers to Phoebe as a deaconess of the church in Cenchreae.

Though the function of the deacon according to Phil 1:1 and Rom 16:1 is somewhat unclear, the word occurs in 1 Tim 3:8,12 as a specific church office. Deacons augmented the service ministry of bishops, according to the context of 1 Tim 3:1-13; however, deacons possessed authority only through service to the church (1 Tim 3:10). A list of requirements for the office of deacon appears in 1 Tim 3. The deacon was to be worthy of respect, monogamous, and a good manager of the family. The author of 1 Timothy also required that a deacon should not be double-tongued, addicted to much wine, or fond of dishonest gain. Finally, deacons were to hold the faith in a pure conscience. Women may have served as deacons in the same manner as men (1 Tim 3:11).

The specific authority of deacons is unclear in 1 Tim 3:8-13; however, in the context of the NT as a whole, the servant role within the church is emphasized. However, a reading of second- and third-century Christian literature confirms the view that the church eventually developed a threefold ministry of BISHOPS, ELDERS, and deacons.

See also BISHOP; CHURCH; ELDER; MINISTER/SERVE; SERVANT.

Bibliography. F. W. Beare, "The Ministry in the NT Church: Practice and Theory," *ATR* 37 (1955): 3-15; H. W. Beyer, "διακονέω, κτλ.," *TDNT*; H. von Compenhausen, *Ecclesiastical Authority and Spiritual Power in the Church of the First Three Centuries.*

—BENNIE R. CROCKETT, JR.

• **Dead Sea.** The spectacular salt lake, measuring ca. fifty-three mi. north-south by ca. ten mi. east-west, located midway between the northern and southern extremities of the JORDAN-Wadi ARABAH rift (PLATES 4, 13, 55). As part of the larger Afro-Arabian rift valley, which extends from east Africa to southeastern Turkey, the Dead Sea—at ca. 1,300 ft. below the level of the Mediterranean—is the lowest point on the earth's surface. In the deepest part of the lake, the northeastern section, the Dead Sea's floor is as much as 2,400 ft. below sea level. The water is quite shallow south of the Lisan, the peninsula that protrudes from the eastern shore. From at least Roman times until mid-nineteenth century, the narrow channel between the Lisan and the lake's western shoreline was fordable. While natural phenomena have caused slight fluctuations in the Dead Sea's water level and surface area, human activities (e.g., irrigation and chemical extraction) also alter the lake's contours.

Along with the Jordan River, three other perennial streams (Zerqa Ma'in, Arnon, and Zered) and numerous springs and wadis replenish the lake's evaporating waters. Since the Dead Sea has no natural outlet and the water sources in its 11,000-square-mi. catchment area carry abundant salts, it has become the world's most saline body of water. Its salinity averages ca. thirty percent, includes high concentrations of calcium chloride and bromine, and allows no significant aquatic life.

The designation Dead Sea is known only in postbiblical sources, but the lake is mentioned frequently in the OT, usually as a geographical boundary, under three names—Salt Sea, Sea of the Arabah, and Eastern Sea. Other non-biblical names include Sea of Asphalt, Sea of Lot, and Sea of Sodom, with the latter two designations connecting the Dead Sea with the narrative in Gen 19. In contrast to this account of judgment, which took place in the environs of a lifeless sea, Ezek 47:1-12 spoke about a future age when the salty lake would flourish with life.

—GERALD L. MATTINGLY

• **Dead Sea Scrolls.** The Dead Sea Scrolls is the name given to a large group of ancient Jewish manuscripts which have been recovered from a series of caves along the northwest edge of the DEAD SEA (PLATE 55). Although many of the manuscripts are fragmentary, their name reflects the fact that the earliest discoveries included seven large leather rolls.

The first scrolls were discovered by accident in the spring of 1947 when a young Bedouin shepherd wandered into a cave looking for a lost animal. By the following spring the scrolls had been authenticated and announced to the world. In the spring of 1949 the cave where the scrolls had been found (later called Cave 1) was identified and excavated. Between 1951 and 1956 archaeologists excavated ruins to the south of Cave 1, known as Khirbet Qumran (PLATE 28), linking the ruins to the scrolls. During the same period, a search for more caves containing manuscripts resulted in the discovery of ten such caves: Caves 2-6 (discovered in 1952), Caves 7-10 (1955), and Cave 11 (1956). In 1955–1958 archaeologists excavated ruins two miles south of Qumran, known as Ain Feshka, linking these ruins to the earlier finds. To date, no further discoveries have been made in the area. On the other hand, the discovery of Caves 1, 6, and 11 by Bedouins, rather than archaeologists, leaves open the possibility that not all of the scrolls have been brought to the attention of the proper authorities. Indeed, it was not until 1967 that the TEMPLE SCROLL, from Cave 11 and the longest of the scrolls yet recovered, was acquired.

Archaeological excavations indicate several stages of occupation on the Qumran site. The Ain Feshka settlement, which was much smaller, follows a similar pattern. Dating of the later stages is aided by the discovery among the Qumran ruins of coins ranging from the reign of John Hyrcanus I (134–104 B.C.E.) to Roman coins celebrating the conquest of the Jews. In the eighth-seventh century B.C.E. the site was an Israelite fortress. Following several centuries of desertion, the site was occupied again from the second century B.C.E. to the first century C.E. This stage involves two main periods of occupation. The first period (ca. 141–107 B.C.E.) consists of two phases. The initial phase involved modest, temporary buildings. The second phase (107–31 B.C.E.) saw massive building activity, which fixed the permanent lines of the settlement. A devastating earthquake and fire resulted in the abandonment of the settlement in 31 B.C.E. The site lay deserted until 4 B.C.E., which marked the beginning of the second main period of occupation (4 B.C.E.–68 C.E.). The site was repaired and rebuilt along the same plan. Evidence of a great fire and the presence of Roman arrowheads and coins signal the destruction of the settlement by the Romans during the Jewish revolt in 66–70 C.E. In the summer of 68 C.E., Vespasian led the Tenth Legion south from Jericho along the Dead Sea, apparently destroying both the Qumran and the Ain Feshka settlements in his wake. The Romans used Qumran as an outpost from 68–73 C.E.

At the height of its occupancy, the Qumran complex included a large building and several smaller ones. In the large building was a fortified tower, which, along with the walls surrounding the settlement, aided in its defense; a kitchen; storage rooms; a large cistern; and several other rooms, one of which contained tables, benches, and inkwells and probably served as a scriptorium. Just to the south of the main building was a large meeting hall with an adjoining pantry, from which over 1000 pieces of pottery were recovered. The settlement also included a pottery complex, a grain complex, a number of large cisterns and smaller pools, and an extensive aqueduct system. No living quarters have been found; the inhabitants presumably lived outside of the walls in tents or huts, or in the nearby caves. Also outside of the settlement are three cemeteries comprising over a 1000 graves: a main cemetery, containing only men, and two secondary cemeteries, which include women and children. The smaller settlement at Ain Feshka to the south was apparently an agricultural and industrial center for Qumran. It included an irrigation system, an enclosure for animals, and what seems to have been a tannery.

Although no manuscripts have been found at either Qumran or Ain Feshka, the connection of the ruins with the manuscripts from the caves seems assured. First, the manuscripts and the ruins are contemporary: the manuscripts were copied during the same period of time that the settlement was occupied. Second, the caves and the ruins are geographically close: all of the caves are within two miles of the ruins and Caves 4, 5, 7, 8, 9, and 10 are within five to ten minutes walking distance. Third, pottery found in the ruins matches pottery found in ten of the caves (Cave 5 contained no pottery). Fourth, writing found on pottery in the ruins matches that found on pottery in Caves 4, 7, and 10. Finally, the character of the ruins, with their cisterns, meeting hall, and scriptorium, provides the logical setting for the ritual washings, sacred meal, and manuscript copying reflected in the scrolls. The presence of the scrolls in the caves is probably the result of the Qumran inhabitants hiding them there in anticipation of the advance of the Roman forces.

The fragmentary nature of most of the Qumran scrolls has made their reconstruction and identification an extremely complicated and tedious process. As a result, many of the fragments have not yet been published. To date, however, about 800 manuscripts have been identified, the most significant finds coming from Caves 1, 4, and 11. Most of the manuscripts are written in HEBREW OR ARAMAIC; Cave 7 contained some GREEK fragments as well (PLATE 48). That some were written in Hebrew attests to a lively literary (as well as oral?) activity in a language previously thought to have been relegated in this period primarily to formal worship and to the rabbinic schools. The manuscripts in Aramaic, the only such literary corpus from this era, confirm the widespread use of Aramaic among Second Temple Jews. The earliest scrolls can be dated by paleography (the study of the formation of letters) to ca. 200 B.C.E.; the latest to the mid-60s C.E. The manuscripts can be classified roughly into four groups: OT books, apocryphal writings, sectarian documents, and miscellaneous writings.

Two of the seven major scrolls discovered in Cave 1 are copies of Isaiah, one of them virtually complete (*1QIsa*[a]). In addition, there are over 170 fragmentary Hebrew manuscripts of OT books, ten of which are in paleo-Hebrew script. There are also Greek fragments of Exodus, Leviticus, and Numbers, and Aramaic targums of Leviticus and Job. The favorite OT books at Qumran were apparently Genesis (fifteen copies), Exodus (fifteen), Deuteronomy (twenty-five), Isaiah (eighteen), and Psalms (twenty-seven); Esther is missing. The importance of these manuscripts for TEXTUAL CRITICISM of the OT cannot be overstated. They predate the oldest manuscripts of the OT in the Hebrew Masoretic tradition by over a thousand years and those in Greek or in any other translation by several centuries. Yet the Qumran manuscripts do not represent a single text form. While some are proto-Masoretic, others are aligned with different textual traditions, including the Old Greek LXX, proto-Lucian, proto-Theodotion, and the Samaritan. Thus, these manuscripts attest to a definite reverence for OT books, but not to the point of insisting on a single unalterable form for the text.

Many of the writings found among the scrolls are apocryphal. Three of the Apocrypha are attested: the Letter of Jeremiah, Tobit, and Sirach. In addition, there are *Apocryphal Psalms*. Some of the writings are related to previously known pseudepigrapha: *Jubilees* is present, as are four of the five books which make up *1 Enoch* (all except the Similitudes) and at least two Testaments (of Naphtali and of Levi; perhaps also Judah, Joseph, and Benjamin) which apparently bear some connection with the *Testaments of the Twelve Patriarchs*. Previously unknown works include, among others, the *Genesis Apocryphon* and related writings, such as the *Book of Giants* and the *Book of Noah*, the *Testament of Amram*, the *Words of Moses*, the *Samuel Apocryphon*, the *Prayer of Nabonidus*, and *Pseudo-Daniel*. That these apocryphal writings were collected by the sect raises the question of why they were preserved and whether or not any of them were composed by the sect, perhaps before its exodus to Qumran. There are at least twelve copies of *Jubilees*, for example, which has strong parallels with the sectarian documents, along with certain differences, and which is cited as authoritative in the *Damascus Rule*. Finally, the presence of these documents, as well as the absence of Esther, raises questions regarding the development of the OT canon.

Another group of documents consists of those which exhibit the distinctive ideas and/or practices of the sect. Several of these writings can be categorized as rules for the community: e.g., the *Manual of Discipline*, the *Rule of the Congregation*, the *Damascus Rule*, and, in a different way, the *War Scroll*, and perhaps the *Temple Scroll*. Other texts are poetical and/or liturgical: e.g., the *Thanksgiving Scroll*, the *Angelic Liturgy*, the *Blessings*, and the *Words of the Heavenly Lights*. A large number of documents are concerned with biblical interpretation: e.g., *Pesharim* (commentaries) on Isaiah, Habakkuk, Nahum, Hosea, Micah, and Ps 37; the *Florilegium* and the *Testimonia*; and *Melchizedek*. This group of writings is especially important for reconstructing the history and nature of the community.

A few of the writings do not fit naturally into any specific category. One document, for example, describes the New Jerusalem. There are also fragments of horoscopes. Most striking is the *Copper Scroll,* a scroll discovered in Cave 3 which is made of copper, rather than leather. It purports to list the hiding places of sixty-four treasures of an enormous magnitude concealed throughout Palestine. Some scholars argue that the *Copper Scroll* is a genuine record of the fortune of the Qumran community, others suggest that it is a listing of the Temple treasury; still others contend that it is imaginary and bears no relationship with the other scrolls, having been placed in Cave 3 sometime after 68 C.E.

The sectarian writings, especially the *Damascus Rule* and the commentaries on Habakkuk, Micah, and Ps 37, give some indication of the origins of the sect. The community was apparently founded by the Teacher of Righteousness (or Legitimate Teacher), who gave leadership to a movement which had begun twenty years earlier, some "390" years after NEBUCHADREZZAR took Jerusalem. The Teacher, a priest, received from God the revelation of his mysteries for the final age and interpreted the Torah accordingly. Breaking with official JUDAISM, he led his followers into exile, where he eventually died. He was opposed by the Wicked Priest (variously called the Scoffer, the Liar, and the Spouter of Lies), who persecuted the Teacher even to the point of pursuing him into exile on the DAY OF ATONEMENT. The Wicked Priest led Israel astray, rebelled against the precepts of God, and defiled the Temple. Ultimately, God delivered him into the hands of his enemies, who killed him.

Most scholars trace the beginnings of the movement to the Hasideans, who opposed the Hellenization policies of Antiochus IV and joined in the revolt of the Maccabees (1 Macc 2:42; 7:13-16). Shortly thereafter, in opposition to the developing Hasmonean dynasty, the Teacher of Righteousness led his followers into the desert. What precipitated this exodus was probably the ascension to the high priesthood of either Jonathan or Simon, both of whom scholars have identified as the Wicked Priest. Although not from the line of Aaron, Jonathan was appointed high priest in 152 B.C.E. by a pretender to the Seleucid throne (1 Macc 10:15-21). In 140 B.C.E. the people, along with the priests, decreed that Simon and his descendants should be high priest until a faithful prophet should arise, with no opposition or private assembly permitted (1 Macc 14:41-47). Either of these incidents could have been offensive to the priest-Teacher, especially if he were of high Zadokite lineage. Not all scholars agree with this reconstruction, however; some deny any connection with the Hasideans and place more of an emphasis on an inner-community split. The cryptic historical references make certainty difficult.

The nature of the Qumran community, however, is more clear. The sect viewed itself as the Community of God which had received his Covenant of Grace. In the last days God had revealed his mysteries to its founder, the Teacher of Righteousness, who was the only legitimate interpreter of the Torah. The members therefore devoted themselves to obedience to the Torah as taught by the Teacher and to the study of the OT scriptures, which they interpreted as being fulfilled in the community. Their methods of interpretation included writing section by section commentaries on OT books, viewed in terms of the history of the sect, and drawing up anthologies of key OT passages on a particular subject. Their outlook was strongly dualistic. They believed themselves to be the sole remnant of Israel, the Sons of Light, who, guided by the Spirit of Truth, would receive everlasting life. God had called them to separate from those outside the community, the Sons of Darkness; led by the Spirit of Falsehood, these would face eternal torment.

Entrance into the community was carefully regulated and involved a two year probationary period. All members were expected to adhere to a detailed code of conduct, and there were various penalties for misconduct. The community had a strict organizational hierarchy: virtually all matters, from the seating arrangement to the order of speaking, were determined by rank. At the top were the priests, the Sons of Zadok, who were themselves ranked according to the perfection of their spirit. Next came the Levites, or elders. Finally, there were the people, who were ranked in Thousands, Hundreds, Fifties, and Tens. Within the larger community there was a Council of the Community, made up of twelve men and three priests. Over the entire community stood the master, or overseer. Each individual was examined annually, at which time his rank could be adjusted upward or downward, depending upon his understanding and behavior.

The sectarians had a communal lifestyle, sharing property and work, studying the Torah, and meeting together for discussion of community matters and ceremonies. Worship was an important aspect of communal life; the sect understood itself as participating in the angelic worship of God. Especially significant was the sacred meal. Ceremonial washings for purification were regular, and emphasis was placed on the use of the solar calendar (cf. *Jubilees, 1 Enoch),* rather than the lunar calendar of official Judaism. Unable to offer sacrifices in the defiled Jerusalem Temple, the community viewed prayer and obedience as acceptable offerings. Other aspects of personal piety included a deep sense of human frailty and sinfulness and thanksgiving to God for his grace and election.

The community had a strong eschatological hope. The members looked forward to the coming of two Messiahs: the Messiah of Aaron, presumably a Priest Messiah, and the Messiah of Israel, presumably a Royal Messiah; the Priest Messiah would be preeminent. In addition, the sect anticipated the coming of the Prophet (cf. Deut 18:18-19) and a heavenly figure, MELCHIZEDEK, who would restore and make atonement for the Sons of Light and execute God's judgment against Belial (SATAN) and his lot. They also awaited a final war, from which, with God's help, they would emerge victorious and after which they would restore the sacrificial cult in Jerusalem.

Most scholars agree that the Qumran community is to be identified with the ESSENES, a sectarian Jewish movement in Palestine noted by the Jewish writers Philo and Josephus and by the Roman naturalist, Pliny the Elder. Three factors make this hypothesis probable. First, no other site has been discovered which could fit Pliny's comment that the Essenes lived on the west side of the Dead Sea between Jericho and EN-GEDI. Second, the excavations at Qumran indicate that the settlement flourished at essentially the same time as did the Essenes. Third, the information which the scrolls provide about the Qumran community is strikingly similar to the descriptions of the Essenes in the classical sources. Whether the Qumran sect was the main Essene headquarters or simply one group of Essenes is impossible to determine. But if this identification is correct, then the scrolls, along with the ruins at Qumran and Ain Feshka, are now the most direct witnesses to this ancient sect.

The importance of the Dead Sea Scrolls for the study of Judaism in late antiquity is beyond dispute. They attest to the rich diversity within Judaism in the Second Temple period and offer new information at almost every point: the languages of the Jewish people, the history of the OT text and canon, methods of biblical interpretation, literary forms, inner-Jewish controversies, as well as practice and theology. In addition, the discovery among the scrolls of apocryphal writings, both known and previously unknown, has played a major role in initiating the current renaissance in the study of Jewish APOCRYPHAL LITERATURE.

The discovery of the Dead Sea Scrolls has stimulated considerable, often sensationalistic, speculation about possible connections between the Scrolls and the origins of Christianity. Most such conjectures (e.g, that Jesus and/or John the Baptist were at one time a part of the Qumran community) have little support. On the other hand, the scrolls serve as important background material, both generally and specifically, for the study of the NT. They exhibit numerous verbal and conceptual parallels with various NT books, most notably the Gospel of John. More general similarities between the scrolls and early Christianity include a communal meal, a water ritual, certain aspects of organization, methods of biblical interpretation, a strong eschatological hope, and an emphasis on the sinfulness of humans and the grace of God. The differences in detail between the Qumran community and the early church are considerable. Yet in a very basic sense they were alike: each was a sect of Jews which gathered around its founder and saw in itself the fulfillment of God's plan for his creation.

See also APOCRYPHAL LITERATURE; CANON; ESSENES; TEXTS/MANUSCRIPTS/VERSIONS; TEXTUAL CRITICISM OF THE OLD TESTAMENT.

Bibliography. M. Black, *The Scrolls and Christian Origins*; M. Black, ed., *The Scrolls and Christianity*; J. H. Charlesworth, ed., *John and Qumran*; F. M. Cross, *The Ancient Library of Qumran and Modern Biblical Studies*, rev. ed.; F. M. Cross and S. Talmon, eds., *Qumran and the History of the Biblical Text*; P. R. Davies, *Behind the Essenes;* ; D. Dimant, "Qumran Sectarian Literature," *Jewish Writings of the Second Temple Period*, ed. M. E. Stone, *Discoveries in the Judaean Desert*, Vols. I-VII; A. Dupont-Sommer, *The Essene Writings from Qumran*, rev. ed.; J. A. Fitzmyer, *The Dead Sea Scrolls: Major Publications and Tools for Study*; W. S. LaSor, *The Dead Sea Scrolls and the New Testament*; E. H. Merill, *Qumran and Predestination*; J. T. Milik, *Ten Years of Discovery in the Wilderness of Judea*; J. Murphy-O'Connor, ed., *Paul and Qumran;* E. Schürer, *The History of the Jewish People in the Age of Jesus Christ*, rev. and ed. G. Vermes, F. Millar, and M. Goodman; K. Stendahl, ed., *The Scrolls and the New Testament*; G. Vermes, *The Dead Sea Scrolls: Qumran in Perspective*, rev. ed. and *The Dead Sea Scrolls in English*, 3rd ed.; B. Z. Wacholder, *The Dawn of Qumran*.

—JOSEPH L. TRAFTON

• **Death.** According to the OT, death occurred when a person's life-giving forces were impaired or gone. At death the vital force (*nepeš*) left (Gen 35:18; 1 Kgs 17:21; Jonah 4:3) and the spirit (*rûah*) returned to God (Eccl 12:7). Neither the *nepeš* nor the *rûah* was viewed as a soul that survived the body. They were simply animating forces that disappeared at death. With the removal of these forces, a person was deprived of breath, the ability to move and the ability to relate to others, especially to God. This was death.

Death was viewed as the normal end to a person's life (Josh 23:14; 1 Kgs 2:2; Job 5:26). Only God was immortal (Ps 90:1-6). Humanity had been created mortal (Gen 3:19) and was prevented by God from attaining immortality (Gen 3:22). Obedience to God might lead to a long life (Deut 30:15-20; Prov 10:2; 11:4) while SIN might lead to a premature death (1 Sam 2:31-36; Job 36:13-14; Ps 55:23), but Israel was too well aware of exceptions (Eccl 7:15-18) to assume that sin was the cause of death. Death was simply the lot of all creatures (Ps 49:12, 20).

SHEOL, located in the depths of the earth (Pss 63:9; 139:8; Isa 7:11), was the abode of the dead. Life did not survive in any form (Job 7:21; Ps 39:13). The dead existed only as shadows of their former selves (Isa 14:9). Although God's power extended to Sheol (Amos 9:2; Ps 139:7-8), God was not there (Ps 88:5; Isa 38:18). Those in Sheol could not praise God (Pss 30:9; 115:17) or even remember God (Pss 6:5; 88:12). The dead knew nothing (1 Sam 28:3-25) and were thus completely cut off from anything that might provide a meaningful existence.

The portrayal of the dead in Sheol certainly underscored the finality and hopelessness of death but it also freed Israel from fearing those who had died. People mourned for the dead by tearing their garments and putting on SACKCLOTH (Gen 37:34; 2 Sam 3:31), sitting on the ground and covering the head with dirt or ashes (Jer 6:26; Lam 2:10), and lamenting (2 Sam 1:17-27). Since the dead had no power, however, there was no need to fear them or worship them. Cutting oneself in an effort to disguise oneself and thus be safe from a dead spirit (Lev 19:28; 21:5; Deut 14:1) or providing food for the dead (Deut 26:14) were not necessary. Similarly, since the dead had no new knowledge, there was no need to seek to consult them (Deut 18:10-11; 1 Sam 28:3-25; Isa 65:4). The dead were cut off from life and unclean (Num 9:6; 19:11). They belonged to another realm and could no longer help or harm those still alive.

Courtesy of the Eisenberg Museum of Biblical Archaeology. Southern Baptist Theological Seminary.

The mummy Sheriyet Mehyet.

Naturally, in ancient Israel these theological understandings of death, taught by the religious leaders, met with opposition, since it is clear that among the population in general there were conflicting views of the power of the dead to affect life on earth. The veneration of ancestors must surely have been a widespread practice. The effort to affirm God's concern for public life and for public morality required this challenge to popular practices reflecting commerce between the world of the living and the realm of the dead.

While death was viewed as the natural end to life, it was hardly something to be eagerly anticipated. Death could be good if it came at the end of a long life (Gen 15:15; 35:29; Judg 8:32; 1 Chr 29:28; Job 42:17) to a man who had chil-

Courtesy of the Eisenberg Museum of Biblical Archaeology, Southern Baptist Theological Seminary.

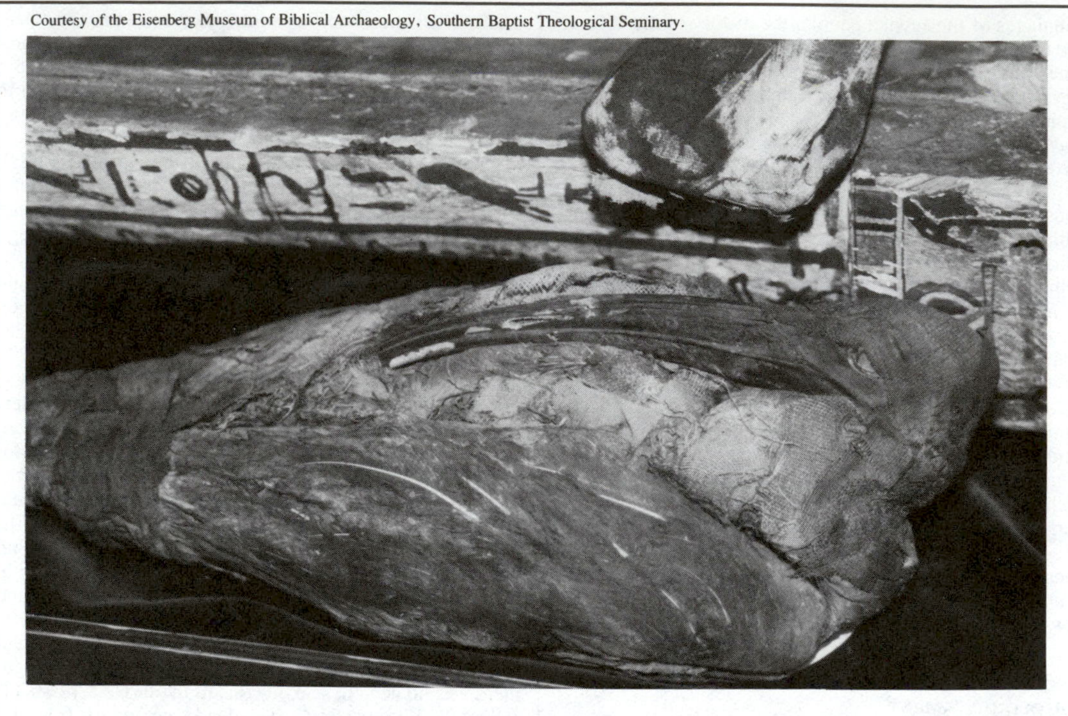

A bird encased with the mummy Sheriyet Mehyet.

dren both to carry on his name (Gen 35:29; Job 42:16) and to bury him (Gen 35:29; 50:7-8). If these criteria were not met, death was an awful tragedy. One who died prematurely (Gen 21:16; Isa 38:1-13), violently (1 Sam 15:32-33), childless (2 Sam 18:18), or without proper burial (2 Kgs 9:30-37; Eccl 6:3) was to be pitied greatly. Such a one had been robbed of a full life and the absence of a belief in an afterlife in which rewards could be received removed all hope.

Israel did not use the term death to refer exclusively to the end of physical life. Death was also used metaphorically. At times death was portrayed as a separate power (Jer 9:21). In other instances it was described as an instrument employed by the heavenly host (2 Sam 24:16; Job 33:22). More commonly, however, death was used to refer to any of those powers that sought to quench life. Illness (Ps 30:3), enemies (Pss 9:13; 55:1-4), and injustice (Ps 116:3) were all manifestations of death as death sought to invade and destroy life. Following this understanding, a person could be said to have died long before his or her body ceased to function (1 Sam 25:37-38; Jonah 2:2-6). Furthermore, in a world in which the powers of life and death were so involved, the decision for life and against death became much more crucial (Deut 30:19).

Several rays of hope shone into Israel's bleak picture of death. Death was often referred to as sleep (Job 14:10-12; Ps 13:3), typically a sleep from which one would not awake (Jer 51:39, 57). Yet the very use of the metaphor of sleep raised the question of whether one could wake from that sleep to something else. According to Daniel, this was a possibility, if not for the whole world, then at least for Israel (Dan 12:2). In addition, Enoch (Gen 5:24) and Elijah (2 Kgs 2:11-12) had not died. If these two had moved into another kind of existence, then perhaps others could as well. Certainly the RESURRECTION of life was not beyond God's power (1 Sam 2:6; Ezek 37:1-14). Similarly, perhaps not even Sheol could terminate the relationship between a person and God. Perhaps God could be a person's "portion" forever (Ps 73:23-26). In the end, Isaiah stated death would be destroyed and a new era would be inaugurated (Isa 25:8). Such ideas tempered the finality and hopelessness of death for Israel and provided the way for the development of the idea of the resurrection embraced by both the PHARISEES (Acts 23:6-7; 24:14-15) and the Christians (1 Cor 15:12-58).

See also CLEAN/UNCLEAN; LIFE IN THE OLD TESTAMENT; MOURNING RITES; RESURRECTION IN THE NEW TESTAMENT; RESURRECTION IN THE OLD TESTAMENT; SHEOL; TOMBS/BURIAL PRACTICES.

Bibliography. L. R. Bailey, Sr., *Biblical Perspectives on Death;* G. Fohrer, *History of Israelite Religion;* E. Jacob, "Death," *IDB;* H. Ringgren, *Israelite Religion;* H. W. Wolff, *Anthropology of the Old Testament.*

—ROBERT C. DUNSTON

• **Death Penalty.** Prescribed for at least twenty-three offenses in the OT. At least six categories of capital offenses can be distinguished: (1) premeditated murder or being the owner of an animal that kills people (Exod 21:14, 29); (2) kidnapping (Exod 21:16; Deut 24:7); (3) PERJURY or a false witness on a capital charge (Deut 18:18-21; 19:15-21); (4) harm to parents (Exod 21:15, 17; Lev 20:9; Deut 21:18-21); (5) certain sexual acts, including incest, ADULTERY, bestiality, sexual intercourse between two males, rape, and coitus during menstruation (Exod 22:19; Deut 22:21-22, 24, 25; Lev 20:10-21); and (6) religious offenses, such as child sacrifice (Lev 20:2); witchcraft and sorcery (Exod 22:18; Lev 20:27); SABBATH-breaking (Exod 31:14; Num 15:32-36); false claim to be a prophet (Deut 13:5, 10); blasphemy (Lev 24:15-16); and a non-Levite's entering the sacred place (Num 1:51; 3:10, 38; 18:7). The forms of execution were burning and/or stoning.

The wide variety of offenses thought to deserve death indicated the Hebrew concern to protect individual lives, preserve family and sexual values, and guard against pagan religious practices. Few would advocate that current capital punishment laws be based upon the biblical lists. There is considerable question as to whether all offenses were actually prosecuted. The theocratic blending of religious rules with socially harmful behavior is also problematic. Some are based on squeamishness or ignorance, as seen in the ban on coitus during menstruation and the concern for the "tokens of virginity." Some betray a bias against women, as in adultery. Others make distinctively religious matters a capital offense, which provided ample justification for religious persecution and the holy wars of the Middle Age.

For good reasons, modern states limit the death penalty primarily to acts of homicide. The Hebrews distinguished between accidental or impulsive killings and premeditated MURDER (Exod 21:12-14; Num 35:16-24). The blood avenger (next of kin) could kill a murderer without incurring GUILT. Killing the murderer was not so much retaliation, punishment or VENGEANCE, as an expression of the belief that innocent blood polluted the land, which belonged to Yahweh (Num 35:33). One who killed accidentally could seek protection in one of six cities of refuge (Num 35:9-11; cf. Deut 4:41-43; 19:2-3), a distinct modification of the general principle that "whoever sheds a person's blood shall have his own blood shed" (Gen 9:6).

Further constraints were established by requiring the testimony of at least two witnesses to impose the death penalty (Num 35:30). The fact that no ransom could be paid to free a murderer (Num 35:31) seemed an effort to reject class distinctions in the administration of JUSTICE.

The sixth commandment seems a further effort to constrain the practice of blood vengeance. It is often argued that "you shall not kill" (Exod 20:13) is intended to forbid homicide. The word for kill is *rāṣaḥ*, which is used for premeditated killing (1 Kgs 21:19; Jer 7:9), involuntary manslaughter (Deut 4:42; 19:3, 4, 6; Num 35:6, 11; Josh 20:3, 5, 6) and killings by the avenger (Num 35:27). The commandment seems to forbid any killing that is not authorized, and thus prohibits executions by tribal codes or blood avengers.

The NT reflects the Jewish belief that adultery and blasphemy are capital crimes (John 8:1-11; 10:31-33). The death penalty was plainly in evidence in Jesus' crucifixion for treason (Matt 27:37; Mark 15:26-27; John 19:15). The fact of Jesus' innocence has served to remind the church of the moral problem at the heart of imposing the death penalty. This irrevocable solution may be an unjust use of power and thus immoral.

Neither Jesus nor Paul seems ever to have explicitly dealt with the morality of capital punishment. But Jesus' rejection of the law of retaliation ("life for a life"—Exod 21:23-25) as part of dealing with the problems of injustice, insult, and injury (Matt 5:38-42), and Paul's dictum that Christians are never to be vengeful (Rom 12:19) seem implicit rejections of vengeance or punishment as sufficient grounds for depriving another of life.

See also ADULTERY IN THE NEW TESTAMENT; ADULTERY IN THE OLD TESTAMENT; MURDER; PERJURY; STONING; VENGEANCE/AVENGER.

Bibliography. W. Eichrodt, *Theology of the Old Testament;* R. L. Honeycutt, "Exodus," *BBC*; "Capital Punishment," *WDCE*; J. H. Yoder, "Expository Articles: Exodus 20:13," *Int* 34/4 (Oct 1980): 394-99.

—PAUL D. SIMMONS

• **Debir.** [dee'buhr] Debir occurs once in the Hebrew Bible as the name of the king of Eglon, one of the five Amorite kings whom Joshua defeated at Gibeon (Josh 10:3). Usually, however, it refers to one of the Canaanite cities conquered by the Israelites at the time of their conquest of Canaan. Alternative names for the city include Kiriath-sepher and Kiriath-sannah (Josh 15:15; Judg 1:11; Josh 15:49). It is listed as a city of Judah located in the hill country (Josh 15:49) and as a Levitical city (Josh 21:15; 1 Chr 6:58 [Heb 6:43]). Probably it is to be identified with present-day Khirbet Rabud, eight mi. south of Hebron (PLATE 10).

The Hebrew Bible provides apparently conflicting traditions concerning the conquest of Debir. Josh 10:38-39 records that Joshua killed all the inhabitants of the city (cf. 11:21 where the inhabitants are called "Anakim"). Yet it is reported twice, in Josh 15:15-17 and Judg 1:11-13, that OTHNIEL conquered the city. According to the latter passages, CALEB had promised the hand of his daughter Achsah to the one who conquered the city. These apparently conflicting traditions may be harmonized by positing a reinhabitation of Debir following Joshua's conquest. More likely, however, these traditions evolved separately and represent independent perspectives regarding the conquest of Debir.

Another Debir, apparently a small village, is mentioned in the description of Judah's northern border in Josh 15:7.

—J. MAXWELL MILLER

• **Deborah.** [deb'uh-ruh] A prophetess and judge *(šôpēt)* during the period of Israel's tribal confederacy (twelfth century B.C.E.). Deborah represents numerous charismatics who rose to leadership in that fluid period when tribes were attempting to establish themselves in Canaan and develop political structures by which they could survive as a united people. Deborah's story is told in Judg 4–5 in both prose and poetry. The prose materials are organized around the typical literary cycle of Judges, moving from disobedience to oppression to repentance to deliverance. Deborah and her general, BARAK, are agents for God's deliverance of Israel from oppression under the northern Canaanites, led by Jabin and his general, SISERA. Either Jabin, king of Hazor, had been restored since earlier destruction by Joshua (Josh 11) or the later historian is drawing upon an earlier tradition. The older poetic version refers only to Sisera.

The narrative moves with a dramatic seriousness seldom matched in Hebrew story-telling. Deborah, the female, is clearly the heroine and Barak, the male, the secondary character. The characterization is intentionally explicit. Deborah says to her reluctant general, "I will surely go with you; nevertheless, the road on which you are going will not lead to your glory, for the Lord will sell Sisera into the hand of a woman" (Judg 4:9). In a patriarchal environment who could miss the point!

The Hebrews met the Canaanites on the famous battlefield, the Plain of Esdraelon (Jezreel), fed by the brook Kishon (PLATE 10). Sisera's forces were routed when the overflowing Kishon caused the Canaanite chariots to mire in the mud. Sisera fled, introducing a sequel story in which the chief character is again female. Jael, supposedly a friend of the Canaanites, invited the weary Sisera into her tent and gave him milk to drink. While Sisera slept the sleep of exhaustion, Jael disregarded her expected Eastern hospitality and drove a tent-peg through his temple.

The poetic version of the story is one of the oldest pieces of Hebrew literature still in existence, coming from very near Deborah's time. The poem is typically called "the Song of Deborah," but it is probably about and not by the prophetess. It is a magnificent poem, utilizing parallelism forms typical of Hebrew and other Eastern POETRY. The song celebrates victory in battle with images of Israel's warrior God undergirding its theme. From heaven the stars themselves champion Israel's cause (Judg 5:20) and God raises "the torrent Kishon" to overwhelm the Canaanites (Judg 5:21). The poem underscores the heroism of Deborah, and also acclaims the praise of Jael. It displays genuine feeling for Sisera's mother as well. Juxtaposed to Jael standing over the fallen body "still at her feet" (Judg 5:27), Sisera's mother peers out the window waiting anxiously for the return of her son. Even the cry that all Israel's enemies perish (5:31) cannot hide empathy for a mother losing her son.

Both the narrative and the poem are important sources for understanding the arduous struggle of Hebrew tribes to carve out their place in Canaan, particularly to control the fertile valleys and trade routes typified in Esdraelon. Further, they are monumental comments on Israel's willingness to preserve in narrative and verse female contributions to their ongoing struggle to possess the land.

See also BARAK; POETRY; PROPHETESS; SISERA; WOMEN IN THE OLD TESTAMENT.

—ROBERT W. CRAPPS

• **Debts.** *See* SABBATICAL YEAR

• **Decalogue.** *See* TEN COMMANDMENTS

• **Decapolis.** [di-kap'uh-lis] Meaning literally "ten-city," the word "Decapolis" is a geographical term referring to an area mostly south and east of the Sea of Galilee (PLATE 20). The region in question was apparently constituted originally of ten Greek cities, nine of which were east of the Jordan River, stretching from DAMASCUS in the north to PHILADELPHIA in the south. Later on, the Decapolis would include more than ten cities, but the original ten were, according to Pliny, Damascus, Philadelphia, Raphana, Scythopolis (the only city west of the Jordan), GADARA, Hippos, Dion, Pella, GERASA, and Canatha.

Many of the cities of that region were founded after the death of Alexander the Great (323 B.C.E.) when his successors, following Alexander's vision of a Hellenized world, established and (re-)built Greek cities throughout the Near East, including Palestine. The new cities attracted Greek-speaking immigrants and were typical examples of Greek culture. Architecturally, they were composed of representative Greek structures, including a colonnaded forum, baths, and amphitheatre, at least one theatre, temples, tombs, and an aqueduct.

In the second century B.C.E., a number of these Greek cities in the Decapolis fell to the Jews in the Maccabean revolution (168–64 B.C.E.). The cities were later liberated from Jewish dominance by the Roman leader Pompey (64–63 B.C.E.), a fact which was widely celebrated by these Greek cities and led to their enthusiastic support of Greco-Roman culture and pro-Roman policies. Pompey placed most of the cities of the Decapolis under the authority of the province of Syria, though two of the cities of the Decapolis (Hippos and Gadara) were later (ca. 30 B.C.E.) given to Herod the Great by Augustus (Octavian), under whose control they remained until Herod's death in 4 B.C.E., at which time they were transferred to the Roman legate in Syria.

Many modern authorities assume that the term "Decapolis" was used in reference to a league or federation, but the ancient sources give little specific information in this regard. Not only are words for "league" or "federation" never used with regard to the Decapolis, but there is no historical record—in either Roman or Greek sources—of any such league having ever been founded. It is of course possible that the "Decapolis" was originally formed as a loosely knit federation whereby the cities of that region joined together as independent political units cooperating for the purpose of their own military and economic advantage. To be sure, the cities of the Decapolis did command major trade routes from east to west and were also stationed along important posts of military significance for the Romans; but every ancient reference to the Decapolis can be easily understood as a geographical designation.

Certainly the Gospels—where probably the earliest, extant references to the Decapolis occur—use the term in a predominantly geographical sense. Matt 4:25 refers to the Decapolis as one of several regions from which multitudes came to see the miracle-working rabbi from Galilee; Mark 5:20 speaks of the Decapolis as the region in which the man from Gerasa enthusiastically reported his encounter with Jesus; and Mark 7:31 refers to the Decapolis as within the compass of Jesus' itinerant ministry. Whatever the source of the term, it was in common use by the time of Jesus as a reference to a region of predominantly independent Greco-Roman cities situated mostly south (though Damascus was included in Pliny's list) and east of the Sea of Galilee.

See also CITY/CITIES; DAMASCUS; GADARA; GERASA; PHILADELPHIA.

Bibliography. S. Thomas Parker, "The Decapolis Reviewed," *JBL* 94/3 (September 1975): 437-41; B. Reicke, *The New Testament Era*.

—ROBERT B. SLOAN

• **Decision Making.** *See* LOT/LOTS (CASTING OF) IN THE BIBLE

• **Deconstruction.** *See* LITERATURE, BIBLE AS

• **Decree.** An official ruling, edict, statute, law, ordinance, dogma, or decision. In the ancient Near East kings usually made their decrees in writing (Ezra 1:1; 6:1-3). They sent special messengers, known as heralds (Dan 3:4), throughout their kingdoms to proclaim the decrees publicly so that all subjects would know to obey them (2 Chr 30:5-6; Esth 8:10; Jonah 3:6-9). Two well-known royal decrees in the Bible are DARIUS's decree to throw into a den of lions anyone who prayed to a god instead of the king himself (Dan 6:7-9) and Caesar Augustus's decree to enroll all the world (Luke 2:1).

As the king of the universe God has made decrees to direct human life (Ps 119:5, 8, 12) and to control nature. The Hebrews understood the laws of the COVENANT at Sinai as God's decree (Exod 19-23). It was the responsibility of Moses to teach the Israelites God's decrees or ordinances (Exod 18:20). Since God has instituted governing authority, the person who opposes a ruling authority resists a decree or ordinance of God (Rom 13:1-2). God has decreed that those who sin against God, society, and themselves shall die (Rom 1:32). With reference to nature, God has a decree to govern the rain (Job 28:26), and a decree to keep the sea in bounds (Prov 8:29). By decree God created the heavenly bodies and established their bounds (Ps 148:1-6).

Religious authorities also issue decrees. The regulations of Jewish law were decrees declared to have been abolished by Christ (Eph 2:15; Col 2:14, 20). The decisions of the JERUSALEM COUNCIL concerning gentile believers (Acts 15:19-20) were decrees or dogmas for the churches to observe (Acts 16:4).

—VIRGIL FRY

• **Dedication, Feast of.** The Feast of (Re)Dedication or Hanukkah, an eight-day festival that begins on 25 Kislev, commemorates the restoration of the Temple and (esp. since 70 C.E.) a historically crucial struggle for religious freedom. The Temple was reconsecrated and the feast established by Judas Maccabeus on 25 Kislev (ca. 14 Dec.) 165/4 B.C.E., reportedly three years to "the very day" after the desecration of the Temple by Antiochus Epiphanes (1 Macc 4:52-59). Excepting Maccabees, Dedication/Hanukkah specifically occurs in the Bible only in John 10:22. Various precursors, however, may be seen in the Hebrew Bible.

The Heb. חֲנֻכָּה (*ḥanukkah*), "dedication/consecration," designates a dedication offering for the tabernacle altar (Num 7:10ff.), and the dedication of the Jerusalem wall (Neh 12:27), the Temple altar (2 Chron 7:9), and the Second Temple (Ezra 6:16-17; Ps 30). In the supposed original Heb. (?) of Maccabees (Gk. ἐγκαινισμός, "renewal"), *ḥanukkah* would have referred to Solomon's dedication of the First Temple (2 Macc 2:9) and the Maccabean rededication of the Second Temple and/or altar (1 Macc 5:56, 59; 2 Macc 2:19; cf. 1 Macc 4:36, 54; 5:1). "Hanukkahs" associated with the Temple thus occur as early as Solomon (1 Kgs 8:65-66; 2 Chron 7:8-9). Hezekiah reconsecrated the Temple in an eight-day ceremony after Ahaz's desecration (2 Chron 29:17). But precursor to the Maccabean rededication may have been the rededication of the postexilic altar (Ezra 3:3-4) and/or the original dedication of the Second Temple (Ezra 6:16ff.). "Hanukkah," however, now specifically designates the crucial event of 165/4 B.C.E. and the annual holiday that still commemorates it.

In 168/7 B.C.E., in reaction to the Jews' resistance to hellenization and specifically their denial of his "divine rights," Antiochus instituted a severe anti-Jewish program. He forbade Jewish religious practices (1 Macc 1:41-64; 2 Macc 6:1-11), made the Temple host to the cult of Zeus, and desecrated the altar with pagan sacrifices (1 Macc 1:54; cf. Dan 9:27ff.)—an intolerable indignity for orthodox Jews. Subsequently the successful Maccabean Revolt culminated with the rededication of the Temple, marking the beginning of an era of relative autonomy for Jews (not fully realized until 152 B.C.E.). Hanukkah marks the anniversary of this victory, whose perpetual observance was established by Judas himself (1 Macc 4:59; cf. 2 Macc 10:5).

Ceremonial relighting of the Temple lamps (1 Macc 4:50) was a prominent feature of the Feast (after the destruction of the Temple, the lighting of candles on an eight-branched menorah at home and at community gatherings). Hence Hanukkah also is called the Feast of Lights, an alternate title Josephus confirms with this rationale: "I suppose . . . because this liberty beyond our hopes *appeared* to us; . . . thence the name [Lights]" (*Ant* 12.7.7).

Hanukkah was to be "in the manner of" the Feast of Booths/Tabernacles (2 Macc 10:6); indeed, 2 Macc 1:9 characterizes Hanukkah as "the feast of booths in the month of Kislev." Hanukkah is celebrated for eight days and includes carrying palms, singing psalms, and the daily recitation of the Hallel (Pss 113-118, cf. esp. 118:27); also included have been the reading of Num 7 and selections from Zechariah (esp. 4:6), gift giving, and other symbolic activities. Today Hanukkah has grown in significance, perhaps in part due to the continuing struggle for Jewish identity and autonomy, and in part because of its calendar proximity to Christmas (which culturally dominates in the West).

See also FEASTS AND FESTIVALS; MACCABEES.

Bibliography. O. S. Rankin, *The Origins of the Festival of Hanukkah*; R. de Vaux, *Ancient Israel*.

—EDD ROWELL

• **Deicide.** *See* ANTI-JUDAISM IN THE NEW TESTAMENT

• **Deir 'Alla, Tell.** [day-ir'-ah-lah"] A large and prominent mound on the eastern side of the Jordan Valley, located ca. seven and one-half mi. northeast of the present confluence of the Jordan and JABBOK (modern Zerqa) rivers (PLATE 3). Tell Deir 'Alla's position in a fertile part of the Arabah (the "Vale of Succoth" of Ps 60:6; 108:7), approximately halfway between the Sea of Galilee and the Dead Sea, made the ancient settlement an important crossroad for north-south and east-west traffic. The identification of Tell Deir 'Alla as biblical SUCCOTH (cf. Gen 33:17; Josh 13:27; Judg 8:5; 1 Kgs 7:46; 2 Chr 4:17), which was made over a century ago, continues to carry the weight of scholarly opinion. The principal dissenter in this site identification is H. J. Franken, the excavator of Tell Deir 'Alla, who associates Succoth with nearby Tell el-Ekhṣaṣ and suggests that Tell Deir 'Alla may have been biblical Gilgal.

Franken's Dutch expedition, sponsored by the University of Leyden, excavated Tell Deir 'Alla for five seasons (1960–1964); the project's attention to stratigraphy and pottery analysis, among other things, has received much praise. The excavations have revealed a long, though intermittent, history of occupation, from the remains of a Chalcolithic village to the abandonment of settlement on the mound in the Persian period. Tell Deir 'Alla's unfortified Late Bronze village, which dated from ca. 1500 to the beginning of the twelfth century B.C.E., contained a large sanctuary. A small Iron Age I walled town was destroyed ca. 900 B.C.E., but the site was reoccupied and its sanctuary rebuilt in the seventh century B.C.E. The town was destroyed in the Persian era, and there was a Roman-Byzantine village immediately east of the tell.

In addition to some inscribed clay tablets from ca. 1200 B.C.E., written in an undeciphered script, Tell Deir 'Alla yielded an intriguing ink-on-plaster inscription that mentions Balaam, the non-Israelite prophet of biblical fame. Though the date, script, and dialect are disputed, this text attests to the importance of the Balaam tradition in this region of Transjordan.

See also BALLAM; SUCCOTH.

—GERALD L. MATTINGLY

• **Deity.** *See* GOD

• **Deliver/Deliverance.** *See* SALVATION IN THE OLD TESTAMENT

• **Demetrius.** [di-mee'tree-uhs] Demetrius was the name of an Ephesian artisan who opposed Paul's preaching (Acts 19:23-41) and an associate of "the Elder" who wrote 3 John.

1. The exact identity of the Ephesian Demetrius is uncertain. He is described in Acts 19:23 as "a maker of silver shrines of ARTEMIS," apparently a reference to his artisan status. However, an inscription from first-century Ephesus mentions a Demetrius who is a ''shrine maker,'' a technical term describing a warden of the temple of Artemis. If Demetrius was an official of the temple of Artemis, Luke misunderstood the technical term identifying Demetrius as referring to one who was a craftsman.

Although excavations at Ephesus have not disclosed the silver shrines of Artemis that Demetrius is supposed to have fashioned, archaeologists have uncovered terra-cotta replicas of the temple, probably used for souvenirs or votive offerings, and some small silver statues of Artemis. So there are indications that artisans produced materials related to the temple and its goddess.

If an artisan, Demetrius was likely the head of the guild that prospered from the presence of the temple. This is why he leads the demonstration against Paul whose preaching threatens the popularity of the goddess. Whether an artisan or a temple official, he has ample reason to oppose Paul.

2. The Demetrius of 3 John is an itinerant missionary associated with the Elder. In his travels, he has been denied hospitality by Diotrephes. The Elder writes 3 John to recommend Demetrius to Gaius and his friends as worthy of their hospitality.

See also ARTEMIS.

Bibliography. E. Haenchen, *The Acts of the Apostles*; A. Malherbe, ''The Inhospitality of Diotrephes,'' *God's Christ and His People,* ed. J. Jervell and W. Meeks; L. R. Taylor, ''Artemis of Ephesus'' *The Beginnings of Christianity: The Acts of the Apostles,* vol. 5, ed. F. J. Foakes-Jackson and K. Lake.

—WILLIAM R. HERZOG II

• **Demetrius the Chronographer.** Demetrius was a Jewish chronicler of the late third century B.C.E., who explored and evaluated the historical writings of the LXX. His history of the Jews survives only in fragments which EUSEBIUS preserved by quoting from Alexander Polyhistor. These fragments address material from the Pentateuch: fragment 1 summarizes the story of the sacrifice of Isaac; fragment 2 examines the patriarchal chronology; fragment 3 endeavors to reconcile the various chronological traditions regarding the genealogy of Moses and Zipporah; fragment 4 summarizes events at Marah and Elim; fragment 5 explains that the weapons of the people of the Exodus were captured from Egyptians destroyed in the flood; and fragment 6 chronicles the history of the time between the Jewish Exile and Demetrius.

The language and style of Demetrius's writings are simple and direct. His reference to Ptolemy IV of Egypt, use of the LXX, and use of a scientific chronological method has prompted scholars to place Demetrius in Alexandria. The examination of earlier chronicles, a focus of historians in Alexandria at this time, and Demetrius's attempts to solve historical or chronological difficulties encountered in those ancient chronicles were in line with an important historical method of the period.

Demetrius's method of answering difficulties has prompted some to consider him an apologist. The evidence would suggest, however, that his apologetic would be implicit at best, since there is no evidence that his chronological findings were used to relate the Jewish culture to the surrounding Hellenistic culture. His contribution seems rather to be the reverse; Demetrius applied the literary methods of the Alexandrian culture to the Jewish historical writings.

Bibliography. J. H. Charlesworth, *The Pseudepigrapha and Modern Research*; J. Hanson, ''Demetrius the Chronographer,'' *The Old Testament Pseudepigrapha,* ed. J. H. Charlesworth.

—STEVEN SHEELEY

• **Democracy.** A system of government in which the authority to rule resides in the people. The Israelites assembled in front of the Tabernacle or tent of meeting to deal with matters concerning the whole nation (Num 8:9; 10:3). The people of a city met at the city gate to decide issues concerning the city (Ruth 3:11; 4:1-4; Deut 21:18-21).

Elders usually represented the Israelites and made decisions on their behalf. Through elders the people demanded of the prophet Samuel the designation of a king (1 Sam 8:1-9). The elders of the Northern tribes made DAVID king when he agreed to rule according to the covenant they made with him (2 Sam 5:1-5). Later, elders in the North refused to make SOLOMON's son, REHOBOAM, king because he would not accept the kingship on their terms (1 Kgs 12:1-20).

Elders represented the Jewish captives in Babylon (Jer 29:1; Ezek 8:1). In the first century C.E., every Jewish community seemingly had elders to represent the people in local government (Luke 7:3). Elders served on the SANHEDRIN, the high court of the Jews (Acts 4:5; 5:27). The Sanhedrin represented the Jews to Roman officials.

The early church had a primitive form of democracy as well. When a dispute arose over the care of widows, the apostles suggested a solution that was adopted by the whole congregation (Acts 6:1-6). When conflict arose in ANTIOCH over gentile converts, the church sent representatives to Jerusalem to settle the issue (Acts 15:1-35). In the early church, elders, also known as bishops or superintendents (Acts 20:17, 28), represented the people of their congregation in decision making (Acts 14:23). The biblical basis for democracy is the intrinsic worth of every human being (2 Chr 19:7; Acts 10:34-35).

See also ASSEMBLY; ELDER; GOVERNMENT; KINGSHIP.

—VIRGIL FRY

• **Demon in the New Testament.** ''Demon'' is a transliteration of a Greek term referring originally to either good or bad spirit beings. (The diminutive form is usually used in the NT.) The term is translated ''devil'' in the KJV, but the RSV uses the word ''demon,'' reserving the word ''devil'' for a Greek term meaning accuser or slanderer. SATAN and ''Beelzebul'' are the most common names applied to the ruler of the demons in the NT.

Classical Greek literature reflects the widespread belief that demons were either good or bad gods possessing supernatural powers with which to harm people. Their anger could be placated through magic. Ancient people feared demons because they inhabited lonely places such as dark, shadowy, deserted areas, places of waste, or ruins of crumbling buildings (cf. Lev 16:6-10; Ps 91:5; Isa 13:21; 34:14; Matt 12:43-45; Luke 4:1-2).

In the OT there are a few references to evil demons (Gen 6:1-4; Lev 16:6-10, 26; Ps 91:5). Occasionally, the demons that appear in the OT are the gods of the foreign nations (Lev 17:7; Deut 32:17; 2 Chr 11:15; Isa 13:21; 34:14; Ps 106:37-38). Yahweh commanded the Israelites not to devote worship to these foreign gods.

Through the influence of the Babylonian and Persian cultures during exile, the Hebrew people adapted foreign concepts associated with demons and evil spirits. Satan, the leader of demons, controlled the present evil world. However, the Hebrews asserted that God had ultimate control over Satan and demons.

According to the synoptic Gospels, demons cause physical disease: blindness, deafness, paralysis, and other maladies. Occasionally, demons declare a knowledge of Jesus' identity (Mark 1:24; 5:7). According to the Gospels, Jesus cast out demons; this is interpreted as evidence of the authority of Jesus and the presence of the Kingdom of God (Mark 3:22-27; 5:1-20; Matt 8:16-17; 12:22-32; Luke 6:17-19; 8:26-39). The synoptic Gospels consistently assert that Jesus possessed authority over Satan (Beelzebul) and the evil spirits that oppressed God's people. Furthermore, Jesus gave to his followers authority over evil spirits and demons (Mark 6:7; Matt 10:1; Luke 9:1), but there are no references in the synoptic Gospels to the disciples' successful exorcism of demons except a summary statement in Mark 6:13.

Paul refers to Satan and evil spirits in highly figurative language in numerous contexts (Rom 8:38; 1 Cor 10:20; Col 1:16; 2:15; Eph 2:2; 3:10; 6:11-12). For Paul, evil forces rule "this age," but all evil forces are under the ultimate control of God. In Colossians Paul affirms that Christ destroyed the power of the evil forces (Col 2:15, 20).

Like Paul, the writer of John's Gospel refers to Satan as the personification of evil (John 13:2, 27), but the use of "the devil" or "demon" also appears in reference to evil (John 7:20; 8:48-49; 10:20-21). Unlike the synoptic Gospels, John's Gospel does not contain a reference to demon exorcism.

See also ANGEL; EVIL; SATAN IN THE NEW TESTAMENT; SATAN IN THE OLD TESTAMENT.

Bibliography. W. Foerster, "δαίμων, κτλ.," *TDNT*; J. M. Hull, *Hellenistic Magic and the Synoptic Tradition*; J. Y. Lee, "Interpreting the Demonic Powers in Pauline Thought," *NovT* 12 (1970): 54-69.

—BENNIE R. CROCKETT, JR.

• Demon in the Old Testament. Although references are rare, belief in demons persisted among the Israelites. According to Israelite theology, GOD was responsible for everything, good or evil (Deut 32:39; 1 Sam 2:6-7; Isa 45:6-7). The God who delivered the people from slavery in Egypt and led them miraculously through the wilderness, also wrestled with and crippled JACOB (Gen 32:24-30), tried to kill MOSES (Exod 4:24), and sent an evil spirit to torment SAUL (1 Sam 16:14). With such a mysterious and unpredictable God, demons were hardly necessary. Apparently, however, belief in demons persisted among the Israelites despite the official theology (Lev 17:7; Ps 106:37).

Israel believed that God was surrounded by a heavenly host. God frequently sent members of this host on earthly errands. The errands could lead to salvation and blessing (Gen 21:17-18) or to destruction (2 Sam 24:16). Although Israel understood that God's heavenly host simply obeyed him, with the exception of the event in Gen 6:1-4, the stage was set for a division of supernatural beings into those who performed good deeds for God and those who performed evil.

Further influences on Israel's ideas concerning demons came from the wilderness and from neighboring religions. The wilderness was a sinister, forbidding place and seemed to be a fitting abode for demons (Isa 34:14). Contact with neighboring religions reinforced the idea of the wilderness as a demonic haunt and introduced other demons (Deut 32:17). Perhaps foreign gods, especially the gods of nations whom Israel had defeated, came to be viewed as demons who had threatened Israel but whom God had conquered.

Despite the possibility for the inclusion of demons earlier in Israel's theology, it was only in the late postexilic period that Israelite theology grappled seriously with the idea. If God was to be viewed solely as good, evil had to come from a different source. Demons led by SATAN became the source of evil. Evidence of this change is not found in the OT but in the Apocrypha (Tob 3:8), Pseudepigrapha (*1 Enoch*), and the NT (Matt 9:34; 12:24).

The OT provides evidence of these stages in the development of the concept of demons. In some cases, phrases may indicate the names of earlier demons (Ps 91:5-6 "terror of the night," "destruction that wastes at noonday") but in other cases specific names are used. The *šēdîm* may have been spirits who could be good or evil but Israelite theology seemed to assume they were evil and unworthy of worship (Deut 32:17 "demon"; Ps 106:37). The *śĕʿîrîm* or "hairy ones" seemed to have been the equivalent of satyrs (Lev 17:7; Isa 34:14). The demons Resheph, Lilith, and Azazel clearly show the influence of the DESERT and other religions upon Israel. Resheph was the Canaanite god of plague and pestilence (Deut 32:24 "burning heat," "plague"; Hab 3:5), Lilith was the Mesopotamian storm demon who in the OT became a night demon of the wilderness (Isa 34:14 "night hag"), and Azazel was the desert demon to whom the scapegoat was sent on the Day of Atonement (Lev 16:8, 10, 26). Demons such as these survived in Israelite thought and practice and eventually found a place in Israel's theology.

See also ANGEL; ATONEMENT, DAY OF; EVIL; SATAN IN THE NEW TESTAMENT; SATAN IN THE OLD TESTAMENT.

Bibliography. G. Fohrer, *History of Israelite Religion*; H. Ringgren, *Israelite Religion*; J. B. Russell, *The Devil*.

—ROBERT C. DUNSTON

• Derbe. [duhr'bee] Located in south-central Asia Minor, in the district of Lycaonia (PLATES 26, 27), Derbe's fame is due primarily to visits made there by PAUL during his missionary journeys (cf. Acts 14:6; 16:1). The exact location of the site is unknown, but since 1956 it has been identified with the mound of Kerti Hüyük, which is about fifteen miles north-northeast of Laranda-Karaman. A second-century C.E. inscription found on this site bearing the name of "Derbe" would seem to confirm this identification.

Little is known of the history of the city, whose political fortunes changed several times. During the first century B.C.E., it was controlled by a local ruler named Antipater, but by the end of the century it was part of the Roman province of GALATIA. One of Paul's traveling companions, GAIUS (Acts 20:4), was from Derbe. The site was apparently abandoned during the Middle Ages.

See also GAIUS; GALATIA; PAUL.

—JOHN C. H. LAUGHLIN

• Descent into Hell. The tradition of a "descent into hell" by Jesus is alluded to enigmatically in the NT and is found in some versions of the Apostles Creed. Indirect references to the descent are given in 1 Peter in the statement that Christ after being put to death "went and preached to the spirits in prison" (3:19) and in the statement that "the gospel was preached even to the dead" (4:6). The core of this descent tradition seems to be that between the crucifixion and the resurrection Jesus descended into the place of the dead where he preached to certain spirits imprisoned there.

The development of this tradition may have been influenced by devotional reflection in the early church: Where was the spirit of Jesus during the interim between his crucifixion and the resurrection? What would be the destiny of those who died before the coming of Jesus? (cf. Acts 2:27; Luke 4:17-18). Some form of the tradition of the descent may have seemed to provide the needed answer.

See also HELL; SHEOL; SPIRITS IN PRISON.

—FREDERICK L. DOWNING

• **Desert.** A wilderness area, rather than pure desert, characterized by wild animals, little vegetation, few areas suitable for agriculture, and in general a dearth of water. The area south of Judah, called the NEGEB, and the wildernesses of the SINAI peninsula are the chief regions called desert in the Bible. In addition, the Rift Valley below the DEAD SEA, the *'ărābâ,* is designated desert or wilderness in several biblical texts.

There is a degree of ambivalence in biblical writers as they treat the desert. On the one hand, the desert continued Israel's trials and testings as they were led from Egyptian bondage to freedom and in the direction of the land of the promise. They frequently were subject to attack by the fierce inhabitants of the desert (cf., e.g., Exod 17), suffered from lack of food and water (Exod 16), and longed for the comforts of Egyptian slavery. On the other hand, the wilderness period was a time of close and intimate communion between the people and God. They ate food from God's table (Exod 16), were faithful and devoted to God (Hos 11; Jer 2), and were under God's constant protection. The desert was the time of revelation (Exod 19–24; 32–34), the scene for the giving of the TEN COMMANDMENTS (Exod 20), and the locale in which the TABERNACLE, its furnishings, and the priestly vestments and instructions were provided (Exod 25-31; 35-40; Num 1–10).

The desert continued to be viewed in this double light. HAGAR could seek refuge from her harsh mistress SARAH (Gen 16), but in turn she would have to depend upon God's care to sustain her in the wilderness. ELIJAH was a person of the wilderness, able to flee there for safety; but he too had to have sustenance from God while seeking his revelation. JOHN THE BAPTIST too, a latter-day Elijah, apparently found the desert to be a place of revelation, while JESUS was in the desert for forty days undergoing temptation by the devil. The desert, in short, is one of the polar images in biblical religion: a place of privation and leanness of life, but for that very reason suitable for special disclosures by God and for training and discipline for mission and ministry in the public world. PAUL speaks of an extended stay in ARABIA prior to his taking up his ministry (Gal 1:17).

See also NAZIRITES; RECHABITES.

—WALTER HARRELSON

• **Desolation, Abomination of.** *See* ABOMINATION OF DESOLATION

• **Deuternomic Reform.** *See* JOSIAH; PREACHING, LEVITICAL

• **Deuteronomist/Deuteronomistic Historian.** [dy*oo*'tuh-ron"uh-mist dy*oo*'tuh-ron'uh-mis"tik] In 2 Kgs 22:3–23:25, there is an account of the finding of a "book of the law" (22:8) in the Jerusalem Temple during renovations authorized in 621 B.C.E. by the young king JOSIAH. In a dramatically told narrative, the king hears and obeys the provisions of this law (confirmed by a word from the prophetess HULDAH), and reverses the religious policies of his grandfather Manasseh. Since the time of Jerome, it has been suggested that Deuteronomy (or at least the legal section of the book) was the law book that justified Josiah's transformation of the cultus of the Jerusalem TEMPLE and his abolition of all cultic activity outside this Temple (23:4-24; cf. Deut 12:1-28).

The legal sections of Deuteronomy (chaps. 12–25), in contrast to their sources in earlier Israelite legal collections (Exod 20–23; Lev 17–26, and the priestly strata of the Pentateuch), seem to reflect an effort to provide a comprehensive law code, formulated from a coherent theological point of view. The opening section is primarily sacral law: sacrifice at the chosen sanctuary (12), apostasy (13), kosher, tithe (14), debt, the firstborn (15), festivals (16), high officials (17), and priests (18). Dominantly civil laws follow, beginning with provisions for accidental homicide (19) and warfare (20), and passing to more complex collections, one dominated by marriage law (21–22), and one alternating purity rules and civil regulations (23–25). These have been discussed in relation to Near Eastern legal codes, such as those of the HAMMURABI dynasty in Babylon.

These sections of Deuteronomy reflect significant legal developments. A comparison of the law limiting the term of slavery for Israelites (Deut 15:12-18) with the older law preserved in the Covenant Code (Exod 21:1-11) is a popular example. The third person form of traditional law ("he shall go out free," Exod 21:2) has been replaced by direct address ("you shall let him go free," Deut 15:12). This direct address adds a rhetorical dimension to law, which accounts for the effect of "your brother" (12) and for the art of persuasion reflected in "for you were a slave" (15), "he has served you six years" (18), "God will bless you" (18), and even the transfer of the "love" that leads to the acceptance of the mark of permanent slavery to the owner (16; cf. Exod 21:5). A tendency toward humaneness has been seen in the requirement that the manumitted slave be compensated for his service (13–14), in the equivalent treatment of male and female slaves ("or a Hebrew woman" displaces the provisions of Exod 21:7-11 [cf. Deut 21:10-14] where prisoners of war are given the rights of a concubine), and in the absence of the provision that a slave-wife and her offspring belong to the "master" (Exod 21:4; see Weinfeld).

The basis for current discussion of Deuteronomy is the hypothesis of Gerhard von Rad that the book is organized upon elements of an ancient tribal "covenant ceremony": a historical recitation of the Sinai story, with instruction and admonition (Deut 1:11); the account of the reading of the law (12:1–26:15); the sealing of the COVENANT (26:16-19); and an enumeration of blessings and curses (chaps. 27–28). American biblical scholars have placed particularly strong emphasis upon this "covenant theology," echoing the structure of Near Eastern treaty/covenant forms in which a powerful king recites the benefits he has provided, binds his vassals to particular obligations, and specifies blessings for those who carry out these obligations and curses for those who fail to carry them out.

The influential study by Martin Noth has seen this work by "the Deuteronomist" (Dtn) as the ideological basis for the "Deuteronomistic history" (Dtr) of Israel from the entry into the land to the Babylonian Exile. This history, held together by speeches and historical reflections (speeches: Josh 1; 23; 1 Sam 12; 1 Kgs 8:14-53; reflections: Josh 12; Judg 2:11-19; 2 Kgs 17:7-41), offers a clear interpretation of history as an expression of God's response to human obedience or disobedience (to deuteronomic principles expressed by authoritative speakers; cf. Deut 29–30). Later, von Rad described a pattern of prophetic word followed by its fulfillment.

Written soon after the beginning of the Babylonian Exile of 587/6 (the reference to the release of Jehoiachin from prison in 2 Kgs 25:27-30 is later), this history interprets the fall of JERUSALEM in relation to the persistence of God's covenant with ISRAEL, and holds out the obligation to obedience in the present situation. Despite recent critical reservations about the magisterial simplicity of Noth's hypothesis, the idea of divine justice as a principal force in the shaping of the course of history is clearly present in this history. As if expressing the criterion in the speech of SAMUEL: "if you will not hearken to the voice of the Lord, . . . the hand of the Lord will be against you and your king" (1 Sam 12:15), the history passes judgment upon each king within the formula that opens and closes each account. With the exception of Hezekiah and Josiah, each king of Judah uniformly "walked in all the sins which his father did before him; and his heart was not wholly true to the Lord his God, as the heart of David his father" (1 Kgs 15:1-8), and every king of Israel "did what was evil in the sight of the Lord, and walked in the way of Jeroboam and in his sin which he made Israel to sin." (1 Kgs 15:33-34; 16:5-6).

Frank Moore Cross has qualified Noth's bleak characterization of the deuteronomistic historian as one who imagines no concrete future beyond the destruction and exile brought about by persistent disobedience, failure to worship only Yahweh, and failure to worship him at the one sanctuary where he dwells. In the refrain, "for the sake of my servant David," Cross sees the historian's affirmation of the persistence of the dynastic promises to Israel, which are not present in Deuteronomy, as the basis of hope for the future.

See also DEUTERONOMY, BOOK OF; PRIESTLY WRITERS; SOURCES OF THE PENTATEUCH.

Bibliography. F. M. Cross, *Canaanite Myth and Hebrew Epic*; A. D. H. Mayes, *Deuteronomy, NCB*; M. Noth, *The Deuteronomistic History, JSOTSupp* 15; G. von Rad, *The Problem of the Hexateuch and Other Essays*; M. Weinfeld, *Deuteronomy and the Deuteronomic School.*

—ROY D. WELLS, JR.

• OUTLINE OF DEUTERONOMY •

The Book of Deuteronomy

- A Outer Frame:
  A Look Backwards (1–3)
- B Inner Frame:
  The Great Peroration (4–11)
- C Central Core:
  Covenant Stipulations (12–26)
- B′ Inner Frame:
  The Covenant Ceremony (27–30)
- A′ Outer Frame:
  A Look Forwards (31–34)

• **Deuteronomy, Book of.** [*doo*'tuh-ron"uh-mee] The last of the five books of the Pentateuch, which in Jewish tradition is commonly called the Torah or the books of Moses. The name Deuteronomy comes from a mistranslation by the LXX translators of a clause in Deut 17:18, which refers to a "repetition (*Deuteronomion* in Gk.) of this law." The Hebrew actually instructs the king to make "a copy of this law." The error on which the English title rests, however, is not serious; for Deuteronomy is in fact a repetition of the Law of Moses as delivered at Mount Sinai (Horeb) in the books of Exodus, Leviticus, and Numbers. It is also the literary bridge connecting the first two major segments of the canon of the Hebrew Bible: the Torah and the Former Prophets (Joshua, Judges, Samuel, and Kings—sometimes called the deuteronomic history).

As a legal document, Deuteronomy is essentially a national "constitution," or what S. D. McBride has called the "Polity of the Covenant People." Though it contains a series of laws, it is not a law code as such. It is essentially a work intended for religious instruction and education in ancient Israel. As such it is a work of extraordinary literary coherence, poetic beauty, and political sophistication. In short, Deuteronomy represents a very early, and a remarkably comprehensive, attempt to reform religion by means of a program of religious education in which every person was to be included, from the king as the head of the nation to every child in every home (cf. 4:9, 10; 6:7, 20; 11:19; 31:13; 32:7, 46).

The book expounds the implications of the historic agreement at Mount Sinai between God and Israel by which the latter became the chosen people. The author's purpose was to maintain the loyalty towards God that Israel professed when the Sinai COVENANT was ratified, so that the people would never be in doubt as to the high moral and spiritual standards demanded by God of the people. The book is essentially an exposition of the great commandment, "You shall love the Lord your God with all your heart, and with all your soul, and with all your might" (Deut 6:5). It was from Deuteronomy that Jesus summarized the entire old covenant in a single sentence (Matt 22:37; cf. Deut 6:5); and from the same he quoted God's revelation in response to each of Satan's temptations (Matt 4:4, 7, 10; cf. Deut 8:3; 6:16, 13).

Deuteronomy is often outlined as a series of three discourses, followed by three short appendices: 1:1–4:43, an historical review of God's dealings with Israel recounting the chief events in the nation's experience from Horeb to Moab, concluding with an earnest appeal to be faithful and obedient, and in particular to keep clear of all forms of idolatry; 4:44–26:19, a hortatory resumé of Israel's moral and civil statutory rulings; and 27:1–31:30, a predictive and minatory section, which begins with a ritual of covenant blessings and curses and concludes with Moses' farewell charge to Israel and his formal commission of Joshua as his successor, following the renewal of the covenant in Moab. Three appendices close the book: the "Song of Moses" (chap. 32), which the great lawgiver taught the people; the "Blessing of Moses" (chap. 33), which forecasts the future of the various tribes; and an account of Moses' death and burial (chap. 34).

The structure of the book may also be described in terms of a five-part concentric design—cf. outline above. The two parts of the "Outer Frame" (chaps. 1–3 and 31–34) may be read as a single document, tied together by the figure of Joshua who appears only in chaps. 3, 31, and 34. The two parts of the "Inner Frame" (chaps. 4–11 and 27–30) may also be read as a single document, joined together by the reference to blessings and curses connected with a cultic ceremony on MOUNT GERIZIM and Mount Ebal (chaps. 11:26-32 and 27:1-14), which are mentioned only in these two contexts within the book of Deuteronomy. At the center of this construction lies the "Central Core" (chaps. 12–26), which is the primary body of instruction in the culture of ancient Israel, sometimes called the deuteronomic law code. This block of material is in turn arranged in "a remarkably coherent five-part structure" (McBride, 239), which is also organized concentrically. In fact, it can be shown that each of these five major parts of the book of Deuteronomy may in turn be analyzed into somewhat similar concentric structures (Christensen, 137-38). According to Kaufman, the organizing principle behind the arrangement of the laws in chaps. 12–26 is the order of the familiar "Ten Commandments" of Deut 5:6-21.

The presence of carefully balanced structures at virtually all levels of analysis within the book of Deuteronomy suggests a rather different model for explaining the form and function of the book from what is often assumed. Such structures are common in works of art, both from antiquity and in the present—particularly in the fields of epic poetry and music. The reason for the similarity is apparently the simple fact that in its essential nature the book of Deuteronomy is itself a work of literary art in poetic form, subject to the restraints of the musical media to which it was originally composed in ancient Israel.

As Bishop Robert Lowth noted 200 years ago, the law codes throughout the Mediterranean world were sung at the festivals in antiquity. The law book we call Deuteronomy was in the hands of the Levites (Deut 17:18) who were commanded by Moses to proclaim it at the Feast of Booths (Deut 31:9). Though we do not know the precise nature of this proclamation of the law, which was handed down within levitical circles, it is likely that it was sung and that this greater "Song of Moses" (i.e., the entire book of Deuteronomy) was taught to the people. J. Lundbom apparently intuited at least part of the picture in his suggestion that it was the "Song of Moses" (chap. 32), rather than the entire Book of Deuteronomy as such, which was found in the Temple in Jerusalem during the reign of Josiah. As the most archaic material in the book of Deuteronomy, this official "Song of Moses" dates from the premonarchic era of ancient Israel in essentially its present form. But that song was imbedded in a much larger "Song of Moses," which we now call the book of Deuteronomy. For generations that song was recited in levitical circles as a primary means of religious education. Eventually it was put in written form and promulgated in Jerusalem as part of a reform movement in the days of King Josiah. Within that movement Deuteronomy became the center of a canonical process that eventually produced the Hebrew Bible as we now know it. That canonical text was recited within the musical tradition of the Second Temple in Jerusalem. The memory of that tradition is still reflected in the Masoretic accentual system of the Hebrew Bible.

When J. van Goudoever commented that Deuteronomy is "the most liturgical book of the Bible" (148), he described the function of the book within a larger cultic pattern in ancient Israel. The Book of Deuteronomy is presented as the Testament of Moses, to be read in preparation for the Passover in Josh 5. In short, the Torah itself is a Passover-story made up of three Passovers: in Egypt (Exod 12), in the wilderness at Sinai (Num 9), and in the promised land (Josh 5). This tradition of three Passovers is the basis of the "Poem of the Four Passovers," known within both the Jewish and Samaritan tradition. This observation bears witness to the memory of the original form and function of the book of Deuteronomy, which is captured in the descriptive phrase "A Song of Power and the Power of Song" in ancient Israel.

See also DEUTERONOMIST/DEUTERONOMISTIC HISTORIAN; LAW IN THE OLD TESTAMENT; TORAH.

Bibliography. D. Christensen, "Form and Structure in Deuteronomy 1–11," in *Das Deuteronomium,* BETL 68 (1985): 135-44; R. Clements, *God's Chosen People: A Theological Interpretation of the Book of Deuteronomy*; R. Clifford, *Deuteronomy: With an Excursus on Covenant and Law*; P. Craigie, *The Book of Deuteronomy*; J. van Goudoever, "The Liturgical Significance of the Date in Dt 1, 3," in *Das Deuteronomium, BETL* 68 (1985): 145-48; S. Kaufman, "The Structure of the Deuteronomic Law," *Maarav* (1979): 105-58; R. Lowth, *Lectures on the Sacred Poetry of the Hebrews*; J. Lundbom, "The Lawbook of the Josianic Reform," *CBQ* 38 (1976): 293-302; A. Mayes, *Deuteronomy*; S. McBride, Jr., "Polity of the Covenant People: The Book of Deuteronomy," *Int* (1987): 229-44; R. Polzin, "Deuteronomy," in *The Literary Guide to the Bible* (1987): 92-101; G. von Rad, *Deuteronomy: A Commentary*; M. Weinfeld, *Deuteronomy and the Deuteronomic School.*

—DUANE L. CHRISTENSEN

• **Devil.** *See* DEMON IN THE NEW TESTAMENT; EVIL; MADNESS; SATAN IN THE NEW TESTAMENT; SATAN IN THE OLD TESTAMENT

• **Dialogue Controversy.** *See* CONFLICT STORY

• **Dialogue of the Savior.** This somewhat fragmentary tractate is the fifth in Codex III from the Coptic library of NAG HAMMADI. It is a revelation dialogue concerned with the eschatological "time of dissolution" (122.2-3), i.e., bodily death and the ascent of the soul. Like other Gnostic revelation dialogues, the *Dialogue* displays such features as questions by interrogators (the Twelve Apostles and MARY), answers by the revealer (the "earthly Jesus"), action by the revealer, and a conclusion. Missing is an initial setting for the dialogue (usually, in Christian Gnostic texts, a post-resurrection appearance of Christ).

The whole may be outlined as follows: (1) Jesus announces his impending departure from earth and teaches the disciples a prayer emphasizing the need to seek freedom from the body through ascetic practice (120.1–122.1). (2) He then instructs the disciples regarding the "time of dissolution" (= the postmortem ascent of the soul past cosmic powers), illuminated Gnostics versus the ignorant, some cosmological wisdom, and the psychology of human beings (mind, soul, body) (122.1–129.16). Next (3), questions from Judas (e.g., about what existed before heaven and earth) introduce a cosmological section that includes typical Gnostic exegesis of GENESIS and explanation of creation as the result of the LOGOS's ordering. This section (127.19–131.18) concludes with Judas's praise of the Lord. (4) Next there are eschatological questions from Mary and MATTHEW, the former being told that gaining immortal life requires keeping Jesus' sayings in the heart. Matthew, in turn, is told he will find the "place of life . . . (and) pure light" in self-knowledge (131.19–132.19). (5) Again, the theme of cosmology is taken up, with the Lord explaining that the Logos sustains everything but that self-knowledge is more important than cosmic knowledge (132.19–134.24). (6) Concluding the Lord's comments about the "time of dissolution" is a passage in which Judas, Matthew, and Mary have a vision of the Abyss of punishment and how good souls are rescued from it. When further visions are requested, however, they are told they must look "within" themselves. The section closes with commissioning of the disciples (134.24–138.2). (7) The last part (138.2–147.22) contains additional questions on eschatological matters based on Gnostic interpretations of Jesus' sayings. Evil powers are overcome when Gnostics are stripped of the "works of femaleness" (= the physical bodies) and are clothed in heavenly garments.

Scholars have identified oral and possibly written sources in the text, including: an apocalyptic vision (134.24–137.3), a CREATION myth (127.23–131.15), an ascent of the soul through heavenly spheres (121.5–122.1), a cosmological wisdom list (133.23–134.24), and a dialogue between the Lord and three disciples (124.23–127.19; 128.23–129.16; 131.19–133.21; 137.3–146.20). The sayings of Jesus found in the last-named are interpretations of traditional sayings that appear earlier than similar ones in John's Gospel.

Two key interpreters (Koester and Pagels) maintain that the tradition of Jesus' sayings in *Dialogue of the Savior* may go back to the late first century C.E. and that the present tractate is "proto-Gnostic." Another (Perkins), however, connects it with the ascetic teaching of the Syrian Gnostic school of the apostle THOMAS.

See also GNOSTICISM; NAG HAMMADI.

Bibliography. H. Koester and E. H. Pagels, "The Dialogue of the Savior (III.5)," *The Nag Hammadi Library in English,* ed. J. M. Robinson and "Report on the Dialogue of the Savior," *Nag Hammadi and Gnosis,* ed. R. McL. Wilson; P. Perkins, *The Gnostic Dialogue: The Early Church and the Crisis of Gnosticism.*

—MALCOLM L. PEEL

• **Diana.** *See* ARTEMIS

• **Diaspora.** *See* HELLENISTIC WORLD; JUDAISM

• **Diatessaron.** [di'uh-tes"uh-ron] Tatian the Syrian wrote in the second half of the second century a work called the *Diatessaron,* "the gospel out of four." It was the first known attempt to create a harmony of the Gospels, which was accomplished by weaving the four accounts into a single narrative.

It is unknown whether the work was orginally composed in Greek or in Syriac, but the Syriac version was very influential both in the East and the West. A single fragment of a Greek text was found at Dura Europa dating from ca. 220, but no manuscript of the complete *Diatessaron* has survived. The work is known through secondary sources: a Syriac commentary on the *Diatessaron* by Ephraem Syrus, as well as an Armenian version of the same; Latin, Arabic, Persian, and Dutch harmonies which were influenced by the *Diatessaron* to various extents. The *Diatessaron* influenced the Old Syriac gospel manuscripts, and, through translation, the Old Latin manuscripts of the NT as well. It is clear that the *Diatessaron* exerted considerable influence in the East until Theodoret of Cyrus (fifth century) removed over 200 copies and replaced them with the four Gospels (Theodoret, *Haer* 1.20).

Tatian had been a student of JUSTIN MARTYR in Rome until the latter's death (ca. 165). Thereupon he moved back to the East where he founded a Gnostic-Encratite sect which rejected marriage, use of meat, and wine (communion wine was replaced with water). The *Diatessaron,* though, does not clearly reflect his heretical views, perhaps due to his method of composition. The omissions from the Gospel text may be explained by the textual exemplars before him, rather than by theological reasons; likewise the occasional apocryphal sayings of Jesus which were included. Apparently the *Diatessaron* was used by both heretical and orthodox groups, at least until Theodoret's time.

Tatian's criteria for the composition of the *Diatessaron* can be seen partially from an examination of the reconstructed work: (a) The Gospel of JOHN had priority over the other texts; next MATTHEW's text seemed to enjoy priority over LUKE and MARK. This is almost the Western order of the Gospels exhibited in Greek Codex D and the Old Latin manuscripts, with which the *Diatessaron* exhibits close affinities. (b) Tatian apparently chose eclectically between parallel texts, following one Gospel, then another. At times he chose not to follow John. For instance, the chronology of the cleansing of the TEMPLE follows the Synoptics (during Passion Week) rather than John's (beginning of Christ's ministry). (c) Gospel narratives are often supplemented with other NT narratives: the death of JUDAS in Acts 1:18 is used to supplement Matt 27:3-10, and the Lord's Supper is supplemented with 1 Cor 11. (d) There is some evidence that Tatian arranged Jesus' ministry around the PASSOVER festivals, and may have grouped materials in what he thought were more logical arrangements, i.e., the events of John 6 are placed before those of chap. 4.

Even though ultimately rejected by the great church in favor of four Gospels, the *Diatessaron* occupies an important place in Gospel research.

Bibliography. B. Altaner, *Patrology*; W. Bauer, *Orthodoxy and Heresy in Earliest Christianity*; J. H. Charlesworth, "Tatian's Dependence upon Apocryphal Traditions," *HeyJ* 15 (1974): 5-17; J. M. Fuller, "Tatianus," *A Dictionary of Christian Biography,* ed. W. Smith and H. Wace; J. Quasten, "The Beginnings of Patristic Literature," *Patrology*.

—GLENN A. KOCH

• **Diatribe.** *See* LITERATURE, BIBLE AS

• **Dibon.** [di'bon] Located about forty mi. south of Amman and two and one-half mi. north of the Arnon River (PLATE 3), Dibon (modern Dhiban) was the birthplace and capital of Mesha, king of Moab. The city is not in the heartland of Moab whose boundaries are usually considered to run from the Arnon River to the Zered; Dibon lies north of this boundary. The MESHA STELE was discovered in Dibon in 1868.

Dibon was excavated from 1950 to 1955 by F. V. Winnett, W. L. Reed, A. D. Tushingham, and W. M. Morton. Remains show that Dibon was occupied in the Early Bronze Age and then had an occupational gap until Iron I. Major finds from Iron I and Iron II included buildings that have been identified as a sanctuary, public buildings, and possibly the royal quarter. If correctly identified, the royal quarter was on a portion of the tell outside the town walls until the time of Mesha. This quarter might well be the *qarḥo* of the Mesha Stele. This level of Dibon was destroyed ca. 582 B.C.E. by the Babylonians. A Nabatean temple was found, but no other structures from that period. Possibly Dibon was then only a pilgrim shrine and not an urban center. Although some Roman coins and two inscriptions have been discovered, there is little architectural evidence of the Roman period. Perhaps Dibon was a fortress guarding the north-south road at that time. Two Byzantine churches and early Islamic structures complete the occupational history of Dibon until the modern period.

—JOEL F. DRINKARD, JR.

• **Didache.** [did'uh-kee] The *Didache,* or *Teaching of the Twelve Apostles,* is a second century Christian document dealing with church order. Reflecting the ecclesiastical life of a local congregation, it belongs to a genre known as church manuals. Other manuals which resemble the *Di-*

dache are the *Apostolic Constitutions* and the *Apostolic Traditions*.

The first part of the *Didache* (1–6) consists of a tradition known as the Two Ways, because the teaching often begins with the phrase: "There are two ways. . . ." Two way theology can be found in a number of Jewish and early Christian documents—The TESTAMENTS OF TWELVE PATRIARCHS; the MANUAL OF DISCIPLINE; the EPISTLE OF BARNABAS and the SHEPHERD OF HERMAS. Traces can be found in the NT, e.g., Matt 6:24, 7:13-14, and James 1:5-8. Sometimes the two ways are expressed as lists of virtues and vices not unlike similar lists found in moral literature of the Greco-Roman world (5:1).

Chaps. 7–11 treat BAPTISM, FASTING and the LORD'S SUPPER. Baptism was done in the name of the Father, Son and Holy Spirit (7:3). It should be done in running water, but failing that, any water would do. Fasting should be done on Wednesdays and Fridays rather than with the hypocrites on Monday and Thursday (8:1). The Lord's Prayer is recommended for praying three times a day. Its form is much like that of Matthew (8:2), except for the doxological ending. "For thine is the power and the glory forever." The Eucharist celebrates the unity of the church, symbolized by the one loaf of bread. It does not recall the death of Jesus, but looks forward to the end-time (10:6). The eucharistic prayer ends with a cry for the end-time. This cry, in Aramaic, *marana tha* (O Lord, come) is a prayer which apparently reflects the end-time orientation of the Jewish Christian community (1 Cor 16:22).

In chaps. 11–13 the manual discusses the protocol for visiting leaders. Apostles and prophets moved from congregation to congregation, though the local community did not always recognize impostors. If they stayed more than two days they were not true prophets. If they asked for money (and food), they must be false. The wandering prophet might stay longer by working for a living, though a true prophet could be paid from the tithe (13:1).

The LORD'S DAY (chap. 14) was celebrated by the breaking of bread (the *agapē* meal) and by holding the Eucharist. Those who come to the meeting are to have confessed transgressions and have been reconciled to friends prior to the worship (cf. Matt 5:23). At the local level (chap. 15) the congregation is advised to appoint BISHOPS and DEACONS to continue the ministry of the prophets and teachers (rather than apostles!). In the final chapter some typical end-time warnings and mandates are expressed.

The local church of the *Didache* had catechetical instruction for initiates (7:1); threefold water baptism (7:3), a eucharistic meal for members only which stressed fellowship (9:4-5); fasts two days a week (8:1); set prayers for the laity (8:3); and regular meetings on the Lord's Day (14:1). It was a church still led by itinerant apostles, prophets and teachers, though local leadership (bishops and deacons) was acceptable.

The discovery of the *Didache* (in 1873, in an eleventh-century manuscript) has had a remarkable influence on our understanding of the early church at a local level. Consequently the date and provenance of the document becomes particularly critical. The document as we know it contains earlier elements. The Two Way material comes from sources prior to this document, even to Christianity itself. The primitive nature of the christology and church organization has brought some to date it before the year 70 C.E. More likely the primitive nature of the documents reflects local practice in contrast to the literature of the church fathers. The *Didache* as we have it should be dated in the early part of the second century. Most place its provenance in Syria, though Egypt has been an option.

See also APOSTOLIC FATHERS.

Bibliography. H. Koester, *Introduction to the New Testament;* R. A. Kraft, *The Didache and Barnabas*; J. Quasten, *Patrology*.

—GRAYDON F. SNYDER

• **Didymus.** *See* THOMAS

• **Dies Irae.** *See* ZEPHANIAH, BOOK OF

• **Diognetus, Epistle to.** [d*i*-og'ni-tuhs] The *Epistle to Diognetus* is an anonymous apology for Christianity now usually included in the APOSTOLIC FATHERS, though of later date. A Diognetus served as tutor to the Emperor Marcus Aurelius (161–80), but it is unlikely he was the "most excellent" person addressed in the apology. The work has been dated anywhere between the mid-second and the mid-third centuries. It reflects some of the polish of third century writings, but most scholars now date it in the late-second century.

The *Epistle to Diognetus* barely survived. In 1870 a fire destroyed the only manuscript of it in a library in Strasbourg. Fortunately the original thirteenth- or fourteenth-century copy had been already duplicated, and it is this transcript which now survives.

Serious question exists about the integrity of the writing. Chaps. 11–12 differ markedly from chaps. 1–10: (1) in being addressed to a believer, (2) in a more positive attitude toward Judaism, (3) in using exact quotations of NT writings, (4) in form and style, and (5) in vocabulary and grammar. Some scholars have attributed the differences to a later author, perhaps Hippolytus (d. 235), but L.W. Barnard has proposed a solution similar to the one P. N. Harrison applied to the Epistle of POLYCARP TO THE PHILIPPIANS—namely, works addressed to different readers at different times by the same author.

The author answered three questions raised by his eminent pagan friend. Why do Christians worship the God of the Jews, to the point of dying for that God, but refuse to worship the gods recognized by the Greeks? Since they worship the Jewish God, why don't they keep Jewish observances? What accounts for the strange character of Christianity and why did this "new race" or religion not appear sooner?

Employing an argument already well honed by Jewish apologists, the writer turned the first question around. Why would Christians worship or die for gods made of stone, bronze, wood, silver, or other perishables which are dumb, blind, without souls, without feeling, without movement, and thus utterly without usefulness to human beings? (2) In response to the second charge, always a troublesome issue for Christians in this period, the anonymous author took care to reply pointedly. Christians do not worship God as Jews do because God has no need of the observances they employ—sacrifices, food laws, sabbaths, circumcision, fasting, and feast days (3-4).

The third question evoked a more positive apologetic. Christians are distinguished from others not by country, language, or most customs, but by manifesting "the wonderful and confessedly strange character of the constitution of their own citizenship" (5). "To put it shortly," the writer summed up, "what the soul is in the body, that the Christians are in the world" (6). Christianity is not of human but of divine origin. The Almighty Creator himself established truth from heaven by the incarnation of the Word. That is why Christians die for their faith (7). Before his coming, human beings had no reliable knowledge of God (8). So great was God's love that God neither rejected nor hated humankind, but gave the Son as a ransom for all, thus covering human sins by his righteousness (9). If you turn to God, who has loved humankind so, you will also gain love for neighbor, including Christians who suffer death for their faith (10).

Bibliography. L. W. Barnard, *Studies in the Apostolic Fathers and Their Background*; J. Quasten, *Patrology*.

—E. GLENN HINSON

• **Disciple Whom Jesus Loved, The.** *See* BELOVED DISCIPLE, THE

• **Disciple/Discipleship.** The disciple is a pupil, a learner, an apprentice. The ancient Greek philosophers had pupils who were to keep alive the ideas of their teachers after their death. Jewish rabbis also developed schools of interpretation which were to be promoted by their learners, and the disciples of JESUS are similar to the disciples of the rabbis. The disciples of Jesus were of a somewhat different nature, however. In contrast to the rabbinic system, Jesus took the initiative and called to himself those he wanted. Moreover, the task of Jesus' disciples was to bear witness about him rather than simply to receive and transmit his teachings. Jesus was more than their teacher; he was their Lord.

John 8:31 is important in understanding the Christian concept of what it means to be a disciple of Jesus. The "true disciple" abides in his word. A disciple is one who "believes in" Jesus (John 2:11; 20:24-29). Matthew states it somewhat differently: the true disciple is one who hears the words of Jesus and puts them into practice (Matt 7:24). This commitment to Jesus shapes the entire life of the disciple. But spiritual fellowship is possible without personal contact with Jesus; all who possess the Spirit abide in Jesus' word and are thus true disciples (John 14:15ff.; 15:26-27). The early church employed the word disciple (as well as other words such as "believer," "brethren," "saints," etc.) to refer to Christians in general and not just to those who knew Jesus personally. The Greek word translated disciple ("learner") could convey the idea that Christianity was simply a philosophical movement, but the notion of intellectual adherence without direct commitment is foreign to NT thinking. A disciple is one who "follows" his master. In the OT era the idea of following could bring to mind the procession of the devotees of pagan cults behind the images of the gods. The concept of following was avoided in describing what it meant to be devoted to Yahweh. The transcendent Yahweh cannot be "followed" in the sense that pagan gods can. In the NT the term "to follow" is used almost exclusively in the Gospels. Disciples leave all to follow Jesus (Mark 10:28; Luke 5:11). To follow him is to participate in the salvation which he offers. To follow him also implies participation in the fate of Jesus (Matt 8:19ff.; John 12:25-26). Furthermore, following Jesus is not simply a private or individualistic attachment to Jesus; it is life in community with others who have heard the same call.

The evangelists do not hesitate to show that Jesus' disciples are capable of serious failure. The disciples lack faith (Mark 4:40), misunderstand the power of Jesus (Mark 5:31), and are described as having hardened hearts (Mark 6:52). Clearly, discipleship is not a life of perfection.

Luke emphasizes certain dimensions of discipleship. Jesus is active in prayer and urges his disciples to follow his example (3:21; 5:16; 9:18; 11:1-13; 23:34). Jesus has women followers (8:1-3; 23:49) and takes the side of the marginal or disinherited in society (7:36-50; 15:1, 2). Luke is particularly interested in the numerous statements from Jesus regarding money and wealth. Wealth appears to be a significant barrier to following Jesus (12:13-34; 14:28-33; 16:19-31; 18:18-27).

See also APOSTLE/APOSTLESHIP; JESUS; RABBI; TWELVE, THE.

Bibliography. J. R. Donahue, "Growth in Grace: Discipleship and the Life of Grace," *SWJT* 28/2 (1986): 73-78; G. Kittel, "ἀκολουθέω, κτλ.," *TDNT;* K. H. Rengstorf, "μανθάνω, κτλ.," *TDNT*.

—JOHN A. WOOD

• **Discipline.** The term "discipline" in various English translations represents two related ideas found in the biblical texts: the negative notion of correction or punishment and the positive concept of instruction, education, and training. The terms normally used in Hebrew and Greek can convey either idea, and these verbs can be used with God or with a human being as subject. Although the biblical words can connote the idea of punishment, they usually, though not always, presuppose that an educational purpose lies behind the disciplinary action; thus they basically are positive in their connotations.

In the OT. Examples from Proverbs demonstrate the wide variety of meanings associated with the idea of discipline found throughout the OT. In addition to the concepts of self-discipline (5:23), reproof (6:23), and chastisement (16:22), discipline often is the practical equivalent of the idea of wisdom (1:2, 3, 7; 3:13; et al.). Moreover, the term frequently refers to the idea of education. This instruction can be that of a parent to a child (e.g., 1:8; 4:1; 13:1) or the more general admonition that might come from any non-parental instructor (e.g., 5:12; 10:17; 12:1). At times such discipline also entails some aspect of corporal punishment, which the Israelites considered essential to the educational process. They would have agreed with the modern maxim: "Spare the rod and spoil the child" (cf. 23:13). As a corrective to wrongdoing, physical chastisement is actually seen as an expression of parental love (13:24).

Out of the context of discipline within the family comes the idea of God as disciplinarian: "As a man disciplines his son, the Lord your God disciplines you" (Deut 8:5b). Recipients of this divine activity can be individuals (Pss 6:1; 39:11), the nation (Jer 5:3), or foreign nations (Ps 94:10). Furthermore, this activity can imply punishment without educational purpose (Ezek 5:15); or, more generally, it can refer to action which seeks the betterment of the recipients (Prov 3:12).

Mediating the concepts of nation and the individual for ancient Israel was the figure of the king. Confident that God in covenant with David had established his line as a permanent dynasty, they recognized a father-son relationship between God and the monarch (Ps 2:7). They also realized that the individual kings were at times ungodly men. Divine punishment meted out to the monarchs was understood to be the appropriate action of a loving parent. Neither the continuation of the dynasty nor the necessity of punishment was in question: "I will be his father, and he shall be my son. When he commits iniquity, I will chasten him . . . ; but I will not take my steadfast love from him" (2 Sam 7:14-15a; cf. Ps 89:32-37). The fact that the king could be chastened but not rejected was evidence both of a filial bond and of the permanency of the covenant relationship.

From the experience of the monarch, the Israelites drew the corresponding conclusion that God's relationship to the nation also was that of parent to child. Though the people of Israel at times needed to be disciplined, the punishment meted out was that from a loving father. In Hosea, this understanding of divine discipline comes to its fullest flower. In individual passages which speak directly of God's punishment of the nation (5:2, 9; 7:12; 10:10) and in the book as a whole, the prophet pictures God as one who chastens those whom he loves, as a father does a son (11:1-2). In purpose, therefore, God's discipline is redemptive, not retributive.

In the NT. In the NT discipline again has a variety of meanings. Although pure punishment is represented in Pilate's scourging of Jesus (Luke 23:16), the terms relating to discipline normally reflect the more positive Greek educational ideal of training with little emphasis on chastisement. The "discipline of the Lord" (Eph 6:4) seems to emphasize instruction and training, rather than some type of corporal punishment. Even correction or reproof can be executed in the Christian community without chastisement: the Lord's servant is to be an "apt teacher, forbearing, correcting his opponents with gentleness" (2 Tim 2:24b-25a).

Hebrews presents the closest parallel to the OT understanding of discipline. Suffering and adversity that befall Christians are to be taken as evidence of God's parental love (12:4-11). Emphasis here is not upon the cause for the discipline, but upon the results of it. God "disciplines us for our good, that we may share his holiness. . . . Discipline . . . yields the peaceful fruit of righteousness to those who have been trained by it" (vv. 10b-11).

See also EDUCATION IN THE NEW TESTAMENT; EDUCATION IN THE OLD TESTAMENT.

Bibliography. G. Bertram, "παιδεύω, κτλ.," *TDNT*; J. A. Sanders, *Suffering as Divine Discipline in the Old Testament and Post-Biblical Judaism*.

—NAYMOND H. KEATHLEY

• **Discourse on the Eighth and Ninth.** Among the eight tractates in Codex VI of the Coptic library of NAG HAMMADI are three that are clearly HERMETIC: *The Discourse on the Eighth and Ninth* (VI.6), the PRAYER OF THANKSGIVING (VI.7), and ASCLEPIUS (VI.8). Hermeticism was a syncretistic, religious-philosophical movement that flourished in Hellenistic Egypt (second and third centuries C.E.) and precipitated a variety of writings attributed to Hermes Trismegistus ("thrice-great"), a Greek title given Thoth, the Egyptian god of wisdom. The *Disc 8–9,* a formerly unknown addition to such writings, purports to be the secret teaching of a "mystagogue" (spiritual leader) to an "initiate" (pupil) regarding mystical ascent and ultimate union with God.

The title of the writing, one derived from its contents (53.24-26; cf. 61.21-22), reflects its distinctive, geocentric cosmology. Nine (or perhaps ten) spheres surround the earth. The first seven are guarded by powers (the planets, the sun, and the moon) which can control human life and interfere with the soul's post-mortem ascent to the highest God. Having successfully passed these seven, however, the soul would attain a beatific vision of the Divine (in the "Eighth"). Ultimately, it would merge in oneness with God (in the "Ninth" or "Tenth" sphere). It is notable that in *Disc 8–9* this ascent is conceived of as *pre-morte* and not *post-mortem*, the soul experiencing spiritual unity with universal Mind and then with God while the initiate still lives.

The tractate opens with a dialogue in which the pupil, after reminding the mystagogue of his promise to do so, formally requests instruction and ultimate experience of the Eighth and Ninth (52.2–53.27). Adding this instruction to his prior attainment of purity (56.27–57.1) and acquisition of knowledge of certain books (54.6-18), the initiate prays for a vision of the ultimate Mind (a penultimate divine Reality—53.28–57.25). Mystagogue and initiate embrace, and afterwards the former has a vision of the Ninth and actually becomes divine Mind (57.26–58.22). Then, the initiate, recognizing the Mind in his teacher (now called Hermes Trismegistus), enters the Eighth sphere, joins a heavenly chorus and sings a "silent hymn" to the Mind (58.22–59.9). The penultimate is achieved when the initiate is fully unified with the Mind and, having become divine, is himself hymned by the chorus of the Eighth (59.15–60.1).

Hermes charges the pupil to remain silent about this vison, and the latter sings a hymn of thanks to God (60.1–61.17). The whole concludes with Hermes' instructions to write an account of the experience on "steles of turquoise" for the "temple of Diospolis." To be included are promises that the contents shall be shared only with those ready for such knowledge and that outsiders will be prohibited from reading it.

References to the town of Diospolis, to writing in "hieroglyphics," to guardian deities with frog and cat faces, and to Hermes Trismegistus all point to Egypt as the place of composition. Also, close affinities of its thought to Tractate XIII of the *Corpus Hermeticum* and to the teaching of the Middle Platonist Albinus make probable a second century C.E. date of composition.

See also HERMETIC LITERATURE; NAG HAMMADI.

Bibliography. D. M. Parrott, J. Brashler, and P. A. Dirkse, "The Discourse on the Eighth and Ninth (VI.6)," *The Nag Hammadi Library in English,* ed. J. M. Robinson and "The Discourse on the Eighth and Ninth: VI.6; 52.1–63.32," *Nag Hammadi Codices V, 2–5 and VI with Papyrus Berolinensis 8502, 1 and 4,* ed. D. M. Parrott (*NHS* 11).

—MALCOLM L. PEEL

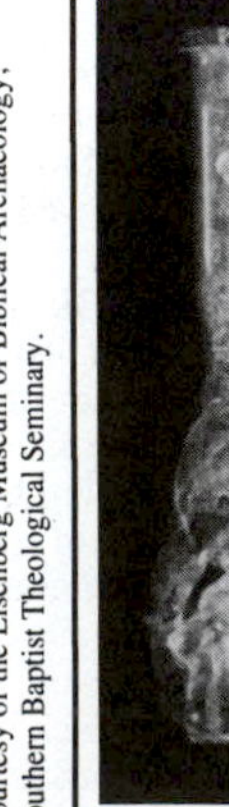

Courtesy of the Eisenberg Museum of Biblical Archaeology, Southern Baptist Theological Seminary.

Glass vial for collecting tears for medicinal purposes.

• **Disease and Healing.** Physical disease has plagued human existence from the dawn of history. Along with the phenomena of disease and suffering have been the corresponding attempts to relieve or to ease the maladies. Since the Bible presents an inclusive view of human life, it is not surprising to find frequent mention of physical disorder and the desire on the part of the afflicted for its alleviation. Both the OT and NT exhibit a sensitivity for those who are suffering. A few allusions are made to curative treatments commonly found in ancient societies. However, healing or the restoration of health is often depicted as a manifestation of God's compassion and power. Health is a gift from God; the Hebrew שָׁלוֹם (PEACE, wholeness) can also mean "health."

In the OT, the words "disease," "sickness," and "illness" with their cognates are employed chiefly to translate the noun חלי (sickness), which is derived from the verb חלה (to be weak). In the NT, the word "sickness" is generally used for the rendering of ἀσθένεια (weakness), μαλακία (misfortune), and νόσος (disease). Even when more specific terms are employed with reference to an ailment, the designation is more descriptive than diagnostic in the medical sense. Some allusion to the symptoms of the malady may be present, but the references are usually general and vague. Hence, difficulties of diagnosis prevail, and it is not always easy to determine the exact nature of the particular ailment. Of maladies described in the Bible, deficiencies in sight and hearing, impairment or loss of the use of limbs, and variant forms of skin diseases are common.

In the OT, disease is often understood from a punitive standpoint as the result of transgression. Deut 28:22, for example, contains a list of diseases said to result from curses given for disobedience. The maladies resemble one another in that they are sudden, severe, epidemic, and fatal. The book of Job shows, however, that the OT is not uniform at this point. Job's disease is not the result of sin. Elsewhere, the descriptions of diseases given in the text indicate certain ailments that were disfiguring and repulsive in their effects (Pss 38:5; 39:9-11; Lev 26:39; Ezek 24:23; 33:10; Zech 14:22). Although the language employed apparently was intended as a warning to the transgressor, the imagery is still relevant to the perceived nature of the diseases.

Allusions to plague and PESTILENCE are also common; at least four outbreaks are recorded among the ancient Israelites during their wilderness wanderings (Num 11:33; 14:37; 16:46; 25:9). Further references to PLAGUES are found in 2 Sam 24:15, 2 Chr 21:14, Ps 91:3, Jer 21:9, and 42:17. Other examples of disease in the OT are included in the narration of the death of prominent individuals: King Asa suffered from diseased feet for two years before his death (2 Chr 16:12-13); Uzziah suffered from LEPROSY (2 Chr 26:21); Jehoram died from a painful intestinal ailment. (2 Chr 21:18-19).

In the NT, diseases are most often described in relation to the healing ministry of Jesus and the apostles. Many kinds of maladies were encountered and cured, such as blindness (Mark 8:22-26; 10:46-52), leprosy (Luke 17:11-19), lameness (Acts 3:6-10; 14:8-10) and paralysis (Matt 9:2-7; Mark 2:3-12; Luke 5:18-25). Compared with other NT writings, the Lukan materials exhibit a greater interest in the precise portrayal of illness. For example, Peter's mother-in-law suffered from "a great fever" (Luke 4:38), and a leper is said to be "full of leprosy" (Luke 5:12). According to some scholars, this Lukan tendency results from the author's profession as a physician. The penal understanding of sickness survived into NT times, but was significantly modified by the teaching of Jesus (John 9) whose first recorded sermon indicates that his earthly ministry was closely tied to the needs of the frail and feeble of body and spirit (Luke 4:18-27).

The Bible provides little information on the treatment of diseases from a medical point of view. In Hebrew history, it is difficult to establish the existence of any state of medical science or a proper order of medical practitioner. The therapeutics that are reported apparently correspond to ancient procedures, as illustrated by the treatment of ailments through local application (Isa 1:6; Jer 8:22; 51:8) and the use of wine and oil (Luke 10:34). A number of hygienic precepts, however, occur in the Pentateuch, including laws regarding personal and communal sanitation. The priests were responsible for declaring the diagnosis of "leprosy" (a generic term including a variety of skin diseases) and, in the case of restoration of health, also the freedom from "leprosy" (Lev 13–14). The Book of Leviticus reflects the religious nature of disease and healing in the OT. The priests were important figures in customs related to disease and healing. Prayers like Ps 6 also indicate that ancient Israel's cult included rituals associated with illness.

In the OT, restoration of health with intervention attributed to the healing of God was somewhat unusual, with most cases clustering around the period of the Exodus and the ministries of Elijah and Elisha. Recovery from leprosy, for example, in the cases of Miriam (Num 12:9-16) and Naaman (2 Kgs 5:8-14) appear to have been miraculous. The son of the widow of Zarephath was raised from the dead by Elijah (1 Kgs 17:17-24), while the same miracle is attributed to Elisha with the son of the Shunammite woman (2 Kgs 4:1-37). In another period, Jeroboam's suddenly palsied hand was healed (1 Kgs 13:4-6) and the recovery of Hezekiah is attributed directly to God (2 Kgs 20:1-11).

The miracles of healing recorded in the OT are few compared to those of Christ in the NT. In the combined narratives of the four Gospels, well over twenty stories of healing of individuals occur. Immediate restoration of health was bestowed in cases where recovery appeared unlikely or problematic. Although related to his compassion for the sufferers, Christ's miracles of healing were not fundamentally different in purpose from other MIRACLES. The miracle stories frequently revealed a christological purpose (Mark 10:46-52; Matt 9:1-8; John 20:30-31). The restoration of the sick formed a part of subsequent apostolic practice as evidenced by several accounts in Acts (3:1-11; 9:33-34, 36-41; 20:9-12).

See also BLINDNESS; CLEAN/UNCLEAN; LEPROSY; MIRACLES; PEACE; PESTILENCE; PLAGUES.

Bibliography. R. K. Harrison, "Disease" and "Healing, Health," *IDB*; E. V. Hulse, "The Nature of Biblical 'Leprosy' and the Use of Alternative Medical Terms in Modern Translations of the Bible," *PEQ* 107 (1975): 87-105; G. J. Wenham, *The Book of Leviticus*, NICOT.

—W. H. BELLINGER, JR.

• **Disgrace.** *See* SHAME

• **Dishonor.** *See* SHAME

• **Diviner/Diviners.** *See* MAGIC AND DIVINATION; ORACLE

• **Divinity of Jesus.** Controversy over the identity and role of JESUS of Nazareth erupted during his three-year public ministry and has continued to the present. Was Jesus the Christ of OT promise and expectation, or was he but a misguided zealot and messianic pretender? The NT makes numerous christological claims for Jesus (cf. John 1:1; 20:28; Rom 9:5; Titus 2:13; Heb 1:8). How can these claims be adjudicated?

Liberal scholars sought by critical study to show that the synoptic Gospels present a merely human Jesus, and that the fourth Gospel and Pauline epistles superimpose a supernatural Christ upon the primitive data. In a sketch of Christianity's beginnings, W. Bousset postulated that Palestinian Jewish Christians revered Jesus only as "Master," but that under the influence of Hellenic savior-cults a pre-Pauline gentile community declared Jesus to be supernatural and worshipped him as Lord. R. Bultmann embellished this notion that NT CHRISTOLOGY is not grounded in the view of Jesus or his disciples, but rather in the theological creativity of the early church. Dispensing almost entirely with any reliable historical portrait of Jesus, he regarded the Gospels as a literary myth aiming to symbolize only an existential experience of new being.

Conservative scholars replied that Paul's theology has its background in Judaism, not Hellenism, and that the messianic claims were evoked by Jesus' life and work; his self-affirmation encompasses key elements of the major christological titles and includes the "I am" declarations of John's Gospel.

C. F. D. Moule adduces decisive evidence that NT christology develops what Jesus and his early followers affirmed. Going back to the primitive Palestinian church is the prayer "Our Lord, come" (1 Cor 16:22; Aramaic, *marana tha*). The term "Master" (*mar*) was used not simply of a human master or rabbi but, as Qumran scrolls attest, of God as well. The Corinthian passage has divinity in view, Moule notes, for one does not "call upon a dead rabbi to 'come.' " Moreover, independently of Hellenic cults, Jews had precedent in the LXX for use of the term "Lord" (*Kurios*).

Jesus' person, teaching, and works, given in the context of OT prophecy, evoked the messianic claims in his behalf. The resurrection of the crucified Jesus supplied the crowning attestation of his divine sonship.

Liberal theologians located Jesus' "divinity" in his unity of purpose with the Father, but perfect moral obedience was God's creational intention for all humankind. The Gospels focus on the divinity implicit in his forgiveness of sins, his miracles, his claim to equal honor with God, his singular entry and exit from the world and coming role as judge of the human race. The NT affirms on the basis of apostolic revelation that Jesus Christ is the divine agent in creation, in redemption, and in the final judgment of humankind and the nations.

See also CHRISTOLOGY; JESUS; LORD IN THE NEW TESTAMENT; MESSIAH/CHRIST; SON OF GOD; SON OF MAN.

Bibliography. O. Cullmann, *The Christology of the New Testament;* I. H. Marshall, *The Origins of New Testament Christology;* C. F. D. Moule, *The Origin of Christology.*

—CARL F. H. HENRY

• **Divorce.** The Bible does not provide a complete and systematic discussion of divorce or MARRIAGE. Texts such as Mal 2:14-16 and Matt 19:6 indicate that divorce is displeasing to God and a violation of what he intended marriage to be (cf. Gen 1:26-27; 2:24). Even so, divorce occurred in biblical times and various OT texts attempted to regulate it.

In the ancient world divorce was the prerogative of the husband since women could not initiate divorce proceedings. Still, the legislation regarding divorce in the OT is primarily intended to protect the woman by either granting or prohibiting divorce. Exod 21:7-11 and Deut 21:10-14 allow a woman to leave a marriage relationship in which she is not provided for or has been rejected. Conversely, Deut 22:13-19 and 22:28-29 prohibit divorce in situations where a woman has been dishonored.

Another concern of OT texts dealing with divorce is the purity of Israel. Deut 24:1-4 recognizes that divorce was occurring and prohibits a woman who has been divorced and remarried from going back to her first husband. Such laxity was viewed as detestable (note, however, 2 Sam 3:14-16; Jer 3:1). Ezra 10:2-17 describes a surprising incident in which divorce is ordered for men who had married foreign wives and were being influenced by idolatrous practices (cf. Neh 13:23f.).

Clearly the OT views divorce as wrong, but the writers view as more important both the protection of the woman from abuse and the purity of Israel's relation with God.

The NT treats divorce in five texts, and all of them are summaries and adaptations of the teaching of Jesus. Three of the texts (Matt 5:32; Luke 16:18; and 1 Cor 7:10) are brief statements of the conclusion drawn in a longer discussion between Jesus and the Pharisees recorded in Matt 19:1-12 and Mark 10:1-12.

All five accounts reject the legitimacy of divorce, but there are differences of wording in each text. The most important differences are: Matthew's inclusion of an "exception" clause permitting divorce and remarriage for "unchastity" (5:32; 19:9); and Mark's extension of the saying about adultery to include a woman who divorces her husband and marries another (10:12). The sequence of the OT quotations and the words "command" and "allowed" are also different in Matt 19:4-8 and Mark 10:3-8.

Both Matthew and Mark say the Pharisees "tested" Jesus by asking him about divorce. The form of the question in Matthew stems from a rabbinic debate over the interpretation of the words "some indecency" (literally "the nakedness of a thing") in Deut 24:1. The conservative school of Shammai focused on the word "nakedness" and interpreted the law as saying that a man could divorce his wife only for unchastity. The more liberal school of Hillel focused on the word "thing" and taught that a man could divorce his wife for any reason, for example, even if she spoiled a dish.

Why the question of the Pharisees was a test or a trap for Jesus is not immediately clear. No doubt the Pharisees knew that Jesus would take a strong stance against divorce, but the test seems to have as much to do with *where* Jesus' statement was made as what was said. Both Matthew and Mark report that this discussion took place across the Jordan. This would place Jesus in the territory of Herod Antipas who beheaded John the Baptist for saying it was not lawful for Herod to marry his brother's wife. The Pharisees' test of Jesus is an attempt to get him to speak out against divorce in Herod's realm and possibly suffer the same fate as John the Baptist. Jesus rejects the legitimacy of divorce, but he directs the attention of his hearers more to God's intention for marriage.

The "exception" clause in Matthew has caused debate with regard to both its origin and its meaning. Even though there are good reasons for believing that the "exception" clause comes from Jesus, the majority of scholars would argue that Matthew has added these words to Jesus' absolute prohibition of divorce. More important is the meaning of the Greek word translated "unchastity" which may include "adultery," "prostitution," "incest," or "any sexual sin.'' The meanings ''any sexual sin'' and ''incest'' are likely possibilities in Matt 5:32 and 19:9 (the meaning ''adultery'' would make Matt 5:32 redundant and the meaning ''sexual unfaithfulness during engagement'' is unlikely). If the meaning is ''any sexual sin,'' Jesus would be agreeing with the school of Shammai. The most likely meaning, however, is ''incest'' (cf. Acts 15:20, 29 [which are based on Lev 17:10–18:29] and 1 Cor 5:1). If ''incest'' is the correct meaning, the ''exception'' clause is not really an exception to the prohibition of divorce. Rather, the statement recognizes that illicit marriages should not be continued.

Paul refers to Jesus' prohibition of divorce, expecting that Christian marriage partners will not divorce. If they should separate, they are to remain single and seek reconciliation (1 Cor 7:10-11). But Paul introduced a ''second exception'' for divorce in a circumstance that Jesus did not address. In 1 Cor 7:12-15 Paul deals with the problem of Christians being married to unbelievers. As long as the unbeliever is content to remain in the marriage relationship, divorce is unacceptable. If the unbelieving spouse chooses to leave, however, the Christian ''is not bound,'' presumably meaning that divorce is permissible. As in Ezra, one's relation with God takes priority over the marriage relation. Whether remarriage is also permissible is not explicit.

In summation, divorce in the Bible is always a violation of God's intention and, therefore, involves sin. Jesus' strong teaching against divorce, however, is not to be viewed as a new legalism. Priority must be given to relation with God and to protection from abuse. Nor is divorce the unforgivable sin. The focus on the necessity of forgiving others (Matt 18:33) just before the discussion of divorce in Matt 19 is hardly coincidental. Divorce is an almost unthinkable option for Christians, but where it occurs, grace must be shown to help people achieve wholeness.

See also ADULTERY IN THE NEW TESTAMENT; ADULTERY IN THE OLD TESTAMENT; FAMILY; MARRIAGE IN THE NEW TESTAMENT; MARRIAGE IN THE OLD TESTAMENT; WOMEN IN THE NEW TESTAMENT; WOMEN IN THE OLD TESTAMENT.

Bibliography. R. H. Charles, *The Teaching of the New Testament on Divorce;* J. A. Fitzmyer, ''The Matthean Divorce Texts and Some New Palestinian Evidence,'' *TS* 37 (1976): 197-226; M. Kysar and R. Kysar, *The Asundered: Biblical Teachings on Divorce and Remarriage;* W. F. Luck, *Divorce and Remarriage: Recovering the Biblical View;* D. W. Shaner, *A Christian View of Divorce according to the Teachings of the New Testament*; B. Vawter, ''Divorce and the New Testament,'' *CBQ* 39 (1977): 528-42.

—KLYNE R. SNODGRASS

• **Donkey.** *See* ASS

• **Dorcas.** [dor'kuhs] Dorcas is the transliteration of a Gk. word meaning ''gazelle.'' According to Acts 9:36-42, a charitable disciple named Dorcas (Tabitha in Aramaic) is raised from death by the prayers of PETER. The news of Dorcas's resurrection caused many to believe throughout JOPPA, a seaport town populated mostly by Greeks in NT times. This story closely resembles that of Jesus' raising the daughter of Jairus (Mark 5:35-43), in which Jesus says, ''Talitha cumi'' (Mark 5:41). Peter says, ''Tabitha, arise.'' Before performing his miracle, Jesus sends the crowd away; similarly Peter dismisses everyone from the room where Dorcas lies dead. Some scholars suggest that both stories are offshoots of the OT resurrection stories of 1 Kgs 17:17-24 and 2 Kgs 4:18-37. Dorcas is one of several women in Luke-Acts praised for good deeds.

—JOE E. BARNHART

• **Dothan.** [doh'thuhn] Biblical Dothan, located ca. sixty mi. north of Jerusalem on the watershed road along the ridge of the central hill country, dominated a fertile agricultural plain (PLATE 13). Its tell with an upper surface of ten acres rises almost 200 ft. above the surrounding plain. A series of archaeological excavations was undertaken by Joseph P. Free for Wheaton College between 1953 and 1960 to clarify the cultural remains of this important site in the tribal area of MANASSEH. The excavations have identified at least eleven strata of what appears to be a continuous occupation from Chalcolithic (ca. 3300 B.C.E.) to Hellenistic times. Biblical references to the site are limited. Joseph's search for his brothers ended with his sale to the Egypt-bound Ishmaelite caravan in the vicinity of Dothan (Gen 37). During the period of the Israelite monarchy, Dothan was fortified because of its strategic location on a major regional road. A punitive raid by the Syrian army was directed at Dothan as a result of Elisha's surveillance and reporting of Syrian army maneuvers (2 Kgs 6:13-14). The Book of Judith mentions Dothan three times in its description of Holofernes' campaign (3:9; 4:6; 7:3).

The original settlement at Dothan near the end of the Chalcolithic period is represented by limited ceramic remains and probably was an unfortified agricultural settlement on the edge of its broad fertile plain. During the Early Bronze Age, however, Dothan became a large urban center with walls four m. thick with segments preserved to two meters height. Two settlement strata have been identified with the Middle Bronze Age. Middle Bronze Age defenses appear to have continued in use during the Late Bronze Age when finds, especially related to tomb burials, reflect a period of prosperity. Excavation of Iron II remains have identified four occupational strata. A large public building, possibly an administrative center of the tenth-ninth centuries, was destroyed by fire, probably during the Aramaean invasion. The second occupational phase saw the rebuilding of this building with the addition of more storerooms at the end of the ninth century and its use to the beginning of the eighth century B.C.E. Structures of the eighth century were destroyed either during Tiglath-pileser III's conquest in 732 B.C.E. or during the fall of the Israelite Kingdom in 721 B.C.E. As a part of the Assyrian province, the town was rebuilt and for a short time from the end of the eighth to the beginning of the seventh century B.C.E. the population maintained close Assyrian affinities that are reflected in the cultural remains. A small Hellenistic settlement was established on the mound's summit. Roman remains are scant. At a much later period in Mameluke times, a large administrative center with possibly six courts and 150 rooms was built on the mound.

Bibliography. J. P. Free, ''The Excavation of Dothan,'' *BA* 19 (1956): 43-48; *BASOR* 131 (1953): 16-20; 135 (1954): 14-20; 139 (1955): 3-9; 143 (1956): 11-17; 147 (1957): 36-37; 152 (1958): 10-18; 156 (1959): 22-29; 160 (1960): 6-15; ''The Seventh Season of Excavation at Dothan,'' *ADAJ* 6-7 (1962): 117-20; D. Ussishkin, ''Dothan,'' *EAEHL*.

—GEORGE L. KELM

• **Doubting Thomas.** *See* THOMAS

• **Doxology.** *See* CURSE AND BLESSING; WORSHIP IN THE NEW TESTAMENT; WORSHIP IN THE OLD TESTAMENT

• **Drachma.** *See* COINS AND MONEY; MONEY

• **Dragon.** *See* TIAMAT

• **Dress.** Garments worn in biblical times remained rather simple and remarkably unchanged during the entire period. From its opening references to leaves (Gen 3:7) and animal skins (Gen 3:21) as body coverings, the Bible goes on to mention a variety of objects for dress. Some articles were worn for usefulness, others for decoration, and others for special occasions. The Bible refers to specific articles of dress, but usually does not describe them with any great detail. Therefore, ancient pictures from tomb walls in Egypt or from stone carvings upon walls or statues in Mesopotamia give us the best depictions. Very few items of clothing have been recovered by archaeologists because the fabrics and fibers tend to decompose over so long a time.

Materials used to make clothing varied. Garments were constructed of wool (Lev 13:47; Deut 22:11), linen (Lev 16:4; 28:42; Jer 13:1; Mark 14:51-52), leather (2 Kgs 1:8), silk (Ezek 16:10, 13), and coarse animal hair (Matt 3:4). Flax and cotton from Egypt were used, too. Garments usually were loose-fitting and flowing.

Five basic articles of clothing were worn by both men and women: (1) outer garment; (2) undergarments; (3) belt, sash, or girdle; (4) footwear; and (5) headgear. Mosaic Law prohibited men from wearing women's clothes and vice versa (Deut 22:5). But the difference in clothes between the sexes was not style. Women's apparel was distinguished by its finer and more colorful materials, sometimes the presence of a veil (Gen 24:65; 38:14), and probably the use of a special headdress.

The outer garment worn by both sexes was long, probably sleeveless "mantle," "robe," or "cloak." Worn on top of everything else, this was the garment torn or "rent" by someone in great distress (Job 1:20; 2:12). It was often decorated with tassels (Num 15:38) or fringes (Luke 8:44). As the outer layer, this mantle could be put to good use. Sometimes it was used to carry things (Exod 12:34; Ruth 3:15; Hag 2:12). At night it was used as a blanket to cover the bodies of the poor and homeless exposed to the cold desert air (Deut 24:12-13; also Jer 43:12). Mantles of distinction were worn by certain individuals as a sign of their office. Kings (Jonah 3:6; Acts 12:21) and prophets (1 Kgs 19:13, 19; 2 Kgs 2:8, 13-14; Zech 13:4; Mark 1:6) are mentioned most prominently.

Courtesy of the Eisenberg Museum of Biblical Archaeology, Southern Baptist Theological Seminary.

Clothespins or stick pins used to hold garments together.

An undergarment worn by both sexes was a sleeved "tunic," "shirt," or "coat," which was next to the skin and fit over the head from the shoulders down to the knees or even the ankles (Gen 37:3, 31-33; Matt 10:10; Luke 6:29). The soldiers who crucified Jesus cast lots for his tunic (John 19:23).

Men also used a "linen garment" which is mentioned several times (Judg 14:12-13; Prov 31:24; Isa 3:23; in Mark 14:51-52 and 15:46 as a modesty drape). Another undergarment worn by males fit next to the skin as a "loincloth" or "waistcloth" (2 Kgs 1:8; Isa 11:5; Jer 13:1).

A "belt," "sash," or "girdle" gathered the clothes together at the waist. Made of folded cloth, it could serve as a money belt (Matt 10:9; Mark 6:8) or a sword carrier (Judg 3:16; 1 Sam 25:13).

Courtesy of the Eisenberg Museum of Biblical Archaeology, Southern Baptist Theological Seminary.

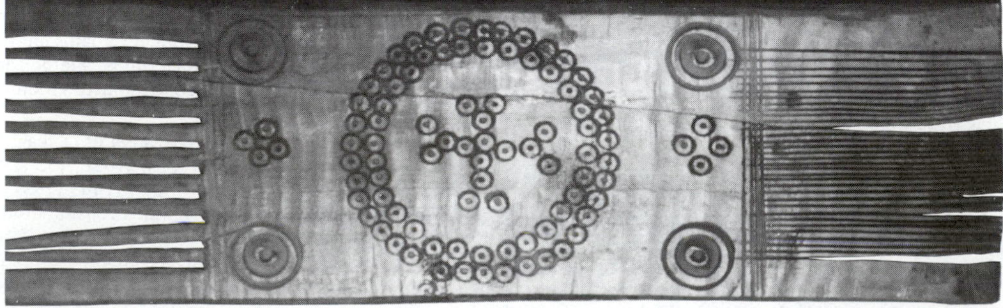

A comb.

Footwear consisted of sandals made of leather with thongs wrapped around the ankle and calf (2 Chr 28:15; Luke 15:22). Women also wore shoes (Cant 7:1; Ezek 16:10).

Headgear is not described in detail. Women sometimes wore a special "headdress" (Isa 3:20) or "turban" (Isa 3:23). Priests wore a special "turban" as well (Exod 28:36-38) along with many other special garments (cf. Exod 28).

Bibliography. J. M. Myers, "Dress," *IDB*; J. B. Pritchard, *ANEP*; C. de Wit, "Dress," *IBD*.

—DONALD W. GARNER

• **Drunkenness.** A state brought about by the excessive use of alcohol.

To the ancient Israelites, wine was a gift from God that had the ability to "gladden the heart" (Ps 104:14-15). The excessive use of the product, however, led to drunkenness, which was roundly condemned by both Testaments.

Proverbs warned that drunkards would be reduced to poverty (Prov 21:17; 23:21) and that their eyes would "see strange things" and their minds "utter perverse things" (Prov 23:33). Drunkenness was neither becoming nor appropriate for a child of God (Rom 13:13; 1 Pet 4:3; Gal 5:21), and no drunkard would inherit the KINGDOM OF GOD. Wine was addicting and caused a false sense of well-being (Prov 23:29-35).

People in leadership positions were to give particular attention to sobriety. Priests and prophets who were "confused with wine" erred in vision and stumbled when giving judgment (Isa 28:7). Lemuel's mother taught him that kings were not to drink wine or strong drink lest they "forget what has been decreed and pervert the rights of all the afflicted" (Prov 31:4-5). In the selection process for bishops, drunkards were to be eliminated (2 Tim 3:3; Titus 1:7).

NOAH and LOT are examples of individuals who were taken advantage of while in a drunken state (Gen 9:20-24; 19:32-36). King Elah was killed while drunk and unable to defend himself (1 Kgs 16:8-10). Ahasuerus, under the influence of alcohol, deposed his queen and set in motion a series of events that led to a major change in his household and government (Esther).

Further advice from Lemuel's mother suggested that those who were dying or in "bitter distress" might drink to "remember their misery no more" (Prov 31:6-7).

Drunkenness is used symbolically to describe a JERUSALEM that has not remained faithful to God (Ezek 23:33).

See also FOOD.

—WILMA ANN BAILEY

• **Dualism.** Belief that the world (or universe) is caused or controlled by two radically conflicting principles or powers, e.g., good and evil, spirit and matter, or the like. The two opposing elements may be coeternal, as Ahura Mazda and Ahriman in later Zoroastrianism; one may evolve or emanate from the other, as the Demiurge from the Boundless One in early Christian Gnosticism; or one may be destined to be overcome by the other in a final cataclysmic struggle, as the demonic empires by the rule of God in Jewish and Christian apocalypticism (Dan 7:11-14; Rev 20:1-15). Dualisms usually perceive the created components in their universe (nature, humankind, society, governments, etc.) as suffering from or reflecting within themselves the warfare of the cosmic powers. However, paradox as such, and duality or polarity (male and female, light and dark, sacred and profane, good and bad, etc.) do not of themselves constitute dualism, though dualistic thought may express itself in such terminology.

Dualism contrasts with *monism* and *pluralism*. None of these concepts can be considered descriptive exactly of classical biblical religion and its fundamental emphasis on both human freedom and the sovereignty of a transcendent and gracious creator God. It was precisely the harsh imperial suppressions of this freedom and their manifest challenge to divine sovereignty—as suffered by the Jews in Palestine under the Seleucids (second century B.C.E.) and by Jews and Christians under Rome (first and early second centuries C.E.)—that are reflected in the apocalyptic dualism of Daniel and Revelation and in many of the writings from Qumran (the Dead Sea Scrolls). The purpose of apocalyptic writing, however, is to assure the reader that the dualism to which it gives expression will finally be overcome.

Early Christian Gnostic dualism, on the other hand—as targeted by polemical citations against it in the NT (e.g., 1 Tim 4:1–5; 1 John 4:2-3) and in the early patristic writings, and now accessible directly in the texts from NAG HAMMADI —appears less concerned with historical crises than with salvation from the perceived evils of finite human existence as such. Gnostic speculation, which took many often quite different forms, typically posited an opposition between spirit and matter, the material created world being understood as the work of a lesser power or "demiurge" that had issued forth—emanated—from the true God and now arrogates to himself the divine role. The human creature is divided between a created self and a spiritual self, and salvation consists in the "knowledge" (*gnosis*) of how this came to be so and of how one's spirit may escape the world and find the way back to its divine source.

The rather special form of GNOSTICISM taught by the second century Christian bishop Marcion held that there are two gods—the creator god of the OT, and the god of Jesus Christ who delivers humankind from that other god and gives eternal life. Although Gnostic Christianity was rejected by the early church councils as incompatible with the classical biblical notion of the worth of creation, confirmed by the incarnation, Gnostic Christ-world dualisms survive in some of the more uncritical, often popular versions of Christian thought competing still today.

Ancient Near Eastern creation myths depicting CREATION dualistically, as a victory by one god over another—e.g., by the Babylonian Marduk over Tiamat (cognate to *tĕhôm,* "the deep," Gen 1:2) or the Canaanite Baal over the god Sea—have left clear traces in the creation vocabulary and imagery of the Bible (Ps 77:16[H 17]; Isa 51:9-10; Job 38:8-11; Mark 4:39). It is the more remarkable therefore that in the face of such traditions OT and NT thought emphatically rejected the relative intellectual convenience of dualistic worldviews in favor of the more difficult paradox of freedom and grace (Job 12:7-9; Isa 45:7; John 1:3; Rev 4:11).

See also MONOTHEISM; SATAN IN THE NEW TESTAMENT; SATAN IN THE OLD TESTAMENT.

Bibliography. U. Bianchi, "Dualism," *EncRel*; J. J. Collins, *The Apocalyptic Imagination*; H. Jonas, *The Gnostic Religion*; E. Pagels, *The Gnostic Gospels*; J. M. Robinson et al., eds., *The Nag Hammadi Library in English*.

—BRUCE T. DAHLBERG

• **Dung.** Animal or human excrement. The fecal matter was used for manuring (Ps 83:10; Luke 13:8) and for fuel (1 Kgs

14:10). Because it was refuse, dung generally was regarded as unclean. Intense destruction and humiliation could be indicated by referring to the remains as dung. Comparison to dung indicated worthlessness or vileness.

Dung as a fuel for cooking was more important in ancient Palestine than was its use as a fertilizer. The dung was gathered and dried prior to its being used as fuel. This heat source was possibly mixed with straw (Isa 25:10), either in a dunghill, in a dung pit, or in the stalls of the animals. Ezek 4:12-15 indicates the uncleanliness of cooking with human dung, but the acceptability of cooking with cow dung. Though not preferred, dung was probably a commonly utilized fuel because it was plentiful. The dung of an animal sacrificed to God was not to be used by humans. Instead, it was burned outside the camp, along with bones, skin, and intestines (Exod 29:14; Lev 4:11; 8:17; 16:27; Num 19:5). After the rebuilding of Jerusalem, the burning of the sacred refuse took place outside of the Dung Gate.

The reduction of a house to a dunghill (Ezra 6:11; Dan 2:5; 3:29) or a sanctuary to a latrine (2 Kgs 10:27) made the place unclean and unacceptable as a place of worship. Utter destruction is symbolized by bodies being like dung on the face of the earth (Jer 8:2; 9:22; 16:4; 25:33). Dung rubbed on the face showed humiliation and uncleanliness (Mal 2:3).

Paul considers all things to be but dung or refuse (Phil 3:7-8) by contrast with the knowledge of Christ.

See also CLEAN/UNCLEAN.

—ROBERT A. STREET, JR.

• **Dura-Europos.** [door'uh-yoor-oh'puhs] The ruins of Dura-Europos are on the west bank of the Euphrates River on the northern edge of the Syrian desert about halfway between Aleppo and Baghdad. About 300 B.C.E., a general of Seleucus I, king of the Syrian Empire, built a fortress city at the site of Dura, identified by some with the plain where Nebuchadrezzar erected an image for all to worship (Dan 3:1). The new city was named Europos after the hometown of Seleucus in Macedonia. Dura-Europos was abandoned in the third century C.E. and was not discovered until 1921. Systematic excavations were conducted on the site in 1922–1923 and 1928–1937. Among the significant finds here were a Jewish synagogue and a Christian church.

The synagogue was originally a private dwelling that served as a house of worship also. About 245 C.E. it was enlarged and made into a regular synagogue. About 253 this building was replaced by a new one. The sanctuary was about twenty-five by forty ft. in size. Entrance was from the east by a larger door on the right for men and a smaller door on the left for women. The absence of foot-rests on the benches between the doors and along the left wall suggests that they were for women. In the center of the west wall was a niche for the Ark of the Law. Beside it was the elder's seat.

The walls all had paintings from top to bottom. Above the niche for the Ark of the Law were paintings of either the temple or a shrine in which the Law was kept, the seven-branched candlestick, and Abraham's near sacrifice of Isaac. Other paintings on the walls portrayed events in the life of the Israelites throughout OT times. These paintings seem to illustrate the covenant relationship between God and Israel from Abraham throughout Israel's history to the fulfillment of the covenant in the messianic age to come.

The church at first was a private dwelling, a house church (cf. Phlm 2). According to writing on a wall, it was constructed in 232 or 233 C.E. Entrance was through a small vestibule into an inner courtyard. Around this court was a series of rooms. One was used as a Christian chapel. Later the chapel was enlarged by opening up two other rooms.

At the west end of the room first used as a chapel was a niche with a basin in it. If this basin were a baptistry, its small size suggests that the mode of baptism may have been pouring instead of immersion. Because immersion was the general practice of the early church, some think the basin was a martyr's tomb.

On the lower part of the wall near the niche was a painting which pictured Adam and Eve standing with a tree between them. Above it was a painting of the Good Shepherd with his flock and with a big ram on his shoulder. Together these two scenes evidently proclaim that sin and death came into human life through Adam and Eve, but that salvation comes through Jesus. Other murals, showing Jesus healing the paralytic (Mark 2:1-12) and his saving Peter from drowning (Matt 14:22-31), also depict Christ as Savior.

Bibliography. E. R. Goodenough, ''Judaism at Dura-Europos,'' *IEJ* 11/4 (1961): 161-70; ''The Paintings of the Dura-Europos Synagogue: Method and Its Application,'' *IEJ* 8/2 (1958): 69-79; M. I. Rostovtzeff et al., *Excavations at Dura-Europos: Final Reports.*

—VIRGIL FRY

• **E.** *See* SOURCE CRITICISM

• **Eagle.** A large bird of prey. The KJV renders the Hebrew noun *nešer* as eagle twenty-six times (plus the two times in Aramaic in Dan 4:30; 7:4). The RSV does likewise, except for Prov 30:17; Lam 4:19; and Hos 8:1, where it is translated vulture. *Nešer* is rendered by the LXX as *aetos,* and by the Vulgate as *aquila.* Although the Heb. word *nešer* may refer to an eagle or a vulture (the context dictates which is meant), it is the griffon vulture that is in mind in most of the biblical references.

The ambiguity of the word *nešer* is often attributed to the inability of the Hebrews to distinguish between the two birds, usually seen at great distances and heights. However, the ambiguity may not be the result of confusing eagles with vultures, but rather may originate in the Hebrews' interest in the birds' similarities. For example, both birds were notably similar in size, strength, and longevity, and in their magnificient flight, regal appearance, nesting patterns, and feeding habits.

Most biblical references employing the word *nešer* (except for Lev 11:13 and Deut 14:12) are metaphorical or illustrative. Some examples are: strength, ''my youth is renewed like the eagle's'' (Ps 103:5); royalty, ''a great eagle with powerful wings, long feathers and full plumage of varied colors'' (Ezek 17:3); tenderness, ''how I carried you on eagle's wings and brought you to myself'' (Exod 19:4-6); speed, ''like an eagle swooping down'' (Deut 28:49); and longevity, ''they will surely sprout wings and fly off to the sky like an eagle'' (Prov 23:5).

Bibliography. G. R. Driver, ''Birds in the Old Testament,'' *PEQ* 87 (1955): 5-20.

—ANTHONY M. TETROW

• **Earthquake.** Palestine has experienced destructive earthquakes in the past because the region is located in an area of several prominent tectonic structures. The rift of the Jordan Valley is a major seismic region capable of generating powerful earthquakes. The two major epicenters of Palestine lie in the Samaritan countryside around Nablus (biblical Shechem) and in the Jordan Valley at Jericho. In Palestine the evidence of collapses and subsequent abandonment resulting from earthquakes is attested at several sites (e.g., HAZOR and TEL DEIR 'ALLA). Earthquakes caused the destruction of structures. Following an earthquake, some cities were renovated while others were abandoned and served as community dumps. Rebuilding was always slow because of the depressed economic situation caused by the earthquake.

The natural force that is displayed in a seismic event terrifies people because it happens unexpectedly and because it threatens them with destruction. Such a phenomenon was considered a manifestation of the divine presence. The combination of thunderstorms and earthquakes was often associated with theophanies (Pss 18:7-14; 29:7-8; Isa 29:6). The revelation of Yahweh amidst thunder, clouds, lightning, and earthquakes evoked fear in the hearts of people and demonstrated that the forces of nature were at his disposal. Yahweh used the forces of nature to manifest himself to Israel and to declare that he was not identical with these natural phenomena; Yahweh was Lord of nature and he used these events to convey a message to his people.

Several earthquakes are mentioned in the Bible and in other historical records. (1) An earthquake at Mount SINAI occurred at the time Yahweh manifested himself to Israel during the establishment of the covenant between God and his people (Exod 19:18). (2) During an earthquake the ground opened and swallowed Korah and the other Levites who challenged Moses (Num 16:31-32). (3) An earthquake in the days of Saul helped his son Jonathan to gain a victory against the Philistines (1 Sam 14:15). (4) An earthquake in the days of Ahab was part of God's manifestation to Elijah at Mount Horeb (1 Kgs 19:11-12). (5) A great earthquake in the days of Uzziah was so powerful that it was remembered many generations later (Zech 14:5) and the prophet Amos began his ministry ''two years before the earthquake'' (Amos 1:1). (6) In 64 B.C.E. a strong earthquake struck Jerusalem causing considerable damage to the Temple and to the walls of the city. (7) In 31 B.C.E., when Herod the Great was king, a severe earthquake ''such a one as had not happened at any other time'' hit Galilee, although it was moderate in Jerusalem (*Ant* 15.5.2). (The Jewish historian Josephus estimated that about ten thousand people died.) (8) The earthquakes of 30 and 33 C.E. caused minor damage to Jerusalem and to the Temple. Either one of these two earthquakes could be associated with the earthquake that occurred at the crucifixion of Christ (Matt 27:51). (9) The earthquake that occurred at the resurrection of Christ (Matt 28:2) was probably an aftershock of the earthquake mentioned above. (10) The earthquake at Philippi contributed to the early release of Paul and Silas from prison (Acts 16:26).

Because an earthquake was considered a manifestation of the power of Yahweh, it was used often in prophetic and apocalyptic literature to portray the calamitous events associated with the judgment of Yahweh.

Bibliography. D. H. K. Amiran, ''A Revised Earthquake-Catalogue of Palestine,'' *IEJ* 1 (1950–1951): 223-42; 2 (1952):

48-62; K. W. Russell, "The Earthquake Chronology of Palestine and Northwest Arabia from the 2nd through the Mid-8th Century A.D.," *BASOR* 260 (Nov 1985): 37-59.

—CLAUDE F. MARIOTTINI

• **Easter.** Derived from *Eostur,* the Norse word for "spring," Easter refers to the Christian festival celebrating Jesus' resurrection. It is the most significant of all Christian festivals, since its celebration focuses upon the consummation of the redemptive act of God in the death/resurrection of Jesus Christ.

The Gospels indicate that the events culminating in the death of Jesus took place during the period of preparation for Passover, a Jewish festival which commemorated the EXODUS from Egypt, and which was celebrated on the evening of 14/15 Nisan. The Gospels indicate further that the death of Jesus occurred on a Friday, "the day before the sabbath" (Mark 15:42). The women to whom the announcement of Jesus' resurrection was first made brought spices "when the sabbath was past," and arrived at the tomb "very early on the first day of the week" (i.e., Sunday; Mark 16:1, 2). Hence, the first day of the week—the day of resurrection—early became a customary time for Christians to assemble for worship and homage to their risen Lord.

Yet while the resurrection was a central conviction, proclaimed and celebrated from the days of the earliest disciples of the risen Lord, there are very few references to an annual festival prior to 300 C.E. Such references as do occur relate to the Christian *Pascha* (Passover), with apparent primary emphasis upon the death of Jesus, in keeping with Passover imagery and terminology. By the fourth century, however *Pascha* clearly referred to celebration of both the death and resurrection of Jesus. According to Eusebius (ca. 260–ca. 340 C.E.), there was dispute as early as the mid-second century regarding the day of the week and of the year on which *Pascha* should be celebrated. Churches in Asia Minor (following the Johannine tradition that the death of Jesus occurred at the time of the slaying of the Passover lambs) celebrated the Christian *Pascha* on 14/15 Nisan, regardless of the day of the week on which this date might fall. Other churches (following the chronology of the synoptic Gospels, and with emphasis upon the Friday/Sunday—death/resurrection sequence of events) employed a different method for calculating the date of the annual festival.

Noting the discrepancy in Christian practice, the provincial Synod of Arles (314 C.E.) had deemed it desirable "that the *Pascha* of the Lord should be observed on one day and at one time throughout the world." The Council of Nicaea (325 C.E.) fixed the date of Easter as "the Sunday immediately following the so-called paschal moon, which happens on or first after the vernal equinox (March 21)." Accordingly, by our present calendar, Easter Sunday may occur as early as 21 March or as late as 25 April.

See also EXODUS; PASSOVER; RESURRECTION IN THE NEW TESTAMENT.

—RAYMOND HARGUS TAYLOR

• **Eating.** *See* FEASTS AND FESTIVALS; FOOD

• **Ebal, Mount.** [ee'buhl] At 940 m. above sea level, Mount Ebal stands taller than its sister mountain, Mount GERIZIM, which rises above the other side of SHECHEM (PLATES 3,13). According to Deut 11:29, Mount Ebal was the site where curses were to be proclaimed and Mount Gerizim was the site where blessings were to be voiced (cf. Josh 8:34). Some traditions considered Gerizim to be the "navel of the earth," while ignoring the taller Mount Ebal.

In October of 1982, Adam Zertal discovered a unique structure located 150 m. below the peak of Mount Ebal. The structure was rectangular (9.5 x 7.1 m.) and constructed out of unhewn stones. Although he originally perceived that he was dealing with an Iron Age farmhouse or watchtower, Zertal eventually decided that he had discovered an early Israelite cultic center. He was easily able to date the structure to Iron Age I on the basis of pottery sherds, scattered in quantity around the site. In addition, the team uncovered a circle of stones in which a fill layer of ash and animal bones was discovered. They also uncovered a rare Egyptian-style scarab with parallels to place it somewhere between the reigns of Ramses II (thirteenth century B.C.E.) and Ramses III (twelfth century B.C.E.).

The zoology department of Hebrew University in Jerusalem concluded that the bones came from young bulls, sheep, goats, and fallow deer which had been burnt in open flame fires with temperatures between 200 and 600 degrees centigrade. Coupled with the lack of remains from pigs, gazelles, and carnivores usually found in non-Israelite Iron Age sites, Zertal believed this was indicative of an Israelite altar. After reading in Exod 27:8 about the hollow interior commanded for the altar in the wilderness, he seemed certain that he had found an altar dating to the entry of the Israelites into Canaan. Upon discovering a ledge, approximately three feet below the top of the structure, he was convinced he had found a parallel to the altar in Exod 27:5. Finally, he argued that the use of the "*beth*" preposition in the Hebrew text of Josh 8:30 suggests that Joshua's altar (built after the fall of Ai) was not built on the top, but rather on the side of Mount Ebal.

Ahron Kempinski argues that Zertal is mistaken. He believes that the structure is representative of three phases of occupation and points to similar construction in a non-cultic Iron Age site at Giloh. He attributed the fill layer to debris from a destruction layer and contended that the intact pottery vessel inside the alleged altar suggested that the "altar" was, indeed, a storage area.

The arguments on either side are far from conclusive, so it seems best to remember Ebal as an important site in early Israel without authenticating the altar.

See also GERIZIM, MOUNT; SHECHEM.

Bibliography. A. Kempinski, "Joshua's Altar—An Iron Age I Watchtower," *BAR* (Jan/Feb 1986); A. Zertal, "Has Joshua's Altar Been Found on Mt. Ebal?" *BAR* (Jan/Feb 1985).

—JOHNNY L. WILSON

• **Ebionites, Gospel of.** [ee'bee-uh-nits] The *Gospel of the Ebionites* is a Jewish-Christian gospel quoted solely by the fourth century father Epiphanius. In his work, *Panarion* (often cited as *Haer*), a "medicine chest" of theological remedies for heresy, he quotes seven passages alleged to be from the *Gospel* (*Haer* 30.13.2-3; 30.13.4; 30.13.6 and 30.14.3; 30.13.7; 30.14.5; 30.16.5; 30.22.4).

Since the fragments are only found in Epiphanius, one wonders where he discovered this information. It has been suggested that he may have seen the work on one of his visits into the region east of the Jordan. He had the habit of depending upon sources for his writings, which are full of interesting and sometimes unique information. Since the fragments of this gospel are given in block quotations, and since their language often differs from the NT text being quoted, most scholars have accepted their authenticity.

The character of this material may be described as follows: (a) The *Gospel of the Ebionites* is reported by the Fathers to be an abridged and falsified MATTHEW, which Epiphanius erroneously called the "Gospel according to the Hebrews" or the "Hebrew Gospel" (*Haer* 30.3.7; 30.13.2); (b) the *Gospel* apparently did not contain a nativity narrative, but began, like MARK, with the appearance of JOHN THE BAPTIST; (c) it seems to have been written originally in Greek, adhering closely to the synoptic Gospels in many places; and (d) since it seems to be familiar with the synoptic tradition, it is to be dated no earlier than the second half of the second century.

The Ebionites, the alleged source of this gospel, were an early Jewish-Christian group remembered for their view that Jesus was "a mere man." They maintained Jewish practices, yet believed that Jesus was a prophet—a human being with no divine essence.

The remains of the *Gospel* do not reflect a strong Ebionitism, although that may be due to their fragmentary nature, or because Epiphanius was confused as to their provenance. The fragments show, however: that Jesus' appointment of disciples was for the leadership of the "congregation of Israel," that the "community" rejected animal sacrifice and espoused vegetarianism, that they held an adoptionist view of the baptism of Jesus, that the Aaronic parentage of John the Baptist was highlighted, and that they justified continuation of the practice of circumcision because Jesus himself was circumcised. These points show a theology and practice similar to that of the Jewish-Christianity described in the CLEMENTINE LITERATURE (*Homilies* and *Recognitions*). Whether that is Ebionite or not is open to serious questions pertaining to definitions of the sect.

The fragments list the names of eight disciples of Jesus, Matthew being the eighth; John the Baptist ate honey but not locusts (vegetarianism?); Jesus reportedly said, "I am come to do away with sacrifices, and if you do not cease sacrificing, the wrath of God will not cease from you"; at the PASSOVER Jesus did not partake because he would have had to eat meat.

The Greek text of the fragments demonstrates the same kind of textual tradition that formed the NT, but contrary to received opinion, the fragments do not show a special relationship to the Gospel of Matthew.

See also APOCRYPHAL GOSPELS; CLEMENTINE LITERATURE; HEBREWS, GOSPEL OF THE; NAZAREANS, GOSPEL OF THE.

Bibliography. G. A. Koch, "A Critical Investigation of Epiphanius' Knowledge of the Ebionites: A Translation and Critical Discussion of Panarion 30," *DA* 37 (Oct 1976): 2253-A; H. J. Schoeps, *Jewish Christianity*; P. Vielhauer, "Jewish-Christian Gospels," *New Testament Apocrypha*, ed. E. Hennecke and W. Schneemelcher.

—GLENN A. KOCH

• **Ebla.** [eb'luh] (Tell Mardikh). One of the largest and most important ancient sites in inner Syria consisting of a mound of some 140 acres about forty-two mi. south of Aleppo (PLATE 1). The site has been systematically excavated since 1964 by a team from the University of Rome under the direction of Paola Matthiae.

The History of Ebla. The excavations of Ebla reveal that the site was occupied from about 3500 B.C.E. (Chalcolithic) to the seventh century C.E. (Byzantine). Of the fourteen levels spanning this period only the four levels IIB1, IIB2, IIIA, and IIIB cover the whole site and represent Ebla's most prosperous and influential period (2600/2400–1600 B.C.E.).

(1) Level IIB1 (2600/2400 B.C.E.–2400/2250 B.C.E.). Though there is some debate over the dates for this period (Matthiae argues for the lower chronology, G. Pettinato and others the higher) we know more of the history and culture of this level than any other. Ebla reached its economic and political heights during this period with the population reaching perhaps as high as 260,000. A large palace complex covering the southern and western slopes of the acropolis was constructed featuring a large porticoed audience hall and a massive tower with stone-inlay stairway. In the administrative wing the royal archives have been uncovered consisting of thousands of cuneiform tablets. Also uncovered were lapis lazuli from Afghanistan, fragments of diorite and alabaster bowls from Egypt, wooden furniture, seal impressions, and small sculptures showing local adaptation of Mesopotamian art of the mid-third millennium B.C.E.

During this period Ebla was ruled by a king (*malikum*) in cooperation with the city "elders" (Sumerian AB x ÁŠ) who represented major family groupings. This king-elders grouping was also recognized in international relations, as evidenced by shipments of textiles sent from Ebla to other cities and addressed to both the king and elders. Under this coalition functioned a variety of officials and workers who performed their duties in the palace acropolis, the four quarters of the lower city, or the outlying network of dependent settlements. It is difficult to fix the boundaries of the kingdom of Ebla but at its height it probably controlled all of northwestern Syria from Hama in the south up to the Euphrates and Balikh rivers. Ebla's political power, however, was undermined by the military expeditions of Sargon and Naram-Sin of Akkad in southern Mesopotamia. Ebla finally fell to the kings of Akkad during the reign of Ibbi-Zikir around 2300 or 2250 B.C.E.

The religion of ancient Ebla was complex. There was the official cult with its three principal deities Kura, Adad, and Shamash. These deities, along with a god named Idakul, are mentioned frequently in documents which record sacrifices performed at the court. But to these must be added the deities of the popular cults which are known from the Eblaite personal names composed with the name of a god. These included such west Semitic gods as Baal, Damu, Lim, Malik, Rasap (Ugaritic Rashap), Kasalu (Ugaritic Koshar), and Kamish (the first-millennium Moabite deity), along with Mesopotamian deities such as Ishtar, Ishar, Dagan, Ada and Il or El. Local deities included the deified Balikh River, and Adamma and Ashtappi, whose names appear a millennium later in the Hurrian pantheon at Ugarit. Also mentioned are *dingir.a.mu* (Sumerian, "the god of my father"; cf. Genesis 43:23) and *dingir.en* (Sumerian, "the [personal] god of the ruler"). It is interesting that Baal does not appear in the official offering lists. This reflects quite a different situation from that at second-millennium Ugarit where Baal is dominant in the official cult. The regular cult of the gods required bread and drink offerings and animal sacrifices. Hymns were sung in honor of the gods and worship was presided over by priests and priestesses. Also attached to the cult were prophets called *mahhu* or *nabi'utum*. The royal family were patrons of the state gods partially underwriting the expenses of the cult.

Ancient Ebla's economy was, of course, predominantly agricultural, with linen (from flax) a very important product. Sheep raising rivaled the linen industry with flocks numbering more than 80,000 belonging to the king alone. Apart from the wool derived from their annual shearing, a large supply of meat was obtained from the 12,000 sheep butchered each year at Ebla.

Another source of income for Ebla was its control of supply routes bringing metals from the Anatolian plateau to the plains of Syria. Full-tin bronzes, gold and silver were the most important of these metals. Records indicate that during the reign of Ibbi-Zikir, Ebla's last king, 1000 pounds of silver and from ten to twelve pounds of gold were received each year. Ebla's trading partners included UGARIT and BYBLOS on the Syrian coast, CARCHEMISH and MARI along the Euphrates, Lagash and Nippur in Mesopotamia, and, to a lesser degree, Iran (Hamazi) and Egypt.

(2) Level IIB2 (2250–1900 B.C.E.). Following the destruction of the IIBl city a smaller settlement was rebuilt. This new occupation belonged to the Early Bronze IVB period and is mentioned in contemporary Mesopotamian sources. Because so little excavation has been done on this level not much can be said of the history and culture of this period. Evidently political power in the region shifted from Ebla to the city of Urshu.

(3) Level IIIA (1900–1800 B.C.E.). This level of occupation fits into the Middle Bronze I period when Amorites were gaining political power in many parts of the Near East. Ebla was rebuilt during this period with heavy fortifications, some of which still stand some twenty-two meters high along the eastern perimeter of the site. These ramparts, four city gates, the ring-shaped lower city and the central acropolis constituted the topography of Ebla. Also constructed in the period were the large Western Palace of the lower city and several of Ebla's major temples (temple D to Ishtar, Bl to Resheph, and N to Shamash). During this period Ebla was probably the most powerful city between Hama and Aleppo and had close ties with Anatolia and Palestine.

(4) Level IIIB (1800–1600 B.C.E.). At the beginning of this period Ebla became a vassal of Aleppo, ruled by Yarim-Lim I. The city, however, did not suffer destruction or attack and maintained a fairly aggressive building program. Structures raised during this period included Sanctuary B2 (probably related to the cult of royal ancestors), Royal Palace E in the north portion of the acropolis, and a royal burial ground constructed out of natural caves beneath the western palace. Two of these tombs (Tomb of the Princess and Tomb of the Lord of Goats) have yielded treasures of significant wealth. Sometime between 1650–1600 B.C.E. Ebla was conquered and destroyed probably as part of the Hittite invasion of Syria under Hattushili I or Murshili I. Ebla declined sharply after 1600 B.C.E., going through prolonged cycles of occupation and abandonment until well into the Byzantine period (500 C.E.).

The Tablets of Ebla. The cuneiform archives of Royal Palace G uncovered during the 1974–76 excavations provide valuable insight into the life and culture of Syria in the third millennium B.C.E. Over 17,000 pieces were found (including almost 2000 complete clay tablets) comprising about 4000 different texts. This corpus can be divided into at least four categories: (1) administrative texts recording expenditures and exchanges involving the palace and its personnel (almost 80% of the texts); (2) lexical texts for the scribes; (3) literary and religious texts; (4) texts bearing on the events of the day (mostly letters and decrees).

Most tablets were found fallen in the debris of two rooms of Royal Palace G, but in a way that makes it possible to reconstruct the original shelving arrangements. All are in the cuneiform script of the mid-third millennium B.C.E. and are written in either Sumerian (the principal written language of southern Mesopotamia in the third millennium) or a hitherto unknown semitic language conveniently labeled "Eblaite."

The archives cover a period corresponding to three dynastic generations totalling approximately forty years: Ar-Ennum, Ibrium, and Ibbi-Zikir. A few documents are connected with the reigns of two previous kings, Igrish-Halam and Irkab-Damu. The entire archive can be dated to approximately the middle of the twenty-fourth century.

There are approximately twenty literary texts, some written in Sumerian, others in Eblaite. Among the latter are equal numbers of original compositions and translations from Sumerian. These texts, along with the Eblaite letters and juridical documents, comprise some of the oldest texts in a SEMITIC LANGUAGE. Of special interest to those who study the history of languages are the approximately 200 lexical texts. These consist of long classified lists of the Sumerian words for objects, animals, birds, fishes, professions and occupations, types of personal names, and geographical names. These Sumerian words were rearranged by the scribes of Ebla who then often added the semitic Eblaite translation. In this manner three large dictionaries of 1500 words were compiled with Sumerian terms and their Eblaite equivalents.

Eblaite as a language is difficult to classify and remains a matter of considerable discussion. Grammatically, Eblaite is perhaps closest to Old Akkadian, the semitic language utilized by the Akkadian Dynasty in southern Mesopotamia, documented slightly later than Eblaite. Some grammatical forms, however, bear closer resemblance to Arabic or South Arabian. Lexically, Eblaite seems closer to the west semitic languages of Ugaritic, Hebrew and Aramaic. Eblaite terms with west semitic cognates include: *'arzatum* (cedar), *badalum* (merchant), *kinnarum* (lyre), and *urpum* (window).

Ebla and the Bible. The importance of Ebla's discovery and excavation for biblical studies is still unfolding. Initial claims about the light which the tablets and remains of Ebla would shed on the early stages of biblical history and culture appear to have been exaggerated. No biblical personalities or events can be identified in the tablets and the term Ebla itself occurs nowhere in the OT. There are in the tablets personal names similar to those found in the Bible (e.g., Ishmael) but these names are also known elsewhere in the Near East. The proposal that the Israelite god Yahweh could be found in the Ebla texts is also now largely rejected. The supposed form *ya,* which occurs as an element in Eblaite personal names, cannot be confidently linked to the Israelite deity and is now understood as a well-established hypocoristic ending in semitic and nonsemitic names. Evidence adduced for the anointing of kings at Ebla in the style of the Bible has been more recently discredited as a misreading of the Ebla tablets. Early claims that the texts mentioned such biblical cities as Jerusalem, Sodom, and Gomorrah also have yet to be demonstrated. Eblaite, though a semitic language, is not so close to biblical Hebrew as once thought and its value for Hebraic studies is still to be determined. To date the value of Ebla's discovery for biblical studies is of a more general nature, serving to clarify further the culture and history of the Syria which was to become Israel's northern neighbor. The urban culture of Proto-Syrian Ebla at approximately 2300 B.C.E. has no parallel outside of Sumer and is the only one known in southwest Asia outside of southern Mesopotamia for the third millennium B.C.E.

Bibliography. A. Archi, "The Epigraphic Evidence from Ebla

and the Old Testament,'' *Bib* 60 (1979): 556-66 and ''Further concerning Ebla and the Bible,'' *BA* 44 (1981): 145-54; S. G. Beld et al., *The Tablets of Ebla: Concordance and Bibliography*; P. Fronzaroli, *The Ebla Language and Semitic Linguistics*; P. Matthiae, *Ebla: An Empire Rediscovered*; L. Vigano, ''Literary Sources for the History of Palestine and Syria: The Ebla Tablets,'' *BA* (1984): 6-16; H. Weiss, ed., *Ebla to Damascus: Art and Archaeology of Ancient Syria*.

—STEPHEN M. HOOKS

• OUTLINE OF ECCLESIASTES •

The Book of Ecclesiastes

I. Theme of the Book: Human Life is Vain (1:1-11)
II. Illustrations of the Theme (1:12–2:26)
  A. Wisdom is vanity (1:12-18)
  B. Pleasure and labor are vanity (2:1-11)
  C. Life itself is vanity (2:12-17)
  D. Vanity itself is vanity (2:18-24)
  E. Religion too is vanity (2:25-26)
III. A Time for All Things (3:1-15)
IV. The Fate of Righteous and Wicked is the Same (3:16–4:16)
V. The Author's Wisdom Collection (5:1–11:10)
VI. Old Age and Death Portrayed (12:1-8)
VII. Conclusion (12:9-14)

• **Ecclesiastes, Book of.** [i-klee′zee-as″teez] One of five *Megilloth,* or ''festival scrolls,'' read in the synagogue during the Festival of Tabernacles.

The author of the text, though not named, is called ''Qoheleth'' (''speaker in an assembly''; 1:1-2, 12; 7:27-28; 12:8-10), a Hebrew term which was translated into Greek as *ekklēsiastēs* (''member of an assembly'') and rendered via the Vulgate into the English title for the work, ''Ecclesiastes.'' Early rabbinic tradition attributed the book to Solomon, since the author is described in the superscription as ''the son of David, king in Jerusalem'' (1:1) and later in the text as the ''king over Israel in Jerusalem'' (1:12). The reputation for wisdom that was associated with Solomon by popular tradition in Israel (1 Kgs 3:12) thus gave a certain authority to the book, as it also did for works such as Proverbs, the *Psalms of Solomon,* the Wisdom of Solomon, and the Song of Solomon, and ultimately assisted Ecclesiastes in its quest for acceptance into the canon.

Several elements of the book suggest that the work in fact derives from an anonymous wisdom teacher (cf. 12:9) during the third century B.C.E., and thus had only a short history prior to its canonization. The text was composed in a late, transitional form of the Hebrew language that reflects numerous pre-mishnaic idioms, Aramaisms, and Persian loanwords. Early manuscripts of the text are relatively free of the type of errors that arise from the transmission of texts over a period of several generations, and there are few divergencies between the Hebrew text and other early versions, including the quite literal translation found in the LXX. Finally, the concerns of the writing are those of the postexilic period, and the author appears well acquainted with thought patterns that were common to the Hellenistic age.

It is doubtful that the text comes from a single author, since several passages reflect redactional tendencies, such as repetitions, contradictions, and irregularities, and since third-person references to the author occur throughout the writing (1:1-2a; 7:27; 12:8-10). These references probably represent additions by a student of the text or, more likely, the concerns of divergent elements within the Jewish wisdom schools of the period, many of which were located in Alexandria, Phoenicia, and Jerusalem. The rationalistic approach of the book and its attack upon traditional religious structures caused anxiety for the adherents of ancient Hebrew orthodoxy, and despite contemporary claims of Solomonic authorship and the acceptance of the book by the sectarian community at Qumran, the rabbinic school of Shammai refused to recognize the book as holy scripture through the end of the first century C.E. Subsequent debate concerning the status of Ecclesiastes in its relationship to scripture continued among Jewish authorities well into the second century (*Yad* 3.5).

With respect to literary form, the book is a compilation of negative exhortations and two-part proverbs, the organization of which is parallel to the genre of early Egyptian ''royal testaments.'' There is a high degree of verbal repetition, and individual discussions are linked through catchword associations. The book contains a marked prologue (1:2-11) and an epilogue (12:9-14), the latter of which probably is not original to the work. The body of the text contains three major sections, which are broadly oriented around the themes of vanity (1:12–6:9), wisdom (6:10–11:6), and age (11:7–12:8). While numerous attempts have been undertaken to determine unifying or cohesive structures and literary patterns within the work, no clear rhetorical schema is readily apparent for the book.

As the primary focus of the book, Qoheleth seeks through empirical observation and deliberation to determine the meaning and role of humanity in existence. There is no appeal to any recognized authority, whether tradition, scripture, or divinity, as a justification for the observations or arguments found in the work. Instead, the author relies upon the perception of life provided by cumulative experience and the self-perceived superiority of personal wisdom. The human situation is the subject of great skepticism, and in many respects the book reflects a form of early existentialism that is without parallel elsewhere in the Bible.

The reader is led through an examination of life that proceeds from and returns to the realization that ''all is vanity'' (1:2; 12:8). The pursuits and toils of humanity, whether for pleasure (2:1-11), wisdom (2:12-17), or wealth (5:10-17), have no ultimate value. Wickedness resides in the places of justice (3:16–4:3) and government (5:18), and death cancels the meaning of righteous endeavors. In many respects the book is an account of the struggle between good and evil—the righteous and the wicked—though no uniform ethical construct ever is established, and it is the very structures of cult and ritual that appear to elicit the greatest despair. The text is dominated by the systematic application of wisdom categories to an investigation of the traditional institutions of ethics and religion. Qoheleth recognizes that all of life exists under the aegis of God, though this God is a rather inaccessible deity whose structuring of reality is incontrovertible, but whose structures are subject to the vagaries of human whim. Otherwise, no divine purpose for human existence or philosophy of history is forthcoming. In the light of these observations concerning reality, life is to be lived for its own benefits: the enjoyment of existence (2:24; 3:22; 8:15); the pleasures of companionship (4:9-12; 9:9); the satisfaction of honest labor (5:12). One detects throughout the book that Qoheleth has intermittently inserted traces of the contemporary doctrine that God is the author of just retribution, much like that belief espoused by the ''friends'' of Job. Since this doctrine flagrantly contradicts the mood of the book, one is led to consider that such passages are designed to show the foolishness of such a doctrine, or are the insertions of a later hand. Instead, Qoheleth concludes that where wisdom and righteousness fail, one must live life on its own terms.

See also WISDOM IN THE OLD TESTAMENT; WISDOM LITERATURE.

Bibliography. G. A. Barton, *A Critical and Exegetical Commentary on the Book of Ecclesiastes*; E. Bickerman, *Four Strange Books of the Bible*; J. L. Crenshaw, *Ecclesiastes, A Commentary*; R. Gordis, *The Word and the Book*; R. B. Y. Scott, *Proverbs. Ecclesiastes*; C. F. Whitley, *Koheleth: His Language and Thought*; J. G. Williams, "What Does It Profit a Man?: The Wisdom of Koheleth," *Judm* 20 (1971): 179-93.

—CLAYTON N. JEFFORD

• **Ecclesiasticus.** *See* SIRACH

• **Economics in the New Testament.** Economics is the study of the use of scarce resources to produce goods and services to meet human needs and wants. Thus economics is concerned with what goods are produced, how they are produced, and to whom they are distributed. The term itself derives from an ancient Greek word that originally referred to the arrangement and management of the private household. It is used in this sense in Luke 16:2-4, where it is translated STEWARDSHIP; it is also used metaphorically to designate both the "commission" of an apostle (1 Cor 9:17) and God's "plan" of salvation (Eph 1:10; 3:9). During the last two centuries, however, the term has come to refer almost exclusively to the *public* structures, institutions, and practices that relate to the production and distribution of goods.

Though in no sense an economics textbook, the NT does reflect at numerous points many of the specific concerns of economics: markets for buying and selling goods outside the household (e.g., Matt 14:15; 25:9; Mark 16:1), the institution of private property (Matt 20:1; 25:14; Luke 15:11-12; Acts 4:34), a monetary system (Mark 12:41; John 2:14-15; Matt 26:15; 28:12), some type of banking (Matt 25:27), the payment of interest (Matt 25:27), a labor market and standard wage for unskilled labor (Matt 20:1-16), and even the suggestion of the profit motive (Matt 25:14-30; Acts 16:16). In contrast to some of these institutions in the larger society is the practice of the early Christian church to hold all goods in common and distribute them based on need (Acts 2:44-45).

The Roman empire of the first century permitted considerable economic diversity, and local economies functioned much as they had prior to Roman rule. Galilee, for example, where the ministry of Jesus began, was a rural agricultural region populated by poor working class people (e.g., farmers, fishermen, carpenters, shepherds, day laborers) and by large numbers of non-working poor (e.g., the blind, the lame, the crippled, the lepers) whose survival depended on charity. Here crops and livestock were primarily for local consumption, and most production (e.g., food preparation, clothing, wine) took place in the home. Many of Jesus' parables reflect this rural Galilean setting (cf. parables in Matt 13 and 20:1-16).

Jerusalem, by contrast, was a major urban center and enjoyed the benefits and liabilities that seem inevitably to inhabit large cities. The economy was shaped by the extraordinary religious significance of the city and depended heavily on the large number of pilgrims and tourists that trekked annually to her gates. Poverty was a serious social problem as great wealth and the generosity of the pilgrims attracted hoards of beggars. As Christianity moved into the larger Greco-Roman world (e.g., to Ephesus, Corinth, Alexandria, Rome), it confronted an even more complex economic order with international standards of currency and sophisticated procedures for buying, selling, and lending.

Economic theory was quite unsophisticated, at least by modern standards, and government intervention was essentially limited to taxation policies. The Romans imposed two basic kinds of taxes: direct and indirect. The direct tax was a poll tax or "head" tax levied annually on each individual (probably the tribute to Caesar mentioned in Mark 12:14); it usually required a census (Luke 2:1-5) and was collected directly by Roman authorities. The indirect taxes (e.g., tariffs, import duties, customs fees) were farmed out regionally to the highest bidders, who were allowed to keep the revenues above what they had contracted to turn over to the government. Such a system was fraught with possibilities for abuse, and many tax farmers or "chief tax collectors" were extremely wealthy. Except for Zacchaeus (Luke 19:2), the tax collectors referred to in the NT were probably not the wealthy tax farmers (the "chief tax collectors") but their underlings hired to do the actual collecting. They were despised as traitors because they were collaborating with foreign occupation forces, and they were probably not wealthy. It is difficult to assess just how oppressive the taxes levied in Palestine actually were since the Jews objected as much to the principle of taxation by a foreign power as to the amount levied (Mark 12:13-17; Acts 5:37).

The society of the Roman empire was highly stratified with huge gaps between the rich and the poor, the few and the many. The very rich usually belonged to one of three groups: (1) the landed aristocracy, (2) royalty (e.g., Herod the Great and his descendants), and (3) members of a religious elite (e.g., the high priestly families of Palestine). The landed aristocrats were often absentee landlords who controlled huge armies of slaves, indentured servants, and hired workers to support their agricultural enterprise whether it be grain, olives, or grapes. Royalty gained wealth through inheritance, taxes, and the confiscation of property. The high priestly families in Jerusalem were supported by inherited wealth and the Temple tax, a half-shekel tax collected annually from every Jew twenty years of age and over in the empire. The rich often lived in conspicuous consumption and were the *raison d'être* of a flourishing long-distance foreign trade with Scandinavia, India, Africa, and points beyond. Overland transportation was quite expensive and hence only luxury items were routinely shipped long distances: precious stones and pearls, silk and cotton fabrics, frankincense, cosmetics, ceramic pieces, and rare woods.

The middle classes of the first century were relatively small but included a broad range of OCCUPATIONS and levels of income. The middle class included merchants, craftsmen (e.g., carpenters, silversmiths, tentmakers), the professions (e.g., lawyers, teachers, physicians), civil servants (e.g., tax collectors), and small entrepreneurs in agricultural industries (e.g., small farmers, shepherds, fishermen). Such occupations required modest amounts of capital or property needed for production (e.g., a boat and net for fishermen; a shop and proper tools for craftsmen; land, oxen, and plow for farmers), and it was this ownership of property that distinguished the middle classes from the lower classes. Some merchants and craftsmen gained considerable wealth, but most of the middle classes existed close to the edges of poverty. Joseph was a carpenter, for example, but still too poor to offer anything other than two doves for Mary's purification (Luke 2:22-24). The social status accorded various occupations was not directly correlated with the income they produced, especially within Judaism. Most manual trades were quite honorable, but physicians were held in low esteem, and Hillel warned that the life of true wisdom was incompatible with that of a merchant. Also, according to the *Mishna,* swineherds, shepherds, and tax collectors were detestable, and, therefore, in the same class with prostitutes, dice-throwers, and usurers.

Just below the middle classes of the first century was a lower working class consisting of day laborers, tenant farmers, servants, and slaves. The day laborers, having no skill or property of their own, simply hired themselves out one day at a time. Jesus' parable of the laborers in the vineyard (Matt 20:1-16) presents an accurate picture of workers waiting in the marketplace to be hired. Tenant farmers had no land of their own but rented land by promising the landowner a substantial portion of their harvest (cf. Matt 21:33-41). The economic significance of slavery was actually declining in the first century and was even less important in Palestine than in some other regions of the empire. But it was still quite profitable for large agricultural enterprises and especially for mining (e.g., copper, silver, gold). Owners were legally bound to provide necessities for their slaves, and hence the lot of slaves was often more comfortable than that of free farmers, day laborers, or indentured servants. Some slaves were highly educated and became prominent teachers, scientists, and poets, and those assigned to household duties often enjoyed many privileges of the wealthy. Within Judaism slavery was strongly opposed by the Pharisees and the Essenes; and while the NT does not attack the institution of slavery explicitly, certainly the logic of the gospel tends inexorably toward the abolition of slavery (Gal 3:28).

At the bottom of the socioeconomic ladder were the widows and orphans and the blind, lame, and paralyzed. Unable to earn a living for themselves and with no publicly funded welfare programs, these depended entirely on charity and the various OT provisions for caring for the poor (Exod 22:21-27; 23:10-11; Lev 19:9-10). Jerusalem was the center of mendicancy in Palestine, both because of the wealth concentrated there and because of the religious traditions that encouraged the thousands of pilgrims to give alms to the poor. These beggars often positioned themselves at locations near the Temple to attract the attention of the pilgrims.

The dependent population also included scribes and teachers who were not permitted to accept fees for their work. They were dependent upon charity or a second job. Hillel, for example, worked as a day laborer while studying to be a rabbi. Jesus and his disciples accepted alms (Luke 8:1-3; 10:7-8), and Paul argued the point that apostles deserve support from the congregation, though he takes pride in not having insisted on this right for himself (1 Cor 9). When Jesus sent his disciples out to preach and heal, he expected them to live off charity (Luke 10:4-8).

Available evidence suggests that the followers of Jesus and members of the early church were drawn primarily from the lower and middle classes. Jesus' family was obviously poor, as evidenced by the two doves offered for Mary's purification (cf. Luke 2:24; Lev 12:8), but as a carpenter Joseph would have belonged to the middle class. Jesus, known as the "carpenter from Nazareth" (Mark 6:3), apparently learned his father's trade, but there is no evidence that he worked as a carpenter during his public ministry. He and his disciples, most of whom were also drawn from the lower middle class, probably lived from a common purse sustained by generous supporters. The people most receptive to Jesus' message of the KINGDOM OF GOD were the poor—the lower working class, the day laborers, the beggars. If the Corinthian church was typical of other NT churches, their membership was also predominantly lower and middle class. However, tensions between rich and poor are reflected in several NT writings (e.g., the Gospel of Luke; 1 Cor 11; Jas 2:1-7), and this probably means that the early Christian movement did include a small minority of wealthy persons.

While the NT does not give a blueprint for the ideal economic order, its teachings are profoundly relevant for Christians concerned about economic issues. The NT is filled with denunciations of the rich (Luke 1:51-53; 6:24-26; 12:13-21; Jas 5:1-6; Rev 18:11-20) and warnings about the dangers of WEALTH (Matt 6:19-21, 24; Luke 12:13-21; 18:24-25). Conversely, it offers hope for the poor (Luke 1:51-53; 4:18; 6:20-21) with justice being portrayed in terms of eschatological reversal (Matt 20:16: "The last shall be first and the first last"). The point is not that the poor are more intrinsically righteous than the rich, nor that wealth is evil in and of itself (cf. 1 Tim 6:10). But wealth is a powerful source of temptation that can destroy one's relationship to God, to neighbor, and even to oneself. Wealth gives the illusion of self-sufficiency (Luke 12:19) and thus produces the haughty arrogance that resists the unconditional love of God. Wealth also tempts one to measure human worth in material terms (Jas 2:1-7) and thus destroys human community by rendering impossible the kinds of relationships that ought to exist between human beings. Some passages call for the total surrender of one's possessions (Luke 12:32-34; 18:22) or a communal sharing of wealth (Acts 2:44-45; 4:32-35), while others stress proper stewardship (e.g., the example of Zacchaeus in Luke 19:1-10). The point is that economic institutions and practices do matter in the life of faith and that they are to be judged in light of their capacity to encourage the proper relationship to God, to neighbor, and to self.

See also AGRICULTURE/FARMING; BORROWING AND LENDING; MONEY; OCCUPATIONS; PUBLICANS; SLAVERY IN THE NEW TESTAMENT; WEALTH.

Bibliography. J. Jeremias, *Jerusalem in the Time of Jesus*; H. Koester, *Introduction to the New Testament,* vol. 1, *History, Culture, and Religion of the Hellenistic Age.*

—MARY JANE GORMAN and JOHN C. SHELLEY

• **Economics in the Old Testament.** The reconstruction of the economy in OT times, that is, the production and distribution of goods and services in the changing social world of Judah and Israel, is hampered by a limitation on data, especially quantitative data, both in the OT and in the archaeological remains. Additionally, the variegated geography of Palestine renders most generalizations about economic life untrue because of the diversity of productive circumstances and widely varying access to interregional and international trade.

Economic Zones. The nature of economic life during OT times in the various regions and subregions of Palestine depended largely upon the extent of involvement beyond the local scene and its impact on the objectives of productive activity (agriculture, pastoralism, crafts and art). When this involvement was minimal, either because of an area's distance or isolation from economic centers (e.g., southern Judah) or geopolitical circumstances (e.g., the low level of international trade during the premonarchical period), economic activity was confined within the radius of the small village and its near neighbors. Agriculture and pastoralism were pursued in ways that increased the subsistence security of the village, always a challenge in this area of great environmental uncertainty. To enhance security, villages diversified crops sown (planting wheat and barley along with vegetables, particularly lentils) and fruit trees planted (olive, fig, and grape vines). They devoted a significant amount of energy to sheep and goat herding especially to provide resources in case of crop failure. Villagers developed social mechanisms to promote and maintain community solidarity (e.g., endogamy, that is, marriage within the clan or tribe). Households stored crops from a year of plenty for a year of want and invested their surplus in larger family size since life was precarious and labor was the key ingredient in making ends meet. Crafts such as clothes-making were carried out within each household, and barter was the exchange mechanism for obtaining other goods: pottery from the village workshop, metals from the more-or-less distant market centers, livestock from nomadic pastoralists. Though the village would fare sometimes better, sometimes worse depending upon natural and political circumstances beyond its control, this zone of economic activity witnessed little or no development throughout OT times. Apart from the everyday objects of its material life, it left little record and falls almost completely outside the gaze of the biblical tradition. The OT contains many direct and metaphorical references to the activities of this village-based economy but the central concerns of these farmers and herders are rarely visible.

During most of the OT period this more local economic zone was related tangentially to a more fully developed and regionally integrated market economy. In this second zone agriculture and pastoralism continued to be practiced but with farmers producing commodities for market rather than exclusively for self-consumption. Other industries (textiles, metallurgy) also contributed significantly to this more diversified and specialized economy. Evidence of this market-oriented economic zone is clear already in the premonarchical period. As told by Judges and Samuel, the story of this period is populated by numerous persons of means whose wealth is ostensibly related to business: for example, NABAL whose specialty is wool production (1 Sam 25) and Abdon whose seventy asses equipped him as a transit trader (Judg 12). The formation of the monarchy was dependent upon and gave impetus to this economic activity. Beginning with the time of SOLOMON, biblical tradition and material and literary remains point to the development of a multifaceted and highly differentiated economy based in a growing number of urban centers. This economy employed money (though not coinage), standardized weights and measures, record keeping, business contracts and perhaps loans; it also involved production centers for certain commodities, markets, warehouses, centralized control, and far-flung trading operations.

Factors Influencing Economic Development. At least five factors influenced the economic development of the monarchical period. Population growth was perhaps the most basic. The expansion of settlement of the hilly regions of Palestine that marked Israel's emergence continued through the monarchical period to the point that the more readily developed land was filled. The economy was forced to shift gears from expansion to intensification, producing more from a limited amount of land in order to feed the growing population. The basic route of intensification of agriculture in this region was terracing and investing in olive groves and vineyards at the expense of grain fields. This trend was abetted by a second key factor, the incorporation of the lowland regions into Israelite control during the process of state formation under David. The integration of these "bread baskets" permitted the highland zone to develop more efficiently into the production of olive oil and wine. The hilly regions began to depend upon the lowlands for the grain that they were not so well suited to produce. The upswing in trade throughout the Mediterranean region and the ancient Near East constituted a third stimulus and whetted monarchical interest in trade both as transit agent and trading partner. This further encouraged the process of intensification and the development of industries, which produced desirable trade commodities. The growth of the monarchical institution itself was a fourth major factor in economic development. The royal house offered a new, non-agricultural locus of employment and spawned a new social class of royal retainers and administrators. Through taxation it drew the productive wealth of the nation into the urban centers where markets for basic needs as well as for luxury items burgeoned. Furthermore, its policies of taxation and procurement, judicial regulation, and land development set the economic agenda for the action for which it attempted to provide security. The monarchy's own agenda was dictated in large measure by a final factor: the emergence of competitor states (e.g., Aram and Moab) and especially the growth of the powerful Assyrian empire, which began to exert its influence within the first century of Israel's and Judah's national lives. Military (e.g., expenditures for armaments and fortifications) and diplomatic matters (e.g., gifts and tribute) played a dominant role in economic decision making.

Role of the Monarchy. Biblical and archaeological evidence for the development of a diversified market-oriented economy during the monarchical period is plentiful. The report of Solomon's activities is the fullest; its details no doubt relate equally well to Solomon's successors on the thrones of Judah and Israel. The royal administration was staffed by various officials (1 Kgs 4:2-6); the territory of the kingdom was divided into districts for taxation purposes (1 Kgs 4:7-20). Solomon is reported to have engaged in trade to acquire essential goods (exchanging wheat and oil for Phoenician timber [1 Kgs 5:1-12; 9:10-14]) as well as for revenue (building ships for maritime trade with Arabia (1 Kgs 9:26-28; 10:14-22); he also engaged in horse trade with Egypt and Cilicia in Asia Minor (1 Kgs 10:26-29). Major cities he is credited with fortifying (HAZOR, MEGIDDO, and GEZER [1 Kgs 9:15]) occupy significant posts on major inland trade routes. The economic role of the Jerusalem Temple for Solomon and his successors was substantial. It served as a locus for the payment of taxes and may have had some banking functions. Moreover, the Temple created the climate for and facilitated business transactions through its guarantee of contracts and teachings with regard to business practices. Economic matters are prominent in priestly instruction (Pss 24:4; 15:4-5).

Though the economic energy of Solomon has left some archaeologically detectable traces, there are few material signs of dramatic economic development during the early monarchy. The following centuries, however, evidence the upsurge of royal involvement in the market-oriented economic zone. In Israel, the ninth century emergence of the Omride dynasty is correlated with the construction of a new capital, SAMARIA, strategically situated close to major trade routes (1 Kgs 16:24). Ivory inlay carvings excavated at Samaria evidence luxury consumption as well as trade contacts with PHOENICIA. The cities of Hazor and Megiddo were expanded and became home to large pillared buildings that functioned as warehouses or markets in these administrative centers. Huge rock-quarried tunnel systems providing an internal supply of water attest to the king's ability to muster large quantities of labor and to the herculean efforts expended to diminish the threat of siege. Ashlar masonry (introduced earlier) and decorative capitals mark a level of royal affluence. In the next century before the destruction of the state at the hands of the Assyrians, the Samaria ostraca—inscribed potsherds recording deliveries of wine and oil to the capital—evidence either taxation or direct monarchical involvement in the production of these commodities. The same century witnessed the widespread use of the innovative beam press, which multiplied the efficiency of extracting oil from olives. The dozens of these rock-carved presses that litter the central hill country demonstrate the expansion of this crucial export industry.

Evidence for economic expansion led by monarchical interests also becomes prominent in eighth-century Judah. Wine jars inscribed with the phrase "belonging to the king" (or "kingly" or "for the king"; Hebrew *lmlk*) and mentioning production or distribution centers point to direct monarchical control of this industry in HEZEKIAH'S era. The growing economic specialization of towns, such as the winemaking center at GIBEON, contributes to a picture of a diversified and regionally interdependent economic system. Because sources for economic information are so incomplete, it is possible to see in this economic growth either the heavy hand of royal control or the operation of free-market forces. Many scholars would stress the overtly political nature of all economic decisions and portray the economy as a nonmarket economy in which decisions on production and distribution were made by central authorities. Others would emphasize the role of supply and demand and the profit motive in shaping economic life. Thus the burgeoning of the wine industry can be viewed either as a state initiated effort to increase the availability of exportable products and help the balance of trade (without regard for its consequences on the family farmers) or as a result of individual entrepreneurs acting to meet demand through risky development (in which many family farmers willingly participated by selling their land).

Prophetic Economics. The intersection between the more local, subsistence-oriented economic zone and the more regional, market-oriented zone provides the substance to much of the prophetic critique of Israelite and Judean leadership and society. The expansion of the market oriented economy placed great pressure upon the land and labor supply of villages. While most families could not tolerate the risk of entering into the regional economy and preferred to maintain the self-reliance of their communities, the growth of this economic zone threatened their ability to carry out their subsistence oriented agriculture and pastoralism. The prophets gave voice to those whose lives and livelihood were caught up in economic processes they could not control. Prominent themes in prophetic criticism relate to the authority's misuse of the judicial system (1 Kgs 21; Jer 8:8-9), commercial practices (Amos 8:4-6), debt bondage (Amos 2:6-8), the expropriation of land (Mic 2:1-2) and unbridled expansion (Isa 5:8-10). Though the prophets themselves probably did not emerge directly out of the village scene, they railed against the distortions of that scene produced by the economic system that villagers hardly understood or could affect. The reality of economic change through the monarchical period is also preserved in the legal literature with its stipulations regarding wages (Lev 19:13), loans (Exod 22:25-28; Deut 15:1-11), slavery (Exod 21:2-11; Deut 15:12-18), rental (Exod 22:14-15), and judicial conduct (Exod 23:3, 6; Lev 19:15) and its more programmatic economic texts such as the institution of the Jubilee (Lev 25). These laws attempt to regulate a diverse economic scene and envision the possibility of restoring a condition of economic equilibrium.

The End of National Life. The tension between the broader economy and the life of the villages of Israel and Judah came to an abrupt end with the military destruction of first one, then the other of these two monarchies at the hands of the Assyrians and Babylonians respectively. Along with the physical destruction and loss of life, the disruption of economic networks and the decapitation of the central administration left the territory in shambles and thrust its remaining inhabitants back on their own local resources. The biblical record pays little heed to the conditions of life after the demise of the political institutions. In the north, the Assyrians repopulated the capital and reestablished some centralized authority, but little is known of its effects (2 Kgs 17:24). In the south, NEBUCHADREZZAR appointed a local administration that attempted to bring about some return to economic normalcy (Jer 40). The fate of those exiled to Babylon apparently permitted full participation in the economic life, including the ownership of property and involvement in commercial activities (Jer 29:5; Ezra 2:68-69). In subsequent years, the return of some exiles and the reconstruction of the Temple and refortification of Jerusalem under the umbrella of Persian rule naturally had economic effects. Judah became a province on the western frontier of the empire. Reform programs with economic tenets attempted to stabilize the religious community of the province, which was apparently fissured by class divisions (Neh 5:1-13). Imperial policy imposed taxes and claimed jurisdiction of economic affairs, and coins were introduced into the country at this time as the prerogative of the Persian rulers. Economic stimuli emanated also from the west as early Greek trading colonies cropped up on the coast. Though sources are limited, Palestine appears to be a scene of social and economic heterogeneity at the end of the OT period.

See also AGRICULTURE/FARMING; COINS AND MONEY: JUBILEE, YEAR OF.

Bibliography. Y. Aharoni, *The Archaeology of the Land of Israel*; A. Malamat, ed., *The World History of the Jewish People,* vol. 4:2, *The Age of the Monarchies: Culture and Society*; M. Silver, *Prophets and Markets: The Political Economy of Ancient Israel*; E. Stern, *Material Culture of the Land of the Bible in the Persian Period 538–332 B.C.*

—DAVID C. HOPKINS

• **Eden, Garden of.** [ee'duhn] A primeval paradise where the first human pair lived. The etymology of Eden is uncertain. The LXX translates it as *paradeisos* ("delight"), suggesting the traditional identification of the garden of Eden with paradise.

The precise term, "garden of Eden," appears only five times in the OT, although it is implied, in varying combinations of "garden" and/or "Eden," thirteen times, first in the Yahwist literature and later in the prophets. Gen 2:15 ("garden of Eden") represents a subtle shift from 2:8 ("garden in Eden"), and from 2:10 ("a river flowed out of

Eden to water the garden''). The term reappears in 3:23-24, where the man is driven out of ''the garden of Eden''; but ''the garden'' is absent from 4:16 (merely ''east of Eden''). In Ezek 36:35, ''the garden of Eden'' is used as a simile for the restoration of Israel, and (as in Joel 2:3) as a contrast to a ''ruined'' place (or ''wilderness'').

Other implied references use ''Eden'' as a synonym for ''the garden of Yahweh'' (Isa 51:3) or ''the garden of God'' (Ezek 28:13; cf 31:9, 16, 18, ''trees of Eden'') and, as above, in contrast to ''wilderness'' and ''desert.'' Isaiah employs the image as a symbol for the restoration of Israel and the passages in Ezekiel imply a primeval state of perfection.

The Yahwist is alone in using the term as an identifiable location, which he clearly places somewhere in MESOPOTAMIA. Attempts to fix a site consistent with contemporary geography, however, are fraught with difficulty. Gen 2:10-14 speak of a river, with its source in Eden, which divides into four rivers. The TIGRIS and EUPHRATES are easily recognizable, but the Pishon and Gihon are more troublesome. Variously identified with the Nile, the Indus, the Ganges, and with unknown Babylonian canals, none of these speculations is easily supportable; and the exact site, if it is meant to be discovered at all, remains an enigma. Indeed, the reference to various rivers seems to be an intrusion into the account and may belong to a different creation story, fragments of which may be preserved in the Ezekiel passages, mentioned above, and elsewhere in the OT. Although connections between the garden of Eden and ancient Near Eastern mythology are possible, they appear to be indirect at best.

The theological significance is less difficult, although, as in all profound stories, meanings can be debated because many may be present. The garden of Eden surely pictures a state of full and free fellowship between God and the creation. The subsequent act of disobedience and rebellion is the central motif of the story and broken fellowship with God is its denouement. What happens in the garden of Eden is, at least, a parable of ''Everyman's'' history. A less important theme, represented by the presence of ''the tree of life,'' may be the squandered opportunity for immortality (cf. the Babylonian stories of Adapa and Gilgamesh). In any case, the twin themes of a life-giving river and a tree of life reappear (without reference to the garden of Eden) in the description of the heavenly city in Rev 22:1-2 (cf. also Ezek 47:1).

See also ADAM AND EVE, LIFE OF; PARADISE.

Bibliography. B. S. Childs, ''Eden, The Garden of,'' *IDB*; J. A. Skinner, *A Critical and Exegetical Commentary on Genesis,* ICC.

—C. EARL LEININGER

• **Edom/Edomites/Idumaea.** [ee'duhm/ee'duh-mitz/id'*yoo*-mee''uh] The people, descendants of the biblical Esau (Gen 36:1-17), are traditionally identified with a region, east of the Arabah, extending approximately 100 mi. from the Wadi Zered to the Gulf of Aqaba (PLATES 11, 13, 21). Though most of its terrain is rugged and mountainous, reaching elevations of over 5,000 ft., oases and limited regions of pasturage and agricultural land were adequate for the establishment of urban centers. During its period of national unity and strength from the ninth-seventh centuries B.C.E., Edom's prosperity was based on commerce and trade, especially the imposition of tolls on caravans moving through its territory.

The time and nature of Edomite tribal consolidation and national unity is unclear. A lack of Egyptian reference to Edom or Seir during the New Kingdom Period suggests either a lack of Egyptian interest or the possibility that Edom had little real political or national significance. Regional references from the fourteenth–twelfth centuries (to the reign of Ramses III) are limited to the Shasu and no specific references to Edomite (or Seirite) towns or rulers are found. Early biblical references similarly are vague. The region of Mount Seir is attributed to the Horites (Hurrians?) in the patriarchal traditions (Gen 14:6). The punitive raid of Chedorlaomer and his northern coalition may have terminated the Horite control in the region. Early Edomite presence may best be understood as a series of clan or tribal units identified with independent ''grazing-rights'' localities (Gen 36:31-39). Small Edomite settlements, later identified with primary urban centers, appear to have developed from these roving tribal groupings. The Israelite confrontation with the ''king'' of Edom during the Moses-led Exodus, however, implies a unification with territorial control from the Kadesh area eastward to the fringe of the Arabian desert (Deut 2:1ff.). Edomite control and a show of military strength are portrayed as adequate to preclude Israelite passage along the king's highway (Num 21:4). Whatever Edom's internal administrative structure, Israel was instructed to recognize the integrity of Edom's territorial and political independence (Deut 2:1-8).

Though the biblical record provides the names of eight kings (Gen 36:31-39; 1 Chr 1:43-51), the nature of the Edomite monarchy prior to subjugation by David and later kings of Israel is unclear. During the period of the Judges, Gideon quelled a Midianite uprising in which Edomites were involved (Judg 6:1–8:28). The initiation of the Israelite monarchy brought the Edomites into conflict with King Saul (1 Sam 14:47). David's conquest of the Transjordan brought Edom under a military administration (2 Sam 8:13-14) which Solomon was not able to maintain (1 Kgs 11:25). However, early in the reign of Jehoshaphat, Edom again is ruled by a military governor of Judah (1 Kgs 22:48). Reference to the king of Edom toward the end of Jehoshaphat's reign (2 Kgs 3:9, 12, 26) seems to suggest renewed Edomite independence, a situation that is assured during the reign of Jehoram. Amaziah (800–783 B.C.E.) defeated the Edomites and destroyed their capital, Sela (2 Kgs 14:7-10; 2 Chr 25:11ff.). The seaport at Elath was rebuilt by Uzziah-Azariah (2 Chr 26:2) and archaeological evidence from the Ezion-geber excavations seems to suggest Israelite control through the reign of Jotham. Renewed Edomite strength is reflected by an invasion of Judah and Edomite control of the port in the time of Ahaz (2 Kgs 16:6; cf. 2 Chr 28:17). The eighth and early seventh centuries were a period of Edomite strength.

Excavations in Edom, and biblical and Assyrian references indicate that the Assyrian period was Edom's most prosperous time, a period of economic expansion. In Assyrian records, Edom is mentioned in Adad-nirari's annals of his expedition to Palestine (810–783 B.C.E.). Qaus-malaku of Edom is identified as paying tribute in the building inscriptions of Tiglath-pileser III (745–27 B.C.E.). A letter from Sargon II's campaign in 712 B.C.E. lists Edom in the revolting coalition of Palestinian states led by Ashdod. Aiarammu, king of Edom, brought tribute to Sennacherib in 701 B.C.E. Qausgabri, a later Edomite ruler, was among the twelve kings required to provide building supplies for Esarhaddon's place at Nineveh, and later pledged allegiance and paid tribute to Ashurbanipal who, in his ninth campaign, pursued Uate, king of Arabia, through Moabite and Edomite territory. Neo-Babylonian and Persian sources make no mention of Edom, though it is clear that the Edomite monarchy continued into the reign of Zedekiah (Jer 27:2ff.). Edom also is mentioned in 1 Esd 4:45, 50.

The deterioration of Judah's power prior to the fall of Jerusalem initiated Edomite encroachment into the Negeb and settlement south of Hebron. Excavations show that a number of sites east of Beersheba, such as Khirbet Gharrah, Khirbet Ghazzel, Tell Milh, Khirbet Meshash, Khirbet Ar'areh (Aroer) and others, some with formidable fortresses, came to an end in the sixth century and were never rebuilt. An ostracon in the archive of Eliashib, recovered at Arad, implies an impending attack from Edom, and so it seems likely that the general devastation of the Negeb and the destruction of Arad and En-Gedi at this time also may be attributed to the Edomites. The next century marked a serious Edomite decline as they increasingly came under Arab control. In the third century B.C.E. Edom was completely overrun and partially assimilated by the Nabataeans.

The end of the Edomite kingdom and the transition to Nabataean control of the region is vague. The latest biblical reference to a king of Edom (Jer 27:3) describes events in 594/3 B.C.E. The Edomite king may have been removed by Nebuchadrezzar or by Nabonidus, but apart from massive deportation (of which we have no literary evidence), the Edomite population clearly survived whatever political changes occurred, including the possible Babylonian sacking of Bozrah, the Edomite capital, destroying its royal administrative and cultic buildings. Evidence from excavations at Umm el-biyarah, Tawilan and Buseirah suggests flourishing communities through the seventh and into the sixth centuries B.C.E. At Buseirah (Edomite Bozrah) excavations on the acropolis have exposed buildings from the Edomite monarchy and Persian periods. A Nabataean inscription on an altar, however, seems to confirm a Nabataean presence. With the exception of a major disaster suggested by evidence of burning and destruction on the acropolis, Bozrah probably retained its administrative role under the Persians. Excavations at other sites, such as Tell el-Kheleifeh, suggest that the Nabataeans were established and in control of trade through Petra by the late fourth century B.C.E.

A northern movement against Judah by the Edomites on the side of the Babylonians in 587 B.C.E. is clearly implied in the biblical text (Obad 11-14; Ps 137; Ezek 35:1–36:15; and 1 Esdr 4:45). The intense animosity of the Jews against the Edomites resulted from the Edomite invasion of the southern frontier and the possible participation in the destruction of Jerusalem. The capture of Elath on the Gulf of Aqaba in 734/3 B.C.E. (2 Kgs 16:6) and defeat of Judah with deportation of captives (2 Chr 28:17) were precursors to Edom's interest in southern Judah (Arad Ostracon #40). The fact that thirty percent of Malhata's Late Iron Age pottery is Edomite and that similar pottery was discovered in the upper stratum of ruins outside the walls of the late preexilic city at Tell Aroer suggest that by the end of the Assyrian period Edomites or people with Edomite affinities were settled among the population of the region south of a line from Arad to Beersheba. Arab pressure from the East and the gradual changeover within Edom from an Edomite to Nabataean population forced a gradual westward move that seems to have extended over several centuries. The Edomite movement among the tribes of Judah's southern border (Kenites, Jerahmeelites, Kenizzites) made infiltration and intermarriage relatively easy. Drawn by the prospect of richer agricultural lands and encouraged by political and economic developments and instability of the Assyrian period, the Edomite move aggravated Judah's vulnerability to imminent Babylonian invasion.

During the events leading up to the Babylonian invasion, it would appear that Edom declined a request from Judah (Jer 27) to participate in rebellion. Edom's nonparticipation seems clear from the fact that Jews had sought refuge in the Transjordan, including Edom, during the Babylonian invasion (Jer 40:11). Apart from a gradual infiltration and failure to assist, Edom appears not to have pressed its advantage militarily during Judah's downfall in 587 B.C.E. However, Edom was accused of doing nothing to help Jerusalem during this crisis (Obad 1-14,15b) and may have participated actively in Jerusalem's destruction.

By the end of the third century B.C.E., the border between Judah and Idumaea appears to run between Beth-zur and Hebron and westward north of Marissa. The lands south of Beth-zur were alien with Idumaeans living in Hellenized cities including Adora, Marissa, Hebron and Beersheba (1 Esdr 4:50; 8:69).

Bibliography. Y. Aharoni, "The Negeb," *Archaeology and Old Testament Study,* ed. D. W. Thomas; W. F Albright, "The Oracles of Balaam," *JBL* 63 (1944): 207-33; J. R. Bartlett, "The Land of Seir and the Brotherhood of Edom," *JTS* n.s. 20 (1969): 1-20, "The Rise and Fall of the Kingdom of Edom," *PEQ* (Jan-June 1972): 26-37, "The Brotherhood of Edom," *JSOT* 4 (1977): 2-27, "The Edomites to Nabataeans: A Study of Continuity," *PEQ* (Jan-June 1979): 53-56 and "Edom and the Fall of Jerusalem, 587 B.C.," *PEQ* (Jan-June 1982): 13-24; C. M. Bennett, "Excavations at Buseirah, Southern Jordan, 1974: Fourth Preliminary Report," *Levant* 9 (1977): 1-10; B. C. Cresson, "The Condemnation of Edom in Postexilic Judaism," *The Use of the Old Testament in the New and Other Essays*; N. Glueck, "Surface Finds in Edom and Moab," *PEQ* (Oct 1939): 188-92; J. Lindsay, "The Babylonian Kings and Edom, 605–550 B.C.," *PEQ* (Jan-June 1976): 23-39; A Musil, *Arabia Petraea* II: *Edom, Pt I*; J. M. Myers, "Edom and Judah in the Sixth-Fifth Centuries B.C.," *Near Eastern Studies in honor of W.F. Albright,* ed. H. Goedicke.

—GEORGE L. KELM

• **Education in the New Testament.** Several fundamental observations are in order as a preamble to a discussion of education in the NT. First, the span of history which will be the focus of attention is brief indeed. With the exception of 2 Peter (which is commonly viewed as of mid-second - century origin), the writings comprising the canonical NT were completed prior to 130 C.E. Understanding the beginning point as the adult ministry of Jesus, the period of history involved would be roughly one century.

Second, the educational efforts of Jesus and his followers were undertaken in two quite disparate pedagogical milieus. Jesus, and his followers who were to remain in and around Jerusalem, were influenced by the universal (for all Jewish children) religious education which had been a primary influence in the preservation of Hebrew culture since the deliverance from Egypt. The central agency of this education remained the home, but Jewish education had, by the time of Jesus' life, grown far more formal with the development of synagogue schools and even elementary schools which taught reading and writing using the Torah as the textbook.

Those early Christians who were to communicate the gospel in the gentile world would have been influenced by the milieu of Hellenistic education. In this setting, schooling was private in nature, largely reserved for the children of wealth and station in life. Education was not religious, but was characterized by philosophical speculation, scientific investigation, aesthetic contemplation, and the cultivation of civic skills.

A third observation concerns the nature of the early Christian community. So long as attention is focused on the century during which the biblical literature was written, one must be aware that Christian doctrine, piety, and ecclesiastical structure were yet to attain the stage of institutional stability. While a fundamental gospel was present and an oral and written tradition were taking shape, a widely accepted and comprehensive content for Christian education would have been difficult to construct. During the NT period, the church, as an institution, was largely unorganized and highly individualistic in nature—as may be seen in the letters of Paul and the Pastorals.

Despite these limitations and difficulties, the record of the first century does permit some generalizations. One of the primary functions of a Jewish religious leader (in Jesus' day, the scribe or RABBI) was to preserve, interpret, and transmit the religious tradition from one generation to the next through TEACHING. Apparently Jesus was seen as fulfilling this role in his public ministry. He was addressed as teacher (Matt 8:19; Mark 9:17; Luke 20:28) and he employed the term with reference to himself (Mark 14:14). In fact, the record indicates a tripartite ministry—Jesus went about teaching, preaching, and healing (Matt 4:23; 9:35). In keeping with the expectations of a religious teacher, he taught in the Temple (Mark 12:35; Luke 19:47) and in the synagogues (Mark 1:21; Luke 4:15). Mark, perhaps, summarizes the centrality of communication through teaching for Jesus' ministry when he wrote: " . . . as his custom was, he taught them" (Mark 10:1).

Jesus' extensive use of PARABLES and the numerous records of his conversational encounters with those who came to him indicate the informal, personal nature of his teaching. As would have been in keeping with his Jewish heritage, his teaching was neither formal nor speculative. But, as skillful a teacher as Jesus may have been, the unique element of his teaching seems to have been associated with the authority compellingly apparent to those who heard him (Matt 7:29; Mark 1:22). In the final analysis, the exceptional quality of Jesus' teaching may not have been a function of method, but of an interpretation which carried the unmistakable imprimatur of religious truth.

It is clear that the ministry of teaching exemplified by Jesus was not lost on his followers. The writer of Acts reports that, on the day of Pentecost, those who believed were taught by the apostles (Acts 2:42). The NT indicates that one of the apostolic functions was teaching (Acts 15:35; Rom 12:5-8; 1 Cor 12:28). Teaching was held in such high regard that it was seen as one of the primary gifts which comprised the total Christian ministry (Rom 12:6-7). The gospel required interpretation if it was to be applicable to life, and teaching was, therefore, a distinct ministry intended to accomplish this interpretation.

Early in the development of the church, there is indication that the worship service included a distinctly didactic element (1 Cor 14:26; Col 3:16). Moreover, as time passed, the need to provide religious instruction for new converts prior to baptism became apparent (this practice was indicated in the earlier documents used to compile the DIDACHE in the second century). This practice of pre-baptism religious instruction came to be known as catechumenal instruction.

By the end of the first century, systematic religious instruction for the children of the faithful was recommended by Clement (*1 Clem* 21:8). It is unclear whether Clement is recommending a new idea or endorsing an established practice, but, whatever the case, religious education was becoming an integral function in the ongoing life of the Christian community.

See also CLEMENT, FIRST; DIDACHE; EDUCATION IN THE OLD TESTAMENT; JESUS; PARABLES; RABBI; TEACHING.

—RICHARD C. MCMILLAN

• **Education in the Old Testament.** The OT did not prescribe for the Hebrews a highly structured system of education. However, the education of children is a recurring theme in the OT. The SHEMA, the Hebrew confession of faith found in Deut 6:4-9, includes a command to teach the Law to the children.

An emphasis on education was part of the ancient near eastern heritage of the Hebrews. The Kingdom of Sumer dominated Mesopotamia from approximately 2500–1500 B.C.E. The Sumerian educational system was primarily for the purpose of producing scribes for the religious, civil, and economic needs of the nation. MARI was a Mesopotamian city-state that flourished during the second millennium B.C.E. Excavations there have unearthed thousands of clay tablets with cuneiform inscriptions. Producing such numerous written documents would have required an extensive network of scribes, trained within an organized educational system. School rooms unearthed at Mari evidence such a system. In Egypt primary education was mostly literacy training. This was followed by a type of apprenticeship during which the student would learn more regarding scribal duties. Proverbs and other tools of Hebrew education are found in most other ancient near eastern cultures.

There are many Hebrew words in the OT that have to do with education and illustrate various Hebrew concepts of the learning process. The word *yāda'*, a form of which is found in Ezra 7:25, is translated "know." To know in this sense means an involvement in the life of the person. Various Hebrew words for "teach" are: *yārâ* (cf. Mic 3:11), which carries the idea of pointing things out; *zāhar* (cf. Exodus 18:20), which communicates the need for admonishment or warning; *lāmad* (cf. Deut 4:10), meaning literally to "goad"; *šānan*, meaning to "teach diligently"—literally to "sharpen" or "pierce" (cf. Deut 6:7). The words for teachers and students (or disciples) were often simply forms of the verbs for teach. In fact, the Hebrew word for the Law, Torah, is a derivative of the above-mentioned verb *yārâ*.

One purpose of education in the OT was training for a separate and holy life. This is the command of God found in Lev 19:2. Holiness and wisdom were not intended to be theoretical, but intensely practical. Those who had truly learned wisdom would live ethically. That is how they could attain the highest good and find meaning in life. This purpose would find expression in instruction to the nation in general and to individuals. It would involve teachings on the LAW and how to maintain the COVENANT with God, as well as practical teachings and wisdom regarding relationships with neighbors.

Another purpose of education was the handing down of the national and religious heritage from generation to generation. This was important throughout the OT. During their early history such transmission was important as the Hebrew people sought to establish a national identity. During the period of the united kingdom (under kings Saul, David, and Solomon) there was the need to legitimize their existence and to call attention to their golden age. The EXILE of later years brought about the need to keep alive the memory of the nationhood that had been and that could be.

Much of the content of education in the OT was the record of God's mighty acts. It was important for the Hebrews to remember what God had done in creation, the calling of Abraham, the Exodus from Egypt, the conquest of Canaan, and other events. In these stories was found evidence of God's choosing them, entering into covenant with them, and setting them apart as a nation. Also in the stories were lessons to be learned regarding the consequences of national and personal obedience and disobedience to God.

The content of OT education included instruction in the day-to-day conduct of life. The core of this instruction was found in the regulations regarding daily personal and religious life found in the Mosaic Law (particularly Leviticus and Deuteronomy, although the TEN COMMANDMENTS—the heart of the Mosaic Law—are first listed in Exod 20. Dietary laws of Lev 11 and feast laws of Deut 16 are other examples.

The WISDOM LITERATURE of the OT, especially Proverbs, took more the form of practical guidelines on how to relate to others and God and how to find meaning in life. Characteristic of this literature is the advice regarding conversation in Prov 15:1 and the summary statement of Eccl 12:13-14.

The primary foundation for education in the OT was the home. Here children were taught to work as well as to worship God. Boys learned a trade from their fathers and girls learned from their mothers the skills necessary to run a household. Both parents were important in the education of all their children.

Much of the tradition of the nation was taught through the observance of the various FEASTS AND FESTIVALS enumerated in the Law. The PASSOVER reminded them of the Exodus, the Sabbath of creation, etc. The rituals associated with these feasts were kept in the home and/or the Tabernacle (later the Temple). Therefore, the education of Hebrew children included the priests as well as the parents.

Other methods of education used memorization and parables. Children were to be taught a little at a time (e.g., note the brevity of the maxims in Proverbs). Parables were brief narratives used to illustrate one central truth. Those involved in the development of these methods would have included the sages (or wise men) and the prophets and prophetesses.

References to "schools" of prophets (1 Sam 10:5 and 19:20) are unclear as to their nature. They may or may not have been vocational training schools.

See also FAMILY; WISDOM IN THE OLD TESTAMENT.

Bibliography. J. Kaster, "Education, OT," *IDB;* D. F. Payne, "Education," *NBD*; W. Barclay, *Educational Ideals in the Ancient World.*

—RONNIE PREVOST

• **Egerton 2, Papyrus.** [eg'uhr-tuhn] Papyrus Egerton 2 is the designation of a fragmentary unknown gospel first published in 1935. The four fragments can be dated with some confidence before 150 C.E. on the basis of the script. To what extent the author was familiar with the synoptics and JOHN is uncertain, but the fragments reflect closer affinities with the latter. If he knew either, he quoted from memory rather than from a manuscript. One fragment has no parallel in any canonical or apocryphal writing.

The first fragment records Jesus' remonstrance of Jewish rulers for their failure to recognize the testimony of the scriptures and MOSES to him along with the reply of the rulers. Analogous exchanges can be found in John, but from two different contexts (John 5:39, 45; 9:29). Similarity of style has led some scholars to propose use of a common source rather than quotation.

The second fragment narrates the unsuccessful efforts of religious leaders to have Jesus stoned by the crowds or to arrest him "because the hour of his betrayal was not yet come." This part sounds Johannine (John 8:59; 10:31; 7:30, 44). Jesus passed "through their midst" and escaped (Luke 4:30; John 10:39). The rest of the fragment reports his healing of a leper and then instructing him to go and show himself to a priest (Matt 8:2-3; Mark 1:40-42; Luke 5:12-13; 17:14).

The third fragment sounds like a variation of the question asked Jesus about paying taxes to Caesar. After complimenting him as a Master "come from God" (cf. Matt 22:16; Mark 12:14; Luke 20:21; John 3:2; 10:25) and his teachings "above all the prophets," his questioners asked, "Is it lawful [? to render] unto kings that which pertains to their rule?" Jesus replied with some indignation, demanding to know why they called him "Master" but did not do what he said (Luke 6:46; 18:9). He capped this off with a quotation from Isaiah: "This people honor me with their lips, but their heart is far from me. In vain do they worship me, [teaching as their doctrines the] precepts . . . " (cf. Matt 15:7-9; Mark 7:6-7).

The fourth fragment has no parallel. Jesus asked a question which is unintelligible in the fragmentary form that has survived. In response to the perplexity of the hearers, he stopped on the edge of the Jordan and stretched out his hand to sprinkle water upon the bank(?) which immediately produced fruit.

Researchers tried early on to connect these fragments with gospels known to us from other sources. Since they contain no hint of docetism, they would not have belonged to heterodox Gnostic literature. Candidates within the orthodox circle mentioned by the church fathers would include the GOSPEL OF THE HEBREWS, the GOSPEL OF PETER, and the GOSPEL OF THE EGYPTIANS. The fact that these fragments show greater affinity for John than for the synoptics excludes the first two, since what is known about them indicates that both stood closer to the synoptics. Available quotations from the *Gospel of the Egyptians* offer no close approximations to the fragments.

See also APOCRYPHAL GOSPELS.

Bibliography. H. I. Bell and T. C. Skeat, *Fragments of an Unknown Gospel* and *The New Gospel Fragments*; C. H. Dodd, "A New Gospel," *BJRL* 20 (1936): 56ff.; J. Jeremias, "An Unknown Gospel with Johannine Elements," *New Testament Apocrypha*, ed. E. Hennecke and W. Schneemelcher.

—E. GLENN HINSON

• **Eglon.** [eg'lon] According to Judg 3:12-30, an extremely obese king of MOAB, named Eglon, led an army of Moabites, AMMONITES, and AMALEKITES into the region that had been known as JERICHO, "the city of palms." This event most likely occurred during the twelfth century B.C.E. and, according to the biblical narrative, the situation existed for eighteen years. The people prayed for a deliverer and God raised up EHUD, a left-handed Benjaminite. Ehud was able to hide a blade approximately fifteen to eighteen inches long on his right side (the implication was that the Moabites would have searched on the left side where a right-handed swordsman would bear his weapon). Ehud told Eglon that he had a message from God for him. As Eglon stood, Ehud buried his blade so deeply in Eglon's stomach that he could not even get the hilt loose. Martin Noth sees the fact that the Benjaminites did not pursue the Moabites past the Jordan after Eglon's assassination as significant. He suggests that this indicates a restoration of a traditional political boundary (i.e., the Jordan River itself) between Moab and Israel. It may be that the references to the idols or carved stones in vv. 19 and 26 reflect the extent of Moabite control when the boundaries were out of the traditional alignment.

See also EHUD; JUDGES, BOOK OF.

Bibliography. M. Noth, *The History of Israel*.

—JOHNNY L. WILSON

• **Egypt.** [ee'jipt] Egypt, a territory in northeastern Africa (PLATE 8), was along with Mesopotamia one of the two centers of civilization in the ancient Near Eastern world. Earliest Egyptian dynasties emerged at the beginning of the third millennium B.C.E. (ca. 3100–2700) and for the better part of 2700 years remained a substantial power in the ancient East. Episodically Egyptian control and influence extended outside African borders, even as far as Mesopotamia in the second millennium, but for the most part life and culture were confined to its own borders.

History. Prior to the third millennium ancient Egypt was two kingdoms. Upper Egypt lay along the last 750 mi. of the Nile River north of a series of treacherous rapids or cataracts. Lower Egypt designates the delta region north of ancient Memphis near modern Cairo. Around 3100 B.C.E. (early dates in Egyptian history remain imprecise) a certain Menes from a ruling family in Upper Egypt united the two kingdoms to form the first Egyptian dynasty. Menes is pictured as wearing a crown bearing symbols of both Upper and Lower Egypt. Subsequent ancient Egyptian history runs through thirty-one dynasties (or thirty by some reckoning), sometimes politically weak, but usually stable.

(1) Dynasties I-VI (ca. 3100–2181 B.C.E.), a period marked by unification of the two lands and increasing consolidation of the divided territory as one kingdom. Governmental power became focused in the pharaoh (a title referring to the chief Egyptian leader, roughly akin to king or emperor). The pyramids (PLATE 40) date to this period; the great pyramid of Cheops, one of the seven wonders of the ancient world, was built during the Fourth Dynasty.

Courtesy of the Eisenberg Museum of Biblical Archaeology, Southern Baptist Theological Seminary.

A collection of scarabs.

Courtesy of the Eisenberg Museum of Biblical Archaeology, Southern Baptist Theological Seminary.

Detail of a scarab.

(2) Dynasties VII-XVII (ca. 2181–1570 B.C.E.), generally a period of weakened Egyptian power marked by lessened pharaonic control and the influx of foreigners. Local provinces rebelled against the absolute power of the pharaoh, but kings of the Eleventh Dynasty were able to maintain Egyptian unity. The last part of the period (ca. 1710–1570) witnessed control by the HYKSOS, who invaded from Asia Minor and ruled the delta region. Native Egyptian rulers controlled the Nile valley but were dominated by the Hyksos. Although details remain obscure, early Hebrew patriarchal contacts with Egypt probably belong to this period.

(3) Dynasties XVIII-XX (ca. 1570–1020 B.C.E.) began with the expulsion of the Hyksos and the return of Egyptian strength under native pharaohs such as Ahmose I and Thutmose III.

A notable pharaoh of the period was Amenhotep IV (1370–1353), also known as Akhen-aton because of his patronage of the Aton cult. Amenhotep, father-in-law of Tut-ank-amen, built a new capital city at AMARNA in Upper Egypt and sought to establish Aton as the sole god, thereby arousing the ire of native priests of Amon, traditionally the high god of Egypt. Egypt, however, survived the disruptive experiment of Amenhotep. His rule was followed by the restoration of the delta capital accompanied by vigorous building under Seti I (1308–1290) and Ramses II (1290–1224). Influence was extended into Syria-Palestine, as evidenced by the first extrabiblical reference to Israel on the stele of Merneptah, successor to Ramses II.

The enslavement of Hebrews and their eventual escape under Moses' leadership belong to the last part of this period.

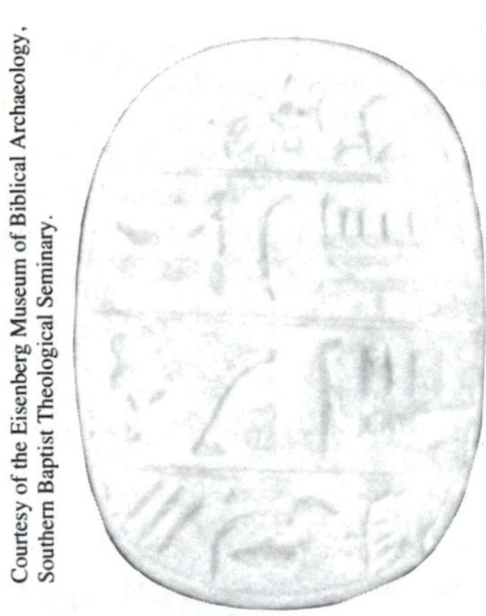
Courtesy of the Eisenberg Museum of Biblical Archaeology, Southern Baptist Theological Seminary.

An inscribed scarab.

(4) Dynasties XXI-XXXI (ca. 1070–333 B.C.E.) were characterized by the political and cultural decline of ancient Egypt resulting in increasing influence from outsiders—Assyrians, Persians, Greeks, and Romans. Occasionally pharaohs attempted to assert Egyptian power, as when SHISAK invaded Palestine (ca. 918) or Necho marched northward to meet Assyrian threats (ca. 609–605), but the days of Egyptian political and cultural greatness were past. For all practical purposes the end of ancient Egyptian history came during the decade of Alexander the Great (333–323) when rule fell to a series of Macedonian rulers (each called Ptolemy).

Geography. As early as the sixth century B.C.E. Greek writers called Egypt "the gift of the Nile." Both Upper and Lower Egypt are defined along the river. The Blue Nile and the White Nile, whose sources lie in interior Africa, merge and flow approximately 1,900 mi. northward to the Mediterranean Sea. After passing the cataracts, the river flows through a fertile valley with limestone cliffs or desert on either side. At places the arable areas extend no more than a mile from the river banks. This narrow trough is Upper Egypt. As the Nile nears the Mediterranean it fans into several streams forming the delta which is Lower Egypt. This area was exceptionally fertile and a prize territory throughout ancient Egyptian history.

The Nile basin was largely hedged in by hostile territory. The Mediterranean to the north, the formidable Lybian desert to the west, the forbidding Red Sea hills and Sinai peninsula to the east, and the threatening cataracts and rough terrain to the south meant that Egyptians were relatively shut up within their Nile tube. This geographical isolation contributed to pride in themselves and encouraged Egyptians to develop stability in their economic and political experience.

Life in this arid region of the world was possible only because of the Nile River, particularly its annual overflow to create fertility amidst the desert and to make agriculture feasible. Upper Egypt has almost no rainfall and Lower Egypt no more than eight inches annually. Hence, their economy and culture depended upon the ability of Egyptians to preserve and utilize the limited water supply. Extensive irrigation systems were developed to water cultivated fields. "Indeed, Egypt was land 'watered by the feet' of those who walked the treadmills of the ever-moving water wheels which lifted precious water to the levels of irrigation canals by which it was lowered to the fields." Small wonder that Egyptians sometimes called this country "the black land" in contrast to "the red land" of the surrounding desert!

In such a tenuous situation Egyptians depended upon the regularity of the Nile. Whether "seven years of plenty" or "seven years of famine" (Gen 41:53, 54), Egypt's prosperity was determined by the Nile's regular overflow to replenish the soil and make agriculture possible. In early July the river typically began to rise and spilled out of its channel for the better part of three months. In early November the waters receded, leaving behind the moist and refertilized soil for the planting of seeds and a springtime harvest. If the inundation went according to schedule, both grain and vegetables in many varieties could be produced and Egypt's reputation as "the bread basket of the ancient world" maintained.

Religion. More is known about official than popular Egyptian religion. Tombs of the pharaohs were usually constructed in the arid areas away from the Nile waters, thereby preserving from decay important and informative inscriptional materials. The moisture along the river where most citizens lived offered little such protection, and details of their daily life have been lost to decay. However, available data make it clear that the geographical isolation and the centrality of the Nile gave Egyptian religion a distinctive flavor. Primarily the Nile and its annual inundation were closely associated with the action of the gods. Egyptians shared with other ancient Easterners a thoroughgoing polytheism. They worshiped many gods whose character and function were not always clearly delineated. Any phenomena, and especially those intimately associated with survival, might be accounted for by the action of a god or even attributed to more than one god.

Hence the dependable inundation which provided ample food and sustained life made its indelible mark on Egyptian myth and ritual. Reason told them that what they saw happening every year must have happened at the beginning. So they conceived of Atum, the creator god, calling order out of the chaotic waters; as the primal water receded, Atum sat on a mound and created other gods and creatures to populate the world. The birth and death of the river were symbolic of the cycle through which life itself passed. The cycle was enacted in the myth of Osiris, who in spite of being treacherously killed, lived on in death and was ultimately avenged by his son Horus. The regular cycle of annual inundation and productivity was a sure sign that the gods continued to act for Egypt's beneficence; contrariwise, disruption in the cycle signaled angry gods.

Further, the Nile's regularity contributed to a sense of stability, confidence, even optimism that characterized Egyptian religion. Since the river's life was the doing of the gods, they obviously favored Egypt over surrounding neighbors whose rivers did not dependably overflow. Although the life of ordinary citizens was not easy in this harsh land, they could depend upon the Nile. Its regularity therefore offered a feeling of confidence that the land would produce, basic needs would be met, and life would go on year to year.

Egyptians' confidence in the Nile—and themselves—must have been enhanced by their geographical situation. Shut up in "a tube, loosely sealed against important outside contact" (Wilson, 11), they were rarely disturbed by outsiders. So protected from intrusion from friend or enemy and with the Nile's annual provision, Egyptians could center attention upon themselves, taking pride and confidence in their land and their gods.

The optimism generated by geographical security and economic confidence doubtless helps explain the role of the Egyptian pharaoh. From the beginning pharaohs were considered as gods—the embodiment of Horus while living, and living on as Osiris after death. As gods the pharaohs' words were absolute law and merited absolute obedience and devoted service. Their death was treated as merely the passing to another existence. Hence care was taken to provide all that might be needed for eternal happiness. At times nobles, officials of the court, and servants were even buried with the pharaoh. Pyramids were constructed as monumental tombs, as everlasting dwelling places for the departed pharaoh, and their burial was accompanied by lavish provisions. In this opulent treatment of the pharaoh Egyptians not only denied the finality of death but also affirmed confidence in themselves and their land as the province of the gods.

Egypt and the Old Testament. The proximity of Egypt and Canaan inevitably brought the two peoples into contact. During times of famine, Hebrews turned to Egypt for survival (cf. Gen 12:10; 42:1-5) and occasionally pharaohs made forays into Canaan to extend their influence or protect their borders. Execration texts including curses upon Canaanite enemies of Egypt (twentieth century B.C.E.), the Tell el-Amarna letters sent from Canaanite princes appealing to Egyptian overlords for help (fourteenth century), and the Merneptah stele (thirteenth century) testify to occasional interchange between the two areas. Some scholars have attempted unsuccessfully to relate the monotheism of the Hebrews to the experiment of Amenhotep IV.

The most obvious and extensive contact between Egyptians and Hebrews occurred during the Hebrew bondage in Egypt and their departure under the leadership of MOSES. Attempts to correlate these histories leave many questions unanswered, but probably patriarchs migrated into Egypt during the Hyksos period, were oppressed by Seti I after the expulsion of the Hyksos, and escaped during the reign of Ramses II.

Whatever the historical reconstruction, the Exodus narrative of the Hebrews (Exod 1–18) intends to show explicitly the superiority of Yahweh, their God, over Egyptian gods, including the divine pharaoh. From the beginning to the end of the story (and with not a little humor) Yahweh, revealed to Moses and Israel on the mountain (Exod 3, 19), overwhelms Egyptian deities supposedly in control of the river. Moses, the future emancipator, is saved from being drowned in the Nile by being floated on the Nile, and a duped pharaoh rears him in the palace (Exod 2:1-10). In plague after plague the inundation of the Nile turns sour at Yahweh's bidding (Exod 7:14-11:10). In territory where they are supposedly in control, the gods of the river are no match for the God of the mountain. Yahweh is even responsible for hardening the heart of the pharaoh. In this fashion the Exodus narrative dramatically caricatures Egyptian religion, thereby underscoring Yahweh's superiority.

Rosetta Stone. Nothing has contributed more significantly to modern knowledge about Egypt than the discovery and decipherment of the Rosetta Stone. Scientists accompanying an expedition of Napoleon Bonaparte to Egypt in 1798 found a slab of black granite containing the same text in three languages: old hieroglyphic, ordinary Egyptian, and Greek. By 1822 a Frenchman, Champollion, had worked through the Greek and ordinary Egyptian inscriptions to decipher the old hieroglyphic picture writing of ancient Egypt. The discovery made it possible to translate volumes of inscriptional material hitherto unreadable. Combined with pioneering archaeological work by the Englishman Sir Flinders Petrie and the American James H. Breasted, this work has unlocked the mysteries of one of the most important areas of the ancient world.

See also AKHENATON; NECHO; NILE; PHARAOH; RAMSES.

Bibliography. J. H. Breasted, *Development of Religion and Thought in Ancient Egypt*; H. J. Flanders, *People of the Covenant;* H. Frankfort, *Ancient Egyptian Religion*; J. A. Wilson, *The Burden of Egypt*.

—ROBERT W. CRAPPS

• **Egyptians, Gospel of the (ANT).** [i-jip'shuhn] The *Gospel of the Egyptians*, not to be confused with a Coptic tractate of the same name found at Nag Hammadi, was apparently an apocryphal gospel used by marginal Christian groups in the second century C.E. in Egypt. The only fragments from this work which have survived are quoted by Clement of Alexandria (*Strom* 3.45, 63, 64, 66, 68, 91-92). These feature a discussion between Salome and Jesus regarding marriage and procreation of children. Salome asks how long death will have power, Jesus replies, "As long as you women bear children." Jesus further states that he had come to "undo the works of the female," and that his kingdom would come "when the two become one and the male with the female is neither male nor female." This espouses an Encratite and/or Gnostic point of view.

The *Gospel of the Egyptians* is named in other patristic sources, but no further hints of its extent or contents are given (Hippolytus, *HaerRef* 5.7.8-9; *2 Clem* 12.2; Clement of Alexandria, *ExcTheod* 67; Epiphanius, *Haer* 62.4). Theodotus believed that the *Gospel* was used by Encratites and Julius Cassianus, while Hippolytus says that it was used by the Naassenes, but Epiphanius links it to the Sabellians. What can be certainly inferred from this is that the book was considered heterodox by the church fathers. Since it was known to Clement of Alexandria it must have been extant in Egypt by the middle of the second century.

Attempts have been made to link the *Gospel of the Egyptians* to other APOCRYPHAL GOSPELS, largely without success. In a variety of ways the GOSPEL OF THE HEBREWS, the GOSPEL OF PETER, and the Coptic GOSPEL OF THOMAS have been discussed as providing a "home" for the fragments of this work. The fact that Salome is named in both the Coptic *Gospel of Thomas* and the *Gospel of the Egyptians* and that Log 22 and *Strom* 3.92 (Clement of Alexandria) parallel each other is striking, but perhaps only circumstantial.

Of greater interest is the relationship between *2 Clem* 12.2 and the *Gospel of the Egyptians*. While *2 Clement* does not assign his statements from the Lord to the *Gospel*, Clement of Alexandria, quoting from the same tradition or a similar one identifies it as the *Gospel of the Egyptians* (*Strom* 3.91-92). This has led to claims that other dominical sayings in *2 Clement* were to be derived from the *Gospel* also (*2 Clem* 2.4; 3.2; 4.2; 4.5; 5.2-4; 6.1-2; 8.5; 9.11; 11.2-4; 11.7; 13.4). In most of these, freely cited canonical quotations can account for the form given, or can be understood as extra-canonical sayings similar to the synoptic tradition.

Similar sayings found in the ACTS OF PETER and the PSEUDO-EPISTLE OF TITUS have led to identifying these apocryphal books with the *Gospel of the Egyptians*, but there is no certainty in these identifications. Since the Greek gospel traditions, in part, were "floating" in the second century, it is extremely difficult to determine the nature of an individual saying tradition.

Schneemelcher's conclusions to his review of the materials is "that apart from the fragments of Clement [of Alexandria] which are expressly declared to be portions of the Gospel of the Egyptians almost nothing can with certainty be claimed for this apocryphal gospel."

See also APOCRYPHAL GOSPELS; CLEMENT, SECOND; PETER, ACTS OF; TITUS, PSEUDO-EPISTLE OF.

Bibliography. M. R. James, *The Apocryphal New Testament;* J. Quasten, *Patrology*; W. Schneemelcher, "The Gospel of the Egyptians," *New Testament Apocrypha,* ed. E. Hennecke and W. Schneemelcher.

—GLENN A. KOCH

• **Egyptians, Gospel of the (NH).** Though a GOSPEL OF THE EGYPTIANS (ANT) was known to the church fathers Clement of Alexandria, Hippolytus, and Epiphanius, another completely different work bearing the same name has surfaced among the tractates in the Gnostic library of NAG HAMMADI. Appearing in two Coptic versions in Codices III.2 and IV.2 (each a different translation from the same Greek original), this *Gospel of the Egyptians* (entitled more correctly, "The Holy Book of the Great Invisible Spirit") is an important document of Sethian GNOSTICISM. It presents a history of salvation featuring the work of Seth, son of the biblical ADAM. Dealt with are the heavenly events (cosmogony) that preceded the birth of Seth, the precosmic origin of his immortal race (or seed), the guarding of this race by heavenly powers, and Seth's coming into the world to effect salvation, especially through baptism. Upon entering the world, Seth puts on the living Jesus as a garment, a Christian touch.

The content of *Gospel of the Egyptians* is divisible into four parts. Part I (III 40.12–55.16 = IV 50.1–67.1) deals with the origin of the heavenly world from a highest God, the "Great Invisible Spirit." From him there evolves a trinity of beings: Father, Mother (Barbelo), and Son. A second description presents each member of this trinity as being composed of eight beings or "ogdoads." There follows the emanation of a pleroma of heavenly powers, down to Adam's great son Seth, who fathers his incorruptible seed.

Part II (III 55.16–66.8 = IV 67.2–78.10) describes the work of Seth-Jesus. Initially, we read of the creation of the Sethian race on earth (earthly counterparts of a heavenly church of angelic beings, the prototypical Sethians). To guard them from dangers sent by Saklas (the Devil/Creator), Seth prays for and obtains 400 ANGELS to protect his race. Not content to leave them alone, Seth, at the wish of the Great Invisible Spirit, descends into the world and suffers its hostilities to redeem his race. He puts on the living Jesus, brings the rite of baptism, and effects a reconciliation of spiritual saints with the pre-existent Father.

Part III (III 66.8–67.26 = IV 78.10–80.15) is a section containing two hymns of praise. Part IV (III 68.1–69.17 = IV 80.15–81–end) designates Seth as author of the entire book and relates that it was deposited on a high mountain (Charaxio) where it remained hidden until the present. At the End it will identify the true race of Seth.

Some scholars suggest the emphasis in *Gospel of the Egyptians* lies upon the concluding hymns and prayers (Part III) which were probably used in connection with the baptism of converts to Sethian Gnosticism. The mythological sections in Parts I and II thus provide a type of justification for the baptismal practice. Others contend that *Gospel of the Egyptians* was originally non-Christian and was later appropriated for Christian Gnostic usage through the addition of details about Jesus. As such, it would preserve one of the earliest forms of the Gnostic myth, the earliest being found in the APOCRYPHON OF JOHN. The provenance and original date of *Gospels of the Egyptians* are unknown, though its usage in Egypt no later than the first half of the fourth century seems probable.

See also APOCRYPHAL GOSPELS; GNOSTICISM; NAG HAMMADI.

Bibliography. A. Böhlig and F. Wisse, *Nag Hammadi Codices III,2 and IV,2: The Gospel of the Egyptians (The Holy Book of the Great Invisible Spirit), (NHS* 4) ed. J. M. Robinson; and "The Gospel of the Egyptians (III,2 and IV,2)," *The Nag Hammadi Library in English,* ed. J. M. Robinson and B. Layton, *The Gnostic Scriptures: A New Translation with Annotations and Introductions.*

—MALCOLM L. PEEL

• **Ehud.** [ee'huhd] The name Ehud (*'ehûd*) appears in the deliverer narrative of Judg 3:12-30 and in the genealogical material of 1 Chr 8:6. The name is formed from the Hebrew word *hôd,* meaning "majesty, honor," which is conventionally used of God's majesty, especially in the realm of nature (cf. Hab 3:3; Pss 8:2 [1]; 104:1; 111:3; 148:13).

The narrative of Judg 3:12-30 is prefaced by a typical rehearsal of Israel's unfaithfulness and consequent oppression at the hands of the MOABITES under their king, EGLON. Following a period of eighteen years, Israel (predictably) "cries out to Yahweh, and then Yahweh raises up a savior" (3:12-15a). The narrative concludes with an equally typical summary concerning the great number of Moabite warriors who were killed (about 10,000) and an idyllic eighty years of rest (i.e., double the traditional forty year generation) that followed the deliverance effected by Ehud (3:29-30).

Within this framework is set the story of Ehud. The characterizations of the named characters in this story already signal the humorous nature of the tale. Ehud's theophoric name bears witness to the majesty of God in creation while he himself is (literally) "hampered in his right hand" (*'iṭṭēr yad yemînô*) or "left-handed" (RSV). The irony of his majestic left-handedness is heightened by the notice that he is a Benjaminite, literally one of the "sons of the right-hand" (3:15a; cf. the similar pun in Judg 20:16). Ehud's royal opponent (who should, of course, be somewhat majestic) is named Eglon, meaning "little calf"; the narrator remarks that he "was a very fat man" (3:17).

The names of the tale's characters are only the beginning of the humor. Other humorous notes include the specially prepared, concealed weapon that the handicapped Ehud strapped to his right thigh (3:16), the twice-told ruse of his announcement of a "word of secret/word of God" for the king (3:19, 20; in Israel, it should be noted, the "word of Yahweh" was public, not secret: cf. Isa 45:19), the setting of Eglon's assassination in the royal privy (3:20), and the detail of how his girth "concealed" Ehud's sword even after the deed (3:22). While Ehud makes good his escape, the final bit of humor in the tale is provided by his majesty's dithering servants (3:24-25). Rallying the Israelite troops from the hill country of Ephraim, Ehud leads them in battle against the Moabites whom Yahweh has already given into their hand (3:26-28).

The Ehud mentioned in the genealogy of 1 Chr 8:6a is very likely to be identified with the hero of Judg 3:12-30.

The reading, "And Gera and Abihud," in 1 Chr 8:3 should probably be emended to read, "And Gera, the father of Ehud." If this common proposal is correct, then it may be concluded that the rubric of 1 Chr 8:6a ("These are the sons of Ehud") refers back to the names recorded in vv. 4-5, thereby relieving Bela from having two sons named Gera.

See also EGLON.

Bibliography. R. G. Boling, *Judges: Introduction, Translation, and Commentary*; M. Noth, *Die israelitischen Personennamen im Rahmen der gemeinsemitischen Namengebung*; J. A. Soggin, *Judges: A Commentary*.

—JOHN KEATING WILES

• **Eighteen Benedictions.** *See* BENEDICTIONS, EIGHTEEN

• **Ekron.** [ek'ruhn] Ekron was one of the cities of the famed PHILISTINE Pentapolis (1 Sam 6:17—ASHDOD, ASHKELON, Ekron, GATH, GAZA). Tel Miqne (also called Khirbet el-Muqanna) has been identified as the site of ancient Ekron. Tell Miqne is located about thirteen mi. east of the modern city of Ashdod and the Mediterranean Sea and approximately twenty-five mi. due west of Jerusalem (PLATES 9, 12). The tell covers nearly fifty acres and is one of the largest Iron Age sites in Israel.

Ekron and its inhabitants are mentioned in thirteen OT passages. All of the Philistine cities remained to be taken according to Josh 13:3. Ekron marked the border of the territory of Judah but was not included in it according to Josh 15:11. But, according to Josh 15:45-46, it was included in Judah's allotment. In Josh 19:43, Ekron was included in the territory of Dan but was never annexed. Reading the verse as "Timnah of Ekron" instead of "Timnah and Ekron" solves the problem of its seeming allotment to two tribes as the smaller city of Timnah was within the territory of Ekron (Judg 14:1ff.). Thus, Ekron was alloted to Judah and Timnah of Ekron was alloted to Dan. Ekron was taken by Judah according to Judg 1:18.

Ekron was the third Philistine city that the captured Ark of the Covenant was taken to (1 Sam 5–6). Ekron was included, with the northeastern part of the Philistine territory, with lands returned to the Israelites during the judgeship of Samuel (1 Sam 7:14). Yet, after David killed Goliath, the Israelites pursued the Philistines to the gates of Ekron (1 Sam 17:52), indicating that Ekron was again a Philistine city. King Ahaziah of Israel sent to inquire of the god of Ekron, BAAL-ZEBUB, whether he would recover from his illness (2 Kgs 1:2-16). Ekron is included also in various lists of nations and peoples to be judged (Jer 25:20; Amos 1:6-8; Zeph 2:4; Zech 9:5-7).

Some scholars say that though Ekron is not mentioned in early Egyptian records, it was a Canaanite city earlier in its history like the other cities of the Pentapolis. Others say that this absence of information argues for the view that the city was founded by the Philistines. If it was established by the Philistines—and this seems fairly certain now—that would change the prevailing concept that the Philistines only overpowered existing settlements rather than beginning their own.

Ekron appears in a list of places captured by Pharaoh Shishak in 918 B.C.E. Ekron was captured by Assyrian King Sargon II in 712 B.C.E. Inscriptions of Sennacherib reveal that Ekron remained loyal to its Assyrian overlord when Judah revolted in 705 B.C.E. Hezekiah of Judah captured King Padi of Ekron and held him hostage for his refusal to join the revolt (cf. 2 Kgs 18:7-8). When Sennacherib campaigned in Judah, however, he forced Hezekiah to release Padi and gave some of Judah's territory to him as a reward for his loyalty. Also according to neo-Assyrian documents, Ikausu, Padi's successor, was not so fortunate and had to pay tribute to Assyrian kings Esarhaddon and Ashurbanipal in the seventh century B.C.E.

Since 1981, Tell Miqne has been excavated by S. Gitin of the W. F. Albright Institute of Archaeological Research and T. Dothan of the Hebrew University. Recent finds include a unique Philistine palace, an industrial complex for olive oil processing, and a massive city wall.

Bibliography. Y. Aharoni and M. Avi-Yonah, *The MacMillan Bible Atlas*; T. Dothan and S. Gitin, "Tel Miqne/Ekron," *Excavations and Surveys in Israel*; A. Mazar, "Israeli Archaeologists," *Benchmarks in Time and Culture*, J. F. Drinkard, Jr., G. L. Mattingly, and J. M. Miller, eds.; W. F. Stinespring, "Ekron," *IDB*.

—TIMOTHY G. CRAWFORD

• **El.** [el] El (אֵל) was the basic or general name for "God" or "deity" used by the semitic peoples of the ancient Near East. The term El represents one of the oldest names used for deity in the ancient world. It appears in ancient Akkadian texts in the form *'ilu* and in Ugaritic texts as *'il*. Though the origin of the term and the root from which it was derived are uncertain, El most likely comes from an ancient root meaning "power," "might" or "active power."

In the OT the word El is used both as a name for God and as an adjective. The adjectival use is seen in expressions like "the power of your hand" (Deut 28:32), and "the mighty cedars with its branches" (Ps 80:10) in which the Hebrew word El is translated "power" and "mighty." Also, El was used in a theophorous sense, that is, it was used to form personal names, such as Eliezer, which means "God is help" (Gen 15:2), and Reuel, which means "friend of God" (Exod 2:18).

El was used by Israel's neighbors, the Canaanites, as the name of the chief god of their pantheon. The Ugaritic texts, the major extrabiblical source on Canaanite religion, describe El as a grandfatherly figure who was revered by the Canaanites as the father of the gods, the father of humans, and the lord of the heavens. Major decisions considered by the other gods in the pantheon had to be approved by El.

In the OT the name El was commonly used in worship by the patriarchs. It usually appeared with other descriptive titles such as EL SHADDAI, El Elyon, El Olam, El Roi, etc. Though the background of these names is obscure, several theories have been proposed concerning their origin. The names were perhaps originally the names of different deities, or names that were used for worship at the various worship centers. While the information is limited, the OT does make reference to the polytheistic strands in ISRAEL's background (Josh 24:14ff.). However, whatever their background, in the OT, they are seen as names for the God of Israel (Gen 33:20), literally "El, the God of Israel," and therefore names for Yahweh, the God of Israel. The important role these names played in patriarchal worship is reflected in Exod 6:2-3. According to this passage the patriarchs did not know God by the name Yahweh. Rather, Yahweh informed MOSES, "I appeared to ABRAHAM, to ISAAC, and to JACOB as "El Shaddai" (Exod 6:3).

El Shaddai seems to be the most commonly used of the El titles during the patriarchal period. It probably meant "God of the mountain" and most likely conveyed the idea of divine might and majesty. It is usually translated "God

Almighty.'' The name appears in Gen 17:1, the account in which the covenant is made with Abraham, as well as other patriarchal narratives (Gen 28:3; 35:11; 43:14; 48:3; 49:25). In addition to the references in Genesis, the name is found in Exodus (6:2-3), Ruth (1:20-21), Psalms (68:14; 91:1), Ezekiel (1:24; 10:5), and twenty-nine times in the Book of Job.

While El Shaddai was not associated with any one particular worship site, the name El Elyon was used in worship at the site of Jerusalem during the patriarchal period. The term Elyon is used in the OT both as an adjective and a noun. Since the noun form means ''the most High,'' or ''the Highest,'' the name El Elyon is usually rendered ''God Most High.'' The association of the name with worship in JERUSALEM is based on the account in Gen 14 in which MELCHIZEDEK is identified as the ''priest of El Elyon'' (Gen 14:18). Because the account refers to pre-Israelite Jerusalem and since the Canaanites spoke of El as the '' most High,'' many suggest that El Elyon was the name of the deity worshiped by the Canaanites in Jerusalem. That the Israelites used the name El Elyon for Yahweh is underscored by Abraham's statement, ''I have sworn to Yahweh, El Elyon'' (Gen 14:22), as well as other references, usually in poetic form, in which the name El Elyon or Elyon is synonymous with Yahweh (cf. Deut 32:8-9; 2 Sam 22:14; Pss 7:17; 9:1-2; 21:7; 91:1-2, 9). Though the name apparently was not used during the greater part of the OT period, references in the Book of DANIEL indicate that the name survived and reappeared in later history; (Dan 3:26; 4:24, 32, 34; 7:18, 22, 25, 27).

The name El Olam meant ''God Everlasting'' and appears only once in this form (Gen 21:33). In the account, Abraham made a covenant with Abimelech after the dispute over a well. The covenant was concluded by Abraham, who planted a tamarisk tree and called on the name of ''Yahweh El Olam.'' Because the event took place at BEERSHEBA, the name is associated with worship at Beersheba during the patriarchal period. While the title El Olam is not found elsewhere in the OT, Olam was used in reference to Yahweh (Isa 40:28; also cf. Ps 90:2), and the attributes of Yahweh (Pss 104:31; 117:2; Isa 54:8; Jer 31:3).

The name El Roi, which probably meant ''God who sees'' or ''God who sees me,'' is found only once in the OT (Gen 16:13). El Roi was the name by which HAGAR addressed Yahweh at the spring Beer-lahai-roi after she fled from SARAH. The idea of ''seeing'' in this name seems to be related to the term ''seer'' (1 Sam 9:9, 11, 18-19). The ''seer'' was a prophetic-type person who declared the word or will of God on the basis of what he saw.

The name El Bethel is found in Gen 31:13 and Gen 35:7; however, the meaning of the name is not clear. Some propose that the name should be translated ''the God of Bethel'' (literally ''El of the house of El''). Others suggest the name meant ''the God Bethel'' because that name appears in the Elephantine Papyri.

The name El Berith (Judg 9:46) meant ''God of the covenant'' and was used in worship by the Canaanites at the site of SHECHEM. Baal-berith (Judg 9:4) was perhaps an alternate or later form of the name. The remains of the temple of El Berith were found in excavations at the site of Shechem.

While the name El was especially popular during the patriarchal period, it is also found in literature from later periods, particularly the poetic literature of Psalms and Job. In these passages the name El was used as a synonym for Yahweh.

See also GOD, NAMES OF.

Bibliography. W. F. Albright, *From the Stone Age to Christianity*; F. M. Cross, ''אֵל,'' *TDOT*; W. Eichrodt, *Theology of the Old Testament*; E. Jacob, *Theology of the Old Testament*; M. H. Pope, *El in the Ugaritic Texts*; H. Ringgren, *Israelite Religion*.

—LAMOINE DEVRIES

• **El Shaddai.** [el-shad'*i*] The generic name for God in the ancient Near East was EL. Combined with a second term, El is made more specific and the divine is described more concretely. ''El Shaddai'' occurs seven times (Gen 17:1; 28:3; 35:11; 43:14; 48:3; Exod 6:3; Ezek 10:5). Perhaps this phrase was the most popular designation for God among the Hebrew patriarchs prior to the name ''Yahweh'' (cf. Exod 6:3).

The precise meaning of ''Shaddai'' is difficult to establish. Commonly translated ''Almighty'' (i.e., powerful), perhaps its root word is the Hebrew term meaning ''devastate, destroy, deal violently with.'' Another suggested translation is ''mountain'' (thus ''God of the Mountain'') based upon an Akkadian word that the Hebrews may have borrowed.

See also BAAL; EL; GOD, NAMES OF.

—DONALD W. GARNER

• **Eldad and Modad.** [el'dad, moh'dad] *Eldad and Modad* is a lost pseudepigraphical work extant in only a single citation in the second-century writing, the SHEPHERD OF HERMAS: ''The Lord is near to those who turn (to him)'' (*Vis* 2.3.4). Evidence from rabbinic sources and from the Targum of Pseudo-Jonathan on Num 11:26 suggests that the book contained references to the end of time, a final war involving GOG and Magog, and the coming of a victorious royal MESSIAH.

Apparently the purpose of the book was to give content to the prophecies of the OT figures Eldad and Modad (Medad) who, according to Num 11:26-29, were the two elders who continued to prophesy in the camp after the other seventy had ceased. Since so little of the book is preserved, it is difficult to say much about its origins, other than that it was evidently composed before the second century C.E., perhaps by a Jew. On the other hand, traditions about Eldad and Modad, as well as the book itself, were widely known in the early church. Epiphanius speaks of the two prophets among the seventy-two, and Pseudo-Jerome identifies them as half-brothers of MOSES. Furthermore, the book is mentioned (as apocryphal) in five ancient canonical lists, the latest being that of Nicephorus (ninth century), with the notation that it contains four hundred lines.

Bibliography. E. G. Martin, ''Eldad and Modad,'' *The Old Testament Pseudepigrapha,* ed. J. H. Charlesworth.

—JOSEPH L. TRAFTON

• **Elder.** Originally an elder was simply an older person. Because wisdom and maturity were frequently associated with old age in the ancient world, the term came to refer to a person of authority.

In the OT elders held authority in the family, tribe, and nation. Elders were prominent in the time of Moses (Exod 3:16; 4:29; 12:21; 17:5). God told Moses to gather seventy of the elders to assist him in leading the Hebrews (Num 11:16-30). Elders appeared in the periods of the judges and the monarchy (Judg 8:16; 1 Sam 15:30; 1 Kgs 8:3). They were especially prominent during and after the Exile (Jer

29:1; Ezra 5:9; 10:14).

The elders were local rulers or magistrates. One of their principal roles was that of judge. The elders met at the city gate to determine guilt or innocence (Deut 22:15). Apparently every town had its own assembly of elders (Deut 19:12). Succoth, for example, had seventy-seven elders at one point (Judg 8:14). The elders considered such issues as murder (Deut 21:1-9), rebellious sons (Deut 21:18-21), a bride's virginity (Deut 22:13-21), and levirate marriage (Deut 25:5-10). They witnessed business dealings (Ruth 4:4) and were involved in military activity (Josh 8:10f.; 1 Sam 4:3). They requested the selection of the first king, Saul (1 Sam 8:4-5), and were active in the reigns of several kings (1 Kgs 12:6; Jer 26:17f.). The elders also helped in the religious life of the Hebrews. They assisted Moses in the covenant ceremony at Mount Sinai (Exod 24:1-2, 9-11) and in some sacrifices (Lev 4:13-21). They are linked at times with the priests (1 Kgs 8:3), and the elders of the priests are mentioned once (2 Kgs 19:2 KJV).

In the Maccabean period members of the SANHEDRIN in Jerusalem were called elders. Local communities of 120 or more could appoint seven elders.

In the NT "elder" can again refer to an older person (Luke 15:25), but it generally refers to leaders in Jewish synagogues or Christian leaders. Each Jewish community had a council or assembly of elders. The Sanhedrin in Jerusalem was a council of seventy leaders which traced its origin to the seventy elders who assisted Moses (*Sanh* 1.6). At Qumran the elders were second in importance only to the priests. In mainstream Judaism the elders were interpreters of the Law. On one occasion Jesus criticized the "tradition of the elders" (Mark 7:1-13; Matt 15:1-20) about ritual cleanliness.

Along with the apostles, elders were leaders in the early church in Jerusalem (Acts 11:30; 15:2, 6, 23; 16:4; 21:18). Paul and Barnabas appointed elders in the churches they founded on their first missionary journey (Acts 14:23). On his third journey Paul met with the Ephesian elders at Miletus (Acts 20:17).

Christian elders were probably ministers. Most scholars agree that elders and BISHOPS or overseers were the same office or task (Acts 20:17, 28). The title elder probably suggests maturity as a requirement for leadership, and bishop or overseer reflects a basic task of the minister. Elders were involved in preaching and teaching (1 Tim 5:17). Peter identified himself as a "fellow elder" when he offered advice to elders (1 Pet 5:1-5). The elders could also be called to pray for the sick and to anoint them with oil (Jas 5:14).

The elder who wrote 2 and 3 John may have been a minister or a highly respected person in the church. The twenty-four elders in Revelation (4:4, 10; 5:5-14; 7:13; 19:4) probably reflect the twelve apostles and the twelve patriarchs or tribes of Israel.

See also BISHOP; DEACON; MINISTER/SERVE.

Bibliography. H. von Campenhausen, *Ecclesiastical Authority and Spiritual Powers in the Churches of the First Three Centuries*.

—WARREN MCWILLIAMS

• **Election.** Refers primarily to God's choice of a people to participate in the divine redeeming purpose and to individuals who perform special functions related to God's chosen people and their mission. Election is emphasized as for witness and service, not primarily for privilege (Exod 19:3-6).

The meaning of Israel's election as the people of God attains classic interpretation in Second Isaiah, where Israel is referred to repeatedly as the servant whom Yahweh has chosen for universal mission: ISRAEL is to be a "light to the nations" so that God's salvation "may reach to the end of the earth" (Isa 49:6).

In the NT the church is understood as God's chosen people (1 Pet 2:9-10). Even more clearly than Israel, the church is invested with a universal mission (Matt 28:18-20; Luke 24:46-49, etc.). Also, in the NT election is related to eternal salvation and is sometimes equated with predestination (Eph 1:3-5; Rom 8:29-30). The elaboration of this concept led to highly abstract and individualistic interpretations of election, especially in Calvinism.

It is important to understand election as God's choice of a people both to participate in and to mediate God's universal redemption. What is most distinctive about the NT concept is the conviction that JESUS Christ is the supremely chosen servant of God, embodying in himself the mission of Israel (Matt 12:18; Luke 9:35; 1 Pet 2:4), and that Christians are chosen in him (Eph 1:4). Christians have no claim to God's election except as they belong to Christ and participate in his mission.

See also CHURCH; COVENANT; ISRAEL; LIGHT IN THE OLD TESTAMENT.

Bibliography. W. Pannenberg, *Human Nature, Election, and History*; H. H. Rowley, *The Biblical Doctrine of Election*.

—E. LUTHER COPELAND

• **Eli.** [ee'l*i*] A judge for forty years (1 Sam 4:18) and the founder of the Elide priesthood. The priest of SHILOH is first encountered in association with HANNAH, the wife of Elkanah the Ephraimite. Hannah prayed for a son at Shiloh, promising to dedicate him to the service of the Lord if the wish were granted. The petition was granted and SAMUEL was born. After Hannah weaned him, Samuel was taken to Shiloh and placed in the care of Eli (1 Sam 1). The boy Samuel began ministering to the Lord at Shiloh in the presence of Eli (1 Sam 2:11).

Eli's two sons, HOPHNI and PHINEHAS, served at the sanctuary but had no regard for their positions. They abused their priestly offices by stealing the sacrificial meat and treating the offerings with contempt (1 Sam 2:12-17). They also used women who served at the TENT OF MEETING for sexual purposes. When Eli reprimanded them and warned them of the consequences of their indecent actions, the sons ignored him (1 Sam 2:22-25).

First Samuel reports that an unnamed man of God gave Eli a warning and spoke a condemnation against his family for Eli's failure to honor God above his sons and for the sons' atrocious actions. The condemnation was that his house would lose its favored status as priests (1 Sam 2:27-36). This story validates the later exclusion of Eli's descendant ABIATHAR from the high priesthood and the establishment of Zadok and his descendants as priests (1 Kgs 2:27). An equivalent denunciation is given as part of the call of Samuel (1 Sam 3).

The beginning of the destruction of the family of Eli took place at the battle of Aphek, where the ARK was captured by the Philistines. During the fighting Phinehas and Hophni were killed. When word of the disaster reached Eli at Shiloh, he fell from his seat by the side of the gate, broke his neck and died (1 Sam 4:1-18). Phinehas's wife gave birth to a son whom she named Ichabod, meaning "no glory," for the glory of God was seen as having departed from Israel with the loss of the ark (1 Sam 4:19-22).

Eli's house was not completely annihilated at this time, however. His descendants through Ahitub, brother of Ichabod and son of Phinehas, continued to be priests at Shiloh (1 Sam 14:3). By the time of David's reign, the Eli priesthood had established itself at NOB where Ahimelech, son of Ahitub, served as a priest (1 Sam 22:11-12). Because of their aid to DAVID, SAUL had Doeg the Edomite kill the priests. Abiathar, one of Ahimelech's sons, escaped (1 Sam 22:16-19). When David became king, he appointed Abiathar as priest. At David's death, SOLOMON expelled Abiathar as priest, exiled him to Anathoth, and completed the word spoken against the house of Eli at Shiloh (1 Kgs 2:26-27).

See also PRIESTS.

Bibliography. H. W. Hetzberg, *I & II Samuel: A Commentary, OTL.*

—ROBERT A. STREET, JR.

• **Eliakim.** *See* JEHOIAKIM; JUDAH, KINGDOM OF

• **Elijah.** [i-lī'juh] An Israelite prophet who ministered during the reigns of AHAB (ca. 869–850 B.C.E.) and Ahaziah (ca. 850–849 B.C.E.). He was a vigorous supporter of his God, Yahweh. Elijah's name, which means either "My God is Yahweh" or "Yahweh is God," reflected his zeal. The DEUTERONOMISTIC HISTORIAN selected certain episodes, a mixture of legend and history, from a cycle of stories about Elijah and inserted his interpretation of this period in 1 Kgs 17–19; 1 Kgs 21; 2 Kgs 1; and 2 Kgs 2:1-12. Elijah's reputation and influence are witnessed in 2 Chr 21:12-15; Mal 4:5-6 (Heb 3:23-24); Sir 48:1-14, several apocalypses bearing his name, the NT, and traditions that grew within the three monotheistic faiths: Judaism, Christianity, and Islam.

The first story (1 Kgs 17–19) abruptly begins with Elijah's proclaiming to Ahab, the syncretistic Israelite king, the beginning of a drought. Upon the instruction of Yahweh, he immediately went to the brook Cherith where he hid from the wrath of Ahab and his Phoenician wife, JEZEBEL, who had been slaughtering the prophets of Yahweh. He stayed there, sustained by the brook, and fed by ravens, until the brook dried up and Yahweh directed him to stay with a widow and her son in Zarephath. When he arrived in Zarephath, he found the widow preparing the last meal she could manage on her meager provisions. However, Elijah assured her that Yahweh would oversee her well-being if she would care for him. She believed him and Elijah's promise proved true. Her son did fall violently ill during this time, but Elijah intervened and implored Yahweh to heal the boy. The boy revived and this restoration provided further proof of Elijah's power and position as a servant of God.

Suddenly, Elijah received another commission; he was to inform Ahab that the drought would soon end. On his way to deliver the message, Elijah encountered Obadiah ("servant of Yahweh"), the head of Ahab's household, searching for suitable pasture for the royal animals. Elijah directed him to return to Ahab and announce Elijah's subsequent appearance. Obadiah was unnerved by this request, for Elijah's unpredictability threatened his life, his position, and his surreptitious protection of the prophets of Yahweh. Elijah swore that he would appear and Obadiah returned and reported to Ahab.

After an initial encounter between Elijah and Ahab during which Ahab placed the blame for the drought on Elijah and Elijah, in turn, blamed Ahab's apostasy, Elijah called for a contest between himself and the 450 prophets of BAAL and the 400 prophets of ASHERAH to be held on the top of MOUNT CARMEL; this contest would decide who was to be God in Israel. Ahab consented and soon the people of Israel, the prophets of Baal, and Elijah were assembled. Elijah suggested that both parties in this contest build an altar complete with a sacrifice, and the god who ignited the sacrifice would be recognized as the true God. Elijah allowed the prophets of Baal to proceed first but their rituals, cries, and self-mutilation did nothing. Then, Elijah prepared his altar and sacrifice, poured water over the whole arrangement, and prayed to Yahweh. Marvelously, the FIRE of Yahweh fell, and even the altar was consumed. In the acclamation of Yahweh's supremacy, Elijah exhorted the people to take the prophets of Baal to the brook KISHON. They were slaughtered there.

As the rain came, Elijah ran before the chariot of Ahab all the way to the royal residence in Jezreel. However, Jezebel greeted the news of Yahweh's victory with renewed resistance to Yahwism and pledged to kill Elijah. Elijah sank into deep depression, fled into the desert, and asked Yahweh to take his life. A messenger sent from Yahweh provided sustenance to Elijah and sent him to Horeb (PLATE 9) for an audience with Yahweh. Upon his arrival at a cave on Horeb, Yahweh pressed Elijah for the reason he was there. Elijah's reply highlighted his zeal at the expense of everyone else, including Yahweh. Subsequently, Elijah witnessed traditional theophanic elements—a strong wind, an EARTHQUAKE, a fire—but none of these elements revealed God. In the silence that followed, Elijah was drawn out of the cave into God's presence. Yahweh once again asked Elijah the reason he was there. Elijah repeated his former answer. Thereupon, Yahweh released this stubborn prophet from his service and sent him to anoint other persons who would complete the war against Baalism. The final act of Elijah's ministry in this story is his enlistment of ELISHA in the active service of Yahweh.

This story has ever been a source of conflicting judgments concerning Elijah. Sirach (48:4) claims: "How glorious you were, O Elijah, in your wondrous deeds! And who has the right to boast that you have?" Yet, PAUL, the apostle, senses the pride and unbelief in Elijah's story when he says: "Do you not know what the scripture says of Elijah, how he pleads with God against Israel? 'Lord, they have killed thy prophets, they have demolished their altars, and I alone am left, and they seek my life.' " But what is God's reply to him? " 'I have kept for myself 7,000 men who have not bowed the knee to Baal' " (Rom 11:3-4). This story continues to teach and maintain its appeal because of its ironic structure; Elijah is the *alazōn* or pretender who is unmasked by the *eirōn* or assassin of pretension. Elijah had eclipsed the will of Yahweh with his own will. For most of the story the two wills had paralleled each other neatly, but when Elijah thought the final victory had been won at Carmel and Kishon, Jezebel met him with a threat; he was discovered and he sank into deep despair. Another ironic account of a willful prophet, the Book of JONAH, mirrors many of the dynamics of this account.

The second story, 1 Kgs 21, picks up the mystery and severity of Elijah and weaves that together with royal greed. Ahab noticed a vineyard below his palace and desired it, as DAVID years before had seen and desired a woman. He offered the owner, NABOTH, another vineyard or a handsome price for the land, but Naboth would not give up the inheritance of his ancestors. This angered and disappointed Ahab, but he did nothing but pout. However, Jezebel ridiculed his timidity and devised a plot by which Naboth would be accused and convicted of defaming Yahweh and the king. For this crime he would be killed.

The plan followed its course; Naboth was killed and Ahab took possession of the vineyard. As he began his inaugural tour of his new property, he met the prophet Elijah, who had been sent by Yahweh to pronounce judgment. When Ahab heard the terms of the judgment he tore his clothes in a dramatic act of repentance. Thereupon, Yahweh instructed Elijah to delay the implementation of the sentence.

The third story, 2 Kgs 1, maintains the fierce monotheism associated with Elijah. The son of Ahab, Ahaziah, was injured in a fall and sent messengers to BAAL-ZEBUB, the god of EKRON, in order to discover the possibility of his recovery. Elijah intercepted the messengers with his measured sarcasm and sent the messengers back with an ominous message—"Is it because there is no God in Israel that you are going to inquire of Baal-zebub . . . ? Now therefore thus says the Lord, 'You shall not come down from the bed to which you have gone, but you shall surely die' " (2 Kgs 1:3b-4). After the king heard the description of the man—"He wore a garment of haircloth, with a girdle of leather about his loins" (2 Kgs 1:8), he knew the man was Elijah. Two times he sent a captain with fifty men to secure Elijah and two times the men were consumed by fire. The third commander exhibited respect for Elijah, so Elijah accompanied him to see the king. Before the king, Elijah repeated his severe judgment; Ahaziah would never recover because he sought the oracle of another god.

The final story, 2 Kgs 2:1-14, links the ministry of Elijah with that of Elisha, just as these two ministries had been linked in 1 Kgs 19:19-21. Elijah began to journey beyond the Jordan to be taken away by Yahweh and Elisha accompanied him. In every town they visited, Elijah instructed Elisha to stay, as he had instructed his young man to stay in Beersheba earlier (1 Kgs 19:3). Elisha, sensing the coming departure, dogged his master's steps. Finally, they crossed the Jordan together. Just before a chariot of fire carried Elijah away, Elijah asked Elisha what he desired. Elisha begged for a double portion of Elijah's spirit, which he indeed received because he saw Elijah depart. He also took Elijah's mantle, which fell to the ground as Elijah was taken, a mantle that seemed to possess magical powers. Then Elisha returned across the Jordan and went on his way.

The Chronicler (2 Chr 21:12-15) includes what might be considered a very fanciful tale. He records a letter sent to JEHORAM, a southern king, from Elijah. This letter condemned the king for departing from the ways of Asa and Jehoshaphat and conducting his policies in the manner of the degenerate kings of Israel. Jehoram's family was threatened with a plague while Jehoram was promised a bowel disease that would kill him.

The prediction included in Mal 4:5-6 builds on the unpredictable nature of Elijah's ministry and the wonder of his departure from his earthly mission. He is identified with the messenger described in Mal 3:1-4, and thereby linked to the purification that precedes the coming of the Lord, or the messianic kingdom. On the basis of such expectations, Jesus is identified with Elijah during his ministry (Matt 16:14; Mark 8:28; Luke 9:8), though Jesus perceived John the Baptist to fulfill that role (Matt 11:14; 17:10-13; Mark 1:2; 9:10-12; Luke 1:16-17; 7:27).

To be sure, the historical Elijah has been obscured in these sometimes patchy or truncated stories laced with historical reminiscence and legendary embellishments, and yet these narratives testify to a person who was fiercely loyal to Yahweh, even though like many humans he was subject to grandiosity. He constantly heeded the call of Yahweh and mirrored Yahweh's surprising presence in his abrupt appearances. He longed for an Israel with an undivided loyalty and he spent his life working toward that goal.

He is remembered in a tangible way in Judaism today. During circumcision, a symbol of the covenant Elijah claimed Israel had broken, an unoccupied chair, the Elijah chair, grants a special solemnity to the ceremony. The cup of Elijah adorns the table of the Passover seder in the event that this mystifying, hidden but living prophet chooses to visit these faithful in this "season of redemption."

See also AHAB; BAAL; ELISHA; JEZEBEL; JOHN THE BAPTIST; MIRACLES; MIRACLE STORY; PROPHET; PROPHECY; THEOPHANY.

—RUSSELL I. GREGORY

• **Elijah, Apocalypse of.** [i-l*i*'juh, uh-pok'uh-lips] Two separate documents carry the title *The Apocalypse of Elijah*. One of these is in rabbinic Hebrew and recounts a revelation from the angel MICHAEL to ELIJAH on MOUNT CARMEL regarding the time of the ANTICHRIST. The other, however, is extant in Coptic, has received a greater amount of scholarly attention, and is the focus of this article. The title to this Coptic document is misleading, as the framework of the document bears little similarity to that of an apocalypse, and it does not claim to be from or to Elijah. The martyrdom of Elijah is treated in an apocalyptic fashion, however, which may explain the title.

As the *Apocalypse* stands it represents a Christian editing of an earlier Jewish document. Both elements are present in the content of the *Apocalypse,* which is a prophecy containing a parenetic section, an apocalyptic timetable, a section concerning the MAN OF LAWLESSNESS, an account of the martyrdom and persecution of the faithful, and the events of the last days. Since the document in its present form exhibits dependence on REVELATION, the Greek text of the *Apocalypse of Elijah* may be dated in the late second to early third centuries C.E.

The redactional nature of the *Apocalypse* renders any clear statement about the impact of this document impossible. The *Apocalypse* does contain elements of Jewish apocalyptic content and style, having some correspondence with the style of DANIEL. Just as clearly, Christian apocalyptic concerns have been interwoven with the Jewish, pointing the final document toward a Christian audience.

See also APOCALYPTIC LITERATURE.

Bibliography. J. H. Charlesworth, *The Pseudepigrapha in Modern Research*; O. S. Wintermute, "Apocalypse of Elijah," *The Old Testament Pseudepigrapha,* ed. J. H. Charlesworth.

—STEVEN SHEELEY

• **Elisabeth.** *See* ELIZABETH

• **Elisha.** [i-l*i*'shuh] Elisha ("God is deliverance") was the disciple and prophetic successor of ELIJAH the prophet. According to our sources, Elisha's long ministry spanned the reigns of the Northern kings Ahab, Ahaziah, Jehoram, Jehoahaz and Jehoash. Elisha was a native of Abel-meholah and appears to have been from a family of considerable wealth.

Information about Elisha is primarily found in a variety

of stories contained in 2 Kgs 1–13. He is introduced, however, in 1 Kgs 19:19-21 where Elijah calls him to the prophetic vocation. This episode appears to be an introduction to a longer narrative that was primarily intended to proclaim that Elisha was indeed the prophetic successor of his master Elijah. In an episode that is reminiscent of JOSHUA's succession of MOSES, Elisha witnesses the translation of Elijah into the heavens after which he receives a "double portion" of Elijah's spirit (2 Kgs 2:1-12). His authority as a prophetic leader is vindicated by a series of miracles performed in the presence of the prophetic disciples. These include the parting of the Jordan (2 Kgs 2:13-14), the purifying of the waters of JERICHO (2 Kgs 2:19-22), the healing of the poisonous stew at GILGAL (2 Kgs 4:38-41), the retrieval of the ax head from the Jordan (2 Kgs 6:1-7), and the production of a limitless supply of oil for a needy widow (2 Kgs 4:1-7). The miraculous powers of Elisha are also portrayed in the stories concerning the multiplication of the loaves (2 Kgs 4:42-44) and the revival of a corpse through mere contact with Elisha's bones (2 Kgs 14:20-21). The unsavory tale about Elisha's calling down bears upon the forty-two children who had taunted his baldness was probably included in the collection in order to magnify Elisha's powers (2 Kgs 2:23-25). But it reads as if it was originally told to children, intended to dissuade them from associating with these prophets who were often regarded by outsiders as madmen (cf. 2 Kgs 9:11).

Of more literary complexity are the satires about the Shunammite woman (2 Kgs 4:8-38; 8:1-6) and the account of the healing of NAAMAN (2 Kgs 5:1-27). The story about the Shunammite woman consists of two episodes. The first tells of the fulfillment of Elisha's prediction that the childless Shunammite woman would bear a son in return for her hospitality toward the prophet (2 Kgs 4:8-17). The next episode narrates how the child is miraculously healed by Elisha after the boy dies from sunstroke (2 Kgs 4:18-37). Like the other miracle stories, this one is intended to highlight Elisha's prophetic powers. But here one detects an interest in emphasizing the prophet's concern to relieve the suffering of this grieving woman.

The episode about the return of the woman's land after her sojourn in the land of the PHILISTINES (2 Kgs 8:1-6) presupposes the previous story about the Shunammite woman, but appears to be an appendix to it. It also portrays Elisha's willingness to extricate the woman from her problems. In this case, however, Elisha's reputation rather than his power is the means by which the desired outcome is achieved.

The story of the healing of Naaman's leprosy urges the teaching that "there is no god in all the earth except in Israel" (2 Kgs 5:15), and that those who believe in Yahweh and yet are forced to worship other gods are forgiven for doing so (2 Kgs 5:18-19). The corollary of this central teaching is that Yahweh's prophets are likewise true. They are not motivated by greed. This latter point is illustrated through Gehazi's actions. He seeks to profit from Naaman's gratitude by receiving payment after Elisha had adamantly refused it. For this sin of greed, Elisha punishes Gehazi and his descendants by afflicting them with leprosy (2 Kgs 5:20-27).

Several stories tell of Elisha's involvement in Israel's military conflicts with traditional enemies. The account of the actions that Israel and Judah took together to quell the Moabite rebellion (2 Kgs 3:1-25a) develops as one would expect, but takes a surprising turn at the conclusion of the story (2 Kgs 3:25b-27). Israel and Judah form an alliance to deal with the problem of Moab's rebellion. But victory becomes impossible when they discover that the wilderness of EDOM does not supply them with water needed to sustain the armies. At the suggestion of JEHOSHAPHAT, the king of Judah, Elisha is summoned to provide an escape from these dire straits. Speaking for Yahweh, the prophet reluctantly agrees to provide the armies with both water and victory over the Moabites. Elisha then instructs the kings to have the valley filled with trenches and predicts that the trenches will be miraculously filled with water. The next morning finds the prophecy fulfilled; and the presence of the water-filled trenches not only provides drink for the armies, but is also instrumental in deceiving the Moabites into believing that Israel and Judah have killed one another. The deception provides Israel and Judah with an easy victory, thereby fulfilling Elisha's prediction that the land of Moab would be decimated (3:19, 25a). With the problem of Moab's rebellion resolved, one would expect the story to conclude here. But it continues on to tell how the king of Moab sought to break through to Edom, his ally (cf. v. 9 which has Edom as an ally of Israel and Judah). Unable to do so, the king of Moab sacrifices his oldest son in desperation. Surprisingly, the sacrifice results in bringing "great wrath upon Israel" and in driving Israel out of Moab (v. 27)!

The other stories involving Elisha are set in the context of Israelite-Aramean conflict. In a story that plays with the motif of "sight" and "blindness," Elisha solves the problem of Aram's raids into Israelite territory (2 Kgs 6:8-23). Through his prophetic second sight, Elisha periodically informed the Israelite king of the location of Aramean troops, which understandably angered the king of Damascus. His attempts to apprehend the prophet were frustrated when Elisha struck the troops blind and directed them to Samaria where they were captured. At Elisha's counsel, the Israelite king treated the prisoners humanely and let them return to Aram, thereby putting an end to the problem of the marauding bands.

The story of the siege of SAMARIA (2 Kgs 6:24–7:20) is somewhat confused and seems to have undergone extensive redaction. The original story (6:24-30; 7:3-16a) tells of how Yahweh delivered Samaria from a dreadful siege by making the Arameans "hear the sound of chariots and horses," causing them to withdraw (2 Kgs 7:6). Into this account have been injected episodes that relate how the king blamed Elisha for the city's problems and how Elisha predicted that the siege be lifted and the royal officer who doubted Elisha's prophecy would die.

In two other stories (2 Kgs 8:7-15 and 2 Kgs 9:1–11:28) Elisha is portrayed as instigating a pair of political coups. In the case of Hazael's coup, Elisha instigates the murder of BEN-HADAD by telling Hazael to assure his master that the king will recover from his illness. At the same time and in contradiction of his message to Ben-Hadad, Elisha tells Hazael that Yahweh predicts that Ben-Hadad will in fact die and that Hazael will replace his master. As a result of the conversation, Hazael murders Ben-Hadad and seizes the throne of Aram. Elisha's role in Jehu's coup is identical. He proclaims that JEHU has been designated by Yahweh as king of Israel, which leads to Jehu's bloody seizure of the throne of Israel.

The account of Elisha's death (2 Kgs 13:14-17, 20a) portrays him on intimate terms with JOASH, the grandson of Jehu. Here Elisha predicts that Joash will enjoy a resounding victory over the Arameans. But the episode seems to have been supplemented with another that explains why

Joash only enjoyed three victories (2 Kgs 13:18-19).

From the numerous and varied stories that Elisha inspired, there can be no doubt that he was a prominent figure in ninth century Israel. Although a few stories seem to be critical of some of his political involvements, most are clearly intended to portray Elisha as Yahweh's spokesman to his generation.

See also ELIJAH; MIRACLES; PROPHET.

Bibliography. R. A. Carlson, "Elisee—le successeur d'ēlie," *VT* 20 (1970): 385-405; J. Gray, *I & II Kings: A Commentary*; H. Gunkel, "Die Revolution des Jehu," *Deutsche Rundschau* 40 (1913): 289-308; J. A. Montgomery, *A Critical and Exegetical Commentary on the Book of Kings*; A. Rofé, "The Classification of Prophetical Stories," *JBL* 89 (1970): 427-44.

—LLOYD M. BARRÉ

• **Elizabeth.** [i-liz'uh-buhth] A daughter of Aaron (i.e., of priestly descent), bearing the same name as Aaron's wife (Exod 6:23) whose name means "God is an oath," i.e., a covenant maker. According to Luke 1:5-7 Elizabeth was the wife of the aging priest ZECHARIAH. Both are described as "righteous before God, walking in all the commandments and ordinances of the Lord blameless." In short, Elizabeth and Zechariah embody the highest form of OT piety.

While barren and of advanced age, Elizabeth gave birth to JOHN THE BAPTIST. These circumstances parallel those of other women in Israel who as a result of divine intervention gave birth to special leaders for Israel (Rebekah, Gen 25:21; Rachel, Gen 29:31; Samson's mother, Judg 13:2ff.; HANNAH, 1 Sam 1:2, 5. This is interesting in view of the popular opinion that barrenness indicated sin or guilt!) There are especially close parallels with SARAH and the birth of Isaac. Both Elizabeth and Sarah are of advanced age. In both cases the announcement of the birth comes to the father rather than the mother. Both Abraham and Zechariah (John's father) find the announcement of the birth of their child hard to believe; however, while Sarah also finds the birth announcement hard to believe, Elizabeth demonstrates no such doubt. There are also interesting parallels in the account of Elkanah and Hannah (cf. 1 Sam 1:1, 3, 13, 17) whose son Samuel was one of the most famous Nazarites of the OT (note the description of John the Baptist as a Nazarite in Luke 1:15). In short it appears that Zechariah and Elizabeth figuratively relive the careers of these two OT sets of parents.

According to Luke 1:36, Elizabeth was a relative of MARY of Nazareth. While the term is too broad to define the precise relationship, tradition has suggested that the two were cousins. It is possible, therefore, that Mary may also have been of priestly descent. During the sixth month of Elizabeth's pregnancy, Mary visited her in a city in the hill country of Judea. When Elizabeth heard Mary's greeting, the baby in her womb leaped for joy (1:41); and filled with the Holy Spirit, Elizabeth welcomed Mary as the mother of her Lord (1:42-44). Thus, just as John would function as the one who pointed the way to Jesus, so his mother Elizabeth is portrayed as the one who points to the significance of Mary's child, Jesus. Some Old Latin manuscripts and a few Western fathers such as Irenaeus and Origin suggest that the MAGNIFICAT of Luke 1:46-55 may have originally been ascribed to Elizabeth.

See also HANNAH; JOHN THE BAPTIST; MARY; SARAH; ZECHARIAH.

Bibliography. I. H. Marshall, *Commentary on Luke*; R. Brown, *The Birth of the Messiah*.

—W. HULITT GLOER

• **Elohim.** *See* GOD

• **Elohist.** [el'oh-hist] One of the literary strata in the Pentateuch identified by the differences in the divine name, place names, religious and moral ideas, and appearance of literary phenomena, such as doublets. The Elohist (E) source uses Elohim for God's name, prefers such places as Horeb, BEERSHEBA, BETHEL and SHECHEM, favors dreams and angels in revelation, and elects to repeat events and teachings. Although its exact origin cannot be fixed, E reflects the period from 850–750 B.C.E. The source probably belonged to all Israel, which E considered a unity before the UNITED MONARCHY.

The study of the literary sources in the Pentateuch began with Witter (1711) and Astruc (1756). These studies later guided Eichhorn, who formulated in 1780 the "older documentary hypothesis" of two continuous sources (J, E) in GENESIS. By 1802, Geddes and Vater suggested their "fragment documentary hypothesis" for the Pentateuch. Next, Ewald and Bleek's "supplementary hypothesis" superseded the "older" view. In 1853, Hupfeld's "newer documentary hypothesis" of Priestly, Yahwist, Elohist, and Deuteronomic sources displaced Ewald and Bleek's conjectures. By 1878, Hupfeld's order of sources was rearranged to JEDP by Reuss, Graf, Kuenen, and Wellhausen.

More recently, Volz and Rudolph have doubted the existence of the Elohist. Volz thought that E and P were commentary on J. Rudolph called P the redactor and E only "interpolations." Wolff attempted to sketch the basic teachings of the Elohist. Without an acceptable *kērygma* (message) the Elohist has a doubtful existence as an independent source.

See also GENESIS, BOOK OF; LITERARY CRITICISM; YAHWIST.

—EDDIE L. RUDDICK

• **Elymas.** [el'uh-mahs] Elymas was a magician and false prophet (Acts 13:6-12), who appears with the proconsul SERGIUS PAULUS when Paul preaches to him. When Elymas opposes Paul, he is blinded temporarily.

Elymas is also called Bar-Jesus. The derivation of "Elymas" and its relation to Bar-Jesus are obscure. The first name given in the Acts account is Bar-Jesus (13:6). In 13:8 another name is given: "Elymas the magician (for that is the meaning of his name)." It would seem that Elymas means magician. In spite of numerous efforts no convincing explanation has linked the two words. Possibly, he was such a well-known magician that his name became synonymous with the practice of magic. It is also possible that Acts 13:8 is simply stating that the Greek form of the name of the Jew is Elymas. This would be in keeping with the Jewish practice of adopting Greek names.

See also SERGIUS PAULUS.

—WILLIAM R. HERZOG II

• **Embalming/Mummification.** Embalming is the process of treating a body to protect it from decay. It was practiced deliberately by the ancient Egyptians, though the process may have been discovered accidentally from early burials in the hot sands. The sand served as a natural desiccant, and would remove most of the moisture from the body so thoroughly that bacterial action was stopped and little decay took place, except around the central body cavity. The Wadi Natron in southern Egypt has natural salts containing sodium carbonate, sodium bicarbonate, sodium sulfate, and sodium chloride. These made a very powerful desiccant and preservative. Some of these early mummies, though not deliberately treated, still have the hair and fingernails preserved.

At least by the Fourth Dynasty, ca. 2600 B.C.E., deliberate mummification was taking place. The word mummy comes from the Arabic word for bitumen, apparently referring to the resins used in the embalming process.

The embalming process began with the removal of the internal organs. These were embalmed separately and then placed in canopic jars along with the body. The body itself was cleansed completely after the removal of the organs. It was then filled with natron solution and allowed to dry thoroughly in the dry sand or in natron crystals. This process took approximately forty days.

The body cavity often had *ushabtis,* and portions of the text of the *Book of the Dead* placed in it. A *ushabti* was a figurine that would accompany the person into the after-life and do the individual's bidding there. The portions of the *Book of the Dead* were placed there to aid the transition to the after-life.

Courtesy of the Eisenberg Museum of Biblical Archaeology, Southern Baptist Theological Seminary.

Tags used to identify the individual being prepared for burial.

Artwork by Margaret Jordan Brown

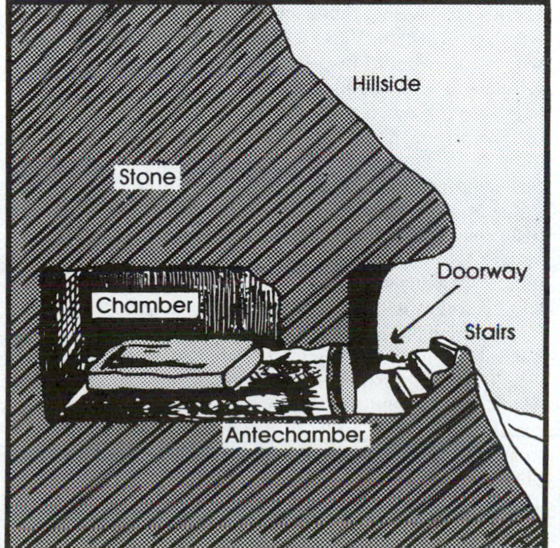

Layout of a typical first-century tomb.

Then the body was coated with aromatic resins and wrapped in linen. Each finger and toe was wrapped individually, then the hands and feet. Finally the entire body was wrapped. A mask depicting the face of the person was placed over the head and shoulders. The mummy was placed in a wooden coffin which was often painted and had inscriptions identifying the person and with additional texts from the *Book of the Dead.* Finally, the wooden coffin was placed in an outer wooden case, which was also decorated.

Mummification continued in Egypt from the Old Kingdom down to the fourth century C.E. After about 600 B.C.E., the process of mummification was in decline. Many of the masks and mummy cases from the later period, especially the Roman period, have quite realistic representations of the deceased. Perhaps it was the rise of Christianity in Egypt that brought an end to the practice of mummification.

—JOEL F. DRINKARD, JR.

• **Emmaus.** [i-may'uhs] Emmaus is mentioned but once, Luke 24:19, in a passing geographical reference which introduces the primary Lucan account of an appearance of the resurrected Jesus. Emmaus was located sixty stadia (seven mi.) from Jerusalem according to the reading followed by the RSV (PLATE 23). Some ancient authorities read "a hundred and sixty stadia." The textual variants and the fact that the location of Emmaus is immaterial to the point of the narrative render a pinpointing of the village impossible. Three suggested locations have gained notice. (1) Josephus identifies an "Emmaus" as a Roman military camp within half the distance noted by Luke; accepting this location would require reading Luke's "seven miles" as a round trip. (2) During the Crusades an ancient fort was found about seven mi. northwest of Jerusalem at the modern site called el-Qubeibeh. While the fort may have existed in the first century, there is no available tradition which gives it a name. (3) Modern Nicopolis, about twenty mi. from Jerusalem on the Joppa road, had the name 'Amwas as late as the Maccabean period. Name similarity and correspondence with the variant reading of "a hundred and sixty stadia" have made Nicopolis ('Amwas) a likely location of Luke's Emmaus.

—RICHARD F. WILSON

• **En-gedi.** [en-ged'*i*] En-gedi was the name of a perennial spring and associated oasis in the Judean wilderness about twenty-five mi. southeast of Jerusalem and about twenty mi. east-southeast of Hebron (PLATE 12). The spring gushes forth some 670 ft. above the DEAD SEA in a gorge which cuts back into the abrupt cliffs which overlook the Sea on its western side. En-gedi is listed in Josh 15:62 as one of the cities of Judah "in the wilderness."

Two major events mentioned in the OT take place at En-gedi. The first occurs when David and his cohorts, on the run from king Saul, hide in wilderness strongholds (1 Sam 22-26). After escaping capture by Saul in the wilderness of Maon, David sought refuge "in the strongholds of En-gedi" (1 Sam 23:29). Here too Saul sought him out, whereupon David and his men hid from Saul in a cave—the very cave, as it turned out, in which Saul unwisely chose to relieve himself. The scene in the cave serves to further enhance the picture of David's loyalty and wisdom and to remind the reader once again of Saul's undeserved and unreasoning hatred of David.

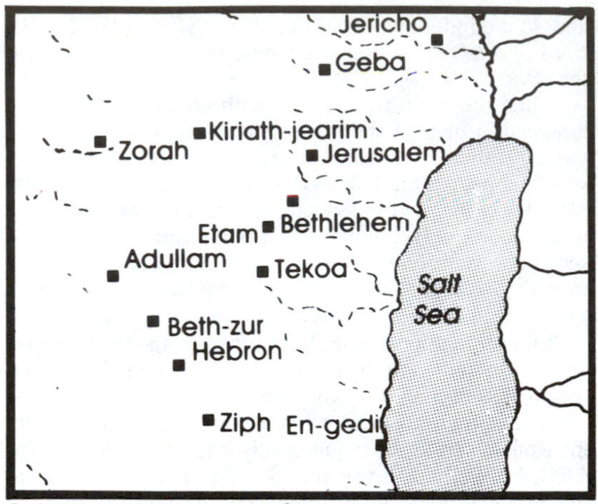

Designed by Margaret Jordan Brown ©Mercer University Press

The second event at En-gedi occurred in the reign of Jehoshaphat and is recorded by the chronicler. According to 2 Chr 20:1-2, "Hazazon-tamar [=En-gedi]" served as a mustering point for the Moabites, Ammonites and Meunites who had come "from Edom, from beyond the sea" (not "Aram" as the Hebrew text has it) in order to make war. While the identification of Hazazon-tamar with En-gedi is not entirely certain, this identification is supported by other geographical clues in the story, and the name Hazazon-tamar ("Palmtree divide") is appropriate for the En-gedi oasis. Since the Hazazon-tamar incident is not mentioned in 2 Kings and the story is legendary in tone, scholars have raised questions about its historicity. This much at least is certain; En-gedi was then as it is now a logical point of entry from the Dead Sea up into the Judean wilderness.

Throughout antiquity the En-gedi oasis was known for the produce of its fertile and well-watered soil. The Song of Songs mentions the fragrant Hynna blossoms of the vineyards of En-gedi (1:14). Its palms are proverbial in Sirach (24:14). Josephus remarks on its fine palms and its opobalsamum (balsum) (*Ant* 9.7). Pliny praises the groves of palm trees at En-gedi as "second only to Jerusalem in fertility" (*NatHist* 5.73). On the other hand, Ezekiel thinks of En-gedi as a place with no fish. In a vision he sees a life-giving river flow out from Jerusalem into the Arabah and on to the Dead Sea; its waters "heal" the sea and fishermen stand beside it "from En-gedi to En-eglaim [just south of Qumran?]" (Ezek 47:9-10).

Archaeological work at En-gedi has focused for the most part on Tell el-Jurn (Tell Goren) located about one half mile south of the spring on a narrow, easily defensible hill. Here were uncovered occupation levels dating from the latter part of the seventh century B.C.E. until the sixth century C.E. In the earliest stratum the excavators found several seals with Hebrew inscriptions. One notable inscription reads, "Uriyahu, [son of] Azaryahu." Additionally, various pottery and metal objects were unearthed that appear to have been used in the manufacture of perfume.

—J. MAXWELL MILLER

• **Encouragement.** *See* BARNABAS

• **Endor.** [en'dor] The site of Endor is mentioned but three times in the OT, first in Josh 17:11 where "En-dor and its villages" is ascribed to the territory of Manasseh in northern Palestine. The traditional location of Old Endor is the modern site by the same name on the north side of a low rise called Little Hermon, about four miles from Mount Tabor and six miles southeast of Nazareth. Ps 83:9-10 presents Endor as the location where SISERA and Jabin with their fugitives were destroyed. The account in Judg 4–5 of this battle led by Barak and Deborah does not mention Endor.

Endor is most famous for its being the home of a necromancer to whom King SAUL turned just prior to his final battle with the Philistines on nearby Mount Gilboa (1 Sam 28). Samuel had died; Saul with his warriors seemed hopelessly besieged by the enemy; no word was forthcoming from the Lord "by dreams, or by Urim, or by prophets" (v. 6). Saul requested his servants to seek out a woman "who is a medium that I may go to her and inquire of the Lord" (v. 7). They replied, "Behold, there is a medium at Endor" (v. 7). Having disguised himself, Saul went at night to request her to "bring up Samuel for me" (v. 11). She did, and the message of the shade of Samuel was as it was before Samuel's death—"The Lord has torn the kingdom out of your hand" (v. 7). Saul collapsed in his anxiety, but later that night recovered sufficiently to return to his battle zone where he died.

—KAREN RANDOLPH JOINES

• **Enemy from the North.** An invader of Palestine who approached from the north, according to the terminology of several of the writing prophets.

Palestine was a land bridge in the ancient Near East. Because the MEDITERRANEAN SEA lay to the west and the Arabian desert to the east, Israel's principal international highways ran north and south. It was therefore from the north or south that Israel's major enemies approached. Occasionally Egypt in the south was a threat; however, most enemies invaded Israel from the north. Several of the writing prophets spoke of Mesopotamian foes—whose lands were actually east or northeast of Israel—as enemies from the north. Such terminology was appropriate because Mesopotamian armies could not march westward across the Arabian desert; they were forced to invade Palestine from the north. Eventually "the north" became a symbol for the place from which evil would come, rather than a term of strict geographic reference.

In connection with his call experience JEREMIAH had a vision of a "boiling cauldron facing away from the north," which represented "families of the kingdoms of the north" who were going to invade Judah (1:13-15). At one time scholars favored the identification of this invader with the Scythians, based on a report in Herodotus's *History* (1.103-6). The invader portrayed in Zeph (1:7-18) also was thought of as the Scythians. However, the majority of contemporary scholars have abandoned this opinion on historical grounds. While most of the passages in Jeremiah that refer to an enemy from the north do not specifically name the invader (1:13-15; 4:6; 6:1, 22; 10:22; 13:20; 15:12), Jeremiah 25:9 associates King NEBUCHADREZZAR of Babylonia and his forces with the enemy from the north.

Jeremiah predicted that an enemy from the north would not only come against Judah but also against Egypt (46:6, 10, 20, 24), Philistia (47:2), and even Babylonia (50:3, 9, 41; 51:48). In addition Jeremiah understood that the harassment of Judah by its northern foe would not be permanent. He foresaw the time when Yahweh would return the exiled Israelites to their homeland from the north (3:18; 16:15; 23:8; 31:8). The latter half of Isaiah also refers to Israel's return from the north (43:6; 49:12).

EZEKIEL built upon Jeremiah's notion of the enemy from the north. He predicted that Tyre would be attacked by the northern enemy Nebuchadrezzar (26:7) and that the wicked chiefs of the north would all die (32:30). He also depicted the eschatological enemy of God's people as a force coming from "the remotest parts of the north" (38:6, 15; 39:2).

Several other prophets also alluded to the concept of an enemy from the north. JOEL termed a locust swarm that would come upon Judah as the "northerner" (2:20). In ZECHARIAH's last vision he saw four chariots that patrolled the earth, one of which went to the north to appease God's wrath in that land (6:6-8). Dan 11 depicts a battle between the Seleucid "king of the north" and the Ptolemaic "king of the south" (11:6-8, 11, 13, 15, 40, 44).

See also ASSYRIA; BABYLONIAN EMPIRE.

Bibliography. B. S. Childs, "The Enemy from the North and the Chaos Tradition," *JBL* 78/3 (1959): 187-98; W. L. Holladay, *Jeremiah 1, Hermeneia*; R. P. Vaggione, "Over all Asia?, The Extent of the Scythian Domination in Herodotus," *JBL* 92/4 (1973): 523-30.

—BOB R. ELLIS

• **Engagement.** *See* MARRIAGE IN THE NEW TESTAMENT; MARRIAGE IN THE OLD TESTAMENT

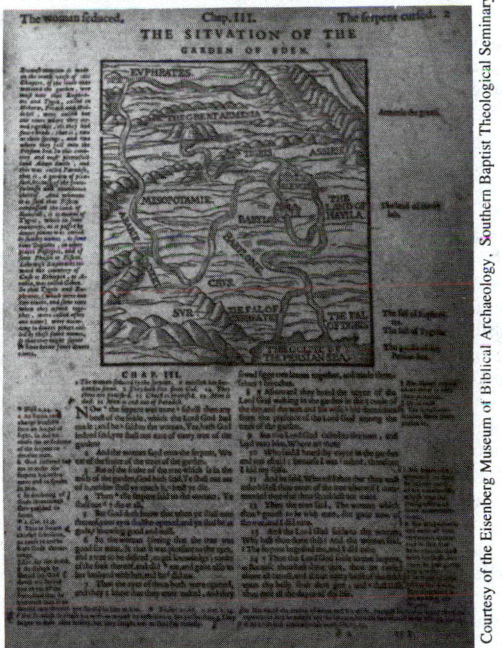
The woman seduced. Chap. III. The serpent cursed. 2

THE SITVATION OF THE GARDEN OF EDEN.

Courtesy of the Eisenberg Museum of Biblical Archaeology, Southern Baptist Theological Seminary.

A page from the Geneva Bible.

• **English Bible, History of.** The first complete Bible to appear in English (1382) is attributed to John Wyclif (ca. 1330–84), known as "The Morning Star of the Reformation" because of his desire to reform the church. Only if everyone knew God's law, he contended, could the church be reformed, and this required that the Bible be translated into the language of the people: "No man was so rude a scholar but that he might learn the Gospel according to his [i.e., its] simplicity." Another "Wyclifite" version appeared after Wyclif's death, but it is uncertain who was actually responsible for the two Bibles, whether Wyclif himself or his colleagues John Purvey and Nicholas of Hereford. An almost word-for-word equivalent of the Vulgate, the Wyclif Bible was the only Bible in English for 150 years; some 107 manuscript copies have survived.

Courtesy of the Eisenberg Museum of Biblical Archaeology, Southern Baptist Theological Seminary.

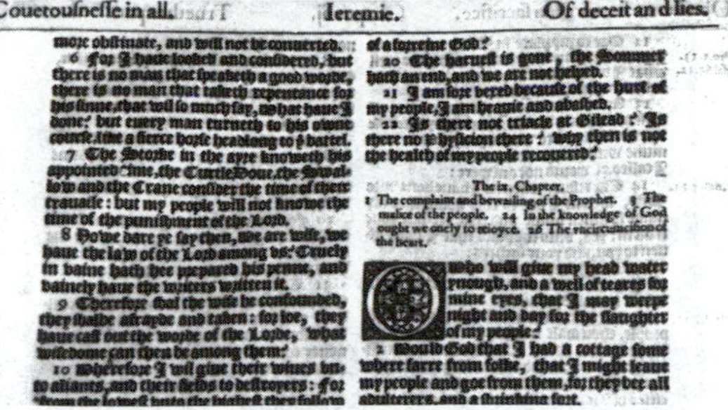
Couetousnesse in all. Ieremie. Of deceit and lies.

more obstinate, and will not be converted.
6 For I haue looked and considered, but there is no man that speaketh a good worde, there is no man that taketh repentance for his sinne, that will so much say, what haue I done? but euery man turneth to his owne course, like a fierce horse headlong to ŷ battel.
7 The Storke in the ayre knoweth his appointed time, the Turtle Doue, the Swallow and the Crane consider the time of their trauaile: but my people will not knowe the time of the punishment of the Lord.
8 How dare ye say then, we are wise, we haue the lawe of the Lord among vs? Truely in vaine hath hee prepared his penne, and vainely haue the writers written it.
9 Therefore shal the wise be confounded, they shalbe afrayde and taken: for loe, they haue cast out the worde of the Lorde, what wisedome can then be among them?
10 Wherefore I wil giue their wiues vnto aliants, and their fields to destroyers: for from the lowest vnto the highest they follow

of a strange God?
20 The haruest is gone, the Sommer hath an ende, and we are not helped.
21 I am sore vexed because of the hurt of my people, I am heauie and abashed.
22 Is there not triacle at Gilead? Is there no Physicion there? why then is not the health of my people recouered?

The ix. Chapter.
1 The complaint and bewailing of the Prophet. 4 The malice of the people. 24 In the knowledge of God ought we onely to reioyce. 26 The vncircumcision of the heart.

O Who will giue my head water ynough, and a well of teares for mine eyes, that I may weepe night and day for the slaughter of my people?
2 Would God that I had a cottage some where farre from folke, that I might leaue my people and goe from them, for they bee all adulterers, and a shrinking sort.

A page from the Bishops' Bible.

William Tyndale, known as "The Father of the English Bible," received his schooling at Oxford (M.A. 1515) and at Cambridge, where he may have studied Greek. Early in his life he became aware of the need for a better translation of the Bible into English. In a debate with various "learned men" he countered the argument that Christians were better off without God's law (the scriptures) than the Pope's laws (canon law) by asserting: "If God spare my life, ere many years I will cause a boy that driveth the plough shall know more of the Scripture than thou dost"—reflecting Erasmus's words in the preface of his 1516 Greek NT. In a more formal way Tyndale expressed his conviction: "I had perceived by experience how that it was impossible to establish the lay people in any truth, except the scripture were plainly laid before their eyes in their mother tongue, that they might see the process, order, and meaning of the text."

Unable to get authorization in England for his translation, in the spring of 1524 Tyndale went to the Continent; after spending almost a year in Wittenberg, he moved to Hamburg and eventually went to Cologne (Aug 1525). There he turned his translation of the NT over to Peter Quentel, a printer, but the city Senate forbade the printing. Tyndale took the printed slips to Worms, and toward the end of Feb 1526 the complete NT was published; copies began to appear in England about a month later. Tyndale's was the first printed English NT and the first English NT to have been translated from the Greek. About 18,000 copies of the original 1526 edition and of the revisions of 1534 and 1535 were printed, of which only two survive. The Bishop of London, Cuthbert Tunstall, bought many copies and burned them publicly. The Lord High Chancellor, Sir Thomas More, denounced the translation as "not worthy to be called Christ's testament, but either Tyndale's own testament or the testament of his master Antichrist."

While living in Antwerp, Tyndale began the work of translating the Hebrew OT: the Pentateuch appeared in 1530, and Jonah in 1531. In May 1535 he was betrayed, arrested by representatives of Emperor Charles V, and taken to Vilvorde, six miles north of Brussels, where he was imprisoned in a fortress. In Aug 1536 he was tried and found guilty of heresy, and on 6 Oct 1536 he was strangled and burned at the stake. His last words were: "Lord, open the King of England's eyes!"

In 1535, before Tyndale's death, a complete English Bible, edited by Miles Coverdale, was published on the

Courtesy of the Eisenberg Museum of Biblical Archaeology, Southern Baptist Theological Seminary.

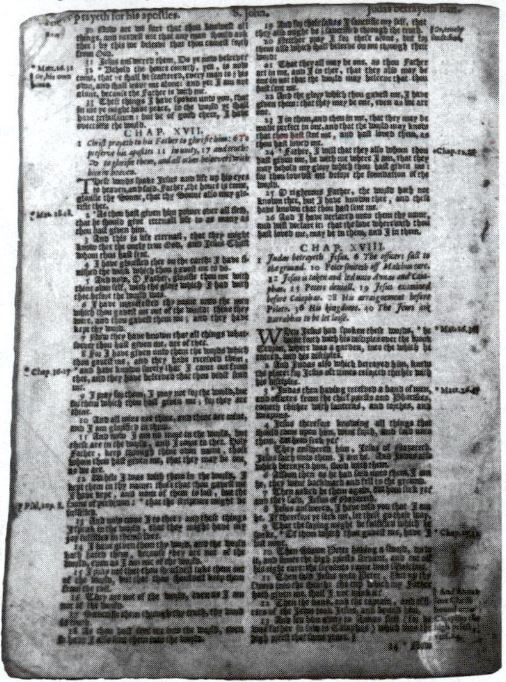

prayeth for his apostles. S. John. Judas betrayeth him.

CHAP. XVII.

1 Christ prayeth to his Father to glorifie him: 6 To preserve his apostles 11 in unity, 17 and truth: 20 to glorifie them, and all other believers with him in heaven.

CHAP. XVIII.

1 Judas betrayeth Jesus. 6 The officers fall to the ground. 10 Peter smiteth off Malchus ear. 12 Jesus is taken and led unto Annas and Caiaphas. 15 Peters deniall. 19 Jesus examined before Caiaphas. 28 His arraignment before Pilate. 36 His kingdome. 40 The Jews ask Barabbas to be let loose.

A page from the 1630 edition of the King James Version.

Continent. The NT was essentially a revision of Tyndale's NT, and Tyndale's translation of portions of the OT was used. The so-called (Thomas) Matthew Bible, edited by John Rogers, was published in 1537 as the first authorized Bible in English. Its Pentateuch and NT were Tyndale's, and his manuscripts of Joshua–2 Chronicles were used. The first Bible completely printed in England (1539), a revision of the Matthew Bible, was the work of Richard Taverner, a lawyer. The Great Bible, so called because of the size of its pages (9x15 inches), was Coverdale's revision of the Matthew Bible; it was printed in Paris in 1539.

During the reign of "Bloody Mary" Tudor (1553–58) no English Bibles were printed in England, and the English Bible could not be used in church services. Among the many Protestant leaders who fled to the Continent was William Whittingham, who became pastor of the English church in Geneva. He translated the NT and served as editor of the OT translation; this Bible, known as the Geneva Bible, was published in 1560 and dedicated to Queen Elizabeth (who had begun to reign in 1558). The first English Bible to have verse numbers, it was printed in Roman type and bound in small octavo size. It became immensely popular among the people: it was the Bible of Bunyan, of Shakespeare, of Oliver Cromwell and his army, of the pilgrims to the New World, and of the Mayflower Compact. It was the first Bible published in Scotland (1579), and was dedicated to its king, James VI. It went through over 150 editions, and remained popular for nearly 100 years. But its extremely Protestant notes were offensive to the bishops, and in 1568 a revision of the Great Bible was published, which became known as the Bishops' Bible, due to the large number of bishops on the committee. In 1570 the Convocation of Canterbury ordered it to be placed in all the cathedrals, and so it became the second authorized version; but it never achieved the popularity of the Geneva Bible.

The King James Bible and Its Successors. When James VI of Scotland became King of England as James I (1603), there were the two Bibles: the Bishops' Bible, preferred by the church authorities, and the Geneva Bible, the favorite of the people.

In 1604, King James convened a meeting of theologians and churchmen at Hampton Court "for the hearing, and for the determining, things pretended to be amiss in the Church." John Reynolds, the Puritan leader, proposed a new translation of the Bible, to replace the two competing Bibles. The king approved, and ordered that "a translation be made of the whole Bible, as consonant as can be to the original Hebrew and Greek, and this is to be set out and printed without any marginal notes and only to be used in all Churches in England in time of Divine Service." He appointed six panels of fifty-four "learned men": three for the OT, two for the NT, and one for the Apocrypha. The first of the fifteen rules drawn up to guide the translators stated: "The ordinary Bible read in the Church, commonly called the *Bishops' Bible,* to be followed, and as little altered as the truth of the original will permit."

The translation was published in 1611; several editions followed, nearly all of which had changes in the text. The most thorough revision was the one made by Dr. Benjamin Blayney, of Oxford, in 1769. Although never formally authorized by Crown or Parliament, this Bible became known as the Authorized Version, popularly the King James Version.

In 1870 the Church of England authorized a revision of the KJV: most of the fifty-four scholars chosen for the task were Anglicans, but there were Baptists, Congregationalists, Methodists, Presbyterians, and one Unitarian in the group. The first rule specified that as few alterations were to be introduced as were consistent with faithfulness. In the NT about 30,000 changes were made, more than 5,000 of them on the basis of a better Greek text. When the NT was published (May 1881), it was enthusiastically received: in the first year three million copies were sold in Britain and the United States. The complete English Revised Version (ERV) appeared in 1885, with an appendix that listed the changes preferred by American scholars. In 1895 the Apocrypha appeared. The Standard American Edition of the Revised Version (ASV) was published in 1901. It removed many archaisms, replaced a large number of obsolescent words, and substituted many peculiarly British words and expressions with those more familiar to Americans.

Rheims-Douai Bible. Although they did not concede that the laity had the right to read the Bible in the vernacular without ecclesiastical approval, Roman Catholic authorities felt the need of an English version officially approved for Catholics. William Allen, a fellow of Oriel College, Oxford, was among the many Roman Catholics who fled England in the reign of Elizabeth I. He settled in Douai, Flanders, where he founded a college to train priests who would eventually go to England. There the translation of the Bible from the Vulgate was begun. In 1578 the college moved to Rheims, where the NT was finished in 1582. Later the college returned to Douai, where the Bible was published in 1609–10. Bishop Challoner of London assisted in a thorough revision of the NT in 1738, and made numerous changes in the whole Bible in the 1749–52 editions. In 1810 the Challoner revision of the Rheims-Douai Bible was authorized for use in America.

Other Translations. Since 1611 many Bibles and over 250 NTs have been published. A few of them deserve mention. After retiring at age sixty, Charles Thomson, who had been Secretary of the Continental Congress, published his translation of the LXX and the NT in 1808, after almost twenty years' work. He has the distinction of having made the first English translation of the LXX and of producing the first English NT to be translated and published in America. In 1862 Robert Young, of Edinburgh (better known for his *Analytical Concordance*), published what is practically a word-for-word equivalent translation of the original. Ferrar Fenton, an English businessman, published his translation of the Bible in 1903, with the claim that it was the most accurate translation ever made, "not only in words, but in editing, spirit, and sense." As late as 1944 a new edition was published. The American Julia E. Smith Parker published her translation of the Bible in 1876; she attempted to use one and the same English word or phrase for every equivalent Hebrew and Greek word.

Modern Era. The modern era of Bible translation into English began in 1901, with the publication of the definitive edition of *The Twentieth-Century New Testament,* in England. This remarkable translation was begun through the efforts of Mrs. Mary K. Higgs, the wife of a Congregational minister, and Mr. Ernest Malan, a signal and telegraph engineer, both of whom were concerned with the fact that the KJV was too difficult for young people to understand. The group that did the work consisted mostly of laywomen and laymen, including Anglicans, Methodists, Congregationalists, Presbyterians, and Baptists. One of their advisors was Richard Francis Weymouth, a classical scholar who was fellow of University College, London. His own translation, *The New Testament in Modern Speech,* was published posthumously in 1902. He wanted to produce a translation that laypeople could understand: "Alas, the great majority of even 'new translations,' so called, are in reality only Tyndale's immortal work a little—often very little—modernized!" He made his translation for private reading, not for public worship.

The most important translation of the early twentieth century was that of the Scottish scholar James Moffatt. He first produced *The Historical New Testament* (1900), followed by *The New Testament: A New Translation* (1913). His OT translation appeared in 1924, and the whole Bible was revised in 1935. He spent the last years of his life as a professor at Union Theological Seminary, New York, and at the time of his death (1944) he was working on a translation of the Apocrypha.

Edgar J. Goodspeed, of the University of Chicago, felt compelled to prepare a NT in American English: "For American readers . . . who have had to depend so long upon versions made in Great Britain, there is room for a NT free from expressions which . . . are strange to American ears." His *New Testament, An American Translation* appeared in 1923. In 1927 a group of scholars headed by J. M. Powis Smith produced a translation of the OT, which in 1935 was published with Goodspeed's NT as *The Bible, An American Translation.* In 1939, with the addition of the Apocrypha, translated by Goodspeed, *The Complete Bible, An American Translation* was published.

Other NT translations worth recording include J. B. Phillips's *The New Testament in Modern English* (1958; revised second edition 1972); William Barclay's *The New Testament: A New Translation* (2 vols., 1968, 1969); Hugh J. Schonfield's *Authentic New Testament* (1955; reissued, with some changes, as *Original New Testament* in 1985), which claims to be the first translation of the NT into English by a Jew.

In 1941 a committee headed by S. H. Hooke of the University of London brought forth *The New Testament in Basic English* (1941), an attempt to make the NT accessible to all who speak or read English. The term "basic" is an acronym for "British American Scientific International Commercial" (English), a list of 850 words compiled by the linguist C. K. Ogden. Another 150 words, fifty of which were special Bible words, were added to this basic vocabulary. The Bible appeared in 1949.

The Watch Tower Bible and Tract Society (better known as Jehovah's Witnesses) published in 1961 a translation of the Bible entitled *The New World Translation of the Holy Scriptures.* It uses "Jehovah" as a translation of the Tetragrammaton in the OT, and displays the Unitarian bias of the Witnesses in its translation, e.g., of John 1:1c, "and the Word was a god."

The Revised Standard Version and After. In 1937 the International Council of Religious Education authorized a revision of the American Standard Version, stating that it should "embody the best results of modern scholarship as to the meaning of the Scriptures, and express this meaning in English diction which is designed for use in public and private worship and preserves those qualities which have given to the King James Version a supreme place in English literature." A committee of thirty-two scholars, headed by Luther A. Weigle, was entrusted with the task. The NT was published in 1946, the Bible in 1952; the edition with the Apocrypha appeared in 1957. An "Expanded Edition," including not only the Roman Catholic deuterocanonical OT books but also *3 and 4 Maccabees,* and Ps 151, appeared in 1977, with the purpose of making this Bible acceptable to Eastern Orthodox Churches.

A landmark in Bible translation was reached in 1970 with the publication of the New English Bible (NT 1961), a translation which broke away completely from the Tyndale–King James tradition. The translators represented nearly all the major Christian Churches in Britain and Ireland, and their chairman, Prof. C. H. Dodd, explained their work as follows: "We have conceived our task to be that of understanding the original as precisely as we could . . . and then saying again in our own native idiom what we believed the author to be saying in his." Using the full resources of the English language, the translators produced a Bible whose language is fresh and natural, although a bit too British, in some places, for American readers. Many of its textual decisions, especially in the OT, have been criticized by scholars as being decidedly idiosyncratic.

Good News for Modern Man. In 1966 *The New Testament in Today's English Version* was published by the American Bible Society. Its main features were the use of "common language," designed to be accessible to all who read English, and the application of what are called "dynamic equivalence" principles of translation (as opposed to "formal equivalence"). The translator, Robert G. Bratcher, was assisted in his task by a panel of specialists; a seven-man committee translated the OT, and the *Good News Bible* was published in 1976; the edition with the deuterocanonical books appeared in 1979.

Several current translations have been motivated, in part at least, by the desire of conservative non-Catholics to produce a translation that would counter what was seen as the liberal bias of the RSV. Conservatives felt a strong need for a modern translation they could trust. *The Amplified Bible* (1965), *The Modern Language Bible* (1969), and the *New American Standard Bible* (1971) were all intended to replace the RSV. Kenneth Taylor's *The Living Bible, Para-*

phrased (1971) occupies a category all its own, but it also reflects a strong conservative bent. With the publication of the *New International Version* in 1978 the goal was finally reached. The intense advertisement campaign that accompanied NIV's publication assured everyone that this is a Bible that can be trusted, for it was produced by people who have "a high view of Scripture," all of whom believe that the Bible, in its entirety, "is the Word of God written and therefore inerrant in the autographs." The success of the NIV indicates that this is the Bible that will be preferred by those who still view the RSV with suspicion; of course many conservatives still prefer the KJV.

Roman Catholic Translations. Roman Catholics have produced a number of modern translations. In 1955 Monsignor Ronald Knox, of Great Britain, published a translation of the Bible from the Vulgate, "in the light of the Hebrew and Greek Originals." It is, conceivably, the last Bible to be translated into English by one person. The English version of the French *La Bible de Jérusalem* was published in 1966 under the title *The Jerusalem Bible*; a revised edition, *The New Jerusalem Bible,* appeared in 1985. American Roman Catholic scholars began a fresh translation of the Vulgate in 1937; the NT appeared in 1941. With the publication in 1943 of the papal encyclical *Divino Afflante Spiritu,* authorizing vernacular translations made directly from the original texts, the translation was begun anew, and *The American Bible* appeared in 1970.

Jewish Translations. One of the earliest Jewish translations of the Pentatuech into English (1785) was done by Alexander Alexander, of Great Britain. Abraham Benisch in 1861 published a translation of the Hebrew Scriptures under the title *Jewish School and Family Bible.* In 1881 another translation was produced by Michael Friedlander, also of England. The first translation of the Hebrew Scriptures into English in the United States was the work of Isaac Leeser (1854); it became the version used in all American synagogues. In 1917 the Jewish Publication Society of America published a new translation produced by Jewish scholars headed by Marcus Jastrow. This translation became the standard Bible in the American Jewish community until the publication of the New Jewish Version, which appeared in stages. *The Torah,* translated by a committee chaired by Harry M. Orlinsky, was published in 1962; *The Prophets,* in 1978; and the final volume, *The Writings,* in 1981. The complete Jewish Bible, in one volume, was published in 1985 under the title *Tanakh.*

Readers of the Bible in English today have a variety of translations that provide them with a clear and faithful record, in their own language, of the great things that God has done.

Bibliography. L. R. Bailey, ed., *The Word of God*; R. G. Bratcher, "Englishing the Bible," *RE* 76/3 (1979): 299-314; F. F. Bruce, *The English Bible*; S. Kubo and W. F. Specht, *So Many Versions?*; *The Cambridge History of the Bible,* 3 vols.; J. P. Lewis, *The English Bible from KJV to NIV*; J. H. P. Reumann, *The Romance of Bible Scripts and Scholars*; H. Wheeler Robinson, ed., *The Bible in Its Ancient and English Versions.*

—ROBERT G. BRATCHER

• **Enoch, First.** [ee'nuhk] *First Enoch* is a composite work containing apocryphal traditions about the biblical figure Enoch (Gen 5:18-24). In its present form it consists of five sections. The first section (1-36), the Book of the Watchers, contains an account of the fall of the group of ANGELS known as the Watchers and their subsequent judgment, and two visions in which Enoch embarks upon journeys to the distant places of earth, where he sees such things as the place of divine punishment, the tree of life, and the TREE OF KNOWLEDGE, from which ADAM and EVE ate. The second section (37-71), the Book of Similitudes (or Parables), consists of three parables which Enoch learns through visions. The first concerns eschatological judgment and reward, the four angels (MICHAEL, Raphael, Gabriel, and Phanuel), and cosmic secrets. The second concerns the Elect One, the SON OF MAN, who will come to exercise final judgment. The third deals primarily with the eschatological judgment which the Elect One will carry out. The third section (72-82), the Book of Luminaries, contains astronomical data which Enoch received from the angel Uriel. The fourth section (83-90), the Dream Visions, consists of two visions which Enoch recounts to his son Methuselah. The first predicts the FLOOD. The second foretells, through extended animal imagery, the history of Israel to the coming of the MESSIAH. The fifth section (91-108), the Epistle of Enoch (or the Book of Admonitions), contains moral exhortations from Enoch to his children, a schematic prediction of history (the Apocalypse of Weeks), descriptions of the woes and blessings that will come with the final judgment, and the story of the birth of NOAH.

The literary prehistory of *1 Enoch* is exceedingly complex and the subject of intense debate. *First Enoch* is extant in its entirety only in a medieval Ethiopic translation. There exist also Greek fragments, a Latin fragment, and, most important of all, Aramaic fragments from Qumran Cave 4 of eleven manuscripts dating from the late third century B.C.E. to the early first century C.E. The Qumran fragments permit several observations. First, all of the sections except the Similitudes are represented at Qumran. Second, the Book of Luminaries found at Qumran is considerably longer than the Ethiopic. Third, two manuscripts probably contained only the Book of Watchers, four only the Book of Luminaries (which is never combined in the manuscripts with any other section), and one only the Epistle of Enoch; three attest to combinations of the Book of Watchers, the Dream Visions, and the Epistle of Enoch. Fourth, there existed a Book of Giants, in which Enoch is a central figure, and which is related to the Book of Watchers. Fifth, there apparently existed a Book of Noah, fragments of which may have found their way into the *Epistle of Enoch* (cf. *1 QapGen*).

It follows from these observations that in its present form, *1 Enoch* is a compilation (and sometimes an abbreviation) of a number of different "Enoch" books which (with the exception of the Similitudes) were composed in Aramaic and which circulated in the last three centuries B.C.E. *The Book of Luminaries,* attested by the earliest Qumran fragment, undoubtedly was written prior to 200 B.C.E.; the *Book of Watchers* ca. 200 B.C.E.; the *Epistle of Enoch* between 175 and 167 B.C.E. just prior to the Maccabean Revolt; and the *Dream Visions* in the late 160s B.C.E. during the Maccabean Revolt. Although the Qumran fragments indicate that these books were being brought together in the first century B.C.E., the suggestion that the *Book of Giants* was combined with them as one of five members of an Enochic Pentateuch (later to be replaced by the Similitudes) is unproven.

The absence of the Similitudes from the Qumran fragments is noteworthy. The Similitudes have long been recognized as a particularly significant section of *1 Enoch.* The picture of an exalted Son of Man who will come to execute judgment has striking parallels with the portrayal of Jesus in the Gospels and may provide important background material (cf. Dan 7) for the Son of Man concept in the NT. The findings at Qumran, however, have given new force to the argument that the section is not pre-Christian at all but rather was composed by a Christian, perhaps as late as the third century C.E. More probable is that the Similitudes stem from Jewish circles other than those close to the Qumran community and date from the first century C.E. Whether they were written before the coming of Jesus or afterwards is debated.

First Enoch is characterized by a number of important theological emphases. There is a highly developed angelology, with an interest in both righteous angels and the Watchers. Furthermore, the portrayal of the Watchers as angels who came down to earth, cohabited with women, and fathered giants, as well as who corrupted humankind by teaching forbidden arts and practices (cf. Gen 6:1-4; *Jub* 5:1-2; Jude 6; 2 Pet 2:4), attests to a strong interest in the origins of evil. There is a constant focus on eschatological punishment and reward, and a keen interest in meteorological and astronomical mysteries, including an affirmation of the solar CALENDAR (cf. *Jubilees*). Finally, the Dream Visions, as well as the Similitudes, depict a certain messianic expectation.

The popularity of the various books of Enoch at Qumran, its early date, and its close parallels with the BOOK OF JUBILEES suggest that the early Enoch books, like *Jubilees*, reflect a proto-Essenic perspective. Certainly the four sections found at Qumran are especially important for illuminating Jewish attitudes in the third and second centuries B.C.E., including the origins of apocalyptic literature, as are the Similitudes for the first century C.E. Speculation about this enigmatic figure from Gen 5:21-24 continued within Judaism, resulting in two other lengthy apocryphal works, 2 ENOCH and 3 ENOCH. It should be noted further that *1 Enoch* attained a certain degree of popularity in the early church. Jude 14-15 quotes from 1:9; the book was also used by the EPISTLE OF BARNABAS, Tertullian, and Origen. Although it was ultimately branded as apocryphal, it continues to be used in the Ethiopic church.

See also ANGEL; APOCALYPTIC LITERATURE; ENOCH, SECOND; ENOCH, THIRD.

Bibliography. R. H. Charles, *The Book of Enoch*; "1 Enoch," *The Apocrypha and Pseudepigrapha of the Old Testament*, ed. R. H. Charles; E. Isaac, "1 (Ethiopic Apocalypse of) Enoch," *The Old Testament Pseudepigrapha*, ed. J. H. Charlesworth; M. A. Knibb, "The Date of the Parables of Enoch: A Critical Review," *NTS* 25 (1979): 345-59; "1 Enoch," *The Apocryphal Old Testament*, ed. H. F. D. Sparks; J. T. Milik and M. Black, *The Books of Enoch*; M. E. Stone, "Apocalyptic Literature," *Jewish Writings of the Second Temple Period*, ed. M. E. Stone; D. W. Suter, *Tradition and Composition in the Parables of Enoch*; J. C. VanderKam, *Enoch and the Growth of an Apocalyptic Tradition*; G. Vermes, "The Ethiopic Book of Enoch," in E. Schürer, *The History of the Jewish People in the Age of Jesus Christ*, rev. ed.

—JOSEPH L. TRAFTON

• **Enoch, Second.** [ee'nuhk] *Second Enoch* is a legendary expansion, in two parts of unequal length, of the story of the biblical figure of Enoch (Gen 5:18-24), and the events leading up to the FLOOD (cf. Gen 5:21-32). The first and longest part concerns Enoch. After preparing him through a dream, two men lead Enoch up through the seven (or ten) heavens, where he sees the rulers who govern the movements of the stars and the weather (first heaven), the FALLEN ANGELS in torment (second), PARADISE for the righteous and the place of eternal punishment for the wicked (third), the movements of the sun and the moon (fourth), the giants whose brothers were the fallen angels (fifth), the ANGELS who regulate the natural order (sixth), and the Lord on his throne surrounded by his heavenly court (seventh). Enoch then writes, at the dictation of an angel, 360 (or 366) books containing all of the secrets of nature. Then God relates to Enoch the CREATION of the world and the FALL. After informing Enoch of what is to come, God sends Enoch back to his family to prepare them for his permanent departure. Enoch describes his visionary journeys, gives a series of moral exhortations, leaves his books, and then is taken up to heaven.

The second section of the book takes the story up to the Flood, focusing on the priesthoods of Methuselah, Enoch's son, and then Nir, the brother of NOAH. God informs both of the coming flood. The book comes to a close with an extended account of the miraculous birth of MELCHIZEDEK to Nir's aged wife Sopanim, prophecies of Melchizedek's central role in God's plan after the flood, and the angel Gabriel's hiding of Melchizedek until the proper time.

Second Enoch is extant in two Slavonic recensions: a longer and a shorter. Scholars are divided over which of the two is closer to the original. The Slavonic is based upon a Greek text, which may have been a translation of a Hebrew or Aramaic original. *Second Enoch* has been dated anywhere between the first century B.C.E., and the ninth century C.E. Both Jewish and Christian authorship have been proposed. Although certainty is far from possible, it seems plausible that *2 Enoch* is a Jewish composition from the first century B.C.E. or C.E.

Second Enoch is characterized by strong monotheistic and ethical concerns. Its emphasis on astronomical (especially calendrical—cf. 1 ENOCH) data, coupled with the requirement of the unusual practice of binding an animal's legs before sacrifice and a focus on the authority of Enoch's writings, suggests a sectarian perspective. The journey through the (seven) heavens (cf. Paradise in the third heaven and 2 Cor 12:2-4) is a familiar Jewish motif, and there is a strong interest in final judgment and the age to come. The speculation about the role of Melchizedek is reminiscent of similar concerns among early Christians (cf. Heb 7) and Essenes (*11QMelch*), although the details are quite different. Finally, its detailed description of the Creation act (long recension) reflects an early concern with relating religion to science.

Bibliography. F. I. Andersen, "2 (Slavonic Apocalypse of) Enoch," *The Old Testament Pseudepigrapha*, ed. J. H. Charlesworth; R. H. Charles and N. Forbes, "2 Enoch, or the Book of the Secrets of Enoch," *The Apocrypha and Pseudepigrapha of the Old Testament*, ed. R. H. Charles; A. Pennington, "2 Enoch," *The Apocryphal Old Testament*, ed. H. F. D. Sparks.

—JOSEPH L. TRAFTON

• **Enoch, Third.** [ee'nuhk] *Third Enoch* purports to record the journey to heaven of Ishmael, a famous rabbi who died shortly before 132 C.E. and who came to be frequently associated with this type of material. Apart from the opening citation of Gen 5:24 concerning Enoch and the recurring "Rabbi Ishmael said," the entire narration is given in the rabbi's own words. The story begins with Ishmael entering six heavenly palaces, one inside the other. Pausing outside of the seventh, innermost palace, he prays that God might grant him to enter without being cast out by the guardian ANGELS. God sends to Ishmael Metatron, the Prince of the divine Presence, who escorts him into the seventh palace and presents him before the throne of glory, where Ishmael is received by God and joins in the heavenly praise. Metatron then identifies himself to Ishmael as Enoch and describes how God took him up from the earth, how he was transformed from a human into an angel, and what his heavenly functions are. The greater portion of the book consists of Metatron's revelations to Ishmael concerning the angelic hierarchy, the divine judgment, and the heavenly worship. Finally, Metatron shows Ishmael the sights of heaven, including the cosmological secrets; the souls of the righteous, the wicked, the intermediate, the patriarchs, the stars, and the punished angels; and the history of the world from Adam to the Messiahs of Joseph and David and the final wars.

Third Enoch is extant in several different recensions in Hebrew, the language in which it was undoubtedly composed. The textual situation is confusing; hence, the date is difficult to determine, with suggestions ranging from the third to the fifteenth century C.E. The earliest material, that relating to Enoch, might go back to first century C.E. Palestinian traditions, but the book's apparent dependence on the Babylonian Talmud suggests that the final redaction was made in the fifth or sixth century in Babylonia. There is no reason to believe that the book records the actual words of Rabbi Ishmael.

Third Enoch is an example of merkabah, or chariot, mysticism. Merkabah mysticism was an esoteric strand within rabbinic Judaism which originated in Palestine during the first century C.E. and which became highly developed, if not widely known, well into the Middle Ages. This movement focused on a mystical ascent into heaven and on the subsequent, often elaborately detailed, descriptions of the heavenly mysteries and the divine throne, typically viewed in terms of a chariot (cf. Ezek 1). It is related to such apocalyptic works as 1 ENOCH, 2 ENOCH, *The Testament of Levi, The Ascension of Isaiah,* and the APOCALYPSE OF ABRAHAM as well as the ANGELIC LITURGY from Qumran, all of which reflect a strong interest in heavenly secrets. The identification of Enoch, about whom there was increasing speculation within Judaism (cf. *1 Enoch, 2 Enoch,* the BOOK OF JUBILEES, the GENESIS APOCRYPHON), with Metatron, the highest of the archangels in the merkabah tradition, is distinctive to *3 Enoch*. Thus, *3 Enoch* serves as something of a bridge between late pre-Christian literature and the classical merkabah tradition.

See also ABRAHAM, APOCALYPSE OF; ENOCH, FIRST; ENOCH, SECOND; ISAIAH, MARTYRDOM AND ASCENSION OF; TESTAMENTS OF THE TWELVE PATRIARCHS.

Bibliography. P. Alexander, "3 (Hebrew Apocalypse of) Enoch," *The Old Testament Pseudepigrapha,* ed. J. H. Charlesworth; H. Odeberg, *3 Enoch*; G. Scholem, *Major Trends in Jewish Mysticism,* 3rd ed.

—JOSEPH L. TRAFTON

• **Epanalepsis.** *See* INCLUSIO

• **Epaphras.** [ep'uh-fras] Epaphras is mentioned in Phlm 23 and Col 1:7; 4:12-13. He was an associate of Paul from COLOSSAE (Col 4:12) and is not to be confused with Epaphroditus who served as the bearer of a gift from the church of Philippi to Paul (Phil 2:25).

Epaphras was instrumental in the spread of the gospel in Colossae (Col 1:7), certainly as a teacher and probably as an evangelist who was crucial in establishing the church. The preferred text in Col 1:7 is "He is a faithful minister of Christ on our behalf" (instead of "on your behalf"), and this suggests that Epaphras was sent by Paul, perhaps during his long stay at Ephesus (Acts 19:8-10), to carry the gospel to Colossae and possibly even to LAODICEA and Hierapolis. With regard to these latter two churches, it is clear that Epaphras had deep concern for their progress and welfare (Col 4:13).

Paul probably wrote Colossians from his Roman imprisonment; at that time Epaphras was also a prisoner (Phlm 23). Epaphras was the source of Paul's information about the Colossian church (Col 1:7); and Paul sends that church his greeting (Col 4:12), noting how much Epaphras cared for them (Col 4:12b-13). Paul had great appreciation for Epaphras and refers to him as "our beloved fellow servant" (Col 1:7). Paul's estimate of Epaphras results in his calling him "a servant of Jesus Christ" (Col 4:12), a designation Paul usually reserved for himself and used once of Timothy (Phil 1:1).

No more is said of Epaphras in the NT, but church tradition records that he later became bishop of Colossae, and after martyrdom was buried under the church of St. Maria Maggiore in Rome.

See also COLOSSAE; COLOSSIANS, LETTER TO THE; LAODICEA.

—HAROLD S. SONGER

• **Epaphroditus.** [i-paf'ruh-dī″tuhs] According to Phil 2:25-30 and 4:18, Epaphroditus was a significant member of the Philippian church who was sent with a gift to Paul during his imprisonment (which is traditionally assumed to have been in Rome). Upon his arrival he had devoted himself tirelessly to attending to Paul's needs and assisting in Paul's mission. Paul calls Epaphroditus his "brother and fellow worker and fellow soldier" and indicates he had risked his own life to fulfill his mission on behalf of the Philippians and had been very near to death. He is now being sent back to the Philippians to relieve their concern and to convey Paul's thanks for the Philippian gift and a report on his condition.

The name Epaphroditus, meaning "handsome" or "charming," corresponds to the Latin *venastus* ("handsome"). It was a very common name during the Roman period, appearing frequently in Greek and Latin manuscripts in the contracted form Epaphras. This has led to the speculation that Epaphroditus is to be equated with the EPAPHRAS of Phlm 23 and Col 4:12. This seems unlikely, however, because this Epaphras seems to have played a significant role in the churches at Colossae, Laodicea, and Hierapolis (Col 4:12-13), and is designated in Col 4:12 as "one of your own."

See also EPAPHRAS; PHILIPPIANS, LETTER TO THE.

—W. HULITT GLOER

• **Ephesians, Letter to the.** [i-fee'zhuhns] From Eph 1:1 we assume that the tenth book in the NT canon was written by the apostle PAUL to the church in Ephesus (PLATES 26, 27) with which he had labored for a considerable part of his missionary career (Acts 19:1-10). There are, however, serious problems connected with the traditional assumptions concerning the origin and destination of the Letter.

Addressees. Certain aspects of the Letter seem strange if it is addressed to the Ephesians with whom Paul had spent over two years. The writer has "heard" of their faith and love (1:15). He must "assume" that they have "heard" of

• OUTLINE OF EPHESIANS •

Letter to the Ephesians

I. Theological: The Church, the New Humanity Composed of Jew and Gentile (1:1–3:21)
   A. Salutation (1:1-2)
   B. In praise of God (1:3-10)
   C. The inclusion of Jew and gentile in the church (1:11-14)
   D. Prayer that readers may grasp what God has done for the church (1:15-23)
   E. Exposition of salvation by grace (2:1-10)
   F. The reconciliation of Jew and gentile in Christ (2:11-22)
   G. Paul's apostolic ministry to gentiles (3:1-13)
   H. Prayer that readers may know God's love (3:14-19)

II. Doxology (3:20-21)

III. Practical: Appeal for the Readers to be Worthy of Their Vocation as God's People (4:1–6:24)
   A. The appeal for genuine unity (4:1-16)
   B. The appeal to forsake the old pagan practices (4:17–5:20)
   C. The appeal to apply Christian principles to the household (5:21–6:9)
   D. The appeal to put on God's armor (6:10-20)
   E. Conclusion (6:21-24)

God's gift to him of his apostolic ministry (3:2ff.) and that they have been instructed in the essentials of the Christian message (4:20). Also, Ephesians does not contain the kinds of personal references we might expect in a letter written to a well-known congregation.

Moreover, the oldest and best manuscript witnesses to Ephesians do not contain the address "in Ephesus" in 1:1. These are the Chester Beatty Papyrus (ca. 200 C.E.) and the great uncials, Vaticanus and Sinaiticus, dated in the fourth and fifth centuries C.E.

In his canon the Gnostic MARCION (ca. 140 C.E.) included Ephesians under the title "to the Laodiceans." This possibility is strengthened by the fact that a letter to the Laodiceans is mentioned in Col 4:16.

A more popular and widespread assumption has been that Ephesians was an encyclical or circular letter, addressed to a number of churches including Ephesus. According to this theory, the original letter contained a blank space to be filled in with the appropriate address by Tychicus, its bearer, before it was delivered to each individual church. As matters now stand, no dogmatic conclusion about the address of the Letter is warranted.

Authorship. The tradition that Paul wrote the Letter is both early and unanimous, so that anyone who challenges it bears the burden of proof. Many modern scholars, however, find the evidence against Pauline authorship so convincing as to be undeniable.

To begin with, a large number of words occur in Ephesians that are not found in the earlier, widely recognized, Pauline writings. Moreover, certain important words found elsewhere in Paul are used with different meanings in Ephesians.

The style of Ephesians is ponderous, characterized by extremely long sentences, by wordiness, and by stringing together genitival phrases. Even the casual reader of the NT restricted to an English translation will readily observe the difference between the style of Ephesians and 1 Corinthians or Romans.

Certain statements in Ephesians do not seem to be coherent with what we know of Paul. Would the Paul who asserted so vigorously that Christ was the only foundation of the church (1 Cor 3:11) have ascribed that function to the apostles and prophets (Eph 2:20)? Would Paul have referred to the apostles as "holy" (Eph 3:5)? The theology of Ephesians, although not unrelated to what we know of Paul, seems to be a development beyond that of the earlier writings. Especially is this true in the doctrine of the church.

Perhaps a greater problem than any mentioned thus far is related to the parallels between Ephesians and Colossians. About one-third of the vocabulary of Colossians is repeated in Ephesians. The parallels are of such a nature, moreover, as to cause many scholars to conclude that they could not have been due to the natural repetitions one finds in the works of the same author. Also, numerous parallels exist between Ephesians and all the other Pauline letters except the Pastorals. These factors have led to the hypothesis that Ephesians was written by an ardent admirer of Paul who was familiar with the earlier writings, especially the Letter to the Colossians.

On the other hand, many scholars still are convinced that Paul wrote Ephesians. They explain many of the characteristics noted above in terms of the unusual nature of the Letter. It consists primarily of prayer and praise. Scholars have shown that the passages of this nature in the other Pauline letters manifest a great deal of similarity with Ephesians. Markus Barth holds that Ephesians was written by Paul and that it was addressed to Christians in Ephesus. The intended readers of the Letter were Christians converted after Paul had left the city.

The Date and Place of Origin. Ephesians is one of the imprisonment letters (cf. 3:1), traditionally ascribed to the time of Paul's imprisonment in Rome after 59 C.E. (cf. Acts 28:14ff.). However, it could also have been written from Caesarea (Acts 23:31ff.) or from some earlier imprisonment (2 Cor 11:23). Of course, if Paul did not write it, these assumptions are not valid.

The Message of Ephesians. The Letter seems to have been written because of the desire of the author to set before the readers a larger vision of their relationship to what God is doing in the universe. As perceived by the author of Ephesians, the redemptive purpose of God, predestined from eternity and executed in and through Jesus Christ, is to overcome the hostility and divisions in the universe by bringing all things together under the headship of Jesus Christ (1:9-10). The church is the concrete evidence that this is his purpose and that it is being executed. It is the "new humanity" created by bringing together Jew and gentile, abolishing the wall of hostility that had divided them (2:14-18).

Ephesians is divided into two distinct parts, each consisting of three chapters. In the first three chapters the author sets forth his vision of the church in God's purpose. In the last three chapters he gives advice to his readers to enable them to live in a way that is worthy of being the church.

See also CHURCH; MARCION; PAUL.

Bibliography. M. Barth, *Ephesians*; F. W. Beare, "The Epistle to the Ephesians: Introduction and Exegesis," *IB*; C. L. Mitton, *Ephesians*.

—MALCOLM O. TOLBERT

• **Ephesus.** [ef'uh-suhs] The origin of the city of Ephesus is shrouded in myth. An old legend says that a group of Atheneans decided to set sail to found a new colony. Before leaving they went to the oracle of Delphi to get her wisdom on the subject. She told them to look for a fish and a wild boar. While sailing along the coast of Asia Minor, they put ashore to camp for the night. As they were frying fish on the beach, one of the fish jumped out of the pan and into a bush. A wild boar hiding there was frightened and ran away. Thus the colonists knew to build the city on that location. The Greek city came into being in 1100 B.C.E. located in the valley between the Koressos and Pion ranges (PLATES 26, 27).

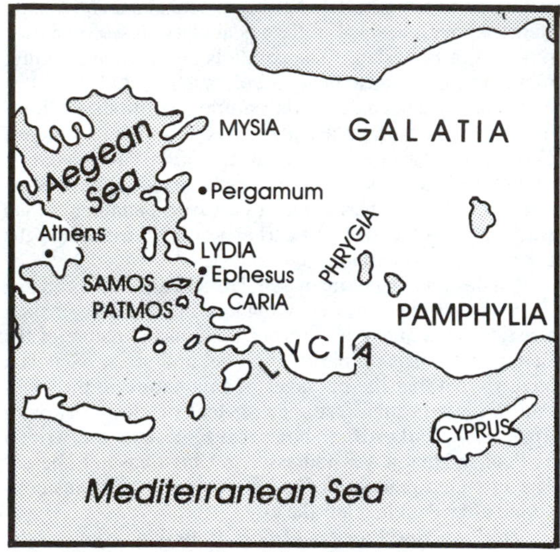

Designed by Margaret Jordan Brown ©Mercer University Press

The Greeks took over the worship of the local goddess, ARTEMIS, and by the sixth century B.C.E. had built a huge temple to her. The temple to Artemis had been constructed following the defeat of Ephesus by the Lydian king, Croesus, in 560 B.C.E. Ephesus was ruled by the Lydians from 560 B.C.E. until 290 B.C.E. During that period Ephesus felt the heavy hand of Alexander the Great in 334 B.C.E. According to a local myth, the grand temple of Ephesus had been burned to the ground by a madman, Herostratus, on the very day that Alexander had been born in 356 B.C.E. When Alexander came to Ephesus, he offered to pay for the rebuilding of the temple, but the local authorities turned him down. Later Ephesus would be ruled by one of Alexander's generals, Lysimachus.

Ephesus came under Roman rule in 133 B.C.E. following a military defeat in the battle of Magnesia in 189 B.C.E. The Romans left their imprint upon the city in terms of beautiful temples and public buildings. A beautiful colonnaded street led from the harbor into the city. It was said that eight chariots could ride abreast on this street, named the Arcadian Road. At the eastern terminus of the road was located the huge amphitheater holding 2,400 people in three ranks of seats (PLATE 59). The great Greek tragic dramas had been performed there since the second century B.C.E. The theater building was most unique in that it had seven thuromata for stage scenery whereas other theaters had only three or five. Thus the number seven took on special meaning in Ephesus.

Of course, the grandest building of all was the temple to Artemis, even today considered one of the seven wonders of the ancient world. It was four times larger than the temple to Athena in Athens. The building was 425 ft. long and 225 ft. wide with 127 columns reaching some sixty ft. high. After much exploration, the English archaeologist John Turtle Wood was able to locate the ruins of the temple in 1869 although very few artifacts were left. Other buildings excavated include the magnificent library of Celsus. The main hall was fifty-five by thirty-six ft. and probably housed about 9,500 rolls in its three levels.

Ephesus was a great seaport city, but ships had to sail down a narrow river channel from the Agean Sea to reach the port. The spring floods along the river tended to deposit silt in the harbor. By the fourth century C.E., Ephesus lost its battle with the silt, and today the city stands several miles from the nearest sea with its harbor being one great wheat field. Yet the city itself is probably the best preserved ancient biblical city.

Bibliography. W. Alzinger, *Die Stadt der Siebenten Weltwunders*; J. Blevins, *Revelation as Drama*; E. Yamauchi, *The Archeology of New Testament Cities in Asia Minor.*

—JAMES L. BLEVINS

• **Ephod.** [ee'fod] The directions for constructing the TABERNACLE and for establishing the cult in the wilderness (Exod 25–31) and the report of their execution (Exod 35–40; Lev 8–9) make reference to the ephod to be worn by AARON while ministering as the HIGH PRIEST (Exod 28:1-35; 39:1-22). The ornate item is depicted as an over the shoulder garment worn on top of a special robe and decorated around the skirt with alternating pomegranates and golden bells. Associated with the ephod was the breastplate containing the URIM AND THUMMIM used for securing oracular responses from the deity (cf. Sir 45:8-12). The ephod described in Exod 28 and 39 was probably that used in the Jerusalem TEMPLE in late preexilic or postexilic times.

In the historical books, reference is made to the ephod as a special priestly attire or accouterment (1 Sam 3:28; 14:3; 23:6, 9; 30:7) used in conjunction with ascertaining the divine will but without any description of its nature.

Some texts refer to the item as if it were a linen waistcloth of some sort, being worn by the lad SAMUEL while serving at SHILOH (1 Sam 2:18), by King DAVID while dancing before the ARK being brought to JERUSALEM (2 Sam 6:14; 1 Chr 15:27), or by any priest as normal attire while serving in a sanctuary (1 Sam 22:18).

Elsewhere, the ephod appears to be a substantial item, some type of cultic furniture or its trappings. In Judg 8:22-27, GIDEON received gold taken in battle and out of this made an ephod, which he set up in Ophrah. Similarly, MICAH in Judg 17:1-5 had an ephod and a TERAPHIM in his shrine along with a graven and a molten image; these were taken by the DANITES and set up in their cult place in Dan (Judg 18:14-20, 27, 30-31). In 1 Sam 21:9, the ephod again appears to be something large and stable enough to conceal a large sword.

In Hos 3:4, the prophet refers to SACRIFICE and pillar, ephod and teraphim as if all these were normal, legitimate elements in Yahwistic worship. (The reference here is probably to the looting of the temple of BETHEL by SHALMANESER V when he arrested King HOSHEA of Israel for treaty infraction; cf. 2 Kgs 17:4; Hos 10:15.)

The term ephod thus appears to have been used to denote special clothing worn by officiants in religious services as well as the elaborate drapery that adorned special cultic paraphernalia or statues, the latter used to symbolize the deity in some fashion and probably in conjunction with determining the divine will (cf. Hos 3:12).

See also DRESS; SACRIFICE; URIM AND THUMMIM.

—JOHN H. HAYES

• **Ephraim.** [ee′fray-im] A term used in three related but distinct ways in the OT. (1) It is the name of the second-born son of JOSEPH and his Egyptian wife Asenath, born to them in Egypt (Gen 41:50-52); the firstborn son is MANASSEH. Ephraim (the name is derived from a verb meaning to be fruitful) receives the larger blessing from his grandfather JACOB, despite the protests of Joseph that Manasseh is the firstborn and deserving of the larger blessing (Gen 48:8-22).

(2) The majority of the biblical references to Ephraim have in mind the tribe that traces its lineage to this grandson of Jacob. The tribe received its allotment of land (Josh 16) in the territory north of the tribe of BENJAMIN and extending northward as far as SHECHEM, southeast to JERICHO, and westward to the Mediterranean Sea. Ephraim and Manasseh, the Joseph tribes, often struggled to maintain their respective lands, with Manasseh proving to be a considerable force in Transjordan, and Ephraim the stronger tribe in western Palestine.

(3) Ephraim, in time, gives its name to North ISRAEL, as is particularly clear in the book of HOSEA (thirty-seven references!). With this shift of terminology from Israel to Ephraim, what was fairly well evident from the books of Samuel, Kings, and Chronicles, has become unmistakable. Ephraim had come to dominate the North Israelite scene to such an extent that its name was synonymous with the entire kingdom first set up by JEROBOAM I (1 Kgs 12) with its capital at Shechem. Even when Shechem had lost political standing first to TIRZAH and then to SAMARIA, Shechem remained a place of important symbolic and ritual meaning. BETHEL was built just north of the tribe of Benjamin and made into the religious capital of the north (1 Kgs 12:29-33). These sites in Ephraim and the connection of priests and prophets with the sites helped to increase the prestige of the tribe in the understanding of Israel's prophets, priests, and (probably) the Levites as well.

JEREMIAH, in dependence upon Hosea, also spoke with great affection of Ephraim, in the name of God (Jer 31:1-20), alternating the designations "Israel" and "Ephraim." Ephraim is God's beloved son, a treasured child. Though the divine wrath has befallen Ephraim, God still loves and yearns for this beloved child (Jer 31:18-20) and will surely find a way to show mercy.

SIRACH (47:21-23) speaks in the same way, identifying North Israel with Ephraim in his reference to the division of Solomon's kingdom that came about in REHOBOAM's day. Probably, Sirach is associating Ephraim with Shechem, the community where the despised SAMARITANS (Sir 50:26) had (and still have) their headquarters and their place of worship.

See also HOSEA; ISRAEL.

—WALTER HARRELSON

• **Ephrathah.** [ef′ruh-thuh] First Sam 17:12 and Ruth 1:2 refer to David and his extended family as Ephrathites from Bethlehem in Judah (PLATE 12); Ruth 4:11 parallels Ephrathah with BETHLEHEM, and Micah 5:2 addresses Bethlehem Ephrathah as a clan (*'elep*, a division within the tribe of Judah; cf. Judg 6:15). The genealogical lists of 1 Chr 2:19, 24, 50, and 4:4 refer to Ephrathah (spelled Ephrath in 2:19), a wife of Hezron (grandson of Judah by Tamar), father of both Ram (who produced the Davidic line), and Caleb. After Hezron's death, Caleb married Ephrathah who bore Hur, "the father of Bethlehem" (4:4) who fathered Salma, also called "the father of Bethlehem" in 2:51. Another (?). Salma was the father of Boaz (husband of Ruth), a great-grandfather of David (2:11; Ruth 4:20-21; Matt 1:4-5; Luke 3:32). The probability, therefore, is that Ephrathah was originally a Judahite clan settled in and around Bethlehem, and that Bethlehem, the village, was a more specific designation within Ephrathah (LXX may interpret correctly when it translates Micah 5:2, "Bethlehem, house of Ephrathah"). As Israel's tribal structure gave way to the monarchy, Ephrathah became identified with Bethlehem and its environs (Gen 35:19; 48:7).

Gen 35:16, 19 and 48:7 state that Rachel was buried near Ephrath(ah) (mistakenly identified by a later editor as Bethlehem), not far from Bethel, while 1 Sam 10:2 and Jer 31:15 locate her tomb in the territory of Benjamin. This Ephrath(ah) could be a town in Benjamin, perhaps the Ophrah (Ephron) of Josh 18:23; but more likely the reference is to a district. First Chr 2:50-51 relates both Bethlehem and Kiriath-jearim, on the border between Benjamin and Judah, to mother Ephrathah, and Ps 132:6 also pairs the two towns. At one time, therefore, the range of the Ephrathah clan probably reached north to Benjamin; but this was forgotten when the Ephrathah district later diminished to the area around Bethlehem with which it became synonymous.

See also BETHLEHEM.

—LAMONTTE M. LUKER

• **Epicureans.** [ep′i-kyoo-ree″uhns] Epicureans were proponents of a philosophical system of thought and conduct which began around 310 B.C.E. and became centered in Athens. They made sensation the standard of truth, the pursuit of genuine happiness the goal of earthly existence, and friendship the environment of fulfillment for its members. Epicureanism spread by way of its disciples through much of the Hellenistic world and achieved its most noteworthy exposition in the writings of the Roman poet, Lucretius (99–55 B.C.E.). Throughout that expansion little if any alterations ever occurred in the doctrine of its founder.

Epicurus, the founder of this highly ethical philosophy, opened his school in 310 B.C.E. In 306 B.C.E. his followers purchased him a home and garden in Athens where he lived and taught until his death in 270 B.C.E. He and his ever increasing community of disciples came to be known as Epicureans and philosophers of the garden.

Epicurus explained the existence of the world through a doctrine of atoms which were in constant movement and responsible for the origin of all living things. Gods existed but were involved in no way in the life of people and, therefore, unnecessary. Hence, religion and its rituals were meaningless. Humans possessed free will and their future was not determined by any power beyond their control. According to Epicurus, the basic condition for the achievement of authentic happiness is freedom from the fear of the gods.

The happiness which Epicureans sought as the goal of human life was not an "eat, drink, and be merry" self-indulgence. Epicurus, as well as his devotees, lived pure and simple lives, abstained from excesses of all kinds, and maintained that sexual intercourse produced more negative than positive consequences. They described the state of happiness as undisturbed tranquillity, which meant the ability to remain unaffected by any and all earthly experiences. The distress of life was negated by the blissful experiences of one's past. True happiness occurred only in this life, for at death the soul dissolved into atoms and possessed no hope nor dread in future existence.

Epicureans magnified friendship as the context out of

which tranquillity arises. They developed organizational brotherhoods aimed at actualizing the happiness of the individual. Reciprocal care, common meals, and memorial festivals served to assist the community member in the attainment of an independence from the gods, other beings, and things. In reality the Epicurean philosophy became a substitute for religion.

Although Epicureanism competed with Stoicism throughout its history, the Epicureans experienced considerable success among the more educated classes through the first century B.C.E. Both Epicureanism and Stoicism, despite their divergent presuppositions and doctrines, had been strongly dependent upon the personal character of their founders. Unlike Stoicism, however, the Epicureans suffered a decline in influence during the period of imperial Rome and received prominence in later centuries only as an object of charges of atheism from both Christians and pagans.

See also HELLENISTIC WORLD; STOICS.

Bibliography. F. C. Grant, *Hellenistic Religions*; N. W. DeWitt, *Epicurus and His Philosophy*; H. Koester, *Introduction to the New Testament*.

—ROBERT M. SHURDEN

• **Epistle/Letter.** Epistles and letters are written messages sent to individuals or groups of people separated from their authors by distance or special circumstances. In antiquity letter writing was a well established mode of communication and assumed many forms ranging from simple personal addresses to elaborate literary masterpieces. Epicurus, Seneca, and Cicero used the epistolary medium for discourse on moral, ethical, and philosophical questions.

In the early church the letter became the most prominent means of elaborating on matters of theology and Christian conduct. Out of twenty-seven NT works, twenty-one are letters, and two of the remaining ones (Acts and Revelation) contain letters. The practice of writing letters was widely continued in primitive Christianity by bishops and influential church leaders such as Clement of Rome, Polycarp, and Ignatius. Thus there came into existence a new epistolary genre called encyclical letters which were meant to convey doctrinal decisions affecting the whole church.

Adolf Deissmann tried to distinguish between letter and epistle. Letters, he suggested, are a private, non-literary means of communication whereas epistles are artistic compositions intended for public dissemination. According to such a definition, Paul's writings were not meant to be literary compositions but simple letters which were not intended for large audiences. Yet many of Paul's letters, even the very personal Letter to Philemon, were in fact written to be shared with the larger community. Most modern scholars refer to NT written communications as letters rather than epistles. The RSV, for example, never mentions the term epistle.

NT letters, however, have been elevated by the early church to a level of spiritual eminence which places them in a unique category eluding traditional definitions. Their permanent use in the church as inspired texts gives them a quality and a meaning never shared with other epistolary documents.

The NT contains several different types of letters. There are general letters (written to churches) and pastoral letters (written to individuals). The general Letters of Paul tend to deal with larger doctrinal issues affecting the community as a whole. The Pastoral Letters (1-2 Timothy, Titus), whose authorship is often contested, belong to the second generation of Christians. They take the form of private communications to Paul's associates. Early Christians regarded the Catholic Letters (James, 1-2 Peter, 1-2-3 John, Jude) as universal and more complete in their teaching. They are encyclical in character, and are often contrasted to Paul's more personal and more local letters. Hebrews is often considered a letter but would qualify more as a treatise containing a long sustained argument in favor of the preeminence of Christianity over Judaism.

NT writers could certainly not foresee that their letters would be collected into a body of canonical literature. Paul's open discussions of scandals and misconduct suggest that he meant to keep a large portion of his writings private. At the same time, the direct nature of the letters attests to their reliability and makes them indispensable for an appreciation of the apostolic age. It is thus understandable that the early church elevated them to the dignity of canonical status.

See also GENERAL LETTERS; LETTERS/INSCRIPTIONS; PASTORAL EPISTLES; PAUL; WRITING SYSTEMS.

Bibliography. A. Deissmann, *Light from the Ancient East*; W. G. Doty, *Letters in Primitive Christianity*; S. K. Stowers, *Letter Writing in Greco-Roman Antiquity*.

—PAUL CIHOLAS

• **Esarhaddon.** [ee'suhr-had″uhn] (Heb. *'ēsar-ḥaddōn*); Assyr. *Ašur-aḫ-iddin* (''Ashur has given a brother'') was king of the Assyrian empire 681-669 B.C.E. Although a younger son of SENNACHERIB, Esarhaddon was chosen to succeed his father by an oracle and installed as crown prince. Nevertheless, when Sennacherib was assassinated by his sons in 681 B.C.E., Esarhaddon was forced to fight a short civil war to gain the throne. The OT reports the patricide and subsequent victory of Esarhaddon in 2 Kgs 19:37 (cf. Isa 37:38).

For most of his reign Esarhaddon was occupied with suppressing rebellions and securing or extending the boundaries of the Assyrian empire. He followed the policy of deportation, exiling traitors from southern Mesopotamia to western parts of the empire (cf. Ezra 4:2). He exacted heavy tribute from Manasseh of Judah who was listed as one of his vassal kings (cf. *ANET,* 291). Ammon, Moab, and Edom, as well as Gaza, Ekron, and Ashkelon were counted among his conquests.

In 675 B.C.E., Esarhaddon invaded Egypt. After four years of setbacks, he defeated the Pharaoh Tirhakah and took Memphis, proclaiming himself king of Lower and Upper Egypt. But as soon as the main Assyrian army withdrew from Egypt, Tirhakah returned to regain Memphis. Esarhaddon died at Haran in 669 B.C.E. on his way to reconquer Egypt.

Manasseh's detention (2 Chr 33:11) probably refers to the rebuilding of Babylon by Esarhaddon. Vassal kingdoms in Syria and Palestine were called upon to supply their share of building materials.

See also ASHURBANIPAL; ASSYRIA.

Bibliography. *ANET*, 289-94.

—STEPHEN J. ANDREWS

• **Esau.** [ee'saw] The son of ISAAC, the twin brother of JACOB, and the grandson of ABRAHAM.

The essentials of the Esau story are found in Gen 25:19–36:43. Major moments in Esau's life include the forfeit of his birthright, marriages, loss of the patriarchal blessing, move to Seir, forgiveness of Jacob, departure again from Canaan, and burial of Isaac. Several motifs from the Genesis account appear also in the traditions of other ancient peoples (e.g., the prenatal struggle of twins). There is archaeological evidence from Nuzi of deathbed wills and of disposal of the BIRTHRIGHT.

Although he may have lived shortsightedly as a younger man, Esau later showed himself to be generous and forgiving (Gen 32-33). To have experienced injustice twice from an opportunistic brother whose very name means "grabber" and then later to affirm that brother is at least some measure of Esau's character.

This burial of animosities suggests that a negativism about Esau in the tradition may derive from a later associating of Esau with the nation of EDOM (e.g., Jer 49:7-10). Such an association would have functioned to explain the existing hostile relations of Edom and Israel-Judah under the monarchy (the book of Obadiah is a denunciation of Edom and a prediction of its destruction). Even though the story of his life is simple enough, the function of "Esau-Edom" in the tradition introduces some complexity about Esau. Just as the older Esau was displaced by the younger but elect Jacob of the same family, with hostilities resolved, so the older Edomites were displaced by the younger but elect Israelites of the same semitic family, but with hostilities unresolved.

The tradition capitalizes on some interesting coincidences and wordplays to enhance the Esau-Edom connection: "Edom" in Hebrew suggests "red," as in the red hills of Seir, the ruddy complexion of Esau, or the red pottage; and "Mount Seir" suggests "hairy," as in Esau's name and appearance.

The mystery of Esau, reflected in the negative handling of the Esau figure, persists in Rabbinical writings (cf. *Jub* 35:13) and into the NT. Overlooking the injustices done to him and his growth toward maturity, the continuing tradition capitalizes on Esau's association with Edom and/or his youthful impetuosity. Paul in his extended section on election (cf. Rom 9:10-13) reflects the negativity, but admits that the rejection of Esau in favor of Jacob was before birth. Such an admission means in Esau's behalf that the choice of Jacob was not then due to any superiority in Jacob's duplicitous character and it overlooks Esau's magnanimity, raising also the question of whether Esau actually lost his heritage through his own choosing or through election. Heb 12:16 represents Esau as one who would abandon the hope of the higher calling in favor of things inconsequential, which also overlooks Esau's relating redemptively to Jacob.

Esau's function, then, in the ongoing tradition (as complicated by the later Edom-Idumaea connection) may have been ideologically convenient for the Hebrews, but it does not seem representative of Esau's personal significance and stature.

See also BIRTHRIGHT; EDOM/EDOMITES/IDUMEA; JACOB.

—DOUGLAS C. BAIN, JR.

• **Eschatology in the New Testament.** [es'kuh-tol″uh-jee] From a combination of two Gk. words: "the last thing" (ἔσχατον) and "teaching," or "word" (λόγος). Eschatology became a technical term in German (and subsequently English-speaking) dogmatic theology during the 1800s, referring to doctrine or teaching about the final things that included DEATH, RESURRECTION, the PAROUSIA (second coming), JUDGMENT, the MILLENNIUM, ETERNAL LIFE, HEAVEN, and HELL. When defined in these terms eschatology can be thought of only in relation to the future and otherworldly matters. But examination of the books of the Bible shows that this understanding is an oversimplification, for certain biblical materials commonly referred to as eschatological are at least as concerned with present existence as they are with the future. Moreover, even when defined strictly in terms of the future, a dogmatic approach to biblical eschatology has problems, for there is no single biblical point of view on the future. For example, some authors are concerned with the future of earthly life, while others seem interested in a world and time beyond the human realm. Indeed the biblical authors show remarkable variety of thinking in this area; and so, biblical eschatology is complex, and the study of it is complicated.

Scholars have, however, found ways of talking about the diverse eschatological thinking of the biblical authors and have coined a number of phrases that describe the complex biblical materials. Thus one reads about (1) prophetic versus apocalyptic eschatology, (2) individual versus national eschatology, (3) individual versus general or universal eschatology, (4) consistent versus realized eschatology, and (5) consistent or realized versus inaugurated eschatology. These phrases are not without liabilities, for frequently the eschatology of a biblical author will not fit neatly into any one category, rather it will be characterized by elements of more than one of these descriptions. But, if these categories are understood as general descriptions that must be nuanced appropriately for each specific biblical author, rather than as absolute and exclusive summaries, they can assist one in understanding the thoughts of the biblical authors about the future/end.

In general, prior to the Babylonian Exile, the prophets of Israel were not interested in individual and otherworldly matters. Instead, preexilic prophets thought, spoke, and wrote of the future of the nation in history. For these biblical authors, the future was the time in which the judgment of God on Israel and its enemies would come about in this world. Therefore divine judgment did not mean the end of the world, but a dramatic alteration of the current patterns of life. God would crush Israel's enemies, or the enemies would execute God's judgment on a sinful Israel (e.g., Isa 1–39; Hosea; Amos; Micah). During the Exile, through the encounter of Israel's religious thought with that of the Babylonians, a less historically-bound form of eschatology evolved, normally called apocalyptic eschatology. The outlook of apocalyptic eschatology is universal rather than national in orientation. In this pattern of thought God acts directly, intervening in history and judging the world in order to bring the current course of history to an end. Beyond this act of judgment lies a new, radically transformed world order (e.g., Isa 40–66, esp. 56–66; Dan 7). In the late pre-Christian period both traditional prophetic eschatology and the newer apocalyptic eschatology informed the outlook of the Jewish people, but the literary sources show that an apocalyptic point of view became increasingly popular.

In the writings of the NT one finds many examples of the apocalyptic pattern of eschatological thought (Matt 25; Mark 13; 1 Cor 7:29-31). Around the turn of the twentieth century Albert Schweitzer argued that the eschatological teaching of Jesus was apocalyptic in character: the whole life, work, and especially teaching of Jesus was a declaration of a future but imminent act of God that would end the present age through judgment and issue in a new era (the KINGDOM OF GOD) where God's will would be done. Schweitzer maintained that Jesus' whole ministry could only be understood as "consistently eschatological" in this apocalyptic sense. Schweitzer's interpretation was opposed by C. H. Dodd who contended that Jesus' teaching and ministry was to be understood in terms of "realized eschatology." Dodd saw the Kingdom of God as already present in Jesus' own ministry, not as a future entity. Other NT scholars have moved to a position between these options, called "inaugurated eschatology," that understands the teaching and ministry of Jesus to possess characteristics of both "consistent" and "realized" eschatologies. Thus, the Kingdom of God is present in the life and work of Jesus, but its fulfillment still lies in the future; and so, one can speak of the "already" and the "not yet" of the Kingdom.

Much of contemporary NT scholarship focuses on the significance of eschatology for the interpretation of various NT writings. Scholars agree on the importance of this subject for accurate interpretation, but the nature of the eschatology of the NT writings is a point of extensive debate. The Book of Revelation is an obvious center of such study, but the Letters of Paul are also scrutinized in terms of eschatology and, to a lesser degree, the remaining books of the NT are presently being interpreted in this way.

See also APOCALYPTIC LITERATURE; DEATH; ESCHATOLOGY IN THE OLD TESTAMENT; ETERNAL LIFE; HEAVEN; HELL; JUDGMENT, DAY OF; KINGDOM OF GOD; MESSIAH/CHRIST; MILLENNIUM; PAROUSIA/SECOND COMING; RESURRECTION IN THE NEW TESTAMENT; RESURRECTION IN THE OLD TESTAMENT; SATAN IN THE NEW TESTAMENT; SATAN IN THE OLD TESTAMENT; SON OF MAN.

Bibliography. J. Bright, *A History of Israel* and *The Kingdom of God;* C. H. Dodd, *The Parables of the Kingdom,* rev. ed.; P. D. Hanson, *The Dawn of Apocalyptic,* rev. ed.; N. Perrin, *The Kingdom of God in the Teaching of Jesus;* F. Richter, *Die Lehre von den letzen Dingen;* J. A. T. Robinson, *In the End, God . . . ;* A. Schweitzer, *The Quest of the Historical Jesus;* G. von Rad, *The Message of the Prophets.*

—MARION L. SOARDS

• **Eschatology in the Old Testament.** [es'kuh-tol"uh-jee] The term "eschatology" is derived from two Greek words: *eschatos,* meaning "last," and, *logos* meaning "word" or "doctrine." Hence, the term generally signifies the doctrine of the end time. In this sense the OT contains very little eschatology except for the mention of the new heaven and the new earth in Isa 65:17-25; 66:22-23 and the visions of the book of DANIEL. Consequently, OT scholars use a broader definition of the term: future expectations so positive for the faithful (usually Israel or some subgroup within the nation) and so discontinuous with the evil conditions of the time of the seer that the future could not emerge through human progress, but could only be introduced by God.

While preexilic prophets predicted the future and spoke of coming judgment, eschatology probably began during the EXILE. The earliest clear voices were those of JEREMIAH, EZEKIEL, and Second ISAIAH (the anonymous author of all or most of Isa 40–55). Second Isaiah, in particular, distinguished the past and God's punishment upon Israel (particularly in the Exile) from the future, when God would restore and bless the people. The experiences of the Exile and Second Isaiah's radical disjuncture between the two epochs set the context for eschatological thinking after the Exile, expressed in Isa 24–27, 56–66, Zech 9–14, and Joel. While each prophet made his own individual contribution to eschatological thinking, it is possible to describe an overall prophetic eschatology.

The circumstances of the Exile saw the people of Israel stripped of their king, their Temple, their national identity and security, and (for those in exile) their land. Not surprisingly, the prophets conceived of the future in terms of God's restoration of what they had lost. The center of their hope was the city of JERUSALEM. No other theme appears so often in OT eschatology as the restoration and even perfection of the city and its inhabitants. The city was conceived of as the center or navel of the earth, to borrow a designation from historians of religion (Ezek 38:12). Its Temple would be the place to which Jews and others alike would come to worship and for heavenly blessing (cf. Isa 25:6; Zech 8:22; 14:16-19 all postexilic; but contrast Isa 19:23-25, which envisions worship centers in Egypt and Assyria as equals to Jerusalem). Temple personnel would be cleansed (Isa 56–66). The city would be restored and perfected by God, even its geography and climate (Zech 14:4-8). Thus, the restoration of Zion served as the center around which eschatological hope grew.

Besides the restoration and elevation of Zion, OT eschatology also included the motif of the redemption and freeing of Israel. The opening verses of Isa 40 tell of the return to Palestine by the exiles, a return that was actually more limited in scope than Second Isaiah seemed to envision. Clearly, though, the eschatological prophets referred to the restoration of the land and the reunification of the northern and southern kingdoms (Ezek 37:11-23), with increased borders (at least in comparison with the truncated postexilic state, Isa 26:15), often ruled by a descendant of David (Ezek 37:24-25; Jer 33:14-26), though perhaps ruled directly by God (Isa 24:23; Zech 14:9). The nations also came in for mention. If the exiles were to be freed and the state of Israel restored, obviously the conquering world powers and the petty kingdoms nearby had to be punished (cf. Isa 62:1-3; Joel 3; Zeph 3:16-20; Zech 9:1-8). Often, though, punishment is not the final word; instead,the remnant of the nations might be included in the future state of affairs (Isa 66:18-21), though normally in a subordinate position to Israel (Isa 25:6-8; Zech 14:16-19).

The redemption and freeing of Israel, the eschatological prophets often said, would be accompanied by the establishment of wonderful, paradisaical living conditions. Isa 65:17-25, building on the depiction of the ideal monarchical state described in Isa 11:1-9, spoke of a transformation of nature in which predators and victims would live in harmony, where carnivores would eat hay, and human life would last 100 years. The earth would produce copiously (Ezek 34:27; 36:30; Isa 27:6; Joel 3:18; Amos 9:11-15). Isa 25:6-8 could even envision the end of death. Jerusalem would undergo vast geographical changes, becoming the mountain at the earth's center through which God's physical and spiritual blessings would come (Ezek 47:1-12; Zech 14:4-8, 10-11). Indeed, Isa 65:17 and 66:22 even envision the re-creation of the cosmos.

The OT prophets also spoke of the transformation of the nation and of the individual person. If Israel was to be rescued from Exile and restored permanently to its homeland, some profound changes had to take place. For one thing, the nation had to be cleansed of past sin. Second Isaiah saw the Exile as Israel's great atonement for preexilic sin, claiming that Israel had paid double (Isa 40:2). In the postexilic period the prophets continued to press Israel for specific kinds of repentance or actions that would in turn bring into being the anticipated new order. For example, in Haggai and Zechariah Israel was commanded to rebuild the Temple; in Isa 27:7-11 and in Joel 1:1-2:17 Israel was commanded to cleanse the cultus. Either in anticipation of these actions or as their consequence, God would forgive the people. This forgiveness could even include the regeneration of the human personality (Jer 31:31-34; and esp. Ezek 36:26-27).

The Book of DANIEL marked the transition to a new kind of eschatology: APOCALYPTIC. Apocalyptic thinking is caused by relative deprivation, i.e., by a disparity between one's perception of one's conditions and one's expectations. Since the writing of Isa 40–55, ancient Israel had anticipated a glorious future, a future not realized as part of the return from the Exile. Some groups, whether priests, exponents of wisdom, or prophets, turned apocalyptic. Apocalyptic eschatology enhanced the disparity between the present evil time and the good age to be introduced by God; it expected the end time almost immediately. To the apocalyptists, evil seemed to have the upper hand, as the world powers brought tribulation upon the righteous. Apocalyptic eschatology looked forward to God's direct intervention to bring this world to an end. Personal survival beyond death was affirmed by some of these apocalyptists (Dan 12:2-3). Apocalyptic eschatology thus appears more deterministic, dualistic, and pessimistic than prophetic eschatology, but remains firmly convinced of God's ultimate victory over evil.

See also APOCALYPTIC LITERATURE; DUALISM; ESCHATOLOGY IN THE NEW TESTAMENT.

Bibliography. G. Fohrer, "Die Struktur der alttestamentlichen Eschatologie," *TLZ* 85 (1960): 401-420; D. Gowan, *Eschatology in the Old Testament;* H. Gressmann, *Der Ursprung der israelitisch-jüdischen Eschatologie;* P. D.Hanson, *The Dawn of Apocalyptic;* J. Lindblom, "Gibt es eine Eschatologie bei den alttestamentlichen Propheten?" *ST* 6 (1952): 79-114; R. Martin-Achard, *From Death to Life;* H.-P. Müller, *Ursprünge und Strukturen alttestamentlicher Eschatologie;* O. Plöger, *Theocracy and Eschatology;* D. S. Russell, *The Method and Message of Jewish Apocalyptic;* G. Wanke, "Eschatologie: Ein Beispiel theologischer Sprachverwirrung," *KD* 16 (1970): 300-312.

—PAUL L. REDDITT

• **Esdras, First.** [ez′druhs] First Esdras (a book in the Apocrypha, known as *3 Esdras* in the Vulgate) narrates the history of JUDAH from JOSIAH's PASSOVER to EZRA's reforms. It covers substantially the same material as that found in 2 Chr 35:1–36:23, Ezra, and Neh 7:6–8:12. The author begins with the Passover celebration of Josiah's reforms (cf. 2 Chr 35:1-19). He then recounts Josiah's death and the reigns of the final kings of Judah, culminating in the fall of JERUSALEM to the Babylonians (cf. 2 Chr 35:20–36:21). Next he shifts to the decree of Cyrus permitting the Israelites to return to Jerusalem and to rebuild the TEMPLE (cf. Ezra 1:1-11), followed by an account of the opposition to the rebuilding program (cf. Ezra 4:7-24). He then tells the story of the three young bodyguards, which is unique to 1 Esdras. There follows a narration of the return itself (cf. Ezra 2:1-70; Neh 7:6-72) and of the reconstruction of the Temple (cf. Ezra 3:1–4:5; 5:1–6:22). Finally, the author relates the story of Ezra (cf. Ezra 7:1–10:44), concluding with Ezra's public reading of the LAW (cf. Neh 7:78–8:12).

For the most part, 1 Esdras is tied closely to its OT parallels. The major exception is the story of the three young bodyguards, which depicts a contest between three bodyguards of King Darius (3:1–5:6). Each is to argue one thing as the strongest in the world; the winner will be honored by the king. The first speaks on behalf of wine; the second praises kings. The third, who is identified as ZERUBBABEL, honors women, then truth. Zerubbabel wins and is given Darius's support to lead the exiles back to Jerusalem.

The origins of 1 Esdras are difficult to determine. It is extant in several ancient languages, the most important being Greek. A Hebrew or Aramaic original seems likely, although a simple translation of the MT is ruled out. A date in the second century B.C.E. seems probable. The story of the three young bodyguards was probably an independent unit, unconnected with Zerubbabel, which was edited into the narrative. The book may have been composed (or perhaps translated) in Egypt. There is an emphasis on Josiah, Zerubbabel, and Ezra, while NEHEMIAH's role is played down. There is also a focus on the Temple. The precise purpose which underlies the composition of the book, however, remains unclear.

The popularity of 1 Esdras is another matter. JOSEPHUS used it, rather than Ezra-Nehemiah, as his main source for the period in his *Antiquities*. It was also used by a number of prominent Church fathers, including Clement of Alexandria, Origen, Cyprian, Eusebius, Athanasius, Chrysostom, and Augustine. Although Jerome criticized the book, it became a part of the Vulgate until 1546, when the Council of Trent rejected it, relegating it to an appendix. The Eastern Orthodox Church accepts 1 Esdras as canonical.

Although it is beset with problems which have defied solution to the present, the importance of 1 Esdras for understanding the history of the OT text, the complexities of the return, and Judaism in the Hellenistic period cannot be overstated.

See also CHRONICLES, FIRST AND SECOND; EZRA, BOOK OF; NEHEMIAH, BOOK OF.

Bibliography. S. A. Cook, "I Esdras," *The Apocrypha and Pseudepigrapha of the Old Testament,* ed. R. H. Charles; J. M. Myers, *I and II Esdras*; C. C. Torrey, *Ezra Studies*.

—JOSEPH L. TRAFTON

• **Esdras, Second.** *See* EZRA, FOURTH; EZRA, FIFTH AND SIXTH

• **Eshbaal.** *See* ISHBOSHETH

• **Espanados.** *See* CHIASM

• **Essenes.** [es′eens] The Essenes were a sectarian Jewish movement in Palestine at the time of Jesus. Details about the Essenes are given by a number of ancient authors, the most important being the Jewish writers PHILO and JOSEPHUS, and the Roman naturalist, Pliny the Elder, all of whom were contemporaries of the Essenes. Although much about the Essenes can be gleaned from these writers, the discovery of the DEAD SEA SCROLLS has brought about a new era in the study of the sect.

There is no scholarly consensus about the origin of the name Essene. The sources fluctuate between *'Essenoi* (Josephus; Pliny: *Esseni*) and *'Essaioi* (Josephus and Philo). Conjectured etymologies include a root meaning of "pious" or "holy" (from the Syriac *ḥaŝen, ḥassayâ*; the Gk. *'osios*; or the Heb. *ḥasîd*), of "healers" (from the Heb. *'āssayâ*), and of "council" (from the Heb. *'ēṣâ*). "Essene" is not found in the Dead Sea Scrolls and, hence, may not have been the sect's own self-designation.

The nature of the Essene movement, however, is quite clear. Viewing the world from a radically dualistic perspective, the Essenes believed that they alone were on God's side. They called therefore for separation from the larger

Caves at Qumran.

Jerusalem museum where many Dead Sea Scrolls are housed.

Jewish society, and their communities were characterized by a rigid hierarchy of leadership under the Zadokite priests, the sharing of all possessions, a detailed code of conduct with appropriate penalties for misconduct, and a strictly regulated initiation procedure. As the community of the new Covenant, the members devoted themselves to the study of the TORAH (especially as interpreted by the Teacher of Righteousness, a key figure in the early development of the sect), and continual worship, which included the observance of a proper calendar, ritual washings, and a sacred meal. They awaited the coming of two Messiahs and a final war, after which they would restore the sacrificial cult in JERUSALEM. Despite their sectarian outlook, the Essenes were admired for their piety and their simple, virtuous lifestyle. Josephus identifies the Essenes as one of the three leading sects among the Jews, along with the PHARISEES and the SADDUCEES (*BJ* 2.8.2; *Ant* 18.1.2).

The primary classical witnesses to the Essenes are Philo (*Hyp* 11.1-18; *EvGood* 12–13), writing in the early decades C.E., Josephus (*BJ* 2.8.2-13 and *Ant* 18.1.5), writing toward the end of the first century C.E., and Pliny (*Nat Hist* 5.15.73), writing in 77 C.E. The numerous patristic witnesses probably have little independent value, with the possible exception of the third century Christian writer Hippolytus (*Haer* 9.13-23), who may have had access to one of Josephus's sources.

By far the most important witnesses to the Essenes are now the Dead Sea Scrolls, along with the accompanying ruins at Qumran. Three factors make probable the hypothesis that those who lived at Qumran and who wrote the Scrolls were Essenes. First, no other site has been discovered which could fit Pliny's comment that the Essenes lived on the west side of the Dead Sea between JERICHO and EN-GEDI (PLATES 28, 55). Second, archaeological excavations indicate that the Qumran settlement flourished at essentially the same time as did the Essenes. Third, the information which the Scrolls provide about the Qumran community is strikingly similar to the descriptions of the Essenes in the classical sources. Whether the Qumran sect was the main Essene headquarters or simply one group of Essenes is impossible to determine. What is certain is that not all of the Essenes lived at Qumran. Both Philo and Josephus relate that Essene communities were scattered throughout Palestine, with about 4,000 adherents. In addition, Philo devotes an entire treatise (*On the Contemplative Life*) to the Therapeutae, which might have been an Egyptian branch of Essenism. The desire for further knowledge about pre-Qumran or non-Qumran Essenism has led to the suggestion that some of the Pseudepigrapha were composed by Essenes, with the best candidates being JUBILEES, parts of 1 ENOCH and perhaps the TESTAMENTS OF THE TWELVE PATRIARCHS.

The origins of the Essenes are obscure. The history of at least part of the sect is illuminated by the archaeological and literary discoveries by the Dead Sea, although the cryptic historical references in the Scrolls do not permit certainty at every point. Most scholars trace the beginnings of the movement to the Hasideans, who opposed the hellenization policies of Antiochus IV and joined in the revolt of the MACCABEES (1 Macc 2:42; 7:13-16). Shortly thereafter, in opposition to the developing Hasmonean dynasty, the Teacher of Righteousness led an exodus of a large group of Essenes into the desert. This group resided at Qumran until 31 B.C.E., when a destructive earthquake, coupled with the demise of the Hasmoneans in 36 B.C.E. and HEROD the Great's support of the sect (Josephus, *Ant* 15.10.4-5), encouraged the group to leave the desert and resettle, presumably, in Jerusalem. Following Herod's death in 4 B.C.E., the sect returned to Qumran. The extent of Essene participation in the revolt against Rome in 66 C.E. is unclear. A certain John the Essene served as a general during the revolt (Josephus, *BJ* 2.20.4), and the Qumran settlement was overrun eventually by the Romans in 68, after which some of the Essenes apparently joined the ZEALOTS in their final and ill-fated stand at MASADA. There is no evidence that the Essene movement survived the war.

The Essenes are never mentioned in the NT. The discovery of the Dead Sea Scrolls, however, has stimulated considerable—and often wild—speculation about possible connections between the Essenes and early Christianity. The conjecture that JESUS and/or JOHN THE BAPTIST had been part of the Qumran community is unconvincing. On the other hand, it is likely that Jesus both knew of and opposed certain Essene teachings (cf., e.g., Jesus' teaching about loving one's enemies [Matt 5:43-44] with the Essenes's command to hate the sons of darkness [*1QS* 1.10]). Numerous parallels have been noted between the Scrolls and various NT books, most notably the GOSPEL OF JOHN. It is plausible that early Christianity gained converts from among the Essenes, perhaps in increasing numbers after the disastrous war of 66–73 C.E. Whatever the case, the existence of the Essenes testifies to the great diversity within Judaism before 70 C.E.

See also QUMRAN, DEAD SEA SCROLLS.

Bibliography. T. S. Beall, *Josephus' Description of the Essenes Illustrated by the Dead Sea Scrolls*; M. Black, *The Scrolls and Christian Origins*; F. M. Cross, *The Ancient Library of Qumran and Modern Biblical Studies*; A. Dupont-Sommer, *The Essene Writings from Qumran*; D. Graf, "The Pagan Witness to the Essenes," *BA* 40 (1977): 125–29; J. Murphy-O'Connor, "The Essenes and Their History," *RB* 81 (1974): 215–44 and "The Essenes in Palestine," *BA* 40 (1977): 106–24; E. Schürer, *The History of the Jewish People in the Age of Jesus Christ*, ed. G. Vermes, F. Millar, and M. Black; G. Vermes, *The Dead Sea Scrolls: Qumran in Perspective* and "The Etymology of 'Essenes,' " *RevQ* 2 (1960): 427–43.

—JOSEPH L. TRAFTON

• **Esther.** [es'tuhr] The legendary Jewish queen of Persia who in the days of Xerxes or Artaxerxes saved the Jewish people by her courage.

—WALTER HARRELSON

• **Esther, Additions to.** [es'tuhr] The translators of the ancient Greek OT of Alexandria, the LXX, evidently felt the need to "improve" on the Hebrew legend of ESTHER by retaining from their sources or even composing six additions to it. Although Jews and most Protestants reckon them as apocryphal, the additions continue to be numbered in the order established by Jerome (340?–420C.E.) in sequence to the last verse of the Hebrew Esther. The additions are numbered chaps. 10–16 in KJV and RSV Apocryphas. NEB includes the entire Greek Esther in the Apocrypha, with chapters 10–16 appearing at their proper place in the narrative rather than separately. NAB and TEV also include the entire Greek Esther, but the additions are marked by letters A-F rather than by numbers.

Addition A is actually the Greek preface to the book of Esther. It begins with a story (Esth 11) about the Jew, MORDECAI, the cousin and adoptive father of the beautiful Esther. Mordecai had a dream about two great dragons squaring off to fight, accompanied by world-wide tumult. A "righteous nation" cried out to God, and from their cry flowed a great river and light effulgent. Esth 12 introduces Mordecai's archenemy, the wicked Haman (simply an "Agagite" from another Semitic tribe in Esth 3:1; cf. 1 Sam 15:8) as "a Bougaean," later clarified (16:10) to mean "a Macedonian," i. e., a generic gentile.

Addition B (Esth 13:1-7) offers the text of the letter which, according to Esth 3:13, the great king ARTAXERXES sent to his provincial governors at the suggestion of Haman, ordering the destruction of the Jews. Written in a style much more elegant than addition A, this is thought to have been composed originally in Greek. Addition C (Esth 13:8-14:19) contains the texts of the prayers offered by Mordecai and Esther after Esther's desperate decision to intercede with the king on behalf of the Jews (Esth 4:15-17). Addition D (Esth 15) follows immediately after these prayers and replaces the canonical text of Esth 5:1-2 with a much enlarged account of Esther's preparations to approach the king with her dangerous request. Addition E (Esth 16) follows Esth 8:12, and, in the same style as addition B, gives the text of the edict there described. In it, the king cancels his earlier order to let Haman kill the Jews, condemns the former even as he goes to considerable lengths to exonerate the latter, and makes much pious reference to the power and justice of God. Finally, addition F (Esth 10:4-11:1) follows immediately upon the end of the Hebrew Esther. In 10:4-13, Mordecai interprets the dream with which the Greek Esther began. He says that the two dragons were Haman and himself, and the spring which became a river accompanied by light was Esther. Esth 11:1, the colophon or concluding inscription, dates the Greek translation at about 114 B.C.E., which many believe to be close to the time of the actual composition of these additions.

The six additions significantly alter the protagonists, the plot, the piety and the purpose of the Book of Esther. First, the hero of the Greek book is God, not Esther. God both reveals the immediate future and saves the Jews. God's name is celebrated in prayer by Esther, Mordecai and the Persian king alike. This "remedies" the most notable "deficiency" of the Hebrew Esther—a feature which alone may have caused the book to be ignored totally by NT writers and apparently not even to be considered a sacred writing by the sectaries at Qumran—namely, the fact that God is never mentioned in it. Second, the Greek plot depicts a struggle much more titanic in its proportions. Now the enemy is a "Macedonian," suggesting that the Jews faced not just local enemies in the Persian diaspora, but the HELLENISTIC WORLD as a whole. Third, the practice of piety is felt in the additions in a way that is not true of the Hebrew book. We hear of prayer and fasting and dietary scruples (14, 17). Finally, the significance of the Festival of PURIM is reassessed. The Hebrew Esther seems to serve largely as a cult legend for that festival. Yet, Purim is mentioned nowhere else in the Bible, nor did the Qumran sectaries include any such feast on their cultic calendar. Perhaps the

Alexandrian community, too, found the emphasis on Purim overdone in the book of Esther and quietly downplayed it by creating a different plot. At their hands it becomes the story of the fulfillment of Mordecai's dream of victory through the powerful guiding hand of the God of Israel.

See also APOCRYPHAL LITERATURE; ESTHER, BOOK OF.

Bibliography. C. A. Moore, *Daniel, Esther, and Jeremiah: the Additions.*

—W. SIBLEY TOWNER

• OUTLINE OF ESTHER •

The Book of Esther

I. Persian Court (1:1-22)
II. Esther Becomes Queen (2:1-23)
III. Haman and His Plans to Destroy the Jews (3:1–4:17)
IV. The Plot Fails (5:1–8:2)
V. The Jews Emerge Victorious (8:3–10:3)

• **Esther, Book of.** [es'tuhr] The festal scroll that is used at the festival of PURIM. It tells the story of the salvation and deliverance of the Jewish people in an attempted extermination during the Persian period. Many modern scholars regard the book as an historical novella that relates a festival legend to explain the origin of Purim, which celebrates a Jewish victory. Some contend that a non-Jewish origin to the festival is being covered up in the story. Others see a dual attempt at explaining Purim and simply entertaining readers with a swashbuckling type of adventure. One things seems evident, however. As B. Childs and J. Crenshaw state, Esther seeks to make "the preservation of the Jewish nation a religious obligation of the first magnitude."

In the book there are at least two and possibly three different plots and stories. One plot is of harem intrigue, with Vashti's refusal to appear before the court and Esther's success in a contest of beauty. Another is a plot of court intrigue. This involves MORDECAI's discovery of a potential revolt, his rise to power, and Haman's defeat by means of Esther's plot.

A third and very interesting aspect of the book is that the events seem to be largely worked out on the human plane. With the lack of direct prayers and references to God, the book almost seems to be nonreligious. In fact, there is no mention of thanksgiving to God after the Jewish salvation. In light of the strict religious nature of much of Judaism, this has led to an idea that Esther may have been penned under the influence of the wisdom literature of the day. The primary reference to any awareness of God's purposes may be found as a veiled reference in Esth 4:14. The wisdom of Esther and Mordecai becomes the focal point as far as the overcoming of impending doom. This may be one reason that there seems to be less regard for Esther than for other biblical books.

As for the content of the book, the stories are woven together in such a manner as to intrigue the reader. The reader is briefly introduced to the historical context of the story by a description of the Persian court under Ahasuerus (Xerxes I). The king is prone to giving lavish banquets at which the beauty of his wives is put on display. When Vashti refuses to appear, she is banished and Esther is chosen to become queen, after concealing her Jewishness. Her guardian, Mordecai, uncovers a plot against the king, which is revealed to Xerxes by Esther. Mordecai is not rewarded immediately, but he will be rewarded later. The new vizier, Haman, dislikes Mordecai and seeks to have him killed through trickery. That, however, is foiled by Esther. She invites Haman to a banquet at which the king is present. When invited to a second banquet, Haman presumes he is to be lavished with honors. Xerxes asks what kinds of honors should be bestowed upon one who has the grand favor of the king. Haman describes the greatest of honors to the king, presuming that he will be the recipient. He is devastated to learn that he is to bestow these on the one whom he hates, Mordecai. Esther reveals her Jewishness to Ahasuerus as well as Haman's schemes to have Mordecai killed. Haman is hanged on his own gallows, Mordecai receives many honors, and edicts are given that save the Jews. The wisdom displayed by both Mordecai and Esther leads to the preservation of the nation.

As previously mentioned, the lack of references to the deity raised some later questions as well as attempts to rectify the situation. In a comparison between the Hebrew and LXX texts, one finds over 100 verses that were added in the LXX additions that attempt to correct the lack of reference to religious piety. Though there were questions about the canonicity of Esther, its inclusion in the canon presumes divine providence both in its inclusion and story.

Some suggest that the lack of reference to God is an attempt to avoid the overuse of the divine name in celebration. Others see this interpreted by later generations as an encouragement that even if the hand of God is not evident, God's providential will still operates for those who will use their wits and work with the deity. A combination of wisdom and integrity brings its just rewards. It seems likely that this latter idea might be the better option for understanding Esther. The descriptions favor a written time frame during Diaspora or the reign of Antiochus IV Epiphanes. This would give hope and encouragement to those who would seek to live rich, creative, and full lives in a pagan environment because of the wisdom given by God.

See also ESTHER; MORDECAI; PURIM.

Bibliography. A. Baumgarten, "Scroll of Esther," *EncJud;* J. Carmody, D. L. Carmody and R. L. Cohn, *Exploring the Hebrew Bible;* B. S. Childs, *Introduction to the Old Testament as Scripture;* J. L. Crenshaw, *Old Testament Wisdom* and *Story and Faith;* W. L. Humphreys, "Esther, Book of," *IDBSupp;* C. A. Moore, *Esther.*

—STEPHEN Z. HEARNE

• **Eternal Life.** In popular religious thought "eternal life" is equated with the idea of life after death, usually in the presence of God. The expression "eternal life" (Gk. ζωὴ αἰώνιος) comes from the NT. It occurs in the Snyoptic Gospels, but it is an especially important theme in the Gospel of John (seventeen occurrences) and 1 John (six times); thus, one may trace the depths of the idea best in relation to the Johannine texts.

"Life" is itself a favorite Johannine term (thirty-six times in the Gospel and thirteen times in the Letters), and without the adjectival modifier "eternal" still designates a special concept. "Life" and "eternal life" indicate something different from and more than "natural life," which is named in the Johannine literature by the Greek word "soul" (ψυχή). Natural life ends in death, but life is viewed positively by the Johannine authors and this probably inspired the development of the phrase "eternal life" as a way of speaking of God's greatest gift to humanity. In developing this idea the author of the Gospel (and in turn the author of the Letters) was not, however, freely inventing a line of thought, rather he was working with and making full use of an existing theme—as is shown in the simple occurrence of the phrase "eternal life" in Mark (10:17,30 par., Matt 19:16,29 and Luke 18:18,30), Matthew (25:46), and Luke (10:25) in relation to future life in the KINGDOM OF GOD (cf. Luke 18:30).

Scholars debate whether Greek or Hebrew, or more particularly Gnostic or rabbinic, thought provides the background out of which the Johannine authors drew inspiration in developing the idea of "eternal life." Though the discussion continues, the current tendency is to favor a Hellenistic Jewish (not purely Greek philosophical or Gnostic) background that interprets "eternal life" as a development of the apocalyptic eschatological idea of *two ages*, "this age" (frequently referred to as "the present evil age") and "the age to come" (cf. *1 Enoch* and *4 Ezra*). In such thought there is both a temporal and qualitative difference between the ages, with the future being superior in duration and quality.

In the Johannine writings the concept of "eternal life" has about it both the notions of temporal (everlasting) and qualitative (abundance) superiority in comparison with natural life, but the use of the phrase in the Gospel and 1 John reveals that the qualitative aspect is foremost in the Johannine thinking. Indeed in the Johannine usage it is clear that "eternal life" is not simply futuristic, for it is the present possession, or better, quality of existence, of those who believe in Jesus. This does not mean there is no future dimension to "eternal life"—it clearly continues beyond death, but the Johannine authors are more concerned with presenting the importance of eternal life as a transformed human existence in the present than with developing teaching about life after death. Thus, contemporary scholars and newer translations use "eternal life" rather than "everlasting life" for the Greek term, taking the emphasis off the durative quality and putting it on the qualitative dimension of the theme.

In essence, for the Johannine thinkers, "eternal life" is the life of God. As God originally breathed natural life into humanity, so God spoke the divine Word of life, the Son of God, Jesus, who was incarnated in order to give eternal life to humankind. For humanity Jesus is life, and through belief in him humans receive his life which is God's own life breathed forth in him. Jesus accomplished the giving of eternal life to believing humans by giving himself in death, so that raised to life, having conquered death, he can communicate eternal life by breathing forth the lifegiving Spirit upon them.

While "eternal life" cannot be destroyed, and so lasts forever, because Jesus has conquered death, the main opponent of eternal life is "sin," not death. Therefore, because believing humans live in the natural world having already received "eternal life" when Jesus bestowed the Spirit upon them, they live opposing sin with no fear of death.

Perhaps the best single statement summary of the meaning of eternal life is John 17:3, "And this is eternal life, that they know thee the only true God, and Jesus Christ whom thou hast sent." Eternal life described as *knowing God* does not refer to mastered factual information or ecstatically communicated spiritual experience, but rather to a thoroughgoing relationship with God in and through belief in Jesus who himself brings the life of God into the lives of human beings.

See also DEATH; EVERLASTING; IMMORTALITY; KINGDOM OF GOD; RESURRECTION IN THE NEW TESTAMENT; RESURRECTION IN THE OLD TESTAMENT; SOUL IN THE OLD TESTAMENT.

Bibliography. C. K. Barrett, *The Gospel According to John*, 2nd ed.; R. E. Brown, *The Gospel According to John;* R. Bultmann, *The Gospel of John* and *Theology of the New Testament;* C. H. Dodd, *The Interpretation of the Fourth Gospel;* A. M. Hunter, *Introducing New Testament Theology;* L. Morris, *New Testament Theology;* F. Stagg, *New Testament Theology*.

—MARION L. SOARDS

• **Ethan.** *See* JEDUTHUM

• **Ethics in the New Testament.** In the most general sense "ethics" is the study of "morals." As a descriptive discipline it seeks to describe fairly and objectively the moral perspectives and practices of a particular group. As a normative discipline, ethics is prescriptive and assumes that some actions are right and others wrong, that some personal qualities are virtues and others vices, that some ways of organizing society are good and others bad. Hence normative ethics seeks to answer questions like the following: "What ought I to do?" "What kind of person ought I to be?" "How ought society to be organized?" Our concern here is to describe the moral perspectives of the NT, while remembering that for Christians these are also normative claims that prescribe how one ought to live.

The ethics of the NT are most fully understood and appreciated in their historical context. Many of Jesus' sayings, for example, have striking parallels in the teachings of first-century rabbis, and early Christianity often drew upon the popular ethical instruction of the Greco-Roman world (e.g., the catalogues of vices and virtues similar to Gal 5:19-23, and the rules for household conduct such as found in Eph 5:21–6:9). But such borrowings were transformed by their setting in the context of God's redemptive love as manifest in the life, death, and resurrection of JESUS Christ and the continuing presence of the HOLY SPIRIT.

While rules, principles, values, and moral quandaries are not absent from the NT, they are not the fundamental stuff of its ethics. Rather, the essence of NT ethics is the new disposition engendered and nurtured by one's encounter with God in Jesus Christ. Ethics is a constituent of Christian faith and cannot be separated or even sharply distinguished from FAITH. NT writers do, of course, appeal to rules and principles, but such rules and principles, and even more general values like love and justice, derive their specific meaning and significance from the gospel story as a whole, especially Jesus' life, teachings, death and resurrection. The ethics of the NT are tied fundamentally to the question of what it means to be a disciple of Jesus.

The ethic of Jesus is part and parcel of his proclamation of the KINGDOM OF GOD, a venerable image of hope for ancient Israel. For the prophets it referred to God's final and decisive act for the salvation of human beings. In the first century it was popularly imbued with exclusivistic and futuristic overtones. But for Jesus the Kingdom was a "coming Kingdom," already "at hand" in his ministry (Mark 1:14-15), impinging directly upon human experience and creating a new world in the midst of the old. The Kingdom both gives and demands a new vision of God, neighbor, and self, a vision in conflict with natural, customary modes of understanding. One cannot put new wine in old wineskins (Mark 2:22).

At the heart of Jesus' proclamation of the Kingdom of God is the God of unconditional, uncalculating love who welcomes even "tax collectors and sinners" (Luke 15:1-32). Such love, designated *agapē* in the NT, reconciles God to human beings and thereby heals the divisions within the self and establishes the possibility of genuine community by breaking down the barriers that separate human beings from each other. Such a vision contrasts sharply with the more "natural" tendency to limit God's love and forgiveness to a particular group, whether defined by race, social status, religious tradition, or the intensity of one's religious commitment. The encounter with such unconditional, uncalculating love may breed resistance, a hardening of the heart based on the selfish fear of losing one's privileged status before God. But it may also lead to REPENTANCE and faith (Mark 1:15), a change so radical that one's whole disposition is transformed. As the grateful acceptance and trustful appropriation of this transforming vision, faith is the context in which the specifically ethical demands of Jesus are to be understood.

At times Jesus' teachings appropriate the language of law (e.g., the antitheses of Matt 5:21-48), and this has led some commentators to find in Jesus' ethic a new legalism, one more demanding than the old, but a legalism nonetheless. To be sure, Jesus' teachings are not contrary to the spirit of the Law (Matt 5:17), but few of his sayings have the precision and clarity of legal rules (compare the regulations of the Covenant Code in Exod 20:22–23:33). Hence Jesus sets forth a morality that, paradoxically, at once fulfills and annuls the morality of Law. The saying "Render to Caesar that which is Caesar's and to God that which is God's" (Mark 12:17), for example, does not offer precise criteria for defining the separate spheres of CHURCH and state (what if Caesar demands more than his due?). But the construction itself gives priority to God's claims, and thus challenges one to rethink the whole issue of how Caesar's claims are related to God's claims. Even the antitheses seem more designed to evoke the new attitude of uncalculating love than to set forth clear precise rules of behavior. The ethic of Jesus then is fundamentally a dispositional ethic based on a new attitude engendered and nurtured by the Kingdom of God.

The parables and other sayings of Jesus are intended both to describe and to evoke this new disposition, often by juxtaposing the old and the new. The old is preoccupied with the letter of the Law and hence insists on precise rules of conduct; the new pushes behind the letter to the spirit of love and mercy that both undergirds and fulfills the Law (Matt 5:22, 28). The old seeks limits to moral responsibility ("And who is my neighbor?" [Luke 10:29]; "How often shall my brother sin against me and I forgive him?" [Matt 18:22]); the new reflects the uncalculating mercy of God that knows no limits (Matt 5:44-45). The old affirms legal restrictions as absolute rights (e.g., the attitude of the unmerciful servant in Matt 18:23-35); the new demands a moral perspective that transcends such self-centeredness (Matt 5:38-42).

The ethical demands of Jesus must be seen as a response to the unconditional, uncalculating love of God. They are not prerequisites for entrance into the Kingdom; nor are they motivated by some innate sense of duty or by desire for reward. Jesus does promise rewards to his followers, but the reward is paradoxical; for the true reward is the gift of acting without thought of reward. In the parable of the great judgment (Matt 25:31-46), for example, the righteous are surprised by their reward, for they have acted without concern for self.

The ethical perspectives developed in the early church were shaped by two powerful forces: (1) the traditions about Jesus and (2) the experience of his resurrection in the Christian community. The resurrection was much more than simply a promise of life after death. It was God's vindication of Jesus and hence a call to mission to continue what Jesus had begun (note Paul's image of the church as the "body of Christ" in 1 Cor 12). It was also a spiritual presence that brought the hoped-for future into the present and created a new attitude and disposition, at once free from the old aeon and in conflict with it.

But these same forces also encouraged FREEDOM and diversity. The Holy Spirit was not only a unifying presence but also the giver of freedom (2 Cor 3:17), and that encouraged multiple images, concepts, and motifs, often complementary, but each with its own approach to Christian ethics. Thus one finds in the NT appeals and exhortations to imitate Christ (Phil 2:6-11), to walk with the Spirit (Gal 5:16-18), to love one another (John 13:31-35), to live with the expectation of Christ's imminent return (1 Cor 7:29-31), to show one's faith through works (Jas 2:14-26), to fulfill one's freedom in love (Gal 5:13-15), to be holy (1 Pet 1:13-21), and to suffer patiently for righteousness sake (1 Pet 2:18-25).

The most complete ethic in the early church was that developed by PAUL. Paul's ethic, articulated in response to several crises, is like a rope with multiple strands. Three will be given attention here: (1) the dialectic of freedom and love, (2) the Christian life as a walk with the Holy Spirit, and (3) the moral character of the Christian community.

Paul's dialectic of freedom and love steers cautiously between the Scylla of legalism and the Charybdis of libertinism. This is developed most clearly in Galatians where Paul challenges the contention that obedience to Law is a prerequisite of salvation, a necessary addition to faith. Paul argues that faith and works of Law are mutually exclusive, for faith is the trustful acceptance of salvation as a gift while the emphasis on works of Law suggests that salvation is a human achievement. Hence the radical ethical corollary of justification by faith: the Christian is free from the Law. Law, of course, has a double meaning: it refers both to the tradition of Moses and to a way of life that seeks to earn salvation. It may seem that Paul has decisively severed the connection between faith and morality, but he argues that faith itself encompasses morality (Gal 5). Freedom from the Law is not license to do as one pleases; rather it marks a new disposition created by the advent of the new age, a disposition marked by new powers of moral discernment and new possibilities of loving one's neighbor. Hence one does not need a law to identify the "works of the flesh" (Gal 5:19-21) or the "fruit of the Spirit" (Gal 5:22-23). Love sets one free and makes one capable of love; freedom fulfills itself in love; love constitutes the fulfillment of the whole Law (Gal 5:1-15). The indicative (you are free from the Law!) is bound inextricably to the imperative (love your neighbor as yourself!).

The Holy Spirit is a second major strand in the ethical thought of Paul, and Paul concludes his argument in Galatians 5 with an appeal to "Walk by the Spirit" (Gal 5:25). In the Greco-Roman world, however, such Pauline phrases as "freedom from the Law" and "walk by the Spirit" were easily misunderstood. In Corinth, for example, "freedom from the Law" becomes license for immoral behavior (1 Cor 6:12-20), and Paul's appeals to the Spirit are misunderstood in terms of a cosmological dualism that extols the spirit and disparages the material world, especially the body. Ethics is a matter of the spirit only and involves an attitude either of indifference or hostility to the body. But Paul insists that the body is the Temple of the Holy Spirit and destined for resurrection (1 Cor 6:19). Christian ethics involves bodily obedience (cf. Rom 12:2). Such dualism of body and spirit also leads to distorted criteria for identifying the Holy Spirit. The Corinthians see the Spirit as manifest in special wisdom (1 Cor 1:10–4:21) and in the gift of tongues (1 Cor 14), both of which become occasions for elitist claims. In his famous poem on love (1 Cor 13) Paul attacks such elitists claims by declaring the vanity of all values without love. The real mark of the Holy Spirit is love.

A third major strand in Paul's ethical thought is the moral significance of the Christian community. Paul's ethic is not individualistic; the community is necessary to sustain the gift of freedom, for freedom needs others to fulfill itself. The community is important both in the sociological sense of maintaining the plausibility of Christian faith in the face of an alien, hostile environment, and in the sense that one experiences salvation precisely in terms of commitment to a community defined by the story of Jesus Christ. Hence Paul's ethic, like that of Jesus, is deeply committed to breaking down the barriers that separate people (Gal 3:28) and to showing the world how human beings can live together in harmony (1 Cor 12–14). This does not amount to a social ethic in the modern sense of addressing social structures and institutions directly. Paul did not mount an attack on slavery, for example. But such social conservatism is probably best understood in terms of Paul's imminent expectation of the Parousia and his tacit realism that the early church lacked the power to effect significant social change. But certainly the logic of Paul's thought—"neither Jew or Greek, neither slave nor free, neither male nor female" (Gal 3:28)—pushes toward a social ethic that unequivocably condemns slavery and other social evils.

Since Martin Luther, much has been made of the contradictions between Paul and the writer of James on the relationship between faith and works (cf. Rom 3:27-31 with Jas 2:14-26). Part of the problem is semantic. James seems to think of faith in a narrower sense than Paul, as something like intellectual assent (cf. Jas 2:19b: "Even the demons believe—and shudder"), and what he means by "works" is close to what Paul refers to as the "fruit of the spirit." Even so, there are significant differences. James is more legalistic than Paul and probably reflects a practical tendency in the early church to swing the focus of ethics back to carefully defined rules and principles. The two agree that faith expresses itself in deeds of love, but James recognizes the value, indeed the practical necessity, of concrete guidelines for daily living. Thus emerges a creative tension between the ethics of character and the ethics of rules. The former is closer to the heart of Christian experience, but moral rules are of practical significance in defining the shape of Christian life. However, such rules do not have a life of their own but derive their substance from the traditions about Jesus and the experience of his resurrection in the Christian community. Rules are appropriate in the service of faith, but neither faith nor ethics can be circumscribed by a catalogue of moral rules.

See also CHURCH AND LAW; FAITH; FREEDOM; HOLY SPIRIT; JESUS; KINGDOM OF GOD; LAW IN THE NEW TESTAMENT; LAW IN THE OLD TESTAMENT; LOVE IN THE NEW TESTAMENT; LOVE IN THE OLD TESTAMENT; PAUL; REPENTANCE; RESURRECTION IN THE NEW TESTAMENT.

Bibliography. V. P. Furnish, *Theology and Ethics in Paul*; J. L. Houlden, *Ethics and the New Testament*; E. Käsemann, *Perspectives on Paul*; L. Keck, *Paul and His Letters*; T. W. Ogletree, *The Use of the Bible in Christian Ethics*; N. Perrin, *Rediscovering the Teachings of Jesus*; R. C. Tannehill, *The Sword of His Mouth*.

—JOHN C. SHELLEY

• **Ethics in the Old Testament.** The study of the moral thought and conduct described in the literature of ancient Israel. While the OT is strictly speaking not an ethical treatise or a moral handbook, it deals extensively with matters of morality and contains vast sections of laws, injunctions, and advice on how the Israelites were to behave in most areas of their life. To identify the ethics of the Hebrew Bible, it is necessary to extrapolate moral claims and values from such diverse literature as proverbs, legal materials, social critiques, stories, poetry, and apocalyptic visions. As with other methods of biblical criticism, one must consider carefully the social and historical contexts and the ancient Near Eastern background for these moral positions, for only in this manner is it possible to understand the variety of stances, both popular and orthodox, evident on many issues.

In the Hebrew Bible ethics is closely associated with theology and religion inasmuch as God is held to be a just, faithful, and compassionate deity who requires of the people a pattern of life reflecting these same moral values. This is given force by describing the divine origin of the laws and by emphasizing God's responses of reward or punishment for the actions chosen by the people. It is obvious from biblical texts that the members of society themselves also sought to engender moral attitudes and to secure social order through the means of inculcation and socialization, law court and punishment, blessing and cursing. Yet moral authority, while exercised directly by parents, leaders, and institutions, derives according to the Bible from God alone. Indeed, precisely because God created the world to be an orderly and harmonious place, morality—acting in harmony with this intended order—can even be thought possible.

Personal Morality. There are six general areas in which the people confronted moral issues throughout biblical times. The first and most basic of these, personal morality is founded on a high valuation of life lived out in this world and in context with others—thus it is neither an otherworldly nor an individualistic type of ethic. Creation texts such as Gen 1–2 and Ps 8 depict humanity as the pinnacle of all creatures, made "in God's image" to represent responsible caretaking of all life in this world. Gen 3 is only the first of many biblical texts emphasizing a person's moral capacity to reason and choose, and then the necessity of bearing the consequences of that choice. Moral character is described in numerous stories and prescribed in especially the wisdom literature (above all in Proverbs and Ecclesiastes): virtues such as magnanimity, bravery, forgiveness, trustworthiness, honesty, moderation, patience, and self-control; and vices such as deceitfulness, hypocrisy, treachery, debauchery, laziness, pride, and envy. That the Israelites did not manage in actuality to attain their own goal of the high worth and rights of people is starkly evident in the lesser status afforded women in comparison to men, the poor in comparison to the wealthy, and slaves in comparison to the free. The prophets relentlessly accused both individuals and the community of injustices, and for JEREMIAH and others the people were so intractable in their immoral ways as to seem almost incorrigible (e.g., Jer 13:23; 17:9-10)—although God is depicted as never abandoning them or giving up hope for their return to moral correctness.

Social Morality. In many respects social morality holds central position in the ethics of the Hebrew Bible. While most laws aimed to control the behavior of individuals, primarily at stake were the consequences of such actions for the community's welfare. Graphically depicting this tie between the one and the many, the disastrous results of Achan's sin struck first the nation and then his own family (Judg 7). The people of Israel, from small village to nation, constituted a social fabric, and divine and human commitment to its preservation was expressed in the much used symbol of the covenant.

The family, the most basic social component, was in need of special protection and enhancement. Structured hierarchically with the father at the head, the family depended for its welfare on the cooperation of all its members. Even with more authority held by the man and despite the practice of polygyny and concubinage, intimacy and companionship between husband and wife were idealized, as is evident in the Song of Songs and elsewhere. The wife had rights of her own, including protection from unjust or arbitrary charges by her husband (e.g., Deut 22:13-21; though also see Num 5:11-31) and receipt of a divorce certificate if the marriage was to be dissolved (Deut 24:1-4). Children were prized in the family, but they could be sold into slavery if the family faced uncontrollable debt. They were obligated to honor their parents (Exod 20:12), especially by supporting them in their old age. Disciplining of children was strict, even with the possibility of death for a son (presumably adult) who refused to heed his parents (Deut 21:18-21). Family members also carried responsibility for their kinfolk: caring for widows and orphans, avenging murder and assault, and redeeming relatives enslaved or inheritance lost because of debts.

The norm in sexual morality was marital intercourse. Prostitution seems in several instances to have been condoned (Gen 38:12-16; Josh 2; Prov 6:26), although the prostitute herself would often be stigmatized. This double standard is evident also in the way adultery was defined: if any man, whether married or unmarried, was discovered to have had intercourse with an unmarried or unbetrothed woman (excluding prostitutes), they would not be punished for adultery yet would have to marry; but the incident would be classed as adultery if a married or betrothed woman was involved, and in that case both man and woman were to be executed (Deut 22:22-24, 28-29). Probably issues of paternity and "ownership" of the woman were decisive in this distinction. Rape was considered vile and deserving of death (Deut 22:25-27; 2 Sam 13). Other forms of sexual activity, including incest, homosexuality, transvestitism, and bestiality, were also regarded as illicit.

HOSPITALITY toward the stranger, who did not possess standing or equal legal rights within the community, was a duty performed by a family, and by taking a person as guest the host became protector and was not to be violated in this role by others in the community (Gen 19:1-11; Judg 19:10-30). The Hebrew Bible does not develop the notion of friendship between two individuals as much as does Greco-Roman literature, although it is portrayed in the story of DAVID and JONATHAN (some interpreters have suggested that 2 Sam 1:26 may allude to a homosexual relationship), negatively in the book of Job where the friends appear less committed to Job than to their own dogmas, and at several points in the wisdom literature both affirmatively (Prov 17:17; 27:10; Sir 6:14-17) and cynically (Prov 19:4, 6-7; 25:17; Sir 6:13; 13:21).

Legal Morality. The ways in which legal conflicts and violations were resolved indicate further moral values at work in the community, not the least being the need to maintain basic order in the society and to curb behavior threatening to it. Primary judicial and penal responsibility resided at the local level, and appeals upwards to the tribal or the national level would occur only in instances lacking precedents or proving too difficult for the local elders to adjudicate (Deut 17:8-13; 1 Kgs 3:16-28). Ruth 4:1-12 provides a description of a case being settled by the elders "at the gate" of the town. Basic to Israel's administration of justice, whether involving civil, criminal, or religious cases, were several principles: trial without delay; presence of witnesses; immediate punishment, set proportionately to the wrongdoing, with imprisonment rarely as an option; restitution of damages to an injured party; blood vengence, although kept within commensurate limits (Exod 21:23-25; Lev 24:19-20) and with "cities of refuge" established for harboring someone guilty of unintentional manslaughter until a trial could occur (Deut 19:1-13; Num 35; Josh 20); little use of maiming (Deut 25:11-12; but note also the "eye for an eye" law) or trial by ordeal (Num 5:11-31), in contrast to practices elsewhere in the ancient Near East; and the need to determine guilt for crimes in order to purge evil from the land (e.g., Deut 21:1-9). Instances of judicial bribery and partiality were not unknown, and the prophets did not hesitate to criticize unjust practices "in the gates" (e.g., Amos 5:10-15).

Political Morality. The Hebrew Bible evidences considerable concern with morality in the political sphere also. Like its neighbors, Israel was inclined to favor hierarchical, monarchic models of governance. One of the accounts of the foundation of the kingdom (1 Sam 8; 10:17-27) describes how the people themselves pressed Samuel to appoint a king over them, while another narrative (1 Sam 9:1–10:16; 11) attributes this form of rulership to God's own will for the people. In the centuries preceding this there may have been more of an anti-statist sentiment as a result of the people's experiences with the oppressive structures of the Canaanite city-states and larger powers such as Egypt. Yet even with the voluntary, often defense-oriented alliances at the local and tribal levels in the premonarchic period, a political hierarchy prevailed with power and authority resting only in the hands of free adult men. Deborah, a judge and deliverer of the people (Judg 4–5), stands out as an exception to this type of male rule. There was some expectation that all tribes should come to each other's aid when necessary (Judg 5:15-17), and evil actions within one tribe could lead to a concerted effort by other tribes to punish the offense (Judg 19–20). This early period, lacking a centralized government, is often described in the book of Judges as a time when all persons did what was right in their own eyes (e.g., Judg 21:25).

After the onset of the monarchy, the king was able to establish systems of court officials, military leaders, bureaucrats, and religious personnel loyal to him. With that came more power to amass wealth and property, construct buildings and monuments, and exercise control over his subjects. Following SOLOMON, the division between the northern and the southern kingdoms reflected to some extent different sets of political values: in the north more popular involvement in the selection of new kings, and in the south more contentment with the principle of dynastic succession. The despotic power of kings is depicted graphically in DAVID's disposal of Uriah (2 Sam 12) and AHAB and JEZEBEL's maneuver to attach Naboth's vineyard (1 Kgs 21). Deut 17:14-20 portrays in a series of moral and religious "oughts" the kinds of behavior that kings sought repeatedly in Israel's history to violate for their own benefit. They thus acted quite similarly to kings in neighboring lands, even though the royal ideology common in the ancient Near East challenged kings to be the protectors of the poor and defenseless. Postexilic Israel, deprived of its political autonomy as colonial subjects successively to Babylonians, Persians, Hellenists, and finally Romans, faced special moral problems associated with partisan factioning among themselves, surviving as a religio-ethnic people (Ezra and Nehemiah), and relating to their foreign rulers (collaboration, resistance, or accommodation; see the books of Esther and Judith).

Warfare in Israel occurred for both defensive and expansionist purposes at various points in history, and the battles were often held to be divinely willed and directed. Israelites presumably fought with the same fierceness and brutality that other warriors in the field demonstrated, including the massacre or enslavement of the enemy. There is, however, another ethic present at certain points in the biblical literature—criticism of ruthless excesses in battle (Amos 1:3–2:3) and a longing for the day when the people will "beat their swords into plowshares" (Isa 2:4; Mic 4:3; yet reversed in Joel 3:10). The notion of peace (*šālôm*) is not understood merely as a political category—the absence of war—but as a much wider state of well-being that should characterize the quality of life for all members in the community.

Economic Morality. The ethics of the Hebrew Bible is most characteristically associated with the economic aspects of Israel's society. At the root is a fundamental concern for those who were vulnerable to economic exploitation or who were greatly worse off than others in the community. Early in their history there was apparently more socioeconomic homogeneity as most of the people lived under similar conditions in village settlements throughout the land and could depend on the help of family and relatives to meet their needs. But with the growth of cities, the rise of the monarchy, the specialization of trades, and the amassing of wealth and power in the hands of a few, a disparity along economic lines resulted, and many persons fell victim to hard times. Such was the situation that prophets such as Amos and Micah faced in the eighth century B.C.E. The legal and prophetic literature is replete with moral imperatives to correct such wrongs against the poor, the widow, the orphan, the stranger, and the slave. Israel was reminded of its own oppression in Egypt and warned not to reproduce such harsh conditions for others in their own midst (Exod 22:21-24). Loans should be available to those in need, with interest charged only against non-Israelite borrowers (Exod 22:25-27; Deut 23:19-20); from several indications this was obviously not the general practice (Ezek 22:12; Neh 5:1-13). SLAVERY, condoned as an economic institution throughout all of Israel's history, produced a class of persons who were exceptionally defenseless in the society, although Hebrew law sought to secure some protection for them, especially for the Israelites who had become slaves in order to repay debts (Exod 21:2-11; Lev 25:39-55; Deut 15:12-18). Other laws and exhortations sought to regulate along more humanitarian lines a wide range of economic practices from land ownership, inheritance, buying and selling, weights and measures, contracts, securities, and taxation, to labor conditions, wages, consumption, restitution of damages, and redemption of persons and property held against debts.

Through the laws of the sabbatical year and the year of JUBILEE (Lev 25 and Deut 15) the Hebrew Bible prescribed a means for securing economic viability for the poor and disenfranchised. Every seventh year debts were to be forgiven and slaves were to be freed, and every fiftieth (or forty-ninth) year inherited land should be restored to a dispossessed family. Beyond a few possible indications (Neh 10:31; 1 Macc 6:49, 53; Josephus, *Ant* 14.202), there is not much evidence that these laws were followed, yet as moral ideals they articulated clearly that persons were not to be left in economic straits with no hope for the future. Justice, the imperative to act responsibly toward others and to seek the release of those suffering from oppression, is represented aptly both in this symbol of the years of release as well as in the ancient tradition of the exodus.

Ecological Morality. The creation accounts in Genesis place human beings in the context of nature—from the grandeur of the cosmos to the intimacy of the garden. A realm of beauty (Pss 8; 19; 29; 104), order (Prov 6:6-8; Jer 8:7), and mystery (Job 38-39; Prov 30:18-19, 24-31), the natural world owes its existence to God just as does humanity, according to the Hebrew Bible, and consequently people's conduct vis-à-vis their environment must be morally responsible. The command to "subdue" and "have dominion over" all living beings on the earth must be understood in terms of the royal ideal in the ancient Near East: not despotic and exploitative rulership, but compassionate and respectful care for all that is under one's charge. Abuse should properly result in the loss of nature's blessings (Job 31:38-40).

The ethic of the Hebrew Bible affirms the goodness of life in this world, the importance of community, and the need for justice and mercy in all contexts. The norms for people's conduct were attributed to their just, compassionate, yet also demanding God. That the Israelites fell short of the ideals is repeatedly apparent: patriarchal and hierarchical subjection, economic exploitation, violence, enmity, discontent. The impact of this ethic on subsequent Judeo-Christian history has been immeasurable—sometimes twisted into legitimating new expressions of injustice and abuse, but richly appropriated also as the guidelines for constructing humane and responsible relations among people and with the world of nature.

See also ECONOMICS IN THE OLD TESTAMENT; FAMILY; PROPHET; THEOLOGY OF THE OLD TESTAMENT.

Bibliography. J. Barton, "Understanding Old Testament Ethics," *JSOT* 9 (1978): 44-64; B. C. Birch and L. L. Rasmussen, *Bible and Ethics in the Christian Life*; H. J. Boecker, *Law and the Administration of Justice in the Old Testament and the Ancient Near East*; J. L. Crenshaw and J. T. Willis, eds., *Essays in Old Testament Ethics*; N. K. Gottwald, *The Tribes of Yahweh: A Sociology of the Religion of Liberated Israel, 1250–1050 B.C.E.*; P. J. Haas ed., *Biblical Hermeneutics in Jewish Moral Discourse, Semeia* 34 (1985); P. D. Hanson, *The People Called: The Growth of Community in the Bible*; W. Harrelson, *The Ten Commandments and Human Rights*; J. Hempel, *Das Ethos des Alten Testaments*; W. C. Kaiser, Jr., *Toward Old Testament Ethics*; D. A. Knight, "Cosmogony and Order in the Hebrew Tradition," *Cosmogony and Ethical Order: New Studies in Comparative Ethics*, ed. R. W. Lovin and F. E. Reynolds; D. A. Knight, "Jeremiah and the Dimensions of the Moral Life," *The Divine Helmsman: Studies on God's Control of Human Events*; J. Muilenburg, *The Way of Israel: Biblical Faith and Ethics*; T. W. Ogletree, *The Use of the Bible in Christian Ethics*; H. van Oyen, *Ethik des Alten Testaments*; D. Patrick, *Old Testament Law*; P. Trible, *God and the Rhetoric of Sexuality*; R. de Vaux, *Ancient Israel: Its Life and Institutions*; J. P. M. Walsh, *The Mighty from Their Thrones: Power in the Biblical Tra-*

dition; H. W. Wolff, *Anthropology of the Old Testament*.

—DOUGLAS A. KNIGHT

• **Ethiopia.** [ee'thee-oh"pee-uh] In ancient sources, the term designates the Nile valley south of Aswan which is properly known as NUBIA. Otherwise, classical sources may use the term more generally to refer to regions south of Egypt as far as Zanzibar. The region occupied by modern Ethiopia was in ancient times part of the Sabaean kingdom of Aksum, ruled by the dynasty descended from Menelik whom tradition recognized as a son of Solomon and the Queen of Saba (= SHEBA).

See also NUBIA

Bibliography. D. R. Buxton, *The Abyssinians*.

—JOHN KEATING WILES

• **Ethiopian Eunuch.** [ee'thee-oh"pee-uhn-y*oo*"nuhk] In Acts 8:26-40, PHILIP successfully witnesses to an Ethiopian eunuch. In earlier times ETHIOPIA referred to any remote area (cf. Amos 9:7), but by the first century C.E., it designated the region directly south of Egypt. The word also had ethnic connotations referring to persons with dark or black skin.

The term eunuch literally means a castrated male. Since such males were used in royal households, the term could be used for royal officials who were not castrated (cf. Jer 52:25 LXX). The repeated description of the Ethiopian as a eunuch (five times) in addition to his identification as the treasurer of Queen Candace makes clear that he was a mutilated male. Even though a eunuch could not become a Jewish PROSELYTE (Deut 23:1), the Ethiopian was so interested in Judaism as to visit Jerusalem and study Isaiah. His conversion to Christianity advances the Lucan theme of the gospel's welcome to those considered outcasts (cf. Luke 51:1-2) and incidentally fulfills Isaiah's prophecy about eunuchs (Isa 56:1-5).

See also ETHIOPIA; EUNUCH; PROSELYTE.

—HAROLD S. SONGER

• **Etiology.** [ee'tee-ol"uh-jee] Etiology (or ætiology) is the study of origins or causes. The word is derived from the Greek *aitia*, which means "cause" and is defined as the science or philosophical discipline which studies causality. When applied to biblical studies, it refers to the use of sagas and legends to explain the origins of some custom, name, place, institution, etc. These stories usually answer the questions, "Why?" and "How?"

Gunkel, Gressmann, and others have demonstrated rather conclusively that many of the traditions of Israel preserved in the sagas and legends of the OT are basically etiological in purpose and origin. Many of these stories are rather incidental—for example, the explanation of why a particular person or place received such a name. However, the Bible contains etiological material that is much more profound. Some of the Genesis stories deal with such subjects as why a man leaves his family and becomes one flesh with his wife, death, the hard lot of the farmer, and why humanity, though one in origin, is so diverse, and why each locality has its own language.

Basing their work on the earlier investigations of Gunkel, most scholars find at least four types of etiological legends and sagas in the OT. (1) Ethnological etiologies seek to explain certain characteristics or circumstances of a tribe or a nation. The location of the Ishmaelites is explained in the story of the flight of Hagar (Gen 21:14-21). The story of Noah's curse placed on Canaan (Gen 9:20-27) gives justification for Canaan's servanthood to his brothers, and thus Canaan's subjection to Israel. Gen 12:1-3, 13:2-13, 27:1-40, and 28:11-17 all serve as explanations for Israel's ownership of Canaan.

(2) Geographical etiologies explain the uniqueness of a locality or a natural phenomenon. The story of Lot and God's punishment of Sodom and Gomorrah serves as a vehicle to explain the desolation of the region around the Dead Sea (Gen 19). Included in the same story is an explanation of how a woman-shaped pillar of salt came into existence.

(3) Etymological etiologies explain the origins of geographical and personal names. Judg 15:9-19 tells the story of SAMSON's arrest by Judeans under Philistine pressure. When he freed himself, he slew a thousand PHILISTINES with the jaw-bone of an ass. Therefore the site was called Ramath-lehi, hill of the jaw-bone. Gen 17:17, 18:9-15, 21:6 are all used as explanations for the name ISAAC (he laughs).

(4) Cultic sites, practices, or objects are also given etiological explanations. The origin of the image of the bronze serpent is given in Num 21:6-9. Gen 28:11-22 serves to explain the sacredness of Bethel. Other passages attempt to explain the existence of religious practices (Gen 17:9-14 and Exod 4:24-26 relate to circumcision; Gen 2:2-3 gives a divine precedent for the Sabbath).

It is generally agreed that many of the etiologies are simply appendages to stories that were already in existence. However, those narratives that begin with etiologies are usually etiological throughout. The old saga about the treaty between the Gibeonites and Israel (Josh 9) and the RAHAB story (Josh 2) serve as examples of stories with attached etiological motifs. Gen 21:22-32, the explanation of the name "Beersheba," is totally etiological in its development.

The historicity of many of the etiologies is suspect and, therefore, each must be confirmed by independent evidence, sources, and archaeological findings. A universal solution is not possible; each narrative must be evaluated on its own merits. This leads to much disagreement among scholars.

See also HERMENEUTICS; SYMBOL.

Bibliography. J. Bright, *Early Israel in Recent History Writing*; N. Gottwald, *The Hebrew Bible—A Socio-Literary Introduction*; O. Eissfeldt, *The Old Testament, an Introduction*.

—JOHN P. DEVER

• **Eugnostos the Blessed.** [y*oo*g-nos'tuhs] In juxtaposition with one another in Codex III of the NAG HAMMADI library are two tractates that display a remarkable literary relationship, *Eugnostos the Blessed* (*3*.70.1–90.12) and the SOPHIA OF JESUS CHRIST (*4*.1–119.18). The former is an older revelatory discourse written by a revered Gnostic teacher, Eugnostos, for his circle. The latter is a Christian Gnostic reworking of *Eugnostos* which both incorporates most of its text and recasts the whole into a dialogue between several disciples and Christ. These two texts provide a classic example of Christianizing editing of an originally non-Christian gnostic writing, a literary demonstration that GNOSTICISM was not simply an intra-Christian phenomenon.

Although it begins like an EPISTLE, with mention of the sender and addressee followed by greetings, *Eugnostos* quickly develops into a monologue in which the author provides knowledge of the God of Truth and the heavenly beings who have emanated from him. Such knowledge, about which the three leading philosophies (Stoicism, Epicureanism, astrology?—70.13-23) have been hopelessly confused, is essential for salvation and makes a person immortal. Such a one will know the difference between the imperishable world of divine aeons and this perishable world.

The teaching offered regarding the hitherto unknown God and the heavenly beings that have evolved from him concerns, first of all, a hierarchy of five highest deities. The highest, "the beginningless Forefather" (75.1-3), is ineffable and can be described only through declaring what He is not (the via negativa) (71.13-23). He is the beginning of all knowledge, the origin of what's manifest. After him are presented the Forefather's reflection, the "Self-Father"; the "Self-Father's" likeness, "Immortal Androgynous Man"; the Immortal Man's male-female son, the SON OF MAN; and the Son of Man's male-female son, "the Savior." The last three, as indicated, all have female counterparts whose names include the component "Sophia." Each of these five highest beings have their own heavenly sphere and retinue of attendants. Second, there is another, similar group of six divine beings who emanate from the first five. From such heavenly beings whose realm is filled with "ineffable joy and unchanging jubilation" (81.14-15) come patterns for the creation of other beings, including 360 Heavens and powers therein (85.1-7). The influence of this heavenly realm is beneficial for those with true knowledge of such divine realities and their evolution.

On grounds of apparent allusions to ADAM (the "Son of Man"—81.12) and possibly to Seth ("Son of Man, Savior"); some would identify the tractate as Sethian Gnostic. However, Seth is never mentioned by name, nothing is said of a primeval fall or split in the Godhead, and there is no mention of the world's creation by an evil Demiurge. The revealed knowledge of the otherwise unknown God received as a gift that brings salvation and immortality is what justifies calling the tractate *Eugnostos* Gnostic, although a more precise identification is precluded. One modern editor (D. M. Parrott) maintains it was written in Egypt. Both he and others would date the non-Christian gnostic tradition in it (at least in its constituent parts) to the first century C.E.

See also GNOSTICISM; NAG HAMMADI.

Bibliography: E. M. Parrott, "Eugnostos the Blessed and The Sophia of Jesus Christ," *The Nag Hammadi Library in English*, ed. J. M. Robinson; D. M. Parrott, "Evidence of Religious Syncretism in Gnostic Texts from Nag Hammadi," *Religious Syncretism in Antiquity*, ed. B. A. Pearson and "The Significance of the Letter of Eugnostos and the Sophia of Jesus Christ for the Understanding of the Relation between Gnosticism and Christianity," *SBLASP*, 1971, Atlanta.

—MALCOLM L. PEEL

• **Eunice.** *See* TIMOTHY

• **Eunuch.** [y*oo*'nuhk] "Eunuch" means an emasculated and impotent man, but the Heb. word translated "eunuch" *sārîs*, is probably an Akkadian loanword from *saresi*, "courtier, officer." The words "eunuch" and "officer" could be closely associated in the ancient world because commonly the king in maintaining his private harem used castrated men in certain capacities of his administration. POTIPHAR, a married man and an "officer (*sārîs*) of PHARAOH, the captain of the guard" (Gen 37:36; 39:1), bought JOSEPH. Pharaoh's chief butler and chief baker are "his two officers (*sārîs*)" (Gen 40:2; cf. v. 7). Eunuchs served in the court of the Babylonian kings (Dan 1:3), as in that of the Persian kings (Esth 1:10), where they served as "chamberlains" to the queen and "guarded the threshold" [served as gatekeepers] of the king (Esth 2:21). The Persian Hegai, "the king's eunuch who is in charge of the women," is mentioned in Esth 2:3, as is Shaashgaz, "the king's eunuch who was in charge of the concubines" of "the second harem" in Esther 2:14. ESTHER's personal eunuch, appointed by the king, was named Hathach (4:5).

Although one "who has a blemish" may not serve as priest (Lev 21:21), including those with "crushed testicles," (v. 20) and "he whose testicles are crushed or whose male member is cut off shall not enter the assembly of the Lord" (Deut 23:1), eunuchs were known also in Israelite royal courts. Ahab summoned "an officer (*sārîs*) to fetch the prophet Micaiah" (1 Kgs 22:9); another king had "an official" at command (2 Kgs 8:6), and some "eunuchs" cared for AHAB's widow JEZEBEL (2 Kgs 9:32). In addition to other officials and warriors, they served as "palace officials" (*sārîs*) in DAVID's court (1 Chr 28:1). When NEBUCHADREZZAR captured Jerusalem, he carried away king JEHOIACHIN's mother, his wives, his officials (*sārîs*), and the nations' leaders (2 Kgs 24:15). JEREMIAH lists "the eunuchs" (*sārîs*) in this group (29:2). Nebuchadrezzar's "captain of the guard," Nebuzaradan, took among others from JERUSALEM "an officer (*sārîs*) who had been in command of the men of war" (2 Kgs 25:19). An Ethiopian eunuch named Ebed-melech, "who was in the king's [Zedekiah] house," saved the life of Jeremiah (Jer 38:7).

Judging from the Levitical and Deuteronomic law and from Jer 38:7, the actual eunuchs as castrated males in the courts of Judah's (and Israel's) kings may have been foreigners. The Jewish men dubbed *sārîs* in Hebrew probably were more properly "officers" or "officials," not "eunuchs" in the technical sense.

In the NT book of Acts, mention is made of an Ethiopian eunuch, "a minister," in charge of the treasure of "the Candace, queen of the Ethiopians" (8:27). On his return home from Jerusalem, the eunuch, having been reading from the Jewish Scriptures, submitted to Christian baptism.

See also SOCIOLOGY OF THE OLD TESTAMENT.

—KAREN RANDOLPH JOINES

• **Euphrates.** [y*oo*fray'teez] The largest river in western Asia, the Euphrates flows over 2800 km. (1740 mi.) from its sources in the Armenian mountains through the Mesopotamian plain to the Persian Gulf (PLATE 2). Because evidence of early civilizations is found along the TIGRIS-Euphrates river valleys, the area has often been called the "cradle of civilization."

The name "Euphrates" can be traced back through several languages (Gk. *euphratēs*; Old Persian *ufrātu*; Heb. *pĕrāt*; Akkadian *purattu*) to the Sumerian *buranunu* meaning "the great river." Scholars have suggested that *buranunu* is a loanword from some pre-Sumerian peoples, and as such belongs to the dark recesses of prehistory prior to 3000 B.C.E.

The course of the Euphrates can be roughly divided into three parts. The upper Euphrates includes the streams of the Armenian highlands. These converge into two branches forming the Euphrates proper north of Malatya, Turkey. The river then enters the Mesopotamian plain about 80 km. (50 mi.) northwest of Haran (Gen 11:31).

At this point, the middle course begins the "great bend" until it flows in a southeast direction towards the Persian Gulf. Carchemish, located at the modern border of Syria and Turkey, guarded an important crossing from northern MESOPOTAMIA to northern Syria. This site served at various times as the capital of the Mitanni, Hittite, and Assyrian Empires. King Josiah attempted to stop Pharaoh Necho II on his march to Carchemish in 609 B.C.E. Four years later, Nebuchadrezzar II defeated Necho there (cf. 2 Kgs 23:29; 24:7).

Farther south, about 80 km. (50 mi.) below the confluence of the Euphrates and the Ḥābūr, is the site of Mari. The culture of Amorite Mari has often been compared to that of the patriarchs in the Bible.

The lower Euphrates enters the flat alluvial plain of southern Mesopotamia approximately 90 km. (55 mi.) north of ancient Babylon. The "Urban Revolution" of civilization began here after people learned how to drain and irrigate the marshy swamps of the region. Sites such as Babylon, Nippur, Erech (Warka) and Ur depended upon its life-giving waters. A LANDSAT satellite photo of the area (Adams, 34) revealed a web of ancient levees. Since annual rainfall was insufficient for crops, irrigation enabled the land to support a dense concentration of people.

Sumerian literature takes note of the river as one of the key elements of daily life. The Babylonian creation account "Enuma Elish" declared that the Euphrates and Tigris rivers originated from the pierced eyes of the slain Ti'amat. "The Legend of Atrahasis," on the other hand, suggested that the two rivers were dug by the gods themselves.

The Euphrates is mentioned by name twenty-one times in the Bible. At other times, the Bible refers to the Euphrates as simply "the river" (*hannāhār*; cf. Deut 11:24). The Euphrates was one of four rivers that flowed in the vicinity of the Garden of Eden (Gen 2:14). It represented one of the borders of the promised land (Gen 15:18; Josh 1:4), Reuben's territory (1 Chr 5:9) and the kingdom of David (2 Sam 8:3; 1 Chr 18:3). The river figured prominently in several of Jeremiah's prophetic oracles (Jer 13:4-5; 46:2-3; 51:63). In Revelation it is related to divine judgments during the tribulation period (Rev 9:14; 16:12).

See also MESOPOTAMINA; TIGRIS.

Bibliography. R. M. Adams, *Heartland of Cities*; G. Meier, "Eufrat," *RdA*; S. A. Pallis, *The Antiquity of Iraq*.

—STEPHEN J. ANDREWS

• **Eupolemus.** [y*oo*-pol'uh-muhs] Eupolemus is the earliest Hellenistic Jewish historian of whom we have any evidence. The five fragments of his writings that have come down to us all derive, most likely, from a single work, the title of which Clement of Alexandria gives as *On the Kings of Judea* (*Strom* 1.153.4). Alexander Polyhistor, a Greek historian of the first century B.C.E. makes use of Eupolemus in his own history of the Jewish people. At least four of the surviving fragments from Eupolemus derive from Alexander Polyhistor as he is cited by EUSEBIUS and Clement. The fifth fragment is found only in Clement, and it is not clear whether he derived it from Alexander or some other source.

The first fragments (Eusebius, *PraepEv* 9.26.1; Clement, *Strom* 1.153.4) identifies Moses as "the first sage," credits him with the invention of the alphabet, and states that "Moses first wrote laws for the Jews." As the first philosopher, the founder of literary culture, and the lawgiver of the Jews, Moses appears as the founder of civilization, from whom other peoples (esp. the Greeks) have received their wisdom. This type of apologetic argument is typical of Hellenistic-Jewish historiography.

The second fragment (Eusebius, *PraepEv* 9.30.1–34.18) is the longest and treats Israelite history from Moses to Solomon, devoting special attention to the construction of the TEMPLE in Jerusalem. Eupolemus glorifies the political significance and power of Israel and magnifies the splendor of the Temple. Clement gives a very brief summary of roughly the same section from Eupolemus's history (*Strom* 1.130.3).

The third fragment (Eusebius, *PraepEv* 9.34.20) contains a brief notice concerning a thousand heavy golden shields produced at the order of Solomon, followed by what is evidently the conclusion of Eupolemus's history of Solomon's reign: "He lived fifty-two years, forty years of which he was a king in peace."

The fourth fragment (Eusebius, *PraepEv* 9.39.2-5) summarizes the conflicts of the prophet Jeremiah with King "Jonachim" (corruption of Joachim?) and King Nebuchadrezzar, although he treats events presented in the Bible as belonging to the reigns of the final three kings of Judah: Jehoiachin, Jehoiakim, and Zedekiah (cf. 2 Kgs 24:1–25:21; 2 Chr 36:5-21).

The fifth fragment (Clement, *Strom* 1.141.4) gives the number of years from Adam to the fifth year of the reign of the Seleucid king Demetrius 158/57 B.C.E., and from the Exodus up to the same date. A final statement concerning the number of years "from this time until the Roman consuls Gnaius and Asinius" (as the text should probably be reconstructed) is in all likelihood not original to Eupolemus.

The fragments give evidence that Eupolemus used the Greek SEPTUAGINT for his work, although it is probable that he also depended at points on the Hebrew text. The date of composition is most likely 158/57 B.C.E. The author's use of not only the Greek but also the Hebrew text of the Jewish scriptures and his orientation to Seleucid rather than Ptolemaic royal chronology point to a provenance in Palestine. It has been suggested that Eupolemus is to be identified with the ambassador of Judas Maccabeus to Rome (1 Macc 8:17ff. and 2 Macc 4:11).

Bibliography. J. R. Bartlett, *Jews in the Hellenistic World*; F. Fallon, "Eupolemus," *The Old Testament Pseudepigrapha*, ed. J. H. Charlesworth; B. Z. Wacholder, *Eupolemus: A Study of Judaeo-Greek Literature*.

—CHARLES H. COSGROVE

• **Eupolemus, Pseudo.** [s*oo*'doh-y*oo*pol"uh-muhs] "Pseudo-Eupolemus" refers to two passages among the fragments of Hellenistic Jewish writers preserved in the *Praeparatio Evangelica* of EUSEBIUS whose contents are similar and whose authorship is disputed. Because the first of these two fragments (*PraepEv* 9.17.2-9) is attributed to the Jewish historian Eupolemus by Eusebius's source, Alexander Polyhistor, scholars who question that attribution label both fragments "Pseudo-Eupolemus." The consensus is that both passages are by one author, probably an unknown Samaritan who wrote in the mid-second century B.C.E. Although both fragments are syncretistic, combining biblical and other Jewish traditions with pagan mythological materials, only the shorter fragment (*PraepEv* 9.18.2) is overtly polytheistic.

In both fragments, ABRAHAM is the focus of attention. He is said to have originated in Babylon as a descendant of the giants, to have been an expert ASTROLOGER, and to have brought the knowledge of ASTROLOGY to Phoenicia and Egypt. The longer and more interesting passage locates

Abraham's encounter with MELCHIZEDEK on Mount Gerizim, the site of the Samaritan temple. It reflects knowledge of a tradition, also found in the DEAD SEA SCROLLS, PHILO, and JOSEPHUS, that a miracle preserved Sarah's chastity in the Egyptian court. Enoch is portrayed as the discoverer of astrology and is identified with Atlas, the mythological figure credited with this discovery by some Greek authors.

The claim that Jewish patriarchs invented and transmitted astrology reflects a larger motif in Hellenistic Jewish apologetics; the Jews are portrayed as responsible for cultural developments that benefit all peoples. Pseudo-Eupolemus regards astrology as one such benefit, displaying none of the ambiguity of Philo and Josephus toward an art so closely tied to pagan religion.

See also ARTAPANUS; ASTROLOGY; CLEODEMUS MALCHUS.

Bibliography. C. R. Holladay, *Fragments from Hellenistic Jewish Authors*; R. Doran, "Pseudo-Eupolemus," *The Old Testament Pseudepigrapha*, ed. J. H. Charlesworth.

—SHARYN E. DOWD

• **Eusebius.** [y*oo*see'bee-uhs] A bishop of CAESAREA Maritima (Palestine), an apologist, and the first church historian. Educated by Pamphilus, his predecessor, he became bishop of Caesarea in 313. An ardent advocate of the Emperor Constantine, he helped define the new stance of Christianity toward the ROMAN EMPIRE after the latter's conversion. In the Arian controversy he played a mediating role, quietly opposing the Nicene formula *homoousios* and subscribing to the deposition of Athanasius by the synod of Tyre in 335. The same year he delivered the official panegyric on Constantine, whom he designated "the friend of almighty God" and "new Moses" and "almost another Christ." He redrew the traditional scheme of history from Abraham to Moses to Christ to read: Abraham–Christ–Constantine. This optimistic view of history contrasted sharply with the more realistic one developed by Augustine in *The City of God*, but it prevailed in Eastern Christian thinking. Eusebius died in 339.

Eusebius stands at the forefront of the golden age of PATRISTIC LITERATURE. A prolific writer with access to the library collected by Origen at Caesarea, he produced several different types of writings—historical, apologetic, biblical, and theological—in addition to his panegyrics entitled *Praise of Constantine* (335) and *The Life of Constantine*. Historical works include *Chronicles*, attempting to prove that the Jewish-Christian tradition was older than any other, the *Church History* (324), and *The Martyrs of Palestine*. Like several other of his compositions, the *Church History* strung facts, excerpts from literature, and historical documents together in loose fashion with decided apologetic purpose. In the earliest version he contended that Christianity's history, especially its stance against a hostile state, proved its divine origin. After Constantine's victory over Licinius in 324 he enlarged and revised the account to accord better with the friendly relationship.

Apologetic writings bear witness to Eusebius's considerable learning. In *Praeparatio Evangelica*, composed between 312 and 322, he tried to demonstrate why Christians preferred the Jewish tradition to paganism, namely, because of the superiority of its "philosophy" to pagan cosmology and mythology. In *Demonstratio Evangelica*, continuing the *Praeparatio*, he argued that Christ had fulfilled OT prophecies and the Law, which had only a preparatory character. A treatise, *On the Theophany*, extant only in Syriac, summarizes the argument in popular style. Only a portion of Eusebius's earliest apology and a few fragments of his twenty-five books against the Neoplatonist Porphyry have survived. He also composed a treatise *Against Hierocles*, governor of Bithnia, who tried to put Apollonius of Tyana forward as the pagan answer to Jesus.

Biblical works have survived only in fragments save for the *Onomasticon*, an alphabetical list of place names that occur in scriptures, annotated as to situation and history. Jerome edited a Latin version. A poor theologian, Eusebius wrote two treatises against Marcellus, Bishop of Ancyra and defender of the Nicene formula, in which he defended Origen's teaching about the subordination of the LOGOS as "ecclesiastical theology."

See also PATRISTIC LITERATURE.

Bibliography. G. F. Chesnut, *The First Christian Histories*, 2nd ed.; R. M. Grant, *Eusebius as Church Historian*; D. S. Wallace-Hadrill, *Eusebius of Caesarea*.

—E. GLENN HINSON

• **Eutychus.** [y*oo*'tuh-kuhs] From a Gk. word (εὔτυχος) that means lucky. Eutychus was a young man from Troas who, according to Acts 20:7-12 was sitting in a window during one of Paul's sermons. As he dozed he fell to his apparent death though Paul declared him alive. Since this story is found in the "we" source of Acts it has been held that a companion of Paul is suggesting that Paul could, in fact, restore the dead. Whether Eutychus actually died has often been debated. Some interpreters suggest that he did not since the distance he fell is not necessarily a fatal distance. Rather, they suggest that the incident is patterned after the prophetic restorations (cf. 1 Kgs 17:21). Perhaps Eutychus was only unconscious and thought to be dead.

—WATSON E. MILLS

• **Evangel.** *See* GOSPEL

• **Evangelist.** While the word "evangelist" figures prominently in early Christian literature, it appears only three times in the NT (Acts 21:8; Eph 4:11; 2 Tim 4:5). The only attested non-Christian usage comes from an inscription at Rhodes referring to a "proclaimer of oracles."

In Acts 21:8 PHILIP is called "the evangelist." He is not depicted as a proclaimer of oracles, but rather as a preacher of Christ to the Samaritans (Acts 8:44) and an announcer of the gospel of Jesus to the ETHIOPIAN EUNUCH (Acts 8:35). He is also described as evangelizing all the towns from Azotus to Caesarea (Acts 8:40). While Philip is the only NT personality called an evangelist, Timothy is instructed to "do the work of an evangelist" (2 Tim 4:5). In 1 Thessalonians Timothy is labeled "our brother and God's servant in the gospel of Christ." Eph 4:11 lists evangelists among the gifts of Christ to the church. Ambiguity as to whether this listing designates the evangelist as a distinct church office stems from the fact that persons holding various offices engaged in the task of evangelism.

Eventually the church came to distinguish the evangelist more precisely. Eusebius, writing in the early fourth century C.E. about the second century, described the evangelists as disciples and zealous imitators of the apostles (*EccHist* 3.37.2; 5.10.2). He also identified as an evangelist Pantaenus, a Stoic philosopher who converted to Christianity, became a missionary to the east, and founded a catechetical school in Alexandria (*EccHist* 5.10). By the third century, "evangelist" was being used for the author of a GOSPEL (Hippolytus, *OnAnt* 5; Tertullian, *AgPrax* 21.23). Eventually the title could be used for the lectionary reader

(*ApChOrd* 19).

The significance of the term "evangelist" becomes clear when related terms are considered. Whereas the noun referring to a person is rare in the NT, the noun "gospel" which pertains to the content of the evangelist's message is common. Also the verb which denotes the act of proclaiming the gospel appears abundantly. In the Greco-Roman world both terms could be used: (1) for the proclamation of the good news of military victory, (2) to signal deliverance from demonic power, (3) in the imperial cult to announce the birth or arrival of the emperor, (4) for the reward given to the herald, and (5) for the offering given to the deity in gratitude for the good news.

While early Christians may have viewed the work of their evangelists in light of these common uses of "good news" terminology, they found the central significance of the concept in the OT. Passages such as Isa 61:1 suggested that the anticipated messianic age, heralded by John the Baptist (Luke 3:18), had dawned in Jesus Christ, whose own preaching announced its arrival (Luke 4:16-21; 7:18-23). Hence, the evangelist was held in the esteem of the herald of Isa 52:7: "How beautiful upon the mountains are the feet of him who brings good tidings."

See also APOSTLE/APOSTLESHIP; CHURCH; PREACHING.

Bibliography. G. Friedrich, "εὐαγγελίζομαι, κτλ.," *TDNT*; M. Green, *Evangelism in the Early Church*.

—SCOTT NASH

• **Eve.** [eev] The first woman, according to biblical tradition. Though the creation accounts of Gen 1:1–2:4a and Gen 2:4b-25 speak of female (1:27) and woman (2:22) respectively, the naming of the woman by her husband in Gen 3:20 allows canonically for the first woman to be known as Eve. The OT thus presents Eve as created by God (Gen 2:21-22) and named by her husband (3:20). She is the mother of three named sons, Cain, Abel, and Seth (Gen 4:1-2, 25-26) and other unnamed sons and daughters (Gen 5:1-5). Indeed, Eve is presented as "the mother of all living" (Gen 3:20), a connection being made to the meaning of her name.

In the ancient world, names carried symbolic meaning, expressing the essence of the one named. For this reason, scholars have sought the origin and etymology of the name Eve (Hebrew, *ḥawwâ*). The name occurs only two times in the OT, Gen 3:20; 4:1. In Gen 3:20 a connection is made between the name and the Hebrew root *ḥāyâ*, "live." On the judgment that "Eve" and "live" are not from the same root, scholars have sought possible cognates in other ancient Near Eastern languages. Popular among them was a theory advanced already by medieval rabbis that saw in the name the Aramaic word *ḥiwyā'*, "serpent." Later scholars took up this theory, going so far as to posit an earlier narrative lying behind the biblical one in which God, man and a serpent deity were the characters. No evidence exists for such a reconstruction. Analogies from Arabic have offered suggestions connected to tribal life, indeed even the possibility that *ḥawwâ* reflects the remnants of a matriarchal tribal grouping. An almost identical parallel, however, is found in the Ugaritic usage of a similar root with the meaning "life," or "something living." This discovery has led to the understanding of the name Eve to be of Canaanite/Phoenician origin, taken over by Hebrew.

The Yahwistic creation narrative (Gen 2:4b–4:26), of which the naming of Eve is a part, contains the rib-story motif. A myth from ancient Sumer concerning the ailing god Enki identifies the healer of his rib, one of his afflicted body parts, as the goddess Nin-ti. A play on words occurs with Sumerian "ti" meaning "rib" as well as "make alive." Thus Nin-ti is the "lady of the rib" and the "lady who makes alive." Though no such word play occurs in the Hebrew, "rib" and "living" are nonetheless connected in the biblical narrative.

Gen 1:27 (P) understands the creation of male and female to be in the image of God. Gen 2:7 (J) knows the creation of *'ādām,* (human being) from the earth (*'ădāmâ*) first. Seeing the loneliness of man, Yahweh creates woman from the man's rib. She is a partner suitable to him, leading to the joyful shout, "bone of my bones and flesh of my flesh" (Gen 2:23).

In a context of disobedience, the harmony of creation is broken. Tempted by the serpent, the woman succumbs to deception and eats the forbidden fruit, giving some to her husband (Gen 3),who is present with her at the temptation. Alienation in her primary functions in life, that of wife and mother, are the woman's punishment. She will know pain at childbirth and subordination to her husband.

The two references to Eve in the NT allude to the Gen 3 context of disobedience. One reference, 1 Tim 2:11-15 argues for woman's silence within the church based on her transgression. A second reference, 2 Cor 11:3 refers to the deception of Eve as an example of how one can be led astray.

See also ADAM; EDEN, GARDEN OF; FALL; SERPENT.

Bibliography. A. S. Kapelrud, "חַוָּה *chavvāh,*" *TDOT*; S. N. Kramer, "Mythology of Sumer and Akkad," *Mythologies of the Ancient World,* ed. S. N. Kramer.

—KANDY M. QUEEN-SUTHERLAND

• **Everlasting.** The term "everlasting" is used in the Bible both in the strict sense of unlimited time and more loosely of simply a prolonged period of time. The Hebrew word which is often translated as "everlasting" originally signified a period of time whose beginning or end (or both) was not fixed. It was used to refer to an especially long period of time, whether in the past (Mic 5:2) or in the future (Lev 24:8). In their attempt to describe God's distinctiveness from the created order and God's mastery over time, biblical writers spoke of God as being everlasting. The duration of God was beyond human comprehension. God was "from everlasting to everlasting" (Ps 90:2).

Since God is everlasting, the attributes of God can also be described as everlasting. Thus, the OT speaks of God's everlasting covenant (Jer 32:40), everlasting salvation (Isa 45:17), everlasting righteousness (Ps 119:142), everlasting name (Isa 63:12), and everlasting love (Jer 31:3). In these instances everlasting carries a qualitative, not merely a quantitative, meaning.

In the NT, a Greek term is used which means basically the same as the Hebrew word in the OT. The word denotes an immense length of time in the past (Luke 1:70) or in the future (Mark 11:14). Punishment for the wicked, as well as reward for the righteous, is described as everlasting (Matt 25:46). The new life (everlasting life) promised to believers (John 3:16, 36; 6:40, 47) is not simply a life of unending duration, but a new quality of life made possible through Christ. Believers already share in this new life in Christ.

See also ETERNAL LIFE.

—MITCHELL G. REDDISH

• **Everlasting Life.** *See* ETERNAL LIFE; EVERLASTING

• **Evil.** The concept of evil is dealt with in both the OT and NT, but a single understanding of the concept cannot be posited. Rather the biblical text offers a variety of connotations that are exemplary of the ongoing struggle of humanity in a search for understanding. In the OT the concept is most often expressed by the Hebrew *ra'* or *rā'â*. The spectrum of meaning is broad, ranging from a description or designation of that which is bad or displeasing (Gen 28:8), to that which is of poor quality or worthless (Jer 14:2), to that which is ethically bad or wicked (1 Sam 30:20). The term is used interchangeably in reference to national or moral evils for, unlike modern thought, these are not distinguished in biblical texts. In its noun usage, therefore, the term can be a reference both to the wickedness perpetrated by humanity (Isa 47:10) and to the calamity or distress that befalls humanity (Jer 36:3).

The Greek rendering of *ra'* or *rā'â* is usually *kakos* or *onēros* in the LXX. In the Greek NT these words offer a vareity of connotations of the term "evil." As in the Hebrew rendering, the significance of these Greek words spans a wide spectrum. Nuances range from that which is bad or displeasing (3 John 11), to wickedness (Rom 1:30), to a personification of evil (Matt 13:19).

The OT record of humanity's struggle with evil reveals the ongoing search for understanding the inconsistencies of its appearances. The expressions of evil in the OT are varied but there are no dualistic tendencies in these expressions. Whether referring to moral depravity or calamity and adversity, the OT writers assert the ultimate control of God over evil (1 Sam 2:6, 7; Isa 45:7). Evidence of the struggle with evil is apparent in the variety of the cries of the psalmists (Pss 17, 44, 73).

Most apparent in the OT, however, is the difficulty of dealing with the DEUTERONOMISTIC principle of RETRIBUTION, a *quid pro quo* theology that maintains that good results from good, evil from evil. Israel, both collectively and individually, had to deal with the inconsistencies of such a theology. If evil is thought of as punishment from God for an individual's or nation's disobedience, then the question inevitably arises concerning apparently undeserved punishment. This question is dramatically posed in the book of JOB. The result is not an explanation or an answer to the question of the origin or appearances of evil. The result is instead an affirmation of God and an assurance that God cares.

In the NT evil is given a different emphasis. The presence of evil is acknowledged, but the emphasis is on its defeat. The question of the origin of evil and the inconsistency of its appearances is, as in the OT, left unanswered, but its demise is reiterated throughout the NT. The NT understanding of evil includes moral connotations and activity that attempts to thwart God's purposes, but unique to the NT is the personification of evil. It is prominent in spirits and demons in the gospel tradition (Matt 12:22-28); it is characterized by *ho ponēros,* the evil one (Matt 13:19).

The overriding message of the NT is the victory over evil by God through Christ. This is seen in Matt 4:1-11 as Jesus resists temptation and in Mark 5:1-20 as he drives the unclean spirits from the Gerasene demoniac. The overwhelming confidence of the victory over evil is dramatically portrayed in the closing book of the Bible. The author of Revelation reassures readers that through the life, death, and resurrection of Jesus the Christ, victory has been won over the powers of evil, and the sufferings of this life fade in the light of the new heaven, the new earth, and the new Jerusalem.

See also SATAN IN THE NEW TESTAMENT; SATAN IN THE OLD TESTAMENT; THEOLOGY OF THE OLD TESTAMENT.

Bibliography. W. Eichrodt, *Theology of the Old Testament,* vol. 1; W. Grundmann, "κακός," *TDNT*; G. Harder, "πονηρός, κτλ.," *TDNT*.

—JUDY YATES ELLIS

• **Evil Spirits.** *See* DEMON IN THE OLD TESTAMENT

• **Exegesis on the Soul.** This fascinating tractate from the NAG HAMMADI library is a mythological narrative of the soul's life in the body, supported by quotations from secondary literature (mostly biblical) and interspersed with exhortations to repentance. The soul is personified as a female who was a virgin and male-female in form when she was alone with the Father. When she falls down to earth and into a body she loses both her androgynous nature and her virginity. The plight of the embodied soul is described graphically: "She becomes female alone and a prostitute, wandering aimlessly, caught in carnality, copulating with whomever she meets." The world is a brothel in which the soul is trapped. The cause of the soul's predicament is not stated explicitly, but there are indications that she bears some blame for it. "I abandoned my house and fled from my maiden's quarters," she cries out to God at one point. Her deliverance lies in fervent repentance. Indeed, repentance is the dominant theme of the treatise and that which gives it a homiletic character. When the soul repents, God sends her a heavenly, male counterpart, the one to whom she was joined before her fall into the body. He is her man, her brother, her bridegroom. Salvation rests in their reunion, which restores the soul's original androgynous nature.

Over half of the document is made up of citations from other works: the OT (Genesis, Psalms, prophets), the NT (Matthew, Luke, John, 1 and 2 Corinthians, Ephesians), I CLEMENT, and Homer's *Odyssey*. The author saw the story of the soul emerging from a proper exegesis of the biblical and classical texts; hence the title, "Exegesis on (or "of" or "concerning") the Soul." For example, the author cites Ezekiel's condemnation of Israel for prostituting herself to the sons of Egypt (16:23-26) and then interprets this allegorically: "But what does 'the sons of Egypt, men great of flesh,' mean if not the domain of the flesh and the perceptible realm and the affairs of the earth, by which the soul has become defiled here?" This definition of "prostitution" as the defilement of the soul by the earth and the flesh is then given apostolic authority by quoting 1 Cor 5:9 and Eph 6:12.

Several interesting metaphors are used to illustrate the soul's salvation. When the soul repents, the Father "will make her womb turn from the external domain and will turn it again inward" like garments that are turned about in water for cleaning. This laundering of the soul is labelled her "baptism."

The soul is also pictured as a woman raging in labor but powerless to beget a child. When the Father sends the bridegroom to her, they are reunited permanently in the bridal chamber, and the soul bears good children. This religious use of marriage imagery is found not only in other Nag Hammadi tractates (e.g., *GosPhil*), but also in biblical and patristic writings.

The soul's salvation is also called a rebirth, and it is dependent solely upon the Father. "Thus it is by being born again that the soul will be saved. And this is due not to rote phrases or to professional skills or to book learning. Rather, "it [is] the grace of the [. . .]."

Exegesis on the Soul cannot definitely be established as Gnostic. Certainly there is much in the tractate that would be appealing to Gnostics and shows affinities with gnostic myth, e.g., the evil nature of the physical world ruled over by an inferior, earthly Father; asexual union as the soul's salvation from the prison of the sexually differentiated body; the forgetfulness of the soul in the world, and the salvific role of remembering. But these features are not exclusively Gnostic. Myths about the soul are widespread in the ancient Hellenistic world and *Exegesis on the Soul* shares features common to other such literature.

In its present form *Exegesis on the Soul* may be said to be Christian, but it is probable that the biblical quotations were added secondarily to a non-Christian document.

Exegesis on the Soul probably originated in Alexandria, Egypt, perhaps as early as the second century. It should be compared with other Nag Hammadi tractactes such as AUTHORITATIVE TEACHING and GOSPEL OF PHILIP.

See also GNOSTICISM; NAG HAMMADI.

Bibliography. B. Layton, "The Soul as a Dirty Garment," *Le Muséon* 91 (1978): 155-69; W. C. Robinson, Jr., "The Exegesis on the Soul," *NovT* 12 (1970): 102-17 and "The Exegesis on the Soul," *The Nag Hammadi Library in English,* ed. J. M. Robinson; R. McL. Wilson, "Old Testament Exegesis in the Gnostic Exegesis on the Soul," *Essays on the Nag Hammadi Texts: In Honour of Pahor Labib* (*NHS* 6), ed. M. Krause; F. Wisse, "On Exegeting 'The Exegesis on the Soul,' " *Les Textes de Nag Hammadi (NHS* 7), ed. J.-E. Menard.

—CAROL D. C. HOWARD

• **Exile.** Used in the Bible to refer to the forced separation of a nation from its homeland (Amos 7:17), the forced separation of an individual from his or her homeland (2 Sam 15:19) and the earthly life of God's people as they await life in heaven (Heb 11:13). Typically, however, "exile" refers specifically to the exile of part of Judah in the land of Babylon during the sixth century B.C.E.

The Babylonian Exile (PLATE 15) of Judah began in 598/7 B.C.E. when NEBUCHADREZZAR crushed a rebellion by Jehoiakim and later deported his successor JEHOIACHIN and most of the royal family, court officials and leading citizens of Judah to Babylon (2 Kgs 24:1-17). A subsequent rebellion by Zedekiah led to the destruction of Jerusalem and a second deportation in 587/6 B.C.E. (2 Kgs 25:1-21). When those who remained in Judah assassinated GEDALIAH, whom the Babylonians had appointed governor, the Babylonians responded by deporting still more Judeans in 582 B.C.E. (2 Kgs 25:22-26; Jer 52:30). The total number of Judeans exiled to Babylon is uncertain but the figure 4,600 given in JEREMIAH is reasonable, although it probably includes only men (Jer 52:28-30). The exiles remained under Babylonian control until CYRUS and the Persian forces took Babylon in 539 B.C.E. In 538 B.C.E. Cyrus issued a decree allowing the Jewish exiles to return home and rebuild their TEMPLE (2 Chr 36:22-23). An early return under Sheshbazzar failed to accomplish much (Ezra 1:8-11) but a subsequent return led by ZERUBBABEL and Joshua succeeded, with the help of the prophets Haggai and Zechariah, in completing the temple in 515 B.C.E. (Ezra 2:1-6:18).

Not much is known about the conditions experienced by the exiles in Babylon, but apparently their existence was not harsh. The exiles were allowed to settle in their own communities (Ezek 3:15), build houses (Jer 29:5; Ezek 8:1), marry (Jer 29:6), and earn a living (Zech 6:9-11). Jehoiachin was regarded as the king of Judah and supported by the Babylonian court (2 Kgs 25:27-30). Despite these humane conditions, the exiles were still prisoners in a foreign land and were ridiculed and tormented by the Babylonians (Ps 137:1-3; Isa 42:22).

During the Exile the Jewish faith was strongly challenged. The Babylonian gods who had apparently defeated the God of Israel and built a huge empire seemed more worthy of worship than the God of Israel (Isa 46:1-2, 9). Some of the exiles even felt that the Exile was caused by their neglect of the more powerful gods (Jer 44:15-19). Even the exiles who clung to their faith in God wondered why Judah had been punished severely (Ezek 18:25) and if Yahweh would ever again be their God (Isa 63:19; Ezek 37:11).

Jewish faith responded powerfully to the challenges. God was the only deity who existed (Isa 45:5); God still ruled history. The Exile was a just punishment upon Judah for its idolatry and disobedience (Jer 7:30-34; Ezek 22:17-22) and as such prefigured the "Day of the Lord." God's mercy was also evident. The land of Judah now enjoyed the sabbath years that had never been celebrated (2 Chr 36:20-21) and the possibility lay open for a new covenant between God and the Israelite people (Jer 31:31-34). In the absence of a temple, tradition and Law became the foci of the Jewish faith (Neh 8:1-8) and the collecting and editing of the sacred writings became imperative. Thus from the calamity and difficulty of the Exile came a faith that could survive and prosper in any nation or circumstance.

See also CYRUS; EZEKIEL.

Bibliography. P. R. Ackroyd, *Exile and Restoration*; J. Bright, *A History of Israel*; R. W. Klein, *Israel in Exile.*

—ROBERT C. DUNSTON

• **Exodus.** [ek'suh-duhs] The Exodus from Egypt, climaxed by Yahweh's marvelous victory at the sea, is a watershed in the actual history of Israel and the recording of that history. The narrative that depicts the Exodus includes the horrible oppression and the marvelous liberation of the people who inherited the promises made long before to Abraham.

The biblical account of the Exodus is both a reflection and a transformation of the actual historical event. The biblical story recollects certain events that took place, but these events have been eclipsed by the merging accounts, i.e., the major traditions of the PENTATEUCH, and the combined effect of these theological perspectives. The transformation arises in the creation of a narrative manifesting the redemptive power of God in what surely would have been viewed as a minor event in the ancient world in which renegades or slaves regularly escaped with no notice. Over time, with the contribution of the distinctive perspectives of several groups, the story developed into the testimony of the whole group bound by covenant to this awesome, powerful, and attentive god, Yahweh.

Historical Roots. Though the story effectively veils the history of this event, scholars are able to date and to reconstitute the chronology and itinerary of the Exodus. Many historians agree that certain biblical texts, e.g., 1 Kgs 6:1, suggest a date for the Exodus. If one accepts the rendering in 1 Kgs 6:1, which claims that 480 years separate the Exodus from the fourth year of Solomon's reign, the date of the Exodus would be ca. 1440 B.C.E. Judg 11:26 echoes this dating when it claims Israel entered into Canaan 300 years before the judge, Jephthah. This date corresponds with the experience of certain Canaanite cities with the unsettling *'apiru,* or *Habiru* as documented in the AMARNA letters; however, the historical reflections of the Exodus and the eventual conquest of Canaan do not parallel the experience of these Canaanite cities. This date is based on numbers that carry symbolic meaning rather than historical reminis-

Courtesy of the Eisenberg Museum of Biblical Archaeology, Southern Baptist Theological Seminary.

A tomb painting depicting brickmaking.

cence. Other texts, such as Exod 12:40-41, which says that 430 years separate the descent of Jacob and his sons from the Exodus, or Gen 15:13-16, which claims Israel will be enslaved 400 years to another nation before it returns in the fourth generation, contradict one another and provide historians with more puzzles to solve rather than data to assimilate.

Many scholars agree, however, that Exod 1:11, which pictures the construction of the "store-cities, Pithom and Ramses," for the Pharaoh, suggests the best possibilities both for the pharaoh of the Exodus and the date of that event. These cities have been identified as Per-Atum and Per-Ramses, which were built during the reign of RAMSES II (1290–1224). His father, Seti I, had begun establishing and erecting fortified cities to protect his territory and to supply provisions to the necessary forces. Ramses II continued this and other building projects. If Exod 2:23 correctly recollects a shift in pharaohs, the Exodus would occur either in the reign of Ramses II (ca. 1250 B.C.E.) or his successor, his son Merneptah (ca. 1220 B.C.E.). However, the "Hymn of Victory of Mer-ne-ptah" (the "Israel Stela") places a group of people known as Israel in Canaan and suggests the Exodus should be dated earlier. On this basis, the pharaoh of the oppression would be Seti I and the pharaoh of the Exodus would be Ramses II, though this conclusion remains unsatisfactory. One could not expect to gain corroboration of the Exodus from Egyptian texts, though there are reports of tribal movements and small groups of escaped slaves, for the event would be too inconsequential or too embarrassing.

The PLAGUES, even though the present arrangement depends on a theological and literary agenda, are rooted in certain features of Egyptian life. Indeed, all these plagues could have natural explanations; certain scholars have prepared schemes whereby the order in the biblical account might actually chronicle an extraordinary collocation of events. Though such a series of events remains a possibility, biblical scholarship largely interprets this attempt to prove the historical accuracy of the biblical account as misdirected. The present narrative primarily presents a composite interpretation of an experience buried in the past but kept alive in the present. These plagues, rooted in history, for the people who leave Egypt, are the signature of their God.

The final event in the series of redemptive actions is the deliverance at the Sea of Reeds (*yam sûp*—wrongfully understood as the RED SEA in the LXX). Depending upon whether one maintains that the Israelites started north from Goshen across the marshy section of Lake Sirbonis but later turned south toward KADESH-BARNEA to miss the fortifications along "the way of the land of the Philistines," or east through the marshy segment of the Bitter Lakes at the northern end of the Gulf of Suez toward Kadesh-Barnea, or south over the marshy end of the Gulf of Suez toward Jebel Musa, a traditional site for Mount SINAI, the Israelite experience recorded a miraculous escape that left the Egyptians crippled and unable to subdue the fugitives (PLATE 9). Again, the possibility of a natural event, e.g., the flow of the tides or the effect of the wind, which allowed these fleeing people to escape the pursuing chariots, remains entirely possible. Yet this story, like that of the plagues, points to an affirmation of Yahweh's power and not the coincidental arrangement of natural forces. One must neither explain away these signs by focusing on their natural character, nor accept the story as an eyewitness account, for both of these procedures overlook the difficulty of knowing what actually happened and the clear possibility of interpreting this narrative even if one does not know what happened several centuries earlier.

From a literary point of view, historical speculation and

reformulation sometimes obscures the literary power of the account. For example, the omission of the Pharaoh's name creates difficulty for the historian. Yet, this occurs again and again in narratives and is quite natural in the literature of a people who thrived on oral stories that could be applied to their predicament. These people knew that the Pharaohs had names, but an unnamed ruler became any ruler who acted arbitrarily and coarsely, while Israel was a very particular group that lived through several hardships. So, in Deut 5:3 when the phrase is heard: "It was not our fathers who . . . , " or in Deut 6:21 when the phrase is heard: "We were Pharaoh's slaves . . . , " the Exodus reveals its timeless nature.

The same would be true in regard to the ten plagues and their ordering. In Pss 78 and 105, the order, the number, and the types of plagues have been altered, surely reflecting different traditions, and also underscoring the literary characteristics of poetic material and the particular contexts in which the material is placed. In Exod 10, the external darkness, which is the ninth plague, prepares the reader for Yahweh's last dramatic deed: the spread of an internal darkness of grief throughout Egypt in the wake of the nocturnal visit of the angel of death and compels the Pharaoh to release the Israelites. In Ps 105, the darkness begins the series of plagues in order to spread the symbolic nature of darkness over the whole account.

The Exodus Account. In a captivating drama a change of fortune must occur to place the protagonist(s) in a troubled situation. Such is the news that a new ruler, unacquainted with Israel's history and threatened by the numbers and success of the Hebrews, ascends to power. He immediately presses them into forced labor by which he plans to decrease their numbers while they build supply cities for his eastern flanks. Pharaoh's plan fails where he most wants it to succeed; the Israelites seem to become more numerous and more vigorous. Thereupon Pharaoh first charges the midwives to kill the male children born to the Hebrews, and later instructs his subjects to do the same.

In the midst of this danger and oppression, a son is born to a couple, both of whom are descended from the house of Levi. The events in the life of the son, who will be named MOSES by Pharaoh's daughter, prefigure many of the episodes in the Exodus that he will manage for Yahweh. His own rescue from the river points to the miraculous rescue later at the Sea of Reeds. His intervention that leads to the death of an Egyptian who was beating a Hebrew and his subsequent flight from Egypt foreshadow his intervention that leads to the freedom of the Israelites. His assistance to the daughters of Jethro (Reuel), the priest of Midian, ironically anticipates the time when a shepherd will deliver the Israelites out of the hand of the Egyptians (in Exod 2:19, they said: "An Egyptian delivered us out of the hand of the shepherds. . . . "). In addition, the birth incident reminds us that water is an important symbol in this story. For Moses, water signals life and providence; for the Egyptians, water stands for death and defeat.

The accession of a new king in Egypt fails to temper the bondage of the Israelites, and their cries for help reach Yahweh. Yahweh then reveals himself to Moses and instructs Moses to serve as his agent in rescuing the people. Moses' response accords with the typical call narrative in the Hebrew Bible; he resists. After Yahweh's first approach, which states that Moses must get the people out of Egypt, Moses responds with two questions: Who am I? (3:11) and Who are you (3:13b)? The second approach provides more information and a plan by which the people may deceive the Pharaoh in order to leave Egypt. Moses again counters with two hesitations: What if they (the Hebrews) do not believe me? and What about my speech difficulties? Yahweh resolves these difficulties and Moses prepares to return to Egypt. On his departure Yahweh further informs Moses that Pharaoh will be stubborn as a means of glorifying the power of Yahweh. These final instructions, along with the curious story of Zipporah's circumcision of her eldest son, anticipate the climactic final plague—the death of the first-born, the act that will break the will of Pharaoh—and the directions concerning the PASSOVER and the law of the first-born.

After Moses and AARON join, they first go to the elders of Israel who are relieved to know that deliverance is near. Moses and Aaron subsequently meet with Pharaoh who alters an earlier question of Moses and defiantly asks: "Who is Yahweh that I should heed his voice and let Israel go? I do not know Yahweh, and moreover I will not let Israel go." Pharaoh not only refuses their request to go to worship for three days in the wilderness; he increases their burdens. This punishment demoralizes the Israelites and strains their relationship with Moses. There follows a lengthy reassurance and recommissioning of Moses (Exod 6:1ff.) and the story moves toward the protracted struggle between the power of Yahweh and the will of Pharaoh.

On the instructions of Yahweh, Moses and Aaron begin to pressure and to threaten Pharaoh so that he will let the people go. The first step, turning Aaron's rod into a serpent, is duplicated by the Egyptian magicians. The magicians' success evaporates as their serpents are swallowed by Aaron's. Yet, as with other signs to come, Pharaoh becomes more intransigent.

With the struggle fully engaged, Yahweh unleashes a series of plagues through Moses, meant to manifest the overwhelming power of Yahweh and intended to force Pharaoh to release the Israelites. The Nile turns to blood, a feat matched by Egyptian magicians; Pharaoh is unmoved. The magicians match the second plague, hordes of frogs. Pharaoh, in order to end this scourge of frogs, promises that the people may go and sacrifice in the wilderness. As soon as the scourge disappears, however, Pharaoh changes his mind, as he will again and again.The magicians fail to replicate the third plague, clouds of gnats, and call this sign the "finger of God" but Pharaoh remains unaffected. The fourth plague, swarms of flies, which do not affect the land of Goshen, prompts Pharaoh to agree initially to the Israelites' demands but only within the land of Egypt. Immediately, Moses reminds Pharaoh that their sacrifices might offend the people of Egypt. Initially Pharaoh agrees to let them go, but ultimately reverts to his original stance. The fifth and sixth plagues, a plague on livestock and boils on humans and animals, misses the Israelites but leaves the Pharaoh unmoved. The seventh plague, hail and lightning, convinces those Egyptians who fear Yahweh to put their livestock under roof and persuades the Pharaoh to let the Israelites go. When Pharaoh refuses to let the Israelites go, an eighth plague, locusts, occurs. When Pharaoh appears to soften, Moses entreats Yahweh who drives the locusts into the Red Sea. The ninth plague, an intensely thick darkness that does not reach the Israelites, presses Pharaoh to allow the people, without their herds, to go to sacrifice. Moses refuses this offer and Pharaoh, overcome with rage, sends Moses away for the last time. Moses announces the last plague, the death of the first-born, then prepares the Israelites for the weathering of this scourge and the exiting from Egypt. The angel of death fills the land of Egypt with sorrow, and the Pharaoh finally allows the Israelites to go.

Combined with this dramatic account of the last plague are regulations concerning the Passover ceremony and the law of the first-born. These rituals, originally separate and rooted in the life of the semi-nomads, represent rites that protected them from the mysterious forces that disrupted their lives. Both ceremonies, and the festival of unleavened bread as well, have been tied to this Exodus event, and thereby their practice and intent have been forever changed.

Characteristically, Pharaoh changes his mind and sends an army to retrieve the Israelites who are caught between the Egyptian army and the Sea of Reeds. The Israelites lose all composure and faith, and, overcome with fear, begin to complain bitterly to Moses and to recall all their misgivings. After the people are quieted, Yahweh directs Moses to raise his staff and then sends a wind to divide the waters. The Israelites hurry across and the Egyptians pursue them. However, the waters rush back and destroy the army so that the Israelites are delivered and Yahweh is glorified. In a victory song (Exod 15:1-18), or, the Song of the Sea, which has been subsequently revised so that this battle and victory take on cosmic significance, Israel celebrates their deliverance and Yahweh's power. Then, the people head toward the mountain where Moses had met this awesome God and where they will bind themselves forever to this God.

Although the narrative traces their trip to Sinai, and the first commandment ties the Exodus to the covenant, the Israelites never quite internalize either the significance of the Exodus or the sense of the covenant. Before Moses can exhibit the tablets of the Law, the people are worshiping a golden calf that they say are the gods that brought them out of Egypt.

Yet other voices keep alive the marvel and consequence of this event of salvation history. BALAAM cannot bring himself to curse a people who has such a God on their side (Num 23:22). Early in his address to Israel, Moses, the eloquent preacher of Deuteronomy, counters the claim that the Exodus was merely a means to place Israel in the hands of its enemies. Moses maintains that the Exodus was redemptive and led to a covenant that brought life to Israel. Therefore, children should be taught that the Exodus established the basis for the way Israel relates to Yahweh and to others and provides fundamental ceremonies, like Passover, which define the life of the people.

The prophets, as they pondered the historical and metaphorical power of the Exodus, certainly perceived the Exodus experience as basic for Israel, just as they saw the Covenant as the standard for their national life. Amos, a prophet of reversals, affirmed that Yahweh redemptively brought the Israelites out of Egypt but their present unrighteousness prepared them for vigorous punishment. The same love that redeems, also punishes. In addition, Amos claimed that the destiny of all nations rested in the providence of Yahweh; he had even brought the Philistines from Caphtor and the Arameans from Kir. Hosea, who saw his relationship with his wife die as she forgot the covenant of marriage, recalled the mighty acts of Yahweh at the Exodus, which the people had effectively forgotten. Ezekiel castigated his people for their rebellion against Yahweh; he claimed that their harlotry had begun before they left Egypt. Yet, in a more hopeful sense, the words of Jeremiah and Deutero-Isaiah envision another exodus, after the people have weathered the humiliation of exile.

The Exodus also finds its way into the literature of Israel's worship; the Psalms exhibit this event in hymns of praise and this motif in pleas for help. Ps 77 recalls the terrors of Yahweh's redemptive action and asks for that same attention in the present. Ps 80 pictures a vine brought from Egypt, planted in Canaan, but jeopardized now by enemies who will succeed unless Yahweh saves it.

Psalms such as 78, 105, 135, and 136 resound with praise for the God who has redeemed and protected them throughout their history. Primarily, the Psalms capture the fundamental emotion of the Exodus, the ecstasy of release, the celebration of redemption, and the recognition of the worth of the forgotten. The praise arising from the Exodus becomes the praise for all times, just as the Exodus remains the event and the paradigm that both energizes and calls to account the people of Israel.

See also EXODUS, BOOK OF; MOSES; PLAGUES; RED SEA/ REED SEA.

Bibliography. B. S. Childs, *The Book of Exodus, OTL;* J. P. Hyatt, *Exodus;* M. Noth, *Exodus, A Commentary, OTL.*

—RUSSELL I. GREGORY

• **Exodus, Book of.** [ek'suh-duhs] The second book of the Pentateuch, known in Hebrew as *we'ēleh shᵉmoth* (["Now these are] the names"), is generally known as Exodus because of the Greek translation (*exodos*) which was followed by the Latin Vulgate. The Greek title testifies to one of the central events of the book, but the events recorded in the Book of Exodus far exceed the account of the deliverance of the Israelites from the oppression of Egypt. This book covers the experience of Israelite slavery, the birth and development of MOSES, the Exodus, the beginning of the wilderness sojourn, the making of the covenant of SINAI, the rebellion of the people, and the renewal of the covenant with the subsequent construction of the Tabernacle and all its furnishings. Throughout this history, several themes guide the presentation: the shift from patriarchal history (Jacob's [Israel's] sons) to Israelite history (the sons of Israel); deliverance; covenant; and Yahweh's central role and character.

The Shift from Patriarchal History to Israelite History. Just as Genesis moved from universal history (Gen 1–11) to patriarchal history (Gen 12–50), Exodus shifts from the history of a family to the history of a people. The first seven verses recount the names of the sons of Jacob and picture the swelling numbers of these sojourners in Egypt. The brothers' families and their tribal character recede as the Israelites are plunged into forced labor or slavery. This shift no doubt reflects the cumulative character of this account, which grew over a long period of time as more historical reminiscences were included and related tribes, which did not experience the cruelty of Egypt or the wonder of the Exodus, developed loyalty to Yahweh.

Deliverance. The supreme paradigm for deliverance in the OT is that of the Exodus from Egypt. However, other instances of deliverance supplement this paradigmatic event. When the Pharaoh sees the success and fecundity of the Israelites, he transforms them into slaves and requires them to work unremittingly. When that fails to decrease their numbers, he instructs the midwives to kill the male babies. When that measure miscarries, for the midwives do not actually comply, he enjoins all Egyptians to murder the male offspring. In this time fraught with danger, Moses' birth occurs and his survival is assured through the courage of his mother, the cleverness of his sister, and the mercy of the Pharaoh's daughter.

• OUTLINE OF EXODUS •

The Book of Exodus

I. Egypt—from Jacob's (Israel's) Sons in Egypt to the Sons of Israel Enslaved (1:1–2:15a)
  A. From favorable conditions to slavery and threat (1:1-22)
  B. Moses' birth, royal care, and exile (2:1-15a)
II. Wilderness—Moses's Commission from Yahweh in the Wilderness (2:15b–4:31)
  A. Moses acquires a wife and an occupation (2:15b-22)
  B. Notation of Yahweh's concern for Israel (2:23-25)
  C. Appearance of God in the burning bush and Moses' call (3:1–4:20)
  D. Yahweh's instructions (4:21-23)
  E. Moses' bizarre encounter with Zipporah (4:24-26)
III. Egypt—Moses' Direction of the Exodus (5:1–15:21)
  A. First encounter with Pharaoh and consequences (5:1-21)
  B. Moses' complaint to Yahweh and the reply (5:22–6:13)
  C. Recommissioning of Moses (6:14–7:7)
  D. Moses and Aaron defeat the Egyptian magicians (7:8-13)
  E. The first nine plagues (7:14–11:10)
  F. Rules for Passover (12:1-28)
  G. The tenth plague and pharaoh's order to go (12:29-42)
  H. Further regulations for passover (12:43-49)
  I. Law of the first born (13:1-16)
  J. Deliverance at the Reed Sea (13:17–14:30)
  K. The Song of the Sea (15:1-19)
  L. Miriam's response (15:20-21)
IV. Wilderness—Murmuring between Oppression and Covenant (15:22–18:27)
  A. Making bitter water sweet (15:22-27)
  B. Providing food (manna) (16:1-36)
  C. Finding water (17:1-7)
  D. Battle with Amalekites (17:8-16)
  E. Jethro's appearance and advice (18:1-27)
V. Sinai—Covenant, Rebellion, Renewal, and Furnishing the Cult (19:1–40:38)
  A. Establishment of the camp and theophany (19:1-25)
  B. The ten words (20:1-17)
  C. The people's reaction (20:18-26)
  D. The Covenant Code (21:1–23:33)
  E. Sealing of the covenant (24:1-18)
  F. Instructions for the establishment of the cult (25:1–31:18)
  G. The golden calf and its consequences (32:1-35)
  H. Yahweh's hesitancy to dwell among his people and Moses' mediation (33:1-23)
  I. The covenant inscribed again (34:1-35)
  J. Construction according to the instructions given for the establishment of the cult (35:1–40:38)

During one of his inspections, Moses spies an Egyptian beating a Hebrew. After he insures the privacy of the location, he kills the Egyptian and thus rescues the unfortunate Hebrew. This act leads to his quick exit from Egypt, but ironically prefigures Moses' role in the freeing of the mistreated Israelites and also the last plague, which will kill all the first-born of the Egyptians and convince the Pharaoh to release the Israelites.

Still breathless from his escape, Moses witnesses a group of shepherds harassing the seven daughters of Jethro, the priest of Midian. Moses chases the shepherds away and helps the women water their flocks. The daughters tell their father: "An Egyptian delivered us out of the hands of the shepherds . . . " (2:19). Eventually, this Hebrew raised among Egyptian royalty will reverse that assertion; Moses will deliver the Israelites out of the hand of the Egyptians.

The bulk of these first fifteen chapters deals with the deliverance of the people of Israel from Egypt. From the moment when Moses reluctantly accepts his commission, complete with the assistance of his brother, AARON, this deliverance is assured. Yahweh, who identifies himself as the God of the Patriarchs, has heard the cries of his people and has determined to act. Yet, the first meeting with Pharaoh clearly reveals that this ruler of Egypt, this god who rules over his people, will not release the Israelites willingly for that would be an affront to his power and a severe depletion of his labor force. There follows a series of nine PLAGUES, some of which leave Pharaoh unresponsive (Nile turned to blood [1], gnats [3], plague on livestock [5], boils [6]) and others which compel the Pharaoh to agree temporarily to Moses' terms (frogs [2], flies [4], hail [7], locusts [8], darkness [9]). Finally, the patience of Yahweh and Moses strained to the limit and the time ripe for the deliverance of Israel, Yahweh unleashes a final plague. Yahweh sends the angel of death who strikes all the first-born of Egypt, but spares the Israelites, for they have dutifully performed the ceremony of the PASSOVER as instructed by Moses. Pharaoh, filled with anger and grief, sends them out of Egypt, but true to his pattern relents and sends his army after them. Yahweh completes the triumphant exit from Egypt when he opens or dries up the Reed Sea so that the Israelites are saved and closes the sea so that the Egyptians are vanquished. Moses and the Israelites respond with a song that glorifies God who delivered them, and Miriam echoes their rejoicing.

The very size of this account testifies to its importance in the life of Israel. More than any other event, the Exodus reveals the determination of Yahweh to remember his promises, and to fulfill his plan. Throughout the OT this event is recalled, e.g., Ps 105:26-38, and is employed to point ahead, e.g., Isa 40:3-5.

No sooner than the strains of the Song at the Sea have died out, the Israelites begin to complain about the hardship of the wilderness to which they have been brought. They forget the agony of Egypt; they remember only the security of slavery, and long to return. Yahweh responds and provides a means to turn bitter water to fresh, to discover sources of fresh water, and to reap a bounty of food, manna from heaven, which they do not deserve. This protection in the wilderness climaxes with the battle between the Israelites and the AMALEKITES who are defeated beneath the upraised arm of Moses, Yahweh's representative.

Whereas these examples of deliverance up to and including the Exodus emphasize the liberating power of Yahweh, and the examples in the wilderness stress the sustaining power of Yahweh, the final example highlights the retributive power of Yahweh. The Israelites build a golden calf in the wilderness just after agreeing to the covenant with Yahweh. For this offense, Yahweh expresses his intention to destroy the people and begin anew with Moses. Moses dissuades Yahweh from that course of action, but does mete out punishment to the guilty people. Yahweh then resolves, for the safety of the Israelites, to send an angel in his stead; his holy presence would consume the people. Moses, who long ago was reluctant to serve as Yahweh's emissary to Pharaoh, now mediates for the Israelites before Yahweh. Moses reminds Yahweh that it is his presence in their midst that sets Israel apart. Subsequently, Yahweh accepts Moses' argument, and the formation of the cult, complete with ordinances, objects, personnel, and tabernacle, proceeds without incident.

Covenant. In this book, the Exodus is inextricably linked with the making of the COVENANT at Mount Sinai; the sense of their liberty under Yahweh remains coupled to the structure of their common life from this time forward, particularly in the prophetic perspective. In the prologue to the first commandment (a part of the first commandment in the Jewish tradition), Yahweh iterates the precipitating cause for a covenant between Israel and himself; Yahweh redeemed this people from bondage. Thereupon Yahweh, in a form resembling treaties in the ancient Near East, offers fundamental laws, the Decalogue (the "ten words"), and complements those with casuistic laws ("ordinances") that address various areas of Israelite life, e.g., the treatment of slaves. This covenant is sealed; Israel accepts or ratifies what Yahweh has offered them. After this ratification, Moses goes to the top of the mountain to receive the tablets of the law and the instruction for the formation of the cult.

Unfortunately, the people, in the absence of Moses, waver in their faith and break the covenant by building the golden calf. Before they even set the new cult up, they sin against Yahweh. Yahweh's reaction is quick and almost final, but with the mediation of Moses the covenant is renewed, the stipulations are inscribed on stone, and the instructions he received earlier on Sinai are followed so that Israel begins to worship in the prescribed manner.

Yahweh. Several roles of Yahweh are reflected in the Book of Exodus. Yahweh is the one who hears the cries of oppression, the one who delivers, the one who covenants, the one who reacts to the breach of covenant, and the one who dwells in the midst of the Israelites. There remain three specific disclosures of the nature of this God; these point to Yahweh's essential character. When Yahweh confronts Moses from the burning bush, Moses asks who it is that sends him to Egypt to perform such a task. The answer conceals as much as it reveals. Yahweh says: "I am who I am" (3:14a). Volumes attempting to explain what Yahweh's response means could be written. Yet the inability to understand this response may be an important clue. Yahweh was beyond names, was beyond control, was beyond human comprehension, but he was not beyond comprehending the plight of the Israelites, he was not beyond controlling the elements for liberation, he was not beyond naming his emissary, Moses. In this exchange, what Yahweh demanded was faith; what Yahweh gave was his presence. The second revelation about Yahweh (33:19b; 34:6b-7) stresses the mercy and compassion, in addition to the holiness and righteousness, of this God who had just witnessed the apostasy of the Israelites. The final description offered in the Book of Exodus emphasizes Yahweh's will to be sovereign ruler over his covenant people (34:14). Yahweh is a jealous god who allows no rivals.

This book reflects the perspective of the final tradition (or source), P, and the preceding traditions, J and E, which he honored. The Yahwist's perspective shows up in the continuing fulfillment of the promises made by God to Abraham, i.e., the tremendous growth of the people in Egypt, and the call to be a responsible people. The ten words stand like the tree of knowledge of good and evil in the midst of this people. As long as they do not eat of it, or as long as they do not violate these fundamental laws, they possess life. The Elohist's emphasis on obedience to the covenant, the horror of apostasy which was realized in the golden calf incident, and the possibility, however difficult, of renewal blended well with the Yahwist's concerns. The priestly perspective, with its regard for a legitimate cult and the presence of Yahweh, surfaced in the wealth of narrative and legal material that instructed the Israelites. P's careful blending of the traditions led to a book that melded together freedom and responsibility, Exodus from Egypt and covenant with Yahweh.

See also EXODUS.

Bibliography. B. S. Childs, *The Book of Exodus, OTL*; W. Harrelson, *The Ten Commandments and Human Rights*; J. P. Hyatt, *Commentary on Exodus, NCB*; E. Nielsen, *The Ten Commandments in New Perspective*; M. Noth, *Exodus, A Commentary, OTL*; W. G. Plaut, *The Torah, A Modern Commentary: Exodus.*

—RUSSELL I. GREGORY

• **Expiation.** [ek-spee-ay'shun] The word "expiation" comes into our religious vocabulary by way of the RSV as a substitute for the word "propitiation" which is used in the KJV and the ASV. However, it is only as a person considers the secondary meanings of the word "expiation" in the dictionary that the term applies to the NT Greek word which is being translated. The Greek verb which is translated "to make expiation" (ἱλάσκεσθαι) appears in Heb 2:17 while the cognate "expiation" (ἱλασμός) is found two times in 1 John (2:2; 4:10). Another cognate often translated "expiation" (ἱλαστήριον) occurs twice in the NT (Rom 3:25; Heb 9:5).

C. H. Dodd made a careful study of the verb and its cognates as they appeared in both classical and *koine* Greek of pagan literature and discovered two meanings. One had to do with placating an angry person or an angry deity. The other centered around the removal of guilt and SIN by performing a sacrifice or paying a fine. Concerning the first meaning he stated that the more common usage was related to placating a person or a god. However, his research on the Greek translation of the OT revealed that the verb and its cognates were never used where God was the object.

With respect to the second meaning Dodd observed that there were many examples in the OT. Thus he concluded that the biblical sense of the words had to do with the performances of acts to remove guilt or defilement. These acts had the force of disinfectants whether it be by washing with water or sprinkling with blood. In the OT lustrations and sprinkling of blood disinfected the priests, the altar, and the people from ritual or moral defilement. On the basis of Dodd's study, the RSV committee substituted "expiation" for "propitiation" in the references above. However, a closer look at some of the references makes that translation questionable.

In Rom 3:25, the word used by Paul (ἱλαστήριον) is used either as a neuter substantive or as an adjective in the accusative case. The translation of the word in the KJV is "propitiation" while the RSV has "expiation." Both William Tyndale and Martin Luther, possibly in reaction to the Vulgate rendering of the word by *propitiatorium,* followed the clue in Heb 9:5 and translated the word properly as MERCY SEAT (Luther, *Gnadenstuhl*). In recent years there has been a return to an emphasis upon this meaning along with an attempt to set it more within the context of the ritual of the DAY OF ATONEMENT.

The importance of the mercy seat in the religion of Israel was fully set forth in Exod 25:17-22. It was at this place that God met his people through the high priest once each year in the ritual of the Day of Atonement. The mercy seat here is defined as the lid of the Ark of the Covenant. From above the mercy seat and between the two cherubim on the Ark God delivered a commandment to Israel through the high priest. This revelation was to be placed in the Ark of the Covenant. It seems clear that Paul was thinking in terms of a spiritual mercy seat, Christ, who was set forth publicly as a demonstration of God's activity in bringing people into a right relationship with himself in contrast to the inaccessible, hidden, and mysterious revelation found in the Levitical sacrificial system. Thus, according to the apostle, God's mercy was supremely revealed in the crucified Christ who is our mercy seat.

Some raise objections to this view because it indicates that Christ is likened to a piece of Temple furniture. However, in John's Gospel Jesus uses a door as a metaphor of himself (10:9). Others say that the verb "put forward" is also against this view. Yet this is the point Paul is trying to get across. God's revelation to the high priest was in secret in the Holy of Holies where nobody but the recipient could make the affirmation, but now God's revelation is made public for all to know. In Christ God revealed his true character in all its splendor and did not hide in a cloud of incense in the Holy of Holies (Lev 16:2).

Strangely enough the KJV translates the verb form in Heb 2:17 with "make RECONCILIATION." Why did not the translators use "make propitiation"? The RSV renders the Greek verb "make expiation." "Expiation" is legitimate provided the translators meant a removal of sin rather than appeasement. At the beginning of Hebrews the author said that Jesus made a purification for sins (1:3). As a merciful and faithful high priest Christ was able to blot out the sin and defilement which blocked our access to God by forgiving sins.

Since the author of 1 John seems to be less influenced by the LXX than any other NT writing, it is difficult to tell whether his use follows the biblical sense as it was commonly understood in secular Hellenistic literature. If it is the secular meaning, it represents the placating of an angry god. However, it is very unlikely that the author would mean this because it is the God of Israel who always does the placating. If the author's use is in the biblical sense, he meant a covering or removal of sin which finally means FORGIVENESS. The TEV translates the term in 1 John 2:2 and 4:10 as a "means by which our sins are forgiven." The NEB renders the word "a remedy for defilement" in both references. The RSV retains "expiation."

To conclude, it seems that the verb in Heb 2:17 (ἱλάσκεσθαι) and the cognate in 1 John 2:2 and 4:10 (ἱλασμός) convey the meaning of removal of defilement or sin and thus indicate forgiveness, while the term in Rom 3:25 and Heb 9:5 (ἱλαστήριον) means mercy seat. In all cases the thought prevails that God by his love and mercy has manifested himself in Jesus Christ to forgive sins.

See also ATONEMENT, DAY OF; ATONEMENT/EXPIATION IN THE NEW TESTAMENT; ATONEMENT/EXPIATION IN THE OLD TESTAMENT; BLOOD IN THE NEW TESTAMENT; BLOOD IN THE OLD TESTAMENT; FORGIVENESS/PARDON; GRACE; JUSTIFICATION; MERCY SEAT; RECONCILIATION; REDEMPTION IN THE NEW TESTAMENT; REDEMPTION IN THE OLD TESTAMENT; SALVATION IN THE NEW TESTAMENT; SALVATION IN THE OLD TESTAMENT; SIN.

Bibliography. C. H. Dodd, *The Bible and the Greeks* and *The Epistle of Paul to the Romans;* A. Nygren, *Commentary on Romans;* A. Richardson, *An Introduction to the Theology of the New Testament.*

—T. C. SMITH

• **Ezekiel.** [i-zee'kee-uhl] Ezek 1:1-3, despite the problem of understanding "the thirtieth year," describes Ezekiel as a priest "among the exiles by the River Chebar" at the time of his prophetic call (593 B.C.E.). The "exile of King JEHOIACHIN" began with his surrender of Jerusalem to the Babylonians (March 597 B.C.E.). According to the account in 2 Kgs 24:12, 14, Jehoiachin became a Babylonian "prisoner" at this time (a king in exile, confined to quarters in the city of Babylon), accompanied by the royal family and the palace officials. The "princes" (patrician urban officials), the "men of valor" (the highest military officers), and the "craftsmen and the smiths" (the skilled technicians) were also among these exiles. They, and possibly others, were given responsibility for expansion or restoration of the system of irrigation canals upon which the prosperity of the Babylonian city-states depended. In the village of Tell Abib (3:15), probably near Nippur, it appears that the exiled patricians had some autonomy in religious and community affairs. The "elders" of the community exercised some kind of leadership over (or among) the agricultural workers (8:1; 14:1; 20:1). The Babylonian policy of replacing the central power structure was intended to discourage further efforts to end the economic drain caused by the payment of regular "tribute" to Babylon. It was assumed that the new officials in Judah, under the rule of Josiah's uncle, Zedekiah, would be more cooperative.

It is generally assumed that Ezekiel was a priest of the Jerusalem Temple. The fact that he was among the exiles of 597 suggests that he was from an aristocratic priestly family, possibly belonging to the old Zadokite line established by SOLOMON (Zadokites appear in Ezekiel only in 40–48). Among the exiles, Ezekiel functioned as a prophet, consulted occasionally by the "elders," and exercising leadership over a group among the exiles. We see his priestly background in the language of the book. The concern with the Temple in Jerusalem, the concern with what is ritually "clean" or "unclean" (cf. 22:23-26), and echoes of the "Holiness Code" give some strength to this assumption.

The scenes with the elders are set in what appears to be his private residence. Like most adults in ancient Israel, Ezekiel was married ("the delight of [his] eyes": 24:15-24). The striking content of the book supports the picture of Ezekiel as an aristocratic priestly intellectual. The metaphors and symbolic actions familiar from the prophetic tradition are used and elaborated in a distinctive fashion. Traditional metaphors, Israel as a vine or bride (15; 16), have been transformed in an astonishing way. In the opening vision (chaps. 1–3), broad learning and a theological audacity are displayed in the elaboration of the metaphor of a thunderstorm: the vision contains symbolism of the Jerusalem Temple, but also of Mesopotamian depictions of the presence of divinity, particularly the wheeled vehicle and the winged genii with especially unnatural combinations of bodies and heads. This broad learning is also demonstrated in the knowledge of Tyrian and Egyptian lore and mythology, used in the characterization of the inevitable end of these nations (chaps. 26–32). There is a distinctive aesthetic, even sensuous quality in Ezekiel's descriptions, indicated by the variety of colors, the tumultuous sounds of wings and wheels, and the brilliant flashes of light that punctuate the narrative. Note also the sweetness of the scroll (3:3) and the indelicate characterizations of the conduct of Jerusalem (16; 23). The substantially elaborated narrative of a simple prophetic action with a clay brick (4–5), shows meticulous elaboration of descriptive and numerical detail. This is typical of Ezekiel's visions (1–3; 8–11; 37; 40–48) and actions (4-5; 12; 21; 24) as well as of the Priestly materials in the Pentateuch. The subtle elaboration of case-law (3:16-21; 18) may also be part of this picture.

Ezekiel deals in a highly symbolic fashion with political tensions: the expectation of restoration among the Babylonian exiles around Jehoiachin, versus the expectation of continued power in Jerusalem court circles. This is compounded by the intrigue of the pro-Egyptian faction in Jerusalem, with its schemes for independence from Babylon (17:1-21; 19:1-9 are fairly specific "allegories" about Zedekiah, JEHOAHAZ, and Jehoiachin—cf. 19:10-14). The first two visions of Ezekiel characterize a major theme in the presentation of his prophetic activity before the fall of Jerusalem in 587/6. The opening vision affirms the presence of the "Glory of God," normally resident in the Holy of Holies of the Jerusalem temple, in the community in exile (1:24-28; 3:22-23). The companion vision (chaps. 8–11), following a harsh characterization of cultic activities in the Temple and a preparation for the destruction of Jerusalem, describes the abandonment of Jerusalem by the "Glory of God" (9:3; 10:4, 18-19; 11:22-23). His symbolic actions (4–5; 12; 21; 24:15-27), focus attention on the inexorable doom of Jerusalem.

For the community in exile, Ezekiel issues a call for responsible obedience to the covenant (cf. chap. 18—note the metaphor of the prophet as "watchman": 3:17-27; 33:1-9). Though he rejects the easy hope offered by the prophets who daub the king's walls with whitewash (13; 22), the weight of his proclamation shifts from disaster to hope after the first refugees bring word of the destruction of Jerusalem in 587/6 (24:26; 33:21). Under the dates of 586–585, we have stirring images of restoration, with the displacement of oppressive rulers (34), the transformation of land and people (36), and the restoration of a united Israel from the desiccated bones littering the plain of Babylon (37). The final vision, the restored city and temple within the recontoured land of Israel (chaps. 40–48, dated in 573), is typically treated as the product of the community that supported Ezekiel and preserved his words.

See also EZEKIEL, BOOK OF; PROPHET; PROPHECY.

Bibliography. W. H. Brownlee, *Ezekiel 1-19, WBC*; M. Greenberg, *Ezekiel 1-20, AncB*; B. Oded, "Judah and the Exile," J. H. Hayes and J. M. Miller, eds., *Israelite and Judean History*; R. R. Wilson, "Prophecy in Crisis: The Call of Ezekiel," *Int* 38/2 (1984) 117-30; W. Zimmerli, *Ezekiel, Hermeneia.*

—ROY D. WELLS, JR.

• **Ezekiel the Tragedian.** The work of Ezekiel the Tragedian (otherwise known as Ezekiel the Poet) exists only in fragments found in the writings of EUSEBIUS, Clement of Alexandria, and Psuedo-Eustathius. Ezekiel's dependence on the LXX and the influence of Hellenistic dramatic forms on his work suggest that Ezekiel wrote in Alexandria during the second century B.C.E., though little direct evidence exists to support or to challenge this conclusion.

Ezekiel's work, fittingly entitled *Exagōgē,* recounts the Hebrew EXODUS from Egypt under the leadership of MOSES. The five act drama, written in iambic trimeter, centers around Moses as the hero. Parts of the biblical account have been adapted to the needs of Ezekiel's narrative, most notably that of allowing an Egyptian soldier to recount the crossing of the RED SEA. These adaptations lend credence to the idea that Ezekiel's drama may have been intended for the stage, since the changes tend to involve events which would have been impossible to present on stage.

The *Exagōgē* is important both for its relationship to the LXX and for the information it provides in the area of Hellenistic tragedy. Ezekiel's dependence on an early recension of the LXX provides evidence for those interested in the literary development of the LXX .The drama's character as a tragedy based on an historical event seems to be a rarity at this point in the development of the tragic genre. Ezekiel's work is also important for its unique blending of the biblical story with the literary form of the Hellenistic tragic drama.

Bibliography. J. H. Charlesworth, *The Pseudepigrapha and Modern Research*; R. G. Robertson, "Ezekiel the Tragedian," *The Old Testament Pseudepigrapha,* ed. J. H. Charlesworth.

—STEVEN SHEELEY

• **Ezekiel, Apocryphon of.** [i-zee'kee-uhl, uh-pok'ruh-fon] The *Apocryphon of Ezekiel* is a lost pseudepigraphon extant in ancient citations of five fragments and one fragmentary manuscript of one of these five. Four of the fragments are very brief. In the fifth, which is found with variations in RABBINIC LITERATURE, a king prepares a wedding feast for his son and invites all in his kingdom except a lame man and a blind man. Indignant, the two plot revenge. The lame man climbs onto the back of the blind man. Using the feet of the blind man and the eyes of the lame man, they enter the king's garden and damage it. The king interrogates them, determines what they have done, and beats them. Their deeds exposed, they blame each other. The point of the story is that since both body and soul work together, final judgment will include both.

The *Apocryphon of Ezekiel* is quoted in a large number of ancient writers, one of whom, Epiphanius (fourth century), specifically speaks of "Ezekiel's own apocryphon" (*Haer* 64.70). The earliest reference is *1 Clem* 8:2-3 (ca. 95 C.E.), where the citation stands without distinction alongside a quotation from Ezekiel. The *Apocryphon* was probably composed in Greek or Hebrew between 50 B.C.E. and 50 C.E. It was popular among Christians, including Gnostics and Manichaeans, and the fragments suggest a Christian redaction of a Jewish original. That such a Jewish writing existed seems confirmed by Josephus's comments that he knew of *two* books of Ezekiel (*Ant* 10.5.1).

See also EZEKIEL, BOOK OF.

Bibliography. J. R. Mueller and S. E. Robinson, "Apocryphon of Ezekiel," *The Old Testament Pseudepigrapha,* ed. J. H. Charlesworth.

—JOSEPH L. TRAFTON

• OUTLINE OF EZEKIEL •

The Book of Ezekiel

Introduction: Ezekiel's Commission (1:1–3:27)
I. Oracles against Judah/Jerusalem (3:22–24:27)
II. Oracles against Other Nations (25:1–32:32)
III. Restoration, Rebuilding of Israel (33:1–48:35)

• **Ezekiel, Book of.** [i-zee'kee-uhl] The book of Ezekiel, with its autobiographical style, its clear narrative setting among the exiles in Babylon, and its explicit chronological organization (from the fifth year [593; 1:2] to the twenty-fifth year [573; 40:1] of Jehoiachin), does not (in contrast with Isaiah and Jeremiah) show obvious marks of editorial, rather than historical, organization. The study of the book in this century, however, has shown consistent interest in the effort to understand the stages through which the book passed before it came to its present form. Though there is no wide support for G. Hölscher's search for the fine prophetic poetry buried within this text, and certainly not for his reduction of Ezekiel's words to 170 verses (thirteen percent of the text, none expressing hope), it is widely assumed that repetitions, explanatory comments, and detailed lists come from the complex process of editing and organizing a written text by later disciples and even by Ezekiel himself.

The overall organization of the book—words of doom for JUDAH and JERUSALEM (1–24), words concerning foreign nations (25–32), and words of hope for ISRAEL and Judah (33–48)—is also found in ISAIAH and in the Greek version of JEREMIAH. The words of doom for Judah open with a description of a vision on the Babylonian plain, based on a traditional Israelite image of the appearance of God in a storm, upon which the "Glory of God" rides to Babylon (1:4-28a). This is followed by a commission to Ezekiel to speak words of "lamentation and mourning and woe" to "a rebellious house," no matter how much he may be opposed (1:28b–3:11). After an interval of seven days, there is a second commissioning to be a "watchman" who warns the city about coming disaster (3:16-21). Oddly, he is then confined to his house in silence (3:24-27). These scenes are a significant element of the organization of the book.

The "glory of God" (chaps. 1–3) reappears in the strange prophetic vision of the cultic improprieties practiced within the Jerusalem Temple (chaps. 8–11), in which the city is prepared for the coming of slaughter and fire. The pantomime of the siege and invasion of Jerusalem (chaps. 4–5), the attack on the rural sanctuaries outlawed by Josiah (chap. 6), and the description of the paralysis of a city under threat of invasion (chap. 7) point to a climax in the death of the official Pelatiah and the departure of the glory of God from the Temple (11:13, 23).

The conclusion of the period of muteness is anticipated at the end of the collection of words against Judah (24:25-27), and is effected when refugees bring the news of the destruction of Jerusalem to Babylon (33:21-22). Similarly, the commission of the prophet as watchman is detailed again at the beginning of the collection of words of hope (33:1-9). In the material bracketed by these references (chaps. 4–24), there are recurrent references to Jerusalem. The prophetic actions of carrying light baggage through a hole in a mud-brick wall, and eating bread and drinking water "with trembling and with fearfulness" (chap. 12), are interpreted as images of exile and invasion for Jerusalem and its ruler. These acts and words intensify the rejection of the religious claims of the new administrators of Jerusalem: "To us this land has been given as a possession" (11:15). The criticism of the hopeful prophetic words of other men and women in the community rejects these words as no more than an effort to lend prophetic authority to royal power schemes (13:1–14:11).

Much discussion of Ezekiel concentrates on the clear picture drawn by the legal series in chap. 18 ("If . . . then"). There, the life-giving power of responsible action overrides all sense of historical doom. The effect of this section of the book is far more complex, with the rejection of the power of virtue to avert disaster (14:12-23) and with the depiction of the limitations imposed by the sin of one generation on the possibilities open to later generations (chap. 20). These reflections alternate with harsh allegories of the city as a burnt vine (chap. 15), and errant wife (chap. 16), and a prostitute (chap. 23). In the allegories of the eagles, the vines, and the transplanted cedar (chap. 17), and the lament over the lion cubs and the vine in the wilderness (chap. 19), there appears to be a severe limitation of hope associated with kings—in Jerusalem or in exile. The words of doom reach a climax in the metaphor of the sharpened sword (chap. 21), the detailed listing of infractions of traditional law (chap. 22), the cooking pot left to burn, and the refraining from mourning rites (chap. 24).

The words against foreign nations, Ammon (25:1-7), Moab (25:8-11), Edom (25:12-14), the Philistines (25:15-17), Tyre (chaps. 26–28), and Egypt (chaps. 29–32) are dated (with the exception mentioned earlier) to the years preceding and following the destruction of Jerusalem in 587/6. In addition, all of these nations played some role in the disaster—note the later words against "Mount Seir" (= Edom, chap. 35) and "Gog and Magog" ("Magog" is formed by reversing and incrementing the letters in "Babylon": bbl/mgg, chaps. 38–39).

The book makes a dramatic turn at this point. Now the watchman is vindicated (33:1-33)—his spectacular words have more than entertainment value (33:32; cf. 20:49). In the extended metaphor of the shepherd who exploits his flock, there is the hope, at long last, for a proper shepherd/king out of the Davidic dynasty who will express the concern of God for his flock (chap. 34). This leads into an image of a transformed people living in an abundantly fertile land, in which the "mountains of Israel" (chap. 36) are contrasted with the blighted "Mount Seir" (chap. 35). The vision of the resuscitation of sun-bleached skeletons (37:1-14), followed by the prophetic action of holding two sticks so that they appear to be one (37:15-28), offers hope for the restoration of a united Israel, with one king and one sanctuary.

The vision of a new Temple (chaps. 40–42)in a paradisiacally transformed land (chaps. 47–48) reflects a vision of the future in which the security and prosperity of the land are guaranteed by a temple governed by divine law (chaps. 43, 44–46), and supervised without royal interference by the traditional Zadokite priests. This vision had a recurrent influence on the history of the postexilic period.

See also PROPHECY; PROPHET.

Bibliography. M. Fishbane, "Sin and Judgment in the Prophecies of Ezekiel," *Int* 38/2 (1984): 151-64; H. G. May, "The Book of Ezekiel: Introduction and Exegesis," *IB*; C. A. Newsom, "A Maker of Metaphors—Ezekiel's Oracles against Tyre," *Int*38/2 (1984): 151-64; W. Zimmerli, *Ezekiel, Hermeneia*.

—ROY D. WELLS, JR.

• **Ezion-geber.** [ee'zee-uhn-ee"buhr] An EDOMITE town at the head of the Gulf of Aqaba on the Red Sea. The scant biblical references identify it as a site on the Exodus route (Num 33:35-36); as Solomon's seaport for trading missions with Africa (1 Kgs 9:26-28; 10:1; 2 Chr 8:17; 9:10, 11); and as the port for Jehoshaphat's fleet that was shipwrecked (1 Kgs 22:48; 2 Chr 20:36).

Attempts have been made to locate Ezion-geber somewhere near modern Elath, i.e., at the oasis of Aqaba on the coast; or on the small off-shore island of Jezirat al-Fara'un. Only the site of Tell el-Kheleifeh (PLATE 12), however, has produced any evidence of Iron Age occupation in the general area. This low mound, in the trough of the Arabah about 550 yards from the shore, now just on the Israeli-Jordanian border, was excavated in 1938–40 by N. Glueck. He not only identified the site with Solomon's seaport of Ezion-geber but claimed to have found evidence of the smelters for Solomon's copper mines. The curious "flues" in the mudbrick walls of the Stratum II fortress, however, are now seen as nothing more than the hollows left by ancient timbers. And further analysis of "crucibles," "slag," and other supposed evidence of ancient metallurgy has shown that most of the evidence is doubtful. Finally, B. Rothenberg's investigation of the copper mines themselves in the nearby Wadi Timnah has demonstrated that they date from the Chalcolithic through the Roman periods. The story of "King Solomon's mines," so widely publicized, was finally abandoned by Glueck himself. Solomon *may* have mined copper in the area, but Tell el-Kheleifeh is not a smelting site; and it may not even be Ezion-geber.

Glueck did not live to publish the site beyond preliminary reports that left most of the data problematic. Recently the material and the site have been re-examined and reworked for publication by G. Pratico, who also had access to Glueck's original field records and diaries. On the basis of the scant evidence thus far published by Pratico (1985), the following picture can be gleaned of Ezion-geber's five levels of occupation.

The first period, Glueck's Phase I, consists of a casemate-walled fortress ca. forty-five m. square, with a single multi-roomed structure in the middle of the otherwise empty space within the enclosure. Unfortunately the only pottery saved from Phase I consisted of sherds of a distinctive coarse-fabric "Negebite" pottery (Glueck's "crucibles"). Even now this pottery can only be dated broadly to the Iron Age, i.e., all the way from about the eleventh to the seventh centuries B.C.E. Glueck's "tenth century" date was evidently influenced by the Solomonic tradition in the Hebrew Bible. More recently other, roughly parallel Negeb forts have been excavated, but their date is also contested and may range anywhere from the eleventh to the ninth century B.C.E. or even later.

Glueck's Phase II–IV plan suggests a basic change to a larger "offsets/insets" fortified settlement, some seventy m. square, enclosed within a solid wall and entered by a typical Iron II three-entryway gate to the south. Within the compound is a single, more prominent building with its own casemate wall—probably still a fort or citadel. From late within this complex probably came Glueck's fine "Jotham" signet ring and the several jars bearing the seal impression of "Qaws'anal, servant of the king" (an Edomite name). The pottery of Phases II–IV, although it cannot be separated out into stratigraphically determined groups, includes "Negebite" wares, many imitations of eighth century B.C.E. Assyrian pottery, and certain common Judaean forms of the eighth to the early sixth centuries B.C.E.

Phase V has scattered post-sixth century B.C.E. sherds, a few as late as possibly the fourth century B.C.E. After this, Tell el-Kheleifeh was abandoned.

Bibliography. N. Glueck, "Ezion-geber," *BA* 28 (1965): 70-87 and "Tell el-Kheleifeh," *EAEHL* 3 (1977): 716-17; G. D. Pratico, "Tell el-Kheleifeh: A Reappraisal," *BASOR* 259 (1985): 1-32.

—WILLIAM G. DEVER

• **Ezra.** [ez'ruh] A Jewish priest and scribe and a Persian governmental secretary during the time of the restoration of Jewish life in Jerusalem after the Babylonian Exile. His story is told in chaps. 7–10 of the Book of Ezra and chaps. 8–9 of the book of Nehemiah. Although these stories do not specifically say so, it is probable that while in exile Ezra and other religious leaders had revised and edited the TORAH, the law codes and stories of Israel's origins found in Genesis, Exodus, Leviticus, Numbers, and Deuteronomy. After the issuance of CYRUS's decree, which encouraged Jews to return to Palestine, Ezra led a group of about 5,000 Babylonian exiles to Jerusalem. He was commissioned by Persian authorities to investigate conditions in Jerusalem to determine if they were consistent with the revised Jewish law that he and other leaders among the exiles regarded as authoritative. Ezra brought a copy of this law with him. He was given power to appoint judges to enforce this Jewish law, which apparently was accepted by the Persians as the appropriate religious and civil code for the province of Judah. He also brought with him donations for the Jerusalem Temple and permission to use Persian state funds to supplement the donations when needed.

When he arrived in Jerusalem he discovered to his considerable dismay that the people had fallen into unacceptable practices. He was particularly concerned about marriages with foreign women involving priests, Levites, and chief officials. In exile, even though surrounded by a foreign culture, the Jews had carefully preserved their distinctive faith and culture by strict observance of the SABBATH, by the practice of circumcision, and by allowing marriage only within the community of Israel. The struggling Jewish community in JERUSALEM had not been strict in these matters; therefore the distinctiveness of Jewish culture so faithfully protected by the exiles seemed greatly endangered there. Ezra went into mourning, fasted, and prayed, citing prophetic prohibitions against mixed marriages. Moved by Ezra's grief the people responded by freely advocating the severe measure of expelling the foreign wives and their children. Ezra as the leading religious official accepted their oaths that they would do as they had covenanted. This was an extreme and exclusive measure unlike the more open orientation to foreign people expressed by other leaders of the exilic and postexilic community (Jonah, for example). Ezra recognized the severity of the action and grieved over the community's loss, but he felt that separation from foreign influences was imperative.

The story in Neh 8–10 tells of a more admirable and much more significant work of Ezra. At the Festival of Tabernacles, celebrating both the beginning of the New Year and the renewal of the covenant with God, Ezra read from the exilic revision of the ancient law that he had brought with him to Jerusalem. The initial response to this reading of the law was grief. The people were instructed not to mourn but to pledge their loyalty to God by observance of his commandments. In effect this was an important, climactic moment in the process of canonization of the Law, the first section of the Jewish scriptures. The at first mournful and then joyful study of and response to the Law continued throughout the days of the Festival of Tabernacles and was followed by further reforms. Ezra thus had led the struggling returned exiles in solemn but joyful renewal of their commitment to God.

See also CHRONICLES, FIRST AND SECOND; EZRA, BOOK OF; NEHEMIAH, BOOK OF.

Bibliography. L. H. Brockington, *Ezra, Nehemiah and Esther*; F. C. Fenshaw, *The Books of Ezra and Nehemiah*; J. M. Myers, *Ezra-Nehemiah*; H. G. M. Williamson, *Ezra-Nehemiah*.

—DAVID A. SMITH

• **Ezra, Book of.** [ez'ruh] The book of Ezra focuses on the release of Jewish exiles by a decree from the Persian ruler

• OUTLINE OF EZRA •

The Book of Ezra

I. Return to Jerusalem under Sheshbazzar and Restoration of the Temple (1:1–6:22)
   A. Cyrus's decree (1:1-4)
   B. Gifts for restoring the Temple (1:5-11)
   C. List of those who returned (2:1-70)
   D. Restoration of the Temple (3:1-13)
   E. Opposition to restoration of Temple and city (4:1-24)
   F. Completion of the restoration of the Temple (5:1–6:22)

II. Ezra's Return and Reform (7:1–10:44)
   A. Ezra's identity and commission (7:1-26)
   B. Preparations for Ezra's departure (8:1-36)
   C. Ezra's reform (9:1–10:44)

CYRUS, the exiles' return under Sheshbazzar to Jerusalem, the construction there of the Temple and its altar, and the arrival of Ezra in Jerusalem and his initial reform dealing with marriages to foreigners. The story is told so as to emphasize three theological themes: God's use of foreign rulers for Israel's sake, opposition from neighboring peoples, and the separation of Israel from foreigners for the sake of the purity of the people of God. These themes are also prominent in the Book of Nehemiah.

Ezra and Nehemiah were treated as one work in early Jewish tradition and in the canon of the Hebrew Bible. Jewish sages attributed them, along with Chronicles, to Ezra, regarded as a second MOSES. Variations of this view have been accepted by some modern scholars, though few still consider Ezra author of the combined works. A larger number accept the unity of Chronicles and Ezra-Nehemiah, but not Ezra's authorship. They suggest a "Chronicler" who based the Chronicles portion of his "history" on the books of Samuel and Kings and added extensive materials from the priestly archives and from his own post-exilic religious circles. The same author then continued his story in Ezra-Nehemiah using a wide variety of other sources, such as letters, court records, royal decrees, lists, memoirs, and genealogies. Depending on the extent to which the Chronicler is thought to have made an original contribution, he is considered either editor or author of "the Chronicler's history," i.e., Chronicles, Ezra and Nehemiah. Those holding this view see Chronicles and Ezra-Nehemiah bound together by a common ideology, uniform cultic ideas and practices, and similar style. Recent scholarship challenges each of these points and finds different themes in Chronicles and Ezra-Nehemiah. For example, a Davidic covenantal theme dominates in Chronicles, an Exodus theme in Ezra-Nehemiah; the harsh attitude toward foreigners characteristic of Ezra-Nehemiah is virtually absent from Chronicles. These thematic differences argue for an origin of Ezra-Nehemiah apart from Chronicles. If so, the author remains unknown to us.

Together the books of Ezra and Nehemiah present a historical problem. Scholars question the date of Ezra's mission, the extent of his relationship with NEHEMIAH, and the sequence of their respective activities. The narrative as it now stands dates Ezra's arrival in Jerusalem to the seventh year (Ezra 7:7) and Nehemiah's to the twentieth year (Neh 2:1) of the Persian king ARTAXERXES, presumably Artaxerxes I. Ezra's reform activities, therefore, preceded Nehemiah's work on the city walls and his reforms. Both men dealt with the problem of marriages to foreign women, with Ezra's measures apparently being more drastic than Nehemiah's. Some scholars suggest that Ezra followed Nehemiah on the grounds that Ezra's religious reform was more appropriate after the city had been restored and fortified and that Nehemiah's marriage reforms would have been unnecessary after the significant religious reforms of Ezra. They further argue the improbability of the Persian appointment of two men with such closely related responsibilities in the same time period. They suggest either that the reference in Ezra 7:7 to the seventh year is a scribal mistake for the thirty-seventh year, or that Nehemiah came to Jerusalem during the reign of Artaxerxes I and Ezra followed during the reign of Artaxerxes II. Thus they claim Nehemiah's work preceded that of Ezra. Such a sequence would answer the above-mentioned objections and also explain the fact that Ezra is mentioned by name only once in the Nehemiah story, and that nothing is said there about his reform. Recent studies, however, prefer the traditional sequence, Ezra before Nehemiah, arguing that reform in Judah would not have gone smoothly, but would have experienced setbacks. Ezra's religious reforms may not have been fully realized until Nehemiah's appointment as governor of Judah enabled him to rebuild the walls of JERUSALEM and reorganize Judah economically. Canonical critics concerned with reading the text as it now stands state that whatever the historical relationship between Ezra and Nehemiah may have been, the explicit intent of the author was to describe the marriage reforms of both men and the building of the wall by Nehemiah as being significant only in light of the community's acceptance of the TORAH. Nehemiah participated with Ezra in instructing the people in the way of the Law and Ezra shared in the dedication of the wall. The author saw the political and religious activities as together contributing to the reconstitution of Jewish life in Jerusalem.

See also EZRA; NEHEMIAH, BOOK OF.

Bibliography. F. C. Fensham, *The Books of Ezra and Nehemiah*; J. M. Myers, *Ezra-Nehemiah*; H. G. M. Williamson, *Ezra, Nehemiah.*

—DAVID A. SMITH

• **Ezra, Fourth.** [ez'ruh] *Fourth Ezra,* an apocalyptic work in Latin manuscripts which, in an expanded form, is called 2 Esdras in the Apocrypha of English Bibles. This early apocalypse later received a Christian introduction and conclusion (chaps. 1–2; 15–16). The name EZRA was popular among Jews who wished to lend authenticity to their writings, which led to a confusing array of books bearing his name. The term "Fourth Ezra" is the English equivalent of *Esdra liber IV,* so identified in Latin manuscripts. These manuscripts vary on the names of the sections which make up the expanded work, but the usual designations are: chaps. 1–2 = *V Esdras*; chapters 3–14 = *IV Esdras*; and chaps. 15–16 = *VI Esdras*. Today *Fourth Ezra* usually means the *Ezra Apocalypse* (chaps. 3–14), but the Latin Vulgate calls all 16 chaps. *IV Esdras*.

The threefold division of the expanded form of *Fourth Ezra* relates to its composition. Six stages may be seen in this process: (1) The central apocalyptic section (chaps. 3–14) was written in Hebrew or Aramaic by an unknown Jew using the pseudonym of Ezra at the end of the first century C.E.. (2) This apocalyptic work was then translated into Greek shortly thereafter. (3) About the middle of the second century a Christian writer added a Greek introduction (chaps. 1–2). (4) A century later another Christian author added chaps. 15–16. (5) The semitic original of chaps. 3–14 perished, as did all of the Greek manuscripts except a few verses in chap. 15. The work survived in several Eastern languages, but most notable was the Latin text of the Vulgate where all sixteen chaps. appeared as *Fourth Ezra* in the appendix. (6) A missing portion of chap. 7 (vv. 36-105) was discovered in a ninth-century Latin manuscript and subsequently included in the Apocrypha. The section was most likely removed earlier for dogmatic reasons.

Part one of the work is the Christian introduction (chaps. 1–2). The author shows God's deliverance and mercy upon the people Israel (1:12-23), but also how he is unhappy with his people and will choose other nations instead (1:24-40; 2:1-14; 33-41). The main section of the book is the Ezra Apocalypse (chaps. 3–14) which has seven visions of unequal lengths. The first is a dialogue between Ezra and the angel Uriel and concerns God's justice and the approach of the new age (3:1–5:20). The second is a complaint that God has been unfair to his people, but the messenger defends God's action as unknowable but righteous (5:21–6:34). The third vision presents a dialogue about God's creation, the messianic age, and the judgment (6:35–9:25). In the fourth vision, Ezra sees a woman who represents the heavenly ZION mourning over the death of her only son (9:26–10:59). The fifth gives the vision of the eagle which stands for the ROMAN EMPIRE (11:1–12:51). In the sixth vision, Ezra sees a man from the sea who is the preexistent MESSIAH (13:1-58). Vision seven has God commanding Ezra to gather a group of scribes and record the scriptures (14:1-48). The Christian appendix contains denunciations against God's enemies and encouragement for the righteous (chaps. 15–16).

In *Fourth Ezra* the writer believes that God is the creator (6:38-54) who is merciful, but also one who will judge (6:1-6). The Messiah will play a large role in this final judgment at which time he will separate the wicked from the true people of God (12:32-34). The whole human race has turned from God and thus is subject to punishment. Even so, God's justice is questioned in dealing with his own people (5:21-30). The apocalypse concludes by affirming that God's ways are unknowable but his will can be followed in the twenty-four books of the scripture which Ezra miraculously preserved (14:27-48).

See also APOCALYPTIC LITERATURE; APOCRYPHAL LITERATURE; EZRA, FIFTH AND SIXTH.

Bibliography. B. M. Metzger, "The Fourth Book of Ezra," *The Old Testament Pseudepigrapha,* ed. J. H. Charlesworth; J. M. Myers, *I and II Esdras: Introduction, Translation, and Commentary*; A. L. Thompson, *Responsibility for Evil in the Theodicy of IV Ezra.*

—W. THOMAS SAWYER

• **Ezra, Fifth And Sixth.** [ez′ruh] *Fifth and Sixth Ezra/Esdras* are the occasional designations of the two Christian additions to the extracanonical Jewish apocalypse variously referred to as *Ezra Apocalypse,* 4 EZRA/Esdras, or 2 Esdras. In modern editions of the OT Apocrypha and/or Deuterocanonicals, 2 Esdr 3-14 represents the original *Ezra Apocalypse* while 2 Esdr 1–2 and 15–16 represent, respectively, *5 and 6 Ezra/Esdras.*

In some older versions 2 Esdr 1–2 and 15–16 appear as one unit designated *5 Esdras*. In some Catholic Bibles *5 and 6 Esdras* appear with the *Ezra Apocalypse* in an appendix to the NT. In modern English versions *5 and 6 Ezra/Esdras* appear as 2 Esdr 1–2 and 15–16 in the Apocrypha of KJV, RSV, NEB, and follows the Deuterocanonicals/Apocrypha in a section entitled "Some Additional Books" in TEV. The Ezra group of writings resists systematic classification of the various titles of the several books, but the accompanying chart indicates *in general* the various designations in the different version families.

The original *Ezra Apocalypse* (2 Esdr 3–14), reflecting the gloomy pessimism following the destruction of the Temple in 70 C.E. probably was written by a Jew in Hebrew (or Aramaic) around 90 C.E. (?). This *Ezra Apocalypse* was circulated alone until around 150 C.E. when a Jewish Christian added a pro-Christian "foreword" in language often resembling that of the canonical Gospels. This Christian "foreword" (2 Esdr 1–2) is a miniature apocalypse that culminates with a vision of the SON OF GOD and those who "confessed the name of God" rejoicing on Mount ZION (2 Esdr 2:42ff.). It has survived primarily in the various Latin versions where it sometimes appears as a part (2 Esdr 1–2) of the *Ezra Apocalypse* and sometimes as a separate unit designated *5 Ezra/Esdras.*

Later, during the third century (ca. 250 C.E. or as late as 270 C.E.), a pro-Christian "afterword" or "appendix" (with verbal echoes of the NT) was added to the Jewish *Ezra Apocalypse.* This "afterword" also has been preserved primarily in the Latin versions, either as part of *Ezra Apocalypse* (2 Esdr 15–16) or as a separate unit designated *6 Ezra/Esdras. Sixth Ezra* is a dismal description of future sufferings comparable to certain OT prophecies and apocalyptic passages in the gospels. Not only the wicked, *6 Ezra* declares, but also the righteous will suffer various calamities: "Behold, the days of tribulation are at hand [throughout, the emphasis is here], but I will deliver you from them" (2 Esdr 16:74).

See also APOCALYPTIC LITERATURE; EZRA, BOOK OF; EZRA, FOURTH.

Bibliography. H. F. D. Sparks, ed., *The Apocryphal Old Testament*; R. H. Pfeiffer, "The Literature and Religion of the Apocrypha," *IB.*

—EDD ROWELL

• **Ezra, Greek Apocalypse of.** The Greek *Apocalypse of Ezra* purports to record the visions which EZRA received after praying and fasting that he might see the mysteries of God. He is taken up to HEAVEN, where he pleads for God's

DESCRIPTION	SEPTUAGINT EARLY	SEPTUAGINT LATE	OLD LATIN AND VULGATE	MOST ENGLISH VERSIONS	OLDER CATHOLIC
"Greek Ezra"	1 Esdras	1 Ezra	3 Ezra	1 Esdras	(appendix)
Ezra (OT)	2 Esdras 1–10	2 Ezra	1 Ezra	Ezra	1 Esdras
Nehemiah (OT)	2 Esdras 11–23	3 Ezra	2 Ezra	Nehemiah	2 Esdras
Ezra Apocalypse	----	----	4 Ezra	2 Esdras 3–14	(appendix)
Ezra Apoc add. 1	----	----	(5 Ezra)	2 Esdras 1–2	(appendix)
Ezra Apoc add. 2	----	----	(6 Ezra)	2 Esdras 15–16	(appendix)

mercy on sinners. There follows a sustained debate between Ezra and God concerning God's justice and mercy. Along the way, Ezra is led down to Tartarus, where he sees various sinners being punished for their sins. He also sees the ANTICHRIST and learns of both his activity and his doom. He catches a glimpse of PARADISE before descending to the depths of Tartarus and seeing all the sinners lamenting their fate. Finally, the angels come to take Ezra's soul. Ezra resists, so God sends his only begotten Son to complete this task. Ezra continues to resist, arguing that there will be no one left to plead for sinners. Eventually, Ezra proposes that he will give up his soul if God will bless all who preserve and heed Ezra's book. God agrees, and Ezra dies and is buried. The book ends with a Trinitarian doxology.

The Greek *Apocalypse of Ezra* is extant in two poorly preserved Greek manuscripts. The apocalypse was probably composed by a Christian between the second and ninth centuries C. E. Its overall lack of consistency and coherence suggests that the book has undergone considerable redaction. It is closely related to other Ezra books, such as 4 EZRA, the VISION OF EZRA, and the APOCALYPSE OF SEDRACH. It also has strong affinities with other early Christian "tours of hell," such as the APOCALYPSE OF PETER and the APOCALYPSE OF PAUL.

The explicitly Christian elements in the apocalypse are noteworthy. In addition to references to "the Christian people" (e.g., 1:6; 2:7), there is mention of PAUL and JOHN (1:20), in connection with virginity, and PETER, Paul, LUKE, and MATTHEW (5:22), in association with Enoch, ELIJAH, MOSES, and "all the righteous and the patriarchs." One of humanity's sins against God is the CRUCIFIXION (2:25; 7:1). There is also a reference to HEROD's slaughter of the innocents (4:11).

Equally striking is the depiction of the Antichrist (4:25-43). There is both a vivid description of his grotesque appearance and an affirmation that his appearance changes from time to time. He attempts to deceive people into believing that he is the son of God. At the final resurrection he will hide in the outer darkness. God will respond by burning up the heaven, the earth, and the sea.

More central is the book's concern for sin and the certainty of divine punishment. Humanity's predicament looks gloomy; God says, "Your sins exceed my kindness" (2:21). Although "Ezra" never receives a clear answer to his questions about God's goodness and overall plan for the human race, he does receive the assurance that the soul of the "elect ones" departs for heaven even though the body departs for the earth (7:2-3).

The Greek *Apocalypse of Ezra* is not to be confused with the *Ezra Apocalypse* known as 4 Ezra (II Esdras 3–14).

See also APOCALYPTIC LITERATURE; EZRA, FOURTH; HELL; SEDRACH, APOCALYPSE OF.

Bibliography. R. J. Shutt, "The Apocalypse of Esdras," *The Apocryphal Old Testament*, ed. H. F. D. Sparks; M. E. Stone, "Greek Apocalypse of Ezra," *The Old Testament Pseudepigrapha*, ed. J. H. Charlesworth.

—JOSEPH L. TRAFTON

• **Ezra, Revelation of.** The *Revelation of Ezra* is a calendologion, a document which predicts the characteristics of the year according to the day of the week on which the year begins. It purports to be a revelation made by the OT figure EZRA to the children of Israel. Its seven brief sections, one for each day of the week, foretell such matters as seasonal weather conditions, the relative abundance of crops and health of livestock, price levels, diseases, natural disasters, warfare, and the fate of kings.

The Revelation of Ezra is a pseudonymous work composed probably in Latin, the language in which it is extant, before the ninth century C.E. in western Europe or north Africa. The presence of the expression the LORD'S DAY suggests that the author was at least a nominal Christian. On the other hand, the document exudes a deterministic perspective: if the year begins on Monday, certain things will occur. There is neither any mention of God nor any allowance for his involvement in the world. Indeed, Nicephorus, patriarch of Constantinople (ca. ninth century C.E.) condemned calendologia as "profane."

Calendologia and similar writings were very common in the Middle Ages. Because of the popularity of the first-century Jewish pseudepigraphon 4 EZRA, prognosticators took the pseudonym "Ezra" more frequently than any other. Indeed, there exist similar "Ezra" documents in Latin, Greek, English, and Old French.

See also ASTROLOGY; SHEM, TREATISE OF.

Bibliography. D. A. Fiensy, "Revelation of Ezra," *The Old Testament Pseudepigrapha*, ed. J. H. Charlesworth.

—JOSEPH L. TRAFTON

• **Ezra, Vision of.** The *Vision of Ezra* purports to be a vision which EZRA received in response to his prayer for courage when he shall witness the judgments of sinners. In his vision seven angels take him on a tour through various levels of HELL. He sees the punishments of many kinds of sinners including adulterous men and women, incestuous mothers and sons, those who did not receive strangers or give alms, those who refused confession or penance, King HEROD because of his slaughter of the innocents, women who violated their virginity before marriage, false teachers, oppressive rulers, disrespectful children, and women who killed their sons conceived in adultery. The angels MICHAEL and Gabriel then lead Ezra through PARADISE and into HEAVEN, where Ezra requests mercy for the sinners. The Lord answers that they are tormented because of their disobedience, but that the elect will receive eternal rest on account of their confession, penance, and abundance in almsgiving.

The *Vision of Ezra* is a pseudonymous work composed probably in Greek between the fourth and ninth centuries, C.E. It is extant only in Latin. References to the LORD'S DAY, BAPTISM, "confession," and "penance" indicate that the author was a Christian. It is closely related to other books connected with Ezra, especially 4 EZRA, the GREEK APOCALYPSE OF EZRA, and the APOCALYPSE OF SEDRACH. It also has strong parallels to other early Christian "tours of hell," such as the APOCALYPSE OF PETER and the APOCALYPSE OF PAUL. Such writings seem to have served the purpose of encouraging righteous living.

See also APOCALYPTIC LITERATURE; PAUL, APOCALYPSE OF; PETER, APOCALYPSE OF.

Bibliography. J. R. Mueller and G. A. Robbins, "Vision of Ezra," *The Old Testament Pseudepigrapha,* ed. J. H. Charlesworth; R. J. H. Shutt, "The Vision of Esdras," *The Apocryphal Old Testament,"* ed. H. F. D. Sparks.

—JOSEPH L. TRAFTON

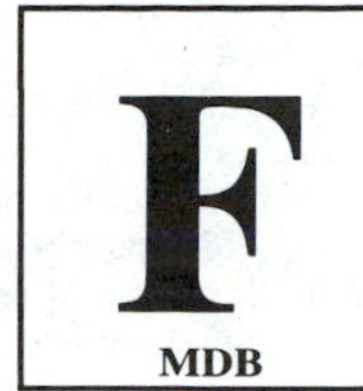

• **Faith.** The word "faith" and related words (believe, faithful, faithfulness) are widely used in the NT. While such words are rare in the Hebrew Bible, the concept of faith there is important, especially for understanding the development of the idea in the NT. The serious student appreciates the range of meanings which attach to the term for and are included in the concept of faith in the Bible. Appreciating this rich variety means not imposing any single understanding on the diverse biblical materials and the varying perspectives of faith contained therein.

Hebrew Bible and Judaism. No Hebrew noun means "faith." The word usually expressing the idea comes from a root (אמן) which can carry the meaning of being firm, faithful, reliable. While the moral character of the one having faith may be part of true faith in God in the Hebrew Bible, the Hebrew term simply means being certain about something or someone, a conclusion supported by the fact that the term is used in a variety of contexts both religious (e.g., Exod 4:1, 5, 9, 31; Ps 78:22; Job 9:16) and nonreligious (e.g., 1 Sam 27:12; 1 Kgs 10:7; Job 15:22) where the reliability of the believer is not an issue. Other "faith" words include a verb which is usually translated "trust" (e.g., Ps 78:22), and a noun which does translate to "firmness" or "faithfulness" but can also be used in both religious and nonreligious contexts (e.g., Hab 2:4; 2 Kgs 22:7).

The meager vocabulary is consistent with the fact that the Hebrew mind tended to think concretely, in contrast with the Greek mind which tended toward abstract conceptual definitions. Moving from a consideration of vocabulary to a more general understanding of the concept of religious faith in ancient Israel, one finds that faith is thoroughly theistic and expressed concretely in stories. That is, faith is illustrated through stories about model individuals and the whole people of God responding positively in OBEDIENCE to God's acts of salvation in history on their behalf. God only is always and absolutely faithful; the people's faithfulness is often contrasted with their faithless disobedience.

The patriarchal narratives and the story of the Exodus-Sinai event stand as the primary pentateuchal expressions of the faithfulness of God and the faith and faithlessness of the people. Regardless of their historicity, a question continually debated, these stories were written much later than the events they allegedly describe, and reflect to a degree Israel's later monotheism and covenant relationship to the one God, a relationship entailing both the privilege of being God's people and the responsibility of conforming to God's will.

The first significant extended narrative about faith and faithlessness is the Abraham cycle of stories (cf. e.g., Gen 12:1-5; 12:10–13:1; 15:1-21; 16:1-4a; 22:1-19), the themes of which are continued through the Isaac, Jacob, and Joseph stories (Gen 12–50). While these narratives focus on individuals, the faith embedded there is reflective of the communal faith of the people of God rather than the individualistically-oriented faith later popular in the Christian religion, in part as a result of Greek influence. God's greatest act of salvation is found in the story of the EXODUS from Egypt and the related stories of God giving the Law at Sinai and leading the people to the promised land (Exodus-Deuteronomy).

In addition to trust and obedience, Israel's faith included WORSHIP. By Solomon's time (ca. 961–922 B.C.E.) Israel was in the process of developing an extensive priestly and sacrificial system which was read back into the stories about the giving of the Law at Sinai. Beginning at least in the eighth century, many of the prophets whose writings found their way into the canon preached against Israel's worship when that "worship" degenerated into hypocritical ceremony devoid of ethical content. Among the prophets, Isaiah speaks more specifically of faith as trust in God in the face of the threat of foreign invasion (e.g., Isa 7:1-9; 28:16; 36-37). Atypically, Deutero-Isaiah (Isa 40–55), along with some Psalms, focuses faith in the direction of the individual.

Postexilic Jewish understanding of faith developed in at least two major directions. First, the element of obedience, always an important component but never the sum total of Israel's faith, moved to center stage. Faith was increasingly understood as keeping TORAH, which included observing the Sabbath and other holy days and, as possible, maintaining the sacrificial system, ideally at the Jerusalem Temple. In part, this move was an attempt to find security in the context of political and cultural uncertainty and the attendant threat to the integrity of Judaism as a people and as a religion. This development continued at least through the beginning of the Christian religion, and can be documented in some of the later books of the Hebrew Bible (e.g., Ezra, Nehemiah), in the Apocrypha, and in the Pseudepigrapha. The rabbis provided authoritative interpretation of the Torah and application of its precepts to every aspect of daily life; their pronouncements on the Torah and on past rabbinic pronouncements were eventually written down in the Mishnah, Talmuds, and other collections. The rabbis equated faith in God and obedience to the Torah, understood as including both the written (Pentateuch) and oral (rabbinic teaching) Torah. After 70 C.E., when the Romans destroyed the Temple, the sacrificial and priestly aspects of

Jewish faith disappeared and Judaism was essentially rabbinic Judaism.

Apocalyptic was a second, very powerful expression of faith, especially during times of persecution. Here faith found release in the people's conviction that their faithful God would certainly and decisively intervene soon to crush the oppressors and restore the fortunes of God's people (e.g., Daniel; noncanonical *1 Enoch*, 2 Esdras).

There were significant exceptions to these trends, as in the more mystical approach of the Hellenistic Jew Philo of Alexandria (20 B.C.E.–49 C.E.), but the thrust was toward and understanding that was practical and legal and/or apocalyptic and away from the earlier, more generalized response to God's saving acts in history.

Classical and Hellenistic Greek Usage. Primary words used by early Christianity to convey the various meanings being discussed were all built from the same stem. These words are the noun "faith" (πίστις), the verb "believe" (πιστεύω), and the adjective (πιστός), which is translated "faithful" or "trustworthy" in the passive sense and "believing" or "trusting" in the active sense. "Unbelief" and "unfaithfulness" were conveyed by adding negative prefixes.

In classical Greek faith meant trust or confidence in, with the object being a wide variety of persons or things. The idea of being certain about something could also be present. Obedience, though not common, could be stressed where the object of faith was a person. In the passive form the word could refer to a thing (e.g., pledge, guarantee, proof) or person (e.g., husband, wife, someone in a contract) as being worthy of trust. The faith word-group was occasionally used with reference to the divine, but often another word for "believe" (νομίζω), rare in the NT, was used in such cases.

In the Hellenistic period, closer to early Christianity, the faith word-group was used in explicitly religious ways. To believe in the gods embraced theoretical conviction as well as piety, sometimes mystically conceived. As religious propaganda, the terms were widely used by various missionary movements, such as mystery cults. Faith in the Isis-Osiris divinities, for example, resulted in mystical union with the gods and eternal life. Non-religious use continued, as with the Stoics where the meaning leaned toward reliability, faithfulness, and harmony, but with reference to oneself and one's moral destiny in the cosmos, not to deity.

It is difficult to generalize; however, it seems that intellectual and individualistic tendencies are more prominent in the Greek context, while obedient and communal tendencies are more prominent in the Jewish.

Jesus and the Synoptic Gospels. Among NT scholars the question of Jesus' understanding of faith has produced more ink than answers. The issue is complicated since the primary sources for the JESUS of history, namely the synoptic Gospels, were written from about 65–90 C.E., that is, some 30–60 years after the Christ-event, and reflect to some degree the developing theology of the church rather than the life and teachings of the historical Jesus. The earliest NT writings, those of Paul, which date in the 50s and 60s, provide practically no information about the historical Jesus. In the Synoptics faith plays a minor role, especially when they are compared to the Pauline and Johannine writings. The noun "faith" and the verb "believe" occur only eleven times in Mark, the earliest Gospel, and, concerning faith, neither Matthew nor Luke add significantly to their source Mark.

Despite the lateness of the sources and the minimal number of references, scholars have probed for the historical Jesus' notion of faith. The most fruitful investigations have concentrated on the synoptic miracle stories where the terms for faith are most common. Scholars once dismissed these stories as later legendary additions to authentic Jesus material. However, form-critical examinations strongly suggest that in his day Jesus was viewed as healer and exorcist, though careful scholars refrain from making judgments about the true nature of the sicknesses and possessions.

Faith plays a crucial role in the MIRACLES, especially the healings, with "Your faith has made you well" being the usual statement found (e.g., Mark 5:34-36/Matt 9:22/Luke 8:48-50; Mark 6:5-6/Matt 13:58; Mark 10:52/Luke 18:42; Matt 8:13; 9:28-29; 15:28; Luke 7:9, 50; 17:19). Attention is called to the importance of faith in other MIRACLE STORIES in other ways (e.g., Mark 4:40/Luke 8:25; Matt 8:23-27; 14:31). Matthew sometimes redacts his source by adding his version of the faith statement (Matt 8:13; 9:29; 15:28) and sometimes he connects faith and understanding (e.g., 16:5-12). Important is the Q saying about the miraculous power of faith, even faith as small as the tiny mustard seed (Matt 17:20/Luke 17:6; cf. Mark 11:22-24/Matt 21:21-22; 1 Cor 13:2; and the Gnostic *GosThom* 48, 106). Faith is mentioned in connection with the forgiveness of sins (Mark 2:5/Matt 9:2/Luke 5:20; Luke 7:50).

It is, then, the incredible power of faith to effect miracles which is emphasized in Jesus' teaching. Noticeably absent is faith directed at Jesus to achieve salvation, traditionally understood. Only twice (Matt 18:6; 27:42) is reference made to having faith in Jesus (Mark 16:16 is not in the best manuscripts, and Mark 9:42 [which is sometimes translated "believe in me"] is also questionable on textual grounds) and in both instances Matthew has added prepositions (me, him) to Mark's version (Mark 9:42; 15:32).

The role of faith in miracles is highlighted when the Jesus exorcism-miracle tradition is compared with similar stories current in Jesus' day. Many details in the Synoptics are paralleled in Hellenistic and Jewish literature; the one thing absent is faith. Because the understanding of faith in the Jesus material is dissimilar to that in Hellenism, Judaism, and (as will be shown) the early church, it is likely that the role assigned to faith in the Synoptics derives from the historical Jesus.

Finally, the main theme of Jesus' teaching was an apocalyptic notion, the KINGDOM OF GOD. Exorcisms and miracles were manifestations of the Kingdom which was being or soon would be established. Faith is not mentioned explicitly with reference to the Kingdom of God, and while speculation about Jesus' faith is precarious, perhaps it can safely be said that for Jesus faith in or on God involved trust that God was acting or would act on behalf of the people, and Jesus so challenged his hearers to have similar trust in God's power and providence. This apocalyptic dimension of his ministry, of which the exorcism-healing tradition was a part, sets Jesus firmly in the Jewish tradition and its conception of faith.

Primitive Christianity and Paul. While attempts have been made to reconstruct the theology of the church in the first ten to fifteen years after Jesus, Paul's letters, the first of which probably date from the early 50s, constitute the primary early witness to the developing theology of primitive Christianity. Set in the context of other critical Pauline themes, faith is, roughly, the appropriate human response to God's graceful salvific act in Christ, a response in which one accepts God's righteousness offered in Christ rather than attempts to earn it through vain self effort. In Paul's theological scheme of things, all persons are separated from God because of sin (Rom 3:23), a reality evidenced among Jews by their having not kept the Law perfectly (e.g., Gal 5:2-3; Rom 2:17-25) and among gentiles by their having not responded positively to the revelation of God in nature (Rom 1:18-23) and conscience (Rom 2:14-16).

The solution to the sin problem—righteousness—is an act of grace on God's part since it is God's righteousness freely offered in Christ. "Justification," Paul's primary word for this salvific process, is itself a version of the word for righteousness and can be translated "make righteous." In any case, salvation is, at least initially, a movement from God to persons rather than vice versa (Rom 1:16-17); so it is God's grace rather than human works of the Law (Gal 2:16; 5:4). The Law reveals sin (Gal 3:23-24; Rom 3:20) but it cannot produce righteousness. The human response to God's offer is to accept the gift (Rom 5:17), to believe on or in Christ (Gal 2:16; cf. Rom 10:9), and to confess Jesus' lordship (Rom 10:9-10). Faith, necessary initially, continues to be essential to the Christian experience (e.g., Gal 4:1-5:1; 5:6, 13-15; Rom 6:5-11).

Some (e.g., Rudolf Bultmann) view faith as the basic grid for understanding Paul's whole theology, but caution is advisable because all of Paul's books were letters written to specific audiences and to address specific issues. In the above summary of Paul's thought all the references about faith derive from two books (Galatians and Romans). By viewing Paul's teaching in light of concrete historical circumstances, his emphasis on faith as opposed to works is understandable, especially the formulations in Galatians. Paul was primarily a church organizer and one of his most troubling problems was with Judaizers—Jewish Christians attempting to convince gentile Christians the latter had to keep the works of the Jewish Law, namely circumcision and dietary prescriptions. In retrospect, this critical issue conceivably could have determined whether Christianity developed as a separate religion or remained a Jewish sect. From a geographical and chronological perspective, the centrality of faith over works of the Law reflects the movement of Christianity deeper into the Hellenistic world and away from its Jewish base.

Paul disagreed with the Judaizers and argued vigorously—in Galatians and Romans—that only faith was required of Jew and gentile. Clearly Paul felt strongly about this, a fact evidenced by the anger exhibited in the Galatian letter. There he claims that the interpretation came directly through a revelation of Christ (1:12), twice damns the Judaizers (1:8, 9), and, lest anyone question the intensity of his anger, says he hopes the knife the Judaizers are using for circumcision slips! (5:12).

The centrality of saving faith in Galatians and Romans and the depth of feeling exhibited in the former book are testimonies to the importance of faith to Paul. On the other hand, the subject of faith rarely appears in his other letters (although the term "the believing ones" is found often). So it is safe to say faith was important, but because Paul did not write a comprehensive and systematic theology, the extent of faith's importance in his total thought is debatable. In a related issue, Paul sometimes (e.g., Gal 3:22; Rom 3:22) uses "faith" in a Greek form that can legitimately be translated either "faith in Christ" or "the faith of Christ." Most scholars think the former translation is the meaning intended, but some argue for the second which, by referring to Christ as a model of faith, perhaps mitigates against overemphasizing human faith.

The significant shift from Jesus to the post-Easter theology of the church should be underscored. Faith in Jesus was limited to a role in the exorcism-miracle tradition; Paul and his brand of primitive Christianity moved faith in Jesus to the center of one's relationship with God. To use a well-worn but apt phrase, Jesus proclaimed the Kingdom of God, the church proclaimed faith in Jesus.

Johannine Literature. Consistent with his preference for verbs over nouns, in John the verb "believe" (in various forms and usually referring to salvific faith) comes to the fore (107 times; only 34 times in all three Synoptics); the noun "faith," very common in the Synoptics and Paul, is absent from John.

Concerning faith, the Fourth Gospel reflects more the developed thinking of the early church than it does that of Jesus. To put it another way, faith in John is more like that in Paul than in the Synoptics, though there are certain distinctive Johannine usages. The form "believe in" or "on," found occasionally in other NT books (eight times), is clearly a favorite (thirty-nine times), and reflects John's stress on the believer's personal trust, active commitment, and total reliance. It is a uniquely Christian idiom; with the possible exception of the Dead Sea Scrolls, this use has no parallels outside Christian literature. The object of "believe in" is usually Christ (thirty-one times, e.g., 3:15-18a; cf 1:12; 3:18b; 14:1).

While the personal dimension, which some relate to possible mystical tendencies in John, is prominent, belief understood more as intellectual assent is also present. One "believes *that*" Jesus is the Christ, the Son of God (11:27), was sent by God (11:42), and is the "I am" (13:19). Although not synonyms, believing and knowing are closely related (e.g., 6:69; 16:30; 17:8; 21-23). Not present in John is the Gnostic notion of two classes of people: persons of faith and a higher class of persons of knowledge.

Compared to the Synoptics, the most distinctive use of faith in John relates to miracles, which John usually calls "signs." In the Synoptics, the miracles—usually called "power acts," a term not found in John—show forth the inbreaking Kingdom of God and are generally performed in response to faith. John has no exorcisms and the seven miracles recorded serve to authenticate the person and mission of Jesus (20:31) and symbolize aspects of John's theology (e.g., 6:1-15; 22-71; 9:1-41; 11:1-57). In other words, in the Synoptics, faith produces miracles; in John, miracles evoke faith. Up to four levels of belief have been identified. Some refuse to see signs and refuse to believe (e.g., 11:47), some see signs but misinterpret Jesus as a wonder-worker only (e.g., 2:23–3:5; 7:3-7), some perceive the true meaning of signs and believe (e.g., 4:53-54; 9:38), and some believe without the aid of signs (e.g., 20:29).

So, in the context of John's "high" Christology, saving faith is understood as believing in Jesus as, or believing that Jesus is, God, the eternal Logos. Consistent with Paul, the object of faith is Christ, though John pays (at least explicitly) little or no attention to the antithesis between faith and works of the Law.

Other NT Writings. As the church moved further away from its vibrant early experience of what it understood to be the risen Lord, and worked to define itself over against "heretical" teaching, perhaps it was inevitable that faith would increasingly be understood, especially in the later documents, as correct doctrine (e.g., Col 1:23; 2:7; 1 Tim 1:10, 19; 4:1; Jude 3). James, in a famous passage always compared with Paul, claims that faith without works is dead

(2:14-22), but in this apparent contradiction with Paul, James uses faith to mean mere intellectual assent to doctrines.

For the author of Hebrews faith is that awareness of the ideal world, including God, which enables one to stand true in the face of persecution (e.g., 3:14; 11:1). Heroes of the Jewish tradition are models of faith (11:1-40). Although reference is made to Jesus as a model of faith (12:1-2), there is very little in the book that is specifically Christian. Noteworthy in Hebrews is the closest thing in the Bible to a definition of faith (11:1).

In all of these other NT writings the christological orientation of Paul and John falls away.

See also ESCHATOLOGY IN THE NEW TESTAMENT; ESCHATOLOGY IN THE OLD TESTAMENT; EXODUS; GALATIANS, LETTER TO THE; GOD; GRACE; HOPE IN THE NEW TESTAMENT; HOPE IN THE OLD TESTAMENT; JESUS; KINGDOM OF GOD; LAW IN THE NEW TESTAMENT; LAW IN THE OLD TESTAMENT; LOVE IN THE NEW TESTAMENT; LOVE IN THE OLD TESTAMENT; MIRACLE STORY; MIRACLES; OBEDIENCE; PAUL; RIGHTEOUSNESS IN THE NEW TESTAMENT; RIGHTEOUSNESS IN THE OLD TESTAMENT; ROMANS, LETTER TO THE; SALVATION IN THE NEW TESTAMENT; SALVATION IN THE OLD TESTAMENT; SIGNS AND WONDERS; TORAH; WORSHIP IN THE NEW TESTAMENT; WORSHIP IN THE OLD TESTAMENT.

Bibliography. J. Barr, *The Semantics of Biblical Language*; H. W. Bartsch, "The Concept of Faith in Paul's Letter to the Romans," *BR* 13 (1968): 41-53; M. A. Beavis, "Mark's Teaching on Faith," *BTB* 16/4 (Oct 1986): 139-42; R. E. Brown, *The Gospel According to John*; R. Bultmann, *Theology of the New Testament*; C. H. Dodd, *The Bible and the Greeks* and *The Interpretation of the Fourth Gospel*; W. Eichrodt, *Theology of the Old Testament*; V. P. Furnish, *Theology and Ethics in Paul*; H. J. Hermisson and E. Lohse, *Faith*; A. J. Hultgren, "The *Pistis Christou* Formulation in Paul," *NovT* 22/3 (Jul 1980): 248-63; J. Jeremias, *New Testament Theology: The Proclamation of Jesus*; W. Kramer, *Christ, Lord, Son of God*; G. E. Ladd, *A Theology of the New Testament*; N. Perrin, *Rediscovering the Teachings of Jesus*; D. E. H. Whiteley, *The Theology of St. Paul*; S. K. Williams, "Again *Pistis Christou*," *CBQ* 49/3 (Jul 1987): 431-47.

—CALVIN MERCER, JR.

• **Faith and Faithlessness.** FAITH is loyalty to God. It is a COVENANT relation based upon belief in the faithfulness of God. God's faithfulness is one of the five greatest attributes of God mentioned in the OT (Exod 34:6). It is therefore always in the background of all teachings about the faithfulness required of humans in relation to God and of all teachings about faithlessness.

Faithlessness is the opposite of faithfulness, and is treated explicitly and implicitly as such throughout the Bible. Deut 32:20 describes a perverse generation as faithless, and this belief promoted the great reformation in the time of Josiah (640–609 B.C.E.). The most influential proclamation of covenant fidelity was in the dialogue of Habakkuk with the Lord of the covenant. Faithlessness as well as faithfulness are involved. In answer to Habakkuk's complaint that God used wicked Babylon to punish his righteous people (1:12-2:1), the Lord declares (2:4): "Behold, he whose soul in not upright in him shall fail, but the righteous shall live by his faithfulness." The RSV and the NIV use the word "faith" instead of "faithfulness" (which they place in a note). But the translation "faithfulness" is nearer the meaning of the original and is very important for understanding why this was so important for the covenant people at Qumran and in the three classical quotations of the passage in the NT (Gal 3:11; Rom 1:17ff.; Heb 2:4).

This essay focuses upon key passages which deal directly and indirectly with the relationship between faith (faithfulness) and faithlessness.

Faith and Faithlessness in Paul. At the very heart of the Pauline canon is the citation of Hab 2:4 in Gal 3:11. In this Letter, the call for the faithfulness of the believer is critical to understanding what has come to be called "justification by faith." It would be better to speak of "righteousness as faithfulness." Believers who become unfaithful are accused of "deserting him who called you in the grace of Christ and turning to a different gospel" (1:6). Those who had received the spirit by "the hearing of faith" were now about to end "with the flesh" (3:1-5). Abraham is typical of all "men of faith who are the sons of Abraham" (3:7). The ethical implication of Paul's view of righteousness as faithfulness is "faith working through love" (5:6). One can "submit again to a yoke of slavery," be "severed from Christ," and "fall out of grace."

Paul's Letter to the Romans makes Hab 2:4 the theme of his gospel as he declares: "For I am not ashamed of the gospel: it is the power of God for salvation to everyone who has faith, to the Jew first and also to the Greek. For in it the righteousness of God is revealed from faith for faith; as it is written, 'He who through faith is righteous shall live' " (1:16f.). Faith as obedience (cf. 1:5; 16:26) is central in all parts of this most important writing on faith. Israel was broken off as branches of a vine because of unbelief; and Gentiles were grafted in because of belief. Gentile believers, too, can be broken off if they do not continue to believe and Israel can be grafted in again in they come to believe (11:17-24). A classic expression of the degrees of faith is found in 12:1-6. Weak believers may stumble and fall by becoming unbelievers (14:13-23). Paul did not hesitate to use the term "law of faith" (3:27) as well as the word of faith (10:8). When Luther added "*allein*" (alone) to his German translation of Rom 3:28 as "faith alone" he put Paul in opposition to James. This was an unfortunate error.

Faith and Unbelief in Hebrews. The use of "full assurance" (πληροφορία) in Heb 10:22 belongs to the important teaching of faith as a pilgrimage from childhood to maturity (5:11-6:3) and from promise to complete fulfillment in the way of faith (11:13-16, 32-40). The Exodus model out of Egypt into the promised land dominates the life of faith: It is not enough to cross the Red Sea unless spiritual life continues from oasis to oasis into the promised land of full salvation.

The five exhortations against APOSTASY in Hebrews (2:1-5; 3:7-4:11; 15:11-6:20; 10:19-39; 12:1-29) are most instructive for the understanding of faith. The second exhortation clearly considers apostasy or falling away the same as unbelief and disobedience. The fifth exhortation in Hebrews which concludes with a comment on Hab 2:2-4 calls the righteous to live by faith. Hebrews clearly distinguishes two types of believers: those who shrink back and are "destroyed" and "those who have faith and keep their souls" (10:39).

Faith and Works in James. The discussion on faith and works in Jas 2:14-26 has been called the "theological core" of James. James seems to be concerned about an early antignosticism, that is, the teaching that one could be saved by faith that was not manifested in works of love. James raised the question: "Can this faith save him" (2:15). His answer is: "So faith by itself, if it has no works is dead" (2:17). Abraham did indeed believe the promise of the Lord in Genesis 15:6, but "faith was completed by works," when, in obedience to the Lord, he was willing to offer his son Isaac in sacrifice (Gen 22:1-14). To make sure that his reader does not assume that Abraham's faith without works merited salvation, he calls on the testimony of Rahab the harlot who received Israel's messengers. He concludes and repeats "for as the body apart from the spirit is dead, so faith apart from works is dead" (2:26). Much criticism that claims that James contradicts Paul has confused the works of love with the works of ceremonial law; but Paul's ethical teaching in Gal 5:6 says much the same as James: "For in Jesus Christ neither circumcision nor uncircumcision is of any avail, but faith working through love."

Faith and Growth in Grace in Second Peter and Jude. The whole of 2 Peter is a polemic against false teachers "who will secretly bring in destructive heresies, even denying the master who bought them, bringing upon themselves swift destruction" (2:1). After many OT examples and some vivid illustrations, the diaspora of believers are warned about the danger of apostasy in which "the last state has become worse for them than the first" (2:20). The conclusion states the theme of 2 Peter: "You therefore, beloved, knowing this beforehand, beware lest you be carried away with the error of lawless men and lose your own stability. But grow in the grace and knowledge of our Lord and Savior Jesus Christ" (3:17f.).

Those who "never fall" are those who grow in grace, supplementing faith with virtue, knowledge, self-control, steadfastness, godliness, brotherly affection, and love. He who lacks these supplements goes "blind and shortsighted and has forgotten that he was cleansed from his old sins" (2 Pet 1:9).

Jude has perhaps been used by 2 Peter too, and the whole question that calls for believers "to contend for the faith which was once for all delivered to the saints" (3) is greatly illuminated by the contrast of apostate persons (3-16) with those who continue in "the faith" of apostolic Christianity (17-23). There are those "who pervert the grace of our God into lasciviousness and deny our only Master and Lord, Jesus Christ." These apostates are "twice dead," dead before they were believers and dead again in apostasy (12), but those who build themselves up in "the most holy faith" keep themselves in "the love of God" and live in the hope of eternal life (20-21) are secure in their salvation. Again the "theological virtues" are the stages in salvation for the spiritually mature. It is promised that the mature believers will be kept from falling by the power of God (24ff.). This teaching is "the faith."

Faith and Perseverance. For Paul, the whole of the Christian life is a walk by faith (2 Cor 5:7); therefore, mature faith increases (2 Cor 10:15). The challenge to the Corinthians was: "examine yourselves, to see whether you are holding to your faith. Test yourselves. Do you not realize that Jesus Christ is in you—unless indeed you failed to meet the test. I hope that you will find out that we have not failed" (2 Cor 13:5-6). The very same word meaning castaway or disqualified is used by Paul when he speaks of his own spiritual discipline (1 Cor 9:27).

In most of the NT there is movement from faith as personal trust to faith as a summary of beliefs. This is most obvious in the Pauline canon. By time the Pastoral Epistles are reached, "faith" is usually "the faith." If there is a corrective to the use of the faith as a noun in the Pastoral Epistles and elsewhere, it is surely found in the Johannine canon. Not once does the Gospel of John use faith as a noun. It is always the verb "I believe" not the noun "belief" or "faith" that is used. Belief is always a process that must be continued as the mark of the true disciple of Jesus. Only once do the Johannine Epistles use the noun "belief" (1 John 5:4). The Book of Revelation does retain the noun four times (2:13, 19; 13:10; 14:12), but the NASB preserves the idea of personal obedience with a translation: "Here is the perseverance of the saints who keep the commandments of God and their faith in Jesus" (14:12).

See also APOSTASY; COVENANT; FAITH.

—DALE MOODY

• **Faithlessness.** *See* FAITH AND FAITHLESSNESS

• **Fall.** This is the name that, in Christian theology, is given to the disobedience of ADAM and EVE in EDEN. This disobedience resulted in an alienation between human beings and God that has affected their relationship throughout time. However, for the Yahwistic writer this account is a means of answering a series of questions, such as: Why is there pain at childbirth? Why is there enmity between snakes and human beings? Why is human life so difficult? The concept of a fallen state for all humankind based on the SIN of Adam and Eve was foreign to the OT mind. The use of this same type of story is found as the backdrop of Ezek 28 concerning the fall of the mighty (i.e., the King of Tyre).

In the story found in Genesis, the eating of the fruit of the tree was a direct challenge to God's authority over and judgment for human beings. They have been given the ability by God to choose between obedience and disobedience. Therefore, the disorder or evil in the world (a world that was declared to be very good) is the result of human frailties, not the working of God. With the assertion of the SERPENT that human beings will become like God and not die, the woman's choice mechanism is now activated. The judgment is made and acted upon, then shared with her partner. The sin is not completed until both have chosen, which shows the social aspect of sin. The immediate consequence seems to be good, for the eyes of the couple are opened. Though physical death did not come immediately, the death of the initially perfect relationship between humankind and God has occurred. Obedience and trust have suffered grievously and the human condition finds itself explained. Yet, though that condition seems to be a common one, the text does not state that the sin will be passed on to each successive generation. In fact, according to Ezek 18, each generation has its own opportunity to overcome or to sin.

In the Christian tradition, Adam, as the type of humanity, sets the tone for the doctrine of humankind and its relationship with God. Human beings were filled with righteousness but also had an inclination toward unrighteousness. In what is also called the original sin, many believe that the first human pair fell and transmitted that corrupted nature to subsequent generations. When Adam fell, he lost the splendor that he had, and because of this sin, all of creation lost its perfection.

The thought of PAUL concerrning the Fall has been influential throughout Christian traditions. When Paul speaks of the universal nature of sin, he is stating an existing reality. Yet, he also speaks of the beginning of that reality in Rom 5:12ff. In this passage, Paul seems to be explaining how in both Adam's sin and Christ's suffering and death, humankind is universally affected. Just as in one man's sin the relationship between human beings and God suffered and death came as punishment for the human tendency to sin, so in one man, Christ, the relationship between humankind and God is set right. Everlasting life becomes the reward for choosing righteousness. Also, in Rom 5:12, not only is death the universal consequence of the first sin, but in the phrase "because all have sinned," Paul contends that all die because of individual sin. Therefore, though death became a reality because of Adam's sin, each person assumes personal responsibility and cannot blame his or her fate on inherited sin. As each person grows into a self-conscious moral individual who places self at the center of the universe, he/she works out an individual heritage in separation from God. Hence, in a sinful world, as each one chooses and fails to live up to God's design and plan, that one vicariously participates in his/her own "fall," which is patterned after the first.

See also ADAM; SIN.

Bibliography. D. M. Baillie, *God Was in Christ*; J. L. Crenshaw, *Story and Faith*; E. E. Halevy, "Adam," *EncJud*; W. G. Kümmel, *The Theology of the New Testament*; H. Ridderbos, *Paul: An Outline of His Theology*; E. A. Speiser, "Genesis," *AB*.

—STEPHEN Z. HEARNE

• **Fallen Angels.** The fallen angels are referred to twice in the NT; in one instance they are described as the angels who sinned (2 Pet 2:4) and in the other as "the angels that left their proper dwelling" (Jude 6). Both references reflect the prevalent first-century Jewish understanding found in the noncanonical works of I ENOCH and JUBILEES and rabbinic writings.

The Jewish tradition apparently was based on the brief reference to "the sons of God" marrying and mating with women in Gen 6:1-4. The tradition is divided as to the reason the angels came to earth; one source relates that two hundred angels descended because of their lust for beautiful women (*1 Enoch* 6:1-6), while another states that God dispatched the angels to earth to instruct persons and that after arriving the angels lusted and fell (*Jub* 4:15). In any case, the result of the angels' mating with humans was massive increase in lawlessness and bloodshed on earth; and the four archangels cried out to God to stop the murderers (*1 Enoch* 9:1). God's response to the angelic prayers was to send one archangel, Uriel, to warn Noah of the coming flood which would destroy the offspring of the fallen angels (*1 Enoch* 10:1-3) and to send another archangel, Michael, to seize and imprison the sinful angels in a place of darkness (*1 Enoch* 10:11-12). The site of the imprisonment is not given a name in the Jewish tradition; but the Greek name for such a place of darkness is Tartarus, hence the NT use of this Greek term in Jude 6 to refer to the "nether gloom" of the angelic imprisonment.

See also ANGEL; ENOCH, FIRST; HELL; JUBILEES, BOOK OF; JUDE, LETTER OF; PETER, LETTERS OF.

—HAROLD S. SONGER

• **False Witness.** *See* PERJURY

• **Family.** "Family" (Heb. *bêt 'āb*, "father's house"; *bayit*, "house"; Gk. *oikia*, "house"), the basic unit of Israelite society during biblical times. The family provided the usual context for economic survival, intimacy, procreation, child-rearing, companionship, and self-identity. At the same time, it contributed to the larger society in judicial, economic, military, political, religious, and informal ways. As a result of these multiple roles, the preservation and protection of the family constituted one of the legal and moral priorities of Israel, and its importance is frequently reflected in the biblical literature.

Through archaeological excavations an ever-increasing amount of information about family life in Israel is coming to light. Dating from the beginning of the Iron Age Period (twelfth century B.C.E.), more than 100 small villages have been discovered in the highland area stretching north to south in Israel, the region that the early Israelites probably first settled. The vast majority of these villages were less than seven acres in size and were comprised in each case of a cluster of families, for a total usually of 100–200 inhabitants. Small villages of this type continued to hold much of the country's population throughout Israel's history, although cities increased in size and number and resulted thereby in different social and economic conditions for the families dwelling there.

Three types of family structure existed throughout Israel's history in both village and city contexts. The smallest was the *nuclear family*, comprised of the parents, their children (with a high infant mortality rate, only two or three children would normally survive), and any slaves that the family was able to afford. Larger was the *extended family*, in which other relatives (e.g., widowed grandmothers, aunts, uncles, as well as unmarried siblings of the household head) lived together with the nuclear family. Beyond this was the *multiple-family household*, differing from the former in that two or more married couples, normally related and each with its own children, resided in a shared compound under the head of the father (or grandfather) or the oldest married brother. This resulted from patriarchal customs: male children married and brought their wives into the family, while daughters went to live with their husbands' families after marriage. At the death of the father, the next generation of parents could either separate and start their own nuclear or extended families, or they might choose to continue this multiple-family structure with the eldest brother as the new household head. Since throughout most of Israel's history and in most geographical localities the family served as the basic social as well as economic unit, a larger household was usually able to meet such needs better than a nuclear family could. Yet it is estimated that, due to the rather high mortality rate, perhaps at any one time not many more than half of the families were the extended or multiple type.

Housing was constructed according to the size and livelihood of the family. Typically a house had two to four rooms, often with a pillared wall that could help support a second floor and also partition off a side room where any animals could be quartered. The largest room or an adjacent courtyard served as the center for food preparation, small craft making, and other family activities. To accommodate multiple-family units, two or more such houses, each with its own separate entrance, were connected around a shared courtyard. If each family member needed on average about ten square meters of roofed space (as is evidenced from comparable cultures in similar climate), the size and layout of these houses would indicate that the nuclear family in Israel generally included four to five persons, while the extended and multiple-family household rarely exceeded fifteen.

Life within the family encompassed the normal activities of work, enjoyment, child-rearing, caring for the elderly, and relating to others in the community. Consistent with the patriarchal nature of the society and apparent in the usual Hebrew word for family (*bêt 'āb* = "father's house"), the primary authority rested with the father, or with the grandfather when several generations lived together. Together with the other household heads in the community—especially in village contexts—he was expected, as an elder, to help in adjudicating legal matters, deciding on political issues at the village and tribal levels, and participating in public religious observances. A man could have more than one wife, and there are ample instances of this in the Hebrew Bible (e.g., JACOB, ESAU, GIDEON, Samuel's father, DAVID, SOLOMON, and other kings; see also Deut 21:15-17), although monogamy was most common if for no other reasons than cost and domestic tranquility.

An adult woman in the family was legally considered to be under the authority of the male head of the household—first her father, then her husband after marriage. If a woman's husband died, she could hope to be cared for by her adult children, or if there were none she would normally return to her father's home or be taken in by the next closest kin. The book of Ruth deals with some of the complexities of these practices, while Deut 25:5-10 prescribes the institution of levirate marriage, according to which a brother of a deceased husband should marry the widow. In the everyday life of the family, the status of the wife, although decidedly inferior to that of her husband, was nonetheless substantial, and Hebrew law ensured her certain rights. The husband could not sell his wife into slavery to pay off debts, unless they both were to be sold. A woman attained prestige especially through bearing children and through the work she did to benefit the family (Prov 31:10-31). The children were required to honor her as much as their father. As a wife, the woman deserved love and respect from her husband, and a high value was placed on good companionship between them. The book of Song of Songs, while not directly dealing with the family, celebrates a relationship between a man and a woman that is based more on mutuality and intimacy than on hierarchy. Divorce, initiated only by the husband, could dissolve the marriage but did not prohibit the woman from remarrying.

Children were highly prized in the Israelite family, not the least because they meant labor resources, continuation of the lineage, protection against various threats to the family, social esteem, and insurance for the parents in old age. The young were probably cared for by the mother in early age. When a boy entered puberty, his father assumed the responsibility for teaching him a trade and preparing him for adulthood, while the mother continued to instruct the girl in domestic skills until her marriage. There is some evidence of actual schools at various points in Israel's history, but generally the family constituted the setting for most education and socialization, including teaching the children the national and religious traditions (Exod 10:2; 12:26-27; Deut 4:9; 6:7). Sons apparently had more rights and privileges than daughters, and the eldest son normally received at least a double portion of the inheritance. The authority of the parents, particularly the father, was absolute. Presumably only as a last resort would children be sold into slavery to pay off family debts, but after the father's death a creditor could demand it (2 Kgs 4:1). Strict disciplining of children is urged for their own benefit (Prov 13:24; 22:15) as well as for the parents' (Prov 29:15, 17; Sir 30:1-13). The commandment to honor one's father and mother (Exod 20:12) was probably directed less toward small children than toward adults, whose responsibility it was to care for their elderly parents, just as they would want for themselves in old age. Similarly, the severe law prescribing death for a stubborn and rebellious son (Deut 21:18-21) may refer to an adult, not a minor, whose behavior is a threat to the family's integrity and survival.

The relationship of families to the larger society follows a pattern of ever-widening circles. A number of families living in proximity together, whether in a village or in a section of a larger settlement, could constitute a *mišpāḥâ*, or "clan." As a group they could meet certain social and economic needs better than an individual family could manage, e.g., food production, manufacture of a variety of domestic goods, trade, protection against external threats. At the next higher level of society was the tribe (*šēbeṭ* or *maṭṭeh*), comprised of many such clans in a more extensive land area; and wider than this in turn was the nation or league of tribes. A prime example of these multiple levels of society is the judicial process of elimination, recorded in Joshua 7, which moved by stages from the tribes down through the clans and (multiple-)family groups and finally to the individual Achan, who was then punished together with his nuclear family.

An indication of the family's importance in Israel is the frequent theological use made of familial images in the Hebrew Bible. Thus Yahweh takes Israel as his bride (Jer 2:2) and keeps her as wife (Isa 54:4-8), even though Israel too often becomes unfaithful to the bond (Hos 1–3; Jer 3:20; Ezek 16). God sustains compassionately from birth (Isa 46:3-4), provides (Jer 3:19) and protects (Ps 146:9) as a father, feeds (Hos 11:4) and clothes as a mother (Gen 3:21), and redeems as the nearest kin (Isa 43:14; Job 19:25; Ps 78:35). The divine purpose is to keep the family Israel together (Isa 63:16) and to ensure its well-being (Deut 32:6). While disciplinary measures will be taken as needed (Deut 8:5; Hos 11:1-7), God will not ultimately abandon the people (Jer 31:9, 20).

In NT times, family life in Palestine, especially in rural villages, continued along lines quite similar to those described for ancient Israel. Domestic architecture was of a comparable style, suggesting parallel patterns in family structure and livelihood. The NT underscores the proper unity intended for a marriage relationship by citing the creation account of Genesis (Mark 10:6-8). Disputes in the Jewish community about divorce gave rise to NT positions more restrictive than those in the Hebrew Bible (e.g., Mark 10:2-5, 9-12; Matt 5:32; cf. Deut 24:1-4). Jesus, also in contrast to the practices of many, showed high esteem frequently for women as well as for children (Mark 10:13-16). In 1 Tim 5:3-6 is advice on what should be expected of widows, depending upon their age, and the requirement of children to care for their elderly widowed mothers is consistent with Israelite practice. Paul urged relationships within the household to be in the form of mutual commitment and subjection to each other (Eph 5:21–6:9; Col 3:18–4:1). With emphasis on the radical claims of the Gospel, however, Jesus announced the divisive effects that his message could have on family ties (Matt 10:35-37; Luke 14:26; 12:52-53), and Paul even advised against marriage at all, if this would be possible for an individual (I Cor 7). Especially notable, however, is the way in which the NT uses the marriage and family models to express the relationship—now not between God and Israel—but between Christ and the church (2 Cor 11:2; Eph 5:23-27, 32; "the household of faith," Gal 6:10).

See also DIVORCE; MARRIAGE IN THE NEW TESTAMENT; MARRIAGE IN THE OLD TESTAMENT; WOMEN IN THE NEW TESTAMENT; WOMEN IN THE OLD TESTAMENT.

Bibliography. L. E. Stager, "The Archaeology of the

Family in Ancient Israel,'' *BASOR* 260 (1985): 1-35; N. K. Gottwald, *The Tribes of Yahweh: A Sociology of the Religion of Liberated Israel, 1250–1050 B.C.E.*; R. de Vaux, *Ancient Israel: Its Life and Institutions*; H. W. Wolff, *Anthropology of the Old Testament*; Y. Shiloh, ''The Four-Room House: Its Situation and Function in the Israelite City,'' *IEJ* 20 (1970): 180-90.

—DOUGLAS A. KNIGHT

• **Famine.** Famine is the severe shortage of food over a long period of time. In the OT, famine is normally caused by the failure of rain and, thus, of the crops. Other causes of famine included repeated insect damage to crops or wartime conditions which prohibited the people from tending their crops. In antiquity, grain could be stored in pits and such stockpiles could sustain a community through one year beyond the year of harvest. However, if the fields did not produce or if the crops could not be harvested the second year, the situation soon got desperate. Perhaps it was such a situation that evoked the lament from Jeremiah, ''The harvest is past, the summer is ended, and we are not saved'' (Jer 8:20). The only recourse in such cases was to go to a region which had food, as the sons of Jacob did (Gen 42:1) when they went to Egypt. Of course, in times when cities were besieged by an enemy the population could not leave to get food. Starvation ensured and, in come cases, the people resorted to cannibalism (2 Kgs 6:24-31). Famine in varying degrees must have been a frequent experience in ancient Israel. It is routinely mentioned along with the sword and pestilence as a common cause of death (Jer 34:17). The prophet Joel describes in vivid detail a locust scourge which devoured the crops and the resulting religious response which sought God's help (Joel 1–2). Even if Joel used the language of famine to describe the destruction wrought by an enemy, it is clear that the ravages of famine provided the imagery. Jeremiah and Ezekiel both viewed famine as a punishment from God sent upon a rebellious people (Jer 14:13ff.; Ezek 5:16). Habakkuk used the worst-case scenario of a famine to assert his faith in God (Hab 3:17ff.).

—JOE O. LEWIS

• **Farming.** *See* AGRICULTURE/FARMING

• **Farthing.** *See* MONEY

• **Fasting.** Fasting, abstaining from food and drink, was practiced by the people of the OT both individually and communally. Most fasts were occasional events, prompted by some crisis in the community or in the life of an individual. People fasted as a sign of mourning at the death of loved ones (1 Sam 31:13; 2 Sam 1:12; 1 Chr 10:12). They fasted also in preparation for receiving divine revelations, as evidenced by the examples of Moses (Exod 34:28), Elijah (1 Kgs 19:8), and Daniel (Dan 9:3; 10:3). Individuals fasted as a means of gaining divine compassion or assistance in the belief that fasting reinforced the urgency of the appeal. This is why David fasted when his newborn child became mortally ill (2 Sam 12:15-23). Ahab fasted as a sign of contrition and in hopes of winning God's approval (1 Kgs 21:27). Nehemiah fasted and made confession for the sins of the Jewish people (Neh 1:4). The author of Ps 35 recounts his experience of fasting and praying for others when they were sick (35:13).

Entire communities also fasted during times of distress or emergency. After the people of Israel had lost a costly battle to the Benjamites, they fasted for a day and offered burnt offerings and peace offerings to God (Judg 20:26). Samuel gathered the Israelites together at Mizpah for a fast as a sign of repentance and a plea to God for aid in their fight against the Philistines (1 Sam 7:6). Jehoshaphat proclaimed a fast throughout all Judah as a part of the people's plea to God for assistance against their enemies (2 Chr 20:3). Ezra led the returning exiles in fasting and prayer as they sought God's protection for their journey to Jerusalem (Ezra 8:21-23).

Apart from these spontaneous fasts, the Jewish people also observed several established fasts which were ordained for the entire community. The earliest and most important regular fast (and the only fast specifically commanded in the OT) was observed on the Day of Atonement. Instructions for the observance of this most holy day include a command for ''afflicting oneself,'' or fasting (Lev 16:29-34; 23:27-32; Num 29:7-11). Later, in remembrance of the destruction of Jerusalem and its accompanying calamities, the Jews set aside four days in the fourth, fifth, seventh, and tenth months as times of fasting and mourning (Zech 7:3-5; 8:19). The fast mentioned in Esth 4:16 became the basis for the fast in preparation for the Feast of PURIM.

Fasting was often accompanied by prayer, especially penitential prayer (Dan 9:3; Neh 1:4), the wearing of sackcloth (1 Kgs 21:27; Neh 9:1; Jonah 3:5), weeping (Neh 1:4; Joel 2:12), and the offering of sacrifices (Judg 20:26; 1 Sam 7:6-10). Most of the fasts mentioned in the OT lasted only one day, ending at sunset (Judg 20:26; 1 Sam 7:6; 1 Sam 14:24; 2 Sam 1:12; 2 Sam 3:35). The fast to mourn the death of Saul and his sons lasted seven days (1 Sam 31:13), although here, too, fasting may have been practiced only from sunrise to sunset each day. Esth 4:16 does mention a three-day fast including both nights and days. The three-week fast of Daniel (Dan 10:2) was likely not a total fast, but an abstaining from certain foods. The author of Ps 109, however, bemoans the physical effect of his prolonged fasting (109:23-25).

Fasting, like other religious observances, was open to abuse. When practiced mechanically, apart from sincere repentance and prayer, fasting became a meaningless ritual. Several of the prophets speak words of warning and judgment against the abuse of fasting (Jer 14:11-12; Isa 58; Zech 7:5-7). Joel, on the other hand, calls for prayer and fasting from all the people as he urges them to repent (Joel 1:14; 2:12, 15).

By the time of Jesus, fasting had become an important exercise of the devout Jew. According to Luke 18:12 the Pharisees fasted twice a week. (Later writings name Monday and Thursday as the Pharisees' days for fasting.) Other texts mention not only the Pharisees, but also the disciples of John the Baptist among those who fasted often (Mark 2:18-20).

Several NT texts reflect Jesus' attitude toward fasting. According to Matt 4:2 Jesus fasted for forty days and nights prior to being tempted in the wilderness. Since he observed other Jewish customs such as prayer and worship in the synagogues (Luke 3:21; 4:15-16; 6:6, 12; 9:18), it is likely that he also fasted during times of spiritual crisis or need. Jesus nowhere condemns fasting, but instead teaches that when one fasts one should do it sincerely and not for public show (Matt 6:16-18). His attitude toward fasting was similar to that of the prophets—fasting, like other religious observances, is valid and beneficial when it is a product of true devotion offered to God.

While Jesus was with his disciples, they did not practice fasting on a regular basis (Mark 2:18). When opponents complained about this, Jesus defended the disciples by pointing out that fasting is not appropriate when the bridegroom is present. Now is the time for joy, not for mourning.

Only two clear references to religious fasting are found in the remainder of the NT. The church at Antioch prayed and fasted when they consecrated Saul and Barnabas as missionaries (Acts 13:1-3). Shortly thereafter, Paul and Barnabas prayed and fasted as they appointed elders for the churches they had established (Acts 14:23). The only instances of fasting in the Letters of Paul probably refer to forced hunger and not voluntary fasting for religious purposes (2 Cor 6:5; 11:27). Fasting as a religious exercise did not die out in the early church, however. Writings from the early centuries of the church attest to the continuance of the practice. The DIDACHE, a manual on Christian morals and church practice written at the end of the first century or the first part of the second century, states that Christians should fast on Wednesday and Friday in contrast to the Jewish fasts on Monday and Thursday (8.1).

See also ATONEMENT, DAY OF; DIDACHE; FEASTS AND FESTIVALS; PURIM.

Bibliography. J. Behm, "νῆστις, κτλ.," *TDNT*; A. Kee, "The Question About Fasting," *NovT* 11 (1969): 171-73; G. F. Moore, *Judaism in the First Centuries of the Christian Era*; J. F. Wimmer, *Fasting in the New Testament*.

—MITCHELL G. REDDISH

• **Fasts.** *See* AB, NINTH OF

• **Fate/Fatalism.** *See* PROVIDENCE

• **Father.** *See* ABBA

• **Feast of Dedication.** *See* DEDICATION, FEAST OF

• **Feast of Lights.** *See* DEDICATION, FEAST OF

• **Feasts and Festivals.** Ancient Israel had a number of feasts or festivals based, as with their neighbors, on observance of the calendar. Often, therefore, the OT refers to "appointed feasts" when the Hebrew text has "seasons, times." The festivals were periods of celebration and thanksgiving accompanied by feasting in great joy. These festivals were of two kinds—the three pilgrim festivals of UNLEAVENED BREAD, WEEKS, and Booths, and other "appointed times" for observances. *Ḥag,* the normal Hebrew word in the OT translated as "feast," means basically a "pilgrim-feast" and is used almost exclusively in that sense. Its underlying verb, *ḥāgag,* means to "make pilgrimage."

One of the "appointed times" was for the New Moon, sometimes listed in close association with the Sabbath (2 Kgs 4:23; Amos 8:5; Hos 2:11; Isa 1:13; 66:23). The New Moon celebration first appears in the OT story of King Saul whose family sat in designated seats to observe the feast (1 Sam 20). The moon was appointed for seasons (Gen 1:14ff. Ps 104:19); the New Moon (*ḥōdeš,* "new moon," "month") occurs every twenty-nine and one-half days and is accompanied by sacrifice more than those for the Sabbath (Num 10:10; 28:1-15). It appears from Amos 8:5 that business dealings were suspended. Although, judging from the Saul story, the New Moon feast may have originally been a family affair, the *ḥōdeš* came to be held at the Temple. The regulations of Ezekiel 46:6ff. and Numbers 10:10; 28:11ff. show as much.

The SABBATH, although it was not a feast day and, like the New Moon apparently was originally a family concern, was a day to be observed. It was a day of rest. In the course of time the day came under cultic regulations at the central sanctuary. "Remember the sabbath day, to keep it holy. Six days you shall labor, and do all your work; but the seventh day is a sabbath to the Lord your God; in it you shall not do any work" (Exod 20:8-10). Observance of the Sabbath was tied to the mighty acts of the Lord: "For in six days the Lord made heaven and earth, the sea, and all that is in them, and rested the seventh day" (Exod 20:11). In Deut 5:15, however, the underlying act of the Lord was the liberating of God's people from Egypt.

Lev 23:24-25 and Num 29:1 introduce an unnamed celebration day heralded by the blowing of trumpets on the first day of the seventh month (Sep-Oct). On this day additional sacrifices were to be offered. The day, apparently beginning the NEW YEAR festivities, is followed on the tenth day of the month by the DAY OF ATONEMENT, and on the fifteenth day by the seven-day feast of TABERNACLES.

The number seven apparently dictates another festal celebration—this time the seventh year, along with the seventh day and seventh month. Every seven years Israel celebrated the fact that the land was the Lord's by allowing the land to rest, that is to lie fallow (Exod 23:11; Lev 25:1-7). In the sixth year the land would provide sufficient food for three years (Lev 25:21), and in the seventh year all Israelite slaves were freed (Exod 21:2-6) and all creditors released from debt (Deut 15:1-6).

Then seven times seven brings the number forty-nine when on the tenth day of the seventh month (Day of Atonement) the trumpet will sound to signify the fiftieth year as one of freedom (Lev 25:8ff.). Often called the YEAR OF JUBILEE, its grants of freedom were essentially those of the sabbatical year (Lev 25:8-55; 27:17-24).

The most important of the three pilgrim feasts was that of PASSOVER and Unleavened Bread. Apparently with an agricultural base, the feast of Unleavened Bread, kept for seven days after a one-day Passover celebration, was distinct from the Passover with its semi-nomadic base. The feasts became combined and came to be celebrated at Jerusalem in the month of Nisan (Mar-Apr).

The Feast of Weeks, known also as the Day of First Fruits (Num 28:26) and Feast of Harvest (Exod 23:16), was a one-day festival held at the end of a cycle beginning at Passover. It was later called Pentecost (literally "the fiftieth [day]") for its observance came fifty days after Passover (Acts 2:1; 20:16). Weeks was a harvest festival celebrated at the time of the wheat harvest (June). As at the other feasts, other festal offerings were made in addition to the regular ones (Num 28:26ff.) The cereal wave offering marked the beginning of the harvest to be ended "seven full weeks" later at this "Feast of Weeks" (Lev 23:15ff.). This period was one to remember the Lord as the source of rain and the earth's fertility (Jer 5:24). On this day offerings of "first fruits" were to be presented (Lev 23:17; Num 28:26); such offerings could apparently be called so because of a later harvest—nearly five months later—observed as the Feast of Booths. The Feast of Weeks seems to be ancient Israel's only festival not "historicized" with a redemptive act of the Lord in history, although it was later associated with the giving of the Torah at Mount Sinai.

The Feast of Booths (or TABERNACLES) marks Israel's third pilgrimage festivity. The seven-day feast began on the fifteenth day of the seventh month, the same month as other celebrations listed above; its original intent was to observe the completion of the agricultural year; thus it could be called the Feast of Ingathering (Exod 23:16). In this period each

Israelite male was to provide himself a booth in which to eat and sleep made from "branches of olive, wild olive, myrtle, palm, and other leafy trees" in the environs of Jerusalem (Neh 8:15). Such practice derived from the custom of farmers to guard their olive trees in September from thieves by watching over them from such booths. The booth became a symbol of Israel's wilderness wanderings, and the two motifs became combined. The relevant Pentateuchal material is found in Exod 23:16; 34:22; Lev 23:33-36, 39-43. Num 29:12-32; Deut 16:13-16. In celebrating the Feast of Booths ancient Israel was celebrating both the completion of the agricultural year and her successful wanderings from her release from Egypt to her promised land.

Other feasts were of a more secular sort: gatherings for feasting and rejoicing within the family (Gen 21:8), or to entertain guests (Gen 19:3), or sometimes as no more than drinking bouts (1 Sam 25:36). The term for such feasts, *mišteh,* "a drinking-feast," would indicate that the festivities might frequently have been accompanied by the drinking of wine.

The great feast described in Isa 25 portrays the "messianic banquet" of the Last Days, an idea that is developed in the Jewish community of later times and in the early Christian community as well.

The major festivals of OT times are also reflected in the NT. The Gospel of John is particularly interested in the importance of pilgrimages to Jerusalem on the occasion of the festival days. Jewish life and thought continues to revolve around the three major festivals. In additions, the festival of PURIM, described in the book of Esther, and the festival of Hanukkah, portrayed in 1 Macc 4, fill out the festival cycle.

See also ATONEMENT, DAY OF; JUBILEE, YEAR OF; MEALS; NEW YEAR'S FESTIVAL; PASSOVER; PURIM; SABBATH; TABERNACLES, FESTIVAL OF; UNLEAVENED BREAD, FEAST OF; WEEKS, FESTIVAL OF.

Bibliography. H. J. Kraus, *Worship in Israel*; T. H. Gaster, *Festivals of the Jewish Year*.

—KAREN RANDOLPH JOINES

• **Felix.** [fee′liks] Antonius Felix was procurator of Judea from 52–59 C.E. Apparently he was a freedman deriving his name Antonius from Antonia, the mother of Emperor Claudius. Acts 23:24-24:27 indicates that he was procurator when Paul was arrested during his last visit to Jerusalem. Fearing for Paul's safety, the Roman commander Claudius Lysias had sent Paul from Jerusalem to Caesarea. It was here that Paul appeared before Felix in face of his accusers from Jerusalem. Perhaps for a bribe, Felix postponed judgment on Paul. When he was removed from office by Nero in 59 C.E. Felix kept Paul in prison and effectively put the burden of deciding the case onto his successor, FESTUS.

The Roman historian Tacitus refers to Felix as a "brutal" ruler who introduced numerous countermeasures aimed at quelling the great social unrest in the province. On one occasion Felix ruthlessly crushed an outbreak led by an Egyptian messianic pretender and killed more than 400 people. But its leader escaped never to be heard from again. This fact may explain the reference in Acts 21:38 where Claudius Lysias mistakenly thought Paul might himself be that leader.

Josephus describes how Felix utilized the services of robbers (known as Sicarii) in the murder of the high priest Jonathan. These and many other excesses and abuses of power became the seeds that finally erupted in the Jewish-Roman War of 66–70 C.E.

Felix owed his position to his brother Pallas who exercised much influence with Emperor Claudius. But finally his own incompetence, immorality, and general mismanagement caused Felix to be recalled to Rome. A delegation of Jews went there to accuse him, but according to Josephus his brother's influence prevented him from being punished.

See also FESTUS; LYSIAS, CLAUDIUS; PAUL.

—WATSON E. MILLS

• **Fellowship.** Fellowship, largely a NT concept, can be understood most fully against the OT background. In the OT there is a COVENANT bond between God and Israel, a bond which God offered, cherished, and maintained. Israel celebrated its covenant relationship with God through cultic practices, keeping of the Torah and maintaining the holy days and feasts. The covenant made Israel distinct from other ancient peoples and provided a unity for all who belonged to the covenant people. At times in the OT this relationship is described with intense tenderness, even when the people of God strain the relationship. In Hos 11:1-9 God refers to Israel as his own rebellious child to whom he should come in anger, but whom he will visit with compassion; and in Exod 19:5 God calls Israel his own treasure among all the peoples. The covenant was a bond between a people and God, not between individuals and the deity. An awed reverence for the deity prevented the Hebrews from pressing the link between God and his covenant community. For them, the God of the covenant had his eternal abode in the heavens; the earth was merely his footstool. Consequently, the OT communities and their writers did not develop a vocabulary of "fellowship" as it appears in the NT.

"Fellowship" as Christians know it really began with the INCARNATION, in the life and ministry of Jesus, when people accepted his offer to become God's children and to live in that father-child relationship. Therefore, Jesus himself was both the binding factor in the new relationship between God and people, and the bond between fellow believers. The NT depicts this fellowship of believers as characterized by joy, hope, and love: joy for God's acceptance of sinners, hope for God's immediate and sure renewal of the world and its perverted order, and love as the true response to God's unmeasured mercy. This community—as Israel which preceded it—would also be characterized by suffering. As a community that awaited the immediate end of the present world order, it was set on a collision-course with non-believers and civil powers that would tolerate no threat (or perceived threat) to their authority and power. The community was propelled by the certainty of its faith and, rather than withdrawing and becoming a secretive cult, it delivered everywhere with boldness the good news message of God's mercy and power.

The NT writers use basically two word-groups to speak of fellowship: words that mean to share or have part in (*metechein* and related words); and the much more frequently used words that mean that which is common or mutually-shared (*koinōnia* and related words). Christian fellowship has two dimensions, the commonality that binds believers together as a body and the relationship that exists between believers and God through Jesus Christ.

The early Christian fellowship was such that the believers held their possessions in common (Acts 2:44; 4:32), meeting the material needs of those within the fellowship (Rom 12:13). Some individual verses speak of their being bound by a common faith (Tit 1:4; Phlm 6) and having a common salvation (Jude 3). The noun "fellowship" (Gk. *koinōnia*) is used in the NT almost exclusively by John (in 1 John) and Paul (who is responsible for thirteen of its nineteen occurrences). John indicates that fellowship is generated through faith in the good news (1 John 1:3) and has ethical demands (1 John 1:7). He speaks of fellowship with other believers, with God the Father, and with Jesus Christ (1 John 1:3).

Paul puts the same idea more formally and confessionally: "God is faithful, by whom you were called into the fellowship of his Son, Jesus Christ our Lord" (1 Cor 1:9). For Paul "fellowship" is the word that describes the mutuality of Christians (Gal 2:9; cf. 2 Cor 8:23; Phlm 17). It is a relationship with the HOLY SPIRIT that motivates one to Christian unity (Phil 2:1; 2 Cor 13:14). It comes from the likeness, the bonding commonality among all believers (2 Cor 13:14), who have Jesus Christ as their Lord, the Holy Spirit as the bonding presence and, God as their loving Father. This comes to striking expression in the statement on Christian unity found in Eph 4:1-6. "Fellowship" even comes to symbolize Christian solidarity in a most tangible form in Rom 15:26, where Paul says regarding the offering he was taking up for the poor Christians in Jerusalem, "Macedonia and Achaia have been pleased to make some contribution (Gk. *koinōnia*)." The term also occurs in 2 Cor 6:14 and 9:13. A somewhat similar use is found in Heb 13:16.

In Paul's writings two other ideas about fellowship stand out clearly. First, Christians share in the fellowship of Christ's sufferings (Phil 3:10), an idea found also in 1 Pet 4:13. This is symbolized by the community through the cup and the bread of the LORD'S SUPPER (1 Cor 10:16; cf. 2 Cor 1:5-7). Paul saw it as the responsibility of the believer in the persecuted communities to bear the burdens of others (Gal 6:2), to support and pray for leaders of the Christian community (Gal 6:6; 1 Thess 5:12-13), and to seek the good of others over one's own good (1 Cor 10:24), for as the old age passed away and the new age dawned, tribulations were to be the lot of believers (1 Thess 3:3). This was due, in part, to their fellowship in Christ's sufferings.

Second, Christian fellowship is a partnership in the spreading of the gospel. The churches did not always live up to this. Paul wrote to the Philippian Christians about how difficult it was for him when no church except theirs aided him (Phil 4:15); yet, he was also grateful for their help (Phil 1:5). In his request for prayer to the Thessalonians he asked them to pray that the word of the Lord might speed on and triumph (2 Thess 3:1). In his Letter to the Romans, Paul requested their assistance on his way to evangelize Spain (Rom 15:23-24).

Christian fellowship was not a state that was enjoyed by believers without effort. It was something to work at, to guard. For one could also be tempted to participate in (have fellowship with) the sins of other people (1 Tim 5:22; 2 John 11 says anyone who aids and abets a heretic "shares [or participates in] his wicked work"). Paul warned the Corinthians that by participating in pagan worship they became partners with demons (1 Cor 10:20).

Fellowship, then, is the reality of life with God in Christ Jesus. It is community with fellow-believers who let Christ be Lord of their fellowship. And it has its source in the incarnation of Jesus Christ.

See also COVENANT; FRIENDSHIP; HOLY SPIRIT; INCARNATION; LORD'S SUPPER.

—RICHARD A. SPENCER

• **Feminist Hermeneutics.** The term feminist hermeneutics refers to various methods of interpretation that are guided by an ideology that values the political, economic, and social equality of the sexes. Standing in a line of hermeneutical theory that recognizes all inquiry to be to some extent subjective and contextually based, feminist theory contends that Western scholarly tradition has been shaped almost exclusively by patriarchal values and concerns. Histories have been reconstructed around male figures and male-oriented events. The quality of literature has been judged from the standpoints of male interests, and interpretations of that literature have further reflected masculine biases. To counteract the partial, incomplete, patriarchal understandings of human life and thought, feminists affirm that the experiences of women as neglected and/or oppressed members of society are valid standards of critical investigation. In other words, for a feminist, the insights of the powerless carry as much credibility as do those of the powerful.

To use a spatial metaphor, the views of the powerful are those from "the top" or from "the front," i.e., from positions of authority and control. The powerless, on the other hand, are confined to seeing more of the "underside," the "backside," the hidden side of life. While patriarchy has perceived itself to be the norm, the standard, the essence of human life, feminism, with its view of the "underside," sees the incongruity of this perception. It is the feminist task to expose the incongruity. Consequently, when a feminist reconstructs history, exegetes a text, analyzes a theory or an argument, she does so with a commitment to critique any tendencies toward patriarchal domination that may manifest themselves in the subject of investigation, whether these be explicit discursive affirmations of male superiority, subtle literary constructions of female inferiority, or attempts to muffle the voices and to conceal the deeds of women in the course of history.

In the field of biblical studies, the feminist investigator encounters an immediate problem: The Bible is patriarchal literature. Among feminists there is no question that the Bible is the product of patriarchal culture and that, as such, it reflects patriarchal bias. Feminists do, however, differ in opinion on the extent and potency of this bias as well as on how this bias should be handled in critical interpretation.

Feminist critics have responded to biblical androcentrism in a variety of ways. Some have rejected the Bible as well as the religious tradition(s) that it represents, claiming that its patriarchal bias keeps it from being authoritative or even relevant to modern women's search for self-understanding.

For feminists who are committed to various Jewish or Christian traditions, however, the centrality of the Bible in those traditions keeps its wholesale rejection from being a viable alternative. Because their religious traditions grant the Bible special authority, their wrestlings with the biblical text have an intensity unequaled in other academic disciplines. The Bible and its related religious traditions have taught the values of personhood, equality, and social justice but at the same time have presupposed a world in which national, social, and gender-oriented chauvinisms are accepted and acceptable. Thus, women stand liberated and subordinated by the same book.

This paradoxical dilemma has produced several different responses. Some feminists find in the Bible a general message of human liberation. For these scholars, the liberating paradigms of the Bible are to be correlated with the feminist critique of patriarchy. While the Bible does not speak directly of women's oppression, analogies can be drawn between the social injustices involving women and any of the injustices against which biblical prophetic voices speak. Affirming an evaluative principle of relevance, this line of feminist thought maintains that the liberating portions of the Bible are authoritative, while texts that fail to promote the fullness of humanity are no longer relevant to the modern situation and, consequently, are not authoritative.

Feminist scholars who have focused on gender-oriented texts have exercised a variety of approaches among themselves. Some have focused on positive portrayals of women in the Bible as countermeasures to texts that portray women as inferior to men. Some critics, on the other hand, have confronted this approach, suspicious of the sexual politics of biblical composers. Who defines positive female qualities? they ask. Are the womanly assets commended in the Bible merely those characteristics deemed valuable by the patriarchy? Other feminists have looked to biblical portrayals of women to discover what can be learned from the analogies between ancient and modern women struggling in an oppressive culture. This avenue of investigation has uncovered glimpses of courage and salvation as well as "texts of terror," tales that call us to grieve over the physical and emotional violence done to particular female characters in the Bible. Another alternative, yet to be explored extensively by feminist biblical critics, is the cross-gender investigation of patriarchy in the Bible. This kind of inquiry might begin with such questions as, does the hierarchy of patriarchy oppress men as well as women? In vigorous competition for male ascendancy, such as can be found in the Bible, do men really treat other men any better than they treat women? Moreover, do women treat other women any better than men treat women?

What is basic for feminist hermeneutics in the field of biblical studies is the recognition that, despite its androcentric leanings, the Bible also makes provision for its own critique, points to its own incongruity. Every characterization of a passive, weak, irresponsible male ridicules "maleness" as an ultimate value. Every message of liberation passes judgment on celebrations of domination. There are, within the biblical materials, perspectives expressed, characters portrayed, and events reported that reflect a knowledge of the "underside," and permit the reader an ironic view of life "at the top."

See also GOD LANGUAGE, INCLUSIVE.

Bibliography. D. N. Fewell, "Feminist Reading of the Hebrew Bible: Affirmation, Resistance and Transformation," *JSOT* 39 (1987): 77-87; E. S. Fiorenza, *In Memory of Her*; E. Fuchs, "The Literary Characterization of Mothers and Sexual Politics in the Hebrew Bible" and "Who is Hiding the Truth? Deceptive Women and Biblical Androcentrism," *Feminist Perspectives on Biblical Scholarship*, ed. A. Y. Collins; R. R. Ruether, "Feminist Interpretation: A Method of Correlation," *Feminist Interpretation of the Bible*, ed. L. M. Russell; K. D. Sakenfeld, "Feminist Uses of Biblical Materials," *Feminist Interpretation of the Bible*, ed. L. M. Russell; M. A. Tolbert, "Defining the Problem: The Bible and Feminist Hermeneutics," *Semeia* 28 (1983): 113-26; P. Trible, *God and the Rhetoric of Sexuality* and *Texts of Terror*.

—DANNA NOLAN FEWELL

• **Fertile Crescent.** The name given by J. H. Breasted to the fertile stretch of land in the form of a crescent from the Persian Gulf to the Mediterranean Sea to Palestine (PLATE

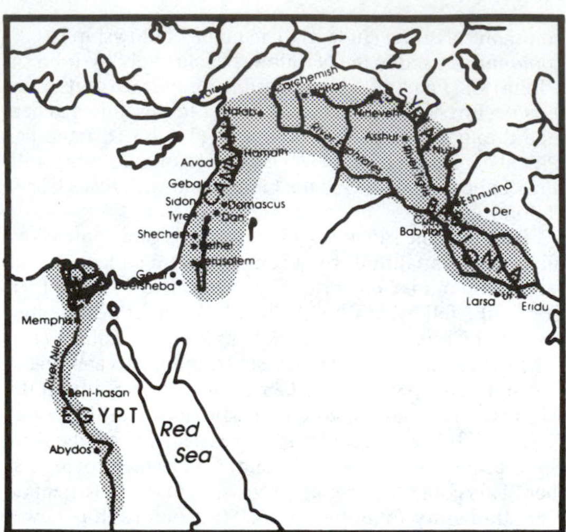

Designed by Margaret Jordan Brown ©Mercer University Press

2). Beginning in the east at the Persian Gulf, the crescent extended northwest to include the valley between the Tigris and the Euphrates rivers, then it continued west to include Syria and the coasts of the Mediterranean, finally it turned south to include Palestine. The territory traversed by this route was followed by the caravans that went from Babylon to Egypt. Today the Fertile Crescent comprises Iraq, Syria, Lebanon, Palestine, and parts of Jordan. The fertility of the land came from the abundance of water provided by the Tigris and the Euphrates, although Syria and Palestine did not receive the benefits of the two rivers. The valley formed by the Tigris and the Euphrates was known as MESOPOTAMIA, the land "between the rivers." Mesopotamia is mentioned several times in the Bible. In the OT it appears five times (Gen 24:10; Deut 23:4; Judg 3:8, 10; 1 Chr 19:6) as a translation of Aram Naharaim, which means "Aram of the two rivers." In the NT it appears in Acts 2:9 and 7:2 in its Greek form "Mesopotamia."

The Fertile Crescent became the cradle of ancient Near Eastern civilization. Great cities and famous ancient cultures developed in these lands: the SUMERIANS, whose culture began around 3500 B.C.E., were the inventors of writing; the Akkadians, who were the first people to form an empire under one ruler; the Mitanni, whose Hurrian population controlled most of the Upper Tigris and the Euphrates ca. 1800 B.C.E.; the ASSYRIANS, the nations that eventually deported the kingdom of Israel into exile; and the Neo-BABYLONIANS, who conquered the kingdom of Judah.

—CLAUDE F. MARIOTTINI

• **Fertilizer.** *See* DUNG

• **Festival.** *See* FEASTS AND FESTIVALS

• **Festus.** [fes'tuhs] Porcius Festus was procurator of Judea from 60 to 62 C.E., though the exact dates of his reign are the subject of much debate primarily because Eusebius dates his reign 56–62 C.E. Most modern scholars, however, favor the dates 60–62 C.E. According to Josephus, Festus's administration was more efficient and competent than that of FELIX, his predecessor. Festus was more appreciative and supportive of the Jewish constituency. He succeeded, for instance, in removing the insurgent Sicarri who were robbing and killing many people.

According to Acts immediately upon assuming power, he addressed the issue of the prisoner PAUL who had already languished in prison for almost two years during the reign of Felix. Festus visited Jerusalem and invited the Jewish authorities to come to Caesarea to present their case against Paul. He offered Paul the opportunity of facing his accusers in Jerusalem; but Paul, sensing the danger, elected to exercise his right as a Roman citizen and he appealed his case to the emperor.

After the appeal had been lodged, King Herod Agrippa II and his sister Bernice visited Caesarea and expressed the wish to hear Paul plead his case. When Paul had finished, Agrippa indicated that Paul could have been given his freedom except for the fact that he had appealed to Caesar. Both Agrippa and Festus agreed that Paul was innocent of any capital crime.

See also AGRIPPA I & II; FELIX; PAUL.

—WATSON E. MILLS

• **Field of Blood.** *See* AKELDAMA

• **Fig Tree.** The fig tree (*ficus carica*) is one of the most important fruit trees in Palestine. It is mentioned more than sixty times in the Bible. The fig tree blooms in the spring. The early figs begin to form in March and ripen by the end of May (Hos 9:10). During the summer the large palm-shaped leaves provide welcomed shade (John 1:48-50). The main crop is ready for harvesting from the middle of August into October. The tree then sheds its leaves and is quite bare in the winter because it has few small branches.

The fruit, which is sweet and high in sugar content, may be eaten fresh (Isa 28:4) or dried into cakes and stored (1 Sam 25:18). Fig cakes were also used in the treatment of boils (2 Kgs 20:7; Isa 38:21).

Adam and Eve covered themselves with fig leaves (Gen 3:7). Along with the olive tree and the vine, the fig tree is mentioned in Jotham's parable (Judg 9:7-15). Jeremiah's parable about the exiles distinguishes good figs and bad figs (Jer 24; 29:17; cf. Matt 7:16; Luke 6:44; Jas 3:12). Sitting under one's vine or fig tree was a common image for peace and security (1 Kgs 4:25; Mic 4:4; Zech 3:10). In contrast, the destruction of fig trees appears frequently in warnings of national crises (Jer 5:17; Hos 2:12; Joel 1:7, 12; Amos 4:9; cf. Rev 6:13).

Jesus tells a parable of an unfruitful fig tree (Luke 13:6-9). A similar parable appears in versions of Aḥiqar (Syriac, 8.35; Arabic, 8.30; Armenian, 8.25), but there the tree is shown no mercy. The fig tree is also featured in the parable at the end of the apocalyptic discourse in the Synoptics (Matt 24:32; Mark 13:28; Luke 21:29).

The cursing of the barren fig tree in Mark 11:12-14, 20-22; Matt 21:18-20 has long troubled interpreters. Luke omits the story, though some suggest that it is derived from the parable in Luke 13:6-9. Mark sandwiches the condemnation of the Temple between the two parts of the cursing of the fig tree, so that the latter interprets his action in the Temple. Since the fig tree was closely linked with the nation's security and destruction, the action is appropriate and prophetic (cf. Jer 8:13). The Temple cult appeared to be prosperous, but like a barren fig tree it bore no fruit.

—R. ALAN CULPEPPER

• **Figures of Speech.** *See* CHIASM

• **Figurines.** *See* IMAGES/FIGURINES

• **Fire.** Earliest allusion to fire is in connection with sacrifice (Gen 4:4). Hebrew Scriptures place the origin of fire in primeval times, but no explanation of its origin as a divine gift is given. Fire often represented the PRESENCE of God, yet the Hebrews never worshiped fire, as did the Persians, nor did they believe fire was one of the basic elements of the universe, as did the Greeks.

The secular uses of fire included cooking (Isa 44:15), heating (Isa 44:16; Jer 36:22; John 18:18), refining metals (Isa 44:12; Jer 6:29; Mal 3:2), burning refuse (Lev 8:17), and providing light (Isa 50:11). In warfare, fire was used to destroy enemy cities (Josh 6:24; 11:11).

In worship, fire consumed the offering and carried the SACRIFICE to God (Gen 8:20-21). The sacred fire of the altar was not allowed to go out (Lev 6:9-13). The cultic fire was a means of maintaining purity and cleanliness (Lev 10:2; Isa 6:6-7).

The association between God and fire is prominent in the OT. The fire of the burning bush (Exod 3:2), the pillar of fire (Exod 13:21-22), and the fire and lightning of Sinai (Exod 19:18) represented God's presence to the escaping Hebrews. Other appearances of God employ fire imagery (Ezek 1). God's sentence upon Sodom and Gomorrah is through fire (Gen 19:24). Judgment is often portrayed by the prophets as involving fire (Amos 1:3–2:5; Mic 1:7; Zeph 1:18). The fiery judgment becomes an eschatological motif in the NT (Mark 9:43-49; Matt 13:40-42; 2 Pet 3:7; Rev 14:9-10). Described as the paradigm of final testing, fire is also said to be the eternal torment for the damned.

—ROBERT A. STREET, JR.

Artwork by Margaret Jordan Brown

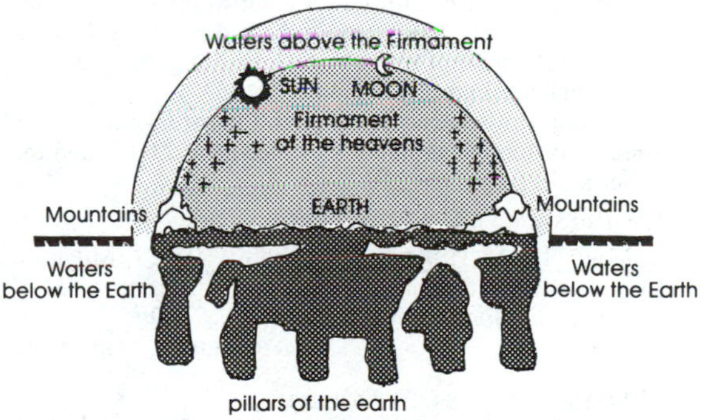

Artist's conception of the firmament above the earth.

• **Firmament.** Derived from the Latin firmamentum, which was used in the Vulgate to translate the Hebrew *rāqîa'*. As the translation implies, the *rāqîa'* was perceived of as a firm object, a "thin sheet stretched out to form the vault of the sky" (Speiser, *Genesis, AncB*, 6). The imagery of a hammered, beaten out, embossed bowl is supported by the Septuagint's use of the Greek stereōma for *rāqîa'*.

Gen 1:6-8 describes the firmament as the expanse that separates the waters above from the waters below and is named HEAVEN or SKY. In Gen 1:14-18 the sun, the moon, and the stars are situated in the heavenly *rāqîa'*. Birds fly across the firmament (Gen 1:20). In Ezek 1:22-26 the firmament is compared to a shining crystal or ice that spreads out above the creatures. A throne is seen above the firmament. The imagery of a sapphire is found in Ezek 10:1. The other uses of the Hebrew word are in Pss 19:1; 150:1; and Dan 12:3.

The Hebrews regarded the firmament as a solid canopy that could be compared to a tent (Ps 104:2) or a hard, molten mirror (Job 37:18). The canopy arched from horizon to horizon and formed a dome or vault above the earth, which the ancient Hebrews regarded as being flat. The purpose of the dome was to keep the cosmic waters from overflowing and flooding the earth. The concept of a domed universe was common among the peoples of the ancient Near East.

See also COSMOLOGY; SKY.

—ROBERT A. STREET, JR.

• **First Day of the Week.** *See* LORD'S DAY

• **First Peter.** *See* PETER, LETTERS OF

• **Firstborn/First Fruits/Firstlings.** As was common in the ancient Near East, the Hebrews believed that the firstborn or the first of the harvest belonged to God, the creator and owner of the universe. To show the sacredness of the objects and the LORD's ownership, the Hebrews presented the first fruits and the firstlings of the flocks to God as offerings or sacrifices. By returning a portion to God, the remainder became available for human use. The offerings for the REDEMPTION of the agricultural crops were known as first fruits and the animals to be sacrificed were called firstlings. A notable exception to such sacrifice of the firstborn is observable in the case of human sacrifice. Though human sacrifice was known among the Hebrews (2 Kgs 16:3; 2 Chr 33:6), it was not widely practiced. Whenever human sacrifice is mentioned in the OT, it is with aversion. Prophetic condemnation of child sacrifice is found in Jer 7:30-34; Ezek 16:20, 21; Mic 6:7. Rather than have such abhorrent sacrifices, laws allowed for a substitution to be made for first-born sons. They were to be redeemed by the dedication of the tribe of LEVI (Num 3:11-13) or the giving of a five shekel tribute (Num 3:44-51).

A firstborn son received special favor in inheriting a double portion of his father's estate (Deut 21:17) and the father's blessing (Gen 27).

See also SACRIFICE; WEEKS, FESTIVAL OF.

Bibliography. V. H. Kody, "Firstborn," *IDB*; J. Milgrom, "Firstborn," *IDBSupp*; J. Milgrom, "First Fruits, OT," *IDBSupp*; J. Morgenstern, "First Fruits," *IDB*.

—ROBERT A. STREET, JR.

• **Flavius Josephus.** *See* JOSEPHUS

• **Flesh.** Most broadly, the term "flesh" is used to refer to the muscles and softer tissues of the bodies of humans and/or animals. The same word may be applied to animal bodies because, like humans, they are finite physical creatures limited by mortality. God, however, is spirit and is therefore superior to "all flesh" (Jer 32:27; see also Isa 31:3).

Animal flesh (often translated "meat") may become food for humans (Gen 9:4) or for other animals (Exod 22:31). Most frequently, animal flesh is mentioned as a sacrificial offering in ritual worship (Exod 29:31; Lev 4:11; 7:15-21; etc.).

"Flesh" can refer to close relationship, kinship, or blood ties among persons (Gen 2:23-24; 29:14; Judg 9:2). Several times "flesh" is mentioned along with "heart" (Prov 4:21-22; Ps 73:26) or "soul" (Pss 63:1; 84:2) to refer to the total person.

"Flesh" may refer to human weakness and frailty (Ps 78:39; 2 Chr 32:8). Or it may indicate the capacity to respond in obedient relationship (Ezek 11:19; 36:26).

See also SOUL IN THE OLD TESTAMENT; SPIRIT IN THE OLD TESTAMENT.

Bibliography. F. B. Knutson, "Flesh," *ISBE*; N. W. Porteous, "Flesh in the OT," *IDB*; H. W. Wolff, *Anthropology of the OT*.

—DONALD W. GARNER

• **Flesh and Spirit.** *Flesh* and *spirit* translate Heb. and Gk. words which are used in the Bible with both literal and figurative meanings. *Flesh* is never used of God in the Bible, but is applied both to human beings and to animals. In a literal sense, *flesh* refers to the flesh of people (Job 2:5; 1 Cor 15:39) and of animals (Lev 4:11; Isa 22:13; 1 Cor 15:39). In reference to people, *flesh* may refer specifically to the foreskin (Gen 17:11) or the male sexual organ (Ezek 16:26; 23:20), or it may refer to the whole body (Prov 4:22; Col 2:1). *Flesh* also connotes relationship to other people (Gen 37:27; Lev 18:6; Rom 11:14).

Flesh has an important nonliteral meaning of human life itself as weak, especially in contrast to God. Job asks God, "Hast thou eyes of flesh? Dost thou see as man sees?" (Job 10:4). Ps 78:38-39 says that God restrained his anger against the Israelite people because "he remembered that they were but flesh."

Spirit refers to the vital power of living people, that which gives life to the body (Ezek 37:1-14; Luke 8:55). Removal of the spirit causes death (Gen 6:3). Num 16:22 and 27:16 call God the "God of the spirits of all flesh."

When *flesh* and *spirit* are used together they refer to the whole personality, the material or outer aspect and the immaterial or inner aspect. In 2 Cor 7:1 Paul writes, "Let us cleanse ourselves from every defilement of body (flesh) and spirit;" and in Col 2:5 he says, "For though I am absent in body (flesh), yet I am present with you in spirit." Here the spirit refers to one's insight, feeling, and will—one's inner life.

Flesh and *spirit* are also in contrast to one another in several passages where flesh is closely connected to sin, and spirit to that divine power from God which produces all divine existence. John 3:6 declares, "That which is born of the flesh is flesh, and that which is born of the Spirit is spirit." Paul declares that attempts to please God in the flesh are not acceptable to God, but rather worship by means of his Spirit (Phil 3:3). Elsewhere Paul relates the spirit to faith and freedom and the flesh to Law and slavery. In Gal 3:3, he asks "Having begun with the Spirit, are you now ending with the flesh?" (see also Gal 5:17; 6:8).

In the NT the apostle Paul gives an ethical sense to flesh. People, as flesh, are contrasted with Spirit and are sinful. They cannot please God without the help of the Spirit. Rom 8 is the classic text in which Paul contrasts life "in the flesh" and life "in the Spirit." Verse 8 says "those who are in the flesh cannot please God." Verse 9 is evidence that to be "in the flesh" is equivalent to not having God's Spirit dwelling in one. *Flesh* in this sense refers to the whole person in his or her distance from God, the attempt to live one's life independently of God. When Paul says in Rom 7:18, "I know that nothing good dwells within me, that is, in my flesh," he is not referring to the physical body. *Flesh* here has the ethical sense of his unregenerate nature. Gal 5:19-21 lists the "works of the flesh." Only five of the fifteen are basically sensual (fornication, uncleanness, licentiousness, drunkenness, and carousing); the other ten include idolatry, sorcery, enmities, strife, jealousies, anger, divisions, and envyings.

Just as *flesh* can refer to the total person apart from God, so *spirit* may describe the total person in relation to God. In benedictions such as Phlm 25, "the grace of the Lord Jesus Christ be with your spirit" and 2 Tim 4:22, "the Lord be with your spirit," one's *spirit* is one's self.

Because the apostle Paul uses *flesh* in both a literal sense and an ethical sense, it is sometimes difficult to know which meaning is intended. In 1 Cor 5, writing concerning a man who is having sex with his stepmother, Paul says, "Deliver this man to Satan for the destruction of the flesh, that his spirit may be saved in the day of the Lord Jesus" (5:5). Some interpreters and translators understood flesh here to be the physical body: TEV—"for his body to be destroyed so that his spirit may be saved"; NJB—"to be destroyed as far as natural life is concerned, so that on the Day of the Lord his spirit may be saved"; Goodspeed—"for his physical destruction, in order that his spirit may be saved on the Day of the Lord." Others understand flesh here in the ethical sense of one's unregenerate nature: NIV—"So that the sinful nature may be destroyed and his spirit saved on the day of the Lord"; Barclay—"This you must do so that this salutory and painful discipline may mortify this man's fleshly desires, so that on the day of the Lord his spirit may be saved."

See also FLESH; HOLY SPIRIT; HUMAN BEING; SPIRIT IN THE OLD TESTAMENT.

Bibliography. F. Stagg, *New Testament Theology*; H. W. Wolff, *Anthropology of the Old Testament*.

—ROGER L. OMANSON

• **Flint.** Flint is a hard, slightly impure variety of quartz, gray to brown or nearly black in color, and abundant in Palestine. Because it fractures along conchoidal lines to produce a smooth (and routinely serrated), sharp, and hard edge, flint was widely used in antiquity to manufacture a variety of tools. Axeheads, knives, picks, scrapers, even sickle blades, and of course spearheads and arrowheads were made of flint from the earliest toolmaking period until long after bronze and even iron began replacing the brittle stone. The abundant variety of flint implements signals the importance of flint remains for dating artifact strata and for determining the age and/or cultural level of the toolmakers of the past.

In the OT "flint" translates two Hebrew words: (1) *ḥallâmîsh* of unknown derivation (but compare Akkadian *elmēšu* "diamond," and perhaps compare the Hebrew *yah^{a}lôm* "diamond/jasper/onyx" [?], apparently—owing to its hardness—from *h-l-m*); and (2) *ṣor,* apparently from *ṣ-r-r* (compare Arabic *ẓarra,* "be sharp/cut," hence "sharp-edged [hard rock]," and Akkadian *ṣurru,* "flint," hence *ṣurtu,* "flint knife"). The former occurs five times and, perhaps excepting Deut 8:15, only in a poetic sense (Deut 8:15; 32:13; Job 28:9; Ps 114:8; Isa 50:7), in RSV translated three times as "flinty" (qualifying "rock") and twice as "flint" (alone), in each instance symbolically of (unyielding) hardness and/or imperviousness. The second Hebrew word occurs at least four and possibly seven times. Zipporah used a "flint" (RSV; KJV, derivatively, "sharp stone") to circumcise her son (Exod 4:25). Later Joshua was commanded to circumcise the people Israel with "flint [RSV; KJV "sharp"] knives" (Josh 5:2, 3). (The notoriety of these specific "flint knives" is marked in LXX by two added notes at Josh 21:42d and 24:31a that Joshua's "stone knives" were buried with him.) While the occurrences in Exod 4:25 and Josh 5:2, 3 designate flint as such, in Ezek 3:9 "flint" is a metaphor or simile for (unyielding) hardness. Other possible occurrences are 2 Sam 2:16 where the site of the "tournament-battle" between the armies of Abner (Saul) and Joab (David) is designated "Helkath-hazzurim," that is, possibly, "the field of *(flint) knives*" (RSV margin, "field of *sword-edges*"; also sometimes read as "field of adversaries" or, following 2:16a, "field of sides); Ps 89:43[H44] where "the Lord" is said to "turn back/blunt the *edge* [that is, the *sharpness*] of the sword" of his servant; and Isa 5:28 where the (eschatological) horses' hooves will be "like flint" (hard, sharp, cuttingly destructive).

Of hermeneutical import regarding "flint," the (prescribed?) use of *flint* knives as late as Joshua (5:2, 3), when metal knives long since had been available, is taken by some—notably Roland de Vaux—as indication of the ancient origins of circumcision. Joshua's use of "flint knives" indeed probably reflects both the antiquity of the rite and the expected conservatism in religious practice.

—EDD ROWELL

• **Flock.** *See* SHEEP

Courtesy of the Eisenberg Museum of Biblical Archaeology, Southern Baptist Theological Seminary.

Tablet seven of the Babylonian creation epic, the Enuma Elish.

• **Flood.** The catastrophic means by which God is reported to have administered divine judgment upon every living thing upon the earth, excluding Noah and those with him on the ark (Gen 6–8). Noah was commanded to build a three-story ark (approximately 450x75x45 ft.) in which he and his wife, their three sons and their wives, and at least two of every living species were to take refuge. Noah obeyed God. Subsequently, he and those with him were saved from destruction. God then commanded them to repopulate the earth, and promised never to bring another such flood.

Flood stories from diverse cultures exist throughout the world; one scholar has documented more than 220 such accounts. Most of the stories differ so radically from the biblical account that no connection is discernible. Notable exceptions, however, are three stories from the ancient Near East.

The oldest of these comes from the Sumerians who invented writing ca. 3300 B.C.E. Only a fragment of a nineteenth century B.C.E. copy of their flood story has survived.

In it King Ziusudra, the Sumerian Noah, described as "humbly obedient" and reverent, was warned that the gods had decreed the destruction of humanity by a flood. After the hero survived the inundation of seven days and seven nights in a huge boat, he made sacrifices to the gods, bowed before Utu, Anu, and Enlil (gods), and was granted "breath eternal."

The oldest Babylonian flood account is the Atrahasis Epic, of which a copy dating to perhaps the seventeenth century B.C.E. is extant. The hero, Atrahasis, learned from the god Ea that Enlil, chief of the gods, planned to destroy humanity with a flood because his sleep was being disturbed. Atrahasis was commanded to build a large boat and bring aboard his family, certain animals, food and other provisions. The flood lasted seven days and seven nights.

The best known parallel to the biblical flood story is found in the Epic of Gilgamesh, where extant *copies* date to ca. 1500 B.C.E. Utnapishtim, the hero of the flood, escaped the deluge of six days and six nights because the god Ea had warned him to build a ship. Aboard the ship he took his family, and wildlife, and in the end received the gift of immortality.

It is clear that there is general agreement between the biblical and other Near Eastern flood stories. Thus, a connection may be assumed, especially since Abraham migrated to Palestine from Ur in Mesopotamia, the homeland of the other stories. Yet there are fundamental differences in the accounts. In the Bible it is human sin that brings judgment, not mere noise disturbing the sleep of the gods. Moreover, the biblical account is monotheistic rather than polytheistic. Above all, the biblical account, with its themes of sin and righteousness, reward and punishment, and judgment and grace, is a story with a moral. Its purpose was to provide divinely inspired insight into the God-human relationship.

Bibliography. J. H. Marks, "Flood (Genesis)," *IDB*; J. R. O'Brien, "Flood Stories of the Ancient Near East," *BI* 13/1 (Fall 1986): 60-65; J. B. Pritchard, ed., *ANET*; H. F. Vos, "Flood," *ISBE*.

—J. RANDALL O'BRIEN

• **Florilegium/Testimonia, Qumran.** [flor'uh-leej"ee-uhm/tes'tee-moh"nee-uh] Among the scrolls found in Qumran Cave 4 are two collections of texts, both written in Hebrew: *4QFlor* and *4QTest*. *4QFlor* is an amalgam of OT texts and interpretations (cf. *11QMelch*). It is extant in twenty-six fragments of four columns, only one of which can be reconstructed to any degree. This column focuses on four passages: 2 Sam 7:10-11a; 7:11b-14a; Ps 1:1; 2:1-2. Other fragments suggest a similar interest in Deut 33:8-11, 12, 19-21; Isa 65:22-23. The pattern follows that of the PESHARIM: first a passage is quoted, then its interpretation is provided. *4QTest,* on the other hand, is simply an anthology. Virtually complete on a single page, it contains Deut 5:28-29 and 18:18-19 (combined as a single quotation); Num 24:15-17; Deut 33:8-11; and a section of a sectarian work, *4QPssJosh*.

The only extant manuscript of *4QFlor* dates from the first half of the first century C.E. There is nothing to indicate that the document itself was composed any earlier. It is usually viewed as an eschatological midrash. God has established a TEMPLE of men in which works of the LAW are offered as sacrifices (cf. Eph 2:19-21; 1 Pet 2:5) in anticipation of the Temple which he will build in the last days. At that time he will raise up the Branch of David and the Interpreter of the Law (a royal MESSIAH and a priestly Messiah? cf. *4QPBless; CD* 6:7; 7:18; *1QSa* 2:12-21) to save the elect of Israel. Although most of the document is lost, its sectarian character is evident: the author interprets the OT passages in terms of his community.

4QTest is considerably older than *4QFlor,* the manuscript dating to 100–75 B.C.E. It is generally viewed as a messianic anthology. Certainly the first three sections—concerning the Prophet like Moses, the Star of Jacob and the Sceptre of Israel, and the blessing of Levi—can be interpreted messianically, each of these quotations referring to a distinct eschatological figure: the prophet, the Messiah of Israel, and the Messiah of Aaron. This approach is complicated by the fact that *CD* 7:18-20 understands the Star and the Sceptre as two separate individuals: the Interpreter of the Law and the Prince of the congregation. The major problem with seeing the document as messianic is the quotation from 4QPssJosh, which deals with an accursed man and, apparently, his two sons. This man is generally equated with the Wicked Priest of the *Pesharim*; thus, the section can be construed as "messianic" in the sense that it deals with (three?) "Antichrist" figures. Without explicit interpretations, certainty is impossible.

4QFlor and *4QTest* are important documents for understanding the use of the OT at Qumran: *4QFlor* for illustrating the interpretive strategies of the community and *4QTest* for providing an example of the way in which the Essenes collected key (and presumably messianic) texts. As a pre-Christian example of such a collection, *4QTest* may shed light on the use of similar testimonia in the NT church. Finally, both documents contribute to the understanding of the history of the OT text prior to the Massoretic Text.

See also DEAD SEA SCROLLS; ESSENES.

Bibliography. G. J. Brooke, *Exegesis at Qumran: 4QFlorilegium in its Jewish Context*; A. Dupont-Sommer, *The Essene Writings from Qumran*; J. A. Fitzmyer, "4QTestimonia and the New Testament," *Essays on the Semitic Background of the New Testament.*

—JOSEPH L. TRAFTON

Courtesy of the Eisenberg Museum of Biblical Archaeology, Southern Baptist Theological Seminary.

A Coptic bread stamp.

• **Food.** The supply of food was sometimes precarious in the biblical world. In EGYPT and MESOPOTAMIA irrigation of land gave more promise of a steady supply of food than in Canaan where the people had to depend upon rain for their crops. Transporting food supplies to outlying areas was difficult. Lack of refrigeration of food also made it difficult to keep food for very long. The wide variety of edibles available in modern times simply did not exist in Canaan. The foods common to all in the Middle East were fruits, vegetables, cereals, and dairy products.

Meat was not part of the daily menu for several reasons.

Some animals, such as pigs and camels, were not eaten by Israelites because they were considered to be unclean. Donkeys probably were not consumed; they were needed for transportation. However, the primary reason lay in the scarcity of meat products. It would be unwise to eat those domestic ANIMALS that could provide cheese, curds, and milk.

Oxen, sheep, goats, fowl (including wild game as well as domestic) and certain kinds of fish were eaten. Royalty ate much better than did common people. SOLOMON's meals were legendary. The average person consumed meat only on special occasions—when guests came, at special family celebrations, or on trips to the Temple. The PASSOVER celebration included the eating of a roasted lamb and the sacrificial system called for the sacrifice and eating of certain animals.

The Jordan River, the Sea of Galilee, and Lake Huleh provided fish. There is little evidence of fish farming in ancient times. Hunting wild game supplemented the meat supply. This would tend to be uncertain (cf. the story of Esau).

The fruits most common were the OLIVE, grape, and fig (Num 13:23). The olive was also made into an oil for cooking and for medication and the grape might be dried into raisins or crushed to make wine. The fig was eaten in its natural state. The palm tree produced dates and the pomegranate was also eaten (Num 20:5). Apples may have been eaten. This, however, is questionable (cf. Joel 1:12; Cant 8:5).

Vegetables included beans, lentils, and cucumbers. Onions, leeks, and garlic are mentioned as foods in Egypt (Num 11:5). Beans and lentils were brought to David as part of his supply of food while in flight from Absalom. Isa 1:8 refers to a cucumber field.

Cereals included barley and a primitive form of wheat called emmer. Due to the scarcity of meat and the seasonal nature of fruit, the people made cereal grains their main supply of food. Several of the grain products could be made into bread, commonly eaten at every meal.

Food in biblical times was usually in scarce supply for the average person. Many laws demand or encourage the feeding of the hungry.

See also AGRICULTURE/FARMING; FAMILY; FAMINE.

—FRED E. YOUNG

• **Food Offered to Idols.** The Greek word translated "food offered to idols" or "food sacrificed to idols" was used by Greek-speaking Jews to refer to sacrifices (usually of animals) which were a regular part of pagan worship (*4 Macc* 5:2; cf. 1 Cor 8:1, 4, 7, 10; 10:19, 28; Acts 15:29; 21:25; Rev 2:14, 20; *Did* 6:3). The meat offered on pagan altars was usually divided into three portions: one portion was burned on the altar, a second was given to the priest, and the third was given to the offerer for consumption within the temple precinct. If the priest did not use his portion, it was sold in the meat market.

A special problem facing the early Christians was whether or not they could eat food previously offered to idols. The importance of this problem becomes evident when one realizes how thoroughly pagan sacrifices permeated all levels of Greek and Roman society. Thus when the church spread to gentile territories, certain food laws were established, including abstinence from eating food which had been sacrificed to idols (Acts 15:29). Soon heretical groups sprang up which not only permitted the eating of such food but also advocated participation in the worship of pagan gods. One such group is strongly condemned in Rev 2:14-15.

In a lengthy portion of 1 Corinthians (8:1-11:1) Paul addresses the issue of eating food offered in pagan sacrifices. He neither appeals nor alludes to the prohibition of Acts 15:29, but instead broadens the discussion to include the question of how believers should use their Christian liberty. Paul is emphatic that the Kingdom of God is not meat and drink, and that Christians are free to eat what they are disposed to, including whatever is sold in the meat market (10:25). Paul also insists, however, that if meat was known to have been sacrificed to idols, then it was not to be eaten lest the more strict ("weaker") believer be offended (8:9-13). In short, Christian liberty must be exercised in love for "the brother for whose sake Christ died" (8:11). Thus, while there is nothing outside a person which going in can defile the person (Mark 7:14-23), and while believers need not make an issue out of meat sold in the market, Christians are to abstain from eating sacrificial meat for the sake of the weaker one's conscience and for their own peace of mind. Above all, everything must be done for the glory of God (10:23–11:1).

In Rom 14 Paul appears to be dealing with the same problem of idol meat, though his treatment in Romans is briefer and couched in more general terms. Possibly the weaker Christians in Rome shared dietary scruples similar to those of their counterparts in Corinth; however, there is no mention in Romans of idols or of food offered to idols. Yet Paul is careful to warn the Roman believers against becoming an occasion of stumbling to a weaker brother through libertarian dietary habits. The discussion proceeds along the same line as in 1 Corinthians—Paul lifts the entire issue to a higher level than mere diet.

See also CORINTHIAN CORRESPONDENCE; LOVE IN THE NEW TESTAMENT; WORSHIP IN THE NEW TESTAMENT.

Bibliography. C. K. Barrett, "Things Sacrificed to Idols," *NTS* 11 (1965): 138-53; G. Fee, "*Eidōluthata* Once Again: I Corinthians 8-10," *Bib* 61 (1980): 172-97.

—DAVID A. BLACK

• **Fool/Foolishness/Folly.** The main Hebrew terms, *nābāl,* "empty-headed" (Ps 14:1), *kĕsîl,* "thick-skulled, dull, stupid" (Prov 1:22), and *'iwwelet, 'ĕwîl,* "simpleton, fool" (Prov 1:7) refer literally to deficient mental capacity. In the LXX, the preferred Greek translation is *aphrōn,* "stupidity, irrationality," which is the negation of *phrēn,* "diaphram, inner organs," which seemed to control breath and emotion, and by extension were regarded as determining consciousness, intelligence, and spirituality. In Plato, *phrēn* is practical, whereas *sophia,* WISDOM, is intellectual. In addition to *aphrōn* (Luke 12:20; 2 Cor 12:11), the NT also used the Greek *mōros* (Matt 5:22; 1 Cor 4:10), a common Indo-European word for "mental deficiency, stupidity" (like the English "moron").

The NT concept depends on OT wisdom. In wisdom, the opposite of the properly ordered "wise" life is the irreverent and disobedient "foolish" life. Mental incapacity is only a small part of the cause—the foolish make themselves foolish. Foolishness is GODLESSNESS: the denial of the power of God, the refusal to fear God, and a failure to practice RIGHTEOUSNESS. Folly is practical atheism (Pss 14:1; 53:1). Pride, greed, thoughtlessness, overconfidence, self-deception, intemperance, and sensuality characterize the fool. Hence, in the NT, calling someone a "fool" is the worst curse (Matt 5:22). Paul reflects the wisdom dialectic: the wisdom of God is the antithesis of worldly wisdom—and so in the eyes of the world Christianity appears as folly (1 Cor 1:20-21). The Christ event is God's "foolishness," which paradoxically is wiser than worldly wisdom (1 Cor 1-3).

See also NABAL; WISDOM IN THE NEW TESTAMENT; WISDOM IN THE OLD TESTAMENT.

Bibliography. G. Bertram, "μωρός κτλ." and "φρήν κτλ." in *TDNT*; D. Georgi, "Folly" in *IDB*.

—JACK WEIR

• **Foreknowledge.** *See* PREDESTINATION

• **Forerunner.** *See* JOHN THE BAPTIST

• **Forgiveness/Pardon.** Forgiveness is primarily an act of grace by which God overcomes or takes away the barriers of SIN that separate God from people, thus making fellowship possible.

OT Usage. The most common Hebrew expression is *sālaḥ,* "to send away" (Lev 4:20, 26; 1 Kgs 8:30, 34; Pss 86:5; 103:3), from which the noun *ṣĕlîḥâ,* "forgiveness," is derived (Neh 9:17; Ps 130:4; Dan 9:9). Words of covering such as *kippēr,* "to cover over" (Exod 29:36; 30:10; Lev 8:15; 16:20; Ezek 43:20; 45:20), and *kāsâ,* "to cover" (Neh 4:5 [Heb 3:37], Pss 32:1; 85:2 [Heb 3]) are also used, along with verbs of removal such as *nāśā',* "to lift up," "take away" (Gen 50:17; Ps 32:5) and *māḥâ,* "to blot out" (Ps 51:1, 7 [Heb 3, 9]; Isa 43:25; 44:22).

The need for forgiveness was based on the belief that Israel's existence depended on its special COVENANT relationship with Yahweh. Since Yahweh is a holy God, Israel's sin continually puts this relationship in jeopardy. The people cannot live without God, but cannot approach God as sinners: thus, forgiveness is necessary. Extensive cultic procedures intended to gain forgiveness are found in the priestly writings. Lev 4–6 describes the sacrifices necessary for the removal of an individual's sin or guilt, while Lev 16 details the ritual for the nation-wide "DAY OF ATONEMENT."

The prophets and other writers emphasized that ritual alone was not sufficient, however. God is indeed eager to pardon (Exod 34:6-7; Ps 86:5; Isa 1:18-19), but expects repentance (2 Chr 7:14; Isa 1:16-17; 55:6-7; Hos 14:1-2 [Heb 2-3]; Joel 2:13) and a willingness to change one's behavior (Deut 30:2; 1 Kgs 8:36). It is not sacrifice God wants, but right living and humble service (Hos 6:6; Mic 6:6-8).

The Exile was understood as God's punishment for a people whose sin was too great to forgive, but later prophets saw the hope of a coming time when God would take the initiative in giving to Israel and to humankind a new covenant and a new heart (Jer 31:31-34; Ezek 36:25-27). Deutero-Isaiah saw this taking place through the ministry of a suffering servant on whom the sins of all would be laid and through whom God would bring about ultimate forgiveness (Isa 53).

Late Pre-Christian Period. Rabbinic Judaism was acutely aware of the omnipresence of sin, understood in both legal and ethical terms, and developed a detailed system that prescribed various means of expiation. The Qumran community also had an intense awareness of sin, which could be forgiven by God's grace, but only when the worshipers turned from their sinful ways in humble repentance (*1QH* 14:24; *1QS* 3:7ff.). The apocalypticism so common to the period led to a lessening of confidence in human abilities and a growing hope for future forgiveness based on God's redeeming action.

NT Usage. The most common words for forgiveness in NT Greek are *aphiēmi* and its cognate noun, *aphesis.* The verb's classical meaning is "to let go," with "to forgive" being a somewhat derived sense: thus only forty-five of its 142 occurrences relate to forgiveness, most of these in the Gospels (Matt 6:12-14; 9:6; Mark 2:7, 10; Luke 23:34; 1 John 1:9). On the other hand, the noun means "forgiveness" in fifteen of the seventeen times it occurs (Matt 26:28; Mark 1:4; Luke 1:77; Acts 2:38). Both of these terms are rare in Paul's writings, as he demonstrates a more developed system containing technical terms such as *dikaioō,* "to justify" (Rom 3:24; Gal 2:16), or *katallassō,* "to reconcile" (Rom 5:10; Col 1:22). As in the OT, circumlocutions include words for covering such as *kalyptō* (Jas 5:20; 1 Pet 4:8) and *epikalyptoō* (Rom 4:7), along with words for removal such as *airō,* "to take away" (John 1:29), *apoluō,* "to release" (Luke 6:37), and *apolouomai,* "to wash oneself" (Acts 22:16). On one occasion (Rom 3:25), *paresis,* "passing over," occurs in the sense of forgiveness, and legal terms such as "ransom" (*lutron*) may also appear (Matt 20:28; Mark 10:45).

The theme of forgiveness is central to the gospels. John came preaching a baptism of REPENTANCE "for the remission of sins" (Mark 1:4), combining the old prophetic call to repentance with a new promise of forgiveness through BAPTISM. Jesus made it clear that God's promised plan of redemption was fulfilled in him: the heart of his work was the forgiveness of humankind (Mark 10:45; Luke 4:18-21). Jesus himself forgave sins (Mark 2:5), and was proclaimed by his followers as the Savior who had come to grant repentance and forgiveness (Acts 5:31). Forgiveness is closely associated with Christ's death on the cross (Mark 10:45; Heb 9:22; 1 Pet 2:24): as the lamb of God he takes away the sin of the world (John 1:29).

Like John, Jesus stressed the prophetic call to repentance (Mark 1:15; Luke 24:47), along with faith. His emphasis on the importance of a subsequent change in the believer's lifestyle is seen in frequent warnings that God's forgiveness to Christians is conditioned by the believer's willingness to forgive others (Matt 6:14-15; 18:21-22; 33-35; Mark 11:25; Luke 11:4; 17:3-4).

The early church interpreted the forgiveness of Christ against the backdrop of the eschatological kingdom that he introduced. Forgiveness is received when one accepts God's judgment through confession of sins (Jas 5:16; 1 John 1:9), repentance (Acts 2:38; 8:22; 20:21; Heb 6:11), and faith (Acts 15:9; Rom 3:22-26; Gal 2:16; Heb 11:6). But this forgiveness does more than just wash away past sins. The believer has died to the old self and has become a new person, no longer under the bondage of sin (Rom 6; Gal 2:19-20; 1 Pet 2:24), but accepted into the eternal kingdom of God (Col 1:13-14).

See also ATONEMENT/EXPIATION IN THE NEW TESTAMENT; ATONEMENT/EXPIATION IN THE OLD TESTAMENT.

Bibliography. R. Bultmann, "ἀφίημι," *TDNT*; W. Eichrodt, *Theology of the Old Testament*; W. A. Quanbeck, "Forgiveness," *IDB*; V. Taylor, *Forgiveness and Reconciliation*; H. Vorländer, "Forgiveness," *DNTT*.

—TONY W. CARTLEDGE

• **Formalism.** *See* LITERATURE, BIBLE AS

• **Form/Gattung.** [gah'toonk] The Bible is composed of diverse types of literature. Any group of writings having well-defined characteristics in common is a type (French *genre;* German *Gattung*). Types of the novel, for example, range widely from detective and romance stories to Stephen King's horror tales and Robert Heinlein's science fiction. Nonfiction works may range from biographies and military manuals to astronomy articles published in astronomy journals. Historical novels purport to combine fact and fiction in a unique manner (sometimes called "faction") designed either to entertain or inform, or both.

Religious literature, including the Bible, is rich in the astounding diversity of its types. The Gospel of Mark in the NT belongs to a *Gattung*, that is, a literary work of a unique kind or *genre*. It is neither strictly a biography nor a work of fiction created primarily to entertain readers. The *genre* of gospel is a special work of literature that draws upon historical accounts, propaganda, visions, poems, exortations, wonder tales, sayings, legends, rituals, curses, benedictions, and other strands of folk life either written or oral. The four Gospels of the NT were written under the control of religious purposes or theological messages. The same may be said of the Book of Judges and other literary works of the OT. They are a special *genre* or *Gattung*. Their authors selected, revised, and adapted material from their culture under the guidance of their overriding purposes and unique messages.

Virtually every "book" of the Bible was composed as much by an editor as by an author, for each "book" was woven together from numerous threads and literary units that came from the editor-author-compiler's tradition. Each creative reworking of the ancient literary units became in a profound sense the fulfillment and development of its written and oral predecessors. The Russian writer Dostoevsky drew material from Charles Dickens and others and then reworked their material with his own genius into a new literary creation. Similarly, biblical writers, drawing from others, created new literary masterpieces. Form critics and editorial (redaction) critics among biblical scholars seek to trace out the various units or forms that the biblical writers appropriated from their culture in order better to grasp the biblical writers's controlling interests and dominant theological messages.

Twentieth-century biblical scholars frequently focus on and isolate small units of literature within larger units in order to study the common structure or type of the smaller units. Detailed comparison of literary types within the Bible with similar types within other ancient literary texts has proved exceedingly fruitful in recent decades. Each larger text is revealed to be unique in the way that it assembles and utilizes the literary subtypes or subgenres available to it. Whenever scholars judge that a major mutation of literary type emerged in antiquity, they are prone to search for the major changes in historical and social conditions or in cultural pressures that triggered the mutation. Hence, increasingly biblical scholarship draws from the disciplines of comparative literature, secular history, and the various branches of the social sciences (especially sociology and anthropology).

See also APOPHTHEGM; EPISTLE/LETTER; GENRE IN THE OLD TESTAMENT; GENRE, CONCEPT OF; GENRE, GOSPEL; GOSPELS, CRITICAL STUDY OF; LITERARY CRITICISM; LITERATURE, BIBLE AS; MIRACLE STORY; PARABLES.

Bibliography. J. M. Robinson, *The Problem of History in Mark and Other Markan Studies;* C. H. Talbert, *What Is a Gospel? The Genre of the Canonical Gospels;* G. A. Wells, *The Historical Evidence for Jesus.*

—JOE E. BARNHART

• **Fornication.** The terms for fornication, while originally used to designate sexual activities associated with a prostitute, came to acquire a more generalized meaning of any kind of illicit or non-marital sexual intercourse. In the OT, various sexual activities are condemned. Among the prohibited sexual relationships are incest, HOMOSEXUALITY, prostitution, bestiality, and adultery. According to the ancient Israelites, adultery was a violation of another man's wife or fiance. A man committed adultery against the husband of the woman, not against his own wife.

The OT does not always condemn prostitution. At least two important figures are described as being prostitutes, yet are never condemned or disparaged for their activities. Rahab, the harlot of Jericho (Josh 2), played a critical role in the story of the Israelites' conquering of that city. Tamar, daughter-in-law of Judah, served briefly as a prostitute to achieve her goal of becoming pregnant. Although Judah initially was furious when he discovered Tamar's deception, she suffered no punishment for her act (Gen 38). On the other hand, many of the sayings in Proverbs warn against association with prostitutes or loose women (5:3-6, 20; 6:23-29; 7:10-27). The imagery in these passages, however, is as much metaphorical as literal. Socially and religiously, prostitutes were viewed as inferior. They were grouped with divorced women and women who had been defiled as persons whom priests were not allowed to marry (Lev 21:7, 14). Any daughter of a priest who became a prostitute was to be burned (Lev 21:9). The Israelites were warned not to allow their daughters to become prostitutes (Lev 19:29).

Premarital sexual intercourse, at least for males, is never explicitly condemned in the OT. The only injunctions given against male premarital sexual activities are those which would include all men, married or single (Lev 18–20; Deut 22:22-30). A young girl, however, was expected to be a virgin at the time of marriage. Proof of virginity could be required, with severe penalties provided for those who failed the test (Deut 22:13-21).

The OT also uses the term "fornication" figuratively to describe Israel's idolatry. Sexual terminology was appropriate to describe religious infidelity because Canaanite religions often utilized sacred prostitutes in worship. Thus, to commit "religious fornication" also often involved actual sexual fornication. This figurative use of the term fornication is found throughout the OT (Exod 34:16; Lev 20:5; Jer 3:1-10; Ezek 16:15-43; 23:1-49; Hos 1:2; 5:3).

In the NT fornication includes all types of sexual immorality. Christians are to avoid fornication, a sin against one's own body (1 Cor 6:18). Abstention from fornication is declared to be the will of God (1 Thess 4:3). Paul lists fornication as one of the works of the flesh (Gal 5:19) and includes fornicators among those who will not inherit the Kingdom of God (1 Cor 6:9-11; cf. Eph 5:5). In the Gospel of Matthew, fornication is the only exception given in the prohibition against divorce (Matt 5:32; 19:9). The author of Revelation uses the term figuratively to describe the rebellion of the people against God (e.g., 2:21; 17:2; 18:9).

See also ADULTERY IN THE NEW TESTAMENT; ADULTERY IN THE OLD TESTAMENT; FAMILY; HARLOT; HOMOSEXUALITY IN THE BIBLE; MARRIAGE IN THE NEW TESTAMENT; MARRIAGE IN THE OLD TESTAMENT; SODOMY.

Bibliography. J. Jensen, "Does *Porneia* Mean Fornication? A Critique of Bruce Malina," *NovT* 20 (1978): 161-84; B. Malina, "Does *Porneia* Mean Fornication?" *NovT* 14 (1972): 10-17; R. Patai, *Family, Love, and the Bible.*

—MITCHELL G. REDDISH

• **Forts/Fortifications.** A system of defensive structures, usually consisting of walls, towers, and gates. Though the majority of the population in the biblical world lived in unwalled villages and farmed the surrounding fields, there was a significant trend towards urbanization beginning in the third millennium B.C.E. These cities, in Palestine and elsewhere, were normally surrounded by fortifications, and they provided a haven for the occupants in times of war (cf. Num 13:28; Deut 1:28). People who lived in unwalled settlements or at some distance from the fortified urban centers were exposed to great danger (cf. Ezek 38:11; Zech 2:4). In addition to the walled towns, there were small isolated forts at strategic locations in most biblical lands; these were built for security purposes and guarded borders, passes, commercial routes, etc. (cf. 2 Sam 8:6; 2 Chr 11:5-11; 17:12; 27:4).

Great ingenuity and expenditure of labor went into the task of building walls, towers, and gates that could withstand the outright attacks and siege warfare of one's enemies. Attention was given to the proper construction of foundations and to the height and thickness of walls, and gate complexes had to be built on a massive scale, since the gateway was, obviously, the weakest point in a town's defensive system. The famous reliefs from SENNACHERIB's palace in Nineveh portray dramatically the Assyrian siege of Lachish (cf. 2 Kgs 18:13-37; 19:8), and the Bible itself is filled with references to sieges of fortified Israelite towns (e.g., Deut 20:20; 2 Sam 20:15; Luke 19:43; 21:20). According to 2 Kgs 17:5, some cities could resist siege for a long time. Because defenses were constructed so well, sometimes the best way to capture a city was to lure its defenders outside the safety of their walls (cf. Josh 8:10-17).

Though walled cities varied in size, the area enclosed by defensive walls in ancient Palestine averaged between five and ten acres, but some were much larger. Naturally, the dimensions of the walls, towers, and gates varied greatly, and the architectural styles changed from period to period. The stone walls built at JERICHO ca. 7000 B.C.E. are the oldest known city fortifications in Palestine and were over six ft. thick. Fortified towns became common by ca. 3000 B.C.E. when city walls were erected around such famous biblical sites as MEGIDDO and GEZER. From the beginning of the third millennium B.C.E. until the arrival of the Romans, cities in the Middle East were almost always fortified. Walls were made of stone and/or mudbrick, with the latter being more commonly used for superstructures; walls typically ranged from fifteen to twenty-five ft. in width and were up to forty ft. high. Solid stone walls were known, but in some periods the ''casemate'' wall was the norm. In the latter, open chambers, which were sometimes filled in with rubble, were sandwiched between two parallel stone walls. A well-known series of casemate walls from ancient Israel, which were found in association with elaborate and strongly built gate complexes, have been found at Solomonic HAZOR, Megiddo, and Gezer (cf. 1 Kgs 9:15). Other famous city fortifications protected Jericho (Josh 6:20), Babylon (Jer 51:44), DAMASCUS (Jer 49:27), and TYRE (Ezek 26:4). Of course, the fortifications of JERUSALEM are mentioned frequently in the Hebrew Bible (e.g., 2 Sam 5:9; 1 Kgs 3:1; 9:15; Ps 48; Neh 1:3; 2:17). It should also be observed that city fortifications were built to accommodate a variety of military or even domestic activities (e.g., 2 Sam 11:20-21, 24; Isa 36:11-12; Josh 2:15). City fortifications were so much a part of the ancient environment that they are mentioned in a striking variety of figurative expressions in the Bible (e.g., 2 Sam 22:2-3; Ps 9:9; Prov 18:11; 25:28; Isa 26:1; 30:13; 60:18).

—GERALD L. MATTINGLY

• **Freedom.** In the NT freedom is always freedom *from* one sphere of obligations and responsibilities *for* another, but never freedom for oneself. As a theological concept freedom means fundamentally freedom in Christ and thus entails obligations to the *Lord* Jesus Christ. This explains the ease with which Paul, for instance, can identify freedom in Christ with being the slave or servant of Christ. Salvation as liberation places one under the sovereign lordship of Christ, who is ''savior'' only insofar as he is ''lord.'' Freedom is conceived in a variety of ways in the NT. At least seven types may be mentioned.

Freedom from Fate. Probably many gentile converts to faith in Christ, such as the converts of Paul's mission, understood themselves as having been liberated from the powers of ''fate'' (cf. Gal 4:8-11). According to the astrological world view pervasive in the Greco-Roman world, human existence is governed by ineluctable forces, typically referred to as ''fate'' or ''necessity.'' While NT writers do not reject the idea of ''necessity,'' they ascribe it to divine providence (cf. Luke-Acts, Paul, and John). Hence, freedom from fate does not mean freedom for self-determination but release from blind and impersonal powers to the Lord of creation, whose sovereign purpose is grounded in justice and love.

Freedom from Sin. Paul views SIN as a power from which believers have been liberated by Christ (Rom 6:1–8:17). This liberation does not exempt believers from struggle against sin. On the contrary, where once they were merely the impotent servants of sin, now they are active participants in the Spirit's battle against ''the flesh'' (Gal 5:13-25; Rom 8:12-13). The Gospel of John closely associates the social metaphors of ethical bondage and freedom with the concept of knowledge (John 8:31-47), which is consistent with the profound Johannine idea that knowing the truth and doing the truth are inseparable (John 8:32; 7:17; 14:20-21). According to James, the gospel means freedom as sovereignty over one's passions. What all three of these NT writers have in common is the conviction that authentic human freedom assumes shape concretely as responsible ethical action.

Freedom from Evil Powers. Closely associated with the idea of freedom from the power of sin is that of liberation from EVIL powers. There is a widespread assumption in the NT that the world is dominated by ''personal'' powers hostile to God (Eph 6:12; John 12:31; 1 Pet 5:8; 1 Cor 15:24-25), which afflict human beings with various evils, from physical ills to social and political oppression. Jesus' healing miracles and exorcisms are viewed as victories over these powers and thus as liberating acts of salvation (Luke 4:18; 13:16; Mark 5:1-14; 7:35). As such,they anticipate the final liberation of the world from the evil powers that dominate it. Paul conceives of the Spirit's activity in a similar way, calling it the ''down payment'' and ''first fruits'' of salvation (2 Cor 1:22; 5:5; Rom 8:23). As a saving presence of divine power the Spirit means ''freedom'' (2 Cor 3:17), freedom as power against ''the flesh'' (Gal 5:1, 13, 16-17; Rom 8:12-15) and freedom experienced in miraculous manifestations of transcendent power (Gal 3:5; 1 Cor 12), which anticipate the final liberation of believers and of the whole creation (Rom 8:18-25). Paul stresses, however, that this liberating or transcendent life in the Spirit flows from the cross (Gal 3:13-14) and is therefore inseparably, if paradoxically, linked with participation in Jesus' death.

Freedom from the Power of Death. According to the author of Hebrews, Christ's death destroys ''the one who has the power of death'' (the devil) and delivers ''all those who through fear of death were subject to lifelong bondage'' (Heb 2:14-15). This deliverance from death touches the psychological sphere as freedom from the anxiety that death as judgment evokes. It affects the ethical sphere as freedom from ''dead works'' (9:14) for authentic service to God. Paul associates the power of death with ''futility,'' from which the whole creation will one day be released (Rom 8:20-21). The word ''futility'' suggests an interrelation between the rule of death over the physical realm and its power over the spirit. For Paul, death is both an expression of divine wrath (''the wages of sin'') and the ''last enemy'' to be destroyed by Christ (cf. Rom 6:23; 1 Cor 15:26). While believers live under the conditions of present earthly existence they remain subject to the power of death as futility, but they are sustained by the life of Christ granted to them in the Spirit. Life in the Spirit, however, is not liberation *from* death but life *against* death. By contrast, John uses the language of freedom *from* death to describe the present situation of believers (5:24). This freedom is understood as an organic unity of knowing and doing the truth (cf. above). Therefore, it assumes shape in the world as conformity to the self-giving way of the cross (15:12-13). Freedom from death means going the way of the seed, which must fall into the ground and die in order to live (12:24).

Freedom from the Law. The idea that believers are free from the Law of Moses is found in both Paul and Luke-Acts. Luke-Acts conceives this freedom as liberation from ''a yoke'' that ''neither our fathers nor we have been able to bear'' (Acts 15:10; cf. 13:39). For Paul freedom from the Law has two aspects. First, it means that believers are not obliged to follow the Mosaic Law because they belong to Christ, whose claims supersede those of the Law. In this sense freedom from the Law is not liberation from the Law, as if the Law were a burden or an evil power. It is like the freedom from obligations that goes into effect when death destroys the relationship in which legal obligations are constituted (Rom 7:2). According to Paul, believers have been crucified to the world, which is structured in ''pairs of opposites,'' and now belong to a world ''in Christ,'' where all are one (Gal 3:27-28; 6:14-15). One pair of opposites that no longer holds in Christ is the distinction, defined and maintained by the Jewish obligation to the Law, between Jew and non-Jew (Gal 3:28). Thus the universality of the new world inaugurated in the gospel spells the end of obligations to the Torah. But Paul also conceives of freedom from the Law as liberation from the curse of the Law and the power of sin. The Law pronounces God's righteous judgment or ''curse'' on sinners and thus seals them in bondage to the power of sin (Gal 3:10-14; 3:21–4:7). Moreover, sin misuses the commandment toward unrighteous ends (Rom 7:7-14). Therefore, Paul views existence under the Law as a context of bondage to sin from which people are liberated by Christ (Gal 3:13-14; 4:4; Rom 8:1-2).

Freedom from Class Distinctions. The Greco-Roman world was marked by social stratification, which distinguished the privileges and arenas of participation appropriate to various members of society. When Paul declares that he is ''free'' in Christ ''from all'' by virtue of his exclusive bondage to Christ, he indicates that he regards himself as no longer obliged to fulfill the social roles and obligations dictated to him by society. In saying that he is ''free from all'' and ''bound to all,'' he indicates that class distinctions no longer determine his existence in Christ (1 Cor 9:19-24). At least in the churches of Paul's gentile mission, this idea of freedom in Christ from class distinction was taken quite seriously and found expression in the famous slogan, ''There is neither Jew nor Greek, there is neither slave nor free, there is neither male nor female'' (Gal 3:28; cf. Col 3:11). Paul maintains that believers are to live out the truth of this slogan in the world by being ready to submit themselves voluntarily to obligations that no longer bind them (1 Cor 7:17-24), in the interest of promoting the gospel. For although believers belong to the new creation, where class distinctions no longer hold, their very freedom in Christ entails obligations to Christ that may under certain conditions require that they not make use of their freedom. The qualified egalitarianism that is reflected in Paul's Letters is not characteristic of the NT as a whole. Although there is evidence that Jesus' own ministry was remarkably egalitarian in certain respects, explicit theological foundations for the idea of ''freedom from class distinctions'' are found only in Paul.

Freedom from Economic and Political Oppression. Many Jews in the first century, particularly those in Palestine, viewed life under Roman rule as a form of political and economic disenfranchisement. Political alliances between the wealthy Jewish aristocracy and the Romans generally worked to the detriment of the Jewish peasantry, who found themselves increasingly overtaxed, divested of land, and forced into debt. It is probably fair to say that most Jews of Jesus' day expected that God would one day ''restore the kingdom (political sovereignty) to Israel'' (Acts 1:6) and that all the nations would stream to pay homage to Zion (Isa 2:2; 60:3). But opinions about how this would be accomplished were quite varied, and it is necessary to distinguish between the speculative ''messianic philosophies'' that arose among the literate (e.g., in scribal circles) and the popular hopes of the peasantry. Although there are certain similarities between these two streams of expectation, the peasants tended to translate their values and religious expectations much more readily into revolutionary activity than did the theologians. The Jewish peasants supported anti-Roman banditry. From peasant ranks activist ''prophets'' and ''kings'' emerged to lead popular uprisings against the Romans and the Jewish ruling class. From among the peasants oracular prophets arose, denouncing oppression and injustice and proclaiming the imminent liberating intervention of God. And it was in the midst of such a volatile social and political climate that a peasant named Jesus of Nazareth came preaching the Kingdom of God.

Although it has often been maintained that Jesus himself rejected the role of a ''political Messiah,'' the matter cannot be settled by deciding between simple alternatives. Jesus did not lead a revolt against Rome, but he was executed as a royal claimant to powers that Rome reserved for Caesar (Mark 15:2, 26; John 19:12-16), and he was crucified along with two ''bandits'' (Mark 15:27). There can be no doubt that many people, including John the Baptist, pinned revolutionary hopes on him, and the synoptic Gospels suggest that although he did not accept the role of political activist, his religious values were revolutionary and his expectation was that God would soon realize the radical Kingdom that he preached. To be sure, it is virtually impossible to distinguish between the views of the historical Jesus and those of a given Gospel writer, each of whom presents Jesus according to his own spiritual lights. The Gospel of Luke is a case in point. As Luke sees it, the mission of Jesus is best summed up in the words of Isa 61:1-2a (Luke 4:18-19), which announce good news to the poor and liberty to those who are oppressed. Although Luke-Acts understands both the ''spiritual'' and the ''social'' aspects of this vision of salvation as belonging to the mission of the church, which lives by the power of the Spirit, there is no evidence in Luke-Acts to suggest that the church either did or is expected to carry out this vision in political, much less revolutionary, terms. Luke-Acts affirms the *value* of socioeconomic liberation for the oppressed, which is central to the prophetic tradition in the Bible, but expects that this liberation must await the final apocalyptic action of God (Luke 21; Acts 1:6-11; cf. Jas 5:1-11).

See also ASTROLOGY; CHURCH AND LAW; ECONOMICS IN THE NEW TESTAMENT; ETHICS IN THE NEW TESTAMENT; EVIL; FLESH AND SPIRIT; HOLY SPIRIT; LAW IN THE NEW TESTAMENT; LAW IN THE OLD TESTAMENT; SATAN IN THE NEW TESTAMENT; SIN; SOCIOLOGY OF THE NEW TESTAMENT.

Bibliography. R. Bultmann, "Freedom," *Theology of the New Testament*; C. H. Cosgrove, "The Divine *Dei* in Luke-Acts: Investigations into the Lukan Understanding of Divine Providence," *NovT* 26 (1984): 168-90; B. Gerhardsson, "*Eleutheria* ('freedom') in the Bible," in *Scripture: Meaning and Method*, ed. B. P. Thompson; R. A. Horsley and J. S. Hanson, *Bandits, Prophets, and Messiahs: Popular Movements in the Time of Jesus*; E. Käsemann, *Jesus Means Freedom*; W. A. Meeks, "The Image of the Androgyne: Some Uses of a Symbol in Earliest Christianity," *HR* 13 (1974): 165-208; G. V. Pixley, "God's Kingdom in First Century Palestine: The Strategy of Jesus," *The Bible and Liberation*, ed. N. Gottwald; W. Wink, *Naming the Powers: The Language of Power in the New Testament*.

—CHARLES H. COSGROVE

• **Freedom in the Old Testament.** *See* LIBERTY

• **Friendship.** The Hebrew noun *rēaʿ*, which is generally translated "friend" exhibits various shades of meaning: "friend" (Deut 13:6 [7]); "lover" (Jer 3:1, 20; Hos 3:1); "companion" (Job 30:29); "neighbor" (Lev 19:18); "fellow human being" (Prov 6:1; 25:8); "another" (1 Sam 28:17). Related occurrences can be rendered as "royal advisor" (1 Kgs 4:5; 1 Chr 27:33); as "playmates" or "companions" of the queen (Ps 45:14; cf. Judg 11:38); as an address (Cant 5:1; cf. Matt 20:13; Luke 12:4); and as "best man" (Judg 14:20; cf. John 3:29).

In the NT *philos* is a friend who is "well-known" (Luke 14:12); a "guest" (Luke 11:6); or a member of a group gathered around a leader (Luke 7:6; Acts 10:24). Jesus is accused of being the friend of sinners and tax collectors (Matt 11:19; Luke 7:34). The disciples are elevated by Jesus to the position of friends (John 15:15). NT friendship involves joy, hospitality, service, and sacrifice (Luke 15:6; John 3:29; Luke 11:5-8).

The Bible affirms the mutual respect and trust of true friendship. The bonds of friendship can often equal or transcend the love and affection uniting members of the same family or clan. Friends may stick closer than brothers or sisters (Prov 18:24; cf. 17:17) and may even lay down their lives for a friend (John 15:13). Scripture does, however, admit the rarity of true friends and admonishes those who falsely practice friendship (Prov 14:20; Jas 4:4).

A notable example of friendship is found in the covenant JONATHAN established with DAVID (1 Sam 18:3). Their friendship was sealed with a gift (1 Sam 18:4) and an oath before the Lord (2 Sam 21:7). David's deep love for Jonathan is expressed in the moving lament of 2 Sam 1:19-27.

See also LOVE IN THE NEW TESTAMENT; LOVE IN THE OLD TESTAMENT.

—STEPHEN J. ANDREWS

• **Fringes.** Tassels originally attached to the corners of an outer garment.

Deut 2:12 lists the basic command to the Israelites to make tassels that were to be placed on the outer garment. Num 15:37-41 expands upon that information. There, Moses was told that the tassels were to be attached by blue cords. These were to be visible so that they might serve as a constant reminder of the commandments that God had given and the obligation of each Israelite to observe them. Although this law was directed to all Israelites, the rabbis later exempted women because as a general rule women were not required to keep positive commandments that were dependent upon a fixed time for their fulfillment.

The Gospel of Matthew records that a woman who had been hemorrhaging for twelve years touched the fringe of Jesus' garment and was instantly healed. Jesus attributed the cure to her faith, not to the touching of the fringes (Matt 9:20; Luke 8:43-44). Apparently this was a common practice since many sick people attempted to do the same thing, and all who were successful were also healed (Matt 14:35-36; Mark 6:56).

Matthew calls attention to certain scribes and PHARISEES who made a practice of lengthening their fringes in order to make a public display of their piety. The faithful are warned not to follow their example because those who exalt themselves will be humbled (Matt 23:5) and have no reward from God (Matt 6:1).

Tassels continue to be worn by Jewish males, particularly in the Orthodox community. The tassels, however, are attached to an undergarment and to the prayer shawl.

See also DRESS.

—WILMA ANN BAILEY

• **Fuel.** *See* DUNG

• **Funerals.** *See* MOURNING RITES

• **Furniture.** The quantity and quality of furniture in the house of an Israelite family varied according to the wealth of the family. The early Israelites lived in tents (Gen 12:8; 24:67; 33:18-19); in large families men and women lived in separate tents (Gen 31:33). Tent furniture (Num 19:8) was very simple. The floor was covered with straw mats or wool rugs. The furniture was utilitarian items such as lamps, pots, jars, kettles, and water bottles. Every home would have a millstone (Deut 24:6), a kneading bowl (Exod 12:34), and a pestle and mortar (Num 11:8). Stoves for baking bread and cooking were made of stones set at the tent door.

With the economic development of Israelite society, most people began to build larger and better houses. Most Israelite houses were built of bricks or stones; they consisted of three or four rooms built around a central court. The houses of peasants were decorated with a limited amount of furniture. Most of their furniture consisted of cooking utensils. Their table was a mat; they slept on rugs, wrapped in their cloaks (Exod 22:26-27). More prosperous families would have an upper chamber containing at least a bed, a chair, a table, and a lamp (2 Kgs 4:10).

Community life in Israelite society was centered around the family. To an Israelite, furniture was a necessary amenity to make life a little easier. Ornate furniture had its origin in Israel when the people came in contact with Canaanite culture. Tables, for instance, are never mentioned in the patriarchal narratives. The early Israelites sat down on rugs to eat (Gen 37:25; cf. Isa 21:5). The first mention of a table is found in Judg 1:7 where a Cannanite king mentions a table used at banquets. An important person would have a larger table to accommodate his many guests (1 Sam 20:24-25, 34). In the NT guests would recline around the table as they ate (Luke 7:36).

Beds for most people would be a reed mat on the floor. Some families would have beds with wooden frames which at times could serve as a litter or stretcher (1 Sam 19:15; Matt 9:2; Luke 5:18). Some beds were expensive, costing enough to pay a debt (Prov 22:27). Ivory was used to decorate homes (1 Kgs 22:39) and furniture. Amos speaks of beds inlaid with ivory (Amos 6:4); Hezekiah, king of Judah, paid part of his tribute to Sennacherib, king of Assyria, with beds and chairs inlaid with ivory. The couches of Xerxes (Ahasuerus) were of silver and gold (Esth 1:6).

Chairs were also found in many houses. There were common chairs (1 Sam 4:13) and royal chairs (Judg 3:20), chairs for dining occasions (1 Sam 20:24-25), formal occasions (1 Kgs 2:19), and for the affairs of government (1 Kgs 10:4-5). Solomon's throne was probably a high-backed chair of wood inlaid with ivory and plated with gold, with arm rests, decorated with lions and bulls (1 Kgs 10:18-20). This kind of royal seat has also been found in the iconography of the ancient Near East.

Every home had a hearth. It was generally a shallow hole in a corner around which a circle of stones was set. Most houses were furnished with different kinds of vessels for storing liquids and grains and for cooking. Bowls, cups, jars, pitchers, juglets, and lamps were common items in almost every household in Israel.

The word "furniture" is also applied to the furnishings of the tabernacle in the wilderness (Exod 25:9) and to the furnishings of the Temple in Jerusalem (1 Chr 9:29).

Bibliography. M. Noth, *The Old Testament World*.

—CLAUDE F. MARIOTTINI

• **Future Life.** *See* ETERNAL LIFE; RESURRECTION IN THE NEW TESTAMENT; RESURRECTION IN THE OLD TESTAMENT; SHEOL

• Gabbatha. [gab'uh-thuh] Occurring only once in the Bible, in John 19:13, the word refers to the paved court where the Roman procurator Pontius PILATE conducted the public trial of Jesus. The site now favored is that adjacent to the TOWER OF ANTONIA, a garrison constructed by HEROD on the northwest corner of the Temple Mount (PLATES 24, 25, 34). Excavations in that area have uncovered 2,500 square yards of pavement made of large flagstones nearly two feet thick with an average length of four feet and width of three and one-half feet. The paved area was on a lofty place, partly roughened for the passage of chariots, but smooth over most of its area. This ancient pavement may be seen today in the basement of the convent of Our Lady of Zion on the VIA DOLOROSA.

See also ANTONIA, TOWER OF; HEROD; PILATE; VIA DOLOROSA.

—WILLIAM F. BROMLEY

• Gabriel. *See* ANGEL

• Gad. [gad] Good fortune; the name of the founder of a tribe in Israel, a prophet, and a pagan god.

1. The seventh son of JACOB, yet the first by LEAH's maid Zilpah (Gen 30:10-11). As such, he was the only full brother of ASHER (Gen 30:12-13). In his final blessing, Jacob promised Gad that he and his descendants would have a troubled life, but that they would ultimately prevail (Gen 49:19).

Gad apparently had seven sons (Gen 46:16) whose descendants later comprised seven separate clans (Num 26:15-18). When the Israelites defeated Sihon and Og, the tribal entities of REUBEN, Gad, and MANASSEH asked to settle that Transjordanian area. MOSES agreed (Num 32) and thus the territory assigned to the Gadites was bounded by the Jordan River on the west, Manasseh on the north, the Ammonites on the east, and Reuben on the south (PLATES 10, 11). Though the area was largely range land except for the Levitical city of HESHBON (Josh 21:34-40), it was strategically located and thus in constant conflict (Judg 10–12; 2 Kgs 10:32-33; 2 Kgs 15:29; Jer 49:1-6).

2. A prophet or "seer" during DAVID's day (1 Chr 21:9). He advised David to leave Moab when Saul was approaching (1 Sam 22:3-5). Later, he offered David a choice of punishments for having taken the census (2 Sam 24:13-15). He also commanded David to purchase the threshing floor of Araunah, the Jebusite (2 Sam 24:18-25). Then, he helped David and NATHAN in organizing the music for the tabernacle (2 Chr 29:25). Finally, he wrote a brief history of David's kingship (1 Chr 29:29).

3. A pagan deity who was worshiped by the Canaanites as the god of good fortune (Isa 65:11).

See also GILEAD.

Bibliography. H. G. Stingers, *A Commentary on Genesis*.

—HARRY B. HUNT, JR.

• Gadara. [gad'uh-ruh] Gadara (modern Umm Qeis) is about six mi. southeast of the Sea of Galilee (PLATE 23). It is mentioned in some manuscripts of Mark 5:1 and Luke 8:26, 37 as the site of Jesus' healing of a demoniac. Gadara was one of the chief cities of the DECAPOLIS and was granted by Augustus to Herod the Great. After Herod's death, Augustus granted the appeal of citizens of Gadara to be placed under the jurisdiction of the province of Syria. The RSV identifies Gergesa as the site of Jesus' healing. Gadara is located too far away from the lake to suit the description of the demoniac as meeting Jesus immediately upon his crossing to the eastern side of the lake. Origen noted that Gadara (and Gergesa) were too far from the lake to be identified as the site of Jesus' healing. He noted that Gergesa was nearby and had a cliff overlooking the Sea of Galilee. For readers interested in relating the story to some specific region, Gergesa (Kursi) is an appealing choice. Kursi provides the only location around the entire Sea of Galilee where a steep place falls precipitously into the water (south of Kursi about a mi.).

See also DECAPOLIS; GALILEE, SEA OF.

—JERRY VARDAMAN

• Gadarene Demoniac. *See* GADARA

• Gaius. [gay'yuhs] A Latin personal name used several times in the NT apparently in reference to four different persons:

1. In Acts 19:29 Gaius (along with Aristarchus) is mentioned as a Macedonean companion of Paul who was attacked by the Ephesian worshipers of the goddess Artemis.

2. Acts 20:4-5 refers to a Christian from Derbe named Gaius who awaited Paul at Troas and accompanied him on his journey to Jerusalem.

3. A Corinthian Christian by the name of Gaius who was baptized by Paul is listed in Rom 16:23 and 1 Cor 1:14. He was apparently a man of prominence since the church met in his home and Paul resided with him on his third Corinthian visit.

4. Third John is addressed to "the beloved Gaius" (1:1).

Chapman (*JTS* 5 [1904] 366ff.) attempts unconvincingly to identify (4) with (1) and (3), and Goodspeed (*JBL* 69 [1950] 381-83) suggests that (3) is the same as Titus Justus of Acts 18:7.

—JOHN COLLINS

• **Galatia.** [guh-lay'shuh] The word Galatia comes from the Greek word for Gauls, the people who invaded and settled in Asia Minor during the late third century B.C.E. The invasion was part of a larger migration of Celtic people in Europe during the last part of the first millennium B.C.E. The term Galatia is used of two different areas during NT times.

Galatia proper (ethnic Galatia) is used to describe the northern part of the central plateau in Asia Minor where the Celtic tribes settled. They invaded Macedonia and Thrace, and were invited in 279 B.C.E. by King Nicomedes of Bithynia to aid him in a war he was in danger of losing to his brother. Later, after completing their service to Nicomedes, the Celts terrorized the countryside. About 275 B.C.E., the Seleucid king Antiochus I finally brought them under control and limited their territory. Attalus I, king of Pergamum, checked their power in 232 B.C.E., and limited their territory even more. During his time the name Galatia was applied to their land.

Living mostly in rural areas, the Galatians were slow to adopt Hellenistic culture. Some writers called them barbarians, but by the first Christian century many of them spoke Greek as well as their native tongue. The chief cities, Ancrya, Pessinus, and Tavium, preserved their ancient Phrygian character and customs.

Provincial Galatia refers to the Roman province which included Galatia proper along with other territory (PLATES 26, 27). In spite of earlier defeats, the Galatians continued to be a military force in Asia, often serving as mercenaries for kings of nearby nations. They sided with Antiochus III, when his Seleucid army was defeated by the Romans in 190 B.C.E. The next year the Romans soundly defeated the Galatians, but leniently granted them independence. In 64 B.C.E., the Roman general Pompey placed them under the rule of Deiotarus and expanded his territory. Later, Mark Antony appointed Amyntas as Deiotarus's successor and gave him additional territory. When Amyntas was killed in 25 B.C.E. his kingdom was bequeathed to the Romans who then gave the name Galatia to the province. This new province included parts of the old kingdoms of Paphlagonia, Pontus, Phrygia, Pisidia, Lycaonia, and Isauria. The southern cities of Pisidian Antioch, Iconium, Lystra, and Derbe were included in its boundaries.

The application of the term Galatia both to the region where the ethnic Galatians lived and to the Roman province causes some difficulties in NT interpretation. Twice in the Book of Acts (16:6; 18:23) Paul is said to have passed through "the region of Galatia and Phrygia." Since the Greek wording is ambiguous, scholars debate whether Luke referred to Galatia proper or to the province of Galatia. The issue is whether Paul ever went as far north as ethnic Galatia.

Disagreement also exists about Paul's use of the terms Galatia and Galatians. The issue is whether the Letter to the Galatians was written to the churches in the north, ethnic Galatia, or to those in the southern region of the Galatian province. Did Paul, like some other ancient writers, restrict "Galatians" to the Celtic people, or did he use the term loosely of the people living in the province, whatever their true nationality? In 1 Cor 16:1, speaking of his offering for the church in Jerusalem, Paul referred to Galatia in its political sense. It is, however, impossible to ascertain how he used the term in the Letter to the Galatians.

See also GALATIANS, LETTER TO THE; ROMAN EMPIRE.

Bibliography. "Galatia," *WBE*; M. J. Mellink, "Galatia," *IBD*; W. M. Ramsay, "Galatia," *DB*; W. M. Ramsay and C. J. Hemer, "Galatia; Galatians," *ISBE*.

—W. T. EDWARDS

• OUTLINE OF GALATIANS •

The Letter to the Galatians

I. Opening (1:1-5)
II. Thanksgiving Parody (1:6-10)
III. Letter Body (1:11–6:10)
  A. Apostolic autobiography (1:11–2:21)
  B. Central argument (3:1–4:30)
  C. Apostolic exhortation (4:31–6:10)
IV. Personal Postscript (6:11-18)
  A. Polemic against the circumcisers (6:11-13)
  B. New creation and the cross of Christ (6:14-17)
  C. Benediction (6:18)

• **Galatians, Letter to the.** [guh-lay'shuns] The Letter to the Galatians is one of the oldest documents of early Christianity and the first extant witness to conflicts in the early church over the role of the TORAH in the religious life of Jewish and gentile believers in Christ. The Letter was composed by PAUL and taken down by a secretary, as is evident from the brief subscription in Paul's own hand appended at the end (6:11-18). It is addressed to a cluster of congregations founded by Paul (4:13) and situated either in the territory of GALATIA in central Anatolia (the north Galatian hypothesis) or, less likely, the area of southern Asia Minor in which the churches of Iconium, Lystra, and Derbe were founded according to Acts 13–14 (the south Galatian hypothesis). The date and place of composition are uncertain. Paul's third missionary journey (ca. 52–56) is a likely possibility, in which case the letter may have been written from Ephesus, Macedonia, or Corinth. The recipients of the Letter are evidently gentiles (4:8-11), but Paul treats them as persons relatively well acquainted with Jewish scripture and tradition. Perhaps there are former "God-fearers" among the Galatian converts to Christ.

The Letter conforms superficially to Graeco-Roman epistolary convention: opening (sender, addressee, greeting), statement of praise or thanksgiving to the gods, letter body, closing. But Paul plays creatively with the perfunctory requirements of the typical epistolary frame, expanding the opening theologically in ways that anticipate the argument of the Letter and making a veritable parody of the customary thanksgiving (cf. Gal 1:6-10 with Phil 1:3-11).

The body of the Letter (1:11–6:10) can be divided into three parts. In the first section Paul presents a selective history of his apostleship, beginning with his call and concluding with a speech he made at Antioch (1:11–2:21). Following this "apostolic autobiography" Paul turns to address the Galatian situation directly for the first time since 1:6-9. Beginning with 3:1 and extending without interruption through 4:11, Paul martials scripture and tradition in an attempt to persuade the Galatians from their present apostasy. After a personal appeal (4:12-20), Paul concludes his theological argument with a reflection on Abraham's two wives and sons (4:21-30), which prepares the way for an extended pastoral exhortation in 4:31–6:10. The Letter concludes with Paul's personal closing statement (6:11-17) and a benediction (6:18).

Galatians is a contribution to a debate that is already under way in the churches to whom Paul writes. Evidently certain teachers have come to Galatia urging the Galatians to get circumcised (6:12-13) and preaching what Paul calls "another gospel" (1:6-10). As "outsiders" to this discussion we must gain access to this circle of conversation in order to understand what Paul is trying to say. The appropriate place for us to enter this circle is the point where Paul first addresses the problem at Galatia both directly and in specific terms. This he does not do until chap. 3, for in 1:6-10 he is direct but not specific and in 1:11–2:21 he is specific but does not focus directly on the Galatian situation.

In 3:1-5 Paul formulates a series of questions regarding the Spirit, the works of the law, and faith. These questions are designed to lead his readers to a conclusion in 3:5, where Paul brings his argument to a close with the words: "Therefore [omitted in most translations], does the one who sustains you with the Spirit and works wonders among you do so because of works of the law or because you heard (the gospel) and believed?" (author's translation). The implied answer, which constitutes the point of this argument, is that life in the Spirit depends not on law-keeping but exclusively on faith in Christ.

If one compares this opening argument with those that follow, paying attention specifically to Paul's conclusions (3:9, 14, 17, 22, 29; 4:7b), a pattern emerges. Each of these conclusions treats the grounds of blessing in Christ. Moreover, it turns out that blessing in Christ is present blessing as embodied concretely in the gift of the Spirit. Paul understands "the blessing of Abraham" (3:8-9), which he also calls "the promise" (3:15-18), to consist concretely in its present manifestation as the Spirit (3:14). Thus, to be an "heir according to promise" by virtue of being in Christ (3:27-29) means being in possession of "the inheritance," which is the Spirit (4:6-7).

We may infer from the repeated point of Paul's argument in 3:1–4:7 that the problem at Galatia concerns the grounds of ongoing life in the Spirit. Can life in the Spirit be promoted by keeping the Mosaic Law, which pronounces life and blessing upon those who do it (Lev 18:5; Deut 30:15-20)? Paul's answer is that life in the Spirit depends exclusively on having entered into the new reality which Christ brings. Paul can describe this entrance in various ways: believing in the gospel (3:2, 5), crucifixion with Christ (2:18-19; 6:14-17), redemption and adoption (3:13; 4:4), "putting on Christ" in baptism (3:27), "justification by faith" (3:6-8, 24; 2:16). Presumably the Galatians have already become accustomed to applying much of this language for belonging to Christ to themselves. Paul reinforces these traditional patterns of Christian self-understanding in the course of demonstrating from the scriptures and early Christian tradition that ongoing life in the Spirit (as sustaining blessing and transcendent power in Christ) depends only on being in Christ and cannot be accessed through any other mode of being or activity.

Paul's central argument is flanked by what we have termed the apostolic autobiography and apostolic exhortation. In the light of Paul's purpose we may now define more precisely the function of these two sections. The autobiographical section accomplishes three purposes in preparation for the central argument of the Letter: (1) it (re)establishes Paul's apostolic authority, (2) it portrays Paul's solidarity with the gentile Christian cause, and (3) it presents Paul as an example of fidelity to the gospel. The exhortation has both a material and a rhetorical function. Materially, it clarifies the relationship between living by the Spirit and living ethically (cf. 5:25). Rhetorically, as pastoral exhortation, it binds the community to the apostle, who now speaks to them as he would under ordinary circumstances, thus creating a mood of normalcy in his pastoral-apostolic relations with the Galatians, as if there were no doubt "that you will take no other view than mine" (5:10). The fact that the Galatians are not included in Rom 15:26 among the churches of Paul's mission that are participating in the offering for Jerusalem may suggest that this confidence was misplaced. For their absence from this list of contributors may indicate that in the end the Galatians rejected Paul's authority and joined the Jewish wing of the church by submitting to circumcision and taking up the Law.

See also CIRCUMCISION; EPISTLE/LETTER; FAITH AND FAITHLESSNESS; FLESH AND SPIRIT; GALATIA; GENTILE/GENTILES IN THE NEW TESTAMENT; HOLY SPIRIT; JUSTIFICATION; LAW IN THE NEW TESTAMENT; PAUL; TORAH

Bibliography. H. D. Betz, *Galatians: A Commentary on Paul's Letter to the Churches in Galatia;* F. F. Bruce, *The Epistle to the Galatians: A Commentary on the Greek Text;* C. H. Cosgrove, "Arguing Like a Mere Human Being: Gal. 3:15-18 in Rhetorical Perspective," *NTS* 34/4 (1988): 536-49 and "The Law Has Given Sarah No Children (Gal. 4:21-30)," *NT* 29 (1987): 219-35; F. Crownfield, "The Singular Problem of the Dual Galatians," *JBL* 64 (1945): 491-500; N. Dahl, "Contradictions in Scripture," *Studies in Paul;* J. L. Martyn, *Galatians;* J. H. Ropes, *The Singular Problem of the Epistle to the Galatians;* E. P. Sanders, *Paul, the Law and the Jewish People;* W. Schmithals, *Paul and the Gnostics;* R. Tannehill, *Dying and Rising with Christ: A Study in Pauline Theology.*

—CHARLES H. COSGROVE

• **Galilee.** [gal'uh-lee] The name Galilee is from the Hebrew term which means circle or district, and in Isa 9:1 the term is given a fuller definition as "Galilee of the nations" (RSV) which meant "Galilee of the gentiles" (NIV). Why a significant part of what constituted the Jewish nation in the first century is called the district of the gentiles in the OT can only be understood from the region's history.

History. The term Galilee was originally applied to a much smaller area than the term included in the first century C.E. In 2 Kgs 15:29 the small area assigned to Naphtali (Josh 19:32-39) is called Galilee. By the time of the Maccabean war in the mid-second century B.C.E., however, the term Galilee designated a much vaster area because Naphtali along with the surrounding tribes of Asher, Zebulun, and Issachar were not able to drive out the land's inhabitants (cf. Judg 1:30-33). By the middle of the second century B.C.E., Jews were a small minority of the population (1 Macc 5:14-23), but the Hasmonean King Aristobulus I (104-103 B.C.E.) radically altered the situation when he conquered Galilee and forced its inhabitants to accept circumcision and the Jewish faith or leave (Josephus, *Ant* 13.11.3). Galilee was no longer the district of the gentiles, but differences between Jews in Galilee and Judea existed. Galileans spoke with a distinct accent (cf. Matt 26:23) and observed different customs in marriage ceremonies.

In the time of Jesus, the boundaries of Galilee (PLATE 23) were well known (cf. Josephus, *BJ* 3.3.1). The southern boundary, dividing it from Samaria, was the Plain of Megiddo or Valley of Jezreel; and the northern edge reached to Lake Huleh. The eastern line was along the Jordan Valley and the western boundary was set by the Phoenician border.

Description. The land in Galilee increases in elevation from south to north, resulting in the area south of the Plain of Ramah (roughly a line from Capernaum to Ptolemais) being known as lower Galilee and the area north of this known as upper Galilee. Galilee enjoyed substantially more annual rainfall than either Samaria or Judea which allowed for intensive agricultural development, especially in the rich valleys and on the terraced hills of lower Galilee. The area also benefited from the fishing industry around the Sea of Galilee and from the tolls collected from the caravans plying the international trade routes that crossed Galilee.

Jesus and Galilee. Jesus spent most of his time in ministry in lower Galilee, particularly in the area at the northern end of the SEA OF GALILEE around CAPERNAUM (cf. Matt 4:13; Luke 4:23) and BETHSAIDA. This ministry also included many of the villages in the area, such as Nain, NAZARETH, and Cana.

Bibliography. K. W. Clark, "Galilee," *IDB*; S. Freyne, *Galilee from Alexander the Great to Hadrian*.

—HAROLD S. SONGER

Designed by Margaret Jordan Brown ©Mercer University Press

• **Galilee, Sea of.** [gal'uh-lee] The lake that is usually termed "the Sea of Galilee" in the NT was known in the OT as the Sea of Chinnereth (Num 34:11; Josh 13:27) or Chinneroth (Josh 12:3). The lake was probably so called from the fortified city of Chinneroth or Chinnereth (Deut 3:17; Josh 11:2; 19:35) which was located on the northwestern shore of the lake and is identified as Tell el-Ureimeh. The lake was later known as Gennesar or Gennesaret and is once so called in the NT (Luke 5:1). The most frequent name in the NT is the familiar "Sea of Galilee" which occurs five times (Matt 4:18; 15:29; Mark 1:16; 7:31; John 6:1). Galilee was originally the name given to a small section of the region (cf. 1 Kgs 9:11), but by the second century B.C.E. it was applied to a much larger area and the lake it included was called the Sea of Galilee. Early in the first century C.E., probably around 25, Herod ANTIPAS built his capital city about midway on the west shore of the lake and named it TIBERIAS in honor of Tiberias Caesar (14–37 C.E.). This imposing and important city soon gave its name to the lake, hence John 6:1 "the Sea of Galilee, which is the Sea of Tiberias" (cf. also John 21:1).

Physical Description. The Sea of Galilee is located in the deep north-south aligned rift valley in which the Jordan River flows (PLATES 23, 25). The lake is mainly fed by the Jordan which gathers water from as far north as Mount Hermon. From the much smaller, marshy Lake Huleh (230 feet above sea level and ten miles north of the Sea of Galilee) the Jordan's waters surge to enter the sea on its northern end with the surface of the lake being approximately 685 feet below sea level. The level of the lake varies by about ten feet annually reaching its fullest in the early spring with the "late rain" (Jas 5:8) and the melting of the Mount Hermon snows.

The Sea of Galilee is rather heart-shaped, being about seven miles wide and thirteen miles long. The mountains rise sharply around the lake with the plain varying in width around the lake shore from less than a mile on the east side to the fertile Plain of Gennesaret almost two miles wide and three miles long on the northwestern shore (cf. Matt 14:34; Mark 6:53). The shallows around the lake are narrow, falling away quickly to depths of about 150 feet. This depth results in storms quickly producing fearsome waves as the height of waves is limited in shallows. Formidable seas could quickly rise in such a deep lake (cf. Mark 4:35-41; 6:45-52).

Fishing Industry. The names of some of the towns around the lake indicate a thriving fishing industry—BETHSAIDA (house of fishing) and Tarichaea (salted)—and both the industry and its product are frequently mentioned in the Gospels (Matt 4:18-22; 13:42-50; Mark 1:16-20; 6:30-44; Luke 5:1-11; Luke 11:11) and in contemporary accounts. The fish found in the Sea of Galilee are similar to those in the Nile River rather than those in the fresh waters of the Mediterranean basin, causing some ancients to speculate that an underground tunnel connected the sea with the Nile (Josephus, *BJ* 3.520).

Bibliography. K.W. Clark, "Galilee, Sea of," *IDB*.

—HAROLD S. SONGER

• **Gallio.** [gal'ee-oh] Junius Gallio Annaeus is mentioned in Acts 18:12, 14, 17 as being the PROCONSUL of ACHAIA with headquarters at CORINTH. He was brother to Seneca, a wealthy and influential philosopher and teacher of Nero. An inscription from Delphi—known as the Gallio inscription—places his service as proconsul ca. 52 C.E. This date is of signal importance in the reconstruction of a Pauline chronology.

PAUL appeared before Gallio on the charge that his teachings were contrary to the law (Acts 18:13), but the case was dismissed because Gallio determined it involved the Jewish law. Apparently he did not wish to become entangled in these discussions.

Later, Gallio returned to Rome where he became involved in a plot against Nero. As a consequence Gallio finally was required to commit suicide.

See also ACHAIA; CHRONOLOGY; CORINTH; PAUL; PROCONSUL.

—WATSON E. MILLS

• **Gamaliel.** [guh-may'lee-uhl] *1*. Rabban Gamaliel I ("the elder") was an honored Pharisaic teacher who was a member of the SANHEDRIN at the time when Christianity was beginning. He was the grandfather of Gamaliel II. Gamaliel I was the most celebrated teacher of his day. He was the first to be called "Rabban" ("our Great One"), rather than "Rabbi" ("my Great One"). Later Jewish tradition said of him, "From the time that Rabban Gamaliel died, respect for the TORAH ceased; and purity and abstinence died at the same time" (*Soṭa* 9.15). Whether or not he was the president of the Sanhedrin is debated, as is the claim that he was a grandson of the famous teacher Hillel. He is mentioned twice in the NT. First, when the Sanhedrin is deliberating about what to do with the apostles, who are preaching about Jesus, Gamaliel advises the council to leave the men alone (Acts 5:27-39). Second, when PAUL addresses the crowd after his arrest in Jerusalem, he says that he had studied at the feet of Gamaliel (Acts 22:3).

2. Rabban Gamaliel II, the grandson of Gamaliel I, was the head of the Jewish academy at Jamnia at the end of the first century (ca. 80–110 C.E.). He played an important role in consolidating Judaism in the aftermath of the destruction of Jerusalem, including standardizing the order of the EIGHTEEN BENEDICTIONS.

See also PAUL; SANHEDRIN.

Bibliography. J. Neusner, *The Rabbinic Traditions about the Pharisees before 70*; E. Schürer, "Torah Scholarship," *The History of the Jewish People in the Age of Jesus Christ,* rev. and ed. G. Vermes, F. Millar, and M. Black.

—JOSEPH L. TRAFTON

• **Games/Play.** In addition to games of running, jumping, tug-of-war (witnessed by an Egyptian relief in a Sixth Dynasty tomb at Saqqarah), wrestling (2 Macc 4:7-17, possibly 2 Sam 2:12-17), and tag, which seem to be present in nearly every culture, there is significant material evidence for board games, stone games, and dice games in the ancient world. In a tomb in ancient Ur (ca. 3000 B.C.E.), Sir Leonard Woolley discovered a board that used seven marked pieces per side. The moves in the game were apparently controlled by "rolls" of six pyramidal dice. Palestinian game boards with similar designs to the one at Ur date from the Middle Bronze Age; the famous tomb of King Tutankamon held a similar wooden game board. The latter followed a traditional style where the board consisted of three tracks of ten squares each. The board itself was the top of a box within which the pieces and dice, pyramids, and/or knuckle bones were kept. Another game board from this time period is "Hounds and Jackals," from a Twelfth Dynasty tomb discovered in Thebes. This board game used a racetrack layout (where pieces travel around the board in a pre-determined pattern) and five ivory pegs per side.

Dice have been found to exist as early as 2000 B.C.E. in Egypt. In fact, dice shaped so that they could be used for cheating have been excavated in Egypt. Early forms of dice were often simple, like knuckle bones. These were the ankle bones of sheep, marked on four faces. Another early form of die was the teetotum. This was a truncated pyramid marked on four sides, which may have been either thrown or spun to determine a move. All early forms of dice seem to bear affinity with the lots or URIM AND THUMMIM (Exod 28:30; Lev 8:8) used by priests and shaman alike to discern the will of the deity.

Another popular type of game in the ancient world is the game of position. In these games, players would place their pieces (usually stones, but sometimes seeds) into lines or patterns in order to capture territory or one's opponent's pieces. At the Egyptian city of Kurna (ca. 1400 B.C.E.), a board design for the game commonly known as "Nine Men's Morris" was found cut into the roof of a temple.

Although board games as such are not mentioned in the Bible, it is interesting to realize that the people of biblical times played such games. These practices might even shed some light on EZEKIEL's "toy soldiers" routine in the streets of Jerusalem (Ezek 4:1-8). The dice used by the soldiers in gambling for Jesus' clothes (Matt 27:35) were probably descendants of those ancient knuckle bones. On the other hand, the Pauline literature is replete with references to athletic events (1 Cor 9:24-27; Phil 3:14; Heb 12:1-2; 2 Tim 2:5).

See also LOT/LOTS (CASTING OF) IN THE BIBLE; URIM AND THUMMIM.

Bibliography. R. C. Bell, *Board and Table Games from Many Civilizations*; R. F. Schnell, "Games, OT," *IDB*.

—JOHNNY L. WILSON

• **Gath.** [gath] Meaning "wine press," Gath was one of the great cities of the Philistine pentapolis (1 Sam 6:17—ASHDOD, ASHKELON, EKRON, Gath, GAZA). Tell eṣ-Ṣafi (or Tel Zafit) has been fairly certainly identified as the site of ancient Gath. Tel Zafit is located about seventeen miles east of the Mediterranean Sea and twenty-four mi. west southwest of Jerusalem (PLATE 12). The tell is 754 ft. above sea level and 325 ft. above the bed of the Wadi Elah which it overlooks. In ancient times the city guarded the main north-south route of the shephelah region running through the plain. Steep slopes of the tell on the north and east reveal white limestone cliffs. The summit of the tell is crescent-shaped and is the site of the ancient acropolis.

Gath and its inhabitants are referred to in twenty OT passages. As in Gaza and Ashdod, some of the ancient race of giants, the Anakim, were said still to dwell in Gath at the time of Joshua (Josh 11:22). The Philistine pentapolis, including the city of "the Gittite," remained to be taken according to Josh 13:3. Gath was the second Philistine city that the captured ARK was sent to and its ruler sent his humiliating guilt offering back with the returning Ark (1 Sam 5–6). Under the leadership of Samuel, the Israelites defeated the Philistines and caused them to return certain cities, including Gath (1 Sam 7:14), though apparently they did not maintain control of it.

Gath was the home of the Philistine giant, Goliath, whom David slew (1 Sam 17). David twice fled to Gath to find refuge from Saul's pursuit; first, he came alone and was not well received (1 Sam 21:10-15); and, later, he came with his followers (1 Sam 27) and apparently almost joined King Achish of Gath against Israel (1 Sam 28:1-2 and 29). After Saul's death, he dreaded the joy that the news would bring to the Philistines (2 Sam 1:20). Tragedy struck when David had the Ark moved. Ironically a man from Gath was chosen to house the Ark for a time and was blessed by its presence (2 Sam 6:10-12; 1 Chr 13:13-14; cf. 1 Sam 5–6). When David fled Jerusalem before Absalom's advance, 600 "Gittites" under the command of Ittai the Gittite, who had come with David from Gath, went with him (2 Sam 15:18-22). Were these perhaps the same "600" who went to Gath with him? (cf. 1 Sam 27:2) Ittai the Gittite was commander of one-third of David's troops when David's forces did battle with those of Absalom (2 Sam 18:2). Gath is again mentioned as the home of great warriors and giants in 2 Sam 21:19-22 and 1 Chr 20:5-8. Shimei, the enemy of David, tracked two missing servants to Gath and was killed for it because Solomon had forbade him to leave Jerusalem (1 Kgs 2:39-41). Hazael the Aramaean captured Gath in his campaign against the south between 837–800 B.C.E. perhaps because of its alliance with Judah (2 Kgs 12:17).

Men from Gath avenged themselves against Israelites who had taken their livestock (1 Chr 7:21). Benjaminites drove off inhabitants from Gath (1 Chr 8:13). David took Gath, temporarily, from the Philistines (1 Chr 18:1). The parallel passage, 2 Sam 8:1, says simply that he took "control of the chief city." Rehoboam, son of Solomon, rebuilt and fortified Gath for the defense of the southern kingdom (2 Chr 11:8). King Uzziah of Judah was victorious against the Philistines and "broke down the wall of Gath" (2 Chr 26:6). Gath is cited in an illustration given to wayward Israel (Amos 6:2; an example of a ruined city?). Micah (1:10) says the devastating news of the destruction of Israel and Judah should not be told in Gath (cf. 2 Sam 1:20; because the Philistines would rejoice or was Gath already a ruin by this time?). It is noteworthy that Gath does not appear in several lists that enumerate the Philistine cities with the enemies of Judah (e.g., Jer 25:20; Amos 1:7-8; Zeph 2:4; Zech 9:5-7). This may be because Gath, which was the closest of the Philistine cities to Judean territory, was closely aligned with Judah by the time of the prophecies or, more likely, it was already abandoned.

Gath was a Canaanite city under the control of Egypt before the days of the Philistines according to the el-Amarna letters. The records of Assyrian King Sargon II record his destruction of the city in his campaign of 711 B.C.E. There seems to be no mention of it after that time.

The site was first identified as Gath in 1887, but has been thought to be the site of other ancient cities. Excavations were carried out for two seasons (1899–1900) by F. J. Bliss and R. A. S. Macalister under the auspices of the Palestine Exploration Fund. The excavations were scattered over the site and could not be extensive because of the village which still exists there. R. Amiran and Y. Aharoni made a survey of the site in 1955.

Bibliography. W. F. Stinespring, "Gath," *IBD*; E. Stern, "eṣ-Ṣafi, Tell," *EAEHL*.

—TIMOTHY G. CRAWFORD

• **Gathering.** *See* CONGREGATION

• **Gattung.** *See* FORM/GATTUNG

• **Gaza.** [gay′zuh] Gaza was one of the cities of the PHILISTINE Pentapolis (1 Sam 6:17—ASHDOD, ASHKELON, EKRON, GATH, Gaza). The ancient site usually identified as Gaza is Tell el-Harube. It lies within the northeast corner of the modern city of Gaza almost three mi. from the Mediterranean Sea and about fifty mi. southwest of Jerusalem (PLATE 12). From 1930–34, Sir Flinders Petrie excavated Tell el-'Ajjul which he identified as ancient Gaza; subsequent studies have determined that identification to be incorrect. Ancient Gaza was the southernmost and westernmost of the great Philistine cities.

The city of Gaza and its inhabitants are referred to in seventeen passages in the Bible (sixteen OT, one NT). Being the southernmost of the Philistine cities, it was used to describe the southwest limit of the lands controlled by Israel (Gen 10:19; 1 Kgs 4:24). Deut 2:23 explains how the "Caphtorim" (Philistines) came from "Caphtor" (Crete) and displaced the earlier residents. Gaza was one of the last cities in which the ancient race of giants (the Anakim) remained (Josh 11:22). It marked the limit of Joshua's conquest (Josh 10:41) and was itself included in the territory allotted to the tribe of Judah (Josh 15:47). Yet all five of the Philistine cities remained to be taken according to Josh 13:3. Judg 1:18 states that it was captured by Judah, but other passages (Judg 16; 1 Sam 6:17; 2 Kgs 18; etc.) make it clear that Judah's control was either incomplete or very transitory.

Midianites raiding Judah devastated the land as far as Gaza (Judg 6:4). Samson hired a prostitute in Gaza and, that night, carried off the city gates which were intended to keep him in (Judg 16:1-3). Later, Samson was carried to Gaza as a blind slave and there died with the Philistine worshippers he killed in the temple of Dagon (Judg 16:21ff.). When the Philistines returned the captured ARK to Israel, the ruler of Gaza sent his bizarre guilt offerings along with those of the rulers of the other cities (1 Sam 6:17). Hezekiah of Judah defeated the Philistines as far as Gaza (2 Kgs 18:8). Gaza is included in lists of nations and peoples to be judged (Jer 25:20; 47:5; Amos 1:6-8; Zeph 2:4; Zech 9:5). An Egyptian king's (simply "Pharaoh" in the text) conquest of the city is used to date an oracle of Jeremiah against the Philistines (Jer 47:1). In the NT, Gaza is mentioned as the terminus of a road starting in Jerusalem (Acts 8:26).

Gaza, known as *pa-Canaan* ("city of Canaan"), is mentioned several times in Egyptian texts found at el-Amarna and Taanach. Its position as an Egyptian administrative center for Egypt's possessions in Canaan is mentioned in documents of Pharoah Thutmose III, ca. 1469 B.C.E. Though it was among the territories allotted to Judah, Gaza seems to have remained Canaanite until the Philistines moved into Palestine and took the area about 1200 B.C.E. It remained Philistine even after its capture by Assyrian King Tiglath Pileser III in 734 and the subsequent, short-lived conquest of the city by Hezekiah of Judah a few years later. Pharoah Necho II captured it in 609 B.C.E. and held it for a brief time.

Under the Persians, Gaza was the site of an important fortress. It was the only city south of Tyre to oppose Alexander the Great in 332 B.C.E. and, because of its resistance, its people were all sold as slaves. Gaza served as an outpost for the Ptolemies until 198, when it was captured by the Seleucid King Antiochus III. It was attacked by the Hasmonean ruler Jonathan in 145 (1 Macc 11:61-62) and taken by Jewish ruler Alexander Jannaeus after a long siege in 96 B.C.E. After the Romans took over the city, it was rebuilt by Pompey in 57 B.C.E., and it flourished. It has continued to survive and prosper under successive rulers—Byzantine, Muslim, Crusader, Mameluke, Ottoman, British, and Israeli—to the present day.

The tell was excavated in 1922 and 1923 by W. J. Phythian-Adams under the auspices of the Palestine Exploration Fund. In 1965 the discovery of an ancient synagogue led to a survey by the Egyptian Department of Antiquities. The Israel Department of Antiquities and Museums excavated the site in 1967.

Bibliography. G. I. Davies, "British Archaeologists," *Benchmarks in Time and Culture,* ed. J. F. Drinkard, Jr., G. L. Mattingly, and J. M. Miller; T. Dothan, *The Philistines and Their Material Culture*; A. Ovadiah, "Gaza," *EAEHL*; W. F. Stinespring, "Gaza," *IDB*.

—TIMOTHY G. CRAWFORD

• **Gebal.** *See* BYBLOS/GEBAL

• **Gedaliah.** [ged′uh-l*i*″uh] A name built upon the Heb. verb "to be great" combined with the personal name of the God of Israel, thus meaning "Yahweh Is Great." At least five persons are mentioned in the OT who bore the name, the most significant being the final ruler of Judah. With his death the Judeans' last effort to maintain self-rule during the Exile was dashed.

Gedaliah was the son of Ahikam and grandson of SHAPHAN. Shaphan was a political leader in Josiah's government who supported Josiah's reform movement (2 Kgs 22–23). He and Jeremiah doubtless established some close ties of friendship that spanned at least three generations. Ahikam, Gedaliah's father, succeeded in sparing JEREMIAH'S life. Evidently, he shared many common values and religious loyalties with him.

Through JEHOIAKIM's and Zedekiah's reign Jeremiah advocated an accommodation with the Babylonians. With the defeat of King Zedekiah, NEBUCHADREZZAR determined to appoint a non-Davidic governor. Gedaliah, Ahikam's son, was his choice. Gedaliah set up his administration at Mizpah where Jeremiah joined him (Jer 40:6).

Gedaliah espoused a policy of cooperation with BABYLON. Some soldiers who had escaped along with some citizens who had sought refuge in surrounding countries returned and joined Gedaliah at Mizpah. He assured them that if they remained faithful to Nebuchadrezzar they would have peace.

King Baalis of AMMON thought that Gedaliah hindered his plans for revolt against Babylon. Doubtless appealing to deep-seated resentment regarding a non-Davidic ruler, he enlisted Ishmael of the royal house to assassinate Gedaliah. Johanan, an officer, offered to slay Ishmael secretly in order to assure peace. Gedaliah, however, rejected his offer as without basis.

Having served about two months, Gedaliah hosted Ishmael and his ten companions. After accepting Gedaliah's hospitality, Ishmael slew him and his Babylonian contingent. Such treason assured swift Babylonian reprisals (Jer 40-41). Though he served but a short time, Gedaliah was worthy of such esteem that his assassination is still recalled on the Jewish calendar as a fast on the third day of the seventh month.

Others who bore the name were: (1) A descendant of Jeduthun. Set apart by DAVID to be a leader of public worship, he specialized in playing the harp (1 Chr 25:3, 9). (2) The grandfather of the prophet Zephaniah. He also was King HEZEKIAH's grandson (Zeph 1:1). (3) A son of Pashhur. An avid nationalist, he served as one of King Zedekiah's advisers. An opponent of Jeremiah's ministry of conciliation with Babylon, Gedaliah assisted in putting Jeremiah into a dungeon where he would have died except for the intervention of Ebed-melech (Jer 38:1-6). (4) A priest of EZRA's day. Along with others he was guilty of having married a foreign wife (Ezra 10:18).

—JERRY WALLACE LEE

• **Gehenna.** [gi-hen'uh] "Gehenna" is derived from a Hebrew word meaning "valley of Hinnom" and refers literally to a valley located west and south of Jerusalem. This valley was part of the tribal boundary between Judah and Benjamin (Josh 15:8; 18:16; Neh 11:30) and was a site where some of the kings of Judah engaged in human sacrifice by fire (2 Chr 28:3; 33:6; Jer 7:31; 32:35). Jeremiah prophesied that the valley of Hinnom would become for the apostates a "valley of slaughter" (Jer 7:32; 19:6, 11, 13; cf. Isa 66:24). In extracanonical Jewish literature and in the NT, Gehenna was used to designate the place/state of torment of the wicked. Routinely translated HELL, Gehenna occurs twelve times in the NT—eleven times in the synoptic Gospels and once in James. Gehenna is qualified twice by "of fire" (Matt 5:22; 18:9); once it is paralleled by "the unquenchable fire" (Mark 9:43); and while various vivid images are used to describe Gehenna, the image of fire is predominant.

The development of the valley of Hinnom as a metaphorical designation in the NT of the (final) state of torment for the wicked can be traced only in the extracanonical literature. *First Enoch* relates a vision of the "Holy Mountain" surrounded by valleys and focuses on the "accursed valley," a place of judgment where in "the last days" the torment of the wicked will be a spectacle before the righteous forever (chaps. 26–27; cf. Isa 66:24). Later Jewish literature reads back into the OT a developed idea of Gehenna. The Talmud lists Gehenna among the seven things created before the world (*Pesh* 54a). Although a certain development of the idea of Gehenna is discernible in extracanonical sources, central aspects of the idea are early OT ideas. The nebulous deep (SHEOL, Deut 32:22; Amos 9:2), the fire of judgment (Gen 19:24; Exod 9:24), and destruction/slaughter as punishment for wickedness (esp. apostasy: Num 25:5; Deut 13:10) are found in the OT. These ideas of deep, fire, and (profane) destruction were all localized and concretized in the accursed valley of Hinnom.

In the NT, the idea of Gehenna is simply stated as understood and accepted. With the exception of Jas 3:6, Gehenna occurs only in the recorded teachings of Jesus, where it is apparent that Jesus assumed his hearers would understand what was meant by Gehenna. In the teachings of Jesus, the traditional images of Gehenna are prominent: deep, or a place/state into which one may be cast (Matt 5:29; Mark 9:45; Luke 12:5); (unquenchable) fire (Matt 5:22; 18:9); and (profane) destruction (Matt 10:28; cf. "the worm" at Mark 9:48). One must distinguish between Gehenna and Hades in the NT, a distinction obscured in the KJV which invaribly translates both as "hell." The distinction in the NT is not always clearly drawn, indicating fluidity in the development of terminology. In the parable of the rich man and Lazarus (Luke 16:19ff.), e.g., the place of fire (Gehenna) appears as a "compartment" of Hades.

While Gehenna is routinely translated as "hell" in most English versions, one must take care not to routinely read back into the NT ideas of "hell" that developed only much later in Christian theology.

See also HELL; SHEOL.

Bibliography. G. W. Buchanan, ed., *Revelation and Redemption: Jewish Documents of Deliverance from the Fall of Jerusalem to the Death of Naḥminides*; J. Jeremias, "γέενα," *TDNT*; F. Lang, "πῦρ," *TDNT*; H. F. D. Sparks, ed., *The Apocryphal Old Testament*.

—EDD ROWELL

• **Gemstones.** *See* JEWELRY

• **Genealogy in the New Testament.** Genealogies were an important aspect of Near Eastern culture and carried out such functions as the preservation of inheritances, land claims, and the preservation of the purity of blood lines. The Gospels of Matthew and Luke contain genealogies designed to trace the descent of Jesus in a way to support the purposes they share and purposes that are unique to each Gospel.

Both Matthew and Luke trace the lineage of Jesus through Joseph. Matthew traces the ancestry of Jesus back to Abraham, but Luke traces it to God through Adam. It is the only known instance of a genealogy being traced to God, and it accents the universality of the meaning of Jesus, the Son of God. Matthew's more Hebraic emphasis is made by tracing the genealogy only to Abraham. It is clear that both writers use the genealogies to strengthen their thematic purposes.

There is artificial construction in both genealogies. Matthew seeks to break his genealogy into three groups of fourteen each, but he has only thirteen names in the final group from the Exile to Jesus. The Lucan genealogy has seventy-three names plus God. Seven, the mystical number of completion, can be seen in both instances. This may have special meaning or it may be a convenient device for memory.

Matthew and Luke use different forms for their genealogies. Luke (3:23) uses a simple genitive, "Jesus . . . being the son (as was supposed) of Joseph, the son of Heli." Matthew (1:2) uses a verbal form, "Abraham was the father of Isaac, and Isaac the father of Jacob." This enables Matthew to add descriptive words such as "DAVID the king," and to include four women, Tamar, Rahab, Ruth, and "the wife of Uriah" (Bathsheba). All of these women had some kind of scandalous or unusual relationship with Jewish men and it is possible that Matthew included them to emphasize the grace of God fulfilled in the Messiah.

Matthew follows the royal line by proceeding from David to Solomon and on to Zerubbabel (the monarchic fourteen), but Luke rejects the royal order by moving from David to his son, Nathan, and from him through a list of unknown names to Shealtiel and Zerubbabel, where the two lists coincide again. Both Matthew and Luke use mostly unknown names in the postexilic lists and their lists do not coincide with each other. Neither coincides with the list of five descendents of Zerubbabel given in 1 Chr 3:19-24.

It is likely that both Matthew and Luke are working with genealogies which were drawn up by Jewish Christians who wanted to affirm Jesus as the Messiah. Matthew begins his Gospel with the genealogy and thus affirms his accent on Jesus as the fulfillment of Jewish expectations. Luke places his genealogy between the Marcan episodes of the baptism of Jesus and the temptation in the desert which gives it the effect of looking backward to divine origins and forward to divine fulfillment.

See also DAVID; KINGSHIP; MESSIAH/CHRIST.

Bibliography. W. F. Albright and C. S. Mann, *Matthew*; R. E. Brown, *The Birth of the Messiah*; J. A. Fitzmyer, *The Gospel According to Luke, I-IX*.

—CARLTON T. MITCHELL

• **Genealogy in the Old Testament.** A written or oral presentation of the descent of a person or group from an ancestor or ancestors. Segmented genealogies present more than one line of descent from an ancestor, while linear genealogies trace only one line. Anthropological research indicates that genealogies function, at the oral stage, to describe kinship, rank, political and legal relationships, geographical location, and obligations within the cultic sphere, particularly in rites for the dead. Linear genealogies often serve to legitimate succession to an office (e.g., priest, monarchy) or some other inheritance, while segmented genealogies generally function to describe the social structure of a society. Oral segmented genealogies rarely extend beyond ten to fourteen generations and average much shorter length, while linear genealogies may stretch a little further. When genealogies are recorded in writing, they usually take on different functions and may extend further.

The OT contains a number of genealogies, including Gen 4:7-22, CAIN through TUBAL-CAIN; 5:1-32, ADAM to NOAH; 10:1-32, the descendants of Noah, also called the table of the nations; and 11:10-26, SHEM to ABRAHAM; all of which seem to function, at least partially, to cover gaps in the time frame of the prehistory. In addition, Exod 6:14-25, LEVI through AARON and PHINEHAS in six generations inclusively, and Num 3:1-2, 17-20, the descendants of Aaron and MOSES, function to legitimate the Aaron line through Phinehas. The longest genealogy occurs in 1 Chr 1:1–9:4, from Adam to the descendants of SAUL, which again serves at least the purpose of bringing the story of God's dealings with humankind down to the time of DAVID, with which the author was concerned. The genealogy from Perez to David, with which the book of RUTH closes (4:18-22), functions to tie King David to the Moabitess heroine of the story, thus serving the more inclusive theology of the author over against the more exclusivistic theology of some contemporaries in the postexilic period who would ban Moabites and many others from the Temple and from inclusion among the people of God. The segmented genealogies presenting the children of Jacob (Gen 35:22-26, 46:8-27) and the lengthy story of their birth (29:31–30:24 and 35:16-21), along with the blessings of Jacob (Gen 49) and Moses (Deut 33), chronicle the shifting fortunes and roles of the various tribes. One should recognize, however, that genealogies are recited for different purposes, so that the differences in the lists do not necessarily prove that they derive from different times.

The word "genealogy" occurs twenty-two times in the singular or plural, all in the books of 1 and 2 Chronicles, Ezra and Nehemiah. Several of these passages indicate how those returning from Exile thought of and utilized genealogies. Fluidity in genealogies was recognized in 1 Chr 5:1, which observes that Reuben was not accorded in the genealogy the prestige among the tribes that his rank as the first born should entitle him to. That discrepancy was explained in terms of a moral failure, suggesting that the genealogy used by the Chronicler was compiled for cultic use in which impurity would be a factor. Further, 1 Chr 5:17 specifically dates a genealogy (or genealogies) from the time of Jotham and Jeroboam (mid-eighth century). Finally, Ezra 2:62 and Neh 7:64 tell of priests who applied for recognition, but were barred from serving because they were not registered in the genealogy of priests.

Bibliography. A. Malamat, "King Lists of the Old Babylonian Period and Biblical Genealogies," *JAOS* 88 (1968): 163-73; R. R. Wilson, *Genealogy and History in the Biblical World* and "The Old Testament Genealogies in Recent Research," *JBL* 94 (1975): 169-89.

—PAUL L. REDDITT

• **General Letters.** In contemporary scholarship seven letters are usually designated as General (or Catholic) Letters: James; 1 and 2 Peter; 1, 2, and 3 John; and Jude. Others argue for only five letters: James; 1 and 2 Peter; Jude; and Hebrews, adding Hebrews because of similarities to the others and placing the Letters which bear the name of John in the Johannine corpus. Continuing debate about what constitutes a "general epistle" reflects the troubled history of these Letters.

Eusebius is the first to apply the term "catholic epistles" (ca. 324) to a collection of Letters: James, Jude, 2 Peter, and 2 and 3 John, which he also designated as "disputed letters," i.e., not having universal acceptance in the church. As the process of formation of a NT canon drew to a close, 1 Peter and 1 John were added to the Catholic Epistle corpus as evidenced by Athanasius's so-called Festal Letter of 367 (Hebrews is designated a Pauline work).

Clearly the designation "catholic" or "general" Letters is a flexible one, although there are certain elements common among the Letters of the corpus. First John and Hebrews (if included in the corpus) lack mention of intended readers but have epistolary closings. Third John is directed to a person, Gaius, while the remaining Letters have vaguely defined audiences: a single congregation in the case of 2 John and community clusters in James, Peter, and Jude. While the audiences may be elusive, one infers that they share a common commitment to a distinctly Jewish-Christian heritage, especially James, Peter, Jude, and Hebrews, over against the assumed gentile heritage which underlies the Pauline corpus. Thus the General Letters provide a necessary perspective on the diversity of the early church. Such are the internal commonalities of these Letters.

Externally, at least two additional shared characteristics may be noted. During the formation of a NT canon only 1 Peter and 1 John among the General Letters escaped dispute. Reasons for hesitancy in accepting the remaining Letters are manifold, yet one issue seems dominant, that of apostolic authorship. James, Jude, and 2 Peter are linked in that Jude draws authority from James (Jude 1:1) and content from 2 Peter. Second and 3 John are written by "the elder" and reflect themes found in the Fourth Gospel and 1 John (undisputed works) as well as in the Book of Revelation. Clear apostolic authority was lacking in these five disputed Letters, according to the judgment of the early church. The inclusion in the canon of the General Letters, however, is a forceful statement of the conviction of the early church that these works are an authentic, authoritative expression of Christian faith.

See also EPISTLE/LETTER; HEBREWS, LETTER TO THE; JAMES, LETTER OF; JOHN, GOSPEL AND LETTERS OF; JUDE, LETTER OF; PETER, LETTERS OF.

—RICHARD F. WILSON

• **Generation.** A rather flexible term used to describe a period of time or a group of people. In its strictest temporal sense, a generation is the period of time between the birth of parents and the birth of their children. The biblical writers reckoned a generation in the legendary antediluvian and patriarchal eras to be as long as 100 years (Gen 15:13-16), but they revised this figure to a more realistic thirty to forty years for later periods (Deut 2:14). At other places "generation" is a more general term and could just as well be rendered "age" (Acts 14:16). The occurrence of the phrase "throughout all generations" as a circumlocution for "forever" is fairly common (Ps 10:6, etc.). Thus the term has no consistent temporal value.

When this term is used to designate groups of people it most often denotes particular levels within a family, such as parents, children, and grandchildren. People within each level belong to different generations (Gen 50:23). In other cases, however, "generation" may designate a group of individuals of varying ages who embody a particular characteristic, such as righteousness (Ps 14:5). Elsewhere the term simply refers to all people living at a particular time (Gen 7:1; Matt 11:16).

While *dôr* is by far the most common word in the OT that is translated "generation," most English versions also render the Hebrew term *tôlēdôt* in this manner. The phrase "These are the generations of . . . " is used by the priestly writer to structure the Pentateuch (Gen 2:4, etc.). In these passages *tôlēdôt* is perhaps better understood as "acccounts" or "genealogies."

See also TIME, BIBLICAL PERSPECTIVES ON.

Bibliography. J. Botterweck, D. N. Freedman, and J. Lundbom, "דּוֹר *dôr*," *TDOT*.

—DAVID H. HART

• **Genesis Apocryphon.** [jen'uh-sis-uh-pok"ruh-fon] The *Genesis Apocryphon* (*1 QapGen*) is a fragmentary retelling of the early chapters of GENESIS. The most poorly preserved of the seven major scrolls discovered in Qumran Cave 1, it is extant in twenty-two columns, only five of which (2, 19-22) are legible to any degree, and eight small fragments, which apparently belonged to the lost beginning of the scroll. Virtually nothing of column 1 (which was not the first column in the original scroll) remains. Columns 2-5, narrated by LAMECH, the father of NOAH, focus on the birth of Noah (Gen 5:28-31). Suspicious that his wife's conception is by one of the fallen angels, Lamech confronts his wife, who denies the charge; he then asks his father Methuselah to inquire about the truth from his father Enoch. In the badly damaged portion that follows, Enoch apparently reassures Methuselah that Lamech is indeed the father (cf. *1 Enoch* 106-107). The very fragmentary columns 6-17, narrated by Noah, tell the story of the Flood and its aftermath (Gen 6–9), apparently concluding with Noah's division of the earth among his three sons (cf. *Jub* 9). Column 18 is lost. By the time the text resumes in column 19, ABRAHAM is the central figure and narrator, a role which he continues until the narration shifts to the third person in column 20. The extant portions of columns 19-22 include an elaborate expansion of the story of Abraham's sojourn in Egypt which resulted in PHARAOH taking SARAH (unsuccessfully) as his wife (Gen 12:10-20). The narrative then moves quickly through the stories of Abraham and Lot (Gen 13:1-13), and the alliance of the four kings and its aftermath (Gen 14), broken up by an extended elaboration of God's promise to Abraham (Gen 13:14-18). The scroll breaks off in the middle of God's promise of an heir to Abraham (Gen 15:1-4).

The scroll, which is written in Aramaic, dates to the period 50 B.C.E. to 50 C.E. Although some scholars argue that the *Apocryphon* was composed during the second century, most opt for a first century B.C.E. date. Nothing in the *Apocryphon* suggests that it is a sectarian composition; the section on MELCHIZEDEK, for example, bears no relationship to the imaginative speculations in *11QMelch*. Yet the *Apocryphon* contains some striking parallels to the BOOK OF JUBILEES and 1 ENOCH, both of which have been found among the Qumran fragments but neither of which appears to have been composed by the Qumran community. The precise relationship of such pseudepigrapha to the Qumran ESSENES remains unclear. Although related to the literary forms of targum and midrash, the *Apocryphon* is neither, being more closely akin to the "rewritten Bible" techniques employed in *Jubilees, 1 Enoch,* the TESTAMENTS OF THE TWELVE PATRIARCHS, and PSEUDO-PHILO.

Perhaps the most significant contribution of the *Genesis Apocryphon* is its value in recovering the form of Palestinian ARAMAIC in use at the time of Jesus. Before the discovery of the *Apocryphon* and other Aramaic texts at Qumran, few witnesses to this period of Aramaic had survived. Now the gap has been filled.

See also DEAD SEA SCROLLS; ESSENES.

Bibliography. J. A. Fitzmyer, *The Genesis Apocryphon of Qumran Cave 1,* 2nd ed.; G. Vermes, "The Genesis Apocryphon from Qumran," in E. Schürer, *The History of the Jewish People in the Age of Jesus Christ,* rev. ed., and "The Life of Abraham (2)–Haggadic Development: A Progressive and Historical Study," *Scripture and Tradition in Judaism,* 2nd ed.

—JOSEPH L. TRAFTON

• **Genesis, Book of.** The first book of the Bible and of the collection of five OT books known as the TORAH or Pentateuch. The title "Genesis" derives from the LXX; the He-

• OUTLINE OF GENESIS •

The Book of Genesis

I. Primeval History: Beginnings (1:1–11:32)
   A. Creation of the universe and of mankind (1:1–2:25)
   B. Beginnings of sin and suffering (3:1-24)
   C. Human beginnings, from Adam to Noah (4:1–5:32)
   D. The flood (6:1–10:32)
   E. The tower of Babylon (11:1-9)
   F. The nations, from Shem to Abram (11:10-32)
II. Israel's Beginnings: the Patriarchs (12:1–50:26)
   A. Abraham and Sarah; Isaac and Rebekah (12:1–25:18)
   B. Jacob and Rachel (25:19–36:43)
   C. Joseph and his brothers (37:1–50:26)

brew title, *bĕrēšît* (''in beginning''), is the first word in the text. The subject matter of Genesis is beginnings, the beginnings of the world and of the people of Israel.

Contents. Genesis can be divided into two major sections: Gen 1–11, the prehistory or primeval history, concerned with the CREATION of the world and of humanity; and Gen 12–50, the patriarchal narratives, concerned with the fathers and mothers of Israel. The patriarchal narratives can be divided into cycles, or complexes, of traditions about ABRAHAM and SARAH; ISAAC and REBEKAH (Gen 12–25); JACOB and RACHEL (Gen 25–36); and JOSEPH and his brothers (Gen 37–50).

Composition. The prevailing understanding of the composition of Genesis holds that Genesis is the end-product of a long history of the transmission of oral and written traditions. This understanding, the so-called documentary hypothesis of Julius Wellhausen (1878), replaced the traditional view of the Mosaic authorship of Genesis and the other books in the Pentateuch. According to the theory, Genesis is composed of three of the four sources identified as components of the Pentateuch. That is, Genesis contains the YAHWIST (denoted by the siglum J), ELOHIST (E), and PRIESTLY (P) sources, with the Deuteronomic (D) source reserved to the book of DEUTERONOMY. The formation of the sources and the composition of the Pentateuch from them are generally dated to the tenth to fifth centuries B.C.E.

With regard to the two major sections within Genesis, only J and P materials have been identified in the primeval history, while all three sources, J, E, and P, have been identified within the patriarchal narratives. For example, in Gen 1–11, the priestly source is found in the creation account in 1:1–2:4a; part of the flood story in 6–9; and the genealogies in 5, 10, and 11:10-32. The Yahwist source consists largely of narrative materials: the garden story in 2:4b–3:24; CAIN and ABEL in 4:1-16; part of the flood story in 6–9; the TOWER OF BABEL in 11:1-9. The three sources found in the patriarchal narratives are more difficult to separate. Generally, however, J and E, parallel sources in these chapters, have been interwoven to form the narrative foundation of the patriarchal stories, while P serves as more an editorial framework, at least after Gen 25.

Thematic concerns. Gen 1–11 describes the creation of the universe and of human life by Yahweh, the God of Israel. The concern of these chapters, however, is not to relate historical-scientific information about creation, but to offer theological insights into the relationship between the creator and the creation. Indeed, much of the material here is ancient legend shared by Israel with its ancient Near Eastern neighbors. Israel, however, refashioned these materials so that its own distinctive understanding of God and the world might be enunciated.

Two themes are primary in Gen 1–11 in describing this relationship between God and the world: the goodness of creation and SIN and judgment. The theme of the goodness of creation is depicted, for example, in creation's perfect response to the Creator's will to create, in God's assertion that creation is good, in the creation of humanity in the image of God as the climax of creation, and in God's blessing on humanity through the injunctions to populate the earth and have dominion over it. The theme of sin and judgment involves the rebellion of humanity against the sovereign authority of the Creator to define the existence of God's creatures. Enunciated primarily in the Yahwist narratives, the theme depicts the attempts of human beings to evade the limits of their finite creatureliness, thus becoming ''like God,'' and God's response to their rebellion—punishment meted out with compassion.

The patriarchal narratives describe the lives of the ancestors of Israel through four generations: Abraham, Isaac, Jacob and Esau, and Joseph and his brothers. These patriarchs cannot be located specifically within ancient Near Eastern history. They are usually considered, however, to be one of the seminomadic peoples present in the ancient Near East in the early to middle part of the second millennium B.C.E.

The primary theme of these narratives is the work of God in establishing Israel as a family among all the families of the earth. This theme is particularly worked out through the motif of the promise of God to each generation of these ancestors of Israel. This promise is to make from the patriarchs a nation of descendants, to give them a land to inhabit, and to make a blessing of them for all the peoples of the earth.

The thematic connection between Gen 1–11 and Gen 12–50 is usually explained in one of two ways. First, the call of Abraham in Gen 12 may be viewed as God's saving response to the sin of Gen 1–11. That is, the promised nation Israel will mediate the blessing of God in the aftermath of sin and judgment. A second link between the two sections of Genesis may be found in the prevailing of the goodness of creation, signaled at the outset by God's affirmation in Gen 1:31 and at the conclusion by Joseph's affirmation of the providence of God in Gen 50:20.

See also COSMOLOGY; CREATION; FLOOD; PATRIARCH.

Bibliography. W. Brueggemann, *Genesis*; G. W. Coats, *Genesis with an Introduction to Narrative Literature*; G. von Rad, *Genesis*; N. Sarna, *Understanding Genesis*; E. A. Speiser, *Genesis*; B. Vawter, *Genesis: A New Reading*; C. Westermann, *Genesis 1–11, Genesis 12–36* and *Genesis 37–50*.

—MARGARET DEE BRATCHER

• **Gennesaret, Lake.** *See* GALILEE, SEA OF

• **Genocide.** *See* ESTHER, BOOK OF

• **Genre in the New Testament.** *See* FORM/GATTUNG

• **Genre in the Old Testament.** [zhahn′ruh] Genre, often called form or type (*Gattung* in German), a traditional structure of literary expression connected with a specific occasion and purpose in the life of the people. A genre is not a literary piece itself but the structure that underlies it and connects it to other literature of the same type and purpose. It is the traditional or conventional form that is common among several generations or groups; what any given author or group does with this stereotypical form constitutes an original contribution. Genres are found in both speech and literature, and they are of singular importance to a people heavily dependent on oral means for transmitting their literary heritage. Present in all parts of the biblical literature, genres contribute considerably to the effort to understand the nature and development of the text.

The study of biblical genres was pioneered by Hermann Gunkel in his commentary on Genesis (1901), where he isolated the smallest and earliest literary units and identified them according to the genres of either saga (mythical, historical, ethnographic, or etiological) or novella. Gunkel later applied the same method to other parts of the Hebrew Bible, especially the prophetic books and the psalms, and he was followed in this by Hugo Gressmann, Sigmund Mowinckel, and many other scholars. Today the study of genre, known by the name of "form criticism," has grown to be one of the most widely used exegetical methods.

Form criticism of a specific text is normally preceded by source criticism (cf. SOURCES, LITERARY), and the results of both these steps are subsequently considered in the work of tradition criticism (see TRADITION IN THE OLD TESTAMENT). The form critic examines four elements in a given text (here a lament or complaint psalm, Ps 64, is used as an example): *structure* or outline of the formal parts (for Ps 64: invocation or cry to God, in v. 1a; petition for help, in vv. 1b-2; reason for the complaint, vv. 3-6; affirmation of confidence or trust, vv. 7-9; prayer or vow or hymn of praise, v. 10); genre, which can be postulated if a similar—though often modified or rearranged— structure can be found in a variety of texts that stem from different authors or groups (e.g., other laments like Ps 64 include those sung by an individual: Pss 3, 6, 22, 102; Jer 20:7-13; and others sung by a group: Pss 60, 74, 79); setting in life (commonly called by the German phrase, *Sitz im Leben*), the typical context in which the genre existed (e.g., the cult, where the lament would be recited by individuals or groups); and intention, the purpose which the genre was meant to serve (for the lament: to express a complaint to God and to solicit divine help).

The seemingly limitless number of genres in the Hebrew Bible can be grouped according to several major categories. Narratives include myth, saga, legend, etiology, history, annals, report, anecdote, novella. The two main legal genres are apodictic law and casuistic law. Songs range from psalm types (such as lament or complaint, thanksgiving song, hymn of praise, liturgy, royal or enthronement psalm, Zion song, and wisdom psalm) to love or wedding songs, work songs, and dirges. Among the prophetic genres are the messenger speech, announcement of judgment or of salvation, woe oracle, salvation oracle, disputation speech, admonition, and various types of reports in prose form. Wisdom genres include proverb, disputation or dialogue, contemplative discourse, riddle, allegory, hymn, onomasticon (list). Most of the genres in the Hebrew Bible have parallels in other ancient Near Eastern cultures, and the form critic attempts to determine points of commonality or distinctiveness. A given genre can be changed as it is transmitted to new generations or groups, sometimes with striking effect—as when the secular lawsuit was adopted by the prophets for the purpose of rhetorically indicting the Israelites or the foreign nations before God (e.g., Hos 4:1-10; Mic 6:1-5[8]; Jer 2:5-13; Isa 41:1-5).

The study of genres has considerable significance for today's task of understanding the biblical text. It allows one to see points of continuity throughout the generations, as well as to appreciate the creative ways in which later persons could adapt the old genres and fill them with new content and novel force. Furthermore, form criticism can help to set guidelines for the interpretation of biblical texts. Thus the meaning of Gen 1–3 will depend largely on whether it is classified as history writing or as a creation myth. Similarly, if a psalm is identified as a lament, one can expect it to contain certain specific elements and serve a set purpose. In this fashion form criticism enables the reader to relate biblical texts to real-life situations of the ancient Israelites, the people who from the outset invested this literature with meaning.

See also FORM/GATTUNG.

Bibliography. G. M. Tucker, *Form Criticism of the Old Testament*; J. H. Hayes, ed., *Old Testament Form Criticism*; R. Knierim and G. M. Tucker, eds., *The Forms of the Old Testament Literature*.

—DOUGLAS A. KNIGHT

• **Genre, Concept of.** [zhahn'ruh] Genre is a French term used to designate literary kinds or types; e.g., tragedy, comedy, epic, history, parable, letter, fiction, poetry, gospel, oracle, apocalypse. From the Renaissance through the eighteenth century, the genres were thought to be fixed and timeless categories which describe all literary works regardless of their author or subject matter, their era, or place of composition. The genres were also ranked in a hierarchy, from epic and tragedy at the top, to lyric and comedy at the bottom. But with the rise of such new forms as the novel and the long descriptive poem, and especially as the Romantics perfected the lyric, the old notion of genre-ranking fell into disuse. Genre is now regarded as a useful interpretive device rather than a criterion for determining the worth of a work.

In a few cases, entire biblical books belong to a single genre: Revelation and Daniel are apocalypses, Psalms is mostly poetry, Amos is a prophetic oracle, Job and Proverbs are wisdom books. But more often the literary modes are mixed. Genealogies are set alongside historical narratives; prayers are blended with hymns; miracle stories are interwoven with parables; legal codes are combined with exhortations; letters are filled with testaments of faith.

In reading scripture no less than in interpreting secular literature, one needs to understand what formal or technical characteristics the text possesses, what literary conventions it observes. Even though the biblical author may not have consciously employed the various genre distinctions, they can often be found to inform the text unawares. Genre criticism is concerned less, therefore, with authorial intention or historical setting than with the text itself as a finished work.

Genre categories are especially useful when interpreting biblical texts that are essentially narrative in type. One must ask who is telling the story, whether the narrator's perspective is omniscient or limited, whether the narrative voice is personal or impersonal, sympathetic or hostile or neutral. Questions about character and plot and mood also arise. Who are the protagonists? What obstacles and opponents must they overcome? How significant is their moral and spiritual development? Around what central conflict, if any, does the action turn, and how is it resolved? What audience does the narrative address, and what atmosphere does it create? Is the natural and historical background rendered solid and life-like, or is it barely sketched for allegorical purposes?

Determining the genre of a text also enables the reader to compare it with similar literary types both within and outside scripture. Jesus' parables, for example, have been likened to comedies and tragedies, the synoptic Gospels to ancient biographies, and the work of the Yahwist to historicized prose fiction. Genre questions thus have more than mere technical and theoretical interest. It makes an enormous difference whether the first chapters of Genesis are read as scientific cosmology, creation myth, or historical saga. To understand the genre of a biblical text, therefore, is to recognize its own suppositions, to enter a life-world other than our own, and thus perhaps to be transformed by the new spiritual order it creates.

See also GENRE, GOSPEL; GENRE IN THE OLD TESTAMENT; LITERARY CRITICISM; LITERATURE, NEW TESTAMENT AS.

—RALPH C. WOOD

• **Genre, Gospel.** [zhahn′ruh] In literary terms, what is a GOSPEL? In the nineteenth and early twentieth centuries similarities between the canonical Gospels and Greco-Roman biographies were recognized and the inference drawn that the Gospels were biographies of the founder of Christianity (Renan, Votaw). In the 1920s a new position was staked out, contending that the canonical Gospels are not biographies, but are the apostolic kerygma (preaching) built up into a vivid narrative form (K. L. Schmidt, R. Bultmann). For nearly fifty years critical orthodoxy held that the Gospels are literarily unique, but by the 1970s a coalition of factors forced a reopening of the case. Chief among them was the recognition by critics that any text standing alone lacks meaning. Such reasoning led criticism to attempt to view the individual text or document in terms of a universal type or genre which is constructed on the basis of an inductive grouping of texts with common features. It is the particular text's participation in the genre that gives it a first level of meaning. A further way of saying something about the meaning of the document as a whole is to note the particular text's transformation of the genre. Recognition of this fact forced NT scholars to ask into what larger context the canonical Gospels fit. In the current discussion there are two very different conceptions of what is meant by genre. Some scholars use genre for classifications that have no necessary ties to a particular time and place: e.g., tragicomedy, parable, fantasy. Others speak of genre in the sense of a literary grouping tied to a particular time, place, and culture: e.g., romance, aretalogy, Greco-Roman history, ancient Mediterranean biography. Since the late 1970s there has been a growing consensus that the canonical Gospels are types of ancient Mediterranean biography, participants in the same large grouping as Philo's *Life of Moses* and Philostratus's *Life of Apollonius of Tyana.* If so, then the canonical Gospels can no longer be regarded as literarily unique. Participation in the ancient biographical genre does not, however, undermine the uniqueness of the canonical Gospels' content any more than the participation of Gen 1 in the genre of ancient Near Eastern creation myth detracts from its uniquely Hebraic witness to the Creator.

See also CANON; GENRE, CONCEPT OF; GOSPEL; GOSPELS, CRITICAL STUDY OF; HERMENEUTICS; LITERARY CRITICISM.

Bibliography. D. R. Cartlidge and D. L. Dungan, *Documents for the Study of the Gospels*; C. H. Talbert, *What Is a Gospel?*; C. W. Votaw, *The Gospels and Contemporary Biographies in the Greco-Roman World.*

—CHARLES H. TALBERT

• **Gentile/Gentiles in the New Testament.** [jen′t*i*l] In English versions of the NT, "gentiles" usually translates a Gk. word (ἔθνη) which normally is rendered "nations." This Gk. word comes from the LXX and translates Heb. words meaning "nations" or "peoples." The singular form may refer to a particular nation, and one of the Heb. words in the singular (עם) is used to refer to Israel as the people or nation of God *par excellence.* The plural of another word (גוֹיִם) designates other peoples with a depreciative nuance. The English word "gentile" comes from a Latin word (*gentilis*), a person belonging to a "clan" or "nation" (*gens*). In the English Bible, it appears almost exclusively in the plural "gentiles," i.e., "nations" or "foreigners" (*gentes,* pl. of *gens*).

OT usage is reflected directly in the NT. "The nations" or "gentiles" (ἔθνη) may designate simply the ethnic distinction between Jews and non-Jews; just as the singular (ἔθνος) is sometimes used for the Jews as the Jewish "nation" (Luke 7:5; John 11:48-52; Acts 10:22). In some contexts "heathen" or "pagans" better captures the intention than "nations" or "gentiles." This holds where "evil passions" are likened to the ways of "the gentiles (ἔθνη) which know not God" (1 Thess 4:5, KJV), rendered "heathen" in some versions. This parallels the OT, "the nations (גוֹיִם) that know thee not" (Jer 10:25). More than ethnic distinction is probably implied in passages dealing with incest (1 Cor 5:1), idolatry (1 Cor 12:2), and anxiety over things (Matt 6:32) perceived as pagan.

Paul sometimes uses "Greeks" and "gentiles" interchangeably (Gal 3:28); but "Greeks" could imply cultural distinction, as in "Greeks and barbarians" (Rom 1:14) or a basic difference in religious mind-set: "For Jews demand signs and Greeks seek wisdom" (1 Cor 1:22).

Non-Jewish Christians are yet termed "gentiles" when simply distinguished from Jews or Jewish Christians, as in "the churches of the gentiles" (Rom 16:4). This usage appears in Paul's rebuke of Peter, who, before the coming of some of "the circumcision" to Antioch, was "eating with gentiles," i.e., uncircumcised, non-Jewish Christians (Gal 2:12). However, non-Jewish Christians may also be perceived as having a new identity "in Christ," now being neither "Jew" nor "Greek" (i.e., gentile). In this view, the distinction between "Jew" and "gentile" is transcended in the creation of a new community "in Christ" (2 Cor 5:16f.; cf. 1 Cor 12:2).

Paul rejected the idea that "all those who are descended from Israel" were really "Israel" (Rom 9:6). "Israel" stood for persons who had entered into covenant relationship with God, not merely the natural descendants of Abraham. Paul distinguished between a Jew outwardly and a Jew inwardly, as between circumcision "in flesh" and "in heart" (Rom 2:28-29; Col 2:11; Eph 2:11). Thus "in Christ," there is "neither Jew nor Greek, there is neither slave nor free, there is neither male nor female" (Gal 3:28). In Eph 2:14-22, Christ is our peace, having destroyed the wall of separation, the cultic "law of commandments and ordinances," creating of the two "one new humanity."

Although the cleavage between Jew and gentile is overcome in Christ, a continuity with Israel holds. These two ideas appear side-by-side in Galatians: "For neither circumcision counts for anything, nor uncircumcision, but a new creation. Peace and mercy be upon all who walk by this rule, upon the Israel of God" (6:15-16). Although "new Israel" or "true Israel" may capture the idea, there has never been but one "Israel of God," those entering into covenant relationship with him, whether Jew or gentile. Historically, Jews have been "near" and gentiles "afar off" (Eph 2:12-13), but neither is "the Israel of God" except through Abraham's kind of faith (Rom 4:16-18). This concept of Christians, Jew and gentile, as the real "Israel" appears variously in the NT (cf. 1 Pet 2:9-10; Jas 1:1).

According to the Gospels, Jesus' attention to non-Jews was limited, his focus being upon "the lost sheep of the house of Israel" (Matt 15:24). However, by practice and teaching, Jesus undercut all arbitrary and secondary tests for identifying the people of God. He began with his own Jewish people and heritage, but what he did there had far-reaching implications for Jews and gentiles. Jesus rejected the cultic distinction between "clean" and "unclean," making the test not what enters the mouth but what comes from the heart (Mark 7:15-23). Eventually his followers came to see that this applies to persons, not just foods (Acts 10:9-16). Jesus rejected the codes which excluded such as the lame, the leper, the blind, the deaf, and a woman with an issue of blood (cf. Lev 15:19-20; 21:18-24; Deut 23:1-6). He went out of his way to affirm these. He scandalized piety by eating with "publicans and sinners" (Luke 15:1). He affirmed as his family anyone doing the will of his Father (Mark 3:35). What was offered the Jews first was intended for gentiles also (Matt 28:19; Acts 1:8; Rom 1:16).

What began as a Jewish community soon included non-Jews. Next, the movement grew from predominantly Jewish to predominantly gentile, and then almost exclusively gentile. Inherent in the gospel is openness to all who will hear it. The Jewish struggle for national survival against the Roman Empire made acute the issue of including uncircumcised gentiles in the fellowship of Jewish Christians who yet were worshipping in the synagogues. Much of this struggle is traced in Acts and Paul's Letters. It was this issue chiefly which caused the parting of Judaism and Christianity, synagogue and church, within the first century. Significantly, in the final book of the NT, when Christians were opposed by the same Roman Empire, the "eternal Gospel" is to be proclaimed to "every nation and tribe and tongue and people" (Rev 14:6). Anyone who thirsts may "take the water of life without price" (22:17).

See also GENTILE/GENTILES IN THE OLD TESTAMENT; JEWS.

Bibliography. G. Dix, *Jew and Greek, A Study in the Primitive Church*; J. Jervell, *Luke and the People of God: A New Look at Luke-Acts;* G. D. Kilpatrick, "The Gentile Mission in Mark and Mark 13:9-11," *Studies in the Gospels,* ed. D. E. Nineham; K. L. Schmidt, "ἔθνος, ἐθνικός," *TDNT*; S. G. Wilson, *The Gentiles and the Gentile Mission in Luke-Acts.*

—FRANK STAGG

• **Gentile/Gentiles in the Old Testament.** [jen'*til*] Distinction is made in the OT between the people of Israel and other peoples. Regularly the word *'am* designates ISRAEL, as in the phrase "people (*'am*) of the Lord," and the words *goyim,* "nations" or "gentiles" (depending on the English translation, RSV, KJV, or NIV, etc.), and *lĕ'ummîm,* "peoples," designate other peoples, i.e., non-Jews. Throughout the OT Israel is represented as living among and in relationship to the nations. Israel's understanding of this relationship was varied and even at times contradictory.

In the primeval traditions of Gen 1–11 all nations are of common descent, the differences between them being attributed to human failures that resulted in broken relationships: rebellion against God (Gen 3), rejection of brother (Gen 4), or human presumption of divine status (Gen 11:1-9). From Gen 12 onward, Israel is set over against the nations as "the people of the Lord." Israel's distinction from the nations was not originally racial, ethnic, or national, but covenantal. As late as the Exodus, Israel was described as a "mixed multitude" (Exod 12:38; the text could, however, refer to a mixed multitude accompanying Israel). Their identity as the "people of the Lord" rested on their willingness to be a servant people through whom God's blessings could be extended to all nations. All nations were the object of God's redeeming purpose (Gen 12:1-3).

Israel's relation to the nations, therefore, in God's purposes, was one of mission. This is the clear intent of God's covenant call to Abram: "Go . . . and I will make of you a great nation, and I will bless you . . . and by you all the families of the earth shall bless themselves" (Gen 12:1-3). This intent is restated in the context of the Sinai COVENANT where Israel is described as a "holy nation" and a "kingdom of priests" to extend torah and covenant blessing to all humankind (Exod 19:3-6). During the monarchy this sense of Israel's being a blessing centered in the Davidic king (Ps 72:17) through whom divine blessing would spread to all nations, and in the Jerusalem cultus seen as a sacred center to which all nations would be attracted to worship the Lord. (Isa 2:2-4; 45:22-24; 51:3-5).

Alongside and contradictory to this sense of mission Israel increasingly felt alienated from and in opposition to the nations. They were seen as a threat to Israel's national destiny and the distinctiveness of Israel's religion, even as enemies of God. When possible they had to be confronted and conquered. The Canaanites and the Transjordan kingdoms had to be defeated to give Israel territory as a nation (Josh 1–11). Their religions had to be eradicated as threats to Yahwism (1 Kgs 18:20-40). Once Israel was established in Canaan its territory had to be expanded and maintained, as represented in the extensive Davidic state as the ideal Israelite state (Judg 20:1; 1 Sam 3:20; 1 Kgs 4:25). All of this was interpreted as God's will for "the people of the Lord." Israel, however, remained a rather small and insignificant nation on the international scene subject to domination by imperial powers like Assyria, Babylon, EGYPT, and Persia. These nations were seen as political and theological threats. Often the prophets interpreted the subjection of one or both of the Israelite states to such powerful nations as God's judgment on the sinful people. This should be understood as an affirmation of God's sovereignty over both Israel and the nations. Israel's misfortune and mistreatment at the hands of the nations fostered a growing sense of isolation and particularism that reached an extreme in the struggles of the postexilic Jewish community to survive when extreme measures were taken to preserve Jews as Jews racially and religiously (Ezra 9–10; Neh 10:30; 13:23-33). At the same time this narrow provincial sense of identity and destiny that rejected the nations was ridiculed and challenged in the wonderfully open-minded stories of RUTH and JONAH; and the earlier and better vision of mission to the nations was revived in the later Isaianic tradition's interpretation of Israel as a servant people whose sufferings in some way redeemed the nations (Isa 42:1-4; 49:1-6; 50:4-11; 52:13–53:12) for whom God had called Israel "to be a light" (Isa 42:6; 60:3).

See also GENTILE/GENTILES IN THE NEW TESTAMENT; JEWS.

—DAVID A. SMITH

• **Gerar.** [gee'rahr] A place-name mentioned in the table of the nations (Gen 10:19), as the site of ABRAHAM's encounter with ABIMELECH (Gen 20:1), and as the site where ISAAC settled (Gen 26:1, 6, 17, 20, 26). The only other biblical reference is in the Chronicles story of a legendary battle between Asa and the Ethiopians (2 Chr 14:13, 14). These references provide no data about the exact location of Gerar. The phrase "valley of Gerar" (Gen 26:17) suggests the vicinity of a stream, but from the OT references nothing can be concluded beyond its location in southern Canaan (PLATE 8).

Scholars have attempted to locate the site, but with limited success. In 1927 Sir Flinders Petrie identified modern Tell Jemmeh as Gerar, but the work of Y. Aharoni in the 1950s supported the identification of Gerar with Tell Abu Hureirah, ca. fifteen mi. northwest of Beersheba in the Negeb (PLATE 3). Excavations demonstrated that the latter site had a long history of occupation and was certainly the location of a settlement during the patriarchal period in Hebrew history; i.e., ca. 1800–1700 B.C.E. Although the identification of this site as ancient Gerar does not necessarily follow from occupancy of the site during the patriarchal period, this possibility has considerable scholarly support.

The description of Abimelech as "king of the Philistines" (Gen 26:1) is anachronistic since the Philistines did not arrive in Canaan until after 1200 B.C.E. During the patriarchal period, the area was dominated by Egypt and only later came under control of the Philistines.

See also ABIMELECH; ABRAHAM; ISAAC.

Bibliography. Y. Aharoni, "The Land of Gerar," *IEJ* 6 (1956): 26-32; E. D. Oren, M. A. Morrison, I. Gilead, "The Land of Gerar Expedition," *ASORN* 36 (1985): 10-12.

—ROBERT W. CRAPPS

• **Gerasa.** [ger'uh-suh] Modern Jerash, Gerasa is located thirty-three mi. southeast of the Sea of Galilee and twenty mi. east of the Jordan River in the mountains of GILEAD (PLATE 12). The extensive remains of this DECAPOLIS city, some 2,000 ft. in elevation, may still be viewed today. The origins of ancient Gerasa may date to the Early Iron Age. Tradition claims Alexander the Great as Gerasa's founder. During the third century B.C.E., the Ptolomies of Egypt administered this area. Antiochus IV refounded the city in the second century B.C.E. and named it "Antioch on the Chrysorrhoas," thus bringing it more prominence. Remains of the many public buildings from the first and second centuries C.E. suggest that Gerasa was one of the most important cities in Roman Arabia. During the fourth century Gerasa became an important Christian city and continued so until the Muslim conquests of the seventh century. Gerasa was left in ruins as a result of an earthquake ca. 747 and was completely deserted about the twelfth century.

The Bible never refers to the city of Gerasa, though there is evidence for "Gerasenes" in manuscripts of both Mark 5:1ff. and Luke 8:26ff. (cf. "Gadarene" in Matt 8:28ff.). These texts, however, refer to the country or territory of the Gerasenes rather than the city. Gerasa could not have been the site for the synoptic stories of the Gerasene demoniac which clearly locate the events somewhere on the eastern coast of Galilee. The modern ruins of the coastal town of Gergesa (Kursi) may have been "the city" from which the demoniac came (Luke 8:27). The presence of a large herd of swine suggests that this district was gentile. Following his encounter with Jesus, the recovered man reported his experience in the city (Luke 8:39), or in the Decapolis (Mark 5:20), located southeast of the Sea of Galilee. Gadara, for which there is also manuscript evidence (cf. KJV of Mark and Luke), and the city of Gerasa were located in the Decapolis.

Bibliography. G. L. Harding, *The Antiquities of Jordan*; C. H. Kraeling, ed., *Gerasa, City of the Decapolis*; G. A. Smith, *The Historical Geography of the Holy Land*.

—CECIL P. STATON, JR.

• **Gergesa.** *See* GADARA

• **Gergesenes.** *See* GADARA

• **Gerizim, Mount.** [ger'uh-zim] The name of a prominent mountain in the hill country of Israel. Only four references to Mount Gerizim by name are found in the OT. These are: the giving of the blessing on Mount Gerizim and the curse on MOUNT EBAL (Deut 11:29; 27:12; Josh 8:33) and Jotham's fable of the trees (Judg 9:7). The Samaritan Pentateuch reads "Gerizim" instead of "Ebal" in Deut 27:4. John 4:21 refers to Gerizim as "this mountain." The importance of Mount Gerizim in the biblical period cannot be measured by the number of times it is named.

Between Mount Gerizim and Mount Ebal to the north lies an east-west valley. SHECHEM and Jacob's well lie at the eastern end of the valley and Neapolis (modern Nablus) lies at the western end. Important north-south and east-west roads crossed at the foot of the mountains. Mount Gerizim stands ca. 2,900 ft. above sea-level and 1,100 ft. above the floor of the valley. On the northern side of Mount Gerizim are at least ten springs. Although Mount Ebal is higher, it has but one spring. Mount Gerizim has had a more significant role than Mount Ebal in the history of Shechem (PLATES 3, 13).

Archaeologists have excavated several ancient structures on Mount Gerizim. The earliest are a shrine from the seventeenth century B.C.E. and a fifty-five foot square temple from the sixteenth century B.C.E. These two are on the northeastern side of the mountain just above Shechem. On the northern peak of Mount Gerizim, at Tell er-Ras, an altar of unhewn stones has been excavated. The altar is thirty ft. high and sixty-six ft. square. It is built on the bedrock, and the stones are laid without cement. The altar is in the middle of a rectilinear courtyard also built out of unhewn stones. This complex of structures was built in the early Hellenistic period and has been identified as the Samaritan temple and the Samaritan altar. According to Josephus (*Ant* 11.8.2, 7; 12.5.5; 13.9.1) the SAMARITAN temple was built on Mount Gerizim with the permission of Darius III and Alexander the Great and it was like the Jerusalem temple. He said it was destroyed by John Hyrcanus in 128 B.C.E. The remains of the altar are still visible from Jacob's well, as they were in Jesus' time (cf. John 4:20). Hadrian built a temple to Zeus Hypsistos in the second century C.E. on top of the remains of the Samaritan temple. From coins and early literary evidence, there were 1,500 marble steps up the northern side of Mount Gerizim to the temple. Zeno built a church on the mountain in the fifth century C.E., and in the following century Justinian built a fortification around the church.

In the early Hellenistic period Shechem became the main city for the Samaritans, and Mount Gerizim was chosen as the site for their temple and altar. Although Shechem has been unoccupied since 107 B.C.E., Mount Gerizim is still revered by the present-day Samaritan community, which celebrates the PASSOVER on the highest peak on the mountain.

See also EBAL, MOUNT; SAMARITANS; SHECHEM.

Bibliography. R. J. Bull, "The Excavation of Tell er-Ras on Mt. Gerizim," *BASOR* 190 (1968): 4-19; O. Eissfeldt, "Gilgal or Shechem?" *Proclamation and Presence*, ed. J. Durham and J. R. Porter; G. E. Wright, *Shechem: The*

Biography of a Biblical City.

—H. PAGE LEE

• **Gershon/Gershom.** [guhr'shuhn/ghur'shuhm] Names used interchangeably (Exod 6:16; 1 Chr 6:1); meaning is uncertain; however, according to Exod 2:22, Gershom is derived from the Heb. *ger,* meaning "sojourner."

Gershom, the oldest son of MOSES and Zipporah, was given his name as a reminder of Moses' Midian exile (Exod 2:22; 18:3). According to the Book of Judges, Gershom had a son named Jonathan, who along with his sons served as priests of the tribe of Dan until the time of the captivity (Judg 18:30). According to the Chronicler, Gershom had a son named Shebuel, listed among the descendants of Levi (1 Chr 23:14-16) and identified as "the chief" (1 Chr 23:16) of a family or clan by that name. Apparently another descendant named Shebuel served as the "chief officer in charge of the treasuries" in the time of David (1 Chr 26:24).

Gershon, the oldest of the three sons of LEVI (Exod 6:16), also called Gershom (1 Chr 6:1), had two sons, Libni and Shimei (Exod 6:17). Libni was also known as Ladan (1 Chr 23:7). The descendants of Gershon were known as the "Gershonites" (Num 3:21; 26:57). As a part of the Levites, the Gershonites were responsible for transporting the different parts of the tabernacle and tent of meeting (Num 3:25-26) during the journey from Sinai to Canaan. They were given thirteen of the cities assigned to the Levites (Josh 21:6).

Gershonites are mentioned in several accounts in later history. Asaph's family was among several prominent families of singers in the temple (1 Chr 6:31-43; 25:1-2). Gershonites are listed among the organized divisions of the temple personnel (1 Chr 23:6-11). They were in charge of the treasury of the house of the Lord (1 Chr 26:20-21; 29:6-8). Also, Gershonites assisted in cleansing the TEMPLE during the reform of Hezekiah (2 Chr 29:12-19).

Gershom, a descendant of Phinehas and head of a family in the Babylonian Exile, returned to Jerusalem from Babylon with EZRA during the reign of Artaxerxes (Ezra 8:1-2).

See also LEVI/LEVITES; MOSES.

—LAMOINE DEVRIES

• **Geshur.** [gesh'uhr] A name perhaps meaning "bridge" or "land of bridges," used in reference to a small country or city-state northeast of the Sea of Galilee, east of the Jordan River, and north of the territory of Bashan (Deut 3:14; Josh 12:5; 13:11) (PLATE 10). The people of Geshur were called Geshurites.

During the conquest, the Israelites did not drive out the people of the small kingdom of Geshur (Josh 13:13). Rather, the people were allowed to stay and the kingdom of Geshur became a part of Israel.

David's wife Maacah, Absalom's mother, was from Geshur. She was the daughter of Talmai, king of Geshur (2 Sam 3:3). After killing AMNON (2 Sam 13:28-29), ABSALOM fled to Geshur and stayed with his grandfather, Talmai, three years (2 Sam 13:37-38). Absalom's exile in Geshur finally ended when David sent Joab to Geshur to seek Absalom's return to Jerusalem (2 Sam 14:21-23). At some point, perhaps during the time of the divided monarchy, the kingdom of Geshur broke away, and along with Aram, participated in raids on Israelite territory in Bashan (1 Chr 2:23).

The term Geshurite is used for a people, or a small clan or city-state, located in the Negeb south of the PHILISTINES, not captured by the Israelites during the conquest (Josh 13:2). David made raids upon the Geshurites of the south during his stay with Achish, the Philistine city-state king of Gath (1 Sam 27:8).

See also ABSALOM.

—LAMOINE DEVRIES

• **Gestures.** A term not found in the Bible; refers to any movement of body, limbs, head, or face expressing an emotion or an idea. Most gestures are natural, nonverbal means of communication, but some in biblical literature were deliberately chosen symbolic actions associated primarily, but not exclusively, with prophetic activity.

Movements of the Body. Standing erect was a position of PRAYER in the case of Solomon (1 Kgs 8:22) and the Pharisees (Luke 18:11). Kneeling, sitting and bowing to the ground expressed the same attitude for David (2 Sam 7:18), Solomon (1 Kgs 8:54), Elijah (1 Kgs 18:42), Daniel (Dan 6:10), and Stephen (Acts 7:60). Sitting in ashes indicated repentance or resignation (Job 2:8; Jonah 3:6). Dancing was an expression of joy and celebration (Exod 15:20; Matt 14:6), but could also signal religious devotion (Exod 32:19; 1 Kgs 18:26; Ps 149:3).

Movements of the Limbs. Bowing the knees indicated WORSHIP and prayer (Ezra 9:5; Ps 95:6; Eph 3:14), but this gesture also served to make a petition (2 Kgs 1:13; Luke 5:8). Shaking knees, on the other hand, showed fear (Dan 5:6). The hands beating on the breast communicated remorse (Luke 18:13; 23:48), while beating others expressed violence (Gen 37:22). Hands lifted toward heaven, or spread forth, or stretched out designated an attitude of prayer (1 Kgs 8:54; Pss 141:2; 143:6; Isa 1:15), but hands (or fingers) could also be pointed in mockery or scorn (Isa 58:9; Hos 7:5). Placed on the head of another, the hands would convey a blessing (Gen 48:14), or a dedication for service (Acts 6:6) or, in the case of a sacrificial animal, consecration (Lev 1:4).

The hands could rend the garments as well as place dust on the head to express grief or consternation (Gen 37:29; 2 Sam 1:11; 13:19; Matt 26:65). Shaking the dust off the garments or feet, on the other hand, signaled rejection (Matt 10:14).

Movements of the Head or Face. The bowed head indicated respect or reverence (Gen 18:2; 1 Kgs 1:16; Ps 95:6), whereas the uplifted head or eyes exuded hope or expectation (Ps 121:1; Isa 60:4) and shaking the head communicated scorn (2 Kgs 19:21; Mark 15:29). The eyes could express pride (Isa 3:16), hatred (Deut 15:9), sadness (Jer 9:1), love (Cant 4:9), and a host of other emotions. The whole head and face could signal scorn (Ps 22:7), but also grace (Ps 31:16) and determination (Luke 9:51). Spitting in the face brought shame (Num 12:14; Isa 50:6; Matt 26:67). Laughing indicated disbelief or disdain (Gen 17:17; 18:12; Luke 8:53). Kissing expressed affection (Ruth 1:14), and pulling the hair or beard indicated intense emotional upset (Ezra 9:3; Neh 13:25; Isa 50:6). Weeping could signal both sorrow and joy (Gen 46:29; John 11:35).

In addition to these common gestures, some others functioned symbolically to communicate certain particular realities or assurances. Moses' uplifted hands assured Israel of success in its war against the Amalekites (Exod 17:11f.). Pulling off one's sandal and giving it to another confirmed a contractual agreement between the two persons (Ruth 4:7-8). Ezekiel ate small portions of food to symbolize the lot of captives and refugees (Ezek 4:9-17).

A public dramatic breaking of a clay pot by Jeremiah pronounced divine judgment upon Jerusalem (Jer 19:1-3, 10-11). Jesus smeared clay made with spittle upon the eyes of a blind man and had him wash it off, to designate the healing of blindness (John 9:6-7).

See also PRAYER/THANKSGIVING IN THE NEW TESTAMENT; PRAYER/THANKSGIVING IN THE OLD TESTAMENT; SYMBOL; WORSHIP IN THE NEW TESTAMENT; WORSHIP IN THE OLD TESTAMENT.

—NIELS ERIK A. ANDREASEN

Artwork by Margaret Jordan Brown

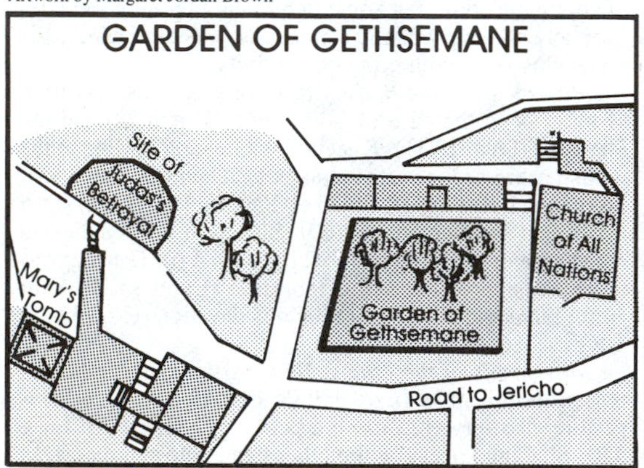

Layout of the Garden of Gethsemane.

• **Gethsemane.** [geth-sem'uh-nee] The name of the place where Jesus agonized in prayer just prior to his betrayal and arrest. Gethsemane appears only twice in the NT (Matt 26:36; Mark 14:32). In the Christian tradition, Gethsemane connotes more than a place; it also alludes to an event. The event is one in which Jesus, alone, wrestles at the depth of his being with issues of ultimate significance for his own future and that of his followers.

Gethsemane is a transliteration of a Greek word that means "oil press" or "oil vat." Each Gospel, in its own way, provides information which permits the location of the site (PLATES 24, 25)in the vicinity of the Mount of Olives (cf. Matt 26:30, 36; Mark 14:26, 32; Luke 22:39-40; John 18:1). John does not mention the Mount of Olives by name, but describes Jesus and the disciples crossing the KIDRON Valley which was the way to reach the Mount of Olives. Even this does not pinpoint the setting with great precision for the Mount of Olives was, in reality, a ridge some two and one-half miles long standing across the Kidron to the east of the Temple mount in Jerusalem.

There is less uniformity among the four Gospels in regards to the character of the place itself. Matthew and Mark use a term that has the sense of a "field" or "piece of land" (Matt 26:36; Mark 14:32). Luke uses a term which has the less precise meaning "place" (Luke 22:40). It is only in the Gospel of John that we learn that it was a garden.

The Gospel of John is the basis for further implications about the character of the setting. In John 18:1, Jesus and his disciples are described as entering the garden. In 18:26 one of the servants of the high priest refers to the garden as a place in which Simon Peter has been. This wording suggests to some a building which may have been referred to as the "oil press." This language has led others to the conclusion that the garden was an enclosed area.

The momentous events at Gethsemane caught the attention and imagination of those who described the events and those who have seriously reflected on them since. Some ancient manuscripts include at Luke 22:44, "and being in an agony he prayed . . . his sweat became like great drops of blood falling down upon the ground." Most likely the writer of Hebrews had the Gethsemane event in mind in certain passages (cf. 5:7-8). Attempts to identify the location have not been universally accepted. One site has been identified as Gethsemane since the fifth century because the olive trees there are so old (PLATE 38); however, they do not go back to the first century. In fact, Josephus noted that all the trees in the vicinity of Jerusalem were destroyed during the siege of Titus (70 C.E.).

See also JERUSALEM; KIDRON; OLIVES, MOUNT OF.

—ROBERT O. BYRD

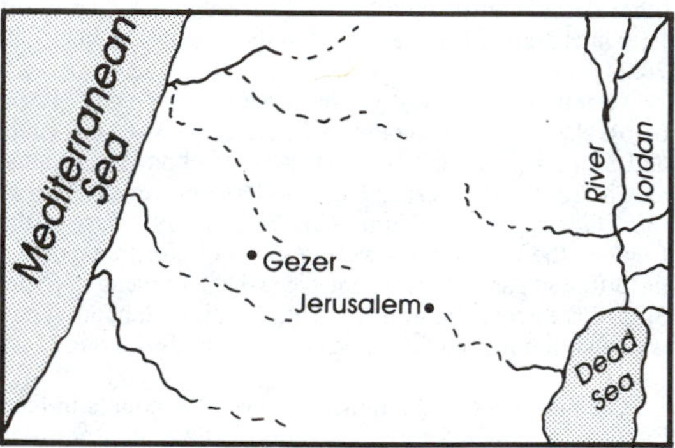

Designed by Margaret Jordan Brown ©Mercer University Press

• **Gezer.** [gee'zuhr] The thirty-three acre mound of Tell ej-Jezer is located five mi. south/southeast of Ramleh, at the juncture of the northern shephelah and the western slopes of the central ridge, guarding the entrance to the valley of Aijalon (PLATE 3). It was identified with the Gezer of the Bible and both Egyptian and Mesopotamian sources by C. Claremont-Ganneau in 1871. Excavations were carried out by R. A. S. Macalister in 1902–1909; A. Rowe in 1934; and W. G. Dever, J. D. Seger, G. E. Wright and others in 1964–1974. The latter excavations were sponsored by Harvard University, the Hebrew Union College—Jewish Institute of Religion, and the Smithsonian Institution. They pioneered newer stratigraphic and interdisciplinary methods, thereby reinterpreting the older results and then setting the entire history of the mound—one of the largest and most significant Bronze-Iron Age sites in Palestine—in larger cultural context.

There are at least twenty-six strata at Gezer, from the site's founding in the Late Chalcolithic period (Stratum 26) ca. 3500 B.C.E. to its abandonment sometime in the first century C.E. The Early Bronze I-II period, ca. 3100–2600 B.C.E. (Strata 25-23), exhibits only an unwalled village, followed by a gap in occupation in Early Bronze III-IV, ca. 2600–2000 B.C.E.

During the Middle Bronze Age, ca. 2000–1500 B.C.E. (Strata 22-18), Gezer grew into one of the most massively fortified Canaanite sites in Palestine, with a massive multi-towered inner wall, plastered embankment (or *glaçis*), and triple entryway south gate and adjoining citadel 5017. Belonging to the latter part of this phase is the well known Gezer high place, an alignment of ten large stelae possibly to be associated with the biblical *maẓẓēbôth*. This period was brought to an end ca. 1482 B.C.E. in a violent destruction, no doubt to be attributed to Pharaoh Thutmosis III, whose inscription on the walls of the temple at Karnak records this victory.

The Late Bronze Age, ca. 1500–1200 B.C.E. (Strata 17-14), is witnessed chiefly by the addition now of the outer wall and a palace on the summit. This would be the Gezer of the several AMARNA letters, which mention three successive kings of Gezer. A decline in the thirteenth century B.C.E. was followed by a localized destruction, probably the work of Pharaoh Merneptah, whose victory stela of ca. 1207 B.C.E. mentions both Israel and Gezer.

According to both archaeology and the Biblical tradition (cf. Josh 10:31-33) Gezer was not destroyed in the Israelite conquest. There are at least five levels on the summit that reflect continued Canaanite occupation, plus the incursions of Philistines, in the twelfth and eleventh centuries B.C.E. (Strata 13-11). The reference in 1 Kgs 9:15-17 to an Egyptian raid, then the ceding of the site to SOLOMON and his refortification, has been dramatically confirmed by the latest excavations. Above a mid-tenth century B.C.E. destruction level is a stretch of double (or casemate) wall and a splendid four-entryway city gate with an outer gateway (Stratum 10). Almost identical walls and gates have been found at Hazor and Megiddo (cf.1 Kgs 9:15-17), as Y. Yadin had already suggested in 1958.

In the Iron II period, ca. 900–600 B.C.E., Gezer was relatively unimportant (Strata 9-5). It was destroyed ca. 734 B.C.E. by the Assyrians as shown both by archaeology and a well known relief of Tiglath-pileser III depicting the siege of the gate. Gezer recovered, however, and was reckoned with Judah until its destruction again by the Babylonians in the early sixth century B.C.E.

The only significant later remains are private houses and the final reuse of the city gate and outer wall, from the Maccabean period (cf. 1 Macc 13:43-48).

Bibliography. W. G. Dever et al., "Excavations at Gezer," *BA* 30 (1967): 47-62, "Further Excavations at Gezer, 1967-71," *BA* 34 (1971): 94-132 and *Gezer I, II, IV, V.*

—WILLIAM G. DEVER

• **Giant.** A being of huge stature, believed by the Hebrews to have lived on the earth from earliest times. Gen 6:4 is often interpreted as saying that giants originated in the marriage of the sons of God (divine beings from the heavenly court) and human women, although in its present form the passage says only that the Nephilim (the fallen ones?) were on earth both before and after the marriages took place. Whatever their origin, the nephilim were thought to be the ancestors of the giants the Hebrews both heard about and met in their conquest of Palestine. The Moabites called the previous inhabitants Emim, meaning the terrible or frightful ones (Deut 2:10). Ammonites spoke of the Zamzummim (Deut 2:20). Another name was Rephaim. All were related as "sons of Anak." The presence of an Anak tribe in Palestine at about 2000 B.C.E. is supported by the Egyptian Execration Texts, which list them as enemies of the pharaoh.

The unbelieving spies cited the presence of giants as one of the reasons the Hebrews should not try to conquer Canaan (Num 13:28, 33). CALEB drove out the three giants named in the spies' report (Num 13:22; Josh 15:14), and JOSHUA destroyed all the Anakim except a remnant in Gaza, Gath, and Ashdod (Josh 11:21). DAVID and his army symbolically completed the conquest when they killed the Philistine giants of Gath (2 Sam 21:16-22; 1 Chr 20:4-8).

The best known of the giants in the OT was GOLIATH, reported in 1 Sam 17 to be about ten ft. tall.

See also GOLIATH.

—ROBERT L. LAMB

• **Gibeah.** [gib'ee-uh] More than one place is called by this name (or some variation of it such as Gibeathah, Gibeath, Geba, or Gibeon) in the Hebrew Bible, and it is not always clear from the context which place is intended or even in some cases whether the name should be translated as a proper noun, "Gibeah," or as an appellative, "the hill."

The most prominent Gibeah was located in the tribal territory of Benjamin, was also called Geba, and is probably to be identified with present-day Jeba eight miles north northeast of Jerusalem (PLATE 11). This Benjaminite Gibeah/Geba is mentioned in the tribal allotment list of Josh 18:28. It attained infamy as the scene of the rape of a Levite's concubine by several Benjaminites and of a resulting punitive military action by the other tribes (cf. Judg 19-21; Hos 9:9; 10:9). It also figures prominently in the stories about SAUL's rise to power and his struggle against the Philistines (1 Sam 13:2–14:46). Eventually it became Saul's capital (1 Sam 22:6; 23:19). Later, Asa would fortify it as a defensive position for Judah's northern frontier (1 Kgs 15:22). Three other Gibeahs also deserve special mention: (1) the Gibeah (or "hill") of Phinehas, probably somewhere near Shiloh (Josh 24:33); (2) the Gibeah near Kiriath-jearim, a temporary resting-place of the Ark (1 Sam 7:1-3; 2 Sam 6:1-3); and (3) the Hivite city GIBEON.

—J. MAXWELL MILLER

• **Gibeon.** [gib'ee-uhn] Related to the Heb. term meaning "hill." Gibeon was a Hivite city at one time (Josh 9:7; 11:19; cf. 2 Sam 21:2); later it is counted as a town of Benjamin's inheritance (Josh 18:25) and a Levitical city (Josh 21:17). Almost certainly it is to be identified with the modern village of el-Jib, six mi. northwest of Jerusalem (PLATE 11).

Gibeon figures prominently in the historical books of the OT: (1) In Josh 9 the Gibeonites send a peace envoy to meet the invading Israelites at Gilgal. Dressed shabbily and claiming to be from a far country, they succeed in making a covenant with Israel. Though Joshua soon discovers the stratagem, its effects are irreversible, and in Josh 10 Israel is obliged to rush to the aid of the Gibeonites who have been attacked by a coalition of local kings. (2) During the time of the shift of power from Saul's house to that of David, the armies of both sides, led by Abner and Joab respectively, face off across the pool of Gibeon (2 Sam 2:12-29). (3) During a famine, David inquires of the Lord and learns that the famine is the result of blood guilt incurred by the house of Saul "because he put the Gibeonites to death" (2 Sam 21:1-2). David expiates this sin by extraditing seven of Saul's sons to the Gibeonites for execution. (4) In 1 Kgs 3:8-15 Gibeon is the place where Solomon offers sacrifices and where Yahweh appears to him in a dream and promises him both wisdom and riches.

Archaeological excavations at el-Jib by J.B. Pritchard in 1956–57 correlate with the OT's description of the city as "a great city, like one of the royal cities" (Josh 10:2), although apparently not during the Late Bronze Age when Joshua's career is usually dated. Among the most notable finds at el-Jib were a pool eighty-seven ft. in diameter and eighty-two ft. deep with a circular stairway descending into it (cf. 2 Sam 2:13; Jer 14:12), a 187-ft.-long water tunnel carved through solid rock to bring spring water into the city even under siege conditions, and numerous jar handles inscribed with the name "Gibeon."

—J. MAXWELL MILLER

• **Gideon.** [gid'ee-uhn] A judge during the premonarchic period. The story of Gideon ("hewer" or "slasher") is found in Judg 6:1–8:35. He was from the clan of Abiezer, part of the tribe of Manasseh. Though counted among the judges of Israel, Gideon is never called by that title. His charismatic call and his role as a military savior, however, clearly identify him as such. His date is difficult to determine, but sometime during the eleventh century B.C.E. is usually suggested.

The traditions concerning Gideon are extremely complex; there is little agreement over the details of the literary sources. Some of the more obvious problems are the following. The hero of the story has a double name: Gideon and Jerubbaal. "Gideon" is most frequently used, occurring a total of thirty-nine times in chaps. 6–8 while "Jerubbaal" occurs only four times (6:32; 7:1; 8:29, 35). But "Jerubbaal" is used exclusively as the father of ABIMELECH in Judg 9. The most common suggestions to deal with this issue are either that Jerubbaal was Gideon's original name, reflecting a period of religious syncretism, or that the names referred originally to two different people. The phenomenon of the same person having more than one name is clearly attested in the Bible, e.g., JACOB/ISRAEL, and JOASH/Jehoash. Monarchs with more than one name were a common occurrence in the ancient Near East.

If the names originally referred to two different people, one of the purposes of the story was to unite them, since in the account as it now stands, they are quite clearly the same person. The question is difficult to decide, but since the biblical editor found it necessary to identify them (cf. Judg 7:1), this may indicate different persons. The popular etiology of Jerubbaal in 6:32 has also been called into question. Whatever the case, the story points to a real conflict between Yahwism and Baalism during this period.

Other complexities abound. There are two etiological legends regarding a tradition of a sanctuary near Ophrah (6:11-24, 33-35; 6:25-32, 36-40). There is also confusion over who participated in the fight against the Midianites. On the one hand, a call is sent out to several tribes (6:33-35), but most of those who respond are sent home for theological reasons (7:2-3). On the other hand, a call is sent throughout Ephraim. They respond by killing the princes of Midian (7:24-25), but they are then said to have been angered by not being invited to join in the fight at all (8:1-3)! Further, Gideon puts God to the test twice (6:17-24, 36-40), and two different campaigns are described, one in Cisjordan (7:1ff.) and another in Transjordan (8:4ff.) (PLATES 10, 47).

No matter what explanation is finally accepted, one can clearly see that the figure of Gideon and the reality of Midianite incursions became the focal points around which these various traditions gathered.

The nature of the Midianite threat is also unclear. Judg 6:2-6 indicates that raids occurred at regular intervals coinciding with Israel's harvest season. Thus the Israelites were forced to hide in caves and thresh grain in secrecy. On the other hand, some scholars suggest that only one invasion took place. Furthermore, Gideon's purpose in one tradition focuses on a blood vendetta against two kings who had killed his brothers (8:18-21), and not a holy war against Midian as a whole. However, he does seem to have secured permanent relief from Midianite pressure (Judg 8:28), which was remembered by later Israel (cf. Isa 10:26; Ps 83:11). Gideon's story also seems to have served as a polemic against the monarchy (cf. 8:22-23).

See also MIDIAN/MIDIANITES.

Bibliography. C. F. Kraft, "Gideon," *IDB*; J. A. Soggin, "Gideon," *Judges A Commentary*; R. de Vaux, "The Judges of Israel," *The Early History of Israel*.

—JOHN C. H. LAUGHLIN

• **Gifts of the Spirit.** The idea of "spiritual gifts" is found only in the NT (though there are numerous instances in the OT where the Spirit of God empowers specific human beings for particular tasks, e.g., Judg 3:10) and especially in the writings of Paul. There are at least five lists of the various gifts found in the NT: Rom 12:6-8, 1 Cor 12:8-10, 1 Cor 12:28-30, Eph 4:7-13, and 1 Pet 4:10-11. Since no two of these lists are identical, it is generally assumed that the lists are not intended to be definitive, but only to indicate the infinite numbers of gifts bestowed by God upon humankind.

Of the gifts that are enumerated, there is wide variety as the following examples indicate:

The Gift of Apostleship. This gift focused upon the way God empowered certain ones through the Spirit to perform specific functions, an "apostle" being one sent forth to declare the gospel. This gift was not strictly confined to one limited group. But it was the prerogative of the Spirit and was not transmitted to other people. The authority resulting from this gift was spiritual and was exercised democratically, not autocratically (Acts 15:6).

The Gift of Prophecy. This gift was characterized by spontaneity and power and may well have included speaking "by revelation" (1 Cor 14:6, 26, 30) in utterances that were fully intelligible without interpretation, as contrasted with speaking in TONGUES, where an interpretation was essential for meaningful understanding.

The Gift of Discerning of the Spirits. The very nature of the gift of prophecy was such that some ("false prophets") would seek to imitate the genuine gift. Paul probably had this gift in mind when he advised the Christians at Thessalonica to "put all things to the test" (1 Thess 5:21, TEV).

The Gift of Teaching. This gift is related to prophecy since the teacher's task was often to explain what the prophet proclaimed. Also the teacher instructed converts and the church generally in faith and practice as well as in the gospel tradition and the scriptures (1 Cor 12:28; Rom 12:7).

The Gift of Exhortation. Those who possess this gift were called upon to encourage others through the persuasive power of love and understanding (Rom 12:8). Thus this ministry functioned largely as one of support.

The Gift of Wisdom. This gift enabled the Christian community to receive and explain the deep things of God (Rom 11:33). Illuminating the plan of God by explaining what certain things mean in their broadest significance was the reason for the Spirit's equipping some for this task by giving them "the word of wisdom" (1 Cor 12:8).

The Gift of Knowledge. Closely related to the gift of wisdom, Paul probably had in mind those words spoken only after long and careful deliberation (cf. 1 Cor 12:8).

The Gift of Speaking in Tongues. Sometimes referred to today as glossolalia, this gift (cf. 1 Cor 12:10) is easily the most controversial. According to Paul, the person exercising this gift addressed himself to God, probably in prayer or praise (1 Cor 14:1-17), and the subsequent "tongue" was not a language at all (1 Cor 14:10-12). In fact, the speech was unintelligible and therefore of no real value to the assembly (1 Cor 14:2-3). Paul indicated that the tongue-speaker lost control of his intellect (1 Cor 14:14-15), and the apostle thus placed certain controls upon the practice (1 Cor 14:27).

The Gift of Interpretation of Tongues. A necessary complement to the gift of tongue-speech, this gift (1 Cor 12:10) would give meaning to the unintelligible speech of the one who was speaking in tongues. While the one speaking in tongues might exercise this gift of interpretation (1 Cor 14:13), usually this gift was given to others (1 Cor 14:26-28).

Various Gk. terms underlie the expression "spiritual gifts" such as πνευματικά and χαρίσματα. The former relates to things spiritual as these are manifested in public worship while the latter refers to all manifestations of God's favor (grace) to humankind. Both are given by God through the HOLY SPIRIT.

Scholars have debated for centuries whether these spiritual gifts were intended for the apostolic age only or whether they have an enduring and permanent place in the expression of Christianity in every age. The twentieth-century rise of neo-Pentecostalism has prompted renewed discussion of this question.

See also APOSTLE/APOSTLESHIP; CORINTHIAN CORRESPONDENCE; HOLY SPIRIT; MIRACLES; PAUL; PROPHECY; PROPHET; PROPHETESS; TEACHING; TONGUES.

—WATSON E. MILLS

• **Gihon.** [gi'hon] According to Gen 2:13, one of the rivers of Eden was named Gihon. Gihon figures most prominently in the OT, however, as the name of a spring at Jerusalem, almost certainly the one known today as the "Virgin's Fountain" in the KIDRON Valley. The importance of Gihon to the ancient city of Jerusalem cannot be overestimated. It was the main source of water for the city in OT times and figures prominently in several of the OT narratives. David gave orders that Solomon should be anointed at Gihon, for example, which suggests that the spring also had sacral importance (1 Kgs 1:33, 38, 45).

Unfortunately, the Gihon spring lay near the base of the Kidron valley some 130 ft. below the level of the ancient city (which sat atop the Ophel ridge). Since it was impracticable to build a defensive wall low enough to include the spring, and thus to insure a reliable water supply in times of siege, it was necessary to construct a water tunnel from within the city walls down to the spring. Archaeologists have uncovered what appears to have been such a tunnel from pre-Davidic times. Indeed this tunnel may have been the means by which David's men gained access to the city (2 Sam 5:8; cf. 1 Chr 11:5-6). This pre-Israelite tunnel carried water from the spring back into the hill for a distance of fifty ft., to a point from where the water could be drawn up a forty ft. vertical shaft. From there the water would have been transported in containers 125 ft. through another sloping tunnel up into the city.

Sometime later, almost certainly during the reign of HEZEKIAH, a more extensive water passage was constructed (2 Kgs 20:20; 2 Chr 32:30; Sir 48:17; cf. 2 Chr 32:1-5; Isa 22:9-11). In light of the report of Hezekiah's rebellion against Assyria in 2 Kgs 18–19, it is possible that the tunnel was constructed in preparation for an Assyrian military retaliation. The tunnel cut a winding path, 1,600 ft. long, through the solid rock of Mount Ophel to bring the spring water to a pool located near the southern end of Ophel (PLATE 37). The happy meeting of the two groups who worked from both ends to cut the tunnel is recorded in an inscription discovered in 1880 on the wall of the tunnel.

The waters of Gihon flow through the tunnel to this day. The pool to which it flows came to be called "the pool of Siloam" and is mentioned in John 9:1-12 as the place where Jesus healed a blind man.

See also SILOAM INSCRIPTION

—J. MAXWELL MILLER

• **Gilboa, Mount.** [gil-boh'uh] A northern spur of the central hill country which extends into the JEZREEL Valley at the southeastern end of the valley, Mount Gilboa is a small range of limestone hills which rise to a height of 1,630 ft. (PLATES 11, 56).

According to Judg 7, Gideon gathered a small force for battle against Midian at the foot of Mount Gilboa ("Mount Gilead" in Judg 7:3 probably should read "Mount Gilboa," cf. 7:1). Mount Gilboa is remembered chiefly, however, as the place where the Philistines defeated Israel and killed Saul and his sons (1 Sam 28:1-4; 31:1-13; cf. 2 Sam 1:1-16). The issue at stake for the Philistines may well have been the control of the southern end of the Jezreel valley and thus access to Beth-shan. Possibly the Israelites (specifically the Manassites; cf. Josh 17:11-13) were expanding from the hill country into the valley and threatening Philistia's control of this important region. After defeating Israel on the slopes of Mount Gilboa, the Philistines exhibited the bodies of Saul and his sons at Beth-shan, a few mi. northeast of Mount Gilboa. Specifically, we are told that they displayed the bodies on the city wall. Thereupon the JABESH-GILEADites, to whose aid Saul had once come (1 Sam 11:1-11), stole the bodies by night and gave them a proper burial (1 Sam 31:11-13). Israel's defeat at Mount Gilboa and the death of Saul and his son Jonathan are memorialized in a poetic lament in 2 Sam 1:19-27.

—J. MAXWELL MILLER

• **Gilead.** [gil'ee-uhd] The ancient name for a mountainous region on the Transjordanian plateau, located between the DEAD SEA and the SEA OF GALILEE. Though the term is not used with great precision in the OT, it can be said that Gilead was north of MOAB and AMMON, which was located on the southeastern side of Gilead, and south of BASHAN; the Syrian Desert formed its eastern boundary. Again, it should be stressed that the frontier between Gilead, Ammon, and Moab is not identified with precision, while Gilead and Bashan are sometimes spoken about without distinction (cf. Josh 17:5; 2 Kgs 10:33; Micah 7:14). In a recounting of the Transjordanian territory taken by the Israelites, Deut 3:10 refers to the tableland (of Moab), Gilead, and Bashan, moving from south to north. Just as the River Arnon divided Moab into two parts, the JABBOK (modern Zerqa) bisected the highlands of Gilead. According to Josh 12:2, SIHON ruled "half of Gilead" (south of the Jabbok = the modern Belqa), and 12:5 says that OG reigned over the other half of Gilead (north of the Jabbok = the modern Ajlun). The northern half of Gilead, which was included in the kingdom of Og, was assigned to the tribe of MANASSEH, and the southern half, which was in Sihon's realm, came under the control of REUBEN and GAD (Deut 3:12; Josh 13:31). Thus, Gilead was the center of the Israelite population on the east side of the Jordan, and the name "Gilead" was sometimes used for Israelite Transjordan in general (e.g., Judg 20:1).

Gilead, which means "stronghold," or perhaps, "rugged" in Hebrew, contains higher and more jagged mountains than Bashan; some of Gilead's peaks have altitudes of

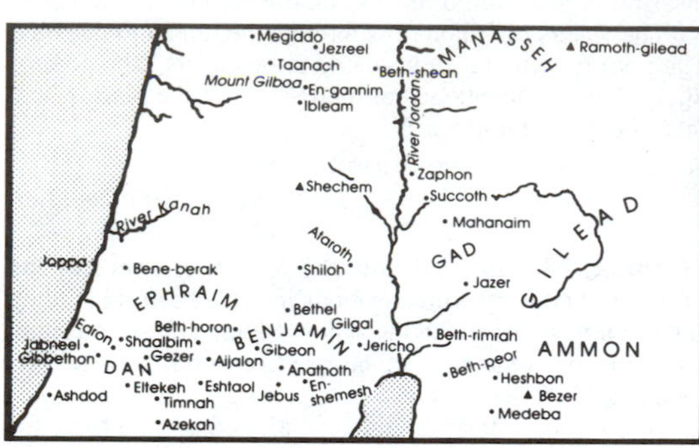

Designed by Margaret Jordan Brown ©Mercer University Press

over 3,000 ft. While these tall mountains are located on either side of the Jabbok, northern Gilead's peaks are generally higher. These limestone hills rest on Nubian sandstone, which is exposed only in the sides of the Jabbok canyon. Gilead was heavily forested in antiquity, especially north of the Jabbok; its scrub oak, carob, and pine forests were sometimes compared with the stands of timber in the Lebanese mountains (Jer 22:6; Zech 10:10). This region is probably most famous because of the biblical references to the medicinal balm of Gilead (Gen 37:25; Jer 8:22; 46:11; cf. Ezek 27:17), though its exact identification is unknown. Grain, olives, and grapes were also grown in Gilead.

While traveling in Gilead, Jacob wrestled with an angel at the Jabbok (Gen 32:22-30). After the Hebrews had incorporated Gilead into their Transjordanian territory, Gilead appears in biblical history most often as a place of refuge (e.g., 1 Sam 13:7; 2 Sam 2:8-9; 17:21-29; cf. Gen 31–21). The prophet ELIJAH was from Tishbe in Gilead (1 Kgs 17:1). According to 1 Kgs 4:7-19, King SOLOMON divided Gilead into two administrative units. This region came under attack from the ARAMAEANS in the ninth and eighth centuries B.C.E. (cf. 1 Kgs 20:23-43; 2 Kgs 13:22; Amos 1:3). In the later half of the eighth century B.C.E., TIGLATH-PILESER III transformed Gilead into an Assyrian province (cf. 2 Kgs 15:29). The region was also made a province in Persian times, and the Romans later subdivided Gilead into Perea and the Decapolis.

In addition to its agricultural importance, Gilead served as a major thoroughfare between north and south, with the King's Highway traversing its highlands. Some of the major OT cities in Gilead were Ramoth-gilead, JABESH-GILEAD, Zarethan, SUCCOTH, MAHANAIM, and Jazer; important places in Hellenistic-Roman times included Gadara, Abila, Pella, and Gerash.

—GERALD L. MATTINGLY

• **Gilgal.** [gil′gal] There was more than one place called Gilgal in ancient Palestine. Especially prominent in the OT narrative is the Gilgal which was located near the Jordan river in the vicinity of JERICHO (Tell es-Sultan). It was at this Gilgal that the Israelites are said to have encamped at the time of their initial entry into the land. Josh 4:19ff. reports that they set up twelve stones as a memorial to the event. Apparently, the name Gilgal was thought to have been derived from this stone memorial, although Josh 5:9 offers another explanation. Gilgal is remembered in the latter passage as the place where those who had not received the sign of circumcision in the wilderness were finally circumcised. Thus "the reproach of Egypt" was "rolled away" from them.

As the narrative continues in the Book of Joshua, we learn that Gilgal served as Joshua's "camp" (Josh 9:6; 10:6, 7, 9, 15, 43). It was there that the Judahites sought him out to request the inheritance promised them by Moses (Josh 14:6). Gilgal also figures prominently in the narratives pertaining to Samuel and Saul. Saul's kingship was reaffirmed at Gilgal (1 Sam 11:14ff.), and his confrontation and break with Samuel occurred there (1 Sam 12; 13:5-15).

It is clear that Gilgal was a prominent cult center in Israel. Judg 2:1ff. reports that a "messenger of the Lord" came from Gilgal to Bochim (Bethel?) to announce judgement on Israel; the book of Judges makes an enigmatic reference to certain "idols" which were at Gilgal (3:19; cf. 3:26); and Hosea and Amos both condemn worship practices at Gilgal (Hos 4:15; 9:15; Amos 4:4; 5:5).

The site of Gilgal cannot be identified with any certainty since the OT provides only an approximate idea of Gilgal's location (PLATE 11), and the ancient name has not been passed down in any modern name in the region. Two possibilities have been considered: Khirbet en-Nitleh, about three miles southeast of Jericho, and Khirbet Mefjer, just over a mile north of Jericho. No clear evidence for an Iron Age occupation has been found at Khirbet en-Nitleh, whereas Khirbet Mefjer has yielded traces of an Iron Age settlement. In view of the OT's description of Joshua's settlement as a camp rather than a city (Josh 10), the search for its remains may be hopeless.

Apparently there was a second Gilgal in the central hill country nearer to Bethel than to Jericho. The clearest evidence of this Gilgal is provided by 2 Kgs 2:1-12, the account of Elijah's parting from Elisha and ascension by a whirlwind into heaven (2 Kgs 4:38). The two prophets travel from Gilgal to Bethel to Jericho, presumably in a continuous, southern direction. The geographical progression suggests a Gilgal located somewhere north of Bethel. Other "Gilgals" are mentioned in the OT in Deut 11:30, Josh 15:7, and Josh 12:23 (the latter instance is usually emended to read "Galilee").

—J. MAXWELL MILLER

• **Glory.** A term applied to God, people, and things, connoting a number of qualities such as renown, splendor, power, worth, and praise.

In scripture the concept of glory is most often connected with the sphere of the divine. Sometimes glory refers to the essence of GOD as a transcendent being (Ps 113:4; Luke 2:9). More often it is connected to the divine splendor or power that people perceive when God is physically manifested.

One means of the revelation of divine glory in the OT is through theophanies, or appearances of God. In them glory is often connected with natural phenomena, such as a cloud, fire, bright light, or storm (Exod 13:21; Ps 18; Ezek 10:4). Glory is manifested at any place where God is present. Therefore, the OT closely links God's glory with the ARK, the Tabernacle, and the TEMPLE (Exod 40:34-35; 1 Sam 4:21-22; 1 Kgs 8:11). In fact, because of God's presence "the whole earth is full of his glory" (Isa 6:3). In the OT divine glory is also connected to events where God is present, including religious ceremonies and mighty acts in history like the Exodus (Lev 9:23; Num 14:22).

In the NT glory is chiefly related to the person and activity of JESUS Christ. Divine glory characterized him before the creation of the world and was manifested in his incarnation (John 1:14; 17:5). That glory was seen by the shepherds at the birth of Jesus and by the disciples as a result of his miracles (Luke 2:9, 14; John 2:11). Jesus' glory was spectacularly demonstrated at his TRANSFIGURATION (Luke 9:28-36 and par.), an event involving cloud and light phenomena reminiscent of the OT. The CRUCIFIXION was also a demonstration of Christ's glory—esp. in the fourth Gosepl—as well as a glorification for God (John 12:23, 28; 13:31-32). Because of his resurrection and ascension Christ now resides at the right hand of God in glory (Acts 3:13; 7:55; Rom 6:4). In the PAROUSIA Christ is to come again in great power and glory (Matt 24:30).

While the Bible most often speaks of glory in connection with God, the term is sometimes related to things and to people. Nature displays glory by virtue of divine CREATION (Ps 19:1; Isa 35:2). Certain human artifacts are so beautiful that they are glorious (Exod 28:40; 1 Chr 22:5). The term "glory" is also applied to the praise that people give to God, as well as the heavenly state that believers will eventually attain (Ps 115:1; Col 3:4; Rev 5:12-13).

When used with reference to people, glory sometimes refers to noteworthy qualities such as wealth, power, or reputation (Gen 31:1; Ps 49:16; Matt 6:29). Human glory can also be an inappropriate pridefulness that is offensive to God (Isa 23:9; cf. Phil 2:3). Because people are created "a little lower than divine," they are crowned with glory and honor (Ps 8:5). However, as a result of sin human beings fail to attain the glory God intended for them to have (Rom 3:23). Only Christ, the second Adam, fulfilled the glory of God in the flesh (Heb 2:9). Thereby he is able to share his glory with his disciples (John 17:22). Christians grow in glory as they are transformed into the image of Christ, and in the eschaton they will achieve full glory by being in the very presence of God (2 Cor 3:18; Col 3:4; 1 John 3:2).

See also GOD; PAROUSIA/SECOND COMING; SHEKINAH; THEOPHANY.

Bibliography. E. Jacob, *Theology of the Old Testament*; G. Kittel and G. von Rad, "δόξα, κτλ.," *TDNT*; A. Richardson, *An Introduction to the Theology of the New Testament*.

—BOB R. ELLIS

• **Glossolalia.** *See* TONGUES

• **Gnosticism.** [nos″tuh-siz′uhm] The word Gnosticism derives from a Gk. noun γνῶσις (*gnosis*), knowledge. The term is used by modern scholars to designate a series of diverse religious movements in the first three centuries C.E. In antiquity the groups so identified designated themselves, and were designated by others, with other names. Some scholars find enough in common among these groups to argue that they should be described as "the Gnostic religion." Others have classified the early movements into types of religiophilosophical systems, e.g., Syrian gnosis, Marcionite Christianity, Valentinianism, the Basilidian movement. On this model the numerous distinct groups, such as the Cainites, Peratae, Barbelo-Gnostics, the Sethians, and the Borborites, to name only a few described in the later Church Fathers, are seen as arising out of the earlier systems.

The movements can be grouped under the rubric "Gnosticism" because they do make certain common assumptions. Essentially the groups are anticosmic, or world-rejecting. While they describe it differently, the CREATION of the world is portrayed in negative terms as driving from an error-prone creator. Hence the highest spiritual reality had nothing to do with the creation of the world, for it was EVIL in its origins. Therefore the world holds humanity trapped in ignorance of its higher spiritual possibilities. Only an emissary sent by the higher spiritual reality into the world can bring the special gnosis that illuminates and liberates. These elements: evil creation, enslavement in the world, emissary from beyond the world, and special knowledge that illuminates are expressed in the Gnostic movements in a variety of different ways. The reader of the original sources may expect to encounter a bewildering array of actors and mythologoumena in the various expressions of this drama of SALVATION.

Extant Original Sources. The ancient sources for these Gnostic movements are of three kinds: patristic reports refuting Christian-Gnostic heretics, original Gnostic writings discovered before 1945, and the NAG HAMMADI codices.

(1) In their treatment of Gnosticism the church fathers concern themselves exclusively with refuting Gnostic heresies that are influencing Christian churches. As far as they are concerned Gnosticism is a Christian heresy. The major sources for the patristic reports are: Irenaeus of Lyons (second century C.E.), *Unmasking and Refutation of the False Gnosis* (*Adversus haereses*); Clement of Alexandria (second and third centuries C.E.), *Miscellanies* (*Stromata*) and *Excerpts from Theodotus* (*Excerpta ex Theodoto*); Hippolytus of Rome (second and third centuries C.E.), *Refutation of All Heresies* (*Refutatio omnium haeresium*); Tertullian (second and third centuries C.E.), *Against Marcion* (*Adversus Marcionem*), *Against Valentinus* (*Adversus Valentinianos*), *The Prescription against Heretics* (*De praescriptione haereticorum*), *Scorpiace* ("a remedy for the scorpion's sting" of the Gnostic heresy); Origen (third century C.E.), *Commentary on John* (*Commentarii in Johannis Evangelium*). *Against Celsus* (*Contra Celsum*); Epiphanius of Salamis (fourth century C.E.), *Medicine Box* (*Panarion*).

These polemical works are also important because, in some instances, they contain quotations from the writings of the Gnostics, such as Valentinus, Heracleon, Basilides, Isidore, and others.

(2) Until the end of the eighteenth century, all that could be known of Gnosticism came from brief quotations from certain Gnostic writings and the extensive polemical reports refuting these movements by their opponents, the church fathers. A modern understanding of the nature of these movements was shaped by their highly polemical reports. Toward the end of the eighteenth century in separate discoveries three ancient codices, containing original Gnostic writings in the Coptic language, were announced.

The Askew Codex was acquired by the British Museum in 1785. It contains four books, the second of which bears a title inserted into the text at a later time: The *Second Book of the* PISTIS SOPHIA. On the basis of that insertion the entire codex has been known by that title. The text, dated to the third century C.E. takes the form of a dialogue between Jesus and his disciples in which Jesus communicates arcane, speculative instruction in response to the disciples questions.

The Bruce Codex was discovered in Upper Egypt in 1769, but not published until 1892. The manuscript contains two Gnostic treatises: the TWO BOOKS OF JEU and the "Untitled Text." The *Two Books of Jeu* are dialogues between the "Living Jesus" and his disciples in which Jesus instructs them in esoteric, arcane gnosis. The "Untitled Text" is a highly speculative religio-philosophical treatise in which Christian elements seem superficial.

The Berlin Codex, discovered in 1896, was not published in its entirety until 1955. The codex has been dated to the fifth century C.E., though the actual composition of the text would have been earlier. It contains four separate writings: the GOSPEL OF MARY, the APOCRYPHON OF JOHN, the SOPHIA OF JESUS CHRIST, and the ACT OF PETER. The first three writings are clearly Gnostic in character. They constitute dialogues between the resurrected Christ and his disciples in which Jesus provides esoteric teaching in response to the disciples' questions. The *ActPet* is not explicitly Gnostic but describes the healing ministry of Peter and holds forth a message of asceticism and self-control.

Most of the material in these three ancient books has been regularly understood to reflect a stage of decline in the vitality and influence of Gnosticism.

(3) The situation with original source material changed in 1945 with the discovery of the Nag Hammadi library. In the library there are fifty-two separate treatises, forty-one of which are known only from the Nag Hammadi texts. The manuscripts were manufactured in the middle of the fourth century C.E., but the texts date from an earlier period. These texts reflect a variety of traditions. A number of texts provide us with instances of non-Christian varieties of Gnosticism; i.e., texts whose narratives betray no evidence of influence from Christian traditions: the APOCALYPSE OF ADAM, the PARAPHRASE OF SHEM, and EUGNOSTOS. Some texts, such as the APOCRYPHON OF JAMES and the TEACHINGS OF SILVANUS, appear to be Christian texts influenced by Gnosticism. Other texts stand in a more Neoplatonic tradition than in a Jewish-Christian tradition, such as ALLOGENES and the THREE STELES OF SETH. In certain other cases, some texts were originally composed as non-Christian texts, but later they were Christianized in an attempt to claim them for use in a Christian-Gnostic context, such as the GOSPEL OF THE EGYPTIANS, the *Sophia of Jesus Christ*, and the TRIMORPHIC PROTENNOIA. Still other texts are associated with Valentinus, such as a VALENTINIAN EXPOSITION; and still others are associated with Greek wisdom literature, such as the SENTENCES OF SEXTUS. A number of texts derive from the Hermetic corpus, such as the DISCOURSE ON THE EIGHTH AND NINTH, and ASCLEPIUS. In short, the texts reflect a wide variety of tradition types originally written at different times from different parts of the ancient world.

The Problem of the Sources. There is significant lack of agreement between the polemical reports of the church fathers about the Gnostics and the Gnostic writings of the Nag Hammadi library. The most extensive and close agreement appears between the report of Irenaeus, *AdvHaer* 1.29 and the *ApJohn.* There is also the problem that the church fathers separate Gnostic groups into clearly defined sects on the basis of specific teachers and distinctive teaching, but in the Nag Hammadi Library one finds side by side in one tractate distinctive teachings that the church fathers attributed to different teachers and sects. While one may sort some of the Nag Hammadi tractates in terms of the sects identified in the reports of the fathers (e.g., Valentinian and Sethian), most of the writings in the library do not fit into the categories of the fathers.

Recent evaluation of the reports of the church fathers concludes that the fathers did not have independent knowledge of most sects, but depended upon the reports of Irenaeus and then upon one another for their information. Where they do appear to have independent knowledge, they frequently do not agree in their description of the same sect.

The Problem of Gnostic Origins. The debate about where and when Gnosticism began is a modern problem. Until the end of the nineteenth century Gnosticism was thought to have been the product of Christian heresy. The early church fathers traced its origins to SIMON MAGUS (Acts 8:9-24) who was acclaimed as the "Great Power" of God. It was from Simon that all heresies originated (Iren., *AdvHaer* 1. 29). Its rapid growth in the ancient world was encouraged by an early Christian fascination with Greek philosophy and mythology. This view of Gnostic origins remained the consensus until the beginning of the twentieth century. The classic statement was made by Adolf Harnack who described Gnosticism as the "acute Hellenization of Christianity." Harnack argued that certain early Christians were led into Gnosticism when they rejected the OT and their Jewish roots, and turned to Platonic DUALISM.

Near the beginning of the twentieth century, scholars of the history of religions, working with the polemical reports of the church fathers argued that evidence pointed toward a non-Christian origin for Gnosticism in the East, in Iranian, Persian, and Mandaean thought.

Near the middle of the twentieth century Hans Jonas, following up on these insights, argued that Gnosticism was produced in late antiquity as the result of a blending of eastern mysticism (a belief in ASTROLOGY, fatalism, and MAGIC) with Greek thought. Hence there was no one single point of beginning, rather Gnosticism derived from the mood or attitude of late antiquity, and it simultaneously emerged in different forms throughout the ancient world.

Others have found the origins of Gnosticism in a kind of radical Judaism. Some argue that it arose among Jewish apocalyptic groups who expected the immediate appearing of the KINGDOM OF GOD. When the TEMPLE at Jerusalem was destroyed in 70 C.E., and the kingdom failed to appear, these sectarian Jews rejected their traditional faith and apocalyptic hopes. It was out of such a shaking of the foundations of faith that Gnosticism emerged. Others argue that Gnosticism derived from the challenge to God's character due to the presence of evil in the world. By definition a righteous God could not be associated with the disorder and evil that one observes in the created order. Such Jews gave up the traditional Jewish view of the goodness of creation and its later corruption through the sin of ADAM and EVE. They rejected the benevolence of the creator and developed out of their traditional faith an anti-cosmic religion of transcendental gnosis.

One problem that has continued to influence the scholarly discussion has been the date of the primary Gnostic sources, principally the texts discovered at Nag Hammadi. Virtually all documents date from the second century C.E. and later. Some have argued that you can find evidence of Gnosticism reflected in the NT. For example, the opponents that Paul debated in 1 Corinthians have been described as Gnostic (cf. 1 Cor 2:14–3:1), and the "Christ Hymn" in Phil 2:5-11 has also been described as an independent piece of tradition quoted by Paul, but deriving originally from Gnostic thought. Scholars who find evidence for Gnosticism in the NT argue that the clearly defined Gnostic groups of the second century would have required a certain amount of lead time in the first century C.E. and earlier to have become so distinctive and widespread in the second century. Further they point out that the church fathers—and Paul—were only concerned to refute heresy in Christian churches. They would have had no interest in non-Christian varieties of Gnosticism that did not impact Christian churches. Hence one could expect Gnosticism in its non-Christian forms to be earlier than the second century C.E. Other scholars, however, take the position: "No texts; no history!" These scholars argue that Gnostic motifs appearing in both the NT and the DEAD SEA SCROLLS simply are not evidence of a fully developed Gnosticism. Gnostic "features" are not sufficient evidence to conclude that there were gnostic groups in the first century. Hence, Gnosticism is not a pre-Christian phenomenon.

The Nag Hammadi library, however, has provided clear evidence of a non-Christian variety of Gnosticism. Such non-Christian Gnostic texts as the *ApocAdam*, the *ParaphShem*, the *StelesSeth*, and *Eugnos* conclusively demonstrate the existence of non-Christian Gnosticism. Hence, while there may currently exist no Gnostic text that can conclusively be dated into the first century C.E. so as to allow an argument for pre-Christian Gnosticism in a temporal sense, there is ample evidence for a "pre-Christian" Gnosticism in a logical sequential sense. Indeed one of these non-Christian Gnostic texts exists both in its non-Christian form (*Eugnos*) and in a later Christianized form (*SophJC*). The Nag Hammadi library may be expected to produce further helpful insights into the problem of Gnostic origins.

Principal Gnostic Systems of the Second Century. Since the time of Irenaeus it has been customary distinguish sects within Gnosticism on the basis of Gnostic teachers and their distinctive teaching. While the Nag Hammadi library raises serious questions about this procedure, it remains the most convenient way to synthesize the material in a brief way.

MARCION and the Marcionite movement are not usually included as a Gnostic sect, but because they share certain features with Gnostic sects, they should be mentioned. Marcion (ca. 150 C.E.), excommunicated by the church at Rome, founded his own church. His movement proved to be a serious competitor to orthodoxy, and survived well past the fourth century C.E. The teaching of Marcion is characterized by his absolute rejection of the Jewish roots of Christianity, i.e., he rejected the creator God of Judaism and the OT. The creator God of Jewish faith he described as a just and righteous God, but he cannot be characterized as merciful and good. On the other hand, Jesus Christ reveals a merciful God of love. Marcion was the first to establish a NT CANON of scripture. It contained an abbreviated form of the Gospel of Luke and ten Pauline letters (without Hebrews and the Pastorals).

Basilides was active in Alexandria, Egypt during the first half of the second century C.E., is the earliest of the Christian Gnostic theologians of that century. All that remains of his considerable literary activity are a few fragmentary quotations preserved in the polemical reports of the church fathers. Among his lost writings are included a gospel and an exegesis of the gospel in twenty-four books. It is reported that he was a disciple of Glaucias, who was described as the interpreter of Peter. His work was continued by his pupil Isidore, of whom also only a few fragments remain. His movement continued into the fourth century. It is not a simple matter to describe the Basilidean system since the two major descriptions of his thought by Irenaeus and Hippolytus are irreconcilable.

The principle difference between the system of Hippolytus and that of Irenaeus is in the conscious rejection of emanation by the system in Hippolytus. According to Hippolytus, Basilides viewed the systems of emanation with their theory of devolution as crude and ineffective. Further, it was the very nature of all existence to strive to rise to the better. No creature would be so unintelligent as to descend. Thus, according to Hippolytus the entire thrust of Basilides' system is upward.

Quotations from the writings of Basilides and Isidore contain only allusions to a cosmogonic system. In these fragments the teaching of Basilides and Isidore deal primarily with ethics.

Valentinus, mid-second century C.E., was the most influential and creative of the Gnostic teachers of his time. The movement he began at Rome survived into the fifth century. His followers claimed that he was a disciple of Theudas, who was described as a disciple of Paul. Until the discovery of the Nag Hammadi library only a few sources for our knowledge of the teaching of Valentinus existed. The patristic sources deal primarily with Valentinianism in its later forms, which they describe as an elaborate system of emanation. For the thought of Valentinus himself we are dependent upon fragmentary quotations preserved in Clement of Alexandria and Hippolytus. The GOSPEL OF TRUTH, a Nag Hammadi text, has been described as a writing of Valentinus. There are also extant excerpts from the writings of some of the disciples of Valentinus: Ptolemaeus, Heracleon, Marcus, and Theodotus. The following Nag Hammadi writings have been identified as belonging to the Valentinian movement: PRAYER OF THE APOSTLE PAUL, TREATISE ON THE RESURRECTION, TRIPARTITE TRACTATE, GOSPEL OF PHILIP, FIRST APOCALYPSE OF JAMES, INTERPRETATION OF KNOWLEDGE, and A VALENTINIAN EXPOSITION.

See also HERMETIC LITERATURE; MARCION; NAG HAMMADI.

Bibliography. (Studies). W. Bousset, *Kyrios Christos: A History of the Belief in Christ from the Beginnings of Christianity to Irenaeus*; C. W. Hedrick and R. Hodgson, Jr., eds., *Nag Hammadi, Gnosticism, and Early Christianity*; H. Jonas, *The Gnostic Religion. The Message of the Alien God and the Beginnings of Christianity*; B. Layton, ed., *The Rediscovery of Gnosticism. Proceedings of the International Conference on Gnosticism at Yale, . . . 1978*; K. Rudolph, *Gnosis. The Nature and History of Gnosticism*; D. Scholer, *Nag Hammadi Bibliography 1948-1969*, updated annually in *NovT* beginning with vol. 13 (1971); R. McL. Wilson, *Gnosis and the New Testament*; F. Wisse, "The Nag Hammadi Library and the Heresiologists," *VC* 25(1971) 205-23; (Texts). H. W. Attridge, ed., *Nag Hammadi Codex I (The Jung Codex) (NHS* 22-23), 1985; A. Böhlig, and F. Wisse, eds., *Nag Hammadi Codices III, 2 and IV, 2: The Gospel of the Egyptians (NHS* 4), 1975; S. Emmel, ed., *Nag Hammadi Codex III, 5. The Dialogue of the Savior (NHS* 26), 1984; W. Foerster, ed., *Gnosis: A Selection of Gnostic Texts*; R. Haardt, *Gnosis. Character and Testimony*; B. Layton, *The Gnostic Scriptures*; D. Parrott, ed., *Nag Hammadi Codices V, 2-5 and VI with Papyrus Berolinensis 8502, 1 and 4 (NHS* 11), 1979; J. M. Robinson, ed., *The Nag Hammadi Library in English*; C. Schmidt and V. MacDermot, eds., *Pistis Sophia (NHS* 9), 1978, and *The Books of Jeu and the Untitled Text in the Bruce Codex (NHS* 13), 1978.

—CHARLES W. HEDRICK

• **God.** *The Idea of God.* Apparently humans everywhere and at all times have concepts of a power, idea, or person that lies behind or beyond everything. This idea or person is called God. People have expressed their ideas about God or insights which have come from God (revelation) in all manner of ways: visual representations (the cave paintings in Lescaux), dramatic arts (the religious precessions at the Pantheon), verbal expressions (the Qur'an), architectural monuments (the cathedrals of the Middle Ages), music (the religious works of J. S. Bach). Since the Enlightenment, Western civilization has sought to find God in the depths of humanity and its inventions; or, more radically, to suppose that human creativity is God or invents the idea of God. Throughout the history of humanity, there have been, as Paul said (1 Cor 8:5), gods many and lords many. The significant thing about this general quest of godness is to realize that it is universal and general and that the notion persists in all communities, primitive or philosophical.

Jewish-Christian Understandings of God. The OT starts with God, a supreme God, as the presupposition of all existence. There are no arguments of proof for the existence of God, as in later Western philosophical discussions. From the beginning it is assumed that in the beginning, God was. In the Bible, God is creator of all things, sustainer of all things, the one who permits all that is, and the redeemer of all things. In the OT, this God is personal. This God takes the initiative in revealing God's self to people. This God is the supreme God. This God forms a covenant community to bless all people. The NT relates this God of the OT uniquely to the person of Jesus of Nazareth. The NT, building upon the OT, unites God's work as creator to the work of God as redeemer. Christians affirm that in the INCARNATION (the coming of Jesus Christ in flesh—as person) God is supremely and finally revealed. This biblical understanding of God came about in many forms over a period of hundreds of years. Following are some materials and viewpoints which went into this picture of God.

The Names of God. NAMES signify people, places, and things. In the modern world, names are mostly just ways of designating objects. In biblical times, the name of a person indicated the power, special qualities, and mysterious, unique essence of that person. Particularly important were divine names which described what God does, what God is like, what powers and mysteries God contains. To call upon the "name of the Lord" is to invoke God's presence and power. To speak in the name of God is to speak on God's behalf with power and authority. The divine names do more than identify and describe. They embody and empower. EL is the primary word for God in the OT. El means strength or power. It is used in several forms (el, elah, eloah). The plural Elohim is used frequently, a phenomenon sometimes called the majestic plural. Although the form is plural the one referred to or who is speaking is singular.

Several other designations for God grow out of compounds of El with other words. The more important of these are: EL SHADDAI, God of the mountains or high places (especially in Job); El Elyon, the high God (Gen 14); El Olam, the God of eternity (Gen 21:33 and the Psalms); El Berith, the God of the Covenant (Judg 9:46); El Elohe-Israel, God, the God of Israel (Gen 33:19-20; Josh 8:30).

A second term for God in the OT is Yahweh (Jehovah) a word related to the Hebrew verb form "I am." The primary instance of the revelation of this name is to Moses at the burning bush (Exod 3). Yahweh becomes the special covenant name of God, in distinction from El, the generic term. Yet, it is not at all certain that Exod 3 refers to a proper name. Ancient peoples felt that to know the name of a god, a person, or a thing was to exercise control over that being. It is probable that the divine voice was saying to Moses, "I am who I am," go and do what you are told. Later generations, especially the prophets, used the term Yahweh as a proper name for God. Still later, the Jewish religious leadership, fearful of violating the commandment against taking God's name in vain, read or spoke Adonai (Lord) instead of Yahweh. Much later critical scholars used the two different designations for God, Elohim and Yahweh, as code terms for assigning different authorship to various parts of the first five books of the Bible.

A third designation for God in the OT is the term Adon or Adonai, usually translated as Lord. The basic idea behind this term is dignity or worth. It is a title conveying respect. Adon is frequently applied to men as leaders. This is parallel to the use of elohim for the supposed deities of other nations and angels. One has to pay close attention to the context when translating the terms. Bible translators often capitalize the terms (Adon and Elohim) when they take them to be referring to the deity and do not capitalize them otherwise.

God is referred to in the OT by a variety of other items most of which are metaphors or similies. God is (like) a rock, expressing strength and solidity. God is (like) a SHEPHERD, a family member, father, brother, kinsman—one who cares for and is related to humans. God is King; God rules. God is supreme and final judge. God is before all things and after all things; God has priority and ultimacy (Isa 43:10). A particularly beautiful way of expressing God's always being there is the poetic phrase "ancient of days" (Dan 7:9).

The Characteristics of God. Descriptions of God in the Bible take the same form as descriptions of created things. Since God is not a created thing, such descriptions must be interpreted with great care. Just as names for God have special sacredness, descriptions about God must be seen as going beyond descriptions of created things.

(1) God is the God who acts. The speech of God (the WORD of the Lord) brings the world and all things in it into being. God said and it was done, done well (Gen 1–2). God's actions deliver the Israelites out of Egypt, establish and preserve a covenant community, commission and vindicate the prophets, send the only-begotten Son, raise Christ to God's right hand, and eventually bring the world to its end. Throughout this great saga of holy history, God is known by what God does.

Biblical notions of God establish God's being from God's doing. The God who is and who is demonstrated by God's own acts takes the initiative in divine/human encounters. God is the God who seeks. God pursues Israel as well as protects her (Hosea; Ps 139). God seeks lost people by patiently waiting, by placing God's self in peril, by vigorously searching (Luke 15). The actions of God are accompanied by the power of God. The God who cares is the God who can. There are spectacular and extraordinary acts of God such as the Exodus, the signs to Elijah, and the deliverance of Jonah. There are also quiet and sustaining evidences of God as expressed in the Psalms. Perhaps the strongest expression of the power of God is God's patience in the face of cosmic and eternal resistance to his purpose in the suffering love displayed through the death of JESUS Christ, and in the face of all suffering.

(2) God knows. Knowing is generally perceived as an intellectual process that comes by reflection or experience. The knowing of God is primarily an interaction with others, Christ, the Spirit, and creation. The Hebraic sense of knowing is to know intimately, to have close and familiar contact with. This is the primary way God "knows" the world and all that is in it. God "walked" in the garden confronting innocent-and-guilty Adam and Eve. God knew Israel in a special way (Hos 11:1). Before the prophets were born God gave purpose to their existence (Jer 1:5). The psalmist is intensely aware that God knows all about the individual (31:7; 44:21) and in a particular way God knows,

is pleased with, the righteous(1:6; 37:18). In this particular sense of knowing as approving and accepting, the Jesus of John's Gospel speaks of God knowing Jesus in a unique and reciprocal way and of God knowing those who relate to God through belief in God's Messiah (John 5, 8, 17). Paul's suggestions about God's foreknowledge (Rom 8; Eph 1) are christocentric and apply to God's purpose in Christ. Later theology created intellectual impasses by discussing God's knowledge as an intellectual cognition. This misunderstanding of the concept of the knowledge of God gave rise either to a predestination stance or to a concept of God's knowledge as limited. Biblical insights about God's knowledge cannot conceive of anything God does not know, and the biblical materials always suppose that what God knows is known in an engaging and intimate way.

(3) God loves; God is love. Jer 31:3 and 1 John 4:8 are mileposts for measuring God. Jer 31:3 uses an intensely physical word for love which means to pant after or desire. OT terms for God are couched in analogies—descriptions of what humans are and what humans can understand (anthropomorphisms). The love of God is a powerful force that creates, pursues, refines. God's love is not just passion; it is also ethical commitment and commandment. Justice (*Mishpat*) is an OT word that connotes love and grace as well as retribution (cf. Deut 10:18-19; Hos 10:12). It gives ethical content to the concept of love. Love is justice and justice that loves is necessary to maintain the righteousness of God. Another OT word for God's love, *hesed,* carries the idea of mercy. It is a term used especially of God's relation to the covenant community.

To the strong desire, ethical pattern, and gracious implications of God's love in the OT are added NT insights. These are: love as fast friendship and family attachment and love which flows outward and reaches out regardless of the worth of the object. *Agapē,* a seldom used word in classical Greek, is invested with Christian content by the redemptive acts of God through Jesus Christ. *Agapē* love is the motivation for the atonement given in Christ (John 3:16). *Agapē* love is the essence of who God is (1 John 4:8). Closely related to love is the fascinating idea of God's wrath. Love and wrath are two sides of the same coin. To reject God's love is to experience wrath. Wrath is not anger as much as it is settled opposition to sin. The major distinction between God's love and wrath is a matter as to where free willed creatures stand in relation to God. To be overwhelmed with a love one cannot receive is to be damned. To be corrected by the displeasure (wrath) of God at one's destructive actions is to be redeemed.

(4) God is holy. The deepest characteristic of God is love. The most distinctive characteristic of God is holiness. To say that God is holy (Isa 6; Matt 6:9) is to say that God is distinct from all creatures. Therefore God offers hope to creation, since the whole creation longs to be other than it is (Rom 8:22-23). Only God is holy in an absolute sense. Other things are holy in a derivative sense (e.g. Sabbath is holy because it is a time set aside to God; Jerusalem is the holy city because it is a place set apart to God; saints are holy because they are people set apart to God). The primary emphasis of holiness is not morality. It is distinctiveness.

God's otherness (transcendence) is affirmed by the idea of God as holy. But the immanence (hereness) of God must be affirmed at the same time. These two basic characteristics are brought together in the two-word title for God, "Holy Father" (John 17:11). God's holiness holds together the love and wrath of God. The requirements of holiness uphold the justice of God. The grace of holiness involves the mercy of God.

(5) Particular NT insights about God. The OT insights, names, and characteristics of God are adopted and enlarged by NT writers. The most distinctive name for God which Jesus used was Father. OT insights about God as Father included the notions of God as Father of Israel and of the King of Israel. Divine parenthood was never seen in scripture as parenthood by physical propagation as found in pagan religions. God was Father of Israel by virtue of the adoptive covenant relationship. In the NT Jesus used the familiar form of father (*Abba*) to refer to God.

The author of John claimed for Jesus a distinctive relationship to God as Father (John 1:18; 3:16, 18). The analogy of father and son is used to describe this relationship. Later Christians, realizing the distinctiveness of this relationship, made a special point to speak of Christ's relationship to God as "begotten not made." The Christian understanding of God inevitably involves a christocentric focus. God is the God of the patriarchs and the "God and Father of our Lord Jesus Christ" (1 Pet 1:3).

Just as the NT expanded the OT meaning of Father, applying it through the focus of the sonship of Christ, so also the NT expanded the idea of God as Spirit. In the OT God's Spirit made the world, came upon certain persons (e.g., the psalmist and the prophets), bestowed power on Israel's kings, and promised a coming Messiah. In the NT, God, the HOLY SPIRIT, bears distinctive witness to Christ and empowers Christ. The Holy Spirit comes upon the church, the body of Christ (Acts 2) and gives gifts for the well-being of the body of Christ (Rom 12; Eph 4; 1 Cor 12–14; Gal 5). God as Spirit (John 4:24) was a specific designation of God. God the Holy Spirit became a special function of God.

The NT so united Father, Son, and Spirit that each of these designations for God was called Lord, the most prevalent title for God in the NT. Later Christians would develop the doctrine of the TRINITY as the fullest historical expression of the Christian God. The NT expressions about God suggest God's actions as three-fold: the Father sends Jesus Christ, the unique Son; the Son bears witness to the Father; the Father and the Son send the Spirit who bears witness to the Son and the Father. God is one. God's manifestations are three. The love of God is first seen through the interactive "bearing witness" to one another of the threefold expressions of God. The NT celebrates this threefoldness in well-known benedictions (2 Cor 13:14) and commissions (Matt 28:19-20).

Distinctiveness of the Biblical Concept of God. The view of God found in the biblical materials has several distinctive insights. The creator/redeemer God of the Bible differs from ideas of God in Eastern religions in that both creation and redemption are functions of the one and same God. The threefold God of Christianity differs from the MONOTHEISM of Judaism and Islam in the variety and complexity of the manifestations of God.

The biblical God is historical, particular, and absolute in a way which challenges the relativism in contemporary religions. Yet, the God of the Bible is styled "the unknown God" who has not left himself without witness in the world and in the pluralistic religious context (Rom 1; Acts 17).

Contemporary Ideas about God. How does the Christian community make the ancient biblical concepts about God meaningful and understandable in the contemporary context? Representing and re-presenting God is a perennial task of the Christian community. A linguistic translation of the Bible from Hebrew, Aramaic, Latin, and Greek into

English, or other modern languages, does not guarantee an adequate comprehension of God. Every age, culture, and context seeks to find in scripture the "God beyond God" who relates to their understandings of God.

A *philosophical* translation of God begins with a philosophical system, acknowledged or unacknowledged, and seeks to interpret the categories of biblical faith in ways that are compatible with that philosophy. The most ancient attempts to perceive God in terms of a philosophical system was the apologetic rationalism of some church fathers (Tertullian) based on the naturalism of early Greek and Roman philosophy. Subsequently Augustine translated the Christian faith in a manner consistent with Neoplatonic philosophy. In the Middle Ages Aquinas "Christianized Aristotle and Aristoteleanized Christianity." Catholic scholasticism was succeeded by classical Protestant rationalism (Melanchthon, Turretin), which is represented today by some adherents of neoevangelical rationalism (Montgomery). Another philosophical perspective of God, sharing wide popularity in the late twentieth century, is process theology (Hartshorne, Cobb, Griffin) based on process philosophy (Whitehead). A third philosophical current used as a way of understanding God is the Christian existentialism of the nineteenth century (Kierkegaard) utilized by twentieth-century theologians (Brunner, Tillich, Niebuhr).

Psychological translations of God take seriously the notion that the knowledge of God and the knowledge of self are inevitably interwoven (the pastoral care movement). Questions arise from this translation as to whether God speaks through the self or is to be identified as the self, the collective consciousness, the meaning of life, etc.

Contemporary *political* modes of interpreting God include the liberation theology movement (Bonino, Boff, Gutierrez) which combines Marxist theory with Christian social activism; feminist theology (Christ, Fiorenza, Ruether) which seeks to see the feminine aspects of God or to move the theological discussion beyond gender; and black theology (Cone, Washington, Roberts, Mbiti) which seeks redress from racism. All of the political interpretations of God describe God as one who is identified with the oppressed.

Some mainstream theologians describe God as "the mystery of creation" (Jüngel), the "crucified God" (Moltmann), and the universal God of the future (Pannenberg). These interpretations of God and a host of lesser known ones give evidence of the fact that the God question and God language (Gilkey) are matters of ultimate concern (Tillich) for the human community.

See also ABBA; BAAL; EL; EL SHADDAI; GOD, NAMES OF; HOLINESS IN THE NEW TESTAMENT; HOLINESS IN THE OLD TESTAMENT; HOLY SPIRIT; INCARNATION; JESUS; JUSTICE/JUDGMENT; KINGSHIP; KNOWLEDGE IN THE NEW TESTAMENT; KNOWLEDGE IN THE OLD TESTAMENT; LORD IN THE NEW TESTAMENT; LORD IN THE OLD TESTAMENT; LORD OF HOSTS; LOVE IN THE NEW TESTAMENT; LOVE IN THE OLD TESTAMENT; MIRACLES; MONOTHEISM; REVELATION, CONCEPT OF; SHEPHERD; SON OF GOD; SON OF MAN; TRINITY; WORD; WORD OF GOD; WRATH OF GOD.

—WILLIAM L. HENDRICKS

• **God Language, Inclusive.** Human beings think through analogy. Although the world is filled with myriads of disparate elements, we learn from early childhood to make sense of the world by constructing networks of relationships among those elements. Midst multitudes of dissimilar "things," we see threads of similarity and with these threads we order and systematize, we categorize and name our world. We name our world through language and what we name it is, for us, what it becomes (cf. Gen 2:19).

When we encounter something that is unfamiliar to us, we naturally try to relate it to what we already know. Reliant upon the language we have used to name our world, we talk of the unknown in terms of the known.

Talking of the unknown in terms of the known is essentially the problem of GOD language. Since we can never fully know what God is like—God will never fit neatly into one of our categories of the world—our language referring to and describing God is always grossly inadequate. By using metaphors and models to talk about God (e.g., God the potter, God the father), we compare God with what we know.

In the modern Judeo-Christian context, God language has fallen prey to both IDOLATRY and irrelevance. First, there has been a tendency to confuse God with the metaphorical language used of God. Certain prominent metaphors and models of God, God the father most particularly, have become idols. We have forgotten that such an image as God the father is an analogy; we have assumed it to be an absolute reality. Second, because of this idolizing of a particular metaphor, many people feel excluded from relationship with the divine. An elevated metaphor that defines God only in terms of one role, one gender, one way of relating, is, for many, an inadequate reflection of how they relate to the divine or of what they need in such a relationship. In short, religious language that idolizes only one way of perceiving the divine becomes irrelevant, meaningless to those who cannot experientially identify with that perception.

Language does not simply reflect our understanding; it shapes our understanding. When we use language to image God, we describe not only God, but ourselves as well. When we think and speak of God, we use categories that we know, human images with which we are experientially familiar. When we use these human images to talk about God, however, the images themselves take on a special quality by their association with the divine: If God is like a father, then fathers are somehow like God. If God is like a king, then kings are like God. If God is conceived as male, then maleness takes on a divine quality.

Many people perceive their relationship to God to be characterized by hierarchy. They use images from their experience, in this case, patriarchal stratification, to express this hierarchy. Through the choice of these particular images, however, hierarchy, then, is reimposed upon human society. The consequence is a circular self-understanding. Human structures are used to express images of human-divine relationships and then those images of human-divine relationships underscore the human structures. The theological impact of the exclusively patriarchal portrayal of God manifests itself in ideology and praxis. There is the permeating view that males are closer to being in the image of God than females (despite Gen 1:27). In turn, this view of male superiority justifies inequitable conduct.

For most people who identify themselves with the Judeo-Christian traditions, the Hebrew and Christian Bibles provide the authority for envisioning God as male. Biblical language about God is primarily gender exclusive. Masculine pronouns are used to refer to God and masculine verb forms are used to tell of divine activity. Most of the biblical images of God are masculine, e.g., God as warrior, king, father. Furthermore, biblical accounts of divine appearances depict God in masculine form (cf. Gen 18; 32).

Not all biblical images of God must be interpreted as masculine, however. It should be noted that we perceive many models of God, e.g., warrior, judge, to be masculine because of our cultural conditioning and not because the images themselves have innate gender-specific orientation. We might well look to the Canaanite myth of the warrior-goddess Anath and the story of the judge Deborah to remind ourselves of our culturally instilled expectations.

Although many divine images in the Bible are sexually ambiguous, some are clearly feminine, just as some are clearly masculine. Of all the biblical feminine images of God, the maternal God appears to be the most common (cf. e.g., Isa 42:14; 49:15; 66:13; Jer 31:20; Deut 32:18). God as mother, like God as father, meets a rather universal human need to view the divine in terms of parenthood. The image of mother and child, however, nuances the divine-human relationship in ways that the image of father and child cannot. In particular, the relation between divine mother and human child has qualities comparable to the physical intimacy and dependency inherent in pregnancy, childbirth, and nursing. "God the father" simply does not connote the same kind of closeness. This is not to say that the image of God the father is flawed; it, like any other image of the divine, is merely incomplete by itself. It does not say all that can be said of divine-human relationships. No image does.

Obviously recognizing the inadequacy of a singular divine image, biblical poets and prophets used a variety of images to depict different ways in which God relates to the world. While they primarily viewed God in masculine terms, their language concedes that the essence of God cannot be captured in masculinity. Through the juxtaposition of differing images, the biblical writers have created multi-dimensional pictures of God that stretch the reader's imagination and sense of wonder. In Isa 42:13-14 the prophet uses sexually diverse images to speak of a new act of liberation:

> The Lord goes forth like a mighty man,
> like a man of war he stirs up his fury;
> he cries out, he shouts aloud,
> he shows himself mighty against his foes.
> "I have been silent for a long time.
> I have kept still, I have restrained myself.
> Like a woman giving birth, I cry out;
> I breathe out and I breathe in together."

In Ps 123:2 the poet compares God to both the master and the mistress of a house:

> Behold, as the eyes of servants
> look to the hand of their master,
> as the eyes of a maid
> to the hand of her mistress,
> so our eyes look to Yahweh our God. . . .

In Luke 15 Jesus tells three parables to illustrate God's attitude toward sinners. With narrative images, he compares God's attitude and response first, to a shepherd who searches for and finds a lost sheep; second, to a woman who seeks her lost coin and who, upon finding it, rejoices; and finally, to a father who welcomes home a wayward child.

If a singular divine image did not satisfy biblical writers, neither should a singular image satisfy us. If biblical writers were not literalists, then we, too, are permitted to be more imaginative in our expressions of God. Our religious language should reflect both similarity and dissimilarity between God and ourselves. Furthermore, religious language should be recognized for what it is: It is an attempt to know God; it is not in itself God.

Inclusive God language is particularly problematic in biblical translation. The value of having translations that reflect as accurately as possible the nature of the original language is undeniable. It is time, however, to reassess the translations that we use in religious contexts. A reassessment does not entail denying the masculo-centric nature of the ancient languages; it does, nevertheless, entail affirming the need for linguistic flexibility in light of modern theological concerns. Just as ancient scribes and rabbis learned, in their synagogue reading, to substitute Adonai when they came across the personal name Yahweh, so, too, we must be willing in our religious contexts to make substitutions for the sake of relevancy.

See also FEMINIST HERMENEUTICS; GOD.

Bibliography. C. Geertz, "Religion as a Cultural System," *Interpretation of Cultures*; S. McFague, *Metaphorical Theology: Models of God in Religious Language*; V. R. Mollenkott, *The Divine Feminine: The Biblical Imagery of God as Female*; R. R. Ruether, *Sexism and God-Talk: Toward a Feminist Theology*; K. Doob Sakenfeld, "Old Testament Perspectives: Methodological Issues," *JSOT* 22 (1982): 13-20; P. Trible, *God and the Rhetoric of Sexuality*and "Postscript: Jottings on the Journey," *Feminist Interpretation of the Bible*, ed. L. M. Russell.

—DANNA NOLAN FEWELL

• **God, Kingdom of.** *See* KINGDOM OF GOD

• **God, Names of.** When God requires Moses to confront the PHARAOH of Egypt and demand that he free the enslaved Israelites, MOSES balks. Amid his many protests Moses requests the name of this deity who seeks so to use him. "God said to Moses, 'I AM WHO I AM.' And he said, 'Say this to the people of Israel, "I AM has sent me to you." ' God also said to Moses, 'Say this to the people of Israel, "The Lord [Heb. YAHWEH], the God of your fathers, the God of Abraham, the God of Isaac, and the God of Jacob, has sent me to you": this is my name forever, and thus I am to be remembered throughout all generations.' " (Exod 3:14-15) After additional support and encouragement Moses agrees to undertake this divine commission.

From the perspective of this particular tradition the name Yahweh is new, but the God who now reveals this as his name is linked to Israel's ancestors. In th OT the name Yahweh is used most often for God, occurring almost 7,000 times, and it has been the object of much speculation. In the passage above it is linked to the Hebrew verb "to be," although the usual pronunciation, "Yahweh," is not the form of the verb that appears in the "I Am" (*'ehyeh*) above. "Yahweh" seems most likely to be a causative form of "to be," with the sense of "to cause to be or happen; to create." Some have suggested that it once was a descriptive epithet attached to El (*'ēl*), a more generic term for the deity (see below). Within Jewish tradition high regard for the sanctity of this name of God led to an avoidance of it on mortal lips. The term "Adonai," "Lord, or my Lord," was substituted for it, thus the use of the form "Lord" in many English translations of the Bible. The term "Jehovah" arose in later Christian circles as a combination of the consonants YHWH with the vowels of "Adonai."

The deity's declaration to Moses in the encounter at the burning bush—"I am who I am"—is a declaration of divine freedom from any possible manipulation or control of the deity through knowledge and use of his name. Naming and names impart power; Exod 3:14-15 makes it clear that

God's gracious sharing of his name does not in any way alter the hierarchical relationship between creator and created. A divine declaration of independence is expressed in this name.

Another tradition refers to the deity as Yahweh from the outset (Gen 2:4b; 4:26). Such an anachronistic reading back of a later name onto an earlier period is not unusual, and a number of additional names for the deity do appear in Genesis and elsewhere. These are all variants of the term *'ēl* and are formed by the addition of a descriptive term or epithet to the word *'ēl* itself. The word *'ēl* can either mean simply "god," or it can serve as the name of the high god of the Canaanite pantheon (compare the English word which as "God" refers to the deity to whom Jews, Christians, and Muslims give allegiance, and as "god" refers to a class of beings). The forms built upon the term *'ēl* are often found in stories that link Israel's patriarchs and matriarchs to significant places in that part of Palestine Israel was later to occupy: El Elyon (God Most High/of the Height) is linked with Jerusalem in Gen 14 and Ps 47; El Roi (God of Seeing) appears to Hagar at a spring in the wilderness in Gen 16; El Olam (God of Eternity) is linked with Beersheba in Gen 21; and El Berith (God of the Covenant) is mentioned in Judg 9. El Shaddai (God of the Mountains/Almighty) is used by priestly traditions in a number of cases (Exod 6:3) as well as in other, generally later, traditions.

It is clear that the Bible expects us to understand that the deity presented under these several *'ēl* designations is the same deity known as Yahweh. Exod 3:14-15 says this explicitly. The same point seems to be made in ABRAHAM's words to the king of Salem in Gen 14:22. "I have sworn to Yahweh God Most High (*'ēl 'elyon*), maker of heaven and earth. . . . " Historically it is possible that the several local manifestations of *'ēl,* the high god of the Canaanite pantheon, who was known (as in Gen 14) as creator of the cosmos, which is comprised of heaven and earth, came in time to be identified with the deity originally linked with Mount Sinai and known as Yahweh. Indeed if, as suggested above, the name Yahweh originated as a descriptive epithet joined to *'ēl,* this identification of deities was natural. A combination of this sort would be encouraged by the Davidic monarchy, which under its founder brought many former Canaanites with their territory into the sphere of Israel. The encounter between Abraham and MELCHIZEDEK, king of Salem (Jerusalem), in which blessing is exchanged, serves as a model for the creative merger of peoples, lands, and gods.

Related to the term *'ēl,* but unique in its use, is the word *'ĕlōhîm.* This term is technically a plural form, and is sometimes used in the OT for several gods, as in the first of the ten commandments in Exod 20:3. This plural form appears over 2,500 times in the OT as a designation of Yahweh, the God of Israel. While there may be polytheistic roots beneath the use of this plural form, it seems to have been understood as an expression of majesty, wholeness, and completeness when applied to the unitary God of Israel and early Judaism.

In the Book of Job and rarely elsewhere another generic term, *'ĕlōah,* is used of the deity. It is striking that this term seems largely confined to material that is least specific in its references to or rootage in particularly Israelite traditions like those dealing with the patriarchs and matriarchs, the exodus and Sinai, the conquest, and the monarchy.

The NT broadly follows these patterns from the Hebrew Bible. The Gk. word *theos* is used more than 2,000 times for the deity, and in the Septuagint, the Greek translation of the Hebrew Bible, this term is used to render *'ĕlōhîm.* A second Greek term, *kyrios,* "Lord," is used in the Septuagint where Yahweh appears in the Hebrew, and this term is used about 100 times in the NT, usually in citations of the earlier Hebraic traditions. Early Christian understandings of JESUS are reflected in the more common application of *kyrios* to him, and in the rare use of *theos* in reference to him as well.

See also NAMES.

—W. LEE HUMPHREYS

• **Godlessness.** A state of characteristic opposition to God; an attitude not just unbelieving, but openly impious and wicked. Several terms are employed in the Bible to convey this broad pejorative complex.

The KJV regularly translated Hebrew *ḥānēp* as "hypocrite(s)" or "hypocritical" (RSV "godless": Job 13:16; 15:34; Prov 11:9; Isa 10:6; etc.). However, more than hypocrisy is meant. The "godless" are those who by act or attitude intentionally set aside the Bible's theological presumption that human beings have a sacred relationship with God.

In the AMARNA texts *ḥanpu* described treasonous "villainy." In Job 36:13 and the Ugaritic texts *ḥanpê-lēb* "godless in heart" is used to indicate a ruthless disposition of deception and dissimulation. The godless are without knowledge (Prov 11:9), speak folly and theological error (Isa 9:17 [MT 16]; 32:6), and have no hope (Job 27:8).

Other terms translated "godless" in the RSV include: *zēdîm* "the proud ones" (Ps 119:51, 69, 78, 85, 122); *bĕliyya'al* "worthlessness" (2 Sam 23:6); and *'ônîm* "powerful ones" (Prov 11:7). The idea of "godlessness" in the OT is also conveyed in the basic concepts behind *rāšā'* "wicked," *'ĕwîl* "ungodly," and *mirmâ* "deceit."

Strictly speaking, in the NT the RSV translates only the Greek word *bebēlos* "profane" as "godless" (1 Tim 4:7; 6:20; 2 Tim 2:16). But *bebēlos* refers in these passages to gnostic teaching. The LXX, however, musters a broad range of Greek words to capture the connotation of Hebrew *ḥānēp.* These words regularly occur in the NT and certainly play a part in the larger biblical complex identifying the "godless." Thus, the godless are *anomos* "outside the law" (1 Cor 9:21); *asebēs* "ungodly" (Rom 5:6); *dolos* "full of deceit" (Rom 1:29); and *hupokritēs* "hypocrites" (Matt 24:51).

See also GNOSTICISM; HYPOCRISY; IDOLATRY.

—STEPHEN J. ANDREWS

• **Gog.** [gog] *1.* In 1 Chr 5:4, a descendant of Jacob's eldest son, Reuben.

2. In Ezek 38 and 39, the name was used nine times to identify the chief prince of Meshech and Tubal. The word Rosh, which is frequently translated as a national name, is a transliteration of the Hebrew word for head or chief. Thus, Gog was the chief prince. He was from the land of Magog, an area associated with Noah's son, Japheth (Gen 10:2).

Gog was portrayed by EZEKIEL as the leader of a confederacy uniting Israel's enemies of the north (Europe), the east (Persia), and the south (Cush and Put of Africa). At some future time when Israel would be reunited in its land and experiencing peace and prosperity, these forces would strike against the defenseless nation. Such a blow was destined to fail, however, for the Lord would intervene to preserve the people and to destroy these enemies. In chaps. 25–32 Ezekiel had dealt with the destiny of Israel's contiguous neighbors. In these chaps. (38–39) he dealt with the fate of distant enemies that had no knowledge or fear of the Lord.

Gog was associated with the land of Magog. This was the land of his origin. The area specified was probably ancient Armenia, located in the vicinity of the Black Sea. The area was also the home of the feared Scythians, known for their ferocity in battle.

3. In Rev 20:8 Gog and Magog were named as two representatives of the world's rebellious nations. They would be deceived by Satan following his release from prison. As in Ezekiel, they are destined for divine destruction.

4. In British legend Gog and Magog were two giants captured and employed as porters at the gate of the royal palace at London's Guild Hall. Their effigies have been replaced twice since they were erected in the reign of Henry V.

See also EZEKIEL.

Bibliography. M. C. Astour, "Ezekiel's Prophecy of Gog and the Cutlean Legend of Naram-Sin," *JBL* 95/4 (1976): 567-79; J. B. Taylor, *Ezekiel: An Introduction and Commentary*.

—JERRY WALLACE LEE

• **Gold.** *See* JEWELRY; SILVER AND GOLD

• **Golden Calf.** *See* CALF, GOLDEN

• **Golden Rule.** A popular title given to Jesus' command to do to others as you wish them to do to you (Matt 7:12; Luke 6:31).

The verse occurs in negative form in widely diverse religious traditions, e.g., Tob 4:15; *EpArist* 207; and Stoic and Confucian literature. Perhaps the most famous parallel is found in the Talmud. Rabbi Hillel was asked by a potential convert to teach him the whole Law during the time in which he could stand on one leg. Hillel responded, "What is hateful to you, do not do to your neighbor. This is the whole Torah. All else is interpretation." (*Sabb* 31a) Such a principle commands one to avoid inflicting harm upon the neighbor. In this negative form, it need not suggest more than prudential, self-regarding motivation for relationships, for common sense can calculate that such intent and practice destroy social harmony. The meaning here, however, is doubtless much more inclusive since Hillel declares it to be the consummate statement of the entire Law.

Jesus states the principle in positive form. One is not only to avoid inflicting pain but is also actively to do the good toward the neighbor. This avoids prudential considerations and modifies the motives which often underlie relationships. When calculation collapses, authentic relation can be realized.

The command appears in Matthew's SERMON ON THE MOUNT and Luke's sermon on the plain. Within these discourses, however, it occurs in different contexts. In Matthew the rule is a summary statement following Jesus' discussion of appropriate expressions of discipleship. In Luke, the verse is set in the midst of Jesus' command that the disciples love their enemies. Matthew, perhaps because of his Jewish-Christian readers, adds "for this is the law and the prophets," suggesting a connection with 5:17. This addition may be relevant as a defense of the disciples whom the scribes accused of defying the Law and the Prophets. Its inclusion also characterizes Jesus' view that unlimited, merciful regard for the neighbor is the ideal intent of the Law and the Prophets. It thus represents a more demanding righteousness than that of the scribes and Pharisees.

The uniqueness of Jesus' principle lies as much in its context as in its content. The statement should not stand in isolation from the larger context of Gospel. Both Matthew and Luke make it clear that both the reason and the resource for such love lies in the nature of God's love. It is God's grace which precedes obedience and makes it possible. In Matthew, this is suggested by the image of the loving parent (the God who stands ready to give abundant good gifts to those who will only ask, 7:11). Likewise, Luke suggests that disciples are to live in the likeness of the God whose kindness is extended even to the ungrateful and selfish (6:35). It is because one's honest goodwill may not, in fact, result in the neighbor's good that one is to be compelled by God-like love. Then God's children will please each neighbor for the other's good and edification (Rom 15:2).

See also SERMON ON THE MOUNT.

—BETTY JEAN SEYMOUR

• **Golgotha.** *See* CALVARY

• **Goliath.** [guh-lɪ'uhth] The PHILISTINE warrior slain by the young DAVID (1 Samuel 17). Described as being "six cubits and a span" (nearly ten feet tall) and coming from Gath (1 Sam 17:4), he probably was one of the Anakim, a tribe of giants whose descendants resided in Gath (Deut 2:10-11; Josh 11:22; cf. 2 Sam 21:22; 1 Chr 20:8). The story in 1 Sam 17 not only related the Israelite victory over the Philistines, but also established the basis for David's later rise to KINGSHIP and demonstrated the power of Yahweh through the humblest of servants.

There is a discrepancy in the biblical narrative at 2 Sam 21:19 where at a later time one of David's warriors, Elhanan, is said to have slain Goliath the Gittite. Although it is possible that this is the earlier tradition and was later applied to David, the story of David's defeat is entirely plausible in the light of his subsequent rise to power and is well established elsewhere in the biblical text (cf. 1 Sam 21:9 and 22:10). In 1 Chr 20:5 Elhanan is said to have slain Lahmi, the brother of Goliath, which may be an attempt to reconcile the discrepancy. On the other hand, Goliath may have become a by-name to describe an otherwise unknown or unspecified giant.

See also DAVID; GATH; PHILISTINES.

—JOHN B. POLHILL

• **Gomorrah.** *See* SODOM/GOMORRAH/CITIES OF THE PLAIN

• **Good News.** *See* GOSPEL

• **Goshen.** [goh'shuhn] *1.* The name of a fertile district in Egypt in which Jacob and his family established their residence at the time of their arrival from Canaan (Gen 46:28) until the time of the Exodus (Exod 8:22). When Jacob arrived in Egypt, Joseph went up from his residence to meet his father in Goshen (Gen 46:29). Goshen was located in the eastern part of the Nile Delta in the area of present day Wadi Tumilat. The land was also known as "the land of Rameses" (Gen 47:11) and "the fields of Zoan" (Ps 78:12, 43). The land of Goshen was assigned by the Pharaoh of Egypt to Joseph's family because it was near Joseph's residence in the capital city, which in the time of the Hyksos, was located in the Delta region (Gen 45:10). The district was good for pasture; from the perspective of Jacob's family, a family of shepherds (Gen 46:34), Goshen was the "best of the land." Pharaoh's herds also grazed there (Gen 47:6).

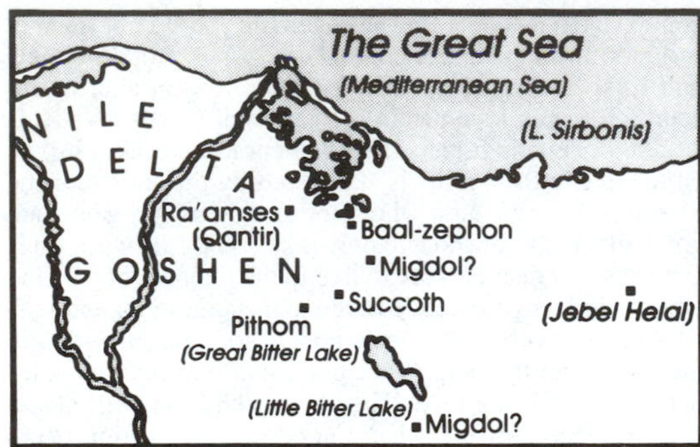

Designed by Margaret Jordan Brown ©Mercer University Press

Egyptian records indicate that it was common for people from Palestine and Sinai to come to Egypt during times of famine to live in the Delta. This fact may demonstrate the possible semitic origin of the word Goshen. The LXX calls Goshen "Gesem of Arabia" (Gen 45:10; 46:34; 47:1). This name indicates that the LXX translators believed Goshen to be a city in the province of Arabia. Goshen is also called by the LXX, *Heroonpolis,* "City of Heroes" (Gen 46:28, 29).

2. A district in southern Palestine (Josh 10:41; 1:16). It was located between the coastal city of Gaza and the hill country of Judah. Its exact location is unknown.

3. A city in the mountains of Judah (Josh 15:51). Its exact location is unknown, however Aharoni has identified it with Tell el-Khuwēilifeh.

—CLAUDE F. MARIOTTINI

• **Gospel.** [gos'puhl] The English word "gospel" is derived from the Old English "godspell," an abbreviated form of "goodspell." The root meaning of "spell" was story. Hence, godspell and its later derivative referred to a good story, or good news. This is consistent with the Greek term used in the NT; the Gk. term (ευαγγέλιον) is composed of a prefix (ευ) meaning "good" and a stem (ἀγγέλιον) meaning "message" which is derived from a word (ἄγγελος) meaning "messenger." The term (εὐαγγέλιον) refers to the good news which is proper to a good messenger. "Gospel," "good news," and "glad tidings" have served appropriately since the Tyndale version as English translations of the Gk. noun. The verbal form which appears frequently in the NT is usually rendered, "to preach" or "to proclaim" the good news (gospel). Therefore, gospel indicates an announcement of a highly favorable experience or event. The verb, likewise, refers to the action of announcing such an event.

In the pre-Christian Greco-Roman world, the word translated "gospel" was used originally with reference to victory in battle. It was employed in two connections: (1) to designate the actual good news of victory and its consequent deliverance, and (2) to designate a reward that was given to the messenger who delivered the good news after the announcement had been verified. For the adherents of the imperial cult the term acquired religious connotations as it was employed in reference to the birth, power, and pronouncements of the emperor-god.

The noun appears infrequently in the Septuagint (LXX), and a distinction is made between the good news itself and the reward for good news by using the singular form for the good news and the plural form for the reward. On the other hand, the verb occurs often in the LXX as a translation of the Hebrew word that denoted the good news of the great victory of Yahweh.

Jesus probably employed the Hebrew verb or its Aramaic equivalent to convey his belief that the KINGDOM OF GOD brought salvation, deliverance, and joy. Later Christian writers employed the Greek noun in order to describe Jesus and what he did and taught to accomplish the transformation of humanity. The good news of the Kingdom proclaimed by Christ became equated with the good news of Christ himself and what he accomplished through his life, death, and resurrection. Paul's use of the term focused on the death and resurrection of Jesus, but Mark confirms that others used the word to describe the entirety of Jesus' life, not just his message or death and resurrection.

During the centuries subsequent to the NT two major developments occurred in the usage of "gospel." Early Christian interpreters employed the term frequently to describe the entirety of the Christian scripture as distinct from the Jewish scriptures. All scripture was viewed as either Prophets (OT) or Gospel (NT). Gospel also became a technical term for the specific books that recorded the story of Jesus' life, message, and redemptive death. Anxious to contend for the singularity of the good news, the documents became entitled "The Gospel according to Mark, Matthew, Luke, and John."

See also EVANGELIST; SCRIPTURE IN THE NEW TESTAMENT.

Bibliography. G. Friedrich, "Εὐαγγελίζομαι, κτλ.," *TDNT*; K. Nickle, *The Synoptic Gospels*; B. H. Streeter, *The Four Gospels*.

—ROBERT M. SHURDEN

• **Gospel Fragments, Papyri.** The discovery of extensive treasures of papyri in Egypt since the third quarter of the nineteenth century has had a significant impact upon NT studies as well as other disciplines. These materials, written in "common Greek," transformed scholarly understandings of biblical Greek and gave extensive insight into the daily life of Egyptians in the Roman period.

Among the documents of common life which were found—deeds, wills, legal contracts, personal letters, inventories, divorce papers, wedding contracts, business doucments—were books and fragments of the NT text as well as fragments of NT apocrypha. The papyri of NT Gospel texts reveal the earliest stratum of extant NT documents.

The latest count gives eighty-eight known NT papyri. Among those which support the Gospels, the majority give texts for MATTHEW and JOHN. Among these is the earliest witness to any part of the NT, papyrus 52 ($\mathfrak{p}^{52}$), which is dated to ca. 125 and contains John 18:31-33, 37-38.

Certain collections of papyri have become known by their owners, or the library which housed them: the John Rylands papyri of the John Rylands Library, Manchester; the Chester Beatty papyri, housed in Dublin; the Bodmer papyri of Cologny (near Geneva). The largest find is the Oxyrhynchus Papyri published in over seventy volumes since 1898 by P. B. Grenfell and A. S. Hunt, et al.

The "early" text of the NT is represented by forty-five papyri and four uncials which were produced between the second and the third/fourth centuries, a stage later supplanted by a "standardized" text. All these papyri are from Egypt, where climatic conditions were ideal for their survival. Their discovery has tended to destroy the theories which dated books of the NT into the middle of the second century. The 𝔭[52] must have been copied shortly after the Gospel of John was written (C.E. 90s). The 𝔭[66] may represent the oldest book (ca. 200) in best condition—some fifty-two pages preserved in entirety (John 1–14) with the rest fragmentary.

Among the papyri were also fragments of APOCRYPHAL GOSPELS. These fragments were of the synoptic type, or Johannine, or showed knowledge of all four gospels. Oxyrhynchus papyrus 840 (*POxy*) is a synoptic type while Papyrus Egerton 2 is a Johannine type, but neither has been identified with a known gospel. Others are *POxy* 1224 containing two sayings of Jesus; *Papyrus Cairensis* 10,735 which speaks of the birth of Jesus and his flight to Egypt; and the Fayyum fragment, which is a piece of the PASSION narrative. These, too, have not been linked with any known gospel due to their fragmentary nature.

POxy 1,654 and 655 have been demonstrated to be fragments of a Greek version of the Coptic GOSPEL OF THOMAS. This work has Greek embedded in the text, indicating that a Greek text stood behind the Coptic. However, these three Oxyrhynchus papyri are not the original from which *Thomas* was translated, but have elicited much scholarly interest in relation to *Thomas* as well as to the GOSPEL OF THE HEBREWS (*POxy* 654), and to the GOSPEL OF THE EGYPTIANS (*POxy* 655 = Clement, *Strom* 3.13, in part).

See also AGRAPHA; TEXTS/MANUSCRIPTS/VERSIONS; THOMAS, GOSPEL OF.

Bibliography. K. Aland and B. Aland. *The Text of the New Testament*; J. A. Fitzmyer, "The Oxyrhynchus *Logoi* of Jesus and the Coptic Gospel According to Thomas," *TS* 20 (1959): 505-60; J. Jeremias and W. Schneemelcher, "Isolated Sayings of the Lord" and "Papyrus Fragments of Apocryphal Gospels," *New Testament Apocrypha*, ed. E. Hennecke and W. Schneemelcher.

—GLENN A. KOCH

• **Gospel Genre.** *See* GENRE, GOSPEL

• **Gospels, Critical Study of.** Two very different objectives have governed the modern, critical study of the Gospels. One aim has been to reconstruct a picture of JESUS using modern, historical methodology. This quest of the historical Jesus has treated the Gospels as the soil containing the ore that, when refined, may yield the gold of reliable historical information about Jesus. This objective demands one cluster of approaches or methods for the study of the Gospels. The other aim has been to discover the theology of the evangelists. This quest of the theology of the Gospel authors has treated the Gospels as themselves the gold to be cherished and appreciated for its inherent value. In the former quest, the Gospels are regarded as a window through which one looks to see something else; in the latter, they are viewed as a mirror which reflects back to the viewer an image of the evangelist's world.

The quest of the historical Jesus was forced upon Christian scholars by the radical treatment of Jesus by H. S. Reimarus and D. F. Strauss. Both Reimarus's eccentricity and Strauss's denial of historicity forced scholars to reassess the Gospel sources. The logic of this history of research may be traced through six stages.

1. Other than the four canonical gospels, what are the sources available for the critical historian's quest for the historical Jesus? There are three possible Greco-Roman sources that are relevant: Pliny the Younger's letter to the Emperor Trajan about 110 C.E.; Tacitus's reference in his *Annals* 15.44 written about 115 C.E.; and Suetonius's *Life of Claudius* 25.4 from about 120 C.E. That there are so few references is not surprising given the fact that such literature comes from the aristocracy who would have had little interest in a despised Jew executed for treason in a remote part of the world. That these references exist, however, is understandable since each involves a disturbance of the public order, a matter of concern to any Roman. Of the three, only Tacitus is of certain value. His statement, "Christus from whom their name was derived was executed at the hands of the procurator Pontius Pilate in the reign of Tiberius," appears to be independent Roman evidence and therefore very valuable. Pliny's information is ultimately derived from the Christians and thus is not independent. Suetonius's sentence about Claudius's expulsion of the Jews from Rome about 49 C.E. is valuable if "Chrestus" really is a garbled reference to Christ ("Christus").

The Jewish evidence concerning Jesus from the early period is limited to JOSEPHUS and the earliest portions of the Talmud. In Josephus's *Antiquities*, there are only two passages with any claim to reliability. The one in 18.3.3, if genuine, must have been interpolated by later Christians for it contains statements that only a Christian could make: "He was the Christ," and "he appeared to them on the third day alive again, the divine prophets having foretold these and ten thousand other wonderful things concerning him." If these Christian assertions are removed, then what remains is a likely statement by Josephus that describes Jesus as a teacher and miracle worker who died on a Roman cross. The other in 20.9.1 is certainly authentic. It mentions Jesus only in passing as it tries to identify the James who was killed at the instigation of the Jewish high priest: "the brother of Jesus who was called Christ, whose name was James." Early evidence from the Talmud is limited. A tradition in *Sanh* 43a speaks of Jesus' crucifixion at Passover time. Another in the same section mentions his having had five disciples. Again, it is not surprising that before Christianity became a power to be reckoned with, the Jewish community would have had little need to refer to its founder. The surprise is the existence of the references that we do have. Taken together with Tacitus, these Jewish texts prove the historicity of Jesus and confirm some key facts about his life found in the Gospels.

The APOCRYPHAL GOSPELS, with the possible exception of the Coptic *Gospel of Thomas*, are of no direct use in the historical reconstruction of Jesus' career. The AGRAPHA likewise are, for the most part, of little use to the critical historian. Paul's letters, the earliest Christian sources, have little to contribute beyond confirming data. The same is true for the rest of the NT outside the canonical Gospels. If one is to know very much about Jesus, it must come from the four canonical Gospels.

2. Once they had recognized that the historian's knowledge about Jesus must come primarily from the four canonical Gospels, scholars found remarkable differences between the first three (Synoptics) and the fourth (John). These differences were of two kinds. First, it was recognized that John and the Synoptics overlapped in only about ten percent of their material. Crucial matter was found in the Synoptics and not in John: e.g., the baptism of Jesus, the temptation of Jesus, Peter's confession at Caesarea Philippi, the transfiguration, the parables, the exorcisms, the last supper viewed as the institution of the Lord's Supper, the agony in the garden, and the cry of dereliction from the cross. Matter crucial to John was missing from the Synoptics: e.g., an early Judean ministry of Jesus, prominent characters like Nicodemus, the Samaritan woman, and Lazarus; certain prominent miracles like the changing of water into wine, the healing of the lame man at the pool of Bethzatha, the imparting of sight to the man born blind, the raising of Lazarus; certain prominent events like the footwashing, the visit of the Greeks to see Jesus, Jesus before Annas at his trial, the beloved disciple, and the appearance to Thomas. This kind of material is complementary and can be explained by the hypothesis that the Synoptics and John each preserve different, but equally accurate, streams of Jesus tradition.

A second kind of difference between John and the Synoptics involves contrast: the Synoptics locate Jesus' public ministry in Galilee except at the end of his career, but John regards Judea as Jesus' homeland and speaks of alternating trips to Galilee; the cleansing of the Temple is first in John and at the end in Synoptics; in the Synoptics Jesus teaches in parables and short pithy sayings, in John his teaching involves long, theological discourses of an argumentative nature; in the Synoptics the theme of Jesus' message is the Kingdom of God, but in John it is eternal life; in the Synoptics Jesus seems to want to keep his messiahship a secret until the very end, in John it is a public claim from the first; the final cause of Jesus' death in the Synoptics is his cleansing of the Temple, in John it is the raising of Lazarus; in the Synoptics Jesus is crucified on the day of Passover, in John it is on the Day of Preparation for the Passover. Moreover, the story of Jesus in the Synoptics is told in terms of exaltation CHRISTOLOGY, whereas in John it is narrated in terms of epiphany Christology. Such differences are not subject to explanation by an hypothesis of different, complementary traditions. Here one is dealing with contrast, and even contradiction.

Prior to D. F. Strauss the differences between John and the Synoptics were explained in such a way that the Fourth Gospel was preferred as an historical source: e.g., Schleiermacher's lectures on Jesus in 1832 were based mainly on John. Strauss's *Life of Jesus* (1835) represented the first attempt to explain the differences between John and the Synoptics in a way that favored the Synoptics in every case. For Strauss, the historian's sources for a knowledge of Jesus were not four but three. His influence continues in the work of Rudolf Bultmann and Günther Bornkamm for whom neither the speeches nor the narratives of John are historically reliable because of their theological tendency. C. H. Dodd's *Historical Tradition in the Fourth Gospel* (1963) is a magisterial attempt to maximize the historical dimensions of John. For him both narratives and speeches have a degree of historical reliability because there are parallels with the synoptic tradition in both. The common consensus, however, remains that the Synoptics are better historical sources than John.

3. In trying to explain the similarities among the Synoptics, scholars of the Enlightenment period disagreed on more than they agreed upon; however, all agreed on the rejection of tradition. Augustine's utilization hypothesis, which saw the Gospels as written in the order Matthew-Mark-Luke, with each successive author using his predecessor(s) was discarded. With reason as their only resource, they applied a succession of hypotheses to the data: first an original-gospel hypothesis, then a fragment hypothesis, then a tradition hypothesis, and finally another utilization hypothesis. In the first half of the nineteenth century the Griesbach hypothesis was supreme: Matthew was written first, then Luke, and finally Mark as an abridgement of the two earlier Gospels. Not until the death of F. C. Baur was it possible for the two-source theory to gain a hearing in any serious way. H. J. Holtzmann in 1863 popularized the priority of Mark; Karl Weizsäcker in 1864 added a hypothetical sayings source also used by Matthew and Luke (first called Q in 1890 by Johannes Weiss). From this time the two-document hypothesis gained popularity. If Matthew and Luke had used Mark and Q as their primary sources, then it was from these two primary sources that any life of Jesus must be written. B. H. Streeter's *The Four Gospels* (1924) was unsuccessful in trying to add to Mark and Q two other written documents, M and L. Those symbols, however, have remained as designations for tradition peculiar to Matthew and Luke, respectively. It is in the form of two primary sources, Mark and Q, supplemented by oral tradition, M and L, that the two-source theory has survived to this point as the dominant explanation of the similarity of the synoptic Gospels.

W. R. Farmer's *The Synoptic Problem* (1963) attempted a revival of the Griesbach hypothesis. Although his adherents are vocal, they are few. The main value of his challenge to the two-document hypothesis is the reopening of the question. Its resolution remains in the future. So unclear are the criteria for deciding the matter that some have simply suspended judgment until further light can he had.

4. Form criticism was a child of disappointment. When it became clear that the earliest written sources, Mark and Q, were at least a generation removed from the events they claimed to narrate, it was deemed desirable to go behind them to the earliest oral traditions about Jesus. When it became apparent that both Mark (Wrede) and Q (Wellhausen) were theologically colored tradition, then it was a necessity. Form criticism took the insights from prior students of folklore and attempted to penetrate back into the period prior to our earliest written sources. Its pioneers in synoptic studies were Martin Dibelius, K. L. Schmidt, and Rudolf Bultmann, who did their work around the time of the First World War. Their work was popularized for the English speaking world by Vincent Taylor's *The Formation of the Gospel Tradition* (1933).

The form critics' conclusions become clear if seen as answers to three basic questions. First, why was the Jesus tradition preserved by the early church? Given the earliest Christians' belief in an imminent end of the world, they would have had no need to preserve historical material for posterity. They did, however, need some of the Jesus material in their daily activities: preaching (1 Cor 15:3-5); worship (1 Cor 11:23-25); catechesis (1 Cor 7:10-11); and apologetics (Mark 12:13-17). The material was useful so it was repeated; in its repetition it became ingrained in the church's corporate memory and was preserved. Second, how was the tradition preserved until its incorporation in the earliest written sources? The form critics contend that it was preserved as oral tradition in single, self-contained, detached units, each one of which was complete in itself. In the early period, there was no connected outline of Jesus' career. Before long, pre-Gospel collections began to form: e.g., a collection of five conflict stories would circulate by themselves in an order in which the hostility to Jesus rises with each successive conflict (Mark 2:1-3:6); a collection of three parables of the Kingdom, each of which contained the key word "seed" (Mark 4:1-34); a collection of five sayings of Jesus held together by key words and link phrases (Mark 9:42-50).

The earliest connected material organized around a chronological principle was the PASSION NARRATIVE.

Somewhere in this oral period, in an informal way resembling the formulation of the Jewish Targums, the originally Aramaic tradition was translated into Greek. That this informal process took place in a variety of settings accounts for some of the variety one finds in duplicate traditions in the Gospels. The Gospels represent the gradual coalescing of the traditions over a period of time. Third, what was the motivation for writing the Gospels? From the number of answers that were given, two are worthy of mention. The success of the Christian mission beyond the bounds of Palestine created needs greater than the ability of the eyewitnesses to meet. The deaths of the eyewitnesses served as a catalyst for the writing of the Gospels in order to preserve their tradition.

If a source critic operating with the hypothesis of the two-source theory attempted to write a life of Jesus from Mark and Q, the form critic recognized as his primary source materials the individual oral traditions that lay behind the Gospels. Still the question had to be resolved: how does one objectively determine whether or not an individual oral tradition comes from Jesus?

5. Three criteria of historicity have been widely used by scholars to determine which individual traditions go back to Jesus. One such criterion claims that when a tradition is found in multiple sources (e.g., Mark and Q; Mark and M; Mark and L; Mark, Q, and Paul) it may be regarded as going back to Jesus. For example, the saying on marriage and divorce is found in Mark 10:11 || Matt 19:9, in Q (Matt 5:32 || Luke 16:18), and in 1 Cor 7:10-11. Not having been created by any one of these three independent sources, the saying in some form must go back very early. The limitation of this criterion is that it can show a tradition is very early, but cannot prove it goes back to Jesus. Another criterion contends that a tradition can be regarded as genuine Jesus material if it shows unmistakable signs of Palestinian origin in language, thought, or topography. Conversely, if a saying shows signs of Hellenistic origins, it obviously cannot go back to Jesus. So, for example, when one notes that the saying on marriage and divorce in 1 Cor 7:10-11 and Mark 10:11-12 allows both the man to divorce the woman and the woman to divorce the man, one knows that this form of the saying comes from a Roman legal context. According to Jewish Law only the man could divorce the woman. The form of the saying that is Palestinian, then, is that which says only the man shall not divorce the woman. The limitation to this criterion also is that it cannot prove that a tradition goes behind the Palestinian church to the Palestinian Jesus. A third criterion, used in conjunction with the other two, is called the negative criterion or the criterion of dissimilarity. It states that if a tradition shows signs of discontinuity with the church that passed it on, then it was not created by the church but goes back to Jesus. For example, in Matt 19:9 and 5:32 the writer added an except clause to the saying about divorce: no divorce except for. . . . In 1 Cor 7:12-15 Paul added an exception to the previously quoted saying about divorce: no divorce except for. . . . The tendency of both Matthew and Paul in Jewish-Christian and gentile-Christian contexts was to make exceptions in the matter of divorce. If the early saying from a Palestinian context absolutely prohibits a man's divorcing his wife, then such a saying shows signs of discontinuity with the church that passed it on. It is, therefore, not likely to have been created by the church but most probably goes back to Jesus.

Once these three criteria have been used together to create a collection of genuine Jesus traditions, if there are other materials that show continuity with them even though they cannot be shown to pass the test of the negative criterion, they may be treated as genuine also. This positive criterion is supplementary to the negative criterion.

From the bricks of oral tradition behind the Gospels that have passed the test of such criteria, the form critic seeks to reconstruct a historian's picture of Jesus. At this point, the question is how the Jesus materials deemed historical are to be fitted together.

6. Lives of Jesus are either arranged chronologically and developmentally or put together topically. The late nineteenth century lives of Jesus operated not only with the two-source theory as a base, but also with two corollaries to the priority of Mark. Mark, they believed, was objective history and yielded developmental information about Jesus. With this view of the sources, they offered a developmental picture of Jesus in which the inner and outer development of Jesus' career were traced. Jesus' outer development was usually described as a movement from initial popularity to ultimate isolation; his inner development was depicted in terms of a messianic consciousness that moved from initial lack of certainty and clarity to ultimate certainty and clarity. The rejection of this type of historical reconstruction of Jesus' career is focused in the work of Rudolf Bultmann. Bultmann, building on the work of W. Wrede and K. L. Schmidt, declared the late nineteenth century quest historically impossible. Wrede had shown that Mark was theologically interpreted tradition, and Schmidt argued that Mark could not provide developmental information about Jesus. There was, then, no way to write a developmental life of Jesus because the sources do not furnish that type of information. Bultmann's *Jesus and the Word* (1926) organized the tradition about Jesus deemed to be authentic in terms of subject matter. Rather than deal with Jesus' life (outer development) and personality (inner development), Bultmann focused on Jesus' message which he arranged in three logical groupings: "The Coming of the Kingdom of God," "The Will of God," and "God the Remote and the Near."

When E. Käsemann called for a new quest of the historical Jesus in 1953, he did not call for a return to developmental lives. Rather he assumed the same view of the sources as had his teacher, Bultmann. The two major contributions of the post-Bultmannians, Bornkamm's *Jesus of Nazareth* (1956) and Conzelmann's "Jesus Christ" (1959), continued Bultmann's logical and topical arrangement of the Jesus material, eschewing all attempts to write developmental lives of Jesus.

The recent quest for the theology of the evangelists began with H. Conzelmann (1954). In his work on Luke he focused his attention on the theology of the author. Two methodological principles were followed. First, he sought to interpret the meaning of the framework, that is, what the arrangement or organization of the Gospel meant. Second, he attempted to interpret the changes which Luke made in his sources, especially Mark. His pioneer work in REDACTION criticism opened the door for other studies on all three synoptic Gospels.

Conzelmann's methodology met with several criticisms. It was objected that not only the changes Luke made in his sources, but also the material he included unchanged from his sources, offered a clue to his theology. Further, it was argued that an evangelist's tendency or theology may be discovered without reference to his sources and changes made in them. This is true for Mark and ought to be for Matthew and Luke also. Even if one assumed no source theory or did not know a Gospel's sources, it would still be profitable and necessary to compare their differences in a Gospel parallel to see how each developed the common tradition in a unique fashion. Modifications in traditional redaction criticism merged with LITERARY CRITICISM as practiced by nonbiblical scholars. the aim became to respect the narrative world of the author and to let it speak on its own terms.

Redaction criticism and literary criticism proved admirably suited to the delineation of the variety of theological motifs in a given Gospel. What eluded either method's grasp was the meaning of a Gospel as a whole. Since all meaning is controlled by context, the question became: what is the context for interpreting a Gospel as a whole? At this point GENRE criticism entered the picture. The meaning of a document as a whole can be discerned in large measure from its participation in and deviation from a larger cluster of similar documents. Especially when genre is understood as a literary category of a particular time, place, and culture is it helpful for interpretation. Then the interpreter has a clue to the social function of such writings.

The claim advanced by K. L. Schmidt and R. Bultmann that the Gospels were literally unique remained critical orthodoxy until the 1970s. Since then, there has been a growing consensus that the Christian Gospels are types of ancient biography. The critical catchword, "The Gospels are not biographies," has been replaced by another: "The Gospels are biographies, albeit ancient ones." This insight has offered the interpreter a preunderstanding with which to approach the Gospel texts as wholes. Genre criticism has become yet another technique to assist in the quest for the theology of the evangelists.

See also FORM/GATTUNG; GENRE, CONCEPT OF; GENRE, GOSPEL; GOSPEL; HERMENEUTICS; INTERPRETATION, HISTORY OF; JOHN, GOSPEL AND LETTERS OF; LITERARY CRITICISM; LUKE, GOSPEL OF; MARK, GOSPEL OF; MATTHEW, GOSPEL OF; REDACTION; RHETORICAL CRITICISM; SOURCE CRITICISM; SYNOPTIC PROBLEM.

Bibliography. G. Bornkamm, *Jesus of Nazareth*; R. Bultmann, *Jesus and the Word* and *The History of the Synoptic Tradition*; H. Conzelmann, *Jesus* and *The Theology of St. Luke*; M. Dibelius, *From Tradition to Gospel*; C. H. Dodd, *Historical Tradition in the Fourth Gospel*; P. C. Hodgson, ed., *The Life of Jesus Critically Examined, by David Friedrich Strauss*; R. N. Longenecker, "Literary Criteria in Life of Jesus Research: An Evaluation and Proposal," in *Current Issues in Biblical and Patristic Interpretation,* ed. G. F. Hawthorne; J. M. Robinson, *A New Quest of the Historical Jesus*; K. L. Schmidt, *Der Rahmen der Geschichte Jesu* and "Die Stellung der Evangelien in der allgemeinen Literaturgeschichte," in *Eucharisterion: Herman Gunkel zum 60. Geburtstag,* ed. H. Schmidt; A. Schweitzer, *The Quest of the Historical Jesus*; B. H. Streeter, *The Four Gospels*; C. H. Talbert, ed., *Reimarus: Fragments* and *What Is A Gospel?*; V. Taylor, *The Formation of the Gospel Tradition*; W. O. Walker, "The Quest for the Historical Jesus: A Discussion of Methodology," *ATR* (1969): 38-56; W. Wrede, *The Messianic Secret.*

—CHARLES H. TALBERT

• **Government.** Israel's government may be classified in four chronological stages: premonarchic, monarchic, postexilic, and Maccabean/Roman. The premonarchic government was tribal, in which the elders and the militia, the chief tribal institutions, made decisions on a variety of matters. Priests also had roles in the government, as shown by Eli and Samuel. National cohesion was quite loose, as depicted in Judg 5 where several tribes do not aid Galilee in its battle, and by Judg 12:1-6 where GILEAD fights EPHRAIM. The administrative organization of the nation was also tribal and familial (Josh 7): families composed clans; clans composed tribes.

Courtesy of the Eisenberg Museum of Biblical Archaeology, Southern Baptist Theological Seminary.

A Sumerian administrative tablet from the reign of Shushin (ca. 2025 B.C.E.)

The monarchy, commonly thought of as Israel's government, lasted for less than 500 years of Israel's 1,300 year history. The monarchy was Israel's form of government during its classical period and was an ideal long after the kings lost power. It is also the government about which we possess the best information in the biblical record. Both parts of the divided kingdom were ruled by monarchies but the two governments were not identical. The Judean monarchy was extremely stable and dynastic. No internal challenges to the Davidic dynasty were ever mounted in Judah. Considerable power was centralized in the hands of the king in the south as exemplified by Solomon's establishment of administrative districts separate from the tribes (1 Kgs 4), the imposition of forced labor on the northern TRIBES (1 Kgs 11:26-28; 12:4), and the permanent housing of the ARK in the TEMPLE (1 Kgs 8). The Judean monarchy emphasized royal institutions over tribal. The northern kingdom, in contrast, preserved tribal powers against encroachments by the kings. Stable dynasties were rare in the north; new kings did not simply inherit power but were ususally chosen by the male citizenry (1 Kgs 12:20; 16:16). The elders of the north also exerted direct influence over their king, as seen in 2 Kgs 20:7-8 where Ahab calls on the elders and "the people" for a declaration of war. These differences in political theory between the two kingdoms are probably the reasons behind the rebellions of Absalom and Jeroboam.

The conquests by ASSYRIA and BABYLON ended the Israelite monarchies and the political realities of the PERSIAN EMPIRE made the monarchy simply an ideal. Under Persian governance, the Jerusalem priests wielded administrative control, probably with the assistance of a council of nobles or "princes." The TORAH, or Pentateuch, was made the civil law of Judah under EZRA, and Judah remained a quiet agricultural theocracy throughout the Persian period.

Judah came under Greek rule when ALEXANDER defeated Persia and for 150 years no changes were made in its local governance. However, in response to the suppression of Judaism by the Greek-Syrian kings, Judea, under the MACCABEES, rebelled and won their independence in 162 B.C.E. Judea remained independent until 40 B.C.E. when HEROD was made king of Judea by Rome. Judea remained under Roman rule up to 70 C.E. when the Temple was destroyed and Judea was abolished as a province.

See also ELDER; KINGSHIP; PRIESTS; TRIBES; UNITED MONARCHY.

Bibliography. P. Ackroyd, *Exile and Restoration*; N. Gottwald, *The Tribes of Yahweh*; B. Halpern, *The Constitution of the Monarchy in Israel*.

—RAY SUTHERLAND

• **Governor.** *See* PROCURATOR

• **Grace.** Grace is the sheer, self-giving love of God toward suffering and sinful humanity. It has no cause outside the love of God himself; it is not dependent on any merit or worth in the recipient. The Hebrew root of the word translated "grace" (חנן) means to "bend down to," suggesting a loving parent bending over a suffering child, or a good Samaritan bending over a wounded man on the Jericho road.

Because it stresses both the divine initiative and human helplessness, grace is a dominant term in the entire sweep of the biblical history of God's activity. It characterizes God's deliverance of his people from Egypt, his provision for them in the wilderness, the establishment of his COVENANT with them, the continuing FORGIVENESS of their sins, and the renewal of the covenant with them. Although it was first and foremost a term for the nature of God's loving care for his creatures, it became a major term for the biblical understanding of human salvation. The biblical use of the idea of grace can be summarized under these two headings: the nature of God and the way of salvation.

The Nature of God. The English word "grace" is related to two OT words, one with the literal meaning "to bend down to" (חָנַן) and another which may be translated "loving kindness" or "steadfast love" (חֶסֶד). The first of these stresses that all loving concern originates with God and that it is in no way dependent on the action, attitude, or intrinsic worth of the recipient. Even the word "love" in most languages can have a self-gratifying dimension to it. Grace defines God's love in utterly self-giving terms. It is as certain as the being of God, and it is not affected by anything outside of the divine nature.

The long experience of the biblical people with the faithfulness of God in the covenant relationship gave rise to the second term. God's grace was not called forth by the obedience of his people, and their faithlessness did not threaten the destruction of the grace of God. However, they learned that grace often took the form of severe discipline, because God's care for them involved punishment, forgiveness, and restoration to relationship. Paul learned the background of this great biblical term from this steadfast grace of God through all kinds of adversity in the experience of Israel. It made it possible to accept the divine "no" to his prayer for removal of his "thorn in the flesh" because he knew from the biblical testimony and his own experience that, indeed, God's "grace was sufficient" for him (2 Cor 12:9).

The Way of Salvation. "Grace" became one of the biggest words in the vocabulary of salvation because of these same two elements: stress upon the divine initiative and affirmation of the divine faithfulness to the relationship.

Like the biblical concept of "election" the doctrine of saving grave has always been plagued by the logical effort to separate the divine choice from the human response. Calvin's doctrine of "irresistible grace" has dominated some reformed theologies to the point that the human being is a passive recipient of the election to eternal life or the reprobation to eternal damnation, without any opportunity whatever for choice or response. Paul understood the inseparable character of gift and acceptance in the wonderful grace of God: "For by grace you have been saved through faith" (Eph 2:8). Exactly because grace is God's gift, unmerited and unearned by the believer, it must be accepted freely by the recipient. If it were in any way coercive or forced, it would deny the very nature of grace. This paradoxical tension in the saving grace of God has called forth the most lyrical and ecstatic expressions of praise on the part of believers from biblical days to the present time. It gives us some of the greatest passages in the Epistles of Paul; it gives us the classic testimony of John Bunyan, *Grace Abounding to the Chief of Sinners,* and the beloved hymn of the converted slave-runner John Newton, *Amazing Grace.* Exactly because it is the purest expression of God's redemptive love in the life of the believer, it is beyond logical analysis.

Christian theologians have catalogued the ways of grace in the salvation of humankind, even though they have not been able to define it adequately. They have stressed "prevenient grace," the loving care of God expressed to human beings through nature, through believing parents or teachers, and through all the means of society and environment by which one may be led to respond to God. This emphasizes the biblical concept of the divine initiative and the sheer unmerited favor of God, since no one can pick his parents or his place to be born and can only be thankful for those gifts which prepared the way for a willing response to divine grace.

Other theologians have stressed "effectual grace," thus balancing the divine initiative with the human response by which grace becomes effective in the life of the believer. Yet,even here, biblical writers and centuries of Christian testimony have affirmed the work of God in the faith response of the believer, so that believers cannot "take credit" for their faith, nor say that God saved them because they believed. The paradox might be stated in this way: human beings cannot take credit for believing in God, yet they are entirely responsible if they reject the grace of God. By the grace of God one is enabled to believe; by one's own choice the grace of God is rejected.

The steadfast love dimension of God's grace is illustrated in the theologian's use of the term "habitual grace." Because God was faithful and steadfast in the covenant relationship, a habitual pattern of trust and growing faithfulness could be engendered in the people. A final description of the "state of grace" in many biblical theologies is drawn from the experience of the covenant people in the Bible. They live in the confident assurance that they have been loved and claimed by God for his very own, and they do not have to be preoccupied with a frantic search for certainty and spiritual security. Rather, they are freed for joyful service in the fellowship of God to a world in desperate need of someone to "bend down to" and to help the suffering, dying, and spiritually destitute.

See also COVENANT; FORGIVENESS/PARDON; GIFTS OF THE SPIRIT; LOVE IN THE NEW TESTAMENT; LOVE IN THE OLD TESTAMENT; MERCY; PROMISE.

Bibliography. J. Daane, *A Theology of Grace*; H. D. Gray, *The Christian Doctrine of Grace*; O. Hardman, *The Christian Doctrine of Grace*; C. R. Smith, *The Bible Doctrine of Grace*.

—WAYNE E. WARD

• **Grain.** The principal grains of the Bible are wheat and barley. It is also apparent that there were inferior forms of wheat such as spelt. In addition, contrary to some versions, corn as is known today (maize) was a grain not known in the Bible. The relatively few dominant Hebrew words for grain in the Hebrew Bible refer specifically to the wheat or barley strains. However, there were many other terms used to describe the grains and the point in processing in which they were found. They were referred to as ears of grain, standing grain, crushed grain, and flour.

Courtesy of the Eisenberg Museum of Biblical Archaeology, Southern Baptist Theological Seminary.

Iron Age bowl, with about one cup capacity.

Concerning wheat, the Heb. *bar* and *ḥita* were the common terms, while the Gk. *sitos* is the NT word for wheat. These terms could be specific designations for the plant "wheat" or generic designations for grain. Note Amos 5:11 where the KJV translates *bar* as wheat, while the NIV translates the Heb. term as "grain." The term *dagan* is another Heb. word for grain. This term was significant for other cultures surrounding ancient Israel since the Canaanite god Dagon was their god of the harvest. The Heb. word for barley is *se'orah,* often connected with the Heb. *se'ar,* the word for hair; the fine strands of barley are similar to hair. Barley ripened before wheat and according to 2 Kgs 7:1 was the lesser of the two in value. Spelt, the Heb. *kussemet,* in Isa 28:25 is used in connection with wheat in the OT, and, as indicated, is apparently a form of wheat. Millet is mentioned once in Ezek 4:9 in the context of a prophetic message.

Wheat and barley were important commodities for ancient Israel; both were used for trade but also for personal consumption. Wheat, the more valuable, was used for human consumption. Its flour was used for making bread loaves. Barley on the other hand was the poor person's meal and was made into small flat cakes. It also was fodder for animals; either the green grain or the ripened kernels could be used. Note 1 Kgs 4:28 where barley was to be provided to feed the horses of King Solomon. The OT speaks of the need for the land owners to leave grain for the poor. Lev 23:22 indicates that the edges of the fields should be left and the harvesters should not gather the gleaning of their harvest. The episode of Ruth gathering the gleaning is an excellent example of this law being effected (Ruth 2:3).

The season for the growing of grains began in October with the harvest being in April-May. This harvest was associated with the feast of first-fruits, the Feast of Weeks. This feast was called to give praise to God who had provided for their harvest. Contrary to the surrounding cultures, the harvest was not produced by sympathetic magic or coercive force upon the god of the grain, but rather by the benevolence and covenant loyalty of their God, Yahweh. The Feast of Weeks is detailed in Lev 23:15–22. As a part of this festive time there were animal and grain offerings, and all work was curtailed in honor of God.

See also FOOD; WEEKS, FESTIVAL OF.

—MARK W. GREGORY

• **Graving/Engraving/Incising.** Terminology used in the OT for engraving, involving a wide range of skills and materials. It can refer to letters incised on a COPPER scroll or into the rock of a cliff (Job 19:24). The Decalogue is said to have been engraved on stone tablets (Exod 32:16; cf. Deut 9:10; 2 Cor 3:7). The jewels on the high priest's breastplate were engraved with the names of the twelve tribes (Exod 28:9-11; 39:6, 14) and his golden headpiece was incised with the words "Holy to the Lord" (Exod 28:36; 39:30). Before casting the golden calf, AARON first prepared it with a graving tool (Exod 32:4). The wooden molding in Solomon's Temple is described as "engraved" with figures of cherubim, palms, and open flowers (1 Kgs 6:18, 29; 7:31). What all these skills of inscribing and carving have in common is the use of a chisel or graving tool. Job 19:24 and Jeremiah 17:1 describe this as being of IRON, but usually the tool was made of copper-bronze. The skilled engraver could work with almost any medium, as the description of a temple artisan in 2 Chr 2:14 indicates.

The most common references to engraving involved the "graven images" prohibited by the Decalogue (Exod 20:4; Lev 26:1; Deut 4:16, 25). These carved idols were regularly distinguished from those that were cast or "molten" (Deut 27:15; Isa 42:17; Nah 1:14). They could be crafted in gold (Jer 10:14), in SILVER (Judg 17:4), in stone (2 Chr 34:7), or in wood (Deut 7:5; Isa 40:20). Since they were objects of worship chiseled from lifeless material by human craftsmanship, they were the brunt of frequent ridicule by the prophets (Isa 44:9-10; Jer 10:14; 51:17).

See also IDOLATRY

—JOHN POLHILL

• **Great Tribulation.** *See* TRIBULATION, GREAT

• **Greece.** *See* ACHAIA; JAVAN

• **Greek Language.** Ancient Greeks referred to themselves as Hellenes. The term "Greek" derives from the Latin *Graecum* ("Greek language"), a cognate of the Latin name *Graeci,* which was in turn derived from *Graioi,* the first Hellenes known to the Romans. As early as 2000 B.C.E., ancestors of the Hellenes began a series of invasions into the Aegean world and within a few centuries dominated what is now known as Hellas (Greece) and part of Asia Minor. Their Hellenic or Greek language took such hold in the Mediterranean world that its literary expression in Modern Greek is in continuity with all known Hellenic works that lie between Homer and Modern Greek. In this article "koine" ("common") refers in general to speech patterns that cross dialectical boundaries, and "Koine" to the specific post-Alexander Common Greek (the Koine dialect).

Greek belongs to a family of languages known as Indo-European. The principal members of this family are Hittite, Tocharian, Indic, Iranian, Armenian, Albanian, Slavic, Baltic, Germanic, Italic, and Celtic. Since the time of Strabo (ca. 64 B.C.E. to 19 C.E.; *Geog* 8.333), it has been fashion-

Courtesy of the Eisenberg Museum of Biblical Archaeology, Southern Baptist Theological Seminary.

Examples of Greek ostraca.

able to differentiate Hellenic peoples and dialects into Aeolic, Doric, and Ionic, but this classification lacks scientific precision. Preferable is the division of the dialects into East Greek and West Greek. This approach takes account of geographical location prior to the great migrations and permits more accurate accounting of the mixture of dialectical features that subsequently took place as a result of trading practices, colonization, or other circumstances.

East Greek consists of the Attic-Ionic, Arcado-Cyprian, and Aeolic groups. These groups comprise the "Old Hellenic" dialects that were dominant in the period represented by the Homeric poems. Ionic was spoken across vast areas of the Hellenic world. Included in the geographical distribution were Ionia itself, the central portion of the west coast of Asia Minor, which was colonized by Hellenes; the adjacent islands, together with their colonies; some of the Cyclades islands, including Naxos, Amorgos, and Paros; and Euboia, including Chalcis with its colonies in Sicily. Its earliest known literary expression is in the poetry of Homer. The Arcado-Cyprian group displays certain features found in the tablets discovered at Pylos, Mycenae, and Knossos, dating from about 1400–1200 B.C.E. and written in Cretan script (Linear B). The Aeolic is represented by Lesbian, Thessalian, and Boeotian. West Greek embraces the Northwest Greek group and the Doric group. Northwest Greek includes Phocian (especially Delphi); Locrian; Elean (Olympia); and the Northwest Greek koine, used especially in Aetolia and other regions under the domination of the Aetolian League. In the Doric group are such dialects as Laconian, Megarian, Corinthian, Argolic, Rhodian, and Cretan, and Coan. Typical of Doric is long alpha, for which Ionic and Attic have eta (e.g., ψυχᾱ vs. ψυχή).

For scientific reasons, comparative study of the dialects of Greece is best done on the basis of inscriptional evidence, and for most of the dialects this is the only available material. In the case of the few dialects that are represented by written works, most of the material is composed in a mixed and artificial form that does not reflect the manner in which people actually spoke at a given time and place. The Homeric poems and the works of Hesiod are a mixture of Aeolic and Ionic. Ionic was featured also in the works of Herodotus, Archilochus, Anacreon of Teos, and the Dorian Hippocrates, a native of Cos. Alcaeus and Sappho use their native Lesbian dialect, and Corinna of Tanagra wrote in Boeotian. The choral lyric, at base Doric, with an admixture of Lesbian and epic forms, became so traditional that it was used even by the Boeotian Pindar and the Ionians Simonides and Bacchylides. Doric was used in the Peloponnese (except Arcadia and Elis); in some of the islands, such as Crete, Melos, Thera, and Rhodes; and in parts of Sicily and in Southern Italy. Pindar and Theocritus affect some Doric features out of regard for its traditional use in the choric ode.

Under the influence of the tragedians Aeschylus, Sophocles, and Euripides, and other literary artists such as Thucydides and Plato, the Attic dialect began to take the ascendancy, and reached its zenith in the works of such writers as Aristophanes, Lysias, and Demosthenes, who well exhibit many of the patterns of the "people's" speech in Athens. Henceforth, literary prose took its cue from Attic.

A number of factors were responsible for protecting the Hellenic world from the linguistic fate that befell much of Europe, especially after the decline of Rome's imperial influence. Indicative of things to come was the post-Homer innovative adaptation of the demonstrative ὅς, ἥ, ὅ for articular use. The works of the great tragedians Aeschylus, Sophocles, and Euripides display a generous hospitality to various dialectical elements. Through some indebtedness to Ionic, even Thucydides endeavored to avoid provincialism. Since fifth-century Athens was the cultural center of Hellas, her linguistic mix of Attic and Ionic Greek itself became a koine or common dialect that was spread beyond her borders through extensive commerce, military actions, and the diplomatic exchange that took place under her hegemony. Other signals of movement toward a common dialect were given in the works of Xenophon and Aristotle, which serve as a linguistic bridge from Attic Greek to what is traditionally known as the Koine, to which the conquests of ALEXANDER gave the final impetus. But prior to Alexander the Great, the most impressive contributing factor to ultimate unity in language was the threat of Persian power: for Hellenes, as never before, experienced a common identity that transcended dialectical boundaries. At the same time, the declining independence of the city-states meant that narrower traditional ties would give way to more spacious conceptions of what it meant to be a Hellene.

Stylish courts tended to set the trend of language, and Hellenes were fortunate that Aristotle was the teacher of Alexander, who demonstrated the truth that Hellenism is primarily a form of civilization. Hellenic refinements and language attended Alexander's march toward India, and the forces of linguistic integration that had already been in motion were reinforced by his zeal for things Hellenic. A century earlier, Aristophanes had non-Athenians speak in their own dialects, and the theater-goers had no trouble understanding them. Now a vast international bureaucracy encouraged communication at two levels: that of the chancery, as primarily exhibited in official inscriptions; and of commercial and personal communication, as reflected especially in papyri.

Ionic and Cyprian could not survive the movement toward standardized language. Doric held out in some rural areas, and numerous inscriptions reveal that the other dialects managed to withstand the tide for a period of from one to three centuries after the Macedonian period. But for the most part, inscriptions throughout the Mediterranean world, from Alexandria to the Bosporus, from Asia Minor to Sicily, conform, even in orthography, to one linguistic pattern. To such an extent did the Koine capture the minds of the world that even in Rome it became the fashion in some quarters to speak Greek, a practice that aroused the indignation of Cicero.

There is no mistaking the Ionic-Attic base of this common or koine dialect, but it is no longer the speech of fifth century Athens. When foreigners begin to use a language, more subtle distinctions in grammar begin to disappear, for speakers learn to get along with a smaller number of inflectional and syntactical devices. Nuances can he expressed through voice patterns and gestures. On the other hand, readers of such language require visual devices, such as punctuation and variety of font, to catch the drift. Since most of the documents from the ancient Greco-Roman world lack such aids to the reader, readers were left with occasional ambiguities.

Most writers and their readers, except antiquarians, readily adapted to the new developments. Attic won out in general, but with loss of many particulars. Gone is the dual, which was already ignored in the sixth century by writers of Ionic and avoided by Thucydides. The optative becomes ever rarer. Instead of saying βουλοίμην ἄν, which would have sounded quaint, one simply declared, ἐβουλόμην. But μὴ γένοιτο has a longer life. The Attic use of -ττ surrenders to -σσ (e.g., θάλασσα for θάλαττα). Among the remnants of the second declension in the NT are the formulaic ἱλεώς σοι (Matt 16:22) and ἵλεως (Heb 8:12). After the loss of Latin in the schools, one hears in modern times such barbarisms as "the media is," "the criteria is," "it's him," and "more unique" or "most unique." Similarly, in the Koine period the violation of concord and other grammatical illogicality was on the increase, and the SEPTUAGINT and the NT parallel what goes on especially in the papyri. Neuter plural subjects, for example, are found with either a singular or a plural verb (cf. Luke 4:41), a practice as old as Homer. Similar formation by analogy leads to a decrease in *mi* verb forms: competing with δείκνυμι is δεικνύω, and ἱστάνω creeps up on ἵστημι. First aorist endings are found in various manuscript traditions in the imperfect forms of ἔχω (e.g., εἴχοσαν, John 15:22; εἴχαμεν, 2 John 5; εἶχαν, Mk 8:7), in a second aorist like ἦλθον (ἦλθαν, Luke 8:35), and in second aorist alongside first aorist forms (e.g., ἔπεσαν, Rev. 7:11; ἔπεσεν 8:10), but the Attic εἶπα was again a forecast. Athens said βασιλίς or βασίλεια in reference to a queen; but, in keeping with a form like φοίνισσα, the Koine promoted βασίλισσα. Luke's lone use of ναῦς in the NT (Acts 27:41) sounds archaic to one who notes the trend from ναῦς to πλοῖον in the papyri. Unfortunately, many of these grammatical phenomena relating to morphology are not noted in the critical apparatus of popular editions of the Greek NT, and some of the manuscript traditions reflect Atticistic scribal interference, a problem that has been insufficiently explored, especially in connection with socio-exegetical study of the NT. Alongside these phenomena are the more frequent use of personal pronouns and decreased use of possessive pronouns; an increase in the use of ὅτι, of prepositions (with some old ones disappearing), of the participle with εἰμί, of the articular infinitive, of the accusative with verbs, of ἐάν and ὅταν with the indicative, and of the comparative for the superlative; and the encroachment of μή on οὐ. Except for the long periodic structure of chancery prose used in official documents and adapted, for example, in 2 Peter and Ephesians (where modern punctuation obliterates the rhetorical reality), Koine sentences tended to be shorter than their classical counterparts, and hypotactic construction gave ground to paratactic. The rapid development of new formations and words in United States speech had its counterpart in the Koine (cf. *BAGD* xiv-xxi). Some of the non-Attic dialects left their mark here and there in the NT, notably in Doric forms, such as ὄρνιξ; λαός and ναός for Attic λεώ and νεώς; οἰκοδομή; ἀλέκτωρ for ἀλεκτρυών; and μοιχᾶσθαι alongside Attic μοιχεύειν.

Because of the composite character of the Koine, it was inevitable that portions of the NT would reflect semitic constructions that had entered into the vernacular of various social groups in the Mediterranean world. Some of these constructions, such as υἱός with a genitive, are to be found, even though with far less frequency, in Greco-Roman authors.

Besides the NT and the LXX, among the chief writings in the Koine are those of Polybius, Strabo, PHILO, JOSEPHUS, Diodorus, Plutarch, Arrian's Epictetus, and Cassius Dio. Lucian, who learned Greek as a second language, is the most distinguished of the "Atticists," who flourished in the second century C.E. and endeavored to reproduce the purity of the earlier Attic. Equally oriented to the past were

Dio Chrysostom, Aristides, Himerius, and Libanius, all of whom affected a florid, periodic style called Asiatic. Notable inscriptional examples are the autobiographical aretalogy and biographical encomium of Antiochus I of Kommagene.

After maintaining its Attic base throughout the Roman domination of the Mediterranean world, the Koine entered its Byzantine phase, with increasing differentiation between scholastic or Attic Greek and spoken Greek. By the twelfth century, the popular dialect resembled the modern Greek of the present day. Since Greeks of that period preferred to identify themselves as *Romaioi* or Romans, rather than *Hellenes,* which many construed as equivalent to "pagans," they called their koine language *Romaic*. To the author of an epic titled *Digenis Akritas,* composed near the beginning of the eleventh century, goes the credit for writing the first text in the popular or modern Greek language. Other important early works are two poems addressed to Emperor Manuel Comnenus in the name of Theodoros Prodromos (fl. 1150). The liberation of Greece in 1821 spelled a resurgence of literary production, whose vitality was signalled by the *Memoirs* of an illiterate general named Makrygiannis (b. 1797), who taught himself to write and gave expression to the people's language in his accounts of the War of Independence. Among the other principal authors are the poets Dionysios Solomos, Kostis Palamas, Andreas Kalvos, Constantinos Kavafis, Odysseus Elytes, Angelos Sikelianos, and George Seferis, and the novelists Nikos Kazantzakis, Elias Venezis, and Kosmas Politis. As in ancient times, a struggle persists for maintenance of a purer form (*kathareuousa,* the "purifying" language) of Greek, with deep roots in ancient literary expression, in the face of developments in the vernacular (δημοτική, the language of the *demos* or "people").

See also ALEXANDER; HELLENISTIC WORLD; JOSEPHUS; PHILO; SEPTUAGINT

Bibliography. *BAGD*; F. Blass and A. Debrunner, *A Greek Grammar of the New Testament and Other Early Christian Literature,* 19th ed.; C. D. Buck, *Introduction to the Study of the Greek Dialects* and *Comparative Grammar of Greek and Latin*; P. S. Costas, *A Short History of the Greek Language*; K. Krumbacher, *Geschichte der byzantinischen Literature von Justinian his zum Ende des ostromischen Reiches (527-1453)*; C. A. Lobeck, *Phrynichi Eclogae Nominum et Verborum Atticorum*; A. Meillet, *Aperçu d'une histoire de la langue grecque*; L. Politis, *A History of Modern Greek Literature*; A. T. Robertson, *A Grammar of the Greek New Testament in the Light of Historical Research*; H. W. Smyth, *Greek Grammar,* rev. G. M. Messing; E. A. Sophocles, *Greek Lexicon of the Roman and Byzantine Periods (From B.C. 146 to A.D. 1100)*; A. Thumb, *Handbuch der griechischen Dialekte.*

—FREDERICK W. DANKER

• **Greetings.** *See* SALUTATIONS

• **Ground.** *See* LAND

• **Grove.** *See* ASHERAH

• **Guilt.** Bearing responsibility for misdeeds, and the acknowledgment of that responsibility. The term *'āšām* also refers to the offering made to expiate inadvertent sin—the guilt offering. Lev 4 gives particulars about these guilt offerings, which are closely related to the sin offerings, also described in Lev 4.

One may become guilty as a result of many breaches of the demands of the deity. Abimelech of Gerar, a foreigner, reproves Isaac for having deceived him, claiming Rebekah to be his sister rather than his wife, and so paving the way for Abimelech to risk the crime of adultery (Gen 26:10). Lev 5 (vv. 2-5) notes these other acts requiring for their expiation the presentation of a guilt offering: failing to testify, touching an unclean thing or human uncleanness, or swearing a rash oath.

The subjective side of guilt is less prominent in the biblical texts than it is in contemporary usage, although it is not by any means absent. Even so, the characteristic term for personal offenses against God is *sin*. While sin produces a sense of guilt and shame, it is the sin that must be confessed before God. The author of Ps 51 acknowledges sin, iniquities, and transgressions, but does not use the term guilt in making confession to God. The prayer for deliverence from bloodguiltiness (Heb. *dāmîn,* "bloods," v. 14, Heb. 16) does show, however, that the sense of guilt, in our sense of the term, was deeply present to the Psalmist.

See also GUILT/GUILT OFFERING; SIN.

—FRED E. YOUNG

• **Guilt/Guilt Offering.** In the OT guilt is primarily a religious concept, not psychological. It is fact more than feeling. Guilt occurred when one transgressed the commandments of God. Thus guilt was closely associated with the idea of SIN. No distinction was made between matters of ritual and morality. One became guilty by touching an unclean thing or human uncleanness (Lev 5:2, 3), through the speaking of a rash oath (Lev 5:4), or by taking the name of the Lord in vain (Exod 20:7). One who committed murder was guilty (Num 35:31; Ezek 22:4). Adam ate the forbidden fruit and tried to hide from God because he experienced guilt (Gen 3:6-11). Thus guilt came from doing acts that were forbidden, or from failing to do what was required.

Guilt was both an individual and a corporate matter. A person would die for the sin that individual committed (Jer 31:30). An entire family or nation might be held responsible for the guilt of one person. When Achan took the things devoted to destruction and hid them under his tent, the army of Israel was defeated (Josh 7:3-11). When his guilt was discovered, he, his family and all his possessions were destroyed by stoning and by fire (Josh 7:24-25).

Often guilt was a personal matter and the result of offenses against God's holiness. Isaiah saw himself as guilty and unworthy to stand in the presence of God (Isa 6:5). David confessed his guilt, seeking the forgiveness of God (Ps 51). Only when guilt was recognized could one confess and have the guilt removed.

Provision was made in the Law for the removal of guilt. Confession of the wrong act was required (Lev 5:5). Where possible, restitution was made to the one wronged (Lev 6:5). A guilt offering was presented to God to remove the guilt (Lev 5:6; 6:6; Ezra 10:19). The guilt offering might vary depending upon the offense. It could be a female lamb or goat or a ram without blemish (Lev 5:6; 6:6; 7:1-7). The guilt offering was in addition to the restitution made for the offense, similar to a fine imposed upon one guilty of a crime.

The NT is the heir of the OT in the understanding of guilt with certain exceptions. There is no thought of guilt coming from ritual violations. Guilt comes from failure to obey the moral commands of God (Jas 2:10).

Words showing the specific idea of guilt are not common in the NT, although the concept of guilt underlies the writings of Paul and others (Mark 3:29; 1 Cor 11:27). More emphasis is placed on individual guilt than corporate. Paul adopted the word for CONSCIENCE, but the word as used by him did not carry the psychological weight that it does for people today. Guilt involved one's relationship with God. Law brought the recognition of guilt (Rom 3:20; 4:15).

Of course no provision is made in the NT for the making of a guilt offering. Rather, guilt is removed through the atonement wrought by Christ. Confession and guilt are the necessary requirements for the removal of guilt. When God forgives one's sins, he at the same time removes the person's guilt.

See also ATONEMENT/EXPIATION IN THE NEW TESTAMENT; ATONEMENT/EXPIATION IN THE OLD TESTAMENT; CONSCIENCE; EVIL; EXPIATION; JUSTIFICATION; RECONCILIATION; SANCTIFICATION; SIN.

Bibliography. P. Tournier, *Guilt and Grace, a Psychological Study*; H. C. Warlick, Jr., *Liberation from Guilt*.

—CLAYTON K. HARROP

• **Habakkuk.** [huh-bak′uhk] A prophet who probably prophesied during the reign of Jehoiakim (609–598 B.C.E.). Nothing is known about his life apart from the book that bears his name. The meaning of the name is uncertain. Some have suggested a connection with the verb found in 2 Kgs 4:16 that means "to embrace." The LXX rendering of the name is akin to an Assyrian word for a plant or a vegetable. According to the apocryphal work Bel and the Dragon, Habakkuk is associated with Daniel. The use of musical terms in the book (3:1, 19) may suggest that Habakkuk was from a levitical family associated with the Temple.

Habakkuk's character is disclosed through his confessional conversations with God. His messages evolved from his own struggle with evil, with God's judgment, with God's silence. With sensitivity and apparent personal torment he reacted to the deeds of violence done to the helpless. He confronted God with cries of "How long?" and "Why?" He boldly questioned God's ways. How could God permit the righteous to suffer at the hands of a cruel, barbaric nation (1:13)? Identified with his people's destiny, he challenged God's actions on the political scene. "Habakkuk, unlike any other OT prophet, was Israel's representative before Yahweh instead of being Yahweh's representative to Israel," according to D. David Garland (*BBC*).

Habakkuk had the prophetic ability to be angry with his people and yet plead for their salvation. He pled for God to "remember mercy" (3:2), even though filled with wrath.

Visual perception stands out in the prophet's work. He "saw" the oracle of God (1:1). He kept watch to see what God would speak to him, and was instructed to record the vision (2:1-2). With eyes of faith the prophet watched from his tower. He saw the certainty and the universality of God's judgment in the events of history.

Two parts of the prophet's message display how Habakkuk's painful anxiety about the course of events subsided in the face of God's coming and actions. The first is the assurance that "the righteous shall live by faith" (2:4). The second appears in the closing verses (3:16-19) to the hymn with which the book ends. God's coming in judgment and in salvation to set the whole cosmos in order leads the prophet to tremble at the glory of God's actions. Waiting quietly for God's day, he expresses assurance that even if all the supports for life—natural and historical—should be removed, the faithful can and should rejoice in God, confident of the salvation that is near at hand.

See also EVIL; GOD.

Bibliography. D. D. Garland, "Habakkuk," *BBC*.

—JIMMIE L. NELSON

• OUTLINE OF HABAKKUK •

The Book of Habakkuk

I. Habakkuk Complains and the Lord Replies (1:1–2:5)
   A. Habakkuk complains of injustice in general (1:1-11)
   B. Habakkuk complains of Babylon's success (1:12–2:5)
II. Five Woes against the Unjust (2:6-19)
III. Habakkuk's Prayer/Hymn Celebrates God's Justice (2:20–3:19)

• **Habakkuk, Book of.** [huh-bak′uhk] The eighth of the prophetic books usually called the "Minor Prophets" or "The Twelve." Habakkuk prophesied during the later prophetic period, which extended to the fall of Jerusalem in 587/6 B.C.E.

The exact date of the prophecy hinges upon the identity of the "wicked" in 1:4 and 1:13b. Traditionally, the "wicked" in 1:4 have been identified as the inhabitants of Judah, and the "wicked" in 1:13b as the Chaldeans, who were already a growing threat to the collapsing Assyrian Empire. Nineveh fell in 612 B.C.E. Jehoiakim, who had been enthroned by Pharaoh Necho, had been ruling for only four years when Egypt was crushed by the Babylonians at Carchemish (605 B.C.E.). The book can be dated between 609 and 598 B.C.E.

The major sections of the book are a dramatic dialogue between the prophet and God, 1:2-2:5; taunt-songs or woes against the Chaldeans, 2:6-19; a prayer of the prophet, 2:20–3:19.

Habakkuk questioned the seeming deaf ear of God in the face of the corrupt social and religious condition of the Israelites. Violence, strife and contention dominated his society. The Law was lifeless. It either was not enforced or was misapplied. The righteous were outnumbered and suffered injustice at the hand of the majority. Why were these wicked not punished? (1:2-4).

The divine silence is broken with an oracle revealing that God is not inactive. A new nation, the Chaldeans (Babylonians), were destroying and enslaving nation after nation; this tyrant nation would be the instrument of God's judgment on Judah (1:5-11).

This answer plunges Habakkuk into deeper perplexity. He has heard the unbelievable (1:5) and expresses the cry of all humanity: Why do the righteous suffer and the wicked prosper? How could God, who is eternal and holy, appoint this oppressor to swallow up those more righteous? The prophet is stunned that God would use this pagan nation to judge the covenant people (1:12-17).

As a watchman climbing his tower to scan the horizon,

Habakkuk looked for God's answer (2:1-2). The impatient prophet was informed that God's judgment was sure but would be according to the divine timetable. "Habakkuk, like all of us, was living 'between the times,' between the promise and the fulfillment. Habakkuk was to wait in faith for God to act. He was assured that judgment on evil would surely come. It will not be late" (Smith).

The oracle the prophet saw, and which was to be engraved on a tablet as a guide for all who read it, is found in 2:4 "Behold, he whose soul is not upright in him shall fail, but the righteous shall live by his faithfulness" (2:4). The character of the righteous in the darkest days will be marked by integrity and trustworthiness.

Habakkuk then delivered a series of woes against the Chaldeans describing a world seemingly out of control and under the domination of evildoers (2:6-10).

The third chapter is a "prayer of Habakkuk." In it God is seen as still in control, a saving God coming to silence all opposing forces. The book closes with the prophet's commitment to faithfulness no matter what the conditions of the world might be (3:16-19).

Bibliography. R. L. Smith, *Micah–Malachi*.

—JIMMIE L. NELSON

• **Hadad.** *See* BAAL

• **Hades.** *See* GEHENNA; HELL; SHEOL

• **Hagar.** [hay'gahr] An Egyptian handmaid or slave of SARAH (Sarai), given as a concubine to ABRAHAM (Abram) when Sarah thought that she would not be able to bear children (Gen 16:1-2). The giving of a concubine for this purpose was a custom at ancient Nuzi and is also reflected in the biblical narrative of Jacob and his wives (Gen 30:3, 9). Hagar is featured in two stories, Gen 16:1-16 and 21:8-21. The first narrative is identified by critical scholars as basically J material with a few P additions, while the second is assumed to be an E tradition.

When Hagar conceived, she began to despise Sarah for her barrenness (Gen 16:4). Sarah in turn became hostile toward Hagar, complained to Abraham, and with his acquiescence began to oppress her helpless slave (Gen 16:5-6). Hagar ran away, apparently trying to return to her home in Egypt. On the way, she was confronted by the angel of Yahweh, who sent her back, instructing her to be submissive to her mistress (Gen 16:7-9). In Abraham's eighty-sixth year, Hagar bore him a son, ISHMAEL, whose name, meaning "God has heard," reflected Hagar's experience (Gen 16:15-16).

Fourteen years later, Sarah bore ISAAC (Gen 21:1-7). At Isaac's circumcision festival, Sarah saw Ishmael mocking Isaac and, fearing for her son's inheritance if not his life, persuaded Abraham to drive Hagar and Ishmael away (Gen 21:8-11). God encouraged Abraham in this, and so Hagar and Ishmael went forth, carrying the provisions given them by Abraham (Gen 21:12-14). Their supplies ran out in the southern wilderness, so Hagar and Ishmael sat down to die (Gen 21:15-16). Again, God intervened and their lives were sustained (Gen 21:17-19). They survived and Ishmael became the ancestor of the ISHMAELITES who wandered in the southern wilderness (Gen 21:20-21).

The Hagar traditions were referred to by Paul in Gal 4:21-31. He treated the story allegorically, with Hagar and Ishmael standing for the old covenant in contrast to the new covenant represented by Isaac, the son of the free woman and Abraham's legitimate heir.

See also ISHMAEL.

—ROBERT L. CATE

• **Haggai.** [hag'*i*] A postexilic prophet whose work is preserved in the short book bearing his name. He is referred to in Ezra 5:1 and 6:14, where he is mentioned along with the prophet ZECHARIAH. He is credited in Ezra with having encouraged the returned exiles to rebuild the Temple in Jerusalem. All of his known prophesying took place within a three-month period in 520 B.C.E. After CYRUS captured Babylon, he issued a decree (538 B.C.E.) allowing Jewish captives to return to Palestine and encouraging them to rebuild the TEMPLE. Some exiles returned under the leadership of Sheshbazzar and ZERUBBABEL, and work on the Temple may have been attempted soon after the return; but in 520 B.C.E. little had been accomplished. The somewhat disorganized political situation, opposition from the indigenous population (Jewish and non-Jewish), and poor agricultural conditions all contributed to this situation. Haggai, however, considered the failure to complete the Temple and fully reestablish worship there as a failure of the people's commitment to God. For him the rather miserable conditions in which the returned settlers found themselves were consequences of the failure to rebuild the Temple, not excuses for not building. Haggai believed that successful and full restoration of Jewish life in Palestine depended on the restoration of the Temple and its cultus. The Temple was the symbol of God's presence with the people; construction of the Temple and participation in its cultus was recognition of and submission to that divine presence. Without this recognition and response, things would continue to go badly for the struggling restoration community. With it, things would go very well and Jerusalem would become a sacred center of blessings in the ideal future age.

See also HAGGAI, BOOK OF; ZERUBBABEL.

—DAVID A. SMITH

• OUTLINE OF HAGGAI •

The Book of Haggai

I. Haggai's Preaching Encouraging Temple Rebuilding and the Result (1:1-15)
   A. "You have neglected the Temple, so God has punished you" (1:1-11)
   B. The success of the work on the Temple (1:12-15)
II. Report of the People's Dissatisfaction with the Rebuilt Temple and Haggai's Reassurance (2:1-9)
   A. "The Temple lacks its former glory" (2:1-3)
   B. "It will have greater glory" (2:4-9)
III. Haggai's Challenge to the Priests to Carry Out Cultic Reform (2:10-14)
IV. Haggai's Promise That with Work Begun and Reform Under Way Blessings Will Follow (2:15-19)
V. Haggai's Promise that Zerubbabel Will Rule As Servant King Over the Ideal Future (2:20-23)

• **Haggai, Book of.** The Book of Haggai [hag'*i*] is a third person record of Haggai's prophetic oracles with various background statements that place the speeches in context. This setting of all of a prophet's recorded oracles in context is unique to the book of Haggai. Rather than being a somewhat disconnected series of oracles like most of the other prophetic books, this book is a short "history" of the success of Haggai's preaching. Haggai's first oracle (1:1-11) has the goal of the construction of the Temple. In this oracle he directly associated the poor circumstances of the people with their neglect of the Temple. This is followed by a report (1:12-15) of the success of the work. His second oracle (2:1-9) reported the people's dissatisfaction with the emerging structure's lack of splendor and encouraged the people about their concern. Reiterating Israel's traditional hope for an ideal future, he assured them that the glory of the new Temple could be greater than that of Solomon's Temple. The presence of God there would be a source of greater blessing. The third oracle (2:10-14) challenged the priests to carry out genuine cultic reform so that the people's worship would be expressive of genuine commitment to God. This was followed by an assurance (2:15-19) that temple construction accompanied by reformation of life and cultus had already begun to bring blessing. Finally, Haggai affirmed Zerubbabel, already Persian governor of Judah, as a future servant king. Civil rule would be administered well by this good descendant of DAVID. Haggai thus connected this worldly activity—building the Temple and reforming its worship—with God's blessing of the Israelite people in the final age. Working for the "kingdom of God" was related to the coming of the kingdom.

See also HAGGAI; POSTEXILIC PERIOD; ZERUBBABEL.

Bibliography. E. Achtemeier, *Nahum-Malachi*; P. R. Ackroyd, *Exile and Restoration*; D. L. Petersen, *Haggai and Zechariah 1-8*.

—DAVID A. SMITH

• **Hair.** Ancient Near Eastern sources provide some clues to the customary hairstyle worn by the people of ancient Palestine. Tomb paintings and reliefs depict semitic men with thick black hair and pointed beards. Women have long black hair bound by a fillet and hanging down the back.

In the OT black hair was admired, and both men and women wore it long (Cant 5:11; 2 Sam 14:26). By NT times, long hair on men was considered shameful (1 Cor 11:14). Beards and hair were dressed, adorned, anointed with oil, perfumed and curled (2 Kgs 9:30; Isa 3:18-24; Ps 23:5; Eccl 9:8; Matt 26:7). The NT, however, advised moderation (1 Tim 2:9; 1 Pet 3:3ff.).

The barber employed a razor in his craft (Ezek 5:1; cf. Isa 7:20). It was a grave insult to shave or pluck out another's hair forcefully (2 Sam 10:4f.; Isa 50:6). It was also considered humiliating to untie a woman's hair in public (Num 5:18; Luke 7:38).

Mourning required shaving the head or beard (Isa 15:2; Jer 16:6), leaving the beard untrimmed (2 Sam 19:24 [25]), or plucking out the hair (Ezra 9:3). During the days of his vow, a Nazirite was not to cut his hair (Num 6:5). At the conclusion of the vow, his hair was offered with a sacrifice (Num 6:18). Offering hair for the dead and cutting the corners of the hair were prohibited (Deut 14:1; Lev 19:27).

Priests were not to shave their heads or allow their locks to grow excessively long (Lev 21:5; Ezek 44:20). Some evidence exists to suggest that prophets were marked by tonsure (1 Kgs 20:35-43; 2 Kgs 2:23). As a sign of age, white hair was regarded with great respect (Lev 19:32; Prov 16:31).

See also NAZIRITES.

Bibliography. J. B. Pritchard, *ANEP*.

—STEPHEN J. ANDREWS

• **Hallelujah.** [hal′uh-*loo*′yuh] The expression "hallelujah" ("praise ye the Lord") apparently derives from a combination of the Hebrew verb *halal* (to "praise, extol") with the first syllable of the tetragammaton (jah = yah of YHWH). Some have suggested that the expression constitutes the earliest form of Hebrew hymnody. Others have suggested that it originated in non-Hebraic cultic or secular usage and was not associated with the divine name.

"Hallelujah" appears as an exhortation to praise twenty-four times in the fifth book of the Psalter. In the RSV it appears at the beginning of Pss 111 and 112; at the end of Pss 104, 105, 115, and 116, and at the beginning and end of Pss 106, 117 (although its appearance here may be an integral part of the psalm and not a liturgical direction), 135 (and in vv. 3, 19 and 20), and 146-50 (with this last psalm, known as the Great Hallel, closing the Psalter). Some manuscripts also include it at the end of Ps 145. Pss 113-18 were referred to as the "Egyptian Hallel" and were used at the great annual pilgrimage feasts (PASSOVER, WEEKS, TABERNACLES, DEDICATION).

The expression appears in non-canonical Jewish writings (Tobit 13:8, *3 Macc* 7:13, several apocryphal psalms) and in later rabbinic literature.

Hallelujah is transliterated *alleluia* in the LXX and in the NT where it appears in Revelation 19:1, 3, 4, and 6 in the triumphal singing of the heavenly multitude. The term functions in Revelation as an expression of praise, rather than an exhortation to praise, and it is as such an expression of praise that hallelujah, or alleluia, has appeared in Christian liturgies since earliest times.

See also WORSHIP IN THE OLD TESTAMENT.

Bibliography. C. Westermann, *The Praise of God in the Psalms*.

—SCOTT NASH

• **Haman.** *See* ESTHER, BOOK OF

• **Hamath.** [hay′math] A major city of Syria in OT times located on the Orontes River (PLATE 1). The ancient site was named Hamath, meaning "citadel" or "fortress," because it was situated on a large mound that could be easily defended. Located on a major trade route, Hamath was an important center of trade. The site, excavated by H. Ingholt from 1932 to 1938, had twelve occupational layers, the earliest dating to the Neolithic Period.

Hamath was the capital of one of several of the independent kingdoms that formed in Syria following the fall of the Hittite empire, ca 1200 B.C.E. It is mentioned a number of times in the OT as well as other ancient Near Eastern texts. The southern edge of Hamath's territory formed the northern boundary of Israel (Num 34:8; Josh 13:5). During David's reign Israel and Hamath shared a friendly relationship. This was due in part to David's defeat of Hadadezer, the king of Zobah, one of Hamath's rival kingdoms (2 Sam 8:3-12). According to the Chronicler, Solomon gained control of Hamath and erected store-cities in the land (2 Chr 8:3-4). Apparently, that control was reestablished at least in part during the reign of Jeroboam II (2 Kgs 14:28).

The size of the kingdom of Hamath is reflected to some degree in the inscription of the Assyrian king, Shalmaneser III, which states that Shalmaneser captured eighty-nine towns in the territory of Hamath. At a later time, the Assyrian king, Sargon II, relocated some of the inhabitants of Hamath in the cities of Samaria (2 Kgs 17:24). Hamath continued to be an important city during the Hellenistic Age. It was renamed "Epiphania" by Antiochus Epiphanes. According to 1 Macc 12:24-25, some of the conflict of the Maccabean Revolt spilled over into the territory of Hamath.

—LAMOINE DEVRIES

• **Hammurabi.** [ham'uh-rah"bee] The sixth and most famous king of the First AMORITE Dynasty of Babylon. Evidence for his reign includes epigraphic and archaeological finds dating from the first half of the second millennium B.C.E.

Name. Hammurabi possessed a not-uncommon Amorite name for his day. At least two kings of Yamhad and one of Ugarit bore the same name. The spelling attested at Ugarit *ʿmrpʾi* suggests a meaning of either "the paternal uncle heals" or "the people heal." It also indicates that an identification of Hammurabi with Amraphel of Gen 14:1, 9 is unlikely, and that Hammurapi is, perhaps, a more accurate spelling.

Date. The date of the First Dynasty of Babylon is crucial because the relative chronologies of the earlier periods of ancient Near Eastern history are based upon it. There exists no absolute control for this period like that provided for Assyrian chronology by the solar eclipse of 15 June 763 B.C.E.

Evidence for the date of Hammurabi includes ancient astrological observations, date-formulae (i.e., the practice of naming a year in the reign of a king after a significant event of that year), king-lists, *limmu*-lists (lists of officials called to serve for one year in a special office) and isolated clues found throughout the entire range of cuneiform documentation. By carefully comparing these materials, scholars have postulated three possibilities. Most scholars choose the middle of these options and place his reign at 1792–1750 B.C.E.

Reign. It was once supposed that Hammurabi was a brilliant statesman and military strategist. The MARI documents, however, have shown that in his early years he was but one of many kings who struggled for power in ancient Mesopotamia. The first twenty-nine years of his reign were devoted to defense, internal administration, canal work, dedications of religious buildings and military engagements of limited consequence. Only in his last fourteen years did Hammurabi become more aggressive and begin to build his empire.

In his thirtieth year he conquered Elam, Assyria, and Eshnunna. Next, he turned his attention to Larsa in the south and Mari in the north. By the end of his reign he had defeated all the kingdoms around him. Yet, having done so, he was not able to maintain what he had acquired, and within one generation after his death, the majority of his empire was lost.

Law Code. In 1902 the French expedition to the ancient Elamite capital, Susa (the Shushan of Daniel and Esther), discovered a black diorite stele inscribed with a prologue, epilogue and 282 laws belonging to Hammurabi. The stele had been carried to Susa after an Elamite invasion of Babylon.

Several of the laws are similar in judgments and regulations to earlier collections of laws (Ur-Nammu, Lipit-Ishtar, Eshnunna). Such codes were written not for judges or government officials, but as literary documents addressed to the gods who would read the text and recognize how just and righteous the ruler had been. In his code, Hammurabi states that when Marduk, the national god of Babylon, commissioned him to guide the people aright, he established law and justice in the language of the land.

In particular, the code of Hammurabi provides striking parallels to some of the biblical laws. A few are almost identical to OT cases, e.g., false witness (Laws 1, 3-4; cf. Exod 23:1-3; Deut 19:16-20), kidnapping (Law 14; cf. Exod 21:16), loss of animals on deposit (Laws 266-67; cf. Exod 22:10-13 [9-12]), rape of a betrothed woman (Law 130; cf. Deut 22:25-27) and personal injuries (Laws 196-97, 200, 209-10; cf. Exod 21:22-25).

In other cases the Code of Hammurabi and biblical law are close but not identical. This group includes cases involving debt slavery (Law 117; cf. Exod 21:2-11; Deut 15:12-18), adultery (Law 129; cf. Deut 22:22-24) and family relations (Law 195; cf. Exod 21:15). Finally, the two formulations both address the same problems, but differ in legal treatments. Examples of this are illegal entry and theft (Laws 21-22; cf. Exod 22:1-4), a wife suspected of adultery (Laws 131-32; cf. Num 5:11-31) and a female debt slave (Law 117; Exod 21:7-11).

The common focus and language of these respective laws have brought into question the originality and independence of the Israelite legal tradition. Some scholars have argued that biblical law was an outright borrowing from Mesopotamia. Others have suggested that Abraham brought this knowledge with him from Ur. Both traditions share a common underlying cultural background. The biblical law affirms Yahweh as the only source of law and righteousness.

See also LAW IN THE OLD TESTAMENT.

Bibliography. C. J. Gadd, "Hammurabi and the End of His Dynasty," *CAH*, 2/1:176-227; S. Greengus, "Law in the OT," *IDBSupp*; H. B. Huffmon, *Amorite Personal Names in the Mari Texts*; T. J. Meek, "The Code of Hammurabi," *ANET*.

—STEPHEN J. ANDREWS

• **Hand.** The basic Heb. word for "hand" (*yad*) can refer to the part of the body known as the hand (also the wrist and arm). Another term, *kāp*, generally means the palm of the hand.

Both *yad* and the Gk. term *cheir* extend beyond literal usage to significant theological meanings. From the image of "holding in the hand" is derived the idea of possession or control. Relatedly, "hand" can refer to that which persons do with the hand(s) or even the persons themselves, or any agent of an action. Through extended metaphor "hand" often means "power," both human and divine. God's saving activity (deliverance, protection) may be described as the work of God's hand. Prophetic inspiration is ascribed to God's putting the divine hand on the spokesman. Negatively, God can turn a hand against people or deliver them into the hands of their enemies.

The hand may also engage in gestures expressive of a variety of feelings or intentions. The reception or bestowal of blessings may be accompanied by gestures of the hands. In the OT the "laying on of hands" may indicate the transference of blessing, guilt, or authority. In the NT, healing may be associated with, or actualized by, the laying on of hands. The Pastoral Epistles relate the laying on of hands to one's empowering and acceptance for church office.

"Hand" may also refer to people, agents, a direction or side, or a part of something. The term *yad* in a few instances refers to a monument.

Bibliography. J. Bergman, W. von Soden, P. Ackroyd, "יָד," *TDOT*; R. C.Dentan, "Hand," *IDB*; E. Lohse, "χείρ," *TDNT*.

—SCOTT NASH

• **Hanging.** For certain heinous crimes, the corpses of executed criminals and public enemies suffered further degradation by being exposed to the elements through hanging or impalement (Gen 40:19; Josh 8:29; 10:26; 2 Sam 4:12).

Far more than mere disrespect for the physical remains of the victim, the act was intended as a public warning and as an extension of punishment.

Deuteronomic precept permitted the hanging of the corpse provided that it was taken down and buried before nightfall (Deut 21:22-23). Prolonged exposure, by hanging or otherwise, was calculated to produce rather gruesome results and thereby to deprive the body of decent burial (Gen 40:19; 2 Sam 21:10; Jer 26:3-9). Deprivation of burial was considered a punishment worse than death (Isa 14:18-21).

According to the Mishnah (*Sanh.* 6.4), the hands of the corpse were tied together and slung over a piece of wood projecting from a beam. An individual thus hung was literally "a curse of God" (*qilĕlat-'ĕlōhîm*, Deut 21:23), which can mean either "an affront to God" (JPSV) or "cursed by God" (RSV). The latter interpretation was transferred by the NT to victims of crucifixion (Gal 3:13; cf. Acts 5:30; 10:39).

In the RSV the ordinary Hebrew word for tree, *'ēṣ*, is translated as "gallows" nine times in the Book of Esther (eight in the KJV). However, since the Persians customarily practiced impalement (Herodotus, *Hist* 3.159; 9.78), Haman was probably impaled on the "tree" he had constructed for MORDECAI (Esth 5:14; 7:9f.; cf. 2:23; 9:13f.).

Death by strangulation as a result of hanging is mentioned only twice in the Bible. Both are suicides: Ahithophel (2 Sam 17:23) and JUDAS (Matt 27:5).

See also CRUCIFIXION.

Bibliography. H. C. Brichto, *The Problem of "Curse" in the Hebrew Bible*; "Kin, Cult, Land and Afterlife—A Biblical Complex," *HUCA* 44 (1973): 1-54.

—STEPHEN J. ANDREWS

• **Hannah.** [han'uh] The Books of 1 and 2 Samuel are introduced with the narrative of Hannah, the barren wife of Elkanah (1 Sam 1:1–2:10, 18-21). Because of the tragedy of Hannah's being childless, her loving husband gave her better sacrifices to offer at their annual pilgrimage to SHILOH (1 Sam 1:3-5, 8). Elkanah's other wife taunted Hannah for her childless state (1 Sam 1:6-7).

In her agony, Hannah vowed to the Lord that if she bore a son, she would dedicate the child to the Lord, making him a NAZIRITE (1 Sam 1:11; Num 6:1-8). Responding to her agony, ELI, the priest at Shiloh, promised that her prayer would be answered (1 Sam 1:17). Shortly afterward, Hannah conceived and then gave birth to Samuel (1 Sam 1:20). She stayed at home from the annual pilgrimages until the child was weaned (1 Sam 1:22-23). Although the length of this period is uncertain, it is generally estimated by scholars that the age of weaning was about three years.

After Samuel's weaning, Hannah took the child to Shiloh where, in fulfillment of her vow, she turned the child over to Eli for service at the sanctuary, leaving him there when the family returned home (1 Sam 1:26-28; 2:11). Hannah carried clothes for Samuel to Shiloh each year on their annual pilgrimage (1 Sam 2:19). After Samuel, Hannah gave birth to five other children (1 Sam 2:20-21).

Some scholars believe that the prayer-psalm of Hannah (1 Sam 2:1-10) was actually much later than the basic narrative. According to this theory, it was inserted in this place by the final editor. Hannah's prayer-psalm eloquently praises God for exalting the lowly and humbling the proud of earth—a theme prominent in OT and NT. Hannah's song finds many echoes in Mary's song, the MAGNIFICAT (Luke 1:46-55).

See also MAGNIFICAT; NAZIRITES; POETRY; SAMUEL; SHILOH.

—ROBERT L. CATE

• **Hanukkah.** *See* DEDICATION, FEAST OF

• **Haran.** [hair'uhn] In the Bible "Haran" stands for several personal and place names. Two different Hebrew roots are involved, although the spelling in most English Bibles does not distinguish between the two. Hence, the name of Abraham's brother and that of the city where Terah, Abraham's father, died (NEB: Harran) appear the same but come from different roots.

Personal Names. (1) A Gershonite, the son of Shimei (1 Chr 23:9). (2) The son of Terah and younger brother of Abraham and Nahor (Gen 11:27-29). The father of Lot and two daughters, Milcah and Iscah, he died in Ur before Terah's departure. (3) One of Caleb's sons by the concubine Ephah (1 Chr 2:46).

Place names. (1) Beth-Haran. An Amorite city taken by the Gadites (Num 32:36). Also called Beth-Haram (Josh 13:27), it is mentioned in Egyptian execration texts of the ninteenth century B.C.E. Most identify it with Tell Iktanu on the Wadi Rameh about twenty-five km. southwest of Amman.

(2) The ancient city located on the Jullab (a tributary of the Balih river) about thirty-five km. southeast of Urfa, Turkey (PLATE 2). Brief investigations of the site began as early as the middle of the ninteenth century. These few explorations were focused mainly on the architectural remains of the Middle Ages. Modern excavation began with a new survey in 1950 and limited digging by the Turkish-Anglo Expedition a year later. In 1959 a deep sounding of ten meters revealed occupational debris from the mid-third millennium B.C.E.

Haran occupied a strategic site at the intersection of several trading routes from Mesopotamia to the Mediterranean. It was listed as a stage on the Old Babylonian merchant itineraries. Even its name in Akkadian, *ḫarrānu* ("journey, caravan") suggests that Haran was an important trading center for Mesopotamian merchants (cf. Ezek 27:23).

At various times, Haran came under the control of the Amorite dynasty of Mari, the Hittite and Mitannian kingdoms, and the Assyrian and Babylonian empires. It was fortified under the Assyrians and briefly served as the headquarters of the depleted Assyrian army after the fall of Nineveh in 612 B.C.E.

Haran, like Ur, was a center of the cult of the moon god, Sîn. The famous temple of Sîn at Haran is mentioned in the Mari texts. The Assyrian kings Sargon and Assurbanipal are known to have contributed to its repair and maintenance. Nabonidus, whose mother was priestess of Sîn at Haran, returned a statue of Sîn from Babylon and installed it there.

Abraham's family stopped at Haran on its way to Canaan (Gen 11:31; cf. Acts 7:2-4). After Abraham's father, Terah, died there (Gen 11:32), Abraham collected his extended family and departed for Canaan (Gen 12:4-5). Later, Jacob fled from Esau's anger to Haran (Gen 27:43). At Haran, he served Laban for the hand of Leah and Rachel, and all his children, except Benjamin, were born there (Gen 29–31).

One of Sennacherib's officials reminded Hezekiah of the sack of Haran in an effort to intimidate him (2 Kgs 19:12; cf. Isa 37:12). Haran is also mentioned in Ezekiel's lamentation for Tyre (Ezek 27:23).

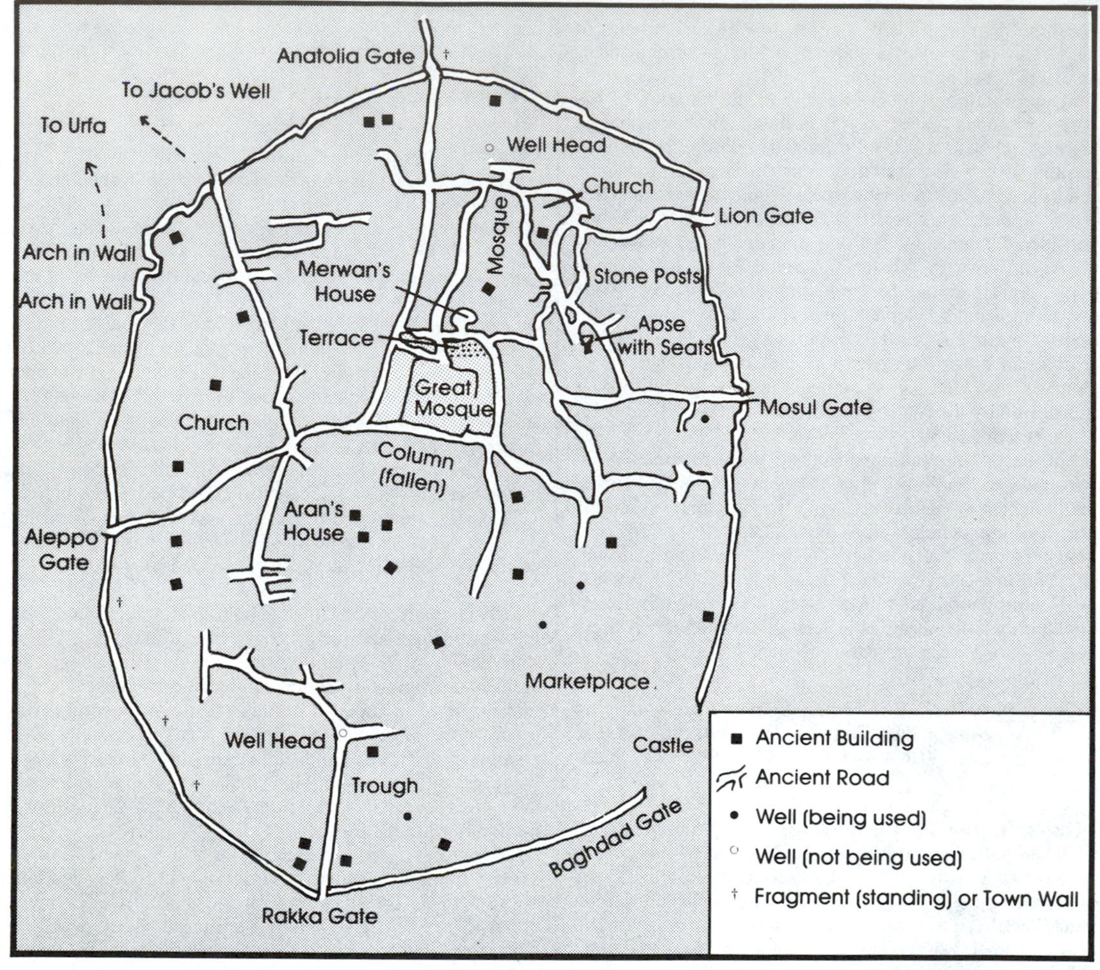

Artist's conception of ancient Haran.

Artwork by Margaret Jordan Brown

See also ARAM-NAHARAIM/PADDAN-ARAM.

Bibliography. J. N. Postgate, "Harran," *RdA*; K. Prag, "The 1959 Deep Sounding at Harran in Turkey," *Levant* 3 (1970): 63-94.

—STEPHEN J. ANDREWS

• **Hardening of the Heart.** A term met especially in the story of the Exodus from Egypt. God is said to have hardened the heart of PHARAOH so that he would not let the Israelites go out from Egypt. Pharaoh is also said to have hardened his own heart. There are also references to a hardening that comes upon Pharaoh's heart, not said to have been deliberately willed by him and not said to have been caused by God.

Such varied terminology probably developed to account for the mystery of divine providence and human freedom. Biblical faith makes clear that God is the director and sovereign of the historical process, even as it makes clear that human beings are responsible for their own conduct. God acts, according to the Bible, to make abundantly clear that sinners who are punished for their sin are in fact grievous sinners. The prophet Isaiah is charged to make the hearts of the people of his day heavy, smear over their eyes, and stop their ears, so that they will not too soon come to repentance and escape God's judgment (Isa 6:10).

Similarly in the Exodus story, God wants Pharaoh's public defeat to be recognizable, his punishment suitable for the crimes done against Israel. God hardens Pharaoh's heart, even as Pharaoh hardens his own heart.

But along the way, as the process continues, hardness descends on Pharaoh, and on Israel in Isaiah's day. It is not the case that divine providence excludes human freedom, for Pharaoh hardens his own heart: his action dovetails with God's action. And neither the individual's act nor God's act excludes a mysterious natural and historical development in which hardness of heart befalls people, not just in virtue of their own personal decisions, and not in relation to claimed divine intervention.

The doctrine of hardness of heart, then, provides a good instance of how biblical faith understood divine providence, human freedom, and a kind of destined leaning in the historical process itself to be related to one another. God directs affairs, but not in such a way as to make automatons of human actors. Human actors have much to say about their fate and fortune, but not to the exclusion of divine intervention. And history itself, social existence in God's world, acts in such a way as to make its own contribution to the fulfilling of human life and divine purpose.

See also PROVIDENCE; ELECTION.

—WALTER HARRELSON

• **Harlot.** *Zōnâ,* a prostitute. In ancient Israel, unmarried harlots were generally tolerated, though not socially acceptable. They had legal rights (1 Kgs 3:16-22) but there were social (Judg 11:1-3) and religious (Deut 23:2) biases against their children. Divorced, widowed, and unmarried women had few ways other than harlotry to support themselves. The Holiness Code forbade fathers from causing their daughters to become harlots (Lev 19:29), a practice most likely associated with poverty. Priests were prohibited from marrying those who had been prostitutes (Lev 21:14).

Although Hebrew scriptures record no laws forbidding men from using the services of harlots, there are strong warnings against the practice (Prov 23:27-28; 29:3). Hosea condemns the double standard that called for punishing harlots while tolerating men who visited them (Hos 4:14).

Inns and taverns often served as brothels in the ancient Near East (cf. Josh 2:1). Harlots often solicited along a country roadside (Gen 38:14-15; Jer 3:2) or in the city square (Prov 7:12). They attracted attention by their clothing, make-up, and jewelry (Jer 4:30; Ezek 23:40; Rev 17:4), as well as their brazen behavior (Prov 7:11-13). They may have had distinctive markings on their breasts (Hos 2:2) and forehead (Jer 3:3). Soothing words (Prov 2:16) and music (Isa 23:16) were "tools of the trade." Egyptian sheets and perfume were used to make the bed more inviting (Prov 7:16-17). Payment was in money, jewelry (Ezek 23:42-43) or other valuable items (Gen 38:15-18; cf. also Luke 15:30).

Harlotry is used metaphorically by the prophets, especially HOSEA (throughout the book), JEREMIAH (Jer 3), and EZEKIEL (Ezek 16, 23). The covenant was conceived as a marriage between Yahweh and the people of Israel. Thus, the interest of the people in other gods was analogous to harlotry. Hosea felt called to marry Gomer, a harlot (Hos 1:2), to symbolize that relationship. He continued to love Gomer despite her unfaithfulness, providing a living parable of God's love. Ezekiel portrays both Israel and Judah as harlots (Ezek 23). Israel (Oholah) was unfaithful so God handed her over to the Assyrians, but even this has not turned Judah (Oholibah) from her unfaithfulness. Fertility elements in Canaanite religions doubtless helped to inspire these images, but they were also used to depict social injustice (Jer 2:33-34; Hos 4:1-10). The Book of Revelation applies the image of harlot to Rome, a woman in jewels and scarlet to whom the kings of the earth come (Rev 17:1-6).

Jesus said that the harlots would enter the kingdom before the religious leaders of his day. This was an attack on the self-righteous, not a condoning of prostitution. PAUL wrote to the Corinthians that they should refrain from immorality, including sexual relations with prostitutes, because their bodies were temples of the Holy Spirit (1 Cor 6:15).

The harlot RAHAB of Jericho, who saved the Israelite spies (Josh 2:1-21), was integrated into the people of Israel (Josh 6:22-25). She is listed in the genealogy of Jesus (Matt 1:5) and the roll call of the faithful (Heb 11:31).

—WILDA W. (WENDY) MORRIS

• **Hasmoneans.** *See* MACCABEES

• **Hazael.** [hay'zay-uhl] Hebrew *ḥăzā'ēl,* "God has seen"; Aramean king in Damascus ca. 841–810 B.C.E., noted for his particularly brutal treatment of Israel. He was to have been anointed by the prophet ELIJAH, but it was Elijah's successor ELISHA who was instrumental in Hazael's rise to power.

Sent to the prophet by the reigning King Ben-hadad to ascertain whether he would recover from an illness, Hazael learned from Elisha that the king would indeed die. The prophet, however, instructed him to report otherwise. Hazael's visit elicited a revelation from God that the future Aramean king would cause Israel great harm. Elisha nonetheless revealed to Hazael that he would succeed BEN-HADAD (2 Kgs 8:7-15). Though the Bible does not indicate that Elisha actually anointed Hazael, the information he supplied undoubtedly had the same effect, for Hazael soon became king. That his ascension to the throne was by arrogation is confirmed by Assyrian records that designate him as "son of nobody," the standard patronym for usurpers.

Hazael was a successful military commander who won significant victories over Israel and Philistia. Capitalizing on the unrest following Jehu's revolt, he seized much of Transjordan from Israel (2 Kgs 10:32-33). He also waged a successful campaign against the Philistine city of Gath followed by a march against Jerusalem (2 Kgs 12:17-18). Jerusalem was spared only when King Jehoash surrendered the contents of the treasury. Though remembered as brutal (2 Kgs 8:12; Amos 1:3), Hazael was nonetheless understood as an instrument used by God to punish Israel for its apostasy (2 Kgs 10:32; 13:3).

See also ARAM/ARAMEANS; BEN-HADAD; ELISHA.

Bibliography. J. Gray, *I & II Kings: A Commentary.*

—DAVID H. HART

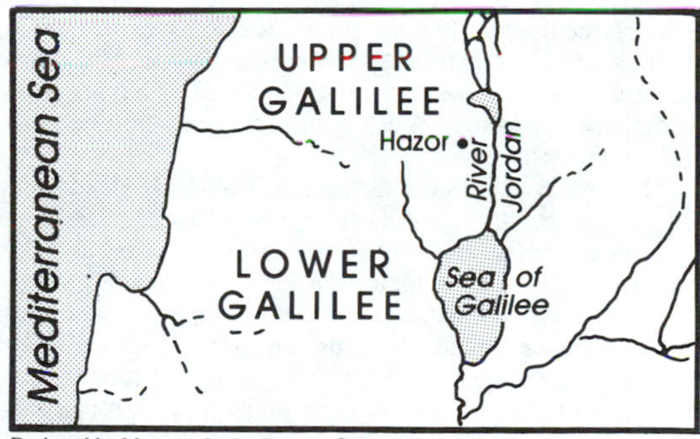

Designed by Margaret Jordan Brown ©Mercer University Press

• **Hazor.** [hay'zor] The 180 acre mound of Tell el-Qedah, flanking the western edge of the Huleh Basin in Upper Galilee, is to be identified with biblical Hazor, "the head of all those kingdoms" (Josh 11:10). Hazor was the major strategic site in northern Palestine (PLATE 13) throughout the Middle Bronze, Late Bronze, and Iron Ages, mentioned not only in the Bible but in the eighteenth century B.C.E. MARI texts, the fourteenth century B.C.E. AMARNA letters, and the neo-Assyrian annals.

Hazor was sounded by J. Garstang in 1928, then extensively excavated by Y. Yadin and others in 1952–58, 1969–72 (PLATE 3). This was the first large-scale modern excavation of the newly formed Israeli school, superbly organized and carried out.

Hazor was only sparsely occupied throughout the Early

Bronze Age (ca. 3200–2000 B.C.E.; Strata 21-18). In the Middle Bronze Age, however, Hazor became the largest fortified Canaanite city-state in Palestine (ca. 2000–1500 B.C.E.; Strata 17-16). Massive defenses of the 180-acre site consist of a cyclopean masonry lower city wall; at least one triple-entryway gate and casemate (or double) upperwall; an elaborate earthen *glaçis* or embankment along the west, with a deep dry fosse and counter-embankment; and even an outer escarpment. Hazor is mentioned in several eighteenth century B.C.E. Mari letters as a partner in an international tin-trading network, and fragments of tablets in a local Akkadian script have been found at Hazor itself.

The Late Bronze Age (ca. 1500–1200 B.C.E., Strata 15-13) is represented principally by the rebuilding of the defenses and domestic areas following the Egyptian destructions ca. 1500 B.C.E. There are also several fine temples constructed now, including the Stele Temple in Area C; a maze-like single-room temple in Area F; and especially the Orthostat Temple in Area H, first a bipartite structure then converted into a classic Syro-Palestinian tripartite temple that is a direct prototype of Solomon's later TEMPLE. A massive destruction toward the end of the thirteenth century B.C.E. brings the huge Canaanite lower city to an end, never again to be extensively reoccupied. This destruction is perhaps to be attributed to the incoming Israelites, as claimed by Josh 11.

The Iron I period sees a squatter occupation consisting mostly of hovels and refuse pits that may reflect the initial Israelite occupation in the twelfth and eleventh centuries B.C.E. (Strata 12-11). By the tenth century B.C.E., Hazor has undoubtedly become the regional capital of the Davidic-Solomonic eighth administrative district, or Naphtali, where Solomon's own son-in-law Bin-Abinadab was governor (cf. 1 Kgs 4:11). Belonging to this period (Stratum 10) are a stretch of casemate wall and splendid four-entryway city gate on the upper city, almost identical to those brought to light at MEGIDDO and GEZER. These are precisely the cities named, with Jerusalem, in 1 Kgs 9:15-17 as having been fortified by Solomon. A destruction at the end has been attributed to SHISHAK, ca. 920 B.C.E.

In Iron II (ca. 900-600 B.C.E.; Strata 9-3) Hazor was again an important regional center, chiefly under Ahab, who is probably to be credited with the principal structures of the acropolis. These include a large colonnaded storehouse; a fortified citadel and residency of monumental proportions; and especially a mammoth, stepped vertical shaft through the bedrock that descended to a gallery sloping farther down to the water-table deep underground. It was this city that was finally destroyed by the Assyrians under Tiglath-pileser III ca. 732 B.C.E. (Stratum 5; cf. 2 Kgs 15:29).

Ruins of ancient Hazor.

In the post-Assyrian period, Hazor declined (Strata 4-3). There are scant remains of the Persian period (Stratum 2), then a final Hellenistic occupation in the Maccabean era (Stratum 1; cf. 1 Macc 11:67).

Bibliography. Y. Yadin, *Hazor, The Rediscovery of a Great Citadel of the Bible; Hazor, the Head of All Those Kingdoms* and "The Israelite Water System at Hazor," *IEJ* 19 (1969): 1-19.

—WILLIAM G. DEVER

• **Headdress.** *See* CROWN/DIADEM/TIARA

• **Healing.** *See* DISEASE AND HEALING

• **Hear, O Israel.** *See* SHEMA

• **Heart.** The word heart appears over 800 times in the Bible. The Heb. *lēb* (לֵב; sometimes *lēbāb* לֵבָב or *libbâ* לִבָּה) and the Gk. *kardia* (καρδία) can be used literally to refer to the physical organ or the center of physical vitality (Hos 13:8; Isa 1:5; Luke 21:34). More often, however, the OT and NT use heart to designate the innermost part of a person.

This more figurative use of heart can focus on different dimensions of the inner life. The heart may be seen as the center of one's emotions, exhibiting the full range of human feelings (Isa 65:14; Jer 49:16; Deut 28:47; 1 Sam 9:20; Rom 1:24; Phil 1:7). The heart may also be viewed as the center of rational activity. Reflection and understanding occur within the heart (Prov 19:8; Isa 65:17; Mark 11:23). In this sense *kardia* in the NT (esp. for PAUL) approaches synonymity with *nous* (νοῦς, mind, intention).

The association of the heart with reflection and intentionality leads to its recognition as the center of volition. One "wills" with the heart (Jer 23:20; Josh 22:5; Luke 21:14; Col 4:8). The heart, therefore, is the place for moral choice. Understandably, the heart is where God confronts the self. In this confrontation the heart may be described as hardened (Exod 4:21), uncircumcised (Deut 10:16; cf. Rom 2:29-31), or renewed (Ezek 11:19; 1 Thess 3:13). The person's moral and religious life roots in the inner self, the heart. By extension both *lēb* (Ps 22:26) and *kardia* (2 Cor 1:22; Col 2:2) can mean "person."

Heart is also used figuratively a few times to refer to the central part of something, such as the sea (Jonah 2:3) or the earth (Matt 12:40).

Bibliography. F. Baumgärtel and J. Behm, "καρδία," *TDNT*; R. Bultmann, *Theology of the New Testament*; R. C. Dentan, "Heart," *IDB*.

—SCOTT NASH

• **Heathen.** *See* GENTILE/GENTILES IN THE NEW TESTAMENT; GENTILE/GENTILES IN THE OLD TESTAMENT

• **Heaven.** In biblical times heaven was believed to be located in the sky where God and the angels dwell (Gen 28:12; Ps 11:4; Matt 6:9). It was acknowledged, however, that the "heaven and the highest heaven cannot contain" God (1 Kgs 8:27) who is omnipresent (Ps 139:8-10). Many in the ancient world assumed there was a hierarchy of heavens (2 Cor 12:2-3), some planes of which were ruled by demonic powers (Eph 6:12), and beyond which Christ was raised when he "ascended far above all the heavens" (Eph 4:10). The reference to the location of heaven was not always taken literally, however. In the rabbinic tradition contemporary with the NT, heaven was thought of as the dimension of God from which salvation emerges and as the source of blessing.

For Christians heaven represents the transformed reality promised by the resurrection of Jesus Christ. There are four dominant images or symbols through which the meaning of heaven has been communicated in Christian tradition. The first is the ecstasy of WORSHIP. There is no need to have a temple in heaven because the worship of the almighty God explodes spontaneously from all creation (Rev 21:22). Living creatures never cease to sing, ''Holy! Holy! Holy!'' and the twenty-four elders cast their crowns before the throne of grace intoning, ''worthy art thou our Lord and God'' (Rev 4).

The desire to experience ecstasy has led to a second significant image of heaven, the beatific vision of the Godhead known as the *visio dei*. The *visio dei* comes into Christian tradition primarily from Plato (*Phaed* 250). The NT, however, is not without its references to seeing God. One of Jesus' BEATITUDES says that the pure in heart will ''see God'' (Matt 5:8), and Paul contrasts present and future by saying, ''for now we see in a mirror dimly, but then face to face'' (1 Cor 13:12). The prospect of apprehending the full truth of God is by no means a dominant motif in the NT.

The third image of heaven is one of rural community: PARADISE. The NT word comes from an old Persian term meaning ''park'' or ''garden'' and, when understood as heaven, depicts plants, animals, and spiritual beings existing together in natural harmony. Its use to designate heaven (Luke 23:43; 2 Cor 12:3; Rev 2:7) usually connotes a return to the Garden of Eden, a state of innocence prior to the fall. It may also connote Plato's isle of the blessed, because the name of that island is the same word used by Matthew's Jesus in the beatitudes to describe the blessings of God's kingdom (5:3). Human alienation from nature will be healed in heaven.

The fourth is the image of urban community: the NEW JERUSALEM, which is a variant on the theme of the KINGDOM OF GOD. The ''heavenly city'' derives from a vision of God's intention to establish an eschatological body politic. It is the new Jerusalem, the capital city of God's new creation whose descent is described in Rev 21:1-4. At the point of earthly destruction and renewal, the new Jerusalem takes up its abode where we are, bringing salvation, the healing of sorrow, the drying of tears, the forgetting of suffering, and the dwelling in safety with God forever.

Political symbols such as the new Jerusalem and the Kingdom of God imply a community of interacting individuals, not simply a sublime knowledge present to the individual soul. Rather than a mystical union, this community is made up of transformed men and women who continue their personal identity and mutual recognition into the resurrection while transcending most of the other categories of this finite and time-bound world. Although, as Augustine made clear, God himself is ''the end of our desires,'' salvation also consists in the redemption of the creation and of the community to be shared by the creatures within it.

See also FIRMAMENT; KINGDOM OF GOD; NEW HEAVEN; NEW JERUSALEM; PARADISE; SKY.

—TED PETERS

• **Heaven, Kingdom of.** *See* KINGDOM OF GOD

• **Hebrew Language.** The Hebrew language is a member of the northwest branch of the semitic family, along with Ugaritic, Phoenician, Moabitic, Aramaic, and Edomite. There are several varieties of the Hebrew language. The biblical language is not called ''Hebrew'' in the OT. It is called ''Canaanite'' (Isa 19:19) or ''language of Judah'' (2 Kgs 18:26; Neh 13:24; Isa 36:11).

Ancient Hebrew inscriptions are: the Gezer calendar (tenth century B.C.E.), the Samaria ostraca (ninth or eighth century B.C.E.), the Siloam inscription (eighth century B.C.E.), and the Lachish letters (sixth century B.C.E.).

The earlier songs and passages of the OT come from the tenth century B.C.E., marking the beginning of the main writing period of the biblical language.

The OT was written in Hebrew—with the exception of portions of DANIEL and EZRA, and a few terms in other books—and is the main source for understanding ancient Hebrew.

Hebrew as Semitic Language. Hebrew uses twenty-two consonants (as does Phoenician), but Ugaritic uses thirty-one signs and Arabic has twenty-eight letters. Hebrew used fewer characters because certain Hebrew letters perform multiple functions.

The letters b, g, d, k, p, and t may contain a dot in the letter's bosom. When that dot is omitted the sounds are bh, gh, dh, kh, ph, and th.

The 'aleph may be a regular consonant, a guttural consonant, or it may be a ''vowel sign'' letter.

The 'ayin serves as a strict consonant or a guttural consonant, but also it is the Hebrew form of either the Arabic 'ayin or ghain; whereas in Arabic there are at least six ''s'' sounding letters, in Hebrew there are three ''s'' letters (if sin and shin are considered as a single consonant); the three ''h'' letters of Arabic appear as one of the two ''h'' letters in Hebrew; the four ''t'' letters of Arabic are found in only two ''t'' letters of Hebrew.

The resh may be a soft or hard ''r.'' It may or may not accept the consonantal doubling; vowel sign letters ('aleph, he, yodh, and waw) may function as consonants, as vowel sign letters, or as portions of diphthongs.

Hebrew Development. When Hebrew was mainly used for conversational communication, there was no need for vowel signs since pronunciation included sounds (vowels) automatically. Written communication brought forth the need for sound indicators; vowel sign letters ('aleph, he, yodh, and waw) were employed. These were used without any consistent pattern. The Masoretes sought to devise a system that would include all of the sounds. The principle of ''one sign for one sound'' for both vowels and consonants was foundational.

Three vowel systems are found in the materials which have been discovered to this date: (1) The Tiberian system, using mainly markings below the consonants, is used in the majority of printed OT. The three classes (a, e or i, o or u) were further divided into four values of sounds, i.e., diphthongs, long vowels, short vowels, and half vowels (shewas). The other two systems were (2) the Palestinian and (3) the Babylonian.

These vowels were developed between the fifth century B.C.E. and the eighth century C.E. and preserve a relatively late tradition. However, the transliterations in the LXX and in Origen guide in recovering the ancient sounds. Also, Jerome sought to recapture the sounds of his Jewish teachers. Since the Arabic language has a more definitive sound structure, the earliest pronunciations of the Hebrew text would reflect Arabic sounds.

Another feature of Hebrew is the use of five final form letters, i.e., when one of these letters (k, m, n, p, or ts) was the last letter of a word it took a different form.

Ancient manuscripts seldom used any word division marks. A few inscriptions made use of a stroke or a dot to divide words. However, there was no commonly accepted pattern of word division.

There was no practice of punctuation marks in ancient manuscripts. The need became so apparent that the Masoretes devised a set of accent markings. (1) Word accentuation enabled the reader to emphasize the proper syllable for pronunciation. (2) Punctuation marks phrased the various elements for thought and pronunciation. Some marks were complete stops, partial stops, or definite pauses. (3) Since these texts were being used in worship, the marks were also directions for cantation.

There was one accent system for the books of prose and a different system for the poetical books of Job, Proverbs, and Psalms.

Hebrew Characteristics. Hebrew is written from right to left, whereas Ugaritic is generally written left to right. Other characteristics include: the ancient writing was consonantal with very little indication of vowels; a regular use of guttural consonants, such as heth and ‘ayin; the base of the linguistic structure is a triliteral root stem (each verb consists of three consonants, and serves as the developing structure for other grammatical forms); the use of emphatic consonants (t, s, k); modification and inflections were formed by prefixes, suffixes, and infixes; writing developed from "defective" to "plene" spelling; there are only a few compound terms, most of which are borrowed expressions (names that contain more than a single integer are known as "sentence names"); and the syntax is very simple and uncomplicated (grammar is the explanation of external elements of the language; syntax is the study of interrelational aspects).

There has not been a continuous use of Hebrew. Much of Hebrew linguistic history is unknown and can only be deduced through written records. Consequently a historical grammar of Hebrew is only tentative. Hebrew grammar can only be descriptive.

Variant forms of the same grammatical form have been preserved. The language grew toward standardized forms from different dialects (cf. Judg 12:6). The scribes/editors preserved the specific forms found in their sources.

Within the Hebrew documents the scholar must confront the fact of linguistic change or growth as noted in suffixes, personal pronouns, use of particles, the development of certain grammatical forms (such as the Hithpa‘el), and the date of writing. Thus an interaction of original author, the one writing, and the reader must take place, leading to a history of the "layers of the text."

Descriptive grammar. The three basic elements of Hebrew are verb, noun, and particle.

(1) In the regular order of a Hebrew idea, action is primary. Hebrew is an action centered language, leading to the fact of inter-action, relatedness of action and/or type of action. Action is primarily expressed within the *verb.*

The verb structure is divided into two categories, i.e., finite (limited by built-in subject, gender, and number) and infinite (unlimited by a subject). The finite forms of the verb are perfect, imperfect, or imperative. Thus, the finite verb established the state of the action. If the writer viewed the action as completed and finished (whether actually or conceptually) a perfect was used. If the writer viewed the action as incomplete, unfinished, or repeated, the form selected would be imperfect. (All imperative forms, being built from the imperfect second person forms, would be by definition unfinished or incomplete, i.e., imperfect).

The verb conveys more nuances and variations of meaning than any other form. The author had available gender, number, and person in each finite form.

Each verbal form also falls into a category of voice, i.e., active or passive. In addition, each verb contained various shades of emphasis within the action. There were three shades into which the writer could frame the scope of action. The most uncomplicated type of action would be "simple." This is seen as *Qal* (simple active) and *Niph‘al* (simple passive and/or reflexive). Then the writer could use an "intense" form of that same action. *Pi‘el* (intensive active) and *Pu‘al* (intensive passive) were used. Also, the writer could use an unusual type of action that came to be known as "causative" action. So, there were *Hiph‘il* (causative active) and *Hoph‘al* (causative passive).

Niph‘al served originally both as a simple passive and as simple reflexive. As the need for greater definition rose, there developed another category known as *Hithpa‘el* that served as intensive reflexive (characteristically active). Earlier Niph‘al incorporated both types of action, but later the ideas of simple passive action and intensive reflexive action were separated into two separate forms.

The Hebrew language did not develop a modal structure of indicative and subjunctive moods. The majority of biblical Hebrew is narrative describing activities within the scope of the writers; it is in the indicative mood.

Certain particles containing a conditional intention were used with the finite verbal structure to connote conditional ideas. The conditional sentences are relatively undeveloped. The different particles used in conjunction with specific verb forms are employed to denote the various types of conditions.

One element of a conditional sentence is the voluntative mood. The voluntative mood expresses the feeling of desire, will, wish, or request. This mood may be indicated by voluntative particles. But it is also expressed in a shortened form of the verb. Since this mood is incomplete, the form of the verb would be an imperfect. The phenomenon of shortening the verb form is "apocopation."

A Hebrew verb may have two causes for apocopation. The imperfect may be prefixed by a "waw consecutive" conjunction which has a tendency to shorten the form due to a possible accent shift. If the imperfect is apocopated due to the waw consecutive, the mood will be descriptive and thus indicative. The other cause of apocopated imperfect verbal form (not caused by waw consecutive) will be in the Semitic mind a voluntative (sometimes called cohortative or jussive).

The infinite forms of the verb are the two infinitives and the participles. These forms are the original basis of nouns.

(2) Descriptions of elements, names that are descriptions of persons, or events are *nouns.* Nouns are categorized in gender (either masculine or feminine). There are two numbers (singular and plural), with an occasional remnant of a dual number. There are three persons (first, second, and third). But there are also other shades of meaning. A noun may be definite or indefinite by the use or non-use of a prefixed definite article.

One of the common uses of nouns together is known as the "construct relationship." This constructs two nouns into a single unit of ideas. This genitive relation may be either possessive, subjective, or objective. These two (constructing) words form one idea; thus there is only one accent. Since the first word loses its distinctive accent, vowel changes due to syllabication will take place. If the new idea is definite, only the second word (the absolute) will have the definite article. Also, since these two words now form a single idea, that idea must be either indefinite (neither word has an article) or definite (only the second word has an article).

Two nouns may be used appositionally and thus one noun modifies the other. In this manner, Hebrew expresses adjectival ideas. There are very few pure adjectives in Hebrew. There are no specific adverbs. Many nouns were used in an adverbial sense.

Hebrew is a very descriptive language. The flow of action may move rapidly or may be held within a specified vista by specific syntactical formations.

When the writer moves the action from one step to another (either rapidly or in planned succession), the phenomenon would be the imperfect form of the verb prefixed by a conjunction and a demonstrative (in the form of waw plus a daghesh forte). Such a succession of imperfects with "waw consecutives" may be governed by any type of grammatical expression, but often by a grammatical perfect. The initial expression sets the pattern of action. But the moving of the action is carried forward by the imperfect with waw consecutive.

This type of formation in early stages was called waw (vav) conversive. It was on this basis that the ancient syntactician projected that the waw "converted" the imperfect into a perfect. This was an attempt to find some kind of sequence of tenses, as dictated by Indo-European grammar. As grammarians investigated further it was clear that the conjunction did not convert the form. So the more accurate title of waw consecutive demonstrated that the action was in consecution. If the writer/speaker desired to stop the action and describe more fully what was involved in the governing (originating) action, the writer would use "a perfect with a simple conjunction" prefixed.

Early grammarians followed the logic that if there was a consecutive prefixed to an imperfect, there could be a consecutive prefixed to a perfect. However, there were two separate forms of the conjunction possible onto an imperfect. But there was only one form of the conjunction ever used with the perfect. In Hebrew thought-pattern there was only one syntactical form of the perfect with waw. When the perfect is related to a previous context by a conjunction or a relative, the action is stopped and conceptualized as finished within the originating form (whether a verbal form or not). This is the device whereby the writer correlates actions. The perfect of correlation preserves the Hebrew thought-pattern, whereas the Indo-European syntax forces the Hebrew thoughts into an Indo-European mold. The Indo-European syntax is much more involved with a sequence of tenses (time) than is Semitic. Hebrew syntax is oriented to the state of action rather than to the time of the action.

(3) *Particles* assist in establishing continuity and/or relations between the verbs and nouns. Within the uncomplicatedness of the Hebrew mind, the writer expressed the ideas uniquely. An interpreter must understand the Hebrew thought-pattern before an attempt is made to establish a smooth Indo-European style. The Hebrew language developed those elements that were needed to convey that thought-pattern.

Later there developed a neo-Hebrew that was a scholastic language, used in the Talmud. Then Modern Hebrew was constructed with an Indo-Germanic base. It differs widely from biblical Hebrew, though it uses much of the same vocabulary. Modern Hebrew uses the same grammatical base but it uses a different syntactical base and thus necessitates a different interpretive methodology.

See also SEMITIC LANGUAGES; WRITING SYSTEMS.

—JOHN JOSEPH OWENS

• **Hebrew/Habiru/Apiru.** [hee'br*oo*/hah-bee'*roo*/ah'pi-*roo*] The term, "Hebrew," is a social designation for the Israelites. It seems likely that the name is derived from the root, *'avar,* meaning to pass beyond, over, or through. This would make sense in light of use of the term by non-Israelites in Gen 39:14, 43:12, Exod 1:16, 1 Sam 4:6, and others, but it is not as clear when Israelites refer to each other as Hebrews (e.g., Deut 15:12 and Jer 34:9). With non-Israelites, the reference would simply be to the Hebrews as foreigners. Hence, they would be from beyond the boundaries of their country and, presumably, the boundaries of their station in society (as in the Joseph narrative recorded in Gen 43:12).

In 1887, Egyptian peasants found tablets in the ruins of Tell-el-AMARNA which would have significant impact upon the meaning of the term, Hebrew. Although it was not immediately obvious, this diplomatic correspondence from the courts of Amen-hotep III and Amen-hotep IV to their vassals to the north used the term *habiru* or *apiru* in such a way that many believed the references designated a non-Israelite ethnic group. Later, studies demonstrated that the term had no ethnic significance, but designated a social or political status, instead.

George Mendenhall observed that the term, *apiru* and the Sumerian logogram, SA.GAZ, appeared together 125 times in the Amarna letters. The context makes it clear that a SA.GAZ is a pejorative reference to a rebel, traitor, or deserter who has thrown off the authority of his former master(s). Since, then, the logogram seems to offer such a clear picture of the group's lack of social status and there is no necessary geographical location for the source of either *apiru* or SA.GAZ, the evidence of the Amarna letters suggests that these groups of people are simply those who have broken off from the authority of the Pharaoh and have become a threat to the stability of the Egyptian empire's vassal states.

The Alalakh tablets list both groups together in their census lists. Here, they are predominantly armed infantry with a solid minority of charioteers. Norman Gottwald has suggested that these may be former *maryannu,* warrior kings, who had been displaced and forced to flee from the city-states where they had once ruled. This finds support even in the Amarna letters, since there are several notes about *apiru* who were hired to form a mercenary auxiliary.

At Mari, two letters from a Yaqqim-Addu add further clarification to the social definition of the term. In one letter Ami-ibal protests that he is not a deserter from the local army, but a refugee who had been forced to migrate (*habaru*) to another place until an individual he trusted came into power and enabled him to return to his homeland. In another, Addu-sharrum claimed that he was a migrant *habiru,* hence immune to extradition. Since Addu-sharrumn was a commander of an armed unit of men, this seems to lend credence to Gottwald's observation that the *apiru* are often armed mercenaries. However, the context of the letters with their concern about the legal status of those who had immigrated casts doubt upon Gottwald's use of the designation as synonymous with outlaws and bandits.

The temptation to identify the Hebrews and the *apiru* as synonymous becomes even more attractive when attention is given to usage of "Hebrew," as in 1 Sam 4:9 where the Philistines are encouraged to battle effectively so they would not become subject to the Hebrews as the Hebrews were once subject to them. This would seem to support the view of Hebrews as rebels, even as the *apiru* in the Amarna tablets were. In 1 Sam 29:3, however, David's men are considered to be Hebrews (i.e., defectors from King Saul's army who had become a mercenary auxiliary for the Philistines).

With such striking parallels between the social status of the *apiru,* which are mentioned in 210 different Near Eastern texts, and the Hebrews as depicted in the biblical accounts, it is no wonder that so many have been anxious to equate the two. Unfortunately, it is not so simple.

Mendenhall and Gottwald utilized this equivalence to build their revolt model of the Israelite entry into Canaan. They posited a situation where the city-states of feudal Canaan were decaying, large population groups deserted the urban sites and migrated to the hill country where they allied with and became absorbed into the tribal confederacy of the Israelites.

This model can be called into question by those who point to the lack of evidence of population movement into the Palestinian hillsides (where the Israelites would have settled according to this model), and note that evidence of continued rebuilding of Canaanite cities after destruction seems to indicate a reluctance to abandon urban civilization. Both of these points would be required to validate the revolt model.

Thus, it is best to see the relationship between the Hebrews of the Bible and *apiru* of the Near Eastern texts as based on social status and pejorative language. The primary meaning of both terms is "refugee" or "outsider." Since many *apiru* were slaves, vassals, or servants who had revolted, it seems reasonable to suggest that the Israelites adapted a non-ethnic slur related to social status and transformed it into a designation of positive value (much like the "Christians" at Antioch). If so, they simply appropriated a generic term for their use.

See also CONQUEST OF CANAAN.

Bibliography. N. K. Gottwald, *The Tribes of Yahweh*; G. E. Mendenhall, *The Tenth Generation*; N. Na'aman, "Habiru and Hebrews: The Transfer of a Social Term to the Literary Sphere," *JNES* 45 (1986): 271-88.

—JOHNNY L. WILSON

• **Hebrews and Hellenists.** [hee'br*oo*s and hel'uh-nists] The names "Hebrews" and "Hellenists" were given by Luke (Acts 6:1) to two distinct groups in the early church in Jerusalem. Both terms are used infrequently in the NT (Hellenists only in Acts 6:1; 9:29 and Hebrews only in Acts 6:1; 2 Cor 11:22; Phil 3:5). Elsewhere NT writers use "Jews" and "Greeks." The numerous attempts at identifying the Hellenists can be reduced to the following: (1) Greek-speaking Jewish Christians having definite affinities with Greek culture; (2) gentile members of the early church; and (3) an early Christian party who rejected the Hebrew law. If the Hellenists were Greek-speaking Jewish Christians (as is probably the case), the Hebrews would be identified as Aramaic-speaking Jewish Christians.

The conflict between Hebrews and Hellenists in Acts 6:1 and the ensuing martyrdom of STEPHEN profoundly influenced the missionary work of the early church and the nature of gentile Christianity.

See also SEVEN, THE; STEPHEN.

—PAUL CIHOLAS

• **Hebrews, Gospel of the.** The *Gospel of the Hebrews* is one of three Jewish-Christian gospels known to the church fathers. (cf. GOSPEL OF THE NAZAREANS and the GOSPEL OF THE EBIONITES.) This gospel is referred to in a variety of ways. Clement of Alexandria (*Strom* 2.9.45, 5) Origen (*John* 2.12; *HJere* 15.4), and Cyril of Jerusalem (in a Coptic translation) speak of it as the "Gospel of the Hebrews." Jerome, however, is not consistent, sometimes calling it the "Gospel of the Hebrews" (*CMic* 7.6; *CEzek* 16.13), the "Hebrew Gospel" (*CEph* 5.4), and the "Gospel according to the Hebrews" or the gospel called "According to the Hebrews" (*CIsa* 40.9; *CEzek* 18.7; *DeVir* 2). He says that it was a "Gospel written in Hebrew speech which the Nazaraeans read" (*CIsa* 11.2), a work which he claimed to have translated into Greek and Latin (*DeVir* 2). There is no certainty that each of these authors was referring to the same work. However, this is the one Jewish-Christian gospel most often mentioned by title.

The *Gospel of the Hebrews* was known in the second century (Eusebius, quoting Hegesippus, *EccHist* 4.22.8), and because it is quoted principally in the third century by Clement and Origen, one presumes the book had an Egyptian provenance. Apart from what Jerome said about a "Hebrew" original, the text is known only in Greek, Latin, and Coptic fragments. No semitic fragments of the work have been found.

The *Gospel of the Hebrews* apparently was almost as long as our canonical MATTHEW, if Nicephorus's count of 2,200 lines is correct (in *OpHist*). The extant fragments suggest that the work possessed an account of Jesus' PASSION and RESURRECTION, some teachings given to his disciples, an account of the baptism, and possibly an account of his preexistence and/or birth. How much was given to each of these areas is not known.

The book's character, however, seems unlike the canonical gospels. It focuses on JAMES, the brother of Jesus, which may be an expansion of the oldest witness to the resurrection (1 Cor 15:7) and/or confusion of the traditions of the two disciples named James. In this gospel James, the Lord's brother, is present at the Last Supper and is a witness of the resurrection, making him the "highest authority in the circle of Jesus' acquaintances" according to P. Vielhauer (Hennecke-Schneemelcher, 2, 160).

Its view of the Holy Spirit seems influenced by Jewish WISDOM LITERATURE where it is a feminine power which has an existence almost apart from God. In the *Gospel of the Hebrews* Jesus is supposed to have said, "My mother, the Holy Spirit, led me away by one of my hairs unto the great Mount Tabor" (Origen, *John* 2.12). And at Jesus' baptism the voice from heaven was that of the Holy Spirit who, addressing Jesus, stated that the first-begotten Son was the eschatological "rest" of Wisdom. Apparently the concept of "rest" was very important in this gospel since the term is found in several of the fragments.

See also APOCRYPHAL GOSPELS; NAZAREANS, GOSPEL OF; EBIONITES, GOSPEL OF.

Bibliography. E. Hennecke and W. Schneemelcher, eds., *New Testament Apocrypha*; A. F. J. Klijn and G. J. Reinink, *Patristic Evidence for Jewish-Christian Sects*.

—GLENN A. KOCH

• **Hebrews, Letter to the.** We do not know who wrote Hebrews; we do not know to whom it was written; we do not know precisely why it was written; we do not even know how to classify the book as a writing. Hebrews is indeed the "riddle" of the NT. In order to gain some understanding of the writing, however, most commentators suggest a

• OUTLINE OF HEBREWS •

The Letter to the Hebrews

- I. Introduction: The Son and Angels (1:1–2:18)
  - A. God's final revelation in his Son (1:1-4)
  - B. Christ higher than angels (1:5-14)
  - C. Admonition (2:1-4)
  - D. Subjection of the world to the Son—the way of suffering (2:5-9)
  - E. The pioneer of salvation made perfect through suffering (2:10-18)
- II. Participation in the House of God and in the Rest along the Way (3:1–4:13)
  - A. Christ's faithfulness over God's house as Son compared with Moses' faithfulness as servant (3:1-6)
  - B. The rejection of Jesus more serious than the rejection of Moses (3:7-19)
  - C. The promise of rest remains but it may be forfeited (4:1-10)
  - D. Exhortation (4:11-13)
- III. The Nature of the Son's High Priesthood (4:14–7:28)
  - A. Christ's high priesthood as encouragement to his people (4:14-16)
  - B. Christ's qualifications as high priest (5:1-10)
  - C. Readers' qualifications and challenge (5:11–6:12)
  - D. The steadfastness of God's promise (6:13-20)
  - E. Christ the perfect eternal high priest according to the order of Melchizedek (7:1-28)
- IV. The Superiority of the Heavenly Reality over its Earthly Copy (8:1–10:18)
  - A. The heavenly sanctuary and the new covenant (8:1-13)
  - B. The ministry of the levitical priests (9:1-10)
  - C. The character of Christ's sacrifice (9:11–10:18)
- V. The Way of the Christian as the Way of Faith (10:19–12:29)
  - A. Privileges and duties of Christians (10:19-25)
  - B. The fate of the willful sinner (10:25-31)
  - C. Call for endurance (10:32-39)
  - D. The faith of past heroes and heroines (11:1-40)
  - E. Exhortation to faithful endurance as sons (12:1-29)
- VI. Concluding Admonitions (13:1-21)
  - A. Ethical injunctions and examples (13:1-8)
  - B. Genuine Christian sacrifice (13:9-16)
  - C. Call for obedience and prayer (13:17-19)
  - D. Prayer and doxology (13:20-21)
- VII. Postscript (13:22-25)
  - A. Personal notes (13:22-23)
  - B. Final greetings and benediction (13:24-25)

specific historical and religious situation which may be seen as the problem or the "question" to which Hebrews is the "answer." Exegesis, however, is often only loosely tied to the specific situation posited. Hugh Montefiore, for example argues that Hebrews was written by APOLLOS to the church at Corinth, especially to the Jewish Christians in that congregation. But his commentary "has been constructed in the hope that it may be of use to those for whom there is as yet no convincing solution to the difficult problems which this Epistle poses" (32). Robert Jewett feels that effective exegesis of Hebrews demands that a particular hypothesis concerning the writer's situation be selected and used in interpretation. He suggests that Hebrews be read as a letter of Epaphras to the churches of the Lycus Valley designed to combat a unique Jewish-Gnostic heresy (evidenced in COLOSSIANS). It would have been written at approximately the same time as Colossians to deal with the same sort of situation.

The suggestion of Helmut Koester that the writing be appreciated not in light of any specific situation but as a "fundamental theological treatise" seems to move away from the historical focus. Instead of moving outside the historical-critical argumentation, however, Koester simply generalizes the historical moment which is used for situating and interpreting the writing. Koester places Hebrews in the "general situation of the churches after Paul's time." Hebrews, then, is interpreted as "a witness for the efforts to develop the Pauline legacy" during the last decades of the first century (272).

This article is designed to survey the conventional historical-critical questions and to suggest a satisfying approach to the interpretation of Hebrews in light of the absence of compelling answers.

The Author. Hebrews is anonymous. In an early period, Hebrews was interpreted as a letter of Paul which was originally written in Hebrew or Aramaic and which was translated by Luke into Greek. Other early traditions name Clement of Rome, Apollos, or BARNABAS as the author. The vocabulary, style, and argumentation of Hebrews lead modern scholars to discount Pauline authorship and to envision the author as a Christian trained in rhetoric and Hellenistic learning. The writing itself is evidence that the writer is a Christian, a very well-educated Christian who uses a sophisticated style of Greek. His or her education and experience involved what we would call *literary* experience. This literary competency is used by the writer in viewing and explicating the OT, the person and work of Jesus Christ, and the place of Christians in the plan of God. The literary ability of the writer is used for religious purposes, but this does not negate the literary character of the writing. Modern critics have suggested as author the names of STEPHEN, PHILIP, PETER, SILAS, Aristion, Prisca, and JUDE.

The Recipients. Christians are being addressed. They are "holy brethren who share in a heavenly call" (3:1). They have been Christians for a period of time—long enough that they ought to be teachers (5:12). They have had a reputation for love and service directed toward other Christians in their need. They are facing difficult days, similar to their early times in Christian life and service. In those early days they suffered, "sometimes being publicly exposed to abuse and affliction, and sometimes being partners with those so treated" (10:33). At that time the Christians addressed in Hebrews "had compassion on the prisoners" and "joyfully accepted the plundering of your property" (Heb 10:34).

In this new period of suffering, the Christians have not yet resisted to the point of shedding their blood (12:4). The fact that the possibility of martyrdom is raised lets us know that the experience they are facing is not trivial, but we learn more about what is happening to the spirit and will of the readers than we learn of the actual cause of their suffering. The writer speaks of the danger of Christians drifting away from the message they have heard, failing to hold fast their confidence and pride, being hardened by the deceitfulness of sin. He warns of the danger of sluggishness. Some of the Christians have begun to neglect regular worship service. They are in need of endurance because they have drooping hands and weak knees (2:1; 3:6,13; 6:12; 10:25, 36; 12:12).

Readers have been sought among Jewish Christians because of the use of the OT and the arguments of the superiority of Jesus and the new COVENANT to Moses and the old covenant. The original readers were regarded for a long time as Jewish Christians living in Palestine, or more specifically in Jerusalem. Since the discovery of the DEAD SEA SCROLLS, some scholars have defended the thesis that readers were former members of the Qumran community—either priests who had been converted to Christianity or former members of the community who had come close to becoming Christians but who had not come all the way.

Some scholars have seen the readers as Jewish Christians outside Palestine—either Jewish Christians spread over the Roman world or Jewish Christians in a particular community (wealthy and cultured Jews at Ephesus, a small conservative enclave of Jewish Christians in Rome, or Jewish Christians in Alexandria or Cyprus who were being induced to espouse nationalistic Judaism).

The fact that the OT was the Bible for the Christian community everywhere—for gentile Christians as well as Jewish Christians—makes it impossible to limit the readers to Jewish Christians in or outside of Palestine. The readers, then, may also be seen as predominately gentile Christians or simply Christians in general who are being warned concerning a general lassitude. These Christians have been located in such places as Corinth, Ephesus, the Lycus Valley, Antioch, Rome, or some other Italian community.

The one bit of information in the book itself which seems to be related to destination is the statement in 13:24 that "those from Italy greet you." It is possible that this is simply a greeting from Italy (perhaps Rome), but it is possible that the author is writing to Rome (or elsewhere in Italy) and sending greetings from Italians who are in his vicinity.

The Date. Since I CLEMENT refers to Hebrews, the writing had to be in existence before the end of the first century. The use made of the Temple in Hebrews (and silence concerning the destruction of the Temple in 70 C.E.) constitutes no justification for dating the writing before 70 because abstract ideas, and not the specific Herodian Temple, are at issue.

What Sort of Writing is Hebrews? How is Hebrews to be read? As a letter? Hebrews lacks the distinctive first-century salutation. Moreover, through chap. 12 the writing is too impersonal to be called a genuine letter (the epistolary ending may have been added by a later hand or by the author to give the writing the characteristics of a Pauline letter or to accompany the writing when it was sent to yet another community). In the last chapter of Hebrews, the writer describes the whole work as a "word of exhortation." The exhortation is made directly but it is also made indirectly in its presentation of Jesus Christ. What is the exhortation? We actually have to move along to the center of the writing to see the exhortation: "Let us leave the elementary doctrine of Christ and go on to maturity. . . . We desire each one of you to show the same earnestness in realizing the full assurance of hope until the end, so that you may not be sluggish, but imitators of those who through FAITH and patience inherit the promises" (6:1, 11-12). The elementary doctrine of Christ has to do both with an inferior concept of the person and work of Jesus Christ and with a superficial Christian faith and life. The maturity to which the writer is encouraging the readers is a christological maturity and a maturity of Christian living.

The Form and Message of Hebrews. Hebrews is a sermon, but it is a particular type of sermon, one which is based on OT Scripture interpreted in a fashion reminiscent of the Alexandrian Judaism represented by PHILO. Hebrews and the other books of the NT looked at OT writings not in the context of the original situations or even in the context of the OT community as a whole. What was sought was not an original dated message to ancient communities. The OT writings were examined in the context of the church to discern the message to the contemporary community. The OT was examined in light of Jesus with the conviction that Jesus opens up the true meaning of the OT. Heb 5:8-10 is an excellent starting point for making sense of the message and form of the entire book. "Although he was a Son, he learned obedience through what he suffered; and being made perfect he became the source of eternal salvation to all who obey him, being designated by God a high priest according to the order of MELCHIZEDEK." The descending and ascending movement described here (although he was Son, he learned obedience through suffering; being made perfect through suffering he became the source of eternal salvation to all who obey him; he is designated HIGH PRIEST) follows the same motif of humiliation and suffering followed by exaltation and glory which pervades the primitive proclamation concerning Jesus. But the method of exegesis is different from that used in other NT writings which make essentially the same point concerning Jesus.

Particular methods are used in Hebrews to allow OT passages to speak to the present: the present is seen as the time of fulfillment of OT promises; specific OT persons, events, or things are seen as types which are related to their counterparts in the age of fulfillment; and OT passages are seen as allegories which refer to the period of fulfillment. In one respect, Hebrews is rather unique among NT books—the assumption and use of a Platonic world view which sees the visible world of phenomena as an exteriorization, an imperfect imitation of the intelligible world. Material and sensible objects are not ultimate; more ultimate and "real" are the archetypes laid up in heaven (the Platonic idealism of Hebrews is so pronounced that some scholars have attempted to defend the thesis that the author of Hebrews had a direct acquaintance with Philo and his attempt to reconcile Greek logic with OT teachings).

The structure of Hebrews is related to its function as a word of exhortation and to its character as an exposition of OT passages. There is an interweaving of theological argument and earnest exhortation (2:14; 3:7–4:11; 4:14-16; 5:11–6:12; 10:19-29; 12:1-17; 13:1-17 all contain explicit exhortations). In the argument and exhortation the Psalter is used extensively. The usual practice is to quote a section of the Psalter and then to use words and phrases from that quotation in the following exposition. At times the argument is elaborated with use of additional OT passages which deal with the same theme. The exegesis of Ps 95:7-11 in the exhortation of 3:7–4:13 contains references to the narrative of the wilderness wanderings; and the exegesis of Ps 110:4 in Heb 7:1-28 refers to the narrative of Melchizedek in Gen 14.

The form of Hebrews is also influenced by the use of the rhetorical device of *synkrisis* (comparison) and the use of the "more or less" type of *a fortiori* argument. In order to show the superiority of a person or object, that person or object may be compared with an outstanding specimen of the same kind. Hebrews shows the infinite worth of Jesus by comparing him with outstanding institutions and figures (angels, Moses, Melchizedek, etc.). The "more or less" argument is essentially the same as that used by the rabbis with the designation *qal-wa-homer* ("light and heavy").

The attempt to outline Hebrews in a definitive way has met with no general agreement. Proposals are based on the major exhortations (seen as standing at the end of the major sections: 1:1–4:13; 4:14–10:31; 10:32–13:17); the christological ideas of the writing; the distinction between the hortatory and christological parts; or on the basis of the scheme of Greek hortatory address. Alexander C. Purdy explains that "no outline can do justice" to the interrelationship of the author's ideas, particularly because of the "subtle and skillful way in which he prepares his readers for the exposition of Jesus as high priest (in 2:17; 3:1), for the discussion of 'God's rest' (in 3:1, 18), and for the Melchizedek speculation (in 5:6, 10; 6:21)" (580).

The different historical situations and the different outlines suggested by commentators constitute not only evidence of the complexity of the book of Hebrews but also evidence that different readers—even critical readers—"concretize" or "actualize" Hebrews in light of their own psychological sets and historical and sociological situations. Hebrews invites readers to interact with the text to relate the text to their own needs in the very process of reading. The outline included here is offered not to enable readers to bypass the active reading which the author of Hebrews expects but to suggest one way of organizing the result of reading and actualizing of the content.

See also ANGEL; APOSTASY; COVENANT; EPISTLE/LETTER; FAITH AND FAITHLESSNESS; HIGH PRIEST; MELCHIZEDEK; PERSECUTION IN THE NEW TESTAMENT; PREACHING; PRIESTS; SUFFERING IN THE NEW TESTAMENT; WORSHIP IN THE NEW TESTAMENT.

Bibliography. M. Barth, "The OT in Hebrews: An Essay in Biblical Hermeneutics," *Current Issues in NT Interpretation: Essays in Honor of Otto A. Piper,* ed. W. Klassen and G.F. Snyder; F. F. Bruce, *The Epistle to the Hebrews: The English Text, with Introduction, Exposition, and Notes*; G. W. Buchanan, *To the Hebrews: Translation, Comment, and Conclusions*; N. A. Dahl, "A New and Living Way: The Approach to God According to Hebrews 10:19-25," *Int* 5 (1951): 401-12; F. V. Filson, *"Yesterday": A Study of Hebrews in the Light of Chapter 13*; J. Hering, *The Epistle to the Hebrews*; F. L. Horton, Jr., *The Melchizedek Tradition: A Critical Examination of the Sources to the Fifth Century A. D. and in the Epistle to the Hebrews*; R. Jewett, *Letter to Pilgrims: A Commentary on the Epistle to the Hebrews*; W. G. Johnsson, "The Pilgrimage Motif in the Book of Hebrews," *JBL* 97 (1978): 239-51; E. Käsemann, *The Wandering People of God: An Investigation of the Letter to the Hebrews*; H. Koester, *Introduction to the New Testament,* vol. 2, *History and Literature of Early Christianity*; F. Lo Bue, "The Historical Background of the Epistle to the Hebrews," *JBL* 75 (1956): 52-57; T. W. Manson, "The Problem of the Epistle to the Hebrews," *Studies in the Gospels and Epistles,* ed. M. Black; W. Manson, *The Epistle to the Hebrews: An Historical and Theological Consideration*; H. Montefiore, *A Commentary on the Epistle to the Hebrews*; A. C. Purdy, "Epistle to the Hebrews: Introduction and Exegesis," *IB*; S. G. Sowers, *The Hermeneutics of Philo and Hebrews. A Comparison of the Interpretation of the OT in Philo Judaeus and the Epistle to the Hebrews*; A. Vanhoye, *A Structured Translation of the Epistle to the Hebrews*; B. F. Westcott, *The Epistle to the Hebrews: The Greek Text with Notes and Essays.*

—EDGAR V. McKNIGHT

• **Hebron.** [hee'bruhn] Located nineteen mi. south of Jerusalem, Hebron (PLATE 13) dominated the southern Judean hill country and the primary route linking Beersheba in the Negeb with Jerusalem, and Shechem and Samaria farther north. Its biblical connection with the name, Kiriath-Arba, may suggest that its foundations were linked to a four-settlement confederacy during the patriarchal period (Josh 14:15). The Canaanite and later Israelite cities were located on a strategic hill (Jebel al-Rumayda) south of modern Hebron. Middle Bronze Age remains have been recovered from a tomb in the wadi nearby. The founding of the town seven years before the building of Zoan in Egypt, according to Num 13:22, not only suggests a date of approximately 1720 B.C.E. (the beginning of Hyksos rule in Egypt), but also may imply a cultural or ethnic tie between the two cities and their populations. Abraham's purchase of the Cave of MACHPELAH from Ephron the Hittite for a family tomb established the importance of Hebron in subsequent Israelite history (Gen 23:1-20).

Toward the end of its Canaanite period, Hebron, as a member of the Jerusalemite confederacy, was visited by the twelve spies (Num 13:22) and participated in the punitive attack against the Gibeonites (Josh 10:3-27). The defeat of Hoham, king of Hebron, in battle against the Israelites was a prelude to its capture by Caleb, son of Jephunneh (Josh 15:13; Judg 1:20) during the Israelite conquest of the southern hill country.

David's mercenary service with Achish, king of Gath, provided opportunity for sharing booty and ingratiating himself among the villages of the Hebron hills. As a result, with Saul's death, David had the support of the southern Judean population in forming his independent kingdom with Hebron as his royal city (2 Sam 2:1-4). After the death of Saul's commander, Abner, and Saul's heir, Ishbosheth, David was anointed in Hebron (2 Sam 5:1-3).

Hebron's importance as an administrative center continued into the united monarchy as a levitical center and city of refuge (Josh 21:13; 1 Chr 6:42). It became a vital part of Rehoboam's defensive system after the division of the kingdom (2 Chr 11:10), and with the reorganization that the division demanded, Hebron continued as a dominant administrative center in the south (2 Chr 11:13-17). Hebron possibly is identified in the royal seals on storage jars of the eighth century B.C.E. as a royal store city where taxes-in-kind were collected for transport to the capital or subsequent distribution to military units or points of need.

With the fall of the Judean monarchy, Hebronites were exiled by the Babylonians. Their city was annexed by the Edomites whose encroachment on Judean territory as far as Beth-Zur already had begun prior to the fall of Jerusalem. A sparse Jewish population may have returned to the Hebron hills during the Persian period (Neh 11:25), but the Edomites dominated the southern hill country. Hebron was reclaimed as a Jewish town during the Maccabean period. An early attack by Judah and the later conquest of Idumaea by John Hyrcanus at the end of the second century B.C.E. forced conversion on the Idumaeans and restored it as a part of the enlarged Judea (1 Macc 5:65).

During the Roman period, Herod the Great built up parts of Hebron including the wall surrounding the Cave of Machpelah. Hebron was captured and plundered by Simeon Bar Giora, the leader of the Jewish Zealots, during the First Jewish Revolt (Josephus, *BJ* 4.529). The Roman commander Cerealius later recaptured the city and burned it down (Josephus, *BJ* 4:554). Though Jews possibly continued to live in the city, they appear not to have participated in the Bar Kochba, or Second Jewish, Revolt of 132–35 C.E.

Bibliography. M. Avi-Yonah, "Greek Inscriptions from Ascalon, Jerusalem, Beisan and Hebron," *QDAP* 10 (1944): 160-69; P. C. Hammond, "Hebron," *RB* 73 (1966): 566-69; 75 (1968): 253-58 and "Hebron," *BTS* 80 (1966): 6-8.

—GEORGE L. KELM

• **Hecataeus, Pseudo.** [*soo'*doh-hek'uh-tee"uhs] Hecataeus of Abdera (fl. ca. 300 B.C.E.) was a Hellenistic author whose undisputed work on Egyptian culture, partially preserved by Diodorus Siculus, contains a sympathetic treatment of the Jews. JOSEPHUS (*Ant* 1.158-59) attributes to Hecataeus a book about Abraham, and Clement of Alexandria (*Strom* 5.113.1-2) quotes from a book *On Abraham and the Egyptians,* which he attributes to Hecataeus. This work is widely regarded as pseudonymous.

In addition, a book called *On the Jews* is attributed to Hecataeus by Josephus, who mentions this work at *CAp* 1.213-14, and quotes from it at 1.183-204 and 2.42-43. Origen also knows about *On the Jews,* although he reports that its authenticity is disputed (*CCel* 1.15). Most, but not all, modern scholars regard this material as pseudonymous. Some hold that all the fragments in Josephus and Clement are by the same author. However, as many as three pseudonymous authors have been seen behind these texts. There is also disagreement as to whether the reference to Hecataeus in *EpArist* 31 is dependent upon a pseudonymous author.

The Pseudo-Hecataeus fragment preserved by Clement consists of a quote, falsely attributed to Sophocles, extolling monotheism and criticizing pagan idols and festivals. The book *On Abraham* may have been the work of a Jewish apologist who attempted to show that pagan poets supported Jewish claims.

The material quoted by Josephus from *On the Jews* includes, among other things, praise of the courage of Jews under persecution, evidence of their hatred of idolatry, and an anecdote about how a Jewish archer debunked the claims of a pagan diviner.

See also JOSEPHUS.

Bibliography. C. R. Holladay, *Fragments from Hellenistic Jewish Authors*; R. doran, "Pseudo-Hecataeus," *The Old Testament Pseudepigrapha,* ed. J. H. Charlesworth.

—SHARYN E. DOWD

• **Heifer, Red.** A "red heifer" has central place in a ritual conducted to obtain the "water for impurity" deemed essential for purifying those persons considered unclean through contact with a corpse. Num 19:1-22 (and tractate *Parah* of the Mishnah) describes the ritual in which an unblemished and unworked reddish cow, along with its blood and dung, was to be burned completely outside the camp. The priest also added cedar wood, hyssop, and scarlet thread to the fire. The resultant ashes were then mixed with spring water to make the "water for impurity" that was sprinkled over the unclean person(s) and/or dwelling(s) on the third and seventh days of their period of contamination. Although not burned on the altar, the red heifer was considered a sin offering because of its role in removing uncleanness (viewed by priests as sin).

The Hebrew text of Num 19 uses the term *pārâ* (cow) and not *'eglâ* (heifer). The LXX, however, refers to the animal in Num 19 as a *damalis* (heifer), as do Josephus (*Ant* 4), Philo, and the *Epistle of Barnabas* (8:1). The author of Hebrews compares the ashes of the heifer (*damalis*) to the blood of Christ that cleanses the conscience from "dead works" (Heb 9:13).

The color "red" (Heb. *ădūmmâ*) in Num 19:2 may indicate a connection with blood. The term may suggest some association with the "reddish-brown" soil, thereby supporting the view of some that the ritual of the red heifer roots in Canaanite attempts to appease evil spirits in the abode of the dead beneath the earth.

See also CLEAN/UNCLEAN.

Bibliography. G. B. Gray, *Numbers, ICC*; J. Milgrom, "The Paradox of the Red Cow (Num 19)," *VT* 31 (1981): 62-72; L. E. Toombs, "Red Heifer," *IDB*.

—SCOTT NASH

• **Hell.** The English word "hell," originally signified the "realm of the dead." It comes unchanged from Old English (cf. Old Norse *Hel,* goddess of the dead). The KJV uses the word "hell" to translate the Heb. SHEOL and the Gk. for Hades, GEHENNA, and Tartarus. With few exceptions, the RSV uses "hell" for Gehenna and Tartarus and transliterates Sheol and Hades. The Hebrew and Greek words have different meanings and should be examined individually.

In the OT, Sheol designated the nebulous realm of the dead inhabited by the "shades" of both the blessed and the damned. There was no developed idea of a place of punishment for the damned. In extracanonical Jewish literature, however, such a development is evident. Hades names the realm of the dead in classical Greek literature (from the Greek god Hades, "the unseen"), and Greek-speaking Jews used this term to translate the OT Sheol. Gehenna was used for the distinct realm of the damned. Gehenna is derived from the Hebrew *gehinnom,* "valley of Hinnom" (at Jerusalem). Jeremiah prophesied Hinnom's judgment and destruction because of forbidden religious practices taking place there (7:30-34; 32:35), and the idea and the word came to be used for eternal damnation.

In the NT, a distinction should be made between Hades (Sheol) and Gehenna. In Matt 16:18, for example, it is "the gates of Hades" which "shall not prevail" against the church of Jesus Christ; thus the reference is not to Gehenna, the place of punishment, but to the realm of the dead, which RSV interprets as "the powers of death."

Gehenna is the term used in the NT to represent the developed doctrine of hell as the eschatological place/state of torment of the wicked. Numerous other terms are included in NT teachings regarding the idea of "hell": "unquenchable fire" (Matt 3:12; Mark 9:43); "the furnace of fire" (Matt 13:42, 50); "the fire and the worm" (Mark 9:48; cf. Isa 66:24); "the eternal fire" (Matt 18:8; 25:41); "eternal punishment" (Matt 25:46); "outer darkness" (with "weeping and gnashing of teeth," Matt 8:12; 22:13; 25:30); "perdition" (John 3:36; Phil 3:19); "the wrath of God" (John 3:36; Rom 2:5; 5:9); "wrath and fury" and "tribulation and distress" (Rom 2:8, 9); "corruption" (Gal 6:8); "eternal destruction and exclusion from the presence of the Lord" (2 Thess 1:9); "the lake of fire (and brimstone)" (Rev 14:10; 19:20; 20:10, 14, 15; cf. Gen 19:24; Ps 11:6; Ezek 38:22); "the pit/abyss" (Rev 20:3); "the second death" (Rev 21:8).

Vivid, graphic descriptions of the specific torments of hell are lacking in the Bible but occur in extracanonical literature, and much later are grotesquely expressed in the art and literature of the medieval church and the Renaissance (e.g., Michelangelo's *Last Judgment,* Tintoretto's *Glory of Paradise,* and Dante's *Divine Comedy*). In the NT, the essence of hell, the eschatological state of the damned, is exclusion (to be cut off, cast out) from the presence of God, which results in ("eternal, fiery") torment.

See also GEHENNA; SHEOL.

Bibliography. M. Burrows, "The Final State of the Wicked," *An Outline of Biblical Theology*.

—EDD ROWELL

• **Hellenistic World.** *The Political Situation* (PLATES 1,

18). The victorious campaign which the Macedonian King ALEXANDER the Great waged against the vast Persian empire beginning in 334 B.C.E. radically changed the ancient Mediterranean world and the Middle East, both politically and culturally. After Alexander died prematurely in 323 B.C.E., his successors fought among themselves for many years. Several successfully carved out manageable domains from the territories conquered by Alexander and founded rival dynastic kingdoms. The more important founders of Hellenistic kingdoms include Ptolemy (whose dynasty controlled Egypt and, until 200 B.C.E., Palestine), Seleucus (the territories between Syria and India), Antigonus (Macedonia), and Lysimachus (Thrace and Armenia). Meanwhile, by 201 B.C.E., Rome had gained complete military control of the western Mediterranean with the conquest of Carthage in North Africa following the First and Second Punic wars (214–205 B.C.E. and 220–201 B.C.E.). Rome continued to expand eastward. In a series of three Macedonian wars (214–205 B.C.E., 200–196 B.C.E., and 148–146 B.C.E.), Rome turned Macedonia and Greece into Roman provinces, and gradually absorbed all of the other major and minor Hellenistic kingdoms. The last to fall was Ptolemaic Egypt which was won by the Romans under Octavian (who later became the Emperor Augustus) in the battle of Actium, on the coast of western Greece, in 31 B.C.E. against Antony and Cleopatra. After the annexation of Egypt, the last of the independent Hellenistic kingdoms, the Mediterranean Sea became, for all practical purposes, a Roman lake. Octavian's victory at Actium and the resultant conquest of Egypt marked the final transitional stage between the Roman republic and the ROMAN EMPIRE, inaugurating a new age of relative peace and prospertiy which lasted for nearly two centuries called the *Pax Romana*. The Roman period, which had begun in 31 B.C.E. lasted until Rome fell in 476 C.E. The eastern half of the empire, with its capital at Constantinople (or Byzantium), survived until it fell to the Turks in 1453. The division of the empire occurred formally in 394 when Valentinian was made emperor of the west, and Valens of the east. The practical Romans absorbed much of Greek civilization and culture, to which they contributed organizational skill, military might, and political know-how. The entire period from Alexander to the deposition of the last Roman emperor is called the Hellenistic period, a term first applied in 1836 to the period following Alexander the Great by the German ancient historian J. G. Droysen. Though Droysen erroneously understood the term "Hellenists" in Acts 6:1 to refer to orientalized Greeks, he correctly regarded the blending or syncretism of Greek and Oriental culture as characteristic of this period.

Hellenistic Culture. Though the ancient world was politically and economically controlled by Rome after 31 B.C.E. Hellenistic culture dominated the ancient world from ca. 300 B.C.E. to ca. 300 C.E. (i.e., from the death of Alexander the Great in 323 B.C.E. to the conversion of Constantine in 312 C.E.). The Roman empire encompassed many native cultures, each vitally concerned with the preservation of its own identity and traditions. The dominance and attractiveness of Hellenistic culture throughout the Mediterranean world proved irresistible to many intellectuals who were natives of one or another of the numerous cultures which had become subject first to the Macedonians, then to their successors and finally to the Romans.

Alexander and his successors consciously used Hellenistic culture as a tool for unifying and pacifying subject peoples. Various segments of conquered populations re-

A coin from the reign of the Seleucid ruler Demetrius I (ca. 162–151 B.C.E.).

Courtesy of the Eisenberg Museum of Biblical Archaeology, Southern Baptist Theological Seminary.

sponded in different ways to political and cultural domination by foreigners. Hellenistic culture proved irresistible to some native members of the upper classes, typically including intellectuals, bureaucrats, religious funtionaries, and aristocrats. In contrast to this largely urban minority, resistance to Hellenism was strongest among rural lower classes. Native intellectuals such as Manetho of Egypt, Berossus of Babylon (both early third century B.C.E.) and Flavius JOSEPHUS, the Jewish historian (late first century C.E.), attempted to defend their native traditions in response to the smothering influences of Hellenism by writing propagandistic historical accounts in Greek emphasizing both the priority and superiority of their respective native cultures.

Palestinian JUDAISM came into direct and permanent contact with Hellenistic culture when Alexander subjected Palestine in 332 B.C.E. on his way to liberate Egypt from the Persians. During the entire third century B.C.E. Palestine was under the political control of the benign Ptolemies. The Seleucids, who wrested Palestine from the Ptolemies at the battle of Panion (200 B.C.E.), pursued a more aggressive policy of Hellenization which incited the Maccabean rebellion in 167 B.C.E. Jews, like many other nativistic cultures, had an ambivalent attitude toward Hellenism. They assimilated some aspects of Hellenistic culture more easily than others. The GREEK LANGUAGE, Greek literary and rhetorical forms, Greek styles in art and architecture, and even Greek names were readily adopted. Yet other aspects of Hellenistic culture were more controversial and even repugnant to Jews with a traditional orientation: religious practices, athletic traditions, forms of entertainment and styles of clothing. While accepted by some liberal members of the upper class including the temple priesthood in Jerusalem, these controversial aspects of Hellenistic culture often met with stiff resistance, even to the extent of armed revolt, on the part of the common people. A type of religious protest literature, called apocalypses, flourished in early Judaism as well as in other native cultures dominated by the Greeks and the Romans.

Hellenistic Language. Philip II of Macedon (who ruled from 359–336 B.C.E.) used Attic Greek as the official language of his court and of his diplomatic correspondence. Under his son Alexander (356–323 B.C.E.), Koine ("common") Greek, a populrized form of imperial Attic, became the language of art, science and literature as well as of administration and commerce throughout the Hellenistic world. The Greek language of the late Hellenistic period can conveniently be divided into two major types, literary and nonliterary Koine. Koine Greek (in contrast to specific dialects like Doric, Aeolic, Ionic or Attic) was a simplified blend of features from Attic and Ionic Greek (dialects of Athens and western Anatolia).

On the basis of the widespread division of Hellenistic Greek into literary and nonliterary Koine, two categories of literature were proposed by late-nineteenth-century German scholars, *Hochliteratur* ("cultivated literature"), produced by and for the educated upper classes of the Greco-Roman world, *Kleinliteratur* ("popular literature"), of which the early Christian literature collectively known as the NT was a prime example. Actually, these categories are ideal types at opposite ends of a complex spectrum of linguistic and literary styles. Recognition of this fact makes it feasible to trace continuities between the patterns and structures of the highest and lowest educational levels. Several scholars have argued for a third kind of Hellenistic Greek between the two extremes of nonliterary and literary Koine. Though there is some disagreement about its exact character, "popular literary Greek" is an appropriate designation of this mediating type of Greek which Lars Rydbeck has labeled *Fachprosa,* "professional" or "technical prose." As the written language of people with some education, it occurs in technical and scientific treatises, in popular philosophical literature, in some of the more literary papyri, and in the NT.

Art and Architecture. The idealism of classical Greek art was gradually transformed during the Hellenistic period into an increasing preference for realism. The emphasis on a more realistic imitation of nature in painting and sculpture determined the subjects selected. Alongside mature men and women, a greater interest is reflected in old age, childhood, and deformity, and to the artistic representation of such emotions as pleasure and pain, and such states as sleep and death. Important developments in sculpture took place during the early Hellenistic period, primarily because of the practice of showing municipal gratitude to benefactors by erecting statues of them in public places. Several artistic styles can be differentiated, each emanating from a major intellectual and cultural center: (1) The Alexandrian style consisted of an impressionistic development of the ideas of Praxiteles of Athens (mid-fourth century B.C.E.), combined with a realistic depiction of the grotesque. (2) The Pergamene style followed the mixed tradition of Scopas (fourth century B.C.E.) and Praxiteles, and is represented by sculptures on the great altar of Zeus from Pergamon depicting the battle between gods and giants. (3) The Rhodian style followed the athletic tradition of Lysippus of Sicyon (late fourth century B.C.E.), and his pupil Chares of Lindos. Rhodes became a major center for bronze casting, while the other centers preferred marble. A typical representative of Rhodian sculpture is the Winged Victory of Samothrace. The creative period of Hellenistic sculpture essentially ended at 146 B.C.E. with the Roman conquest of Greece. Thereafter the Roman demand for enormous quantities of Greek sculpture led to large-scale copying of older works, and Greece became a center for statue manufacturing.

The many new cities founded by Alexander and his successors led to a blossoming of Hellenistic architecture, building, and town planning. By the beginning of the fifth century B.C.E. the physical requirements of Greek cities included an acropolis, walls, an agora, a theater, a gymnasium, and temples. some Hellenistic architectural features include the preference for the Corinthian order with its baroque features (rather than the Doric or Ionic orders), the preference for rectilinear rather than curvilinear forms, and the creative use of interior space. There was, in addition, an emphasis on the facade and a tendency to view a building within the setting of other buildings rather than as an isolated work of art (a characteristic of the classical period).

Literature. Both Hellenism and Judaism preserved cultural traditions and ideals of the past through approved collections of classical literature. Works written many centuries before the Christian era (such as Homer and the Hebrew Bible) continued to exert far reaching influences. While Greek literary classics exerted a broad influence on Hellenistic and Roman culture, in Judaism biblical literature was particularly influential. Yet both cultures were traditional in that cultural and religious values of the present were regarded as anchored in the paradigmatic past as mediated by approved literature. Literature produced from the second through the fourth centuries C.E. was also oriented to the past, since the traditional character of both Hellenism and Judaism ensured the preservation of earlier literary genres, forms, and styles in later literary activity. Throughout Greek history there was a tendency to single out the most accomplished authors of various literary genres (the most important of which were epic, lyric, and dramatic poetry). Much of this scholarly activity centered at the museum of Alexandria (founded by Ptolemy I) which boasted a great library founded by Ptolemy II (when destroyed by fire in 47 B.C.E. it contained about 700,000 books). Aristophanes of Byzantium (ca. 257–180 B.C.E.), a famous grammarian and librarian at the Alexandrian museum, apparently drew up lists of selected or approved authors (cf. Quintillian 1.4.3; 10.154-59). Since the late-eighteenth century classical scholars have used the term "Alexandrian canon" for the catalog of more than eighty classical authors, which included five epic poets, ten orators, nine lyric poets, five tragic poets, and so on. The Alexandrian canon had both positive and negative effects on ancient literature. The works of approved authors were read in schools and by the educated, they were copied, recopied and commented upon, and thus preserved for posterity. The works of unapproved authors, however, were neglected and eventually lost. Hellenistic literary culture regarded the works of approved authors as models worthy of emulation. An orator who wanted to describe a contemporary battle turned to Herodotus, Thucydides, and Xenophon for their descriptions.

The *Iliad* and *Odyssey* had an enormous influence on Hellenistic and Roman culture, not only on the art, literature, and philosophy of the educated, but also on the common people. Homer has been called "the Bible of the Greeks." This religious analogy is appropriate since both the *Odyssey* and the *Iliad* claimed to be products of the divine inspiration of the Muse, and the author himself was often called "the divine Homer." Homer was central to the educational system, and at the primary level exercises in writing and reading were based on Homeric texts and large portions were memorized. This was reinforced by frequent public recitals of and lectures on the Homeric epics. In religion, Homer provided the Greeks with basic conceptions of the gods of the Olympian pantheon. With regard to private religious practices, oracles were derived from Homeric texts, and Homeric verses were used on magical amulets. Since the purpose of education was character formation, Homer became the primary source for moral and political guidance. Homer was also regarded as a practical guide in the areas of rhetoric, warfare, and housekeeping. The Greeks thought that virtually every rhetorical and literary genre was anticipated by Homer. According to Menander Rhetor (third century C.E.), in his discussion of the many subtypes of epideictic oratory, "It is necessary to elaborate on the starting-points received from the poet [i.e., Homer], after understanding the basic scheme the poet has transmitted to us."

From the late first century through the third century, there was a widespread nostalgia for the past among both Greeks and Romans. This archaism, which was particularly characteristic of the programmatic rhetorical movement called the Second Sophistic, took several forms. Widespread attempts to imitate the language and literary style of the Attic prose writers of the classical period (450–330 B.C.E.) is called linguistic Atticism. The preference for literature written in Attic or Atticistic Greek contributed to the neglect and eventual loss of most Hellenistic literature from the late fourth century B.C.E. through the late first century C.E. Thematic archaism was also prevalent. Greek historians focused on the period of Alexander or earlier, and in so doing both neglected and depreciated the events of the more recent past. Orators declaimed on themes from the classical past, such as "Athens the greatest city," and "Alexander the greatest Greek." Archaism was both the cause and result of emphasizing literary models of the classical past. Dissatisfaction with the political and cultural realities of the present was another contributing factor which encouraged both linguistic and thematic archaism.

Native intellectuals in states subject to the Greeks, and then the Romans, used the Greek language and literary genres to explain the history and traditions of their cultures to the Greeks as well as to themselves. The Babylonian priest Berossus wrote a history of Babylon entitled *Babyloniaka* (early third century B.C.E.), dedicated to Antiochus I, in which he interpreted Babylonian history and traditions for the Greek world. Similarly, Manetho, an Egyptian high priest from Heliopolis and a contemporary of Berossus, did the same for Egyptian history in *Egyptiaka,* a history of Egypt written in Greek dedicated to Ptolemy II. In Rome, one of the first historians was Q. Fabius Pictor (late third century B.C.E.) who wrote his *Histories* in Greek to communicate Roman policies and institutions to the Hellenistic world.

Jewish Hellenistic literature, written primarily in Greek using Hellenistic literary forms and traditions, is the best-preserved Hellenized nativistic literature from the Greco-Roman period. The history of early Jewish literature reflects the increasing domination of Hellenistic literary culture. The penetration of Hellenistic culture into Palestine from the late fourth century B.C.E. on makes it difficult to determine whether particular Jewish writings arose in Palestine or the Diaspora. The SEPTUAGINT, a translation of the Jewish scriptures from Hebrew to Greek during the early third century B.C.E. in Alexandria for Greeks as well as for diaspora Jews, is one important indicator of the impact of Hellenization upon Judaism.

Religion and Philosophy. The political and cultural unity imposed on increasingly larger segments of the ancient Mediterranean world and the Near East, first by the Greeks and then by the Romans, resulted in a period of great creativity in the areas of both religion and philosophy. Previously isolated ethnic traditions came into contact with one other and affected each other in a variety of ways. Religion for the ancients was not an isolatable component of culture but an integral feature which permeated life and thought generally. Cults in the Hellenistic world tended to focus on myth and ritual to the virtual exclusion of theology and ethics. Further, all of the great religious traditions had centers both in their ancestral homeland as well as in a diaspora population of immigrants who worshipped native deities in foreign lands.

Several distinctive forms of religion and religious traditions flourished in the Hellenistic world, including (1) ruler cults, (2) state cults, and (3) MYSTERY RELIGIONS. The ruler cults, which first developed in the Hellenistic kingdoms, provided a religious and political framework for the various national groups united under regional Greek monarchies, and eventually the Roman empire. The Ionian cities of western Anatolia had proclaimed the divinity of Alexander when he liberated them during his campaign against the Persians. Of the mainland Greeks, however, only the league of Corinth voted divine honors to Alexander (324 B.C.E.). Later the Athenians voted divine honors to Antigonus and Demetrius Poliorketes in 307 B.C.E. By 270 B.C.E. Ptolemy Philadelphos had founded a cult celebrating the divinity of both his wife Arsinoe and himself. The deification of rulers was a grateful municipal response to individuals of great merit. Rome adapted features of the Hellenistic ruler cults to the needs of an enormous empire. Julius Caesar was posthumously deified in 42 B.C.E. Thereafter living emperors took the title *divi filius* ("son of god") referring to their imperial dynastic predecessors (thereby legitimating their own rule), and deceased emperors thought worthy of the honor were enrolled with the gods of Rome by an act of the senate. The imperial cult, particularly strong in such eastern provinces as Asia, became a way for provincial expression of loyalty and patriotism.

The traditional state cults of the Greek and Roman cities continued to flourish but were weakened by the subjugation of the *polis* ("city-state"), first to leagues and then to empires. Since the primary function of state cults had been to ensure national prosperity by promoting peace with the gods, the subjugation of cities to larger political units meant that the quest for prosperity had to be pursued at a higher level, such as the ruler cults.

The growing concern of individuals for their own welfare and salvation encouraged the proliferation of mystery religions. The Greek terms *mysterion* and *mystes* mean "secret ritual" and "initiant." Mystery cults, then, are essentially voluntary associations of people who have experienced a secret ritual initiation thought to guarantee prosperity in this life and happiness in the life to come. The Eleusinian mysteries, centering in the worship of Demeter and Persephone, is the oldest known Greek mystery religion. Many oriental cults moved westward with native immigrants and were transformed into mystery cults. Among the more prominent of these are the cults of Isis and Osiris, Cybele and Attis and Aphrodite and Adonis.

Numerous philosophical schools and traditions, many of which originally centered in Athens, flourished in major urban centers throughout the ancient Mediterranean world during the Hellenistic period. While Greek philosophy in the classical period tended to focus on three main divisions of logic, physics, and ethics, during the Hellenistic period the quest for the *summum bonum* ("the greatest good") resulted in a growing emphasis on ethics. The major philosophical traditions of the Hellenistic world all sought legitimation by tracing their traditions back to Socrates (469–399 B.C.E.). The major competing schools of Hellenistic philosophy include Platonists, Aristotelians, EPICUREANS, CYNICS, STOICS, and Skeptics.

See also ALEXANDER; CYNICS; EPICUREANS; GREEK LANGUAGE; MACCABEES; MYSTERY RELIGIONS; ROMAN EMPIRE.

Bibliography. E. L. Bowie, "Greeks and Their Past in the Second Sophistic," *Studies in Ancient Society,* ed. M. I. Finley; J. B. Bury et al., *The Hellenistic Age*; G. Dickens, *Hellenistic Sculpture*; D. R. Dudley, *A History of Cynicism from Diogenes to the 6th Cent. A.D.*; S. K. Eddy, *The King is Dead: Studies in the Near Eastern Resistance to Hellenism (334–31 B.C.)*; J. Ferguson, *The Heritage of Hellenism* and *The Religions of the Roman Empire*; F. C. Grant, *Roman Hellenism and the New Testament*; R. M. Grant, *Gods and the One God*; E. S. Gruen, *The Hellenistic World and the Coming of Rome*; M. Hadas, *Hellenistic Culture*; A. A. Long, *Hellenistic Philosophy: Stoics, Epicureans, Sceptics*; A. J. Malherbe, *Moral Exhortation, a Greco-Roman Sourcebook*; A. Momigliano, *Alien Wisdom: The Limits of Hellenization*; A. D. Nock, *Conversion: The Old and the New in Religion from Alexander the Great to Augustine of Hippo*; F. E. Peters, *The Harvest of Hellenism: A History of the Near East from Alexander the Great to the Triumph of Christianity*; P. Petit, *Pax Romana*; J. H. Randall, Jr., *Hellenistic Ways of Deliverance and the Making of the Christian Synthesis*; J. M. Rist, *Stoic Philosophy*; W. W. Tarn, *Hellenistic Civilisation*; F. W. Walbank et al., eds., "The Hellenistic World," *CAH* 7/1; F. W. Walbank, *The Hellenistic World*.

—DAVID E. AUNE

• **Hereafter.** *See* ESCHATOLOGY IN THE NEW TESTAMENT

• **Herem.** *See* BAN

• **Hermas, Shepherd of.** The early Christian document *Hermas,* or *Shepherd of Hermas,* was known to the early church fathers. The MURATORIAN CANON, a list of canonical books from about the third century, says Hermas was written by the brother of Pius, bishop of Rome about 140–154. Despite much speculation the author remains unknown. It was written in Rome and involves the Roman church. The document was composed over a longer period of time. It is divided into five Visions, twelve Mandates, and ten Similitudes. Visions 1–4 were composed during a threatened persecution, probably under Trajan (98–117). Vision 5–Similitude 8 and Similitude 10 were written by the same author to describe REPENTANCE to wavering Christians. Similitude nine was written to unify the entire work and to threaten those who had been disloyal. This last phase must have occurred before IRENAEUS (ca. 175). A preferred date would be 140.

There are no complete Greek texts of *Hermas.* The great fourth century manuscript of the Greek Bible, Codex Sinaiticus, contains only the first quarter of *Hermas.* When all the texts are put together still 107.3–114.5 is missing, and must be supplied by the Latin text in the Vulgate.

In the first Vision Hermas has a desire for a certain woman (Rhoda) and then is accosted by an elderly woman (the CHURCH) about his sin. In the second Vision Hermas learns repentance is possible. Hermas sees the church as a tower in the third Vision. The tower is built on a foundation of APOSTLES, BISHOPS, teachers, and DEACONS. The fourth Vision takes the form of an apocalypse in which the church is threatened by an unusual beast. The twelve Mandates, introduced by the fifth Vision, consists of admonitions regarding faith, innocence, truthfulness, chastity, repentance, patience, ill temper, self control, doublemindedness, grief, cheerfulness, and evil desire. The ten Similitudes are analogies or PARABLES with similar concerns. The Similitudes build analogies on two cities, trees, vineyards, shepherds, sticks, mountains, a tower, and a garment.

Hermas reflects a local type concern for morality much like the EPISTLE OF BARNABAS and the DIDACHE. Like them *Hermas* contains a Two Way theology (36–39), though his system depends on two angels rather than two impulses (36.1) and he stresses self-control more than right choice. As in other Two Way systems doublemindedness (*dispychia*) and doubt are the primary sins (39.1-12).

From the beginning Hermas was caught in a struggle over APOSTASY. Hermas speaks for the possibility of one postbaptismal repentance. Even within the document some argue against any repentance for the Christian (31.1), while others count on the continuing mercy of God (43.4). Hermas holds to both—a strict morality with a merciful God (31.2-7).

The Christology of *Hermas* has often been called adoptionist (cf. 59). There is little christological reflection in the book. Most NT Christological functions are performed by angels or the HOLY SPIRIT (12.1; 25.2). The complete dwelling of the Spirit in the Son so pleased God that the Son was taken as a divine partner (29.5-7).

The *Shepherd of Hermas* paints a remarkable picture of the second century church at Rome. We find among the Christians good and evil, faith and hypocrisy, wealthy and poor—all the qualities of every day Christian life. The church is not in danger, but it has reached certain interior accommodations. In addition to postbaptismal repentance, for example, in the parable of the elm and the vine (Similitude 2) the elm tree, representing the wealthy of the congregation, gives financial support to the congregation, while the vine, supported by the elm, represents the poor who pray for the congregation.

The form of Visions, Mandates, and Similitudes share much with similar Jewish material. Yet direct use of either OT or NT can only be lightly attested. Many of the analogies, such as the garment, the willow, the elm and vine, and the empty jars, have no biblical counterpart. A number of significant details, such as the elderly woman of Vision 2, or the virgins of Similitude 9, come from the Greco-Roman milieu.

See also APOCALYPTIC LITERATURE; APOSTASY; APOSTOLIC FATHERS.

Bibliography. G. F. Snyder, *The Shepherd of Hermas*; J. Quasten, *Patrology*.

—GRAYDON F. SNYDER

• **Hermeneutics.** [huhr′muh-ny*oo*″tiks] The theologian S. Kierkegaard once observed that "it is no use remembering a past that cannot be made present." Spanning a period of well over one thousand years from their earliest writings to the latest, both the Hebrew scriptures and the Greek writings of the Christian Bible engage continually in the vital exercise of making the past present. Through this activity the past informed each new present even as that present reformed the past for those who produced and treasure this material. In fact, the very emergence of a "Bible" as a fixed set of writings or scripture, as well as the authority accorded it as canon within the synagogue and the church, may broadly be perceived as one very important result of this continued engagement between past and present. The Bible itself, in whatever form, exemplifies, illustrates, and is itself the product of processes that can be called "hermeneutical."

The word "hermeneutics" comes from a Greek term meaning "interpretation, explanation, translation." As applied to the Bible it has been used to refer both to the principles by which a text is understood in terms of its original context or historical setting, and to the principles and procedures by which a text from one context is made meaningful in another. While hermeneutics encompasses both exegesis and interpretation, the emphasis generally falls on the latter, on making texts meaningful in the present. Since the last century the term came to be used specifically of the techniques, rules, and principles by which the Bible, recognized as the product of ancient Israel, early Judaism, and the early Christian church, could be made meaningful to readers and hearers in a modern west that is so distant from the ancient Near East and the early Mediterranean world.

How could material designed to address people who lived in times and places remote from ours, with their own distinct concerns, perceptions, and sensibilities, be made to address people who live in contexts so distant and different from the material's original home? How, for example, might prophetic oracles, once addressed to the tiny nation Israel as it struggled to survive amid the tensions created by the ongoing conflict between the superpowers of Assyria and Egypt, meaningfully address the citizens of one of the world's superpowers in the twentieth century of the Common Era? How might instruction regarding sexual and other relationships that originated in tribal Israel speak to men and women in a society transformed by new technologies, mores, family and communal life styles, as well as distinct individual values? Can letters addressed to small Christian communities struggling to set roots in a Jewish and Greco-Roman world (Should one eat meat or animals sacrificed to idols? Should one observe Jewish dietary regulations?) also address fundamental concerns of churches firmly rooted in the establishments of twentieth-century Main Street U.S.A.? "Hermeneutics" is the term applied to the ways people wrestle with questions such as these, and to the methods developed to allow ancient texts to speak across centuries and vast expanses of space.

It is recognized that already within the Bible a complex hermeneutic is apparent, both within and between the testaments. Two examples can serve as illustrations, one drawn from the Hebrew Bible itself and one linking the OT and the NT.

(1) In the oracles of the great prophet of Israel's exile, the so-called "Second Isaiah," the following remarkable passage is found: "Thus says the Lord, who makes a way in the sea, a path in the mighty waters, who brings forth chariot and horse, army and warrior; they lie down, they cannot rise, they are extinguished, quenched like a wick: Remember not the former things, nor consider the things of old. Behold, I am doing a new thing; now it springs forth, do you not perceive it? I will make a way in the wilderness and rivers in the desert" (Isa 43:16-19). The context of this saying is one of radical discontinuity between past and present, between Israelite nationhood and exile that followed the destruction of that nation by NEBUCHADREZZAR of Babylon. For many the traditions of Israel's past seemed dead—consider the poignant cry in Psalm 137: "How can we sing the Lord's songs in a foreign land?" This prophet of the Exile accents the disjunction between old and new in v. 18: "Remember not the former things." Yet it is precisely with a host of echoes of the past, and especially its paradigm story of the EXODUS, that he introduces the God whose command is given in v. 18. Vv. 16-17 reverberate with strains of canonical (Exod 15:1-10) and no doubt other celebrations of Yahweh's triumph over Egypt's PHARAOH when he delivered his chosen people from bondage into freedom. Paradigms from the past are recalled even as the charge is given: "Remember not the former things."

Then a new act of God's deliverance, one that is just now springing forth, is presented in terms of a march through a transformed wilderness to a new ZION and a new nation Israel. Once again echoes are heard from the past: of the first wilderness trek to nationhood and freedom; of the first Zion and its Temple. The exiles' new identity is to be built upon this announced future, a future whose contours are etched in themes drawn from the past. The past informs the exiles' present and their hopes for the future, even as their present crisis reforms their memory of the past. The God who once delivered will deliver again. Exile in Babylon is experienced as the old Egyptian bondage and slavery, from which Israel will pass as it once did, in a march over a highway through a wilderness transformed this time toward new nationhood and freedom. The past appears in this oracle as a *type* for the future in which it is to be realized. This mode of interpretation or appropriation of the heritage can therefore be called "typology." Typology is one of the fundamental principles shaping both inner-biblical and later hermeneutics.

(2) If the Second Isaiah found in his people's memories of the past a typology for the future of the exiles, PAUL at one point states that the Hebrew past provides an "allegory" that casts radical new light on the transformed situation of humanity in relation to God, brought about by God himself through the death and resurrection of JESUS. An example is found in his letter to the church of Galatia in a context in which Paul struggles with the relationship between law and grace, obedience and faith, a struggle that informs much of this letter as well as the one to the Romans. In Gal 4:21-31 he states that the situation of ABRAHAM, who had two wives and two sons, one born to a slave woman and one to a free, is an allegory: these women are two covenants. Hagar the slave is Mount Sinai, "she corresponds to the present Jerusalem, for she is in slavery with her children." By contrast "the Jerusalem above is free, and she is our mother." The persecution of the free by the child of the slave, the "one born of the flesh," corresponds to the present situation faced by Christians—"so it is now." This provides a basis for casting out the "slave and her son" in favor of the "son of the free woman." Traditions from Gen 16 and 21 are here read and recast dramatically in light of the very new situation faced by the early church. A reading of the Genesis material dealing with Abraham, HAGAR, SARAH, and their sons in its own context will reinforce the fundamental ways in which PAUL has reshaped it and given it a new tone as well as new significance. He struggles in this letter to make sense, not only of the severe tensions between Jewish and Christian groups, but more fundamentally of the role of the Torah now that he recognizes the crucifixion and resurrection of Jesus as God's paradigmatic act to restore human beings to Him. In the old paradigm that Paul valued as a Jew, Mount Sinai and the giving of Torah followed the Exodus as a response to God's grace; now it, and the "Old Israel" based in it, must somehow be shown to be not only preparatory for, but, for a time at least, replaced by the "New Israel." Material from the Abraham

stories in Genesis provided Paul with ground for reflection on this complex of issues when it is read as what Paul himself identifies as "allegory."

The typological reading of the past by the Second Isaiah and the allegorical reading of the heritage by Paul are but two modes and examples of inner-biblical hermeneutics. Others include fundamental recastings of earlier traditions (note the ways Chronicles reshapes and edits the material from Samuel and Kings), juxtaposition of texts (two accounts of origins in Gen 1:1-2:4a and 2:4b-3:24 are set side by side in a way that invites the playing of their distinct perspectives one upon the other), supplementation of older texts in ways that formatively alter their context and thrust (note that the oracles of the ISAIAH of Jerusalem were linked with those of the Second Isaiah and with still later material to make up the Book of Isaiah).

Clearly the period of wilderness wandering in Israelite history was remembered in one way by JEREMIAH (2:2-3) and in another by those who gave shape to the Torah. Someone sought to shape the reader's appreciation of "the Preacher" and at the same time to temper their reading of his words in Ecclesiastes by providing an addendum to the book in 12:9-14. The author of Dan 9 provided new calculations regarding Jeremiah's seventy years for the desolation of Jerusalem (Jer 25:11-12; 29:10), in light of his and his colleague's experiences in the days of persecution under Antiochus IV in the second century B.C.E. Ps 22 provided motifs and themes taken up in the gospel traditions of the church for the presentation of the crucifixion. The motif of a suffering servant in Isa 40–55, and especially 52:13–53:12, was used by early Christians to add nuances to the designation MESSIAH, as it was applied to JESUS, in their attempt to give words to what they experienced as God's actions in him that had so fundamentally transformed their lives.

In time a canon of scripture was fixed by both synagogue and church, a process J. A. Sanders describes as a movement from sacred story, that could be adapted as retold in new times and contexts, to a sacred text, that while fixed in its wording demanded ever new interpretation. Various modes of interpretation emerged.

Some interpreters appear to operate on the principle that behind what may be generally secondary or superficial differences in periods and places, human beings are essentially the same; they struggle with the same basic issues and concerns, and share fundamental perceptions and sensibilities. Strides in historical and related studies, especially those of the last century, have provided a more fundamental appreciation of the profound ways particular contexts, cultures, and languages, shape individuals. This has made us aware of the potential gap between the present and the context out of which biblical and other ancient texts emerged, as well as the rich variety of situations and communities through which they have passed as they have been treasured. Principles of interpretation have changed as the biblical texts have grown, been collected and fixed in their every word. For the fixed text still demands interpretation in new settings. Some methods employed in earlier periods, including some utilized within the biblical tradition itself, may appear suspect or even bizarre today. But even they point to a necessity that is as alive today as ever to seek direction, guidance, perspective, comfort and correction from the past.

An early example of new interpretations that appear alongside the original material, which is left unaltered, are biblical commentaries among the DEAD SEA SCROLLS found at Qumran. These cite a brief portion of a biblical book and then provide a sentence or two of interpretation that generally applies the material to the life and times of the community that produced these commentaries. These interpretations were called *pesharim,* a term with connotations of solving a puzzle or even untying a knot. Sometimes the implications and meanings of ancient texts for the present were not to be found on the surface of the texts themselves, and one had to dig deeply into them. This might especially be the case if one lived in a community that was in a constant state of red alert for God's climactic breaking into human history, a community that perceived itself as a spot of purity in an evil and corrupt world, and a community that knew it was to be at the human center of God's new creation. For example, Hab 2:3—"If it seems slow, wait for it; it will surely come, it will not delay"—was interpreted in this way: "This is addressed to the men of truth, the men who carry out the Law, who do not relax from serving the Truth even though the final moment be long drawn out. Assuredly, all the times appointed by God will come in due course, even as He has determined in his inscrutable wisdom."

This small monastic community of Jews living near the northwest corner of the Dead Sea was not the only group who found themselves living in an unstable present, awaiting God's new creative action, and which looked for direction, a sense of place, meaning, comfort, and challenge to the scriptures they received from the past. According to the Gospel of Luke (24:27), Jesus spoke with two apostles who did not recognize him on the road to Emmaus: "And beginning with Moses and the prophets, he interpreted to them in all the scriptures the things concerning himself."

Canonization of scripture is itself a grand example of the hermeneutical necessities and activity of early Judaism and Christianity in the last centuries B.C.E. and the first three centuries C. E. The fixing of a CANON and of the text of scripture was a formative stage in a hermeneutical process already long underway. In fact, the very shape of their Bibles reflects distinct Jewish and Christian hermeneutics and contexts for remembrance.

(1) The Hebrew Bible moves from Torah (Genesis–Deuteronomy) and former prophets (Joshua–2 Kings) to the so-called writing prophets (Isaiah, Jeremiah, Ezekiel, and Book of the Twelve) and finally to the Writings. It ends with the Chronicler's work in the striking order of Ezra, Nehemiah, and only then 1 and 2 Chronicles. This particular Bible ends therefore with the assurance of the restoration of Jerusalem and a Jewish community in the Palestinian homeland, in part through the efforts of CYRUS, the king of the Persian empire. The goal is renewal of the cultic establishment in Jerusalem, as constituted by the Torah which presents it as modeled on patterns already established in the wilderness. There is closure in this looping back to origins at Mount Sinai. What most naturally follows from this is the Jewish Mishnah and Talmud, which are broadly comprised of interpretation, application, and supplementation of that Torah. While rooted in the paradigmatic encounter with God at the sacred mountain following the Exodus from bondage toward freedom, Mishnah and Talmud present rich appropriations and adaptations of Torah that developed well into the first centuries C.E.

(2) The Christian OT begins in the same manner as the Hebrew Bible, but places 1 and 2 Chronicles, Ezra, Nehemiah (in that order), along with Esther, after the former prophets, then presents the other Writings, and concludes with the writing prophets. Its last words are those of the lit-

tle book of Malachi, which looks not only back to Horeb (Siani) and MOSES (4:4) but ahead, especially to the new appearance of that quintessential prophet ELIJAH just before the "great and terrible day of Yahweh comes" (4:5). This final thrust captures nicely the whole prophetic expectation of a radically new act of God that is yet to come. This is quite distinct from the closure provided by the Jewish Hebrew Bible as it looks back to God's mighty acts in the Exodus and at Mount Sinai. The shape of the Christian OT demands a NT that sets forth God's new saving acts in Jesus the Messiah whose coming is heralded by the Elijah-like figure of JOHN THE BAPTIST.

In time, within both Judaism and Christianity, rules, principles, and patterns of interpretation were more and more consciously crafted, clarified and articulated, for example, in seven rules by Hillel or thirteen rules by a Rabbi Ishmael. Distinct emphases would be found in different circles: allegory was the mode preferred by third-century Alexandrian Christian communities in Egypt (and by Jews living there earlier), while an emphasis on literal meanings and on typology dominated in the Christian communities of Antioch on the Syrian coast. Philosophical and literary issues, as well as findings from communication theory, have shaped discussions of hermeneutics, especially in the last century. However it is clear that a range of hermeneutical procedures is apparent already in the Bible itself, and the distinct shapes it assumed in the synagogue and church are already testimony to a rich hermeneutical legacy.

J. A. Sanders has spoken of the canonical process or canonical hermeneutics as taking place within a matrix of tensions determined by a pole of stability and a pole of adaptability. Hermeneutics works by various principles to maintain a balance between continuity and change, between the old and the new, in which the past informs and shapes the present as the present reforms and sometimes even transforms the past. The field of tensions defined by stability and adaptability, and between past and present, is already apparent in the biblical tradition. Both the shapes of sacred scripture and later interpretations witness to the beginning of a process still alive in communities that find themselves enlivened by their biblical heritage.

See also CANON; HISTORY OF INTERPRETATION.

Bibliography. P. J. Achtemeier, *The Inspiration of Scripture* and *An Introduction to the New Hermeneutics*; J. Barr, *The Bible in the Modern World*; J. Barton, *Reading the Old Testament*; B. S. Childs, *Introduction to the Old Testament as Scripture, The New Testament as Canon: An Introduction* and *Old Testament Theology in a Canonical Context*; W. L. Humphreys, *Crisis and Story*; T.J. Keegan, *Interpreting the Bible*; J. A. Sanders, *Torah and Canon, Canon and Community* and *From Sacred Story to Sacred Text*.

—W. LEE HUMPHREYS

• **Hermetic Literature.** [huhr-met′ik] The Hermetic literature is a body of non-Christian texts reflecting a religious statement drawn from Greek philosophy and Near Eastern traditions. They are so named because in many of them Hermes Trismegistus (Thrice-Greatest Hermes), a Greek name for the Egyptian god Tat or Thoth, appears as a revealer of mysteries. The writings appear to date from the second and third centuries C.E., and were probably composed in Egypt.

Much of the Hermetic literature is of an occult nature, dealing with ASTROLOGY, alchemy, and MAGIC, but of more importance is an array of writings which purport to teach mysteries concerning God, the universe, human nature and salvation. God is light and the source of good; material is darkness and evil. Humanity is mortal in body but immortal in soul. The WORD, also called Mind and SON OF GOD, mediates between God and creation, and the Mind in humanity makes redemption possible. Salvation is bestowed through knowledge (*gnosis*), and by means of an ecstatic experience, results in deification. Hermetism is thus a rather elevated religious expression of Greco-Roman paganism.

The major source is the *Corpus Hermeticum,* consisting of some seventeen or eighteen tractates. This collection has long been known. The books contained in it are of different origins and do not reveal a perfect consistency in their teaching. The most famous of these tractates is the first, *Poimandres.* Here an unnamed person receives a revelation from a god, Poimandres, who tells of the creation of the world and primal man. This creature, seeing his reflection in the Waters below, desired to create one like himself, descending into a lower order of creation to do so. Humanity is thus created, mortal in body, but partially immortal. At death the soul rises, gradually abandoning physical and moral hindrances, until it comes to rest in God. Becoming God is thus the end of those who have attained knowledge (*gnosis*).

The thirteenth tractate in the corpus, *On Rebirth,* has, along with *Poimandres,* been involved in discussions of the background of the Gospel of John. Here, Hermes speaks to his son Tat, answering the question of what happens when one becomes God. Such a person must be born again. Tat, mystified by how one can be born again, asks further questions, and Hermes reveals the process. After instruction and self-preparation, there must be solemn meditation, as a climax to which there occurs the ecstatic mystical experience of rebirth.

The tractate ASCLEPIUS, closely associated with the *Corpus Hermeticum,* is another important witness to the Hermetic tradition. Until the discovery of the NAG HAMMADI codices, it was known only in a Latin translation.

Codex VI of the Nag Hammadi library contains in Coptic translation fragments of three Hermetic works, *The* DISCOURSE ON THE EIGHTH AND NINTH, the PRAYER OF THANKSGIVING, and chaps. 21–29 of the forty-one chapters of *Asclepius.*

In addition, fragments of and quotations from other Hermetic sources are found in a variety of ancient Christian sources in Greek, Latin, and Syriac.

Most of the Hermetic writings are revelatory literature. In them Hermes generally appears teaching mysteries which have been revealed to him. The setting is Egyptian. Supposedly the mystical lore of ancient Egypt is being transmitted, thus giving the ideas, at the time of their writing, an exotic appeal. In fact, other than the identification of Hermes with Tat, there is very little genuine Egyptian influence evident. The substance is basically a popularized mysticism drawing from a syncretism of STOIC and Platonic philosophy seasoned with a bit of Near Eastern exoticism. This orientation was common enough in the centuries before and after the turn of the era, and something similar to it is known in the work of the Jewish philosopher PHILO of Alexandria.

Judaism has had an influence on the Hermetic literature, stronger in some books than in others. This influence is not from orthodox Jewish thought and practice. It is mediated rather through a familiarity with certain canonical sources such as Genesis (reflected in the cosmogony of

Poimandres), as well as apocryphal writings known in heterodox Jewish communities, probably in Egypt.

The relation of Hermetism to Christianity has been much discussed, particularly since there is a quite striking similarity in thought and vocabulary between some of the Hermetic books and the Johannine literature. Themes such as rebirth, the imagery of light and darkness, and the place of the Word as Son of God appear in both, yet some particularly significant Hermetic terms do not appear in John, words such as mystery, knowledge (*gnosis*), and IMMORTALITY. The consensus today is that both the Hermetic writings and the Johannine tradition are drawing from a common and older theological terminology, and that there is no direct connection between the two in either direction. While the Hermetic authors must have known Christianity, there is little if any discernible distinctive Christian influence on the writings.

More problematic is the relation to GNOSTICISM. The Hermetic literature is often discussed in works dealing with Gnosticism, and *Poimandres* is anthologized in collections of Gnostic sources. And of course the Gnostic library of NAG HAMMADI contains fragments of Hermetica. There are obvious and fundamental similarities, e.g., salvation comes thorugh the knowledge (*gnosis*) of God. But there are differences as well. There is no REDEEMER figure in the Hermetic writings; Hermes appears as a mystagogue, to instruct and induct one into mysteries, but not as a savior. The DUALISM characteristic of Gnosticism is not as pronounced in Hermetism, seasoned as it is with some Stoic pantheism. There is some sense of social obligation in the religious teaching of Hermetism. And while Gnosticism is known to have flourished in communities of initiates, for which the Gnostic texts served as sacred writings, there is no evidence that the Hermetic literature ever represented a canonical scripture for defined groups. Indeed it has been argued, though not unanimously, that there never existed identifiable religious congregations of Hermetists in the sense of Gnostic conventicles or Christian churches. The literature was for readers rather than for worshipers. However, the Hermetic *Prayer of Thanksgiving* from Nag Hammadi has reopened this question; it appears to be a liturgical prayer given prior to a ritual embrace and a cultic meal. Many scholars prefer to use the terms "semi-Gnostic" or "Gnosticizing" to refer to the Hermetica.

The Hermetic literature appears to represent a pagan Gnosticism in which religious salvation is necessary and, through knowledge of the mysteries, attainable, but without a redeemer figure. For Gnosticism as known from the church fathers, the Nag Hammadi library, and other sources, Christianity was a catalyst in the shaping of the tradition, and Jesus was accorded a role as Savior.

From the Renaissance through the eighteenth century there was considerable interest in the Hermetica as a source of esoteric religious insight on the part of some European writers, who often combined Hermetism with kabbalism. In modern times, however, interest in the Hermetic writings has been of a scholarly nature.

See also DUALISM; GNOSTICISM; MYSTERY; MYSTERY RELIGIONS; PHILO; WORD.

Bibliography. There is no satisfactory English translation of the Hermetica, but one may consult (with caution) W. Scott, *Hermetica*; *Poimandres* is available in W. Forester, *Gnosis* and in R. Haardt, *Gnosis: Character and Testimony; and Studies;* C. H. Dodd, *The Interpretation of the Fourth Gospel* and *The Bible and the Greeks*; G. V. Moorsel, *The Mysteries of Hermes Trismegistus*; H. R. Willoughby, *Pagan Regeneration*.

—ROGER A. BULLARD

• **Herod.** [her'uhd] Herod is the name of a family whose members controlled Palestine from the middle of the first century B.C.E. to the end of the first century C.E. At least six, perhaps seven, members of this family (excluding women) are mentioned in the NT, three of which are called Herod (Herod the Great [Matt 2:1-19]; Herod ANTIPAS [Mark 6:14-29 and others] Herod Agrippa I [Acts 12:1-23]).

The first and most famous member of this family was Herod the Great, who was born ca. 73 B.C.E. The stage for his rise to power was set by his father, Antipater, who was an Idumean. A shadowy figure whose past was unclear even in antiquity, Antipater rose to power during the first half of the first century B.C.E. by taking advantage of the internecine warfare between Aristobulus and Hyrcanus II, the sons of Alexander Jannaeus and Alexandra.

The second son of Antipater, Herod proved himself a capable leader as governor of Galilee, a position made possible by his father's standing with Rome. When civil war broke out again between the families of Aristobulus and Hyrcanus, Herod manipulated the situation so that he was named King of Judea by the Romans. After a three year war with Antigonus, the son of Aristobulus, Herod reigned as king for over thirty years (37–4 B.C.E.). His rule is usually divided into three periods: 37–25, consolidation; 25–13, prosperity; 13–4, domestic strife.

During the first period, Herod secured his position by eliminating anyone who might contest his own authority. Those so disposed included members of his own family, among whom were his wife, Mariamne I, and her mother, Alexandra. In addition, Herod himself drowned his brother-in-law, Aristobulus. During these first years he also took vengeance upon the Sanhedrin for the latter's treatment of him when he was governor of Galilee.

During the second period of his reign (25–13 B.C.E.), Herod engaged in a remarkable building program. Among his many accomplishments were theaters, royal palaces, numerous fortresses, and even entire gentile cities, which he built or rebuilt. The best known of the latter was CAESAREA Maritima, which included a harbor he had constructed. But the most famous of his architectural masterpieces was the rebuilding of the Temple in Jerusalem. This ambitious project, the remains of which can still be seen, was begun around 20 B.C.E. It was not fully completed until 62 C.E., just before its destruction by the Romans during the war of 66–70. It was this Temple that was known by Jesus and his disciples.

This period also saw Herod's total disregard for Jewish Law. This can be clearly seen in his introduction of games to honor Caesar. Politically he was a significant and successful ruler who enjoyed considerable favor with Rome.

But if Herod was successful politically, his personal life was an unmitigated disaster. As Josephus succinctly (and mildly!) put it: "In revenge for his public prosperity, fortune visited Herod with troubles at home" (*BJ* 1.22.1). Troubles indeed! Herod had no fewer than ten wives and at least fifteen children, ten of whom were sons. His house was filled with plots, lies, counterplots, and machinations of all descriptions as each child tried to discredit his rivals and ingratiate himself to Herod. Such was Herod's temperament that he had no scruples against killing his own children, and he did so on several occasions. Thus it was said that it was safer to be Herod's pig than Herod's son.

Because of Herod's merciless and ruthless behavior, he

is often judged a villain, and perhaps rightly so. Still he managed to bring peace and prosperity to a significant part of the Roman Empire during a most turbulent time. That he was able to accomplish this in spite of his domestic troubles was no mean achievement.

The stories of the Herodians in the NT are not designed to add to a knowledge of history. Most of what is related concerning them is not in Josephus; and where the two sources coincide, there are differences. The NT accounts must be read in light of the evangelistic purposes of their authors.

The birth of Christ is described as having occurred during the time of Herod the Great (Matt 2:1-19; cf. Luke 1:5). The chronological reference may be valid, but the accounts of the visit of the Magi and the slaughter of the innocents are otherwise unattested and should be read as part of a theological and not historical introduction to the story of Jesus.

When Herod died, his kingdom was divided among three of his sons. Archelaus, who is mentioned only once in the NT (Matt 2:22), was made ethnarch of Judea but was replaced by a procurator in 6 C.E. Another son, PHILIP, was made tetrarch of the territory east and northeast of Galilee (cf. Luke 3:1). He plays no role in the Gospels, and little is said of him in Josephus except that he built the city of Caesarea Philippi (cf. Mark 8:27). Philip apparently married his niece Salome, who was the daughter of Herodias and Philip's half-brother Herod (Philip and Herod are apparently confused in Mark 6:17 and Matt 14:3).

The Herod about whom the most is related in the Gospels is ANTIPAS who was made tetrarch of Galilee. Herod Antipas was the full brother of Archelaus. He is condemned by JOHN THE BAPTIST (Mark 6:14-29; Matt 14:6-8) for marrying Herodias, the wife of his half-brother. Two other stories involving Antipas are found only in Luke. In one, Antipas is called a "fox" by Jesus (13:31-33), and in the other, Jesus is sent by Pilate to Antipas for interrogation (23:6-12).

Two other members of Herod's family are prominent in the NT. A grandson, Agrippa I (called Herod in the text; cf. Acts 12:1-23) managed, by 41 C.E., to gain control of as much territory as had his grandfather. Acts relates how Agrippa killed James and arrested Peter only to be killed himself by an angel.

Paul appeared before Agrippa's son, also named Agrippa (Acts 26:1-32). Little is known of this Agrippa after about 61 C.E. But with his death ca. 100, the Herodian dynasty came to an end.

See also AGRIPPA I AND II; ANTIPAS; CAESAREA; HERODIAN FORTRESSES; JOHN THE BAPTIST; MACCABEES; SAMARIA; TEMPLE/TEMPLES; TETRARCH; TIBERIAS.

Bibliography. F. V. Filson, *A New Testament History;* Josephus, *BJ;* A. Momigliano, "Herod of Judea," *CAH* 10:316-39; S. Perowne, *The Life and Times of Herod the Great.*

—JOHN C. H. LAUGHLIN

• **Herod Antipas.** *See* ANTIPAS

• **Herod the Great.** *See* HEROD

• **Herod, Palace of.** A fortress-palace was built by Herod the Great in Jerusalem just to the south of what is today known as the Jaffa Gate, extending north-south along the western city wall. On the northwest of the palace were three strongly fortified towers called Hippicus, Phasael, and Mariamne. Josephus described Herod's Palace as "A palace . . . which exceeds all my ability to describe it" (*BJ* 3.4.4).

Remains of Herod's Palace area are still visible at the Citadel to the right of the Jaffa Gate in old Jerusalem. The Tower of Phasael, popularly known as David's Tower, rests on bedrock and its Herodian ashlar masonry is preserved to a height of twenty meters. Recent excavations in the southwestern section of old Jerusalem, including the Citadel and the Armenian Garden, have uncovered remains of the foundation platform on which Herod's Palace was built.

See also HEROD; HERODIAN FORTRESSES; JERUSALEM.

—FREDERICK L. DOWNING

Herodium, a Herodian fortress at Masada.

• **Herodian Fortresses.** The dominion of Herod ("the Great") was characterized by a remarkable chain of fortresses, strategically located for control of the Jordan Valley. A total of either nine or ten such fortresses were either built or remodeled by Herod.

The fortress Alexandrium, the northernmost, was located on Mount Sartaba, some twenty-five mi. north of the northwestern tip of the Dead Sea and east of Nablus (ancient Shechem). About fifteen mi. to the south, on the summit of the traditional "Mount of Temptation" just above old Jericho, was the fortress Docus. Still further south, on the site of Herod's new Jericho, the fortresses Threx and Tauros lay alongside the Wadi Qilt. Some uncertainty surrounds these two in that the fortress Cypros is described as being in this same vicinity. One possibility is that Pompey destroyed Tauros and Herod rebuilt it, naming it after his mother Cypros. Still further south, approximately five or six mi. west-southwest from Qumran, and only slightly more southeast of Jerusalem, lay the fortress Hyrcania. Next came the fortress which bore Herod's own name (Herodium), situated seven or eight mi. south of Jerusalem and approximately four mi. southeast of Bethlehem. The last of the chain west of the Jordan, MASADA, was located just off the western shore of the Dead Sea above the springs of Engedi.

On the eastern side of the Jordan Valley were the fortresses Machaerus and another Herodium. The former, famous as the place where JOHN THE BAPTIST was imprisoned, lay just north of the rift where the Arnon flows into the Dead

Sea. The location of the latter is uncertain.

Most of these fortresses were originally built by Herod's Maccabean predecessors and rebuilt by Herod. Of the ten (or nine), Josephus mentions Alexandrium, the Herodium southeast of Bethlehem, and Hyrcania as being erected by Herod (*Ant* 16.2.1), but some scholars think Hyrcania was built by John Hyrcanus.

Regardless of how many fortresses Herod actually built, he left his mark upon each one. Common features stamp them as the work of a single school of military architecture. They were all of stone construction on top of a mountain and protected by a steep ascent almost impossible to scale. Each contained vast cisterns for storing rainwater. Aqueducts brought additional water from neighboring hills or, where available, springs. Each fort contained four towers of unequal height, with an artificial ditch separating the fort from the surrounding hill. These are the major features which the label "Herodian" denotes.

The superb military strategy in the construction of these fortresses is reflected by the fact that each fortress could signal at least one other fortress. No less than four (Herodium, Machaerus, Docus, and Cypros) could signal directly to Jerusalem.

See also HEROD; MASADA.

Bibliography. J. S. Minkin, *Herod;* S. Sandmel, *Herod.*

—JOE E. LUNCEFORD

• **Herodians.** [hi-roh'dee-uhns] In the NT, the Herodians are paired with the PHARISEES and depicted as antagonistic toward Jesus. The term occurs only in Matthew and Mark. Three times the references are undisputed (Mark 3:6; 12:13; and Matt 22:16). The Herodians may also be mentioned in Mark 8:15. Most Greek manuscripts read, " . . . leaven of Herod" but a few have, " . . . leaven of the Herodians."

The name implies a supportive stance toward HEROD the Great and/or his family. One obvious conclusion is that those described by this term would favor Roman rule. The only instance in which this faction is mentioned in the accounts of both Matthew and Mark is in the context of a challenge to Jesus by them (and the Pharisees) on the question of whether Roman taxes should be paid. For this reason, some have concluded that "Herodians" may be a negative epithet used for Jews who willingly paid Roman taxes.

The connection made in the Gospels between the Pharisees and the Herodians is an enigma. Generally, the Pharisees steadfastly avoided political entanglements of any kind. Could the evangelists be drawing attention to the broad range of opposition created by Jesus?

See also HEROD; PHARISEES.

—ROBERT O. BYRD

• **Herodium.** *See* HERODIAN FORTRESSES

• **Heshbon.** [hesh'bon] Biblical Heshbon in MOAB is almost certainly to be identified with modern *Tell Ḥesbân,* six miles southwest of Amman (PLATE 12). According to Num 21:21-30 and Josh 12:2, the incoming Israelites in the late thirteenth century B.C.E. conquered the Amorite King SIHON here in his capitol, then assigned the area to the tribe of Reuben and Gad (Josh 13:27; Num 32:37). The site was apparently refurbished by Mesha in the late ninth century B.C.E., as suggested by prophetic oracles against Moab. Although it is not mentioned in the NT, Heshbon (now Esbus) appears in Hellenistic and Roman sources; and it continues to be an important town into the Byzantine and Islamic periods.

Excavations were carried out in 1968–1978 by Andrews University under the direction of S. Horn, R. Boraas, L. T. Geraty, and others, partly in the hope of authenticating the biblical tradition of the Transjordanian conquest. No remains of the Late Bronze Age were found, however, and there was only scant occupation in the twelfth-eleventh centuries B.C.E., as witnessed by pockets of Iron I sherds on bedrock. Indeed, not before the late eighth century B.C.E. was Heshbon a significant Iron Age site. That leaves the biblical period of the Judges and the United Monarchy (cf. 1 Kgs 4:19), as well as the era of King Mesha of Moab in the ninth century B.C.E., without witness, at least on present evidence. However, the inter-disciplinary and ecological orientation of the exemplary project has shed much light on other periods.

The late eighth and early seventh centuries B.C.E. are represented by a buttressed wall following the scarped rock near the summit, possibly a defense wall. A large plaster open reservoir may be tentatively connected with the reference in the Song of Songs (7:4) to "pools in Heshbon, by the gate of Bath-rabbim."

The later seventh and sixth centuries B.C.E. have produced some of the best stratified examples yet found of the distinctively painted "Ammonite" pottery of Transjordan, as well as nearly a dozen ostraca in Ammonite and Aramaic, mostly economic dockets. The Iron II remains would provide a historical setting for the oracles against Moab in Isa 15:4; 16:8, 9; Jer 48:2ff., which mention Heshbon specifically.

There are scattered Persian period and early Hellenistic remains, then more substantial evidence from Late Hellenistic (ca. 198–63 B.C.E.), including a major defense wall on the summit which illuminates the tradition that Heshbon was ruled by Alexander Jannaeus (ca. 103–70 B.C.E.). The Early Roman period at Heshbon, now called "Esbus" and colonized by Herod, is particularly well represented. Substantially heavier occupation is attested by a large defensive wall with towers, an extensive plastered roadway and public plaza, and several nearby tombs (one with a rolling-stone door). The earthquake of 31 B.C.E. may have interrupted occupation for a time. The Late Roman period (ca. 135–324 C.E.) sees the construction of a large municipal building near the summit and rare coins of Elagabalus (218–222 C.E.). The heavy plastered roadway and plaza are built up further, perhaps in connection with Esbus' position on the Roman *via nova Traiana,* part of the frontier system known as the *Limes Arabicus* (ca. second through sixth centuries C. E.).

In the Byzantine era both the summit wall and the plastered roadway/plaza continued in use, as did the earlier tombs. The "North Church" on the summit is now constructed, reflecting the mention of the site in Eusebius. Esbus was, in fact, a Christian bishopric, and Bishop Gennadius attended the Council of Nicea in 325 C.E. The church continues in use with alterations and additions until the Persian conquest in 614 C.E., and possibly even into the early Islamic period.

The Umayyad period (661–750 C.E.) and 'Abāssid period (750–969 C.E.) are represented by scattered sherd material, followed by a gap. In the Ayyūbid/Mamluk period, however (1174–1516 C.E.), Heshbon has produced one of our best-stratified sequences of pottery. In addition to other domestic remains, there are tombs and a fine bath. Modern *Hesbân* is only a tiny village around the slopes of the mound.

Bibliography. R. S. Boraas and L. T. Geraty, eds., *Hesh-*

bon 1974 and *Heshbon 1976*; R. S. Boraas and S.H. Horn, eds., *Heshbon 1971* and *Heshbon 1973*; L. T. Geraty, "Heshbon: The First Casualty in the Israelite Quest for the Kingdom of God," H. B. Huffmon, F. A. Spina and A. R. W. Green, eds., *The Quest for the Kingdom of God*; J. A. Sauer, *Heshbon Pottery 1971* and "Transjordan in the Bronze and Iron Ages: A Critique of Glueck's Synthesis," *BASOR* 263 (1986): 1-26.

—WILLIAM G. DEVER

• **Hezekiah.** [hez'uh-*ki*"uh] (Hebrew "God strengthens.")

1. A very important king of JUDAH, 727–698 B.C.E., remembered as one of the few good kings in the OT. His reign is contrasted with the idolatry and apostasy of his father AHAZ and his son MANASSEH. Reflecting his importance, the biblical material about Hezekiah is extensive and includes 2 Kgs 18–20, 2 Chr 29–32, and Isa 36–39. However, there are numerous difficulties in interpreting and reconstructing this material.

One difficulty is the chronology. Though the total reign of twenty-nine years (2 Kgs 18:2) is widely accepted, there are two different dates that are current. The first date, 716/5–687, emphasizes the synchronism in 2 Kgs 18:13 when SENNACHERIB invades Judah in 701 and makes earlier synchronisms part of Hezekiah's coregency with his father Ahaz. The second date, 727–698, emphasizes the synchronism in 2 Kgs 18:10 which correlates the sixth year of Hezekiah with the ninth of HOSHEA and the fall of SAMARIA in 722/1. Furthermore, this higher chronology works back from the Babylonian capture of Jerusalem in 597 and does not extend Hezekiah's reign much beyond 700 because that would not allow sufficient time for Manasseh's reign, 697–642. No chronological certainty is possible, but here the second date of 727–698 will be followed.

The three main biblical passages referring to Hezekiah are significantly different. Isa 36–39 is quite similar to 2 Kgs 18–20 and seems to be derived from it. Both accounts emphasize Hezekiah's successful confrontation with Sennacherib, his illness and recovery, and the visit of the envoys from MERODACH-BALADAN. A brief mention of Hezekiah's reform, and the tribute he paid to Sennacherib appears in 2 Kings; Isaiah adds a song of thanksgiving after recovery from his illness. The account in 2 Chr 29–32 is quite different with only about a dozen verses that are strictly parallel to 2 Kgs 18–20. Here the emphasis is on Hezekiah's reform, which is extensively described. Much less attention is given to Sennacherib's invasion, 2 Chr 32:1–23, and only brief mention is made of Hezekiah's illness and the visit of envoys from Babylon.

When Hezekiah came to the throne, he inherited his father's vassalage to ASSYRIA. Assuming the earlier chronology, he ruled during the entire reign of SARGON II, 721–705, who campaigned in the area of Judah in 720, 716, and 713 to keep his vassals in line. At the same time Merodach-Baladan, a Chaldean rebel, had successfully revolted against Sargon and controlled Babylon from 721–710. Probably close to the time of the third campaign of Sargon, Merodach-Baladan's envoys from Babylon visited Hezekiah (2 Kgs 20:12-19). Hezekiah showed them everything. Undoubtedly, Assyria viewed this treatment of a rebel quite negatively. ISAIAH also condemned Hezekiah for granting these visitors such privileges and predicted a future exile to Babylon.

There are many other indications that Hezekiah was planning a revolt against Assyria. He strengthened the military (2 Chr 32:5–6), laid up provisions (2 Chr 32:28–29), fortified JERUSALEM (2 Chr 32:5), and built a tunnel to carry water from the Gihon Spring under the city to the western mount (cf. 2 Kgs 20:20). His religious reform may also date to this time though the biblical text is unspecific. It included removing high places (local sanctuaries), breaking the pillars, cutting down the ASHERAHS, and breaking into pieces the bronze serpent (Nehushtan) that MOSES had made (2 Kgs 18:4). Hezekiah also sent letters throughout EPHRAIM and MANASSEH in the north inviting them to celebrate the PASSOVER with the rest of the country (2 Chr 20:1ff.). It is obvious that religious reforms had political overtones in the sense that Hezekiah was attempting to revive nationalistic inclinations. This would inevitably lead to a revolt against the Assyrians (2 Kgs 18:8). The right time came after the death of Sargon II in 705 when Assyria was in turmoil with revolts in Babylonia and Anatolia as well as in Aram-Palestine. Sennacherib replaced Sargon in 705 and suppressed the rebellion of Merodach-Baladan in Babylon. In 701 he marched to Aram-Palestine down the Phoenician coast into Philistia. According to the Prism of Sennacherib, he states that he conquered forty-six walled cities under Hezekiah's control. While on his campaign he sent a diplomat to Jerusalem to get Hezekiah to surrender (2 Kgs 18:13-36). The diplomat used the most persuasive political propaganda he could to get Hezekiah and the people of Jerusalem to surrender. Undoubtedly, Sennacherib did not want to besiege the city of Jerusalem for three years as Assyrian forces had done to Samaria twenty years earlier. Sennacherib claims to have shut up Hezekiah as "a prisoner in Jerusalem, his royal residence, like a bird in a cage." Yet Hezekiah, with the support of Isaiah, would not surrender. Miraculously the angel of the Lord killed 185,000 Assyrian troops and Sennacherib withdrew. Though the size of the Assyrian army seems to be exaggerated, a dramatic deliverance of Jerusalem is likely on the basis of later history. By JEREMIAH's day the inhabitants of Jerusalem considered their city and its temple to be invincible (Jer 7, 26). The dramatic deliverance from Sennacherib is a likely origin for this attitude. Nevertheless, a dramatic deliverance was not enough to give Hezekiah independence. Both he and his son Manasseh continued to be vassals of Assyria since it was nearing the peak of its power after 700.

Probably before Sennacherib's invasion, Hezekiah became severely ill (2 Kgs 20:1-11). Isaiah predicted his death and instructed the king to prepare for death. Instead Hezekiah prayed and wept. The result was that God promised him a fifteen year extension of his life and the deliverance of Jerusalem from the Assyrians. Isaiah proceeded to heal him with a cake of figs placed on the boil, and gave Hezekiah a sign from the Lord that the shadow would go back ten steps.

Hezekiah's men are remembered for their preservation of the proverbs of SOLOMON (Prov 25:1). Hezekiah is also listed in the genealogy of JESUS (Matt 1:9–10).

2. An ancestor of ZEPHANIAH (Zeph 1:1) who could have been identical with King Hezekiah above.

3. An ancestor of some of the exiles who returned from Babylon with ZERUBBABEL (Ezra 2:16; Neh 7:21). Probably he is also the one who, with NEHEMIAH, set his seal on the covenant (Neh 10:17).

4. The KJV spelling of Hizkiah (1 Chr 3:23), a descendant of the royal family of Judah.

See also ISAIAH; PASSOVER; SENNACHERIB; SILOAM INSCRIPTION.

Bibliography. J. Bright, *A History of Israel*; R. B. Dillard, *2 Chronicles, WBC*; J. M. Miller and J. H. Hayes, *A History of Ancient Israel and Judah*; J. B. Pritchard, *ANET*; J. D. W. Watts, *Isaiah 34–66, WBC*.

—JAMES C. MOYER

• **Hezekiah's Tunnel.** *See* SILOAM INSCRIPTION

• **High Place.** A worship site or place of worship used by the Canaanites and the Israelites as well as other ancient Near Eastern peoples. The Hebrew word, "high place," had a semitic origin and literally meant "back" or "ridge." The usage of the term changed during the OT period. At first, "high place" referred to an open-air worship site located on a hill, mound, or an elevated surface. As worship or cultic activities became more institutionalized and associated with buildings, "high place" was used in reference to the worship center or SANCTUARY.

High places were associated especially with the Canaanites. The typical high place was located on a wooded hill or ridge and was equipped with a variety of installations including altars, incense altars, pillars, sacred groves or poles, corpses, graven IMAGES (cf. Exod 34:13; Lev 26:30; Num 33:52; Deut 12:2-3; Ezek 6:3-6). Canaanite high places were most likely equipped for rituals of worship for their gods including Baal, Ashtoreth, Asherah, and Anath.

On the one hand the Israelites were commanded to destroy the high places of the Canaanites (Num 33:52; Deut 12:2-3). On the other hand the Israelites worshiped at high places themselves, high places that would be destroyed if Israel was disobedient (Lev 26:30). In some instances Israel's high places were used for the worship of Yahweh (2 Chr 33:17), and in other instances they were used for the worship of the gods of Israel's neighbors.

High places are well documented in the history of Israel. Samuel offered sacrifices at a high place (1 Sam 9:12-14). The high place in this instance was located on a ridge or hill (1 Sam 9:11, 25). In addition to offering sacrifices, a variety of rituals were performed at the high place including musical processions such as those of the roving band of prophets at the high place at Gibeath-elohim (1 Sam 10:5). Gibeath-elohim and Ramah must have been the sites of major high places during the time of Samuel and Saul (1 Sam 9-10; 19:18-24). While many high places were in use during the reign of David and Solomon (1 Kgs 3:2), the major high place was located at GIBEON (1 Chr 16:39; 1 Kgs 3:3-4). The high place at Gibeon was perhaps the high place of the royal family prior to the building of the temple. It was the site at which the tabernacle and altar of burnt offering were located (1 Chr 21:29). Solomon built high places dedicated to the gods Chemosh, Molech (1 Kgs 11:5-8), Ashtoreth (2 Kgs 23:13), and perhaps others, gods of the wives he had received through marriage alliances with neighboring countries.

References to high places reflect their usage in both the northern and southern kingdoms. Jeroboam I built "houses on high places" and appointed a non-levitical priesthood for them (1 Kgs 12:31). According to the deuteronomic history, high places were built in every town (2 Kgs 17:9) and were centers of idolatry that resulted in the decline and fall of the Northern Kingdom (1 Kgs 17:7-18). Both Amos and Hosea denounced the high places in the North (Amos 7:9; Hos 4:13;10:8).

High places were no less present in the Southern Kingdom. During the reign of Rehoboam, high places and male cult prostitutes were prominent throughout Judah (1 Kgs 14:23-24). Other kings from Judah who either fostered or permitted worship at high places include Asa (1 Kgs 15:14), Jehosophat (1 Kgs 22:43), Jehoram (2 Chr 21:11), Jehoash (2 Kgs 12:3), Amaziah (2 Kgs 14:4), Uzziah (2 Kgs 15:4), Jotham (2 Kgs 15:35), Ahaz (2 Kgs 16:4), and Manasseh (2 Kgs 21:3). The reforms of Hezekiah and Josiah represent major attempts at removing them. While Hezekiah "removed the high places, and broke down the pillars and cut down the Asherah" (2 Kgs 18:4), his son Manasseh "rebuilt the high places" (2 Kgs 21:3). Josiah's reform was more thorough and extensive (2 Kgs 23:4-20). He not only removed the high places of Judah and Jerusalem (2 Kgs 23:5, 8, 9, 13) but also the high places that remained at Bethel (23:15), and Samaria (23:19-20). Like the earlier prophets, those who prophesied at the time of the fall of Judah denounced worship at the high places (Jer 7:31; Ezek 20:28-29).

Archaeological excavations have added a new dimension to the present day knowledge of "high places." While many of the earliest high places built on the upper part of a ridge or hill have not survived the centuries, several unique high places have been found including those at the biblical sites of Megiddo, Hazor and Samaria.

Bibliography. W. F. Albright, *Archaeology and the Religion of Israel*; Y. Yadin, *Hazor*.

—LAMOINE DEVRIES

• **High Priest.** In the Letter to the Hebrews we find a description of Israel's high priest, which must be characterized as a "glossy print": MOSES installed AARON as the high priest in the wilderness and from then on there was a high priest functioning as long as the nation lasted.

The scriptures themselves, however, present difficulties with this view: (1) The term itself *kōhēn haggādôl*) is only used four times in preexilic texts (Lev 21:10; Num 35:25-28; Josh 20:6) and Sabourin (143) suggests it "must have been introduced by later editors." Generally the term appears in postexilic literature: Haggai, Zechariah, Nehemiah. (2) There is no hint of a high priest functioning during the first centuries of Israel's history, certainly not at the time of the judges. It was a prophet-judge, SAMUEL, who clearly was the religious leader under King SAUL. DAVID and SOLOMON were not only kings, but also religious leaders (cf. Ps. 110:4). They sacrificed in the sanctuaries, and they appointed and dismissed priests.

It is clear, however, that as life became more complicated and the reasons for approaching the deity grew complex, the priests gained power as their skills became more in demand. They became numerous and better organized. However, their leader is only called "chief priest" (*kōhēn hārō'š*). During the royal period there are several hints at rivalry between the kings and the priests (2 Kgs 11; 2 Chr 26). Ezekiel's vision of the new Temple and its new priesthood shows that the priests gained power during the Exile. In the future they were to be closest to Yahweh and his Temple. The prince was only to serve as provider to the Temple and its functionaries (Ezek 44–48). The title "high priest," however, does not appear in his book. The tension between kings and priests is acute in the Books of Haggai and Zechariah. Zech 4 presents a vision of a lamp stand which is fed by two olive trees, and the prophet was told that these were "two anointed ones," apparently the king and the priest, who accordingly now were equal. There was a blossoming of royal hopes when Zerubbabel was governor. He was seen as the one to fulfill the messianic prophecies of old (Hag 2:21-22; Zech 6:12-13). But he disappeared and with him the last hopes of kingship. From then on the priests dominated the arena. It is likely that ideas from kingship influenced the new political arrangement. The high priest is the most important man in the nation, and his title from now on is "the high priest," (*hakōhēn haggādôl*).

In the second century B.C.E. the Jews gained their freedom under the leadership of a priestly family, the Maccabees. Their leaders took the title "high priest" but tragically were soon contaminated by the power of the office. The Qumran community was formed in protest against this priestly tyranny.

After the Romans conquered the region, the priests still held the power in the land. This is evidenced in the stories about Jesus, especially his crucifixion. One is obliged, however, to ask if the people would have been any better off without the supremacy of the high priests.

See also PRIESTS.

Bibliography. R. E. Clements, *God and Temple*; A. Cody, *A History of OT Priesthood*; E. O. James, *The Nature and Function of Priesthood*; H. J. Kraus, *Worship in Israel*; L. Sabourin, *Priesthood*; R. de Vaux, *Ancient Israel, Its Life and Institutions.*

—REIDAR B. BJORNARD

• **Higher Criticism.** *See* INTERPRETATION, HISTORY OF

• **Hilkiah.** [hil-kiʹuh] A Hebrew name attributed to several individuals in the OT, most or all of whom are of Levitical or priestly families. Evidence from recent ostraca discoveries suggests that the original form of the name was probably Hilkiyahu. The name means "Yahweh is my portion." The name appears thirty-three times in the OT and refers to some identifiable individuals: a descendant of Merari, a Levite (1 Chr 6:45); a second Merarite, a doorkeeper of the Tabernacle (1 Chr 26:11); father of Eliakim, one of King HEZEKIAH's officials (2 Kgs 18:18, 26, 37; Isa 22:20, 22); father of Gemariah, one of those who carried Jeremiah's letter to the exiles (Jer 29:3); JEREMIAH's father, a priest from ANATHOTH (Jer 1:1); the high priest charged by King JOSIAH to commence the temple repair that evoked Josiah's Reformation (2 Kgs 22–23; 2 Chr 34–35). The name appears several other times, primarily in genealogical passages. Some or all of these may refer to those listed above.

See also LEVI/LEVITES; PRIESTS.

Bibliography. J. H. Hayes and J. M. Miller, eds., *Israelite and Judean History.*

—BRUCE C. CRESSON

• **Hill Country.** In the OT and NT, several words refer to "hill" or "hills." No single term exists for "hill country." Thus the translation of these terms is largely determined by the context of the passages in which they occur. The biblical terms for "mount" or "mountain" are often translated as "hill" (compare the KJV and RSV of Gen 36:8, 9) and, especially in the poetic parts of the Bible, the terms for "hill" and "mountain" are used parallel to each other (cf. Ps 72:3 and Isa 30:17). Thus the site of the temple could be referred to as Mount ZION or the hill of the Lord (Pss 74:2; 15:1). In general, the hill country is that land which lies on either side of the central mountain ridge of the northern and southern biblical kingdoms.

In the north the hill country of Ephraim and Manasseh formed the core of the kingdom as did the hill country of Judah in the south. On the east there is a sharp descent into the Jordan Valley or the basin of the Dead Sea. In general the barren land on the east side of the southern hill country is referred to as wilderness. On the west the hill country is broken by valleys that carry major roads through the lowlands to the plain.

The major cities of biblical times tended to dominate the ridge line of both kingdoms (Mispah, BETHEL, and SHILOH in the north; JERUSALEM and HEBRON in the south).

In addition to the purely geographical references to the hills, the hills are often referred to as the site of corrupt worship. For Hoṣea, Jeremiah and Ezekiel, especially, the hills were the center of Israel's sin (Hos 4:13; Jer 2:20; Ezek 6:13). The sacred hill top sites may have been corrupt in the eyes of the prophets because they were outside Jerusalem and, thus, illegal, but it is more likely that these places were associated with one or more of the fertility religions associated with the baals.

—JOE O. LEWIS

• **Hinnom, Valley of.** [hinʹuhm] The Valley of Hinnom (Heb. *ge-hinnōm*) is a deep, narrow depression to the south and southwest of JERUSALEM (PLATES 24, 25). During OT times the valley marked part of the boundary between the tribes of Benjamin and Judah (Josh 15:8; 18:16), and during NT times it marked the immediate south and southwest limits of the expanded city. In Joshua (15:8; 18:16) and Nehemiah (11:30) the term is merely a place-name. Elsewhere in the OT it occurs with reference to a specific site in Hinnom, a place of child sacrifice in worship of the pagan deity Molech (2 Kgs 23:10; Jer 32:35).

Hinnom was the site of child sacrifice particularly during the reigns of Ahaz and Manasseh (2 Chr 28:3; 33:6) and during the time of Jeremiah (7:31-32; 19:2, 6; 32:35). Josiah abolished the rite by desecrating the site (2 Kgs 23:10), but the pagan practice was revived when his reform movement waned. Jeremiah cursed the site and declared that it would be known no longer as Hinnom but as the "valley of slaughter" where the "sons of Judah" had slaughtered their children and they themselves would be "slaughtered" for their apostasy. Jeremiah declared that Hinnom would be accursed as the place where corpses of slain idolaters would be discarded (7:32-33; 19:6-7, 11, 13). Hence, from the name of this accursed place of such profane associations (*ge-hinnōm*), there developed during the especially apocalyptic postexilic period a designation of the place/state of fiery destruction of the wicked—*Gehenna.*

The presence of Jewish and Christian tombs from the Roman period indicates that Hinnom later became a burial ground, and tradition cites it as the location of the "Field of Blood" (Matt 27:3-10; Acts 1:19) or "potter's field" (Matt 27:10). The reputable Jewish grammarian and biblical exegete David Kimhi (ca. 1160–1235) described the Valley of Hinnom as one of Jerusalem's garbage dumps where "unclean" corpses were discarded and where fires burned continuously. Kimḥi's description is discounted by some as lacking *conclusive* archaeological evidence, yet it certainly conforms to first-century allusions to *Hinnom* as a perpetually burning, maggot-infested pit of putrefaction. In sum, Hinnom was a well-known figure of abomination, judgment, and destruction (Jeremiah), and thus a ready metaphor for an eschatological place/state of punishment—*Gehenna.*

See also GEHENNA; HELL; JERUSALEM.

Bibliography. J. Jeremias, "γέεννα," *TDNT*;

J. Montgomery, "The Holy City and Gehenna," *JBL* 27 (1908): 24-47.

—EDD ROWELL

• **Historical Criticism.** *See* INTERPRETATION, HISTORY OF

• **History of Interpretation.** *See* INTERPRETATION, HISTORY OF

• **History Writing.** *See* KINGS, BOOKS OF FIRST AND SECOND; LITERATURE, BIBLE AS

• **Hittites.** The term "Hittite," which occurs in Akkadian, Egyptian, Ugaritic, and biblical Hebrew, refers to at least four distinct ethnic groups of the ancient Near East.

1. The original "Hattians" comprised part of the indigenous population of the central Anatolian plateau before ca. 2,000 B.C.E. We know these peoples, however, almost entirely from the stamp they left on their successors, the later "Hittites."

2. The rise of the Hittites proper to power in the second millennium B.C.E. began with the immigration of groups of Indo-Europeans from the north into central Anatolia sometime before 2,000 B.C.E. At first these non-semitic newcomers simply identified themselves with the city of Nesha and called their language *našili*. But as they came to dominate the area and to assimilate with the native Hattians, they established their capitol at former Hattuša (PLATE 1) and designated their kingdom as "Hittite." Throughout their hegemony (ca. seventeenth to thirteeth centuries B.C.E.) these Hittites continued to reflect in part the language, culture, and religion of their predecessors.

The Hittites were formerly known only from the mention of them in the Bible. Then the name turned up in the ninteenth century in Egyptian and cuneiform sources. The exact identity of these Hittites remained in dispute, however, until 1906, when German excavations under Hugo Winckler began at the site of ancient Hattuša, near modern Bogazköy, in central Turkey near Ankara. Thousands of CUNEIFORM tablets came to light the first season, some in Akkadian and immediately legible, many others in a new script and language. By 1915 a Czech Assyriologist, Hrozný, had succeeded in deciphering Hittite, and the new discipline of Hittitology was born.

The German excavations at Bogazköy have continued, interrupted only by the two world wars, and thus far more than forty volumes of Hittite texts have been published. The site itself boasts a vast lower and upper city, with towered city walls and multiple gates; a bridge across to a neighboring hilltop citadel; monumental palaces, administrative complexes, several temples, storerooms, and domestic installations.

The Hittite kingdom can be divided into the old Hittite period (ca. 1700–1400 B.C.E.), and the Hittite Empire (ca. 1400–1190 B.C.E.). Apparently the first king of the former was Labarna, but we have no texts until the time of Hattšili I (ca. 1650–1620 B.C.E.), who extended Hittite power well into Syria. Under his grandson Muršili, the Hittites took Aleppo and even sacked Babylon ca. 1595 B.C.E., thus bringing the dynasty of Hammurabi to an end. Telepinu (ca. 1525–1500 B.C.E.) consolidated power by entering into treaty relations with the Hurrians, another Indo-European people who had now risen to power in upper Mesopotamia and Syria and who would continue as powerful rivals of the Hittites during their own zenith under Mitannian kings in the fourteenth century B.C.E.

After a brief decline, the Hittite Empire witnessed a revival, especially under Šuppiluliuma I (ca. 1380–1346 B.C.E.), who defeated the Mitannian king Tušratta, recaptured Aleppo, and reorganized Syria under vassal kings at Aleppo, Carchemish, Ugarit, and elsewhere. There was little challenge to Hittite expansion southward until ca. 1300 B.C.E., when Ramses II met Muwatalli near Qadesh on the Orontes in a standoff battle. The aftermath was a treaty that we have recorded in two extant versions, one Hittite and one Egyptian, each claiming a decisive victory. The last Hittite military ventures were battles fought against the invading SEA PEOPLES off the coast of Cyprus ca. 1200 B.C.E. After that, the Hittite kingdom collapsed, coinciding with the end of the Bronze Age everywhere in the ancient Near East.

3. The old area of Hittite control in the southeast, in Syria, survived, and in the early Iron Age it became the arena of the Aramaean peoples and the petty kingdoms they established as they became sedentary. Hittite influence was still sufficiently strong, however, that it is seen in the Aramaic language and culture. This neo-Hittite entity, as it is called, is particularly evident in the art and architecture of Iron Age north Syria, at sites like Karatepe, Sam'al, Carchemish, Tell Halaf, Aleppo, Tell Der'a, and others that are now relatively well known archaeologically. Here Syrian kings executed monumental inscriptions in a developed form of the old, alternate Hittite hieroglyphic script. And down to the mid-first millennium B.C.E., they still bore names resembling those of the former Hittite kings of Hattuša.

4. The latest mention of Hittites is found exclusively in the Hebrew Bible. These references are not, of course, to the Hittites of Anatolia during the second millennium B.C.E. (although a memory of them, like the Amorites, may lie behind the biblical tradition; cf. Ezek 10:3). The biblical Hittites are, rather, a late and very minor element in the ethnic mix of Iron Age Canaan. They were probably assimilated foreigners who traced their ancestry back to the early Iron Age neo-Hittite sphere in north Syria, not entirely fancifully. Thus the Bible refers to Syria as the land of the Hittites and speaks of Hittite kings there (2 Kgs 7:6; 2 Chr 1:17; e.g.,). But all the Hittites specifically mentioned as living among the Israelites, in fact, bear good semitic names, such as Ephron, Zohar, Judith, Beeri, Basemath, Elon, Adah, Ahimelech, and the hapless Uriah. It has been noted that the Assyrian annals of Sargon II, in the eighth century B.C.E., refer to a "land of Hatti" in southern Palestine, and to the citizens of the Philistine city of Ashdod as "Hittites." These references, however, are not precise enough to enable us to recognize a distinct, separate ethnic group in these latest Hittites.

The classic era of Hittite culture in the second millennium B.C.E. may have made a lasting impact on ancient Israel in more than one way. A few Hittite words closely resemble Hebrew, such as those for wine, oak, and others; but these may simply go back to long-distant common linguistic prototypes. The numerous deities of the Hittite pantheon are scarcely attested directly anywhere in the Hebrew Bible. But recently it has been suggested that the formula "El, Maker of (Heaven and) earth" (*el . . . qoneh . . . arets*) may reflect "Kunirtsu," a Hittite deity (cf. Gen 14:19).

A much more direct legacy may be detected in the well-known Hittite suzerainty treaties, which many recent scholars have seen as providing the cultural background, if not the direct prototypes, of much of the covenant material in the Hebrew Bible. V. Korošec, G. Mendenhall, K. Baltzer, D. J. McCarthy, and others have drawn parallels between the basic categories of these Hittite treaties and such biblical formulae as the Decalogue and the Holiness Code, even the fundamental framework of the book of Deuteronomy. Common features include: (1) the suzerain's titulature; (2) the historical background; (3) the stipulations of the treaty; (4) a clause requiring the preservation, public display, and periodical rereading of the covenant; (5) a list of divine witnesses; (6) curses for violating the covenant and blessings for obeying the stipulations.

Bibliography. O.R. Gurney, *The Hittites;* H. A. Hoffner, "The Hittites and Hurrians," *Peoples of Old Testament Times,* ed. D. J. Wiseman; D. McCarthy, *Treaty and Covenant.*

—WILLIAM G. DEVER

• **Holiness Code.** *See* LAW IN THE OLD TESTAMENT

• **Holiness in the New Testament.** Holiness is a term that refers to the essential quality of God or the divine. God is "holy" and so are people, institutions, actions, and things closely associated with God.

The NT writers affirm the notion of holiness found in the OT although the holiness of the physical Temple in Jerusalem is somewhat deemphasized. Rather the concept of the "holy" Temple is restated metaphorically (1 Cor 3:17; 6:19). The NT uses holiness in specific ways: (1) God is addressed by Jesus as holy Father (John 17:11); (2) Jesus is called holy on numerous occasions, a notable one being in Mark where the unclean spirit "confesses" Jesus to be the Holy One of God (Mark 1:24). In the birth narrative of Luke, the angel who announces Jesus' birth indicates that the child will be a "holy" child (1:35). In the post-resurrection era, Jesus' disciples refer to him as "holy" (Acts 3:14; 4:27, 30); (3) Those who comprise the Christian community are themselves called "the holy ones" by Paul (Rom 1:7; 1 Cor 1:2). The Christian community is called a "holy nation" (1 Pet 2:9) and holiness is required of its members because God is holy (1 Pet 1:16); (4) The HOLY SPIRIT comes upon those who believe in Jesus Christ.

See also HOLY SPIRIT; PURITY; SAINT/SAINTS; SANCTIFICATION.

—WATSON E. MILLS

• **Holiness in the Old Testament.** The Hebrew word translated "holiness" is *qōdeš* and connotes separateness or distance. The word *qdš* occurs in several ancient semitic languages with apparently the most elemental meaning being that of "separateness." The etymology of the word is uncertain, but at its earliest stage it already had come to have its full meaning in a religious context. Normally in ancient semitic languages, including biblical Hebrew, a noun derives its meaning from its underlying verb. The reverse may be true for *qōdeš*. The verb *qādaš* simply means "to be *qādôš* [holy]." So the term *qōdeš* has to do with a feeling, a dynamic state, separated from action; a feeling of separateness, differentness, and remoteness. In the ancient world, as in the OT, the idea of morality was not at all involved. By means of this word, dealings are made with the primitive, primary, and basic reactions of humanity to the mystery over against which all of human life is set.

In the OT some thing or some place is holy because it is related to God. Only in relation to the divine is it holy, meaning that it has been set apart for GOD. The Bread of the Presence was holy bread (1 Sam 21:6). The altar for sacrifice was holy (Exod 29:37), as were its utensils (Exod 30:28-29). Other places may be set apart as sacred: Sinai (Exod 19:23); the tabernacle with its furniture (Exod 40:9); and the Sheep Gate of NEHEMIAH's Jerusalem (Neh 3:1). Priests were holy (Exod 29:1), as were their vestments (Exod 28:4). The first-born of human being and of animal was to be consecrated to the Lord (Exod 13:1-2). Eleazar was consecrated to care for the ARK as it began its twenty year stay in the house of his father Abinadab (1 Sam 7:1). In short, a long list of persons, things, and places could be listed that were holy, or consecrated to the Lord in one capacity or another.

The term *qādēš* is used in the OT of temple-prostitutes, male and female, forbidden in Israelite law: "There shall be no cult prostitute of the sons of Israel" (Deut 23:17). Nonetheless, in the administration of King REHOBOAM there were "male cult prostitutes in the land" (1 Kgs 15:12; 22:46). JEHOSHAPHAT removed them (1 Kgs 22:46), as did the later King Josiah (2 Kgs 23:7). HOSEA referred to female cult prostitutes in eighth-century B.C.E. Israel (Hos 4:14). In such cases the term "holy one(s)," male or female, in the OT can be used, obviously not in the sense of moral or acceptable, but as "separated to" even beyond the OT approval.

All sacredness comes from God, for God and God alone occupies and sustains the realm of otherness. Holiness in this sense is not one divine attribute, even the most significant; in the most technical sense, this is the only pure quality of God. God acts out of such attributes as love, righteousness, etc., but only one attribute is indicative of the nature of God. When the Lord swears by God's own holiness (Amos 4:2) the oath rests upon God's essence. The Holy is insulated from the ordinary. MOSES was admonished, "Do not come near; put off your shoes from your feet, for the place on which you are standing is holy ground" (Exod 3:5). Consequently, Mount Sinai, while awaiting the divine visit, cannot be touched upon penalty of death (Exod 19:12).

Such also would be the fate of those touching holy vessels or the altar (Num 18:3), and the Ark of the Covenant (1 Sam 6:19; 2 Sam 6:7). "Mortals shall not see me [God] and live" (Exod 33:20). This unbridgeable gulf (sometimes dangerous) between the human and the divine is clearly stated in Hos 11:9, "I am God and not man, the Holy One in your midst."

The word "holy" is often directly related to the character and name of God. The seraphim of Isa 6 chant in the Temple of the enthroned and elevated Lord, "Holy, holy, holy is the Lord of hosts" (v. 3). The prophet of the Exile characteristically labeled God "the Holy One of Israel" (e.g., Isa 41:14, 16, 20; 43:3, 14, 15). This means that "besides me there is no god" (Isa 44:6). Consequently the question and answer, "Is there a God besides me? There is no rock; I know not any" (Isa 44:8). Numerous other times the OT knows the Lord as "Holy One" (e.g., Jer 50:29; 51:5). Thus one understands why that which is holy is always associated with God.

The opposite to *qādôš* is not evil, but *ḥōl* "common": "you are to distinguish between the holy (*qōdeš*) and the common (*ḥōl*)" (Lev 10:10). The same contrast between the words occurs in 1 Sam 21:5. Ezekiel chastens the priests for having "made no distinction between the holy and the common" (22:26); the restored temple in Ezekiel's vision "had a wall around it . . . to make a separation between the holy and the common" (42:20); the priesthood of this new Temple is to "teach my people the difference between the holy and the common" (44:23); the land of Israel will be divided between a "holy" use and an "ordinary" use

(48:15).

Holiness in the OT points to the extraordinary, the uncommon, indeed the unique when referring to God. Therefore, the name of the Lord must not be taken "in emptiness" (Exod 20:7), and everything and every being associated with the divine is of extreme importance. God is that *mysterium tremendum* (Otto) whose personal name was not to be pronounced, but whose character of otherness always stood over against the common ways of humanity.

See also GOD.

Bibliography. E. Jacob, *Theology of the Old Testament;* R. Otto, *The Idea of the Holy;* N. Snaith, *The Distinctive Ideas of Old Testament*.

—KAREN RANDOLPH JOINES

• **Holy Ghost.** *See* HOLY SPIRIT

• **Holy Orders.** *See* ORDAIN/ORDINATION IN THE NEW TESTAMENT

• **Holy Sepulchre.** *See* CALVARY; CHURCH OF THE HOLY SEPULCHRE

• **Holy Spirit.** *The Old Testament.* Although pervasive in the NT, the term "Holy Spirit" appears only three times in the OT (Ps 51:11; Isa 63:10, 11). This term brings together two OT ideas which originally were independent of one another, "holiness" and "spirit." The two ideas were not only distinct but pointed in opposite directions. Holiness pointed to God's otherness and separation from all else, and spirit pointed to God's dynamic action in relation to his created world. Thus initially, holiness implied the transcendence of God, and the Spirit of God implied his immanence. Only as each idea developed in the OT were they eventually brought together in the term "Holy Spirit."

The holy as first perceived was something separated or withdrawn from ordinary life. The holiness of God was something mysterious, powerful, awesome, withdrawn, and not directly approachable. From the idea of the holiness of God came that of holy places, times, rites, offerings, and persons qualified to perform holy rites and make holy offerings to a holy God. This idea of holiness originally had no moral or ethical reference, but these ideas emerged and became emphatic in the prophets (e.g., Amos 2:7; Isa 6:1-5; Hab 1:12f.; 3:3; Hos 11:8-12).

Possibly the earliest reference in the OT to Yahweh as the holy God appears in the story of the Ark of the Covenant, where God slew seventy men because they "looked into the ark of the Lord [Yahweh]" (1 Sam 6:19). The question was posed, "Who is able to stand before the Lord, this holy God?" (v. 20). In this perception of God as holy, he is complete otherness and unapproachable in his majesty and power.

With this idea of holiness, God may be approached only through holy rites, with holy offerings at holy places (shrines, altars, temples), at holy times (seasons, days, hours), by holy men (cultic priests, male only). The architecture of the Temple in Jerusalem reflected this perception of holiness, with its Holy of Holies representing the presence of God, to be entered by the high priest alone, once a year with the ATONEMENT offering. A graduated sense of holiness was likewise reflected in the divisions of the Temple: outer court open to gentiles and animals, the court for Jewish women, the court for Jewish men, the Holy Place for Jewish priests, and finally the curtained-off Holy of Holies (cf. Matt 27:51).

The idea of spirit had its own independent development in the OT. The Hebrew word for spirit stood for wind or breath and then for spirit within God or human beings, and even in "the living creatures" (Ezek 1:20f.; 10:17). The word spirit appears over 370 times in the OT, and "the Spirit of God" or "Spirit of the Lord" is pervasive. In OT usage, the Spirit of God may imply his presence, "Whither shall I go from the Spirit? Or whither shall I flee from thy presence?" (Ps 139:7), or his dynamic action (Gen 6:3; Judg 14:6, 19; Joel 2:28f.). In early usage it was restrictively the dynamic power of God, but the term came to serve also the idea of God's revelatory and redemptive activity, as implied in "Not by might, nor by power, but by my Spirit, says the Lord of hosts" (Zech 4:6). The more comprehensive work of the Spirit is seen in Isa 11:2-3, "And the Spirit of the Lord shall rest upon him, the spirit of wisdom and understanding, the spirit of counsel and might, the spirit of knowledge and the fear of the Lord." The Spirit of God is the source of human life in its physical, intellectual, and moral aspects (e.g., Job 32:8; 33:4; 34:14ff.; Ps 104:30; Isa 11:2; Zech 4:6).

In the OT, "the Spirit of God" does not imply a person separate from God. In Ps 139:7, Spirit is a synonym for God (cf. Isa 31:3). In Gen 1:1ff., there is an interchange between "God" and "the Spirit of God": "In the beginning God created the heavens and the earth . . . and the Spirit of God was moving over the face of the waters . . . And God said, 'Let there be light!' . . . " The Spirit of God is God acting in the created world. The "Spirit of God," "his Spirit," "thy Spirit," and "Holy Spirit" are all references to God himself, with no implication of plurality or division. Such usage does not undercut monotheism, foundational to OT theology: "Hear, O Israel: The Lord our God is one Lord" (Deut 6:4). The Holy Spirit is not a separate person within deity.

Significantly, in the three occurrences of "Holy Spirit" in the OT, the concern is for moral behavior and not separation. This seemingly appears in Isa 63:10, "But they rebelled and grieved his holy Spirit." Ps 51 is explicit, concerned throughout with cleansing from sin and renewal of "a new and right spirit within" along with the prayer, "Cast me not away from thy presence, and take not thy holy Spirit from me" (v. 11).

Both in direct linkage with God and in strong moral reference, this OT usage of Holy Spirit anticipates the more pervasive NT usage. Thus two originally independent ideas, holiness as the otherness and separation of God from ordinary life (transcendence) and spirit as God's action in his world (immanence), are brought together. The ultimate expression of the creative tension between God's transcendence and immanence appears in Jesus Christ, "the Word became flesh" (John 1:1, 14).

The New Testament. The term "the Holy Spirit" appears almost 100 times in the NT, and the idea is even more prevalent through interchanging terms: the Spirit, the Spirit of God, the Spirit of the Lord, the Spirit of Christ, the Spirit of JESUS, and the Holy Spirit. In English, Holy Ghost and Holy Spirit render the same Greek term. The term Holy Spirit appears throughout the NT. It is most prominent in the Lucan writings, thirteen times in his Gospel and forty-three times in Acts. (When all terms for "the Spirit" are considered, the Lucan emphasis is less distinctive.)

In the NT, the Holy Spirit represents the presence of God, active and powerful in revealing, convicting of sin, judging, guiding, empowering, comforting, enlightening, teaching, restraining, and otherwise. Every step in the Christian life may be attributed to the work of the Holy

Spirit, from conversion (John 3:6) to such maturity as reflects "the fruit of the Spirit" (Gal 5:22).

The Holy Spirit is personal in the NT, but not a person separate from God. The oneness of God is as firm in the NT as in the OT. Jesus himself affirmed the oneness of God, building the love commandment upon Deut 6:4 (Mark 12:29f.). The oneness of God is explicit in Paul and other NT writers (Rom 3:30; 1 Cor 8:6; Gal 3:20; Eph 4:6; 1 Tim 1:17; Jas 2:19; Jude 25; John 17:3). The Holy Spirit is not a third God nor one-third of God. The Holy Spirit is God himself, present and active within his world. Significantly, "Spirit of God," "Spirit of Christ," and "Christ" are interchanged in Rom 8:9-11.

The coming of the Holy Spirit upon the disciples on the day of Pentecost is pivotal in Acts, and this is to be given its full significance for the intention of Acts: the disciples spoke in tongues, in such a way that each person understood in that one's native language; about 3,000 persons were saved; the church was united in FELLOWSHIP; they were moved to generosity in giving to the poor; and they were fearless in the face of opposition (Acts 2–4). Breaking through the language barrier on the day of Pentecost foreshadowed the crossing of greater barriers separating Jews from non-Jews. Luke shows the overcoming of such barriers to be the work of the Holy Spirit. Tongues at Corinth later were the opposite: unintelligible to all but the initiated, divisive within the church, and repelling outsiders (1 Cor 12–14).

The Holy Spirit did not first come at Pentecost. The Holy Spirit is prominent in the Gospel of Luke, characterizing the piety of some devout Jews before the birth of Jesus (Luke 1–2). John the Baptist was filled with the Holy Spirit while yet in his mother's womb (1:15). The Holy Spirit came upon the virgin Mary (1:35). Elizabeth was filled with the Holy Spirit (1:41) as was Zechariah (1:67). The Holy Spirit was upon Simeon, and he came "in the Spirit" into the Temple (2:25-27). The Holy Spirit came upon Jesus at his baptism (Mark 1:10; and par.). Jesus gave assurance that the heavenly Father will "give the Holy Spirit to those who ask him" (Luke 11:13), with no implication that the gift was not immediately available or dependent upon BAPTISM or laying on of apostles' hands. Thus, both OT and NT witness to the presence of the Holy Spirit before Pentecost. The new at Pentecost was the completed work of Jesus, culminating in his death and resurrection. This was the mighty plus with which now the Holy Spirit continued the work of God begun in creation (Gen 1:1f.).

"Baptized with the Holy Spirit" (Acts 1:5), for the Holy Spirit to "come upon" someone (Acts 1:8), and to be "filled with the Holy Spirit" (Acts 2:4) are interchangeable. These are stylistic differences, not theological distinctions. Luke employs the identical terms for Elizabeth, Zechariah, and Simeon as for the disciples at Pentecost. No single pattern appears in the NT as to the sequence of baptism, laying on of hands, or the presence of apostles for the coming of the Holy Spirit upon a person. The Holy Spirit comes upon anyone with the faith to ask (Luke 11:13).

In the Gospel of John, the Holy Spirit is known also as the Paraclete, one called alongside as comforter or counselor (14:16). He is also "the Spirit of truth" (14:17; 15:26; 16:13), reminding Jesus' followers of the things Jesus had spoken (14:26), bearing witness to Christ (15:26), and guiding Jesus' disciples in further truth (16:13). The Holy Spirit convicts the world of sin, righteousness, and judgment (16:8-11). He is the spirit of truth, opposite to the spirit of error (1 John 4:6). Essentially, the Holy Spirit is the continuing divine presence which became incarnate in Jesus Christ. Thus, the followers of Jesus are not left orphans by the physical withdrawal of Christ. Before his ascension, Jesus promised: "I will not leave you desolate; I will come to you" (John 14:18). The Holy Spirit is the continuing divine presence, known in Jesus as one who could be physically seen, heard, and touched (1 John 1:1).

The presence of the Holy Spirit in a human life is not characteristically evidenced in some exotic way, like speaking in tongues, but in inner qualities of character and outward ministry. The fruit of the Spirit includes love, joy, peace, patience, kindness, goodness, faith, gentleness, and self-control (Gal 5:22). Where the Spirit is there is freedom (2 Cor 3:17), love (Rom 5:5), peace and joy (14:17), hope, joy, and peace (15:13). The work of the Spirit is known in the fellowship of the church (2 Cor 13:14). It is by the Spirit that we know the deep things of God (1 Cor 2:10-13). In scripture, those who "spoke from God" are ones "moved by the Holy Spirit" (2 Pet 1:20ff.). Being "filled with the Spirit" is evidenced not in self-serving ways but in ministry to others. When filled with the Holy Spirit, Zechariah preached (Luke 1:67). Filled with the Holy Spirit, Barnabas sold a field and gave the money to care for the poor (Acts 4:36ff.; 11:24). Stephen, "full of faith and of the Holy Spirit" (Acts 6:5), gave his life for his witness to Christ. Empowered by the Holy Spirit, Jesus' followers are to be his witnesses to the end of the earth (Acts 1:8). With the Spirit upon Jesus, he proclaimed his vocation in terms of ministry to human need at every level (Luke 4:18ff.), inclusive of persons as far away as a Sidonian widow (4:26) and a Syrian leper (4:27).

See also BAPTISM; BAPTISM OF FIRE; CREATION; FELLOWSHIP; FLESH AND SPIRIT; GOD; HOLINESS IN THE NEW TESTAMENT; HOLINESS IN THE OLD TESTAMENT; INCARNATION; JESUS; REVELATION, CONCEPT OF; SANCTIFICATION; TONGUES; TRINITY.

Bibliography. C. K. Barrett, *The Holy Spirit and the Gospel Tradition;* W. Eichrodt, *Theology of the Old Testament;* R. Otto, *The Idea of the Holy*; H. W. Robinson, *The Christian Experience of the Holy Spirit;* N. H. Snaith, *The Doctrine of the Holy Spirit*; F. Stagg, *The Holy Spirit Today*.

—FRANK STAGG

• **Holy War.** Although the technical term, holy war, is not used in the OT, there are clear-cut guidelines that indicate how the "wars of the Lord" (Num 31:14; 1 Sam 18:17; 25:28) were to be fought. Yahweh is declared to be a "man of war" (Exod 15:3) who does the fighting for Israel (Deut 20:4), because the battle itself belongs to the Lord (1 Sam 17:47). In addition, the title LORD OF HOSTS (i.e., of armies) is used more than 200 times in the OT to express God's ultimate power and authority.

In actual practice, Israel was supposed to allow potential enemies outside the promised land a chance to negotiate a treaty (Deut 20:10-18), while offering no quarter whatsoever to their predecessors in the promised land itself (Deut 7:16). This was extremely pragmatic in that Israel's primary objective was to occupy and settle the land of God's promise with no risk of any residual heathen contamination.

In order for a conflict to be considered "holy," it needed to meet several criteria. First, there needed to be assurance that God had ordained the battle (Num 31:3; Josh 6:2; 8:1; Judg 7:7). Second, the warriors who would participate in the battle had to be ceremonially CLEAN (Num 31:19-24;

1 Sam 21:4; 2 Sam 11:11). Third, the military leaders needed to possess a special gift of God's presence, usually referenced with " . . . and the SPIRIT of the Lord came upon . . . " that leader (Judg 6:34; 11:29). Fourth, the use of the ARK as a symbol of God's presence in battle (Josh 6:4, 12; 1 Sam 4:4) and references to the Lord's delivering Israel's enemies into their hands (Judg 3:28; 7:15; 1 Sam 7:8) work together to suggest the theological emphasis of holy war (i.e., God fulfilling the promise to give Israel a land through His mighty acts). Indeed, the emphasis on the miraculous that appears in the accounts and the historical hints about small forces, coupled with notes on the use of ruse and surprise, would suggest that the Israelites' presence in battle was secondary. They were, evidently, present primarily to actualize the promise by fighting alongside the divine warrior. The celebrative nature of holy war with its ritual songs and shouts also emphasizes the cultic aspects of the experience.

Finally, there are strict instructions concerning the BAN (*ḥerem*). The root verb, *ḥāram,* carried the idea of dedication, separation, and prohibition. This idea corresponded theologically to the Israelites' perception that God's HOLINESS was such that the common (unclean) neither could nor should be allowed in the divine presence. The "consecration" of the spoil to the Lord, whether it involved people, animals, or possessions, demonstrated that holy war was not a partial procedure for Israel. The people were thorough and made certain that God's enemies were annihilated, along with any evidence of their worship of false gods. To separate the chosen people further from the contagion of their enemy, the warriors had to remain outside the main camp of Israel for the typical seven day purification period in order to cleanse themselves, their weapons, their clothing and their tools (Num 31:16-24). The ban's restrictions against keeping the spoils of war, as well as its ritual demand for purification, puts the aggressive acts of war into the category of SACRIFICE. Israel had to relinquish its claims on the spoil in order to participate in the peace and prosperity to come as a result of the ritual obedience implied in both participating in battle and obeying the proscriptions of the ban.

Once the land of promise had actually been conquered and the monarchy was well established, the ideals and traditions of holy war were superficially followed, but warfare more and more became an instrument of national policy wielded by the king. As the monarchy divided and the religious dimension to Israel's warfare was lost, the Deuteronomic movement began to idealize holy war as an extremely important symbol of trust in God's sufficiency. The eighth century PROPHETS seized on this theological point in order to preach against dependence on military might or political acumen (Hos 7:11; Isa 31:1). Now, the prophets indicated, the very contamination from other nations that holy war was designed to protect Israel from (Josh 23:12-13) had become their lifestyle. Hence, God would treat Israel itself as one of the nations and would allow the nations to make war against it (Amos 3:11-12; Hos 10:3-10).

In the NT, the concept of holy war has been spiritualized into an eschatological struggle between the CHURCH, as it seeks to actualize the ultimate victory of Christ over SATAN, and the forces of evil (1 Cor 10:3-4; Eph 6:12; 1 Tim 1:18-19). As with ancient Israel, God's promises of ultimate victory and God's marvelous rewards are still available to obedient soldiers. However, the battle is no longer physical. It now takes place on a more essential level.

See also BAN; HOLINESS IN THE OLD TESTAMENT; THEOLOGY OF THE OLD TESTAMENT.

Bibliography. J. Bright, *The Authority of the Old Testament*; P. C. Craigie, *The Problem of War in the Old Testament*; P. D. Miller, *The Divine Warrior in Early Israel*; L. E. Toombs, "War, Ideas of," *IDB*; R. de Vaux, *Ancient Israel*.

—JOHNNY L. WILSON

• **Holy Week.** *See* PASSION NARRATIVE

• **Homicide.** *See* MURDER

• **Homosexuality in the Bible.** Biblical imagery has been an enduring part of the anti-homosexual polemic of both church and society in the western world. Numerous laws and court decisions through the centuries have cited biblical precedent as an authority in actions directed against homosexual activity on the assumption that the biblical tradition speaks forcefully and unequivocally against such activity.

In reality, the biblical record on this issue is subject to more than one interpretation. There are only a few specific references to homosexual activity, and their meaning and relevance for issues raised in the modern world are not agreed upon by all.

Homosexuality in the Old Testament. (1) Lev 18:22 and 20:13, from the sixth century B.C.E. priestly Holiness Code (Lev 17–26), are the only specific condemnations of homosexual acts in the OT. The Holiness Code forbids acts that are "abominations" (*tô'ēbâ*), that is, ritual uncleanness or sins associated with idolatrous gentiles (cf. 2 Kgs 16:3; Isa 44:19). The reference to homosexual acts may, therefore, be regarded as a reference to otherwise unknown sexual acts associated with pagan shrines.

(2) The KJV used the word "sodomites"—usually regarded as equivalent to homosexuals—in Deut 23:17-18, 1 Kgs 14:24, 15:12, 22:46 and 2 Kgs 23:7. There is, however, no justification for such a translation. The term in question, *qādēš,* simply means a male cultic figure, probably a prostitute, whose functions parallel the female cultic figures also mentioned in the texts. There is no indication of homosexual activity in the texts.

(3) The Sodom story in Gen 19:1-26 (cf. Jud 19–21) has been interpreted as referring to homosexual acts. Derrick S. Bailey and others have argued that the demand by the men of Sodom to "know" Lot's guests had no inherent sexual connotation. Most commentators disagree, citing the substitute offer of Lot's daughters as having clear sexual implications. If homosexual acts were intended, however, they were clearly of a certain type—i.e., same sex rape which was intended to show the dominance of the men of Sodom over these strangers. (A similar story appears in the Egyptian myth, "The Contending of Horus and Seth," where Seth dominated Horus by raping him.) OT references to the moral indignation felt toward Sodom—Ezek 16:49-50, Isa 1:10, 3:9, Jer 23:14, Wis 10:8, 19:4, Sir 16:8—refer to moral and social corruption, cynical selfishness, and lack of justice in Sodom, but make no reference to sexual sins of any sort. It is only in the first century C.E. (Philo and Josephus), when Jews were coming into contact with the homosexual practices accepted in the Hellenistic world, that the Sodom story was interpreted in terms of sexual sins. These sexual references were not, however, necessarily homosexual. Sodom's sin is described as "licentiousness" and "lust of defiling passion" in 2 Pet 2:4-10, while Jude 6-7 refers to their indulging in "strange flesh" (as in the

Book of Jubilees, most likely a reference to the potential sexual relationship between humans and angels).

Homosexuality in the New Testament. NT references to homosexuality came at a time when even Hellenistic writers (e.g., Seneca and Plutarch) were increasingly critical of the exploitation and self-indulgence of homosexual acts directed against slaves and young boys.

(1) 1 Cor 6:9-10 (cf. 1 Tim 1:10) are often regarded as referring to homosexual acts, but in fact the exact nature of what is condemned is not clear. In 1 Cor 6:9-10 two terms are used. *Malakoi* (μαλακοί) has as a basic meaning "soft" or "weak," and there is no compelling reason to translate the term as "effeminate," which is a euphemism referring to the subordinate partner in a homosexual relationship. While not a technical term for pederasty (the love, including sexual love, of young boys), *malakoi* is occasionally used in the first century C.E. to describe people involved in pederastic practices. "Thus the use of *malakos* would almost certainly conjure up images of the effeminate call-boy, if the context otherwise suggested some form of pederasty" (Scroggs, 65). *Arsenokoitai* (ἀρσενοκοῖται) is a combination of words meaning "male" and "sexual intercourse," but the precise nature of this sexual activity is not known for certain. Boswell points out that, as late as the twelfth century, Peter Cantor's listing of passages condemning homosexuality did not list either 1 Cor 6:9-10 or 1 Tim 1:10—a strange omission if general homosexual activity is the clear meaning of the language. The passages may be taken to refer to male sexual activity such as prostitution, or pederasty, but whether such prostitution included homosexual prostitution is less certain. What is reasonably clear in these texts is the condemnation of exploitive sexual acts such as prostitution (whether heterosexual or homosexual) and the use of children as sexual objects by adults.

(2) Rom 1:26-27 is the only unquestionable reference to homosexual acts in the NT. Here same sex acts that are contrary to nature (παρὰ φύσιν), or contrary to human custom, are seen as the result of a denial of God's sovereignty. Modern applicability of this passage, however, depends upon the weight one gives to the social context of this passage and the possibility that Paul is alluding to the abusive, exploitive forms of homosexual behavior—e.g., the holding of slaves as sexual objects, sex with young boys—characteristic of the disbelieving Hellenistic world.

Both OT and NT writers would certainly have assumed heterosexual relations as a social and religious norm. Heterosexual marriages were arranged early and usually without consultation with children. Biblical references to sexual activity (e.g., Gen 1–3) take for granted that they are heterosexual.

Homosexual activity associated with pagan worship and exploitative homosexual activity are clearly condemned. What is not clear, because it was not an issue in the biblical period, is whether involuntary homosexual orientation—the idea of a sexual orientation that is not voluntarily chosen is as recent as the nineteenth century—or committed, loving relationships between consenting persons of the same sex was to be condemned. Contemporary answers to these questions are based on theological and social considerations and are not simply and directly derived from the biblical material itself.

Bibliography. D. S. Bailey, *Homosexuality and the Western Church Tradition*; D. L. Bartlett, "A Biblical Perspective on Homosexuality," *Homosexuality and the Christian Faith,* ed. H. J. Twiss; J. Boswell, *Christianity, Social Tolerance and Homosexuality*; M. Douglas, *Purity and Danger*; J. Nelson, *Embodiment*; J. N. Ostwalt, "The Old Testament and Homosexuality," *What You Should Know About Homosexuality*, ed. C. W. Keysor; R. Scroggs, *The New Testament and Homosexuality*; D. Williams, *The Bond That Breaks: Will Homosexuality Split the Church?*

—T. FURMAN HEWITT

• **Hope in the New Testament.** Hope is one of the abiding virtues of Christian faith (1 Cor 13:13). The NT employs hope (ἐλπίς, ἐλπίζω) some seventy-nine times (forty-eight noun forms, thirty-one verbal forms). In addition to this language, the concept of hope is central to the life and thought of the NT.

The Language of Hope in the NT. The language of hope belongs primarily to Paul and Acts. The synoptic tradition rarely uses these words. The term is missing entirely from Mark and from the Q (sayings) traditions. Matthew has the term only once (12:21 = Isa 42:4). Luke makes use of the term on three occasions (6:34; 23:8; 24:21), but two of these are commonplace.

One rarely finds the term in the Johannine tradition. The fourth Gospel employs the term once (5:45). The Johannine Epistles have three instances (1 John 3:3; 2 John 12; 3 John 14), but only 1 John 3:3 carries theological significance. The Book of Revelation makes no use of this word. The term appears occasionally in the General Letters.

(1) Hope as a past and future heritage based on the acts of God (Luke 24:21; Acts 2:26 [Ps 16:9]; 23:6; 24:15; 26:6-7; 28:20; Rom 4:18; 5:2; 8:20, 24-25; 1 Cor 15:19; 2 Cor 1:10; 3:12; Gal 5:5; 1 Thess 2:19; 4:13; 2 Thess 2:16; 1 Tim 1:1; 4:10; Eph 1:18; 4:4; Col 1:5, 23, 27; Titus 1:2; 2:13; 3:7; Heb 3:6; 6:11, 18; 7:19; 10:23; 11:1; 1 Pet 1:3, 13, 21; 3:15; 1 John 3:3). This use of hope is rooted conjunctly in the past and in the future. This idea is historically grounded in the acts of God with little emphasis given to emotive or psychological aspects of hope. The future aspects of this hope are almost wholly apocalyptic—in dramatic fashion, God will break into history with judgment and redemption. The retrospective aspects of this hope point to the ancient promises of God to Israel. This is the predominant use of the term hope in the NT. This understanding of the term is developed primarily in Acts and in Paul.

In Acts, this dually focused hope is central to the gospel which Paul preaches. Paul is placed on trial (Acts 26:6) and is bound in chains to Rome "because of the hope of Israel" (Acts 28:20). Acts links this hope to the end-time actions of God—to the apocalypse and to the resurrection. Paul declares to the council that "with respect to the hope and the resurrection of the dead I am on trial" (Acts 23:6). Paul proclaims this future hope as a Jewish heritage (Acts 25:15).

Paul's own writings confirm Luke's portrait. For Paul, hope is an ancient heritage rooted in God's actions in behalf of Israel; this is the hope given to Abraham (Rom 4:18). At the same time, this hope will only be fulfilled with the end-time redemption of God's people and God's creation (Rom 8:18-25). This hope is linked distinctly to the future resurrection (1 Cor 15:19; 2 Cor 1:10; 2 Thess 4:13-18). For Paul, this future of hope fills the present with FAITH, with patience, and with comfort (Gal 5:5; 2 Thess 4:18).

Paul's conception of hope is altered somewhat in 2 Thessalonians, Colossians, Ephesians, and the Pastoral Epistles (1, 2 Tim, Titus). Hope is here linked to eternal life (2 Thess 2:16; Titus 1:2; 3:7), to heaven (Col 1:5), to a present experience of glory (Eph 1:16-23), and to the doctrines of God and Christ (1 Tim 1:1; 4:10; Col 1:27; Titus 2:13). In these writings, the stark apocalyptic hope of Paul has been transformed into a reflective pastoral eschatology.

Hebrews emphasizes hope as a future attainment which shapes the present life of the believer. The hope of the future brings steadfast assurance (3:6; 6:11; 10:23; 11:1) and leads the believer into the presence of God (6:19; 7:19). For Hebrews, this future hope revitalizes the believer in the midst of present difficulties.

Hope as the future action of God is also prominent in 1 Peter. This hope is established by God through the resurrection of Jesus Christ, yet this heavenly salvation is to be revealed in the last times (1:3-5, 13, 21). This end-time hope leads to faith and to a sober witness (1:21; 3:15).

Within the Johannine tradition, 1 John 3:3 speaks of the future hope of believers. This hope looks to the appearance of Jesus at the end of time and exhorts believers to ethical purity.

(2) The hope of the gentiles fulfilled in Jesus Christ (Matt 12:21 [Isa 42:4]; Rom 15:12 [Isa 11:10]; Eph 2:12; Col 1:27). This usage builds upon the ancient hope given to Israel in the mighty deeds of God. The hope of Israel becomes, by extension, the hope of the gentiles. This transition is a present reality, having occurred in the ministry of Jesus (Matt 12:21; Rom 15:12) or through the risen Christ (Col 1:27; Eph 2:12).

(3) Absolute use of hope as a Christian virtue (Rom 5:4; 12:12; 15:4, 13; 1 Cor 13:7, 13; 1 Thess 1:3; 5:8; 2 Thess 2:16; Col 1:5; Heb 11:1). In this concept, hope becomes a realized virtue in the life of the believer. Here, the past and future elements of hope converge in the present experience. Typically, this use of hope is absolute—without reference to another object or event. Frequently the language employed for this concept is hymnic, poetic, proverbial, or formulaic (Rom 5:4; 12:12; 15:13; 1 Cor 13:7, 13; 1 Thess 1:3; 5:8; 2 Thess 2:16; Col 1:4-5; Heb 11:1). Faith, hope, and LOVE form a trilogy of Christian virtues in various passages (1 Cor 13:13; 1 Thess 1:3; 5:8; Col 1:4-5). While this category of hope is rooted in future events (1 Thess 5:8), the focus falls on the present work of hope in the life of the believer.

(4) Immediate hopes related to Christian ministry (Rom 15:24; 1 Cor 16:7; 2 Cor 1:7, 10, 13; 5:11; 8:5; 10:15; 13:6; Phil 1:20; 2:19; 2:23; Phlm 22; 1 Tim 3:14; 2 John 12; 3 John 14). Hope is a practical matter related to the ongoing Christian ministry. In particular, this use relates the immediate hopes of the minister for believers.

(5) Hope as daily confidence (John 5:45; 1 Tim 5:5; 6:17; Heb 3:5; 10:23; 11:1; 1 Pet 3:5). Here hope provides the confidence, faith, and trust which govern daily life.

(6) Commonplace use of hope (Luke 6:34; 23:8; Acts 16:19; 24:26; 1 Cor 9:10). Here hope is used in an everyday manner, with no special theological sense.

The Concept of Hope in the NT. In spite of limited use of the term for hope, the NT makes frequent use of the concept of hope. This concept is central to all parts of the NT.

(1) The synoptic tradition. In the synoptic Gospels (Matthew, Mark, and Luke), the concept of hope is built around Jesus' present announcement of the Kingdom of God and around Jesus' future coming as the Son of man. In Mark 1:14-15, Jesus announces that the Kingdom of God is at hand. Jesus preaches the gospel of God and demands repenting and believing. Mark insists that Jesus' story is the fulfillment of the prophetic hope of the OT (Mark 1:1-3). This ancient hope is renewed as Jesus proclaims the nearness of the Kingdom. Mark characterizes Jesus as one who teaches with authority (Mark 1:22), then demonstrates this authority through Jesus' mighty deeds (Mark 1:23-39). However, Jesus' ministry of hope can only be understood in light of his destiny in Jerusalem—to die on the cross (Mark 10:45). Jesus will be crucified, yet he will be raised (Mark 8:31; 9:31; 10:33-34). The resurrection of Jesus brings a new stage of hope. The disciples who abandoned the crucified Jesus will meet the risen Lord in Galilee (Mark 14:28; 16:7). For Mark, the ultimate hope for believers is rooted in the Parousia (end-time appearance) of Jesus, the returning Lord. The Son of man will come in power and glory to gather the elect from the corners of earth and heaven (Mark 13:24-32; 14:60-62). Without using the language of hope, the Gospel of Mark carefully articulates the concept of hope. The hope of Israel is fulfilled in Jesus—in his life, in his death and resurrection, and ultimately in his return.

Matthew and Luke develop this understanding of hope found in the Gospel of Mark. Matthew draws specific lines between Jesus and the hopes of Israel. Matthew's genealogy shows that Jesus is the son of Abraham and the son of David (1:1-17). Jesus is Immanuel—God with us (1:23)—and this fulfills the promise of Isaiah. Matthew employs citation formulas to show Jesus as the fulfillment of the OT promises (e.g., 1:22; 2:5, 17, 23; 3:3; 4:14; 8:17; 12:17-21; 13:14-15, 35; 15:7; 21:4, 13, 16, 42). Matthew picks up the portrait of Jesus as one who teaches with authority (7:28 = Mark 1:22). Matthew demonstrates this power in what Jesus teaches, particularly in the sermon on the mount (chaps. 5–7). For Matthew, the hopes of Israel are fulfilled in the ministry of Jesus, the mighty teacher of the Kingdom of God. Matthew also picks up from Mark the hope of the resurrection appearances. Matthew shows this hope fulfilled in Galilee (28:16-20). The risen Lord will accompany the church in its mission, and this hope extends to the end of the age. Matthew also embraces the ultimate hope rooted in the Parousia of the Son of man (19:28; 24:29-31; 26:64). Thus, the Gospel of Matthew takes over the concept of hope and develops it in a distinct manner.

Luke also presents Jesus as the fulfillment of the hopes of Israel. Pious Jews such as Elizabeth, Zechariah, Mary, Simeon, and Anna recognize that Jesus represents the hopes of Israel (chaps. 1–2). For Luke, the ministry of Jesus fulfills God's promises through the prophets. Luke 4:14-30 and 7:22-23 provide a paradigmatic portrait of Jesus' ministry. Jesus brings good news (gospel), healing, and release. The Jubilee Year of God's favor has come to Israel. Today the OT is fulfilled in their hearing. Thus, Luke gives a distinct interpretation of the same truth: in Jesus, the hopes of Israel come to completion. Luke follows Mark in further linking the concept of hope to the resurrection of Jesus. For Luke, it is the risen Lord who defines hope for believers. The risen Lord interprets the life and death of Jesus as the fulfillment of Moses and the prophets (24:25-27; 24:44-48). The risen Lord promises the Spirit for the mission of the church (24:49; Acts 1:8). Finally, Luke also proclaims the ultimate hope which roots in Jesus' Parousia (21:25-28; 22:69; Acts 1:11).

While the term for hope is rare in Matthew, Mark, and Luke, the concept of hope abounds. Building on the framework of the Gospel of Mark, each of the Synoptics narrates the hope which centers in Jesus. In his earthly ministry, in his death and resurrection, in his promised appearing, the hopes of the past and the future are realized in Jesus, the Lord of the church.

(2) Acts. For Luke, the movement begun in Jesus is completed in the mission of the early church. Beginning in

Jerusalem with the power and presence of the risen Lord, the church moves outward under the guidance of the Spirit. Luke locates the hopes of both Israel and the gentiles in the mission activity of the early church. Under the power of the Spirit, the church fulfills the promises of the OT, extends the ministry of Jesus, proclaims the risen Lord, and draws upon the hope of Christ's return.

(3) The Pauline tradition. For Paul, Jesus also represents the hopes of Israel. The conversion/calling of Paul establishes a radical christological perspective from which to view the history of Israel. For Paul, the saving activity of God is no longer centered in the legal framework of the Law or in the ritual framework of Jewish worship (circumcision, Temple, food laws). Instead, God's saving activity centers in the Messiah. This Messiah is Jesus, who was crucified in Jerusalem and seen alive by early followers. For Paul, the central focus of this saving activity is the cross and resurrection; this is the scandalous gospel Paul preaches. The revelation on the Damascus road is that the hope of Israel is in the crucified and risen Messiah. This revelation becomes for Paul both a conversion and a calling, and it serves as the center of his message and mission. Paul knows or says little of the earthly ministry of Jesus. Hope centers instead on the risen Christ. The resurrection of Christ is a dramatic apocalyptic sign which marks the beginning of the new age. By faith in what God has done in the risen Christ, one becomes a new creation and a participant in this new age. While the resurrection of Christ provides hope as a present reality for believers, the resurrection of believers is a future, apocalyptic event. For Paul, hope ultimately centers around the returning Lord and the resurrection of the dead.

(4) The Johannine tradition. In the fourth Gospel, Jesus represents a hope which is unchanging. Jesus embodies a hope which precedes Abraham and issues from the very nature of God (John 8:58). Jesus' status is the same in creation, in incarnation, in glorification: he is the eternal *Logos* who reveals the Father and brings eternal life to all who believe. For the fourth Gospel, all of the hopes of past and future are realized in the present moment of existence when one makes a choice to believe. Thus, the resurrection and its hope is not a future mystery, as in Paul, but a reality already present in Jesus (John 11:25-26). Faith brings the hope of eternal life, but this life is already present in the experience of the believer (John 3:36). This christological understanding of hope and life also shapes the Johannine Letters. Faith provides eternal life—a reality already present in the lives of those who are children of God.

The Book of Revelation offers a radically different understanding of hope. Probably written in a situation of conflict and persecution, Revelation offers a hope which is wholly futuristic and apocalyptic. While this hope inspires ethical and moral living, the reality of this hope belongs to the future, apocalyptic acts of God. The vision of this hope employs apocalyptic images and events, but it centers ultimately in God's actions in Christ This hope guides the churches and the believers through the stormy trials of the present age.

(5) Hebrews. Hebrews links the future hope and the present life of the believer. For Hebrews, the certain hope of the future inspires believers to live faithful, steadfast, righteous lives. Jesus, through his earthly ministry and death, has entered into the presence of God to serve as a priestly mediator of this hope. The present suffering and obedience will give way to a heavenly hope; this encourages believers to "run with perseverance the race that is set before us . . . " (Heb 12:1-2).

(6) The General Letters. The concept of hope is employed on occasion in the General Letters. James speaks primarily of ethical and moral conduct—on how one is to live out the life of faith. Nonetheless, this ethical exhortation is set within the context of the near return of the Lord (Jas 5:7-9). This end-time hope shapes the daily living of those who wait in hope upon the Lord.

In 1 Peter, hope is a present experience through the resurrection of Jesus, but also a future experience waiting to be revealed from heaven (1 Pet 1:3-5). Because of this, believers are to be sane, sober, and righteous in the midst of the present fiery ordeal. Jude and 2 Peter share a common understanding of hope focused around the end-time appearance of the Lord.

Conclusion. Both the language and the concept of hope are central to the thought of the NT. For the NT, hope is theological—it roots in the actions of God. In particular, the acts and promises of God for Israel provide the foundation for hope. For the NT, hope is christological; God's promised hope is realized in Jesus the Messiah. Various aspects of Jesus' story are shown to be the prophetic fulfillment of the OT hope. In his coming, in his life and death, in his resurrection, Jesus brings these ancient hopes to reality for both Jews and gentiles. Ultimately, this hope is eschatological—it will be fulfilled with the end-time appearing of Jesus Christ as Lord. Christians are encouraged to see and experience the present impact of such hope. Hope is to fill the life of the believer with faith, with encouragement, and with steadfast endurance. This hope is God's eternal, abiding heritage for the children of God.

See also FAITH; LOVE IN THE NEW TESTAMENT.

Bibliography. C. E. Braaten, *The Future of God* and *Eschatology and Ethics*; A. Brieger, *Die urchristliche Trias Glaube-Liebe-Hoffnung*; E. Brunner, *Eternal Hope,* and *Faith, Hope, and Love*; R. Bultmann and K. H. Rengstorf, "ἐλπίς, ἐλπίζω," *TDNT*; W. H. Capps, ed., *Hope Against Hope* and *The Future of Hope*; K. P. Donfried, "Hope," *HBD*; J. Macquarrie, *Christian Hope*; M. D. Meeks, *Origins of the Theology of Hope*; P. S. Minear, *Christian Hope and the Second Coming* and "Hope," *IDB*; J. Moltmann, *The Experiment of Hope, The Future of Creation, The Future of Hope,* and *Theology of Hope*; D. Moody, *The Hope of Glory*; C. F. D. Moule, *Meaning of Hope*; A. Pott, *Das Hoffen im NT*; R. Reitzenstein, "Die Formel 'Glaube, Liebe, Hoffnung' bei Paulus," *NGG* (1916): 367-416; J. A. T. Robinson, *In the End, God* and *Jesus and His Coming*; E. Walter, "Glaube, Hoffnung und Liebe im Neuen Testament," *Leben aus dem Wort* 1 (1942).

—EDWIN K. BROADHEAD

• **Hope in the Old Testament.** A variety of OT words may express the meaning "hope" or "to hope." The most frequent noun meaning "hope" is *tqwh*. The nouns, *mqwh, twḥlt,* and *śbr* occur less frequently with this meaning. The verbs related to these nouns, *qwh, yḥl* and *śbr,* all have the basic meaning "to wait" and may also sometimes mean "to hope." The verbs *bṭḥ* "to trust," *ḥkh* "to wait, await," and *ḥyl* "to wait with anxious longing," as well as some of their related nouns, occasionally should be understood as "to hope" or "hope." (In more than seventy places the LXX translates forms of *bṭḥ* as "hope.")

In spite of the large vocabulary of "hope" in the OT the meaning and use of the concept are not as varied as in English. In the OT "hope" or "hoping" in and of itself, without an object, is not of any value. It is not an optimistic frame of mind or an attitude of courage that life rewards and other people admire. Occasionally in the OT hope is a calculated probability, something that one may reasonably expect to come to pass (e.g., Esth 9:1; Job 6:8; 7:2; Isa 5:2, 4, 7; in every one of these examples, however, the expectation is, in fact, not fulfilled). Even rarer are references in which hope is equivalent to "dreams" or "desires," those longings that extend beyond the limits of sober expectation (e.g., Prov 13:12). Hope may exist simply because one is alive (Eccl 9:4) or because there is still time and opportunity to improve one's life (Prov 19:18). These are everyday uses of "hope" in the OT, without reference to God as its source or its object.

The majority of OT references teach that hope is available to persons living in relationship with God. Hope connects persons to the future, to what is on the other side of one's current situation of distress, or to one's posterity. OT hope rests on the belief that one's future is in God's hands. The relationship with God in which such hope may exist is generated and sustained by confession and forgiveness of sin, by experiencing and remembering God's redemption, by living the life of wisdom in the fear of God, by obedience to God's word, and by belief in God's promises. The basic object of hope is life, its fullness in the present and its possibilities for the future. Life comes from God. Both the attitude of hope and its concrete realization are good gifts from God.

Many of the sayings in the Books of Proverbs and Job teach that a fool's hope is futile. The problem does not lie with the things hoped for, since they are never identified, but with the foolish person's failure to live in the fear of God. Only the righteous person's hopes are happily fulfilled (Prov 10:28; 11:23; 23:18; 24:14). The hopes and expectations of the wicked are terminated at their death (Prov 11:7). JOB's friends, in their efforts to persuade Job to acknowledge his sin and set things right with God, use the argument that if one is righteous, one has hope (Job 4:6; 5:16; 11:18). The only "hope" a godless person will see realized is death, the negation of hope (Job 8:13-14; 11:20; 27:8). Job agrees that God is the source of hope, but he knows that even though he is righteous God has taken away his hope (Job 7:6; 13:15; 14:19; 19:10; 30:26). Job's only "hope" is to die (Job 6:8-9), yet he voices the hope beyond hope that God would be present even in the realm of death (Job 14:13-15; cf. Isa 38:18).

The vocabulary of hope occurs most frequently in psalms, especially psalms of lament, both in the Book of Psalms and in psalmic passages elsewhere in the OT. In situations of deep distress and in the face of the encroaching power of death, God's people cry out individually and corporately to the Lord, the hope of Israel (e.g., Pss 9:18; 38:15; 71:5; Jer 14:8). The psalmists confess that God alone is the source of hope, and reliance on anyone or anything else is vain (Pss 62:5; 33:18-22; 146:5; Isa 64:4; Ezek 19:5; Mic 5:7; 7:7). Psalms expressing hope describe God as creator (Pss 33:6-8; 104; 146:6), as the source of life (1 Chr 29:14-15; Ps 33:19; 104:29), as savior (Pss 31:2-5; 33:20; 71:3, 15; 78), and as the just and powerful ruler of the world (Pss 33:4-5, 11; 62:11-12; 78; 145:10-18; 146:7-9; 147; Isa 30:18). In Ps 119 God's word, in commandment and promise, is the basis and object of the faithful person's hope (vv. 119:43, 49, 74, 81, 114, 147). The divine quality most often associated with hope is God's steadfast love (*hsd*—Pss 31:7; 33:18, 22; 42:8; 62:12; 130:7; 145:8; 147:11; Lam 3:21-22). Hope issues in praise of God, whose compassionate Lordship provides humanity with the sole basis for living in hope (Pss 42:5, 11; 43:5; 71:14).

Repentance, confession of sin, and God's merciful forgiveness are prerequisites for hope because through them a person or a nation is restored to life in right relationship with God (Ezra 10:2; Pss 39:7-8; 130:3-6; Jer 14:7-8; Lam 3). The ultimate value of fellowship with God meant for OT faith that hope could exist even in the face of imminent and unavoidable death (Ps 130:7). Life with God, no matter how short its duration, could be both the source of hope and its fulfillment.

The vocabulary of hope is rare in the prophets and the remainder of the OT, in spite of the fact that hopeful expectation of fulfillment is implicit in believing God's promises. Prophets themselves waited in hope for God's appearing (Isa 8:17; Dan 12:12; Hab 2:2-4). Even the false prophets hoped that God would fulfill their lying words (Ezek 13:6). The destruction of their land and exile in Babylon left the people of Israel without hope because there seemed to be no future for the nation (Jer 31:15; Ezek 37:11). Nevertheless, God's promise through the prophets included restoration of fellowship with God, return to the Land, and the gift of hope (Jer 29:10-14; 31:16-17; Ezek 37:12-14).

See also FAITH AND FAITHLESSNESS; LOVE IN THE NEW TESTAMENT.

Bibliography. J. Moltmann, *Theology of Hope*; C. F. D. Moule, *The Meaning of Hope*; W. Zimmerli, *Man and His Hope in the Old Testament*.

—PAMELA J. SCALISE

• **Hophni.** [hof'n*i*] Brother of PHINEHAS and son of the high priest ELI, served as a priest of the Lord at SHILOH (1 Sam 1:3). Unfavorably described, Hophni and Phinehas "did not know the Lord" (1 Sam 2:12), abused their privileges as priests (1 Sam 2:13-16), and "despised the offering of the Lord" (1 Sam 2:17). Their reproachable character, unrestrained by an aging Eli, was further defamed by reports of licentiousness at the sanctuary (1 Sam 2:22). Because of this immorality and the abuse of the priestly office, a curse was pronounced on the house of Eli first by an unnamed prophet (1 Sam 2:26-36) and later by a young SAMUEL (1 Sam 3:11-14). Along with his brother, Hophni later accompanied the Ark of the Covenant into battle against the Philistines at Aphek/Ebenezer. Both died in the battle and the Ark was captured (1 Sam 4:11).

See also ELI; PHINEHAS; PRIESTS; SAMUEL.

—W. H. BELLINGER, JR.

• **Horeb, Mount.** [hor'eb] An alternate name for Mount Sinai. Though the sacred mountain on which Moses received the Ten Commandments is generally called SINAI, seventeen times it is referred to as Horeb (nine times in Deuteronomy). It was here that ISRAEL entered into covenant with GOD (Exod 19–24). The people encamped at the foot of this mountain, after their departure from EGYPT, while MOSES spent forty days on Mount Sinai/Horeb with God receiving the words, ordinances, and commandments that became known as the Law or Torah. While Moses was on the mountain, the people turned to Aaron and persuaded him to make the golden calf, which they worshiped (Exod 32). In his anger at their idolatrous action, Moses shattered the two stone tablets (v. 19) on which God had written the Ten Commandments. He later ascended the mountain a second time (Exod 33–34) and received another copy of the commandments. He was then permitted to see the glory of God from "a cleft of the rock" (Exod 33:17-23).

Some 400 years later the prophet ELIJAH journeyed forty days from BEERSHEBA to "Horeb the mount of God" in his flight from the wicked queen JEZEBEL (1 Kgs 19). Like

Moses before him, Elijah encountered God in a cave on the mountain. But this time God was not to be found in the wind, earthquake, and fire, but rather in "a still, small voice" (vv. 12-13). Mount Horeb thus played a pivotal role in the OT story on two different occasions. It is interesting to note that both Moses and Elijah appeared again on a mountain in the NT, together with Jesus at his transfiguration (Luke 9:28-33). In a symbolic sense, that mountain too is "Horeb the mountain of God."

The two different names for the mountain, along with two series of related terms and concepts, led scholars to posit at least two major versions of the original experience of Moses in terms of the documentary hypothesis. Of the four primary written sources of the Pentateuch isolated by these scholars, the term Horeb belongs to E (Exod 3:1; 17:6; 33:6) and D (Deuteronomy).

In some passages Horeb seems to designate an area larger than Mount Sinai (Deut 4:10; 9:8; 18:16), for Moses struck the rock in the region of Horeb (Exod 17:6), but not on Mount Sinai, which was reached later (Exod 19:1). Other attempts to distinguish between Horeb and Sinai have led some to identify two separate peaks in the same range. According to Deut 1:2, it is an eleven day journey (on pilgrimage?) from Horeb to Kadesh-Barnea in the Negeb of southern Israel.

The traditional location of Mount Horeb is Jebel Musa ("Mountain of Moses," 7,363 ft.) in southern Sinai, where the present Monastery of Saint Catherine has been located since 527 C.E. Here one finds a sizeable plain below the mountain, together with an adequate water supply—the traditional well of Moses, by which Moses met the daughters of JETHRO (Exod 2:15-19). If the biblical events did not actually take place here, they certainly should have—as anyone can testify who has climbed the 3,700 "steps" to the top of the mountain for the traditional sunrise experience. In fact some tourists choose to spend the night in "Elijah's cave" on the top rather than make the climb in the dark.

See also SINAI.

—DUANE L. CHRISTENSEN

• **Horn.** *See* SHOPHAR

• **Horn/Horns of the Altar.** "Horn" (Heb. *qeren,* Gk. *keras*) may refer to the actual horn of an animal or to objects made from animal horns (e.g., flask, 1 Sam 16:1). Certain musical instruments were called "horns" (Josh 6:5). More common terms are *yôbēl* = trumpet and *šōpār* = ram's horn. Horn-like projections could be called "horns" (e.g., hills, Isa 5:1).

In both testaments "horn" is used figuratively to indicate some sense of "power." One's power may be described as "horn" (Deut 33:17), or the one possessing the power may be called a "horn" (Dan 8:20-21). Apocalyptic animal imagery depicts degrees of power through horn symbolism (Dan 8:7; Rev 13:1). God can exalt or cut off one's "horn" (Ps 75:10). The hopes of God's people rest in God as their "horn of salvation" (2 Sam 22:3; Ps 18:2) or in God's raising up a "horn of salvation" to deliver them (Ps 132:17, quoted in Luke 1:69). Association of "horn" with sexual power and fertility may root in phallic semblance (Ps 132:17).

The "horns of the altar" may represent a convergence of literal and figurative meanings. Ancient deities and divinely inspired persons were often depicted with horns or horned headdresses. These depictions may reflect association with radiating sunlight, as well as the "power" of horn imagery (and may relate to the matter of MOSES' "horned" appearance in Exod 34:29). Altars to ancient deities were adorned with the horns of sacrificed animals. Eventually four raised cornerstones became the "horns of the altar" (Exod 27:2). Propitiatory blood was to be applied to these horns (Exod 30:10). Clinging to the "horns of the altar" might provide asylum (1 Kgs 2:28). "Cutting off" the horns of the altar represented Yahweh's rejection of Israel's cultus and the loss of divine security (Amos 3:14).

See also MUSIC/MUSICAL INSTRUMENTS; REFUGE, CITIES OF.

Bibliography. J. R. Conrad, *The Horn and the Sword: The History of the Bull as Symbol of Power and Fertility*; L. J. Coppes, "קֶרֶן *qeren,*" *TWOT*; W. Foerster, "κέρας," *TDNT*.

—SCOTT NASH

• **Hosea.** [hoh-zay'uh] The son of Beeri. No other details of his early life are mentioned. His name means "salvation," a common Hebrew name found in various forms. Hosea lived in the Northern Kingdom of Israel; his ministry covered approximately the last quarter-century of the nation's existence (750–724 B.C.E.). Jeroboam II was the ruler when Hosea began to prophesy. References to King Hoshea's submission to Assyria (Hos 5:13; 8:9-10) and captivity (Hos 13:10-11) indicate that the prophet witnessed the end of the Northern Kingdom.

Hosea was commanded by God to marry Gomer, the daughter of Diblaim. She bore three children, to whom Hosea gave symbolic names, indicating the growing alienation of God from the Israelite community that had turned its back upon the deity and was worshiping God through the popular fertility rites introduced through Canaanite influences. Gomer, apparently a product of this society, became for Hosea a symbol for Israel, God's bride, who abandoned her true lover and husband for the worship of Baal. When Gomer left her husband, Hosea was commanded to bring her back, discipline her, and let the relationship once more be restored (Hos 3). Chaps. 1–3 of the Book of Hosea provide this story of God's love for errant Israel, a love that will not be put off, finally, by the faithlessness of the beloved. It is not certain just how much the story in Hosea 1–3 parallels the actual life of the prophet Hosea, but clearly the emphasis falls not on the broken family relations of the prophet but upon the broken relationship between God and people that the prophet first announced and then spent his life seeking to heal.

In other respects, however, Hosea is just as much a prophet of judgment as was his near contemporary Amos. Hosea fiercely attacked the priests and the prophets who were "feeding on the sins of the people" and neglecting to teach them knowledge of God (Hos 4:1-6). He insisted that what God demanded of Israel was not sacrifice but steadfast love, not burnt offerings but knowledge of God (Hos 6:6). The social crimes that left the people exposed to violence on every side were grimly pointed out by a prophet who could see little prospect for them unless God took special and unprecedented action.

Hosea is remembered for his belief that such unprecedented action was near at hand. Although Israel had sinned greatly, even from its youth (Hos 11:1-4), the very heart of God was touched with compassion by the people's great need and misery. God was God, not a human being. God was the Holy One in their midst. God by rights should bring disaster on such a faithless people, but God was moved by love to forgive (Hos 11:5-9). This same display of love is eloquently portrayed in Hos 2 under the image of God the loving husband who insists on forgiving and restoring the errant wife. And it stands out also in the picture of a stubborn son, Ephraim, who will not assist at the coming birth of new life to mother Israel, but refuses to let new birth happen (Hos 13:12-13).

Hosea's influence on the prophet Jeremiah is massive. Much of the message of Jeremiah seems to have been fashioned out of Hosea's language and imagery. Hosea's portrayal of the love of God for sinners, a love that is not sentimental and by no means uninterested in public and private justice, has left its mark on the entire Bible. Hosea is the prophet of divine love that will not give up on the sinner.

See also BAAL; HARLOT; LOVE IN THE OLD TESTAMENT; PROPHECY.

—WALTER HARRELSON

• OUTLINE OF HOSEA •

The Book of Hosea

I. Hosea's Marriage and Family: Symbol of God's Relationship with Israel (1:1–3:5)
   A. God's judgment against a faithless people (1:1–2:1)
   B. Warnings and promise (2:2-23)
   C. A husband's (Hosea's and God's) love (3:1-5)
II. Israel's Unfaithfulness and God's Judgment (4:1–14:9)
   A. Indictment for infidelity and warnings of judgment (4:1–6:6)
   B. Judgment against Israel for continued and unrepentant sin (6:7–13:16)
   C. Final call to repentance and promise of restoration (14:1-9)

• **Hosea, Book of.** The first book of those prophetic books usually called the minor prophets or "The Twelve." Hosea was the only one of these prophets native to the Northern Kingdom of Israel. Contemporaries were ISAIAH and MICAH who lived and prophesied in Judah, and AMOS who lived in Judah but delivered his messages in Israel.

Hosea began his ministry toward the end of JEROBOAM II's reign (786–746 B.C.E.). The Assyrian menace, foreseen by Amos, was now a reality. TIGLATH-PILESER III became king of Assyria in 745 B.C.E. By 743 B.C.E. Israel was paying tribute to the Assyrian ruler (2 Kgs 15:19-20). After Jeroboam's death the succession to the throne was by regicide. Zechariah was slain by SHALLUM, then MENAHEM killed Shallum. Menahem's son PEKAHIAH was slain by PEKAH who established an anti-Assyrian coalition. The Syro-Ephraimite war against Judah was a result of this coalition (Isa 9:8-12; Hos 5:8-11). In 733 B.C.E. Tiglath-pileser deported much of the population and seized most of Israel's territory. The city of Samaria was saved when HOSHEA ben Elah assassinated Pekah, paid heavy tribute to Assyria and assumed the throne as the vassal-king of Tiglath-pileser (5:13; 8:9f.).

Not content to remain a vassal, Hoshea sought Egyptian support for revolt (9:3; 11:5; 12:1). Hoshea withheld tribute when SHALMANESER V succeeded Tiglath-pileser. In 724 B.C.E. Hoshea was stripped of his power and imprisoned. Israel's armies were defeated and the siege of Samaria began (chaps. 13–14).

Hosea's messages reflect the events of the last quarter century of Israel's existence (750–724 B.C.E.).

There are two major sections of the book. The first section is the marriage of Hosea and Gomer (chaps. 1–3). The second section is composed of a series of oracles on God's judgment against Israel (chaps. 4–14).

Interwoven in the first section is Hosea's experience with Gomer and the Lord's experience with Israel.

"Yahweh's word" (1:1) was the revelation that Hosea proclaimed but also that which directed his own life. He was directed to marry "a wife of harlotry, and have children of harlotry. . . . So he went and took Gomer the daughter of Diblaim" (1:2, 3). This command has been interpreted in various ways.

Earlier commentators interpreted the marriage allegorically. The allegorical approach is considered necessary in order to eliminate the moral difficulty of the marriage of the Lord's prophet to a harlot. However, the style is that of a narrative, not an allegory. Simple facts are presented, such as the weaning of a child (1:8). Gomer and Diblaim are names of real people and have no symbolic value.

Most interpreters accept the historicity of the marriage and the birth of the children. However, there is a difference of opinion concerning Gomer. Some consider Gomer to be a harlot before marriage, possibly a cult prostitute. Others insist that Gomer was not a harlot before marriage but deeply influenced and attracted by the spirit of harlotry that dominated her society. The latter view is more consistent with the analogy drawn between Hosea's experience with Gomer and the Lord's experience with Israel. Gomer bore three children whose names were prophetic of the Lord's judgment of the Israelite people. "JEZREEL," the name of the first son, was the region where JEHU massacred the family of AHAB (2 Kgs 9–10). Not only the dynasty of Jehu but the institution of kingship for Israel was doomed. The second child, a daughter, was named Loruhamah, which means "no mercy," symbolizing the plight of Israel. The mercy of the Lord was removed from the nation. The second son, Loammi, "not my people," was the most intense judgment of all. The nation Israel was not distinct from the other nations. The Lord had divorced Israel.

Gomer left Hosea for her "lovers." She sank into the harlotry of the land. Hosea was commanded to "go again, love a woman" (3:1). The prophet's love for Gomer moved him to redeem her and to restore her. Hosea had already become aware of the Lord's unchanging love for Israel. Hosea's experience of love was based upon his prior understanding of the Lord's undeserved helping and healing love. The Lord's message, which the prophet proclaimed, was lived out in his life.

The second section of the book (4–14) portrays the spiritual adultery of Israel. The unfaithfulness of kings, priests, and people is presented in staccato fashion. Their "loyalty is like a morning cloud and like the dew which goes away early" (6:4b). The people have no knowledge of God in the land (4:1). This "knowledge" means an intimate personal relationship with the Lord. The "spirit of harlotry has led them astray" (4:12). The Lord demands more than shallow repentance and ritual. "For I desire steadfast love and not sacrifice, and the knowledge of God rather than burnt offerings" (6:6).

The judgment and salvation cycle is evident in this section. Chap. 11 ends a series of judgments with the declaration of the Lord's extraordinary loving-kindness. There is hope for the future. Chap. 14 contains an exhortation for Israel to return to God (14:1-3) and a promise. God will heal their unfaithfulness and love them freely (14:4).

See also HOSEA; PROPHECY.

Bibliography. J. Mays, *Hosea, A Commentary*; H. Wolff, *Hosea*.

—JIMMIE L. NELSON

• **Hoshea.** [hoh-shee'uh] A name by which five different OT people were known. Hoshea was the original name of Joshua (Num 13:16) and was the name of the eighth-century prophet whose name is more commonly spelled Hosea. The third Hoshea was the last king of Israel (reigned 732-724 B.C.E.), who assassinated PEKAH (736–732 B.C.E.) as part of a conspiracy (2 Kgs 15:30). According to a fragmentary text by the Assyrian emperor TIGLATH-PILESER III (744–727), the people of northern Israel overthrew Pekah and Tiglath-pileser installed Hoshea as king. In 2 Kgs 17:2 Hoshea was not judged as severely as were previous kings, but vv. 3-6 describe his vassalage to SHALMANESER V (726–722) and the fall of Samaria. The other two men named Hoshea were a chief officer DAVID placed over Ephraim (1 Chr 27:20) and a levitical priest who endorsed NEHEMIAH's covenant (Neh 10:23).

See also JOSHUA.

—PAUL L. REDDITT

• **Hospitality.** A necessary practice in the ancient world. Inns were scarce and even when found were not often places where God-fearing people wanted to stay. The Bible and the early church fathers thus spoke often of the necessity and sacredness of giving and accepting hospitality.

In the OT the practice of hospitality involved danger. A traveling stranger might be someone in genuine need, or an enemy. At times an effort might be made to determine whether a STRANGER should be welcomed or not (Josh 2:2-3). Similarly, a host might be a warm, caring person or an enemy (Judg 4:17-21). Despite such potential dangers, hospitality was usually offered and accepted. There was less danger in sharing food and fellowship with an enemy than in raising the enemy's anger by withholding hospitality.

Typically a stranger would enter a city, go to an open place, and wait for an invitation from someone to lodge for the night (Gen 19:1-3; Judg 19:15-21). The one who offered hospitality treated the stranger well. The stranger's animals were cared for, water was provided for him to wash his feet and he was provided with a meal and rest (Gen 18:1-8; 19:1-3; 24:31-33). Protection was also provided for the stranger even if it put the host and his family in peril (Gen 19:6-9; Judg 19:22-24). Hospitality thus went well beyond simply providing for basic needs. Perhaps through such meticulous care, the host hoped to turn aside an enemy's wrath (2 Kgs 6:11-23) or even turn an enemy into a friend (Prov 25:21-22).

Obviously the faith and experience of ISRAEL played an important role in Israel's understanding of the need to show hospitality. For much of their early history, the Israelites had been strangers in foreign lands. God told the people to remember this fact and to treat all strangers with love and respect (Exod 22:21; Lev 19:34; Deut 10:18-19). Beyond simple obedience to God, showing hospitality might lead to a blessing from God (1 Kgs 17:1-24; 2 Kgs 4:8-37) for one might actually be entertaining God (Gen 18:1-15). Conversely, to refuse to show hospitality or to abuse the stranger not only disobeyed God but also could set into motion a chain of events leading to curse and destruction for Israel (Judg 19:22–20:48). Clearly God's command to love was to take precedence over selfish desires or fears.

In the NT the practice of hospitality is amply attested. JESUS had no apparent place of residence (Matt 8:20) and relied on the hospitality of others (Mark 14:3; Luke 8:3; 10:38; John 12:1-2). When Jesus sent his disciples out two by two, they also depended upon hospitality (Matt 10:5-15; Mark 6:7-11; Luke 10:4-11) as did PETER (Acts 10:5-6), PAUL (Acts 16:15; Rom 16:23; Phil 4:14-18), and other missionaries (Acts 18:27; 3 John 5-8) in the early days of the church. During times of persecution hospitality provided by Christians for Christians was especially important since it offered protection and encouragement through fellowship and worship (Acts 10:7).

Jesus set the example as both host and guest. He stressed being a good NEIGHBOR (Luke 10:29-37) and then demonstrated it by feeding the crowds (Mark 6:41-44) and washing the disciples' feet (John 13:1-17). Hospitality indicated one's commitment to Christ and one's awareness that to serve one's neighbor was to serve Christ (Matt 25:31-46). A Christian was to show hospitality to anyone, especially those who could not repay (Luke 14:12-14). As a guest a Christian was not to seek a place of honor (Luke 14:8) or a better place to stay (Mark 6:10). One was to eat what was set before one (Luke 10:8) and be thankful.

Showing hospitality could be dangerous to the host and abused by the guest. The possibility of persecution could make one reluctant to offer hospitality, but usually the risk was taken in order to obey Christ (Acts 10:22-23). Abuse of Christian hospitality by people claiming to be Christian preachers was probably the more real problem. Christian communities were encouraged to test those who came seeking hospitality (1 John 4:1; 2 John 7-11). A person might be examined to determine whether his or her doctrine was sound (2 John 10) or a letter might be accepted as proof of a person's character and commitment (1 Cor 16:10; Eph 6:21-22). Even when a community had been deceived, however, the community probably felt that it had followed Christ's example of love and care.

The NT churches were encouraged to practice hospitality (Heb 13:2; 1 Pet 4:9) and did. People both close at hand (Acts 2:44-45) and far away (Rom 15:26-27; 2 Cor 9:1-2) were cared for. Jesus' teaching that to care for anyone was to care for him lived on in the church (Gal 4:14) and undoubtedly served to bond the Christian communities together as one.

In the early church, the DIDACHE (*Did* 11) reflects the hospitality practiced by the early church. A Christian preacher was to be welcomed and cared for but for no more than two days. One who would stay a third day would be regarded as a false prophet who was taking advantage of the community. When the Christian preacher left he might request bread to care for his physical needs on his journey. Bread was to be given to him but if he asked for money he revealed himself as a false prophet. Similar rules applied to offering hospitality to any Christian (*Did* 12).

The early church carried on Christ's ministry with enthusiasm. CLEMENT praised the Corinthian church for its hospitality (*1 Clem* 1:2) and Aristides stated that all Christians practiced hospitality (*Apol* 15:7). John Chrysostom wrote that the church of Antioch cared for 3,000 virgins and widows, in addition to foreigners, patients and prisoners (*HMatt* 66 on Matt 20:29.30.3). Such ministry undoubtedly was a strong witness for Christ.

See also ETHICS IN THE OLD TESTAMENT; STRANGER.

Bibliography. V. H. Kooy, "Hospitality," *IDB*; B. Metzger, "Hospitality," *HBD*.

—ROBERT C. DUNSTON

• **Household Gods.** *See* IMAGES/FIGURINES; LABAN; SCULPTURE; TERAPHIM

• **Huldah.** [huhl'duh] The name of a woman of Jerusalem who was a prophet during the reign of JOSIAH (639–609

B.C.E.). When the book of the Law was discovered in the Temple during the eighteenth year of Josiah's reign, the king ordered his chief officials to "inquire of Yahweh," in other words, to seek an oracle. Intercession with Yahweh was perhaps also expected because the provisions of the book had not been followed. It was to Huldah that they turned. Her oracle, as reported in 2 Kgs 22:15-20 predicts the downfall of the kingdom of Judah after the death of Josiah. The king himself was promised a peaceful death. Since the oracle is in deuteronomic language some commentators attribute it to a later editor. However, there is reason to believe that Huldah may have been a part of a deuteronomic circle centered in Anathoth. The oracle must have taken essentially its present form before the death of Josiah, since its predictions concerning his peaceful death were not fulfilled.

It has long been suggested that there is a close association between the "book of the law" discovered in the Temple and the deuteronomic law code (Deut 12–26). If so, Huldah's concerns embraced both cultic sin and social injustice within a call for an attitude of obedience to God. As presented in 2 Kgs 22:1–23:30, the discovery of the book and the oracle of Huldah provide the impetus for the cultic reforms of Josiah. However, according to 2 Chr 34:3-7, the reform was begun in the twelfth year of his reign, six years before the discovery of the book. If the later chronology is correct, Huldah played a less important role in the Josianic reforms than 2 Kings implies. In either case, however, her validation of the importance of the deuteronomic regulations and her words of judgment resulted in a renewal of the covenant and in at least some momentum for reform (2 Kgs 23:1-25; 2 Chr 34:29-33).

Huldah may have been a cult prophet. More likely she was an official royal prophet. Some scholars have alleged that the reform was carefully staged, and the officials turned to Huldah knowing she would provide an oracle that would be supportive. Huldah, with her husband, Shallum, keeper of the wardrobe (for palace or Temple?) lived in the area of Jerusalem built for Temple and palace personnel.

According to the Mishnah (*Mid* 1.3), the southern gates to the Temple Mount were called Huldah Gates. The so-called "Double Gate" and "Triple Gate," both of which have long been sealed, are in approximately the same locations as the Herodian Huldah Gates. Jewish tradition suggests that Huldah was related through her husband to JOSHUA. R. R. Wilson, on the other hand, thinks that she may have been the wife of Jeremiah's uncle (cf. 2 Kgs 22:14; Jer 32:7).

See also PROPHET; PROPHETESS; WOMEN IN THE OLD TESTAMENT.

Bibliography. D. L. Christensen, "Huldah and the Men of Anathoth: Women in Leadership in the Deuteronomic History," *SBLASP*; R. R. Wilson, *Prophecy and Society in Ancient Israel*.

—WILDA W. (WENDY) MORRIS

• **Human Being.** A term that distinguishes the human species from all other creatures. There is no specific biblical word that is its exact equivalent, although *'ādām* in the OT and *anthrōpos* (person), *anthrōpinos* (human), and *kata sarka* (according to the flesh) in the NT in certain contexts approximate its meaning. Other words that are applied to human beings in the OT are *nepeš* (soul, life, self), *ruaḥ* (spirit), *leb* (heart), and *bāśār* (flesh). Equivalent NT words are *psuchē* (soul, breath), *pneuma* (spirit), *kardia* (heart), and *sarx* (flesh; translated in some versions as "human being," e.g., Matt 24:22, Rom 3:20; 1 Cor 1:29). However, none of these words is used exclusively in the scriptures as the exact equivalent of "human being."

Human beings are part of the created order, yet are unique in the order of creation. This uniqueness is expressed in the only biblical term that distinguishes human beings from all other creatures: "image of God" (Gen 1:26). It is not used of any other beings; however, nowhere in the scriptures is "image of God" clearly defined. Many answers have been proposed for the questions, "What distinguishes human beings from other creatures?" "What unique characteristics distinguish us from all other creatures as being created in the 'image of God' "?

Some attempts have been made to link the "image and likeness" (Gen 1:26) to a physical resemblance since God is frequently described in anthropomorphic terms (e.g., eyes, arms, voice, etc.), but such language may only be an accommodation to the limitations of human understanding and vocabulary. The most frequently noted distinction between human beings and other creatures is the ability to make moral choices, i.e., to distinguish between right and wrong. This discernment would imply that human beings are the only ones of all created beings who will be held accountable by God for their actions.

Other unique qualities of human beings include the ability to think about the past and to pass on the benefit of experience to the next GENERATION. This involves the ability to store up knowledge through memory, arrange it rationally and logically, come to new insights, and then communicate meaningfully to someone else what has already been learned. Other creatures adapt to their environment, but human beings are constantly attempting to adapt their environment to their needs and desires. That which is called civilization is constantly being modified (not always necessarily for the better!) because of this unique quality found only among humans. The mastery of tools is essential to the development of civilization; no other creature has been known to develop and use tools.

Human beings, having been created in the image and likeness of God, reveal that stamp of the divine by their capacity and desire to know God. Created from the dust of the earth (Gen 2:7) in the weakness of flesh but as spiritual beings, humans have a capacity for the divine and a desire to have communion with God through WORSHIP, by whatever name they call God. This quality is evidenced by the fact that all peoples of all times, however primitive or sophisticated, have developed cultic expressions of individual and corporate worship. The ability to know God has at times in history been perverted by a determination to reject God or to become a god. No other creature demonstrates an awareness of the divine or a desire to please, imitate or rebel against God.

Another distinctive quality of human beings based on their reasoning powers and the image of God within them is the urge to speculate about life after death and to develop beliefs about it. They are self-aware creatures with the ability to think introspectively. Not only do they remember the past, but they have hope for the future and an innate desire to live indefinitely. Closely related is the ability of the human creature to think philosophically about the meaning of LIFE, suffering, good and EVIL, the best way to live life, etc.

The ability to reason has resulted in another distinctive characteristic of human beings, i.e., the tendency to place arbitrary values on material things such as gold and silver, works of art, LAND, gems, houses, etc., and to preserve and pass on these values to the next generation. The biblical injunction that gives human beings dominion over the rest of creation implies an obligation to use and manage material things responsibly (Gen 1:28; 1 Cor 4:2).

Human beings are able to communicate their inmost feelings and reveal their inner self, aspirations, hopes, and fears as other creatures apparently cannot. Humans can enjoy intimate relationships with one another, not observed in other creatures. It has been said that they were made to love; only another person can satisfy the deepest needs of one's human nature (Gen 2:18-20). Growing out of this desire for intimate, meaningful relationship is the institution of marriage, a commitment that is unique to persons. The scriptures emphasize the responsibilities as well as the privileges of relationships (e.g., Gen 4:9-10; Exod 22:21-22; Amos 5:24; Matt 19:19; Luke 19:29-37; Eph 5:22–6:9).

Biblical evidences that affirm the uniqueness of human beings include the following: (1) man and woman are depicted in the scriptures as the climax and crown of creation (Gen 1–3); (2) though a part a nature, only the human creature has been given authority over the rest of creation (Gen 1:28-29; 2:19-20); (3) the human creature is the only one of God's created beings with whom God desires to have fellowship (Gen 3:8; 5:24; Matt 23:37); (4) Christ took on the form of humanity in the incarnation in preference to the form of any other creature (Phil 2:5-11); (5) human beings are the only creatures held accountable before God (Rom 3:4; 6:23; Heb 9:27); (6) human beings of all created beings are promised eternal life in the scriptures (John 3:16).

See also CREATION; ETHICS IN THE NEW TSTAMENT; ETHICS IN THE OLD TESTAMENT; IMAGE OF GOD.

Bibliography. G. C. Berkouwer, *Man, The Image of God*; W. Dyrness, *Themes in Old Testament Theology*; W. Eichrodt, *Man in the Old Testament*; J. G. Gibbs, "Human," *ISBE*; A. R. Johnson, *The Vitality of the Individual in the Thought of Ancient Israel*; N. W. Porteous, "Image of God," *IDB*; H. W. Wolff, *Anthropology of the Old Testament*.

—F. B. HUEY, JR.

• **Humiliation.** *See* SHAME

Likeness of a nobleman hunting in the marshes.

• **Hunting.** The pursuit of wild animals, birds, or fish for food, clothing, or tools, or for sport. Except for the prominence given, both actually and symbolically, to fishermen and fishing in the NT gospels, there are few direct references in the Bible to actual hunters and hunting. Of those few, the chief examples appear in the Book of Genesis.

Among the traditional descendants of Noah, Nimrod is remembered as "a mighty hunter before the Lord" (Gen 10:8-9) and also as the builder or conqueror of several principal cities in Babylon and Assyria (vv. 10-12). Later Jewish tradition held Nimrod to have instigated construction of the tower of Babel (Gen 11:1-9; cf. Josephus, *Ant* 1.4.2-3). The tradition possibly reflects an inference that Nimrod's hunting prowess threatened rebellion against the covenant between God and Noah and all life—the sign of which was God's own bow (*qešet*, "archer's bow"; Gen 9:12-17). The fourteenth-century B.C.E. *Tale of Aqhat*, from Canaanite Ugarit, finds its human hero, Aqhat, contending with the goddess Anat for possession of a specially-made hunter's bow.

Ishmael, Abraham's son by Hagar, after being sent away with his mother into the wilderness, "grew up [and] lived in the wilderness, and became an expert with the bow" (Gen 21:20).

Jacob's brother, Esau, "a skilful hunter, a man of the field," was loved by his father Isaac, "because he ate of his game" (Gen 25:27-28). It was while Esau hunted game, to prepare a meal for his father, that Jacob contrived to cheat Esau out of their father's blessing (Gen 27:1-40).

The portrayal of David as clubbing bears and lions that attacked his father's sheep (1 Sam 17:34-37) is not a portrayal of hunting, strictly speaking, though a hunter's skill is certainly implied in striking Goliath with a stone from a sling. The sling, whirled about the head until the slinger releases the stone, is still today a hunter's weapon in that region, where, by the ancient standard, a practiced user can "sling a stone at a hair, and not miss" (Judg 20:16).

The ostrich who "rouses herself to flee [and] laughs at the horse and his rider" (Job 39:18) may imply pursuit by a hunter on horseback. Pritchard's standard anthology of pictures includes ancient Assyrian and Egyptian bas-reliefs of hunters on horseback and others hunting from horse-drawn chariots; their weapons are either bows and arrows, or spears (hunting-spears are mentioned as the weapons of Nebuchadrezzar in Jdt 1:15). Some of these reliefs picture game being driven by beaters into pits or deadfalls. S. W. Helms has shown that driving gazelles into trap corrals has been a hunting practice from neolithic times at least down to the recent past in the Transjordan.

Beyond the foregoing examples, hunting or the weapons of hunting would seem to occur only as metaphors in the Bible. David complains that Saul seeks his life "like one who hunts a partridge in the mountains" (1 Sam 26:20). Deliverance from the "snare of the fowler [bird hunter]" is a common figure for deliverance from danger (Pss 91:3; 124:7; cf. Hos 9:8). For Job, "God . . . has closed his net about me" (Job 19:6). The wisdom sage's advice is to "pursue wisdom like a hunter" (Sir 14:22).

The Bible's relative paucity of reference to hunting may well reflect a difficulty inherent to the postexilic Jewish ethos—the difficulty of reconciling the adventitious circumstances attendant upon the killing of game with a ritual imposition, on the hunter, of strict procedures for the slaughter of animals intended for food (Lev 17:10-16; see esp. 17:13, for the hunter)—the quarry might die before it could be properly bled. That postbiblical rabbinical tradition discouraged the activity of hunting, particularly as a sport, appears to be well documented.

Bibliography. J. K. Anderson, *Hunting in the Ancient World*; S. W. Helms, "Paleo-Beduin and Transmigrant Urbanism," *Studies in the History and Archaeology of Jordan*; "Hunting and Animals," *ANEP*; L. I. Rabinowitz, "Hunting," *EncJud*; E. A. Speiser, *Genesis, AB*; L. E. Toombs, "Hunting," *IDB*.

—BRUCE T. DAHLBERG

• **Hurrian.** *See* NUZI

• **Husband.** *See* MARRIAGE IN THE NEW TESTAMENT

• **Hushai.** [hoosh'*i*] Identified as a "friend" of DAVID (2 Sam 15:37). "Friend" was apparently a royal title (cf. 1 Kgs 4:5). When ABSALOM revolted against his father, Hushai followed David from the city, showing his loyalty to the king. David, however, sent Hushai, along with Zadok and Abiathar, back to Jerusalem as his agents. Hushai's task was to refute the advice of the wise counselor Ahithophel. Ahithophel advised Absalom to pursue David from Jerusalem at once, not allowing him to reach safety elsewhere. Hushai, however, reminded Absalom of David's fighting prowess and advised him to round up a large army before attacking the king. Further, Hushai warned David of Ahithophel's counsel, sending word through the priests, Zadok and Abiathar. Absalom followed Hushai's advice, giving David time to escape to MAHANAIM and muster his army.

See also DAVID; FRIENDSHIP.

—PAUL L. REDDITT

• **Hyksos.** [hik'sohs] The Hyksos were Asiatics who invaded and controlled EGYPT sometime during the Middle Bronze Age III (1750–1550 B.C.E.). According to Manetho (third century B.C.E.), a Ptolemaic historian known through the writings of Josephus, the Hyksos founded the fifteenth dynasty and ruled Egypt for over a 100 years (1650–1542 B.C.E.). Manetho translated the word "Hyksos," which he applied originally to the leaders of this group, to mean "shepherd kings," but modern scholars believe the word is simply the Greek from of the Old Egyptian "kikau-khoswet" which means "rulers of foreign countries."

What ethnic elements comprised the Hyksos and when and how they entered Egypt are questions for which there are still no definitive answers. The study of Hyksos names (e.g., on scarabs) indicates that their basic composition was semitic. Whether or not their makeup also included Indo-European and/or Hurrian elements is still debated. Some scholars relate their appearance in Palestine and Egypt to the Horite movement that spread over the Levant during the first half of the second millennium B.C.E. There is also no agreement on how they managed to gain control over Egypt. Some suggest it was done in a single assault, while others believe it was done in stages.

Whatever the case, by the end of the eighteenth century (a commonly suggested date is 1720 B.C.E.), they were well established in the Nile Delta, having built a capital city at Avaris (PLATE 8). The location of this city is probably indicative both of the close relationship they maintained with Palestine, from which they had come, and also of the fact that they were never in full control of Upper Egypt which remained in the hands of Theban princes during this time.

It is from within this latter group that the Egyptians' struggle to overthrow the Hyksos began in the sixteenth century with the efforts of Ka-mose, the last Upper Egyptian ruler of the Seventeenth Dynasty. But it would be Amosis (ca. 1552–1527), the founder of the eighteenth dynasty, and the brother of Ka-mose, who would rid Egypt of these "foreigners" for good. By 1540 he had succeeded in driving them back into Palestine, pursuing them as far as Sharuhen (probably Tell el-Farah, south) where, after a three-year siege, he drove them out.

The full extent of Hyksos domination is still unclear, but the evidence certainly points to Egypt, Palestine, and at least parts of Syria. That they possessed a distinctive culture of their own, however, has been seriously questioned by recent studies that have raised doubts regarding their association with the massive rampart fortifications found at most major cities during this period, and with other cultural remains previously attributed to them. Some scholars do credit them with the introduction of the war chariot and composite bow into the region.

Politically they organized Palestine into a city-state system producing a feudal society with its concomitant uneven distribution of wealth. Nevertheless, Palestine experienced one of its most prosperous periods under Hyksos rule. Along with the Horites, and other ethnic groups, the Hyksos formed the population met by the Israelites and other peoples who entered Canaan in the thirteenth century B.C.E.

Finally, it should be noted that some scholars locate the story of Joseph (Gen 37–50) during the period of Hyksos domination in Egypt. But this is debatable and demands a historical evaluation of the biblical story not shared by other experts.

See also EGYPT.

Bibliography. J. Bright, *A History of Israel*; W. C. Hayes, "The Hyksos Infiltration and the Founding of the Fifteenth Dynasty," *CAH* 2/1: 54-60; T. O. Lambdin, "Hyksos," *IDB*; J. V. Seters, *The Hyksos*; R. de Vaux, *The Early History of Israel*.

—JOHN C. H. LAUGHLIN

• **Hymn.** Sacred poetry set to music and used in both private and corporate worship. The word "hymn" technically does not appear in the OT and has only scant use in the NT but the practice of singing praises to God is common throughout the Bible.

The Psalms of the OT reflect a form of the hymn used both in Temple worship and in more informal times of devotion. The singing and chanting of Psalms in worship were often accompanied by virtually all types of musical instruments known in the ancient Near East. These ranged from stringed instruments and pipes to trumpets and cymbals (Ps 150). The OT narrative includes songs used on particular occasions to mark a significant religious experience. The song of MOSES and MIRIAM (Exod 15) celebrated the deliverance of ISRAEL from EGYPT and the song of HANNAH (1 Sam 2, probably a psalm of national thanksgiving) marked the giving of the child SAMUEL to the Lord. Work songs (Num 21:17-18), wedding songs (Cant 3:6-11; 7:1-6), and funeral dirges (2 Sam 1:17-27) indicate that Israel's life was replete with singing. The use of psalms as a form of hymn appears also in the Apocrypha in writings such as The Song of the Three Young Men and The Prayer of Manasseh.

The Hebraic heritage of NT persons accounted for the inclusion of psalms as a major part of the hymnody in the Christian scriptures. In the infancy narratives the MAGNIFICAT (Luke 1:46-55), BENEDICTUS (Luke 1:67-79), and NUNC DIMITTIS (Luke 2:29-32) served as hymns that became integral parts of the Christian liturgical tradition. At the Last Supper JESUS and his disciples sang a hymn before they departed from the upper room (Mark 14:26) to go to Gethsemane. This hymn was probably the Hallel, the Pss 113–118, which Hebrews sang at principal festivals.

PAUL and SILAS, imprisoned in Philippi during a missionary journey, sang hymns as a devotional act (Acts

16:25), perhaps indicating the frequent use of hymns in private Christian worship (Jas 5:13). Fragments of several early hymns appear in the NT (Eph 5:19; Phil 2:6-11; 1 Tim 3:16). These hymns appear to have both devotional and doctrinal significance for the early church. Primitive doxologies likewise appear in 1 Tim 6:15-16 and Rev 4:8, 11.

The apostle Paul encouraged the church at Colossae to sing "psalms, hymns, and spiritual songs" as acts of thanksgiving to God. Some interpreters view these designations as early categories of hymnody ranging from liturgical psalms and hymns to spontaneous spiritual songs that may have been ecstatic. Such interpretations are instructive but without biblical support.

After the passing of the apostolic era the early church began to preserve and develop its hymns, giving preference to songs of praise to Christ. The earliest collection of Christian hymns in a hymn book was the Odes of Solomon, which dates from the first half of the second century. Hymns were widely used to teach doctrine in the early church, as attested by the frequent use of hymns among heretical groups such as the Gnostics and Arians and by the care orthodox Christianity gave to selecting suitable hymns for worship.

See also BENEDICTUS; MAGNIFICAT; NUNC DIMITTIS; POETRY; PSALMS, BOOK OF; WORSHIP IN THE OLD TESTAMENT; WORSHIP IN THE NEW TESTAMENT.

Bibliography. O. Eissfeldt, *The Old Testament: An Introduction*; D. P. Hustad, "The Psalms as Worship Expressions: Personal and Congregational," *RE* 81 (1984): 407-24.

—STEVEN SIMPLER

• **Hymn Scroll.** *See* THANKSGIVING SCROLL/HYMN SCROLL

• **Hymns/Creeds.** Part of the heritage of the early church was its use of psalms in WORSHIP. Psalms played a great part in the ritual of the Temple and in the services of the synagogues in the diaspora. It was natural that early Christians would seek to express their praise to God by such means.

Evidence for the use of psalms and hymns in the life of Jesus can be found in the synoptic Gospels. Jesus was greeted with words from the Book of Psalms at his entry into Jerusalem (Mark 11:9 and par.). When he and his disciples had finished their last supper together, they sang a hymn (Mark 14:26 and par.).

The Book of Psalms was widely used by the early church. Citations from the Psalms are frequent in NT writings. This song book of the Jewish community served as a resource for both the worship and the teaching of the church.

Hymns as well as psalms were an important part of Christian worship. In the Letters to the Colossians and Ephesians, reference is made to "psalms and hymns and spiritual songs" (Eph 5:19; Col 3:16). In Paul's list of elements found in the worship of the Corinthian church, hymns were given first place (1 Cor 14:26). Paul and Silas sang hymns in the Philippian jail (Acts 16:25).

Although no clear distinction can be made between the three types of songs referred to in Ephesians and Colossians, Christians not only used OT psalms but also developed for themselves their own special hymns of praise addressed to Christ. Examples of such hymns have been preserved in the NT.

No precise list of hymns in the NT can be made because scholars have not come to agreement on the question of criteria. Among the criteria suggested for identifying hymns are the following: use of introductory formulas; parallelism; use of a relative pronoun at the beginning (e.g., Phil 2:6; 1 Tim 3:16); descriptive participles; the use of conjunctions introducing indirect discourse or causal clauses; and vocabulary differing from the context.

In spite of a lack of agreement, scholars have identified hymns and hymnic material on the basis of criteria listed above. The birth narratives of Luke contain hymnic passages similar to OT hymns (Luke 1:46-55, 68-79); these are hymns addressed to God.

Other prominent passages which appear to meet the requirement for hymns are: Phil 2:6-11; Eph 5:14; Col 1:15-20; 1 Tim 3:16; and 2 Tim 2:11-13. While most recognize these as hymns, or fragments of hymns, there is little agreement about their origin and whether they contain secondary additions. For example, was the hymn of Phil 2 composed by Paul or did he use a hymn composed by someone else? Were the words "death on a cross" added by Paul as an explanation?

Other passages are suggested as being hymnic. Revelation contains many hymns (4:11; 5:9b-10, 12-13; 11:17-18; 15:3-4; 19:6-8). Debate still occurs concerning the prologue of the Gospel of John (1:1-18). Did a pre-Christian hymn, perhaps in honor of John the Baptist, or an early Christian hymn lie behind this passage? Certainly there are hymnic aspects to the material.

The use of hymns was widespread in the church and important in its life and worship. Hymns served as a means of expressing praise to God and to Christ. They were also means of expressing the beliefs of the people, their creeds.

Creedal material in the NT differs from the highly developed creeds of the church from the third and fourth centuries. They are materials which express the faith of the community, perhaps having their origin in the early years of the church. Expressed most frequently in the writings of Paul, they were received from those who were Christians before him.

It is generally agreed that the earliest confession of the Christians was "Jesus is Lord" (Rom 10:9; 1 Cor 12:3) or "Jesus is the Christ" (1 John 2:22). This does not exclude the confession of the one God, a confession shared with their fellow Jews. The distinctive claim of Christians, however, was that Jesus was Lord. Some argue that this confession developed in the Hellenistic church, but there is growing agreement that the claim goes back to the church in Palestine.

It may be that 1 Cor 15:3ff. is the oldest piece of creedal material that we can clearly identify. Paul had received the tradition—as is indicated by the technical terms used for receiving and passing on the tradition. The use of "that" four times suggests quotation marks. Five statements are made in this passage: "Christ died for our sins in accordance with the scriptures"; "he was buried"; "he was raised on the third day in accordance with the scriptures"; "he appeared to Cephas"; and "he appeared to the twelve."

A central element of the creeds was reference to the death of Christ (cf. 1 Tim 2:5-6 and 1 Pet 3:18). The death of Christ for sin was apparently part of the regular preaching and teaching of the church. Along with this was an emphasis upon the resurrection. The creedal material refers not only to what Christ had done but also to what God had done in raising him from the dead (Rom 4:24; 2 Cor 4:14; Eph 1:20-22; 1 Pet 1:21). Closely connected with the idea of resurrection was that of exaltation to the right hand of God (Rom 8:34).

Another piece of early creedal material is Rom 1:3-4. Indications that this is material Paul received from others are that it reflects ideas which he did not commonly express and omits other ideas which were prominent when he was freely expressing himself. These verses place emphasis upon Jesus as Lord, upon his human descent from David, and upon his being designated or appointed Son of God at his resurrection.

From the evidence in the NT, it seems that Christians from the earliest time expressed the common elements of their faith in similar ways. These expressions are embedded in the NT writings, preserved as pieces of creedal, traditional material by the later writers.

See also BAPTISM; BENEDICTUS; MAGNIFICAT; MUSIC/MUSICAL INSTRUMENTS; NUNC DIMITTIS; POETRY; PSALMS, BOOK OF; WORSHIP IN THE NEW TESTAMENT; WORSHIP IN THE OLD TESTAMENT.

Bibliography. G. Delling, *Worship in the New Testament;* D. Guthrie, *New Testament Theology;* M. Hengel, "Hymn and Christology," *Papers on Paul and Other New Testament Authors,* ed. E. A. Livingstone; A. M. Hunter, *Paul and His Predecessors;* C. F. D. Moule, *Worship in the New Testament;* V. H. Neufeld, *The Earliest Christian Confessions;* J. T. Sanders, *The New Testament Christological Hymns.*

—CLAYTON K. HARROP

• **Hypocrisy.** In Classical and Hellenistic Greek, the verb which can be translated literally "to play the hypocrite" originally meant "to explain" or "to interpret." The nouns "hypocrisy" and "hypocrite" signified "answer" and "actor" respectively. Later the terms were used metaphorically to compare human life and conduct to the stage and the work of an actor. Additional words were required to indicate whether the comparison had a positive, neutral, or negative connotation.

The LXX used the terms in a negative sense exclusively, but not with the meaning "pretense." Greek-speaking Jews used the words to refer to evildoers, deceivers, godless people, or those who commit apostasy (Job 34:30; 36:13; 2 Macc 5:25; 6:21). The NT continued the Jewish use of the word group (cf. Mark 12:15; Matt 22:18; Luke 20:23), with the exception of Luke 20:20 where the scribes and high priests sent spies who "played the hypocrite" or "pretended to be sincere."

—RON FARMER

• **Hypostasis of the Archons.** [h*i*′puh-stas″sis, ahr′kohns] *The Hypostasis of the Archons,* from Codex II of the NAG HAMMADI documents, is of two literary types. The first part is a Gnostic interpretation of the Genesis account of creation, while the latter part is a revelation discourse between a heavenly mentor, Eleleth, and an earthly questioner. It has been suggested that this reflects the editorial combination of two sources. There are few Christian touches in the book, and it is possible that most of the material stems from a Gnosticism rooted in Judaism. There may be affinities with the Sethians or Ophites. Like all the Nag Hammadi documents, it is assumed to have been written in Greek and translated into Coptic. It is tentatively dated to the third century C.E.

An ignorant power proclaims himself as the only God, whereupon a voice calls him Samael, god of the blind, The archons (rulers) make a man from the dust of the earth, in their image which they have seen in the water, but they cannot make the man live. The Spirit accomplishes this by settling in him. The archons have this ADAM name the animals, and command him not to eat of the fruit of the TREE OF KNOWLEDGE of good and evil. While Adam sleeps, the archons create a woman from his side. They fall in love with her and try to rape her, but they succeed only in raping her image, while the real woman laughs at their blindness.

The serpent appears as an instructor, tempting the woman to eat the fruit and obtain knowledge. Both the man and woman eat, and realize that they are spiritually naked. The Great Archon confronts the pair and curses Adam, the woman, and the serpent, and cast them out of PARADISE. The story of CAIN AND ABEL is then told in a form fairly close to that of Genesis. Adam and EVE, who is now named, have a son and a daughter, the undefiled virgin.

The archons determine to annihilate humanity with a flood, but the ruler of the forces commands NOAH to build an ark. A female figure, Norea, appears, wishing to board the ark, but being forbidden, burns it with her breath. Norea, identified as daughter of Eve, is now accosted by the archons, but she prays for help to the God of the All. An angel, Eleleth, appears, who says he will instruct her.

Here the narrative shifts to the first person, and a revelation discourse ensues. Eleleth assures his listener, presumably Norea in present text, that the archons will not prevail. They originated in the desire of Sophia (Wisdom) to create something on her own. A lion-like androgyne is formed, who arrogantly proclaims himself the only god, and proceeds to create seven androgynous offspring, to whom he proclaims himself as god. Zoe (Life), daugher of Sophia, corrects him. This archon is Ialdabaoth, corresponding to the creator God of Genesis. He is cast into Tartaros, while his son Sabaoth repents, and praises Sophia and Zoe, who transport him to the seventh heaven. The jealous Ialdabaoth now brings envy and death into being. Eleleth's fearful listener is reassured that those whose souls came from imperishable light are immortal, and after an eschatological trampling of the evil powers they will know the truth, the Father, and the Holy Spirit, and praise the Father and Son forever.

Strong Gnostic themes are seen in this book, especially in the picture of the Jewish God as a lesser, jealous deity, and the picture of the serpent as a beneficent figure bringing knowledge (*gnosis*) to humanity against the will of the jealous demiurge.

See also APOCALYPTIC LITERATURE; COSMOLOGY; GNOSTICISM; NAG HAMMADI; ORIGIN OF THE WORLD, ON THE; PISTIS SOPHIA.

Bibliography. R. Bullard, *The Hypostasis of the Archons*; W. Foerster, *Gnosis: A Selection of Gnostic Texts*; B. Layton, "The Hypostasis of the Archons," *HTR* 67 (1974): 351-426 and 69 (1976): 31-102; E. Pagels, "Exegesis and Exposition of the Genesis Creation Accounts in Selected Texts from Nag Hammadi," *Nag Hammadi, Gnosticism, and Early Christianity,* ed. C. Hedrick and R. Hodgson, Jr.

—ROGER A. BULLARD

• **Hypsiphrone.** [hip-sif′roh-nee] *Hypsiphrone* is a highly fragmentary treatise from Codex XI of the NAG HAMMADI documents. It is apparently a revelation discourse delivered by Hypsiphrone, She of High Mind, describing her descent into the world.

See also GNOSTICISM; NAG HAMMADI.

Bibliography. J. D. Turner, "Hypsiphrone," *The Nag Hammadi Library in English,* ed. J. M. Robinson.

—ROGER A. BULLARD

• **Iconium.** [*i*-koh'nee-uhm] Located in south-central Asia Minor (modern Turkey), Iconium was the capital of Lycaonia during the Greek and Roman periods (PLATES 26, 27). The area was settled by the Phrygians around 1200 B.C.E. Even though some ancient authors, such as Pliny and Cicero, refer to the city as being Lycaonian, the inhabitants spoke the Phrygian language and apparently regarded themselves as Phrygians.

The city was rarely politically independent, and by the first century C.E., it was part of the Roman empire. It was famous for its beauty and its economic prosperity which was due in most part to its strategic location on major trade routes and to its rich agricultural products. In late Roman and Byzantine periods it became a large and wealthy city. Iconium is first mentioned in the fourth century B.C.E. by the Greek author, Xenophon. In his famous work, *Anabasis*, he describes the travels of the Persian king, Cyrus, who visited Iconium.

By the time of the NT, Iconium, along with such other cities as ANTIOCH of Pisidia, LYSTRA, and DERBE, belonged to the Roman province of GALATIA. According to Acts 14, PAUL visited Iconium on his first missionary journey and had considerable success preaching there to both Jews and gentiles. At the same time, Jewish opposition forced him and BARNABAS to flee the city for their lives. TIMOTHY, recruited by Paul on his second mission through the area (Acts 15:40–18:21), was apparently well-known and respected in Iconium (cf. Acts 16:1-2). The setting of the apocryphal story of Paul and the woman Thecla is also located in this city.

See also ANTIOCH; BARNABAS; DERBE; GALATIA; GALATIANS, LETTER TO THE; LYSTRA; PAUL, ACTS OF; TIMOTHY.

Bibliography. W. M. Ramsey, *The Cities of St. Paul*.

—JOHN C. H. LAUGHLIN

• **Iddo.** [id'oh] *1.* A descendant of Gershom the son of Levi (1 Chr 6:21; it appears that he is called Adaiah in 6:41).

2. Iddo, the son of Zechariah, was David's officer over the tribe of Manasseh in Gilead (1 Chr 27:21).

3. The father of Ahinadab, one of Solomon's twelve district officers (1 Kgs 4:14).

4. A prophet active during the reigns of Solomon, Jeroboam I, Rehoboam, and Abijah.

5. The father or grandfather of the prophet Zechariah (cf. Zech 1:1, 7; Ezra 5:1; 6:14). He may be the Iddo named as a priest who returned from Babylon with Zerubbabel (Neh 12:4; cf. 12:16), or the two may be different individuals.

6. A leader in Casiphia who sent a group of Temple servants to Ezra to return with him to Jerusalem (Ezra 8:15-20).

—JEFFREY S. ROGERS

• **Idolatry.** Israel's prohibition against images in the worship of her God stands in stark contrast to her culture. People of the ancient Near East commonly accepted that fertility was as much a result of their participation in agriculturally oriented religions as conscientious cultivation of the soil. Sacred objects such as stone pillars, images of fertility gods and goddesses, and sacred poles (*Asherim*) were all part of this religious practice. A household image of the earth goddess would have been regarded as important for farming as a strong plow. Given this cultural mindset, it is not surprising that archaeologists have discovered numerous fertility figurines in Hebrew settlements, for the average worshipers of Yahweh had difficulty excluding such commonly accepted cultural practices from their lifestyle. It would seem very natural to these Hebrew folk, even great heroes of faith like AARON (Exod 32) and GIDEON (Judg 8:24-27), to adapt local images to the worship of Yahweh. Thus in Israel's law it was necessary not only to prohibit the worship of other gods (Exod 20:3), but also prohibit the use of images in the worship of Yahweh (Exod 20:4).

Unless this image-oriented milieu is taken seriously, modern readers will fall into several common misunderstandings of Israel's prohibition against idolatry. First, the prohibition against idols was not a claim for a rationally sophisticated religion versus primitive religions. Ancient Near Eastern writings indicate an awareness of the difference between gods themselves and the images that represented the gods or that the gods temporarily inhabited. Second, the notion that Israel advocated a spiritual religion versus the material one of idolatry draws on a distinction that was foreign to the ancient Near East including the Hebrew people. OT narratives often describe manifestations of Yahweh associated with material objects, e.g., burning bush, pillar of fire, the Ark of the Covenant. Third, it is a gross oversimplification to portray Israel as consciously rejecting Yahwism through involvement with idols. Israel easily fell into the polytheism found among Canaanite neighbors (e.g., Exod 20:23, NEB) or the past (cf. Josh 24:14; Gen 31:14-32) while maintaining that Yahweh was the chief god. Israel adapted images for what was perceived to be a justifiable syncretistic devotion to Yahweh; but images legitimately used by Yahwism in one era—e.g., MOSES' brazen serpent (Num 21:8-9), sacred pillars (e.g., Judg 3:19), sacred trees (Josh 24:26) and the enigmatic ephod (e.g., 1 Sam 23:6-7)—were rejected as idolatrous by later eras. Perhaps, as Lev 26:1 suggests, the issue was whether or not the sacred object became the focus of worship ("bow down to them"). Or, perhaps the issue had been the object's resemblance ("likeness") to humans or creatures as the Decalogue suggests (Exod 20:4; Deut 5:8), though as the problem of idolatry increased, all ritual objects became suspect.

JEROBOAM's use of bull images is a good illustration of Israel's struggle. Sanctioned by Yahweh's prophet AHIJAH, Jeroboam led the northern tribes in rebellion against the oppressive tyranny of Judah (1 Kgs 11:29–12:15) and sought to provide his nation its own Yahwistic identity in contrast to the Jerusalem Temple cult of Judah. He designated DAN and BETHEL as centers of worship and set up a "golden calf" at each sanctuary (1 Kgs 12:26-33), probably to represent Yahweh's throne in much the same way as the Ark of the Covenant functioned in the Jerusalem Temple (e.g., 2 Kgs 19:15). There is evidence that Canaanite religions also employed the bull image as the throne of an invisible god (Albright, 203, 229-30). Israel's bull images were later condemned as idolatrous by the prophet HOSEA (e.g., 10:5; 13:2) and the DEUTERONOMISTIC HISTORIANS (e.g., 1 Kgs 14:9; 2 Kgs 10:29). The latter also provide a story about the origin of the sanctuary at Dan, clearly identifying it as a place with a history of idolatry (Judg 17–18).

Living with Canaanite neighbors led to an ongoing temptation to embrace Baalism (e.g., Judg 2:11-13; 1 Sam 7:3-4; 1 Kgs 18:20-40), but the problem was fueled by SOLOMON and later kings who married daughters of foreign monarchs to seal military alliances and trade agreements (1 Kgs 11:1-8) and allowed their queens to support their native religions (e.g., JEZEBEL, 1 Kgs 16:31-33; 21:25-26). Monarchy-supported idolatry reached its zenith during the long reign of MANASSEH, who placed "the graven image of ASHERAH" in the Temple itself (2 Kgs 21:1-9).

A century earlier the prophet Hosea had lambasted not only idolatrous practices but their deeper problem: image-religion is basically motivated by human materialistic desires and thereby attempts to manipulate the deity for selfish ends (2:5; 7:14; 10:1). Some commentators (e.g., Harrelson, 64-70) have noted that Hebrew scriptures speak of one legitimate image or representation of God: humanity (Gen 1:26-28). Thus Hosea was intolerant of even traditional sacred objects associated with Yahweh worship (Hos 3:4-5), for image-oriented religion encourages human energy to be invested in craftsmanship and in ritual attention to the images (Hos 13:2) rather than right living (cf. 6:6). Hosea and other eighth-century prophets also denounced Israel and Judah's trust in weapons of war (Hos 10:13) in terms parallel to their denunciation of idolatry (cf. Isa 2:7-8; Mic 5:10-15). Later the prophet EZEKIEL would identify the connection between Israel's infatuation with Assyrian military might and her attraction to Assyria's false gods (cf. chap. 23).

The concerns of these prophets were codified into more specific prohibitions against idolatry in the deuteronomic collection of laws. Not only are graven images prohibited, but also worship of heavenly bodies (Deut 4:19) as well as objects like sacred pillars (16:22) and trees, which had an ancient tradition among the Hebrews (cf. Gen 21:33; 28:18; Exod 24:4; Josh 4:4-9; 24:26; 1 Sam 7:12). This had been anticipated by HEZEKIAH's reform, which had destroyed pillars and the brazen serpent (2 Kgs 18:4). Images are not only prohibited because Yahweh says so (Deut 5:8); there are logical reasons as well. Idols are inconsistent with the nature of Yahweh, who is not seen but heard (Deut 4:12-18). Thus Moses is portrayed as having only heard God, though other traditions had described Moses' seeing God at least to some degree (Exod 19:11; 24:9-11; 33:18-23; Num 12:8). Also, idols are products of wood and stone made by human hands (Deut 4:28), and they are powerless to do anything (4:32-33). King JOSIAH's reform of Judah sought a rigorous application of deuteronomic prohibitions (2 Kgs 22–23).

The prophet JEREMIAH—who lived though Josiah's reform efforts, the subsequent return to idolatry and corruption, and even the downfall of Judah—provided one of the most thorough indictments of idolatry. He allowed that the prohibition against idolatry went against human custom (10:2-5) and the desires of the human heart (9:13-14), but this in no way excused it. God had summoned Israel to follow God's law, but Israel had stubbornly continued in idolatry (16:10-13). Idols are mere creations of human hands, without power, and ridiculous objects compared to Yahweh, the creator (10:11-15). Jeremiah's denunciation of the rampant idolatry was fierce: e.g., "they have polluted my land with the carcasses of their detestable idols" (16:18). He had no patience with the syncretism that allowed images in the Temple (7:30; 32:34). Recalling the exclusive relationship commanded by God, Jeremiah, like Hosea, equated idolatry with adultery, abandoning Yahweh in favor of other lovers (3:1-9). In contrast to these idols who have no feelings, God is moved to grief and anger (8:18-19).

After the collapse of Judah the prophet Ezekiel recalled his nation's history as one littered with idolatry (chap. 20). Not only the nation, but also individual hearts were estranged from God because of idolatry (14:4-8). By describing the materials and process of idol-making (Isa 44:9-20), Deutero-Isaiah ridiculed these creations of human hands that have to be moved by lowly beasts (46:1-7) in contrast to the power and care of Yahweh. Similarly, a narrative about the Philistine god Dagon in 1 Sam 5:1-5 humorously contrasts the powerlessness of an idol with Yahweh.

With Israel's development of monotheism it was only a short move to claim that any loyalty other than to Yahweh was idolatrous. The Book of Job juxtaposes trust in wealth with worship of the heavenly bodies (Job 31:24-28). Centuries later JESUS would personify material desire as a competing loyalty with God: "You cannot serve God and money" (Matt 6:24). In Eph 5:3-5 and Col 3:5-6 greed is identified as a form of idolatry. A story in Acts depicts the Ephesian populace rioting against Paul's missionary work because it threatened the economic well-being of the silversmiths and others who benefited from the Artemis cult's popularity (Acts 19:23-41).

After the Exile the Jews' resistance to idolatry was encouraged by the threat of assimilation into gentile culture. The heroic resistance of three young Jews in Exile to idol worship is offered by the Book of Daniel as a model for Jews in conflict with the evils of gentile culture (chap. 3). In 4 B.C.E. young Jewish men cut down the golden eagle that HEROD the Great had placed over the Temple gate (Josephus, *BJ* 2.33.2-4). During the reign of Pontius PILATE (26–36 C.E.), Roman soldiers brought their standards (with images of Caesar on them) into Jerusalem. There was a large scale protest by the Jews, and eventually Pilate backed down and had the standards removed (Josephus, *BJ* 2. 9.2-3). This was the tension-ridden milieu in which Jesus lived.

Wisdom of Solomon, a first century B.C.E. Jewish writing from Egypt, which was read by many early Christian communities, claimed that idolatry "[I]s the beginning, cause, and end of every evil" (14:27). In the same vein PAUL argues that humanity's practice of idolatry is "without excuse" as humanity abandoned the clear evidence of knowledge of God in favor of idols resembling animals and humans (Rom 1:19-27). God left humanity to the natural consequences of worshiping and serving "the creature rather than the creator." Paul's address to the Athenians in Acts 17:22-29 is more tolerant of the ignorance from which idolatry stems, though no less insistent that it is false and requires repentance and conversion to the true God. Paul includes idolatry in lists of vices (Gal 5:19-21; 1 Cor 5:9-11).

A common theme in early Christian writings called for shunning idols (2 Cor 6:16-18; 1 John 5:21; 1 Cor 10:14; *Barn* 20:1; *Did* 5:1; 6:3). In 1 Thess 1:9-10 Paul recalls how his readers "broke with idolatry when you were converted to God and became servants of the real, living God." The question of accommodation to this culture is well illustrated by the controversy concerning eating meat that had been sacrificed to idols (and then sold in the marketplace). Did eating this meat or participating in civic feasts that consumed this meat constitute idolatry? Though he explicitly rejects participating in pagan rituals (1 Cor 10:14-22), Paul states that since those idols are not real, sacrificing meat to them is meaningless; and therefore eating it is without significance for one's conscience. Paul warns that this theological distinction might not be understood by new Christians. Thus out of a pragmatic concern for the faith community and care for fellow Christians, the meat offered to idols should not be eaten if it will undermine the faith of the "weak" (1 Cor 8:7-13; 10:14-33). In Rev 2:13-28 the issue is not pragmatic but a matter of faithfulness to God and a rejection of Satan. The idols are not gods, but they have a demonic reality (9:20)—an idea Paul also embraced (1 Cor 10:14-22)—and therefore under no circumstances should one eat meat that has been offered to idols.

As these early Christians read their scriptures (Jewish scriptures), they saw themselves as Israel once again living in a pagan world with the lure of popular idolatry. Thus to compromise with Greco-Roman culture was akin to the religious syncretism of BALAAM in Num 25:1-2; 31:16 (cf. Rev 2:13-17; Jude 11; 2 Pet 2:15). Toleration only led to immorality (Rev 2:20). Whether it be the desire to participate in trade guild feasts that were held in pagan temples (probably the issue in Rev 2:18-21) or to succumb to the coercion to participate in the emperor cult, the choice was God or Satan (Rev 13:11-17; 14:9-12; 20:4). The Romans regarded the emperor cult simply as a sign of patriotism and necessary for social order, whereas Christians denounced it as idolatrous and demonic.

See also IMAGE OF GOD; IMAGES/FIGURINES; MONOTHEISM.

Bibliography. W. F. Albright, *From Stone Age to Christianity: Monotheism and the Historical Process;* C. K. Barrett, "Things Sacrificed to Idols," *Essays on Paul;* E. Bevan, *Holy Images: An Inquiry into Idolatry and Image-Worship in Ancient Paganism and in Christianity;* W. Eichrodt, *Theology of the Old Testament*; R. Grant, *Gods and the One God: Christian Theology in the Graeco-Roman World;* W. Harrelson, *The Ten Commandments and Human Rights*; J. L. Mays, *Hosea, A Commentary*; D. Patrick, *Old Testament Law;* A. Phillips, *Ancient Israel's Criminal Law: A New Approach to the Decalogue;* C. R. North, "The Essence of Idolatry," *Von Ugarit nach Qumran;* R. de Vaux, *The Bible and the Ancient Near East.*

—DAVID NELSON DUKE

• **Idumaea.** *See* EDOM/EDOMITES/IDUMAEA

• **Ignatius.** [ig-nay'shuhs] Ignatius, whose writings are included in the APOSTOLIC FATHERS, was Bishop of ANTIOCH and was martyred at Rome during the reign of Trajan (98–117). Virtually nothing is known about Ignatius apart from what his seven letters reveal about his last days. EUSEBIUS fixed the date of martyrdom in the tenth year of Trajan (108), but modern historians have disputed this. It is probably safest to say that he was escorted as a prisoner from Syria to ROME to suffer martyrdom sometime during Trajan's reign. On the way he composed seven letters, four from SMYRNA and three from Troas. From Smyrna he wrote to Christian communities in EPHESUS, Magnesia, and Tralles to thank them for emissaries they had sent to greet him and to the church of Rome to exhort the Romans not to do anything to prevent his martyrdom. From Troas he dispatched letters to Polycarp, Bishop of Smyrna, and to the churches of Smyrna and PHILADELPHIA to thank them for their hospitality and asking them to send messengers to Antioch to congratulate them on the ending of a conflict.

The seven letters of Ignatius were revised and enlarged and six other letters added about 380. In the Middle Ages four Latin letters were also tacked onto the Ignatian corpus. Printed in Latin in 1498 and in Greek in 1557, this longer collection was not challenged until 1646, when six of the original letters were published. In 1689 the letter to the Romans appeared. Protestant scholars, however, questioned the authenticity of even the seven letters until the late-nineteenth century when Theodore Zahn, F. X. Funk, J. B. Lightfoot, and Adolf Harnack made an irrefutable case for them.

As one would expect of letters written at approximately the same time with similar purpose, these letters are repetitious. The most distinctive is the letter to the Romans. Ignatius complimented the church of Rome highly, noting its preeminence in the whole region. Although his encomium is somewhat excessive in its praises, there can be little question that he ascribed a special place to this church. He hoped to see the Romans, but he was writing to make sure they would not try to save him from wild beasts. They should pray for him, above all, that he would remain faithful. "Suffer me to be eaten by the beasts, through whom I can attain to God. I am God's wheat, and I am ground by the teeth of wild beasts that I may be found pure bread of God" (*Rom* 4.1). The psychological state of the BISHOP at this point has evoked a considerable discussion. It was not enough that he experienced abuse from the company of ten Roman soldiers who guarded him on the way to Rome; he longed, rather, to be devoured by the beasts. If the latter hesitated to consume him, he would "force them" to do so, for by that he could be assured of attaining to Jesus Christ. The Romans, therefore, must not interfere. "Suffer me to follow the example of the passion of my God," he pleaded (*Rom* 6:3). He no longer had any desire for the things of this world nor for life itself. Roman efforts to avert his death would be a token of hatred and not of love. If they were friends, they would pray for him and for the church in Syria.

In the other six letters Ignatius offered thanks for assistance and responded to divisions among the churches of Asia Minor. The exact nature of the problem is debated. Ignatius mentioned both docetism, that is, the belief that Jesus only "appeared" to be human but was actually not, and Jewish tendencies which caused rifts in Christian communities. Some scholars have theorized two separate groups, one Gnostic and the other Jewish, perhaps ESSENE, but the mixture of allusions in each of the letters probably argues for a syncretistic movement which combined some elements of both. In Asia Minor at this time there were Jewish cults of this sort—the Zeus-Sabazios Cult and that of Cerinthus. Among other things, Ignatius charged, the heretics denied the INCARNATION, death, and RESURRECTION of Jesus; rejected the Eucharist or LORD'S SUPPER because of the same docetism (*Smyrn* 7.1); yet lived in a Jewish fashion—evidently meaning by observance of Jewish customs (*Magn* 8.1).

Ignatius saw the remedy for schism or heresy in commitment to the bishop. "Do nothing without the bishop!" is a constant refrain. From the vigor of his exhortation most scholars conclude that the churches of Asia Minor, and indeed that of Antioch and Syria, had not yet developed the monarchical episcopate Ignatius proposed but were in transition. The letters contain clear evidence of some kind of serious questioning of Ignatius's authority which may have increased his desire for martyrdom. When he reached Troas, he received the good news that the Church of Antioch had settled the controversy and asked the church of Philadelphia to send a DEACON to congratulate them (*Philad* 10.1). Churches should not baptize, celebrate Eucharists, hold agape-feasts, or perform marriages without the bishop's presence or approval (*Smyrn* 8). Presbyters and deacons served under and at the direction of the bishop, who should be honored as God.

Against docetism Ignatius underscored each time the true humanity of Jesus as well as his divinity. "There is one Physician, who is both flesh and spirit, born and yet not born, who is God and man, true life in death, both of Mary and of God, first passible and then impassible, Jesus Christ Our Lord" (*Eph* 7.2). Against the "Judaizers" he insisted that "Jesus Christ is our only teacher, of whom even the prophets were disciples in the Spirit and to whom they looked forward as their teacher" (*Magn* 9.1-2).

Ignatius was the first Christian writer to use the term "Catholic Church" (*Smyrn* 8.2) to designate Christians everywhere. He held a high view of the Eucharist, calling it "the medicine of immortality, the antidote against death, and everlasting life in Jesus Christ" (*Eph* 20:2). It symbolized the incarnation, "the flesh of our Lord Jesus" (*Philad* 4.1; *Smyrn* 7.1).

Considerable discussion has arisen over the sources of Ignatius's thought. He quoted or alluded to Paul's letters numerous times and knew Matthew's Gospel. He never quoted John, although his thought parallels it at many points. He may have known the Johannine tradition in some earlier form. He also reflected some Gnostic influences. He depended on a Syrian tradition of his day.

See also APOSTOLIC FATHERS; BISHOP.

Bibliography. L. W. Barnard, *Studies in the Apostolic Fathers and Their Background*; V. Corwin, *St. Ignatius and Christianity in Antioch*; R. M. Grant, *Ignatius of Antioch;* J. Quasten, *Patrology*; W. R. Schoedel, *Ignatius of Antioch: A Commentary on the Letters of Ignatius of Antioch.*

—E. GLENN HINSON

• **Illness.** *See* DISEASE AND HEALING; MADNESS

• **Illyricum.** [i-lihr'i-kuhm] Illyricum (PLATE 1) was the Roman name of a province on the Adriatic Sea, north of Macedonia and west of Thrace (modern Yugoslavia and Albania). Ancient writers spoke of the wildness of the Illyrians and the piracy practiced when they descended out

Designed by Margaret Jordan Brown ©Mercer University Press

of their mountain regions. This activity brought them into conflict with the Romans who began conquest of Illyricum in the third century B.C.E. and integrated it fully in the empire only in the first century C.E. under Tiberius.

Paul spoke of having preached the gospel "from Jerusalem and as far round as Illyricum" (Rom 15:19), but it is not clear that he was actually in Illyricum. The language used by Paul would be accurate if he had come within sight of Illyricum on his westward journey through Macedonia (cf. Acts 20:1-2).

—HERBERT O. EDWARDS, SR.

• **Image of God.** Used in the OT to indicate the distinctiveness of persons in God's created order. What constitutes human uniqueness has been the subject of considerable theological discussion ("reason," "soul,", "free will," etc.), but this is not the focus of the biblical materials. The phrase comes from the priestly tradition in Gen 1:26-27; 5:1-3; 9:1-7, and its meaning is nowhere specifically clarified, thus permitting later speculation to go beyond the priestly idea.

According to Gen 1, human beings were created in the image of God. The most obvious meaning is physical resemblance, but the writer clearly intends more, suggesting a more complex relationship between Creator and human creation. It is difficult to determine what the priestly writer meant specifically. Negatively, no dualistic definitions of humanity are intended. Whole persons are made in God's image; the image of God is not an implanted characteristic. Further, the reference is not to something "lost" in the FALL. After the FLOOD, humans remained in the image of God (Gen 9:6) as much as before the Fall.

Positively, both Gen 1:26-27 and 9:1-7 use image of God to indicate that humans are both different from and superior to other animals. Beasts of the earth are made "according to their kinds" (1:25), but humankind (*'ādām*) is in God's image to ". . . have dominion . . . over all the earth, and over every creeping thing that creeps upon the earth" (1:26). Such dignity belongs equally to male and female (1:27). The opening paragraph of Gen 9 further defines the role of animals to be to serve humans. Yet the created is not equal to the Creator. Persons are in the image of God; they are not God. In the wider narrative, one dimension of sin is aspiring to usurp the deity's role (Gen 3:5). Thus minimally in describing persons in the image of God the priestly writer intends to affirm a superiority over other creation and an inferiority to God as Creator. In larger perspective, the writer places human beings in intimate association with God, able to be in relationship to God, to pronounce God's name. The capacity to speak is probably a part of what it means to have been created in the image and likeness of God.

In the NT, particularly in Paul's writings, the meaning of image of God is transformed to apply to JESUS as the Christ. Accordingly, Christ "is the image of the invisible God" (Col 1:15) or "the likeness of God" (2 Cor 4:4); that is, a reflection of the prototype. Believers take on God's image as they are "conformed to the image of his Son" (Rom 8:29). Thus for Paul, being in God's image is more a matter of salvation than creation.

See also CREATION.

—ROBERT W. CRAPPS

• **Images/Figurines.** Images and figurines were common features of religious life in the ancient Near East. Archaeological excavations have uncovered carved or molded figures from almost every occupation level. There is also textual evidence from Mesopotamia and Ugarit for the practice of making images for use in local temples. The image symbolized the deity's PRESENCE for the local devotees who would come "to see the face" of their god and pray. Images were not only used at shrines, but have also been uncovered in the remains of houses (cf. Laban's "household gods" in Gen 31:30ff.).

There are several Hebrew words (for example, *semel, pesel,* and *ṣelem*) which may be translated by "image," "figurine," or "statue." Often, however, the most appropriate translation is the pejorative term "idol." By and large, the use of images or figurines in worship is strictly forbidden in the OT. The second commandment declares, "You shall not make for yourself a graven image, . . . you shall not bow down to them or serve them, for I the Lord your God am a jealous God . . . " (Exod 20:4-5a; cf. Deut 5:7-9).

Nevertheless, numerous texts suggest that foreign cultic practices, including images and figurines, were present in Israel and Judah from early times until at least the period of JOSIAH's reforms (cf. Gen 35:2ff.; Exod 32; Josh 24:14; Judg 6:25-27; 17:1-13; 1 Kgs 12:26-33; 14:9-10; 2 Kgs 17:16-18, 29-33; 22:17; 23:4-20; Isa 2:18; 17:7-8; Jer 2:28; Hos 4:12-13, 17; 6:10; 8:4-6; 11:2; 13:1-3; 14:8; Amos 5:25-27; Mic 1:7). Such practices are almost always viewed negatively as the cause of the downfall of the people, a king, of Israel, or as that which threatens Judah's existence. For example, included among the list of sins which led to the fall of Samaria in 722/1 B.C.E. is the statement, "they served idols, of which the Lord had said to them, 'You shall not do this' " (2 Kgs 17:12).

These strong prohibitions indicate that the influence of foreign religious practices was a serious problem in ancient Israel. In spite of this there are some few texts which refer to images without this polemic. Moses erected the "bronze serpent," though it was not an object of worship, but a device for healing (Num 21:8-9). Later Hezekiah destroyed it because the people burned incense to it (2 Kgs 18:4). The story of Micah's molten image, later set up at Laish (Dan), is presented in Judg 17 without negative comment. The Ark of the Covenant was decorated with cherubim which may have symbolized Yahweh's glory (Exod 25:18-20).

It is not surprising that archaeological evidence of images of Yahweh has not been forthcoming. There are, however, OT texts, similar to Mesopotamian texts, which refer to seeing the deity or image of the deity in the sanctuary. For example, Ps 17, a prayer for deliverance from personal enemies, concludes with the statement, "I shall behold thy face in righteousness; when I awake, I shall be satisfied with beholding thy form" (v. 15). Ps 63:2 states, "I have looked upon thee in the sanctuary, beholding thy power and glory." These rare references to seeing Yahweh in the context of the sanctuary may simply relate an idiom for "worship in the Temple." Yet when compared with similar Mesopotamian texts they may reflect vestiges of an older usage when images were employed in the worship of Yahweh. In spite of this similarity, the prohibition of images in Yahweh worship prevailed as is strongly indicated throughout the OT.

Representations of God were also objectionable to early Christians. The NT mentions images or idols (εἰκών) in connection with gentile paganism. Paul found Athens "full of idols" (Acts 17:16). He forbids Christians from participating in ceremonies which may honor pagan gods or idols (1 Cor 8:4, 7; 10:14; 12:2; cf. Acts 15:19-20; 1 John 5:21).

See also IDOLATRY.

Bibliography. F. Nötscher, *"Das Angesicht Gottes schauen" nach biblischer und babylonischer Auffassung*; A. L. Oppenheim, "Verse Account of Nabonidus," *ANET*; J. B. Pritchard, *Palestinian Figurines in Relation to Certain Goddesses Known through Literature*; G. von Rad, "εἰκών," *TDNT*; A. Spycket, *Les Statues des Culte dan les Textes Mesopotamiens des Orîgnes a la Ire Dynastie de Babylone*.

—CECIL P. STATON, JR.

• **Immanuel.** [i-man'*yoo*-uhl] This name occurs as "Emmanuel" in Matt 1:23 and means "God with us." Immanuel occurs in the prophecy of ISAIAH during the Syro-Ephraimitic crisis of ca. 735 B.C.E. (7:14). The prophet was seeking to give King Ahaz the assurance that God was with him as he faced the terror of invading armies. The prophecy was later picked up and utilized by Matthew and the early Christians as pointing to the virgin birth of JESUS. They saw in it not only that teaching but also the assurance that, with the birth of Jesus, God had uniquely invaded history and was now truly with us.

The Hebrew word that was used for the young woman in Isa 7 is *'almâ* and merely refers to a woman who is of marriageable age. The OT does have a word that means virgin, *bĕtûlâ*. The term *'almâ* says nothing about a woman's virginity. It is used in the OT of both virgins and nonvirgins (Gen 24:43; Exod 2:8; Prov 30:19; Ps 68:25; Cant 1:3; 1 Chr 15:20).

However, when the LXX translators translated this passage from Hebrew into Greek, they clearly translated this Hebrew word with a Greek word that does mean virgin, *parthenos*. They may have made a mistake; they may have been inspired to correct what Isaiah had originally said; or they may have seen something in this passage that caused them to make this choice. The latter is most likely because in this passage it is the woman who named the child, a task normally done by the father. If they had not made this choice, more than seven centuries later the passage would have brought no comfort to JOSEPH who was seeking to understand what had happened to Mary, his betrothed. Regardless of how the Isaiah passage is understood, Jesus was clearly born of a virgin, as Matthew teaches.

The Immanuel of Isaiah's prophecy has been interpreted as pointing to a child of King Ahaz, a child of the prophet's, or some other child whose birth would have been known both to the king and the prophet. In such arguments, Jesus was the ultimate fulfillment of the hope, even if the hope is perceived as more limited in its original expression. Isaiah's hope appears to have been much larger than any of these suggestions.

At the time of Ahaz, Isaiah was assuring his king that he was not alone in facing the crisis that confronted him. In the foreshortening of prophecy, Isaiah missed the date of the birth of Immanuel. However, within the time of which he spoke, God had intervened and the crisis was over. Truly, Ahaz and his people could well have declared, "God is with us." Even more so can Christians say the same since the coming of Jesus.

No evidence has been found that Jesus was ever called Immanuel as a personal name. On the other hand, that name has brought comfort and hope to all his followers with its assurance and hope.

See also ISAIAH, BOOK OF.

—ROBERT L. CATE

• **Immortality.** The word "immortality" literally means "not subject to death." The nearest Hebrew equivalent is an expression in Prov 12:28 meaning "no death" (although the text is uncertain). The equivalent Greek expression is found in 1 Cor 15:53, derived from a combination of terms meaning literally "not to die." Another term meaning "incorruptible" or "imperishable" is found in 1 Cor 15:53 and Rom 2:7.

Although the Hebrew scriptures do not contain a clear teaching about the afterlife of the individual, and certainly no doctrine of the immortality of the soul, they do supply foundations on which the later Jewish and Christian beliefs were to be built. As the perception of Yahweh, the covenant God of Israel, progressed from polytheism through henotheism to monotheism, beginning in the age of the patriarchs and coming to maturity in the preaching of the great prophets, so the understanding of Yahweh came to assume God's creatorship, sovereignty, immutability, and supremacy over death and decay. Yahweh is a living God (Pss 18:46; 84:2; Hos 1:10) and to find God is to find life (Amos 5:4). Again, the increasing doubt concerning the adequacy of the deuteronomic doctrine of two ways (Deut 28; cf. the former prophets and Proverbs) whereby good is rewarded and evil is punished in this life, led naturally to the projection of a future life wherein the scales would ultimately be balanced. Further, it was not possible for Hebrew thought to escape the various teachings about personal immortality so prominent in the cultures of the Egyptians, Babylonians, Persians, Hellenists, and others with whom Israel came into constant contact.

The Hebrews accepted death as ordained by God (Gen 3:3-19), a mark of human creatureliness (Isa 40:6-8), and they believed that when humans die they go to the grave (Sheol) and remain there as mere shades—shadows of what was, has-beens. A future may be hoped for, however, in the bearing of children, in the reputation that remains, and most of all in the survival and prosperity of the covenant people of God to which one belongs (Isa 40; Ezek 37). Nevertheless, after the Babylonian Exile and in early Judaism glimmers of hope and speculation began to appear (Job 19:2; Dan 12:2; Wis 1:15; 2:23-24; 3:4-8). Among the Jews at the time of Jesus, the question of the afterlife was disputed between the Pharisees and the Sadducees (Mark 12:18-27; Matt 22:23-33; Luke 20:27-40).

The NT shows that belief in the possibility of individual immortality was a basic element of Christian faith from the beginning (1 Cor 15). Paul emphasized that faith regularly in his writings and he based it primarily on his experience of the risen Christ (Gal 10:11-17) and on the available testimony of many witnesses. The canonical Gospels contain the accounts of the resurrection of Jesus, and the earliest Christian community was the direct result of the apostles' proclamation of that event (Acts 2:24, 32). References to the resurrection of Jesus and its effect on the believers are so numerous that they cannot be listed here. They permeate the whole text. In brief summary, their teachings may be stated as follows: the one God is the source of life; human sin has caused alienation and a universal condition of mortality; because of his mercy God in Christ has defeated the power of death; those who respond to God's grace by faithfulness receive the renewal of life and are in Christ, participating in the eternal life of God.

It is important to note that the Bible does not teach the idea of the natural immortality of the soul, as found in most Hellenistic thought. Rather, the soul is the whole self, however divided for thoughtful analysis, and it is mortal—subject to death and in a condition of spiritual death. Immortality is thus a gift, derived from God's gracious nature and based upon the death and resurrection of Jesus Christ, which is the earnest of the resurrection of the believer to eternal life.

See also ETERNAL LIFE; FLESH AND SPIRIT; RESURRECTION IN THE NEW TESTAMENT; RESURRECTION IN THE OLD TESTAMENT; SOUL IN THE OLD TESTAMENT.

Bibliography. K. Stendahl, ed., *Immortality and Resurrection*; P. Benoit and R. Murphy, eds., *Immortality and Resurrection*; J. Baillie, *And the Life Everlasting*.

—J. WILLIAM ANGELL

• **Impalement.** *See* HANGING

• **Incarnation.** The term incarnation comes from the Latin *incarnatio*. It entered the Christian theological vocabulary from the Latin translation of John 1:14, "the Word became flesh." Incarnation is a broad religious concept in which it is maintained that the divine has taken bodily form. Several religions have utilized the concept: Hinduism regarded Rama as the god Vishnu incarnate, and ancient Egyptian religion viewed the gods as incarnate in humans and animals.

In contrast to these occasional incarnations, Christianity has made incarnation its central doctrine. That JESUS is God incarnate informs every tenet of the faith, from creation to eschatology. It particularly involves the doctrine of salvation, for the incarnation of God in Jesus remains the key for understanding how the estrangement between humans and God is remedied.

The Gospel of John introduces the word incarnation and is also responsible for setting the problem in universal perspective. John linked Christian incarnation to the Logos of Hellenistic speculation. The eternal and divine rationality of the universe is linked to the particular person of Jesus. Many of the theological struggles of the church can be seen as the result of competing ideas about the relationship between the universal Logos and the particular individual Jesus. The biblical writers themselves offered no systematic speculation about this interrelation and appear to have been of several minds.

Spirit Incarnation. The most Jewish understanding of incarnation appears in several passages of the NT and is clearly set forth in the identifying formula Paul cited in Rom 1:3-4: Jesus Christ, "who was descended from David according to the flesh and designated SON OF GOD in power according to the Spirit of holiness by his resurrection from the dead." Here, as in several other passages (1 Tim 3:16; 1 Pet 3:18; and 2 Tim 2:8), two stages in the life of Jesus define incarnation—life in the flesh followed by life in the Spirit.

NT authors differ as to when these stages occur. In the Romans passage incarnation occurs with resurrection. The synoptic Gospels regard the Spirit as installed in Jesus by the descent of the Spirit at his baptism; and the infancy stories of Matthew and Luke push the incarnational infilling back even further to the activity of the Spirit upon Mary in supernatural conception. Finally, the Christ hymn of Phil 2:5-11 connects incarnation by Spirit with the concept of pre-existence (cf. 1 Pet 1:20; 2 Tim 1:9-10).

The strength of this idea of incarnation is the maintenance of the distinction between God and man which later results, in the thought of Tertullian and others, in the doctrine of two natures. The incarnation occurs by overlaying divinity upon humanity, rather than by the assimilation of one to the other. God has moved upon the man Jesus by the Spirit; and he is, as a result, God incarnate.

Divine Substance Incarnation. Less Jewish and more Hellenistic is the essentialist view of incarnation. For the Greeks something's essence was its permanent identifying substance. When applied to incarnation, this concept became the dominant one in Christian tradition. It is not completely absent in the NT, appearing especially in John's writings, in the prologue to his Gospel, in the proclamation of Jesus' unity with the Father (10:30), and in the confession of Thomas (20:28).

Essentialist incarnation emphasizes the presence of a divine substance in Jesus. The result is a man whose essence is divine. Of course, the problem for this view is the difficulty of maintaining two substances in one particular in a way that the divine substance does not extinguish the human or transmute it into something nonhuman.

Some views of Christ as mediator present problems in this regard. As mediator Jesus occupies a position between God and humankind. Here interest is focused upon an independent third party who provides a connection between the divine and human but is precisely neither. Thus, Jesus is God incarnate as the unique God-man. Christ is a HIGH PRIEST without progenitor or progeny. He is helper for faltering humanity. Hebrews and 1 Timothy particularly speak of Jesus in these terms: Heb 8:6, 9:15, 12:24, and 1 Tim 2:5.

Appearance Incarnation. Incarnation as appearance takes two forms. The first views the divine in Jesus as the mere appearance of God without a union of the two. An extreme form of this approach claims that God appeared in the figure of Jesus of Nazareth, but not in an indissoluble way. Thus, for docetic CHRISTOLOGY, God is present in Jesus but there is no union, no coincidence of the human and divine (for early rejections of incarnation as mere appearance see Col 2:8-9 and 1 John 4:1-3).

The second form of incarnation as appearance emphasizes that the event of Jesus is the self-revelation of the divine. God has appeared to men in the life of Jesus, but not as mere epiphany. The divine is identical with the particular human. Jesus did not simply bear witness as did the Baptist (John 1:6); he is himself the appearance of God as life and light and word (John 1:1-5).

This view overcomes the dualism inherent in any statement of incarnation. Incarnation is neither a second stage of nor a second substance in Jesus. God's revelatory appearance in Jesus unifies the human and divine. From this unity three affirmations flow. First is the biblical affirmation that the divine in Jesus is God's self-revelation (2 Cor 4:6). The initiative is with God, not man, not even Jesus. Second, the self-revealing appearance of God cannot take place in two or more ways. He, who is the same eternally, cannot show himself in a plurality of revelations (John 14:6-7; Heb 1:1-4).

The third affirmation is central for the concept of incarnation: the revealer and the revealed are identical. Were this not the case, the events of Jesus' life would obscure, not make clear, the divine. Jesus made this point in his response to the Baptist's query about messiahship, "Go and tell John what you have seen and heard . . . " (Luke 7:22). In the human actions of Jesus God appeared in self-revelation, a fact at which the Jews took offense (John 1:45; 7:52). Thus, John depicts Jesus affirming to the Baptist, "Blessed is he who takes no offense at me" (Luke 7:23), i.e., at the identity of Jesus and God.

See also CHRISTOLOGY; GNOSTICISM; JESUS; JOHN, GOSPEL AND LETTERS OF; LOGOS/WORD; MEDIATION/MEDIATOR IN THE NEW TESTAMENT; MESSIAH/CHRIST; RELIGIONS OF THE ANCIENT NEAR EAST; RELIGIONS, HELLENISTIC AND ROMAN; SALVATION IN THE NEW TESTAMENT; SALVATION IN THE OLD TESTAMENT; SON OF GOD.

Bibliography. D. M. Baillie, *God Was in Christ;* E. Brunner, *The Christian Doctrine of Creation and Redemption;* R. Bultmann, *Theology of the New Testament.* vol. 2; O. Cullmann, *Christ and Time* and *The Christology of the New Testament;* W. Pannenberg, *Jesus—God and Man.*

—DON H. OLIVE

• **Incense.** Usually a combination of aromatic spices, gums, and resins prepared for burning to produce fragrant odors. In the biblical writings incense is most often associated with worship. In the OT Temple there was a specific "altar of incense" in the "holy place" of the Temple. In the NT there are only a few references to incense. Perhaps the most important is in the story of the MAGI who brought frankincense and myrrh, usually contained in incense, to worship the Christ child (Matt 2:11).

The primary word for incense in the OT refers to the smoke produced by burning of sacrificial offerings but later came to be associated specifically with "incense" offerings. The biblical formula for incense to be used in worship is given in Exod 30:34ff. It was composed of equal parts of stacte, onycha, galbanum, and frankincense. These were to be blended with a seasoning of pure salt. This became an exclusively sacred compound; manufacture for personal use was expressly forbidden. "Whoever makes any like it to use as perfume shall be cut off from his people," Exod 30:38 warns. The sanctity of this incense was further established in the restrictions regarding its use. Only the high priest, specifically excluding any others, could present the incense offering on the golden altar twice daily, morning and evening.

The significance and sanctity of the incense was indicated also by the fact that the high priest was to take a censer for burning incense with him upon entering the Holy of Holies on the Day of Atonement (Lev 16:12, 13).

Incense was used along with burnt offerings, presented on the brazen altar. Lev 2 specifies that frankincense was to be added to meal or cereal offerings. It is often speculated, though it was not a stated requirement, that incense was added to animal sacrifice to create the "pleasing odor" that arose to Yahweh.

Some spices originated in the area of ancient Canaan, but most came by trade routes from Arabia (and perhaps farther east) and from Africa. These were for the most part extremely costly commodities, often more valuable than silver or gold.

Incense burners have been discovered in many excavations, showing evidence of the frequency of incense use. It is only in recent years that incense burners from the period of the Hebrew kingdoms have been clearly documented. It is impossible in most cases to determine whether usage was cultic or secular.

See also WORSHIP.

Bibliography. M. Haran, "The Uses of Incense in Ancient Israelite Ritual," *VT* 10 (1960): 113-29; D. Edelman, "The Meaning of *Qitter*," *VT* 35 (1985): 395-404; L. Y. Rahmani, "Palestinian Incense Burners of the Seventh to Eighth Centuries B.C.E.," *IEJ* 30 (1980): 116-22.

—BRUCE C. CRESSON

• **Inclusio.** [in-kl*oo*'zhee-oh] From a Latin term meaning to "shut off" or "confine," this technical term is used in rhetorical criticism to indicate the return to the opening phrase or idea at the close of a composition (the descriptive terms "cyclic composition" or "ring composition" are also used for this device). Presence of this rhetorical device assists in the determination of the limits of a literary unit. The repetition, of course, may be redactional or the work of the original author. Examples are numerous: Jas 2:14-16 begins and ends with the words "What does it profit." "Vanity of vanities, says the preacher; all is vanity" in Eccl 1:2 and 12:8 serves to tie together the material through 12:8.

The rhetorical device known as *epanalepsis* (repetition of the beginning at the end) is repetition of a phrase or idea at the end of a sentence or a clause (instead of an entire text) such as: "Rejoice in the Lord always; again I will say, rejoice" (Phil 4:4). The *inclusio* and *epanalepsis* tend to make texts stand apart from their surrounding. The *anadiplosis* (repetition of an end at the next beginning) does just the opposite by having the last word or phrase repeated in the first word or phrase in the next sentence. An example is: "I will lift up mine eyes unto the hills, from when cometh my help. My help cometh from the Lord which made heaven and earth" (Ps 121:1, KJV).

See also RHETORICAL CRITICISM.

—EDGAR V. MCKNIGHT

• **Inheritance in the New Testament.** The word inheritance is used in the Bible in a theological or symbolical sense to affirm the relationship between God and his people (Deut 9:26,29; Jer 10:16; Ps 28:9; Gal 3:7-14). The theological perspective of the OT is essential for appreciating the NT use of the concept.

In the OT, from the first, the land of CANAAN was promised as an inheritance by God to Abraham and his seed (Gen 12:7). This land was a gift of God to Israel, even though its possession required effort.

When the Israelites went into exile they were disinherited from the land. This disinheritance meant more than just the loss of a little strip of territory. In a deeper sense it meant the loss of spiritual blessings as a consequence of national sin.

The idea of a restored inheritance, taught by the prophets, suggested the glorious anticipation of the messianic age. In that period the people, not by works which they had done, but by God's grace, would recover that which they had lost. The COVENANT which they had broken would be renewed.

In fact, the idea of inheritance underwent a process of both narrowing and expansion. On the one hand, instead of the whole people, only a REMNANT is to inherit the promises. On the other hand, the inheritance expands to include not only Canaan but the nations (Isa 54:3; Ps 2:8; Dan 7:14).

In Mark 12:1-11 Christ claims to be the heir of God. This identification of Christ as heir is fundamental to the use of inheritance throughout the NT. This is seen in Heb 1:2 and implied in Rom 8:17. The MESSIAH, through whom the disinheritance should be brought to a close and the covenant renewed, was naturally regarded as the supreme heir of all the promises and privileges implied in the old covenant. As the Messiah's unique relation to the Father became more clearly defined, the idea of his inheritance indicating his unique birth and universal supremacy became enlarged and expanded.

Rom 8:17 states also that those "in Christ" are joint heirs with Christ of the inheritance. Since Christ is the only begotten Son, the inheritance is his by right. However, the believer receives this inheritance by grace through ADOPTION in Jesus Christ. The word "adoption" thus occurs in connection with inheritance in Rom 8:15, 23, and Gal 4:5.

As God's heirs, according to the NT, we are in a real sense currently "owners" of all the good things tangible or intangible to be found in God. The blessings we receive now are from the rich store of his wealth, distributed in his will but truly our own. One day we will possess fully what we currently own (Rom 8:17-23; 1 Cor 15:50; Heb 11:13; 1 Pet 1:3-4).

See also ADOPTION; COVENANT; ESCHATOLOGY IN THE NEW TESTAMENT; ESCHATOLOGY IN THE OLD TESTAMENT; KINGDOM OF GOD; REMNANT.

—JOHN P. NEWPORT

• **Inheritance in the Old Testament.** The distribution of rights, position, and property at the death of an individual to appropriate heirs. Inheritance was of great concern in the biblical world. Specific laws and customs governing inheritance are set forth both in the Bible and documents from neighboring contemporary cultures. In the Bible, the term is used to describe the passing of an estate of material value (land and other property) from parent to child or some other heir. It is also a theological term: the land was considered an inheritance from God (i.e., the tribal inheritances allotted to the Israelite tribes on the occupation of Canaan); in the NT the Kingdom of God was the inheritance of those who by faith became the children of God.

The references to inheritance in the Book of Genesis reflect legal practices and customs prevalent among the various peoples of the ancient Near East. Usually property was handed down from father to son with the first-born receiving a share double that of his brothers. In the ancient Near East the practice of ADOPTION was common in the case of a childless (or son-less) family. In some cases the adopted son could inherit the estate, but this usually required marriage into the family. Perhaps adoption was concerned with providing care for the childless adults in old age more than with continuation of a family name.

In the OT law property was to remain among the blood-kin. Inheritance passed to sons, with the eldest receiving a double portion. If there were no sons, daughters could inherit the estate, but in this case they were forbidden to marry outside the clan or tribe of the father. If there were no children the property was passed to the father's brothers; if none of these, then to his paternal uncles. In case none of these existed, then title passsed to "his kinsman who is next to him of his family" (Num 27:8-11). An unusual instance was the sharing of inheritance of daughters with their brothers in Job 42:15. In a culture in which polygamy was practiced, it is important to note that children of concubines or slaves had the same inheritance rights as other offspring as long as they were acknowledged by the father.

The most frequent references to inheritance in the Bible are in the divine-human relationship. In the covenant with Abraham (Gen 12; 15; etc.) and with the nation (Exod 19, etc.) the land was promised to the Israelite people in response to their pledge to obey the voice of Yahweh and to keep Yahweh's covenant. This land was divided among the tribes and came to be viewed as an inheritance carrying with it obligations in the covenant. It was subject to divinely set regulations, especially to keep it as a family possession. For this purpose the rules of inheritance noted above were established, as were the YEAR OF JUBILEE regulations in which every fiftieth year land was to revert to its original owner or the owner's heirs.

In the NT little is said concerning inheritance of physical property. The emphasis is more spiritual: the meek shall inherit the earth (Mark 5:5), eternal life can be inherited (Luke 18:18), and the righteous inherit the Kingdom of God (1 Cor 6:9).

See also LAND.

Bibliography. C. Gordon, *The Code of Hammurabi*; N. H. Smith, "Daughters of Zelophehad," *VT* 16:124-27; E. Davies, "Inheritance Rights and Hebrew Levirate Marriage," *VT* 31:138-44, 257-68; R. K. Harrison, "The Matriarchate and Hebrew Regal Succession," *EvQ* 29:29-34.

—BRUCE C. CRESSON

• **Iniquity.** *See* SIN

• **Inscriptions.** *See* LETTERS/INSCRIPTIONS

• **Insects.** *See* CREEPING THINGS

• **Inspiration.** *See* BIBLE, AUTHORITY OF; SCRIPTURE IN THE NEW TESTAMENT; SCRIPTURE IN THE OLD TESTAMENT

• **Intercession.** *See* PRAYER/THANKSGIVING IN THE NEW TESTAMENT

• **Intermediate State.** The state of existence between death as an individual phenomenon and the resurrection of the body at the final eschatological consummation. The backdrop of the concept is found in the development of the OT concept of SHEOL. Originally perceived as either the grave or the realm of the dead where there is the absence of all we know as life, Sheol came to be seen as an intermediate state due to the development of the apocalyptic vision of a final consummation and judgment. In the late B.C.E. period Sheol, translated in the NT as Hades, came to be distinguished from PARADISE, an intermediate resting place for the righteous. This development seems to be reflected in the parable of the rich man and Lazarus (Luke 16:19-31), Jesus' promise to the dying thief (Luke 23:43), and Rev 6:9-11.

While the NT clearly teaches that believers are "with Christ" immediately after death (Phil 1:23; 2 Cor 5:8; 1 Thess 5:10; Luke 23:43), it gives little attention to the nature of this existence. Some have likened it to the experience of sleep (i.e., "soul sleep") in which the waking person is unaware of the passing of time. Others have seen it as a conscious existence. On the basis of 2 Cor 5:1-10 some believe that at death the believer receives an intermediate body which will be exchanged at the final consummation for the SPIRITUAL BODY described in 1 Cor 15. On the other hand, some see this text referring to the "spiritual body" of 1 Cor 15, and argue that at the time of death the "natural body" is replaced immediately by the "spiritual," resurrection body. Still others argue that the soul exists in a disembodied state until the resurrection. Those adhering to the notion of a conscious existence see it as a state of joy and blessedness in God's presence (i.e., Paradise) for the righteous, while for the wicked it is a time of suffering and separation from God (i.e., Hades; cf. Luke 16:23; 1 Pet 3:19; 2 Pet 2:9). Some have seen it as a time of punishment and/or purification in preparation for the final consummation (i.e., purgatory, apocatastasis).

Objections to the notion of an intermediate state have focused on those views which posit a dichotomy between body and soul or engender an individualistic, privatized eschatology which does not acknowledge the significance of the final eschatological consummation of the Kingdom of God.

See also ESCHATOLOGY IN THE NEW TESTAMENT; ESHATOLOGY IN THE OLD TESTAMENT; PARADISE; SHEOL; SOUL IN THE OLD TESTAMENT; SPIRITUAL BODY.

—W. HULITT GLOER

• **Interpretation of Knowledge.** The *Interpretation of Knowledge,* from Codex XI of the NAG HAMMADI documents, provides an unusual glimpse into the life of a Gnostic Christian congregation. The writer, obviously a person of repute, interprets the death of Jesus, the unity of the church, and the equality of believers from a Gnostic viewpoint. The writing is a homily of sincere pastoral concern, perhaps, as has been suggested, for oral delivery. The text is fragmentary in places, but enough remains for a striking picture to emerge. This Gnostic circle clearly honors the Gospel of Matthew and the writings of Paul; there are reminiscences of Johannine themes.

The world, we are told, is a place of unfaith and death. Faith removes us from this realm, dominated as it is by evil powers who keep us imprisoned in the flesh. Removed from unfaith and death, we live in the locale of faith, the church. The Savior died a vicarious death on behalf of this "church of mortals," but the evil powers split the church into factions.

The Savior's teaching is recalled through references to the gospel. It is through him who humbled himself and suffered disgrace that we receive glorification, forgiveness, and grace. Christ is our brother, sent by the Father in love for us.

The writer apparently faces a situation in which his audience is divided over the question of spiritual gifts, such as prophecy. It is much like the situation addressed by Paul in 1 Corinthians, and the Pauline metaphor of the church as the body of Christ is used to make an appeal for unity. Each member of the body is significant in its own way. We should acknowledge our gifts, share them, and in unity pursue our task as combatants for the Word, overcoming every sin to receive a victor's crown.

The author may be associated with Valentinian GNOS-

TICISM, and may here be promulgating a view of Christian unity broader than the catholic church would recognize. The church is the body of those who have faith, not an institution which through its offices mediates salvation. This position, held in the church catholic, led the orthodox to describe those outside its structures as heretical—not of the body of Christ. But the Gnostic author of this book, unconcerned with institutions and offices, finds room for all.

See also GNOSTICISM; NAG HAMMADI.

Bibliography. E. Pagels and J. D. Turner, "Interpretation of Knowledge," *The Nag Hammadi Library in English*.

—ROGER A. BULLARD

• Interpretation, History of. As a sect of Judaism, Christianity inherited a variety of approaches to interpretation of the OT. By the time of Jesus, Jewish scribes had developed an intricate set of rules of interpretation known as the "Rules of Hillel," whose influence can be seen in Jesus' and Paul's interpretation of the OT and possibly in other early Christian writings. The Qumran sect employed what is known as the *Midrash Pesher* method, applying texts directly to their own situation, whose influence also appears in early Christian interpretation. In the Diaspora, PHILO of Alexandria borrowed Stoic allegorical methods of interpreting Homer and applied them to the Pentateuch so as to enhance the appeal of Judaism to non-Jews. Hebrews in the NT and writings by the Christian Platonists of Alexandria, Clement and Origen, betray direct indebtedness to Philo.

It is somewhat risky to try to evaluate Jesus' approach to scripture. Insofar as we can tell from the canonical Gospels, he shared rabbinic methods to some extent. Like the rabbis he considered scripture authoritative and inspired, regarded Moses as the author of the Pentateuch and David of the Psalms, and strongly emphasized the vitally religious portions rather than the lesser cultic prescriptions. At the same time he differed from the rabbis in his underlying outlook. He did not hesitate to criticize scripture in light of his own highest utterances and pointed to himself as the fulfillment of scripture. He came up with strikingly original interpretations, for instance, concerning the imminence of the KINGDOM OF GOD and the application of certain passages to his own ministry as the "signs" of fulfillment. In this he showed affinity for the *Midrash Pesher* method of Qumran.

Paul's use of the OT resembled that of Jesus in rejection of legalism and viewing of the OT as a book of hope. It differed from Jesus' use in Paul's more radical rejection of the LAW in light of Christ's death and resurrection and in being more theological. As a rabbi, he would be expected to use rabbinic methods, valuing every word (cf. Gal 3:16 "not to seeds, but to seed"). He employed both typology (1 Cor 10:6) and allegory (Gal 4:22-26). Some parallels can be seen to Philo's exegesis, especially in the freer outlook and use of terminology of Greek rhetoric than was customary among the rabbis. Furthermore, he viewed the OT christocentrically, e.g., as leading up to Christ himself and to the foundation of the church as Israel under a new covenant.

In general, other early Christian writings of the first century followed the example of Paul. They interpreted the OT typologically and sometimes allegorically. Typology depended on actual historical parallels between old and new, Israel and church, whereas allegory could take the literal and historical rather lightly. Most writers searched the OT scriptures for their testimony to Christ. This was especially true of Hebrews and Matthew, both of which built their argument around Jesus' fulfillment of OT types.

The Second Century. The OT still remained the Bible of the church during the second century, MARCION's repudiation of it notwithstanding; but the words of Jesus and thence the "memoirs of the apostles" assumed increasing importance as scripture. By the mid-to-late second century the churches possessed a core of a NT CANON—the four canonical Gospels, Acts, thirteen Letters of Paul, 1 John, and 1 Peter being almost universally used in public worship. Although the NT gradually assumed an authority greater than the OT, methods of interpreting the latter were applied to the NT also.

The EPISTLE OF BARNABAS (ca.130) used typology or allegory to show that the OT had validity only if interpreted in terms of the gospel and disregarded history. Marcion, rejecting the OT completely, interpreted it literally to emphasize its crudeness. Justin (ca. 150) repudiated Marcion's effort to detach Christianity from the OT. A native of Flavia Neapolis (modern Nablus) in Palestine, he showed some familiarity with rabbinic methods. He avoided allegorical exegesis and favored historical and christocentric approaches.

The Gnostics laid aside the caution shown by some early interpreters and resorted readily to allegorical interpretation not only of OT but also of NT writings. In his *Letter to Flora* the Valentinian scholar Ptolemaeus divided the Law into three categories: (1) that given by God, (2) that imparted by Moses, and (3) that made by the elders. Even the most important part, however, had different sections: "genuine precepts" untainted by evil, sections containing evil and unrighteous things, and typical and symbolic portions.

IRENAEUS, educated under both Polycarp of Smyrna and Justin, was the first to work out a theory of the relation between the two Testaments (ca. 180–190), arguing that the God in both is the same. He sharply criticized the Gnostics and Marcion for disregarding the context of a passage and for interpreting clear and obvious passages by dark and obscure ones. In practice he fell into some of the same pits the Gnostics did, particularly in the use of allegory. What saved him from their fanciful excursions was adherence to the rule of faith as preserved in churches founded by apostles.

The Alexandrian School. At Alexandria, Philo's use of allegorical method to demonstrate that the OT contained the highest and most noble in Hellenistic thought blazed the trail for Christian use of that method. A Valentinian Gnostic named Heracleon produced the first commentary on one of the Gospels, a fanciful work which has survived in fragmentary form through Origen's quotations in his *Commentary on John*.

No writings by the founder of the Alexandrian school, Pantaenus, have survived, but his immediate successor, Clement (fl. 180–202), was the first to justify and explain the allegorical method, albeit not systematically. Clement found as many as five senses in scripture: (1) historical, usually the stories of biblical history; (2) doctrinal, moral, religious, or theological, in which biblical statements could be directly appropriated; (3) prophetic, including both explicit prophecies and "types"; (4) philosophical, including "cosmic" and "psychological" meanings; and (5) mystical. Clement made faith in Christ, his person, and his work, the guiding principle.

Clement's successor, Origen, first at Alexandria (202–32) and later at Caesarea (232–54/5), set forth the principles of Christian allegorization in his treatise on *First Principles*. Origen stressed the ultimate mystery of the scripture. They contain three senses: literal, moral, and mystical-allegorical. Not all scripture will have a literal meaning, though, for God could not demand or do some things attributed to God in the OT. Since God never utters an idle word, however, all scripture must have a spiritual meaning. To be certain one is interpreting correctly, one must rely on God, collect and compose spiritual truths, observe the use of words, compare similar texts when one is literal, the other spiritual, and be guided by the rule of faith. Without the use of allegory one may make many mistakes.

The Antiochene School. The Alexandrian school exerted wide influence, but the church as a whole displayed a considerable reluctance to use the allegorical method, particularly in view of abuses by the Gnostics. In the third century Nepos, an Egyptian, wrote a *Refutation of the Allegorists*. The most consistent opposition, however, came from the school of Antioch, perhaps under influence of the synagogue. Theophilus of Antioch (ca. 175) interpreted Genesis in Jewish fashion. Lucian (d. 312), founder of the Antiochene school, edited a text of the OT probably derived from Jewish sources. Dorotheus, head of the school, studied Hebrew. Proximity to the holy land encouraged attention to the historical sense of scripture.

The Antiochenes took up the cudgels against allegorical interpretation. Eustathius, Bishop of Antioch from 324 to 330, attacked Origen's allegorical exegesis. Diodore, Bishop of Tarsus (d. 390), composed an antiallegorical work entitled: *What Is the Difference Between Theory and Allegory?* Theodore, Bishop of Mopsuestia (392–428), wrote a treatise on *Allegory and History against Origen.* Both sides appealed to Gal 4, the Sarah and Hagar story, the Alexandrians insisting it defended their method, the Antiochenes denying it. The latter contended that Paul's interpretation of scripture was comparison, not allegory, despite his use of that word. For them the prophets really foresaw the coming of Christ and there was no allegory in what they said.

Theodore of Mopsuestia distinguished between prophecies he considered really messianic and those genuinely historical. Books which have no prophetic element should be excluded from the scripture! Theodore thus rejected Job, the wisdom writings, and some of the historical books in the OT and the Catholic Epistles and James in the NT as merely human writings. In 553 the Council of Constantinople ordered his exegetical writings burned. He was charged with responsibility for the error of Nestorius and for denying some scriptures which the church judged canonical.

The Antiochene tradition of interpretation had one of its best representatives in John Chrysostom (ca. 347–407), the most eminent preacher of his day. A pupil of Diodore, he did not reject allegorical interpretation completely, but, as a rule, he restricted himself to typology. The historical meaning supplies the outline, typology the final form of the portrait.

Jerome (ca. 342–420), the greatest biblical scholar of the late fourth and early fifth centuries, was an Origenist in his early years. When the Origenist controversy erupted about 399, however, he began to move away from allegorization. He continued down this path steadily thereafter, partly because of his textual studies and partly because of his growing knowledge of Jewish exegesis. Apollinaris of Laodicea, condemned for heresy at Constantinople in 381, taught Jerome historical method.

Antiochene influence faded during the Middle Ages, but it appeared in two handbooks on interpretation: Adrian's *Introduction to the Divine Scriptures* (ca. 425) and Julius Africanus's *Regulative Institutes of the Divine Law* (ca. 550). The latter distinguished typology from prophecy and systematized Theodore of Mopsuestia's typology along Aristotelian lines. Unlike Theodore, however, he did not reject any canonical books but rather divided them into classes: (1) those with perfect authority, (2) those of moderate authority, and (3) those with no authority.

The Middle Ages. The Western (Latin) Church moved gradually toward an authoritative mode of interpretation in which allegorical method played a significant role. The basic rule laid down by Irenaeus—e.g., to interpret in line with the faith of the church—was expanded by TERTULLIAN (ca. 200) in the assertion that only the church has a right to interpret scriptures. The true scriptures are found only where the truth of Christian discipline and faith are found, for the church had scriptures before heretics did, just as it had the truth before they perverted it. In a treatise on *Christian Doctrine* (ca. 397) Augustine separated himself from the allegorical method which he had adopted under influence of Ambrose, Bishop of Milan (374–397). The interpreter must explain the mind of the writer of scriptures rather than set forth personal opinions. This requires one to distinguish between literal and figurative statements and, if in doubt, "consult the rule of faith." Ultimately the interpreter's authority is scripture itself and the tradition of the church. In 434 Vincent of Lerins set forth the famous principle concerning the catholic sense of interpretation: "That which has been believed everywhere, always, by all."

The method of interpretation changed little during the Middle Ages. In the divorce between biblical and dogmatic theology, scriptures came to be used chiefly in catena as proofs. In the schools theologians consulted the fathers and, in the late Middle Ages, Jewish authorities. Although this gave some pull toward historical interpretation, the weight fell more heavily on the allegorical. Interpreters found four meanings in scripture: historical, allegorical, analogical or mystical, and moral or tropological. Allegorical interpretation, however, declined in the late Middle Ages as Aristotelian thought impacted the schools. Thomas Aquinas turned out to be the most notable exponent of a historical approach. He did not reject allegorical method, but he taught that spiritual truths are inculcated under the likeness of material things. He argued that the several senses assigned to each scripture text only confuse and deceive. His critique sowed the seeds for modern study of scriptures with their emphasis on study of languages and context and objectivity in research.

The Reformation. By the sixteenth century Europeans had developed a more critical approach to interpretation in the process of attempting to recover Greek and Latin classics. As the Renaissance moved northward, humanist scholars applied methods used on the classics to the Bible. John Wyclif (d. 1382) insisted on a literal and grammatical interpretation and presided over translations of the entire Bible. Erasmus published a Greek NT in 1516 and wrote critical notes on much of the NT. The famous Complutensian Polyglot initiated by Cardinal Ximenes was in process of publication between 1515 and 1522. Johann Reuchlin established a scientific basis for the study of Hebrew with the publication of *Rudiments of Hebrew* in 1506. In Oxford, John Colet, who became Dean of St. Paul's Cathedral in 1504, influenced Erasmus through his studies of the NT. In France Jacques Lefevre d'Etaples issued a revised Latin translation of the letters of Paul with commentary which reflected advances toward modern biblical criticism.

Luther ceased allegorical interpretation after 1517 and insisted thereafter on the "one simple solid sense" of scripture. He viewed historical and grammatical interpretation as the means to an understanding of Christ. Interpretation must be done in faith, however, thus leading to a "spiritual interpretation," what the Bible says to experience. The Bible can be understood in terms of itself, scripture interpreting scripture.

John Calvin, a humanist scholar before his conversion to the evangelical cause, interpreted both literally and typologically. Interpretation, Calvin said, need not be christocentric. Faith is primary. Scriptures are themselves the authority for faith. Calvin exerted a strong influence in England, where the Puritans sought to effect a "further reform" along lines laid down by Calvin in Geneva. The Puritans insisted, as Calvin did, on taking the scriptures in their plain and obvious sense and repudiated allegorical or spiritual interpretation.

Modern Critical Interpretation. Modern critical interpretation began in the nineteenth century, but it was rooted in the Enlightenment of the seventeenth century with its confidence in the powers of human reason, progress, and essential goodness. Advances in science and technology encouraged application of critical scientific method to study of historical documents, including scripture. The idealistic philosophy of G. W. F. Hegel (1770–1831) supplied a framework for more liberal interpretation as Hegel undercut all sense of divine revelation. Søren Kierkegaard (1813–55), although accepting the dialectical method of Hegel, vigorously opposed him on the matter of revelation. According to his existentialist philosophy, God confronts human beings in their particular situations.

Modern historical-critical work began with Hermann Samuel Reimarus's famous essay *On the Purpose of Jesus and His Disciples,* published in 1778, a work running more than 4,000 pages. Reimarus still left some room for the supernatural, but full developed rationalism soon followed and opened the way to mythological interpretations. Some scholars even denied the historicity of Jesus. In 1863 Ernest Renan drew together the results of German critical scholarship of the eighteenth and nineteenth centuries to produce his own liberal *Life of Jesus.*

Modern interpretation of scripture has developed largely in response to challenges posed by such criticism. Doubts about Jesus' historical existence aroused interest in auxiliary studies: the history of the times, religions, geography of the ancient world, archaeology, languages, rabbinic literature and thought, apocalyptic. New methods were developed in order to aid in the resolution of problems posed by radical criticism. F. J. A. Hort, a distinguished NT scholar at Cambridge, and Bishop B. F. Westcott spent years (1852–1881) on the preparation of a Greek NT and in development of the science of textual criticism. In Germany Julius Wellhausen (1844–1918) devoted the greater part of his life to higher criticism, completely transforming OT criticism with his documentary hypothesis concerning Genesis in 1885. In later years he applied the same method to the NT, thus opening the way to source criticism. Almost simultaneously, Hermann Gunkel turned the attention of scholars to the study of the forms of oral tradition lying behind the sources with the publication of a commentary on Genesis (1909). The German "history of religions school," which flourished between 1880 and 1921, had a powerful impact through comparison of OT and NT documents with those of other religions.

In these developments, interpretation moved away from the grammatico-historical approach based on a theory of verbal inspiration. During the 1950s, scholars began to focus more on the theology of biblical writings as reflected especially in the salvation history school of Oscar Cullmann and Walter Eichrodt. During the 1970s, they shifted their accent to literary approaches in the study of the history of traditions and the Bible as story. As a result of ecumenical developments following the Second Vatican Council, however, some scholars renewed interest in what ancient concern for the Bible as canon would mean for interpretation.

Throughout the modern era, Roman Catholic interpretation paralleled Protestant interpretation to some extent. Pope Leo XIII (1878–1903) opened the way for biblical criticism in the encyclical *Providentissimus Deus,* establishing the Pontifical Biblical Commission. Reaction against and condemnation of Roman Catholic Modernism by Pope Pius X in 1907, however, cast a pall over the work of scholars such as Alfred Loisy (1857–1940), who pursued historical-critical studies with zeal. In 1943, Pius XII gave renewed impetus in *De spiritu sancto* which carried over into postwar scholarship. When Pope John XXIII announced the Second Vatican Council shortly after taking office, Catholic biblical scholars stood ready and waiting, for they had already joined Protestants in many common endeavors.

Higher criticism has not been favorably received by all. During the late nineteenth and early twentieth century, conservative Protestants gathered their forces to stem the tide of liberalism, particularly in biblical studies. Although fundamentalists could allow "lower criticism," that is, textual, they viewed "higher criticism" as a threat to the inspiration and authority of the Bible. Originally they spoke of "plenary verbal inspiration," but today most use the term "inerrancy" to describe the Bible and insist on the Bible's accuracy on historical, scientific, or philosophical as well as theological matters. The progress of modern biblical interpretation, however, has led to its acceptance even among very conservative scholars.

See also BIBLE, AUTHORITY OF; BIBLE; HERMENEUTICS; JESUS; NEW TESTAMENT USE OF THE OLD TESTAMENT; PAUL.

Bibliography. E. C. Blackman, *Biblical Interpretation*; *The Cambridge History of the Bible*; F.W. Frederic, *History of Interpretation*; R. M. Grant, *A Short History of the Interpretation of the Bible*; R. P. C. Hanson, *Allegory and Event*; J. L. Kugel and R. A. Greer, *Early Biblical Interpretation*; G. W. H Lampe and K. J. Woollcombe, *Essays on Typology*; S. Neill, *The Interpretation of the New Testament, 1861–1961*; J. M. Robinson and J. B. Cobb, eds., *The New Hermeneutic,* New Frontiers in Theology 2; B. Smalley, *The Study of the Bible in the Middle Ages*; J.D. Wood, *Interpretation of the Bible: A Historical Introduction.*

—E. GLENN HINSON

• **Irenaeus.** [*i'*ruh-nee″uhs] Irenaeus (ca. 135–202) was bishop of Lyons, missionary, anti-heretical writer, and definer of catholic theology. Educated at the feet of the venerable Polycarp, bishop of Smyrna, he accompanied the latter to ROME for a confrontation with Anicetus over the Asian custom in observing EASTER on 14 Nisan, the Jewish PASSOVER. There he did further study with JUSTIN MARTYR. He escaped the pogrom in Lyons and Vienne in 177 by being sent to Rome on official business. Already a

PRESBYTER, he returned to Lyons when he succeeded the ninety-year-old Pothinus, who was martyred. He promoted vigorous missionary activities throughout Gaul. His most important contribution, however, lay in the response he made to the threat posed by MARCION and GNOSTICISM. He issued a stern rebuke to Victor, Bishop of Rome (189-99), when the latter rashly excommunicated Christians of Asia because they observed Easter on 14 Nisan. Later tradition celebrated him as a martyr, but this is uncertain. He probably died about 202.

Two major writings of Irenaeus—*Refutation and Overthrow of Knowledge Falsely So-called* (usually called *Against Heresies*) and *Proof of the Apostolic Preaching* as well as letters and fragments of other works have survived. Composed at the request of a friend, usually dated about 185 to 189, *Against Heresies* is somewhat disjointed. In book 1 Irenaeus outlines the systems of Valentinus and, more briefly, other Gnostics. In book 2 he attempts a fuller refutation of the Valentinian system with its elaborate COSMOLOGY. In book 3 he constructs his argument for catholic teaching based on scriptures and tradition. In book 4 he continues a refutation of Marcion that he began in book 3, arguing especially for the oneness of OT and NT depictions of God. In book 5 he sustains catholic teachings on such doctrines as RESURRECTION, INCARNATION, and "last things." *Proof of the Apostolic Preaching,* long lost but rediscovered in an Armenian translation in 1904, is a catechetical treatise designed to introduce inquirers to Christian faith. The first part focuses on theological issues, the second on christological, citing "proofs" chiefly from the OT.

Irenaeus rejected the view of his teacher Justin Martyr that the seminal LOGOS inspired both Greeks and Jews and placed his emphasis on scripture, regarding the Greek OT as canonical in its entirety and using the core of the present western CANON of the NT. Although he criticized the Gnostics for allegorical interpretation, he frequently lapsed into it himself. Ultimately he placed his confidence in the tradition committed to the churches founded by apostles, citing the list of bishops of the Roman church as the example *par excellence*. He considered the "living voice" a constantly renewed understanding of the Christian heritage, the true authority.

Irenaeus's theology reflects a strong Pauline slant. In opposition to Marcion and the Gnostics he affirmed Jewish monotheism. Through the Son and the HOLY SPIRIT (or the WORD and WISDOM), the "two hands of God," God created the world directly *ex nihilo* and continues to inspire and reveal. According to Irenaeus's famous recapitulation theory, Jesus reversed the effects of the "Fall" by overcoming the powers of sin, death, and the devil that hold humankind in thrall through obedience to God. To sustain this, Irenaeus contended that Jesus lived fifty years rather than thirty, thus experiencing every phase of human life. Like his mentor Justin, Irenaeus emphasized human free will, though he acknowledged that the Fall attenuated it. In ESCHATOLOGY he was a chiliast or millenarian who, against the Gnostics, attached great importance to resurrection of the flesh.

See also PATRISTIC LITERATURE.

Bibliography. E. G. Hinson, "Irenaeus," *EncRel*; J. Lawson, *The Biblical Theology of Saint Irenaeus*; G. Wingren, *Man and the Incarnation: A Study of the Biblical Theology of Irenaeus*.

—E. GLENN HINSON

• **Iron.** By virtue of the fact that meteorites are composed chiefly of iron, ancient people had access to this prized metal long before its smelting procedure was unravelled. Although the second most abundant metal, iron rarely is found in its pure form except in meteorites or as small specula in basaltic rocks. Bronze tools and weapons long predated those of iron because the smelting of iron was a much more difficult process.

Apparently, the discovery of the iron smelting process was made by the Hittites in Asia Minor about the middle of the second millennium B.C.E. Supporting this view is the fact that the word for "iron" in Akkadian, Hebrew, Ugaritic, and Aramaic seemingly derives from Hittite. The early spread of the metal is difficult to trace archaeologically because iron rusts away so quickly. The OT traces the beginning of ironworking to one Tubal-Cain (Gen 4:22), identified in genealogy as a descendant (as were Meshech and others) of Japheth and therefore from Asia Minor (Gen 10:2), Hittite territory. Ezekiel said of Tyre that Meshech and Tubal traded "vessels of bronze for your merchandise" (27:13). Jeremiah also mentioned "iron, iron from the north, and bronze" (15:12), associating metalworking (including that of iron) with northern territory.

The introduction of iron into ancient Palestine is usually attributed to the PHILISTINES who arrived there shortly after 1200 B.C.E. and therefore soon after Joshua's conquest. Iron was in the booty taken from the Midianites in Moses' time (Num 31:22), and Moses commanded that "no iron tool" should be used in working stones for an altar on Mount Ebal (Deut 27:5). Furthermore, the "Canaanites who dwell in the plain," those in Beth Shan and in the nearby Jezreel Valley (Josh 18:16), Joshua could not expel (in contrast to Canaanites in the hill country) "because they had chariots of iron" (Judg 1:19).

Whether or not the Philistines introduced iron into Palestine, they had a large supply of it and discouraged ironworking among the Hebrews. The Philistine Goliath's iron spearpoint weighed 600 shekels (sixteen pounds; 1 Sam 17:7), and Philistine smiths had to be used to repair the tools of the Hebrews doubtless made of bronze (1 Sam 13:19-22). The Hebrews were hampered in their lack of iron weapons, while Jabin, the king of Hazor, had 900 iron chariots (Judg 4:3). David dispelled the Philistines, and iron became more common with the Israelites. David came to possess "great stores of iron for nails for the doors of the gates and for clamps" (1 Chr 22:3). He compelled conquered Ammonites "to labor with saws and iron picks and iron axes" (2 Sam 12:32).

In the chronology of Palestinian archaeology, the term "Iron Age" usually refers to the years near 1200–600 B.C.E. Iron Age I is 1200–900 B.C.E.; Iron Age II is 900–600 B.C.E.; some use the term "Iron Age III" to refer to the period 600–300 B.C.E., but most call this "The Persian Period."

See also METALLURGY.

—KAREN RANDOLPH JOINES

• **Isaac.** [*ī'*zik] The second of an oft-cited trio of patriarchs from Israel's early period: "ABRAHAM, Isaac, and JACOB" (Exod 3:6; Jer 33:26; Acts 7:8).

The name has the form of a verb and means, "he laughs." There are three folk explanations of it (not intended to be grammatically or historically correct): (1) mother SARAH and her friends rejoice at the child's birth (Gen 21:1-6); (2) Sarah is amused at the announcement of the unlikely impending birth (18:9-15); and (3) father Abraham laughs skeptically at the announcement (17:15-19). Advocates of the documentary hypothesis have usually assigned these explanations, respectively, to the sources E, J, and P (thus, the last of them would be a reflection of the despair of the exilic community). It has been plausibly conjectured, based upon the form of other names in the ancient Near East where the subject of a verb is the deity, that the original meaning of the name was, "he (i.e., God) rejoices (at the birth)."

The biblical account of his life is as follows. Isaac was born as the result of a divine promise to Abraham that he would be the ancestor of a great and blessed nation (Gen 12:1-3; 15:1-6), but only after a delay that created doubt on the part of Abraham (16:1-2; 17:1, 15-19; 21:1-3). He is to be the recipient of the promise, even in the presence of a half-brother (16:1-6; 21:8-21). Abraham's faith is severely tested by the near sacrifice of Isaac (22:1-19, an episode that figures prominently in the thought and art of both synagogue and church). For a wife, REBEKAH is chosen from among relatives in upper Mesopotamia rather than a local Canaanite woman (24:1-67), and this leads to the birth of twins, ESAU and Jacob (25:19-26). God's promise is repeated to him (26:1-5), and Isaac settles down in the southern part of Canaan (26:6-33). When he blesses his sons, a ruse leads the younger (Jacob) to receive the stronger wording (27:1-40), thus signifying that it is through him that the promise is to be realized. Isaac died at the age of 180 years (35:28-29) and was buried in a family tomb (49:30-31).

His name, like that of son Jacob, came to be used for the totality of a nation of descendants (i.e., the Northern Kingdom; Amos 7:9, 16). NT writers cite the patriarchal list (Acts 7:8), relate his birth in the context of the divine promise (Rom 9:6-11; Gal 4:28), and mention his near sacrifice (James 2:21).

Some modern interpreters (e.g., M. Noth) have suggested that the three patriarchs, rather than being individuals in a biological line, originated as names of clans who settled in Canaan at different times: Jacob as a settlement of Arameans in the north of Canaan, and Abraham and Isaac as an earlier settlement in the south (Amorites?). Thus, the traditions about these clans-become-individuals would have initially been preserved in such southern sanctuaries as BEERSHEBA (Gen 21:31; 22:19) and Beer-lahai-roi (24:62; 25:11), where a deity designated as "the Fear of Isaac" (31:42, 53, RSV; NAB, "the Awesome One of Isaac") may have been worshiped.

See also BEERSHEBA; PATRIARCH.

Bibliography. M. Noth, *The History of Israel*.

—LLOYD R. BAILEY

• **Isaac, Testament of.** The *Testament of Isaac* is a legendary account of the events leading up to the death of ISAAC. It begins with God sending the archangel MICHAEL to prepare Isaac for his departure. Isaac comforts JACOB, who overhears the conversation, and gives a series of moral exhortations to those who gather to hear him. Then an angel takes him up in a vision. First, Isaac sees sinners being punished; then he is taken to heaven, where he sees ABRAHAM and the heavenly worship of God. Finally, God sends his chariot for Isaac's soul, Isaac gives final directives to Jacob, and his soul is taken to heaven. The narrative is prefaced and concluded with some comments on the annual celebration of the death of Isaac.

The *Testament of Isaac* is extant in Coptic, Ethiopic, and Arabic, but was probably composed in Greek, presumably in Egypt. In its present form it is Christian, but it might go back to a Jewish original, perhaps written in the second or third century C.E. It is closely related to the TESTAMENT OF ABRAHAM and the TESTAMENT OF JACOB, being dependent on the former and a source for the latter.

The *Testament of Isaac* is most significant for shedding light on medieval Coptic Christianity, especially its annual celebration commemorating the death of Isaac. It has a strong moral emphasis, a concern for showing mercy, and a focus on human sin and God's forgiveness. There is also a brief tour of HELL (cf. GREEK APOCALYPSE OF EZRA). The document seems intended to encourage righteous living.

See also TESTAMENTS, APOCRYPHAL.

Bibliography. K. H. Kuhn, "The Testament of Isaac," *The Apocryphal Old Testament*, ed. H. F. D. Sparks; W. F. Stinespring, "Testament of Isaac," *The Old Testament Pseudepigrapha*, ed. J. H. Charlesworth.

—JOSEPH L. TRAFTON

• **Isaiah.** [*i*-zay'yuh] The name Isaiah means "Yah (or "Yahweh") is salvation." The name is essentially the same as Joshua, Jesus, and Hosea. It also carries the same content as Elisha, although with El instead of Yah. The name expressed the hope and faith of his parents that their God would in some way effect salvation or deliverance for the people through their son. If ever a hope proved to be inspired, this was one, for Isaiah proclaimed God's message of salvation to the people of Judah in the latter third of the eighth century B.C.E.

Isaiah was the son of Amoz (1:1), not to be confused with AMOS, the prophet from Tekoa, although he was probably born during the time of that prophet's ministry. A tradition recorded in the Talmud suggests that Isaiah was a nephew of Judah's King AMAZIAH, and thus a cousin of King UZZIAH. While this tradition is unsubstantiated, it might serve to explain the easy access that Isaiah had to the royal court throughout his ministry. He also showed a very intimate knowledge of the intrigues within the royal household, as well as a detailed awareness of the intricacies of international diplomacy as practiced by the kings of Judah.

Isaiah was said to be the author of "the acts of Uzziah" (2 Chr 26:22). The ability to write in those times was not common. That this particular work was attributed to him might identify him as an official court scribe. While either the tradition or this deduction may be true, neither is necessarily so. However, either or both would explain his familiarity with the royal house and the official goings-on.

Isaiah was called to be a prophet during the time of mourning following the death of King Uzziah (Isa 6:1). The last datable event from his long ministry is in 701 B.C.E., the time of the Sennacherib crisis (36:1–37:38; 2 Kgs 18:13–20:19). However, another tradition suggests that Isaiah was martyred by the evil King MANASSEH, who had the old prophet tied in a hollow log and sawn in two. It may be to this tradition that the author of Hebrews refers (Heb 11:37). In any case, Isaiah's ministry extended from ca. 742 B.C.E. to the end of the eighth or the beginning of the seventh century B.C.E.

Isaiah was married to a prophetess (Isa 8:3), and they had at least two children. In the manner of his contemporaries, his children bore names that expressed his faith. Maher-shalal-hash-baz ("The Spoil Speeds, the Prey Hastens," 8:1-4) and Shear-jashub ("A Remnant Shall Return," 7:3) carried names that stressed the two major themes of his early messages. They carried a warning that the crisis of temporal judgment was immediately upon the people of Judah, but that God would ultimately deliver a portion of the people from the forthcoming exile and destruction.

Isaiah's ministry was the lengthened shadow of his call. Overcome with grief, and perhaps with anger, at the death of his beloved Uzziah, Isaiah was in the Temple at a time of worship, possibly wondering what kind of God would have taken Uzziah in such a way. As the smoke of the incense and sacrifice filled the air, he received a vision of Yahweh, perceiving him as he really was and not as the prophet had imagined him to be. His vision revealed to him the awesome holiness of Yahweh. From that time on, the most common phrase used by Isaiah to describe Yahweh was "the Holy One of Israel." In becoming aware of God's holiness, the prophet also became aware of his own sinfulness, as well as that of his people. Confessing his sin, he was cleansed by God. This cleansing is described in terms that reflect the pain that may accompany such a purging. All of these themes played a major part in his subsequent preaching: the sinfulness of people before God, the cleansing forgiveness of God, and the agony that for Israel was going to accompany the purging judgment.

At this point, the prophet sensed that Yahweh was seeking for someone to share this message of sin, judgment, and hope with God's people. Isaiah offered himself (Isa 6:8). With no reluctance, the young man plunged headfirst into Yahweh's ministry. No reluctance is ever found on the part of this prophet from and to Jerusalem. This is even more amazing in light of the fact that Yahweh revealed the essentially fruitless nature of the prophet's mission (6:9-10). He was offered the hope that only a few of his people would hear and respond (6:13). With the impetus of that call, Isaiah set forth on his forty-year mission for God.

The ministry of the prophet falls into four rather distinct sections. First, he was intensely involved in the Syro-Ephraimitic crisis of 735 B.C. E. He apparently had begun with the proclamation of judgment and a call for righteousness in ca. 742 B.C.E. In confronting King AHAZ, he urged him to trust in Yahweh rather than in his own political, military, and diplomatic plans (7:1-12). Isaiah promised the king a deliverance by God.

Upon Ahaz's refusal to heed, Isaiah then went into the second stage of his ministry, a time of withdrawal (8:16-18). During this time he apparently devoted himself to his disciples, training them and waiting for God to send him forth again. The third stage began with the accession of King HEZEKIAH, ca. 715 B.C.E. Under Isaiah's leadership, he apparently broke the alliances of his father with Assyria. Unfortunately, these were supplanted by alliances with Egypt, which Isaiah also opposed. It was during this time that for three years Isaiah went naked and barefoot, dressed as a captive, as a warning (20:1-6).

The final period of the prophet's ministry is dated in the time of the Sennacherib crisis, ca. 701 B.C.E. In this crisis, in spite of the overwhelming force of the Assyrian king, the prophet offered hope to Hezekiah that God would deliver Jerusalem from the expected catastrophe (37:33-38). And so God did. Following this, Isaiah passed from the stage of history. He had served God and his people with dependability and faithfulness.

See also ISAIAH, BOOK OF; PROPHET.

Bibliography. R. L. Clements, *Isaiah 1–39, NCB;* J. D. W. Watts, *Isaiah 1–33, WBC.*

—ROBERT L. CATE

• **Isaiah, Book of.** The first of the latter prophets in the MT and the first of the so-called major prophets in the English versions; the Book of Isaiah has probably had more superlatives applied to it than any other book in the OT. It is one of the three longest books in the Bible, along with Jeremiah and Psalms.

• OUTLINE OF ISAIAH •

The Book of Isaiah

I. Selections from Sermons Dealing with Judah and Israel (1:1–12:6)
  A. The setting (1:1)
  B. Accusation against Judah (1:2-31)
  C. Past and future contrasted (2:1–4:6)
  D. The song of the vineyard (5:1-30)
  E. Isaiah's call (6:1-13)
  F. The Immanuel prophecy (7:1–8:22)
  G. Messianic names and nature (9:1-7)
  H. Divine wrath (9:8–10:34)
  I. The shoot of Jesse (11:1-16)
  J. Praise for God's salvation (12:1-6)
II. The Foreign Prophecies (13:1–23:18)
III. The Little Apocalypse (24:1–27:13)
  A. The present world doomed (24:1-23)
  B. Yahweh's magnificent victory (25:1-12)
  C. Divine provision for the future (26:1-21)
  D. Ultimate redemption (27:1-13)
IV. Divine Wisdom and Human Folly (28:1–33:24)
  A. Contrasting attainments (28:1-29)
  B. Empty religion attacked (29:1-24)
  C. Revelation to rebellious people (30:1-33)
  D. Folly of foreign alliances (31:1-9)
  E. The righteous king (32:1-20)
  F. Praise to God (33:1-24)
V. Yahweh's Fury and Blessing (34:1–35:10)
  A. The day of vengeance (34:1-17)
  B. The highway in the wilderness (35:1-10)
VI. Historical Interlude (36:1–39:8)
  A. Sennacherib's attack (36:1–37:38)
  B. Hezekiah's illness (38:1-22)
  C. The Babylonian envoys (39:1-8)
VII. God's Great Redemption (40:1–55:13)
  A. Good news to Zion (40:1-11)
  B. God's nature revealed (40:12–41:29)
  C. The first servant song (42:1-9)
  D. The new song and Yahweh's redemption (42:10–44:8)
  E. Empty idols and the great redeemer (44:9–47:4)
  F. Judgment upon Babylon (47:5-15)
  G. The fulfillment of redemption and judgment (48:1-22)
  H. The second servant song (49:1-13)
  I. The abundance of Divine blessing (49:14-26)
  J. The third servant song (50:1-9)
  K. Invitation to share in redemption (50:10–51:23)
  L. The bearers of good tidings (52:1-12)
  M. The fourth servant song (52:13–53:12)
  N. Vindication of Yahweh's servants (54:1-17)
  O. The fifth (?) servant song (55:1-13)
VIII. Yahweh's New People (56:1–66:24)
  A. Judgment and redemption (56:1–59:21)
  B. The awesome glory of God (60:1–65:16)
  C. The new heavens and the new earth (65:17–66:24)

Any measure that can be applied causes it to be classified as one of the more significant books in the OT. Its very length first leads to this conclusion. Further, more copies of it have been found among the DEAD SEA SCROLLS than of any other book except Deuteronomy. It is quoted more by JESUS and the NT writers than any other book, with more than four hundred references having been identified. Finally, the messianic prophecies, popularized by Handel's "Messiah," and the songs of the suffering servant have been treasured by Christians over the centuries.

The POETRY of the book is exalted, being some of the most uplifting in the Bible. The literary genius of the author or editor is unquestioned, and it ranks with the few truly great literary masterpieces of the world. For all of this perhaps its major appeal lies in its characterization of the messiah. In the first half of the book we see the messiah as king. In the latter half, we see him as suffering servant.

Unity of Isaiah. The authorship and unity of the Book of Isaiah has been more seriously debated than that of any other biblical book. The passages that have been most frequently questioned as having come from the original author, or from the lips of Isaiah if he were not the original writer, are listed below.

(1) The lyric psalm following the vision of the messianic kingdom (12:1-6); (2) The oracle against Babylon (13:1–14:23); (3) The oracle against Moab (15:1–16:14); (4) The oracles against Babylon, Edom, and Arabia (21:1-17); (5) The so-called "little apocalypse" (24:1–27:13); (6) The oracle to Jerusalem (33:1-24); (7) The oracle of judgment and restoration (34:1–35:10); (8) The historical appendix or insertion, essentially parallel to 2 Kgs 18:13–20:19 (36:1-39:8); (9) The section dealing with God's great redemption (40:1–55:13); (10) The section on the new people of God (56:1–66:24); (11) Other less significant and shorter passages; Isa 40:1–55:13 is frequently called Deutero-Isaiah and 56:1–66:24 is identified as Trito-Isaiah. Sometimes both are considered to be one unit with the entire section, 40:1–66:24, being called Deutero-Isaiah.

Divisions of Isaiah. (1) The issues regarding unity can generally all be found, with only minor exceptions, in Isa 40–66. Those supporting the disunity point out that nowhere in these chapters is Isaiah ever identified as the author. Further, the attitude changes radically, with the first part of the book, i.e., Isa 1–39, being concerned with confrontation and rebuke, while the latter half deals with comfort and assurance. The mood of the first part is gloom while the mood of the second part is hope and light. In addition, in the latter part of the book the destruction of Jerusalem is presupposed as an accomplished fact. Yet, this catastrophe is merely anticipated in the first part. Further, in the latter part both the prophet and his people are in Exile, while the Exile is far in the future in the first part.

In the latter part, Cyrus, king of Persia is twice named without any introduction or explanation, although he clearly lived more than a century and a half after Isaiah of Jerusalem and would obviously have been unknown to the people of Judah in the eighth century B.C.E. Further, the fall of Babylon is seen in the immediate future in 40–55 and in the past in 56–66. Yet Babylon was not even a threat, much less an enemy, in the lifetime of Isaiah of Jerusalem.

In addition to this internal evidence from the Book of Isaiah, the Bible twice refers to the edict of Cyrus that allowed the Jews to return home from Babylon as being in fulfillment of the prophecy of Jeremiah (2 Chr 36:22-23; Ezra 1:1-4). Such a reference to Jeremiah's prediction of a return from exile after seventy years is surprising if a direct reference to Cyrus by name had been available from the preaching of Isaiah. Further, Jeremiah only barely escaped death following his prediction of the destruction of the Temple (Jer 7:26). That he was delivered at all was due to the discovery of a one-verse reference in the prophecy of Micah (Mic 3:12). This entire episode becomes difficult to understand if the material in Isa 40–66 had been available, for it presupposes the destruction of the Temple (44:26, 28; 49:19; 51:17-20; 52:9; 60:10; 63:18; 64:10-11). The people of Jeremiah's day showed no awareness of any of these passages.

Furthermore, those who support a non-Isaianic authorship of these chapters point to differences in style and theology. Numerous words and phrases found in one section are not found in the other. "The Lord, Yahweh of Hosts," "remnant," and "to stretch out the hand," are all quite common in chaps. 1–39, but do not appear in 40–66. Further, "in that day" occurs more than thirty times in chaps. 1–39 and only once in 40–66. On the other hand, "all flesh," "to choose," "chosen," and "I, Yahweh [or some other name for God]" do not occur in chaps. 1–39, while appearing with frequency in 40–66. "Redeem" is found more than twenty times in chaps. 40–66 but only once in 1–39. Among the theological differences that have been noted is the fact that in chaps. 1–39 God's majesty is emphasized, the messiah is king, and Yahweh is related to Israel through a covenant commitment. In contrast, in chaps. 40–66 God's infinity is stressed, the messiah is suffering servant, and Israel is related to Yahweh through his redemptive choice.

Those who support the unity of the book point out that the Bible always treats the book as a unit. No ancient manuscript, including the Dead Sea Scrolls, has been found that makes a division between chaps. 39 and 40. A division does occur in the Dead Sea Scrolls between chaps. 33 and 34. Those who support the unity of the book also point out that different purposes require different vocabulary, emphases and style. The supporters of unity also point out that Isaiah could have envisioned the future under inspiration and produced a message for those who were in exile at that time. The issue, however, is not whether or not God could have done this but whether or not he did do this.

The general conclusion shared by the majority of scholars is that Isa 40–66 was the product of a group of disciples who had immersed themselves in the proclamations of Isaiah of Jerusalem and who sought to proclaim their mentor's concerns in a new day and in a different life situation. If this theory is correct, then biblical references to this material as being from Isaiah have to be understood as literary references only.

Regardless of the issues of whether or not chaps. 40–66 came from eighth-century Isaiah, no one disagrees with the setting that this material addresses. Isa 1–39 focuses upon Judah and Jerusalem in the eighth century B.C.E.; 40–55 addresses the exiles in Babylon just prior to the return in 539 B.C.E.; and 56–66 deals with those who are back in Jerusalem after the return.

(2) The commentators who have maintained that the material in chaps. 40–66 did not come from Isaiah of Jerusalem but from an unknown prophet or school of prophets in the exilic period have also pointed out that chaps. 34–35 bear a remarkable similarity to 40–66 in theology and style. They clearly bear more similarity to chaps. 40–66 than to 1–33. However, this very similarity has been used by proponents of Isaianic unity as evidence for that unity, since chaps. 34–35 are obviously in the first part of the book.

At the same time, the similarity between 2 Kgs 18:13–20:19 and Isa 36–39 has created a great deal of discussion regarding unity. Four options exist. The Book of Isaiah copied from Kings, the author(s) of Kings copied from Isaiah, both copied from a third (unknown) source, or a unique miracle of inspiration occurred. The latter option is possible, but it does not appear to have been God's normal (or even abnormal) way of inspiring scripture. It is also possible that both used a third source, but no evidence of such a source exists at this time. For a long time, those who supported separate authorship for chaps. 1–39 and 40–66 suggested that the Isaianic chapters were copied from Kings to give the significant details of the latter part of Isaiah's ministry, thus serving as a conclusion to the first part of the book and an introduction to the latter part.

However, with the discovery in the Dead Sea Scrolls that a break occurs between chaps. 33 and 34, supporters of a separate authorship for the two parts of the book are now frequently suggesting that the second section really begins with chap. 34 rather than with chap. 40. This hypothesis suggests the author or editor of the second part of the book began his new work with an oracle of judgment and restoration, followed it with a summary of Isaiah's latter ministry, and then moved on into the body of chaps. 40–66. The major message of restoration and deliverance found in chaps. 40–66 was based upon the hope which Isaiah's own ministry had established. Proponents of this theory usually suggest that the author of Kings borrowed this material as one of his sources, even as he used other historical data for the creation of his work.

In general then, those who support an independent authorship for chaps. 40–66 now usually support an independent authorship for chaps. 34–39. Some disagreement exists among them as to whether or not chaps. 34–39 is in itself a unity. On the other hand, those who hold a literary unity of the book are forced to admit some literary affinity between the Kings and Isaiah material. In general, these usually suggest that the Isaiah material was inserted here by a later editor, borrowing it from Kings. However, proponents of this hypothesis have never offered a satisfactory explanation as to why it was inserted at this point.

(3) The material in chaps. 24–27 has been identified as the "little apocalypse" of Isaiah. Debate continues whether or not Isaiah of Jerusalem authored this section.

Those who deny it to Isaiah, do so on the basis of its advanced theology, such as the resurrection from the dead (26:19) and the elements of APOCALYPTIC LITERATURE present (apocalyptic literature is a very late OT phenomenon). The characteristics identified as apocalyptic are the concepts of a universal judgment, the shutting up of the heavenly host, and the catastrophic inbreak of God's kingdom.

On the other hand, those who support the unity of Isaiah point out that many of the characteristics of apocalyptic literature found in Daniel and Revelation are not present in these chapters. Obviously, any literary genre must have a beginning; supporters of unity in Isaiah suggest that Israel's apocalyptic traditions begin here.

If this material did come from eighth-century Isaiah, it is a strange thing that it went so long unnoticed. It was at least a century and a half—and possibly three or more centuries—before any similiar literature appeared in Israel. Further, the hope of even a limited resurrection was absent until later in Israel's theological development. Those who insist that it was late suggest that it came from the exilic or postexilic eras, although they are not able to agree among themselves any more precisely.

(4) Isaiah's oracle against Moab, chaps. 15 and 16, is quite similar to the one found in Jer 48:28-39. Many interpreters have denied that Isaiah of Jerusalem authored the oracle, claiming that it belonged originally to Jeremiah and was later enlarged and inserted in Isaiah. One can argue equally well that Isaiah wrote the oracle and that Jeremiah recast it for his time. A third case, just as strong, can be made that the two prophets took an anonymous oracle and reinterpreted it, each in his own time. Arguments from silence, however wield little persuasive power. Further, so little is known of Moabite history that it is impossible to identify a specific occasion from which such an oracle might have arisen.

(5) The oracles against Babylon, Edom, and Arabia—Isa 13, 14, and 21—are normally denied to eighth-century Isaiah for some of the same reasons that chaps. 40–66 are. The basic problem is that Babylon was no threat to Judah in the eighth-century B.C.E. The bitterness here expressed toward Babylon, Edom, and Arabia seems to presuppose the destruction of Jerusalem in 587/6 B.C.E., as well as the atrocities and oppression that followed. With no explanation given, this material would have been meaningless to the contempories of Isaiah of Jerusalem. In order to get around this difficulty, some have suggested that these oracles were originally addressed to Assyria and related enemies and later reinterpreted by Isaiah's disciples. In general, those who have difficulty with chaps. 40–66 also have difficulty with chaps. 13, 14, and 21. Those who have no problems with chaps. 40–66 have no problem here either.

(6) The lyric psalm, Isa 12, and the oracle to Jerusalem, Isa 33, do not sound at all like the preaching of Isaiah recorded in chaps. 1–11. The poetry appears to be more exalted than that found in the sermons. Further, some have suggested that it sounds somewhat like that found in chaps. 40–66. Each of the poems is brief, giving scant basis for a detailed analysis. The material in chap. 12 does not appear to be greatly different from some things found in chaps. 1–11. Since the break in the Dead Sea Scrolls occurs between chaps. 33 and 34, the evidence appears to be quite insufficient to deny these two chapters to Isaiah of Jerusalem.

Message of Isaiah. The book of Isaiah contains some of the most memorable sermons and poetry to be found anywhere in the world's literature. The writer who produced this material towers over his time.

The message of the book of Isaiah is one of the more profound of the OT. The author(s) viewed God as the awesome Holy One of Israel, but also saw him as the great Redeemer. Intensely aware of the prophet's own sinfulness and that of his people, the book of Isaiah also affirms the unbelievable love of God. Out of the love comes God's judgment as well as his redemption.

As a part of God's future for his people, the book points to the messiah who will rule on the throne of David in righteousness. But he also points to the suffering servant, the One who brings healing through his own suffering. The message of the book is so magnificent that it was no wonder that Jesus himself began his ministry by quoting from it.

> The Spirit of the Lord God is upon me,
> because the Lord has anointed me
> to bring good tidings to the afflicted;
> he has sent me to bind up the broken hearted,
> to proclaim liberty to the captives,
> and the opening of the prison to those who are bound;
> to proclaim the year of the Lord's favor. . . .
> —Isa 61:1-2; cf. Lk. 4:16-19

See also APOCALYPTIC LITERATURE; DEAD SEA SCROLLS; ISAIAH; MESSIAH/MESSIANISM; POETRY; PROPHECY; PROPHET; REMNANT.

—ROBERT L. CATE

• **Isaiah, Martyrdom and Ascension of.** The *Martyrdom and Ascension of Isaiah,* often referred to simply as the *Ascension of Isaiah,* is considered part of the OT pseudepigrapha. In its present form, extant in full only in an Ethiopic translation from the original Greek, the *Ascension* is a Christian work from the third or fourth century C.E. that incorporates a much older Jewish legend about the martyrdom of ISAIAH the prophet at the hand of the evil king MANASSEH.

This legend, in which Isaiah meets his death by being sawed in half, is found in the first five chapters of the present work: 1:1–3:12 and 5:1-16 (3:13–4:22 is a Christian interpolation). The death of Isaiah is not discussed in the OT; this martyr story probably arose during the persecution of the Jews by Antiochus Epiphanes in 167–164 B.C.E. Such stories encouraged Jews to be faithful to the COVENANT, even to the point of death (cf. 1 Macc 6–7). Since the story about Isaiah's martyrdom was known to Justin (*Trypho* 120:5), to Tertullian (*DePat*, 14; *Scorp*, 8), and probably to the author of HEBREWS (11:37), it may have been written down by the first century C.E. It was probably composed in Hebrew and later translated into Greek, but if so, the original has been lost. It is thus impossible to know how thoroughly the Jewish story has been reworded by the subsequent Christian editor(s).

The two reports, chaps. 3:14–4:22 and 6:1–11:43, are overtly Christian in content. The first, sometimes called the "Testament of Hezekiah," has been interpolated into the martyrdom. It is not a testament, but a report of Isaiah's vision before his arrest. It describes the life, death, and resurrection of the Beloved, the corruption of the church, the reign of the ANTICHRIST (Beliar), and the second coming. Some scholars find an allusion to the Nero *redivivus* myth in the description of the antichrist as a "murderer of his mother" who is responsible for the deaths of "some of the twelve" (4:2-3; cf. Rev 13:3; 17:11; Suetonius, *Nero* 57; Tacitus, *Hist* 2.8f.). This would suggest a late first century C. E. date for the composition of 3:14–4:22. Such a date is supported by the view of the corruption of the church as a sign of the second coming (3:21-31), a position also found in the PASTORAL EPISTLES, 2 Peter, and 1 CLEMENT.

Perhaps the final stage of composition consisted of the addition of the longer vision report, chaps. 6–11, and the editing of chaps. 1–5 to accommodate the addition. This vision is cast in the form of a tour of heaven, a common device in ancient apocalypses (cf. 2 ENOCH; REVELATION). Isaiah is transported through the levels of heaven to the seventh heaven, where he sees the righteous in their robes, singing praises to God while they await the thrones and crowns to be awarded them at the end of time. An interesting aspect of the theology of this vision report is that Christ and "the angel of the Holy Spirit" both worship "the Lord," indicating a subordinationist view of the TRINITY (9:40). Isaiah sees Christ's descent to earth (where his true nature is not recognized), his miraculous birth, his CRUCIFIXION, RESURRECTION, and ASCENSION back through the heavens in triumph. The Christology of chaps. 6–11 reflects the descending/ascending redeemer pattern, and has docetic tendencies (e.g., 9:14: "they will think that he is flesh and a man"). Study of Gnostic materials has uncovered a number of parallels to aspects of the vision report in chaps. 6–11. It is thought that this portion of the *Ascension of Isaiah* dates from the second century C.E. and that the final combination and editing process was completed in the third or fourth century.

Bibliography. J. H. Charlesworth, *The Pseudepigrapha and Modern Research*; M. A. Knibb, "Martyrdom and Ascension of Isaiah," *The Old Testament Pseudepigrapha*, ed. J. H. Charlesworth; G. W. E. Nickelsburg, *Jewish Literature Between the Bible and the Mishnah.*

—SHARYN E. DOWD

• **Ishbosheth.** [ish-boh'shith] A son of Saul, also known as Eshbaal (cf. 1 Chr 8:33; 9:39). Under the leadership of ABNER, Ishbosheth sought to reign over the kingdom after Saul's death (2 Sam 2:8-10). However, he was followed only by the northern tribes and then for only two years. After that he was murdered (2 Sam 4:5-8).

During the early period of the Hebrew settlement in CANAAN and continuing into the time of the monarchy, many names in Israel were compounded with BAAL. It is possible that, at least for some, this name may have been used merely as another name for Yahweh, since it means "Lord." On the other hand, it may have indicated a deep involvement with the worship of the Canaanite Baals (Baalim). In either instance, its usage indicates a strong Canaanite influence upon ISRAEL.

Until recently, most interpreters assumed that later prophetic or deuteronomistic influence upon Israel caused a scribal change of the name from Eshbaal ("Man of Baal") to Ishbosheth ("Man of Shame"). This supposedly reflected a belief that it was a shame for any Hebrew to have been so involved with the Baal worship to have a name compounded with Baal.

In recent discoveries, however, other cognate languages have revealed a linguistic root indicating that *bosheth* may have derived from a root referring to the genitals, to sexual potency, and ultimately to pride. In Hebrew, it later came to mean "shame," apparently because of its sexual connotations. It is possible that as it was used in the name Ishbosheth it may have carried a reference to sexuality and thus was a parallel to Baal, the god of the Canaanite fertility cult. In this case, Ishbosheth and Eshbaal may have been almost synonymous. At the present state of linguistic knowledge, it is impossible to state with certainty what precise connotation of the name was intended by the biblical author.

See also BAAL.

Bibliography. M. Tsevat, "Ishbosheth and Congeners," *HUCA* 46:1-87.

—ROBERT L. CATE

• **Ishmael.** Ishamel, which means "God (El) hears," is the name of five different men in the OT, the most prominent of whom was the first son of ABRAHAM (or Abram) and the progenitor of the ISHMAELITES (Gen 25:13-16; 1 Chr 1:28-31). The birth of Ishmael is recorded in Gen 16. The infertile wife SARAH (or Sarai) offered her maid HAGAR to Abram as a concubine. One text from the city of NUZI casts light upon this arrangement. In Hurrian society a wife who had borne no children should secure for her husband a concubine, whose offspring would be considered the child(ren) of the wife herself. More problematic is Sarah's conduct in 21:8-21. According to the Code of Hammurabi, a priestess who because of her rank could not have children could give her husband a concubine. If the concubine failed to remain subservient, she could be reduced to slavehood again, but she could not be sold. Sarah may have acted within contemporary (though not biblical) morality by dealing harshly with Hagar, but her demand for Abraham to expel Hagar was excessive. It was the provision of God, not the morality of Sarah, that rectified matters.

Many scholars see as doublets Gen 16 (usually attributed to the Yahwist) and Gen 21:8-21 (often considered Elohistic). In both stories Sarah and Hagar quarrel, Abram must choose between the women, and Hagar leaves. As the stories now stand, Gen 21:8-21 is dated approximately sixteen years after Gen 16, the circumcision of Ishmael at age thirteen (17:25) and three years of ISAAC's life (21:8) having intervened. Since the dating system in the Pentateuch is considered priestly, scholars often question its accuracy. Within 21:8-21 one finds no definite indication of Ishmael's age, but vv. 14-15 seem to presuppose a young, almost helpless child. In fact, v. 14 might mean that Abraham put Ishmael on Hagar's back, and v. 15 clearly assumes a child too small to help his mother search for water. Conversely, there are differences between the accounts. In Gen 16 Sarah dealt so harshly with Hagar that she chose to leave, while in Gen 21 Abraham ordered Hagar to leave. Also, Gen 16 ends abruptly with the birth of Ishmael, while Gen 21 only treats Ishmael's early boyhood. Thus, even if these narratives originally constituted a doublet, they have been edited to fit different contexts. Both stories were highly sympathetic toward Ishmael as Abraham's son, while still emphasizing Isaac as the one through whom God's covenant would be passed on.

Ishmael is mentioned only twice more. In Gen 25:9 he assists Isaac in burying their father Abraham, and in 28:9 ESAU, hoping to please his parents by taking a relative as his wife, marries Ishmael's daughter.

The second Ishmael, the son of Nethaniah, assassinated Gedaliah, the governor of Judah after the fall of Jerusalem in 587/6, a number of Jews and Shechemites, and a small force of Babylonians garrisoned at Mizpah, and then escaped to AMMON (2 Kgs 25:23-25; Jer 40–41).

The other men named Ishmael were the third of six sons of a Benjaminite named Azel (1 Chr 8:38; 9:44), the father of a man named Zebadiah, governor of the house of Judah (2 Chr 19:11; 23:1), and a priest who had married a foreign wife (Ezra 10:22).

See also ABRAHAM; ISAAC; ISHMAELITES; SARAH.

Bibliography. G. von Rad, *Genesis, a Commentary*; E. A. Speiser, *Genesis*; H. C. White, "The Initiation Legend of Ishmael," *ZAW* 87/3 (1975): 269-305.

—PAUL L. REDDITT

• **Ishmaelites.** [ish'may-uh-*l*its] Gen 25:12-18 lists twelve tribes whose eponymous ancestors were the children of Ishmael. Their habitat is located in the desert regions to the south and east of Canaan. They are pictured once as caravaneers trading in gum, balm, and myrrh (Gen 37:25). A related group of people, also linked genealogically with ABRAHAM through Keturah (Gen 25:1-4), were the Midianites. Aside from their apparent interchangeability in the Joseph story, sometimes attributed to different sources (Gen 37:27, 28; 39:1), the Midianites of Gideon's story seem to have been identified as Ishmaelites (Judg 8:24). Continuing contacts between Israel and the Ishmaelites are indicated by the notices that Jether the Ishmaelite was the father of Amasa, David's nephew, and that one of David's officials was Obil the Ishmaelite (1 Chr 2:17; 27:30).

See also ISHMAEL; MIDIAN/MIDIANITES.

—JOHN KEATING WILES

• **Ishtar.** *See* QUEEN OF HEAVEN

• **Israel.** [iz'ray-uhl] The precise original meaning of this name remains uncertain. The folk etymology of the term in Gen 32:22-32 leaves uncertain whether the root *śrh* is to be understood as "strive, struggle" ("he struggles with God ['el]" or "God struggles") or "to have dominion over" ("he has dominion over God [or a divine being]" or "God has dominion"). The association of the name with *śrh* or *śwr* (a by-form of *śrr*), suggesting the idea of dominion, is indicated by Hos 12:5 (cf. Hos 8:4 and Judg 9:22). *Miśrah,* from *śrh,* in Isa 9:5-6 clearly indicates "dominion, authority." Thus, it would appear that the name should be connected with the idea of dominion/rule, rather than with the idea of struggle or striving. Less likely is the association of the name with the verb *yšr* "to be upright" found in the name Jeshurun, used as a synonym for Israel in Deut 32:15; 33:15, 26; and Isa 44:2 (so Nahmanides and other medieval Jewish interpreters). Such an association understands Israel ("he who is upright with God") as an antonym to Jacob ("deceitful, crafty"). Even less probable is Philo's view that the name is an abbreviation for *'iš-ra'ah-'el,* "the one who saw God."

The terms Israel and Israelites (children of Israel) were used with a number of different but related referents in the Bible and in biblical times. Among these are (1) a secondary name for the patriarch JACOB, (2) the "descendants" of the patriarch Israel/Jacob, (3) a tribal grouping in central Palestine in premonarchical times, (4) a kingdom composed primarily of northern tribal groups ruled by SAUL, (5) the monarchical state and its citizens ruled by DAVID and SOLOMON, (6) the northern state that separated from Davidic authority at the death of Solomon, (7) the cooperative union between the Kingdom of Israel, with its capital in SAMARIA, and Judah, with its capital at JERUSALEM, during the ninth and eighth centuries, (8) Judah and Judeans as the remnant of the old union of north and south after the Assyrian capture of Samaria in 722/1 B.C.E., and (9) adherents of various forms of Hebrew and OT religion (including its use as an early Christian self-designation).

Interestingly, the term "Israel" is practically never used as a geographical or territorial designation, indicating that the term was not geographical but religious and political in origin. Biblical references to the land of Israel are infrequent and late (cf. 2 Kgs 5:2; 2 Chr 30:25; 34:7; Ezek 27:17; 40:2). Only one ancient Near Eastern text refers to the "land" of Israel. In describing his battle at Qarqar (in 853) with a coalition of western powers, the Assyrian king Shalmaneser III (858-824) refers to King Ahab of the land of Israel (*Sir-'i-la-a-a*).

(1) Two biblical narratives report the change of Jacob's name to Israel, one associated with PENUEL in Transjordan (Gen 32:28) and the other with BETHEL in the central hill country, west of the Jordan (Gen 35:10). The renaming of Jacob to Israel may indicate the combining of two patriarchal figures (a Transjordanian Jacob and a west Jordan Israel?) revered by two originally separate peoples or else a nationalizing of the ancestral figure of Jacob by "identifying" him with the political entity Israel.

(2) Israelites or the children of Israel refer to the people who were members of the tribal and political entity bearing the name "Israel." They are idealistically depicted in the scriptures as one genealogically related group, namely, as the descendants of the twelve sons of the patriarch Israel/Jacob (cf. Gen 30:1-24; 35:16-20; 48:1-20). The description of these descendants as the offspring of four different women (LEAH, RACHEL, Zilpah, and Bilhah) and the diversity in the lists of the sons/tribes (Gen 49; Num 1:20-2:31; 26:1-65; Deut 33; Judg 5) suggest a diverse background for the people and a fluidity in the groups understood as belonging to Israel at any particular time.

(3) Reference to a people called Israel appears in a hymnic inscription set up in Egypt by Pharaoh Merneptah in the last decade of the thirteenth century, or shortly before the year 1200 (cf. *ANET*, 378). This "Israel" was located in the northern hill country of Palestine, and is

probably to be identified with the Ephraim/Manasseh/Benjamin tribes that occupy center stage in the Book of Judges. These tribes were settled in the central hill country of Palestine, primarily north of Jerusalem and south of the Esdraelon Plain, with some spillover into Gilead, east of the Jordan. More loosely associated with this group were the Galilee-Jezreel tribes of Asher, Naphtali, Issachar, and Zebulun and the Transjordanian tribes of Reuben and Gad.

The leaders of this Israel appear to have been tribal elders and occasional savior figures such as DEBORAH, BARAK, GIDEON, and JEPHTHAH. These savior figures were of diverse background with diverse patterns of leadership. The name Israel used of this tribal affiliation, containing a reference to the deity EL, suggests that at least some of the elements that made up early Israel originally venerated the god El in a special way (cf. Gen 33:20; 35:7; 31:13) and that Yahweh, a militant deity under whose banner they fought (Exod 15:3; Num 10:35-36; Judg 7:20), only secondarily became the dominant tribal deity.

Recent sociological approaches to early Israelite history have concluded that the earliest Israel was a conglomerate of peoples, composed of indigenous local villagers, displaced persons, and social refugees as well as migrant groups entering Canaan from the outside. The social upheavals and disruption of trade throughout the eastern Mediterranean seaboard ca. 1250–1100 B.C.E. created the conditions in which the tribal-based entity Israel arose in the Palestinian hill country. Archaeological evidence supports this hypothetical view and suggests no major invasion of the central hill country of Canaan and no massive destruction of biblical proportions at the time but only continuity of the previous culture with degeneration in material artisanship.

The individual tribe in the Israelite affiliation was distinguished by geography, common life styles, real and conjectured kinship, and the shared need of physical protection. As the Book of Judges indicates, the cooperation of two or more tribes was generally the consequence of confronting a common enemy.

(4) The appearance of greater external threats and gradual internal political evolution toward more centralized and perduring leadership eventually led to the establishment of kingship and the founding of Israel as a monarchical state. The external threats were posed by peoples from Transjordan, such as the Moabites, Ammonites, and Midianites, and by the Philistines from southwest Palestine. Early stages in this process and the gradual evolution of tribal life toward more stable and continuing leadership can be seen in the role of the family of Gideon (Judg 6–9) and the figure of Jephthah (Judg 11:1–12:10).

Like Abimelech and Jephthah (cf. Judg 9:4; 11:3), SAUL rose to prominence at the head of a small personal army capable of rallying tribal support, defending Israelite territory, and protecting the people from external plunder and attack (cf. 1 Sam 11; 13:1–14:46). Under Saul's leadership, monarchy became and continued to be the fundamental pattern of Israelite government.

The general territorial extent of Israel at the time of Saul is reflected in the description of the kingdom inherited by his son (or grandson?) ISH-BOSHETH (2 Sam 2:8-9). "All Israel" at the time consisted of Gilead (territory around Mahanaim in Transjordan), the Asherites (probably an enclave of the tribe of Asher in southwest Ephraim; cf. 1 Chr 7:35-45), Jezreel (the hill country abutting the Jezreel Valley), Ephraim, and Benjamin. Either before or at the time of Saul's death, DAVID had established an independent kingdom in Judah although Saul certainly seems earlier to have enjoyed the support of Judeans (cf. 1 Sam 23:7, 19; 24:1; cf. 1 Sam 15:1-12). Thus Saul's Israel was limited to the central Palestinian hill country south of the Valley of Jezreel, limited terrain in central Transjordan, and portions of the Judean hill country.

(5) Under David and Solomon, the state of Israel expanded to incorporate extensive territory in Transjordan, the region of Galilee, and all of "greater" Judah. Although the editorial glorification of the Solomonic state claimed that Solomon "ruled over all the kingdoms from the Euphrates to the land of the Philistines and to the border of Egypt" (2 Kgs 4:21) and that "he had dominion over all the region west of the Euphrates from Tiphsah to Gaza, over all the kings west of the Euphrates" (2 Kgs 4:24), other and more realistic texts suggest a much more limited territory. The traditional expression "from Dan to Beersheba" (2 Sam 17:11; 1 Kgs 4:25) is probably more descriptive of the extent of the Israelite state.

Two texts, perhaps based on authentic records, indicate something of the territorial dominion claimed by David and Solomon. Even these texts, however, cannot be taken as reflective of firm boundaries of a kingdom totally ruled by these two monarchs since boundaries in ancient times were often idealized phenomena, realistic only when a king could collect taxes and muster troops from the citizenry of an area. (a) 2 Sam 24:1-10 reports on David's census, which began at the River Arnon (the traditional northern border of Moab), extended to north of Dan, and reached westward to the territories of Tyre and Sidon. Whether any or how much of the Mediterranean coastal region belonged to Israel at the time remains uncertain. (b) 1 Kgs 4:7-19 preserves a list of Solomonic officers appointed to serve over twelve Israelite districts (in its present form, the text does not include Judah as one of the twelve districts) to supply provisions for Solomon's table and fodder for his horses (1 Kgs 4:27-28). The territory of these districts conforms with what can be known about the territory included in David's census and the list provides greater specificity about cities and regions. Obviously between Saul's time and the reign of Solomon, vast areas of Palestine had been brought under Israelite control.

Israel's economic well-being during the reigns of David and Solomon was in no small measure the product of Phoenician largess. Numerous texts speak of Israel as beneficiary of Phoenician expertise (2 Sam 5:11; 2 Kgs 5:1-12; 9:26-28; 10:11, 22) and even of Solomon's balance of trade deficits and concession of territory to Hiram of Tyre (1 Kgs 9:10-14). With its lack of natural resources, limited population, and restricted access to world markets, Israel's periods of reasonable prosperity were dependent upon cooperative participation with outside, more resourceful powers.

(6) Following the death of Solomon (probably in 927), the northern tribes broke away from the Davidic state protesting against the oppressive policies of the Jerusalemite monarchy (1 Kgs 12:1-20). This northern group assumed the name Israel which, as already noted, had earlier designated a political entity in the central highlands (see no. 3 above) even though the Judeans could continue to be called children of Israel (cf. 1 Kgs 12:17). The northern tribal elders meeting at SHECHEM selected JEROBOAM I (927–906), a former Solomonic official, as their new king (1 Kgs 11:26-28; 12:20). As part of his royal program, Jeroboam established two major cult centers, at Bethel and Dan, and thus at important points near the two extremities of his kingdom

(1 Kgs 12:28-33).

Warfare between Israel and Judah developed after the split (1 Kgs 15:6) but was probably limited to skirmishes fought to establish the boundary between the two states, a boundary that lay within the old territory of the tribe of Benjamin and only a few miles north of Jerusalem. The Egyptian invasion of Palestine by pharaoh SHISHAK (1 Kgs 14:25-28) no doubt diverted attention from local hostilities for a time.

In comparsion with Judah, the northern kingdom of Israel possessed greater territory, a large population, the largest cities, and a location more open and accessible to international trade and political relationships. Probably all territory east of the Jordan passed out of Israelite control early in the rule of Jeroboam, climaxing a process of attrition already begun under Solomon (1 Kgs 11:1-25).

The reign of the family of Jeroboam came to an end in its second generation when Baasha assassinated King NADAB and exterminated all the royal house (1 Kgs 15:27-30). Border warfare between Israel and Judah flared anew. When Baasha sought to fortify the town of Ramah, the Judean king Asa bribed the Aramean king of Damascus to attack Israel from the northeast. This counterattack diverted Israelite forces and allowed Asa to fortify the towns of Geba and Mizpah as permanent border points (1 Kgs 15:17-22).

(7) In the second quarter of the ninth century, Israel and Judah entered a period of cooperative alliance which lasted, with only intermittent interruptions, until PEKAH's takeover in Samaria in 734. After OMRI's coup and his success in a four-year civil war (1 Kgs 16:8-23), JEHOSHAPHAT, his southern counterpart, "made peace with" (or "submitted to") the king of Israel (1 Kgs 22:44). "Israel" now became a bipartite state with two monarchs, but with clear dominance belonging to the northern king.

The following factors indicate the close union of the two kingdoms. (a) The royal houses intermarried. Athaliah, an Omride princess but whose parents remain uncertain (2 Kgs 8:18, 26), was married to JEHORAM son of Jehoshaphat. (b) Although Assyrian texts make references to practically all the kingdoms in Aram-Palestine, no Assyrian text mentions Judah until 734 indicating that Judah was subsumed under "Israel" (cf. *ANET* 279, 281, 282). (c) For a time, both Israel and Judah were ruled simultaneously (ca. 851–840) by a king named Jehoram. Rather than two kings with the same name, this was probably the same person, namely, the Davidic Jehoram, son of Jehoshaphat. (d) When King AMAZIAH of Judah challenged the Israelite king at Bethshemesh, a traditional Judean site, he was severely defeated (2 Kgs 14:8-14). Amaziah's effort was probably an attempt to assert Judean independence from Israel. (e) Two contemporary prophets refer to the bipartite kingdom of Israel: Mic 1:14 speaks of the "kings of Israel" (probably Jotham of Judah and Jeroboam II of Israel) and Isa 8:14 refers to "both houses of Israel."

Under Omri and AHAB, Israel reached a level of territorial expansion and wealth equal to the time of Solomon, as archaeological remains have indicated. Portions of Transjordan and Galilee were retaken from Aram (cf. 2 Kgs 14:25 and the Mesha Inscription, *ANET*, 320-21) and the port of Elath was restored to Judean control (2 Kgs 14:21-22). As in the days of Solomon, Israel's prosperity was a by-product of good relations with outside powers. Israel became a cooperative partner in a Aramean-Palestinian alliance of powers that joined to protect eastern Mediterranean interests against Assyrian dominance (cf. *ANET*, 278-79 for the alliance that halted the Assyrian king Shalmaneser III at Qarqar in 853). With such ecumenical economic arrangements, ecumenism in religion also prevailed, as indicated by an inscription set up in Aramean territory by an Aramean monarch but dedicated to Baal Melqart, a Phoenician deity (cf. *ANET*, 501). With Omride intermarriage with and economic ties to the royal house of Tyre, some acknowledgment of the Phoenician Baal occurred in Israel as well (1 Kgs 16:31-32) but to the chagrin and consternation of the prophet Elijah and his supporters.

Following its defeat by Shalmaneser III in 845–844 and the usurpation of the Aramean throne by HAZAEL (cf. *ANET*, 280-81), the Aramean-Palestinian alliance disintegrated. Hazael attacked Israel probably to regain territory in the northern Transjordan previously lost to the Omrides (2 Kgs 8:28-29; 9:14b-15a). When Shalmaneser III was again in the region, in 841–840, JEHU, the commander of the Israelite army, led a coup against the wounded King Jehoram and, paying tribute, placed Israel under the custody and protection of the Assyrians (*ANET*, 281). Jehu moved to gain control of the country and stabilize his rule. The Israelite and Judean monarchs along with other members of the royal house were killed, Samaria taken, and much of the national leadership killed (2 Kgs 9:1–10:17) in what must have taken considerable time and great civil strife although the scriptures describe these events as if they occurred in a matter of days.

Jehu's submission to the Assyrians established an international policy for Israel that lasted for over a century. Throughout the reign of Jehu and the four successors from his house (JEHOAHAZ, Jehoash [or JOASH], JEROBOAM II, and ZECHARIAH) as well as during the rule of MENAHEM and his son PEKAHIAH, the offical stance of the government in Samaria was pro-Assyrian. None of these seven monarchs ever adopted an anti-Assyrian posture or joined the western alliance against Assyria. Two consequences followed from this policy. (a) When Assyria was strong and active in the west, Israel enjoyed prosperity and territorial expansion (again through the help and intervention of an outside power) and was weak and economically distressed during Assyrian decline. (b) Israel—and Judah, which shared a common foreign policy—was militarily and economically isolated and became the object of local harassment when anti-Assyrian sentiment was strong in the west.

Throughout much of the reign of Hazael (ca. 844–806), Israel and Judah were subject to Aram (the Elisha narratives in 2 Kgs 3-8; 13:14-19 and the battle narratives in 1 Kgs 20 and 22 probably describe conditions during the reign of Jehu and his two immediate successors). From 838 until 806, Assyrian power was basically absent from the west and Israel and Judah were dominated by "Greater Aram" ruled by Hazael (2 Kgs 11:32-33; 12:17-18; 13:3, 7, 22). In the fifth year of his reign (806–805), the Assyrian king Adad-Nirari III (810–783) began to reassert Assyrian authority in the west (*ANET*, 281-82) and Israel's fate took a turn for the better (2 Kgs 13:24-25). Under Jeroboam II (788–748), Israel and Judah recovered economically and territorially for a time, retaking all of Galilee, parts of Transjordan, and reacquiring control of the seaport of Elath (2 Kgs 14:21-25; 2 Chr 5:11-22). The Hebrew text of 2 Kgs 14:28 speaks of how Jeroboam II "returned Damascus and Hamath to Judah in Israel" but this text is corrupt and probably should be understood as referring to the fact that Jeroboam II reconquered territory in Galilee and Transjordan held by Hamath and Damascus during the days of Jehu, Jehoahaz, and Jehoash. For a time, the house of Israel was again, in cooperation with Assyria, a power in the eastern Mediterranean world.

In the late 760s and throughout the 750s, Assyrian power waned and Israel too entered a phase of decline. A revitalized anti-Assyrian coalition in the west led by Rezin of Damascus pressured Israel-Judah (Amos 1:3-15; Isa 9:12). PEKAH, killed in 731–730 (2 Kgs 16:29-30) after a rule of twenty years (2 Kgs 16:27), apparently led a portion of Israel to break away from Jeroboam's kingdom in 751–750 and threw in their lot with Rezin and the anti-Assyrian coalition (2 Kgs 15:37). From the 750s until the final fall of Samaria in 722/1, civil strife and civil war plagued Israel constantly.

The Jehu dynasty in Samaria ended with the assassination of Zechariah (2 Kgs 15:8-10). The assassin, Shallum, perhaps anti-Assyrian politically, was quickly attacked and killed by Menahem who secured his hold on the throne with the assistance of Assyria, now ruled by Tiglath-pileser III (744–727), an aggressive and successful monarch (2 Kgs 15:17-20). Menahem ruled over only the old tribal territory of Ephraim and Samaria, the capital city. Major portions of Israelite territory, including Galilee and Transjordan, were now under the control of Aram and Pekah (Isa 9:1; 2 Kgs 15:29) and much of Judah was sympathetic to the anti-Assyrian cause (Mic 1:10-16; Isa 8:6). In 734, the anti-Assyrian Pekah assassinated Menahem's successor, PEKAHIAH, seized the throne in Samaria, and brought the entire north into the anti-Assyrian coalition (2 Kgs 15:23-25). King AHAZ was expected to follow the lead of the north since the Jerusalemite king was an inferior power to the Samarian monarch. When Ahaz refused to take up arms against Assyria, Pekah and Rezin moved against Jerusalem to depose Ahaz and exterminate the Davidic house and to place a cooperative Tyrian prince, the son of Tabeel, on the throne of Judah (2 Kgs 16:5; Isa 7:6). The siege of Jerusalem failed and the dynasty of David survived, as Isaiah promised (Isa 7:3-17), for Tiglath-pileser moved into Aram-Palestine late in 734 or early in 733 and the siege was lifted.

The Assyrians fought the western coalition for three years and defeated its leading powers—Aram, Phoenicia, Philistia, and the Arabs. In his third campaign (732–731), Tiglath-pileser killed Rezin and incorporated the sixteen districts ruled by him into the Assyrian empire (*ANET*, 282-84). HOSHEA was recognized as ruler over Israel and the Assyrians left the task of defeating Pekah and the anti-Assyrian Israelites to Hoshea and his supporters, probably including Ahaz (2 Kgs 15:30; Hos 1:11).

Hoshea (730–722/1) presided over the last days of Israel's existence as a nation although he was apparently unable to control the anti-Assyrian fervor in the north. He joined a revolt against the Assyrians, probably before the death of Tiglath-pileser III, which was suppressed by Shalmaneser V, probably in his accession year (before Nisan 726). Later, Israel rebelled again and sent to Egypt for help (in 726). Hoshea was subsequently arrested (725) but rebellion continued in Samaria. The city was placed under siege (in 724–723) and fell to Shalmaneser in late 722 or early in 721 (2 Kgs 17:1-6; 18:9-10). Shalmaneser V died before the final disposition of Samaria. Rebellion flared anew and Sargon II took Samaria again, in his second year (720–719), and presided over the rebuilding of the city and its incorporation into the Assyrian empire (*ANET*, 285). Israel ceased to exist as a political entity.

(8) After the demise of the Northern Kingdom and its incorporation into the Assyrian empire as the province of Samerina, Judeans continued to use the name Israel as a self-designation. This was only natural since they had been part of the house of Israel not only during the times of David and Solomon but also throughout much of the ninth and eighth centuries and now survived as the remnant of Israel. Jeremiah, for example, uses the name Israel both for the old Northern Kingdom and for his contemporaries in Judah. The name, when applied to Judeans, was used primarily in a spiritual or religious sense since the political entity of the Davidic kingdom was clearly known as Judah (cf. *ANET*, 287, 291, 294). In the Jerusalem cult, as reflected in the psalms, Yahweh was worshiped as the God of Israel; the expression "Yahweh of Judah" never appears.

(9) The terms Israel and Israelite was used in postexilic and later times to refer to Yahweh worshipers and adherents to Jewish religion in various forms. Even Samaritans in the diaspora, as indicated in a Delos inscription, could refer to themselves as Israelites. Adherents to apocalyptic communities such as the early church could speak of themselves as the true or new Israel (cf. Gal 6:16; Jas 1:1; 1 Pet 1:1).

See also JUDAH, KINGDOM OF; KINGSHIP.

Bibliography. G. W. Ahlström, *Who Were the Israelites?*; R. B. Coote and K. W. Whitelam, *The Emergence of Israel in Historical Perspective*; G. A. Danell, *Studies in the Name Israel in the Old Testament*; J. H. Hayes and P. K. Hooker, *A New Chronology for the Kings of Israel and Judah*; J. M. Miller and J. H. Hayes, *A History of Ancient Israel and Judah*; W. T. Pitard, *Ancient Damascus*; S. Sandmel, *The Several Israels*; L. M. White, "The Delos Synagogue Revisited: Recent Fieldwork in the Graeco-Roman Diaspora," *HTR* 80 (1987): 133-60.

—JOHN H. HAYES

• **Israelite.** [iz'ray-uh-l*i*t] A term that can be applied to anyone who is one of the people of Israel, and thus a descendant of one of the sons of the patriarch JACOB (Israel). Israel, or the sons or children of Israel, as a designation appears to have been applied to the people first and only later did the term Israel come to be applied to the land where they dwelt. The term also appears to have been used of the people who worshiped the God of Israel (regardless of their descent), and thus became a religious or cultic designation. Thus, Israelite designated a descendant of Jacob and a worshiper of Yahweh. Only infrequently, if at all, was Israelite used to identify a person from the land of Israel.

The Merneptah stele (ca. 1220 B.C.E.) contains the first nonbiblical reference to Israel. There the determinative is used that identifies a people rather than a land or a kingdom. However, the court records of SHALMANESER III of Assyria refer to King Ahab as an Israelite, where the determinative indicates a nation or land. That is not surprising, for he was ruler over the Northern Kingdom.

In the era of the divided monarchy, when "Israelite" appears to refer to a person's geographical background, it is used of inhabitants of the Northern Kingdom only. It is only in the postexilic period that the term is used to refer to people from the southern part of the land. Even then, the reference appears to be more cultic than geographic.

See also ISRAEL; JEWS.

Bibliography. J. B. Pritchard, *ANEP*.

—ROBERT L. CATE

• **Issachar.** [is"uh-kahr'] The fifth of Jacob's sons by LEAH and the ninth son altogether; the first of Leah's second set of children (Gen 29:32–30:18). The name is explained as meaning "man of reward" (Gen 30:18). Issachar was the eponymous ancestor of one of the twelve tribes of Israel.

As a tribe, Issachar is frequently listed with Zebulun (Leah's sixth son), as are Ephraim and Manasseh (Deut 33:18-19; 1 Chr 2:1). In the tribal territories as assigned in the Book of Joshua, Issachar and Zebulun have adjacent regions to the north of Manasseh (Josh 19:10-23). Mount Tabor was on the border between the two and was apparently shared as a common worship center (Josh 19:22; Deut 33:18-19).

In the blessing of Jacob, which is set forth as a prophecy, Issachar is described as a strong ass, heavily loaded with saddle baskets on each side and unable to rise (Gen 49:14). The blessing goes on to describe him (them) as having willingly submitted to enslavement in the midst of his (their) pleasant land (Gen 49:15). The tribe's territorial allotment had a number of Canaanite cities in it. When this is connected with some of the Canaanite correspondence from Tell el AMARNA, it appears possible and perhaps likely that some and perhaps all of the Issachar tribe was enslaved by some of these Canaanite city-states. Canaanite inhabitants would have held on to their territory, among some of the richest in Canaan, for as long as possible.

In the period of Deborah, the tribe of Issachar was able to throw off their Canaanite suzerains and became leaders in driving them out from the northern territories (Judg 5:15). Issachar's tribal allotment was an independent administrative district under Solomon (1 Kgs 4:7, 17), indicating that it had gained its full place among the tribes.

See also TRIBES.

—ROBERT L. CATE

• **Ithamar.** [ith'uh-mahr] The youngest of Aaron's four sons (Exod 6:23). When the older sons Nadab and Abihu offered to God a fire contaminated by incense, they were burned (Lev 10:1-7), with Eleazar and Ithamar assuming the roles of priests. In the traditions Eleazar overshadowed Ithamar. Eleazar had charge of the Kohathites, who cared for the holiest objects, including the Ark, the altars, and the sacrificial vessels (Num 3:31-32). Ithamar controlled the Gershonites and the Merarites, who were responsible for the Tabernacle and its framework (Num 3:21-26, 33-37; 4:21-33). Also, 1 Chr 24:3-6 traces the line of Eleazar through Zadok and of Ithamar through Abiathar. While both lines were recognized, the line of Eleazar included more "chief men." The PRIESTLY WRITERS emphasized the Zadokites, and Ezekiel recognized only them as priests.

See also PRIESTS.

—PAUL L. REDDITT

• **Ittai.** [it'*i*] A Gittite who helped lead DAVID's fight against ABSALOM; a warrior who belonged to David's bodyguard.

When Absalom revolted against his father, King David (2 Sam 15–18), David fled from Jerusalem. Among those who remained loyal to David were six hundred Gittites (i.e., inhabitants of Gath), who had followed David from their city, presumably when he left the service of Achish (1 Sam 29:6-10). Ittai expressed the loyalty of the Gittites to David (2 Sam 15:21). When David had mustered his army to attack Absalom, he divided it into thirds and placed Ittai over one third, alongside Joab and his brother Abishai (2 Sam 18).

A second warrior named Ittai, son of Ribai, a Benjaminite from Gibeah, belonged to David's bodyguard, a cadre of select fighters called "the thirty" (2 Sam 23:29), who may have served as a council of war.

—PAUL L. REDDITT

J

MDB

• **J.** *See* SOURCE CRITICISM; YAHWIST

• **Jaazaniah.** [jay-az′uh-ni″uh] "Yahweh hears"; a common OT name, found also on several LACHISH ostraca and a seal from Tell en-Nasbeh. In the OT the name refers to these four:

1. A Maacathite military commander who joined GEDALIAH, governor of Judah, at Mizpah (2 Kgs 25:23). This was probably the same as Jezaniah (Jer 40:8) and the Jezaniah of Jer 42:1 (Azariah, RSV, to agree with spelling in Jer 43:2).

2. A son of Jeremiah (not the prophet) and one of the RECHABITES taken by the prophet Jeremiah to the Temple where he asked them to drink wine (Jer 35:3).

3. A son of Shaphan, one of seventy elders seen by EZEKIEL in a vision offering incense to idols in Jerusalem (Ezek 8:11).

4. A son of Azzur, one of twenty-five people Ezekiel saw in a vision (Ezek 11:1) at the east gate of the Temple.

—F. B. HUEY, JR.

• **Jabbok.** [jab′uhk] Jabbok, a perennial stream and the valley it has cut across the Transjordanian plateau. The Jabbok, which is mentioned in the OT a number of times, is identified with the modern Wadi Zerqa (or Nahr ez-Zerqa). Along with the YARMUK, ARNON (Wadi el-Mujib), and ZERED (Wadi el-Hesa), the Jabbok is one of the four major canyons that drains Transjordan's highlands. In addition to the Yarmuk, which enters into the Jordan River a short distance south of the SEA OF GALILEE, the Jabbok is one of the two major permanent streams that empties into the Jordan on the east. The Jordan/Jabbok confluence is located ca. twenty-four mi. north of the Dead Sea, just north of biblical Adam (PLATE 5). Thus, in the same way that the Arnon canyon divides Moab into two parts, the Jabbok bisects Gilead (cf. Deut 3:12, 16; Josh 12:2-6).

The Jabbok rises at Rabbath-Ammon (RABBAH, PHILADELPHIA), "the city of waters," where URIAH the Hittite was killed (2 Sam 11:16-17; 12:27). From Rabbath-Ammon, the river follows a circuitous course for ca. sixty miles before it enters the Jordan, flowing northeast, north, northwest, and west, consecutively. The OT cities of SUCCOTH, PENUEL, and MAHANAIM were located along the Jabbok's course.

Though the highlands of GILEAD are composed largely of limestone, red Nubian sandstone is exposed in the sides of the Jabbok canyon. Its narrow valley is cultivated, and the Jabbok's gradual descent led to its use as a route of access between the plateau and the Jordan Valley; this use seems to be reflected in the account of Gideon's pursuit of the Midianites (Judg 8:4-9).

Gen 32:22-32 is probably the best known biblical episode in which the Jabbok appears, the account of JACOB's wrestling with an angel at Penuel, near a ford of the river. It is possible that the Hebrew word for "he wrestled" is a pun on the name Jabbok. Reference to the Jabbok ford (Gen 32:22) points to the river's potential as a territorial boundary. The canyon was, in fact, the boundary between Ammon and Israel (e.g., Num 21:24; Deut 2:37), between Reuben/Gad and Transjordanian Manasseh (e.g., Deut 3:16), and between the kingdoms of Sihon and Og (e.g., Josh 12:2).

—GERALD L. MATTINGLY

• **Jabesh-Gilead.** [jay′bish-gil″ee-uhd] Jabesh-Gilead was a settlement in the Transjordan area closely related to the reign of SAUL. It was a settlement in the mountainous area north of Gilead and southwest of Ramoth-Gilead, and east of the Jordan in the area given to the half-tribe of Manasseh. The land of Gilead, the general area in which Jabesh-Gilead is located, served as a center for Israelite population in the Transjordan (PLATE 10). Jabesh-Gilead is most often associated with Wadi Yabis (River Jabesh) which flows into the Jordan some twenty mi. south of the Sea of Galilee. Wadi Yabis reflects the preservation of a name through a geographical feature. Two major sites have been associated with Jabesh-Gilead. The first is Tell el-Maqlub which overlooks the north bank of the wadi in the hill country of Gilead. The primary evidence for such an identification is a reference in Eusebius to Jabesh-Gilead (*Onom* 100.12). Eusebius states that Jabesh-Gilead was a village some six mi. from Pella on the road to Gerasa. The second option is to identify the site of Jabesh-Gilead with a combined site of two tells further west on the wadi. The joint site of Tell el-Mezbereh and Tell Abu-Kharaz is at a point closer to the Jordan where the wadi broadens and leads into the Jordan Valley. Such a site is closer to Bezek and Beth-Shan, cities west of the Jordan, related to Jabesh-Gilead in biblical narrative. Evaluation of surface level potsherds shows a long period of occupation for the second site (from ca. 3200 B.C.E. to the Roman and Byzantine periods). The predominant potsherds dated from the thirteenth through the sixth centuries B.C.E.

Biblical references to Jabesh-Gilead closely relate this settlement to the life of King Saul and the city of GIBEAH in Benjamin. The first biblical references to Jabesh-Gilead come in the enigmatic story surrounding Judg 21:9-14. All Israel had fought and destroyed Gibeah of Benjamin and the other Benjaminites for the apparent rape and death of the concubine of a Levite. This warfare resulted in the near extermination of the Benjaminites. However, the assembly determined that Jabesh-Gilead had not responded to the call to war. In response, Jabesh-Gilead was destroyed except for 400 virgins given to the remaining Benjaminites. This story reflects the intertribal conflicts of Israel and shows the ties binding Jabesh-Gilead and the tribe of Benjamin. Saul's first military action as king of Israel was to break the siege of Nahash the Ammonite (1 Sam 11:1-11), who had threatened to humiliate Israel by the subjugation of Jabesh-Gilead and the mutilation of its inhabitants. In both stories, all Israel was called to war by dismembered body parts which were circulated to the tribes. The body parts of the concubine were used in the Judges story, and in Samuel, Saul's oxen served this function. In response to the death of Saul and the disgraceful treatment of the remains of Saul and his sons, men of valor from Jabesh-Gilead rescued their bodies. In a night-time raid on Beth-Shan, the bodies were taken from the city walls and returned to Jabesh-Gilead, where the bodies were burned and buried (1 Sam 31:1-13 || 1 Chr 10:1-12). After David is notified of Saul's death, he commends the valor of the men of Jabesh-Gilead and assures them of no reprisal (2 Sam 4:4-5). This was an apparent attempt to win their support for his kingship over all Israel in light of the conflict between Abner who set Ishbosheth as king over Israel (2 Sam 8–10). The last mention of Jabesh-Gilead is when David returns the bodies of Saul and his sons to Benjamin and the tomb of Kish, Saul's father in Zela in response to the actions of Rizpah, the daughter of Aiah, Saul's concubine (2 Sam 21:12-14).

Bibliography. Y. Aharoni, *The Land of the Bible,* rev. ed.; D. Baly, "Jabesh-Gilead," *HDB*; H. G. May, "Jabesh-Gilead," *IDB*.

—DAVID M. FLEMING

• **Jacob.** [jay'khuhb] An Israelite personal name that refers to two persons in the Bible.

1. The third of a trio of patriarchs: "Abraham, Isaac, and Jacob" (Exod 3:6; Acts 7:8), father, son, and grandson.

The name has the form of a verb whose ancient meaning cannot be precisely defined, although two folk-explanations have been handed down. (1) Since he was born holding the heel (*'aqēb*) of his twin (ESAU), he was called "Jacob" (*Ya'aqōb*), as if the verb meant, "He grabs the heel" (Gen 25:24-26). (2) When he cheated his brother, the latter remarked upon the appropriateness of the name: "He has ousted me [*ya'qebēnî;* RSV "supplanted"] twice" (Gen 27:36). In nonbiblical names, the verb is sometimes combined with the name of a deity (e.g., "May the God [name] *'-q-b* [protect?]"). Was this the original form and meaning of the patriarch's name?

After a crucial event, he was given the name "Israel" (Gen 32:22-28; cf. 35:9-10). Such changes, designating a new status, are otherwise attested (Gen 17:5, 15; 41:45; Acts 13:9).

Genesis sketches his life as follows. He was born as the result of ISAAC's prayer that the promise would be realized despite REBEKAH's barrenness (25:21-26; cf. 12:1-3). Following conflict with Esau, he fled to his mother's relatives (25:29-34; 27:1–29:1), where LABAN tricked him into marrying LEAH and thus forced him to work another seven years for the daughter whom he preferred, Rachel (29:2–30:24). He tricked Laban in turn, and then departed for his parental home (30:25–33:19). In order to commemorate the place where he had received divine assurances, he erected an altar at BETHEL (35:1-15; cf. 28:10-22). When he learned that his son JOSEPH, thought to be dead, was an official in Egypt, he and his clan settled down there (37:1–47:12). As death approached, he blessed each of his sons (tribes; 48:1–49:27). Then he died, was embalmed, and carried to the ancestral tomb in Canaan (49:28–50:13).

Variations and repetitions have led some modern interpreters to discern in the Jacob stories the same three literary strands that are thought to run from Genesis through Numbers (the so-called J, E, and P sources of the documentary hypothesis). Others have proposed the existence of four once-independent thematic collections, which grew in the following order: Jacob and Esau stories, Jacob and Laban stories, holy places and divine appearances, and stories of Jacob's descendants.

"Jacob" and "Israel" are used not merely for the patriarch but also for the community that claimed descent from him (e.g., the former at Isa 2:5, the latter at 1 Kgs 4:1).

Some modern interpreters (e.g., M. Noth) have suggested that the three patriarchs, rather than being related biological individuals, originated as the names of groups that settled in Canaan at different times. Jacob, for example, is called an "Aramean" (Deut 26:5), as is Laban (Gen 28:5; 31:20, 24), and this people seems to have arrived in Canaan in the twelfth century B.C.E., whereas other groups (possibly associated with the names Abraham and Isaac) may have arrived much earlier. The Jacob stories usually involved sanctuaries in the north of the country (whereas Abraham and Isaac are in the south), where a deity known as "the Mighty One of Jacob" (Gen 49:24) may have been worshiped.

2. The father of Joseph the husband of Mary (Matt 1:15, 16).

See also ESAU; ISRAEL; LABAN; LEAH; RACHEL.

Bibliography. M. Noth, *The History of Israel*; C. Westermann, *Genesis 12-36*.

—LLOYD R. BAILEY

• **Jacob, Blessing of.** Sometimes referred to as "The Testament of Jacob," Gen 49:2-47 is a collection of oracles about each of the twelve tribes of Israel. It is often noted as Jacob's blessing because of its proximity in the present text to the blessing of MANASSEH and EPHRAIM at the end of chap. 48 and because of its ties to the magical understanding of blessing wherein a father passes his power of fertility and prosperity to a particular son in a ritual of word and symbolic action. In Gen 49, however, the words ascribed to Jacob are not strictly "blessings." Some, in fact, seem almost like curses. REUBEN is censured because of an alleged sexual indiscretion, SIMEON and LEVI are condemned because of the violence they perpetrated on SHECHEM (Gen 34), ISSACHAR is portrayed as a slave, and Gad is promised a future as victims of raiders. NAPHTALI is promised lovely offspring, Zebulun is predicted to become a maritime nation, and DAN, JOSEPH, and BENJAMIN are expected to be mighty military forces.

The focus of the blessing seems to be JUDAH, however. The passage uses royal imagery (lion, scepter, staff) and notes how his brothers will be subservient to him. This royal emphasis would suggest a tenth century date for collecting these traditions together. The rationale behind the collection would be to lend authority to the monarchy.

See also CURSE AND BLESSING; KINGSHIP; MAGIC AND DIVINATION; TESTAMENTS, APOCRYPHAL.

Bibliography. E. A. Speiser, "Genesis," *AncB*.

—JOHNNY L. WILSON

• **Jacob, Ladder of.** The *Ladder of Jacob*, presumably a Jewish work originally, is an elaboration of Jacob's dream at Bethel, with great attention given to the description of the dream as well as the inclusion of Jacob's lengthy prayer of thanksgiving. The document concludes with an angel's revelation of events surrounding the coming of the Christ and the last days. This last chapter is an obvious Christian addition to the Slavonic *Ladder*.

The text must be reconstructed from portions found in the Slavonic *Explanatory Palaia*, a retelling of the OT stories with commentary. Care must be taken to note the anti-Jewish polemic of the *Palaia* in its use of the Jewish *Ladder*.

Although the document is found only in the Slavonic language, the original was most likely a Jewish text written in Greek to an audience with some knowledge of Hebrew. This has led some to posit a Palestinian provenance in the second century C.E. There is no external evidence to support or deny this assumption.

Five themes characterize the *Ladder of Jacob*. The most prominent theme is a belief in one God who is Lord, although Jewish MONOTHEISM is not clearly presented. A second characteristic is the presence and prominence of angels; the archangel Sariel appears also in the DEAD SEA SCROLLS. A third characteristic is the personification of the voice speaking to Jacob; the voice has taken a place on the stage rather than merely being heard. An anti-astrological orientation provides a contrast to the TREATISE OF SHEM. Finally, an apocalyptic vision seems to pervade the text.

See also APOCALYPTIC LITERATURE.

Bibliography. J. H. Charlesworth, *Pseudepigrapha in Modern Research*; H. G. Lunt, "Ladder of Jacob," *The Old Testament Pseudepigrapha*, ed. J. H. Charlesworth.

—STEVEN SHEELEY

• **Jacob, Prayer of.** The *Prayer of Jacob* is a little known document which has been preserved in only one papyrus, dating from the fourth century C.E. The document seems to have been written in Greek, and parallels with other documents suggest that the *Prayer* was composed by a Jewish magician in Egypt during the second century C.E. The *Prayer* consists of four invocations (including an invocation of the Father as Creator and the one who sits "upon the mountain of holy Sinaios"), three petitions (one of which invokes the secret name of God), and one injunction ("Say the prayer of Jacob seven times to the North and East").

The *Prayer* exhibits similarities with the genres of Gnostic documents and magical charms, but falls short of identification with either genre. The magical nature of the document is clear, though. Hebrew is highly respected, yet misunderstood by the author, while the name of God is considered to possess great power. The *Prayer* falls short of being a magical charm in that it gives no indication that the angels of God can be summoned to give aid through the incantation of the prayer. The *Prayer* differs from canonical documents in that the name of God has become efficacious in itself; the biblical writers had seen the power of God's name as an extension of God's power.

This document combines the name of JACOB with the idea of being as an angel on earth and having received immortality. This combination provides an important hermeneutical parallel with the pseudepigraphical PRAYER OF JOSEPH.

See also GNOSTICISM; MAGICAL PAPYRI.

Bibliography. J. H. Charlesworth, *The Pseudepigrapha in Modern Research* and "Prayer of Jacob," *The Old Testament Pseudepigrapha*, ed. J. H. Charlesworth.

—STEVEN SHEELEY

• **Jacob, Testament of.** The *Testament of Jacob* is a legendary account of the events leading up to the death of JACOB. It begins with God sending the archangel MICHAEL to announce to Jacob that his death is near. Another angel then appears to prepare Jacob for his death. Jacob makes JOSEPH swear to bury him in the tomb of his father; then he blesses EPHRAIM and MANASSEH, and then his own twelve sons. He is taken up to the heavens, where he sees the places of both punishment and reward. Then he dies and his soul is taken to heaven. With PHARAOH's permission, Joseph buries his father in Canaan and then returns to Egypt. The narrative is prefaced and concluded with some comments on the annual celebration of the death of Jacob.

The *Testament of Jacob* is extant in Coptic, Ethiopic, and Arabic, but was probably composed in Greek, presumably in Egypt. In its present form it is Christian, but it might go back to a Jewish original, perhaps written in the second or third century C.E. It is dependent on the TESTAMENTS OF ABRAHAM and ISAAC; yet it is more closely tied to the GENESIS narrative than they are.

The *Testament of Jacob* is most significant for shedding light on medieval Coptic Christianity, especially its annual celebration commemorating the death of Jacob. Its ethical injunctions are less integrated with the narrative than in the *Testament of Isaac*, being found primarily in the concluding section. The document seems intended to encourage righteous living.

See also TESTAMENTS, APOCRYPHAL.

Bibliography. K. H. Kuhn, "The Testament of Jacob," *The Apocryphal Old Testament*, ed. H. F. D. Sparks; W. F. Stinespring, "Testament of Jacob," *The Old Testament Pseudepigrapha*, ed. J. H. Charlesworth.

—JOSEPH L. TRAFTON

• **Jacob's Well.** According to tradition, Jacob's well is located at the foot of Mount Gerizim ca. 1,300 ft. southeast of the edge of ancient SHECHEM. Jacob's well is first mentioned in the Bible in the account of Jesus' conversation with a Samaritan woman (John 4). The account indicates the general location of the well: "So he came to a city of SAMARIA, called SYCHAR, near the field that Jacob gave to his son Joseph" (4:5). Acknowledged by Jews, Samaritans, Christians, and Muslims, the location of the well is one of the best-attested in Israel. This site corresponds with locations given by EUSEBIUS in the *Onomasticon*, with the descriptive statements made by the Pilgrim from Bordeaux, and with the placement on the Madeba Map.

Today, the site is marked by an unfinished Greek Orthodox basilica which provides access to the ancient well, estimated to be about seventy-five ft. deep. Although this well is generally assumed to be the one referred to in John, the only evidence of its antiquity beyond the time of Jesus lies in the gospel tradition that "our father Jacob gave us the well, and drank from it himself, and his sons, and his cattle" (John 4:12).

See also EUSEBIUS; GERIZIM, MOUNT; SAMARIA; SAMARITANS; SHECHEM; SYCHAR.

—FREDERICK L. DOWNING

• **Jairus.** [jay-*i*-ruhs] Jairus is the name given by Luke (8:41) and Mark (5:22) to the anonymous ruler in Matt 9:18 whose twelve-year-old daughter was restored to life by Jesus after he healed the woman who had a hemorrhage for twelve years. The gospel account is remarkable because the account of the hemorrhaging woman is encased by the narrative of Jesus' miracle. The accounts have in common the number twelve and the commendation of faith.

Jairus is one of three synagogue rulers identified by name in the NT. Others are Crispus (Acts 18:8) and Sosthenes (Acts 18:17).

See also MIRACLE STORY; MIRACLES.

—JOHN R. DRAYER

• **James.** [jaymz] A version of JACOB, James was a common name in the first-century communities of faith, both Jewish and Christian. The NT makes note of four persons named James: two of the twelve disciples, the leader of the Jerusalem church, and the father (or brother) of one of the disciples.

James, the Son of Zebedee. The Synoptics identify James the son of ZEBEDEE, and his brother John, as one of the first group of disciples Jesus called (Matt 4:18; Mark 1:19; Luke 5:10). These sons of Zebedee, James and John, were also given the nickname "sons of thunder" (Mark 3:17) perhaps as a reflection of their volatile personalities (cf. Luke 9:54). The sons of Zebedee and Peter comprise the inner circle of Jesus' disciples, witnessing the transfiguration (Mark 9:2-8 and par.) and asked to go deeper into the garden with Jesus the night of his arrest (Mark 14:33 and par.). Acts includes this James among those of the Jerusalem church (Acts 1:13) and reports his death at the hand of Herod (12:2).

James, the Son of Alphaeus. There was a second James in the company of THE TWELVE, according to the Synoptics (Matt 4:18; Mark 1:19; Luke 5:10). Nothing more is said of James the son of Alphaeus in the NT, although the Synoptics suggest his mother was a witness at the crucifixion (Mark 15:40 and par.). Mark alone identifies the mother as that of James "the less," perhaps a comparative reference to James the son of Zebedee.

James, the Brother of Jesus. The most prominent James in the NT is James, a brother of Jesus (cf. Mark 6:3; Matt 13:55) and the head of the Jerusalem church. Paul provides the link between the brother of Jesus and the Jerusalem church leader (Gal 1:19; 2:12) and alludes to James's apostolic authority (1 Cor 15:7). The Book of Acts further establishes the importance of this James in connection with the reporting of the arrest of Peter (Acts 12:17), the outcome of the Jerusalem Council (Acts 15), and Paul's final visit to Jerusalem (Acts 21:17-18). This James, sometimes called "the Just," is most often associated with the Letter of James. The Letter of Jude, which claims to have been written by a "brother of James," also draws some authority from this James.

James, Father or Brother of Judas. Luke alone identifies two of the Twelve as having the name Judas (Luke 6:13-14 and Acts 1:13); the Lucan Judas, not Iscariot, is either a son (RSV) or brother (KJV) of James. Any further statement about this James is conjecture.

See also APOSTLE/APOSTLESHIP; DISCIPLE/DISCIPLESHIP; JACOB; JOHN THE APOSTLE; JUDAS; TWELVE, THE; ZEBEDEE.

—RICHARD F. WILSON

• **James, Apocryphon of.** Purportedly written by JAMES, brother of Jesus of Nazareth, this "revelation dialogue" was unknown prior to its discovery in the "Jung Codex" (Codex I) of the Coptic library of NAG HAMMADI. The author claims to have incorporated within his letter an "apocryphon" ("secret writing") which contains a final discourse of the risen Christ with James and the apostle PETER following the RESURRECTION and just prior to the Lord's ascent into heaven "in a chariot of spirit" (14:26–15:6). This teaching of Christ, originally intended for future elect "children" but held selfishly by the first disciples until now, must be kept hidden from the unworthy and shared only with the "few," the Lord's "sons" (16:26-30). James and Peter seek to ascend into heaven after Christ but are prevented that they may return and share the secret teaching with the rest of the twelve.

In the dialogue between the Savior and his disciples we learn that Jesus descended to earth to save his "sons" by teaching them to cultivate the "Kingdom within" themselves (12:30-31; 13:17-19), to hold fast to the teaching given them, to know themselves (i.e., "be filled with the Kingdom"—12:18-30), and thus to "save themselves" (7:10-11; 11:4). "Faith" must complement "knowledge" in this process, and one is to be prepared for martyrdom, even volunteering for it (4:22–6:21)—a strikingly heterodox view! Ultimately, true "sons" will follow Christ in his ascent to "the Majesty" (= Godhead), "stripping themselves" that they may "clothe themselves" (14:35-36). These "sons" (the writer and his circle) have separated themselves from the community of the great church (i.e., the orthodox, those "pretenders to the truth and falsifiers of knowledge," 9:24ff.) and perceive themselves to be the true community.

Though the *Apocryphon* is found in a codex containing clearly Gnostic writings (GOSPEL OF TRUTH, TREATISE ON THE RESURRECTION, TRIPARTITE TRACTATE), debate continues over whether it is Gnostic. The initial editors held that some of its doctrine and vocabulary link it to the Valentinian school of Gnosticism, e.g., its tripartite anthropology (spirit, soul, flesh), the 550 days of Christ's appearances between his resurrection and ASCENSION, "diminution" ("a loss" of Spirit) and "being filled." Other scholars find additional Gnostic ideas in such concepts as "drunk" versus "sober" (3:9-10), "awake" versus "asleep" (3:11-12; 9:33-34), devaluation of the soul compared to the spirit (4:8-22), "knowledge" (8:26), conflict with hostile archons (8:35-36), the "light that illumines" in the "defiling" and "dark" world (13:20; 10:1-5). Still others, however, noting that most of these ideas appear in non-Gnostic, heterodox and even orthodox Christian writings, conclude the document is non-Gnostic. The discussion continues, with increasing numbers evaluating it as Gnostic.

The author, adopting the pseudonym of James and claiming (falsely) to have written this text in "Hebrew," has supposedly composed it in Jerusalem. However, the similarity of its ideas to those of Clement of Alexandria, Origen, and SECOND CLEMENT has led some to place its composition in Egypt. It has been variously dated between the second and the third century, with cessation of all official persecution of the church in 314 C.E. marking the latest possible date of composition.

See also GNOSTICISM; NAG HAMMADI.

Bibliography. M. Malinine, H.-Ch. Puech, G. Quispel et al., *Epistula Jacobi Apocrypha*; F. E. Williams, "The Apocryphon of James," *The Nag Hammadi Library in English,* ed. J. M. Robinson and "The Apocryphon of

James,'' *Nag Hammadi Codex I (The Jung Codex). Introductions, Texts, Translations, Indices,* ed. H. W. Attridge.

—MALCOLM L. PEEL

• **James, First Apocalypse of.** The *First Apocalypse of James* is the second of four apocalypses in Codex V of the NAG HAMMADI documents. It is followed in the collection by a SECOND APOCALYPSE OF JAMES. Both are actually entitled simply *Apocalypse of James*; the additions ''first'' and ''second'' are scholarly conventions to distinguish the two. The *First Apocalypse of James* has been dated ca. 200 C.E., largely on the grounds that one section seems to demonstrate Valentinian influence.

The *First Apocalypse of James* belongs to a category of the APOCALYPTIC genre known as revelation discourse in which a heavenly mentor reveals mysteries (cf. MYSTERY) to an earthly listerner, who often asks questions. This document is typical of other Gnostic apocalypses in that narrative is at a bare minimum—simply a framework for the revelatory dialogue. In a sense, this treatise consists of two such apocalypses or discourses, one before the crucifixion of Jesus and another after his resurrection, both delivered to James by Jesus. The JAMES here is not the disciple, but James the Just, known in the NT as the Lord's brother. The known prominence of this James in Jewish Christianity suggests that the work has affinities with Jewish Christianity, although this has been disputed. A connection with Syria may be suggested by the mention of Addai, the alleged founder of Syrian Christianity. The document exists in Coptic, although like the other Nag Hammadi documents it is thought to have been composed in Greek.

Suffering is the theme of the document. It opens with Jesus revealing to James the nature of the highest God—He Who Is—unnameable, ineffable. Jesus predicts his own death at the hands of the evil powers. James is told that he too will be seized, but that he should leave Jerusalem, since many evil powers reside there. Jesus reveals that there are seventy-two heavens, which James will not be able to number until he casts away blind thought and the bonds of flesh. When he does, he can reach Him Who Is. James asks how he can ever reach that goal, with so many evil forces arraigned against him. Jesus reassures James that it is actually he, Jesus, against whom the powers are armed, but promises that after he has been seized he will reveal everything, so that people may have faith. Jesus then bids James farewell, and ''fulfilled what was fitting.''

Several days later the risen Jesus appears to James on a mountain. James, troubled at how Jesus has suffered, is assured that he has not in fact suffered at all. But he does predict that James will suffer on his behalf, that he will encounter (after death) heavenly toll-collectors who will challenge him on his upward ascent, but Jesus instructs him how to respond to them. (The content of this instruction is the section identified with Valentinian GNOSTICISM.) James is told to reveal these things to Addai, who will write them down. At this point the text becomes rather fragmentary, but Jesus takes his departure from James. The ending may have described the martyrdom of James.

The book thus reassures the Gnostic believer that although the soul must endure suffering (the fate of Jesus and James prefigure that of the soul), redemption is certain. The concern with martyrdom is unusual in a Gnostic document.

See also APOCALYPTIC LITERATURE; GNOSTICISM; MYSTERY; NAG HAMMADI.

Bibliography. F. T. Fallon, ''The Gnostic Apocalypses,'' *Semeia* 14 (1979): 123-58; W. Schoedel, ''Scripture and the Seventy-two Heavens of the First Apocalypse of James,'' *NovT* 12/2 (Apr 1970): 118-29, ''The (First) Apocalypse of James,'' *Nag Hammadi Codices V, 2-5 and VI,* ed. D. Parrott (*NHS,* 11), and ''The First Apocalypse of James,'' *The Nag Hammadi Library in English,* ed. J. M. Robinson.

—ROGER A. BULLARD

• OUTLINE OF JAMES •

The Letter of James

- I. Chapter 1
  - A. Address and greeting (1:1)
  - B. The Christian way of dealing with trials (1:2-4)
  - C. The relationship of wisdom, prayer, faith, doubt, and stability (1:5-8)
  - D. The transience of earthly wealth (1:9-11)
  - E. Distinctions among trial, temptation, and sin (1:12-15)
  - F. God, the source of all good (1:16-18)
  - G. Hearing, responding, and self-control (1:19-21)
  - H. On hearing and doing God's word (1:22-25)
  - I. One illustration (not a definition) of pure religion (1:26-27)
- II. Chapter 2
  - A. Belief in Christ rejects partiality toward the rich (2:1-7)
  - B. Christian love for the ''neighbor'' rejects such partiality (2:8-9)
  - C. Love for neighbor illustrated as a kind of Christian ''law'' (2:10-13)
  - D. James' view on the relationship of faith and works (2:14-26)
- III. Chapter 3
  - A. Teachings related to the use of the tongue (3:1-12)
  - B. An illustration of true wisdom (3:13-18)
- IV. Chapter 4
  - A. On personal individual piety in contrast to a ''worldly'' life (4:1-10)
  - B. Relationship to others based on awareness of the law, the lawgiver, and judge (4:11-12)
  - C. Sin of presumption vs. true humility (4:13-16)
  - D. The sin of omission (4:17)
- V. Chapter 5
  - A. Judgment on rich people (5:1-6)
  - B. The virtue of patience (5:7-11)
  - C. Oaths forbidden (5:12)
  - D. Prayer and healing (5:13-18)
  - E. On reclaiming sinners (5:19-20)

• **James, Letter of.** The Letter of JAMES begins like other letters in the NT, but it is quite different from all other letters. Addressed to ''the twelve tribes in the Dispersion,'' it is very general, whereas letters usually named individuals and came to focus on specific issues related to them or to their congregations.

What Kind of Literature? NT scholars usually refer to James as a diatribe or a paranesis. Paranetic literature is the more general ethical exhortation designed as moral instruction, and one is reminded a bit of the proverbs. Paranetic writing is not usually well outlined; it moves quickly from one issue to another and often returns to a subject which has already been covered.

James is cast in the form of a letter to the Christian community at large, similar to 1 Peter in many ways, but quite different from other epistles.

Authorship. The Letter identifies the author as ''James, a servant of God and of the Lord Jesus Christ.'' The name is actually Jacob, but English translations employ the name James so as to reserve the name Jacob for the OT patriarch.

Traditionally, the church identifies this James as the half brother of Jesus who is prominent in the Jerusalem church (Acts 15:13-21; 21:18-25; Gal 1:19). James, the brother of Jesus, lived in Nazareth (Mark 6:3), and apparently, along with other siblings, Joseph, Judas, Simon, and sisters, did not understand or accept Jesus during his lifetime. Evidently, James the brother of Jesus became a believer later. He did receive a resurrection appearance and appears as an apostle (1 Cor 15:7). This is the James who was obviously the leader in the Jerusalem church in Acts 15.

The other men named James in the NT are James the son of Zebedee, an apostle (Matt 4:21); James the son of Alphaeus, an apostle (Matt 10:3); and James the father of Judas (Luke 6:16). No serious case for the authorship of this Letter has been made for any of these men named James. Tradition, although late and not well documented, focuses on James the brother of Jesus.

Arguments in favor of James the brother of Jesus are: (1) His relationship to Jesus would have been a factor to encourage the canonization of the Letter. (2) His prominence in the Jerusalem church is well known. (3) He was martyred in the seventh decade of the first century (notes in Josephus would suggest a date of 60–62 C.E.; the second century Hegesippus dated James's death after the beginning of the Jewish revolt ca. 66–67 C.E.). (4) Only this James is well known enough to be seriously considered; James the son of Alphaeus evidently died about 42 C.E. (Acts 12:2). (5) The Judaistic flavor of the writing suggests a native Palestinian as author.

There are numerous arguments against the belief that James the brother of Jesus was the author. (1) There was strong resistance to the inclusion of the Letter in the NT. Its acceptance was late. Such resistance is hard to explain if it had been written by this James. (2) There is no internal evidence to relate the author to Jesus' family. (3) The literary style, paranesis, and the superior type of Greek employed suggest to many that a peasant from Galilee could not have written it. Some commentators such as Burton Scott Easton consider it inconceivable that this James could have written it.

It appears to the present writer that, in light of our evidence, the best case is for James the brother of Jesus. Tradition favors him; there is no rival. A scribe's assistance could account for the Greek style, but why could not a Palestinian Galilean learn Greek? A date about 60–62 C.E. would fit the other evidence including knowledge of Paul's theology and letters. The Hebrew nature of the book is certainly understandable. In short, its theology is almost exclusively the high moral teachings of first-century Judaism, basic OT thought.

There are distinctively Christian themes in the book, however, to justify its inclusion. James is a "servant of God and of the Lord Jesus Christ" (1:1). Reference is made to "the faith of our Lord Jesus Christ, the Lord of glory" (2:1). The early Christian hope of the coming of the Lord is mentioned twice (5:7, 8). To be sure, James does not mention great Christian themes such as atonement, the death of Christ, resurrection, etc., but the nature of his Letter may explain such omissions.

Doctrinal and Thematic Emphases. The writing is not a systematic composition. It switches subjects quickly without transition and often returns to a subject such as the rich. It must be read for the truth taught in each brief statement.

The writing includes, incidentally, the great biblical themes: God the Creator and Father (2:19; 3:9); one universe (1:17); God is holy (1:13); gives good gifts to us (1:17); is the source of all good (1:5, 17); our ways are in his hands (4:15); God is merciful (5:11); hears prayers (1:5; 4:2; 5:13-18); and forgives sins (5:15, 20); and the book sees salvation as JUSTIFICATION (2:21).

James deplored hypocrisy, sham, and pretense of any kind. His exhortations reflect an appreciation for the Hebrew prophets. He also believed that God and the Christian life were incompatible with the cultural world of his time. His repeated condemnations of the rich and powerful suggest a kinship with Amos and suggest a serious flaw in contemporary American Christian understanding.

See also FAITH AND FAITHLESSNESS; GENERAL LETTERS; JAMES; JUSTIFICATION; LAW IN THE NEW TESTAMENT; LOVE IN THE NEW TESTAMENT; WEALTH; WISDOM LITERATURE; WISDOM IN THE NEW TESTAMENT.

Bibliography. W. Barclay, *The Letters of James and Peter*; P. Davids, *The Epistle of James*; M. Dibelius, *James*; B. Easton, "The Epistle of James: Introduction and Exegesis," *IB*; S. Laws, *A Commentary on the Epistle of James*; J. W. Roberts, *The Letter of James*; J. H. Ropes, *A Critical and Exegetical Commentary on the Epistle of St. James*; E. M. Sidebottom, *James, Jude, 2 Peter*; H. S. Songer, "James," *BBC*.

—MORRIS ASHCRAFT

• **James, Protevangelium of.** [proh'toh-i-van-jel"ee-uhm] The *Protevangelium of James* is an APOCRYPHAL GOSPEL dealing with events leading up to the birth of MARY as well as the birth of Jesus. The title, attached to the document only since the sixteenth century, suggests events predating the story in the canonical gospels. The work was composed in the late second or early third century. Its popularity is suggested by the existence today of over thirty manuscripts in Greek, plus versions in Syriac, Georgian, Armenian, Ethiopic, Slavonic, and Coptic. The book was condemned in the West, and consequently no Latin manuscripts survive.

The JAMES to whom the book is ascribed is apparently the Lord's brother, who writes soon after the death of HEROD. Some early sources, however, seem to have some other James in mind, and it cannot be certain that by Herod the author intends Herod the Great or Herod Agrippa. Certain misinformation in the book about Jewish customs would point to a gentile author.

The book begins with the rich Joachim bringing offerings to God. He is upbraided by a fellow Jew for this presumption, since he is childless. Thereupon he enters the wilderness to fast until God grants his prayer for a child. Meanwhile his wife Anna is also praying, in a poetic lamentation of her childlessness. An angel announces to Anna that she will bear a child, and Anna immediately devotes the child, whether male or female, to God for life. Joachim has also experienced an annunciation that his wife has miraculously conceived; he returns, and is joyously greeted by his wife. Mary is the child born, and she is brought up in the TEMPLE, as was SAMUEL. Her parents leave her there at the age of three. When she reaches puberty, the priests determine to select a husband for her from among Jewish widowers. A miraculous sign indicates that JOSEPH has been chosen by God. Joseph has misgivings because he has sons already, and is old, but he receives Mary out of fear of consequences should he refuse.

Since Mary is of the house of DAVID, the priests give

her the task of weaving a veil for the Temple. While she is at work, an angel announces to her that she will give birth while still a virgin, and that the child will be the SON OF GOD. Joseph does not discover Mary's pregnancy until the sixth month, and in spite of Mary's protests of innocence is distraught. An angel reassures him in a dream, but the priests are not reassured until both Joseph and Mary drink the "water of conviction" (Num 5:11-31).

After Augustus's decree, Joseph and Mary trek to BETHLEHEM, but the child is born on the way, in a cave near town. For the birth of Jesus, Joseph secures the help of a midwife, whose hand is severely burned when she doubts Mary's virginity and seeks to test her state. She is healed by touching Jesus. The story of the wise men follows, with Mary wrapping Jesus in swaddling clothes and putting him in a manger to hide him from Herod's wrath after he decrees the death of the infants. Meanwhile, ELIZABETH, mother of JOHN THE BAPTIST, takes her child off into the hills for hiding. Herod is furious that the child has escaped, and the book closes with John's father, Zacharias, suffering martyrdom.

The *Protevangelium of James* is a work of unusual literary merit when compared to other infancy gospels. The purpose of the work is clearly the glorification of Mary. The importance of the book lies in its early statement of the themes that would later be developed in both East and West concerning the virgin Mary. Although the book was condemned in the West, its influence can be seen not only in Christian art, but in the theological development culminating in the Catholic dogma of the Immaculate Conception, proclaimed in 1854. The tradition found in some Christmas carols that Joseph was an old man when he married Mary stems from this book, as does the early view that the brothers of Jesus in the NT were actually sons of Joseph by a former marriage.

See also APOCRYPHAL GOSPELS; MARY; VIRGIN BIRTH.

Bibliography. O. Cullmann, "The Protevangelium of James," *New Testament Apocrypha*, ed. E. Hennecke and W. Schneemelcher.

—ROGER A. BULLARD

• **James, Second Apocalypse of.** The *Second Apocalypse of James* is the third of three apocalypses from Codex V of the NAG HAMMADI documents. It is preceded in the codex by a FIRST APOCALYPSE OF JAMES. Both works are actually entitled *Apocalypse of James*; "first" and "second" are scholarly conventions to distinguish the two. The *Second Apocalypse of James* has strong associations with Jewish Christianity, though this has been disputed. While the tractate is clearly Gnostic, it does not deal with Gnostic themes with a heavy hand, and cannot be associated with any of the recognized Gnostic sects of the second century. On the other hand, there are few allusions to anything in the NT. These observations lead to a tentative dating in the second century. Like the other Nag Hammadi tractates, it is assumed to have been written in Greek and translated into Coptic. The JAMES referred to in the title is James the Just, known in the NT as the Lord's brother, a leading figure of Jewish Christianity.

Although entitled an apocalypse, it is actually a revelation discourse, and can be called an apocalypse only in the sense of other Gnostic apocalypses, which typically contain little if any narrative and consist essentially of discourse. The actual form of this book, however, is a written report made by a priest Mareim to Theuda, father of James. (The *First Apocalypse of James* also denies that James is blood relative of Jesus.) The content of most of this report is a revelatory discourse delivered by James himself, opening with a description of himself as one rich in knowledge (*gnosis*). He indirectly reports revelatory words of Jesus, and describes an appearance of Jesus to him. Jesus therein identifies James as an illuminator, a redeemer blessed by the heavens. Jesus kisses James, and invites him to stretch out his hand to him, but when James reaches, Jesus disappears. James then appeals to his audience to renounce their way and walk with him so as to become free, and receive the mercy of a kind Father.

A final section deals with the death of James. It is argued that this section was originally the closing part of a separate document. In it the manner of James's stoning is described, and there is a prayer of some length in which James prays for deliverance. The prayer itself may have a separate origin; there is nothing in it to demand an association with James, or for that matter, with Gnostic sources. It could be a prayer of anyone facing death.

The prayer is one of several passages in this document that betray a consciously artistic structure, almost hymnic in nature. Another of these sections is the passage in which Jesus speaks of James as the illuminator-redeemer.

The treatment of James in the treatise is of special interest. In the martyrdom section, he is simply the martyr, and the description given of his death has strong ties to Jewish and Jewish-Christian traditions. But in the previous, and longer, discourse section he not only receives from Jesus a special revelation, he is the one who guides the Gnostics into heaven and grants them their reward. It has been observed that James functions for this author very much as PETER did in orthodox Christianity as keeper of the keys of the Kingdom. Here James has become virtually a Gnostic redeemer figure.

See also APOCALYPTIC LITERATURE; GNOSTICISM; NAG HAMMADI.

Bibliography. F. T. Fallon, "The Gnostic Apocalypses," *Semeia* 14 (1979): 123-58; C. Hedrick, "The (Second) Apocalypse of James," *Nag Hammadi Codices V, 2-5 and VI*, ed. D. Parrott (*NHS*, 11); C. Hedrick and D. Parrot, "The Second Apocalypse of James," *The Nag Hammadi Library in English*, ed. J. M. Robinson.

—ROGER A. BULLARD

• **Jannes and Jambres.** [jan'iz, jam'briz] *Jannes and Jambres* is a legend based upon the references in Exod 7–8 to the anonymous Egyptian magicians who opposed MOSES. The fragmentary nature of the text permits only a rough reconstruction of the story. Apparently while consulting his magical tools Jannes is visited by two angels who have been sent to take him to Hades. Granted a reprieve of fourteen days, Jannes entrusts a secret book to his brother Jambres. After being called to oppose Moses before the king, Jannes is struck with a painful ulcer and acknowledges that he has opposed the power of God. Following Jannes' death Jambres begins to practice MAGIC and calls up the spirit of his brother. Jannes informs Jambres of the justice of his punishment, describes the hopeless situation of existence in the netherworld, and warns Jambres to live a good life. The ending is lost.

Jannes and Jambres is extant only in Latin and Greek fragments. It was probably composed in Greek before the third century C.E. Whether the author was a Christian or a Jew is unclear, but he apparently drew upon earlier traditions about these two magicians (cf. *CD* 5; 2 Tim 3:8-9). There are many stories about them in later Jewish, Christian, and pagan literature. *Jannes and Jambres* (Latin, *Mambres*) is mentioned by Origen (third century) and, under the title *Penitence of Jannes and Jambres,* by the so-called Gelasian Decree (sixth century). It may have been written to encourage righteous living through fear of divine punishment.

Bibliography. M. R. James, *The Lost Apocrypha of the Old Testament*; A. Pietersma and R. T. Lutz, "Jannes and Jambres," *The Old Testament Pseudepigrapha,* ed. J. H. Charlesworth.

—JOSEPH L. TRAFTON

• **Japheth.** [jay'fith] Japheth—"may God enlarge"—was one of NOAH's sons. He had two brothers, SHEM and Ham (Gen 5:32; 6:10; 7:13; 9:18, 23, 27; 10:1-2; 1 Chr 1:4-5). He and his wife were two of the eight people who were delivered from the destructive waters of the flood (Gen 7:7; 1 Pet 3:20). Soon after that, he and his brother Shem covered their father's nakedness when Noah succumbed to strong drink (Gen 9:20-23). As a result of this incident, Noah declared that CANAAN and his descendants would become subservient to the descendants of his uncles, Shem and Japheth. Then Noah blessed Shem, but also indicated that God would enlarge Japheth so that he would ultimately inhabit the tents of Shem (Gen 9:27).

Apparently, Japheth was fruitful, for he had at least seven children who became the ancestors of the people who lived to the north and west of Palestine (in the modern territory of the Anatolia and the Aegean). Though all his descendants are not yet clearly identifiable, they include: Gomer (the ancestor of the Cimmerians), Magog (of the Lydians), Madai (of the Medians), Javan (of the Ionians and later the Greeks), Tubal (of the Tabalians), Meshech (of the Phrygians), and Tiras (of the Etruscans). Thus, Japheth primarily became the ancestor of the modern day Indo-European family of nations. Because of this, some have interpreted Noah's PROPHECY in Gen 9:27 to mean that the gospel would come first to the descendants of Shem (that is, the Hebrews), but then spread rapidly through the descendants of Japheth.

See also NOAH.

Bibliography. U. Cassuto, *From Noah to Abraham,* part 2; D. Neisman, "The Two Genealogies of Japheth," *Orient and Occident,* ed. H. A. Hoffner.

—HARRY B. HUNT, JR.

• **Jashar, Book of.** [jay'shur] The *Book of Jashar*—Heb., "one who [or that which] is upright or righteous"—is a collection of ancient songs that celebrate the deeds of the heroes (ones who are upright) of early Israel. Since there is no extant manuscript of the book, the nature of the collection has to be determined from the three biblical quotations that purport to come from this collection. Joshua's command to the sun and the moon (Jos 10:12-13) and David's lamentation over Saul and Jonathan (2 Sam 1:19-29) are attributed directly to the *Book of Jashar*. Also, in the Septuagint (LXX) text of Kings, the dedicatory sentence of Solomon (1 Kgs 8:12ff.) is attributed to this ancient collection. From this information about the *Book of Jashar*, two inferences may be drawn. First, the source was probably well known in ancient Israel. Secondly, the text itself was most likely a collection of poems and songs that were transmitted primarily in an oral fashion and may not have been committed to writing before the monarchial period in Israel.

See also WARS OF THE LORD, BOOK OF THE.

—HENRY L. CARRIGAN, JR.

• **Javan.** [jay'vuhn] A grandson of NOAH and son of JAPHETH, Javan is named in Gen 10:2 and 1 Chr 1:5 along with six brothers—Gomer, Magog, Madai, Tubal, Meshech, and Tiras. He was the father of Elishah, Tarshish, the Kittim and the Rodanim or Dodanim (Gen 10:4; 1 Chr 1:7) who were described as ancestors of people living along coastal areas or on islands (Gen 10:5).

The Hebrews used this same name to designate a gentile area. Isa 66:19 connects the term with Tarshish, Pul, Lydia, and Tubal, and associates them with distant islands whose inhabitants were unfamiliar with the Lord (cf. Ezek 27:13, 19). A survey of all the pertinent passages (including Dan 8:21; 10:20; 11:2) indicates that the Hebrews equated Javan with Greece, or perhaps more specifically Ionia, and that they believed Javan's descendants settled the area.

—WALTER E. BROWN

• **Jebus/Jebusites.** [jee'bus/jeb'*yoo-sitz*] Jebus, the city inhabited by the Jebusites, is identified as Jerusalem in Josh 15:8, 63; 18:28; Judg 1:21; 19:10; 2 Sam 5:6; and 1 Chr 11:4. It was located on the eastern hill of the city, between the Kidron and Tyropoeon Valleys, south of the peak on which SOLOMON later built the Temple. DAVID captured the city from the Jebusites, apparently by entering the city through its water shaft (2 Sam 5:6-8), and made it his capital.

The name "Jebus" seems to have been derived from the name of the people themselves, and perhaps to have had limited application to the city; it was applied to the city between the time of the conquest and the monarchy. The name "Jerusalem" is known from Egyptian execration texts as early as the first quarter of the second millennium B.C.E. The site itself was occupied as early as the beginning of the third millennium, as proved by the discovery of pottery found in a cave near the Gihon Spring. In the second millennium, the inhabitants constructed a wall with bastions well down the eastern slope of Ophel and dug a water shaft to the Gihon. The execration texts show that Jerusalem was an important urban center alongside Shechem by the nineteenth or eighteenth centuries. The best information about pre-monarchical Jerusalem comes from the Amarna letters, correspondence between Palestinian rulers and the Egyptian Pharaohs Amenophis III and Amenophis IV (King Akhenaton, 1379–1362 B.C.E.). Six letters were sent to Amarna by Abdi-Hiba (or Abdu-Heba), prince of Jerusalem, proclaiming his loyalty to the Pharaoh and complaining about the Habiru (renegades who attacked Palestinian towns and villages). Adoni-zedek headed a confederacy of five Amorite kings (Josh 10:5) who attacked the city of Gibeon, attempting to break its coalition with Israel. JOSHUA defeated the coalition, but returned to GILGAL rather than occupying Jerusalem (10:43). Judg 1:8 records another episode in which the tribe of Judah torched the city, but 1:21 acknowledges that the tribe of Benjamin could not expel the Jebusites from the city. David was the first Israelite to occupy the city permanently.

Who were these Jebusites? Unfortunately, no one can say with certainty. One theory is that they migrated to central Palestine as part of a Hurrian (biblical Horite or, more likely, Hivite) movement, settling in Jerusalem in the early Middle Bronze period (ca. 1950 to 1550 B.C.E.). Another theory is that the city was occupied by Amorites (cf. Josh

10) until the defeat of the city by Judah and that it was resettled by Jebusites who were related to the Hittites (cf. Ezek 16:3), after the destruction of the Hittite Kingdom by the SEA PEOPLES. All that one can say with confidence is that the Jebusites were one of the traditional peoples living in Palestine, whose land (according to Israelite belief) Yahweh promised to give to the people of Israel (cf. Deut 7:1). In the table of nations (Gen 10:15-18) the Jebusites are listed as the descendants of Canaan, indicating that the OT knew them only as inhabitants of Palestine and did not connect them with any outside nation.

See also CONQUEST OF CANAAN; JERUSALEM.

Bibliography. W. S. LaSor, "Jerusalem," *ISBE*; B. Mazar, "The Early Israelite Settlement in the Hill Country," *BASOR* 241 (Winter 1981): 75-85 and *The Mountain of the Lord*.

—PAUL L. REDDITT

• **Jedidiah.** *See* SOLOMON

• **Jeduthun.** [ji-dy*oo*'thuhn] A levitical singer of DAVID's time associated with Asaph and Heman (1 Chr 16:37, 41-42; 25:1, 6; 2 Chr 5:12). That he may also have been called Ethan is indicated by 1 Chr 6:31-47 and 1 Chr 15:16-17 where Ethan is listed with Asaph and Heman in the place of Jeduthun. The superscriptions of Pss 39, 62, and 77 may originally have read "upon the hands of Ethan," either indicating a melody or connecting the psalms to the choir led by Jeduthun (or Ethan) in David's time.

All references to Jeduthun are in Chronicles, which has as its purpose showing that the restored TEMPLE was a continuation of a great heritage from MOSES and David. The three traditional fathers of Temple MUSIC are said to have been present when David moved the Ark to Jerusalem (1 Chr 16:37, 41; 25:1-6), and their sons, forming into professional guilds, continued their work.

Jeduthun and Asaph are said to prophesy (1 Chr 25:3) " . . . with the lyre in thanksgiving and praise to the Lord," and both Jeduthun and Heman are called seers (1 Chr 35:15; 2 Chr 25:5) but the Chronicler is careful to note that their work was done under the order and direction of David. They were not great independent prophets like SAMUEL or AMOS. Their work does, however, remind the reader how dance and perhaps music were used earlier to stir up religious fervor (1 Sam 10:5; 19:20-24; 2 Kgs 3:15).

Jeduthun is the father of Obed-edom who combined gatekeeping with music (1 Chr 16:37-43). Descendants of other outstanding musicians such as Korah (1 Chr 6:37) and Asaph (1 Chr 6:39) were also gatekeepers.

See also DANCING; LEVI/LEVITES; MUSIC/MUSICAL INSTRUMENTS.

—ROBERT L. LAMB

• **Jehoahaz.** [ji-hoh'uh-haz] "Yahweh has grasped"; alternately spelled as "Joahaz." The name given to three kings of Judah and one king of the northern kingdom of Israel.

1. Another name for Ahaziah, the sixth king of Judah (843/2 B.C.E.; 2 Chr. 21:17; 22:1; 25:23). "Jehoahaz" employs the divine name as a prefix, while "Ahaziah" employs the divine name as a suffix.

2. The eleventh king of Israel (815–802 B.C.E.), the son and successor of JEHU (2 Kgs 13:1-9). He perpetuated the idolatrous practices JEROBOAM I had instituted in the Northern Kingdom. As a result God gave the kingdom over to a harsh Aramean oppression. A deliverer saved ISRAEL from that oppression after Jehoahaz entreated God's favor.

3. Another name for AHAZ, the eleventh king of Judah (735–715 B.C.E.), according to an inscription of the Assyrian king TIGLATH-PILESER III. The name "Ahaz" may have been an abbreviated form of "Jehoahaz."

4. The sixteenth king of Judah (609 B.C.E.), the son and successor of JOSIAH, who was also known as Shallum (2 Kgs 23:31-34; 1 Chr 3:15; 2 Chr 36:1-4). The people of the land made Jehoahaz their king after Josiah was killed in a battle with Pharaoh NECHO II of Egypt. Necho, who had gained control of Judah, deported Jehoahaz to EGYPT. An older brother of Jehoahaz, JEHOIAKIM, was placed on the throne. While Jehoahaz ruled only three months, his actions were "evil in the sight of the Lord," according to 2 Kgs 23:32.

See also AHAZ; SHALLUM.

Bibliography. J. Bright, *A History of Israel*; D. W. Thomas, ed., *Documents from Old Testament Times*.

—BOB R. ELLIS

• **Jehoiachin.** [ji-hoi'uh-kin] Jehoiachin—"Yahweh establishes," alternately spelled as "Jeconiah" and "Jechoniah"—was the eighteenth king of JUDAH (2 Kgs 24:8-17; 2 Chr 36:9-10); he also was known as Coniah (Jer 22:24, 28).

Jehoiachin assumed the throne of Judah in 598 B.C.E. at age eighteen (2 Kgs 24:8; however, cf. 2 Chr 36:9). He became king at a desperate time in Judah's history. His father, JEHOIAKIM, had rebelled against the lordship of NEBUCHADREZZAR, king of Babylonia. As a result, Nebuchadrezzar invaded Judah and besieged JERUSALEM late in 598 B.C.E. Soon thereafter Jehoiakim died, leaving his son on the throne. In March of 597 B.C.E., the Babylonians conquered Jerusalem and took Jehoiachin and a large contingent of leading Judeans into captivity. Nebuchadrezzar placed Jehoiachin's young uncle, Zedekiah (Mattaniah), on the throne (2 Kgs 24:17). While Jehoiachin's reign lasted only three months, it was "evil in the sight of the Lord," according to 2 Kgs 24:9).

Jehoiachin hoped to return to his throne from the Babylonian Exile; however, as JEREMIAH predicted, neither he nor any of his sons regained the monarchy (Jer 22:24-30). While in captivity Jehoiachin was placed in a position above the other exiled kings by Evil-merodach (Amel-Marduk), Nebuchadrezzar's successor (2 Kgs 25:27-30). In spite of his captivity Jehoiachin was evidently considered by the Babylonians and the exiled Judeans to be the legitimate claimant to the throne of Judah (cf. Ezek 1:2). Jehoiachin's name appears in Matthew's genealogy of JESUS (1:11-12).

See also JUDAH, KINGDOM OF; NEBUCHADREZZAR.

Bibliography. J. Bright, *A History of Israel*; D. J. Wiseman, *Chronicles of the Chaldaean Kings*.

—BOB R. ELLIS

• **Jehoiada.** [ji-hoi'uh-duh] Jehoiada (Heb. "Yahweh knows") was HIGH PRIEST who served during the reigns of Ahaziah, Athaliah, and JOASH. Jehoiada was the husband of Jehoshabeath and uncle of Joash (2 Chr 22:11). Jehoiada's own son, Zechariah, died at the command of Joash for condemning the king's APOSTASY (2 Chr 24:20-22). Jehoiada's most noteworthy accomplishment was the removal of Athaliah from the throne of Judah. She had seized rule by killing the royal successors after her son Ahaziah was killed during Jehu's insurrection. Due to the efforts of Jehoiada and his wife Jehoshabeath, Joash was spared from

Athaliah's purge and the pious couple secretly raised the child in the Temple precincts. In the seventh year of Athaliah's rule, Jehoiada organized and led an overthrow that succeeded in removing Athaliah and placing Joash on the throne. Jehoiada's virtually nonviolent transfer of power stands in sharp contrast to the bloody massacres that JEHU committed to seize the throne of Israel some seven years earlier.

Jehoiada served as a counselor to Joash thereafter. We are told that "Jehoash [Joash] did what was right in the sight of Yahweh all of the days in which Jehoiada the priest instructed him" (2 Kgs 12:2; 2 Chr 24:2). When the Temple was not repaired due to an inadequate means of administrating the Temple funds, Jehoiada instituted a new method of collecting funds for the repair of the Temple (2 Kgs 12:7-9). According to 2 Chronicles, Jehoiada died at the age of 130 and was buried with the Judean kings in the city of David (2 Chr 24:15-16).

Other biblical characters named Jehoiada are: the father of Benaiah (2 Sam 8:18); the priestly leader of the Aaronides who supported David at Ziklag (1 Chr 12:27); the son of Benaiah and grandson of Jeoiada who succeeded Ahithophel as David's counselor (1 Chr 27:34); a priest who during the time of Jeremiah was charged to watch over the prophecies given in the Temple (Jer 29:26); and the son of Paseah who helped repair the Old Gate during Nehemiah's reconstruction of Jerusalem's wall (Neh 3:6).

See also PRIESTS.

—LLOYD M. BARRÉ

• **Jehoiakim.** [ji-hoi'uh-kim] Jehoiakim (Heb. "Yahweh raises up"), alternately spelled "Joakim" or "Joacim," was the name of both a king of Judah and a priest of Jerusalem.

Jehoiakim was a son of JOSIAH and the seventeenth king of Judah, who reigned 609–598 B.C.E. (2 Kgs 23:34–24:6; 2 Chr 36:4-8). Jehoiakim, also called Eliakim, was placed on the throne by the Egyptian Pharaoh NECHO II when he seized control of Palestine in 609 B.C.E. Jehoiakim replaced his younger brother King JEHOAHAZ, who was taken captive to EGYPT.

Because of the large tribute demanded by Necho, Jehoiakim imposed heavy taxes upon the Judeans. He also exploited the nation's depleted resources by building a new palace for himself (Jer 22:13-19). Jehoiakim reversed the reforms of his father, allowing idolatry to flourish. The prophets JEREMIAH and Uriah condemned his rule (Jer 26:20-23; 36:11-32). Jehoiakim responded by persecuting Jeremiah and executing Uriah.

King NEBUCHADREZZAR of Babylonia seized control of Palestine in 605 B.C.E., after defeating the Egyptians at CARCHEMISH. Although Jehoiakim submitted to Nebuchadrezzar in the beginning, he later rebelled, evidently hoping for Egyptian support. In 598 B.C.E. Nebuchadrezzar invaded Judah and besieged Jerusalem. Before he captured the city, Jehoiakim died, leaving his young son JEHOIACHIN on the throne.

Another Jehoiakim was a priest at Jerusalem to whom the Babylonian captives sent an offering, according to the apocryphal book of Baruch (1:7).

See also KINGSHIP.

Bibliography. J. Bright, *A History of Israel*; D. J. Wiseman, *Chronicles of the Chaldaean Kings*.

—BOB R. ELLIS

• **Jehoram.** [ji-hor'uhm] Jehoram (Heb. "Yahweh is exalted"), alternate form Joram, was the name of at least three OT persons.

Jehoram, the king of ISRAEL who ruled ca. 849–842 B.C.E., was the son of AHAB and JEZEBEL, and the younger brother of Ahaziah whom Jehoram succeeded after Ahaziah's fatal fall from his upper chamber (2 Kgs 1:2-18). Although he did not abandon his parents' patronage of Baalism, Jehoram seems to have made concessions to Yahwism (2 Kgs 3:2). Indeed, on one occasion Jehoram was anxious to obtain the help of Elisha, even though the prophet had rebuked him for the Baalism he sponsored (2 Kgs 3:13). Jehoram defended ISRAEL against the aggression of HAZAEL (2 Kgs 8:28-29; 9:14-15) but was assassinated by Jehu ben Nimshi, one of his officers, near JEZREEL, where he was recovering from a wound received in battle (2 Kgs 9:15-26).

The second Jehoram referred to in the OT is the king of Judah who ruled ca. 849–842 B.C.E. He was thirty-two years old when he succeeded his father JEHOSHAPHAT. Jehoram followed the religious policies of Israel, being influenced by his wife Athaliah, the daughter (or sister) of Ahab (2 Kgs 8:16-18). During his reign, Libnah and EDOM successfully revolted, even though Jehoram went to battle against the Edomites (2 Kgs 8:20-22; 2 Chr 21:8-10). According to Chronicles, after Jehoram secured the throne, he killed his six younger brothers along with some rulers of Israel (2 Chr 21:4). Chronicles also reports that in fulfillment of Elijah's prophecy, the PHILISTINES and the Arabs deported Jehoram's possessions and his family and that Jehoram himself was struck with sickness (2 Chr 21:11-18). His death was not lamented. He was not honored with the customary burial rites nor was he interred in the tombs of the Judean kings (2 Chr 22:19-20).

Chronicles mentions a third Jehoram, one of Jehoshaphat's priests who participated in implementing the reforms of the king (2 Chr 17:18).

See also HAZAEL; ISRAEL; JUDAH, KINGDOM OF; KINGSHIP.

—LLOYD M. BARRÉ

• **Jehoshaphat.** [ji-hosh'uh-fat] Jehoshaphat was the son of Asa (and Azubah, daughter of Silhi) who succeeded his father as king of Judah; he reigned for twenty-five years (1 Kgs 22:41-42). According to 1 Kgs 22:44, he established peaceful relations with the Northern Kingdom of Israel (though the actual end of warfare between the two probably occurred during the reign of his father—cf. 1 Kgs 15:17-22). He controlled the neighboring Transjordanian state of Edom (1 Kgs 22:47) and attempted unsuccessfully to revive the shipping trade on the Red Sea from which SOLOMON had profited (1 Kgs 22:48-49; cf. 1 Kgs 9:26-28; 10:22). He is also credited with having continued the religious reforms of his father (1 Kgs 22:46). The details of Jehoshaphat's reign are sketchy and disputed.

First Kgs 22:2-38 places him alongside AHAB, king of Israel, in a battle against the ARAMEANS at Ramoth-Gilead in the Transjordan, where Ahab is reported to have been mortally wounded (however, 1 Kgs 21:27-29 and 22:40 imply that Ahab died of natural causes). Recent scholarship has tended to view 1 Kgs 22:2-38 as a prophetic narrative that was originally told of anonymous kings and was only secondarily identified with Ahab and Jehoshaphat. Thus, its value to the historian remains in question (to move this account to the period of the dynasty of Jehu, as many of these scholars do, is simply to recreate on the basis of slightly different criteria the attempt of the biblical writer to place the narrative in a logical historical context). Jehoshaphat is placed alongside Joram, king of Israel, at war against MESHA, king of Moab, who had rebelled against Israel after the death of Ahab (cf. 2 Kgs 1:1; 3:4-27 and the "Moabite Stone" [*ANET*, 320-21] where the account is given from Mesha's point of view).

A much more extensive account of the reign of Jehoshaphat is found in 2 Chr 17:1–21:1. It emphasizes the military strength, peace, and prosperity of his reign (2 Chr 17:1–18:1), his promulgation of the law (17:3-9), his institution of judicial reforms (19:5-11), and his piety and utter confidence in God in the face of a threat to the security of the kingdom (20:1-30). As is the case with the material in the Books of Kings, the particulars of these accounts have been disputed. However, there is sufficient archaeological and textual evidence to suggest that the Chronicler was drawing on reliable sources for his depiction of Jehoshaphat's military and administrative restructuring (17:1-2) and his judicial reforms (19:5-11).

Another Jehoshaphat, the son of Ahilud, was a high official under DAVID (2 Sam 8:16; 20:24) and Solomon (1 Kgs 4:3). Jehoshaphat the son of Paruah was Solomon's administrative officer in the district of Issachar (1 Kgs 4:17). Jehoshaphat the son of Nimshi was the father of JEHU, who overthrew the dynasty of OMRI and became king of Israel (2 Kgs 9:2, 14). A variation on this name ("Joshaphat") is given as the name of one of David's mighty men (1 Chr 11:43) and as the name of one of the priests who blew the trumpets in the procession that brought the Ark of God into Jerusalem (1 Chr 15:24).

See also JUDAH, KINGDOM OF.

Bibliography. W. F. Albright, "The Judicial Reform of Jehoshaphat," in *Alexander Marx Jubilee Volume*; F. M. Cross, Jr. and G. E. Wright, "The Boundary and Province Lists of the Kingdom of Judah," *JBL* 75 (1956): 202-26; H. G. M. Williamson, *1 and 2 Chronicles*.

—JEFFREY S. ROGERS

• **Jehoshaphat, Valley of.** In Heb. the "valley of Yahweh-judges," it is mentioned only in Joel 3:2, 12, referring to the site of Yahweh's coming trial and judgment on the wicked and persecuting nations. It is probably also referred to twice in Joel 2:14 as the "valley of decision." This judgment oracle is set in "the times when I restore the fortunes of JUDAH and JERUSALEM" (Joel 3:1). The text of Joel gives no topographical location, but traditional interpretation has located it in the environs of Jerusalem, often specifically in the KIDRON Valley, which bounds the eastern side of the city of Jerusalem. Perhaps it refers to a valley named for King Jehoshaphat, but more likely it is a prophetic oracular affirmation of divine judgment on nations wickedly opposing the purpose of Yahweh, and without specific geographical location.

Bibliography. A. Negeb, *Archaeological Encyclopedia of the Holy Land*; G. W. Wade, *Micah, Obadiah, Joel, and Jonah*,

—BRUCE C. CRESSON

• **Jehovah.** *See* GOD; GOD, NAMES OF

• **Jehu.** [jee'hyoo] The son of JEHOSHAPHAT, the son of Nimshi, Jehu became king of Israel (841 B.C.E.) in a bloody *coup d'etat* (2 Kgs 9:1–10:17) that overthrew the dynasty OMRI had established approximately forty years earlier. Reigning for twenty-eight years (2 Kgs 10:36), he founded a dynasty that ruled Israel for nearly a century.

A military officer stationed at Ramoth-Gilead in the northern Transjordan, Jehu was designated king and anointed by an emissary of the prophet ELISHA and acclaimed king by the army. He immediately hurried to JEZREEL, where Joram the king was recuperating from wounds sustained in battle (cf. 2 Kgs 8:28-29). There Jehu killed Joram and ordered the deaths of Ahaziah, king of Judah (who was visiting Joram), and JEZEBEL, Joram's mother. He was also responsible for the extermination of the entire lineage of Omri and of forty-two Judean princes whom he encountered on his way to assume power in Samaria. When he arrived in the capital city, he announced a great assembly to offer sacrifices to the Canaanite deity BAAL; as soon as the sacrifices were completed, he instructed his soldiers to slay all the worshipers of Baal and to demolish the sanctuary (2 Kgs 10:18-27).

Jehu's rise from military officer to monarch appears to have been spurred by a combination of religious and political factors. In addition to his massacre of the worshipers of Baal, his connections to Elisha (2 Kgs 9:1-3) and the fanatical Rechabites (2 Kgs 10:15-16; cf. Jer 35:1-19) suggest that he was part of a religious backlash against the tolerance of Baalism by the dynasty of Omri. He was probably also associated with a reaction against the anti-Assyrian politics of his predecessors. On the "Black Obelisk" of SHALMANESER III, king of Assyria, he is pictured paying tribute under the caption, "Jehu ruler of (Beth-)Omri," in 841 B.C.E. This acceptance of Assyrian overlordship reveals an obvious change of policy, since Ahab (the father of Joram, whom Jehu overthrew), is named in the annals of Shalmaneser as a leading participant in an anti-Assyrian coalition at the battle of Qarqar on the Orontes River in 853 B.C.E.

Jehu's political realignment had its drawbacks, since a pro-Assyrian policy was at least implicitly anti-Aramaean. Thus, when Assyrian pressure on the Aramaean kingdom was reduced after 838 B.C.E., the Aramaean king Hazael turned his forces against Israel and took over almost all Israel's Transjordanian holdings (2 Kgs 10:32-33) and campaigned as far south as the Philistine coastal plain (2 Kgs 12:17-18). Although in 2 Kgs 10:30 Jehu is commended for his zeal in exterminating "the house of Ahab," in Hos 1:4-5 he is condemned for the violence of his actions. He (along with every king of Israel) is also condemned for allowing worship to continue at the northern sanctuaries of Dan and BETHEL (2 Kgs 10:29, 31).

Another Jehu, the son of Hanani, was a prophet who announced the end of the house of Baasha, king of Israel (1 Kgs 16:1, 7, 12). It is reported in 2 Chr 19:2-3 that a prophet by the same name reprimanded Jehoshaphat, king of Judah, for his association with Ahab, king of Israel.

Jehu was also the name of a descendant of Jerahmeel (1 Chr 2:38), a descendant of SIMEON (1 Chr 4:35), and one of DAVID's mighty men at Ziklag (1 Chr 12:3).

Bibliography. M. C. Astour, "841 BC: The First Assyrian Invasion of Israel," *JAOS* 91/3 (1971): 383-89; J. M. Miller, "The Fall of the House of Ahab," *VT* 17 (1967): 307-24; M. Weippert, "Jau(a) mar Humri—Joram oder Jehu von Israel?" *VT* 28/1 (1978): 113-18.

—JEFFREY S. ROGERS

• **Jephthah.** [jef'thuh] One of Israel's Judges. The name Jephthah (*yiptāḥ*), meaning "he [God] opens," appears as a personal name in Judg 11–12, 1 Sam 12:11, and in the NT at Heb 11:32 (*Iephthae*). Josh 15:43 mentions a village in the shephelah named Iphtah (= *yiptaḥ*).

After a preface heightening Israel's apostasy and consequent plight (Judg 10:6-18), Jephthah is introduced as a son of Gilead (usually a region, not a person) and a nameless harlot. Having fled from his brothers who had disinherited him and settled in the land of Tob where brigands gathered around him (11:1-3), Jephthah is invited to return to Gilead and become the leader in the struggle against AMMON. He negotiates with the elders of Gilead to be their "head," is made their "head and leader," and takes an oath at Mizpah (11:4-11). Jephthah first resorts to diplomacy, but this is rejected by the Ammonites. War follows. After Jephthah's dreadful vow, the war is brought to a successful conclusion for the Israelite groups in Gilead and Manasseh (11:12-33).

Jephthah's successful leadership in war against the Ammonites is followed by two episodes of his violence against Israelites. In fulfillment of his vow to sacrifice whoever would come forth to meet him upon the successful prosecution of the war, he sacrifices his virgin daughter, his only child. Jephthah's response to Ephraimitic complaints over not being called to war against the Ammonites is war against EPHRAIM (11:34–12:6).

The summary statement in Judg 12:7 is part of the list comprised by Judg 10:1-5 and 12:7-15. Convention designates these figures minor judges in distinction from the deliverers called major judges. This notice records a six year term for Jephthah the Gileadite and his burial "in his city in Gilead" (12:7).

The interruption of the list of minor judges by the deliverer narratives concerning Jephthah is variously explained. Assuming that the minor JUDGES held a nonmilitary office for the administration of justice in Israel, while the deliverers filled a different role, some have argued that the appearance of Jephthah in both these roles prompted the narrators of Judges to extend the activity of judging to other deliverer figures (cf. 3:10; 4:4; 15:20; 16:31). Others have argued from the same literary fact that minor judges were considered to have been military deliverers (cf. the judge Tola; 10:1, 2); the difference between major and minor judges is, therefore, the outcome of literary, not social, history.

The simple observation that Israel's premonarchic political leaders were of various kinds should prompt greater caution regarding socio-historical reconstruction of premonarchic Israelite life. Jephthah's appearance in three different roles ("leader," "head," one who "judged Israel") may not be any more remarkable than that DEBORAH is designated as a "prophetess" who "judged Israel" (4:4) and a "mother in Israel" (5:7). Associated with cities are "officials" (8:14; 9:30; 10:18) and a "king" (9:16). GIDEON's title is never even given. ELI, a priest, is styled as one who "judged Israel" (1 Sam 4:18), and SAMUEL fills all the important pre-monarchic roles of Israelite leadership: priest, prophet, judge, deliverer.

See also JUDGES, BOOK OF; SACRIFICE.

Bibliography. R. G. Boling, *Judges: Introduction, Translation, and Commentary*; A. J. Hauser, "Minor Judges: A Re-Evaluation," *JBL* 94 (1975): 190-200; J. M. Miller and J. H. Hayes, *A History of Ancient Israel and Judah*; M. Noth, *Die israelitischen Personennamen im Rahmen der gemeinsemitischen Namengebung*; J. A. Soggin, *Judges: A Commentary*.

—JOHN KEATING WILES

• **Jerahmeel.** [ji-rah'mee-uhl] Also Jeremiel, a personal and tribal name, Jerahmeel means "El (God) is merciful, has pity."

The Jerahmeelites are first encountered in 1 Sam 27:10 and 30:29, where they are among the tribes friendly to David during the period of his residence in ZIKLAG. Seemingly they were among those semitic clans like the KENITES who had migrated to southern Judah from the southern wilderness around KADESH. In the genealogy of Judah in 1 Chr 2, the name Jerahmeel appears six times, where he is identified as the son of Hezron, the grandson of Judah. The genealogy probably reflects the absorption of the Jerahmeelites into Judah after they had been pushed northward by the increasing pressure of the EDOMITES from the south.

As a proper name, Jerahmeel appears two other times in the OT. A Jerahmeel is listed in the genealogy of LEVITES in 1 Chr 24:29, and another Jerahmeel appears in Jer 36:26, who is identified as an officer and perhaps relative of King JEHOIAKIM. Finally, in the APOCALYPTIC LITERATURE, a Jeremiel (Ramael) appears as the archangel who presides over the resurrection (*1 Enoch* 20:8; 2 Esdr 4:36; *2 Bar* 55:3).

See also TRIBES.

Bibliography. J. Bright, *A History of Israel*; T. K. Cheyne, "Jerahmeel," *EB*.

—JOHN POLHILL

• **Jeremiah.** [jer'uh-mi'uh] Jeremiah, son of Hilkiah, of ANATHOTH, ministered as a prophet in JERUSALEM from the thirteenth year of JOSIAH (627/6 B.C.E.) until after Judah fell to Nebuchadrezzar, king of Babylon in 587/6.

Sources. The prophetic ministry of Jeremiah is the source of the various traditions found in the biblical book of Jeremiah as well as in several apocryphal and post-biblical works (the Book of BARUCH and the LETTER OF JEREMIAH, in the Apocrypha; several apocalypses of Baruch, the *Paraleipomena of Jeremiah*, the *Midrash to Lamentations*, part of the Lives of the Prophets, plus several rabbinic legends). A lament, on the occasion of Josiah's death, attributed to Jeremiah is noted in 2 Chr 35:25, but has not been preserved. Tradition has also identified Jeremiah as the author of Lamentations and 1 and 2 Kings.

Although the primary purpose of the Book of Jeremiah is not biography, the book includes several narratives of incidents in the prophet's life plus poetic laments attributed to him (the "confessions"). There is more of this material in Jeremiah than in any other prophetic book. Commentators have used these passages to reconstruct a chronology of Jeremiah's life, date his speeches, and describe his spiritual development (e.g., Bright and Holladay). Other interpreters deny any possibility of recovering the historical Jeremiah. According to Carroll (47), for example, it is only the editorial framework that attributes the poetic oracles to Jeremiah, and, since the biographical narratives are also a product of editorial activity, no part of the book can be connected directly to any particular person. A third approach suspends judgment on the search for the historical Jeremiah and seeks to analyze the role of the diverse and sometimes contradictory biographical and autobiographical material in the message of the book (e.g., Polk). The purpose of the OT books of the prophets is to make the divine word known so that God's people will believe and obey it. The traditions about the prophets' lives serve this purpose.

Most prophetic books begin with headings that locate the prophet's ministry in the reigns of Israel's or Judah's kings. The oracles in the book can then be understood as an interpretation of God's dealings with the people of Israel during a particular historical period (e.g., Mic 1:1). This coordination with Israel's historical traditions is sometimes made more explicit by the inclusion of portions of the books of Kings (e.g., Isa 36:1–38:8; 38:21–39:8 = 2 Kgs 18:13–20:19). Narratives of the prophets' dealings with the kings or other officials give evidence of the leaders' response to the divine word (e.g., Amos 7:10-17).

Headings and other narrative elements connect the divine message to the prophets' experience. Typical formulas introduce books and oracles as the word of the Lord that "came to" the prophet, or that he "saw." Call narratives identify the divine authority behind a prophet's ministry and the source of the preaching (e.g., Isa 6). Vision reports (e.g., Amos 7:1-9; 8:1-3) and accounts of symbolic actions (e.g., Ezek 12:1-20) involve the prophets as more than mouthpieces for the divine word. Sometimes a prophet's entire way of life becomes a vehicle for the message (e.g., Hos 1–3). Accounts of the prophets' prayers on behalf of Israel or for themselves demonstrate their intimate relationship with the Lord and their love for God's people (e.g., Amos 7:1-6; Hab 3:1-19).

The Book of Jeremiah contains all of these features. The presentation of Jeremiah in his book resembles the figure of MOSES in the Pentateuch. In both cases, the biographical material addresses the issue of authority: Was this person called and commissioned by God? Are his words of law or prophecy truly from God? Does his message retain its authority even in written form and in distant times and places? Both Moses and Jeremiah satisfy the requirements for true prophets described in Deut 18:15-22.

Background and Family. Jeremiah was born into a priestly family in Anathoth. Although this town was located only about three mi. north of Jerusalem, it lay within the territory of the tribe of Benjamin. Centuries earlier it had been the home of ABIATHAR, who was appointed priest in Jerusalem by David as a representative of the priestly families of the northern tribes (2 Sam 8:15; 1 Kgs 2:26-27). Abiathar was a descendant of ELI, the priest at Shiloh (1 Kgs 2:27), and he may have been an ancestor of Jeremiah.

The Book of Jeremiah does not say that Jeremiah ever functioned as a priest. It also gives no indication of how his father Hilkiah was affected by Josiah's religious reforms. There is no way to determine whether he officiated at a local shrine which was torn down (2 Kgs 23:8-9) or if he was a supporter of the reform who gained thereby the opportunity to serve in the Temple (Deut 18:6). Jeremiah later preached against the unfaithful priests in Jerusalem (e.g., 5:30-31; 6:13-14) and they, in turn, were among his persecutors (e.g., 20:1-6).

The dates of Jeremiah's birth and death are unknown. The heading of the book places the beginning of his ministry in the thirteenth year of JOSIAH (627 B.C.E.). In the call narrative he resists God's commission by claiming, "I am only a youth" (1:6). Two different interpretations of these data have been proposed. The most frequent conclusion is that Jeremiah was a teenager when he was called to prophesy in 627. His estimated date of birth would then be ca. 645–640 B.C.E. (e.g., Bright, lxxxvii). Another understanding is based on 1:5, which places Jeremiah's call before his birth. According to this calculation, he was born in 627 (Holladay, 1). The book's interest in the day of Jeremiah's birth appears only in contexts that reflect upon the suffering caused by his ministry. He laments the fact that he was ever born (15:10; 20:14-18). The end of his life is not reported in the Bible, but a later legend claims that he was stoned to death in Egypt (*LivProph* 2:1).

Jeremiah's marital status became part of his message. God commanded Jeremiah not to marry and have children (16:2). Without descendants, he was cut off from the future. His isolation was compounded by a divine command not to participate in community feasts or mourning, as a sign that there would be no weddings to celebrate and no one to bury the dead when God's judgment fell upon Judah (16:5-9). His way of life prefigured the fate of Jerusalem and Judah which his oracles announced.

The men of Anathoth threatened to kill Jeremiah if he continued to prophesy (11:21-23). Like the suffering righteous person in the Psalms, Jeremiah found his neighbors, and perhaps his family, plotting against him (e.g., Pss 41:9; 69:8). Their punishment would be death (11:22-23; cf. Amos 7:16-17).

The Book of Jeremiah presents a prophet who knew the ministry of HOSEA, another prophet from the northern tribes. Both prophets portrayed Israel as God's unfaithful wife, a harlot lacking steadfast love and failing to acknowledge God's provision for her (Jer 3:1-5, 20; 2:4-8, 13; Hos 1–3). God's love for Israel was like a parent's for a child (Jer 3:19; Hos 11:1). Jeremiah and Hosea pled with God's people to repent (Jer 3:22-25; 14:7-10, 19-22; cf. Hos 6:1-3; 14:2-3), and promised that one day they could truly know the Lord (Hos 2:22; Jer 31:34) (Thompson, 81-85).

The covenant between the Lord and Israel, mediated by Moses, was fundamental to Jeremiah's ministry. The specifically Deuteronomic perspective on law and covenant is evident throughout the book, and especially in the prose portions (Nicholson). The canonical Book of Jeremiah presents him as a prophet like Moses who preached the word given him by God, and mediated a renewed or new covenant with Israel. In Deuteronomy, Moses interprets the covenant for the generation after Sinai, and in the Book of Jeremiah, the prophet applies the terms of the deuteronomic covenant to the people in the last years of the kingdom of Judah (Cazelles, Holladay, and Hyatt in Perdue and Kovacs, 89-128; 313-24). If the deuteronomic traditions were preserved and developed in the northern tribes, then Jeremiah could have been trained in this theology from an early age (Wilson, 231-51).

Place in History. Jeremiah's ministry began in 627 B.C.E. (1:1). That very year, ASHURBANIPAL, king of Assyria, died, and the empire began to weaken. Nationalistic movements began in many subject states, including Judah. Josiah's program included political, military, and diplomatic efforts aimed ultimately at restoring the united kingdom of David. In 621 B.C.E. repair work on the Temple turned up a scroll of the Law which guided the reformation of religious life (2 Kgs 22:8–23:3). The Book of Jeremiah does not give any explicit information about his involvement in the reform movement. From the viewpoint of the completed book, Josiah's reform was obsolete. Repentance and renewed commitment were short-lived and inadequate to stem the tide of judgment.

Josiah's reform came to an abrupt end in 609 when he was killed in an unsuccessful attempt to prevent the Egyptian army from joining forces with the Assyrians against Babylon. JEHOAHAZ became king in Jerusalem, but the victorious Egyptians gained control of Palestine and replaced him with his older brother, JEHOIAKIM (22:11-12). Chap. 26 sets the Temple sermon in this year (7:1-15; 26:4-6). Repentance and obedience might have reversed the threatened judgment on Israel for failing to heed God's prophets. Instead, the priests and prophets attempted to execute Jeremiah for preaching against Zion. He was saved when the elders argued that the prophet Micah had not been put to death for bringing a similar message (26:10-19, 24).

In 605 the Babylonians, under Nebuchadrezzar, defeated the Egyptians and Jehoiakim became their vassal. That year was also a major turning point in Jeremiah's ministry. At God's command, he dictated to Baruch a collection of his oracles from the previous twenty-three years. Jeremiah was barred from the Temple, but, in the hope that Judah would recognize the Babylonians as the threatened "foe from the north" (4:5-31) and would repent, he sent Baruch to read the scroll aloud (36:1-8). Jehoiakim responded by burning the scroll. The opportunity to turn back the divine judgment was lost, and Jeremiah's prophecies of doom would be fulfilled by the hand of Nebuchadrezzar (25; 36:27-32).

Jehoiakim's rebellion in 600 led to the siege of Jerusalem. By the time the city fell in 598/7, Jehoiakim had died and had been succeeded by his son, JEHOIACHIN, who was taken into exile with other leaders of Judean society. The Babylonians placed ZEDEKIAH, a brother of Jehoiakim, on the throne. Within a few years he was plotting rebellion with the neighboring states and the false prophets were promising the imminent return of the exiles who had been taken to Babylon. The Lord's message through Jeremiah to Judah and the other nations was to submit to Babylonian rule. The exiles were told to settle down for a long sojourn in Babylon (seventy years). False prophets in Judah and in Babylon opposed Jeremiah's ministry (chaps. 27–29).

In 589 Zedekiah led Judah in its final revolt. Throughout the subsequent siege, in public and in private, Jeremiah urged surrender. His message did not change when an Egyptian army caused Nebuchadrezzar's forces to withdraw temporarily. At that time he attempted to leave Jerusalem to take possession of his property in Anathoth (32:6-15) but he was arrested on suspicion of desertion to the enemy and remained in custody until the city fell (chaps. 37–38). Charged with sedition, he was left in an empty cistern to die, but Zedekiah permitted his rescue (chap. 38).

In the midst of the divine judgment on Judah, Jeremiah proclaimed God's message of hope for the future. A collection of oracles (chaps. 30–31) and Jeremiah's purchase of a field in his home town (chap. 32) made known God's promise to restore Israel to life in the land.

The Babylonian forces under Nebuchadrezzar devastated Jerusalem and destroyed the Temple in 587/6. Thousands of educated Judeans were deported to Babylon, but, given a choice, Jeremiah elected to remain in the land, which had been made a Babylonian province (chaps. 39–40). When Gedaliah the governor was assassinated by a member of the Judean royal family, part of the remaining population fled as refugees to Egypt, taking Jeremiah and Baruch with them. Jeremiah's last oracles were spoken against the Judean fugitives in Egypt.

Suffering Prophet. Jeremiah's suffering became part of the message of the book. Silencing Jeremiah was part of Israel's sin (7:23-26; 26:4-6; 29:19; 35:15; 36:28-31; cf. Amos 7:16-17). Accounts in the narratives and the confessions telling of Jeremiah's imprisonment and of attempts to kill him serve as evidence of Israel's rebellion and the justness of God's judgment. They also serve to justify Jeremiah. Unlike Moses, the prototype of all true prophets (Deut 18:15-22), Jeremiah failed to lead Israel to repentance or to turn aside God's wrath (cf. Exod 32–34). God had commanded Jeremiah not to intercede for the people (7:10; 14:11-12; 15:1-4). Instead of prayers of intercession, the book records psalms of lament (the "Confessions") and other prayers that express Jeremiah's anguish about the message he had to bring (e.g., 17:14-16). These prayers also reflect God's own pain and sorrow at Israel's rebellion and the judgment that must follow. The ministry of Jeremiah, as presented in the book, led later generations to repent and to trust God for their future.

See also EXILE; JEHOIAKIM; JEREMIAH, BOOK OF; JOSIAH; PROPHET.

Bibliography. J. Bright, *Jeremiah, AncB*; R. P. Carroll, *Jeremiah, OTL*; W. L. Holladay, *Jeremiah, Hermeneia*; E. W. Nicholson, *Preaching to the Exiles*; T. Polk, *The Prophetic Persona: Jeremiah and the Language of the Self*; J. A. Thompson, *The Book of Jeremiah, NICOT*.

—PAMELA J. SCALISE

• OUTLINE OF JEREMIAH •

Outline of Jeremiah

I. Prophecies against Judah and Jerusalem (1:1–24:10)
  A. The call (1:1-19)
  B. Early sermons (2:1–4:4)
  C. The enemy from the north (4:5–6:30)
  D. The temple sermon (7:1–8:3)
  E. Oracles, prayers, confessions (8:4–24:10)
II. Prophecies against the Foreign Nations (25:1-38)
III. Oracles, Judgments, Promises, and Stories from Various Periods of Jeremiah's Life (26:1–35:19)
  A. The temple sermon (26:1-24; see 7:1–8:3)
  B. The struggle with false prophets (27:1–29:32)
  C. Israel's future; the new covenant (30:1–31:40)
  D. Jeremiah buys a field (32:1-44)
  E. Judah's coming glory (33:1-26)
  F. Jerusalem under siege (34:1-22)
  G. Jeremiah and the Rechabites (35:1-19)
IV. Jeremiah's Sufferings (36:1–45:5)
  A. Baruch reads a scroll (36:1-32)
  B. The fall of Jerusalem (37:1–40:6)
  C. The rule of Gedaliah (40:7–41:18)
  D. Flight to Egypt (42:1–43:7)
  E. Prophecies in Egypt (43:8–44:30)
  F. Jeremiah and Baruch (45:1-5)
V. Oracles against the Foreign Nations (46:1–51:64; see also chap. 25)
VI. Historical Appendix (52:1-34)

• Jeremiah, Book of. The Book of Jeremiah is the second book of the prophets in the Christian canon and the second of the latter prophets in the Hebrew Bible (Talmud Baba Bathra 14b–15a indicates that Jeremiah was once ordered first among the latter prophets, immediately following 1 and 2 Kings). The book contains the prophetic traditions that originated in the ministry of Jeremiah, son of Hilkiah ca. 627–585 B.C.E.

Literary Forms. The Jeremiah traditions are preserved in a variety of literary forms, including speeches in poetry and prose, and biographical and historical narrative. Sigmund Mowinckel's description of four sources, based on that of Bernard Duhm, is still a useful starting point for the literary analysis of the book. Mowinckel's source A is poetry. He included oracles, without introductions or conclusions, which are now found in chaps. 1–25. The message of these oracles was one of judgment on JUDAH and JERUSALEM.

Within Mowinckel's source A one group of passages deserves to be singled out. Scattered through chaps. 11–20 are a series of poems usually labeled confessions (11:18–12:6; 15:10-11, 15-21; 17:14-18; 18:18-23; 20:7-13, 14-18). Like the laments in the PSALMS, these prayers express the individual's anguish and complaint to God. The confessions give voice to the agony of one forced by God to deliver a message of doom to his own people (e.g., 15:17-18; 17:16) and to the pain he suffered at the hands of those who despised the divine word (e.g., 11:19; 18:20; 20:10). A few other passages may also be understood as the prophet speaking for himself rather than for God (e.g., 4:19-21; 5:3-5; 8:18–9:1). The confessions have usually been read as windows on the soul of Jeremiah, revealing the spiritual struggles of one particular servant of God. Recently, however, less individualistic interpretations have been proposed. The stereotyped form of expression in the confessions provides the basis for the hypothesis that these laments were spoken by the prophet as a cultic commentator for the people and also for the alternate conclusion that these prayers were only secondarily attributed to Jeremiah. The present form of the book, however, presents the confessions as an integral part of Jeremiah's message. Their function within the book may be analogous to and an extension of the call narrative (1:4-19).

Source B consists of narratives of Jeremiah's ministry that are similar, to the accounts of prophetic activity found in 1 and 2 Samuel. Most of the B source narratives appear in chaps. 26–45. Source C includes speeches or sermons in prose. The style of this material resembles that of DEUTERONOMY and the DEUTERONOMISTIC HISTORY. It is often described as wordy or monotonous. The relationship of B and C material to the author(s) of the deuteronomistic history and the companion issue of Jeremiah's affinities to deuteronomic theology have been the subjects of intense scrutiny, but no consensus has emerged. The logical possibilities include the following: (1) Jeremiah himself authored the B and C prose. This is the traditional view, which also attributes the authorship of 1 and 2 Kings to Jeremiah. (2) Jeremiah was a member of the deuteronomistic school who preached in prose (C) as well as poetry (A). His secretary, BARUCH, or some later disciple(s) composed the biographical narratives (B) based on what they knew of his life and work. (3) Jeremiah was not himself a deuteronomist, but the persons who preserved his words interpreted his message as being compatible with deuteronomic theology and cast the traditions in deuteronomic language and forms. (4) The style of Jeremiah B and C and of the deuteronomistic history is simply typical of Hebrew prose of their period and cannot be used as evidence of a particular theological stance.

Mowinckel's source D consists of poetic oracles of future hope found in chaps. 30–31. Subsequent scholarship has researched the origin and development of each of these sources and their relationship to one another, but no generally accepted solution has been achieved. In the present form of the book, material of all four types has been combined in various configurations over a lengthy period of development.

Two other blocks of material complete the book. Oracles against foreign nations (chaps. 46–51) announce divine judgment on the ancient Near Eastern superpowers and on Judah's neighboring states. Chap. 52 duplicates 2 Kgs 24:18–25:21 and adds statistics from the official records of the Judean exile.

Composition. Numerous indications of the process of composition can be found in the Book of Jeremiah. Units of like material have sometimes been joined on the basis of a common theme or catch-word connection. So, for example, the poetic oracles in chap. 2 all denounce Israel's apostasy, and the narratives in chaps. 27–29 each deal with the danger of false prophets. In other places the collections bring together a mixture of types. In 18:1–20:18, prose speech, biographical narrative, poetic oracle, and confessions are combined. This extended collection is then linked to chap. 21 by the repetition of the name PASHHUR (20:1-6; 21:1). A collection may have a title, as does 23:9-40 which begins, "concerning the prophets. . . . " Chap. 25:1-13a, on the other hand, clearly marks the conclusion to a more extensive collection that begins with chap. 1. The language of 1:15-19 is echoed in 25:3-9 and 25:3 refers to the starting date given in 1:2. To complicate matters further there are numerous duplications of passages (e.g., the Temple sermon in chaps. 7 and 26). These few examples demonstrate that the book of Jeremiah can only properly be described as a collection of collections or an anthology of anthologies that is the product of a complex process of development.

The arrangement of the book as a whole continues to provide a challenge for its interpreters. The order may be based loosely on literary types. Mowinckel's A source is found only in chaps. 1–25 and his B source is almost entirely confined to chaps. 26–45. Yet other poetic oracles appear in chaps. 30–31 (source D) and in chaps. 45–51 (oracles against the nations), B material is used in chaps. 19–20, and prose speeches (C) occur throughout the book. Some parts of chaps. 26–45 are dated, but the dates and circumstances of most oracles in chaps. 1–25 can only be inferred from their contents. Chronological order has not been followed in either case. In general terms, but not in every particular, it is possible to see an arrangement according to message. The thrust of chaps. 1–25 is the announcement of divine judgment on Judah. Chaps. 26–45 give more space to promises of a hopeful future in the midst of the final years of danger, destruction, and dispersion. The oracles announcing God's judgment upon the other nations, especially Babylon, imply a future turn of events in Israel's favor. The interpretative effect of the book's arrangement has yet to be convincingly defined. It is likely to be discerned in subtle shaping of the Jeremiah traditions rather than in the broad outline of the book.

According to the book, portions of Jeremiah's message were committed to writing during his lifetime. Chap. 29 records a letter from Jeremiah to the Judean exiles in Babylon, which consists of a series of oracles introduced and punctuated by formulas typical of oral delivery ("Thus says the Lord . . . " and "utterance of the Lord"). In 30:2 God commands the prophet to write down a collection of oracles that had already been delivered. This document presumably consisted of all or part of the material now in chaps. 30–31. A similar command is recorded in 36:2, and the execution of this commission is described in some detail. In 605 B.C.E. God instructed Jeremiah to write on a scroll the divine words spoken to him since the days of Josiah. Baruch wrote the scroll at Jeremiah's dictation and then read it aloud in the Temple. The specific content of this scroll is unknown. Most commentators believe that it is to be found in chaps. 1–25, since the dates in their concluding summary (25:3) match those in 36:1-2, and the description of the scroll as divine threats of disaster (36:3) suits the oracles in chaps. 1–25. After King JEHOIAKIM destroyed the first scroll, Jeremiah dictated a second copy, to which additional similar sayings were added (36:32). These three incidents illustrate the function of preserving prophetic preaching in written form. The truth of God's word can be measured by comparing the prophecy to subsequent fulfillment (30:3) according to the standards set in Deut 18:21-22. In written form prophetic preaching can address persons in places where the prophet cannot go because of distance (the exiles were in Babylon, chap. 29) or resistance (Jeremiah had been barred from the Temple, 36:5-6). God's word through the prophets maintains its authority and effectiveness across distances of time and space.

Text. The Hebrew text of Jeremiah differs significantly from the LXX. It is about 2,700 words longer. Some of the additional words are part of phrases that explain or expand a name or idea (e.g., MT "Jeremiah the prophet" usually corresponds to LXX "Jeremiah"). Other phrases provide headings, offer clarifications, or insert references to material found elsewhere in the book. In other cases whole passages found in the Hebrew text are missing from the Greek (e.g., 33:14-26). The LXX regularly omits the second occurrence of doublets (e.g., 8:10b-12, which duplicates 6:13-15). Scribal error cannot account for all of these omissions. Furthermore, some material is arranged quite differently in LXX than in the MT (e.g., 23:7-8 appears at the end of the chapter in LXX). The oracles against the nations are found at the end of the MT—in chaps. 46–51. The LXX, however, places them in the middle, following 25:13, and arranges them in a different order, with Babylon in third place instead of last.

The best explanation for these variations is that two different Hebrew texts of Jeremiah existed in the last centuries B.C.E. The LXX is a translation of the shorter version while the MT preserves the longer version. Evidence for this theory is provided by a fragment discovered in Cave 4 at Qumran, which appears to be part of a Hebrew scroll of the shorter text.

Contents. (1) Beginning with Jeremiah's call to be a prophet to the nations who would "pluck up" and "tear down" but also "build" and "plant," this section (chaps. 1–25) proceeds with oracles of indictment and doom, and reports of visions and symbolic actions, which make known God's threat to destroy Judah and Jerusalem for their sin. The promise of eventual restoration is also adumbrated within these chapters (3:12-18; 16:14-15; 23:1-8; 24:1-10).

The Israelites are indicted for unfaithfulness, idolatry, foolishness, violation of the covenant, and reliance on the temple as a guarantee of divine protection. Judah's kings and prophets are also castigated for oppressing God's people and particularly for rejecting God's word given through Jeremiah. The oracles in these chapters threaten destruction of the land and the temple, and decimation of the people by conquest and deportation. The invading "foe from the north" of the early chapters is identified later as Babylon.

Circumstances in Jeremiah's life function as part of the divine message. God's command not to marry or to celebrate weddings and mourn at funerals (16:1-9) prefigures the social dislocation in store for the people of Judah. Accounts of persecution (e.g., 11:21; 20:1-6) and the confessions function as further evidence of the people's sin.

(2) Prophetic speeches are set within a narrative framework that spans the period from the beginning of Jehoiakim's reign, through the fall of Jerusalem in 587/6 B.C.E. and Jeremiah's forced flight to Egypt (chaps. 26–45). The Judean prophets and kings opposed Jeremiah and threatened his life because he preached submission to Babylon, God's chosen agent of judgment. When the conquest was complete, survivors spurned God's offer of deliverance from the Babylonians and fled to Egypt. Chaps. 30–33 comprise a "Book of Consolation," a collection of oracles promising Israel and Judah restoration to their land and a new covenant with God.

(3) Oracles against Egypt, Philistia, Moab, Ammon, Edom, Damascus, Arab tribes, and Elam conclude with a collection of sayings against Babylon. God's judgment on Babylon initiates the ingathering of the exiles (chaps. 46–51).

(4) Chap. 52 duplicates 2 Kgs 24:18–25:30 and adds information on the number of persons deported in 598/7, 587/6, and 582 B.C.E. It describes the defeat of Jerusalem, the plundering of the Temple, the fate of ZEDEKIAH, and the release of JEHOIACHIN from prison many years later.

See also DEUTERONOMIST/DEUTERONOMISTIC HISTORIAN; JEREMIAH; PROPHET.

Bibliography. J. Bright, *Jeremiah, AncB*; R. P. Carroll, *Jeremiah, OTL*; W. L. Holladay, *Jeremiah, Hermeneia*; J. A. Thompson, *The Book of Jeremiah, NICOT*.

—PAMELA J. SCALISE

• **Jeremiah, Letter of.** The Letter of Jeremiah, one of the books of the Apocrypha, is not a letter nor was it composed by Jeremiah. It is a homily directed against the worship of idols, and its author chose to appropriate the authority of the prophet JEREMIAH, perhaps because Jer 29 mentions a letter written by the prophet to those in Babylonian EXILE. The document's argument against idolotry is persistent and repetitive. Jews confronted by idols are exhorted to worship only the Lord, since the idols are only man-made objects of wood, gold, and silver and are powerless to do anything. Therefore, each strophe ends with the refrain, "Therefore they evidently are not gods; so do not fear them."

SECOND MACCABEES (ca. 100 B.C.E.) refers to the Letter, and a Greek manuscript of the Letter dating to about the same period was discovered at Qumran. Internal evidence, however, points to a date around 317 B.C.E. A logical reconstruction would have the Letter composed in Hebrew during the late fourth century B.C.E. with the Greek translation occurring between that time and the first century B.C.E. Evidence regarding the place of composition is inconclusive, but the author may have been writing from Palestine, addressing Jews in the diaspora who were encountering idols.

The Letter has been preserved as part of the CANON in Christian manuscripts, although it was ultimately removed from the Hebrew canon. It occupies various positions in the manuscripts and has been attached both to Jeremiah and to BARUCH. In the Catholic Bible and the KJV the Letter of Jeremiah constitutes the last chapter of Baruch rather than appearing as a separate book.

See also APOCRYPHAL LITERATURE; BARUCH; JEREMIAH.

Bibliography. C. A. Moore, *Daniel, Esther and Jeremiah: The Additions*; G. W. E. Nickelsburg, *Jewish Literature Between the Bible and the Mishnah*.

—STEVEN SHEELEY

• **Jericho.** [jer'uh-koh] Jericho, "city of the palm trees" (Deut 34:3), is unquestionably to be identified with the ten-acre mound of Tell es-Sultan (PLATE 3), near the copious spring of the same name on the northern outskirts of the oasis and the modern city, some six mi. north of the shore of the Dead Sea (PLATES 10, 49). The site was investigated by C. Warren in 1867, then dug extensively by E. Sellin and C. Watzinger in 1907–09, and again by J. Garstang in 1930–36. Finally, modern stratigraphic methods were first introduced in Palestine at Jericho by the large-scale excavations of Kathleen Kenyon in 1952–58.

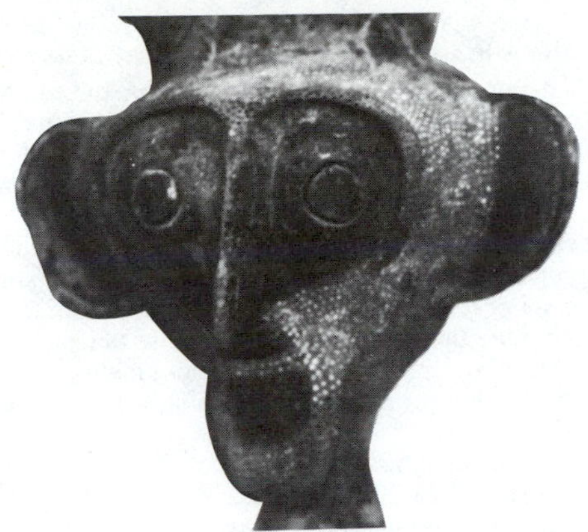

A human-face vase from Jericho.

Jericho is one of the most important Neolithic sites in the Levant, and is represented by thick deposits of all four of the known phases (first designated here). Following a thin Mesolithic or "Natufian" occupation of the tenth and ninth millennium B.C.E. is Pre-Pottery Neolithic A (or Neolithic 1), ca. 8500–7650 B.C.E. To this phase belongs an astonishing stone defensive tower ca. nine m. high, set into a mudbrick city wall—the oldest defensive system in the world by at least five millenia. Pre-pottery Neolithic B (Neolithic 2), ca. 7650–6000 B.C.E., sees the growth of a permanent, agriculturally-based village of rectangular mudbrick houses. A series of stylized plaster human figures, as well as detached and plastered human skulls, suggests the nature of the cult. Some of the earliest known pottery characterizes the next two phases, Pottery Neolithic A-B (Neolithic 3-4), but the overall culture declines now (ca. 6000–4000 B.C.E.).

After a gap of several hundred years, Kenyon's "Proto-Urban" period spans what other scholars would term the Late Chalcolithic-Early Bronze I horizon, ca. 3400–3100 B.C.E. There are scant domestic remains on the mound, but a number of successive burials in caves contain rich deposits of distinctive red-burnished and red-painted pottery contemporary with the late Pre-Dynastic (or Gerzean) period in Egypt. Kenyon argued for successive increments of newcomers from outside Palestine, but the differing pottery styles she describes do not suggest anything more than slightly divergent local ceramic traditions.

The first urban era in Palestine, the Early Bronze II-III period, ca. 3100–2600 B.C.E., sees Jericho evolving into a large fortified town, with as many as seventeen successive phases of the mudbrick city wall. The town collapses, like nearly all other urban sites in Palestine, by the beginning of Early Bronze IV at latest (ca. 2300 B.C.E.). Some continued occupation of the area, however, probably by pastoral nomads, is attested by nearly 350 shaft-tombs in the vicinity of the mound, mostly with secondary disarticulated burials, degenerate Early Bronze Age pottery, and copper weapons and implements.

Middle Bronze Age Jericho, ca. 2000–1500 B.C.E., was again a prosperous fortified urban center. Inside the new city walls near the gate was an area of well laid out shops and residences along a street ascending the terraced hillside. The numerous off-site tombs of this period have yielded fine wheel-made pottery, sophisticated bronzes, Egyptian-style scarabs, carved ivory inlays, and alabasters, as well as spectacularly preserved wooden furniture, baskets, textiles, and even remains of foodstuffs. Apparently natural gases seeping into the tombs through fissures in the rock of this earthquake-prone area rendered organic substances inert and thus preserved them. Jericho was probably destroyed ca. 1500 B.C.E. in the Egyptian raids accompanying the expulsion of the HYKSOS from Egypt, like nearly every other site thus far excavated in Palestine.

The Late Bronze Age at Jericho is poorly represented. Recovery may have begun before ca. 1450 B.C.E., but occupation ceased sometime before ca. 1350 B.C.E. Garstang had dated a massive mudbrick city wall to the fifteenth century B.C.E. and thus adduced it as evidence of the Israelite destruction claimed in Josh 6 (relying, of course, on the date of ca. 1446 B.C.E. for the Exodus as typical of the scholarship of that day). Kenyon, however, showed conclusively that this was the city wall of the last urban Early Bronze phase, ca. 2300 B.C.E. at latest. She found no city walls at all of the Late Bronze Age, and only a few tombs and scant domestic occupation of the Late Bronze IIA phase, ca. 1400–1350 B.C.E. Tell es-Sultan in the time of JOSHUA seems to have been abandoned already for a century or so, calling into question either the identification with biblical Jericho, or (more likely) the simplistic reading of the Joshua tradition as history in the more modern sense.

Not until about the ninth century B.C.E. was the site reoccupied. This may be connected with the references to Jericho in the time Ahab and Elijah-Elisha (1 Kgs 16:35; 2 Kgs 2:4; cf. Josh 6:26). The eighth and seventh centuries B.C.E. apparently saw a continual buildup of Israelite and Judean Jericho, but after the Babylonian destruction in the early sixth century B.C.E. the site lay abandoned.

The Jericho of the NT period spread elsewhere in the large, fertile oasis. The references to Jesus' baptism nearby (Matt 3:15-17), his temptation in the wilderness (Matt 4:11), or his miracles and parables in the town (cf. Mark 10:46-52; Luke 19:1-28) cannot be placed in an archaeological context, however. The only well attested remains are found at three small mounds along the north and south banks of the Wadi Qelt just west of the modern town. Here American excavations in the 1950s and more extensive Israeli clearance in the 1970s–1980s has revealed a spectacular complex that is clearly the winter palace of HEROD the Great, incorporating earlier structures of Alexander Jannaeus (103–76 B.C.E.). This extensive complex includes elaborately decorated residential quarters, audience chambers, swimming pools, baths, as well as terraced patios and gardens laid out along the river bank. Wooden beams are extremely well preserved. The *opus reticulatum* brickwork of some structures is in a style rarely encountered outside the Italian mainland. In the foothills to the north have been found several ossuary burials like those known otherwise chiefly in Herodian Jerusalem, several with names allowing us to reconstruct a three-generation Goliath family of unusual height.

Still another Jericho of the oasis belongs to the Islamic period, where the unfinished (?) Hisham's Palace of the Omayyad period (661–750 C.E.) has brought to light expressive gypsum carvings, decorative panels, and figural representations of both humans and animals, the latter somewhat surprising in Islamic art. Elaborate baths nearby exhibit some of the finest mosaics of this period ever found in Palestine, especially a well known scene featuring a sacred tree flanked by animals.

See also CONQUEST OF CANAAN.

Bibliography. R. Hachlili, "The Goliath Family in Jericho: Funerary Inscriptions from a First-Century A.D. Jewish Monumental Tomb," *BASOR* 235 (1979): 31-66; K. Kenyon, *Digging Up Jericho;* E. Netzer, "The Hasmonean and Herodian Winter Palaces in Jericho," *IEJ* 25 (1975): 89-100.

—WILLIAM G. DEVER

• **Jeroboam I.** [jer'uh-boh"uhm] The first king of the Northern Kingdom (Israel) after the division of the Davidic Kingdom, he reigned ca. 922–901 B.C.E. In keeping with ancient Near Eastern custom, Jeroboam may have chosen this name when he ascended the throne, since it apparently means, "May the People [nation] multiply." Thereby he would anticipate rivalry with the remainder of the Davidic state (Judah).

There are two accounts of his premonarchical days. According to the Hebrew text (followed by English Bibles), he was the son of Nebat and Zeruah (a widow), a member of the tribe of Ephraim, whom King SOLOMON had appointed to oversee construction projects that were done with forced labor (1 Kgs 11:26-28). His apparent dissatisfaction with such policies may have brought him to the attention of the prophet AHIJAH, who announced, with the symbolic action of tearing a garment, that God would rip a major portion of the state from the control of the Davidic dynasty and convey it to Jeroboam. Subsequently, Jeroboam fled to Egypt for his life and remained there until the death of Solomon (11:29-40). Upon his return, and subsequent to the arrogance of King Rehoboam (Solomon's son), the ten Northern tribes proclaimed Jeroboam as their king (12:1-20).

The other account is found in a supplement that follows 1 Kgs 12:24 in the Greek text (LXX, where the book is designated as 3 Kgs). In pro-Judean tones, it declares Jeroboam's mother (here named Sarira) to be a harlot; he aspires to kingship, rather than being summoned to it; while in Egypt, the Pharaoh provides him with a wife from the royal family, apparently to delay his departure; the child who died following the prophet Ahijah's subsequent rejection of Jeroboam was the result of this marriage; and a prophet named Samaias tore a garment to symbolize the division of the Davidic Kingdom, just as had Ahijah of Shiloh previously.

Upon becoming king, Jeroboam moved quickly to fortify his realm, perhaps fearing EGYPT (1 Kgs 14:25) and JUDAH (15:6). He then provided places of worship for his citizens (foremost being DAN and BETHEL) as replacements for the Judean national sanctuary at Jerusalem. This included the erection of images in the form of golden calves, the appointment of nonlevitical priests (he himself served in this capacity), and the revision of the liturgical calendar (12:25-33). Such actions, unorthodox from a Judean point of view, earned him a ceaseless litany of condemnation by the Judean editors of the Books of Kings, who attributed the ultimate demise of the Northern Kingdom to them (13:33-34). Even in his own lifetime, they reported, the prophet Ahijah had announced the death of Jeroboam's son, the extinction of his line, and the defeat of his nation by the Assyrians (14:7-16). (Ahijah's anger may have been aroused, in part, by the fact that Jeroboam had favored Dan and Bethel as religious centers rather than Ahijah's sanctuary at SHILOH.)

The parallel and much later account in Chronicles is even more pro-Judean in tone, and gives details (perhaps exaggerated) of the struggle between Jeroboam and King ABIJAH of Judah (the son of Rehoboam; 2 Chr 10:2-16; 12:15–13:20).

See also AHIJAH; CALF, GOLDEN; IDOLATRY; REHOBOAM.

Bibliography. J. Bright, *A History of Israel,* 2nd ed.; M. A. Cohen, "The Role of the Shilonite Priesthood in the United Monarchy of Ancient Israel," *HUCA* 36 (1965): 59-98.

—LLOYD R. BAILEY

• **Jeroboam II.** [jer'uh-boh"uhm] An energetic and able king of Israel who reigned ca. 786–746 B.C.E.; son and successor of Joash (Jehoash); father of king Zechariah. Upon attaining the throne, he apparently chose this name (possibly meaning "may the people [nation] multiply") in admiration of his country's first monarch whose success he hoped to imitate.

Scant detail of his long and successful reign is provided by 2 Kings (14:23-29), since its editors are pro-Judean and denounce him summarily "because he did not depart from all the sins of Jeroboam [I] the son of Nebat, which he made Israel to sin" (v. 24). We are merely told that "He restored the border of Israel from the entrance to Hamath (or Lebohamath) as far as the Sea of the Arabah" (v. 25; cf. Amos 6:14), including the recovery of Damascus (v. 28), just as the prophet JONAH had anticipated (v. 25). The result was the restoration of the boundaries of the Davidic-Solomonic state (1 Kgs 8:65; cf. Num 34:1-9). In the previous century-and-a-half, much of that territory had been lost by the emergence of the states of Aram (Syria), Ammon, Moab, and Edom (2 Kgs 3:4-27; 8:20-22; 12:17-18; 13:3-23), although Jeroboam's father had reversed the trend (2 Kgs 13:25).

Scattered details of Jeroboam's campaigns are preserved in the book of the contemporary prophet AMOS (e.g., 6:13, concerning the reclamation of cities in Gilead).

This remarkable resurgence of national power was not entirely the result of Jeroboam's administrative and military abilities, however. Israel's perennial enemy from the north, the Arameans, had been crippled by repeated campaigns by the Assyrians. They apparently are the "savior" of Israel, mentioned at 2 Kgs 13:5. When the Assyrians were not able to continue their pressure upon Syro-Palestine, this created a power vacuum into which Jeroboam (as well as his contemporary, King UZZIAH of Judah) could expand.

The result was a period of peace and prosperity such as Israel had not known since Solomonic times. Territorial expansion brought new land, an increase in agricultural produce, new ports and trade routes, and additional revenues from taxation and tolls on caravans. Thus the prophet Amos, a contemporary, speaks of affluent families who own both winter and summer houses (3:15), of the importation of ivory, of feasting and relaxing to music (3:15; 6:4-6). Archaeological remains from the capital city (Samaria) support the prophetic description.

Such prosperity fostered the widening of socioeconomic gaps, the oppression of the poor, the perversion of justice in the courts, and the resurgence of Baalism (a religion tied to an agricultural economy). These were departures from Israel's ancient ideals and provoked stern rebuke from the prophets Amos (2:6-8; 3:13-15; 4:1-3; 6:1-7) and Hosea (2:1-13), who anticipate that the deity will not allow it to continue.

With the death of Jeroboam, the fate that the prophets had anticipated began to unfold. Within twenty-five years, the state of Israel ceased to exist.

See also AMOS, BOOK OF.

Bibliography. J. Bright, *A History of Israel,* 2nd ed.

—LLOYD R. BAILEY

• **Jerubbaal.** *See* GIDEON

• **Jerusalem.** [ji-*roo'*suh-luhm] Jerusalem is a holy city to three major religions, Judaism, Christianity, and Islam. The name Jerusalem first appears in historical documents in Egyptian execration texts dated to the nineteenth century B.C.E. as Rushalimum. Earlier occurrences to Shalem in the EBLA tablets from the twenty-fourth to twenty-second centuries B.C.E. may refer to Jerusalem, but this is not certain at present. From the AMARNA tablets of the fourteenth century B.C.E. the name is given as Urusalim. The name probably meant originally "foundation of Shalem" (Shalem is the name of a god). This essay will consider Jerusalem from its beginnings through the Byzantine period, the periods of the OT, NT, and early church.

Geography and Prehistoric Settlement. The city of Jerusalem is situated about thirty-six mi. east of the Mediterranean on the eastern edge of the ridge of the central hill country at an elevation of about 2,500 ft. (PLATES 7, 11, 12, 24, 25). The MOUNT OF OLIVES to the east of Jerusalem has an elevation of over 2,700 ft. Jerusalem itself is located on a quadrilaterally shaped plateau. Two hills, one on the east and the other on the west, surrounded on three sides by valleys form the basic topography of Jerusalem. The KIDRON Valley lies to the east of the eastern hill, and separates it from the Mount of Olives. The HINNOM Valley runs to the west and south of the two hills. It joins the Kidron valley at the southeast end of the eastern hill. The third valley is the Tyropoeon or Central Valley which runs between the two hills. The western hill is about 200 ft. higher than the eastern hill, 2,500 ft. compared to 2,300 ft. in elevation.

The site was undoubtedly chosen for habitation because of the presence of water nearby and the natural defense afforded on three sides by the valleys. The GIHON spring (the name means "gushing") emerges well down the slope on the eastern slope of the eastern hill (PLATE 37). Although the spring constantly provides water, the flow does gush and subside. Furthermore Jerusalem sits near the junction of two important roads, the north-south road which followed near the crest of the central hill country and linked HEBRON with SHECHEM and the east-west road from JERICHO to the coastal plain where it linked with the coastal road, Via Maris.

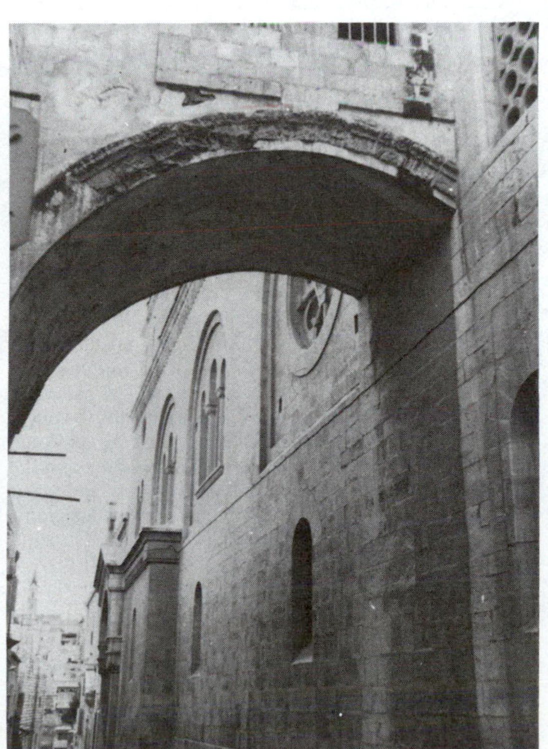

Ecce Homo Arch in Jerusalem.

Although evidence from south of Jerusalem indicates human habitation since the Paleolithic Age, ca. 50,000 B.C.E., permanent habitation apparently began in the Chalcolithic period. Pottery from that time has been found in Jerusalem, although no structures that old have been found to date.

Amorite, Canaanite, and Jebusite Remains. The earliest houses thus far discovered in Jerusalem belong to the Early Bronze Age. Shiloh discovered at least two houses belonging to that time period on the eastern hill, the site of the old Canaanite-Jebusite city of Jerusalem. This early settlement apparently had no wall. But Benjamin Mazar has argued that retaining walls he dates to this period suggest an urban center.

The Middle Bronze Age finds are much more extensive, though settlement was limited to the eastern hill, Ophel. This was the Jerusalem of MELCHIZEDEK, if Jerusalem is to be identified with the SALEM of Gen 14. This was also the first period the Canaanite-Jebusite city had a wall. The MB IIA wall dating to about 1800 B.C.E. was about eight ft. thick. This wall, repaired and rebuilt frequently, continued in use for over 1,000 years in some sections. The wall was built about two-thirds of the way down the Kidron (eastern) side of Ophel. The spring Gihon lay outside the Jebusite wall, a fact surprising at first notice. Yet to have placed the wall any lower in the valley so as to include Gihon would have left defenders on low ground, below attackers on the opposite hill. Access to the spring from inside the walls was provided by cutting an oblique passage in bedrock 92 ft. long and 26 ft. deep. At the end of the passage a 40 ft. vertical shaft reached water level. Rope drawn buckets could be let down the shaft to get water. DAVID's soldiers may have gained access to the city by coming up through this shaft and passage (2 Sam 5:8). Above the MB walls in the northern part of the Jebusite city, some rather massive terraces were found. Shiloh has suggested that these terraces were constructed by the Jebusites to provide additional building space on top of the slope. They were the foundations or support structures for the Jebusite citadel. Shiloh argues that the term Ophel meant acropolis or upper city. Thus the chief administrative center of the Jebusite city probably lay above these terraces. Unfortunately nothing now remains of those buildings.

Late Bronze Age Jerusalem is the city of the Amarna letters. Six of the letters are from Abdi-hiba, king of Jerusalem. He complained to the pharaoh about rebellion in Canaan. Some of the city-states were disloyal to the pharaoh and were allied with the *habiru.* A letter from another city-state described how all the other local rulers had turned against that city-state (and against Egypt) except for Abdi-hiba.

Jerusalem in the Middle and Late Bronze Ages was approximately eleven acres in size. Although considerable pottery from the period has been found, few houses or structures have been located. Shiloh has suggested that the terrace system was expanded in the Late Bronze Age giving a larger platform for the citadel.

David and Solomon. Jerusalem did not finally fall into Israelite hands until the time of David. (The account of its destruction in Judg 1 may reflect a defeat, but not the actual capture of the city by the Hebrews.) As mentioned above, 2 Sam 5 records the capture of Jerusalem by the Hebrew army under JOAB. Jerusalem was of strategic importance because it was a major Jebusite center lying between the territory of Judah and the rest of the territory of Israel. Although technically a part of the tribal allotment of Benjamin (Josh 18:16), the city had never been incorporated into either Israel or Judah. A Jebusite city-state in the heart of the kingdom presented too many risks to be left unchallenged. However, once Jerusalem was captured, it provided an ideal site for the capital of the now unified monarchy. It was a ''neutral'' capital that belonged to neither tribal group. Since it lay on the border between Judah and Israel, it was an ideal compromise location for the capital. Jerusalem, already rich in Canaanite traditions, was to become the administrative, political, and religious center for the united monarchy. David could by decree or move of residence make Jerusalem the administrative and political center. But to assure that it would also become the religious center, David retrieved the chief cult object of the confederacy, the ARK of the covenant, from obscurity in Kiriath-jearim and brought it to Jerusalem (2 Sam 7). With this action and the building of the Temple by Solomon, Jerusalem's place in Israelite history was certain.

Little is known of David's building activities in Jerusalem. Apparently he did construct a palace (2 Sam 5:11), but its location is not known. The city remained much as it had in Jebusite times. David did repair the city and its walls (PLATE 36) including the *millo* (1 Chr 11:8). Although the term *millo* is much debated, it probably refers to the stone terraces and foundations that supported the Jebusite acropolis area.

It was Solomon who turned Jerusalem into a royal capital with his building projects. Solomon extended the city northward from its Jebusite limits, more than doubling its size and adding the huge palace-Temple complex (1 Kgs 3). The site of the TEMPLE mount was identified as MOUNT MORIAH in 2 Chr 3:1, often further identified with the Gen 22 reference where Abraham was to offer Isaac. Although no architectural remains of the palace-Temple complex have been found, the biblical account gives ample description to suggest its impressive size and splendor. In all likelihood the platform for the complex and any extant remains lie buried under the remains of the larger Herodian platform supporting the Dome of the Rock and Al-Asqa Mosque (PLATE 35). The Temple had interior dimensions of 60 cubits length, 20 cubits width, and 30 cubits height (1 Kgs 6:2). Assuming the longer royal cubit was used for this royal complex, the interior size would have been about 105 ft. by 35 ft. by 52 ft. high. The Temple itself was only one part of the much larger complex (PLATE 22). The palace buildings were considerably more extensive than the Temple and took longer to complete. Just one part of the palace, the Palace of the Forest of Lebanon was 100 cubits long, 50 cubits wide and 15 cubits high (1 Kgs 7:2), or nearly three times the size of the Temple interior. Solomon used Phoenician craftsmen supplied by Hiram, king of Tyre, for constructing the palace-Temple complex and supplying its furnishings.

While no remains from these structures have been found, both Kenyon and Shiloh found fallen ashlar blocks that may have come from royal or administrative buildings of this period. Kenyon also found a Proto-Aeolic column capital that probably came from a public building of this period or slightly later.

Divided Monarchy to End of Monarchy. At some point during the divided monarchy, the population of Jerusalem grew beyond the bounds of the eastern hill, Ophel. Avigad has found houses and household objects on the western hill along with an Israelite wall from the eighth century B.C.E. This wall has been traced for over 200 ft.; it was about 22 ft. thick and still stands in places to a height of 10 ft. At least one defensive tower was excavated along the wall. Shiloh also found that Israelite houses were built outside the wall on Ophel during this period. It is possible that some of this expansion occurred during the long and peaceful reign of UZZIAH, or perhaps it reflects the migration of refugees from the collapse of the Northern Kingdom in 722/1 B.C.E. The settlement on the western hill is probably the Mishneh or Second Quarter (2 Kgs 22:14).

HEZEKIAH is said to have built a new wall as well as repairing the existing walls; he also strengthened the *millo* (2 Chr 32:2-5). But the major achievement of Hezekiah was the water tunnel which bears his name (2 Kgs 20:20; 2 Chr 32:3) undertaken because of the Assyrian threat of 701 B.C.E. This tunnel brought water from the spring Gihon on the east slope of Ophel to the pool of Siloam on the southwest slope of Ophel inside the defensive wall. The tunnel was about 1,750 ft. long and followed a snake-like course. It was cut by teams working from the two ends. Shiloh has recently surveyed the tunnel and spring; he found that the Gihon was only one foot higher than the Siloam pool end of the tunnel, an average fall of only one inch every 146 ft. An inscription found in the tunnel, the SILOAM INSCRIPTION, describes the completion of the project.

One other water system for Jerusalem should be mentioned. Along with the earlier Jebusite shaft and the Siloam tunnel system, there was a stone-cut channel that brought water along the slope of Ophel from Gihon to the area of the Siloam pool. In addition to bringing water to the pool, this channel also had openings that allowed irrigation of the fields in the Kidron Valley. The date of this system is not known, but it is usually thought to predate Hezekiah's tunnel, and may even be Jebusite.

Although Jerusalem survived the Assyrian threat during Hezekiah's reign, SENNACHERIB, the Assyrian ruler, did conquer most of Judah and boasted in an inscription that he left Hezekiah surrounded like a bird in a cage. The city was not so fortunate just over a century later. In 598 B.C.E., the Babylonians under NEBUCHADREZZAR invaded Jerusalem and Judah, carrying off King JEHOIACHIN and most of the royal family into captivity. ZEDEKIAH was placed on the throne by the Babylonians. He subsequently revolted; the Babylonians returned, and in 587 B.C.E. conquered and destroyed Jerusalem (2 Kgs 25:10). Excavations on the western hill have unearthed numerous arrow and spear points as evidence of the destruction. Likewise Kenyon's and Shiloh's excavations on Ophel showed massive destruction and burning from this Babylonian assault.

Exilic through Hasmonean Periods. Jerusalem lay in ruins during the Exile. Although some people still lived in the city, there is no evidence of rebuilding during this period. The victory of CYRUS over the Babylonians in 539 B.C.E. permitted the return of exiles to their homeland. Few of the Jewish exiles returned. Those who did return in 538 B.C.E. under ZERUBBABEL did begin rebuilding the Temple, though apparently only the foundations were completed. It was only at the impetus of prophets such as

HAGGAI that the project was taken up again by the returnees in 520 B.C.E. The Second Temple was completed in 515 B.C.E. The comment that elders who remembered the Solomonic Temple wept when they saw the foundations of the Second Temple (Ezra 3:12) makes one wonder if they wept for joy or in disillusionment over the new structure. The walls of Jerusalem remained in ruins until the time of NEHEMIAH, about 445 B.C.E. (Neh 2–3), when he received permission from the Persians and persuaded the people to rebuild the walls. During this period only Ophel was occupied, and even the walls of Nehemiah were located higher up the slopes of Ophel than the Middle Bronze through Iron Age walls.

The reforms of EZRA and Nehemiah brought about considerable tension within the populace. The calls for a purified religion permitting no outside elements and even demanding the divorce of foreign wives ran counter to the desire of those who wanted to adopt some of the culture of the Persians and Hellenists. Ultimately a stadium and gymnasium were built in Jerusalem (1 Macc 1:14). However, extreme attempts to force Hellenism on all the Jews, especially by Antiochus IV (Epiphanes), resulted in the Maccabean revolt and the Second Commonwealth period ruled by the Hasmoneans. Antiochus IV even built a fortress overlooking the Temple mount called Akra. The Maccabees captured Jerusalem in 164 B.C.E., but did not capture the fortress Akra until 141 B.C.E.

With the rise of the Maccabees, Jerusalem grew again. Once again it included the western hill as well as Ophel. Josephus reports that the Hasmoneans built a palace on the western hill. Portions of the Hasmonean city wall and a defense tower on the western hill have been excavated. Although few Hasmonean buildings have been recovered, numerous pottery and other material remains have been found.

Herodian Period. The Romans entered Jerusalem in 63 B.C.E. and put an end to the independent Hasmonean rule. HEROD came to the throne, placed there by the Romans, in 37 B.C.E. The Herodian period marked the greatest building program Jerusalem had known (PLATE 34). First he rebuilt the Hasmonean walls adding three monumental towers, Mariamne, Phaesalis, and Hippicus. Then he built a massive palace-administrative complex on the western hill. Later the palace housed the Roman PROCURATORS and was called the *praetorium.* Herod strengthened the northern defenses of the city by constructing a second wall from the north of the western hill to a new fortress (Antonia) he constructed just north of the Temple mount on Ophel.

The crowning achievement of Herod's building program was the rebuilding of the Temple. He extended the platform supporting the Temple south, more than doubling its size. The present Haram esh-Sharif platform, basically identical with Herod's platform, has outside dimensions of 1,041 ft. (north), 1,556 ft. (east), 929 ft. (south) and 1,596 ft. (west). The southeast corner of the Herodian platform survives today to a height of about 130 ft. Immense ashlar stones were used in the foundation of this platform. One of the stones was 46 ft. long, 10 ft. wide, 10 ft. high and weighs 415 tons. Other ashlars 39 ft. long, weighing 350 tons, and 36 ft. long, weighing 325 tons, have been found.

Excavations outside the southern and western walls of the Temple platform have revealed something of the splendor of the Temple. From the west a massive arched bridge linked the Temple mount with the western hill. On the south a large open plaza had several sets of steps leading up to the Huldah gates, with internal stairs then giving access to the Temple platform. Herod built colonnades all around the Temple platform. Avigad has excavated several residences of the Herodian period on the western hill, including one palatial mansion covering over 6,000 sq. ft. and overlooking the Temple mount. Avigad suggests that this mansion may have belonged to one of the high priestly families.

Herodian Jerusalem was virtually all destroyed during the war with Rome of 66 to 70 C.E. The climax came in 70 C.E. with the arrival of three Roman legions. Jerusalem was captured and the Temple destroyed by Titus on the 9th of Ab, 70 C.E., according to Rabbinic tradition the very same day the Babylonians had destroyed the Solomonic Temple. The western part of the city held out longer, but fell in the early fall of 70 C.E. Only the Temple platform and portions of the tower Phaesalis remained standing.

After 70 C.E. After Titus's conquest, most of Jerusalem remained in ruins. Certainly none of the administrative centers were rebuilt. Continued rebellions, culminating in the BAR KOCHBA revolt of 132–35 C.E., led to a harsh suppression by Hadrian. Jerusalem was razed to its foundations. Hadrian then built a new Roman city, Aelia Capitolina, primarily on the western hill. Aelia was laid out following typical Roman city plans. The discovery of the Byzantine *cardo* (the main north-south street of Roman cities) at Jerusalem lends evidence to a Roman plan for the city Aelia. Indeed, the Byzantine *cardo* may have been a rebuild of the earlier *cardo* of Aelia Capitolina. Recent excavations at the Damascus gate have uncovered portions of the Roman gateway opening into a large semi-circular plaza.

With the rise of Constantine as emperor and the advent of Christianity to an official status in the empire, great interest developed in the Holy Land. Great numbers of pilgrims flocked to Jerusalem and many churches were built. The walled city of Jerusalem reached its greatest extent during the Byzantine period. The MEDEBA mosaic map, found on the floor of a Byzantine church in Medeba, Jordan, depicts many of these churches. It also clearly depicts the colonnaded *cardo* of the Byzantine period. A section of that *cardo* has been excavated. It was paved with large flagstones and had a drain to carry away rainwater. The street was 37 ft. wide flanked by two colonnaded and roofed porticoes, each 16 ft. wide. Portions of arches, columns, and column capitals have been recovered along the *cardo.* This was the Jerusalem of the early church prior to the Islamic conquest.

Bibliography. N. Avigad, *Discovering Jerusalem*; K. Kenyon, *Digging Up Jerusalem* and *Jerusalem: 3000 Years of History*; W. H. Mare, *Archaeology of the Jerusalem Area*; B. Mazar, *The Mountain of the Lord*; Y. Shiloh, *Excavations at the City of David, I, 1978-1982*; Y. Yadin, ed., *Jerusalem Revealed, Archaeology in the Holy City, 1968-1974.*

—JOEL F. DRINKARD, JR.

• **Jerusalem Council.** The Jerusalem Council is the title usually given to the head-on confrontation between PAUL and the Judaizers around 49 C.E.. Paul and BARNABAS returning from the first missionary journey to Asia Minor were summoned to Jerusalem to appear before the church. The major concern seemed to be Paul's preaching to the gentiles and accepting them into the church without requiring circumcision.

Luke, in the Book of Acts, presents the conference in a more formal setting (Acts 15). In contrast Paul gives a more personal, informal description in Gal 2. In Acts 15, the church at Antioch appointed Paul and Barnabas to go up to

Jerusalem to discuss primarily the issue of circumcising gentiles (15:2). Their opposition came from believers who belonged to the party of the Pharisees and insisted on circumcision of gentile converts. Both Peter and James spoke out in favor of Paul's gospel. The church agreed that circumcision should not be required of gentiles. A letter was sent out to all the churches calling for gentile converts to abstain from meat offerings to idols, meat with blood in it, and unchastity, but the burden of circumcision would not be required (15:29).

In Gal 2, Paul's trip to Jerusalem seems to be more of a personal visit to defend his gospel. Paul took Titus, a gentile, along as a test case. Titus was not forced to be circumcised (Gal 2:5). Peter, James, and John, pillar apostles, gave Paul and Barnabas the right hand of fellowship (Gal 2:9). The meeting resulted in a two-fold mission—Paul would go to the gentiles and Peter to the Jews. The only other stipulation mentioned in Galatians is an offering to be collected by Paul for the Jerusalem poor.

The Jerusalem Council, whether formal or informal, freed the church from becoming a sect of Judaism. The door was opened for gentiles to enter the church freely.

See also APOSTLES, ACTS OF THE; BARNABAS; GALATIANS, LETTER TO THE; PAUL.

Bibliography. G. Bornkamm, *Paul.*

—JAMES L. BLEVINS

• **Jeshua.** [jesh'*yoo*-uh] An Aramaic form of the name JOSHUA, meaning "Yahweh is salvation." It occurs only in postexilic biblical literature, which supports the later origin of the name. Joshua, the son of Nun, is referred to in one passage as Jeshua (Neh 8:17).

Several people bear the name Jeshua in the OT but the best known is the high priest who returned from Babylonian Exile with ZERUBBABEL (Ezra 2:2; Neh 7:7). The biblical sources are not consistent in rendering his name, however. Haggai (Hag 1:1) and Zechariah (Zech 3:1) both refer to him as Joshua. Jeshua and Zerubbabel were instrumental in rebuilding the altar at the old Temple site (Ezra 3:2) and later in rebuilding the Temple itself (Ezra 5:2).

With the exception of a Jeshua whose nonpriestly clan returned from Exile with the high priest Jeshua and Zerubbabel (Ezra 2:6) and a Jeshua whose son helped rebuild the walls of postexilic JERUSALEM (Neh 3:19), most of the men who bear the name Jeshua are priests or Levites. A certain Jeshua was the head of the ninth division of priests during DAVID's reign (1 Chr 24:11) and may have been the ancestor of the high priest Jeshua of postexilic Judah. A Levite named Jeshua who helped in the distribution of the priests' and Levites' allowances during HEZEKIAH's reign (2 Chr 31:15) may have been the ancestor of the Levite Jeshua who helped interpret the law that EZRA read to the people (Neh 8:7).

Jeshua was also the name of a town in southern Judah that was occupied by some of those who returned from exile in Babylon (Neh 11:26). The town was approximately ten mi. northeast of BEERSHEBA.

See also PRIESTS.

Bibliography. B. T. Dahlberg, "Jeshua," *IDB*; "Jeshua," *HBD*.

—ROBERT C. DUNSTON

• **Jesse.** [jes'ee] The grandson of BOAZ and Ruth and the father of DAVID (RUTH 4:17). Jesse was a prosperous farmer and a respected member of the community of BETHLEHEM in the land of Judah (1 Sam 16:1, 20). His family was a large one, consisting of eight sons (1 Sam 17:12—seven sons according to 1 Chr 2:13-15) and two daughters (1 Chr 2:16). When Jesse's youngest son David came to SAUL's attention, Jesse was already an old man (1 Sam 17:12), but he lived long enough to survive an exile in Moab (1 Sam 22:3-4) and apparently to see his son become king.

Jesse was associated with the messianic ruler by Isaiah, who declared that when the Davidic dynasty of his era was gone, God would raise a new dynastic line from the "stump of Jesse" (Isa 11:1,10). This line would grow from the root of the Davidic dynasty without repeating the errors of the Davidic dynasty.

See also DAVID; MESSIAH/MESSIANISM.

Bibliography. E. R. Dalglish, "Jesse," *IDB*; Y. Gitay, "Jesse," *HBD*.

—ROBERT C. DUNSTON

• **Jesus.** [jee'zuhs] The evidence for the life and teaching of Jesus of Nazareth comes almost entirely from Christian sources: the four canonical Gospels, a few scattered references in the Letters of Paul and the other NT books, and the apocryphal gospels (especially those which preserve sayings of Jesus unknown in the canonical Gospel tradition). Contemporary pagan and Jewish sources have very little to say about him. What they do say focuses not on the name "Jesus" but on the designation "Christ" (misunderstood in Roman sources as a proper name). The Roman historian Tacitus, in referring to the Christians, mentions that "they got their name from Christ, who was executed by sentence of the procurator Pontius PILATE in the reign of Tiberius. That checked the pernicious superstition for a short time, but it broke out afresh—not only in Judea, where the plague first arose, but in Rome itself" (*Ann* 15.44). A more problematic notice is that of Suetonius, to the effect that the emperor Claudius "expelled the Jews from Rome, on account of the riots in which they were constantly indulging at the instigation of Chrestus" (*Claudius* 25.4). Confusion exists not only over the spelling of the name but over the fact that Suetonius is referring to events in Rome almost two decades after the date of Jesus' death as determined from the canonical Gospels.

The Jewish historian Josephus knew that "Christ" was a title (meaning "Messiah" or "Anointed One") and not a proper name, yet he has little more to say: James, stoned to death by Jewish authorities about 62 C.E., is identified as "the brother of Jesus the so-called Christ" (*Ant* 20.200). A more extensive reference in Josephus is open to serious question because it seems to have been edited later by Christian scribes (*Ant* 18.63-64), yet there is ample ground for believing that Josephus refers once again in that passage to Jesus as "the Christ," with the additional information that Jesus was a teacher, that he performed "suprising works," that Pilate condemned him to the cross, and that the movement continued after his death.

This is about all the data that "secular history" (i.e., history not written by committed Christians) can provide. There is no historical controversy over the fact that Jesus was known as "Christ," that he was (as the creeds say) "crucified under Pontius Pilate," and that the movement he started spread and flourished despite his death. In Christian theology each of these facts was interpreted in a distinctly Christian way: the designation "Christ" meant that Jesus was not only the Jewish Messiah but the divine SON OF GOD; his death on the cross was understood as a sacrifice or atonement for sins; the continuation of the movement was attributed to his resurrection from the dead and his exaltation to heaven as Lord of all. The first two of these are theological confessions made on the basis of faith; they cannot be argued pro or con historically. The third is also a theological confession, but one based on certain historical claims not accepted by everyone: i.e., that the tomb of Jesus was found empty and that he was seen alive by his disciples after his death. Those claims are of interest to historians as well as theologians, but only after they have investigated a more controversial side of the man Jesus, the teaching and the miracles to which Josephus refers.

If by the "life of Jesus" we mean only a sequence of events, it is hardly surprising that historians must settle for something less than absolute certainty. It would be hard to establish a precise chronology or itinerary for the career of anyone who lived nineteen centuries ago. Even the Gospels are divided in their testimony as to whether Jesus' ministry was conducted mainly in Galilee (Mark, Matthew, Luke) or in Jerusalem (John). When NT scholars speak of great uncertainty in our knowledge about Jesus (by the use of such expressions as "the quest for the historical Jesus" or "the search for the real Jesus"), they are usually referring not to a sequence of events but to Jesus' teaching. Did he say what he is represented as saying in the synoptic Gospels? In John? In both? In the non-canonical collections (e.g., the *Gospel of Thomas* or the *Apocryphon of James*)? What was his attitude toward the Jewish law? Did he accept it, reject it, or reinterpret it? If we assume that he proclaimed the KINGDOM OF GOD, or Kingdom of Heaven, what did he mean by this phrase? If we assume that he taught in parables, why did he adopt this method? What was his attitude toward war and violence? Was he more like a biblical prophet, a Jewish apocalyptic visionary, a rabbi, a wisdom teacher or sage, a political revolutionary, a Gnostic who renounced the world, or what? Most crucial for theologians (at least for many of them) is what did he teach about himself? Did he call himself the Christ? Did he claim to be the Son of God, as he is said in John's Gospel to have done? And beyond the matter of his teaching, did Jesus perform MIRACLES of healing? Did he perform exorcisms on those believed to be demon-possessed? Did he turn water into wine, multiply the loaves, walk on the Sea of Galilee? Is it possible for a twentieth-century person even to consider believing such things? The study of Jesus' life is a veritable minefield in which many individuals and groups, Christian and non-Christian alike, have strong vested interests. The world continues to ask, "What is the truth about Jesus, and where is it to be found?"

Some scholars have tried to distinguish the actual words of Jesus from words attributed to him after the fact by his followers by a so-called criterion of dissimilarity, i.e., sayings attributed to Jesus can be accepted as authentic if they are without parallel either in the Jewish world of his time or in the writings of Christians after his death. Other sayings can then be accepted if they agree or if they are natural extensions of these core pronouncements. Still other sayings may be authentic, but cannot be so proven. Such an approach effectively places Jesus of Nazareth outside the chain of cause-and-effect that is the essence of human history and of the history of thought. Consequently, though many scholars claim to be using this method in reaching their conclusions about Jesus, few if any actually do. A better method is to take our sources at face value, with emphasis on features about which several sources are in agreement and with some caution about features where the special interests of one particular source or Gospel seem to have been at work in shaping the tradition. Yet there is no ground a priori for bias against any of our sources, whether one of the Synoptics, or John, or even a noncanonical source such as the *Gospel of Thomas*.

Who Was "Jesus of Nazareth"? A good starting point is the account of Jesus' baptism in the Jordan River by the desert prophet JOHN THE BAPTIST (Mark 1:9-11) (PLATE 54). It is unlikely that Jesus' followers after his death would have made up a story in which he submits to another's authority and receives a rite of washing that was "for the forgiveness of sins" (Mark 1:4). That this incident was a problem for some Christians can be seen not only from Matt 3:14-15 (where John says, "I need to be baptized by you"), but from the careful avoidance in Luke and John of any explicit statement that John baptized Jesus (cf., e.g., Luke 3:19; John 1:32-34; the Baptist's role in Luke-Acts and John is rather that of a witness to who Jesus is). Because of such tendencies, the evidence of Mark's Gospel that Jesus came to receive John's baptism is to be accepted as historical. Jesus must have found something appealing in the proclamation of John the Baptist that the last judgment was very near and that everyone, religious and irreligious alike, must repent of their sins and submit to a new cleansing in preparation for that great day.

All that is said about Jesus' origin in the story of his baptism is that he came to the river "from Nazareth" (Mark 1:9). Nothing is known of Nazareth from the OT or later Jewish sources, even though "Jesus of Nazareth" was a designation that followed him to the day of his death (cf. John 19:19). More information was needed about Jesus' origins. Both Matthew and Luke place alongside the link with Nazareth another tradition, to the effect that Jesus was born in Bethlehem, the "city of David," as a descendant of David's royal line. Matthew devotes a whole chapter to showing how this child born in Bethlehem ended up as an adult in Nazareth, described sarcastically by his enemies as a "Nazarene" (lit., "Nazairite," Matt 2:23). The play on words calls attention simultaneously to Jesus' obscure origins and to the stark contrast (in the eyes of many) between his supposed holiness (like the Nazairites of the OT) and his practice of keeping company with sinners, prostitutes, and tax collectors (cf. Mark 2:17). Luke, while confirming Matthew's testimony that the family was of the royal line of David (Luke 1:32-33; 2:4), admits that Nazareth was the family home of Jesus' parents all along (1:26-27). He reconciles the Nazareth and Bethlehem traditions on the grounds that a Roman census brought the holy family back to their ancestral city just before Jesus' birth (Luke 2:1-7).

Despite the birth stories in Matthew and Luke, Jesus in his own time was known to his contemporaries not as a native of Bethlehem and a messianic claimant from the line of King David, but as a humble Nazarene. Whatever their merit as history, the birth stories were not public knowledge during Jesus' lifetime, perhaps because (as Luke puts it) "Mary kept all these things, pondering them in her heart" (Luke 2:19; cf. v. 51). Even in the Gospel of John, Jesus' first disciples introduced him as "Jesus of Nazareth, the son of Joseph" (John 1:45), and were answered with words that early Christian preachers would hear many times from skeptical Jewish audiences: "Can any good thing come out of Nazareth?" (1:46). In Nazareth itself, the people among whom he had grown up said of him incredulously, "Is not this the carpenter, the son of Mary and brother of James and Joses and Judas and Simon, and are not his sisters here with us?" (Mark 6:3; cf. Luke 4:22). And in neighboring Capernaum they asked, "Is not this Jesus, the son of Joseph, whose father and mother we know? How does he now say, 'I have come down from heaven'?" (John 6:42). The marvelous accounts of Jesus' birth, whatever their value as genuine history, cannot be presupposed in attempting to make sense of the Gospel records of his life and teaching.

The same is true of the spectacular events associated with Jesus' baptism in the Jordan River, the descent of God's Spirit on him like a dove and the voice from heaven announcing "You are my beloved Son; with you I am well pleased" (Mark 1:10-11 ‖ Matt 3:16-17 ‖ Luke 3:21-22). There is no evidence that anyone except Jesus—and possibly John the Baptist—either heard the voice or saw the dove. Consequently those around him did not assume that he was the "Son of God"—whatever they might have understood by that designation. Ironically, the first intimation that he was more than simply "Jesus of Nazareth" comes neither from his family, nor from his disciples, nor from the religious leaders of Israel. It comes from the devil, in the story of Jesus' temptation as recorded in Matthew and Luke, and from the demons and the demon-possessed, in a number of remarkable stories in the Gospels. Just as the devil challenged Jesus twice in the desert as "Son of God," so in the course of his ministry the demons repeatedly confronted him with such words as "What have you to do with us, Jesus of Nazareth? . . . I know who you are, the Holy One of God" (Mark 1:24), or "What have you to do with me, Jesus, Son of the Most High God?" (Mark 5:7). Though the programmatic accounts of Jesus' birth and baptism establish his identity once and for all for the benefit of the Christian reader of the Gospels, the issue is raised first in his ministry by the powers of evil!

The temptation narrative affords yet another clue to the ministry of Jesus as a whole (PLATE 41). His answers to the devil's challenges, drawn from scripture, are centered not on himself but on "the Lord your God" (e.g., Matt 4:4, 7, 10). The God-centered character of his message continues as he begins his ministry in Galilee: "The time is fulfilled, and the kingdom of God is at hand; repent, and believe in the GOSPEL" (Mark 1:15; cf. Matt 4:17). The Kingdom of God, or Kingdom of heaven, becomes the dominant theme of Jesus' proclamation and teaching from this point on, at least in the first three Gospels. Though much attention has been given to what Jesus meant by the "Kingdom," the controlling word in the announcement is not "Kingdom" but "God" (or "heaven," which was for the Jews an indirect way of referring to God). Mark even refers to this proclamation as "the gospel of God" (Mark 1:14; cf. also Paul in 1 Thess 2:8, 9; Rom 1:1). Even in John's Gospel, Jesus is represented as reminding his hearers again and again that he has come not to glorify or proclaim himself, but solely to make known "the Father," or "the One who sent me" (e.g., John 4:34; 5:19, 30; 6:38; 7:16-18, 28; 8:28, 42, 50; 14:10, 28).

As to his own identity, Jesus seems not to have wanted that question raised prematurely. He silenced the demons (e.g., Mark 1:25, 34; 3:12) and told the people he healed not to tell anyone (e.g., Mark 1:43-44; 7:36a). But the more he urged silence, the faster his reputation spread (e.g., Mark 1:45; 7:36b). Some wondered if Jesus might be the Messiah who would deliver his people from Roman rule—just as some had wondered about John the Baptist (Luke 3:15; John 1:19-21). But according to all the Gospels, Jesus was as reluctant as John had been to play out that role. Once in Galilee, when the crowds tried to "take him by force to make him king," Jesus fled to the hills (John 6:15). Instead of claiming the titles of either "Messiah" or "Son of God," Jesus had a way of using the emphatic "I" in pronouncements in which it was not grammatically necessary (as, e.g., Matt 12:28), and a habit of referring to himself mysteriously in the third person as SON OF MAN. The latter expression (*bar enasha* in the Aramaic language that Jesus spoke) meant simply "a certain man," or "someone," yet in some Jewish sectarian circles it had been used to designate a heavenly figure who would represent the people of God and gain their deliverance (cf., e.g., Dan 7:13; *1 Enoch* 46.3). Moreover, Jesus often seemed to speak and act with the authority of God himself. In his teaching he boldly stated, "You have heard that it was said . . . but I say to you" (Matt 5:21, 27, 31, 33, 38, 43). And so radical was his reinterpretation of the Jewish Law that he is represented as prefacing the first of his sermons with the disclaimer, "Do not think that I have come to abolish the law or the prophets; I have not come to abolish them but to fulfill them" (Matt 5:27). Because of such speech and such behavior, the crowds who heard him "were astonished at his teaching, for he taught them as one having authority, and not as their scribes" (Matt 7:29) (PLATE 23).

The Teaching of Jesus. The two reference points for the teaching of Jesus were, first, the Jewish scriptures and, second, his own vision of God and of God's Kingdom. The former interest he shared with all Jewish teachers of his time; the latter he had in common with such biblical prophets as Ezekiel and Daniel, and with the later Jewish visionaries who produced such apocalyptic works as *1-2 Enoch, Testament of Moses, 4 Ezra,* and *2 Baruch.* For the Jesus of the Gospels, the two interests cannot be separated. His appeal to scripture can be seen in the temptation narratives of Matthew and Luke, and in a variety of controversy stories in which he is seen taking issue with current biblical interpretations on many subjects (e.g., sacrifice, the laws of purity, divorce, or the Sabbath). His vision of God and of the Kingdom is seen both in his PARABLES about life in this world (e.g., Mark 4; Matt 15; Luke 8), and in his vivid descriptions of the glory and judgment of God in heaven at the last day (e.g., Matt 8:11-12; 25:31-46; Mark 14:62; Luke 10:18). In either case, ordinary perceptions of reality are radically transformed.

This transformation is evident early in Jesus' ministry in the BEATITUDES with which he begins the SERMON ON THE MOUNT in Matthew's Gospel. Speaking of the crowds from all over Palestine crying out to him in their confusion and pain (Matt 4:24; 5:1), Jesus reveals that he saw them not as they were then, but with the eyes of love, as God saw them. They were the "poor" for whom God's Kingdom was intended, "mourners" to be comforted, and the "meek" who would inherit a new earth. They were a people hungry and thirsty for justice whose hunger would be more than satisfied by God's grace. For the present they were "harassed and helpless, like sheep without a shepherd" (Matt 9:36); it was to them that Jesus believed himself sent (Matt 15:24), and to them in turn that he sent his disciples. They were the "lost sheep of the house of Israel" (Matt 10:6), the nucleus of a restored Israel, and Jesus is said to have appointed twelve of his followers to rule over Israel's twelve tribes (Matt 19:28 ‖ Luke 22:29-30; cf. Acts 1:15-26).

These "lost sheep" were not all the Jews of Palestine, but specifically those not normally expected to benefit from the coming of the Messiah. For their carelessness about the law, many of them were regarded by their fellow Jews as enemies of God, but it was Jesus' conviction that God loved his enemies, and that consequently he and his disciples must love them too (Matt 5:38-48). When he was challenged for enjoying table fellowship with social outcasts (known to religious Jews as "sinners"), Jesus replied, "Those who are well have no need of a physician, but those who are sick; I came not to call the righteous, but sinners" (Mark 2:17). When the religious authorities murmured, "This man receives sinners and eats with them" (Luke 15:1-2), he told three parables to demonstrate that God's joy at the recovery of all such "sinners"—tax collectors, prostitutes, shepherds, soldiers, and all others despised by the pious in Israel—was greater than any joy "over ninety-nine righteous persons who need no repentance" (Luke 15:7; cf. vv. 25-32).

Such an unrestrained celebration of God's mercy on sinners must have seemed to the religious leaders of Jesus' day a lowering of ethical standards and a compromise of the holiness of God. Though there is little evidence that Jesus included non-Jews among the "sinners" to whom he was sent, the principle, "not to the righteous, but to sinners," made the proclamation of the good news of the Kingdom of God to the gentiles after his death a natural extension of his own practice. And in Jesus' own vision of the future, "many will come from east and west and sit at table with Abraham, Isaac, and Jacob in the kingdom of heaven, while the sons of the kingdom will be thrown into the outer darkness" (Matt 8:11-12). In that day twelve uneducated Galileans would "sit on twelve thrones, judging the twelve tribes of Israel" (Matt 19:28; cf. Luke 22:30). Such is the magnitude of the reversal of present circumstances that comes to expression in the sayings and parables attributed in the Gospel tradition to Jesus of Nazareth.

The kingdom that Jesus proclaimed, like the kingdom his hearers were expecting, was a future kingdom, but Jesus saw it impinging on the present in the repentance and transformation of "sinners" and in the healings and exorcisms God was performing through him (cf., e.g., Matt 12:28 || Luke 11:20). Jesus' teaching as recorded in the Gospels is alive with metaphors and parables of this kind. Depending on our own presuppositions we can regard them as the product of his ingenuity, creativity, or imagination. Or we can attribute them to his prophetic vision of God and of God's future for Israel and the world. Intimations of Jesus the visionary can be found not only in the accounts of his baptism, where he sees a dove descending and hears a voice saying "You are my beloved Son," and in the temptation, where he converses with SATAN, but in a brief passing reminder to his disciples that "I saw Satan falling like lightning from heaven" (Luke 10:18; for other possible examples, cf. Luke 11:49; 12:49-50). At any rate, the parables of Jesus continue to illumine Christian believers and fascinate scholars like wheels within wheels, or wells without bottoms, for they embody the insight of someone who saw things differently and continually turned human expectations and human values upside down. When this is understood, it is not so strange after all that Jesus was crucified.

Conflict in Jesus' Ministry. Opposition to Jesus and his teaching began rather early, according to Mark, at Capernaum (PLATE 52), where the Pharisees and Herodians began to plot ways of getting rid of him (Mark 3:6; cf., in a Jerusalem setting, John 5:16-18). The stated issue was Jesus' willingness to perform healings on the Sabbath (Mark 3:2; cf. 2:24; John 5:16), but it is possible that the healings themselves provoked opposition even apart from the Sabbath question. According to Luke, Jesus looked for hostility—and found it—in his home synagogue at Nazareth when he announced good news to the poor (Luke 4:16-30). Again, Jesus' healings were the issue: "Physician, heal yourself! Do here in your home town what we have heard you did in Capernaum" (Luke 4:23).

Opposition to Jesus came to a head in connection with his practice of exorcism. Religious leaders from Jerusalem came to Galilee to investigate him, and concluded that he was himself "possessed by Beelzebub, and by the prince of demons he casts out the demons" (Mark 3:22; cf. Matt 12:24 || Luke 11:15). Jesus replied that his healings of the demon-possessed were a sign rather that Satan's power was broken and the Kingdom of God was decisively at work in him: " . . . no one can enter a strong man's house and plunder his goods, unless he first binds the strong man; then indeed he may plunder his house" (Mark 3:27; cf. Matt 12:29; Luke 11:21). As Jesus saw it, the "strong man" (Beelzebub or Satan) was now bound, his "house" was being robbed and his captives set free.

In one way this crisis in Jesus' ministry simply confirmed his victory over Satan in the desert after his baptism. Yet it also demonstrated that the "temptation" was by no means over. The Beelzebub controversy, triggered by his healing and saving activity, set a grim precedent for Jesus' relationship with the Jerusalem authorities, and made his eventual arrest and execution almost inevitable. According to Mark, it was from that time on that Jesus began to speak "in parables" (Mark 3:23). There is no doubt that Mark emphasizes (perhaps overemphasizes) the dark side of Jesus' use of this remarkable teaching method (Mark 4:10-12), yet it is likely that parables served as Jesus' way of distinguishing those who were ready to see reality in a new way from those who were not. Parables unfolded his vision of the Kingdom of God to his followers while effectively hiding it from his enemies.

John's Gospel suggests that Jesus may even have used the imagery of his kingdom parables (e.g., the image of planting and growth) to hint at his own eventual arrest and execution on the CROSS (John 12:24, 32). In all the Gospels, in a variety of other images and metaphors (e.g., "drinking the cup," Mark 10:38; a shepherd risking his life for a flock of sheep, John 10:15; spreading fire over the earth, Luke 12:49), and sometimes in quite explicit language (e.g., Mark 8:31; 9:31; 10:33-34), Jesus is said to have announced to his disciples that he would be arrested and tried by the religious leadership in Jerusalem, die on the cross, and rise again from the dead. Even though the Gospel writers may have sharpened these predictions after the fact in light of the fulfillment, there is good reason to believe that Jesus defined his mission from the start, at least in certain respects, as that of the "servant of the Lord" described in Isa 40–66 (e.g., the citation of Isa 61:1-2 in Luke 4:18-19). As his ministry moved toward its completion, the vicarious suffering of the servant (cf. Isa 51:13–53:12) came into ever sharper focus for Jesus (cf., e.g., Mark 10:45; 14:24). He is represented also as comparing himself to the stricken shepherd of Zech 13:7 (Mark 14:27), and, at the end, to the righteous sufferer of the biblical psalms (e.g., Mark 15:34; Luke 23:46; John 19:28). In the drama of his last meal with his disciples, he told them that only his death could guarantee the coming of the kingdom he had proclaimed (Mark 14:22-25 || Matt 26:26-29 || Luke 22:14-20; cf. 1 Cor 11:23-26).

Jesus' anticipation of his own death is of course debated among scholars. The belief of the early church that Jesus was the Son of God could have led the Gospel writers to assume that he knew the end of his life almost from the beginning, and to avoid at all costs the notion that he was taken by surprise at any point (cf., e.g., John 10:17-18). And the belief of the church that Jesus' death was a sacrifice for human sin could have led them to assume that already during his lifetime Jesus interpreted it as such. But the bitterness of the Beelzebub controversy early in Jesus' ministry suggests that an early death at the hands of the religious authorities was a reasonable and realistic expectation. And there is no disputing Jesus' fondness for striking metaphors of conflict (e.g., Mark 3:27), and for surprise violent endings to rather conventional stories (e.g., the death of a bridegroom at his own wedding, Mark 2:20; the murder of a landlord's son by his tenant farmers, Mark 12:8; an unfaithful servant being "cut in half" by his angry master, Matt 24:51). Is it so strange that someone who saw the world in such "large and startling figures" (Flannery O'Connor's term for an artist's or writer's vision) might have included himself and his own fate in his image-making? The church's contribution to the tradition was probably not to create Jesus' anticipation of his death and resurrection, but to make explicit after the fact what was already implicit in some of his own metaphors and parables. Justice must be done, however, to the fact that when Jesus was arrested and executed, and especially when he appeared alive to his disciples afterward, they were by no means prepared for what happened. The predictions Jesus made are therefore best understood as indirect rather than direct, couched in metaphor rather than literal common speech (cf., e.g., John 16:19-22, 25).

The Death and Resurrection of Jesus. The immediate provocation for Jesus' arrest seems to have been his act of driving the money changers out of the Jerusalem Temple (e.g., Mark 11:15-17; cf. John 2:13-22). This, combined with certain pronouncements he is supposed to have made against the Temple, aroused the Jewish authorities to act decisively against him. During his last week in Jerusalem, Jesus had predicted the Temple's destruction (Mark 13:1-2 || Matt 24:1-2 || Luke 21:5-6) and according to some witnesses had claimed that "I will destroy this temple that is made with hands, and in three days I will build another, not made with hands" (Mark 14:58; cf. Matt 26:61). Distorted as these charges may have been, there was a grain of truth in them, for even the Christians attributed to him the statement, "Destroy this temple, and in three days I will raise it up" (John 2:19), as well as a promise to Peter that "on this rock I will build my church, and the gates of hell will not stand against it" (Matt 16:18). Jesus' intention to establish a new community as a "temple," or dwelling place of God (cf. 1 Cor 3:16-17) was perceived by some as a very real threat to the existing community of Judaism and to the Temple that stood as its embodiment, even though Jesus himself probably had in mind a restoration, not a replacement, of Israel (cf. Matt 19:28 || Luke 22:30). On this basis Jesus was arrested and charged as a deceiver of the people.

A preliminary hearing before the Jewish Sanhedrin, or ruling council, seems to have ended inconclusively, despite Jesus' reference to himself before the high priest as "Son of man sitting at the right hand of power, and coming with the clouds of heaven" (Mark 14:62; cf. Dan 7:13). The high priest called his pronouncement blasphemy and the Council agreed that such words deserved death, yet there is no evidence that Jesus was formally tried and convicted of anything. If he had been, he would have been stoned to death like Stephen in Acts 7, or as the woman caught in adultery was about to be stoned according to some manuscripts of John 7:53-8:11. If Jesus had been stoned to death without a formal conviction it would have been murder, and murder was forbidden by the Decalogue (cf. John 18:31b, "we are not allowed to kill anyone," probably a reference to the Jews' own law, not to something prohibited by the Romans).

Lacking a conviction by their council, a small group of Jewish priests decided to send Jesus to Pontius Pilate, the Roman governor, with charges against him that would be taken seriously by the Romans: "We found this man perverting our nation, and forbidding us to give tribute to Caesar, and saying that he himself is Christ, a king" (Luke 23:2). Jesus' execution is therefore attributable neither to the Jewish people as a whole nor to the Sanhedrin. The blame rests instead with an unspecified group of priests (presumably including the high priest) who manipulated the Romans into doing what their own law would not allow them to do, and with the Romans, who allowed themselves to be so manipulated. Consequently Jesus died by CRUCIFIXION, a distinctly Roman rather than Jewish method of execution, and his own metaphorical words about being "lifted up" (poorly understood at the time he uttered them) came ironically to realization (cf. John 3:14; 8:28; 12:32; 18:31).

The story of Jesus does not end with his death. His body is said to have been placed in a new tomb belonging to a secret disciple named Joseph (Luke 23:50-56; John 19:38-42) (PLATE 39). There are several accounts of what happened after that. All four Gospels agree that two days later some women who had remained faithful to Jesus discovered the stone over the tomb's entrance rolled away and Jesus' body gone. According to Mark a young man then told the women to tell the rest of Jesus' disciples to go and meet Jesus in Galilee, just as he had promised them (Mark 16:7; cf. 14:28). The most reliable manuscripts of Mark's Gospel end the story there, leaving the rest to the reader's imagination. In Matthew the women carried the news to the disciples, who went accordingly to a mountain in Galilee. There the risen Jesus appeared to them as a group and commanded them to make more disciples, teaching and baptizing among the gentiles (Matt 28:16-20). In Luke the risen Jesus appeared to his disciples not in Galilee but in the vicinity of Jerusalem on the same day he was raised (Luke 24:13-51). Luke adds in the Book of Acts the surprising information that the appearances of the risen Jesus went on over a period of forty days in which he continued to instruct them about the Kingdom of God. John has an appearance of Jesus on EASTER day in Jerusalem to one of the women, Mary Magdalene, another on the same day to ten gathered disciples, another a week later (still in Jerusalem) to the same group plus Thomas (John 20:10-31), and a fourth appearance, at an unstated time, by the Lake of Galilee (John 21:1-14).

These varied accounts cannot be convincingly integrated into one coherent account. Whatever the facts, and whatever their precise order, the disciples' experience of what they took to be the resurrected Jesus transformed them from a scattered and fearful band of refugees into the nucleus of a powerful movement able to challenge and change forever the Roman empire within a few decades. Many theories have been proposed as to exactly what happened. Theologians—and some historians—are often more comfortable with the resurrection as a matter of faith than of fact. But because the historical impact of the resurrection experience is undeniable, it is hard to avoid asking about the historical causes of that experience. Is it conceivable, for example, that Jesus' disciples could have stolen his body, lied about what they had seen, and risked their lives for a lie? If Jesus' enemies stole the body, would they not have produced it when the disciples began to preach that Jesus was alive? These are the kinds of questions that Christian apologists have asked for a long time, and they have not been convincingly answered. Some have replied that the reports of the empty tomb are not essential to the story, and that Christian faith rests not on those reports but on the appearances. Yet Matthew already in the first century emphasized the importance of the empty tomb by recording an attempt by the priestly authorities to bribe Roman soldiers into saying that Jesus' disciples came secretly and stole his body (Matt 28:11-15). And Luke has Peter arguing in the first Christian sermon that "the patriarch David . . . both died and was buried, and his tomb is with us to this day" (Acts 2:29). The force of the argument depends on the assumption that the tomb of Jesus was also known and publicly acknowledged to be empty. Clearly the resurrection faith of the early Christians rested on reports both of an empty tomb and of resurrection appearances. Paul places great emphasis on listing those to whom the risen Jesus "appeared" (1 Cor 15:5-8), but only after he has clearly stated that Jesus "died," "was buried," and "was raised the third day" (1 Cor 15:3-4)—the "third day," presumably, because that was when the tomb of Jesus was found empty. Though it would be an exaggeration to claim that the physical resurrection of Jesus is a proven fact, yet the historical evidence in its favor is extremely strong.

In one respect at least, the resurrection of Jesus is a barrier to understanding the Jesus of history, because of the uncertainty over whether some sayings in the Gospels are to be attributed to Jesus during his lifetime or to the "Risen One" (i.e., to Christian prophets after the resurrection speaking in Jesus' name). Yet in the last analysis, Jesus' resurrection pointed his followers toward, not away from, his career as a real figure in history. The resurrection impelled his disciples to remember, preserve, and keep alive the record of his deeds and words. Several of the accounts of Jesus' resurrection emphasize the need to verify that this divine stranger was "the same Jesus" the disciples had known as a friend and companion on earth (e.g., Luke 24:30-31, 36-42; John 20:27). In all the early Christian sources, the meaning of the resurrection is that the story of Jesus of Nazareth goes on. Mark makes the point with the promise that Jesus will reunite his scattered followers and lead them into Galilee (Mark 16:7). Matthew does it with the risen Jesus' concluding words, "I will be with you always, even to the end of the age" (Matt 28:20). Luke does it with the entire Book of Acts, tracing the spread of the message of Jesus and the Kingdom of God all the way to Rome. John does it with his promise that the Holy Spirit will continue the work of Jesus, and with his picture of the Spirit coming on the disciples from the mouth of Jesus himself (John 20:21-22). The methods are different, but the point is always the same: Jesus' story is not over, for his ministry goes on wherever his name is confessed and his teaching obeyed.

See also BEATITUDES; CROSS; CRUCIFIXION; DIVINITY OF JESUS; EASTER; GOSPEL; GOSPELS, CRITICAL STUDY OF; JOHN THE BAPTIST; KINGDOM OF GOD; LORD IN THE NEW TESTAMENT; MESSIAH/CHRIST; MIRACLE STORY; MIRACLES; PARABLES; PILATE; RESURRECTION IN THE NEW TESTAMENT; SERMON ON THE MOUNT; SON OF GOD; SON OF MAN; TOMB OF JESUS.

Bibliography. G. Bornkamm, *Jesus of Nazareth*; H. Conzelmann, *Jesus*; C. H. Dodd, *The Parables of the Kingdom*; D. Flusser, *Jesus*; J. Jeremias, *New Testament Theology: The Proclamation of Jesus*; M. Kähler, *The So-called Historical Jesus and the Historic Biblical Christ*; G. E. Ladd, *The Presence of the Future*; T. W. Manson, *The Teaching of Jesus*; B. F. Meyer, *The Aims of Jesus*; J. R. Michaels, *Servant and Son*; C. L. Mitton, *Jesus: The Fact Behind the Faith*; G. O'Collins, *The Resurrection of Jesus*; J. Pelikan, *Jesus Through the Centuries*; J. Riches, *Jesus and the Transformation of Judaism*; E. Schillebeeckx, *Jesus: An Experiment in Christology*; A. Schweitzer, *The Quest of the Historical Jesus*; E. Stauffer, *Jesus and His Story*; W. B. Tatum, *In Quest of Jesus*; V. Taylor, *The Life and Ministry of Jesus*; G. Vermes, *Jesus the Jew*.

—J. RAMSEY MICHAELS

• **Jesus' Tomb.** *See* TOMB OF JESUS

• **Jethro.** [jeth'roh] Priest of Midian and the father-in-law of MOSES (Exod 3:1; 4:18; 18:1-2, 5-6, 12). He is known as Hobab the Kenite in the tradition found in Num 10:29-32 and Judg 4:11 and may be identified with Reuel in Exod 2:18. These various names reflect either the interchange of clan names or a misunderstanding on the part of the biblical editor when compiling disparate stories about the relationship between Moses and the Kenites, a subtribe of the Midianites.

Moses' flight from Egypt after killing an Egyptian led him to the desert region of MIDIAN in the SINAI. There he met his future wife at a well. She was Zipporah, one of seven daughters of Jethro/Reuel, the priest of Midian. Moses aided the daughters in watering their flocks and protected them from the other shepherds (Exod 2:17-19). For this service he is granted hospitality and becomes a shepherd in the household of his new father-in-law (Exod 3:1).

This idyllic existence ends with Moses' call before the burning bush to lead his people out of Egypt (Exod 3:2–4:23). Interestingly, Moses does not mention this encounter or the revelation of Yahweh's plans to Jethro. It is only when Moses and the people return to Mount Sinai after the Exodus that Jethro reappears in the narrative. He brings Zipporah and Moses' sons out to meet him (18:5). However, he also makes a statement of faith declaring that "Yahweh is greater than all gods" (Exod 18:11).

Jethro's declaration is prefaced in the narrative by the statement that he had "heard of all that God had done for Moses and for Israel his people" (v. 1). Parallels to this statement of faith in the power of Yahweh are found in the stories of RAHAB (Josh 2:10-11) and the Gibeonites (Josh 9:3-10). This suggests a narrative pattern of "hearing" followed by a statement of faith and the establishment of a covenant (Exod 18:12; Josh 2:12-14; 9:15-16). It also weakens the contention that Jethro was in fact a priest of El or Yahweh and had introduced the worship of that god to Moses. Rather, Jethro's statement and his making a sacrifice can be seen simply as a thanksgiving offering to one that he perceives to be a powerful deity who has rescued his son-in-law and his people (Exod 18:11-12).

While the Israelites were encamped near Sinai, Jethro is portrayed as also offering some administrative advice to his son-in-law. Moses had been exhausting himself hearing all of the disputes of the people. Jethro makes the useful suggestion of delegating authority to trustworthy and experienced men (Exod 18:13-26), and thus providing a precedent for future administration of justice within the tribes and the nation (cf. Num 11:16-22, 24-25; Deut 1:9-18, which do not mention Jethro's suggestion).

Traditions vary on the departure of Jethro from the Israelite encampment. Exod 18:27 has him simply slip away after giving thanks for Moses' return and offering advice to help him organize the people. Num 10:29-32 contains Moses' request that Hobab/Jethro remain with them as a guide through the wilderness. The Kenites join in the settlement (Judg 1:16), but some eventually resume their nomadic and separate existence (Judg 4:17).

See also KENITES; MIDIAN/MIDIANITES; MOSES.

Bibliography. H. Reviv, "The Traditions Concerning the Inception of the Legal System in Israel: Significance and Dating (Exod 18:12-27; Num 11:16-25; Deut 1:9-17)," *ZAW* 94/4 (1982): 566-75; J. Van Seters, "Etiology in the Moses Tradition: The Case of Exodus 18," *HAR* 9 (1985): 355-61.

—VICTOR H. MATTHEWS

• **Jeu, Two Books of.** [jee'uh] The Bruce Codex, a 156-page papyrus book acquired by the Scottish traveller James Bruce in Egypt in 1769 and kept today in Oxford's Bodleian Library, include *Two Books of Jeu.* The title does not appear in the manuscript and, in fact, differs from a title found at the end of the first book (53.25), "The Book of the Great Logos corresponding to Mysteries." However, on the basis of their content and double citation (158.18ff. and 228.35) under the name "the two books of Jeu" in another Gnostic text from approximately the same period, PISTIS SOPHIA, Carl Schmidt of Berlin designated pages 1-88 the *Books of Jeu.* In the text "Jeu" is identified as the "true God" emanated from the highest divine being, "the Father."

Cast in the form of a Gnostic revelation dialogue in which the "living" (= "resurrected") Jesus responds to questions of the Twelve and some holy women, the two books have the following content. In Book I (chaps. 1–41), Jesus reveals how his Father emanated "Jeu," who, in turn, brought forth twenty-eight other emanations who have authority over "treasuries," i.e., heavenly repositories of divine knowledge (*gnōsis*) and blessing. The form (or type), mystical name, character, and number of most of the twenty-eight emanations are described with the help of diagrams and cryptic signs. There follows a fragmentary hymn of praise to the "First Mystery" who caused "Jeu" to form the twenty-eight emanations. Jesus resumes teaching about the sixty divine "treasuries," their names, and their entry. He also provides an awe-inspiring and all-powerful Name that will allow the disciples, upon its utterance, to enter all treasuries and pass to the place of the true God. Book I concludes with a hymn of praise sung by Jesus and his disciples as they ascend through the "treasuries."

In Book II (chaps. 42–52) Jesus teaches the disciples the mysteries of the "Treasury of Light," the sphere of the highest "invisible God" and state of ultimate blessedness. These mysteries cleanse their souls of sin and enable them to ascend, after death, to this "Treasury." Jesus gives his disciples "three baptisms" (of water, fire, and the Holy Spirit), the "Mystery" that removes the wickedness of the (world-ruling) Archons, and a "spiritual unction" or sealing. This equips them with all they need for their final, heavenly trip. They are then fortified with controlling knowledge of the names of the demonic archons who would impede their souls, and they are given the "seals," "passwords," and formulae that guarantee safe ascent. After a stern warning that such secret information is not to be shared with the unworthy, the whole closes with a hymn sung to the Father by Jesus and his disciples, as well as a partial description of the passage of the soul.

Most scholars believe the Coptic text of the "Books of Jeu" is a translation from a Greek original composed in Egypt, probably in the early to mid-third century. It represents a late form of Christian GNOSTICISM, somewhat cumbersome and tedious, which possibly emanates from certain Barbelognostics with Encratite (world-denying) tendencies.

See also GNOSTICISM; PISTIS SOPHIA.

Bibliography. H.-Ch. Puech, "The Two Books of Jeu," in *New Testament Apocrypha,* ed. E. Hennecke and W. Schneemelcher; C. Schmidt and V. MacDermot, *The Books of Jeu and the Untitled Text in the Bruce Codex,* ed. R. McL. Wilson.

—MALCOLM L. PEEL

Courtesy of the Eisenberg Museum of Biblical Archaeology, Southern Baptist Theological Seminary.

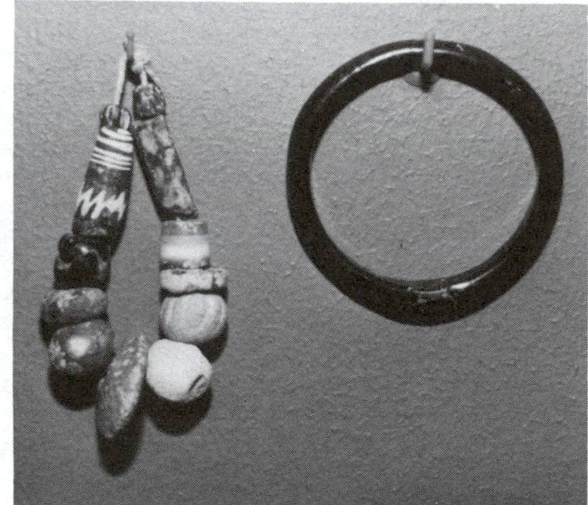

Roman bracelet and necklace.

• **Jewelry.** Body ornaments usually made of precious or semiprecious materials. Archaeological and textual evidence from the ancient Near East reveal a wide variety of media for the production of jewelry. Gold and silver, commonly associated with the sun and moon and believed to possess magical properties, were of course highly prized. Electrum, an alloy of these two metals, was also used. However, it was bronze that was utilized most often, especially in Palestine where the inhabitants were of modest means. These metals were all ideal candidates for the manufacture of jewelry because of their relatively low melting points and malleable nature.

Nonmetallic materials included faience, gemstones, bone, glass, and ivory. Egyptian faience, manufactured by glazing over granules of quartz, was extremely popular and spread around the Mediterranean, making its way to Palestinian sites such as Lachish and Megiddo. A number of gemstones were known and used in jewelry, and the OT makes reference to several of them. The catalog of jewels on the priestly breastplate representing each of the twelve tribes (Exod 28:17-20; 39:10-13) is difficult to translate but probably includes carnelian, topaz, emerald, carbuncle, lapis lazuli, onyx, amber, agate, amethyst, chrysolite, beryl, and jasper. This same list less three gems is found also in Ezekiel's protrait of the King of Tyre (Ezek 28:13). Rev 21 is dependent upon these priestly stones but adds crystal and pearls as well in its description of the new Jerusalem. From these passages it is clear that the number of stones known and used in the biblical world was considerable.

Courtesy of the Eisenberg Museum of Biblical Archaeology, Southern Baptist Theological Seminary.

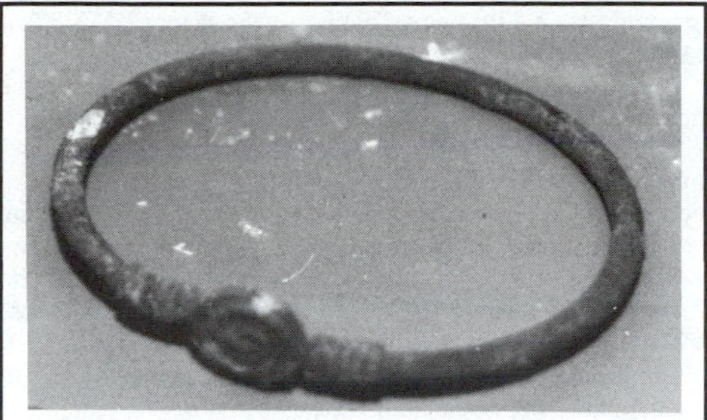

A bracelet from the Roman period.

While such prized materials were utilized by the prosperous, common animal bones were used by the poor to make jewelry. Some bone pendants have been uncovered at Iron Age Megiddo, Gezer, and Lachish, but the largest numbers have come from the economically depressed Beit Mirsim. It seems that such crude jewelry was scorned by the wealthier members of society.

Ancient Near Eastern jewelers were quite skilled. The priestly outfit detailed in Exodus consists in part of braided gold cords and stones engraved with the names of the twelve tribes and set in fine gold filigree. Exquisite inlaid jewelry has been uncovered in Egypt, Palestine, Syria, and Mesopotamia. Fine examples of granulation have also been unearthed. The artisans who produced these items were in such demand that they were often carried off as booty in war. Thus it is sometimes difficult to limit a design to a particular region.

The forms of jewelry were as varied as the materials used for its manufacture. The most complete catalog of jewelry in the Bible is found in Isa 3:18-23. It mentions anklets, headbands, pendants, bracelets, armlets, amulets, signet rings, and nose rings. Elsewhere there is mention of earrings (Gen 35:4, etc.), chains (Gen 41:42, etc.), and beads (Num 31:50). Material remains from Syria and Palestine confirm the textual evidence. Ugarit has yielded earrings of gold and lapis lazuli, and excavators at Megiddo have uncovered headbands, bracelets, and pendants. Other sites have surrendered tassel earrings, rings, necklaces, and headdresses. Often jewelry took the shape symbolic of a particular deity. The moon crescent, sun disk, and star of Ishtar were all popular forms.

Jewelry in the ancient Near East served not only as ornamentation; it had many practical uses. In a time before coinage became widespread, jewelry served as a convenient medium of exchange and a means of storing wealth. It was included in dowries (Gen 24:53) and taken as spoil in battle (2 Chr 20:25). King Hezekiah's treasury is said to have contained precious stones (2 Chr 32:27). Exchanges of money in the OT such as the purchase of Joseph by the Ishmaelites (Gen 37:28) probably entailed the transfer of jewelry along with other forms of precious metals.

Certain types of ornamentation were worn as signs of high office. The priestly attire has already been mentioned. Nobility too had its symbols. Both Joseph (Gen 41:42) and Daniel (Dan 5:29) are awarded gold chains indicative of their political positions. The armlet was perhaps also a royal ornament. It is brought by the Amalekite along with the crown as evidence of King Saul's death (2 Sam 1:1-10). The signet ring was used by people of high standing to authenticate their instructions. Its unique impression verified the source of a document. Such rings are included in the catalog of Isa 3, which no doubt condemns the excesses of the upper class.

Certain items of jewelry were thought to possess magical properties because of their association with deities. Both figurines and symbolic representations of the gods were common. In an age when infant mortality was high and crops failed more often than not, there was naturally an emphasis on fertility deities. Such an emphasis found expression in amuletic jewelry.

Particularly popular were Ashtarte pendants. These might take the form of a fertility goddess with a prominent pubic area or more often the shape of a triangle representing the female genitalia. They could be suspended from a cord around the neck or from a girdle about the waist. In the latter case the pendant would cover the pubic area of its wearer. Such ornamentation, it was thought, would guarantee fertility. These pendants have been discovered at various sites, most notably Ajjul.

Courtesy of the Eisenberg Museum of Biblical Archaeology, Southern Baptist Theological Seminary.

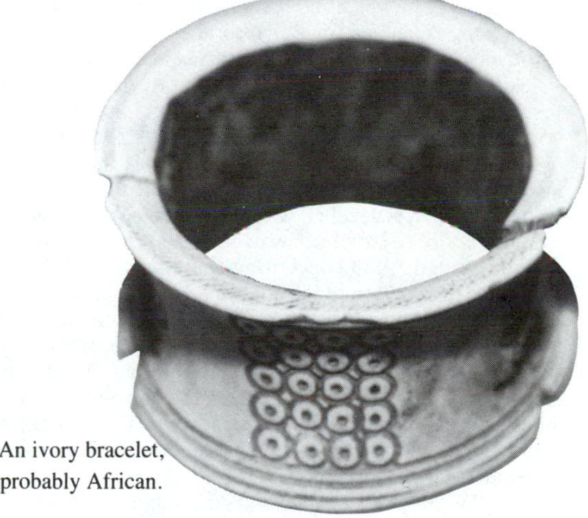

An ivory bracelet, probably African.

Jewelry as such is not condemned in the Bible. The author of the Song of Songs describes the woman bedecked with jewels (1:10, 11) and compares the man to fine jewelry (5:14). The prophet Ezekiel speaks figuratively of how God has adorned Israel with jewelry (16:11, 12). Both men and women are depicted in the Bible as enjoying the use of body ornaments. It is only with excessive use that jewelry is viewed negatively, whether it be the excesses of the idolaters who trust in amulets, the wealthy whose exorbitant jewelry comes at the expense of the poor, or the harlot who adorns herself to ply her trade.

See also DRESS; MAGIC AND DIVINATION; METALLURGY

Bilbiography. G. I. Davies, *Megiddo*; K. R. Maxwell-Hyslop, *Western Asiatic Jewelry c. 3000-612 B.C.*; E. Platt, "Bone Pendants," *BA* 41/1 (March 1978): 23-28, "Jewelry of Bible Times and the Catalog of Isa 3:18-23," *AUSS* 17 (1979): 71-84, 189-202, and "Triangular Jewelry Plaques," *BASOR* 221 (Feb 1976): 103-11; D. Ussishkin, "Lachish: Key to the Israelite Conquest of

Canaan?," *BAR* 13/1 (Jan/Feb 1987): 18-39.

—DAVID H. HART

• **Jews.** [*jooz*] The term for the ethnic-racial descendants of ABRAHAM and adherents of the religion centered on the Mosaic Law; it was used especially by gentiles and/or persons outside of Palestine, and was particularly common beginning in the postexilic period. The term is used in the OT (2 Kings, Zechariah, Jeremiah; extensively in Ezra, Nehemiah, and Daniel). Diaspora Jews, including PHILO, came to use the term, as did JOSEPHUS. It is rarely used in the synoptic Gospels (fifteen times, often in the speech of gentiles), but is frequent in JOHN (sixty-eight times), Acts (seventy-nine times), and Paul's Letters (thirty-five times). In John the term often designates only those Jewish leaders who particularly opposed Jesus (cf. 1 Thess 2:14-16). Paul also used the term for persons of faith in Christ Jesus, even if they were not ethnic Jews (Rom 2:28-29; cf. Rom 9:6-8; 1 Cor 10:18; Rev 2:9; 3:9).

See also ISRAELITE.

—DAVID M. SCHOLER

• **Jezebel.** [jez'uh-bel] Daughter of the Phoenician king Ittobaal, or Ethbaal (1 Kgs 16:31). Jezebel married AHAB, son of Omri, who became king of Israel. Their marriage sealed a treaty in which merchandise from Phoenician trade routes was exchanged for agricultural produce from Israel, and the two countries allied themselves against Aram.

Some scholars doubt the historicity of the account of Jezebel's securing the vineyard of NABOTH for Ahab by suborning witnesses and providing faked legal documents (1 Kgs 21:1-16). This incident, however, is indicative of the conflict between Israelite and Canaanite ideas of kingship and property. Jezebel, who advocated royal privilege, paid lip service to Israelite law even as she perverted it. Elijah confronted Ahab concerning this injustice, and predicted the destruction of his house (1 Kgs 21:21).

Jezebel encouraged the spread of the cult of BAAL (doubtless Melqart, the Tyrian Baal) and his consort, Asherah (= Astarte). The altar Ahab built for Baal and an Asherah in SAMARIA (1 Kgs 16:32-33) likely provided more than just a place of worship for Jezebel or Phoenicians at court. It may have been a state-sponsored cult for Canaanite residents of Israel.

The 850 prophets of Baal and Asherah under Jezebel's patronage (1 Kgs 18:19) may have engaged in propagation of the cult. It is reported that Jezebel killed prophets of Yahweh (1 Kgs 18:4, 13). Elijah, her main antagonist, arranged the slaughter of the prophets of Baal. Jezebel's zeal may have been due to her having grown up in the house of a priest, if JOSEPHUS is correct (*CAp* 1.18).

As Queen Mother, Jezebel exerted influence during the reigns of her sons Ahaziah and Joram (2 Kgs 9:22). She also may have influenced events in Judah under Athaliah, who was evidently raised by Ahab and Jezebel. (The Hebrew text of 2 Kgs 8:26 and 2 Chr 22:2 identifies her as the daughter of Omri whereas 2 Kgs 8:18 and 2 Chr 21:6 call her the daughter of Ahab.)

Jezebel died a violent death around 845 B.C.E. when JEHU and his partisans—at the instigation of ELIJAH—revolted against the rule of Joram. Jezebel met death with dignity. She was thrown from a window, trampled by horses, and eaten (except for her skull, feet, and palms of her hands) by dogs (2 Kgs 9:33-37). This fulfilled the prophecy of Elijah (1 Kgs 21:23).

The name Jezebel, as it has been transmitted in the text of the Hebrew scriptures, may reflect a deliberate distortion of a name meant to honor Baal. If Gray is correct, the original was a cultic cry, "where is the Prince?" The distorted form means "no nobility."

In Rev 2:20 Jezebel is the symbolic name for a false prophet. Her name has come to symbolize evil.

In Jewish tradition Ahab is sometimes exonerated at her expense (*Sanh* 10:2, 28b). According to one tradition, she decorated his chariot with lurid pictures in order to excite her husband (*Sanh* 39b). There is, however, a tradition that whenever Jezebel saw a funeral procession passing, she followed the cortege, joining in the mourning. Likewise, when a wedding procession passed, she would join the celebration. Because of this, the horses that trampled her to death spared her hands and feet.

See also AHAB; BAAL; ELIJAH; IDOLATRY; JEHU; NABOTH.

Bibliography. P. R. Ackroyd, "Goddesses, Women, and Jezebel," *Images of Women in Antiquity,* ed. A. Cameron and A. Kuhrt; L. Bonner, *The Stories of Elijah and Elisha as Polemics against Baal Worship*; S. B. Frost, "Judgment on Jezebel, or a Woman Wronged," *TT* 20 (1964): 503-17.

—WILDA W. (WENDY) MORRIS

• **Jezreel.** [jez'ree-uhl] *1.* A town in Judah, whose location is unknown (Josh 15:56), from which came Ahinoam, one of David's wives (1 Sam 25:43).

2. A son of Etan, a descendant of Judah (1 Chr 4:3), who may be the personification of the town with the same name or its eponymous ancestor.

3. The first son of Hosea (Hos 1:4) named symbolically in anticipation of the judgment to come upon the house of Jehu for the latter's bloodbath at Jezreel (2 Kgs 9:17-26; 10:1-11).

4. A border town in the territory of Issachar (Josh 19:18) identified with the modern village of Zer'in, which is located at the foot of MOUNT GILBOA. Jezreel is listed as one of the towns in the fifth district of Solomon's administration (1 Kgs 4:12), but its importance dates from the time of the Divided Monarchy. Commanding a view of the valley to which it gave its name, the town was strategically located on the main roads between the Mediterranean coast and the Jordan Valley and from Judah to Galilee.

The Israelites encamped there before their battle with the Philistines (1 Sam 29:1, 11) and Ishbaal, Saul's son, controlled it for a brief period before losing Israel to David (2 Sam 2:9). Ahab (ca. 871–852 B.C.E.) had a royal residence in Jezreel (1 Kgs 21:1) beside which was the garden of Naboth; and Joram, Ahab's son, retreated to the town to nurse his wounds received in battle against Hazael of Syria (2 Kgs 8:29). The town was the scene of a major portion of Jehu's bloodbath in which Joram, Jezebel, and many others were murdered and to which the heads of Ahab's seventy sons were sent from Samaria.

5. Valley of Jezreel. Jezreel is the name given to the valley that separates GALILEE from SAMARIA, the western end of which is sometimes called "Esdraelon" (PLATE 56). On its eastern end, it lies between the Hill of Moreh to the north and Mount Gilboa to the south. Drained by the River Jalud in the east, and by the River KISHON in the west, it is one of the most fertile areas of Palestine. It is over forty mi. long and varies in width from less than a mi. to more than six.

The valley is a major corridor through Palestine from Egypt to Asia and from the Mediterranean to the Transjordanian Plateau. This passage has been used by traders and by armies from earliest to most recent times. In the OT period, the Canaanites at first controlled the valley (Josh 17:16), and it was destined to be the scene of many historic battles.

Here, Deborah and Barak defeated the Canaanite forces of Sisera (Judg 4–5), and from Jezreel Gideon routed the coalition of the Midianites and Amalekites (Judg 6:33–7:23). From Jezreel came the news of the deaths of Saul and Jonathan, both of whom had died on nearby Mount Gilboa (2 Sam 4:4; cf. 2 Sam 1:21; 1 Sam 31:1-13). The prophet Hosea places the fitting punishment of Israel here (1:5), and centuries later, Josiah, the young king of Judah, met his death in the Valley of Jezreel close to Megiddo. Finally, this valley became the apocalyptic symbol for the location of the war to end the world (Rev 16:16).

See also ARMAGEDDON.

Bibliography. B. T. Dahlberg and G. W. Van Beek, "Jezreel," *IDB*; G. A. Smith, "Esdraelon," *The Historical Geography of the Holy Land.*

—JOHN C. H. LAUGHLIN

• **Joab.** [joh'ab] Joab, along with Abishai and Asahel, were sons of Zeruiah and nephews of David (1 Sam 26:6). He joined the forces of the fugitive DAVID, and soon became captain of the 600 men who followed David. From this troubled beginning stemmed the eventual establishment of the kingdom of David, a kingdom that rested on the superlative nature of David's leadership and the passion, skill, and wisdom of Joab.

Joab's career reveals a man who dedicated his military prowess to Yahweh (2 Sam 10:12) and to his leader, David. His superb military strategy generally depended upon speed and ingenuity. On one occasion when he was confronted on the one side by the Arameans and on the other side by the Ammonites, he devised a war plan that not only carried the day but led to a COVENANT of peace from the Arameans (2 Sam 10:9-19). It was during this period that David neglected his duty as commander of the forces of ISRAEL and stayed in JERUSALEM. Not only did this make his direction of the army more distant, but David's adultery with BATHSHEBA led to the death of URIAH the Hittite who was exposed to certain death by Joab on the order of David. After ABSALOM had been in exile for several years, Joab sensed that David missed his son greatly. Joab convinced "the wise woman of Tekoa" to serve as an instrument of reconciliation (2 Sam 14:1ff.). Ironically, Absalom's return eventually led to a rebellion that endangered the life and rule of David (2 Sam 15:10). In the battle that decided the fate of that rebellion, Absalom, helplessly hanging from a tree by his long hair, was spied by one of the soldiers. When he told Joab and testified to his unwillingness to slay Absalom, the son of David, the one person David specifically wanted spared, Joab retorted: "I will not waste time like this with you (1 Sam 18:14)." He subsequently went and thrust three darts into Absalom's heart. His ten armor bearers then surrounded Absalom and killed him. On another occasion after he had chased Sheba, who had rebelled against David, to the city of Abel of Bethmaacah, he bargained with a wise woman, who saved her city by surrendering the head of Sheba (2 Sam 20). Joab's opposition to the census of David was the last recorded incident in which he tried to counsel David against an act that might anger Yahweh. David prevailed and suffered some harsh consequences.

Joab possessed an unruly side that eventually led David on his deathbed to instruct Solomon to execute him. After Abner, the former commander of Saul and present commander for Saul's son, ISHBOSHETH (Ishbaal), had secured a covenant with David, Joab met with ABNER and killed him. There can be no doubt that Joab had reason to suspect that Abner was filled with deceit. Besides, Abner had killed Joab's brother, Asahel, in a skirmish when the forces of David were contesting the forces of Ishbosheth (2 Sam 2:23). Yet, David would have no part of the blame for Abner's death and passed the curse on to Joab (2 Sam 3:29), for this son of Zeruiah proved, at times, "too hard" (1 Sam 3:39) for David. Following the death of Absalom and the harsh criticism by Joab of David's ungrateful behavior, David appointed Amasa as his new commander over the army of Israel. However, Amasa in his first assignment as the new commander, i.e., the rebellion of Sheba, delayed in his duties and placed David's kingdom in jeopardy. David then assigned the role to Abishai, Joab's brother. When Amasa finally caught up with the troops, Joab, during a gesture of friendship, killed Amasa (2 Sam 20:9). Finally, Joab was a part of the group that supported the succession of ADONIJAH, the next son in line to the throne of David. Curiously enough, a woman, Bathsheba, who was coached by a man, NATHAN, foiled the plans of Adonijah and set the stage for Joab's demise. Perhaps the feeble David saw his support of Solomon to be a way of asserting his will one last time and clearing away the persons who had served him well, but not always as explicitly as possible. Joab was one of those persons.

The narratives that detail Joab's role in the rise and success of David ultimately display a certain ambivalence on Joab's part toward David. One can be certain that he loved his leader well and served him continuously. There is no indication that he used for his own benefit the incriminating information he possessed. Even his passionate acts, which David condemned, furthered the career of David. Yet, he made a crucial error that cost him his life: he supported Adonijah. However, his life apparently had lost its worth to David long before. If anything, the story of Joab reveals either the genius of David's strategy—playing one over against another—or the selfishness of David's manipulation.

See also ABSALOM; ADONIJAH; DAVID; KINGSHIP.

—RUSSEL I. GREGORY

• **Joanna.** [joh-an'uh] The name Joanna is the feminine equivalent of the name John. According to Luke 8:1-3 Joanna was one of a number of women who, having been healed by Jesus of "evil spirits and infirmities," provided for the disciple band "out of their means." She was the wife of the otherwise unknown Chuza, an official in the service of HEROD Antipas. While his precise office cannot be ascertained, he may have been a high official in Herod's court. According to Luke 24:1-10 Joanna was one of the women who discovered the empty tomb and became one the first heralds of the resurrection as they returned from the tomb and "told all this to the eleven and to all the rest" (Luke 24:9). The fact that Joanna and Chuza are mentioned by name suggests they were well known in the early church and may evidence the existence of disciples among the aristocracy.

—W. HULITT GLOER

• **Joash.** [joh'ash] The name of eight people in the OT, including two kings, one Israelite, the other Judean. (1) The father of GIDEON (Judg 6:11). Joash maintained an altar to BAAL at Ophrah (6:25) but defended Gideon when the latter destroyed it (6:31-32). (2) A son of AHAB, king of Israel (1 Kgs 22:26). The prophet Micaiah ben Imlah was put in prison under Joash's keeping after the former delivered an oracle of doom against Ahab (1 Kgs 22:13-23). (3) A Judean from the house of Shelah (1 Chr 4:22). (4) One of DAVID's mighty men (1 Chr 12:1-3). From Gibeah in Benjamin, Joash was ambidextrous. (5) A Benjaminite from the household of Becher (1 Chr 7:8). (6) A steward in David's household in charge of the stores of oil (1 Chr 27:28).

(7) The eighth king of Judah (2 Kgs 11-12; cf. 2 Chr 22–24). Joash was the son of Ahaziah who was a victim of the purge of JEHU (2 Kgs 9:27-28). Following the death of Ahaziah, his mother Athaliah, the grandmother of Joash, usurped the throne of David. She eliminated the members of her son's family, except for the young Joash who was saved by his aunt, Jehosheba, Ahaziah's half sister. For six years the child, along with his nurse, remained hidden in the temple (2 Kgs 11:1-3). When he was seven years old, JEHOIADA, the priest, after careful planning, crowned Joash king and had Athaliah put to death (11:4-16). Joash is said to have reigned for forty years (ca. 837–797 B.C.E.).

One of Joash's main tasks was to repair the temple. But the effort failed due to the ineffectiveness of the priests in charge of the repairs. To remedy the situation, Jehoiada fixed a special box to collect money to pay for the repairmen. While this action corrected the abuses of the priests, no funds were found with which to replace the temple vessels (2 Kgs 12:4-16). This tradition of the paucity of Temple funds seems contradicted by the last act of the king, which was to pay off HAZAEL, king of Aram, who was poised to attack Jerusalem. Part of the payment is said to have come from the treasuries of the Temple (12:17-18).

Joash met his death at the hands of conspirators; their motives for killing him are not given by the editor(s) of the Books of Kings (12:19-21). There are several significant differences between the accounts of Joash in Kings and in Chronicles (cf. 2 Chr 22:10–24:27). Most scholars believe the Kings account is the more reliable.

(8) The twelfth king of North Israel (2 Kgs 13, 14; 2 Chr 25). According to Kings, Joash became king of Israel in the thirty-seventh year of Joash of Judah and reigned for sixteen years (2 Kgs 13:10; ca. 800–785). His reign is linked to the death of ELISHA and to wars with Aram (cf. 2 Kgs 13:14-19). Specifically, he is said to have defeated Benhadad of Aram three times (13:25). There are considerable historical problems here, but an Assyrian inscription from the time of Adad Nirari III (810–783 B.C.E.), and the Aramaic inscription of Zakir, king of Hamath and La'ash, provide an important broader background from which to understand the biblical text.

The Assyrian text, dated to around 805 B.C.E., records an invasion by Adad-Nirari III into the west that included Israel and Aram. The text claims that Adad defeated the king of Damascus. The Zakir inscription, which is dated to the early part of the eighth century B.C.E., also records a victory by Zakir over "Bar-hadad bar Hazael, king of Aram." This Bar-hadad is almost certainly the Ben-hadad of 2 Kgs 13:24. While the Bible attributes Joash's victories to Yahweh's help (cf. 2 Kgs 13:23), the form of that help would now appear to be the weakening of Aram at the hands of other enemies.

Joash also defeated AMAZIAH, king of Judah (2 Kgs 14:11-14), and destroyed part of the wall of Jerusalem. Under the rule of Joash's son, JEROBOAM II (ca. 785–745), Israel attained its greatest achievements.

Bibliography. J. Pritchard, *ANET*; M. Black, "The Zakir Stele," *Documents From Old Testament Times*, ed. D. W. Thomas; J. M. Miller and J. Hayes, "The Century of the Jehu Dynasty," *A History of Ancient Israel and Judah.*

—JOHN C. H. LAUGHLIN

• **Job.** [johb] The name Job is well attested in the ancient Near East, appearing in Egyptian execration texts, the AMARNA tablets, Ugaritic literature, and documents from MARI and Alalakh. Its meaning seems to be "inveterate foe" or "enemy," presumably as an occupation or in the passive sense. The sixth-century prophet Ezekiel mentions Job in connection with Noah and Daniel, each of whom is remembered as having saved others through his intercession. In all probability, this Daniel, cited by Ezekiel, belongs to Ugaritic legend, as the spelling makes clear (*dn'l* rather than *dny'l*). Therefore, Ezekiel implies that a tradition about three ancient worthies circulated in the Exile, in some ways reminiscent of the seven sages in ancient Sumer.

The prominence of the name throughout the Fertile Crescent and the memory of folk heroes do not suggest that the Job of the Bible was an historical person. Job is a fictional character, the invention of the author of the book, although by name linked to a figure of legendary fame. This statement also applies to Job's children, the three friends, and the interloper, all fictional characters. The tendency of later readers to treat Job as a real person testifies to the realistic presentation of his struggle.

In a sense, two different kinds of Job make their appearance in the book. The first, patient in the midst of cruel treatment, sat for the portrait that the Epistle of James lifts up for exemplary conduct. The second, impatient to the point of blasphemy, is the disputant with Eliphaz, Bildad, Zophar, and God (he does not respond at all to Elihu). The patient Job in the prose account receives God's badge of honor, in addition to earning the same praise from the narrator. This Job has impeccable credentials. He has personal integrity (*tām*), moral uprightness (*yāšār*), religious fervor (*yĕrēʾ ʾĕlōhîm*), and innocence (*sār mērāʿ*). The only chinks in his formidable armor are a suspicion about his children and impatience with his wife's solution to his troubles. In his humble faith, he brought nothing into the world and will return naked to mother earth (or Sheol, if *šāmâ* functions euphemistically). Similarly, the Lord gives and takes away, for both of which the proper response is praise. Small wonder this Job receives God's affectionate title, "my servant," and ends his days in enviable style, surrounded by new children and grandchildren.

The other Job bears little resemblance to this one of pious remembrance. From the outset he curses the day of his birth, the nearest thing to cursing God. Until the end he maintains innocence, with the consequence that God must be guilty. Between these two emotional points Job grows increasingly angry, charging his three friends with ineptness as comforters and accusing God of attacking him viciously and of hiding so that Job cannot achieve vindication. Caught in a quandary of his own making, he undercuts the very premise that allows him to complain about his personal condition. In short, if God lacks justice, as Job claims to be the case, then Job has no basis on which to seek redress for wrongs perpetrated against him. This pitiful creature struggles to achieve vindication in the courts, for he knows he is innocent. His plight evokes fleeting thoughts of a powerful advocate who will force God to face Job in a higher court, and in the end Job pronounces an oath of innocence designed to force the deity to answer. Confident that a sinner cannot stand before the creator, Job dares God to appear.

Job's response to the speeches from the tempest indicates that he understands the implications of the rapturous description of nature and its creatures. Not one word is spoken about human beings, whereas God's excitement over these wild creatures seems boundless. No wonder Job recognizes his smallness and abandons titanic ambitions. God's further exuberance over mythic creatures of chaos, Leviathan and Behemoth, evokes yet another admission of finitude. Astonishingly, Job concedes that his prior knowledge of God came indirectly, as if by rumor, and acknowledges that his present knowledge derives from direct vision, which prompts him to submission of some sort. Does he now reject the serious charges against God's manner of running the universe? Or does he abandon his fruitless effort to force a trial in which the Creator appears as defendant?

The former Job, the pious one, gave rise to a devotional text, *The Testament of Job*. Here the hero possesses magical powers to recognize a disguised Satan and passes these powers along to his daughters. This Job also feeds the hungry and protects the dignity of the poor; he also enjoys the love of a wife who sells her hair to feed her sick husband. The defiant Job probably prompted the warning in Ecc 6:10 against struggling with one who is stronger. This impatient Job has many modern admirers—philosophers, poets, and literary critics.

The biblical Job is probably a non-Israelite, an Arab dwelling in the land of Edom. His friends also represent foreign lands, with the exception of Elihu, who gives voice to traditional Jewish wisdom. The setting for this story about Job appropriately fits the patriarchal period. Although Job's suffering resembles that of Jewish exiles, the reference seems much wider. Job stands for the suffering of extraordinarily virtuous people from every land. He does not represent everyone, however, for few can boast such moral credentials. The religious question posed by this fictional character extends beyond "Why do the innocent suffer?" to an even more penetrating query, "Can religion survive adversity?" The issue of disinterested righteousness, then, is that to which Job lent his name.

See also WISDOM IN THE NEW TESTAMENT; WISDOM IN THE OLD TESTAMENT; WISDOM LITERATURE.

Bibliography. C. Duquoc and C. Floristán, eds., *Job and the Silence of God*; G. Gutiérrez, *On Job: God-Talk and the Suffering of the Innocent*; N. C. Habel, *The Book of Job*; J. G. Janzen, *Job*; M. H. Pope, *Job*; A. de Wilde, *Das Buch Hiob*.

—JAMES L. CRENSHAW

• OUTLINE OF JOB •

The Book of Job

I. Prologue: God Assents to the Testing of Job (1:1–2:13)
II. Job's Lament (3:1-26)
III. Dialogue between Job and His Three Friends (4:1–27:23)
IV. Poem on the Inaccessibility of Wisdom (28:1-28)
V. Job's Oath of Innocence (29:1–31:40)
VI. The Speeches of Elihu (32:1–37:24)
VII. God's Answer to Job from the Whirlwind (38:1–41:34)
VIII. Job's Response and Repentance (42:1-6)
IX. Epilogue: Job Is Vindicated and His Fortunes Are Restored (42:7-17)

• **Job, Book of.** The single word that serves as title to this book in the Hebrew canon is *'yōb*, "enemy." It is a word that provides not only the name of the central character of the book, Job, but also the central theme of Job's relation to GOD. The issue is stated bluntly in 13:24: "Why do you hide your face from me and count me as your enemy (*lĕ'ôyēb*)?" For Job, God seems hidden, painfully absent in a time of crisis and need. It is a response Job understands to be appropriate when directed toward opponents and violators of God's will, but not towards those who, like Job, are "blameless and upright" (cf. 1:9). Thus Job's anguished cry raises the question that the whole of the book that bears his name strains to answer, "Why?" Why do the innocent suffer? And why does God seem absent when they do?

As if to insist that attention not be diverted from this all important theological issue to questions of lesser importance, the Book of Job gives little attention to matters of historical detail. Nowhere is the author of the book or the date of its writing identified. It is often suggested that the author belonged to the intellectual elite of the day, perhaps working out of the same wisdom tradition responsible for such books as PROVERBS and ECCLESIASTES. Despite some rather certain connections with this tradition, however, it is clear that both the themes of Job and the literary styles that carry them cannot be restricted to any one tradition. With respect to date, a postexilic setting is usually recommended, thus suggesting that the kinds of questions Job raises are to be associated primarily with the period following the destruction of Jerusalem in 587/6 B.C.E. when the stablizing institutions of society and religion could no longer support the full weight of theological assumptions. Yet it is clear from extrabiblical texts that the problem of innocent suffering did not emerge for the first time either in the Book of Job or in the land of Israel. Texts from Sumeria, Babylonia, and Egypt, the oldest dating to the beginning of the second millennium B.C.E., suggest that by the time of the writing of Job, considerable attention had been devoted to this most fundamental issue.

The book in its present form consists of five major sections: (1) a prose prologue (1–2); (2) three cycles of dialogue between Job and his friends (3–31); the speeches of Elihu (32–37); (4) Yahweh's speeches (38–42:6); and (5) a prose epilogue (42:7-17). The contrast between the narrative style of the prologue, epilogue, and the poetry that dominates in chaps. 3–42:6, and more importantly, the stark contrast in the portrayal of Job, suggest that different authors and differing perspectives have shaped the individual sections. Even so, despite the different influences at work here, it is the arrangement of these chapters into their present order that produces the message of the Book of Job in its most compelling and troubling form.

Taken together, the prologue and epilogue present Job as an exemplary model of faith. He is introduced as "blameless and upright," a God-fearer, and as one who "turned away from evil" (1:1). This assessment is twice affirmed by God in precisely the same terms (1:8; 2:3), thus making it unequivocally clear that Job's innocence is beyond question. The strength of Job's character is further manifest in his passive and pious acceptance of the horrendous calamities described in these opening chapters. For him there is no mystery in these experiences: "Shall we receive good from God and not evil?" (2:10). The question is raised without doubt about the answer, and whenever any response other than the one modeled by Job is suggested, it is rejected and dismissed immediately (2:9-10). The reward for such faithfulness is restoration and divine blessing (42:10-17).

In the poetic chaps. (3–42:6) the portrayal of Job is quite different. Job's initial response is to curse the day of his birth and to wish for death's relief from his miserable days (3:3). Three cycles of speeches follow (4–14; 15–21; 22–31) in which one by one Job's friends Eliphaz, Bildad, and Zophar offer explanations for Job's suffering. With a variety of approaches the friends each seek to affirm the conventional wisdom, which understands suffering as always linked to punishment for sin. The Elihu speeches (32–37), though usually understood as interpolations, offer similar explanations. All of these explanations Job rejects, protesting repeatedly his innocence (e.g., 6:28-30; 9:21; 10:7; 16:17; 23:10, 12; 27:2-6), and lashing out at his friends for their worthless arguments that turn truth into lie in order to protect God (e.g., 13:4, 7).

Job's primary struggle, however, is not with the friends but with God, who through all of Job's suffering remains silent and distant. Job's quest for God leaves him vulnerable before two contrasting experiences. On the one hand, God seems nowhere to be found. Job moves forward and backward, in this direction and that, but God is absent (e.g., 23:8-9). He cries out, but God does not answer (cf. 19:7; 30:20; 31:35). On the other hand, God's presence is all too real for Job, hunting him like some vicious beast set to ravage its prey (10:16-17; 16:7-15), hemming him in so that he cannot escape and setting nets for his capture (19:8-12). Before this stalking God, Job sees himself as both enemy and victim.

The climax of the drama comes with two speeches from Yahweh (38–39; 40:6–41:34) and accompanying responses from Job (40:1-5; 42:1-6). With the severity and power of hurricane force winds (cf. 38:1; 40:6) God comes, not answering the questions Job had been hurling heavenwards, but with divine interrogations that overwhelm and silence the sufferer. Job can only acknowledge that before this all powerful Creator, he is too small (40:4). Against such a formidable opponent, Job will press his case no further (40:5; 42:6). In neither response is there any admission of guilt, only submission to the unparalleled power and sovereignty of God. The dialogue between creator and creature ends, yet the troubling "Why?" questions with which it all began remain unanswered.

Nevertheless, in its final form the Book of Job offers clear counsel and profound encouragement to those who would dare to follow Job's lead. Job had demanded justice. What he was granted was communion (cf. 42:5-6). It is significant that such an unqualified intimacy with God occurred for Job in the midst of his struggle with suffering. It is the counsel of the epilogue that such intimacy comes only to those who struggle honestly, who risk pressing the outermost boundaries of what tradition recommends as appropriate response to God, who dare question and protest and challenge the sovereign God of the universe. It will be these who can expect a hearing from God (cf. 42:8), not those who know only how to parrot answers without understanding the questions (cf. 42:7).

See also JOB; SATAN IN THE OLD TESTAMENT; SUFFERING IN OLD TESTAMENT.

Bibliography. J. Crenshaw, "Popular Questioning of the Justice of God in Ancient Israel," *ZAW* 82 (1970): 380-95; M. B. Crook, *The Cruel God: Job's Search for the Meaning of Suffering*; R. Davidson, *The Courage to Doubt*; J. Gray, "The Book of Job in the Context of Near Eastern Literature," *ZAW* 82 (1970): 251-69; N. Habel, *Job, OTL*; W. L. Humphreys, *The Tragic Vision and the Hebrew Tradition*; M. Tsevat, "The Meaning of the Book of Job," *HUCA* 37 (1966): 73-106.

—SAMUEL E. BALENTINE

• Job, Targum of. The *Targum of Job* is an ancient ARAMAIC translation of JOB, fragmentary manuscripts of which have been found at Qumran in Caves 4 and 11. The longer and more important of the manuscripts, *11QtgJob*, consists of twenty-seven large fragments, a number of smaller fragments, and a small scroll. The fragments contain portions of Job 17:14–36:33 in twenty-eight columns. The end of the manuscript, still in scroll form, contains parts of Job 37:10–42:11 in ten columns. A single fragment in two columns, *4QtgJob*, contains parts of Job 3:5-9 and 4:16–5:4. In all, about fifteen percent of the text of Job has survived. Although copied by different scribes, both manuscripts date from the first half of the first century C.E. The *Targum* is unrelated to a fifth century C.E. targum by the same name.

The *Targum of Job* seems to be a generally faithful translation of a Hebrew text which was apparently similar to the MT. The date of the translation (as opposed to the date of the manuscripts) is somewhat problematic. Careful study of the Aramaic indicates that it is closely related to, but later than, the Aramaic of DANIEL and earlier than the Aramaic of the GENESIS APOCRYPHON. Assuming a date for Daniel in the first half of the second century B.C.E. and a date for *1QapGen* in the first century B.C.E., scholars have generally dated the *Targum* to the second half of the second century B.C.E. But the Aramaic of Daniel, notoriously difficult to date on linguistic grounds, might be as early as the late sixth century B.C.E. Thus, an alternate date of 250–150 B.C.E. has been suggested for the *Targum*. In any event, the *Targum of Job* is the oldest known targum.

Nothing in the *Targum* suggests that it is a sectarian composition. Its significance therefore does not lie in shedding light on the peculiar doctrines and practices of the ESSENES, other than that they used it. Rather, its importance is fourfold. First, it is a witness to the Hebrew text of Job at a stage prior to the MT. Thus it contributes to a better understanding of the history of the OT text. Second, it is a witness to the early existence and use of Aramaic translations of the OT. Thus it contributes to a better understanding of the origins and history of the targums. Third, it is a witness to a particular stage in the development of Aramaic. Thus it contributes to a better understanding of the history of the Aramaic language. Fourth, it is a witness to a form of Aramaic still used in Palestine in the first century C.E. Thus, it contributes to a better understanding of the language spoken by Jesus.

According to a rabbinic tradition, Rabbi GAMALIEL I (first half of the first century C.E.) condemned a targum of Job. Although certainty is impossible, it may be that Gamaliel was shown a copy of the *Targum* being used in Qumran and rejected it because of its association with the Essenes.

See also DEAD SEA SCROLLS.

Bibliography. J. A. Fitzmyer, "Some Observations on the Targum of Job from Qumran Cave 11," *CBQ* 36 (1974): 503-24; T. Muraoka, "The Aramaic of the Old Targum of Job from Qumran Cave XI," *JJS* 25 (1974): 425-43; M. Sokoloff, *The Targum to Job from Qumran Cave XI*.

—JOSEPH L. TRAFTON

• Job, Testament of. The *Testament of Job* is a retelling, with considerable differences, of the story of JOB, primarily by Job himself. The book takes the form of a testament, that is, a set of final exhortations from an aged father to his children. The story, purportedly told by Job's brother Nereus, begins with Job, ill and desiring to settle his affairs, calling together his seven sons and three daughters. He recounts for them his former wealth and piety; how SATAN had retaliated against him for destroying an idol's temple; the loss of his possessions, children, and health; his wife's subsequent humiliation and eventual death; the coming of the three kings, Eliphas, Baldad, and Sophar, and their interaction with him; Elihu's Satan-inspired insult; and God's response, involving the forgiveness of the three kings, the rejection of Elihu, and the restoration of Job. Job then gives some concluding exhortations and divides his possessions among his sons. To each of his daughters he gives a multicolored cord, a protective amulet of the Father, which changes their hearts and enables them to speak ecstatically in the dialect of angels. Finally, Job's soul is taken away in a heavenly chariot and his body is buried, to the ecstatic blessings of his daughters.

The *Testament of Job* is extant in Greek, Slavonic, and Coptic (in part). Although a semitic original is possible, the strong linguistic affinities between the testament and the SEPTUAGINT version of Job suggest that it was composed in Greek, probably during the first century B.C.E. or C.E. Whether the author was a Jew or a Christian is debated. An ESSENE or, more likely, Egyptian Theraputae milieu has been suggested, and it is possible that the testament was redacted by Montanists at the end of the second century C.E. It may have been known by Tertullian (cf. 20:8-9 and *DePat* 14:5), and it is listed as apocryphal by the so-called Gelasian Decree (sixth century).

The differences between the *Testament* and canonical Job are striking. Satan's attack on Job is seen as retaliation for Job's destruction of an idol's temple. God, in fact, forewarns Job of such eretaliation while promising to restore Job if he endures patiently. Thus, Job's suffering does not surprise him, and his patience never wavers. Also, Job's wealth and concern for the poor are described at length. His wife's humiliation and ultimate consolation receive much attention. The role of Job's three friends is greatly diminished, as is that of Elihu, who speaks for Satan. God's response to Job, so crucial in the canonical Job, is merely alluded to. Finally, the elaborate concern for the multicolored cords and their effect on Job's daughters is unique to the testament, as is the description of Job's death.

Other noteworthy features of the testament include a strong otherworldliness (e.g., 33:3-9; 48–50), a firm hope in the RESURRECTION alongside a body/soul DUALISM (cf. 4:9 and 52:10-11), and a strong interest in women (e.g., female servants and widows, as well as Job's wife and daughters).

See also JOB, BOOK OF; SATAN IN THE OLD TESTAMENT; TESTAMENTS, APOCRYPHAL.

Bibliography. J. J. Collins, "Testaments," *Jewish Writings of the Second Temple Period,* ed. M. E. Stone; R. P. Spittler, "Testament of Job," *The Old Testament Pseudepigrapha,* ed. J. H. Charlesworth; R. Thornhill, "The Testament of Job," *The Apocryphal Old Testament,* ed. H. F. D. Sparks.

—JOSEPH L. TRAFTON

• **Joel.** [joh'uhl] A Hebrew name meaning "Yah(weh) is God." Little is known about the men named Joel. For the most part, the name simply appears in lists found in postexilic collections of tribal genealogies, levitical lists, and lists of civil and military leaders.

1. A descendant of REUBEN and father of Shema (1 Chr 5:4, 8).

2. A descendant of Issachar (1 Chr 7:3).

3. A chief of the tribe of GAD in Bashan (1 Chr 5:12).

4. A levitic ancestor of SAMUEL (1 Chr 6:36).

5. Samuel's elder son, appointed by Samuel as a judge, but rejected by the people for bribery and injustice (1 Sam 8:2). According to Chronicles, he is also the father of Heman, one of the levitical singers appointed by DAVID (1 Chr 6:33; 15:17).

6. The brother of NATHAN and one of David's "mighty men" (1 Chr 11:38).

7. One of the chiefs of the Levites who helped bring the ARK to Jerusalem at the time of David (1 Chr 15:7, 11; also probably 1 Chr 23:8).

8. A Levite in charge of the Temple treasury (1 Chr 26:22).

9. A Benjaminite officer in charge of the half tribe of Manasseh in Gilead (1 Chr 27:20).

10. A prince in the tribe of Simeon at the time of Hezekiah (1 Chr 4:35).

11. A Levite who assisted in the cleansing of the Temple under Hezekiah (2 Chr 29:12).

12. An Israelite whom EZRA required to divorce his foreign wife (Ezra 10:43).

13. A leader in Jerusalem following NEHEMIAH's repopulation of the city (Neh 11:9).

14. The prophet Joel, son of Pethuel (Joel 1:1). The Book of Joel gives no further information about the prophet, although the contents of the book gives clues to his times and character.

See also JOEL, BOOK OF.

—JOANNE KUEMMERLIN-MCLEAN

• OUTLINE OF JOEL •

The Book of Joel

I. A summons to fast and lamentation (1:1-20)
II. The Day of the Lord; the enemy from the North (2:1-11)
III. Summons to repentance (2:12-17)
IV. Promise of restoration (2:18-29)
V. Judgment upon the nations (2:30–3:17)
VI. Restoration for Israel and judgment on enemies (3:18-21)

• **Joel, Book of.** The second book of the minor prophets. Little is known about the prophet Joel other than that he was the "son of Pethuel" (Joel 1:1). Other information about him can only be inferred. References to liturgical actions (lamentation, fasting, solemn assemblies) and use of liturgical forms (laments, calls to worship, blessings) reveal Joel's knowledge of the Temple and its WORSHIP; thus, many scholars believe that Joel may have been a prophet connected with the worship in the Temple at Jerusalem. Joel's vivid description of the locust plague also reveals his knowledge of the land and nature.

The Book of Joel gives no clear historical references. Consequently, scholars have dated it from 835 to 312 B.C.E.; the generally accepted date is from 400–350 B.C.E. Similarly, the book gives no clear indication of its setting. However, the many references to the Temple, Zion, and Jerusalem suggest Jerusalem as the location for Joel's prophecies.

The Book of Joel is divided into two parts: 1:1–2:17 and 2:18–3:21. The first part describes a locust plague and its effects. This section alternates descriptions of the locusts' attack and destruction (1:4, 6-7, 10, 12, 17-20; 2:3-10) with calls to various groups in the community to lament, fast, and repent (1:5, 8-9, 11, 13-14; 2:12-17). Throughout this first part, the significance of the locusts gradually expands; they evolve from a natural disaster to a sign of God's judgment and the coming Day of the Lord (1:15; 2:1-2, 10-11).

The second part of the Book of Joel develops this theme of the Day of the Lord. It describes both the destruction coming to the enemies of God and of God's people and the blessing awaiting the faithful and repentant.

For God's enemies, the Day of the Lord will be a day of gloom and terror; a time when they will be driven away, judged, sold into slavery, and made a desolation (2:20, 30; 3:2-8, 12, 14, 19-20). On this day, God will avenge all the acts they committed against God and against God's innocent people.

For the faithful and repentant, however, the Day of the Lord will be a time of blessing (2:32). Enemies will be driven away; wine, oil, and grain will again be plentiful; and God will be in the midst of the people (2:18-27). The climax of the Day of the Lord will be a new outpouring of God's spirit on all people. Communication between humanity and God will be restored and people will once again prophesy, dream dreams, and see visions.

Classified as one of the minor prophets, the Book of Joel is significant for three reasons. Use of earlier prophetic traditions, such as AMOS's view of natural disasters as God's punishment (Amos 4:6-12) and of the Day of the Lord as a day of darkness and gloom (Amos 5:18-20), and ISAIAH's prophecies about turning swords into plowshares (Isa 2:4, here reversed) show the influence of previous prophetic traditions. Secondly, Joel's use of vivid imagery strongly influences the literary style of the pre-Christian period. Lastly, Joel outlines many basic beliefs of apocalyptic theology: natural disasters as signs of the coming end; separation of the faithful from the enemies of God; a final judgment; and a final era of peace guaranteed by God's presence on earth in the midst of the people.

See also APOCALYPTIC LITERATURE; JUDGMENT, DAY OF; SPIRIT IN THE OLD TESTAMENT.

—JOANNE KUEMMERLIN-MCLEAN

• John the Apostle. This John is one several mentioned in the Bible. He was one of the earliest disciples of Jesus. Considerable knowledge about him may be gleaned from the NT, both by direct reference and by inference. Early Christian tradition supplies more information about him, much of it of questionable value. The following will summarize that evidence.

New Testament Evidence. The apostle John is mentioned by name three times in Matthew, ten in Mark, seven in Luke, nine in the Acts, and once in Galatians, making a total of thirty times. However, when the duplications in the synoptic references are eliminated, the total is reduced to twenty-three. The name does not occur in the Gospel of John except that there are five references to the "disciple whom Jesus loved," assumed by many to be the apostle. In addition, the Apocalypse names a John four times, and tradition has identified him as the apostle. Thus the NT references to John number either 23, 30, 35, or 39, depending upon the assumptions made.

The synoptic Gospels record that John and his brother, JAMES, were the sons of ZEBEDEE and Salome. Since Salome was apparently the sister of Mary, the mother of Jesus, the brothers were first cousins of Jesus. James and John were also partners with Simon Peter in a fishing business in the Sea of Galilee. Mark refers to "hired servants" of Zebedee and his sons, suggesting a family of prominence. Their home was in Capernaum of Galilee, not far from Nazareth, the home of Jesus. Mark further suggests that Salome, with her family's means, was one of those women who ministered to Jesus in Galilee and accompanied him to Jerusalem at the time of his death (Mark 15:41).

James and John, along with Peter and Andrew, were the first of THE TWELVE called by Jesus. Apparently, James, John, and Peter were the closest to Jesus during his ministry, present at the raising of the daughter of Jairus (Mark 5:37), at the transfiguration (Mark 9:2 and par.), and at the agony of Jesus in the Garden of Gethsemane (Mark 14:33 and par.). However, Jesus rebuked the sons of Zebedee when they sought the destruction of a hostile Samaritan village (Luke 9:54), when they forbade an outsider who was casting out demons (Mark 9:38), and when they, or Salome for them, asked that they have the highest rank in the kingdom (Matt 20:20-24; Mark 10:35-41). Jesus may have indicated their impetuosity by calling them "Boanerges, that is, sons of thunder" (Mark 3:17). John and Peter were also sent by Jesus to prepare the Passover feast on the night of the betrayal (Luke 22:8).

In Acts, John appears four times: among the eleven in the upper room following the ascension of Jesus (1:13); in the account of a confrontation with the religious authorities at the Temple, where he and Peter were imprisoned and threatened (3–4); when John was sent with Peter to Samaria to investigate the evangelism of Philip (8:14); and when Herod executed his brother James (12:2).

Paul refers to John along with James and Peter as "pillars" of the church who welcomed his work among the gentiles (Gal 2:9).

The Evidence of Tradition. There are varying references to John in the extant writings of the early Christian centuries. Some of it is hearsay, some contradictory. Eusebius quotes from Papias, Polycrates, Apollonius, and Irenaeus. Earlier traditions are also passed on by Justin Martyr, Irenaeus, Tertullian, the Muratorian Fragment, and Clement of Alexandria. These witnesses are the basis of the belief that John lived in Ephesus after leaving Jerusalem, was banished to Patmos for a period, was released under Nerva (98), and died a natural death in Ephesus during the reign of Trajan (98–117). The same traditions claim that he wrote the Fourth Gospel, the three Epistles of John, and the Apocalypse in later years. The latter claims have been debated for centuries because the internal and external evidence is ambiguous.

See also APOSTLE/APOSTLESHIP; BELOVED DISCIPLE; DISCIPLE/DISCIPLESHIP; JAMES; JOHN, GOSPEL AND LETTERS OF; REVELATION, BOOK OF; TWELVE, THE; ZEBEDEE.

Bibliography. W. F. Howard, *The Fourth Gospel in Recent Criticism and Interpretation*; L. Morris, *Studies in the Fourth Gospel;* R. H. Strachan, *The Fourth Gospel.*

—J. WILLIAM ANGELL

• John the Baptist. According to the NT, John the Baptist was born of priestly lineage (Luke 1:5-7) about the same time as Jesus and lived in the wilderness (Luke 1:80, cf. Mark 1:4). (Some interpreters have understood John's association with the wilderness as evidence that he was affiliated with the Essenes.) According to Luke, he was physically related to Jesus through the kinship of their mothers (Luke 1:36); however, there is no evidence that he knew Jesus prior to their adult lives. According to the Gospel of John, Jesus and John ministered simultaneously for a brief duration (John 3:25-30); the synoptic Gospels, nevertheless, place the public ministry of Jesus after the arrest of John (Mark 1:14; Luke 3:18-23a). John was arrested and eventually executed by Herod ANTIPAS. The Gospels indicate that Herod's motive was to silence the Baptist's preaching against the ruler's sexual immorality (Mark 6:17; Luke 1:19). Josephus states that Herod executed John because he feared that the Baptist's preaching would spark an insurrection.

The message of John the Baptist is summarized in Mark 1:4-8; Luke 3:7-9, 16-17; Matt 3:7-12; and Luke 3:10-14. (The fourth Gospel's summation of John's preaching is overlain with distinct Johannine interpretation.) The following features characterized John's message. First, he preached a radically eschatological message. The judgment of God was coming, which was to be wrathful toward and utterly destructive of the ungodly (Luke 3:7-9, 17). The only way to prepare for the wrath to come was through REPENTANCE, which John understood in the traditional Jewish sense of the total transformation of priorities and values, accompanied by a radical change in lifestyle (Luke 3:8-9). Second, John's message proclaimed a redefinition of the people of God. He utterly rejected the idea that one's physical descent as a Jew would spare one from the wrath of God (Luke 3:8). Only the repentant would be spared from God's judgment. John invited all to such repentance, be they the multitudes, the tax collectors, or even the soldiers (Luke 3:10-14).

Third, John believed that his role was preparatory for the coming of one greater than he (Matt 3:11; Mark 1:7; Luke 3:16; John 1:26-27). Precisely whom John envisioned as this coming one is open to debate. Some have suggested that John was speaking of God himself who was about to come to manifest his judgment and salvation. Others believe that John was looking for a messianic deliverer to serve as God's agent in manifesting the kingdom. If so, there is no evidence that John was looking for a nationalistic redeemer who would bring political liberation from the Romans. The evidence does seem clear that John did not view the man Jesus of Nazareth as this coming one until after Jesus appeared to John to be baptized (Matt 3:13-17; John 1:32-34). Even then, the NT indicates that John was still not certain that Jesus was the one to come, for while the Baptist sat in prison awaiting execution, he sent his disciples to Jesus to ask him concerning this very question (Luke 7:18-23; Matt 11:2-5). Given John's assumptions that the coming one would manifest the righteous wrath of God and bring judgment down upon the enemies of God, it is not surprising that the Baptist had genuine questions about Jesus' status given the latter's inclination to associate with the ungodly and unclean. Nonetheless, this coming one was to be the one to complete the work which John had begun. It would be this coming one who would offer the BAPTISM of both fire and spirit (Luke 3:16). This is probably to be understood to mean that the coming one would manifest the wrathful judgment of God on the unrepentant (fire baptism) and the new life and salvation of God on the repentant (spirit baptism).

The meaning of John's baptism is complex. There is no question that John associated the ritual of immersion with the act of repentance (Mark 1:4; Luke 3:3; cf. Matt 3:6). Given John's Jewish foundations it is possible that the baptism was understood as a ritual bath which washed away the defilement of former sin. Some scholars have noted that gentiles who wished to convert to Judaism were required to undergo such a ritual bath. The fact that John insisted that even Jews participate in a similar ritual is consistent with his message that being a descendant of Abraham was not sufficient for entrance into the Kingdom of God. In the face of the coming judgment, Jews stood on an equal footing with gentiles: the Jews would also face judgment if they did not repent and receive the cleansing bath.

Jesus held John in high regard (Luke 7:24-35; Matt 11:7-19). He submitted to John's baptism (Mark 1:9-11 and par.), indicating that Jesus embraced as his own John's message that the new age which was about to dawn demanded total surrender to the claims of God's righteousness (Matt 3:15). Jesus affirmed that John was a prophet (Luke 7:26), yet more than a prophet, since John came prophesying that the time of eschatological fulfillment was actually coming upon the world (Luke 7:26-27). Jesus' statement that "he who is least in the kingdom of God is greater than [John]" (Luke 7:28b) could be understood to mean that Jesus viewed John as the end of the line of prophets who, though great, paled in significance when compared to the new age of salvation which was dawning. Hence, Jesus, like John, saw the Baptist's role as preparatory.

John's impact continued long after his death. Not only was he consistently given an important preparatory role by succeeding Christian generations, he had followers in his own right. He had disciples during his ministry (Luke 7:18; Mark 2:18; John 3:25-30), and Acts speaks of persons who had submitted to John's baptism throughout the Roman Empire (Acts 18:25; 19:3). In light of such texts as John 1:8, 20, and 3:28-30, many believe that the Gospel of John was written in part to challenge followers of the Baptist who, even in the late first century C.E., believed that John was the final messenger of God. There exists to this day in modern Iraq a religious group which some argue can be traced to followers of the Baptist.

See also ANTIPAS; BAPTISM; DEAD SEA SCROLLS; ELIJAH; ELIZABETH; ESSENES; REPENTANCE; ZECHARIAH.

Bibliography. C. H. Kraeling, *John the Baptist;* T.W. Manson, "John the Baptist," *BJRL* 36 (1954): 395-412; W. Wink, *John the Baptist in the Gospel Tradition.*

—J. BRADLEY CHANCE

• **John, Acts of.** The *Acts of John* is one of a group of writings classified as APOCRYPHAL ACTS, a popular genre which served to entertain the reader through the presentation of the miraculous exploits of prominent figures, in this case the apostle JOHN.

The *Acts of John* was written in Greek in the third century, and almost seventy percent is still preserved in a variety of Greek and Latin manuscripts. Based on the geographical settings within the *Acts,* its probable origin, while not certain, is Asia Minor. Syria also has been proposed as an alternate site of origin. The author is unknown; however, later church fathers ascribed this work, along with the rest of the apocryphal *Acts,* to an author named Leucius Charinus.

The Council of Nicea of 787 rejected the *Acts* as a heretical composition, based on its allegedly Gnostic and docetic tendencies. The docetic character is illustrated whenever John discusses leaning upon the breast of Jesus. John recounts that at times Jesus felt solid and firm while at other times he was soft and immaterial. GNOSTICISM is illustrated in the appearances of the heavenly Christ who helps reveal special knowledge to the uninitiated.

The basic outline of the *Acts* is a brief travel narrative. Most of John's activity takes place in EPHESUS, with a brief trip to SMYRNA and LAODICEA. The legends told of John involve an abundance of miracles, such as raising the dead, healing the sick, reading thoughts, and the destroying of the temple of Artemis at Ephesus. One of the most unusual accounts is John's encounter with bedbugs that interrupt his night's sleep. He responds to this intrusion by commanding the bedbugs to assemble in one single spot until morning. The bedbugs dutifully obey.

The author uses several images and phrases from the canonical Gospels. He presents the image of John leaning on the breast of Jesus, and presents another transfiguration scene attended by himself, Peter, and James. A recurring theme is the designation of LOGOS (Word) for Christ. Jesus is described, just as in the canonical Gospel of John, in metaphorical language as the door, mirror, lamp, and way.

The lack of a martyrdom scene distinguishes this work from most of the apocryphal Acts in which the conclusion focuses on the hero willingly giving up his life. The scene of John's death is peaceful. He simply instructs some men to dig a deep trench, offers up a lengthy prayer concerning his purity from women, and then lies down and dies.

The emphases of the *Acts of John* are within the ascetic tradition. The numerous miracles and the speeches and prayers of John picture the proper relationship of men and women as one of a nonphysical union. The desire for one of the opposite sex is seen as lustful and a proclivity for the things of this world.

See also APOCRYPHAL ACTS.

Bibliography. K. Schäferdiek, "The Acts of John," *New Testament Apocrypha,* ed. E. Hennecke and W. Schneemelcher.

—DAVID M. MAY

• **John, Apocryphon of.** The *Apocryphon of John,* a Coptic Gnostic revelation discourse, is known in long and short recensions. The long form is found in Codices II and IV from NAG HAMMADI; the short form is found in Codex III as well as in a manuscript known as the Berlin Codex. It was apparently widely known in antiquity. Several of the church fathers, particularly Irenaeus, seem to have been familiar with the Gnostic mythology found in this document, if not with the tractate itself. These traditions are thus at least as old as the late second century C.E., but little more can be said about the dating of the book itself. All the manuscripts are in Coptic, though it is assumed to have been composed originally in Greek.

The *Apocryphon of John* tells of the creation, fall, and salvation of humanity through a Gnostic interpretation of the early chapters of Genesis. Some of the themes found here are similar to those in the HYPOSTASIS OF THE ARCHONS and ON THE ORIGIN OF THE WORLD. The slim narrative framework for this apocalyptic discourse is an appearance of the risen Jesus to his disciple John.

As John is pondering in grief, a light shines from heaven, the earth quakes, and a child appears, who is transformed into an old man, identifying himself to John as the incorruptible Father, Mother, and Son. He then proceeds to reveal the heavenly secrets. The supreme being is described as a unity for whom even the word "God" is inadequate. This being produces, as the story begins, a female entity, Barbelo, in answer to whose prayers foreknowledge, incorruptibility, eternal life, and truth come into existence. Christ appears as the firstborn of the invisible Spirit and Barbelo. Twelve powers (aeons) come forth, and Perfect Man comes into being from the will of Christ and the Spirit.

Sophia (Wisdom), last of the twelve aeons, generates on her own a lion-faced serpent, Ialtabaoth, the First Archon, who creates a multitude of powers and angels, to whom he proclaims that he is the only God, a jealous God. Sophia, seeing this, remorsefully repents of having tried to create without the consent of the Spirit.

Hearing a voice from above saying that Man exists, Ialtabaoth sees the Perfect Man's image in the water, and bids all the powers help create in that image a man, whom they will call ADAM. A long passage ensues in which the creation of each part of the body is attributed to some particular ANGEL. The supreme being, through the First Archon's angels, moves Ialtabaoth to breathe breath into the motionless body of the man they created. When he does so, he unwittingly bestows on him a higher wisdom than his own. Adam is then cast down to the lowest region, but the supreme being sends Adam a helper, Zoe (Life), to teach him how to return to his heavenly origins. The archons place Adam in PARADISE where he was to eat of the trees of death and deceit, but Christ induces Adam to eat of the TREE OF KNOWLEDGE (*gnosis*). When John reacts in astonishment, Christ replies that the serpent taught people to eat of the wickedness of sexual activity, birth, and begetting.

Ialtabaoth, in an unsuccessful attempt to gain the divine light that is in Adam, creates a woman from Adam's rib, whom Adam recognizes as his counterimage. The pair is instructed in perfect knowledge. Ialtabaoth throws them out of Paradise, and seduces EVE. Two sons are born, Eloim and Yave. The First Archon thus succeeds in creating sexual desire, thus making salvation more difficult.

John asks if all souls will be saved. Christ replies that those on whom the irresistible Spirit of Life descends will be saved, but not those on whom the opposing spirit descends. Yet he goes on to allow for the eventual salvation even of these, when their power gains more strength than the evil spirit. Souls are not reincarnated. In spite of the Mother-Father's mercy, the spirit of evil came into existence because of the activity of the First Archon. He blinded the creation, and arranged a flood to destroy it, but NOAH and many others escaped by hiding in a luminous cloud (not an ark). The archon's angels raised children by human women, and thus the human race became enslaved, mingling in its nature the divine spirit and the spirit of evil. But finally Christ descended to the realm of darkness to waken humanity and remind them of their origins.

Jesus now tells John that he is returning whence he came, but commands John to write these things and make them known. When Christ disappears, John reports to his fellow disciples.

See also APOCALYPTIC LITERATURE; GNOSTICISM; NAG HAMMADI.

Bibliography. F. T. Fallon, "The Gnostic Apocalypses," *Semeia* 14 (1979): 123-58; S. Giversen, *Apocryphon Johannis*; R. McL. Wilson, *Gnosis and the New Testament*; F. Wisse, "The Apocryphon of John," *The Nag Hammadi Library in English,* ed. J. M. Robinson.

—ROGER A. BULLARD

• **John, Gospel and Letters of.** Called the "spiritual Gospel" by Clement of Alexandria, the Gospel of John has long been recognized as distinctive from the other three (the synoptic) Gospels. It preserves a tradition of Jesus' "signs," words, and crucifixion that seems to be independent of the synoptic Gospels. The Gospel of John has exerted a profound and pervasive influence on Christian theology, especially through its depiction of Jesus as the *logos* (Word) that became flesh.

Both John and the Synoptics give historical accounts of the ministry of Jesus from his baptism through the resurrection appearances, and both provide theological interpretation. Although the sequence in the Gospels varies, in both John and the Synoptics one finds the cleansing of the Tem-

• OUTLINE OF JOHN •

The Gospel of John

I. The Prologue (1:1-18)
II. Jesus before the World (1:19–12:50)
  A. Introduction: the first disciples (1:19–2:11)
  B. The revelation of eternal life: Cana to Cana (2:12–4:54)
  C. Revelation and judgment at the festivals (5:1–10:42)
  D. Withdrawal and return (11:1–12:50)
III. Jesus with His Own (13:1–20:31)
  A. The farewell discourse (13:1–17:26)
  B. The trial of Jesus (18:1–19:16a)
  C. The death of Jesus (19:16b-42)
  D. The resurrection of Jesus (20:1-29)
  E. Conclusion (20:30-31)
IV. Epilogue (21:1-25)
  A. The catch of fish (21:1-14)
  B. The commissioning of Peter (21:15-23)
  C. The postscript (21:24-25)

ple, the feeding of the five thousand and the crossing of the sea, healing miracles, the anointing of Jesus by a woman, the entry into Jerusalem, and similarities in the accounts of the arrest, trials, crucifixion, and discovery of the empty tomb. The differences between John and the Synoptics are equally pronounced. In John the Kingdom of God, which is the major theme of Jesus' teachings in the Synoptics, appears only in John 3:3, 5 and 18:36. In its place, the kingship of Jesus becomes a primary theme of the trial and death of Jesus. In the Synoptics Jesus teaches in pithy sayings and parables; dialogues and long discourses dominate in the Gospel of John, where Jesus sounds more like the author of the Johannine Epistles than the Jesus of the synoptic Gospels. In the Synoptics Jesus spends all but the last week of his ministry in and around Galilee. John probably gives us a more accurate picture of the ministry of Jesus by recording several trips back and forth between Galilee (John 2; 4; 6), Samaria (John 4), and Judea (John 2–3; 5; 7–10; 11ff.). Whereas Jesus heals lepers and casts out demons in the Synoptics, neither lepers nor demons are mentioned in John; and the miracles that are reported are interpreted as signs that point to Jesus' identity as the Son of God. Clearly, John's account provides a different and extraordinarily valuable perspective on the significance of Jesus' life, his teachings, and his death and resurrection.

Authorship of the Gospel. From the latter part of the second century, church tradition has held that the Gospel, Letters, and Revelation were written by the apostle John, who lived to an advanced age in Ephesus. That tradition, however, is suspect on the grounds that the differences among the five writings make it highly unlikely that one person wrote all five, and the fact that the claim of apostolic authority helped the church rescue the Gospel of John from its use by the Gnostics. The author of the Book of Revelation claims the name "John" (1:1, 4, 9; 22:8), but he does not identify himself as an apostle.

Irenaeus, Bishop of Lyons in Gaul (ca. 130–200 C.E.), gives us the following account: "Afterwards, John the disciple of the Lord, who also had leaned upon His breast, did himself publish a gospel during his residence at Ephesus in Asia (*AdvHaer* 3.1.1; cf. Eusebius *EccHist* 5.8.4). Is this John, "the disciple of the Lord," the apostle? In the course of weighing the evidence, Eusebius himself comments at one point: "This confirms the truth of the story of those who said that there were two of the same name in Asia, and that there are two tombs at Ephesus both still called John's" (*EccHist* 3.39.6). At least one of the Johns was probably the author of Revelation, but whether he was the apostle—and what his relationship to the Gospel was—is still debated.

The Gospel itself tells us that it is the testimony of the BELOVED DISCIPLE, but it does not identify the beloved disciple by name. At the end of the Gospel we read that he is the one who has borne witness and written these things; "we" know that his testimony is true; and "I" do not suppose the world could contain the books if everything were written down (21:24-25). From these verses we see the influence of the beloved disciple, a community that accepted his teaching, and an editor who speaks in the first person.

The Gospel scarcely mentions James and John, the sons of Zebedee (21:2), and we hear nothing of the three significant events in the synoptic Gospels at which only Peter, James, and John were present with Jesus: the raising of Jairus's daughter, the transfiguration, and the agony in Gethsemane. The beloved disciple appears only in John 13 and subsequent chapters, and he is known by the high priest in Jerusalem (18:15).

On the basis of the Gospel alone, one might conclude that the beloved disciple was Lazarus, who was from Bethany (so he could have been known by the high priest more easily than a Galilean fisherman), and who is introduced as "he whom you love" (11:3). Because he had been raised from the dead, the Johannine community could easily have thought that the Lord intended that he would not die again (21:23).

Life Setting of the Gospel. The Gospel of John probably originated in a community that had been forced out of the synagogue (9:22; 12:42; 16:2). At first a group of Christian Jews remained within the synagogue, but eventually differences over the observance of the Law and the claim that Jesus was the Christ resulted in their being expelled from the synagogue. They rallied around the beloved disciple, who had been an eyewitness to the ministry of Jesus; and their identity as Christians was defined by their response to his teaching and preaching. In him they saw the Paraclete, the HOLY SPIRIT, at work in their midst.

The evangelist—either the beloved disciple himself or one of his followers—collected the traditions about Jesus, weaving together the signs material, the discourse material, and the passion narrative to form a first edition of the Gospel. The evangelist himself or another member of the Johannine community then enlarged the Gospel in a second or subsequent edition(s) by inserting material such as the prologue, John 15–17, and the references to the beloved disciple. At some point the sequence of chaps. 5 and 6 was reversed, and the cleansing of the Temple was moved to the beginning of the ministry of Jesus so that the raising of Lazarus could serve as the event that triggered Jesus' arrest. The Gospel once concluded at the end of John 20, but an editor added John 21, resolving the question of the roles of Peter and the beloved disciple and giving the Gospel a second ending.

Date of the Gospel. In view of evidence for such an extended process of composition, we can speak only of a date at which the Gospel reached its final form. The Gospel rests on early tradition reaching back to Jesus, but it was composed over a period of decades. Most interpreters conclude that the Gospel was completed by 90–100 C.E. The earliest fragment of a manuscript of the NT contains a few verses from John. Found in Egypt, it is dated between 125–150 C.E.

Life Setting and Date of the Letters. The three Letters were probably written by another member of the Johannine

• OUTLINE OF FIRST JOHN •

The First Letter of John

I. The Prologue: The Word of Life (1:1-4)
II. Light among God's Children (1:5–2:27)
  A. The incompatibility of light and sin (1:5–2:2)
  B. Love as a test of knowledge (2:3-11)
  C. Conflict with the world (2:12-17)
  D. Conflict within the community (2:18-27)
III. Righteousness among God's Children (2:28–4:6)
  A. The hope of the righteous (2:28–3:10)
  B. The love of the righteous (3:11-24)
  C. The two spirits (4:1-6)
IV. Love among God's Children (4:7–5:12)
  A. The true nature of love (4:7-21)
  B. The true nature of faith (5:1-12)
V. The Epilogue (5:13-21)

• OUTLINE OF SECOND JOHN •

The Second Letter of John

I. Greeting: In Truth and Love (1-3)
II. Request: Love Those Who Walk in Truth (4-6)
III. Warning: Do Not Receive Those Who Spread Deception (7-11)
IV. Closing: The Fulfillment of Joy (12-13)

• OUTLINE OF THIRD JOHN •

The Third Letter of John

I. Greetings to a Beloved Brother (1-4)
II. Praise for Gaius's Hospitality (5-8)
III. Criticism of Diotrephes' Defiance (9-10)
IV. Praise for Demetrius's Truthfulness (11-12)
V. Peace for "the Friends" (13-15)

community shortly after or during the late stages of the composition of the Gospel. The three Letters seem to come from a single hand, that of the Elder (2 John 1; 3 John 1), toward the end of the first century or in the opening years of the second century.

First John and 2 John reflect a division within the Johannine community and related churches. First John 2:19 refers to those who "went out from us." Later we read that "many false prophets have gone out into the world" (1 John 4:1). These false prophets may be recognized because they do not confess "Jesus Christ has come in the flesh" (4:2). The primary issue seems to have been the INCARNATION. The false prophets who had gone out from the community did not deny the divinity of the Christ; they denied that the Christ had come in flesh. The Gospel was written "that you may believe that Jesus is the Christ, the Son of God" (John 20:31), but now that confession is no longer sufficient.

The false prophets diminished the significance of Jesus' death and held a thoroughly realized eschatology which denied any future judgment of believers. Because they believed in Jesus as the Christ, they had been born from above. They had crossed from death into life (1 John 3:14), so they had already been raised to eternal life. The judgment is now, in how one responds to Jesus (John 3:19-21), so they were without sin (1 John 1:6, 8, 10; 2:1; 3:9). The Elder also complained that this group had failed to practice love for their fellow Christians (1 John 2:4-10). Perhaps they had refused to share their goods with needy believers (1 John 3:17).

In response, the Elder calls the community back to the affirmation of the incarnation, the command to love one another, the significance of the death of Jesus, and the reality of the resurrection and future judgment.

Literary Form and Primary Themes of the Gospel. The Gospel of John falls naturally into four basic sections. The first chapter constitutes a poetic and prose introduction to the Gospel. Chaps. 2–12 record Jesus' signs and public ministry. Chaps. 13–20 contain the footwashing; the farewell discourses; the prayer of consecration; the arrest, trials, and death of Jesus; the discovery of the empty tomb; and appearances to Mary Magdalene and the disciples.

The prologue introduces Jesus as the *logos*. This concept has deep roots in both Jewish and Greek thought. The opening words echo the first verse in Genesis. The wisdom tradition had identified WISDOM as the one through whom God had created the world (Prov 8:22), and all wisdom was believed to be contained in the law. Wisdom had been personified, so it was a short step to affirm that Jesus was the Wisdom of God that had become flesh. Greek readers would have understood that Jesus was the incarnation of the rational principle of the universe that the Stoics spoke of as the *logos*.

The prologue may have originally been a hymn to the *logos* into which prose sections have been added. John the Baptist is introduced as a witness to Jesus (John 1:6-8, 15), and Jesus' superiority even to Moses is defended (John 1:17). Jesus is the revealer who has revealed the Father. Those who accept him as the revealer have become the "children of God" (John 1:12).

Like the Synoptics, John begins with the baptism of Jesus. John the Baptist's only role is to bear witness to Jesus, and even the baptism of Jesus is reported in John's testimony. Followers of John could not argue, therefore, that John was first and that Jesus was his disciple, so John was the greater.

The changing of water to wine (2:1-11) introduces the ministry of Jesus as the beginning of the new life of the messianic age. Jesus is immediately brought into conflict with the Jewish authorities (2:12-25), so that all of the rest of the Gospel contains elements of a trial narrative.

Nicodemus, a teacher of the Jews, comes to Jesus at night, and Jesus instructs him about the necessity of birth from above (3:1-12). Here we meet a typical Johannine device. Jesus speaks in metaphorical, enigmatic sayings. His dialogue partners do not understand because they seize on the literal meaning of his words, and thereby the evangelist educates the reader to look for the metaphorical or symbolic significance of what Jesus does and what he says.

John 2–4 follows a progression parallel to the early chapters in Acts, as Jesus moves from the Temple to dialogue with a Pharisee, to interaction with a fringe group in the Judean wilderness (John the Baptist), to Samaria, and finally to a royal official (who may have been a gentile). The section begins and ends in Cana of Galilee and develops the theme of Jesus as the bringer of life from above.

The Samaritan woman learns—without any sign, though she has none of the advantages of Nicodemus—that Jesus is the giver of life and that this life is sustained by "living water," which must represent the Spirit of Jesus' revelation of the Father. The relationship between belief and life is then dramatically illustrated by the healing of the royal official's son (4:43-54).

Following the healing of the man at the Pool of Bethesda (5:1-18), the evangelist explains that "the Jews" sought to kill Jesus because he violated the Sabbath and blasphemously claimed that God was his Father. The rest of John 5 reads like a trial scene, as various witnesses are introduced in Jesus' defense.

The feeding of the multitude (John 6) becomes the basis for an extended discourse on Jesus as the bread of life. Jesus reenacts the Exodus experience, feeding the multitude in the wilderness and crossing the sea. But he himself is the bread from heaven, and one must feed on him to sustain the life he gives. This challenge was too much for most of Jesus' followers, however, so they abandon Jesus. Only the twelve are left—and one of them will betray Jesus.

John 7 and 8 present Jesus as the water of life and the light of the world against the background of the FEAST OF TABERNACLES, at which these two symbols were especially significant. These chapters show us an escalating hostility against Jesus. The revelation forces one either to accept Jesus or reject him, and so it sifts all humanity into two camps. The debate with the Jewish authorities reaches its most intense and hostile level in these chapters. Jesus debates with them his identity as the Son of God and their identity as the children of Abraham.

In John 9 Jesus, the light of the world, brings sight to a man born blind. The blind man is an "everyman" figure. We are all born blind and must be given sight. Sin consists not in being born blind but in refusing to see.

The next chapter develops the themes of Jesus as the good shepherd and his followers as those who hear his voice. At the feast of Hanukkah (DEDICATION), Jesus presents himself as the one in whom the glory of God may be seen. Consistently, therefore, Jesus fulfills and replaces the Jewish festivals. He is the reality to which they point.

As a result of the hostility against him, Jesus withdraws from Jerusalem (10:40-42), but he goes back to Judea—knowing that the authorities mean to kill him—in order to raise Lazarus, his friend, from the grave. Jesus, therefore, lays down his life for his friends (see John 15:13-15; 3 John 15). The raising of Lazarus also emphasizes that those who believe in Jesus already have eternal life; it is a quality of life in relationship to God that begins now and continues forever.

Mary anoints Jesus' feet (12:1-8), ironically anointing Jesus as king and preparing for his burial. At the close of chap. 12 Jesus pronounces judgment on the world in a final soliloquy. Because "his own" did not receive him, Jesus turns to those who did believe in his name (1:11-12) in the chapters that follow.

John's account of Jesus' last evening with the disciples is peculiar in that it does not report the giving of the bread and the wine. At the last supper Jesus, knowing that his death was imminent, washed his disciples' feet. The footwashing illustrates the meaning of his death for them and provides a lesson on how they are to relate to one another (13:1-20).

In the farewell discourses Jesus teaches the disciples about the meaning of his death as his return to the Father, the coming of the Paraclete (Holy Spirit), and the persecution they will experience. The original discourse concludes at the end of chapter 14—"rise let us go hence" (14:31). The same themes are treated in the next two chapters. Then Jesus prays for himself, for the disciples, and for those who would believe as a result of their witness (17:1-26). He prays for the sanctity and unity of all who believe in his name.

In the garden there is no agony. Jesus is now supremely in control. The disciples do not abandon Jesus; he lays down his life for them. While Peter is busy denying Jesus, Jesus repeatedly stands by his witness to the truth. Jesus is tried before Annas and Caiaphas, though part of this trial is given earlier (11:47-53), and then he is taken to Pilate. The Roman trial is presented in seven scenes, with the Jews outside—because they will not defile themselves by entering a gentile house—and Jesus inside. Pilate bounces back and forth between the two. Neither will give in, and in the end Pilate hands Jesus over to be crucified and wins from the Jews the confession that they have no king but Caesar. Actually, however, Pilate, not Jesus, has been on trial; and he stands condemned because he refuses to confess what he knows to be true, namely that Jesus was "the king of the Jews."

The crucifixion is for John the exaltation or enthronement of Jesus as king. It is the first step in Jesus' return to the Father. Jesus' identity is heralded in Hebrew, Latin, and Greek: "The King of the Jews." The soldiers divided his garments; Jesus brings his mother and the beloved disciple into a new relationship with one another; he thirsts, and then when he is satisfied that his mission is complete, he lays down his life.

Jesus dies at the time the PASSOVER lambs were slaughtered; he was the true "lamb of God" (cf. 1:29, 36). No bones were broken, but his side was pierced (19:34-37). Joseph of Arimathea and Nicodemus then give him a kingly burial (19:38-42).

On the first day of the week Mary Magdalene finds the tomb open and tells the disciples. Peter and the beloved disciple race to the tomb, and the beloved disciple "saw and believed" (20:8).

Jesus then appears to Mary, to the disciples without Thomas, and a week later to the disciples with Thomas. The risen Lord commissions the disciples and breathes the Holy Spirit on them. Thomas's climactic confession, "My Lord, and my God," is followed by a final beatitude on all who will believe without seeing (20:28-29). A statement that the Gospel was written "that you may believe that Jesus is the Christ, the Son of God, and that believing you may have life in his name" (20:31) provides what may once have been the conclusion of the Gospel.

Chap. 21 reports an appearance of the risen Lord to a group of seven disciples while they were fishing. Following the Lord's instructions the disciples enclose a great catch of fish. Symbolically, Peter draws the untorn net full of fish to the risen Lord, and together they eat a meal of bread and fish around a charcoal fire (cf. 18:18; 21:9). Peter is then challenged to tend the flock. Like the good shepherd, he will lay down his life for the sheep; but the beloved disciple will bear a true witness. An editor's note draws the Gospel to a close again (21:24-25).

Literary Form and Primary Themes of the Letters. First John was written by the Elder to the Johannine community about the threat posed by those who had departed from it. Because 1 John takes up relatively few themes and weaves them together in a spiral fashion, using transitional statements to link paragraphs together, it is difficult to outline. One common pattern highlights the three statements "God is light" (1:5), "He is just" (2:29), and "God is love" (4:8).

Three times in the first chapter we read "if we say" followed by a statement denying sin (1:6, 8, 10). Similarly, three times early in chap. 2 the Elder rejects the claims of those who say they know Jesus but do not follow his commands (2:4, 6, 9). Paradoxically, the Elder later claims that those who have been born from above cannot sin (3:6, 9). Both the Elder and his opponents share the ideal of perfectionism, but the Elder realizes that believers can and do sin.

The opponents claim to be sinless already.

Repeatedly, the Elder exhorts the community to "believe in the name of his Son Jesus Christ and love one another, just as he commanded us" (3:23). Those who do not believe that Jesus has come in flesh (i.e., the incarnation; cf. 4:2) and have gone out from the community (2:19) show that they have violated both of these fundamental commands.

In response to the teachings of these false prophets, the Elder reaffirms the importance of the confession of sin, the death of Jesus, and the future coming of Jesus.

The second Letter seems to have been written to one of a network of churches linked to the Johannine community. In it the Elder warns "the elect lady" and her children of the danger of the false teachers who have gone out from the community. He instructs them not to receive anyone who does not "abide in the doctrine of Christ" (2 John 9-10).

The third Letter concerns difficult relations with another sister church. The challenge of this letter for modern readers is to understand the roles of the Elder, Gaius, Diotrephes, and Demetrius in the affairs that are referred to in passing. Diotrephes seems to have been a leader of the church who has ceased to receive the messengers sent by the Elder. His reasons for this action are open to speculation and debate. Gaius continues to receive messengers, such as Demetrius, who is commended to him.

See also BELOVED DISCIPLE; GNOSTICISM; GOSPELS, CRITICAL STUDY OF; HOLY SPIRIT; INCARNATION; JOHN THE APOSTLE; LOGOS/WORD; REVELATION, BOOK OF.

Bibliography. Surveys of Johannine Scholarship: W. F. Howard, *The Fourth Gospel in Recent Criticism and Interpretation*; R. Kysar, *The Fourth Evangelist and His Gospel: An Examination of Contemporary Scholarship*. Commentaries: C. K. Barrett, *The Gospel According to St. John*; G. R. Beasley-Murray, *John*; R. E. Brown, *The Gospel according to John*; R. Bultmann, *The Gospel of John*; C. H. Dodd, *The Interpretation of the Fourth Gospel*; E. Haenchen, *John*; B. Lindars, *The Gospel of John*; D. M. Smith, *John*; R. Schnackenburg, *The Gospel according to St. John*. Monographs and Articles: R. E. Brown, *The Community of the Beloved Disciple*; O. Cullmann, *The Johannine Circle*; R. A. Culpepper, *The Johannine School* and *Anatomy of the Fourth Gospel: A Study in Literary Design*; P. D. Duke, *Irony in the Fourth Gospel*; R. T. Fortna, *The Gospel of Signs: A Reconstruction of the Narrative Source Underlying the Fourth Gospel*; B. Lindars, *Behind the Fourth Gospel*; J. L. Martyn, *History and Theology in the Fourth Gospel*; J. Painter, *John: Witness and Theologian*; D. M. Smith, *Johannine Christianity: Essays on Its Setting, Sources, and Theology*; J. Staley, *The Print's First Kiss: A Rhetorical Investigation of the Implied Reader in the Fourth Gospel*. The Letters of John: R. E. Brown, *The Epistles of John*; R. A. Culpepper, *1, 2, 3 John*; C. H. Dodd, *The Johannine Epistles*; I. H. Marshall, *The Epistles of John*; S. S. Smalley, *1, 2, 3 John*.

—R. ALAN CULPEPPER

• **Jonadab.** [joh'nuh-dab] Name meaning "Yahweh is liberal"; alternate form—Jehonadab.

The first Jonadab mentioned in the OT is the son of Shimeah, nephew of DAVID, and "friend" of AMNON. Jonadab, who is described as " a very shrewd man" (2 Sam 13:3), sought to help Amnon's depression over Tamar by formulating a clever plan that would provide Amnon with an opportunity to have his way with TAMAR (2 Sam 13:5). Amnon's rape of Tamar eventually incited ABSALOM to avenge his sister. Absalom's slaying of Amnon gave rise to a rumor that the princes who had accompanied Amnon were also killed, but Jonadab informed David that only Amnon had been killed as a result of Absalom's desire to avenge his sister (2 Sam 13:30-32).

Jonadab, the son of Recab, was a zealous Yahwist and the founder of a group who refused to participate in an agriculturally-based life style. Jonadab's well-known "zeal for Yahweh" is indicated by JEHU's desire to have Jonadab witness Jehu's murder of the worshipers of BAAL (2 Kgs 10:15-16, 23). The group that Jonadab founded apparently clung to a pre-sedentary concept of Yahwism in protest to what they perceived to be an accommodation to Canaanite religion. At the instructions of Jonadab, they refused to plant or to own vineyards, drink wine, grow crops, build houses, or live within a city (Jer 35:6-11). JEREMIAH contrasted the group's loyalty to their founder with Judah's continual disobedience to Yahweh (Jer 35:14). The prophet also proclaimed that because of the obedience of Jonadab's followers, Yahweh promised that Jonadab "shall never lack a man to stand before me" (Jer 35:18-19).

See also ABSALOM; AMNON; RECHABITES; TAMAR.

—LLOYD M. BARRÉ

• **Jonah.** [joh'nuh] The name Jonah (Heb. *yônâ*, Gk. *Iōnas*) means dove in Hebrew. Jonah the son of Amittai is briefly mentioned in 2 Kgs 14:25, where he is said to be a native of Gath-Hepher, a village about three mi. northeast of NAZARETH in the territory of Zebulun. Apparently active during the reign of king JEROBOAM II (786–746 B.C.E.), he is often called a nationalistic prophet because his only known oracle predicted the expansion of the northern kingdom "from Lebo-hamath" (north of Damascus in the Valley of Lebanon) "as far as the Sea of the Arabah" (the Dead Sea), and was fulfilled when Jeroboam II recovered these formerly Israelite territories.

Jonah the son of Amittai also appears as the central character in the fifth book of the minor prophets, which bears his name. Here, Jonah is portrayed as a recalcitrant prophet who has memorable adventures on the high seas and inside the belly of a fish before reluctantly prophesying to Nineveh, with surprisingly spectacular results. Most modern scholars regard this as a literary rather than a historical account, suggesting that either some historical tradition about Jonah, or perhaps his known nationalistic fervor, led the later author to choose this prophet as the appropriate vehicle for his marvelous message on the inclusive love of God for all nations.

Jonah appears in the NT in Jesus' reference to the "sign of Jonah" (Matt 12:39-41; 16:4; Luke 11:29-30, 32). This "sign" had a dual significance, serving both to predict Jesus' three day stay in the tomb and consequent resurrection, as well as to condemn the unbelief of "this evil generation" which would not follow the Ninevites' example of repentance.

The apocryphal book of 1 Esdras mentions a Levite named Jonah who was charged by EZRA with having a foreign wife (1 Esdr 9:23). In the parallel text of Ezra 10:23, however, he is called Eliezer.

See also JONAH, BOOK OF.

—TONY W. CARTLEDGE

• **Jonah, Book of.** The Book of Jonah appears canonically in the midst of the minor prophets, but in every other way it stands apart. While other prophetic books focus on speeches of the named prophets, the Book of Jonah concentrates on the prophet's actions, and they are not envia-

• OUTLINE OF JONAH •

The Book of Jonah

I. Jonah's Call, Disobedience, and Punishment (1:1-17)
II. Jonah's Repentance and Deliverance (2:1-10)
III. Jonah's Preaching Mission in Nineveh (3:1-10)
IV. God's Mercy on Nineveh and Rebuke of Jonah (4:1-11)

ble. Jonah's single prophetic speech is limited to five words in the Hebrew text: "Yet forty days and Nineveh will be destroyed!" (3:4).

While the traditional view ascribes authorship to Jonah son of Amittai (2 Kgs 14:25, cf. JONAH) sometime in the eighth century B.C.E., modern scholars generally argue for a later date, citing evidence that Assyria is only a distant memory to the author: Nineveh "*was*" (3:3); the title "King of Nineveh" (3:6) was not used by contemporaries; the legendary size of the city (3:3 implies a diameter of about sixty mi.) does not square with the findings of archaeologists (a *circumference* of only eight mi.). In addition, philological study has revealed a number of words or phrases which show late Hebrew or Aramaic influence. These factors, along with a consideration of the most likely historical situation, make it probable that the book belongs to the late fifth or early fourth centuries B.C.E.

The most common question about Jonah—whether he truly was swallowed by a big fish—is really a part of the larger question of the book's literary type. Those who take it as a historical narrative cite 2 Kgs 14:25 and Jesus' reference to Jonah (Matt 12:39-41 and par.) as evidence, although neither is compelling. Jonah's known nationalistic bent would make him an ideal foil for a later author to use in criticizing postexilic Israel's isolationism, and Jesus' use of a popular story as an illustration implies no more historicity than one would ascribe to the "good Samaritan." One should note that it brings no dishonor to the book to question its historicity in every detail—to honor scripture truly, one should seek to read it as it was intended to be read.

The Book of Jonah has been identified as historical narrative, didactic fiction, mythical allegory, and instructive short story. The story's brevity, tight structure, vivid images, surprise elements, and didactic purpose are most like the features of a parable, while the extreme intolerance of Jonah, which contrasts so sharply with the charitableness of the gentile sailors and the deep contrition of the Ninevites, adds a strong element of satire.

The structure of Jonah falls neatly into two corresponding halves (chaps. 1–2; 3–4). Both sections begin with a chapter in which Jonah is first called to proclaim God's word in Nineveh. Then he comes into contact with gentiles who are incredibly responsive and immediately turn to worship Yahweh (chaps. 1; 3). The second chapter of each section finds Jonah alone and in dialogue with God (chaps. 2; 4).

The story's elements of surprise and contrast are especially notable. When called to go eastward to Nineveh, Jonah embarks on a ship bound for Tarshish, a location as far *west* as was known in ancient times (1:1-3). When God unleashes such a storm that even seasoned sailors panic, Jonah first sleeps (1:4-5), then passively allows himself to be thrown into the sea (1:12-15), which immediately becomes calm (1:15). Jonah is then swallowed by a great fish (1:17), but remains healthy and calm enough to compose a psalm of thanksgiving (2:2-9, often thought to be secondary) before being safely deposited on land three days later. When the call to proclaim Nineveh's destruction is repeated, Jonah reluctantly goes (3:1-3), and does not even reach the heart of the city before the entire metropolis from king to cattle repents in dust and ashes (3:4-9), leading God to have mercy and call off the destruction (3:10). Far from being pleased, Jonah wishes to die because (now we learn!) he really wants these pagans to suffer (4:1-3). After setting up a flimsy booth in which to pout and observe the city, Jonah finds joy in a plant which miraculously grows up in a day (4:5-6), but again he wishes for death when the plant dies just as quickly (4:7-10). God's concluding question (4:11) seems abrupt, but it is in reality, a masterful stroke, vividly contrasting Jonah's bitter and selfish attitude with the compassionate nature of God (cf. Exod 34:6). The book thus opposes any attitude of superiority or exclusiveness on Israel's part, and reminds the nation of God's universal and redemptive love for all peoples.

See also JONAH.

Bibliography. L. C. Allen, *Joel, Obadiah, Jonah, and Micah*; T. Fretheim, *The Message of Jonah*; H. W. Wolff, *Obadiah and Jonah*.

—TONY W. CARTLEDGE

• **Jonathan.** [jon'uh-thuhn] A personal name meaning "Yahweh has given"; alternate form—Jehonathan.

The first Jonathan cited in the OT was the son of Gershom, descendant of MOSES. According to Judg 17–18, Jonathan was a Levite from BETHLEHEM who was taken in by Micah to be his priest (Judg 17:8-13; 18:30). While serving Micah, Jonathan gave a favorable oracle to some Danite spies who were seeking a place to settle. Later, when a Danite war party sought to capture Laish, they took the priestly accouterments from Micah and persuaded Jonathan to join them and to serve as their priest. After securing Laish (renamed Dan) for themselves, they installed Jonathan and his sons as priests of DAN (Judg 18:30).

Jonathan, the son of Saul, is the most familiar biblical character with this name. In 1 Samuel, Jonathan is portrayed as an inspiring and effective leader and as the devoted friend of DAVID. In both of these facets of his character, Jonathan stands in contrast to his father SAUL.

How Jonathan once turned certain defeat into victory is portrayed in the account of Israel's battle with the PHILISTINES at MICHMASH (1 Sam 13:1–14:46). In an act of bravery and faith, Jonathan and his armor bearer defeated a Philistine garrison encamped south of Michmash. When Saul learned that the Philistines were retreating, he mounted an attack that inspired the previously intimidated Israelites to join, resulting in the defeat of the enemy.

The following episode pictures Saul's misguided leadership. During the course of the battle, Saul had unwisely laid an oath upon the people that no one should eat until victory had been won. Jonathan, who was absent when the oath was issued, had eaten some honey for strength. When he later learned of his father's oath, he accused Saul of "troubling the land" (1 Sam 14:29). It was later discovered that Jonathan had violated the oath, and Saul intended to have him executed. But the people intervened and saved Jonathan, insisting that he had won a great victory for Israel and should not be killed (1 Sam 14:45).

Jonathan is also portrayed as one who was deeply devoted to David, his potential rival to the throne. Jonathan once succeeded in reconciling David and Saul (1 Sam 19:1-7). When Saul's wrath against David again emerged, Jonathan agreed to sound out his father's disposition and to warn David if Saul intended him harm (1 Sam 20:1-42). The arrangements were confirmed with a solemn oath of mutual loyalty (1 Sam 20:12-17).

When David learned that Saul and Jonathan had fallen in battle (1 Sam 31:2-4), he expressed his profound grief in the beautiful dirge found in 2 Sam 1:19-27.

A third Jonathan, son of Abiathar, served as a courier of information provided by Hushai, David's spy, during the rebellion of Absalom (2 Sam 15:30-37; 17:17-18). During the rivalry of Adonijah and Solomon for the throne, Jonathan also informed Adonijah and his party that Solomon had been made king (1 Kgs 1:41-48).

Other biblical characters named Jonathan are: David's uncle and counselor and scribe (1 Chr 27:32); the son of Shimei and brother of David, who slew a "giant" at Gath (2 Sam 21:20-21; 1 Chr 20:6-7); the son of Shammah (or Shagee) the Hararite, mentioned as one of David's "Thirty" (2 Sam 23:32; 1 Chr 11:34); the son of Uzziah, who was in charge of David's storehouses (1 Chr 27:25); a scribe whose house served as a prison for Jeremiah (Jer 37:15, 20; 38:26); the father of Ebed (Ezra 8:6); the son of Asahel, who opposed Ezra's proposal to investigate foreign marriages (Ezra 10:15); the head of the clan of Malluchi (Neh 12:14); and the son of Shemaiah (Neh 12:35).

See also DAVID.

—LLOYD M. BARRÉ

• **Joppa.** [jop'uh] Joppa, located in the Plain of Sharon thirty-five mi. from Jerusalem (PLATE 23), was the principal seaport of Jerusalem. Joppa is built on a rock 116 ft. high which projects from the coastline to form a cape. The modern name of Joppa is "Jaffa," and it has been annexed to the southern end of Tel Aviv, the cultural, social, and commercial center of modern Israel.

Joppa is first mentioned in historical records in a list of towns conquered by Thutmose III during his first campaign in the mid-fifteenth century B.C.E. Old Egyptian records speak of the beautiful gardens and productive fruit trees of Joppa. Artisans in Joppa came to be known for their work in leather, wood, and metal.

In biblical times Joppa was in the territory allotted to the tribe of Dan (Josh 19:46). Due to the Philistine invasion, however, Joppa became a major northern city on the Philistine Plain, and the Israelites did not take effective control of the city until the reign of King David. Solomon developed the natural port of Joppa to serve Jerusalem. Many of the cedars from Lebanon used by Solomon to build the Temple came through the port of Joppa (Ezra 3:7). In the book of Jonah, Joppa is the seaport from which Jonah sailed to avoid preaching to the Ninevites (Jonah 1:3).

Though many Israelites returned to Jerusalem after the decree of Cyrus in 538 B.C.E., it is doubtful that Joppa was again controlled by the Israelites. During the fifth century B.C.E. Joppa and Dor were ceded to the king of Sidon. At the destruction of Sidon by Artaxerxes III (ca. 358–338 B.C.E.), Joppa became an independent city.

Joppa, along with the entire coast of Syria, was taken by Alexander the Great on his march from Tyre to Gaza in 332 B.C.E. The citizens of Joppa suffered greatly during the wars of the Diadochi after Alexander's death. The city was finally taken by Ptolemy I after the battle of Ipsus in 301 B.C.E., and it remained in Egyptian hands until 197 B.C.E. when it was brought into the Seleucid kingdom by Antiochus III, the Great.

In 168 B.C.E. Antiochus IV Epiphanes landed in Joppa on his way to plunder the Temple and to enforce his program of Hellenization. Shortly thereafter 200 Jews were drowned after being enticed onto boats in the harbor. Judas Maccabeus fought back by burning the harbor, but he could not take the city. Joppa was later taken by the Jewish high priest Jonathan and his brother Simon and remained under Jewish control for almost a hundred years until Pompey captured Joppa for Rome in 66 B.C.E. The city became the site of a Jewish revolt against Rome which Vespasian stopped by burning the city in 68 C.E. Since then the city has been rebuilt several times.

A Christian community arose in Joppa during NT times. This was where Peter raised Tabitha (Dorcas) from the dead (Acts 9:36-42). Peter also had a vision while in Joppa to go see Cornelius. This incident became the beginning of his ministry to the gentiles (Acts 10; 11:5-17).

—ROBERT RAINWATER

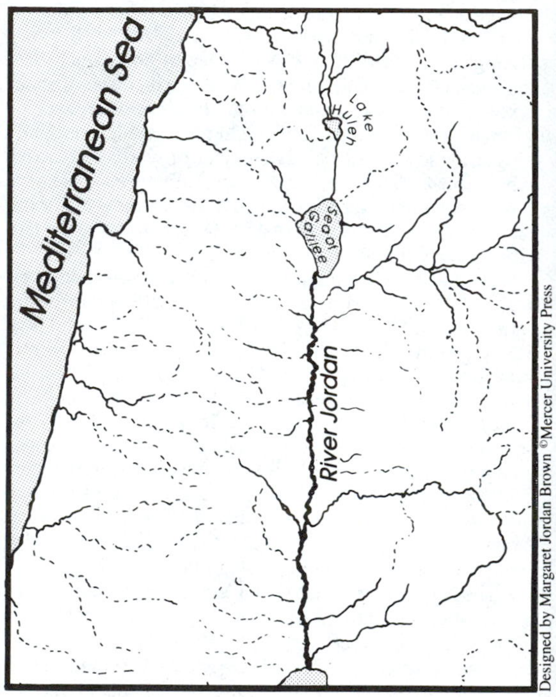

Designed by Margaret Jordan Brown ©Mercer University Press

• **Jordan River/Valley of the Jordan.** The Jordan Valley is part of the Great African Rift, which extends from northern Syria about 3,500 mi. to the Zambesi in southeast Africa. It is situated on a geographical fault caused by the east to west contraction of the limestone crust of the earth during the Eocene era. The plate tectonics produced the steep slopes of the current Jordan Valley.

The Jordan River is the largest and most important river in Palestine, extending from the slopes of Mount Hermon in the north to the DEAD SEA. It is formed from the joining of four rivers that have their point of origin in the Mount Hermon basin, some one thousand ft. above sea level—the Hasbani, the Liddani, the Banyasi (Banias), and the Bareighit rivers. These four rivers merge about seven mi. north of where Lake Huleh used to be, forming the Jordan River proper. By the time the Jordan reaches Lake Huleh, it has fallen to within seven ft. of sea level. In the next ten and one-half mi. it traverses on its way to the SEA OF GALILEE, it falls to 695 ft. below sea level. When it reaches the Dead Sea, it has descended to 1,294 ft. below sea level. While its length from the Sea of Galilee to the Dead Sea is only sixty-five mi., the river's actual course is some 200 mi. as it meanders in contorted loops. The valley itself varies from three to fourteen mi. in width. Since the river descends at a rate of about nine ft. per mi., the current was swift and turbulent, prior to the construction of modern dams on its tributaries, and irrigation projects, which restrict the flow of water. In ancient times, it presented a formidable barrier, as attested in the Book of Joshua (cf. Josh 3:15).

The meaning of the word "Jordan" is debated. The most prevalent explanation for its etymology is that it comes from the Hebrew word *yarad,* meaning "the descender." Others have regarded it to be of Indo-Aryan origin, formed from the words *yor* (year) and *don* (river), signifying the "perennial river." Still others have argued that it may be related to the Arabic root *wrd,* "to come to," denoting the river as a source of water for the surrounding populations.

The OT uses several terms to denote the Jordan River, most frequently "the Jordan" with the definite article. Another termination is "the ARABAH," which denotes the Jordan Valley from the Sea of Galilee to the Dead Sea, but also includes the Wadi el-Arabah that reaches to the gulf of Aqaba. Elsewhere it is called the "jungle" or "pride of the Jordan" (Jer 12:5; Zech 11:3). It is also designated by "the districts of the Jordan" in Josh 22:10-11, and the "valley of Jericho" in Deut 34:3.

The Jordan Valley is a diverse geographical region, which Aharoni divided into five geographical zones: the Huleh Valley; the Sea of Galilee, the Jordan Valley proper, the Dead Sea, and the Arabah. The lower Jordan is further divided into two terraces. The broad, upper terrace is a broken and desolate slope called the *Ghor* (rift). Below this level (as much as 150 feet in some places) is the lush, fertile and narrow flood plain called the *Zor* (thicket).

The climate in the Jordan Valley is diverse. Some parts are a veritable wilderness, while others, particularly the lower Zor region, are decidedly tropical in nature. The valley receives rainfall only between October and March. While the northern part receives about fifteen in. per year, the southern region receives only six in. It is a hot region, with mean summer and winter temperatures of 87 and 58 degrees in the north and 107 and 62 degrees in the south. Near JERICHO, temperatures of 130 degrees have been recorded. However, not all of the Jordan Valley is a hot desert "which devours its people" (cf. Deut 32:22-24). The "Jungle of the Jordan" is a tropical region that abounds in flora and fauna, capable of supporting tamarisks, poplars, and acacias. Until the nineteenth century it was the habitat for lions, ibex, leopards, and boars (cf. Jer 4:7; 5:6; 12:8; Amos 3:4).

In terms of human habitation, the Jordan Valley represents one of the first settled valleys of the ancient Near East. Glueck found more than seventy ancient settlements in the east valley, many of which date from the Early Bronze Age. Since then more than fifty other sites have been discovered in the northern half of the valley, some of which date to the Neolithic and Chalcolithic periods. The earliest evidence for a settled population has been traced to before 70,000 B.C.E. Many of these sites bear witness to advanced cultures, such as the recently discovered temples at Tell Kittan (Early Bronze Age).

In the OT, the Jordan River is best known as the eastern boundary of the promised land. The first mention of the Jordan occurs in the story of Abram and LOT. Upon seeing the lush area of the valley, Lot chose the "whole plain of the Jordan" (Gen 13:10-11). In the CONQUEST account, the Jordan was the first major obstacle for the Israelite tribes. The Bible reports that this formidable obstacle was overcome by means of a miracle or act of providence—the waters of the Jordan stood in a heap at Adam (Josh 3:18). Earthquakes in this region have produced such phenomena on other occasions. On 8 Dec 1267 a landslide blocked the river for ten hours. The same thing reoccurred in 1927 (for twenty-one hours). At other times, the river is passable at the numerous fords which sprinkle the river (fifty-four according to M. Har-El). These fords have played various roles in the subsequent military endeavors of Israel and Judah (cf. Judg 12:3; 1 Sam 11:11; 31:12; 2 Sam 17:22). Elsewhere in the OT the Jordan figures prominently in the miracles of Elijah and Elisha, who divided the Jordan at Jericho (2 Kgs 17:3-5; 2 Kgs 2:13-15).

In the NT, the Jordan plays a significant role in the early chapters of the Gospels. John the Baptist preached and baptized there (Matt 3:5; Mark 1:5; Luke 3:3). There too Jesus received his baptism (Matt 3:13; Mark 1:9-11; Luke 3:21). In later church hymnology, the Jordan symbolizes the rewards of the blessed in the afterlife. As such, the Jordan River carries metaphorical power and spiritual significance for the believing community.

Bibliography. Y. Aharoni, *The Land of the Bible;* E. Eisenberg, "The Temples at El Kittan," *BA* 40 (1977): 77-81; N. Glueck, "Some Biblical Sites in the Jordan Valley," *HUCA* 23 (1951): 105-28 and *The Jordan River;* M. Har-El, "The Pride of the Jordan—The Jungle of the Jordan," *BA* 41 (1978): 65-75; M. Ibrahim, J. Sauer, and K. Yassine, "The East Jordan Valley Survey, 1975," *BASOR* 222 (1976): 41-66; E. Smick, *Archaeology of the Jordan Valley*; E. Yamauchi, "Jordan," *TDOT*.

—DUANE L. CHRISTENSEN

• **Joseph.** [joh'sif] The name Joseph appears in biblical narrative in both the OT and the NT. The Heb. word *yôsēp* may be a derivation from the Hebrew root *ysp* meaning "he adds" (Gen 30:24), or (as explained in Gen 30:23) from *'sp* meaning "take away." The Gk. rendering is *Josēph,* an alternate form being *Josēs.*

Five OT personages bear the name Joseph. The four less prominent include: (1) Joseph the father of Igal, the spy sent by MOSES from the tribe of Issachar to investigate the land of Canaan (Num 24:7); (2) Joseph son of Asaph, set apart by DAVID as one of several musicians (1 Chr 25:2); (3) Joseph son of Binnui, one of many who had taken foreign wives (Ezra 10:42); and (4) Joseph son of Shebaniah, a priest (Neh 12:14).

The fifth and most prominent Joseph in the OT literature is Joseph, the son of JACOB and RACHEL and the main character in Gen 37–50. Joseph was the eleventh of the twelve sons of Jacob and the elder of Rachel's two sons. Born in Paddan-aram, the baby was named *yôsēp*. The explanation in Gen 30 is a play on the Hebrew words *ysp*, add again, and *'sp*, take away. (Yahweh "took away" the barrenness of Rachel and he "added to" her prosperity and happiness.) This indication of divine activity introduces a story highlighted by divine favoritism.

The story begins with a description of seventeen year-old Joseph and of the favorable relationship he has with his father Jacob (Gen 37:3) and the unfavorable relationship with his brothers (Gen 37:4, 8, 11). The jealousy of the brothers, aroused by the paternal favoritism shown in Joseph (Gen 37:3) and deepened by Joseph's dreams foreshadowing a time when the brothers would bow in obedience to him, led them to sell Joseph into slavery to some Midianite traders passing through their fields.

The brothers returned home taking with them Joseph's

coat, which they had dipped in goat's blood, and a report that their brother had been slain by a wild animal. Joseph, meanwhile, was taken down to EGYPT by the Midianite traders who sold him to POTIPHAR, an officer of Pharaoh.

In time Joseph became a trusted servant of Potiphar (Gen 39:2-4) and served the household well until Potiphar's wife, unhappy with her failure to seduce the handsome servant, made false accusations against Joseph and had him imprisoned.

During his imprisonment Joseph gained the trust of the jailer and was given charge over the other prisoners. There he successfully interpreted the dreams of two prisoners, officers of Pharaoh; one of the officers remembered Joseph's ability and two years later Joseph was asked to interpret the dreams of the Pharaoh. The Pharaoh recognized the wisdom of Joseph and appointed him to a rank second only to the king (Gen 41:39-49).

The Pharaoh's dreams were a foreshadowing of a famine that would plague Egypt and surrounding lands. Preparations were made to guard against this tragedy. The famine came as predicted by Joseph's interpretation; his brothers in Canaan also were among the many who were left without food. When Jacob learned of the food supply in Egypt, he sent some of his sons to buy grain. Unknowingly they came before Joseph with their request.

Joseph recognized his brothers but did not reveal his identity to them. He began a test of their character. He accused them of being spies and demanded that they go back to their father and return with their youngest brother. Nine of the brothers were allowed to make this trip, but Simeon was held in prison until they returned (Gen 42:6-25).

Reluctantly Jacob allowed his youngest son, BENJAMIN, to travel to Egypt. Again Joseph tested his brothers, this time accusing them of stealing his wine goblet. This time, however, he did not delay their anguish. Instead, he revealed himself to his brothers, forgave them for past wrongs, and encouraged them to return for their father and come back to dwell with him in Egypt (Gen 44:3–45:15).

As the Joseph story ends, the family is reunited, settled and prospering in GOSHEN. Even after the death of Jacob, the brothers have Joseph's assurance that no harm will come to them (Gen 50:19-21).

The Joseph story in the OT (Gen 37–50) is the longest of the patriarchal stories (Gen 12–36). The narrative unity of Gen 37–50 (with the exception of chap. 38) distinguishes it from the episodic nature of the other patriarchal traditions. The absence of call, promise, and revelation (such as are found in Gen 12:1-3; 26:2-5; 28:13-14) also differentiates this patriarchal narrative.

The Joseph story is considered by some to be a part of the wisdom literature of the OT. G. von Rad suggests that the development of character of Joseph is consonant with some of the didactic writings in such wisdom literature as Proverbs and Job.

Whatever the genre, however, this distinctive narrative is a bridge between the patriarchal traditions in Canaan and the Moses tradition in Egypt.

NT literature also has several men who bear the name Joseph. Two are mentioned as the ancestors of Jesus (Luke 3:24, 30); one is a follower of Jesus called Barsabbas, surnamed Justus, who, along with Matthias, is put forward as a possible replacement for JUDAS (Acts 1:23); a fourth NT Joseph, mentioned in Acts 4:36, is a Levite, surnamed Barnabas, who sold his field and offered his money to the apostles. In Matt 13:55 Joseph, the son of MARY and the brother of JESUS, is introduced (this could be the same person mentioned in Matt 27:56 and in Mark 15:40, 47 as *Joses*).

Joseph of Arimathea figures more prominently than the aforementioned characters. His story appears in Matt 27:57-60, Mark 15:42-46, Luke 23:50-53, and John 19:38-41. A wealthy man and member of the SANHEDRIN, Joseph from Arimathea requested permission from PILATE to remove the body of Jesus after the crucifixion. Having thus obtained permission, Joseph removed the body, enshrouded it in clean linen, and placed it in a new tomb.

The most prominent Joseph in NT literature is Joseph, husband of Mary. The Gospels of Matthew and Luke provide most of the information about this Joseph; John refers to him twice (1:45; 6:42); Mark makes no direct reference to him.

The description of Joseph in the Gospels of Matthew and Luke is almost exclusively limited to the birth/infancy narratives. The differences in these two are illustrative of the intentionality of each writer.

The birth/infancy narrative of Matthew (1–2) begins with a genealogy in which the author carefully traces the lineage of Jesus from ABRAHAM through three sets of fourteen generations. The intentionality of this writer is not a presentation of an historically precise record of lineage; rather the intentionality is a presentation of the guidance of God through history from Abraham to DAVID to Joseph to Jesus.

Joseph is an important character in the birth/infancy narrative of Matthew. The writer of this Gospel presents Joseph as a compassionate and righteous man, unwilling to bring shame to his betrothed (Matt 1:19-24), and willing to marry her even though he discovers that she is about to bear a child. Joseph is an obedient servant of the Lord, open to the guidance and direction provided by dreams and angelic messengers (Matt 1:20; 2:13, 20ff.). This obedient servant takes Mary as his wife, flees Bethlehem to save his family from the wrath of HEROD, and finally settles in NAZARETH.

Joseph is given less emphasis in the Lucan narrative. This more maternal account, though limited in the amount of information presented about Joseph, does provide another view of this NT figure.

As Joseph is mentioned throughout the narrative the emphasis is on his devotion to the Law. He is shown presenting the child, Jesus, for the rites of circumcision and purification (Luke 2:21-27), and making annual pilgrimages to Jerusalem for the Passover (Luke 2:41).

The author of the Lucan narrative provides a genealogy of Jesus in 3:23-38. Unlike the Matthean genealogy, this tracing of the lineage of Jesus is from Jesus to Joseph and all the way back to ADAM. Once again it is important to note that the intentionality is not a presentation of biological descent but of theological descent.

Joseph is not mentioned in any of the NT writings beyond the early portions of the narratives; it is therefore assumed by many that he died prior to the years of Jesus' ministry.

See also JACOB; MARY.

Bibliography. S. Sandmel, *The Hebrew Scriptures, An Introduction to Their Literature and Religious Ideas*; E. Schweizer, *The Good News According to Luke* and *The Good News According to Matthew*; G. von Rad, *Genesis* and "The Joseph Narrative and Ancient Wisdom," in *The Problem of the Hexateuch and Other Essays;* C. Westermann, *Genesis,* trans. D. Green.

—JUDY YATES ELLIS

• **Joseph and Asenath.** [joh'sif, as'uh-nath] *Joseph and Asenath* is a legendary account of how the OT patriarch JO-

SEPH came to marry the Egyptian daughter of Potiphera, the priest of On (Gen 41:45) (the transliteration *Asenath* follows the MT אָסְנַת, as in RSV and most English translations; *Aseneth* follows the Greek of LXX and *JosAsen*, 'Ασεννεθ/'Ασσενεθ). The story opens with the introduction of Asenath, a beautiful, reclusive eighteen-year-old virgin who despises men and devotes herself to the gods of Egypt. Upon learning during the seven years of plenty (Gen 41:47-49) that Joseph intends to visit, her father proposes to Asenath that he give her to Joseph in marriage. Asenath, scornful of Joseph, flatly refuses and retires to her chamber. But after witnessing the arrival of Joseph in all his royal glory, she regrets her decision and prays to the God of Joseph for mercy. Upon being introduced to Joseph, she becomes disheartened when he tells her that there can be no romantic involvement between Jews and pagans. After his departure, Asenath turns away from her gods, repents in sackcloth and ashes for seven days, and confesses her sins to God. God sends an ANGEL, who informs her that her prayers have been answered. Upon his return Joseph is smitten with Asenath, and they are married. Desiring Asenath as his wife, Pharaoh's son plots to kill Joseph. After being spurned by Simeon and Levi, he enlists the aid of Dan, Gad, Naphtali, and Asher. Led by Levi and Benjamin, the other brothers thwart the plot. Asenath intercedes for the offending brothers, who are spared, and the kingship passes to Joseph, who rules for forty-eight years.

JosAsen is extant in a number of ancient languages, including Syriac, Armenian, Latin, Slavonic, Rumanian, and most importantly, Greek. There are several different recensions, the relationship among which is unclear. Beyond an agreement that it was probably composed in Greek, the book's origins are debated. It has been dated from the second century B.C.E. to the fifth century C.E. Asia Minor, Palestine, Syria, and Egypt have been proposed as the place of origin. It has been viewed as a Jewish composition, a Christian composition, or a Christian redaction of a Jewish composition. Attempts have been made to tie it to such groups as the ESSENES and the Therapeutae. It has been seen as a missionary tract and a Hellenistic romance. It may well have been written to aid Hellenistic Jews in understanding the place of Judaism in the larger society.

JosAsen contains a number of striking themes. The centerpiece of the story is the conversion of Asenath, with its related emphasis on repentance, confession of sin, and new birth/eternal life. Connected with this are several references to eating "blessed bread of life," drinking "a blessed cup of immortality," and being anointed with "blessed ointment of incorruptibility" (the Eucharist and baptism?). Also, there is a strange, and lengthy, section involving Asenath, the angel, and a honeycomb. There are numerous parallels to the NT: e.g., not repaying evil for evil (cf. Rom 12:17), being rescued from the lion's mouth (cf. 2 Tim 4:17). Whatever its origins, *JosAsen* became a favorite book throughout Christendom for centuries after its composition.

See also JOSEPH.

Bibliography. C. Burchard, "The Importance of Joseph and Aseneth for the Study of the New Testament," *NTS* 33 (1978): 102-34 and "Joseph and Aseneth," *The Old Testament Pseudepigrapha*, ed. J. H. Charlesworth; D. Cook, "Joseph and Aseneth," *The Apocryphal Old Testament*, ed. H. F. D. Sparks; H. C. Kee, "The Socio-Cultural Setting of Joseph and Aseneth," *NTS* 29 (1983): 394–413.

—JOSEPH L. TRAFTON

• **Joseph, History of.** The *History of Joseph* is a Hellenistic Jewish expansion of the biblical story of JOSEPH. Written in Greek, this work is extant only in fragmentary form, making the date and provenance difficult to establish. Egypt has been suggested as the place of origin.

Although the fragments are difficult to decipher, the surviving portion of the work seems to focus on the narrative of Gen 41:39-42, i.e., from Joseph's rise to power in Egypt through his encounter with his brothers and their return to Jacob, leaving Simeon behind in prison. An interesting aspect of the *History* is the repetition of the phrase "Joseph remembering Jacob," which occurs six times in the extant fragments. It has been suggested that the repetition of this phrase points to a period of persecution or other hardship when it was considered important to remind Greek-speaking Jews of their threatened heritage.

There is a tendency to ascribe to Joseph a more exalted position than is his in the biblical version of the story. He is portrayed as ruler, savior, and provider of food for the Egyptians. The most striking instance of this tendency occurs in the conversation between Jacob and the nine sons who return from Egypt the first time. Here, it seems, Jacob is said to pray to "the God of Joseph," a phrase which clearly serves to elevate Joseph to the status ordinarily reserved for Abraham, Isaac, and Jacob.

See also JOSEPH.

Bibliography. G. T. Zervos, "History of Joseph," *The Old Testament Pseudepigrapha*, ed. J. H. Charlesworth.

—SHARYN E. DOWD

• **Joseph, Prayer of.** The *Prayer of Joseph* is a lost pseudepigraphon extant in only three fragments. The longest fragment is based upon Gen 32:22-31, where JACOB wrestles all night with an unidentified adversary and subsequently is given the name "Israel." In this fragment, narrated by Jacob, the focus is on the identity of the two combatants. Jacob is identified as Israel, an ANGEL of God who descended to earth and tabernacles among people, a ruling spirit, the firstborn of every living thing, the archangel of the power of the Lord, the chief captain among the sons of God, and the first minister before the face of God. His adversary is the angel Uriel, who is envious of Jacob's lofty status. The second fragment, a single sentence, seems to be part of an elaboration of Jacob's blessing of Joseph's sons in Gen 48. The third fragment is apparently a paraphrase of the first. None of the fragments indicate why the title of the book attributes it to JOSEPH.

The three fragments of the *Prayer of Joseph* are preserved in the writings of Origen (third century). According to the stichometry of Nicephorus (ninth century), the book contained eleven hundred lines. Some scholars argue that the document was composed in Greek by a Christian in Egypt during the first or second century C.E.; others suggest that the author was a Palestinian Jew who wrote in Aramaic during the first century C.E. The fragmentary nature of the book makes certainty impossible.

See also MAGICAL PAPYRI.

Bibliography. J. Z. Smith, "Prayer of Joseph," *The Old Testament Pseudepigrapha*, ed. J. H. Charlesworth; "The Prayer of Joseph," *Religions in Antiquity*, ed. J. Neusner.

—JOSEPH L. TRAFTON

• **Josephus.** [joh-see'fuhs] Flavius Josephus was a Jewish historian of the first century C.E. and a major source for our knowledge of Jewish history during the Greco-Roman period. In his autobiography and other writings enough information has been transmitted to piece together a fairly accurate picture of this prophet-historian of the Jews. In 37 C.E. Josephus was born in Jerusalem of a rich and distinguished family. His father, Matthias, had the advantage of belonging to one of the aristocratic priestly families which ran the affairs of Jerusalem and Palestinian Jewry during the Roman occupation. Josephus was endowed with a keen intellect, an amazing memory, a compelling charm, and an ability to adapt to all circumstances of life.

Instead of joining the aristocratic SADDUCEES he threw in his lot with the PHARISEES, but only after he had tried the Sadducees and ESSENES as well. At the age of nineteen he studied with all three religious parties. Apparently he spent more time with the Essenes before finally becoming a Pharisee because he affirmed that he had been a disciple of Bannus for three years. (Bannus was a hermit and so presumably a member of the Essene group.) The writings of Josephus reflect an admiration for the Essenes and their way of life. While he mentions the popularity of the Pharisees, he was also critical toward them.

In 64 C.E. Josephus went to Rome to plead for the liberation of certain priests who had been sent there by FELIX, the procurator, in order to be tried by Nero. Through Alityrus, a Jewish actor, Josephus gained access to Poppaea, Nero's wife, who was sympathetic to Judaism. The mission of Josephus was successful because Poppaea was able to liberate the priests. His visit to Rome fully convinced him of Roman military supremacy and at the same time the futility of his own people's attempt to revolt against the empire.

When Josephus returned to Judea, he was shocked by the state of ferment and unrest in his country. In just a short time the Jews were plunged into a war against the Romans that lasted four years. He was opposed to the revolt of 66 C.E., but there was nothing he could do to restrain the ZEALOTS. In fact he was forced to participate in the rebellion and was named governor of Galilee. Josephus accepted the post in Galilee more as a move to intervene and prevent the war than to confront the Roman forces. Josephus put up a good front for military operations against the Romans by fortifying Tiberias, Taricheae, and Jotapata; however, it was quite evident that his heart was not in the fight.

In the spring of 67 C.E. Josephus, deserted by his army in Galilee, retreated to the fortified town of Jotapata. After a seige of forty-seven days the fortress fell to Vespasian who was in command of over 60,000 troops coming from Ptolemais. The Zealots with Josephus at Jotapata demanded that all Jews commit suicide rather than be taken prisoner. But Josephus and a companion refused to kill themselves. They hid in a cave and later surrendered. They were brought before Vespasian, and Josephus predicted that the Roman general would become the emperor of Rome. This came true two years later. Vespasian had decided to send Josephus to Rome in irons, but after the prediction made in his behalf he changed his mind and allowed Josephus to be an adviser in the war on the Zealots.

In 69 C.E. Vespasian left his son Titus in charge of Roman forces in Palestine and went to Rome to be proclaimed emperor and successor to Nero. Josephus was with Titus at the seige of Jerusalem in 70 C.E. He acted as an interpreter and also advised the Jews to surrender. When the city fell, Josephus was able to save a number of prisoners including his own brother. When Titus went to Rome to participate in the triumph, Josephus accompanied him. Vespasian, now emperor, bestowed many honors on the Jew who had predicted that he would be emperor. He gave Josephus an annual pension, granted him Roman citizenship, and permitted him to use the family name of Flavian as part of his own.

In Rome Josephus devoted himself to studies and literary pursuits. His first literary work, completed about 78 C.E., was *The History of the Jewish War*. It was written in Aramaic and later translated by him into Greek. This history described the sequence of events from the time of Antiochus IV (Epiphanes) in 175 B.C.E. until the conquest and destruction of Jerusalem in 70 C.E. plus the aftermath of the war with the seige of MASADA in 73 C.E. Copies of the history were sent to Vespasian and Titus.

In 93 C.E. Josephus published *Jewish Antiquities,* a history of Israel from the beginning until 70 C.E. The first ten of the twenty books gave an account of the history of Israel found in the OT, from creation to the Babylonian Exile. Very little was recorded about the postexilic period due to lack of sources. His coverage of the Maccabean period was more detailed. Three books of the history were devoted to the reign of HEROD the Great. The last three books gave the reader the reasons for the rebellion of 66-70 C.E. The historical reliability of the document is frequently open to question due to the untrustworthiness of Josephus's sources and his own disposition to exaggerate; however, the work contains important historical data.

Josephus was noted for two other works. One was an *Autobiography*. This was essentially a defense of the action he took in Galilee in the winter of 66–67 C.E. It was also his defense against Justus of Tiberias, who had written a book saying that Josephus was the instigator of the rebellion whereas he in fact opposed it. The other work was an apologetic entitled *Against Apion*. The first book of this apology is written against those Greeks who did not believe Josephus's account of Jewish history. Book two of the document is more especially against the anti-Jewish calumnies of Apion of Alexandria and Apollonius of Molon.

Bibliography. N. Bentwich, *Josephus;* W. R. Farmer, *Maccabees, Zealots, and Josephus*; H. St. J. Thackeray, *Josephus, the Man and the Historian*; W. Whiston, trans., *The Works of Flavius Josephus*.

—T. C. SMITH

• **Joses.** [joh'siz] The name Joses (Gk. JOSEPH) is associated with three individuals in the NT.

1. One of the brothers of Jesus (Mark 6:3; cf. Matt 13:53, "Joseph").

2. The brother of JAMES the Younger, whose mother, Mary, stood by the cross of Jesus and came to his grave (Mark 15:40, 47).

3. The original name of BARNABAS, a co-worker of Paul (Acts 4:36).

See also BARNABAS; JAMES; JOSEPH.

—HERBERT O. EDWARDS, SR.

• **Joshua.** [josh'*yoo*-uh] A personal name derived from the Hebrew verb "to save" (hence meaning: "[The god] Yahu [i.e., Yahweh] delivers"). It was later shortened to Jeshua (from which Jesus is derived) and Hoshea. In its older form, it designates four persons.

1. A man from Bethshemesh in whose field the Ark of God, pulled on a cart by cattle, came to rest after it had been sent away by the Philistines (1 Sam 6:1-16).

2. A governor of Jerusalem at the time of King Josiah (2 Kgs 23:8).

3. A priest at the time of return from Exile (Hag 1:12, 14; Zech 3:1; 6:11).

4. The son of Nun, military successor to Moses, and the major figure in the account of Israel's settlement in the Land of Canaan. He is called Hoshea at Num 13:8 and Deut 32:44.

The son of Nun is first mentioned in connection with military leadership against the Amalekites (Exod 17:8-13), following which he is called MOSES' "servant" who accompanies him part-way up the sacred mountain (24:12-13; 32:17). Thereafter, he also serves in a religious capacity at the Tent of Meeting (33:11) and was one of the leaders chosen to gather intelligence about the "promised land" (Num 13:1-8). Because he and CALEB did not share the pessimism of their contemporaries (Num 14:1-10), they alone were allowed to live to see the promise realized (14:30; 32:12). Thus, Joshua was commissioned as Moses' successor to lead the people across the Jordan (27:18-23; Deut 31:7-9).

The account in the Book of Joshua begins with God's encouragement of Joshua, a rousing speech by the latter to the tribes, and their promise to obey his leadership (chap. 1). Thereafter, descriptions of his activities often seem patterned after those of Moses so as to solidify his role as the latter's successor (e.g., the parting of a body of water, 3:7–4:24; the transcription of "the law of Moses" onto stones, 8:30-35; and a Deuteronomy-like final summary of God's acts and a call to faithfulness, 24:1-28).

After the successful occupation of the Land (chaps. 1–12) and the partitioning of it among the twelve tribes (chaps. 13–22), Joshua died at the ideal age of 110 and was buried on his allocation of property (24:29-30).

In the Pentateuch (Gen–Deut) it is clear that Moses' priestly successor is to be his brother AARON (Exod 28–29, 39–40; Leviticus in its entirety). Such priestly leadership, even in the secular sphere, was actualized in the post-exilic age (sixth century, B.C.E. onward) until the reinstitution of monarchy at the time of the Maccabees (second century). In order to disenfranchize priestly leadership thereafter, it was sometimes taught that it was Joshua who was to transmit cultic materials instead of Aaron (Mishnah, *Pirke Aboth*, 1:1). Such a royal power play, by means of biblical stories, was made possible, in part, by the fact that Joshua had sometimes been portrayed as a royal figure (e.g., God's Spirit rests upon him, Num 27:18; cf. 1 Sam 16:13 concerning David; he leads the people in a covenant ceremony, Josh 24; cf. 2 Sam 5:3 concerning David).

See also JOSHUA, BOOK OF.

—LLOYD R. BAILEY

• **Joshua, Book of.** The sixth book of the Bible, which describes Israel's emergence as a political power in the Land of CANAAN. The title has been assigned by tradition because JOSHUA, the successor of MOSES, is the major actor with whose death the work ends. It does not, therefore, indicate authorship.

The book may be divided into the following thematic sections. (1) The transfer of leadership to JOSHUA (1:1-18). (2) Entry into and conquest of Canaan (2:1–12:24). That the conquest was not total, however, is clear from succeeding chapters and from Judges. (3) Distribution of the land among the tribes (13:1–22:34). (4) Joshua's farewell address (23:1–24:28), death, and burial (24:29-33).

Traditionally, the book has been classified in one of two ways: (1) either by the synagogue as among the former prophets (Joshua–2 Kings), so-called because that body of material reflects the prophetic emphasis upon God's judgment, or (2) by the Christian community as part of the "historical books" (Joshua–Esther), so-called because of their concentration upon happenings in a chronological fashion.

• OUTLINE OF JOSHUA •

The Book of Joshua

I. The Conquest of Canaan (1:1–12:24)
   A. Preparation for invasion (1:1–2:24)
   B. Crossing Jordan and setting up for attack (3:1–5:15)
   C. Campaigns of conquest (6:1–12:24)
II. The Division of the Conquered Land (13:1–22:34)
   A. East of Jordan (13:1-33)
   B. West of Jordan (14:1–19:51)
   C. Cities of refuge (20:1-9)
   D. Cities of the Levites (21:1-45)
   E. Eastern tribes return to their territories (22:1-34)
III. Conclusion (23:1–24:33)
   A. Joshua's farewell (23:1-16)
   B. Covenant renewal at Shechem (24:1-28)
   C. Joshua's death; burial of Joshua and of Joseph's bones (24:29-33)

Modern interpreters have proposed two understandings of its origins. In either case, at some time removed from the events described, individual accounts were gathered, arranged, and supplemented with theological reflection in order to give a sustained and educational portrait of Israel's past. (1) It is the conclusion of the story that begins with Genesis, and thus it depicts the actualization of the deity's oft-repeated promise of land to the descendants of the patriarchs (e.g., Gen 12:7). Thus, the first six books of the Bible (a Hexateuch) have a unity, even if compiled in stages (so von Rad). (2) It is the continuation of the story of Israel's history in the land of Canaan, which begins with Deuteronomy and concludes with 2 Kings. That is, it is part of the once independent "Deuteronomic History" (so Noth).

The second of these alternatives is now usually accepted by interpreters. The historical portrait by the "Deuteronomic Historian," if taken seriously by readers during the exile (587–539 B.C.E.), would give an understanding of why the land was gained and lost, and would perhaps engender hope for the future. The goal of the "History" was not to present a sterile recitation of objective happenings but rather to state the theological facts (from a prophetic and deuteronomic point of view).

The role of the Book of Joshua within the larger "History" would be to stress that the land had been the deity's to grant as a free gift (and thus the deity's to repossess in case of dissatisfaction with the tenants). This theological assertion is bolstered by minimizing details of Israel's warfare in a protracted struggle: the land was transferred to the recipients of the promise with a minimum of effort and in a relatively short time. Likewise, any accommodation with the Canaanite inhabitants is minimized, in order to stress that acceptance of foreign ideas and practices not only led to the exile but also was not to be tolerated after a return to the homeland.

See also CONQUEST OF CANAAN; DEUTERONOMIST/DEUTERONOMISTIC HISTORIAN.

Bibliography. T. Fretheim, *Deuteronomic History*; G. von

Rad, *The Problem of the Hexateuch and Other Essays*; J. A. Soggin, *Joshua*.

—LLOYD R. BAILEY

• **Josiah.** [joh-si'uh] The most highly praised of all the kings of Judah; ascended the throne at eight years of age (2 Kgs 22:1) and had a fruitful reign of thirty-one years (640–609 B.C.E.). He followed the two-year reign of his father Amon who was assassinated by his servants. By necessity or inclination Amon had followed the policy of capitulation to Assyria adopted by MANASSEH his father.

During this time Judah, like most of the ancient Near East, had been under the domination of the then most powerful nation, Assyria. Subservience to Assyria necessitated, in addition to other requirements of vassalage, the symbolic incorporation of Assyrian religious cults. The historian's criticism of such idolatrous religious syncretism was directed toward those who "burned incense to . . . the sun, and the moon, and the constellations, and all the hosts of the heavens" (2 Kgs 23:5).

Winds of change were blowing, however, and a coalition of Medes and Babylonians now represented a major threat to ASSYRIA. Events that were to follow left Assyria's energy and military forces totally absorbed with the defense of its southeastern border. Assyria's imminent defeat made Babylonia the new, if short-lived, master of the region. Confronted with increasing Assyrian weakness, Josiah found the circumstances ripe for the assertion of Judean political independence and religious renewal. Both were inextricably intertwined.

While workmen were "repairing" the TEMPLE, probably an indication of religious reform already begun, HILKIAH the high priest reported the discovery of a lost "book of the law" (2 Kgs 22:8). The validity and authority of this newly-found book of the covenant was authenticated by HULDAH the prophetess. Upon hearing the contents read, most probably the heart of the later canonical book known as DEUTERONOMY, Josiah was moved to embark on the sweeping religious reforms that its message demanded.

Whether an authentic sermon from MOSES to the Israelites before their entry into Canaan, as was supposed, or a work written later to provide the stimulus and authority for such reforms, what is clear is that Josiah's Deuteronomic reformation was radical and all-encompassing. Vestiges of Baalism and Assyrian objects of worship in the very Temple itself were thrown out. Idolatry in all its forms was repudiated and the high places where it was practiced were torn down, not only in Judah but in the territory of the former northern kingdom of Israel as well. He also "broke down the houses of the male cult prostitutes which were in the house of the Lord" (2 Kgs 23:7) and forbade consulting with mediums and wizards. Idolatrous priests were eliminated, worship was centralized in JERUSALEM, a COVENANT renewal ceremony was held, and the long-nelgected observance of PASSOVER was reinstituted.

Josiah's political ambitions both contributed to the religious reform and were enhanced by it. He apparently sensed correctly that Babylonia controlled the future and thereby Judah's fortunes. Pharaoh Necho of Egypt was marching northward to shore up the tottering forces of Assyria's last king, Asshur-Uballit, then engaged in mortal combat against Babylonia. Josiah's motive in marching against Pharaoh Necho is not certain. Clearly a victory would establish hegemony over the region once more. A new David presiding over a newly united Israel might conceivably be the result. In any case, his hopes were dashed by his untimely death in the resultant battle against the Egyptians at MEGIDDO in 609 B.C.E. Judah's last hope for a restoration of the nation to its former greatness died with him.

In evaluating his reign the historian understandably concluded: "Before him there was no king like him . . . nor did any like him arise after him" (2 Kgs 23:25).

See also DEUTERONOMY, BOOK OF; DEUTERONOMIST/DEUTERONOMISTIC HISTORIAN; HILKIAH; HULDAH; PASSOVER.

—BERNARD H. COCHRAN

• **Jotham's Fable.** [joh'thuhm] Jotham's fable (Judg 9:8-15) is a virtually perfect example of this poetic literary device, common in ancient Near Eastern WISDOM. Despite the popularity of fables, especially fables about plants and animals, only a few have been preserved in the OT, perhaps due to their magical and superstitious elements. Less full-blown biblical examples include Jehoash's insult to Amaziah (2 Kgs 14:9), Nathan's story to David (2 Sam 12:1-4), and Ezekiel's fables of the eagle and the lioness (Ezek 17, 19). A widespread form of ancient intellectual activity, fables are not widely used today, perhaps because they utilize the unreal and the fabulous in presenting their truths. SOLOMON, consistent with the Wisdom tradition about him, spoke of "trees" and of "beasts" (1 Kgs 4:33) and so perhaps was a fabulist.

A fable is a form of poetic, didactic narrative using metaphors and symbolic codes in which plants, animals, minerals, seasons, tools, parts of the body, and so forth boast of their greatness and importance. Like parables, many of the elements in a fable lack specifically identifiable meaning, yet usually present a single truth, reality, insight, or moral. Unlike parables, fables cloak the everyday in the fantastic and the unreal. Often in fables the disclosure involves cruelty. Of course, since trees and animals do not really talk, the content of the fable does not literally happen; but the narrative is imaginatively told in order to convey the truth in a forceful way. Fables become didactic when the speaker applies the account to a specific social, political, or biographical situation, thereby giving the fable allegorical features and insuring a correct interpretation.

Jotham's fable is a political satire that probably in its original setting was opposed to all forms of monarchy. The sole survivor of Abimelech's brutal murder of the sons of Jerubbaal (or GIDEON), Jotham jeeringly spoke the fable to Shechem as a warning against Abimelech's tyranny. In spite of Abimelech's violent coup, SHECHEM had made him king. In the fable, the trees are the Shechemites and the useless bramble is ABIMELECH. Seeking a king, the trees approach the olive tree, the fig tree, and the vine—all in vain. Finally, they appeal to the bramble, who alone is willing to be their king but who cruelly promises violence and war (fire). The fable insults both the treacherous Abimelech and the fickle Shechemites. But, in a broader sense, it ridicules the very notion of absolute monarchy.

See also ALLEGORY; KINGSHIP; WISDOM IN THE OLD TESTAMENT; WISDOM LITERATURE.

Bibliography. G. von Rad, *Wisdom in Israel*.

—JACK WEIR

• **Journey Toward Jerusalem.** *See* TRAVEL NARRATIVE

• **Joy.** Pleasure, happiness, or gladness that all people experience generally, but which people of faith experience in distinctive ways. Joy may spring from common human experiences such as a fitting reply (Prov 15:23), harvest time

(Isa 9:3), a marriage (Isa 62:5), the birth of a child (John 16:21), or just an unexpected event (Acts 12:14). But real and enduring joy issues from a proper relationship with God (Pss 4:7; 16:11).

Joy or rejoicing may also belong to the cultic and ritual life of a people. Such was the case in ancient Israel. Just as there was ritual mourning, so there were occasions for rejoicing and displaying joy before God, even when personal feelings might have been anything but joyful. Even so, the OT stresses strongly the delight that the people of Israel were to take in the good life that God had provided them. Rejoicing on the occasions of the major festivals of Passover/Unleavened Bread, Weeks, and Booths was particularly stressed. Here too, it is clear that true joy derives from a proper relationship with God.

The heart of the NT message is that the God of joy came into the world as a human being, JESUS Christ. His birth was announced as "good news of great joy for all people" (Luke 2:8-12). His life was saturated with a joy that he intended his followers to experience fully (John 15:11; 16:24; 17:13). And although his death brought untold sorrow temporarily, his resurrection created joy that endures to the present day (Matt 28:8), perpetuated by his continuing presence with believers through the HOLY SPIRIT (Acts 13:52; Rom 14:17; Gal 5:22; 1 Thess 1:6).

Although people who have God's joy are not exempt from sorrow altogether, they need not be overwhelmed by it. The unhappiness experienced following disobedience has a positive import. It is God's way of turning them back toward a better life and restored happiness (Pss 32:1-5; 51:10-12; 2 Cor 7:8-11). Difficulty, particularly that caused by one's faith, can be endured with gladness following Jesus' example (Heb 12:2), because physical and material losses translate into spiritual gains (Jas 1:2-8; Heb 10:34; Rom 8:18). Even the sorrow produced by death cannot last because believers share in the confidence of resurrection (1 Thess 4:13-18; 1 Pet 1:3-9).

See also DANCING; FEASTS AND FESTIVALS; WORSHIP IN THE OLD TESTAMENT.

—WALTER E. BROWN

• **Jubilee, Year of.** [joo'buh-lee] The year of Jubilee, or "the Jubilee," refers to a special observance of every fiftieth year among the people of Israel. Scriptural references come primarily from Lev 25 and 27, with one other mention in Num 36:4. The year of Jubilee has the literal translation, year of the Ram's Horn. Thus, the occasion received another designation, year of the Trumpet. The ram's horn or trumpet, *yôbel,* was used by the priests for the year of Jubilee and very special occasions (cf. Exod 19:13; Josh 6:5; Isa 27:13). Jubilee became a transliteration of *yôbel.* By contrast *šôpār* indicates the horn used for less significant purposes and by others who were not priests. The appearance of *šôpār* in Lev 25:9 may indicate a later use of the other word for ram's horn.

The time for the year of Jubilee began with "the trumpet sound throughout all your land" on "the tenth day of the seventh month, in the day of atonement" (Lev 25:9). Originally the day of atonement was a day of the new year season in the autumn; later, the new year started in the spring, so that the first month became the seventh month. The year of Jubilee came at the conclusion of "seven weeks of years" or forty-nine years (25:8). Lev 25:10, 11 schedules the observance of the special year after the forty-nine years for each fiftieth year. The pseudepigraphical book of Jubilees, probably written in the second century B.C.E., places the year of Jubilee during the forty-ninth year.

Liberty under the Lord, Yahweh, stands out as the main theme. Lev 25:10 urges Israel to "proclaim liberty throughout the land to all its inhabitants." The theology of the land pivots around the statement of the covenant Lord in Lev 25:23, "the land is mine." A great transition faced the Hebrews as they anticipated moving from Mount Sinai in the wilderness to the land of promise located among the Canaanites.

Every seventh year the land was to receive the benefit of a SABBATH and lie fallow (Lev 25:2-7). Then, in each fiftieth year, the land would not be tilled and planted for a second consecutive year (25:11-12). Everyone had an obligation to live on what the fields and vineyards produced "of themselves" (25:11). The people could not store produce that came from the land during this time. Ownership of land reverted to the original owner without exchange of money or other goods (25:25-55).

Laws pertaining to ownership of persons carried great significance during the year of Jubilee. Slaves would have freedom (25:10). Hebrews could have other Hebrews as servants, but not own them as slaves. The purpose underlying the observance was that reconciliation with the land and the inhabitants would open the way for liberty to become a reality.

Little evidence supports the idea that Israel faithfully observed the year of Jubilee. The people of the land seem to have minimized the observance of the year of Jubilee, which would have been attributed to the widespread unfaithfulness of Israel to the Lord. Consequently, the year with perhaps the greatest potential became obsolete and functioned mainly as a reference for a unit of time for the people of Israel. One should not, however, overlook the symbolic importance of the year of Jubilee as a sign of God's insistence that liberty be proclaimed and observed in the land.

See also CALENDER; FEASTS AND FESTIVALS; LIBERTY; SABBATICAL YEAR.

Bibliography. R. E. Clements, "Leviticus," *BBC*; S. Joenig, "Sabbatical Years and the Year of Jubilee," *JQR* 59 (1969): 222-36; N. Micklem, "Leviticus," *IB*.

—OMER J. HANCOCK, JR.

• **Jubilees, Book of.** [joo'buh-leez] The *Book of Jubilees,* or the *Book of the Divisions of the Times into Their Jubilees and Weeks* (as it was known at Qumran), is an apocryphal account of the things that were revealed to MOSES during his forty days and nights on Mount SINAI (Exod 24:12-18). The narrative begins with a prologue, in which God commands Moses to write a book to assure his descendants that God has not abandoned them despite their transgression of the COVENANT. Then God instructs the angel of the presence to reveal to Moses sacred history, beginning with the creation. The rest of the book contains the angel's revelation, which is drawn from the "heavenly tablets" and which essentially consists of a creative retelling of Gen 1 through Exod 14.

The literary strategies of the author are noteworthy. At times he simply follows the OT text. Other times he deletes material, especially stories which cast the patriarchs in a bad light, such as ABRAHAM identifying SARAH as his sister in the presence of foreign rulers (Gen 12:10-20; 20:2-7). Sometimes he condenses stories, such as the FLOOD (5:20-32; cf. Gen 6:13–8:19). Other times he rewrites them considerably, such as the sacrifice of ISAAC (17:15–18:16; cf. Gen 22:1-18). Typically he adds material: frequently details, such as the identification of Cain's wife as his sister (4:9), often supplementary stories, such as those about Abraham's youth (11:14–12:14), but especially legal material, such as the institution of the FEAST OF WEEKS and the solar calendar after the flood (6:17-38) or the laws of incest (33:10-17). The result is a dramatically rewritten narrative (cf. 1 ENOCH; *1QapGen;* PSEUDO-PHILO) with definite theological tendencies.

The most striking features in *Jubilees* concern the reckoning of time. Two features stand out. First, the contents of the book are dated in terms of JUBILEES—forty-nine-year periods made up of seven "weeks" of years (cf. Lev 25). For example, Eve bears Cain in the third week of the second jubilee and Abel in the fourth. Noah takes a wife in the first year of the fifth week of the twenty-fifth jubilee. The book ends with Moses being informed that forty-nine jubilees, one week, and two years have now passed; after forty more years (i.e., at the close of the fiftieth jubilee), the Israelites will enter Canaan, after which other jubilees will pass before the people and the land are purified permanently. Second, the book commands that all feasts be dated according to the solar CALENDAR of 364 days (divisible by seven) so that they will be held on the same day of the week each year (6:32-35). There is a corresponding polemic against the 354-day lunar calendar, which is not divisible by seven and, hence, changes the feast days from year to year, thus profaning them (6:35-38).

There are other significant theological emphases in *Jubilees*. The author takes pains to root various legal precepts, as well as the major feasts, in the time of the patriarchs, thereby underlining the eternal validity of the LAW. Penalties for breaking certain precepts are particularly severe. There is a strong emphasis on the importance of CIRCUMCISION and the SABBATH, and a definite preeminence given to the priestly tribe of LEVI. There is a highly developed angelology, including a class of angels, the Watchers, who come down to earth and father giants and evil spirits through women (cf. Gen 6:1-4; *1 Enoch* 6–10; Jude 6); the leader of the evil forces is Mastema. There is a sustained polemic against following gentile practices. Although the author frequently mentions the transgressions of the Israelites, little besides his polemic against the lunar calendar suggests a sectarian perspective. To be sure, the author intends for his book to be understood as given by divine revelation, but it is a revelation of the "orthodox" position to which his people will soon return.

Jubilees is extant in Hebrew, Greek, Syriac, and Latin fragments; it is preserved in its entirety only in Ethiopic. It was composed in Hebrew, "the language of creation" (12:26). The Ethiopic is a translation of a Greek rendering of the Hebrew. The presence of fragmentary manuscripts of *Jubilees* at Qumran, the earliest dating from ca. 100 B.C.E. and the direct citation of *Jubilees* in CD 16:2-4 (ca. 100 B.C.E.) attest to its early date. Certain elements in the strong polemic against following the practices of the gentiles suggest the period of Jewish hellenization during the reign of Antiochus IV (3:31; 15:33-34; cf. 1 Macc 1:11-15). Depending on how they understand other apparent historical allusions, scholars place Jubilees either just prior to the Maccabean Revolt (170–165 B.C.E.) or, more likely, right after it (161–140 B.C.E.).

Of special interest is the question of the relationship of *Jubilees* to the Qumran community. The fact that at least twelve copies of *Jubilees* have been recovered from the Qumran caves attests to its popularity there. It is cited as authoritative in the DAMASCUS RULE, is closely related to the GENESIS APOCRYPHON, and has strong parallels with Qumran theology (e.g., priestly supremacy) and practice (e.g., the solar calendar). Yet there are differences: *Jubilees,* for example, does not have the vocal antiestablishment perspective of the sectarian scrolls. Given the probable date of *Jubilees,* it is best to see it as a proto-Essene writing which was produced before the split which led to the formation of the Qumran community. It is noteworthy that *Jubilees* appears to be dependent on certain traditions which have been recorded in *1 Enoch,* parts of which have also been found at Qumran.

Jubilees is an especially important document for understanding Jewish attitudes towards the Law and the calendar in the second century B.C.E., as well as for gaining insights into Jewish methods of biblical interpretation. If it is indeed a proto-Essene work from the Maccabean period, it constitutes an invaluable witness to both the diverse Jewish responses to the issues of the day and the prehistory of the Qumran community.

Bibliography. R. H. Charles, *The Book of Jubilees* and "The Book of Jubilees," *The Apocrypha and Pseudepigrapha of the Old Testament*; G. L. Davenport, *The Eschatology of the Book of Jubilees*; J. C. Endres, *Biblical Interpretation in the Book of Jubilees*; A. Jaubert, "The Calendar of *Jubilees*," *The Date of the Last Supper*; G. W. E. Nickelsburg, "The Bible Rewritten and Expanded," *Jewish Writings of the Second Temple Period,* ed. M. E. Stone; C. Rabin, "Jubilees," *The Apocryphal Old Testament,* ed. H. F. D. Sparks; J. C. VanderKam, *Textual and Historical Studies in the Book of Jubilees*; G. Vermes, "The Book of Jubilees," *The History of the Jewish People in the Age of Jesus Christ,* rev. ed., ed. E. Schürer; O. S. Wintermute, "Jubilees," *The Old Testament Pseudepigrapha,* ed. J. H. Charlesworth.

—JOSEPH L. TRAFTON

• **Judah, Kingdom of.** [*joo'*duh] Judah proper consisted of the southern part of the central Palestinian hill country (Mount Judah) between JERUSALEM and HEBRON from which the tribe living there received its name. The kingdom of "Greater Judah," created by DAVID, was more extensive geographically, including territory southward to BEERSHEBA and westward to include the shephelah, and more extensive ethnographically, incorporating the Calebites, Korahites, Kenizzites, Jerahmeelites, Kenites, and Simeonites. After a stint of service to the PHILISTINES (1 Sam 27), David and his private army moved into Hebron where he was anointed as king over "the house of Judah" (2 Sam 2:1-4a). Although the biblical narrative places this event after the death of SAUL, the chronological references in 2 Sam 2:8-11 suggest that David may have established himself in Hebron while Saul was still alive. "Greater Judah" was no doubt created during David's seven-and-one-half-year rule in Hebron.

When David became king over Saulide territory, Judah became part of greater Israel (2 Sam 5:1-5). With the death of SOLOMON and the secession of the North from the United Kingdom, the Davidic Kingdom again consisted of the state of Judah.

From Rehoboam to Jehoshaphat (ca. 926–878). REHOBOAM not only had to bear the brunt of Solomon's economic and public labor policies but also to suffer the consequences of his own and his advisers' ineptitude in handling the succession to the throne (1 Kgs 12:1-20). After the North rebelled against the policies and ideology of the Davidic family, Rehoboam was able to retain control of only

Judah and apparently a portion of southern BENJAMIN. According to 2 Chronicles, Rehoboam heavily fortified his kingdom (11:5-12) and settled members of the royal family throughout the land (11:23). The location of his fortified cities, scattered throughout his kingdom rather than just at its borders, indicates that they were intended to provide as much for internal security against his own subjects as for external security against invaders. In the fifth year of his reign, the Egyptian pharaoh SHISHAK (Sheshonq) campaigned in Palestine, probably to buttress his authority at home and to insure Egyptian influence in regional trade (1 Kgs 14:25-26). At this time, or perhaps at the death of Solomon, Judah lost control of the seaport at Elath.

Military conflict between Israel and Judah, probably limited border strife, was characteristic of the period from Rehoboam to JEHOSHAPHAT (1 Kgs 14:30; 15:6, 16, 32) and constitutes a major topic of the narrative about Asa (1 Kgs 15:16-22). The latter resorted to paying the Arameans to intervene in the struggle on his behalf.

From Jehoshaphat to Athaliah (ca. 877–840). During the early part of this period, Judah was dominated by Israel ruled at the time by the Omrides who participated in the western anti-Assyrian coalition and shared in the economic well-being this internationalism produced. Jehoshaphat inaugurated a policy of Judean submission to the north (1 Kgs 22:44). Second Chr 17–20 provides an account of Jehoshaphat's activities, which stresses the prosperity of his reign, his military strength and triumphs, and his religious and administrative reforms; no doubt the consequences of cooperation with the Omrides.

JEHORAM, the son of Jehoshaphat, succeeded his father (probably in 852) at a time when an injured Omride, Ahaziah, was ruling in Samaria (2 Kgs 1:2, 17). With the latter's death (probably in 851), Jehoram of Judah apparently ascended the throne in SAMARIA as well. Although the later biblical editors assumed Jehoram to be a brother to Ahaziah, it seems more probable that one and the same Jehoram ruled over both kingdoms (contrast 2 Kgs 3:1; 8:16, 25 with the Hebrew of 1:17). If this was the case, then for a time a Davidic king again ruled over both Israel and Judah. Under Jehoram, Judah lost control over Edom, and even one Judean town (Libnah), for reasons unknown, asserted its independence from Jerusalem (2 Kgs 8:20-22). Jehoram had serious conflict with Aram, now ruled by the aggressive HAZAEL. When Jehoram was wounded in battle against Aram, his son Ahaziah apparently assumed the kingship in Jerusalem (2 Kgs 8:25-29). Both Jehoram and Ahaziah, along with other members of the royal family, were killed in JEHU's coup that brought him to the throne in Samaria (2 Kgs 9:24, 27; 10:12-14).

Judah during the Reign of the House of Jehu. As the new ruler of Israel, Jehu placed his kingdom under the protection of the Assyrians (*ANET*, 281), a move that characterized the international policies of Samaria for over a century or until PEKAH seized the Samarian throne in 734. With the deaths of Jehoram and Ahaziah, Athaliah (839–833) seized the throne in Jerusalem (2 Kgs 11:1), perhaps saving it from Israelite usurpation, and reigned for seven years until she was toppled in a coup led by the high priest JEHOIADA (2 Kgs 11:2-20). Jehoash or JOASH (832–803), a youngster seven years old, was placed on the throne (2 Kgs 11:21). During much of Jehoash's reign, Judah was a vassal to Aram.

Following SHALMANESER III's last western campaign in 838, in his twenty-first year (*ANET*, 280), the Assyrians were not directly involved in Aramean-Palestinian politics for over three decades. During this time, Hazael dominated practically all Aram-Palestine in his "Greater Aram" including Israel and Judah (2 Kgs 10:32-33; 12:17-18; 13:3-7, 22).

Beginning in the fifth year of Adad-Nirari II (810–783), Assyria again became active in the west (*ANET*, 281-82) and the fortunes of Israel and Judah took a turn for the better (2 Kgs 13:4-5, 14-19, 24-25). AMAZIAH (802–786) of Judah won a victory over the Edomites (2 Kgs 14:7) but his efforts to assert independence from Israel led to Judah's defeat by Jehoash of Israel, the seizure and plunder of Jerusalem, the destruction of part of Jerusalem's fortifications, and the capture of Amaziah and probably his being held as a hostage for a time in Samaria (2 Kgs 14:8-14).

Judah under UZZIAH/AZARIAH (785-760) shared in the renewed prosperity characteristic of the early reign of JEROBOAM II, a prosperity consequent upon Assyria's presence in the west (2 Kgs 14:21-28; 2 Chr 26:1-15). After Uzziah was smitten with leprosy, he was replaced on the throne by JOTHAM (759–744) although Uzziah probably lived until late in 734 (cf. Isa 6:1).

The latter part of Jotham's reign witnessed a radical weakening of Judah and the kingdom was placed on the defensive (2 Chr 27). The following factors contributed to this condition. (1) Assyria was torn by internal trouble, plagues, and civil strife, and its authority became inconsequential in the west. (2) A strong anti-Assyrian coalition developed in Aram-Palestine and placed increasing pressure on pro-Assyrian Israel and Judah (Hos 1:4-5; Amos 1:3-15). (3) Jeroboam II was confronted with an anti-Assyrian rival to the throne in the person of Pekah who apparently under Aramean influence led a group in defection from Samaria beginning in 751–750, twenty years prior to his death in 731–730 (note the reference to his twenty-year rule in 2 Kgs 15:27b). Pekah and REZIN not only harassed Israel but Judah as well (2 Kgs 15:37). (4) Many Judean towns threw their support to the anti-Assyrian coalition and thus against Jerusalem (Isa 3:16-4:1; 8:6; Mic 1:8-16).

Judah and the Assyrian Empire. Jotham and his successor AHAZ (743–728) continued to support the pro-Assyrian policies of Samaria during the reigns of MENAHEM (746–737) and PEKAHIAH (736–735). When Pekah seized the throne in Samaria in 734, Ahaz refused to follow the new Israelite monarch in supporting the anti-Assyrian coalition. Ahaz asserted Judean independence from Israel (Isa 9:2) and Rezin and Pekah moved to depose Ahaz, exterminate the Davidic family (2 Kgs 16:5; Isa 7:3-6), and bring Judah completely into the anti-Assyrian coalition, a policy favored by most Judeans (Isa 8:6). The appearance of TIGLATH-PILESER and the Assyrian army in the west late in 734 or early in 733 rescued Ahaz and Jerusalem.

The kingdom of Judah remained pro-Assyrian and avoided any involvement in the rebellions against Assyria in the 720s during which Samaria was captured, part of its population deported, and the region incorporated into the Assyrian empire (2 Kgs 17:1-6; 18:1-12). At the beginning of his reign, the new Assyrian king SARGON II (721–705) instituted a policy of cooperation with the Egyptian Delta princes in opposition to the Ethiopians in Upper Egypt. HEZEKIAH (727–699), as a cooperative pro-Assyrian, seems to have profited from this arrangement (cf. 1 Chr 4:39-43; Isa 19:16-25).

During the Ashdod revolt (ca. 714–711), Judah became involved in anti-Assyrian activity (*ANET*, 289) much to the chagrin and opposition of Isaiah (Isa 20; 22). Apparently, Hezekiah's illness in his fourteenth year (2 Kgs

18:13; 20:6) coincided with this revolt and leadership fell to the monarch's subordinates, Shebna and Eliakim (Isa 22:15-25).

In 705, following Sargon's violent death on the battlefield in Anatolia, Hezekiah, supported by Isaiah (Isa 24–27), helped lead a revolt against Assyria. This revolt was planned in advance with the cooperation of the Ethiopian (twenty-fifth) Dynasty which had gained dominance over the Delta in about 712. Hezekiah's religious reform and efforts to centralize Yahwistic religion in Jerusalem (2 Kgs 18:4; 19:22; Isa 27:9) were probably carried out to avoid the defection of Judean cities which had plagued Ahaz. The reform policies of Hezekiah were probably embodied in the earliest form of the book of DEUTERONOMY, which either served as the basis of his reform or was written down as a summation of his program. The anti-Assyrian revolt, however, was a failure. The western powers were defeated, Hezekiah had to pay special tribute, and Judean territory was reduced (*ANET* 287-88; 2 Kgs 18:13-16), although Jerusalem was not taken nor Hezekiah forced to abdicate.

Hezekiah was succeeded by his young son MANASSEH who reigned for fifty-five years (698–644). Judean policy returned to one of submission to Assyria and the Deuteronomic policy of religious centralization in Jerusalem was reversed. The editors of the Kings material on Manasseh (2 Kgs 21:1-18) depict him as one of the worst of Judah's monarchs because of his reversal of Hezekiah's policies and his religious programs contrary to Deuteronomy. Assyrian texts (*ANET* 291, 294) indicate Manasseh's participation in projects carried out by ESARHADDON (680–669) and his support of, if not presence on, an invasion of Egypt by ASHURBANIPAL (668–627) to expel the Ethiopians (664–663). With the expulsion of the Ethiopians from Lower Egypt and the establishment of the Twenty-sixth Dynasty in Egypt, renewed cooperation between Assyria and the Delta Egyptians ensued.

Manasseh's successor, AMON (643–642), was assassinated by some of his officials after only a two-year rule (2 Kgs 21:19-26). His assassination was probably motivated by an anti-Assyrian movement in Judah at a time when several Transjordanian kingdoms and Tyre were in revolt (*ANET* 297-98). The coup was suppressed by the people of the land who placed the eight-year old JOSIAH on the throne.

Judah as an Egyptian Vassal. Josiah (640–610) was able to carry out a major reform of Judean/Jerusalemite religion in his eighteenth year, and thus became a great hero to the editors of Kings (2 Kgs 23:4-14, 21-23). It is doubtful whether he was able to exercise much political freedom and territorial expansion except to incorporate the territory around BETHEL into his kingdom (2 Kgs 23:15-18). During his reign, Egypt and Assyria shared control over Palestine and the lower eastern Mediterranean seaboard (cf. Jer 2:16-18, 36-37). Egypt had become more dominant in the eastern Mediterranean seaboard as Ashurbanipal had become more involved elsewhere. The Babylonian Chronicles indicate that the Egyptians were fighting against the Babylonians in Mesopotamia itself in support of their Assyrian allies (at least by 616 B.C.E. when the extant chronicles resume after a break). This suggests Egyptian dominance throughout Palestine and Aram and the vassalage of the Judean monarch to the Egyptian pharaoh.

Josiah was killed at MEGIDDO in 610 by Pharaoh NECHO II (610–595) who had only recently assumed the throne (2 Kgs 23:28-31). What precipitated this killing remains unknown (compare 2 Chr 35:20-27). The expression "went to meet him" (2 Kgs 23:29), which describes Josiah's movement to Megiddo, would not normally indicate hostile intent.

The Judeans enthroned JEHOAHAZ II as Josiah's replacement without Egyptian approval. Egypt imposed a stiff penalty on its vassal, deposed Jehoahaz, and replaced him with JEHOIAKIM, his brother (2 Kgs 23:31-35). The latter appears to have been a fairly oppressive monarch or at least one with whom the prophet JEREMIAH had serious differences (cf. Jer 22:15-23; 36:20-32).

In the years that followed the enthronement of Jehoiakim (608–598), the Kingdom of Judah was caught up in the international struggles between Egypt and Babylonia. The external pressures on the kingdom were paralleled by internal party factions—pro-Babylonian and pro-Egyptian—that further unraveled the fabric of Judean society. These factors were also exacerbated by religious and nationalistic sentiments that accelerated the nation's plunge into tragedy.

Judah as a Babylonian Vassal. At the battle of CARCHEMISH in the summer of 605, the Babylonian crown prince, NEBUCHADREZZAR (604–562), routed the Egyptian army (cf. Jer 46:2). After Nebuchadrezzar sacked Ashkelon in Chislev (Nov/Dec) 604, Jehoiakim submitted to Babylonian vassalage (cf. Jer 36:9-10). After three years (604–601), he rebelled against Babylon (2 Kgs 24:1) when Nebuchadrezzar's invasion of Egypt during Chislev 601 suffered defeat (*ANET,* 564). More than three years passed before the Babylonians attacked Jerusalem in force (sometime after Chislev 598; *ANET,* 564). Jehoiakim died, apparently shortly after the city was put under siege, and was replaced by JEHOIACHIN who surrendered to Nebuchadrezzar when the latter put in an appearance at the siege (2 Kgs 24:8-12). A Babylonian text notes that the city was "taken" on what corresponds to 16 March 597 (2 Adar in Nebuchadrezzar's seventh year).

Nebuchadrezzar returned home with some Judean exiles (Jer 52:28b) for the new year festival, but apparently decided not to leave Jehoiachin on the throne and subsequently had him and other deportees brought to Babylon (2 Kgs 24:12b-16; 2 Chr 36:9-10). A new "king of his liking" (*ANET,* 564), ZEDEKIAH, was placed on the throne in Jerusalem.

Under Zedekiah (596–586), pronationalist and pro-Egyptian factions began pushing for rebellion against Babylonia in the king's first year (Jer 27–28). Revolt was eventually precipitated following a triumphal visit to Palestine-Phoenicia by the Egyptian pharaoh Psammetichus II (595–589) in his fourth year (592–591). Zedekiah was eventually captured and Jerusalem fell to Nebuchadrezzar's forces in July 586 after a siege begun about January 587 (2 Kgs 25:1-7). The Temple and much of the city were burned about a month later (2 Kgs 25:8-12). The Davidic Kingdom of Judah ceased to exist.

The nature of the Judean political situation under Babylonia immediately after 586 remains uncertain. Biblical texts report that GEDALIAH and the pro-Babylonian faction, of which the prophet Jeremiah was a primary spokesperson, were placed in charge of affairs (2 Kgs 25:22; Jer 40:7). No text stipulates the office to which Gedaliah was appointed. Possibly, the Babylonians experimented for a time with a non-Davidic Judean monarch with Mizpah as the royal seat (cf. Jer 41:8-10).

See also DAVID; ISRAEL.

Bibliography. J. Bright, *A History of Israel*; J. H. Hayes and P. K. Hooker, *A New Chronology for the Kings of Israel and Judah*; J. M. Miller and J. H. Hayes, *A History of Ancient Israel and Judah*; M. Noth, *The History of Israel*; J. A. Soggin, *A History of Israel.*

—JOHN H. HAYES

• **Judaism.** [*joo'*duh-iz-uhm] The name given to the religion and culture of the Jewish people following the EXILE in 587/6 B.C.E. "Judaism" is derived from Judah, the fourth son of JACOB after whom the Southern Kingdom in ISRAEL was named in the OT. When the Israelites returned to their homeland, which was now the Persian district of Judah, after the Exile, they were called Judahites (hence Jews) and their religion and culture was called Judaism. In the days of the kingdom, the religion of the people is customarily called "Israelite religion"; in the earliest period "Hebrew religion" is used. Yet this should not obscure the fact that in a broader sense all of the OT is part of the history of the Jewish people.

To understand the development of Judaism it is necessary to identify two distinct periods in the history of the Jewish people separated by the destruction of JERUSALEM by the Romans in 70 C.E. The first period begins with the Persians, who conquered the BABYLONIAN EMPIRE and permitted the exiled Jews to return to Palestine, beginning ca. 538 B.C.E. The Persian policy of religious toleration, coupled with the stability of the PERSIAN EMPIRE for 200 years, afforded the Jews ample freedom to reestablish their religion in the wake of the debacle of the Exile. After the defeat of the Persians in 331 B.C.E. by ALEXANDER the Great, Palestine came under the rule of Alexander and his Greek successors. The policies of these kings, first the Ptolemies (301–198 B.C.E.) and then the early Seleucids (198–175 B.C.E.), included religious freedom for the Jews. But things changed with the ascension of Antiochus IV in 175. Antiochus's attempt to suppress Judaism led to the revolt of the MACCABEES (167–142 B.C.E.) which resulted in political independence for the Jews in 142. From the family of Judas Maccabeus, one of the early leaders of the revolt, came the new nation's leaders, the Hasmonean dynasty. Jewish independence lasted until 63 B.C.E. when the Roman general Pompey captured Jerusalem in the name of ROME. Chafing under heavy taxation and incompetent Roman governors, and with the memory of the Maccabean revolt still alive, the Jews rebelled against Rome in 66 C.E. The war ended in disastrous defeat for the Jews in 70 C.E. Judaism would never be the same after 70. The Jews' capital, Jerusalem, was burned; their TEMPLE was destroyed; many of their institutions, such as the SANHEDRIN, were gone; and their hopes were shattered. A new period in the history of Judaism had begun. The equally disastrous rebellion of BAR-KOCHBA in 132–135 C.E. only served to give further impetus to this new direction.

The first period under consideration, sometimes called the Second Temple period or, in its later stages, the late pre-Christian period, is characterized by a number of features. Central is TORAH (the LAW), the divine instruction given by revelation to Israel through MOSES on Mount SINAI. Torah is contained in the five books of Moses—i.e., the Pentateuch—and governs Jewish life and piety. Obedience to Torah was of first importance to Jews. It was upon Torah that the returning Jews were grounded by EZRA. Furthermore, it was because of the necessity of interpreting the Torah for application to everyday life that there arose the professional order of Torah scholars, or scribes, often called RABBIS or sages. These scholars, among whom were the famous Hillel and Shammai, commonly attracted schools of disciples and frequently attained a high degree of public visibility. Their interpretations of Torah were passed along by their disciples from one generation to the next, with the teachings of successive rabbis added to their own. Thus, there developed oral traditions of interpretation alongside the written Torah.

Also important was the Temple. Many of the commandments in Torah involved the offering of sacrifices. This ritual could be performed only in the Jerusalem Temple, which was rebuilt soon after the return from the Exile. The right to offer sacrifices was given exclusively to the PRIESTS, who served as mediators between the people and God in these required acts of obedience and, thus, were viewed by the people as spiritual leaders. The priests were strictly organized, with the high priest at the head. For the HIGH PRIEST were reserved certain acts of the highest cultic significance, such as the offering of the sacrifice on the DAY OF ATONEMENT. In addition to the ongoing private sacrifices, public sacrifices were held twice a day in the Temple, and there were supplementary sacrifices on the SABBATH and during the great festival periods (PASSOVER, Pentecost [WEEKS], TABERNACLES, and DEDICATION), as well as for new moon, NEW YEAR, and the Day of Atonement. The influx into Jerusalem of large numbers of pilgrims coming for the great festivals was common.

Jewish worship was not limited to the Temple. With the renewed emphasis on Torah after the Exile came the rise of a new institution: the SYNAGOGUE. Unlike the Temple, which was limited to a single place, synagogues could be established wherever there were a sufficient number of Jews. Synagogues were primarily houses of religious instruction. Jews in an area would gather on the Sabbath for public prayer, the reading of a passage from Torah (and typically from one of the Prophets), and an exposition or sermon. As ARAMAIC replaced HEBREW as the common language of the Jews in Palestine, the scripture reading came to be followed by an interpretive Aramaic translation, or targum. In addition to offering sacrifices and participating in synagogue worship, typical Jewish piety included such things as observing the Sabbath, fulfilling the regulations concerning cultic purity, and carrying out formal rituals such as the daily recitation of the EIGHTEEN BENEDICTIONS.

During most of this period the Jews were under the control of foreign rulers. Yet the Jews generally had a certain amount of freedom in regulating religious, and often civil, matters. Throughout much of this period authority was concentrated in the hands of the leaders of the clans, or elders, and the priests. The high priesthood, in particular, came to be an office of immense prestige and importance. By the first century B.C.E. the Sanhedrin had become the chief governing body for Jewish internal affairs. Centered in Jerusalem and made up of seventy-one members drawn from the priests, the elders, and the scribes, and with the high priest at its head, the Sanhedrin was the supreme tribunal on matters concerning Jewish law.

For many Jews, matters such as Temple worship and the actions of Sanhedrin were but distant realities. The Exile had scattered Jews outside of Palestine. Those who returned to Palestine were a minority; most remained in their new homes. Eventually those Jews who lived outside of Palestine came to be known as Jews of the dispersion, or the diaspora. Such Jews struggled with maintaining their traditional religion in the context of a foreign culture. Compromises were made at times, but the distinction between diaspora Jews and those in Palestine should not be overdrawn. To be sure, Jews in Egypt or in Rome, for example, took on a particular character. But communication between the Jews of Jerusalem and those of the diaspora served both as a unifying feature within Judaism as a whole and as a check on possible diaspora excesses. Furthermore, foreign influence was not limited to the diaspora; Greek influence in Palestine, which began in the Persian period and intensified after Alexander, had an impact on the development of Judaism in Palestine as well. Thus, Jews of the diaspora studied Torah, gathered together for synagogue worship, and even made pilgrimages to Jerusalem. In addition, since they could no longer read Hebrew, they produced the Greek translation of the scriptures known as the Septuagint (LXX).

The commonality of features in Judaism before 70 C.E. should not overshadow its widespread diversity. All agreed that Torah was central, but disagreements arose over how it should be interpreted. Few denied the importance of the sacrificial cult, but some questioned the legitimacy of how it was being carried out. Further disputes arose over such matters as the proper attitude towards the Roman overlords and who should be the spiritual leaders of the people. Ultimately, the very question of the true identity of Israel was at stake. A host of groups, such as the PHARISEES, the SADDUCEES, the ESSENES, and the various unnamed groups reflected in the Pseudepigrapha arose, competing with one another for the allegiance of the people, and, hence, the right to define Judaism on their terms. This diversity, combined with the lack of a clear victor in this period, suggests that before 70 there was no single "normative" or "official" Judaism; rather, there were many "Judaisms."

The fall of Jerusalem in 70 C.E. marks the beginning of the second period in the development of Judaism. With the Temple destroyed, the sacrificial cult, so important for six centuries, had abruptly ended, along with the authority of the priests. In the wake of such a significant rebellion, the recognized authoritative body in Judaism, the Sanhedrin, could no longer be tolerated by the Romans. All who had participated in the war and survived had seen their hopes dashed. Two questions concerning the future of Judaism now arose. First, who would exert the leadership necessary for confronting the new conditions? Second, given the changed situation, what form would Judaism now take?

The leadership void was filled by the Pharisees. With the permission of the Romans, the Pharisees, who had not generally taken part in the war effort, set up schools for the continued study of Torah and its application to the Jewish people. The pioneer in this movement was Rabbi Yohanan ben Zakkai, who established an academy at Jamnia after the war. Torah scholars such as GAMALIEL II gathered together to formulate a Judaism which could exist without the Temple cult. Thus, they found counterparts to the various elements of the sacrificial system: the Temple would be replaced by the holy people; the priesthood by the holy man; the sacrifices by the holy way of life of the people. The holy way of life included religious duties, acts of kindness and grace beyond those commanded, and, especially, studying Torah. All Jews, therefore, would become like the sages. Torah was now understood to include not only the written Torah given to Moses but also the oral Torah—i.e., the interpretations of the written Torah which had been passed along in the scribal schools. This oral Torah was codified around 200 C.E. by Rabbi Judah the Holy into the Mishnah. After 70, therefore, a normative Judaism took shape. To be sure, in the early part of this period there remained some diversity, to which pseudepigrapic books such as the APOCALYPSE OF ABRAHAM and FOURTH EZRA attest. Similarly, nationalistic sentiment led to a second revolt under Bar Kochba in 132. But with the failure of the revolt, Rabbinic Judaism emerged victorious over all of its competitors. The rabbinic tradition, with its vast literary production of which the Mishnah was only the beginning, has served as the foundation of Judaism ever since.

As a product of the return from the Exile, Judaism therefore forms the religious and cultural contexts within which the later books of the OT must be read. Narratives such as Ezra and NEHEMIAH, as well as the prophets HAGGAI, ZECHARIAH, and MALACHI, illuminate the beginnings of Judaism. But an understanding of Judaism, especially in its two periods, is perhaps even more important for the study of the origins of Christianity. Jesus was a Jew, and his disciples were Jews as well. In fact, for a while early Christianity was little more than one more Jewish group striving to define Judaism on its own terms. Given the diversity within Judaism during this period, Jews, for the most part, seem to have tolerated the Christian movement as yet another sect. After 70, however, the Pharisaic attempts to define and standardize the religion resulted in the Jews taking a firmer stand against Christianity. Even with the gentile mission well established, certain Christian communities, such as those of MATTHEW and JOHN, seem to have been still strongly Jewish after 70. But now the clashes with the Jews, who viewed Christians as heretics, were sharper, and Jewish Christians were forced to face the possiblity that their new faith was indeed a new religion.

See also APOCRYPHAL LITERATURE; RABBINIC LITERATURE.

Bibliography. J. H. Charlesworth, *The Old Testament Pseudepigrapha and the New Testament* and *Jesus Within Judaism*; D. Daube, *The New Testament and Rabbinic Judaism*; W. D. Davies, *Paul and Rabbinic Judaism* and *The Setting of the Sermon on the Mount*; W. D. Davies and L. Finkelstein, eds., *The Cambridge History of Judaism*, 4 vols.; M. Hengel, *Jews, Greeks, and Barbarians* and *Judaism and Hellenism*; M. McNamara, *Palestinian Judaism and the New Testament*; G. F. Moore, *Judaism in the First Centuries of the Christian Era*; M. J. Mulder, M. E. Stone, and S. Safrai, eds., *The Literature of the Jewish People in the Period of the Second Temple and the Talmud*; J. Neusner, *From Testament to Torah: An Introduction to Judaism in Its Formative Age, Judaism: The Evidence of the Mishnah,* and *Judaism in the Matrix of Christianity*; E. P. Sanders, *Paul and Palestinian Judaism*; S. Sandmel, *Judaism and Christian Beginnings*; S. Safrai and M. Stern, eds., *The Jewish People in the First Century*; E. Schürer, *The History of the Jewish People in the Age of Jesus Christ*, rev. and ed. G. Vermes, F. Millar, and M. Goodman; M. E. Stone, *Scriptures, Sects, and Visions: A Profile of Judaism from Ezra to the Jewish Revolts*; V. Tcherikover, *Hellenistic Civilization and the Jews*.

—JOSEPH L. TRAFTON

• **Judaizers.** *See* OPPONENTS OF PAUL

• **Judas.** The name Judas is the Gk. form of the Heb. *Judah*. The best-known Judas in the Bible is Judas Iscariot, but other individuals also bore the name.

1. Judah, the son of Joseph, an ancestor of Jesus who lived before the Exile (Luke 3:30).

2. Judah, the fourth son of Jacob (Matt 1:2-3).

3. Judas Maccabeus, third of the five sons of the priest Mattathias (1 Macc 2:1-5). In 166 B.C.E. Judas assumed the military leadership of the Jews (1 Macc 2:66; 3:1).

4. Son of Chalphi and one of the two captains who stood by Jonathan Maccabeus at Hazor when everyone had fled to safety (1 Macc 11:70).

5. A son of Simon Maccabeus (1 Macc 16:2).

6. Judas of Galilee, who, in the days of the enrollment, raised a revolt; he and his followers all perished (cf. Luke 2:2; Acts 5:37).

7. Judas Iscariot, an apostle of Jesus and the treasurer of the group. He received thirty pieces of silver for leading the soldiers to Jesus in the Garden of Gethsemane (Matt 26:47-50). For the death of Judas, compare Matt 27:3-10 and Acts 1:16-21.

8. Judas, son of James, and apostle (Luke 6:16; John 14:22).

9. Judas of Damascus, in whose home Saul stayed until Ananias arrived to speak to him (Acts 9:11).

10. The writer of the Letter of JUDE (a shortened form of Judas) identifies himself simply as the "brother of James." It is assumed he was also the brother of Jesus.

See also JUDE; MACCABEES, THE.

—HERBERT O. EDWARDS, SR.

• **Jude.** Jude is the shortened form of the name JUDAS and is given in the salutation of the LETTER OF JUDE as the author: "Jude, a servant of Jesus Christ and brother of JAMES" (v. 1). The traditional view is that Jude is to be identified with the Judas described as one of the "brothers of the Lord" in Matt 13:55 and Mark 6:3. Many scholars regard the authorship of the letter as pseudonymous. Others question why a pseudonymous author would choose the name of such an obscure individual.

See also JAMES; JUDAS; JUDE, LETTER OF.

—RON FARMER

• OUTLINE OF JUDE •

The Book of Jude

I. Salutation (1-2)
II. Statement of Purpose (3-4)
III. Judgment against False Teachers (5-16)
IV. Warnings (17-19)
V. Exhortations (20-23)
VI. Doxology (24-25)

• **Jude, Letter of.** The short Letter of Jude is noted for its sharp rebuke of licentiousness, its predilection for triadic formulations, and its superb benediction.

Author. The writer identifies himself as JUDE the brother of JAMES and, by implication, the brother of Jesus (Matt 13:55; Mark 6:3). Many notable scholars hold that the Letter is pseudonymous, that is, penned by an unknown author who gave his work greater credibility by attaching to it the name of one of Jesus' brothers. Christians can affirm either position with intellectual integrity and spiritual fidelity.

Date. Suggestions of date are found in v. 3, where the writer looks back to the apostolic age as past, and in v. 17, where the readers are reminded of words spoken to them by the apostles. Two issues influence the date assigned to the Letter. The first question relates to authorship. If the Letter was written by Jude, then the date must be confined within the reasonable limits of his lifetime, i.e., 65–80 C.E. If the author was not Jude, then the writing may be placed any time within the lifespans of those who had heard the apostles, i.e., 90–140 C.E.

The second issue concerns the relationship of Jude to 2 Peter. Nearly all of the subject matter in Jude is common to 2 Peter and the organization of the material is similar. Three theories have been proposed to explain these parallels. The first holds that Jude borrowed from 2 Peter. Evidence for this contention rests on comparisons of Greek verb tenses. In 2 Peter warnings are voiced in future tenses. In Jude almost verbatim warnings are given in aorist (past) tenses (cf. 2 Pet 3:3 and Jude 18). Advocates of this view generally propose an early date for the Letter.

The second theory maintains that 2 Peter depends on Jude. Support for this opinion comes from literary and stylistic comparisons. Jude's letter is harsher in tone and appears to have been written with greater spontaneity than 2 Peter. Most significant is the impression that the author of 2 Peter intentionally excises Jude's references to apocryphal literature. Both Jude and 2 Peter allude to the pseudepigraphic *Assumption of Moses,* but 2 Peter removes the name of Moses (cf. Jude 9 and 2 Pet 2:11). In addition, while Jude directly cites the Book of *Enoch* (also in the pseudepigrapha; *1 Enoch* 1:9, cf. Jude 14-15), 2 Peter omits reference to Enoch entirely. Proponents of this theory usually assign a late date to the Letter.

A third theory suggesting a common source, either oral or written, has little support and few adherents.

Recipients and Purpose. The Letter was written to the church at large. Its purpose was to warn Christians about libertines who were leading the church into error. Jude describes the heresy he is combating in very general terms. Some scholars have identified it as a form of Gnosticism or a proto-Gnostic Jewish dualism. The most that can be gleaned from internal evidence is that the heresy involved simple antinomianism and a practical infidelity.

See also ENOCH, FIRST; GNOSTICISM; JUDAS; JUDE; PETER, LETTERS OF.

Bibliography. A. E. Barnett, "The Epistle of Jude: Introduction," *IB*; D. Guthrie, *New Testament Introduction;* B. Reicke, *The Epistles of James, Peter and John.*

—WILLIAM BRUCE PRESCOTT

• **Judea.** [*joo*-dee'uh] The NT term for the territory of Judah. In the OT, JUDAH is the term used to refer to the territory assigned to the tribe of Judah (PLATE 11). Ultimately, it was used for the territory of the Southern Kingdom. After the fall of the Northern Kingdom, Judah is used to refer to the territory of the entire nation. It became the name assigned by the Persian empire to the province. After the Maccabean revolt, the term came to include almost all of what we now call Palestine. When the Romans captured the land, they changed the name to the *Provincia Judaea.* It was from this designation that the NT name actually came.

Obviously, the territory called Judea had varying boundaries throughout the entire biblical period. However, it always appears to have centered upon Hebron or Jerusalem and to have included a major north-south highway called the water-parting route. There is also a major road heading eastward, descending from Jerusalem to Jericho and then on across the Jordan.

This region is bordered on the west by the Philistine plain, on the southwest by the rolling hill country known as the shephelah, on the south by the desert wilderness known as the Negeb, and on the east by the Jordan rift, which includes the Jordan River and the Dead Sea. Beyond the sea lies the Transjordan plateau. The land is extremely hilly and very fertile. It is good for vineyards and orchards, as well as grain fields in the area of Bethlehem. The far south has less rain and was used mainly for grass lands for flocks.

See also JUDAH, KINGDOM OF; ISRAEL.

Bibliography. Y. Aharoni, *The Land of the Bible*. D. Baly, *The Geography of the Bible*.

—ROBERT L. CATE

• OUTLINE OF JUDGES •

The Book of Judges

I. Summary of Events, from Joshua to the Judges (1:1–2:5)
II. Introduction to the Judges (2:6–3:6)
III. Stories of the Judges and Their Time (3:7–21:25)

• Judges, Book of. The Book of Judges bridges the gap between the initial possession of the land under JOSHUA and the final establishment of the monarchy in Israel. Through a series of dynamic stories the book surveys a turbulent period in Israel's early history. Chap. 1, assumed by many scholars to contain early traditions, relates the attempts of various tribes to occupy their allotted territory. Since not every tribe enjoyed complete success, the Israelites secured their hold on the land gradually over an undisclosed period of time.

The opening of chap. 2 lays the foundation for the central section of the book. The basis for the relationship between God and Israel is, in fact, the covenant made by the Lord with Israel's ancestors. Failure to keep this covenant brings punishment; faithfulness brings blessing. The basic principle forms the outline for the telling of the stories of the judges of Israel. When the people turn away from God, they are oppressed by their neighbors, but when they are faithful, a deliverer leads them to victory and freedom. Judg 3–16 illustrate this formula in the stories of OTHNIEL, EHUD, DEBORAH, GIDEON, JEPHTHAH, and SAMSON.

After each deliverance, the writer makes a summary statement concerning the years that the land had rest or the years that a particular person judged the land. The exception to this pattern is the reference to Shamgar, who is said to have delivered Israel. No time period is given, and little is known about this character.

A second group of individuals, referred to as minor judges, is also found within the book. This group includes Tola, Jair, Ibzan, Elon, and Abdon. These persons do not deliver Israel, but are reported to have judged.

The exact nature of the office of judge is unclear, but it apparently involved giving decisions in difficult, judicial matters and providing military leadership in time of need. Some leaders exercised both functions (Deborah; Jephthah), while others functioned in only one role or the other. The deliverers acted primarily as military leaders while the minor judges functioned in a judicial role. ABIMELECH (Judg 9) does not fit clearly into either the role of deliverer or judge and may be included because of his relationship with Jerubbaal (Gideon), as is explained in Judg 9:1.

The second major section of Judges, chaps. 17–21, contains a collection of stories that reflects the turmoil prior to the establishment of the monarchy. This chaos is underlined by the phrase "there was no king in Israel" (17:6; 18:1; 19:1; 21:25). The material could once have been part of a collection of stories used to illustrate the need for the monarchy in Israel.

The judges have traditionally been viewed as leading a united Israel and serving consecutively in office. Two aspects of the book raise questions about that understanding. If the judges served one after the other, the number of years attributed to them is difficult to fit into the chronology of the period. Secondly, some of the individual stories mention smaller groups instead of all Israel and indicate that only some of the tribes were initially involved (Judg 6:35; 7:23-24; 12:1; 15:9-10). This observation has led to the conclusion that the judges may have been local tribal leaders who exercised authority over a particular territory in times of trouble. If the judges were local leaders, then their times in office could have overlapped in various parts of the country.

Israel in the period of the judges was a loose confederation of tribes. No central religious shrine or central political structure is found in the Book of Judges. This lack of authority is emphasized especially in chaps. 17–21. Although the material has been edited at a later date, it does present some fascinating vignettes of life and customs from this early transitional period in Israel's history.

The development of the Book of Judges into its present form has been the subject of considerable debate among scholars. At one time many scholars traced sources from the Pentateuch through Joshua and Judges, but this view is no longer widely accepted. The majority now sees the book as related in some way to the deuteronomistic history—that is, the overview of Israel's history stretching from Deuteronomy through 2 Kings.

The covenant formula is clearly articulated in Deut 7:9-11, 11:13-17, and 30:15-20. This principle then becomes the basis for interpreting and explaining the events in Israel's history. Nowhere is this principle from Deuteronomy more clearly evident than in the varying periods of deliverance and oppression in the Book of Judges.

Using the covenant formula as a basis, the writer of Judges arranges the various traditions about the judges into a unified story that not only retells the past but explains why these things happened as they did. It was once maintained that this editorial process took place after the fall of Jerusalem in 587/6 B.C.E. In recent scholarship, a two-stage process with one edition before the Exile and a second edition after the fall of Jerusalem has been suggested.

Readers of the Book of Judges have opened up a new realm of study with the application of literary analysis to the narratives of Judges. A careful reading of the stories involved reveals skillful use of repetition, anticipation, dialogue, and other artistic techniques. These techniques are used, not just to display literary skill, but to communicate the message of the book.

The basic religious viewpoint of the Book of Judges is clear. Israel was not always at rest because the people were not always faithful to God. Eventually Israel degenerated into a chaotic state that required the strong leadership of a king. A more subtle message may be found in the type of leadership that is presented in the portraits of the judges. If there had been more leaders like Deborah or Gideon, leaders who did not grasp for personal power and glory, Israel's later history could have been different indeed.

See also DEUTERONOMIST/DEUTRONOMISTIC HISTORIAN.

Bibliography. R. G. Boling, *Judges, AncB*.

—PHILLIP E. MCMILLON

• Judgment. *See* JUSTICE/JUDGMENT; PESTILENCE

• Judgment Hall. *See* GABBATHA

• Judgment Seat. The judgment seat (βῆμα) was a throne-like speaker's platform used by kings and royal officials for public pronouncements. The word is also translated as "tribunal" or even "throne." The word is typically used in the NT for the judgment seat. In Acts 18:12, Paul was brought before the judgment seat of Gallio at Corinth. This raised throne or platform has been excavated in the marketplace at Corinth. The *bēma* of Pilate is also mentioned in Matt 27:19 from which Pilate judged Jesus.

The term judgment seat is also used by Christian writers to refer to the judging activity of Christ. "For we shall all stand before the judgment seat of God" (Rom 14:10b).

See also GALLIO; JUDGMENT, DAY OF; THRONE.

—JAMES L. BLEVINS

• **Judgment, Day of.** Throughout the Bible God is portrayed as a judge. In much of the material focused on the early history of Israel in the OT God is depicted as being steadily involved in judging the daily activities both of individuals and Israel as a nation (e.g., Gen 38:1-10; Exod 4:24-26; Josh 2). In later prophetic literature God is routinely declared to stand in judgment of Israel, rewarding obedience and punishing disobedience of the divine will (e.g., Isa 1; Jer 5; Hos 2; Amos 7). At times the prophets announced impending crises that would come as acts of God's judgment, and in that the realizations of these divine judgments lay in the future, one could describe the crises as eschatological (cf. Jer 4; Hos 10; Joel 2). But, in other strata of OT prophetic literature, there appears a concept that was previously unknown, i.e., the idea of a final day of judgment by God (sometimes called "the Day of the Lord") that would bring human history to an end through a universal assize (Dan 7 and 12; but cf. Isa 24). The notion of a day of judgment is one of the chief characteristics of the kind of eschatological thinking that evolved in Israelite religious thought during the Babylonian Exile; and the literature from the postexilic period is replete with this kind of thinking and teaching. Usually this pattern of thought is designated apocalyptic eschatology.

The apocalyptic eschatological concept of a day of judgment, itself a development of the concept of God as judge, continued to develop in at least two ways. First, most often God (Yahweh = the Lord) is the judge on the day of judgment, but in a few instances in the OT one finds that God's messiah or other representative is said to be the one enacting judgment in God's behalf (Isa 11; Jer 23; Dan 7). Second, in the earliest prophetic portraits of the day of judgment there is no concept of the judgment of each individual human, but as apocalyptic eschatological thinking evolved, the idea of the judgment of each individual in the context of a final, universal day of judgment became the norm. A striking part of this innovation was the development of the concept of the resurrection of the dead, so that not only are the living brought under God's judgment, but also the dead who at the day of judgment are raised to life. This understanding of the day of judgment occurs in the OT in a fully explicit form for the first time in Daniel (cf. esp. chaps. 7 and 12). Then, in the Jewish literature from the late pre-Christian period (*1 Enoch* 47; *4 Ezra* 7) and in the NT (Matt 25; 1 Thess 4–5; Rev 20) one regularly finds references to the day of judgment where the event is portrayed as the universal judgment of each individual human, both the living and the resurrected dead. Examination of pertinent passages shows that the thinking about the day of judgment became increasingly elaborate.

In the NT, there are two texts that preserve language reflecting the original thinking about the day of judgment with God as the judge (2 Pet 3:12; Rev 16:14); but even here, as elsewhere throughout the NT (e.g., 1 Cor 15; 1 Thess 4–5; 2 Thess 2; Heb 9), the day of judgment is bound to the idea of the parousia of the risen Jesus, i.e., the second coming of Christ. Since in the NT the day of judgment occurs when Christ returns in glory, it is Christ who sits in judgment at the grand assize. Nevertheless, it is God's judgment that is enacted, as was the case when God's messiah acted as God's agent of judgment in the OT. In the NT the judgment brings a separation. While there are several metaphors for the distinction that allows this separation—wheat versus tares, good fish versus bad fish, sheep versus goats, foolish versus wise—the real distinction is of the sinful from the righteous. No longer is one's national identity of primary significance; rather, it is the condition of one's own life as determined through one's relation (or lack thereof) to Jesus Christ.

While the day of judgment brings an end to human existence as it is currently known and experienced, it is clear that the various biblical authors do not view the outcome of the judgment as a void. Beyond the day of judgment, the biblical authors agree there is something new: a new age, a new creation, a new Jerusalem, a new heaven, and a new earth—all of which are ways of naming the fully realized form of the Kingdom of God. This positive imagery dominates the biblical scenes of the day of judgment, but the converse of these images is also present in certain of the passages describing the day of judgment, e.g., the imagery of destruction, perdition, or hell.

See also APOCALYPTIC LITERATURE; ESCHATOLOGY IN THE NEW TESTAMENT; ESCHATOLOGY IN THE OLD TESTAMENT; HEAVEN; HELL; KINGDOM OF GOD; PAROUSIA/SECOND COMING; RESURRECTION IN THE NEW TESTAMENT; RESURRECTION IN THE OLD TESTAMENT.

Bibliography. B. Anderson, *Understanding the Old Testament*, 4th ed.; F. Büchsel, "κρίνω, κτλ.," *TDNT*; W. Eichrodt, *Theology of the Old Testament*; L. Goppelt, *Theology of the New Testament*; F. Stagg, *New Testament Theology*.

—MARION L. SOARDS

• **Judgment, Last.** *See* JUDGMENT, DAY OF; PAROUSIA/SECOND COMING

• **Judith, Book of.** [*joo'*dith] The Book of Judith is an apocryphal story, told with great literary skill, about a threat to the Israelites which was negated by the daring exploits of a beautiful widow named Judith. The story, which is set "in the twelfth year of the reign of NEBUCHADREZZAR, who ruled over the Assyrians in the great city of Nineveh" (1:1) at a time when the Israelites "had only recently returned from the captivity" (4:3), falls into two well-balanced parts. In the first part (1–7), Nebuchadrezzar, angry when Syria and Egypt fail to assist him in his victorious campaign against the Medes, entrusts his chief general Holofernes with the task of taking revenge on the recalcitrants. After making elaborate preparations, Holofernes begins a brutal march through the condemned region, where many cities capitulate without resistance. The Israelites, on the other hand, prepare to fight back. When Holofernes learns of the Israelites' actions, he inquires as to what sort of people they are. Through a summary of OT history, Achior, the leader of the Ammonites, informs Holofernes that as long as the Israelites do not sin, God will protect them. Angered at this counsel, Holofernes hands Achior over to the Israelites and besieges the town of Bethulia. As the residents plead that they be allowed to surrender, Uzziah, the chief magistrate of the town, convinces them to wait five days to see if God will act. With the suspense appropriately heightened, the book now shifts to the second part (8–16) with the introduction of the heroine. Judith, a pious and beautiful widow, unhappy with the deal struck between Uzziah and the people, castigates the leaders for their lack of faith and receives permission to embark upon a secret plan. After praying for God's assistance, Judith adorns herself in a comely fashion and departs with her maid by night to Holofernes' camp, where she arouses quite a stir. Judith informs Holofernes that she has fled the town because its residents are about to sin and thus will lose God's protection. She requests asylum and promises to tell Holofernes when the people sin, which God will reveal to her. After three days, Holofernes invites her to a banquet with the intention of possessing her. Alone at last with Judith, Holofernes passes out, drunk. With Holofernes' own sword and a prayer for strength, Judith cuts off his head and gives it to her maid. With Holofernes' head concealed, Judith and her maid slip out of the camp, return to Bethulia, and display their prize. The peoples' spirits are restored, and Achior converts to Judaism. In the morning Holofernes' body is found and his army panics. The Israelites rout the fleeing Assyrians and plunder their camp. Judith is honored, sings a song of thanksgiving to God, and retires to her home, where she lives the rest of her days as a widow.

Several features of Judith stand out. First, it is a finely crafted story, filled with suspense, marked by careful character development, and rising to an unforgettable climax. The author was a master of irony. Second, although it reads like a factual account, from the opening verse it is replete with historical blunders of the first magnitude. It is highly unlikely that so skillful an author was unaware of these blunders; their presence must be deliberate. But if so, then the author does not purport to be writing a true story at all; the work must be some sort of didactic fiction (cf. TOBIT). Third, Judith seems to be a rather ambiguous heroine: she is pious to a fault, yet she saves her people through lying, deceit, and murder! It is safe to say that whatever difficulty later readers have had with Judith's methods, they did not bother the author.

Judith is extant in a number of ancient versions, the most important being Greek and Latin. It was probably composed in Hebrew. The date of Judith is problematic. Some scholars, noting the strong Persian elements in the book, have suggested that it was composed in the fourth century B.C.E. Others have emphasized Hasmonean parallels and have called for a date near the end of the second century B.C.E. It is possible that a story from the Persian period was rewritten during the Hasmonean period, but it seems more likely that the book is a literary unity and, while set in the former period, dates from the latter. Whether or not the story rests upon an original historical kernel, albeit with considerable literary embellishment, about a Jewish woman who saved her people by assassinating an enemy leader, cannot be known.

The religious perspective of Judith has also been debated. Although it has been typically labeled Pharisaic, an origin among the SADDUCEES has also been suggested. Given the great diversity within Judaism in the last two centuries B.C.E., it is better to leave the question open while acknowledging that the author affirms a fairly traditional focus on the importance of prayer, devotion to God, and the TEMPLE cult, combined with an openness to the conversion of gentiles. Although Judith is the heroine, the author emphasizes that it is God who has given Israel the victory (cf. 9:9-10; 13:13-18; 16:2-5). Perhaps this latter point is the key to understanding the purpose of the book: to present Judith as a model of a courageous individual—a widow no less—whose boldness in the face of overwhelming odds was honored by God.

Never regarded as canonical by Jews, Judith received a mixed reaction in the early church. Some, such as Clement of Alexandria, Augustine, the Council of Nicea, and the Council of Carthage accepted it; others, such as Origen, Athanasius, Cyril of Jerusalem, and Gregory of Nazianzus did not. Eventually it was accepted into the CANON of both the Roman Catholic Church and the Eastern Orthodox Church; it was rejected by Protestants. Canonical or not, with its daring heroine and shocking climax Judith has made a distinctive and lasting impact on art and literature.

See also APOCRYPHAL LITERATURE.

Bibliography. L. Alonso-Schökel, "Narrative Structures in the Book of Judith," *Protocol Series of the Colloquies of the Center for Hermeneutical Studies in Hellenistic and Modern Culture,* 11; A. E. Cowley, "The Book of Judith," *The Apocrypha and Pseudepigrapha of the Old Testament,* ed. R. H. Charles; J. Craghan, *Esther, Judith, Tobit, Jonah, Ruth*; T. Craven, *Artistry and Faith in the Book of Judith*; J. C. Dancy, *Judith*; M. S. Enslin and S. Zeitlin, *The Book of Judith*; C. A. Moore, *Judith*; G. W. E. Nickelsburg, "Stories of Biblical and Early Post-Biblical Times," *Jewish Writings of the Second Temple Period,* ed. M. E. Stone; G. Vermes, "The Book of Judith," *The History of the Jewish People in the Age of Jesus Christ,* rev. ed., ed. E. Schürer.

—JOSEPH L. TRAFTON

• **Justice/Judgment.** The range of issues addressed by the terms justice and judgment is broad indeed. As an introduction three important perspectives should be considered: (1) justice/judgment as defined essentially by *law*; (2) justice/judgment as *more than legal definition*; and (3) the quest for *divine justice,* particularly as framed in the issue of theodicy.

Justice and Law. The judicial framework of justice/judgment (Hebrew *mišpāṭ*) is most evident in the association with law or commandment. Thus God's *mišpāṭîm* are those laws given through Moses (Exod 24:3) which the people are to hear (*šmʿ*, e.g., Deut 5:1; 7:12), keep/obey (*šmr*, e.g., Lev 18:5, 26; Deut 7:11; 11:1; 12:1) and do (*ʿśh*, e.g., Lev 18:4; Deut 11:32; 26:16). These laws are true (*'ĕmet,* Ps 19:10), good (*tôb,* Ps 119:39), right (*yāšār,* Ps 119:137), and righteous (*ṣedeq,* Ps 119:75) and thus commend themselves to careful observance, for in living according to God's laws people bring themselves into conformity with God's will. The reward for such obedience is the blessing of God (cf. Deut 28:1-14); the consequence for disobedience, God's punishment (cf. Deut 28:15-68).

A judicial nuance is also present in a number of cases where *mišpāṭ* is appropriately rendered "decision," in the sense of a legal ruling by a judge. One may come before the king (e.g., 2 Sam 15:2, 6) or a judge (e.g., Judg 4:5) for such a decision, or one may appeal the case directly to God (e.g., Num 27:5; Job 13:18; 23:4). In all these cases *mišpāṭ* refers to both the process involved in the decision making (cf. Ps 1:5) as well as the content of the decision rendered. The content is described as positive for those who are innocent and therefore have a legitimate claim, or negative for those who are in the wrong, in which case the decision has the character of legal punishment. When God executes justice (*ʿāśâ mišpāṭ*) in this latter sense, it is the opponents of God who are punished (e.g., Exod 12:12; Num 33:4). The righteous wait expectantly for such judgments on their enemies (e.g., Pss 119:84; 149:9) and indeed count it as their right (cf. 1 Kgs 8:45, 49, 59; Mic 7:9; Pss 9:4; 140:12; 146:7) for maintaining obedience before the God who is proclaimed in faith as the judge of all the earth (Gen 18:25; cf. Judg 11:27; Isa 33:22; Pss 82:8; 96:13; 98:9).

Justice and Righteousness. While justice/judgment is

List of Plates (Maps, Charts, and Photos)

[PLATE 1]

BIBLICAL WORLD

BIBLICAL WORLD

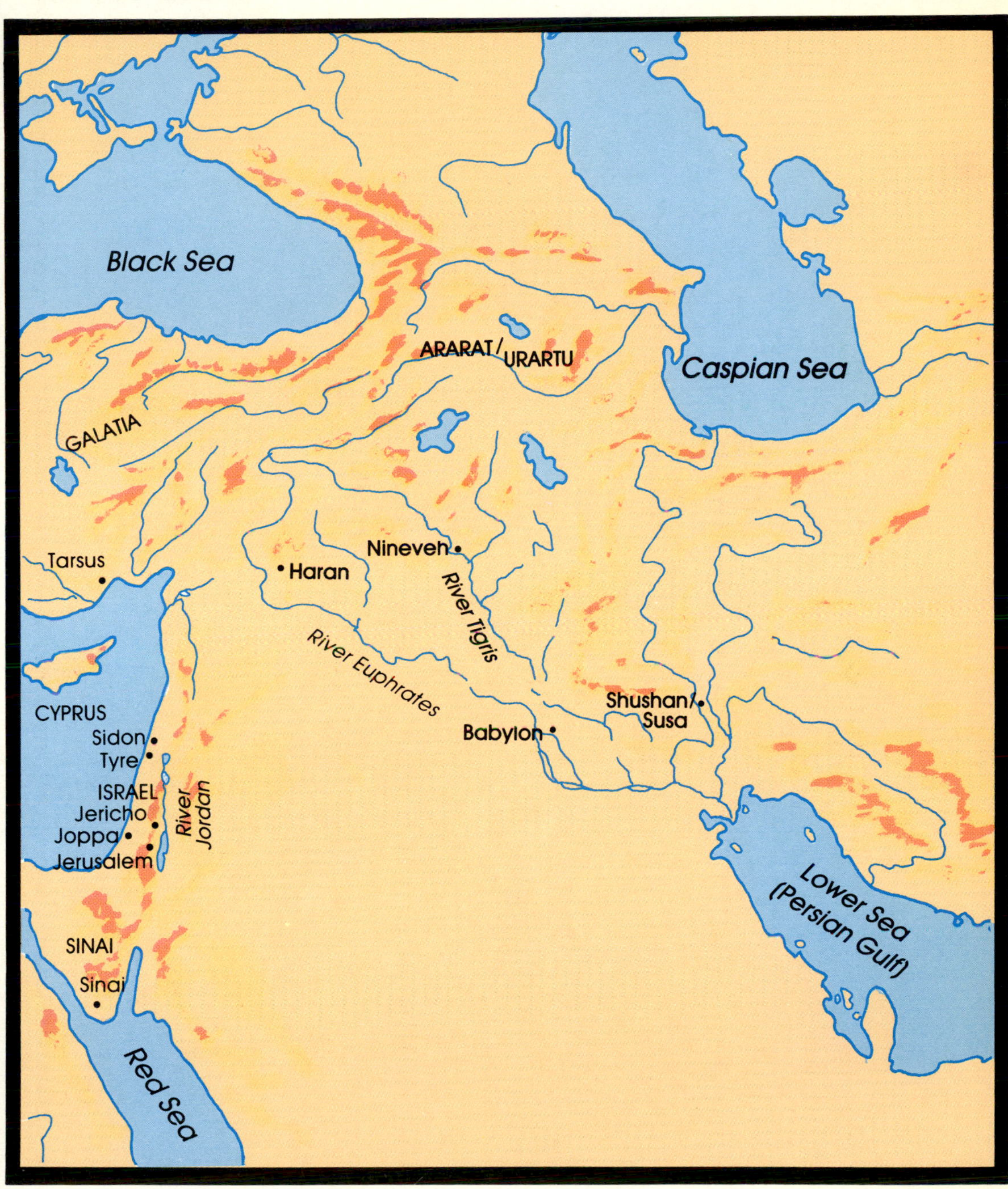

Artwork by Margaret Jordan Brown © Mercer University Press

[PLATE 2]

Caspian Sea
Black Sea
MEDIA
Ecbatana
(Malamir)
ELAM
Susa
Zagros Mountains
GUTIUM
Lower Sea (Persian Gulf)
FERTILE CRESCENT
SUMERIA
BABYLONIA
Lagash
Isin
Ur
Erech
Kish
Sippar
Agade?
Cuthah
Babylon
Borsippa
River Diyala
River Adhaim
Lake Urmia
Lake Van
ASSYRIA
Gt. Zab
Arbela
Little Zab
Calah
Nineveh
River Tigris
River Habor
(Tell Halaf)
Euphrates
River
Mari
ARARAT
MITANNI
Haran
Carchemish
(Zinjirli)
Tadmor
QarQar
ARABIA
(KEDAR)
(Dumah)
(Tema)
(Dedan)
HITTITE EMPIRE
Ankuwa
Taurus Mountains
River Halys
River Sangarius
ARZAWA
River Orontes
Kedesh
Damascus
Ugarit
Hamath
Arvad
Gebal
Berytus
Sidon
Tyre
Acco
Dor
Joppa
Ashkelon
Shechem
Jerusalem
Jericho
Hebron
Beer-sheba
Kadesh-barnea
MIDIAN
Red Sea
SINAI
Lower Egypt
Alashiya, Kittim (Cyprus)
The Great Sea (Mediterranean Sea)
Rhodes
Troy
MINOANS
Knossos
Caphtor (Crete)
Phaistos
Athens
Argos
Mycenae
Pylos
PUT
Memphis
Heracleopolis
River Nile
Beni-hasan
Akhetaton
Upper Egypt
Abydos
EGYPT
Syene
1st Cataract

[PLATE 3]

ARCHAEOLOGICAL SITES
The Great Sea
River Abana
Damascus
River Pharpar
Sidon
Zarephath
Tyre
PHOENICIA
LEBANON
Mount Hermon
Abel-beth-maachah
Dan
ARAM
Kedesh-naphtali
Hazor
Sea of Galilee
GALILEE
River Kishon
Mount Carmel
Gath-hepher
Jokneam
Dor
Shunem
Megiddo
Jezreel
HAVVOTHJAIR
Beth-arbel
Ramoth-gilead
Taanach
ISRAEL
Ibleam
Dothan
River Cherith
Socoh
Tirzah
Mount Ebal
Shechem
Succoth
AMMON
Mount Gerizim
Penuel
Mahanaim
Aphek
Tappuah
Shiloh
Zarethan
Joppa
River Jordan
Ephron
Gilgal
Bethel
Rabbathammon
Bethhoron
Jericho
Shaalbim
Mizpah
Jabneel
Ekron
Gezer
Gibeon
Geba
Gibbethon
Aijalon
Ramah
Elealeh
Timnah
Kiriath-jearim
Heshbon
Ashdod
Zorah
Jerusalem
Libnah
Medeba
JUDAH
PHILISTIA
Azekah
Etam
Bethlehem
Baal-meon
Socoh
Adullam
Tekoa
Dead Sea
Moresheth-gath
Mareshah
Ataroth
Beth-zur
Lachish
Hebron
Tell el-Hesi
Dibon
Adoraim
Ziph
En-gedi
Tell Beit Mirsim
Gerar
MOAB
Arad (Tell-el-Milh)
Beersheba
Nimrim
Kir-hareseth

Artwork by Margaret Jordan Brown © Mercer University Press

[PLATE 5]

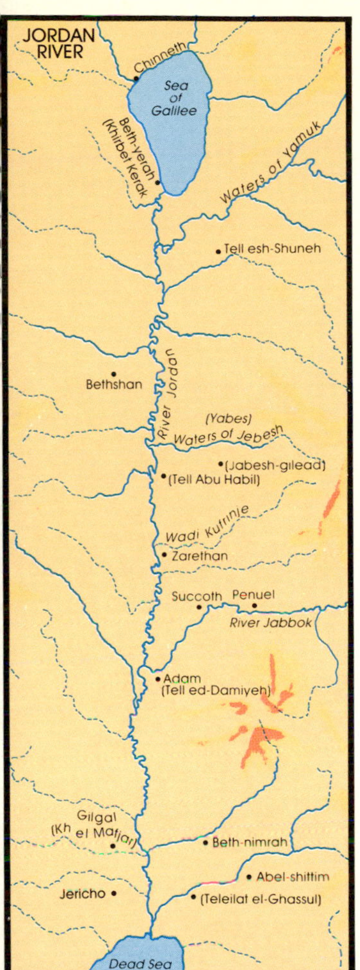

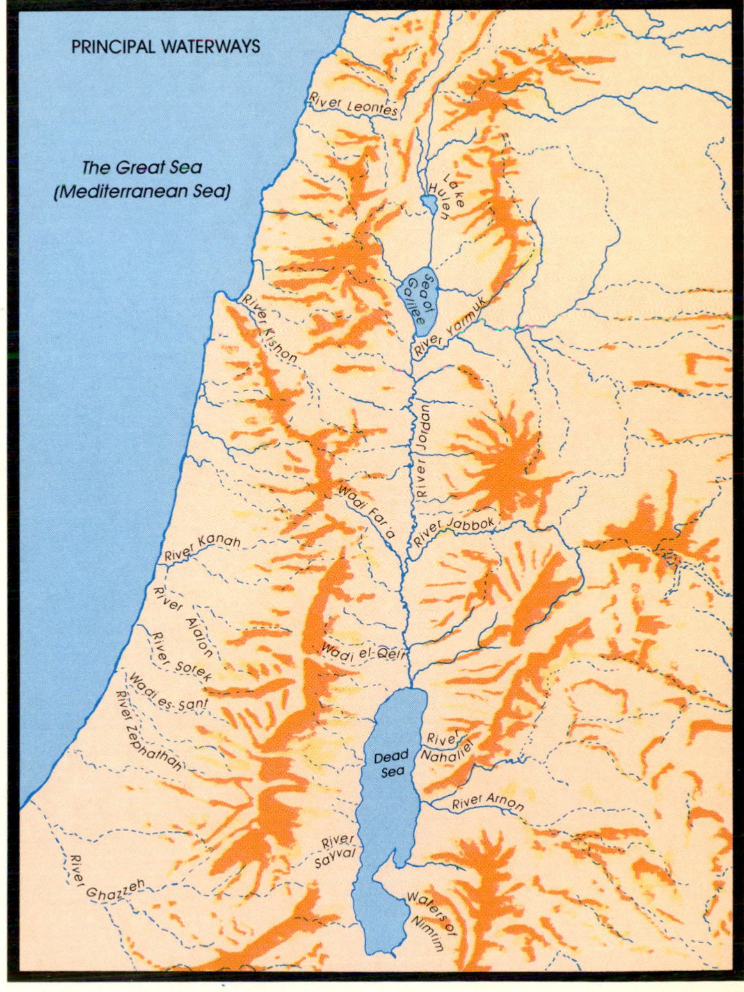

Artwork by Margaret Jordan Brown © Mercer University Press

[PLATE 6]

ECONOMICS
The Great Sea
Trade-Caravan-Export Center
Coin Minting
Sidon
Mount Lebanon
Mount Hermon
Trade-Caravan-Center
Damascus
Tyre
Dan
Port City
Acco
Hazor
Sea of Galilee
Galilee
Bashan
Ashtaroth
Hauran
Dor
Wadi Yarmuk
Megiddo
Ramoth-gilead
Bethshan
Trade Center
Plain of Sharon
Gerasa (Jerash)
Samaria
Metalwork
Trade-Caravan-Center
Shechem
Succoth
Port City
Joppa
Gilead
River Jordan
Rabbah/Philadelphia
Bethel
Caravan Center
Jericho (OT)
Ashdod
Jerusalem
Worship Center
Gaza
Lachish
Dead Sea
Trade-Caravan-Center
Metalwork
Hebron
Gerar
En-gedi
River Arnon
Judea
Beersheba
Kir-hareseth
Zoar
River Zered
Negeb
Kadesh-barnea
Punon
Wadi Arabah
Port City
Elath
B Barley
Cs Camels
Ct Cattle
Dp Date Palm
D Dyes
Fg Figs
Fs Fish
Fr Forests
G Grapes
H Honey
Ol Olives
Io Iron Ore
Co Copper Ore
Py Papyrus
P Pomegranates
S Salt
Sp Sheep
T Textiles
W Wheat

VEGETATION
Acco
Hazor
The Great Sea
Sea of Galilee
River Jordan
Jerusalem
Dead Sea
En-gedi
Beersheba
Kadesh-barnea
WOODLANDS
SCRUB
DESERT
DUNES

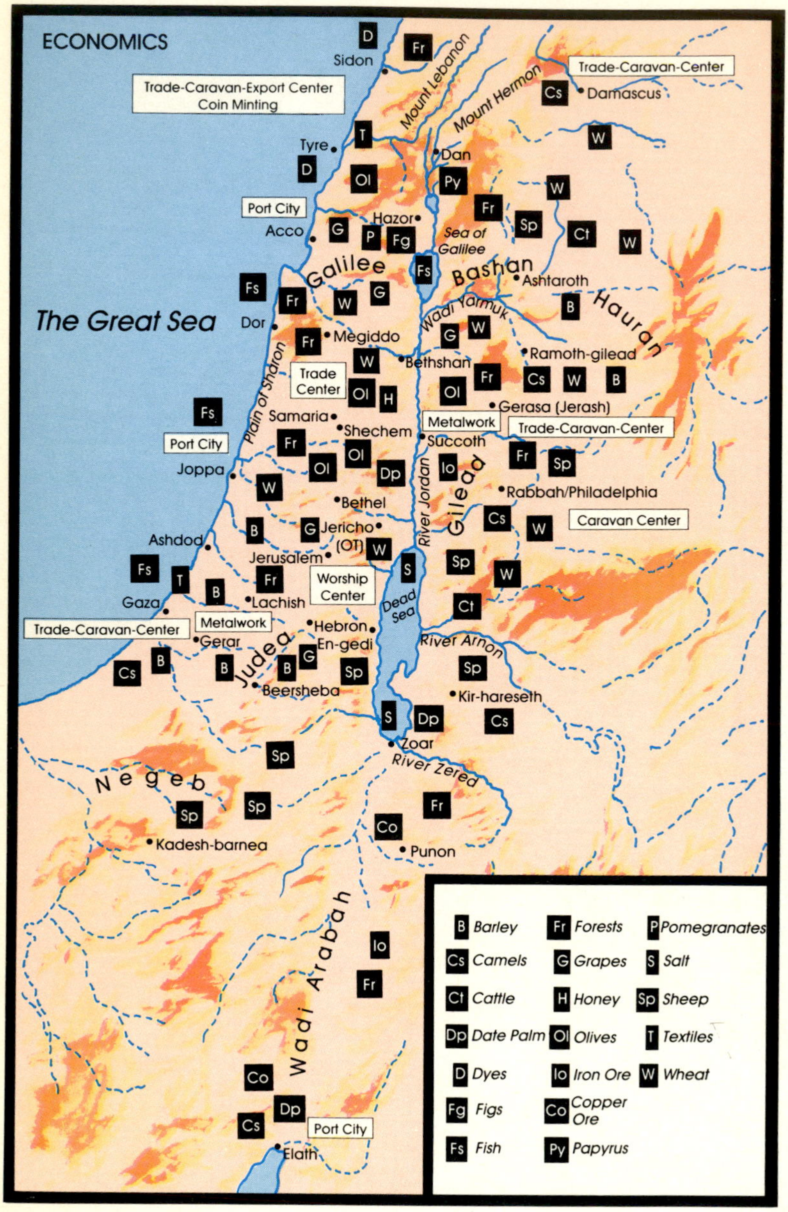

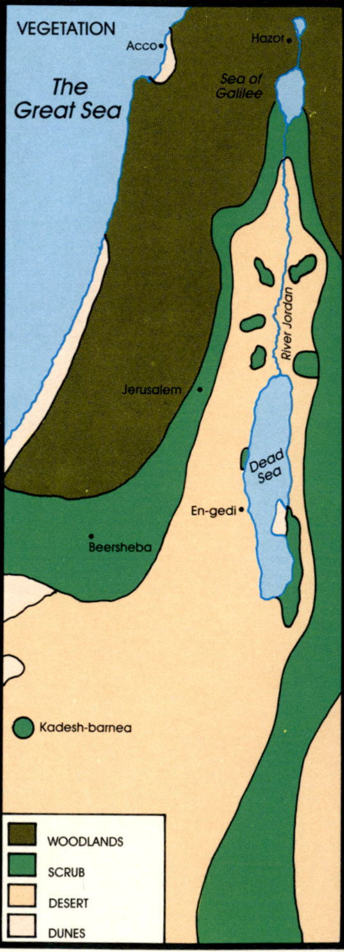

Artwork by Margaret Jordan Brown © Mercer University Press

[PLATE 7]

Artwork by Margaret Jordan Brown © Mercer University Press

MACEDONIA
THRACE
Black Sea
EPIRUS
BITHYNIA
Aegean Sea
Ilium
HELLAS
Sardis
(ASIA MINOR)
Tarsus
CRETE
CYPRUS
The Great Sea
(Mediterranean Sea)
Cyrene
CYRENAICA
Damascus
Sidon
Tyre
SYRIA
Jerusalem
Gaza
Alexandria
Sais
Pelusium
Heliopolis (On)
Memphis
Oracle of Amon
ARABAH
SINAI
LOWER EGYPT
Oxyrhynchus
Hermopolis
EGYPT
Akehetaton
(Tell El-amarna)
UPPER EGYPT
Ptolemais
Nag Hammadi
Thebes
(Karnak, Luxor)
Syene
Red Sea
Nile River
NUBIA
EGYPT AND NUBIA

[PLATE 9]

Artwork by Margaret Jordan Brown © Mercer University Press

CONQUEST
AND
SETTLEMENT
The Great Sea
Zarephath
Damascus
Mount Hermon
River Pharpar
Ahlab
Tyre
Dan
DAN
Kanah
NAPHTALI
Kedesh
Hammon
Achzib
ASHER
Hazor
Sea of Galilee
BASHAN
Accho
Beth-anath?
ARGOB
Karnaim
Ashtaroth
ZEBULUN
Mount Carmel
Aphek
Hammath
River Yarmuk
HAVOTH-JAIR
ISSACHAR
Sarid
Dor
Megiddo
Edrei
MANASSEH
Ramoth-gilead
Beth-shan
MACHIR
Ibleam
Dothan
Mahanaim?
MANASSEH
Tabbath
River Jordan
Shechem
Succoth
River Jabbok
AMMON
Aphek
Joppa
Zeredah
Shiloh
GAD
EPHRAIM
Lod
Rabbath-ammon
Beeroth?
Bethel
Gilgal
Jericho
DAN
Gezer
BENJAMIN
Debir
Heshbon
Jerusalem
Mount Nebo
Ashdod
Libnah
Medeba
Ashkelon
Bethlehem
Baal-meon
PHILISTINES
Addulum
Gath
Dead Sea
REUBEN
Lachish
JUDAH
Kiriathaim
Gaza
Hebron
Dibon
Debir
En-gedi
CALEB
River Arnon
CHERETHITES
CRETANS
Ziklag?
SIMEON
Sharuhen
MOAB
Beersheba
KENITES
Kir-hareseth
Aroer
JERAHMEEL
Rehoboth
River Zered
Bozrah
Hazor-addar?
Punon
SEIR
Kadesh-barnea
EDOM

TRIBAL TERRITORIES
The Great Sea
Sidon
Zarephath
Ahlab
Tyre
Kanah
Laish/Dan
Kedesh
ASHER
NAPHTALI
Achzib
Achshaph
Hazor
Acco
Beth-anath
Rehob
Kabul
Aphek
ZEBULUN
Sea of Galilee
Golan
Rimmon
Bethelem
Gath-hepher
Jabneel
BASHAN
Beth-shemesh
ISSACHAR
Endor
Dor
Shunem
Megiddo
Jezreel
MANASSEH
Ramoth-gilead
Taanach
Beth-shan
Mount Gilboa
En-gannim
Ibleam
MANASSEH
River Jordan
Mount Ebal
Zaphon
Mount Gerizim
Shechem
Succoth
River Kanah
Mahanaim
Ataroth
GILEAD
Joppa
Bene-berak
Shiloh
GAD
Jazer
EPHRAIM
Bethel
Gilgal
Beth-horon
BENJAMIN
Beth-nimrah
Ekron
Shaalbim
Jericho
AMMON
Jabneel
Gibbethon
Gezer
Aijalon
Gibeon
DAN
Gibeah
Anathoth
Beth-peor
Heshbon
Eltekeh
Eshtaol
En-shemesh
Bezer
Ashdod
Timnah
Jebus
Medeba
Azekah
Ashkelon
PHILISTINES
Tekoa
Dead Sea
REUBEN
Gath
Mareshah
Kedemoth
Gaza
Lachish
Beth-zur
Hebron
Kiriathaim
Dibon
JUDAH
Ziph
Aroer
Juttah
River Arnon
Ziktag
SIMEON
En-rimmon
Jattir
Sharuhen
MOAB
Beersheba
Moladah
Hormah

Artwork by Margaret Jordan Brown © Mercer University Press

Artwork by Margaret Jordan Brown © Mercer University Press

HIGHWAYS
The Great Sea
(Mediterranean Sea)
Sidon
To Ugarit
Mount Lebanon
To Kadesh, Hamath, Riblah
Damascus
To Hamath, ALeppo, Tadmor/ Paimyra
Tyre
River Leontes
Dan
Mount Hermon
The King's Highway
Hazor
Sea of Galilee
Acco
Ashtaroth
Waters of Yarmuk
Dor
Megiddo
Ramoth-gilead
Ibleam
Bethshan
River Jordan
Socoh
Tirzah
Samaria
Shechem
Mahanaim
Aphek
Succoth
Adam
Shiloh
Joppa
Bethel
Rabbah
Lod
Gilgal
Ai
Aijalon
Heshbon
To Dumah
Ashdod
Beth-shemesh
Jerusalem
Ashkelon
Dead Sea
Gaza
Hebron
Lachish
En-gedi
River Arnon
Gerar
Arad
Beersheba
Kir-hareseth
To Pelusium/Sin
The Way of the Sea
Zoar
The King's Highway
Negeb
Oboth
Bozrah
To Heliopolis/ On The Way to Shur
Kadesh-barnea
Punon
Petra
Wadi Arabah
The King's Highway
To Memphis/Noph
To Tema, Dedan
Ezion-geber (Elath)

Artwork by Margaret Jordan Brown © Mercer University Press

Black Sea
Caspian Sea
MESOPOTAMIA
ASSYRIA
BABYLONIA
CANAAN
EGYPT
The Great Sea (Mediterranean Sea)
Red Sea
Lower Sea (Persian Gulf)
BABYLONIAN EMPIRE
River Euphrates
River Tigris
River Nile
Tarsus
Carchemish
Harran
Halab
Nineveh
Asshur
Nuzi
Ugarit
Hamath
Arvad
Tadmor
Gebal
Sidon
Damascus
Tyre
Dan
Eshnunna
Der
Cuth
Babylon
Nippur
Shechem
Bethel
Jerusalem/Moriah
Mamre/Hebron/Machpelah
Sodom and Gomorrah
Zoan
Gerar
Beersheba
Erech
Larsa
Ur
Eridu
Memphis
Beni-hasan
Abydos

[PLATE 16]

Black Sea
Caspian Sea
The Great Sea (Mediterranean Sea)
Lower Sea (Persian Gulf)
Red Sea
PERSIAN EMPIRE
PERSIS
ELAM
MEDIA
BABYLONIA
ASSYRIA
ARMENIA
ARABIA
KEDAR
COMMAGENE
CAPPADOCIA
MOSCHI (MESHECH)
COLCHI
PAPHLAGONIANS
DASCYLIUM
CIMMERIANS
PHRYGIA
IONIA
LYCIA
PAMPHYLIA
CILICIA
PHOENICIA
AMMON
JUDAH
MOAB
EDOMITES
SINAI
EGYPT
ETHIOPIA
(CUSH)
MACEDONIA
THRACE (SKUDRA)
THESSALY
PELOPONNESUS
Caucasus Mountains
River Cyrus
River Araxes
Lake Urmia
Lake Van
River Tigris
River Euphrates
River Halys
River Nile
Mount Ida
Hellespont
Sinope
Trapezus
Pteria?
Gordion
Lesbos
Mytilene
Sardis
Ephesus
Salamis
Marathon
Athens
Sparta
Crete
Rhodes
Xanthus
Melitene
Tarsus
Issus
Haran
Arpad
Aleppo
Thapsacus
Hamath
Tadmor
Salamis
Soli
Citium
Cyprus
Amathus
Arvad
Gebal
Sidon
Tyre
Damascus
Samaria
Ashdod
Gaza
Jerusalem
Zoan
Sais
Tahpanhes
Heliopolis
Memphis
Sela
Dumah
Hermopolis
Coptos
Abydos
Thebes
Edfu
Yeb (Elephantine)
Syene
Tema
Dedan
Nineveh
Arbela
Asshur
Arrapkha
Rages (Rhagae)
Ecbatana (Achmetha)
Bisitun (Behistun)
Eshnunna
Der
Gabae (Isfahan)
Babylon
Borsippa
Nippur
Susa (Shushan)
Erech (Uruk)
Ur
Larsa
Parsagarda (Pasargadae)
Persepolis

[PLATE 17]

Artwork by Margaret Jordan Brown © Mercer University Press

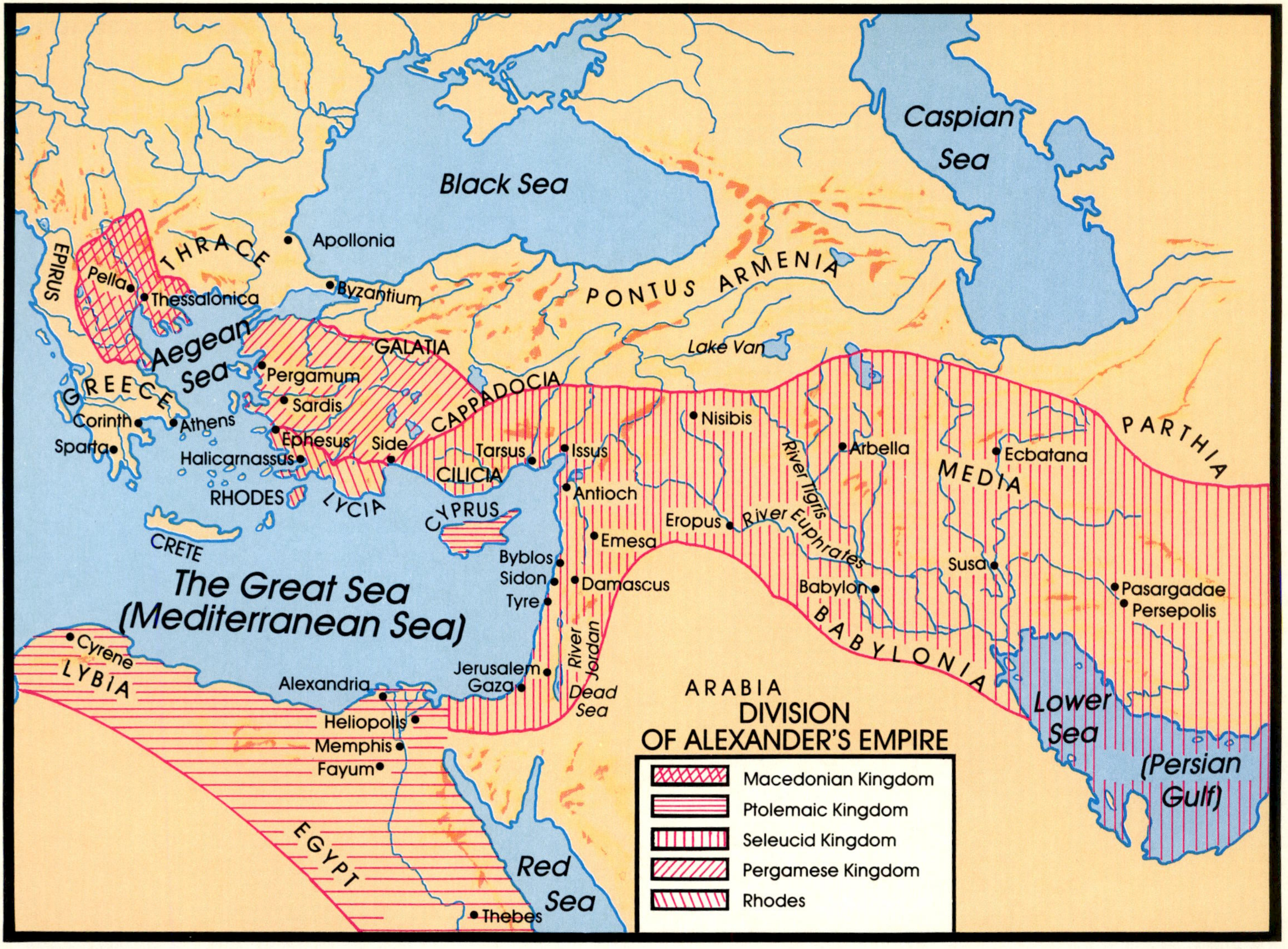

Artwork by Margaret Jordan Brown © Mercer University Press

ISRAEL
UNDER THE MACCABEES
Judean Boundaries Before 166 B.C.E.
A Conquests of Jonathan, 160–134 B.C.E.
B Conquests of Simon, 142–134 B.C.E.
C Conquests of John Hyrcanus, 134–104 B.C.E.
D Conquests of Aristobulus I, 104–103 B.C.E.
E Conquests of Alexander Jannaeus, 103–76 B.C.E.
Maximum Maccabean Holdings
The Great Sea (Mediterranean Sea)
PHOENICIA
GALILEE
SAMARIA
JUDEA
IDUMEA
PHILISTIA
GAULANITIS
GALAADITIS
TOBIADS
NABATAEANS
AKRABATTENE
River Leontes
Mount Hermon
Tyre
Paneas
Cedasa (Kedesh)
Hazor
Seleucia
Ptolemais (Acco)
Sea of Galilee
Arbela
Gamala
Carnaim
Hippos
Sepphoris
Gaba
Mount Carmel
Mount Tabor
Philoteria
River Yarmuk
Abila
Dion
Gadara
Edrei
Plain of Esadraelon
Dora
Scythopolis (Beth-shan)
Ephron
Strato's Tower
Narbata
Pella
Plain of Sharon
Samaria
River Jordan
Amathus
Gerasa
Ragaba
Apollonia
Capharsaba
Pharathon
Shechem
Mount Gerizim
River Jabbok
Alexandrium
Joppa
Ramathaim
Gedor
Beth-dagon
Timnah
Gophna
Lydda (Lod)
Adida
Ephraim
Bethel
Dok
Tyrus
Philadelphia (Rabbah)
Beth-horon
Elasa
Mizpah
Jamnia (Jabneh)
Gazara
Caphar
Jericho
Emmaus
Michmash
Cedron
Heshbon
Samaga
Azotus (Ashdod)
Ekron
Jerusalem
Qumran
Hyrania
Medeba
Bethbasi
Ascalon
Bethzacharia
Adullam
Tekoa
Marisa
Beth-zur
Dead Sea
Machaerus
Anthedon
Gaza
Adora
Hebron
En-gedi
River Arnon
Raphia
Masada
Arad
Beer-sheba
Charachmoba
Zoara
River Zered

[PLATE 20]

ROMAN EMPIRE
Oceanus Atlanticus
BRITANNIA
Londinium
GERMANIA INFERIOR
GALLIA
BELGICA
LUGDUNENSIS
GERMANIA SUPERIOR
RAETIA
NORICUM
PANNONIA
DACIA
Mare Caspium
TARRACONENSIS
AQUITANIA
ALPES COTTIAE
NARBONENSIS
ALPES MARITIMAE
ILLYRICUM
DALMATIA
MOESIA
Pontus Euxinus
ARMENIA
LUSITANIA
HISPANIA
Massilia
Tarraco
THRACIA
BITHYNIA & PONTUS
CORISICA
Roma
MACEDONIA
CAPPADOCIA
ASSYRIA
BAETICA
SARDINIA
ASIA
GALATIA
MESOPOTAMIA
Carthago
CILICIA
MAURETANIA
SICILIA
Athenae
TINGITANA
Syracusae
LYCIA
Antiochia
CAESARIENSIS
AFRICA
Mare Internum
CRETA
SYRIA
Damascus
Hierosolyma
JUDAEA
ARABIA
Cyrenne
Alexandria
CYRENE
AEGYPTUS

RULE OF HEROD THE GREAT
The Great Sea
(Mediterranean Sea)
River Leontes
Tyre
PROVINCE OF SYRIA
Huleh
GAULANITIS
TRACHONITIS
BATANAEA
AURANITIS
Ptolemais (Acre)
LOWER GALILEE
Bethsaida
Sea of Galilee
River Yarmuk
Hippos
Dion
Sepphoris
Nazareth
Gadara
River Kishon
Caesarea
Scythopolis/Bethshan
Pella
SAMARIA
Sebaste/
Samaria
Wadi Fara
Gerasa
River Jabbok
River Kanah
Antipatris
Alexandrium
Phasaelis
Joppa
River Aialon
River Jordan
PERAEA
AMMON
JUDAEA
River Sorek
Wadi el-Qelt
Cyprus
Jerusalem
Wadi es-Sant
River Zephathah
Bethlehem
Qumran
Hyrcania
Herodium
River Nahaliel
Dead Sea
Machaerus
Hebron
River Arnon
IDUMEA
River Sayyal
Masada
River Ghazzeh
Fortified Locations

SOLOMON'S TEMPLE

ARTIST'S CONCEPTION

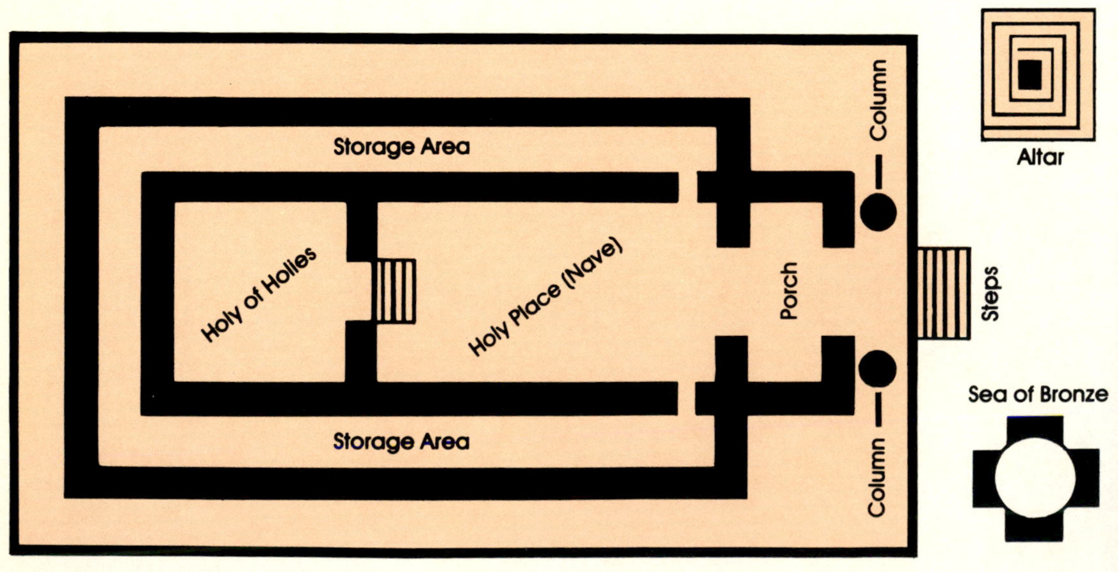

LAYOUT

[PLATE 23]

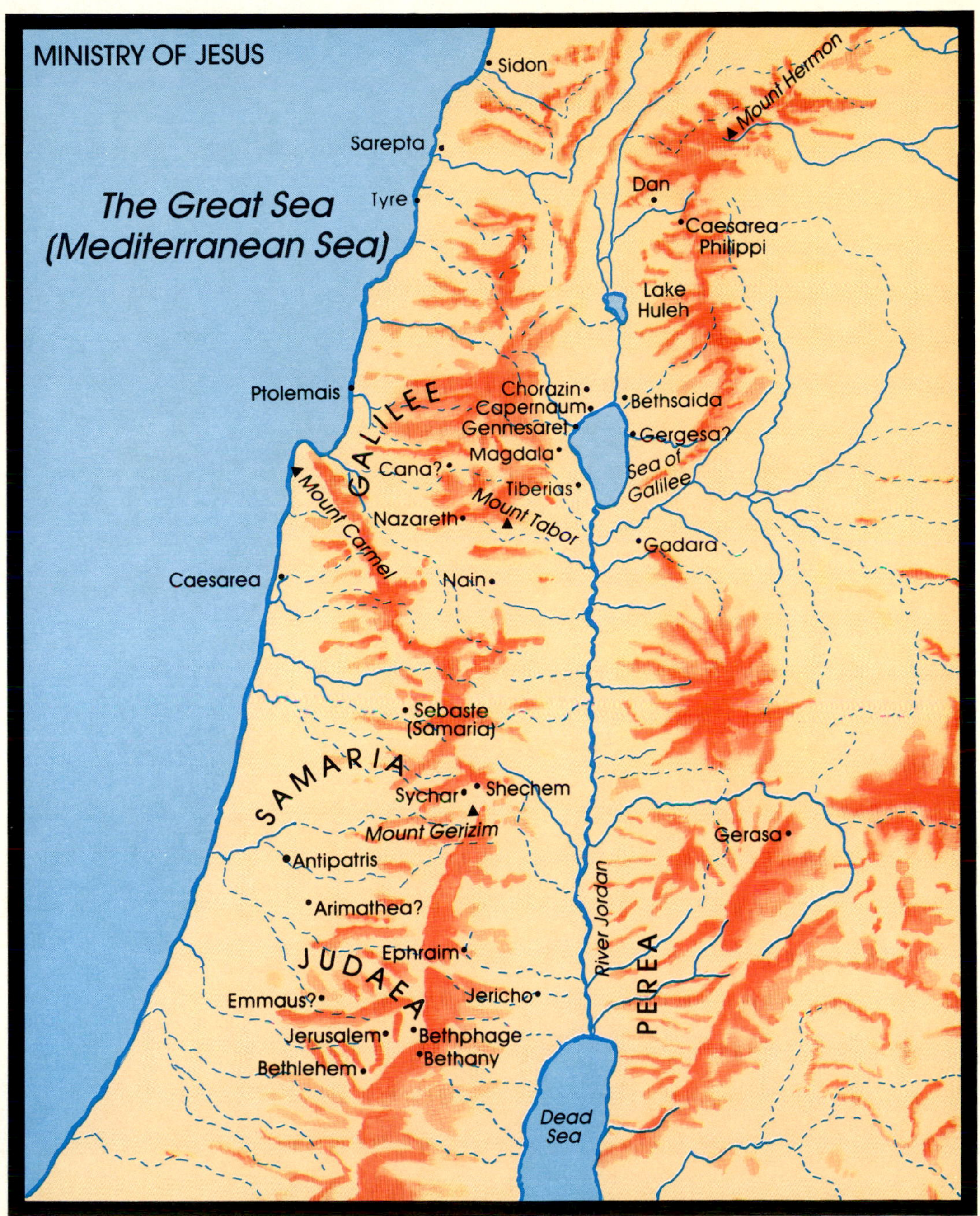

Artwork by Margaret Jordan Brown © Mercer University Press

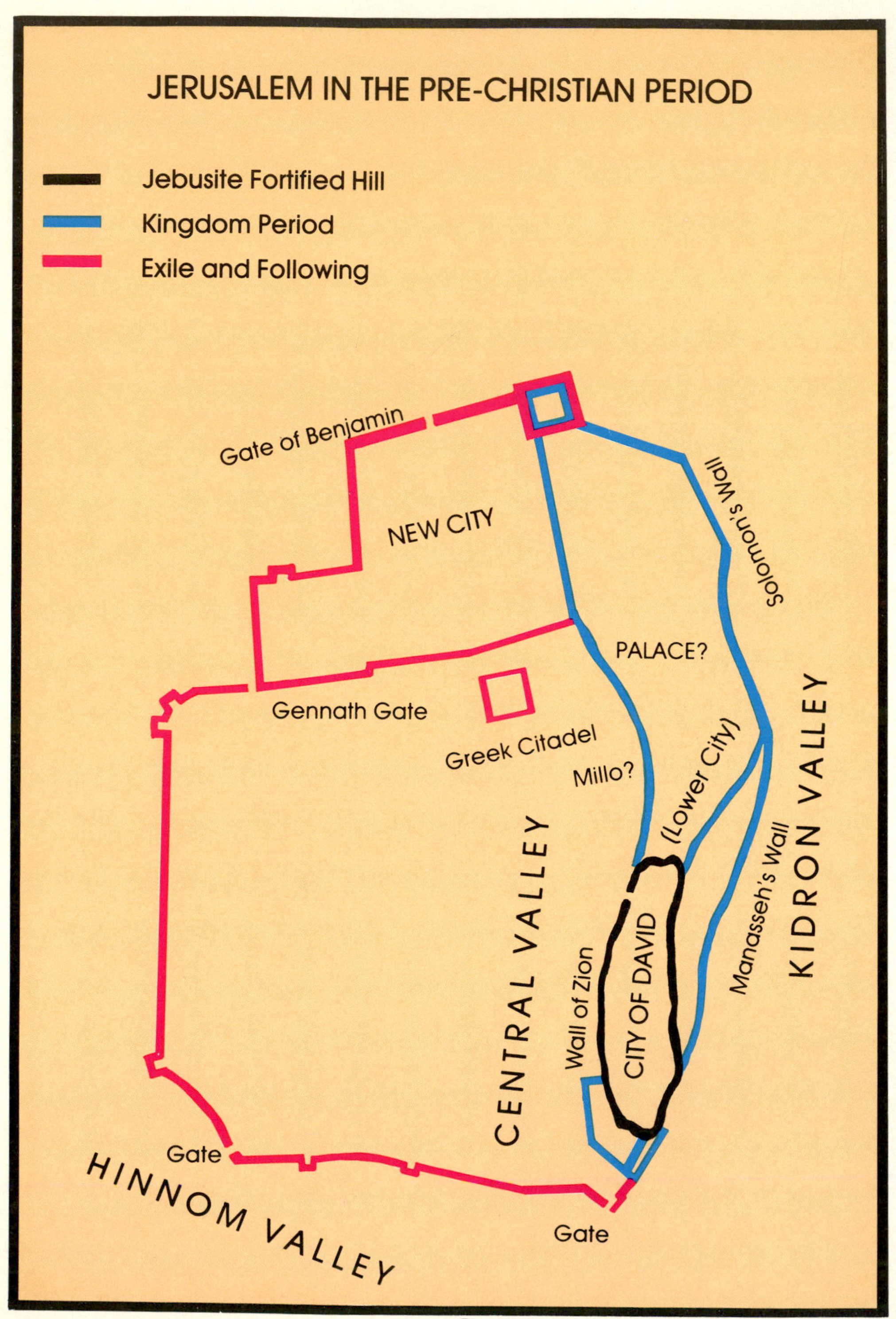
JERUSALEM IN THE PRE-CHRISTIAN PERIOD
Jebusite Fortified Hill
Kingdom Period
Exile and Following
Gate of Benjamin
NEW CITY
Solomon's Wall
PALACE?
KIDRON VALLEY
Gennath Gate
Greek Citadel
Millo?
(Lower City)
CENTRAL VALLEY
Manasseh's Wall
Wall of Zion
CITY OF DAVID
Gate
HINNOM VALLEY
Gate

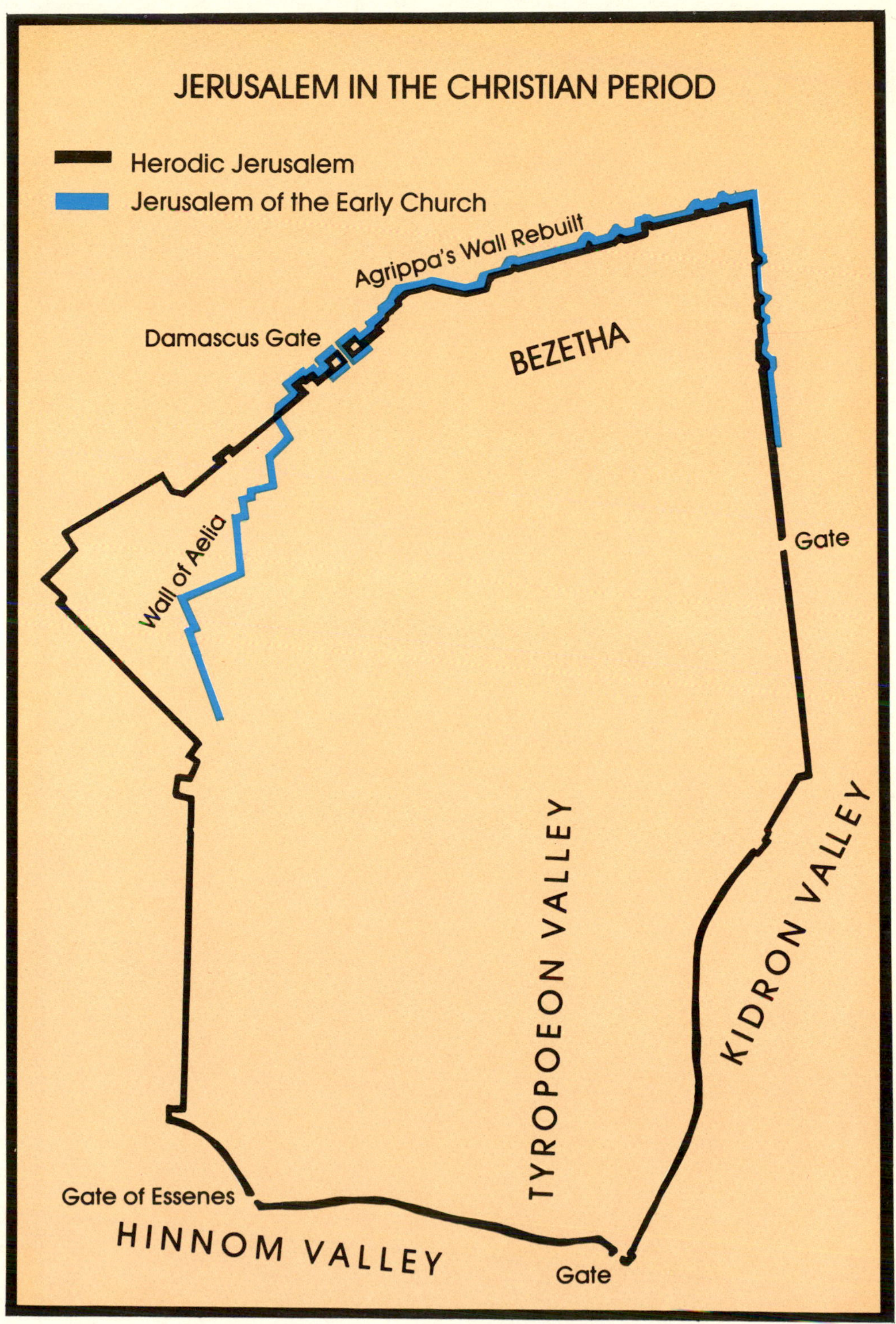
JERUSALEM IN THE CHRISTIAN PERIOD
Herodic Jerusalem
Jerusalem of the Early Church
Agrippa's Wall Rebuilt
Damascus Gate
BEZETHA
Gate
Wall of Aelia
TYROPOEON VALLEY
KIDRON VALLEY
Gate of Essenes
HINNOM VALLEY
Gate

Artwork by Margaret Jordan Brown © Mercer University Press

Artwork by Margaret Jordan Brown © Mercer University Press

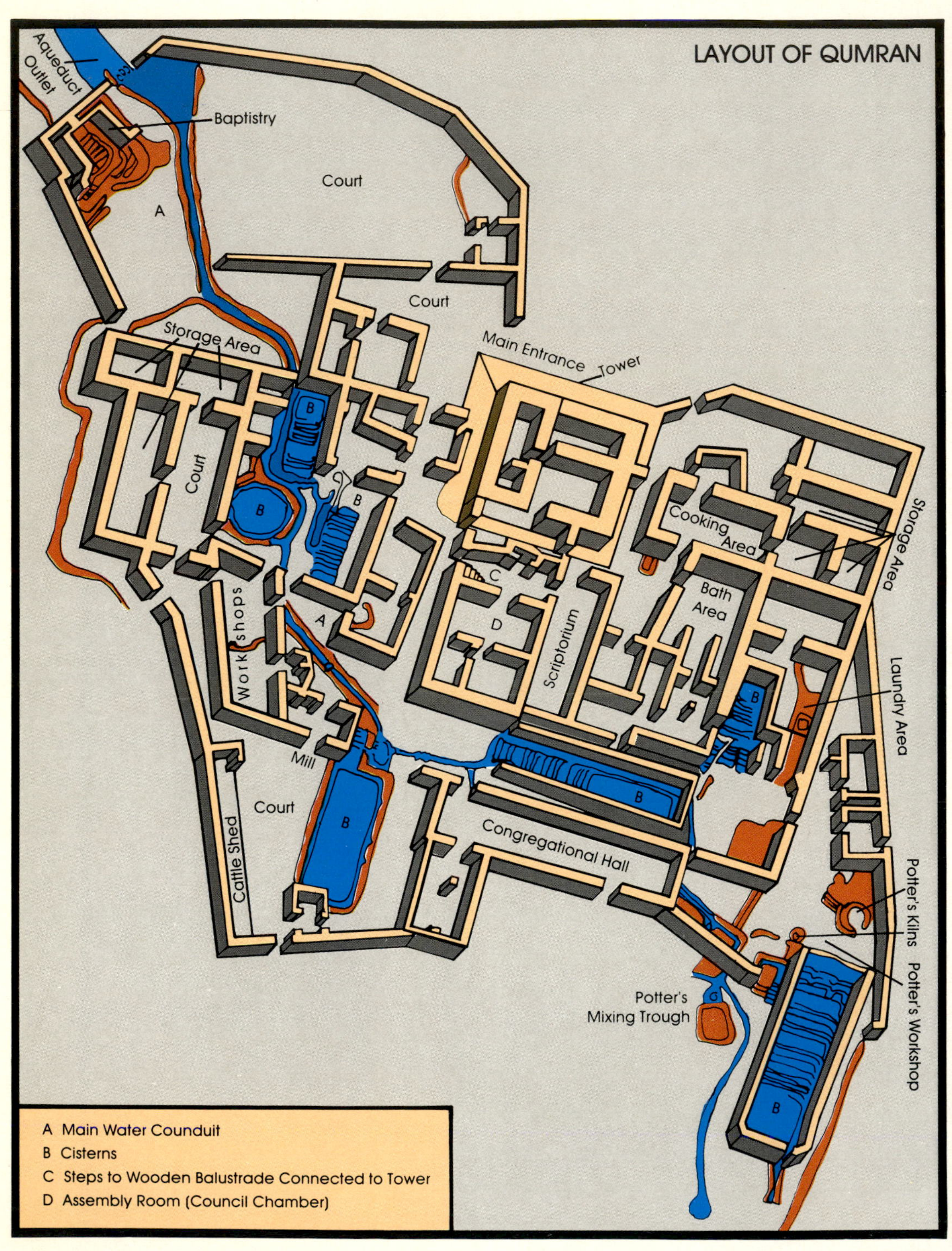
LAYOUT OF QUMRAN
Aqueduct Outlet
Baptistry
Court
A
Court
Storage Area
Main Entrance
Tower
Court
B
B
B
Cooking Area
Storage Area
C
Bath Area
A
D
Scriptorium
Workshops
Laundry Area
B
Mill
B
Court
B
Congregational Hall
Cattle Shed
Potter's Kilns
Potter's Workshop
Potter's Mixing Trough
B
A Main Water Counduit
B Cisterns
C Steps to Wooden Balustrade Connected to Tower
D Assembly Room (Council Chamber)

Artwork by Margaret Jordan Brown © Mercer University Press

CHRONOLOGY OF THE BIBLICAL PERIOD

I. Before the Patriarchs, –ca. 2000 B.C.E. (Cf. "Table of Archaeological Periods," ARCHAEOLOGY, p. 55.)

II. Beginnings of "Hebrew" History, ca. 2000–1020 B.C.E.

A. The patriarchal age; migrations; "Canaan" under Egyptian influence, ca. 2000–1500

B. Backgrounds and birth of Hebrew nationalism, ca. 1700–1020.

[Hebrews]		*[Egypt]*	
1. "Hebrews" sojourn in Egypt	ca. 1700–1300	Hyksos dominate Egypt	after ca. 1710
		Eighteenth Dynasty, Egyptian resurgence	1570
Movement into Egypt began ca. 1700,		Egyptian independence under Ahmose I	1570–1546
and "Hebrews" continued migrations throughout period		Thutmose III	1490–1435
		Religious revolution (Amarna period)	1370–1353
Hebrews oppressed by Egyptians		Nineteenth Dynasty, prosperity, building	1310
		Seti I	1308–1290
2. Moses and "exodus" from Egypt	ca. 1280	Ramsès II	1290–1224
3. Joshua and "conquest" of Canaan	ca. 1250–1200	Twentieth Dynasty	1200
4. Amphictyony	ca. 1200–1020	Ramses III	1175–1174
Hebrews struggle with Canaanites	ca. 1100	Defeat of "sea peoples"; Philistines settle in Canaan	
Philistines dominate Southern Canaan by Saul's time		End of Egyptian empire	1065

III. Hebrew Monarchy, ca. 1020–(597)587 B.C.E.

A. United Monarchy .... 1020–922 B.C.E. Saul, 1020–1000; David, 1000–961; Solomon, 961–922

B. Divided Monarchy .... 922–(597)587 B.C.E. (*See also* "Kings of Israel and Judah," CHRONOLOGY, p. 149.)

[Judah]		*[Israel]*		*[Egypt]*	
Rehoboam	922–915	Jeroboam I	922–901	Shishak invades Judah	918
Abijah	915–913				
Asa	913–873	Nadab	901–900		
		Zimri	876		
		Tibni (coregency)	876–?		
		Omri (coregency)	876–869	*[Syria]*	
		Ahab	869–850	Battle at Qarqar	853
Jehoram/Joram	849–842	Ahaziah	850–849		
Ahaziah	842	Jehoram	849–842	Hazael	ca. 842–806
Athaliah	842–837	Jehu	842–815		
Joash/Jehoash	837–800	Jehoahaz	815–801		
Amaziah	800–783	Joash	801–786		
Uzziah (coregency)	783–742	Jeroboam II	786–746		
Jotham (coregency)	750–735	Zechariah	746–745		
		Shallum	745	Rezon	ca. 740–732
		Menahem	745–736	Fall of Damascus	732
		Pekahiah	736–735	*[Assyria]*	
Ahaz	735–715	Pekah	735–732	Tiglath-pileser	745–727
		Hoshea	732–722	Shalmaneser V	727–722
		Siege of Samaria by Assyria	724–722	Sargon II	722–705
		Fall of Samaria	722/1	Conquest of Samaria	722/721
Hezekiah	715–687			Sennacherib	705–681
				Siege of Jerusalem	701
Manasseh	687–642			Esarhaddon	681–669
Amon	642–640			Ashurbanipal	(?)699–633
Josiah	640–609			Assuretililani	(?)633–629
				Sinsharishkun	(?)629–612
				Fall of Ninevah to Bablonia	612
				[Egypt]	
Battle at Megiddo	609	[N.B. regarding Judah, Babylon: Nebuchadrezzar first captured Jerusalem in 597, deported Jehoiachin and others, and installed Zedekiah as puppet king. Zedekiah rebelled; Nebuchadrezzar recaptured Jerusalem in 587/6—routinely called the "fall of Jerusalem."]		Necho	609–593
Josiah killed by Necho of Egypt				*[Babylon]*	
Jehoahaz	609			Nabopolassar	626–605
Jehoiakim	609–598			Nebuchadrezzar	605–562
Jehoiachin (Jehoiakin)	597			Battle of Charchemish	605
Zedekiah (puppet king)	597–587			(Final) Conquest of Palestine	587/6
(Final) Fall of Jerusalem	587/6				

IV. Exile and Return, (597)587/6–333 B.C.E.

[Judah]		*[Babylon]*	
Judah in exile in Babylon	(597)587/6–538	Amel-marduk	562–560
		Neriglissar	560–556
		Nabonidus	556–539
		Fall of Babylon to Persia	539
		[Persia]	
Edict of Cyrus; captives return to Jerusalem	538	Cyrus	539–530
		Cambyses	530–522
Rebuilding of temple in Jerusalem	520–516	Darius I	522–486
		Xerxes I	486–465
Nehemiah governor of Judah	445	Artaxerxes I	465–424
Mission of Ezra	428	Xerxes II	423
		Darius II	423–404
		Artaxerxes II	404–358
		Artaxerses III	358–338
		Arses	338–336
		Darius III	336–331
		Persia conquered by Greece	331

CHRONOLOGY OF THE BIBLICAL PERIOD

V. The Hellenistic Period, 333–63 B.C.E.

Near East controlled by Macedonian empire under Alexander the Great (331–323); then Ptolemies and Seleucids vie for territories, with Egypt under control of Ptolemies and Syria under Seleucids.

[Palestine]		*[Egypt/Ptolemies]*	
Judah under the Ptolemies	323–198	Ptolemy I	323–285
		Ptolemy II	285–246
		Ptolemy III	246–221
		Ptolemy IV	221–203
Battle of Panium; Seleucids gain Palestine	198	Ptolemy V	203–181
		Egypt controlled by Rome	after 180
		[Syria/Seleucids]	
Palestine ruled by Seleucids	198	Antiochus III	223–187
Maccabean Revolt	167	Antiochus IV Epiphanes	175–163
Judas Maccabaeus leads Jews	166–160		
Religious emancipation of Jews	165		
		Antiochus V	163–162
Jonathan, high priest	160–142	Demetrius I	162–150
		Alexander Balas	150–145
		Demetrius II	145–139/8
Simon, high priest	142–134	Antiochus VI	145–142/1
Jewish political independence	142	Tyrpho, claimant of Syrian throne	142/1–138

VI. Jewish Political Independence, 142–63 B.C.E.

Simon, high priest	142–134		
John Hyrcanus, high priest (and king?)	134–104		
Aristobulus I, high priest and king	104–103		
Alexander Janneus, high priest and king	103–76	Cleopatra VII	69–30
Alexandra, queen; Hyrcanus II, priest	76–67	Antipater active in Palestinian affairs	67–43
Aristobulus II, king and high priest	67–63	Pompey (Rome) captures Jerusalem	63

VII. The Roman Period, 63 B.C.E.–ca. 135 C.E.

Rome appoints Hyrcanus ethnarch and high priest	63	Julius Caesar defeats Pompey at Pharsalus	48
Antipater, under Roman grant, rules Palestine	ca. 55–43	Julius Caesar assassinated	44
Herod and Phasael named tetrarchs	41	Octavian/Antony defeat Brutus/Cassius at Philippi	42
Parthian thrust into Palestin	41–37	Battle of Actium, Octavian defeats Antony	31
Herod the Great, king of Palestine	40(37)–4	Death of Cleopatra and Ptolemy XV	30

[Rulers in Palestine]		*[Roman emperors]*		*[Events]*	
Herod the Great, king	37–4	Augustus	31 B.C.E.–14 C.E.	Herod begins rebuilding temple	20–19
Archelaus, ethnarch	4 B.C.E.–6 C.E.	(= Octavian, Julius Caesar)		Birth of Jesus	8–6 B.C.E.
Philip, tetrarch	4 B.C.E.–34 C.E.				
Herod Antipas, tetrarch	4 B.C.E.–39 C.E.				
[Procurators of Judea]					
Coponius	6–9 C.E.				
Ambibulus	9–12	Tiberius	14–37 C.E.	John the Baptist preaching	27–28 C.E.
Annius Rufinius	12–15			Jesus baptized by John	27 or 28
Valerius Gratus	15–26			Jesus crucified	29 or 30
Pontius Pilate	26–36				
(Cf. "Outline," PAUL, p. 660; cf. also "Dates," CHRONOLOGY, p. 150.)				Conversion of Paul	35 (or 32)
Marcellus	36–37	Caligula	37–41	Peter imprisoned by Agrippa	41–44
Marullus	37–41	Claudius	41–54		
Herod Agrippa I ("king")	41–44			James, son of Zebedee, executed	44
Cuspius Fadus	44-46			Paul in Galatia	49
Tiberius Alexander	46–48			Jews banished from Rome	49
Ventidius Cumanus	48–52			Paul in Corinth	50–52
Herod Agrippa II ("king")	50–?			Paul in Ephesus	52–55
M. Antonius Felix	52–60	Nero	54–68	Paul arrested in Jerusalem	56
Porcius Festus	60–62			Paul in Rome (death, 60+)	58–60
Albinus	62–64			Death of James, Jesus' brother	62
Gessius Florus	64–66			Death of Peter	(?) ca. 64
First Jewish Revolt	66–73	Galba	68	Flight of Christians from Jerusalem	66–69
		Otho	69		
		Vitellius	69		
		Vespasian	69–79	Jerusalem and temple destroyed	70
		Titus	79–81		
		Domitian	81–96	Council of Jamnia	90
		Nerva	96–98	Ignatius martyred in Rome	ca. 107
		Trajan	98–117	Pliny (Younger), gov. of Bithynia	111–113
Bar Kokhba Revolt	132–135	Hadrian	117–138	Jews defeated, dispersed	132–135

*The chronology broadly follows the scheme proposed by W. F. Albright (cf. *BASOR* no. 100 [December 1945]: 16-22) as developed, e.g., in *The Westminster Historical Atlas to the Bible*, ed. G. E. Wright and F. V. Filson (rev. ed., 1956).

Regarding dates during the time of Paul, cf. PAUL. Also cf. Marion L. Soards, *The Apostle Paul: An Introduction to the Writings and Teaching*.

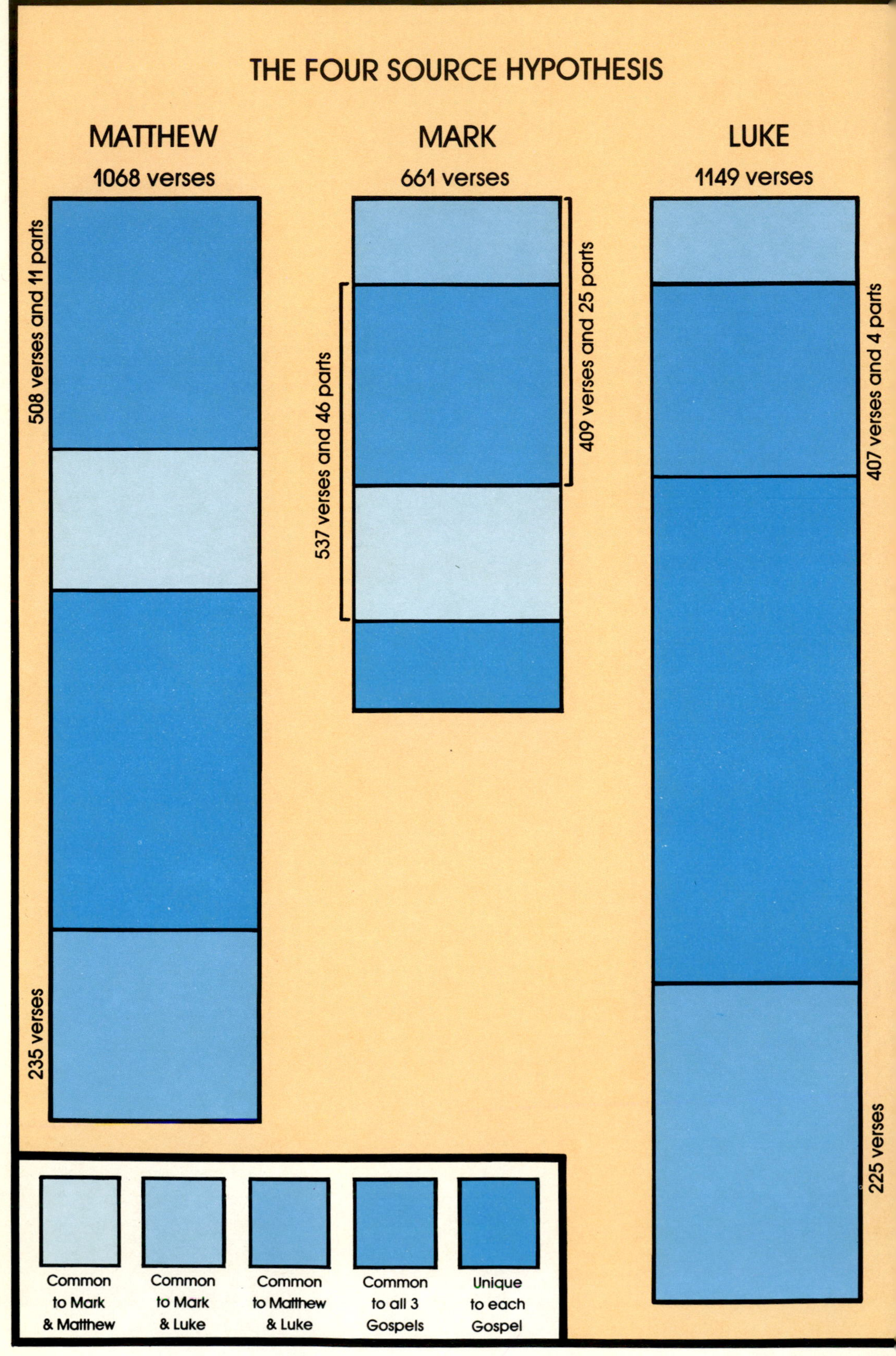
THE FOUR SOURCE HYPOTHESIS
MATTHEW
1068 verses
MARK
661 verses
LUKE
1149 verses
508 verses and 11 parts
235 verses
537 verses and 46 parts
409 verses and 25 parts
407 verses and 4 parts
225 verses
Common to Mark & Matthew
Common to Mark & Luke
Common to Matthew & Luke
Common to all 3 Gospels
Unique to each Gospel

[PLATE 33]

A satellite view of Palestine. Courtesy of the National Aeronautics and Space Administration.

A scale model of first-century Jerusalem viewed from northeast to southwest, with the pools of Bethesda and the Fortress of Antonia in the foreground.

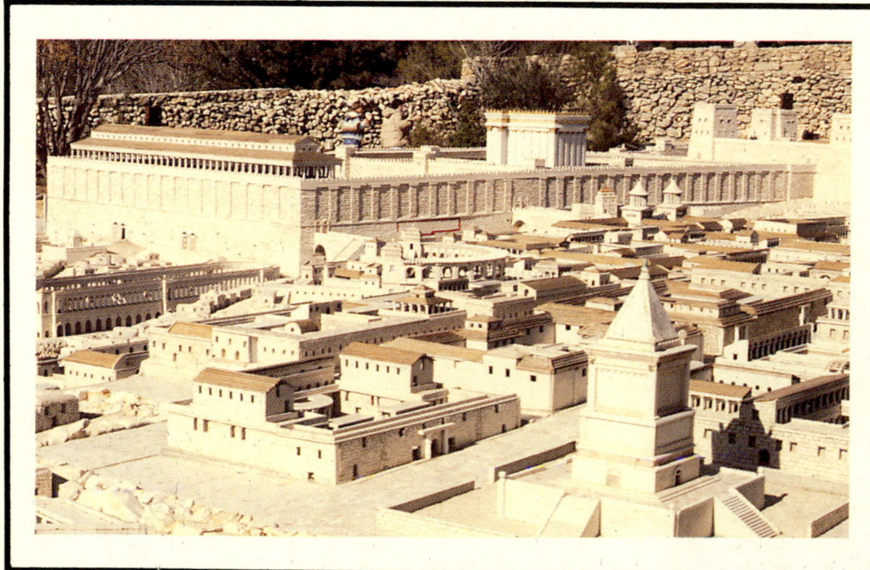

A scale model of first-century Jerusalem viewed from southwest to northeast, with the tomb of David in the foreground and the Temple platform in the background.

Dome of the Rock (*Qubbat al-Sakhra*) or Mosque of Omar in Jerusalem, built 688-691 C.E.

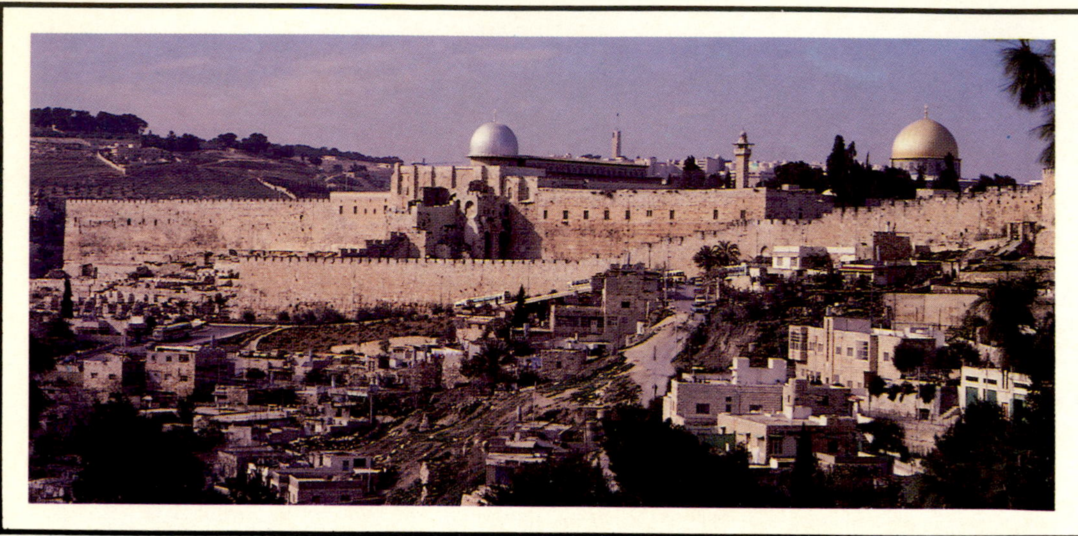

The Old City of Jerusalem showing the wall and portions of the Temple Mount.

The southeast corner of the Temple platform and Old City wall, often called the Pinnacle of the Temple (the lower courses of the wall are Herodian masonry).

[PLATE 37]

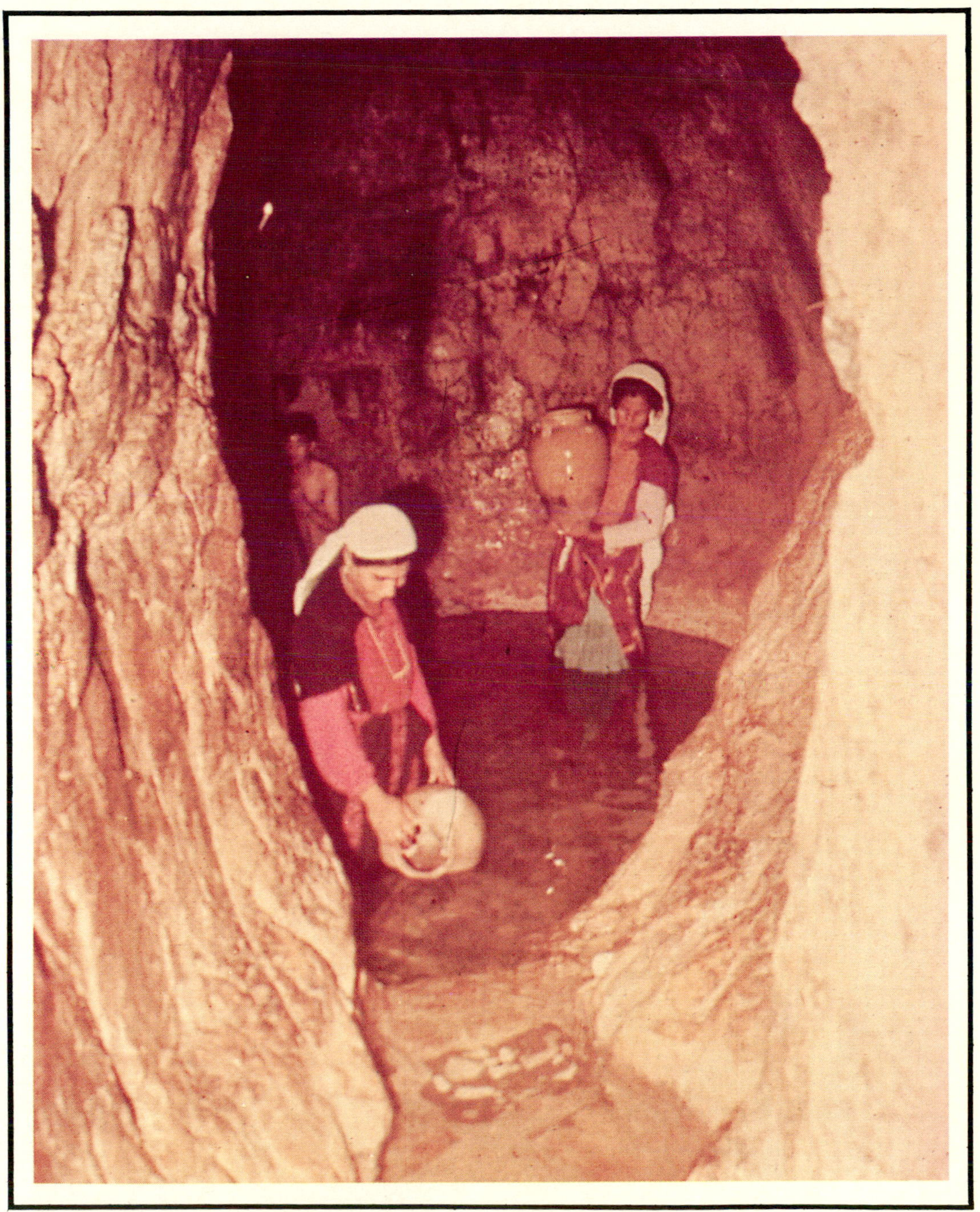

Gihon Spring from which ''Hezekiah's Tunnel'' transported water to the Pool of Siloam within the walls of the city.

Garden of Gethsemane.

Church of All Nations.

Detail of mosaic on the Church of All Nations depicting Jesus as the link between humankind and the Creator.

[PLATE 39]

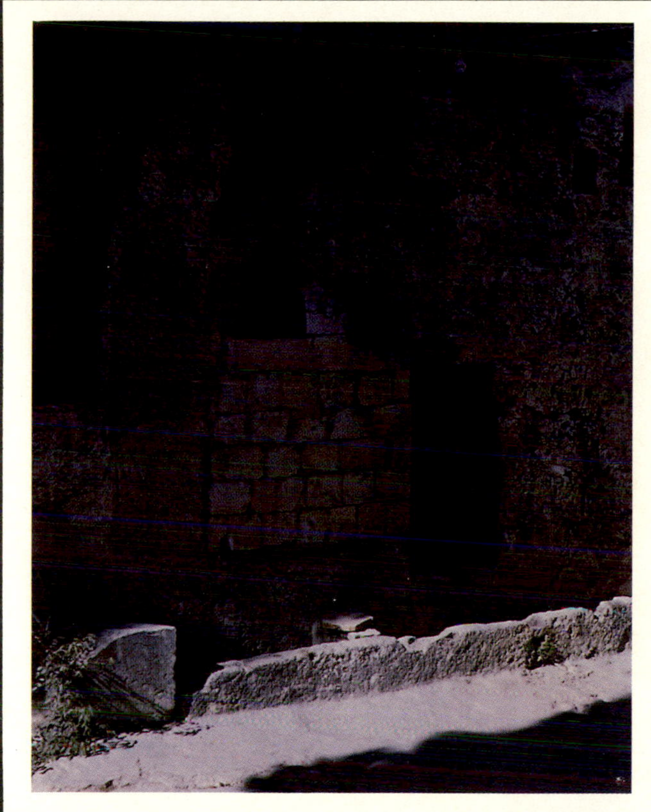

Garden tomb, near the site identified as Golgotha by General Charles Gordon in 1883.

Gordon's Calvary, north of the Damascus Gate.

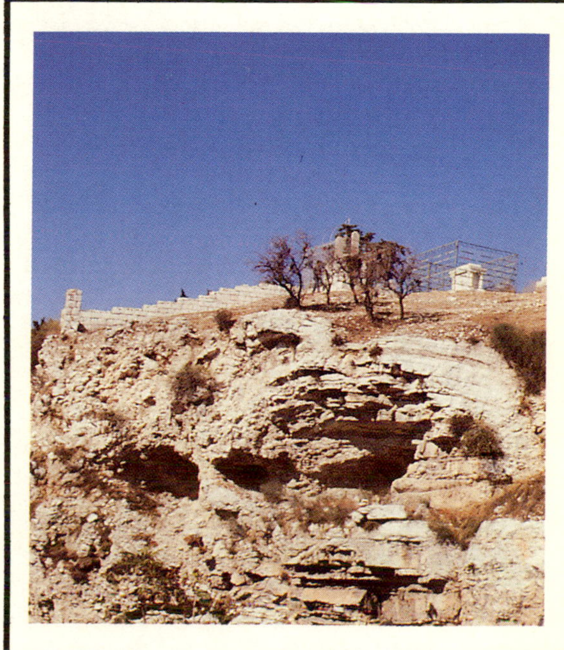

Houses along the Nile, south of Thebes.

[PLATE 41]

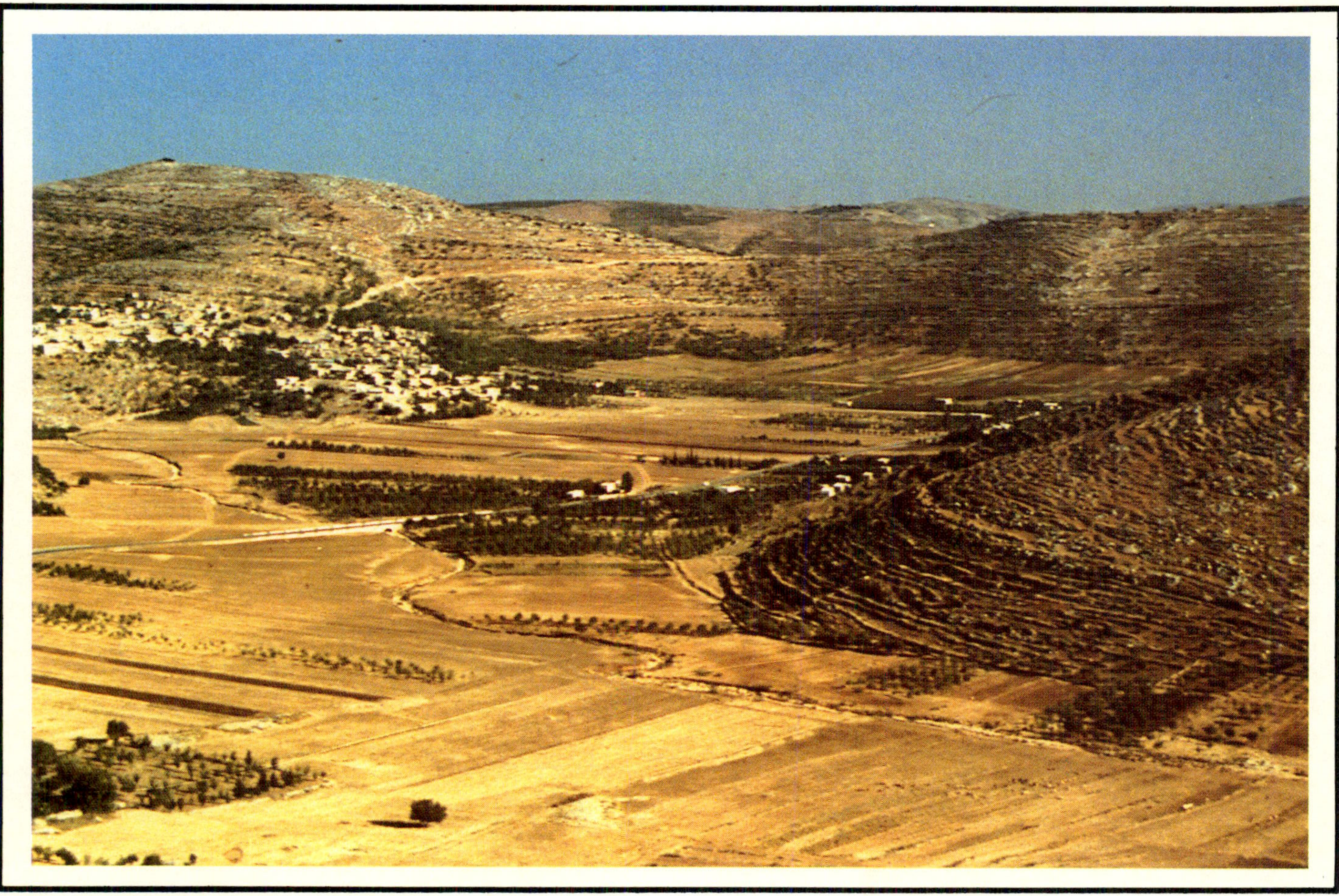

Fields southeast of Bethlehem, traditional site of the shepherds' fields (Luke 2:8).

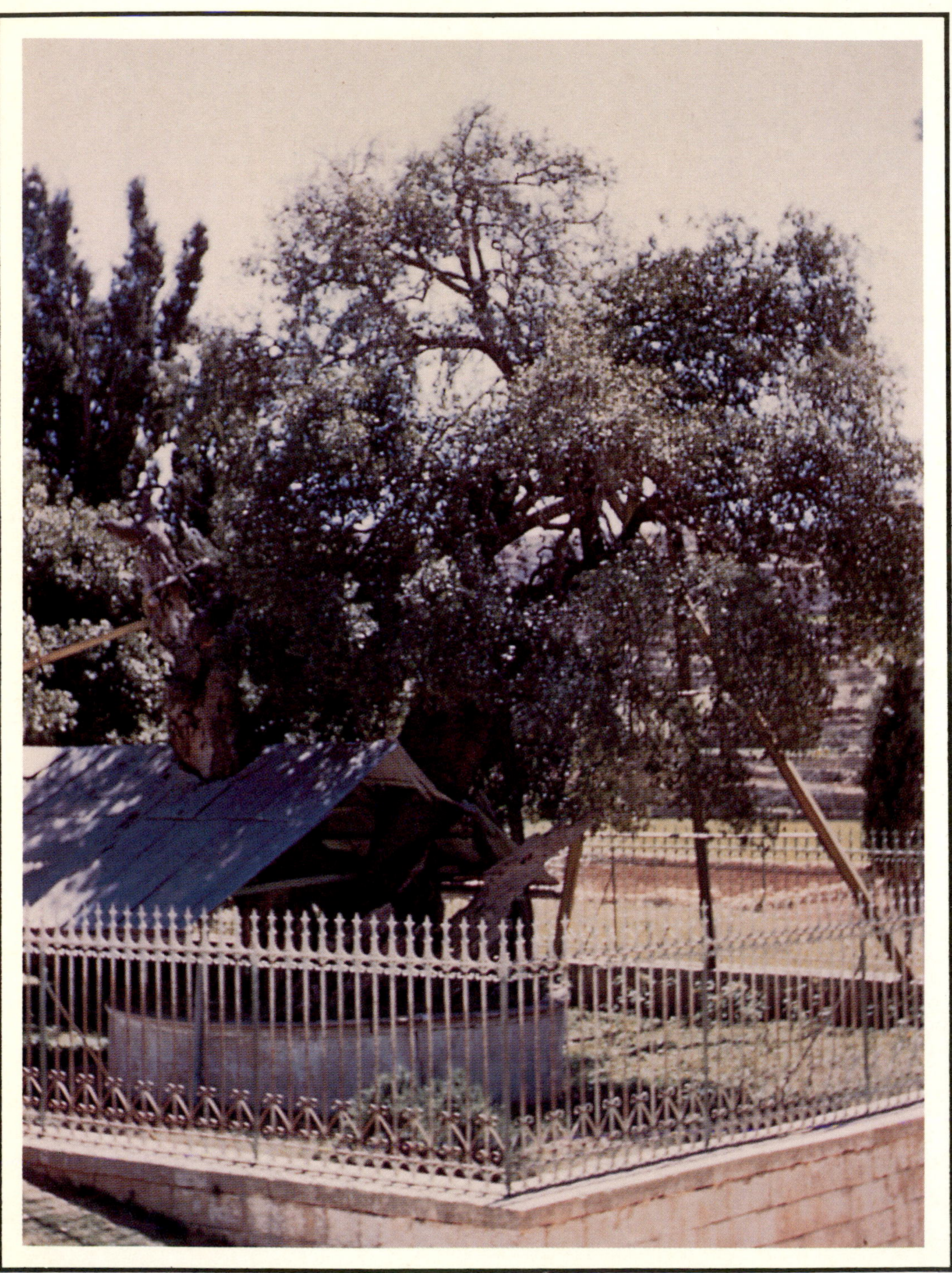

Traditional site of the oaks of Mamre where three visitors called on Abraham and Sarah (Gen 18:1-15).

[PLATE 43]

Camels foraging in the Negeb.

[PLATE 44]

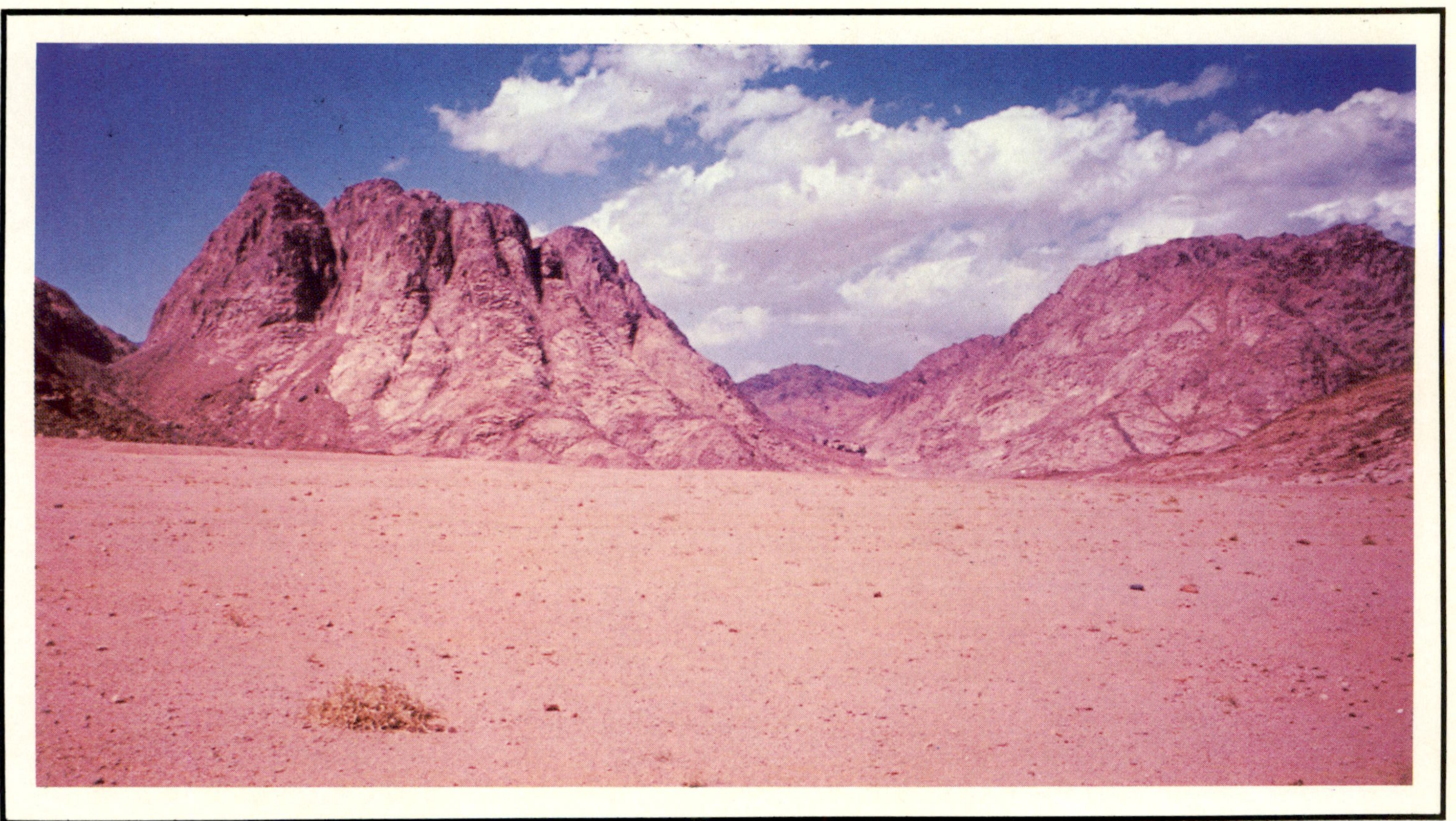

Traditional Mount Sinai (Jebel Musa) in the southern Sinai Peninsula.

A side view of the Khazneh or ''Treasury'' at ancient Petra (capital [?] of Edomites and Nabataeans), showing the building cut into the stone face of the cliff.

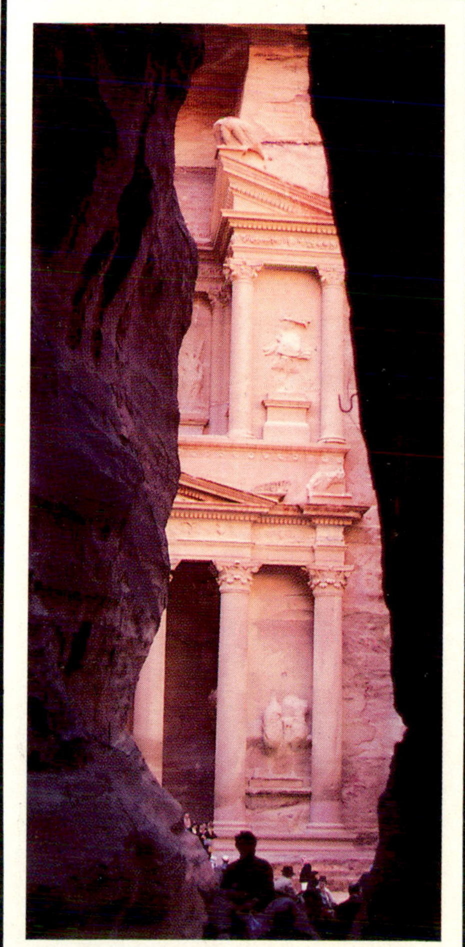

The narrow Siq, the natural passageway leading to Petra with the Khazneh in the background.

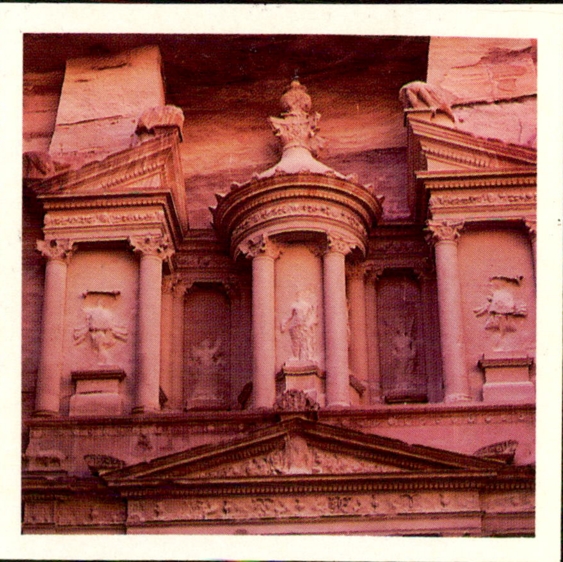

A front view of the Khazneh or ''Treasury'' at Petra, showing the façade (notice the column capitals, and statues in the upper story).

Masada, as seen from the east, where Herod built a fortress which was occupied by Zealots during the First Jewish Revolt (portions of the "snake path," the only access in antiquity, can be seen on the slope).

Excavations revealing the lower portions of Herod's palace built on the north end of Masada.

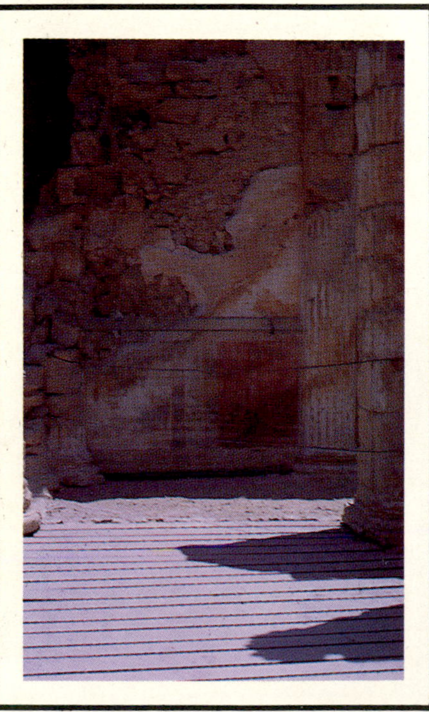

The lower palace area at Masada showing columns cut out of the rock face.

[PLATE 47]

The Dead Sea, looking east toward Transjordan.

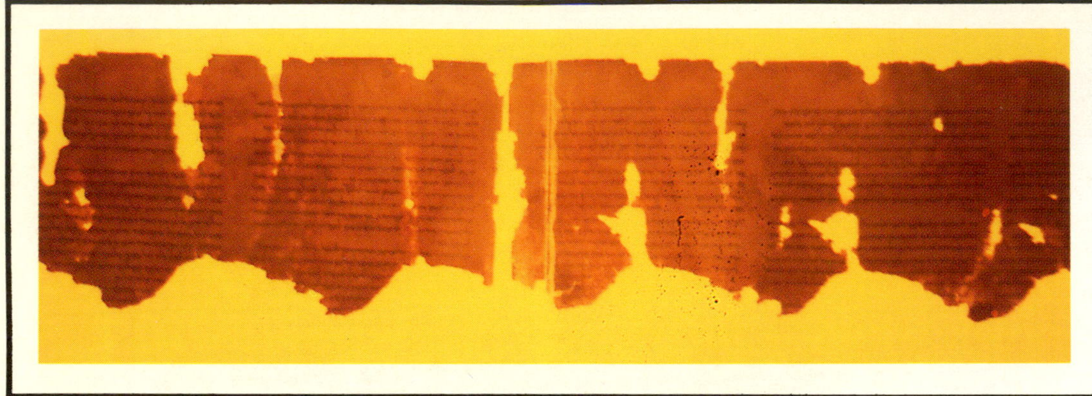

The War Scroll (*1QM*), one of the Dead Sea Scrolls, describing the final battle between the Children of Light and the Children of Darkness.

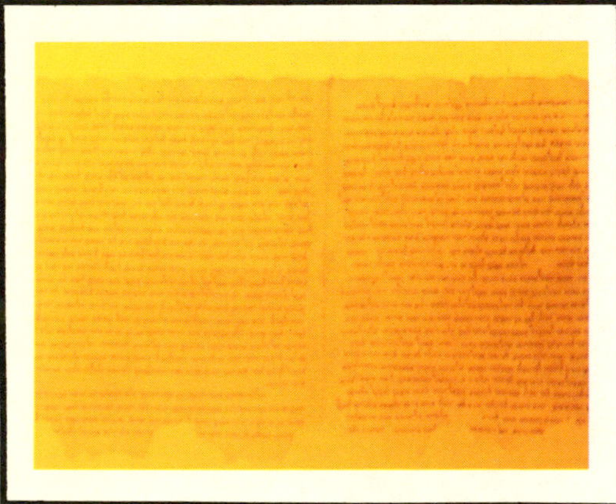

The Manual of Discipline (*1QS*), one of the Dead Sea Scrolls, giving rules for the life of the Essene community that produced the scrolls.

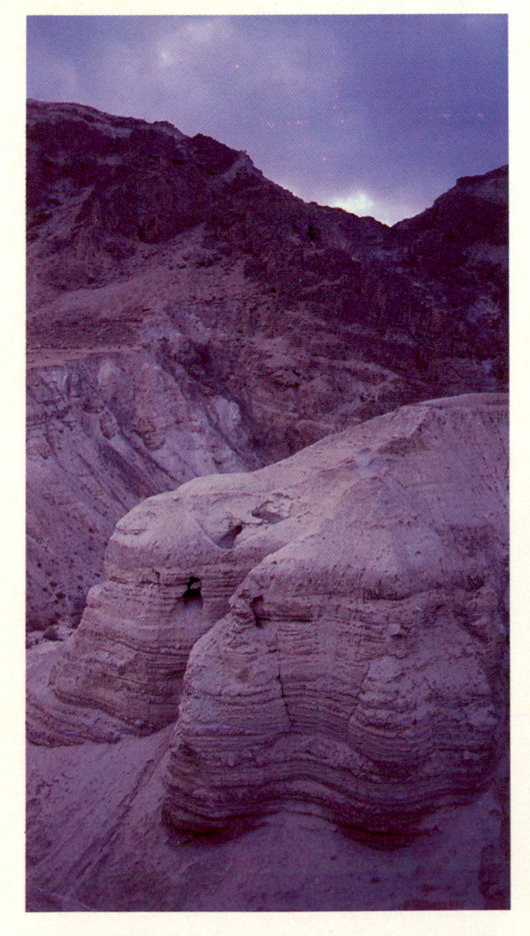

Wadi Qumran to the left, with Cave IV of the Dead Sea Scrolls discovery visible on the promontory in the center.

The traditional Mount of Temptation from the plain near Jericho.

Tell of Old Testament Jericho.

A section of the Roman aqueduct at Caesarea that brought water from the foothills of Mount Carmel eight to twelve mi. away.

An inscription mentioning Tiberius and Pontius Pilate found at Caesarea.

[PLATE 51]

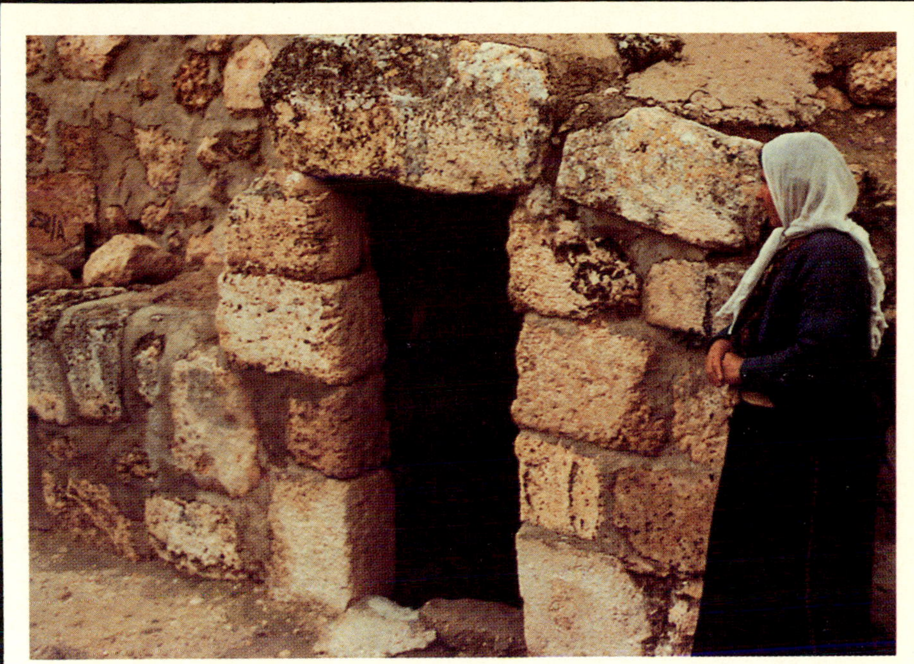

The traditional tomb of Lazarus (John 11).

Façade of the temple at Abu Simbel in Upper Egypt (built by Ramses II, 1279-1212 B.C.E.), near the Aswan high dam on the Nile.

Ruins of the Capernaum synagogue, dating no earlier than the late second century C.E.

The Step Pyramid (*mastaba*) of King Djoser (Zoser) of Egypt (Dynasty III, 27th century B.C.E.) at Saqqara, across the Nile from ancient Memphis—the first great stone pyramid.

Fishing on the Sea of Galilee.

A view of Transjordan's eastern hills across the Sea of Galilee.

The Transjordan as seen from the central hills, with the Sea of Galilee in the foreground.

The upper Jordan River.

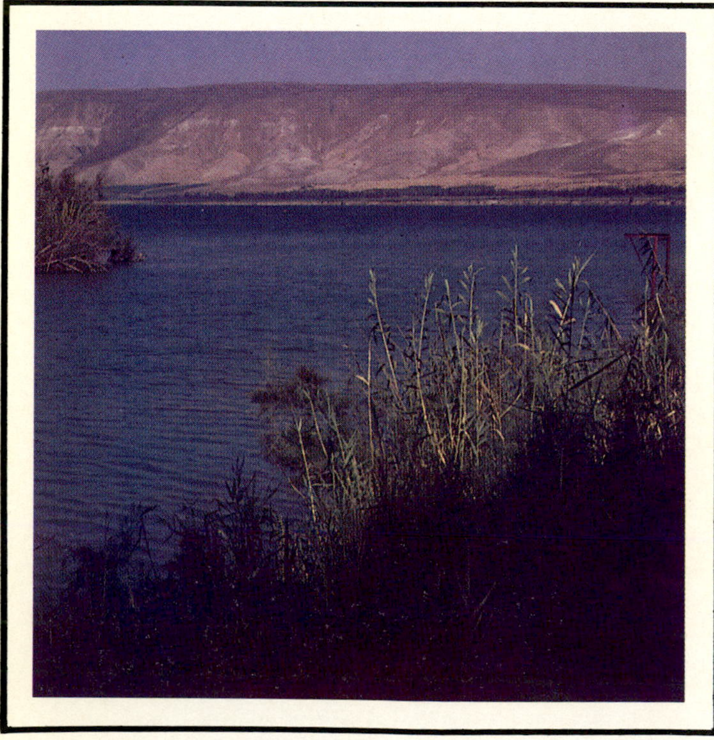

Source of the Jordan River with the Sea of Galilee and eastern highlands beyond.

The southern end of the Sea of Galilee.

The valley of the Jordan River.

[PLATE 56]

Plain of Esdraelon, viewed from the top of the mound of Taanach (Judg 5:19).

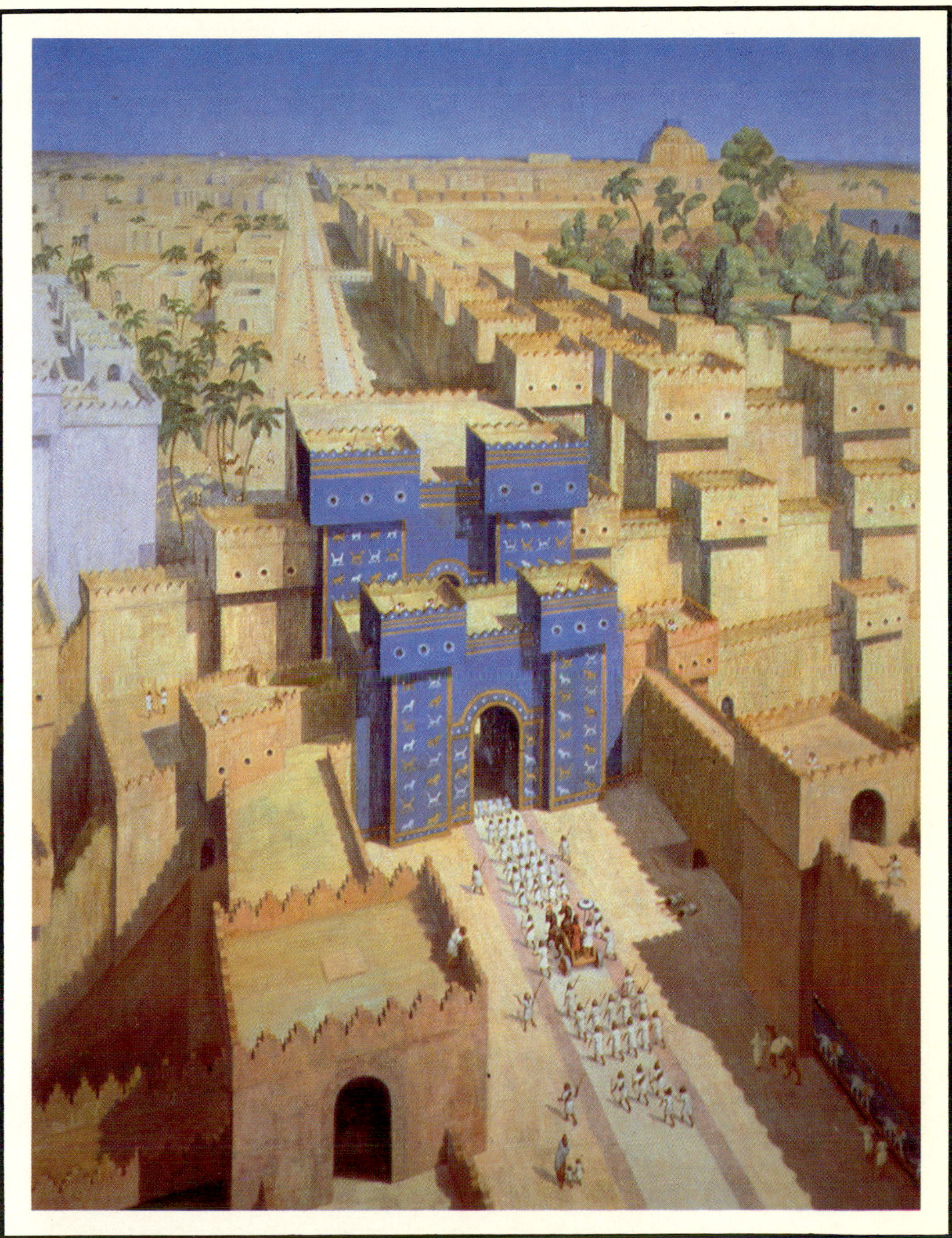

Artistic rendition of the Ishtar Gate and Procession Way in Babylon, 7th-6th century B.C.E. (Nebuchadrezzar II).

[PLATE 58]

A sphinx from Nineveh.

A lion from the
Processional Street in
Babylon.

Views of the unique amphitheater at Ephesus with seven *thuromata* or windows, and seating 24,000-25,000.

The Acropolis of Athens, with the Parthenon (5th century B.C.E.).

The west end of the Parthenon.

The Acropolis, viewed from downtown Athens.

[PLATE 61]

The Necropolis (cemetary) overlooking the Kidron valley.

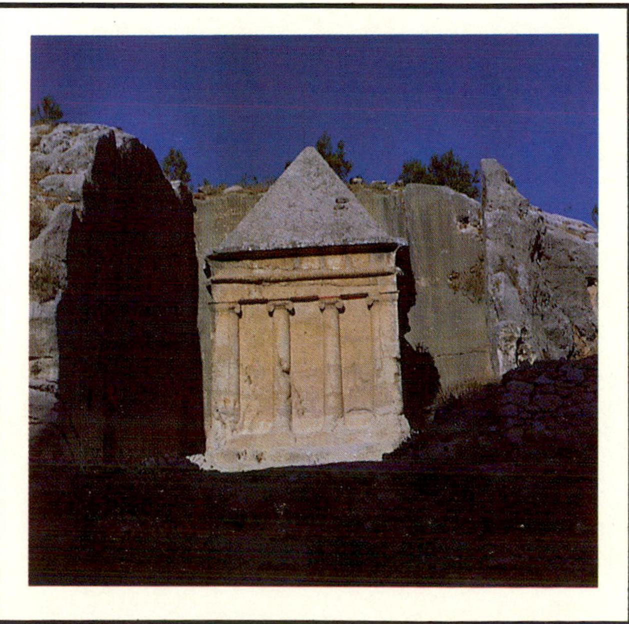

The traditional site of the tomb of Zechariah in the Kidron Valley.

The Acrocorinth (sometimes called the ''acropolis'' of Corinth), viewed through the remains of a sixth-century B.C.E. temple of Apollo, overlooking Corinth.

surely to be understood in a judicial sense, it is clearly the case that in the OT neither idea can be limited simply to a question of legal definition. This is especially clear in the frequent collocations of "justice" (*mišpāṭ*) and RIGHTEOUSNESS (*ṣĕdāqâ*). God is a lover of righteousness and justice (Ps 33:5), characteristics which, when coupled with God's unending love (*ḥesed*) and compassion (*raḥămîm*), serve as the cornerstones of God's rule (Ps 89:14; cf. Jer 9:23; Hos 2:19 [MT 2:21]; 12:6 [MT 12:7]). The people of Israel are to follow in the way of God by doing righteousness and justice (Gen 18:19), and their leaders, especially their kings, are charged to implement policies that nurture and secure these qualities in the lives of those for whom they are responsible (2 Sam 8:15; Ps 72:1-2; Jer 22:3; cf. 1 Kgs 3:7-9). Such policies are prominently described with reference specifically to social concerns, namely caring for the poor and the needy (Ps 72:2, 4), securing the welfare of the alien, the orphan, and the widow (Jer 22:3). Faithful attention to these concerns determines God's evaluation of one's true loyalties.

It was primarily the prophets who sounded the charge that Israel's kings (e.g., Jer 22:13-19) and official leaders (e.g., Mic 3:1-12; cf. Jer 2:8; 5:31; 6:13-14; 8:8-12) had failed to live up to this high standard of justice. Certainly the prophetic condemnations focused on the breaking of the Law. This is especially clear in their attacks on such clearly prohibited offenses as bribery, idolatry, and murder (e.g., Jer 7:3-15). But it is also the case that the prophets concerned themselves with behavior which, under the letter of the law, may not have been illegal. They were particularly concerned, for example, with false attitudes that would permit one to observe faithfully the formalities of worship while at the same time plotting to defraud and cheat their neighbors (Amos 8:4-6; cf. 2:6-8; 5:10-12; Mic 3:9-12). Such behavior makes a mockery of justice (Amos 5:7; 6:12), and God will not abide it (cf. Amos 5:21-24; Mic 6:6-8). Gradually the prophets come to look toward the future when the ideal King will at last embody the true justice that is God's (Isa 11:1-4) and toward the new Jerusalem where programs of social reform will assure that justice can be achieved outside the Temple and not only within it (Ezek 45:8-17; 46:16-18).

God's Justice. In a still broader sense, what is at stake in the issue of justice becomes especially clear in those OT texts that raise pointed and probing questions about God's justice. It is evident that there is a standard of justice which is expected of God, in essence that God will faithfully discriminate between the righteous and the wicked (cf. Ps 1), and that God for the most part acts consistently in accordance with this standard, even when external circumstances may raise doubts (e.g., Gen 18:22-25; Ezek 18:1-32). And yet it is also clear that God is in no way bound to human standards of justice. On the one hand this results in magnanimous and undeserved forgiveness from a God whose compassion and mercy override the requirement of justice (e.g., Exod 33:19; Hos 11:8-9; Jonah 4:1-5, 9-11). But on the other hand it leaves many an innocent sufferer groping for answers where none seem available. The OT unashamedly recounts the hard and pressing questions of many of these sufferers, most notably in the significant tradition of lament that runs throughout Israel's encounter with God (e.g., the lament psalms, the confessions of Jeremiah, Job). In their pursuit of relief, or at least understanding, these hurl at God questions and complaints, anger and frustration, even doubt and scepticism, in the hope of finding some clue to the mystery of God's justice. In the end God proclaims, "I am God" (Hos 11:9) and "I am creator" (cf. Job 38–41). Within this proclamation, and within its testimony to God's ultimate sovereignty, the quest for divine justice must find its way.

See also ETHICS IN THE NEW TESTAMENT; ETHICS IN THE OLD TESTAMENT; SUFFERING IN THE OLD TESTAMENT.

Bibliography. R. Adamiak, *Justice and History in the Old Testament: The Evolution of Divine Retribution in the Historiographies of the Wilderness Generation*; J. Barton, "Natural Law and Poetic Justice in the Old Testament," *JTS* 30 (1979): 1-14; H. J. Boecker, *Law and the Administration of Justice in the Old Testament and in the Ancient Near East*; W. Brueggemann, "Theodicy in a Social Dimension," *JSOT* 33 (1985): 3-25; J. Crenshaw, "Popular Questioning of the Justice of God in Ancient Israel," *ZAW* 82 (1970): 380-95; L. Epsztein, *Social Justice in the Ancient Near East and the People of the Bible*; B. Johnson, "מִשְׁפָּט, *mišpāṭ*," *TWAT*; J. Mags, "Justice: Perspectives from the Prophetic Tradition," *Int* 37 (1983): 5-17; P. Miller, *Sin and Judgment in the Prophets*.

—SAMUEL E. BALENTINE

• **Justification.** The biblical teaching of justification by faith was the main doctrine of Christianity for the Protestant reformers and has retained its place of prominence in Protestant denominations since the sixteenth century. The reformers rediscovered in the Bible, especially in the Letters of PAUL to the Galatians and the Romans, the reality that one is justified by God apart from any works of merit. Key passages which state this fact are Rom 3:21-31, Gal 3:11, and Eph 2:8-9. The writings of Paul contain the clearest biblical teaching regarding justification by faith.

Though Paul's teaching clearly has direct meaning for the individual sinner who wants to know how to become acceptable to God, the context in which Paul developed his teaching regarding justification by faith was the conflict in the first-century church between Judaizing Christians who insisted that gentile converts should be circumcised and obey Jewish food laws and those who did not so believe. As Stendahl says, "Paul's doctrine of justification by faith has its theological context in his reflection on the relation between Jews and gentiles, and not within the problem of how *man* is to be saved, or how man's deeds are to be accounted . . . " (26). Similarly Dahl claims that "the framework which Paul uses to locate the doctrine [of justification by faith] is social and historical rather than psychological and individualistic" (110).

In brief, Jews and Judaizing Christians argued that gentiles may become part of God's chosen people by becoming part of the Jewish people. Since circumcision was a sign of God's covenant with his people, gentile Christians should therefore be circumcised. Paul argued in Romans and Galatians that Christ makes salvation available for everyone who has faith, whether Jew or gentile. Gentile Christians therefore do not need to become Jews. The teaching of justification by faith enabled Paul to affirm the universality of the gospel. Unfortunately in the history of the church, the social context in which Paul developed his teaching was forgotten once the church became a gentile church. The doctrine of justification by faith has become limited to personal religious experience and salvation. A careful study of Paul's Letters in their historical setting reveals an often neglected social dimension in the doctrine of justification by faith.

This doctrine is based on the assumption that all people are sinners and need to be saved (Rom 3:9-18). It is also based on the belief that God is righteous/just, faithful, and truthful (Rom 3:1-8); he keeps his commitments. And God's commitment to Abraham was the following: "Scripture, foreseeing that God would justify the gentiles by faith, preached the gospel beforehand to Abraham, saying, 'In you shall all the nations be blessed' " (Gal 3:8). So Paul's teaching of justification by faith is not primarily anthropological, i.e., answering how the guilty sinner can be saved. It is primarily theological, defending God's moral integrity. God has not required of gentiles something different than he required of the Jews or of Abraham. Abraham was saved through faith, not through works of the Law (Rom 4). Similarly all people—Jews and gentiles—are justified through faith. The coming of Christ showed God's righteousness, his moral integrity, in that through the death of Christ God made salvation available for all through faith, just as he had promised to Abraham (Gal 3:6-9, 14-18).

Justification is entirely an act of God (Rom 8:33) and is based on the death of Jesus Christ, "who was put to death for our trespasses and raised for our justification" (Rom 4:25). Paul writes that "God shows his love for us in that while we were yet sinners Christ died for us. Since, therefore, we are now justified by his blood, much more shall we be saved by him from the wrath of God" (Rom 5:8-9).

The imagery of justification is a legal one, but as the parallelism between Rom 5:9 and 5:10 demonstrates, justification and RECONCILIATION are different metaphors describing the same reality. To reconcile means to put an end to enmity; to justify means to put an end to legal contention. Much discussion of the doctrine of justification throughout the history of the church has focused on whether justification confers on the believer a new status or a new character. Does justification bear the stamp of a legal conception (a status) rather than of an ethical conception (a real change in character)? Or in other words does justification mean that believers have only a new standing before God and are considered righteous, or are they also made righteous?

Since English has no verb "to rightwise" or "to rightify," we use the Latin, "justify." But "to justify" in English does not mean "to make right." Biblical words for justification, however, are used for making right in the sense of rectifying a relationship. So justification is the action by which God rectifies the relation between himself and people.

See also RIGHTEOUSNESS IN THE NEW TESTAMENT; RIGHTEOUSNESS IN THE OLD TESTAMENT.

Bibliography. G. Bornkamm, *Paul;* N. A. Dahl, *Studies in Paul;* F. Stagg, *New Testament Theology;* K. Stendahl, *Paul Among Jews and Gentiles.*

—ROGER L. OMANSON

• **Justin Martyr.** [juhs'tin-mahr"tuhr] Justin Martyr was an early Christian apologist. Born of pagan parents in Flavia Neapolis (modern Nablus) around 100 C.E., he manifested a serious religious interest from an early date. After studying with STOIC, Peripatetic (Aristotelian), Pythagorean, and Platonist teachers, he experienced a conversion from Greek to Hebrew truth. As a philosopher-evangelist, he taught in Rome during the reign of Antoninus Pius (138–161). His students included Tatian (fl. 160–175), the founder of the Encratite sect, and IRENAEUS (ca. 130–202), Bishop of Lyons and anti-heretical writer. Betrayed by a CYNIC philosopher named Crescens, he suffered martyrdom early in the reign of Marcus Aurelius (161–180), probably between 163 and 165.

Although a prolific author, only three of Justin's writings have survived, two apologies addressed to gentiles and his *Dialogue with Trypho, a Jew*. In his *First Apology*, addressed ca. 150 to the Emperor Antonius Pius, Justin wove together a refutation of stock pagan charges against Christianity and a positive case for it as the "true religion." He demanded a halt to punishment of Christians for the name alone and called for an impartial investigation of stock charges—atheism, immorality, treason, social aloofness, and theological absurdity. Rather than opposing Greek thought without qualification, he acknowledged that the divine LOGOS had inspired both Greek philosophers and Hebrew prophets. The truth which they received in a partial and incomplete form, however, became incarnate in Jesus of Nazareth. Christianity, therefore, is the true philosophy.

In his *Second Apology*, a brief work addressed to the Roman Senate, Justin pled a case for three Christians condemned to death by the prefect Urbicus, explaining why all Christians do not just commit suicide if they love death so much. They remain alive because they have a mission—to save the human race by instructing them in divine doctrines. This is why God delays the judgment. Christians do not differ from others in whom the divine Logos dwells except in the fact that they possess the whole truth. By dying, they prove the validity of their faith.

In the *Dialogue with Trypho* Justin ostensibly recorded a debate which took place in Ephesus between himself and a Jew named Trypho shortly after the BAR-KOCHBA rebellion (132–135). Since he quoted from the *First Apology*, however, the *Dialogue* in its present form cannot be a Moreover, some scholars have argued that the writing was not an apology to Judaism at all but to gentiles who used Jewish arguments against Christianity (as Celsus did in his *True Discourse* ca. 175). Others have suggested that he wrote it to prop up wavering Christians. The *Dialogue* consists of four parts: (1) an account of Justin's conversion (1–10), (2) an explanation as to why Christians do not keep the whole LAW (11–31), (3) an answer to Jewish claims about Jesus (32–114), and (4) an argument for the gentile mission based on the OT.

Although not a brilliant thinker, Justin made a significant contribution by presenting Christianity as a philosophy. Previously it had competed mainly with oriental religions. Since the philosophies of this day also served religious purposes, Justin widened the Church's appeal. In his presentation he contributed significantly to Christianity's self-understanding.

See also PATRISTIC LITERATURE.

Bibliography. L. W. Barnard, *Justin Martyr: His Life and Thought*; E. G. Hinson, "Justin Martyr," *EncRel;* E. F. Osborn, *Justin Martyr*.

—E. GLENN HINSON

• **Justus.** [juhs'tuhs] Justus is the commonplace Latin surname borne by three men in the NT. Little is known about the individuals beyond the scant details in each reference.

1. Joseph BARSABBAS Justus is mentioned as the losing candidate to fill Judas's apostleship (Acts 1:23). Matthias won the casting of lots. Neither Justus nor Matthias is mentioned further.

2. Titius Justus is identified as a worshipper of God in Corinth who received Paul into his home adjacent to the synagogue which Paul abandoned in choosing to go to the gentiles (Acts 18:7).

3. Jesus Justus is one of a trio of Jewish Christians who comforted Paul during the imprisonment described in Col 4:11.

—JOHN R. DRAYER

• **Kadesh-Barnea.** [kay′dish-bahr″nee-uh] The home of the Hebrews for a period of nearly a generation during the wilderness wandering period. It is located both in the Wilderness of Paran (Num 13:26) and in the Wilderness of Zin (Num 20:1). Perhaps Kadesh lay in a remote wilderness region known by both names, or near the boundary of these two regions. Clearly, Kadesh-Barnea must have had abundant water for the Hebrews to stay here for a lengthy period. From here the spies went out through the land of Canaan (Num 13:1-26), and the Hebrews tried an abortive campaign against the land from the south and were defeated by the Amalekites and Canaanites (Num 14:40-45). Here too Miriam, Moses' sister, died and was buried (Num 20:1). The site is also known as Meribah, strife, because the people rebelled against God there (Num 20:2-13). Kadesh is mentioned in Gen 14:7 where its former name Enmishpat, spring of judgment, is also given. Kadesh lay on the southern border of the tribe of Judah, between the Arabah and the Brook of Egypt.

Several biblical references help with the general location of Kadesh-Barnea, but precision isn't possible. Deut 1:2 locates Kadesh as eleven days journey from Mount Horeb by way of Mount Seir. Unfortunately, neither of these mountains can be identified with certainty. Nor are the border descriptions mentioned above of much help. The best suggestions are for a strong water supply in the wilderness area of northern Sinai. The two sites most frequently identified with Kadesh-Barnea are Ein Qedeis and Ein el-Qudeirat, with the consensus favoring Ein el-Qudeirat.

Ein el-Qudeirat was first surveyed by C. L. Woolley and T. E. Lawrence in 1914 (PLATES 3, 9). It was later surveyed by Nelson Glueck, Roland de Vaux, and Yohanan Aharoni. In 1956 Moshe Dothan excavated there and in 1976–79 Rudolph Cohen excavated the site. While it is not certain that Ein el-Qudeirat is the site of Kadesh, the location seems compelling. This site has the most abundant water supply in the northern Sinai. It lies on the junction of two major roads, the Way of Shur from Edom to Egypt, and the road from Eilat and the central Negeb to Arad and Hebron.

The major find was a fortress, twice rebuilt, that probably guarded Judah's southern border from the tenth century B.C.E. to the sixth century B.C.E. The fortress is about 135 ft. by 200 ft.

However no remains from the wilderness wandering period have been found. While it is quite possible that no structural remains would survive, especially if the Hebrews were tent dwellers, it is surprising that no pottery or other remains have been found.

—JOEL F. DRINKARD, JR.

• **Kenaz/Kenizzites.** [kee′naz/ken′uh-*zits*] A clan or tribe located in southern Judah and associated with the Edomites as well as with Judah. Individuals bearing the name Kenaz are mentioned in Gen 36:11 and 1 Chr 1:36 (one of Esau's descendants); in 1 Chr 4:15 (a member of the tribe of Judah and a descendant of Caleb; cf. Num 32:12; Josh 14:6, 14); and in 1 Chr 4:13 (again a member of the tribe of Judah and a brother of Caleb; cf. Josh 15:17). The Kenizzites are connected with Caleb, called a Kenizzite (Num 13:12), and Caleb in turn is closely associated with Hebron and with the tribe of Judah.

See also CALEB.

—WALTER HARRELSON

• **Kenites.** [ken′*its*] A nomadic group that engaged in both pastoralism and the working of metal. Their principal area of operations was in the rocky, semi-arid region between Arad and the Gulf of Aqabah. Their activities as itinerant smiths brought them into friendly contact with several other tribal groups, and thus they are sometimes closely associated with both the Midianites and the Amalekites. For instance, MOSES' father-in-law JETHRO/Hobab is identified as both a Midianite (Exod 18:1; Num 10:29) and a Kenite (Judg 1:16; 4:11).

The Kenites are first mentioned in Gen 15:19 in the list of those peoples who were to be displaced by the patriarchs and their descendants. For the most part, however, the Kenites are portrayed in a favorable light by the biblical writers (with the possible exception of Balaam's prophecy in Num 24:21-22). Their allegiance to the Israelites is first established through Moses' marriage (Exod 2:15-21). Suggestions, however, that Jethro/Hobab instructed Moses in the worship of Yahweh or provided him with the model for Israelite legal administration (cf. Exod 18:6-26) go beyond present evidence. Continued relations between the two groups extend into the wilderness wanderings in which Hobab accompanies Moses as a guide (Num 10:29-33; contra Exod 18:27). During the settlement period, Judg 1:16, the Kenites are described as leaving their territory to join the tribe of Judah in the conquest of southern Canaan.

Despite their close relations with other peoples, the Kenites apparently preferred to remain neutral whenever possible. Thus, Heber the Kenite continued his normal routine, remaining at peace with Jabin, the king of Hazor, while the Israelites, under Deborah and Barak, were at war with this king (Judg 4:17). The actions of Heber's wife, Jael, while celebrated by the Israelites in Deborah's Song (Judg 5:24-27), would have caused bad feelings elsewhere and may have restricted his clan's activities as smiths in regions outside of Israel (cf. Jacob's reaction to the raid on

SHECHEM in Gen 34:30).

It may be that during the early monarchy, the PHILISTINES expelled the Kenites and other smiths from Israelite territory as a way of weakening their rivals and making them more dependent on Philistine technology (1 Sam 13:19, 22). In spite of the constant hostilities between Israel and its neighbors, good relations between Israel and the Kenites appear to have remained constant. Thus, in 1 Sam 15:6, Saul allowed the Kenites to depart the territory of the Amalekites before he launched a war against that perennial enemy of Israel.

David also dealt kindly with the Kenites during the period before he became king. While he was serving as a mercenary chieftain for the Philistine King Achish of Gath, David raided villages in the NEGEB, some of which were in the territory of the Kenites (1 Sam 27:8-10). Subsequently, however, he distributed a portion of the loot he had taken in these raids to political friends in Judah, including some living "in the cities of the Kenites" (1 Sam 30:29).

No further mention of these people is found in the biblical text after this point. It can thus be assumed that they lost their tribal identity as the Israelite monarchy grew to control more territory and the various aspects of the economy within the kingdom.

See also AMALEK/AMALEKITES; MIDIAN/MIDIANITES.

Bibliography. J. M. Miller and J. H. Hayes, *A History of Ancient Israel and Judah.*

—VICTOR H. MATTHEWS

• **Kerygmata Petrou.** [ker'ig-mah'tah-peh"tr*oo*] The *Kerygmata Petrou* or *Preachings of Peter*, is one of the Jewish-Christian sources contained in the basic writing which underlies the pseudo-Clementine *Homilies* and *Recognitions*. This source has been reconstructed variously from *Recog* 3.75 which has been described as the table of contents; from the *Epistula Petri* (the *Letter of Peter* prefixed to the *Hom*); and from the *Contestatio* (often listed as chaps. 4 and 5 of the *Epistula Petri*). The *Kerygmata Petrou* has received more attention than any other supposed source behind the CLEMENTINE LITERATURE.

The early literature spoke of the *Kerygmata Petrou* as Ebionite, defined as the Jewish-Christian element opposed to Pauline Christianity. While this view has not completely died in modern times, its force has diminished. The *Kerygmata Petrou* should not be reduced to such a simple term as Ebionite, however one defines that group of Jewish-Christians. That the *Kerygmata Petrou* is broadly Jewish-Christian is certain, but there are mixtures of Jewish practice, Elkasaite theology, Gnostic elements, etc., in it.

The *Kerygmata Petrou* was produced in the area of Coele-Syria, where also the basic writing originated. The use of a NT canon which did not include the catholic epistles nor the Revelation of John seems to point to this geographical area. Also the document knows Galatians and 1 Corinthians, which were first in the Syrian corpus of Pauline Letters. Scholars are therefore convinced that the *Kerygmata Petrou* originated in the East. A date in the third century seems probable.

If Georg Strecker's views are correct, this Jewish-Christian source for the basic document of the pseudo-Clementines espoused the following ideas: (1) the true prophet was the bearer of revelation. There were seven incarnations of the "true prophet" beginning with Adam and culminating with Joshua/Jesus; (2) opposed to the true prophet was female prophecy which accompanies him as a partner. EVE was the first representative; following such leads to error and death; (3) the true prophet points out the false pericopes which have been added to the LAW: passages which speak of many gods, anthropopathisms, references to sacrifice, to the temple, and to kingship, all of which have falsified scripture; (4) Jesus chose only twelve apostles, therefore PAUL was not an APOSTLE. He was the arch-enemy of PETER, and the representative of female prophecy. His treatment of the Law was not approved by JAMES, the Lord's brother, therefore it was false; (5) the laws of purity, including baptism, were upheld. Apparently the *Kerygmata Petrou* makes a distinction between BAPTISM and the lustral baths required by Jewish law. It may be that it had already substituted baptism for circumcision, although that is not clearly indicated.

The *Kerygmata Petrou* shows a Jewish Christianity which was syncretistic, but was apparently not viewed as heretical by the majority church.

See also CLEMENTINE LITERATURE.

Bibliography. G. Strecker, "The Kerygmata Petrou," *New Testament Apocrypha*, ed. E. Hennecke and W. Schneemelcher, and "On the Problem of Jewish Christianity," in W. Bauer, *Orthodoxy and Heresy in Earliest Christianity*, ed. R. Kraft and G. Krodel.

—GLENN A. KOCH

• **Keys of the Kingdom.** This phrase occurs only in Matt 16:19 where Jesus promises to PETER "the keys of the kingdom of heaven." In Isa 22:22 "the key of the house of David" is conferred upon Eliakim, King Hezekiah's steward, symbolizing the authority to grant admittance and exercise control over the palace. In Rev 3:7 this passage is applied to Christ who exercises such authority over the heavenly kingdom. A similar view may underlie the passage in Matthew. Peter, as the recipient of the keys, exercises authority as Christ's representative.

In Matt 23:13 Jesus condemns the scribes and Pharisees because they "shut the kingdom of heaven against men." Luke 11:52 describes this action of the scribes as taking away "the key of knowledge." By failing to teach accurately the ways of God to the people, the scribes and Pharisees have locked them out of the Kingdom. Jesus' statement to Peter indicates that now the responsibility to proclaim and teach the message of the Kingdom, and thus to effect admittance into the Kingdom, belongs to Peter and not to the scribes and Pharisees.

The power of the keys is further indicated in the second half of Matt 16:19 in the statement about "binding" and "loosing." To bind and loose in rabbinic usage meant to declare certain activities permitted or prohibited, to impose or remove a ban of excommunication. To have the keys of the Kingdom is to have the power to bind and loose. The authority of binding and loosing is also granted to the disciples as a whole (Matt 18:18). Thus, by their teaching and proclamation of the gospel, as well as by their disciplinary decisions, the disciples "open" or "close" the KINGDOM OF GOD to their hearers. To those who hear the gospel and respond positively, the Kingdom is opened; to those who fail to hear, the Kingdom is closed.

See also KINGDOM OF GOD; PETER.

—MITCHELL G. REDDISH

• **Kidron.** [kid'ruhn] A valley on the edge of the city of JERUSALEM, the Kidron Valley extends several miles, beginning as a plateau north of Jerusalem then heading southward along the entire eastern edge of the city. It thus forms a natural boundary between the eastern portions of Jerusalem and the MOUNT OF OLIVES. South of the city, the Kidron Valley intersects the Hinnom Valley, then follows a wandering course southeastward to the Dead Sea. For centuries the portion of the valley adjacent to Jerusalem has remained dry except during periods of heavy rainfall, though it is likely that prior to the late eighth century B.C.E. and the diversion of waters surrounding Jerusalem by King Hezekiah (2 Chr 32:3-4), a perennial brook flowed through the valley. It is difficult to be certain of this however, since the bed of the valley in ancient times was many feet below the present surface level.

The topography of the Kidron Valley, as well as its close proximity to Jerusalem, have made it a particularly useful area. For example, it has been utilized as a burial site throughout its history (2 Chr 34:4; 2 Kgs 23:6). Even today both ancient and modern tombs are visible on its slopes. In addition, the valley has been used as a deposit for certain pagan objects of worship stripped from Jerusalem during major reform periods in Judah's history. Our earliest notice of this practice is given in connection with the reign of King Asa (911–870 B.C.E.). As a portion of the reforms carried out during his reign, Asa cut down an image of the Canaanite goddess Asherah, and burned it in the Kidron Valley (1 Kgs 15:13; 2 Chr 15:16). Similar actions were taken in later centuries, particularly in connection with the far-reaching reforms of Hezekiah (715–687 B.C.E.) and Josiah (640–609 B.C.E.). The indication of the OT texts here is that the valley functioned as a dumping ground for such idolatrous objects or, on occasion, such objects were burned, with the remaining ashes scattered over the valley or cast in the brook Kidron (2 Kgs 23:4-12; 2 Chr 29:16; 30:14).

The Kidron Valley is also mentioned in the OT with respect to the confrontation between King David and his son Absalom (2 Sam 15:23). Being forced to flee for a time from Jerusalem, David is said to have crossed the brook Kidron during his flight into the wilderness. The underlying suggestion here, that the Kidron is regarded as the traditional boundary of the city, is reflected years later during Solomon's effort to secure his father's throne. Solomon is said to have placed a certain Shimei under protective custody in Jerusalem, by warning him not to cross the Kidron Valley (1 Kgs 2:37).

The single NT reference to Kidron is found in John 18:1, where the fourth evangelist tells us that, prior to his arrest, Jesus took his disciples and crossed the Kidron Valley on his way to Gethsemane.

See also JERUSALEM; OLIVES, MOUNT OF.

Bibliography. R. M. Mackowski, *Jerusalem City of Jesus;* G. F. Owen, *Jerusalem.*

—MICHAEL D. GREENE

• **Killing.** *See* MURDER

• **Kingdom of God.** *1.* It is paradoxical that even though the expression Kingdom of God does not occur in the OT, L. Köhler could affirm that the one fundamental statement in the theology of the OT is "God is the ruling Lord" (30). For that affirmation, "God is the ruling Lord," is largely what Jews meant by "Kingdom of God." In the Bible Kingdom is a dynamic word. The Heb. *malkuth,* Aramaic *malkutha,* and Gk. *basileia* all signify "royal power," just as the English term "kingdom" originally meant the authority and power of a king, not a country or people ruled by a king. Accordingly, in the biblical tradition the primary notion of Kingdom of God is God's exercise of his royal power (cf. 2 Chr 29:11; Rev 12:10).

The great paradigm of God's exercise of his sovereign power is the EXODUS. The events from the deliverance of the Jews from the slavery of Egypt to their establishment in the promised land were viewed as the pattern of God's future acts of royal power. Prophets therefore looked for a second Exodus (cf. Isa 51:9-11; Hos 2:16-25), which would bring about a greater deliverance than that from Egypt for the "inheritance" of the Kingdom of God under the rule of his representative, the Messiah (cf. Isa 9:2-7; Jer 25:5-6; Ezek 34:22-24).

2. The hope of the Kingdom of God was maintained by the apocalyptic writers of Israel, although their conceptions of its nature diverged considerably. They emphasized the transcendental aspects of God's works, and looked for God to come and directly intervene in this world's affairs to end wickedness and to introduce the age of righteousness, peace, and life. Frequently these writers give expression to the prophetic expectation of God's establishment of his rule in this world under the King-Messiah (e.g., *PssSol; 1 Enoch* 6-36, 83-90). Others looked for the Kingdom in a renewed universe, as in the *Similitudes of Enoch*, wherein the SON OF MAN is a heavenly figure, associated with God in judgment and rule. Yet others see precedents for both anticipations in the OT: they looked for a Kingdom set in this world, to be followed by the Kingdom in a new creation. *Fourth Ezra* has a startling example of this concept: the Messiah is said to rule for 400 years, after which he and all humanity will die, the world will return to primeval silence, and a new world will appear (7:26-44). *Second Baruch* more cheerfully asserts that the Messiah's rule "will stand forever, until the world of corruption is at an end" (40:3).

Various passages in the Qumran writings have links with all three interpretations; the community that preserved them, however, had most in common with the Book of Daniel. One feature is noteworthy: the community apparently believed that the Kingdom was already among them, in that they participated in the eschatological salvation (*1QH* 3:19-23), belonged to the heavenly Jerusalem (*1QH* 6:23-27), and enjoyed the hidden paradise later to be revealed (*1QH* 8:4-8). As in other respects, the beliefs of this community present significant precedents for the faith of JESUS and his Church.

3. According to Mark 1:14-15 the theme of the preaching of Jesus was the Kingdom of God. His message is summarized as: "The time is fulfilled, and the kingdom of God is at hand; repent, and believe in the gospel." This appears to mean that the time of waiting for the fulfillment of God's promise is over, and God is now initiating his royal saving work in the world. Luke does not reproduce this summary, but he provides a concrete example of it. His account of the ministry of Jesus commences with the visit to Nazareth. Jesus reads Isa 61 to the people; the passage uses the imagery of the year of Jubilee (Lev 25) as a picture of the emancipation of God's people when he brings his Kingdom into the world. Jesus' exposition of it is condensed into a single sentence: "Today this scripture has been fulfilled in your hearing" (4:21). G. B. Caird commented on that: "He has not merely read the scripture; as King's messenger he has turned it into a royal proclamation of amnesty and release" (86).

Frequently the Gospels set forth the "acts of power" (*dunameis,* MIRACLES) of Jesus as manifestations of the Kingdom of God. Matt 11:5 gives Jesus' reply to John the Baptist's question as to whether he was "the coming one"; it is virtually a citation of Isa 35:5-6, which describes in glowing colors the transformation God will bring when he comes to save his people. In effect, therefore, Jesus is saying, "It's all happening *now*—and that answers your question!" When accused by his opponents of being in league with the devil Jesus told a parable, indicating that only one who overcomes a strong man can take away his goods (Mark 3:27); his release of Satan's victims takes place because he has overpowered him. Matt 12:28 (= Luke 11:20) draws the consequence: "If it is by the Spirit ["finger," Luke] of God that I drive out demons, then the kingdom of God has come upon you." For other sayings of Jesus which set forth the same message cf. Matt 11:12-13; 13:16-17; and Luke 17:20-21. Such sayings show that God's royal saving action has begun in Jesus. They do not mean that the Kingdom has no future. On the contrary Jesus often spoke of the future manifestation of the Kingdom, as in the prayer he taught his disciples (Matt 6:9-10) and the beatitudes (Matt 5:3-12). Many of his PARABLES depict the Kingdom of God initiated in his ministry in relation to its future consummation, notably the parables of Mark 4 and Matt 13. In all these the tacit assumption is that Jesus is the mediator in the present of the Kingdom awaited in the future.

The Son of man sayings proceed precisely on that premise, for the Son of man is the representative of the Kingdom of God (as in Dan 7:13). G. Vermes and J. Jeremias have shown that "Son of man" can be used in place of "I." That is an illuminating item, but it does not eliminate the significance of the expression in eschatological contexts (cf., e.g., Luke 12:8-9). Such Son of man sayings as Mark 2:10, 28, and Matt 11:18-19 are consonant with the presence of the Kingdom in Jesus' ministry. The Son of man's actions in relation to the Kingdom in the immediate future is seen in utterances which intimate its coming through his death and resurrection (Mark 8:31; 9:31; 10:45; Luke 22:15-20). The role of the Son of man in the consummation of the Kingdom of God is illustrated in Mark 14:62; Luke 17:22-37. The interrelation of these sayings indicates that the process of the coming of the Kingdom of God is unitary: it comes through the progressive operations of the Son of man.

The foregoing review of the teaching of Jesus on the Kingdom of God assumes the substantial authenticity of the Kingdom sayings in the synoptic Gospels. This is questioned by some recent scholars, primarily through a conviction that the apocalyptic views ascribed to Jesus in the Gospels were alien to him. It is urged that Jesus was a Galilean, open to the thought of the world beyond Palestine; his concept of the Kingdom of God was personal, akin to the notions of wisdom, freedom, and independence characteristic of the Greek idea of kingdom (cf. the Stoic maxim, "Only the wise man is a king"); his teaching is best understood as a critique of contemporary society in the Cynic mode. The representation in the *Gospel of Thomas* of the Kingdom in terms of knowledge of one's true identity is accordingly closer to Jesus than the apocalyptic utterances of the Gospels. This proposal to interpret Jesus in the light of Hellenistic religious thought entails minimizing his relationship to the OT and contemporary Judaism and ascribing to his followers a serious misrepresentation of his essential message; neither procedure is plausible. The portrayal of Jesus' Kingdom teaching in the Gospel traditions is a consistent whole, and at one with the most characteristic teaching of Jesus and the events of his ministry. On critical grounds the recorded teaching of Jesus on the Kingdom of God in the Gospels is rightly viewed by the vast majority of NT scholars as bedrock tradition.

4. The Gospel of John mentions the Kingdom of God in one saying only, John 3:3, repeated in an explanatory fashion in 3:5 (although cf. also 18:36). This phenomenon is comparable to the lack of mention of Kingdom of God in the OT: its reality is present throughout the Gospel. The entire ministry of Jesus, with its signs and its climax in the "lifting up" of Jesus on the cross to heaven, forms the eschatological event whereby the Kingdom comes. John 3:3 is explained in light of the Spirit's new creative activity (vv. 5-6) and the redemption of Christ, through which the ETERNAL LIFE of the Kingdom of God is made available to humankind (3:14-15, 16). This is the distinctive mark of the Fourth Gospel, namely the offer of the life of the Kingdom of God through Christ, which is yet to be known in its fullness in God's future (cf. 5:25-29; 11:25; 14:3, 18-20, 23; 17:24-26).

5. The coming of the Kingdom of God in the "Christ-event" is assumed in the primitive kerygma, as is traceable in the letters of the NT. The affirmation that it all happened "according to the scriptures" (1 Cor 15:3-4) emphasizes that it took place in fulfillment of God's purpose to establish his Kingdom. The hymns of the NT celebrate the enthronement of Christ (Phil 2:6-11; Col 1:15-20; 1 Tim 3:16). For Paul the new creation became reality in the risen Lord, so that to be "in Christ" is to participate in it (2 Cor 5:17).The believer has been transferred into the Kingdom of Christ (Col 1:13) and rejoices in its blessings now (Rom 14:23). The Holy Spirit is the guarantee of participation in the final Kingdom (Eph 1:13-14). Accordingly, the goal of Easter is that God may be "all in all" in a universe subjected to him by the Son (1 Cor 15:20-28).

6. The Book of Revelation shares the same stance as the rest of the NT, namely that the turn of the ages occurred in the death and resurrection of Jesus (cf. esp. chap. 5; and 1:5-6; 12:1-12). If the expectation of the future manifestation of the Kingdom dominates the book, it is because the author sees in the contemporary worship of the emperor of Rome the precursor of the adulation of the Antichrist, whose bid for world sovereignty must be replaced by the Kingdom of God and of his Christ (for the expression see Rev 11:15). The Revelation appears to teach that the Kingdom initiated by Christ's redemptive work will find its culmination in history, in its establishment in power on the earth at his parousia (19:11–20:6); this understanding, related to the prophets and to contemporary Jewish interpretation, anticipates a kind of sabbath of history which will give way to the eighth "day," in which time will be no more (cf. 2 *Enoch* 32-33; *Barn* 15). The vision of the city of God in Rev 21:9–22:5 is set in deliberate contrast to the depiction of the city of Antichrist in chap. 17. The author may well have seen in the city the context of the Kingdom of God in history and in the new creation. From the Easter exaltation on, the Kingdom of God "comes down" from heaven to earth, but as hidden reality until its unveiling at the parousia of Christ.

See also ESCHATOLOGY IN THE NEW TESTAMENT; ESCHATOLOGY IN THE OLD TESTAMENT; ETERNAL LIFE; EXODUS; JUDGMENT, DAY OF; MESSIAH/CHRIST; MIRACLES; PARABLES; PAROUSIA/SECOND COMING; RESURRECTION IN THE NEW TESTAMENT; RESURRECTION IN THE OLD TESTAMENT; SON OF MAN.

Bibliography. G. R. Beasley-Murray, *Jesus and the Kingdom of God;* M. Buber, *Kingship of God;* G. B. Caird, *The Gospel of St. Luke;* R. H. Charles, *A Critical History of the Doctrine of a Future Life;* B. Chilton, *God in Strength: Jesus' Announcement of the Kingdom;* C.H. Dodd, *Para-*

bles of the Kingdom; K. Koch, *The Rediscovery of Apocalyptic;* L. Köhler, *Old Testament Theology;* W. G. Kümmel, *Promise and Fulfillment: The Eschatological Message of Jesus;* G. Ladd, *The Presence of the Future;* N. Perrin, *The Kingdom of God in the Teaching of Jesus;* R. Schnackenburg, *God's Rule and Kingdom.*

—G. R. BEASLEY-MURRAY

• **Kingdom of Heaven.** *See* KINGDOM OF GOD

• **King James Version.** *See* ENGLISH BIBLE

• **Kings of Israel and Judah.** *See* CHRONOLOGY IN THE OLD TESTAMENT

• OUTLINE OF KINGS •

The Books of Kings

I. David's Last Days and Death (First Kings 1:1–2:46)
II. Solomon's Reign (3:1–11:43)
III. The Divided Kingdom (12:1–2 Kings 17:41)
 A. Rehoboam and Jeroboam (12:1–13:34)
 B. The struggles of northern and southern kings (14:1–16:34)
 C. Elijah and the kings of Israel (17:1–21:29)
 D. Micaiah son of Imlah (22:1-53)
 E. Elijah and Elisha (2 Kings 1:1–8:29)
 F. The Jehu revolution (9:1–10:36)
 G. Athaliah is overthrown in Judah (11:1-21)
 H. Struggles of northern and southern kings (12:1–17:41)
IV. Judah, Assyria, and Babylonia (18:1–25:30)
 A. Hezekiah and Assyria (18:1–20:21)
 B. Manasseh and Amon (21:1-26)
 C. Josiah (22:1–23:30)
 D. Josiah's successors; the fall of Jerusalem (23:31–25:30)

• **Kings, Books of First and Second.** The Books of Kings contain the story of the kingdoms of Israel and Judah from DAVID's death until the final loss of Judean political independence to the Babylonian empire. The two present works are the continuation and conclusion of the deuteronomic history which is comprised of Joshua, Judges, Samuel, and Kings.

Kings is a composite work compiled by editors who selected, arranged, and commented on material derived from earlier sources. These sources from which the editors drew came from widely divergent backgrounds and were the product of various groups within Israel. As a result they exhibit varied views of history, theological purposes, political theories, and literary styles. Three of the sources from which the editors drew are named and cited in Kings, referring the reader to them for further information. The two works most commonly cited are called "The Book of the Chronicles of the Kings of Israel," and "The Book of the Chronicles of the Kings of Judah." These works are cited thirty-three times in Kings and are found in conjunction with nearly all of the kings, with only two Israelite and four Judean kings lacking such citations. The full nature and contents of these works are not fully discernible from the limited extracts that have been incorporated into Kings, but the titles may imply that they are extracts from royal archives. The material preserved from them is not incompatible with official records of the time and primarily consists of official records of the kings or accounts based on official records. The third named source in Kings is "The Book of the Acts of Solomon," which appears to be a work very similar in nature to the "Books of the Chronicles," but pertaining only to SOLOMON's reign.

Another source used heavily by the compilers of Kings is the body of stories concerning the prophets, particularly the northern prophets. This source is unnamed by the compilers of Kings, probably due to the nature of the material. It is unlikely that all the stories concerning the northern prophets are from the same source. Several styles are evident in the stories, which show much evidence of long oral transmission, and they are likely drawn from several differing prophetic groups, and do not constitute a single source. The chief cycle of these stories concerns the two greatest of the northern prophets, ELIJAH and ELISHA, and has been incorporated into Kings essentially as a block in 1 Kgs 17–2 Kgs 10. Other prominent prophets are seen in 1 Kgs 11–14 (Ahijah), and 1 Kgs 22 (Micaiah). Except for some individual Elisha stories, these prophetic narratives deal primarily with the interaction between prophets and kings. This probably reflects the compilers' concern with the impact of the prophets on political events.

Another unnamed source is possibly seen in 2 Kgs 12:4-16; 2 Kgs 16:10-18; and 2 Kgs 22:3–23:24, each of which deals with major modifications to the Jerusalem Temple. These accounts possibly represent extracts from Temple records.

The purpose of the compilers in editing these sources into a connected narrative was not to eliminate inconsistencies but to put the stories into chronological order and to introduce some similarity and continuity among the theologies and philosophies presented in the source materials. The method used to maintain this continuity is the construction of a framework into which the stories are placed. This framework consists of a formulaic introduction to the reign of each king and contains the relevant known personal data, an evaluation of the king's administration from the religious vantage point of the editors, and ending with a notice of the king's death and the name of his successor, if succeeded by his son. The editors generally restrict their comments to this framework and seem to have made few changes in the stories. As a result each source retains its own character, style, and point of view, with the fortunate result that many groups and factions of Israel speak to us in Kings, not just the compilers.

The purpose of the compilers of Kings and the deuteronomic history is not to record history in the current sense. The stories were intended to serve as vehicles for the theological purposes of the compilers; thus the focus of the work is not on historical accuracy but on theological teaching. This lack of primary emphasis on history is shown in several ways. The citations to fuller histories show that the compilers used only those materials that fit their theological purpose. Two of Israel's most successful and prominent kings, OMRI and JEROBOAM II, receive only passing mention, and one of the most significant events in Israel's history, the battle of Qarqar, is ignored.

One of the purposes of Kings is to interpret certain aspects of Israel's history according to the standards of the deuteronomistic historian, especially in the areas of the centralization of Temple worship in Jerusalem and in maintaining that worship free from foreign influences. All of the Israelite kings were adjudged to have done evil because they did not recognize the sole legitimacy of the Jerusalem Temple. Most Judean kings were also labeled as evil since they allowed worship at the "high places" as well as at Jerusalem. Only Asa, JEHOSHAPHAT, HEZEKIAH, and JOSIAH were given approval. Therefore, the kingdoms were found wanting in the eyes of the editors. This failure was the basis for another of their purposes: explaining the fall of Judah and Israel in theological terms. The negative judgment of the compilers regarding Israel and Judah allowed them to see the defeat of the nation not as a defeat of their God but as his victory; God allowed his agents to conquer his people as punishment for their sins. Another recurrent theme related to Kings' theological purpose was the fulfillment of prophecy. A main point of the prophetic stories is that all of God's prophecies are fulfilled; any that have not yet proven true will be accomplished in the future. The implication, as seen in 2 Kgs 25:27-30, is that 2 Sam 7, the prophecy of an everlasting Davidic dynasty, is still in effect, and the Davidic monarchy will be restored.

See also DEUTERONOMIST/DEUTERONOMISTIC HISTORIAN.

Bibliography. J. Gray, *I and II Kings, A Commentary, OTL*; G. H. Jones, *1 and 2 Kings, NCBC*.

—RAY SUTHERLAND.

• **Kingship.** The concepts of God and humanity, and the relationship between them, are affected by the biblical view of kingship. In the OT this takes the form of praising Yahweh as king and defining his relationship with the human king of Israel. The idealized human king eventually led to the messianic hope. In the NT, the OT categories of kingship are understood in terms of Jesus' messiahship and in the concept of the Kingdom of God.

God is described as king in several ways in the OT. He is most commonly seen as king of Israel. There is some disagreement over how early in its history Israel came to think of God as king, but it is generally agreed that its formulation was very old, going to a time when Israel did not claim that there were no other gods but Yahweh, but only that there were no others for Israel (Exod 20:1-3). In time this view expanded until Yahweh was considered also to be the king of the whole world (Jer 10:7; Zech 14:9). In the Psalms we find God presented as king over the gods (95:3; 103:19-22); this may reflect the old henotheistic view in which Yahweh was one god among many. His original kingship over Israel was rooted in his special relationship with her, grounded in his saving acts in the liberation from slavery in Egypt and in the establishment of the covenant on Mount Sinai (Exod 19:6; Deut 33:5).

Because God was the original king of Israel, the introduction of human kings was not easy. Judges presents a picture of a disorganized people unable to make any real headway against the enemies who populated their land, largely because there was no king (19:1; 21:55). Israel was united not by any sort of political organization but by acceptance of a COVENANT with Yahweh. The tribes were guided by village elders in day-to-day affairs (Judg 11:5) and by leaders especially empowered by the spirit of God during military crises (Judg 3:10). No king was needed because Yahweh reigned over Israel (Judg 8:22-23). Charismatic deliverers provided leadership during emergencies, which was a sufficient arrangement for sporadic fighting against the Canaanites and other groups but was inadequate to meet the threat from the powerful PHILISTINES. This led to the introduction of a human king over Israel (ca. 1000 B.C.E.).

The Books of Samuel present two views of the development of the kingship. One sees the establishment of the monarchy as a gift of God (1 Sam 9:16). According to this interpretation the king will rule "the people of Yahweh" and save them from their enemies (1 Sam 10:1). The other view, however, treats the monarchy as developing out of the desire of the people to be like the other nations (1 Sam 7:13-14; 8:19-20). According to this view, the monarchy was a blasphemous rejection of God's kingship (1 Sam 8:7) and a source of hardship for the nation (1 Sam 7:11-18). This bipolar evaluation of kingship continued throughout Israel's history: on the one hand the monarchy provided the glories of David (2 Sam 7:8–9), while on the other the abominable apostasy of Manasseh was also its product (2 Kgs 21). The successes were more than matched by the failures. Every king of the Northern Kingdom was found wanting, in the judgment of the OT accounts.

Kings provided security by giving dependable leadership and conducting a consistent foreign policy. They led the armies when military action was necessary. The monarch was responsible for maintaining domestic justice and occasionally for adjudicating difficult legal cases (2 Sam 14:47; Ps 101). He had cultic responsibilities as well, officiating at sacrifices, supplications, and blessings on important occasions (2 Kgs 3:4; 19:14-19; 2 Sam 6:18). The king could discipline the priests (1 Kgs 2:26-27) and even reform the cult when necessary (2 Kgs 18:1-8): the TEMPLE itself was built through royal sponsorship (1 Kgs 5:1-6). The health and welfare of the nation was considered to be bound up with the reign of the monarch (Ps 72). The loss of the monarchy in the Exile was a devastating blow (Lam 4:20).

Saul, the first king, was more like the charismatic deliverers than like the later kings (1 Sam 11:6-8; 22:6-8). His successor David set the standard for kingship. His personality and actions left a permanent mark on the way Israel viewed its kings. He was the unifier, the poet, the conqueror of Jerusalem. God made a covenant with him to establish his throne and his seed forever (2 Sam 7:8-16). He and the kings after him were to be sons of God (2 Sam 7:14). Passages celebrating the king as the firstborn (Ps 89:27) begotten son of God (Ps 2:7), who sits at his right hand (Ps 110:1), may be misinterpreted as evidence of divine kingship in Israel. Divine kingship was accepted in some of the ancient Near East. The Egyptian Pharaoh was worshipped as the incarnation of a god. In Babylon the king became divine through adoption, but he was not worshiped, although his divine mediation with the gods of the pantheon was crucial to the well-being of both people and land. Certainly Israel's king enjoyed a special relationship with God as the divine instrument in governing Israel; the Lord's anointed should not be killed (1 Sam 26:9) or cursed (Prov 24:21-22). He was nonetheless a man, under God's judgment (Deut 17:14-20), and whatever blessings his reign brought were from God (Ps 132:11-18). Although not a god, he was the vehicle for God's ruling of his people. This high view of kingship under God inevitably led to disappointment in the reigning kings. None was perfect, and so the ideal king always remained as a hope for the future. Aided by the fall of the monarchy, the inherent hope related to kingship became messianic hope, the belief that an ideal son of David would come to lead his people into a time of peace and justice (Isa 11:1-9; Ezek 34:24; Hos 3:5).

The OT view of kingship is understood in the NT: God is the true king whose kingdom is in the hands of his Son (John 1:49). Jesus Christ is both the charismatic, spirit-filled leader and the anointed king, proclaiming the kingdom of God to all who will hear and accept it. The justice and peace of the idealized kingdom in the OT (Isa 11:6-9; Mic 4:1-4) is actualized in the KINGDOM OF GOD (Luke 4:18-20). Like the ideal kingdom of the OT, the sovereignty of God is both present in the power of Christ (Matt 12:28) and in those who have faith (Rom 4:1-5) and at the same time future in its fulfillment on earth (Matt 24:14).

See also KINGDOM OF GOD; JOTHAM'S FABLE; MESSIAH/MESSIANISM.

Bibliography. W. Eichrodt, *Theology of the Old Testament;* H. Frankfort, *Kingship and the Gods*; J.D. Levenson, *Sinai and Zion*; S. Mowinckel, *He That Cometh*; G. von Rad, *Old Testament Theology*.

—CAROL STUART GRIZZARD and MARVIN E. TATE

• **Kinship.** *See* INHERITANCE IN THE OLD TESTAMENT

• **Kiriath-Jearim.** [kihr'ee-ath-jee"uh-rim] A town located about eight mi. north of Jerusalem on the border between Judah and Benjamin (PLATE 13). The name means "city of forests." The town is known by many names in the Bible: Kiriath (Josh 18:28), Kiriath-baal (Josh 15:60), and Baale-Judah (2 Sam 6:2). It was one of the four Hivite cities that joined forces to deceive Joshua at the time of the Israelite conquest. Convincing Joshua that they had come from a distant land, they gained the protection of a covenant with Israel and thus avoided destruction (Josh 9).

Kiriath-jearim was the site for the resting of the ARK for twenty years after its return to Israel by the Philistines (1 Sam 7:1-2); it was then taken to Jerusalem by David (2 Sam 6).

URIAH, a prophet from the time of Jeremiah whose message was akin to that of Jeremiah, came from Kiriath-Jearim. He was executed by King Jehoiakim, apparently on the charge of treachery.

See also ARK.

—FRED E. YOUNG

• **Kiriath-sepher.** *See* DEBIR

• **Kish.** [kish] Name of four men in the OT; also a city in Mesopotamia.

Of the four men, Kish the father of SAUL is mentioned most often, though information about him is scarce. Kish was a wealthy man (1 Sam 9:1, 3) from GIBEAH (1 Sam 10:26) in the land of Benjamin (1 Sam 9:1, 21). When his son Saul was chosen by lot to become king, Kish was undoubtedly present, yet quite in the background (1 Sam 10:20-24). The only other information given concerning Kish is that he, and later Saul and JONATHAN, were buried in a tomb at Zela in Benjamin (2 Sam 21:14). The OT is even unclear as to whether his father was Abiel (1 Sam 9:1) or Ner (1 Chr 8:33; 9:39). Some have suggested these passages indicate two different men named Kish, but that seems doubtful.

The other three men who bear the name Kish are a Levite who lived during DAVID's reign (1 Chr 23:21-22), a Levite who assisted in cleansing the temple during HEZEKIAH's reign (2 Chr 29:12), and a Benjaminite ancestor of MORDECAI (Esth 2:5).

Kish also was a dominant Sumerian city in the Early Dynastic period (ca. 2850–2360 B.C.E.) in Mesopotamia. According to the Sumerian king list, Kish was the city where kingship was restored after the flood. Excavations at Kish have uncovered evidence of a flood, but the flood was too late and too limited to support either the biblical or Sumerian flood story. The great king SARGON rose to power in Kish and established the Akkadian Empire (ca. 2350 B.C.E.).

See also SARGON; SAUL; SUMERIA/SUMERIAN.

Bibliography. E. R. Dalglish, "Kish," *IDB*; L. E. Pearce, "Kish," *HBD*.

—ROBERT C. DUNSTON

• **Kishon.** [ki'shon] (Heb. *qîšôn.*) The river in Israel that drains the western part of the Valley of JEZREEL (Esdraelon), emptying into the Mediterranean about two mi. northeast of the foot of MOUNT CARMEL (PLATE 13). "The torrent Kishon" is celebrated in the Song of DEBORAH as one of the decisive forces enabling the tribes of Israel, under Deborah and Barak, miraculously to defeat the Canaanites (Judg 5:21; cf. 4:7, 13). Ps 83:9[H10] recalls events at the Kishon as precedent for expecting victory over another enemy in a different crisis.

It is not clear exactly where along the Kishon's twenty-five-mi. course this battle took place; but "at TAANACH, by the waters of MEGIDDO" (Judg 5:19) suggests a location along its upper length. In this region the Kishon is a dry wadi bed in the summer, but it can be torrential during the winter rains. That the Canaanite SISERA "alighted from his chariot and fled away on foot" (Judg 4:15) implies that the chariots were bogged in the mud of the flood plain, and the more lightly equipped Israelites gained the upper hand.

Today the swampy areas along the Kishon have been drained; those sections of the river that flow in winter may reach a width of twenty ft. For its last six mi. or so, the Kishon becomes a perennial river, and near its end at the coast it is about sixty-five ft. wide. At the mouth itself, an enlarged modern harbor has been dredged, to supplement the port facilities at nearby Haifa.

Bibliography. M. Avi-Yonah, "Kishon," *EncJud*; D. Baly, *The Geography of the Bible*; J. B. Pritchard, ed., *The Harper Atlas of the Bible*; G. W. Van Beek, "Kishon," *IDB*.

—BRUCE T. DAHLBERG

• **Knowledge in the New Testament.** The NT affirms the Greek notion that knowledge is something to be grasped by the mind (Rom 1:18-23; 12:2). But it also preserves the Hebrew idea of knowledge as experience and personal relationship. True knowledge of God can never be acquired apart from an intimate relationship. Although the NT frequently implies that all human beings are capable of knowing God, a true knowledge of his work in Christ is given only to those in whom the Holy Spirit operates (1 Cor 2:12-14; Eph 3:4-5). Paul regarded the ultimate knowledge of God as a spiritual gift not available to all (1 Cor 12:8; 13:2, 8; 14:6; 2 Cor 6:6; 11:6).

The Gospels suggest that Christ alone possesses true knowledge and can mediate it to whomever he chooses (Matt 11:27). Especially in the writings of John is there a complete identification of FAITH, love, and knowledge, the knowledge which is linked with eternal life (14:7, 9, 17; 8:55; 17:3; 1 John 3:6). The Johannine identification of faith and knowledge, however, is conditional on intimacy with the Father (17:25; 7:29; 8:55; 10:15) and on an enduring commitment which leads to the possession of TRUTH (8:31-32). The ministry of Christ consists in disclosing and mediating God's knowledge (14:1-17; 17:1-6).

In Paul, there is only one ultimate basis for knowledge, namely the risen Lord who has revealed God's eternal plan of salvation. To know God also implies the realization that we were known by him from all eternity (1 Cor 13:12; Gal 4:9). God can be known because he has chosen to reveal himself in creation (Rom 1:19-20). But there is a larger, deeper, and more mysterious element of knowledge which only the more mature Christian can aspire to (Rom 11:33-36; Eph 1:17; 4:13; Phil 1:9; 3:8; Col 1:10). Paul often describes knowledge as God's mystery (Rom 11:25; 16:25; 1 Cor 15:51; Eph 1:9; Col 1:25-27) and considers himself a privileged recipient of it (Eph 3:1-5; 6:19). Since a full apprehension of God's MYSTERY is not available, even to the most enlightened Christian, human knowledge remains incomplete and imperfect (1 Cor 13:12).

Any discussion of knowledge in the NT must note that sacred authors often wrote in opposition to GNOSTICISM (the religion of gnosis or knowledge) which was based on an initiation of the believer into the higher truth of a religion which stands above both faith and natural reason. The Gnostics turned knowledge into a mysterious possession which could lead the believer to full redemption. NT thought concerning knowledge often borrows the very language of Gnosticism. The *Gospel of Thomas* quotes Luke 11:52 where Jesus strongly rebuked the scribes and Pharisees for having taken away the key of knowledge and for having invalidated religion for everyone in the process. When, in Col 2:8, Paul takes a strong stance against philosophy, he most probably means Gnostic speculation. Paul and John constantly remind their readers that knowledge, taken by itself, leads away from God. True knowledge must spring from faith and be rooted in the historical revelation of God in Christ.

For Paul, knowledge was a gift of grace not to be confused with the esoteric tenets of other religious doctrines (1 Cor 1:5-6; 12:8; 2 Cor 8:7). Apart from faith, even the most perfect expression of human knowledge cannot provide a lasting and redemptive understanding of God's relationship to the world.

See also FAITH; FAITH AND FAITHLESSNESS; GNOSTICISM; KNOWLEDGE IN THE OLD TESTAMENT; MYSTERY; OBEDIENCE; REVELATION, CONCEPT OF; TRUTH.

—PAUL CIHOLAS

• **Knowledge in the Old Testament.** In Hebrew, the act of knowing is much more important than the resultant knowledge. The verb *yāda'*, "know," in its variant forms and meanings occurs much more frequently than its derivative noun, *da'at*, "knowledge." Its meaning is much more experiential and relational than the "head knowledge" that was so important to the Greeks, and that has dominated western civilization.

Human beings achieved the ultimate knowledge, knowledge of God, only because of the choice God makes to be revealed to humankind. The God-like knowledge, "both good and evil," was not to be attained apart from the gift of the Creator, according to the profound story of the beginning of this relationship in the Garden of Eden (Gen 2–3). It is more important to say that God knows human beings than it is that they know God and one another.

That God knew Abraham meant God had "chosen" him (Gen 18:19, Heb. "known"). In a remarkable dialogue with the Lord, Moses asked to know more intimately the one who already knew him (Exod 33:12-23). This was when God made known the divine ways to MOSES (Ps 103:7a; cf. Exod 34:5-7). God knew DAVID in the promise to his "house" (2 Sam 7:19-21), God knew the hearts of Israelites (all people) who prayed toward Solomon's Temple (1 Kgs 8:33-39), and God knew the way to wisdom that human beings did not know (Job 28:12-18, 20, 23).

The Lord knew JEREMIAH before he was born, and appointed him to be a prophet (Jer 1:5). This was similar to the wondrous ways the Lord had known the Psalmist (Ps 139, esp. vv. 13-16).

Human beings know one another in the most intimate of relationships, the sexual act (Gen 4:1; 19:8; 24:16). The varieties of meaning of the verb "know" include: "learn to know," "perceive," "find out and discern," "discriminate," "know by experience," "recognize, admit, acknowledge, confess," "consider," "be acquainted with, take notice of, regard," "know how, be skillful in," and "have knowledge, be wise."

The noun knowledge has other shades of meaning as well: "perception," "skill," and especially "discernment, understanding, wisdom" in the wisdom literature. Knowledge of God can include faith and obedience in covenantal relation to God. That God knows the people Israel is not only a privilege, but a responsibility (Amos 3:1-2). This covenantal use of the word was related to its use in ancient Near Eastern international treaties between an overlord and his vassals. Kings in Israel were responsible for such knowledge (Jer 22:16), and so were priests (Hos 4:1, 4-6). God is the true overlord of all nations (Ps 46:10). In the prophetic literature, knowledge of God was particularly important in Hos 6:6, Jer 31:34, Ezekiel 6:7, and some 43 other passages: "And you shall know that I am the Lord." This formula, which is at least as old in prophetic speech as the anonymous prophets of King Ahab's day (1 Kgs 20:13, 28), is a recognition or acknowledgment of the Lord's sovereignty even beyond the borders of Israel (Exod 7:5).

Perhaps the most distinctive meaning of the verb is to know the Lord in personal relationship, with the connotation of a faith relationship and covenantal obedience (1 Sam 3:7; Job 19:25; Prov 2:5; 9:10; Hos 2:2-9; and Jer 9:24; 31:34). The most interesting use of the noun is the reference to the suffering servant of the Lord in Isa 53, who is acquainted with (literally, known of) grief (v. 3), and by whose knowledge (experience of suffering) the righteous servant shall make many to be accounted righteous (v. 11).

See also KNOWLEDGE IN THE NEW TESTAMENT.

Bibliography. C. F. H. Henry and R. K. Harrison, "Know, Knowledge," *ISBE*; H. B. Huffmon, "The Treaty Background of Hebrew YADA," *BASOR* 18 (1966): 31-37; O. Piper, "Knowledge," *IDB*.

—M. PIERCE MATHENEY

• **Korah.** [kor'uh] *1.* Korah, the son of Izhar, was the progenitor of the levitical family of Korahites (Exod 6:21, 24). An influential family (perhaps originally from Judah—cf. 1 Chr 2:43) in the hierarchy in the Jerusalem TEMPLE, the Korahites are variously referred to as being "in charge of the work of the service" in the Temple (1 Chr 9:19), gatekeepers of the Temple (1 Chr 9:19, 23; 26:1) and singers (2 Chr 20:19; cf. 1 Chr 6:33-37). The famed singer Heman is a descendant of Korah. The titles of Pss 42, 44–49, 84–85, 87–88 probably indicate that these psalms are from a Korahite collection or hymnal, or were performed according to a Korahite style or tradition of psalm-singing. The prominence of the Korahites is underlined by the note in 1 Chr 9:19 pointing to their historical position in charge of the camp of Yahweh in the wilderness. In Num 16:1-40, Korah is the leader of a rebellion against the authority of MOSES and the priestly prerogative of AARON. Interwoven with the account of the rebellion of Dathan and Abiram against Moses' leadership, this incident depicts a struggle between priestly and Levitical interests in Israel. Korah accuses Moses and Aaron of laying an exclusive claim to holiness (v. 3), a charge that Moses answers with the countercharge that the Levites are not satisfied with the ministry assigned to them but aspire to the priesthood as well (vv. 8-10). The incident ends with a clear specification of priestly privilege (vv. 31-40).

2. Korah, the son of Esau by his Hivite wife Oholibamah, is named as a chief (or clan) of Edom (Gen 36:18).

See also MUSIC/MUSICAL INSTRUMENTS; PRIESTS.

—JEFFREY S. ROGERS

• **Kuntillet 'Ajrûd.** [*koon*'ti-let-aj"*rood*] Arabic, "the hill of 'Ajrûd"; also called Ḥorvat Teiman (Heb. "the Teman ruin"). An isolated hilltop site in the northeastern Sinai desert, excavated in 1975–76 by Israeli archaeologist Zeev Meshel and dated, on the basis of associated ceramic and paleographic evidence (pottery types and script types, respectively), to the late ninth or early eighth century B.C.E. The site is of considerable importance for the information it provides on Israelite religion and culture during the divided monarchy.

The principal feature of Kuntillet 'Ajrûd is the partially preserved, fieldstone walls of a small building complex which, during a relatively brief period of use, evidently functioned as a combination caravansarai and religious shrine for travelers through the area. Recovered from debris on floors of the small rooms and inner courtyard of the major building were pieces of fallen wall-plaster and broken pottery—much of the latter proving to be restorable—bearing painted inscriptions, designs, and drawings in various states of preservation and chiefly religious in content (cf. below). Included among the material-culture remains were pieces of textiles—most of them linen; some, wool. Previously, textiles had not been recovered from this period in the region's history. The discoveries are still under intense study, but preliminary publication of them has made clear that they open a new and important window onto eighth-century Israelite and Phoenician religion.

The Site. Both the Arabic and Hebrew names of the site are relatively modern; its name in biblical times is unknown. It can be noted, however, that although shallow wells do lie near the base of the hill, "wells" does not translate " 'Ajrûd," as implied in some recent publications. " 'Ajrûd" occurs elsewhere, also, as the place name for an ancient castle eighteen km. northwest of Suez along the road to Cairo, where the term goes back to the twelfth century C.E., its meaning uncertain and long debated. Since both sites with the name 'Ajrûd lie on a route of pilgrimage to Mecca, E. Rüppell's suggestion that the term is an Arabic corruption of (a possibly French?) *Hajji route* (Hajj road) is not implausible.

Situated on the rising western end of a narrow plateau or small butte overlooking the Wadi Quraiya, which crosses the region in a wide shallow valley from east to west, Kuntillet 'Ajrûd is fifty-three km. south of 'Ein el-Qudeirat (biblical Kadesh-Barnea), or about 150 km. south of Gaza, and lies on the ancient main route from that northern region down to 'Elat and into the southern Sinai (PLATE 8). Landroutes between Egypt and Arabia also pass nearby. It was first brought to the attention of Westerners by E. M. Palmer and C. F. Tyrwhitt Drake, explorers of the northern Sinai for London's Palestine Exploration Fund. Only very briefly described, and designated "Contellet Garaiyeh" in Palmer's report, it was their campsite for 28-29 January 1870 (misstated 1869 in some references). They did a small probe into a "wall . . . of sun-dried bricks" and noted broken storage jars "built into the wall," one of the jars being "marked on the shoulder with a Phenician [*sic*] *aleph*." They gave but a single morning to their investigation, however, before moving on, and definitive archaeological excavation there was to await the project led by Meshel.

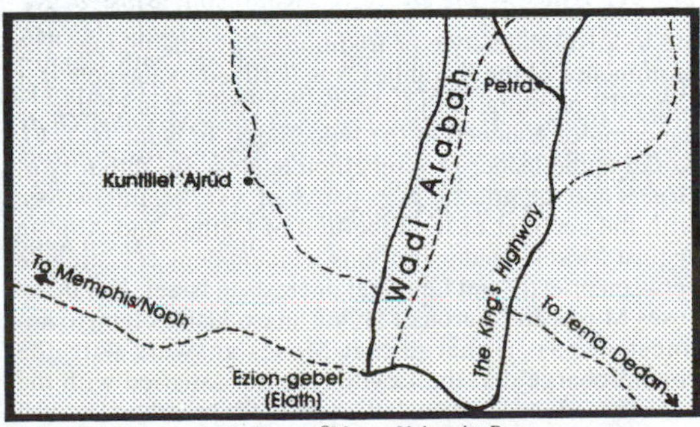

Designed by Margaret Jordan Brown ©Mercer University Press

In his 1978 Israel Museum Catalogue notes on Kuntillet 'Ajrûd, Meshel cites the visit to 'Ajrûd by Alois Musil in 1902 and notes, as possibly significant, the latter's being accosted and briefly detained by local Bedouin for "trespassing on their holy place." Probably, however, this does not reflect 'Ajrûd's brief period as a cultic site in ancient times. Musil looked only for caves on the hill and did not visit the building ruins, which he saw only at a distance and which he understood served as a Bedouin cemetery. The latter detail doubtless accounts for the "tradition of holiness attached to the place" by the Bedouin who confronted Musil, but a tradition apparently unknown to Bedouin now, some seven decades later, as noticed by Meshel.

That 'Ajrûd for a period during the late ninth or early eighth centuries B.C.E. served as some kind of cultic center for travelers from the north (Israel and Judah; perhaps Phoenicia also) is indicated by the provenance established for the pottery vessels and by the form and subject matter (including personal-name forms) of the remarkable painted inscriptions and drawings. A possible further indication is the high proportion of linen cloth found among the TEXTILE fragments at 'Ajrûd. Linen was a material prescribed especially for priestly garments (e.g., Lev 16:4).

The Inscriptions. Among several inscriptions preserved on a restored, much-decorated, three-ft.-high pithos (large storage jar; plural: pithoi) is one that is a blessing or benediction addressed to at least two persons and that includes the phrase (as transliterated from the paleo-Hebrew consonantal script) . . . *brkt 'tkm lyhwh šmrn wl'šrth*, "I bless you [plural] by Yahweh Shomron [i.e., 'Yahweh of Samaria'] and by his Asherah." One of several inscriptions on a second pithos translates as, "I bless you by Yahweh of Teman and his Asherah." (In these examples, "his Asherah" translates *'ašērātōh*, where the masculine-singular possessive suffix, *-ōh*, is an early Hebrew form that appears only occasionally in the later biblical masoretic text [e.g., Jer 2:3a].) Other inscriptions, in black or red ink on wall plaster now fallen and broken so that only parts of the written lines are legible, include such phrases as "blessed be their day . . . "; "Yahweh favored . . . "; and "in the ways of El . . . blessed be Ba'al in the day of. . . . " A large stone bowl weighing over four hundred pounds is inscribed on its rim with *l'bdyw bn 'dnh brk h' lyhw* . . . ("[Belonging] to 'Obedyau son of 'Adnah, may he be blessed by Yahwe[h]").

The Drawings. The first blessing noted above, inscribed on the first pithos, has beneath it a painted line-drawing of two bovine-faced humanoid figures wearing tall head-dresses, standing side by side, arms akimbo, with a third figure seated to the viewer's right and playing a lyre.

A second drawing on this vessel shows a stylized "tree of life," flanked by two ibexes, and below it a striding lion—both known to be symbols associated with the cult of Asherah (cf. below). A third drawing on the same vessel is of a cow licking her suckling calf. The second pithos exhibits a drawing of five standing or processing human figures with faces turned upward and arms raised as if in prayer or supplication. Also on this second pithos are line-paintings of a cow and of a man drawing a bow. These and the other pictures are crudely executed, and the disposition of them on the pithoi and in relation to each other shows no special order or plan; however, they are not mere local inventions, peculiar to this site. For all their crudity, many of them are recognizable representations of images and symbols known from other ancient sites and monuments in the Near East.

Interpreting Kuntillet ‘Ajrûd. In the Canaanite texts from Ugarit (ca. 1365–1180 B.C.E.), Asherah is the goddess Atirat, consort of the creator-god El. In some biblical references to Asherah, several centuries later, she is understood to be the consort of Baal (e.g., 1 Kgs 18:19; 2 Kgs 21:7). At ‘Ajrûd, however, Asherah—if indeed the goddess is meant—appears to be considered the female consort of Yahweh, and if that is the correct interpretation of these inscriptions, the association of Asherah with Yahweh—along with many other names and motifs in the drawings and texts at ‘Ajrûd—provides tangible evidence for that popular religious syncretism in Israel and Judah which was fought against by the now classical prophets of Yahweh from Elijah onwards, and proscribed by the religious reforms of Hezekiah (2 Kgs 18:4) and Josiah (2 Kgs 23:4-20).

Scholarship at present is divided as to whether in fact ASHERAH in the ‘Ajrûd texts refers precisely to the goddess, to an image of her, or to some cult object such as a sacred tree or pole, or even a sacred grove. Confusing the issue, biblical references to Asherah (plural, Asherim and Asheroth) can be found for each of these meanings (e.g., Deut 16:21; Judg 3:7; 1 Kgs 16:33). Whether the three human-like figures on the first pithos (above) include representations of Asherah, or Yahweh, or the popular Egyptian deity Bes—all three have been suggested at one time or another—or none of these, is debated and remains under careful comparative study with what is known of such images and motifs from other sources. Linguists point out that personal names in ancient Hebrew do not take a modifying possessive pronoun or noun; therefore "his [Yahweh's] Asherah," on such a premise, must refer either to an inanimate cult object (the sacred pole or tree), or to a generic Asherah—i.e., a particular local manifestation of the goddess, not the supreme goddess herself—or to "Asherah" as some kind of actualizing attribute of Yahweh, but not as another deity. However, the many biblical references to the popular worship of other deities, alongside that of Yahweh (1 Kgs 18:19; 2 Kgs 23:13), and to the confusion of them with Yahweh (1 Kgs 18:21; Hos 3:16) together with the explicit association, at ‘Ajrûd, of Yahweh with at least El and Baal, suggest that the linguistic premise may itself require some qualification. Z. Zevit has proposed reading an alternative form for the final syllable in "Asherah" that, if accepted, would obviate the difficulty.

Of considerable interest in this context is the 1977 publication by A. Lemaire of an inscription from an eighth-century B.C.E. tomb at Khirbet el-Qôm, near Hebron in Judah, which invokes Yahweh together with "his Asherah" in a blessing-formula like that found at ‘Ajrûd. Of relevance, also, is a recent proposal by J. G. Taylor that Yahweh is associated with Asherah in the Asherah-iconography known from a tenth-century incense stand found at Ta‘anach.

It has been suggested, finally, by Meshel and others, on the basis of terms cognate to "asherah" in other ancient semitic languages, that it can also refer to a *cella,* i.e., a holy place or shrine, and that such might be the meaning of the term in the ‘Ajrûd inscriptions. That "Yahweh's asherah" was invoked, along with Yahweh, by travelers, in expressions of thanksgiving and blessing, would make sense if it meant Yahweh's holy place as that which, physically, gave sanctuary and relief to those engaged in what must have been a difficult, not to say life-threatening journey in that austere desert region. This hypothesis, however, considers only the inscriptions; it does not help to explain the drawings, in at least some of which the images and symbols are those known to be associated elsewhere with particular deities.

See also RELIGION OF ISRAEL; RELIGIONS OF THE ANCIENT NEAR EAST.

Bibliography. P. Beck, "The Drawings from Ḥorvat Teiman (Kuntillet ‘Ajrûd), *Tel Aviv* 9 (1982): 3-86; M. D. Coogan, "Canaanite Origins and Lineage: Reflections on the Religion of Ancient Israel," *Ancient Israelite Religion,* ed. P. D. Miller et al.; W. G. Dever, "Asherah, Consort of Yahweh? New Evidence from Kuntillet ‘Ajrûd," *BASOR* 255 (Summer 1984): 21-37; J. A. Emerton, "New Light on Israelite Religion: The Implications of the Inscriptions from Kuntillet ‘Ajrûd," *ZAW* 94 (1982): 2-10; J. Gunneweg et al., "The Origin of the Pottery of Kuntillet ‘Ajrûd," *IEJ* 35/4 (1985): 270-83; A. Lemaire, "Les inscriptions de Khirbet el-Qôm," *RB* 84 (1977): 595-608, and "Who or What Was Yahweh's Asherah?" *BAR* 10/6 (Nov/Dec 1984): 42-49; P. K. McCarter, Jr., "Aspects of the Religion of the Israelite Monarchy," *Ancient Israelite Religion,* ed. P. D. Miller et al.; Z. Meshel, *Kuntillet ‘Ajrûd: A Religious Center from the Time of the Judaean Monarchy on the Border of Sinai* and "Did Yahweh Have a Consort? The New Religious Inscriptions from the Sinai," *BARev* 5/2 (Mar/Apr 1979): 24-35; J. Monson, general consultant, *Student Map Manual. Historical Geography of the Bible Lands,* §§2-6; A. Musil, *Arabia Petraea*; S. M. Olyan, *Asherah and the Cult of Yahweh in Israel*; E. H. Palmer, *The Desert of the Exodus*; J. B. Pritchard, ed., *The Harper Atlas of the Bible*; E. Robinson, *Biblical Researches in Palestine, Mount Sinai and Arabia Petraea*; J. G. Taylor, "Yahweh and Asherah at Tenth Century Taanach," *Newsletter for Ugaritic Studies* 37/38 (Apr/Oct 1987): 16-18; J. H. Tigay, *You Shall Have No Other Gods: Israelite Religion in the Light of Hebrew Inscriptions*; Z. Zevit, "The Khirbet el-Qôm Inscription Mentioning a Goddess," *BASOR* 255 (Summer 1984): 39-47.

—BRUCE T. DAHLBERG

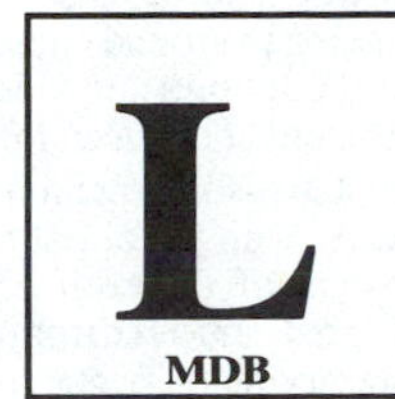

• **L.** *See* SOURCE CRITICISM

• **Laban.** [lay'buhn] A personal and place name, derived from a verb meaning "to be white." Places might be so named because of the color of the soil or because of unusual snowfall (e.g., Mount Lebanon). The personal name is likely a shortened form (nickname) of *Labana-ila*, "the White One [the Moon] is god," a name known from sources outside the Bible.

The Place. A location in the Sinai Peninsula, mentioned in connection with the site of Moses' final speech (Deut 1:1). It may be the same as Libnah (Num 33:20), but the precise location has not been determined by modern geographers.

The Person. An Aramean who lived in the vicinity of Haran (now in southeastern Turkey) and who was a relative of the patriarch Abraham (Gen 11:24-30; 24:15, 29). Two episodes have been preserved concerning his interaction with relatives in Canaan.

When ABRAHAM sought a wife for his son ISAAC, he sent a servant to his relatives in upper Mesopotamia (Gen 24). Relying upon an omen, the servant chose REBEKAH, who turned out to be the sister of Laban. It was this brother (rather than the father) who played the major role in welcoming the guest and arranging for Rebekah's decision concerning the proposed marriage. (This is in keeping with what is known from ancient nonbiblical sources about marriage customs among the Hurrian population of the area.) Some modern interpreters have detected, in Laban's delays in the procedure (v. 55; cf. v. 30), hints of the craftiness that characterizes his behavior in the following episode.

JACOB, the son of Isaac, having defrauded his brother ESAU, fled for safety to his mother's family in upper Mesopotamia (Gen 27–29). There Laban welcomed him and agreed that Jacob marry his younger daughter (RACHEL) in return for seven years of service. At the agreed time, however, Laban tricked him into marrying the older daughter (LEAH) and required another seven years for Rachel (Gen 29). After Jacob had fathered twelve children and expressed a desire to return to his homeland, he decided upon a means of dividing the flock so as to give himself a fair share. Laban then sought to take unfair advantage, but Jacob found a way to secure an even larger percentage (Gen 30) and departed with it without Laban's knowledge (Gen 31:1-18). Rachel, apparently in order to ensure her husband's legal right to a portion of Laban's estate, surreptitiously took along some small figurines ("household gods"), the possession of which perhaps would legitimate his claim.

Upon learning that Jacob had outsmarted him and had apparently stolen the images, Laban pursued Jacob's group for days, intending to regain possession. Finally, however, cautioned by the deity, unable to find the figurines, and unwilling to deprive his descendants of security, he entered into a formal agreement of peace with his son-in-law (Gen 31:19-55).

Some modern interpreters have suggested that, behind this story of individual action, there is a memory of a border agreement between Israelites and Arameans. In any case, Israelite hearers of the account as it now stands would not only have been amused by Jacob's cleverness (his name, after all, means "trickster"), but also reminded that God had acted graciously even to such a person as he had been, and thus to them as his descendants.

See also ARAM/ARAMEANS; JACOB.

Bibliography. G. von Rad, *Genesis*; C. Westermann, *Genesis 12-36*.

—LLOYD R. BAILEY

• **Lachish.** [lay'kish] According to historical sources, Lachish was an important city during both the Canaanite and Israelite periods. Before the 1930s the city was generally identified with Tell el-Hesi, a site located in the Coastal Plain some fifteen mi. northwest of Gaza. But in 1929 W. F. Albright proposed Tell ed-Duweir as the location of the ancient city. His proposal was dramatically confirmed by the discovery there in 1935 of the so-called "Lachish Letters" by James L. Starkey. Further confirmation of this location comes from Eusebius, who, in his *Onomasticon,* located Lachish seven Roman mi. from Eleutheropolis (modern Beth-Govrim). Tell ed-Duweir is

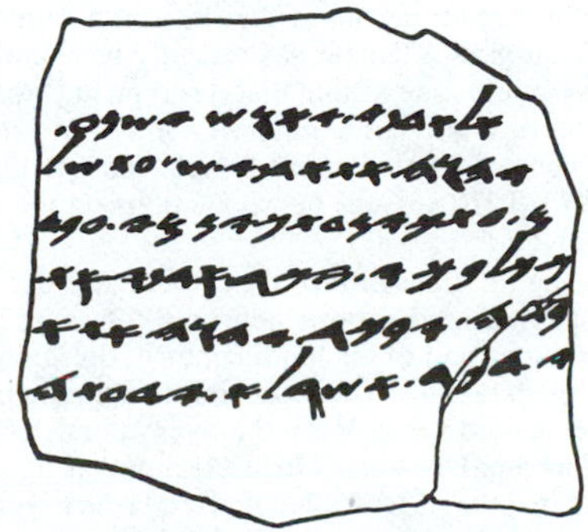

Lachish Letter No. 2.

an imposing mound some thirty acres in size at its base narrowing to around eighteen acres on its summit. It is located in the foothills of Judah about thirty mi. southwest of Jerusalem and fifteen mi. west of Hebron (PLATE 13).

Lachish is mentioned in both biblical and nonbiblical texts, with the oldest reference coming from the AMARNA letters of Pharaoh Amenophis IV (fourteenth century B.C.E.). SENNACHERIB destroyed the city in 701 B.C.E., preserving his account of the victory in elaborate bas-relief on the palace walls in Nineveh.

There are numerous references to Lachish in the OT. The first is in the context of the Israelite conquest of Canaan and records the destruction of the city by JOSHUA (Josh 10:1-32). The city is not mentioned again until the time of Rehoboam (ca. 928–911 B.C.E.) who is said to have built Lachish along with other Judahite cities (2 Chr 11:5, 9). In the eighth century B.C.E., King Amaziah was killed at Lachish after fleeing from a rebellion in Jerusalem (2 Kgs 14:17-20; 1 Chr 25:27). Sennacherib's attack against the city is recorded in the OT (2 Kgs 18:13ff.; 2 Chr 32:9ff.; Isa 36:1ff.), and the city played an important role in Judah's defense during the Babylonian campaign in the sixth century (Jer 34:7). During the postexilic period, Lachish apparently was resettled again (Neh 11:30).

The excavation of the tell did not begin until 1932 when the Welcome-Marston Expedition was organized under the direction of James L. Starkey. Unfortunately, the excavation came to a tragic end when Starkey was murdered in 1938. Two brief seasons of excavation were conducted at the site in the summers of 1966 and 1968 by Y. Aharoni who excavated the so-called "Solar Shrine"; and a long-term excavation was begun in 1973 under the direction of David Ussishkin.

Thus far the excavations have revealed that a troglodyte community existed on the site from the late Chalcolithic period (fourth millennium B.C.E.) through Early Bronze II (twenty-seventh century). During Early Bronze III, the caves were used for graves. Most of the evidence for the Middle Bronze Age (2200–1550 B.C.E.) comes from tombs, though during Middle Bronze II B (1750–1550) the city was fortified with a glacis and moat. An important discovery from this period is a Canaanite inscription found on an eighteenth–seventeenth century dagger. It is one of three such Canaanite inscriptions known from the Middle Bronze Age II.

In the Late Bronze Age, the city reached its peak. During this time, a small building was constructed in the dry moat near the northwest corner of the mound. Known as the "Fosse Temple," it was built in the sixteenth or fifteenth century and went through three phases before being destroyed by fire at the end of the thirteenth century. But its identification as a temple has recently been called into question by studies suggesting that it served the more humble function of a potter's workshop. However, what may be the remains of a Late Bronze temple came to light during the 1973–1976 seasons of excavations on the summit of the mound.

Following the Late Bronze Age, there appears to have been an occupational gap for nearly 300 hundred years. During the latter half of the tenth century, the site was occupied by the Israelites. The most significant remains from this period, called Level V by the excavators, have been identified as a palace-fort. This building was apparently constructed in three stages (called A, B, C) which correspond to Levels V, IV, and III, respectively. Ultimately reaching dimensions of more than 250 ft. in length and 116 ft. in width, the building has been described by the excavator as "the largest, most massive, and most impressive building of the Iron Age known in the Land of Israel. . . ." The Level V phase of the building was destroyed by fire, perhaps during the campaign against Israel by Shishak of Egypt.

During the Level IV (900–750 B.C.E.) occupation, Lachish became a royal Judean fortified city. To this period belong the two city walls, a gate complex and palace-fort B. It has been suggested that this phase of the city's history was brought to an end by an earthquake. To Level III belong the final stage of the palace-fort and a great shaft which was dug on the eastern side of the mound. Measuring seventy-five ft. square and sixty-six ft. deep it may have been intended as a water source (cf. the monumental water sources at Megiddo and Hazor) or a stone quarry. This level suffered catastrophic destruction, the remains of which lie under three ft. of ashes. But the date of this destruction is greatly disputed. The present excavator associates it with the Assyrian conquest of 701 B.C.E. But other scholars have insisted that it be dated to the time of the first campaign against Judah by Nebuchadnezzar in 598/7 B.C.E. In any case, after the destruction of Level III, the palace-fort was abandoned and the city gate rebuilt. All scholars are agreed that this phase of the city's history (Level II) was brought to an end in 587 by the Babylonians. From this period come the famous "Lachish Letters," eighteen of which were found in one room of the destroyed city-gate complex. The generally accepted interpretation of the letters is that most of them were sent to the military commander at Lachish by a subordinate stationed in a garrison somewhere between Lachish and Jerusalem. But Y. Yadin believed the letters were composed at Lachish itself in preparation of a letter that was to be sent to Jerusalem.

The last period of occupation, Level I, was during the postexilic period. The few remains from this period suggest that the site was abandoned ca. 150 B.C.E. The Solar Shrine, identified as a Jewish cult center, dates to the Hellenistic phase of this Level.

Bibliography. Y. Aharoni, *Investigations at Lachish: The Sanctuary and the Residency (Lachish V)* and "Lachish, the Excavation of the Solar Shrine," *EAHL* 3 (1977): 747-49; C. Clamer and D. Ussishkin, "A Canaanite Temple at Tell Lachish," *BA* 40/2 (1977): 71-76; P. J. King, "Lachish," *HDB*; O. Tufnell et al., *Lachish II: The Fosse Temple*; H. Torczyner et al., *Lachish I: The Lachish Letters*; D. Ussishkin, "Lachish, the 1973-75 Excavations," *EAEHL* 3 (1977): 750-53 and *Excavations at Tel Lachish 1973–1977*.

—JOHN C. H. LAUGHLIN

• **Ladder of Jacob.** *See* JACOB, LADDER OF

• **Laish.** *See* DAN/DANITES

• **Lamb.** *See* SHEEP

• **Lamb of God.** The lamb of God is a title for Jesus that appears only in John 1:29, 36, although the image of Jesus as a lamb occurs in Acts 8:32, 1 Pet 1:18-20, and twenty-eight times in Revelation.

JOHN THE BAPTIST identifies Jesus as "the lamb of God that takes away the sin of the world" (John 1:29). Three contexts for interpreting this title have been proposed: (1) the apocalyptic lamb, (2) the suffering servant, and (3) the paschal lamb.

The Apocalyptic Lamb. The figure of a lamb (or ram) appears in Jewish apocalyptic literature representing the agent of God who crushes evil and delivers God's people (*TJos* 19:8; *1 Enoch* 90:38). Similarly, in Revelation the lamb overcomes evil (17:14), overcomes death (5:5-6), opens the scroll (4:7ff.), and leads the people (7:17) as the Lord of lords and King of kings (17:14; 19:16). This context has been championed especially by C. H. Dodd. The Greek term used consistently for "lamb" in Revelation (ἀρνίον) is not the same as that used in John 1:29 (ἀμνός).

The Suffering Servant. The NT speaks of Jesus as the suffering servant, an image derived from the servant songs in Isaiah. Isa 53:7 likens the servant to "a lamb that is led to the slaughter," and this verse is specifically applied to Jesus by Acts 8:32. The accounts of the baptism of Jesus also evoke Isa 42:1—"my servant . . . my chosen, in whom my soul delights; I have put my spirit upon him." Moreover, just as the servant bears the sins of many (Isa 53:4, 12), so the lamb of God takes away the sin of the world (John 1:29). This interpretation has been defended by Joachim Jeremias, who argues (with questionable support) that the Aramaic word for "servant" could also mean "lamb."

The Paschal Lamb. C. K. Barrett maintains that the primary background for this title is the Passover lamb, which, however, was not technically a sin offering. Nevertheless, paschal imagery is important in John's account of the crucifixion: Jesus dies at the time the priests began to sacrifice the Passover lambs (John 19:14; cf. Exod 12:6); Jesus is offered wine from a sponge raised to him on hyssop (John 19:29; cf. Exod 12:22; Rev 5:9); and none of Jesus' bones were broken (John 19:36; cf. Exod 12:46).

See also EXPIATION; JOHN THE BAPTIST; JOHN, GOSPEL AND LETTERS OF; REVELATION, BOOK OF; SIN.

Bibliography. J. Jeremias, "ἀμνός, ἀρήν, ἀρνίον," *TDNT*.

—R. ALAN CULPEPPER

• **Lamech.** [lay'mik] A personal name found in genealogies in Genesis, 1 Chronicles, and Luke. In the genealogy in Gen 5:1-32 (attributed to the priestly source), he is the son of Methuselah (v. 25) and the father of NOAH (vv. 28-29). This line is adopted in 1 Chr 1:3-4 and Luke 3:36-37. However, in the genealogy in Gen 4:17-26 (usually attributed to J, the Yahwist), Lamech is the son of Methushael (v. 18) and the father of sons Jabal, Jubal, Tubal-cain, and a daughter, Naamah (vv. 20-22). The similarity of the names in the two genealogies in Genesis suggests that they are related, but it is not clear whether they both derive from a single list or whether two originally disparate lists have become similar by association with each other. The Genesis lists also have some striking similarities with Mesopotamian traditions of the history of culture found in the Sumerian king list, the Eridu Genesis, and the Harab myth; but the precise nature of the relation between the Mesopotamian and biblical materials is not entirely clear. In Gen 4:19-22, Lamech, through his two wives, Adah and Zillah, is presented as the progenitor of a generation of great cultural development: his sons become the ancestors of the herders, musicians, and smiths. Lamech himself becomes the epitome of human vengefulness: in his song in vv. 23-24, he boasts of killing in return for being struck, of avenging "seventy-sevenfold" in place of the sevenfold vengeance promised to protect his ancestor CAIN (Gen 4:15). This endless vengeance of Lamech is transformed in the words of JESUS into endless forgiveness in Matt 18:22.

—JEFFREY S. ROGERS

• OUTLINE OF LAMENTATIONS •

The Book of Lamentations

I. A Dirge over the Fallen City of Jerusalem (1:1-22)
  A. Jerusalem's ruin portrayed (1:1-11)
  B. Zion laments its fate (1:12-22)
II. God's Judgment upon Jerusalem (2:1-22)
  A. God's judgment and its effects (2:1-10)
  B. Reactions of the people (2:11-12)
  C. Zion addressed (2:13-19)
  D. Zion appeals to God (2:20-22)
III. Zion Laments and Meditates over Its Ruin (3:1-66)
IV. Meditation over the Ruin of Zion (4:1-22)
V. A Plea to God for Mercy (5:1-22)

• **Lamentations, Book of.** [lam'en-tay"shuhns] Five lament poems articulating grief, confession, and HOPE in reaction to the destruction of JERUSALEM and the TEMPLE by the Babylonians in 587/6 B.C.E. Chaps. 1 and 2 are divided between the lament of the poet (vv. 1-11) and of the personified city ZION (vv. 12-22). In chap. 3, the anonymous "I am the [man]" wrestles with God's RETRIBUTION and goodness. The poet, in chaps. 4 and 5, leads a communal lament, ending (5:20-22) with the characteristic lament question, "Why?" These poems were probably used liturgically in annual public ceremonies of FASTING and commemoration on the site of the ruined Temple during the EXILE (cf. Zech 7:1-7; 8:19; Jer 41:5).

The Hebrew title of Lamentations is *'êkâ* ("how"), a mournful exclamation which begins the first, second, and fourth poems (cf. Isa 1:21; Jer 48:17). In the Babylonian Talmud (*Bathra* 15a) the book is titled *qînōt* ("laments" or "dirges"), which the LXX and Vulgate translate respectively as *threnoi* and *threni*. Whereas in the Hebrew canon Lamentations stands third among the five *Megilloth* (festival scrolls) in the Writings, English translations, following the LXX, place the collection after the prophet JEREMIAH and expand the title to "Lamentations of Jeremiah." Most contemporary interpreters challenge this ancient tradition, and speak instead of anonymous eyewitness authors or of a redactor of independent compositions.

Literary Analysis and Date. The first four of the five poems in Lamentations are acrostics. In chaps. 1 and 2, the first line of each three-line verse begins with the successive letters of the Hebrew alphabet; in chap. 4 the first line of each two-line verse is arranged alphabetically. Chap. 3 offers a more compact acrostic in that each of the three lines within each verse begins with the same letter of the alphabet. Chap. 5 is not an acrostic, but its twenty-two one-line verses correspond to the number of letters in the Hebrew alphabet.

In chaps. 2–4, the second part (B) of each line (A + B) of POETRY is often disproportionately shorter than the first part. This imbalance has traditionally been termed *qînâ* (dirge) meter, i.e., a long line of three accents followed by a grief-shortened line of two accents. Such "limping" or "sobbing" meter supposedly expresses the anguish of mourners. Interpreters today disagree over how meter is to be measured and whether or not meter is what characterizes Hebrew poetry.

Most agree, however, that the acrostic form of Lamentations allows for the expression of the full gamut of emotions, "from A to Z," over Jerusalem's destruction, facilitating a "comprehensive grief catharsis" (Gottwald) that leads to hope. The formality and compactness of the acrostic form channels and reinforces emotions rather than forces thoughts about the disaster into any systematic progression. The terse poetry repeats key terms like *'êkâ* ("how!") and "days of old" (1:7; 2:17; 5:21), thereby underscoring the tragic reversal of past joy into present tragedy.

The influence upon Lamentations of the funeral song (e.g., 2 Sam 1:17-27) and of the individual and communal lament can be seen in the personification of Jerusalem/Zion as bereaved mother and widow who confesses the collective sins of the people and calls upon God to end her suffering, and in the anonymous "I" who suffers in chap. 3. Although Zion sings dirges, God is not dead; God lives as the wrathful agent of Jerusalem's destruction (1:5, 12; 2:5-6; 4:22; 5:19). Unfortunately, as is true throughout the OT, the experience of mothers and wives becomes symbolic in Lamentations for the experience of the city Jerusalem and the people of Judah, especially in their punishment by God; it is an experience of vulnerability, infertility and powerlessness (1:1, 8, 19, 21; 2:13, 18; cf. 4:21-22, re: Edom) and a sexist insult to women.

Many interpreters see a chiastic structure in chaps. 1–5, with chap. 3 as the core (from mid-Exile), chaps. 2 and 4 as eyewitness, vivid accounts of the catastrophe, and chaps. 1 and 5 as later, more distanced and general descriptions (from the end of Exile). Perhaps the laments were collected because of some event like the release from Exile or the rebuilding of the Temple, following Mesopotamian practice. Gottwald agrees that 3:25-27 constitutes the center of the book as a statement of faith and hope with its triple acrostic repetition of "good." He questions, however, the idea of a chiastic structure because of the affinities between chaps. 1 and 2 (each with laments of the poet and personified Zion) and chaps. 4 and 5, both communal laments.

Lamentations has been read by Jews since 70 C.E. on the ninth of AB (midsummer) as part of their festal calendar to commemorate the fall of the Second Temple to the Romans. The book has also been taken up into Christian liturgies for Holy Week in reference to Jesus' suffering. But in its original setting, Lamentations carried out "the task of historical 'grief work,' " linking lament to the historical crisis of Exile.

Author. Jeremiah has traditionally been seen as the author of Lamentations because he is the weeping prophet who prophesied the destruction of his people and of the Temple (Jer 7:29; 9:10, 19; 27:1-15). Second Chr 35:25 also associates him with the composition of dirges for King JOSIAH. Yet Lamentations shares neither Jeremiah's perspective on foreign alliances (Lam 4:17; Jer 2:18, 36) nor his view of the king (Lam 4:20; Jer 24:8-10—contra Habel). Some interpreters argue for "unity of authorship" from a contemporary of Jeremiah, or for a final redactor. Though the poems share vocabulary, style, and the acrostic form, they can each stand as self-contained, independent compositions.

Debate also surrounds the question of streams of tradition in Lamentations. Because it expresses crushed hopes for Judah's king, views Jerusalem's sins in a general way, and hints that God's judgment is too severe (2:20; 3:43-44; 4:20; 5:7), Lamentations is seen to reflect the popular (i.e., nonprophetic) ideology of the monarchic period (Glatt and Tigay). Gottwald argues that several sources—prophetic and DEUTERONOMISTIC, royal, priestly, and wisdom—commingle in the collection. The prophetic and deuteronomistic come to expression in the view that Judah's sins and false prophets caused the catastrophe (1:8-9; 2:14); confession is necessary in light of God's righteous judgment (1:18; 3:39-42; 4:22; 5:16). The WISDOM tradition emerges clearly in chap. 3, in which God is seen as transcendent, and suffering is recognized as a mark of retributive discipline; God's JUSTICE is affirmed and waiting and hope are counseled. The royal David/Zion tradition emerges in the surprise of passersby over the ruin of Jerusalem (2:15-16; 4:12) and of the Temple (1:10; 2:6-7, 20) and in the communal lament over the king as God's anointed (4:20).

Themes. Grief predominates in the Lamentations collection, articulated in terms of humiliation by a scornful enemy (1:7, 9, 21; 2:15), anguish of the elect (2:1, 20; 4:2; 5:2), scope of the destruction (1:1; 2:7, 9, 15; 4:12; 5:14), and pervasive famine (1:1; 2:11-12, 20; 4:5, 9-10). God as enemy and perverse shepherd is seen (2:5-6, 8, 21; 3:2), tearing and slaying "without sparing" (2:2, 17, 21; 3:43). Israel identifies the catastrophe with the DAY OF THE LORD as a time of judgment against Israel (1:12; 2:1, 22). God's wrath was justly provoked by the sins of the people and their leaders, and these sins are confessed repeatedly (1:18, 20, 22 by Zion and 5:7, 16; 3:42 by the people). A restrained hope emerges as a resolution of grief, anticipating Second Isaiah by praying for what Second Isaiah boldly asserts (3:57-58; 4:22; cf. Isa 40:2). Grief resolution also awaits the punishment of the nations (1:21-22; 3:52-66). Resolution centers in chap. 3, with its complaint and recollection of God's merciful character and sovereignty.

See also AB, NINTH OF; EXILE; POETRY.

Bibliography. D. Hillers, *Lamentations, AncB*; D. Glatt and J. Tigay, "Lamentations of Jeremiah," *HBD*; R. Gordis, *The Song of Songs and Lamentations*; N. Gottwald, "Lamentations," *HBC* and *Studies in the Book of Lamentations*; R. Klein, *Israel in Exile*; J. Kodell, *Lamentations, Haggai . . .* ; A. Laffey, *An Introduction to the Old Testament: A Feminist Perspective*; G. Wood, "Ruth, Lamentations," *JCB*.

—DENISE DOMBKOWSKI HOPKINS

• **Laments.** *See* MOURNING RITES

• **Lampstand.** *See* ZECHARIAH, BOOK OF

• **Land.** Terms that may be translated "land" sometimes have the meaning "soil" or "ground," and sometimes "earth," or "world." Context dictates the particular meaning. The term *'ereṣ*, for example, can mean either earth or land, while the term *'ădāmâ* may have the meaning earth, land, ground, or soil, depending on the context. One of the most pervasive uses of the term *'ereṣ* is in the expression "land of Israel," or "land of Egypt," and the like.

Land in the Ancient World. Land was of fundamental importance in the ancient world. Very early, tribes and families would lay claim to particular grazing and farming lands and would jealously guard their rights to these in perpetuity, passing the rights along to their descendants in accordance with the prevailing legal and customary arrangements. Land was quickly identified with the state, as is evident from Mesopotamian and Egyptian records, and was granted by the rulers to those who served them well. Maintaining one's ownership of land was no simple matter, for those with power and authority were skillful in finding ways to wrest the land from its owners.

One graphic story of this sort appears in the Elijah stories (1 Kgs 21)—the story of NABOTH's vineyard. The king of Israel, AHAB, wanted the vineyard of Naboth and sought to buy it from him or to exchange another property for it. Naboth was adamant that he would not sell his patrimony, not even to the king. Queen JEZEBEL took charge when she found her husband sick with longing for this plot of land: she hired perjurers to say under oath that Naboth had blasphemed God and spoken treason against the king. Naboth was executed on this false testimony, and Ahab had his vineyard.

Religious Significance of Land. But the story also shows how significant land was for Israelite religious thought. ELIJAH the prophet arises to challenge the king for his misdeed—both for taking the vineyard from a person who was rightly insistent upon keeping his family property and for his part in Naboth's false condemnation and execution.

Family land represented one's part of the promise God made to the ancestors, Abraham, Isaac, and Jacob. The earliest of the words of promise to Abraham (Gen 12:1-3) speaks of Abraham's going to an unknown land that God will identify as the promised destiny of Abraham. There God will bless him, bring him fame, protect him, and—through him—bring blessing to "all the families of the earth" (12:3).

Land and blessing are intertwined in these stories of Israel's forebears. God is bringing blessing to Abraham and his descendants, according to early Yahwistic tradition, out of divine love and without regard to any merit on Abraham's part. Central to that blessing are land and descendants, the two clearly interdependent. One critical aspect of this promise is the way that the narratives of the Pentateuch (the first five books of the OT) present the land as God's own, which God is giving to Israel as a possession. It is at one and the same time God's land and the land that God is giving, or granting, to Israel.

DEUTERONOMY works out the terms on the basis of which the land—Yahweh's land—will be Israel's land: Israel must be faithful to Torah; must not worship the foreign deities of the land; must treat the land with respect, acknowledging Yahweh's ownership; and must never suggest that its own might or power secured the land. The land was sheer gift of grace, but the gift, once given, carried with it the gravest of demands for obedience to the divine covenant, faithfulness to God's Torah (cf. Deut 8 and Josh 24 in particular).

Threats to the Possession of the Land of Israel. Israel's prophets, from the time of AMOS onward until the fall of Jerusalem in 587/6 B.C.E., brought theological denunciations of the people of Israel for their failure to fulfill the demands for obedience to the divine will. HOSEA could even speak of the land's languishing (or mourning) as a result of the people's sin (Hosea 4:1-3). When the community perpetrated injustice on the land, the land itself could serve as a witness against the perpetrators (cf. Gen 4:10, where the blood of the murdered ABEL cries out from the ground against the murderer CAIN).

Thus it is not surprising that the prophets would threaten the people with destruction by invading armies and eventually with exile from the land (Amos 5:27; Jer 5). The land is held in trust for the Lord; when the people fail God, the heritage is gravely threatened.

The Land and the Cult. Israel's cultic life also served to maintain the people's hold upon the land and to protect the land from spoilation. Careful regulations are provided in Israelite law for the maintenance of the purity and health of the land. The SABBATICAL YEAR assures that the land will have its "sabbath" every seventh year (Exod 23:10-11; Deut 15). The JUBILEE YEAR also involved release from debts and the restoration of encumbered family property to the family (Lev 25). In times of warfare, the land was to be protected from depredations such as the cutting down of its fruit trees (Deut 20:19-20), and it was also to be protected from the defilement of excrement (Deut 23:12-14) and all the more from the defilement that came from homicide (Deut 21) or from exposure overnight of a criminal who had been executed (Deut 21:22-23).

Indeed, in general, the community's worship, its observance of dietary laws, its continuing respect for the Lord's presence in the land all aimed at the assuring of the continued health and productivity of the land. Observance of the SABBATH, the three major festivals (PASSOVER/Unleavened Bread, WEEKS, and TABERNACLES), the sabbatical and jubilee years, and other appointed feasts and fasts maintained the health of God's land, the land of the promise, a land that was intended from the first to flow with "milk and honey" (Exod 3:8).

The Land as Promised Land. The land of Canaan is described with language that seems to contemporary readers to be excessive. One would suppose from the language of Deut 8 that Canaan was almost like the Garden of Eden (cf. esp. vv. 7-9). Ps 104 also portrays the earth in similar terms: water is abundant, there is food for human beings and animals, and harmony obtains between the animal and the human communities. This kind of description rests on an understanding of how the land of Canaan was intended by God to be; it is what Canaan would have been if Israel had remained faithful to God. Israel's narrators and poets and prophets continue to maintain this picture of the land in its intended divine character as they describe the day of fulfillment that awaits the community. In Gen 49 (vv. 8-12), in the blessing of Judah, the bounty of the land is vividly portrayed, as a descendant of Judah is promised to appear on the scene soon. Amos 9 closes with a promise of abundance beyond human imagining in the day that lies ahead for Israel (vv. 13-15). And a number of the prophets portray the day of consummation in similar terms. The desert will rejoice and blossom (Isa 35), the land and its trees will produce with such bounty that famine will be known no more (Ezek 36:28-32), and the whole of the natural world will rejoice along with rejoicing Israel (Isa 55).

The threats to the land will be overcome in the day of God's consummation of the divine work on earth. When that happens, the poor and the dispossessed will again have their opportunity for life on earth of the kind purposed by God from the beginning. This message of good news for the poor and the dispossessed dominates in the NT. Jesus' first sermon as reported in Luke 4:16-19 picks up the OT promise of freedom in the year of release (Isa 61:1-3) and affirms that the day of consummation is now ready at hand. The inheritance of land becomes more and more identified with the new kind and quality of community life among the Christian believers, as is evident especially in Galatians and Hebrews, an inheritance that is finding realization within the community already, and still awaits the coming of the Son of man for its public display.

It is particularly important for Jewish and Christian understanding, however, that the notion of land as God's gift to the people not be so spiritualized that the notion of a geographical locale be set aside entirely. One can see in the creation of the state of Israel how vital—even for secular members of the community—the biblical notions of land remain. Israel's future under God is tied to fulfillment of human needs on this earth. Israel awaits a new ZION, a new ruler from the line of DAVID, a new COVENANT, and indeed a new heaven and earth. The fulfillment of the divine promises, which is tied to the demand that Israel be faithful to God's covenant, involves such concrete realities as food and clothing and shelter and hope. Land thus remains an essential ingredient in the hope of Israel, and Christian hope, while less closely tied to a particular locality, is equally concrete in its affirming what fulfillment of God's purposes for all humankind entails.

See also COSMOLOGY; ESCHATOLOGY IN THE OLD TESTAMENT; INHERITANCE IN THE OLD TESTAMENT; JUBILEE, YEAR OF; PROMISE; SABBATICAL YEAR.

Bibliography. W. Brueggemann, *The Land*; W. Kickel, *Das Gelobte Land*.

—WALTER HARRELSON

• **Language of the New Testament.** *See* GREEK LANGUAGE

• **Laodicea.** [lay-od'i-see″uh] The city of Laodicea was founded in the third century B.C.E. (ca. 250) by the Seleucid ruler Antiochus II, who named the community after his wife, Laodice. Also known as Diospolis or Rhoas (Pliny, *NatHist* 5.105), the city was established as a Seleucid stronghold on a plateau above the Lycus River in southwest Phrygia (western Asia Minor), six mi. southwest of Hierapolis and about ten mi. northwest of COLOSSAE (cf. PLATES 26, 27). Laodicea lay at the crossroads of two ancient trade routes. The first route ran from the ports of Miletus and Ephesus in the west through Pisidian Antioch to Syria in the east; the other extended from the southern port of Attalia through Philadelphia to Pergamum in the north. The city soon developed into a center of commerce and trade, and a strong banking industry arose out of this prosperity (Cicero, *AdFam* 3.5.4). By the second century B.C.E., Laodicea began to mint its own coinage, which bore the images of Zeus, Asclepius, and local river deities. Laodicea also was known for the development of a special eye salve and for its famous linen and wool industry, which featured a fine, black wool from the flocks of sheep that grazed in local pastures (Strabo, *Geog* 12.8.16). Destroyed by an earthquake ca. 60 C.E., the city was able to rebuild completely through the power of local wealth, without the assistance of Rome (Tacitus, *Ann* 14.27).

Laodicea came under the control of Pergamum in 190 B.C.E., from which it was obtained by Rome in 133 B.C.E. Under the domination of the Roman empire, the population consisted primarily of Jews, Syrians, Romans, and other Romanized natives. It is assumed from Col 2:1 and 4:13-16 that the first-century church in Laodicea was in close contact with other local congregations, especially those at Colossae and Hierapolis. The "letter from Laodicea" that is mentioned in Col 4:16 is believed by some scholars to have been received in Laodicea. The church of Laodicea was the last of seven congregations addressed by the author of Revelation (1:11; 3:14-22), who frames images of the community there in reference to the prosperity of the city: the phrase "neither cold nor hot" (v. 15) parodies the warm waters that were brought to Laodicea via an aquaduct from local springs; the reference to "white garments" (v. 18) shames the renowned glossy, black wools of the region; the allusion to "salve to anoint your eyes" (v. 18) mocks the noted ophthamological expertise of the city.

The role of Laodicea in the development of early Christianity grew dramatically in subsequent years, and no doubt was influenced by the prosperity of the community. The Laodicean Bishop Sagaris was martyred ca. 166 C.E. The city also hosted the Council of Laodicea in 367, which opposed the Montanist and Quartodeciman movements and which accepted twenty-six books (minus Revelation) into the NT canon. The modern Turkish town of Denizli currently stands at the spring waters near the site of Laodicea, which itself was abandoned in the thirteenth century. The ruins of the ancient city are known today as Eski Hissar, and remain unexcavated.

See also COLOSSAE; COLOSSIANS, LETTER TO THE; REVELATION, BOOK OF.

Bibliography. D. Magie, *Roman Rule in Asia Minor*; W. M. Ramsay, *The Cities and Bishoprics of Phrygia*; M. J. S. Rudwick and E. M. B. Green, "The Laodicean Lukewarmness," *ExpTim* 69 (March 1958): 176-78.

—CLAYTON N. JEFFORD

• **Laodiceans, Epistle to the.** The *Epistle to the Laodiceans* is a short piece purporting to be a letter from PAUL to LAODICEA. Col 4:16 refers to a letter "from Laodicea," which the Colossians are enjoined to have read in their church. Grammatically, the phrase "from Laodicea" could mean that the letter was written *by* the Laodiceans or *from* Laodicea, but the context suggests that the letter was written by Paul *to* the Laodiceans. We do not know whether any of the early Christian writers who refer to or discuss this "Epistle of the Laodiceans" had genuine knowledge of it. The MURATORIAN CANON (ca. 200 C.E. ?) mentions an epistle to the Laodiceans "forged in Paul's name for the sect of MARCION" (lines 63-65), although according to Tertullian the Marcionites regarded EPHESIANS as the Laodicean epistle (*AdvMarc* 5).

The only extant pseudo-Pauline letter to the Laodiceans is a writing by that name preserved in numerous manuscripts of the Latin Bible. No evidence of a Greek text has been discovered, although Lightfoot detects Grecisms in the Latin version and certain Greek fathers refer to a letter to the Laodiceans. Many of the church fathers explicitly rejected this Latin *Epistle to the Laodiceans.* But Gregory the Great regarded it as authentic (*Moralia* 35.20.48), and its presence in many collections of the Latin Bible from the sixth to the fifteenth century suggests its widespread acceptance during the Middle Ages. Adolf von Harnack and Gilles Quispel have sought to demonstrate that the writing has a Marcionite slant, but the epistle is in fact theologically rather colorless, amounting to little more than a string of pious phrases lifted from Paul's other letters, notably PHILIPPIANS, and exhibiting nothing of the sustained argumentation and development of thought so characteristic of Paul.

Bibliography. J. B. Lightfoot, *St. Paul's Epistles to the Colossians and to Philemon,* 3rd ed.; W. Schneemelcher, "The Epistle to the Laodiceans," *The New Testament Apocrypha,* ed. E. Hennecke and W. Schneemelcher.

—CHARLES H. COSGROVE

• **Last Judgment.** *See* JUDGMENT, DAY OF

• **Last Supper.** *See* SACRAMENTS

• **Last Words.** *See* PARENTAL BLESSING

• **Last Words of David.** The ancient poem found in 2 Sam 23:1-7 functions as a testament to DAVID, similar to those "Last Words" for JACOB in Gen 49 and MOSES in Deut 33. David's "Last Words" follow a royal psalm in 2 Sam 22 (=Ps 18), just as the "Last Words of Moses" follows the Song of Moses in Deut 32. Because the patriarchs were near death (Jacob in Gen 49 and Moses in Deut 33), such last words were dynamic and potent, giving divine authority to their predictions.

Materials such as the "Last Words of David" are thought to have been accumulated in such collections as the *Book of the Wars of Yahweh* (Num 21:14) and the *Book of the Upright* or *Jashar* (Josh 10:13; 2 Sam 1:18). These larger units appeared when the clans became united. Depending on their origin, some of these poems reflect later antimonarchical viewpoints, while others mirror an earlier promonarchical outlook. The "Last Words of David" represent one of those promonarchical sources.

The introduction (vv. 1-3a) to the "Last Words of David" contains a historical resumé that connects the themes of chap. 22 with the composition. Styled like the oracles of BALAAM in Num 24 and Agur in Prov 30, the poem's prophetic character is emphatic. God's spirit fills Yahweh's anointed with the Divine Word.

The second component (vv. 3b-4) reflects the theme of 2 Sam 2–5, "David under the Blessing." These couplets, in the form of a wisdom saying, contrast the ways of the upright and the godless, confidently declaring God's blessings to be on the righteous dynasty of David.

The final segment mirrors 2 Sam 9–24, "David under the Curse." The promise to David in 2 Sam 7 is qualified. David's sin led to his loss of blessings, but the messianic promise to his house remained. Thus, the "Last Words of David" form a vital part of the main theme, introduced in the "Song of Hannah" in 1 Sam 2, repeated in the dynastic promise in 2 Sam 7, and concluded in 2 Sam 23. David's sin cost him, but the curse of sin did not nullify the eternal promise of God.

See also DAVID; SAMUEL, BOOKS OF FIRST AND SECOND.

Bibliography. B. Childs, *Introduction to the Old Testament as Scripture*; W. Harrelson, "Creative Spirit in the Old Testament: A Study of the Last Words of David (2 Sam 23:1-7)," *Sin, Salvation and the Spirit*, ed. D. Durken; A. R. Johnson, *Sacral Kingship in Ancient Israel*; J. R. Porter, "Old Testament Historiography," *Tradition & Interpretation*, ed. G. W. Anderson.

—EDDIE L. RUDDICK

• **Laughter.** Expresses enjoyment, skepticism, or mockery and ridicule. The WISDOM writer apparently had the first idea in mind when he said that God had set a time for laughter (Eccl 3:4). Examples are celebration of the thrill of FREEDOM (Ps 126:2) and the revelry of a feast (Eccl 10:19). However, the wisdom writer also questioned the value of laughter (Eccl 2:2). In doing so, he hinted at a truth that other writers emphasized—laughter is foolish if it prevents serious reflection on life's true values (Eccl 7:3, 6). The Gospel writer pronounced a blessing on those who mourned out of a desire for God and for divine righteousness. In due time, they would laugh (Luke 6:21, 25; cf. Jas 4:7-9).

The clearest example of skeptical laughter is ABRAHAM and SARAH's response to the Lord's promise that they would have a son. Because of their age and impotence, they both found amusing the prospect of having sexual pleasure and producing their own son (Gen 17:15-18; 18:10-12). But God carried out the divine promise, and the proud parents named their son ISAAC, which means "he laughs." No doubt, when they called his name, they often laughed with enjoyment about what God had done (Gen 21:1-7).

Probably the majority of the laughter recorded in the Bible expresses different levels of mockery and ridicule. Chaldeans laughed at fortified cities (Hab 1:10). Lady Wisdom laughs at the fool (Prov 1:26). People laughed at Jesus (Mark 5:40; Luke 8:53). However, here, just as in the Isaac event, God has the last laugh (Pss 2:4; 37:13; 59:8), and God is always the author of the true laughter of enjoyment.

See also JOY; WORSHIP IN THE OLD TESTAMENT.

—WALTER E. BROWN

• **Law in the New Testament.** "Law" is used in the NT in a variety of ways. The term can refer to any part or all of the OT (1 Cor 14:21), all or part of the Pentateuch (Matt 11:13), specific commands (1 Cor 9:8-9), the will of God (Rom 8:7), and Jewish tradition (Acts 22:3; cf. 1 Cor 9:20). Some would translate "law" (νόμος) as "principle" in texts like Rom 3:27, but this is debated. Because of the various nuances of the term, care should be taken in interpretation to determine how "law" is being used in each specific context.

Law occupies a different role in the NT than it had in the OT and Judaism. In both the OT and Judaism the Law stands at the center of the relation between God and the people. In the NT JESUS Christ occupies this position. His coming clearly marks the end of an era. However, the OT Law is still a major focus of the NT writings, and one ought not conclude that the Law is no longer in force. The same writers who declare that change has taken place with the coming of Christ also affirm the continuing validity of the Law (Luke 16:16-17).

Understandably then, many of the 193 references to law in the NT appear in contexts of debate. The conflicts between Jesus and the religious leaders of Judaism often centered on interpretation of the Law. Many of the debates within the early church were over the relevance of the OT Law for Christians. Especially well known are Paul's confrontations with "Judaizers" who wanted to make gentile Christians observe the Jewish Law. In fact, over half of the occurrences of "law" in the NT are in Romans and Galatians.

The OT did not teach salvation by works and was not inherently legalistic. The Law in the OT was an expression of the COVENANT relation with God. In fact, the meaning of TORAH is primarily "instruction" or "direction."

Likewise Judaism was not inherently legalistic and did not necessarily teach salvation by works. Salvation was not so much earned as it was a result of being born Jewish or converting to Judaism. In the NT era Jews focused more on those aspects of law that separated them from other races. Consequently emphasis was placed on circumcision, Sabbath keeping, food laws, and rituals of purity. The desire for purity led Jews to place a "fence" around the Law to lessen the danger of transgression. This "fence" was an explanation and application of the Law to every part of life. While there were many godly Jews, this type of devotion led often to legalism because the intent of the Law was frequently lost.

Jesus and the Law. All four Gospels present Jesus as expressing a very positive attitude toward OT Law (even though Mark never explicitly uses the word "law"). Jesus asserted that he came to fulfill the Law, not destroy it (Matt 5:17). He stressed the permanence of the Law (Matt 5:18) and expected that people should obey it (John 7:19). When people asked him how to find eternal life, he instructed them to obey the commandments (Matt 19:17; Luke 10:26-28). The Gospel writers themselves seem to hold this same high view of the Law. They understood that the Law pointed to Jesus (John 1:45).

At the same time Jesus is presented as one who broke

the Law as far as the Jews were concerned. He repeatedly violated their understanding of the Sabbath. He ate with tax collectors and sinners, which for Jews was defiling. He set aside their understanding of the Law on issues like divorce, food laws, and ritual cleansings.

Jesus was not, however, a new lawgiver. He came as the authoritative interpreter of the Law. Like the prophets before him, Jesus took the Law much more seriously than most of the Jewish people. He told the people that their righteousness had to exceed that of the Pharisees (Matt 5:20). Then in the antitheses ("You have heard it said, but I say to you" sayings) of Matt 5:21-48 Jesus explained the true intent of God's Law. Where murder and adultery had been viewed as violations of the Law, Jesus argued that attitudes of anger and lust were violations as well. Where people had used the OT to legitimate divorce, Jesus prohibited it. Where people had used oaths as ways of avoiding the truth, Jesus required truth all the time. Where people used the OT to legitimate retaliation, Jesus asked people to turn the other cheek and show mercy.

All these teachings about law are based on two assumptions: that God's people should take their character from God; and that the Law is encompassed in the love commands. Since God displays mercy and goodness even on the unrighteous, his people should too. They are to love even their enemies (Matt 5:44-45). They are to be perfect as their heavenly father is perfect (Matt 5:48). This is not a call to perfectionism; it is a call to follow God.

Jesus' focus on the Law is not some form of legalism. Like Judaism before him and Paul and James after him, Jesus summarized the Law with the love commands. The essence of the Law is "You shall love the Lord your God with all your heart, and with all your soul, and with all your mind," and "You shall love your neighbor as yourself" (Matt 22:37, 39). All else is commentary. That is why the "golden rule" is seen as a summary of the Law and the Prophets (Matt 7:12) and why Jesus could tell the Pharisees that they had neglected the weightier matters of the Law: justice, mercy, and faith (Matt 23:23).

The question still must be asked whether Jesus did not violate the OT Law itself in addition to violating the Jewish understanding of the Law. Some would see Jesus' teaching on divorce as a contradiction of Deut 24:1-3, but this text does not legitimate divorce. It recognizes that divorce occurred and attempted to prevent a woman from remarrying her first husband after the death of, or divorce from, a second husband. The only place where Jesus appears to contradict the OT is in his statement "Not what goes into the mouth defiles a man, but what comes out of the mouth, this defiles a man" (Matt 15:11). While Matthew refers this saying to eating with unwashed hands, the Marcan parallel adds the comment, "In saying this, Jesus declared all foods clean" (Mark 7:19). At least in Mark, Jesus implies that the violation of OT food laws is not defiling; rather what defiles is sinful actions and speech.

This change is indicative of Jesus' approach to the Law. He was not tolerant of the Law's concern for external purity and separation. He focused on the Law's concern for inner righteousness and for proper relations between people and with God. His was an ethic of principle rather than an ethic of rules, and the dominating principle for him was the love command.

Paul and the Law. PAUL's comments on the Law have caused debate right to the present time. Hardly anything derogatory was said about the Law by other NT writers, but Paul made surprisingly negative statements about the Law. In his theology the Law brings a curse (Gal 3:13), is not a means to being declared righteous before God (Rom 3:20), works wrath (Rom 4:15), actually leads to the increase of sin (Rom 5:20), is associated with sin to create transgression and death (Rom 7:8-11), is the power of sin (1 Cor 15:56), becomes a tyrant from which people need to be freed (Rom 7:1, 6), and has a ministry of condemnation (2 Cor 3:9).

At the same time Paul made the most positive statements about the Law. The Law is holy and the commandment is holy, righteous, and good (Rom 7:12). The Law is spiritual (Rom 7:14) and gives knowledge of sin (Rom 3:20). The righteous requirement of the Law is to be fulfilled (Rom 8:4) and doing the Law as opposed to merely hearing it is a factor in being declared righteous (Rom 2:13). Contrary to what is often asserted, Paul did not argue that Christ brought the Law to an end. In Rom 3:31 Paul asserted that his understanding of faith did not nullify the Law; rather it established the Law. Rom 10:4 is the verse cited most often to show Paul viewed the Law as obsolete, but this verse should probably be translated "For Christ is the *goal* (τέλος) of the law for righteousness to everyone who believes" (cf. the use of "goal," τέλος, in 1 Tim 1:5).

Paul quoted the Law as validation for his arguments (Gal 3:13). He expected people to obey its ethical injunctions and saw the Law as encapsulated in the command to love one's neighbor as one's self (Rom 13:8-10). Paul did not explain how he made distinctions in the Law, but he clearly did. He saw the love command as universally binding, but he rejected the Law's focus on circumcision, food laws, and sabbath keeping. Apparently those items that separated Jews from gentiles were the items he saw as no longer binding. The Law was no longer determinative; Jesus Christ was. In fact, Paul saw Christian acts of love as fulfilling the "law of Christ" (Gal 6:2).

One key to understanding Paul's statements on the Law is in seeing the context in which Law is placed. When viewed in connection with sin and the flesh (by which Paul means humanity apart from God), the Law is negative. It brings people to subjection and death. But this is contrary to God's intention. The Law has, in fact, become a tool that sin has commandeered to cause rebellion and transgression (Rom 7:7-13). When, however, the Law is viewed (as God intended) in connection with faith and God's Spirit, then the Law is positive and is to be lived (Rom 8:4).

While most of Paul's references to law refer in some way to the OT, he also speaks of the "law written on the heart." By this he means the moral conscience that is available to all humans. Paul's statements are a recognition that some people who had not encountered the revelation in the OT still had come to similar moral beliefs and practices.

Other NT Writers. The Book of Hebrews is the only NT writing to comment explicitly on the cessation of the sacrifices detailed in the OT Law. (However, note Matt 12:6-7 and 1 Cor 5:7-8.) The writer of Hebrews had a positive view of the OT Law, but saw it as the shadow of the good things coming in Christ (10:1; cf. Col 2:17). He understood the old priesthood of Aaron as replaced by a new one, that of Christ. Christ offered the one perfect sacrifice, and therefore, no other sacrifice is necessary (10:1-18). The change in priesthoods effected a change in the Law (7:12) so that the first covenant of God with Israel was replaced with the new covenant prophesied in Jer 31:31-34 (8:8-13). The laws in this covenant are placed in the minds and written on the hearts of God's people. The prophecy of Jer 31 has been fulfilled by the work of Christ.

The author of James agreed with Paul that Christians

should be doers of the word and not hearers only (1:22; cf. Rom 2:13). The Law is to be performed. Pure and untainted religion is embodied in the care of widows and orphans and in keeping oneself undefiled from the world (1:27). The focus on doing, however, does not lead to legalism or a view of the Law as drudgery. The author was enamored with the Law. Surprisingly, he described the Law as the perfect law of liberty, meaning the law that gives freedom. Into this law one should inquire and in it one should remain (1:25). Doing leads to happiness. The Law is "the royal law" and is summarized by the command to love one's neighbor as oneself (2:8). Christians are to live with the recognition that they will be judged on the basis of this law of liberty (2:12).

Conclusion. The NT evidence indicates that the Law has a much more positive role in the lives of Christians than Reformation theology has often allowed. The understandings of law as external form, as legalism, or as a way to earn salvation were never legitimate. The Law is always susceptible to being used by sin to foster rebellion and pride. The OT Law was only a shadow of the good things coming in Christ. But the intention of the Law always has been found in the commands to love God and neighbor. The high call of the Law to orient one's being and actions around the love of God and neighbor is a call that still needs to be heard.

See also COVENANT; JESUS; LAW IN THE OLD TESTAMENT; PAUL; TORAH.

Bibliography. R. Badenas, *Christ the End of the Law: Romans 10:4 in Pauline Perspective*; R. Banks, *Jesus and the Law in the Synoptic Tradition*; C. L. Blomberg, "The Law in Luke-Acts," *JSNT* 22 (1984): 53-80; C. E. B. Cranfield, "St. Paul and the Law," *SJT* 17 (1964): 43-68; W. D. Davies, *Torah in the Messianic Age and/or the Age to Come*; D. P. Fuller, *Gospel and Law: Contrast or Continuum?*; R. A. Guelich, *The Sermon on the Mount*; H. Hübner, *Law in Paul's Thought*; J. Jervell, "Law in Luke-Acts," *HTR* 64 (1971): 21-36; R. S. McConnell, *Law and Prophecy in Matthew's Gospel*; D. J. Moo, "Paul and the Law in the Last Ten Years," *WTJ* 49 (1987); S. Pancaro, *The Law in the Fourth Gospel*; H. Räisänen, *Paul and the Law*; E. P. Sanders, *Paul, the Law, and the Jewish People*; G. S. Sloyan, *Is Christ the End of the Law?*; S. G. Wilson, *Luke and the Law*.

—KLYNE R. SNODGRASS

• Law in the Old Testament. The distinctive character of OT law becomes clearer after first recognizing three components of law shared in common by almost every law tradition, including that of the OT. One of these components is of course a body of particular laws or statutes—a society's specification of whatever obligations and practices it requires of its members as necessary to their life in community. The articles of the United States Constitution are an example. In the OT, the collections of law in its first five books (the Pentateuch) are an example of a special kind.

A second component is the shaping effect particular historical and cultural experiences of a society, including its religious beliefs, had upon its law. This may also include founding events, lived history, ethos—all that forms a society's distinctive self-understanding. The historical record and statements of principle contained in the Declaration of Independence exemplify this second component of law. In the OT Pentateuch, it is represented by the epic narrative in which the law collections are embedded, and from which many of the individual laws explicitly take their rationale (e.g., Exod 20:2-3; 22:21[20]; 23:9; Lev 19:33-36; Deut 26:5-11).

A third component is the formal, informal, and sometimes *ad hoc* judicial procedures by which law is interpreted and by which, even before formal law exists, disputes and complaints are adjudicated, creating precedents that become a source of law. These may be carried out by persons of recognized authority or simply by consensus in an assembly of the people. In this way is built cumulatively a society's tradition of what is lawful and susceptible to legislation. An example in American history is the impromptu shipboard assembly that drew up the Mayflower Compact of 1620. Illustrations of this role in the OT are many and varied, e.g., Deborah (Judg 4:5), or David (1 Sam 30:24-25).

What distinguishes OT law first of all is the striking way these three elements are now combined and their interrelation made explicit in a single work. This is the Pentateuch (traditionally, "the Five Books of Moses"), forming the first of Judaism's three main divisions of the Hebrew scriptures and entitled, from its content, *tôrâ* (hereinafter, TORAH). Classically this term has been translated as "law" (Gk., *nomos*; Latin, *lex*). It is often held that law is a poor translation of *torah* since the latter's meaning extends so far beyond the subject of laws and legalism. This however describes a relatively recent and reductionist view of law that misrepresents torah because it misrepresents the true dimensions of law.

The Vocabulary of Law in the OT. Derived from the verb *yôrâ* (hiphil form), "teach," perhaps related originally to a root homonym meaning "shoot" or "throw," and associated therefore with the casting of lots to determine divine judgment and direction (Josh 18:6), the noun torah acquired early the inclusive meaning of "authoritative teaching," "direction," "instruction," or even "tradition," whether human (Prov 1:8) or divine (Deut 33:10). During the postexilic period Torah came to signify the Pentateuch itself and its content, comprehending the whole of God's revelation through Moses at Sinai—not only the laws but also the epic story of Israel as a people of God, as well as traditions about the creation of the cosmos and the beginnings of the human race. Torah is indeed a comprehensive term, though in more than a few of its occurrences it refers simply to particular laws or legal decisions (Gen 26:5; Lev 26:46; Ezek 44:5).

Of the dozen or so Hebrew words in the OT vocabulary of law none carries so many connotations as torah. Each of the others signifies respectively some distinct type or element of law; on occasion, even something like natural law. These terms and their most typical translations (RSV) are as follows: *'ēdût* and cognates *'ēdâ* and *tĕ'ûdâ*, "testimony" (Exod 31:18); *piqqûd*, "precept," (Ps 119:15); *miṣwâ*, "commandment" (Deut 8:1, 2); *'imrâ*, "word" (Ps 119:11); *mišpāṭ*, "ordinance" (Exod 21:1) *ḥōq* and *ḥuqqâ*, "custom" (Judg 11:39), "due [of priest]" (Lev 10:13), "statute" (Exod 18:16; Lev 3:17), "fixed order [of nature]" (Jer 31:36), "[ritual] ordinance" (Exod 13:10; Ezek 44:5); *dābār*,"word" (Exod 24:3; Amos 3:1), "commandment" (Deut 10:4); *mišmeret*, "charge [assigned duty]" (Deut 11:1); and *dāt* (Persian loan-word in postexilic Hebrew and Aramaic), "law [of the king or of God]" (Ezra 7:26).

A concept basic to OT law, "covenant" (*bĕrît*), receives a separate discussion elsewhere (cf. COVENANT). Israel took over the concept to describe the relationship between itself and God, as well as the resultant obligations, i.e., its law (Exod 19:4-6; 24:3-8).

The Individual Laws. Following Albrecht Alt, biblical scholarship has generally recognized at least two major law types in the Pentateuch: casuistic (or case) law, and *apodictic* law. The distinction is based more on form than on content.

Case law typically takes the form, "If such and such occurs or is done, the one responsible shall be dealt with in such and such a way." Case law considers the circumstances and degrees of responsibility involved in an offense—e.g., the difference between premeditated and unpremeditated murder (Exod 21:12-14), or between an owner who knows and one who does not know that an ox gores (Exod 21:28-32).

Apodictic ("undisputed") law typically takes the form of a categorical directive or prohibition, "You shall . . . " or "You shall not . . . " as in the TEN COMMANDMENTS (Exod 20:2-17). Apodictic law is thought to be distinctive though possibly not unique to Israel in the ancient Near East—whether true analogies occur in certain Hittite treaty texts is debated.

Alt also included among the apodictic laws those that begin with a "whoever" clause, as illustrated by Exod 21:15 ("Whoever strikes his father") or 21:16 ("Whoever kidnaps anyone" [author's translation]), followed by the prescribed penalty. The first two words in English represent a single participial verb form in Hebrew, such laws therefore being categorized as the "participial" type. It has been suggested that this form is in fact closer to case law, since it considers the possible case of violation and prescribes sanctions—unlike laws in the apodictic mode, which simply direct or prohibit and only rarely hint at sanctions (cf. Exod 20:7; 23:7).

The significance of this typological distinction in OT law is disputed. One suggestion is that apodictic law states policy while case law applies it. It is not always clear, however, what apodictic law, if any, might be the particular "policy" behind particular case laws, and certain apodictic examples—e.g., the prohibition against boiling a kid in its mother's milk (Exod 23:19b)—would seem originally to have derived from policy rather than to have articulated any. Another suggestion is that the apodictic form predominates in ritual or cultic law and the casuistic in civil law, but numerous exceptions occur (Exod 22:21; 23:6, 10-11). The distinctiveness of apodictic law may rather lie in its relative simplicity and lack of reference to sanctions—the implication being that, at least in their original cultural milieu, such laws appeared axiomatic and their validity self-evident; to anticipate violations by stipulating punishment would diminish the law's apodictic force. Case law, anticipating cases, demands exercise of discernment and discrimination to determine motive and the degree of guilt (Deut 17:8). Conceivably, then, the two types find some analogy in the modern distinction between "situation ethics" and "ethics of principle." At any rate, the biblical law codes do not appear to rank one type over the other in terms of claim on the hearer or reader.

Another type of law is the ritual malediction or curse (Deut 27:15-26). That a curse replaces more prosaic penalties or punishments implies circumstances in which other means of enforcement are unavailable or violators might avoid detection. A curse was expected to have its effect whether a violator was detected or not.

Law Elsewhere in the Ancient Near East. Archaeological discoveries in the nineteenth and twentieth centuries include a number of legal texts from Near Eastern kingdoms that flourished at various times before and during the period of the Hebrew patriarchs and the rise of Israel. Laws in the Pentateuch and in these recovered texts show some striking points of comparison. The most representative of these law texts, along with other contemporary literature, are brought together in English translation in a now standard anthology edited by James Pritchard. The laws are thought not to have functioned as statutory law for their respective lands or governments but appear rather to be illustrative law, "case studies," to suggest how cases might be handled, not necessarily how they must be.

Resemblances between the ancient Near Eastern laws and OT case law are often close, as in the following examples among many from the great law code of the Old Babylonian King HAMMURABI (1792–1750 B.C.E.): laws on theft (Hammurabi 6-13; Exod 22:1-4); on care of an orchard (Hammurabi 60; Lev 19:23-25); on the goring ox (Hammurabi 250-51; Exod 21:28-32); and on retaliation (Hammurabi 196-201; Exod 21:24).

In view of their shared features the differences between Israel's and its neighbors' law traditions are the more striking. The rarity if not absence of the apodictic form in the extra-biblical texts has been noted. In addition, the variety and diversity of subject matter ranging across the Pentateuchal collections, and the sweep of historical and religious development implied there plainly exceed anything comparable to be found in the extant Near Eastern legal material. The Near Eastern parallels, in their respective prologues—where these survive—invariably portray the king as promulgator and sponsor of the law and its mediator between heaven and the royal realm. The Pentateuch in its present form represents its law with rich symbolism as having been received outside of Israel's land and well before the rise of the kingdom in Israel. After Moses, the priest and not the king remains mediator of the law (Deut 33:10; Mal 2:4-7). The rich component of cultic legislation in Pentateuchal law and the artless way in which narrative and law interact throughout the Pentateuch, resulting in a truly singular literary form, are quite unlike anything in the comparative material cited above. Nevertheless, the similarities between Israel's case law and that of its neighbors indicate the existence of a certain amount of widely shared legal tradition in the Near East upon which Israel drew materially though selectively in the development of its own law.

The Law Collections of the Pentateuch. The laws of the Pentateuch form no monolithic or homogeneous system but are gathered into a number of shorter and longer series or codes, each reflecting its own distinctive cultural and historical context and background ("code" is a somewhat inaccurate designation, but the usage is conventional and retained here for convenience).

(1) "The Decalogue" or "Ten Commandments" (Exod 20:1-17; Deut 5:6-21). "Decalogue," from the Gk., translates literally the Heb. "ten words [*dĕbārîm*]," as in Deut 4:13; 10:4. Its apodictic gravity, simplicity and brevity suggest this law series is the oldest in the Pentateuch, quite possibly going back to Moses.

(2) "The ritual decalogue" (Exod 34:11-26). These are ten apodictic cultic laws (taking vv. 11-16 as prologue), described as the Ten Commandments (Heb. "ten words") written after Moses had destroyed the first tables of stone (Exod 34:1, 27-28 with 32:15-19). Reflecting a settled agricultural background, a relatively well organized cult order, and a monarchic ideology (34:24), these laws may derive from ninth or eighth century Judah.

(3) "Litany of twelve curses" (Deut 27:15–26). Twelve maledictions upon any violator of eleven laws (the twelfth curse recapitulates the whole). An early ceremony associated with ancient Shechem, between Mount Gerizim and Mount

Ebal (vv. 12-13), forty-one mi. north of Jerusalem.

(4) "The Covenant Code" (Exod 21:1–23:33; possibly including also 20:22-26). So named from association with the covenant ceremony of Exod 24:3-6 (the titles used for this and the following "codes," respectively, are modern conventions). It is a mixture of cultic and civil law, and of both apodictic and case law, reflecting a background possibly that of the early monarchy. The "angel" (*mal'āk*), literally "messenger," of Exod 23:21, 23, appears to be responsible for enforcement of this law and may be a priestly figure; cf. the priestly messenger (*mal'āk*) and his instruction (*tôrâ*) in Mal 2:7.

(5) "The Deuteronomic Code" (Deut 12–26). Many of its laws are found in the Covenant Code or elsewhere in the Pentateuch, but much of its content is new. The constraints placed on the king (17:14-20) imply the monarchic period. Other features, including the emphasis on sacrifice only at one central temple (not identified in the code), suggest this as the "book (scroll) of the law" (*sēper hattôrâ,* 2 Kgs 22:8, 11) on which JOSIAH based his religious reform not long before Jerusalem's fall to Babylon (2 Kgs 22:3–23:25). Not part of the Deuteronomic Code itself but preserved in the sermonic introduction to it is the apodictic SHEMA (from the opening Hebrew word, "Hear . . . "), a confession of faith central to Jewish worship down to the present (Deut 6:4-9; cf. Mark 12:29-30).

(6) "The Holiness Code" (Lev 17–26). So named today from its emphasis on holiness as motivation for observing the law (19:2; 20:26), though that is scarcely peculiar to this code (Exod 19:6; Num 16:3; Deut 7:6). On the meaning, in this context, of holiness—a much misunderstood term—cf. the discussion of Lev 11 under "The Priestly Code," below. The laws of this code are grouped together more or less according to subject matter—sacrifice; prohibited sexual practices; what defiles a priest—including physical conditions perceived to disqualify a priest (chap. 21); the liturgical year; and much else.

The proscription in Lev 18 of certain kinds of sexual relations is explained there by ascribing such customs to the non-Israelite peoples among whom Israel once lived or will live (Lev 18:1-2), who are said to defile the land by these practices (Lev 18:24-30), though this begs the question of why they were considered defiling. The stress on holiness in this context (Lev 19:2) gives the most likely clue to the logic at work, analogous to that for the distinction between clean and unclean animals (cf. discussion of Lev 11, below).

For the most part, Lev 19 is concerned with social bonds and with ethics, echoing the Exodus Decalogue tradition (Lev 19:11) and focusing on love for one's neighbor (v. 18) and for the resident alien (v. 33). Even ecology is a concern (vv. 23-25). The Holiness Code is now incorporated into the longer Priestly Code.

(7) "The Priestly Code." Believed to be the work of the latest editors or redactors of what was becoming the Pentateuch in the postexilic community in Babylon, the so-called Priestly Code is scattered in shorter and longer segments through the Pentateuch, though its consistent interest in rite and ritual ("priestly" matters), coupled with a distinctive rhetorical style (fastidious repetition of the same terminology for a given object or idea each time it is mentioned, avoiding synonyms) makes it easy to recognize. Its law sequences belong to a long strand of legal and narrative material (called today the priestly source, or P) traceable intermittently through the first four books of the Pentateuch, beginning with the creation story (Gen 1:1–2:4a) and ending with Num 36.

The laws of the Priestly Code deal with the sanctity of blood as the seat of life, commanded in God's covenant with Noah (Gen 9:1-7; cf. Lev 17:10-11; 19:26); the ritual law of circumcision, commanded in God's covenant with Abraham (Gen 17:1-14); institution of the feasts of PASSOVER and UNLEAVENED BREAD (Exod 12:1-20, 24-27a); cultic instructions concerning the Tabernacle and its furnishings, priestly vestments, the consecration of priests, and related matters (Exod 25–31); and finally, in Exodus, an account of how the preceding cultic instructions, with some elaboration, were carried out (Exod 35–40). Much of this has to be seen as P's idealization of the worship in the wilderness period as a prefiguration of the much later Jerusalem Temple and its liturgy. The law and covenant traditions placed in Genesis likewise must be seen as constructs of the priestly theology rather than as objective history; earlier contributors to what is now Genesis (whatever is not from P) appear to know nothing of them.

The largest sequence of priestly law, including the Holiness Code, occupies all of Leviticus. It is a stately compendium of ritual order dealing with sacrifices, priestly ordination, animals permissible for food, clean and unclean conditions of the body and of human dwellings, and much else. Chap. 16 prescribes Israel's annual DAY OF ATONEMENT (Yom Kippur).

Some law sequences in their present form in Leviticus appear intended less for the instruction of priests than for contemplation by readers, to persuade them of the beauty and drama of the liturgical order and to show that holiness has its liturgical expression. The SACRIFICES in chaps. 1–7, for example, are described in a measured language that lends itself to visualization and contemplation of what takes place. The repetition of certain rubrics at regular intervals is aesthetically satisfying (1:9b with vv. 13b and 17b, or 4:2 with vv. 13, 22, and 27).

The rationale behind the Priestly Code is suggested by the seemingly arcane dietary rules of Lev 11 (cf. Deut 14:3-20) that distinguish between clean and unclean animals (cf. CLEAN AND UNCLEAN). The rules have been explained as early notions of hygiene, as allegories, or simply as preferences of taste; however, their key plausibly is the one stated with the rules themselves: they are for keeping Israel holy (Lev 11:44-45). Clean is associated with the holy, which in turn describes separateness, not in the negative sense of arrogance or hostility but in the positive sense of being distinct, having one's own irreducible identity. Among the animals of Lev 11, the unclean are those of mixed or confused identity: if for example birds typically fly and quadrupeds walk, a quadruped that flies—the bat (v. 19)—is perceived as having a confused identity; it is unclean. The birds listed as unclean (vv. 13-19) swim or dive or in some other way do not behave like birds. The choice of which physical or behavioral details establish identity in a given example may today seem subjective or quaint, but the principle is clear: the animal perceived as "ordered" has its holiness and is clean; the animal having a blurred identity is contaminating and to be avoided (the interpretation follows that of Mary Douglas: cf. bibliography). The ordered character of creation and its creatures is a distinguishing theme in the priestly source, beginning with its highly ritualized account of creation (Gen1:1–2:4a) and ending with its last tradition in the Pentateuch—the ordinance against mixing the tribal inheritances (Num 36:7).

Divine Law in the OT. Ezra's law book—the Pentateuch or a substantial part of it—brought from Babylon to

Jerusalem early in the fourth century B.C.E. (Ezra 7:1-6), is described as "the book of the law (*tôrâ*) of Moses which the Lord had given to Israel" (Neh 8:1). It is presented as an object of reverence among the returned exiles in Jerusalem (Neh 8:5-6). Moreover, Artaxerxes, king of Persia, commands and empowers Ezra to "appoint magistrates and judges" and to enforce "the law (*dāt*) of your God and the law (*dāt*) of the king" (Ezra 7:25-26).

The king's equation of divine law and royal law was not in itself unusual; throughout the ancient Near East law was understood to originate with deity. In this general respect the laws of the Pentateuch are not unique; the law "written with the finger of God" (Exod 31:18; Deut 9:10) is an arresting image, but theologically not radical in its time. However, for the Jews as a distinct people, led to reject the polytheisms around them, the relation between their law and that of their immediate neighbors, and between their law and that of the imperial powers to which they were subject, was a perennially pressing problem. This explains the passion for holy separation from the neighboring nations that is behind Ezra's shorter prayer of confession (Ezra 9:10-15), and behind the complaint with which his "great confession" ends (Neh 9:36-37). Fidelity to the law remained a critical issue for Jewish survival in Palestine during the Hellenistic period, a century before the advent of Roman rule (Dan 1–12, esp. chap. 11; 1 Macc 1–4; 2 Macc 3–7).

Therefore, that Israel's law is understood as divine law is taken more or less for granted and is scarcely an issue in the OT. What does matter there deeply is the practical meaning of the Law in terms of Israel's faith and life. How had the Law become known? How could it be known now? Who had access to it? Where was it rightly practiced? Answers to these questions run a gamut in the OT from the symbolic to the literal and from the intimately personal to the forensic and confrontational. For some of its exponents the Law was wholly supernatural; for others it was present to the human mind and accessible to the understanding.

Early traditions in Exodus, for example, relate how the Law was given to Moses by God, written on two tables of stone. They emphasize the mystery and portent of the encounter but show no great concern for consistency of detail (compare Exod 24:12; 31:18; 32:15-16; 34:1; 34:17-28: the contradictions are apparent). The more literal-minded Deuteronomist presents a thoroughly harmonized and self-consistent narrative, declaring that both sets of tables contained the same Decalogue (Deut 5:6-21; cf. Exod 20:1-17); both were written by God, and the surviving second set is in the ARK of God (Deut 4:13; 5:22; 9:9-10, 17; 10:1-5). The contrast between the impressionism of Exodus and the didacticism of Deuteronomy is evident.

A completely contrasting notion of divine law involves use of the sacred lot to anticipate the outcome of some fateful event (Num 27:21; 1 Sam 14:37; 23:2), or to discover culpability or guilt (Exod 28:30; 1 Sam 14:41). The lot (*gôrāl*; Lev 16:8-10), of which URIM AND THUMMIM (Exod 28:30) was a particular form, presupposed a wholly supernatural and transcendent divine will, discoverable only through circumvention of human and other creaturely factors by casting lots. "The lot (*gôrāl*) is cast into the lap, but the decision (*mišpāṭ*) is wholly from the Lord" (Prov 16:33). This is the logic behind the Book of Esther, where, though God is never mentioned in the book, Haman's attempt to insure the success of his evil plot against the Jews is foredoomed by his reliance on the lot (Esth 3:7; 9:24). The sacred lot (Gk. *klēros*) appears also in the NT (Acts 1:24-26).

The prophetic literature focuses less on law and laws than on the immediate "word" (*dābār*) of God as the apodictic command for the time and place in which the prophet speaks. Isaiah's "Bind up the testimony (*tĕʿûdâ*), seal the teaching (*tôrâ*) among my disciples" (Isa 8:16) refers presumably to his own teaching. The prophets can allude to the objective law entrusted to the priests (Hos 4:1-2; Jer 2:8; Malachi, *passim*) but usually their appeal targets an interior law (*tôrâ*) "written on the heart" (Jer 31:33; Isa 51:7; cf. Mic 6:8). For Elijah, the divine word is described as "a still small voice" (1 Kgs 19:12), though a literal translation is truer to the mystery: "a voice of thin silence" (*qôl dĕmāmâ daqqâ*). For Jeremiah, the prophet is no passive conduit of someone else's words but one from whom is required a discriminating choice of words by which to articulate the divine word: "If you utter what is precious, and not what is worthless, you shall be as my mouth" (Jer 15:19b). Ezekiel suggests the possibility of having to judge the validity even of laws ascribed to God, declaring as the word of God that "I gave them statutes (*ḥuqqîm*) that were not good and ordinances (*mišpāṭîm*) by which they could not have life" (Ezek 20:25). Ezekiel's own visionary "ordinances (*ḥuqqôt*) of the temple of the Lord and all its laws (*tôrôt*)" (Ezek 44:5; cf. 40–48), whatever their purpose, never became binding as law.

The OT WISDOM LITERATURE refers often to law (e.g., Prov 28:4) but not explicitly to the Law of Moses. Law appears to belong naturally to the social order (Prov 13:14; Eccl 12:11). Knowledge of it begins in reverence and humility (Prov 1:7). The man Job, a non-Israelite, measures himself by a very high ethic without reference to a particular law tradition (Job 31:1-40). The magisterial Ps 119, meditating on the law of the Lord, does not refer specifically to the Law of Moses nor does it refer necessarily to any written law code; the psalm often suggests a notion of law closer to the wisdom tradition (e.g., vv. 18-19, 27, 64, 89, etc.; cf. bibliography for a relevant study by Jon Levenson). An explicit identification between WISDOM (*ḥokmâ*) and Pentateuchal law (*tôrâ*) is not clearly seen until the deuterocanonical (OT Apocrypha) wisdom literature (Prologue to Sirach; Sir 24:23; Bar 3:9–4:1). The development was anticipated, however, by the Deuteronomist, for whom the Law of Moses replaced the wisdom of the nations (Deut 4:5-8).

Little is said directly in the OT about any role for the king as mediator or promulgator of law, though the Deuteronomic Code is explicit about responsibilities of the king *under* the law (Deut 17:14-20). An editorial theme in Judges, on the other hand, implies that the monarch in Israel was the only reliable guarantor of order (Judg 17:6; 18:1; 19:1; 21:25), and certain prophetic oracles associate the king positively with the law (Isa 9:7; Jer 23:5; Ezek 37:24). A postexilic governor of Judah—Zerubbabel, a descendant of David—seems to have been the focus of such sentiment (Hag 2:23), but he unexplainedly disappears from the scene. 1 Sam 8:11-17 describes as a warning the "ways of the king" (*mišpaṭ hammelek*), i.e., the king's prerogatives, reflecting probably the nation's experience under Solomon. The opposition between monarchy and theocracy posited by 1 Sam 8:7 is of course the theological view of a priesthood; such views may account in part for the paucity of connections between king and law in the Pentateuchal tradition, in which priestly editors had the final hand.

Significant references to the law process appear in the Pentateuch and elsewhere in the OT that are not explicitly associated with the Sinai revelation or with deity at all. Examples include Moses as judge and legislator, prior to Sinai (Exod 18:13-27); Joshua as lawgiver (Josh 24:25-26); legal rulings by priests and judges (Deut 17:8-23); Deborah as judge (Judg 4:4-5); the rite (*ḥōq*) remembering Jephthah's daughter (Judg 11:39c-40); and David's booty law (1 Sam 30:24-25). The Pentateuchal stories themselves often turn tacitly on points of law familiar to the culture in which the stories are told: Hagar's surrogate motherhood (Gen 16:2) reflects family-law attested in the Mesopotamian Nuzi tablets (fifteenth century B.C.E.; cf. bibliography). Joseph's brothers deceive Jacob with Joseph's bloodstained coat as evidence both of his death and of their innocence (Gen 37:31-33), following by analogy the prescription of Exod 22:13 [12] (cf. Hammurabi Code, 266).

Taken together, the highly diverse sources and understandings of law in the OT suggest that it be appreciated for the paradox of faith and history that it is. The Law revealed through Moses and the body of law that Israel itself developed over the course of its history are presented in the OT finally not as two realities but one. The Law is described with the language of revelation—the fire, the cloud, the thick darkness, the voice (Deut 5:22)—yet it is preserved and displayed in the OT in such diversity of form and context as to show unmistakably its genesis and long growth in Israel's society. It should be apparent that this carries implications for OT law as a resource for ethics. Because it is historically conditioned, no law or interpretation of law can be considered privileged simply by its being attributed to divine origin. The corollary is that because it is given out of Israel's historic faith, the law can truly function as torah—teaching—an empowering resource instead of an overpowering dictate.

See also COMMANDMENT; LAW IN THE NEW TESTAMENT; LOT/LOTS (CASTING OF) IN THE BIBLE; TEN COMMANDMENTS; TESTIMONY.

Bibliography. A. Alt, "The Origins of Israelite Law," *Essays on Old Testament History and Religion,* trans. R. A. Wilson; H. J. Berman, *Law and Revolution*; D. Daube, *Studies in Biblical Law*; M. Douglas, "The Abominations of Leviticus," *Purity and Danger*; W. J. Harrelson, "Law in the OT," *IDB*; H. Kleinknecht and W. Gutbrod, "νόμος," *TDNT*; J. D. Levenson, *Sinai and Zion* and "The Sources of Torah: Psalm 119 and the Modes of Revelation in Second Temple Jerusalem," *Ancient Israelite Religion,* ed. P. D. Miller, Jr. et al.; H. P. Nasuti, "Identity, Identification, and Imitation: The Narrative Hermeneutics of Biblical Law," *JLR* 4/1 (1986): 9-23; M. Noth, "The Laws in the Pentateuch: Their Assumption and Meaning," *The Laws in the Pentateuch and Other Studies,* trans. D. R. Ap-Thomas; D. Patrick, *Old Testament Law*; J. J. Petuchowski, "Not By Bread Alone," *Heirs of the Pharisees,* repr. in *Understanding Jewish Theology,* ed. J. Neusner; J. B. Pritchard, ed., *ANET*; G. von Rad, *Old Testament Theology,* 1, trans. D. M. G. Stalker; J. A. Sanders, *Torah and Canon*; E. A. Speiser, "New Kirkuk Documents Relating to Family Laws," *AASOR* 10 (1930): 31-33 and *Genesis, AncB*; P. Ricoeur, "Toward a Hermeneutic of the Idea of Revelation," trans. D. Pellauer, *Essays on Biblical Interpretation.*

—BRUCE T. DAHLBERG

• **Lawlessness.** *See* SIN

• **Lawlessness, Man of.** *See* MAN OF LAWLESSNESS

• **Lawyer.** *See* SCRIBE IN THE NEW TESTAMENT

• **Lazarus.** [laz'uh-ruhs] Lazarus is a shortened form of the common name Eleazar, which means "God helps." The name appears in two contexts in the Gospels. In Luke 16:19-31, Jesus tells the parable of the rich man and Lazarus. In John 11:1-44, Jesus raises Lazarus, the brother of MARY and MARTHA, in Bethany.

No connection between these two occurrences of the name can be demonstrated, but the parallels are provocative. In the parable both Lazarus and the rich man die. Lazarus goes to the bosom of Abraham, while the rich man is in torment. At the end the rich man appeals to Abraham to send Lazarus back to warn his brothers, but the response is, "If they do not hear Moses and the prophets, neither will they be convinced if some one should rise from the dead" (16:31).

In John, Jesus raises Lazarus from the dead. Many of the Jews believed, but some reported Jesus to the Pharisees. In John it is the raising of Lazarus rather than the cleansing of the Temple that leads to Jesus' arrest (cf. 11:8, 16, 47). Lazarus is also with Jesus at a meal following his resuscitation (12:1) and when Jesus enters Jerusalem (12:9-11).

A further parallel between Luke and John may be seen in that Lazarus is identified as the brother of Mary and Martha in John. The only other reference to Mary and Martha in the Gospels is in Luke 10:38-42. In both Luke and John, Martha serves while Mary is at Jesus' feet. In Luke Mary listens to his teaching. In John she is identified as the one who anointed Jesus' feet (11:2; 12:1-8; cf. Luke 7:37-38). As a result of these similarities, it has often been suggested that the account of the raising of Lazarus in John was developed from a parable like that found in Luke.

Interpreters have also suggested that Lazarus may have been the BELOVED DISCIPLE. Again, the evidence is intriguing but not conclusive. Lazarus is referred to as "he whom you [Jesus] love" (John 11:3). The beloved disciple does not appear in John until after the raising of Lazarus (cf. 13:23). John 21:20-23 reports that "the brethren" believed that the beloved disciple would not die, which would be understandable if he had already been raised from the dead.

Lazarus was from Bethany, near Jerusalem. The beloved disciple was known by the family of the high priest in Jerusalem (John 18:15)—a point that is more easily explained if the beloved disciple were not a Galilean fisherman but a member of an influential family in Bethany. The Gospel of John also gives more attention to Jesus' ministry in Judea than do the Synoptics. Finally, there is the suspicious—but perhaps meaningless—detail that both Lazarus and the beloved disciple are remembered as being at the table with Jesus (John 12:2; 13:23; 21:20).

See also BELOVED DISCIPLE; MARTHA; MARY; RESURRECTION IN THE NEW TESTAMENT.

—R. ALAN CULPEPPER

• **Leader.** *See* PRINCE/CAPTAIN

• **League.** *See* AMPHICTYONY/CONFEDERACY

• **Leah.** [lee'uh] The first of JACOB's two wives and ancestor of the tribes of Israel, Leah was daughter of LABAN, Jacob's uncle (brother to REBEKAH, Jacob's mother), and elder sister to her co-wife RACHEL. Gen 29:15 provides the only personal information about her, that "her eyes were weak" (Heb. *rakkôt,* "tender, weak") and describes Rachel as "beautiful and lovely." The description of Leah is unclear. The implied contrast between the sisters, however, has suggested to interpreters either that Leah's eyes lacked luster (a disparagement) or that they were soft, or tender (a compliment), but no match for Rachel's loveliness.

Leah became Jacob's wife through deceit on the part of

her father. Jacob had worked in Laban's service for seven years in order to marry Rachel, but Laban substituted Leah—probably veiled as was the custom—for Rachel on the wedding night. When the deceit was discovered the next morning, Laban defended his action by asserting the custom of the eldest daughter in a family marrying first. Laban then arranged Jacob's marriage with Rachel at the end of Leah's week-long marriage feast, in return for another seven year's service.

As the first wife, Leah should have held the senior position, but Rachel, the favored wife, seems to have been more prominent. The report in Gen 29–30 of the birth of Jacob's children, the ancestors of the tribes of Israel, develops the theme of the rivalry between the sisters. Leah was mother to six sons—Simeon, Levi, Judah, Issachar, and Zebulun—and a daughter, Dinah. Leah had given birth to four sons when an infertile Rachel obtained two sons by sending her maidservant, Zilpah, to Jacob. Leah responded by sending her maidservant, Bilhah, who would also give birth to two sons. The births of Leah's last two sons and daughter and Rachel's firstborn son, Joseph, followed upon Leah's buying sleeping privileges with Jacob from Rachel in exchange for MANDRAKES, an aphrodisiac.

According to Gen 49:31, Leah was buried in the family burial cave at MACHPELAH in Canaan.

See also JACOB; LABAN; MANDRAKE; RACHEL.

—MARGARET DEE BRATCHER

• **Lebanon, Mount.** [leb′uh-nuhn] Mount Lebanon is part of an extended mountain range, and is one of the two mountain ranges reaching through what is now modern Lebanon, extending from the Amanus range in the north to the Sinai in the south. The Lebanons are the most western mountain range parallel to the coastal plains adjacent to the Mediterranean Sea. The Anti-Lebanons are further to the east, roughly parallel to the Lebanons. The region was populated in antiquity by the Canaanites and the Phoenicians. The Phoenicians constructed major maritime centers, such as BYBLOS, TYRE, and SIDON, for the purpose of trade. In the ninth and eighth centuries B.C.E., Tyre and Sidon, with the rest of southern Phoenicia gained political and economic unity and power. More properly, Mount Lebanon refers to the range of mountains north of Palestine with the Nahr el-Kebir serving roughly as a southern boundary from Upper Galilee (PLATE 1).

Just east of Mount Lebanon is the Beqa‘ Valley, which runs parallel to the Lebanon range, known in antiquity as Coele-Syria. This region provided land conducive to easy settlement in contrast to the Mount Lebanon region with its rough terrain, high cliffs, and deep wadis. The Beqa‘ Valley served as a major transportation route from Mesopotamia, through Palestine's Jezreel Valley, on toward Egypt. The Anti-Lebanon range is further east and runs roughly parallel to the Beqa‘ and Mount Lebanon. Mount Hermon is at the southern end of the Anti-Lebanons. Together, the Lebanon and the Anti-Lebanon ranges are the major summits of the Levant.

The term Lebanon is derived from the Hebrew word for white. This name is given to the snow covered mountains which dominate the horizon for most of the year, especially in the winter time (cf. Jer 18:14). The notable attributes of the Lebanon range are its white peaks, and the forests of cedar and cypress. Lebanon was known in the ancient Near East as a major source of wood and wood products in antiquity. Exportation of these products reached from Egypt to Mesopotamia and Israel. The wood products were used for major public works. It was used for building temples, palaces, and shipbuilding. Tyre, Sidon, and Byblos served as the major ports for the exportation of timber harvested from the mountains of Lebanon.

The cedars of Lebanon are referred to in the Hebrew Bible (cf. Judg 9:15; 1 Kgs 4:33; 5:6-14; 7:2; 2 Kgs 19:23; Isa 2:13; 10:34; 14:8; Jer 22:23, etc.). Their strength and beauty are regularly noted as the glory of Lebanon (e.g., Isa 35:2). Judgment upon Lebanon is talked about in terms of cutting down or burning up Lebanon's cedars (e.g., Isa 2:13). Mount Lebanon is referred to in terms of its snow, its imposing summit, and as a region composing the hill country. Hos 14:5-7 refers to Lebanon in terms of its wood products, its fragrance, and its wine. Ps 92:12 uses the cedars of Lebanon as a metaphor for the imposing growth of a righteous person. Of great significance in the Hebrew Bible is the trade between Lebanon for its cedar and other wood products for major building projects. Special notice is made of the source of wood for Solomon's building of the Temple and the palace of Solomon (e.g., the House of the Forest of Lebanon; cf. 1 Kgs 5:6-14; 7:2; 10:17, 21; 2 Chr 2:8, 16; 8:6; 9:16, 20). Also of interest is the usage of Lebanon's cedar exported from Tyre and Sidon for the Second Temple following the Exile (Ezra 3:7).

—DAVID M. FLEMING

• **Lebbaeus.** *See* THADDAEUS

• **Legend.** *See* MYTH

• **Lending.** *See* BORROWING/LENDING

• **Leprosy.** Leprosy is an indefinite and general word for an eruptive scourge, or a morbid, whitish scaliness on the skin. It is recognized by either swelling or an eruption or spot. The priestly literature deals with the subject at length in Lev 13–14.

Leviticus instructs the priest to examine the afflicted person to observe whether the spot is spreading or not, whether it is deep or superficial, and whether the hair is discolored or not. Raw flesh is considered unclean and spots that spread are unclean. The leprosy may follow a boil or a burn; it may be in the beard or the hair; it may cause itching.

The leper must wear torn clothes, cover his mouth, and cry, "Unclean," in the presence of others. Also the leper must be quarantined "outside the camp."

Leprosy may be discovered in a garment of wool or linen, or of leather. It will appear as mold, mildew, or discoloration. The damaged garment must be washed, and if the leprosy does not disappear, it must be burned.

Leprosy may be cured, and Lev 14 gives elaborate directions for cleansing the leper and certifying his recovery of health. This includes bathing, shaving, bringing a sacrifice of two birds, and later, two lambs. The recovered patient must be touched with consecrated oil on the ear, thumb, and big toe. A sin offering, burnt offering, and cereal offering must be brought.

A house with leprosy will show mold, rot, or fungus. The evidences of the contamination must be scoured off and removed. If the condition persists, the affected wood or stone must be removed and destroyed.

The following instances of leprosy may be noted: Moses is given leprosy in the hand, as a sign of God's power and authority exercised through Moses, the leprosy is removed as soon as it is given (Exod 4:6); Miriam is turned white as a divine judgment for her opposition to Moses (Num 12:10);

Gehazi is stricken with leprosy as a judgment on his disobedience to Elisha (2 Kgs 5:27); four lepers in Samaria discover the flight of the Syrians, and give the news to the suffering Israelites (2 Kgs 7:3-15); Naaman is afflicted with leprosy, though still active and working, and is not isolated (2 Kgs 5:1-14); Uzziah suffered with leprosy sent as a judgment of the Lord and had to live in quarantine while his son Jotham served as regent in his father's place (2 Kgs 15:5); ten lepers are healed by Jesus and are directed to go to the priest to get the medical clearance (Luke 17:12-19).

The identification by modern medicine of the disease or diseases described in the Bible is difficult. Several diseases are at least related to biblical leprosy. Could the biblical cases be identified with any of the following? *Elephantiasis graecorum* is a dreadful disease which attacks the skin and mucous membranes and finally the joints, causing fingers and toes to gradually drop off. G. H. A. Hansen discovered the bacillus which causes the disease, "microbacterium leprae." *Psoriasis vulgaris* is a scaly, noncontagious disease called "dry tetter" which resembles the descriptions given of some of the cases of leprosy reported in the Bible. *Psoriasis guttata* is a disease which causes scattered patches of dry, scaly skin, called "white leprosy."

Clearly, the exact nature of the biblical leprosy is not known, and none of the modern types of disease is exactly identified with the biblical disease (or diseases). The biblical term for leprosy seems to be broadly generic, covering skin diseases of many types. Whatever its precise nature, leprosy was a dreaded plague, bringing horror and despair, and provoking anguished and desperate supplications.

—WILLIAM H. GEREN

• **Letter.** *See* EPISTLE/LETTER

• **Letters/Inscriptions.** Recent years have witnessed the recovery of an abundance of inscriptional material from Syria-Palestine. Probably the most exciting was the recovery of the EBLA (Tell Mardikh) archives. Not only was this find significant because of its size (over 4,000 tablets that were complete or nearly so, and a total of over 17,000 fragments) and age (the majority of texts date to about 2400–2250 B.C.E.), but also because it provides significant historical data for the Old Canaanite period especially concerning a previously unknown kingdom in North Syria. Although not nearly so spectacular, many significant finds have also been made of inscriptions in the alphabetic scripts of Palestine.

Palestinian Inscriptions. While it is true that the quantity of finds of alphabetic scripts has not been as great as for the cuneiform archives, nevertheless many additional inscriptions in HEBREW, ARAMAIC, MOABITE, AMMONITE, EDOMITE, and PHOENICIAN have been recovered in Palestine. To date, the largest single corpus of Palestinian inscriptions is from ARAD where 112 Hebrew, 85 Aramaic, 2 Greek and 5 Arabic inscriptions were unearthed. In addition 13 inscribed weights and 9 *lmlk* impressions were found. The longest single inscription from Palestine is the fragmentary DEIR 'ALLA text.

The list of major inscriptions now known from Palestine must include at least the following from the period of the Hebrew monarchy, about 1000–586 B.C.E.: Gezer calendar, MESHA STELE, Amman Citadel inscription, KUNTILLET 'AJRUD ostraca, SAMARIA ostraca, SILOAM tunnel inscription, Shebna tomb inscriptions, Deir 'Alla inscription, Tell Qasile inscriptions, Meṣad Ḥashavyahu inscriptions, HESHBON ostraca, Gibeon jar handles, Arad ostraca, Lachish ostraca, Tell Siran bottle, Khirbet el-Qom inscriptions, Khirbet Beit Lei inscriptions, and a number of inscriptions from various excavations in Jerusalem (the most exciting probably being the Ketef Hinnom silver amulets bearing a variant form of the Aaronic benediction [Num 6:24-26] and dating to about 700 B.C.E.). From the earlier periods, one must include the Proto-Sinaitic inscriptions, Proto-Canaanite inscriptions from Lachish and Beth-Shemesh, the Izbet Ṣartah ostracon, and a number of inscribed javelin heads. Later finds include the Samaria papyri, Naḥal Ḥever, Wadi Murabbaat, and Qumran (DEAD SEA SCROLL) material.

The value of these inscriptions for historical reconstructions and biblical interpretation is inestimable. A few examples will show the value of these inscriptions. The Mesha Stele provides much new information about King Mesha of Moab, previously known only from a few references in the OT. Furthermore, the stele also mentions

Courtesy of the Eisenberg Museum of Biblical Archaeology, Southern Baptist Theological Seminary.

Siloam tunnel inscription.

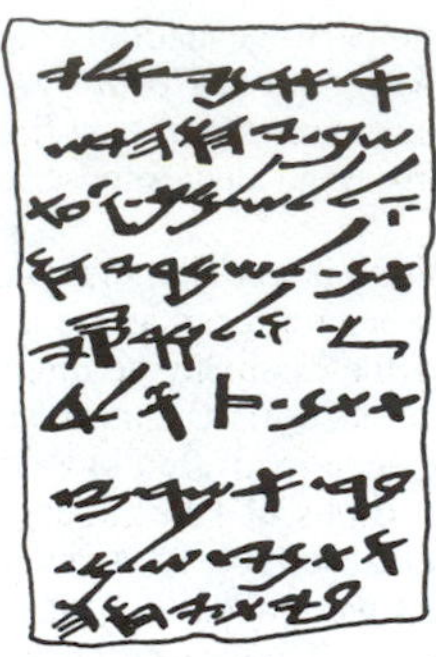

An Arad ostracon.

OMRI, king of Israel, and provides a correspondence between the reigns of these two kings. Israel's God, Yahweh is mentioned on the stele, along with CHEMOSH, Moab's god. The language of the Mesha stele is very close to the Hebrew of the OT, so it provides very helpful parallels in studying the Hebrew language during the period of the monarchy. The Meṣad Ḥashavyahu ostracon provides insights into the situation at the time of Josiah. The inscription illuminates the biblical command concerning garments taken in pledge (Exod 22:26-27). In the inscription a peasant complains that his garment has been taken without cause (apparently by an overseer) and he requests its return. A second matter of interest from the inscription is the availability of writing for a peasant. Either the peasant was literate, or scribes were readily available, even to a poor peasant. In either case, it is apparent that a relatively small matter was put in writing and brought to higher officials for redress.

Letter Form. Among the many inscriptional finds from Palestine have been a number of letters. A study of these letters has shown that they have significant features in common.

(1) Sender: Some letters begin with the name of the person sending the letter. This feature is not very common in Hebrew letters however. Arad 16 begins in this manner: "Your brother Hananyahu sends (greeting) concerning the well-being of Elyashib and the well-being of your household."

(2) Recipient: Most Hebrew letters begin with the name of the recipient. Since letters would typically be sent by messenger, one must assume the recipient would know the sender from the messenger, or would recognize the writing or seal affixed to the letter. A typical recipient formula is simply "To ______" (the name of the person intended). Often the relative rank of the recipient to the sender is indicated, for example, "To my lord Yaush" (Lachish Letter 2), in which the sender is definitely addressing a superior.

(3) Greeting: Most Hebrew letters included a greeting. Arad 16 mentioned above shows a common form of greeting. At times the greeting may be quite elaborate. Often Yahweh is invoked to bring well-being (*shalom*) and blessing on the recipient and the entire household.

(4) Transition: Many letters use a specific word to indicate the transition from greeting to the formal body of the text. Typically the Hebrew word *v'at,* "and now" marks the transition. This transition can readily be seen in Arad 18: "To my lord Elyashib, may Yahweh ask concerning your well-being. And now, give . . . ."

(5) Body: The body of the letter contains the purpose of the letter, perhaps a message, a report, a command, or a response to a previous communication.

(6) Closing greeting: None of the Hebrew letters from the period of the monarchy have this feature. But it does appear in Aramaic letters and later letters from the Bar Kochba period. *Shalom,* "well-being," is a typical closing word.

(7) Signature: Again none of the Hebrew letters from the period of the monarchy have this feature. But it does appear in several later letters. Obviously the signature is unnecessary in those letters which have the sender's name as the first element.

This letter form remains relatively unchanged into the NT period. Even the epistles of the NT show many of the same elements as the much earlier Hebrew letters. Note, for example, the elements in the Letter to the Galatians:

Sender: "Paul an apostle" 1:1
Recipient: "to the churches of Galatia" 1:2
Greeting: "Grace to you and peace" 1:3
Transition: (missing)
Body: "I am astonished" 1:6–6:10
Closing greeting: "See with what large letters I am writing with my own hand . . . The grace of the Lord Jesus Christ be with you." 6:11-18

The study of Hebrew letter forms can aid in interpreting NT materials by offering additional comparative texts.

Hebrew letters also indicate frequently the relationship between the sender and the recipient. One example has been noted above, as a sender addressed the recipient as a superior, "my lord." The sender who is of lesser status would use such terms as "your servant" and "your son." It is unclear whether all references to a son describe kinship, or may refer to the relative status of the two individuals. When the two individuals are of equal status, the term "my brother" was used. The use of this kinship term to indicate relative status without necesitating kinship suggests a similar use of the term "son." Furthermore, the use of kinship terms to indicate status may open anew discussion of kinship terms in the Bible.

See also MESHA STELE; SEMITIC LANGUAGES; SILOAM INSCRIPTION; WRITING SYSTEMS.

Bibliography. J. A. Fitzmyer, "Some Notes on Aramaic Epistolography," *JBL* 93 (1974): 201–25; D. Pardee, *Handbook of Ancient Hebrew Letters*.

—JOEL F. DRINKARD, JR.

• **Levi the Apostle.** *See* MATTHEW

• **Levi/Levites.** [lee'vi/lee'vits] The Heb. form *lēwi* serves as the personal name for the third son of Jacob and Leah (Gen 29:34) and for the adjective, Levite. Levi is also the name of one of Jesus' disciples (Luke 5:29), also called MATTHEW. The noun *lēwi* means a binding or a garland; the verb *lāwâ* means to cling to, to join, be joined to.

The traditional view is that Levi was the son of JACOB, and thus father of one of the twelve tribes. In the beginning it was a wild and warring tribe (Gen 34:25, 30; 49:5-7). Later its descendants distinguished themselves as fierce Yahweh-believers (Exod 32:25-29) and so the service of God at the sanctuaries was given to them.

Some passages raise questions about this traditional interpretation: (1) Exod 4:14—"Is there not AARON, your brother, the Levite?" If Levite only means to be of the tribe of Levi, why is it used in this way? Does MOSES need to be reminded of his tribal origins? (2) Judg 17:7—"Now there was a young man of Bethlehem in Judah, of the family of Judah, who was a Levite, and he sojourned there." The man is a Judahite by birth, and his profession is to be a priest, a Levite. Both these passages, then, speak of the Levites as a trade-guild. They are the persons with the know-how in religious matters (cf. esp. Deut 33:8-11). (3) In Num 3:5-9, the Levites seem to be a group with special skills; they are mentioned over against Aaron and his sons, although according to Gen 29:34 they are all of the same tribal family. (4) The scriptures throughout speak of the Levites as priests and temple personnel. This needs to be taken seriously. (5) When DAVID conquered Jerusalem, there was a JEBUSITE priesthood under the leadership of ZADOK. David, with shrewd talent for leadership, took his priest of many years, ABIATHAR the Levite, and placed him alongside Zadok to be responsible for the religious life in his new capital. All was well during David's reign. But when he died, Zadok took the upper hand, and Abiathar was expelled (1 Kgs 1–2). The Levites never succeeded in gaining equality again. When Ezekiel, himself a Zadokite priest, drew his blueprint of the new Temple with its priesthood, the Zadokites were priests of first order. The Levites were made gate-keepers, assistants at sacrifices and Temple-singers, and this is in effect after the return.

But what about the tradition that the Levites, who originally were sons of Jacob, emerged into a full-fledged priesthood? It appears more correct to view it in this way: (1) There was originally a tribe, Levi, which took part in the Exodus and the conquest, but this tribe died out. (2) The Levites, originally scattered persons with religious know-how, developed into an organized tradeguild, gained respect, and served at the many local sanctuaries throughout the country. And because Levi was the word covering both, it was natural for the priestly guild to claim the venerable term and to establish direct ties to their forefather, Levi.

See also PRIESTS.

Bibliography. R. E. Clements, *The People of God*; A. Cody, *A History of OT Priesthood*; R. de Vaux, *Ancient Israel, Its Life and Institutions*.

—REIDAR B. BJORNARD

• **Leviathan.** [li-*vi*'uh-thuhn] A mythological sea monster.

God's battle with the chaos monster is an important metaphor in the Bible for speaking of the origins and maintaining of creation. Leviathan is one of the names (cf. Rahab, Tannim, Yam, Behemoth, and Tehom) given to this many-headed sea monster who was defeated by God prior to the creation of the world (Ps 74:12-14; Isa 27:1). Though defeated in primeval time, Leviathan continues to lurk in the cosmic ocean, seeking occasion to destroy the created order (Job 3:8). In the celebration of the NEW YEAR'S FESTIVAL, God annually subdues this monster and then ascends the divine throne as ruler of the cosmos. By this victory God sustains creation and preserves the structures of life against the threat of destruction (Job 41:1-34, where the crocodile is an earthly representation of Leviathan). The closest parallel to Leviathan is the seven-headed dragon, Lotan, of Canaanite myth who contended with BAAL for rulership of the earth. Leviathan and Lotan come from the same semitic root.

The images of the mythical battle between God and the chaos monster were also used to speak of the struggle between the people of God and their historical enemies (Ezek 29:1-16; 32:2-8; Hab 3:1-19), though the specific occurrence of the name Leviathan is not found in these contexts. In APOCALYPTIC LITERATURE, the images of the cosmic battle are used to speak of God's final defeat of Leviathan at the end of time (*2 Esd* 6:52, *2 Bar* 29:3-8).

See also TIAMAT.

Bibliography. C. H. Gordon, "Leviathan, Symbol of Evil," *Biblical Motifs*, ed. A. Altman; M. K. Wakeman, *God's Battle with the Monster*.

—LEO G. PERDUE

• **Levirate Marriage.** *See* MARRIAGE IN THE OLD TESTAMENT; NAOMI; TAMAR

• OUTLINE OF LEVITICUS •

The Book of Leviticus

I. Laws Concerning Sarifice (1:1–7:38)
II. The Consecration of Priests (8:1–10:20)
III. Ritual Cleanness and Uncleanness (11:1–15:33)
IV. Observance of the Day of Atonement (16:1-34)
V. Law on Holiness: The Holiness Code (17:1–26:46)
VI. Laws on the Payment of Vows and Tithes (27:1-34)

• **Leviticus, Book of.** [li-vit'i-kuhs] The third book of the Bible, included in the first division of the OT designated as the TORAH or Pentateuch. As its title suggests, the work deals principally with the levitical priests and their duties. Although the Hebrew title comes from the first word in the book, *wayyiqrā'* (and he called), the LXX's designation, "the levitical book," is an apt description of the book's content and purpose. Leviticus is a manual instructing the levitical priests and legislating the means by which relationship between God and people is to be facilitated. While the regulations focus on the priests, few of the laws are reserved for them alone.

The Book of Leviticus developed over a period of time, and various sources have been used in its composition. Its legislation reflects customs from the time of the monarchy and the First Temple and from earlier periods. The final form of the book, however, is usually associated with the priestly tradition that took shape during the Babylonian Exile or the postexilic era.

Leviticus is placed in the literary/historical framework of ancient Israel's sojourn at Sinai. Most of the book contains legislation; only four narratives appear. The most important of these narratives is the ordination of the Aaronistic priests (Lev 8–9), which records the fulfillment of the instructions given in Exod 29:1-35 and 40:12-15. Other narratives, apparently connected with the legislation as illustrations, include the punishment of Nadab and Abihu (Lev 10:1-11), the ritual error of Eleazar and Ithamar (Lev 10:16-20), and the stoning of the blasphemer (Lev 24:10-14, 23). The remainder of Leviticus, however, sets forth by means of legislation the way of priestly approach to a holy God.

A general consensus among scholars exists concerning the structure of the book. Chaps. 1–7 deal with the sacrificial system; chaps. 8–10 describe the inaugural service at the sanctuary; chaps. 11–16 give laws of impurities; chaps. 17–26 stipulate laws of holiness; and chap. 27 is an appendix on various gifts to the sanctuary. There is logic to this structure. The priests begin to offer sacrifice as a part of worship in chaps. 8–10. Chaps. 1–7 give guidance for that task; the remainder of Leviticus concerns preparation for worship.

The first section of Leviticus, chaps. 1–7, is a manual of sacrifice that explains the five types of sacrifice and how they are to be offered. The whole burnt offering (chap. 1) was the only sacrifice entirely consumed on the altar. The donor actively participated in the ritual for this sacrifice.

Its purpose is given in Lev 1:4: " . . . and it shall be accepted for him to make atonement for him." The cereal or grain offering (chap. 2), a gift from the staple of daily food, emphasized the recognition of God as the sustainer of daily life. The "peace offering" (chap. 3) was a shared offering in which part of the sacrifice—the fatness—was consumed by fire and part was eaten by the people. The purification or sin offering (Lev 4:1–5:13) involved the use of the blood of the animal to cleanse the sanctuary and its instruments from the contamination of sin. The reparation or guilt offering (Lev 5:14–6:7) was for the purpose of compensation of trespass upon the property of God or another person. Lev 6:8–7:38 provides further instruction on sacrifice for the priests. As a whole, these sacrifices were gifts to God signifying that God had given all things to the people. As a sign of continuing relationship, the offerings facilitate atonement and communion between a redeemed people and a holy God.

Following the historical narrative of chaps. 8–10, which depicts the Aaronic priests being inducted into service and the inaugural service at the sanctuary, the next section of Leviticus contains more instructions. Chaps. 11–16 concern laws of impurity designating what is clean and unclean. The ordinances include dietary laws (chap. 11) that prohibit foods of various kinds among land animals, fish, birds, and winged insects. Ritual purification after childbirth (chap. 12) is directed. Hygienic precepts are given regarding disease (Lev 13–14) and sanitation (chap. 15). The priests were instructed to identify and isolate those with contagious disease. The section concludes with instructions concerning the great DAY OF ATONEMENT (chap. 16), the most significant worship day of the year for ancient Israel. Its elaborate ritual removed any impurity that might have remained uncleansed. Although scholars have several views regarding the rationale for the CLEAN/UNCLEAN ordinances of Leviticus, the only basis for this conduct in the laws themselves was holiness. That which was clean promoted acceptability for worship, while association with the unclean made one unacceptable for worship.

The final portion of Leviticus (chaps. 17–27) is often called the Holiness Code because of its key word, *qādôš* (holy), and because it stresses holiness in life and worship. The section alternates between moral and ritual laws emphasizing that the people are to live differently from other nations since they are "set apart" to God. Penalties are described for illicit relations and pagan cultic practices that reflect identity with the Canaanites (Lev 18–20). The people were given instructions on how to be holy and how to live in a distinctive manner bearing witness to their relationship with God. Separation from idolatrous and immoral practices that pollute the land is a goal of this section. The life of holiness is associated with God: "You shall be holy . . . for I am holy" (Lev 19:2).

Further legislation in this section directs ritual concerning sacrifices and stipulates restrictions placed upon the priests to guard against moral and ritual defilement (Lev 17: 21-22). Sacral calendar events such as festivals (chap. 23) and sabbatical and jubilee years (chap. 25) are described. Several miscellaneous statutes are included (chap. 24). Chap. 26 cautions the people that neglect of these duties constitutes severing their relationship with God and threatens the community's future. Leviticus concludes with an appendix to the holiness section that describes vows, tithes, and gifts to the sanctuary (chap. 27).

As a people, ancient Israel had been made holy by God's act of ELECTION and promise to bless the community by dwelling in its midst. Leviticus is "torah" or instruction, teaching the people how to respond properly to God in worship and life and thus continue to enjoy God's presence. The response must be commensurate with God's holiness.

See also CLEAN/UNCLEAN; PRIESTLY WRITERS; SACRIFICE; TORAH; WORSHIP IN THE OLD TESTAMENT.

Bibliography. R. E. Clements, "Leviticus," *BBC*; G. H. Davies, "Leviticus," *IDB*; M. Noth, *Leviticus: A Commentary, OTL*, rev. ed.,; G. J. Wenham, *The Book of Leviticus, NICOT*.

—W. H. BELLINGER, JR.

• **Liberation.** *See* FREEDOM

• **Liberty.** The primary focus of the OT concept and ancient Israelite social practice of liberty is economic. The Hebrew terms for liberty (FREEDOM) and liberate (set free) denote emancipation from slavery. They extend metaphorically beyond this literal sense, but do not include the familiar associations of the modern concept of liberty (freedom of religious, political, and intellectual self-determination [human rights]). Slaves appeared in ancient Israelite towns as a consequence of financial insolvency (indentured servitude or debt-bondage), sale by the family, military conquest, and probably an international slave trade. The biblical legal literature regulates but does not attack the institution of slavery. It focuses most prominently on debt slavery of community members. Debt slaves "go forth to freedom" (Heb. *ḥopšî*) after seven years of service (Exod 21:2-6; Deut 15:12-18). Permanently injured slaves (of any kind) are freed as compensation for their injury (Exod 21:26ff.). LEVITICUS legislates the release of debt slaves in the YEAR OF JUBILEE when "you shall proclaim liberty (Heb. *dĕrôr*) throughout the land to all its inhabitants" (25:10), a motto cast into the American liberty bell.

Jer 34 recounts a single instance of a proclamation of emancipation (*dĕrôr*) for all community members held as slaves. Under the stressful conditions of the Babylonian siege of Jerusalem, King Zedekiah arranged the release (*ḥopšê*) of slaves who were summarily re-enslaved probably when the siege was temporarily lifted. JEREMIAH castigates the slave holders with an ironic proclamation of their liberty: liberty to destruction. The Hebrew word for "freedom," *ḥopšî*, is also used metaphorically to refer to the liberation death provides for slaves (Job 3:19) and the tax-exempt status that a monarch might confer upon a subject in recognition of special service (1 Sam 17:25).

In the Jeremiah text (34:13) as well as elsewhere in the slavery laws (Lev 25:42; Deut 15:15) appeal is made to Israel's experience of slavery and God's rescue from the Egyptian house of bondage as the underlying motives for compliance. The OT concept of liberty is inextricable from this confession of divine deliverance. The theological thrust of liberty comes across most clearly in the expansions of its application beyond literal slavery to apply to those who are oppressed (Isa 58:6) or in captivity (Isa 61:1). The surrounding verses define the states from which God demands liberation to hunger, homelessness, and hopelessness. Isa 42:7 uses Exodus language to announce the liberation of people to theological insight. In these texts, the OT repudiates bondage to human masters and structures. It views liberation as a movement into bondage to the divine master and God's commandments (Deut 6:20-25). Bonded service to God, the keeping of Torah, is viewed as the ultimate source of human liberty (cf. Ps 119:45).

See also FREEDOM; SLAVERY IN OLD TESTAMENT; SLAVERY IN THE NEW TESTAMENT.

Bibliography. R. de Vaux, *Ancient Israel*; W. Harrelson, *The Ten Commandments and Human Rights*.

—DAVID C. HOPKINS

• **License.** *See* FREEDOM

• **Life after Death.** *See* ETERNAL LIFE; RESURRECTION IN THE NEW TESTAMENT; RESURRECTION IN THE OLD TESTAMENT

• **Life in the New Testament.** In the NT, several different words are translated life. One word (ζωή) is used for human existence and another (βίος) is used for the conduct of life. Yet another word (ψυχή) is often used for a person as a living being. In a general sense, life in the NT simply means the span of one's natural life ending in natural death. Life can simply signify health (Mark 5:23). The support of such life (βίος) is food, clothing, shelter, etc. In the parable of the prodigal son, the prodigal comes to the father and asks him to divide up his living (βίος) (Luke 15:12). At the end of the story, the father exclaimed, "For this your brother was dead, and is alive (ζωή)."

In the NT, life is always conditioned by being "in the flesh." Thus death becomes a very vital part of life. Natural life is given of God. Yet there is a spiritual life that is promised and qualified with the adjective "eternal." This latter life is given to believers at the RESURRECTION of the dead. Such endless life is not an intrinsic part of being human but rather is a unique act of God. The model for human resurrection is God's action in raising Jesus Christ from the dead. In Christ, death has been once for all conquered. Because of this action in Christ, eternal life is for the Christian a present experience as well as a longed-for future event.

Paul's View of Life. For Paul, life was always lived in a particular sphere—in the flesh (Rom 8:13), in love (Rom 14:15), or in sin (Rom 6:2). Thus Paul always viewed life as a walk, for one always leads one's life in a particular way. Life can go astray in the sense that one can live only for oneself instead of surrendering oneself. True life is found only in the righteousness of God. Because of human sin, man has never possessed valid life but it must be presented to him as a gift of God.

By the grace of God, life becomes possible in the person of Jesus Christ (Rom 3:25). Through faith in Christ, human beings receive this gift of eternal life. Paul often contrasted "life in the flesh" with "life in Christ" (Rom 8:12). Paul viewed this life as a present reality. In baptism, the believer dies to sin and becomes one with Christ. The believer must live life in Christ, and the gospel becomes life. Yet Paul also looks forward to receiving a spiritual body on the resurrection day.

John's View of Life. For John, Christ is the revealer who is life himself and thus can reveal life to human beings; one who accepts this life possesses it here and now and "has passed from death to life" (5:24b). The present moment is even more radical for John than for Paul. He who believes has eternal life. Those who respond in faith have the future life now. Futuristic eschatology seems to fade in importance.

Abiding in Christ, however, for John is not some mystic state but involves abiding in love (15:9-17). There is a strong ethical message in John. Love for one another is always a criterion of faith. The commandments of God are placed upon the believers (John 5:24). Because the divine life is in the believer, then the whole world can be influenced by the gospel. This life is not the possession of a few but given by God for all people who will believe.

See also DEATH; ETERNAL LIFE; IMMORTALITY; LIFE IN THE OLD TESTAMENT; RESURRECTION IN THE NEW TESTAMENT.

Bibliography. R. Bultmann, "ζάω, κτλ.," *TDNT*.

—JAMES L. BLEVINS

• **Life in the Old Testament.** The existence of a person on this earth in relationship to the living God who gives this existence meaning. Life is manifested in the breath (*nĕšāmâ*, twenty-four times) and in the BLOOD (*dām*, 360 times) because breath and blood belong to God. Life without a steady bond to God is no life at all. That does not mean, however, that any notion of the sanctity of human life in and of itself existed in ancient Israel. The sixth commandment ("You shall not kill," Exod 20:13; Deut 5:17), for example, intends to say simply that life belongs to God, not that it is inviolate.

Life is often contrasted with DEATH (Gen 47:19), which is accepted as God's inevitable will (2 Sam 14:14; Ps 103:15-16). SHEOL, the "pit" in the bowels of the earth to which the dead go to exist as shades of their former selves, does not prolong life or increase its value (Job 3:12-19). The dead in Sheol are cut off from the cultic community and from God (Pss 6:5; 30:9; 88:11-12; 115:17; Isa 38:10-11; cf., however, Ps 139:7-8). The only OT reference to individual life after death is Dan 12:2, which springs from Jewish apocalyptic thought of the second century B.C.E.; the dry-bones-come-to-life of Ezek 37 function simply as a metaphor for the renewed existence of the nation after Exile.

Both *ḥayyîm* and *nepeš* in the OT can be translated as "life." *Ḥayyîm* often refers to the physical sense of life-span, of the days or years of one's lifetime (Gen 23:1; Exod 1:14; Ezek 7:23; Eccl 2:3; Pss 49:18; 104:33). Long life is seen as God's good gift and desire for all (Gen 15:15; Prov 3:16; Judg 8:32; Ps 91:16). *Ḥayyîm* connotes not merely survival but well-being and happiness on this earth in relationship to God (Prov 3:13-18; 13:10; Pss 16:11; 133:3). DEUTERONOMY and WISDOM associate life with the keeping of God's commandments (Deut 5:16; 16:20; 30:15-20; Prov 4:4; Ps 119:144; cf. also Exod 20:12; Lev 18:5; Ezek 18:1-9); life and human responsibility and choice are correlative. Consequently, sinners must repent in order to live (Ezek 33:11; Ps 49:10). Much of Christian anthropology, taking its lead from Augustine's doctrine of the FALL and of original sin, stresses the pain of life as a result of God's curse on the sinful human beings in the garden (Gen 2–3:19), a view challenged by contemporary biblical anthropologists, feminists, and liberationists who stress becoming rather than being as the biblical category.

Nepeš can also mean "life" itself, especially when it designates the organ of vital needs of a person (i.e., the throat for eating and breathing) necessary for a person's continued existence (Ps 30:3; Prov 19:8). If one asks for one's own or another's life, one asks for the *nepeš* (2 Kgs 1:13; Esth 7:3; 1 Kgs 3:11; cf. Jonah 4:3). "To seek someone's life" (*biqqēš nepeš*) is literally "to seek someone's *nepeš*" (Exod 4:19; 1 Sam 20:1; 2 Sam 4:8; 1 Kgs 19:10; Jer 4:30; 11:21). In Deut 12:23, "the blood is the *nepeš*" (life); a complete identification of blood and life commands that the blood (life) not be eaten with the FLESH (cf. Lev 17:11; Gen 9:4-5). To kill means to kill the *nepeš* (Lev 24:17-18; Exod 21:23-24; 1 Kgs 20:39).

Nepeš is not some indestructible core of being over against one's physical life that can live when cut off from that life. *Nepeš* does not mean SOUL; one does not *have* a *nepeš* but *is* a *nepeš*, and lives as a *nepeš* (Lev 17:10; 20:6; 22:4; Gen 2:7). The *nepeš* as the life of human beings remains at God's disposal (1 Sam 25:29; Pss 16:10; 30:3; 49:15).

See also DEATH; HUMAN BEING; RESURRECTION IN THE OLD TESTAMENT; SHEOL.

Bibliography. W. Harrelson, *The Ten Commandments and Human Rights*; O. Piper, "Life," *IDB*; H. W. Wolff, *Anthropology of the Old Testament*.

—DENISE DOMBKOWSKI HOPKINS

• **Life, Eternal.** *See* ETERNAL LIFE

• **Life, Everlasting.** *See* ETERNAL LIFE

• **Life, Future.** *See* ESCHATOLOGY IN THE NEW TESTAMENT; ETERNAL LIFE; GEHENNA; HELL; SHEOL

• **Light in the Old Testament.** Physical light, as the first act of creation, existed prior to the formation of the heavenly luminaries (Gen 1:3, 5, 14ff.). This light was called day and was set apart from the darkness. The OT sometimes appears to have regarded daylight as separate and distinct from sunlight (Isa 30:26; Eccl 12:2). Morning light arrives prior to the rising of the sun (Judg 16:2; 2 Sam 17:22).

The sun, moon, and stars function as regulating sources of light controlling the seasons, the days, and the years (Gen 1:14-18). Like the sun, the moon gives light (Isa 60:19; Jer 31:35). Artificial light emanates from fire (Ps 78:14) and lamps (Jer 25:10).

To see the light of day means to possess life (Job 3:16). The dead see the light no more (Ps 49:19 [20]), but those who are healed are brought back to the light of the living (Ps 56:13 [14]; Job 33:28, 30). The light of life is reflected in the eyes (Ps 38:10 [11]; Prov 29:13) as is the light of joy and vitality (Prov 15:30; Ezra 9:8). Light stands for well-being and success (Job 18:5-6; 22:28; Prov 13:9) and finally, the light of one's countenance (face) indicates favor and goodwill (Job 29:24; Prov 16:15).

Light symbolizes the gift of God's salvation (Isa 60:1ff.). In this context "to see the light" means to experience deliverance (Isa 9:2 [1]). God is the light of the faithful (Ps 27:1; Mic 7:8) and of Israel (Isa 10:17). To walk in the divine light means to follow God's commandments (Isa 2:5; cf. Prov 6:23). God's light protects and illuminates (Isa 42:16; Ps 43:3). The servant of the Lord is called to be a light unto the nations (Isa 42:6; 49:6).

See also LIGHT/DARKNESS IN THE NEW TESTAMENT.

Bibliography. S. Aalen, "אוֹר," *TDOT*.

—STEPHEN J. ANDREWS

• **Light/Darkness in the New Testament.** In the OT light was viewed as an independent entity apart from the heavenly bodies. Only in the period of the Exile did light become associated with heavenly bodies (Isa 60:19). In the creation story (Gen 1:1-3) light came into existence before the creation of the sun and moon. Thus the Genesis writer dealt a severe blow to star worship. Light was seen as the gift of God. In the beginning, God created the light from the DARKNESS which enshrouded the earth.

In the OT light is used extensively to describe the person of God. Light emerges from the face of God and falls upon his people (Num 6:25; Ps. 4:6; Ps 31:16). "Who coverest thyself with light as with a garment" (Ps 104: 2). According to his will, God can break this light and send darkness upon Egypt and cause the sun to stand still (Josh 10:12-13). God's light is the essence of his action in the world. He appears in a cloud of light or a fiery pillar to bring about his will.

In later Judaism, a more fully developed theological use of light/darkness took place. Then one encounters more the concept of salvation/perdition in connection with light/darkness. In Isaiah we find the statement: "I form light and create darkness, I make weal and create woe, I am the Lord, who do all these things" (45:7). Here cosmology and soteriology are combined. Darkness came to mean a basic ignorance of God's saving action and became the source of sin and evil. "The murderer rises in the dark, that he may kill the poor and needy; and in the night he is as a thief" (Job 24:14).

The NT picks up on this OT salvation/perdition theme of light/darkness. Light has the function of carrying out God's salvation purpose. Matt 4:16, "The people who sat in darkness have seen a great light" is a quotation of Isa 9:2. God's light is viewed as a gift given to men for revelation, illumination, or salvation (Heb 6:4; 10:32). Light in the NT has conquered darkness (John 1:5). Thus, there is a strong eschatological aspect of light/darkness in the NT. The day will come when the children of light will rule the world (Col 1:12). Darkness will never prevail again (1 John 2:8). Darkness can be viewed as the state of not receiving Christ's revelation or receiving it and turning away from it.

This eschatological note of light/darkness was also present at Qumran and is reflected in the Dead Sea Scrolls. An end-time conflict is foreseen between the children of light and the children of darkness (*1QM*). The future conflict has present significance in that the children of light should separate themselves from the children of darkness (*1QS* 1:3-4). In modern Jerusalem, the Dead Sea Scroll Museum has been constructed out of black stone and white stone to symbolize the light/darkness antithesis so popular at Qumran. The white and black stones might well also symbolize a dominant theme throughout Judaism and Christianity.

See also DARKNESS; LIGHT IN THE OLD TESTAMENT.

Bibliography. H. Conzelmann, "φῶς, κτλ.," *TDNT*.

—JAMES L. BLEVINS

• **Lights, Feast of.** *See* DEDICATION, FEAST OF

• **Literary Criticism.** Literary criticism is a broad term used to describe at least two separate approaches to the study of the Bible. The older use of the term has to do with studies relating to authorship of books, their literary relationships, and the possible sources lying behind them. This type of literary criticism is primarily historical and is concerned with how and why biblical writers composed their works as they did. The zenith of this branch of literary criticism was reached in form criticism, which seeks to get behind the literary sources to the traditions from which they came, and redaction criticism, which investigates how units of the tradition were put together. These two disciplines were the forerunners of the second use of literary criticism.

The more recent approach of literary criticism has to do with the analysis of the Bible as literature is studied. Literary critics hold that one should read the Bible as one would study a work of art, a poem, or a work of fiction. Rather than examining the factors that led to the writing of the Bible, this method claims to focus attention on the text itself. The biblical writers are seen as artists or poets, not so much concerned with creating works of history or theology as with recreating the mystery of the sacred story, drawing together the central values of its culture and faith. Following Aristotle's analysis of poetical language as moving beyond the ways people normally speak to the engagement of the imagination, literary critics place emphasis on the reader's imaginative interaction with the text.

Literary criticism is similar to form criticism in that it pays attention to the forms of the text. Unlike form criticism, which is concerned with the origin and historicity of the form, literary criticism puts its emphasis on the form itself. Some of the forms identified are: (1) The story, in which the reader becomes aware of and interacts with the author, the narrator, and the development of the plot and characters. This form includes the parables as well as the Gospels, Acts, and other NT writings. In fact, the entire Bible can be seen as a profound story with the happy ending that God will prevail. (2) The proverb and the aphorism, metaphorical in language, which through paradox and/ or irony challenge the reader's understanding of a particular experience or truth. Literary critics, observing a sense of disorder in the modern world, feel that these forms are the best way to provide a sense of divine or moral order which shapes the outcome of human actions. (3) The letter form, following the style of informal ancient letters, is poetic in nature and engages the reader's imagination in an intimate relationship with the heart of the gospel.

There is not consistent classification of forms among literary critics, nor is there a single approach among them. Since literary criticism is abstract in nature, its proponents offer no clear methodology by which to practice the discipline. They do agree, however, that the text is not an object to manipulate; it is instead a living work of art which profoundly communicates to the reader who, with appreciation and imagination, interacts with the text.

See also FORM/GATTUNG; GENRE, CONCEPT OF; GENRE, GOSPEL; GOSPELS, CRITICAL STUDY OF; INTERPRETATION; NEW TESTAMENT AS LITERATURE; RHETORICAL CRITICISM.

Bibliography. W. A. Beardslee, *Literary Criticism of the New Testament*; D. Jasper, *The New Testament and the Literary Imagination*; E. V. McKnight, *The Bible and the Reader: An Introduction to Literary Criticism.*

—W. T. EDWARDS

• **Literature, New Testament as.** *See* NEW TESTAMENT AS LITERATURE

• **Literature, Bible as.** *Introduction.* The expression "Bible as literature" may appear strange to persons accustomed to viewing the OT and NT as divine revelation. So long as the written word was thought to bear the imprint and authority of its presumed author, those who cherished the Bible saw no need to emphasize its literary merit. Once the focus shifted to the human process that brought the Bible into existence, interest in its literary quality naturally flourished. The result has evoked the claim that a shift in paradigm has taken place, the historical giving way to the literary. Actually, both perspectives appear viable in current research, for diachronic and synchronic analyses of the Bible have their enthusiastic promoters.

The adjective "good" is implicit in the expression "Bible as literature." Judgments differ widely on the extent of meritorious literature in the Bible, although most critics agree that the Book of Job holds its own in any canon of world literature. High marks usually go to a small number of additional biblical works, for example, Ruth, the Joseph narrative, Deutero-Isaiah, and Hebrews. Brief poems throughout the Hebrew Bible achieve exquisite heights of imagery and evocative power. Many critics think that the vast majority of the literature in the Bible, however, does not belong in a repository for *belles lettres*. Nevertheless, modern interpreters have begun to demonstrate the remarkable ingenuity of biblical authors, and this research into ancient narrative and poetic technique may require radical reassessment of the Bible as literature. At the very least, current literary investigations will undoubtedly clarify the criteria by which to judge sacred literature.

Several ancient texts leave no doubt that rhetoric played a significant role in the oral and written word. Egyptian wisdom literature includes eloquence as one of its cardinal virtues, along with a sense of timeliness, restraint, and integrity. "The Tale of the Eloquent Peasant" attests to the popularity of the right word for the occasion and emphasizes the desirable consequences of eloquence. The Bible also praises those persons who speak effectively, a persistent theme in Proverbs. The observation that pleasant speech increases persuasiveness (Prov 16:21) may refer to the speaker's ability, but it may also indicate kind words rather than eloquence. Similar ambivalence shrouds Ezek 33:32, which describes the people's reaction to the prophet's mode of delivery or actual message. To them Ezekiel resembled a skillful singer or musician.

One of the finest examples of rhetoric in the Hebrew Bible occurs in the story about David's domestic difficulties. The counselor Hushai sought to buy time for a fleeing David by persuading Absalom to muster a substantial army before pursuing his father. Hushai played on the memory of David's expertise as a soldier, the psychological impact of rumor, and Absalom's ego. Feigning loyalty to the rebel son, Hushai envisioned himself among a vast army that would fall on David like dew, and failing that, dragging the city that conceals David into the valley "until not even a pebble is found there" (2 Sam 17:7-13).

Such examples, which could easily be multiplied, indicate that an artistic use of language characterizes a considerable portion of the Bible. Furthermore, a striving for eloquence is no accidental feature but belongs to the essence of this literature. Reading the Bible is therefore an aesthetic experience as well as, at least for many, a devotional one. By necessity, stammering speech often results from the effort to communicate the numinous. Encounter with the Transcendent One cannot easily be conveyed by mortals, and the Bible never loses sight of this fact. That is why "broken testimony" best describes the content of the Bible, and this brokenness refers to more than such things as its alien worldview, prescientific and nonphilosophical nature, and its theocentricity. As the author of Num 12:6-8 perceived, ordinary human beings catch only fleeting glimpses of the transcendent realm, grasping that reality partially and enigmatically.

Stylistic Features. Perhaps that element of mystery partially explains one of the most important features of biblical style, its allusive quality. The biblical story proliferates meaning, or in the words of Erich Auerbach, it is "fraught with background." Words and images danced in the reader's imagination, evoking active participation in the canonical process itself, and once the story or poem took final shape, elicited commentary again and again through the centuries. The pregnancy of biblical imagery resulted from something more than a world view now obscured by time. Ancient readers who shared the ethos of the Bible also appreciated its allusiveness, for they recognized the psychological power of the unspoken, as an ancient curse formula illustrates dramatically ("May thus happen to you . . . and more!").

Another aspect of biblical style, the use of repetition, enhances this allusiveness. Hebrew poetry is marked by balanced lines in which the second half of a line repeats the content of the first, albeit in different words, or says something just the opposite, or carries the thought a step further after returning to a portion of the original idea. Scholars designate these three types of parallelism synonymous, antithetic, and stair-step (or ascending) respectively. Virtually all Hebrew POETRY has at least one kind of parallelism. Such repetition also characterizes Ugaritic literature, which has extensive affinities of language with the OT. Dozens of paired words occur in both bodies of literature, and the occasional reversal of the sequence—placing the "b" word in the "a" position—may have rhetorical significance.

Another form of repetition, leading words, extends beyond poetry to prose. Certain ideas lend unity to a composition, focusing the hearer's or reader's thoughts on one or more words. This device may be restricted to a brief unit, such as the fivefold use of *lēb* (heart) in Ps 73, or it may reach from beginning to end of a substantial literary work. Repetition occurs also in refrains or refrain-like formulas, often called repetets. The priestly account of creation in Gen 1:1-2:4a concludes each day's activity with the observation that "God saw that it was good; and there was evening and morning, a . . . day," and the same solemn device marks prophetic, psalmic, and wisdom literature. For instance, Amos uses refrains freely in the oracles against the nations ("For three transgressions of . . . and for four I will not cause it to return") and in his poignant liturgy of wasted opportunity ("Yet you did not return to me"). To conclude each verse, Ps 136 employs the refrain, "For his steadfast love endures forever," and Eccl 3:2-8 repeats "a time to (or for)" twenty-eight times, while also using formulaic expressions such as "Utter futility and shepherding (or chasing) the wind."

Sometimes a literary feature seems to combine both the allusiveness of Hebrew literature and its repetitive character. A fondness for puns may derive from this particular aspect of plays on words, whether the intent is to reinforce prophetic oracles ("And he [God] looked for justice, but behold, bloodshed; for righteousness, but behold, a cry"—*mišpāṭ/miśpaḥ, ṣĕdāqâ/ṣĕʿāqâ*) or to demonstrate linguistic agility ("Therefore its name was called Babel, because there the Lord confused [*bālal*] the language of all the earth"). Occasionally an author permits such similarities in sounds to cascade mightily, as in Isa 24:16-17a (*rāzî-lî rāzî-lî ʾoy lî bôgĕdîm bāgādû ûbeged bôgĕdîm bāgādû paḥad wāpaḥat wāpāḥ* . . .).

Other stylistic techniques give the impression of conscious striving for completeness, whether through alphabetic poems or ring composition. The former, acrostics, are governed by the Hebrew alphabet, although considerable variety does occur in the way the poems use the twenty-two letters. Comparable complexity occurs also in Mesopotamian acrostics. The Hebrew Bible has acrostics with as many as eight lines beginning with the same letter of the alphabet (Ps 119) and as few as one (Prov 31:10-31), with variations such as the first letter in three lines (Lam 1 and 2), each initial letter in three lines (Lam 3), the first letter in two lines (Lam 4) and twenty-two lines without alphabetic sequence (Lam 5).

Ring composition, often called INCLUSIO, opens and closes with the same word or phrase. Another way of signaling completion, this device lends coherence to a larger unit. A particularly striking example in Eccl 1:2 and 12:8 gives thematic emphasis to the futility of all things, at least as perceived by this book's author. CHIASM, a variant of inclusio, uses the *abba* structure. For example, Eccl 3:8 observes that there is "a time to love and a time to hate; a time for war, and a time for peace." Here love corresponds to peace, hate to war, and the chiastic form extends over the entire poem, 3:2-8.

Especially rich in metaphor, biblical literature describes the deity as shepherd and envisions people as God's sheep. Or the Bible refers to God as parent-husband and describes Israelites as obedient or disobedient children. Alternatively, the ancient writers imagine God as king and depict human beings as subjects. This metaphorical thinking extended beyond Israel's borders, for her neighbors pictured the deity in similar ways, prompting Thorkild Jacobsen to describe Mesopotamian religion under metaphors for nature, royalty, and parent. Biblical prophets often depict God in harsh terms, using metaphors to underscore destructive power. For instance, Hosea calls God a cancer, a moth, a lion, a vulture, but the prophet also thinks of the deity as parent, dew, and physician. Harlotry, Hosea's metaphor for the people's conduct, enjoys widespread usage in the Bible, particularly in Ezekiel.

A substantial portion of the Bible uses the narrative form, often thought to reflect the perspective of an omniscient narrator. Hebrew stories naturally develop plots, describe characters, and reflect changes in point of view. As plots unfold they convey information that no human being could possibly know, and they presuppose sovereign control over events. Names often offer clues about character, as do specific actions the narrator chooses to record. Various means of shifting the point of view allowed storytellers to change perspectives at important junctures. Dialogue and quite ordinary vocabulary such as *hinneh* (behold) often signal such a shift. Reported narration, in which the same material occurs twice, with slight modification, slows down the pace of a narrative and heightens tension as well.

Dialogue frequently unfolds with subtle nuances, sometimes punctuated by silence like that enveloping Abraham and Isaac on the journey toward a distant mountain. Rich in anticipation, this story presses toward what Frank Kermode has called the "sense of an ending." What somebody says has revelatory power, whether allowing others to see weakness of character or enabling them to witness remarkable strength. The narrator also offers clues about character in subtle ways. Samson's father uses faltering syntax to indicate sheer terror in the presence of a divine messenger, and Amnon abruptly dismisses his dishonored sister, "Up, out!" The NT uses diatribe as an effective means of defending the peculiar theology and lifestyle that came to characterize Christians. In the Synoptics Jesus speaks like a lowly Galilean, whereas the Gospel of John has him talk like an exalted communicator of divine mystery.

In one instance the Bible permits dialogue to form on the lips of an ass, and abstractions such as Wisdom also have the ability to speak. This personification, dependent on *maʿat,* the goddess of order in Egypt, vies with its opposite, Folly. Both Wisdom and Folly argue their case before vulnerable youth, using rhetorical strategies appropriate to the high stakes involved in the seduction of life or death. Other poetic personifications stop short of speech, although the abstractions behave like human beings capable of love and hate. Righteousness and Truth kiss one another; Death's manifestations—Sword, Pestilence, and Famine—wield destruction.

The tendency to stretch the credulity of hearers or readers has virtually no limits. The narrator describes the event of creation as if observed by an eye-witness, informs us about God's innermost thoughts, and turns ordinary events into dramatic episodes. The escape of a small group of people from Egyptian bondage becomes the backdrop for a cosmic drama between competing gods, and the symbol of exodus comes to stand for the decisive creative act by which Yahweh defeats chaos and establishes order. Some NT authors go farther in this respect, for they claim that Jesus had no human father and that he conquered death, which will eventuate in cosmic victory over evil ("And there was no more sea").

Not all biblical stories that strain one's ability to believe actually aim to generate acceptance at face value. Irony often functions in tales of the fantastic. The book of Jonah uses irony freely—from the name, Jonah, son of faithfulness, to the final divine rebuke. This sober look at a disreputable prophet moves from irony to satire. Elsewhere prophets use satire to poke fun at the foolish conduct of the Israelites. Isaiah's poignant plea to a forgotten harlot shows the power of such language: "Take a harp, go about the city, O forgotten harlot! Make sweet melody, sing many songs, that you may be remembered" (23:16).

Biblical authors excel in the art of introducing an element of surprise into stories, but apparent coincidence operates under God's watchful eyes. Joseph's brothers intended evil for him but God turned the episode into something beneficial. Ruth happened to glean in the fields of Boaz, although the narrator practices understatement here. The Bible often advances a theory of peripety, whereby a person anticipates something but encounters its opposite. The book of Esther employs this device to good effect, as when Haman prepares a gallows for his enemy Mordecai but dies on it himself.

In Archibald MacLeish's *J.B.*, the character who plays Satan complains that God never laughs in the Bible. That observation may be technically true, but humor certainly belongs to the OT. The royal decree in Esther that every man shall rule his household must surely have evoked laughter, even if modern readers cannot always detect the factors that amused ancient audiences. In the Book of Jonah an endangered ship thinks it is about to break apart, animals don sackcloth and abstain from food and water, and a great fish, nauseous from Jonah's pious psalm, vomits the prophet onto land. Biblical humor sometimes extends to sex. The Gazites surround a harlot's house, intending to capture an exhausted Samson, but, to their dismay, the hero emerges from the sexual act fully invigorated, leaving their town gateless and thus exposed to attack.

The narrative strategy of juxtaposition functions in the Bible to unite texts separated in narrative space and time. Linguistic clues link the two passages, such as the similarity in commands and repetition of divine promise in the call of Abraham and the story about the offering of Isaac. Between the two texts, prefigurement enters the picture, for the banishment of Hagar and Ishmael points to the sacrifice of another son. The prominence of promise in the Bible encourages the practice of prefiguring, for God's people look to the future for a decisive act of redemption. Exodus gives way to a new exodus, creation to a new creation, covenant to a new covenant. Each time the old order pales when compared with the new, and the NT reckons that human imagination cannot fathom what God has planned for the righteous. Anticipation, then, lies at the heart of the Bible.

Literary Forms. Form and style are integral to the message of the Bible. The literary genres within the OT and NT, like stylistic devices, resemble those found in non-canonical literature of the time. Both prose and poetry flourish in the Bible, along with scattered examples of epic prose such as the framing narrative in Job. Poetry has its own forms, as does prose. The NT consists of gospel, letter, and apocalypse, each with variations. Luke carries the story beyond the period of Jesus' ministry, also recording the origins of the church. Paul's "occasional" letters to local churches differ greatly from the Letter to the Hebrews, and Mark's little apocalypse can hardly compare formally with the Johannine Book of Revelation.

Within the larger forms of gospel, letter, and apocalypse one finds many types of literature: pronouncement stories, aphorisms, parables, hymns, blessings, woes, prayers, catalogues of virtues and vices, visions, and so forth Extended metaphors transform some parables into allegories, and symbolism turns the Gospel of John into esoteric teaching, a point vividly illustrated by the futile conversation between Jesus and Nicodemus, a classic example of two people talking past each other.

The forms in the Hebrew Bible range from authoritative statute ascribed to the deity and transmitted by the great lawgiver, Moses, to popular aphorisms claiming no warrant beyond their internal logic. Legal statutes assumed one of two types, apodictic or casuistic. The former type imposed an absolute imperative on individuals, whereas the latter kind referred to hypothetical cases and stated the consequences, whether fines or physical punishment. In short, God's heavy hand provided the warrant for apodictic law ("Thou shalt not . . . ") and the human court handled casuistic offenses. Within WISDOM LITERATURE, aphorisms or sentences (truth sayings) vied with instructions, which used imperatives and offered reasons for obeying, either warnings or promises of reward.

Prophetic and priestly oracles occur often, with visions enlivening some prophetic books like Amos and Ezekiel. The phenomenon of prophecy itself combined these two ways of understanding communication between the hidden realm and human beings, for prophets bore both names, *nābî'* (one called or one who proclaims) and *ḥōzeh* or *rō'eh* (seer). The latter aspect of prophecy naturally culminated in apocalypse, which abounds in the elaborate visions and symbolism of Deutero-Zechariah and Daniel that appear strange to the modern age.

The Psalter, often called Israel's hymn book of the Second Temple, contains liturgical expressions of communal and private devotion. Hymns celebrate God's creative and redemptive power, laments complain about circumstances that threaten to overwhelm believers, thanksgiving psalms extol the praises of Israel's God who either has already acted to deliver or who will surely do so soon. Torah psalms and didactic compositions explore the wonders of divine instruction, even when the lessons result from painful experience and never fully explain life's perplexities (Pss 49, 73). Royal psalms and pilgrimage psalms show how this literature is firmly rooted in daily life.

This discussion of literary forms only scratches the surface, for law, prophecy, and wisdom use numerous literary types. To mention only a few, wisdom literature makes skillful use of prayer, hymn, allegory, riddle-like questions, numerical sequences, particles of existence, dialogue, autobiographical narrative, reflection, example story, royal fiction, extended metaphor, negative confession, benediction, and malediction. Canonical prophets varied their oracles and visions by introducing entrance liturgies, confessions, prayers, complaints, discussion, liturgical compositions, dirges, and so forth. The legal material comprises only a portion of the Torah, which also has patriarchal narratives, legends, genealogies, etiologies, curses, and the like. Letters, documents, popular songs, wedding songs, annals, anecdotes, fables—the list is virtually endless.

Furthermore, the Bible uses literary conventions, or type scenes, that leave the impression of déjà vu. Three different accounts of the ancestress in danger witness to the fondness for this theme. Meetings at a well, appearances of an angelic visitor to announce good tidings, response to bad news, the defeat of a strong man by a woman, a portentous dream that unfolds as described, and much more make up Israel's type scenes. It appears that storytellers picked and chose various items from the building blocks at their disposal, adding their own individual contributions in the act of composition. Formulaic patterns enabled them to treat familiar matter in unfamiliar ways, for each author brought special gifts and interests to address a particular audience. Endless stylistic devices assured individuality despite literary conventions that pushed toward uniformity.

Some biblical authors went beyond mere use of type scenes, borrowing actual literary sources and reshaping them to meet a new social context. The Pentateuch seems to derive from four literary strata, each having a different author and originating over the course of several centuries. Similarly, the synoptic Gospels rely on a source that goes by the letter Q. The prophets Micah and Isaiah share a vision of an era when instruments of war will be put to peaceful use, and Israel's historiographers draw on several sources that lend credibility to their theological understandings of national history.

The likelihood of literary sources in various biblical texts raises the possibility that some larger literary units came about through a lengthy process of editing. The prophetic book of Isaiah, for example, arose as a result of at least three different editors or redactional circles. Likewise, the book of Jeremiah combines prophetic oracles, prose sermons exhibiting deuteronomic influence, and biography. Such editorial activity occurred also in the composition of wisdom literature, as the several collections in Proverbs and the secondary passages in the Book of Job demonstrate. In the case of Ecclesiastes, two epilogues show that wisdom, like prophecy, constituted a living tradition. An admirer of Qoheleth, the Hebrew name for the author of Ecclesiastes, appends an endorsement of the teacher's collected words, but another epilogist cautions against uncritical acceptance of the skeptic's observations on life.

The Hebrew Bible reveals signs of editorial desire to attribute the majority of the Torah and Writings to three persons, regardless of indications that they could not have written the texts assigned to their names. Moses was believed to have written the Torah, David was credited with writing most of the Psalms, and Solomon was thought to have composed the wisdom literature. The unknown author of Ecclesiastes adopts the persona of King Solomon, at least in the first two chapters, and this artifice extends to Song of Songs and Wisdom of Solomon, despite the latter's use of Greek rather than Hebrew. Moreover, editorial glosses and superscriptions entered the biblical text for centuries, making it virtually impossible to ascertain the date of any given literary unit. Although the fixing of the canon slowed the process, copiers of the text continued to add marginal glosses, some of which eventually entered the biblical text itself.

Contemporary Literary Theory. The task of recognizing literary artistry in the Bible requires intuition to the extent that close reading is a humanistic enterprise. The goal of close reading, creating a countertext, necessitates attention to every facet of grammar and syntax. A literary critic reads a text in the same way a composer reads a musical score. The literary critic repeats the act of composition, pausing at each stage to determine the many possibilities open to the author. Aesthetic criticism leaves little to chance. Ideally, its practitioners notice every choice of vocabulary, the position of subjects and predicates, the vehicle and tenor of metaphors, the use of monologue or dialogue, the delaying of key words and the forceful heaping up of others. Such analysis is informed by familiarity with style and rhetoric in other texts on a similar theme.

Close reading is only one way of creating a countertext. Another way proceeds by comparative study, both within the Bible and outside it. Ancient Near Eastern texts serve as comparison and contrast for any study of the OT, and Greco-Roman or rabbinic literature offers valuable comparative texts for students of the NT. Often the same theme is dealt with several times within the Bible; for example, the Day of the Lord, the idea of a hidden God, the centrality of the city of God, Jerusalem, and the attributes of God as declared to Moses in Exod 34:6-7 occur in several different contexts, and the selective use of these themes is noteworthy. In many cases biblical authors reflect on the same themes that occur in extrabiblical sources, and the different nuances reveal much about biblical writers. The creation and flood traditions, the Job literature, the proverb collections, the erotic songs, the miracle stories, and the apocalyptic images suggest that biblical writers were thoroughly immersed in their culture. For this reason, literary analysis of the Bible casts its net rather widely. Insofar as much western literature drew inspiration from the Bible as well as Greek classics, comparison on a wider scale seems entirely appropriate. Furthermore, great literature from all cultures explores fundamental human problems and aspirations, making a comparison with biblical texts both informative and salutary.

The Bible lends itself to study in several different ways, four of which merit discussion here: formalism, structuralism, reader-response criticism, and deconstructionism. The first, formalism, emphasizes the text itself as the decisive factor in interpretation. The second, structuralism, stresses the capacity of the reader to penetrate beneath the surface level of what is spoken or written to the deep structures of thought. The third and fourth, reader-response criticism and deconstructionism, concentrate entirely on readers rather than the meaning of texts, insisting that authorial intention and the original sense of a text do not mandate a single meaning that astute readers must discover.

Comparison of numerous Russian folktales led Vladimir Propp to isolate certain narrative sequences that make up a given kind of folktale, the fairy tale. Some stories had additional components that were not essential to the action sequence, leading to the conclusion that stories contained both obligatory and optional components. Study of these formal elements has thrown light on, among others, the Book of Ruth, the patriarchal narratives, and Tobit. Formalism necessitates the isolating of formal elements of biblical stories and putting them on a grid that represents an artificial construct. To some extent, form critics do the same thing, for they construct the essential elements of a literary type on the basis of several different texts.

Structuralists make a fundamental assumption that all thinking rests on binary opposition which must be mediated by a third category that participates in both realms but belongs to neither. Highly dependent on de Saussure's distinction between a sign and what it signifies, structuralism operates with a view of language that distinguishes surface levels from deeper structures of discourse. The mind automatically registers the surface meaning of what is said and decodes it, producing a hidden level of meaning. Patterns exist in speech, and the goal is to discover the different configurations of a given discourse. Some features are culture distinct, like the patterns on carpets from Persia, Greece, or China; others have universal distribution. This tension explains structualists' intense interest in philosophy and anthropology.

The complete shift to the reader takes place in affective criticism, which concentrates on the emotive reaction to texts. The old axiom that "ninety per cent of what one sees lies behind the eyes" implies that readers' responses to texts depend more on what they bring to the experience of reading than on the actual contents of written texts. The emphasis falls on the total experience of reading a text or listening to a speaker, not on one final meaning. The actual sense of a text includes a reader's understanding of the way that plot unfolds or the poem constructs its images, the questions a reader poses to the text, the conjectures emerging during the process of reading, and the resolution of the difficulties created by tensions within the text.

Deconstructionists believe that every act of reading creates a new text, hence no definitive interpretation exists for any text. How one reads a given text depends on a host of factors, and that particular combination occurs only once. All readings possess a certain tenuousness, for the meaning of a text must be permanently deferred. The essence of a text, its openness, accords with a philosophical relativism that has come to characterize the modern intellect. One could read the David stories from the perspective of Saul, the Exodus event from that of the Egyptians, the story of the Judges from the viewpoint of the Canaanites, Judas' betrayal of Jesus from the perspective of a Zealot, and Paul's theological treatises from that of Jews contemporary to him. The many legitimate agendas of modern interpreters—evangelical and liberal, feminist, liberation theology, black—seem to reinforce the view that readers create their own text, to the extent that they manipulate it to wrench from the ancient word something quite modern.

The literary approach to the Bible promises to illumine the sacred text in new ways. Time alone will tell whether the enthusiasm over the Bible as literature will pass like so many fads. In the interim, countless readers encounter one surprise after another as they view the text through new lenses. The time is ripe for aesthetic readings and holistic (or total) interpretations of texts previously dissected so thoroughly that their beauty and complexity vanished from sight.

See also BIBLE AND WESTERN LITERATURE; HERMENEUTICS.

Bibliography. R. Alter, *The Art of Biblical Narrative* and *The Art of Biblical Poetry*; R. Alter and F. Kermode, eds., *The Literary Guide to the Bible*; A. Berlin, *Poetics and Interpretation of Biblical Narrative*; J. A. Clines, D. M. Gunn, and A. J. Hauser, eds., *Art and Meaning: Rhetoric in Biblical Literature, JSOTSup* 19; J. L. Crenshaw, *Samson: A Secret Betrayed, a Vow Ignored*; N. Frye, *The Great Code: The Bible and Literature*; E. L. Greenstein, "Literature, the Old Testament as," *HBD* and "Theory and Argument in Biblical Criticism," *HAR* 10 (1986): 77-93; D. M. Gunn, *The Story of King David, JSOTSup* 6; T. R. Henn, *The Bible as Literature*; J. Magonet, *Form and Meaning*; R. Polzin, *Biblical Structuralism*; A. Preminger and E. L. Greenstein, *The Hebrew Bible in Literary Criticism*; H. N. Schneidau, *Sacred Discontent: The Bible and Western Tradition*; M. Sternberg, *The Poetics of Biblical Narrative*; P. Trible, *God and the Rhetoric of Sexuality*; M. Weiss, *The Story of Job's Beginning*.

—JAMES L. CRENSHAW

• **Lives of the Prophets.** The *Lives of the Prophets* is a collection of biographical sketches, in varying lengths, of OT prophets. In its earliest form it probably contained material about twenty-three prophets: ISAIAH, JEREMIAH, EZEKIEL, DANIEL, the twelve minor prophets, Nathan, Ahijah the Shilonite (1 Kgs 11:29-39), the "man of God" who came to Jeroboam at BETHEL (given the name of "Joad"; 1 Kgs 13:1-32), Azariah the son of Oded (2 Chr 15:1-7), ELIJAH, ELISHA, and Zechariah the son of Jehoiada (2 Chr 24:20-22). The prologue promises to give "the names of the prophets, and where they are from, and where they died and how, and where they lie." Some of the entries do little more than that; the section on JOEL, for example, consists of a single sentence. Others add information about the prophet's life, ranging from a little (cf. the sections on HOSEA, OBADIAH, NAHUM, ZEPHANIAH, HAGGAI, Ahijah, and Azariah) to a lot (cf. the sections on Isaiah, Jeremiah, Ezekiel, Daniel, JONAH, and HABAKKUK). Typically, the additional material is extracanonical, and some of it is paralleled in other apocryphal writings, such as Jeremiah's hiding of the Temple vessels (cf. 2 Macc 2:4-8; *4 Bar* 3:8-20), his being stoned (cf. *4 Bar* 9:22-31), Isaiah's being sawn in two (cf. *MartIsa*), and Habakkuk's visit to Babylon to feed Daniel (cf. Bel). The stories are frequently miraculous: Isaiah performs a water miracle at Siloam; Jeremiah prays the asps and crocodiles out of Egypt; Ezekiel reproduces the Red Sea miracle (cf. Exod 14:21-29) in Exile; Elijah's father has a vision when Elijah is born; the golden calf in GILGAL bellows at Elisha's birth. Also, a prediction by the prophet, frequently concerning the TEMPLE, the end, or both (cf. the entries on Jeremiah, Ezekiel, Daniel, Jonah, and Habakkuk) is often recorded.

The *Lives of the Prophets* is extant in a number of ancient languages, including Syriac, Ethiopic, Latin, Armenian, and most importantly, Greek. Although its origins are difficult to determine, it is plausible that the work was composed by a Palestinian Jew in Greek during the first century C.E. It became popular among Christians, who sometimes added sections on NT figures such as Zechariah, SIMEON (Luke 2:25-35), and JOHN THE BAPTIST, and who are presumably responsible for Jeremiah's predictions of the VIRGIN BIRTH, the infant in a manger, and gentiles worshiping a piece of wood, all of which are found in the earliest extant Greek recension.

The motivation behind the collection is not altogether clear. The fact that several of the prophets were martyred (Isaiah, Jeremiah, Ezekiel, Micah, Amos, and Zechariah, the son of Jehoiada) raises the possibility of an early Jewish veneration of martyrs. The author's keen interest in where the prophets are buried might suggest a more general veneration of the saints (cf. Jesus' accusation in Matt 23:29 about building the tombs of the prophets and adorning the monuments of the righteous). Perhaps the author intended simply to bring together extracanonical traditions about the prophets.

Bibliography. D. R. A. Hare, "The Lives of the Prophets," *The Old Testament Pseudepigrapha,* ed. J. H. Charlesworth; D. Satran, "The Lives of the Prophets," *Jewish Writings of the Second Temple Period,* ed. M. E. Stone; C. C. Torrey, *The Lives of the Prophets.*

—JOSEPH L. TRAFTON

• **Locusts.** *See* JOEL, BOOK OF

• **Logos/Word.** [loh'gohs] The Gk. term *logos* usually appears in the NT with such meanings as "word," "speech," "reason," "report," "account," "reckoning," or "judgment." However, *logos* conveys a highly specialized theological meaning in John 1:1, 14 and in Rev 19:13; in these texts *logos* traditionally is translated as "Word."

Among Greek philosophers, *logos* has a rich heritage. For Heraclitus (sixth century B.C.E.), *logos* was an eternal principle which gives order to the universe. On the other hand, Chrysippus (282–209 B.C.E.), a Stoic philosopher, used *logos* to refer to a purposeful and guiding reason, by which he implied deterministic reason. Other STOICS used *logos* for the rational principle in the mind, which is expressible in speech. PHILO, a Jewish interpreter of the OT during the first century C.E., understood *logos* to refer to an intermediary between God and the universe. Interpretations of *logos* in John 1:1, 14 and Rev 19:13 in terms of an abstract philosophical background overlook Jewish antecedents of *logos*. In the LXX, the term *logos* is used to translate an OT word signifying God's creative and life-giving power (Deut 32:46-47) or the ability of God's word to heal (Ps 107:20). An obvious parallel to John 1:1 that indicates the creative ability of God's spoken word is Gen 1:1-26 (cf. Ps 33:6).

According to John 1:1, 3, 14, the creative Word of God not only was preexistent and essentially God, but also became flesh in the person of Jesus. Rather than speaking through the prophets (Heb 1:1-2), God revealed himself through a person (John 1:14). According to Isa 55:11, God's word does not return to him empty or without accomplishing his will. Jesus, the Word (self-expression of God), accomplished the work of his Father (John 5:17, 19-23, 36).

Although the prophets spoke of and communicated "the word of the Lord," *logos* in John 1:1, 14 is personified. This personification of *logos* in John parallels the use of WISDOM in the OT and in the Apocrypha. Prov 1:20-33, 8-9, Sir 24, and Wis 7:22–11:1 illustrate the personification of Wisdom, and many functional parallels exist between Wisdom's personification in those texts and in John 1:1, 14. For example, both Wisdom and the Word dwell among God's people, both act as God's agents of creation, both are the reflection of the glory of God, and both bring light and life to God's people. However, neither the OT nor the Apocrypha refers to Wisdom as having the same essence as God.

According to Rev 19:13, a title given to the rider on the white horse is "the Word of God." "The Word of God" is the Christ who avenges the persecution of God's people. "The Word of God" defeats the heathen, the monster, and the kings of the earth by means of his authoritative word (Rev 19:15-21).

See also CREATION; INCARNATION; JESUS; JOHN, GOSPEL AND LETTERS OF; PROPHET; STOICS; WISDOM IN THE OLD TESTAMENT.

Bibliography. R. E. Brown, *The Gospel According to John I-XII*; C. H. Dodd, *The Interpretation of the Fourth Gospel*; A. Debrunner, et al., "λέγω, κτλ.," *TDNT.*

—BENNIE R. CROCKETT, JR.

• **Lois.** *See* TIMOTHY

• **Lord in the New Testament.** In the NT, the English word lord usually translates the Gk. word *kyrios*. Technically an adjective, the word is derived from a noun meaning "force," "power," or "cause." The dominant meaning of *kyrios* is "having power," especially legal or legitimate power; consequently, possible renderings include "lawful," "valid," "authorized," and "empowered." *Kyrios* as a noun was rare at first, another noun meaning "owner" or "lord" in the sense of unconditional or absolute power being more common in classical Greek. Beginning in the fourth century B.C.E. *kyrios* was used with two related meanings: (1) the lord or lawful owner of slaves, the lord of subject peoples, the master of the house, and (2) the legal guardian of a wife or girl. In koine Gk. *kyrios* was used almost interchangeably with the alternative term meaning absolute power. By the NT period, *kyrios* became the most frequently used word, perhaps because it did not contain the element of arbitrariness. *Kyrios* was a common title of respect (e.g., used for officials, philosophers, physicians, husbands, and fathers).

Although the adjective form was used of the Greek gods during the classical period, the noun form was first used to refer to deity in the LXX. During the Hellenistic period *kyrios* increasingly was used of the gods, particularly in Egypt, Syria, and Asia Minor where the term corresponded to native usage.

In the LXX *kyrios* is used to translate a Hebrew title of courtesy and respect when addressing superiors. The major use (over 6,150 occurrences) of *kyrios,* however, is as a substitute for the TETRAGRAMMATON (YHWH = Yahweh). Whether *kyrios* is a creative attempt by the translators or the rendering of an already existing Hebrew substitute is debated.

Much debate surrounds the origin of the use of *kyrios* as a christological title in the NT. Three suggestions have been proposed. Noting the LXX usage, some scholars argue that the designation is meant to assign to JESUS the OT attributes of God. Others maintain that as the early church expanded, exposure to the Hellenistic cultural usage prompted gentile Christians to adopt the term. Still others suggest that the term is a translation of a title (*mārā*) applied to Jesus by the earliest Aramaic-speaking Christians (1 Cor 16:22; cf. Rev 22:20); *kyrios,* then, was used in the translation of the primitive Christian confession—Jesus is Lord. Whatever the origin, certainly each of the proposals contributed to the development of the *kyrios* Christology.

Kyrios occurs approximately 740 times in the NT (usually referring to Jesus) and in every document except Titus and the Johannine Letters. Because most of the NT references to God as *kyrios* occur in quotations from the LXX, the following discussion will be restricted to the application of the term to Jesus.

Many of the applications of *kyrios* to Jesus in the Gospels merely reflect the term's use as a title of respect (e.g., Matt 8:6, 21). Occasionally, however, the term expresses Christian faith (e.g., John 20:28). Often in narrative sections the evangelists, especially Luke, refer to Jesus simply as "the Lord," reflecting the common post-Easter usage of the term (e.g., Luke 7:13, 19).

Acts continues the Lucan usage of the title "the Lord." Although some of these occurrences are in prayers which do not indicate that Jesus is being addressed (e.g., 1:24; 4:29), other instances clearly refer to Jesus (e.g., 2:36; 10:36). On several occasions the longer "Lord Jesus" and "Lord Jesus Christ" occur (e.g., 4:33; 11:17). The frequency of *kyrios* in Acts demonstrates how natural it was for the early church to refer to Jesus in this manner. Of particular importance for understanding the early Christian conception of the lordship of Jesus is 2:30-36 which links with *kyrios* the resurrection, the ascension, and the title Christ.

Kyrios is a common designation for Jesus in the Pauline literature. Most scholars agree that 1 Cor 12:3; 16:22; Rom 10:9; and Phil 2:11 indicate that the lordship of Jesus was an aspect of the pre-Pauline tradition. Paul did, however, expand and elaborate on the theme. For Paul, Jesus' lordship includes creative and sustaining functions (1 Cor 8:6), extends to the dead as well as the living (Rom 14:9), and provides salvation to all who call on his name (Rom 10:13). The transfer of these OT functions of God to Jesus suggests that Paul understood *kyrios* in terms of its LXX usage. He does, however, distinguish Jesus from God. God has delegated the rule of the cosmos to Jesus for a particular time—from the exaltation to the parousia—and for a specific end—the completion of the saving work, the subjection of the powers (1 Cor 15:24-28). Also prominent in Paul is the Lord-servant motif. Paul understood himself and Christians in general to be slaves of the Lord Jesus (Rom 1:1; 14:8; 1 Cor 7:22). In fact, Christians have been "purchased" by Jesus (1 Cor 6:19-20; 7:23). Paradoxically, only when people render him service do they experience genuine freedom (Gal 5:1, 13).

Most of the occurrences of *kyrios* in the Epistle to the Hebrews are in OT quotations. Against this background the instances where the reference is to Jesus stand in bold relief (2:3; 13:20). In 1 Peter the lordship of Jesus is stressed to encourage the suffering readers to remain steadfast (3:15); this is especially clear in the use of OT quotations (3:12). Both Jude and 2 Peter use the expression "Lord Jesus Christ" (Jude 17; 2 Pet 1:8), and 2 Peter frequently has the distinctive "Lord and Savior Jesus Christ" (1:11). Contrary to the rest of the NT, the Revelation of John generally applies the title to God (4:8, 11). Nevertheless, three times *kyrios* is used of Jesus (11:8; 17:14; 19:16).

See also GOD, NAMES OF; JESUS; LORD IN THE OLD TESTAMENT; MARANATHA; TETRAGRAMMATON.

Bibliography. W. Bousset, *Kyrios Christos*; O. Cullmann, *The Christology of the New Testament*; W. Foerster and G. Quell, "κύριος, κτλ.," *TDNT;* R. H. Fuller, *The Foundations of New Testament Christology*; R. H. Fuller and P. Perkins, *Who Is This Christ?*; F. Hahn, *The Titles of Jesus in Christology*; K. G. Kuh, "μαρανάθα," *TDNT*; I. H. Marshall, *The Origins of New Testament Christology*; K. H. Rengstorf, "δεσπότης, κτλ.," *TDNT*.

—RON FARMER

• **Lord in the Old Testament.** In the OT "Lord" is used in both a general and a specific sense. Generally the term refers to persons who command honor and respect, as when members of the tribes of Gad and Reuben said to MOSES, "Thy servants will do as my lord commands" (Num 32:25). In the same manner Philistine leaders are called "lords" (Judg 3:3; 16:5, 8, 18, 27, 30; 1 Sam 5:8), JOSEPH's brothers acknowledge him as master (Gen 44:7, 9, 16, 18-20, 22, 24), and the Book of Daniel so designates nobles given a feast by BELSHAZZAR (Dan 5:1). Such references carry no implications of divinity, but are meant to designate superiors who possess authority and therefore merit exaltation and honor.

The Hebrew word BAAL was also used to refer to a person of authority or to a master (Num 21:28; Isa 1:3). Yet since the name came to be associated with Canaanite fertility deities, this usage does not seem to have been widespread among the Hebrews and even condemned by the prophet Hosea (2:16).

In some English versions of the OT (notably RSV) Lord (all capitals) is typically a translation of YHWH (most probably vocalized "Yahweh"). The TETRAGRAMMATON is the third person form of the verb "to be." Although the form frequently appears in the OT text, the name came to be regarded as too sacred to pronounce. When the Masoretes added vowels to the consonantal text, they indicated that the Heb. word *Adonai* (Lord) should be substituted. Ancient Greek and Latin translators of the Hebrew text preserved this substitution rule. The form "Jehovah" used in the ASV is of late medieval origin, combining the consonants of the tetragrammaton and the vowels added by the Masoretes.

According to Exod 3:13-15, the name Yahweh was introduced to Moses at SINAI (Horeb) on the occasion when he was summoned to be the agent for emancipating Hebrews from Egyptian bondage. In a theophany of a bush burning but not consumed, the divine name was revealed to Moses. Since Israel shared an ancient view that a person's name conveyed personhood, the EXODUS report is crucial for understanding Israel's conception of deity and the meaning that the nation gave to God's name.

The Exodus narrator interprets Yahweh to be derived from the verb "to be," and treats it as a first person form because Yahweh is the speaker. In response to the question, "What is his name?" God says to Moses, "I am who I am" (Exod 3:13, 14). However, the Exodus narrator chooses only one of the possible translations of the verb form. Granting the translator's formulation in the first person, other options include, "I am what I am," "I will be what I will be," and "I cause to be what is."

Since the Book of Exodus underscores Israel's God as the source of all that happens, the idea of cause in the last option surely became part of Hebrew mentality (so W.F. Albright). The story of Israel's deliverance in Exod 1–19, with one of its climaxes in the burning bush episode, underscores Yahweh as the chief agent in events working to Israel's advantage—even in areas of Egypt's supposed supremacy. With not a little humor the narrator reports how Yahweh dupes the pharaoh and Egyptian gods. Israel's deity enables Moses to escape from the pharaoh's plan to slay Hebrew infants by cradling him on the Nile and even having Moses reared in the pharaoh's palace (Exod 2:1-10). Egyptian gods supposedly control the inundation of the NILE, but Yahweh, the mountain deity of Sinai, turns inundation into PLAGUES (Exod 7–11). At the burning bush Moses complains that he is inadequate, but Yahweh reassures him that the cause is Yahweh's (Exod 3:12, 16-17, 20-22) and provides both signs and spokesman.

Hence, whatever the linguistic roots of the word Yahweh (Lord), its meaning for Israel was grounded in the Exodus event as the deity's mighty act. Facets of meaning grew out of this fundamental historical orientation—cause of events, irresistible power, dependability, unapproachable mystery. Divine mystery is emphasized symbolically by a burning bush that is not consumed. Yahweh's fullness and permanence are elaborated in God's summary statement, "Say to this people of Israel, The Lord, the God of your fathers, the God of ABRAHAM, the God of ISAAC, and the God of JACOB, has sent me to you: this is my name for ever and thus I am to be remembered throughout all generations" (Exod 3:15).

A frequent phrase in OT references to Israel's deity is "Lord of hosts" (KJV "Lord Sabaoth"). The phrase appears about 267 times and enjoyed an established history in Israel. Apparently it originated with sanctuary rituals at Shiloh during the period of tribal confederacy, about 1200–1000 B.C.E. (1 Sam 1:3, 11). Sometimes the phrase is used with the article, as "Lord of the hosts" (e.g., Hos 12:5; Amos 3:13); at other places the article is absent, "Lord of hosts" (e.g., 2 Sam 5:10; 1 Kgs 19:10; Jer 5:14). These references with and without the article also include the expansions, "Lord God of hosts" or "Lord God, the God of hosts."

The hosts over which the Lord is assumed to be authoritative are variously interpreted to mean the armies of Israel or the heavenly bodies or angelic beings. Whichever is correct, the expanded forms minimally suggest the extensiveness of divine sovereignty.

The LXX translated both Yahweh and Adonai in the OT with the Gk. word *kyrios*, lord. The Greek label is often a general word of respectful address, but in early Christianity sometimes expressed religious faith, especially in reference to Jesus. An early Christian using a confessional phrase such as "the Lord Jesus Christ" (1 Thess 1:1; 1 Cor 8:5-6) would have concluded an intimate relationship between Jesus and Yahweh of the OT.

See also ARK; GOD, NAMES OF; HOLY WAR; LORD.

Bibliography. W. F. Albright, *From the Stone Age to Christianity*.

—ROBERT W. CRAPPS

• **Lord of Hosts.** One of the most common divine titles in the OT, occurring some 267 times. The term does not occur at all from Genesis to Judges. It appears first in 1 Sam 1:3, 11 where it is defined (17:45) by the parallel statement "The God of the armies of Israel." This may indicate that the term was originally associated with the ARK and the HOLY WAR theology.

The term "hosts" is also connected in the OT with the heavenly bodies (Deut 4:19; 17:3) and the ANGELS of heaven (Ps 148:2). In this connection the term refers to God's leading the heavenly armies. This seems to be the usage with the prophets, who employ the term some 247 times.

In the LXX, the term is usually translated *kyrios pantokrator*, "The Lord, the ruler of all things," which gives an even more generalized meaning to the title. This LXX rendering occurs in the NT in 2 Cor 6:18 and nine times in Revelation. The Hebrew form of the title appears in Rom 9:29 and Jas 5:4 as *Kyrios Sabaoth*.

See also ARK; GOD, NAMES OF; HOLY WAR.

Bibliography. G. von Rad, *Old Testament Theology*.

—JOHN POLHILL

• **Lord's Day.** The first day of the Christian week, the Lord's day is the day on which early Christians began to worship, rather than on the Jewish SABBATH, as a means of joyfully celebrating the resurrection of Jesus. "Lord's" is an adjective meaning "belonging to the lord," and was commonly used in the Greco-Roman world in the sense of "belonging to the emperor" or "imperial." In addition, the Romans had a monthly "Sebaste day" to honor the emperor. This usage could have provided the analogy for the Christian use of Lord's day, but Christians would have more likely chosen the designation as a protest against the emperor cult.

In the NT, "Lord's day" is found only in Rev 1:10 where John describes the circumstances of his apocalyptic vision. He was in the spirit on the Lord's day. This reference is usually, but not always, taken to mean that John was worshiping on Sunday. Although some take the expression as an eschatological reference to "the Day of the Lord," and others maintain that it refers to Easter, the chief celebration of the resurrection, the traditional view is more probable since in the writings of the church fathers "Lord's day" refers to the first day of the week.

Apparently Christians began to worship on the first day of the week quite early, although no clear evidence exists about when the shift was made. That the first day of the week received special emphasis because of the Lord's resurrection is clear. The resurrection accounts in all four Gospels (Matt 28:1; Mark 16:2; Luke 24:1; John 20:1) emphasize that the resurrection took place on the first day of the week, probably reflecting an already existing practice of worshiping on the first day. In John's Gospel, the appearances of Jesus on two successive "first days" (John 20:19, 26) furnish a hint that the first day was the regular day for worship when John wrote. Paul instructed the Corinthians (1 Cor 16:2) to set aside money on the first day of the week for the offering he was collecting. Some interpreters, feeling that the act was connected with some system of wage paying customary in the gentile world, believe that the money was set aside at home rather than when the church was gathered. If so, this verse would not be a reference to worship on the first day of the week. Yet, early in the second century there existed a wide-spread custom of collecting offerings for the poor during worship on Sunday. Thus, Paul was likely referring to public worship on the first day of the week, another indication that the practice must have begun earlier.

According to Acts 20:7ff., the church met on the first day of the week for the purpose of breaking bread. This obvious reference to the Lord's Supper indicates both that the church's worship on the first day of the week and that the Lord's Supper were already institutionalized. Thus the Lord's Supper and the Lord's day were both part of the church's celebration of the resurrection of Jesus. Another clue that the two events were observed together at an early stage of the church's life in honor of the resurrection is found in the only other NT occurrence of the adjective "Lord's" (1 Cor 11:20) where it is a modifier of "supper."

Writings of the early Christian fathers show that the practice of worshiping on the first day of the week was common by the turn of the first century. The *Didache* (14.1), a late first-century writing, indicates that Christians assembled for worship on the Lord's day, and Ignatius (*Magn* 9.1) early in the second century declared that Jewish Christians no longer kept the Sabbath but worshiped on the Lord's day.

Acts indicates that, at first, Christians continued to keep the Jewish Sabbath. Yet, they also worshiped on the first day of the week. Paul attended synagogue Sabbath services while on his mission tours (Acts 13:14; 16:13) and worshiped the risen Lord on the first day of the week (20:7ff.). Yet, when Christianity spread into the gentile world, observance of the Jewish Sabbath by gentile Christians gradually disappeared. Paul counseled the Colossians (2:16) not to have regard for Sabbath observances which are a shadow of the future and told the Romans (14:5ff.) that every day is sacred to the Lord. Second-century Christian writers indicate that the Sabbath was not observed by Christians. Ignatius seems to have contrasted the Sabbath with the Lord's day which he called Christ's special day.

There is no indication that the earliest Christians thought of the Lord's day as superceding the Sabbath or that the Lord's day assumed the features of the Jewish Sabbath. Later Christians, however, did consider the Sabbath as part of the Law which Christ had superseded. They did not deem it necessary to abide by the restrictions of the Jewish Sabbath on either Saturday or Sunday. Not until medieval times was such a transfer made. Existing in a pagan culture, gentile Christians worshiped on the Lord's day and then went about their normal routines, including work. In the fourth century, Constantine, following the analogy that Roman law provided for the suspension of work on festive days, decreed that the Christian's Lord's day should have the same standing.

Evidently in the early days it was common, but not necessary, for worship services to be held at night. Acts 20:7ff. describes an evening service. Pliny, the governor of Bithynia, in his letter to Trajan about punishment of Christians, stated that they met on Sunday mornings before dawn and again in the evening for a corporate meal. In the weekly worship, the emphasis was on the Lordship of Christ, demonstrated by the label Lord's day and by the celebration of the Lord's Supper. The supper, usually referred to as the "breaking of bread," was probably a regular evening meal followed by the Lord's Supper (1 Cor 11:17ff.). The NT also indicates that preaching, prayers, and hymns were significant parts of the service from the earliest times (Acts 20:7ff.; 1 Cor 14:16-23; Eph 5:19).

Christians did not use "Sunday" as a designation for the day of worship until the fourth century, although Justin Martyr (ca. 150) in his *Apology* (67) used the expression "day of the Sun" as a means of communication with the non-Christians. There were several means of determining the calender in the Greco-Roman world. Gentile Christians adopted the Jewish seven-day calender, itself a modification of an old Babylonian planetary calender, rather than the confusing Roman way of reckoning. As time passed they combined the two calenders, maintaining the religious connotations of the Jewish calender while adopting the names of the pagan calender. When "Sunday" was adopted after Constantine made it a legal holiday, it was not an attempt to combine Christian worship with that of the sun god. Rather, Sunday signified both the day of the resurrection of the Lord and the time of the new creation made possible by the resurrection.

See also SABBATH.

Bibliography. G. B. Caird, *The Apostolic Age*; J. S. Clemens, "Lord's Day," *DCA*; A. Deissman, *Light from the Ancient East*; J. B. Lightfoot, *The Apostolic Fathers*; W. Rordorf, *Sunday*.

—W. T. EDWARDS

• **Lord's Prayer, The.** The Lord's Prayer is the name ascribed to the prayer of Jesus found in Matthew (6:9-13) and Luke (11:2-4). The two prayers differ in setting, length, and text. In the former version, the occasion for the prayer is a discourse on religious practices, including prayer, which have become meaningless, routine formalities. In the latter, one of Jesus' disciples asks that he teach them how to pray as John the Baptist had taught his disciples. In both settings, it is given as a pattern for all who wish to learn the meaning and practice of prayer. It is generally recognized that the original form of the prayer is that found in Luke (which has only five petitions) and that the Matthean text (with seven petitions) is a liturgical composition, growing out of its use in the worship of the early church. Textual differences may be accounted for by the fact that the prayers arose and were translated in two different worshipping communities.

According to Jeremias (who is working from the Lucan version) the earliest form of the prayer is the following:

Father,
Hallowed be thy name.
Thy kingdom come.
Give us each day our bread for tomorrow.
And forgive our sins, for we also forgive
everyone who is indebted to us.
And let us not succumb to the trial.

In Matthew's text (the more familiar version) there are three "Thou-petitions," centered in GOD, and four "We-petitions" which are focused upon human needs. The petitions are framed by an opening address and a concluding doxology.

The Address. The original Aramaic word ABBA is used in the invocation and is translated "Father." It suggests the familiar, tender yet respectful, relationship of child to parent. Not only does Jesus address God in this intimate way, but he also gives his disciples the astonishing privilege of using this word themselves. Matthew, following traditional Jewish piety, adds the phrase "who art in HEAVEN." The word "our" implies that the prayer is for the Christian community.

The Thou-Petitions. The first three petitions (the third is omitted in Luke), or "Thou-petitions," are expressed in passive verb forms. The passive voice was widely used as an indirect way of referring to God's activity. Hence, the three petitions (for the hallowing of God's name, the coming of his Kingdom, and the doing of his will) refer to acts of God rather than to Christian acts of commitment. The name expresses God's essential nature, and it is this that God is asked to sanctify. God's nature as holy is then expressed in God's rule through the coming of the Kingdom, understood both as having already dawned in the world in Jesus and also as God's eschatological reign. Matthew's addition "Thy will be done" is an expansion of the previous petition, for when God fully carries out his will in the world, the Kingdom will have fully arrived.

The We-Petitions. In these petitions, God is asked to meet the needs of the Christian community by providing the gracious gifts of daily bread, forgiveness, and deliverance from evil.

In the fourth petition, the word which is translated "daily" has long perplexed biblical scholars. It may refer to bread for tomorrow, or it may suggest the spiritual bread of the messianic banquet. It may, indeed, refer to both, for daily bread is a symbol of the messianic meal and in that meal we are reminded of the sanctity of our daily bread.

In the fifth petition, the petition for forgiveness, Matthew uses the word "debts" while Luke prefers the word "sins." Matthew's Jewish audience understood sins as debts owed to God. Luke's use of "sins" would make the concept more intelligible to gentile readers. The word "trespasses," used in some versions, is not found in the prayer itself but, rather, in Matt 6:14-15, a statement of Jesus which is attached to the prayer. The word "as" ("as we forgive our debtors") does not imply that God's forgiveness is conditioned by our first having forgiven. Instead, it suggests that the profound grace of God's forgiveness can become fully operative only in the life of one who has forgiven.

The sixth petition ("lead us not . . . but deliver us . . . ") is the only one that is formulated in the negative. The word translated TEMPTATION may also mean trial or testing. Indeed, in all but one of the twenty-one places the word occurs in the NT, it means the latter. This petition is a prayer for perseverance in trial. It is not a petition to be spared trial but to be enabled to overcome trial. The plea "lead us not into temptation" could be taken to imply that it is God who tempts us. But this suggestion is forcefully rejected in Jas 1:13: "Let no one say when he is tempted, 'I am tempted by God'; for God . . . tempts no one." The second half of this petition ("but deliver us from evil") is recorded only in Matthew. The Greek may be translated either as "evil" (idea, impulse) or "the evil one" (Satan). Both uses are found in the NT, and it cannot be determined with absolute certainty which meaning is intended here.

The Doxology. The doxology is absent altogether in the Lucan version of the prayer, and it does not appear in the oldest mss. of Matthew. The earliest witness to a doxology in the Lord's Prayer comes from the *Didache* where it appears in a shorter form: "For Thine is the power and the glory forever." This addition to the prayer was probably the result of liturgical development, serving as a concluding expression of praise for God's sovereignty.

The Uniqueness of the Prayer. Proximate parallels to many of the petitions of the Lord's Prayer can be found in the Jewish *Kaddish* and the EIGHTEEN BENEDICTIONS. The prayer of Jesus, however, has radically modified their meaning. In using the word "Abba," the Son reflects the intimacy of his unique relationship with his Parent. And through his life and work, the faithful community is drawn into a new relationship with God. The Kingdom has broken into the world through him, and his disciples are empowered, individually and corporately, with his Spirit in their journey toward its consummation.

See also ABBA; BENEDICTIONS, EIGHTEEN; GOD; HEAVEN; KINGDOM OF GOD; PRAYER/THANKSGIVING IN THE NEW TESTAMENT; SERMON ON THE MOUNT; SIN; TEMPTATION.

Bibliography. M. Dibelius, *The Sermon on the Mount*; P. B. Harner, *The Lord's Prayer* and "Matthew 6:5-15," *Int* 41/2 (1987): 173-78; J. Jeremias, *The Lord's Prayer*; C. Laymon, *The Lord's Prayer in Its Biblical Setting*.

—BETTY JEAN SEYMOUR

• **Lord's Supper.** "Lord's Supper" is a term derived from Paul's writings (1 Cor 11:20) which describes the practice in the early church of commemorating the last meal which JESUS and his disciples ate together on the evening before his CRUCIFIXION. The word "supper" (δεῖπνον) modified by "Lord's" (κυριακός) appears only this one time in the NT. That Paul linked the practice to which he was referring to this meal is clear from the context.

Each of the four Gospels mentions a last meal (Matt 26:17-29; Mark 14:12-25; Luke 22:7-38; John 13:1-38). The texts describing the Supper differ in several ways, including the chronology, the sequence of events during the meal, and the instructions given by Jesus to the disciples. Because of the theological significance of the Supper, scholarly debate has focused on a number of issues raised by the diversity of the texts.

One important issue is whether the meal was a Passover meal or not. According to Jeremias (20) the Synoptics agree that the meal occurred on the first day of the PASSOVER celebration, a day which began with the eating of the meal reenacting the original Passover experience of the Israelites in Egypt. John, on the other hand, says that it occurred on the day of preparation for the Passover, and, therefore, it was a regular evening meal.

Although all four Gospels place the experience in the context of the Passover season, understanding the meal as a Passover meal affords a wealth of symbolic reference by which to understand the meaning of the experience both to the original participants and to modern interpreters of the text. Of particular importance is the connection between Jesus' impending sacrificial act and the eating of lamb with the meal in commemoration of the lambs that were sacrificed in behalf of the Israelites in Egypt.

Courtesy of the Eisenberg Museum of Biblical Archaeology, Southern Baptist Theological Seminary.

A Coptic communion cup made of ivory.

Another important issue is to what extent the texts represent the original words and experiences of Jesus and the disciples and to what extent they represent the perspectives of the writers and the later practices of the early church. In 1 Cor 11:17-33, where Paul discusses the Supper, he is describing a ritual practiced by Christians of his day. He is critical of their method of observing the Supper and of behavior they exhibited during the time before and after the observances. The text implies that he had in mind a preferred method of observing the Supper and an interpretation of the significance of the Supper in the life of the church.

Paul introduces his "better way" by indicating that he had received it from the Lord. Because his account varies from those of the Gospels, the question emerges as to how the tradition regarding the Supper was handed down in the decades following the event. Barrett (264–66) discussed what Paul meant by "received from the Lord," concluding that though complete certainty is not possible, a combined effort of human tradition and divine authority may have been at work.

The Gospels were written after 1 Corinthians, and their account of the Supper is of great importance in seeking to reconstruct how the practice and interpretation of the Supper evolved during the first few decades after the original event.

Jeremias concludes that there are three distinct lines of tradition, especially regarding the words of Jesus at the Supper. These are the Marcan (also used by Matthew), the Pauline-Lucan, and the Johannine. In spite of the distinct features of each, he believes that all three accounts preserve the words of Jesus in an "essentially reliable form" (189-203).

John 6:52-59 is not included in an account of the Supper itself, but it clearly is related to a discussion of the meaning of the Supper. It is distinguished from the other

Gospels by its use of the verb for "eat" (τρώγω). Here a verb used infrequently elsewhere in the NT is used four times within a few verses to describe the process by which the flesh (bread) is to be eaten. The verb can be translated as gnaw, munch, or eat (audibly). John may have chosen this word to counter any Gnostic tendencies that would spiritualize the Supper rather than let it remain a physical experience. Culpepper (197) sees John's choice of verbs as giving added meaning to the experience of partaking of the Supper and to the power of the symbol of bread throughout the Gospel.

The meanings of the Supper for modern readers of the text are derived from a complex interaction of the words, the physical objects, and life experiences, especially traditions which have produced the various ritual forms of the Supper today. One common element for all readers is that the physical properties of bread and wine have remained relatively constant. In spite of the enormous changes between the first century and our own, we can share something of their experience by eating the bread and drinking the wine. The Supper thereby provides a symbol by which individual believers may enrich their own personal faith and link themselves to other believers, past and present.

Virtually all Christian groups celebrate the Lord's Supper in some fashion, and it serves as a potential force for unity among Christians. At the same time controversy over the significance of and manner of celebrating the Supper remains one of the chief barriers to closer cooperation among Christians.

See also CRUCIFIXION; JESUS; PASSOVER; SACRAMENTS; WORSHIP IN THE NEW TESTAMENT.

Bibliography. W. F. Arndt and F. W. Gingrich, *BAGD*; C. K. Barrett, *The First Epistle to the Corinthians*; A. Culpepper, *Anatomy of the Fourth Gospel*; A. J. B. Higgins, *The Lord's Supper in the New Testament*; J. Jeremias, *The Eucharistic Words of Jesus*; A. Schweitzer, *The Problem of the Lord's Supper*.

—STUART R. SPRAGUE

• **Lot.** The grandson of Terah, the son of Haran, and the nephew of Abraham (Gen 11:27-32; 12:4-5). Lot was a somewhat tragic figure who always appeared in Abraham's shadow. The biblical writer portrayed Lot in association with Abraham; Lot's disastrous history is the counterpart to Abraham's success.

Lot was dependent upon Abraham, since Abraham was the head of the household; the dependence thus reflects the normal pattern of clan and family relationships. This motif of dependence and weakness continues, however, throughout the entire narrative. Lot's wealth seems to have derived from his association with Abraham (Gen 13:1-5).

Abraham, not Lot, initiated a solution to the problems among their herdsmen (Gen 13:5-9). Even after Lot went his own way, Abraham rescued him from the captors of Sodom (Gen 14:13-16), then God saved Lot from the destruction of Sodom because of Abraham (Gen 18:16-33; 19:29).

Lot's "friendship with the world" is a foil for Abraham's friendship with God. When they decided to separate, Abraham let Lot choose his own direction. Lot chose what looked good to him, but it was a wicked place (Gen 13:10-13). Abraham, willing to trust God and take second choice, received, immediately after Lot's departure, God's promise of all he could see in every direction (Gen 13:14-18).

Lot apparently rose to some prominence in Sodom (he sat in the city gate, a status that involved giving counsel and advice). He lived in his own permanent house (Gen 19:1-4). Abraham lived in a tent but counseled directly with God (Gen 18:1-2, 22-23; Jas 2:23). Lot's hesitancy to leave the city where he had invested his life and stored his treasures is in contrast to Abraham's willingness to follow wherever the Lord might lead (Gen 19:16-22; Heb 11:8-10).

Lot's fruitlessness is shown in contrast to Abraham's fruitfulness. Lot left Abraham for Sodom, a materially fruitful place, but eventually had to leave the city with only his life and two other people. Immediately after Lot departed for Sodom, the Lord promised Abraham, who stood in a desert, more descendants than he could count (Gen 19:14-15, 26; 13:14-17).

As they were leaving Sodom, Lot's wife took one last, longing look at the city against the angel's advice and was turned to a pillar of salt, producing a scene of death, desolation and grief. Sarah, Abraham's wife, though physically incapable of becoming pregnant, gave birth to a wonder child, producing a scene of life, potential, and celebration (Gen 19:26; 21:1-7).

Lot's tragic end is a foil for Abraham's bright future. The last picture of Lot showed him an old and frightened man, living in a cave with his two daughters. They used him to get pregnant so that their family would survive, and he did not even know it (Gen 19:30-35). Meanwhile, Abraham saw the birth of Isaac, the beginning of the realization of all God's promises to make him a great nation (Gen 21:1-7; 22:1-18). Lot faded out of view just as Abraham's future broke over the horizon.

Lot appears in a positive light only when compared to the extremely wicked residents of Sodom (Gen 19:1-8). The NT writer reflected this idea in affirming that Lot was a righteous man (2 Pet 2:7-8).

See also ABRAHAM; SODOM/GOMORAH/CITIES OF THE PLAIN.

—WALTER E. BROWN

• **Lot/Lots (Casting of) in the Bible.** Throughout the ancient Near East, as well as among the Hebrews in the OT and in a minor way among the Christians of the NT, the casting of lots was a significant way to determine the answer to questions or issues. Stones of various shapes and colors (perhaps the forerunners of dice) apparently were shaken, then tossed. This random selection process, when done properly, was considered to be evidence of the divine will (Prov 16:33).

Such use of the lot determined the answer to all sorts of issues. Among these were guilt (Jonah 1:7), the choice of a ruler (1 Sam 10:19-24), the division of land (Josh 14:2; 18:10-11; 19:1), and the choice of the proper animal for sacrifice (Lev 16:7-10). This casting of the lot was not considered to be magic or witchcraft, for these practices were condemned (Deut 18:10-12), while the use of lots was not.

In the NT, the early Christians used the lot to determine the successor to Judas (Acts 1:23-26). That they do not appear to have used this method elsewhere may be due to the descent of the HOLY SPIRIT at Pentecost (Acts 2:4). Thereafter, the Spirit's presence guided them in their decisions. In addition to the Christians, the Roman soldiers cast lots to divide the clothing of Jesus (Matt 27:35; Mark 15:24; Luke 23:34; John 19:24).

It is possible that the URIM AND THUMMIM were two

stones carried in the breastplate or ephod of the high priest to be used for the casting of lots (Exod 28:30). It appears that a priest with an ephod holding these stones was usually needed to make major decisions (1 Sam 23:4, 9, 11, 12). The Bible also notes that this approach to reaching a decision was not always successful (1 Sam 28:6).

See also URIM AND THUMMIM.

—ROBERT L. CATE

• **Love in the New Testament.** Love is the most important of the abiding Christian virtues (1 Cor 13). Both the language of love (ἀγαπάω, ἀγάπη, ἀγαπητός, φιλέω) and the concept of love are central to all parts of the NT.

Love and Israel. The story and thought of the OT centers around the covenant made between Yahweh and the people of Israel. Yahweh will be the God of Israel and Israel will be the people of God. The framework for this covenant relationship is articulated in the Torah—the laws and commandments which guide the covenant life of Israel. Nonetheless, the Law is not the foundation of the covenant. Instead, the OT covenant is founded upon the steadfast love (*ḥesed*) of God. This foundational love is realized in the mighty acts of God in Israel's history, particularly in creation and the EXODUS from Egypt. This steadfast love binds Israel to God as a bride: "And I will make for you a covenant on that day. . . . And I will betroth you to me for ever; I will betroth you to me in righteousness and in justice, in steadfast love, and in mercy. I will betroth you to me in faithfulness; and you shall know the Lord" (Hos 2:18-20). This gift of God's steadfast love demands from Israel a response of obedience: "So you, by the help of your God, return, hold fast to love and justice, and wait continually for your God" (Hos 12:6). Israel is to respond to the love of God with unwavering loyalty. Thus, the *Shema* forms the central command of the OT: "Hear, O Israel: The Lord our God is one Lord; and you shall love the Lord your God with all your heart, and with all your soul, and with all your might" (Deut 6:4-5). From this command grow the various guides to worship in the OT. In addition, Israel is to respond to God's steadfast love by treating other humans with justice and compassion: "you shall love your neighbor as yourself: I am the Lord" (Lev 19:18). From this requirement grow the ethical demands of the OT. Thus, the life and identity of Israel is rooted in the steadfast love of Yahweh. From this steadfast love grow the covenant, the commandments, and the FAITH of the OT.

Love in the Synoptic Tradition. The use of love in the synoptic Gospels draws upon this OT concept. The concept of love in the Synoptics primarily reflects the demands of the *Shema* and Lev 19:18. When asked which commandment is the greatest, Jesus quotes Deut 6:4-5, then adds to it Lev 19:18: Love God and love your neighbor (Mark 12:29-31; Luke 10:27; Matt 22:37-39). Thus, Jesus affirms the OT link between worship and ethics, but his interpretation is still more radical. Jesus extends the understanding of neighbor beyond the borders of Israel and beyond the bounds of kinship: Jesus demands love of the enemy (Matt 5:43-48; Luke 6:27-36). From within this christological perspective, the Synoptics provide a radical interpretation and application of the OT concept of love—both its gifts and its demands. To practice this type of love for neighbor and enemy bears evidence of one's love for Jesus and for God (Matt 25:31-46; Luke 7:47).

In a different direction, the Synoptics use the term "beloved" (ἀγαπητός) as a title for Jesus. Taken from Isa 42:1, this reference links Jesus uniquely to the work of God as the beloved Son of God. This phrase is used as a term of revelation which bears witness to the distinct identity of Jesus. Thus, the title is used at the baptism of Jesus (Mark 1:11; Matt 3:17; Luke 3:22) and at his transfiguration (Mark 9:7; Luke 9:35). In addition, this title is used to speak of the faithful ministry of Jesus in Matt 12:18 and in the parable of the vineyard (Mark 12:6; Luke 20:13).

Pauline Tradition. In Pauline thought, the central concept of love is interpreted and applied to various aspects of the human situation. The Pauline use of love falls into seven primary categories. (1) The extension of the covenant love of the OT (Rom 13:8-10; Gal 5:14). Like the Synoptics, Paul uses love to reflect the demands of the *Shema* and Lev 19:18. In this way, Paul draws upon the central theology of the OT: Yahweh's steadfast love requires love of God (Deut 6:4-5) and love of neighbor (Lev 19:18). Thus, Paul's multifaceted interpretation of the concept of love is rooted first in the OT concept of the gift and demand of God's love. (2) The love of God, Christ, the Spirit for us (Rom 5:5, 8; 8:35, 37, 39; 9:13, 25; 15:30; 1 Cor 16:22 [φιλέω]); 2 Cor 5:14; 13:11-14; Eph 2:4; 3:19; 6:23; Col 1:13; 3:12; 1 Thess 1:4; 2 Thess 2:13-16; 3:5). (3) Our love for God, Christ, the Spirit (Rom 8:28; 1 Cor 2:9; 8:3; 2 Cor 9:7; Gal 2:20; Eph 6:24; Phlm 5). (4) Love between Christians (2 Cor 2:8; 8:7-8, 24; 11:11; Eph 1:15; 4:2; Col 1:4; 1 Thess 3:12; 4:9; 2 Thess 1:3; Phlm 5, 7; Titus 3:15[φιλέω]). (5) "Beloved" as a title for Christians (Rom 1:7; 11:28; 12:19; 16:5, 8, 9, 12; 1 Cor 4:14, 17; 10:14; 15:58; 2 Cor 7:1; 12:19; Eph 5:1; 6:21; Phil 2:12; 4:1; Col 1:7; 4:7, 9, 14; 1 Thess 2:8; 1 Tim 6:2; 2 Tim 1:2; Phlm 1,16 [cf. Col 3:12]). (6) Love between wife and husband (Eph 5:25, 28, 33; Col 3:19). (7) Love as the preeminent Christian virtue (Rom 12:9; 14:15; 1 Cor 4:21; 8:1; 13:1-4, 8, 13; 14:1; 16:14, 24; 2 Cor 2:4; 6:6; Gal 5:6, 13, 22; Eph 1:4; 3:18; 4:15, 16; 5:2; Phil 1:9, 16; 2:1, 2; Col 1:8; 2:2; 3:14; 1 Thess 1:3; 3:6; 5:8, 13; 1 Tim 1:5, 14; 2:15; 4:12; 6:11; 2 Tim 1:7, 13; 2:22; 3:10; Titus 2:2, 10; Phlm 9).

Paul primarily speaks of love as a Christian virtue. This use builds upon Paul's careful description of the way love operates between God and humans and between humans and other humans (categories 1–6). Thus, the steadfast love of God from the OT is displayed in God's love for us. This leads to our love for God, to love within the Christian community among the "beloved," to love within the family. Paul incorporates each of these aspects into his concept of love as the virtue which most characterizes the life of the believer.

For Paul, love is the greatest of the three enduring virtues (1 Cor 13:13; 1 Thess 1:3; 5:8; Col 1:4-5). This love is more than passive emotion. Love is closely linked to faith in various passages (1 Cor 13:13; 1 Thess 1:3; 5:8; Col 1:4-5; Gal 5:6, 13, 22; 1 Tim 1:14; 2:15; 6:11; 2 Tim 1:13; 2:22; 3:10; Titus 2:2; Phlm 5). Love is one of the active fruits of the Spirit (Gal 5:22). Faith works through love (Gal 5:6). Christians serve one another through love (Gal 5:13). Thus, love serves as the link between faith and ethics: love is the basis of ethics, the very expression of faith.

Paul gathers the whole of Christian faith around the presence and practice of love in the life of the believer. Various gifts of faith and ministry are meaningless apart from the active presence of love (1 Cor 13:1-3). Love produces active righteousness (1 Cor 13:4-7). Love is unfailing and unending (1 Cor 13:8-13). Love fulfills the whole demand of the Law (Gal 5:14). Love is the aim of the Christian life (1 Cor 14:1).

Johannine Tradition. Love is the central concept in Johannine thought. Love is the key to the Johannine doctrine of God: "God is love" (1 John 4:8,16). Love is the key to the relationship between Jesus and the Father: "the Father loves the Son, and has given all things into his hand" (John 3:35). Love is the key to Jesus' ministry in behalf of believers: "As the Father has loved me, so have I loved you; abide in my love" (John 15:39). Love is the key to the believer's relationship with Jesus: "He who has my commandments and keeps them, he it is who loves me; and he who loves me will be loved by my Father, and I will love him and manifest myself to him" (John 14:21). Love is the key to relations between Christians: "This is my commandment, that you love one another as I have loved you" (John 15:12). In Johannine thought, love is the operative power behind Christian existence.

The Johannine use of love builds upon the OT. Without quoting directly from Deut 6:4-5 or Lev 19:18, the Johannine traditions provide extended exposition of the OT concept of God's redemptive love. Like the covenant, Johannine thought is rooted in the steadfast love of God. While the OT describes this love through God's mighty acts in history, Johannine thought understands love as an eternal attribute in God's nature: God is love. In agreement with the OT, Johannine thought understands God's love as the foundation of all faith.

Johannine thought understands God's foundational love in a radical christological perspective: God's love is expressed distinctly in the sending of the Son (John 3:16). Through the mission of the Son, the love of the Father is made available to believers: "he who loves me will be loved by my Father, and I will love him . . . " (John 18:21). Thus, the way one responds to the Son is decisive: "He who believes in the Son has eternal life; the one who does not obey the Son shall not see life, but the wrath of God rests upon him" (John 3:36; cf. 8:42). In Johannine thought, love is the key for understanding both God and God's presence in Jesus Christ.

Beyond this, the Johannine traditions focus the ethical implications of this divine love. This concern is prominent in the Johannine Letters, where division among believers seems to be a crucial issue. When the love of God abides in a human life, that life undergoes transformation. The gift of God's love carries with it an ethical demand: "This is my commandment, that you love one another as I have loved you" (John 15:12). One's love for God is evidenced in one's love for others (John 13:34, 35; 15:12, 17; 1 John 2:10; 3:10, 11, 14, 23; 4:7, 11, 12, 19, 21; 5:1, 2; 2 John 5). Absence of this love points to the absence of God (1 John 4:8, 20). In this manner, Johannine thought draws upon the central focus of the OT as expressed in Deut 6:4-5 and Lev 19:18. In particular, Johannine thought builds upon the connection made by Jesus between love for God and love for neighbor (Mark 12:29-31; Luke 10:27; Matt 22:37-39). Within this framework, believers are addressed as the "beloved" (1 John 2:7; 3:2, 21; 4:1, 7, 11; 3 John 1, 2, 5, 11). The beloved—those loved of God—are to love others (1 John 4:7).

Thus, God's love is the center of the Johannine world. Johannine thought encompasses theology, Christology, anthropology—God, Christ, humanity—in it's exposition of love. First John 4:7–12 expresses this in summary form.

Other Traditions. Love is used in various ways in other parts of the NT. In Hebrews, love is an activity of God (Heb 1:9; 12:6), but love is also present among believers (Heb 6:10; 10:24). The ethical teaching of James draws upon Jesus' twofold command to love. Christians are to love God (Jas 1:12; 2:5), and they are to love the neighbor (Jas 2:8). In 1 and 2 Peter a similar focus emerges. Christians are to love Christ (1 Pet 1:8) and to love one another (1 Pet 1:22; 2:17; 4:8; 5:14; 2 Pet 1:7). In Jude, Christians are loved by God (Jude 1), and they are to keep themselves in the love of God (Jude 2, 21).

The Beloved. The NT employs the term for "beloved" in two distinct ways. Various passages use this term to reflect Isa 42:1 (Mark 1:11; 9:7; 12:6; Matt 3:17; 12:18; Luke 3:22; 9:35; 20:13; 2 Pet 1:17). These passages employ the term as a distinct title for Jesus: he is God's beloved Son. Outside of the Synoptics and 2 Pet 1:17, the NT uses "beloved" as a title by which Christians refer to other Christians.

Conclusion. The language and the concept of love are central to the thought world of the NT. The use of love in the NT is rooted in the central OT concept of God's steadfast love. God's love serves as the foundation of the covenant and as the basis of the faith and ethics of Israel. The NT builds its use of love upon this foundation. In various places direct reference is made to the OT framework. The *Shema* of Deut 6:4-5 is cited in Mark 12:29-31; Luke 10:27; Matt 22:37-39. The command of Lev 19:18 is cited in Mark 12:29-31; Luke 10:27; Matt 22:37-39; Rom 13:8-10; Gal 5:14; Jas 2:8. At these points, the NT concept of love builds explicitly on the OT heritage.

More frequently, the NT builds upon the OT concept of love in an implicit, indirect manner. Through various means and devices the NT explores the implications of God's steadfast love for the life of the believer. The theological implications are considered, and love is seen to be indicative of the activity and nature of God. When the christological implications are explored, the sending of the Son is seen as the ultimate act of God's love. The question of salvation is considered; God showed divine love for us in that while we were yet sinners Christ died for us (Rom 5:8). The question of community is addressed; Christians are joined into the fellowship of the "beloved" and are commanded to love one another. The relationship to the world is considered; those loved of God are to love even their enemies. This exploration and application of the OT concept of love leads to a conclusion which lies at the center of NT thought: love is the enduring, defining characteristic of the Christian life.

See also FAITH; HOPE IN THE NEW TESTAMENT; HOPE IN THE OLD TESTAMENT; LOVE IN THE OLD TESTAMENT.

Bibliography. G. Bornkamm, "The More Excellent Way," *Early Christian Experience*; A. Brieger, *Die urchristliche Trias Glaube-Liebe-Hoffnung*; H. Conzelmann, *First Corinthians*; K. P. Donfried, "Love," *HBD*; V. P. Furnish, *The Love Command in the New Testament*; G. Johnston, "Love in the New Testament," *IDB*; T. Merton, *Love and Living*; J. Moffatt, *Love in the New Testament*; Mother Teresa, *Love, A Fruit for all Seasons*; R. Niebuhr, *An Interpretation of Christian Ethics* and *Love and Justice*; A. Nygren, *Agape and Eros*; H. Preisker, *Die urchristliche Botschaft der Liebe Gottes*; R. Reitzenstein, "Die Formel 'Glaube, Liebe, Hoffnung' bei Paulus," *NGG* (1916): 367–416; L. Schottroff, et al., *Essays on the Love Commandment*; E. Stauffer, "ἀγαπάω, κτλ.," *TDNT*; P. Tillich, *Love, Power, and Justice*; E. Walter, "Glaube, Hoffnung und Liebe im Neuen Testament," *Leben aus dem Wort*, 1; B. B. Warfield, "Love in the New Testament," *PTR* 16 (1918).

—EDWIN K. BROADHEAD

• **Love in the Old Testament.** In the OT the verb *'āhēb* and its related nouns are the primary terms meaning "love" (related terms, such as *ḥesed* "steadfast love," will not be discussed here; cf. LOVING KINDNESS). In the LXX, the ancient Greek translation, words from the root *'hb* are translated by forms of *agapaō/agapē* "love." The usage of *agapaō* in the LXX helped to shape the distinctive NT meaning of the term.

The most basic use of "love" in the OT is in the relationship between woman and man. Within marriage, love includes sexual relations and also affectionate regard expressed in other ways, such as personal loyalty and willingness to act for the other's benefit (e.g., RACHEL and JACOB, Gen 29:20; Delilah and SAMSON, Judg 14:16; 16:4,15; HANNAH and Elkanah, 1 Sam 1:5; the foreign wives and SOLOMON, 1 Kgs 11:2). A loving marriage was part of the life of wisdom (Prov 5:19; 15:17; Eccl 9:9). The Song of Solomon celebrates the longings and joys of intimate love, but even in this book one discovers the awareness that love involves a devotion that endures beyond erotic satisfaction (Cant 8:6).

Biblical narratives illustrate the destructive power of uncontrolled and uncommitted sexual passion. The rape of Dinah by Shechem and of TAMAR by AMNON began with love, but violence transformed the passion to hatred (Gen 34:3, 7; 2 Sam 13:1, 14, 15). In PROVERBS, the strange woman who seduces young men represents folly, and the pleasures she offers lead to death (Prov 7:18, 22-23, 27).

Illicit love serves as a powerful metaphor for Israel's infidelity to God. Beginning with HOSEA (2:5, 15; 3:1; 9:1) and also in the other prophets (Isa 57:8; Jer 2:25, 33; Ezek 16; 23), Israel was condemned for taking "lovers" by forging alliances with the foreign nations and worshiping other gods. These unfaithful relationships with foreign powers, which were entered into for quick gratification and security, resulted in humiliation and rejection (Hos 2:7; Jer 22:20; 30:14; Lam 1:2, 19; Ezek 16:35-43). This adultery contrasts with Israel's early love for God, like a bride's love for her husband (Jer 2:2).

Among members of a FAMILY or a household, love motivates action for the good of the other. A father loves his own son and disciplines him (Prov 13:24). Because Ruth loved NAOMI she stayed with her to provide her first with food and then with a new family (Ruth 4:15). A Hebrew slave who chose to remain in servitude with his slave-wife and their children rather than go free alone loved his master (Exod 21:5; Deut 15:16). ABRAHAM's great love for ISAAC did not, however, stand in the way of his obedience to God (Gen 22:2). In Hosea, God expresses love for Israel like that of a parent for his or her child (Hos 11:1, 4, 8, 9).

One of the OT words meaning "friend" is a form of the verb "love." Such a friend is someone who loves. True friends are allies whose loyalty, affection and commitment to one's well-being are assured (Esth 5:10, 14; 6:13; Prov 17:17; 18:24; 27:6; Jer 20:4, 6). Individuals may be friends of God in this sense (Judg 5:31; 2 Chr 20:7; Isa 41:8). In contrast, friends may turn out to be insincere and self-serving hangers-on (Prov 14:20; 18:24). The pain of being abandoned by friends contributed to the suffering of Job and the psalmists (Job 19:19; Pss 38:11; 88:18).

The friendship of DAVID and JONATHAN offers the clearest example of love between friends. In spite of David's being in direct competition with him for the throne, Jonathan loved David as himself (1 Sam 18:1). The two friends made a covenant to which David remained loyal even after Jonathan's death (1 Sam 18:3; 2 Sam 9). Jonathan betrayed his father and his own royal ambition in order to save David's life (1 Sam 20). David marvelled that such a self-sacrificing love, offered freely and maintained faithfully, could exist without the passionate bond of a sexual relationship (2 Sam 1:26).

The OT commandments to love one's neighbor (Lev 19:18) and the stranger as oneself (Lev 19:34) are rooted in God's love for Israel and for the resident foreigner (Deut 10:18-19). The categories "neighbor" and "stranger" include every person an ancient Israelite might encounter. These commandments extend from the natural affection and commitment within the family to encompass the rest of humanity. Love can be commanded because loving actions appropriate to a loving relationship are deeds of will, not the spontaneous products of emotion. Commands prescribing such loving actions toward neighbors and strangers constitute much OT law. The command to love one's neighbor came to function as a summary of the Law (Mark 12:28-34).

Love for an object, activity, or ideal involves a desire for, or attachment to, the beloved object that directs one's actions and may determine one's whole way of life. Israel was warned against loving things such as sleep, pleasure, money, lying, false oaths, violence, death and evil (e.g., Pss 4:3; 11:5; 52:4; Prov 8:36; 20:13; 21:17; Mic 3:2; Zech 8:17). Israel and her leaders were indicted for loving to wander and to oppress, and for their love for bribes, false prophecy, strange gods, and shame (e.g., Isa 1:23; 57:8; Jer 5:31; 8:2; 14:10; Hos 4:18; 12:7). Love for things pertaining to God, and which God loves, too, such as Jerusalem, wisdom, salvation, justice, righteousness, and peace is part of one's love for God (e.g., Pss 11:7; 33:5; 37:28; 40:16; 99:4; 146:8; Prov 4:6; 19:8; Amos 5:15; Mic 6:8; Zech 8:19). To love God's name is to love God (Pss 5:11; 119:132; Isa 56:6).

The language of love had a place in public life and diplomacy. The people's admiration for David is called love (1 Sam 18:16, 22). Kings were warned not to love those who hated them or God (2 Sam 19:6; 2 Chr 19:2). Hiram of Tyre and the Queen of Sheba praised Solomon, saying that his reign was evidence of God's love for Israel (1 Kgs 10:9; 2 Chr 2:11; 9:8). Their diplomatic compliment also contains a theological truth.

In the ancient Near East, treaties between states often required that the vassal king love his overlord (cf. Hiram's love for David, 1 Kgs 5:1). In the OT, the covenant relationship between Israel and God required all Israelites to love the Lord God with all their "heart, soul, and might" (Deut 6:5; 11:1, 13, 22; 13:3). One who loves God keeps God's commandments (Deut 10:12-13; 19:9; 30:16, 20; Josh 22:5; cf. John 14:21). God is repeatedly described as the one who keeps covenant and steadfast love with "those who love him and keep his commandments" (Exod 20:6; Deut 5:10; 7:9; Neh 1:5; Dan 9:4). Within this covenant relationship the love for God's law voiced so many times in Ps 119 (e.g., v. 159) almost becomes the equivalent of loving God.

God's love for Israel was the origin of the covenant relationship. Divine choice or election of individuals and the nation as a whole is identified with God's love (Deut 4:37; 7:8; 10:15; Ps 78:68; Isa 43:4; 48:14; 63:9; Mal 1:2). Even Israel's disobedience and unfaithfulness did not destroy God's love (Hos 14:4). The Lord said, "I have loved you with an everlasting love; therefore I have continued my faithfulness to you" (Jer 3:13).

See also COVENANT; FRIENDSHIP; LOVING-KINDNESS.

Bibliography. J. Bergman et al., "אָהַב *'āhabh*," *TDOT*; N. Lohfink, *The Christian Meaning of the Old Testament*; W. Moran, "The Ancient Near Eastern Background of the Love of God in Deuteronomy," *CBQ* 25 (1963): 77-87; L. Morris, *Testaments of Love*.

—PAMELA J. SCALISE

• **Love Apples.** *See* MANDRAKE

• **Loving-Kindness.** Found about thirty times in the KJV as one of nine or ten different translations for the Heb. word *ḥesed*. *Ḥesed* occurs over 245 times in the OT and is frequently rendered "mercy" in the KJV (ca. 120 times; cf. MERCY) and "steadfast love" in the RSV (ca. 177 times). The English term loving-kindness is attributed first to Miles Coverdale, but it has been employed primarily in the Psalms and always with reference to God in most of the English versions up until the time of the RSV.

The basic meaning of *ḥesed* springs from interpersonal relationships inherent in FAMILY and clan society. *Ḥesed* is that mutual "loyal love" or "kindness" shared between relatives (Ruth 1:8), between host and guest (Gen 21:23) and between friends (1 Sam 20:8, 14). By extension, "kindness" is demonstrated between a monarch and subjects (2 Sam 2:5) and between strangers in unique circumstances (Gen 40:14).

Ḥesed is reciprocal. In return for her act of "kindness," RAHAB expected the same from the Israelite spies (Josh 2:12, 14). Mutual responsibility in a COVENANT also assumed some measure of *ḥesed*, though the institution of a covenant was not a prerequisite for its demonstration (Gen 21:23, 27). Finally, acts of "kindness" are ultimately repaid (Prov 3:1-5).

Yahweh's nature is to keep covenant and show "kindness" (Exod 34:7; Deut 7:9, 12); to give (Mic 7:20), remember (Ps 25:6), and take away (Jer 16:5) *ḥesed*. Recipients of God's "kindness" include individuals (Gen 32:10-11) and groups (2 Sam 2:5-6) as well as Israel (Exod 15:13). All nations have seen God's *ḥesed* revealed in the history of Israel (Ps 98:2-3). Yahweh's "steadfast love" endures forever (Ps 136).

See also LOVE IN THE OLD TESTAMENT.

Bibliography. N. Glueck, *Ḥesed in the Bible*; K. Sakenfeld, *Faithfulness in Action;* H. Zobel, "חֶסֶד," *TDOT*.

—STEPHEN J. ANDREWS

• **Luke.** [l*oo*k] Luke was the fellow traveler of Paul and the traditional author of the third Gospel and the Acts of the Apostles. His name (Gk. *Loukas*) is probably an abbreviation of the Latin *Lucius*. Luke is mentioned by name only three times in the NT, all in letters attributed to Paul: Col 4:14; Phlm 24; 2 Tim 4:11. The most important of these is the passage in Colossians, where Luke is called "the beloved physician" and is apparently distinguished from Paul's other co-workers "who are from the circumcision" (Col 4:11). That the writer of Luke-Acts was educated and could have been a physician is borne out by the vocabulary of Luke and Acts, as well as by the character of the contents of both writings. In the LETTER TO PHILEMON, sent to the same place as Colossians, Luke joins Paul's other "fellow workers" in sending greetings to Philemon. Finally, in 2 Tim 4:11 Paul writes, "Only Luke is with me," and asks Timothy to join him with Mark.

If Colossians and Philemon were written by Paul when he was a prisoner in Rome, then Luke must have accompanied Paul on his voyage as a prisoner to Rome, as described in Acts 27 and 28. These two chapters comprise one of the three WE-SECTIONS in Acts (beginning in Acts 16:10; 20:5 and 27:1) in which the author identifies himself as a participant in the narrative. If Luke was the author of Acts, then he must have joined Paul at Troas in 50 C.E. and traveled with him to Philippi (Acts 16:10-18). Here he appears to have been left behind, only to be picked up again some seven years later on Paul's trip to Jerusalem with the offering for the Judean Christians (Acts 20:5–21:18). It is conceivable that Luke was the "true yokefellow" whom Paul asks in Phil 4:3 to help resolve the differences between Euodia and Syntyche. Later still, possibly during Paul's second imprisonment in Rome, Luke is alone with Paul (2 Tim 4:11)—which may imply that Luke served as the amanuensis of Paul if the latter wrote 2 Timothy. This agrees with an early Christian tradition (the so-called Anti-Marcionite Prologue to Luke) that Luke the physician remained a faithful coworker of Paul until the apostle's martyrdom. What happened to Luke after this cannot be determined with certainty, but according to the same tradition Luke continued to serve the Lord without wife or child until he died in Boeotia in Greece at the age of 84.

Some scholars identify Luke with one or both of the bearers of the name Lucius in Acts 13:1 and Rom 16:21. In Acts, however, there is no evidence to connect this Lucius with Luke the physician (Lucius was a common name in the Roman world). The Lucius mentioned in Romans as one of Paul's "kinsmen" is distinguished from Timothy, who is called "my fellow-worker." It is difficult to see how the gentile Luke could be regarded as a relative of Paul by kinship or race.

See also APOSTLES, ACTS OF THE; LUKE, GOSPEL OF; WE-SECTIONS.

Bibliography. C. K. Barrett, *Luke the Historian in Recent Study*; S. G. Wilson, *Luke and the Pastoral Epistles*; W. K. Hobart, *The Medical Language of St. Luke*.

—DAVID A. BLACK

• **Luke's Travel Narrative.** *See* TRAVEL NARRATIVE

• **Luke, Gospel of.** The Gospel of Luke is the first part of a two-volume work, the second part of which is the ACTS OF THE APOSTLES. Both the third Gospel and Acts are dedicated to THEOPHILUS, and Acts 1:1 refers to "the first book" and summarizes the contents of the Gospel. Similarity in style and theological perspective seal the case. The work was probably divided in the second century when the third Gospel was included in the fourfold Gospel, leaving Acts to circulate alone. Because of the original unity of Luke-Acts, interpretation of the third Gospel must refer to Acts, just as interpretation of Acts must take into account the Gospel of Luke.

Prior to the 1940s Luke was generally regarded as a historian and research on the third Gospel focused on SOURCE CRITICISM. Since the mid-fifties there has been a "new look" in Lucan studies. Luke is now seen as a theologian of stature who consciously planned and produced his work, and the third Gospel is regarded as a theological document with a distinctive view of Christian faith and life. Dimensions of this outlook include the following.

Christology. Luke's picture of Jesus is many-sided. On the one hand, Jesus' story is told as the model of what Christian life should be. Unlike Greco-Roman biographies, with which Luke has many affinities, Luke tells the story of Jesus in developmental terms: from his dedication to God as an infant (2:22-24), to his affirmation at twelve

• OUTLINE OF LUKE •

The Gospel of Luke

I. The Prologue (1:1-4)
II. Prophecies of Future Greatness (1:5–4:15)
  A. Annunciation of the birth of John (1:5-25)
  B. Annunciation of the birth of Jesus (1:5-25)
  C. Visit of Mary and Elizabeth (1:39-56)
  D. Birth and early life of John (1:57-80)
  E. Birth and early life of Jesus (2:1-52)
  F. Adult ministry of John (3:1-20)
  G. Prelude to Jesus' public ministry (3:21–4:15)
III. Anointed with the Holy Spirit (4:16–9:50)
  A. For the whole person in the whole world (4:16-30)
  B. Called and commissioned (4:31–5:11)
  C. The difference Jesus makes (5:12–6:11)
  D. Transcending the times (6:12-49)
  E. The breadth and power of Jesus (7:1-17)
  F. Confirmed forgiveness (7:18-50)
  G. The Word of God at work (8:1-21)
  H. Universal power and vested interests (8:22–9:6)
  I. A foreshadowing of sufferings to come (9:7-50)
IV. Guidance on the Way (9:51–19:44)
  A. Costs of discipleship (9:51–10:24)
  B. On loving God and the neighgbor (10:25-42)
  C. Prayer: for what and why? (11:1-13)
  D. Healing in biblical perspective (11:14-36)
  E. Mealtime controversies (11:37-54)
  F. Possession, preparedness, and repentance (12:1–13:21)
  G. Wrong responses to the good news (13:22–14:35)
  H. The response of elder brothers (15:1-32)
  I. The use and misuse of wealth (16:1-31)
  J. The possibility of an impossible demand (17:1-10)
  K. Eschatology, faith, and prosperity (17:11–18:30)
  L. On being part of the people of God (18:31–19:44)
V. Martyrdom and Vindication (19:45–24:53)
  A. Tested in the Temple (19:45-21:4)
  B. On persecution and perseverence (21:5-38)
  C. Mealtime farewells (22:1-38)
  D. A model for martyrs (22:39–23:25)
  E. Innocent and obedient (23:26-56a)
  F. Victory, presence, and mission (23:56b–24:53)

of the parental decisions made about him at his birth (2:41-51), to his empowering by the Spirit prior to his adult ministry (3:21-22; 4:18-21), to his suffering-rejection-death in obedience to God (chaps. 9–23), to his resurrection-ascension-exaltation (chap. 24). On the other hand, Jesus' story is cast in the pattern of exaltation CHRISTOLOGY: Jesus lives the life of a benefactor, is raised from the dead, and rules from heaven as Lord until his return as messianic judge. Birth narratives precede Jesus' virtuous life so as to preclude any attempt to understand his life, and that of a disciple, in a legalistic fashion. Jesus' life is God's act. By derivation, the life of a disciple that passes through the five stages must also be God's act.

Eschatology. The third Gospel, together with Acts, tells its story in terms of a history of SALVATION that runs from Israel to Jesus to the apostolic age to the postapostolic age. The career of Jesus sets the example for the apostles and both together are normative for the period after the apostles. This history of salvation, however, is not a substitute for an imminent ESCHATOLOGY. An expectation of an imminent end is found in Luke. From the Lucan vantage point, all the stages of holy history have already taken place except the end (21:9-32), that cosmic event which occurs at the end of a series of unfolding stages. This cosmic eschatology is complemented by an individual eschatology which holds that at death a believer goes to PARADISE to be with Jesus (23:43). The history of salvation most likely serves to show the dignity of the Christian movement because of its links to and roots in the ancient Jewish tradition.

Soteriology. The third Gospel does not connect Jesus' death with the forgiveness of sins. Jesus' death is viewed as the martyrdom of a righteous man which serves as the model for Christian suffering. As such, it is part of the divine plan (24:25-27). It is also viewed as a sacrifice that seals the bonds of the new COVENANT (22:20b). Forgiveness flows from the word of the earthly Jesus (5:24; 7:48) and from the exalted Christ (Acts 5:31). Salvation applies almost exclusively to the present. It includes healing as well as forgiveness, and is associated with faith. It comes about not only through the hearing of the word but also through contact with the miraculous. Luke has a very positive evaluation of the evangelistic benefits of miracle, though he is not so naive as to reduce being saved to being healed (17:11-19). Salvation is intended for all peoples. The Gospel, along with Acts, aims to show that the inclusion of the gentiles in the Christian movement was rooted in the OT (2:32; 3:6; 4:25; cf. Acts 14:27; 15:15; 28:25-29) and intended by the founder of Christianity (24:47; 10:1; 7:1-10; cf. Acts 1:8).

Prayer. Two primary emphases may be discerned. First, prayer is desirable among Christians as they wait for the PAROUSIA because it enables them to escape from temptation and be found faithful at the judgment (22:46; 21:36;18:1-8; 11:1-13). Second, prayer is the instrument by which God directs the course of holy history, both in the career of Jesus (3:21:22; 6:12; 9:18; 9:28; 22:42) and in the life of the church (22:31-32; cf. Acts 1:14; 4:31; 10; 13:1-3).

Possessions. Vested financial interests outside the church resist the gospel (8:37; cf. Acts 16:19-23; 19:25-29). Within the people of God the wise use of possessions for the corporate good has priority (chap. 16). The principle of reciprocity in their use must be broken (6:34).

Women. Luke pays special attention to women. Women are frequently set alongside men in various ministries: as guarantors of the facts of Jesus' life, as servants among Jesus' disciples, in prophesying, in prayer, in hospitality, in teaching (cf. Acts 18:26).

Clarification of these various theological tendencies of the third Gospel has been the focus of research in the past generation during which REDACTION criticism has been the favored method of study. Less attention has been given to the traditional introductory questions such as the following.

Authorship. As early as Irenaeus (ca. 180 C.E.; cf. *AdvHaer* 3.1.1) the third Gospel was attributed to Luke, the companion of Paul mentioned in Phlm 24; Col 4:14; and 2 Tim 4:11. The MURATORIAN CANON, Tertullian, Origen, EUSEBIUS, and Jerome continue the identification. The ancient title, "Gospel according to Luke," is found at the end of the Gospel in the oldest extant manuscript of it ($\mathfrak{p}^{75}$), a papyrus codex from 175–225 C.E. Given the patristic attitude that a canonical Gospel had to have as author an APOSTLE or an apostolic man, modern scholars are reserved about this patristic evidence. Although the third Gospel is itself anonymous, some have attempted to use its connections to Acts to find internal evidence about authorship. The WE-SECTIONS (Acts 16:10-17; 20:5–21:18; 27:1–28:16) have been regarded as the personal memoirs of a companion of Paul. Because of the similarity of style and content between these sections and the rest of Acts, it has been claimed that a companion of Paul was also the author of Acts and, by extension, of the third Gospel. Two arguments have undermined such claims. First, in antiquity such "we" sections were widely used as a literary technique in narratives that were by no means produced by eyewitnesses (cf. Lucian, *A True Story*). Second, there are so many differences between the Paul of Acts and the Paul of the genuine epistles that it is difficult to believe a companion of Paul could have written Acts: e.g., the Christology of Paul in Acts fits the exaltation pattern (Acts 13:32-33) whereas in the letters it fits the epiphany pattern; the eschatology of Paul in Acts assumes his death and history's continuation thereafter (Acts 20:25) while the epistles assume that Paul will be alive when the parousia occurs; the Paul of Acts is not a letter writer, contrary to the apostle of the letters. The matter of authorship is moot.

Date. The third Gospel is most likely dated between 80 and 100 C.E. In Luke 1:1-4 the evangelist says he is not an eyewitness but is recording material passed down to him. He is at least a second generation Christian (cf. Heb 2:3). Acts ends with Paul in prison in Rome. So, if Luke and Acts were written at the same time, Luke cannot be earlier than the early 60s. Acts 20:25 reflects a knowledge of Paul's death, so a date must be after 64. If one assumes the two-source theory, then the Gospel must be after 65–75. Luke 21 echoes the fall of Jerusalem in 70 C.E. It is difficult to date the Gospel much before 80 C.E. Acts shows no knowledge of Paul's Letters. Since they were collected, edited, and published near 100 C.E., Acts must be prior to that event. Luke and Acts were known to MARCION and Justin so they cannot have been written much after 100 C.E. Since the Western text is very early—at least mid-second century—if Luke-Acts is late, there is no time for these textual variants to arise. It is difficult then to date Luke much beyond 100 C.E.

Place of Writing. The so-called Anti-Marcionite Prologue to Luke says that Luke composed this Gospel entirely in the regions about Achaia. This tradition is continued in Jerome's *Commentary on Matthew* and in Gregory of Naziansus (*Oratio* 33.11). An alternate tradition may be reflected in the Pseudo-Clementine *Recognitions*' location of Theophilus in Antioch (10.71). Modern attempts to localize the Gospel in Caesarea, the Decapolis, or Asia Minor have all lacked convincing evidence. All that can be said with certainty is that its author lived outside Palestine. Locale is not decisive for interpretation and so is a matter of some indifference.

Text. There are two textual traditions of great antiquity for Luke and Acts, the Alexandrian (e.g., א, B, $\mathfrak{p}^{75}$) and the Western (e.g., D and some old Latin mss.). The Western text has created interest especially in those places where its readings are briefer (e.g., 5:39; 7:71; 10:42; 11:35-36; 12:19; 19:25; 22:19b-20; 24:6; 24:12; 24:31; 24:40; 24:51; 24:52). Although an earlier generation of scholars tended to regard these Western readings as original, since the discovery of $\mathfrak{p}^{75}$ scholarly preference inclines towards the Alexandrian text throughout.

Sources. The sources of the third Gospel have been a matter of dispute since the mid-60s. The reigning two-source hypothesis which holds that Luke used Mark, Q and L tradition has been challenged by a revival of the Griesbach hypothesis: Matthew was written first, Luke used Matthew, and Mark used Matthew and Luke. Although the majority of NT scholars continue to espouse the two-source hypothesis, enough question has been created by the challengers that some have simply suspended judgment until further evidence is available. The interpretation of the third Gospel in its present form is not dependent on any source theory, but the quest for the historical Jesus demands some working hypothesis about sources.

Genre. Recent scholarship has raised once again the question of the genre of Luke. After a generation or two that rejected all claims that Luke was a biography, in the past decade there has been a growing consensus that Luke is indeed a biography, albeit an ancient one.

See also APOSTLES, ACTS OF THE; CHRISTOLOGY; CHRONOLOGY; ESCHATOLOGY IN THE NEW TESTAMENT; GOSPELS, CRITICAL STUDY OF; INTERPRETATION, HISTORY OF; LUKE; PAUL; Q; REDACTION; SOURCE CRITICISM; THEOPHILUS; WE-SECTIONS; WOMEN IN THE NEW TESTAMENT.

Bibliography. P. J. Achtemeier, "The Lucan Perspective on the Miracles of Jesus: A Preliminary Sketch," *JBL* 94 (1975): 547-62; H. Conzelmann, *The Theology of St. Luke*; J. A. Fitzmyer, "Papyrus Bodmer XIV: Some Features of Our Oldest Text of Luke," *CBQ* 24 (1962): 170-79; I. H. Marshall, *Luke: Historian and Theologian*; P. T. O'Brien, "Prayer in Luke-Acts," *TB* 24 (1973): 111-27; K. Snodgrass, "Western Non-Interpolations," *JBL* 91 (1972): 369-79; C. H. Talbert, *Reading Luke* and *What Is A Gospel?*; J. B. Tyson, "Source Criticism of the Gospel of Luke," *Perspectives on Luke-Acts*, ed. C. H. Talbert; R. Zehnle, "The Salvific Character of Jesus' Death in Lucan Soteriology," *TS* 30 (1969): 420-44.

—CHARLES H. TALBERT

• **Lydia.** [lid'ee-uh] Lydia was a seller of purple cloth who was converted by Paul in PHILIPPI and played a key role in the foundation of the church there.

Acts 16:14 explains that Lydia was from the city of THYATIRA, which was located in a western region of Asia Minor called Lydia. Information about Thyatira helps one understand her occupation and religious inclinations. The city was famous for its dyeing, and inscriptions have been discovered honoring the guild of dyers in Thyatira. They were especially famed for the manufacture of a luxurious purple dye. This dye was probably extracted from Mediterranean mollusks. Eight thousand of these mollusks were required to produce just one gram of dye so the dye was very expensive and used to color woven materials and cloths. A less likely possibility is that the purple dye was obtained in Thyatira from the madder root. Whatever the source of the dye, Lydia imported the dyed purple fabrics from her hometown of Thyatira and sold them in Philippi for a profit. Her business probably made her wealthy. Acts 16:15 indicates that she owned her own home and it was large enough to accomodate other family members and several guests as well. The absence of any reference to a husband indicates that Lydia was single—widowed, divorced, or never married.

Lydia was also a "worshipper of God" or a "God-fearer"—a pagan who worshipped the one Jewish God instead of the multitude of Greek, Roman, and Oriental gods, but who had not yet become a full-fledged Jew. Since Thyatira had a Jewish colony, Lydia may have begun worshipping the one God there. Apparently there was no synagogue in Philippi, but she and several other women met by the Gangites River outside the city to worship. Paul and his companions met them there during Paul's second missionary journey. After he explained the good news of Jesus Christ to them, Lydia accepted Paul's message and was baptized with her household (including relatives, children and/or slaves).

One result of her conversion was that she immediately

opened her home to the missionaries. They stayed with Lydia until they were arrested and imprisoned (Acts 16:16-39). Before leaving Philippi to continue their missionary journey, Paul and Silas made a point of visiting Lydia. She is an excellent example of one early Christian who was not poor, but rather who used her wealth to help spread the gospel. Paul did not specifically mention her name in his later Letter to the church at Philippi, but it is possible that her financial resources enabled the Philippians to send the monetary aid to Paul which he mentions in Phil 4:14-18.

See also PAUL; PHILIPPI; THYATIRA.

Bibliography. F. W. Foakes-Jackson, and K. Lake, eds., *The Beginnings of Christianity:* Part I: *The Acts of the Apostles*; E. Haenchen, *The Acts of the Apostles: A Commentary*; I. H. Marshall, *The Acts of the Apostles*.

—MARK J. OLSON

• **Lying.** The Bible uses many words to represent the sinful act of mishandling or misrepresenting truth. In the OT, the most common words are *kāzav* (often used with the root idea of deliberate deception and unreliability), *šeqer* (utilized regularly in the legal sense of fraud), and *kaḥaš* (most often representative of negation or denial). Other words utilized in the OT to express a dishonest or deceptive act/state are: *remiyyâ* and *mirmâ* (both are nouns meaning treachery and containing a root idea of corruption), *beged* (translated treachery and related to a noun for a garment or covering, suggesting a "cover up"), *šāw'* (conveying the idea of emptiness or vanity as a wrong performed against being), and *kaḥad* (meaning to hide or conceal).

In the NT, the most important terms used to describe untruth as a false assessment of reality or as a threat to authentic being are: *pseudos* and *pseudomai* (the generic words for lies and lying, which are used in the NT as the diametric opposite of the truth and "doing" the truth as a lifestyle), *planaō* and *planē* (which express error with the idea of wandering or being misled from the truth), and *apataō* (meaning beguile and with the connotation of seducing one into deception). Other NT terms include: *dolos* (craftiness), *dolioō* (to deceive), and *paralogizomai* (to cheat).

Bibliography. H. Conzelmann, "ψεῦδος, κτλ.," *TDNT*.

—JOHNNY L. WILSON

• **Lysias, Claudius.** [klaw'dee-uhs-lis"ee-uhs] Lysias was military commander in JERUSALEM when PAUL was "arrested" (Acts 21:31-36). Apart from his part in Paul's arrest, little is known of Lysias. In the Acts narrative, however, Lysias is described as coming to Paul's rescue when the missionary's life was endangered by the mob (Acts 21:27-36). Lysias as military commander has Paul "arrested," or perhaps taken into protective custody. After taking Paul into the TOWER OF ANTONIA, Lysias discovers Paul's Roman citizenship (Acts 22:24-29). During the ensuing dialogue, Lysias admits that he "bought this citizenship for a large sum" (Acts 22:28), possibly indicating that he gained his citizenship through emancipation from slavery. After having Paul examined by the SANHEDRIN and later learning of a plot against Paul's life, Lysias has Paul sent to FELIX, the territorial PROCURATOR, along with a letter summarizing the incident.

See also ANTONIA, TOWER OF; FELIX; JERUSALEM; PAUL; PROCURATOR; SANHEDRIN.

—FREDERICK L. DOWNING

• **Lystra.** [lis'truh] Lystra was a town located in central Asia Minor some twenty mi. southeast of Iconium and in the Roman province of GALATIA (PLATES 26, 27). It was visited by Paul on his first missionary journey (Acts 14:6).

The exact location of Lystra was determined in 1885 by the discovery of a large stone altar with an inscription giving the Latin name of the town and stating that it was a Roman colony. This identification was confirmed by the finding of coins. Lystra had been given the status of a colony in 6 B.C.E. by the emperor Augustus. It served primarily as a military outpost, giving protection against the mountain tribes of the area. A minor military road connected Antioch with Lystra and Derbe.

While Greek was spoken, the most common language was a native dialect (Acts 14:11). The town contained some Greek and Roman residents. The majority of the population were native Lycaonians, characterized by superstition and lack of education. Few Jews lived in the town. Ancient tradition stated that the gods Zeus and Hermes had taken human form and visited the region (Acts 14:8-18).

TIMOTHY was a resident of Lystra (Acts 16:1). His mother was a Jew and his father Greek. He was probably converted during Paul's first visit to the town, and was chosen as a traveling companion when Paul returned a second time. Lystra played only a minor role in subsequent Christian history.

No excavation work has been undertaken at Lystra. There are indications that it was inhabited from the third and second milleniums B.C.E.

See also GALATIA; PAUL; TIMOTHY.

Bibliography. W. M. Ramsay, *The Cities of St. Paul*.

—CLAYTON K. HARROP

• **M.** *See* SOURCE CRITICISM

• **Maccabees.** [mak′uh-beez] The Maccabees were the Jewish leaders who spearheaded the revolution in 167 B.C.E. that resulted in the formation of an independent Jewish state in JUDEA that endured until 63 B.C.E. when it fell under Roman domination. The term "Maccabee" was actually a nickname for one of the bravest of the early leaders of the revolution, Judas (or Judah); and as he was of the house of Hasmon, the term Hasmonean is sometimes used interchangeably with Maccabean. The early Jewish sources refer only to the Hasmoneans, while the early Christian sources refer to the Maccabees with the term appearing first in the writings of Clement of Alexandria (second century C.E.) who refers to the "Books of the Maccabees." Clement probably used this designation because the exploits of Judas, called Maccabee, are so prominent in the two books. Scholars generally view the Maccabean period as that in which Judas and his brothers were leaders and designate the period, beginning with John Hyrcanus, the son of one of the brothers, as Hasmonean.

Three primary sources are used by historians in reconstructing the events of the Maccabean period. The most reliable of the sources are 1 MACCABEES and the *Jewish Antiquities* of Flavius JOSEPHUS. The book of 2 MACCABEES deals with events paralleling the first eight chapters of 1 Maccabees, but is generally viewed as a less trustworthy source.

The Jewish Revolt in Judea. The reasons for the Jewish revolt (167–164 B.C.E.) against the ruling Seleucid kingdom of Syria are complex, but all relate to the Jewish perception that they were being forced to choose between loyalty to their non-Jewish overlords and loyalty to their God.

The earliest to emerge of these reasons related to changes in the Jewish high priesthood. The HIGH PRIEST since the time of EZRA had been the leader of the Jewish community, both politically and religiously. He inherited his office and held it for life according to the legislation in Num 25:10-13. When non-Jewish powers came to rule Judea, the most important function of the priest was, from their point of view, his paying them the money they demanded as taxes from a captive people. The right to collect taxes which the high priest held was a profitable one; powerful, wealthy Jews gained this right by bribing the overlords, creating a deep division in the Jewish aristocracy. As the struggles for power among Jewish leaders grew, a man named Jason was appointed high priest through bribery by Antiochus IV in 175 B.C.E., replacing his brother, Onias III, the current high priest. Three years later, Menelaus, who was not even of the priestly line, offered a larger bribe and was appointed in place of Jason. To the Jews it was clear that the gentile overlords were in these actions setting aside the laws of God in the TORAH.

The second reason Jews felt forced to choose between their God and their gentile overlords was the rapidly increasing visibility of Hellenistic customs and practices that were perceived as incompatible with Jewish faith. ALEXANDER the Great had envisioned one world empire held together by a unity of language and culture, and the area around the Mediterranean had moved substantially in this direction by the early second century B.C.E. Hellenistic influence had made substantial inroads into Judea. Greek dress, language, architecture, and life styles were apparent in both GALILEE and Judea. Those Jews most loyal to their Seleucid overlords were the most open to Hellenistic ways because this was the path to acceptance by those in power and thus the path to wealth and privilege. Many Jews, however, resisted such innovations and saw themselves as a separate group—the Devout or Hasidim—over against the compromising Jews whom they termed the Hellenists.

The third and precipitating reason for the Jewish revolution was the decision of the Seleucid king, Antiochus IV (175-163), to consolidate his empire by ruthlessly enforcing Hellenism on all persons in his domain. Desperately needing money to finance the military machine needed to hold his empire together and expand it, Antiochus looted the Jerusalem TEMPLE in 169 B.C.E., slaying many Jews in the operation. One year later he sought to add Egypt to his domain but was stopped by ROME. Seeing his hopes for expansion dashed, Antiochus escalated his plans for the consolidation of his empire. He appointed his own tax collector who plundered Jewish villages, he set up a garrison in Jerusalem called the Akra, he forbade Jews to observe their practices related to the SABBATH and to CIRCUMCISION (1 Macc 1:41-51); and he decreed the execution of anyone found possessing a Torah scroll. To symbolize the demise of JUDAISM, he built a pagan altar in Jerusalem and in 167 B.C.E., or 25 Kislev (which falls in December), a pig was sacrificed on it to Zeus. Jewish reaction was divided; those who gladly embraced Hellenism were not too dismayed, but others saw the suppression of Judaism as a challenge to God, calling the sacrifice "the abomination that makes desolate" (Dan 11:31).

The Struggle for Religious Freedom. The Jews who sought to be loyal to the Torah resisted the enforced Hellenization, and some were martyred; but passive resistance quickly was replaced by active rebellion. When the representatives of Antiochus arrived at the little village of Modein (PLATE 19), about eighteen miles northwest of Jerusalem, they demanded that a priest named Mattathias offer a heathen sacrifice. He refused, and killed both the king's officer and a Jew who volunteered to make the sacrifice. Along with his five sons—John, Simon, Eleazer, Judas, and Jonathan—he took refuge in the rugged hill country, joining others who had fled there to be able to practice their religion.

Soldiers from the Syrian garrison in Jerusalem hounded the refugees, and they were determined to fight—even on the Sabbath if necessary (1 Macc 2:4)—for their religious freedom. Mattathias led in consolidating the resistance and was quickly supported by many loyal Jews, including the zealous Hasidim. He roamed the region, circumcising children, killing Jews who had lapsed from their faith, and encouraging resistance to the Seleucids.

In the spring of 165, Mattathias died after recommending that his son Judas be their commander. Judas was called "Maccabee" (hammerer) which probably means "the warrior quick to strike." His early leadership was marked by recurrent victories because the Seleucids underestimated the strength of the guerrilla forces. In 165 a large Seleucid force led by three generals—Ptolemy, Nicanor, and Gorgias—was sent against Judas, who by this time had a regular army with designated officers (1 Macc 3:55). The Jews were so outnumbered that defeat seemed assured; slave dealers were already present in the Syrian camps to buy the Jewish captives. With a brilliant strategy of ambush, Judas defeated a part of the Seleucid force and the remainder fled, giving the Jews a total victory. After further victories and diplomatic negotiations, the Jews were granted amnesty. Judas then directed his efforts to resuming the temple services. He occupied Jerusalem, except for the hostile garrison (Akra) and proceeded to purify the temple by erecting a new altar in place of the defiled one and replacing the sacred vessels of the temple with new ones. A great celebration marked the rededication of the Temple which occurred on 25 Kislev, 164 B.C.E.—exactly three years after its desecration. The Jews decided to establish the celebration—the Feast of the Dedication (cf. John 10:22) or Hanukkah—as an annual one, which rather ironically shows the pervasive influence of Hellenism as previous Jewish feasts were set by OT law (Lev 23:4-8).

The Struggle for Political Independence. With the achievement of religious freedom in Judea, the task of Judas seemed at an end; but other Jews were being persecuted by gentiles in Gilead and Galilee and pleaded for assistance. Judas led forces to Gilead and Simon to Galilee, rescuing the faithful and bringing them safely back to Judea. These successes led Judas to dream of political consolidation for the Jews; he continued his military exploits, not only to deliver Jews, but to extend Jewish power. When Judas laid siege to the Syrian garrison in Jerusalem, the internally troubled Seleucid empire took action, sending General Lysias against Judas with a huge army. In the ensuing battle, Eleazer (one of the five sons of Mattathias) was killed; the Jews were defeated and fled to Jerusalem where they were besieged. Their defeat seemed assured, but Lysias had to capitulate and return to ANTIOCH to deal with internal Seleucid affairs in a deteriorating empire. Judas was pardoned, designated as the king's agent in Judea, and religious freedom was affirmed, although the Syrian garrison in Jerusalem remained. The career of Judas, although seemingly secure, was quickly threatened. The appointed high priest, Alkimus, was strongly pro-Syrian; and Judas drove him out of Jerusalem, causing him to appeal for Syrian aid. An initial Syrian victory was followed by Judas driving Alkimus out again. This time General Nicanor led the army against Judas, but he was slain and his death was celebrated annually by the Jews as the Day of Nicanor until the seventh century. This was Judas's final victory—an avenging army faced him with his army having dwindled to eight hundred soldiers. Judas died at Elasa in 161 B.C.E.

The nationalist Jewish movement which Judas had led since the rededication of the temple in 164 B.C.E. seemed doomed as the Seleucids ferreted out his supporters. A small group of them, however, elected Jonathan, a brother of Judas, as leader and tried to continue the fight. For years almost nothing occurred to further the cause for freedom; but Jonathan and Simon, the two surviving brothers of Judas, slowly expanded their base of support in Judea against the pro-Seleucid (Hellenistic) Jewish group. Jonathan shrewdly exploited the internal struggles for power in the Seleucid empire to his advantage, and a significant event for Jewish freedom occurred in 153 B.C.E. when Jonathan, promising Jewish military support, was appointed high priest by Alexander Balas, a rival of Demetrius for the Seleucid kingship. This marked the end of the pro-Syrian (Hellenistic) Jewish power in Judea and opened the way for the rapid escalation of the Jewish nationalistic movement. Jonathan continued to exploit the internal political struggles of the Seleucids for Jewish advantages, and his increased power resulted in his being treacherously captured in 143 B.C.E. by Tryphon who feared that Jewish military strength was a threat to the stability of the Seleucid empire.

At an assembly called by Simon, the Jewish people elected Simon, the last remaining son of Mattathias, as their leader. He immediately began to strengthen the fortifications in Jerusalem. Tryphon soon executed the captured Jonathan, and Simon became high priest. Simon, like Jonathan, took shrewd political advantage of the unrest in the Seleucid kingdom; and as Tryphon and Demetrius struggled to gain ascendancy, Simon promised Demetrius his support if the Judean Jews were exempted from tribute; Demetrius agreed. This exemption ended the Seleucid domination and gave the Judean kingdom its autonomy. Jews, recognizing this, began to use their own chronology and to date treaties according to the year of Simon, High Priest and Prince of the Jews.

Simon knew that Demetrius had granted what he could not deliver if Tryphon triumphed, and he moved swiftly to consolidate his position by conquering the city of Gazara, replacing its Gentile inhabitants with loyal Jews, and by laying successful siege to the Syrian garrison (Akra) in Jerusalem, entering the fortress with celebrations in June of 141 B.C.E. Simon's reign was marked with peace because the Seleucids were occupied with their own internal affairs, and the Jewish state prospered.

In 140 B.C.E. it was determined by the Jews in assembly that Simon would be the high priest, ethnarch (ruler), and military commander of the Jews "until a trustworthy prophet should arise" (1 Macc 14:41). This meant that Simon and his descendants would rule until God indicated otherwise; this was the foundation of the Hasmonean high priestly and princely dynasty. This decision of the Jews was ratified by the Romans in a treaty in which Simon's position was recognized by Rome, but Simon's reign did not end in peace. His son-in-law, Ptolemy, plotted to seize the kingship and assassinated Simon and two of his sons in 135 B.C. at a banquet he had arranged in their honor. Ptolemy then sought to do away with the third and only surviving son, John

Hyrcanus; but he escaped his assassins and secured his position in Jerusalem before Ptolemy could arrive. Hyrcanus, the first son of one of the Maccabean brothers to rule, consolidated his kingdom, and the hereditary Hasmonean dynasty endured until 63 B.C.E. when it fell to Rome.

The Contribution of the Maccabees. Mattathias along with his three sons—Judas, Jonathan, and Simon—courageously and shrewdly fought for freedom for the Jewish people. Their success was due in large part to the deterioration of the Seleucid empire, which never employed its full force against the Jews and which was in such disarray that political advantage could be taken at crucial times. The Maccabees were remembered and revered by all Jews in later generations. The ZEALOTS in the time of Jews looked to them as models of courage and faith in a struggle with Rome which they, like their Maccabean ancestors, perceived to be a clear choice between loyalty to God and dominion by gentiles. In addition, the accomplishments of the Maccabees are remembered annually by Jews everywhere in the celebration of Hanukkah.

See also HELLENISTIC WORLD; MACCABEES, FIRST; MACCABEES, SECOND.

Bibliography. M. Avi-Jonah and J. Kausner, "The War of Liberation," *The World History of the Jewish People,* vol. 6, *The Hellenistic Age,* ed. A. Schalit 147-210.

—HAROLD S. SONGER

• **Maccabees, First.** First Maccabees is a Jewish book relating the revolt of the MACCABEES in the second century B.C.E. While it was never accepted by Jews as part of the CANON, Roman Catholics consider it a book of the OT. Protestants count it among the APOCRYPHAL LITERATURE.

Importance of 1 Maccabees. First Maccabees is valuable as the principal source for reconstructing the political and cultural history of the Jews in Palestine from 167–134 B.C.E. The book is also of great importance in understanding how a loyal Jew in 100 B.C.E. understood and perceived the dynasty of the Hasmoneans that was established in 135 B.C.E.

The value of 1 Maccabees for understanding the NT is in the fact that first century Jews, having lost their independence in 63 B.C.E., were keenly aware of what courageous ancestors had done. These treasured memories fueled their aspirations for another earthly kingdom, shaped their hopes for what God would do, making it difficult for them to accept and understand the heavenly kingdom proclaimed by Jesus (John 6:14-15; Acts 1:6-8).

Content. First Maccabees focuses on the thirty-four year period from 167–134 B.C.E. in which the Jews in Palestine gained their political independence and established a ruling dynasty— the Hasmoneans. The book begins with a summary of how the Seleucid power in Syria was extended to Palestine after the death of ALEXANDER the Great and then recounts the persecution of the Jews under the Seleucid ruler, Antiochus IV (175–164 B.C.E.), who was seeking to unify his empire. The Jewish practices of CIRCUMCISION and keeping the SABBATH were conspicuous, marking them off from gentiles, and Antiochus focused on these features of Judaism, along with others, forbidding their observance (1:1-64). First Macc 2 recounts the initial Jewish act of rebellion by the aged priest Mattathias which resulted in his leaving the village of Modein with his five sons to seek refuge in the hill country. They were soon joined by many other Jews who would rather fight than give up observing the LAW (2:1-48). Just before he died, Mattathias conferred leadership of the growing army of resistance on his son Judas, nicknamed the Maccabee. Almost half of 1 Maccabees is devoted to recounting his exploits (3:1–9:22).

After several battles in which Judas displayed high skills as a strategist (cf. esp. 4:1-25) against Seleucid military forces (3:1-4:35), the Jewish community gained respite from attack, and the TEMPLE in Jerusalem was cleansed and its rituals resumed in a great celebration on 25 Kislev (which falls in December), 164 B.C.E., three years to the day from its desecration by Antiochus IV (1:54-59; 4:52-59). Religious freedom could not be maintained without consolidation, and Judas continued the fight. After a number of encounters with Seleucid forces, Judas was killed near Mount Azotus and the leadership passed to his brother Jonathan in 161 B.C.E.

Jonathan carried on the struggle, again gaining a time of respite for the Jewish people (9:23-73). Jonathan assumed the high priesthood and cleverly played off the contenders for the Seleucid throne to Jewish advantages (10:1-12:23), finally being treacherously murdered by Trypho, usurper king of Syria in 142 B.C.E. (12:46-48; 13:23-24).

Simon, another brother of Judas, assumed leadership by cleverly promising support to Demetrius, who claimed the Seleucid throne. Simon negotiated release from the obligation to pay tribute. This was the equivalent of political freedom (13:36-40); "and the people began to write in their documents and contracts, 'In the first year of Simon the great high priest and commander and leader of the Jews' " (13:42). The resulting peace is extolled in a psalm of praise for Simon (14:4-15), and he was confirmed as "their leader and high priest forever" (14:41)—a pledge that his children should inherit his rule (cf. 14:48-49). Simon and all of his sons but John Hyrcanus were treacherously murdered by his own son-in-law, who sought the leadership of the Jewish state. The Hasmonean hereditary dynasty, begun with Simon, was continued as John Hyrcanus became high priest and leader in 135 B.C.E. (16:11-24).

Authorship and Date of First Maccabees. The author of 1 Maccabees is unknown but his basic perspective is clear—the author was a Jew, deeply committed to observing the OT laws, ceremonies, and rituals. He disdained those who abandoned Jewish customs for gentile ways (1:41-43) and saw God at work in the deeds of the Maccabees and their followers, delivering his people as he did in OT history (cf. 3:50-64; 4:30-33; 8:41-42; 14:4-15).

The author also is clearly supportive of the newly established dynasty, making it clear that God had chosen to work through their leadership and theirs alone to achieve victory over the gentiles (5:55-62). That the author supported the change from a designated leadership (2:66-68; 9:28-31; 13:1-8) to a hereditary Hasmonean dynasty with the ascension of John Hyrcanus is also clear in the highest praises being heaped on Simon (14:4-15, 41-49) and the way in which John Hyrcanus is described (13:53; 16:2-3, 23-24).

The date of the writing of 1 Maccabees is clearly after the reign of John Hyrcanus (cf. 16:23-24), placing it later than 106 B.C.E., and before the Romans were seen as enemies (8:1-32), placing it clearly before 63 B.C.E. The way in which the reign of John is referred to would suggest the book was composed shortly after his death, perhaps around 100 B.C.E.

See also APOCRYPHAL LITERATURE; MACCABEES; MACCABEES, SECOND.

Bibliography. H. W. Attridge, "Historiography," *Jewish Writings of the Second Temple Period,* ed. M. Stone; W. H. Brownlee, "Maccabees, Books of," *IDB*; J.A. Goldstein, *I Maccabees*; E. Schürer, *The History of the Jewish People in the Age of Jesus Christ*, rev. G. Vermes et al.

—HAROLD S. SONGER

• **Maccabees, Second.** Second Maccabees relates Jewish history from ca. 180 B.C.E. to 161 B.C.E. Much of it parallels material in the early chapters of I MACCABEES. It is not a continuation of that book. Jews have never considered 2 Maccabees part of their CANON, but Roman Catholics include it in the OT. Protestants count it among the APOCRYPHAL LITERATURE.

Importance. The value of 2 Maccabees is that it is the only written account in existence describing the situation in Jerusalem at the time Antiochus IV (175–164 B.C.E.), the Seleucid king of Syria, was forcing Hellenistic culture on the Jews. In addition, it parallels and offers alternative sequences of a number of events in the Maccabean rebellion from its beginning to the victory of Judas over Nicanor (161 B.C.E.).

Second Maccabees is also helpful in understanding portions of the NT. The references to suffering and martyrdom in Heb 11:35-38 are illuminated by 2 Macc 6:10–7:42 (cf. 10:6). The fact that Judas and others ate what grew wild to avoid defilement (5:27) throws light on the diet of John the Baptist (Mark 1:6). The frequent references to heavenly warriors (3:25; 5:2-4; 10:29-31) provide an understanding of the Jewish background for Jesus' statement about the heavenly legions (Matt 26:53) and many of the scenes in Revelation which involve horsemen and warriors.

Content. Second Maccabees begins with two letters (1:1-9; 1:10-2:18), calling upon the Jews in Egypt to celebrate the feast of the dedication of the TEMPLE (Hanukkah) with their Palestinian colleagues. The author next candidly confesses dependence on the five volumes of history written by Jason of Cyrene and indicates that his purpose is to condense them into one volume (2:19-32).

The first episode recounted sets the stage for much of the remainder of the book as the attempt of Heliodorus, a Syrian official, to seize unlawfully the gold and silver deposited in the Temple—some by widows and orphans (3:10)—for safekeeping is thwarted by a heavenly warrior with weapons of gold. Heliodorus only escapes with his life because of the intercession of the HIGH PRIEST, Onias (3:1–4:6). The sanctity of Jerusalem is soon under threat again, as Jason obtains the priesthood from Onias by bribery, and immediately seeks to shift "his countrymen over to the Greek way of life" (4:10). Further deterioration of the Jerusalem situation, as the author viewed it, occurred under Menelaus who outbribed Jason and assumed the high priesthood for himself (4:23-50). In the downward spiral of the misfortunes of the Jerusalem Jews, the lowest point is reached in the next episode when the Seleucid king, Antiochus IV, massacred Jerusalem citizens, entered the temple (defiling it with a gentile presence), took the sacred vessels of gold, and plundered the temple treasures (5:1-27). The king then launched an attack on Judaism, seeking to unify the Jews into his kingdom which primarily followed a Hellenistic style of life. The SABBATH and CIRCUMCISION were forbidden and pagan gods were honored in Jerusalem, resulting in mounting Jewish resistance and eventuating in martyrdoms (6:1-7:42).

But the Jewish fortunes now reversed because "the wrath of the Lord had turned to mercy" (8:5). Judas Maccabeus achieved victory after victory over the gentile forces, defeating Nicanor, Timothy and Bacchides, and others (8:1-9:29). Finally, Judas and his followers were able to enter Jerusalem, purify the sanctuary and re-establish worship in the Temple (10:1-9). Further attempts by the Seleucids to recover their power in Jerusalem were repulsed, and the book closes with the death of the arch-enemy of the Jews, Nicanor (10:10–15:37).

Sources and Perspective. The author of 2 Maccabees indicates that he has abridged the five-volume work of Jason of Cyrene into one volume and that his purpose was ". . . to please those who wish to read, to make it easy for those who are inclined to memorize, and to profit all readers" (2:25). Jason's work has not survived except in this abridgement, and the explanation for the disagreements in the sequences of events where 2 Maccabees parallels 1 Maccabees (1 Macc 1:10–7:50) continues to be debated by scholars, although there is general agreement that 1 Maccabees is the more reliable source. Equally puzzling is the reason for the book's rather abrupt ending with the death of Nicanor (2 Macc 15:37-39).

The perspective of the author is that God is actively at work in the world, both directly through his angels (2:24-26; 5:1-4; 10:29-31; 11:6-13; 15:23) and less directly through his faithful servants (2:17; 12:16), to preserve the sanctity of the Temple (cf. 2:22; 5:15-20; 14:31-36; 15:18, 34) and to maintain his justice in rewarding the righteous (7:23; 8:18; 8:36; 13:44-45) and punishing persons for sins (1:17; 2:34; 4:38; 5:18-20; 6:14-16; 7:37-38; 9:5-29).

Authorship and Date. The author of 2 Maccabees is unknown. The date of the work cannot be fixed precisely, but it is clear that it was written prior to the Roman domination of 63 B.C.E. because the Jews are still in control in Jerusalem (15:37). The first letter to the Jews in Egypt (1:1-9) cites the Seleucid year of 188 which would be 124 B.C.E., the earliest date for the letter. The letter was thus written in the period from 124–63 B.C.E., and scholars disagree as to where the book should be placed in this period.

See also APOCRYPHAL LITERATURE; MACCABEES, FIRST; MACCABEES.

Bibliography. H. W. Attridge, "Historiography," *Jewish Writings of the Second Temple Period,* ed. M. Stone; W. H. Brownlee, "Maccabees, Books of," *IDB*; E. Schürer, *The History of the Jewish People in the Age of Jesus Christ,* rev. G. Vermes, et al.

—HAROLD S. SONGER

• **Maccabees, Third.** *Third Maccabees* is a historical romance set in the reign of Ptolemy IV Philopator of Egypt (221–204 B.C.E.). It has nothing to do with the Maccabean period. This anonymous Hellenistic Jewish narrative is similar in language, style, and emphasis to SECOND MACCABEES and the LETTER OF ARISTEAS; the author was probably an Alexandrian Jew, writing in the early first century B.C.E. The book has canonical standing in Eastern Orthodoxy.

The narrative relates two crises in the relationship between Ptolemy IV Philopator and his Jewish subjects. In both situations, God intervenes miraculously in response to the prayers of the Jews, exemplified in each case by a model prayer placed by the narrator on the lips of a priestly representative.

The first crisis occurs when Ptolemy, returning from his victory over Antiochus the Great at Raphia (217 B.C.E.), visits Jerusalem and decides to enter the inner sanctum of the Temple. This horrifies the Jews, who, unable to dissuade him, appeal to God to prevent the sacrilege. Simon, the high priest, reminds God of previous mighty acts and of God's obligation to hear prayers offered in the temple.

God strikes Ptolemy to the ground, temporarily paralyzed.

This miraculous solution to the first crisis provokes the second, however, as Ptolemy determines to avenge himself on the Jews. He tries to force the Jews to join the cult of Dionysus, but most resist.

Ptolemy issues a decree commanding the arrest and deportation of all Jews in Egyptian territory. The Jews are imprisoned in a stadium in Alexandria, where Ptolemy plans to have them trampled to death by drunken elephants. Each time the execution is scheduled, however, the Jews pray to God for deliverance and God causes Ptolemy to forget to give the fatal order. Finally, it looks as though time has run out for the Jews. The elephants are about to be turned loose upon them. They prostrate themselves before God, led in prayer by the venerable priest Eleazar, whose prayer is constructed much like that of Simon. In response to the prayers, God sends two angels, visible to everyone except the Jews, who turn the elephants back upon the Egyptian army. Ptolemy has a change of heart and issues another decree, ordering that the Jews be set free and returned to their homes.

The narrative concludes with an account of a festival, held at the expense of the king, at which the Jews celebrate their deliverance with banqueting, singing and dancing. The text states that this festival was established as an annual event to commemorate God's act of salvation (6:36). The Jews are given permission to execute all those of their number who had apostasized to escape persecution.

A major purpose of *3 Maccabees* seems to be etiological; it explains the origin of a festival celebrated by Alexandrian Jews. It is not known how much of the account has any historical basis. The stories of God's powerful response to prayer are intended to provide edification and encouragement for the Jewish community. At the same time, the Jews are presented to outsiders as loyal citizens whose worthy beliefs and practices are misrepresented by pagans with base motives.

See also ARISTEAS, LETTER OF; LITERATURE, APOCRYPHAL; MACCABEES, SECOND.

Bibliography. H. Anderson, "3 Maccabees," *The Old Testament Pseudepigrapha,* ed. J. H. Charlesworth.

—SHARYN E. DOWD

• **Maccabees, Fourth.** *Fourth Maccabees* is probably the most recent of the Hellenistic Jewish documents bearing the title "Maccabees"; it should be dated during the first half of the first century C.E. It is found in Codex Sinaiticus and Codex Alexandrinus, but not in the Vulgate. It has not been regarded as canonical by any Christian community, though it is highly regarded in Eastern Orthodoxy. The author is unknown.

Although he apparently used 2 MACCABEES as a source, the author of *4 Maccabees* has produced an entirely different kind of document. Whereas 2 Maccabees is a narrative about the atrocities, martyrdoms, and battles of the Maccabean period, *4 Maccabees* is a philosophical discourse in support of the thesis that "devout reason (εὐσεβὴς λογισμός) is master of the passions" (1:1). In fact, it is thought that the original title may have been "On the Supremacy of Reason." The heroic martyrdoms of Eleazar, the seven brothers, and their mother are illustrations offered in support of the argument.

The discourse demonstrates a strong Stoic influence in its advocacy of the life of reason, but it parts company with Stoicism by asserting the more Jewish view that reason controls the passions, but does not eliminate them; since God created the passions they are not intrinsically evil. The author of *4 Maccabees* argues that since reason chooses a life of wisdom and since the Jewish LAW is the repository of all wisdom, it is only through a life of obedience to the Law that one may attain to the virtues admired by the Greeks. In this way, the writer achieves the dual purpose of hellenistic Jewish apologetics: the defense of the Jewish way of life to gentiles who might criticize it and to Jews who were tempted to abandon it for the attractions of Greek culture.

After a brief account of the divine punishment of Apollonius, a Syrian governor who tried to plunder the treasury of the Jerusalem temple (cf. similar accounts with different villains in 2 Macc 3; *3 Macc* 1:6–2:24), the author proceeds to describe the attempts by Antiochus IV Epiphanes to hellenize the Jews. First the old priest Eleazar, then the seven brothers and their mother, refuse to eat pork or sacrifices made to idols and are horribly tortured and killed. The tortures are described in even more gory detail than that provided by 2 Maccabees and the speeches of the martyrs are even more courageous and defiant. The author devotes considerable space to the mother. Her steadfastness proves his point, because if "even a woman" could endure the sight of her sons being tortured, then surely "we must concede that devout reason is sovereign over the passions" (16:1-2). After the mother's speech, the author closes his discourse with a doxology.

The idea that the suffering of the martyrs atones for the sins of the nation, implied by 2 Macc 7:37-38, is explicit in *4 Macc* 6:29 and 17:21, where the deaths of the martyrs are understood as a ransom (ἀντίψυχον) the concept of expiation (ἱλαστήριον) occurs in 17:22. Whereas 2 Maccabees emphasizes the hope of the bodily RESURRECTION, the author of *4 Maccabees* appeals to the Greek idea of the IMMORTALITY of the soul.

See also APOCRYPHAL LITERATURE; MACCABEES, SECOND; STOICS.

Bibliography. H. Anderson, "4 Maccabees," *The Old Testament Pseudepigrapha,* ed. J. H. Charlesworth.

—SHARYN E. DOWD

• **Macedonia.** [mas'uh-doh"nee-uh] Macedonia was one of the major areas of Paul's mission work. It was a province located in what is now northern Greece and southern Albania (PLATES 26, 27). The Aegean coastal plain on the east of Macedonia gives way to a mountainous interior with deep river valleys before reaching the Adriatic coast on the west. The climate of the interior produces cold winters and hot summers. The region was much valued for timber and precious metals.

The earliest inhabitants were influenced by people from Anatolia (modern Turkey) who brought copper-working skills (ca. 2800 B.C.E.). The first Greek-speaking peoples came to the region between 1900–1600 B.C.E. and settled there and in ACHAIA (Greece) to the south. Perdiccas established the first Macedonian dynasty in the seventh century B.C.E. During the period of the Persian empire, Macedonian timber and silver were in great demand and trade flourished. Philip II rose to leadership in Macedonia by 358 B.C.E. He united the tribes and cities of Macedonia and came to be the ruler of Greece as well. Recent excavations at Vergina have unearthed what must certainly be the tomb of Philip II, yielding a richly decorated shield, a sword, and the remains of a scepter and crown.

The most famous Macedonian, ALEXANDER the Great, was the son of Philip II and his third wife, Olympias. Tutored by Aristotle and schooled in military tactics by his father, Alexander set out on conquests that changed the world. After the half-century of instability which followed Alexander's death (323 B.C.E.), Antigonus II Gonatus (276 B.C.E.) established a dynasty which lasted until Rome took over the area in 168 B.C.E. The Romans divided Macedonia into four republics, breaking up the unity, and it was not until the territory was united again to form a Roman province in 148 B.C.E. that it began to play a significant role once more. From Macedonia, Rome extended her control to Greece, devastating many Greek cities, including Athens and Corinth, and incorporating the whole territory into the province.

In 27 B.C.E. Caesar Augustus separated the territory again into Macedonia and Achaia (names which they bear in the NT). The Roman road, the Via Egnatia, transversed Macedonia from the Adriatic Sea on the west to the Aegean on the east. THESSALONICA (the seat of the Roman administration), PHILIPPI, NEAPOLIS and Nicopolis were all on the eastern part of this well maintained thoroughfare.

Paul was called to Macedonia in a vision at Troas during his second missionary journey (Acts 16:9). He established churches in Philippi, Thessalonica, and BEREA (Acts 16-17). On his third journey he sent helpers to Macedonia while he was in Asia (Acts 19:22) and later traveled through it himself (Acts 20:1-3). Three letters were written to churches in Macedonia—Philippians, 1 and 2 Thessalonians. Macedonian Christians, though persecuted, showed exemplary character (1 Thess 1:2-8; 2 Cor 8:1-5). They took part in Paul's collection for the church in Jerusalem (Rom 15:26) and some of them accompanied Paul to deliver it (Acts 20:4). One Macedonian, Aristarchus, was with Paul on his journey to Rome to stand trial (Acts 27:2).

See also ACHAIA; ALEXANDER; AMPHIPOLIS; BEREA; NEAPOLIS; PAUL; PHILIPPI; THESSALONICA.

Bibliography. J. Keil, "The Greek Provinces," *CAH* 11:555-605; N. G. L. Hammond, *History of Macedonia*; F. W. Walbank, "Macedonia and the Greek Leagues," *CAH* 7:446-81.

—JOE R. BASKIN

• **Machaerus.** *See* HERODIAN FORTRESSES

• **Machir.** [may'kihr] Name of an early tribe in Israel, identified also as the son of MANASSEH in Gen 50:23. A distant relative of Machir was ZELOPHEHAD, the father of four daughters who were granted the right of inheritance because their father died in the wilderness without sons (Num 27:1-11). Machir conquered territory in Transjordan formerly held by Gilead and was allotted the conquered land by Moses (Num 32:39-40). In Judg 5:14, Machir is mentioned along with Ephraim, Benjamin, and Zebulun as a supporter of DEBORAH and Barak in the battle against Sisera. Here, Machir appears to be a locality in western Palestine.

A second Machir appears in 2 Sam 9:4-5 and 17:27. He lived in Lo-debar, where he for a time gave a home to Jonathan's son MEPHIBOSHETH. He later came to David's support in Transjordan when David was fleeing from Absalom.

See also DEBORAH: MANASSEH; ZELOPHEHAD.

—FRED E. YOUNG

• **Machpelah.** [mak-pee'luh] From a Heb. root apparently meaning "double," the proper name Machpelah refers to the location of the burial site purchased by ABRAHAM for SARAH and for his family. The specific reference speaks of either the "cave of Machpelah" (Gen 23:9) or the "field of Machpelah" (Gen 23:17). Whether Machpelah was only a place name or was a personal name (i.e., the cave/field belonging to Machpelah) is unclear. The LXX understands Machpelah as a comon noun "double," probably in the sense of "the double cave."

At the death of Sarah, Abraham, who was then living in HEBRON, purchased from Ephron the Hittite both the field and the cave of Machpelah for 400 shekels of silver (Gen 23:1-20). The passage is lengthy, taking pains to show that Abraham, a sojourner in the land rather than a citizen, purchased this land for his family burial plot. The implication is that this is the only land Abraham owned in Canaan. Also buried at Machpelah were Abraham (Gen 25:9), Isaac and Rebekah (Gen 49:31), Jacob (Gen 49:31-33; 50:12-13) and Leah (Gen 49:81).

Machpelah is located "east of" or "in the vicinity of" MAMRE (Gen 23:17, 19). It is more fully located as "the cave of the field of Machpelah east of Mamre (i.e., Hebron) in the land of Canaan" (Gen 23:19).

The traditional location of Machpelah is the Harem el-Khalil within the modern town of Hebron and somewhat east of the site of the ancient mound of Hebron. The wall around the site was built by Herod, with upper courses added at later times. A church was built in the enclosure in the fifth or sixth century C.E., and the patriarchal tombs were described by travelers in the sixth century. The present cenotaphs come from the Abbasid or Omayyad and Mameluk periods.

—JOEL F. DRINKARD, JR.

• **Madness.** Various forms of mental disorders, especially of the more extreme types. Examples of mental disorders rarely appear in either the OT or the NT. The most notable OT example is SAUL (1 Sam 16:14-16, 23; 18:10; 19:9). His condition is attributed to "an evil spirit from God" and he is said to have "raved within his house" (1 Sam 18:10). The Hebrew term used to describe his condition means "to prophesy" (cf. the prophets of BAAL on Mount Carmel, 1 Kgs 18:29). An older usage of this term refers to an ecstatic or emotional form of prophecy. When Saul joined a band of such prophets after he had been anointed by Samuel, the common folk raised questions about his judgment, if not his sanity ("Is Saul also among the prophets?" 1 Sam 10:11). That God is said to be the source of such a condition is in keeping with the preexilic view that God was the source of everything.

In the NT, the Gerasene demoniac(s) (Mark 5:1-20; Luke 8:26-39; Matt 8:28-34) is described as having an "unclean spirit." The Talmud had four tests for madness: spending the night in a grave, tearing one's clothes, walking around at night, and destroying anything given. This man met all four tests. In contrast to the OT, where such illness was said to be caused by God, it was now attributed to demons.

See also DEMON IN THE NEW TESTAMENT; DEMON IN THE OLD TESTAMENT; DISEASE AND HEALING.

—JOHN H. TULLOCK.

• **Magadan.** *See* MAGDALA/MAGDALENE

• **Magdala/Magdalene.** [mag'duh-luh/mag'duh-leen] Magdala, a town on the western shore of the SEA OF GALILEE between TIBERIAS to the south and CAPERNAUM to the north (PLATE 23), was undoubtedly the home of Mary Magdalene, a disciple of Jesus (Luke 8:2) who was an important witness to Jesus' death, burial (Mark 15:40, 47; 16:1;

Matt 27:56, 61; 28:1; John 19:25; cf. Luke 23:55-56), and resurrection (Luke 24:10; John 20:1, 18; cf. Mark 16:9).

Magdala is not mentioned in the NT apart from the reference in the name of Mary Magdalene, which denotes "woman from Magdala." In some NT manuscripts Magdala occurs as a variant reading for Dalmanutha in Mark 8:10 and for Magadan in Matt 15:39, a parallel text, but these are uncertain, later scribal identifications.

Magdala, probably modern Mejdel, is usually identified with Migdal Nûnyâ (Tower of Salted Fish) of the Babylonian Talmud, Migdal Ṣeb'iyâ (Tower of Dyers) of the Palestinian Talmud, and Tarichaeae (Place of Salted Fish) of Josephus (*BJ* 2.595-637; 3.443-502). Tarichaeae was the place of Josephus' headquarters in the Jewish revolt against Rome which began in 66 C.E. According to Josephus, Tarichaeae had 40,000 people, a fleet of 230 boats and a hippodrome.

Modern excavations at Mejdel have uncovered what are probably first-century C.E. Roman ruins and streets and, perhaps, a very small Jewish synagogue.

Mary Magdalene's prominence as a witness to Jesus' resurrection is reflected in the importance she assumes in Gnostic Christian literature in the second and third centuries C.E. In writings such as the *Gospel of Thomas*, the *Gospel of Philip*, the *Gospel of Mary*, and *Pistis Sophia*, she is represented as a sophisticated theological interpreter of Jesus and often as his favorite disciple.

See also CAPERNAUM; GALILEE, SEA OF; MARY; TIBERIAS.

Bibliography. C. M. Grassi and J. A. Grassi, *Mary Magdalene and the Women in Jesus' Life*.

—DAVID M. SCHOLER

• **Magdalene.** *See* MARY

• **Magi.** [may'jī] According to Herodotus (ca. 450 B.C.E.) magi (the plural of *magus*) were a priestly caste among the sixth-century Medes who specialized in interpreting the significance of human affairs through the observation of celestial phenomena (7.37) and the interpretation of dreams (1.107-108, 120, 128; 7.19). When the Persians conquered the Medes (ca. 550 B.C.E.), the magi apparently adopted the Zoroastrian religion of their conquerors, transforming it to the extent that they became its priests. Cicero (*On Divination* 1.91) indicates that no one was able to assume the throne of Persia without mastering the scientific discipline of the magi. In subsequent centuries the term came to be loosely applied all across the Mediterranean world to those adept in various forms of secret lore and magic. Thus by the first century C.E. it was applied to those of a particular class rather than to those of a particular culture or citizenship.

In the early Greek translations of the Book of Daniel the term is used for those thought to have the power of interpreting dreams and visions (Dan 1:20; 2:2; 4:7; 5:7). The first-century Jewish philosopher PHILO knows of scientific magi but also uses the term for charlatans and magicians (*SpecLeg* 3.18.100-101). Josephus, a first-century Jewish historian, mentions a magus from Cyprus named Atomos who was attached to the court of the Roman proconsul Felix at Caesarea (*Ant* 20.7.2), and the NT mentions Elymas Bar-Jesus, a magus and Jewish false prophet from the city of Paphos on the island of Cyprus who was associated with the Roman proconsul Sergius Paulus (Acts 13:6-12). Such references indicate the significance of such figures in the Greco-Roman world. The NT also mentions Simon, a magus who had "amazed" the nation of Samaria with his magic (Acts 8:9-24). Thus the term had come to refer to those engaged in all manner of astrology, magic, and fortune-telling.

Matthew records the visit of magi from the East (traditionally thought to be Persia, Babylonia, or Arabia) who worshiped the newborn Jesus. The fact that their pilgrimage was prompted by celestial phenomena (i.e., the star, 2:2) suggests that they were astrologers. Upon learning from the chief priests and scribes of the Jewish people that Christ should be born in Bethlehem (according to Mic 5:2), Herod sent the magi to "search diligently" for the child and return to report to him the child's exact location. Having been led by the star to the exact location, the magi worshiped the child and presented gifts of gold, frankenscense, and myrrh. Being warned of Herod's intention to harm the child in a dream, they did not report their discovery to him, but returned home another way.

While the biblical narrative provides no other details, later tradition in the Eastern church has suggested that there were twelve magi. The Western tradition that there were three is probably based on the mention of three gifts (Matt 2:11); to the three have been attributed the names of Caspar, Melchior, and Balthasar. The popular tradition that the three were kings is probably derived from Isa 60:3. Other OT texts which may have influenced the tradition are Num 24:17 and Pss 68:29; 72:10. Since the fourth century C.E. the Festival of Epiphany has celebrated the manifestation of the Christ child to the magi. Matthew's inclusion of the visit of the magi in the narrative of Christ's birth clearly functions to emphasize the adoration of Christ by gentiles and the tribute offered to Christ by adherents of the best of pagan lore and religious perceptivity.

See also ASTROLOGER; ASTROLOGY; STAR OF BETHLEHEM; WISDOM IN THE OLD TESTAMENT.

Bibliography. R. Brown. *The Birth of the Messiah*.

—W. HULITT GLOER

• **Magic and Divination.** The practice of divination attempts to contact supernatural powers to attain answers to questions that usually involve the future and lie beyond human control. Such practice was widely known in the ancient Middle East, especially among the Babylonians, who refined it into a highly technical and respectable discipline. Ezek 21:21 records, "For the king of Babylon stands at the parting of the way, at the head of the two ways to use divination; he shakes the arrows, he consults the teraphim, he looks at the liver."

The early Babylonians and then the Assyrians employed several different methods in the practice of divination. The Babylonians commonly used hepatoscopy, divination by the liver. By virtue of being considered the seat of life, the liver of a sacrificial animal could be carefully observed by specially trained priests to determine the future activities of the gods. For this purpose the priests underwent ceremonial cleansings in preparing to interpret the livers, which were carefully divided into zones, each zone containing its own secrets. Such action was taken before proceeding on any matter of real gravity. In Palestine and in Mesopotamia models of animal livers apparently used as instructional tools in teaching the science of hepatoscopy have been uncovered.

Other methods of divination included augury (foretelling the future by natural signs, especially the flight of birds), hydromancy (divination by mixing liquids; cf. Gen 44:5),

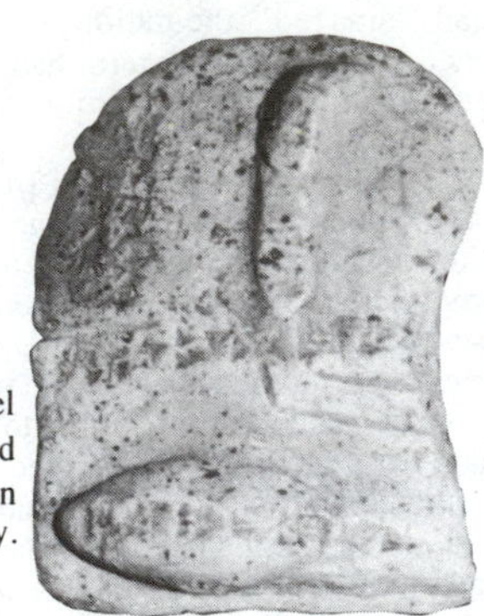

A model of a liver used in liver divination or hepatoscopy.

Courtesy of the Eisenberg Museum of Biblical Archaeology, Southern Baptist Theological Seminary.

casting lots (Jonah 1:7-8), astrology (2 Kgs 21:3-5), necromancy (consulting the dead, 1 Sam 28:7-19), observing the URIM AND THUMMIM (1 Sam 28:6), and by consulting the teraphim (Ezek 21:21).

The use of magic is often recorded in the literature of the ancient Middle East in reference both to gods and human beings. The gods themselves were understood to be superhumans, thereby themselves subject to the higher power of magic. In *Enuma Elish,* the Babylonian creation epic, the god of wisdom, Ea, killed his father Apsu, god of the fresh river waters, after reciting a spell. In the same epic, Marduk, the leader of the pantheon, went into battle against Tiamat, goddess of the chaotic sea, with a talisman of red paste in his mouth. Likewise, Tiamat relied on the recitation of a charm to cast a spell before entering the mortal struggle with Marduk. To demonstrate his supreme position in the godhead Marduk, through the magical power of his word, caused a piece of cloth to vanish and to reappear. In order to assure her reappearance on the earth, Ishtar, the goddess of love and fertility, donned charms before descending into the underworld.

Similar beliefs in magic are evident in ancient Canaanite myths. The supreme Canaanite deity El acted to heal the ill king Keret by working magic. The goddess Anath effects through magical means the restoration to the earth of her dead brother BAAL. She also attacked Baal's murderer, Mot, the god of death, splitting him, winnowing him, burning him, grinding him, and sowing his body in the ground. Such action, doubtless some form of cultic rehearsal, insured the germination in the earth of the apparently dead seed. Paghat, the daughter of the legendary King Daniel, is said to observe the movement of water and of the stars.

The OT often attests to the practice of magic by the Hebrews themselves, reflecting how entrenched it was. SAUL, the first Hebrew king, is said to have "put the mediums and the wizards out of the land" (1 Sam 28:3), but even he later sought out a necromancer (1 Sam 28:7). JEHU responded to the question of Joram, king of Israel, as to whether he came in peace, "What peace can there be so long as the harlotries and the sorceries of your mother JEZEBEL are so many?" (2 Kgs 9:22). Isa 2:6 accuses the house of Jacob of being "full of diviners from the east and of soothsayers like the PHILISTINES." Isa 3:2-3 reflects that the society attaches the same importance to "the diviner," "the skillful magician," and "the expert in charms" as to "the mighty man and the soldier, the judge and the prophet." Consequently, king MANASSEH could make public use of such services (2 Chr 33:6). The people acted in a similar fashion. Jeremiah admonishes his people not to heed "your [false] prophets, your diviners, your dreamers, your soothsayers, or your sorcerers" (27:9; cf. 29:8).

Although varying kinds of divination and magic are reported to have been practiced widely and often in ancient Israel and among her neighbors (Deut 18:9-14; 1 Sam 6:2; Isa 19:3; Ezek 21:21; Dan 2:2), Israel herself was clearly and firmly admonished to have no part in such activities. "You shall not practice augury or witchcraft" (Lev 19:26); "Do not turn to mediums or wizards; do not seek them out to be defiled by them" (Lev 19:31); "If a person turns to mediums and wizards playing the harlot after them, I will set my face against that person and cut him off from among his people" (Lev 20:6); "A man or a woman who is a medium or a wizard shall be put to death; they shall be stoned with stones, their blood shall be upon them"(Lev 20:27); "When you come into the land which the Lord your God gives you, you shall not learn to follow the abominable practices of those nations. There shall not be found among you any one who burns his son or his daughter as an offering, any one who practices divination, a soothsayer, or an augur, or a sorcerer, or a charmer, or a medium, or a wizard, or a necromancer. For whoever does these things is an abomination to the Lord; and because of these abominable practices the Lord your God is driving them out before you. You shall be blameless before the Lord your God. For these nations, which you are about to dispossess, give heed to soothsayers and to diviners; but as for you, the Lord your God has not allowed you so to do" (Deut 18:9-14); "You shall no more see delusive visions nor practice divination" (Ezek 13:23).

See also MAGICIANS.

Bibliography. J. B. Pritchard, ed., *ANET*.

—KAREN RANDOLPH JOINES

• **Magical Papyri.** [puh-pi'ri] The magical papyri are a collection of diverse ancient Greek, Demotic, Egyptian, and Coptic magical texts written from the third through the sixth centuries C.E., nearly all of which have been preserved by virtue of the dry climate of Egypt. Eight of the more extensive magical papyri appear to be books of magical recipes once owned by practicing magicians, and fragments of many other such books have also survived. A relatively small number of papyri (about three dozen) appear to have been prepared for a particular person and for a specific purpose (much like modern prescriptions). Magical papyri and magical books of various kinds were doubtless widely distributed throughout the ancient Mediterranean world (cf. Acts 19:19), but nearly all of them have perished. The extant magical papyri therefore have a largely Greco-Egyptian character. Yet there are other important sources for Greco-Roman magic which have been preserved on more durable materials. These include magical gems and amulets (of which about 5,000 examples have survived) as well as lead curse tablets (the so-called *defixiones tabellae*). Since these sources, together with scattered references in ancient Greek and Latin literature, reveal many points of contact with the magical papyri, it is probable that the papyri represent a Greco-Egyptian variation of an international and eclectic form of magic. The conservative nature of the rituals, formulas, prayers and hymns preserved in the papyri suggest that Greco-Egyptian magic had taken on a fairly stable form by the first century C.E. Palaeographical evidence suggests that several of the papyri were in fact written as early as the first century C.E.

Most of the texts included in the corpus of magical papyri contain detailed instructions for the performance of rituals involving the recitation of carefully prescribed formulas, prayers, and hymns, and the preparation of various concoctions, sacrifices and paraphernalia, all for achieving very particular goals within a private setting. The distinguishing features of all magical papyri is that they consist of religious texts containing instructions for the performance of private instrumental rituals. The procedures of spells (the Greek term is πϱάξεις, "actions") are designed to accomplish a variety of specific goals. There are five major categories of spells which are found in the magical papyri: (1) erotic magic, (2) revelatory magic, (3) protective and apotropaic magic (the usual function of magical gems and amulets), (4) aggressive and malevolent magic, and (5) general purpose procedures, such as those for procuring the services of an assistant deity (πάϱεδϱος δαίμων). These magical procedures generally consist of three major sections: (1) preliminary preparations (often including various types of purification, perhaps including abstention from sexual intercourse); (2) invocation (ἐπίκλησις); and (3) sacrificial ritual (πϱᾶξις). Among the more striking and pervasive features of the magical papyri are the frequent use of *voces magicae*, i.e., lengthy sequences of vowels and consonants with no discernible meaning (e.g., the frequently occuring palindrome ἀβλαναθάναλβα), and the elaborate use of divine names as part of invocation rituals. Many of these were borrowed from Judaism, including Iao (the divine name which occurs most frequently), Sabaoth, Adonai, and Eloe or Eloai.

See also MAGIC AND DIVINATION.

Bibliography. H. D. Betz, ed., *The Greek Magical Papyri in Translation Including the Demotic Spells*; G. Luck, *Arcana Mundi: Magic and the Occult in the Greek and Roman Worlds*; A. D. Nock, "Greek Magical Papyri," *Essays on Religion and the Ancient World*, ed. Z. Stewart; M. Smith, "Relations between Magical Papyri and Magical Gems," *Papyrologica Bruxellensia* 18 (1979): 129-36.

—DAVID E. AUNE

• **Magicians.** People who used varying means to practice magic are often mentioned in literature from the ancient Middle East. Such practice was also widespread in the culture of the ancient Hebrews as is seen in the historical books of the OT. This explains why OT law repeatedly prohibited the practice and why the prophets waged such a zealous struggle against it.

It was the Canaanites and Philistines inside the borders of Palestine as well as the Babylonians and Egyptians without who resorted to the use of numerous forms of magic and divination. Laban practiced divination (Gen 30:27). Balak the Moabite hired the Mesopotamian magician BALAAM to curse Moses' group of Hebrews (Num 22–24). The Philistine magicians requested guidance as to how to treat the troublesome Ark of the Covenant (1 Sam 6:2). Isaiah referred to "diviners from the east" and "soothsayers like the Philistines" (2:6).

Any and all forms of magic and divination are forbidden by OT law and are punishable by death. "You shall not permit a sorceress to live" (Exod 22:18); "You shall not practice augury or witchcraft" (Lev 19:26); "Do not turn to mediums or wizards" (Lev 19:31); "If a person turns to mediums and wizards, playing the harlot after them, I will set my face against that person" (Lev 20:6); "A man or a woman who is a medium or a wizard shall be put to death; they shall be stoned with stones, their blood shall be upon them" (Lev 20:27). Such magicians and sorcerers are placed in the same category as those offering human sacrifice (Deut 18:10-11; cf. 2 Kgs 17:17).

Such resorting to magic is in sharp contrast to inspired prophecy. Following the adamant prescription against any form of magic in Deut 18:9-14, and in contrast to it, is the promise of the Lord to raise up a prophet. Prophetic inspiration, not magic and divination, provides insight into the will of the Lord; therefore, magicians are like false prophets (Ezek 13:17-19). Israel's false prophets see false visions and divine lies, saying, " 'Thus says the Lord' when the Lord has not spoken" (Ezek 22:18). Micah puts the diviners and false prophets in the same group (3:7, 11). The Lord "frustrates the omens of liars, and makes fools of diviners" (Isa 44:25). The false prophets, says the Lord, "are prophesying lies in my name. . . . They are prophesying to you a lying vision, worthless divination, and the deceit of their own minds" (Jer 14:14). "So do not listen to your prophets, your diviners, your dreamers, your soothsayers, or your sorcerers" (Jer 27:9). Ezekiel speaks of "flattering divination" (12:24).

The NT takes the same view. PAUL called the magician Bar-Jesus "you enemy of all righteousness, full of all deceit and villainy" (Acts 13:10); he compares sorcery to immorality, licentiousness, and idolatry (Gal 5:19-21). At PHILIPPI Paul met a slave girl "who had a spirit of divination and brought her owners much gain by soothsaying" (Acts 16:16). Considering her possessed, Paul ordered the spirit to leave her, whereupon she ceased to divine and her owners fell into consternation.

See also MAGI; MAGIC AND DIVINATION; SIMON MAGUS.

—KAREN RANDOLPH JOINES

• **Magnificat.** [mag-nif'uh-kat] The hymn of praise that appears in Luke 1:46-55 traditionally has been called the Magnificat after the initial word of the first line of the Latin translation: *Magnificat anima mea Dominum* ("My soul magnifies the Lord"). This is the best known of several psalms that are found in the first and second chaps. of Luke, all of which are related by virtue of their hymnic structure: the BENEDICTUS (1:67-79); the Song of the Angels (2:13-14); and the NUNC DIMITTIS (2:18-32). The format of the hymn is structured around a series of couplets that are gathered into four separate sections: introduction (vv. 46b-47); first strophe (vv. 48-50); second strophe (vv. 51-53); conclusion (vv. 54-55). Although the Song of HANNAH in 1 Sam 2:1-10 serves as a model upon which the Magnificat is constructed, numerous OT allusions occur throughout the verses.

The hymn is ascribed by the overwhelming majority of biblical manuscripts to the mother of Jesus, MARY, but three Old Latin texts and several patristic authors (Irenaeus, Origin, and Niceta of Remesiana) attribute the words to the person of ELIZABETH. There are several arguments in support of Elizabeth as the speaker. The circumstances of Elizabeth are much closer to those of Hannah than are the circumstances of Mary. So too, it is quite possible that the hymn may be the product of a circle of disciples that gathered around JOHN THE BAPTIST. While the original Lucan text simply may have omitted the name of the speaker, the consensus of scholarship is that the passage should be associated with the figure of Mary.

The Magnificat is a hymn of praise and thanksgiving in honor of the salvific acts of God. It focuses upon the theme of divine justice—the low are exalted, the mighty are felled, the Messiah is the agent of this supreme reversal of fortunes. The first section of the song describes the mercy that the Lord distributes to the impoverished of society; the second section praises the divine justice that God exacts upon the mighty on behalf of the lowly. In each instance, the covenant of faithfulness between God and the elect of God is demonstrated, both with respect to the individual (Mary) and with respect to society (Israel).

Scholars debate the semitic origins of the hymn, though it bears the marks of Hebrew meter and incorporates numerous idioms that are drawn from the OT. The work is most likely the product of Jewish-Christian origins, and probably was received into the Gospel of Luke from an earlier tradition. It reveals an in-depth understanding of the messianic hope that is found in OT prophecy, yet displays the intense self-examination of the early church. The Lucan emphasis upon a renewed and living covenant between God and the new Israel is emphasized in the figure of Mary, who represents the rise to exaltation from humble beginnings. This rise is couched partly in militaristic language, which is reminiscent of the eschatological and nationalistic faith of the Maccabees (vv. 51-52). Its culmination, however, occurs in the figure of Jesus, who is the present fulfillment of God's covenant with Abraham and the key to salvation both for Jews and for gentiles.

See also ELIZABETH; HANNAH; HYMN; HYMNS/CREEDS; JOHN THE BAPTIST; MARY; MUSIC/MUSICAL INSTRUMENTS.

Bibliography. S. Benko, "The Magnificat: A History of the Controversy," *JBL* 86/3 (Sep 1967): 263-75; R. E. Brown, *The Birth of the Messiah: A Commentary on the Infancy Narratives in Matthew and Luke*; J. A. Fitzmyer, *The Gospel According to Luke, I-IX*.

—CLAYTON N. JEFFORD

• **Mahanaim.** [may'huh-nay″im] A place name from the root *ḥnh,* meaning to encamp against, settle down for the night, or encamp for the purpose of protecting. It is found in a number of cognate languages and occurs, in various forms, over 140 times in the OT. The verb is found mostly in the simple form.

Mahanaim is a dual form and means "two camps" or "twin encampment." One early reference to Mahanaim is in Gen 32:1-2 in which JACOB, after leaving LABAN at Mizpah, is described as having encountered the divine Lord. He called the site Mahanaim, the two armies (PLATE 11). It was located within the territory of GAD (Jos 13:24-26; 21:38). At Mahanaim ABNER made ISHBOSHETH king over Israel; and from Mahanaim, he marched to fight with the soldiers of JOAB (2 Sam 2:8-13). DAVID included Mahanaim in his travels (2 Sam 17:24-29; 19:32), and SOLOMON appointed one of his officials to serve in Mahanaim (1 Kgs 4:14).

See also ISHBOSHETH.

—FRED E. YOUNG

• **Maiden.** *See* VIRGIN

• **Malachi.** [mal'uh-k*i*] The name traditionally given to the prophet responsible for the BOOK OF MALACHI. In all likelihood, the prophetic book is anonymous. No other occurrence of this term appears, and nothing is known of the author of the Book of Malachi other than what is found in the book itself.

See also MALACHI, BOOK OF.

—WALTER HARRELSON

• OUTLINE OF MALACHI •

The Book of Malachi

I. God's Love for Israel Contrasted to Israel's Faithlessness to God (1:2-5)
II. Disputation on Corrupt Worship and Imperfect Sacrifices (1:6-14)
III. Failure of Priests to Teach the Law Faithfully (2:1-9)
IV. Disputation on Divorce and Marriage to Foreign Wives (2:10-16)
V. Disputation on God's Justice (2:17)
VI. The Messenger of the Covenant (3:1-5)
VII. Disputation on Corrupt Worship and Withholding Tithes (3:6-12)
VIII. Rebuke Against Those Who Question God's Faithfulness and Blessing on Those Who Fear God (3:13–4:3)
IX. Concluding Commandment (4:4) and Promise (4:5-6)

• **Malachi, Book of.** The Book of Malachi closes the collection of prophetic literature in the Hebrew scriptures and is the last book of the Christian OT. The word *malachi* means "my messenger" and is probably not a proper name, designating instead the role played by the book's prophetic spokesman as God's advocate. The term is similarly used in Mal 2:7 and 3:1, but probably not of the same person. The reference in 2:7 is to the responsibility of priests to be teachers of God's law and their failure to meet that responsibility. The "messenger" of 3:1 plays a role as spokesman of final judgment. This future role distinguishes him from the author of the book. Even if, as some argue, Malachi is a proper name we know nothing further about the prophet than what we learn from the book itself, which is that he is God's advocate in a disputation with the priests and people of the postexilic community during difficult times.

The setting of the book is the first half of the fifth century B.C.E., between the restoration of the Temple and its cultus and the cultic and social reforms of EZRA and NEHEMIAH. The expectations of HAGGAI and ZECHARIAH for an ideal future had not been realized; instead the newly restored cultus was already being abused. The situation described, cultic abuses and lowering of social standards, fits the period just before the reforms of Ezra and Nehemiah.

The form of the book is different from all other prophetic books. It is a series of discourses or disputations presented in a series of rhetorical questions and answers. The prophet as God's advocate states a principle that incites objections from the priests or people. The prophet then reaffirms the original principle and adds words of judgment. This rhetorical discourse form derives either from the procedures in the law courts or from the teaching methods of Israel's wisdom tradition.

Malachi began with a contrast between God's love for ISRAEL, demonstrated by the choice of JACOB and rejection of ESAU, and Israel's faithlessness to God (1:2-5). The author then illustrated Israel's ingratitude by referring in succession to the offering of unacceptable animals for sacrifice, animals they would not dare present to the governor (1:6-14); to the failure of the priests to be faithful teachers (2:1-9); to divorce and marriage with foreign wives (2:10-16); to the people's questioning of God's justice (2:17). Next is announced the coming of God's messenger of judgment to judge and purify the faithless priests and people (3:1-5). The widespread withholding of tithes is condemned, but blessings are promised if the people met their obligations to God (3:6-12). Some of the people still objected that nothing was gained by serving God (3:13-15). Others, however, in response to the prophet's charges, declared their faith in God and were recorded as having done so (3:16-18). Judgment was then pronounced on the arrogant objectors and blessing on those who responded in obedience (4:1-3). The book ends with a commandment to keep the law and a final promise of the return of ELIJAH as God's messenger for the last days to prepare Israel to meet God on the day of final judgment (4:4-6). This commandment and this promise are considered by many to be editorial appendices to Malachi added as conclusions to the entire prophetic collection. There is no compelling reason to regard them as editorial additions. As appropriate conclusions to Malachi they are also appropriate as the final words of the OT prophetic literature.

Bibliography. E. Achtemeier, *Nahum-Malachi*; P. R. Ackroyd, *Exile and Restoration*; R. Mason, *The Books of Haggai, Zechariah and Malachi.*

—DAVID A. SMITH

• **Mamre.** [mam'ree] Mamre was an Amorite leader who fought with Abraham against Chedolaomer and the four eastern kings (Gen 14:18-24). He is said to have had two brothers, Eshcol and Aner (Gen 14:13, 24).

Mamre is also a place name, the site where Abraham built an altar (Gen 13:18) and then lived when he came into southern Canaan (PLATE 11). Mamre is noted for its trees, translated as oaks or terebinths (Gen 13:18; 18:1). The place Mamre is named for the Amorite leader, apparently because the area belonged to him (Gen 14:13). It is also said to be located near HEBRON (Gen 13:18). Mamre is also located near MACHPELAH, the burial grounds Abraham purchased at Sarah's death to become the family burial plot (Gen 23:17, 19). The clearest biblical location, and one which shows the nearness of the various places may be found in Gen 23:19 which speaks of the burial cave Machpelah as "in the cave in the field of Machpelah near Mamre (which is at Hebron) in the land of Canaan."

The site of Mamre is usually identified with Ramat el-Khalil less than two mi. north of Hebron (PLATE 42). Josephus mentions at Mamre a terebinth which he says had existed since creation. It was under this tree that Abraham entertained the angels (Gen 18). Herod built enclosure walls around the traditional site of Mamre and Hadrian completed the walls. A Christian basilica was built there by Constantine's mother-in-law.

—JOEL F. DRINKARD, JR.

• **Man.** *See* HUMAN BEING

• **Man of God.** *See* PROPHET

• **Man of Lawlessness.** The man of lawlessness is a specific individual designated by 2 Thess 2:3-11 as the son of perdition who must appear at the outbreak of apostasy prior to the PAROUSIA of Christ. Whereas the heavenly Christ is portrayed as humbling himself to take on human form (Phil 2:7-9), the earthly lawless one is portrayed as attempting to promote himself to the place and rank of God. According to 2 Thess 2:3,5, the second coming of Christ has not taken place because the man of lawlessness has been prevented by a restraining agency (impersonal in v. 6, but personal in v. 7). Major interpretations as to the restrainer's identity are: (1) the rule of law represented by the Roman empire and the emperor; (2) SATAN; (3) a special agent of God or Satan; and (4) a spirit, force, or person known to the first-century readers but unknown to contemporary readers. The author's message is that both the lawless one and the power that restrains him are the instruments of God, who has already secretly released the force of lawlessness to be made manifest in due time. The eventual appearance of the lawless one will lead to his confrontation with the Lord Jesus, who will extinguish him "with the breath of his mouth." Some scholars (e.g., Dibelius) detect in this phrase a primitive conception of the magical power of the breath, a theme expressed in a passage in Lucian (*The Liar,* 12) where the Babylonian magician gathered together all the snakes from an estate and blew upon them, "and straightway every one of them was burnt up by the breathing." Other scholars believe the author is alluding to Isa 11:4 and 2 Esdr 13:1-11.

The appointed role of the lawless one is that of perpetuating the delusion of those in the great rebellion ("the apostasy") against righteousness. His works of deception will be attended by powerful signs and wonders. The motif of a lawless one clearly began within Jewish literature before the Christian era. The phrase "the apostasy" (or "the religious revolt") was well-known to the early Christians. It goes back at least to the time of Antiochus IV, who ruled from 175 until 164 B.C.E. (1 Macc 1:10). Antiochus, who tried to force Hellenism upon the Jews, became in the apocalyptic tradition a type-figure of self-deification and grandiose revolt against God and divine law. The lawless one became in APOCALYPTIC LITERATURE a kind of earthly incarnation of Satan, whereas in 2 Thessalonians he is an evil parallel to the incarnation of God in Christ. If Christ is destined to be exalted, the lawless one is doomed to destruction.

Paul and his disciples spoke of believers wrestling not against flesh and blood, but against principalities, powers, world rulers of darkness, and the spiritual hosts of wickedness in the heavenly places (Eph 6:12; Rom 8:22, 38-39).

The term ANTICHRIST does not appear in Paul's writings. There is thematic kinship between the concept of the antichrist and the lawless one. Some scholars connect the lawless one with Belial/Beliar, which rabbinic tradition interpreted as "outside the yoke of the law." In Qumran literature and 2 Cor 6:15, however, Belial/Beliar is a synonym of Satan, rather than a human mortal in whom Satan is incarnate.

See also ANTICHRIST; APOCALYPTIC LITERATURE; SATAN IN THE NEW TESTAMENT; THESSALONIANS, LETTERS TO THE.

Bibliography. J. E. Frame, *The Epistles of St. Paul to the Thessalonians, ICC.*

—JOE E. BARNHART

• **Manasseh.** [muh-nas'uh] One of the twelve TRIBES of Israel, and the name of at least four different men in the OT.

1. The older son of JOSEPH, born in EGYPT (Gen 41:51), was named Manasseh. According to the priestly genealogy of Joseph (Num 26:28-37), Manasseh fathered MACHIR, who in turn fathered GILEAD.

2. The tribe descended from Manasseh was destined to be overshadowed by the tribe of EPHRAIM, as the story of Jacob's blessing of Joseph's two sons showed (Gen 48). Similarly, the blessing of MOSES bestowed upon the Joseph tribes flocks ten times larger for Ephraim than for Manasseh (Deut 33:17). The tribe numbered 32,200 in the first census list (Num 1:34-35), increasing to 52,700 in the second (Num 26:34). As Israel approached Canaan, the daughters of Zelophehad, descendants of Manasseh, asked Moses for an inheritance of their own, which they received. This incident provides the basis for a law in ancient

Israel that allowed a man's daughters to inherit his property if he had no sons (Num 27:1-11). In Num 36:1-12, however, the daughters of Zelophehad were required to marry men from Manasseh, so that land belonging to the tribe of Manasseh would not be lost to that tribe through marriage.

The tribal allocation for Manasseh is complicated. In what may be early traditions, Machir inherited land in Transjordan north of the land of Gilead (Num 32:39-40, although the region is itself called Gilead) and Joseph inherited the hill country of Ephraim, which turned out to be too small, requiring the tribe to expand northward (Josh 17:14-18). The story of the altar built by the tribes of Transjordan (Josh 22) suggests more differentiation between Machir and Manasseh than the story now reflects. These traditions have been reworked and superseded by another tradition, which views Machir as the son of Manasseh and attributes the land of Machir to Manasseh. The Transjordanian half of Manasseh participated with Gilead and REUBEN in the crossing of the Jordan (Josh 4:12) and in the battles with the Canaanites as Moses had commanded (Josh 12:6) (PLATE 11).

3. Manasseh the king (reigned 697 [687?] to 642 B.C.E.) was twelve years old when he ascended to the throne, and his sinful monarchy necessitated God's punishing Judah (2 Kgs 21:11-16; cf. Jer 15:4). Not even the reforms instigated by his grandson Josiah (reigned 640–609) could atone for the state-sponsored worship of Assyrian gods and human sacrifice practiced by Manasseh. The Chronicler speaks of Manasseh's exile and subsequent repentance, return to Jerusalem and reforms (2 Chr 33:11-16). Scholars find a meeting between Manasseh and his Assyrian overlord quite possible, whether in Babylon must remain open, but point out that neither 2 Kings nor Jeremiah reports any conversion of Manasseh.

4. Ezra 10:30, 33 records the divorces of two different men named Manasseh from their non-Judean wives. Also, Judg 18:30 mentions a priest who officiated at the shrine in Dan with its golden calf. Indications in the Hebrew text, however, suggest that the priest's grandfather was really Moses, not Manasseh, and an editor had changed the reference, probably to remove any possible stigma from the lawgiver.

See also MACHIR; TRANSJORDAN; TRIBES.

Bibliography. E. Danelius, "The Boundary of Ephraim and Manasseh in the Western Plain," *PEQ* 89 (Jan 1957): 55-67; 90 (Jan 1958): 32-43; 90 (July 1958): 122-44; E. L. Ehrlich, "Der Aufenthalt des Königs Manasse in Babylon," *TLZ* 21 (July 1965): 281-86; A. Memaire, "Galaad et Makir: Remarques sur la tribu de Manassé à l'est du Jourdain," *VT* 31 (Jan 1981): 39-61.

—PAUL L. REDDITT

• **Manasseh, Prayer of.** No one knows who wrote the short, penitential Prayer of Manasseh, nor can much more be said about when it was written than that it appeared after the work of the Chronicler (ca. 300 B.C.E.). That date seems certain because it supplies the text for the prayer of entreaty which, according to that writer, the wicked Judean king MANASSEH (697–643 B.C.E.) offered to God while he was a captive of the Assyrians in Babylon. The king's prayer and even his captivity were unknown to the writer of the earlier account of Manasseh's reign (2 Kgs 21:1-18), who found nothing of redeeming merit in this king's life and in fact attributed the downfall of Judah to his sins (2 Kgs 24:3-4). In 2 Chr 33:12-13, however, Manasseh's pious prayer was sufficient to restore him to God's favor and subsequently to his throne in Jerusalem; the powerful prayer itself was preserved in the "Chronicles of the Seers" (2 Chr 33:19). That document is lost, but a later writer filled in the gap by offering this fifteen-verse text.

The structure of the Prayer of Manasseh follows the timeless pattern of penitential prayer: an invocation of the God of the PATRIARCHS (v. 1) is followed by an ascription of praise to God, the creator and the forgiver of sinners (vv. 2-8). Then come confession of sin (vv. 9-12), entreaty for forgiveness (v. 13a, b), and assurance of pardon and doxology (vv. 13c-15).

The prayer shares the ideas of postexilic Judaism in its reference to the sinlessness of the patriarchs ABRAHAM, ISAAC and JACOB (v. 8); and in its images of contrition ("I am weighted down with many an iron fetter," v. 10; "I am unworthy to look up and see the height of heaven," v. 9; "do not condemn me to the depths of the earth," v. 13) which are reminiscent of the fate of the fallen angels in 1 ENOCH. Furthermore, it shows marks of kinship with such other second to first century B.C.E. apocryphal texts as the PRAYER OF AZARIAH and the *Song of the Three Young Men,* Judith 9:2-14, and TOBIT 3:2-6, 11-15. The Prayer was apparently unknown to the fourth century C.E. translator of the Latin Bible (Vulgate), Jerome, and it is only weakly attested in the tradition of the LXX. Among the earliest LXX manuscripts it is found only in the fifth century C.E. Codex Alexandrinus. Yet it achieved canonical status in eastern Christianity, and continued to be treasured in the west as a model of spiritual discipline. The KJV translators and most other English Bibles placed the Prayer in the Apocrypha, just before 1 Maccabees; however, in spite of its whitewash of the wicked king Manasseh, it was esteemed enough by the Calvinistic translators of the Geneva Bible to be placed among the canonical books between 2 Chronicles and Ezra—and then labelled "apocryphe"! In this version it was known to Shakespeare, John Bunyan, and the English and American Puritans, some of whom loved the quiet beauty and sincerity of this psalm.

See also APOCRYPHAL LITERATURE; MANASSEH.

—W. SIBLEY TOWNER

• **Mandaeans/Mandaeism.** [man-dee'uhns/man-dee'iz-uhm] The Mandaeans are a Gnostic sect which has survived since the early Christian era in Iran and Iraq. Scholars debate the date and circumstances of origin. Between 1900 and 1950 some scholars (R. Reitzenstein and R. Bultmann) based their arguments for pre-Christian GNOSTICISM on evidence of Mandaeans, but others (esp. British) just as strongly dismissed Mandaean evidence because of the lateness of the known sources. Many of the latter argued for Babylonian origins in the third century C.E. or later. Since 1950, translation of further Mandaean sources by M. S. Drower, K. Rudolph, and R. Macuch has shifted the weight of scholarship toward a Palestinian origin as early as the first century C.E. or before. The most important evidence for this theory comes from the *Haran Gawaita,* translated by Drower and published in 1953. After a prologue this work reported that "Haran Gawaita receiveth him and that city in which there were Nasoraeans, because there was no road for the Jewish rulers. Over them was King Ardban. And sixty thousand Nasoraeans abandoned the Sign of the Seven and entered the Median hills, a place where we were free from domination by all other races." Crucial here is the reference to King Ardban (Artabanus). If Persian king Artabanus IV is meant, the exodus from Palestine occurred ca. 80-81 C.E.; if Artabanus V, ca. 213–224. Since the earliest Mandaean manuscript dates from the sixteenth century, arguments for an early date based on colophons and scripts are somewhat shaky.

Mandaean ideas are, if anything, more difficult to explicate than their history. E. Yamauchi proposed that the original Palestinian "Nasoraeans" (1) were non-Jews superficially acquainted with the OT; (2) were antagonistic to Jews; (3) spoke an Aramaic dialect and were somewhat familiar with Nabataean script; (4) probably dwelt in Transjordan and worshipped the god of the Hauran range east of Galilee; and (5) may or may not have known JOHN THE BAPTIST, whom the Mandaeans honor, but definitely had no firsthand knowledge of Christ or Christianity. Retaliatory attacks of Jews on gentiles in the area east of Galilee on the eve of the war with Rome (66 C.E.) forced them to flee to ANTIOCH. Around 100 C.E. they accepted the teachings of Menander, the Gnostic leader, about achieving immortality through BAPTISM. Subsequently they moved eastward to Haran and then to Adiabene (the "Median Hills" referred to in the *Haran Gawaita*). As Christian influence grew in this area, they migrated southwards to the marshes of Mesopotamia, where they converted an indigenous Aramaean population. Several thousands still live today in this part of Iran and Iraq.

Like most Gnostic systems, Mandaeism is highly syncretistic. It is in many respects similar to Manichaeism, with which it evidently crossed paths, but it has absorbed characteristics from other cults and cultures which give it special features. Marriage, rejected by many Gnostic sects, for instance, is virtually mandated: "If a man has no wife, there will be no Paradise for him hereafter and no Paradise on earth," Mandaean priests insist. Similarly, baptism, though somewhat like the Christian rite, is not only the symbol of life but life itself and is administered several different ways and repeated. Understandably, therefore, debate about Mandaeism will continue.

See also MANI/MANICHEISM.

Bibliography. E. S. Drower, *The Mandaeans of Iraq and Iran: Their Cults, Customs, Magic Legends, and Folklore*; E. M. Yamauchi, *Gnostic Ethics and Mandaean Origins, Pre-Christian Gnosticism,* and "The Present Status of Mandaean Studies," *JNES* 25 (1966): 88-96.

—E. GLENN HINSON

• **Mandrake.** Mandrakes (*Mandragora officinarum*) are stemless perennial plants with large rosetted leaves, found in uncultivated fields throughout the eastern Mediterranean region. The root is fleshy and usually forked, making the whole plant look like a human body. Accordingly, the mandrake was used for magical purposes, especially to procure fertility. A milder relative of the deadly nightshade, the mandrake was also used for both its narcotic and its purgative effects.

Mandrakes appear twice in the Bible, Gen 30:14-16 and Cant 7:13. In the former the matriarchs vie for JACOB's approval (by overcoming their infertility). LEAH's son REUBEN has mandrakes, which Leah trades to RACHEL for a night with Jacob. The story concerns magical means for enriching the family. In the latter passage the scent of the plant (which is malodorous to western people) is primary, though the fertility motif is certainly not absent.

See also JACOB; LEAH; PLANTS OF THE BIBLE; RACHEL; REUBEN.

Bibliography. M. Zohary, *Plants of the Bible*.

—LOREN D. CROW

• **Manger.** A manger, crib, or stall, as the Heb. and Gk. terms are variously translated (2 Chr 32:28 [LXX]; Job 6:5; 39:9; Prov 14:4; Isa 1:3; Hab 3:17; Luke 2:7, 12, 16; 13:15) is an animal feeding trough. Troughs were frequently hollowed from limestone and were approximately three feet long, adequate in size for placement of an infant.

The Lucan account of the birth of Jesus indicates that it took place in an area where animals were kept and that the infant was placed in a manger "because there was no place for them in the inn" (2:7). Although no location is specified in Luke, tradition going back to the second century C.E. locates the place of Jesus' birth in a cave. The present Church of the Nativity in BETHLEHEM evolved from a basilica which the Emperor Constantine erected over a cave believed to be the place of Jesus' birth.

—JOHN R. DRAYER

• **Mani/Manichaeism.** [mah'nee/man"uh-kee-iz'uhm] Mani was the founder of a dualist sect which takes its name from him. Born 14 April 216 C.E. in Babylonia of wealthy and influential parents, Patik and Miriam, he developed a keen interest in the religion of "those who practice ablutions," possibly the MANDAEANS, who would probably have gained a considerable following in the area by this time. At age twelve, Mani had his first revelation in which he learned he was the twin of "the Living Paraclete." On the basis of this revelation he developed his whole set of ideas and renounced the baptist community he belonged to up to this time.

Mani began his mission ca. 240. Appointed an apostle by an angel, he proceeded to India, where he came under Buddhist influence. From there he went to Persia, Babylonia, Maisan, and Khuzistan. In Khuzistan he experienced anew his missionary vocation. Going from there to Babylonia proper, Media, and Persia, he established contact with Shapur the Great (241–272), becoming a part of his royal retinue, and accompanied him in his wars against Rome. He enlisted Shapur's brothers, Mirsah and Peroz, as patrons. With their support Mani and Manichaeism seem to have become the king's favorite, but Zoroastrianism, the "fire cult," had a strong proponent at court in the person of Karter, under whose leadership Zoroastrianism became the official religion of Persia. Thereafter the state wreaked havoc on Manichaeans, Christians, Buddhists, and adherents of other religions.

Under Shapur I, however, Mani enjoyed royal support for his mission efforts in Ctesiphon, the capital, Egypt, Parthia, and Abzakhya, a province east of the Tigris. Shapur's son, Hormizd I (273–274), accorded Mani similar respect and gave the same encouragement to his mission, but he reigned only a year. Bahram I (274–277), a second son, however, did not. He vetoed Mani's evangelistic efforts then underway at Hormizd-Ardashir in the Province of Susiana. Mani was obliged to turn back to Ctesiphon, where religiopolitical interests combined to effect his downfall at court. Zoroastrians accused him of teaching contrary to their law, an offense punishable by death. On 19 January 276 Bahram ordered him fettered and imprisoned. Weakened by harsh treatment, he died on 14 February. Followers buried his mutilated corpse in Ctesiphon.

Mani's teachings combined elements of several cultures and religions. According to a polemical source, in his mission work Mani dressed in the garb of Mithra, but he signed his letters, "Mani, Apostle of Jesus Christ." He also claimed Buddha and Zoroaster as his predecessors.

At its heart Manichaeism was profoundly dualistic.

There are two eternal principles: God or light; matter or darkness. Originally separated from one another, these two have become mixed up with one another as a result of a kind of cosmic fall. If redemption is to occur eventually, the world must pass through three epochs: the stage when light and darkness were separated, that when they have become blended into one another, and that when the blended elements will have again been separated. For the individual redemption requires liberation from the body and return to the realm of light. Jesus appeared as the REDEEMER, who, united with the souls of all persons, suffered for them.

Manichaeism gained a considerable following in the fourth century. Among the notable adherents, though never a full member of the sect, was Augustine (for nine years, 374–383). Manichaeism exerted an influence in subsequent centuries on medieval sects such as the Paulicians, Bogomils, Patarenes, and especially the Cathars, who, about 1200, numbered in the millions in southern France and northern Italy.

See also DUALISM.

Bibliography. L. J. R. Ort, *Mani: A Religio-Historical Description of His Personality*; S. Runciman, *The Medieval Manichee: A Study of the Christian Dualist Heresy*; G. Widengren, *Mani and Manichaeism*.

—E. GLENN HINSON

• **Manna.** [man'uh] In Exod 16:15, the children of Israel are fed a bread-like substance from heaven and declare it *mān hû'* (either "What is it?" or perhaps "It is manna.") because they did not know *mâ hû'* ("What it was"). In spite of the awkward etymology, the context makes it clear that the bread was intended to be God's gift of bread to provide for the Israelites' needs in the wilderness. It was an egalitarian gift in the sense that those who gathered much had no surfeit and those who gathered a small amount had no shortage. Indeed, even the fact that one could not save the leftovers encouraged the Israelites to understand the manna as God's regular provision.

From early in the twentieth century onward, scholars have noted the similarities between the manna and a secretion of the *tamarix gallica mannifera* trees of the west Sinaitic peninsula that occurs annually during May and June. A plant lice (*trabutina mannipara*) punctures the fruit of the tamarisk tree and after digesting the fruit juice, excretes a yellowish-white substance that melts during the day, but solidifies in the cool periods of night and morning. It has a sweet taste, is best harvested in the morning, does not keep, and attracts ants. It is easy to see how this phenomenon could depict God's miraculous provision to the wilderness wanderers.

See also PLANTS OF THE BIBLE.

Bibliography. B. Childs, *The Book of Exodus, OTL*.

—JOHNNY L. WILSON

• **Manual of Discipline.** The *Manual of Discipline* (*1QS*), or the *Rule of the Community,* is one of the foundational documents of the Qumran community. Twelve copies of the *Manual* have been identified among the DEAD SEA SCROLLS (PLATE 48). The longest, the best preserved of the seven major scrolls from Cave 1, contains eleven columns. It dates from 100–75 B.C.E. The other copies are fragmentary: one manuscript from Cave 5 and ten manuscripts (not yet published) from Cave 4, including three dating to 100–75 B.C.E. The *Manual* begins by setting forth the aims of the community. Next comes the ritual for entrance into the community, followed by a meditation on the Two Spirits: the Spirit of Truth and the Spirit of Falsehood. Next comes the Rule proper, including regulations for joining the community, for community life, and for the organization and assembly of the community; a penal code; and guidelines for the Master of the community. The *Manual* concludes with a hymn of thanksgiving.

The *Manual of Discipline* provides the most complete picture available of the Qumran community. The *Manual* depicts its members as the Sons of Light; outsiders are the Sons of Darkness, from whom they have been called to separate. They have united together as the Community of God which has received his Covenant of Grace. They live a communal life, sharing property and work, studying the LAW, and meeting together for discussion of community matters and ceremonies, such as the communal meal. Regulations involve everything from slander and lying to sleeping or spitting in the Assembly. The community has a strict organizational hierarchy; virtually all matters, from the seating arrangement to the order of speaking, are determined by rank. At the top are the priests, the Sons of Zadok, who are themselves ranked according to the perfection of their spirit. Next come the Levites, or elders. Finally, there are the people, who are ranked in Thousands, Hundreds, Fifties, and Tens (cf. Exod 18:25). Within the larger community there is a Council of the Community, made up of twelve men and three priests. Over the entire community stands the Master, or Overseer. Each individual is examined annually, at which time his rank may be adjusted upward or downward, depending upon his understanding and behavior. Entrance into the community is carefully regulated. The initiate first takes an oath, in the presence of the entire community, to obey the Law as it is interpreted in the community and to separate from the Men of Falsehood. He is examined by the Master and, if pronounced fit for the discipline, admitted into the Covenant to begin receiving instruction in the rules of the community. During the first year he does not partake of the communal meal, and he keeps his property separate from that of the community. At the end of the first year he undergoes a second examination. If he is allowed to continue, he embarks upon a second probationary year, during which he does not partake of the communal drink and his property is held in trust by the community. At the end of the second year he undergoes a third examination. If he is found acceptable, he becomes a full-fledged member of the community and is given a rank, and his property is merged with that of the community.

The *Manual* also gives insight into some of the fundamental doctrines of the community. The meditation on the Two Spirits illuminates the sect's basic dualistic outlook. God has created for people Two Spirits in which to walk until the End: the Prince of Light/Angel of Truth/Spirit of Truth and the Angel of Darkness/Spirit of Falsehood (cf. 1 John 4:6). Those who walk according to the Prince of Light will receive everlasting life; those who follow the Angel of Darkness eternal torment. The spirit to which people belong is determined by God's choice, not theirs. This thought is expressed clearly in the hymn that concludes the *Manual*: with a deep sense of human sinfulness, the psalmist affirms that people cannot establish their own steps; their hope must be solely in the mercy of God. The Manual also reveals the messianic expectations of the sect. Three figures are anticipated: the Prophet and two Messiahs—the Messiah of Aaron, presumably a priestly Messiah, and the MESSIAH of Israel, presumably a royal Messiah (cf. *1QSa*; *4QTestim*; *CD* 6:7; 7:18).

A number of concepts in the *Manual* have striking NT parallels. The centrality of the sacred meal (and drink) calls to mind the importance of the LORD'S SUPPER in the early church and a reference to being sprinkled with purifying water has led some to think of BAPTISM. Aspects of the organizational structure (elders, overseer) are reminiscent of that found in the PASTORAL EPISTLES. The dependence on God's grace has been linked by some to JUSTIFICATION by faith. In addition there is list of attitudes that characterize those led by each of the Two Spirits (cf. Gal 5:19-23), a call to love the Sons of Light (cf. Jn 13:34) and to hate the Sons of Darkness (cf. Matt 5:43-44), and identification of the sect as the Way (cf. Acts 9:2), the use of Isa 40:3 to justify a movement in the wilderness (cf. Mark 1:2), the notion of prayer as sacrifice (cf. Heb 13:15), and an interpretation of the cornerstone of Isa 28:16 (cf. 1 Pet 2:4-8).

The *Manual of Discipline* was probably composed between 150–100 B.C.E. Its literary history has been much debated. Given its age and its centrality to the community, some scholars have suggested that its author was the Teacher of Righteousness, a suggestion which has not proved persuasive. Others have argued that it is a composite document, drawing from several independent sources. The publication of the manuscripts from Cave 4 will prove important for a more adequate assessment of its literary history. Its relationship with the DAMASCUS RULE is also problematic. There are strong ties in tone and detail; yet there are differences. Scholars are divided as to which was written first. Whatever the case, the importance of the *Manual* for understanding the Qumran community cannot be overstated.

See also DEAD SEA SCROLLS; ESSENES.

Bibliography. W. H. Brownlee, "The Dead Sea Manual of Discipline," *BASORSup* 10-12; A. Dupont-Sommer, *The Essene Writings from Qumran*; A. R. C. Leany, *The Rule of Qumran and Its Meaning*; L. H. Schiffman, *The Halakhah at Qumran* and *Sectarian Law in the Dead Sea Scrolls*; G. Vermes, "The Writings of the Qumran Community," in E. Schürer, *The History of the Jewish People in the Age of Jesus Christ,* rev. ed.; P. Wernberg-Møller, *The Manual of Discipline*.

—JOSEPH L. TRAFTON

• **Maranatha.** [mair'uh-nath"uh] Maranatha is the oldest recorded prayer of the early church. It is preserved in its Aramaic form in 1 Cor 16:22 and *Did* 10:6, and a Greek translation appears in Rev 22:20. The term may be divided as either *marana tha* or *maran atha,* and may mean either "Our Lord, come!" or "Our Lord has come." The former is more likely.

The preservation of the Aramaic prayer, like *amen* or *abba,* confirms both its antiquity and its importance for the church. The prayer reflects the early transference of the term "Lord" (*mar*) from God to Jesus.

At the conclusion of 1 Corinthians the prayer follows the pronouncement of a curse ("anathema") on those who do not love the Lord. It has been suggested both that the prayer reinforced the curse and that it introduced the celebration of the LORD'S SUPPER.

The reading of 1 Corinthians may have taken the place of a sermon. At the end of the sermon believers may have exchanged a kiss of greeting (Rom 16:16; 1 Cor 16:20; 2 Cor 13:12), excluded unbelievers, and invited the presence of the Lord as they prepared to eat the bread and drink the wine (cf. *Did* 10.6-7). The Supper itself, therefore, looked back to the "last supper," celebrated the presence of the Lord with the community, and looked forward to the messianic banquet at the Lord's coming.

The earliest preserved prayer reflects a high Christology, a set liturgical pattern, and both eschatological and eucharistic emphases in the church's worship.

See also LORD IN THE NEW TESTAMENT; LORD'S SUPPER.

Bibliography. K. G. Kuhn, "μαρανα θά," *TDNT*; C. F. D. Moule, "A Reconsideration of the Context of *Maranatha*," *NTS* 6 (1959-60): 307-10.

—R. ALAN CULPEPPER

• **Marcion.** [mahr'shuhn] Marcion, the son of the bishop of Pontus in northern Asia Minor, was born about 80 C.E. Our knowledge of him comes from remarks made about him by opponents until the time of his death (about 160) and down into the third century, including Justin, Irenaeus, and Tertullian. His brilliant mind and organizational skills were at the heart of a major controversy in the church in the period from 135 to 150. Central for Marcion was his understanding of Jesus as the messenger and agent of God's love and mercy toward humanity, and especially the poor. In his careful study of what at that time was the only authoritative body of scripture for the church—the Jewish scriptures which came to be called the OT—he found what he considered to be an unacceptable representation of God as causing evil and effecting punishment, of using evil men to achieve his purposes, and as binding his people to obey his laws or suffer dire consequences. He felt that the Christian efforts to avoid these conclusions about the God of the Jews were misguided, and rejected the allegorical methods by which the explicit meaning of the Jewish Bible was adjusted to fit with Christian insights.

Marcion took as central for faith the writings of PAUL and the GOSPEL OF LUKE, although he felt that in their present form both had been altered to try to accomodate them to aspects of the Jewish scriptures. He formulated, therefore, an official list of Christian scriptures, which consisted of an expurgated version of Luke, and the letters of Paul, with some significant passages omitted. The birth and childhood stories were taken out of Luke, because they tied Jesus in with the God of the OT. The middle section of GALATIANS was also dropped (Gal 3:16–4:6), because it associated the new covenant community with the OT figure, ABRAHAM. The letters he took to be by Paul were those in our present NT from Romans through 2 Thessalonians, plus Philemon. The PASTORALS were not included, and scholars have raised the question whether he even knew them. These conclusions of Marcion's about the scriptures were reached by him after he left Pontus and took up residence in Rome, where he seems to have engaged in extended and detailed study of the OT.

The result of his studies was that he began to teach these ideas and to organize Christian communities on the basis of these convictions. Within a few years, there were Marcionite churches from Rome and Carthage in the western part of the Mediterranean world to Asia Minor, Syria and Mesopotamia. His reading of Paul's declaration in Gal 3:28 that "in Christ there is neither male nor female" led him to conclude that there should be equal opportunity for women in the church. But even more radical was his teaching that there should be no participation in sexual activity among its members, since sexual identity had been abolished in Christ. Other ascetic standards were fostered in the Marcionite churches, so that they celebrated the eucharist with water rather than wine.

His rejection of the OT and his ASCETICISM had a very

different base than those ideas did in the Gnostic teachings of this period. The Gnostics divided the universe into realms of spirit and matter, and some of them saw asceticism as a way of triumphing over the material world. But for Marcion, the rejection of the God of the OT was not for his role as creator, but for having given the Law, and for reported schemes involving wicked agents (like David, who arranged to steal the wife of his competitor for the kingship). Marcion wanted to focus Christian faith and life on the love of God in Jesus as disclosed through a revised Luke and the Letters of Paul.

Although the major reaction to Marcion was one of violent hostility on the part of the bishops, his ideas did force the main body of the church to draw up its own authoritative list of scriptures, and to develop ways of interpreting the OT within a framework of Christian understanding. Christian theology also had taken seriously the concepts of love and mercy, rather than stressing law and ecclesiastical authority.

See also CANON; GNOSTICISM; PAUL.

Bibliography. E. C. Blackman, *Marcion and His Influence*; A. Harnack, *Marcion: The Gospel of the Alien God*; R. J. Hoffman, *Marcion: On the Restitution of Christianity*; J. Knox, *Marcion and the New Testament*.

—HOWARD CLARK KEE

• **Marduk.** *See* MERODACH/MERODACH-BALADAN; MORDECAI; RELIGIONS OF THE ANCIENT NEAR EAST.

• **Mari.** [mah'ree] Mari was one of the most important cities in Mesopotamia in the third and early second millennia B.C.E. The site of Mari, present-day Tell Hariri, is located near the Euphrates River, about seven mi. north of Abu Kemal in southeastern Syria, near the Iraqi border (PLATE 2).

Mari was located at the intersection of two main caravan routes, one that connected the Upper Euphrates with Syria and the other that went from the Persian Gulf to the Mediterranean coast. For this reason, Mari became a center of commerce, a rich city with an international population and a strong political power in its day. The site of Mari was discovered when villagers unearthed a headless statue at Tell Hariri. Excavations were initiated at the site in 1933 under the auspices of the Louvre Museum and under the direction of André Parrot. The work at Tell Hariri continued until 1936, being halted by the beginning of World War II. It was resumed in 1951 and halted by war in 1956. Since then, more than twenty campaigns have been conducted by Parrot and Jean Margueron.

The existence of Mari was known from cuneiform texts from Sumer; the city was also mentioned in a Babylonian text from the time of HAMMURABI (ca. 1765 B.C.E.). The history of Mari goes back to the third millennium B.C.E. The city itself was founded at the end of the fourth millennium; it was conquered by Eannnatum of Lagash ca. 2500 B.C.E. and again by Sargon of Akkad ca. 2350. Mari was under the control of the rulers of UR until Ishbi-Irra of Mari was able to gain independence from Ur. After several years of obscurity, Mari entered its final period of glory in the nineteenth and eighteenth centuries B.C.E. under the dynasty of Yaggid-Lim and Yahdun-Lim. Yahdun-Lim was killed by Shamshi-Adad of Assyria, who placed his son Yasmah-Adad as ruler of Mari. When Yasmah-Adad died, Zimri-Lim, son of Yahdun-Lim, who had taken refuge in Allepo, regained control of Mari (ca. 1779) and ruled until 1760 when Hammurabi, king of Babylon conquered Mari. Zimri-Lim ruled as a vassal of Hammurabi until Mari was finally destroyed by the Kassites in 1742 B.C.E.

The results of the excavations have provided ample material for archaeological studies. Among the discoveries were the temples dedicated to the gods Dagon and Shamash and to the goddess Ishtar, and several palaces dating from the early third millennium (pre-Sargonic) to the early second millennium B.C.E. (Old Babylonia Period). The most important of these palaces was the royal palace finished by Zimri-Lim, the last king of Mari. His palace complex contained about 300 rooms, covering more than fifteen acres. Some rooms of the palace were decorated with sculptures, wall paintings, and other ornamentations. One of the paintings, the "Investiture of the King," was decorated with trees, streams of water, and winged creatures, reminiscent of the Eden story (Gen 2).

Among the many rooms excavated, Parrot discovered the throne room, several audience rooms, a scribal school, and the royal residence with bathrooms and lavatories. There were also servants' rooms, kitchens, bakeries, wine cellars, and even an ice-storage room. Inscriptions were found in stones, jewelry, seals, and cylinders. One of the most important discoveries was the royal archives with more than 20,000 tablets, most of them written in Akkadian. The importance of these texts to biblical studies lies in the fact that the culture of Mari is part of the northwest semitic culture, the same culture to which the OT belongs. In addition, these texts give evidence that there were two languages in Mari. One of them was the language of the palace, used in official correspondence and business transactions by the nobility and by the scribal officials; and another, a more popular language, was used by the lower class. Most of the tablets deal with economic and administrative matters. They provide valuable information about legal customs and cultural practices such as nomadism, military structures, tribal organizations, and the position of women in Mari society. They also provide necessary information to reconstruct the political and economic life of the city.

The texts found at Mari provide some interesting parallels with the biblical texts. The texts mention several important cities in Palestine and Syria. Among them are Laish, the city conquered by the tribe of DAN in northern Israel (Judg 18:1-31); HAZOR, an independent city-state that became an important Israelite city; and UGARIT, a Canaanite city-state. Personal and place names in the Mari texts are similar to names found in the patriarchal narratives. The texts mention the cities of HARAN and Nahur (NAHOR). The names of these cities are comparable to personal names found in the patriarchal narratives (Gen 11:22-32). The texts also mention the Habiru, a group of people found in the Amarna tablets (fourteenth century B.C.E.) who have been compared to the Hebrews of the OT by some scholars.

Customs reflected at Mari are also similar to patriarchal customs. Covenants at Mari were ratified by the killing of an ass, a practice similar to the pact between the Shechemites and Jacob (Gen 33:19; 34:1-3). The texts contain references to prophecy. Prophets were inspired by their gods to communicate divine messages to a third party. These oracles were often received by dreams. The prophet, as a representative of the god, delivered the message to the king in the name of his god in the same manner as the prophets of Israel spoke to the king in the name of Yahweh. The prophetic oracles at Mari, however, differed from the prophetic oracles of the OT because they lacked the intense moral content of biblical prophecies. At Mari the oracles were concerned for the most part with the proper care of the gods and their temples. Some oracles promised success in battle while others contained threats of defeat in case of noncompliance with the wishes of the deity.

These parallels between Mari and the biblical texts should not be used to prove or disprove the antiquity of biblical traditions. Rather, they demonstrate that some practices in the OT find a common background with similar practices in Mesopotamia.

Bibliography. A. Malamat, "Mari," *BA* 34 (1971): 2-22 and *BA* 47 (1984): 70-120.

—CLAUDE F. MARIOTTINI

• **Mark.** Mark is known as "John whose other name was Mark," "John called Mark," and "John," or "Mark." The KJV has Marcus in Col 4:10 and Phlm 24. Traditionally, he is regarded as the author of the GOSPEL OF MARK.

Mark's early life as a Christian is unknown. The view that he was the "young man" of Mark 14:51 and that the UPPER ROOM was in his home has been theorized by some interpreters. It is known that he was a Jew and the son of MARY, a leading Christian woman at Jerusalem who possessed a large house where the early believers gathered (Acts 12:12).

John Mark was chosen as a companion of BARNABAS and Saul (PAUL) when they returned to Antioch after their famine-relief visit to Jerusalem (Acts 12:25). He accompanied them on their first missionary journey as a helper (Acts 13:5). At Perga he left them and returned to Jerusalem for an undisclosed reason (Acts 13:13). Mark's failure to complete the trip led later to the estrangement of Paul and Barnabas. The latter wanted to take Mark with them to re-visit the Christians converted on the first trip, but Paul refused, separated from Barnabas, and chose Silas as a partner. Barnabas took Mark to Cyprus, giving his cousin (Col 4:10) a second chance.

Mark is not heard of again for about ten years. He appears several times in Paul's Letters. Col 4:10-11 and Phlm 24 indicate that he was a fellow worker with Paul in Rome. In 2 Tim 4:11 Paul, in prison for a second time, asks Timothy to bring Mark to him "for he is useful to me for ministry."

The final reference to Mark comes from PETER in Rome. He refers to him as "my son" (1 Pet 5:13). Thus, Mark is depicted as being the companion of both Paul and Peter.

Early church tradition confirms Mark's relationship with Peter. Papias (60–130 C.E.) and Clement of Alexandria (150–215 C.E.) tell us that he served as Peter's interpreter and wrote his Gospel from Peter's remembrances. The early church historian Eusebius (ca. 325 C.E.) states that Mark was the first evangelist to Egypt and the first bishop of Alexandria.

See also BARNABAS; MARK, GOSPEL OF; MARY; PAUL; PETER; UPPER ROOM.

Bibliography. W. L. Lane, *Commentary on the Gospel of Mark.*

—J. A. REYNOLDS

• **Mark, Gospel of.** Most scholars believe that Mark was the earliest of the four NT Gospels. The Gospel was written anonymously and derives its authority from its witness to Jesus Christ and not from the identity or credentials of the author. The earliest testimony about the Gospel claims that it was written by MARK. It comes from PAPIAS, the Bishop of Hieropolis (ca. 140): "Mark, having become the interpreter of Peter, wrote down accurately whatever he remembered of the things said and done by the Lord, but not however in order" (Eusebius, *EccHist* 3.39.15).

• OUTLINE OF MARK •

The Gospel of Mark

I. Jesus and the Announcement of the Kingdom of God (1:1–3:6)
  A. John the Baptist; the temptation (1:1-13)
  B. Jesus' ministry begins (1:14-45)
  C. Conflict with religious authorities (2:1–3:6)
II. Jesus' Ministry in Galilee (3:7–8:21)
  A. The gathering of the crowds (3:7-35)
  B. Parables; miracles (4:1–5:43)
  C. Hardening of hearts (6:1-6)
  D. Miracles and teachings (6:7–7:37)
  E. Jesus misunderstood (8:1-21)
III. Jesus' Teaching on Discipleship (8:22–10:52)
  A. Opening of blind eyes (8:22-26)
  B. First prediction of death (8:27–9:29)
  C. Second prediction of death (9:30–10:31)
  D. Third prediction of death (10:32-45)
  E. Opening of blind eyes (10:46-52)
IV. Jerusalem; the Passion (11:1–15:41)
  A. Entry into Jerusalem (11:1-11)
  B. Controversies in the Temple (11:12–12:44)
  C. Teaching about the end (13:1-37)
  D. Jesus' final deeds (14:1-42)
  E. Trial and crucifixion (14:43–15:41)
V. Burial and Resurrection (15:42–16:8)
  A. Burial (15:42-47)
  B. Empty tomb (16:1-8)
VI. The Long Ending (16:9-20)

There would be no reason to attribute the Gospel to Mark, a relative unknown and not an apostle, unless some basis existed for this fact. Whether the Mark mentioned in 1 Pet 5:13 and the Mark who was a fellow worker of Paul (Acts 12:25; 13:4, 13; Col 4:10; Phlm 24; and 2 Tim 4:11) are identical with the author of the Gospel is debatable since Marcus was a common name.

Date and Origin. Many scholars have connected the origin of the Gospel with Rome. This cannot be proved, but it does appear that Mark was not written in Palestine. The fact that Jewish customs are regularly explained (7:3-5, the washing of hands) indicates that the audience was not familiar with them. Phrases in Aramaic, the language of Palestine, are always interpreted, even the familiar *Abba* (14:36). A Roman origin is suggested by the number of words in the Gospel transliterated from the Latin. The designation of the Greek woman from the region of Tyre as Syrophoenician (7:26) is a Roman distinction that differentiates her from a Libyphoenician from Carthage. In 12:42, the coinage of Palestine, two *lepta,* is explained in terms of Latin coinage. The allusions to persecution in Mark also fit well a Roman context after the Neronian atrocities. Except for isolated local confrontations, Christians had been relatively ignored and could worship in peace. Things changed dramatically after a disastrous fire swept Rome in 64 C.E. destroying ten of the city's fourteen wards. The emperor, Nero, attempted to squelch rumors that he was responsible with a program of tax relief, food giveaways, and rebuilding. When the rumors persisted, he found a scapegoat in the Christians. The Roman historian, Tacitus, reports the mass arrest of Christians. Admission to being a Christian led to death. Many Christians are said to have informed on others, and many were convicted.

Mark can be understood as a pastoral response to this situation. In a context of suffering and martyrdom, he wrote to show the similarity between what Jesus faced and what the Roman Christians faced. The passion of Jesus takes up one-half of the Gospel. Hengel concluded that Mark was written after the persecution of Nero and before the destruction of Jerusalem in the year 69. He wrote: "The time in which the evangelist is living is coloured by the vivid experience of fearful persecution, an expanding mission, the danger of being led astray, and the tumult of war threatening the whole empire" (25). Just as Jesus was falsely accused of being in league with the devil (Mark 3:21, 30), the Christians were misrepresented as atheists and haters of mankind. Just as Jesus was framed by false witnesses (14:56-59), they were framed by false accusations. Just as Jesus was betrayed by an intimate friend, one of the twelve (14:43-46), they were betrayed by intimates. They could read that Jesus predicted that this very thing would happen (13:1-13). Jesus spoke openly of persecution that would come not only to him but also to his disciples and warned about the need to stand up to it. He warned that those who have no root in themselves endure for awhile and then, when affliction or persecution arises on account of the word, immediately they fall away (4:17). He insisted that bearing one's cross was an integral part of discipleship (8:34-38). He warned that they would be salted with fire and that salt that loses its savor cannot be resalted (9:49-50). He promised his followers rewards but only with persecutions (10:29-30). The persecuted Christians could read about the disciples being swamped by the waves, but when Jesus got into the boat the wind ceased (6:45-51). They learn that Jesus' spiritual presence not only brings peace; his behavior under the most severe persecution sets an example for the community. He made his bold confession before the authorities (14:62; 15:2). He endured the bone-tipped flagellum of the guards in silence (15:15). At the end, a Roman soldier confesses, "Truly this man was the Son of God" (15:39).

Subject to vicious gossip as well as hostility (cf. 1 Pet 2:15; 3:13-16; 4:12), the church needed to be firmly grounded in the origin of their faith so that they could respond to calumny and so that they would not be led astray by false prophets. It is possible that Mark compiled a written record from what Peter had preached and from other traditions to meet this need. This seems to be more likely than the theory that the evangelist sought to correct misinterpretations of Jesus.

Christology: Who Is Jesus? Even though Jesus is identified in 1:1 as the Christ, the title is inadequate to express who Jesus truly is in Mark partly because of the political baggage associated with the term (cf. 13:22). The Christ is to be the son of David, a royal figure (12:35-37); and the high priest interrogates Jesus as a royal pretender (14:61). The chief priests mock him on the cross as the Christ, the King of Israel (15:32). Peter's confession that Jesus is the Christ (8:29) is silenced by Jesus because Peter lacks understanding of how Jesus is to be the Christ (8:30-33).

Jesus never uses this title; instead, he, and he alone, refers to himself as the Son of man. Jesus asserts that the Son of man has authority to forgive sins (2:10), is the lord of the Sabbath (2:28), will suffer, die, and be raised (8:31, 38; 9:9, 12; 10:33), will give his life as a ransom (10:45), and will return in power (13:26; 14:62). In Judaism, the Son of man was associated with power, glory, heavenly exaltation, and judgment. In Mark, he is associated with power blended with suffering.

Mark portrays the humanity of Jesus throughout the Gospel. Jesus is moved to anger (3:5; 10:14). He sleeps (4:38). He marvels at unbelief (6:5) and sighs deeply in frustration (7:34; 8:12; 9:19). He also trembles (14:33) and feels God-forsaken (15:34). Mark, however, just as plainly understands Jesus to be the Son of God. This is clear from that fact that he is identified as the Son of God at climactic moments in Mark, the baptism (1:9-11), the transfiguration (9:7), and the crucifixion (15:39). From the very beginning the evangelist portrays Jesus as the Son of God walking the earth. He demonstrates his supernatural power over the demonic (1:23-28). He heals diseases (1:29-34), including the cleansing of leprosy (1:39-45), something that only God could do (2 Kgs 5:7); and he forgives sins, also something that only God could do (2:1-10).

Jesus as Miracle Worker. Mark devotes proportionately more space to the miracles of Jesus than the other Gospels. The miracles are not simply deeds of loving-kindness but demonstrations of the divine wrath against Satan, and all the supernatural beings in Mark recognize this. Jesus did nothing to stir up publicity or provide spectacles through miracles, but they do reveal his power to destroy the tyranny of the demonic, to loose the shackles of unforgiven sin, and to rescue and save his people.

The term "messianic secret" was first employed by William Wrede in 1901 to explain why Jesus repeatedly tells people not to tell what he has done or who he was. Wrede contended that this was a device invented by the author to cover up the fact that the historical Jesus never made messianic claims for himself and was not recognized as the Messiah by his disciples until after the resurrection. This conclusion is belied by the fact that Jesus was condemned by the Romans as a messianic pretender, and it is unlikely that the resurrection convinced the disciples of Jesus' messiahship had they not had some inkling of it before his death. The commands to keep silent after the healings are not consistent and have more to do with the secret of Jesus' divine sonship than his messiahship. In 9:9, Jesus charged the disciples to tell no one about the transfiguration until the Son of man should have risen from the dead. This is because the ministry and identity of Jesus could only be understood after his death and resurrection. The secret is a secret of faith.

Jesus as Teacher. Jesus' teaching characterizes the central thrust of his activity since both the noun and verb are prominent in Mark. Jesus is one who teaches. Jesus has compassion on the crowds and expresses this through his teaching them.

Discipleship. Mark intends to instruct his church on the true nature of discipleship. He does this by candidly depicting the failures of Jesus' disciples. Although the disciples have been given the mystery of the Kingdom (4:11), they consistently misunderstand Jesus' teaching and actions in spite of private tutorials. They particularly fail to understand the necessity of Jesus' suffering. Each time Jesus plainly predicts his passion, the disciples manifest in some way their incomprehension. Jesus then takes this as an opportunity to expound further on the nature of true discipleship (8:31-38; 9:30-37; 10:32-45). The disciples display a delight in power, glorious achievements, and personal ambition; and they want a messiah who is beyond suffering and death and who will then offer them all of their hearts' desires. Jesus, instead, is a messiah who goes willingly to death and requires his disciples to accept the cross not only as a means of salvation but also as a way of life.

The Ending of Mark. Three different endings to Mark exist in the manuscript tradition: the ending at 16:8, a shorter ending (printed in a note in the RSV and NEB), and the longer ending, 16:9-20. "For they were afraid" (16:8) is an unusual way to end the Gospel. But the other endings do not appear to be original to Mark on the basis of the evaluation of the manuscript evidence and because they betray non-Marcan linguistic traits. Why the Gospel ends at 16:8 will probably never be known for certain.

Summary. 1:14–3:5: The beginning of Jesus' ministry in Galilee marked by divine miracles and controversies that climax in the resolve to kill him.

3:7–8:22: The gathering of the crowds, appointment of the Twelve, teaching in parables, healing and feeding miracles that climax in a lack of understanding and the hardening of hearts.

8:23–10:45: The teaching on discipleship that begins and ends with the opening of the eyes of the blind.

11:1–13:37: The entry into Jerusalem and the final controversies in the Temple that climax in eschatological instruction.

14:1–15:39: The passion of Jesus that climaxes in the confession of the centurion.

15:40–16:8: The burial of Jesus that climaxes with the account of the empty tomb.

See also GOSPEL; GOSPELS, CRITICAL STUDY OF; MARK; SYNOPTIC PROBLEM.

Bibliography. P. J. Achtemeier, *Mark*; H. Anderson, *The Gospel According to Mark*; C. E. B. Cranfield, *The Gospel According to St. Mark*; M. Hengel, *Studies in the Gospel of Mark*; W. H. Kelber, *Mark's Story of Jesus*; W. L. Lane, *Commentary on the Gospel of Mark*; E. Schweizer, *The Good News According to Mark*.

—DAVID E. GARLAND

• **Mark, Long Ending of.** In most of the Greek manuscripts of the GOSPEL OF MARK the Gospel concludes with a section (16:9-20) in which the risen Christ is reported to have appeared to Mary Magdalene, then to two unnamed disciples, and finally to the eleven disciples. He rebukes them for their unbelief, commissions them for a world mission, asserts that faith and baptism are essential for salvation, and promises the gifts of exorcisms and tongues, as well as the ability to handle serpents or drink poison without harm. Then follows a brief account of the ASCENSION and enthronement of Jesus, and of the disciples' launching of the universal mission as well as its confirmation by signs.

In the oldest and best manuscripts of Mark (Codex Vaticanus and Codex Sinaiticus), however, as well as in the writings of some of the most learned of the church fathers (Clement of Alexandria, Origen, Eusebius), and in several of the ancient translations of the NT (Sinaitic Syriac, many Armenian, Ethiopic and Georgian texts), Mark ends with 16:8. This ending is even more abrupt in Greek than in English translations, since the final word is a conjunction (γάρ, meaning "for"), which normally introduces another clause. Translated literally, the text reads, "They were afraid, for. . . ." Significantly, it is precisely at 16:8 that Matthew and Luke diverge from each other in their respective accounts of the resurrection appearances.

How are we to account for this abrupt ending? The BOOK OF DANIEL has had a pervasive influence on Mark, not only in Mark 13, where there are direct references to such features as "the desolating sacrilege" (Dan 9:27; Mark 13:14), but in the latter part of the book, where Daniel's reaction to the visions of the end of the age are fear and trembling (Dan 10:7-10), exactly as in Mark 16:8. The probability, therefore, is that this is how Mark intended to end his gospel; the promise of deliverance has been given, and the inner core of his followers respond with fear and astonishment.

The other Gospel writers, who used Mark as their basic source, were not content with this open-ended conclusion in 16:8, but each provided his own independent ending, as is apparent from a study of Matthew, Luke and John. Apparently, those who were copying Mark were uncomfortable with his seemingly abrupt finish to his Gospel, and drew upon the other Gospels and upon independent tradition to provide what seemed a more satisfactory conclusion. Mark 16:9-20 differs from the rest of Mark in both literary style and vocabulary. The following literary links are evident: Mark 16:9, cf. Luke 8:2; Mark 16:9-11, cf. John 20:11-18; Mark 16:12, cf. Luke 24:13-35; Mark 16:14, cf. John 20:19-23; Mark 16:14-16, cf. Matt 18:16-20; Mark 16:19, cf. Luke 25:50-51.

Two other endings which were supplied for Mark in the early church are (1) a brief conclusion found in some late manuscripts and ancient versions: "But they reported to Peter and those with him all that they had been told. And after this Jesus himself sent out by means of them, from east to west, the sacred and imperishable proclamation of eternal salvation." (2) In one ancient manuscript, Codex Washingtonianus, there is some additional material inserted after Mark 16:14 which speaks of the ongoing conflict with, and the final triumph over the power of Satan. None of these added materials matches in vocabulary or attempts to remedy what was regarded as the abrupt ending with which Mark had brought to a close his original gospel.

See also MARK, GOSPEL OF; TEXTUAL CRITICISM OF THE NEW TESTAMENT.

—HOWARD CLARK KEE

• **Mark, Secret Gospel of.** In 1958, while cataloging old manuscripts and books in the Orthodox Monastery of Mar Saba near Jerusalem, Morton Smith of Columbia University discovered a fragment of a letter claiming to be from Clement of Alexandria (ca. 150–215 C.E.). The fragment consisted of two-and-a-half pages of Greek text written in a late-eighteenth-century hand on both sides of the last page and inside the back cover of a 1646 edition of the epistles of IGNATIUS of Antioch. The heading of this text read: "From the letters of the most holy Clement, the author of the *Stromateis,* to Theodore." Since no letters of Clement had previously been found, its potential importance was great. That potential was enhanced by the fact that the writer quoted from a hitherto unknown *Secret Gospel of Mark* (*SMark*), an amplified form of the canonical Gospel which was purportedly composed by the evangelist himself!

The letter's contents are divisible into a scribal heading (cited above); the letter proper (containing an attack on the second-century Carpocratian Gnostics and an explanation of three existing versions of Mark's "Gospel"); and quotations from both *SMark* and Carpocrates' additions to that Gospel. Following commendation of the unknown "Theodore" for silencing "the unspeakable teachings" of the Carpocratians, the author gives him more complete information about the "divinely inspired Gospel according to Mark" to which these heretics appeal.

While with the apostle PETER in Rome, MARK wrote the canonical Gospel (Mark I) as an introductory work for catechumens. After Peter's death, Mark moved to Alexandria and from his own and Peter's notes wrote an enlarged version of this Gospel, which contained "knowledge" for "those . . . being perfected" (Mark II or *SMark*). At his death Mark left this composition to the Alexandrian church where it was guarded, "being read only to those . . . being initiated into the great mysteries." But Carpocrates duped an elder of the church into giving him a copy of *SMark* and interpolated it with his own, false teachings (Mark III). This expanded *SMark* became the authoritative source for Carpocratian Gnostic teaching. Theodore should know of Mark II's existence but never acknowledged it publicly. It was "secret."

The author then quotes a passage from *SMark* that parallels Mark I (10:32-34) and recounts a story resembling Jesus' raising of LAZARUS (John 11:1-44). Included are Jesus' meeting in BETHANY a woman whose brother had died; his immediate visit to the brother's garden tomb from whence a great cry comes forth; his rolling the stone from the tomb door, raising the brother, and receiving the youth's loving response; and his accompanying the raised youth to the latter's home. After six days' stay, Jesus gives him instruction, receives him wearing a linen cloth over his nakedness, stays the night with him, and teaches him "the mystery of the Kingdom of God." There follows another passage from Mark I (10:35-46), after which *SMark* speaks of the presence in JERICHO of the youth's sister, Jesus' mother, and Salome—all of whom Jesus "did not receive."

Prior to the partial citation of Mark 10:46, the author notes that in discussing the young man's initiation by Jesus, Carpocrates has added (in Mark III) the words "naked man with naked man." Also, he is reported to have added still other "falsifications" to *SMark*.

The story of Jesus' raising of the young man at Bethany is not unlike other apocryphal tales resulting from second-century harmonization of canonical gospel stories. Also, Carpocrates' addition, suggesting some homosexual act in connection with initiation, recalls reports about this teacher's licentiousness based—in part—on his own corrupt exegesis of Gospel material (so Irenaeus, *AdvHaer* 1.25.4-5). But what has attracted major attention to *SMark* is the interpretation by M. Smith of its significance for understanding the development of early Christianity. His conclusions are: (1) that the writing containing *SMark* is a genuine letter of Clement of Alexandria; (2) that the story of the raising and initiation by Jesus is drawn from an Aramaic source used in common by Mark and John, though in an earlier version of Mark than the canonical one; (3) that this Aramaic source preserves a record of a secret, nocturnal baptismal rite administered by the historical Jesus to his inner circle of disciples, a rite known in *SMark* as "the mystery of the Kingdom of God"; (4) that Jesus, a magician and supposed divine being who possessed the HOLY SPIRIT, brought about—by means of this baptism-initiation union with himself—admission into the Kingdom through a hallucinatory heavenly ascent and liberation from the Mosaic Law (= libertinism). Smith then explains that in the post-Easter, pre-Pauline church an esoteric branch of Christianity preserved and used Jesus' secret rite. It was retained in *SMark* and certain libertine Gnostic sects, including that of Carpocrates. In turn, an esoteric branch of the church, made up of those never initiated into the "mystery of the KINGDOM OF GOD," held the new faith was principally concerned with ethical-social transformation. This exoteric view found expression in our canonical Gospels. Finally, Pauline Christianity represented a safe, balanced compromise of the esoteric and exoteric. This explains the dominant place his writings assume in the CANON.

Such a radical reconstruction of Christian origins has found little acceptance among scholars, though most accept Smith's demonstration of Clement's authorship of the letter and admire his erudition. Especially telling have been such criticism as the synoptic Gospels' complete silence about and John's explicit denial of (4:2) Jesus' practice of BAPTISM, as well as *SMark*'s omission of any explicit mention of baptism or accompanying ritual. Also, Smith's reconstruction requires the acceptance of his extensive creative speculation regarding gaps in our historical knowledge (e.g., his claim that while in the Garden of GETHSEMANE Jesus actually performed a nocturnal baptism on the unnamed, nude young man mentioned in Mark 14:51-52). Further, the existence of a lost Aramaic source known to Mark and John has been rejected as too speculative, the echoes of these Gospels being better explained by borrowing from them by the author of *SMark*. Smith's approach also lacks sophisticated use of modern methods of literary analysis, e.g., redaction and form criticism. This has resulted in occasional uncritical syntheses of traditional and late redactional materials. Then, it is highly unlikely, as Smith claims, that Jesus and the early Christians, though accused of magic, were persecuted primarily for this. Other social, religious, and political factors played more decisive roles. Moreover, Smith's understanding of the views of Jesus and Paul on the law is questionable, for does radicalization of the law necessarily equal libertinism? Finally, Smith's discussion of Jesus' teaching on the Kingdom of God omits any consideration of the PARABLES of the Kingdom and also too easily assumes the singular occurrence of the phrase "the mystery of the kingdom" (Mark 4:11 and par.) derives from the historical Jesus.

In sum, the *SMark* is a NT apocryphal writing partially quoted in an authentic letter of Clement of Alexandria. It was probably known in certain circles in the Alexandrian church, as well as by the Carpocratian Gnostics. However, it adds nothing new to our knowledge of the historical Jesus.

See also GNOSTICISM; MARK, GOSPEL OF.

Bibliography. P. Achtemeier, review of M. Smith, *Clement of Alexandria and a Secret Gospel of Mark,* and *The Secret Gospel, JBL* 93/2 (1974): 625-28; R. M. Grant, "Morton Smith's Two Books," *ATR* 56 (1974): 58-64; M. Smith, *Clement of Alexandria and a Secret Gospel of Mark* and *The Secret Gospel: The Discovery and Interpretation of the Secret Gospel According to Mark.*

—MALCOLM L. PEEL

• **Market/Marketplace.** Marketplaces, open spaces near the gates of the city, were the centers of communal life in biblical times. Buying, selling, and trading took place in the market; however, many other activities also occurred there. The men or elders of a city met in the marketplace to decide important matters or to witness transactions (Deut 25:7; Ruth 4:1).

The marketplace is mentioned more prominently in the NT than in the OT. Jesus compares those who are impossible to please with children sitting and playing in the marketplace (cf. Matt 11:16; Luke 7:32). Men go to the market to look for work (Matt 20:3) and to seek the approbation of their neighbors (Matt 23:7; Mark 12:38; Luke 11:43; 20:46). Mark records people bringing their sick friends and relatives to the marketplace, hoping that Jesus might pass by and heal them (6:56). Acts 16:19-20 describes the use of the marketplace as a courtroom. The marketplace, as in Athens, was also a place of public disputation (cf. Acts 17:17).

See also STOICS.

—HERBERT O. EDWARDS, SR.

• **Marriage in the New Testament.** The OT concept of monogamy as the divine ideal (Gen 2:21-24) is presumed in the NT writings. The proscription against incestuous marriage (Lev 18:6; Deut 27:20-23) is also supported by John the Baptist (Matt 14:3-4; Mark 6:17-18; Luke 3:19) and Paul (1 Cor 5:1).

Jesus. Although Jesus was never married, he clearly endorsed marriage, and as a guest at a wedding celebration he created wine when a shortage was made known to him (John 2:1-11). He cites Gen 1:25 and 2:23-4 in support of God's creation of man and woman for a oneness together which should not be severed by DIVORCE (Mark 10:6-9; Matt 19:4-6). In Mark 10:11-12, Luke 16:18, and 1 Cor 7:11, Jesus is quoted as saying that one's divorce of mate and remarriage and one's marriage to a divorced person are adulterous. In two places, however, Matthew cites one exception as a ground for divorce—unchastity (5:32; 19:9). Jesus holds strongly to monogamy and says that the deuteronomic allowance of divorce (24:1) was a result of the hardening of Israel's heart (Mark 10:5; Matt 19:8).

Jesus clearly stresses the priority of commitment to him and to the Kingdom of God over commitment to marriage and family (Matt 10:37; Luke 14:26). Matt 19:12 suggests that one's commitment to the Kingdom can lead to one's avoidance of marriage and Luke 14:20 suggests that marriage is sometimes used as an excuse from total commitment. He also states that in the resurrection there will be no marriage (Mark 12:25; Matt 22:30; Luke 20:35).

As in the OT, the beautiful image of marriage is used by Jesus to set forth some important teachings. Against the OT expectation of a future marriage of Yahweh with Israel (Hos 3:1-5; Isa 54:4ff.; 62:4f.; Ezek 16:7f.), Jesus refers to himself as the bridegroom (Mark 2:19f.; Matt 9:15f.; Luke 12:35-40) and a king giving a marriage feast for his son (Matt 22:1-14; Luke 14:16-24).

Paul. Strong support of marriage and a desire that Christians remain single and devote their full lives to God are found in Paul's writings.

Monogamy is the ideal for Pauline teachings on marriage and family. Marriage was created by God and is good, and is not to be rejected if received with thanksgiving (1 Tim 4:3-4). He presumes bishops and deacons (1 Tim 3:2,12) and elders (Titus 1:6) to have been married and to have children. He stresses the true oneness that should characterize a marriage and views the sexual relationships as indicative of the oneness that should constantly prevail, except for mutually agreed brief periods for prayer (1 Cor 7:3-5). He holds free love to be a violation of God's intent (1 Cor 7:10-11) Believers should remain married to unbelievers for the benefits to the children and the hope that the believer's influence may bring the spouse to belief. Should the unbeliever separate from the believer, however, it appears the believer is free to remarry (1 Cor 7:10-15). Widows and widowers also are free to remarry believers (1 Cor 7:9,39; Rom 7:2-3). Young widows should marry and have children (1 Thess 5:14). He predicts that false teachers in the future would forbid marriage (1 Tim 4:3).

Whether or not Paul was ever married is open to question. He makes no mention of having had a wife or child, although a Jewish male was expected to marry and have children. He even states that the apostles were married (1 Cor 9:5). Whether he was a widower or bachelor, by the time he writes 1 Corinthians, he is single (7:7), and views the states of both the married and the unmarried as individual gifts of God. He does express his wish that all could be like himself so that they could devote their full lives to God (7:7-8, 27-35, 40). Also, the pressures of the time can make marriage difficult and undesirable (7:26-31). He strongly supports marriage for the average person, but wishes all could be single like himself for the sake of the Kingdom.

While acknowledging the equality of all in Christ, including male and female (Gal 3:28), he also acknowledges a hierarchy of God, Christ, man, and woman (1 Cor 11:3). Both husbands and wives have responsibilities toward each other (1 Cor 7:2-5; Eph 5:21-33; Col 3:18-19; Titus 2:4-6; cf. 1 Pet 3:1-7).

Paul uses the beautiful divinely intended union of man and woman in marriage symbolically to convey some of his messages. Although admitting he is speaking foolishly, he says he betrothed the Corinthian Christians to Christ "as a pure bride to her one husband," but fears that like Eve they may be led away from that single union in Christ (2 Cor 11:2-3). The image of Christ as the bridegroom to the church, who loved his bride and gave himself up for her sanctity, is used as the model for husbands toward their wives. Christ and his church are one, and the married are to be one (Gen 2:24; Matt 19:6); Christ's unselfish love is to pattern their love for each other (Eph 5:21-33). Again, as death frees one from the legal marriage bond, so Paul views his readers' marriage to the Law as cancelled by their death to it through the body of Christ for a marriage to him (Rom 7:1-6).

Other NT References. Heb 13:4 calls for marriage to be held in honor and for the sexual fidelity of spouses. 1 Pet 3:1-7 expresses a hope that believing wives may be able to lead unbelieving husbands into the faith by their reverent and chaste behavior, like 1 Cor 7:12-14.

The Gospel of John and the Johannine Letters make no mention of marriage, except Jesus' providing wine at a marriage feast (John 2:1-11) and John the Baptist's reference to himself as the friend of the bridegroom (John 3:28-29). The Book of Revelation, however, uses the image of marriage several times. The 144,000 redeemed on Mount Zion with the Lamb are those who are chaste, who have not defiled themselves with women (14:1-5). The doomed Babylon is portrayed as a queen guilty of fornication with the kings of the earth (18:1-3, 7-9), and one of her many punishments is that "the voice of the bridegroom and bride will be heard in you no more" (18:23). In contrast, the awaited marriage of the Lamb and the bride is climactic for Revelation. The bride is portrayed as having made herself ready for the wedding, being clothed in fine linen, which is "the righteous deeds of the church" (19:7-8). Therefore, "Blessed are those who are invited to the marriage supper of the Lamb" (19:9). The holy city, new Jerusalem, is portrayed as coming out of heaven from God, prepared as a bride adorned for her husband (21:2). A closing statement in the Bible has the Spirit and the Bride awaiting this wedding with a longing, as well as a plea to the readers, "Come!" (22:17). The Bible opens and closes with a marital union concept.

See also DIVORCE; WOMEN IN THE NEW TESTAMENT; WOMEN IN THE OLD TESTAMENT.

—HENRY JACKSON FLANDERS, JR.

• **Marriage in the Old Testament.** In the OT the deepest relationship between one man and one woman. Marriage was the general practice in the OT and is regularly presupposed in the NT. The creation account of Gen 2:4bff. indicates of the man that woman, not animals and birds, was "a helper fit for him" (literally "a helper like in front of him," v. 20). The literal Hebrew denotes woman's closeness and parallelism to the man, and the account of her creation from his rib underscores this point, while explaining Adam's statement that she "is bone of my bones and flesh of my flesh'' (v. 23). Thus the summary statement: ''Therefore a man leaves his father and his mother and cleaves to his wife, and they become one flesh'' (v. 24).

The usual practice of monogamy seems reflected in numerous OT references. In OT law the singular ''wife'' commonly is used (Exod 29:17; 21:5; Lev 18:8, 16, 20; 20:10; 21:13; etc.). The Book of Proverbs, centering on how to build a good life, never mentions polygamy, but often refers to ''wife'' (12:4; 18:22; 19:13; 31:10; etc.). Ecclesiastes admits many activities, including having ''many concubines'' (Eccl 2:8), to be meaningless, whereas the sane and rewarding approach to a happy life is to ''enjoy life with the wife whom you love'' (9:9). MALACHI sharply condemns faithlessness to ''the wife of your youth . . . though she is your companion and your wife by covenant'' (2:14).

However, having more than one wife is known in OT records. Bigamy is assumed in the law of Deut 21:15ff. Elkanah had a wife in addition to HANNAH, Samuel's mother (1 Sam 1:2). Sarai, having borne her husband Abram no children, furnished him her Egyptian maid HAGAR as a second wife to bear him a son (Gen 16:3). Jacob married two sisters, LEAH and RACHEL (Gen 29:15ff.), who in turn furnished him wives in face of the absence or cessation of childbearing (Gen 30:1-13). The kings could have many wives, as did DAVID (2 Sam 5:13), SOLOMON (1 Kgs 11:1, 3), REHOBOAM (2 Chr 11:21), and the Persian king (Esth 2:3, 14). Even so, the normal pattern in old Israel was monogamy. Bigamy could be established by so-called levirate (from Latin *levir,* ''brother-in-law'') marriage, which dictated that the closest male relative of a sonless deceased was to marry the widow in order to produce a son (Deut 25:5).

No certain age for marriage is laid down in the Bible, but probably the groom normally was between the ages of 14 and 18 and the bride between 14 and 16. The initiation of the marriage process began with the selection by the groom's father of the bride (Gen 38:6), although the son could make his own selection while his father merely negotiated (Judg 14:3). However, perhaps due to his family's absence, JACOB negotiated for himself in choosing to marry Rachel (Gen 29:18). Similarly, the approval of the woman's father and/or brothers was sought (Gen 24:51), but REBEKAH was consulted for her consent (Gen 24:58). The father, if living, normally made the decision (Exod 2:21; Josh 15:17; 1 Sam 18:27). In the extraordinary case of the Moabitess RUTH, NAOMI, in the absence of Ruth's family, arranged for her marriage (Ruth 3:1-4).

These preliminary negotiations held by the families of the prospective bride and bridegroom were followed normally by the presentation of gifts or a payment called the *mōhar*. Then began the customary betrothal, about which the Bible offers no complete set of rules. The woman was then considered a wife, although consummation of the marriage came later. The payment of the *mōhar* was inseparable from the betrothal (2 Sam 3:14; 1 Sam 18:25). The betrothal ceremony seems merely to have been a feast (Judg 14:10) or celebration attended by family and friends. On this occasion the purchase money was paid (Gen 24:53-54) and the bride blessed by her father or brothers with the benediction that she be favored with many children (Gen 24:60; cf. Ruth 4:11-12). A time period of uncertain length, probably a few months, intervened between the betrothal ceremony and that of marriage (Deut 20:7).

Because marriage was a private affair between two persons and their respective families, the marriage ceremony required no publicity and never involved the priests. Among the upperclass at least, the mother of the bridegroom perhaps provided him a matrimonial crown (Cant 3:11). Wearing sumptuous clothes (Isa 61:10), the groom, with a company of family and friends (Cant 3:6-11; Judg 14:11; Matt 9:15), left his home (Ps 19:5) and met his bride at her home, where she too was accompanied by family and friends. She was beautifully dressed, decorated with jewels (Jer 2:32; Isa 61:10; Rev 21:2), and her face was veiled (Gen 29:25; Cant 4:1). The procession (which might be at night, Matt 25:6-10) was accompanied by music and songs (Jer 7:34; 16:9; 25:10; Ps 45:15), as the groom led the bride to his home (Ps 45:15; cf. Cant 4:8). A feast was served, apparently at the house of the groom or that of his parents (Matt 22:10; cf. John 2:1, 9). Details of the marriage ceremony are unknown, but it may have been here also that the benediction was given that the bride bear many children. The marriage could now be consummated, and the bride could be escorted by her father to the nuptial chamber (Gen 29:22-23; Judg 15:1). The festivities lasted for a week or more (Gen 29:27; Judg 14:12).

The figure of marriage appears often in the Bible to portray God's relation to the Israelite people. ''Your Maker is your husband'' (Isa 54:5). Israel is not to be labelled ''forsaken,'' but ''My delight is in her''; her land is not to be named ''Desolate'' but ''Married'' (Isa 62:4). The entire book of HOSEA is built around the image of God as the husband of wayward ISRAEL. In the books of the prophets Israel's idolatry is likened numerous times to a wife's infidelity (Isa 1:21; Jer 3:1-20; etc.). And the church is called the bride of Christ (2 Cor 11:2; Rev 19:7; 21:2, 9; 22:17).

See also FAMILY; WOMEN IN THE NEW TESTAMENT; WOMEN IN THE OLD TESTAMENT.

Bibliography. E. Neufeld, *Ancient Hebrew Marriage Laws.*

—KAREN RANDOLPH JOINES

• **Mars Hill.** *See* AREOPAGUS

• **Marsanes.** [mahr-suh-neez'] Although its fifty-four pages are quite fragmentary, enough of this first (and perhaps only) tractate from Codex X of the NAG HAMMADI library is preserved to make possible identification of it as a formerly unknown *Apocalypse of Marsanes.* The title, ''Marsanes,'' the probable reconstruction of the last line of text (68.18), is most likely the proper name of a Gnostic prophet mentioned in two early writings. In one, ''The Untitled Text'' in the Codex Bruce from fourth–fifth century Coptic Egypt, ''Marsanes'' is the ''perfect man'' who saw and revealed the highest ''Father's . . . invisible, perfect Triple-Power'' (7.9-21). In the other writing, *The Refutation of All the Heresies* (40.7.6), Epiphanius of Salamis (315–403 C.E.) mentions a certain prophet Mardianos (=Marsanes) whom the Archontic Gnostics believed was taken into heaven and returned to earth three days later.

In the best-preserved portion of the manuscript (1-10) is recounted the visionary experience of Marsanes in ascending to and descending from the highest level of the divine world. In ascending, the seer passes through thirteen levels of reality or ''seals'' (2.12–4.23). These range from ''worldly'' and ''material'' levels of bodily existence (2.16-21) to the 13th ''seal'' of the unknown ''Silent One,'' the invisible Three-Powered One, the highest Deity (4.12-23). Then (4.24–5.26) the visionary (probably Marsanes himself) claims that he has gained knowledge of all within the higher, intelligible world.

In 6.1-16 is described the descent and ascent of a savior, ''the Self-Begotten One,'' who, like Marsanes, saved a multitude ''through his revealing work.'' Next (6.17-8.12) follow questions of Marsanes which reflect his intellectual ascent to and praise of the "Silent," "Three-Powered One" (6.18-19). The prophet also sees the male-female virgin Barbelo who has fallen from perfection by becoming female and notes her return from "duality" to the primal state by becoming solely male again—the ultimate goal of all Gnostics (8.13–9.27). Finally, the ascent of the "Invisible Spirit," a savior, is offered as the model of those who obtain true knowledge (9.28–10.29). Marsanes invites all who dwell on earth to gain this knowledge that they may ultimately receive the "crown" of victory (10.13-23).

In the other best-preserved section of text (24-42) there appears discussion of the alphabet and combinations of letters which indicate various "shapes" of the human soul and "names" of gods and angels. It is possible that mastery of such information would assist Gnostics in their own heavenly ascent. The whole reflects considerable knowledge of Greco-Roman astrological and zodiacal speculation, Platonic discussion regarding "shapes" of souls, technical discussion of Greek grammar, Pythagorean reflection about numbers, and the (probable) magical use of wax images and emeralds.

Marsanes exhibits no traces of direct Jewish or Christian influence. Its Sethian Gnostic provenance is made clear by its close affinities with other Sethian writings from the Nag Hammadi library: the THREE STELES OF SETH, ZOSTRIANOS, and ALLOGENES. The type of Platonic influence upon its thought (akin to that of Iamblichus of Chalcis) may point toward a date of third century C.E. Place of composition is unknown.

See also ALLOGENES; GNOSTICISM; NAG HAMMADI; SETH, THREE STELES OF; ZOSTRIANOS.

Bibliography. B. A. Pearson, "Marsanes," *The Nag Hammadi Library in English*, ed. J. M. Robinson, "*NHC* X,*1*: Marsanes. Introduction and Translation," *Nag Hammadi Codices IX and X. The Coptic Gnostic Library*, ed. B. A. Pearson (*NHS* 15) and "The Tractate Marsanes (*NHC* X) and the Platonic Tradition," *Gnosis: Festschrift für Hans Jonas*, ed. B. Aland.

—MALCOLM L. PEEL

• **Martha.** Martha is first mentioned in Luke 10:38ff. as living in "a certain village" with her sister MARY. The Lucan record presents Martha as worried and upset about many things in her frantic efforts to be a good hostess to Jesus. Mary, however, is depicted as sitting and listening to Jesus and leaving all the chores to her sister. Finally, Martha complained to Jesus about her sister's inactivity. His reply indicated that Martha's anxiety over all the household chores was causing her to miss the most important thing—fellowship with the Lord. He rebuked her for letting many good things take priority over the best.

The next appearance of Martha is in John's account of the raising of her brother, LAZARUS (John 11). John specifies her village as BETHANY, which was located less than two mi. from Jerusalem.

Jesus, after a four-day delay, came to Bethany in response to the sisters' request for help for Lazarus. Martha was the first to hear of his arrival and at once went out to meet him. Later, she told Mary that Jesus had come. Hearing this, she ran and fell at his feet. Thus, John's description of the two sisters is similar to that of Luke.

The last appearance of Martha is in John 12:2-8 (cf. parallel accounts in Matt 26:6-13; Mark 14:3-9). The setting is a dinner in the house of Simon the Leper. Simon's relationship to Martha, Mary, and Lazarus is not known. One theory is that he was their father. The relationship must have been very close for they are in Simon's house with Martha serving again. Mary, true to her character, anointed Jesus with a very expensive perfume. This time there is no record of anxiety or complaining on the part of Martha.

See also BETHANY; LAZARUS; MARY.

—J. A. REYNOLDS

• **Martyr.** *See* WITNESS

• **Martyrs/Martyrdom.** *See* PERSECUTION IN THE NEW TESTAMENT; PERSECUTION IN THE OLD TESTAMENT

• **Mary.** Six or seven women in the NT bear the name Mary, depending upon whether two of these are the same persons.

1. Mary Magdalene, one of the most prominent followers of Jesus, derived her name from her home town in Magdala. Apparently she was the leader of a group of women who followed Jesus and contributed financially to his mission (Mark 15:40, 47; 16:1; Matt 27:55-56; Luke 8:2-3; 24:10). She participated in the Galilean ministry, witnessed the crucifixion and burial, anointed his body, was first at the tomb (Mark 16:1; John 20:1), according to the Fourth Gospel was first to see the risen Christ (John 20:14), and was first to report the empty tomb (Mark 16:1-7; John 20:1-2). She is often wrongly identified with the sinful woman of Luke 7:36-39 who anointed Jesus. Of all women, more is said of Mary Magdalene during Jesus' ministry and death than any other.

2. Mary of Bethany, the sister of MARTHA and LAZARUS, appears in two Gospels. In Luke 10:38-42 she is more attentive to Jesus' teaching while Martha "serves." In John 11:28-37 her grief over Lazarus moves Jesus deeply, and she anoints Jesus with costly ointment (12:1-8). Apparently Mary attached herself closely to her family and friends, and Jesus defended her on two occasions against those who would alter this trait within her (Luke10:40-42; John 12:4-8).

3. Mary, the mother of JAMES the Younger and JOSES, was active with Mary Magdalene in the ministry of Jesus (Mark 15:41; Luke 8:3; 23:55; 24:10), and appears in accounts of the crucifixion, burial, and resurrection of Jesus (Mark 15:40, 47; 16:1; Luke 23:55–24:10; Matt 27:55-56). She may have been the mother of James the son of Alphaeus and possibly is the same as Mary of Clopas.

4. Mary of Clopas appears only in John 19:25, at the cross of Jesus. Clopas most likely refers to her husband. She may have been the same as the previous Mary, mother of James and Joses, and may be the "other Mary" who appears in Matt 27:61 and 28:1.

5. Mary, mother of John MARK, was a hostess for the gathered church in Jerusalem (Acts 12:12). Her son was a companion of Paul and most likely the author of the Gospel of Mark.

6. Mary of Rome (or Ephesus) was a worker in the Roman (or Ephesian) congregation greeted by Paul (Rom 16:6). The place of residence of this Mary depends upon the destination of Rom 16.

7. Mary, the mother of Jesus, is referred to in two statements by Paul. He declares that Jesus was "born of a woman, born under the law" (Gal 4:4). Paul does not introduce the virginal conception of Jesus into the account, either because he was not aware of it or it did not suit his purpose to mention it. Paul also refers to "James the Lord's brother," suggesting that Mary had another son (Gal 1:19).

Infancy stories involving Mary are found only in Matthew and Luke, and they are by intention highly theological. Both Gospels affirm the virginal conception. In Matthew an angel revealed to JOSEPH that the conception was of the Holy Spirit (1:20). Matthew connects Mary with the genealogy by naming four women who, although they had unusual marital unions, were used in God's messianic plan (1:3-6). Mary is the instrument of the fulfillment of prophecy (1:23; cf. Isa 7:14) and maintains a state of virginity until after the birth of Jesus (1:25). In contrast to Luke, Matthew then shifts the focus to Joseph, to whom both Mary and the child are entrusted (2:13-14, 20-21). Joseph takes them into Egypt to escape Herod (2:13-15) and finally back to Galilee after the death of Herod (2:19-23).

Luke's infancy story places Mary in a more central position and records extensive episodes surrounding the announcement, the birth of Jesus, and even events after the birth. In Luke the angel appears to Mary, not Joseph (1:26-38). A lengthy narrative describes this announcement and Mary's response, which is finally acceptance (1:38). She then travels to see her kinswoman ELIZABETH in Judea (1:39-56). In the dialogue with Elizabeth, Mary responds with the MAGNIFICAT (1:46-55). Mary eventually delivers the child in Bethlehem, where angels and shepherds come to pay homage (2:8-20). Luke also relates the purification of Mary and the consecration of her firstborn (2:22-24). Mary is seen as a pious woman of the common folk obedient to God and his law (2:39). An elderly man, SIMEON, and an aged prophetess, ANNA, rejoice over the coming of the Messiah (2:25-40). A final episode in Luke's narrative is the trip to Jerusalem when Jesus is twelve years old. Even though Jesus has a higher loyalty to God, he is obedient to his parents (2:51).

References to Mary in accounts of the ministry of Jesus are not as favorable as in the infancy narratives. In the Beelzebul controversy, Jesus' mother and brothers apparently try to restrain him (Mark 3:32), and in the preaching in the synagogue after his family is mentioned, Jesus says, "A prophet is not without honor, except in his own country, and among his own kin, and in his own house" (Mark 6:4). The parallel passages in Matthew and Luke are softer and more favorable to Mary (Matt 12:46-50; 13:53-58; Luke 8:19-21; 4:16-24), especially in Luke (cf. 11:27-28). In Mark 6:3, where brothers and sisters are mentioned, these seem to be natural children by Mary and Joseph, but those holding to Mary's perpetual virginity consider them as children of Joseph only (cf. *ProtJames* 9.2). By this time Mary is apparently a widow since Joseph never makes an appearance during Jesus' ministry. Although no writer explicitly states that Mary did not believe in Jesus during his ministry as the Gospel of John does about his brothers (John 7:5), it does not appear that Mary followed him during his ministry. Jesus resisted attempts by his family to direct his ministry (Matt 12:46-50; Mark 3:32; Luke 8:19-21; John 2:3-11), and once said to Mary, "O woman, what have you to do with me?" (John 2:4). However, John's Gospel also records Mary's presence at the cross, and she becomes at the end a model of faith in Jesus and the ideal mother for the leader of the new community, the "beloved disciple" (John 19:25-27).

The woman in Rev 12:1-6 who brings forth the Messiah is not Mary but the people of God—Israel and the Church, who bring forth Christ. Later apocryphal and patristic works expanded on the biblical view of Mary, but in none of these is there reliable information beyond that which is in the NT.

See also ANNA; ELIZABETH; JAMES; JESUS; JOSEPH; LAZARUS; MAGNIFICAT; MARK; MARTHA; SIMEON.

Bibliography. R. Brown and others, *Mary in the New Testament*; V. Eller, "Mary: Protestantism's Forgotten Woman," *ATR* 62 (1980): 146-54; M. J. Evans, *Woman in the Bible*; E. Moltmann-Wendel, *The Women Around Jesus*; R. R. Reuther, *Mary—The Feminine Face of the Church*; E. Stagg and F. Stagg, *Woman in the World of Jesus*.

—W. THOMAS SAWYER

• **Mary, Gospel of.** The *Gospel of Mary* is an APOCRYPHAL GOSPEL of Gnostic origin, dating from the second century. Only fragments remain, partly in the original Greek and partly in Coptic translation. The MARY intended is Mary Magdalene.

What survives consists of two parts, which may represent different sources. The fragments begin at a point where the risen Christ speaks with his disciples before leaving them, giving them the command to preach the gospel of the Kingdom. The disciples are distressed at his departure, but Mary arrives and comforts them.

In the second part, Peter asks Mary to reveal the mysteries the Savior had revealed to her. She responds with a description of the ascent of the soul through hostile spheres. Andrew and Peter refuse to believe that the Savior revealed such secrets to a woman. This reduces Mary to tears, but Levi defends her.

The second part is reminiscent of Gnostic gospels such as the APOCRYPHON OF JOHN, in which there is a dialogue between the questioner and a revealer.

See also APOCRYPHAL GOSPELS.

Bibliography. H.-Ch. Puech, "Gnostic Gospels and Related Documents: the Gospel of Mary," *New Testament Apocrypha,* ed. E. Hennecke and W. Schneemelcher.

—ROGER A. BULLARD

• **Mary, Questions of.** The "Questions of Mary" refer to what were apparently two sources used by certain Gnostic groups, the "Great Questions of Mary" and the "Little Questions of Mary." All we know of these is the little told by the fourth century heresiologist Epiphanius (*Pan* 26.8.1-3). The "Great Questions" was apparently used by circles of libertine Gnostics to justify obscene sexual practices that constituted their rites of redemption. MARY Magdalene appears as a recipient of a secret revelation from Jesus.

Epiphanius simply mentions the "Little Questions." We know nothing about the work.

Bibliography. H.-Ch. Puech, "Gnostic Gospels and Related Documents: The Gospel of Mary," *New Testament Apocrypha,* ed. E. Hennecke and W. Schneemelcher.

—ROGER A. BULLARD

• **Masada.** [muh-sah'duh] The site of a fortress built by HEROD the Great and later occupied by Jewish ZEALOTS during their revolt against the Romans. The fortress occupies the top of a free standing rock situated some 1,300 ft. above the western side of the DEAD SEA across from the boot-like projection of land on the eastern shore known as the Lisan (PLATES 8, 46). Its surface is shaped roughly like a lengthwise cross-section of a football, measuring 1,900 ft. from tip to tip and 650 ft. across the middle. All sides rise vertically from the base limiting access in ancient times to switchback footpaths. Masada is not mentioned in the Bible but is famous in Jewish history because 960 Zealots occupied the fortress and chose to die by their own hands rather than allow the Romans to capture them in 73 C.E. after a three-year siege. The Jewish historian, Josephus, described the terrible end of this revolt and, as a result, it has become a national shrine for Israelis who commemorate their sacrifice.

The Israeli archaeologist Yigael Yadin excavated this site in two seasons, 1963–64 and 1964–65, using thousands of volunteers. Although Josephus had described the fortress and its buildings, many thought the descriptions to be inaccurate. Generally speaking, the excavation confirmed the accuracy of the ancient historian's description and demonstrated that building activity began with Herod the Great and ended in the fifth or sixth centuries C.E. when Byzantine monks erected churches on the mountain top. In between these two periods the Romans and the Zealots left their marks on the site. The outline of nine Roman camps which surrounded the base of the mountain are still clearly visible to the visitor standing on top. Visible, too, is the massive earth fill on the west side which enabled the Romans to gain access at last to the summit.

The most spectacular remains at this site are those of Herod's buildings. Especially magnificent is the "hanging" three-tiered palace which Herod had built on the very northern-most tip of the mountain. Built in three levels, it was literally perched over the edge of the mountain. The upper level contained living quarters with a semi-circular porch area overlooking the sea below. Its rooms had beautiful mosaic floors and brilliantly painted plaster walls and ceilings. The middle level contained a circular building, perhaps with double rows of columns supporting the roof. The lowest level, a terrace some forty-five ft. below the middle level, is remarkable for its well preserved painted walls designed to look like marble panels. Even more remarkable is the small Roman bath on this level with its cool, warm, and hot rooms. The cost of building and sustaining this structure must have been tremendous both in terms of money and in human effort and life.

Other structures from this period can only be mentioned briefly. Moving from north to south, the excavation uncovered a large bath house just behind the northern palace. The large bath was especially ornate with the same separation of cool, warm, and hot rooms and a system for conducting the heat from an adjacent room. The hot air not only heated the floor of the hot room but rose through clay pipes in the walls to heat the entire room. Water poured on the floor produced steam. The warm room between the hot and cool rooms received ornate treatment by the builders with tiled floors and a richly painted ceiling.

Several large store rooms and an administrative building surrounded the bath complex. And beginning at the storage rooms, a double wall, known as a casemate wall, ran around the entire top of the mountain some 4,200 ft. The two walls were over thirteen ft. apart with over a hundred rooms built into this space. Many towers and four gates were spaced at intervals around the wall.

Another large palace complex, the largest of the buildings on the mountain top, occupied the middle of the western wall. Apparently this palace was the actual center of life in Herod's period. Three other small palaces were built south of this major building complex. A small swimming pool lay between the western palace and one of the small palaces. Water for the baths and the swimming pool came from huge cisterns as large as three story buildings which trapped rain water.

A small building on the northwest wall has been identified as a synagogue, oriented toward Jerusalem. While it may have been a synagogue before the Zealots arrived, it was clearly redone to serve for worship by them. In addition, ritual baths were discovered which had been constructed in conformity with the Jewish ceremonial law.

The Roman occupation of the site following the death of the defenders caused little change on the top of the mountain. However, in the Christian era, Byzantine monks lived at Masada and two structures remain as evidence of their practice of a different faith on this site. A church with portions of the walls still erect and its apse, easily identifiable, stands between the storerooms in the north and the western palace. Yadin's excavation uncovered the floor of this church and revealed a lovely mosaic pattern distinctive of the Byzantine period. Nearby a small building apparently served the monks as a workshop for creating the mosaic floor.

The Byzantine monks who probably left in the seventh century C.E. apparently were the last to live on Masada before modern times.

See also HERODIAN FORTRESSES.

Bibliography. K. N. Scoville, *Biblical Archaeology in Focus*; Y. Yadin, *Masada: Herod's Fortress and the Zealots' Last Stand* and "Masada," *IDBSupp*.

—JOE O. LEWIS

• **Maskil.** [mas'kil] From the root *śkl*, meaning to prosper, consider or instruct. The word occurs mostly in the intensive and causative forms of the verb in the OT. Maskil appears in early and late writings and refers both to men and to women.

Maskil is found in the introduction to at least ten Psalms and within many biblical passages. Attributed to various authors, these Psalms contain a certain type of WISDOM. They were written by wise persons who knew how to enable the worshiper to approach the deity appropriately and by so doing bring about a good response.

In late Jewish times the *maskil* type of literature became more and more prominent. Some authorities hold that several canonical Psalms were written by these wise ones.

See also PSALMS, BOOK OF.

—FRED E. YOUNG

• **Masora/Masoretes.** *See* TEXTS/MANUSCRIPTS/VERSIONS

• **Mastema.** *See* BAAL-ZEBUB/BAAL-ZEBUL

• **Mattaniah.** *See* ZEDEKIAH

• **Matthew.** [math'y*oo*] Matthew is included in all the lists of the original twelve disciples of Jesus (Matt 10:3; Mark 3:18; Luke 6:15; Acts 1:13). The account of his call is given in Matt 9:9, Mark 2:14, and Luke 5:27. All three accounts state that the man was a tax collector (cf. Matt 10:3). Matthew's Gospel gives his name as Matthew, while Mark and Luke state that his name was Levi. The details of the accounts in the three Gospels are so similar that it is assumed they record the call of the same man. Why do the accounts give different names? One suggestion is that the man had two Hebrew names. Another is that his name was Levi and Jesus gave him the name Matthew. A third suggestion is that his name was Matthew and that he was from the tribe of Levi.

Mark 2:14 states that Levi was a son of Alphaeus. The lists of disciples give JAMES, the son of Alphaeus. If Matthew and Levi were the same person, then Matthew and James were brothers.

Matthew was a minor official in the service of Herod

ANTIPAS at Capernaum. The border between Galilee and the regions governed by Herod Philip was near Capernaum. In contrast to tax farmers who received their position by promising to pay a fixed amount of money, Matthew probably collected custom tolls on merchandise carried on the Damascus-Mediterranean highway. He would also have been involved in collecting tariffs placed upon fish exported from the Sea of Galilee as well as taxes on other activities in the region.

Nothing is said in the Gospels about Matthew's integrity. Tax collectors had a reputation for dishonesty in first-century Judaism. Many opportunities for illegal profits were presented. Tax collectors were also looked upon as traitors because they were collecting taxes for a foreign power (Rome) even in such a situation as Matthew who worked in the employ of one who was a Jew. They were considered to be outside the Law and religiously unclean.

His work as a tax collector at Capernaum must have given Matthew opportunities to see and hear Jesus. Therefore when Jesus summoned him, he was ready to leave everything (Luke 5:28) and follow him. The call was followed by a meal where Jesus seems to have served as host and other tax collectors and sinners were guests. This may have taken place in the home of Matthew. If so, he must have accumulated some wealth.

Early tradition states that Matthew was the author of the Gospel which bears his name. Papias stated that Matthew wrote the oracles of the Lord in Hebrew. Opinions differ as to whether Papias was referring to the Gospel of Matthew.

After the list of disciples in Acts, Matthew disappeared from the pages of the NT. According to tradition, after he spent a number of years in Palestine he went to Ethiopia and then to other lands to preach. The traditions do not agree about his death. One account states that he died a natural death, while another claims he was martyred.

See also APOSTLE/APOSTLESHIP; DISCIPLE/DISCIPLESHIP; JAMES; MATTHEW, GOSPEL OF; PUBLICANS; TWELVE, THE.

Bibliography. R. Brownrigg, *The Twelve Apostles*; E. J. Goodspeed, *Matthew, Apostle and Evangelist*; E. G. Kraeling, *The Disciples*.

—CLAYTON K. HARROP

• Matthew, Gospel of. *Authorship*. The Gospel of Matthew is traditionally attributed to an individual mentioned in the Gospel itself, a tax collector named MATTHEW who left his collector's booth to follow Jesus as a disciple and then (with other tax collectors and "sinners") entertained Jesus in his home for a meal (Matt 9:9-13). This tax collector, identified as Levi in Mark (2:14-17) and Luke (5:27-32), is named Matthew in the Gospel bearing that name, and thereby given an identity as one of Jesus' twelve apostles (cf. Matt 10:3). The earliest known identification of Matthew as the author of this Gospel comes from Papias, a bishop in Asia Minor in the second century, quoted in the fourth century by the church historian Eusebius. After discussing Papias's testimony to Mark's Gospel, Eusebius adds more briefly that "about Matthew this was said, 'Matthew collected the oracles in the Hebrew dialect; each interpreted them as he was able' " (*EccHist* 3.39.16). The difficulty is that Matthew's Gospel as we have it today is written in Greek (like all the NT), not Hebrew, and more importantly, gives no evidence of being a translation from Hebrew. Either Papias was not referring to the Gospel of Matthew that we possess, or he was mistaken, or the word "dialect" does not refer to language, but to Matthew's literary or rhetorical structure—viewed as a distinctly Hebrew or Jewish structure.

• OUTLINE OF MATTHEW •

The Gospel of Matthew

I. Preparation for the Gospel (1:1–4:16)
   A. The Genealogy of Jesus the Messiah (1:1-17)
   B. The Birth of Jesus: "God with us" (1:18-25; cf. Isa 7:14)
   C. From Bethlehem to Nazareth (2:1-23)
   D. From Nazareth to the Jordan River (3:1-17)
   E. From the Jordan to the desert (4:1-11)
   F. The return to Galilee (4:12-16)
II. Jesus and the Gospel of the Kingdom (4:17–16:20)
   A. Narrative introduction (4:17-22)
   B. First discourse: the sermon on the mount (4:23–7:29)
   C. Narrative: nine (ten) miracles (8:1–9:34)
   D. Second discourse: the mission (9:35–11:1)
   E. Narrative and controversies (11:2–12:50)
   F. Third discourse: parables of the Kingdom (13:1-53)
   G. Narrative: the identity of Jesus (13:54–16:20)
III. Jesus and the Passion (16:21–28:20)
   A. Narrative introduction (16:21–17:27)
   B. Fourth discourse: life in the new community (18:1–19:1a)
   C. Narratives and discourses: the journey to the Temple (19:1b–23:39)
   D. Fifth discourse: the destruction of the Temple and the end of the world (24:1–26:2)
   E. Narrative of the Passion (26:2–28:20)

In any event, Papias' testimony set the tone for others to follow: Matthew was consistently seen as the author and was assumed not only to have been the most Jewish of the Gospel writers, but to have written his Gospel in Hebrew or Aramaic. Matthew came to be regarded as the earliest of the Gospels (e.g., by Augustine), and consequently stands at the front of the canonical NT. In the face of a growing consensus among nineteenth- and twentieth-century scholars that Mark was actually the earliest Gospel and that Matthew was a revision of Mark, there were those (particularly in the Roman Catholic tradition) who ingeniously suggested an original Aramaic Matthew prior to Mark, even while recognizing Mark as a source for the Greek Matthew. But the Aramaic Matthew has never been found, and even if it were found, its relationship to Greek Matthew would still have to be demonstrated. The identification of this Gospel with Matthew the tax collector, though possible, is unproven. The Gospel is anonymous, even though for convenience it continues to be referred to as "Matthew."

The Jewishness of Matthew. The Gospel of Matthew is most profitably studied as a literary creation in itself, not as a second edition of Mark, and certainly not as the translation of a supposed Hebrew original. It does, however, exhibit a characteristically Jewish style and structure. It appears to be the product of first-century Jewish Christianity, but a Jewish Christianity significantly attuned to the Greek-speaking gentile world. The Jewishness of Matthew is immediately evident in the genealogy (1:1-17), where the descent of Jesus is traced from ABRAHAM through DAVID to the time of the Jewish Exile in Babylon, and from there to "Joseph the husband of Mary, of whom Jesus was born, who is called Christ" (v. 16). In keeping with the fondness in Jewish APOCALYPTIC LITERATURE for dividing history into periods, Matthew notes fourteen generations from Abraham to David, fourteen from David to the Exile, and fourteen from the Exile to Jesus, forty-two generations in all. If Jewish history is viewed as a "jubilee" of forty-nine generations (cf. Lev 25:8-12; Isa 61:1-2; Luke 4:18-19), then this is Matthew's way of saying that history is now entering its last phase, and that the KINGDOM OF GOD is not far off (cf. Matt 3:2; 4:17; also 24:22, "for the sake of the elect those days will be shortened"; 28:20, "I am with you always, to the close of the age").

The list of Jesus' ancestors is of course a Jewish list, except for four gentile women: Tamar (v. 3), Rahab (v. 5), Ruth (v. 5), and Uriah's wife (v. 6). Two of the names, Tamar and Ruth, are probably attributable to Matthew's apparent dependence on the Book of Ruth (4:12, 18-21), while Rahab is drawn in because in Matthew's tradition (otherwise unattested in Jewish tradition) she was mother to Boaz, who married Ruth. Matthew's point closely parallels the point made by the Book of Ruth. Ruth tells the romantic story of a gentile woman who, it turns out, was the great-grandmother of David the king! Matthew mentions no less than three gentile women in David's ancestry, and a fourth in the ancestry of the son of David, Jesus the Messiah. The fourth, Uriah's wife, stands as an ironic reminder of David's sin and repentance. Though Matthew wants to place Jesus unmistakably in the Jewish messianic line, he insists at the same time that the line is not pure in the strictest terms of the Jewish Law. Gentiles too had a place in the events that led to the Messiah's coming. After Jesus' birth, a group of gentiles ("wise men [magi] from the east") came to worship the child born "king of the Jews" (2:1-2, 9-12). When a gentile centurion comes to faith (without even asking Jesus to compromise his Jewishness by entering a gentile home), Jesus says, "Not even in Israel have I found such faith. I tell you many will come from east and west and will sit at table with Abraham, Isaac, and Jacob in the kingdom of heaven, while the sons of the kingdom will be thrown into the outer darkness; there men will weep and gnash their teeth" (8:10-12). Still, Jesus keeps insisting that "I was sent only to the lost sheep of the house of Israel" (15:24; cf. 10:5-6), and at first hesitates to heal the daughter of a Canaanite woman who cries out to him as "son of David" (15:22-26; cf. the foreign women in Matthew's Davidic genealogy). But when the woman persists, Jesus grants her request and commends her great faith (15:27-28).

On the one hand, Jesus in Matthew's Gospel remains for the most part within the limitations of Judaism, and emphasizes in the strongest possible terms the eternal authority of the Jewish Law: "Think not that I have come to abolish the law and the prophets; I have not come to abolish them but to fulfill them. . . . Till heaven and earth pass away, not an iota, not a dot will pass from the law until all is accomplished. Whoever then relaxes one of the least of these commandments and teaches men so, shall be called least in the kingdom of heaven; but he who does them and teaches them shall be called great in the kingdom of heaven" (5:17-19). Even regarding the contemporary interpreters of the Law, he acknowledges that "The scribes and the Pharisees sit on Moses' seat; so practice and observe whatever they tell you, but not what they do; for they preach, but do not practice" (23:2-3).

On the other hand, Jesus' vision (according to Matthew) looks beyond the present to a day when salvation will reach gentiles as well as Jews (cf., e.g., 4:15-16, "Galilee of the Gentiles—the people who sat in darkness have seen a great light"; 12:21, "in his name will the Gentiles hope"), or even gentiles instead of Jews (cf., e.g., 8:10-12 as quoted above; also 21:43, "the kingdom of God will be taken away from you and given to a nation producing the fruits of it"). At the end of the age, "when the Son of man shall sit on his glorious throne," Jesus and his disciples will exercise judgment over both the Jews ("you . . . will also sit on twelve thrones, judging the twelve tribes of Israel," 19:28) and the gentiles ("Before him will be gathered all the nations [gentiles], and he will separate them one from another as a shepherd separates the sheep from the goats," 25:32). The terms of judgment on Israel are unstated, but the gentiles are judged on the basis of how they have treated the disciples of Jesus that would be sent to them as missionaries ("As you did it to one of the least of these my brethren, you did to me," 24:40). The judgment of Israel and of the gentiles in Matthew presupposes that there has been a mission to both Israel and to the gentile world, a mission that would continue until the end of the world and the full establishment of the Kingdom of God. In the case of Israel, Jesus tells his disciples early on that "you will not have gone through all the towns of Israel, before the Son of man comes" (10:23). In the case of the gentiles, he says in his last discourse, "this gospel of the kingdom will be preached throughout the whole world, as a testimony to all nations [gentiles]; and then the end will come" (24:14; cf. 26:13), and after his resurrection to his disciples, "All authority in heaven and on earth has been given to me. Go therefore and make disciples of all nations [the gentiles], baptizing them in the name of the Father and of the Son and of the Holy Spirit, teaching them to observe all that I have commanded you; and lo, I am with you always, to the close of the age" (28:18-20). The placement of the latter pronouncement at the very end of Matthew's Gospel suggests that here is where the emphasis lies. This passage, in fact, affords the decisive clue to the Gospel's purpose.

The Purpose of Matthew. The task of Jesus' disciples according to Matt 28:18-20 is to "make disciples of all nations" and in connection with this undertaking baptize and teach. What they are to teach is made explicit in the words, "all that I have commanded you" (v. 20). They are to teach the teachings of Jesus himself, and it is a fair inference that the teachings the author has in mind are the teachings preserved in the Gospel of Matthew itself. The inference is confirmed by the fact that Matthew has arranged the teachings of Jesus topically in five long discourses (i.e., chaps. 5–7, ethics; chap. 10, missionary instructions; 13:1-52, the nature of the Kingdom of heaven; chap. 18, relationships in the believing community; chaps. 24–25, the destruction of Jerusalem and the close of the age). Each discourse is terminated with a summary, "And it came to pass when Jesus had finished" (each summary a little different depending on the setting: 7:28-29; 11:1; 13:53; 19:1; 26:1). Although the summary may have been traditional in early Christian accounts of Jesus' teaching (cf. Luke 7:1), Matthew has made it a key to his arrangement of the material to be taught; it appears that the first summary (7:28-29) may have served as a model for the others. From one standpoint, then, Matthew's Gospel appears to be a catechism or teaching book for the use of Jesus' disciples in carrying out the mission to the gentiles commanded in 28:18-20. Another such early Christian teaching book is the second-century *Didache,* or *The Teaching of the Lord through the Twelve Apostles to the Gentiles.* Matthew too calls attention to the role of the apostles in connection with the mission to the gentiles, even though he calls them "disciples" rather than "apostles," and even though they are eleven rather than twelve (28:16; they are "apostles" only in 10:2).

The main thing distinguishing Matthew from the *Di-*

dache is that Matthew is not simply a teaching book, but a Gospel as well, following the precedent of Mark. A glance at the outline shows that after a narrative introduction (1:1–4:16), Matthew alternates narrative and discourse at least from 4:17 to the end of chap. 18. Only after Jesus leaves Galilee do the categories become somewhat blurred (esp. in a series of exchanges between Jesus and various questioners in the Jerusalem Temple in 21:23–23:36). Matthew wants to do two things at once for gentiles interested in Christianity: to tell the story of Jesus, and to pass the teaching of Jesus along to those who need to hear and obey it.

The first section of Matthew (1:1–4:16) is entirely narrative. The genealogy is followed by an account designed to reconcile Jesus' birth in Bethlehem (in keeping with widespread Jewish expectations, 2:5-6), with the known fact that Nazareth was his childhood home (cf. Mark 1:9). The author brings the infant, with his parents, from Bethlehem to Egypt (2:13-19), back to Judea again (2:19-21), and finally to Galilee and "a town called Nazareth" (2:22-23). Each step of the journey is explained by the will of God revealed in dreams (2:13, 19, 22; cf. v. 12), and also by the claim that everything that happened was a fulfillment of scripture 2:15, 18, 23). This claim, made first in connection with the birth and naming of Jesus (1:23), keeps recurring throughout the Gospel, in 4:14-16, 8:17, 12:7-21, 13:35, 21:4-5, and 27:9-10 (ten times in all), each quotation introduced with a formula stating (with slight variation) that "this happened so that the scripture might be fulfilled"). Matthew seems to have taken his cue for this formula from Mark 14:49, where Jesus at his arrest in Gethsemane says, "Let the scriptures be fulfilled." The parallel in Matthew resembles the characteristically Mathean formula: "this has taken place that the scriptures of the prophets might be fulfilled" (26:56; cf. v. 54).

Most of the scriptures to which Matthew calls attention throughout his Gospel are not (like the one cited by Herod's advisors in 2:5) passages that the Jews customarily associated with their expectations of the Messiah. They are distinctly Christian proof texts, although introduced on the basis of the same kind of reading of the scripture to which the Jewish rabbis were accustomed. Matthew wants to emphasize that not only the coming of Jesus, but everything that happened to him in his birth, ministry and death, was part of the divine plan (cf. Jesus' words to John the Baptist in 3:15), and therefore in many specific instances foretold in the God-given scriptures of the prophets. But for whom was this emphasis important? Was it for a Jewish audience, to convince the Jews out of their own scriptures that Jesus was the Messiah? This seems plausible, but it is also likely that many of the texts Matthew cites would have seemed farfetched to a Jewish audience that was not already disposed to acknowledge Jesus as the Messiah. They would have been less convincing, for example, than Matthew's genealogy, or the testimony of Jesus' birth in Bethlehem the city of David. Another possibility is that the scripture citations were brought in for the benefit of gentile converts, to make certain that in believing in Jesus they would take seriously as well the Jewish scriptures that so marvelously foretold Jesus' coming. Especially if Matthew's Gospel was written as a teaching book for gentiles, the latter alternative is the more likely one. It would have been all too easy for gentiles to accept Jesus the Jew as their Lord and Savior while ignoring the Jewish scriptures and to some extent even the Jewish God. For Matthew, this is simply not an option. As a Jew, he wants Judaism to fulfill its destiny as heir to the promise given to Abraham in Gen 12:3 that through him all the nations would be blessed. As a Jewish Christian involved in mission and ministry to gentiles, he wants to insure that the Jewish heritage and the Jewish scriptures are not abandoned as the Christian message moves quickly across significant cultural barriers.

See also ABRAHAM; APOSTLE/APOSTLESHIP; CHURCH AND LAW; DAVID; DISCIPLE/DISCIPLESHIP; GENTILE/GENTILES IN THE NEW TESTAMENT; GENTILE/GENTILES IN THE OLD TESTAMENT; GOSPEL; GOSPELS, CRITICAL STUDY OF; KINGDOM OF GOD; LAW IN THE NEW TESTAMENT; MAGI; MATTHEW; MESSIAH/CHRIST; SERMON ON THE MOUNT; SYNOPTIC PROBLEM; TEMPTATION OF JESUS.

Bibliography. E. P. Blair, *Jesus in the Gospel of Matthew*; G. Bornkamm, G. Barth, and H. J. Held, *Tradition and Interpretation in Matthew*; J. A. Broadus, *A Commentary on the Gospel of Matthew*; R. E. Brown, *The Birth of the Messiah: A Commentary on the Infancy Narratives in Matthew and Luke*; W. D. Davies, *The Setting of the Sermon on the Mount*; R. H. Gundry, *Matthew: A Commentary on His Literary and Theological Art*; D. R. A. Hare, *The Theme of the Jewish Persecution of Christians in the Gospel according to Matthew*; D. Hill, *The Gospel of Matthew*; J. D. Kingsbury, *Matthew: Structure, Christology, Kingdom* and *The Parables of Jesus in Matthew 13: A Study in Redaction Criticism*; E. Krenz, "The Extent of Matthew's Prologue," *JBL* 83 (1964): 409-14; R. S. McConnell, *Law and Prophecy in Matthew's Gospel*; J. P. Meier, *Law and History in Matthew's Gospel* and *The Vision of Matthew: Christ, Church, and Morality in the First Gospel*; J. R. Michaels, "Apostolic Hardships and Righteous Gentiles: A Study of Matthew 25:31-46," *JBL* 84 (1965): 27-37; A. Plummer, *An Exegetical Commentary on the Gospel according to St. Matthew*; K. Stendahl, "Quis et Unde? An Analysis of Mt. 1–2," *JCU* (1964): 94-105; M. J. Suggs, *Wisdom, Christology, and Law in Matthew's Gospel*; W. G. Thompson, *Matthew's Advice to a Divided Community* (1970).

—J. RAMSEY MICHAELS

• **Maundy Thursday.** [mawn'dee] Maundy Thursday is an important celebration of the church observed during Holy Week. The word "maundy" comes from the Latin word *mandatum,* translated command or mandate. The command in question comes from John 13:34, "a new commandment (*mandatum*) I give to you, that you love one another." These words were uttered by Jesus following the last supper and the washing of the disciples' feet.

Thus, Maundy Thursday commemorates the last supper of Jesus with his disciples, the night before his death on the cross. By the fourth century, the Council of Hippo (393) established Maundy Thursday as the Lord's institution of the Eucharist. In the Roman Catholic tradition, Maundy Thursday is one of the most complex holy days. Seven events are celebrated: (1) Tenebrae ("darkness"), special services conducted as a mourning and reenactment of the events surrounding the death of Christ; (2) reconciliation of penitents; (3) the Mass; (4) consecration of the oils; (5) stripping and washing of the altar; (6) feet washing; and (7) the loving cup.

—JAMES L. BLEVINS

• **Meals.** The names and times for daily meals are not given in the OT. There are, however, terms for meals in the NT: *ariston* is lunch, *deipnon* dinner, or chief meal. One learns from Exod 16:12 that there were two meals eaten daily, one in the morning and one at twilight. Food and drink formed part of the meal. For most persons, meat was on the menu only for the evening meal on special occasions. The morning meal was modest, consisting of few items. Fruit and bread were common for breakfast, while the evening meal was more substantial.

Special meals usually took place in the evening, but there are some references to meals that occurred during the day. Such meals, however, were apparently banquets or feasts. With the coming of special guests, the fatted calf would be slaughtered (e.g., Gen 18:1- 8). Wines and rich delicacies were consumed at such banquets. Amos pictures banquets with individuals lying on beds made with ivory inlay, eating the best of foods, drinking wine from bowls, and singing songs (Amos 6:4-6). Revelry and hilarity set the tone at such banquets.

Banquets would take place on the occasion of the arrival of a guest (e.g., Gen 19:3), at harvest festivals (e.g., Judg 9:27), at a wedding, or on the occasion of the ratification of a treaty. Ordinary meals involved only the members of the family, but banquets and feasts might bring large numbers of persons together. Probably, only males would be invited to such banquets. Forms of entertainment included music, song, dance, and even the posing of riddles or the telling of stories. The prophets, the author of Proverbs, and Paul roundly denounced the debauchery and riotous behavior that took place at such banquets.

Special seating and choice portions might be reserved for special persons at banquets. Joseph gave Benjamin five portions, showing his special status (Gen 43:34), and Samuel reserved a special part of the meal for Saul to eat (1 Sam 9:23-24). The manner of seating was important. Abraham stood while his three guests sat (Gen 18:8). Guests of honor were placed at the head of the table (1 Sam 9:22). Members of the family were seated according to age (Gen 43:33). Sometimes, important guests would be seated on either side of the host. James and John asked Jesus for these choice spots when Jesus claimed his place at the last day (Mark 10:37), but Jesus encouraged his disciples to take the lower seats, waiting to be invited to assume a place of greater honor.

Early custom involved reclining at the meal. Chairs and stools probably were used by some at later times. Amos castigated those who reclined at ease on their couches (6:4-6). Using the right hand for eating was important, since the left hand was normally used for other bodily functions and thus should not be used for eating. Eating without washing one's hands was unacceptable.

It is not clear just how the food was served. There are references to the host's doing the serving, but there are also references to servants who did the serving. Bread was served before wine was passed, a custom reflected in the last supper of Jesus.

Cooking utensils are mentioned, but there are no references to eating utensils. Persons normally ate with their fingers, using portions of bread to dip into liquid food or to pick up portions of meat or vegetables.

Meals also have a symbolic importance in biblical times. The Passover meal was symbolic of Israel's liberation from Egyptian bondage and had to be prepared and eaten in the way prescribed so as to recall the events of Israel's leaving Egypt on the first Passover night. The LORD'S SUPPER, foreshadowed in Jesus' last meal with the disciples, is observed as symbol of Christ's death and resurrection. It is a participation in Christ's death but also a sharing of Christ's resurrection.

Sacrifices were also occasions for shared meals, where the family gathered to enjoy its share of the sacrifice and where the communion between God and the family and its individual members would be felt profoundly by the faithful. While some sacrifices were offered wholly to God, most of them involved a shared meal with the deity.

The last great meal to be celebrated is the Marriage Supper of the Lamb, in which heaven and earth join in the celebration of the final triumph of the Lord (Rev 19:9).

See also BANQUET; FOOD; SACRIFICE.

—FRED E. YOUNG

• **Meat.** *See* FLESH

• **Meat Offered to Idols.** *See* FOOD OFFERED TO IDOLS

• **Medeba.** [med'uh-buh] A town in northern MOAB approx. fifteen mi. southeast of the northern edge of the DEAD SEA (PLATE 12), Medeba is mentioned only five times in the OT. Num 21:27-30 relates an ancient taunt song which reports that Sihon, the Amorite king, captured Medeba and additional Moabite territory. Shortly after this Israel defeated Sihon and conquered the territory Sihon had taken from the Moabites (cf. Num 21:21-26). This conquered territory, including Medeba, was later allotted to the tribes of Reuben, Gad, and half of Manasseh (Josh 13:9, 16).

First Chr 19:7 may suggest that during the time of David Medeba belonged to the Ammonites, whose land lay to the north of Moab. There the Syrian army, allies of the Ammonites, encamped before their defeat at the hands of Joab, Abishai, and David's army (cf. 1 Chr 19:1-19). The final biblical reference to Medeba is found in Isa 15, an oracle against Moab; "Over Nebo and over Medeba Moab wails" (v. 2), presumably because of a defeat at the hands of the Assyrians. Medeba is also mentioned on the Moabite Stone which says that Omri took Medeba and Israel dwelt there for forty years before Mesha recaptured and rebuilt it.

Medeba was important during Maccabean times and later was a center for Christianity. It continues to be occupied even today, largely because of its rich farm lands and its location along the King's Highway which runs through Transjordan.

Bibliography. Y. Aharoni, *The Land of the Bible: A Historical Geography*.

—CECIL P. STATON, JR.

• **Media/Medes.** [mee'dee-uh/meeds] An ancient land and people in northwest Iran who in later OT history were associated with the Persians. The land of Media was located southwest of the Caspian Sea and northeast of the Zargos Mountains, a mountain range that ran parallel to the Tigris River. Ecbatana was the capital of Media. The land of Media was made up of mountainous terrain. The people of Media used the fertile valleys for agricultural purposes. Because Assyrian records from the eighth century B.C.E. speak of the Medes supplying the Assyrians with horses, it may be assumed that the Medes specialized in the production of horses.

While the origin of the Medes is obscure, they were descendants of an Indo-European branch of people. In the Bible, Media is listed in the Table of Nations as Madai, one of the Sons of Japheth (Gen 10:2). Like their origin, the history of the Medes is somewhat obscure and imprecise. Two sources provide the most important information concerning Median history, namely, ancient Assyrian inscriptions and the writings of the Greek historian, Herodotus, though the reliability of the latter is questioned and debated at points. References to the Medes begin to appear in Assyrian inscriptions during the reign of Shalmaneser III, king of Assyria about 858–824 B.C.E. According to his annals, Shalmanesar III invaded several regions east of Assyria including the land of the Medes. The Medes are also mentioned in the records of Assyrian kings from later periods, including those of Shamshi-Adad V, Tiglath-pileser III, Sargon II, and Sennacherib. According to Assyrian records, Tiglath-pileser III (745–727 B.C.E.) carried out several campaigns against the tribes of Media and gained control of their territory. Assyrian claims that 65,000 men were captured, though most likely embellished for propaganda purposes, nevertheless suggest that a significant onslaught of the region took place. Assyrian records indicate that Sargon II fought against the Medes and their neighbors and succeeded in making them vassals. According to the Bible, some of the Israelites deported by the Assyrians at the time of the fall of Samaria were relocated "in the cities of the Medes" (2 Kgs 17:6; 18:11).

The history of the development of the Median empire is obscure in the early stages. Herodotus attributes the unification of the Medes to Deioces, who is recognized as the first ruler of the nation. The city of Ecbatana (Ezra 6:2) was built under his encouragement. The Median rulers who followed Deioces were Phraortes, Cyaxares and Astyages. Of these, Cyaxares, who ruled ca. 625–585 B.C.E., played a formative role in shaping both the history of Media and that of the ancient Near East. Cyaxares halted the Scythian advance on Media, established Media's independence as never before, and dealt the final blows that resulted in the downfall of the Assyrian empire. As an ally with Nabopolassar of Babylon, Cyaxares played a major part in the fall of the Assyrian sites of Asshur in 614 B.C.E., Nineveh in 612 B.C.E., and Haran in 610 B.C.E. Cyaxares was succeeded by his son Astyages, who was defeated by the Persian king Cyrus the Great, ca. 550 B.C.E. Although a province of Persia, Media's influence and identity continued.

Media's influence in the ancient world is demonstrated in a number of ways. References to "the laws of the Medes and Persians" in the books of Esther (1:19; 8:8) and Daniel (6:8) suggest that Media shared in a legal system that was considered firmly established and unalterable. The prophecies of Isaiah and Jeremiah identify Media as an instrument of divine judgement against Babylon (Isa 13:17; Jer 51:11, 28). Apparently the Medes had an administrative structure that was highly regarded and adopted at least in part by others. For instance, the term "satrap," an administrative title for the governor of a province used by the Persians in the time of Darius I, originated with the Medes. References to Media or its people appear in the Apocrypha (1 Macc 6:56; 14:1-3) and the NT (Acts 2:9).

See also PERSIAN EMPIRE.

Bibliography. J. M. Cook, *The Persian Empire*.

—LAMOINE DEVRIES

• **Mediation/Mediator in the New Testament.** Mediation is the means by which transcendence is related to finitude and divine holiness is related to sin. Mediation is the action by which humanity experiences or is given awareness of God, which it otherwise would not have due to finitude or sinfulness. Even religions of immanence—the view that God exists within nature—have mediators; for example, poets are mediators of nature's power because of their imaginative ability to evoke from nature a vivid presence of God. In Acts 17:22-31, Paul quotes a pagan poet to acknowledge this mediatorial power. Normally, however, mediation signifies a person or group which acts to bring about a relationship between two partners which otherwise would not occur.

In the NT, mediation is assumed rather than directly defined or described. The noun appears six times (Gal 3:19-20; 1 Tim 2:5; Heb 8:6; 9:15; 12:24) and the verb once (Heb 6:17). The idea is everywhere present, however, and is usually described in other ways, such as COVENANT, RECONCILIATION, or SALVATION. The partners in the covenant which God mediates to humanity are not equal, for God, the sovereign and merciful creator, redeemer, judge, and lord, establishes and keeps the covenant, even when we break or ignore it.

"For there is one God, and there is one mediator between God and men, the man Christ Jesus" (1 Tim 2:5). Fundamental for the NT is the view that Jesus Christ completes in his unique person and activity what had been promised under the old covenant; and Col 1:15-20 declares that Jesus was the preexistent Lord at creation and now upholds the cosmos until the end. Thus, from beginning to end, Jesus, the Word, mediates power to exist to all that is. He not only proclaims God's love and mercy; but in him, the proclaimer becomes the proclaimed. He is the second Adam who succeeds in obedience to the Law, where the first Adam had failed (e.g., Matt 4:1-11); he is greater than Moses, for he not only received and taught the Law, he fulfilled it (John 1:17; 5:46). Further, Jesus not only revealed God, as the OT prophets did; he was (and is) the revealed God himself.

The mediator of the one covenant of God with his people, the HIGH PRIEST (Heb 9:11-28), propitiates God's wrathful judgment through his sacrificial death on the cross as a "ransom for many" (Rom 3:25; Mark 10:45); he is also God himself doing this (2 Cor 5:19). He is the mediator through his reconciling of humanity to God by his obedient life and atoning death, which continues the mediation of the covenant that God began in creation. This mediation is sustained now through Christ's intercession for us at God's right hand; and the Holy Spirit internally mediates God to us until he who is centrally called mediator, Jesus Christ, comes again.

See also HIGH PRIEST; RECONCILIATION.

Bibliography. E. Brunner, *The Mediator*; J. Denney, *The Death of Christ*; H. D. MacDonald, *The Atonement of the Death of Christ*.

—JOHN S. REIST, JR.

• **Mediation/Mediator in the Old Testament.** The process of using an intermediary or a "third party" between two people or parties; a mediator is the person or object that does this. Mediation and mediators are used in many situations—to establish or maintain relationships between parties, to provide information between one party and another, to intervene on behalf of one party with another, to negotiate between parties, and to reconcile separated or conflicting parties or people.

In religion, mediation is one of the ways in which humans are able to come into contact with the divine. In contrast to a direct and personal relationship with the divine, mediation emphasizes the use of a third party or object to serve as go-between for humans and the divine. This go-between functions in two ways—first, as a figure or object representing GOD to humanity, and second, as a figure or object representing humanity to God.

Not all religions stress the concept of mediation, nor does a particular religion always stress the concept in the same way at all times. Emphasis on the need for mediation and mediators between God and humanity arises when certain theological understandings of the nature of the divine world, of God, of humanity, and of the relationship between the two creates the need for mediation. When a theological system includes a radical separation between the realms of the divine and the human, mediation is often proposed as a way to bridge the gap between the wholly other and transcendent world of the divine and the material and physical world of humanity. Communication or relationship between the two occurs through a person or an object that is able to operate in, and is acceptable to, both worlds. In this understanding, the material world, while seen as separate and different from the divine world, is not necessarily seen as sinful or corrupt. In religious systems relying heavily on the theological concept of mediation, there are cases, however, where the world is seen as corrupt and sinful. In these cases, mediation is not simply a way of bridging the gap between the human and divine worlds; rather, it is the only possible way to establish connections between the holy world of the divine and the sinful and corrupt world of humanity.

Although the concept of mediation and mediators is present in both the OT and NT, the terms themselves are seldom used. The term "mediator" does not appear in the Hebrew OT. The Gk. term for mediator, *mesites* is used six times in the NT: two times referring to an intermediary who communicated the law to humanity (Gal 3:19, 20) and four times referring to the work of JESUS, either as a mediator of the *covenant* between God and humanity (Heb 8:6; 9:15; 12:24) or simply as a mediator between God and humanity (1 Tim 2:5).

In the OT, many figures and objects serve as mediators between God and humanity: (1) particular individuals such as the patriarchs, MOSES, the judges, and EZRA; (2) holders of particular offices such as priests, prophets, teachers and the king; (3) certain general figures such as diviners and magicians; and (4) suprahuman beings such as angels, the "Servant of the Lord," and the MESSIAH.

Most of the major OT leaders are presented as mediators. The patriarchs received dreams, auditions and messengers from God on behalf of their clan; in return, they offered prayers and sacrifices to God for the clan. Moses served as a mediator not only between God and the Hebrews, but also between the Hebrews' God and Egypt's PHARAOH. Military leaders such as JOSHUA and the judges, filled with the "Spirit of the Lord," led the people into battle. Late in Israel's history, leaders such as Ezra continued the tradition of mediation between the people and God by recommunicating the word of God and renewing the covenant.

In addition to particular individuals, holders of certain offices also served as mediators. The most prominent of these offices was that of priest. The priest's role as mediator consisted primarily of offering sacrifices and leading TEMPLE worship, but priests also taught the sacred traditions to the people (cf. Deut 33:8-11). Prophets of various types received the word of God and communicated it to the people. Teachers found God in the search for wisdom and taught their students to do so; kings served as the primary political representative between the people and God.

There were also several popular figures who mediated between the people and God. Many of these figures are associated with practices such as magic and divination. Although generally condemned in the OT, they seem to have been accessible to people and used by them as a source of contact with God.

Lastly, in the later periods of Israelite religion, suprahuman mediators became increasingly important. Angels became prominent as messengers between God and humanity. In Isaiah, the Suffering Servant of the Lord atones for Israel and reconciles God and humanity. Finally, the Messiah is a figure who functions as the ultimate mediator.

In addition to these various figures, the OT also knows of many objects that mediate between God and humanity: (1) "concepts" such as the covenant and the Torah; (2) material objects such as the ARK, TEMPLE, and sacrifices; (3) aspects of God such as God's Face, Name, and Glory; and (4) hypostases such as Wisdom, the Word of God, and the Spirit of God.

In the NT, JESUS is the primary mediator. Jesus functions in several ways: as a source of knowledge of the nature and will of God; as a means of overcoming the separation between humanity and God; and as a means of establishing and maintaining a continuing relationship between people and God.

Finally, in addition to Jesus, the NT also sees the HOLY SPIRIT as a mediator. According to Acts, the Holy Spirit is critically involved at Pentecost, and both 1 Corinthians and the Gospel of John see God's help and presence in the world continuing through the Holy Spirit.

See also MAGIC AND DIVINATION; MESSIAH/CHRIST.

—JOANNE KUEMMERLIN-MCLEAN

• **Mediterranean Sea.** [med'i-tuh-ray"nee-uhn] The Mediterranean Sea is an arm of the Atlantic Ocean which separates Europe from North Africa and the Middle East. Between its extreme ends, the Mediterranean is 2300 mi. long. The width varies from 100 to 600 mi. with an average of 400 mi. The total surface area of the Mediterranean is 1,158,000 square mi.—twice the size of the Caribbean or four times the size of the state of Texas. The temperature varies from 54-57 degrees Farenheit during the winter to 72-75 degrees during the summer in the western part of the sea. In the eastern part the temperature varies from 57-62 degrees during the winter to 75-82 degrees during the summer.

The sea is referred to approximately 380 times in the Bible. The Mediterranean is referred to as "the Great Sea," "the Western Sea," or simply "the sea" (it was also referred to once as "the Sea of the Philistines" in Exod 23:31, because it was remembered they had come from across the Mediterranean Sea, [Deut 2:23]). Thirteen times (Num 34:6, 7; Josh 1:4; 9:1: 15:12, 47; 23:4; Ezek 47:15, 17, 19, 20; 48:28; Dan 7:2) it is called "the Great Sea." Four times (Deut 11:24; 34:2; Joel 2:20; Zech 14:8) it is called "the Western Sea" or literally "the sea behind" since the orientation of the ancient Israelites was toward the east. These designations were to distinguish it from the other seas in the region: the Red Sea with its extentions up either side of the Sinai peninsula (the Reed Sea and the Gulf of Elat), the Sea of Galilee, and the Dead Sea (also known as "the Salt Sea" or "the Sea of the Arabah"). The vast number of references are simply to "the sea." Though many of these may be fairly easily determined as references to the Mediterranean, many more are ambiguous.

The Mediterranean Sea is alluded to in the Bible for several reasons (the following references are representative rather than exhaustive). It signified vast distances (Deut 30:13; Job 11:9; Ps 65:5). It was used to designate the western boundary of the territory of the tribes of Israel (Josh 15:4, 46; 16:3, 8; 17:9, 10; 19:29). It was a means of transport for materials (1 Kgs 5:9; 2 Chr 2:16; Ezra 3:7; 1 Kgs 18:43, 44).

The Mediterranean Sea even represented the differences between the power of man and the power of God. God created the sea (Pss 95:5; 146:6; Acts 4:24; 14:15). God's power quiets the sea (Job 26:12; Ps 107:29; Jonah 1:15). God controls or "covers" the sea by his power (Job 36:30; 38:8; Pss 72:8; 89:9; Isa 10:26; 50:2; Jer 31:35; Jonah 1; Zech 9:8; Hab 3:15). The fish and animals in the sea tremble in anticipation of God's presence (Ezek 38:20). The sea roars in praise and anticipation of God's coming for judgement (Pss 96:11; 98:7). In contrast, the sea is untamed by man (1 Chr 16:32; Job 7:12; Jude 1:13; Rev 7:1ff). Also, some of its creatures, though obedient to God, are much more powerful than man (Job 41).

The sea was generally an unknown to the ancient Hebrews. Some say that the desert origin of the Hebrews caused them to fear the sea. It might have been because the Israelite coast of Palestine was virtually devoid of safe harbors. Though sailors and ships are mentioned in several places (Ps 107:23; Prov 23:34; 30:19; Ezek 27:9, 29; Jonah 1), these are definitely or probably all references to sailors and ships of other peoples. First Kgs 10:22 and 2 Chr 8:19—the great merchant voyages to Tarshish when Solomon was king—are exceptions, but were undertaken with the Phoenicians who were great sailors (also, the location of "Tarshish" is very problematic). In the NT, the journeys of Paul indicate that the Mediterranean Sea was well travelled (Acts 13:13; 17:14; 18:18; 27–28).

Bibliography. J. R. MacDonald, "Mediterranean Sea," *Encyclopedia Americana*; W. L. Reed, "Great Sea," *IDB*.

—TIMOTHY G. CRAWFORD

• **Medium.** *See* MAGIC AND DIVINATION

High Place at ancient Megiddo.

• **Megiddo.** [mi-gid'oh] Identified with modern Tell el-Mutesellim, the mound of Megiddo is located about twenty mi. southeast of Haifa (PLATE 13). The ancient city guarded the pass through the Jezreel valley, the scene of many battles, both ancient and modern. The mound was occupied almost continuously from the Chalcolithic (fourth millennium B.C.E.) through the Persian periods (fourth century B.C.E.).

Even though important Early Bronze and Middle Bronze Age cities existed here, Megiddo is not mentioned in historical texts until its defeat at the hands of the Egyptian Pharaoh, Thutmosis III (ca. 1468 B.C.E.). The city is also mentioned in a Taanach Letter of the late fifteenth, and in the AMARNA correspondence of the fourteenth century B.C.E.

In the OT, Megiddo is listed as one of the cities defeated by JOSHUA (Josh 12:21); and it was "by the waters of Megiddo" that DEBORAH is said to have defeated the coalition of the Canaanite kings (Judg 5:19). However, both the biblical (cf. Josh 17:11; Judg 1:27) and archaeological evidence indicate that Israelite control of the city probably does not antedate the mid-tenth century. During that time Megiddo was the leading city in SOLOMON'S fifth district (1 Kgs 4:12), and, along with Hazor and Gezer, was fortified by him (1 Kgs 9:15). The city was an important Israelite stronghold throughout the period of the divided monarchy until its defeat by Tiglath-pileser III in 733/32 B.C.E. During the revolt of Jehu (mid-ninth century), Ahaziah, king of Judah was killed at Megiddo (2 Kgs 9:27), as was Josiah over two hundred years later in 609 (2 Kgs 23:29-30; cf. 2 Chr 35:20-27). The lack of any biblical references to the city after this time indicates a diminished role during the last years of Israel's history. Because of the many battles fought there in antiquity, the author of Revelation (16:16) made ARMAGEDDON ("the mountain of Megiddo") the location of God's final battle against the forces of evil.

The site was first excavated between 1903 and 1905 by J. Schumacher on behalf of the German Oriental Society. Between 1925 and 1939, the Oriental Institute of the University of Chicago sponsored a major excavation under the direction of C. S. Fisher, P. L. O. Guy, and G. Loud. In order to reexamine the controversial stratigraphy of the Iron Age, Y. Yadin conducted several seasons of work between 1960 and 1971.

Because of the circumstances surrounding the American excavation (i.e., incomplete and inadequate publications; methodology used), there is considerable confusion over both the dates and content of many strata. The dates have in many cases been amended by later scholars and these will be followed here.

The original excavators identified twenty strata on top of the mound, some of which were subdivided, yielding a total of twenty-five levels of occupation. The earliest material, a few flints and bones found in a cave, was dated to the pre-Pottery Neolithic period and was assigned Stratum −XX. Stratum XX proper, consisting of a few mud-brick houses, was dated to the Chalcolithic period. While there is confusion over the dating of some of the Early Bronze Age strata, modern scholars generally assign Strata XIX-XV to this period. To Stratum XIX (3150–2850 B.C.E.) belong the earliest buildings of any significant size. Also discovered were some of the earliest known examples of local Palestinian art: stone drawings of men and beasts. A sacred area was also thought to have been found which continued in existence throughout the long history of the Bronze Age.

Strata XVIII-XVI are confused but were dated by the excavators to the Early Bronze Age II-III (2850–2350 B.C.E.). The major architectural discovery from these strata is a great wall, twenty-five feet thick which fortified the city. It is the first and largest city wall ever built at Megiddo. To Strata XVII-XVI (EB III: 2650–2350 B.C.E.) belongs the largest open-air altar yet found in Palestine. Made of small stones and surrounded by a temenos wall, it is twenty-five feet in diameter and five feet high. The city of Stratum XVI was destroyed but the altar continued in use during the last city of the Early Bronze Age (Stratum XV). Also dated to Stratum XV are three new temples of the broad-house type.

To the Middle Bronze Age (2200–1550 B.C.E.) are assigned Strata XIV-X. Stratum XIV, a transitional period between Middle Bronze I and Middle Bronze II, represents a decline in the material culture of the city. Buildings are small and poorly constructed and the round altar was no longer used. During the time of Stratum XIII (Middle Bronze II-A), a new city wall was built of mud brick. Associated with this wall is the earliest city gate known from Megiddo; it was large enough for pedestrians only. It is believed that during this period, the city was under Egyptian control. Strata XII-X represent the Middle Bronze Age II-B period (1750-1550). While the city plan of Stratum XII differed radically from that of Stratum XIII, there is a close similarity of plans from Stratum XII through Stratum VII-A (twelfth century). This would indicate cultural continuity during this time. During the time of Stratum XI a new stone wall was built with a glacis. This wall was used until the end of the Bronze Age. The first of a series of palaces was built near the city gate in Stratum X. This new gate measured thirty-six by fifty-nine ft. and had an entrance nine ft. wide.

To the Late Bronze Age (1550–1200 B.C.E.) belong Strata IX-VI B. This was one of the most prosperous periods in the city's history as reflected in the various treasuries of gold vessels, jewelry, and especially carved ivories found in the palaces from Strata VIII and VII B. Also generally assigned to this period, is a large fortified temple. The city of Stratum VII-B suffered a violent destruction, but at whose hand is unclear.

The first Iron Age city, Stratum VI B-A, dates to the last half of the twelfth century and was very meager compared to its Bronze Age predecessors. There is some evidence that this phase of the city's history was destroyed by the Philistines.

To Strata V B-A and IV B-A belongs the most controversial stratigraphical problem at Megiddo: the question as to which architectural features belong to the time of David and Solomon and which to the period of Omri (ninth century). The American excavators stripped away almost completely the first four strata of the mound. This made it very difficult to know with confidence which ruins should be assigned to which levels. To try to clear up this stratigraphical confusion, Y. Yadin began excavating anew at Megiddo in 1960.

As a result of his work, Yadin concluded that Stratum V B–V A should be dated to ca. 1000–950 B.C.E. (i.e., during the time of David and the first part of the reign of Solomon). He further concluded that remains from Strata V A–IV B belong to the Solomonic period. The most important of these ruins is the massive six-chamber gate, a casemate wall, and palaces 1723 and 6000. Yadin dated Stratum IV A to the Omride period and assigned to it the so-called "Solomonic Stables," which probably were store-houses or army barrracks. In addition, he also redated the large water tunnel from the thirteenth–twelfth century of the original excavators to Stratum IV A. While many scholars have accepted most of Yadin's conclusions, others, such as D. Ussishkin, still date the gate to Stratum IV A. This period of the city's history was brought to an end by Assyrian conquest in 733/32 B.C.E.

The city of Stratum III (ca. 732–630) reflects Assyrian influence and was followed by an open, unfortified city (Stratum II) that is believed to have been destroyed by Necho in 609. The last historical gasp of this great city (Stratum I) was during the following Persian period and ended around 350 B.C.E. when the mound was abandoned.

Bibliography. Y. Aharoni, "Megiddo," *EAEHL* 3 (1977): 830-47; N. L. Lapp, "Megiddo," *HBD*; A. Negev, ed., "Megiddo," *AEHL*; J. B. Prichard, *ANET* and "The Megiddo Stables: A Reassessment," *Near Eastern Archaeology in the Twentieth Century,* ed. J. A. Sanders; J. N. Schofield, "Megiddo," *Archaeology and Old Testament Study,* ed. W. Thomas; D. Ussishkin, "Was the 'Solomonic' City Gate at Megiddo Built by King Solomon?," *BASOR* 239 (1980): 1-18.

—JOHN C. H. LAUGHLIN

• **Melchizedek.** [mel-kiz'uh-dek] Canaanite king-priest who blesses Abram and accepts his tithe after Abram liberated Lot and the king of Sodom from Chedorlaomer (Gen 14:18-20). Melchizedek is mentioned once more in the OT (Ps 110:4) in conjunction with the establishment of an everlasting Davidic line. The meanings of the OT references are obscure at best. In Heb 5:6, 10; 6:20; 7:1, 10, 11, 15, 17, 21, the author constructs an argument for the superiority of Jesus as priest in relationship to Melchizedek (KJV "Melchisedec"). Following Ps 110, Jesus is linked to David and Melchizedek; since Abram paid a tithe, Melchizedek is superior; Levi was present in the loins of Abram; therefore, Jesus is a priest superior to the levitical line.

Bibliography. F. F. Bruce, *The Epistle to the Hebrews*; G. Buchanan, *To The Hebrews*; M. Dahood, *Psalms III, 101-150*; G. von Rad, *Genesis,* rev. ed.; A. Weiser, *The Psalms*; C. Westermann, *Genesis 12-36*.

—RICHARD F. WILSON

• **Melchizedek (11Q).** *Melchizedek* (*11QMelch*) is a fragmentary collection of OT texts and interpretations centering around the mysterious OT figure by the same name (Gen 14:18-20). The document is extant in fourteen fragments of a single manuscript discovered in Qumran Cave 11. The manuscript, written in Hebrew and dating from the second half of the first century B.C.E., contained at least three columns, only one of which can be reconstructed to any degree. Whether the entire document focused on MELCHIZEDEK, or whether these columns were part of a longer document that presented history in terms of jubilee years (cf. *4QPEzek*), is unclear. The surviving fragments interpret certain verses (vv. 9, 10, 13) of Lev 25, which give regulations for the YEAR OF JUBILEE. This jubilee is viewed as the tenth (and last) jubilee, which is a time of salvation (understood in terms of Isa 52:7 and 61:1-2) and judgment (understood in terms of Ps 7:8-9 and 82:1-2). The key figure in this final jubilee is MELCHIZEDEK, who will restore and make atonement for the Sons of Light and who will execute God's judgment against Belial and his lot.

11QMelch seems to be an eschatological midrash, similar to *4QFlor*. In its concern to interpret the OT in terms of the Qumran community, it also has affinities with the PESHARIM. The extant fragments do not relate Melchizedek explicitly to the classic OT texts: Gen 14:18-20 and Ps 110:4. Rather, he is portrayed as a heavenly figure whose role is similar to that attributed to the archangel MICHAEL in *1QM* 17:5-8, leading some scholars to suggest that the two be equated. He also bears a close relationship to the Prince of Light (*1QM* 13:9-10; *1QS* 3:20; *4QMess*) and the Angel of Truth (*1QS* 3:24-25). He probably was a key figure in the fragmentary *4QMess* as the heavenly adversary of Melchiresha, the ruler of the darkness, and may have been identified in the ANGELIC LITURGY as the highest of the seven chief angels.

Of special interest are possible connections between *11QMelch* and the NT. The most striking NT parallel is the speculation about Melchizedek in Heb 5 and 7. The differences between the portrayals of Melchizedek in the two documents, however, diminish the probability of a direct relationship between the two. Also noteworthy is the key role that Isa 61:1-2 plays in both *11QMelch* and Luke 4:16-21 in defining the missions of Melchizedek and Jesus, respectively. In addition, scholars have pointed to the possible significance of *11QMelch* for shedding light on the concepts of the SON OF MAN in the Synoptics and the paraclete in John.

11QMelch contributes to an understanding of the distinctive theology of the Qumran community, especially its ESCHATOLOGY, angelology, and messianism. It also illumines the interpretive strategies of the sect. It provides further a rare example of ancient Jewish speculation about Melchizedek (cf. 2 ENOCH) and an example of a jubliee-based calendrical system (cf. also *Jub*; *TLevi*). Finally, it sheds light on Jewish exegetical methods in this period and on the history of the text of the OT prior to the Massoretic Text.

See also DEAD SEA SCROLLS; ESSENES.

Bibliography. J. A. Fitzmyer, "Further Light on Melchizedek from Qumran Cave 11," *Essays on the Semitic Background of the New Testament*; F. L. Horton, *The Melchizedek Tradition*; P. J. Kobelski, *Melchizedek and Melchireša'*.

—JOSEPH L. TRAFTON

• **Melchizedek (NH).** *Melchizedek* is a Coptic GNOSTIC tractate from Codex IX of the NAG HAMMADI documents. Much of the text is fragmentary. Like the other Nag Hammadi tractates, it is assumed to have been composed in Greek. Egypt was probably the place of composition, possibly in the second century C.E.

The book centers on the priest-king MELCHIZEDEK of Gen 14:18-20, who is also referred to in Heb 5:5–7:28. The first part of the work contains a revelation given Melchizedek by a heavenly instructor, Gamaliel. It concerns the passion and resurrection of the Savior, and warns against docetic interpretations of his suffering. There is instruction on the names of the aeons, the origins of the lower world, and a fragmentary interpretation of Adam and Eve. Melchizedek is told not to reveal these MYSTERIES unless it is revealed that he should.

Melchizedek then prays to the Father, who has raised him from ignorance and death into life; he affirms his own priesthood and declares himself offered as a sacrifice. This is a prelude to his baptism. Melchizedek then recites, apparently as part of the baptism, a doxology to the Father and to the aeons, named individually. After this, he speaks of repeating in himself the passion of Jesus, of being crucified and raised again. Once more there is a warning against revelation of these mysteries to the fleshly. A closing sentence declares that when the brothers belonging to the generations of life had said these things, they were transported above the heavens.

Influences from the DEAD SEA SCROLLS, the NT, and rabbinic lore have been noted here in the figure of Melchizedek as teacher of wisdom, eschatological HIGH PRIEST and MESSIAH. Particularly striking is the picture of Melchizedek recapitulating the work of Christ. It has been plausibly suggested that the book is a gnostic ritual of initiation, in which, after instruction in the mysteries, the initiate assumes the role of Melchizedek, confessing himself raised to life, offering himself as a sacrifice, undergoing baptism while reciting a roll of holy names, and finally identifying himself with Christ himself as a redeemed redeemer. This interpretation gains strength from parallel situations in ancient magical literature, particularly the Egyptian *Book of the Dead*.

See also APOCALYPTIC LITERATURE; GNOSTICISM; MYSTERY; NAG HAMMADI.

Bibliography. B. Pearson and S. Giversen, "Melchizedek," *The Nag Hammadi Library in English*, ed. J. M. Robinson; B. Pearson, "The Figure of Melchizedek in the First Tractate of the Unpublished Coptic-Gnostic Codex IX from Nag Hammadi," *Studies in the History of Religion* 31:100-108 and "Anti-Heretical Warnings in Codex IX from Nag Hammadi," *NHS* 6:145-54.

—ROGER A. BULLARD

• **Memorial.** *See* NAMES; WITNESS

• **Menahem.** [men'uh-hem] The son of Gadi, who came from TIRZAH to SAMARIA and assassinated SHALLUM, the king of Israel, and began his own reign. Menahem's reign was one of terror. He sacked the city of Tappuah and killed all of the pregnant women in the city. This was a custom of the times intended to prevent boys (destined to become soldiers) from being born.

Menahem ruled over Israel in Samaria for ten years. His record was one of evil practices. Pul (TIGLATH-PILESER) attacked Israel during the reign of Menahem. Menahem paid an indemnity of 1,000 talents of silver, and Pul left him in charge of the kingdom. The indemnity was raised by a tax on the wealthy in Israel. Menahem was succeeded by his son Pekahiah (2 Kgs 15:13-22).

See also SHALLUM.

—FRED E. YOUNG

• **Menander, Syriac.** [sihr'ee-ak-muh-nan″duhr] *Syriac Menander* (*SyrMen*) is a loose anthology of WISDOM sayings, similar in form to PROVERBS or SIRACH. It provides practical guidelines for living, covering a wide range of topics including parents, children, marriage, eating and drinking, possessions, friends, and old age. It consists of two parts: a short "Epitome" and a longer section of "Sentences."

The collection is attributed pseudonymously to Menander, the famous writer of New Comedy at Athens (ca. 300 B.C.E.). Whether it was composed in Syriac, the only language in which it is extant, or Greek is uncertain. The third century C.E. seems to be a reasonable suggestion for its date.

Perhaps the major issue relating to *SyrMen* is the nature of its religious character. It is typically classified as Jewish. Indeed, there is a strong focus on God, for example, as creator, as active in human affairs, as one who hates the wicked, and as one who listens to prayer. He is to be praised and feared. On the other hand, similar notions can be found in Greek writers. Absent from this document are specifically Jewish concerns such as the covenant or references to OT figures and stories. In addition, there is one non-judgmental reference to polytheism (11.263-64). Thus, the question of whether this collection was composed by a Jew, a strongly Hellenized Jew, or a Greek, remains open at present. Whatever the case, *SyrMen* is an excellent example of ancient oriental wisdom.

See also WISDOM LITERATURE.

Bibliography. T. Baarda, "The Sentences of Syriac Menander," *The Old Testament Pseudepigrapha*, ed. J. H. Charlesworth.

—JOSEPH L. TRAFTON

• **Mene, Mene, Tekel, Parsin.** [mee'nee-mee'nee-tek'uhl-pahr"sin] Enigmatic words inscribed on the wall of BELSHAZZAR's banquet hall in Dan 5. Though Belshazzar's sages are unable to interpret the writing, DANIEL by divine assistance reveals the message of doom sent by God. This tale contrasts Belshazzar's behavior with that of his predecessor Nebuchadrezzar. They both are guilty of overt pride, but Belshazzar, unlike NEBUCHADREZZAR, refuses to humble himself before God. As a result, he must suffer divine judgment.

The consensus is that the phrase contains the Aramaic words for the weights mina, shekel, and half-mina and sums up the worth of successive Babylonian rulers following Nebuchadrezzar. Daniel, however, makes a pun by interpreting the phonetically similar verbs "number" (*mĕnâ*), "weigh" (*tĕqal*), and "divide" (*pĕras*) (vv. 26-28). The final verb allows for a further wordplay on "Persia" (*pāras*). Daniel's interpretation and the textual evidence of the versions, which assume only three words, suggest that the first "mene" is superfluous. Most scholars agree, but at least one critic has argued plausibly that the first "mene" is to be taken as a participle and is original to the ARAMAIC text. Thus the phrase could be rendered "numbered a mina, a shekel, and two half-minas." Nonetheless, the original meaning of the phrase was perhaps lost by the time Daniel was composed. Indeed, Daniel seems oblivious to it. The names of the rulers referred to are thus uncertain, though the two half-minas probably refer to NABONIDUS and his son Belshazzar, who for a time shared regency.

See also BELSHAZZAR; DANIEL, BOOK OF; SYMBOL.

Bibliography. O. Eissfeldt, "Die Menetekel-Inschrift und ihre Deutung," *ZAW* 63 (1951): 105-14.

—DAVID H. HART

• **Mephibosheth.** [mi-fib'oh-sheth] An Israelite personal name, apparently meaning "From the mouth of the Potent One" (that is, sanctioned by the deity who is known for his sexual potency). Reference thereby is made to the Canaanite fertility deity, Baal. While this name was acceptable in early Israel, later generations used the word *bosheth* in the sense of "shame," and thus understood the name in a negative sense (the oft-repeated modern suggestion that the element *bosheth,* with the meaning "shame," has been substituted for Baal by later generations, is without merit).

1. A son of King SAUL, who (along with other family members) was handed over to the Gibeonites to be executed. This DAVID did, at Gibeonite request, in return for Saul's slaughter of Gibeonite citizens in violation of a treaty (2 Sam 21:1-9; cf. Josh. 9:1-15).

2. A grandson of Saul (2 Sam 4:4) whom David exempted from the Gibeonites' request for retribution (2 Sam 21:7). Previously, although an heir to the throne, he had not pressed his claim. When David emerged as Saul's successor, he welcomed Mephibosheth and dealt kindly with him "for JONATHAN's sake" (2 Sam 9; cf. 1 Sam 20:42). Even when Mephibosheth was maliciously depicted as seditious, David acted with restraint (2 Sam 16:1-4) and Mephibosheth was ultimately cleared of blame (2 Sam 19:24-30). At 1 Chr 8:34, he is referred to as Meribbaal (possibly originally Meribaal, "Beloved of Baal").

See also DAVID; JONATHAN; MERIBBAAL.

—LLOYD R. BAILEY

• **Merab.** *See* MICHAL

• **Merari.** [mi-rah'ri] The third son of LEVI and brother of Gershon and Kohath (Gen 46:11; Exod 6:16; Num 3:17; 1 Chr 6:1), one of the seventy persons who accompanied Jacob in the migration to Egypt (Gen 46:11). Although little else is known about Merari personally, a significant levitical family, the Merarites, descended from Merari and his two sons, Mahli and Mushi (Exod 6:19; Num 3:20; 1 Chr 6:1). As a family, the Merarites are mentioned occasionally throughout the history of the Exodus, conquest, monarchy, and restoration.

The references during the time of Exodus come from the priestly tradition. During the Exodus, the Merarites were numbered at 6,200 males from a month old and upward and 3,200 from thirty to fifty years old. They were stationed to the north of the Tabernacle and assisted with its care and transit (Num 3:33-37; 4:42-45). Their appointed charge was to carry the less important items of the Tabernacle such as frames, pegs, and cords (Num 3:36-37; 4:31-32; 10:17), for which they were given four wagons and eight oxen (Num 7:8).

In the occupation of Canaan, the Merarite family was assigned twelve cities among the tribes of Reuben, Gad, and Zebulun, including two cities of refuge (Josh 21:7, 34-40).

The references during the time of monarchy and restoration come from the chronicler. During the monarchy, 220 Merarites, under Asaiah as chief, accompanied the Ark of the Covenant as David brought it to Jerusalem (1 Chr 15:6). Certain others served as musicians (1 Chr 15:6, 16-17) and doorkeepers (1 Chr 26:10, 19). The Chronicler also reports that the Merarites participated in the successive cleansings of the Temple under Hezekiah (2 Chr 29:12) and Josiah (2 Chr 34:12). After the Exile, Merarites assisted Ezra as Temple ministers (Ezra 8:18-19).

See also LEVI/LEVITES.

—W. H. BELLINGER, JR.

• **Mercy.** Several different Heb. and Gk. roots are found in the Bible's rich vocabulary of mercy. None of these can be limited to only one translation. For example, the KJV translates the Hebrew word *ḥesed* as "mercy" 120 times (RSV "steadfast love"). In doing *ḥesed* an attitude of mercy is often implied (Exod 15:13; Ps 31:7). Nevertheless, *ḥesed* is better translated "kindness" (cf. LOVING-KINDNESS). KJV "mercy and truth" (*ḥesed we'ĕmet:* 2 Sam 15:20; Ps 25:10; etc.) is a hendiadys meaning "lasting kindness."

The Heb. root *ḥānan,* "be gracious," requires at times the sense of extending mercy (Deut 7:2; Pss 51:1; 123:2-4). Mercy in this case is the undeserved and gracious favor of the superior to the inferior. *Rāḥam* and its derivatives express the emotional aspect of mercy, the feelings of compassion and pity (Exod 33:19; Isa 30:18). The noun *raḥămîm,* "compassion," first referred to the bowels, the seat of feeling (Gen 43:30; 1 Kgs 3:26; cf. RSV "heart"). Both *ḥāmal* (Exod 2:6) and *ḥûs* (Deut 7:16) mean "to have pity or compassion" (cf. Jer 13:14; 21:7).

In the NT the specific notion of mercy is rendered by *eleos* (Matt 9:13; Eph 2:4) and *oiktirmos* (Rom 12:1; Heb 10:28). The verb *splagchnizomai* meant "to be moved with compassion" (Matt 9:36; Luke 15:20).

God is the father of mercies (2 Cor 1:3; cf. Ps 86:15) and God's compassion is extended over all creation (Ps 145:8-9). By virtue of God's own mercy, and not because of any personal righteousness, God saved us (Titus 3:5). Jesus was moved to compassion on many occasions (Matt 20:34; Mark 1:41; etc.). Christians are called to be compassionate and merciful (Luke 6:36; Col 3:12).

See also JUSTICE/JUDGMENT; LOVE IN THE OLD TESTA-

MENT.

Bibliography. K. D. Sakenfeld, *Faithfulness In Action: Loyalty in Biblical Perspective.*

—STEPHEN J. ANDREWS

• **Mercy Seat.** A rectangular slab of gold that sat on top of the ARK of the Covenant.

Exod 25:17-21 records Yahweh's instructions to MOSES for the construction of the mercy seat, and Exod 37:6-9 contains a description of Bezalel's labor in making it. The mercy seat was made of pure gold, measuring two-and-one-half cubits by one-and-one-half cubits (approximately three ft. nine in. by two ft. three in.). Its thickness is not known. Two gold cherubim figures were attached to the mercy seat, one at each end. These figures faced each other with their heads looking downward and their wings outstretched over the mercy seat. The mercy seat sat atop the Ark of the Covenant, which was kept in the Holy of Holies in the Tabernacle and later in the Temple (Exod 26:34). The Ark and the mercy seat were hidden from sight by a veil that hung over the opening to the Holy of Holies (Exod 26:33).

The mercy seat had two primary functions. One was that Yahweh, when speaking with Moses at the tent of meeting, was present above the mercy seat and between the two cherubim (Exod 25:22; 30:6; Num 7:89). Consequently, the Ark of the Covenant with the mercy seat was considered to be the throne or footstool of God on earth (Pss 99:1, 5; 132:7).

The second major function of the mercy seat was related to the DAY OF ATONEMENT (Lev 16:1-28). On that day the Holy of Holies was filled with a cloud of incense in order to obscure the appearance of the mercy seat. The HIGH PRIEST then slaughtered a bull and carried some of its blood into the Holy of Holies. With his finger he sprinkled the blood on the east side of the mercy seat and in front of it in order to atone for his own sins and those of his household. Next the high priest slaughtered a goat and also sprinkled some of its blood on and before the mercy seat in order to atone for the sins of the people and any uncleanness that may have defiled the sanctuary.

Scholars have debated the etymology and the literal meaning of the Hebrew word *kappōret,* translated as "mercy seat" in most English versions. One theory is that the verbal root behind the word originally meant "to cover," based on an Arabic cognate. This theory suggests that the word *kappōret* literally means "a place of covering (sin)." The majority of contemporary scholars accept another theory, one that proposes that the verbal root behind this Hebrew word has the meaning "to wipe clean" or "to make atonement." Therefore, the literal meaning of *kappōret* is "a place of atonement." Such an idea is reflected in the LXX, which translates the Heb. word with the Gk. term *hilastērion,* meaning "a place of propitiation" or "a propitiatory." This Gk. word is used in Rom 3:25 to speak of the propitiatory action of Christ's death.

See also ARK; ATONEMENT/EXPIATION IN THE OLD TESTAMENT; TEMPLE/TEMPLES.

Bibliography. G. R. Driver, "Studies in the Vocabulary of the Old Testament," *JTS* 34 (Jan 1933): 33-44; R. R. Nicole, "C. H. Dodd and the Doctrine of Propitiation," *WTJ* 17/2 (May 1955): 117-57; G. J. Wenham, *The Book of Leviticus, NICOT.*

—BOB R. ELLIS

• **Meribbaal.** [mer'ib-bay"uhl] Heb. meaning uncertain, though it may be translated "hero of Baal" or "loved by Baal." The grandson of Saul and the crippled son of Jonathan whose name also appears in the form, Mephibosheth. The name appears to have been altered from Meribaal ("hero of Baal") to Meribbaal ("opponent of Baal") to Mephibosheth ("he who scatters shame" or "from the mouth of shame") as a consequence of the struggle between the Hebrews and the Canaanite BAAL worshippers. The use of Baal as an affix for proper names does not appear uncommon during the time of Solomon (witness "Ittobaal"), but such usage disappears in texts written after the ninth century B.C.E. It is interesting that the name Meribbaal survives in the genealogies of 1 Chr 8:34 and 8:40 (a late, postexilic writing) while the name Mephibosheth appears as the "original" name in 2 Sam 4:4 and 3:6.

See also DAVID; ISHBOSHETH; JONATHAN; MEPHIBOSHETH.

—HENRY L. CARRIGAN, JR.

• **Merneptah.** *See* ISRAEL

• **Merodach/Merodach-baladan.** [mi-roh'dak/mi-roh'dak-bal"uh-duhn] Merodach, also known as Marduk and Bel, the creator god of the ancient Babylonians. His exploits were chronicled in the *Enuma elish,* the creation epic of ancient Babylon, dating most likely from the last half of the second millennium B.C.E. Merodach, like the other Babylonian divinities, sprang from Apsu and Tiamat. He was elected by the gods to fight for them against Tiamat, who participated in a rebellion against the rest of the pantheon, instigated by a god named Kingu. Merodach and Tiamat were chosen as the combatants by their respective forces, and Merodach slew the goddess. He split her body in half, creating the heavens with half of her torso and the earth and its creatures with the other half.

Merodach or Bel is mentioned several times in the OT. Jer 50:2 and 51:44 predict the demise of Merodach before God as part of the downfall of the BABYLONIAN EMPIRE. Likewise, Isa 46:1 ridicules Merodach and Nebo (Nabu, the son of Merodach) as worthless idols who must be carried about by human beings and who could not aid their devotees. In the Apocrypha one of the additions to the book of Daniel is named BEL AND THE DRAGON. This addition contains two stories, one about the priests of Bel who ate the provisions set out daily for Bel and claimed the god was devouring the food. Daniel trapped them, thus proving Bel was no god.

The name Merodach was used in two compound names that appear in the OT: Evil-merodach, the son of Nebuchadrezzar, who ruled Babylon from 562–560 B.C.E. and who elevated King Jehoiachin in Exile (2 Kgs 25:27), and Merodach-baladan. Merodach-baladan was the leader of a Chaldean tribe named Bit-Yakin that lived in southeast Babylonia. When Shalmaneser V died (722 B.C.E.) and was succeeded by Sargon II (Assyrian Emperor from 721 to 705), Merodach-baladan gained control over Babylonia and, with the aid of the king of Elam, rebelled against ASSYRIA. Sargon II was occupied with military campaigns in Asia Minor and then northwestern Iran, leaving Merodach-baladan in control of Babylonia for twelve years. Sargon II defeated Merodach-baladan in 710 B.C.E., driving him south to Dur-Yakin. When Sennacherib succeeded Sargon II, Merodach-baladan revolted again and ruled Babylon a second time for nine months before Sennacherib defeated him.

Merodach-baladan sent envoys to Hezekiah, who showed them all his treasury (cf. 2 Kgs 20:12-19; Isa 39:1-8; and 2 Chr 32:31). Hezekiah's indiscretion led Isaiah to predict that the Babylonians would one day return to take what they had seen. In the texts as they now stand, this episode is placed after the siege of Jerusalem by Sennacherib in 701, but it is dated quite generally "at that time." If Merodach-baladan was indeed king of Babylon when he sent the envoys, the episode would have occurred between 715 (ascension of Hezekiah) and 710 (defeat of Merodach-baladan by Sargon II) or in 703 during his nine-month second reign. Either date is preferable to one after 701, when the tribute Hezekiah paid would have left him few riches to exhibit.

See also BABYLONIAN EMPIRE; IDOLATRY.

Bibliography. J. H. Groenboek, "Baal's Battle with Yam: a Canaanite Creation Fight," *JSOT* 33 (1985): 27-44); J. B. Pritchard, ed., *ANET*; J. Reade, "Mesopotamia Guidelines for Biblical Chronology," *SMS* 4/1 (May 1981): 1-9.

—PAUL L. REDDITT

• **Mesha.** [mee'shuh] A personal and place name that appears in the OT four times.

1. In Gen 10:30, a place in Yemen or southeast Arabia; a portion of the heritage of the descendants of Shem.

2. In 1 Chr 2:42, Mareshah (Heb. *mesha*) was the firstborn of Caleb, of the lineage of Judah.

3. In 1 Chr 8:9, Mesha was a descendant of BENJAMIN.

4. In 2 Kgs 3:4, Mesha was a king of MOAB, during the time of AHAB, Ahaziah, and JEHORAM (kings of Israel).

The spelling of the Hebrew names in Gen 10:30 and 1 Chr 8:9 is very similar. But it differs substantially from that of 1 Chr 2:42 and 2 Kgs 3:4.

The facts about Mesha come from 2 Kings and the Moabite Stone (the MESHA STELE). Mesha (king of Moab) was a subject of Ahab (king of Israel; 2 Kgs 3:4). He was called a "*nqd*," i.e., an owner of a breed of sheep known for its excellent quality of wool (Amos 1:1). He paid an annual tribute of 100,000 lambs and the wool of 100,000 rams.

Mesha rebelled against the descendants of Omri after the death of Ahab. Mesha laid the groundwork for his revolt by capturing the towns of Nebo, Ataroth, and Jahaz. He erected inhabited fortifications at Medeba, Beth-diblathen, and Baal-meon on the northern border.

To quell this revolt, JEHORAM, grandson of OMRI and son of Ahab, sought the assistance of JEHOSHAPHAT, king of Judah, and the king of Edom. The three kings attacked Mesha from the south, cleverly and laboriously avoiding the heavily fortified northern boundary. They besieged Kirhareseth. When Mesha saw that the fight was hopeless, he offered his eldest son for a burnt offering to his god, CHEMOSH.

—JOHN JOSEPH OWENS

• **Mesha Stele.** [mee'shuh-stee"lee] The MESHA Stele is the most important inscription yet discovered in the Moabite language. The stele was discovered in 1868 in the village of Dhiban, ancient DIBON, by F. A. Klein, a missionary sent by a British Missionary Society. The inscription was at the time complete, a thirty-four line memorial stele carved on black basalt. Because the local bedouin thought the inscription might be hollow and contain valuable treasure or to give all the clans a portion, the stele was broken. Only about two-thirds of the stele has been recovered. The original is now located in the Louvre Museum, Paris. Fortunately, a squeeze impression was made of the inscription before it was broken, thus almost all the text can be restored reliably.

The inscription dates to the reign of Mesha, king of MOAB, mentioned in 2 Kgs 3. The stele is usually dated to the latter period of Mesha's reign, about 835 B.C.E. The language and script of the inscription are Moabite. The language is virtually identical with biblical Hebrew, the major difference being that a plural is formed with an *–n* rather than with an *–m* as in Hebrew. The script is quite similar to Hebrew and Phoenician of the same time period, but does indicate that national scripts had developed by this period.

The Mesha Stele (also known as "Moabite Stone")

The inscription contains a summary of the military campaigns of Mesha to enlarge his empire, especially against Israel, and his building projects. The Israelite King OMRI is mentioned as is the name of the Hebrew deity, Yahweh. The Moabite deity CHEMOSH is mentioned in terms identical to those the Bible uses of Yahweh. Chemosh was angry with his land and so he permitted Omri to oppress Moab. But then Chemosh allowed Mesha to be victorious and overcome all his enemies and regain the land. Mesha then built a sanctuary for Chemosh and located the stele in that sanctuary. Later in the inscription it is mentioned that Mesha had placed under the ban (*ḥrm*) an entire community for Chemosh.

Mesha had his capital in Dibon, even though Dibon is located north of the Arnon River, the traditional northern border for Moab. He built there a sanctuary for Chemosh because Chemosh had given him and his people deliverance. From excavations in Dibon, scholars have found remains of what may be the royal quarter and sanctuary built by Mesha and called *qarḥo* on the inscription.

The Mesha stele is an important historical witness for the mid-ninth century B.C.E. But it must be used with caution; one cannot ascertain the arrangement of the material, whether chronological or some other pattern.

In 1958, a fragment of another inscription of Mesha was found in Kerak, Jordan. It contains portions of three lines and mentions Chemosh by name, and has the words "king of Moab." On the basis of the epigraphy, the inscription is dated to the reign of Mesha.

See also MESHA; MOAB.

—JOEL F. DRINKARD, JR.

• **Mesopotamia.** [mes'uh-puh-tay"mee-uh] The Gk. rendering of the Heb. *'aram naharaim* ("Aram of the two rivers") coined at the time of Alexander the Great to denote the region between the Tigris and the great bend of the middle Euphrates. In the Bible, Aram-naharaim probably refers more specifically to the region between the upper Euphrates and Khabur rivers. The term was later extended to cover the whole of the valleys of the EUPHRATES and TIGRIS from the foothills of the Taurus Mountains south to the Persian Gulf, and from the Syro-Arabian Desert east to the Zagros Mountains (PLATE 1). In preclassical antiquity the two halves of Mesopotamia in this broader sense were known as BABYLONIA (the south) and ASSYRIA (the north, though with some variation). In the most ancient usage southern Mesopotamia was comprised of Sumer and Akkad. Geographically, Mesopotamia today corresponds largely with modern Iraq.

The southern part of Mesopotamia, to about fifty mi. north of Baghdad, is an alluvial plain, very productive when adequately irrigated. North of this, between the Tigris and Euphrates, is a low plateau, the Jazira ("island"). East of the Jazira is fertile undulating terrain watered by the Greater Zab and Lesser Zab rivers. This area, with the city of Ashur on the west bank of the Tigris, formed the heartland of ancient Assyria.

The climatic feature important for the ancient cultural development of the region is that only in northern Mesopotamia (the heartland of Assyria and the north of the Jazira) is rainfall adequate for agriculture. Elsewhere irrigation is necessary, demanding skilled control of the rivers. The control and management of these water resources was a major factor in the economics and politics of southern Mesopotamia.

The earliest substantial evidence of agricultural settlements in Mesopotamia comes from the sixth millennium B.C.E. Beginning about 4000 B.C.E. (the Uruk period) civilization began to flourish in Mesopotamia. The emergence of cities, major religious and political institutions, and writing over the next 1,500 years have earned for the region the title "cradle of civilization."

The peoples and kingdoms of ancient Mesopotamia played an important role in the history of biblical Israel. Aram-naharaim was the place where the biblical patriarchs lived before they went to Canaan. It includes HARAN, the city to which Abraham migrated after leaving UR. It is the region to which Eliezer was later sent to find a bride for Isaac (Gen 24:10). The prophet Balaam came from Mesopotamia to curse Israel at the hire of Balak (Deut 23:4). Cushanrishathaim ruled Mesopotamia when he oppressed Israel during the period of the Judges (Judg 3:8-10). In the time of David, Mesopotamia provided charioteers and horsemen to support his Ammonite enemies (1 Chr 19:6). From the mid-ninth to the mid-sixth centuries B.C.E. Israelite politics were influenced greatly by the empires of Mesopotamia, who ultimately subjugated Israel and Judah. The neo-Assyrians, under Shalmaneser V and Sargon III, were responsible for the destruction of Samaria in 722 B.C.E., while their successors the neo-Babylonians, under Nebuchadrezzar, did the same to Jerusalem in 587/6 B.C.E.

—STEPHEN M. HOOKS

• **Messenger.** *See* ANGEL

• **Messiah/Christ.** [muh-s*i*'uh] *Messiah* is the transliteration of a Heb. word (מָשִׁיחַ) which means "the anointed one." The word occurs thirty-nine times in the OT, most frequently in reference to the kings of Israel and Judah who were anointed on accession to office. The king was often called "the Lord's anointed" (2 Sam 19:21). In postexilic writings, the term was occasionally used of the high priest (Lev 4:3). In both instances, the term signifies divine authorization. The LXX translates the term with the Gk. equivalent (χριστός) which means "the anointed one" and which is transliterated as "Christ."

The roots of later Jewish and Christian messianism are difficult to trace, but certainly one of the more influential contributing elements is the promise that David's dynasty will be permanent (2 Sam 7:4-16; Pss 2, 18). Later parts of the OT expect a descendant of DAVID who will establish an ideal reign of peace, prosperity, and righteousness (Isa 9:1-7; 11:1-9; Jer 23:5-6; Ezek 34:23-24; 37:24-25; Amos 9:11-12; Mic 5:2-5a; Hag 2:21-23; Zech 4:6-10; 9:9-10). Yet the title "the anointed one" or "messiah" is not used with reference to this messianic figure. Moreover, in some OT books this future age is established directly by God (Joel 2:28–3:21; Zephaniah).

The postexilic period proved disappointing to those expecting the imminent arrival of the idyllic future. Corruption and exploitation continued; priests and Davidites struggled for power, with the high priest emerging as the "anointed"; the canonized Pentateuch with its laws replaced the prophets and their eschatological vision. As a result, messianic expectation lay dormant.

Under Seleucid rule, especially that of Antiochus IV Epiphanes, the authority of the priesthood was shattered, and Hellenism was forced upon the people. Loyal Jews found four solutions to the problem: (1) The Hasidim had faith in God's power to save, but were ready to die rather than violate God's law. (2) The apocalyptic movement revived the prophetic vision. (3) The Hasmoneans instigated armed revolt. (4) The Pharisees developed a form of Judaism which shifted the focus from earthly to heavenly rewards and punishments.

Under the Hasmoneans, messianism revived. The combination of the priesthood and monarchy during this period influenced the nature of this messianic expectation. Several writings mention two messiahs, one Davidic and the other Aaronic (priestly); frequently the priestly figure is supreme (*TLevi* 18; *TRev* 6; *lQSa* 2:19-20). The cruelty of the later Hasmoneans and the subsequent Roman conquest sparked a revival of Davidic messianism (*PssSol* 17–18). Messianic expectations remained vivid until the end of the second Jewish revolt (135 C.E.). The paucity of messianic material in the Mishna probably reflects the rabbinic concentration on the Law and opposition to the false hopes raised by Zealots and apocalyptic groups, hopes which had cost the Jewish people dearly at the hands of the Romans.

No systematic statement of Jewish messianic expectations during the late Hasmonean and Roman periods is possible due to the confusing abundance of viewpoints. Some of the literature stresses the Davidic Messiah. This strain of the tradition is nationalistic and this-worldly. The Messiah is to usher in a golden age for Israel with Jerusalem as the center of the world. In many respects, this line of thinking continues the eschatological vision of the OT prophets. Other literary works stress the SON OF MAN. This strain of the tradition is universal and otherworldly. The Son of man, who is of heavenly origin, will appear at the end of time as judge. The eschatology of this understanding is clearly apocalyptic rather than prophetic. The conflict between the this-worldly and otherworldly expectations was harmonized in some writings by portraying the messianic kingdom as the end of the present age. This earthly kingdom was to last for a specific period of time (40, 400, 1,000, and 2,000 years are suggested by various authors) and be followed by the new (otherworldly) age.

Some authors calculated the time; others said only God knew. Some felt God would act when sin was at its peak. Others were confident that the Law must first be kept; in fact, some thought that the Messiah was present but unrecognized due to the sins of Israel. Some authors affirmed that a forerunner would reveal the Messiah; Enoch, Moses, the prophet like Moses, and (most frequently) Elijah are honored with this function. Noteworthy in light of the later Christian understanding is the fact that although the Messiah might suffer in his effort to establish his Kingdom or die at the end of the Kingdom period, no Jewish author proposes a Messiah who suffers and dies for the sins of all people.

In this climate of messianic multiplicity, Jesus began his ministry. The diversity of messianic expectations alone would dictate that not all Jews would view him as Messiah. To complicate matters, the Christian conception differed markedly from any that had been espoused before. This novel understanding was made possible by a fusion of the following: (1) the promise to establish the throne of David forever; (2) the prophetic linkage of an ideal Davidic king with an idyllic future; (3) the Pharisaic belief in the world to come and the resurrection; and (4) the Pharisaic method of free interpretation of scripture.

''Christ'' occurs 529 times in the NT. Apparently, Jesus did not use the term, probably due to the difference between his self-understanding and the messianic expectations of the day. When the disciples recognized him as the Messiah, he commanded them to keep it secret and responded with teachings about the necessity of suffering (Mark 9:27-31). A reinterpretation of messiahship was needed.

In light of the resurrection, the early Christians were confident that Jesus was the Christ (Acts 2:30-36); in fact, this was the theme of their preaching and teaching (Acts 5:42; 1 Cor 15:3-5.) The Pauline literature reveals that among gentile Christians ''Christ'' became a proper name. Consequently, ''Christ'' came to include everything the early Christians knew and believed about Jesus. His self-understanding, ministry of service and suffering for others, and resurrection led them to understand messiahship not in earthly, national, political terms, but rather in terms of freeing people from the enslaving and dehumanizing effects of sin and overcoming the ultimate enemy, death. Thus, ''Christ'' took over the functions of the messianic king, the messianic high priest, the prophet like Moses, the suffering servant, the Son of man, the righteous one, and other such titles.

See also ANOINT; DAVID; ESCHATOLOGY IN THE NEW TESTAMENT; ESCHATOLOGY IN THE OLD TESTAMENT; JESUS; KINGDOM OF GOD; SON OF GOD; SON OF MAN.

Bibliography. W. Bousset, *Kyrios Christos*; O. Cullmann, *The Christology of the New Testament*, rev. ed.; R. H. Fuller, *The Foundations of New Testament Christology*; R. H. Fuller and P. Perkins, *Who Is This Christ?*; W. Grundmann et al., ''χρίω, κτλ.,'' *TDNT*; F. Hahn, *The Titles of Jesus in Christology*; I. H. Marshall, *The Origins of New Testament Christology*.

—RON FARMER

• **Messiah/Messianism.** [muh-si'uh/mes''ee-uhn-iz'uhm] The concept of messiah is found in both OT and NT, but the many connotations of the word, resulting from its evolution throughout the history of the testaments, defy simple definition. Messiah means ''the anointed one,'' but this often misunderstood and misinterpreted concept must be viewed in light of the history of Israel and in light of the story of JESUS of Nazareth. Even then it is impossible to reconstruct a concise and lucid history of the term, but a clearer understanding of the intentionality of the text can result.

In the OT the word is expressed by the Hebrew noun *māšîaḥ* from the verbal root *mšḥ* anoint. The noun *māšîaḥ* meaning the anointed, occurs thirty-nine times in the OT. The term is most often reserved for kings (1 Sam 12:3; Hab 3:13; Ps 28:8), but is also used to describe the high priest (Lev 4:3; 6:22), CYRUS of Persia (Isa 45:1), and the patriarchal ancestors (Ps 105:15). Such variety is illustrative of the fluidity of the term; however, a survey of OT writings reveals that a development from a present messiah of the Davidic line to a more nebulous concept of messiah in an indefinite future is consonant with the influence of historical events in the life of Israel. The messianic concept of the people of Israel has clear political origins and this political aspect of the concept must be examined in order to understand correctly the concept reflected in the NT.

In the NT the Gk. rendering of *māšîaḥ* is *christos*, though it is also transliterated as *messias*; both examples of transliteration, however, are followed by an explanation including the Gk. *christos*. Originally a title, *christos* came to be regarded as a personal name appended to Jesus. Jesus Christ came to be regarded as ''The Messiah,'' but this new interpretation cannot be understood without first understanding the nature of messianism and messianic expectation which preceded him.

The concept of messiah in the OT spans a continually changing spectrum. In preexilic and exilic Israel the term messiah is most often a reference to a Davidic king. Distinctive forms of messianic movement begin with SAUL (1 Sam 9:16), then are carried to DAVID and his successors. Legitimation of kingship in Israel rests on the promise to David revealed in the NATHAN prophecy (2 Sam 7:8-16). A Davidic monarchy is promised to be established by Yahweh as an eternal dynasty.

The act of royal anointing was an act borrowed from (or at least influenced by) Israel's neighbors, but Israel's preexilic monarchy refashioned the concept. Kingship as previously known to Israel had been oppressive, but as monarchy became Israel's form of self-government a new idea was introduced. David and his successors are referred to as *měšîaḥ Yhwh,* the anointed of Yahweh. Israel's concept of kingship rests upon divine appointment.

Thirty of the thirty-nine occurrences of the term in the OT denote Hebrew kings. The origins of the messianic idea inextricably bind *māšîaḥ* to royal ideology. Furthermore, when thus used as a royal title the term is always written *měšîaḥ yhwh* (anointed of Yahweh) or with a pronominal suffix referring to Yahweh. The origin and authority of the anointing is divine, not human.

The royal psalms (2, 18, 20, 72, 89, for example) are celebrations of this relationship of Yahweh and king; they reflect the promise made in the Nathan prophecy. Originally the psalms may have been written for specific occasions within the Davidic reign, but these specific occasions that gave rise to the psalms are transcended as the reading of *māšîaḥ* is broadened to include any monarch of the Davidic line. Ps 72 is particularly illustrative of the hope of Israel for salvation through a Davidic king.

The successive failures of the Davidic kings to deliver Israel led inevitably to disillusionment, and as optimism waned a different concept of messiah emerged. This redirected hope can be seen in Isa 9:1ff. Mic 5:1-6 is another example of expression of hope for a restoration of a dynasty the equal of David's (these expressions are visions of an ideal king and are often used by successive generations as expressions of hope).

The messianic concept undergoes further change in postexilic Israel when there is no longer a Davidic line. The hope now moves to an indefinite future. This is evidenced in the writings of ZECHARIAH (9:9ff.) and HAGGAI (2:20-23). Israel's expectations can no longer be centered on a king in a continuing line of monarchs, but although the hope becomes more difficult to discern at this period in Israel's history, it still remains. At some point in the indefinite future Yahweh will raise up an anointed one to save Israel.

It is difficult to trace clearly the transition from OT messianism to NT messianism. The development of the term messiah continues into NT times.

The Gk. word for *māšîaḥ* is *christos*. The titular aspect of *christos*, a confession of the redactors, quickly becomes a cognomen for Jesus. NT literature, therefore, reveals an evolution from the concept "messiah" to "The Messiah." *Christos* as a title is frequently attributed to Jesus, but it should be noted that the preference in self-designation is the title, SON OF MAN (Mark 8:31; Luke 9:22).

The Gospels affirm the messiahship of Jesus in a variety of ways. The birth/infancy narratives of Matthew (Matt 1; 2) and Luke (Luke 1; 2) affirm the messiahship. Mark's affirmation comes most clearly on the lips of PETER (Mark 8:29) and on the lips of Jesus himself before the high priest (Mark 14:61, 62), but Mark's "messianic secret" emphasizes the incompleteness of one's understanding of Jesus as messiah unless seen through the lens of the cross. This presentation of the suffering of Jesus lends new meaning to the concept of messianism. The fulfillment prophecies in Matthew represent a new understanding of OT messianic scriptures (Matt 1:22; 2:6).

The messiahship of Jesus is also affirmed in the apostolic preaching of the first century (Acts 2:36; 4:27; 10:38; 17:3). Here, as well as in Pauline literature, it is recognized that the history of Jesus of Nazareth gives new form to the messianic hope.

This refashioning of the concept of messiah in light of the history of Jesus moves the reader from the Jewish idealizations of messiah. The Jewish idealizations of a Davidic messiah, whether in the present or some indefinite future, are political. Jesus does not correspond to the hoped-for political messiah; politically he has no power; his is a path of suffering. The temptation narratives (Matt 4:1-11; Luke 4:1-13) illustrate his nonconformity with typical messianic characteristics. Jesus presents a messiahship with qualifications (Mark 8:31; Matt 21:4, 5; 26:64; Luke 22:67).

It is difficult to equate Jesus with the messiah of Jewish expectation, for Jesus, The Messiah, transcends the expectations of Israel. He is not a conqueror of nations, but instead he is a conqueror of death. He is "the anointed one" who is an amalgamation of the royal messiah, the priestly messiah—and more. The kingdom that he ushers in is not the expected one; the salvation he offers is unique.

It is in the light of these histories (that of Israel and Jesus of Nazareth) that the OT language of messianism is melded with the NT concept of messiah. The transition from messiah to the Messiah is a radical change, and much care must be taken to understand and appreciate the term messiah/Messiah in its wide spectrum of meaning and application.

See also JESUS; KINGSHIP; SON OF MAN; SON OF GOD.

Bibliography. J. Becker, *Messianic Expectation in the Old Testament*; A. Bentzen, *King and Messiah*, ed. G. W. Anderson; J. Durham, "The King as 'Messiah' in the Psalms," *RE* 81 (Summer 1984): 425-35; W. Grundmann, "χρίω, κτλ.," *TDNT*; J. Klausner, *The Messianic Idea in Israel*; S. Mowinkel, *He That Cometh*; G. A. Riggin, *Messianic Theology and Christian Faith*.

—JUDY YATES ELLIS

• **Messianic Rule.** *See* RULE OF THE CONGREGATION/MESSIANIC RULE

• **Messianic Secret.** *See* MARK, GOSPEL OF

• **Metallurgy.** Metallurgy is the technology of metals, usually involving in the ancient world a smelting process in which metals are extracted from ores. The OT lists the metals known in ancient Palestine as gold, silver, bronze, iron, tin, and lead (Num 31:22). Gold, found in the native or metallic state as nuggets in the sands and gravels of river beds, was probably the first metal used because of its softness and because it does not require smelting. Gold could easily be shaped, often for jewelry or other items of decoration, but probably due to gold's scarcity the earliest known metal objects for usage are of COPPER.

Copper ore appears in many parts of the world, sometimes in quantity, and often in a high state of purity. Copper from such ore, although soft, can be hammered into hardness for use as weapons or tools. However, as more of the surface ore was used and the ore had to be mined, it contained more and more impurities and was harder. This more impure copper or copper ore is often incorrectly called BRONZE, and was itself harder and more easily cast. Thus came the deliberate mixing of ores to obtain a more desirable product. The superiority of tin as an alloying material was soon appreciated. Initially, a tin content of five percent or less was used, but the final optimum portion seemed to be in the ten to twelve percent range. This mixture is "bronze" in the correct sense. Copper mixed with tin is less brittle, and because tin often had to be imported from a distance bronze was rather expensive.

Overlapping the time when bronze was used, IRON was being produced. However, the production of iron was a slow process because it involves a technique much more elaborate than that of copper. A more complex furnace is required with temperatures sufficiently high to melt both the iron and the slag. Futhermore, bronze could be cast, but initially articles of iron were made only under the hammer. In time came the discovery (probably by the Hittites) that in the continued heating of iron to a red heat in a mass of glowing charcoal it was converted to a much harder metal due to absorption of carbon. Thus, steel came to be.

Definitive dates in ancient Middle Eastern history for the transitions in usage from one metal to another are far from being precise. However, the Chalcolithic Age ("copper stone age") is near 4000–3000 B.C.E., the Bronze Age near 3000–1200 B.C.E., and the Iron Age to follow. Chronological terminology, usually at about 600 B.C.E., changes to Persian Period, Greek Period, Roman Period, etc.

Deut 8:9 labels Palestine, to be "a land whose stones are iron, and out of whose hills you can dig copper." On both sides, especially on the east, of the Wadi Arabah, south of the DEAD SEA, copper ore, mainly malachite, was mined in ancient times. Some of the veins of ore may geologically be connected with those in the Sinai Peninsula and contained up to forty percent metal. Early in its history, Egypt obtained copper from Sinai, and later from the Arabah. As early as 2000 B.C.E. at Edomite Punon exploitations began.

A number of Iron Age (1200–600 B.C.E.) mining and smelting camps in the Arabah attest to an extensive exploitation of the area for copper and iron ore. The exact location of most iron mines is uncertain, but iron slag at the smelting camps indicates that iron as well as copper was mined there. The largest smeltery presently known was at Mene'iyyeh located some twenty-one miles north of the Gulf of Aqaba and on the west side of the Arabah. This site is also called Timna' (PLATES 3, 9). About fifty-two mi. further north, about sixteen miles south of the Dead Sea, and on the east side of the wadi lay a smelting center containing the ruins Khirbet en-Nahas, Khirbet el-Gheweibeh, and Khirbet el-Jariyeh, all named after tributary wadis nearby.

The mining and smelting of the copper ore in the Arabah were done first almost certainly by the KENITES living in the area. From them almost certainly the Hebrews learned methods of metallurgy. In addition to needing access to the Gulf of Aqaba, probably one of the major causes for tensions between the ancient Hebrews and Edomites was control of the copper mines in the Arabah. Excavations in the area at Timna' by Nelson Glueck in 1941 uncovered evidence of a copper smeltery. Not far away Reno Rothenburg in 1971 discovered a group of copper mines extending in various directions for hundreds of yards. Some mines were fifty feet deep. Ore was hoisted from them by ropes. Associated with these mines was a large, circular smeltery. Copper ore may have been mined there as early as the Chalcolithic Period, but its primary date of use was about 1400 B.C.E. An iron ore mine was also discovered. Nelson Glueck's identification as a smeltery of a structure at Tel el-Kheleifeh (Ezion-geber) excavated between 1938–1940 has been abandoned.

See also BRASS/BRONZE; COPPER; IRON.

—KAREN RANDOLPH JOINES

• **Metaphor.** *See* PARABLES; LITERATURE, BIBLE AS

• **Micah.** [mi'kih] An eighth-century Judean prophet. His name is a shortened form of Micah-Yah(weh) (Who is like the Lord?). Micah's name asks a rhetorical question demanding the answer, "No one!" His book describes a unique God who offers a unique way of life devoted to the principles of justice, righteousness, and peace. Consequently, students over the centuries have asked "Micah-Micah?" (Who is like Micah?); for, while perhaps not unique, Micah is the epitome of the Hebrew prophet, and appears among the so-called minor (Latin for shorter) prophets due only to the brevity of his book, not the importance of his message.

Micah probably came from Moresheth-Gath, a village outside the city of Gath, in Judah's relatively rural Shephelah valley, which was populated by shepherds and small farmers. His dedication to the plight of the "little people," whom God had favored and protected ever since the Exodus of the slaves from Egypt, as well as his copious use of shepherding and agricultural imagery, suggests that Micah himself was likely a small landowner. The editorial introduction (1:1) that places the prophet's activity within the reigns of the eighth-century Judean kings Jotham, AHAZ, and HEZEKIAH may well be correct, if he began his career addressing SAMARIA before the northern kingdom of Israel fell in 722/1 (cf. 1:2-9) and later turned his focus to JERUSALEM.

A true prophet (3:8; 7:7), Micah was filled with a word from God that he declared to his contemporaries even though it was unpopular and controversial. He contrasted himself to the pseudo-prophets (2:11; 3:5-7) who simply told the rich and powerful what they wanted to hear. For his social and religious criticism he was persecuted (2:6), ridiculed (7:10), and rejected (7:1-5).

Indeed, his book comes to us in the form of a lament at the "funeral" of his country. This word from God so permeated the prophet's life, and he so identified with it, that he was not only a preacher (2:6) but also an activist who probably acted out his funeral dirges (cf. chaps. 1 and 7)—just as Jeremiah marched yoked and Isaiah paraded in the nude—as a social demonstration of his protest. Finally, this preacher-activist was a poet who loved metaphor (e.g., 3:5-7; 7:1-4), puns (e.g., 1:10-16), and humor (e.g., 1:7; 2:11). Either he or his editors even included a clever play on his own name at the end of the book (7:18).

Micah, the social and religious critic, became the first Hebrew prophet to predict the destruction of Jerusalem (3:12) because of its nationalism, militarism, and injustice; and although he probably expected Assyria to be God's instrument of discipline, his words were eventually fulfilled by Babylonia in 587/6. Yet Micah, the visionary poet, saw beyond that disaster to an international community of justice, righteousness, and peace, wherein all humans "shall beat their swords into plowshares, and their spears into pruning hooks; nation shall not lift up sword against nation, neither shall they learn war any more" (4:3; cf. Isa 2:4). These words, inscribed on a statue at the United Nations in New York, a gift from the U.S.S.R., keep alive the vision of Micah and of his contemporary, Isaiah.

See also MICAH, BOOK OF.

Bibliography. W. Brueggemann, *The Prophetic Imagination*; A. J. Heschel, *The Prophets*; H. W. Wolff, *Micah the Prophet*.

—LAMONTTE M. LUKER

• OUTLINE OF MICAH •

The Book of Micah

I. Oracles against Judah and Jerusalem (1:1–3:12)
- A. Judgment against Israel and Judah (1:1-9)
- B. Assyria invades Judah (1:10-16)

II. Judgments and Promises for Israel (4:1–7:20)
- A. Zion's coming glory (4:1-5)
- B. Zion's coming victories (4:6-13)
- C. The ruler from Bethlehem (5:1-5a)
- D. Israel's coming victories (5:5b-9)
- E. Judgment against Judah (5:10-15)
- F. The demands of covenant faith (6:1-8)
- G. Judgment against Judah (6:9-16)
- H. Prayer of lamentation (7:1-7)
- I. Liturgy of confession and trust (7:8-20)

• **Micah, Book of.** The Book of Micah consists of numerous short oracles that have been joined into longer poems. Some of the short oracles may come from a period later than Micah, and the longer poems may also have been shaped by Micah's disciples, but the entire book now makes a forceful statement that seems both literarily and theologically unified.

The first poem (1:2-9) recalls the God of the Exodus who fights for the "little people" against oppression (Exod 15:4) and who is now descending to destroy SAMARIA and JERUSALEM unless they repent of their faithlessness to God. A small upper class had become wealthy by taking advantage of the common people, a situation completely contrary to the spirit of the Exodus and of Hebrew religion. The ruling class expressed their sin of faithlessness through their unethical conduct, arrogance, pagan religious practices and the worship of their own military might, wealth, and political power. Thus Micah, spokesman and demonstrator for God, laments and enacts the "funerals" of Israel and Judah. The next poem (1:10-16), a dirge replete with puns, commemorates the deaths of a series of small towns in the shephelah as God the Divine Warrior (under the guise of SENNACHERIB in 701) marches toward Jerusalem.

Micah 2:1-5 opens with the funeral cry, "Alas!" (or "Woe!") and refers to the coming "end" of the upper class, especially the business persons and large landowners, because of the way they have taken advantage of those less well off than themselves; in v. 4 these leaders join in their own dirge. A rare glimpse of how those attacked respond to the prophet ("Do not preach!") is provided in 2:6-11; while 2:12-13 announces that God must cull his people, and form them into a kingdom of God headed by an ideal messiah (human king).

Chap. 3 again attacks the leaders of society, those Micah calls the "heads"—the political, economic, and religious leaders. Blessed with power, it is their responsibility to lead society down the paths of justice, righteousness, and peace. They have not done so, and because of them (v. 12) their unjust, unrighteous, and militaristic society will fall. In this poem the clergy (the seers, v. 7) lead the lamentation through the mourning gesture of covering the lip.

Following the stern criticism of chap. 3, 4:1-7 offers an energizing vision of hope for how the nation, indeed the world, could be if it lived under the kingship of God, by transforming the leveled Mount Zion of 3:12 into the symbolic mountain capital of an international kingdom of God. The collection of oracles in 4:8–5:4 contrasts the real and the ideal and culminates in a messianic hope for the kingdom of God. The national lamentation continues in 5:1 which should be translated: "Now you are lancing yourself, daughter of lancers." Lancing was a common Canaanite funerary practice, and in a brilliant pun, daughter of lancers (soldiers) refers to militaristic Jerusalem.

The portrait of the nation "then and now" progresses in 5:5-15. The hope is for an age of peace (the kingdom of God) ruled symbolically by a reformed Zion that stands ready to defeat any evil that threatens. But first, the present reality: Zion's own idolatries must be destroyed.

So far it seems no one will listen, but the persistent prophet calls once more in chap. 6 for the nation to listen, this time in the form of a mock court setting. The divine warrior, who sits now as king and judge, holds court with the nation. Unfortunately, the defendant is unrepentant and guilty: the sentence is served in the closing verses.

Chap. 7, a lament for a nation that has brought on itself the judgment of God, concludes with both a trust in a future when the people will again let God rule, and a hymn of praise to this king who not only criticizes and disciplines but also forgives, renews, and heals.

See also MICAH.

Bibliography. L. C. Allen, *The Books of Joel, Obadiah, Jonah and Micah*; D. R. Hillers, *Micah*; J. L. Mays, *Micah*.

—LAMONTTE M. LUKER

• **Micaiah Son of Imlah.** [mi-kay'yuh, im'luh] A ninth-century prophet who appears in only one OT story (1 Kgs 22:1-38; cf. 2 Chr 18:1-34).

After the 400 ecstatic court prophets told AHAB and JEHOSHAPHAT that they would win at Ramoth-Gilead, Jehoshaphat, who was still apprehensive, inquired about the possibility of consulting another prophet of Yahweh. Ahab reluctantly summoned Micaiah ben Imlah, whom he hated, because Micaiah always prophesied evil concerning the king.

The fear that bad things might happen simply because Micaiah predicted them was shared by the officer sent to bring Micaiah. He urged the prophet to let his word be like the unanimous victory oracle given by the 400, fearing that the words of one lone dissenter might release forces that would jeopardize the victory believed to be assured by the oracle of the brotherhood.

Although Micaiah swore to the officer that he would prophesy only what Yahweh told him to say, when he came before the two kings he at first repeated the victory oracle of the court prophets. Micaiah's rhetorical sarcasm (later to be used by Jeremiah [28:6] to show contempt for Hananiah's oracle of weal) annoyed Ahab, who insisted that Micaiah speak only the truth.

Micaiah then related to Ahab two visions. In the first vision, he saw Israel scattered like sheep without a shepherd, revealing that Ahab would die at Ramoth-Gilead. In the second, Micaiah saw Yahweh on the divine throne surrounded by the heavenly host. Yahweh was in council with angelic advisers about how to entice Ahab to his death at Ramoth-Gilead. Yahweh accepted the offer of one of the spirits to "go forth and be a lying spirit in the mouth of all his prophets" (v. 22). The purpose of the vision was to explain why the court prophets had lied to Ahab in the first place. It is noteworthy that Micaiah does not accuse the 400 of being false prophets, as Jeremiah or Ezekiel would have done later. To Micaiah they are true prophets who have been inspired by Yahweh to tell a lie. Early prophecy was so monistic that all events good and evil were attributed to Yahweh (cf. Amos 3:6). The concept of the lying spirit sent by Yahweh and his council may be compared to the "evil spirit from Yahweh" in 1 Sam 16:14ff., and to the adversary (the SATAN) in Job 1–2 and Zech 3. Micaiah's clear warning to Ahab relieved God of any charge of deceiving Ahab, although the lying spirit had enticed him.

Zedekiah, spokesman for the 400, slapped Micaiah and demanded to know how Yahweh's spirit went from Zedekiah to Micaiah. Micaiah's cryptic answer alludes to unnamed horrors that will befall Zedekiah: "on that day when you go into an inner chamber to hide yourself" (1 Kgs 22:25). The futile efforts of human beings to hide from the Day of Yahweh are mentioned by Isaiah (2:10, 19) a century later.

In a vain effort to nullify his oracle of doom, Ahab placed Micaiah in prison on a starvation diet. Ahab disguised himself at Ramoth-Gilead, but to no avail. Yahweh's inexorable word released from the mouth of Micaiah reached the doomed king in the form of what looked like a random arrow. Micaiah's fate was left untold.

See also AHAB; JEHOSHAPHAT; LYING; PROPHET.

Bibliography. J. L. Crenshaw, *Prophetic Conflict*; S. J. De

Vries, *Prophet Against Prophet*; J. Lindblom, *Prophecy in Ancient Israel*.

—EMMETT W. HAMRICK

• **Michael.** [mi'kay-uhl] The name Michael means "who is like El (God)?" and is attributed to eleven different biblical characters: (1) the father of the Asherite spy Sethur (Num 13:13); (2) two Gadites otherwise unknown (1 Chr 5:13, 14); (3) a levitical musician who was an ancestor of Asaph (1 Chr 6:40); (4) a son of Izrahiah of the tribe of Issachar (1 Chr 7:3); (5) a Benjaminite, son of Beriah (1 Chr 8:16); (6) a military commander who joined David at Ziklag (1 Chr 12:20ff.); (7) the father of Omri of Issachar (1 Chr 27:18); (8) a son of King Jehoshaphat murdered by his brother Jehoram upon the latter's ascension to the throne (2 Chr 21:1-4); (9) a descendant of Shephatiah and father of Zebediah, the latter returning from Babylonia to Judah with Ezra (Ezra 8:8); and (10) the archangel Michael.

The archangel Michael is sometimes referred to as the patron or guardian angel of Israel. He is mentioned as a "prince" over Israel in Dan 10:13, 21, and 12:1, and is involved in cosmic warfare against the demonic powers that influence the leaders of Israel's enemies. According to Dan 12:1, he will be instrumental in the final deliverance of God's people.

Jude 9 alludes to a dispute between the "archangel Michael" and the devil about the body of Moses, apparently referring to an account appearing in the pseudepigraphical *Assumption of Moses*. In Rev 12:7 Michael leads the angels in the battle that results in Satan's fall from heaven.

See also ANGEL.

—W. HULITT GLOER

• **Michal.** [mi'kuhl] The name is apparently a shortened form of Michael, meaning "Who is like God?" She was the younger of SAUL's two daughters (1 Sam 14:49), who loved DAVID and was engaged to him after her father reneged on a marriage between David and Saul's older daughter Merab (1 Sam 18:17-19). Since David had no money and since Saul wanted to rid himself of David, Saul demanded as a bride price the foreskins of one hundred Philistines, which David doubled (18:20-27). When Saul sent men to David's house to kill him, Michal saved him by lowering him out a window, making a dummy to put in bed and telling the assassins David was ill. Saul demanded to know why she had tricked him, so she lied, telling him David forced her to help him escape. In revenge (or perhaps because David had abandoned her) Saul gave Michal to Paltiel as a wife (1 Sam 25:44; 2 Sam 3:15).

After David became king of Judah and lived at Hebron, ABNER offered to make peace between David and ISHBOSHETH, Saul's son who ruled Israel in name only from MAHANAIM. David demanded that Abner bring Michal back to him. David may have loved her, or resented the slight of losing her to another man. He also probably wanted her back to strengthen his claim to Saul's throne through Michal. Either this reuniting did not constitute remarriage in the eyes of the author of 2 Sam 3, or the author overlooked the prohibition against the practice (Deut 24:1-4). Unfortunately for Michal, this second phase of their marriage ended as tragically as the first. When David brought the ARK of the Covenant from KIRIATH-JEARIM (or Baale-judah; 2 Sam 6:1–2), he leaped and danced before the Ark, apparently in some sort of ritual that resulted in immodesty. Michal saw him "and despised him in her heart" (2 Sam 6:16; 1 Chr 15:29). When she chastised David for his behavior, he saw in her remarks resentment that he had replaced her father. The author then notes that Michal remained childless. One should probably conclude from the statement that David ceased having relations with Michal, though it is possible the author meant to say that God made her infertile.

The name Michal appears one last time in the Hebrew text of 2 Sam 21:8, but since it mentions five daughters most scholars read the name Merab, following a few Hebrew manuscripts and the LXX.

See also DAVID; SAUL.

Bibliography. H. W. Hertzberg, *I and II Samuel, OTL*; P. K. McCarter, "I Samuel," and "II Samuel," *AncB*.

—PAUL L. REDDITT

• **Michmash.** [mik'mash] A village located in the rugged hill territory of the tribe of Benjamin, seven miles northeast of Jerusalem (PLATE 11). Michmash is located opposite Geba on the northern bank of Wadi Suwainet. This strategic position occupied by the village of the pass into the Jordan Valley enabled SAUL and JONATHAN to gain a major Israelite victory over the Philistines at the site (1 Sam 13–14). In Isa 10, the prophet announces in an oracle that the Assyrians will "store their baggage" at Michmash on their march to conquer Jerusalem. According to lists recorded in Ezra (2:7) and Neh (7:31; 11:31-36), Michmash was inhabited after the Exile. In the Maccabean period, the village became the seat of Jonathan's government of reform, very likely because of the increasing Hellenization of Jerusalem (1 Macc 9:73).

See also JONATHAN; PHILISTINES.

—HENRY L. CARRIGAN, JR.

• **Middoth.** *See* NEW TESTAMENT USE OF THE OLD TESTAMENT

• **Midian/Midianites.** [mid'ee-uhn/mid'ee-uh-nits] Listed as the fourth son of ABRAHAM by his wife Keturah in Gen 25:1, 4; 1 Chr 1:32-33. He and his sons were sent eastward (Gen 25:6) to separate them from the covenantal heir Isaac and to form one of the tribes of the northern Arabian desert.

The territory occupied by the Midianites stretched from the Northern Hijaz, east of the Gulf of Aqaba, to the northern portions of Transjordan (PLATE 9). The biblical record associates them with several other groups (Kenites, Amalekites, Ishmaelites) and nations (Amorites, Edom, Moab). These associations are based upon prolonged social and economic contact—not tribal affiliation. Like most of the peoples of this area they engaged in a mixed economy of transhumant pastoralism and terraced irrigation farming. Until the end of the second millennium they also were involved in the incense trade from Arabia to Mesopotamia.

Contact between the Hebrews and the Midianites is first found in the sale of JOSEPH as a slave into Egypt. Having found Joseph in an unguarded pit, the Midianites sold him to POTIPHAR (or to the Ishmaelites, Gen 37:28), a military official in Pharaoh's court (Gen 37:36). More intimate contact occurs when MOSES marries into the family of JETHRO/Reuel, the priest of Midian (Exod 2:15-22). The later identification of Jethro as a Kenite (Judg 4:11, called Hobab in this account) may suggest that the Kenites were a subtribe of Midian, but it is more likely that through close association, they simply were merged in the mind of the biblical editor (cf. Num 10:29).

The collapse of several Near Eastern states after the incursions of the SEA PEOPLES (after 1200 B.C.E.) contributed to the movement of the incense road farther east and a greater utilization of camels as the primary carriers of goods. The economic activities as well as the tribal territories of the Midianites would have become more restricted to northern ARABIA (1 Kgs 11:18) as new kingdoms developed in TRANSJORDAN and CANAAN. The enmity between the Israelites and the Midianites in the wilderness suggests the beginning of what became a wider conflict later. Fearful that the people would adopt the god of the Midianites, Moses ordered the execution of the leaders of the idolaters; and a priest, PHINEHAS, killed an Israelite and his Midianite concubine to save the people from foreign religious contamination (Num 25). Subsequently, a raid was made against the Midianites that resulted in a massacre of all but the women and children (Num 31:4-12).

During the settlement period, GIDEON's raid against the Midianites (Judg 7:2–8:28), while dependent on the editorial framework of the Book of Judges, describes how their settlements east of the Jordan were added to Israelite territory and how the Midianites were driven out. The conflict of peoples is further enhanced by a conflict between their gods. Gideon had torn down an altar to BAAL in his village (Judg 6:25-32) and then had taken the crescent earrings (symbols of their god) from the vanquished Midianites and their camels and melted them down to form an EPHOD (Judg 8:24-27). This follows the same theological precedent as the incident at Peor in Num 25.

Midianites continued to engage in trade during the first millennium, according to Assyrian records as well as the Bible (Isa 60:6). Their domestication of the camel allowed them to operate in a wide area to the north and east of their traditional territories. It is possible that they eventually merged with the Arab tribes who later formed the Nabataean kingdom (cf. Ezek 25:4-11).

See also ISHMAELITES; JETHRO; KENAZ/KENIZZITES.

Bibliography. W. J. Dumbrell, "Midian: A Land or a League?," *VT* 25 (1975): 323-37; E. A. Knauf, "Midianites and Ishmaelites," *Midian, Moab, and Edom,* eds. J. F. A. Sawyer and D. J. A. Clines; E. J. Payne, "The Midianite Arc in Joshua and Judges," *Midian, Moab, and Edom,* eds. J. F. A. Sawyer and D. J. A. Clines.

—VICTOR H. MATTHEWS

• **Midrash.** *See* NEW TESTAMENT USE OF THE OLD TESTAMENT; RABBINIC LITERATURE

• **Mighty Men.** *See* DAVID

• **Milcom.** *See* AMMON/AMMONITES; MOLECH

• **Miletus.** [m*i*-lee'tuhs] Miletus (PLATES 26, 27) was an important ancient seaport and commercial center in southwestern Asia Minor (modern Turkey). Because of its location at the mouth of the Maeander River, it may be assumed that Miletus was founded for coastal shipping. Although destroyed ca. 1200 B.C.E., Miletus was probably not abandoned by Greeks who had made it into a fortified outpost two centuries earlier. Ionian immigrants were most important in the reinforcement of Miletus after it was destroyed, and by the seventh century B.C.E., it was the leading center of Ionian naval enterprise.

The Persians controlled Miletus for at least two periods, but in 334 B.C.E. it was freed by Alexander the Great and became a major Hellenistic port.

During the Hellenistic and Roman periods (323 B.C.E.–325 C.E.) the city had four harbors and three market areas, of which one was the largest of the Hellenistic world. Archeological excavations have revealed remains of a large granary, a shopping area 600 ft. long (the gift of Antiochus I of Syria), temples of Apollo Delphinus and Athena, stadiums, and the largest open-air theatre in Asia Minor (an inscription in the theatre reads: "Place of the Jews, who are also called the God-fearing").

Paul's visit on the third missionary journey (Acts 20:15-38) took place during the period of Miletus's prosperity. Paul sent to Ephesus for the elders to come to Miletus where he delivered a farewell message. Paul may have visited Miletus a second time (2 Tim 4:20), leaving his companion Trophimus. Silt deposited by the Maeander River changed the coastline so that Miletus (modern Palatia) is presently located five mi. inland.

—ROBERT K. GUSTAFSON

• **Military.** *See* SOLDIER; WEAPONS/WARFARE

• **Millennium.** [muh-len'ee-uhm] From a combination of two Latin words: *mille,* "thousand," and *annus,* "year." Millennium designates a period of 1,000 years. Specifically in relation to the Bible, millennium names the 1,000 years mentioned in Rev 20:1-10, esp. vv. 2-6, when SATAN is bound and shut up in "the pit," a time during which the resurrected martyred (Christian) saints reign with Christ before the final onslaught of Satan and, then, the final judgment.

Historically Christians have been divided sharply about the interpretation of this 1,000 year period, taking one of three basic positions. *Premillennialists* maintain that the 1,000 years is a literal time between the second coming of Christ and the final judgment. This group subdivides further into two schools of thought: "historical premillenialists" understand the millennium as a historical extension of the work of Christ in history, a phase between the era of the church and the full form of the KINGDOM OF GOD; "dispensationalists" regard the millennium as a distinct period, not a phase in the ongoing work of God in history, wherein all unrealized OT prophecies to Israel will be perfectly fulfilled. *Postmillennialists* contend the 1,000 year period is a literal time in history prior to the coming of Christ, as yet not realized, when the proclamation of the gospel will be exceptionally well-received. *Amillennialists* interpret the millennium as a literary device typical of APOCALYPTIC LITERATURE (a genre which has clearly influenced the writing of the Book of Revelation), symbolizing the growth of faith during the period of the church on earth and the binding of Satan as a symbol for the work of Christ during this ministry, passion, and in his death and resurrection.

Three further observations are necessary in relation to a consideration of the millennium: First, the only passage in the Bible that makes explicit mention of the millennium is Rev 20:1-10. Second, it is probably true that the idea of a 1,000 year reign of Christ as presented in Rev 20 is a development of the basic OT prophetic notion of a future messianic era, but the use of prophetic passages from the OT in developing millennarian doctrine is illegitimate; for, in fact, the passages cited have nothing to do with a 1,000 year reign, but rather anticipate the coming (first coming) of the Messiah and/or the ultimate consummation of the work of God in the Christ in the age to come, i.e., in the full and final form of the Kingdom of God—in other words, the OT has no concern with the idea of a millennium. Third, most millennarian teaching shows no interest in or knowledge of the historical context in which, and in relation to which, the Book of Revelation was written. This disregard for the historical situation of John of Patmos and his readers usually leads to serious misinterpretation of the passage in Rev 20. The author of Revelation plainly states that the events to which he refers "must soon take place" (Rev 1:1). He addresses lukewarm Christians (Rev 3:1,15-16) in an atmosphere of persecution (Rev 1:9; 2:2,9,13,19) clearly issuing admonition and encouragement (Rev 1–3). The content and imagery of the whole book relate to the purposes established in the early chapters of the work. Understood in this manner, the millennium is a promise of Christ's steadfastness and an example of the security believers have, despite adversity, through their faith in Christ. Whether the millennium is understood as a symbol or as a precise period of future time is not so much decided by a careful reading of the text as it is by the attitudes and methods of study that one brings to the text. Moreover, no matter what interpretation one chooses to defend, one must realize that Rev 20 is concerned to portray Christ and his victory, in which the faithful believers have a share, not to communicate special information that puts the readers in a privileged position if the millennium is correctly understood.

See also APOCALYPTIC LITERATURE; ESCHATOLOGY OF THE NEW TESTAMENT; ESCHATOLOGY OF THE OLD TESTAMENT; KINGDOM OF GOD; MESSIAH/CHRIST; MESSIAH/MESSIANISM; REVELATION, BOOK OF; SATAN IN THE NEW TESTAMENT; SATAN IN THE OLD TESTAMENT

Bibliography. G. R. Beasley-Murray, *The Book of Revelation*; G. B. Caird, *The Revelation of St. John the Divine*; S. J. Case, *The Millennial Hope*; N. Cohn, *The Pursuit of the Millennium,* rev. & expanded ed.; A. Y. Collins, *The Apocalypse*; F. Stagg, *New Testament Theology*.

—MARION L. SOARDS

• **Minister/Serve.** The terms occur in both the OT and NT in a range of meanings. The Hebrew terms *šārat* and *'ābad* (or cognates thereof) are the most common OT words, the former ordinarily translated "minister," the latter "minister" or "serve."

Usually the terms refer to priestly actions: AARON and his sons would "minister in the holy place" (Exod 28:43); the LEVITES would "minister to their brethren in the tent of meeting" (Num 8:26). "Serve" can also carry non-priestly meanings. JOSHUA was the "minister of Moses" (Num 11:28; Josh 1:1). Esau would "serve" Jacob (Gen 25:23). At Shechem the Israelites covenanted to "serve the Lord" (Josh 24.21).

The principal NT terms are *diakoneō* and *douleuō,* the former as a verb "to serve" or as a noun, "servant" or "deacon," the latter meaning "be a slave." In KJV the former was usually rendered "minister," the latter, "serve," but in RSV, renderings vary. Although "minister" suggests "waiting upon," "assisting," or "aiding one in need" ("when did we . . . not minister to thee?": Matt 25:44), "minister" also names a special Christian vocation: "minister of Christ," or of the "gospel" (Col 1: 7, 23).

The Greek term *diakonos,* often rendered "minister," is translated DEACON in special passages. *Douleuō,* "to serve," or literally "to be a slave to," usually carries the simple idea of "serving" another, but often has a spiritual connotation: "You cannot serve God and mammon" (Matt 6:24); "serve the Lord" (Rom 12:11).

—ROLLIN S. ARMOUR

• **Miracle Story.** In the biblical material, the miracle story tells of a mighty act of God. In the Gospels it is generally a story about Jesus which recounts such a mighty act, often characterizing it as an aspect of the inbreaking of the KINGDOM OF GOD.

In form-critical study of the NT, scholars use miracle story more specifically to denote a literary form. Comparing the miracle stories in the Gospels with such stories in other literature of the period, they have defined and characterized the form.

For the form critic, a miracle story is an extended narrative about a miracle. It is not simply a brief context involving a miracle, the purpose of which is to provide a setting for a saying of Jesus; such brief forms are called apophthegms, paradigms, or pronouncement stories. Likewise, the miracle story is not to be confused with the miracle event, for such an event is a divine mystery; rather it is the story of an event. Like other literary forms, the laws governing its style are elastic, yet the miracle story has definite characteristics, not all of which may be present in any one example.

Although form critics often divide them into several types, miracle stories usually consist of three parts. First the situation is described, giving an account of some need. For example, in stories of healing, the condition of the patient is described, emphasizing the seriousness or the length of the illness and the inability of others to help. Often the story also tells of the skepticism of others regarding Jesus's ability to help.

In the second part, the miracle is recounted. The NT miracle story differs from others of the period in that it gives few details at this point, possibly because it was believed human language was not capable of expressing such a divine mystery. Likewise, when healing words are spoken, they are sometimes given in an unknown or foreign tongue. Occasionally no one is allowed to be present. However, in demon possession, often the demon senses the presence of one who has power over him and disputes with him before coming out.

Finally, the response is indicated. A person healed often gives some indication of the fact, such as walking. Demons that have been expelled sometimes engage in spiteful or destructive acts. And witnesses express wonder or approval.

The miracle story forms an essential part of the gospel tradition, being a part of the missionary teaching of the early church. Its interest is more theological than historical, for it seeks to deepen the understanding of Jesus as one who has power and authority over nature, the demonic, sin, and death, and to set forth the implications for the life of those who choose to follow him. Although it has similarities with other miracle stories of the period, the NT miracle story is distinct, for it reflects the faith of the early church that the power of God had decisively broken into the world in Jesus Christ.

See also KINGDOM OF GOD.

Bibliography. R. Bultmann, *The History of the Synoptic Tradition* and "The Study of the Synoptic Gospels," *Form Criticism: Two Essays on New Testament Research*; H. C. Kee, "Miracle Stories, NT," *IDBSupp*; A. Richardson, *The Miracle Stories of the Gospels*; V. Taylor, *The Formation of the Gospel Tradition*.

—G. THOMAS HALBROOKS

• **Miracles.** The term miracle is used to indicate an extraordinary event which is believed to be the result of divine intervention, interrupting the normal or expected course of things. Miracles are recorded in the Bible, and this article will deal first with the kinds or types of miracles in the scriptures. The second section will treat how miracles have been understood and interpreted, and the final section will deal with crucial elements in the contemporary Christian understanding of miracles.

Miracles occur in both the OT and NT, but they are not all the same kind. For this reason, it is helpful to group the miracles in categories for perspective. They are frequently placed in categories that reflect contemporary thought and classified under such headings as nature miracles, healing miracles, theophanies, and so forth. A better approach is, however, to group the miracles in categories that reflect the biblical settings; and this is the pattern followed in the following discussion.

Miracles in the OT. Miracles in the OT are portrayed as God acting directly, as God acting through his chosen agent whom he empowers, or as God acting in conjunction with his agent who announces what God intends to do. These different ways in which miracles occur appear in the various categories of miracles in the OT.

Most of the miracles in the OT are events in which the motifs of judgment and deliverance are interwined. In the crossing of the sea (Exod 14:10-29), for example: "Thus the Lord saved Israel that day from the hand of the Egyptians; and Israel saw the Egyptians dead upon the seashore" (Exod 14:30). In most miracles of this type, Israel is delivered and her enemies destroyed (e.g., Exod 19:12-28; Josh 10:11; 10:12-14; 2 Kgs 6:24-7:20); but in some of them the judgment and deliverance is confined to Israel. In the deliverance from death of those bitten by the fiery serpents, for example, the serpents were sent because the people spoke against God; but the people were delivered from death by looking on the bronze serpent Moses prepared (Num 21:4-9).

Two other large groups of miracles contain one of these motifs: judgment or deliverance. Disobedience results in judgment as, for example, the plague which God sent because of Israel's worship of the golden calf (Exod 32:35; cf. also Gen 20:1-18; Lev 10:1-3; Num 11:1-3; 2 Sam 6:7). Miracles of deliverance include persons being saved from death (Gen 5:24; 1 Kgs 17:17-24), illness (2 Kgs 5:1-19), poison (2 Kgs 4:38-41), lions (Dan 6:19-24), and hostile armies (Exod 17:8-13).

Another large group of miracles is composed of miracles of sustenance in which God provides food (Exod 16:13-31) or water (Exod 17:1-7) for both animals and persons (cf., also Judg 15:18-20; 1 Kgs 17:8-16; 2 Kgs 3:13-20; 4:1-7).

Two other types of miracles are found in the OT. One group contains miracles of call (Exod 3:1-22), revelation (Exod 19:16–20:20), or instruction (Num 22:21-35); and the other group is composed of miracles of assurance. Miracles of this type include the fleece of Gideon (Judg 6:36-40) and Hezekiah's sundial (2 Kgs 20:1-11).

When one views the miracles in the OT as a whole, it is important to note that they are clustered rather than evenly distributed. Most of the miracles are recounted in the context of Israel's deliverance from Egypt, journey in the wilderness, and entrance into Canaan. Most, but not all, of the remaining miracles are related to the careers of Elijah and Elisha.

Miracles in the NT. The NT, although less than one-third the length of the OT, contains about the same number of miracles. In addition to miracle stories, the NT has summary statements of many miracles being performed by both Jesus (e.g., Mark 1:32-34; Luke 9:11) and the apostles (Acts 5:12-16; 19:11-12). Miracles were also performed by the early Christians as Paul's reference to some Christians being given the gifts of healing and miracles demonstrates (1 Cor 12:9-10; cf. Gal 3:5). Miracles in the NT are thus not limited to the period of the ministry of Jesus, but he performed most of the miracles. The majority of the miracles of Jesus are healing miracles (cf., e.g., Mark 1:40-45; 3:1-6; Luke 13:10-13); but miracles of deliverance from storms (Mark 4:35-41) and death (Luke 7:11-17) occur as well as miracles of instruction (Mark 11:12-14), sustenance (Mark 6:34-44; 8:1-9), and call or affirmation (Luke 5:1-11; John 1:47-50). Miracles of judgment which are frequent in the OT are not reported in relation to the ministry of Jesus (cf. Luke 9:51-56), but do occur in Acts (cf. 5:1-11; 13:4-11).

In addition to the miracles related to the ministry of Jesus, the NT reports miracles related to the birth, death, and resurrection of Jesus and miracles related to the spread of the gospel in Acts. These include miracles of judgment, as mentioned above, and miracles of deliverance (Acts 12:1-11; 28:3-6), instructions or revelation (Acts 2:1-42; 10:9-29), healing (Acts 3:1-16; 28:7-10), and affirmation (Acts 16:9-10; 18:9-10). The largest group of miracles is composed of miracles of healing, just as in the ministry of Jesus.

Interpretation of the Miracles of the Bible. Frequently one encounters the assertion that persons living prior to the scientific age when the laws of nature were not understood all believed in miracles and that miracles only raise questions for modern persons. This is not accurate: miracle stories occur in literature preceding the time of Jesus, and these stories were believed by some and flatly denied by other classical writers who felt miracles were impossible. Neither is it accurate to affirm that religious people believe in miracles while the irreligious do not. A glance at the way in which the miracles of the Bible have been interpreted suggests that a person's presuppositions about the nature of reality are more crucial in how one deals with the miraculous.

Since the establishment of Christianity, the majority of Christians have accepted the miracle stories at face value, believing that miracles could and did occur. Some, however, have had intellectual difficulty in accepting miracles and, in struggling with the question of the reality of supernatural events, developed ways of understanding miracles that seemed to them to allow one to maintain faith in Christ and yet to deny that he worked miracles. Two basic approaches have been taken. The first approach is to acknowledge that the Bible does contain miracles and to explain how they became included by affirming that these stories were added by the writers in an honest effort to establish the truth of the scriptures. Some representatives of this approach seek to trace the stories of healings or miraculous feedings in other literatures to discover the sources of the biblical stories (e.g., Richard Reitzenstein and Rudolf Bultmann), but others have been quick to point out that viewing the miracles as accretions to the narrative overlooks the way in which the theme for the miraculous is woven inseparably into the biblical revelation.

The second approach which seeks a compatibility between belief in Christ and unbelief regarding miracles acknowledges that there are miracles stories in the Bible, but affirm that they do not have to be understood as supernatural events. This has been done in two ways. The first is to allegorize the miracles and make them testify to spiritual values (R.C. Trench). The story of the healing of a blind man is thus transformed into a story which teaches us that Jesus can open the eyes of our understanding to see God as we ought instead of in our sin-blinded way. Likewise, the stilling of the storm is transformed into a message about Christ's ability to calm the storms we pass through in life and to give us peace in turmoil. The second way persons have avoided interpreting miracles as supernatural events is to show how the event could have occurred. The story of the feeding of the five thousand (John 6:1-14) is thus explained: all were hungry; and all had food hidden in their cloaks but were afraid to let others know it lest theirs be taken. When Jesus set a lad before him who unselfishly gave up his lunch, all were ashamed, brought out their food, and had more than enough. Such interpretations of miracles fail because they neither do justice to the stories as told nor are able to explain the reactions of observers (cf. John 6:14).

Crucial Dimensions in a Christian Understanding of Miracles. Some persons have felt it adequate to deal with the miracles of the Bible by simply affirming their belief in them. But it is clear that miracles raise more questions than the one of belief, even though this matter is crucial for those whose presuppositions thrust this question to the center. All of the miracles in the Bible need to be understood in the light of the revelation about their meaning that occurred in Jesus Christ, and this requires that the following perspectives be kept in mind in understanding any miracle.

(1) To label an event as a miracle requires faith in God because a miracle is more than a mysterious unexplainable wonder. A miracle is God acting in history outside of what would be the expected outcome of events, and this event which is not understandable by natural explanation is perceived as God acting. A miracle is then a faith understanding and does not compel belief. The miracles of Jesus did not force all the observers to believe he was God's son (Mark 3:22). The disputes about the credibility of miracles are not, therefore, confined to the modern or scientific age; and the Christian need not be surprised that what she or he attributes to God will be assigned by others to unknown or other causes.

(2) Miracles are always to be understood as SIGNS (Exod 10:1-2; Luke 2:12; John 20:30; Acts 2:22). A sign is an event that points to crucial realities for existence, and unbelief cannot comprehend (Matt 12:38-39). Miracles are thus deeds which speak; they speak of God's love as they provide deliverance, sustenance, or healing; they speak of God's demands as they express judgment or provide instruction; and they speak of God's ultimate intentions for our existence as they restore the dead to their loved ones and health to the incapacitated.

(3) The supreme miracle is the coming of God's son in human form to redeem persons and the certification of the incarnation is the resurrection. When one believes that God raised Jesus from the dead, which is essential to Christian faith (1 Cor 15:12-19), one has understood the ultimate miracle. This belief about who Jesus was places all individual miracles in their proper context for evaluation.

See also MAGIC AND DIVINATION; MIRACLE STORY; SIGNS AND WONDERS; THEOPHANY.

Bibliography. J. Kallas, *The Significance of the Synoptic Miracles*; H. Lockyer, *All the Miracles of the Bible*; N. van der Loos, *The Miracles of Jesus*.

—HAROLD S. SONGER

• **Miriam.** [mihr'ee-uhm] A Hebrew name applied to two OT figures, the best known being the sister of MOSES.

Moses' sister is listed both in Num 26:59 and 1 Chr 6:3 as a child of Amram. Her mother was Jochebed. Both parents were descendants of LEVI. While not identified by name in the narrative of Moses' infancy, Miriam must have been the sister who watched over the basket in the Nile (Exod 2). She secured Moses' mother as his nurse.

After the drowning of the Egyptians in the sea, Miriam, called the PROPHETESS, led the women in celebration (Exod 15:20-21). Later, as the Israelites neared Canaan, she and AARON rebuked Moses for marrying a Cushite woman, challenging Moses' position as the prophet of Yahweh. It is reported that God punished her with LEPROSY, but Moses intervened on her behalf, and she was restored after seven days (Num 12). She died at Kadesh (Num 20:1) and was buried there. She was remembered as an example in cases of leprosy (Deut 24:9) and as a leader of Israel (Mic 6:4).

The other Miriam is mentioned only in the genealogy of 1 Chr in an uncertain text 4:17, that fails to distinguish whether the person was male or female or who was the immediate ancestor. Some translations rearrange the text to relieve the uncertainty.

The name Miriam becomes *Maria(m)* in Greek.

See also AARON; DANCING; LEPROSY; MARY; MOSES; POETRY; PROPHETESS; RED SEA/REED SEA.

—MICHAEL FINK

• **Mishnah.** *See* RABBINIC LITERATURE

• **Missing the Mark.** *See* SIN

• **Mite.** *See* MONEY

• **Mittani.** *See* NUZI

• **Mixed Marriages.** *See* EZRA

• **Moab/Moabites.** [moh'ab/moh'uh-bits] Moab was the name of a small kingdom in ancient Transjordan. The occupants of this region were called Moabites or, collectively, Moab. Moabite territory was situated on the Transjordanian tableland that rises immediately to the east of the DEAD SEA, with the deep ARABAH providing an effective boundary between Judah and Moab. The northern limit of Moabite land shifted from time to time, depending on political and military circumstances; the HESHBON vicinity was the effective boundary in times of Moabite strength, while the ARNON gorge separated Moab from enemies to the north in times of Moabite weakness. Moab's eastern extent was set by the Syrian Desert, the effective limit of the agricultural zone. The Zered canyon was the southern boundary of the Moabite kingdom, which separated the latter from the land of EDOM (PLATE 10).

The terrain of Moab may be described as gently rolling tableland, but numerous streams drain the plateau and have cut deep ravines that open into the Dead Sea valley. The plateau's western side has a higher elevation than the lower desert fringe on the east; the western half of the plateau receives more rainfall and is, therefore, better suited to agriculture. Moab has always been famous for its pasturage (cf. 2 Kgs 3:4), but its soils and climate also allow for the growing of wheat and barley. Also famous is the so-called King's Highway, which has fords on the Arnon and ZERED and cuts right across the Moabite plateau (cf. Num 21:21-22; Judg 11:17).

The origin of this semitic people is described in a straightforward way in Gen 19:37—the Moabites descended from Moab, the son of LOT and his older daughter. According to Deut 2:10-11, the Emim were the pre-Moabite occupants of this region. Archaeological investigations in Moab indicate that there was a significant population in the third millennium B.C.E., the Early Bronze Age. Though Glueck's view concerning an occupational gap in

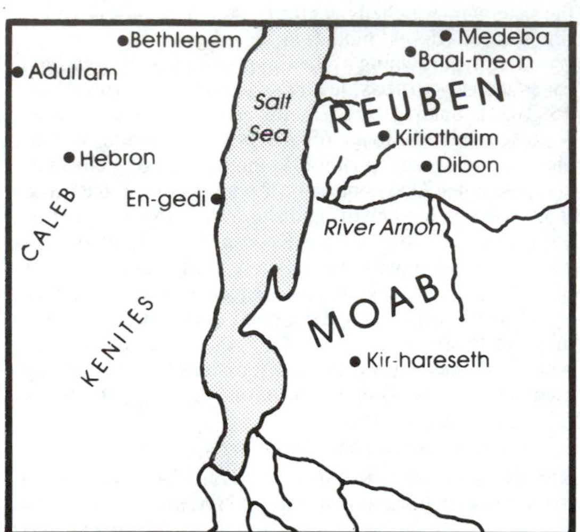

Designed by Margaret Jordan Brown ©Mercer University Press

Moab during much of the second millennium B.C.E. has been revised, it does appear that there was a decline in population during the Middle Bronze Age and the early part of the Late Bronze Age. Whatever explanation is given for this phenomenon must also take into account the appearance of a Moabite kingdom, beginning sometime ca. 1300 B.C.E. near the time of the Hebrew migration through Moabite territory. Unfortunately, an understanding concerning the establishment of this small kingdom, which lasted from ca. 1300–600 B.C.E., is quite limited. It must be stressed that this kingdom was not, at the time of their first contact with the Hebrews, a fully formed political unit with a centralized army, etc. Bits of information are provided by archaeology and textual sources.

According to Num 21:13 and 26, the Moabites did not control the region north of the River Arnon at the time of the Hebrew migration, since the Amorite King Sihon had assumed power in this area and ruled from Heshbon. Num 21:21-32 reports that the Hebrews soundly defeated SIHON when he refused them permission to pass through the Moabite realm. The famous episode involving the Mesopotamian diviner, BALAAM, occurred when King Balak of Moab feared the presence of such a powerful force of Israelites in his territory (Num 22–24; Josh 24:9). Ultimately, the Hebrew tribes of REUBEN and GAD occupied Sihon's territory, with the Arnon serving as the new boundary between Israel and Moab proper (Num 32). The Moabite plateau on the northern side of the Arnon was, thereafter, a source of contention between the Israelites and Moabites.

In the period of the Judges, the Moabite king EGLON, oppressed the Hebrews, an indication that Moabite power had increased once more, but he was assassinated by EHUD (Judg 3:12-30). Northern Moab came under the control of Israel once again by the time of JEPHTHAH (Judg 11:26), but the Book of RUTH points to a time when Israel and Moab lived in peace. The latter story also reflects one kind of reaction to famine in antiquity—migration to another land where climatic conditions were more favorable.

The age of SAUL and DAVID, the late eleventh through mid-tenth centuries B.C.E., witnessed the return of a bitter hostility between Israel and Moab. According to passages such as 1 Sam 14:47 and 2 Sam 8:2, it would seem that Israel was usually more powerful, a situation that continued into SOLOMON's reign. Most interesting is the biblical reference to the presence of Moabite women in Solomon's harem (1 Kgs 11:1), which caused him to build a high place for the Moabite god, Chemosh, at Jerusalem (1 Kgs 11:7, 33).

The Moabites exerted their independence once again at the beginning of Israel's divided monarchy, but kings OMRI and AHAB subjected their traditional foes to Israelite control once again in the ninth century B.C.E. One of the most important discoveries in the history of Syro-Palestinian archaeology, the MESHA STELE (or Moabite Stone), which dates to ca. 830 B.C.E., provides important illumination on this relationship (cf. 2 Kgs 3). Without question, King Mesha is the best known figure from Moabite history, although knowledge of him is tantalizingly scanty. After his day, Moab's conflicts with the surrounding nations (e.g., Israel, Judah, Edom, and Assyria) were brought to an end with the Babylonian invasion, when King NEBUCHADREZZAR destroyed the Moabite kingdom at the opening of the sixth century B.C.E. (cf. Ezek 25:8-11). The age-old conflict between Moab, Israel, and Judah is highlighted by the numerous prophetic indictments leveled against the Moabites (e.g., Isa 15–16; Amos 2:1-3; Jer 9:25-26; 48:1-47; Zeph 2:8-11).

Following the Babylonian conquest, the kingdom of Moab never reappeared. The former Moabite territory eventually came under Persian control, but we know very little about this period. A variety of Arab peoples moved into southern Transjordan, a process that had been underway since before the Babylonian invasion, but the NABATAEANS emerged by the fourth century B.C.E. as the dominant inhabitants of this region. Since the Jewish community sought to observe the law of Deut 23:3–6, people of Moabite ancestry were still identified in postexilic times (cf. Ezra 9:1; Neh 13:1, 23).

While knowledge of Moabite religion is limited, it is safe to say that there were many similarities between the religious practices of Canaan, Israel, and Moab, among others. By the time that the Moabite kingdom emerged, however, there were distinctive features in the beliefs and rituals of Moab. Most important was the worship of the national or ethnic god, Chemosh, though it is now known that this deity was part of a much older semitic pantheon. Num 21:29 and Jer 48:46 refer to the Moabites as the "people of Chemosh," and the frequent references to this god in Moabite personal names and in the Mesha Stele point to Chemosh's role in personal and national life.

Num 22–24 indicates that the Moabites sought divine guidance and that diviners and oracles were highly respected. Moabite religion included a priesthood (Jer 48:7) and a sacrificial system (Num 22:40–23:30; 25:1-5; 2 Kgs 3:27; Jer 48:35). What has been identified as a Moabite sanctuary has been uncovered at Dhiban (ancient DIBON); both the Mesha Stele and the Hebrew Bible (cf. 1 Kgs 11:7-8; 2 Kgs 23:13) indicate that such structures existed.

Bibliography. A. H. van Zyl, *The Moabites*; J. R. Bartlett, "The Moabites and Edomites," *Peoples of Old Testament Times*, D. J. Wiseman, ed.; N. Glueck, *The Other Side of Jordan*, rev. ed; J. A. Dearman, ed., *Studies in the Mesha Inscription and Moab*.

—GERALD L. MATTINGLY

• **Moabite Stone.** *See* CHEMOSH; MESHA STELE

• **Molech.** [moh'lek] The term, which was a form of SAC-

RIFICE in ancient Israel, is usually mistakenly identified as an Ammonite deity (1 Kgs 11:7) to whom human sacrifice was offered (2 Kgs 23:10; Jer 32:35). Earlier scholars had suggested that "Molech" (Heb. *mōlek*) was the result of combining the consonants for "king" (*melek*) with the vowels of "shame" (*bōšet*), thus expressing contempt for the Canaanite god. This etymology and the apparent equation of Molech/Milcom with "the abomination of the Ammonite" in 1 Kgs 11:5, 7, 33 were enough to identify Molech/Milcom with a certain *malik* or *muluk* deity found in Akkadian texts and also as a theophoric element in personal names (2 Kgs 17:31).

However, Punic inscriptions from 400–150 B.C.E. imply that the word *mlk* (pronounced *molk*) is a general term for "sacrifice" or "offering." Hence, the OT passages where *mōlek* occurs (Lev 18:21; 20:2-5; 2 Kgs 23:10; Jer 32:35) should be interpreted as saying that adults caused children to pass through the fire "for or as a sacrifice" rather than "to Molech." Other evidence from inscriptions also connects this term with human sacrifice.

Furthermore, the LXX rendering of 1 Kgs 11:7 suggests that "Molech" is a scribal error that should be read as "Milcom." Hence, the identification of Molech with the Ammonite god Milcom cannot stand. In fact, Molech is not a deity at all but a word meaning "sacrifice."

Child sacrifice did occur in the OT. Human sacrifice, however, was abhorred by the people of Israel (2 Kgs 3:27). Child sacrifices were offered to BAAL (2 Kgs 17:17; Jer 32:35), to the Host of Heaven (2 Kgs 21:5-6) and to other foreign gods (2 Kgs 17:31), though the practice probably was rare outside Israel as well as within Israel. The law of Moses demanded the death of anyone who offered a human sacrifice (Lev 18:21; 20:2-5).

See also AMMON/AMMONITES; IDOLATRY; SACRIFICE.

Bibliography. W. F. Albright, *Archaeology and the Religion of Israel*, and *Yahweh and the Gods of Canaan*.

—STEPHEN J. ANDREWS

• **Molten Image.** *See* GRAVING/ENGRAVING/INCISING; IMAGES/FIGURINES

• **Monarchy.** *See* UNITED MONARCHY

• **Money.** Money refers to that which is generally accepted as a medium of exchange, a measure of value, or a means of payment. In the NT era money was identified almost exclusively with coinage, i.e., minted metals of fixed weight and purity. Barter, of course, was still widespread, but the use of money was well-established throughout the Roman empire.

Though often obscured by English translations, the NT mentions a variety of coins and reflects the fact that several different currencies circulated in the Roman Empire. Coins of the imperial monetary system established by Augustus figure most prominently. The imperial currency was based on the old Attic standard of Alexander the Great and included coins minted in three metals—gold, silver, and copper (cf. Matt 10:9; Rev 9:20). The silver denarius is mentioned more frequently than any other coin (Matt 18:28; 20:2, 9, 10, 13; Mark 6:37; 14:5; Luke 7:41; 10:35; John 6:7; 12:5; Rev 6:6). Considered a fair wage for one day's labor (Matt 20:1-16), the denarius enjoyed wide circulation for two major reasons: Roman troops were paid in denarii and the census tax (Mark 12:14) had to be paid in denarii. Thus when Jesus asked for a coin during his confrontation with the Pharisees and Herodians over paying taxes to Caesar, he was handed, appropriately, a denarius (Mark 12:16). The imperial currency also included two copper coins that are mentioned in the NT, the ass (Matt 10:29; Luke 12:6) and the quadrans (Matt 5:26; Mark 12:42). A single denarius was worth sixteen asses or sixty-four quadrans.

Alongside the imperial currency were old Greek coins and various provincial issues that, though supervised by the emperor, retained traditional Greek denominations (e.g., *talent, mine, stater, drachma, lepton*). The value of the talent (Matt 18:24; 25:15-28) varied over time, but in the NT period one talent was approximately equal to 6,000 denarii. In what appears to be the same parable as found in Matt 25:15-28, Luke uses "mine" (RSV "pound") instead of "talent" (1 talent = 60 mines). The stater, found in the story of Jesus and the payment of the Temple tax (Matt 17:2), was a large silver coin equal to four drachmas. (The RSV, which renders "stater" as "shekel," reflects Exod 30:13 where the requirement of the Temple tax is given in shekels. Since there were no Jewish shekels minted during Roman occupation, the preferred means of payment for the Temple tax was the Tyrian shekel, a large silver coin minted in Tyre that was approximately equal in weight and value to the stater.) The Greek drachma, found only in Luke 15:8-9, was a silver coin roughly equivalent to the denarius. The lepton (KJV "mite," RSV "copper coin" in Mark 12:42) was the smallest of the Greek coins, and it had a value one-half that of the Roman quadrans, the smallest of the Roman coins.

The Greek word for silver was the generic term for money (e.g., the "love of money" in 1 Tim 6:10 is literally the "love of silver"), but the word could also refer to silver coins, usually those larger than the denarius or drachma. Thus the thirty pieces of silver given to Judas (Matt 26:15; 27:3, 5, 6, 9) and the "sum of money" (KJV "large money") used to bribe the guards at the tomb (Matt 28:12) may have been staters or Tyrian shekels.

No Jewish coins are specifically mentioned in the NT, but archaeological evidence suggests that copper coins from the Maccabean period and from the reign of Herod the Great circulated widely in Palestine. Unlike the imperial coins, which, according to Jewish tradition, violated the second commandment with their pictures of gods, goddesses, and emperors, these Jewish issues were stamped with non-offensive images.

See also COINS AND MONEY.

—JOHN C. SHELLEY

• **Money Changers.** *See* MONEY

• **Monogamy.** *See* MARRIAGE IN THE NEW TESTAMENT

• **Monotheism.** [mon″uh-thee-iz′uhm] A word derived from the Greek words, *monos* (alone or single), and *Theos* (God), expressing belief in one GOD. It is considered by many to be the unique contribution of biblical faith to the history of religious thought. A monotheistic faith is characteristic of Judaism and Christianity, but a survey of biblical literature reveals that the faith of Israel was not monotheistic from its inception and the monotheism of the NT is enhanced by the revelation of God in JESUS.

In the ancient Near East the existence of divine beings was universally accepted; therefore, the questions that arose concerning deities were not concerned with the reality of existence but with the nature of the reality.

Israel's monotheism may be said to be a development in an unfolding relationship between Yahweh and Israel—a flowering from the uniqueness of God to a firm expression of Yahweh's existence and the non-existence of other gods. This flowering is a difficult one to trace, but it is possible to capture glimpses of Israel's relationship to God at various stages in its history and begin to formulate a rough idea of the development.

Throughout its history, Israel's neighbors could best be described as polytheistic. The religions of most of these neighbors were nature religions and as such included the recognition and worship of a plurality of deities. These polytheistic cultures provided the setting for the development of Israel's faith.

In the patriarchal traditions of Genesis it appears that the seminomadic tribes each had a deity upon which to call (Gen 24:27; 31:5, 53). As the stories of the patriarchs unfold it is important to note that although the names of Canaanite deities were associated with particular places, the God of the patriarchs was not bound to a certain location.

The point at which the uniqueness of Israel's God is first made clear is in the Mosaic tradition, especially in connection with the EXODUS event. This salvific activity of God in history offers several unique characteristics.

The very name revealed to Israel, *yhwh*—known technically as the TETRAGRAMMATON—is indicative of the uniqueness. This clearly distinguishing appellation suggests that there is only one; no others bear this name.

A second unique characteristic revealed in this Mosaic tradition is the demand for sole allegiance from Israel (Exod 20:3). The introductory verse of the Decalogue reminds Israel that it was Yahweh who brought her up from Egypt, out of bondage; it is in view of this act of deliverance that the commandments are given, commandments that delineate the appropriate response to such a god. It is clear from Exod 20:3 that Yahweh is to be the only god for the community of Israel, but such a statement must still be viewed in terms of a polytheistic culture. Yahweh is a jealous god (Exod 20:5) and will not tolerate shared allegiance.

A third unique characteristic expressed here is the prohibition of images (Exod 20:4). The uniqueness of Yahweh cannot be captured in any form that the people can fashion. This is in striking contrast to typical Near Eastern cults of this period in which deities were represented in a great variety of forms.

It becomes apparent that the faith of the Mosaic tradition does express a realization of the uniqueness of Yahweh, but because the existence of other gods is not denied, this belief should not yet be viewed as monotheism.

Progression from polytheism to monotheism is marked by struggles to resist worship of other gods and to hold fast to the requirements set forth in the decalogue. OT literature includes many instances of Israel's battle to be strong in allegiance to Yahweh and to resist seduction by other deities (e.g., Exod 32:1-8; Judg 2:1-13).

With the ELIJAH story (1 Kgs 18:1-46) a monotheistic viewpoint is emerging. It echoes the challenge in Josh 24, but Elijah's affirmation of God as expressed in 1 Kgs 18:24 stretches beyond the challenge of JOSHUA. This affirmation finds expression in the prophecies of AMOS, JEREMIAH, and ISAIAH.

The eloquent poetry of Deutero-Isaiah brings the idea of monotheism to fullest expression (Isa 40:18, 25; 41:21-29; 43:10; 44:6-8; 46:9). The writer of Deut 6:4-9 records the monotheism in permanent credal form. Known as the SHEMA, it clearly expresses Israel's faith: "Hear, O Israel, the Lord our God is one Lord." The OT view of God is seen to have developed from comprehension of and relationship to a god who is unique to Israel—to Yahweh, God of creation and controller of all nations and history.

This monotheistic faith of Israel is foundational to that expressed in NT literature as supremely revealed in Jesus. NT literature is brimming with affirmations of God's sovereignty and control and the expression of this through the life of Jesus of Nazareth. The credal affirmation of monotheism expressed in Deut 6:4-9 is echoed in NT literature (Mark 12:28-30; Matt 22:34-40; Luke 10:25-28) as Jesus espouses this as the greatest of all commandments.

Although the emphasis in NT literature is on the special revelation of God in Jesus, there is no transference of worship from God to Jesus. There is, instead, a presentation of the INCARNATION as a means of providing a closer relationship to the one God.

The affirmations of the one God are not lost among the NT stories of the life and teachings of Jesus; rather they are reaffirmed and then enhanced by the possibility for a more intimate relationship with the Father through the Son. Jesus affirms the creator God, sustainer God in such passages as Luke 12:22-32 and Matt 6:25-35 as he describes the tender care of the Father for the lilies of the field and the birds of the air. Jesus' prayer in the final hours of his life expresses clearly his desire that the people know the Father, "the only true God" (John 17:3). The more personal expression of monotheism in NT literature expresses the more intimate communion made possible through the incarnation of God in Jesus Christ.

See also GOD; POLYTHEISM; SHEMA; TEN COMMANDMENTS; TETRAGRAMMATON.

Bibliography. R. E. Clements, *Old Testament Theology*; W. Eichrodt, *Theology of the OT*; H. H. Rowley, *From Moses to Qumran*; W. Schmidt, *The Faith of Old Testament Theology*; G. von Rad, *Old Testament Theology*; C. Westermann, *Elements of Old Testament Theology*.

—JUDY YATES ELLIS

• **Mordecai.** [mor'duh-k*i*] A personal name found in two late OT references. The Israelites often had both a Hebrew name and a non-Jewish name. Mordecai appears to be a parallel to the name Marduk or Merodach, the chief Babylonian deity. Marduk represented the victory over the gods of chaotic waters. A dramatization of that mythic victory highlighted the Babylonian new year festival each spring.

The first Mordecai appears in a list of men who returned to Jerusalem after the EXILE (Ezra 2:2; Neh 7:7). The list in Ezra 2:2 states that these persons returned with ZERUBBABEL. While that may be correct, at least two considerations seem noteworthy. First, the list follows the statement in Ezra 1:8, 11 that Sheshbazzar led a group of exiles from Babylonia to Jerusalem. Second, Nehemiah, about 445 B.C.E., may have been referring to the well-known persons. Thus, the list may actually be a compilation of several groups who returned from exile. Twelve names in Neh 7:7 evidently represent a second exodus for the tribes of Israel (cf. 1 Esdr 5:8).

The second and more familiar person with the name of Mordecai occurs in the Book of Esther. Esth 2:5-7 describes him as a Jew who lived in the Persian capital of Susa, a descendant of Kish from the tribe of Benjamin, an exile who accompanied Jeconiah (Jehoiachin), and a foster-father of Hadassah or Esther. NEBUCHADREZZAR carried Jeconiah (Jehoiachin), king of Judah, into captivity in 597 B.C.E. If Ahasuerus, the king named in the story, was Xerxes (485–464 B.C.E.) or Artaxerxes II (404–361 B.C.E.) then Mordecai's age would be about 130 to 150 in this story. The reference to Kish probably did not mean that Mordecai was the great grandson of Kish; rather, this genealogy seems to relate Mordecai to Kish, father of SAUL. The conflict in the story between Mordecai and Haman, a descendant of King Agag and the Amalekites (Esth 3:1) may be a throwback to the long-standing enmity between the Israelites and the Amalekites (cf. Exod 17:8-16; 1 Sam 15:7-9). Mordecai accepted the responsibility for Hadassah, who was an orphan. He enabled her to become a member of the king's harem. When the king needed a new queen he chose Esther. Her Jewish identity remained hidden.

Haman developed a plot to destroy Mordecai and other Jews. Mordecai confronted Esther with a great risk to enter into the presence of the king without invitation. She heard the challenge in words that have become a famous statement, "Who knows whether you have not come to the kingdom for such a time as this?" (Esth 4:14). Esther accepted his request, called for a three-day fast, and said to Mordecai, "Then I will go to the king, though it is against the law; and if I perish, I perish" (Esth 4:16). Esther revealed her Jewish identity and informed the king about Haman's wicked plot. In the meantime the king had issued orders for Haman to reward Mordecai for uncovering an earlier assassination plot on the king's life. The gallows that Haman intended for Mordecai became the method of death for Haman (Esth 7:10). Mordecai received Haman's position as chief minister of the king.

After the destruction of the enemies of the Jews, a feast of joy and celebration named PURIM was instituted. An alternate designation for this feast was the Day of Mordecai (2 Macc 15:36). The feast presents an intense contrast in the loud responses, "cursed be Haman" and "blessed be Mordecai."

See also ESTHER; ESTHER, BOOK OF; PURIM.

Bibliography. B. W. Anderson, "Introduction and Exegesis of Esther," *IB*; R. B. Bjornard, "Esther," *BBC*; T. H. Gaster, *Festivals of the Jewish Year*.

—OMER J. HANCOCK, JR.

• **Moriah, Mount.** [muh-ri'uh] The OT contains only one reference to Mount Moriah (2 Chr 3:1). The writer mentioned Mount Moriah as the location where SOLOMON built the TEMPLE (PLATE 12). This site previously had been Araunah's (Ornan's) threshing floor that DAVID had bought to use as a place of sacrifice to stop a plague on his people. After the Lord appeared to him and the plague ended, David declared that the house of the Lord would be built on this same site (2 Chr 21:1–22:1).

The general area lies today in a Muslim tract called the Noble Sanctuary. The more specific site is occupied by a Muslim shrine called the Dome of the Rock (PLATE 35), completed in 691 C.E.

Authorities generally agree on this identification of Mount Moriah, but they do not agree regarding the association of the "Mount" with the "region of Moriah" (Gen 22:2). The Chronicler cites no specific connection between the two, but may have implied it. The fact that the designation of the Temple site as Mount Moriah appears nowhere else adds weight to this suggestion.

Some objections to the linking of Mount Moriah and the region of Moriah are that (1) Jerusalem is not far enough from south Philistia to require a three day trip, and (2) the Temple hill is not visible until one gets rather close.

Answers to these objections are that (1) Jerusalem is about eighty km. from south Philistia, a distance that could require a three day trip, and (2) in Genesis, the stress is not on a specific mountain, but on a region called Moriah. In addition, some of the heights of Jerusalem are visible at a distance.

Josephus, an ancient Jewish historian, asserted that Mount Moriah was the same as the place where ABRAHAM prepared to sacrifice ISAAC. This identification was also accepted by the Rabbis and by Jerome. Muslim faithful point out "Abraham's place" inside the Dome of the Rock. The Samaritans, however, equated the place of Abraham's act with MOUNT GERIZIM, their holy place.

The suggestion that the specific location within the region of Moriah and Mount Moriah itself are one and the same makes sense on theological grounds. In the first instance, Abraham was ready to make a supreme sacrifice of obedience because of his faith in the Lord. As a result, the Lord revealed himself to Abraham and reaffirmed his covenant promise. In the second instance, the Temple is to be built, and it will be the place where the Lord will reveal himself in a special way and worshipers will offer sacrifices that demonstrate their faith in the Lord and the covenant promises.

See also JERUSALEM.

Bibliography. G. A. Barrois, "Moriah," *IDB*; J. Finegan, *Light from the Ancient Past*; T. C. Mitchell, "Moriah," *IBD*.

—WALTER E. BROWN

• **Mosaics.** [moh-zay'iks] A mosaic is a decoration usually made of small pieces of stone, called *tesserae* (glass, clay, and marble are also used) and inlaid to form patterns of pictures on floors, walls, ceilings and even furniture and other personal items. The earliest mosaics known, made of cone-shaped tiles, come from Mesopotamia and date between the fourth and second millennia B.C.E.

By comparison, the oldest mosaics known from Palestine are those in Herod's (37–4 B.C.E.) palaces at MASADA. These include both black and white as well as multicolored patterns.

The art of mosaics reached its peak in the Byzantine period (324–640 C.E.) and is especially represented in the churches and synagogues built during this time. One of the finest examples of a mosaic pavement in a synagogue is that found at Hammath Tiberias which dates to the fourth century C.E. The mosaic is divided into three panels, a common practice in the following century. Usually the first panel in such pavements contains a biblical scene of salvation such as the sacrifice of Isaac by Abraham. At Hammath Tiberias, this panel is replaced with dedicatory inscriptions. The middle panel, surprisingly, contains a zodiac with Helios, the sun god, at its center. In the corners of this panel the symbols of the four seasons of the year are also included. The third panel, closest to the Torah shrine, normally contains the ark of the Law and cultic objects such as the menorah, the shofar, and incense shovel.

Another type of mosaic decoration (e.g., at Maon), consists of representations of animals, birds, fruits and scenes of rural life. This type is even more common in the churches of this period and is distinguished from those of the synagogues only by the distinctive Jewish cultic objects included in the latter.

Another common mosaic decoration is that of geometric or conventional designs. This type exists in the synagogues found at Jericho and elsewhere. Recent excavations of other synagogues, such as those at En-Gedi and in the Beth-shan Valley, include excerpts from the Talmud.

The mosaics in the Christian churches also show a wide variety of types. The earliest remains consist mainly of geometric patterns, but a notable exception to this practice is in the pavement of the Church of the Loaves and Fishes at Heptapegon. Dating to the last half of the fourth century, this mosaic, preserved in the nave, contains scenes of the Nile including a variety of plants and animals. On the other hand, the mosaic in a fifth century church at Gerasa contains only geometric designs. Still different is the sixth century mosaic in the church at Kursi (Gergesa) on the eastern shore of the Sea of Galilee. Here the decoration is a geometric design with panels containing animals and fowls. The latter have been badly damaged by later iconoclasts. Conspicuously absent from most Christian mosaics are representations of human form.

From a sixth century church in MEDEBA, Jordan, comes a very unusual mosaic map of Israel. Originally containing two and a half million *tesserae,* the map contains valuable geographical and topographical information of Palestine.

Beautiful early Arab mosaic art can be seen in the famous Dome of the Rock in Jerusalem (PLATE 35). Completed in 691 C.E., the mosque is covered with mosaics both inside and out.

Occasionally Mosaics are also found in private houses. A good example comes form a Jewish villa at Beth-shan which contains scenes from the *Odyssey*.

Bibliography. M. Avi-Yonah, *The Madaba Mosaic Map*; M. Dothan, "Tiberias, Hammath," *EAEHL* 3 (1977): 819-23; H. Frankfort, *The Art and Architecture of the Ancient Orient*; A. Negev, ed., "Mosaics," *AEHL*.

—JOHN C. H. LAUGHLIN

• **Moses.** [moh'zis] Moses (Moshe), to whom the Pentateuch is credited, dominates the bulk of the first five books of the Hebrew Bible. His name reflects, like the story of JOSEPH, a genuine but surface knowledge of Egypt for it mirrors names like Thutmose, which means "The god Thut is born." That his name appears to leave out the name of the god born, from an Egyptian perspective, fits the story of this man who seems oblivious of his heritage until he encounters a vibrant god in the barrenness of the wilderness. From the time he meets Yahweh at Sinai in the wilderness, he directs for Yahweh the major events that create and identify the people of Israel. Yet, this central position in Israelite history and tradition does not mean that the historical Moses is near. The advent of modern biblical scholarship—which has recognized that the biblical material is not strictly history, biography or autobiography, but an inspired, creative, and interpretative combination of traditions—has spawned the quests for the people who figured prominently in the biblical story. As a result, the historical Moses proves as elusive as the historical Jesus. Some scholars, e.g., Martin Noth, have argued that Moses was linked to every tradition but rooted in none of them so that Moses seemed a creation, or, at least a later addition. Many, and not conservatives alone, have answered this perspective with skepticism. They agree that Moses has attracted certain traditions and that his role has magnified with time, but there had to be some person who burst into the history of Israel and contributed a surge of creative energy that still excites believers in Judaism, Christianity, and Islam. Moses is witnessed through the thick, opaque glass of the Hebrew Bible; he may never be seen clearly, but his reflection or his outline is there. Many great persons, including Moses and Muhammed, the founder of Islam, assume a great many roles and perform a great many tasks, some in part, some fairly completely, and lay the groundwork for a great many other responsibilities. The result is that, as the endeavor continues, more and more is attributed to them. Just as a seed gives way to the growing and maturing plant, the historical person recedes as that person's significance for an institution develops.

Outline of Moses' Life. According to the biblical narrative, a boy was born among the Hebrew slaves at a time when the Pharaoh wanted every male offspring in that prolific community killed. Moses' family succeeded in hiding him for some time, but circumstances forced them to take a dramatic risk. In a way somewhat reminiscent of the story of Sargon (*ANET*, 119), his mother placed him in a basket calked with pitch and floated him down the Nile near the bathing place of Pharaoh's daughter. The royal lady discovered the child, pitied him, and made arrangements for his care, which included, at the suggestion of Moses' watchful sister, her hiring Moses' mother as the wet nurse. Subsequently, Moses grew up in the house of Pharaoh and enjoyed the privileges there.

One day during an inspection, Moses spotted an Egyptian guard beating one of the slaves. Moses killed the guard. Later, when he realized from the taunt of one of two Hebrew slaves, whom he stopped from fighting, that his murder was public knowledge, he fled to the desert much like Sinuhe, an Egyptian official (*ANET*, 18ff.). Soon, he rescued a group of women victimized by shepherds at a well and subsequently married one of them. He welcomed the opportunity to serve her father, JETHRO (also known as Reuel or Hobab in other traditions), as a shepherd. This second phase of Moses' life moved smoothly until he experienced a THEOPHANY that introduced him to Yahweh. At this meeting, Yahweh convinced a reticent, doubtful Moses to return to Egypt in order to liberate the Hebrew people.

Moses' fear realized itself immediately on his return. The Pharaoh, vehemently opposed to the depletion of his labor force, complicated Moses' task by increasing the work of the slaves. This additional hardship damaged Moses' fragile credibility with his people who complained to him again and again, even later during the wilderness sojourn, when the way proved difficult. Moses therefore attempted to reject his commission. Yahweh comforted and encouraged Moses so that he reaffirmed his commitment. Eventually, after a series of PLAGUES, which exhibited the power of Yahweh but also were met by the intransigence of Pharaoh, and a tenth plague, the death of the first-born of Egypt, Pharaoh freed the Hebrews. Moses led them triumphantly out of Egypt, even though at the last moment Pharaoh tried to reverse his decision. In fact, the decisive act of the exodus occurred at the Reed Sea (RED SEA in many translations) where the Israelites crossed on dry land but the Egyptians perished in the returning waters.

With an urgency that sprang both from his eagerness to weld this people to the God who proved himself so mightily during the Exodus and also from the constant irritation of this demanding and impatient people, Moses quickly brought the Israelites to SINAI (Horeb, PLATES 9, 44). There Moses received the covenant, which would bind this people and this god together forever. Like a magnifying glass, the sojourn at Sinai and the COVENANT concluded there focused the history of Israel into one special moment or one fundamental event that fulfilled some of the history and determined the rest of history for this people; here the Israelites, the descendants of Abraham, and Moses, and Yahweh were moving toward the realization of the ancestral promises and beyond. However, before the covenant was completed but not before the people had endorsed it, they committed apostasy. They claimed that they believed Moses, who had been gone so long atop the mountain, might be dead; accordingly, they constructed a GOLDEN CALF to act as their god. Yahweh almost destroyed the people, but Moses interceded and convinced Yahweh to forgive them.

When the covenant was finally complete, Moses led the people by stages toward the promised land. Moses' administrative skills and his mediating capacities were tested at every point. Several people, e.g., KORAH, and also his brother AARON and his sister MIRIAM, challenged his authority. Ultimately, when the people reached the border of Canaan, the promised land, they decided on the basis of a spy report that the land of Canaan was too difficult to conquer. Moses condemned their faithlessness and instructed them that a whole generation, with the exception of a few faithful persons, must die so that the land of Canaan would be overtaken by persons faithful to Yahweh. Reacting to that news, they made an unsuccessful raid on the Amalekites and the Canaanites. Even Moses could not cross into the promised land, for earlier, at Meribah, he acted contrary to Yahweh's instruction. Indeed, the people could not conquer this land alone, but with Yahweh nothing could stop them.

The BOOK OF DEUTERONOMY relays the last portrait of Moses actively leading the people. The faithless generation lie in their wilderness graves; their children stand on the threshold of the new land. Moses delivers a series of hortatory addresses, reviewing their history, repeating the Law given at Sinai (though there are new sections that complement and extend the legal traditions found in Exodus, Leviticus, and Numbers), and renewing the constant message of Moses—"Choose Yahweh and one chooses life." With these messages, a song of praise, and a blessing, Moses climbs to the top of Mount Pisgah, views Canaan, and dies.

Moses as Deliverer. Though Moses is inextricably linked both to the Exodus from Egypt and the covenant at Sinai, Moses is associated first with the Exodus. He was a party to that oppression and his rescue while a baby from the cruelty of Pharaoh prefigured his role in delivering the Hebrews. Later, as a young man, he would save an Israelite from certain death at the hands of an Egyptian guard and also the daughters of Jethro, the priest of Midian, from the brutality of some shepherds. But the Exodus was the deliverance for which his upbringing in Egypt and his experience in the wilderness had prepared him. His feeling of obligation, his sense of justice, and his relationship with this persuasive and zealous god, Yahweh, spurred him back to the challenges he would find in Egypt. Even though the story of Moses retains his reservations about his qualifications, his story clearly depicts him as a person who was born for such a task, for such a time.

Moses as Wonderworker. Moses was no magician for he lacked the ability to manipulate his surroundings, but he initiated miracles and performed signs that revealed the presence of a powerful God, Yahweh. Before he returned to Egypt, he expressed hesitancy about his credibility before the Israelites. Yahweh fitted him with three wonders—turning his rod into a serpent, altering his hand to one beset by leprosy, and changing some water from the Nile into blood—to testify to Moses' authenticity. When the Egyptian ruler proved obdurate, Yahweh authorized Moses to introduce a series of plagues in order to break Pharaoh's will. The eventual helplessness of the Egyptian magicians, the relentless pressure of the first nine plagues, and the overwhelming sorrow caused by the last plague, broke the Pharaoh's resolve to retain these Hebrew slaves. Yet Moses managed one final miracle, the crossing of the Reed Sea, as he raised his hands to cause the sea to recede so the deliverance "by Yahweh's uplifted hand" could be consummated. On another occasion, Moses would watch another army defeated as he held his arms aloft with the help of Aaron and Hur (Exod 17). Throughout the wilderness sojourn, Moses performed necessary wonders to assure the continued well-being of the people. Yet, all these miracles, with Moses as the agent of their occurrence, pointed to the power and beneficence of Yahweh, the God who claimed that he would be with his people and watch over them.

Moses as Lawgiver. The connection between Moses and the Law (TORAH) recorded in the Hebrew Bible derives from the role of Moses played in forging a covenant between the God of the Exodus and the liberated people. Moses, attentive to the fear and the sense of unworthiness felt by the people, climbed to the top of Sinai, received the stipulations of the covenant between Yahweh and Israel, and delivered them to the people. This law he received, which became known as the written Law of Moses, continued to grow in the traditions so that several bodies of law exist in the confines of the Hebrew Bible. Eventually, a new corpus was accepted as binding as well—the oral Law of Moses included in the Talmud. Just as the miracles were not actually the miracles of Moses, the Law was the Law revealed by Yahweh the Lawgiver. But Moses stands forever in the Hebrew Bible and in sculpted visions as the person holding the ten words (commandments). Covenants that bind two persons together are known by the privileges and responsibilities required of the two parties. Moses, the person who could safely go up to the top of Sinai, received the stipulations of the covenant between Yahweh and Israel and delivered them to the people.

Moses as Intercessor/Mediator. Moses did not possess a natural talent for this task; he slowly developed his skills. His first attempt to mediate between a harsh Egyptian guard and a helpless slave failed. Shortly afterward, his effort to reconcile one Hebrew with another led ultimately to Moses' flight from Egypt, not to a resolution of the argument. Perhaps in the desert he learned to listen, to observe, and to reflect, so that at the burning bush he began to understand how to balance commitment with personal gifts. Up to this point, his story greatly parallels that of Joseph, who lived a privileged life as a youth. His brothers became so jealous that they almost killed him and eventually, sold him into slavery. During that time of forced exile from his family, Joseph learned from his struggles. So Moses, too, learned during his exile from home the skills for mediation.

Though he tried to reason with the Pharaoh upon his return to Egypt in order to secure the freedom of the Hebrew slaves, Moses' arbitration was doomed from the beginning. The awesome power of Yahweh served as the point of that episode and not the insightful intercession of Moses. The supreme example of Moses' mediation surfaces in Exod 32–34. While Moses was receiving the Law on MOUNT SINAI, the people built a golden calf. Yahweh immediately reacted and informed Moses, in a manner reminiscent of the time of Noah, that his stubborn, faithless people would be destroyed and Moses would be the beginning of a new nation. Moses dissuaded Yahweh by musing on the possible reaction of the Egyptians to this act and by referring to the covenant with Abraham, Isaac, and Jacob (here called Israel). Yet, even when Yahweh changed his intention, i.e., repented of the evil, he informed Moses that an angel would be leading them. Moses realized that there must be consequences for this idolatrous act. In a manner resembling the practices associated with holy warfare and the punishment meted out to Achan at Jericho (Josh 7), he commissioned the LEVITES to go through the camp to punish the camp. In addition, a plague affected the rest of the people.

Moses was still troubled by Yahweh's distancing himself from the people. He continued to argue with God; Moses did not want to be the start of a new people and he did not want to go any farther if Yahweh was not in their midst, or totally committed to them. Moses' argument convinced Yahweh and he pledged his presence. Subsequently, Moses asked to see Yahweh's face, but Yahweh declined; he hid Moses in the cleft of the rock to protect his life and allowed Moses to see his back.

The mediation continued as Moses climbed back up to the top of Sinai; the broken treaty had to be restored. When he returned, his face, absolutely radiant from the communion with Yahweh, had to be veiled in the presence of the people. Moses reported the stipulations, including the instructions for the implementation of the wilderness cult, to the people and they began to enforce them. Unfortunately, along with the reprieve of the people, this mediation marked the loss of an originally privileged relationship that was forever lost; the covenant had been breached but repaired by means of a fervent and fearless mediator. Furthermore, a paradigm of atonement lay in this lengthy account.

Moses continued this role throughout his tenure as leader. Whenever the people became disgruntled, they would long for Egypt. Yahweh's natural response would be disgust, e.g., when Yahweh sent fiery serpents to afflict the people (Num 21:4ff.). Moses stood always in the middle, working on a solution that allowed for justice and mercy. On another occasion following the report of the spies sent to view Canaan, the people were overcome with doubt and fear (Num 14). They wished to return to Egypt; Yahweh wished to destroy them there. Moses interceded for the people. Yahweh did not destroy them, but he promised that a new generation would conquer the land. Moreover, when the people did try to conquer the land, Yahweh absented himself from the battle, so that they met defeat. According to one tradition, during one of these incidents Moses' anger overcame him. He struck a rock to bring water to the people, but this act contradicted Yahweh's instructions (Num 20:10ff.). For that unnecessary act, Yahweh barred Moses from the promised land. Even Yahweh's mediator had to stay within certain bounds. However, a tradition reflected in Deut 3:26 interpreted Moses' exclusion as the supreme selfless act of a mediator; Moses stayed behind so that the people who tried Yahweh at every step of the way could enter the land.

Moses' ability to supplicate his God and to mete out the necessary punishment secured his reputation as a mediator. Later generations of storytellers would allude to his skill and commitment. The story of ELIJAH casts a negative judgment on the prophet as a mediator; he travels to Horeb not to argue for his people, sinful though they be, but to impress Yahweh with his own righteousness (I Kgs 19:14). Yahweh exposes Elijah's arrogance and strips him of his responsibility. JEREMIAH, in order to underscore the absolute depravity of his audience, declares that not even Moses could convince Yahweh to forgive them (Jer 15:1).

Moses as Administrator. When Moses was not overseeing the extraordinary events of the Exodus, receiving the covenant, or meeting the persistent demands of the people, he was managing their everyday existence. In particular, with a group this large, he had to administer justice, e.g., the case of the daughters of Zelophehad (Num 27:1ff.) and periodically assess the people by means of a census (Num 1:1ff.). However, the true mark of his administrative skill lay in his ability to take advice and to implement it. Soon after the Exodus, Jethro, Moses' father-in-law, witnessed the enormity of Moses' task (Exod 18:13ff.). He suggested that Moses appoint persons to assist him. Moses accepted this suggestion and delegated his authority so that the people relied on a hierarchy of leaders, with Moses' attention directed only to the most pressing issues. Later, Moses appointed seventy elders who received a portion of the spirit that rested upon Moses (Num 11). They relieved Moses of a part of the responsibility and bother of the Hebrew people.

As administrator, Moses was not spared the constant complaints of the people. Neither was he spared the sporadic challenges to his authority. He confronted his brother Aaron and his sister Miriam when they spoke against him (Num 12). He subsequently interceded on Miriam's behalf when she was afflicted with leprosy as a punishment. Moses swiftly handled the untoward cultic behavior of Nadab and Abihu (Lev 10), just as he would later manage the insolence of Korah, Dathan and Abiram (Num 16). However, Moses correctly praised the behavior of Eldad and Medad; their acts exhibited the spirit of Yahweh, not arrogance. Though on many occasions Moses would have given up his responsibility readily, obligated by the divine commission, he continued with his task as an able administrator who dealt speedily with matters that warranted dispatch and more slowly with matters of concern; he also delegated authority when necessary, so that all matters received due consideration.

Moses as Military Commander. Moses never distinguished himself as a military leader like JOSHUA; his work remained preliminary to the CONQUEST OF CANAAN. Yet, he did preside over the battles before the Hebrews entered into the promised land. While Joshua fought Amalek with the warriors of Israel, Moses stood on the top of the hill (Exod 17:8ff.). If his hands were lifted, symbolic of the uplifted hand of Yahweh who delivered his people, the people prevailed; if his hands dropped, the enemies prevailed. With the help of Aaron and Hur, Moses kept his hands raised until Joshua secured the victory. Furthermore, Moses led the people in their battles against Sihon, the king of the Amorites, and against the Midianites. The only skirmish that Moses did not oversee was the ill-fated clash with the Canaanites that the people mounted after Moses berated them for their lack of faith (Num 14:40ff.).

Moses as Priest. Similarly, Moses was not a priest but he received the instructions about the priesthood in his stint upon Sinai. His brother Aaron was the first priest and the beginning of the priestly succession. For as long as Moses led the people, he assisted the priesthood by securing all the materials for the construction of their mobile cult and completing the instructions given to him. Without the Law from Sinai and Moses' regimented implementation, the cult would have foundered from the first.

Moses as Prophet. Though prophecy was linked closely with the period and the institution of monarchy, Moses was considered the archetype of the PROPHET. His call narrative contained the elements of divine commission and human hesitation. After his acceptance of his task, he acted courageously and relied almost completely upon Yahweh. He certainly performed signs and wonders, which accomplished his task and testified to the redemptive presence of Yahweh. However, tradition elevated Moses more than any other prophet, for his role was pivotal in the formation of Israel. This perspective was reflected particularly in the narrative concerning the rebellion of Aaron and Miriam. Prophets receive their messages in dreams and visions, but Moses spoke with Yahweh face to face. In another text, Moses' special position lent weight to the criteria for true and false prophecy. Moses was regarded as the standard for prophecy even though he lived long before the line of prophets remembered in the Hebrew Bible; he set up the standard for prophecy by the life he lived for Yahweh and by means of the covenant law he received from Yahweh (cf. Deut 18:15-16; 34:10-12).

Moses as Preacher. The Book of Deuteronomy contains the work of a group that creatively exhorted the people. They picked up the sense of Moses and renewed his message to their contemporaries. They placed Moses at the threshold of a land he would never enter, with the children of the people he had led from slavery to freedom, from insecurity to covenant. There, on that boundary, Moses reviewed their history, restated the covenant stipulations, and recalled the people to their covenant obligations. The hortatory style is unmistakable; the message is clear. Moses urged the people to choose obedience to Yahweh, even in the face of supreme danger, and thereby to choose life. He did not hesitate to picture the other alternative, rebellion, or disobedience, and its consequence, death, but his definite call addressed a people who could choose to obey and to make a difference in their personal and national life.

Moses as Author. Tradition claims that Moses wrote the entire Pentateuch. Though historical-critical work indicated the impossibility of that feat, Moses' role in the eventual creation of the Pentateuch remains undisputed. His life and work served as fertile soil in which traditions could grow and multiply. His historic place and vision allowed his authority to be borrowed again and again. The Book of Deuteronomy contains more than his sermons; Deuteronomy contains a song and a blessing, creating other contexts from which Moses, through other inspired authors, continued to speak.

Moses' continuing high place in the biblical tradition is reflected in later writings. Among these are the oral law of Moses, which is contained in the Talmud; the pseudepigraphical writing *The Testament of Moses,* which recounts the events of the end of time; the Gospel of Matthew, which grants a Mosaic cast to the life of Jesus in order to underscore the authority of Jesus' teachings leading to the fulfillment of the law of Moses; Paul's use of the Torah and the imagery surrounding Moses to address the issue of the Jews' place in God's plan (Rom 10:5ff.) or to argue for the preeminence of Christian truth (2 Cor 3:12ff.); the Book of Hebrews, which lists Moses among the truly faithful; and the Islamic belief that Moses prophesied the coming of Muhammed, who was to be another great man of faith like Moses.

Moses as Servant of Yahweh. This role includes all the rest and best describes Moses (Exod 14:31). Whether Moses was releasing the plagues of Egypt, receiving the Law upon Sinai, interceding for the people before an angry deity, delivering the judgment for the sins of the people, dealing with the newest complaint of the assembled people, or addressing the people who stood on the border of their new land, Moses performed for Yahweh. What he did, he did for the greater glory of Yahweh so that the promises to Abraham, Isaac, and Jacob could finally be realized. What he accomplished, he accomplished at the request of Yahweh, for Yahweh. This resolve—to point to God rather than the accomplishments of humans—was reflected in the tradition that recorded the poignant final episode of Moses' life. Yahweh buried Moses in an unspecified place (Deut 34:5ff.); his grave could never become a place of pilgrimage. Moses served his God so that Yahweh's will could be done and Yahweh's deeds could be praised. That accomplishment remains the true legacy of this servant; through his life the splendor of Yahweh, his overlord, is revealed.

See also EXODUS, BOOK OF; PLAGUES; RED SEA/REED SEA.

Bibliography. M. Buber, *Moses*; B. S. Childs, *The Book of Exodus, OTL*; W. Harrelson, *The Ten Commandments and Human Rights*; J. P. Hyatt, *Exodus*; M. Noth, *Exodus, A Commentary, OTL*; J. B. Pritchard, ed., *ANET*; G. von Rad, *Moses*; M. Walzer, *Exodus and Revolution.*

—RUSSEL I. GREGORY

• **Moses, Assumption of.** *See* MOSES, TESTAMENT OF

• **Moses, Testament of.** The *Testament of Moses* is a Jewish pseudepigraphon that purports to be MOSES' farewell speech to JOSHUA. Moses passes on his authority to his successor and predicts the history of Israel into the Herodian period, when the final consummation is expected. The work is extant only in one Latin palimpsest, probably a translation from a Greek translation of a semitic original.

In its present form the *TMos* can be dated to the early first century C.E., since chaps. 6 and 7 refer to HEROD the Great and his sons. Some scholars regard this material as a later interpolation, and date the original work in the Maccabean period. Ancient lists of non-canonical works include both a *TMos* and an *Assumption of Moses.* The extant work was once thought to be the *AsMos,* but it is now generally referred to as the *TMos.*

The author held a Deuteronomic view of history; the EXILE is understood as a punishment for sin. The postexilic period is seen as a time of renewed APOSTASY, punished by persecution in the author's present. It is anticipated that the martyrdoms of the righteous, represented by the mysterious Taxo and his seven sons, will be followed by their final vindication, the defeat of the devil, and the punishment of the enemies of Israel. The message is one of encouragement to oppressed Jews: the creator is in absolute control of history and will not allow God's people to be crushed forever.

See also DEUTERONOMIST/DEUTERONOMISTIC HISTORIAN; TESTAMENTS, APOCRYPHAL.

Bibliography. J. Priest, "Testament of Moses," *The Old Testament Pseudepigrapha,* ed. J. H. Charlesworth.

—SHARYN E. DOWD

• **Mount of Olives.** *See* OLIVES, MOUNT OF

• **Mount, Sermon on the.** *See* SERMON ON THE MOUNT

• **Mourning Rites.** Public expression of grief was commonly expected and carried out in ancient Egypt, Mesopotamia, and Palestine, often with the same methods. Moses' people expressed their grief that the Lord would not accompany them into Canaan by wearing no ornaments (Exod 33:4). JOAB obtained a woman from Tekoa to pretend to be a mourner by wearing "mourning garments" and omitting anointing herself with oil (2 Sam 14:2). Other manifestations of self-neglect while mourning included allowing the hair to hang loose and tearing one's clothing, although Aaron and two of his sons were commanded not to do so (Lev 10:6). When DAVID heard that ABSALOM had killed all his sons, he and his servants "rent their garments" and David "lay on the earth" (2 Sam 13:31). Other such indications of lament included fasting, putting on sackcloth, praying with the head bowed on the chest, and going about bowed down (Ps 35:13-14). Other common methods were pouring dust or ashes on the head (2 Sam 15:32), shaving the head (Jer 7:29), cutting oneself (Jer 16:6), weeping (2 Sam 1:12), and pulling hair from the head and beard (Ezra 9:3). Usually, as seen in numerous OT examples, a combination of many of the procedures listed above was used (Jer 41:5; Ezra 9:3,5; Gen 37:34; Job 1:20; 2 Sam 3:31-32; 13:19; 15:32).

It was imperative to combine burial procedures of the deceased with appropriate rites of lamentation, as with a son of Jeroboam (1 Kgs 14:13,18). JOB expected that wicked men's "widows make no lamentation" (27:15). It was a serious situation for a deceased person neither to be mourned nor buried (Jer 16:4,6), for this paralleled the donkey's plight (Jer 22:18-19; cf. 25:33). Members of the family of the deceased lamented: his sons for JACOB (Gen 50:10), ABRAHAM for SARAH (Gen 23:2), BATHSHEBA for Uriah (2 Sam 11:26), but, due to the Lord's command, not EZEKIEL for his wife (Ezek 24:16-17). Others affected by a death joined in lamentation: all Israel for SAMUEL (1 Sam 25:1; 28:3), David and his men for SAUL and JONATHAN (2 Sam 1:12), and JOAB for ABNER (2 Sam 3:31).

Such laments were included in the funerary ritual, usually set to a halting or crippling beat of 3:2,3:2 or the *qînâ* beat, and played on musical instruments, the preferred one probably being the flute (Jer 48:36; Matt 9:23). The Hebrew verb *sāpad* ("wail, lament") describes this act, and its noun, *mispēd* ("wailing"), has the connotation of a shrill cry.

Other exclamations of grief are *hôy* or *hō,* "ah, alas, ha," usually expressing intense dissatisfaction and pain. The urban and wailing Israelites will cry "alas, alas" when calling "the farmers to mourning, and to wailing those who are skilled in lamentation" (Amos 5:16). The unnamed old prophet from Bethel interred "in his own grave" the body of "the man of God" killed by a lion and "mourned over him, saying, 'Alas, my brother' " (1 Kgs 13:30). JEREMIAH said of King JEHOIAKIM, "They shall not lament for him, saying, 'Ah my brother!' or 'Ah sister!' They shall not lament for him saying, 'Ah Lord!' or 'Ah his majesty!' " (Jer 22:18). Burning incense accompanied mourning for the king: "As spices were burned for your [Zedekiah] fathers, the former kings who were before you, so men shall burn spices for you, saying, 'Alas, lord!' " (Jer 34:5). Thus, ISAIAH can say of Judah, "Ah, sinful nation" (1:4).

Mourning for the dead began at death (Matt 9:23) and normally lasted seven days (Gen 50:10; 1 Sam 31:13; 1 Chr 10:12; Job 2:12:13). However, it continued for thirty days for MOSES and AARON (Num 20:29; Deut 34:8) and seventy days for Jacob, following Egyptian custom (Gen 50:3). Probably, most of the mourners, especially the professional ones, were women.

See also DEATH; SACKCLOTH.

—KAREN RANDOLPH JOINES

• **Mummification.** *See* EMBALMING/MUMMIFICATION

• **Muratorian Canon.** [myoor'uh-tor"ee-uhn] The Muratorian Canon is an early list of books to be accepted as NT scripture, possibly the oldest such list we possess. It is traditionally dated ca. 200 from Rome but some scholars argue for an Eastern provenance a century later. In 1740 Ludovici Muratori published this list which he had found in an eighth century manuscript collection of theological tracts stored in the Ambrosian Library of Milan. In addition to naming the books, the document offers brief observations about the origins of each. Since Luke is described as the third of the Gospels, the original list must have begun with Matthew. A fragmentary sentence—which must refer to Mark—describes the author as making records of reports of the sayings and activities of Jesus given by the disciples, "at which however he was present and so he has set it down."

Luke is identified as a physician, who travelled with Paul and was fully instructed by him. Luke was not an eyewitness of Jesus, but on the basis of his own point of view reported all that he could ascertain about him. On the other hand, John was chosen by the other "disciples and bishops" to write down everything about Jesus concerning his birth, death, resurrection, his associations with the disciples, his coming in humility and his future coming in glory. The resulting account was reviewed by the other apostles, but embodies John's own point of view, since as he reports in his letter (1 John 1:1): he has seen, heard, and handled the Word of Life. The acts of all the apostles are reported by Luke, although he omits the martyrdom of Peter and the journey of Paul to Spain. Neither of these events is reported in other NT writings.

The document attributes to both Paul and John seven letters (John's are included in Revelation). The Pauline letters mentioned are Corinthians, Ephesians, Colossians, Thessalonians, Romans, Philippians, Galatians, but the writer goes on to observe that in his generosity Paul wrote additional letters to the Corinthians and the Thessalonians, to Titus, Philemon, and twice to Timothy. Significantly, he notes that these latter letters are "for the ordering of ecclesiastical discipline" in the church universal. At the same time he lists letters forged in Paul's name (to the Laodiceans and the Alexandrians) which are not accepted by the church as a whole as authentic and authoritative, "for it will not do to mix gall and honey." The list of authoritative works to be read in the churches concludes with Jude, two letters of John—and the WISDOM OF SOLOMON! Two apocalypses are also included, those of John and Peter, although the author acknowledges that some do not accept the APOCALYPSE OF PETER. The SHEPHERD OF HERMAS is said to be widely used, but is not to be on the official list of writings, either among the prophets (OT) or the apostles (NT). Emphatically rejected are the Gnostic writings, such as those of Valentinus and MARCION. Not mentioned are 1 and 2 Peter, James and 3 John.

This list of writings authorized for public reading in the churches corresponds in general to those mentioned by the church fathers in the second to the fourth conturies, but the differences in detail show that there was not during this period a commonly agreed upon set of writings which comprised the NT.

See also CANON.

—HOWARD CLARK KEE

• **Murder.** Willful or premeditated homicide. One of the stipulations of God's covenant with Noah after the flood enunciates the basic principle that underlies the biblical position concerning homicide: "Whoever sheds the BLOOD of man, by man shall his blood be shed; for God made man in his own image" (Gen 9:6). Human life is sacrosanct because of its relationship to the divine, and human society must ensure by means of the severest punishment that this sanctity is respected. The Decalogue also lays absolute claim to this respect for human life in the commandment, "Thou shalt not kill" (Exod 20:13; Deut 5:17).

While these texts prohibit killing, state the theological basis for the principle, and name an appropriate punishment, they do not carefully define the conditions in which one may be said to have committed murder, nor do they make allowance for unwitting or accidental homicide. Israel's major law codes, however, explore the legal implications of the prohibition against homicide. Only once does OT law announce, without qualification, the principle that homicide is punishable by death (Lev 24:17). Every other treatment of homicide in the law codes dwells particularly upon the task of differentiating between intention and accident.

The simplest treatment of the issue of intention in homicide cases is found in the first of a catalog of capital offenses in Exod 21:12-25. These laws identify the offenders ("the one who strikes," "the one who steals"), sometimes state the results of the offender's actions (someone dies), and stereotypically pronounce the death penalty upon the offender ("he shall surely die"). The first of these laws, which deals specifically with homicide, further describes the circumstances in which the death penalty may be imposed. It is necessary to establish premeditation by means of the criterion of preparation: If the offender ambushed the victim, premeditation could be assumed. Premeditation could also be established if prior motive could be demonstrated. In the event that premeditation could not be determined, the killer was to be permitted refuge (cf. below). If, however, the killing could be classified as murder with clear intent, even the place of refuge was to be considered ineffectual for the killer. Two aspects of this law are particularly interesting. First, the concern for clear criteria for distinguishing murder from manslaughter is evident. Only murder deserves capital punishment. Second, the command to apprehend and execute the murderer, even if the fugitive has already reached sanctuary, seems to emphasize the urgency of carrying out sentence in cases of capital homicide. It is too great an offense to be left unpunished.

Four texts (Deut 4:41-43; 19:1-13; Num 35:9-34; Josh 20:1-9) describe the establishment of cities of refuge, where the unintentional killer may be kept safe from the "kinsman-avenger," a near-relative of the victim, whose duty it was in ancient Israel to even the score with the killer. Deut 19 and Num 35 offer information pertinent to an understanding of the details of the OT's position with regard to homicide. Deut 19 opens with a statement of God's saving activity in the conquest (v. 1), goes on quickly to dictate the establishment of three cities to which killers may flee (v. 2), and directs the preparation of adequate roads to these cities (v. 3). Criteria for establishing accidental homicide are outlined (v. 4) and particularized by the citation of a hypothetical case (v. 5), that of an ax-head flying off its handle and striking a mortal blow to the owner's co-worker. The purpose of the cities of refuge, according to 19:6-9, is to protect such an unintentional killer from the victim's kinsman-avenger. The killer who kills accidentally, without previous intention ("he was not at enmity with him in times past"), is innocent and must be protected "[lest] there be blood-guilt upon you" (v. 9).

The reference to blood-guilt and the protective attitude taken toward the unintentional killer must not be understood as leniency toward murder. If prior motive can be demonstrated, the killer (who is, therefore, a murderer) who nevertheless seeks refuge is to be surrendered to the kinsman-avenger (vv. 11-13): "your eye shall not pity him, but you shall purge the guilt of innocent blood from Israel, so that it may be well with you" (v. 13).

Several elements introduced in the account of the establishment of cities of refuge in Num 35:9-34 reflect a truly judiciary approach to the problem of accidental manslaughter. One emphasis of the account is the refinement of the term used for "killer." Exod 21 and Deut 19 use the term neutrally to refer simply to the act of killing a person, without further specifying whether the killing involved criminal intent. Num 35:11 and 15 employ the term technically to mean the accidental killer, while 35:16-18 clearly state that only the killer who demonstrated intention is a "murderer." Second, the judicial function of the assembly in assessing the guilt of a killer (35:12, 24), which reflects the beginnings of a developed judicial system, is new to discussions of the refugee. Third, tests for intentionality are expanded from the two of Deut 19 (ambush and prior intent), to four: The killer who kills "by mistake" is innocent 35:11, 15). The killer who uses a lethal weapon (35:16-18), lies in ambush (35:20), or acts upon a standing quarrel (35:21) is a murderer. Fourth, several questions of legal, technical, and procedural nature are treated: rules concerning evidence and witnesses, the length of the term of asylum and the impermissibility of ransom (or bail in modern terms).

The danger inherent in allowing the shed blood of an innocent to go unavenged, which motivated the requirement of strict application of the death penalty in murder cases, and the interest in providing asylum and protection to the accidental killer (and thereby avoiding the spilling of innocent blood), were great enough to require that provision be made for cases in which blood had been spilt under unknown circumstances. Deut 21:1-9 outlines in detail a ritual procedure designed to provide appropriate atonement for the blood of the slain. The text describes such a situation (a corpse found with no sign of the circumstances of the death—21:1), and strings together a series of specific actions to be taken as steps in the ritual (21:2-6), including a ritual statement to be made by the participants to the effect that they are ignorant of the circumstances of the death of the deceased (21:7-8). The death of the calf called for in the text is meant in some way as an atonement for the spilt blood of an innocent and the washing of hands as an absolution of guilt.

The OT, then, advocates a very high respect for human life. The murderer who means to kill must be punished for an action that strikes at the very heart of human society and that destroys one made in the very image of God. All other killers, however, must be protected. The loss of precious human life in an accident cannot be compensated by further shedding of blood. The desire for revenge must be controlled.

JESUS, too, addressed the issues of intention and revenge, extending the OT position to even more radical limits. In his SERMON ON THE MOUNT discussion of the law concerning murder (Matt 5:38-42), Jesus argued that not only the act of murder, that is, homicide with intent, is contrary to God's will, but the very intent to do harm, itself. "You have heard that it was said to men of old, 'You shall not kill; and whoever kills shall be liable to judgment.' But I say to you that every one who is angry with his brother shall be liable to judgment . . . " Jesus' call to love without limit precludes the desire to do even the enemy harm (Matt 5:43-48). In the same sermon, Jesus rejects altogether the applicability of the principle of revenge in the Kingdom of God. Not only are the innocent to be protected from vengeance, but the wrongdoer also: "You have heard that it was said, 'An eye for an eye and a tooth for a tooth.' But I say to you, Do not resist one who is evil. But if any one strikes you on the right cheek turn to him the other also . . . " (Matt 5:38-39).

See also BLOOD IN THE OLD TESTAMENT; ETHICS IN THE NEW TESTAMENT; ETHICS IN THE OLD TESTAMENT; LIFE IN THE OLD TESTAMENT; NOACHIC LAWS; REFUGE, CITIES OF.

—MARK E. BIDDLE

• **Music/Musical Instruments.** Music, both vocal and instrumental, and the use of musical instruments played a vital role in the experiences of daily life and WORSHIP in ancient Israel. However, the story of the development of the art and the precise meaning of some of the terminology is still open to discussion.

Music in the Ancient Near East. Music was an important part of life and culture not only in ancient Israel, but among other ancient Near Eastern people as well. Some of the earliest information available comes from the two great centers of culture, namely, Mesopotamia and Egypt. The information consists of inscriptions on clay tablets, cylinder seals, and panels, as well as, in some instances, the actual remains of instruments themselves. An old Sumerian clay tablet from ca. 3000 B.C.E., found at the site of Uruk, depicts in pictographic form, a boat-shaped harp, apparently the type of harp used by the Sumerians of that day. Furthermore, a harp of this type, along with other instruments including, a set of silver pipes and nine richly decorated lyres were found among the funerary objects of Queen Pu-Abi and her retinue (ca. 2650 B.C.E.) in the royal cemetery at Ur, the hometown of Abraham. A shell panel, originally a decorative inlay of one of the lyres, features an animal orchestra which includes a donkey playing a lyre, a bear clapping and singing, and a jackel providing rhythm with a percussion instrument and a sistrum. Cuneiform textual evidence indicates that by the end of the third millennium B.C.E. the Sumerians had produced HYMNS dedicated to their gods, their kings, and their temples. According to Assyrian and Babylonian resources new developments in music flourished in Mesopotamia during the second and first millennia B.C.E. Scribal lists as well as reliefs suggest that new instruments appeared along with the older standard forms. Hymns to the gods, lamentations, and liturgies multiplied. Technical terms concerning the performance of the music were developed and added. And distinctions between ordinary and specialized musicians began to appear.

Likewise the history of the development of music in Egypt is similar to that of Mesopotamia with some of the earliest iconographic depictions of instruments dating back to ca. 3000 B.C.E. and continuing down into the Roman period. In Egypt, as in Mesopotamia, the art work is supplemented with actual discoveries of instruments such as end-blown flutes, clarinets, oboes, harps, lyres, trumpets, wooden clappers, bronze cymbals, bells, rattles, as well as others.

Music in Ancient Israel. In the OT, the origin of music is attributed to Jubal a descendant of Cain, whose name is similar to the Hebrew word for ram, *yobel,* the animal from whose horns the *shophar* was made. Jubal is identified as "the father of all those who play the lyre and the pipe" (Gen 4:21).

Music was an important part of daily life in ancient Israel. It played a vital role in family functions such as farewell parties (Gen 31:27) and homecomings (Judg 11:34). Apparently numerous daily activities were accompanied by singing, such as, well digging (Num 21:17-18), the work of the watchman (Isa 21:12), work in the vineyard (Isa 27:2-5), treading in the winepress (Jer 25:30; 48:33), and harvesting activities (Isa 16:10). Battles and struggles in warfare were commemorated in songs (Num 21:27-30). The "Book of the Wars of the Lord" (Num 21:14-15), to which the biblical writer makes reference, may have been a collection of songs of this type. A number of songs of this type appear in the OT including the song of Miriam (Exod 15:21), the song of Deborah (Judg 5), Samson's song (Judg 15:16), and the song of the women in the time of Saul and David (1 Sam 18:7).

Of all the figures in Israel's history, David is especially associated with music. He was recognized as an inventor of instruments (Amos 6:5), a skilled musician (1 Sam 16:16), the court musician of Saul (1 Sam 19:9), and a dancer at special religious events (2 Sam 6:14-15).

Music played an important role in the religious activities of ancient Israel. The early bands of roving prophets used musical instruments such as the harp, tambourine, flute, and lyre in their processions (1 Sam 10:5). During the early stages of prophetism, minstrels performed as the prophet engaged in prophesying (2 Kgs 3:11, 15). But the major developments in Israel's sacred music came from her worship, worship that was focused on sacrifice and eventually institutionalized in the TEMPLE. Perhaps the earliest forms of Israel's sacred music consisted of nothing more than the accompaniment of a trumpet (Num 10:10). Apparently the greatest developments came with the monarchy and the building of the Temple. Though discussion continues about his role in these matters, David is identified as the one who initially organized the levitical musicians and singers (1 Chr 15–16), groups that later were a part of the professional staff of the Temple. Temple music accompanied sacrifices (2 Chr 29:20-30). It included the singing of hymns of praise and thanksgiving to music produced by a wide array of instruments, such as the trumpet, lyre, harp, flute, and cymbals (Pss 98:1-6; 150:1-6). But that all ceased with the destruction of the Temple (587 B.C.E.) and the Babylonian Exile.

During the period of captivity in Babylonia, the Jews remembered Jerusalem and its Temple worship as they were forced to perform for their captors (Ps 137). With the building of the Second Temple, music was restored and placed under the direction of the descendants of the original levitical musicians (Ezra 2:41). The levitical musicians of this period, who in a sense formed a type of music guild, took responsibility for the organization of the Psalter and its captions or headings.

The OT writers make reference to a number of musical instruments. While the precise meaning of many of the biblical terms remains ambiguous, a number of the instruments have been identified. Often the identifications have been made with the assistance of archaeological discoveries, as well as the writings of the rabbis, and early church fathers. Modern scholarship often divides the instruments into about four major categories: the "idiophones" consisting of instruments made of material that produces sounds like the cymbal, rattle or sistrum, the gong, and the bell; the "aerophones," or instruments that are blown, including the flute or pipe, the clarinet, the horn, the trumpet, and the *shophar* horn; the "membranophones," or instruments with a stretched hide or membrane that produces the sounds, such as the tambourine, and drum; and the "chordophones,'' or stringed instruments like the lyre, lute, and harp.

Instruments used in biblical times were made of materials that might be called the natural resources of ancient Israel. These materials include cured animal horns, bones, skins, and intestines, as well as metals, such as brass, plant materials including wood and reeds, pottery, and stone.

A study of the biblical terms for the instruments is a highly complex one, however, a number of the basic terms form the core of the study. The most frequently mentioned instrument in the OT is the *shophar,* the horn (Judg 3:27). The instrument, made of a ram's horn, was heated and bent to the shape of a right angle. A *qeren* (Josh 6:5), which referred to an animal horn, must have been used as a synonym for *shophar*. The *hasosera,* trumpet (Num 10:2-10), was made of metals like silver or bronze, and was used especially to summon a group. The *kinnor*, David's harp (1 Sam 16:23), was actually a lyre. The lyre, the most common stringed instrument, had a rectangular or trapezoidal shape. A lyre appears in the Egyptian tomb painting at Benihasan depicting the Amorite nomads. The *nebel,* the second most common stringed instrument and always mentioned along with the lyre, was most likely a type of lyre or harp. The term is usually translated harp, and at times, lute (Ps 150:3). The *asor,* which appears only in Psalms, was most likely a ten-stringed harp (Ps 33:2). The *khalil,* often translated flute (1 Sam 10:5) or pipe, was a type of double clarinet or double oboe. It consisted of two pipes made of reed, metal, or ivory. The *ugab,* which appears in Gen 4:21; Job 21:12; 30:31; Ps 150:4, most likely was a kind of pipe. The *toph,* often translated timbrel or tambourine (Exod 15:20; 2 Sam 6:5), was a small hand drum or tambourine that did not have jingles. The terms *mesiltayim* or *selselim* (2 Sam 6:5; 1 Chr 13:8) refer to cymbals. Ancient cymbals were round flat plates, usually about five to seven in. in diameter and made of bronze. The *menaanim* (2 Sam 6:5), translated castanets, clappers, rattles, or sistrums, were noise makers. *Paamon* (Exod 28:33) were small bells attached to garments, while *mesillot* (Zech 14:20) were bells attached to the harnesses of horses.

Music in the New Testament. While the NT has relatively few references to music or musical instruments in comparison to the OT, nevertheless, music must have played a vital role in the early Christian community. Apparently, Jesus, the twelve disciples, and other followers attended the temple and synagogue services where they shared in Israel's rich musical heritage (Mark 3:1; Luke 4:16; 20:1). Also, the Gospels provide some glimpses of Jesus and his disciples singing (Mark 14:26). During the period following Jesus' earthly life and ministry, early Christians engaged in the singing of "psalms and hymns and spiritual songs'' (Eph 5:19; Col 3:16) in their meetings. The important role singing played in the early Christian community is reflected further in Revelation (cf. 4:10-11; 5:9-10). The NT makes reference to a number of musical instruments, including the *aulos* (1 Cor 14:1), a flute (cf. *khalil* above); the *kithara* (1 Cor 14:7; Rev.5:8), a type of lyre, but translated harp; the *salpinx* (Matt 24:31), a trumpet; the *kumbala* (1 Cor 13:1), a cymbal; and the *chalkos* (1 Cor 13:1), a gong.

Bibliography. "Ancient Musical Instruments,'' *BAR* 8/1 (Jan/Feb 1982): 19-41; J. W. McKinnon, *Music in the Ancient World*; O. R. Sellers, "Musical Instruments of Israel,'' *BA* 4/3 (1941): 33-47; A. Sendrey, *Music in Ancient Israel*.

—LAMOINE DEVRIES

• **Mystery.** The word "mystery" comes from a Greek word used in MYSTERY RELIGIONS to mean the secret revealed to an initiate. These mystery religions spread into Greece and the Roman Empire in the late Hellenistic age as persons sought identification with the gods and assurance of immortality. The initiates were taught mysteries which they were obliged to conceal. An important question is the relation of Christianity to the mystery religions. Related to this question is the NT use of the term "mystery.''

The Hebrew OT did not have a word which was the exact equivalent of the Greek word. There is, however, the idea of secret knowledge which the Lord revealed (Isa 48:3, 6; Amos 3:7). In Daniel and later books, the secret knowledge is that a new age will come when God will rule over a perfect earth.

In the NT, the term is used in relation to a wide range of subjects. Mark 4:11 (Matt 13:11 || Luke 8:10) uses the term which is translated "secret." "And he said to them, 'To you has been given the secret of the kingdom of God, but for those outside everything is in parables.' '' Pauline literature uses the term twenty-one times with a variety of references: God, faith, or religious knowledge (Rom 11:25; 1 Tim 3:9; 1 Cor 2:1; 13:2); the gospel (Rom 16:25; 1 Tim 3:16); the future (1 Cor 2:7; 15:51; Col 1:26 ff.); apostles' responsibility for sharing the secrets (1 Cor 4:1); secrets and speaking in tongues (1 Cor 14:2); something wicked to be revealed (2 Thess 2:7); Christ now revealed to gentiles (Col 2:2-3; 4:3; Eph 1:9; 3:3-4, 9; 6:19); and a secret couched in symbolic language (Eph 5:32). References in Revelation concern the future (10:7) and secrets using symbolic language (1:20; 17:5, 7).

Often it is asked whether the idea of mystery came into Christianity from a Greek or a Hebrew background. Arguments for Greek influence include the fact that mystery cults had a fairly large following in Greco-Roman times; the prominence of "mystery" in contemporary and earlier Greek religions; several prominent terms in Pauline literature used also by mystery cults; the use of the term in the LXX; the fact that NT writers addressed gentiles as well as Hebrews; the fact that the Hellenistic Judaism of Paul's time came to be seen by some persons as "the greatest mystery"; and Greek influence on Christianity through Judaism.

Arguments for Hebrew influence include the confession that Hebrew prophets and apocalyptists were divinely-chosen channels for God's revelations; the opinion that the concept and the word "mystery" in Hebrew writing were adequate background for the concept and the word in Christian writing; the fact that Pauline typology comes extensively from the OT, e.g., 1 Cor 10:1ff.; Paul's understanding of Christian secrets as revealed to all rather than just the initiated; the evidence that in the mystery religions there was nothing corresponding to Pauline "faith"; Paul's restrained use of terms from mystery cults; the opinion that since leadership in Hellenistic Judaism denounced the mystery cults, use of cultic concepts was a scheme for advancing Judaism rather than being a case of domination by Greek concepts; and limitation of similarity between the Christian mystery and pagan mysteries.

What we can safely recognize is that the mystery cults were an element in the environment of Hellenistic Judaism and the early gentile church, that writers would be open to their influence, and that some Greek mystery terms were used in the Judeo-Christian writings probably to attract gentile attention. Hebrew writings provided background for NT use of "mystery"; NT writers, therefore, would not have depended solely on Greek sources.

See also APOCALYPTIC LITERATURE; ESCHATOLOGY IN THE NEW TESTAMENT; ESCHATOLOGY IN THE OLD TESTAMENT; GNOSTICISM; HELLENISTIC WORLD; MYSTERY RELIGIONS; PROPHECY; PROPHET; VISION.

Bibliography. R. E. Brown, "The Semitic Background of the New Testament MYSTERION," *Bib* 39 (1958): 426-48 and 40 (1959): 70-87; W. D. Davies, *Paul and Rabbinic Judaism;* J. A. Robinson, *St. Paul's Epistle to the Ephesians.*

—PHILIP R. HART

• **Mystery Religions.** The phrase "MYSTERY religion" is used as a general description for a diverse group of ancient Hellenistic private cults and hellenized oriental cults which shared a number of common features. Most Greco-Roman mystery cults were profoundly affected by (and sometimes explicitly modeled after) the mysteries of Eleusis, referred to by the Greeks as simply "*the* mysteries" (τά μυστήρια). The Gk. term μύστης means "initiant," and the verbs τελεῖν and μύειν mean "to be initiated." The cognate term μυστήριον therefore, means "initiatory ritual," and refers to the secret rites which provide the focus for such mystery cults. In contrast to the public celebrations of traditional state cults which were primarily concerned with national prosperity, mystery religions were private voluntary associations (joined by undergoing a secret ritual of initiation), and which primarily focused on individual SALVATION (including prosperity in this life and happiness after death). Yet with the single exception of the mysteries of Mithras, all of the gods worshiped in the Greek mystery religions also had public or state cults (e.g., Demeter, Persephone, Dionysus).

General Features of Mystery Cults. In the ancient Mediterranean world mystery cults originated in two quite different ways. Native Greek mystery cults were connected with specific locations (e.g., the mysteries of Eleusis and Samothrace). Oriental mystery cults (such as the mysteries of Isis and Cybele) were hellenized exports of various Levantine and Near Eastern native cults which moved westward with the immigrants from those regions. As the name implies, mystery religions centered on secret rituals of initiation. The oaths which initiants took never to reveal the content of these initiatory rituals were so effective that to this day scholars have only vague ideas about the character of such rituals. The experience of ritual initiation can be broken down into three constituent elements: (1) *Dromena* ("things enacted") refers to the cult drama which acted out the MYTH on which the cult was based. (2) *Legomena* ("things spoken") refers to the recitation of the central myth which provided an explanation of the cult drama. (3) *Deiknumena* ("things shown") refers to the ritual objects which were displayed before the initiant. Mystery religions did not transmit doctrines to the initiants (a task more appropriate to the philosophical schools), for as Aristotle observed (*On Philosophy,* frag. 15), initiants into the mysteries did not need to learn but to experience. The result of this experience was the conviction that the initiant would enjoy prosperity in this life coupled with a happy afterlife. Often the secret rituals of the mystery cults involved a surrogate experience of death, through the ritual reenactment of the death of one of the deities central to the cult. The survival of the initiate could be interpreted as a rebirth (cf. Apuleius, *The Golden Ass* 11.16), i.e., as a guarantee of happiness and prosperity both in this life and the life to come.

Mystery religions were once widely thought to center in a god who represented or personified the annual decay and revival of vegetation, and who is born, dies and rises to new life annually. Yet a careful investigation of the category of dying and rising gods (e.g., Attis, Adonis, Tammuz, Osiris), indicates that while the conception of the death of such deities was a notion widely held in antiquity, the notion of their resurrection is rarely, if ever, encountered.

Though many types of mystery cults flourished in the Greco-Roman world (e.g., the mysteries of Dionysus, Samothrace, Aphrodite and Adonis, Kubaba-Cybele and Attis, and Mithras), the following discussion will focus first on a native Greek mystery cult (the Eleusinian mysteries), and then on a hellenized oriental mystery cult (the mysteries of Isis).

The Eleusinian Mysteries. The mysteries of Eleusis were both the oldest and most influential mystery cult in the ancient world; they were celebrated as early as the fifteenth century B.C.E. (though the archaeological evidence is ambiguous) to 395 C.E. when the site was destroyed by the Goths. The priestly personnel of these mysteries, including the Hierophantai ("bearers of sacred objects") and the Dadouchoi ("torch bearers") were traditionally drawn from the Eumolpidai and Kerykes clans. The Homeric *Hymn to Demeter,* probably composed before 550 B.C.E., is the earliest literary evidence for the cult of Demeter at Eleusis. This hymn contains the etiological myth which provides the basis for the ritual of initiation. The myth centers in the abduction of Persephone, the daughter of Demeter, by Hades, the god of the underworld, to be his wife. Grieving and fasting, Demeter sought for her daughter for nine days. Finally Helios the sun god, who sees all, revealed what had happened. In anger, Demeter abandoned Olympus and visited the house of Celeus, lord of Eleusis, incognito and was hospitably received by Metaneira the queen of her daughters. Demeter continued mourning and fasting until Metaneira gave her a beverage consisting of meal, water and mint. Demeter became a nurse for Metaneira's son Demophoön, whom she (unsuccessfully) tried to make immortal. Demeter then revealed who she was and Celeus instituted a cult in her honor. In anger over her abducted daughter, Demeter caused a drought which deprived people of food and the gods of sacrifices. Zeus therefore sent Hermes to fetch Persephone from Hades. Hades let her go, but first offered her a taste of pomegranate which insured her return to the underworld. Again reunited with her mother Demeter, the fact that Persephone had tasted food in the underworld made it necessary that she return there to spend one-third of every year.

By the early Christian period, initiation into the Eleusinian mysteries involved three separate and progressive stages (cf. Clement of Alexandria *Strom* 5.70.7). Candidates for the Greater Mysteries held on 15–22 Boedromion (Sept-Oct) must first have been initiated into the Lesser Mysteries held at Agrae near the Ilissos in Athens during the month Anthesterion (though this was originally a separate festival). The Eleusinian mysteries themselves consisted of two stages, the first level of initiation was called initiation and the participants initiants, while the second level was called beholding, and the participants were designated beholders. The sacred ritual objects (the things shown to the initiants on the final day of the festival) were brought to the Eleusinion in Athens on the fourteenth of Boedromion. On the fifteenth, called *Agyrmos* ("gathering"), the initiants (who came from all over the Greek world) gathered at the Stoa Poikile in the Agora where a formal invitation, and warning, was announced to those gathered. There the initiation fee was paid (by the fourth century B.C.E. it was fifteen drachmas, ten days' wages). Initiants were led and instructed by mystagogues (initiation guides). On the sixteenth initiants were ritually purified by bathing in the sea, and after returning to Athens were anointed with the blood of a sacrificial pig. On the nineteenth, the sacred objects were escorted by the initiants back along the Sacred Way to Eleusis, fourteen mi. from Athens. The procession stopped at every temple and shrine along the route and made the appropriate sacrifices to various gods and heroes, arriving at Eleusis at night with the aid of torches. The focus of the celebration occurred on the sixth day (the twentieth of the month) on which the initiants broke their fast by drinking a mixture of barley and water called *kykeon*. The culminating ceremony began in the evening at the Teslesterion or "hall of initiation," in the center of which was a sacred room called the Anaktoron. The sacred object revealed to the initiant was in all probability simply a head of wheat (Hippolytus, *Haer* 5.8.39). At the conclusion of the Homeric *Hymn to Demeter,* a beatitude is pronounced upon all initiants; "Happy is the one who, of those on the earth, has beheld these things; but the one who has no part in the holy rites has another destiny as he wastes away in gloomy darkness." Though the ritual is tantalizingly concealed in this myth, it appears that Demeter's grief and fasting and drinking *kykeon* are paradigmatic in that those ritual moments are reenacted by the worshiper. This is reflected in Clement of Alexandria's preservation of this Eleusinian formula: "I fasted, I drank *kykeon,* I have taken from the *kiste* [a container in which sacred objects of Eleusis were stored] and when my task was completed, deposited into the basket and out of the basket into the *kiste*" (*Protrept* 2.21.2; cf. Arnobius 5.26).

The Mysteries of Isis. Isis and Osiris (the ruler of the dead) were two of nine genealogically arranged major Egyptian deities comprising the Heliopolitan Ennead, referred to in the Pyramid Texts of the Fifth and Sixth Dynasties (ca. 2340–2200 B.C.E.). In Egyptian myth, Isis was both the sister and wife of Osiris and the mother of Horus. An elaborate myth involving Isis and Osiris can be reconstructed from the Pyramid Texts of the Fifth and Sixth Dynasties (2501–2181 B.C.E.). In this myth, Osiris was violently murdered by Seth, his brother and arch rival, and mourned by his sisters Isis and Nephthys. Herodotus (2.61, 132) describes the ritual lament of thousands of Isis worshipers. Isis, with her attendant Anubis (the god of embalming), searched far and wide for the body of Osiris. Isis conceived Horus by the deceased Osiris, and gave birth to Horus who fought with Seth and ascended the throne (Isis herself represents the throne). Finally Osiris was resuscitated when Isis breathed life into his nostrils. This myth provided the basic ideology of Egyptian kingship. The coronation of the new Pharaoh (the incarnate Horus, successor to the murdered Osiris) celebrated the renewed triumph of divine order over chaos. The deceased ruler had become Osiris in the underworld. Yet Osiris was never thought to return to life in this world, but rather to attain life in the next world (various funerary texts entertain the undesirable possibility of a second death). Yet this Egyptian cult was never a mystery religion since individuals are not initiated after experiencing a secret ritual.

The Hellenized mystery cult of Isis probably arose in Alexandria and was in all probability deliberately modeled after the mysteries of Demeter at Eleusis. By the early Ptolemaic period (early third century B.C.E.) the public cults of Isis and Serapis [developed from Osiris] had been transplanted by Egyptian immigrants throughout the Mediterranean world. The most extensive version of the myth is preserved by the Greek writer Plutarch in *De Iside et Osiride* 12-19 (a less detailed version is found in Diodorus Siculus 1.14-22). The myth related by Plutarch exhibits striking parallels to the Greek myth of Demeter, a fact which is perhaps not surprising since in accordance with the common *interpretatio Graeca* Demeter was identified with Isis and Dionysus with Osiris (cf. Herodotus, *Hist* 2.123, 156). Osiris became ruler of Egypt but was tricked by Typhon (Seth) into getting into a coffin. Typhon nailed down the lid and threw the coffin into the Nile. Eventually it drifted to Byblos on the Phoenician coast. Isis, who searched everywhere for her husband, eventually found the coffin at Byblos. After returning to Egypt with the coffin, Typhon stole the body and cut it into many pieces which he scattered around Egypt (thereby accounting for the many cult centers of Osiris). Isis gathered the pieces together and before embalming it had sexual relations with the dead Osiris and conceived Horus.

An almost perfectly preserved Iseum (temple of Isis), built before 79 C.E. has been excavated at Pompeii, where murals depict various aspects of Isiac ritual. The most detailed ancient discussion of Isiac initiation is found in *Metamorphoses* 11 where Apuleius describes the initiation of his protagonist, Lucius, into the mysteries of Isis. After a preliminary ritual bath of purification, Lucius fasts for ten days. He was then led into the inner sanctum of the temple of Isis, and reportedly reached the threshold of the underworld, was face to face with the gods below (including Persephone) and the gods above and moved across the elements of the cosmos. Finally at midnight he saw a great light. Although the nature and content of this religious experience is only hinted at in the narrative of Apuleius, it is at least clear that Lucius is presented as undergoing a ritual experience of death which in some way guarantees happiness and prosperity both in this life and in the life to come.

Bibliography. S. Angus, *The Mystery Religions: A Study of the Religious Background of Early Christianity*; U. Bianchi, *The Greek Mysteries*; W. Burkert, *Ancient Mystery Cults, Greek Religion,* and *Homo Necans: The Anthropology of Ancient Greek Sacrificial Ritual and Myth*; J. Campbell, ed., *The Mysteries: Papers from the Eranos Yearbooks*; F. Cumont, *The Mysteries of Mithra*; F. Cumont, *Oriental Religions in Roman Paganism*; J. Ferguson, *The Religions of the Roman Empire*; J. Godwin, *Mystery Religions in the Ancient World*; F. C. Grant, *Hellenistic Religions: The Age of Syncretism*; J. G. Griffiths, *Apuleius of Madauros: The Isis Book* and *Plutarch's De Iside et Osiride*; B. Metzger, "Bibliography of Mystery Religions," *Aufstieg und Niedergang der römischen Welt,* ed. W. Haase, II, 17/3: 1259-1423; G. E. Mylonas, *Eleusis and the Eleusinian Mysteries*; A. D. Nock, *Conversion: The Old and the New in Religion from Alexander the Great to Augustine of Hippo*; H. W. Parke, *Festivals of the Athenians*; R. Reitzenstein, *Hellenistic Mystery-Religions: Their Basic Ideas and Significance*; N. J. Richardson, *The Homeric Hymn to Demeter*; J. Z. Smith, "Dying and Rising Gods," *EncRel*; F. Solmsen, *Isis among the Greeks and Romans*; M. J. Vermaseren, *Cybele and Attis: The Myth and the Cult*; R. E. Witt, *Isis in the Graeco-Roman World.*

—DAVID E. AUNE

• **Myth.** The word "myth" derives from the Gk. *mythos,* meaning "word," or "speech." This "word" refers to a reality of inhabitants, space, and time quite different from the ordinary world of everyday life. *Mythos* tells a story whose major character or characters are superhuman beings. The world inhabited by these divine beings is understood as sacred (heaven, temples, and the like). This means it is separated and marked off from the ordinary world of human dwelling. Mythic time refers to beginnings when things first came into existence; e.g., when the human world was created. Mythic time is a time prior to history, thus existing before human beings. The popular notion that myth refers to something that is untrue is a misconception. Rather, through the power of the imagination cultures present what they consider to be fundamentally real.

Mythos may be contrasted to another Greek term, *logos,* which also means "word." Unlike *mythos,* however, *logos* refers to reasoned discourse based on sense experience, analysis, critical reflection, and debate. The frame of reference for *logos* is the everyday reality of human beings, often formulated in history, science, and law. *Logos* expresses what is true and sensible in everyday life. This world of *logos* is that of human beings, and its time is their history, present, and projected future.

Myth is characterized by four features: sacred space, times, events, and speech. The terms "sacred" and "holy" refer to reality that is distinguished from the everyday, i.e., the profane or the secular, world. Something is considered sacred, or set apart, if it is associated in some way with a divine being. And because it is sacred, it is permeated with power. The sacred possesses great power, power both beneficial and destructive. Knowing what is sacred and how it may be approached is thus a matter of life and death for those who believe in the reality of the holy.

A sacred space may be a temple, region, e.g., heaven, rock, tree, spring of water, mountain, or the like. The space is sacred because a deity occupies its space, dwells there on occasion, or may take up residence there again. The space may be accessible to human beings or denied human contact depending upon the decision of the deity. Even so, the power of the sacred is something to be feared. Before the burning bush, Moses removes his sandals, not merely as a sign of respect or obedience, but as a recognition that he has unwittingly entered into sacred space and is threatened by its power.

Myth also speaks of sacred times that are different from the ordinary moments of human life. Ordinary time is usually understood as a steady succession of unrepeatable moments, measured by clocks and calendars: seconds, hours, days, weeks, months, and years. This is the time of everyday activities. Ordinary time is sometimes called linear time, because it denotes the succession of moments. Sacred time, by contrast, is an eternal now, i.e., a time that collapses past, present, and future into one unending moment. Thus, in one sense, the act of creation, a common mythic theme, is not a once-for-all event prior to human history, but an eternal action. Furthermore, sacred time envelops divine events that are repeatable. This is the cyclical view of time, comparable to the repetition of the seasons. Many cultures celebrate a festival of the new year when the world is believed to be renewed by repeating its beginnings.

Sacred events are also separated from the everyday world of human dwelling. These divine actions include the creation of the world and humanity, the origins of social institutions and values, directing the course of history, saving the elect, and bringing the world to an end. Sometimes these actions involve what modern understanding would consider to be miraculous. But in the world of mythic imagination, divine beings speak objects into existence, breathe life into lifeless beings, divide rivers, and flood the earth with the waters of chaos.

Most celebrated by human communities are those sacred events that are life-giving and redemptive in character. Thus the act of creation is often central, for this is the event that originated and continues to sustain the structures of life for existence. Divine actions that created a people, provided them sustenance through the gifts of land and food, and redeemed them from threats are remembered and celebrated. Humans are even taught to imitate certain actions of divine beings, for through imitation these human actions partake of the power of the sacred, are given their validity, and become successful. For example, the construction of a house is thought to imitate the creation of the cosmos, when the divine architect planned and built the earth. Indeed, the proper construction of the house is an activity anchored within the very order and life-sustaining power of the creation itself.

A fourth feature of myth is sacred language. Myth narrates the reality it describes into existence. Its language is power-laden. When properly used, say in the recitation of the story of creation, the great drama of the origins of life is replayed. CREATION is spoken into existence once again, renewed by vital power.

With regard to content, myths may be placed into three major categories: cosmogony (genesis or beginning of the world), redemption, and eschatology (the end of time). Cosmogonic myths tell the story of beginnings, including the world and the variety of phenomena that makes up present reality. Redeemer myths tell of divine saviors who come to save humanity or a select group from destruction. Eschatological myths depict the end of the present world and the establishment of a new and better world. Often the new world is a return to the original creation in its perfection and bliss.

Why do human communities construct and tell myths? A common misconception is that myths are prelogical attempts by primitive peoples to explain how various things originated or why certain things happen. If this were true, the explanations of myths would now be obsolete in the world of modern science. Yet this is not a view held today by those who study myths. It is true that myths may answer a variety of questions. Why does this event occur? Why are certain things forbidden or allowed? Why do people suffer and die? and so forth. Yet the fundamental purpose is not to answer questions, but rather to preserve the existence of a human community. Human life is ever subject to catastrophes, ranging from war to famine to plague. Myths are created by human cultures in order to preserve and sustain those important elements of a community's common life. These important elements include social institutions, laws and values, religious beliefs and practices, and economic systems. Myths anchor these elements in a reality believed to be more secure and enduring. The sacred power of mythic reality is released in ritual, drama, and story telling in order to secure the existence of a human community and its essential traditions.

Another important purpose of myth is to provide a model for human existence. Significant human actions necessary for the community to survive imitate the activities or follow the commandments of deities. Such essential actions as love-making, reproduction, farming, war, and legislation are grounded in sacred actions and/or commandments of divine beings. Through imitation expressed in actual conduct (e.g., the act of marriage) and rituals that symbolize divine action or commandments (e.g,. the marriage ceremony performed in a church or a synagogue), humans participate in divinely legitimated activities and experience well-being.

Myths are not the dead relics of past cultures. All societies have their myths that embody their cherished values and beliefs. In America politicians often speak of this nation's destiny to lead the free world. This view is not unlike the Babylonians' assertions that their god, Marduk, chose Hammurabi to rule an empire. Even nontheistic societies have their myths. For example, Marxist countries speak of economic determinism as an historical process that will inevitably lead to a paradise of a classless, stateless society in which all people will have what they need to exist. In Marxist ideology, however, a supreme being is replaced by an historical process. Myths continue to exist, because they express and establish what human cultures consider to be most fundamentally real and true.

See also HERMENEUTICS; RELIGIONS OF THE ANCIENT NEAR EAST; RELIGION OF ISRAEL; RELIGIONS, HELLENISTIC AND ROMAN.

Bibliography. A. Dundes, ed., *Sacred Narrative*; M. Eliade, *Myth and Reality*; J. W. Rogerson, *Myth in Old Testament Interpretation*.

—LEO G. PERDUE

• **Naaman.** [nay'uh-muhn] A personal name, with the meaning "pleasantness," borne by two persons in the Bible: *1*. The grandson of Benjamin (son of Jacob) and father of the Naamite clan (Gen 46:21; Num 26:40; 1 Chr 8:4, 7).

2. The commander of the army of the king of Aram (RSV, SYRIA) who was healed of leprosy by the Israelite prophet Elisha, as narrated in 2 Kgs 5.

Naaman is described as a valiant soldier held in high esteem by the king because of his military victories, but afflicted with LEPROSY. His wife's Israelite maid, though herself a captive of Aramean raids into Israel, had compassion upon him and suggested that there was a prophet of Samaria in Israel who could heal him. The Aramean king, upon hearing Namaan's request to go to Israel to seek out this prophet, enthusiastically encouraged him and gave him a letter of introduction in which he asked the king of Israel to heal his commander.

Naaman set out for Israel with horses and chariots laden with expensive gifts of silver, gold, and clothing. The Israelite king (most probably Jehoram) became alarmed at the request of the letter, interpreting it as a ruse by Aram to pick a quarrel with him and provoke a war. ELISHA, learning of the king's distress, requested that the king send the commander to him so that he would "know that there is a prophet in Israel" (v. 8). When Naaman arrived at Elisha's house, the prophet sent a messenger who told him that if he dipped seven times in the Jordan River he would be cured of his leprosy. Naaman left in a rage, offended that Elisha did not come out to him personally and insulted at being asked to wash in the Jordan when, as he complained, there were far better rivers in Aram. At his servants' insistence, however, he complied with the prophet's instructions and was completely cleansed of his disease.

Immediately upon his healing, Naaman became a confirmed believer in the Israelite God. He went before Elisha and stated his confession of faith: "Now I know that there is no God in all the world except in Israel" (v. 15). He then requested two mule loads of Israelite soil to take back with him to Aram upon which to offer sacrifice and worship the Lord. Further attesting to the sincerity of his conversion, he requested forgiveness for the gestures he would have to perform, as acts of patriotism, in accompanying the king of Aram into pagan temples to observe the rituals of worship of the Aramean god RIMMON.

To show his gratitude, Naaman attempted to lavish upon Elisha the expensive gifts that he had brought for him in exchange for the healing. The prophet, however, declined his generosity, thus indicating to Naaman that the blessings of the Lord are free. When his servant Gehazi, through devious means, acquired some of the gifts for himself, Elisha confronted him, saying that the leprosy of Naaman would never depart from him or his descendants.

Jesus alluded to Naaman's cure as an example of God's gracious concern for a non-Israelite (Luke 4:27).

See also DISEASE AND HEALING; LEPROSY; MIRACLES.

—ROBERT B. BARNES

• **Nabal.** [nay'buhl] A wealthy Calebite from Maon who herded his sheep and goats in Carmel (1 Sam 25). The name means "fool." During the time of sheep shearing, DAVID, operating a kind of protection racket, sent ten servants to Nabal requesting provisions for payment. When Nabal not only refused their request, but acted in a rude and insulting manner, David took 400 of his warriors to seek revenge. The certain massacre was averted when ABIGAIL, the beautiful wife of Nabal, heard of David's plans and intervened with provisions and supplications. Because of her actions, David did not carry out his attack. When Abigail related the turn of events to her husband, who had just awakened from a night of drinking and feasting, he became ill and died ten days later. Upon learning of his death, David took Abigail as his own wife. She eventually bore him a son, Chileab (2 Sam 3:3).

This carefully crafted story functions at several levels. At the most obvious, it explains how David came to have another man's wife as his own without violating established standards of conduct (cf. his behavior in 2 Sam 11 after he became king!). The story also served to win him loyalty from the Calebites who at that time were still separate from Judah. But its most important function was to show how David's destiny was in the hand of Yahweh and not his own. Thus Abigail's speech not only anticipates David's rise to kingship (v. 30) but also saves him from an act of vengeance (vv. 33-34), which is the prerogative of Yahweh alone.

See also ABIGAIL; DAVID.

—JOHN C. H. LAUGHLIN

• **Nabataeans.** [nab'uh-tee"uhnz] A fascinating, if imperfectly known, Arab people who occupied much of the territory surrounding Palestine from late in the OT period until well beyond the era in which the NT was written. Though they are often overlooked, the Nabataeans played a major role in the military, political, commercial, and agricultural activities of the pre-Christian and NT periods. Most of the popular awareness of this remarkable people centers around PETRA, but there is much more to Nabataean history and culture than this spectacular site in southern Jordan. Likewise, the pivotal role of this Arab people in the geopolitical configuration of the intertestamental period and the first century C.E. goes far beyond the few specific references to the Nabataeans in 1–2 Maccabees and the single reference to them in the NT.

The semitic name for the Nabataeans was *Nabatu,* but they were known in Gk. as *Nabataioi* (1 Macc 5:25; 9:35). By Josephus's day, their kingdom was known as Nabatene. On historical and linguistic grounds, the identification of Nabataeans with either the Ishmaelite tribe of Nabaioth (Gen 25:13; 28:9; 36:3; 1 Chr 1:29; Isa 60:7) or with the Aramaic tribe of Nabatu (called Nabaiati in Assyrian texts from the eighth to seventh centuries B.C.E.) is no longer valid.

In general terms, the Nabataeans were found in the lands to the east and southwest of the DEAD SEA (PLATES 13, 17). At the climax of their political and cultural achievement, in the first century C.E., Nabataean Arabs occupied parts of the Negeb, Sinai, Egypt, southern Syria (Hauran), Transjordan (especially Edom and Moab), and northern Arabia. Avraham Negeb has identified the four major Nabataean regions as (1) northern Arabia, (2) Edom and Moab, (3) Hauran, and (4) Sinai, the Negeb, and Egypt. Of course, not all of these areas were colonized or even occupied by the Nabataeans with the same intensity at all periods in their history. Their settlement and/or use of any area depended on the extent of their commercial and agricultural activities in a given period and was conditioned by the international politics of the day.

In addition to the mute archaeological sources that pertain to the Nabataean civilization, there is a small number of written sources from which to draw more specific information. Unfortunately, there are no extant historical texts of any significant length written by the Nabataeans themselves. There is, of course, a wealth of epigraphic evidence left by this Arab people; thousands of Nabataean Aramaic inscriptions from all over their realm have been discovered. Very few of these inscriptions are of any appreciable length, with the Turkmaniyeh Tomb Inscription from Petra being the principal exception; most of the short texts are funerary or votive in nature, or are graffiti or coin inscriptions. No Hellenistic or Roman writer has provided us with a systematic treatment of Nabataean history. Occasional reference is made to a certain Uranius, the author of a book entitled *Arabica,* but we know nothing about him or his work. This means that our most important sources of historical data on the Nabataeans remain the writings of Diodorus Siculus (some of whose account was drawn from Hieronymous of Cardia, an eyewitness to important events in Nabataean history), Josephus (who drew his Nabataean information from Nicolaus of Damascus), and Strabo, though there are references to the Nabataeans in other ancient sources as well.

Scholars now speak in terms of some familiarity with approximately 1,000 years of Nabataean history, with the bulk of knowledge relating to the period between ca. 100 B.C.E. until ca. 200 C.E. Naturally, details about most of their prehistory are lacking, but a scholarly consensus locates the original Nabataean homeland in Arabia, though there are many suggestions as to which part of the peninsula (e.g., western shore of the Persian Gulf, Dedan, Qedar). While the steps in the lengthy process are still unknown, it is certain that the Nabataeans, along with other Arab tribes, began to enter southern Transjordan even before the neo-Babylonian invasion of the early sixth century B.C.E. The gradual demographic shift put pressure on the Edomites (later known as Idumaeans), who began to move into southern Judah and the Negeb in the sixth century B.C.E., a process that accelerated with the collapse of Judah. Under the Persians and Alexander the Great, the Edomite/Idumaean and Nabataean infiltration into southern Palestine and Transjordan continued with little or no interference. While the Nabataeans were originally a nomadic people, they eventually developed a sedentary lifestyle as they took up agriculture and began to control the international trade routes that crossed the regions in which they had settled.

The first historical account of the Nabataeans is Diodorus Siculus' record of the unsuccessful invasion of Nabatene by the Greek general, Antigonus I, in 312 B.C.E. While this is the official beginning of Nabataean history, it also tells us something about the economy of this people; Diodorus refers to the loot that the Greeks captured in this raid, wealth that was already amassed at Petra because of the caravan trade. The next historical reference to the Nabataeans is found in 2 Macc 5:8, where mention is made of Nabataean/Hasmonaean relations in 169 B.C.E. Most important is the fact that this text brings us to the beginning of the Nabataean dynastic monarchy, which began with ARETAS I. Though our knowledge of their list of kings is incomplete and, occasionally, the subject of serious disagreement, the Nabataean dynasty ran along the following lines: Aretas I (ca. 169 B.C.E.; cf. 1 Macc 5:25; 2 Macc 5:8), Aretas II, Obodas I (ca. 95 B.C.E.), Rabbel I (88–86 B.C.E.), Aretas III Philhellene (87?–62 B.C.E.), Malichus I (62–30 B.C.E.), Obodas II (30–9 B.C.E.), Aretas IV (9/8 B.C.E.–40 C.E.), Malichus II (40–70 C.E.), and Rabbel II (70–106 C.E.). Much of the history of Nabatene is told in terms of power struggles and military conflicts between the Nabataeans and the Hasmonaeans, Rome, and HEROD the Great; their story would include references to greed, intrigue, and a constant desire for territorial expansion and commercial control.

One of the most interesting episodes in Nabataean history has to do with Herod the Great, who was half Nabataean through his mother, Kypros (a heritage which his Jewish subjects never forgot). Malichus I was allied with Julius Caesar against Pompey, a status that the Nabataean king had attained through the dealings of Antipater, Herod's father. Herod clashed with the Nabataeans on more than one occasion, including the time when Malichus refused to provide him sanctuary during Herod's fight against the Parthians.

The death of Obodas II brought Aretas IV to the throne in 9/8 B.C.E., a position he held for nearly a half century, until 40 C.E. He was unquestionably the most powerful monarch the Nabataeans ever had, and Nabatene reached its cultural and commercial apogee during this reign. The daughter of Aretas IV was given in marriage to Herod's son, Antipas, though Antipas later divorced her so he could marry Herodias. Under Aretas IV, the Nabataeans exercised some kind of control over Damascus, a situation that is reflected in the NT reference to Paul's escape from the Syrian city (2 Cor 11:32). Scholars have long debated the meaning of this reference to an "ethnarch" at Damascus who was under the jurisdiction of King Aretas, but no satisfactory solution has been put forward.

During the reign of Malichus II, Nabatene declined, and Rabbel II witnessed the annexation of the Nabataean realm into the newly formed Province of Arabia, in 106 C.E. Bostra, in southern Syria, was designated as the new capital, and Petra began to decline in commercial significance, since the trade routes had shifted to the west and north of the former Nabataean capital. The Nabataeans continued to live in the same areas, but they were no longer identifiable at the time of the Islamic expansion in the seventh century B.C.E.

Since the European discovery of Petra by Burckhardt in 1812, much of the interest in the Nabataeans has focused on this spectacular ruin in southern Transjordan. With over 500 funerary monuments, the architecture of Petra is certainly distinctive, as is Nabataean art and architecture elsewhere. One type of Nabataean pottery is famous because of its beautiful painting and delicacy. No less remarkable, however, were the Nabataean skills in water management and agriculture, expertise that is easily observable in the publications of the major excavations at Nabataean sites in the Negeb, especially Oboda, Mampsis, and Elusa. The techniques that the Nabataeans used to exploit this arid environment have been studied by modern settlers and scientists.

Though the Nabataeans were of Arab origin, their official written language was ARAMAIC, the *lingua franca* of much of the Near East during the first millennium B.C.E. The abundant but usually brief Nabataean inscriptions are written in an elongated cursive version of Aramaic capital letters. This was a distinctive dialect and script of Aramaic, known as Nabataean Aramaic. For many years, it was suggested that Arabic had been abandoned by these immigrants by the fourth century B.C.E., but some scholars now believe that the Nabataeans not only continued to speak Arabic but wrote it as well, in addition to using Aramaic for more formal occasions.

At the head of a long list of gods and goddesses stood the Nabataean god Dushara, who was sometimes identified with Greek Dionysus and Zeus; the origin of this deity is unknown, but the Nabataeans might have brought his cult from their Arabian homeland. Allat was the leading goddess in the pantheon, which also included Allah, Allahi, El, Baal, el-Uzza, and other deities. Noteworthy Nabataean temples have been discovered at Wadi Ram, Petra (Qasr Bint Faraun), Khirbet et-Tannur, Dhat Ras, Qasr Rabba, and Dhiban. Nothing is known about the relationship between the Nabataeans and Christianity.

Bibliography. I. Browning, *Petra*; N. Glueck, *Deities and Dolphins: The Story of the Nabateans*; P. Hammond, *The Nabataeans—Their History, Culture and Archaeology* and "New Light on the Nabateans," *BAR* 7/2 (1981): 22-41; A. Kasher, *Jews, Idumaeans, and Ancient Arabs*; J. Lawlor, *The Nabataeans in Historical Perspective*; A. Negev, *Nabatean Archaeology Today*; J. Starcky, "The Natabaeans: A Historical Sketch," *BA* 18 (1955): 84-106.

—GERALD L. MATTINGLY

• **Nablus.** *See* SHECHEM

• **Nabonidus.** [nab'uh-ni''duhs] [Akk. *Nabû-na'id*—"Nabu is exalted"] The last king of the neo-Babylonian (Chaldean) Empire (555–539 B.C.E.). Although he is not mentioned in the OT, his son and coregent BELSHAZZAR is named by Daniel as the king of Babylon when it fell to Cyrus in 539 B.C.E.

Not of royal lineage, Nabonidus ascended the throne as the result of a palace conspiracy. During his first three years he conducted successful military campaigns in Syria, Cilicia and northern Arabia. Like other neo-Babylonian rulers, Nabonidus distinguished himself as a builder and restorer of temples. It was his religious zeal, however, for which he is most remembered. He devoted his only daughter to the moon-god and restored the temples to Sin at Ur and Haran. Early in his reign Nabonidus made a concerted effort to exalt Sin above all other deities. This move offended the Babylonians and resulted in opposition from the priests of Marduk.

For ten years Nabonidus chose to live some 500 mi. from Babylon at Teima, an oasis in northern Arabia. The reason for the move is not clear but "The Prayer of Nabonidus" an Aramaic text discovered at Qumran in 1953, suggests that illness may have been a factor. As Nabonidus departed to Arabia, he entrusted the kingship to his son Belshazzar. This may explain why Daniel mentions Belshazzar, not Nabonidus, as the king of Babylon and why Daniel is exalted to the third, not second, position in the kingdom (Dan 5:1, 7, 16, 29). Nabonidus returned to Babylon in his seventeenth year to meet the invasion of Cyrus. It was too late. The city fell in 539 and the neo-Babylonian empire came to an end.

—STEPHEN M. HOOKS

• **Naboth.** [nay'both] Typical of the fearless rural land holders of ancient Israel, Naboth possessed a vineyard near the palace of AHAB in the valley of JEZREEL. Ahab's desire for Naboth's vineyard led to a series of events that were to reap bitter fruit in the northern kingdom (1 Kgs 21). When the king sought to purchase the vineyard or to trade other land for it, he was turned down by Naboth. The land was perceived as being the divine gift to God's forebears and posterity. Recognizing the validity of Naboth's position, Ahab gave in to Naboth's decision but went home to pout.

Reared in a different culture, Queen JEZEBEL, Ahab's wife, could not understand this affront to royal authority. She secured two men of low character who perjured themselves and accused Naboth of blasphemy (1 Kgs 21:8-14). He was tried and condemned, and he and his family were executed by stoning. At this point, Ahab seized the land. It has been suggested that he may have been a distant relation of Naboth's and thus was entitled to the land. However, there is no evidence to suggest that his seizure of the land was anything more than simple use of royal authority.

The prophet ELIJAH met Ahab at Naboth's vineyard as Ahab inspected his new property. He condemned the king for his sin (1 Kgs 21:17-20). In that confrontation, he predicted the end of Ahab's line and the king's own death at the place of Naboth's execution. Later, Jehu's killing of Joram, Ahab's son and successor, was understood as the final fulfillment of this prophecy (2 Kgs 9:24-26).

See also AHAB; INHERITANCE IN THE OLD TESTAMENT; JEZEBEL; KINGSHIP; LAND.

—ROBERT L. CATE

• **Nadab.** [nay'dab] A name meaning generous, noble. Nadab was the name given to the following Hebrew Bible personalities: The eldest of AARON'S four sons (Exod 6:23; 1 Chr 6:3). He participated in ratification of the Sinai Covenant (Exod 24:1, 9). Later designated a priest (Exod 28:1), Nadab died childless (Num 26:60-61; 1 Chr 24:2) after a ritual offense. The exact nature of the offense is uncertain (Lev 10:1; Num 3:2, 4).

The king of Israel who succeeded his father, JEROBOAM I (1 Kgs 14:20). He was assassinated in Baasha's coup (1 Kgs 15:25-31), the first of a series of destabilizing dynastic changes in Israel.

One of the sons of Jeiel and Maacah in the Benjaminite genealogy, this Nadab was either an uncle or great-uncle of King Saul (1 Chr 8:30; 9:36).

A Jerahmeelite, son of Shammai (1 Chr 2:28, 30) and

descendant of JUDAH through his daughter-in-law, Tamar.

A nephew of Ahikar (Tob 11:18-19), Tobit's nephew (Tob 1:21-22; 2:10), and betrayer of Ahikar (Tob 14:10-11, probably an allusion to the older "Story of Ahikar").

See also ABIHU.

—C. EARL LEININGER

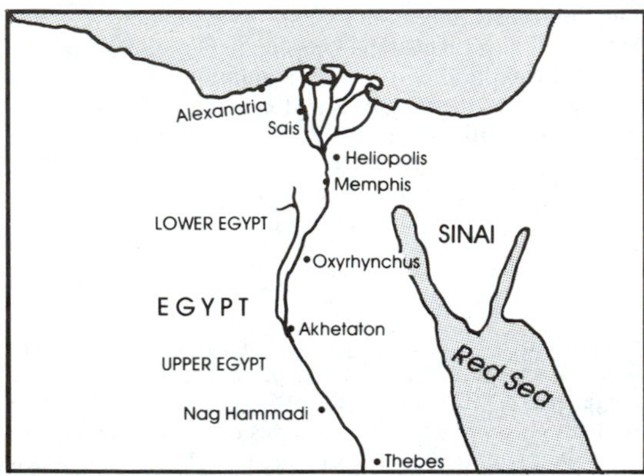

Designed by Margaret Jordan Brown ©Mercer University Press

• **Nag Hammadi.** [nahg'huh'mah"dee] The Egyptian town of Nag Hammadi located about 369 mi. south of Cairo, became internationally famous through the discovery near there in 1945 of one of the most important ancient manuscript collections ever found, the Coptic Gnostic library of Nag Hammadi. Consisting originally of thirteen leather-bound codices written on papyrus (forerunners of modern books with sewn quires), the library contains fifty-two writings which shed invaluable light on the history of early Christianity and the religious spirit of the Greco-Roman world from the second to the fourth centuries.

To Prof. James M. Robinson of the Institute for Antiquity and Christianity (Claremont University Center) goes credit for uncovering details of the original discovery and coordinating full publication in 1977 of photographic facsimiles and English translations of its 1,156 surviving pages. According to his report, in December 1945 three brothers from the al-Samman clan—Muhammad, Khalifah, and Abū al-Majd Alī—had travelled some six km. north of their hamlet of al-Qaṣr to the foot of a prominent line of cliffs overlooking the Nile River, the Jabal al Ṭārif. Their purpose was to obtain "sabakh," a nitrate-rich gravel found in the talus slopes of such cliffs and used as a low-grade fertilizer in peasant gardens. While digging near a huge boulder, they uncovered a large, sealed, clay jar which, when broken open, yielded the leather envelopes containing the codices. Depressed at not finding treasure in the jar, Muhammad Alī took the codices to his home. His mother, believing them worthless and needing fuel for her oven, burned some of the pages and probably the leather cover from Codex XII. Later, an itinerant English teacher saw one of the manuscripts and recognized its potential value. This led to the eventual transfer of the collection to Cairo, later acquisition of the whole by antiquities dealers and private collectors, seizure of the codices by the Egyptian Department of Antiquities, and their final deposit in the Coptic Museum in Cairo in October 1946. Over the following thirty-one years until their full publication, the vicissitudes of Egyptian political life and scholarly jealousies prevented access to most of the texts. Since 1977, however, all have been published and more than a decade has been devoted to study and interpretation of the library.

Of the fifty-two surviving tractates (some in very fragmentary condition), six are duplicates (APOCRYPHON OF JOHN—two copies, GOSPEL OF THE EGYPTIANS (NH), EUGNOSTOS, GOSPEL OF TRUTH, ON THE ORIGIN OF THE WORLD) and six others were known prior to discovery of the Nag Hammadi library (*ApJohn*, SOPHIA OF JESUS CHRIST, PLATO'S REPUBLIC 588B-589B, PRAYER OF THANKSGIVING, ASCLEPIUS, SENTENCES OF SEXTUS). The remaining forty tractates, however, were unknown prior to the discovery. All are written in the Coptic language, the final stage of classical Egyptian whose alphabet is a mixture of uncial Greek letters and demotic (hieroglyphic) characters. Two principal dialects are represented, Sahidic and Subachmimic from southern and central Egypt, respectively. Both, however, are mixed and may represent fairly early stages of dialectical development or considerable cross-fertilization from other dialects.

A majority of these texts are Gnostic, emanating from that widespread, syncretistic religious movement first identified and vigorously combatted by Christian heresiologists and the Neoplatonists. While variations clearly exist in content, most texts in this library share some basic views: (1) a cosmic and theological DUALISM, which views the earthly world as an alien place, the production of an inferior and ignorant God, the very opposite of a heavenly, pleromatic realm of the highest, unknown God of Light and Truth; (2) an anthropomorphic dualism or tripartism, which holds that trapped within the material, human body is a "spark" or "fragment" of the highest God; (3) a Redeemer-Revealer figure, who descends from the highest God, reveals the divine nature of those willing to hear, and makes known the way of ascent and salvation; (4) a saving *gnosis* or "knowledge," which is not learned but received as a gift from the Redeemer, which enlightens the hearer regarding his/her divine nature, and which empowers the recipient to experience salvation; and (5) an ethic, which in the Nag Hammadi texts is ascetic and world-denying rather than libertine.

Some of the tractates have been identified with particular Gnostic sects described by such heresiologists as IRENAEUS Hippolytus, Epiphanius. Thus, the designation "Valentinian" has been given to the first four texts from Codex I (APOCRYPHON OF JAMES, GOSPEL OF TRUTH, TRIPARTITE TRACTATE), another from Codex II (GOSPEL OF PHILIP), and several from Codex XI (VALENTIAN EXPOSITION). Other texts in which the figure of Seth is prominent as the revealer of *gnōsis* have been attributed to "Sethianism." These include *ApJohn,* HYPOSTASIS OF THE ARCHONS, *GosEg,* APOCALYPSE OF ADAM, THREE STELES OF SETH, ZOSTRIANOS, MELCHIZEDEK (NH), THOUGHT OF NOREA, MARSANES, ALLOGENES, TRIMORPHIC PROTENNOIA. There are additional texts that cannot be clearly identified with any particular Gnostic sect, such as the collection of sayings of Jesus in the GOSPEL OF THOMAS, a striking literary parallel to the lost Q source used by the evangelists Matthew and Luke, or THUNDER, PERFECT MIND which contains self-revelations similar to those of Jesus in the Fourth Gospel.

The eclectic character of the Nag Hammadi library is attested, however, by the presence within it of writings from that non-Christian, Hellenistic, religio-philosophical movement of Egypt known as Hermeticism. These include DISCOURSE ON THE EIGHTH AND NINTH, *PrThanks,* and *Asclepius.* Surprising, too, are the occurrences of non-

Gnostic texts, such as a portion of Plato's *Republic*, the pagan wisdom collection *SentSextus*, the Christian wisdom writing excerpted in later Christian monastic literature attributed to St. Antony (TEACHINGS OF SILVANUS) and the AUTHORITATIVE TEACHING. A pervasive ascetic and mystical emphasis may account for the existence of these texts in the library, an emphasis congenial to Christian Gnostics who probably collected them.

Diverse, too, are the literary types found in the library. These include: "gospels"—*GosTruth, GosThom, GosPhil, GosEg* (all of which resemble NT APOCRYPHAL GOSPELS rather than canonical gospels); "acts"—ACTS OF PETER AND THE TWELVE APOSTLES and most of LETTER OF PETER TO PHILIP; "letters"—TREATISE ON THE RESURRECTION, EUGNOSTOS, and the introduction of *EpPetPhil* (none of which consciously imitate the Pauline letter form); "apocalypses"—APOCALYPSE OF PAUL, FIRST APOCALYPSE OF JAMES, SECOND APOCALYPSE OF JAMES, APOCALYPSE OF ADAM, APOCALYPSE OF PETER (NH) (which offer divine revelations of the future or accounts of heavenly, visionary journeys); "dialogues"—*SophJC* and DIALOGUE OF THE SAVIOR (featuring conversation between the risen Christ and his disciples); "secret books" or "apocrypha"—*ApJas* and *ApJohn* (which intermingle revelation discourse with apocalypse); "speculative cosmogonic tractates"—*OrigWorld* and *Eugnostos*; "wisdom literature"—*SentSextus* and *TeachSilv* (which resemble the canonical PROVERBS); "revelation discourses"—*TrimProt* and *Thund* (in which the divine revealer speaks in the first person); and "exegesis"—EXEGESIS ON THE SOUL (an interpretation of the soul's fate in the world).

Used pieces of papyrus glued into the leather covers of Codices I and VII to thicken and stiffen them (i.e., "cartonnage") contain place names, dates, and content helpful for reconstruction of the library's probable origins. The names include "Chenobos [keia]," site of the conversion of St. Pachomius, founder of communal monasticism in fourth century Egypt. Also, in Codex VII's cartonnage are receipts of a monk named Sansnos, overseer of monastery cattle. Further, dates among these receipts include 333, 341, 346, 348 C.E. A major Pachomian monastery was located at Chenoboskia (Monastery of St. Palamon) and a great Basilica of Pachomius existed at Pabau in this same era—both within sight of the Jabal al-Ṭārif where the discovery occurred. All this circumstantial evidence points toward the probability that some Christian monks with eclectic, Gnostic tastes collected the library in the early fourth century, probably making needed copies at the nearby monastery. (It is clear, however, that some of the tractates are much older than these fourth century copies of Greek originals.) Then, in 367 C.E. when Bishop Athanasius of Alexandria sent throughout the monasteries of the upper Nile his Festal Letter naming those twenty-seven writings in the NT CANON acceptable for Christian faith and demanding that other writings were to be destroyed, the eclectic monks of Chenoboskion probably buried their unacceptable books for safekeeping. They most likely intended to recover them when the "heat" was off!

The importance of this library lies in its (1) providing historians with firsthand information about the Gnostics' teaching, information previously available mainly from distorted and polemical writings of the church heresiologists; (2) clarifying that Gnosticism did not arise solely from within Christianity but also existed in non-Christian and even heterodox Jewish spheres as early as the late-first or early-second century; (3) illuminating the background against which the church worked out her creeds, canon, and standards for ordination; and (4) casting light on the general development of Christianity in Egypt and of the Coptic language spawned by that movement.

See also GNOSTICISM.

Bibliography. D. N. Freedman, ed., *BA* 42/4 (Fall 1979); G. MacRae, "Nag Hammadi," *IDBSup*; J. M. Robinson, "Introduction," *The Nag Hammadi Library in English* and *The Facsimile Edition of the Nag Hammadi Codices*.

—MALCOLM L. PEEL

• **Nadan.** *See* AHIQAR

• **Nahor.** [nay'hor] A name with four distinct meanings.

1. Nahor is one of the sons of Serug, a descendant of Shem, one of the sons of NOAH (Gen 11:22-25). He is also identified as the father of Terah and the grandfather of Abraham in this context.

2. Nahor apparently became a family name, used by other members of the family, for ABRAHAM's brother was also called Nahor (Gen 11:26). He married a niece, the daughter of Haran, and became the father of eight sons (Gen 11:29; 22:20-24). He also had four sons by a concubine.

3. Through his sons, this Nahor became the father of a people who were made up of twelve tribes or clans (Gen 22:20-24). The Hebrews never forgot their relationship to these tribes. These ultimately made up the Semitic tribes known as the ARAMEANS.

4. Nahor also appears to be the name of a city (Gen 24:10). It has been suggested that this was not the actual name of the city but merely descriptive of the fact that it was a city belonging to Abraham's brother. Such a view is unlikely, because Nahor is also mentioned, in ancient texts from Mari, as a city. The location of this city appears to be somewhat north or west of the biblical city by that name. It is probable that both names merely reflect the ancient heritage of the Nahor tribes in that region.

See also ARAM/ARAMEANS.

—ROBERT L. CATE

• **Nahum.** [nay'huhm] The name of the seventh-century prophet responsible for the book that bears his name. The name means "comforted," or "consoled," and probably is a shortened form of the name "Nehemiah," "The Lord has comforted." The prophet was active toward the end of the seventh century B.C.E. From the BOOK OF NAHUM one may conclude that he was a devout Yahwist, fiercely supportive of the Israelite community in its time of great danger, and skilled in laying out oracles of judgment against the foes of God's people.

See also NAHUM, BOOK OF.

—WALTER HARRELSON

• OUTLINE OF NAHUM •

The Book of Nahum

I. God's Judgment on Nineveh (1:1-10)
II. Celebration of the Fall of Nineveh (1:11–3:19)
   A. Assyria is doomed (1:11-15)
   B. Description of Nineveh's fall (2:1-13)
   C. A taunt song: woe to bloody Nineveh (3:1-19)

• **Nahum, Book of.** [nay'huhm] Standing seventh in the minor prophets, the Book of Nahum preserves the message of a prophet named Nahum, from the city of Elkosh (location unknown). Nahum's message centered on God's coming punishment of Nineveh (the capital city of the Assyrian empire) for its sin and brutality.

The prophet must have flourished after the destruction of the Egyptian city of Thebes by the Assyrians in 663 B.C.E., since 3:8 looks back on the fall of Thebes and asks Nineveh if she deserves a better fate. On the other hand, Nahum looks forward to the fall of Nineveh (unless one understands chapters two and three as prophecy after the fact), thus setting 612 (the date of the destruction of Nineveh) as the latest date. A precise date between 663–612 is not possible, but a date closer to the end than the beginning of the period seems likely. Under ESARHADDON (Assyrian ruler from 680–669) and ASHURBANIPAL (668–627) the Assyrian empire reached its greatest size, solidified by the destruction of Thebes. By the end of Ashurbanipal's lengthy reign, however, the Assyrian empire was disintegrating. MEDIA (under Cyaxares) and Babylon (under Nabopolassar) broke away from ASSYRIA and attacked her. Nahum may well have delivered his threats against Nineveh within the context of this disintegration.

The Book of Nahum opens in 1:2-9 with a hymn in the form of a partial alphabetic acrostic that runs from *aleph* to *mem* (with a slight textual emendation in v. 9). In 1:2-5 the hymn proclaims God's nature as patient, but moral, and therefore certain to punish the guilty. In 1:6-9 the hymn depicts the punishment itself. It is possible, of course, that Nahum wrote half of an acrostic as an introduction to his message, but it does not seem likely. What seems more probable is that Nahum or a later editor prefaced Nahum's messages with a hymn borrowed from somewhere else, but which prepares the reader for the messages of God's WRATH upon Nineveh that follow in chapters two and three. The intervening six verses, 1:10-15 (H 1:10–2:1), seem to represent several different perspectives, causing scholars to suggest several ways of understanding the verses. (1) Several scholars have attempted unsuccessfully to rewrite the Hebrew text and extend the acrostic even further. (2) Others find evidence of a litany offered by several different groups. (3) It is not impossible that verses originally directed against Jerusalem have been reworked (by Nahum? by someone else?) into threats against Nineveh.

The theme of the book is God's punishment, which will be directed against Assyria for its cruelty. In announcing such punishment, Nahum articulated the judgment of God upon sin and cruelty. Assyria certainly proved itself guilty of both, and Nahum was justified in condemning it. On the other hand, the tone of Nahum appears to be one of glee at Nineveh's coming destruction. Nahum is not a false prophet predicting peace when there was none (Jer 6:14), much less did he predict that which did not come true; but he was a nationalistic prophet, thundering the destruction of the enemy Assyrians.

See also ASSYRIA.

Bibliography. K. J. Cathcart, *Nahum in the Light of Northwest Semitic*; H. Schulz, *Das Buch Nahum: eine redaktionskritische Untersuchung, BZAW* 129; A. van Selms, "Alphabetic Hymn in Nahum," *Biblical Essays,* ed. A. H. van Zyl.

—PAUL L. REDDITT

• **Names.** "What's in a name?" Shakespeare has Juliet ask. Ancient Israelites would respond: "A great deal!" They would not agree with the apparent disparagement of the power of names that follows—"A rose by any other name would smell as sweet." Personal and place names from the Bible, as well as those found in material excavated throughout the biblical world, have meanings and provide compelling revelations of the sensitivities and convictions of those who gave them and possibly those who bore them. A name is often an abbreviated or brief sentence; it is common for a name to be an overtly religious expression.

In naming a child parents might express a wish (EZEKIEL = may God [*'ēl*] strengthen), a conviction (ELIJAH = my God is *Jah* [Yahweh]; DANIEL = my judge is God), a statement about this child (Elnathan = God has given), an emotion (ASHER = happy !; ISAAC = laughter—a play on SARAH's reaction to the news that in her advanced age she would bear a child). A place name might capture a special characteristic of a locale: BETHEL = house of God; JERUSALEM = foundation of salem/peace; Ramah = height; Carmel = garden/orchard. Some personal names were also plant or animal terms: JONAH = dove; DEBORAH = bee; TAMAR = palm. Some seem to suggest some quality of the bearer: NABAL = brute/fool.

Naming plays a variety of important roles in biblical narratives. Giving and listing names appears sometimes as the climax or denouement of a story. In Ruth the occasion is joyous for Ruth and her mother-in-law (Ruth 4:13-17), an important continuation of a most distinguished famous line (4:18-22). By contrast, the naming of Ichabod (1 Sam 4:19-22) by Phinehas's wife—the old priest Eli's daughter-in-law—captures the deep sense of devastating loss and endings that mark the capture of the Ark by the Philistines, the death of Eli and termination of this line, and the departure of Yahweh's glory from Israel. The tensions, conflicts and emotions of LEAH and RACHEL are effectively depicted in the naming of the children they and their maids bear (Gen 29:31–30:24). The designation of BENJAMIN as Ben-Oni (= son of my sorrow) by his mother Rachel is tragically telling (Gen 35:16-20). JOSEPH gives his two sons by his Egyptian wife names that reveal his personal perspective of his fate in a narrative that centers on the external course of his rise to power in Egypt (Gen 41:50-52).

The names of some significant figures reflect events in their lives. The name MOSES, actually based in an Egyptian verb meaning "to give birth" (Rameses = [the sun god] Ra gave birth), is explained in Exod 2:10 through a pun on the Heb. verb *māšâ,* "to pull out," reflecting the child's rescue from the Nile. Places also receive names reflecting significant events that there took place in the lives of important figures. Penuel is named through JACOB's nocturnal wrestling match there, from which he emerged with his own new name, "Israel," stating that he had seen God face to face (Gen 32:27-30; Peniel = face of God). The valley named Achor (trouble) is the locale where Achan and his family were executed, pointing up the trouble he brought on the invading Israelites when he took dedicated spoil from captured Jericho (named for the moon).

Names connote status; a change in name can mark a change in status. Jacob's change in name points up his changed affluence and psychological state as he reenters the land of promise. Many years earlier he fled ESAU ("hairy") with nothing but his staff; he now returns rich in herds and family to another confrontation with Esau. The change in the condition of ABRAHAM's wife is testified by the change in form of her name from Sarai to Sarah, which is accompanied by this notice from God: "I will bless her and she shall be a mother of nations; kings of peoples shall come from her" (Gen 17:16). As early Jews found themselves dispersed among the nations and living in the two worlds of the Jewish community and a larger foreign environment, some came to have two names, one denoting their ethnic religious identity and one their lives in the larger Persian, Greek, or Roman world. Daniel and his colleagues had both Jewish and gentile names (Dan 1:6-7), as does ESTHER (= the Babylonian deity Ishtar), known also as Hadassah (Esth 2:7), and as later would PAUL/Saul. Jesus is a hellenized form of the Jewish JOSHUA (Yahweh saves).

Biblical names often reveal religious sensitivities and may even allow one to tap into more popular patterns of ancient Israelite and early Jewish and Christian religious perspective. Many names have a shortened form of Yahweh, the proper name of Israel's deity. This appears as *Ja-/Jeho-* or *-iah/-jah* (the Y of Yahweh becomes J in English transcriptions of names). Others were composed with the words *'ēl* or *baal,* both of which can be ambiguous, for *'ēl* can simply mean "God" and refer to Yahweh or it can be the name of the high god of Canaan's pantheon, while *baal* is both the name of the popular Canaanite storm god of fertility and also means "lord/master/owner" and might be a title of Yahweh (some scribes were so sensitive to the pagan possibilities in *baal* that they altered names in which it appears, for example, with the word *bosheth*, meaning "shame;" thus SAUL's fourth son is named Ishbaal in 1 Chr 8:33 and 9:39, but is called ISHBOSHETH in 2 Sam 3:14-15). It is most striking that in spite of regular prophetic denunciation of their people's propensity for other deities, a large majority of Hebrew names with a divine element contain a form of Yahweh, while there are remarkably few that clearly use the name of another god. The many names on epigraphic material uncovered by archaeologists are in line with biblical evidence. Whatever attraction other deities had—and clearly they exerted some—did not spill over into the naming and religious sensitivities reflected in this very human activity.

A wide range of qualities of the deity finds expression in biblical names. Yahweh saves (Joshua), is exalted (Adoniram), is good (Tobiah), remembers (Zechariah), is righteous (Zedekiah), blesses (Berechiah), loves (Jedidiah), is mighty (Amaziah), judges (Daniel), hears (Shemaiah), builds (Benaiah), is a father (Abiel) or a brother (Ahiah), is strong (Uzziah), and cannot be compared to anyone or anything (Micaiah/Micah/Michal/Michael). The list could go on and on through most of the religious and theological themes of the Hebraic tradition.

The privilege to give names is the power to define the named and is an expression of authority. ADAM (whose name means "human being") is depicted in Gen 2:19-20 naming all other creatures formed by the deity: an effective expression of human lordship over creation. It must be noted that a perspective that views man as authority over woman is a condition of the fallen order and not the ideal in God's creation (in 2:23 Adam does not name woman but describes her and the essential link between man and woman). On another level, God's protective lordship is especially directed to Israel as he engraves its name on the palm of his hand (Isa 49:16). Finally, it must be noted that the deity makes his name Yahweh known to Moses, but only in a context that underscores divine freedom from any manipulation of that name to control him by mortals: "I am who I am."

See also GOD, NAMES OF.

—W. LEE HUMPHREYS

• **Naomi.** [nay-oh'mee] The mother-in-law of Ruth. The name means "my pleasantness," "my grace," "my joy." Naomi is mentioned only in the BOOK OF RUTH, where she sometimes overshadows Ruth. During the period of the Judges, Naomi leaves BETHLEHEM during a time of famine, with her husband Elimelech and their two sons. They settle in MOAB, where the sons marry. Elimelech and both sons die, leaving Naomi a childless widow and Elimelech without heir. Naomi decides to return home. Her daughters-in-law begin the trip with her. Three times Naomi tells them to return to Moab, but Ruth insists on accompanying her. Arriving in Bethlehem, Naomi expresses her bitterness and emptiness. Ruth goes to the fields to glean. She happens upon the field of Boaz, a distant relative of Elimelech, who is kind to her. Naomi devises a bold, dangerous plan. As a result, Boaz redeems the property of Elimelech and marries Ruth. Their son, Obed, is the grandfather of David.

Naomi perceives herself to be full when she leaves Bethlehem (despite the famine) and empty when she returns (1:21). As a woman in a male-dominated environment, the loss of her husband and sons deprives her of her social status and identity. Upon her return, she tells the women to call her Mara (bitterness) rather than Naomi. From this point, however, her bitterness recedes and she and Ruth take responsibility for their own lives and for each other, until their plan succeeds.

There is a close identification between Naomi and Ruth in the story. Ruth's identification with her mother-in-law is made clear in her vow (1:16-17), in which she promises to go wherever Naomi goes, live where she lives, worship her God, die where she dies and be buried there. This is matched by the declaration of the women of the neighborhood, who say of Obed, "A son has been born for Naomi." Naomi "nurses" the child (4:16), probably a poetic way of expressing grandmotherly care. If the reader is to think of the practice of levirate marriage, Ruth is seen as a stand-in for Naomi.

Naomi and Ruth alternate as central character in the story. They represent older and younger generations, native Israelite and foreigner. In some Jewish traditions, Naomi is said allegorically to represent the Jewish people when God's face is hidden from them, whereas Ruth represents the Jewish people pledged to renewed fidelity to God. If, as some suggest, the purpose of the book was to encourage Jews to return from exile, Naomi serves as a model and encouragement to those who are undecided. If an aging widow (and young foreign widow) can return and find blessing, all exiles should return!

Theologically, Naomi appears to accept the view that whatever happens, whether suffering or blessing, is from the hand of God (1:8-9, 14, 20-21; 2:19).

Many modern commentators consider the Book of Ruth to be a short story. This does not exclude the possibility that the characters, including Naomi, were real people or that the story was based on a historical incident. Such questions remain open.

See also MARRIAGE IN THE OLD TESTAMENT; RUTH, BOOK OF.

Bibliography. E. E. Campbell, Jr., *Ruth. A New Translation with Introduction and Commentary*; H. Chertok, "The Book of Ruth—Complexities Within Simplicity," *Judm* 35:3 (1986): 290-97; J. M. Sasson, *Ruth*; P. Trible, "A Human Comedy," *God and the Rhetoric of Sexuality*.

—WILDA W. (WENDY) MORRIS

• **Naphtali.** [naf'tuh-*li*] The sixth son of JACOB, the second son of Bilhah, RACHEL's maid (cf. Gen 30:7-8).

The story of the birth of Jacob's sons is told in Gen

29:31–30:24. Rachel had remained childless, while her sister Leah had borne four sons. In desperation, Rachel gave her maid to Jacob, planning to adopt Bilhah's children as her own. When Naphtali was born, Rachel said that she had fought (*naptûlē*) with her sister, thus deriving the name Naphtali.

The tribe Naphtali was the subject of two blessings in the Pentateuch. Stanley Gevirtz has reconstructed the textually difficult Gen 49:21 as a taunt for Naphtali's future fall from freedom to political subservience and translates: "Naphtali a mountain-ewe was born, who gives (birth to) lambs of the fold." Deut 33:23 spoke of the territory the tribe was to inherit, and may have emphasized that the Sea of Galilee belonged to Naphtali. In the wilderness the size of the tribe was listed first as 53,400 soldiers (Num 1:43) and then at 45,400 (Num 26:50). Naphtali pitched camp north of the Tabernacle and marched at the rear of the company. In Josh 19:32-39 Naphtali was allotted land lying south of Mount Lebanon, west of the Jordan and the Sea of Galilee, in the hill country east of Asher (PLATE 11). It was bounded on the south at the tip of the Sea by Issachar and to the southeast by Zebulun.

In the premonarchical period Naphtali answered two calls to battle. In Judg 4 Naphtali, accompanied by Zebulun, answered the call of its native son BARAK to wage war against Sisera, general of Jabin's army. In the song of Deborah (Judg 5:18) Naphtali was mentioned as faithful and heroic, but the tribe's role seems rather diminished in Judg 5 as opposed to Judg 4. In the GIDEON story Naphtali, along with Manasseh, Asher and Zebulun, responded (Judg 7:23) to Gideon's call to battle (Judg 6:35). Neither of these accounts reflects a second-class status for Naphtali as a tribe, though the story of the birth of Naphtali to a concubine instead of a full wife might suggest less importance for Naphtali than for the tribes said to descend from the full wives Leah (Reuben, Simeon, Levi, Judah, Issachar and Zebulun) and Rachel (Joseph and Benjamin).

Naphtali receives little mention in the monarchical period. According to 1 Chr 12:34, 40, Naphtali participated in electing David by sending troops and food. 1 Kgs 4:15 lists Ahimaaz as the officer over Naphtali under Solomon's redistricting program. Solomon also employed Hiram of Tyre (1 Kgs 7:13-14), whose mother came from Naphtali, to fashion the bronze work on the Temple. Further, Naphtali (along with Dan) was attacked by Ben-hadad of Damascus during a battle between Israel and Judah during the early years of the divided monarchy in the reigns of Asa, king of Judah (913–873), and Baasha, king of Israel (900–877; cf. 2 Chr 16:4; Isa 9:1). Second Kgs 15:29 records the sacking of Naphtali, along with Gilead and Galilee, by Tiglath-Pileser III (Assyrian emperor, 745–727), in 733–732, during the aftermath of the insurrection of Israel and Aram against Assyria.

See also TRIBES.

Bibliography. C. H. J. de Geus, *The Tribes of Israel*; S. Gevirtz, "Naphtali in the 'Blessing of Jacob'," *JBL* 103/4 (Dec 1984): 513-21; M. Noth, *The History of Israel*.

—PAUL L. REDDITT

• **Narrative.** *See* LITERATURE, BIBLE AS; NEW TESTAMENT AS LITERATURE

• **Nathan.** [nay'thuhn] Heb. *nātān,* "He [God] has given"; the name of a prophet associated with the courts of DAVID and SOLOMON .

Nathan does not fit the pattern of the charismatic prophets seen in SAMUEL, ELIJAH, and the sons of the prophets. He was related to the political life of the monarchy and seems to have been part of the government. He appears for the first time in 2 Sam 7. Nothing is said about his origin or how he became attached to David's court. Some scholars have associated him with the original Jebusite population of Jerusalem, while others associate him with the Ephraimite prophetic traditions of the northern tribes. According to 1 Chr 29:29 and 2 Chr 9:29, he wrote the chronicles of the reigns of David and Solomon, which indicates that the traditions of ISRAEL associated him with the collections of old tribal materials that form the basis of the stories of David. Nathan is also said to have been involved in the development of music in the worship of Israel (2 Chr 29:25).

When David proposed to build a TEMPLE for God in Jerusalem, Nathan first approved, but then after receiving a divine revelation he rejected David's request (2 Sam 7:1-17). According to Nathan, David was not to build the temple, but a son who would succeed David on the throne would build a temple for God while God would build a dynasty for David. This prophecy of Nathan, which promises the establishment of an everlasting dynasty for David, became the focus of messianic hope for the postexilic community.

Nathan also played an important part in the events following David's affair with BATHSHEBA and the death of Uriah, her husband (2 Sam 11). Nathan confronted the king by relating a story in which a poor man's only lamb was taken away by a rich man. When David declared that the rich man should die, Nathan accused David of being guilty of murder (2 Sam 12:1-25). Jewish tradition has preserved the memory of this event in the title of Ps 51. Later, when Bathsheba conceived a son by David, she called his name Solomon, but Nathan called him Jedidiah, "Beloved of Yahweh" (2 Sam 12:25). This event demonstrates the prophetic influence in Israel: the prophets could confront the kings for their crimes and make them responsible to the laws of Israel.

In the struggle between ADONIJAH and Solomon for the succession of David's throne, Nathan took Solomon's side, while Adonijah had the support of Joab the commander of the army, of Abiathar the priest (1 Kgs 1:7), and of the royal officials of Judah (1 Kgs 1:9). Solomon also was supported by ZADOK the priest, BENAIAH the commander of the mercenary army, and David's mighty men (1 Kgs 1:8). When Adonijah was crowned king by his supporters, Nathan advised Bathsheba how to approach David when she asked the king to fulfill his promise to choose Solomon as his successor. When his plan succeeded, Nathan and Zadok, by command of David, anointed Solomon as the new king over Israel (1 Kgs 1:5-48).

Other biblical characters named Nathan were: (1) David's third son, born in Jerusalem (2 Sam 5:14; 1 Chr 14:4). His descendants are mentioned as joining in lamentation on the Day of Yahweh (Zech 12:12). He is also listed in the genealogy of Jesus (Luke 3:31); (2) a man from Zobah, the father of Igal. Igal is listed as one of the thirty mighty men of David (2 Sam 23:36); (3) the brother of Joel, one of the officers in David's army (1 Chr 11:38); (4) the father of Azariah, the chief of the district prefects under Solomon (1 Kgs 4:5). This Nathan sometimes is identified with Nathan the prophet; (5) the father of Zabud, who served as King's Friend under Solomon (1 Kgs 4:5). This Nathan is listed as the son of an Egyptian slave (1 Chr 2:34-36); and (6) a man who returned from the Exile in Babylon. He promised to divorce his wife because she was not a Jew

(Ezra 10:39).

See also BATHSHEBA; DAVID; PARABLES; PROPHECY; PROPHET; SOLOMON.

Bibliography. J. Lindblom, *Prophecy in Ancient Israel*; R. R. Wilson, *Prophecy and Society in Ancient Israel*.

—CLAUDE F. MARIOTTINI

• **Nation/Nations.** *See* GENTILE/GENTILES IN THE NEW TESTAMENT; GENTILE/GENTILES IN THE OLD TESTAMENT; PEOPLE/PEOPLES

• **Nationalistic Prophecy.** *See* NAHUM, BOOK OF

• **Natufian Culture.** [nah-toof'yan] Natufian is the term used to describe a people and culture of ancient Palestine during the Mesolithic or Epipaleolithic Age from about 10000 to 8000 B.C.E. The name is derived from the Wadi en-Natuf, one of the sources of the Yarkon River located about nine mi. northeast of Lod. The same culture has been discovered at other sites in Palestine including the MOUNT CARMEL caves, 'Eynan, Kebara, Naḥal Oren, Wadi Kharaitun, and Yonin Cave.

The Natufian culture is noted for its fine microlithic TOOLS and its movement toward food production and permanent settlement. The Natufians inhabited both caves and open-air sites, often occupying the same site continuously for long periods of time. The site of 'Eynan at the shore of the former Lake Huleh had circular stone huts with stone basements. These huts ranged from sixteen to thiry ft. in diameter and several had hearths, grindstones, and mortars and pestles remaining in place. The large quantity and size of the utensils suggests a transition to agriculture. Evidence from other Natufian sties suggests a concomitant move toward the domestication of animals, especially gazelles and goats. Tools were made of stone and bone, and include sickle hafts, awls, points, fishhooks, barbed harpoons, borers, gravers, scrapers, needles, and arrowheads. Larger tools included axes, adzes, and picks, probably for agricultural use.

The Natufian culture has also provided a number of artistic works, primarily small sculptures of animal and human forms. The sculpture often decorated tools, especially sickle hafts, and may have had a magical purpose. Human figurines especially represented fertility motifs. Other art work had decorative and geometric patterns.

The Natufians carefully buried their dead. A relatively large number of Natufian burials has been located, perhaps because they buried their dead within the caves or settlements where they lived, and they continued to use the same settlement for a long period. In most burials the individual was placed in a contracted or fetal position. Grave goods included pendants, necklaces, headdresses, and anklets. From a similar time period, the Shanidar cave in northern Iraq has the earliest evidence of flowers being buried with a body. The presence of such items suggests the concern for a proper burial, and the accompaniment of personal items with burial. A number of collective burial sites have been located, including several with megalithic monuments. The purpose of these sites has been disputed, since some of the remains show evidence of beheading.

Bibliography. E. Anati, *Palestine Before the Hebrews*; D. A. E. Garrod and D. M. A. Bate, *The Stone Age of Mount Carmel*.

—JOEL F. DRINKARD, JR.

• **Nazareans, Gospel of the.** [naz'uh-reenz] The *Gospel of the Nazareans* is an apocryphal Jewish-Christian gospel known through fragments given by the church fathers, particularly Jerome. This gospel was the product of a group called either the Nazoreans, Nazareans, Nasoreans, or Nasareans, a name used of Jesus (Matt 2:23) and of early Christians (Acts 24:5). It is uncertain whether this group was an orthodox offshoot of Christendom or a heretical group.

Their gospel was reported to be an Aramaic version of MATTHEW's Gospel. Both IRENAEUS (*AdvHaer* 3.1.1) and EUSEBIUS (*EccHist* 3.24.6 and 5.8.2) speak of an original Aramaic version of Matthew. Whether these were identical is unclear.

The church fathers also speak of a GOSPEL OF THE HEBREWS and a GOSPEL OF THE EBIONITES. How these relate to the *Gospel of the Nazareans* is also quite difficult to judge. At present, most scholars view these as three distinct gospels, the *Gospel of the Nazareans* being viewed as a Hebrew/Aramaic targum of Matthew's Gospel. Fragments of this gospel do not reveal heretical tendencies, but provide interesting variants to the text of Matthew: Matt 6:11—"Give us this day our bread of tomorrow"; Matt 7:21—"If you are in my bosom and do not the will of my father in heaven, I will cast you out of my bosom"; Matt 12:13—The man with the withered hand was a mason who wanted to be healed so that he could resume work; Matt 19:16ff.—one of two rich men was told by Jesus to sell all and give to the poor. The man began to scratch his head because Jesus' words did not please him; Matt 27:51—At Jesus' crucifixion the veil of the temple did not split but the lintel of the temple collapsed.

See also APOCRYPHAL GOSPELS.

Bibliography. A. F. J. Klijn and G. J. Reinink, *Patristic Evidence for Jewish-Christian Sects, NovTSupp* 36; P. Vielhauer, "Jewish-Christian Gospels," *New Testament Apocrypha*, ed. E. Hennecke and W. Schneemelcher.

—GLENN A. KOCH

• **Nazareth.** [naz'uh-rith] Nazareth (PLATE 23) lies about fifteen mi. west of the southern tip of the Sea of Galilee and twenty mi. east of the Mediterranean Sea. Rising about 1,300 ft. above sea level, it is situated on the northern ridge above the JEZREEL valley and just west of MOUNT TABOR. Because of its isolation from economic centers and trade routes during JESUS' day, the village of Nazareth did not participate in the major rhythms of Galilean commerce. Its marginality probably contributed to the apparent disdain for the village expressed in Nathanael's response to Philip, "Can anything good come out of Nazareth?" (John 1:46). Its small size perhaps influenced Jesus to focus his ministry in Galilee in villages and hamlets such as Capernaum, Bethsaida, and Chorizon.

The origin of Nazareth cannot be precisely determined. Archaeological digs have found no evidence for the existence of a community at Nazareth during the centuries preceding the birth of Jesus. In addition, ancient Jewish texts make no mention of Nazareth. The earliest record of Nazareth is found in the Gospels and Acts, and the first non-Christian reference dates from approximately 170 C.E. The name "Nazareth," however, probably means "guard-place," which suggests that it was established as an outpost for one of the cities, perhaps Sepphoris, along trade routes to the north.

At the beginning of his Gospel, Mark indicates that Jesus had left Nazareth in order to be baptized by John the Baptist in the Jordan River. According to the Gospel of Luke,

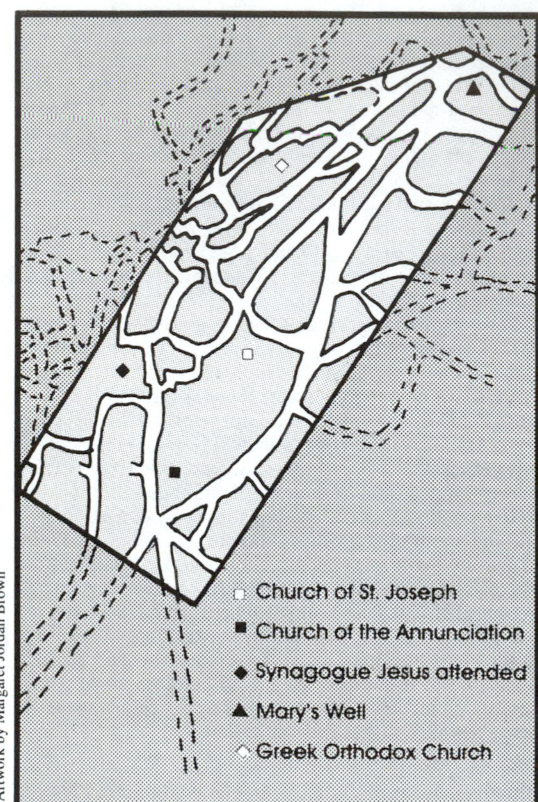

Artist's conception of ancient Nazareth.

the angel Gabriel went to Nazareth, the home of JOSEPH and MARY, to announce the forthcoming birth of Jesus (Luke 1:26). Subsequently, Luke identifies Nazareth as the place to which Mary, Joseph, and Jesus returned after his birth in Bethlehem and as the place where Jesus grew up (Luke 2:39ff.; cf. Matt 2:23).

Luke's emphasis on the home of Jesus as Nazareth—the isolated outpost—reinforces his theme of Jesus ministering primarily to the outcasts of Jewish society. Only Luke (4:16) specifies that as an adult Jesus returned to Nazareth; parallel passages in Matthew (13:54) and Mark (6:1) tell of Jesus returning to his "own country." Luke indicates that the return occurred at the outset of Jesus' ministry, while Mark and Matthew suggest that it took place just before the death of John the Baptist. The evangelists agree that on that occasion Jesus went to the synagogue on the sabbath and read from the prophet Isaiah about the Lord anointing the chosen servant to preach good news to the poor, to proclaim the release of captives, and to set the oppressed free (cf. Isa 61:1). After identifying himself with the anointed servant, Jesus angered the crowd by praising former prophets' ministries to foreigners. Threatened by the crowd, Jesus departed from Nazareth and never returned to his home town.

See also JESUS; JOSEPH; MARY; SEPPHORIS.

Bibliography. G. Bornkamm, *Jesus of Nazareth*; J. F. Strange, "Diversity in Early Palestinian Christianity: Some Archeological Evidences," *ATR* 65 (Jan 1983): 14-24.

—JOSEPH L. PRICE

• **Nazirites.** [naz'uh-rits] A religious group noted for its steadfast allegiance to Yahweh. The Heb. verb root (*nzr*) means to dedicate, or to consecrate. The noun identified one who was separated. The term also was related to the Hebrew verb (*ndr*), to vow. The role of a Nazirite was assumed by making specific vows of separation and abstinence.

The origins of the Nazirites is obscure. In the ancient world most religions had devotees. Baal worship in Canaan had both male and female adherents who served as cult prostitutes. They were constant threats to Yahweh worship. The Nazirite movement was an effort to resist such Canaanization of Yahweh worship.

In Num 6:1-21 Moses regulated the solemnization of the Nazirite vows. Although only Levites could serve at Yahweh's altar, certain members of other tribes deeply desired to be devoted to Yahweh. Such persons, male and female, could fulfill that desire as Nazirites.

Nazirites willingly assumed three vows of abstinence. First, they totally abstained from alcoholic drink. This was a costly vow to one who lived where drinking water was unsafe and diluted wine was the normal drink. The Nazirite rejected all products coming from a vineyard.

Second, Nazirites abstained from cutting their hair. The hair was considered to be an expression of the person's life as was his or her blood. Long hair was a visual symbol and reminder that the Nazirite was holy (Num 6:5), separated to God.

Third, Nazirites were to avoid any defiling contact with the dead. To do so annulled the vow. When contact occurred, Nazirites had to go through a seven-day cleansing period, shave their hair, and begin their vows anew.

These vows usually were self-assumed. In the case of SAMSON (Judg 13:5) and SAMUEL (1 Sam 1:11), they were made by one's parents. In such cases, however, the individual doubtless agreed to such vows at some later point. The length of the vows varied from some stated period to the whole of one's lifetime. While some assumed the obligations for life, most undoubtedly made them for a relatively brief period. The completion of the vow was to be marked by a detailed religious ceremony.

JOHN THE BAPTIST's lifestyle has led some interpreters to identify him as a Nazirite, but the evidence is far from conclusive. PAUL's vow (Acts 18:18; 21:26), which was concluded by cutting his hair at the Temple, was doubtless the completion of a Nazirite vow. According to Eusebius, JAMES, the Lord's brother, was remembered as a Nazirite. Such persons by their lives served to call others to a deeper commitment to the Lord.

See also HOLINESS IN THE NEW TESTAMENT; HOLINESS IN THE OLD TESTAMENT; SAMSON.

Bibliography. W. Eichrodt, *Theology of the Old Testament*; R. K. Harrison, *ISBE*; R. de Vaux, *Ancient Israel: Religious Institutions*.

—JERRY WALLACE LEE

• **Neapolis.** [nee-ap'uh-lis] Located ten mi. from PHILIPPI on the north coast of the Aegean Sea (PLATES 26, 27), Neapolis was the city from which Paul disembarked on his second missionary journey to begin his mission work in Europe after having the vision of the Macedonian (Acts 16:11). He probably went through it again on his third missionary journey (Acts 20:1), and left from there on his last voyage to Troas (Acts 20:6).

From its founding in the seventh century B.C.E., the city was known as Neapolis—new city. Located on a promontory, it had harbors on both sides, giving it a strategic location adjacent to the ancient coast road joining Asia and Europe. From 350 B.C.E. Philip of Macedonia had used it as a harbor for Philippi, and in 42 B.C.E. Brutus and Cassius had used the harbor as a base in the battle of Philippi with Octavian and Antony.

At the time of Paul's visits, Neapolis was part of the Roman province of MACEDONIA, dependent on Philippi, and the residence of some of its leading citizens. The gospel had early success there, causing the city later to be renamed Christopolis.

Today it is the modern town of Kavalla. There remain ruins of the ancient city wall, a temple of the city's patron goddess Parthenos, and an aqueduct that is probably of Roman origin. Behind the Greek Orthodox Church of St. Paul near the seashore, a stone supposedly marks the place where Paul first set foot on the continent of Europe.

See also MACEDONIA; PHILIPPI.

Bibliography. J. Finegan, *The Archeology of the New Testament: The Mediterranean World of the Early Christian Apostles* and "Neapolis," *IDB*; H. F. Vos, "Neapolis," *ISBE*.

—G. THOMAS HALBROOKS

• **Nebuchadrezzar.** [neb'uh-kuh-drez″uhr] Also known as Nebuchadnezzar, Nabuchodonosar, or Nabuchodonosor, Nebuchadrezzar was king of BABYLONIA for forty-three years, 605–562 B.C.E. (the name has been standardized to "Nebuchadnezzar" in most English translations but "Nebuchadrezzar" is the form truest to the original). He was the son of Nabopolassar and the father of Amel-Marduk (the "Evil-Merodach" of the OT, 2 Kgs 25:27; Jer 52:31). His name in neo-Babylonian—Nabu-kudurri-uṣur—means either "(may the god) Nabu protect my boundary stone" or "O Nabu protect my offspring." Nebuchadrezzar's name is mentioned ninety-one times in the OT.

His first campaign into Syria-Palestine, including Judah, came in 605 B.C.E. while he was still only crown prince in charge of one of his father's armies. After defeating the Egyptians at Carchemish on the Euphrates River and at Hamath on the Orontes River, Nebuchadrezzar pursued them all the way back to the border of Egypt (cf. Jer 46:2ff.). By this move, Nebuchadrezzar wrested control of Syria and Palestine from Egypt (cf. 2 Kgs 24:7). He was able to hold Syria but Palestine largely remained a no-man's land between Babylonian controlled Syria and Egypt.

During Nebuchadrezzar's campaign into Palestine, King Jehoiakim of Judah was very willing to accept his sovereignty, but rebelled only three years later (2 Kgs 24:1–2). Nebuchadrezzar made campaigns into Palestine the next few years to recapture vassals such as Ashkelon (604 B.C.E.) who were trying to revolt, probably under the prompting of Egypt. In December of 601, both he and the Egyptian Pharaoh Hophra suffered numerous casualties in battle but it was the Babylonian army that was forced to return home in order to regroup and reequip for a year and one-half. Egyptian Pharaoh Hophra recaptured Gaza and continued to pressure Judah to revolt. Nebuchadrezzar conducted a thirteen year siege of Tyre from either 598/7 to 585/4 B.C.E. or 588/7 to 573 B.C.E. (Ezek 26:7ff.; 29:18).

According to the historian Josephus, Jehoiakim of Judah did pay tribute to Nebuchadrezzar when he appeared with a newly strengthened army in 599. Jehoiakim revolted from Babylon in late 598, died in December (perhaps a political assassination) and was succeeded by his son Jehoiachin (this seems to be the case although there is difficulty reconciling it with Dan 1:1-2 which says that Jehoiakim rather than Jehoiachin was the one taken prisoner first by Nebuchadrezzar). By this time, Nebuchadrezzar was already on his way from Babylon to suppress the revolt. Jerusalem was taken in March of 597 after a short siege. Jehoiachin was replaced by his uncle Mattaniah (whose name was changed to Zedekiah). Jehoiachin, his family, and state and military officials totalling 3,000 people were taken captive to Babylon according to the Babylonian Chronicle (Jer 22:25; 24:1; 29:1-2; Dan 1:18; 2–4). The OT adds 1,000 craftsmen and 7,000 soldiers to the total taken away. Heavy tribute was also levied: parts of Solomon's Temple and palace were carried off as booty (2 Kgs 24:10-17; 2 Chr 36:7, 10; Ezra 1:7; 2:1; 5:14; 6:5; 7:6; Esth 2:6; Jer 28:3ff.; Dan 1:2; 5:2ff.).

Nebuchadrezzar suppressed a revolt in Babylonia in 595 B.C.E. It is possible that Jews were involved in this and that it provides the background for Jeremiah's prophecy in 29:21-22. The Babylonian Chronicle records at least one military campaign for virtually every one of Nebuchadrezzar's first eleven years on the throne. Unfortunately, the Chronicle is not extant for the last thirty-three years of his reign.

Though Zedekiah had sworn by God to be loyal to Nebuchadrezzar, he rebelled against him and the final assault on Jerusalem began in January of 588 B.C.E. (Jer 21:2, 7; 32:1–2; 34:1; 37:1ff.). Though Zedekiah appealed to Egypt for help, it apparently made only a half-hearted effort which did no more than draw away a few troops from the siege of Jerusalem. The Babylonians destroyed the Temple in August of 587 and took the city one month later, destroying it (2 Kgs 24:17–25:21; 2 Chr 36:18-21; Jer 39:1-14).

The attempt was made to designate a province of Judah under a governor named Gedaliah with support from the prophet Jeremiah. Gedaliah was slain and Jeremiah was carried off by the fearful Jews to Egypt (Jer 43–44). Shortly thereafter, in 581, Nebuzaradan—commander of the Babylonian imperial guard—arrived in Judah, carried away another 745 captives, and annexed Judah to the province of Samaria (2 Kgs 25:22–26; Jer 52).

Nebuchadrezzar was seen as the instrument of God to punish Judah in numerous OT passages (1 Chr 6:15; 2 Chr 36:17; Ezra 5:12; Jer 25:9 and 27:6, where he is called "my servant"), but later he or his descendants were to be punished for what they had done to Judah (Jer 50:17-18; 51:34-35).

Despite his military campaigns, Babylonian royal inscriptions show Nebuchadrezzar in remarkably few warlike stances. He strove to be known as a just king and his moral qualities were emphasized. He claimed a divine vocation (cf. Jer 1:4) as did most kings. Also, he claimed to be a reformer, redressing the rights of the poor against the abusive rich and attempting to do away with the practice of bribery.

Bibliography. Y. Aharoni and M. Avi-Yonah, *The Macmillan Bible Atlas*; A. L. Oppenheim, "Nebuchadrezzar," *IDB*; D. J. Wiseman, *Chronicles of Chaldean Kings* and *Nebuchadrezzar and Babylon*.

—TIMOTHY G. CRAWFORD

• **Necho.** [nee'koh] Necho II was pharaoh of Egypt from ca. 610–595 B.C.E. during the twenty-sixth dynasty. His reign marked a period of Egyptian expansion into Syria-Palestine begun by his father Psammeticus I (ca. 664–610 B.C.E.).

Necho is best known as the Egyptian pharaoh who killed

the Judean king JOSIAH at MEGIDDO in 609 B.C.E. (2 Kgs 23:9). Necho was advancing through Syria-Palestine to aid the remnant of the Assyrian army against the Babylonians. The Assyrian capital of Nineveh had fallen to the Babylonians three years previously in 612 B.C.E. Yet portions of the Assyrian army had continued to fight against the Babylonians from the Upper Euphrates area. At first glimpse it seems surprising that an Egyptian would come to aid the Assyrians, for only about fifty years earlier an Assyrian army under ASSHURBANIPAL had invaded Egypt, reached and sacked Thebes, the capital. But now Assyrian power was broken. Apparently Necho was seeking to assert Egyptian control over Syria-Palestine and hoped that supporting a weak Assyrian army might produce a buffer area between Babylon and Syria-Palestine in the Upper Euphrates.

Josiah, knowing he was seriously outnumbered, set his forces in the pass at Megiddo to prevent Necho's passage north. No threat from Necho is mentioned in the text of 2 Kings. Second Chronicles even states that Necho tried to dissuade Josiah from pursuing the battle, stating that he had no quarrel with Judah (2 Chr 35:20-24). Perhaps Josiah was asserting Judean independence, or perhaps he was supporting Babylon, or perhaps he realized if Necho was successful, Egypt would make Judah a vassal anyway. In any case, Josiah determined the time and place of the battle. Josiah was killed in the battle, and Necho marched on northward.

Necho's battle with Babylon was inconclusive. But on his march back southward through Judah, Necho removed Josiah's successor Jehoahaz, took him as prisoner to Egypt, and placed Jehoiakim on the throne (2 Kgs 23:33-34). Jehoiakim was required to pay heavy tribute to Egypt (2 Kgs 23:35). Necho again fought Babylon in 605 B.C.E. at Carchemish and was decisively defeated. Syria-Palestine then came under Babylonian control.

Necho was able to mount a major expedition to Nubia and to halt a Babylonian incursion into Egypt in 601–600 B.C.E. He apparently engaged in much trade along the coasts of the Red Sea, and, according to Herodotus, sent ships to circumnavigate Africa. He also began a canal along the Wadi Tumilat to link the Nile with the Red Sea.

—JOEL F. DRINKARD, JR.

• **Negeb.** [neg'eb] The word Negeb in its modern usage indicates all of the Southern part of the state of Israel. Roughly, this territory is triangular in form, one side the north-south line along the Wadi el-Arabah from the DEAD SEA to Elat on the Gulf of Aqaba, one side the line between Elat and the proximity of Gaza, and the third side a less than definite line from Gaza just north of BEERSHEBA to the Dead Sea (PLATES 1, 4, 43). Because this section of western Palestine lies south of the hill country, the word Negeb in the OT sometimes simply means south instead of referring to a certain area. Abram is said in Gen 12:9 to have journeyed "toward the Negeb" (RSV "the South" in KJV, cf. 13:14; 28:14). This same connotation is intended when the word refers to the southern side of the Tabernacle (Exod 26:18; 36:23) or to the south side of a city (Num 34:5) or valley (Josh 15:7).

Some usages of the word in the OT, however, refer to a clearly defined region in Judah (Josh 15:21-32). The inheritance of Simeon is located in this region (Josh 19:1-9). There are OT references to the Negeb of the Jerahmeelites and of the Kenites (1 Sam 27:10) and to the Negeb of the Cherethites and of Caleb (1 Sam 30:14). All of these areas belong to the same general region later included within the kingdom of Judah. The "watercourses of the Negeb" (Ps 126:4) almost certainly refers to this more restricted Negeb of Judah, as does Jeremiah's term "cities of the Negeb" (13:19; 32:44; 33:13; cf. Obad 19-20). Rather than being desert, this area is relatively well-watered, suitable for both agriculture and grazing. The territory south of Beersheba, however, in what today is normally called the Negeb, becomes more and more desert-like, making farming without irrigation impossible. The southernmost parts are called *midbar,* "wilderness, desert," in the OT.

In the Negeb proper the dry climate posed a serious obstacle to sedentary occupation, allowing it to flourish for rather short periods of time. These periods of occupation reoccurred about once each 1,000 years—the first in the transitional period between the Chalcolithic and Early Bronze Ages (ca. 3000 B.C.E.), the second near the beginning of the Middle Bronze Age (ca. 2100 B.C.E.), and the third in the period of the Hebrew monarchy (ca. 1000 B.C.E. onward). Fortunately for archaeologists, the dry climate, the rather intermittent human occupation, and the remoteness of the ruins have made them best preserved from their periods in Palestine. Also, a good deal of inscribed material, so rare in Palestine, has been recovered there. The excavations of the city of ARAD have been the most significant in the area.

Bibliography. Y. Aharoni, "The Negeb," *Archaeology and Old Testament Study,* ed. D. W. Thomas; D. Baly, *The Geography of the Bible.*

—KAREN RANDOLPH JOINES

• **Nehemiah.** [nee'huh-mi''uh] Nehemiah was a Jew who was a cupbearer, a very important official, to the Persian king ARTAXERXES I. The cupbearer's close association with the royal household probably required that he be a eunuch. If so this would have put Nehemiah at a disadvantage as a leader of Jews who excluded all impaired or defective persons from participation in the religious congregation (cf. Deut 23:1). Nehemiah's great success in spite of this disadvantage is a credit to his exceptional abilities as a military, political, and religious leader, to his prophetic sense of social justice, and to his personal goodness and kindness. He was a strategic leader in the restoration of Jewish life in Judah after the Babylonian Exile.

At his own request, but with obvious advantages to the Persians, Nehemiah was sent to the postexilic community in Judah as governor with authority to fortify Jerusalem and to correct political, cultic, and social practices that were weakening the province of Judah. For Persia his success would strengthen a weak point on its western frontier. For the Jews it meant the strengthening and purification of Jerusalem as a sacred city. The Temple had been rebuilt and, if some of EZRA's work preceded Nehemiah's, significant cultic reforms were under way. Jerusalem,however, was still unfortified and was sparsely populated. Nehemiah's first work was to organize and direct the rebuilding of the city wall. This activity was opposed and threatened by local leaders led by Sanballat of Samaria and Tobiah of Ammon. Therefore, Nehemiah also organized and directed the defense of the people who were repairing the walls. Neither ridicule (Neh 4:1-6), false accusations to the Persians (6:1-14), nor clandestine threats and attacks (Neh 4:10-23) prevented the successful completion of this work. When it was finished Nehemiah led in the dedication of the wall (Neh 12). Since the refortified city was still sparsely populated, Nehemiah and the other leaders arranged for one-tenth of the people who lived in the countryside to move into Jerusalem. These people were chosen by lot and willingly moved into the city. Work on the walls combined with generally poor agricultural conditions caused a food shortage for the poor, who were also being abused by the noble class. With prophetic anger Nehemiah corrected the abuses and from his own resources, which must have been extensive, provided for the needy, thereby encouraging others to do the same (Neh 5).

Nehemiah accomplished all of this during a twelve year tenure as governor (445–433 B.C.E.) after which he returned to Persia. Some years later he came back to Judah for a second term as governor. He discovered several cultic abuses that the leaders in Jerusalem condoned or participated in. These abuses posed several threats to the religious integrity of the Jewish community. Tobiah the Ammonite, who had earlier opposed Nehemiah's work on the walls, was quartered in the Temple precincts with the permission of the priest in charge. Nehemiah abruptly expelled him and had the quarters cleansed. LEVITES who earlier had moved to Jerusalem in connection with Nehemiah's attempts to strengthen the population of the city were so poorly supported that many of them had moved back to their rural homes. Nehemiah brought them back from their farms and arranged for their support. The SABBATH had become commercialized. Vendors, both Jewish and foreign, traded on the Sabbath both inside the city and along the walls outside. Nehemiah had the city gates closed against vendors on the Sabbath and drove away those who traded along the walls. Many Jews, including some priests, had married foreigners. Nehemiah physically attacked some of these Jews and demanded an end to further intermarriage. Because Nehemiah was both layman and eunuch he must have been supported by important religious leaders in accomplishing these reforms. His success is a measure of his character and abilities and of his authority as Persian governor of Judah.

In addition, if Ezra preceded Nehemiah in Jerusalem and if they worked together for a time, Nehemiah participated in an exceptional celebration of the FESTIVAL OF TABERNACLES (Neh 7:72-10:39). This celebration focused on Ezra's reading of the Law (TORAH), which he had brought with him from Babylon, the community's acceptance of its requirements as God's law for them, their renewal of their covenant with God, and a strong commitment to support the Temple services and servants, the priests, Levites, and Temple singers. This was Ezra's great achievement and this account belongs more to the Ezra tradition than to the Nehemiah tradition. Nehemiah is mentioned as a participant (8:9; 10:1). The extent, however, to which the two men's work overlapped, if at all, is much debated. Many scholars believe that it makes more sense historically to separate the work of the two men with Nehemiah's activity preceding that of Ezra. They date Nehemiah's governorships between 445 and 430 B.C.E. and Ezra's return to Jerusalem in 398 B.C.E. The canonical sequence, Ezra preceding Nehemiah, does raise some questions, especially about the ways in which the two men dealt with Jewish marriages to foreigners. Recent scholarship, however, seems inclined to accept the canonical sequence, the purpose of which is to represent Ezra's presentation of Torah and its acceptance by the restoration community as giving meaning to all the other accomplishments of Ezra and Nehemiah.

See also CHRONICLES, FIRST AND SECOND; EZRA; NEHEMIAH, BOOK OF; JERUSALEM; SANBALLAT.

Bibliography. L. H. Brockington, *Ezra, Nehemiah and Esther*; F. C. Fenshaw, *The Books of Ezra and Nehemiah*; J. M. Myers, *Ezra-Nehemiah*; H. G. M. Williamson, *Ezra-Nehemiah*.

—DAVID A. SMITH.

• OUTLINE OF NEHEMIAH •

The Book of Nehemiah

I. Nehemiah's Account of His Work in Jerusalem (1:1-7:5)
   A. Editorial introduction (1:1)
   B. Report from Jerusalem and Nehemiah's prayer of response (1:2-11)
   C. Nehemiah's commission from Artaxerxes (2:1-10)
   D. Nehemiah's inspection of the city walls (2:11-16)
   E. Rebuilding the walls in the face of political opposition and economic and social problems (2:17–6:19)
   F. Measures taken to repopulate the city (7:1-5), continued in 11:1-36.
II. A Census List (7:6-73a)
III. Ezra's Cultic Reforms (7:73b–10:39)
   A. Reading the law (7:73b–8:12)
   B. Celebration of the Feast of Tabernacles (8:13-18)
   C. Public fast and Ezra's prayer of contrition (9:1-37)
   D. Renewal of the covenant with God (9:38–10:39)
IV. Nehemiah's Account of His Work in Jerusalem Continued (11:1–13:31)
   A. The repopulation of the city (11:1-36)
   B. A list of the exiles who returned with Zerubbabel (12:1-26)
   C. Dedication of the restored walls (12:27-43)
   D. Arrangements for support of temple servants and services (12:44-47)
   E. Cultic reforms (13:1-31)

• **Nehemiah, Book of.** [nee'huh-mi"uh] Nehemiah forms the second part of a single book, Ezra-Nehemiah, in the Hebrew scriptures. This work continues the story told in CHRONICLES. Many scholars attribute both Chronicles and Ezra-Nehemiah to the same author, traditionally thought to be Ezra, but considered in modern scholarship to be a later anonymous author who compiled various sources into a comprehensive cult oriented narrative of Israelite history. Recently some scholars have argued for a separate authorship of Ezra-Nehemiah on grounds of a different theological perspective from that in Chronicles. In either case Ezra-Nehemiah completes the story in the Chronicles narrative. The focus is on the return to JERUSALEM from the Babylonian EXILE and the restoration of Jewish cultic and civil life in Judah. The Book of Nehemiah focuses on Nehemiah's accomplishments during two terms as Persian appointed governor of Jerusalem and on Ezra's presentation of the Law to the restored community followed by the ritual celebration of its acceptance. The author of Ezra-Nehemiah freely compiled his narrative from memoirs of Ezra (cf. Ezra 7–10; Neh 8–10) and memoirs of Nehemiah (chaps. 1–7; 11–13), Aramaic texts of Persian court records and decrees, letters, genealogies, and lists of various kinds. The Nehemiah memoirs leave the impression of a genuinely pious appeal to God to look with favor on the work of his faithful servant Nehemiah.

The resultant story is of Nehemiah's heroic and generous efforts to restore Jerusalem's fortifications, enlarge its population, provide for the people's physical needs, and to carry out certain cultic reforms. The narrative of these accomplishments is interrupted by the somewhat intrusive account of Ezra's cultic reforms and of the covenant renewal based on the public reading and acceptance of the Law that Ezra had brought with him from Babylon.

The canonical arrangement of the materials in Ezra-Nehemiah represents Ezra's return to Jerusalem and his reforms there as preceding Nehemiah's return. Nehemiah is mentioned in connection with Ezra's reading of the Law (Neh 8:9) and Ezra in connection with the dedication of the walls (Neh 12:36), implying that the two leaders worked together for some time. This chronological sequence has been questioned on the grounds that two men with similar responsibilities would not have been appointed by the Persians to overlapping terms of office and that the reforms of Ezra, especially in the case of marriage to foreign women, were more severe than those of Nehemiah and must have come later. Many scholars, therefore, argue that Nehemiah's work preceded that of Ezra. Although there are some difficulties with the canonical sequence, its clear intention is to present Ezra's cultic reforms, especially the presentation of the Law, and Nehemiah's civil reforms as complementary to each other. Recent scholarship is inclined to accept this sequence as fairly accurately representing the actual historical situation. The work of the two leaders is viewed as complementary and the differences in their treatment of the problem of mixed marriages is attributed to the unsettled and changing situation in postexilic Jerusalem.

See also CHRONICLES, FIRST AND SECOND; EZRA; NEHEMIAH.

Bibliography. L. H. Brockington, *Ezra, Nehemiah and Esther*; F. C. Fenshaw, *The Books of Ezra and Nehemiah*; J. M. Myers, *Ezra-Nehemiah*; H. G. M. Williamson, *Ezra-Nehemiah*.

—DAVID A. SMITH

• **Nehushtan.** *See* SERPENT

• **Neighbor.** The common term for neighbor is based on a verb meaning "associate with." The extended family virtually assured that those who lived closest to a person would be related in some way or another. The command in the Holiness Code to "love your neighbor as you love one another" (Lev 19:18) assumes that the neighbor is a fellow Israelite since it is followed by an additional admonition to love the "stranger who sojourns with you" (Lev 19:34); but even here it is assumed that the stranger has established a special kind of relationship and is not just any stranger.

In the NT, Jesus makes Lev 19:18 part of his summary of the Law, combining it with Deut 6:4-5, known in Jewish tradition as the SHEMA. His admonition to "love your neighbor as you love yourself" is greeted by the question, "And who is my neighbor?" His response is to tell the parable of the good Samaritan (Luke 10:29-37) in which he expands the traditional definition of neighbor rather radically. Set against the background of mutual animosity and distrust that characterized Jewish-Samaritan relationships, Jesus casts his victim as a Jew and the compassionate hero of the story as a hated Samaritan. Being a neighbor means that one does not let any barrier prevent one from going to the aid of a human being who is in need, regardless of the person's background.

See also ETHICS IN THE NEW TESTAMENT; ETHICS IN THE OLD TESTAMENT; FAMILY; LOVE IN THE NEW TESTAMENT; LOVE IN THE OLD TESTAMENT; STRANGER.

—JOHN H. TULLOCK

• **Nephilim.** *See* GIANT

• **New Birth.** The term "new birth" is one of many phrases used to designate a spiritual change in which a condition of estrangement and alienation from God is overcome as a result of God's reconciling activity. Though the specific phrase is found infrequently in the Bible, the ideas suggested by the term are important in Christian tradition and are reflected in numerous ways within the NT.

Of course the idea of newness, and even the notion of a renewal of life, is by no means foreign to OT faith. It appears in the psalmist's expressed desire for God to place within him "a new and right spirit" (Ps 51:10). Similar concepts are reflected in various prophetic materials (e.g., Jer 31:31-34; Ezek 36:26-28; Isa 65:17-25), though here the specific concern is more in terms of national, and even eschatological renewal, rather than individual renewal. Within the covenant context these ideas are to be noted in connection with Jeremiah's hope for a new covenant (Jer 31:31-34).

In the NT the concept of new birth finds its most explicit expression in the context of Jesus' conversation with a Jewish leader named Nicodemus (John 3:1-9). Here, in the dialogue style for which the fourth Gospel is known, the Johannine Jesus tells Nicodemus that one cannot see the KINGDOM OF GOD unless one is born anew. Nicodemus mistakenly understands Jesus to mean that one must be physically born a second time, and it is only with some extended explanation that Jesus makes clear he is speaking of a spiritual rather than a physical rebirth. In this instance spiritual renewal is also directly connected with baptism.

Similar ideas can be found throughout the Pauline Letters.For example, in Rom 6 Paul speaks of spiritual renewal as a dying and rising with Christ in baptism. He even characterizes the Christian's present conduct in the world as that of "walking in the newness of life" (6:4). Of course such ideas as are reflected here and throughout the Pauline corpus by the use of such similar phrases as "new life in the Spirit" (Rom 7:6) and "new creation" (2 Cor 5:17; Gal 6:15) can only be understood properly in the full context of Paul's theological reflection. For Paul, the imagery suggested by such concepts includes the newness of life made possible for all of creation, inasmuch as the power of sin, death, and the Law is overcome through the death and resurrection of Jesus. As Paul says in 2 Cor 5:17, if anyone is in Christ, he is a "new creature."

Ideas reflective of spiritual rebirth and regeneration can also be found in various NT texts from the post-Pauline period. One may note, for example, the further connection of these ideas with Christian baptism (Titus 3:5; Col 2:11-13), as well as the conviction that new birth is made possible through the resurrection of Jesus and through the living word of God (1 Pet 1:3, 23).

See also CONVERSION; ETERNAL LIFE; FAITH; FAITH AND FAITHLESSNESS; KINGDOM OF GOD; REPENTANCE.

—MICHAEL D. GREENE

• **New Criticism.** *See* LITERATURE, BIBLE AS; NEW TESTAMENT AS LITERATURE

• **New Heaven.** The phrase "new heaven" appears four times in the Bible (Isa 65:17; 66:22; 2 Pet 3:13; Rev 21:1) as part of a longer phrase, "new heaven(s) and new earth," which always refers to the renewal of the creation in the last days. Similar references occur in the Apocrypha and pseudepigrapha (*2 Esdr* 7:75; *2 Bar* 32:6; *1 Enoch* 45:4-5) where the focus is the same.

Biblical writers believed that sin had affected the entire cosmos. So the writer of Ephesians argued that Christians were contending against both unjust rulers and heavenly hosts of wickedness (Eph 6:12). Paul believed that the whole creation had been "subjected to futility" and was "groaning in travail" under its burden (Rom 8:18-25).

The heavens so affected are also referred to as "the air" in Eph 2:2, "the prince of the power of the air." This may be why Paul depicts Thessalonian believers being swept up "in the air" to meet the Lord. When the Lord appears even the dwelling places of the demons will be safe (1 Thess 4:16-17).

Paul used APOCALYPTIC imagery to describe Christian life as a new creation in which "the old has passed away, behold, the new has come" (2 Cor 5:17). But this conviction about present reconciliation did not replace the future HOPE. Instead it heightened expectation as 2 Pet 3:11-13 attests.

The new heaven would bring what human life could not give: the cessation of grief, pain, and death (Rev 21:2-4). So it remained a symbol of the completeness of the creation after "the former things have passed away" (Rev 21:4).

See also HEAVEN; HOPE IN THE NEW TESTAMENT; HOPE IN THE OLD TESTAMENT.

Bibliography. E. Best, *The First and Second Epistles to the Thessalonians*; G. B. Caird, *The Revelation of St. John the Divine*; A. Farrer, *A Rebirth of Images: The Making of St. John's Apocalypse*.

—WILLIAM R. HERZOG II

• **New Jerusalem.** The concept of the new Jerusalem reached its apocalyptic, spiritual climax in the Book of Revelation. The concept began with the prophetic idea of the reformation and transformation of the earthly city of Jerusalem. The vision of a "new Zion" in Isa 40–55 and Ezekiel's prophecy of the political and religious restoration of Israel (Ezek 40–48) were major OT contributions to this development. The idea of a new Jerusalem can also be found in Jewish literature (cf. *2 Esdr* 10:25-28; *2 Bar* 4:3), as well as in the NT (cf. Gal 4:26-27; Phil 3:20; Heb 12:22).

The failure of the prophetic hope for a new Jerusalem to materialize politically led ultimately to its spiritualization by the author of the NT Book of Revelation. As described in Rev 21, the new city comes down out of heaven from God (v. 10), a description without parallel in the other literature. Elaborate symbols are used to indicate its completeness and perfection, including its measurements, which are multiples of twelve (cf. 21:12, 16, 17). Furthermore, it is described as a perfect cube (v. 16), the same as the Holy of Holies in the first Temple (1 Kgs 6:20). This city, however, has no Temple for in its entirety it is symbolic of the presence of God, who is its Temple (v. 22).

That the author also intends the new Jerusalem to be identified with the Church, the bride of Christ, is made clear in 21:2. Thus Christ will dwell with his perfect and pure bride forever.

While some scholars detect the influence of the astrological zodiac on the author, especially in the description of the twelve jewels (Rev 21:19-20), the primary influence is clearly biblical. This concept of the new Jerusalem has nourished Christian eschatology for nearly two thousand years.

—JOHN C. H. LAUGHLIN

• **New Moon.** *See* SABBATH

• **New Testament as Literature.** NT writings follow the rules or conventions not only of the Greek language but also of secondary literary "languages." Biblical scholars in general have discovered the value of viewing the Bible as literature, and NT scholars are sharing in this discovery. This essay will first of all survey the literary conventions of the NT writings and then discuss broader implications of viewing the NT as literature.

Literary Conventions of the NT. A beginning point in examining the nature of the NT as literature is the distinction between narrative and nonnarrative discourse or didactic material. The four Gospels, Acts, and the Book of Revelation (to a large extent) are in narrative form and follow the conventions of narrative. The remaining material follows various epistolary and rhetorical didactic conventions. The narrative of the Gospels is to be read differently than didactic epistolary works.

Identification of the specific genre of each writing is important, for each genre has its own conventions. The Book of Revelation is an apocalyptic writing and it may be appreciated by seeing it in relation to apocalyptic sections of the NT. But the conventions of the apocalypse are best seen by comparing it with the OT Book of Daniel and various nonbiblical apocalypses. It is helpful to note the common characteristics of the four Gospels and to read each Gospel in light of those conventions. But distinction must also be made between the conventions shared by the first three Gospels and those unique to the Gospel of John. In a sense, each Gospel (and each NT writing) is unique and demands reading in light of its unique nature, but attention to common characteristics is important as a beginning point.

The epistolary material of the NT follows the conventions of ancient letters. Of course, care must be taken to distinguish between the genuine letters which follow the conventions in a standard fashion and those following the letter form in a more or less creative fashion. Paralleling the epistolary conventions are Greco-Roman rhetorical conventions which were followed in composition of speeches and letters.

Smaller forms are to be found within each of the larger units. These range from figures of speech to extended literary units. Best known are the forms which have been identified by NT form critics following the distinction between narrative and discourse. The PASSION NARRATIVE is an intermediate form standing between the gospel genre and the smaller forms. To determine conventions to be followed in reading and interpreting a passion narrative, the passion narratives of the four Gospels may be compared and then passion stories outside of the Gospels may be utilized. Pronouncement stories are short stories which tell of isolated events in the life of Jesus and which contain pronouncements suitable for sermons. Miracle stories in the NT follow the style of similar stories from ancient to modern times, giving the history of the illness, the technique of the miracle, and finally the success of the miraculous act. Miracle stories may be compared with other miracle stories and with pronouncement stories which use accounts of miracles as the narrative framework for a pronouncement. Legends are religious narratives of saintly men and women, and myths are narratives which describe the many-sided interaction between transhuman persons. Discourse material includes the PARABLES and sayings such as proverbs, prophetic and apocalyptic sayings, and laws and community regulations.

The form critics combined historical and literary interests when they studied the Gospel tradition. They were concerned for those forms which could be connected with a particular life setting. A literary approach is less concerned with a sociological or historical life setting and more concerned with the literary form and function of the unit. A literary approach, then, will examine the smaller forms in light of their relationship with each other within the larger literary unit. It places the units within larger literary complexes. Miracle stories in the Gospel of Matthew and pronouncement stories in the Gospel of Mark, for example, combine to form larger literary units. Parables and sayings of Jesus have been combined into larger literary units in the well-known five discourses of the Gospel of Matthew.

A literary approach to a particular book of the NT is not content with specifying genre and examining the individual units and their combinations in light of literary affinities. It is concerned with examining the literary coherence of the entire unit. The beginning point of the contemporary literary contextualizing of biblical writings may be seen as the emphasis upon the literary work as a unity to be understood essentially in terms of that literary structure. In literary studies in America, this emphasis resulted from New Criticism, which desired to explain a work by considering it as an autonomous whole with a significance and value determined apart from any external reference. When the new critical principle is applied to biblical literature, the biblical text is interpreted as a structural unity, with each part seen as integral to the whole and as modifying the meaning of the whole. Interpretation, then, involves bringing all parts of the texts into a meaningful relationship to the entire text. This involves the linear (or syntagmatic) relationships within a text. But it also involves metaphoric (associative or paradigmatic) relationships. Whenever possible, that is, one unit in the text is seen as standing in a metaphoric relation to other units and to the total work. A literary approach, therefore, does not begin by dissecting a book of the NT into different sources, but considers the book as a unity. Each part of the text is studied in relation not to the historical setting and activity of the author or editor but on its own in relation to other parts. With narrative, for example, plot is important. Plots are arrangements of events into a beginning, a middle, and an end, which together form a completed whole. The events in the plot move toward the resolution of some conflict, and plots are often characterized by the sort of conflict (physical, character, and moral and spiritual) that is resolved in the story. Ingredients of stories are characters (even when the conflict is not essentially between characters), settings, and the strategies for moving the story along in an interesting way and involving the reader in the story.

A literary approach to the Gospel of Mark, for example, will attempt to discern some plot developing from a beginning to a ending. It will attempt to discern relationships of significance between and among the units. Readers who have been influenced by the form-critical attention to the individual units may attempt to escape the ambitious task of relating the series of actions in Mark 1:4–3:35 to each other. The conclusion of the story of Jesus' healing on the Sabbath ("The Pharisees went out, and immediately held counsel with the Herodians against him, how to destroy him" [3:6]), however, encourages the reader to organize the segments into a story which will conclude with the passion. The early stories of Jesus' success in chaps. 1–3 serve as motivation for the plot of his enemies against Jesus recounted in chap. 3. The chapter on parables (4) with its emphasis on the "secret" of the Kingdom of God relativizes such a passion-directed processing. The reader may even despair of making any sense of the materials as a whole. Later on in the Gospel, moreover, the reader is encouraged once again to tie segments together as the author specifies relationships. In Mark 8:19, the Jesus of the Gospel of Mark questions the disciples about events recorded earlier in the Gospel: "When I broke the five loaves for the five thousand, how many baskets full of broken pieces did you take up?" They said to him, "Twelve." "And the seven for the four thousand, how many baskets full of broken pieces did you take up?" And they said to him, "Seven." And he said to them, "Do you not yet understand?"

Readers are encouraged by the Jesus of the Gospel of Mark to see metaphoric relationships. In the stories of feeding, the remaining broken pieces serve effectively as a symbol for the abundance of bread. But the question of Jesus indicates that another meaning is to be discerned as well. The reader who wants to discover that meaning must see metaphoric relationships between different episodes. The text refers the reader back to the stories of miraculous feedings (6:35-44; 8:1-8). But by means of the repetition in 8:18 of the quotation about seeing but not understanding (which came first in 4:12), the reader is invited to re-examine and find deeper meaning in the parable of the seed in 4:3-9. The reader may see connections between this parable and the miraculous feedings which had escaped detection at first.

But the reader must go further, for to make sense of these relationships is to overcome the failure to understand Jesus' identity. The reader continues to read the Gospel in light of this perspective. Immediately after the discussion in the boat, comes the central part with Jesus' own answer to the question of who he is (8:27-29). The threefold announcement of his arrest, execution, and resurrection as the completion of his way of life is connected with the theme of seeing and understanding by the framework of the two stories relating the healing of a blind man in Mark. The theme of the first story (8:22-26) is the development of "seeing" into "looking intently" and movement from seeing men that "look like trees" to "seeing everything clearly." The story suggests various ways of seeing, a way of seeing which causes one to misinterpret what one sees and a way of seeing which is both clear and comprehensive. The theme of the second story (10:46-52) is the connection between seeing on the one hand and following Jesus on the way on the other.

Literary Study of the NT as a New Paradigm. The study of the NT as literature must be seen as something new in the history of interpretation. It may be compared and contrasted with the study of the NT as dogma and as history. With the dogmatic approach of the ancient and medieval church, the essential character of the Bible was its nature as a sign of God, a communication intrinsically far above the pitch of human minds but available as a sign. The critical and historical approach resulted from a transformation of worldview in the Enlightenment. The historicality of literary documents and of other cultural phenomena replaced the framework provided by the theological conceptualization of the ancient and medieval world. Cultural documents and artifacts are bound up not with a preexisting world, of which the artifacts are an exteriorization. They are to be understood precisely within the temporally and spatially limited context of their origins.

Literary approaches are not satisfied with the reduction of biblical texts to "causes" in the Neoplatonic and historical-critical perspectives. Texts are viewed in light of linguistic and literary relationships, but there is no attempt to reduce texts to linguistic and literary systems. Instead of a simple one-to-one cause and effect model, literary critics emphasize the multiplicity of relationships and interdependence or mutual "causation."

When the NT is viewed as literature, historical and

dogmatic factors are not ignored. The historical factors, however, are seen as circumstances of origin, and the discovery of such circumstances is not seen as the ultimate goal of NT study. The dogmatic aspects are not ignored, but they are coordinated not with an ancient or modern dogmatic system. A contemporary literary approach is concerned with translating doctrinal emphases into terms which are relevant for the modern reader and consistent with the nature of the NT text as literature.

The practical use of the biblical texts in ancient and modern times does not mean that a literary approach is impossible or inappropriate. At one period in literary study, the view of literature separated it from other uses of language. The reality of literature was seen as a world of its own. Literature, then, was essentially independent of historical, social, and economic realities. The aim of literary study was to explain why a particular work of art was beautiful. Judged in light of this particular literary ideology, the Bible could not be approached as literature. But this ideology is no longer self-evident in literary criticism. All sorts of texts may be read as literature regardless of their original functions. Moreover, literary and nonliterary functions coexist. Giving attention to aesthetic, emotive, and conative functions of biblical texts does not deny that biblical texts had particular practical functions and continue to have such functions. In the real life of a culture, texts must often carry out different functions at the same time in order to be effective. In order for an icon to be perceived as a religious text, it must also be a work of art. The reverse is also true. In order to be perceived as a work of art, the icon must have the religious function that is proper to it. Placing the icon in a museum, in a certain sense, violates the effect of the unity of the two functions.

From the perspective of the literary paradigm in its broadest sense, the question as to the role and function of the NT arises. With the dogmatic approach, the function of the Bible was to provide doctrine, and the NT was the ultimate source of doctrine. The OT was preliminary. With the historical approach, the Bible provided historical answers to historical questions. The development of an evolutionary approach reinforced the significance of the NT over against the OT. A role and function of the NT consistent with a literary view of the Bible will begin with the Bible as a whole. It is possible to see the entire Bible in literary terms as kerygmatic. That is, the Bible as a whole and in its individual units is proclamation and actualization of good news.

The question of function is related to the matter of genre in terms of the Bible as a whole. The biblical writings (OT and NT) share a common narrative plot at the most profound level. This common plot may be perceived by utilizing the four-fold organization of basic motifs, or "pregeneric elements of literature," at work prior to the development of ordinary literary genres. (The four seasons of the year have been used in explicating the motifs.) These elements are comedy (the mythos of spring), romance (the mythos of summer), tragedy (the mythos of autumn), and irony and satire (the mythos of winter). The Bible contains stories that reflect all of these plots and their modifications and combinations. Romance is the successful quest, and the complete form of the romance has a preliminary stage of a perilous journey with its minor adventures, a crucial struggle in which either the hero or his opponent or both must die, and the exaltation of the hero who has proved himself to be a hero even if he does not survive the conflict. But the thrust of the Bible is in the direction of the comic. The standard shape of comedy is a u-shaped pattern in which the action is first of all brought to a low point by a series of misfortunes and then sent to a happy conclusion by some fortunate twists in the plot. The normal pattern of action for comedy the desire of a young man for a young woman, resistance of this desire by some opposition, and a twist at the end of the plot, which enables the hero to have his will.

The comic pattern is obvious in the stories of the failure, captivity, and redemption of the people of God. An essentially comic perspective is evident in the narrative accounts of Israel and Jesus Christ. It is also evident in nonnarrative material of the Bible. A literary approach to the NT allows use of the resources of the OT in a different fashion than did the dogmatic and historical approaches. The biblical writings as a whole present a view of the world which is at odds with the view of life as romance, as a quest in which the universe is the creation of humankind. The Bible is the epic of the creator, not of the creature.

The question of the sacred is an important question which must be raised in a literary approach to the NT as literature. With the world view which operated with the dogmatic approach, there was no question concerning the divine. The divine was essential. With the Enlightenment, a view of the world developed in which the criterion of reality is the order of nature as the source of sense experience. This view of the world has resulted in what is known as the "death of God." There is no criterion in the natural world which can serve as the basis of judgment of the sacred. It is possible that with the new world view operating with a literary approach to the Bible, God may be conceptualized once again. The world which is disclosed in the biblical texts, in fact, involves a sacrality which enables human experience to be fulfilled. But the sacred is not approached as a "thing" as would be required in the critical approach growing out of the Enlightenment. John Macquarrie's suggestion that Exod 3:14 be translated as "I let be what I let be" allows us to conceive of the sacred which is related to the world but which is not to be reduced to the world. God *is* in a dynamic and creative sense. The very fact of God is the condition that there are any beings or properties of beings. We may speak of the experience with the sacred as grace insofar as it supports and strengthens human existence and helps the overcoming of the fragmentariness and impotence of this existence. The sacred is judgment as it lays claim on humans and exposes the distortions of their existence. As it brings new understanding of ourselves and of the wider life within which we live, we may call this "revelation." The Bible approached as literature discloses a world in which the sacred makes sense. It invites its readers to share such sense and such a world.

When the Bible is seen as a kerygmatic offering of such a world, as the proclamation of this good news in the comic genre, the reader's interaction with the Bible is seen as an essential factor in biblical literature. The reader's interaction may result in a special kind of knowledge. This knowledge is not essentially dogmatic information. It is not essentially historical data. It is a "knowledge" which affects relationships of individuals with other individuals, of individuals with themselves, and of individuals with the sacred. The emphasis on the role of biblical literature in the life of the reader does not mean that the text is minimized. On the contrary, the text is taken just as seriously as before. But taking the text seriously in a reader-oriented literary approach does not mean distancing the text so that it becomes and remains ancient and strange. It means situating the text in a fashion that it is able to speak to the reader in his or her contemporary idiom. Readers come to texts and are able to make sense because there is some correlation of textual factors and factors in the reader's world. Characters, events, and situations in the text are not unlike those in the reader's world. But the text often challenges the conceptions and ideologies with which the reader begins, and the reader modifies or recreates his world ideologically. Since world and self do not exist in isolation, however, the reader's self is being redefined in the process. Experience with the text is an experience which alters needs and possibilities.

The sort of knowledge which is provided by the Bible as literature is expanded. This knowledge is not simply knowledge of facts which can be determined from the biblical narrative and discourses, detached from the texts, and then reattached to dogmatic and historical systems of the reader's own day. The knowledge gained is the kind that is obtained by viewing biblical texts in light of their integrity as linguistic and literary creations and by examining the world disclosed in the texts and the world of values and meanings presupposed by the world of the text. The sacred is experienced in creative interaction with the biblical text. This experiential knowledge may influence the reader more intimately than convention biblical knowledge. A sensitive reader may, in fact, be "creating" a new world in the process of reading.

See also APOCALYPTIC LITERATURE; APOPHTHEGM; BIBLE AND WESTERN LITERATURE; BIBLE IN AMERICA; EPISTLE/LETTER; FORM/GATTUNG; GENRE, CONCEPT OF; GENRE, GOSPEL; INTERPRETATION, HISTORY OF; LITERARY CRITICISM; LITERATURE, BIBLE AS; MIRACLE STORY; PARABLES; PASSION NARRATIVE; PROVERB/RIDDLE.

Bibliography. M. H. Abrams, *The Mirror and the Lamp: Romantic Theory and the Critical Tradition*; R. Alter, *The Art of Biblical Narrative*; R. Alter and F. Kermode, eds., *The Literary Guide to the Bible*; Augustine, *On Christian Doctrine*; G. B. Caird, *The Language and Imagery of the Bible*; B. S. Childs, *The New Testament as Canon: An Introduction*; F. Dreyfus, "Exégèse en Sorbonne, Exégèse en Eglise," *RB* 81 (1975): 321-59; R. M. Fowler, "Irony and the Messianic Secret in the Gospel of Mark," *Proceedings: Eastern Great Lakes Biblical Society* 1 (1981): 26-36; N. Frye, *Anatomy of Criticism: Four Essays, The Great Code: The Bible and Literature,* and *The Secular Scripture: A Study of the Structure of Romance*; S. A. Geller, "Were the Prophets Poets?" *Prooftexts: A Journal of Jewish Literary History* 3 (1983): 211-21; W. Iser, *The Act of Reading; A Theory of Aesthetic Response*; J. L. Kugel, *The Idea of Biblical Poetry: Parallelism and Its History* and "On the Bible and Literary Criticism," *Prooftexts: A Journal of Jewish Literary History* 1 (1981): 217-36; E. V. McKnight, *The Bible and the Reader: An Introduction to Literary Criticism, Meaning in Texts: The Historical Shaping of a Narrative Hermeneutics,* and *Postmodern Use of the Bible: The Emergence of Reader Oriented Criticism*; J. Macquarrie, *Principles of Christian Theology*; D. Robertson, *The Old Testament and the Literary Critic*; L. Ryken, *How to Read the Bible as Literature*; M. Sternberg, *The Poetics of Biblical Narrative: Ideological Literature and the Drama of Reading.*

—EDGAR V. MCKNIGHT

• **New Testament Chronology.** *See* CHRONOLOGY

• **New Testament Greek.** *See* GREEK LANGUAGE

• **New Testament Theology.** *See* THEOLOGY OF THE NEW TESTAMENT

• **New Testament Use of the Old Testament.** The use of the Jewish scripture by NT writers has been one of the leading storm centers of biblical scholarship during this century. The issue is not whether the earliest church used the sacred writings of the synagogue; clearly it did, and to a significant extent. In fact, the only Bible known to JESUS and his first followers was a collection of those books which came to be known to later Christians as the OLD TESTAMENT. Even a cursory reading of the NT reflects the pervasive interaction between Christian faith and the OT. Clearly the OT was a primary authority by which the early believers anchored and clarified their faith in Jesus of Nazareth as God's Messiah.

Nor does any modern scholar disagree that the writers of the Christian scripture interpreted their Bible in the mainstream of contemporary Jewish HERMENEUTICS. The OT was an interpreted authority. That is, its authority for the believing community, Jewish or Christian, was felt only when (and if) the biblical text was reinterpreted and made meaningful for the new context of faith. The character of earliest Christianity was Jewish, then, not only because it shared the same Bible but also because it shared the same biblical hermeneutics.

Yet, Christians interpreted the Jewish scriptures differently than did Jews; indeed, the wedge which finally separated Christians from the synagogue was the dispute over how scripture should be interpreted for Israel. Christians contended that the Bible should be rendered in light of their claim that rabbi Jesus from Nazareth was in fact the Christ of God; that through him GOD had already set into motion an age during which the scriptural promises concerning God's salvation would be fulfilled. Although Jews and Christians were loyal to the same God, and defended their theological convictions by appealing to the same collection of sacred writings and by utilizing the same hermeneutical methods, their disagreements about Jesus were so basic that disunity became inevitable.

This ancient dispute frames the real issue at stake in the modern discussion. There is something of a consensus over the character of NT usage of the OT as well as over those Jewish methods employed by NT writers for adapting their biblical text to the new situation they believed was inaugurated by Jesus and continued in the tribes of Israel grounded upon his twelve apostles. The real issue at stake is *how* the Bible's authority is actually used by the NT writers, and whether the NT's use of the OT has any continuing theological or hermeneutical value for today's church. After summarizing the consensus and our emphasis within it, we will enter into the modern debate and offer a perspective on the hermeneutics of the NT writers which might continue to inform the hermeneutics of today's church.

The NT Use of the OT. Typically, OT texts and images appear as citations or are alluded to in the NT. If a biblical text is cited by a NT writer, often it is introduced by a formulaic phrase which identifies its canonical author ("For God says . . . "). A few such formulas are less general and envisage a particular community's theology or CHRISTOLOGY. For example, the language of "fulfillment" tied to the "prophetic citations" of Matthew's Gospel ("This was to fulfill the words of the prophets . . . ") reflects the central belief of Matthew's church that Jesus from Nazareth fulfills the Law and Prophets (Matt 5:17-20). Biblical citations are tied, then, to a particular writer's understanding of how a living God addresses the new situation brought about by the advent of God's Christ.

Sometimes two or more texts from different OT books are combined to form a single utterance of a particular prophet (Matt 27:9) or even from an unknown source (Jas 4:5); or several texts are combined to form a scriptural catena which concentrates and authorizes a particular point of interpretation or argumentation (Heb 1:5-12). Biblical writers often altered biblical texts, or substantially altered their original meaning, when contemporizing it for a particular audience (2 Cor 3:16). Such textual reforms were the hermeneutical vehicles of new meanings allowing the biblical texts to address a new situation in light of the church's conviction that something new (and messianic) had happened in the life of Jesus.

Although his "source" thesis has now been abandoned by the majority of biblical scholars, C. H. Dodd argued that these citations quoted a certain body of uncontested Jewish scripture (e.g., the "servant" passages from Second Isaiah) which in turn "testified" to Jesus as God's Christ, thereby building "the substructure of NT theology" (127). The real issue in the debate with Dodd is not from where (and the biblical field is much broader than Dodd contended), but rather for what reason is the OT cited—since quotation always involves interpretation. Indeed, the same texts are sometimes used by different authors with very different meanings for very different reasons (notice, e.g., how differently Paul [Rom 4:2-5] and James [2:21-24] employ Gen 15:6!).

While citations, especially when preceded by formal introductions, offer us the clearest examples of the NT's use of the OT, there are also countless allusions to familiar OT phrases, persons, and stories found throughout the NT. In fact, we would contend that this more pervasive and subtle use of the OT points to a more profound understanding of the OT: the WORD OF GOD takes the form of promise in the OT which is in fundamental continuity with its NT form of fulfillment. That the NT writers continually "found" OT analogies to their memories about Jesus and his apostles, and to the crises facing their audiences, caused them to frame their convictions about Jesus and their compositions to their audiences against a biblical backdrop.

Since quotations are most often derived from convictions about the significance of the Christ event, such quotations might be construed as an apologetical collection of "proof-from-prophecy" verses, representing a "NT within the OT." In this sense, the OT comes to contribute nothing to the writer's (or reader's) understanding of Jesus' messianic mission. Allusions, on the other hand, represent a more comprehensive and "natural" merging of the OT with the NT, reflecting Augustine's saying, "the New lies hidden in the Old, and the Old is made plain in the New."

The pervasiveness of the OT in the NT, found at the allusory level, is detected only when the reader is sensitive to biblical phraseology, to OT types, or to catchwords which link OT to NT. Much like devout people of every age, NT writers were so informed by their reverent reading and hearing of scripture that they formed habits of thought and language characterized by the natural interweaving of their words and insights with the people and passages of scripture. Sometimes we find large blocks of the OT alluded to by NT writers through familiar phrases which carry significant theological freight. For example, C. F. Evans pointed out that Luke linked his narrative of Jesus' journey to Jerusalem (Luke 9–18) to Deut 1–26 linguistically by familiar catchwords. The evangelist's purpose according to Evans was to make this theological point: Jesus fulfills the Deuteronomic promise (18:18) of an eschatological "prophet like Moses." Such allusions reflect a midrashic hermeneutic, typical of virtually every NT writer (cf. below), which facilitated a devotional and edifying reading of the whole OT.

Further, OT types utilized by NT writers as normative historical modes of God's saving activity allude to particular episodes in which the OT type has a significant role in the biblical narrative of salvation's history. Thus, whether the types are persons (e.g., Moses, Elijah, Adam), institutions (e.g., cultus, monarchy), events (e.g., Exodus, wilderness, Exile) or covenant mediators (e.g., priest, king) the OT type alluded to by the NT writer links the narrative of God's salvation of Israel to the salvation of the church as one continuous narrative.

Midrash: the NT Interpretation of the OT. Scholars generally agree that NT writers not only used the Jewish scriptures as their biblical authority but utilized contemporary Jewish hermeneutics to find meaning in the sacred texts for their audiences. The NT writers were concerned not so much with original meanings but with the new meanings hidden within a particular text. This more dynamic and devotional interpretation of scripture is called "midrash," which means "to seek" (from the Heb. verb, *darash*). The purpose of the interpreter's search (and resulting commentaries) is the clarification of God's Law (*halakah*) and gospel (*haggadah*) for the biblical community in light of its current crises of faith and life. Such clarifications make it possible to find and enter into the *shalom* promised by God for that Israel which trusts God's gospel and obeys God's law.

While midrash refers to a particular genre of rabbinic commentary on the biblical text (e.g., Rom 4:3-25 on Gen 15:6 and Ps 32:1-2), formed when certain exegetical rules (*middoth*) are followed, it is also clear that it refers to an interpretive act which seeks to adapt the sacred text to life. Both citations of and allusions to the Jewish scriptures represent the writer's activity in discerning those meanings in selected biblical texts or phrases which nurture and direct the formation of his audience's faith. Thus, midrash is more than a commentary on a text; it is the use of a biblical text thought to enshrine the very truth from God in a way which allows the text to interpret the living context of the faithful. Midrash is more than a technique for interpreting the biblical text; it involves certain convictions about God and about the Bible's role within a believing community as its religious authority. The assumption that the Word of God is heard through interpretation is justified not because certain midrashic *middoth* are followed; rather, it is derived from the assurance that the community and its interpreter share fundamental convictions about the function of their Bible and about the nature of the theological truth it enshrines.

Many scholars seek to locate the generally recognizable methods of Jewish exegesis (including allegory, targumic translation, typology, pesher-midrash, and even literal-historical) in the NT, classifying them according to agreed-upon technical descriptions of each. Such a concern, however, sometimes obscures the overarching reality that all are really midrashic in spirit; that is, all biblical interpretation and every method utilized proceeds from the conviction that the scriptures contain a current word from God for the interpreter and each member of his audience. Especially since the discovery of the *testimonia* at Qumran (*4Q Testim*), scholars have emphasized the particular importance of the *pesher* (or, interpretive) midrash to underscore this more implicit, edifying element of Jewish hermeneutics. As is well known, the midrashim of Qumran are similar to that found in the NT in that both presume that scripture contains a theological (usually eschatological) meaning, made relevant by present events or circumstances, which is found by a reconstruction of the text itself and the abrogation of its original meaning. This is true, however, in every NT use of the OT. NT writers, believing that the eschaton had dawned in Christ, discovered their kerygmata in OT texts and utilized all current methods of exegesis in locating new meanings appropriate for the life and faith of their Christian audiences.

Of course, such an understanding of NT exegesis emphasizes the fluid and relative character of biblical meanings. Was there no ongoing body of beliefs and behaviors which so focused the act of midrash that a stability of theological meaning was maintained from OT to NT? Dodd contended that the kerygma, or preaching, of the earliest church provided its exegetes with such a center. Thus, for him, the NT *testimonia* which pointed to OT passages were the yield of a certain methodology of biblical exegesis which yielded in turn a certain kerygma, the very foundation of Christian theology. Against Dodd, however, we would contend that it was the church's theocentric (not christocentric) kerygma, and not the OT, which provided the starting point for the NT use of the OT. Different biblical meanings for diverse Christian contexts, derived from the application of different midrashic methods, all had a common center: all meanings bear witness to the salvation of God through Jesus Christ which was proclaimed as true by the church's apostles.

In our opinion, the shift from a christocentric to a theocentric center is critical as well for an adequate understanding of the NT's view of the OT as promise. If one argued that all the allusions to and quotations of the OT found in the NT were formulated from those convictions about Jesus, then the OT would function usefully only as a prophecy of the life and work of Jesus as Christ, without continuing authority for the post-Easter community. The tendency would be to move dangerously closer to the Marcionite heresy. Clearly Jesus' kerygma, and the unifying kerygma of the early church, however, were theocentric: God saves through Christ those who turn to God in repentance and faith. The result, then, is that at the outset of midrash exists the firm conviction that the God of Israel is the God of Jesus; and the Jewish scriptures which tell the story of God's salvation in Israel's history is but the "first" testament of what God continues to do in Christ. The scriptural citations and allusions are really evidences of a belief that God has continued his salvation of Israel in the history of the church. All the midrashim of NT writers, explicit and implicit, envisage precisely that theocentric perspective.

The NT Use of the OT: a Canonical Perspective. The general contour of this consensus has been shaped by the historical interpretation of the NT. The practical significance of this yield for today's church, however, is viewed by most critics rather negatively. The seemingly subjective, pastoral character of the NT use of the OT does not appeal to the modern exegete. To take into the biblical text what one ultimately derives from it is an affront to modern canons of objectivity. Further, the primary importance the historical critic posits for the text's original, or authentic meaning, as well as the distinction drawn between the text's original meaning and its significance for the interpreter's own faith and life, is reversed by the NT's concern for those meanings which are also relevant for the interpreter's faith and life even though different from the original intent and meaning of the OT. The tendency of modern biblical criticism is to lock the Bible's normative meaning into its original meaning, often neglecting its possible significance for today's church.

In reaction against these tendencies of historical criticism, some scholars, such as Brevard Childs and James Sanders, are now calling for a postmodern hermeneutic which acknowledges the Bible's authorized function as the church's canon which evaluates the truth of theological and ethical claims in every age. While the results of an historical interpretation of the Bible are not abandoned, they are filtered through and given new importance by this canonical perspective. Indeed, a canonical interpretation for the Bible is less a technique and more a way of viewing the hermeneutical enterprise.

Such a perspective is framed in two different ways by the NT use of the OT. First, NT writers read their Bible as sacred scripture; it was the book of and for a believing community. Their interpretations of the OT assumed that the Bible would fulfill its sacred function as the nurturing, correcting word of the Lord only when it was read by real persons in real congregations facing real crises of faith and life. The stance of biblical criticism to explain the text in abstraction from the living context of faith is thereby corrected by the stance of the biblical writers themselves. The exegete is not a technician, but a member of a worshiping community who comes to the sacred texts in faith. Further, the NT use of the OT reminds the hermeneut that biblical interpretations must always be related in meaningful ways to the community of faith if they are to bear the Word of God.

Second, while midrash is a hermeneutics of adaptation which seeks to contemporize the biblical text for a particular context of faith, NT writers were always constrained by certain stable/stabilizing convictions about a covenanting God and a covenanted people. Midrash is not theologically arbitrary! It rather is an interpretative act which calls attention to those theological convictions which provide a coherent center for the Bible's message. Methodologically, midrash seeks to relate the biblical text to the community in theologically significant ways—to help it understand what it means to believe and to behave as God's people ought. The NT use of the OT reminds the modern exegete that biblical interpretation must always make clear in an increasingly ambiguous world the eternal truth of God's gospel.

See also CANON; CHRISTOLOGY; GOD; HERMENEUTICS; JESUS; MESSIAH/CHRIST; OLD TESTAMENT; SCRIPTURE IN THE NEW TESTAMENT; WORD OF GOD.

Bibliography. D. L. Baker, *Two Testaments: One Bible*; R. Block, "Midrash," *Dictionnaire de la Bible: Supplement*; C. H. Dodd, *According to the Scriptures: The Substructure of the New Testament*; E. E. Ellis, "How the New Testament Uses the Old," *New Testament Interpretation: Essays on Principles and Methods*; C. F. Evans, "The Central Section of St. Luke's Gospel," *Studies in the Gospels*, ed. D. E. Nineham; M. D. Goulder, *Type and History in Acts*; M. Miller, "Targum, Midrash, and the Use of the OT in NT," *JSJ* 2 (1971): 29-82.

—ROBERT W. WALL

• **New Year's Festival.** A great celebration throughout most of the ancient Near East inaugurating the new year. In Israel the earliest calendar was agricultural. Thus the New Year was set at the first cutting of the crop. King SOLOMON adopted a solar calendar, and new year's day was set on the day of the autumnal equinox in the month of Ethanim (1 Kgs 8:2). Later, after the Exile, a lunar calendar was adopted, and the new year's day was set to be on the first day of the seventh month (Lev 23:23-25).

The celebration was begun by the blowing of the shophar (*šôpār*), an instrument made of a ram's horn. The king ascended his throne, and peace and prosperity were established. Closely connected with this was the agricultural setting. The drought of summer had been threatening life like the ancient powers of chaos—rivers and lakes dried up, the grass withered, the trees went limp and the animals languished—so the great festival was held with all the pomp and circumstance the local priesthood could muster. Processions were held, one of the most important being that of the king to his throne. (In some periods the king's reign was seen to begin on this day, even if he had taken over earlier in the previous year at the death of his predecessor.) Sacrifices were brought in abundance to petition the gods to reestablish fertility and prosperity and peace in the land.

The celebration was in some places connected with a view of a dying and rising deity, such as Baal in ancient Ugarit. His death was tied to the drought and his resurrection to the lifegiving spring rains.

It was on the basis of such a general religio-historical view that Sigmund Mowinckel connected the new year festival in Israel to Israel's God. He argued this out of his understanding of the so-called enthronement Psalms (93; 97; 99 and probably also 95; 96; 98; Heb. *yhwh mālak*). Mowinckel suggested that these psalms were used at a festival for Yahweh's enthronement, which took place at new year. The deity ascended to the throne, and peace and prosperity were again guaranteed. Mowinckel insisted that the expression *Yahweh Malak* must be understood to mean "Yahweh has again taken the reign." Such a theory is quite plausible. We do know that Israel followed Mesopotamia in its understanding of time, that the names for the 12 months are almost the same, and that the main festivals are the same. Many have accepted Mowinckel's theory. Others, like A. Weiser and K. Bernhardt, reject it.

See also CALENDAR; FEASTS AND FESTIVALS; TIME, BIBLICAL PERSPECTIVES ON.

Bibliography. S. Mowinckel, *The Psalms in Israel's Worship*; N. Snaith, *The Jewish New Year Festival*; R. de Vaux, *Ancient Israel, Its Life and Institutions.*

—REIDAR B. BJORNARD

• **Nicodemus, Gospel of.** *See* PILATE, ACTS OF

• **Nicolaitans.** [nik'uh-lay"uh-tayns] The origin and character of the Nicolaitan heretical movement is obscure. The sect is mentioned twice in the BOOK OF REVELATION. In his letters to the seven churches of Asia John referred to the existence of Nicolaitans in EPHESUS and PERGAMUM (Rev 2:6, 15). The Ephesian Christian community had rejected the heretical teaching while the minority of the church in Pergamum had been attracted to it. Though the same immoral practices were prevalent in the church of Thyatira, John does not attribute these evils to the Nicolaitans (Rev 2:20-25). Rather he blamed a prophetess by the name of Jezebel who beguiled the Christians into engaging in illicit sexual intercourse and sacrificing food to idols. Thus it is apparent that three of the churches of the province of Asia were afflicted by this heresy.

The Nicolaitans taught that Christians were free to eat food offered to idols and to practice fornication in the name of religion. John compared the sect to the teaching of Balaam (Num 25:1-2). While the Israelites were wandering in the desert, Balaam taught Balak, king of Moab, how to lead the Israelites astray into pleasure and vice. Paul alludes to the subtle plan of Balaam in 1 Cor 10:8 as a warning against a libertine group in the church of Corinth.

Two theories have been advanced concerning the origin of the name of the Nicolaitan sect. One comes from the tradition of the church fathers and the other is sheer speculation. Irenaeus said that the Nicolaitans were the followers of Nicolaus, the proselyte of Antioch, who was one of the Seven appointed by the apostles of Jerusalem in Acts 6:5 (*AdvHaer* 1.26.3; 3.11). A second theory is that Nicolaus is a Greek translation of the Hebrew word Balaam. However, the attempt to show that Nicolaus and Balaam are equivalents has failed.

See also EPHESUS; PERGAMUM; REVELATION, BOOK OF.

Bibliography. W. M. Ramsay, *The Letters to the Seven Churches of Asia*; H. B. Swete, *The Apocalypse of St. John*; F. J. A. Hort, *The Apocalypse of St. John I–III*; P. Carrington, *The Meaning of Revelation.*

—T. C. SMITH

• **Nile.** [n*i*l] The Nile River is the longest river in the world. From its most distant source along the White Nile, it runs 4,187 mi., emptying into the Mediterranean on the Egyptian coast. Running through Uganda, Sudan, and EGYPT, the system drains a basin of about 1,107,227 square mi. The Blue Nile, with sources in the Ethiopian highlands, joins the White Nile at the city of Khartoum. About 200 mi. downstream from Khartoum, the system is joined by the Atbara River. From that point to its mouths on the Mediterranean, about 400 mi., the system has no more tributaries.

The traditional boundary between Upper (= Southern) and Lower (= Northern) Egypt is marked by the delta region which begins about twelve mi. below Cairo. The delta is about 120 mi. across at its widest point. In modern times there are two main branches of the delta, each about 146 mi. long, but it had seven major branches in ancient times.

The regular rising and falling of the Nile has from ancient times marked off the Nile Valley from the desert on either side, making it an early center of civilization. From the First Cataract (ancient Syene; cf. Ezek 29:10) north to the delta, the cultivable land created by the annual flooding of the Nile is only ten to fourteen mi. across, sometimes becoming as narrow as 1,500 ft. The dependence of Egypt upon this seasonal inundation justified Herodotus in his description of Egypt as "the gift of the Nile" (*Hist* 2.5).

Although it is now known that this seasonal flooding is due to the tilting of the earth on its axis, the ancients marveled at the Nile's habits. Diodorus Siculus gave expression to this ancient wonder: "The rise of the Nile is a phenomenon which appears wonderful enough to those who have witnessed it, but to those who have only heard of it, quite incredible. For, while all other rivers begin to fall at the summer solstice and grow steadily lower and lower during the course of the following summer, this one alone begins to rise at that time and increases so greatly in volume day by day that it finally overflows practically all Egypt" (*Hist* 1.36).

Just as other ancient peoples, the biblical writers knew of the significance of the Nile for the life of Egypt. This is certainly the point of the plagues beginning with the smiting of the Nile, the very heart of Egyptian life. Various passages show knowledge of its seasonal inundations (Isa 23:10; Jer 46:7, 8; Amos 8:8; 9:5), its importance in international grain trading (Isa 23:3), and the dependence of Egypt upon its relative predictability (Isa 19:7, 8). The varying usage of the Hebrew designation *ye'or* (sing.) and *ye'orim* (pl.) probably indicates knowledge of the Nile and its seven branches in the delta region.

See also EGYPT.

Bibliography. W. Fitzgerald, *Africa: A Social, Economic and Political Geography of Its Major Regions*; E. Ludwig, *The Nile: The Life-Story of a River*.

—JOHN KEATING WILES

• **Nimrud/Calah.** [nim'*roo*d/kay'luh] Nimrud is the modern name given to the site of one of the major ASSYRIAN cities, known in ancient times as Calah. It is located on the east bank of the TIGRIS River just north of the confluence of the Tigris and the Upper Zab (PLATE 1).

Calah was founded by Shalmaneser I about 1250 B.C.E. It became the capital of Assyria in the Neo-Assyrian period during the reign of Ashur-naṣir-apli II who greatly enlarged the city. His city wall was nearly five mi. long and enclosed 900 acres. The city remained the capital until the late eighth century B.C.E. when the capital was moved, first to Khorsabad, then to Nineveh. Ashur-naṣir-apli built a large palace in Nimrud, excavations have shown that it covered over 4,000 square ft. (An inscription from Nimrud describes the feast Ashur-naṣir-apli gave at the completion of the palace. Over 69,000 guests were invited from across the kingdom to celebrate for ten days. They consumed 1,000 oxen, 14,000 sheep, 1,000 fatted sheep, 10,000 each of birds, fish, and loaves, 10,000 containers each of wine and beer!) This palace had both public or reception rooms and the family's private rooms. The throne room was flanked by winged lions and bulls and decorated with reliefs showing hunting scenes.

SHALMANESER III, Ashur-naṣir-apli's son and successor, built a large palace-fort at the site which served as his administrative center. This fort had barracks, workshops, storage rooms and a palace. It was Shalmaneser's treasury to store spoils from his campaigns and tribute received from vassals. From here Shalmaneser began his campaigns into Syria-Palestine including the invasion which led to the Battle of QARQAR in 853 B.C.E.

The Black Obelisk which relates tribute paid by Jehu of Israel to Shalmaneser was discovered here at Calah. It was from Calah that TIGLATH-PILESER III launched his attacks on Israel and Judah.

Other major remains include a ziggurat and temples to Nabu, Ninurta, and Ishtar. Significant finds have included hundreds of cuneiform tablets, reliefs depicting military campaigns, winged human-headed lions which guarded the palace doorway, and numerous delicately carved ivories showing local and imported artistry. The city was destroyed by the Medes in 614–612 B.C.E.

Nimrud was first excavated by Henry Layard from 1845–1851 and again from 1949–1963 by M. E. L. Mallowan and D. Oates for the British School of Archaeology in Iraq.

See also ASSYRIA.

—JOEL F. DRINKARD, JR.

• **Ninth of Ab.** *See* AB, NINTH OF

• **Noachic Laws.** [noh-ay'kik] Moral requirements that must be observed by everyone, whether Jew or gentile. Jewish rabbis discussed the seven so-called Noachic or Noachide laws as part of the larger question of God's relation and revelation to mankind both before and outside of the covenant with Israel at Sinai. According to the Talmud, God gave Adam six mandates obligatory upon all humankind: five prohibitions (against idolatry, blasphemy, murder, adultery, robbery), and one positive command (to establish courts of justice). When God was reconstituting life on earth after the great flood, he gave to Noah and his descendants, and thus to the entire human race, an additional prohibition, namely, not to eat flesh cut from a living animal (until then meat was forbidden to human beings; Gen 9:3-4). The rabbis said these seven laws were binding on all humankind until Sinai, and upon all non-Israelites since. Israelites, of course, had the much more detailed Mosaic Law. In addition to "the seven laws of the sons of Noah," the Noachic laws, the Talmud speaks of numerous other laws against such things as eating an animal's blood, emasculating animals, and practicing sorcery, but usually these are subheadings under the seven major mandates.

The Talmud says that gentiles who obey the Noachic laws are not only pious in the sight of God, but are to be protected by Jewish law when under Jewish jurisdiction. They also will participate in the blessings of the world to come. Meanwhile, the commands were to be strictly enforced, the penalty for transgression being execution. The application of these laws was to be sometimes more severe and sometimes less severe than similar laws for Jews. For example, a Jew who stole items below the value of the smallest Palestinian coin was not to be charged with a crime, although the theft was a capital offense for a Noachide. On the other hand, a major sin such as idolatry or adultery committed by a Noachide under duress was no basis for charges, but such offenses were to be avoided by a Jew even upon pain of martyrdom.

The rabbis appear to have sometimes differed as to whether the seven mandates were to be considered part of natural law intended for all non-Israelites or as laws for non-Jewish residents living under Jewish jurisdiction. The terminology and rationale carry the universal and natural law themes; however, the discussions of enforcement presume a Jewish jurisdiction. The rabbis also discussed the status of Christianity and Islam, since both came under the Noachic principle, and found both conforming; however, until the late Middle Ages some rabbis felt that Christianity's belief in the Trinity violated the requirement of absolute monotheism. In the seventeenth and eighteenth centuries theoreticians of natural law, both gentile and Jewish, often cited the principle of Noachic law as a basis for universal natural law.

The Noachic laws are thought by many to stand behind the compromise reached at the JERUSALEM COUNCIL (Acts 15:1-29), where gentile converts are required to abstain from idolatry, from unchastity, from eating what has been strangled, and from blood (Acts 15:20-29).

See also JERUSALEM COUNCIL.

Bibliography. S. Berman, "Noachide Laws," *EncJud* 12:1189-91; H. Revel, "Noahide [*sic*] Laws," *UnivJewEnc* 8:227-28.

—ROLLIN S. ARMOUR

• **Noah.** [noh'uh] Hero of the flood account and related stories, as conveyed by the Bible, early Jewish and Christian literature, and the Qur'an.

When the deity could no longer tolerate human violence, the decision was made to cleanse the world by means of a universal FLOOD (Gen 6:5–9:19). The sole survivors were to be Noah and his family, because he was "a righteous man." At God's direction, a vast ship was constructed and pairs of all land animals were brought aboard so that there could be a new beginning. The deity then caused it to rain for "forty days and forty nights. . . . All flesh died that moved upon the earth." When the waters had abated, God pledged that such an event would not be repeated and created the RAINBOW as a sign of the promise. However, since human nature remained unchanged, two restrictions were placed upon subsequent behavior (9:3-6).

The Bible outlines a series of cultural beginnings in Gen 4 (city building, music, etc.), and then continues the list with Noah as the founder of vine cultivation (Gen 9:20-27). The name, Noah, (as interpreted by his father), seems to allude to this agricultural innovation (5:28-29). His subsequent drunkenness leads to a reprehensible act that brings a curse upon his grandson. The story explains how one line of Shem's descendants (Israel) rose to political power while Ham's (Canaan) declined.

While the flood story is silent concerning Noah's attitude toward his neighbors' impending destruction, subsequent generations assumed that he not only had exhorted them to ethical lives but also had warned them of the flood (2 Pet 2:5). Such belief is asserted in the NT, by the historian Josephus *(Ant),* and in the late B.C.E. Jewish literature (cf. *Jub* 7:20-39). This conclusion may have arisen from an interpretation of the episode preceding the flood story: God limited a human's lifespan to 120 years. That figure may have referred to the amount of time remaining before the flood, time in which to repent.

No compelling meaning for the name Noah has yet been advanced. It most often has been related to the verb "to rest" *(n-w-ḥ),* perhaps loosely related to the proposal of father Lamech: "this one shall bring us relief *(nḥm)* . . . " (Gen 5:29). Others have proposed that it is associated with the subsiding of the flood, or to his long life (under the assumption that the verb *n-w-ḥ* can mean "to be extended"), or even that his name is related to that of a deity.

Noah's age (950 years) is in keeping with the extraordinary lifespans in Gen 1–11. Modern readers, thinking only of biological age, may wonder how persons could have lived so long. Biblical authors, however, often thought in terms of a system of numbers. One system of counting in the ancient Near East (the Sumerian) was constructed on base-60, whereas the modern Western one is place-notation constructed upon base-10. The ages in Gen 1–11 are calculated in months in multiples of 60. Thus, Noah's 950 years yields 11,400 months, reflecting $(60^2 \times 3) + (60 \times 10)$. Not surprisingly, the flood is placed to begin in Noah's 600th year, that is, in his (60×10) year or his $(60^2 \times 2)$ month!

See also FLOOD; NUMBERS/NUMEROLOGY; RIGHTEOUSNESS IN THE NEW TESTAMENT; RIGHTEOUSNESS IN THE OLD TESTAMENT.

Bibliography. L. R. Bailey, *Noah, the Ark, and the Flood*; J. P. Lewis, *A Study of the Interpretation of Noah and the Flood in Jewish and Christian Literature.*

—LLOYD R. BAILEY

• **Noah Covenant.** *See* COVENANT WITH NOAH

• **Noahide Laws.** *See* NOACHIC LAWS

• **Nob.** [nob] A city in the territory of the tribe of Benjamin (Neh 11:32; PLATE 11), called in the days of King SAUL "the city of the priests" (1 Sam 22:19). Ahimelech was the priest in charge of "the bread of the Presence" (1 Sam 21:6) which he gave to the fugitive DAVID and his men who pretended to be on a secret mission from King Saul. It would seem that Nob had succeeded SHILOH as the leading sanctuary of the period. Other special objects there included holy vessels, GOLIATH's sword, and the ephod. When Saul learned of Ahimelech's aid to David, he ordered all the eighty-five priests of Nob to be slain, a task carried out by the Edomite Doeg when Saul's servants refused. In addition Doeg put Nob "to the sword; both men and women, children and sucklings, oxen, asses and sheep, he put to the sword" (1 Sam 22:19). There was one escapee, ABIATHAR, whom later David elevated as priest in Jerusalem.

The city Nob appears to have been just north of JERUSALEM, although archaeological evidence is lacking. Isa 10:28-31 mentions several cities, including ANATHOTH, which the Assyrian invader will trample. Then "this very day he will halt at Nob, he will shake his fist at the mount of the daughter of Zion, the hill of Jerusalem" (v. 32). Apparently, Nob is on a height between Anathoth (ca. three mi. north of Jerusalem) and Jerusalem. Mount Scopus, less than a mi. north of Jerusalem, the only direction from which the city was vulnerable and a campsite of the later Roman invader Titus, is the most likely candidate, for there the shaking of the fist would be visible. But an even more suitable site in this regard is the Mount of Olives, just to the northeast across the Kidron Valley.

See also ABIATHAR; DAVID.

—KAREN RANDOLPH JOINES

• **Nomad.** [noh'mad] A nomad, a pure nomad, is one who has no fixed residence and who wanders from place to place, but usually within a well-defined territory and often seasonally for the purpose of securing food. Some of these pure nomads are hunters and gatherers, others will produce rapidly maturing crops, and many move in search of grazing land for their herds of animals. The OT probably knows little if anything of such pure nomads. The closest terms Hebrew had for nomad, were several which meant "wanderer," such as the judgment on Cain: "you shall be a fugitive and a wanderer" (Gen 4:12) and the place of his exile, Nob, "Wandering" (Gen 4:16). Pure nomadism in the ancient Near East was a late arrival, dependent primarily on the domestication of camels, which seems to have been achieved only in the first millennium B.C.E.

At the outset, a discussion of several additional terms is required, terms closer to what Israel knew: seminomadism, transhumance, and pastoral nomadism. The seminomad is one who lives usually in portable or temporary dwellings, often tents or mud huts, practices seasonal migration most frequently with herds of animals, but regularly has a base dwelling at which some crops are cultivated. Transhumance is the seasonal movement of herds, usually sheep, between lowland and highland pastures either under the care of herders or accompanied by the whole population. Pastoral nomadism is another term describing the same combination of herding and seasonal movement. It is usually a synonym for seminomadism or transhumance, and will be so understood in this essay.

Many of the wandering peoples known to the Hebrews such as the AMALEKITES, EDOMITES, KENITES, MIDIANITES, and ISHMAELITES, belong to the pastoral nomad type. Even the Hebrews themselves may have practiced this type of life style at times. The patriarchs, at least to the extent that they may be regarded as historical, may have been pastoral nomads. Some of the migration described in Genesis seems to follow the seasonal pattern expected of pastoral nomads. Furthermore, the description of the patriarchs as having vast herds of animals and living for the most part in the more marginal lands of the Negeb and hill country away from the major agricultural centers fits the pastoral nomad.

The Iron I Age, from about 1200–1000 B.C.E., considered to represent the period of Israelite settlement in the hill country, shows a mixed economy based on agriculture and pastoralism. This could indicate a continuing existence of a transhumant culture or the gradual sedentarization of pastoral nomads. Israel at the period of the monarchy, and indeed throughout that region for most of its history, was a mixed population some completely urban, a few completely nomadic, and many mixing agriculture with pastoral living.

—JOEL F. DRINKARD, JR.

• **Norea, Thought of.** [noh'ree-uh] The second tractate of Codex IX in the NAG HAMMADI library is an ode to Norea, a figure who appears in a wide variety of Gnostic literature as the daughter of ADAM and EVE, the wife/sister of Adam's son Seth, or as the wife of NOAH or his son SHEM. Though lacking the regularity of meter of a Greek poem, *Norea* possesses some of the characteristics of semitic poetry (balanced structure, repetition, parallelism). The text is a translation from Greek into Coptic.

The contents of *Norea* are clarified by comparison with the experience of Sophia (personification of the highest God's "Wisdom") in the Nag Hammadi tractate the HYPOSTASIS OF THE ARCHONS, the late Gnostic text PISTIS SOPHIA, and the mythology of Valentinian GNOSTICISM (Irenaeus, *AdvHaer* 1.2.5-6). In each case, Sophia finds herself outside her rightful place in the heavenly Pleroma (the fullness of beings who constitute the highest Godhead). She cries for help, wanting to be restored to her original place. Divine intermediaries hear and effect her restoration. Sophia's experience parallels that of souls which have fallen into human bodies on earth from the transcendent and divine realm. Their salvation involves their own cries for release, the saving work of divine intermediaries, and the souls' reintegration into the Pleroma.

The structure of *Norea* reveals the influence of the story of Sophia. First, in 27.11-20 there appears an initial prayer, calling upon the highest, triadic Godhead: the "Father of All," the Mother (or "Ennoia of the Light"), and the Son (or the "Nous dwelling in the Heights"). Second, Norea cries for help to regain "rest" among the Holy Ones and is subsequently delivered (27.21–28.12). She is restored to her proper "place" (=the Pleroma). Third, there is a description of Norea's activity within the Pleroma (28.12-23), including her saving work of "speaking with words of Life," existing in the "Exalted One's" presence, and glorifying him. Finally (28.24–29.5), we read of Norea's own salvation with the assistance of four "luminaries" and how, through her "thought" (29.3) or saving *gnosis,* her spiritual kin ("all the Adams that possess the thought of Norea"—29.1-3) are to be reunited with the Godhead. As female savior and as a Gnostic redeemer figure, she saves others and simultaneously saves herself!

Several distinctive motifs make clear that *Norea* is to be classified as a Sethian Gnostic writing. These include: the presence of Norea, wife/sister of Seth; the mention of the triadic Godhead (Father, Son, and Mother); and the naming of four luminaries or illuminators (93.20-22). It is a Gnostic text, however, which lacks any trace of direct influence from either Judaism or Christianity. No final solution seems possible regarding the tractate's authorship, the precise identity of the Gnostic sect from which it arose, or its place of composition. In that the Coptic version seems to have been copied not later than 350 C.E., the original Greek version was probably written in the late second or early third century.

See also GNOSTICISM; NAG HAMMADI.

Bibliography. S. Giversen and B. A. Pearson, "NHC IX,2: The Thought of Norea: Introduction, Notes, Transcription, and Translation," *Nag Hammadi Codices IX and X: The Coptic Gnostic Library,* ed. B. A. Pearson (*NHS* 15); B. A. Pearson, "The Figure of Norea in Gnostic Literature," *Proceedings of the International Colloquium on Gnosticism,* ed. G. Widengren; "The Thought of Norea," *The Nag Hammadi Library in English,* ed. J. M. Robinson.

—MALCOLM L. PEEL

• **North Galatia.** *See* GALATIA

• **Nubia.** [ny*oo*'bee-uh] Nubia is that part of the Nile valley which extends northward from about 16° north latitude to include Aswan and the First Cataract. The traditional boundary between Lower Nubia and Upper Nubia is the Second Cataract. Ancient Egyptian sources refer to Lower Nubia as the land of *Wawat* and Upper Nubia as the land of *Kush.* Non-Egyptian sources from antiquity refer to the whole region beyond Egypt's traditional southern boundary at Aswan as Kush (=biblical Cush) or ETHIOPIA.

The area was effectively occupied by Egypt only in the Middle Kingdom (ca. 2000–1700 B.C.E.) when a series of forts were built through the area of the Second Cataract, a canal was opened at the First Cataract to allow easy navigation to the south, and campaigns against the land of Kush were successfully pursued. Probably due to Hyksos pressure, the area became thoroughly Egyptianized by the end of the period of Egyptian humiliation. With the rise of the New Kingdom (1580–1100 B.C.E.), Egyptian influence in Nubia was much broader, taking hold as far upstream as the Fourth Cataract.

The earliest Nubian state of which there is certain evidence was established in Upper Nubia sometime before the mid-eighth century B.C.E. with its capital at Napata near the Fourth Cataract. The rulers of this state were probably native to the area. The Nubian ruler Kashta moved north and invaded Egypt. He was succeeded by Piankhy who completed the conquest of Egypt. It is to these figures that the founding of the Twenty-fifth Dynasty (often called the Ethiopian Dynasty) is to be traced. The most famous of these Kushite pharaohs is probably Taharqa, mentioned in the Bible as "Tirhaka king of Ethiopia" (2 Kgs 19:9; "*melek kush*").

Taharqa may have been encouraged by the withdrawal of Sennacherib II from Syria-Palestine in 701 B.C.E. for he set up his capital in the delta city of Tanis from where he could more conveniently meddle in Syro-Palestinian politics. The Assyrian monarch Esarhaddon invaded Egypt, forcing Taharqa to retire to Memphis which soon fell to Esarhaddon. Taharqa himself escaped to Upper Egypt and within a short time had reestablished Kushite power in Egypt. Esarhaddon's successor, Ashurbanipal, took up the campaign to secure Egypt for the Assyrian empire and invaded Egypt once again. This invasion ended with a decisive Assyrian victory, sealed with the destruction of Thebes (663 B.C.E.), which was still recalled by the prophet Nahum at the close of the century (Nah 3:8). Following this defeat, the Kushite rulers, ruling from their old capital city of Napata, were confined to their homeland in Upper Nubia.

The capital was later moved to Meroë, situated between the Sixth and Fifth Cataracts. The existence of early graves at this city may indicate that a branch of the royal family had been in residence at this city already as early as Piankhy. The establishment of the capital at this city has not been dated with certainty, but it must have been before Herodotus (late fifth century B.C.E.) for he knows of Meroë but never mentions Napata. It may be that the move was occasioned by the campaign of Psammetichus II against Kush (591 B.C.E) during which Napata was detroyed.

Ruling from Meroë, the Kushite kingdom maintained its authority and independence for centuries. Lower Nubia was later ruled by the Ptolemaic kings, and the Meroitic empire was confined to Upper Nubia. During the Roman period, the areas between the First and Second Cataracts was established as a Roman Protectorate, but was invaded in 23 B.C.E. by the Meroitic queen, Kandake. "Kandake" was the Meroitic title for queens, but it came to be taken as the personal name of the queen (cf. Acts 8:27, Candace). The Roman commander Petronius led the retaliatory campaign which was successful in extending Roman power to the Fourth Cataract. Lower Nubia remained a nominal subject of Rome, but it enjoyed quite a bit of independence. It seems that Rome's primary interest in holding Lower Nubia was in securing a buffer zone for protection against raids in Upper Egypt.

See also ETHIOPIA.

Bibliography. W. B. Emery, *Nubian Treasure: An Account of the Discoveries at Ballana and Qustul*; W. A. Fairservis, *The Ancient Kingdoms of the Nile and the Doomed Monuments of Nubia*; P. L. Shinnie, *Meroë: A Civilization of the Sudan*; J. Simons, *The Geographical and Topographical Texts of the Old Testament: A Concise Commentary in XXXII Chapters*.

—JOHN KEATING WILES

• **Numbering.** *See* CENSUS, DAVID'S

• OUTLINE OF NUMBERS •

The Book of Numbers

I. Preparations for Leaving Sinai (1:1–9:23)
   A. Census and camp arrangements (1:1–4:49)
   B. Final preparations: various laws and the second passover (5:1–9:23)
II. The Wilderness Journey: From Sinai to Moab (10:1–21:20)
III. Conquests and Preparations for Life in the Land (21:21–36:13)

• **Numbers, Book of.** The fourth book of the Pentateuch, also commonly known as the fourth book of MOSES. The name is derived from the Latin title *Numeri,* which is a translation of the Gk. *Arithmoi.* The title reflects the emphasis on numbers present in the book, especially in the census lists of chaps. 1 and 26. The Hebrew title is *bĕmidbār*, meaning "in the wilderness," which comes from the fourth word in the first verse. The Hebrew name better describes the content of the book, a recollection of Israel's experience in the wilderness. The book may be divided into three major parts: Israel at SINAI (1:1–10:10); Israel in the wilderness, south of Palestine (10:11–21:9); and Israel in EDOM and MOAB (21:10–36:13).

The Book of Numbers is a collection of stories that demonstrate the unfaithfulness and rebellion of Israel against God and God's chosen leader, Moses. Jewish and Christian traditions believed until recently that the book was written by Moses. The advent of literary criticism has demonstrated that Numbers is composed of several sources that incorporate much historical material handed down and rewritten to meet the theological needs and concerns of later generations. The book incorporates a number of legal, liturgical, and statistical materials into a historical narrative that seeks to portray Israel as the people of God. Numbers is a compilation of different traditions by the Yahwistic, the Elohistic, and the priestly communities. The Priestly community contributed most of the material and gave the final form to the work in postexilic times.

Numbers seems to lack a consistent arrangement of its contents, but several theological emphases are seen throughout the book. First, the book presents Israel as the people of God marching towards the land of promise. The life of the community was centered around the tent of meeting (2:1-34), which bore witness to the divine presence among the people. Israel was a community on the march whose goal was the land promised by Yahweh. Israel's greatest sin was the refusal to enter the land (14:1-38) and to accept the divine intent (21:4-9). Second, the book addresses the problem of authority in the community. There are several episodes dealing with the problem of legitimate authority and the prominence of Moses as leader of the community. Moses' authority was challenged by AARON and MIRIAM (12:1-16), by the Levite clan of Korah (16:1-35), and by the community (11:4-6; 12:1-2; 14:2-3). Third, the book deals with the murmuring of the people about their misfortunes and their rebellion against God. The people complained about food (11:1-35), about the lack of water (14:1-12), and about the report of the spies (14:1-12). They also committed apostasy at Baal-peor (25:1-12).

One special problem in the book is the census figures in chaps. 1 and 26. These two figures have been interpreted in different ways. Some scholars have taken the numbers literally. However, the numbers would imply a population of two to three million people. Given the conditions of the wilderness, the demography of the area, and the intimation that Israel was a small people (Num 13:27-29; Deut 7:6-7), such an interpretation is improbable. G. E. Mendenhall has proposed the view that the figures represent a military list giving the number of men available for military duty. Others have seen the number as a census list from the time of the monarchy.

The Oracles of Balaam (Num 22:41–24:25) bless Israel. Inscriptions from *Tell Deir 'alla* in Jordan describe BALAAM, the son of Beor, as the leader of a religious community in Transjordan.

See also BALAAM; CENSUS/ENROLLMENT; TORAH.

Bibliography. M. Noth, *Numbers, OTL*; P. J. Budd, *Numbers, WBC*.

—CLAUDE F. MARIOTTINI

• **Numbers/Numerology.** A *number* is the name of a quantity. A *numeral* is a symbol for a number. *Numerology* is the symbolic use of numbers for esoteric knowledge. In the Bible, numbers are used to quantify, and they are used to symbolize a nonquantifiable figure. A mediating, rhetorical usage of numbers may also be observed in which quantification is present, but more important purposes lie in the numbers' ideological significance.

Numbers and Arithmetic. Ancient peoples used various ways to represent quantities. Numbers were written as words; the acrophonic variant of this system was to represent the number by the phonetic symbol for the initial sound of the number word. Numerals were also used, or number values were assigned to letters of the alphabet. These systems were used side by side. At Ugarit, for example, administrative and economic documents used numerals, while words were used in literary documents.

Hieratic (Egyptian) numerical symbols on ostraca from Samaria, Arad, and elsewhere demonstrate preexilic Israelite use of numerals. If Israelite writers followed the convention known from Ugarit, the absence of numerals in the OT may indicate that materials which appear to be administrative documents were preserved as literary documents. Maccabean coins are the earliest evidence for Jewish use of the alphabetic system. The acrophonic system is nowhere in evidence in the Bible.

The OT preserves examples of basic arithmetic operations such as addition (Gen 5), subtraction (Gen 18:28), multiplication (Lev 25:8), and division (Exod 21:35). In addition, Israel used simple fractions such as 1/2 (Num 15:9), 1/3 (Num 15:6), 1/4 (Lev 23:13), 1/5 (Lev 6:5 [Heb 5:24]), 1/6 (Ezek 4:11), 1/10 (Num 28:5), 2/10 (Num 15:6), 3/10 (Num 15:9), 1/50 (Num 31:30), 1/100 (Neh 5:11), and 1/500 (Num 31:28). Clearly, numbers are used in the Bible to quantify. In such cases, the biblical writers certainly intended to represent some exact quantity. Historical judgment must, of course, be exercised as to the accuracy of such quantifications.

Numbers and Rhetoric. Numbers may also be used rhetorically. The final tally of Job's possessions (42:12) bespeaks more than mere quantification. Taken with the figures for length of life in 42:16, they are more than an "audit." They indicate that the restoration was a double portion of new life (cf. Pss 90:10; 128:6).

The common sequence x/x + 1 is more concerned with emphasis than counting. Often this pattern does make the figures "come out right" (cf. Prov 30:15-31), but this is not always obvious (cf. Job 5:19; 33:14, 29). Other times, the pattern may be used for stylistic reasons alone (e.g., Amos 1:3–2:16).

Many interpreters argue that certain numbers carry meanings beyond quantity. The number SEVEN signifies completeness and perfection. Others which may mean more than mere quantity are *ten,* TWELVE, *forty,* and *seventy.* No single rule can be given for such significance-laden numbers. Each case must be weighed on its own merits.

The number *ten* derives its comprehensive significance from the ten fingers. Its pedagogical value is obvious from the fact that the TEN COMMANDMENTS (Exod 34:28) can be counted in various ways, but that however they are counted, Jewish, Roman Catholic, and Protestant traditions always come out to ten. Job uses the number *ten* comprehensively, not quantitatively, to refer to his friends' tenfold reproach (Job 19:3).

Whatever its prehistory, the biblical importance of the number *twelve* derives from its usage in the expression "the twelve tribes of Israel"; it is often noted that the tribes named are more than twelve, but that the various lists are adjusted to make them "come out right" to the number *twelve.* (Judg 5 is exceptional in this regard.) Similar observations could be made about the NT lists of the twelve disciples/apostles (cf. Matt 10:1-4 and par.). Acts 1:15-26 indicates that the number itself was felt to be significant. It came to indicate the whole people of God as summed up in their leaders.

The numbers *forty* and *seventy* may often be round numbers. The rains of Noah's flood fall for forty days and nights (Gen 7:12), the wilderness and wanderings are forty years (Deut 1:3), Moses spends forty days on the mountain (Exod 24:18), and Elijah and Jesus fast for forty days (1 Kgs 19:8; Matt 4:2), the Ninevites are given forty days to repent (Jonah 3:4). *Seventy* is the traditional number for a group of the elders of Israel (Exod 24:1; Num 11:16), the number of rulers' "sons" (Judg 9:2; 2 Kgs 10:1), and the number of years of Israel's punishment at the hands of Babylon (Jer 25:11). In terms of people, *seventy* probably refers to "a larger group of people taken as a whole" (Fensham). Dan 9:2 and 24 show that the number *seventy,* if taken as a precise quantification of years, demands re-interpretation.

Numbers and Esoterica. Although numerological senses have been suggested for John 21:11 and Gen 14:14, the only clear use of numbers to refer to something esoteric is the well-known 666 of Rev 13:18. This is the sum of numerical values assigned to the letters of a human name. Nero is the most likely of the countless suggestions. The Hebrew transcription of the Greek form of his name, which would give the value of 666, is attested in a scroll from Murabba'at; moreover, the Hebrew transcription of the Latin form of his name would explain the variant reading of 616 in some manuscripts.

Otherwise, various systems of interpretation find remarkable numerical relationships in the biblical text. Such numerical relationships are taken to be mathematical evidence of the rationality of scriptural teachings (Philo). Others argue that the striking numerical phenomena which they see in the biblical text constitute mathematical proof of the inspiration of scripture (Lucas and Washburn, or Luna). All such speculative systems stand under the ancient observation of Iamblichus regarding such numerological speculations, which the Greeks called *geometria:* " . . . in this way we could easily transform anything into any number, by dividing or adding or multiplying" (cited by Sambursky).

See also SEVEN, THE; TWELVE, THE.

Bibliography. Y. Aharoni, "The Use of Hieratic Numerals in Hebrew Ostraca and the Shekel Weights," *BASOR* 184 (1966): 13-19; J. J. Davis, *Biblical Numerology*; F. C. Fensham, "Numeral Seventy in the Old Testament and the Family of Jerubbaal, Ahab, Panammuwa and Athirat," *PEQ* 109 (1977): 113-15; D. R. Hillers, "Revelation 13:18 and the Scrolls from Murabba'at, *BASOR* 170 (1963): 65; J. Lucas and D. Washburn. *Theomatics: God's Best Kept Secret Revealed*; M. Luna, *The Number 7 in the Bible: Thousands of Amazing Facts Concerning the Sacred Number: A Scientific Demonstration of Divine Inspiration of the Bible*; H. R. Moehiring, "Arithmology as an Exegetical Tool in the Writings of Philo of Alexandria," *SBLASP* 13 (1978): 191-227; O. Neugebauer, *The Exact Sciences in Antiquity,* 2nd ed.; S. Sambursky, "On the Origin and Significance of the Term Gematria," *JJS* 29 (1978): 35-38; W. H. Shea, "Date and Significance of the Samaria Ostraca," *IEJ* 27 (1977): 16-27.

—JOHN KEATING WILES

• **Nunc Dimittis.** [noonk'di-mit"is] Along with the MAGNIFICAT (Luke 1:46-56), the BENEDICTUS (Luke 1:67-79), and the Gloria in Excelsis (Luke 2:14), the Nunc Dimittis (Luke 2:29-32) is one of the four poems or songs in Luke's birth and infancy narrative. Emphasizing the uniqueness and significance of Jesus, the songs also depict the happiness and joy surrounding his birth. The occasion of the Nunc Dimittis was twofold. One was the purification of Mary (Lev 12:2-8) and the second was the presentation of Jesus as a firstborn (Exod 12:2, 12-16; Num 18:15,16). Both reflect the fact that Joseph and Mary were faithful followers of the Mosaic Law.

Also faithful to the Jewish past, yet hopeful of its future, was Simeon, a "righteous and devout" and, apparently, aged man. As one "looking for the consolation of Israel," he personified the spirit of messianic expectation in first-century Judaism. In the infant Jesus, elderly Simeon saw the promised Messiah of Israel, the "Lord's Christ." Holding in his arms this fulfillment of an ancient hope, Simeon spoke in poetry. Traditionally known in the church by the first two words of the Latin translation ("Now let . . . depart"), the Nunc Dimittis, although brief, contains a major theological theme found in Luke and Acts. That theme is the universal nature of the gospel of Jesus Christ. Drawing heavily from the message of Isaiah (Isa 52:10; 42:6; 49:6), Simeon saw Jesus as God's servant, bringing salvation to all people. Jesus was "a light" to the gentiles to bring them out of darkness. And as the fulfillment of divine promise, Jesus was the "glory" of Israel. Luke's gospel was inclusive, not exclusive; it was universal, not racial, regional or national. Simeon sings this song of universalism at the beginning of Jesus' life.

See also BENEDICTUS; HYMN; MAGNIFICAT; SIMEON.

—WALTER B. SHURDEN

• **Nurse.** A term used in the KJV for a person (either male or female) who nurtures a child, and by all English translations for a wet nurse (in the former case, the Heb. verbal root *'-m-n,* "to support," is used, and the RSV sometimes renders the noun by "foster fathers" rather than KJV's curious "nursing fathers" [Isa 49:34]; in the latter case, the root *y-n-q,* "to suckle," is used).

Israelite women usually nursed their own children (Gen 21:7; 1 Sam 1:23; 1 Kgs 3:21), but various circumstances might lead to the services of a wet nurse (Gen 24:59; Exod 2:7, 9). Such persons, rather than temporary hirelings, might become esteemed members of the family group (Gen 35:8). Weaning was sometimes regarded as a significant transition, to be observed with a feast (Gen 21:8).

Nurture of children (whether the care of older ones or the suckling of infants) provided analogies and metaphors for describing other types of relationship. Hence, MOSES' concern for the people in the wilderness might be compared with that of a "nurse" (Num 11:12), as might monarchical protection (Isa 49:23) and PAUL's attitude toward a congregation (1 Thess 2:7).

See also FAMILY.

—LLOYD R. BAILEY

• **Nuzi.** [n*oo'*zee] An ancient city in northern Mesopotamia. It was located at the modern site of Yorghan Tepe, about eight mi. from Kirkuk in northeast Iraq (PLATE 1). Excavations at the site were conducted between 1925 and 1931 by Edward Chiera and Robert H. Pfeiffer under the joint sponsorship of the University of Pennsylvania, Harvard University, and the American Schools of Oriental Research.

Excavations at the site have revealed that in the third millennium B.C.E., the place was called Gasur. The city reached its zenith during the fifteenth and the fourteenth centuries B.C.E. under the control of the Hurrians (biblical Horites). The Hurrians were a nonsemitic people who came from Armenia. They established their presence in Anatolia, Mesopotamia, Syria, and Palestine. They organized the Mitanni kingdom of which Nuzi was a dependency. At the site of ancient Nuzi archaeologists found thousands of clay tablets, most of them written in Akkadian with some Hurrian words. These documents were discovered in the palace and in private homes. Some of these documents cover four or five generations of the same family, providing a complete file of wealthy individuals.

The texts reflect Hurrian customs and legal practices of the fifteenth century B.C.E. The documents include business records, wills, adoption and marriage contracts, and statements detailing the sale and transfer of lands, goods, and people. Although these documents are somewhat later than the time of the patriarchal narratives, they reflect legal customs and social practices that were common in the social world of the patriarchs.

In Nuzi, a property owner who had no son could adopt someone to be the heir of his properties. The adopted son could be a relative, a freeborn man, or a slave. The adopted son would care for the man in his old age, provide him with burial, and continue the affairs of the family. A similar situation is reflected in ABRAHAM's adoption of Eliezer of Damascus, although the practice of adoption is not found in Israelite law. Abraham had adopted Eliezer, a slave born in his house, to be his heir (Gen 15:2-3). According to Nuzi law, if a son was born to this same property owner, then the legitimate son would become the rightful heir. God's answer to Abraham was that Eliezer would not be Abraham's heir but his own son, born of SARAH, would be the heir (Gen 15:4).

Another practice at Nuzi is similar to the events between Abraham and Hagar. In Hurrian society if a woman was unable to conceive a son, she had the right to provide her husband with a slave as a secondary wife. The son born of this union would become the heir and would be considered the son of the true wife. The action of Sarah, requesting Abraham to take Hagar as wife, explains her words to Abraham: "I shall obtain children by her" (Gen 16:2). Rachel and Leah, when they became unable to conceive also gave their servants, Bilhah and Zilpah to JACOB (Gen 30:1-13). A similar regulation is found in the Code of Hammurabi, however only the priestess is mentioned in reference to this right.

Another custom at Nuzi that finds parallel in the biblical narratives is the law of inheritance. At Nuzi, the laws of inheritance indicated that when a father died, his eldest son would receive a double portion of his father's inheritance. Deut 21:15-17 parallels this Nuzi legal custom. In Israel, a son would receive a double portion of the inheritance upon his father's death. In Nuzi, oral blessings and deathbed wishes had a legal status when uttered in the presence of witnesses. Thus, when ISAAC blessed Jacob his blessing had a binding character over his sons. At Nuzi, an individual could sell or transfer his birthright since Hurrian society did not consider chronological age the single criteria for determining inheritance. One text found in Nuzi describes a man who transferred his inheritance to his brother in exchange for three sheep. Gen 25:31-34 describes how Esau sold his rights as firstborn for food. In Hurrian society, the right of the firstborn was at the discretion of the father and he could revoke this right at will. In Gen 48:13-20, Jacob, in spite of the protest of Joseph, blessed Ephraim over Manasseh, even though Manasseh was the firstborn.

Two laws that at one time were considered to be valuable parallels to the patriarchal stories, now have been reevaluated in the light of publication of new texts dealing with family laws. First, earlier scholars believed that the custom of a brother adopting his sister provided authentic parallels to Abraham's representing Sarah as his sister to Pharaoh (Gen 12:10-16) and to Isaac's portraying Rebekah as his sister to Abimelech (Gen 26:6-11). New research into family law at Nuzi indicates that the law that allowed a brother to adopt his sister did not grant him marital rights over her. The rights of an adopting brother ceased with the marriage of his sister to another man. Second, earlier scholars believed that possession of household gods symbolized the right of inheritance. At the death of the head of a household, the household images were given to the primary heir, but evidence shows that a secondary heir could also receive the family images. New evidence tends to demonstrate that when the head of a household died, other images were made to take the place of the household gods.

The Nuzi texts also provide useful information on the Habiru. At Nuzi, the Habiru appear as underprivileged foreigners who sold themselves to their patrons for protection and food for themselves and their families, and for rations for their animals. The names of the people who are classified as Habiru appear to be Akkadian, although some of the Habiru had Hurrian names. The social position of the Habiru at Nuzi seems to reflect the same conditions found at a later time in Palestine as revealed in the AMARNA letters.

These parallels between Nuzi social and legal practices cannot be used to authenticate the biblical narratives about the patriarchs as some have done. The patriarchal narratives and the Nuzi texts are separated by two to three hundred years. However, it can be said that some of the social practices of the patriarchs reflect some of the practices in Mesopotamian society.

Bibliography. C. H. Gordon: ''Biblical Customs and the Nuzi Tablets,'' *BA* 3 (1940): 1-12; M. H. Morrison, ''The Jacob and Laban Narrative in Light of Near Eastern Sources,'' *BA* 46 (1983): 155-64; B. L. Eichler, ''Nuzi,'' *IDBSup*.

—CLAUDE F. MARIOTTINI

• **Oath.** A statement by means of which a person guarantees that a promise will be kept or that the truth has been spoken. Ordinarily a deity was invoked as the guarantor (Amos 8:14), with the expectation that divine retribution (often expressed in the form of a curse) would follow in case of perjury: ''May the god ______do thus-and-so to me, if this oath is not kept.'' Normally in ancient ISRAEL it was Yahweh (''the Lord'') who was thus invoked, and the actual content of the curse was often suppressed (e.g., Ruth 1:17; 1 Sam 14:44; 1 Kgs 2:23; but see the full form at Num 5:21-22; Ps 7:3-5). The deity was thought to be impelled to protect the divine name from profanation by acting against the perjurer (Lev 19:12). Symbolic acts such as a raised hand (Dan 12:7), the grasping of a sacred or potent object (e.g., the genitals of ABRAHAM, Gen 24:1-3), or sacrifice (in the case of a COVENANT, Gen 15:7-18), often accompanied an oath.

The Hebrew word for ''oath'' is related to the number SEVEN, whose sacred character likely is derived from an ancient Heptad of deities (''The Seven'') in whose name oaths were often taken. Hence, ''to swear'' originally meant ''to invoke The Seven.'' This may be related to the seven lambs that were utilized in Abraham's covenant with ABIMELECH (Gen 21:22-31).

Since oaths might be taken rashly to one's regret (Judg 11:9-35), and since the use of the divine name came to be forbidden (note the substitutes in Matt 23:16-22), some groups within Judaism frowned upon taking them (including Jesus, Matt 5:33-37; the Essenes, so Josephus, *BJ* 2.8.6; but contrast Paul's use of them, 2 Cor 1:23; Gal 1:20; Phil 1:8).

See also BEERSHEBA; CURSE AND BLESSING.

Bibliography. S. Blank, ''The Curse, Blasphemy, the Spell, and the Oath,'' *HUCA* 23 (1950-1951): 73-95.

—LLOYD R. BAILEY

• **Obadiah.** [oh'buh-di''uh] A common Hebrew name, Obadiah means ''servant of the Lord'' and is the name given to the shortest book among the Hebrew prophets. Whether it was the name of a prophet or is symbolic for the role of the nation of ISRAEL in exile is open to debate, though certainly the title may serve both purposes.

Obadiah is the name of a dozen other persons referred to in the OT, the most prominent of whom was an official in the court of King Ahab (1 Kgs 18) who protected many prophets from persecution and death at the hands of Queen Jezebel. The prophet Elijah appeared to Obadiah and sent him to Ahab to arrange a meeting between the prophet and the king.

—LAMONTTE M. LUKER

• OUTLINE OF OBADIAH •

The Book of Obadiah

I. God's Judgment on Edom (1-10)
II. Reason for the Judgment: Edom's Mistreatment of Judah (11-14)
III. The Day of the Lord and Its Outcome (15-21)

• **Obadiah, Book of.** The poem that is the Book of Obadiah probably was composed during the EXILE in Judah not long after the fall of JERUSALEM when Edom not only gloated while its sibling-nation was defeated by Babylon, but also helped itself to the plunder and even rounded up Jewish fugitives and turned them over to the enemy (vv. 11-14). The legends of the brothers JACOB, ancestor of Israel, and ESAU, ancestor of Edom, in Gen 25–36 reveal the tribal relations the two nations had shared at their origins and help explain the intense feelings of betrayal that the Hebrew poet expresses in Obadiah. Formally, the poem is similar to the genre ''foreign nation oracle'' against Edom (cf. Isa 34; Ezek 25:12-14; 35); it has special affinities with Jer 49:7-22, and its background is echoed also in such exilic passages as Lam 4:21-22 and Ps 137:7-9.

Even as Esau was an eponym for Edom in the legends of Genesis, so Edom in the exilic and postexilic literature was much more than simply a country; Edom became a symbol for human arrogance opposed to God (vv. 3-4), hatred and betrayal opposed to love and faithfulness, a symbol of EVIL. Hence the bitterly somber tone of the poem, which is constructed in two parts, vv. 1-14 and 15-21, around three major Hebrew traditions, the Day of the Lord, the Kingdom of God, and the suffering servant.

Contrasted with the day of Jerusalem's fall described in vv. 11-14 is the eschatological Day of the Lord when God shall act (vv. 8 and 15-21). The Day of the Lord grew out of Israel's holy war tradition and was the day on which the God of the Exodus would defeat all forces of oppression, often, of course, identified with Israel's enemies. The eighth-century prophets turned the tradition on its head by claiming that because of Israel's oppression of its own people, the Day of the Lord would be a day in which God fought against his own nation (e.g., Amos 5:18-20). And yet the concept never lost its original implications, and especially in light of the Exile became that Day in which God would defeat all powers of evil and establish a universal kingdom of justice, righteousness, and peace.

The kingdom is described in vv. 15-21. As usual in Hebrew ESCHATOLOGY, Mount Zion is its symbolic capital (vv. 17 and 21; cf. Mic 4). Also typical are its boundaries, which are those of the empire of David (vv. 19-21; cf. Gen 15:18; Mic 7:12). Even as v. 1 had resounded international outrage against Edom's evil, so vv. 15-16 announce judgment on international evil; but v. 17 holds out universal hope: "there shall be those that escape" from around the world—the righteous who wish to join in the Kingdom of God and who make the pilgrimage to Zion, its center.

The third theme of Obadiah, servant of Yahweh, is summed up in its title. Israel in exile is the servant who suffers on behalf of the world, symbolically offering sacrifice and making God's kingdom possible. This, too, is an exilic theme expressed in Second Isaiah's suffering servant songs (Isa 42:1-4; 49:1-6; 50:4-11; 52:13–53:12). It would be combined with the idea of the Kingdom of God by Jesus and the early church to produce the concept of the king who suffers on behalf of his people.

See also EDOM/EDOMITES/IDUMAEA; OBADIAH.

Bibliography. L. C. Allen, *The Books of Joel, Obadiah, Jonah and Micah*; B. Childs, "Obadiah," *Introduction to the Old Testament as Scripture*; J. Muilenburg, "Obadiah, Book of," *IDB*.

—LAMONTTE M. LUKER

• **Obed-Edom.** [oh'bid-ee"duhm] A proper name meaning "servant of Edom"; it appears in the OT twenty times, borne by several different men.

The best known Obed-edom lived in the time of DAVID. When David was moving the Ark of the Covenant to Jerusalem, tragedy struck and Uzzah was killed. The king placed the Ark in "the house of Obed-edom the Gittite" (2 Sam 6:10) where it remained three months, "and the Lord blessed Obed-edom and all his household" (v. 11). "Gittite" refers to someone from GATH, but probably not the one in Philistia because it is unlikely a Philistine would be permitted to house the Ark. Obed-edom probably was from Gath-rimmon in the tribal territory of DAN.

All Obed-edoms in the OT were associated with the Ark or the Temple, as musicians (1 Chr 15:24), gatekeepers (15:18; 16:38; 26:4-5, 15), and later as custodians of Temple vessels in the reign of AMAZIAH, king of Judah (2 Chr 25:24).

—D. C. MARTIN

• **Obedience.** Submission to the will of another; compliance with God's law.

The Hebrew word for obedience is also translated "to hear." Genuine hearing includes obedience. God speaks and the faithful response is to hear and obey. Failure to comply with God's word is evidence of deafness (Ps 115:6; Isa 6:9-10). The same theme is developed in the NT with the exhortation that he "who has ears to hear, let him hear" (Matt 11:15; Mark 4:9; Luke 14:35).

In the OT, morality is equated often with obedience to God's commandments (Exod 19:5, 8; Deut 28:1; 30:11-14; Eccl 12:13; Isa 1:2; Jer 2:4; 7:21-28). The promises of the covenant are predicated upon obedience (Exod 15:26; Lev 20:22-24; Deut 6:1-3). The dominance of the obedience motif is reflected in the ranking of obedience as more important than sacrifice (1 Sam 15:22; Jer 7:21-23).

In the NT the obedience theme centers on Christ's submission to God. In the gospels, doing the will of his father was Christ's food (John 4:34). In Christ's temptations and passion experience, the theme is his obedience to God (Matt 4:1-11; 26:36-39; Luke 22:39-42). PAUL sees Christ as the one who, unlike ADAM, was obedient to God (Rom 5:18-21). Through Christ's obedience, believers are justified before God (Rom 5; 6:16; 2 Cor 10:5-6).

—DANIEL B. MCGEE

• **Obeisance.** The act of paying homage, showing respect, or demonstrating submission, usually indicated by some form of bowing. The most widely used Greek word for this act was *proskuneō,* whose etymology seems to have meant "to kiss reverently." This gesture seems to have involved full prostration on the ground and kissing the other's feet, whether it be a sovereign, a master, a parent, or a cultic idol.

It is questionable whether, among the Hebrews, obeisance involved the act of kissing. It certainly included bowing. Jacob bowed seven times before Esau (Gen 33:3), David three times before Jonathan (1 Sam 20:41). Characteristically, obeisance is described as prostrating oneself with one's face to the ground (Gen 43:26-28; 48:12; 1 Sam 24:8; 25:23; 2 Sam 14:33; 15:5; Ruth 2:10). Obeisance was done before a king or a superior (1 Sam 24:8; 1 Kgs 1:16, 23, 31; Gen 37:7-10; 42:6). Also, one shows obeisance to God's prophet (1 Sam 28:14; 2 Kgs 2:15; 4:37). Surprisingly, only rarely was someone described as showing obeisance to God (Gen 24:26, 48; Isa 60:14).

The picture in the NT is different, where the object of obeisance was always something actually or supposedly divine. References to *proskunēsis* are most frequent in the Gospels, Acts and Revelation, occurring only three times in all the Letters (1 Cor 14:25; Heb 1:6; 11:21). Jesus was often approached with the gesture (Matt 2:2; 8:2; 9:18; 14:33; 15:25; 20:20). Obeisance was reserved for deity, and Peter refused it from Cornelius (Acts 10:25-26) as did the angel in Revelation (19:10; 22:8-9). One could indeed prostrate oneself before false gods (Rev 13:4, 8, 12, 15; 14:9, 11), but true worship was to fall down before the Lord of Lords (Rev 4:10; 5:14; 7:11; 11:16; 19:4).

See also GESTURES; WORSHIP IN THE OLD TESTAMENT.

Bibliography. H. Greeven, "προσκυνέω," *TDNT*.

—JOHN POLHILL

• **Occupations.** The wide spectrum of activities by which people in Palestine maintained themselves varied along with the history of the region and the economic development of the Near Eastern and Mediterranean worlds. Many of these diverse occupations and their methods are referred to in the Bible. Constant throughout time were occupations devoted to the needs of family and home. From the earliest times through the end of the NT period the largest portion of the populace of Palestine provided its own needs directly through its own production. Depending upon their locations, families were engaged in farming, fishing, hunting and shepherding to provide their food. Fishing was a limited occupation in OT times (Amos 4:2) but increased in importance with the rise of fish in the diet of Hellenistic and Roman times. Farming and shepherding are interdependent activities and were carried on in tandem in most villages, though neither agricultural specialists nor nomadic pastoralists were completely absent from the picture. AGRICULTURE focused on the essential grains and pulses as well as crucial fruits such as figs, olives, and grapes, which required only simple processing. SHEEP and goats were the primary focus of pastoral energies and were utilized mainly for milk and wool. Masonry and carpentry to provide shelter were also household prerogatives, as were wool-washing, SPINNING AND WEAVING for clothes. Food storage such as drying figs and food preparation such as bread baking were also carried out in the domestic context. Imitation provided the only training necessary for these occupations.

Ideally, production levels were set by the needs of the family and the village. But the autonomy of the family and village was regularly undercut by political power that extracted taxes and rents from their production.

Specialization was also a part of the lives of villagers. Both within and among villages pottery making, smithing (Jer 6:29-30; Isa 54:16), and craftwork were carried on as primary occupations by certain families. Especially fine or special purpose items might also be produced by experts. Pottery workshops probably existed in every village. PRIESTS and prophets (1 Sam 7:16; 9:6ff.) were religious specialists who earned their livelihood through the practice of their trades. Occupational specialization possessed a hereditary character. Jesus is reported to be the son of a village carpenter (Matt 13:55).

In urban environments this specialization was greatly heightened both in terms of the diversity of occupations and the percentage of persons engaged in them. Most of the biblical references to occupations presuppose this urban diversity. Jeremiah visits a potter (Jer 18:2) and is able to draw upon this familiar sight in his diatribe. Loaves of bread come to him from the baker's street (Jer 37:21). Goldsmiths and perfume makers are among those whom Nehemiah directs in building the city walls (Neh 3:8), and Ephesus boasts a guild of silversmiths (Acts 19:24). Paul was a tentmaker and makes contact in unfamiliar cities with members of his trade (Acts 18:3). Isaiah meets with the king at the fuller's field, doubtlessly the pungent place where wool was washed commercially. The city of Samaria provides the backdrop for Amos' denunciation of the deceitful business practices of the grain merchants who represent what was likely a diverse retail marketplace. Supplying these markets, i.e., feeding the urban demand for essentials such as food and luxury items such as imported dishes, increased the level of specialization in the surrounding countryside. Farms could produce wine and olive oil for market instead of a diverse repertoire of foods for self consumption. These market-oriented farms became places of employment for landless day laborers and these workers as well as the estate owners themselves came to rely upon the markets for their foodstuffs. Commercial transport of farm produce to the cities for sale and for the import-export business involved many in transit trade (Ezek 28).

The urban centers housed the political and religious institutions that structured society and directed its economic systems. These institutions added broadly to the kinds of occupations available. First Sam 8 lists the needs of the incipient Israelite monarchy: armed forces, agricultural workforce, armament manufacturers, palace personnel. It warns that these positions would be filled involuntarily, and it is probably true that conscripts or slaves performed many of the occupations involving hard labor. The grand building projects of the royal house from Solomon's time to Herod's involved huge inputs of physical labor for quarrying, transporting, erecting, and finishing limestone blocks (2 Chr 2:2). The remains of these projects, most notably the Omride citadel at Samaria and the Herodian Temple Mount, are ample testimony to the highly developed nature of stone masonry. As with other skills, there is little known about the organization of this profession. Apart from the mass of persons employed to carry out the wishes of the state, there were also the ranks of the officials and functionaries of court and Temple, which were the professions par excellence in Biblical times. The list of Solomon's cabinet ministers (1 Kgs 4:2) signals the growth of a bureaucracy that would provide occupations for professional SOLDIERS, priests, prophets (1 Kgs 22:6), secretaries (also known as SCRIBES), advisers and lower officials. These state officials often bear the brunt of prophetic denunciation (Mic 3; Jer 8:8-12). When Palestine was incorporated into the rule of an empire, some would become imperial agents, such as the tax/toll collector Zacchaeus (Luke 19). Like the priesthood, it is probable that most political and religious functions were maintained within the confines of certain families.

Determining how the various occupations were regarded by the persons who engaged in them and by others is complicated by the urban-managerial orientation of the biblical tradition. There is, for example, an unmistakable elitism in Sirach's description of the wisdom of the scribe as compared to the plow-handler, artisan, smith and potter (Sir 38:24–39:11). Unlike the basic Roman cultural stance, however, work itself seems to have been highly valued both in Israelite and early Jewish times (Gen 2:15; Ps 104:23; Prov 6:6-11). Legal stipulations recognize the plight of the day laborer (Deut 24:14-15; Lev 19:13). Some descriptions of those who toiled for their livings arouse sympathy for the oppressed (Job 24:10-12) and recall the hard service of Israel's bondage in Egypt (Exod 1:14). Jesus' view of labor is embedded in his proclamation of the reversals of the kingdom: laborers in the fields will find a liberation from the toil of cultivation yet share in the harvest (Mark 4:26-29).

Bibliography. R. deVaux, *Ancient Israel,* vol. 1, "Social Institutions"; M. Elat, "Trade and Commerce," *The Age of the Monarchies: Culture and Society,* ed. A. Malamat; D. E. Oakman, *Jesus and the Economic Questions of His Day.*

—DAVID C. HOPKINS

• **Offering for the Saints.** *See* CONTRIBUTION FOR THE SAINTS

• **Og.** King of Bashan. The defeat of Og, king of Bashan, at Edrei in the northern Transjordan is among the most celebrated victories in the accounts of Israel's conquest and settlement (cf. Num 21:33-35; Deut 3:1-11; Neh 9:22; Ps 135:11). Og is referred to both as "the last of the Rephaim" (e.g., Deut 3:11), a legendary race of giants, early inhabitants of Palestine (cf. Deut 2:10-11; 2 Sam 21:16-22), and as an "Amorite" (e.g., Deut 4:47); but this latter designation is doubtful, probably due to his secondary association with SIHON, king of Heshbon. Although "Og" may not be a personal name at all and "Bashan" is the name of a geographical region rather than a kingdom, Og was clearly a figure of some repute in Israel (and Ammon—cf. Deut 3:11); otherwise his defeat could not have served as it does to legitimize Israel's claim to the territory of the northern Transjordan.

See also BASHAN; SIHON.

—JEFFREY S. ROGERS

• **Oholah/Oholibah.** [oh-hoh'luh/oh-hoh'li-buh] Names given by the prophet EZEKIEL to SAMARIA and JERUSALEM respectively. The names appear in Ezekiel's ALLEGORY of judgment against Judah (Ezek 23). The apparent meaning of Oholah is "her tent," and of Oholibah is "my tent (is) in her." The names may denote Israel's early history of living in tents, or its worship in tents at pagan shrines, or perhaps the people's historical link to the TABERNACLE in the wilderness.

Although the existence of shrine tents is uncertain, Israel did live in tents in its early period and there was some form of tabernacle in the wilderness. The allegory thus could point to living in tents, understood positively, prior to the introduction of the worship of BAAL (Hos 2:12-13 [H 2:14-15]). The allegory could, however, use the reference to tents in a negative way, placing additional emphasis on Israel's early unfaithfulness (Ezek 23:3, 19, 27).

Behind the allegory there lies the Israelite understanding that God desires to dwell ("tabernacle" or "tent") with the people of God (Exod 33:10; Num 9:17; 12:5, 10), but that the divine presence will be withdrawn if Israel persists in sin (Ezek 10).

See also EZEKIEL.

Bibliography. W. Eichrodt, *Ezekiel, A Commentary*.

—WALTER E. BROWN

• **Oil.** In the biblical world, oil for various uses was extracted from two sources. In parts of Mesopotamia the people made their oil from sesame seeds, but in Palestine it seems that oil was produced only from olives. OLIVE oil was one of the main products along with wine, wheat, barley, honey, and figs. The olive tree flourished in Palestine, especially in Galilee, Perea, and the Decapolis. Many of the trees have survived for centuries. Some affirm that the olive trees in Gethsemane date back to the Arab invasion of 637 C.E. Still others believe that they were there in the time of Christ. It is very doubtful that they are that old.

Several methods were used in biblical times to extract oil from olives. One method was by treading on the olives after they had been dumped into a vat (Mic 6:15). A second way to get the oil from the olive was by means of pestle pounding: workers took a pestle and beat the olives in a mortar. This was called "beaten oil" and was very fine (Exod 27:20). It was used for the lamps to burn continually in the Temple. A third method was the oil press, in which the remaining pulp from the two other procedures was mashed to get the rest of the oil. Large oil presses have been discovered at Debir and Beth-shemesh dating from the tenth to the sixth century B.C.E.

The most frequent use of oil in the OT was anointing. The king (1 Sam 10:1; 16:1; 2 Kgs 9:3; 11:12), the priest (Lev 8:30), and the PROPHET (Isa 61:1) were anointed with oil to show that they had been chosen by God and separated to him for a particular purpose. Olive oil was also used to smear the shield of a warrior (Isa 21:5; 2 Sam 1:21). This action was probably symbolic of dedication to Yahweh.

There are few biblical references to the use of oil in preparation of foods (1 Kgs 17:12; 1 Chr 12:40); however, it is assumed that many foods were cooked in oil just as butter and shortening are used today. Another important function of olive oil was to give illumination. Oil was poured into a lamp in the shape of a saucer with pinched lips which held the wick. Olive oil was widely used for medicinal purposes, especially for healing wounds (Isa 1:6; Mark 6:13; Jas 5:14; Luke 10:34). Olive oil was also mixed with the cereal offering as part of the daily burnt offering ceremony.

See also ANOINT; FOOD; KINGSHIP; OINTMENT/PERFUME; OLIVE; PRIESTS; PROPHET.

Bibliography. R. J. Forbes, *Studies in Ancient Technology*; G. E. Wright, *Biblical Archaeology*; J. Finegan, *Light from the Ancient Past*.

—T. C. SMITH

• **Ointment/Perfume.** Ointments and perfumes were widely enjoyed in biblical times. Both generally consisted of some type of oil mixed with various aromatic spices, although there were also dry perfumes in powdered form. In the arid heat of the Near East, oil was a welcome emollient and moisturizer, whereas the fragrances served to mask body odors.

The art of ointment-making and perfumery is very old. The industry was practiced in Egypt, Persia, Babylonia, Syria, Palestine, Greece, and Rome. The quest for raw materials (often from such exotic places as Arabia, Africa, and India) and markets fostered thriving, profitable trade routes. The caravan of Ishmaelites to whom Joseph's brothers sold him were carrying spices from Gilead to Egypt (Gen 37:25).

In Palestine the most common base was olive oil, which by itself could be used as an ointment. Various spices were added to the oil both to thicken it and to provide fragrance. The whole mixture was then boiled (Job 41:31).

Ointments and liquid perfumes were stored in long, slender flasks, often ornately carved and preferably made of alabaster (Mark 14:3; Luke 7:37), a soft stone. The neck of the sealed container would be broken in order to pour out the contents (Mark 14:3).

The high cost of many ointments is reflected in the Bible. King Hezekiah's treasures included, alongside the silver and gold, his "spices" and his "precious oil" (2 Kgs 20:13). The "very expensive ointment" (Matt 26:7) with which Jesus was anointed in Bethany was reckoned by the disciples to have been worth approximately a year's wages (Mark 14:5; John 12:5). The "pure nard" which it contained was derived from the roots of a plant grown in distant India.

Cosmetically, ointments were liberally applied to the body after bathing (Ruth 3:3; 2 Sam 12:20). The Bible frequently refers in particular to anointing the head (Ps 133:2; Matt 6:17). It is twice reported that Jesus' feet were anointed (Luke 7:38; John 12:3). Perfumes were used by both sexes to make themselves more attractive (Esth 2:12; Cant 1:3, 12; 3:6; 4:10) as well as to scent clothing (Cant 4:11; Ps 45:8) and to enhance the allure of the harlot's bed (Prov 7:17).

It was a sign of lavish hospitality, especially at banquets, to anoint the heads of guests (Ps 23:5; Luke 7:46). Nero had dining rooms specially equipped to spray perfumes on his guests.

Medicinally, ointments were used in dressing wounds (Isa 1:6; Luke 10:34) and in various preparations for specific ailments (Rev 3:18).

Ointments were profusely employed in funeral preparations. King Asa was buried "with spices and various kinds of aromatics compounded into an ointment" (2 Chr 16:14 NASB). According to John (19:39-40), the body of Jesus was wrapped in linen with "a mixture of myrrh and aloes, about a hundred pounds' weight." According to Mark (16:1) and Luke (23:56; 24:1), the women who discovered the empty tomb had gone there intending to anoint Jesus' body with spices and ointments.

Ointments also figured prominently in religious ceremonies. Formulas are given for "sacred anointing oil" (Exod 30:23-25) and for the holy incense (Exod 30:34-35). The former was used in consecrating the sanctuary, its furnishings, and the priests; the latter was burned twice daily on the incense altar in the holy place. Kings also were anointed to their office (1 Sam 10:1; 16:13; 1 Kgs 1:39; 2 Kgs 9:6).

Jesus' anointing in Bethany involved treatment as an honored guest, consecration to his messianic task, and preparation of his body for burial.

See also COSMETICS.

Bibliography. W. A. Poucher, *Perfumes, Cosmetics and Soaps*; Theophrastus, *Concerning Odours*; J. Toutain, *The Economic Life of the Ancient World*.

—DONALD N. PENNY

• **Old Testament.** The term "Old Testament" is a Christian designation used to denote the first part of the Christian BIBLE in contrast to the second part, namely, the NT. In contemporary Protestant usage, the OT (of thirty-nine books) contains the same writings as the Hebrew or Jewish Bible (of twenty-four books), but not in the same sequential order.

The use of the term "testament" for these writings is derived from Latin where the word denoted a last will. The Latin usage is itself based on the fact that the Greek translators rendered the biblical Heb. term *bĕrît* (COVENANT) with *diathēkē* ("will, testament") rather than *synthēkē* ("covenant"; used only in Wis 12:21 in the sense of covenant). Technically, it would have been more logical to speak of the writings of the old and new covenants rather than testaments. Perhaps *diathēkē* was used by the Greek translators rather than *synthēkē* for theological reasons, because the latter was understood as referring to an agreement arrived at after discussion and often by parties of equal rank. The translators wished to avoid any idea of such conditionality for the covenant.

Reference to Judaism and Jewish scriptures as the old or first covenant in comparison to Christianity as the new covenant are already found in 1 Cor 11:25; 2 Cor 3:6, 14; Heb 9:15-18, and are probably dependent upon Jer 31:30-32. The expression "book of the covenant" may have been current in Judaism at the time of the early church to denote Jewish scriptures (Exod 24:7; 2 Kgs 23:2, 21; Sir 24:23; 1 Macc 1:56-57; cf. 2 Kgs 22:8, 10) and thereby influenced the Christian choice of terminology.

Melito, bishop of Sardis (ca. 170 C.E.), already referred to the ancient writings of the Law and the Prophets as the OT. By the time of Tertullian (ca. 160–220) and Origen (ca. 185–254), the terminology of OT for Jewish scriptures and NT for Christian scriptures was in current usage. Origen refers to "testimonies drawn from the scriptures which we believe to be divine, both from what is called the OT and also from the New, endeavoring to confirm our faith by reason" (*OnPrin* 4.1; Greek version). No single designation for the Hebrew scriptures has been characteristic of Judaism. The term "the books" (*Ha-Sĕpārîm* in Heb., *ta biblia* in Gk.) was frequently employed in both Hellenistic (cf. Dan 9:2; *Letter of Aristeas* §316; *Prologue to Sirach* 1; 1 Macc 12:9; 2 Macc 8:23; Josephus, *Ant* 20.261) and rabbinic literature (*m.Meg* 1.8; *Git* 4.6; *Kelim* 15.6; and elsewhere). The Greek form, via the Latin, has supplied us with the word "Bible."

Like the word "scripture," terms derived from the verbs for "write" (*ktb* in Heb.; *graphō* in Gk.) were frequently employed, sometimes in the singular (*m.Taan* 3.8; *Sanh* 4.5; *'Abot* 3.7, 8, etc; *Letter of Aristeas* §§155, 168; John 2:22; Acts 8:32; 2 Tim 3:16; etc.) and other times in the plural (*m.Yad* 3.5; Mark 12:24; 1 Cor 15:34 etc.). The adjective "holy" was sometimes used to modify such writing(s) (*m.Šab* 16.1; *Erub* 10.3; *Yad* 3.2; Philo, *OnFF* 1.4; Josephus, *Ant* 1.13; 10.210; Rom 1:2; *1 Clem* 45:2; 53:1; etc.).

The term *miqra'* ("reading") was used in rabbinic literature (*m.Ned* 4.3; *'Abot* 5.21; etc.) and was widely popular in the Middle Ages. The acronym TaNaKh, presently in wide usage (cf. the recent Jewish Publication Society translation), is derived from the first letters of the three divisions of the Hebrew Bible—Torah (Law), Nebi'im (Prophets), and Kethubim (Writings).

Various Forms of the OT. What is the Bible in Judaism and the OT in Christianity exists in several forms. The Protestant OT contains the same books with the same contents as the Jewish Bible but orders many of the books in a different sequence. The Roman Catholic OT includes all the books found in the Hebrew Bible but varies in two ways in addition to the ordering of the books. First, the BOOK OF ESTHER includes 107 verses not found in the Hebrew text distributed in six places throughout the book (before 1:1; after 3:13; 4:17; 8:12; 10:3; plus a colophon) and the BOOK OF DANIEL includes 174 verses not found in the Hebrew-Aramaic text: the PRAYER OF AZARIAH and the *Song of the Three Young Men* (sixty-eight verses inserted following 3:23), SUSANNA (sixty-four verses, variously located; in the Vulgate as chap. 13), and BEL AND THE DRAGON (forty-two verses, in the Vulgate as chap. 14). Second, the Catholic OT, affirmed at the fourth session of the Council of Trent (8 April 1546), includes the books of TOBIT, JUDITH, WISDOM OF SOLOMON, Ecclesiasticus (or SIRACH), BARUCH (associated with the BOOK OF JEREMIAH), and 1–2 MACCABEES. (The Greek Orthodox Church at the Synod of Jerusalem [March 1672], in question three to its eighteen decrees, affirmed the canonicity of the Wisdom of Solomon, Judith, Tobit, Bel and the Dragon, Susanna, 1–3 Maccabees, and Sirach. Debate over the extent of the canon has occurred in recent years in the Greek Orthodox church. In 1950, the Holy Synod of the Greek church sanctioned an edition of the OT which includes the books of the Catholic OT plus 2 Esdras and 3 MACCABEES with 4 MACCABEES printed as an appendix.)

How are these differences even among Christians over the extent of the OT to be explained? Basically, three main approaches to this issue have been taken. (1) The Protestant reformers in reverting to a shorter canon argued that the original Hebrew Bible was the OT of Jesus and the early church and that the other books (called apocryphal by Protestants, sometimes deutero-canonical by Catholics) were incorrectly added. Although used in the early church, the latter works were considered "ecclesiastical" (useable in the church) but not canonical. (2) Catholics (and Orthodox) have argued that the long canon was recognized in early church councils and historically has generally been the OT of the church. (3) In 1719, Francis Lee, in completing J. E. Grabe's edition of the LXX, proposed that both canons existed in Judaism at the time of the early church, a proposal later advanced independently by J. S. Semler (1771). The shorter Hebrew (or Palestinian) canon was assumed to have been accepted by Palestinian Jews and the longer (or Alexandrian) canon, in Greek form, was the Bible of Hellenistic Jews in Egypt and the diaspora. Discussion over the extent of the OT in the early church was thus concerned with the differences between these two canons.

Some General Considerations on the Extent of the OT. Recent study on the canonization process and the contents of the OT in both early Judaism and Christianity is characterized by a diversity of opinions. The following positions, however, although not unchallenged, appear feasible. (1) Writings that never became part of any canon were occasionally called "scripture" or "inspired." (2) The development of a closed OT canon involving a list of included works, and by implication excluded works, was a long process in both Judaism and Christianity in which no decisive once-for-all actions were taken in antiquity. (3) The idea that ancient Judaism developed two OT canons—Palestinian and Alexandrian—should be given up. (4) Jesus and the early church did not inherit a closed canon of scripture from Judaism (for a different opinion, cf. Leiman and Beckwith). At the time of Jesus and the early church, however, the Law/Pentateuch existed as both authoritative and as a closed work. The existence of a rewritten form of Gen 1:1–Exod 12:50 (the BOOK OF JUBILEES) and of the TEMPLE SCROLL from Qumran indicates that even in early Judaism pentateuchal material could be rather freely recast and expanded. Some regulations in Chronicles, Ezra, and Nehemiah, declared to be according to the Law/the Book of Moses, etc. (cf. Ezra 6:7-18; Neh 10:35-37; Callaway), have no counterpart in the Law/Pentateuch. This indicates that the expression "Law of Moses" was an elastic concept and could be applied to prescriptions and formulations not found in the pentateuch or elsewhere in the Bible. (5) Writings designated "the Prophets" were certainly in use along with the Law as inspired and authoritative works (cf. *Prologue to Sirach*; 2 Macc 15:9; Matt 5:17; 7:12; 11:13; 22:40; Luke 16:16; 16:29; John 1:45; Acts 13:15; 24:14; 28:23; Rom 3:21). What was alluded to in the reference "the Prophets," however, remains uncertain (cf. Barton). In *4 Macc* 18:10-19 and Josephus *CAp* 1.37-43 "the books of the prophets" are more extensive than what came to compose this section of the Hebrew scriptures. Sir 44–49 (written ca. 180 B.C.E.), however, seems to be familiar with the prophetical books, both the so-called former prophets (Joshua–2 Kings) and the latter prophets (Isaiah–Malachi) and even the designation "the book of the twelve" (49:10 = Hosea–Malachi).

(6) By the end of the second century C.E., the standard Hebrew canon had evolved with its three-fold division of Law, Prophets, and Writings. Discussions on the exclusion and inclusion of Proverbs, Song of Songs, Esther, Ecclesiastes, and Ecclesiasticus (Sirach) continued but consensus favored all but the latter (*m.Ed* 5.3; *Yad* 3.5; *b.Meg* 7a) so that the final canon included twenty-four works (2 Esdr 14:44-46).

(7) Early Christians inherited a variety of books from Judaism, probably most already in Greek translation, which was far more inclusive than what became the Hebrew canon. These were used and quoted as authoritative by the authors of the NT and the early church fathers. Eventually, the church debated the extent of the canon and produced its own OT. A number of church fathers were aware that Judaism possessed a canon with fewer writings than were employed as scripture in the church (Justin, *Trypho* 68.7-8; Tertullian, *AppWo* 1.3) and some—Melito of Sardis, Origen, Athanasius, Cyril of Jerusalem, and especially Jerome—argued for a Christian OT identical with the Jewish canon or expressed doubts about the full authority of the extra books. The uncertainty about what constituted the OT is aptly reflected in the oldest Christian codices of the Bible: Codex Vaticanus contains no books of Maccabees, Codex Sinaiticus has 1 and *4 Maccabees*, while Codex Alexandrinus contains all four books of Maccabees. Although the Council of Laodicea (ca. 360 C.E.) favored a Christian OT paralleling the Jewish canon, later councils dominated by the western fathers supported the longer canon (at Hippo in 393; Carthage in 397 and 419). Augustine offered a rationale for excluding such works as *1 Enoch*, which he presumed to date from pre-Mosaic times (their great antiquity raises suspicion about their genuineness), and for including the so-called apocrypha (*ChrDoc* 2.8.12-13; *CivDei* 18.38). To support the latter, he appealed to the legend of the miraculous translation of the Hebrew scripture into Greek (based on the *Letter of Aristeas*) and declared inspired not only the Hebrew writings but also books not found in the Hebrew canon (Tobit, Judith, 1–2 Maccabees, Wisdom of Solomon, and Sirach).

Until the time of the Reformation and the Council of Trent, the longer canon was in general use throughout the Western church. Some copies of the Vulgate even included works not accepted at the Council of Trent (1–2 Esdras and Prayer of Manasseh). At the same time, knowledge of and support for an OT identical with the Hebrew were not unknown (Gregory the Great, John of Damascus, Hugh of St. Victor, Nicholas of Lyra, Cardinal Cajetan). The Wyclif Bible (1382) contained only the shorter canon as did Catholic Bibles published in Germany (1527) and France (1530). Renewed interest in Hebrew and the Jewish canon by Renaissance humanists and the reformers' dislike for the content and certain doctrines in the books of Maccabees (purgatory in 2 Macc 12:44-45) led to the exclusion of the "apocrypha" from the OT (first systematically argued for by Carlstadt in 1520).

The Nature of the OT. The OT is a diverse collection of writings coming from various periods in Israelite history. At the same time, it represents only a selection of the literature produced in ancient Israel. The OT itself mentions works from some of which passages are said to have been excerpted but works that have not survived: the BOOK OF THE WARS OF THE LORD (Num 21:14), the BOOK OF JASHAR (Josh 10:13; 2 Sam 1:18), the chronicles of King David (1 Chr 27:24) and Solomon (1 Kgs 11:41) as well as the kings of Israel and Judah (1 Kgs 14:19, 29 and frequently in the Books of Kings), a book of laments (2 Chr 35:25), and so on. Many of these works probably did not survive because of conditions in the country (war, plundering, exile, the nature of the writing material, and so on). Others may have simply perished from neglect or from being superseded by other works. Various reasons lie behind why those works that survived did so and were incorporated into the OT: study texts preserved by scribal and priestly guilds, liturgical material constantly used in worship, historical texts giving expression to and explaining the nation's past, works expressive of and authenticating ongoing theological positions, moral texts offering counsel on the art of living, texts appealing to human interests and expressive of human experience, and so on. Most of these texts were no doubt imbued with sanctity since their contents in one way or another were identified with the will and word of God.

The Hebrew OT is structured according to a tripartite pattern—the Torah (Genesis–Deuteronomy), the Prophets (the former—Joshua–2 Kings—and the latter—Isaiah–Malachi), and the Writings (the remainder, including Ruth, Chronicles, Ezra–Nehemiah, Esther, Lamentations, and Daniel). The Hebrew OT is structured so as to give prominence to the Torah, which assumes primary authority and in light of which the other books are to be read and understood. The middle (Prophets) and end (Writings) are to be interpreted in light of the beginning. Placing the Books of Chronicles at the end of the Bible, however, preserves an eschatological outlook since 2 Chr 36:22-23 looks forward to the rebuilding of the Temple.

The Christian OT is structured according to a quadripartite pattern—the Law, the historical books, the poetic and didactic books, and the Prophets. Such a structure highlights a futuristic/eschatological reading of the material. The old looks forward to the new. The beginning and middle parts are to be read in light of the end.

See also BIBLE; CANON; ESSENES; HERMENEUTICS; SEPTUAGINT.

Bibliography. J. Barton, *Oracles of God: Perceptions of Ancient Prophecy in Israel after the Exile*; R. Beckwith, *The OT Canon of the NT Church and its Background in Early Judaism*; P. R. Callaway, "The Temple Scroll and the Canonization of Jewish Law," *RevQ* 13 (1988): 239-50; O. Eissfeldt, *The OT: An Introduction*; S. Z. Leiman, *The Canonization of Hebrew Scripture: The Talmudic and Midrashic Evidence*; N. M. Sarna, "Bible," *EncJud* 4 (1971): 814-36; J. A. Soggin, *Introduction to the OT*; A. C. Sundberg, Jr., *The OT in the Early Church*.

—JOHN H. HAYES

Artwork by Margaret Jordan Brown

Olive branch.

• **Olive.** The olive tree is an evergreen with leathery leaves shaped like the blade of a lance, dark green on top and silver underneath. They may grow to a height of forty feet, although most are kept pruned to make harvesting easier. The tree blooms in the spring and the fruit matures some six to eight months after the blossoms drop off, around October. The olives are green when they first appear and gradually blacken as they get riper. Some may be picked green and soaked in a salt water solution to be eaten as treats but most in ancient times were allowed to ripen for maximum oil production. The harvesters would beat or shake the trees to make the olives fall. Deut 24:20 directed the Israelites to leave all the fruit which did not fall off easily for "the resident alien, the orphan, and the widow." The olives would be taken to a press made of two circular stones, one of which would rotate on top of the other to crush the fruit. The pulp would then be put into bags to be squeezed or trodden to release every possible ounce of oil.

Olive trees may be grown from seeds, but these do not produce well and must be grafted onto older trees. The other way to start a new tree is to cut a slip from an older tree and root it. The new plants grow slowly and take fifteen to twenty years to reach full production. Once begun, however, they are hardy, withstanding drought and heat, and growing well in the poor, rocky soil found in many parts of Palestine. The trees also produce for a very long time; some have been found in the eastern Mediterranean area which are over 2,000 years old. Without fertilizing and irrigating, however, the trees are likely to bear good crops only every other year.

The olive has been raised by the inhabitants of the Mediterranean basin since ancient times. It is thought to have been cultivated first in Syria and then spread to the other parts of the area around the sea; evidence of olive production on Crete has been found dating back to the fourth millennium B.C.E. Among Semitic people, it soon became one of the three most important staples (along with grain and wine). The Israelites used the oil for cooking, for treating wounds, for oiling tools, for lamp fuel, and for ceremonial anointings.

The olive, since it is an evergreen, served as an image of perpetual usefulness (Ps 52:8). The rhythm of the harvest was used by the prophets as a lesson on the impending judgment: Isa 17:6 compares the gleanings to the remnants of the nation after judgment, Isa 24:13 uses the bare boughs as symbols of desolation, and Jer 11:16-17 describes God's wrath by the image of olive trees burned by a besieging army. Since the oil was used to anoint kings, the olive tree was symbolic of dignity (Judg 9:9) and was used in Zech 4 to represent God's two anointed messengers (cf. Rev 11:4). Paul, in Rom 11, uses the grafting process to represent the inclusion of the gentiles into the covenant God made with the Jews.

—RICHARD B. VINSON

• **Olives, Mount of.** The Mount of Olives was called by several other names in ancient times. Luke 12:37 calls it Olivet, the Romans referred to it as Mount Scopus, and in the Talmud it is named "Mount of the Ointment." It is a ridge to the east of JERUSALEM, about two and one-half mi. long and extending 230 ft. above the Temple Mount (PLATE 23). It has three peaks; one lies northeast of the city, and is the tallest. This peak is thought by some scholars to be the site of NOB, a sanctuary where the priest Ahimelech served in the time of Saul (1 Sam 21:1). The central peak is directly opposite the site where the Herodian Temple stood. The KIDRON Valley lies between the city and the third southernmost slope, which scholars believe is the site of the "Mount of Corruption," so named because Solomon allowed his foreign wives to worship their gods there. The whole hill was covered with olive groves in ancient times, and so gained its name.

The mount is mentioned twice in connection with David, if the connection with Nob is correct. When still a rebel against Saul, David fled to Nob and talked Ahimelech into giving him bread and a weapon. When Saul discovered what had happened, he ordered Ahimelech, all his family, and all the inhabitants of Nob killed. The second episode names the Mount of Olives explicitly, stating that David left Jerusalem following the rebellion of Absalom and "went up the ascent of the Mount of Olives" (2 Sam 15:30).

The mount had a sanctuary to the Lord on one of its summits in the time of David (2 Sam 15:32), and it also was the spot where the ceremony of the red heifer (Num 19) was conducted. The mount also figures in a prophecy from Zechariah, which predicts that the hill will split from east to west on the Day of the Lord (Zech 14:4). GETHSEMANE, an olive orchard on the central summit, was a favorite spot for Jesus to meet with his disciples (John 18:2). Jesus be-

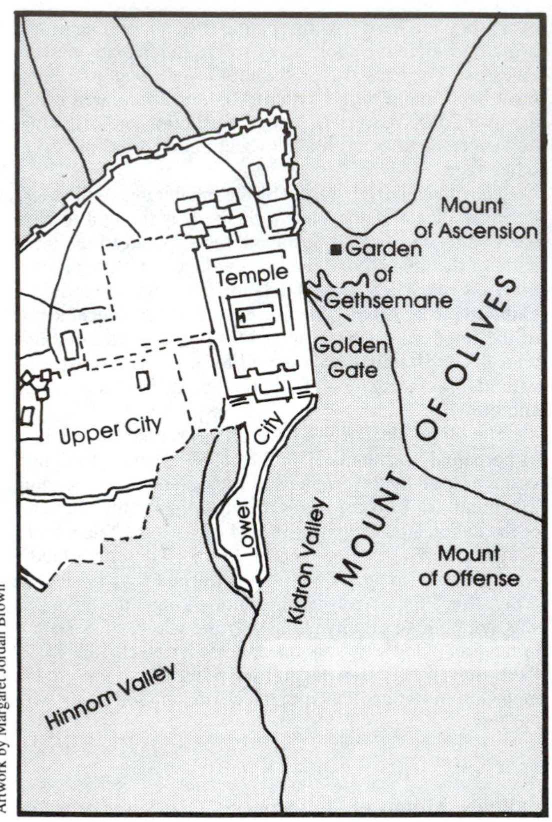

Jerusalem and the Hinnom and Kidron valleys in relation to the Mount of Olives.

gan his entry into Jerusalem on Palm Sunday from the mount (Mark 11:1) and would have crossed it daily during his last week, as he went back and forth from BETHANY to Jerusalem. Later that week, Jesus sat on the mount as he instructed his disciples regarding the destruction of the Temple and the coming of the SON OF MAN. Acts 1:12 also implies that Jesus ascended into heaven from the mount.

The Romans camped on the Mount of Olives to conduct their campaign against Jerusalem in the war of 66–70 C.E. Later Christians built monasteries and churches on the summits, commemorating the various sacred spots. Three examples are the Church of All Nations, located on the traditional site of Gethsemane, the Dominus Flevit, a tear-shaped church on the spot where Jesus is said to have wept over Jerusalem (Luke 19:41), and the Mosque of the Ascension. There are also many ancient Jewish, Christian, and Muslim graves on the southern end of the mount and across the Kidron on the slopes leading up to Jerusalem, due to the belief that the Kidron will be the site at which God judges the world on the Day of the Lord.

See also BETHANY; GETHSEMANE; JERUSALEM; KIDRON; NOB.

Bibliography. G. A. Barrois, "Olives, Mount of," *IDB*; J. Murphy-O'Connor, *The Holy Land*.

—RICHARD B. VINSON

• **Omri.** [om'rı] The name of four individuals in the OT, the most notable being the king of Israel who reigned ca. 876–869 B.C.E.

Omri, Israel's king, was possibly a non-Israelite since his father's name was not given. A general under Elah, he was chosen king by the army at Gibbethon after Elah's assassination. His ascension to the throne was hampered by Zimri, the general who had murdered Elah. The opposition of Zimri was dealt with swiftly. Omri marched to Tirzah, the capital of Israel, and Zimri, seeing his hopeless situation, committed suicide. Other tensions existed, for Tibni, the son of Ginath, was proclaimed king by half of the people. The resulting civil war lasted about four years but Omri emerged triumphant.

The exact length of Omri's reign is uncertain. Omri came to the throne in the thirty-first year of Asa of Judah and was succeeded by AHAB in Asa's thirty-eighth year (1 Kgs 16:23, 29). This gives Omri a reign of eight years, not twelve as stated in 1 Kgs 16:23. This difficulty can be reconciled by recalling the national disorder after the death of Elah. Zimri, who ascended to the throne in the twenty-seventh year of Asa, ruled for only seven days (1 Kgs 16:15). Omri and Tibni were also proclaimed kings in the same year. The four years of civil war have been counted as part of Omri's reign in 1 Kgs 16:23.

According to the account in 1 Kgs 16:15-29, Omri had little importance. Apart from the war with Tibni, there are few details of his reign, yet a few facts can be gleaned concerning Omri's deeds. A Phoenician alliance was established when Omri married his son Ahab to JEZEBEL, the daughter of the king of Sidon (1 Kgs 16:31). The civil war, which had existed with Judah since Rehoboam, was brought to a close by the marriage of Athaliah, Omri's granddaughter (2 Kgs 8:26) or daughter, to JEHORAM (Joram) of Judah. Omri also founded Samaria as the capital of Israel. The entire Northern Kingdom eventually became designated as Samaria. Omri founded a dynasty that lasted four generations, until the time of JEHU (842 B.C.E).

Though Omri brought peace to Israel through alliances, the writer of Kings dismisses him as evil (1 Kgs 16:25-27) and refers the reader to the Book of the Chronicles of the Kings of Israel for more information. (This work is not the canonical 2 Chronicles, for Chronicles has no mention of Omri's reign.)

Extrabiblical references provide additional insight into the monarchy of Omri. The Moabite Stone, also known as the MESHA STELE, indicates that Omri oppressed Moab and conquered Medeba. The Black Obelisk of SHALMANESER III indicates the strength of the Omri dynasty by referring to Jehu, who overthrew the dynasty, as "son of Omri" or as "king of the country of Omri."

The other persons bearing the name Omri were a Benjaminite of the family of Becher (1 Chr 7:8), a Judahite and son of Imri belonging to the family of Perez (1 Chr 9:4), and a son of Michael and an officer over the tribe of Issachar during the reign of David (1 Chr 27:18).

See also SAMARIA.

Bibliography. J. A. Soggin, *A History of Ancient Israel*; H. B. Maclean, "Omri," *IDB*; J. M. Miller and J. Hayes, *A History of Ancient Israel and Judah*.

—ROBERT A. STREET, JR.

• **Onesimus.** [oh-nes'uh-muhs] Onesimus was a slave mentioned in Paul's Letters to Philemon and Colossians. His name means "useful" (which explains the pun in Phlm 11). After running away from his master Philemon, who lived in or near Colossae, he met Paul while Paul was imprisoned. Paul converted him to Christianity and sent him back, accompanied by TYCHICUS and bearing an intercessory letter for his master.

As a runaway, Onesimus was liable to severe punishments, including death, according to the whim of his owner, so Paul felt the need to ask Philemon for clemency for the slave. Some writers think Paul also hinted for Onesimus's emancipation, hoping that Philemon would do more than forgive (Phlm 21). On the other hand, Paul may have been suggesting that Philemon send the slave back on a permanent loan, since Paul's plans for continuing his apostolic work while in prison required helpers (Phlm 12-14). Neither of these theories can be substantiated, but it must be assumed, since the letter was preserved, that Philemon treated Onesimus kindly.

There was an Onesimus who was the bishop of Ephesus around 110–117 C.E. and many commentators believe that this was the same Onesimus mentioned in the NT. This theory, though attractive, rests on slim evidence. Onesimus was a common slave name, and the parallels between Paul's letter and a later document which mentions Bishop Onesimus are phrases which occur frequently in Greek letters of exhortation. It is safer to say that it is impossible to trace Onesimus's fate beyond his return to Philemon.

See also PAUL; PHILEMON, LETTER TO; SLAVERY IN THE NEW TESTAMENT.

—RICHARD B. VINSON

• **Ophel.** *See* JEBUS/JEBUSITES; JERUSALEM

• **Opponents of Paul.** From his Letters, it is obvious that PAUL had many opponents and enemies. Much internal evidence points to a group termed the Judaizers, who composed the right wing of the Jerusalem church as the major opponents of Paul. They viewed him as a "Johnny come lately" to the Christian movement—one who possessed little knowledge of the historical Jesus. They attacked him especially at the point of not being one of the twelve disciples.

The major issue, however, separating Paul and the Judaizers was the one concerning the CIRCUMCISION of the gentile converts. Judaizers emphasized three major points: (1) salvation belonged to the children of Abraham; (2) gentiles could become adopted children of Abraham by accepting the initiatory rite of circumcision; and (3) converts should keep the Jewish Law with particular emphasis on the food laws, feasts, and fasts.

The great Tübingen critic, F. C. Baur, did much to emphasize the Judaizers as Paul's major opponents. As early as 1831 Baur raised questions concerning Paul's relationship to the Jerusalem disciples in reference particularly to the "Christ party" at Corinth (cf. 1 Cor 1:12). Baur believed that even the most casual reader of the NT would notice the tension that existed between Paul and the Jerusalem church. Baur underlined that tension to the point of almost warlike proportions. Baur saw the conflict as between Paul, the champion of the gentile movement, and JAMES along with PETER, the leaders of the Jerusalem church. These Jerusalem apostles and other members of their party followed Paul around on his various journeys. They attempted to correct his false teaching. In Baur's view, the majority of the NT books tried to cover over this conflict— especially the Book of Acts. Baur, in addition, viewed GALATIANS as Paul's major reply to his Judaizing opponents.

Other evidence points to GNOSTICISM as the background of Paul's opponents. Walter Schmithals has been the chief advocate of identifying Paul's opponents as Gnostic Jewish Christians. He based his theory on evidence that there were more than two parties in early Christianity: the Pauline and the Jerusalem apostles. He argued for a syncretistic group of Jews who had modified their Judaism with Gnosticism. He associated the Gnostic concept of primal man with the Messiah or Christ. Schmithals felt that the various Gnostic Christian sects evolved out of Gnostic Jewish sects. In fact he concluded that Judaism had been the most important mediator of Gnosticism to the West.

Schmithals pointed to Gal 4:9-10 as good support for his Gnostic theory. There Paul warned the Galatians not to return to the weak and beggarly elemental spirits. The reference to the worship of "elemental spirits" should be considered an evident overtone of Gnosticism. Gnosticism fostered a worship of those spirits through cultic practices (days, months, seasons) which would propitiate them.

W. Luetgert and J. H. Ropes took the position that Paul was opposed by two groups rather than one. Paul was caught between the legalists on one hand and the libertines on the other. The legalists called him too conservative. The Ropes-Luetgert school made much of Gal 5:11. There Paul declared, "But if I, brethren, still preach circumcision; why am I still persecuted?" In their view, this would certainly not be a charge leveled at Paul by Jews from Jerusalem. The accusation that Paul was "preaching circumcision" would be made by a more liberal group such as the libertines. Paul viewed the libertine theology as much a threat as the Judaizers. The libertines felt that the Jewish Law was not binding on them, and this attitude led to moral license. They accused Paul of giving in to the Judaizers and the authority of the Jerusalem church.

The two-front theory also recognized the role and influence of the Judaizers. Unlike Baur, Luetgert-Ropes rejected the identification of the Jerusalem Twelve with the Judaizers as Jewish Christians loosely connected with the church or even legalistic gentiles.

Johannes Munck concluded that Paul's opponents, especially in Galatia, might have been gentile converts rather than Jerusalem Jews. Paul converted the gentiles without insisting on circumcision. Later these converts encountered the demands of the Law as revealed in the Jewish scripture. Some felt that they were not true Christians because they had not received the seal of the covenant, circumcision. Thus they voluntarily accepted this rite and started preaching it to their fellow brothers. At the same time, they called into question the apostolic authority of Paul. These gentile Judaizers felt that the Jerusalem apostles were still preaching circumcision and the Law. Thus there was a call to return to the orthodox teaching of Jerusalem and a mandate to brand the Pauline gospel as heresy.

Who were Paul's opponents? A multitude of answers have been given over the years by NT scholars. Were they the Jerusalem Twelve, gentile Christians, Jewish Gnostics, Jewish Christians at Jerusalem or some combination of these groups? Perhaps, the answer depends on whether one were in Galatia or Corinth. The Jerusalem Judaizers seem to be the best choice for Galatia. It is hard to oppose F.C. Baur at that point. Although he exaggerated his case, he saw the basic theological cleavage between Paul and the Jerusalem church. At Corinth, the opponents seem to have more of a Gnostic background. The so-called Christ party was a group that separated the body from the soul. These enthusiasts believed that what you did in the body could not affect the soul. This attitude led to the excesses at Corinth. The best approach to the problem, then would be to see many Pauline opponents coming from a multitude of backgrounds. Only the study of the context of the writing can allow one to point to one group over against another.

See also CIRCUMCISION; GNOSTICISM; JAMES; PAUL; PETER.

Bibliography. F. C. Baur, *Paulus*; W. Luetgert, *Gesetz und Geist*; J. Munck, *Paul and the Salvation of Mankind*; J. H. Ropes, *The Singular Problem of the Epistle to the Galatians*; W. Schmithals, *Gnosticism in Corinth*.

—JAMES L. BLEVINS

• **Oracle.** The message of a god through a PRIEST, a diviner, or a PROPHET. The term may also refer to the place where oracles were received (e.g., the oracle of Delphi). The message might be received through the sacred LOTS, URIM AND THUMMIM (1 Sam 14:41), through divination by various means, or (most characteristically in Israel) through a prophet.

The prophetic oracle was usually poetic in form, limited in length, oral in presentation, and had one central focus. It was delivered with a sense of divine compulsion and urgency, focusing on a situation that was of immediate concern to the prophet, one that he was convinced should be of immediate concern to his hearers as well.

The prophets were convinced that God had spoken directly to them, hence the characteristic expression, "Thus says the Lord" (cf. Amos 1:3, 6, 9, 11). This communication from God could either be by sound or by sight. Visions were oracles received through the sense of sight, since most visions originated in something the prophet saw (cf. Amos 7; Jer 1:11-19.)

Prophets were speakers, not writers. They gave the oracles orally at whatever time and place they deemed appropriate. It might be in the presence of a ruler (Nathan to David, 2 Sam 12:1-7); in the city (Amos 7:12, 13); or in the precincts of the Temple (Jer 26:1). The writing down of the oracles was left to disciples (Isa 8:16; Jer 36). Regardless of how received or delivered, the oracle was the Lord's word, not the prophet's.

Oracles were also known in the NT. A healing oracle apparently was received by Paul (2 Cor 12:9), along with other kinds of oracles (cf. 1 Cor 15:51-52; 1 Thess 3:4).

See also PROPHECY; LOT/LOTS (CASTING OF) IN THE BIBLE; MAGIC AND DIVINATION; URIM AND THUMMIM.

—JOHN H. TULLOCK

• **Oral Tradition.** The passing along of the biblical materials by word of mouth, prior to the writing down of these materials—narratives, poetic utterances, wisdom sayings, lists, and the like.

Important distinctions made in recent discussions should be noted. The tradition that is being passed along is called the *traditum*. The process of passing along the tradition is called *traditio*. The group or individual responsible for passing along the tradition is called the *tradent*. It should also be noted that tradition is passed along orally and in writing. It is passed along, moreover, in ways other than speaking or writing, as the life of the community is embodied in institutions, customs, rituals, artifacts, and the like. Here, however, we are concerned with oral tradition as contrasted with the written biblical record.

Oral and Written Traditions. When did the writing down of biblical tradition begin? The majority judgment is that the preserving in written form of large blocks of biblical tradition began in the tenth or ninth century B.C.E., when the great narratives of J and E were produced to tell the story of Israel's beginnings. These were followed by early collections of the lives of the judges and of the beginnings of kingship, so that by the time of the early monarchy, many of the oral traditions of ancient Israelite history and legend had already been set out in written form destined to endure, though suffering editorial rearrangement over time. Behind these written collections lay the period of passing down tradition orally: the traditions of the beginnings of humankind (Gen 1–11), of ABRAHAM, ISAAC, JACOB, and JOSEPH (Gen 12–50), and the Exodus and wilderness stories and the careers of Israel's judges. Not until about the tenth century were these large blocks of biblical tradition available in written form.

After the appearance of such written materials, however, oral transmission of tradition continued, and the oral traditioning process (the *traditio*) affected the contents of the written collection. During the Babylonian Exile, and in the early years of the return, the written form of the tradition gained such solidity that oral transmission of the materials ceased materially to affect the contents of the written text.

For approximately 400 years, written and oral traditions would have existed side by side, with writing slowly becoming the definitive way to pass the tradition along. When one looks at the final result, one can recognize that biblical tradition is the product of this long process of traditioning, in which the story of God's dealings with Israel existed first in story form, then in the form of written recording of some of the stories but not of others, then as written record of major blocks of tradition, which would have been affected to some extent by the continuing passing along of traditions orally, and finally as fully written records.

Oral Tradition and the Babylonian Exile. Other scholars have stressed the enormous influence of the Babylonian Exile on the writing down and standardizing of traditions normally passed along orally until the Exile threatened their loss. Tradition was to be passed along orally; that was the normal way of recording for the community the story of God's saving deeds. The prophet JEREMIAH spoke to the people under normal circumstances; only when he was forbidden the opportunity to deliver his message orally did he resort to writing (Jer 36:1-8). The written word, moreover, had less effect, it would seem, than an oral presentation might have had, for Jehoiakim simply cut up the scroll and burned it, piece by piece, as it was read (Jer 36:23-26).

The biblical record was handed down by word of mouth until danger of its being lost forced it to be recorded; so it was claimed by some scholars. The Bablylonian Exile was the greatest threat to Israel's continued existence, and during the Exile, systematic efforts began and continued to preserve the biblical heritage. Various collections probably existed in written form prior to the Exile, but primarily the biblical record was an oral record until events required that it be recorded on manuscripts. But once the record was made and assented to, the written record thereafter dominated as the authoritative record of Israel's history under God.

The former view seems to be the more probable one. It is certainly true that the Babylonian Exile was a time of refining and recasting biblical traditions, written and oral. But the probabilities are that much of biblical tradition was already in written form as the exiles were taken from Jerusalem and Judah in 597 and 587/6 to Babylon, there to live in hope and anticipation of return to their homeland.

Oral Rendering of the Tradition. It is still the case that the written record is most effectively received and obeyed as it is presented in the living voice of those appointed to read it aloud. Oral tradition is tradition at its best and most effective. The later institution of the synagogue became central for the hearing of sacred tradition, read aloud and commented upon by the community's leaders (cf. Luke 4:16-21).

See also FORM/GATTUNG; INTERPRETATION, HISTORY OF; Q; REDACTION; TRADITION IN THE OLD TESTAMENT; TRANSMISSION HISTORY.

Bibliography. D. A. Knight, *Rediscovering the Traditions of Israel*; E. Nielsen, *Oral Tradition.*

—WALTER HARRELSON

• **Ordain/Ordination in the New Testament.** Ordination is the ceremony of laying on of hands to set apart and certify candidates who have been chosen to fulfill various ministerial offices. Among the variety of Christian traditions, different styles or procedures of the ceremony have developed. In some traditions the BISHOP alone lays hands on the çandidate, while in other traditions all ordained persons of equal or higher ministerial rank consecutively or concurrently lay their hands on the head of a candidate and offer prayers for the candidate.

In both the OT and NT the practice of laying on of hands derives its significance from the particular context in which it occurs. Consequently, not all ritual acts of laying on of hands signify ordination. In the OT the laying on of hands is performed on the animals for cultic sacrifice, some of which are used in ordination rituals of the Aaronic priesthood (Exod 29:10-28), and on scapegoats (Lev 16:21). In the NT the laying on of hands is used by Jesus in healing miracles. At other times it is associated with the receipt of gifts of the Spirit (Acts 8:14-18; 9:17-18), sometimes after the laying on of hands by elders (1 Tim 4:14) or by Paul (2 Tim 1:6).

The first recorded Christian ordination took place when THE TWELVE apostles identified and commissioned THE SEVEN (Acts 6:1-6) to serve tables and attend to the needs of widows so that the Twelve could devote their full energies to the preaching of the gospel. The early church also ordained Saul and Barnabas and dispatched them to missionary work (Acts 13:1-3). By the end of the apostolic age, three ministerial offices—bishop, ELDER, and DEACON—required ordination. Now among the plurality of Christian traditions, no consensus exists about what ministerial offices require ordination.

Questions about the significance of ordination generate disagreement among the various traditions of Christianity. Roman Catholics, Orthodox, and Anglicans regard ordination (the conferring of holy orders) as a sacrament, an act through which the grace of God is imparted. Most Protestant traditions, however, consider ordination to be a human response in faithfulness to the experience of divine grace.

Since biblical times the roles of women in ministry have also been the subject of controversy; and prospects of their ordination have called into question patriarchal attitudes about the subordination of women to men. The silence of the NT specifically on the ordination of women continues to be a subject of debate, although Paul clearly stated that in Christ there are no ethnic or gender distinctions (Gal 3:28). He also noted that women were his missionary colleagues (Rom 16:3). Patriarchal attitudes about the subjugation of women to men in Christian families and ministries are reflected in Ephesians and the Pastorals (Eph 5:22ff.; 1 Tim 2:11f.). The Protestant affirmation of the priesthood of all believers, however, challenges all social and cultural restrictions imposed as criteria for ordination.

See also BISHOP; DEACON; ELDER; MINISTER/SERVE; SACRAMENTS; SEVEN, THE; TWELVE, THE; WOMEN IN THE NEW TESTAMENT.

Bibliography. M. Carson and J. J. H. Price, "The Ordination of Women and the Function of the Bible," *JPH* 59 (Summer 1981): 245-65; M. W. Shepard, Jr., *The Worship of the Church*; J. E. Steely, "Ministerial Certification in Southern Baptist History: Ordination," *BHH* 15 (Jan 1980): 23-29.

—JOSEPH L. PRICE

• **Ordain/Ordination in the Old Testament.** Ordination in the OT has to do with the consecration of the PRIESTS, a ceremony described in Exod 29 and Lev 8. The intent was to signify that the priests had been set apart for the sacred purpose of serving God in the cult and of leading in divine worship.

At the entrance to the tent of meeting before the congregation of people, MOSES led in the first ordination of priests, involving AARON the high priest and his sons as regular priests (Lev 8). Presumably, the listed procedures were carried out later at the Temple entrance. Having washed the priests with water, Moses placed on Aaron as high priest his special regalia, including a breastpiece containing the URIM AND THUMMIM (cf. Exod 28 for more detail of priestly garments). Anointing olive oil was sprinkled on the tabernacle and its contents; it then was poured on the head of Aaron only.

Certain sacrifices were involved. After Aaron and his sons had laid their hands on the "head of the bull of the sin offering" (Lev 8:14), Moses killed it, using its blood to purify the altar. Similarly, then Moses sacrificed "the ram of the burnt offering" (v. 18). Next, Moses "presented the other ram, the ram of ordination" (v. 22), which he killed. Moses placed in the hands of Aaron and his sons pieces of unleavened bread, which he then removed and "burned them on the altar with the burnt offering, as an ordination offering, a pleasing odor, an offering by fire to the Lord" (v. 28).

The one OT analogy to the Christian custom of ordination is in the transfer by Moses of his authority to JOSHUA (Num 27:15-23), signified by the laying on of hands.

The term "ordain" is used frequently in English translations of the Bible to render Hebrew words that have to do with establishing, ordering, or setting in place.

See also ORDAIN/ORDINATION IN THE NEW TESTAMENT.

—KAREN RANDOLPH JOINES

• **Ordinance.** *See* LAW IN THE OLD TESTAMENT

• **Origin of the World, On the.** *On the Origin of the World* is a modern title given to an untitled Coptic Gnostic tractate found in Codex II of the NAG HAMMADI documents, as well as fragmentarily in Codex XIII. It has obvious affinities with the THE HYPOSTASIS OF THE ARCHONS, which it follows in Codex II. This treatise deals with events before creation, as well as with creation itself, but is essentially a thoroughly Gnostic interpretation of the primeval history of GENESIS. The writer speaks in the first person, occasionally addressing the reader. It is a conscious attempt to present an orderly explanation of Gnostic COSMOLOGY, and to some extent soteriology and ESCHATOLOGY, perhaps for the reading public. No identification can be made with any particular Gnostic group. The material found here has been drawn from a rich variety of sources, including the traditions of Egypt. This suggests Alexandria as a possible place of composition. The well-developed GNOSTICISM indicates that this may be one of the later Nag Hammadi documents, dating to the third century or even the fourth. It is assumed, like the other Nag Hammadi tractates, to have been composed in Greek and translated into Coptic.

In primordial times PISTIS SOPHIA (Faith-Wisdom) comes into being, and then creates the lion-like androgynous archon (ruler) Ialdabaoth, who begets other archons and boasts of being the only God. Pistis rebukes him, saying that an immortal Man of Light existed before him. She then withdraws into light. Sabaoth, Ialdabaoth's son, praises Pistis, whereupon the jealous father creates seven maleficent beings: wrath, grief, etc. Zoe (Life), who is with Sabaoth, counters with seven beneficent beings: peace, truth, etc. Ialdabaoth then sees a light revealing the immortal Man of Light. Pronoia, female counterpart to Ialdabaoth, creates a Light ADAM. Sophia brings EVE into existence independently. It is after Eve appears that Ialdabaoth creates an earthly Adam, who does not come alive until Sophia sends her breath into him, but still he cannot rise. Eve is sent as an instructor to raise Adam. She bids him rise, which he does, praising her as mother of the living because she gave him life.

The evil archons attempt to defile her, meanwhile putting Adam into a forgetful sleep, convincing him later that Eve was made from his rib, and that he is her master. Eve escapes the archons by going into the TREE OF KNOWLEDGE, leaving an image of herself with the earthly Adam. The archons command this Adam and Eve not to eat from the tree of knowledge. An instructor, however, convinces them to do so, and when they eat, the light of knowledge (*gnosis*) shines on them. The archons cast the pair out of PARADISE, to keep them from the TREE OF LIFE. Angry, Sophia chases the archons from their heavens and relegates them to the sinful world, where they are responsible for the existence of many demons who will lead humanity astray until the advent of the True Man.

The narrative ends at this point, followed by a brief soteriological section, ascribing salvation ultimately to the Immortal Father. A brief apocalyptic passage closes the book, with light victorious over darkness.

See also APOCALYPTIC LITERATURE; COSMOLOGY; GNOSTICISM; HYPOSTASIS OF THE ARCHONS; NAG HAMMADI; PISTIS SOPHIA.

Bibliography. R. L. Arthur, trans., in R. H. Arthur, *The Wisdom Goddess*; H.-G. Bethge and O. Wintermute, ''On the Origin of the World,'' *The Nag Hammadi Library in English,* ed. J. M. Robinson; P. Perkins, ''*On the Origin of the World:* A Gnostic Physics,'' *VC* 34/1 (1980): 36-46.

—ROGER A. BULLARD

• **Orphica.** [or'fuh-kuh] Sometimes referred to as Pseudo-Orpheus, Orphica is a Jewish imitation of Orphic poetry, probably dating from the early second century B.C.E. It is composed in archaizing Greek hexameters and is apparently an attempt to represent Orpheus, the patron of Greek poetry and of an ancient mystery cult, as a proponent of Jewish MONOTHEISM and a witness to the greatness of MOSES.

The poem is quoted by Eusebius (*PraepEv* 13.12.15) and, in a shorter version, by Pseudo-Justin (*Mon 2* and *Cohort 15*). Clement quotes portions of the poem in the *Strom* and *Protrept* and a version is extant in a theosophical text of the fifth century C.E.

In the longer version, the first eight lines and the last four lines purport to be admonitions delivered by Orpheus to his son and pupil Musaeus; they echo the terminology of the MYSTERY RELIGIONS and provide a frame for the rest of the poem. The central section is in three parts. Lines 10-16a interpret ''an ancient saying,'' about the nature of God: ''He is one'' (Deut 6:4) and ''there is no other'' (Isa 45:5). The interpretation emphasizes God as the source of all that is, stressing God's transcendence, but asserting that God is present in everything, even in EVIL and SUFFERING. Lines 16b-25 assert that mortals are incapable of seeing God in this life and lines 26-41 are a report of the one exception to this rule: Moses, a ''unique man'' experienced a vision of God (or an apotheosis?) and received revelations from God ''in aphorisms, in the form of a double law.''

The Christian apologists quoted this hymn to prove that even the pagan Orpheus bore witness to the truth of scripture.

Bibliography. M. Lafargue, ''Orphica,'' *The Old Testament Pseudepigrapha,* ed. J. H. Charlesworth.

—SHARYN E. DOWD

• **Othniel.** [oth'nee-uhl] A minor judge. Within the tradition that preserves stories of the tribe of Judah, CALEB is remembered as a successful warrior who acquired territory for the tribe of Judah in the northern NEGEB. He offered the hand of his daughter, Achsah, in marriage to the one who could conquer Kiriath-sepher (Debir) for Judah. Othniel, a son of Kenaz, Caleb's brother, captured Kiriath-sepher. At Othniel's urging, Achsah requested from her father Caleb land and springs of water, both essential for survival in the Negeb. The Book of Judges also records a notice of Othniel's successful freeing of Israel from the hands of Cushan-rishathaim, king of Mesopotamia, bringing peace to the land for a period of forty years. There is some question, however, about the Mesopotamian king since he is not otherwise known.

These Judahite stories are of interest in that they are preserved in Josh 15:13-19 and Judg 1:11-15; 3:7-11, which give evidence of having been shaped by the northern traditions of the Elohist and DEUTERONOMIST—both of whom give central position to JOSHUA, a warrior from Ephraim.

See also JUDGES, BOOK OF.

—WILLIAM R. MILLAR

P

MDB

• **P.** *See* PRIESTLY WRITERS; SOURCE CRITICISM

• **Pact.** *See* COVENANT

• **Paddan-Aram.** *See* ARAM-NAHARAM/PADDAN-ARAM

• **Palace of Herod.** *See* HEROD, PALACE OF

• **Palestine, Geography of.** [pal'uh-st*i*n] The study of the geography of Palestine offers a vital perspective on biblical history and literature. The life of the communities of this region is marked by a high degree of direct dependence upon the natural givens of earth and sea. The landscape of Palestine endowed life with a highly regional character in biblical times. Politics and history possessed unavoidable geographical dimensions. And the literary record of that history, while rarely engaging in a description of its environmental setting, presupposes a familiarity with the lay of the land, the location of boundaries, the hierarchy of villages and cities, and the usual way to get from here to there. Geographical study aids in the recovery of these features.

Palestine: Name, Location and Boundaries. The name "Palestine" derives ultimately from the name of its southern coastal region inhabited in biblical times by the PHILISTINES. The Greek form of the name (*Palaistine*) was used as a designation for the larger region by the historian Herodotus and Syria Palaestina became the name of the Roman province which encompassed most of the area that can be called Palestine today. Biblical names for this territory include CANAAN (Gen 12:5) and the Land of ISRAEL (*eretz yisrael;* 2 Kgs 5:2). Contemporary use of any of these designations for this area has unavoidable political overtones.

Palestine is located at the eastern end of the MEDITERRANEAN SEA and at the western end of the FERTILE CRESCENT which encompasses the agriculturally usable land stretching from the head of the Persian Gulf, northward along the routes of the Tigris and Euphrates rivers to the Anatolian plateau, and bending southward along the eastern Mediterranean coast. Jumping over the barren SINAI peninsula, this cradle of the earliest Near Eastern civilization reaches to the valley of the Nile. Thus Palestine constitutes both a land bridge connecting Egypt and Mesopotamia, the two major centers of ancient Near Eastern civilization, and a port of entry for contact between this sphere and the Greek and Roman civilizations of the Mediterranean (PLATE 2).

Well-defined boundaries compress Palestine into a narrow strip of land bordered on the west by the Mediterranean Sea and on the east by the Arabian Desert. The desert of the Sinai peninsula marks the southern boundary while less than 250 km. to the north, the frontier is set by the final reaches of the LEBANON and Anti-Lebanon mountains. Thus Palestine encompasses the whole of contemporary Israel, the Gaza Strip, the West Bank, plus the eastern portions of Jordan, the Golan Heights, and southern hills of Lebanon. Its total area is small, comparable to the size of the state of Maryland.

Principal Features. Three features of the geography of Palestine stand out as being of prime significance for understanding its human occupation and history. Though small in total area, Palestine boasts a remarkable diversity. The geological history of the area has produced a complex landscape that can aptly be described as fragmented. The diversity extends to landforms, elevation, natural vegetation, soils, and climate and introduces a high degree of regionalism into the life and history of its inhabitants. Unlike Egypt or Mesopotamia, Palestine's major river, the Jordan, does not serve to unify this complex map. As a consequence of this variegated landscape broad generalizations about the nature of life in Palestine are ruled out. Political unification of the region has always been fraught with difficulties and, when achieved, has never been long-lived.

Limited natural resources constitute a second determining characteristic of Palestine. The land does not possess any great mineral wealth, only some pockets of iron ore east of the Jordan and copper in the south. Forests of small trees and dense undergrowth satisfied limited local building needs, but were cut down for fuel rather than harvested for lumber. The region's predominantly limestone rocks provided most of the material for construction. The amount of level land for agriculture was restricted in most areas, and the Mediterranean climate, while well suited for farming, was highly erratic and caused significant hardships three or four years out of ten. The possibilities for irrigation were strictly limited, and not all of the region receives sufficient rainfall for dry farming. A variable border of aridity (at 200 mm. of rainfall) runs through the land marking the juncture between the desert and the sown areas. Under these limitations of natural resources, the success of settlement in the area was often marked by the ability to cope with economic failure.

The location of Palestine at the place where the Mediterranean and Near Eastern worlds, especially commercial worlds, overlap represents a third and most decisive feature of its geography. Politically, Palestine was rarely exempt from larger struggles which it could do little to control. Campaigning armies of the empires often crossed its soil. By virtue of its position it participated in the larger world of commerce as a transit agent or trading partner or, exceptionally, a broker. Major trade routes funneled through Palestine from four directions: from Europe through the

Phoenician ports, from Egypt along the Mediterranean coast, from Arabia and East Africa through the Gulf of Aqaba, and from Mesopotamia skirting the Arabian desert. The prosperity of Palestine depended in large measure upon the political and economic situation in these distant lands and upon its relationship with other more active traders such as the Phoenicians.

Topography and Regions. The landscape of Palestine is generally described as consisting of four or five north-south oriented strips. Moving inland from the Mediterranean the strips one encounters are: the coastal plain; the highlands which form the region's backbone; the Jordan (or Rift) valley which slices deeply through the center of Palestine; and the Transjordanian plateau (PLATE 4). This is a convenient description and is accurate inasmuch as most commercial traffic runs along the north-south pathway and to the extent that the deep Jordan valley has impressed its north-south orientation upon the region. Nevertheless, this emphasis on north-south movement obscures the countervailing geological fracturing which repeatedly breaks the north-south flow as well as the vital role of east-west movement in the history and life of the region. The most obvious break in the north-south flow is created by the JEZREEL valley. This broad plain links the Bay of Acco with the Rift valley and is geologically part of a larger depression that includes the valleys of Lower GALILEE and the SEA OF GALILEE and continues on the Transjordanian side in the form of the YARMUK valley. In the south the Beersheba basin similarly cuts through the mountainous zone linking the Gaza region on the coast with the ZERED valley on the other side of the Jordan. These physical features of the landscape of provided the major corridors of lateral movement. Since variations in climate and vegetation are generally much more radical along the east-west line than the north-south and since controlling diverse ecological zones was a high priority in the economy of Palestine during most periods, east-west movement was crucial even where the terrain was not so conducive.

The Costal Plain. The coastal plain is a good barometer of the variegated character of the Palestinian landscape since it offers no less than three clear divisions along its length. The clearest break is made by the promontory of MOUNT CARMEL which extends the Highland zone to the very edge of the Mediterranean, cutting the plain in two. North of Mount Carmel the Bay of Acco offers the only significant natural harbor on an otherwise smooth coastline. Acco, called Ptolemais in Greek and Roman times (Acts 21:7), sits at the northern extremity of the bay and is buffered by a wide plain that continues the Jezreel valley and offers good agricultural circumstances. Toward the south, the bay itself is punctuated by a number of shallow streams which formed swamps in biblical times. The KISHON river drains into the bay at its southernmost end. Moving to the north of Acco, the costal plain abruptly narrows at Rosh ha-Niqra beyond which it offers very little level land but more opportunities for harbors which, like TYRE, were put to good use by the seafaring Phoenicians.

South of Mount Carmel the proximity of the hills to the sea provides room for only a narrow strip of land. The coastal plain broadens conspicuously south of the Tanninim River into the plain of Sharon. Extending southward to the Yarqon River, the Sharon plain posed difficulties for its ancient inhabitants by virtue of marshes which trapped water draining from the inland region behind a hardened ridge of former coastline. On the inland side of the marshes, the plain was home to a forest of deciduous oak trees (Tabor oaks). Commercial traffic across the plain was intense, however, since it offered exclusive access to the major northward passes through the Carmel range, like the one controlled by MEGIDDO. Its coastline boasted two seaports, one natural harbor where the ancient city of Dor was located, and the other a humanly engineered harbor at the Roman provincial capital of CAESAREA, built by Herod in the final decades of the first century B.C.E.

The coastal plain maintains its width south of the river Yarqon, but becomes more of a fertile farming region owing to the presence of rich soils especially in the basin around Lod and southward throughout the Philistine plain until agriculture is ruled out by growing aridity. The southern section is home for the five cities of the Philistines: ASHDOD, EKRON, GATH, GAZA, and the harbor city of ASHKELON. The main road from Egypt (the "Way of the Sea") passed directly through this region, turning inland at the port city of JOPPA to continue its path through APHEK (Antipatris) and northward through the Sharon. Because of its fertility and strategic location, this section of the coastal plain was hotly contested and usually found itself under the sway of the Egyptians.

The Shephelah. Inland from the Philistine plain sits a singular foothills region between the coastal plain and the highlands of Judea proper. Known as the Shephelah (lowlands), this area of rolling hills runs from the Ajalon Valley in the north to the Wadi Shiqma in the south (a "wadi" is a seasonal stream usually possessing a dry bed some portion of the year). It consists of higher and more fertile eastern and lower western sections separated by a series of north-south running valleys. Drainage from the hills has cut rounded east-west valleys which intersect the north-south running valleys and provide access to the interior. The famous city of Lachish sits at precisely such a crossroad controlling access to the southern reaches of the Judean hills and contributing to its status as the second most important city in the Judean nation. Because of its location and the transitional character of its topography, the shephelah figures prominently in the struggles of the Philistines and the Israelite inhabitants of the highlands to secure lifespace during the early biblical period. Judean kings often found themselves engaged with invading armies who chose to attack Jerusalem via the western approach through this region.

Judean Highlands. From the coastland through the shephelah the altitude gradually increases until it achieves the average 700 m. height of the Judean hills. With a few peaks breaking the 1,000 m. mark, this region presents a fairly compact mountain range possessing clear borders with the shephelah to the west and the Judean desert to the east. It presents a tripartite structure with the JERUSALEM hills at its center surrounded in the north and south by the higher BETHEL and HEBRON hills. The Hebron hills are the largest in terms of area and constitute a broad plateau that trails off into the Negeb in the form of two elongated spurs. These hills are fairly isolated from the coastal plain by the steep escarpment that forms their western border. The city of Hebron occupies a central position astride the main road that ran north through the highland regions toward BETHLEHEM and Jerusalem and the east-west way to Lachish and the coast. The northern section of the Hebron hills receives fair amounts of rainfall but this diminishes to the point of aridity as one passes southward into the Negeb.

The fairly imprecise boundary between the Hebron hills and the Jerusalem saddle to the north is signaled by a decline in elevation and a widening of the crest of the hills to the east and west. The Jerusalem saddle is more strongly dissected than its southern neighbor. Wadis cut to the heart of the area from both east and west. Yet they do not cut off the north-south flow of traffic and between the wadis continuous spurs provide good possibilities for ascent into the hills. From the coastal plain, the Nahal Sorek and the Nahal Ayalon were well-traveled routes, the latter eventuating in "Ascent of BETH-HORON" that was followed by many invading armies ("nahal" is the Heb. equivalent of the Arabic "wadi"). The single large expanse of level land in these hills occurs in the neighborhood of GIBEON, a town along this ascent eight km. north of Jerusalem. Jerusalem itself sits at about the same latitude as the northern end of Dead Sea so that travelers crossing the Rift valley would find the city an ideal way station on the way up from or down to Jericho. North of the plain of Gibeon, the contours of the Bethel hills begin their rise. The hills are broader than the rest of the region and no shephelah accompanies them on the west. Nonetheless, the pattern of dissection produced by the wadis has deeply carved this area, slicing nearly completely through it. As a result, travel northwards along the watershed is more arduous and must cross a number of valleys. Access from the coastal plain is also minimal leaving the area somewhat cut off so that it served a disputed boundary zone between the Judean and Israelite nations during the days of the monarchy.

The Judean Desert. Flanking the Jerusalem saddle and Hebron hills to the east, an arid zone produced by the rainshadow effect of the highlands makes a step-like descent to Dead Sea depression. The steps of the Judean desert give order to its highly diverse landscape of plateaus, hills, and gorges and provide zones of distinct characters: a semi-arid zone offering possibilities for permanent occupation; an area, known in the Bible as the Judean wilderness, comprising two levels and suited to pastoral pursuits; and a final barren terrace ending in a continuous and precipitous escarpment that drops to the shore of the Dead Sea. The Judean desert frequently provided a place of retreat and refuge as indicated in the narratives of David's flight from Saul and by the histories of the fortress MASADA and the DEAD SEA SCROLL community of Qumran during the Greek and Roman periods. Economically, the oasis of EN-GEDI was regularly occupied and known for its perfume industry.

The Negeb. This broad region consists of the southernmost extension of the mountainous backbone of Palestine from which emerges a plateau that slopes gently all the way to the coastal plain. The northern border of the Negeb is marked by the BEERSHEBA and ARAD basins and the wadi system that drains these to the west. In the south the Negeb hills reach down to the tip of the gulf of Aqaba and the border between the Negeb and the Sinai peninsula runs roughly along a line connecting the tip of the gulf with the Wadi el-Arish that runs to the Mediterranean coast. The deep canyon of the Nahal Zin bisects the Negeb into a higher and more mountainous southern subregion known as the central Negeb hills and a more habitable northern Negeb hills. The northern section begins above the Rift valley in a series of mountain folds angled to the northeast. The mountains bear two prominent craters, scars produced by a unique type of erosion, between which passed an important highway descending via the "scorpion pass" to the valley below. The mountains decline progressively toward the west giving way to the Beersheba and Arad basins and a plateau region drained by the Nahal Besor. South of the Besor a large area of sand dunes points toward the coast. The city of Beersheba occupies the central place astride routes connecting the coastland with the Rift valley and initiating the main road heading north into the highlands.

South of the Nahal Zin the central Negeb highlands present a forbidding landscape undergirded by a geological structure of great complexity. One of its five mountainous folds is incised over half its length by the immense Ramon crater. Near their border with the Sinai the central Negeb hills offer a home to the oasis of KADESH-BARNEA (Num 13, 20) whose precise location is a matter of dispute. At the top of the gulf of Aqaba Nubian sandstone forms a part of the southernmost tip of the highland mountains. The copper in this sandstone was mined as far back as the fourth millennium B.C.E.

The Samarian Highlands. Reversing directions and moving north, the border between the Judean and Samarian highlands is recognized in a slight turning of the axis of the hills toward the northeast and the appearance of numerous basins among the hills. The first of these, the valley of SHILOH makes a good reference point and marks the beginning of a highly discontinuous zone that constituted the heartland of the Israelite nation. Six subregions are readily seen. At the center of the region stand the western Samarian hills dominated by a high core of mountains including MOUNT EBAL and MOUNT GERIZIM that rise above the city of SHECHEM. This central block is sliced through by a series of intersecting valleys which provide significant agricultural possibilities and through which ran the major communications routes of the region. To the southwest of Shechem the hills that extend toward the Sharon section of the coastal plain offer little potential for settlement. But to the northwest valleys are prominent and filled with alluvial or readily plowable chalky soils. The city of SAMARIA (Sebaste) perches on a rounded hill overlooking one of these basins. The run of the West Samarian hills continues in the form of the Gilboa range which pokes its crescent shape out into the Jezreel valley that borders the hills to the north. The eastern section of the Samarian hills shows the influence of its turn closer toward the Rift valley. It is severely cross-faulted by branches of the valley, the most prominent of which is the Wadi Faria which dominates the northern section of the hills. Narrow at its head inside the hills, the wadi assumes the shape of a broad plain by the time it exits into the Jordan valley, providing the possibility of irrigated agriculture and smooth transit.

Three distinct subregions join together to form the Carmel range that breaks toward the coast north of the western Samarian valley of Dotan. The three subregions are demarcated by two wadis that provided the crucial passes through which flowed traffic between the coastal plain and the Jezreel valley. The Nahal Iron marks the northern boundary of the Iron hills that initiate the Carmel range. This pass directs its traffic toward the gate-keeping city of Megiddo. North of the North Iron, the Menashe hills offered better circumstances for agriculture than their southern neighbors. The Nahal Yoqne'am created the second major pass through the hills, with the city of Yoqne'am situated at its opening into the Jezreel valley, and marks the boundary with the Mount Carmel heights. This subregion comprises a nearly triangular section of hills which offers a steep escarpment to Jezreel and leaves but a thin sliver of coastal plain to the west. Its highest elevations occur away from the sea at its center and southeast corner where the Horn of Carmel (traditionally the site of 1 Kgs 19) overlooks the Jezreel.

The Valley of Jezreel constitutes the sixth subregion that can be considered amongst the Samarian highlands though it is quite distinct geologically. Known also as the Esdraelon or Megiddo plain and filled with alluvial soils, this valley offers the largest expanse of flat farmland in Palestine. The Jezreel also provided ideal terrain for chariot armies who fought for control of the strategic and commercial value inherent in the international routes that traversed it. The battle between DEBORAH and BARAK and a coalition of Canaanite cities (Judg 4–5) represents the most famous of the engagements fought on this battleground. Late in the history of the Judean monarchy, King Josiah lost his life near Megiddo in a conflict with the Egyptian king NECHO II. The Jezreel is drained ineffectively by the perennial Nahal Kishon and much of it was probably flooded during the highpoint of the rainy season and may have remained marshland. Settlement kept to its edges and in addition to Megiddo and Yoqne'am already mentioned, included the cities of TAANACH (also along its western rim), Beth-Haggan at its southernmost indentation into the hills, Jezreel, and BETH SHAN, the ancient gatecity to the Jordan valley. Called Scythopolis in NT times, this city was at one time the main city of the Decapolis (Mark 7:31).

The Galilean Highlands. The Galilean highlands rise abruptly to the north of the Jezreel valley and form the most variegated mountain region of Palestine. The coastal plain and Rift valley mark their western and eastern boundaries while the gorge of the Litani river north of Tyre sets their northern limits. The dominant determinant of Galilean topography is multi-directional geologic faulting that gives the landscape a predominantly east-west trend and shapes five distinct subregions. The Bet Kerem valley offers the most obvious dividing line, severing the higher northern subregion, Upper Galilee, from its southern neighbor, Lower Galilee. The two subregions earn their names; some mountains of Upper Galilee break through the 1,200 m. elevation mark while all of Lower Galilee stays below 600 m.

Lower Galilee presents three distinct subregions. At its center a ladder-like sequence of mountain ridges and wider basins offers the best possibilities for settlement. In NT times, the major city of the region, SEPPHORIS occupied a central position hugging the skirts of the chalk hills. Just north of Sepphoris, a major communications route connected Acco on the coast with the southern end of the Sea of Galilee and points east via the city of Hannathon and the large Bet Netofa valley. MOUNT TABOR is the southern outlier of this subregion's hills. Strips of land to the east and west of central Lower Galilee were less welcoming of settlement. The rounded hills of western Lower Galilee, also known as the Allonim hills, decline toward the coast and the Jezreel whose western door they nearly close. Yet most of the subregion is covered by a thick crust of limestone that inhibits soil formation and the appearance of springs. Eastern Lower Galilee consists of a series of plateaus of basalt that issued from the subregions's now extinct volcanic cones. The major valley of the area is created by the drainage of the Nahal Yavneel into the Rift valley. Its western border with the Rift valley is marked by steep escarpments, limiting communication.

Within Upper Galilee eastern and western subregions can be distinguished. Both present more complex topographies than their southern neighbors. Few of Lower Galilee's broad basins remain. Instead, a jumble of valleys, gorges, ridges, and isolated peaks leaves the region without any unifying feature and creates a highly discontinuous area well-suited to an independent lifestyle. The larger western subregion is dominated in the south by the Meron mountain block which boasts the highest peaks in western Palestine. To the west of this block which is itself heavily dissected by the upper tributaries of the Nahal Keziv, a loose belt of basins has been preserved. Upper Galilee stretches towards the coast in a sequence of nearly parallel narrow mountain ridges. The most prominent of these ridges, the Hanita, slices right through the coastal plain and protrudes into the sea at Rosh ha-Niqra. North of the Hanita, which marks the present border between Lebanon and Israel, the ridges turn more to the northwest and broaden considerably as the central mountains give way to rounded hills and finally to a thin strip of coastal plain that leads northward to Tyre.

The deep gorge of the Nahal Amud marks the dividing line between western and eastern Upper Galilee and constitutes an obstacle to communication which further fractures the area. On its east, the greatest uniformity is found north of the latitude of the Hanita ridge where a broad band of chalk hills is drained by a northward-running tributary of the Litani River. The hills merge with the limestone of eastern Upper Galilee on the east and climb slowly to become a long ridge running northward to the end of the Huleh basin and presenting its face to the valley floor. This plain is itself cut off from the southern section of Eastern Upper Galilee by faulting that intrudes from the Rift valley and creates a number of distinct plateaus. In this area the descent to the Rift valley is frequently stretched out over a sizeable horizontal distance providing easier access to the Valley floor and level agricultural lands. The major city of HAZOR occupied a position on this descent where traffic flowing down into the valley met traffic flowing along it. The hills of eastern Upper Galilee culminate in the Zefat mountain block, topped by Mount Kena'an at 955 m. Cutoff from the west by the North Amud, a major mountain route passed over the shoulder of these hills toward the Sea of Galilee.

The Rift Valley. The Rift valley represents one of the world's most dramatic geological formations, a tectonic tear in the surface of the earth extending southward from the borders of Turkey to the long lakes of East Africa. Sheltering the Sea of Galilee, Jordan River and Dead Sea, this valley sets the basic north-south orientation of Palestine. Along its continuous run of some 500 km. from the skirts of Mount Hermon in the north to the tip of the Gulf of Aqaba, it shelters Palestine's major bodies of water and river as well as numerous diverse hospitable and inhospitable terrains. It is the area of Palestine which has changed most radically since ancient times, witnessing the enlargement of the Dead Sea, the drainage and disappearance of the Huleh Lake and swamps, hydroelectric projects, and intensive agricultural settlement. The Jordan River traverses approximately one-third of the Rift valley. Its sources lie in the springs at the foot of Mount Hermon, the final peak of the Anti-Lebanon range. The northern tip of the Rift valley, where it gives way to basalt and limestone hills, has long been a natural frontier and a key strategic and commercial location. In Israelite times the long-tenured city of DAN took up its position the northwest edge of the valley. Nearby, CAESAREA PHILIPPI (Paneas) was made capital of the region in Jesus' day. East-west traffic across the Rift valley was shunted to these towns by the tangled swamp and small lake that filled the Huleh valley to their south. Though highly productive today, this area was usable only as hunting grounds in the past. Through the basalt rim of this valley the Jordan River reemerges and descends rapidly though a narrow valley toward its entrance at the northern edge of the Sea of Galilee.

Also known as the Sea of Chinnereth, Sea of Tiberias or Lake of Gennesaret, this pear-shaped body of fresh water measures eighteen km. long by twelve km. wide and sits in a depression bordered mostly by steep slopes. Besides supporting the fishing industry, its year-round warm temperatures produced by an altitude ca. 200 m. below sea level make the environs propitious for farming. The amount of level land is limited, however, with the largest area offered on the northwest shore, anchored in OT times by the seaside site of Kinneret. In NT times fishing dominated the livelihood of the area's inhabitants and a dozen villages and towns populated the shore. These included TIBERIAS, MAGDALA, Chinnereth, CAPERNAUM, Chorazin (somewhat inland), Bethsaida, and Gergesa, many sites familiar from the Gospels. At the southern end of the Sea, the Jordan exits and begins its meandering course, traveling by twists and turns over 300 km., three times the length of a straight line connecting it to its Dead Sea goal, and negating its potential as a transit route. The Jordan is not a mighty river, averaging only ten m. in width and three m. in depth. Yet it has often cut its course deeply into the plain so that it is difficult to cross and its waters—saline to begin with—are not readily accessible for irrigation purposes. Apart from a small triangle of land where the Jordan exits the Galilee, the Rift valley through which it passes offered possibilities for settlement only where valley branches brought water from the hills on either side. Draining the hills of the BASHAN, the Yarmuk is the most voluminous of the handful of tributaries that make life possible on the eastern flanks of the Rift valley where such towns as Pella and Succoth made their homes. On the western side the broader valleys of Beth Shan (Scythopolis) and Nahal Faria offered the most important loci for settlement. The Beth Shan valley was particularly important for its connection with the Jezreel valley and the trade routes that passed through it. Between these two valleys the Jordan River flows through a narrow corridor which broadens to the south. A major crossing of the valley is located at this point where the JABBOK river drains the hills of GILEAD. Despite its breadth, the plain is nearly desolate until the oasis of Jericho crops up around the site of a prolific spring. Opposite JERICHO, the plains of MOAB are well watered. The Jordan River ends its flow in Dead, or Salt, Sea. Presently some eighty km. long and sixteen km. broad, this sea at the lowest point on the surface of the earth possesses no outlet: evaporation removes water leaving a high concentration (some twenty-five percent) of salts behind. The sea can support no life, but its mineral wealth —its salts, sulphur, and bitumen—has long been exploited. A number of springs issue forth on its shores and these locations have also provided long tenured occupations. En-Gedi is the most prominent site on the west. The cliffs of the eastern side end nearly at water's edge except in the south where wadis provide water for a level area of shore behind the Lisan peninsula. In ancient times, the sea probably came to an end at this point and the smaller southern lobe of the sea did not exist.

South of the Dead Sea the Rift valley continues its run to the northern tip of the Gulf of Aqaba that leads to the Red Sea. Here the city of Ezion-Geber opened up trade with South Arabia and the eastern coast of Africa and in OT times was caught in a tug of war between Israel and Edom. The Rift bears the name ARABAH over this stretch and it constitutes a true desert, punctuated by a few springs but otherwise devoid of occupation. The major path of communication crossed at the Ascent of the Scorpions which led westward between the two craters of the northern Negev Highlands toward the Mediterranean. Forts guarded this route in many periods.

Transjordanian Plateau. The Transjordanian plateau makes a steep and wall-like ascent along the entire length of the Rift valley. It maintains its height as it stretches eastward into the Arabian desert, leaving a north-south running strip of agricultural and pastoral land between thirty and fifty km. broad. The plateau is dissected into five geographical and infrequently political divisions by wadis which cut deep canyons on their way to the Rift valley. North of the Wadi Yarmuk a basaltic plateau, known biblically as the Bashan and in modern times as the Golan Heights, runs toward the foot of Mount Hermon. Varying in altitude between 400 and 850 m., it is characterized by fertile volcanic soils and good rainfall patterns, making its broad plains a veritable granary. Traffic traversed the Bashan on the way to Damascus and points east. In Roman times the region included the important city of Gadara, whose position on chalk hills south of the Yarmuk shows that the river was no firm boundary. South of the Bashan the region of Gilead is marked by a more discontinuous topography of limestone hills and includes the greatest portion of the territory drained by the east-west flowing sections of the next major wadi system, the Jabbok. Precise boundaries of between Gilead and Ammon, the region to the south and east, are difficult to fix and it is not surprising that Israel, AMMON and MOAB competed for control of this productive region with its forests and good agricultural possibilities. Rammoth-Gilead was a northern border town often in dispute between Israel and Syria. The OT locates PENUEL, Mizpah, and MAHANAIM in this area in connection with the story of Jacob. Jabesh-Gilead on the Jabbok sat at the heart of the territory, while in Roman times Gerasa was one of the most magnificent cities of the province.

The chief city of the territory of Ammon was RABBATH-AMMON, present day Amman, which lay at the edge of the desert on the tail of the Jabbok. The region surrounding Rabbath-Ammon consisted of rounded chalk hills and the broad valley of the Jabbok, though its geographical borders are not well defined. Owing to its readily defended hilltop position and copious springs, the Ammonite capital provided a crucial stopping-off point on the main north-south roads connecting Ezion-Geber and the Arabian peninsula with Damascus. The heartland of Moab consists of a more well-defined region, encompassed by the wadis ARNON and Zered. The plain to the north of this core was often Moabite as well, along with the towns of HESHBON and MEDEBA. The Moabite capital was located at Kir-Hareseth which, like the other cities mentioned, occupied a position along the main north-south road known as the King's Highway that had to traverse the deep gorge of the Arnon near the towns of DIBON and Aroer. The plateau itself rises toward the south where it reaches heights above 1,200 m.

The plateau continues to climb south of the Wadi Zered, and the mountains at the center of the region of EDOM achieve the highest summits in Palestine, over 1,700 m. The main settlement of the region hugged the western border of the heights both to the north and south of an incursion of the Rift valley that divides the region in two. To the north Bozrah was the focus of Edomite settlement during the late Iron Age, while to the south the Nabatean cities of PETRA and Beidha were renown. The settlement of the region was based upon commercial transit activity with the highland settlements serving as the bases of inter-regional authority. In Roman times the Nabataeans extended this authority northward toward Damascus, southward into the Arabian peninsula and westward to the Mediterranean.

Bibliography. D. Baly, *The Geography of the Bible*; O. Efrat and E. Efrat, *Geography of Israel*; M. Miller and J. Hayes, *A History of Ancient Israel and Judah*; J. Rogerson, *Atlas of the Bible*.

—DAVID C. HOPKINS

• **Paltiel.** *See* MICHAL

• **Papias.** [pay'pee-uhs] A bishop of Hierapolis in Asia Minor sometime in the first half of the second century. According to IRENAEUS (*AdvHaer* 5.33.4) Papias had heard JOHN, the disciple of the Lord. He was also reputed to be a companion of the martyr POLYCARP. His writing consisted of a five-volume work called *Interpretation of the Lord's Oracles*. Fragments remain from Irenaeus, EUSEBIUS and a few other sources.

The fragments of Papias have been very important for reconstructing the history of the NT CANON. We learn from him that "Mark, having been Peter's translator wrote all that he remembered accurately but not in order as to what was either said or done by the Lord" (Eusebius, *EccHist* 3.39.15).

In regard to the GOSPEL OF MATTHEW he says, "Now Matthew made an ordered arrangement of the oracles in the Hebrew language, and each man translated them as he was able" (Eusebius, *EccHist* 3.39.15). Apparently Papias believed Matthew was responsible either for an oral form of Matthew or an Aramaic composition which was prior to our Greek.

Papias was deeply interested in the ORAL TRADITION. He make a point of seeking out what the ELDERS had to say: "And if by chance someone should come who had actually attended the elders, I examined the words of the elders, what Andrew or Peter or Philip or Thomas or James or John or Matthew or any of the Lord's disciples, and that which Aristion and the elder John, the disciples of the Lord, were saying. For I assumed that what is derived from books does not profit me so much as what is derived from a living and abiding voice" (Eusebius, *EccHist* 3.39.3-4).

Perhaps this interest in oral tradition, rather than written materials, caused Eusebius to speak of Papias as one limited in intelligence. The intense millenarianism of Papias may also have annoyed Eusebius (*EccHist* 3.39.11-13). In any case the statement has caused many to suppose the author of the GOSPEL OF JOHN was this very elder mentioned by Papias (cf. 2 John 1; 3 John 1).

See also CANON; ELDER; EUSEBIUS; ORAL TRADITION.

Bibliography. W. R. Schoedel, *Polycarp, Martyrdom of Polycarp, Fragments of Papias*; J. Quasten, *Patrology*.

—GRAYDON F. SNYDER

• **Papyrus.** [puh-pi'ruhs] Papyrus is an aquatic plant of the sedge family which grows in a wide distribution in the marshy areas of the Egyptian delta. The plant looks very much like a stalk of corn. When cut, the stalk was divided into pieces of about twelve in. in size. Each piece was then cut open and the core of the pith removed. These pieces of pith were then pressed into ribbon-like sections and laid out in a crisscross pattern. The layers were pressed together to form a sheet of paper-like writing material. The papyrus was then polished with stones or shells and several sheets joined together to form a SCROLL. In 2 John 12, a Gk. word (χάρτης) describes a roll of papyrus used for writing a letter. This is the only biblical reference to the papyrus paper.

The typical papyrus scroll could extend some thirty-two ft. Dowels made of wood or stone were attached to the ends of the scroll to aid in unrolling it. Ancient writers also made use of the CODEX, a loose-leaf book of numerous papyrus sheets. They were piled one upon another, folded down the middle, and fastened together. The codex became more popular in that the scribe might write on the front and back rather than on the one side of the scroll. The Christian church made extensive use of the codex in preserving its sacred writings. However most of the surviving codices are written on parchment (made from animal skins) rather than papyrus. Thousands of parchment biblical fragments have been found in contrast to the small number of papyrus ones.

A papyrus plant.

Artwork by Margaret Jordan Brown

In writing on the papyrus sheets, an ink was used made from a carbon base of soot, gum, and water. The oldest biblical papyrus fragments were found in 1947 among the DEAD SEA SCROLLS (dating from 250 B.C.E. to 50 C.E.). The earliest NT papyrus fragment, found by C. H. Roberts in 1935, dates to the first half of the second century. It contains thirty words from John 18. Chester Beatty came across other old papyrus fragments in 1930 which included a variety of NT references. In 1956, Martin Bodmer found a papyrus copy of most of the Gospel of John dating back to 200 C.E.

The ancient Egyptian papyrus writings predate all of the biblical fragments. The oldest extant copy at Cairo contains the records of the fifth-dynasty king, Assa. The British Museum contains a papyrus roll 135 ft. long dating back to Rameses II (ca. 1170 B.C.E.). The library at Alexandria (destroyed by fire in 47 B.C.E.) was said to include 700,000 papyrus works. Thus much information has come down to the modern world on those somewhat fragile pieces of papyrus.

Papyrus is also mentioned in several places in the Bible outside the context of writing material. In Exod 2:3, the infant Moses was placed in a floating basket made of "bulrushes." The plant which the writer had in mind was probably the papyrus. In ancient Egypt many small boats and sailing vessels were constructed from papyrus, (Isa 18:2). The Book of Job (8:11) speaks of the papyrus plant: "Can the papyrus grow up without marsh?" (NASV). Isa 35:7 speaks of the new age when the desert would become a place for papyrus.

See also CODEX; SCROLL; TEXTS/MANUSCRIPTS/VERSIONS; WRITING SYSTEMS.

—JAMES L. BLEVINS

• **Parables.** If one would understand JESUS, it has been said, one must understand his parables. As much as a third of the teaching of Jesus in the Gospels is expressed parabolically. If his encompassing theme was the KINGDOM OF GOD, Jesus' characteristic medium was the parable. An effort at reaching an understanding of the nature of parables and their appropriate interpretation can be guided by means of a triangular model requiring careful attention from three relatively distinct angles of vision: literary, historical, and theological. Various advanced methods of biblical analysis are requisite for the undertaking.

The Parable as Literature. At the outset, the literary form of the parables must be considered. Though in the original instance the actual parable of Jesus was an oral event presented courageously by Jesus as a public storyteller, the modern reader receives each parable as a literary form in a literary gospel. The etymology of the Gk. word for parable (παραβολή) is telling for both instances. The word derives from a preposition (παρά) meaning "beside" or "alongside"; and a verb (βάλλω) meaning "to throw." Hence a parable by derivation indicates the function of throwing alongside, one thing juxtaposed to another in comparison.

The meaning of the word "parable" cannot be derived simply from the Greek, however. The OT background is important. In the OT, a term for sayings is used (מָשָׁל) which has a broad semantic field. It includes parables in the narrow sense, but also such things as taunts, legal axioms, and rules of conduct. John Drury (*The Parables in the Gospels*) points out that Ezekiel contains examples of virtually all of the different categories of Hebrew sayings (מָשָׁל). There are figurative, popular sayings (16:44; 18:2-3), elaborate historical allegories (chaps. 15, 17), enacted allegories (24:3), songs of derision (chaps. 27, 28, 31, 32), and prophetic oracles throughout. The LXX uses the word parable to translate the inclusive Hebrew term regularly, and the word parable in the NT actually covers a wider category than the actual parables of Jesus. The word appears forty-eight times in the synoptic Gospels and twice in Hebrews.

Biblical parable should be distinguished but not divorced from allegory. An allegory is a series of pictures or cryptograms in a story symbolizing a series of truths in another sphere. Each detail in the allegory functions as a separate metaphor. Madelein Boucher (*The Parables*) defines allegory broadly as "an extended metaphor in narratory form." For each detail of the story there is a hidden meaning. Distinguished literary allegories include John Bunyan's *Pilgrim's Progress* and Jonathan Swift's *Tale of a Tub*. The parable on the other hand has one main point. Ian T. Ramsey (*Christian Discourse*) characterizes parable as leading to a "disclosure point," while allegory correlates two areas of discourse. Dan Via (*The Parables*) points to the greater internal coherence of the parable. The primary distinction between parable and allegory turns upon the singular internal juxtaposition characteristic of the parable.

Adolf Jülicher in his groundbreaking volumes *Die Gleichnisreden Jesu* rightly reacted to the ancient tendency to allegorize the parables in the service of ecclesiastical theology. The tendency to read such allegorical interpretations into the text, such as viewing the reference to the two denarii paid to the innkeeper by the so-called good Samaritan (Luke 10:35) as a coded reference to two members of the Trinity, was discredited critically by his scholarly influence.

However, subordinated allegorical dimensions do exist within the parables. One finds stock metaphors for God such as king, for example. Furthermore, there is consensus that a parable such as that of the sower (Mark 4:1-9; par.) was a "commentary on the campaign" in Galilee. The curious slandering of allegory and the distancing of Jesus from it is strangely overdone. Prejudice against allegory has been rebutted effectively by Raymond Brown, "Parable and Allegory Reconsidered" in *New Testament Essays*. On the other hand, even though the parable of the sower has an allegorical cast, the classic juxtaposition remains. The first three fields (Mark 4:3-7) are contrasted with the fourth because absolutely no fruit results in the first three instances while a bountiful harvest develops from the good soil (v. 8).

Various classes of parable within the synoptic Gospels can be set out (classic parables do not appear in the Gospel of John). C. L. Mitton (*The Good News*) pictures Jesus' ability to turn ears into eyes: "Sometimes it is a still picture, like a single cartoon; at other times it is a series of moving pictures like a short story presented on a film." Classification begins with the extensive number of parabolic sayings, such as throwing "pearls before swine" (Matt 7:6) or serving two masters (Matt 6:24). These sayings are prominent in Matthew's Gospel and may be thought of as "parable germs" (A. B. Bruce), one-liners with a picturesque appeal to the imagination.

Simple parables represent a picture elaborated into a story. They grow out of a typical experience and appeal to common sense. They often illumine the Kingdom of God and open with an introductory formula ("The Kingdom of God is like . . . "). These extended similes include the paired parables (Matt 13:44-45; Luke 14:28-32; 15:3-10).

Parabolic stories or narratives derive from a specific situation and frequently begin with reference to a "certain" (τις) person. Luke reports numerous narrative parables, such as the unjust steward (16:1-8), the rich fool (12:16-21), and the good Samaritan (10:30-37). A narrative parable amounts to a dramatic story composed of one or more scenes drawn from daily life yet focused on an unusual, decisive circumstance. They are unique events rather than frequent situations.

The parables partake of some of the narrative patterns in folk literature. Rudolf Bultmann (*The Synoptic Tradition*) mentioned the law of end stress, repetition, antithesis of two types, economy in description, and single perspective. John Donohue (*The Gospel in Parable*) isolates four elements of narrative: meaning, character, plot, and point of view. Dan Via (*The Parables*) suggests the creative application of the dramatic categories of comic and tragic to certain parables. Scenes in narrative parables are actually juxtaposed, as in the instance of the three scenes in the parable of the unmerciful servant (Matt 18:23-34) and of the two scenes in the parable of the rich man and Lazarus (Luke 16:19-31). Jülicher and others also advocate the category of *exemplum* (example story), not a comparison but an example to emulate, but it is not universally accepted. The question whether the parable of the good Samaritan is an example or comparison is vexed. The admonition "go and do likewise" (v. 37) leans toward *exemplum,* but the critical questions, "Which of these three . . . " (v. 36) assumes a comparison. The hearer must make a personal judgment drawn from an internal juxtaposition of three travelers as they related to a wounded traveler. The category of example story should be used only with great reticence.

Other literary considerations include common metaphors present in scattered parables. John Crossan (*In Parables*) calls attention to parables containing the common metaphor of master/servant which reflect a time of critical reckoning. Peter R. Jones (*The Teaching of the Parables*) highlights the householder parables that feature an authority figure whose purpose is resisted or even rejected yet whose will is ultimately achieved.

Jones also calls special attention to the prominence of direct discourse and the category of the refusal parable. The latter relates to those parables that express the intention of a character not to do what is requested: "I do not will" (οὐ θέλω). Examples include the elder brother (Luke 15:23) and the wedding guests (Matt 22:3). Direct discourse is also immensely important in many parables in bringing the stories to life. Through the conversation the parable often makes its point, sometimes through a soliloquy. Surely Jesus delivered these conversational lines in an animated fashion. Furthermore, the function of numerous parables as questions involves the audience (Luke 17:7-10; 16:1-8; 12:20; Mark 12:9).

A famous literary definition of a parable devised by C. H. Dodd in *The Parables of the Kingdom* deserves consideration: "At its simplest the parable is a metaphor or simile drawn from nature or common life, arresting the hearer by its vividness or strangeness, and leaving the mind in sufficient doubt about its application to tease it into active thought." Note the definition's emphasis upon the hearer.

The Parables in Jesus' History. The parables of Jesus illuminate and are illuminated by Jesus' historical context. Many parables grew out of conflict. The parables functioning as questions, usually for Pharisees and sinners, expose the suppositions of Jesus' critics, explain his ministry, and extol the Kingdom of God. Some were parables of the times that interpreted the specific moment of historic crisis precipitated by Jesus' presence. Other occasions included scholarly debate (e.g., Luke 10:25-37), leading to a midrashic parable, and formal teaching settings (Mark 4:1-2).

The fact that Jesus presented the story during a momentous shifting of the aeons affects the meaning and requires response to the parabolist as well as the parable. The teller as well as the tale is crucial. Sometimes "christological penetration" is discernible within the parable (e.g., Mark 3:23-27). The parables are not merely clever stories but proclamations of the gospel inviting a decision.

There are interesting historical antecedents in the OT, especially the prophetic parables. The most instructive comes from the prophet Nathan's parable to King David (2 Sam 12:1-4). A. T. Cadoux (*Parables of Jesus*), sensitive to the importance of the prophets' use of parables, pointed out how both Jesus' parable to Simon the Pharisee and Nathan's parable brought the hearer to self-condemnation before he saw where he was being led. Note also other parables in the OT (Isa 28:23-29; 5:1-7; Eccl 9:13-16; Amos 7:8-9; Ezek 15:1-8; Judg 9:7-15).

Some scholars picture Jesus only in idyllic pastoral scenes beside lakes drawing parables from agriculture. The impression of Jesus conducting a largely rural ministry may be abetted by attention to selected parables drawn frequently from farming and infrequently from fishing. Jesus, however, grew up a scant four miles from the city of Sepphoris, replete with marketplace and lawcourts. Tiberias, also a Greco-Roman city, was situated along the Sea of Galilee. Jesus grew up in the shadow of a Greco-Roman urban culture. Hence he could speak pictorially not merely of lost sheep (Luke 15:3-7) and of rural rich fools (Luke 12:16-21) but also of urban situations. He portrayed a metropolitan judge (Luke 18:1-8), for example, and a Pharisee and a tax collector praying in the Temple (Luke 18:9-14). His parable about the talents (Matt 25:14-30; Luke 19:12-27) deals with urban life, referring to banks and the earning of interest. In his parable about a banquet (Luke 14:16-24) the host commanded his servant to go into the "streets and lanes of the *city*" (v. 21). The parable regarding an unmerciful servant (Matt 18:23-35) also draws upon urban life, and the account of the wicked tenants (Mark 12:1-11) has an agrarian content but an urban application. These glimpses of urban life corroborate the growing recognition of the Greco-Roman influence even in Galilee and the urban aspect of the historical ministry of Jesus.

In the historical ministry of Jesus enacted parables may also be found (Luke 15:1; 19:1-10; Mark 3:13-19; 11:1-11, 12-14, 15-19). Edward Schillebeeckx in his book *Jesus* also portrays Jesus himself as a kind of living parable, opening up the possibility of a new and different life. The Jesus parable displays how God cares for the oppressed, the poor, the blind, and sinners.

Parable as Theology. The parables do contain a continuous theme, the great thesis on the Kingdom of God (βασιλεία τοῦ θεοῦ). They portray the nature of the Kingdom (Mark 4:26-29), the grace (Luke 18:9-17), the crisis (Luke 12:54-56), and the conditions, such as forgiveness (Matt 18:23-35), compassion (Luke 10:25-37), and responsive hearing (Matt 7:24-27).

In *Jesus and the Kingdom of God* George Beasley-Murray establishes the Kingdom as present in the ministry of Jesus in such parables as the strong man bound (Mark 3:27), the treasure and the pearl (Matt 13:44-46), and the laborers in the vineyard (Matt 20:1-16). The Kingdom as future is proclaimed in the judge and the widow (Luke 18:1-8) and the talents and the pounds (Matt 25:14-30; Luke 19:11-27). Jesus inaugurated the Kingdom, but the consummation remains in the future. The seed parables are decisive: the seed is sown, therefore, the harvest will follow.

The parables in content may be characterized in different ways—as eschatological: urgency due to the intervention of God; existential: illumination of human existence; ethical: the values of the Kingdom; and evangelistic: a call to decision.

The model of the triangle focuses discussion of the nature of the parable in terms of its literary aspects, historical roots, and the theological meanings.

See also JESUS; KINGDOM OF GOD.

Bibliography. K. Bailey, *Through Peasant Eyes* and *Poet and Peasant*; A. B. Bruce, *The Parabolic Teaching of Christ*; M. Boucher, *The Parables*; J. Donohue, *The Gospel in Parable*; C. H. Dodd, *The Parables of the Kingdom*; J. Drury, *The Parables in the Gospels*; J. Jeremias, *The Parables of Jesus*; G. Jones, *The Art and Truth of the Parables*; P. R. Jones, *The Teaching of the Parables*; A. Jülicher, *Die Gleichnisreden Jesu*; S. Kistemaker, *The Parables of Jesus*; E. Linnemann, *Jesus of the Parables*;

C. Smith, *The Jesus of the Parables*; R. Stein, *An Introduction to the Parables of Jesus*; D. Via, *The Parables*.

—PETER RHEA JONES

• **Paraclete.** *See* ADVOCATE/PARACLETE; HOLY SPIRIT

• **Paradigm.** *See* APOTHEGM

• **Paradise.** Paradise is an ancient Persian word which appears in the Bible with the original meaning of park or walled garden and with a derived meaning related to concepts of life after death.

In the OT the word paradise appears three times (always in the original sense): Neh 2:8 (king's forest), Eccl 2:5 (parks), and Cant 4:13 (orchard). The derived sense of paradise as the abode of the righteous dead developed in later Jewish and Christian thought. In early traditional Jewish theology all the dead descended to SHEOL, a shadowy underworld. Eventually the Jews postulated separate destinies for the wicked and the righteous, and in the Apocrypha the concept of paradise was contrasted with GEHENNA (2 Esdr 7:36). Although paradise was beyond human knowledge in the present (2 Esdr 4:1-12), it would be revealed eventually (2 Esdr 7:36). Like Eden, paradise contained the TREE OF LIFE (2 Esdr 8:52-54).

In the pseudepigrapha differing concepts of paradise are expressed. Paradise was in the third heaven (*2 Enoch* 8a) or on earth (*1 Enoch* 32). In the *Testament of Levi* a new priest will open the gates of paradise and remove the sword, allowing the saints to eat of the Tree of Life (18:10-11). Paradise was considered either the abode of the righteous prior to resurrection or their eternal destiny after resurrection. This state would be like the original garden of Eden. Several sources noted the presence of trees in paradise. In *1 Enoch* Gabriel is named as the guardian angel of Eden or paradise (20:7). Enoch and Elijah were taken directly to paradise without dying (*1 Enoch* 60:8; 89:52).

Paradise is used three times in the NT, generally reflecting later Jewish thought. In Luke 23:43 Jesus told the penitent thief that "today you will be with me in Paradise," implying that the righteous dead go immediately to paradise. In Luke 16:19-31 Jesus told of Lazarus being taken to Abraham's bosom, apparently also referring to the abode of the righteous after death. Some identify paradise and Abraham's bosom with heaven, the final abode of the righteous. Others see paradise as a separate section of Hades which has been removed to the third heaven since the resurrection and ascension of Jesus (cf. Eph 4:8).

In 2 Cor 12:3 Paul referred to himself as a man caught up into paradise. Probably Paul located paradise in the third heaven (12:2), reflecting some late Jewish thought (*Apoc Mos* 37:5). How Paul's experience in paradise related to the issue of an INTERMEDIATE STATE is a matter of scholarly debate. Sometimes Paul suggested that death was immediately followed by communion with God (Phil 1:23; 2 Cor 5:8). Elsewhere he suggested that time elapsed between death and the resurrection (1 Cor 15:51-57).

In Rev 2:7 the church at Ephesus was told about the possibility of eating of the tree of life in the "paradise of God." Here paradise seems to be part of the consummation of history (cf. Rev 22:1-5). The restoration of an Eden-like paradise was part of Jewish hope (Isa 51:3; Ezek 36:35). In the second century B.C.E. the tree of life was associated with the Jerusalem Temple (*1 Enoch* 25:4-7).

See also DEATH; GEHENNA; HEAVEN; HELL; RESURRECTION IN THE NEW TESTAMENT; RESURRECTION IN THE OLD TESTAMENT; SHEOL.

Bibliography. H. Bietenhard and C. Brown, "Paradise," *NIDNT*; R. H. Charles, *Eschatology: The Doctrine of a Future Life in Israel, Judaism and Christianity*; C. R. Smith, *The Bible Doctrine of the Hereafter*.

—WARREN MCWILLIAMS

• **Parallelism.** The complex network or feeling of correspondence between adjacent lines, parts of lines, and/or words. The nature of this correspondence varies because parallelism activates all the levels of language at once: lexical (vocabulary), semantic (meaning), grammatical (syntax and morphology), and phonological (sounds). It cannot be restricted to one level of language or another, although the semantic and grammatical are the most evident aspects of parallelism and have historically received the most attention. No one formula can account for all parallelism. Parallelism is a common feature of all language, both prose (cf. Gen. 21:1) and poetry, although it is more predominant, balanced, and terse in poetry (Gen 4:23-24).

The history of the study of biblical parallelism has been shaped by Bishop Robert Lowth's "Lectures on the Sacred Poetry of the Hebrews" delivered in 1753. Lowth identified *parrallelismus membrorum* ("the parallelism of the clauses") and distinguished three types of semantic parallelism: synonymous (interpreted as a restatement, or saying the same thing twice), antithetical (a negation or opposite statement), and synthetic (a catchall category of sequence and combination). Lowth's legacy has been a narrow, static view of parallelism as simple repetition. Most contemporary scholars, viewing parallelism through the prism of linguistics, have abandoned the Lowth model, especially as developed by his successors. They argue instead for dynamic movement and interplay within and between lines. Parallelism does not always make its correspondence explicit; complete correspondence on all linguistic levels is rare. Thus parallelism can become the vehicle of figurative, metaphorical language. Parallelism in itself does not have meaning but contributes to and structures the meaning of a text, as well as draws from that meaning.

See also POETRY.

—DENISE DOMBKOWSKI HOPKINS

• **Parchment.** Parchment is a writing material made from sheep or goat skins. The name "parchment" was probably derived from PERGAMUM, the name of the place where parchment was first produced by Eumenes in the first half of the second century B.C.E. The skins were soaked in lime water to remove the hair. Then they were scraped, washed, stretched on frames, and dried. Finally, they were rubbed down with fine chalk or pumice. Unlike leather, parchment was not tanned. Skins had long served as writing materials, but this new method of production made it possible to write on both sides of the skins which, in turn, made the book form—CODEX—more practical.

Although more expensive, parchment eventually replaced PAPYRUS as a writing material because it was more durable and the ink could be scraped off and the parchment reused. An even finer form of parchment, vellum, was made from the skins of young or stillborn calves, kids, or lambs. Most of the great manuscripts of the Bible between the fourth and the sixth centuries C.E. were written on vellum. After the sixth century, the quality of vellum deteriorated when the demand became so great that high-grade skins were difficult to find.

Parchment is referred to one time in the Bible (2 Tim 4:13), where Paul instructs Timothy to "bring the cloak that

I left with Carpus at Troas, also the books, and above all the parchments.'' Paul is pictured as being in prison at the approach of winter. He needed his cloak; but even of more importance than physical comfort were the books and the parchments. The emphasis placed upon the parchments in the letter indicates that they must have been important, perhaps parts of the LXX. Evidence for this is the frequent use of the word translated parchment as a technical term for a codex. Although there is no way to know precisely the nature of the parchments envisioned, they were pictured as prized possessions of Paul. This reference to parchments throws light on the writing materials used in the early church and demonstrates how important books were to early Christian leaders.

See also CODEX; PAPYRUS; PERGAMUM; WRITING SYSTEMS.

—W. T. EDWARDS

• **Parental Blessing.** The biblical concept of ''blessing'' (Heb. *bĕrākâ*; Gk. *eulogia*) designated some special good or benefit conferred by God. This benefit could, however, be requested of God by a third party as in the case where a divine blessing, to be distinguished from the BIRTHRIGHT or INHERITANCE, was requested on behalf of a child by a parent. For example, JACOB tricked ISAAC into granting blessing of prosperity and dominance (Gen 27:28-29), the source of which was clearly to be God.

In the patriarchal narratives, the theory behind the parental blessing, normally greater for the first-born (Gen 27; but cf. Gen 48:13-19), seems to have been rooted in the notion of imitative MAGIC, where rituals or words have a life and power of their own that evokes a response from the gods. From this idea the Hebrews retained the idea that words have within them the power to bring about the fulfillment of the promise contained in the words. Because a word was considered a reality, a thing of power in itself, a blessing once uttered could not, as Isaac noted (Gen 27:33), be retracted.

Parental blessings, particularly valued at the end of a father's life (Gen 27; 48), were accompanied by a ritual such as a laying on of hands or a kiss, thus adding to the tangible nature of the spoken word.

By the Christian era the concept of parental blessing had evolved to become an invocation of God's love, mercy, and care and had become less a notion of automatic action, although it was still considered that the prayers and blessings of certain holy persons had more efficacy than those of others.

See also BIRTHRIGHT; CURSE AND BLESSING; INHERITANCE IN THE NEW TESTAMENT; INHERITANCE IN THE OLD TESTAMENT; MAGIC AND DIVINATION.

Bibliography. J. Pedersen, *Israel: Its Life and Culture*.

—T. FURMAN HEWITT

• **Parousia/Second Coming.** [puh-*roo'*zhee-uh] The Gk. word παρουσία means ''arrival,'' ''coming,'' or ''presence.'' In Greek literature the word most often indicates the reaching of a destination in the normal course of life, but parousia was frequently employed in reference to a special appearance or visitation by a ruler or god; and so, in the Greek world the word could be understood to have a technical force. Transliterated into English the word parousia functions as a technical term for the coming of Christ at the end of human history, as depicted in the NT.

Usually, in popular speech, this advent of the resurrected JESUS is referred to as the second coming. But, the phrase, second coming, does not occur in the NT, although Heb 9:28 (''Christ . . . will appear a second time . . . to save those who are eagerly waiting for him'') comes close to using the phrase. The first preserved occurrence of ''second coming'' in relation to the return to earth of the resurrected Jesus is found in Justin Martyr's *Dialogue with Trypho* (chap. 14), from the middle of the second century. Yet, the Christian expectation of the coming of Christ at the end of history is traceable to the earliest traditional material in the NT. First Thessalonians (4:13–5:11), perhaps the earliest preserved writing in the NT, offers extensive explicit teaching concerning this coming, as does the later letter, 1 Corinthians (chap. 15).

Moreover, in his letters Paul drew upon traditional material from the belief and worship of the early church that was itself formed earlier than the writing of the letters, and in this traditional material one finds testimony to the fervent early Christian conviction that the resurrected Jesus would return. In 1 Cor 16:22 Paul writes, ''If any one has no love for our Lord, let him be accursed. Our Lord, come!'' The enthusiastic utterance, ''Our Lord, come!'' translates into English from Greek the word MARANATHA, which is itself a transliteration into Greek of two Aramaic words. Scholars understand Paul to be using a phrase (*maranatha*) from the worship of the oldest Christian community in Palestine, and in this petition (''Our Lord, come!'') one sees that the earliest Aramaic-speaking Christians strongly anticipated the coming of Christ.

While there is debate whether or not the early Christians believed that Christ would necessarily come soon (an expectation described as ''the imminent parousia''), it is clear that the anticipation of Christ's coming was a consistent part of early Christian belief. As noted, the earliest traditional material and writing in the NT record this hope, but what is likely the latest document in the Christian canon, 2 Peter (3:12), maintains this same expectation. Furthermore, the Book of Revelation bears extensive testimony to the early Christian anticipation of the coming of Christ. In Rev 22 Christ is portrayed as saying, '' 'And behold, I am coming soon' '' (v. 6); then, he repeats, '' 'Behold, I am coming soon . . . ' '' (v. 12). In response to these declarations, the Spirit and the Bride (the Church) say, '' 'Come' ''; and the one who hears the reading of the Revelation is directed to say, '' 'Come' '' (v. 17). Finally, Christ reiterates his promise, '' 'Surely I am coming soon,' '' to which the writer, John of Patmos, adds, ''Amen. Come, Lord Jesus'' (v. 20).

These and similar passages demonstrate the eschatological character of early Christianity. The basic belief of early Christians had a future dimension that focused hope in relation to the fulfillment of God's work in Christ at the end of history. This hope was both personal, related to the person of the risen, glorified, and returning Lord Jesus Christ, and universal, relating to the work of Christ in his return which would affect all of creation as his power and glory dominated the entire cosmos.

In analyzing the teaching of the NT writers concerning the parousia, it is striking that the parousia thinking of the early church made no direct use of the language of the historical Jesus, who spoke according to the Gospels about the future coming of the SON OF MAN. Rather, the early church formed terminology related to the parousia that excluded the Son of man. One finds instead references to the coming (or ''day'') of Christ, the Lord, the Lord Jesus, the Lord Jesus Christ, and God; so that the historical Jesus alone is found referring to the coming of the Son of man in Christian scripture.

Finally, Christians have interpreted the idea of the parousia in two distinct manners, understanding the pertinent texts in quite different fashions. Some conclude that the parousia will be a literal, singular, observable appearance of the glorified Christ at a specific moment in the future; thus, they anticipate the event. Others interpret the parousia as a metaphor for the perpetual, gradual process of permeation of this world's social structures by the increasingly victorious spirit of Christ; thus they point to signs of the current occurrence of the parousia and celebrate it as a past, present, and future event.

See also ESCHATOLOGY IN THE NEW TESTAMENT; JESUS; JUDGMENT, DAY OF; KINGDOM OF GOD; MESSIAH/CHRIST; MILLENNIUM; RESURRECTION IN THE NEW TESTAMENT; SON OF MAN.

Bibliography. C. K. Barrett, *The First Epistle to the Corinthians*; G. R. Beasley-Murray, *Jesus and the Future*; E. Best, *A Commentary on the First and Second Epistles to the Thessalonians*; G. B. Caird, *The Revelation of St John the Divine*; A. Oepke, "παρουσία, πάρειμι," *TDNT*; J. A. T. Robinson, *Jesus and His Coming*.

—MARION L. SOARDS

• **Pashhur.** [pash'huhr] A proper name appearing fourteen times in the OT. If Egyptian in background, it means "portion of [the god] Horus"; if Hebrew, it comes from a verb meaning to tear to pieces.

Pashhur, son of Immer, was a priest and "chief officer in the house of the Lord" (Jer 20:1). He strongly disagreed with the unpatriotic preaching of JEREMIAH. He beat him and "put him in the stocks that were in the upper Benjamin Gate of the house of the Lord" (v. 2), then released him the next day. Jeremiah told Pashhur that the Lord changed his name to "Terror on Every Side" (v. 3).

Another Pashhur in Jeremiah's day was the son of Malchiah. He was sent by Zedekiah, last king of Judah, along with Zephaniah the priest, to ask Jeremiah to "inquire of the Lord for us, for NEBUCHADREZZAR the king of Babylon is making war against us" (Jer 21:2). Jeremiah again predicted utter destruction for Jerusalem (vv. 3-14). This Pashhur had a son, Gedaliah. Both are called princes or officials (Heb. *śārîm*, 38:4) and both were involved in throwing Jeremiah into "the cistern of Malchiah, the king's son" (v. 6).

Other Pashhurs and their descendants are among the exiles to return to Jerusalem (cf. 1 Chr 9:12; Ezra 2:38; 10:22; and Neh 7:41; 10:3; 11:12). All were of priestly families. One had six sons, all married to foreign wives, who agreed to divorce them (Ezra 10:22). This same Pashhur may have been one of "those who set their seal" under Nehemiah to put away their foreign wives (Neh 10:1, 3).

See also JEREMIAH; TEMPLE/TEMPLES.

—D. C. MARTIN

• **Passion, The.** Passion is the technical term for the suffering, trial, and crucifixion of Jesus, especially the events of the last week of his ministry as recorded in the Gospels. Because the resurrection is an inseparable part of that event, it is often embraced in the comprehensive use of the term.

Reformation theologies, especially those shaped by John Calvin, tended to focus exclusively upon the death of Christ as a propitiation for human sin, satisfying the wrath of God or preserving the divine honor. Such a transactional view of the significance of the suffering of Jesus has been highly modified in recent theologies by broader emphasis on the incarnation of Christ, his entire servant ministry, and his continuing ministry "at the right hand of the Father."

Jesus' own self-designation, SON OF MAN, found more than eighty times in the synoptic Gospels, refers in more than half of those occurrences to his earthly suffering, rejection, and approaching death. This makes his entire incarnate life and mission a ministry of suffering. Thus it shifts the emphasis from a transaction between the Son and the Father at Calvary's CROSS, to a life-style of crossbearing and suffering for the Christian disciple. This is reinforced by the strong influence of the suffering servant image of Isaiah in the Gospel portrait of Jesus and in the early Christian interpretation of the life of Jesus in the Epistles.

Contemporary emphasis upon the passion of Christ as a comprehensive interpretation of his life and ministry has caused a broad reevaluation of the rejection of the doctrine of "patripassianism" by the early church. This doctrine that the Father suffered in the death of Christ was soundly rejected in the early centuries of the church because it seemed to threaten the distinctive roles of Father and Son, especially in a more transactional view of the atonement. But the broader emphasis upon the entire incarnational ministry of Jesus as the involvement "of the Godhead bodily" in the suffering and death of Jesus has revived a doctrine of "theopassianism," the suffering of God. It serves as an important corrective, both in preserving the unity of God and in drawing the Christian into the passion of Christ by crossbearing discipleship, symbolized in baptism and fulfilled in a servant ministry of sacrifice and suffering in the world.

Paul even sees Christians as completing "what is lacking in Christ's affliction" (Col 1:24), as he is doing in his own suffering. He may be remembering his encounter with Christ on the road to Damascus: "Saul, Saul, why do you persecute me?" (Acts 9:4). In the suffering of the Christians, Christ was suffering; in the church, the body of Christ, the passion of Christ continues. This broader emphasis upon the passion of Christ has enriched the doctrine of God who identifies with the suffering of humanity and the practice of Christian discipleship as the sharing of Christ's continuing ministry of suffering in the world.

See also CROSS; EXPIATION; PASSION NARRATIVE; SON OF MAN; SUFFERING IN THE NEW TESTAMENT; SUFFERING IN THE OLD TESTAMENT; TRIAL OF JESUS.

Bibliography. F. W. Dillistone, *The Significance of the Cross*; P. T. Forsyth, *The Cruciality of the Cross*; J. Knox, *The Death of Christ*; L. Morris, *The Cross of Jesus*.

—WAYNE E. WARD

• **Passion Narrative.** The passion narrative consists of the Gospels' accounts of Jesus' experience during the week that climaxed with his CRUCIFIXION and resurrection (Mark 11–16; Matt 21–28; Luke 19–24; John 12–21). Traditionally Christians have referred to the period from Palm Sunday to Resurrection Sunday (EASTER) as Passion or Holy Week.

The synoptic Gospels indicate that Jesus explicitly predicted his passion on three occasions: (1) Mark 8:31-32 || Matt 16:21 || Luke 9:22; (2) Mark 9:31-32 || Matt 17:22-23 || Luke 9:43-45; and (3) Mark 10:32-34 || Matt 20:17-19 || Luke 18:31-34. At other points he indirectly pointed to his death (e.g., Mark 10:45). The disciples are portrayed as not fully understanding the significance of his death until after the resurrection.

Several major events in the passion narrative are recounted (with minor differences) by two or more Gospel writers. The Synoptics, of course, have more points in common. Events common to two or more accounts are the plot by the chief priests and elders to kill Jesus, the anointing of Jesus at the house of Simon the leper, Judas's agreement to betray Jesus, the preparations for the Passover meal, the Passover meal, Jesus' designation of Judas as the betrayer, the prediction of Peter's denial, the initiation of the LORD'S SUPPER, Jesus' prayer in the garden of Gethsemane, the arrest, the appearances before Jewish and Roman officials, Peter's denial, the scourging, Jesus' journey to Golgotha, the crucifixion, Jesus' death, and his burial in Joseph of Arimathea's tomb.

Each Gospel writer highlighted certain details and events. For example, Mark noted Jesus' use of the Aramaic *Abba* in his prayer in Gethsemane (14:36), the young man who fled naked from Gethsemane (14:52), and Simon of Cyrene as the father of Alexander and Rufus (15:21). Matthew noted Judas's suicide (27:3-10; cf. Acts 1:18-19), the dream of Pilate's wife (27:19), the people's acceptance of blame for Jesus' death (27:24-25), and the opening of the tombs in Jerusalem (27:52-53). Luke highlighted the innocence of Jesus (23:4, 14, 15, 22, 41, 47), the disciples' discussion of greatness (22:24-30), Jesus' mention of swords for the disciples (22:35-38), Jesus' appearance before Herod Antipas (23:6-12), and Jesus' words to the women on the way to Golgotha (23:27-31). Although John's Gospel has the same basic sequence as the synoptic Gospels, he highlighted several different events. John alone discussed the foot washing (13:1-20), the new commandment (13:34), the farewell discourses, including the role of the counselor (paraclete) in 14:1–16:33, the high priestly prayer (17), the identification of Malchus as the man whose ear was cut off by Peter (18:10-11), Jesus' appearance before Annas (18:12-14), the soldiers' plan to break Jesus' legs and the piercing of his side (19:31-37), and the role of Nicodemus in the burial (19:39).

One of the traditional features of the study of Jesus' passion is the SEVEN WORDS FROM THE CROSS: Jesus' request for divine forgiveness for his executioners (Luke 23:34), his promise to the penitent thief (Luke 23:43), his expression of concern for his mother and BELOVED DISCIPLE (John 19:26-27), his cry of abandonment (Mark 15:34; Matt 27:46), his expression of thirst (John 19:28), his sense of accomplishment (John 19:30), and his committing of his spirit to God (Luke 23:46).

See also ADVOCATE/PARACLETE; CRUCIFIXION; EASTER; JUDAS; PASSION, THE; PETER; SEVEN WORDS FROM THE CROSS.

Bibliography. R. Leivestad, *Christ the Conqueror*; V. Taylor, *The Passion Narrative of Luke*; E. Haenchen, "History and Interpretation in the Johannine Passion Narrative," *Int* 24/2 (Apr 1970): 198-219.

—WARREN MCWILLIAMS

• **Passover.** The Heb. noun translated "Passover" is *pesaḥ* from the verb *pāsaḥ,* meaning "to pass or spring over," also "to limp." Some have suggested that a ritual dance may lie in the background, for the verb is used to describe the cultic dance of the Canaanite prophets in their contest with ELIJAH (1 Kgs 18:21, 26). However, in light of Exod 12:23 the most persuasive position considers the etymology as having to do with a "gracious passing over" by "the destroyer" [death]. The sense of "spare" is basic.

The most extensive block of OT literature dealing with the Passover is contained in Exod 12:1–13:16; in addition, several other passages treat the subject: Deut 16:1-8; Lev 23:5-8; Num 9:1-14; 28:16-25; Ezek 45:21-25. Like these, other sections deal with the closely related FEAST OF UNLEAVENED BREAD (Exod 23:15, 18; 34:18, 25). All relate the Passover feast as a remembrance of the EXODUS of the ancient Hebrews from Egyptian bondage amid divine signs and wonders. Three months later, the people enter into a covenant with God at Mount SINAI. Exod 12 first establishes the date of the celebration—"the first month of the year" (v. 2), often known as Abib (Exod 13:4; 23:15; 34:18; Deut 16:1), which means "fresh young ears" of barley (Exod 9:31). Later in the OT (Neh 2:1; Esth 3:7) the month took the Babylonian name Nisan. The first month falls in March/April.

At evening of the 14th of Abib, the beginning of the 15th, each man (if with a small household joining with his neighbor, Exod 12:3-6) killed from his herd a sheep or goat, smearing some of its blood on the doorposts and lintel of the house. It was roasted and eaten that night with bitter herbs (Exod 12:8). Not a bone of the animal was broken; it was eaten only in the house (Exod 12:46) and in haste, demonstrating the participants' readiness for departure, with their loins girded, sandals on their feet and staffs in their hands (Exod 12:11). Such also was the significance of the unleavened bread, time being too short for dough to ferment (Deut 16:3; Exod 12:39). Any portion of the animal remaining until the morning was to be burned (Exod 12:10). Because "it is the Lord's passover" (Exod 12:11), God was to see the blood on the houses of the participants and spare them the plague of death brought on "all the first-born of the land of Egypt" (Exod 12:12). This apparent family observance is always to be honored: "This day shall be for you a memorial day, and you shall keep it as a feast to the Lord; throughout your generations you shall observe it as an ordinance for ever" (Exod 12:14).

From the time of the reformations of King JOSIAH ca. 621 B.C.E. until 70 C.E., all Jewish males observed three pilgrim festivals at Jerusalem—those of Unleavened Bread, Weeks, and Booths (Deut 16). Although the Passover and the Feast of Unleavened Bread originally were two separate festivals, they had been combined by 621 B.C.E. so that the Passover also became a pilgrim festival observed at JERUSALEM. The Passover-Unleavened Bread festival, begun with the observance of its chief feature, the passover meal, lasted for seven days, during which nothing leavened was eaten (Exod 12:15). On the first and last days there was "a holy assembly" and no work was to be done (Exod 12:16). It is also said of the Unleavened Bread festival, "On this very day I brought your hosts out of the land of Egypt: therefore you shall observe this day throughout your generations, as an ordinance for ever" (Exod 12:17). On the second day of the festival the priest waved before the Lord a sheaf of the first-matured barley (Lev 23:10-11). During each day of the festivals of Passover—Unleavened Bread, there were to be sacrifices, animal and cereal, in addition to the regular ones (Lev 23:8; Num 28:19-23).

The origin of the Passover motif lay probably in the seminomadic realm, while that of the Unleavened Bread feast came from the agricultural realm. The ritual of the Passover perhaps began when in the spring primitive seminomads at night left their campsites hastily for the cultivated areas after having sought protection by means of the rites of a common meal and warding off of demons with animal blood smeared on the openings of their tents. The Feast of Unleavened Bread, also in the spring, was a ceremony of agriculture whereby only new, unleavened bread was eaten. In Hebrew tradition the two were given a more historical setting and combined as spring rituals.

Problems confront the attempt to determine whether in old Israel the celebration of the Passover was a family or cultic affair. King Josiah ca. 621 B.C.E. commanded his people to celebrate the Passover in Jerusalem where, apparently (cf. 2 Chr 35), the priests would slaughter the animals and return their carcasses to the individual families: "For no such passover had been kept since the days of the judges who judged Israel, or during all the days of the kings of Israel or of the kings of Judah" (2 Kgs 23:22; cf. 2 Chr 35:18). This seems to indicate that the Passover as a pilgrim and sanctuary feast was not an absolute innovation, but a reinstitution of an old custom predating the monarchy. There is evidence of one premonarchical observance of the Passover—that of JOSHUA and his people at GILGAL, later to become the site of a significant Israelite sanctuary (Josh 5:10-11). It may have been that in the period of the judges immediately following Joshua, the Passover Feast was a pilgrim and sanctuary feast, a practice abandoned by the kings until Josiah reintroduced it at Jerusalem and combined it with that of Unleavened Bread. An objection to this interpretation is that according to 2 Chr 30:1ff., King HEZEKIAH, after the fall of the Northern Kingdom, invited the Israelite survivors to participate in the Passover rituals at Jerusalem. Since the chronicler almost certainly was writing in the period when SAMARITANS and Jews had no dealings with one another, this story may be an invitation on the Chronicler's part for them to return to the fold.

With the destruction of the Temple in 70 C.E. the Passover ceased to be a sacrificial rite and continued as a celebration of God's redemptive character. Today the *Seder*, "order of service," features a ritual designed to retell the biblical story of the Exodus. Among other procedures, it involves the eating of unleavened bread (*matzah*) and bitter herbs (e.g., horseradish) to commemorate the bitterness of servitude, and *haroseth*, a mixture of chopped apples, nuts, raisins and cinnamon, to symbolize the mortar used by the enslaved Hebrews to build the store-cities of Pithom and Raamses (Exod 1:11).

See also EXODUS; FEASTS AND FESTIVALS; UNLEAVENED BREAD, FEAST OF.

Bibliography. T. H. Gaster, *Festivals of the Jewish Year*; H.-J. Kraus, *Worship in Israel*.

—KAREN RANDOLPH JOINES

• **Pastoral Epistles.** *General Characterization.* From the time of the earliest church fathers, it has been recognized that the two Epistles to TIMOTHY and that to TITUS comprise a distinct grouping. All three designate PAUL as author. All three are addressed to individual coworkers of Paul. The three deal with similar circumstances—the organization of the churches, the threat of false teachers, the importance of exemplary Christian behavior in the world. The actual term "Pastoral Epistles" is of recent origin, however, being first suggested by D. N. Berdot and Paul Anton in the early eighteenth century. The term "pastoral" is not altogether accurate, as Timothy and Titus are depicted in these Epistles as the representatives of the apostle Paul to the churches of EPHESUS and CRETE and not as the "pastors" of the churches. The term is useful insofar as there is a definite "pastoral" concern to provide for adequate leadership in the organization and ministry of churches.

These three Epistles are missing in the earliest listing of Paul's Letters, that of Marcion from the mid-second century. It is also sometimes argued that the earliest extant manuscript of Paul's Letters, $\mathfrak{p}^{46}$, did not contain the Pastorals, although this is a conjecture based on missing leaves of the papyrus and is contested. It is in any event certain that by the last quarter of the second century, they were consistently included among the Letters of Paul in such widespread witnesses as the MURATORIAN CANON from Rome, Irenaeus from Gaul, and Tertullian from North Africa. No church father ever questions their authenticity. Pauline authorship went unchallenged until the early nineteenth century, when J. Schmidt and F. Schleiermacher questioned whether Paul wrote 1 Timothy. In 1812, Eichhorn questioned all three, arguing that their language and style was not that of the other Pauline Letters. In the mid-nineteenth century, F. C. Baur argued for rejecting Pauline authorship on the basis that the false teaching combatted in the Pastorals was a developed GNOSTICISM and the Epistles were thus composed in the second century. In 1921, P. N. Harrison argued against Paul's authorship of the Pastorals by an elaborate analysis of vocabulary and style, which has influenced many British and American scholars to question their authenticity.

The question of authenticity thus tends to consume most critical study of these three Epistles. In virtually unavoidable circularity, one's view on this question tends to influence the position taken on other introductory matters, such as date, setting, and purpose. In an attempt to aid the student to follow these issues inductively, the discussion below will begin by characterizing these epistles on their own terms before moving to the arguments for and against authenticity.

Characterization. Although the Pastorals have much in common, there are significant differences between them. The similarities between 1 Timothy and Titus are particularly strong, the latter being almost a précis of the former. There are some differences also. The false teaching attacked in Titus, for example, is more explicitly Jewish. Second Timothy really stands apart from the other two. The language is less distinct from the other Pauline Letters and the content differs, with far more detail about Paul's personal affairs. It can almost be characterized as Paul's last testament.

First Timothy. First Timothy is the least personal of the three. Paul gives very little information about his own current circumstances (only 1:3), and completely omits his customary exchange of greetings at the close. Judging from the scant information of the Epistle, Paul seems to be writing from Macedonia. He has left Timothy in Ephesus with the duty to correct false teachers who are leading the people astray (1:3-7). Three matters comprise the main content of the Letter. First is the false teaching which propounds "myths and genealogies" (1:4; 4:7). This seems to have involved some sort of interpretation of the Jewish Law (1:7-10), forbidding marriage and advocating abstinence from certain foods (4:3). The teachers may also have forbidden the drinking of wine (5:23). The false teaching is described in general terms, such as "shipwreck of the faith" and a "seared conscience" (1:19-20; 4:1-2). It loves to create dissension and is avaricious (6:3-10). This overall description of the teaching is so general as to defy specific identification with any early Christian movement. Some scholars have sought to identify it with Marcionism (esp. 5:1-5) or with second-century Gnosticism, but no explicit theological deviations are delineated, and there is really no evidence for a heresy more developed than the sort of false teachings combatted in 1 Corinthians and Colossians.

A second major element of the content is the focus on CHURCH organization. Chaps. 2 and 3 are devoted to this,

• OUTLINE OF 1 TIMOTHY •

The First Epistle to Timothy

I. Epistolary Introduction (1:1-2)
II. Personal Words to Timothy (1:3-20)
  A. The danger of false teachers (1:3-11)
  B. Personal appeal to Paul's own example (1:12-17)
  C. Renewed appeal to wage war on the false teachers (1:18-20)
III. Advice Relating to Church Order (2:1–3:16)
  A. The centrality of prayer (2:1-7)
  B. The deportment and role of women (2:8-15)
  C. Qualifications of a bishop (3:1-7)
  D. Qualifications of deacons (3:8-13)
  E. The centrality of Christ (3:14-16)
IV. Combatting False Teaching (4:1-16)
  A. Prophecy of false teachers to come (4:1-5)
  B. Combatting the false teaching (4:6-10)
  C. The minister's example (4:11-16)
V. Discipline within the Church (5:1-22)
  A. The proper manner of discipline (5:1-2)
  B. Regulations regarding widows (5:3-16)
  C. Regulations regarding elders (5:17-22)
VI. Miscellaneous Concluding Exhortations (5:23–6:19)
  A. Care for one's personal health (5:23)
  B. Ultimate transparency of sin and holiness (5:24-25)
  C. The deportment of slaves toward their masters (6:1-2)
  D. The avarice of the false teachers (6:3-10)
  E. The importance of Timothy's example (6:11-16)
  F. The proper use of and attitude toward wealth (6:17-19)
VII. Epistolary Conclusion (6:20-21)
  A. Final personal warning to avoid the false teaching (6:20-21a)
  B. Epistolary benediction (6:21b)

dealing with public prayer, the role and position of women in the congregation, and the qualifications for BISHOPS (''overseers'') and DEACONS. Chap. 5 returns to the theme of church regulation, dealing particularly with the enrollment of WIDOWS. Many scholars see this as referring to an official order of older (''real'') widows responsible to the younger widows in the church, but the reference may only be to an official roll of those widows who are eligible for the charity of the church. The discipline of ''elders'' is treated in 5:17-22. At least some of the ELDERS are involved in preaching and teaching, and they receive some sort of remuneration. The final major component of the Letter is Paul's advice to Timothy as Paul's representative in securing the order of the churches and integrity of their teaching. He is to confront the false teaching by holding true to his calling in waging the ''good warfare'' (1:3, 18). He is responsible for promoting sound teaching (4:6; 6:2b) and the orderly performance of public worship (4:11-16). Above all, he is to set a good example in his own deportment and commitment to the faith (4:12; 6:11-16).

Titus. In many respects, Titus is almost a reduced version of 1 Timothy. The same three concerns are found as in 1 Timothy—the threat of false teaching, the concern with church order, and the importance of Titus's example. Within these, however, there are significant differences. The treatment of the false teaching points more explicitly to its Jewish color; not only is it said to involve quarrels over the Law (3:9), its teachers are described as ''the circumcision party'' (1:10) and its teachings as ''Jewish myths'' (1:14). Likewise, there are differences in the treatment of church order. Titus is instructed to appoint ''elders'' in every church in 1:5, but the description of the elders' qualifications flows

• OUTLINE OF TITUS •

The Epistle to Titus

I. Epistolary Introduction (1:1-4)
  A. Summary of Paul's gospel (1:1-3)
  B. Address and benediction (1:4)
II. Titus's Task (1:5-16)
  A. Appointment of elders/bishops (1:5-9)
  B. Countering false teaching (1:10-16)
III. Instructions to Groups in the Christian ''Household'' (2:1-10)
  A. The general rule of sound doctrine (2:1)
  B. Advice to various groups (2:2-10)
IV. Advice for the Whole Community (2:11–3:11)
  A. The basis of Christian deportment in God's gracious activity in Christ (2:11-15)
  B. Relationships toward outsiders (3:1-8a)
  C. The importance of good deeds (3:8b)
  D. Avoidance of false teaching and factiousness (3:9-11)
V. Personal Conclusion (3:12-15)
  A. Instructions to Titus (3:12-14)
  B. Exchange of greetings and concluding benediction (3:15)

into that of a ''bishop's'' qualifications at 1:7. Elders and bishops thus seem to be interchangeable terms for the same office. A more obvious difference is the treatment of the various age groups in the church. Titus is concerned with the example and character of each group (2:1-6), 1 Timothy with the proper way to relate to them (5:1-2). Also there is the difference that 1 Timothy focuses on roles and relationships within the church. Titus emphasizes the deportment of Christians toward outsiders; slaves are thus to ''adorn the doctrine of God'' by their good behavior (2:10) and there is certainly an evangelistic concern behind the exhortations to set a good example before all (3:1-2) and to show good deeds toward all (3:8). Unique to both Epistles are their confessional statements—the christological hymn of 1 Tim 3:16 and the ''gospel summaries'' of Titus 2:11-14; 3:4-7.

The most obvious differences between the two are in the personal references. Paul is writing to Titus who has been left behind on the island of Crete (1:5) just as Timothy had been left at Ephesus (1 Tim 1:3). The work seems to be fairly new, and Titus is given the task to appoint elders/bishops for each of the churches (1:5). Paul warns Titus about the false teaching of the ''circumcision party'' and the vulnerability of the none-too-reliable Cretans (1:10-13). The address of the Letter is somewhat elaborate and contains a summary of the gospel (1:2-4), in the fashion of the Letter to the Romans. The conclusion is more characteristically Paul's than that of 1 Timothy, containing the customary exchange of greetings and a few words about the apostle's present circumstances. Evidently Zenas the lawyer and Apollos are with Titus on Crete, and Paul urges him to supply them adequately for their journey when they depart (3:13). Apollos was a coworker of Paul, familiar from 1 Corinthians and Acts; we know nothing more of Zenas. Paul evidently intends to send Artemas and Tychicus to Titus soon (3:12), perhaps to relieve him of the work on Crete so that he may be free to visit Paul. Tychicus is also a known coworker of Paul (Acts 20:4; Col 4:7; Eph 6:21); Artemas is not mentioned elsewhere. The place from which Paul is writing is not specified, but he expresses his intention to spend the winter on the Adriatic coast at Nicopolis (3:12). The concluding benediction of the Epistle is identical to that of 1 Timothy.

• OUTLINE OF 2 TIMOTHY •

The Second Epistle to Timothy

I. Personal Introduction (1:1-18)
  A. Salutation (1:1-2)
  B. Paul's thanksgiving and prayer for Timothy (1:3-7)
  C. The example of Paul's own circumstances (1:8-18)
II. Appeal to Endure Suffering (2:1-13)
  A. Fighting as a soldier of Christ (2:1-7)
  B. Following the example of Christ (2:8-13)
III. Appeal to Combat False Teaching (2:14-4:5)
  A. Avoiding the error of the false teachers (2:14-19)
  B. Setting the proper example (2:20-26)
  C. Characteristics of the false teaching (3:1-9)
  D. Responding to the false teaching (3:10-4:5)
IV. Personal Conclusion (4:6-22)
  A. Paul faces death with assurance (4:6-8)
  B. Paul's relationship with his coworkers (4:9-13)
  C. The opposition to Paul (4:14-16)
  D. Paul's confidence in the Lord's deliverance (4:17-18)
  E. Personal greetings (4:19-21)
  F. Concluding benediction (4:22)

Second Timothy. Taken as whole, 2 Timothy is quite distinct from the other two Pastorals. The concern for church organization has slipped into the background, and the primary exhortations to Timothy deal with his personal example and leadership in combatting the false teaching. There is an emphasis on enduring persecution which is lacking in the other two (2:3; 4:11-13). The false teaching is treated at much greater length, and the situation seems more threatening. The Epistle is rich in personal detail and is written in a livelier, less wooden style than the others.

Paul's situation has changed. He is now in prison in Rome (1:8; 2:17) and writing Timothy, who is evidently still in Ephesus (4:12). His style is quite personal. Timothy is no longer his "child in the faith" (1 Tim 1:2) but his "beloved child" (1:2), and the apostle speaks fondly of Timothy's mother and grandmother (1:5). He speaks of his opposition in Asia; Phygelus and Hermogenes have abandoned him (1:15), and Hymenaeus and Philetus have veered from the truth (2:17). In 1 Timothy Paul had already referred to his confrontation with Hymenaeus (1:20), who was evidently put out of the church along with one Alexander, who may well be the same as the coppersmith mentioned in 2 Tim 4:14. Paul reflects on his past missionary endeavors (those of his first journey, 3:11), and looks toward an uncertain future. He has reason to believe that his death is imminent, but he has fought the good fight and is ready with confidence to face the righteous judge (4:6-8). The closing personal references are almost a catalog of familiar coworkers of Paul—Demas, Titus, Luke, Mark, Tychicus. New are Crescens and Carpus. From the reference to the latter (4:13) we learn that Paul had recently been in Troas and left his coat and papers there. The whole tone of this section is discouraged. His companions have either deserted him or are busy elsewhere. Old enemies like Alexander continue to plague his thoughts (4:14-15). No one supported him in his first trial (4:16), but God delivered him then, and will again, even though it be for the heavenly Kingdom (4:17-18). The whole passage 4:6-18 reads like a final testimony of the apostle. The final verses contain the customary exchange of greetings to such well-known Ephesian Christians as Priscilla and Aquila (Acts 18:26), Trophimus (Acts 21:29), and Onesiphorus, who had recently visited Paul in prison (1:16-18). The concluding benediction resembles more that of Galatians and Philippians than the other Pastorals.

Along with the many personal matters, the false teaching occupies the major space of 2 Timothy. Apart from stereotypical descriptions of these teachers as being guilty of every conceivable vice (3:2-5), they are described as lovers of dissension (2:23) who particularly prey on weak women (3:6-7). The most specific new thing one learns about them is their claim that the resurrection has already occurred (2:18). The major antidote which Paul recommends to Timothy is sound teaching and setting a good example (1:13-14; 2:14-15; 3:14-17; 4:2-4). An example of such teaching is the little confessional gem preserved in 2:11-13.

Authorship. Many scholars continue to question whether Paul could have written the Pastorals in their present form. In general, their arguments involve historical and linguistic considerations. Historical questions are of three types. First is the problem of fitting the personal remarks of the Pastorals into a chronology of Paul's ministry. Timothy's ministry in Ephesus, Paul's establishment of work on Crete, and his plans to winter in Nicopolos are among many such details which cannot be fit within the outline of Paul's ministry that appears in Acts. Advocates of Pauline authorship agree, and tend to solve the problem by postulating that the Pastorals were written after Paul's release from his "first" Roman imprisonment (Acts 28:30-31). It is argued that Paul returned to ministry in the East and that 1 Timothy and Titus were written during this period. Second Timothy is dated subsequently, upon a second and final imprisonment in Rome. The NT gives no evidence for the outcome of Paul's first Roman imprisonment nor for any subsequent ministry, other than such a conjecture based on the Pastorals. Advocates of such a view appeal to later Christian writings, particularly to *1 Clem* 5:7, which speaks of Paul's ministry having reached the "limits of the West." From this one could infer a release from prison and mission work west of Rome, but Clement's remark could be an inference from Romans 15:24 and does not mention further work in the East anyway. Such arguments from Pauline chronology are indecisive on both sides. Paul's ministry is not easy to construct from the NT evidence. The picture of Acts is itself quite selective. Paul is said to have spent eighteen months in Corinth on the second journey, two and a half to three years in Ephesus on the third, but only the scantiest information is given about the events of those periods. Acts is silent on matters Paul mentions in his Letters, such as the second visit to Corinth and the ministries to the Lycus valley and Illyricum. It would not be wholly impossible to fit the data of 1 Timothy and Titus within the long periods of ministry in Corinth and Ephesus.

A second historical consideration involves the nature of the heresy combatted in the Pastorals, which had both Jewish and Gnostic traits. Few today would follow the nineteenth century scholars who argued for Marcionism or developed second-century Gnosticism. Apart from an ascetic strain and a speculative tendency involving "myths and genealogies," the only specific information on the false teachers is their belief that the resurrection had already occurred (2 Tim 2:18). Some contemporary scholars argue that the teaching is moving toward the sort of speculation combatted in the Johannine Letters and reflects a development of the last quarter of the first century, subsequent to Paul. Proponents of Pauline authorship are quick to point out that Paul himself encountered among the Corinthians a "realized eschatology" whose emphasis on the Spirit rendered the resurrection superfluous, and speculation and asceticism were at the heart of the Colossian teaching. Perhaps more significant is the fact that in the Pastorals Paul does not argue directly against the specific tenets of the teachers as in 1 Corinthians and Colossians but merely accuses them of opposition to "sound doctrine."

A final historical argument deals with the church organization reflected in the Pastorals. It is highly doubtful that those scholars are correct who cast Timothy and Titus in the role of monarchial bishop. Nor can one appeal to the actual officials of the church as a development beyond Paul. Only two offices appear in the Pastorals—elders/bishops and deacons, and Paul addresses both in Phil 1:1. The detail with which they are treated is another matter. There is emphasis on their formal ordination, their qualifications, the procedure of disciplining them—even their material support. Considerable attention is given to the proper maintenance of the church's charity to widows. There is great concern that Christians present a good image to the outside world, and there is the impression that the elaborate advice to Timothy concerning his own personal example might be designed as a model for leading elders. Such considerations have led many to feel that the structure of the churches in the Pastorals is later than Paul, becoming more formalized, more adjusted to "life in the world," as opposed to the more eschatologically-oriented, "charismatic" churches of Paul's ministry. Proponents of Pauline authorship respond that there is no structural detail which goes beyond the other Pauline Letters and that these, i.e., the Pastorals, are specifically designed to assist Timothy and Titus in church organization and thus have an emphasis different from that of the Letters addressed to congregations.

Whereas such historical, developmental arguments are not conclusive in deciding the issue, many feel that linguistic considerations tell decidedly against Paul's authorship of the Pastorals. It was this which led Schleiermacher and Eichhorn to raise the first questions. P. N. Harrison continued this with his elaborate charts that document the uniqueness of the Pastorals' vocabulary and style. It is not just the large number of words unique to the Pastorals, but the fact that different words are used for familiar concepts from the other Pauline Letters. Even the particles, the little transitional words which tend to be habitual and particularly indicative of one's style, differ in the Pastorals from the other Pauline Letters. The Greek student who has cut his teeth on Romans, Philippians, and Corinthians, is quick to realize that the Pastorals are a "different world." Closely akin to this is the consideration that the argument of the Pastorals tends to be more stilted and less fresh. There is constant reference to "sound teaching," "good doctrine," "the deposit." Many feel that this reflects a later generation when the concept of tradition is stronger, when the church is moving toward a definition of orthodoxy. Proponents of Pauline authorship usually respond to such arguments by pointing out that there is an emphasis on tradition in undisputed Pauline Letters as well, such as Jesus' teaching on divorce and the *paradosis* on the Lord's Supper and the resurrection. They also note the large number of unique words which one can isolate in any individual Pauline Letter and attribute this to the occasional nature of the Epistles. They add to this the uniqueness of the Pastorals in being addressed not to churches but to Paul's coworkers who are familiar with Paul's teaching and have no need of its repetition, only to be reminded to remain true to it. Despite the rejoinders of the Pauline advocates, the style of the Pastorals is in degree far more different than the differences between other Pauline Letters. This has led many proponents of Pauline authorship to postulate that the Pastorals were entrusted to an amanuensis, or secretary. Various candidates have been proposed—Tychicus, Luke—but no specific candidate has found a large following. In any event, it would have had to have been an amanuensis given a great deal of freedom, for the differences in conceptuality cannot be explained on the basis of variation in taking dictation. A "mediating" theory that has gained considerable following is that of P. N. Harrison. Noticing that in the passages which deal with Paul's personal situation there is less difference from the style of Paul's other Letters, he suggested that the Pastorals were constructed around such passages, which are fragments of genuine Pauline Letters.

One final argument of those who defend Pauline authorship should be mentioned, because it constitutes a major problem for the assumption that the Pastorals are the product of a later Paulinist who wrote under Paul's name in addressing problems of his own day. Simply put, it is the question "Why three?" Given the striking similarity in content between 1 Timothy and Titus, why should Titus have been written at all? It is certainly more conceivable that Paul would have written two coworkers the same things than to see a later age constructing two "general epistles" that deal with the same thing. And why the elaborate personalia of 2 Timothy in an epistle which in addition to the personal references mainly treats only the false teaching, and that in a manner which does not go beyond the other two? This question of the setting for three such epistles has as yet to be adequately addressed by those who argue pseudonymity.

Conclusion. The remaining items which customarily go into an introduction to a NT letter are inextricable from the question of authorship. Those who argue for Pauline authorship generally date them roughly between 62-67 C.E., after a release of Paul from his first Roman imprisonment. First Timothy and Titus are seen as written at the same time; it is usually suggested, from Macedonia. Second Timothy comes at the end of the period. Paul writes from a second Roman imprisonment and awaits his trial, which most likely will lead to his martyrdom. Those who argue pseudonymity are by necessity generally not very specific in treating matters of setting. Asia Minor has been suggested because of the centrality of Ephesus in the Letters. A date in the last decade of the first century or first decade of the second is generally suggested. No alternative suggestion for authorship has found wide support, and the idea that the Pastorals come from a "Pauline school" has been generally rejected.

See also BISHOP; CHURCH; CRETE; DEACON; ELDER; EPHESUS; EPISTLE/LETTER; GNOSTICISM; LAW IN THE NEW TESTAMENT; PAUL; TIMOTHY; TITUS.

Bibliography. M. Dibelius and H. Conzelmann, *The Pastoral Epistles*; E. E. Ellis, "The Authorship of The Pastorals: A Resume and Assessment of Recent Trends," in *Paul and His Recent Interpreters*; G. D. Fee, *1 and 2 Timothy, Titus*; P. N. Harrison, *The Problem of the Pastoral Epistles*; J. N. D. Kelly, *A Commentary on the Pastoral Epistles*.

—JOHN B. POLHILL

• **Patmos.** [pat'muhs] One of the smallest Aegean islands, is ten mi. long and six mi. wide and lies off the coast of Turkey (PLATE 20). The island is very rocky and barren and, is situated in a volcanic zone. Patmos's only claim to fame has been its association with the Book of REVELATION. The Romans often used remote islands for political banishment. The reference to Patmos in Rev 1:9 fits the picture of banishment at hard labor. Eusebius (*EccHist* 3.18.1) reported that John was banished to Patmos in 95 C.E. by the Emperor Domitian and released eighteen months later.

Early historical references to Patmos are very few. The island was first mentioned by Thucydides in the fifth century B.C.E. Later (first century B.C.E.) the name Patmos appeared in the works of the Roman geographer, Strabo. In the first century C.E. as we have seen from Revelation, the Romans probably used the island for political banishment. In 1088 C.E., Patmos became the home of the Monastery of St. John, the Theologian. The monastery was founded by Christodoulus and located on the second highest hill on the island.

This monastery soon beckoned the leading religious scholars of the Mediterranean world. A center for the study of the Christian religion emerged supported liberally by the Byzantine emperors. After the surrender of Constantinople to the Ottoman Turks in 1453, the island and monastery came under the protection of Pope Pius II in 1461 and Pope Leo X in 1513. However, even under Turkish rule the island progressed well.

In 1821 Patmos gained its independence from the Turks. This period of freedom lasted only eleven years, for in 1832 the island was returned to the Turks by treaty. In 1912, Italy annexed the island and finally gave it to Greece at the end of World War II. Patmos stands just off shore from Turkey and hundreds of mi. from the capital of Greece, Athens.

The island is divided into two equal parts which are linked by a narrow isthmus of land. The major port on the island is Skala situated at the foot of the monastery mountain. On the mountain, today, stands the grotto of Revelation marking the place of John's writing of the Apocalypse, and chapels in honor of St. Anna, St. Nicholas and St. Artemius.

Inside the grotto, one sees a small couch chiselled out of the rock where it is said that John rested his head. Above the couch is a cross hewn out of wood by John. To the right the visitor may see a rocky bookstand on which the scroll of Revelation was written. The rock face of the cave is split from north to south above the rock couch on which John rested. Tradition says the rock was split when John heard the words of God, "I am the alpha and omega." The Monastery of St. John, itself, has always been well-known for its library of nine hundred manuscripts and two thousand old books. The oldest manuscript there is Codex 67, dating from the sixth century and containing a fragment of the Gospel of Mark.

Bibliography. F. V. Filson, "Patmos," *IDB*; O. F. A. Meinardus, *St. John of Patmos*; Strabo, *Geography*, 5 and 6.

—JAMES L. BLEVINS

• **Patriarch.** [pay'tree-ahrk] (Gk. *patria* "family, clan" + *archē* "ruler") Broadly speaking, any of the forefathers of the Israelite nation. Genesis presents two groups of patriarchs: the "antediluvian" (those living before the flood) and the "postdiluvian" (those living after the flood). In the NT, David and the twelve sons of Jacob are included in this broader category (Acts 2:29; 7:8, 9). However, both the OT and the NT tend to restrict the term to refer to the three patriarchs par excellence, ABRAHAM, ISAAC, and JACOB, when speaking of the religious heritage of Judaism and Christianity.

The Problem of the Patriarchal Narratives. Since the late nineteenth century, advocates of the documentary hypothesis have regarded the patriarchal narratives as a major problem in the reconstruction of Israel's history. It was assumed that history could be reconstructed with confidence only on the basis of contemporary records. And since the documentary hypothesis proposed that the oldest stratum of the Pentateuch (J) should be dated to the early monarchial period of Israel's history, it was obvious that the patriarchal narratives were not contemporary with the events of which they told.

Thus, Wellhausen concluded that from the narratives "we attain to no historical knowledge of the patriarchs, but only of the time when the stories about them arose in the Israelite people" (Wellhausen, 318-19). Hence, the patriarchs were considered to be little more than eponymous ancestors of clans or free creations of unconscious art.

The development of form criticism and the results of archaeological investigations in Mesopotamia and Syria in the early decades of this century suggested that a modification of the previous view was necessary. The J and E documents were now seen to be the repositories of very ancient traditions—traditions that were transmitted orally or in writing but that ultimately antedated the period of their redaction in monarchial times.

Exponents of this synthesis claimed that striking parallels from extrabiblical materials from NUZI, MARI, Alalakh, and other Mesopotamian sites confirmed and dated the stories of Abraham, Isaac and Jacob to the first half of the second millennium B.C.E. (Albright, 236-49; cf. Bright, 67-103). Thompson and Van Seters have recently criticized this position. Their strictures against forcing parallels are well noted (cf. M.J. Selman, 105ff.). Still, the basic attraction of this synthesis has a wide appeal, and especially so among those who do not accept the documentary hypothesis (Harrison, 105-13).

The Structure of the Patriarchal Narratives. Gen 12–50 contains the primary accounts of Abraham, Isaac and Jacob and some of their descendants (Gen 37–50 deals with the fortunes of Joseph). The accounts appear to be inserted into a preexistent framework defined by the recurring formula, "These are the generations (descendants) of . . . " (cf. 2:4; 5:1; 6:9; 10:1; 11:10; 11:27; 25:12, 19; 36:1, 9; 37:2). The role of this formula in Genesis is not totally clear.

The narrator appears more interested in presenting the movement of an intertwined theme than strictly detailing the personal history of a patriarch. The ebb and flow of the narrative is so complex as to make its subdivision difficult. Nevertheless, with reference to the three patriarchs mentioned above the text may be generally divided as follows:

1. The Story of Abraham, 11:2–25:18
2. The Story of Isaac and Jacob, 25:19–50:26

Abraham and Jacob function as major protagonists in the stories, while the role of Isaac is secondary.

Theme of the Patriarchal Narratives. The major theme of the patriarchal narratives is introduced in the call and election of Abraham in Gen 12:1-3. To Abraham, a childless immigrant, Yahweh offers land (v. 1), posterity (v. 2), and blessing (v. 2f.). Subsequent circumstantial and human complications threaten the fulfillment of these great promises. These complications provide tension, movement and unity to the narratives. Thus, anticipation of the working out of God's promises gently drives the reader along from the call of Abraham (Gen 12) to the death of Joseph (Gen 50).

For example, Abraham's seed is to become a great nation (12:2). Sarah, however, is childless (11:30). The land of Canaan is promised to Abraham and his descendants (12:1, 7), but the Canaanites possess it (12:6). Abraham is to be a blessing (12:2-3), but his lapse in Egypt (12:10-20) and again at Gerar (20:1-18) bring plague and the threat of death to innocent persons. This pattern of PROMISE and fulfillment is repeated throughout the patriarchal narratives.

Secondary to the theme of promise and fulfillment is the covenant established between God and Abraham in Gen 15:7-21 and 17:1-21. Both passages affirm the certainty of God's promise of land (chap. 15) and posterity (chap. 17). The covenant promises are reaffirmed to Isaac (26:2-5) and Jacob (28:13-15; 35:9-12).

The Religion of the Patriarchs. Unfortunately, the source materials in Gen 12–50 provide little information about the religious practices of the patriarchs. They built altars, made sacrifices and covenants, and prayed. Circumcision, vows, the payment of tithes, and ritual purification also played important roles in the practice of their faith.

While his ancestors appeared to be polytheistic in faith (31:19-35; 35:2), Abraham possessed a single-minded devotion to the God who called him (12:1-3) and made a covenant with him (15:7-21). The frequent identification of this patron deity of the clan as "the God of Abraham" (31:53), "the God of Isaac" (28:13) and the more developed formula "the God of Abraham, the God of Isaac, and the God of Jacob" (Exod 3:6) underscores the personal characteristic of the patriarchal faith.

A. Alt ("The God of the Fathers") argued that the oldest names for the patriarchal deities in Genesis were "Fear of Isaac" (31:42) and "Mighty One of Jacob" (49:24). These two deities along with another, "the God of Abraham," were three different anonymous gods worshipped by different tribes or groups of clans in their nomadic period. Later, a pooling of the history of these tribes as they arrived in Canaan identified the patriarchal deities with each other and the local El gods of the Canaanite shrines and brought about the genealogical relationship of the tribal fathers. Only in the development of premonarchial religion was Yahweh identified as the national God of all Israel.

Alt's view, which has gained currency in most of the standard histories of OT religion, has been effectively challenged by F. M. Cross. According to Cross, the god worshipped by the patriarchs was not anonymous but rather the high god of Canaan, El. Such epithets as El Shaddai, El Elyon, and El Olam were not secondary additions to the tradition after the settlement in Canaan, but represent the original name of the God worshipped by the patriarchs. The formula "the God of Abraham" was employed to emphasize the special relationship between Abraham and his God, El Shaddai. Cross affirmed that a basic continuity existed between the God of the patriarchs and the God of Moses because Yahweh was essentially an abbreviation of an epithet of El. However, texts such as Exod 3:13-15 and 6:3 appear to suggest that the name Yahweh was a new revelation to Moses.

See also GENESIS, BOOK OF; GOD, NAMES OF; SOURCE CRITICISM; SOURCES OF THE PENTATEUCH.

Bibliography. A. Alt, "The God of the Fathers," *Essays on Old Testament History and Religion*; W. F. Albright, *From the Stone Age to Christianity*; J. Bright, *A History of Israel,* 3rd. ed.; F. M. Cross, *Canaanite Myth and Hebrew Epic*; S. R. Driver, *An Introduction to the Literature of the Old Testament*; R. K. Harrison, *Introduction to the Old Testament*; M. J. Selman, "Comparative Customs and the Patriarchal Age," *Essays on the Patriarchal Narratives,* ed. A. R. Millard and D. J. Wiseman; T. L. Thompson, *The Historicity of the Patriarchal Narratives*; J. Van Seters, *Abraham in History and Tradition*; J. G. J. Wenham, "The Religion of the Patriarchs," *Essays on the Patriarchal Narratives,* ed. A. R. Millard and D. J. Wiseman; D. J. Wiseman, "Abraham Reassessed," *Essays on the Patriarchal Narratives,* ed. A. R. Millard and D. J. Wiseman.

—STEPHEN J. ANDREWS

• **Patristic Literature.** [puh-tris'tik] Writings composed by early Christian apologists, theologians, bishops, and others during the first several centuries. Up to about 200 C.E. most of this literature was written in Greek. Thereafter, as Christianity spread from urban centers to more remote parts of the world, writers used the vernacular: Latin, Syriac, Armenian, Georgian, Gothic, and others. The earliest writings reflect the modest cultural background of converts to Christianity in the ROMAN EMPIRE, where Christianity enjoyed its most notable success. By the last quarter of the second century, however, the quality improved steadily. Patristic literature reached its "golden age" after the conversion of Constantine as floods of better educated persons poured into the churches. Although the barbarian invasions, beginning already in the third century, diminished the output and quality of literature in the West, Greek literature thrived from the fourth century on. So too did Syriac and other writings until the Muslim conquests in the seventh century.

To Around 200 C.E. Several different types of literature appeared during the second century. A miscellaneous collection of second century writings has become known as the APOSTOLIC FATHERS, presumably because the authors were believed to have known the APOSTLES. These usually include a letter of I CLEMENT, a letter from a presbyter-bishop of ROME to the Corinthians concerning a schism there (96 C.E.); seven letters of IGNATIUS, bishop of Antioch, to churches who had hosted him during his journey through Asia Minor, to Polycarp of SMYRNA, and to the church of Rome (110–17 C.E.); a letter of POLYCARP TO THE PHILIPPIANS that served as a cover letter for the letters of Ignatius (115–35); the SHEPHERD OF HERMAS, an apocalyptic work addressing the problem of forgiveness of sins committed after BAPTISM (ca. 140); an early sermon known as SECOND CLEMENT (ca. 140); an early Christian manual called the *Teaching of the Twelve Apostles* or DIDACHE that contains first-century matter but was published in its present form in the second century; a treatise on interpretation of the OT entitled the EPISTLE OF BARNABAS (ca. 130); the MARTYRDOM OF POLYCARP, the earliest Christian martyrology (156); and an apology of uncertain date called the EPISTLE TO DIOGNETUS.

Second-century authors penned several apologies or defenses of Christianity, ranging from modest to poor quality. An apology by a certain QUADRATUS, supposedly a disciple of the apostles, addressed to the Emperor Hadrian (117–38) in response to persecution in Asia Minor has survived only in a quotation by EUSEBIUS. Aristo of Pella's defense of Christianity against Judaism (ca. 140) and Apollinaris of Hierapolis's of four apologies are lost. Surviving apologies include those written by the Athenian philosopher Aristides, also addressed to Hadrian (ca. 140); JUSTIN MARTYR's two apologies and his *Dialogue with Trypho* (ca. 150); Tatian's *Address to the Greeks* (ca. 175); Athenagoras's *Supplication for Christians* (ca. 175–80); Theophilus of Antioch's apology addressed *To Autolycus* (ca. 180); Melito of Sardis's *Apology* directed to the Emperor Marcus Aurelius (161–80); and Clement of Alexandria's *Protrepticus* (ca. 190). Such works show steady refinement and tightening of the argument as Christianity drew more cultured and better educated converts into its ranks. Apologists had to defend Christianity against numerous charges raised by both Jews and Gentiles. Jews objected to the use of the Greek OT (SEPTUAGINT), the idea of a crucified messiah, the claim that Jesus was the messiah, the claim that Jesus was divine, the doctrine of resurrection, and Christian rejection of the ritual law. Gentiles raised charges of moral debasement, social aloofness, theological absurdity, atheism (i.e., by not believing in the gods), and responsibility for the calamities befalling Rome. Besides answering such charges, apologists ridiculed POLYTHEISM and argued in favor of MONOTHEISM, constructing a case for Christianity as the "true philosophy." The LOGOS spoke truth through OT prophets and through Greek philosophers, but became incarnate in Jesus of Nazareth (so Justin and Clement of Alexandria).

Some antiheretical literature also appeared during the second century in opposition chiefly to GNOSTICISM, Marcionism, and Montanism. The Gnostics, now much better known because of the discovery of the ancient library at Chenoboskion or NAG HAMMADI in Egypt, were themselves prolific. The most important second-century opponent of heresy was IRENAEUS, bishop of Lyons (d. ca. 202). In a treatise usually entitled *Against Heresies* (185–89) he outlined the Valentinian system and proceeded to refute it along with others on the basis of reason (book 2), tradition and the teaching of the apostles (book 3), the sayings of Jesus (Book 4), and last things (book 5). He borrowed much of his material from Justin, with whom he had studied in Rome but from whom he diverged in emphasizing biblical theology more strongly than reason. He also relied on Hegesippus, a convert from Judaism whose largely anti-Gnostic *Memoirs* have perished, for his concept of a chain of doctrine preserved in apostolic churches. Irenaeus also put together a handbook for introduction of inquirers to the Christian fold under the title of *Proof of the Apostolic Preaching*, discovered in an Armenian version in 1907.

A sizeable body of popular literature made its appearance during the second century. A collection of hymns written in Syriac circulated with the title of THE ODES OF SOLOMON. APOCRYPHAL GOSPELS, ACTS, and epistles were produced by both orthodox and heterodox writers. The GOSPEL OF THE EGYPTIANS, composed some time after 150, was considered canonical in Egypt. The PROTOEVANGELIUM OF JAMES fictionalized Jesus' childhood. A GOSPEL OF THOMAS, discovered at Nag Hammadi, contains 114 sayings of Jesus, some possibly dependent on the canonical Gospels but most independent of them. The fictionalized ACTS OF PAUL, according to Tertullian, resulted in the defrocking of the priest who composed them about 160. The ACTS OF THOMAS, dating from early third century, romanticized the missionary exploits of the apostle in India. In addition to the so-called *Epistle of Barnabas*, unknown authors of this period produced apocryphal letters under the name of Paul and an EPISTLE OF THE APOSTLES, which purports to give Jesus' last instructions before the ascension.

The Third Century. The scope and quality of Christian literature improved noticeably during the third century. Particularly significant was the development of Latin literature in the West.

One of the earliest Latin treatises, preserved as the eighth book of Tertullian's *To the Nations* in a single manuscript of the ninth century, was the highly polished apology by Minucius Felix, a lawyer residing in Rome, entitled *The Octavius*, which argued for Christianity from a strictly philosophical point of view. The date is somewhat uncertain, but the work has enough similarities to Tertullian's apologies to suggest a common date about 200 C.E.

The most prolific and gifted Latin writer of the third century was Tertullian of Carthage (d. after 220). Converted to Christianity ca. 195, he remained a Catholic Christian for several years and then, ca. 206, became a member of the Montanist sect. In later years he separated from the latter and headed a sect named after himself. A skillful controversialist, Tertullian composed several types of literature. (1) He wrote at least four apologies: *To the Nations* (197), *The Apology* (late 197), *The Witness of the Soul*, and *To Scapula* (212). His *Apology* was apparently a more polished version of his appeal *To the Nations*. (2) He penned numerous polemical or theological treatises—*Prescription for Heretics* (ca. 200): five books *Against Marcion*; a treatise *Against Hermogenes*, a Gnostic; another *Against the Valentinians*; a remedy for *The Scorpion's Sting*, i.e., the Gnostics (213); an essay on *The Flesh of Christ* against Gnostic Docetism (210/12); a defense of the Christian doctrine of *The Resurrection of the Flesh*, again opposing Gnostics; a treatise *Against Praxeas*, one of the Modalists, spelling out a doctrine of the TRINITY and making the first use of the term; a treatise on *Baptism*; and another on *The Soul* (210–13), directed against Gnostics. (3) He also composed numerous practical treatises: an encouragement addressed *To the Martyrs* (197 or 202); a treatise forbidding Christians to participate in *The Public Spectacles* (197–200); another on *Prayer*, composed for new converts; an essay on *Patience* (200–203); treatises on discipline, a more lenient one written in his Catholic period (ca. 203) entitled *Penance* and a more rigorous one composed in his Montanist period (after 206) entitled *Modesty*, in which he refused to permit forgiveness of sins after baptism; a work on *The Dress of Women* (197–201); an appeal *To His Wife* to remain unmarried should he die (203); two treatises belonging to the Montanist period prohibiting second marriages absolutely—*Exhortation to Chastity* (207) and *Monogamy* (ca. 217); a composition on *The Veiling of Virgins*, requiring nuns to wear veils in public as well as in church services; a treatise on *The Crown (of a Soldier)* forbidding Christians to enter military service (211); a diatribe against idolatry by involvement in various types of public service—art, teaching, military service; another against *Flight in Persecution*; a defense of Montanist practices of *Fasting: Against the Catholics (Psychics)*; and a short apology for his wearing of the philosopher's *Pallium* (toga).

Hippolytus, schismatic bishop of Rome (d. 235), was the last westerner to write in Greek rather than Latin. His most noteworthy surviving work is *The Apostolic Tradition* composed at the time of his separation from the Church of Rome in 217. Sharply critical of Sabellianism or Modalism, which he attributed to Popes Zephyrinus (199–17) and Callistus (217–22), Hippolytus wrote two major antiheretical works, *Syntagma* or *Against All Heresies* and *Philosophumena* or *Refutation of all Heresies*, but only the latter is extant. He also penned several exegetical studies—a *Commentary on Daniel* (ca. 204), a *Commentary on the Canticle*, treatises on the *Blessing of Jacob* and the *Blessing of Moses*, and a homily on the *Narrative of David and Goliath*. A major theological writing on *The Antichrist*, written ca. 200, has survived in Greek, his *Chronicle* of world history from creation to 234 in Latin. An apology *Against the Nations* is known only from a quotation in John of Damascus.

Novatian, leader of the schism bearing his name, wrote two letters to Cyprian of Carthage on behalf of the Roman Church and several treatises which survived under other names. His essay *On the Trinity* (before 250) attacking the Monarchians is one of the most important theological writings of the third century. Other writings dealt with *Jewish Foods*, the *Public Spectacles*, and *The Value of Modesty*.

Cyprian, bishop of Carthage (248–58), carried on an extensive correspondence which gives much insight into church affairs during the third century, especially regarding the Novatianist schism. In addition, he wrote several treatises directed to a variety of issues: a personal reflection on becoming a Christian addressed *To Donatus*; an early apology *That Idols Are Not Gods*; a collection of proof texts on various subjects entitled *Three Books of Testimonies to Quirinus* (249–50); a treatise on *The Unity of the Church* in response to the Novatianist schism; another on *The Lapsed*, arguing for cautious readmission of those who apostatized during persecution; practical treatises on *The Dress of Virgins* (249), *The Lord's Prayer, The Value of Patience, Envy and Jealousy*; and pastoral essays on *The Mortality*, during a plague (252), and *Good Works and Almsgiving*. Cyprian was the most influential western writer from Tertullian to Augustine.

Little has survived of the writings of Victorinus of Pettau (d. 304), a *Commentary on the Revelation* and a short treatise on *The Creation of the World*. However, the West boasted two apologists in the early fourth century. Arnobius, bishop of Sicca in Numidia (North Africa), wrote seven books *Against the Nations*, a work showing modest competence. Lactantius, a teacher of rhetoric in Nicomedia, Diocletian's new capital city, and later tutor of Constantine's son Crispus, composed several essentially apologetic writings. His principal work was *The Divine Institutions*, the first comprehensive presentation of the Christian faith in Latin (304–13). In addition, he prepared an *Epitome* of the *Institutions*, a treatise on humankind as *The Work of God* (303–304), *The Wrath of God* (after 313), *The Deaths of Persecutors* (316–21), a poem on *The Phoenix Bird*, and other writings now lost.

In the Greek East the school of Alexandria pumped life into the literary enterprise. Founded by Pantaenus in the second century, it rose to prominence under Clement (fl. 180–202, d. 211/216) and Origen (185–232 in Alexandria, 232–254/5 in Caesarea Maritima). In addition to the apology mentioned earlier, Clement wrote a basic textbook for new converts entitled *The Instructor*, a wide-ranging work for more advanced seekers called *Stromata* or *Things*, a homily on Mark 10:17-31 exploring *How the Rich Person Can Be Saved*, notes excerpted from a Valentian Gnostic named Theodotus and from prophetic writings, and some exegetical treatises now lost. Like Justin, Clement had a high regard for Greek philosophy.

Origen was the most prolific and gifted author in Christian antiquity. Although many of his essentially exegetical studies have perished or suffered radical alteration at the hands of early translators, a considerable body of writings has survived, most from his Caesarean period. His first work, *First Things*, penned while he was still in Alexandria (220–30), was the earliest Christian manual of theology. At Caesarea he wrote a treatise on *Prayer* (ca. 232–33); an *Exhortation to Martyrdom* addressed to two friends who had suffered persecution in 235; a lengthy apology for Christianity *Against Celsus* (ca. 248), whose *True Discourse* offered a harsh critique around 178–80; and several letters, only two of which have survived. Biblical studies, by far the largest part of his vast output, included a six-column edition of the OT, the *Hexapla*, giving the Hebrew text, transliteration, and Greek translations of Aquila, Symmachus, the LXX, and Theodotion (ca. 248); commentaries on almost all the books of the Bible, of which portions on Matthew, John, the Song of Songs, and Romans have survived; sermons on much of the OT and some of the New, although most exist only in Latin translation and much is lost. In 1941 a record of Origen's *Disputation with Heracleides* and a treatise on the *Pascha* were found at Tura.

Origen had both friends and critics and eventually suffered formal condemnation. One of his contemporary correspondents in Palestine was Julius Africanus (d. after 240), author of the first Christian chronicle of the world, only fragments of which are extant, and a hodgepodge called *Embroideries*. Origen's student Dionysius, bishop of Alexandria (247–264/5), wrote extensively, but little has survived. Gregory Thaumaturgus, bishop of Neocaesarea in Cappadocia, delivered a *Panegyric* about his teacher in 238 as he left Caesarea and wrote a few other brief treatises. Most critics of Origen represented the Antiochene "School" founded by Lucian (d. 312). They included Methodius, the most successful of Origen's critics, and an anonymous author of a work on *Correct Faith in God*.

This age of martyrs produced a number of accounts of martyrdoms: *The Passion of Saints Perpetua and Felicity* (202/3), *The Martyrdom of the Virgin Potamiana and the Soldier Basilides* (202/3), *The Proconsular Acts of Cyprian* (258), *The Acts of Saint Maximilianus* (295), *The Acts of Saint Marcellus, The Acts of Saint Felix* (303), *The Acts of Saint Dasius* (303/4), *The Acts and Testament of the Forty Martyrs* (320), and Eusebius's *Martyrs of Palestine* (303–311).

The Fourth Century and After. Christian literature expanded appreciably during the period following Constantine's conversion. In the East its quality shot upwards as better educated persons swelled the ranks of the churches. Space will permit mention of a few major contributors and their chief works.

Eusebius, bishop of Caesarea in Palestine (d. 339), is best known for his *Church History* (324), a mine of primary sources, but he composed numerous other historical, apologetical, and biblical writings. Historical writings consisted of *Chronicles* of world history, a *Life of Constantine*, a panegyric in *Praise of Constantine*, and *The Martyrs of Palestine*. Apologetic works consisted, among other things, of the *Preparation for the Gospel*, and the *Demonstration of the Gospel*, arguing the superiority of Christianity to Judaism; a treatise *Against Hierocles*, Governor of Bithynia, who placed Apollonius of Tyana above Christ; and a treatise now lost criticizing the Neo-Platonist Porphyry. Among biblical works Eusebius's *Onomasticon*, listing biblical sites, is the most important. Numerous later authors updated the *Church History* of Eusebius: the most important of these were Socrates, who extended it to 439; Sozomen, who added an account from 324 to 425; and Theodoret of Cyrus, who updated from 325 to 428 with a strong antiheretical slant.

The Arian controversy which developed soon after Constantine's conversion occasioned an outpouring of literature from both sides. Few Arian writings have survived, but much is extant from the hands of opponents. Chief among the latter was Athanasius, bishop of Alexandria. Athanasius penned numerous anti-Arian treatises, the most important of which were his *Oration on the Incarnation of the Word* (ca. 318), *Three Orations against the Arians* (ca. 335/6), an *Apology against the Arians* (357), a *Letter concerning the Decisions of the Nicene Synod* (350–51), and a *History of the Arians for Monks* (ca. 358). He wrote also a *Life of Saint Anthony* (ca. 357), the model of early hermits, and the famous *Thirty-Ninth Festal Letter of 367,* in which he listed the twenty-seven books now in the NT as alone canonical.

The Great Cappadocians rank close behind Athanasius in order of importance in the East. Basil (ca. 330–79), bishop of Neocaesarea, wrote important theological treatises *Against Eunomius,* a strict Arian, and on *The Holy Spirit* (375). His most significant efforts, however, may have been two monastic rules and his 365 letters which are revealing of church life in his day. Gregory (329–ca.390), bishop of Nazianzus, is known for his forty-five orations, letters, and poems. Gregory, bishop of Nyssa (d. 394) and younger brother of Basil, made his impact on spirituality through a treatise on *The Life of Moses* and *Sermons on the Lord's Prayer*.

Cyril of Jerusalem (d. 386) is noted for his *Mystagogical Catecheses,* twenty-four sermons delivered in Jerusalem in 348 or 350. Epiphanius, bishop of Salamis (d. 403), penned many books on a variety of themes, the most important of which is his *Panarion* or *Medicine Box.* Theodore, bishop of Mopsuestia (d. 428), the greatest exegete of the Antiochene school, wrote commentaries on all books of the Bible. John Chrysostom (d. 407) left many exegetical homilies of the literal/typological type and several influential treatises, notably one on *The Priesthood.*

For the West the most important figures were Ambrose, Jerome, and Augustine. Ambrose, bishop of Milan (339–97), played a prominent role in Augustine's conversion through allegorical sermons. His *Duties of Ministers* represented the first comprehensive presentation of Christian ethics from a strongly Stoic standpoint. In theological writings Ambrose introduced eastern thinking, especially of the Cappadocians. Jerome (d. 419/20) is best known for his Vulgate edition of the scriptures, produced by commission of Pope Damasus. In addition, he translated writings by others, commented on several OT and NT writings, composed several theological polemical writings, wrote biographies, extended Eusebius's *Chronicle,* and left many sermons and letters. The towering theologian in the West was Augustine, bishop of Hippo (354–430). More than eighty treatises have survived, including his classic *Confessions* (397–400), *The Trinity* (399–419), and *The City of God* (413–26). Most of this vast corpus as well as a large number of letters emerged in the context of controversy with Manichaeans, Donatists, Pelagians, and pagans during his long tenure as bishop of Hippo (395–430).

See also MARCION; APOSTOLIC FATHERS.

Bibliography. B. Altaner, *Patrology*; H. von Campenhausen, *Men Who Shaped the Western Church* and *The Fathers of the Greek Church*; F. L. Cross, *The Early Christian Fathers*; E. J. Goodspeed, *A History of Early Christian Literature*; P. de Labriolle, *History and Literature of Christianity from Tertullian to Boethius*; J. Quasten, *Patrology*.

—E. GLENN HINSON

• **Pentateuch.** *See* TORAH

• **Paul.** [pawl] Paul was a first-century non-Palestinian Pharisaic Jew who changed from being a persecutor of the earliest Christian church to become one of the most effective and influential missionaries in all of Christian history. He called himself an "apostle of Jesus Christ" to "the Gentiles," and, while it was primarily to non-Jews that he preached, his message had a profound impact even on the originally Jewish portion of early Christianity.

Paul's Life. (1) Sources for the study. The NT and other early Christian literature seem to provide a wealth of sources for reconstructing the life of Paul. Over one-half of the Book of Acts is an account of Paul's career from the time he was a persecutor of the church through his imprisonment in Rome toward the end of his life. Thirteen letters in the NT bear Paul's name as their author. Outside the canon of the NT many volumes of early Christian literature present themselves as other "letters" by Paul or offer further accounts of his "acts."

(a) Problems. When one turns to the early Christian literature in order to ascertain the life of Paul, one immediately encounters three serious problems. First, extensive as the sources are, they provide *insufficient data* for writing a "life" of Paul. For example, little, if anything, is known about Paul's birth, childhood, and early manhood; indeed, we do not even know with absolute certainty when, where, and how Paul died. Much remains shrouded in mystery, for the sources are simply inadequate for producing a Pauline biography.

Second, one must establish the *authenticity* of the sources. For example, no contemporary scholar judges that Paul wrote any of the number of extrabiblical letters that are attributed to him, correspondences like the *Epistles of Paul and Seneca*, Paul's *Letter to the Laodiceans*, and *3 Corinthians*. Clearly these were produced by others in the name of Paul. Moreover, because of matters of history, vocabulary, style, and theology, many scholars (frequently the majority) judge that as many as six of the thirteen Letters in the NT attributed to Paul were written by his colleagues and students, not the apostle. These are 2 Thessalonians, Ephesians, Colossians, 1 and 2 Timothy, and Titus. Only seven Letters are judged undisputedly to be authentic. Thus, many scholars conclude that all of the NT Letters attributed to Paul are not of equal value for reconstructing the life of the apostle.

Third, it is sometimes *impossible through harmonization to reconcile statements* made in even the most reliable sources. For example, Acts 9 recounts that when Paul was struck down on the road to DAMASCUS, he was "immediately" active there (in Damascus) preaching in the synagogues that Jesus was the Son of God. After "many days," Acts says, he went to Jerusalem in an effort to join the disciples; but they were afraid of him, because they doubted his sincerity, and so, they avoided him. Then, one learns from Acts that BARNABAS took Paul to the apostles who accepted him. The result was that Paul preached, going in and out among the Jerusalem Christians and even down to CAESAREA, so that "the church throughout all Judea and Galilee and Samaria had peace and was built up" (Acts 9:31).

In contrast, Gal 1:11-24 (esp. vv. 15-24) is a statement by Paul declaring his independence as an apostle. He avers here that the gospel he preached did not come from any human, instead it came through a revelation by God of the risen Jesus Christ. Paul claims he was ordained by God, that he did not confer with "flesh and blood," i.e., any human agent. He insists that when he was called by God he did not go up to Jerusalem to the apostles for their approval but went to Arabia and later returned to Damascus. He says that after three years he visited Cephas (Simon Peter) in Jerusalem for fifteen days; but he declares that he saw "none of the other apostles except James the Lord's brother'' (Gal 1:19). Indeed, Paul claims that he departed after this visit ''still not known by sight to the churches of Judea'' (Gal 1:22).

Frequently accounts of early Christianity provide a harmonization of these passages. But this is bad method! One cannot simply take a secondary source (here, Acts) and derive from it a framework into which a primary source (here, Galatians) must be made to fit. The result of such harmonization is abusive of primary material and produces a distorted picture of early Christianity.

(b) Methods. There is a way to work through the rough spots in the reconstruction of Paul's life, but in order to do so, one must be guided by sound method. Briefly stated, the critical method that guides most contemporary Pauline studies is this:

(i) The primary sources always have priority. Moreover, the soundest basis for understanding Paul is laid by using the seven undisputed Letters of Paul: Romans, 1 Corinthians, 2 Corinthians, Galatians, Philippians, 1 Thessalonians, and Philemon. The other Letters may be consulted in an ancillary capacity—though they add little if anything to one's knowledge of Paul's life.

(ii) The secondary source, Acts, may be used cautiously as a supplement to the primary materials when it is not in conflict with the Letters. Indeed, agreement of the primary and secondary materials gives one certainty, for the author of Acts shows no knowledge of Paul's Letters or even that Paul wrote letters.

(iii) Other early Christian documents are almost useless for the purpose of reconstructing Paul's life. These works are highly legendary in character. They illustrate matters that are best regarded as debatable or unknown. For example, extrabiblical early Christian literature offers competing stories about Paul's death. This diversity probably indicates that the exact manner of Paul's death was not widely known among subsequent Christians and that because of their curiosity these later Christians formulated a variety of accounts by interpreting freely, using pious imagination, the evidence that was available to them.

(c) Results. By taking the autobiographical material in Paul's Letters, comparing that information with Acts, and then considering the extrabiblical sources, one distinguishes two kinds of material. First, one isolates reliable information that allows one to compose Paul's story in outline. This account is nothing like a biography, the sources do not provide such extensive information; but one gets an impression of the man and develops a sketch of his career as an apostle. In the form of a sentence outline, the sketch appears as follows:

(i) The man's name was Paul, a Greek name.

(ii) He had a Jewish name, Saul. (Having two names was not uncommon for Jews who lived outside Palestine in the first century.)

(iii) Paul was born in TARSUS, a city in southeastern Asia Minor.

(iv) He came from a family of PHARISEES of the tribe of Benjamin and was named for the tribe's most illustrious member, King Saul.

(v) Paul's Letters show familiarity with both *rabbinic* methods for interpretation of scripture and *popular Hellenistic philosophy* to a degree that makes it likely that he had formal education in both areas.

(vi) He was probably, as an adult, a resident of Damascus.

(vii) He was an active persecutor of the early Christian movement (probably because he perceived it to be a threat to Torah obedience).

(viii) Paul became a Christian, an apostle, through a dramatic revelation of Jesus Christ.

(ix) His first years as a Christian, spent in Arabia, are a mystery.

(x) Three years after his call Paul went to Jerusalem to visit; he saw Peter and James.

(xi) Later (after fourteen years), he returned to Jerusalem for a meeting often referred to as ''the Jerusalem Conference'' or ''the Apostolic Council.''

(xii) Paul was a vigorous evangelist, traveling and preaching in Achaia, Arabia, Asia, Cilicia, Galatia, Judea, Illyricum, Macedonia, Syria, and making plans for Italy and Spain.

(xiii) On the mission field he: worked with a group of trusted colleagues (Aquila, Prisca, Silvanus, Sosthenes, TIMOTHY, TITUS, and others); supported himself with his craft, tentmaking; was often in danger and abused; and suffered from a ''thorn in the flesh.''

(xiv) Along with evangelization, Paul worked among his non-Palestinian congregations on a major project, a collection for the ''poor'' in Jerusalem, which he hoped would reconcile the non-Law-observant Christian givers and the Law-observant Christian recipients.

(xv) While actively engaged in evangelization of a region, Paul wrote to churches he had founded earlier in other areas to address problems experienced by those congregations.

(xvi) Paul's clear self-perception was that he was an ''apostle of Jesus Christ to the gentiles,'' i.e., one sent to proclaim the good news of Jesus Christ among non-Jews.

(xvii) One probably loses sight of Paul in the primary sources as he is imprisoned in Caesarea writing to Philemon and to the church at PHILIPPI (cf. the chronological sketch below). Nevertheless, with all but certainty one may conclude that while in prison (under Felix and then Festus), he appealed to be tried before Caesar (Nero) and was sent to Rome for a hearing. Subsequently, he died there as a martyr.

Even in this material there is some uncertainty. For example, because of the ambiguity of his statements, when Paul says ''then after three years'' (Gal 1:18), and ''then after fourteen years'' (Gal 2:1), one cannot be sure exactly what he means. He could be indicating two points in time, both dated from his call—to paraphrase, ''then three years after my call,'' and ''then fourteen years after my call.'' But, he could mean ''then three years after my call,'' and ''then fourteen years later''—in other words, *seventeen* years.

A second kind of information isolated in this study is that information in the secondary sources about which the interpreters of Paul must express reservations. For example, Acts 2:3 informs the reader that Paul was brought up in Jerusalem at the feet of GAMALIEL—in other words, Paul was a student in Jerusalem of one of the most famous rabbis in Jewish history. But, Paul himself never mentions these credentials. This is striking, for there are places in his Letters where he lists his ''Jewish'' credentials at length. The mention of Gamaliel in these listings would have amplified Paul's point concerning his former zeal for and status in Judaism, but he does not mention the connection. It is possible that Paul studied with Gamaliel in Jerusalem, but since he does not mention this himself, it is safest to omit this item when reconstructing his life. Moreover, from Paul's own Letters Paul himself says he ''went up to Jerusalem to visit'' and that he ''returned to Damascus'' (Gal 1:18, 17).

From this manner of reference, serious students of Paul's life and work understand that he was, as an adult, a resident of Damascus, not Jerusalem. Even more problematic is the claim in Acts that Paul received an endorsement from the apostles in Jerusalem. Not only does Paul not say this, he flatly denies it in Galatians.

In conclusion, by delineating and practicing a sound method for the use of sources in the reconstruction of Paul's life, one achieves valuable results. On the one hand, one exposes information that allows a more sophisticated reading of the NT documents in relation to one another. On the other, one develops a sketch of the life of Paul. This sketch may, through the conservatism of the method, be a minimal one; but it is absolutely reliable, admitting no debatable material. The sketch will be useful for the remainder of this study.

(2) The pattern of Paul's life and work. Toward the end of his ministry Paul says, "I have been able to bring to completion [the preaching of] the gospel of Christ from Jerusalem around as far as Illyricum" (Rom 15:19). In modern terms he claims to have preached the "good news" from Israel through Lebanon, Syria, Turkey, Greece, as far as portions of Bulgaria, Albania, and Yugoslavia. How could Paul have done this in twenty to twenty-five years of his ministry?

The usual image of Paul is of an energetic, tenacious, individual preacher, but one should recognize that Paul's missionary activity was team work. His Letters reveal that he coordinated the activity of a systematically organized band of missionaries and that his method was fairly consistent. Paul would move with a group of seasoned missionary colleagues to the capital city of a Roman province. Upon arrival he and his associates would approach the local SYNAGOGUE, and if possible set up a base therein for the proclamation of the gospel. If no synagogue existed, the team would seek out the "God-fearers," i.e., gentiles who were attracted to the theology and morality of Judaism but who had not become full converts. If there were no God-fearers, Paul and his companions would take the message to the local marketplace. In the process of moving into a city Paul would gather any Christians who already lived there and incorporate them into the missionary enterprise, thereby expanding his staff. While Paul seems to have remained in the capital city and its immediate area, his fellow workers appear to have dispersed themselves throughout the other cities, towns, and villages of the region in order to establish satellite congregations. Paul would remain in one location until the job he set out to do was done (he was in CORINTH a year and a half and in EPHESUS two years and three months) or, more often, until he became embroiled in a controversy that forced him to leave the region. Paul then moved on to repeat this process in a new location. But, he did not loose contact with the churches he founded. Indeed, he paid checkup visits to the churches when he deemed it necessary. Moreover, he used the writing of letters as a part of his missionary strategy, employing the written communication (like a modern "bishop's letter") to influence and build up the congregations he addressed.

Some scholars attribute this method of organizing missionary work to the church at Antioch of which Paul was a member, and which itself was extremely active in early Christian missionary work. This may be the case; or, if Paul was a Jewish missionary before he was Christian, perhaps he adapted the technique from Jewish missionary activity. It may even be that Paul devised the strategy himself. Knowing the source of Paul's missionary style would be enlightening, but not knowing this does not detract from understanding Paul's work and appreciating its effectiveness.

(3) Chronological outline. In attempting to map a Pauline chronology—i.e., to locate times and places in the life of Paul—one immediately finds a lack of real detail for the task. Moreover, even with regard to some of the available details there are uncertainties. For example, how long was Paul in Arabia (Gal 1:17)? Or when he writes in Philippians and Philemon that he is in prison, in what city is the prison located? And when he says he is confident of his impending release, is he merely being optimistic? or does he have some reason to believe he will be freed? or is he playing a bluff to motivate those to whom he writes?

Because of the lack of specific information and in light of the difficulties associated with using what material is available, many scholars argue that no more than a relative dating of Paul's Letters is possible. And even here there are problems, for the preserved copies of Paul's Letters are not dated. Moreover, the claims of some scholars to recognize developments in Paul's thinking from one Letter to another are not persuasive, being locked in as they are to the presuppositions that Paul's thought evolved and that he could not change his mind.

From these cautionary remarks one might gather that the prospect of working out a Pauline chronology is bleak. But, these warnings should not completely deter an attempt at correlating dates and places for Paul's career. Indeed, one firm date for Paul's activity is ascertainable (though recent work by Jewett, Luedemann, and Murphy-O'Connor draws conclusions that differ from this scholarly consensus). From Acts 18:12-18 one learns that Paul was in Corinth when GALLIO was proconsul. An inscription found at Delphi (an ancient Greek town) permits dating of Gallio's term as proconsul to the period from May of 51 C.E. to May of 52 C.E. By correlating Acts and the Delphic inscription, one learns when Paul could possibly have appeared before Gallio. At the earliest it was the summer of 51 and at the latest the spring of 52. Scholars mount arguments for both extremities, but they have not settled the issue which is perhaps unresolvable. Since there is nothing in Acts 18:12 to indicate that Gallio had taken office only recently (Acts 18:11 is a simple atemporal summary and does not indicate past time), for convenience we will make use of the later date—although recognizing that one may adjust the ensuing reconstruction by moving back the dates almost one year.

The information concerning Paul's imprisonment in Caesarea under Felix and then Festus is another "definite" moment in Paul's life. Some scholars correlate the information in Acts 24–26 with other material from Roman history concerning the family of Felix, but this is quite complicated and the case is fraught with difficulties, even improbabilities, and is merely speculative. Thus it is best to use the information in Paul's Letters and Acts to work forward and backward from the dating of Gallio's proconsulship. Also to be considered are the conditions for travel in the ancient Greek world. For example, those who traveled on foot, as Paul no doubt did, could cover about twenty miles per day; few sea voyages took place during March, April, May, September, and October, and from November through February the Mediterranean was effectively closed for travel. Taking all these factors into the calculation, one achieves the chronological outline below.

(The conclusion that Paul did not write the six disputed Letters lies behind this particular reconstruction. The decisions concerning the authorship of these Letters are not

• OUTLINE OF PAUL'S LIFE •

35 (or 32)	Paul is called by God's revelation of Jesus Christ (problem of "three" and "fourteen")
35–38	Missionary activity in Arabia (Gal 1:17) and Damascus (2 Cor 11:32)
38	Paul visits with Peter and (James) in Jerusalem (Gal 1:18)
38–48	Missionary activity in Cilicia and Syria (Gal 1:21)
48	So-called Apostolic Council in Jerusalem (Gal 2:1-10; Acts 15)
48 or 49	Incident with Peter and others in Antioch (Gal 2:11-14)
49	Missionary activity in Galatia (Acts 16:6)
50	Missionary activity in Philippi, Thessalonica, and Beroea (Acts 16:11–17:14)
Late 50	Travel to Corinth via Athens (Acts 17:15; 18:1); writing of 1 Thessalonians
Late 50 to May 52	Missionary activity in Corinth (Acts 18:11)
Summer 52	Travel to Caesarea; then Antioch; then passing through Asia Minor he paid a second visit to Galatia on the way to Ephesus (Gal 4:13; Acts 18:18-23)
Late 52 to spring 55	Missionary activity in Ephesus (Acts 19:1, 8-10, 22); writing of Galatians, 2 Cor 6:14–7:1; 1 Corinthians, and the letters preserved in 2 Cor 8 and 2:14–6:13; 7:2-4
(54)	Visit to Corinth (presupposed in 2 Cor 13:1)
Late 54–55	writing of letter preserved in 2 Cor 10–13
Summer 55	Travel through Macedonia to Corinth; writing of letter preserved in 2 Cor 1:1–2:13; 7:5-16, and of the final "Collection Letter," 2 Cor 9
Late 55 to early 56	Stay in Corinth; writing of Romans
56	Travel to Jerusalem with the collection; arrest and imprisonment
56–58	Imprisonment in Caesarea; writing of Philippians and Philemon
58	Felix replaced by Festus; Paul appeals to Caesar and is sent to Rome
58–60	Imprisonment in Rome (Acts 28:30)
60+	Martyrdom

related to chronology, however; and those who conclude that Paul did write the disputed Letters can easily factor their conclusions into this account of Paul's life by locating 2 Thessalonians shortly after 1 Thessalonians, late in 50 or early in 51 C.E. from Corinth. Furthermore, most scholars who accept Colossians, Ephesians, and the Pastoral Epistles as authentic Pauline letters usually and most aptly regard them as coming from the time of Paul's Roman imprisonment. If one concludes that any or all of these is/are genuine Pauline correspondences, one may set the Letter[s] in the period 58–60+ C.E.)

Paul's Letter Writing. Since Paul's Letters are what remain directly from his labors as an apostle, one should examine them in terms of their organization and style to see if they offer further insight into the character of their author. To perceive the genius of Paul's Letters it is helpful to know something about letters and letter writing in antiquity.

(1) Ancient letters. Education, commerce, and travel in the Hellenistic era created a context for letter writing. There was even a semiprofessional class of letter writers called scribes or amanuenses. Letters moved surprising distances in Paul's day. The first "traveling" letters were official communication regarding governmental and military matters, but with improved conditions all sorts of letters were produced. These included public decrees by rulers, official letters between authorities, business letters, friendly communications, and brief notes of all sorts.

In Paul's day, as today, letters were written in standard forms. Normally, there were five sections to the letter: (1) a Salutation in three parts which name the sender, the addressee, and offer a greeting; (2) a Thanksgiving; (3) the Body of the letter; (4) Final Instructions (Parenesis); and (5) the Closing in two parts which offers final greetings and the parting word. The letters are frequently dated and addressed.

(2) Paul's modifications to standard letter form. It is helpful to compare Paul's briefest letter, Philemon, as an example of Paul's letter writing style, with the standard form of the Hellenistic letter. When this is done, one readily recognized how Paul's Letter are similar and dissimilar to other letters of his day.

Salutation

Sender(s):

"Paul, a prisoner for Christ Jesus and Timothy our brother"

Recipient(s):

"to Philemon our beloved fellow worker and Apphia our sister and Archippus our fellow soldier and the church in your house"

Greeting:

"Grace to you and peace from God our Father and the Lord Jesus Christ."

Thanksgiving

"I thank my God always when I remember you (singular, indicating Philemon) in my prayers."

Body of the Letter

Paul discusses the return of Onesimus, a runaway slave.

Final Instructions (Parenesis)

Throughout the letter Paul has exhorted Philemon: "receive him" (v. 17); "charge that to my account" (v. 18); "refresh my heart in Christ" (v. 20). His final instructions are in v. 22, "prepare a guest room for me."

Closing

Greetings:

"Epaphrus, my fellow prisoner in Christ Jesus, greets you (singular) [and] Mark, Aristarchus, Demas, and Luke, my fellow workers."

Parting word:

"The grace of the Lord Jesus Christ be with your spirit."

Yet, as similar as the Letters of Paul are to other Hellenistic letters, one should notice how Paul subtly altered the style of the standard letter for his own purposes. These alterations reflect the peculiarly Christian character of Paul's Letters and reveal how thoroughly his relationship with Jesus Christ affected him. Indeed, God's revelation of the risen Christ gave Paul a new emphasis and left its stamp on everything he did, even the writing of letters. It is instructive to view the anatomy of some of Paul's changes of the form of a standard letter. For example, *in the opening* of his Letters Paul identifies himself in relation to God and Christ. Moreover, he identifies those to whom he writes in terms of their own roles as Christians. Furthermore, he alters the language of the normal greeting and expands it into a lofty but practical wish for the recipients. The usual salutation in Hellenistic letters is the word *greetings*. But, Paul does not send his readers "greetings"; he salutes them by saying, "grace and peace." The words *greetings* and *grace* resemble one another in Gk.: "greetings" = *chairein* and "grace" = *charis*. Thus, Paul's salutation begins with a wordplay that reveals the effects of God's activity, and he develops his altered greeting by coupling a common Jewish greeting, "peace" (*shalom*), with "grace."

Finally, one should recognize that Paul was not a casual letter writer. His are not simple friendly communications. He wrote to address specific situations that existed in particular churches. With his Letters he sought to extend his influence (often in an authoritative fashion) in order to assure desired results. He always strives to build up the congregation addressed. Thus, for Paul the letter was an instrument of his apostleship.

Paul's Religious Background and Thought. (1) Judaism. Paul the Christian had once been Paul the Jew. It is clear from both his own Letters and the story of his ministry in Acts that Paul was not merely a Jew but a Pharisee. He boasts from time to time in his Letters of his Jewish past in rebuttal to other missionaries who caused problems in the churches that he had founded (see Phil 3 and 2 Cor 11). In so doing Paul reveals that prior to being a Christian he was a zealous Pharisee. Acts 22:3 preserves a tradition that associates Paul with Rabbi Gamaliel I, one of the most influential figures in first-century Judaism. While Paul does not mention this striking association when rehearsing his Jewish credentials, the association of Paul with formal rabbinic education seems likely, for in his writings Paul manifests signs of "rabbinics": He does midrashic exegesis of the Hebrew Bible; he demonstrates a clear perception of the Law as the heart of Judaism; and the contrast he draws between Christ and the Law shows his disavowal of human, systemic righteousness which he had once practiced with confidence and contentment. These features of Paul's writings locate him within the stream of first-century Pharisaic Judaism; they do not, however, amount to evidence for the assertion that Paul was a Rabbi.

(2) Hellenism. As it is clear that Paul's past was in Pharisaic Judaism, it is also certain that Paul was a Hellenized Jew. According to Acts he was born outside Palestine in the Greco-Roman trade city of Tarsus. Indeed Paul's own writings show signs of Hellenistic education. The basic mastery of the skills of reading, thinking, argumentation, and expression in writing are the hallmarks of Hellenistic education. Moreover, the Letters are filled with telltale signs of Paul's Hellenistic heritage: From his quotation of Jewish scripture one sees that Paul read the Bible in its Greek version, the LXX. Paul is thoroughly familiar with the conventions of popular Hellenistic philosophy and methods of literary interpretation. Moreover, he calls himself Paul (Gk. *Paulos*), not Saul (Heb. *Sāul*); and his metaphors are drawn from the Greco-Roman world of sports and military.

(3) Debate. These observations illustrate a basic problem for those seeking to understand Paul; namely, what background best accounts for Paul's own understanding of what he did and said? Formerly scholars drew hard lines between three areas that putatively influenced Paul. Since he was certainly a Pharisee, rabbinic or Palestinian Judaism was thought to provide the key to interpreting Paul. His use of apparently technical language in reference to tradition he had received and delivered (1 Cor 15:3) to the churches he founded was taken to indicate his self-understanding and his attitude toward the tradition itself. Moreover, Paul's practice of midrashic exegesis (cf. Paul on Exodus in 1 Cor 10 or on Abraham in Gal 3) was thought to reveal his approach to the OT while his concern with the contrast between Christ and the Law was determined by his past participation in Pharisaism.

Yet, other scholars argued that Hellenism was the most appropriate background for viewing and interpreting Paul. That Paul did allegorical exegesis was said to show still another attitude and approach toward the Hebrew Bible (see Paul on Sarah and Hagar in Gal 4). Furthermore, it was held that by casting Paul in the context of Hellenism one found the prerequisite cause for understanding such basic Pauline notions as the sacraments and Christology. Since Paul was thoroughly Hellenistic in heritage, this meant that he would interpret baptism and the Lord's Supper in relation to the practices of Hellenistic MYSTERY RELIGIONS, and he would have understood Christ in terms of a general, Hellenistic myth of a descending and ascending redeemer figure.

(4) Apocalyptic thought. A third approach to Paul designated apocalyptic Judaism as the determinative background for understanding his writings. Paul's language bespeaks an apocalyptic perspective in focusing on wrath, judgment, and the day of the Lord. He displays a yearning for the messianic age that characterized all apocalyptic writing. He shows an awareness of living on the boundary of two worlds, one dying and one being born. Further he has a sense of special urgency derived from the apocalyptic conviction that his generation is the last. The clearest sign of Paul's thoroughly apocalyptic perspective is the presence of his writings of the dualistic doctrine of two ages. This doctrine maintains that the age to come breaks into the current age supernaturally through God's intervention and without human agency.

Scholars now recognize that these backgrounds are not exclusive of one another and that each makes a contribution to a balanced reading of Paul, for Paul was influenced by and drew upon all of them. Nevertheless, the question remains whether one of these is dominant.

It is becoming increasingly clearer through the work of several contemporary scholars (e.g., Beker, Käsemann, and Martyn) that the apocalyptic element provided Paul with the basic framework of his thought and determined his comprehension of the world around him. What is this apocalyptic perspective? When scholars are called upon for clarification one finds that remarkably different understandings of "apocalyptic" exist. In Gk. *apokalypsis* means "revelation." Paul uses this word to refer to his original encounter with the risen Jesus Christ (Gal 1:13). That dramatic revelation was the occasion of Paul's call. Moreover, it was the time and means of Paul's being taught or given the basis of the gospel which he preached (Gal 1:11-17). This disruptive intervention of God into Paul's life bespeaks the pattern of thought typical of first-century apocalyptic Judaism.

Apocalyptic is a special expression of Jewish eschatology that was characterized by the dualistic doctrine of two ages. On the one hand there is "the present evil age," and on the other there is "the age to come." The "present evil age" is the world of mundane realities in which human beings live; the "age to come" is the supernatural realm of the power of God. There is no continuity between these ages. Indeed, apocalyptic Jewish thought held that at some future moment "the age to come" would break into the human realm by a supernatural act of God. In this moment of God's intervention the "present evil age" would pass away and "the age to come" would be established as a new reality, ordained and directed by God. Apocalyptic Judaism held that by this act of God evil would be annihilated and those who were righteous would be redeemed. Thus "the age to come" was the hope of those who believed in God but found themselves oppressed by the forces of evil in the present world. In Jewish apocalyptic literature the authors usually claim to live in the last days of "the present evil age." Their message to readers is the joint promise and warning that the intervention of God is about to happen.

Throughout his Letters Paul's language and patterns of thought reveal elements of this apocalyptic eschatology. For example, Paul frequently uses apocalyptic language: "destined . . . for wrath," "the wrath to come," "the wrath of God," "the day of wrath," "the day of the Lord Jesus Christ," "the day of salvation," "redeemed," "redemption," "this age," "the rulers of this age," "the present evil age," and "the ends of the ages." Moreover, Paul reveals in his Letters the conviction that he and his readers are part of the last generation of humanity (1 Thess 4:13-18, esp. v. 17; 1 Cor 15:51-57).

Paul does not use the phrase "the age to come," and so some scholars deny the thoroughgoing apocalyptic character of his thought. But he speaks in distinctively Christian phrases of the same idea when he says, "a new creation" and "the Kingdom of God." This difference in phrases indicates a slight, but fundamental, alteration on the part of Paul. He transforms the pattern of Jewish apocalyptic thought described above into a particularly Christian pattern of apocalyptic thinking which permeates all of his writings. In other words, Paul the apostle articulates an apocalyptic perspective that has been modified in light of the Christ-event.

Jewish apocalyptic eschatology thought in terms of two ages. These were distinct; one age ended and the other began by an intervening act of God. Paul has a similar, but distinct, view of time that stamps his entire thought process. He maintains the temporal dualism characteristic of Jewish apocalyptic, but he modifies the scheme in light of the Christ-event so that there are two distinct ages that are separated and joined by an interim.

For Paul the first temporal epoch is "the present evil age" (Gal 1:4; 1 Cor 2:6-8). This age is ruled by the god of this world (2 Cor 4:4), namely Satan, and by the elemental spirits of the universe (Gal 4:3; 1 Cor 2:8). Under the influence of its rulers this age is at odds with God (1 Cor 15:24-28; Rom 8:37-39). Nevertheless, this age is passing away (1 Cor 7:31). The second epoch is the "new creation" (Gal 6:14; 2 Cor 5:17). This new age comes as God in Christ defeats the forces in opposition to him (Gal 6:14; 1 Cor 7:31; Rom 5:21), and it is established as the *regnum dei,* apparently an age of glory (1 Thess 2:10-12; 1 Cor 15:20-28; 2 Cor 4:17; Rom 5:2, 21).

The present exists as the juncture of the ages or as a mingling of the ages (1 Cor 10:11; 2 Cor 5:16). Here 1 Cor 10:11 is important. In this verse Paul describes himself and other humans as those "upon whom the end<u>s</u> of the age<u>s</u> have met." Modern translations often obscure Paul's idea in this phrase, translating it as does the RSV, "upon whom the end of the ages has come." This rendering implies that Paul stands at the end of time and looks back at the ages (something like dispensations?) that have gone before—indeed, he does not. Paul perceives that he and other humans live at the juncture of the ages. This juncture came about as a result of the cross of Christ (1 Cor 1:17-18) and it will conclude, marking the absolute end of the present evil age, at the coming of Christ from heaven (1 Thess 2:19; 3:13; 4:13-18; 1 Cor 15:23-28).

Paul was called and he thought, worked, and preached in this interim. Much of Paul's message derives from his understanding of this juncture, for, as noted, it came about as a result of the cross of Christ (1 Cor 1:17-18). In essence Paul said:

(a) Sin has been defeated (Gal 1:4; 1 Cor 15:3; Rom 4:25).

(b) Death has been condemned (1 Cor 15:54-57; Rom 8:31-39).

(c) The Law has been exposed for what it is (Gal 3:24-25; Rom 7:7-12).

(d) Christ has discharged humanity from the curse of the Law (Gal 3:13-14; Rom 7:4-6).

(e) Although the battle goes on toward God's final victory, creation has been reclaimed by God (1 Cor 15:20-28; Rom 8:18-25).

(f) God's sovereignty has been established (Rom 8:31-39).

(g) Creation presently awaits the grand assize (1 Thess 5:2-11; 1 Cor 6:2-3; 15:20-28; 16:21; Rom 8:18-25), and while the Kingdom of God has *not yet* been fully established in glory, this is *already* the messianic age in which, for now, everything is to be viewed from the vantage point of the cross (2 Cor 5:16).

See also ACTS OF THE APOSTLES; ANTIOCH; BARNABAS; CAESAREA; CORINTH; DAMASCUS; EPHESUS; EPISTLE/LETTER; ESCHATOLOGY IN THE NEW TESTAMENT; FAITH; GALLIO; GAMALIEL; GENTILE, GENTILES IN THE NEW TESTAMENT; JERUSALEM COUNCIL; JUSTIFICATION; LORD'S SUPPER; MESSIAH/CHRIST; MYSTERY RELIGIONS; ONESIMUS; PHARISEES; PHILIPPI; PRISCILLA/AQUILA; RABBINIC LITERATURE; SILAS; SYNAGOGUE; TARSUS; TIMOTHY; TITUS.

<u>Bibliography</u>. J. C. Beker, *Paul the Apostle: The Triumph of God in Life and Thought*; G. Bornkamm, *Paul*; W. Bousset, *Kyrios Christos*; R. Bultmann, *Theology of the New Testament*; W. D. Davies, *Paul and Rabbinic Judaism*; W. G. Doty, *Letters in Primitive Christianity*; E. E. Ellis, *Paul and His Recent Interpreters*; E. Käsemann, *Perspective on Paul*; L. E. Keck, *Paul and His Letters*; J. Knox, *Chapters in a Life of Paul*; G. Luedemann, *Paul, Apostle to the Gentiles*; J. L. Martyn, "Epistemology at the Turn of the Ages: 2 Corinthians 5:16," *Christian History and Interpretation,* ed. W. R. Farmer et al.; W. A. Meeks, *The First Urban Christians* and *The Writings of St. Paul*; J. Murphy-O'Connor, "On the Road and on the Sea with St. Paul," *BR* 1 (Summer 1985): 38-47; C. Roetzel, *The Letters of Paul*; E. P. Sanders, *Paul and Palestinian Judaism*; A. Schweitzer, *Paul and His Interpreters*; M. L. Soards, *The Apostle Paul: An Introduction to His Writing and Teaching*; P. Vielhauer, "Apocalypses and Related Subjects," *New Testament Apocrypha,* ed. E. Hennecke and W. Schneemelcher.

—MARION L. SOARDS

• **Paul and Seneca, Letters of.** [pawl, sen'uh-kuh] According to Augustine (354–430), the Roman philosopher Seneca (ca. 4 B.C.E.–65 C.E.) wrote a series of letters to the apostle PAUL (Augustine in *Ep* 153.14 *ad Macedonium*). Jerome (ca. 342-420) speaks of a mutual correspondence (*DeVir* 12). Although there is no convincing evidence that Paul and Seneca knew one another personally, much less that they corresponded with one another, a spurious correspondence known as the *Letters of Paul and Seneca* does exist in Latin. This collection is probably the one to which Jerome refers, since Jerome's single reference to the contents of Seneca's letters to Paul agrees materially with a line in the eleventh letter of the pseudonymous collection. According to Jerome the correspondence between the apostle and Seneca was "read by many," and Jerome himself includes the philosopher in his list of saints. Since the Latin apologist Lactantius (ca. 240–320) speculates that Seneca would have become a Christian had someone shown him the way (*DivInst* 6.24.13-14), it is unlikely that the correspondence was in existence when Lactantius expressed this opinion (ca. 304–11). Therefore, it appears that the letters were composed sometime between 311 and 392, the date of Jerome's *DeVir*. The last two letters in the collection (13 and 14), however, may have been written at a later date, since they exhibit a different style.

The letters abound in exaggerated flattery and are for the most part uninteresting, evidencing none of the thought of either man. Among other things the letters promote the idea that Seneca interceded with Nero himself on Paul's behalf and even brought the apostle's writings to the emperor's attention, who is said to have been very impressed with them. The author's purpose in concocting this fictional correspondence was probably two-fold: (1) to exalt the apostle by making him the intimate of the most famous and politically influential philosopher of his day, and (2) to provide a justification for interpreting Paul in the tradition of STOIC moral philosophy. The epistolary genre is well-suited to the first aim. In antiquity one of the principal uses of the letter was to maintain friendly relations (φιλοφρόνησις), and mutual friendship is the dominant theme of the Seneca-Paul correspondence. This is especially evident in the fourth letter, which consists of only a few lines to the effect that Seneca's thoughts are with Paul and that he looks forward to seeing him again in person. The second aim is reflected in the very choice of Seneca as Paul's intellectual confidant. In the first letter the renowned Stoic philosopher refers to the "wonderful exhortations for the moral life" that are contained in Paul's writings, as if the apostle, like Seneca himself, had produced "moral epistles." Thus Paul is esteemed by the author of the fictional correspondence, and presumably also by the Italian believers who read these epistles, as the first Christian moral philosopher in the classical tradition.

Bibliography. A. Kurfess, "The Apocryphal Correspondence between Seneca and Paul," *New Testament Apocrypha,* ed. E. Hennecke and W. Schneemelcher; J. N. Sevenster, *Paul and Seneca.*

—CHARLES H. COSGROVE

• **Paul, Acts of.** The *Acts of Paul* is a NT apocryphal work written around the beginning of the second century. While authorship is unknown, the geographical setting of this work suggests that the author resided within the general vicinity of Asia Minor. This assessment corresponds with Tertullian's view that the author was an elder in Asia Minor who lost his eldership because he penned this particular work.

The compositional nature is best described as a loose collection of PAUL'S exploits and preaching. What is most characteristic of this collection is the legendary and hyperbolic nature of Paul's deeds. The accounts which the author collected combine many different traditions and vary greatly in detail and locale. While three popular accounts of Paul's deeds circulated independently, such as the *Acts of Paul and Thecla,* the *Martyrdom of Paul,* and the apocryphal Corinthian letters, all of these accounts are best classified as parts of the whole known as the *Acts of Paul.*

The *Acts* is a fragmentary work with no complete copy preserved. Its reconstruction has been greatly assisted by a Greek papyrus at Hamburg and a Coptic papyrus at Heidelberg. The tentative reconstruction portrays the journey of Paul as: Damascus, Jerusalem, Antioch, Iconium, Antioch, Myra, Sidon, Tyre, Smyrna, Ephesus, Philippi, Corinth, Italy, and Rome.

The journey motif is grounded in the extraordinary and miraculous deeds which Paul performs. Paul is able to heal the blind, escape from life threatening situations, baptize a lion, and on many occasions bring the dead back to life. Unlike the canonical accounts, with which a comparison may be drawn, the *Acts of Paul* shows little restraint in attributing to him extraordinary powers and investing him with heroic characteristics.

The fantastic and entertaining deeds of Paul account for the popularity of this work in the early churches. It is cited by such church fathers as Origen, Hippolytus, and Cyprian. While the work was never held to be explicitly heretical, it nevertheless did not enjoy canonical status. The exaggerated tales, which accounted for its popularity, helped obstruct it from achieving such status. Also some church fathers, such as Tertullian, objected to the *Acts* on the grounds of the large role which women played as followers, teachers of doctrine, and administers of sacraments.

The purpose of the *Acts of Paul* is not necessarily polemical in nature; the book is more accurately described as a teaching tract. It was an entertaining method for portraying to the readership of the second-century moral values in regard to sexual purity and the proper relationship to the world.

The work also perpetuated a portrait of Paul which was larger than life. This is illustrated by its account of the martyrdom of Paul, a graphic reminder to the reader that when one did not compromise with the world death was a likely result. This type of martyrdom, however, is to be embraced as a sign of faith in God. As Paul states at his execution: "Believe in the living God who raises up from the dead both me and all who believe in him!"

See also APOCRYPHAL ACTS.

Bibliography. S. L. Davies, "Women, Tertullian and the Acts of Paul," *Semeia* 38 (1986): 139-43; E. M. Howe, "Interpretations of Paul in the Acts of Paul and Thecla," *Pauline Studies,* ed. D. A. Hagner and M. J. Harris; W. Schneemelcher, "Acts of Paul," *New Testament Apocrypha,* ed. E. Hennecke and W. Schneemelcher.

—DAVID M. MAY

• **Paul, Apocalypse of (ANT).** The *Apocalypse of Paul* is a late Christian apocalypse from ca. the fourth or fifth century C.E., and unrelated to a Coptic work of the same name from NAG HAMMADI. It purports to be the record written by Paul of his vision when he experienced the third heaven (1 Cor 12:2). The vision is composed of two sections. The first part involved a description of the place in which the righteous reside, i.e., HEAVEN. The second part pictures the place of punishment reserved for sinners and the godless, i.e., HELL.

This particular apocalypse was a popular work in the early church because of its vivid presentation of heaven and hell. It was not, however, universally appreciated or used. Augustine, e.g., considered its content unacceptable for church usage. The extant copies of this apocalypse consist of a few Greek fragments, a portion in Coptic, and a full text in Latin. While allegedly written by PAUL, it is in fact much later, as is evident from the nature of ecclesiastical concerns that it expresses. The author drew many of his images from a stock of Greek traditions, such as a journey by boat over Lake Acherusia.

The *Apocalypse* begins an account of its discovery in a marble box which also contained Paul's walking shoes. After this introduction, the content of the apocalypse details a vision of heaven seen by Paul. In a tour of heaven, Paul is greeted by the major and minor prophets, and the patriarchs. The climax of this heavenly pilgrimage is Paul's arrival at the city of Christ where DAVID is the main singer. While Paul sees many major figures in heaven, he also sees the obscure, such as the babies killed by HEROD the Great.

In contrast to the city of Christ, which is filled with light, rivers of wine, oil, milk, honey, and songs of praise and rejoicing, the vision of hell is one of torment and depression. A guiding principle there is that each person's punishment is commensurate to his or her sin. While many of the punishments involve fire, the punishment for those who harmed widows, orphans, and the poor was the cutting off of hands and feet and being placed naked in ice and snow. The punishments which Paul witnesses are so ghastly that he pleads for respite for the tormented sinners who are then given a temporary reprieve from their torments on Sunday.

The *Apocalypse of Paul* was significant in the early church for two reasons. First, the vision of hell which Paul described is one which motivated the reader by fear and dread. The portrayal of those tormented in hell was a graphic warning for any who might be tempted to commit sins in this world. Furthermore, the depiction of specific ecclesiastical groups within the punishment hierarchy of hell is an indictment of perceived corruption within the church.

Second, while the OT and NT stories were insightful in describing the lives of righteous and suffering figures, they often ended abruptly and later readers had an insatiable curiosity to know what else happened, where those people are now, and what heaven is like. The *Apocalypse of Paul* helped fill in the gaps for later Christian readers.

See also APOCALYPTIC LITERATURE; HEAVEN; HELL.

Bibliography. R. Casey, "The Apocalypse of Paul," *JTS* 34 (1933): 1-32; H. Duensing, "Apocalypse of Paul," *New Testament Apocrypha,* ed. E. Hennecke and W. Schneemelcher; M. Himmelfarb, *Tours of Hell: An Apocalyptic Form in Jewish and Christian Literature.*

—DAVID M. MAY

• **Paul, Apocalypse of (NH).** The Coptic *Apocalypse of Paul* from Codex V of the NAG HAMMADI documents is the first of four apocalypses in that codex. It has no relation to a previously known APOCALYPSE OF PAUL (ANT) written in Greek and known in other versions, though the subject matter is somewhat similar. Epiphanius mentions an *Apocalypse of Paul* used by Gnostics, but it is impossible to say whether there is any connection between it and this document. The date and provenance of this tractate cannot be determined, but it is probably no later than the second century. Like all the Nag Hammadi documents, it is assumed to have been written in Greek and translated into Coptic.

The first lines of the work are lost, but at the beginning of the recoverable text, PAUL, traveling to Jerusalem, meets a child who identifies himself as a spirit who will accompany him to the heavens to meet his fellow apostles. He invites Paul to open his mind. Passing through the third heaven, they come to the fourth where they are joined by the twelve apostles. In this fourth heaven Paul sees a soul brought from the land of the dead to judgment, flailed and accused by three witnesses to whom he must answer. Going on to the fifth heaven, he sees angels with whips drive souls on to judgment. At the sixth heaven a bright light shines down, and Paul has the toll collector there admit them to the seventh heaven, where all is brightness. An old man dressed in white and seated on a throne challenges Paul's ascent. Paul says he is going to the dead to lead captive the captivity of Babylon. The old man bids Paul see the powers surrounding him, and asks how he thinks he can escape. At the spirit's direction, Paul gives a sign, whereupon the seventh heaven opens, and Paul and the apostles rise to the eighth, the ninth, and finally the tenth heaven, where Paul greets his fellow spirits.

The theme of Paul's ascent is clearly based on 2 Cor 12:2-4, providing a Gnostic interpretation of Gal 1:11-17 and 2:1-2. The child-spirit is probably an epiphany of the risen Christ. The scenes in the fourth and fifth heavens where souls are directed to judgment are syncretistic, incorporating motifs from Jewish APOCALYPTIC, Greek mythology, and popular ASTROLOGY. The old man in the seventh heaven is surely the lesser God of Judaism (cf. Dan 7:13), and may indicate the origin of this work among an anti-Jewish group. All the lower heavens represent realms of evil, through which a soul must pass to reach the goal of the tenth heaven.

There is some scholarly discussion as to whether this or any of the Gnostic apocalypses should properly be considered in the genre of apocalyptic, or rather as a dialogue of revelation. Certainly this document is typical of other Gnostic apocalypses, in that narrative matter is decidedly secondary to discourse.

See also APOCALYPTIC LITERATURE; GNOSTICISM; NAG HAMMADI.

Bibliography. F. T. Fallon, "The Gnostic Apocalypses," *Semeia* 14 (1979): 123-58; W. Murdock and G. MacRae, "The Apocalypse of Paul," *Nag Hammadi Codices V, 2-5 and VI* (*NHS*, 11), and "The Apocalypse of Paul," *The Nag Hammadi Library in English,* ed. J. M. Robinson.

—ROGER A. BULLARD

• **Paul, Prayer of the Apostle.** The *Prayer of the Apostle Paul* is a brief piece opening Codex I of the NAG HAMMADI documents, also known as the Jung Codex. Ascribed to Paul, it is a Gnostic prayer in the name of Jesus Christ for light and mercy, for the gifts of the Spirit, for authority, healing, and redemption. Similarities to prayers in the HERMETIC LITERATURE and magical texts have been noted. There is a direct reference to 1 Cor 2:9, which is given a Gnostic interpretation.

See also GNOSTICISM; NAG HAMMADI.

Bibliography. D. Mueller, "Prayer of the Apostle Paul," *The Nag Hammadi Library in English,* ed. J. M. Robinson.

—ROGER A. BULLARD

• **Paulus, Sergius.** *See* SERGIUS PAULUS

• **Pavement.** *See* GABBATHA

• **Pay/Payment.** *See* WAGES

• **Peace.** Times of war and their aftermath give birth to quests for peace that seek to go beyond the simple absence of conflict. The Heb. word *šālôm* in its fullness represented a vision of peace and spiritual well-being that was grounded in covenantal relationship with Yahweh and was reflected in all dimensions of life: economic, political, biological, and religious.

The development of this search for peace reached a critical stage during and after the Babylonian invasion of Judah in 587/6 B.C.E. The resulting destruction and fall of Jerusalem precipitated a profound quest for peace as people of ancient Israel looked to their leaders for answers and direction. Where was God's activity in the events? Was it possible to find ways to move from the despair of no meaning to better times?

The three major social institutions in place at the time of the fall to which people looked for answers were: the TEMPLE with its PRIESTS; the palace with its wise men; and the prophetic schools, popular PROPHETS who gathered around themselves disciples who studied and passed on the prophet's teachings. Several writings and major editions of collections of writings can be traced to these years. From them we get a sense of ancient Israel's various understandings of peace.

The Temple and the Priests. Scholars generally agree that the final priestly edition of the first four books of the Bible (Genesis, Exodus, Leviticus, Numbers) is to be dated to the time of the fall of Jerusalem and early EXILE. With the Temple no longer operative it was essential to do whatever was necessary to preserve the truths of tradition for future generations. The priestly contribution to Israel's understanding of peace can be thought of as holding on to what is known: in times of trouble, to turn to these values and insights preserved in tradition, those truths that have withstood the test of time. The priestly editor organized tradition around the central idea of God's eternal covenant with the faithful Israelite people. There had been signs in Israel's past of that eternal relationship. It was evident in the stories of heroes who, because of their FAITH in similar difficult times, stood as models for subsequent generations: NOAH and the flood with the sign of the RAINBOW, God's promise never to abandon humanity again; ABRAHAM and his journey to an unknown land armed only with the promise of blessing and the sign of circumcision; MOSES who spent most of his life facing the difficulties of the wilderness. And yet, ISRAEL was born in the wilderness; that was where Moses received the Law and the Sabbath as signs of God's eternal commitment to the Israelite people. Indeed, creation itself (Gen 1:1) was to be conceived as God's power to bring order out of chaos. The source of peace, then, in the eyes of the priests was to be found whenever people gathered around scripture on the SABBATH—wherever they were—to remember God's mighty acts on their behalf. If they remembered and were like Noah, Abraham, and Moses, a new day would come.

The Palace and the Wisemen. There are those who date the Book of Job to the period of the Exile and read the trials of Job as a means of struggling with the problems of a fallen Judah. Judah, too, was once powerful and rich (as under David) but gradually all was lost. Whereas it was possible to understand the wicked being punished for their sins, the wisemen knew of those who did live righteous lives. They, too, were suffering. Was God fair in the events of 587/6 and after? In Job 42:5-6, after much struggle to understand, Job confessed, "Then I knew only what others had told me, but now I have seen you with my own eyes. I am ashamed of all that I have said and repent in dust and ashes." Could it be that the wisemen were affirming through Job that in the quest for peace there would be times when easy doctrinal answers do not fit the powerful evidence of present experience? In humility we must learn to accept our finiteness and with it the painful reality of not always understanding. Some things, including peace, are discovered only by experience.

Job's comforters, in pressing him to identify his sin, were the voice of the DEUTERONOMIST solution. Many have dated the final editing of that great collection of literature (Deuteronomy, Joshua, Judges, 1-2 Samuel, 1-2 Kings) to this same period under discussion. The controlling idea in this collection of writings is that God's covenant with the Israelite people is conditional. Their argument was that, in our search for peace, if we break covenant with Yahweh, we should not be surprised that the curses of the covenant will bring punishment, even destruction. The central thrust of the deuteronomist's work is to document how over and over again leaders and people "did what was evil in the eyes of the Lord." Implied in the argument is the assumption that if one identifies and confesses the sin, God in his benevolence will restore the broken relationship. It was this doctrinal solution that Job (the wisemen?) regarded as too easy and pressed God for further answers.

The Prophets. The prophets as a group tended to look to the future for a solution. This needs to be qualified by noting that the prophets were restating the Mosaic theology of a conditional covenant over against the theology of an eternal covenant being developed and nurtured by the royal theologians (priests and kings). Jeremiah reminded those at the temple that saying "peace, peace" when basic covenantal responsibilities were being neglected does not bring peace (Jer 6:14). Most of Jeremiah's ministry was spent tracing the fall of Judah. But toward the end, when others were convinced that all was lost, Jeremiah envisioned a time of restoration. He bought some land. He described a new covenant to be written on the heart rather than simply in those buildings that were so important to the royal theologians.

EZEKIEL was one carried off in the first deportation to Babylon. He, too, spent his early ministry interpreting the fall of Judah. But, in Exile, he envisioned that day when the nation would be resurrected (Ezek 37–39). Consistent with his priestly background and social location among the established leaders of preexilic Judah, his vision of restored Israel included a rebuilt Temple and the restoration of the legitimate priesthood (Ezek 40–48).

The writings of Isaiah 40–55 may reflect the social location of poorer Judahites left back in Palestine during the days of Exile. Their quest for peace and the restoration of Israel focused less on buildings and more on values of peace and JUSTICE. Their images of better times included plenty of food and wealth, security, and lack of fear. All levels of the social order would benefit in the new kingdom. It was Isaiah who perceived God's power to restore peace (*shalom*) and wholeness even in the suffering of his servants (Isa 53:5).

In all of the above traditions, peace involves the establishment of a secure life on this earth, a life marked by sufficient food, clothing, and shelter; by meaningful work and the opportunity for rest from work. Peace in the OT means more than the absence of warfare; it means a life lived in association with family and neighbors that is marked by blessings human and divine.

Among the divine blessings anticipated on the day when God brought peace to the whole world was a renewal of God's own presence among the people and the opportunity to rejoice in that presence. Thus, biblical *shalom* did involve spiritual goods as well as material ones.

In the NT, Jesus appears to have been guided by the Isaianic vision, locating God's redemptive activity among the poor (Luke 4:18). Jesus' vision of peace was inclusive and recognized the healing power of God in suffering. For Christians, Jesus would be the king who fulfilled another of Isaiah's visions: "Of the increase of his government and of peace (*shalom*) there will be no end" (Isa 9:7).

See also HOLY WAR; JUSTICE/JUDGMENT; RECONCILIATION.

—WILLIAM R. MILLAR

• **Pearl.** Pearls were valued highly in the ancient world, and the word became a figure of speech for something of supreme worth. In Judaism the pearl was a metaphor for a valuable saying. The form of Jewish preaching with its use of many Bible verses was compared to a string of pearls, and Job 28:18 states that the price of wisdom is above pearls.

In the NT the pearl is a simile for religious truth and the Kingdom of heaven (Matt 7:6; 13:45-46) and an eschatological motif depicting the glory of the future Jerusalem (Rev 21:21). However, the pearl is also referred to as that which symbolizes worldly values (the great harlot in Rev 17:4) and as inappropriate as an ornament for modest women (1 Tim 2:9).

—VERNON R. MALLOW

• **Pekah.** [pee'kuh] The next to the last king of ISRAEL, ascended to the throne upon his assassination of Pekahiah. Pekah appears to have reigned from about 740 to 732 B.C.E., although he is said to have reigned for twenty years (2 Kgs 15:27). Various explanations have been offered for this discrepancy in the length of his reign. Since Pekah was supported in his rebellion by the people of Gilead, a Transjordan region, it is possible that he had been reigning there for the entire period. Further, since he reversed the pro-Assyrian policies of his two predecessors, it is also possible that he discounted the years of their reigns, claiming that period as his own.

Upon his accession, he immediately instituted an anti-Assyrian policy, joining in a coalition with the Arameans (RSV Syrians) under their king, Rezin. They tried to get AHAZ of Judah to join with them in an attempt to overthrow the Assyrian suzerainty.

When Ahaz of Judah refused to join this coalition, Pekah and Rezin marched against Judah, seeking to depose Ahaz and install their own puppet upon the throne of Judah (735 B.C.E.; Isa 7:1-17; 2 Kgs 16:1-9; this has come to be known as the Syro-Ephraimitic crisis). They were unsuccessful in this effort, however.

In the meantime, King Ahaz had sent tribute to TIGLATH-PILESER III of Assyria, asking for help in overthrowing this coalition. Such help was not long in coming. In 732 B.C.E., the Assyrians defeated the Arameans, seizing some of the territory of Israel. At about the same time Hoshea assassinated Pekah and claimed the throne for himself.

See also ISRAEL.

Bibliography. R. L. Cate, *These Sought a Country: a History of Israel in Old Testament Times*.

—ROBERT L. CATE

• **Pekahiah.** [pek'uh-hi"uh] A personal name meaning "Yahweh has opened [the eyes]." Pekahiah succeeded his father MENAHEM to the throne of Israel and ruled from ca. 738–737 B.C.E. As a result of following his father's pro-Assyrian policies, Pekahiah was assassinated by one of his officers, Pekah ben Remaliah, in the "keep" of the king's castle (2 Kgs 15:25). The assassination may have had the support of Damascus since Pekah and Rezin later formed an alliance against Judah (2 Kgs 15:37; 16:5). The mention of Argob and Arieh in 2 Kgs 15:25 may refer either to conspirators or to victims. But 1 Kgs 4:13, which names Argob as a place, makes it more likely that both Argob and Arieh are place names that have been transposed from names listed in 2 Kgs 15:29.

—LLOYD M. BARRÉ

• **Pentecost.** *See* WEEKS, FESTIVAL OF

• **Penuel.** [peh-ny*oo*'uhl] Also Peniel; in Hebrew it means "Face of God." A city in east Palestine located on the river JABBOK (modern river Zerqa) and commanding the entrance into the Jordan Valley. In Gen 32:24-32, Jacob names the site Penuel, for it is in this place that he witnesses "God face-to-face." During the campaigns of the judges, GIDEON, while pursuing the Midianites, is refused food by the citizens of Penuel. This refusal so angered Gideon that he returned to destroy the town and kill its inhabitants (Judg 8:4-17). Thus, in 1 Kgs 12:25, the writer can claim that JEROBOAM built the city, perhaps in retreat from the invasion of Pharaoh SHISHAK, who probably included Penuel (Pernoual) in his list of conquests. In 1 Chr 4:4 and 8:25, Penuel appears as a personal name rather than as the name of this site.

See also JABBOK; JACOB.

—HENRY L. CARRIGAN, JR.

• **People/Peoples.** Three Heb. words appear in the OT to refer to "people" or "peoples," either as one nation or many: *'am*, usually with the idea of a related unit; *gôy*, people of the world with no special bond of kinship; *lĕ'ōm*, "people" in general and used late for the main part. All three terms may refer to ISRAEL or to gentile nations.

Israel is carefully positioned among the people of the world in the uniquely arranged table of nations in Gen 10. Here more than seventy different ethnic groups are divided along racial lines as descended from Noah's three sons, Shem, Ham, and Japheth. Israel's ancestors came from Shem so that Israel understood itself to be historically and culturally related to other peoples. The world's population was once unified, having one language, but in trying to make a name for themselves they were confused in language and scattered "over the face of all the earth" (Gen 11:8). Immediately, in Gen 11, the genealogy of SHEM is followed to Israel's father ABRAHAM, in whom "all the families of the earth shall bless themselves" (Gen 12:3); thus in the course of time Israel became "as a covenant to the people, a light to the nations" (Isa 42:6).

Frequently in the Bible the identity of the nation Israel is seen vis-à-vis the nations of the world. A coronation prayer for the Israelite king was, "May men bless themselves by him, all nations call him blessed" (Ps 72:17). SOLOMON's prayer at the temple dedication included imploring the Lord to hear at the temple the prayer of "a foreigner who is not of thy people Israel" so that "all the peoples of the earth may know thy name and fear thee" (1 Kgs 8:41, 43). JEREMIAH maintained that if Israel should return to the Lord, "then nations shall bless themselves in him, and in him shall they glory" (4:2). In Second Isaiah a theme similar to that of Isa 45:22 is repeatedly heard: "Turn to me and be saved, all the ends of the earth."

The NT clearly delineates how the promise to Abraham and the mission of Israel are being fulfilled. Jesus' ancestry derived from ADAM himself (Luke 3:38), and Israel's mission to the nations is consummated when "standing before the throne and the Lamb" there appears "a great multitude which no man could number, from every nation, from all tribes and peoples and tongues'' (Rev 7:9).

See also GENTILE/GENTILES IN THE NEW TESTAMENT; GENTILE/GENTILES IN THE OLD TESTAMENT.

—KAREN RANDOLPH JOINES

• **Perea.** [puh-ree'uh] The word Perea is derived from the Greek equivalent of the Heb. phrase ''beyond the Jordan'' (Isa 9:1), and designates the region east of the JORDAN RIVER which was inhabited in OT times by the peoples of MOAB, AMMON, and GILEAD. Perea is used frequently by Josephus to refer to this region, but is never used in the NT which prefers the longer form ''beyond the Jordan'' (cf. Matt 19:1; Mark 10:1).

Perea was part of the larger territory ruled over by HEROD the Great until his death in 4 B.C.E. Following Roman confirmation, both Perea and GALILEE were given to Herod's son, Herod ANTIPAS and remained under his control throughout the time of Jesus. Perea extended from the DEAD SEA in the south nearly as far as Pella in the north. The boundary in the west was the Jordan River and in the east the territory of the Nabataeans (PLATES 47, 54, 55). The district was predominantly Jewish by Jesus time.

In the NT both John the Baptist and Jesus visit the territory of Perea. John baptizes at Bethany, ''beyond the Jordan'' (John 1:28). Both Mark and Matthew suggest that among the crowds which followed Jesus during his early ministry there were many from ''beyond the Jordan'' (Mark 3:7-8; Matt 4:25). Mark and Matthew both report that Jesus and the disciples went into Perea after leaving Galilee for the last time. There for some time Jesus ministered to the large crowds that followed him (Mark 10:1ff.; Matt 19:1ff.).

Bibliography. Y. Aharoni and M. Avi-Yonah, *The Macmillan Bible Atlas,* rev. ed.; G. A. Smith, *The Historical Geography of the Holy Land.*

—CECIL P. STATON, JR.

• **Pergamum.** [puhr'guh-muhm] Pergamum is located some fifteen mi. inland and two mi. north of the Caicus River (PLATE 20). It is situated on a hill some 900 ft. above the river plain. Thus its location is one of the most spectacular of the seven cities mentioned in REVELATION. Pergamum's history can be traced back into the Archaic period. During the height of Persian power, Pergamum was ruled by a Persian viceroy, Congylus. Alexander the Great arrived on the scene in 334 B.C.E. and Pergamum fell under Greek power. Following the death of Alexander in 323 B.C.E., his general Lysimachus took control of Pergamun and western Asia Minor and ruled until his death in 281 B.C.E. Philetaerus took over power and founded the Pergamene monarchy. His adopted son Eumenes (263–241 B.C.E.) reigned following his father and became the country's first King. There followed a 150-year period or golden age for Pergamum from 283–133 B.C.E. The city grew very powerful and wealthy and ruled over that part of the world. It has been called one of the most brilliant cultural centers of the Greek world.

In 133 B.C.E. the last Pergamene king, Attalus III died and willed his kingdom to the Roman empire. The Romans then proclaimed the kingdom of Asia a province and made Pergamum the capital city. The city was allowed its own senate and free elections as well as the power of the sword to decide life and death type sentences. The city was one of the first to practice city zoning. The poorer people were located at the foot of the 900-ft. mountain, the next district was for shops, and the next zone for the rich and their villas. Finally the top of the mountain was crowned with all the public buildings and temples.

One of the most spectacular of the numerous temples was the one dedicated to Zeus. The altar is more than an altar, for it is in reality a large colonnaded building some 18 ft. tall shaped in the form of a horseshoe, spanning an area of 120 by 112 ft. The foot of the altar contains a frieze depicting the war between the gods and the giants. In the 1930s, the altar was removed by German archaeologists and taken to Berlin where it was the main attraction at the newly opened Pergamum museum. Thus today only the base of the altar may be seen on the site at Pergamum.

The library was one of the most prominent public buildings of Pergamum. During the reign of the Pergamene kings, a great love of books was developed. A beautiful library building was erected; it contained a reading room 44 by 52 ft. The library contained some two hundred thousand volumes at the time that it was given to Cleopatra of Egypt. During the reign of Eumenes II, the leaders of the city developed treated animal skins as a writing material, parchment. Our word PARCHMENT comes from the word Pergamum.

Another outstanding public building was the Asclepion located in the valley. The temple building might be called one of the first hospitals in the Greek world. The worshipers believed that the god, Asclepius revealed to the sick the necessary cure through the means of dreams. The sick were taken to a special sleeping chamber where they were given drugged wine and put to bed. Asclepius would then reveal to them their cure. The symbol of the temple were two snakes entertwining around a column. Galen, 130–200 C.E. was a native of Pergamum.

Bibliography. J. Blevins, *Revelation*; F. A. O. Meinardus, *St. John of Patmos*; E. Yamauchi, *The Archeology of New Testament Cities in Western Asia Minor*.

—JAMES L. BLEVINS

• **Perjury.** Deliberate lying on the part of a person who has taken an oath to tell the truth. Perjury was taken quite seriously in the biblical world; the punishment for this crime was severe.

The Decalogue prohibits the bearing of false witness against one's neighbor (Exod 20:16; Deut 5:20). It was also forbidden to swear falsely by God's name, for such an act caused the name to be profaned (Lev 19:12). Jeremiah pointed out the hypocrisy of those who swear falsely and then go into the Temple proclaiming deliverance (Jer 7:9-10).

Since a word backed by an oath had to be accepted as true in matters of interpersonal disputes (Exod 22:10-11), proof to the contrary led to punishment for the individual involved. Lev 6:1-7 says that a person who obtains something by false swearing must restore what was taken plus a fifth of its value and bring a guilt offering to the priest in order to make atonement for the sin committed. Deut 19:16-21 (cf. Exod 23:1) demands that those who falsely accuse others of a crime receive the punishment that they intended for their victims. There was to be no pity for such people; they were to serve as examples to others so that such evil would never again be committed in Israel.

The NT reports that during the trial of Jesus, many false witnesses spoke, but their testimony could not stand because they could not agree on the facts of what took place or what was said (Mark 14:56-59; Matt 26:59-60).

Paul reminded Timothy that the law was given, not for the just, but for the lawless, including those who commit perjury (1 Tim 1:10).

See also LYING; TESTIMONY; WITNESS.

—WILMA ANN BAILEY

• **Persecution in the New Testament.** Political and religious persecution was a reality in the ancient world. The history of the Jewish nation is characterized by persecution in various forms. By the first century C.E. Palestine was occupied by the Romans whose presence had alleviated some forms of oppression but added others. Christianity was born into an atmosphere of oppression and persecution.

Traditionally, those who have addressed the subject of persecution during the NT era have paid careful attention to the official persecutions of Christians under PAUL, HEROD, Nero, Domitian, and Trajan. More recent evaluations of the religious and political atmosphere within the Greco-Roman world have questioned the severity (and sometimes the reality) of such persecutions, especially those of Nero and Domitian. Much of the evidence of oppression during NT times comes from Christian writings; very little corroborating evidence can be found in non-Christian sources. Religious persecution of Christians was a reality, however, and took both official and unofficial forms.

The narratives of the NT portray early conflict between Christians and the Jewish authorities. Jesus' conflict with the Jewish authorities led to his CRUCIFIXION. The Gospels certainly place the blame for that crucifixion at the feet of the Jews, even though they are also quite clear that the Roman government actually executed Jesus. In Acts, the Jewish persecution of Christianity intensified. Paul is introduced during Stephen's martyrdom (Acts 7:58). Stephen's death inaugurated a systematic oppression of Palestinian Christians, and Paul led the fight to stamp out "the Way" (Acts 8:1).

Acts also narrates the official persecution of Christian leaders in Jerusalem by Herod Agrippa (Acts 12:1-5). Peter was imprisoned; James was executed. Herod may well have been acting on his own, though he imprisoned Peter because he wanted to please the Jews, which implies some Jewish influence in the ongoing official persecution of Christians (Acts 12:3). The fourth Gospel also indicates that Christians had been forced out of the synagogues, a less drastic, but every bit as official, form of religious persecution (John 9).

Acts is less clear about official Roman persecution of Christians elsewhere in the empire. That Christians were affected by Claudius's edict which expelled Jews from Rome in 49 C.E. is very possible (Acts 18:2). This persecution should not be construed as official persecution of Christians. Claudius's edict concerned the Jewish inhabitants of Rome; persons such as Aquila and Priscilla were forced to leave Rome because they were Jewish, not because they were Christian. Acts seems to have gone to great lengths to argue for a harmonious relationship between the government and the church. This apologetic purpose seems to have been aimed as much at convincing the church that the government was helpful to the Christian mission as it was aimed at convincing the government that the church could be trusted to uphold the laws of society.

Ecclesiastical tradition has long claimed that the martyrdom of Peter and Paul in Rome took place during a period of intense persecution of Christians by Nero. The Roman historian Tacitus also mentioned Nero's persecution of Roman Christians following the fire of 64 C.E. Quite likely the Christian population of Rome, not well received in Roman society because of its dislike of the Roman lifestyle, was used by Nero as a scapegoat. Nero was himself blamed for the fire which left many homeless; perhaps he blamed the fire on the Christians to quell the rumors of his own guilt. This persecution was probably limited to the area of Rome itself.

Many have proposed an official persecution during the reign of Domitian (cf. *1 Clem* 1). Such a proposal is usually part of the solution to the dating of the Book of Revelation. Once again, the historical evidence indicates a more local persecution which resulted in the imprisonment of John, rather than an organized pogrom against believers in the empire. In fact, the clearest record of any official persecution of Christians for their faith came during the reign of Trajan (98–117 C.E.), as both the Christian bishop IGNATIUS of Antioch and a Roman official (Pliny the Younger) wrote about an official attempt to discourage the practice of Christianity.

More common was an unofficial type of persecution (Heb 10:32ff.; 1 Pet 3:13ff.). The exclusive nature of Christianity invited problems with the surrounding society. Christians increasingly found themselves in conflict with the Jewish community, as the church desired or was forced to establish a separate identity from the synagogue. Anti-semitism was a first-century reality, and often the survival of the church outside of Palestine demanded such separation. Christians were also reluctant to become involved in the social activities of Greco-Roman cities, many of which had strong pagan religious overtones. For that reason, they were considered antisocial, a charge which could very easily be construed as anti-civil as well.

Another subtle form of unofficial persecution was economic deprivation. In a world which boasted of upward social and economic mobility, many Christians were unable to succeed economically because of the political and religious nature of business. All aspects of Greco-Roman social life were strongly connected to pagan worship practices. In addition, the Christians considered coins which bore the image of the emperor to be idolatrous; therefore, engaging in commerce was often difficult. Furthermore, refusal to worship according to the imperial cult separated Christians from society and earned them the distrust of other citizens who were vitally concerned with the imperial religion which was woven into the fabric of the empire.

The persecutions of Christians by Jewish and Roman officials have been the focus of much scholarly attention. While one can see evidence of such persecution, one must admit the relative lack of proof that such persecutions were pervasive. First-century persecution of Christianity was often unofficial, and the NT Epistles stress the need for Christians to maintain their reputation as valuable members of society, even in the face of such persecution.

See also ANTI-JUDAISM IN THE NEW TESTAMENT; CRUCIFIXION; HEROD; PAUL; PETER, LETTERS OF; RELIGIONS, HELLENISTIC AND ROMAN.

Bibliography. F. W. Beare, "Persecution," *IDB*; A. Y. Collins, *Crisis and Catharsis: The Power of the Apocalypse*; J. H. Elliott, *A Home for the Homeless: A Sociological Exegesis of 1 Peter*; B. Reicke, *The New Testament Era*; P. W. Walaskay, *"And So We Came to Rome": The Political Perspective of St. Luke*.

—STEVEN SHEELEY

• **Persecution in the Old Testament.** "Persecution" comes from verbs in Hebrew and Greek, both of which basically mean to pursue. The pursued felt persecuted by pursuers. Common uses of the Greek and Hebrew verbs implied pursuit to inflict harm.

Whether pursuit was, indeed, persecution depended on the point of view of the pursuer or the pursued. Not all pursuit was persecution. Persecutors believed themselves to be preservers of truth or initiators of reform; recipients of their harm believed them to be oppressors. Oppression was directed toward those faithful to a cause to make them change or to destroy their cause. It was a systematic effort to put down or eliminate a cause by social pressure, even to the point of using violence.

Jesus perceived persecution in the OT as a constant element in Israel's history. He spoke of "the blood of all the prophets" and of "the blood of Abel to the blood of Zechariah" (Luke 11:50-51), also saying, "For men so persecuted the prophets who were before you" (Matt 5:12).

Three major eras of persecution in the OT are prominent. The first was that of the Egyptians against the Hebrews. The cause was fear: "The people of Israel are too many and too mighty for us," the Pharaoh said (Exod 1:9), so "they set taskmasters over them to afflict them with heavy burdens" (v. 10). "The people of Israel groaned under their bondage . . . and God heard their groaning" (2:23-24). With Moses' help, God delivered the Israelite people from that oppression.

A second era of suffering was in the days of the judges. Most of it was brought on by the Israelites themselves: "And the people of Israel did what was evil in the sight of the Lord . . . and he gave them over to plunderers" (Judg 2:11, 14). Yet "the Lord raised up judges, who saved them out of the power of those who plundered them" (v. 16).

The third era was during the prophets and the events leading up to the Exile. Jeremiah was the prime example. He was put in stocks (20:2), confined (32:2), beaten and imprisoned (37:15), and put in a cistern to die (38:6). He prayed, "Take vengeance for me on my persecutors" (15:15). Jerusalem was invaded by the Babylonians; "her pursuers [persecutors?] have all overtaken her in the midst of her distress" (Lam 1:3). Even God was blamed: "Thou hast wrapped thyself with anger and pursued [persecuted?] us, slaying without pity" (3:43).

A strong belief foundational to the OT understanding of persecution was that God was in charge. God was asked to judge persecutors (Ps 119:84) and would punish persecutors (Deut 30:7). Only God could and would deliver the persecuted from their persecution (Pss 31:15; 142:6).

Another era of persecution against Jews arose in the later pre-Christian period. It reached its worst with the oppression of Antiochus IV (Ephiphanes). He tried to force Hellenism onto the Jews; their resistance for religious reasons resulted in severe persecution. Judas Maccabaeus led them to independence and relief from oppression.

See also PERSECUTION IN THE NEW TESTAMENT.

—D. C. MARTIN

• **Persepolis.** [puhr-sep'uh-lis] The impressive site of Persepolis was a ceremonial city built by DARIUS, king of the PERSIAN EMPIRE in the late-sixth century B.C.E. It was one of several royal residences in this period of Persia's history. Other residential cities were SUSA, Babylon, and Ectabana. It is known that Persepolis existed under Persian domination from the time of Darius I to Darius III, who was the last of Achaemenian kings. The campaign of Alexander the Great overcame Babylonia, Susa, and Persepolis. Persepolis, which was destroyed by fire in 330 B.C.E., continued to exist under Seleucid and Parthian rule.

Persepolis is located approximately fifty km. North of modern day Shiraz (PLATE 16), which serves as a hub for tourist travel in the Southwest Iranian area. The ancient site was originally called Parsa during the Achaemenian rule; the Greek name was Persepolis, while the current Iranian name of the ruins is Takhti-i Jamshid, which means "the throne of Jamshid."

The ruins of Persepolis indicate a magnificence of planning and design that would have very few equivalents in its time. The primary features of the complex include: a tremendous terrace with drainage and water channels pre-cut into the foundations; the Apadana, the meeting hall of Darius, which probably was finished by Xerxes; the massive staircase of the Apadana lined by murals chiseled in the stone; and the Hall of one hundred columns, the throne room of Xerxes. The importance of Persepolis is demonstrated by the splendor of the ruins; however, Persepolis fell short of being the primary site of administrative and economic concentration. For these functions, Susa was the more important city.

—MARK W. GREGORY

• **Persian Empire.** [puhr'zhuhn] The Persian empire at its height encompassed a considerable domain. From the Greek Isles, to the mighty Egypt, to western India—all fell under its sway. From where did this people, the Persians, come, and how did this aristocratic and far-reaching government develop?

The origin of the Persian people may be found in the introduction of two groups of people into the ancient Iranian plateau, which is found in the middle of important crossroads from the Near East and Central Asia to India and Asia Minor. The settling of this area cannot be dated with certainty but apparently occurred sometime in the eleventh century B.C.E. The infiltration of groups of nomadic people spawned the future first-millennium peoples. Two groups became the precursors of the Medes and the Persians.

By the ninth century B.C.E., there are cuneiform tablets that refer to peoples known as the *Parsua* and the *Mada*, Persians and Medes. While these references give an indication of separate peoples, apparently these groups were not completely stabilized. There are indications that especially the Persian group was still migratory. Eventually the Persian group settled in the area known in antiquity as Pars. This area is located northeast of the Persian Gulf in southwest Iran.

Persia's birth into a unified people found fruition under the leadership of Achaemenes, ca. 700 B.C.E. With this ruler the formation of a dynasty was introduced that eventually brought Persia to its highest stages. Under the leadership of Achaemenes and his successors, Persian territory expanded to include Anshan and other western areas. Indeed, it was from the Elamite capital of Anshan that a Persian ruler revolted against Astyages, who was the Median overlord. With this revolt of Cyrus II in 549 B.C.E., Persia began its zenith years. This properly began the Achaemenian dynasty.

Cyrus II, who ruled from 559–530 B.C.E., greatly expanded the Persian empire in the West. Assyria, Cilicia, and Sardis all fell under Persian domination. Cyrus now controlled the area from the Persian Gulf to the Aegean Sea. The Babylonian empire, which may have originally assisted Cyrus II in his revolt against Astyages, now would become a victim of his greatly increasing power. In 539 B.C.E., the Babylonian empire fell under the conquest of Cyrus. Apparently the Babylonian empire under the rule of Nabonidus and his son Belshazzar had rapidly disintegrated. They had undercut their religious and political foundations. The Persians and the Babylonians fought at Opis on the Tigris River, with the Persian victory here, the city Babylon soon fell without a struggle. It is said that disgruntled Babylonians aided in the overthrow. Regardless, it is this conquest that provides the impetus for the historic return of the Hebrew people from the Exile. Cyrus, rather than continuing the practice of dislocation of captured peoples actually allowed those peoples to return to their homelands. The edict of Cyrus is found in Ezra 1:1-4, where the testimony includes a pronouncement that God himself had given Cyrus all the kingdoms of the earth, and that a house of the Lord should be rebuilt in Jerusalem. Thus the prophecy of Isaiah was fulfilled that the exiled people of God would return to Jerusalem. Cyrus II, a non-Israelite, was used by God to effect this restoration.

An archaeological account has been recovered that gives similar information. From the "Cyrus Cylinder," a cylindrical cuneiform inscription, credit for the victory of Cyrus is given to the Babylonian god Marduk who supposedly ordained Cyrus to his task. The cylinder tells of the humane efforts of Cyrus; not only did he return the Israelites to their homeland, but also other peoples were allowed to relocate and take their gods with them. This quite unusual behavior began a dynasty that would last for two centuries, and would only experience demise with the coming of Alexander the Great.

Cyrus died in 530 B.C.E. and was succeeded by his son Cambyses II. Cambyses continued the expansion plan of his father. He conquered Egypt, Cyprus, and the Greek islands, but stopped at Nubia (PLATE 16). While these campaigns were in progress, unrest developed at home. An impostor, Gaumata, posing as the dead brother of Cambyses tried to take advantage of Cambyses' absence. Revolts occurred in Media, Armenia, and Babylonia. Gaumata's rule, however, was short lived; it lasted approximately six months. Cambyses, aware of the unrest, began the return to Babylon. Records indicate that he died en route while in Syria; it has been ascertained that he committed suicide. He was succeeded by DARIUS I in 522 B.C.E. Darius captured and killed Gaumata and shortly thereafter in the royal city of Ecbatana was pronounced king. Within a short period of time Darius had regained control of the empire. Administration under Darius was well organized and beneficial to the empire. He began building programs and even instituted the building of the temple in Jerusalem. Ezra 6 records the search for the Cyrus decree which indicated that the house of the Lord in Jerusalem should be rebuilt. Then according to the word of Darius, the building should commence.

Darius's achievements are demonstrated in his efficient rule over the empire. He developed a system of twenty satrapies, which divided the kingdom into manageable portions. The center of the empire, however, was not a separate satrap, and was not included in taxation. It had a favorable position. On the other provinces taxation was standardized so that the relative wealth of each satrap could be tapped. A coin system was established which assisted in the taxation process and which also greatly enhanced trade. In addition, he sent special envoys throughout the empire to watch over his interests. He likewise structured an hierarchial system of the military so that all separate military forces from each satrap were directly responsible to him. Other important features from this period include the enhancement of the road system. In particular, from Sardis to Susa, 111 post stations were formed to promote rapid journey. Major roads were patrolled to make them safe, and an imperial courier system was developed to make possible rapid communication from one side of the empire to the other. The building program begun by Darius was extensive. Royal cities were built at SUSA, Ecbatana, and PERSEPOLIS. A channel connecting the lower Nile to the Red Sea was completed. It is evident that Persia had come into its own. Darius ruled from 522 to 486 B.C.E. The successors of Darius were only able to maintain the size and prestige of the Persian empire. Persia had reached the peak of its expansion.

Xerxes I reigned following Darius I, from 485 to 465 B.C.E Xerxes is known from the Biblical text in Esther as Ahasuerus. The setting of the Book of Esther is placed in Susa where Xerxes reigned. Xerxes campaigned against the Greeks with some success. However, he was assassinated in 465 B.C.E. and succeeded by his son Artaxerxes.

ARTAXERXES (465–425) quickly asserted authority after the death of his father even though revolts were occurring in Syria and Egypt. He apparently maintained amicable relations with the Hebrew people. He was succeeded by another member of the royal family who reigned as Darius II (423–404). At this time the mountainous peoples of the Armenian and Assyrian ranges began to trouble the empire. Darius II, on the way to battle with them, died in Babylonia. His son Artaxerxes II followed him (404–359 B.C.E.). Artaxerxes II successfully defended his throne against Cyrus the Younger. However, his continual problem was with the Egyptians, who for sixty years remained his nemesis. He was never able to bring Egypt into submission. Artaxerxes III (359–338) resumed the battle against Egypt and met with success only in 343 B.C.E. Artaxerxes III and his son, Arses, were poisoned by Bagoas, his vizier. The last of the Achaemenid dynasty was Darius III (336–330 B.C.E.). Darius III was defeated by Alexander in 330 and shortly thereafter died. The Persian empire, when it had at last regained the massive splendor of its earlier kings, tumbled to its knees.

ALEXANDER the Great had moved through Cappadocia, Cilicia, Syria and down to Egypt, liberating the provinces as he went. From Egypt in 331 B.C.E. he moved northeast into the heart of the Persian empire gaining Susa and Persepolis. Persepolis, which epitomized the Persian civilization was burned in 330 B.C.E. Darius III had planned a last stand but was killed in July 330 B.C.E. by two of his satraps. His successor was quickly subjugated and the Persian empire was at an end.

The grand Persian empire contributed much to the ancient Near East. It is obvious that the coinage system was very influential and that at least in some periods there was a unification of the Near Eastern area that was unrivaled. The influence upon the Palestinian-Syrian area would have been important since that area remained a province of the empire. In addition, the influence of the Persian empire upon the Greek civilization may have been quite significant. There are indications that both in medicine and philosophy Persian thought found some acceptance. It is known that the Persian court contained Greek scientists and physicians. The extent of this influence, however, can be postulated only tenuously.

Two matters remain in discussing the Persian empire: religion and language. The religion of Persia included a variety of deities, even though there were overtones of monotheism. It has been noted that there are some correlations between Iran and India with relation to major deities. The gods Mitra, Varuna, and Indra are known to both religious systems. In Persia a tendency toward monotheism was demonstrated by the elevation of one God, Ahura-mazda. Yet in the teachings of Zarathushtra there are strong indications of a dualistic universe in which "truth" is contrasted with "falsehood." Zarathushtra, a prophet of Persia in the sixth century B.C.E., founded the movement known as Zoroastrianism. His teachings are known from the *Gatha*, which is contained in the *Avesta*, the body of material from which this dualistic philosophy comes. A very important emphasis of these teachings was the free will of mankind to choose between truth and falsehood, good and evil. In the period of the Achaemenian dynasty there was evidently a pantheon of gods, but the issue of what was the official religion of Persia is highly debated. It is evident that Zoroastrianism remained strong, even when there was a later revival of the Mithras cult.

It is known that the religious background of the NT era contained influence from Persian religion. Mithraism found common acceptance in the Roman empire in the early Christian time. This "mystery" religion was dispersed throughout the empire by many soldiers who embraced its tenets. These tenets included rites of baptism and lessons of accountability; Mithraism often came into conflict with the rapidly expanding Christian faith.

With regard to the language system, Old Persian, a syllabic script, became the initial prominent language of the unified Persian empire. It is known that another dialect, Avestan, was used in the composition of certain religious documents. However, with the demands of an expanding and diversified empire, the necessity of an official language such as ARAMAIC became apparent. Therefore official correspondence with provinces was conducted in Aramaic, while the Old Persian script was partially retained for royal inscriptions. In the Common Era, up until approximately 700 C.E., dialects such as Pahlavi, Parthian, and Sogdian were used. Modern Persian developed in the late first millennium and utilized Arabic script.

See also CYRUS; MEDIA/MEDES.

Bibliography. A. Bausani, *The Persians: From Earliest Days to the Twentieth Century*; G. C. Cameron, *History of Early Iran*; A. T. Olmstead, *History of the Persian Empire*.

—MARK W. GREGORY

• **Person of Christ.** *See* JESUS

• **Personification.** *See* LITERATURE, BIBLE AS

• **Pesharim, Qumran.** [koom′rahn-pesh″uhrim] Among the DEAD SEA SCROLLS are continuous commentaries on OT books. Fifteen such commentaries, called *Pesharim*, have been identified. All are fragmentary. Each of the *Pesharim* is extant in a single Hebrew manuscript, giving rise to the suggestion that many, if not all of them, are autographs. The manuscripts date from the second half of the first century B.C.E. to the first half of the first century C.E. The name *Pesharim* is the plural of the Hebrew word *pesher* ("interpretation"), which introduces the section of interpretation following each OT citation.

The commentators believed that the OT books were full of mysteries which were fulfilled in the history of the community. The meaning of these mysteries was hidden until God revealed them to the Teacher of Righteousness and some of his followers; hence, the need for interpretation. The *Pesharim* are therefore filled with enigmatic historical allusions, which probably reflect three periods in the community's history. The first period involved the Teacher of Righteousness, the Man of Lies, and the Wicked Priest. The identification of these figures has been a major controversy in Qumran research. The second period involved the Lion of Wrath, those who seek smooth things, Ephraim and Manasseh, and Demetrius the king of Greece. These passages probably concern the reigns of Alexander Jannaeus (103–76 B.C.E.), Salome Alexandra (76–67 B.C.E.) and Hyrcanus II and Aristobulus II (67–63 B.C.E.). The final period is the time of the Kittim, presumably the Romans.

The Pesharim are thus of distinctive importance, along with the DAMASCUS RULE, in any attempt to reconstruct the history of the Qumran community. In addition, their particular interpretive strategy, found elsewhere among the scrolls (cf. the thematic, or noncontinuous, *pesharim*: *4QFlor* and *11QMelch*), makes a significant contribution to an understanding of Jewish exegetical methods in this period and has striking similarities to the interpretive strategies used by some of the NT writers (e.g., Matthew). Finally, the OT citations in the *Pesharim* make an important contribution to an understanding of the history of the text of the OT prior to the Massoretic Text.

See also DEAD SEA SCROLLS; ESSENES.

Bibliography. W. H. Brownlee, *The Midrash Pesher of Habbakuk*; M. P. Horgan, *Pesharim: Qumran Interpretations of Biblical Books*; G. Vermes, "The Writings of the Qumran Community," in Emil Schürer, *The History of the Jewish People in the Age of Jesus Christ*, rev. ed.

—JOSEPH L. TRAFTON

• **Pestilence.** Pestilence is usually a designation for fatal DISEASE sent by God as punishment upon the unfaithful, sinful, and disobedient. The term for pestilence (Heb. *deber*, Gk. *loimos*) is a general designation for any epidemic disease; whereas the words for PLAGUE (Heb. *maggēpâ, makkâ, nega', negep)*, which seem to be synonyms, refer literally to a "blow," "stroke," or "touch," and by extension mean wounds, hurts, injuries, and torments. Of the ten plagues (Exod 7–12), only the disease on the cattle is labelled a pestilence (*deber*) (Exod 9:15), although Amos 4:10 describes a later pestilence as being "after the manner of Egypt" (RSV). The diseases that are called plagues usually involve bubonic phenomena (cf. 1 Sam 5–6) and so would also technically be pestilences. Whereas plagues are unusual and hence more likely to be viewed as direct strokes of divine judgment, pestilences usually are more typically epidemics of Palestine, such as dysentery, smallpox, typhus, typhoid, and cholera. In the prophets, "sword, FAMINE, pestilence" often occur together (Jer 14:12; 24:10; Ezek 6:11, etc.), suggesting a siege and the diseases of a contaminated water supply. In one passage (Hos 13:14), the KJV and RSV translate *deber* as "plague."

Pestilence was a threat to Pharaoh (Exod 9:15) and both a warning and punishment to the rebellious Israelites in the wilderness (Num 14:12; 16:46; etc.). In his prayer dedicating the Temple, Solomon asked God to remove pestilence when the nation repents (1 Kgs 8:37). The prophetic formula "sword, famine, pestilence" associates pestilences with judgment and sieges, and this formula probably underlies the NT usage in Luke 21:11.

See also DISEASE AND HEALING; PLAGUES.

—JACK WEIR

• **Peter.** The surname Peter appears 155 times in the NT in reference to a disciple of Jesus and means "stone" or "rock." According to Mark 3:16, Luke 6:14, and John 1:42 Jesus himself gave this name to his disciple. The Aramaic equivalent is Cephas which is found only once in the Gospels (John 1:42) and eight times in Galatians and 1 Corinthians (Paul uses the name Peter only in Gal 2:7-8). Peter's Aramaic given name was Symeon (15:14; 2 Pet 1:1); its Gk. equivalent is Simon (fifty times). These figures include the combinations Simon Peter (twenty times) and Simon who is called or named Peter (seven times).

The Aramaic name of Peter's father was Jonah (Matt 16:17), and its Gk. equivalent was John (John 1:42; 21:15-17). John 1:44 says that Peter's home was in BETHSAIDA, whereas Matt 8:14, Mark 1:29, and Luke 4:38 indicate that he had a home in CAPERNAUM. The two villages were only a few miles apart near the Sea of Galilee. He and his brother ANDREW were fishermen by trade (Mark 1:16). He was married and evidently took his wife with him at church expense during some of his missionary travels (Matt 8:14; Mark 1:30; Luke 4:38; 1 Cor 9:5). His brother Andrew was a follower of JOHN THE BAPTIST before he began to follow Jesus (John 1:35-42), and it is probable that Peter was also. Acts 4:13 does not indicate that he was illiterate, only that he did not have rabbinical training. His native language was Aramaic, but as a native of "Galilee of the gentiles" he could certainly speak Greek.

The Gospels, Acts, and Pauline Letters picture Peter as the leader of the apostles. His name heads each of the lists of the apostles (Matt 10:2; Mark 3:16; Luke 6:14; Acts 1:13). He was one of the so-called inner circle of the apostles (e.g., Mark 5:37; 9:2; 13:3; 14:33). He was their spokesman and representative (e.g., Mark 9:5; 10:28; 11:21; 14:29).

There is, however, some difference in emphasis among the sources. Mark's description is often uncomplimentary, the most notable instances being 8:33 where Jesus calls Peter "Satan" and perhaps 14:71 where the meaning may be that Peter invoked a curse on Jesus rather than himself. Luke omits both of these. Matthew includes the curse but omits the characterization of Peter as Satan. Indeed, Matthew exalts Peter more than any other NT writer, especially in connection with Peter's confession of Jesus at CAESAREA PHILIPPI not only as the Messiah but as the Son of the living God (16:16). The promise of Jesus to build his church on Peter and/or his confession and similar confessions is unparalleled.

In addition to omitting most of Mark's derogatory statements, Luke honors Peter by his unique accounts of the miraculous catch of fish (5:1-11), Jesus' prayer for Peter (22:31-32), and a resurrection appearance to Peter (24:34). Moreover in the first half of Acts Peter is the leading character without a trace of criticism. Peter is the most frequently mentioned disciple in John's Gospel, but in terms of significance he takes second place to the BELOVED DISCIPLE. The latter is the disciple who most closely follows Jesus and is the model for others. In the Pauline Letters Peter is acknowledged as a leader of the Jerusalem church (Gal 2:7, 9), a source of information about Jesus (if that is the meaning of Gal 1:18), the apostle to the Jews (Gal 2:7-8), and the subject of a resurrection appearance (1 Cor 15:5), but he is also rebuked for wavering about accepting gentile Christians as equals (Gal 2:11-14).

For about a decade Peter was the leader of the Jerusalem church. Then he became an itinerant evangelist in Palestine (Acts 9:32; 11:18). At this point JAMES the brother of Jesus assumed the leadership. Acts 12:17 would seem to imply that James was already the leader when Peter was forced to flee for his life in 44 C.E. Certainly James was the leader when the Jerusalem Council met (Acts 15). About that time Peter was at Antioch (Gal 2:11). First Cor 1:12, 3:22, and 9:5 may indicate that Peter came to Corinth. First Pet 1:1 may indicate that he ministered in Asia Minor and 5:13 that he came to Rome (Babylon is almost certainly a code name for Rome). Of his other movements the NT mentions nothing.

Two NT books claim to have been written by Peter. The authorship of 2 Peter was disputed in the early church, and that of both is disputed by contemporary scholars.

Early Christian tradition confirms the implication of 1 Pet 5:13 that the apostle went to Rome; it also claims that he founded the church there, served as its first bishop, and died a martyr's death during the persecution of Nero in 64 or 65 C.E. (cf. John 21:18-19; 2 Pet 1:14-15). Some of the sources give Paul an equal role in founding the church, which is certainly false (there was already a church in Rome when Paul wrote to it, and at that time he had never visited the city). The claim of Peter founding the church and serving as its first bishop may be questionable, but there is nothing improbable about the claim that he died as a martyr in Rome.

A part of the early Christian tradition is the APOCRYPHAL LITERATURE which was falsely ascribed to Peter. This includes the *Preaching of Peter* (KERYGMA PETROU),the APOCALYPSE OF PETER, the GOSPEL OF PETER and the ACTS OF PETER.

See also ANDREW; ANTIOCH; APOCRYPHAL LITERATURE; CAPERNAUM; GALATIANS, LETTER TO THE; KERYGMA PETROU; PETER AND THE TWELVE APOSTLES, ACTS OF; PETER, ACTS OF; PETER, ACT OF (BG); PETER, APOCALYPSE OF (ANT); PETER, APOCALYPSE OF (NH); PETER, GOSPEL OF; PETER, LETTER OF TO PHILIP; PETER, LETTERS OF; TWELVE, THE.

Bibliography. R. E. Brown, et al., *Peter in the New Testament;* F. F. Bruce, *Peter, Stephen, James, and John;* D. W. O'Connor, *Peter in Rome;* O. Cullman, *Peter: Disciple-Apostle-Martyr*.

—JAMES A. BROOKS

• **Peter and the Twelve Apostles, Acts of.** The first tractate (*AcPet12*) in Codex VI of the Coptic Library of NAG HAMMADI is a hitherto unknown story about the apostle PETER, ten other disciples (not twelve as the title wrongly asserts), and Jesus Christ in the postresurrection but preascension period. The story, which has literary similarity to early Christian APOCRYPHAL ACTS of the apostles from the second and early third centuries C.E., is based on two allegories: Jesus as a foreign pearl merchant and Jesus as a physician who heals souls. The writing emphasizes, in Encratitic fashion, the need of disciples to renounce possessions, become poor, and avoid rich men who can lead the faithful astray. This is understood as proper preparation of disciples for their apostolic ministry.

The story may be divided into four parts. In the first (1.1–2.10), Peter tells how the disciples, fulfilling the Lord's commission, set sail in a ship and landed at a strange island city named "Habitation." In part two (2.10–5.18), as Peter is going to inquire about lodgings, he meets a pearl merchant (actually Jesus in disguise); the two greet each other as "brother and friend." Peter next observes responses to the merchant's efforts to sell his pearls: those of the rich (sceptical and rejecting) and those of the poor (interested and inquiring). After acknowledging the poor cannot afford to buy a pearl, the merchant indicates he will give them one for nothing if they will come with him to his city (the "the journey of faith"). Peter also learns from the merchant that his name is "Lithargoel," that is, "the light, gazelle-like stone'' (i.e., ''a pearl'').

Part three (5.19–8.11) deals with the journey of Peter and friends to the ''City of Nine Gates,'' dwelling place of Lithargoel. The disciples are told to avoid ''robbers and wild beasts'' on the journey by renouncing possessions and by fasting. The disciples journey to the city of Lithargoel and arrive in joy and peace. Finally, in part four (8.11–12.19), the disciples meet Lithargoel coming out of the city disguised as a physician. He reveals he is actually Jesus Christ (9.1-19). The disciples worship him and pledge again to do his will. The Lord-physician gives them medicine and commands them to return to Habitation to teach believers and give the poor what they need to live, that is, the ''name'' of Christ, the most precious knowledge. Then, Jesus commands the disciples, as ''physicians of the soul,'' to ''heal the heart.'' He also exhorts them to avoid showing partiality to the rich and afterward departs.

Debate continues over whether this tractate is Gnostic. Some identify the tractate with an ascetically-inclined Petrine school of GNOSTICISM and note its similarities of content to the Gnostic LETTER OF PETER TO PHILIP. Others, observing that *AcPet 12* appears in a codex whose other writings are not Gnostic, lacks distinctive Gnostic teachings, and is typical of Christian apocryphal acts of the second century, hold it to be non-Gnostic. Its provenance is unknown, as is its authorship.

See also GNOSTICISM; NAG HAMMADI; PETER, LETTER OF, TO PHILIP.

Bibliography. D. M. Parrot and R. McL. Wilson, ''The Acts of Peter and the Twelve Apostles,'' *The Nag Hammadi Library in English*, ed. J. M. Robinson; P. Perkins, *The Gnostic Dialogue*; R. McL. Wilson and D. M. Parrott, ''The Acts of Peter and the Twelve Apostles: VI.*1*: 1.1–12.22,'' *Nag Hammadi Codices of V, 2–5 and VI. with Papyrus Berolinensis 8502, 1 and 4*, ed. D. M. Parrott (*NHS* 11).

—MALCOLM L. PEEL

• **Peter, Acts of.** The *Acts of Peter* (*ActsPet*) is an apocryphal work written in Greek around the second or third century. Like most apocryphal works, authorship and the point of origin remain obscure. No internal or external evidence reveals the identity of the author. Because of the social setting within the book, however, Asia Minor has been suggested as a likely geographical point of origin.

For the early churches the *Acts of Peter* was a widely circulated work. Its popularity was based in part upon the reputation of the apostle PETER whose allegedly supernatural deeds it reports. After the Nicene Council of 787, however, its use waned in most of the churches because of official sanction against it.

Several Greek fragments of this work survive and the complete *Acts* is found in a sixth or seventh century Latin manuscript, the *Actus Vercellenses*. The work is a composition which connects several different episodes in the life of Peter. The one major feature which serves to bond the separate episodes into a coherent narrative is the miraculous deeds allegedly performed by Peter.

Among the various legendary traditions which this apocryphal *Acts* ascribes to Peter are the healing of the blind, a temporary healing of his paralyzed daughter, and the restoring of life to the dead. A major portion of this work is devoted to the contest and final denouement between Peter and SIMON MAGUS in Rome. This particular challenge and riposte episode supplements the encounter between Peter and Simon in the canonical Acts of the Apostles (8:9-24). The *Acts of Peter* climaxes with a martyrdom scene in which the apostle gives up his life. His Roman crucifixion is reminiscent of Jesus' crucifixion in the Gospels with the exception that Peter is executed on a cross in an upside down position.

Several prominent teaching features are implicit in an analysis of the *Acts*. For example, the work conveys a paradigmatic image of the struggle between God and SATAN. This dualistic struggle is illustrated by their respective representatives, Peter and Simon Magus. The power which Simon wields is used to perform miracles with which he could mislead people. In the final contest with Peter, Simon is shown to have powers which are subordinate to the spokesperson of God. In any dualistic struggle with agents of evil, the power of God as displayed by his messenger is always superior.

Another teaching emphasis is a concern over sexual morals, particularly refraining from sexual relationships, even those within marriage. This Encratic emphasis in Peter's preaching is portrayed by the author as the one element which ultimately leads to Peter's execution, since the concubines of AGRIPPA began practicing sexual abstinence on account of Peter's message.

The *Acts* functions not as a detailed theological treatise concerning specific doctrines, but as a form of entertainment and vivid uncomplicated teaching. The author arranged and worked with the legendary traditions about Peter in order to promote proper sexual behavior and extol the power of God. The purpose, therefore, of the *Acts of Peter* is to present the social environment of the day as one which needs to be approached cautiously and without compromise.

See also APOCRYPHAL ACTS.

Bibliography. H. Koester, ''The Miracle-Working Apostles in Conflict with the World: The *Acts of Paul* and the *Acts of Peter*,'' *History and Literature of Early Christianity*; W. Schneemelcher, ''The Acts of Peter,'' *New Testament Apocrypha*, ed. E. Hennecke and W. Schneemelcher; R. F. Stoops, Jr., ''Patronage in the Acts of Peter'' *Semeia* 38 (1986): 91-100.

—DAVID M. MAY

• **Peter, Act of (BG).** The *Act of Peter* (*ActPet*) is a short story about the chief apostle and his paralytic, virginal daughter. Surviving only in a Coptic translation of the original Greek text, it is the fourth writing in Papyrus Berolinensis 8502, a codex acquired in Cairo in 1896 for the Berlin Museum. Subsequent study has convinced most that *ActPet* was originally part of the missing introductory portion of the apocryphal ACTS OF PETER now preserved in a Latin manuscript.

The APOCRYPHAL ACTS (e.g., the ACTS OF JOHN, Peter, PAUL, ANDREW, THOMAS) were excluded from the NT canon. Their original popularity was due to their capacity to entertain, instruct, morally edify. Rather than theological discussion, however, such *Acts* focused on miraculous acts and marvels of all description. Such is the case with *ActPet,* whose heroine, Peter's daughter, is miraculously stricken with an infirmity that both preserves her chastity and simultaneously converts to faith her would-be rapist.

The story unfolds at Peter's home in Jerusalem where he is healing the sick on a Sabbath. One in the crowd boldly questions why Peter has healed many but has neglected to cure the paralysis crippling his God-fearing daughter who lies nearby. To persuade those present of God's power to overcome evil, Peter in Jesus' name commands the girl to arise. She does, walks to her father, and thereby elicits praise of God. Then Peter commands her to return to her place, and she relapses into her paralytic state. Claiming this reversal "beneficial," Peter then offers an explanation throughout most of the remaining text.

He states that when the daughter was only ten, her great beauty attracted the amorous advances of many and especially a rich man named Ptolemy. Having his many proposals for marriage declined, Ptolemy apparently abducted Peter's daughter. The apostle's prayer for her, however, resulted in her being stricken with paralysis before Ptolemy could have intercourse with her. As a result, Peter's daughter was preserved from "defilement, [and] pollution, and [destruction]" (135.12-14). Ptolemy, blinded from grief, contemplated suicide. A divine light, however, led him to Peter's house where he regained his sight and converted to faith in Christ (135.17–138.10). Thereafter he lived in chastity, did good for many, and died leaving some land to Peter's daughter. The land was sold, and all proceeds were give the poor (138.12–139.17). Thus, says Peter, God providentially cares for his own. At the end, the apostle gives bread to the crowd and enters his house.

The text is not Gnostic but has Encratite tendencies. The Encratites were second and third-century Christians whose extreme asceticism led to their condemnation as heretical. They rejected wine, meat, and often marriage—especially extolling chastity and sexual purity. Since the *Acts of Peter* (of which *ActPet* is a part) was used by the author of the apocryphal *Acts of Paul* and since the latter was cited by Tertullian ca. 190 C.E., the text can be dated as early as 180–190 C.E. It may have been composed in Asia Minor or Rome, though no certainty on this matter is possible.

See also APOCRYPHAL ACTS.

Bibliography. J. Brashler and D. M. Parrott, "The Act of Peter (BG,4: 128,1–141,7): Introduction and Translation," *Nag Hammadi Codices V,2–5 and VI, with Papyrus Berolinensis 8502,1 and 4,* ed. D. M. Parrott (*NHS* 9), and "The Act of Peter (BG 8502, 4)," *The Nag Hammadi Library in English,* ed. J. M. Robinson; W. Schneemelcher, "The Act of Peter," *New Testament Apocrypha,* ed. E. Hennecke and W. Schneemelcher.

—MALCOLM L. PEEL

• **Peter, Apocalypse of (ANT).** The *Apocalypse of Peter* is an apocryphal work which reports the words of Jesus to his disciples regarding two events: the destruction of the present age and the fate of sinners and hypocrites as well as the righteous. In the first section the destructive judgment of God comes upon the cosmos by fire. The last section, however, concerns the ultimate fate of humanity after death. A disproportionate amount of space is devoted to the fate of sinners and hypocrites in a place of punishment (HELL), while there is only a brief account of the righteous in the place of bliss (HEAVEN).

This work is the oldest of all the apocryphal apocalypses dating from the early part of the second century. It is probably also the most significant of all the apocryphal apocalypses since it served as a model for later apocalypses such as those of Paul and Thomas. In the second century, this work was popular with many in the churches, as is illustrated by its inclusion within the MURATORIAN CANON (200 C.E.). Even as late as the fifth century, the *Apocalypse of Peter* continued to be read in some churches on Good Friday. It has survived today in both Greek and Ethiopic manuscripts. It is to be distinguished from a Coptic work of the same name found at NAG HAMMADI.

The *Apocalypse*'s description of the place of punishment, hell, is one in which the eternal punishment fits the earthly crime. Blasphemers are hung by their tongues, murderers are placed in a pit with venomous snakes, those who charged excessive interest are placed in blood and boiling mire up to their knees, and those who procured abortions are forced to stand in excrement which reaches their throats. A full range of punishments are prescribed for a variety of disobedient social groups: children who dishonor their parents, disobedient slaves, sorcerers and sorceresses, and unmarried women who have lost their virginity.

The *Apocalypse* played a significant role in the early Christian world by providing a vivid didactic lesson on the punishments one might experience. It functioned as a pointed reminder to any who might contemplate straying from the prescribed Christian pattern of life about the consequences their actions might entail. A recurring theme is that those who experienced pleasure in their earthly life will experience pain in the afterlife. The converse is true for those who experienced pain in this world.

The *Apocalypse* also functioned as a catharsis for those readers who in life might suffer at the hands of corrupt lenders, liars, abusive parents, or others. Some, such as aborted children and the victims of murder, would be allowed to participate in or watch the torment of their earthly antagonists.

The *Apocalypse of Peter* is significant because it reveals how the early Christian community conceptualized hell and heaven. It also illustrates the different strata of sins which the early community considered particularly offensive. The influence of the images portrayed in the *Apocalypse* goes beyond the immediacy of the early Christian centuries. For example, Dante Alighiere drew many of his pictures of punishment for the *Inferno* from the images described in the *Apocalypse of Peter*.

See also APOCALYPTIC LITERATURE; HELL; PAUL, APOCALYPSE OF (ANT); THOMAS, APOCALYPSE OF.

Bibliography. R. James, "The Recovery of the Apocalypse of Peter," *CQR* 159 (1915): 1-36; M. Himmelfarb, *Tours of Hell: An Apocalyptic Form in Jewish and Christian Literature;* C. Maurer, "Apocalypse of Peter," *New Testament Apocrypha,* E. Hennecke and W. Schneemelcher.

—DAVID M. MAY

• **Peter, Apocalypse of (NH).** The Coptic *Apocalypse of Peter* from Codex VII of the NAG HAMMADI documents, has no relation to a previously known APOCALYPSE OF PETER extant in Ethiopic and partially in Greek. Like all the Nag Hammadi tractates, it is assumed that this *Apocalypse of Peter* was composed in Greek and translated into Coptic. Like other Gnostic apocalypses, this document is a revelation discourse with only the barest narrative framework. Its content is a revelation granted to PETER and interpreted by Jesus, the Savior. It clearly belongs to a time when lines between orthodoxy and heresy were sharply drawn and the institutions of the orthodox church established. For this reason it is dated to the third century, making it among the latest of the Nag Hammadi documents. Alexandria has been suggested as its provenance.

The scene is the Temple, where the Savior pronounces blessings on those who belong to the Father and summons Peter to become perfect, a foundation for the "remnant" whom he has called to knowledge (*gnosis*). Peter fears for his life on seeing priests and people rushing up to kill them, but the Savior reassures him that they are blind, with no guide. A great light descends on the Savior, who then interprets what Peter is seeing and hearing. A series of prophecies ensues in which the writer, speaking of events in the past, has Jesus predict the fragmentation of early Christianity into various groups opposing the writer's own gnostic community. Some of these prophecies clearly refer to the orthodox church; others may refer to competing Gnostic groups. Particularly, bishops and deacons (in orthodoxy) are singled out as dry canals, falsely claiming divine authority. All these other groups are imitation fellowships—counterfeits.

Peter then has a vision of Jesus seized and crucified, but laughing. The Savior explains that a fleshly substitute is actually being fixed to the tree, while the living Jesus laughs. Another vision ensues in which the laughing Savior is filled with a holy spirit, surrounded by light and angels. This no doubt corresponds to the resurrection of orthodox Christian tradition, but the vision is here interpreted in a gnostic fashion: the living Jesus becomes one with the light and spirit of the intellectual fullness (*pleroma*). Jesus urges courage and faithfulness on Peter, promising to be with him so that no enemy can prevail against him.

The book clearly employs a motif typical of apocalyptic—hope and reassurance for the benefit of a community beset and despised by what had become Christian orthodoxy. The Gnostics are here assured of their divine origin and destiny, as opposed to the counterfeit existence of non-Gnostic mortals. The social setting in which the book was written is thus one of the clearest among all the Gnostic writings. The book rejects the orthodox presentation of martyrdom as of saving value, and explains the suffering of the Gnostics as the perfection of the genuine brotherhood. Only the fleshly can die.

See also APOCALYPTIC LITERATURE; GNOSTICISM; NAG HAMMADI.

Bibliography. J. Brashler and R. Bullard "The Apocalypse of Peter," *The Nag Hammadi Library in English*, ed. J. M. Robinson; S. K. Brown and C. W. Griggs, "The Apocalypse of Peter: Introduction and Translation," *BYUS* 15/2 (1975): 131-45; F. T. Fallon, "The Gnostic Apocalypses," *Semeia* 14 (1979): 123-58.

—ROGER A. BULLARD

• **Peter, Gospel of.** The *Gospel of Peter*, an apocryphal gospel from the second century, was known to various church fathers of the third through fifth centuries. Although they refer to it by name, they do not supply quotations from it. Hence, the text of this "gospel" was unknown until modern times.

Origen (*CMatt* 10.17) affirms that it contained the tradition in which the brothers of Jesus were said to be sons of Joseph by a former marriage. Judging from Origen's remarks, some Christians of his time thought highly of this work.

Eusebius of Caesarea also knew of this gospel, referring to it in two ways: (a) through the writings of Serapion, bishop of Antioch (ca. 190); and (b) through its relationship to the development of the NT CANON.

Eusebius (*EccHist* 6.12.2) quotes from a work by Serapion indicating that some people in the parish of Rhossus in Syria had been led astray by this gospel's heretical notions, which Serapion identified as docetic, i.e., Christ's body was not real, but only appeared so. Serapion apparently found many things in the *Gospel of Peter* which agreed with the canonical gospels, but some additions had been made which, in his estimation, rendered the work unacceptable for Christian use.

Eusebius further states (*EccHist* 3.3.2) that several writings attached to Peter's name, including the *Gospel*, were to be rejected by the church because no church father made use of quotations from them. This is an overstatement regarding some of the writings, but not in respect to the *Gospel of Peter*. In his famous statement on the formation of the NT canon (*EccHist* 3.25.6) Eusebius refers to the works cited and/or written by heretics and includes the *Gospel of Peter*. These "fictional" works, said Eusebius, were to be cast out since they were not in accord with orthodoxy.

Jerome (*DeVir* 1) also denounced the *Gospel of Peter* as apocryphal, and therefore to be rejected, along with other spurious writings circulating under Peter's name.

Finally among the early witnesses, Theodoret (*Haer* 2.2) indicated that a book by the same title was used by the Nazareans, "who regard Christ as a righteous man." He probably meant by such a statement that the *Gospel of Peter* presented a docetic view of Christ.

It was not until 1886–87 that an eighth-ninth century fragment identified with the *Gospel of Peter* was found in a monk's tomb at Akhmim in Upper Egypt. The fragment is part of the passion narrative beginning with Jesus' trial before Herod and Pilate and culminating with the resurrection. Since the fragment had ornaments at the beginning and end of the text, the copyist has indicated that he knew nothing of a more extensive text. Unfortunately, this does not allow us to judge Origen's statements regarding the brothers of Jesus, or to judge whether the *Gospel of Peter* was originally as full a gospel as the canonical models.

The fragment has several unique features: Joseph of Arimathea begs the body of Jesus from Pilate before the crucifixion but PILATE must beg it from HEROD, who has sentenced Jesus to death (vv. 3-5). Jesus' only word from the cross is "My power, O power, thou hast forsaken me!" (19; resulting from changing the Hebrew/Aramaic aleph-lamedh-yodh, אלי, "my God" to aleph-yodh-lamedh-yodh, אילי, "my power"?). Pilate appointed a certain Petronius to guard the tomb (31). Petronius and some Jewish elders and scribes who had come to the tomb (38), were witnesses of the resurrection; what they saw was two men descending from heaven and entering the tomb. Three exited, two supporting the third, and the cross followed. A voice from heaven asked if "Thou hast preached to them that sleep," and the cross answered in the affirmative (39-42). The end of the resurrection narrative reflects Mark 16:8, the women fleeing from the tomb in fear (57). The narrative then concludes with the disciples, Peter, Andrew, and Levi, going fishing (60), as in John 21, although there is not much of that account intact in the fragment.

The fragment does not clearly reveal a Gnostic theology, although its peculiarities could be understood from Gnostic preconceptions. It does, however, have a strong anti-Jewish flavor in that the Jews, the elders and the priests perceive the great evil which they did to themselves in the crucifixion; also it is stated that the soldiers were commanded to say nothing of the resurrection lest they fall into the hands of the Jews and be stoned.

Its docetic tendencies are quite subtle. While on the cross Jesus held his peace "as if he felt no pain" (10). It may also be that his cry from the cross was interpreted in a docetic way. Was "my power" for "my God" an innocent variant reading of the semitic consonantal text, or an intentional misreading to support a theological position? It is not clear.

Its author(s) certainly had a knowledge of the canonical fourfold Gospel tradition, as well as John 21, usually viewed as an addendum to John. Maurer is certainly correct when he says that what distinguishes the *Gospel of Peter* from the NT Gospels is its ''massive apologetic reasoning.'' Ocular testimony is preferred to the testimony of belief (Hennecke-Schneemelcher I, 181). All of this demonstrates that the *Gospel of Peter* was a product of a community which had to stake out claims for the uniqueness of Jesus in striking ways, moving away from the reticence of the gospel narratives toward the realm of the magical and the fantastic.

The *Gospel of Peter* enjoyed a substantial influence in Syria, as noted above by Serapion, and where it, or the traditions it represented, were taken up, directly or indirectly, by the Syrian *Didascalia,* The *Teaching of the Apostles*. Strecker has noted ''surprising agreements'' between the two works: Herod, rather than Pilate, had Jesus crucified; Pilate was exonerated in the condemnation of Jesus; the resurrection was dated on the night preceding Sunday; and fasting was emphasized during holy week.

Based on the witness of Serapion and the evidence linking the *Didascalia* and the *Gospel of Peter,* it is reasonable to believe that the *Gospel* was produced in Syria in the second century. Also, if the conjecture regarding the confusion between ''my God'' and ''my power'' is correct, Syria is a likely area in which such an interpretation might reasonably have taken place.

See also APOCRYPHAL GOSPELS; NAZAREANS, GOSPEL OF THE.

Bibliography. W. Bauer, *Orthodoxy and Heresy in Earliest Christianity*; P. Gardiner-Smith, ''The Gospel of Peter,'' *JTS* 27 (1926): 255ff. and ''The Date of the Gospel of Peter,'' *JTS* 27 (1926) 401ff.; E. Hennecke and W. Schneemelcher, eds., *New Testament Apocrypha*; J. Quasten, *Patrology*.

—GLENN A. KOCH

• **Peter, Letter of, to Philip.** The *Letter of Peter to Philip* is a Christian Gnostic text from the NAG HAMMADI library. Only part of the text is in letter form. That part constitutes less than twenty lines at the beginning of the text. Following the letter is a revelation discourse, a genre of literature developed by Gnostics in which Jesus appears after the resurrection and instructs his disciples. In this revelation discourse, Jesus summarizes Gnostic teaching concerning the deficiency of the aeons, his own mission, and the struggle between his followers and the ''powers.'' After the discourse, the text records conversation among the apostles, their preaching and healing activities in Jerusalem, and further appearances of Jesus.

In the letter, PETER asks PHILIP to come together with the other apostles in order to locate themselves for preaching the gospel. Philip had been separate from the others and unwilling to come together (a possible reference to Acts 8:1-8), but in response to Peter's request, which is made ''according to the orders of our God, Jesus,'' Philip joyfully complies. The matter of ''locating'' themselves is not mentioned again until the conclusion when the apostles separate ''into four words in order to preach,'' a possible reference to the four Gospels or to geographic regions. This is one indication of some kind of tension between persons, groups, or traditions represented by ''Peter'' and ''Philip'' that the author resolves in favor of ''Peter.'' In the content of the writing there are other indications that the author's historical setting was one of conflict. The apostles pray for strength because ''men seek after us to kill us.'' The hostile powers fight with the ''inner man'' and are to be combatted by coming together and teaching. And a central concern of the text is the necessity of suffering.

The *Letter of Peter to Philip* is part of a large body of Petrine literature, both canonical and apocryphal, produced by early Christian circles. Other such Gnostic writings reflect a similar situation of controversy over the status of Peter. The emerging orthodox church had a strong hold on Peter traditions. Peter is often painted as an opponent of Gnosticism and a champion of orthodoxy, both in patristic and Gnostic sources (e.g., *GosMary, GosThom, PistS*). But in the *Letter of Peter to Philip,* Peter is portrayed as a true Gnostic, thus giving apostolic authority to the author's understanding of the Christian message. Of course, the genre of revelation discourse provides the ultimate sanction for the author's message by placing it in the mouth of the risen Jesus. And in this case, the chain of tradition is traced back to the earthly Jesus, because the risen Jesus states at several points that he is only repeating what he already taught in his embodied state, ''because of your unbelief.'' Moreover, it is stressed that the revelations are given to the whole gathering of apostles, rather than to a few. These emphases may be a response to patristic criticism that Gnostics taught new and private material.

The author of the *Letter of Peter to Philip* is clearly familiar with the NT, especially Luke-Acts. He does not quote passages literally, but alludes to them often: e.g., ''It is necessary that they bring you to synagogues and governors so that you shall suffer''; ''Peace to you all and everyone who believes in my name''; '' . . . let your prayer be known. And he, the Father, will help you.'' The prologue of John's Gospel may be in the background of one passage (136.16–137.4). The literary model for the *Letter of Peter to Philip* comes from the *Acts* genre and derives many narrative details from the opening chapters of the canonical Acts of the Apostles: the disciples gather together, receive a revelation from the risen Christ who then ascends into heaven, they go to Jerusalem to preach and heal, and then separate from each other to preach at the command of the Lord. Peter even preaches a type of ''Pentecost sermon.''

The *Letter of Peter to Philip* provides one glimpse of Gnostic Christology. Jesus is the light from the Father, the illuminator, who was sent down into the world of darkness and was crucified. But Jesus was ''a stranger to this suffering.'' Those who hearken to Jesus' call are given authority and become themselves ''illuminators in the midst of dead men.''

The original Greek version of the *Letter of Peter to Philip* probably dates from the late second or early third century.

See also GNOSTICISM; NAG HAMMADI.

Bibliography. G. P. Luttikhuizen, ''The Letter of Peter to Philip, and the New Testament,'' *Nag Hammadi and Gnosis* ed. R. McL. Wilson (*NHS*, 14); M. W. Meyer, *The Letter of Peter to Philip*; D. M. Parrott, ''Gnostic and Orthodox Disciples in the Second and Third Centuries,'' *Nag Hammadi, Gnosticism, and Early Christianity,* ed. C. W. Hedrick and R. Hodgson, Jr.; P. Perkins, *The Gnostic Dialogue*; C. M. Tuckett, *Nag Hammadi and the Gospel Tradition: Synoptic Tradition in the Nag Hammadi Library*; F. Wisse, ''The Letter of Peter to Philip,'' *The Nag Hammadi Library in English,* ed. J. M. Robinson.

—CAROL D. C. HOWARD

• OUTLINE OF FIRST PETER •

The First Letter of Peter

I. Opening and Greeting (1:1-2)
II. Blessing (1:3-12)
III. Exhortation to Holy Living (1:13–2:10)
IV. Social Code for Christian Households and Encouragement for Suffering Believers (2:11–4:11)
  A. Preamble to the social code (2:11-12)
  B. Social code for Christian households (2:13–3:7)
  C. Conclusion to the social code (3:8-12)
  D. Guidance for Christians who suffer for the faith (3:13–4:6)
  E. Summary exhortation and doxology (4:7-11)
V. Encouragement in the Face of Suffering (4:12-19)
VI. Exhortation to Constancy under Suffering (5:1-11)
VII. Epistolary Conclusion (5:12-14)

• **Peter, Letters of.** The Petrine Letters—1 and 2 Peter—are two of seven NT letters known as Catholic or General Letters (the others are James, 1, 2, 3 John, and Jude), so designated because they are addressed not to any single church or recipient, but to the larger Christian community, and thus valuable for the universal (catholic) church. The Letters are important as evidences of early Christian history and theology.

First Peter. First Peter was apparently known and used by the church in the East earlier than in the West. It was quoted by Polycarp in his *Letter to the Philippians* (ca. 135), accredited to PETER by Papias (first quarter of the second century) and Irenaeus (ca. 185), and used freely by Clement of Alexandria (ca. 200). In the West, it was omitted from the MURATORIAN CANON (the Christian scriptures accepted by the church at Rome about 180–190) and first appeared as accepted scripture in the writings of Tertullian (ca. 200–210). This is all the more striking, as much scholarship cites Rome as the place where the Epistle was written.

The author identifies himself as "Peter, apostle of Jesus Christ" (1:1) and a "fellow elder and witness of the sufferings of Christ" (5:1). Traditionally, this has been taken as a certification that the Letter came from Jesus' first disciple. Most modern scholars hold that the real author used Peter as a pseudonym. The style of the work is very literary, with traces of rhetorical expertise, deliberate rhythm and artistry, and a familiarity with the LXX, hardly from Peter (who was "illiterate" or "uneducated," according to Acts 4:13). Whether the linguistic elegance derives from Silvanus (SILAS), the scribe of the Letter (5:12), is unresolvable. The Letter has Pauline traits: the use of "in Christ" (3:16; 5:10, 14), the view of Jesus' death as a ransom (1:18-19), and the use of a social code (2:13–3:7) similar to those in Colossians and Ephesians. This is in tension with the report of the intense theological differences between Paul and Peter given in Gal 2. First Peter lacks any evidence of first-hand knowledge of Jesus, no mention of his life, ministry, teachings, no parables, no miracles, not even echoes of his striking proverbs. The phrase "witness of the sufferings of Christ" is so general that it might be said by anyone for whom the passion of Jesus was his/her personally redeeming experience. Finally, the persecutions described in 1 Peter appear to be general and official, such as those inflicted on Christians under Domitian, well after Peter's death.

If Peter wrote this Epistle, it should be dated about 64. Those who consider it to be from another author (or even from a Petrine school) date it late in the first century, about 90–95. Crucial to the question of dating the Letter is the reference in 4:16 to their suffering as Christians. From the earliest days of the church Christians were subject to abuse and suffering for their faith; however, widespread and legally sanctioned persecution of Christians as Christians began only under Domitian in the 90s.

The Letter mentions as its place of origin "Babylon" (5:13), a first-century symbol for Rome in apocalyptic literature (cf. Rev 14:8; 16:19). Early church tradition maintains that Peter went to Rome, served, and died there. The parallels between 1 Peter and *1 Clement* (the letter of the bishop of Rome to the Corinthians about 96) show a possible Roman connection. And the greetings extended from "Mark" (5:13) also strengthen the proposal that 1 Peter came from Rome (Mark was with Paul in Rome: Col 4:10; Phlm 24).

The readers are addressed as "exiles of the Dispersion in Pontus, Galatia, Cappadocia, Asia, and Bithynia" (1:1), Christians dwelling in the more northern part of Asia Minor. Nevertheless, the exhortation to holiness and steadfastness under persecution, the reminder of the great hope laid up for God's people, and the encouragement to center one's life in Christ apply to Christians everywhere. The writer also addressed the readers as "exiles," chosen, destined, and sanctified, a description of who they were, not where they were. As God's people, this world for them was an alien place, because their home was with God. Consequently, they were encouraged to fortitude during their temporary sojourn or exile (cf. 1:17; 2:11).

The recipients were, in all likelihood, gentiles. They were called on to avoid "the passions of [their] former ignorance" (1:14), reminded that they were "ransomed from [their] futile ways inherited from [their] fathers" (1:18) and called "out of darkness into his marvelous light. Once . . . no people but now . . . God's people" (2:9-10), and reminded that joining in with what gentiles do was a thing of the past (4:3-6).

First Peter addresses two crises: temptation and persecution. The pagan society in which the readers lived posed a constant threat. Many religions, cultures, and cults were active and attractive. The Christian community survived by its close fellowship (Christ is here portrayed as shepherd and the church as a flock, 5:2-4). Moral perils at hand were to be avoided: passions of ignorance (1:14); futile ways (1:18); malice, guile, insincerity, envy, slander (2:1); passions of the flesh (2:11); evil (2:16); superficial and showy adornment (3:3); reviling (3:9); licentiousness, passions, drunkenness, reveling, carousing, lawless idolatry, wild profligacy (4:3-4); murder, theft, wrong-doing, mischief-making (4:15). The writer exhorts the exiles by pointing to Jesus as redeemer and spotless example, and by calling them to respond to Christ with resolute conviction (2:24).

While persecution appears to be a focus throughout the Letter, in 1:1–4:11 persecution is only potential; but, from 4:12 on, it is real. While 1:6 says "you may have to suffer," and 3:14 "even if you do suffer," beginning with 4:12 the language shifts to "you share Christ's sufferings" (4:13), "let those who suffer . . . " (4:19). The danger they faced was intense. They were in peril of losing their well-being and their lives. That may be concluded fairly by the intense exhortation given and by the author's use of the example of Christ's suffering and death as their model.

By means of sermonic material (1:3–4:11) and admonitions (4:12–5:11), this Epistle aims to exhort the readers to be steadfast in God's grace (5:12), in the face of persecution, temptation, alienation, and social oppression. The readers are encouraged to be constant both for the sake of their witness for Christ and for the future hope for what they would receive (an imperishable, undefiled, unfading inheritance; the salvation of their souls; God's approval; and his blessing: things hoped for which are kept in heaven for those who suffer and persevere for Christ).

A striking feature of 1 Peter is its theology and ethics. Suffering is viewed as a testing, purifying experience, to be met with humility and love. A social code (2:13–3:7, a feature which early Christians adopted from Stoic philosophers) instructs in correct living within given social roles. The writer starts from a point of radical eschatological hope when he offers his ethical guidelines: "the end of all things is at hand" (4:7). Irrespective of that starting point, it is quite problematic to modern readers that he calls for submission to all governmental powers and for slaves to be patient about being beaten (using Christ's passion as example), that he calls women "the weaker sex" and gives proscriptions against immoderate female attire, that his advice to husbands fosters patronizing, sexist roles, that he teaches a doctrine of Jesus' preaching in the world of the dead to people who died in Noah's day, and that his remarks about baptism are extremely sacramental. Apart from those factors, 1 Peter contains some of the richest expressions of Christian hope and piety in the NT. Its exhortation is consistent in putting Christ as the focus of Christian living, duty, and hope.

• OUTLINE OF SECOND PETER •

The Second Letter of Peter

I. Opening and Greeting (1:1-2)
II. Exhortation to Holy Living (1:3-11)
III. Reminder of the Inspired Tradition Guaranteed by Apostolic Testimony and the Sacred Hope Given by Inspired Prophets (1:12-21)
IV. Warning about and Execration of False Teachers (2:1-22)
V. Exhortation on the Parousia and the Apocalypse (3:1-13)
VI. Concluding Exhortation to Holiness and Steadfastness (3:14-18)

Second Peter. Probably the latest work in the NT to be written, 2 Peter was also the latest to be accepted as a part of the Christian Bible. It was not used by the apostolic fathers, not quoted by the church fathers until 250 (by Firmilian of Caesarea), not accepted by Eusebius, and questioned by Jerome, Erasmus, and Calvin. Its inclusion in the church canons cannot be dated with confidence before the late fourth century and in Syria before the sixth century. This is surprising to the general reader, since the author names himself "Simeon Peter" "an apostle" (1:1), claims to have been present at the transfiguration (1:17-19), and links this writing with 1 Peter (3:1). The church fathers were unconvinced of these claims to authority.

Many factors prevent most modern scholars from accepting 2 Peter's claim to be from Jesus' first disciple. First, the work is a Jewish-Greek writing which makes an artificial effort at imitating Hellenistic authors. The style is a mixture of Hebraisms and secular Hellenistic traits. It uses a Hebrew-affected style of grammar and identifies the author with the strangely Hebraizing spelling "Simeon." There is also an apparent use of terms used in Hellenistic religions ("divine power" 1:3; "godliness" 1:3, 6, 7; "knowledge" 1:2, 3, 8; 2:20; "divine nature" 1:4; "self-control" 1:6; "eye-witnesses" 1:16; "corruption" 1:4; 2:12, 19; "brotherly affection" 1:7. Such a Hellenistic inclination is contrary to all we know of Peter from the Gospels and Acts.

Second, there is an almost unquestionable use of Jude as a source by the writer. Both writings address the PAROUSIA as a matter of teaching, and attack false teachers. Even more important is the high degree of similarity between the two in specific subject matter, choice of vocabulary, and even the order of ideas. Evident throughout the works, this is especially clear in 2 Pet 2:1-19 and Jude 4:16, where false teachers are described and OT allusions are drawn in exactly the same way by both writers. Since Jude was almost certainly written after Peter's death and 2 Peter after the Letter of Jude, 2 Peter could not have come from Simon Peter. Moreover, it is inconceivable that the first disciple, the first to address Jesus as "Christ," the rock on which the church would be built, this member of the inner circle of disciples, would have to rely on Jude for his message.

Third, this is the only book in the NT that confronts heretical teaching against the parousia. Other writings confront heretical teachings about the parousia, but not teachings that the parousia would not occur. Such a heresy arose in the church during the second century when Gnostics with libertine anti-spiritualism opposed the doctrine of the parousia. The writing, thus, appears to come from a time much later than the lifetime of Peter.

Fourth, the work exhibits aspects of early Catholicism characteristic of the late first and early second centuries. The concept of apostleship held by the writer and the reference to "all [the] letters" of Paul (3:16) as if they were a collected body of works ranked as "scriptures" along with other "scriptures" indicate a time much later than the days of Peter. The "early Catholicism" in evidence here is one of the work's assets as a piece of history. Most scholars consider 2 Peter to be a pseudonymous letter, the latest written NT book, dating perhaps as late as 140–150.

Since authorship is uncertain, no certain place can be designated as its point of origination. In the address, no place-name advises us of its destination either. Such places as Palestine, Egypt, Rome, or Asia Minor have been proposed; but all proposals are guesses.

The purposes of the work are clearer and easier to decipher. The author intends to warn the readers about the heresy of false teachers who make light of Jesus' coming (1:16; 3:3ff.) and to protect them from the immoral ways of those libertines who are in their midst (3:17). The opponents he confronts are not two groups but one. False teaching and immoral living are interrelated.

The writer assails the false teachers who appear to have had a genuine conversion at some point (2:20-22), but who misuse Paul's Letters (3:16) and teach error that probably derived from private or idiosyncratic interpretations (1:20). Such practice amounts to denying Christ (2:1, 20-22). The author's purpose is to stabilize the readers (3:17), so that they will not lose their "entrance into the eternal kingdom of our Lord and Savior Jesus Christ" (1:11). To achieve this, he attacks the ways and teachings of the heretics and also repeats his injunction for the readers to remember their heritage. They are founded on a trustworthy revelation that God promised and gave through inspired prophets, guaranteed through apostolic witness, certified by the work of the Holy Spirit, and will vindicate at the coming of the Lord. He launches an excited assault on the immorality of the heretics. Their assumed freedom is another slavery. Their ways will incur God's wrath. Their final state will be worse than if they had never come to Christ.

Second Peter is significant because of the view it gives us of emerging Catholicism in the second-century church.

It is equally as valuable as evidence for the lively contest the early church engaged in when deciding on what scriptures should be admitted to the canon, based primarily on the standard of apostolic authorship.

See also APOSTLE/APOSTLESHIP; CANON; EPISTLE/LETTER; JUDE, LETTER OF; MURATORIAN CANON; ETHICS IN THE NEW TESTAMENT; PAROUSIA/SECOND COMING; PERSECUTION IN THE NEW TESTAMENT; PETER; SILAS; SUFFERING IN THE NEW TESTAMENT.

Bibliography. E. Best, *1 Peter. New Century Bible Commentary*; J. L. Blevins, "Introduction to 1 Peter," *RE* 79 (1982): 401-13; J. N. D. Kelly, *A Commentary on the Epistles of Peter and Jude*; W. G. Kümmel, *Introduction to the New Testament*; E. G. Selwyn, *The First Epistle of St. Peter*.

—RICHARD A. SPENCER

• **Peter, Preaching of.** *See* KERYGMATA PETROU

• **Petra.** [pe'truh] Petra is fifty mi. south of the Dead Sea. It is in a basin one mi. long and one-half mi. wide. The entrance is from the east through a narrow, twisting gorge that runs 6,000 ft. between two red sandstone cliffs 500 ft. high. Petra was the capital city of Nabataea, the greatest commercial empire of the ancient Near East in NT times.

The NABATAEANS apparently originated in the northwestern Arabian Desert. They began to move into Edom after the fall of Jerusalem to Babylon in the early part of the sixth century B.C.E. as the Edomites migrated into southern Judah and the Negeb or southern Palestine. In 106 C.E. Rome incorporated Petra into the Roman empire. The Crusaders had a fortress at Petra. When it fell to the Muslims near the end of the twelfth century, Petra disappeared from the historical record until its rediscovery in 1812 by a Swiss explorer named Burckhardt. Systematic archaelogical investigations began in 1929.

Petra is a beautiful city, even in ruins. Almost all of its structures have been cut into the red sandstone cliffs. The Khazneh Far'um ("the treasury of the Pharaoh") is most likely the tomb of a Nabataean king. Its facade is 92 ft. wide and 130 ft. high. Its color is marble white in the sunlight, red in the moonlight, and deep mahogany in the shadows. On a ledge 700 ft. high is an open-air sanctuary, a high place, dedicated to Dushura, the chief god of Petra. Steps cut into the rock lead up to this high place. The high place consists of a rectangular court with two altars on one side. One apparently was for burnt offerings and the other for blood libations. There is also a Roman amphitheater with seats carved out of the rock to accommodate 3,000 to 5,000 spectators.

There was a small Christian community in Petra. A Greek inscription (447 C.E.) refers to the consecration of a chapel by the bishop of Petra, who actually lived at Kerak nearby. Christianity continued in the form of monasticism as late as the Crusades.

The Bible does not mention Petra. Yet some identify it with the Edomite city of Sela which Amaziah of Judah captured in the early part of the eighth century B.C.E. (2 Kgs 14:7-10). The fact that Sela in Hebrew and Petra in Greek both mean "rock" makes this identification attractive. Moreover, there is in Petra a huge rock 950 ft. high on whose summit a fortress once stood. Passages in the OT speak of a rock (*sela*) in Edom in a way to suggest the rock fortress in Petra (2 Chr 25:11-12; Jer 49:16-17; Obad 3-4). Pottery evidence, however, shows that the Edomites first occupied this rock fortress considerably later than the reign of Amaziah. Also, the tombs in Petra are all later than the Edomite occupation of the city. Thus the identity of Sela with Petra must be abandoned.

Unlike the OT, the NT does refer to Petra indirectly. King ARETAS IV, who ruled from Petra (9 B.C.E.–40 C.E.), attempted to seize Paul in Damascus shortly after his conversion (2 Cor 11:32-33).

Bibliography. C. M. Bennett, "The Nabateans in Petra," *Arch* 15 (1962): 233-43; P. C. Hammond, "Petra," *ISBE*; A. Kennedy, *Petra, Its History and Monuments*.

—VIRGIL FRY

• **Pharaoh.** [fair'-oh] Pharaoh is the Hebrew form of the Egyptian word "Per-o," which originally meant "the great house." But by the beginning of the Eighteenth Dynasty (sixteenth century B.C.E.), pharaoh was used as a title for the king himself. The pharaohs of Egypt had five official titles, the final two of which preceded the king's most commonly used names which were enclosed in elliptical shaped rings called cartouches. The name following the fourth title, called the *prenomen,* was the pharaoh's throne name and paid honor to the god, Re, as in the names "Neb-maat-Re" or "Menkheperre." The name following the fifth title, the *nomen,* was the personal or family name such as "Ramses," a name popular during the Nineteenth and Twentieth Dynasties. Thus the full name of Thutmose III (ca. 1452–1425 B.C.E.) was: (1) Horus: Mighty Bull, Appearing in Thebes; (2) the Two Ladies: Enduring of Kingship; (3) the Horus of Gold: Splendid of Diadems; (4) the King of Upper and Lower Egypt: Enduring of Form is Re (i.e., "Menkheperre"); (5) the Son of Re: Thoth is Born" (i.e., "Thutmose"). These titles clearly reflect the Egyptian belief that the pharaoh was a god.

As the king of Egypt, the pharaoh had many symbols of his authority including at least five different types of crowns. The *Red Crown* of Lower Egypt (northern Egypt) is known to have existed as early as 3000 B.C.E. and had a flat top with a long extension in the rear. The *White Crown* of Upper Egypt (the southern section of the country extending to the Sudan border), sometimes called the *White Crown of Osiris,* was conical shaped, usually with a knob on the top. This crown too has a long history and appears on king Nar-Mer of the First Dynasty. After the unification of the two kingdoms, in the protodynastic period (3200–2800 B.C.E.), the *Double Crown,* representing both kingdoms, was worn. The *Blue Crown,* made of cloth or leather, was normally worn in battle and was popular during the period of the New Kingdom (ca. 1546–1085). The *nemes,* a royal headcloth, extended down over the shoulders to the breasts. It was worn by both kings and queens as early as the Third Dynasty (ca. 2700–2650). A characteristic motif on many of these crowns is the *uraeus* or coiled cobra. Other symbols of Egyptian royalty include the crook, flail, mace and curved sword or scimitar.

While the pharaoh filled many roles, his main task was the administration of his empire. But the day-to-day responsibilities were delegated to various administrators, in particular, the vizier, who was the highest minister in the bureaucracy. Up to the time of Thutmose III there was only one vizier but this king introduced two, to administer Upper and Lower Egypt respectively. The main responsibility of the vizier was to administer the tributes that came to Egypt from other rulers (cf. the story of Joseph in Genesis).

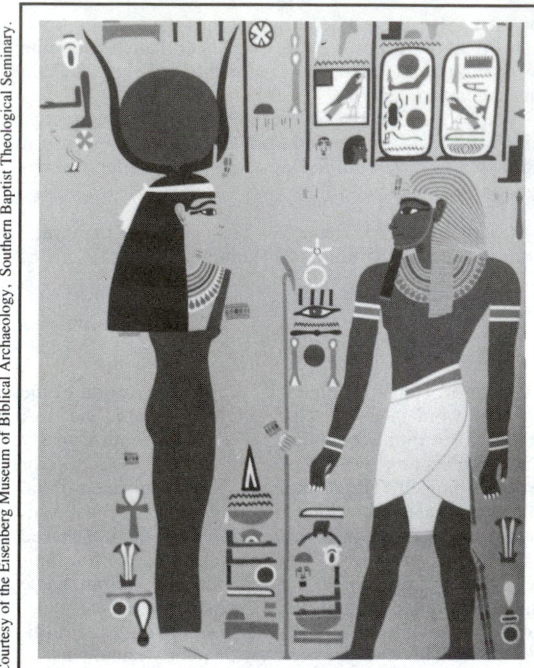

Courtesy of the Eisenberg Museum of Biblical Archaeology, Southern Baptist Theological Seminary.

Painting from the tomb of Pharaoh Horem-Heb.

Even though the word pharaoh occurs many times in the OT, only in four or five instances is the king identified by name:

1. SHISHAK. Sheshonk I (ca. 945–924) was the founder of the Twenty-Second Dynasty. He gave refuge to Jeroboam during the time of Solomon, but captured Jerusalem, raiding the Temple, in the fifth year of the reign of Rehoboam, Solomon's son (1 Kgs 11:24; 14:25-26; 2 Chr 12:1-9). There is speculation that Shishak may also have been Solomon's father-in-law (cf. 1 Kgs 3:1) but this is doubtful.

2. Tirhakah. Called the "king of Ethiopia" (2 Kgs 19:9; Isa 37:9) Tirhakah (Tahaqa, Twenty-Fifth Dynasty, ca. 690–664) is said to have supported Hezekiah of Judah against the Assyrian king, Sennacherib. However, since Tirhakah was not the pharaoh in 701 B.C.E., the usual date given for Sennacherib's attack, the biblical reference may reflect a second, later campaign against Jerusalem by the Assyrian king. On the other hand, another pharaoh may have been involved in the 701 siege. If the former was the case, then the biblical editors have combined two campaigns of Sennacherib into one.

3. NECHO. Necho II (Twenty-Sixth Dynasty, ca. 610–595) is famous for having killed the Judean king, Josiah, in 610/09, when the latter fought him near Megiddo (2 Kgs 23:29; 2 Chr 35:20-24). Necho placed Josiah's son, Jehoiakim, on the throne (2 Kgs 23:30-35; 2 Chr 36:1-4), but suffered defeat at the hands of Nebuchadrezzar at Carchemish in 605 B.C.E. There is also a tradition that claims that Necho tried, unsuccessfully, to dig a canal linking the Nile River with the Red Sea.

4. Hophra. A pharaoh of the Twenty-Sixth Dynasty (ca. 589–570), Hophra urged Zedekiah of Judah to revolt against the Babylonians (Jer 37:5). The prophet Jeremiah said that he would be given into the hands of his enemies just as Zedekiah had been given to Nebuchadrezzar (Jer 44:3). This prophecy was fulfilled when Hophra was forced from his throne in 569 and finally killed in 566.

5. So. Called "the king of Egypt," So is said to be the pharaoh to whom the Israelite king, Hoshea (730–722), appealed for help just prior to the destruction of Israel by Assyria (2 Kgs 17:14). However, since no pharaoh with this name is known from this period, the reference is not clear. Some scholars suggest that Osorkon IV (ca. 727–720) is meant, while others interpret the word as an epithet with the meaning of "Saite," referring to the Saite Dynasty of the seventh-sixth centuries B.C.E. On the other hand, the word in the Hebrew text can be repointed to read "Sive" and may refer to an Egyptian commander.

Other unnamed pharaohs play an important role in the biblical traditions. Included among these are the pharaohs in the stories of Abraham (Gen 12:14-20) and Joseph (Gen 39–50). In addition, the unknown pharaoh during the Hebrew enslavement (Exod 1–2) is often identified with Seti I (ca. 1291–1279) or Ramses II (ca. 1279–1212). Ramses is also most often identified as the pharaoh of the Exodus (Exod 5–12). Other unnamed kings of Egypt include the pharaoh(s) in the story of Hadad of Edom (1 Kgs 11:14-22), and the pharaoh who gave the city of Gezer as a dowry to his daughter when she married Solomon (1 Kgs 3:1; 7:8; 9:16, 24; 11:1). This latter pharaoh is sometimes identified as King Siamun of the Twenty-First Dynasty.

See also EGYPT; NAMES.

Bibliography. J. C. H. Laughlin, "Ancient Crowns," *BI* (Spring 1984): 46-51; J. Pritchard, *ANEP*; G. Steindorff and K. C. Seele, *When Egypt Ruled the East*; J. Wilson *The Culture of Ancient Egypt* and "Egypt," *The Intellectual Adventure of Ancient Man*, by H. Frankfort, Mrs. H. Frankfort, J. Wilson, T. Jacobsen.

—JOHN C. H. LAUGHLIN

• **Pharisees.** [fair'uh-seez] The Pharisees were a Jewish religious party which flourished during the last two centuries B.C.E. and the first Christian century. The primary sources of information about them are the Jewish historian JOSEPHUS, the NT, and RABBINIC LITERATURE. They are not mentioned in the OT or the apocryphal literature, although the *Psalms of Solomon* is often identified as a Pharisaic work. Josephus describes them as one of four Jewish sects—the others being the SADDUCEES, the ESSENES, and the Zealots—and says that there were about 6,000 of them.

Name. The most likely meaning of the name is "separatist." From whom or what the Pharisees were separated, however, is most uncertain. Among the suggestions are the heathen during the time of Ezra and Nehemiah, the Hellenistic compromisers during the period of Seleucid rule, the Maccabeans when the revolt became more political than religious, the common people who did not keep the LAW, and ceremonial uncleanness in general. Inasmuch as the name was probably given them by their enemies, the third suggestion seems to be the most likely.

Less likely explanations of the name include "interpreters" and "Persianizers." The latter implies that they derived some of their ideas from Persian religion.

History. The origin of the Pharisees is obscure. Their spiritual ancestry may go back to the period of the Restoration when under the influence of Ezra the Law became the dominant element in Judaism. As an identifiable party, however, their origin is probably to be traced to the late Maccabean or early Hasmonean period. There is general agreement that they grew out of the Hasidim, who remained faithful to the Law despite the willingness of many Jews to Hellenize and despite the religious persecution of the Seleucid Syrian ruler Antiochus IV. Josephus first mentions them in connection with his description of the time of JONATHAN (161–142 B.C.E.). He describes them as a well-established party during the time of John Hyrcanus (135–104) and relates the beginning of the estrangement between them and the Hasmoneans. The rupture reached its climax in a civil war during the reign of Alexander Janneus (103–76), but their fortunes were restored and their influence reached an all-time high during the reign of his successor Alexandra Salome (76–67). They again fell from favor during the reign of the last of the Hasmonean priest-kings, ARISTOBULUS II (67–63). Except for the last year or two of his reign HEROD the Great (37–4) tolerated them because of their popularity and willingness to stay out of politics. Of their relationships with the Roman governors we have little information. During the first Christian century the Pharisees constituted a significant minority in the SANHEDRIN. Several times Josephus emphasizes their popularity with the masses. Most of them seem to have opposed the revolt against Rome in 66–70 C.E. Although the party as such perished as a result of that revolt, Pharisaic and scribal ideals survived in the Rabbinic Judaism which was formulated at Jamnia during the following decades.

Beliefs and Practices. The Pharisees were middle-class "laymen" who were committed to obeying the Law as it was interpreted by the SCRIBES. The scribes were scholars who were primarily concerned with interpreting and applying the written Law. The purpose of this was to make the Mosaic Law relevant to changing situations. In doing so they produced a tradition constituting a second body of Law, which until the third Christian century existed only in oral form. This oral tradition came to be as important as the written Law—perhaps even more so! The Pharisees therefore were devoted practically more to the legalistic traditions of the scribes than to the biblical Law. This is their most important characteristic, and in this they differed greatly from both the Sadducees and Jesus. Pharisaic legalism and traditionalism are reflected in such passages as Matt 9:14; 15:2; 23; Mark 7:1-5; and Luke 18:11-12.

The Pharisees believed in the work of divine providence in such a way as to take a mediating position between free will (the emphasis of the Sadducees) and determinism (the emphasis of the Essenes). Another Pharisaic distinctive was belief in future life, bodily RESURRECTION, rewards and punishment, and a messianic kingdom. The Sadducees denied all these things. The Pharisees also developed an elaborate concept of angels and demons, something else which distinguished them from the Sadducees. The Pharisaic belief in resurrection and angels is attested in Acts 23:8.

The Pharisees were organized into small brotherhoods or fellowships. They were closely related to the SYNAGOGUE. One could almost say that the synagogue was a Pharisaic institution. They were in no sense a political party; as long as the government permitted them freedom of worship, they were indifferent as to politics.

The Pharisees in the NT. The name appears sixty-eight times in the synoptic Gospels, nineteen in John, nine in Acts, and in Philippians (3:5) where PAUL admits to having been a Pharisee (also Acts 23:6). In the NT the Pharisees are often described as the opponents of Jesus and the early church. Jesus criticized them for substituting their traditions for the revealed will of God, their lack of compassion, their contempt for the common people who could not obey the Law as carefully as they did, and for their failure to practice what they preached. It is important to note that they are also criticized in rabbinic literature. It must not be thought, however, that all Pharisees were hypocrites. Nicodemus and GAMALIEL were Pharisees. The Pharisees of Luke 13:31 helped Jesus. A few became Christians, although some of these tried to hold on to their former religion (Acts 15:5). It is obvious from the above description of beliefs and practices that Christianity has much in common with the Pharisees. Pharisaism represented one of the better elements in first-century Judaism.

See also CLEAN/UNCLEAN; ESSENES; GAMALIEL; JOSEPHUS; LAW IN THE NEW TESTAMENT; LAW IN THE OLD TESTAMENT; MACCABEES, SADDUCEES; SANHEDRIN; SCRIBE IN THE NEW TESTAMENT; SCRIBE IN THE OLD TESTAMENT.

Bibliography. J. Bowker, *Jesus and the Pharisees*; L. Finkelstein, *The Pharisees*; J. Neusner, *From Politics to Piety, the Emergence of Pharisaic Judaism* and *Rabbinic Traditions about the Pharisees before 70*; E. Rivkin, *Hidden Revolution*.

—JAMES A. BROOKS

• **Philadelphia.** [fil'uh-del"fee-uh] One of the seven churches of the Book of Revelation (1:11 and 3:7), Philadelphia was a city in the Roman province of LYDIA in western Asia Minor (PLATES 26, 27). It was located on a plateau at the base of Mount Tmolus in the Cogamis River valley that led west to SARDIS, the ancient capital of Lydia.

Built by Attalus II (159–138 B.C.E.) and named for his brother its strategic setting was one of the reasons for its location. The Pergameme kings needed a good communication route from PERGAMUM through Sardis and Philadelphia on to the south.

In Roman times the city belonged to the district of Sardis, the leading city of Lydia. In the first century it was a stage on the main line of imperial communication coming from Rome by Troas, Pergamum, and Sardis passing through Philadelphia and on to the east. In the larger region, EPHESUS was the great administrative center; Philadelphia along with the other churches of Revelation was a center for postal delivery and for judicial administration. The seven cities were located on the road which led from Ephesus northwards through SMYRNA and Pergamum and then wound southwards through THYATIRA, Sardis, Philadelphia, and LAODICEA, forming a somewhat circular route.

Philadelphia gained renown through a major disaster. In 17 C.E. an unusually strong earthquake destroyed twelve cities in the great Lydian Valley, including Sardis and Philadelphia. The city experienced frequent shocks for some time afterwards causing many inhabitants to remain outside the city, a situation which probably had not disappeared when the Book of Revelation was written.

The city regained its prosperity. It was an important place for coinage especially in the reign of Augustus. Its staple export was wine, its coins showing the head of Dionysos. It also had some industry in textiles and leather, and some part of its prosperity derived from its hot springs. From the time of Caracalla in the early third century the city was called Neokoros ("temple warden") because of its connection with the cult of the emperor. By the fifth century it had developed wealth and become known for its festivals and pagan cults which gained it the name of little Athens.

The church at Philadelphia appears to have been somewhat feeble (Rev 3:8), yet it stands second only to Smyrna in point of merit in the list. There is no hint of heresy within the church, although John warned against disunity and the preaching of the Judaizers, as did Ignatius a few years later. In contrast to the letters that precede and follow in Revelation, the letter to Philadelphia gives neither rebuke nor warning for this church, but simply commendation and exhortation.

Philadelphia's importance increased during Byzantine and medieval times, and during the fourteenth century it stood practically alone against the entire Turkish power as a free, self-governing Christian city amidst a Turkish land, withstanding two sieges, but finally falling in 1391. It is now the modern city of Alashehir and is still to a large extent Christian.

See also EPHESUS; LAODICEA; LYDIA; PERGAMUM; REVELATION, BOOK OF; SARDIS; SMYRNA; THYATIRA.

Bibliography. G. R. Beasley-Murray, "Revelation," *NCB*; J. Finegan, *The Archeology of the New Testament: The Mediterranean World of the Early Christian Apostles*; M. J. Mellink, "Philadelphia," *IDB*; W. M. Ramsay, *The Letters to the Seven Churches of Asia*.

—G. THOMAS HALBROOKS

• OUTLINE OF PHILEMON •

The Letter to Philemon

I. Introduction (1-3)
II. Words of Praise for Philemon (4-7)
III. Appeal for Onesimus (8-22)
IV. Closing Words (23-25)

• Philemon, Letter to. [fi-lee'muhn] Philemon is a Letter of PAUL addressed to Philemon and the church that met in his house. It was written while Paul was in prison, probably at the same time as Colossians (assuming Paul wrote that Letter). Since Paul was imprisoned for a number of years and in at least two places (Caesarea and Rome), Philemon cannot be dated precisely, but is generally placed in the latter part of Paul's ministry. Since ONESIMUS is mentioned in Col 4:9, most commentators assume that Philemon lived in or near COLOSSAE and that Colossians and Philemon were sent simultaneously by the hand of TYCHICUS (Col 4:7) and Onesimus.

Philemon is an intercessory letter, asking Philemon to receive Onesimus, his runaway slave, with clemency. After the salutation, Paul introduces the ideas of "sharing" (v. 6), "comfort" (v. 7), and "refreshment" (v. 7) in his thanksgiving prayer. Since it is typical Pauline strategy to introduce topics in a non-argumentative section that later become the basis of his appeal, readers may anticipate an appeal for Philemon to encourage and refresh Paul in a particular way.

Philemon was within his rights as a slave owner to punish Onesimus in whatever way suited him, and Paul never directly challenges that. Instead, he moves back and forth from his position of authority within the church to the basic equality of Philemon, Onesimus, and Paul under Christ's Lordship. In vv. 8-9, Paul establishes his relationship with Philemon: he has the right to command, but will set that aside for love's sake. He begins his request in v. 10, only to interrupt it with commendations for Onesimus, who is indeed his useful (a pun—the name means "useful") and dearly beloved child. Paul next explains why he sent Onesimus home. Actually, the law required him to do so, but Paul makes a virtue of necessity, again emphasizing subtly his superior status as evangelist.

Vv. 15-16 have led to much of the discussion surrounding Philemon. At the least, these verses are Paul's attempt to see God's providence in Onesimus' escape, since it led to Onesimus' conversion by Paul. However, Knox and more recently Petersen argue that these verses imply that Paul expects Philemon to free Onesimus. Petersen notes that "Paul never calls Onesimus 'your slave,'" so there is nothing to balance the "no longer as a slave, but . . . as a beloved brother . . . both in the flesh (i.e., in the world) and in the Lord (in the Church)." Other interpreters argue that since Paul does not openly ask for manumission of Onesimus, Philemon should be balanced by other Pauline passages that do not question the legitimacy of slavery (Col 3:22-25) and that urge slaves to be content with their present status (1 Cor 7:17-24).

Whatever the answer to this, Paul closes the Letter on an authoritative note. Paul offers to repay Onesimus's damages, but reminds Philemon that he, too, is a debtor to Paul and needs to repay what he owes (vv. 19b-20). Confident of Philemon's obedience, Paul announces a visit in the near future to insure it.

See also COLOSSIANS, LETTER TO THE; ONESIMUS; PAUL; SLAVERY IN THE NEW TESTAMENT.

Bibliography. J. Knox, *Philemon Among the Letters of Paul*; N. Petersen, *Rediscovering Paul: Philemon and the Sociology of Paul's Narrative World*; S. Stowers, *Letter Writing in Greco-Roman Antiquity*.

—RICHARD B. VINSON

• Philip. [fil'ip] The name Philip was borne by two prominent NT personalities: Philip the apostle and Philip the EVANGELIST, also known as Philip the DEACON.

The synoptic Gospels and Acts do not refer to Philip the apostle except in their lists of disciples (Matt 10:3; Mark 3:18; Luke 6:14; Acts 1:13). The Gospel of John indicates that the apostle Philip came from Bethsaida and gives four reports from his life: (1) his long-standing knowledge of Israel's messianic hope and his enthusiasm as a new disciple which are evident in his successful attempt to bring Nathanael to Jesus (1:45-51); (2) his particular role in the feeding of the multitude reported in John 6 and the way in which he responded to Jesus' testing of him; (3) the occasion at which some Greeks wanted to see Jesus (12:20-22) and asked Philip to introduce them to him; and (4) his request made to Jesus in the Passion narrative. As doubt began to trouble the disciples in that narrative, Philip entreated Jesus by saying: "Lord, show us the Father, and we shall be satisfied" (14:8). Jesus gently rebuked him but also answered him by delivering a marvelous homily on the meaning of his presence among them.

Our knowledge of Philip the evangelist comes from the Book of Acts which indicates that Philip was one of THE SEVEN Hellenist leaders (Acts 6). After the martyrdom of STEPHEN, he left Jerusalem and fled to SAMARIA where he started a successful mission later sanctioned by the apostles in Jerusalem (8:14). SIMON MAGUS is said to have been one of his converts (8:13). In the role he played in the conversion of the ETHIOPIAN EUNUCH Philip revealed his unique gift as a prominent evangelist of the early church (8:26-40).

Two decades after the beginning of the mission to the gentiles, Paul was a guest in the home of Philip in Caesarea (Acts 21:8). There, Paul, Philip, and his four daughters who had the gift of prophecy, contemplated together the end of the first stage of the missionary work of the early church. It was then that Paul reflected on the events which would bring his preaching to an end.

A substantial body of apocryphal literature centers around Philip. A Gnostic GOSPEL OF PHILIP was discovered at Chenoboskion in 1946. The *Acts of Philip*, a very late work of the early church reports his martyrdom and crucifixion at Hierapolis. Philip also occupies a prominent place in the *Pistis Sophia*, a Gnostic document of the fourth century.

NT records clearly distinguish between two different Philips: the apostle and the evangelist. Those records are more reliable than later traditions of the church which know of only one Philip with the qualities of both NT personalities. Unfortunately we know nothing more about Philip the apostle than what is reported in the Fourth Gospel. Philip the evangelist seems to have led a much more eventful life with great missionary achievements amidst difficulties and persecutions. According to some traditions, his last Christian duties were as bishop of Tralles before suffering martyrdom at Hierapolis.

See also APOSTLE/APOSTLESHIP; BETHSAIDA; DEACON; DISCIPLE/DISCIPLESHIP; ETHIOPIAN EUNUCH; EVANGELIST; PHILIP, GOSPEL OF; SEVEN, THE; SIMON MAGUS.

Bibliography. E. G. Kraeling, *The Disciples*.

—PAUL CIHOLAS

• **Philip, Gospel of.** Significant for the light it sheds on SACRAMENTS ("mysteries") observed by early Valentinian Gnostic communities is the thirty-five page *Gospel of Philip*, the third tractate of Codex II in the NAG HAMMADI library. Rather than having a literary form similar to the four canonical Gospels, however, the *Gospel of Philip* is an anthology of extracts drawn from different writings. Included are seventeen sayings of Jesus (with several not found in the NT), biblical interpretations, aphorisms, narrative dialogue, defensive statements, and categorical assertions of dogma. Also found are several stories about Jesus, such as that which asserts his father JOSEPH made the very cross of wood on which his son was crucified (73.8-15).

No discernible outline governs the arrangement of excerpts, and abrupt changes in thought and random sequencing predominate. Occasionally, two excerpts are placed together on the basis of a catchword (e.g., "death" or "die" in 52.2-21) or the association of similar ideas (e.g., "bridegroom" and "bridal chamber" in 67.2-27). To bring some order to the whole, scholars have—on the basis of content and style—numbered the excerpts. Lack of agreement over exact divisions of the text, however, has led scholars to prefer to refer to Coptic page and line numbers.

Certain themes reappear throughout. Included are the need to experience spiritual RESURRECTION prior to physical death (56.15-19; 56.26–57.21; 66.7-20; 73.1-7), speculation regarding the meaning of Jesus' names (54.5-15; 56.3-12; 62.6-15; 63.21-24), separation of the sexes (ADAM and EVE) as the source of death and their reunion as life (68.22-24; 70.9-21; 76.6-16).

Especially important is mention of five "mysteries" or "sacraments": "BAPTISM, chrism, Eucharist, ransom, and bridal chamber" (67.27-29). Baptism, by immersion, denotes initiation into the mysteries of Gnostic wisdom and confers IMMORTALITY (61.12-20; 65.25-30; 69.4-26; 73.1-7; 75.21-24; 77.7-14). Chrism, anointing with oil of the olive tree, is even more important than baptism and confers immortality (73.15-19; 74.12-21). Eucharist, reception of the bread and cup, enables the Gnostic to receive "the perfect man" (75.14-21), anticipate union with his "angel image" at death (58.10-14), and receive perfection and ETERNAL LIFE (57.3-8). "Ransom" or "redemption," details of which are not given, is compared to entry into "the holy of the holy" in the Jerusalem TEMPLE. It may denote, as in Marcosian Valentinianism—a final rite for the elect prior to their last ascent to the Pleroma (heavenly Godhead) (52.35–53.13; 69.23-27; 85.21-31). The "Bridal Chamber," the most important sacrament and one uniquely Valentinian occurs in a specially prepared chamber, with accompanying prayers, for those being perfected in "spiritual marriage." Its purpose is to anticipate reunion of the individual's spirit with its angelic counterpart and with the Pleroma at the End of time (67.9-18; 69.14-28; 70.5-9; 74.36–75.2; 81.34–82.26; 86.4-9.)

The author is unknown, though the subscript title of the work attributes it to one of the twelve apostles, PHILIP (86.18-19). The place of composition is also a puzzle, though an interest in etymologies of Syriac words in the text (63.21-23; 56.7-9) has led some to identify it with Syria. One editor (Isenberg) dates it in the latter half of the third century.

See also APOCRYPHAL GOSPELS; GNOSTICISM; NAG HAMMADI.

Bibliography. W. W. Isenberg, "(The Gospel According to Philip) Introduction," *Nag Hammadi Codex II, 2-7, together with XIII, 2 Brit. Lib. Or.4926(1) and P. Oxy. 1, 654, 655*, ed. B. Layton, *NHS* and "The Gospel of Philip," *The Nag Hammadi Library in English*, ed. J. M. Robinson; B. Layton, "The Gospel according to Philip," *The Gnostic Scriptures: A New Translation with Annotations and Introductions*.

—MALCOLM L. PEEL

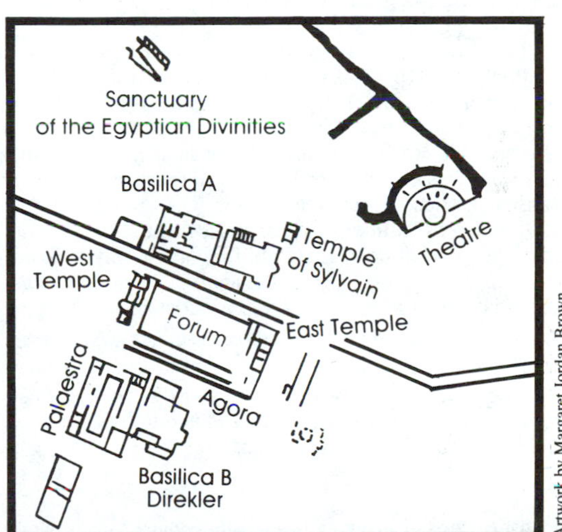

Layout of ancient Philippi.

• **Philippi.** [fi-lip'*i*] Philippi was located on the Gangites River (a tributary of the Strymon) about nine mi. from the Aegean Sea and the port of NEAPOLIS (PLATE 23). The site was originally occupied by settlers who came into MACEDONIA from the island of Thasos and was at first called Krenides which means "fountains." No doubt this name was given because of the many fountains or springs in the vicinity. In its early days Philippi was a very prosperous city due to the gold mines nearby.

In 356 B.C.E. Philip II, king of Macedon and father of ALEXANDER the Great, seized the city and named it Philippi in honor of himself. Philip increased the population by bringing in Greek settlers. When Macedonia was divided into four districts in 167 B.C.E. by the Roman consul Aemilius Paulus, Philippi was placed in the first district, and AMPHIPOLIS became the capital of the district. When the districts were dissolved, the seat of government for all of Macedonia became THESSALONICA. This was the situation in Paul's day.

In 42 B.C.E. a famous battle was fought near Philippi. The combined forces of Octavian and Antony defeated the army of Cassius and Brutus. When the city was taken, Octavian declared Philippi a Roman colony. Some of the soldiers of Octavian and Antony who were about to retire remained in Philippi. This set a precedent because from that time many veterans in the Roman army retired in this city. At first the colony bore the official title *Colonia Julia Philippensis,* but after Octavian was designated Augustus in 27 B.C.E., it was renamed *Colonia Augusta Julia Philippensis.*

The population was made up of Thracians, Greek descendants from the settlers brought in by Philip II, and Romans who were encouraged by Octavian and Antony to settle there. As a Roman colony Philippi had the right to autonomous government, immunity from imperial tribute, and the same privileges as Roman citizens. It was Rome in miniature. The people worshiped many gods and goddesses. The early settlers worshiped the Thracian god Liber Pater and the goddess Bendis. In addition to these deities they had the Greek Athena; the Roman Mars, Jupiter, and emperor cult; the Anatolian Cybele; and the Egyptian Isis and Serapis. Philippi was strategically located astride the Via Egnatia, a vital military and commercial road that stretched across northern Greece from the Aegean to the Adriatic at Corcyra.

On his second missionary journey PAUL preached in Philippi (Acts 16:12-40). LYDIA, a woman from Thyatira, was his first convert. He also exorcised the spirit of Python from a slave girl who was being used by her owners. As a result of this act he and Silas were beaten and thrown into prison. It was here that Paul witnessed to the jailer after an earthquake had shattered the prison. The church that Paul established in Philippi was dear to the heart of the apostle. IGNATIUS of Antioch visited Philippi on his way to Rome to die as a martyr in 107 C.E. Polycarp in the middle of the second century wrote a letter to the Christians in Philippi.

See also LYDIA; MACEDONIA; PAUL; PHILIPPIANS, LETTER TO THE.

Bibliography. J. Finegan, *Light from the Ancient Past;* K. Lake and H. J. Cadbury, *The Beginnings of Christianity,* vol. 4; G. E. Wright, *Biblical Archaelogy.*

—T. C. SMITH

• **Philippians, Letter to the.** [fi-lip'ee-uhnz] PAUL wrote this Letter to the church he had founded at PHILIPPI, a Roman colony in MACEDONIA. The circumstances under which this congregation was established are described in Acts 16:12-40. The warmth of the relationship between apostle and congregation makes this Letter one of the most attractive compositions in all NT literature.

Paul was a prisoner when he wrote (cf. 1:7, 13, 14, 16). The serious nature of this imprisonment is seen from such vv. as 1:20-23, 30, 2:17, and 3:11. These passages suggest that Paul's life was held by a slender thread and that he had no certainty of release. At the same time, his fate is not definitely settled. He believes that, if it is God's will, he will be spared (1:19). One of the main factors in his hope is that his presence is needed by the Philippians, and he looks forward to a return visit to see them (1:24-26). Nonetheless there is a tension in his writing which reflects a perturbed state of mind about his future, even if he knows that his life and death alike are in God's hands (1:20-23).

What prompted him to write? A natural answer would be his desire to tell his friends how he was faring in jail and what expectations he had for the future days. Paul shows this concern to keep in touch with the Philippians in 1:12-14. Evidently there was some misunderstanding about the reason for Paul's imprisonment, and he wished to clear up a possible rumor that he was simply a political prisoner.

In addition, Paul had some special reasons to be grateful to his friends in this church. They had sent gifts to him repeatedly, throughout active ministry (4:10-20), and in the recent past they had commissioned a man named EPAPHRODITUS to bring a gift, presumably of money. Epaphroditus had come with the church's gift and, because of sickness, he had been unable to return to Philippi. Naturally the church members were anxious to know why he had stayed on with Paul. Paul will therefore entrust the Letter to him, and praise him for his service to Christ, which had been costly in terms of his health. At the same time he will say "thank you" to the church for their gifts. (Some scholars think that 4:10-20 which mentions the gift is a separate letter.) Generosity was a mark of this Macedonian congregation (2 Cor 9:1-5).

The Letter is more than an expression of Paul's gratitude. It contains bitter warnings against opponents who are not identified—though they are described. In 3:2 Paul abruptly directs his attention to some people who are bent on destroying his apostolic work. Exactly who these people were is debated. But it seems that they were Jewish

• OUTLINE OF PHILIPPIANS •

The Letter to the Philippians

I. Address and Salutation (1:1-2)
II. Paul's Thanksgiving and Confidence (1:3-7)
III. An Apostolic Prayer (1:8-11).
IV. Paul's Great Ambition and Joy (1:12-26)
  A. Unexpected results of his imprisonment (1:12-14)
  B. Motives—sincere and mixed (1:15-18)
  C. Paul's dilemma, and confidence, in life and death (1:19-26).
V. Exhortation to the Christian Community (1:27–2:18)
  A. Exhortation to unity and courage in the face of alien influences (1:27-30)
  B. Exhortation to harmony and humility in the face of factiousness (2:1-4)
  C. The "Way" of Christ (2:5-11)
  D. Exhortation applied, and the example of Paul (2:12-18)
VI. Future Plans (2:19-30)
  A. The commendation of Timothy (2:19-24)
  B. The commendation of Epaphroditus (2:25-30)
VII. Warnings and Encouragements (3:1-21)
  A. Paul's warning and claim (3:1-3)
  B. Paul's autobiography (3:4-14)
  C. Paul's call for unity in conviction and conduct (3:15-17)
  D. Sectarian teachers to be shunned (3:18-19)
  E. The Christian's true inheritance (3:20-21)
VIII. Encouragements, Appreciations, Greetings (4:1-23)
  A. Encouragements to steadfastness and unity: appreciation of service (4:1-3)
  B. Encouragements to prayer and noblemindedness (4:4-9)
  C. Appreciation of the Philippians' gifts (4:10-20)
  D. Greetings (4:21, 22)
  E. Benediction (4:23)

Christians who dogged the apostle's footsteps and tried to impose a series of Jewish rituals on his gentile congregations. This is the reason why he so vehemently denounces them. (Again, some commentators believe that 3:1b is the beginning of a separate Pauline letter.) After a powerful statement of his understanding of what it means to be a Christian (3:8-14), he returns to sound another warning against opponents. The opponents described in 3:18, 19 are most likely Jewish, and they may be the same as the people described in 3:2. However, several scholars are convinced that these descriptions better fit a body of professed Christians whom the later church called Gnostics. They claimed to possess a religious knowledge of a secret kind which enabled them to treat physical appetites with indulgence and excess. Paul therefore calls them the enemies of the cross (3:18) and exposes what he regards as false teaching and practice.

Inside the life of the Philippian church all was not well. In some way Paul had learned of a spirit of selfishness and dissent (2:1-4, 14) along with quarrelsomeness (4:2). He gently promotes harmony between factious members. Possibly there was a sense of false pride in the achievements of some Christians in Philippi which Paul wanted to correct by stressing the importance of constant progress in the Christian life (3:12-16).

At the time he wrote this Letter Paul's active ministry was restricted, but imprisonment did not mean inactivity. He was able to look beyond the confines of his prison cell to express thanks for those who in their freedom were proclaiming Christ (1:15-18), even though they were motivated by wrong objectives. The verses may mean that they were deliberately antagonizing the Roman authorities by a political version of the gospel message and so compounding Paul's difficulties as a prisoner. This would explain the need for him to stress that he was no political prisoner who was guilty of social crimes or subversive designs.

The passage in 2:6-11, an early HYMN of Christ's acceptance of suffering that led to his exaltation, is inserted to show how God can bring triumph out of obedient devotion to his will. Perhaps a suffering apostle and a persecuted church were so contrary to what some had expected of the Christian life that they were beginning to doubt. Paul must clear up this matter (1:27-30). He does so by showing that loyalty to the gospel often entails such trials as both he and they were facing. But God is in it with them, and he will bring them through. They should not be cowered or give in; he wants to be proud of them even if he has to pay the price of his apostolic service in death (2:14-18).

Hope still burns brightly, and he moves on to make future plans (2:19-24). These plans include the sending of TIMOTHY as his personal messenger and the anticipation that he himself will be able to see them soon. Depending on the place where Paul was a prisoner, we can say that that hope was attained either after his release from imprisonment in Rome at the end of the two years of Acts 18:30 (see the witness of 1 Tim 1:3), or earlier if his detention was in Caesarea (Acts 24:27) or Ephesus (Acts 19:1-41). The last view is attractively presented by several modern scholars who argue that Paul spent some time in an Ephesian jail where his life was threatened (cf. 1 Cor 15:32; 2 Cor 1:8-11). Thereafter he was released, and the narrative in Acts 19:22; 20:1-5 records both the visit to Timothy and the later visit of Paul to Macedonia.

See also GENTILE/GENTILES IN THE NEW TESTAMENT; GNOSTICISM; MACEDONIA; PAUL; PHILIPPI.

Bibliography. F. W. Beare, *A Commentary on the Epistle to the Philippians*; J. F. Collange, *The Epistle of St. Paul to the Philippians*; R. P. Martin, *Philippians*.

—RALPH P. MARTIN

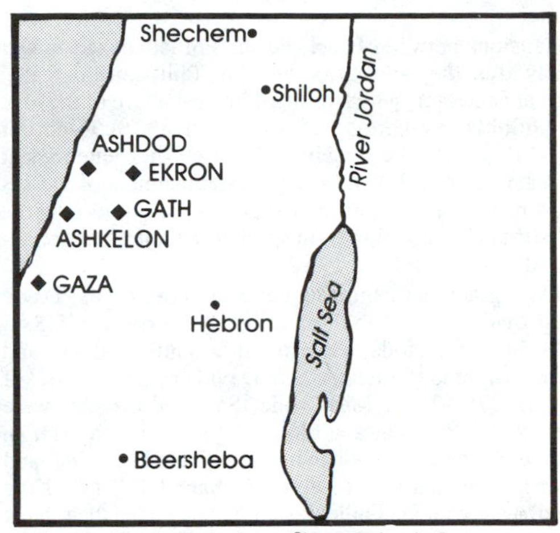

Designed by Margaret Jordan Brown ©Mercer University Press

• **Philistines.** [fi-lis'teenz] A nonsemitic people who migrated to the southeastern Mediterranean from the Aegean basin in the early twelfth century B.C.E., thereby becoming a major rival of Israel. The Philistines' Hebrew name was *pelishtim*, and their conquered territory was called *eretz pelishtim* (''land of the Philistines'') or *pelesheth* (''Philistia''). The name ''Palestine'' is derived from *Palastinoi*, a Greek designation for the Philistines' descendants.

Though it is probable that the Philistines migrated to Egypt and coastal Palestine during a great ethnic upheaval near the close of the thirteenth century B.C.E., a more specific origin remains uncertain. The Philistines were part of the movement involving a number of SEA PEOPLES, including the Tjekker who, along with the Philistines, fought Rameses III ca. 1190 B.C.E. Following an Egyptian victory, many of these Aegean warriors settled along Canaan's southern coast—Philistia. The Bible points to the Philistines' Aegean origin by linking them with Caphtor, which is almost certainly CRETE (Jer 47:4; Amos 9:7; cf. Gen 10:14; Deut 2:23; 1 Chr 1:12).

Most scholars suggest that the use of the term ''Philistines'' in Gen 21:32, 34 and 26:1, 8, 14–18 is anachronistic, since the name does not appear in nonbiblical sources before ca. 1200 B.C.E. It is, of course possible that Aegean peoples had migrated to Canaan at an earlier time and that a biblical editor later applied the ethnic label, Philistine, to them, as in Gen 10:14; Exod 13:17; 23:31; Josh 13:2-3.

The Philistine league of city-states (i.e., GAZA, ASHDOD, ASHKELON, GATH, EKRON) was located along Palestine's southern coast between Gaza and modern Tel Aviv (PLATE 12). This region was agriculturally and commercially rich, but the Philistine expansion into Canaan's interior led to an inevitable conflict with the Israelites, who were expanding into Canaan from the east. Josh 13:2-3 and Judg 3:1-3 say that the Lord used the Philistines ''to test'' Israel; this test consisted of a bitter rivalry that lasted from the mid-twelfth century B.C.E. until ca. 965 B.C.E. (i.e., until King DAVID's victory over the Philistines). The Bible contains numerous references to conflicts between the Israelites and the Philistines, beginning with praise for Shamgar's slaughter of 600 Philistines with an ox goad (Judg 3:31). Among the most famous narratives in the OT is Judg 13–16, the story of Samson and his relations with the Philistines, a passage which also recognizes the importance of strength and military prowess in the Hebrew–Philistine encounter.

Tensions between Israel and the Philistines led to war shortly after the call of SAMUEL. The Philistines defeated Israel at Ebenezer, which resulted in the capture of the ARK and Shiloh's destruction (1 Sam 4–6; cf. Ps 78:56-66; Jer 7:12-14). Later, the Israelites defeated their enemies at Mizpah (1 Sam 7:3-14). With the establishment of SAUL's kingship and a regular army, Israel was victorious over the Philistines (1 Sam 13–14), in spite of the latter's more advanced weapons (cf. 13:19-22).

During another campaign between these rivals, David killed GOLIATH and the Philistines were routed (1 Sam 17:41-54), an episode that resulted in Saul's jealousy and David's flight to Philistia, where David became a vassal of ACHISH (27:1–28:2). Meanwhile, Saul and his sons were killed by the Philistines at Mount GILBOA (1 Sam 31), an event which caused David to break with the Philistines and assume his monarchy at Hebron (2 Sam 1:1–2:11). King David's war with the Philistines ultimately ended their threat to Israel (cf. 2 Sam 5:17-25; 8:1; 21:15-22; 23:8-39). When Solomon came to power, he exacted tribute from Philistia's city-states (1 Kgs 4:21), an indication of the extent of David's victory.

Throughout the history of the divided monarchy, hostility between Israel and the Philistines continued, albeit sporadically (cf. 2 Chr 17:11; 21:16-17; 26:6-7; 28:18; 2 Kgs 18:8). Because of this continued conflict, the prophets leveled serious indictments against the Philistines (cf. Amos 1:6-8; Zeph 2:4-7; Joel 3:4-8; Isa 14:28-31). In the last reference, Isaiah warned the Philistines about Assyrian expansion, a process that had begun to be felt in Philistia in the ninth century B.C.E. After Assyria's collapse, Philistia joined Egypt in an anti-Babylonian alliance, but Nebuchadrezzar deported the Philistine rulers and people (cf. Jer 25:20; 47:2-7; Zech 9:5-6), thereby terminating Philistia's independence.

In addition to the OT and extrabiblical texts, archaeological excavations in Philistia continue to supplement our knowledge of this important people. Most Philistine sites are located in the coastal plain and foothills of southern Palestine; evidence from these sites agrees with the written sources in placing the most important part of the Philistine story between ca. 1200–1000 B.C.E. Even the distinctive pottery of the Philistines, which reflects their Aegean origin, disappears by ca. 1000 B.C.E.

The locations of Gaza, Ashkelon, and Ashdod are certain. Ancient Ekron is almost certainly identified with the site of Khirbet Muqanna (Tel Miqne), but the location of Philistine Gath is uncertain, though it might have been at Tell es-Safi. Excavations at Philistine sites such as Deir el-Balah, Tell el-Batashi, Tell GEZER, Tell Jemmeh, and Tell Qasile have yielded much data on Philistine pottery, architecture, burial practices, trade, and religion. For example, it is now clear that the anthropoid clay coffins, once associated with the Philistines, represent a custom of the Egyptians who lived in Palestine.

According to the written evidence, there were three Philistine gods—Dagon, Ashtaroth, and BAAL-ZEBUB. Dagon had temples in Gaza (Judg 16:21, 23-30), Ashdod (1 Sam 5:1-7), and probably in Beth-shan (1 Chr 10:10; cf. 1 Sam 31:10). Temples for the worship of Ashtaroth were located in Ashkelon, according to Herodotus I.105, and probably in Beth-shan (1 Sam 31:10), while Baal-zebub had a temple in Ekron (2 Kgs 1:1-16). The excavation of Tell Qasile, at Tel Aviv, resulted in the discovery of a series of superimposed Philistine temples, structures that contain both Canaanite and Cypriote-Greek features.

It is important to observe that the names of the principal Philistine gods are semitic, an indication that the Philistines had adopted the deities—or at least the names of deities—worshiped by the Canaanites. Other common features of Philistine religion include sacrifice (cf. Judg 16:23) and the consultation of priests, diviners, and soothsayers (cf. 1 Sam 6:2-9; Isa 2:6). Portable idols were carried into battle (cf. 2 Sam 5:21), and 1 Sam 5:1–6:21 indicates that the Philistines recognized the existence of other national deities.

To date, no written text can be attributed to the Philistines with any degree of certainty, though there are several undeciphered inscriptions with Cypro-Minoan or Cypro-Mycenaean script that might be Philistine. Most of the Philistine names in the OT are semitic, but the names Achish and Goliath have parallels in Crete and western Anatolia. Furthermore, it is likely that several Hebrew words were borrowed from the language of the Philistines. While these Aegean immigrants assimilated much from Hebrew and Canaanite culture, including language, Neh 13:23–24 indicates that there was still a language barrier between the Ashdodites and the Judaeans in postexilic times.

Bibliography. T. Dothan, *The Philistines and Their Material Culture* and "What We Know about the Philistines," *BAR* 8 (1982): 20–44; K. A. Kitchen, "Philistines," in *Peoples of Old Testament Times,* ed. D. J. Wiseman.

—GERALD L. MATTINGLY

• **Philo.** [fi'loh] Philo of Alexandria was a Jewish philosopher, and one of the most energetic Jewish writers of all time. He was born about 20 B.C.E. of a wealthy and well-known family. His brother was Alexander, an important financial officer in the Jewish community, which made up one-half of the population of the city. Since Alexander was one of the richest men in the world, it is assumed that Philo had wealth in his own right. Unlike Alexander he was not attracted to the type of political or social life that wealth might acquire. From his early days Philo was more interested in the religion of his people.

Alexandria in Philo's day was a hotbed of intellectual excitement. In the first century C.E. the city's library housed the largest collection of papyrus rolls in the world. Orientalism, Hellenism, Romanism, and Judaism came together in Alexandria, and each made a contribution to the world that was far-reaching and profound. In this environment with its amalgam of philosophical thought a Jew like Philo found it necessary to defend Judaism against POLYTHEISM, scepticism, and atheism. To do this he had to be skilled in Greek thought and Oriental mysticism in addition to having more than just an ordinary knowledge of his own Jewish religion.

Philo attempted to combine Greek thought and learning with Judaism. He borrowed from the metaphysics of Plato, the numbers of Pythagoras, the LOGOS/WORD idea and ALLEGORY from the STOICS, and mysticism from the HELLENISTIC WORLD. He learned from all of them, but insisted that MOSES was greater than any. In fact he believed that the philosophers of Greece had taken their systems of thought from Moses, in whom all truth was found. Although his style, terminology, and pattern of thought were

Greek, he remained loyal to Moses and the traditions of Israel. He sought a syncretism of elements selected from Greek philosophy, Oriental mysticism, and Jewish theology. In his thirty-eight works, a library in themselves, Philo referred to the Pentateuch about a thousand times and alluded to the Psalms and Prophets on twenty-six occasions. He contributed immeasurably to Judaism by means of his view of scripture, his allegorical interpretation, and his *logos* doctrine.

Philo's Concept of Scripture. His view of inspiration was mechanical, and in this respect he followed Plato. The record of revelation was written in the condition of ecstasy when all human powers were obliterated. The oracles of the prophets came by means of divine ventriloquism. God spoke to the prophets as passive instruments. Philo assumed that all scripture was divine. He was probably acquainted with the Hebrew text of the scriptures, but he based all his arguments on the Greek translation of the Hebrew scriptures, the LXX, which was completed about two centuries before his day. He considered this text verbally inspired and correct. Philo attributed to the Greek translation a veneration and faith so profound that he considered it as having been written by God.

Philo's Allegorical Method of Interpretation. Since there were some passages in the Pentateuch difficult to understand, some historically improbable, some having contradictions and inconsistencies, and others presenting the character of God in a bad light, Philo resorted to allegory to make a case for God's revelation. The allegorical method was not an invention of Philo; he borrowed it from the Stoics in Alexandria. Allegory is an interpretive method in which a text has a symbolic meaning beyond the literal sense. For the educated class this was a way to remain faithful in an established religion without accepting the absurd and ridiculous. Those who used this method of interpretation believed that all revelation was a divine cryptogram which served the dual purpose of concealing truth from the unworthy and unveiling it for the worthy.

Philo contended that a text had two meanings: the plain or literal and the underlying or spiritual. He rejected the plain meaning when the text presented a contradiction or something unworthy of God. Before the advent of modern biblical criticism Philo recognized that there were two accounts of the CREATION of humanity in GENESIS. To overcome the contradictions he interpreted the two stories allegorically. He interpreted the original ADAM in Gen 1:27 as a heavenly creation unmixed with material things, but in Gen 2:7 the human soul was mixed with clay when God fashioned the earthly Adam. Thus Philo made a distinction between an archetypical Adam and an earthly Adam.

Philo's Logos Doctrine. Although Philo was influenced by the Stoics' concept of the *logos*, the Word, as a pervading force in the universe and humanity, he did not restrict himself to the Stoic understanding of the term. On the contrary he used *logos* more in the sense of Plato's archetype. For Philo the *logos* was most like God because it was a primal emanation. On some occasions he referred to the *logos* as second God. In fact the *logos* possessed the creative and ruling powers of God. There seems to be nothing in his works that would lead to the belief that Philo considered the *logos* as a person. Apparently what he did was to make an extreme extension of the personification of WISDOM IN THE OT without actually accepting personalization.

For most of his life Philo enjoyed peaceful days, but in 39–40 C.E. he led a delegation of Jews to Rome in order to plead the cause of Alexandrian Jews against Flaccus, the governor of Egypt who was persecuting them to gain the favor of the antisemitic element in the city. Gaius Caligula was emperor at the time. Caligula treated Philo and his companions with contempt, and they were afraid they would be put to death. This incident had a terrible effect on Philo. He was never able to get over this, and his declining years were spent in a mystical and contemplative way of life.

Philo died ca. 49 C.E., but not without making an indelible impression on intellectual history. In addition to rendering a service of Judaism with his apologetic approach, he laid the foundation for the Alexandrian school of interpretation that came to great prominence in Christians such as Clement and Origen. He also wielded a tremendous influence on the Western church through Augustine, Jerome, and Ambrose.

See also ALLEGORY; HELLENISTIC WORLD; INTERPRETATION, HISTORY OF; WORD.

Bibliography. J. Drummond, *Philo Judaeus*; E. R. Goodenough, *An Introduction to Philo Judaeus*; S. Sandmel, *Philo's Place in Judaism*.

—T. C. SMITH

• **Philo, Epic Poet.** The author of the Greek epic *On Jerusalem* is referred to either as Philo the Epic Poet or Philo Epicus to distinguish him from the philosopher, PHILO of Alexandria. Fragments of the epic are preserved by Eusebius in his *Preparation for the Gospel* (*PraepEv*). Since Eusebius is quoting from Alexander Polyhistor (fl. ca. 50 B.C.E.), Philo should be dated prior to the first century B.C.E. The provenance is unclear; Alexandria is a possibility.

A total of twenty-four verses of Philo's epic have survived. They are composed in pretentious Greek hexameters in imitation of the epics of the Alexandrian period. The vocabulary is obscure and difficult to translate. The first two fragments (*PraepEv* 9.20.1) concern the binding of ISAAC and his miraculous rescue (Gen 22). Only here in the whole corpus of Jewish literature is the epithet "thunderer" applied to God (cf. *Iliad* 13.521). The third fragment (*PraepEv* 9.24.1) extols God's faithfulness to ABRAHAM, Isaac, JACOB, and JOSEPH. The emphasis is on Joseph as an interpreter of dreams.

The title of the epic, *On Jerusalem*, seems particularly appropriate for the fourth, fifth, and sixth extant fragments (*PraepEv* 9.37.1-3), which are devoted to a description of the marvelous water-supply system of the city. These fragments are of importance not primarily because of their contents, but because they represent an attempt by a Hellenistic Jewish poet to celebrate the sacred places and events of his people in the same grand manner used by the Greek conquerors to magnify their culture and their heroes.

Bibliography. H. Attridge, "Philo the Epic Poet," *The Old Testament Pseudepigrapha*, ed. J. H. Charlesworth; C. R. Holladay, *Fragments from Hellenistic Jewish Authors*.

—SHARYN E. DOWD

• **Philo, Pseudo.** [*soo'*doh-fi''loh] When the writings of PHILO of Alexandria were translated into Latin, a document was included among them that later came to be called *Liber Antiquitatum Biblicarum (Biblical Antiquities)*. It is a narrative about the history of Israel from ADAM through the death of SAUL. Philo's authorship is now denied by virtually all scholars. The work is a mixture of biblical material, interpretation, and legend. It seems to reflect the milieu of Palestinian Judaism around the end of the last century B.C.E., and may stem from a Hebrew original.

In some places Pseudo-Philo condenses the biblical narrative into a few lines, as in the case of the JOSEPH stories of Gen 37–50 (=*LAB* 8:9-10). But KENAZ, who is merely mentioned as OTHNIEL's father in Judg 3:9, 11, expands into a major military and cultic leader under the pen of Pseudo-Philo (chaps. 25–28). Some stories that were important to the biblical writers are missing; although the PLAGUES against the Egyptians are listed, the origin of PASSOVER is omitted.

The purpose of the legendary material that the author has woven into the account is sometimes difficult to discern, but certain patterns can be observed. There is a tendency to provide names for characters left unnamed in the Bible, and to make connections between characters. Thus, SAMSON's mother is named Eluma; the Benjaminite who brought to Eli the news of the loss of the Ark (1 Sam 4:12-18) was Saul; JACOB's daughter Dinah became Job's wife; GOLIATH was DAVID's distant cousin, because he was descended from RUTH's ''sister'' Orpah.

Pseudo-Philo makes some attempts to eliminate contradictions from the story line; Saul had to ask who David was after Goliath's death despite their prior acquaintance because an angel had changed David's appearance. The two biblical accounts of Saul's death are harmonized so that Saul falls on his sword, but does not die until he is killed by the passing Amalekite, who happens to be the son of Agag whom Saul spared in disobedience to SAMUEL. Some of the additions are found only in Pseudo-Philo, while others also appear in RABBINIC LITERATURE and other Jewish writings. Pseudo-Philo knows the legend that a miraculous well of water followed Israel throughout the wilderness wanderings—a tradition found in a number of Jewish sources and appropriated by Paul (1 Cor 10:4).

Jewish heroes are glorifed beyond the biblical portrayal; MOSES was born circumcised and his exclusion from the promised land was not because of any sin, but to prevent him from seeing the idols there. There is some tendency to magnify the role of the women in the narrative. Jael's murder of Sisera is expanded into an elaborate narrative (perhaps under the influence of the story of JUDITH). Three chapters are devoted to DEBORAH. She is designated ''woman of God,'' perhaps a play on the common phrase ''man of God.'' The sacrifice of JEPHTHAH's daughter is compared to the near-sacrifice of ISAAC; she makes a long and courageous speech and God pronounces her ''wise in contrast to her father.'' Upon her death she goes to ''the bosom of her mothers.''

Bibliography. D. J. Harrington, ''Pseudo-Philo,'' *The Old Testament Pseudepigrapha,* ed. J. H. Charlesworth.

—SHARYN E. DOWD

• **Phinehas.** [fin′ee-huhs] A personal name. The name Phinehas is Egyptian meaning ''the dark-skinned one.'' There are three men so named in the OT.

1. Phinehas, a priest, the son of Eleazar and grandson of AARON (Exod 6:25; 1 Chr 6:4). He was the ancestor of EZRA (Ezra 7:5) and of Gershom, a priestly companion of Ezra (Ezra 8:2). His home was in the hill country of EPHRAIM (Josh 24:33). During a time of apostasy an Israelite man was having intercourse with a Midianite woman during the fertility rites of BAAL. Phinehas demonstrated his zeal for Yahweh by killing them both with one spear thrust. This act ended a plague sent on Israel for such apostasy. For this deed Phinehas was rewarded with a ''perpetual priesthood'' (Num 25:6-15) and was remembered among the heroes of faith (Ps 106:30; Sir 45:23-24; 1 Macc 2:26, 54). MOSES sent him with the troops in a subsequent holy war against Midian (Num 31:6). Later, in the time of JOSHUA, Phinehas negotiated a dispute with the tribes of Eastern Palestine about an altar these tribes built on the western side of the Jordan frontier. This act is represented as apostasy, but may have been a claim by the Eastern tribes to territorial rights west of the river (Josh 22:10-34). When Benjaminites wronged a Levite from Ephraim by ravishing his concubine, Phinehas advised Israel to continue to war against Benjamin until they were punished (Judg 20:27-28). Late tradition designated Phinehas as chief of the Levitical gate keepers, an office associated with the office of high priest (1 Chr 9:17-10).

2. Phinehas the son of ELI and brother of HOPHNI (1 Sam 1:3). He and Hophni abused the priestly office (1 Sam 2:12-17) and were killed in battle with the PHILISTINES (1 Sam 4:11). The wife of Phinehas bore a son whom she named Ichabod, ''no glory,'' as a symbol of the depth to which Israel had fallen (1 Sam 4:19-22). This Phinehas was grandfather of Ahijah, or Ahimelech, a priest in the time of SAUL (1 Sam 14:3) and great grandfather of ABIATHAR priest to DAVID.

3. Phinehas father of a certain Eleazar who returned from Babylon with Ezra (Ezra 8:33; 1 Esdras 8:63).

—DAVID A. SMITH

• **Phocylides, Pseudo.** [s*oo*′doh-foh-sil″uh-deez] Phocylides was an Ionic poet of the sixth century B.C.E., famous in antiquity for his practical maxims. Few of these sentences survive, and the poem of 230 lines (hexameters) that has come down to us under his name is almost certainly pseudonymous. This poem, referred to as *The Sentences of Pseudo-Phocylides*, was written in Greek by someone who knew both the LXX and popular Hellenistic ethics. It consists of one-sentence ethical rules, such as ''Do not tell lies, but always speak the truth'' (7) and ''Long hair is not fit for boys, but for voluptuous women'' (212), grouped together somewhat loosely on various moral and sapiential topics (justice, mercy, the love of money, life and death, etc.). Van der Horst has shown that at least half of the verses have material equivalents in Greek maxims.

There are a number of indications that the author of Pseudo-Phocylides was a Hellenistic Jew. In addition to echoes of the LXX, the work contains verses that closely parallel certain passages in PHILO's *Hypothetica* and JOSEPHUS's *Against Apion,* two works that are representative of Jewish apologetic literature. It also appears to advocate, if in a somewhat veiled fashion, the so-called NOACHIC LAWS, which Jews (at least of a later period) regarded as binding upon all of humanity. It affirms the existence of one God (54), a hallmark of Jewish faith, and at one point expresses hope in a physical RESURRECTION (103), another distinctively Jewish belief. Nevertheless, there are no overt references to the Jewish LAW in the poem, and none of the sentences presupposes Jewish national particularities. It has been suggested that Pseudo-Phocylides represents a kind of nonproselytizing Jewish apologetic literature. As such it may be designed to win the respect of cultured pagans for Jewish ethics. One can also imagine it serving the needs of cultured Hellenistic Jews by providing them with a ''universal Jewish ethic'' that was materially consonant with popular Hellenistic moral philosophy and at the same time gave the appearance of indebtedness to the LXX. Or, in view of the pseudonym and the dearth of explicit reference to Jewish laws, it may be that the author has no interest in promoting Jewish values but endeavors to present a "common ethic" (cf. *SibOr* 3.758), that is, a universal ethic in the Greek tradition. In short, the fact that at points the poem shows influence from Jewish literature and tradition tells us something about the identity of its author, but it does not provide a sure clue to the purpose of the work.

Considerations of style and content suggest that the poem was written sometime between 50 B.C.E. and 100 C.E., perhaps in Alexandria. Alexandria was a center of Hellenistic-Jewish culture, and Philo, with whom Pseudo-Phocylides shares many affinities, carried out his work there. An Alexandrian provenance is also suggested by the poem's polemic against human dissection (102). As far as we know, human dissection was practiced only in Alexandria, where it served the study of human anatomy.

Bibliography. J. H. Collins, *Between Athens and Jerusalem: Jewish Identity in the Hellenistic Diaspora*; M. Gilbert, "Wisdom Literature," *Jewish Writings of the Second Temple Period*, ed. M. E. Stone; P. W. van der Horst, *The Sentences of Pseudo-Phocylides: Introduction, Translation, and Commentary*.

—CHARLES H. COSGROVE

• **Phoenicia.** [fi-nish'uh] A Middle Eastern country located along the eastern shore of the Mediterranean during the biblical era (PLATE 1). The land was originally known by its Hurrian name Canaan (or "land of purple") because it was famous for its purple dye. However, by about 1200 B.C.E. Greek traders had renamed it Phoenicia (a Greek translation of the word CANAAN). Though at first the terms must have been used interchangeably, they soon came to identify two completely different places, with Phoenicia referring to the sea coast and Canaan the hill country. However, like many other countries of the ancient Near East, the land and its people were sometimes simply known by the name of its capital or one of its major cities (Arvad, Tripolis, BYBLOS, Beirut, Sidon, ZAREPHATH, Tyre, or ACCO).

Phoenicia was a small country located just northwest of Palestine. Its natural boundaries included: the Mediterranean Sea on the west, the mountains of Lebanon on the east, Mount Cassius on the north, and Mount Carmel on the south. Thus, though the country extended along the coastline some distance (at least 130 miles), its width varied from almost nothing where the mountains touched the sea, to several miles where they receded inland. This quite naturally left the country segmented and thus led to the formation of independent city states, which were loosely united.

What land there was between the sea and the mountains was quite fertile and thus readily produced abundant crops (such as wheat, barley, figs, dates, olives, and grapes), as well as great forests (which contained trees such as cedars, pines, oaks, and firs). In addition to this, the sand from the areas of Sidon and Tyre was perfect for use in the making of glass. Moreover, the large sea snail murex (from which the reddish-purple dye was made), was plentiful in that part of the Mediterranean. Thus, though small, the land was not only able to sustain its own people, but also to provide many products for export.

Ivory artifact from Phoenicia.

The Phoenicians controlled not only Palestine's main north-south trade route (the Via Maris), but also two of the eastern Mediterranean's main harbors (TYRE AND SIDON). Thus, they became one of the most distinguished trading and seafaring peoples in the history of mankind. They not only exported their own goods (such as cedar, glass, purple dye, wine, jewelry, and metal products), but also trafficked in other goods (such as wool, gold, silver, ivory, ebony, and spice). Undoubtedly, such an interchange of goods and ideas not only led to their own industrialization, but also to their colonization of other parts of the Mediterranean (such as Cyprus, Africa, Sicily, and Spain). However, their strategic location as well as the wealth which it produced left them as a target for every world power.

The earliest history of the land is very difficult to reconstruct. Archaeological data from the site of Byblos (ancient Gebal) seems to indicate that the land was occupied as early as 3000 B.C.E. However, this civilization was replaced by a more advanced one which was dominated by the Amorites (ca. 2500 B.C.E.) Their domination lasted until ca. 1800 B.C.E., when because of the struggles within Mesopotamia, Phoenicia was left relatively unnoticed. Unfortunately, this vacuum was quickly filled, first by the HYKSOS, and then by the Egyptians. However, if the AMARNA letters are any indication, the Egyptians really had to struggle to keep control of the land. Finally, their domination was broken when the SEA PEOPLES invaded ca. 1200 B.C.E.

Although the sea peoples destroyed several cities (including Ugarit, Arvad, and Sidon), they left the land basically free from foreign influence and somewhat united under the king of Tyre. During this time of freedom, Hiram I (the king of Tyre) managed to align himself with both King David (2 Sam 5:11) and his son Solomon (1 Kgs 5:1). As a result of these treaties, he not only provided the material, but also many of the craftsmen used to build the Temple and royal palace (1 Kgs 5:1-12; 2 Chr 2:3-16). Furthermore, he also assisted Solomon with his maritime endeavors (1 Kgs 9:27). Even after the division of the kingdom, Hiram's successor, Ethbaal, managed to keep the relationship between the two peoples strong by marrying his daughter, Jezebel, to Ahab (1 Kgs 16:30-31). As might be expected, Jezebel carried her Baal worship with her (1 Kgs 18:19).

About this time (875 B.C.E.), the Assyrians began to exert their influence on the land. Apparently, Asshur-nasir-pal II was the first Assyrian to exact tribute from the Phoenicians, but he was quickly followed by Shalmaneser III, Adad-nirari III, Tiglath-pileser III, Sargon II, Sennacherib, Esarhaddon, and even Asshurbanapal. Though the names and faces changed, the picture was much the same during the Neo-Babylonian era (particularly under Nebuchadrezzar II). Yet, despite all their loss of revenue and the occasional destruction of their property, the Phoenicians did manage to maintain their identity. Thus, when the Persians took over (in 539 B.C.E.) and began to treat them kindly, they once again prospered. However, after a while, the people of Sidon decided to revolt. Artaxerxes III was furious and thus quickly destroyed the city (351 B.C.E.). Soon after that, the Persians gave way to the Greeks. During this process, Alexander the Great attacked Tyre and destroyed it (332 B.C.E.). As a result, Phoenicia remained under Greek influence until the time of Pompey (ca. 64 B.C.E.), when he made it a part of the Roman Empire. Then, although the cities continued to exist, the national entity gradually faded away.

Phoenician religion was basically just a continuation of the earlier Canaanite religion. Like its predecessor, it was polytheistic in nature. The greatest of their gods was BAAL, who is generally thought to have been a fertility god; in Phoenicia he seems to have been closely identified with some of their other gods (such as the storm god—Hadad, the sun god—Shamash, and the god of the netherworld—Reshep). The primary female deity and consort of Baal was Astarte, or Ashtoreth (a well-known mother and fertility goddess).

Undoubtedly, such polytheistic tendencies and the practices that went with them (such as temple prostitution and child sacrifice) were part of the reason for the biblical prophets' strong condemnation against Phoenicia and their prediction of its ultimate judgment (Isa 23:1-18; Ezek 26:2–28:23). Despite such rampant paganism, the religious toleration which was practiced there made it a fertile field for the spread of the gospel (Luke 6:17; Acts 11:19; 15:3; 21:2-3).

Bibliography. W. F. Albright, "Role of the Canaanite in the History of Civilization," *The Bible and the Ancient Near East,* ed. G. E. Wright; D. R. Ap-Thomas, "The Phoenicians," *People of Old Testament Times,* ed. D. J. Wiseman; D. B. Harden, *The Phoenicians*; S. Moscati, *The World of the Phoenicians.*

—HARRY B. HUNT, JR.

• **Pilate.** [pi'luht] Pontius Pilate was the Roman PROCURATOR of JUDEA, 26–36 C.E., subject to some degree to the Roman legate in Syria (PLATE 20). Meager information about him outside the NT is found in PHILO, JOSEPHUS, Tacitus, and on a dedication inscription found at Caesarea in 1961. For instance, Tacitus recorded that Pilate condemned "Chrestus" to death (*Ann* 15.44).

Pilate's procuratorial duties were judicial, military, and financial. His judicial authority was unrestricted in both civil and criminal cases against ordinary provincial persons. Popular reactions, however, could lead to an imperial review. Pilate's military powers related primarily to control of Jewish citizens who felt that submission to Rome was apostasy. The approximately 3,000 soldiers he commanded were recruited mostly from Samaria and Caesarea and were often the most barbarous inhabitants of the province. Financial duties of Pilate included collection of taxes, including customs.

In the NT Pilate was prominent in the condemnation of Jesus. Jewish leaders, wanting Jesus removed and yet desiring to maintain leadership of the people, involved Pilate in the trial. This established Roman responsibility for the crucifixion. The NT recorded Pilate as not regarding Jesus as dangerous to the state but condemning him to avoid Jewish wrath (Luke 23:13-24).

Evaluation of Pilate's career has been both negative and positive. The Jewish sources represent Pilate negatively. Philo wrote that the conduct of his office was marked by corruption, violence, ill-treatment, and numerous illegal executions. Philo and Josephus record instances of the offense of Jewish traditions by Pilate. He was the first procurator of Judea to use pagan religious symbols on coins. Roman standards bearing the emperor's image were brought into Jerusalem and votive shields inscribed with the emperor's name were placed in the royal palace. Pilate used Temple funds to build an aqueduct, and his forces quelled what he erroneously thought was a revolt by Samaritans, killing and capturing some of them. The massacre of Samaritans caused such a reaction that Pilate was summoned to Rome.

Christians considered his condemnation of Jesus to be Pilate's greatest misjudgment. The NT presents Pilate as reluctantly condemning Jesus (Mark 15:12-15; Luke 23:13-24; Matt 27:22-24; John 19:12-15), and the Jews as taking the blame (Matt 27:25). Current interpretations of these accounts include the view that Christianity was embarrassed by the tradition which blamed Pilate for Jesus' death, and that as the church spread westward it shifted the blame onto the Jewish people. Also, Pilate is defended by the claim that his decision as recorded in Matthew, Mark, and Luke fit well into the Roman legal framework. Without any defense by Jesus himself, Pilate has no option but to convict him. It is also pointed out that since TIBERIUS kept Pilate in office for ten years, he must have found no serious fault in his administration.

As nothing substantive is known about Pilate's early life, nothing is known of his last days. Josephus wrote that Pilate was summoned to Rome to justify himself in regard to the Samaritan massacre, but that Emperor Tiberius died before Pilate arrived. He was not reappointed as procurator of Judea.

See also JUDEA; PASSION NARRATIVE; PROCURATOR; TRIAL OF JESUS.

Bibliography. C. K. Barrett, *The New Testament Background: Selected Documents*; F. V. Filson, *A New Testament History*; E. Lohse, *The New Testament Environment.*

—PHILIP R. HART

• **Pilate, Acts of.** The *Acts of Pilate* is a name given to a composite work dating from no earlier than the mid-fourth century, consisting of two main parts probably not joined before the fifth century. It is sometimes referred to as the *Gospel of Nicodemus* because of this man's prominence in the book.

The first portion (1–16), is essentially a passion gospel in two parts. The first, the *Acts of Pilate* proper (1–11), is an elaborate account of Jesus' trial before PILATE, his crucifixion and burial. It is characterized by fanciful episodes designed to minimize the guilt of Pilate in Jesus' death and to emphasize the responsibility of the Jews. The second part (12–16) concerns debates in the SANHEDRIN about the resurrection and ascension of Jesus, with witnesses (a priest, a rabbi, a Levite) testifying that they had seen Jesus rise into heaven. Joseph of Arimathea is an important figure in this portion.

The second main section of *Acts of Pilate* is an elaborate description of Christ's DESCENT INTO HELL (cf. 1 Peter 3:19).

The work survives in Greek and Latin manuscripts, with the first portion also extant in Coptic, Armenian, and Syriac. Many manuscripts have unique additions, one of them being an alleged letter written by Pilate to the Emperor Claudius, giving an account of Jesus' trial. There is no evidence that Pilate ever made such a report, but it was widely assumed in antiquity that he must have. Apparently there were several fabrications of such a report. JUSTIN MARTYR (second century) refers to one as a valid document. Christian versions of Pilate's report may well have been written in reaction to pagan forgeries of such a report.

The *Acts of Pilate* was quite popular in the Middle Ages. In the West it was sometimes taken seriously as a witness to the passion of Christ, and influenced European art and literature. In the East the tendencies to exculpate Pilate led to his veneration as a saint and martyr in the Coptic Church.

See also APOCRYPHAL GOSPELS.

Bibliography. J. Quasten, *Patrology*; F. Scheidweiler, "The Gospel of Nicodemus, Acts of Pilate and Christ's Descent into Hell," *New Testament Apocrypha*, ed. E. Hennecke and W. Schneemelcher.

—ROGER A. BULLARD

• **Pirke Aboth.** [pihr-kay'ah-voht'] *Pirke Aboth* (*Sayings of the Fathers*) is a collection of ethical and religious maxims attributed to Jewish teachers ranging from the third century B.C.E. to the third century C.E. The opening section of the document traces the transmission of TORAH from SINAI to the destruction of JERUSALEM in 70 C.E. The first links in the tradition are simply named: MOSES, JOSHUA, the Elders, and the "men of the Great Synagogue" at the time of EZRA. Afterwards, the author lists important rabbis along with quotations representative of their teachings. Two sages are listed first, then ten in pairs, ending with Hillel and Shammai (from whom developed the two major Rabbinic schools), then three more, concluding with Simeon ben Gamaliel, one of the leaders during the siege of Jerusalem. The next section focuses primarily on the teachings of Yohanan ben Zakkai, the central figure in the preservation of the tradition following the fall of Jerusalem. The next section contains, in no particular order, various teachings attributed to forty other rabbis from the first three centuries C.E. The document concludes with a series of ethical reflections arranged primarily numerically and without ascription to particular rabbis.

Pirke Aboth is not an independent work, nor is it a unified composition. Rather, it is a part of the great codification of Jewish traditions that was carried out by Rabbi Judah the Holy at the end of the second century C.E. and which is known as the Mishnah. *Pirke Aboth* stands near the end of *Neziqin*, the fourth of the six orders of the Mishnah. It might have been compiled originally as a conclusion to the Mishnah, designed to validate the authority of the Mishnah by demonstrating its unbroken connection with the tradition which began at Sinai. It certainly gives the impression of being the product of several editors.

At the heart of *Pirke Aboth* is Torah, the divine instruction given by revelation to Israel. The importance of Torah for the individual's destiny is seen in the words of Hillel: "Who has gained for himself words of Torah has gained for himself the life of the world to come" (2:8). But the study of Torah also gives blessing in the present: "When two sit and there are between them words of Torah, the SHEKINAH [i.e., the divine presence] rests between them" (3:3; cf. Matt 18:20), and "Everyone who receives upon him the yoke of Torah, they remove from him the yoke of the kingdom and the yoke of worldly occupation (3:7; cf. Matt 11:29-30). *Pirke Aboth*, then, is a classic document for understanding the importance of Torah in Judaism.

Pirke Aboth has gained a unique place in Jewish literature apart from its presence in the Mishnah. It has become a regular part of Jewish liturgy, being the only complete work of any kind contained in the Jewish prayer book. It has even been seen as containing the essential teaching of true piety: "He who would become 'Hasid' should fulfill the words of Aboth" (*BQam* 30a).

See also RABBINIC LITERATURE.

Bibliography. R. T. Herford, *The Ethics of the Talmud: Sayings of the Fathers*; C. Taylor, *Sayings of the Jewish Fathers*, 2nd ed.; B. T. Viviano, *Study as Worship: Aboth and the New Testament*.

—JOSEPH L. TRAFTON

• **Pistis Sophia.** [pis'tis-soh-fee"uh] The name *Pistis Sophia* (*Faithful Wisdom*) has been given the whole of the fourth-century parchment Codex Askew. Obtained in 1773 in London by Dr. A. Askew, this 174-leaf codex is today found in the British Museum. Its name comes from the major theme of the first part: Sophia, emanation of the highest God, is portrayed as fallen, repentant, and delivered from chaos through her faithful response to Christ's saving work. She is described in the SOPHIA OF JESUS CHRIST (Berlin Codex 8502, 3) as heavenly consort of the SON OF MAN, his female nature who is "mother of all things."

Study of the codex has shown its four sections are divisible into two groups: Books I-III (¶¶ 1–231.9), which contain a typical Gnostic revelation dialogue between the Risen Christ and his disciples said to occur in Jerusalem in the twelfth year of his pre-ascension appearances. Most date composition of these books between 250–300 C.E. and would apply the title *Pistis Sophia* only to them. Book IV (¶¶ 232.1–254.8), however, unfolds on the days immediately following the Resurrection. Jesus' teaching occurs on the seashore, in a heavenly region known as the "Midst," on a Galilean mountain, and in "Amente" (the Underworld). Most date this Book 200–250 C.E., earlier than the *Pistis Sophia*.

In Books I–III we learn that during eleven years of post-Resurrection appearances, Jesus has instructed the disciples in lesser mysteries. Now, during the twelfth year, the luminous Revealer will teach them the supreme mystery. Following a marvelous ascent into and descent from "the places out of which I came forth" (I,6.22-23), Jesus shares with his disciples secret knowledge about heavenly regions and especially about the fall, repentance, and his ultimate redemption from chaos of *Pistis Sophia*. In gratitude, she offered a series of hymns to the "First Mystery." Each hymn is followed by an interpretation by a disciple of a selected OT psalm. Much dialogue is concerned, as well, with the mysteries of the light, the origin of sin and evil, the need for repentance, the types of post-mortem punishment awaiting sinners. Throughout, forty-six questions are put to Jesus, some thirty-nine by Mary Magdalene alone. Also, there are several citations from the TWO BOOKS OF JEU and of five ODES OF SOLOMON, Syrian and possibly Gnostic hymns from the second century.

The second writing (Book IV) contains discourses by the risen Jesus on heavenly powers, as well as an account of visions and rituals enjoyed by the disciples. A pervasive concern is with repentance in a Gnostic sense. The revelation ends with Jesus' description of punishments for various sins and his prayer in Amente for compassion. Throughout, disciples and holy women intervene with questions.

The *Pistis Sophia* represents a late (third century) and less original form of GNOSTICISM, one preoccupied with traditional formulae and interpretations needed for heavenly ascent. Although the myth of Pistis Sophia's fall and redemption (representative of humanity in general) may be influenced by earlier Valentinian Sophia-speculation, its form in Books I–III is difficult to identify with any specific Gnostic sect. Egypt seems clearly the place of origin.

See also GNOSTICISM; JEU, TWO BOOKS OF; SOPHIA OF JESUS CHRIST.

Bibliography. H.-Ch. Puech, "Pistis Sophia," in *New Testament Apocrypha,* ed. E. Hennecke and W. Schneemelcher; K. Rudolph, *Gnosis: The Nature and History of Gnosticism*; C. Schmidt and V. MacDermot, *Pistis Sophia,* ed. R. McL. Wilson (*NHS*, 9).

—MALCOLM L. PEEL

• **Pity.** Pity belongs to a semantic field that includes such concepts as concern, MERCY, and compassion, and denotes both feelings and actions of sympathy and concern for, even identity with, others in trouble or desperate straits. A number of Hebrew and Greek verbs and related parts of speech are translated as "pity" in modern versions. Hebrew terms include *ḥûs, ḥāmal, ḥānan, naḥam,* and *riḥam.* Greek terms include *eleaō, eleeō, oiktirō,* and *splagchnizomai.* Pity is an affection that may be possessed by and characteristic of both humans and the divine.

Several deuteronomic texts warn against allowing the eye to pity as if pity, for even the wrongdoer, was such a normal reaction as to require persistence for its avoidance: inhabitants of Canaan are to be destroyed (Deut 7:16), apostasizing family members are to be stoned (13:6-11), the murderer executed (19:11-13), malicious witnesses subjected to the consequences of their false accusations (19:15-21), and women guilty of causing genital injury punished (25:11-12), and all without showing pity. In certain circumstances one should act without pity, act unaffected by what one sees, according to these texts.

On the one hand, under normal conditions, humans are expected to show pity towards those in distress and desperate conditions or to those less fortunate and less privileged. Not to show pity is characteristic of the wicked (2 Sam 12:6; Ps 17:10; Amos 1:11). In certain circumstances, pity is to be expected (Job 19:21-22; Pss 69:20; 109:12). The Hebrew king who had a special responsibility for the powerless, the poor, and the oppressed is praised for having pity on the weak and needy (Ps 72:12-14).

Pity and lack of pity are both ascribed to the deity. In judgment, God acts without pity (Jer 13:14; 15:5; 20:16; Lam 2:17; 3:43; Ezek 5:11; 7:4, 9; 8:18; 9:5, 10; Hos 1:6, 7; 2:4; Zech 11:5). On the other hand, pity from God is requested (Ps 90:13). Acts of REDEMPTION are spoken of as acts based on divine pity (Ps 102:12-13; Isa 49:10; 63:9). Ps 103:13 describes God as one who pities the God-fearers as a father naturally pities his children. One of the emphases of the Book of JONAH is to stress God's willingness to show pity, on even the dreaded Ninevites when there are acts of contrition (Jonah 4:10-11).

In the NT, Jesus is depicted acting out of a feeling of pity (Matt 20:34) and as a response to the request for pity (Mark 9:22).

See also LOVE IN THE OLD TESTAMENT; MERCY.

—JOHN H. HAYES

• **Plagues.** Exod 7–12 contains the combined traditions of the priestly and Yahwistic elements of the Pentateuch concerning the ten "plagues" (9:14). These plagues were sent by the Lord upon the unwilling Egyptian PHARAOH to force him to liberate the enslaved Hebrew people. The J document seems to preserve seven of these "signs and wonders" (7:3), while P contains the complete ten. The extended Ps 78 recalls the "signs in EGYPT" (v. 43) but includes only seven of the plagues, while Ps 105 follows the P source in recounting all ten of the "signs . . . in the land of Ham" (v. 27).

The first nine plagues were natural phenomena with which the Egyptians in historical times had been acquainted. Yet they are to be understood not as random occurrences, but as testimonies ("signs") to the divine activity and intent. In the first six plagues an understandable sequence of events could perhaps be seen. The first plague, the transformation of the NILE into blood, was duplicated by the Egyptian MAGICIANS and is often taken to be based on the Nile's becoming a dull red with the presence of tiny organisms often found after its annual flooding by the month of September. Plague two, a scourge of frogs also repeated by the Egyptians, has been known to occur several times in Egypt, and could have been encouraged by the decaying organic matter of the first plague. The remaining eight plagues the Egyptian magicians could not repeat. A large number of decaying dead frogs could bring about the kind of PESTILENCE seen in the next four plagues: gnats on people and beasts (third, 8:16-19); swarms of flies (fourth, 8:20-32); sickness and death to all the livestock of the Egyptians (fifth, 9:1-7), but "not one of the cattle of the Israelites was dead"; the sixth plague involved MOSES' casting ashes or dust into the air before Pharaoh (9:8-12). The dust settled throughout the land, causing sores or boils "on man and beast throughout all the land of Egypt." The result of these plagues, as with all of the first nine, was that "the Lord hardened the heart of Pharaoh, and he did not listen" (9:12).

Plagues seven through nine involved, instead of disease and death, disturbances of nature. A severe hailstorm accompanied by lightning and thunder (9:13-35) "struck down everything that was in the field throughout all the land of Egypt, both man and beast; and the hail struck down every plant of the field, and shattered every tree of the field" except "in the land of Goshen, where the people of Israel were" (vv. 25-26). In the eighth (10:1-20) the Lord brought a wind from the east containing "a dense swarm of locusts as had never been before" (v. 14) which "ate all the plants in the land" (v. 15). A deep darkness for three days, "a darkness to be felt" (10:21), was the ninth scourge (10:21-29). None but the people of Israel could see one another. Probably, this was a duststorm caused by the hot wind, called Khamsin by the Arabs, coming from the Sahara.

The tenth and decisive plague leading to the release of the Hebrews was the death of all the firstborn of Egypt (11:1–12:30). Here the direct intervention of the Lord is involved, not diseases and natural phenomena. The Hebrews were instructed to smear the blood of an animal on the doorposts and lintels of their houses so that death, "the destroyer," would not enter them. Thereafter, "at midnight the Lord smote all the first-born in the land of Egypt" including "all the first-born of the cattle" (12:29). Then Pharaoh released Moses' people; the "signs" of the Lord had proved to be effective.

The term "plague" is also used for other disasters that befell Israel and the surrounding nations. One most severe plague was the forms of skin disease that went under the name of leprosy.

See also EXODUS; LEPROSY; PASSOVER; PESTILENCE.

—KAREN RANDOLPH JOINES

• **Plants of the Bible.** The study of plants in the Bible has been plagued by modern concepts of *genus* and *species.* The ancients probably had no such concepts. They were much more concerned with a plant's uses and appearance than with its genetic relationship to other plants. Thus we should not be surprised to find that a single word may designate what to us are very different plants.

Field and Garden Crops. (1) Barley (Heb. *śĕʿōrâ,* Gk.

krithē). The barley harvest comes about a month earlier than the wheat harvest (early- to mid-spring), so the first fruits would have been offered during the Passover festival, rather than at Pentecost with the wheat. Barley was less highly esteemed than wheat (about half as valuable; Rev 6:6), normally being reserved for animal food. However, barley is somewhat hardier than wheat, and so is often cultivated in more extreme climates.

(2) Beans (Heb. *pôl*). The standard variety of bean in biblical times was the hardy broad bean. The plant stands erect, and grows to be about three feet tall. Its large flowers, mostly white in color, bloom in late spring; the pods ripen in summer with several seeds each. Beans are included in the list of standard victuals in 2 Sam 17:28, and are one of the ingredients in Ezekiel's bread (Ezek 4:9) for his "siege."

(3) Cucumber (Heb. *qiššu'â*). Listed favorably as one of the items that the Israelites ate while in Egypt (Num 11:5), the cucumber was and still is a staple of that land. A similar word, *miqšâ*, may be related, having the meaning "cucumber field" in Isa 1:8 and Jer 10:5. The cucumbers of this area are larger, sweeter, and juicier (much more like melons) than their European relatives. The gourd (Heb. *paqqu'ōt*), a similar plant, is also found in abundance in Palestine. The Temple had ornaments shaped like the gourd (1 Kgs 7:24).

(4) Emmer (Heb. *kūssemet*). Emmer is a variety of wheat which, like the other wheat of ancient Palestine, is quadraploid (having four rows of seeds). The Hebrew word has traditionally been translated "spelt"; but this is a hexaploid variety, and was probably not grown in ancient Palestine. Emmer is inferior to durum wheat since its grains are hulled, though it is somewhat hardier.

(5) Grapevine (Heb. *gepen*, Gk. *ampelos*). Vines have been cultivated from very ancient times, at least since the Early Bronze Age (ca. 3000 B.C.E.). The fruit of the vine, the grape, is a berry whose color—like that of its juice—derives chiefly from its membranous skin, the inside being almost colorless. In modern Palestine white grapes are most common; however, in antiquity the red grape may have been more prevalent, as evidenced by the expression "blood of grapes" (Gen 49:11; Deut 32:14). The vine is a creeping plant with very long, slender branches that are usually propped up with sticks. Harvest comes over the entire summer season, from July to October. The grapes were eaten raw, dried into raisins, or pressed into juice, which was then either boiled into a thick syrup or fermented in wine. The natural yeasts of the grape will begin to ferment it into wine in about three days; and it is unlikely that the ancients knew any way to keep it from fermenting.

The gathering and pressing of grapes was an occasion of great joy and festivity, so it is easy enough to understand how the vine became a symbol of abundance and blessing in the OT. The blessing of Jacob, for example, lauds the Judean monarchy by envisioning an abundance of wine (Gen 49:11).

(6) Lentil (Heb. *'ădāšâ*). This plant is small, with slender stems much like the common pea plant. Its flowers are violet; and its fruit, the pea-like lentil, grows each in its own pod. It is used in soups or pastes, or under extreme circumstances in breads (Ezek 4:9).

(7) Wheat (Heb. *ḥiṭṭâ*). Durum wheat was, and still is, the most common crop in Palestine. It grows ideally in climates with a moderate, moist winter. Planted just before or after the early rains (October), the wheat grows during the winter and spring, ripens in early summer, and is harvested in June or July. Durum wheat stands erect, its grains remain on the stalk until harvest, and its kernels have no hulls, so it is easy to harvest and to thresh.

Wild wheat also grows in abundance in Palestine, and in some areas is harvested, though its brittle stalks and heads make this difficult since the grains fall to the ground before or during harvest. The generic term *dāgān* "corn, grain" is distinct from American corn, referring generally to all cultivated grains.

Fruit-producing Trees. (1) Almond (Heb. *šāqēd*). The almond tree, related to the peach tree, grows wild in Palestine and may in fact have been first domesticated there. It is grown mostly for its seed, which is quite delicious. The tree may also have been thought to hold magical qualities (Gen 30:37). The blossoms of the almond tree are the first in Palestine to set on (in early February). Thus the verbal root *šqd* "to watch" has some logic to it, since the almond blossom's white or pink brilliance is a harbinger of spring in Israel (cf. Jer 1:11).

(2) Apricot/Apple (Heb. *tappûaḥ*). It is uncertain exactly how to translate this word. Scholarly opinion falls into two camps: apple and apricot. Neither is certainly attested as having been grown in Palestine during the biblical period. Both are round, fleshy fruits with sweet aroma and taste. The trees blossom in spring with an abundance of pink or white flowers. The fruits ripen throughout the fall.

(3) Date Palm (Heb. *tāmār*, Gk. *phoinix*). The palm tree is striking for its shape. Its tall, straight trunk can grow to nearly 100 feet without any branches. The top of the tree is crowned with a sphere of gigantic leaves that look something like huge feathers. The fruit (dates), which ripens at the end of summer into brown, sweet berries, hangs in clusters from the top of the tree. Dates were either dried and eaten whole, pressed into cakes, or their juice fermented into liquor. The unique contour of the tree is depicted in Israelite and other Near Eastern art, often as a symbol for uprightness (cf. Judg 4:5). In the NT the leaves (wrongly called "branches") are waved before Jesus on his entering Jerusalem (John 12:13).

(4) Fig (Heb. *tĕ'ēnâ*, Gk. *sukē*). The fig tree, a small deciduous tree with large leaves, provides one of the most important crops in Palestine. If well-tended the tree yields two harvests per year. The first harvest ("early figs") ripens in June; the second ("late figs") in August/September. The fruit contains numerous seeds, which contribute to its unique texture. Because of their high sugar content figs were pressed into cakes and dried, either for storage for the fruitless months or for export.

(5) Olive (Heb. *zayit*, Gk. *elaia, agrielaios*). This gnarly, slow-growing evergreen grows best on rocky, dry soil, as is found in the mountainous regions of Judah and Israel. The fruit is gathered when fully ripe (September), and either eaten raw or, more commonly, pressed for oil (the expression *'eṣ šemen* "oil tree" may refer to the olive). The olive was one of the "seven species" with which the land was blessed (Deut 8:7), and is used as a symbol of prosperity and peace (Heb. *šālôm*; cf. Gen 8:11). Two olive trees—the "two witnesses" of Revelation—are even said to "stand before the Lord of the Earth" (Rev 11:4; cf. Zech 4:3, 12-14).

(6) Pomegranate (Heb. *rimmôn*). The pomegranate is a small, bushy deciduous tree with thick, often thorny, foliage. The flower is fragrant and showy—usually either red or yellow/white in color—and, as the fruit ripens, becomes a crown-shaped appendage to it. The fruit is about the size and shape of a large orange, with a tough outer rind that

ranges in color from brownish-yellow to red. The fruit consists of hundreds of seeds, each of which is surrounded by its own sweet, juicy pulp. The seeds are separated into layers inside the fruit by an inner rind. Because of the multitude of seeds in each fruit, the pomegranate became a symbol of fertility in many of the cultures of the ancient world. In Israel it adorned Temple furnishings, and was counted with grapes and figs among the chief blessings of the land (Num 13:23).

(7) Sycamore (Heb. *šiqmâ*, Gk. *sukomorea*). The sycamore is a light-wooded tree whose fruit is similar to the fig, though of lesser quality in sugar content and taste. The thick branches grow out of the trunk quite close to the ground, which makes it easy to climb (Luke 19:4). In antiquity it was a common tree with little value (1 Kgs 10:24), but today would be extinct if not for human intervention.

Spices and Herbs. (1) Bitter Herbs (Heb. *mĕrōrîm*). This designation occurs in connection with the Passover meal (Exod 12:18; Num 9:11) and parallel to "gall" (Lam 3:15). The exact identification of the term is uncertain, but Mouldenke and Zohary identify it with herbs like endive, chicory and reichardia, though they do not limit the category to those plants.

(2) Cassia (Heb. *qĕṣî'â*). The cassia, a native of East Asia, often grows to be forty feet tall. The oil, which is distilled from the tree's leaves, is aromatic and was one of the ingredients in the oil with which the "tent of meeting" was anointed (Exod 30:22-32). In addition, the large leaves, bark, and immature fruits are used as flavoring agents.

(3) Cinnamon (Heb. *qinnāmôn*, Gk. *kinamōmon*). The cinnamon tree is an evergreen, native to Ceylon and the coast of India, that grows to be twenty to thirty feet tall. Its bark is peeled off and sold in short tubes as a spice. It was exported into most parts of the ancient world. In Israel it was used as a spice, a perfume, and an ingredient in the sacred oil (Exod 30:23).

(4) Coriander (Heb. *gad*). It is not certain that the Hebrew word is to be identified with coriander, but this seems to be the best alternative. The two instances of the word in the OT (Exod 16:31; Num 11:7) are for comparison with manna. The coriander plant, which is fairly common in Palestine (though not in the desert), is an annual herb of the carrot family. The entire plant has a strong characteristic smell: the leaves are often used as a spice and the oil from its seeds is extracted for perfume and medicine.

(5) Henna (Heb. *kōper*). This plant is referred to twice in Cant (1:14; 4:13; perhaps also 7:11) as a particularly sweet-smelling plant. The flowers may have been worn by the wealthy in a sachet around the neck; and the leaves may also have been used as a cosmetic. The henna bush grows either wild or cultivated, especially in the warm oases of Palestine.

(6) Hyssop (Heb. *'ēzôb*, Gk. *hussōpos*). The hyssop is a many-stemmed, hairy shrub, whose stems can grow to three feet tall. In biblical times it was tied in bunches and used in rites of purification, since the plant's hairs retain the purifying liquid (Exod 12:21-22; Ps 51:7; cf. John 18:28-30). The plant is also gathered for use as a spice.

(7) Mustard (Gk. *sinapi*). It is fairly certain the Greek word refers to the Black Mustard plant, which is quite common in the Galilee region. It is an annual herb that, though having very small seeds, grows to seven feet or more. This fact is the basis of Jesus' parable about the reign of God (Matt 13:31 = Mark 4:30 = Luke 13:18).

Medicinal and Magical Plants. (1) Aloes (Heb. *'ăhālîm, 'ăhālôt*, Gk. *aloē*). Aloe is the aromatic resin that

An aloe plant.

comes from the leaves of the aloe plant. This resin was imported into Israel, making it expensive. In the OT it is used primarily as an erotic scent (Prov 7:17; Cant 4:14). It has also long been known as a medicinal plant.

(2) Balm (Heb. *ṣŏrî*). The term "balm" probably refers to the gum of the balsam plant (though Zohary links it with the *Storax*), which is native to the tropical portions of South Arabia. The gum, which is extracted from the branches (the seeds are also used as spices), was used as a spice, as an aromatic oil, and as a cure for snakebite or other ills.

(3) Mandrakes (Heb. *dûdā'îm*). The mandrake is a common plant in the fields and steppes of the biblical world. The roots are shaped like a human body, which gave rise to its use in magic to induce love and conception (Gen 30:14-16). The plant is stemless, with large leaves around purple flowers.

(4) Wormwood (Heb. *la'ănâ*, Gk. *apsinthos, cholē*). "Wormwood" probably, though not certainly, refers to the artemisia shrub, which grows commonly in the deserts of Palestine. The leaves are strongly aromatic, and their juice can be deadly if taken by itself; but in small proportions it is a medicine against intestinal worms, a fact reflected in its name. Wormwood often symbolizes the pain of God's judgment.

Forest Trees. (1) Acacia (Heb. *šiṭṭâ*). It is almost certain that the word shittim (KJV) refers to common acacia, an evergreen tree that attains twenty to thirty feet in height. Its branches are long and spindly, ending in yellow flowers. A member of the mimosa family, its wood is excellent for building (Exod 26:15).

(2) Aleppo Pine (Heb. *berôš*). There is general agreement that *berôš* usually refers to the Aleppo pine, a species native to the forests of Syro-Palestine and not found outside the Mediterranean region. It is a stately, fast-growing tree (reaching up to eighty feet) that grows in areas where many other trees will not grow. As the tree grows the upper branches inhibit the light, killing the lower branches. Its straight wood makes good timber.

(3) Algum (Heb. *'almūggîm, 'algūmmîm*). The Hebrew *'almūggîm* (= *'algūmmîm*, the last two radicals having been transposed) has been variously identified. It is often rendered "sandalwood"; but "Red Saunder" (Mouldenke, Zohary) and "Juniper" have also been proposed. No identification is certain.

(4) Cedar (Heb. *'erez*). The cedar, which for the most part refers to the "cedar of Lebanon," was renowned in ancient times for its long-livedness, great height, perdurability as timber, and fragrance. Though it once grew in abundance in the Lebanon Mountains, it is now nearly extinct through millennia of human abuse. A tall, stately tree (up to 100 feet tall and eight feet in diameter; cf. Ezek 31), it becomes increasingly pyramid-shaped with age, with branches that reach out in what appear to be layers.

(5) Cypress (Heb. *tĕ'aššûr*). The identification of this tree is far from certain. RSV translates "pine," others translate "cypress" or "cedar." Some botanists favor the box tree, an evergreen with oblong leaves, which may be found in the Lebanon. But the cypress, an evergreen with spreading branches, achieving up to fifty feet in height, is much more common to Palestine, and is to be preferred.

(6) Gopher (Heb. *gōper*). The phrase "gopher wood" is used only once in the OT, as the material from which Noah was to build the ark (Gen 6:14). It is quite uncertain what material is meant. It has been argued that the word is a loan word for "cypress," or perhaps "bitumen." In any case, it seems that some kind of tree is meant, since the Hebrew "tree" (*'ēṣ*) is used in connection with it.

(7) Myrtle (Heb. *hădas*). The myrtle is a tree or shrub native to Asia Minor (in areas of moist soil) which achieves a height of about five feet. Its dense foliage has led some scholars to equate it with the Heb. *'ēṣ-'ābôt,* "leafy tree." Probably because of its pleasant scent, the plant is used in the Jewish Festival of Booths (Neh 8:15).

(8) Oak Tree (Heb. *'ēlôn, 'allôn*), Terebinth Tree (Heb. *'ēlâ, 'allâ*). The Hebrew root of these words may be related to that for "god" (*'ēl*), thus possibly referring to any tree of gigantic proportions, or even hinting that these trees had a cultic use (Hos 4:13). Both the oak and the terebinth are large, sturdy trees, of which most varieties are deciduous, and which have a long life. Both are mainly trees of the steppe, midway between the arable land and the desert. The wood of both is quite hard and somewhat knotty. As such a sturdy tree, each can be symbolic of strength or durability (Amos 2:9), or of pride (Isa 2:13).

(9) Plane Tree (Heb. *'armôn*). The plane tree is quite common in Palestinian forests that have a permanent river, and may once have been even more common. It is a tall tree with dense foliage and large, dark green leaves. The bark peels off easily (the Heb. word is related to *'ārōm,* "naked"), which may have been the reason for Jacob's using it in magic (Gen 30:37).

(10) Poplar (Heb. *'ărābâ*). The Euphrates poplar is a common tree in the forests along the Jordan River. The rendering "willow" for this word is made less likely since the Arabic cognate is used of the poplar. The tree is tolerant to salt, and so can grow in areas of brackish water. It is one of the four species used at the Festival of Booths (Lev 23:40).

(11) Tamarisk (Heb. *'ēšel*). The tamarisk is a large, leafless evergreen tree indigenous to Palestine, especially to the Arabah and to wadis and salt marshes of the dry areas. The branches are soft and green. Zohary believes that the term for "cedar" (Heb. *'erez*) is occasionally (e.g., Lev 14:4) to be translated "tamarisk." A bush-like variety grows in the wadis of the desert whose honey-like drippings are probably what the Israelites referred to as "manna" (Heb. *man*; the Bedouin still call this *mann*).

(12) White Poplar (Heb. *libneh*). The Hebrew suggests that this tree is white; but it is debated whether it is the white poplar or the storax. In Hos 4:13 it appears to be a large tree such as the white poplar, and not a shrub like the storax. The white poplar, a native of Syria and Lebanon, grows tall and straight with white bark.

Shrubs, Weeds, and Thistles. (1) Broom (Heb. *rōtem*). Because this word is so clearly related to the Arabic *ratam* "broom," its identification is not questioned by scholars. The broom is a small bush with many spindly branches, making good kindling and hot coals (Ps 120:4).

(2) Juniper (Heb. *'ărô'ēr*). The translation of this word is uncertain, so that many elect to translate it "shrub." On the basis of the Arabic many scholars accept its identification as the Juniper, a shrub usually less that fifteen feet high, which is found in Palestine only isolatedly in the desert (Jer 17:5-6). The trunk is thick; the leaves are tiny, scale-like growths that cover the thin branches.

(3) Nettle (Heb. *ḥārûl*). This is the generic Hebrew word for any kind of thorny weed, though occasionally scholars have proposed more specific identifications such as chick pea. Nettles are annual plants growing in neglected areas and in unweeded gardens (Prov 24:31ff.).

(4) Tumbleweed (Heb. *galgal*). The Hebrew literally means "wheel," and so the plant in question, though this is debated, is probably the tumbleweed. The tumbleweed is famous for its "tumbling" before the wind (Isa 17:13). The plant grows on a small stem that breaks off when dry, leaving the round calyx to blow about.

(5) Weeds (Gk. *zizanion*). It is usually thought that the weeds referred to in Jesus' parable (Matt 13:24-30) are *lolium,* annual plants that, until they bear fruit, look almost exactly like wheat. The grains are smaller than those of wheat, and so are separated at threshing.

Other Plants. (1) Flax (Heb. *pēšet,* Gk. *sindōn*). Flax is an herb growing up to three feet tall, with a showy blue flower at the top. The seed is rich in oil. In biblical times the plant was harvested whole, dried, cut open, and combed, and the fibers woven into cloth. In the NT the words for flax usually mean "cloth."

(2) Lily (Heb. *šôšan,* Gk. *krinon*). Scholars debate the identification of these words. Zohary is quite sure they refer to the white lily. Others are less sure, preferring to speak of a word that can apply to a variety of different flowers. The white lily is a bulbous herb with thin leaves growing all along a stem, culminating in a white flower. The white lily often symbolized beauty and purity (Cant 2:1-2; Matt 6:8) or fertility.

(3) Reed (Heb. *qāneh,* Gk. *kalamos*). There are several kinds of reeds that grow in Palestine, but most common is a large (up to ten feet) plant that in Palestine grows chiefly by the Jordan (the Nile is famous for it). Out of the stalk grow large leaves; and the whole is topped with a white plume. The hollow stem breaks easily (2 Kgs 18:21), but in dense growths can be a considerable obstacle. A similar plant, the cattail (Heb. *sūp*), is thought to have given its name to the Hebrew *yam-sūp* "sea of reeds" crossed by Moses and his group (Exod 13:18).

The most common metaphor for which plants are used in the Bible is that of fertility and abundance. The vine, pomegranate, and olive are especially symbolic of this abundance. Often depicted by personifying a growing plant, this abundance is provided by God (Jesus' parable of the mustard plant—of something small that becomes large—lies within this tradition); and should one take it for granted or become haughty, it can be taken away (Ezek 17, 31; Ps 80). In times of prosperity everyone sits "under one's own vine and fig tree." With respect to trees of great antiquity or height, a kind of eternality or longevity is sometimes in view. Ps 1 contrasts a tree planted by a stream on the one hand, and chaff on the other, between something enduring and something fleeting. The "tree of life" in Gen 3 also illustrates this use of plant imagery. Sometimes peculiar characteristics of a given plant can be used in a metaphor. In Jotham's fable (Judg 9:9-20) several plants are asked to become "king" over the rest. After several "noble" plants (olive, fig, vine) refuse, the nettle (Heb. *'āṭād*), a plant of no use to anyone, accepts the offer—a poignant commentary on power. Plants, like humans, have a multitude of differences. It is for this reason that they serve as useful analogies on such a wide variety of subjects.

See also AGRICULTURE/FARMING; FOOD.

Bibliography. G. Dalman, *Arbeit und Sitte in Palaestina*; F. Lundgren, *Die Benutzung der Pflanzenwelt in der alttestamentlichen Religion*; H. N. Moldenke and A. L. Moldenke, *Plants of the Bible*; M. Zohary, *Plants of the Bible*.

—LOREN D. CROW

• **Plato, Republic 588B-589B.** [play'toh] This brief tractate from the NAG HAMMADI library is a Coptic translation from Greek of a short passage from Plato's *Republic* (588B-589B). The identity of the Coptic text as a translation from Plato was not recognized immediately, owing in part to the damaged manuscript (the top few lines of each page are largely illegible), to the unexpected nature of such a find, and most importantly, to the fractured nature of the translation. Whether the inaccuracies are due to the translator's lack of language skills or to a deliberate intention to render a Gnostic interpretation of the passage is debatable.

The passage chosen for translation is a parable told by Socrates on the nature of justice and injustice. The human soul is pictured as the union of three creatures: a many-headed beast (symbolizing human desires), a lion (symbolizing emotions), and a man (symbolizing reason). The person who does injustice feeds the beast and lion but starves the man, and thus destroys the soul. The man who does justice, on the other hand, allows the human part of the soul to be in control, and this produces reconciliation among the elements. In other words, when rationality rules, justice is served.

Why was this particular passage from Plato chosen for translation and inclusion in the Nag Hammadi collection? First, it should be noted that this passage was popular in late antiquity. EUSEBIUS, the church historian, quotes it in a work called *Preparation for the Gospel* (12.46.1-6). Stoic and Neoplatonic philosophers also allude to it. The passage may have been included in anthologies of edifying quotations that were known to circulate in late antiquity. If the Coptic translator was acquainted with the passage from such an anthology, he may not have even known the text was from Plato. But beyond the availability of this Platonic passage, the Gnostics or monastics who copied and preserved the Nag Hammadi library certainly would have been attracted to the passage's theme of justice, the tripartite psychology, and its ethical rigor. Moreover, if the translation is indeed a gnosticizing interpretation of Plato, this is in keeping with Gnosticism's syncretistic character. Platonic influence on Gnostic teaching is evident in other texts. But the themes of the passage would have held wide appeal, so it is difficult to establish on this basis that the translation is gnostic. Investigations into possible hermetic tendencies of the translation have also been made, especially because the text is included in a codex with several clearly hermetic works (DISCOURSE ON THE EIGHTH AND NINTH, ASCLEPIUS, PRAYER OF THANKSGIVING).

The lion is a widely used symbol for both good and bad forces in many traditions: Judeo-Christian, Greek philosophical, and Gnostic. Biblical authors, for instance, use the lion to describe Yahweh, Israel, and Christ on the one hand, and their enemies or the devil on the other hand. Likewise for Plato, the lion-like part of the soul could be a force for good or evil. Wild emotions destroy a person, but they can be tamed and made an ally of reason. In Gnostic interpretation, however, the lion almost always symbolizes evil. In some Gnostic texts, the lion represents the evil creator god (e.g., *ApJohn, HypArch*). In other texts, the lion represents the evil passions, especially sexual desires, which are the creation of this evil god and must be eradicated (e.g., *GosThom* 7). The Nag Hammadi fragment from Plato's *Republic* illustrates the latter anthropological usage of the lion. The text is a moralistic homily urging the just man to "cast down every image of the evil beast and trample them along with the images of the lion."

See also GNOSTICISM; HERMETIC LITERATURE; NAG HAMMADI.

Bibliography. J. Brashler and D. M. Parrott, "Plato, Republic 588B-589B," *The Nag Hammadi Library in English*, ed. J. M. Robinson; H. M. Jackson, *The Lion Becomes Man: the Leontomorphic Creator and the Platonic Tradition* (*SBLDS* 81); *Nag Hammadi Codices V,2-5 and VI with Papyrus Berolinensis 8502. 1 and 4,* D. M. Parrott, ed.

—CAROL D. C. HOWARD

• **Pleasing Odor.** *See* INCENSE

• **Poetic Fragments, Hellenistic Jewish.** During the Hellenistic Period Jews of the diaspora composed numerous books in Greek literary genres, including epic poems. They also edited authentic fragments of Greek poetry and wrote brief passages of poetry in imitation of classical style under classical pseudonyms. The motivation for reworking and composing such fragments was to supply evidence from Greek literature that the best of Greek wisdom was found already in Jewish scripture and tradition, from which the Greeks were said to have derived it.

These fragments of pseudo-Greek poets, together with some genuine excerpts from classical poets, were collected in anthologies (*gnōmologia*), and much later early Christian fathers made considerable use of these anthologies in mounting their own case that "Judeo-Christian" faith precedes the wisdom of the Greeks, who they claimed were dependent upon Moses and the Jewish scriptures for many of their ideas. In fact, we owe our knowledge of these fragments to Christian authors: Clement of Alexandria (ca. 150–215), EUSEBIUS (ca. 263–339) and Pseudo-Justin (date uncertain). Clement cites Hecataeus's work *On Abraham and the Egyptians* as the source for one of his quotations. It is likely that this writing is a pseudonymous work composed by a Hellenistic Jew (cf. Josephus *Ant* 1.159), but we should not assume, as some scholars have, that Pseudo-Hecataeus composed any of the pseudonymous verses that he quotes. The fragments known to us from Clement and Pseudo-Justin may derive from a single *gnōmologion* dating from the third to second century B.C.E.

The fragments defend cardinal Jewish beliefs regarding the holiness of the seventh day (the SABBATH), the nature of GOD, CREATION, and ESCHATOLOGY. For example, a number of the fragments defend the oneness of God and link it closely with faith in God as creator. In Greek religion the acclamation "one God" typically meant allegiance to a single deity above all other lords. But Jews defended the oneness of God above all other gods by affirming that one God created all things. Thus, one of the fragments attributed to Sophocles declares, "God is one, one in very truth, who fashioned heaven and the broad earth." To defend the idea of eschatological judgment another passage from Sophocles is adduced. This fragment announces a final cosmic conflagration and mentions "two ways" in Hades, "one for the just and one for the impious." The second theme is also presented in a fragment from the comic poet Diphilus.

It is difficult to discern the purpose of the original Jewish anthologies, since the poetic material is extant only in the works of Christian authors who introduce it with their own introductions and comments. One can speculate, however, that the collections served a number of uses. They could have been used apologetically to win respect from pagans for the Jewish faith. One can also imagine Hellenistic Jews who valued Greek learning and culture delighting in proofs to the effect that the "best" of Greek wisdom is already found in Jewish scripture.

Bibliography. H. Attridge, "Fragments of Pseudo-Greek Poets," *The Old Testament Pseudepigrapha,* ed. J. H. Charlesworth.

—CHARLES H. COSGROVE

• **Poetry.** Literature in which balanced PARALLELISM and terseness are perceived to be predominant. Since biblical poetry lacks features that mark classical verse as poetry, such as quantitative meter and regular rhyme, parallelism within and between lines and words serves as its primary identifying feature. Terseness also identifies biblical poetry; it is a condensing and compressing of the poetic message into brief clauses of often no more than three or four words containing the bare essentials of meaning. Parallelism activates a network of linguistic correspondences within and between lines, thereby increasing the feeling of their connectedness, while terseness creates a correspondence in the number of parts so that the parts and lines appear balanced in length or rhythm. Parallelism and terseness together create the perception of the poetic couplet or brief, two-part sentence form that is the essence of poetry. This form gives poetry the feeling of regularity, closure, and completeness akin to the final "click" of rhyme. Perception is a crucial part of the process of all language. One perceives the dominance of parallelism in poetry not only because of its quantity, but because of its terseness.

Extent. Though it has been argued on the one hand that the entire Bible is written in poetic verse, and on the other hand, that there is no precise distinction between biblical prose and poetry, Psalms, Proverbs, Job, Canticles, Lamentations, much of the prophets, and portions of the Pentateuch, Daniel and Ecclesiastes are generally recognized as poetry in the OT. Only a few passages are perceived as poetry in the NT, e.g., the MAGNIFICAT and prophecy of Zechariah in Luke 1, the NUNC DIMITTIS in Luke 2, the HYMN in Phil 2, and parts of Revelation, along with fragments of poetic lines quoted by NT authors, e.g., 1 Cor 15:33; Acts 17:28. Poetry also appears in the APOCRYPHA, pseudepigrapha, and the DEAD SEA SCROLLS.

Form and Its Effects. The short, two-part sentence form or couplet is the basic unit of Hebrew poetry. The two parts are separated by a slight stop or pause (indicated by /). The second part is usually a continuation of the first in some way, and ends in a full pause or stop (indicated by //):

__________ / __________ //

This binary form is the rule in biblical Hebrew, while the three-part or ternary sentence is the exception. A confusing range of terminology is used to talk about this form. Each part of it is variously called line, stich or stichos (row, line), hemistich (half line), colon (part, member), verset, or A or B. The two parts together are called line, distich (two stichs), stich, bicola, verse, or couplet. This binary form, or line, exhibits a varied correspondence or intensity of parallelism between its two parts (which will be called A and B; so Kugel).

The medial pause in a line has too often been seen as an "equals" (=) sign; it is rather simply a pause or comma, or perhaps better, a double arrow (‹——›; so Kugel). That is, B comes after A, adding to it, particularizing or expanding it (Muilenburg), as well as looks back to A to connect to it; B thus exhibits both "retrospective" and "prospective" qualities. The afterwardness of B gives it its "emphatic" character; it parallels or seconds and reinforces A and gives to the poetic line the feeling of closure and completeness akin to the final "click" of rhyme (Kugel), as for example in Job 3:3.

Sometimes an obvious correspondence exists between A and B, the latter a seeming restatement of the former, as in Ps 146:2. Yet A and B can also be quite unequal in length and seem to be parallel, as in Ps 124:6. Most poetic parallelisms fall somewhere in between these two extremes in varying paralleling intensities. In proverbs and sayings, however, the whole point of the form is finding the precise connection between the seemingly unrelated A and B, as in Eccl 7:1. The "sharpness" of this proverb, that is, "the potential subtleties hidden inside juxtaposed clauses," is the highest form of parallelism (Kugel).

Terseness also contributes to the poetic effect of the binary form or line. Parallelism and terseness together create our perception of "oneness forged out of twoness" (Berlin) and of the regularity of poetry. Terseness constantly presses toward compactness and ellipsis. The most frequent grammatical omissions are the definite article *ha-*, the relative particle *'ašer,* and personal suffixes on nouns, verbs and prepositions, as for example in Ps 118:22.

The compactness, simplicity, and shortness of A and B, which are usually clauses of only three or four words, forces us to consider their connectedness, particularly when their relationship is left unstated. One cannot reduce the "telegraph style" (Kugel) that is terseness, however, to metrical formulae or statistical analyses of length or syntax because terseness, like parallelism, is variable.

Parallelism. The history of the study of biblical parallelism has been shaped by Bishop Robert Lowth's eighteenth century "Lectures on Hebrew Poetry" and his Isaiah commentary. Lowth identified *parallelismus membrorum* ("the parallelism of the clauses") and distinguished three types of semantic parallelism as the essence of Hebrew poetry: synonymous (interpreted as a restatement or saying the same thing twice), antithetical (a negation or opposite statement), and synthetic (a catchall category of sequence and combination). Lowth's work has served for over 200 years as the model that scholars fleshed out and identified. Recently, however, the model has come under attack, particularly from linguists.

Parallelism is the complex network or feeling of correspondence between adjacent lines, parts of lines, and/or words. The nature of this correspondence varies; it cannot be restricted to one level of language or another, although the semantic and grammatical aspects of parallelism are most evident and have historically received the most attention. Parallelism activates all the aspects of language at once—lexical (vocabulary), grammatical (syntax and morphology), semantic (meaning), and phonological (sounds) on the levels of the word and the line (Berlin). Their interplay and integrated effect contribute to the feeling of a pervasive parallelism.

(1) The grammatical aspect of parallelism. Inflection or formation of verbs, nouns, adjectives, etc. within a line (morphology) and the combination of parts within A and B and of A and B with each other (syntax) mark the grammatical aspect of parallelism. An exact grammatical correspondence in which the syntax and morphology of A and B are the same, or repeated, is rare; see Ps 103:10. Usually B substitutes something morphologically different for what appears in A, as in Ps 33:2, where a pronoun is substituted for a noun.

> Praise *the Lord* with the lyre /
> With the ten-stringed harp sing to *[him]* //

Often, too, verbs from the same root but different conjugations or aspects are paired in A and B, as the *qal/niph'al* in Ps 24:7—

> *Lift up,* O gates, your heads /
> and *be lifted up,* O eternal doors //

Alternation also frequently takes place between *qtl-yqtl* forms (the Hebrew "perfect" and "imperfect") as in Ps 92:4—

> For you, O Lord, *have made me glad*
> by your work /
> in the works of your hands *I (will) exult* //

Scholars have traditionally viewed these morphological alternations, and others such as shifts from A to B in person, number, gender, definiteness and case (not in terms of case endings but nouns as nominative or accusative) as simply stylistic devices for variety. Rather, they are examples of morphological parallelism that serve to differentiate and integrate A and B. Kugel argues that the *qtl/yqtl* alternation, for example, indicates an intermeshing of actions in the same way as subordinating phrases function in English.

Common syntactical parallelisms include transformations from A to B of nominal (without a finite verb) to verbal (with a finite verb), as in Mic 6:2b—

> For the Lord has a quarrel with [his] people /
> and with Israel [he] will dispute //

Also occurring are positive-negative transformations, as in Prov 6:20—

> Guard, my son, the commandment of your father /
> and do not forsake the teaching of your mother //

Other transformations involve grammatical mood, i.e., a contrast of the indicative and interrogative, e.g., Pss 6:6; 73:25. These transformations challenge the emending of texts because of so-called grammatical "inconsistencies."

(2) The lexical and semantic aspects of parallelism. These two aspects are intertwined. The lexical aspect refers to specific words or word groups that are paired in A and B, while the semantic deals with the relationship between the meanings of A and B; words, of course, affect that relationship. The discovery of the Ugaritic poems at Ras Shamra in 1929 led to the collection by Dahood of "fixed word pairs," i.e., parallel terms that occur in both the Bible and Ugaritic texts. It also generated theories about oral composition—poets drew upon a stock of fixed pairs for their oral composition of parallel lines (Culley). This hypothesis finds little support today (Yoder). Rather, word pairs are viewed as the products of normal word associations (Berlin, O'Connor).

Some words are paired frequently with others to make a single merismatic phrase: "day and night" for example, meant "all the time" (Kugel). Further, a word may elicit a parallel word or be paralleled by itself, i.e., repeated, as the comparison of 2 Sam 22 and Ps 18 shows. Also, a word may elicit many different associations, depending upon the poet's artistry, the requirements of the context and how stereotyped it has become. One cannot predict word associations in biblical parallelism but can only explain and categorize them according to rules of linguistics.

The semantic aspect of parallelism has received the most attention because of Lowth's tripartite model. But as Kugel argues, "Biblical parallelism is of one sort, 'A, and what's more, B' or a hundred sorts: but it is not three." Scholars today tend to see a more dynamic movement within a line than Lowth did. Parallelism does not always make the semantic relationship between A and B explicit. As Kugel argues: "A is so, and what's more, B." B in its connection to A has an "emphatic, seconding character"; B carries A further, echoing, defining, restating, contrasting it, *"it does not matter which."*

Alter prefers to speak of the movement of meaning within a line as "heightening," or "intensification." His "rule of thumb" is that a general term occurs in A and is specified or concretized or focused or intensified in B, as in Prov 3:10 (the verbal movement shows intensification, the noun movement specification/concretization)—

> Then your barns *will be filled* with *plenty* /
> and your vats *will be bursting* with *new wine* //

In this light, ellipsis, which occurs when the subject or verb appears in A but is "gapped" (missing) and only implied in B, is no longer seen as an example of "incomplete" or defective parallelism. Rather, ellipsis is one way in which B "seconds" or "intensifies" A by isolating terms for attention, as in Lam 3:19—

> *Remember* my affliction and my bitterness /
> the wormwood and the gall //

Semantic parallelism is rarely complete or explicit; "language resists true synonymity" (Alter). Not only can B "second" or "intensify" or complete A, but sometimes B can cause us to see A in a new way. Scholars speak of this dual semantic function of parallelism in different ways: as disambiguation (or redundance) and ambiguity (Berlin) or as the perception of disharmony which prompts semantic modifications (Alter). This dialectical tension of semantic parallelism is evident in the "intensification" of numbers, as in Deut 32:30a (cf. Ps 62:12; Gen 4:24)—

> How could *one* chase a *thousand*/
> and *two* put *ten thousand* to flight//

The dialectical tension is also evident in the movement from a standard, common, literal term in A to a more literary, figurative, metaphorical term in B (Alter), as in Gen 4:23 (cf. Prov 26:9; Eccl 7:1; Ps 88:12-13; Jer 48:11)—

> *Ada and Zilla, hear* my voice /
> *Wives of Lamech, give ear* to my speech //

Parallelism can serve as the vehicle for figurative language and metaphor; cf. Isa 1:9-10.

(3) The phonologic aspect of parallelism. Traditionally, the study of sound parallelism in biblical poetry has been relegated to the secondary status of poetic "technique," i.e., alliteration, assonance, onomatopoeia, or paranomasia (wordplay or punning), as in Amos 8:2 (*qáyiṣ*/basket, paired with *qēṣ*/end). Contemporary scholars focus upon the repetition and contrast of sounds in parallel lines,

and more specifically on sound pairs, i.e., "the repetition in parallel words or lines of the same or similar consonants (at least two sets) in any order within close proximity" (Berlin).

Sound may play a part in certain lexical combinations, for example, desert-wilderness (*mdbr-'rbh*) in Jer 2:6. Some sound pairs also show grammatical and semantic correspondence, as in Ps 122:7—

May there be peace [šlwm] in your ramparts /
Tranquility [šlwh] in your citadels //

Other sound pairs show no lexical and/or semantic correspondence, but occur in addition to a word pair or in place of one, as in Job 36:15. This shows that sound pairing is more than coincidental. Most sound pairs are not naturally associated word pairs or automatic responses "but a one-time nexus between sound and sense" (Berlin); the "unexpectedness" of their combination creates their effect.

(4) Summary. Given the different aspects of language that may be activated by parallelism, it is clear that no one formula can account for all possible parallelisms within and between poetic lines. One can identify, however, formal principles that may make parallelism perceptible and interesting to a reader or listener. Parallelism itself does not have meaning; parallelism does, however, help to structure the text and its meaning. Each parallelism fits into its context, and participates in and contributes to the meaning of the text as a whole.

Meter and Poetry. There is no word for "poetry" in biblical Hebrew, yet ever since Lowth, parallelism has been equated with poetry. Lowth himself argued that meter was the basis of biblical poetry but was lost to us because of the uncertainties of Hebrew pronunciation; its existence and structure, however, could be inferred from parallelism. Since Lowth, scholars have either persisted in the belief that meter characterizes Hebrew poetry (disagreeing over how meter is to be measured), or they have taken parallelism as a substitute for meter and its regularity. Many scholars today argue, however, that the rough equality of lines and the rhythm or meter of poetry are not accidental but also not metrical, i.e., not a product of syllable, accent, or word quantities; rather meter is a product of parallelism and cannot be understood apart from it. Textual emendation for the sake of meter is generally rejected today. Terse parallelism, not meter, distinguishes poetry from prose.

See also PARALLELISM.

Bibliography. R. Alter, *The Art of Biblical Poetry*; A. Berlin, *The Dynamics of Biblical Parallelism*; U. Cassuto, *Biblical and Oriental Studies*; T. Collins, *Line-Forms in Hebrew Poetry*; F. M. Cross and D. N. Freedman, *Studies in Ancient Yahwistic Poetry*; P. Craigie, "The Problem of Parallel Word Pairs in Ugaritic and Hebrew Poetry," *Semitics* 5 (1979): 48-58; R. Culley, *Oral Formulaic Language in the Biblical Psalms*; M. Dahood, "Poetry," *IDBSupp* and *Psalms I, II, III*; S. Geller, *Parallelism in Early Biblical Poetry*; N. Gottwald, "Poetry, Hebrew," *IDB*; G. B. Gray, *The Forms of Hebrew Poetry*; J. Kugel, *The Idea of Biblical Poetry*; R. Lowth, *Lectures on the Sacred Poetry of the Hebrews* and *Isaiah: A New Translation with a Preliminary Dissertation and Notes*; J. Muilenburg, "A Study in Hebrew Rhetoric: Repetition and Style," *VTSupp* 1 (1953): 97-111; M. O'Connor, *Hebrew Verse Structure*; T. H. Robinson, *The Poetry of the Old Testament*; B. H. Smith, *Poetic Closure: A Study of How Poems End*; D. Stuart, *Studies in Early Hebrew Meter*; P. Yoder, "A-B Pairs and Oral Composition in Hebrew Poetry," *VT* 21 (1971): 470-89.

—DENISE DOMBKOWSKI HOPKINS

• **Poimandres.** *See* HERMETIC LITERATURE

• **Politarch.** *See* THESSALONICA

• **Polycarp, Martyrdom of.** [pol'ee-kahrp] The *Martyrdom of Polycarp* is one of the oldest martyr accounts from the postapostolic church, and is included in editions of the APOSTOLIC FATHERS. It purports to record the martyrdom of Polycarp, the bishop of SMYRNA. The document takes the form of a letter from the church at Smyrna to the church at Philomelium and to the church at large. After a brief introduction noting that Polycarp's martyrdom has brought "the persecution" to an end, the writer provides a general description of the persecution, followed by contrasting portraits of Germanicus, who faces martyrdom nobly, and Quintus, who after volunteering for martyrdom recants out of fear. The rest of the document is devoted to Polycarp. Pressured by other Christians who are concerned for his safety, Polycarp initially withdraws to a farm. But when he learns through a vision that he must be burned alive, he goes willingly when his pursuers come for him. He is taken to the stadium, where the proconsul tries to persuade him to renounce Christ. Polycarp refuses and is condemned to be burned alive. The flames do not touch him, however, and the executioner must kill him with a dagger. His body is then burned, and the Christians gather his bones and deposit them in a suitable place. The document concludes with a request to the church at Philomelium to pass the letter along to other churches.

MartPol is extant in Latin, Syriac, Coptic, Armenian, and most importantly, Greek, the language in which it was undoubtedly composed. The antiquity of the book is confirmed by the fact that most of it is preserved by EUSEBIUS (*EccHist* 4.15). In the textual tradition there are appended to the document several supplements, the value of which is debated. One dates the martyrdom, with scholars understanding the reference either as 23 February 155, or 22 February 156. Another traces the transmission of the text from IRENAEUS, who was a younger contemporary of Polycarp, to Gaius, then to Socrates, then to Pionius, an early fourth century martyr who supposedly wrote the *Life of Polycarp*.

Although some scholars argue for a certain amount of interpolation by later Christians, most agree that *MartPol* is a genuine account written by an eyewitness to Polycarp's death. It therefore sheds valuable light on the persecution of early Christians, including the charge that Christians were atheists, the guilt attached to the mere name "Christian," the opportunities for accused Christians to recant, and the types of tortures which awaited those who did not. It also provides an early example of a growing tendency to hold martyrs in high esteem, even attesting to the practice of commemorating the "birthday" of one's martyrdom. The developing martyrology of the early church produced many similar—and sometimes quite fantastic—writings which served to inspire Christians of every generation, but perhaps no martyr's words ever surpassed the simple eloquence of those of Polycarp: "For eighty-six years I have served him, and he has done me no wrong; how can I blaspheme my King who saved me?" (9:3).

See also APOSTOLIC FATHERS.

Bibliography. K. Lake, ed., *The Apostolic Fathers*; J. Lawson, *A Theological and Historical Introduction to the Apostolic Fathers*; W. R. Schoedel, *Polycarp, Martyrdom of Polycarp, Fragments of Papias*.

—JOSEPH L. TRAFTON

• **Polycarp, to the Philippians.** The letter of Polycarp to the Philippian church is a document from one of the important Christian figures of the early second century. Polycarp of Smyrna is known from several notices in EUSEBIUS, IRENAEUS, and Tertullian, as well as from the MARTYRDOM OF POLYCARP, and the letter of IGNATIUS to Polycarp. Polycarp is seen as a bridge figure between the apostolic era and the next generation. Irenaeus (Eusebius, *EccHist* 5.20.6) said that Polycarp had sat at the feet of JOHN, and that he was appointed to his position at Smyrna by the APOSTLES themselves (3.36.1).

Irenaeus further noted (Eusebius, *EccHist* 5.20.8) that Polycarp wrote several letters to neighboring Christian congregations, but today only the letter to the Philippians survives. The Christian community at Philippi had asked Polycarp for copies of the letter of Ignatius (13:2). Apparently Polycarp attached them to this letter. A second occasion for the letter was the apparent abuse of office by a certain elder (11:1-2).

The letter contains many quotations and echoes of biblical materials from both the OT and the NT as well as from the books of TOBIT and I CLEMENT.

For one who is apparently writing shortly after the death of Ignatius (ca. 117), which he mentions, he demonstrates a significant use of NT materials. It is remarkable that he knew the collection of the Letters of Paul (3:2), but makes no mention of a collection of four Gospels.

Polycarp's letter to the Philippians presents a Christianity not unlike that of the Pastoral Epistles, evincing a strong morality, anti-docetism, reverence for tradition, and concern for the poor. Some have even suggested Polycarp wrote or edited the Pastoral Epistles.

There are nine Greek manuscripts of the letter, all of which end at 9:2 (evidently deriving from a single source). The complete letter occurs in a Latin version, though chaps. 9 and 13 are found in Eusebius (*EccHist* 3.36.13-15).

See also APOSTOLIC FATHERS; PASTORAL EPISTLES; POLYCARP, MARTYRDOM OF.

Bibliography. P. N. Harrison, *Polycarp's Two Epistles to the Philippians*; J. Quasten, *Patrology*; W. R. Schoedel, *Polycarp, Martyrdom of Polycarp, Fragments of Papias*.

—GRAYDON F. SNYDER

• **Polygamy.** *See* ADULTERY IN THE OLD TESTAMENT; MARRIAGE IN THE NEW TESTAMENT; MARRIAGE IN THE OLD TESTAMENT

• **Polytheism.** [pol″ee-thee-iz′uhm] The belief in and worship of multiple gods and goddesses. Polytheism was the most common system of religion in the ancient world. All the major civilizations of the ancient world were polytheistic, as were the minor nations with whom the people of the Bible came into closest contact.

Polytheism functioned in the ancient world in a number of ways. Polytheism offered a logical and meaningful explanation for differences in the world. Various parts of the physical world (earth, sun, etc.) were identified as different gods or goddesses themselves or were considered to be under the control of different deities. Various natural forces and political events (floods, war, etc.) were explained as the work of different deities. Finally, conflicting or unequal human experiences (fortune, disaster, etc.) were seen as caused by different deities. In polytheism, diversity in the human world simply reflected diversity in the divine world.

Diversity within polytheism was controlled by systems that related the different deities to each other. Gods and goddesses were often grouped into families and generations, with stories—myths—explaining their relationships. In this way, the various deities became part of a larger and more inclusive whole.

By incorporating diversity into this larger system polytheism allowed change while offering stability. Exchanges through trade, war, and conquest were common in the ancient world. As different cultures came into contact, cultures and religions changed. Old gods and goddesses acquired new names and powers. Deities gained or lost importance. Old beliefs and practices were combined with new ones. As a result, in spite of the varying fortunes of individual deities, the system as a whole provided stability.

Finally, the wide range of deities in polytheism individualized religion. People in the ancient world worshiped gods and goddesses of love, war, the home, the state, etc. Each of these deities attracted different people—or the same person in different situations. Also, polytheism offered gods and goddesses who shared the worshipers' specialized interests and who were able to meet specific needs in specialized ways.

Polytheism was a constant factor in the world of the Bible. Although fundamentally rejected in the Bible, traces of it appear there: in Canaanite names for God (EL, Elyon); references to the worship of BAAL and ASHERAH; the acknowledgment of angels and spirits; and the recognition of other gods' control of other lands.

The worldview of polytheism differed significantly from the monotheism that arose in ancient Israel. Polytheism explained differences by attributing them to different deities; biblical monotheism saw them as varying aspects or elements of a single deity. Polytheism saw the world as controlled by varying and often conflicting forces; biblical monotheism saw the world as ultimately controlled by a single force. Lastly, polytheism created coherence and unity by relating different gods and goddesses; biblical monotheism sought coherence and unity behind the diverse world in the coherence and unity of the one Creator.

See also GOD; IDOLATRY; MONOTHEISM.

—JOANNE KUEMMERLIN-MCLEAN

• **Poor.** A wide variety of words in the OT delineate the experience of poverty in ancient Israel. These terms convey the range of negative social and psychological implications, such as humiliation, oppression, vulnerability, and helplessness. Concurrently, the poor, in contrast to the rich, are also depicted as more likely to be humble, devout, and innocent of the worst crimes against humanity, though they may lack knowledge of the Torah (Jer 5:4).

Sociohistorical Overview. In a peasant economy, like that of ancient ISRAEL, the great majority of people did little more than subsist on small family farms. Prior to the sixth century, goods were bartered, and money consisted of weighed metal objects, including jewelry, wire, and metal ingots. So, the poor are identified as those who cannot either provide their own food and shelter or barter for it. They must depend on the generosity of others if they are to remain free persons, Otherwise, they are forced to seek a lower social and legal status by becoming slaves or hired servants. The more fortunate were able to reside with their relatives and might be treated with the hospitality accorded hired servants, sojourners, or visiting strangers (Lev 25:35, 39-40).

From the earliest period of tribal confederacy, Israel and the surrounding nations followed certain humanitarian laws and customs aimed at protecting persons who lacked independent means of survival. This diverse group included widows, orphans, lepers, slaves, hired servants, visiting strangers, and others. The rise of the monarchy in Israel after 1000 B.C.E. shifted the balance of power. While ancient Near Eastern kings routinely swore to be benevolent to the destitute, the increase in trade with other nations greatly increased the prosperity of the ruling elite. Heavy taxation and the desire among the wealthy to accumulate land led to various ways around laws protecting small farm owners. By the eighth century some Israelite prophets railed against the rich who bought up small farms, depriving whole families of any independent means of support. In the seventh century, the reforms of the Judean Kings HEZEKIAH and, later, JOSIAH, centralized government and made an impressive attempt to redress some of these injustices. The Assyrian defeat of northern Israel was interpreted as God's response to the crimes of IDOLATRY and abuse of the poor. When Judah was itself defeated by the Babylonians in the sixth century, wealthy landowners and national leaders were deported and only an impoverished Judean population was left in the land. The Babylonians allowed these people to do forced labor as "vinedressers and plowmen" (2 Kgs 25:12 = Jer 52:16). Only with the later reconstitution of Israel under the Persians was the nation reestablished with a codified TORAH, including in it many of the ancient laws regarding the poor.

The Poor in the Context of Scripture. In the narratives of the Torah (Genesis to Deuteronomy) people are portrayed most often as agriculturalists or semi-nomadic herders. The poor do not exist as a distinct class of persons in the early narratives. Animals as well as people could be poor in the sense of being deprived of food or good health (cf. Gen 41:19). However, in the story of the Hebrew enslavement, an ethnic group of people becomes systematically deprived, oppressed, and life threatened. In the various law codes of the Torah, the memory of this slavery and deliverance is cited as motivation for just treatment of the poor who include sojourners, servants, widows, and orphans (e.g., Exod 22:21-24[H20-23]; Lev 25:42; Deut 15:15; 24:18, 22). Just as Hebrew slaves cried out of bondage and God responded to liberate them (e.g., Exod 3:7-10; Deut 26:6-8), so the poor and needy may call out to God and bring the charge of sin upon their oppressors (Deut 24:14; cf. Exod 22:27[H26]). Whoever responds to the poor will receive God's blessing (Deut 15:10).

Besides this direct association of the memory of slavery with Israel's future response to the poor, there were extensive provisions in the various laws to protect poor persons. The poor were to be treated impartially in courts and daily life (Exod 23:3; Lev 19:15; Deut 1:17; cf. Job 34:19); money or food given to them should not be considered loans (Exod 22:25[H24]; Lev 25:37; Deut 24:12-13); fields were to be left for them to glean for food (Exod 23:11; Lev 19:10; 23:22); and they could bring less to sacrifice during ritual offerings and feasts (Lev 5:7; 12:8; 14:21; cf. Exod 30:11-15). As already mentioned, a number of laws in the Holiness Code of Lev 25 governed treatment of the people who become destitute and must sell their land or rely on others for survival.

Deut 15 expresses uniquely the dilemma regarding the future existence of poor Israelites in the promised land. On the one hand, obedience to the revealed law will insure the blessing of God so "there will be no poor among you" (v. 4). On the other hand, only a few verses later is the admission that "the poor will never cease out of the land" (v. 11a). The inevitability of their presence provides a reason for being generous to them (v. 11b), and that response is, again, linked to memory of God's mercy to the Hebrew slaves in EGYPT (v. 15). In sum, the Torah repeatedly draws an analogy between the plight of the poor and the Hebrew experience of oppression in slavery. While some persons may be poor through lassitude and disobedience, the focus in the Torah is on the typical poor who through circumstances outside of their control become destitute and potentially subject to neglect or abuse.

The trampling, oppression, extortion, and selling of the poor into slavery form a repeated indictment among the prophets (Amos 2:6-7; 5:1-12; 8:4-6; Isa 3:13-24; Jer 5:26-29; Mic 2:1-2). These activities are incriminating evidence that Israel has disregarded God's demand for justice. In the Writings, certain Psalms illustrate the cries of the oppressed poor, reminiscent of the Torah. In them, poor persons can presume the special concern of God who will act as their legal advocate and liberator (Pss 10; 34; 37; 70; 82 [cf. Isa 41:17]; Job 5:16; 29:12, 16; 34:28; 36:15). From another perspective, the WISDOM LITERATURE abounds with observations about the conditions of the poor. While laziness or perversity accounts for some poverty (Prov 10:4; 13:18; 20:13; 28:19), the poor are mostly victims of social prejudice (Prov 18:11, 23; 19:4, 6-7; 22:7; Eccl 5:8; 9:13-16). Oppression of the poor is condemned in language reminiscent of the Torah (Prov 14:21, 31; 21:13; 22:22-23; 28:27). However, the motivation cited for one's care for the poor pertains only to duty, personal happiness, and justice, without any reference to Israel's unique memory of once being slaves.

While poverty was never sacralized, riches are consistently viewed as a common source of corruption (Ezek 7:19-20). Occasionally in biblical narrative, a lack of wealth is viewed positively as a sign of potential humility, which is a highly regarded trait. DAVID conveys this characteristic when he tells SAUL, "I am a poor man and of no repute" (1 Sam 18:23). Conversely, SAMUEL's judgment of David takes the form of a juridical parable in which the victim is "the poor man" (2 Sam 12:1-4). Finally, the remnant of Judah in Babylonian Exile can be called "a people humble and lowly" (Zeph 3:12) and these left in Jerusalem are "the poorest of the land" (2 Kgs 24:14; Jer 52:16 = 2 Kgs 25:12). In the present form of the biblical prophets, certain promises convey confidence, like that of Deut 15:4, that an age will dawn when all the poor will be lifted up and set free, and will attain God's desired gift of land and prosperity (Isa 29:19; 61:1-4).

See also JUSTICE/JUDGMENT; PROPHET; SLAVERY IN THE NEW TESTAMENT; SLAVERY IN THE OLD TESTAMENT; WEALTH.

Bibliography. C. Brown, *The Rich, The Poor—and the Bible*; T. D. Hanks, *God So Loved the World: The Biblical Vocabulary of Oppression.*

—GERALD T. SHEPPARD

• **Porcius Festus.** *See* FESTUS

• **Postexilic Period.** (538–330 B.C.E.) The period, following the Babylonian EXILE (587–538 B.C.E.), initiated by Persia's defeat of the Babylonians.

In 539/8 B.C.E., CYRUS of Persia issued an edict of toleration which allowed and encouraged Jewish exiles to return to Jerusalem, to rebuild the Jerusalem temple, and to renew the rites associated with worship there. This period marks the rebuilding work of EZRA and NEHEMIAH. Some of the significant literature of the period is Isa 40–66,

ZECHARIAH, HAGGAI, Ezra, and Nehemiah.

In addition, the postexilic period marks the beginnings of the development of Judaism. Among the features of this development are the concern with legal traditions (especially those dealing with ritualistic matters), the concern with the written word (the priestly editing of the TORAH occurs during this period), and the institution of a priestly class (a class that is, in some ways, a precursor to the rabbinic movement of the second century B.C.E.). Some of the biblical texts that reflect these developments are Lev 17–26 (the Holiness Code) and Gen 1:1–2:4a.

See also EZRA; HAGGAI; NEHEMIAH; PRIESTLY WRITERS; ZECHARIAH.

—HENRY L. CARRIGAN, JR.

• **Potiphar.** [pot′uh-fuhr] An official in Egypt to whom JOSEPH was sold by some Ishmaelite (or Midianite) traders. Joseph had been sold to the traders by his brothers (Gen 37ff.). In Egypt, Joseph became so successful that Potiphar "made him overseer of his house and put him in charge of all that he had" (Gen 39:4). Joseph is said to have been "handsome and good-looking" (39:6), so that the wife of Potiphar invited Joseph to lie with her (Gen 39:7). Once, while attempting to coerce an unwilling Joseph to comply, she was left with his garment in hand. This garment she later used to persuade her husband that Joseph had made improper advances toward her, which resulted in Joseph's imprisonment, a story reminiscent of parts of the Egyptian "Story of Two Brothers."

Potiphar is called in Gen 39:1 a *sārîs,* normally translated as "eunuch," but here is best rendered as "officer."

See also EGYPT; EUNUCH; JOSEPH.

—KAREN RANDOLPH JOINES

• **Potter's Field.** *See* AKELDAMA

• **Pottery Chronology.** The ability to date Palestinian pottery—and thus the strata or earth layers in the mounds that contain it in such abundance—has challenged archaeologists from the beginning of the discipline in the mid-nineteenth century. It was not until 1890 and the work of the brilliant Nestor of the discipline, Sir William Flinders Petrie, that the fundamental principles of ceramic typology were discerned. Working for only a few weeks at Tell es-Hesi, where Palestinian archaeology began (PLATE 3), Petrie observed intuitively that the pottery of each of his eight levels or strata differed not only in ware and manufacture and decoration, but particularly in the basic form of each vessel. Moreover, the changes in pottery over time seemed to follow consistent and continuous principles of evolution. If these principles could be charted on the basis of carefully controlled stratified examples, even tiny sherds or bits and pieces, then a "type-series" could be devised for each vessel-form. Thus a relative chronology could be worked out, which Petrie called "sequence" dating (currently known as "seriation"). Then, through comparative study with whole pots of each type found elsewhere in datable contexts (for example in Egyptian royal tombs), a network of synchronisms would eventually yield a corpus of Palestinian pottery dated in an absolute or precisely fixed chronology. So significant was his new tool that Petrie pronounced pottery "the essential alphabet of Palestinian archaeology."

Petrie's pioneering insights were not worked out systematically, however, (or even pursued by himself) until much later. The pottery chronology of F. J. Bliss and R. A. S. Macalister at mounds in the Judean Shephelah from 1898 to 1900, for example, remained poorly elaborated and was off by as much as four centuries for some periods.

As more mounds were dug, Petrie's initial attempt to build up a complete corpus (or catalogue) of pottery types was taken up by others. This ambitious work was never completed, however.

It remained for W. F. Albright, the "father of biblical archaeology," to reduce what had been largely guesswork to more exact science, especially in his epoch-making work at Tell Beit Mirsim from 1926–1932. Here Albright, separating earth-layers more carefully and observing every nuance of ceramic change with a masterly eye and a computer-like memory, gradually learned his pottery so well that by the mid-1930s, Albright and some of his leading proteges like Nelson Glueck could date the common pottery of Palestine to the century. Often they could even be precise enough to correlate pottery-bearing destruction layers with specific historical events known from texts, such as the Assyrian destructions in 734–722 B.C.E.

The work of Albright was continued by students like G. E. Wright, whose 1937 dissertation *The Pottery of Palestine from the Earliest Times to the End of the Early Bronze Age* was a landmark study. Wright himself later directed a number of ceramic dissertations at Harvard, such as Paul W. Lapp's *Palestinian Ceramic Chronology 200 B.C.–A.D. 70* (1961), and at least a half-dozen others, mostly unpublished; an exception is D. P. Cole, *Shechem II. The Middle Bronze IIB. Pottery,* 1984, a Drew University dissertation based on Wright's excavations. Wright also experimented with refined pottery dates by coupling detailed American-style ceramic analysis with more meticulous British stratigraphic digging techniques at Shechem in 1956–1968. This tradition then continued at Gezer in 1964–1973 under Wright's former students W. G. Dever, J. D. Seger, J. S. Holladay, and others.

The four Gezer final report volumes published thus far (1970, 1974, 1987), as well as much of the current American archaeological fieldwork in both Israel and Jordan, epitomize the American school of ceramic typology. Meanwhile, the Israelis have built up considerable expertise of their own, and indeed, apart from a very few foreign specialists, they dominate the field today. They have stressed the importance of the recovery and restoration of whole forms more than sherds, based on larger (but sometimes less precise) exposures in the field. They have also noted the significance of regionalism, which Albright had downplayed somewhat. The standard handbook—the only compendium even approaching Petrie's old notion of a corpus—is that of the Israel Museum's Ruth Amiran, *Ancient Pottery of the Holy Land.*

More recently there has been perhaps less emphasis on the strictly typological approach to ceramic analysis. This is partly because typology, i.e., the mere cataloging of pottery forms, had tended to become an end to itself, and often too narrow an objective. It was also partly because the very success of the pioneer generation in dating pottery so well had left little but the refinement of details, which was less challenging. Today, Palestinian pottery is studied not only for chronological clues, but also as evidence for trade and international relations, as a witness to technology, as a measure of esthetic and artistic development, and above all as a unique indicator of cultural contact and cultural change. Nevertheless, all of the other aspects of ceramic analysis are dependent upon a firmly fixed chronology.

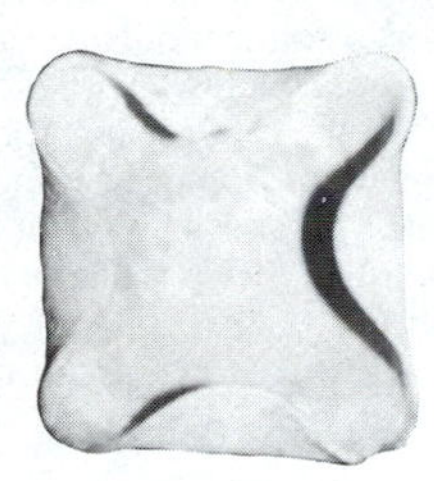

A Middle Bronze II lamp.

A Middle Bronze-Late lamp.

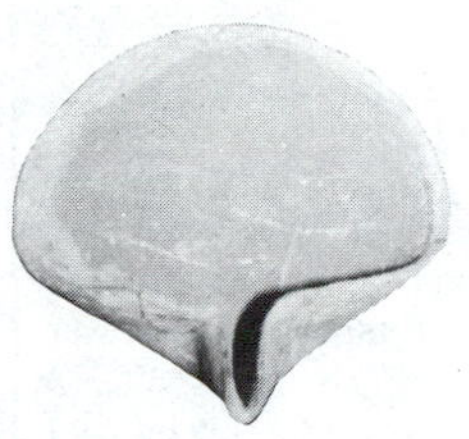

A Late Bronze-Iron I lamp.

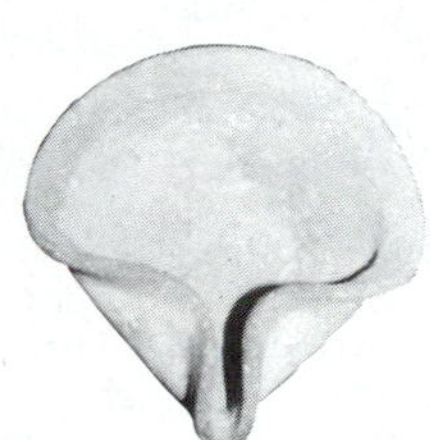

An Iron II lamp.

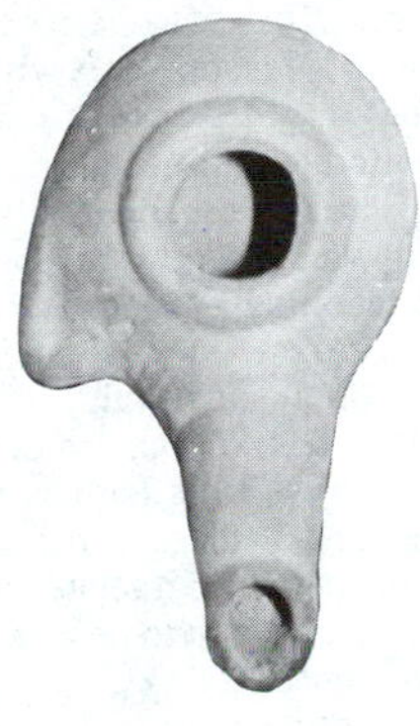

A Persian Period lamp.

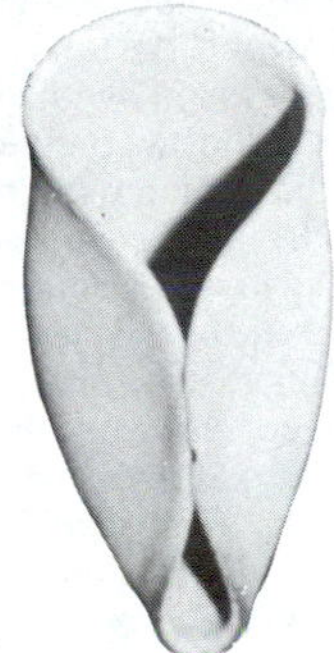

A Hasmonean lamp.

A Herodian lamp.

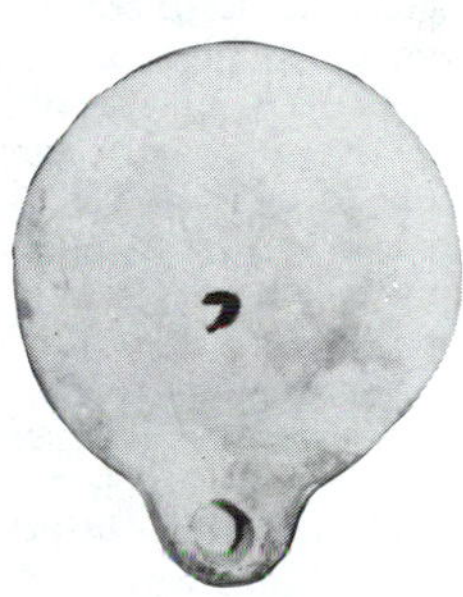

A Roman lamp.

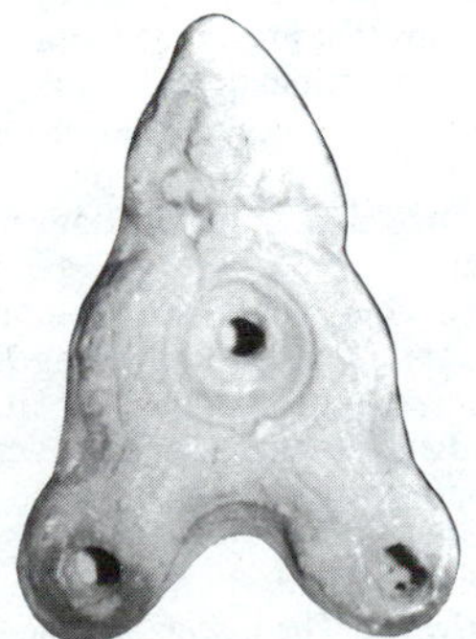

An atypical Hellenistic-Roman two-spouted lamp.

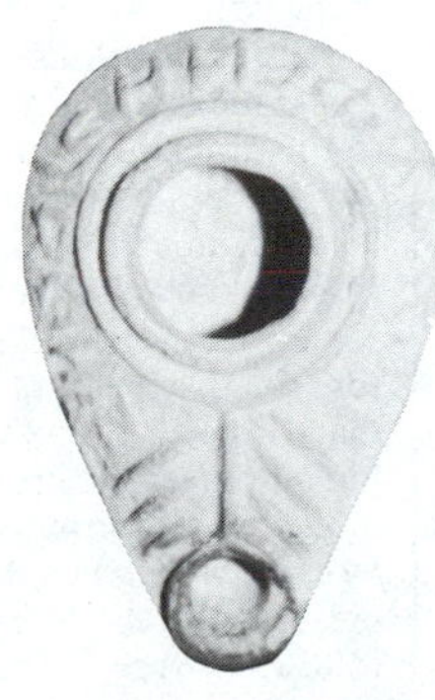

A Byzantine lamp with inscription: "The light of Christ shines for all."

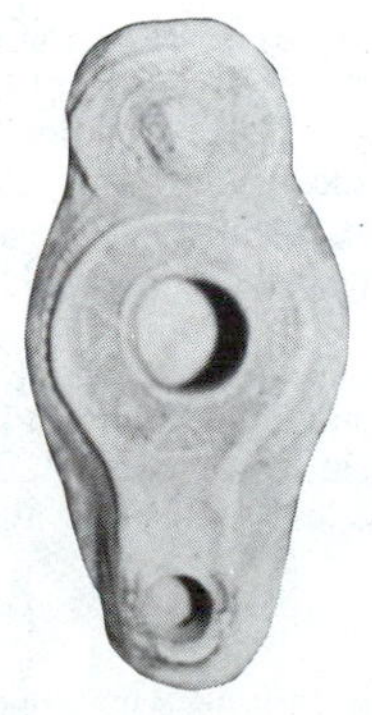

A Byzantine lamp with a face on the handle.

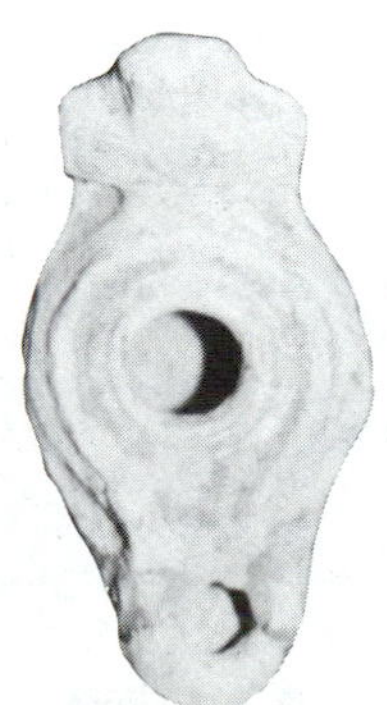

A Byzantine lamp with a cross on the handle.

Courtesy of the Eisenberg Museum of Biblical Archaeology, Southern Baptist Theological Seminary.

Bibliography. R. Amiran, *Ancient Pottery of the Holy Land.*

—WILLIAM G. DEVER

• **Pound.** *See* MONEY

• **Power.** Force, might, strength; the ability to do, to create, and to carry out one's will. See Isa 41:21-24, 46:8-11, and 48:3-5, where the real test of a god is to recall the past or predict the future and bring about an announced new thing; only the Lord can do this. God is the ultimate source of all power (1 Chr 29:11f.). God is all-powerful; all power derives from the almighty.

God's power is most evident in creation: "It is he who made the earth by his power" (Jer 51:15); "By the word of the Lord the heavens were made" (Ps 33:6; Gen 1–2).

God is incomparable and has unlimited power, "Whatever the Lord pleases he does, in heaven and on earth" (Ps 35:6; cf. 115:3). God asked Abraham, "Is anything too hard for the Lord?" (Gen 18:14); Jeremiah stated, "Nothing is too hard for you" (32:17); and Job declared, "I know that you can do all things" (42:2).

God's power is creative and also recreative. Its most gracious expression is in redemption and deliverance with the Exodus as the classic example. Israel was "brought forth out of Egypt with great power and with a mighty hand" (Exod 32:11). The plagues ultimately were redemptive: "That you [Egyptians] may know that I am the Lord in the midst of the earth" (Exod 8:22).

God shared power. A psalmist declared that the Lord "gives power and strength to his people" (Ps 68:35). God told Moses, "See that you do before Pharaoh all the miracles that I have put in your power" (Exod 4:21). Moses was complimented after his death "for all the mighty power and all the great and terrible deeds that [he] wrought in the sight of all Israel" (Deut 34:12).

God's power in action was expressed as a "mighty hand and outstretched arm" (Deut 5:15; cf. Jer 32:17). Unlimited power was implied in God's question to Moses, "Is the Lord's hand shortened?" (Num 11:23). Isaiah stressed the universal redemptive quality of God's power: "The Lord bared his holy arm before the eyes of all the nations; and all the ends of the earth shall see the salvation of our God" (52:10). God is universally sovereign, one "who rules by his might forever, whose eyes keep watch on the nations" (Ps 66:7).

God's power was recognized and expressed in names and titles given him by his people. Jacob spoke of God as the "Mighty One of Jacob" and "God Almighty" (Gen 49:24-25). God told Abraham and Jacob, "I am God Almighty" (Gen 17:1; 35:11). The psalmist and Isaiah also spoke of God as "the Mighty One of Jacob" (Ps 132:2; Isa 49:26; 60:16).

The Lord is all-powerful because there is no other god, no other source of power. God said, "See now that I, even I, am he, and there is no god besides me" (Deut 32:39; cf. Isa 45:5-7). God's power is exclusive; any and all other power is derived from God.

—D. C. MARTIN

• **Praetorian Guard.** [pri-tor′ee-uhn] The praetorian guard refers to military and other personnel attached to a Roman governor or emperor. Paul's reference in Phil 1:13 (τὸ πραιτώριον) is probably correctly translated "praetorian guard" (RSV). Many scholars combine this reference with Paul's allusion to "Caesar's household" in Phil 4:22 to support the theory that Philippians was written during Paul's imprisonment at Rome. However, the phrase originally referred to a place, initially the headquarters of a Roman general and later the residence or palace of the governor of a province (cf. Mark 15:16; John 18:28, 33). Moreover, the phrase may refer to soldiers outside Rome. Thus, Paul's use of the phrase is not conclusive proof of the Roman origin of Philippians. On the other hand, it could certainly refer to the imperial guard of Rome. Instituted by Emperor Augustus, the praetorians became a powerful force in Roman political life until abolished by Constantine in the fourth century.

—WALTER B. SHURDEN

• **Praetorium.** *See* GABBATHA

• **Prayer, The Lord's.** *See* LORD'S PRAYER

• **Prayer of Manasseh.** *See* MANASSEH, PRAYER OF

• **Prayer of Thanksgiving.** *Prayer of Thanksgiving* is a brief, untitled hermetic text from the NAG HAMMADI library. It is the seventh tractate in the sixth codex, a codex that includes other hermetic works (DISCOURSE ON THE EIGHTH AND NINTH, and ASCLEPIUS). The prayer is written in the first-person plural and issues repeated praises and rejoicing to God, who gives knowledge that illumines and deifies the human recipients: "Thou has made us divine through thy knowledge." This knowledge along with God's kindness, love, affection, and teaching are available to everyone and everything. God is addressed with numerous titles: Father, undisturbed name, intellectual light, womb of every creature, womb pregnant with the nature of the Father, eternal permanence of the begetting Father. It is possible that *Prayer of Thanksgiving,* because it bears no title and is placed directly after the hermetic tractate, *Disc 8–9,* was intended by the scribe who copied it to be a prayer for the knowledge revealed in that previous text.

The prayer has only a brief narrative context. It begins with a heading, "This is the prayer that they spoke," and concludes with the statement, "When they had said these things in prayer, they embraced each other and they went to eat their holy food which has no blood in it." This conclusion provides rare evidence for the existence of hermetic communities with cultic practices (liturgical prayer, ritual embrace, and a cultic meal). The other classic hermetic writings do not render much knowledge about the religious/social life of the groups that preserved them.

At the end of the prayer is a scribal note that may refer to this tractate or to the one that follows. The scribe remarks that he is unsure what discourses to copy because "very many have come to me" and he is uncertain which may be known to the reader(s).

This prayer was known in Greek and Latin versions before the discovery of the Coptic version in the Nag Hammadi library. In the Greek version the prayer is part of a longer prayer located in a magical text. The Latin version of the prayer forms the conclusion to a work from the *Corpus Hermeticum* called *Asclepius* (part of *Asclepius* is also preserved in the Nag Hammadi library in the tractate that follows *Prayer of Thanksgiving*). The Greek and the Coptic versions of the prayer correspond closely while the Latin version has been expanded.

See also HERMETIC LITERATURE; NAG HAMMADI.

Bibliography. J. Brashler, P. A. Dirkse, and D. M. Parrott, "The Prayer of Thanksgiving," *Nag Hammadi Library in English,* ed. J. M. Robinson.

—CAROL D. C. HOWARD

• Prayer/Thanksgiving in the New Testament. The writers of the NT express the concepts of giving thanks and being thankful in different ways. A common way was by use of forms of a noun which customarily meant GRACE (χάρις), but which also connoted "thanks" ("to have thanks"—Luke 17:9; 1 Tim 1:12; 2 Tim 1:3; Heb 12:28; "with thanks" or "thanksgiving"—1 Cor 10:30; Col 3:16; and Paul's doxological "thanks be to God"—Rom 6:17; 1 Cor 15:57; 2 Cor 2:14; 8:16; 9:15). Also used were forms of a word which carried the explicit meaning "give or giving thanks" (εὐχαριστεῖν; used in the NT thirty-eight times as a verb, fifteen times as a noun, and only in Col 3:15 as an adjective).

Virtually all expressions of thanks in the NT are directed to God. Thanks offered to people are rare (Luke 17:9, 16; Acts 24:3; Rom 16:4). In one passage, thanksgiving is offered to "Christ Jesus our Lord" (1 Tim 1:12), though thanks are offered elsewhere to God through Jesus Christ (Rom 1:8) or in the name of the Lord Jesus Christ (Eph 5:20). All other thanksgivings in the NT are directed to "God" (twenty-one times), to the "Father" (John 11:41; Col 1:12), to "God the Father" (Eph 5:20; Col 3:17), to "Father, Lord of heaven and earth" (Matt 11:25, par. Luke 10:21), to "God the Father of our Lord Jesus Christ" (Col 1:3), to "my God" (Rom 1:8; Phil 1:3; Phlm 4), to "our God" (Rev 7:12), to "thee, Lord God Almighty" (Rev 11:17), to him who is seated on the throne (Rev 4:9). In numerous other thanksgivings God is clearly the recipient, although that goes unsaid.

The principal means of offering thanks was prayer. The NT writers refer to different types of prayers (supplication, intercession, a specific request, thanksgiving, and to "prayer" in general). The prayer of thanksgiving might be offered to God directly (as the thanks Jesus offered in John 11:41, "Father, I thank thee") or obliquely (most of the instances in the NT fall into this category, since the documents are letters to readers or narratives in the third person. Even when Paul breaks forth with doxology, he presents it to his readers).

The customary Jewish prayer of thanksgiving, called *Berakah* ("blessing"), followed the form "Blessed art thou . . ." or "Blessed is he who . . ." and was offered on both common and special occasions. This type prayer was doubtless practiced by Jesus and Paul (cf. Matt 15:36 and par.; Matt 26:27 and par.; Acts 27:35). Examples are to be found in the NT (cf. Luke 1:68; Rom 1:25; 9:5; 2 Cor 1:3; 11:31; Eph 1:3-14; 1 Pet 1:3). Paul was so accustomed to this Jewish way of giving thanks that for him "to bless" and "to give thanks" were interchangeable.

Other means of thanksgiving besides prayer were also appropriate. The Colossians were enjoined to sing psalms, hymns, and spiritual songs with thankfulness in their hearts (Col 3:16). They were to offer every word or deed in the name of the Lord Jesus, giving thanks to God (Col 3:17). Thanksgiving was not a religious exercise, but an attitude of the inner person undergirding the perspective of all aspects of the believer's life. It could even be offered in unintelligible tongues; however, Paul disparaged that (1 Cor 14:16-18).

Thanks are offered to God for a variety of causes. Gratitude and praise are given for all people (1 Tim 2:1); for cherished fellow believers (Phil 1:3; 2 Tim 1:3); for mutual Christian concern (2 Cor 8:16); for generosity among believers (2 Cor 9:11); for all the foods which God created (1 Tim 4:3); for the blessing of answered prayers (2 Cor 1:11); for the life-transforming work God does in Christ (Rom 6:17); for God's making sinners sufficient for sharing the blessed promises he gives his people (Col 1:12); for strength to serve God (1 Tim 1:12); for victory over death, sin, and law (1 Cor 15:57); for God's sure and victorious sponsorship of those who serve Christ (2 Cor 2:14); for an imperishable relationship with God (Heb 12:28); and for Jesus Christ, God's inexpressible gift (2 Cor 9:15).

Paul regularly included a "thanksgiving" section in his epistles (except 2 Corinthians and Galatians). He would thank God for the readers and by expressing what prompted his gratitude, encourage them. He was thankful for the faith of the Romans which was widely acclaimed (Rom 1:8), for the faith and love of Philemon (Phlm 4) and the Thessalonians (2 Thess 1:13) and the faithful saints (Eph 1:15), for the faith, love, and hope of the Colossians (Col 1:3-5), for the work of faith, labor of love, and steadfastness of hope of the Thessalonians (1 Thess 1:3), for the grace of God given to the believers in Corinth (1 Cor 1:4), that the Thessalonians accepted the gospel as a divine word and not a human proclamation (1 Thess 2:13), that they remained sound even under persecution (1 Thess 3:6-9), and that God gave them the privilege of experiencing his saving work at the beginning (2 Thess 2:13).

At the heart of thanksgiving is an understanding of the divine-human relationship. People who are whole and recreated recognize their indebtedness to God and his praiseworthiness, and so give thanks. People who are distorted in sin do not honor God or give him thanks (Rom 1:21) because of their wrong understanding of themselves and God. Even believers have to guard themselves against the sinful thinking that focuses on evil and to practice thankfulness instead (that is, act on a proper understanding of self and God, Eph 5:1-4).

Constancy in thanksgiving is widely attested and encouraged as the proper mode of living for believers. This is not a formal demand to practice something otherwise alien to the believer, but an encouragement to actualize and nurture the proper relation to God which believers know. Paul gave thanks to God "always" for his brothers and sisters in Christ (1 Cor 1:4; Col 1:3; 1 Thess 1:2; 2 Thess 1:3; Phlm 4), without ceasing (1 Thess 2:13; Eph 1:16); at every mention or remembrance of them (Phil 1:3). His own attitude of thanksgiving is evident (a word of thanksgiving is present in every chapter of Colossians—1:3, 12; 2:7; 3:15-17; 4:2, and in almost every chapter of 1 Thessalonians—1:2; 2:13; 3:9; 5:18). He called on others to "be thankful" (Col 3:15), to live in Christ "abounding in thanksgiving" (Col 2:7), to be steadfast in prayer with thanksgiving (Col 4:2), to give thanks always and for everything in the name of the Lord Jesus Christ (Eph 5:20), and to give thanks in all circumstances (this was directed to new believers undergoing harsh persecution), because that is God's will (1 Thess 5:18). While awaiting his own execution or release in Roman imprisonment, he wrote, "Have no anxiety . . . with thanksgiving let your requests be made known to God" (Phil 4:6). When we live as people set free and recreated, we will not be anxious, but thankful.

The final purpose of thanksgiving is to give glory to God (2 Cor 4:15; 1 Cor 10:31). That was the purpose of Christ and should be the purpose of those blessed by God through Christ. For thanksgiving to accomplish that end, it must be genuine and not false (Luke 17:15-16 and 18:11-12 are example of true and false thanksgiving, respectively).

Thanksgiving both expresses and nurtures a right understanding of and a right relationship to God. In giving thanks the divine-human communion is complete: God who graciously gives and blesses becomes the recipient of gratitude and blessing freely offered.

See also GESTURES; GRACE; LORD'S PRAYER; MARANATHA; WORSHIP IN THE NEW TESTAMENT.

Bibliography. H. Conzelmann, "εὐχαριστέω, κτλ.," *TDNT*; J. Jeremias, *The Eucharistic Words of Jesus*; P. Schubert, *Form and Function of the Pauline Thanksgivings*.

—RICHARD A. SPENCER

• **Prayer/Thanksgiving in the Old Testament.** In the OT prayer is a primary means of communication which binds God and people into intimate and reciprocal relationship. In the broadest sense such communication may be achieved through act as well as word. As act, prayer is manifest in a variety of nonspeech approaches to God, e.g., song, sacrifice, dance, any one of which deserves its own place in the study of prayer. Prayer as word consists of the special speech directed from people to God. More specifically it is the texts of such communication that are preserved in the OT. It is prayer in this second, more restricted sense that is discussed here.

Certain criteria may be proposed for identifying prayers. At a first level, certain key expressions may be prefaced to or included within a person's speech which serve to distinguish it as prayer, e.g., "to pray" (*pll*), "to entreat or petition" (*'tr, pg'*), "to call on the name of God" (*qr' bšm yhwh*). Very often, however, such clear indicators are lacking, and one must search for other reasons to justify the label "prayer." For example, perhaps the majority of recorded prayers begin with the simple statement "and *X* said to God," an introduction that resembles in theologically significant ways the conversational style of discourse employed between persons of equal stature. What distinguishes these conversational prayers from other forms of more casual exchange is the weighty nature of their content. What is communicated to God is not something peripheral or insignificant. Rather it is a subject of fundamental, often desperate, concern which if left unaddressed may leave the one who prays without adequate understanding, or worse, with a level of uncertainty that threatens to undermine trust in God.

A further distinction may be made between prose prayers and those poetic in style. The former function as integral parts of narrative contexts and derive their meaning directly from what precedes and follows them in a specifically defined situation. They therefore give the impression of being nonrepeatable. Poetic prayers usually lack this specificity of context, and because of their conventional language lend themselves particularly to a wide range of interpretations and use. Both types occur throughout the OT, the former more frequently where narrative is the primary literary style, especially in Genesis through 2 Kings, the latter in the Psalms and to a lesser extent in the Prophets, where poetry is the norm.

Prose prayers are usually petitions. Some are quite brief, containing little more than the petition itself, which may or may not receive immediate divine response (e.g., Gen 15:2, 3, 8; Judg 13:8; 2 Sam 15:31; 1 Kgs 6:17, 18, 20). In these cases the petition usually consists of a request for something concrete and practical, the granting of which can be verified (e.g., information, a child, healing). Some petitions are presented with lengthy elaborations that serve to provide added incentive for divine response (e.g., 2 Sam 7:18-29; 1 Kgs 8:22-61; 2 Kgs 19:15-19). In these lengthier prayers petitions are usually of a more abstract nature, e.g., for blessing, remembrance, hearing. In postexilic prayers the petition for forgiveness emerges as paramount (Dan 9:3-19; Ezra 9:6-15; Neh 1:5-11; 9:5-37).

A particularly noteworthy feature of a number of prose prayers is the petition for divine justice (Gen 18:22-33; Exod 32:7-14; Num 11:11-15; 14:13-19; Josh 7:7-9; 1 Kgs 17:17-24). Set within the context of some rupture in the relationship with God, these prayers occur at crucial junctures that are perceived as unfair and on occasion labelled bluntly as "evil" (e.g., Exod 32:12, 14; 1 Kgs 17:20). In the aftermath of these prayers the crisis is presented as having been averted or resolved. Thus the narrative sequence—crisis, prayer, resolution—suggests an important role for prayer as a literary and theological vehicle for addressing and resolving issues related to God's justice.

The Psalms represent the largest collection of poetic prayers in the OT, although poetic addresses occur often in narrative contexts as well (e.g., 1 Sam 2:1-10; 2 Sam 22:2-51; Jonah 2:1-9; and the confessions of Jeremiah: Jer 11:18-23; 12:1-6; 15:10-21; 17:14-18; 18:18-23; 20:7-13, 14-18). A distinguishing feature of these prayers is their formulaic language that renders them appropriate for repetition by a variety of persons in a variety of contexts.

Two types of prayer dominate in the Psalms, lament and praise. Lament prayers are more frequent than any other single type, comprising more than one quarter of the collection (e.g., Pss 13; 22; 42–43; 44; 79; 88). When considered along with the confessions of Jeremiah, and the laments of Habakkuk (Hab 1:2-17) and Job, these lament prayers provide a profound witness to a tradition that promoted and encouraged the practice of bringing before God even the most difficult and despairing of circumstances. The general pattern of these prayers—invocation, lament, petition—provides in itself a means of both articulating and coping with these circumstances.

Prayers of praise also follow a general pattern. Following an opening summons to praise, the heart of the prayer consists of a listing of reasons for praising God, often quite elaborate and extensive. Finally the prayer concludes as it began, with a statement of praise (e.g., Pss 8; 33; 96; 100; 117; 136; 145–150). There is in these prayers a profound sense of preoccupation with God that renders petitions for self inappropriate.

The prayers of the OT are an important, though much neglected, witness to what transpired between the people of ancient Israel and the God who called them into faith. They suggest that life in relation to God was not to be lived on the level of monologue alone, with God always speaking, leading, commanding, punishing, forgiving, etc., and humanity always the passive recipient. Instead Israel had an important role to play. In the dialogue of faith Israel was sometimes petitioning, other times praising, often times complaining, but almost never silent. It was Israel's divinely designated role to participate as partner with God in the accomplishing of the divine will, frequently even addressing God with language suggesting that something like peer status was permitted. Perhaps even more astonishing, certainly less comprehensible, is the portrayal of these ancient prayers as not only addressing God but also as influencing God. They praise, and God is pleased. They lament, and God is moved to compassion. They challenge and protest and question, and God listens and responds. Such prayers are a witness and a summons to a divine-human relationship that has consequences in both heaven and earth.

See also GESTURES; LORD'S PRAYER; PSALMS, BOOK OF; WORSHIP IN THE OLD TESTAMENT.

Bibliography. S. Balentine, "Prayer in the Wilderness Traditions: In Pursuit of Divine Justice," *HAR* 9 (1985): 53-74; S. H. Blank, "Some Observations Concerning Biblical Prayer," *HUCA* 32 (1961): 75-90; W. Brueggemann, *The Message of the Psalms*; R. Clements, *In Spirit and in Truth: Insights from Biblical Prayers*; M. Greenberg, *Biblical Prose Prayer as a Guide to the Popular Religion of Ancient Israel*; M. Haran, "Priesthood, Temple, Divine Service: Some Observations on Institutions and Practices of Worship," *HAR* 7 (1984): 121-35; F. Heiler, *Prayer. A Study in the History and Psychology of Religion*; H. G. Reventlow, *Gebet im Alten Testament*; C. Westermann, *Praise and Lament in the Psalms*.

—SAMUEL E. BALENTINE

• **Preacher.** *See* EVANGELIST

• **Preaching.** "Preach" translates a Greek word (κηρύσσω) which described the actions of heralds. These were people employed by royal, civic, and religious authorities to make announcements, to call assemblies together, to publish rules and decrees through towns, to offer prayers at public assemblies, to deliver written or oral notices to other important persons, and to be announcers at games or religious festivals. Certain priests of the mystery religions and the Cynic philosopher-preachers also used "preach" to describe what they did. The CYNICS provide an especially good parallel for the NT, because they saw themselves as God's heralds, criticizing improper living and offering advice on how to attain the good life.

Although the word "preach" is rarely used in English translations of the OT, it is clear that there were persons who fulfilled heraldic functions in ancient Israel. The OT speaks of fasts, festivals, and messages "proclaimed" to armies, kings, and towns (Lev 23; Deut 20; 1 Kgs 21:8). The word "proclaim" is also used by the prophets to describe their own activity (Isa 61:1-2; Jer 3:12; Joel 3:9; Amos 4:5); this fits with other evidence which shows that one way Israel viewed the prophetic role was as God's messenger.

In the NT, "preach" is used to describe the actions of Jesus and the apostles. Scholars use the corresponding noun, the Greek word *kerygma,* to denote the content of the early Christian preaching. Paul, our earliest witness to the kerygma, used "preach" and "evangelize" as equivalent terms, showing that his main interest was in starting new churches and making new converts. Sometimes he used "preach" without any object (Rom 10:14), but most often he wrote that he preached "Christ" (1 Cor 1:23; 2 Cor 1:19) or "the gospel" (Gal 2:2; 1 Thess 2:9). In a few passages, Paul indicated that he tried to follow traditions about Christ and the gospel which he had received; putting these together, we can see that Christians before Paul preached the death and resurrection of Jesus, his messianic status, his imminent return, and the belief that all these things happened "according to the scriptures" (Rom 1:2-4; 1 Cor 15:1-7). Paul wrote repeatedly that he put most stress in his own preaching on the cross and its implications for the nature of salvation.

The synoptic Gospels show Jesus, the Twelve, and John the Baptist preaching. John's preaching is uniformly described as a call for repentance and ethical reform in view of the coming of the Day of the Lord; the link between John and Jesus probably means that Jesus' early preaching included the same themes. All three Synoptics say that Jesus preached the gospel, and that he did so in synagogues in Galilee. All three also make a point of using the same word to describe the activities of the disciples and their Lord, showing that they believed there was continuity between Jesus' preaching and the church's kerygma. Their message was doubtless similar but not identical to his. Jesus, to judge from the material available in the Gospels, focused on the arrival of God's reign in his own ministry, but not on his own messianic status. Even if Jesus predicted his own death, which many scholars doubt, he still did not concentrate on his death and resurrection as much as the authors of the NT.

Beyond these similarities among the Synoptics, there are differences. Matthew almost always uses the phrase "the gospel of the kingdom" to note what Jesus preached, and uses a triad of "teaching in their synagogues, preaching the gospel of the kingdom, and healing every disease" as a general summary of Jesus' early ministry. Matthew also restricts "preach" to Jesus and the Twelve, as part of his program of grounding the beginnings of the church in Jesus' life. Mark, on the other hand, allows others to preach; three times persons who had experienced or witnessed miracles preached about Jesus' deeds, in defiance of Jesus' explicit command to keep silence. Mark also tends to use "preach the gospel" without any qualifier. This strengthens the connection between Jesus' preaching and the preaching of Christians in Mark's time. Luke accomplishes the same purpose differently; he uses "preach" and "evangelize" as equivalent terms, and stresses repentance and forgiveness of sins as the content of Jesus' preaching. Thus, when one reads the Gospel of Luke and then Acts, one is struck by the smooth continuation of the basic message.

The Johannine writings, which use the term "preach" only once (Rev 5:2), tend to stress that Jesus "manifested God's glory" and that his disciples "testified" or "confessed" to the true nature of God which Jesus showed them. They also say that the apostolic testimony led to faith and to the creation of churches (John 21:24; 1 John 1:1-3). These terms are the Johannine functional equivalents to "preaching." Perhaps they also indicate that the Johannine "gospel" focused on Jesus as a revealer of God's inner being.

The rest of the NT uses a wide variety of terms to refer to preaching. In Hebrews, the act is described by the common word "speak" (1:2; 2:3; 13:7). First Peter uses this term also (4:11), as well as "make a defense" (3:15), "preach" (3:19), and "evangelize" (4:6). Second Pet 1:16, arguing against heretical teachers, asserts that the apostles "made known . . . the power and coming of our Lord Jesus Christ," and Jude 3 refers to the faith "once for all delivered to the saints." The difference in the vocabulary is a result of changing situations in which these early Christians tried to present the gospel. First Peter seems to be addressed to a community which the author believes will soon be persecuted, while 2 Peter and Jude are polemics written against opponents inside the church. The emphasis in preaching therefore changed; 1 Peter and Jude made a point of connecting the gospel to the apostles.

See also EVANGELIST; GOSPEL; TEACHING.

Bibliography. C. H. Dodd, *The Apostolic Preaching and Its Developments*; G. Friedrich, "κῆρυξ, κτλ.," *TDNT*.

—RICHARD B. VINSON

• **Preaching, Levitical.** According to the narratives of 1–2 CHRONICLES, EZRA, and NEHEMIAH, LEVITES had a preaching role in addition to their duties in the sanctuary. Neh 8 describes an occasion in which the Levites "helped the people to understand the law . . . they gave the people the sense, so that the people understood the reading" (Neh 8:7-8). Other sections of the OT describe the roles of the

Levites differently, so that some scholars see in these passages the work of an editor or school of editors protesting the postexilic trend limiting the priesthood to the descendants of AARON OF ZADOK. Gerhard von Rad also theorized that these passages preserve evidence of a real reform of the TORAH undertaken by the Levites prior to the exile; in his theory the Levitical reform was one of the sources for the material in DEUTERONOMY.

See also JOSIAH; LAW IN THE OLD TESTAMENT; LEVI/LEVITES.

—RICHARD B. VINSON

• **Preachings of Peter.** *See* KERYGMATA PETROU

• **Predestination.** Predestination is the belief that God has foreordained the events of history according to his own predetermined plan. In the history of the Christian church, few doctrines have given rise to as much controversy. The first major debate was that between Augustine and Pelagius in the fifth century. Continuing for centuries, debate reached its height in the Reformation period between the interpreters of John Calvin and those of Jacobus Arminius. Essentially, the discussion has centered on the relationship between God's sovereign will and human responsibility. Theologians have tended to fall largely either into the camp of Calvin or that of Arminius.

Calvin maintained that because God is sovereign, salvation is totally his action. Individuals can believe only as they are given the ability to do so by God. Thus, God has predetermined who will be saved before the foundation of the world. GRACE is irresistible to those who have been elected. NT texts like Eph 1:4-5, 2 Tim 1:9, John 15:16, Rom 9–11, 1 Pet 1:2, John 6:37, 17:9, and 13:18 have been used to support this view. The logical extension of this understanding of predestination is that God has also chosen beforehand those who will be lost (double predestination).

Calvin's doctrine of predestination was rigorously challenged in Holland by Jacobus Arminius and his followers. Arminius argued that individuals have the capacity to believe and that God has given them the freedom to accept or reject his grace. God is not a tyrant who arbitrarily decides who will be saved and who will be damned. Instead, he has created men and women with a freedom and dignity to choose, and he honors the choices made.

In light of these theological discussions, it is important to look at the biblical evidence. The word predestination comes from a Greek word which means "to pre-horizon, to mark out beforehand." Its basic meaning is "to set limits." It is used figuratively to mean "to fix, to appoint."

That God is sovereign over human affairs is seen in OT texts like Gen 8:20-22, 9:12-16, and Exod 3:17. Earthly kings and empires may rebel against him, but they do not frustrate his purposes. They often unknowingly carry them out (Isa 44:28–45:4).

Yet, God is not pictured as a despot but rather as one who has placed limits on himself in his COVENANT with Israel. God's sovereignty is seen in his choice of Israel to be his priests to the world. The emphasis in the OT is that God has taken the initiative in calling Israel.

God's ELECTION of Israel, however, in no way relieved human responsibility. In fact, it accentuated it. Amos 3:1-2 is a prophetic warning to the people of Israel who had forgotten their responsibility. By choosing Israel instead of other nations of the world, God held Israel more accountable than them.

This tension between divine and human will is seen further in the NT. Predestination here must be understood in two senses. The verb is used most often in reference to the work of Christ. The sending of Jesus into the world was definite, purposeful, and predetermined by God. Jesus' coming was God's ultimate revelation of himself to the world.

Yet, in the life and ministry of Jesus, one immediately becomes aware of the interplay between the divine and human wills. Jesus is not presented in the Gospels as a player whose every move is made according to a divine script. In his temptations (Luke 4:1-13), he faced real options. Otherwise, his temptations are a sham.

His prayers were for real guidance and help (Luke 22:39-44). His death, although ordained by God, was the result of conscious, deliberate choices made by a self-serving Sanhedrin, jealous Pharisees, a cowardly Pontius Pilate, and a confused Judas Iscariot. Nowhere in the NT are these people presented as helpless pawns who were just fulfilling the roles assigned to them by divine decree.

In Acts 3:13-15, Peter attributes the death of Jesus to responsible human beings who made conscious choices to serve their own interests. At the same time, he affirms God's control by saying that puny human beings, no matter how apparently powerful, could not thwart his purposes in history. God's sovereignty is seen no more clearly in that he raised Jesus from the dead.

This same tension between divine and human will is seen in the second sense of predestination in the NT. Texts like 1 Thess 5:9 and Rom 8:28-30 describe the believer's being predestined in Christ. The theological debate has centered most often on the meaning of foreknowledge, especially in the Romans passage. Medieval theology came to equate foreknowledge with predetermined events. Foreknowledge was understood as little more than fatalism.

In the NT, God's foreknowledge is not fatalism. It seems to mean simply that God has taken the initiative in SALVATION. God loves man before man loves God. Texts like 1 Cor 8:3 and 1 John 4:7-21 show this relationship between foreknowledge and God's initiative in loving man.

In Jesus, God has done something that man could never do for himself. Salvation is purely an act of God (Eph 2:8-9). God's initiative, however, in no way lessens human responsibility. Texts like Gal 4:8-9, Phil 2:12-13, and Eph 2:10 seem to place the divine and human wills in tension in salvation.

Perhaps the greatest perversions of truth have been born when one takes biblical truth and reduces it to logical propositions. One must remember that logic is a human invention designed to explain reality.

The biblical writers appear to affirm two things which seem illogical to us. God is sovereign. Salvation is from first to last his work. He alone controls history. One's standing before God is on the basis of God's grace, not human effort or goodness.

At the same time, the Bible affirms that God has given us the right to reject him. Part of being human is the ability to make deliberate choices which God honors.

These two affirmations of truth place us in a tension. When we confess that Jesus is Lord, we affirm that God's purposes in history will not be frustrated by the forces of evil. Yet, we also affirm that he bids us each day to be his people in concrete ways, and we can reject his invitation to our own hurt and loss.

See also ELECTION; PROVIDENCE; SALVATION IN THE NEW TESTAMENT; SALVATION IN THE OLD TESTAMENT.

—LOYD MELTON

• **Preexistence.** *See* CHRISTOLOGY

• **Prefect.** *See* PROCURATOR

• **Presbyter.** *See* ELDER

• **Presence.** The Bible speaks of the divine presence in several ways. God's constant care for the world makes it fruitful (Ps 65:1-13), and yet at times GOD seems to be absent (Mark 15:34); at still other times God comes in glory (Ezek 1). The biblical presentation of presence encompasses all of these understandings.

During the wilderness period ISRAEL perceived God's presence inhabiting the tent of meeting (Exod 40:34-38) and the ARK of the covenant (Exod 25:21-22). These were vehicles of God's intermittent or "coming" presence; rather than being God's permanent abode, they were vehicles of presence with a purpose. The tent was an ordained place for dialogue between God and humanity, while the Ark was the vehicle of Yahweh's leading presence with the hosts of Israel. These movable emblems of Yahweh's presence were suitable for a people on the move, but after Israel's settlement in the land more permanent sanctuaries were developed.

When the TEMPLE was built in Jerusalem, the transitory divine presence as needed came to be understood as God's abiding presence in the Temple (1 Kgs 8:12-13; Pss 48:1-2; 132:13-14). Eventually this led to a widespread belief that Yahweh's presence with Israel was an absolute guarantee, whatever the nature of the nation's response to God (Jer 7:1-15). The ZION theology sought to regularize the unpredictable freedom of Yahweh stressed by the intermittent presence in the tent and Ark. When the Temple was destroyed this concept of presence was destroyed as well. To deal with this loss, Israelite theologians worked with the older concepts of divine presence in the name and glory of Yahweh. In SOLOMON's prayer at the dedication of the Temple in 1 Kgs 8, Yahweh's dwelling place in heaven is stressed. Yahweh's "name" would be present in the Temple, i.e., the effective presence would be through the use of the name of God in WORSHIP. The glory of Yahweh is closely associated with the Temple and the Tabernacle (Exod 40:34-38; Num 20:6; Ps 24:7-10). The "glory" of God designates an awe-inspiring presence. EZEKIEL's visions of the glory of God leaving the Temple (Ezek 10:18-19; 11:22-23) and returning (Ezek 43:1-5) show how this theology dealt with the Exile: Israel's behavior caused Yahweh to withdraw the divine presence, but it was later returned as of old. The loss of the Temple was not the destruction of God's habitation but of a place where God had chosen to be.

The concepts of God's presence as coming and leading are not contradictory to the experience of the abiding presence. God may appear suddenly, but is also present with the people of Israel, although there are occasions when God withdraws from human perception (e.g., Isa 1:12-15; 45:15; Ps 22:1-21). On these occasions the presence of God is experienced in a dreadful silence (cf. Amos 8:11-14; Mark 15:34). There is a certain tension between these views, as often happens when human beings try to describe God, but they each deal with part of the experience of God and are each needed to understand how the Bible expresses God's presence.

In the NT literature the fulfillment of the presence of God is seen in JESUS Christ, the revealer of God's nature. In Christ and the HOLY SPIRIT we see both the constant hidden-but-present aspect (Matt 28:20; Rom 8) as well as the sudden coming in power (Acts 2) of God's presence. The seeming paradox is resolved in the experience of believers (1 John 5:19-20).

See also GOD; THEOPHANY; WORSHIP IN THE NEW TESTAMENT; WORSHIP IN THE OLD TESTAMENT.

Bibliography. M. Haran, *Temples and Temple Service*; N. D. Tryggve, *The Dethronement of Sabaoth*; S. Terrien, *The Elusive Presence*.

—CAROL STUART GRIZZARD, MARVIN E. TATE

• **Priestly Writers.** Religious leaders who sought to preserve and enhance their priestly tradition through the composition of the P (priestly) material in 444 B.C.E. and its editing into the biblical text.

During the early part of the nineteenth century, when the concepts of evolution (particularly that of things developing linearly from the simple to the complex) were gaining popularity, several Old Testament scholars (such as H. B. Witter, J. G. Eichhorn, W. M. L. DeWette, H. Hupfeld, K. H. Graf, and A. Kuenen) became convinced that the Pentateuch was composed from several sources (J, E, D, P) each of which was more elaborate than the former. The last of these sources, that of the priestly writers (P), was the most complex and thus became that which held them all together. The main popularizer of this theory was Julius Wellhausen in his *Prolegomena to the History of Israel*.

Wellhausen believed that the priestly system had gradually developed from a very simple family-oriented system to a very elaborate and centralized system under JOSIAH (Ezek 44:6-16). However, during the Exile many of the political and social gains of the priesthood were in danger of being lost. Thus, the returning priestly writers sought to compose a document (P) that would trace their origin back to MOSES and thus give more validity to them (Exod 25–31; 35–40) and their efforts (Lev 1–7; 17–26). This document (including parts of Genesis, Exodus, Numbers, and most of Leviticus) was then superimposed over the other three Pentateuchal sources to make a unified story. This theory has been and continues to be called into question.

Among the chief challenges of recent date are two that stand out. Some materials found in the Pentateuch, including those in the priestly tradition, are recognized today to come from very ancient times. A *process* of handing down the materials from very ancient times, until finally the traditions were put into written form, seems better to account for the origin of the materials preserved by the priests.

The second challenge focuses upon the artful way in which the traditions of the Pentateuch, with all their unevennesses, have been put together. Newer literary studies of the Pentateuch have called into question the rather "bookish" form of earlier literary criticism of the Pentateuch, including critical work on the priestly writings.

See also LITERATURE, BIBLE AS; SOURCE CRITICISM; SOURCES OF THE PENTATEUCH; TRADITION IN THE OLD TESTAMENT.

Bibliography. S. R. Driver, *Introduction to the Literature of the Old Testament*; R. K. Harrison, *Introduction to the Old Testament*; R. J. Thompson, *Moses and the Law in a Century of Criticism Since Graf.*

—WALTER HARRELSON

• **Priests.** One of the most important mediators between God and the community and between God and individual worshipers.

Etymology. The term "priest" evolved via Middle English from the Greek *presbyteros,* an elder. The Hebrew *kōhēn* may come from the verb *kûn,* to stand, perhaps "to stand before the Lord." The Arabic term *kâhin* has a more restrictive meaning: "soothsayer."

General View of Priests. From time immemorial humankind has been preoccupied with existence itself and with coexistence with the environment. Especially when this was threatened, as in natural catastrophes such as earthquakes, drought, floods, pestilence and diseases, then ways and means were sought to ameliorate these forces. From before historical time many of these forces were felt to be divine powers, which were therefore to be approached in awe and reverence. But as the environment was quite variegated, and these forces were encountered in so many ways, it seemed obvious that there were many gods. So it became a problem to know to whom human beings were to relate. Even if they contacted the right god or goddess, how were they to approach him or her?

It was here that the "holy men and women" came to assistance. They have been mainly of three kinds: the miracle maker, the shaman, and the priest. The priests were people that either through training and/or inherited position or through divine appointment were acceptable to the deities, so that they could come close to them, and either by sacrifices of various kinds or by skilled methods intercede for the one who wanted to pray but did not dare approach the deity for fear that something wrong could be done that would worsen the situation. These kinds of experts can be found in all religions throughout the world. And because they were called upon predominantly during periods of catastrophes, over the years they acquired great powers, and often came to rival that of the secular powers, such as chieftains, kings and even emperors.

Description of Priests in the OT. In ancient ISRAEL a priest was called kohen (*kōhēn*). We meet such a person in Gen 14 where ABRAHAM pays homage to MELCHIZEDEK, priest of Salem. His high esteem is obviously based on his priestly function. One reads of no priestly activity among the Hebrews in EGYPT. The family father was the one who officiated at the encounters with the deity, as we can clearly see in the story about the first PASSOVER (Exod 12). But it did not take long before the family needed the help of people with the specialized knowledge; therefore, soon after Israel had settled in Canaan, priesthoods were established both at SHILOH and at NOB. These priests were described as Levites. There naturally developed rivalry between these different priesthoods and their sanctuaries.

The priests really came into power after DAVID had chosen Jerusalem to be his capital and had established his main sanctuary there. David joined the Levites, who had been faithful Yahweh-worshippers, and the Zadokites, the priesthood of the god Salem in Jerusalem (note the name!) into a religious coalition (whether this was on the basis of syncretism is hard to say, but it is very likely; compare, for instance, how the names of Yahweh and El were united to cover one deity later on). All went well during David's reign, probably because he held together the different groups by his strong personality. But when he died, his son, King SOLOMON, soon expelled the Levites and left the priestly functions to the Zadokites (1 Kgs 1–2). The Levites had to be satisfied with serving at the many local sanctuaries throughout the country. Many scholars believe that the Book of Deuteronomy is best understood as a claim for a place in the sun by the Levites.

As originally the family father was the primary religious functionary, so now in the nation the king was the main officiator. He represented the people to their God, and he represented God to the people. There are statements about royal activity at the altar (2 Sam 6; 1 Kgs 8, 12; 2 Chr 26:16-17).

But it seems evident that the power of the priests grew during the royal period (1000–587 B.C.E.). Actually, the two functions needed and supported each other. How intimately this was the case is clear from the stories in 2 Kgs 11. It was always necessary to approach the deity in the correct manner. The priests were the specialists, and they guarded their secrets with zeal (2 Chr 26:16-17). A clear indication of their importance is seen in the high number of priests and Levites listed in the books of EZRA and NEHEMIAH. As the years passed they developed an elaborate system of position and rank of tasks and responsibilities. At the time of the return from EXILE, the people had a HIGH PRIEST, who according to the prophets HAGGAI and ZECHARIAH, was equal to the prince in power and status. And because Judah never again obtained a king, the high priest, for all practical purposes, was the leading person in the nation, something we see substantiated during the time of the Maccabees and at the time of JESUS.

The priesthood was further divided into "families," who had their special tasks to perform at the Temple. Mainly we read of two divisions: the priests and the Levites. The priests were the ones "to stand before God," to serve at the altar and carry out whatever was needed in God's presence. The Levites, who originally also had been priests of Yahweh in Israel, were now relegated to the lower level, to take care of all the menial tasks at the Temple. They were responsible for the slaughter of the sacrificial animals. They were gatekeepers and Temple singers.

The priests were of great importance for the religious life in Israel. They were teachers and guides. Deut 33:8-11 tells how they were to instruct the people in the law of God. Often they would have traditions on which to build their advice to the people who asked. Or they might cast lots, the Urim and Thummim, in order to obtain a yes or a no answer from the deity. In the early days "The Law" was either (a) divine oracles spoken by the priests under inspiration (at this time they were not greatly different from the prophets in mode of performance) or (b) tradition built up over the years by generations of priests. Naturally, this body of material grew, generally stored in the memories of the priests, and in the end, after the Exile, "The Law" was completely written down and consisted of the Pentateuch or "The Five Books of Moses," clearly the most sacred and authoritative part of the Hebrew Bible.

The psalms present an interesting base for a study of the priesthood. There can be little question that the priests had a great deal to do with whatever happened around the sanctuaries, and yet the priests were not mentioned in the psalms.

Sacrifices were brought, and, from what may be learned in the books of Exodus, Leviticus and Numbers, the priests were the ones officiating and conducting the proceedings. It seems curious, then, that priests would inspire the attitude that God has no delight in sacrifice and that he would not be pleased with burnt offerings (Ps 51:16). And yet there is no reason to deny that such spiritual sensitivities could indeed exist among the priests. After all, they were living and working in Yahweh's presence. They were prone to reflect on his majesty and grandeur and to become aware of the distance between almighty God and the offerings they presented.

The psalms also list the requirements for a life within the COVENANT. There are clear lists that are supposed to be—so to speak—nailed to the gate of the Temple area. These appear in Pss 15, 19, and 24. This clearly is material proffered by the priests to the people. Also, when one reads of the love for the law of God as it is expressed in Ps 119, one is clearly hearing the thought of a person with priestly responsibilities. A few times, the person praying in the psalms expressed the hope of remaining in the house of God forever (Ps 23), and one must wonder whether the speaker is a king or a priest. The common people did not have access to the Temple proper. By and large, it can be assumed that the high cultic sense of Yahweh's presence expressed in the psalms is a creation of the Israelite priests.

In biblical studies it is customary to underrate the priests in favor of the prophets. However, it is probably fair to say that if it had not been for the faithful work of generation after generation of priests, the prophets would have had no congregations to address.

Priesthood in the NT. In the NT the term priest (*iereus*) is predominantly used for the representatives of the Jewish faith, who resisted the activities of Jesus. They were the leaders of the Jewish community and understood Jesus to be a threat to the *status quo*. The term is also used for the functionaries of pagan gods, as in Acts 14:13. In the Letter to the Hebrews the term priest is employed to describe Jesus the Christ as he provides atonement for his people and as he serves in the Heavenly Tabernacle. In the Book of Revelation the term is used twice to portray the activity of the redeemed who are called "priests of God and the Christ" (Rev 1:5-6; 20:6). It is, therefore, difficult to say that the term priest is central and essential to the structure of the church in the NT.

The English word priest, however, stems from the Gk. *presbyteros*. This word is used several times in the Book of Acts and in the Pastoral Letters to describe the "elders," i.e., the leaders of local congregations. It is an ongoing discussion between the established church denominations (Greek Orthodox, Roman Catholic, Anglican, Lutheran, et al.) on the one hand, and the more independent congregational type churches (e.g., Baptists) on the other hand, whether this term presbyter, our priest, is to be seen as a fully worthy successor to the OT *kōhēn* and the NT *iereus*.

Priests in the Christian Churches. It seems as if the authors of the NT made a clear distinction between those who served as religious functionaries, whom they called *iereus*, and those who were leaders of the new faith communities, whom they called presbyters. A problem has arisen in our culture because one normally translates the old religious functionary's title (Heb. *kōhēn*) with "priest," a word that evolved from "presbyter." The possibility of confusing the two, therefore, has been very near at hand, and it actually has taken place in some circles. It is an example of how beliefs under certain circumstances may change within a family of languages.

Whatever the actual and original meaning of the title priest, there can be little question that, in many religions, the priests have served an important function toward enhancing the spiritual and emotional well-being of their respective peoples.

See also ELDER; LEVI/LEVITES; TEMPLE/TEMPLES; WORSHIP IN THE OLD TESTAMENT.

Bibliography. A. Cody, *A History of Old Testament Priesthood*; S. I. Curtiss, *The Levitical Priests*; I. Engnell, *Studies in Divine Kingship in the Ancient Near East*; S. Gayford, *Sacrifice and Priesthood*; G. B. Gray, *Sacrifice in the Old Testament*; A. H. J. Gunneweg, *Leviten und Priester*; S. H. Hooke, *Prophets and Priests*; E. O. James, *The Nature and Function of Priesthood*; G. Landtman, *The Origin of Priesthood*; J. Pedersen, *Israel, Its Life and Culture*; L. S. J. Sabourin, *Priesthood*; R. de Vaux, *Israel, Its Life and Institutions*; A. C. Welch, *Prophet and Priest in Old Israel*.

—REIDAR B. BJORNARD

• **Prince/Captain.** In Israel, someone holding an office of high political or military authority. Four Hebrew words are commonly rendered "prince" in the English versions. In early usage, the term *nāgîd* is used almost exclusively to designate a king, or someone who later became king. SAMUEL anoints SAUL as *nāgîd* in 1 Sam 9:16 and 10:1. DAVID is called *nāgîd* in 1 Sam 13:14 and 25:30 and SOLOMON is declared *nāgîd* by David in 1 Kgs 1:35. In later usage in Chronicles the term referred to any kind of leader.

The Hebrew *nādîb* is used mostly in poetry and seems to denote nobility or aristocracy rather than leadership. Another term is *nāśî'*, which in early usage commonly denoted tribal chiefs (Gen 17:20; 23:6; 34:2), but was used by Ezekiel as a euphemism for "king" and in the postexilic period referred to the aristocracy (Exod 16:22; Josh 9:15-18; 1 Chr 2:10).

A word commonly used as "prince" or "captain" is *śar*, which could be used for leaders of many sorts, but particularly for a military leader (1 Sam 12:9; 22:2; 1 Kgs 2:5; 16:9). *Śar* also was used to refer to the king's civil officials (1 Kgs 4:2; Jer 34:21).

Sons of the kings were not called princes in Israel. There seems to be no Hebrew word for that specific position.

See also RULER.

—RAY SUTHERLAND

• **Principalities and Powers.** The expression "principalities and powers" is related to several words in the Greek NT, usually used in combination with one another: principalities (ἀρχαί), authorities (ἐξουσίαι), powers (δυνάμεις), and lords (κυριότητοι). The most common phraseology is principalities and powers (αἱ ἀρχαὶ καὶ αἱ ἐξουσίαι; Luke 12:11; 20:20 [sing]; 1 Cor 15:24; Eph 3:10; 6:12; Col 1:16; 2:10, 15; Titus 3:1; cf. 1 Pet 3:22). The singular form of the word translated authorities (ἀρχή, fifty-five uses) is frequently used for "beginning" but in combination with ἐξουσία it designates power (eleven uses) either in the sense of "dominion" or "authority." No significant difference in meaning between authorities (ἀρχαί) and powers (ἐξουσίαι) in NT usage can be demonstrated. The derivative term ruler (ἄρχων) denotes an "authority" either human (twenty-seven uses) or supernatural (ten uses). The human designations range from political rulers (Matt 20:25) to Jewish religious leaders (Matt 9:18, 23; Luke 18:18). Frequently, the devil is termed the ruler of demons (ἄρχων τοῦ κόσμου τούτου; John 12:31; 14:30; 16:11; cf. 1 Cor 2:6-8; Eph 2:2).

In NT usage, the expression principalities and powers can refer to human authorities (Luke 12:11; Rom 13:1; Titus 3:1) in line with its Hellenistic meaning (*TDNT* 2:571). In its major (Pauline) uses, however, the expression refers to superhuman powers which operate in this world, thus extending its complex Jewish background (cf. Dan 7 and 10). Debated is the connection of principalities and powers with angels. Passages like Rom 8:38 (neither angels nor principalities; οὔτε ἄγγελοι οὔτε ἀρχαὶ) and 1 Pet 3:22 (angels and authorities and powers; ἀγγέλων καὶ ἐξουσιῶν καὶ δυνάμεων) establish a linkage. Principalities and powers are perceived as personal beings following the pattern in Jewish apocalyptic writings. Are they possibly good forces as well as evil forces? They certainly belong to the created order which exists through and for Christ (Col 1:16); they are counted among "all things" which were reconciled to God through Christ's death (Col 1:20). Possibly Col 2:15 and Rom 8:38 pick up on the juridical role of accuser in Zech 3:1-5. Clearly, the principalities and powers represent part of the demonic opposition to the community of faith in Eph 6:12. Christ has triumphed over them in his death and resurrection, but his reign will not be complete until they have been finally brought under subjection at the close of the age (1 Cor 15:24; 1 Pet 3:22).

Modern scholarship has differed over the present-day significance of the biblical concept. Gordon Rupp (*Principalities and Powers*) accepts the supernatural meaning for Paul but applies them to the great historical forces which have made playthings of the "little people" in every era (11). Hendrik Berkhof (*Christ and the Powers*) argues for a Pauline "demythologizing" of the Jewish apocalyptic sources from heavenly angels to structures of earthly existence. G. B. Caird argues in *Principalities and Powers, A Study in Pauline Theology* for a naive Pauline superstition permeating the apostle's understanding which must be "demythologized" along the lines of Berkhof's position. Somewhat similar is the position of Markus Barth in *The Broken Wall* and also in his commentary on Ephesians in the *Anchor Bible*. Other scholars, such as A. J. Bandstra (*The Law and the Elements of the World*) and W. Carr (*Angels and Principalities*) have argued for the continued understanding of supernatural powers at work in our world.

See also ANGEL; DEMON IN THE NEW TESTAMENT.

Bibliography. G. Delling, "ἄρχω, κτλ.," *TDNT*; W. Foerster, "ἔξεστιν, κτλ.," *TDNT*; H. Schlier, *Principalities and Powers in the New Testament*; W. Wink, *Naming the Powers: The Language of Power in the New Testament* and *Unmasking The Powers: The Invisible forces that Determine Human Existence*.

—LORIN L. CRANFORD

• **Prisca and Aquila.** *See* PRISCILLA AND AQUILA

• **Priscilla and Aquila.** [pri-sil'uh, ak'wi-luh] Wife and husband, Paul's companions in missions and vocation: Acts 18:1-3, 18-19; Rom 16:3-5; 1 Cor 16:19; 2 Tim 4:19. Both names are originally Latin, indicating Roman connections.

Acts indicates that Aquila was a Jew originally from Pontus, but nothing is said about Priscilla's race. Some infer from the silence of Acts that she was not Jewish, but Roman. Early citizens of Rome, they were expelled by Emperor Claudius ca.49–50 C.E. because of Jewish unrest, which Suetonius says was "at the instigation of *Chrestus*" (*Lives* 25.4), perhaps a reference to Christ.

In CORINTH, PAUL met Priscilla and Aquila who by trade were leather-workers ("tentmakers," Acts 18:3). Thus began a close relationship as Paul lived and worked with the couple at Corinth for one to two years (Acts 18:11, 18).

When Paul journeyed to Jerusalem, he left the couple in EPHESUS where they continued their evangelism. They instructed APOLLOS, a Jew from Alexandria, in the "way of God" more accurately, for he knew only John's baptism and facts about Jesus. First Corinthians (written in Ephesus) mentions Aquila and Prisca and "the church in their house" (16:19), and Rom 16 indicates that the couple "risked their necks" for the sake of Paul (16:4). Paul regularly uses "Prisca" instead of "Priscilla," and his references usually place "Prisca" before "Aquila," probably because she was more important for the Christian community—whether by virtue of nobility, personality, or spirituality is unclear. Luke's reversal of the traditional order of names (cf. Acts 18:2 and 18:18, 26) when the couple left with Paul to Ephesus and instructed Apollos may indicate that she better understood the gospel. Various authorities suggest that she wrote Hebrews. Certainly, she was one of the significant women in the early church along with LYDIA of Philippi and Phoebe of Cenchreae.

See also APOLLOS; CORINTH; DECREE; EPHESUS; PAUL; WOMEN IN THE NEW TESTAMENT.

—FRANK LOUIS MAULDIN

• **Prison.** Although it would appear that imprisonment was not known until the Persian period (cf. Ezra 7:26), the OT often mentions the practice of confining persons, both outside and inside Israelite culture. POTIPHAR had JOSEPH imprisoned "where the king's prisoners were confined" (Gen 39:20), a place said to be "in the house of the captain of the guard" (Gen 40:3). Reference is made to persons who are "in custody" (40:4), and who have been placed "into the dungeon" (40:15; 41:14). The PHILISTINES bound SAMSON "with bronze fetters; and he ground at the mill in the prison" (Judg 16:21). The king of Assyria captured HOSHEA, the northern kingdom's last and treacherous king, and "bound him in prison" (2 Kgs 17:4). Evil-merodach, in his first year as Babylon's king, "graciously freed JEHOIACHIN king of Judah from prison" (2 Kgs 25:27) so that he could "put off his prison garments" (v. 29). Another Babylonian prison is mentioned in Jeremiah 52:11 in which King NEBUCHADREZZAR placed the blinded Zedekiah. However, King ARTAXERXES of Persia lists imprisonment as a punishment (Ezra 7:26).

The Israelites also had their places of confinement. An unnamed son of an Israelite woman and an Egyptian "blasphemed the Name, and cursed" (Lev 24:11), so that he was placed "in custody, till the will of the Lord should be declared" (v. 12). Likewise, in the wilderness "a man gathering sticks on the sabbath day" (Num 15:32) was taken "in custody, because it had not been made plain what should be done to him" (v. 34). Certain persons regarded as potential problems to civil order were imprisoned in the period of the monarchy. Zedekiah had the vociferous MICAIAH held "in prison" with "scant fare of bread and water" (1 Kgs 22:27). Such was the case also with JEREMIAH when Jerusalem's city elders imprisoned him in "the dungeon cells" (37:16) that were "in the house of Jonathan the secretary" (v. 15). The conditions there were life-threatening, so that Jeremiah later successfully pleaded with Zedekiah to commit him to "the court of the guard" where he received daily a loaf of bread (v. 21). It was here that later Jeremiah was cast into a cistern with mire, apparently to starve, but was rescued by Ebed-melech (38:1-13). Jeremiah "remained in the court of the guard until the day that Jerusalem was taken" (38:28). This "court of the guard," apparently in the palace area, allowed prisoners outside contact (Jer 32:2-8; 33:1).

Both Roman and Jewish prisons are mentioned in the NT. The high priest and his party of Sadducees at Jerusalem "arrested the apostles and put them in the common prison" (Acts 5:18), apparently awaiting interrogation. Such had been the case with PETER and JOHN in Acts 4. Jesus taught to "make friends quickly with your accuser . . . lest . . . you be put in prison" (Matt 5:25). Paul confessed to having earlier imprisoned Christians and beaten them (Acts 22:19). Imprisonment as a method of coercion could be used by the Romans (Matt 18:30). JOHN THE BAPTIST was imprisoned by the Romans and executed (Matt 14:3-10). The Roman procurator's palace at Caesarea (Acts 23:35) had rooms for confinement, as did the Fortress Antonia at Jerusalem (Acts 23:10).

See also REFUGE, CITIES OF.

—KAREN RANDOLPH JOINES

• **Prison Epistles.** Four of the thirteen NT Letters which bear Paul's name as author are known as prison Epistles or captivity Letters. In Philippians (1:7, 13-14), Colossians (4:3, 10, 18), Ephesians (3:1; 4:1; 6:20), and Philemon (1, 9, 10, 13, 23), the writer refers to imprisonment as a circumstance out of which the correspondence emerged. Second Timothy also originated from prison (1:8, 16; 2:8). However, a later date of origin and common features with 1 Timothy and Titus require that it be viewed among the pastoral Letters.

The location of the writer's imprisonment is not stated in the prison Letters. Since the fourth century, church tradition has claimed that they were written by Paul between 60 and 62 C.E. as he waited in a jail in Rome for the result of the appeal to Caesar. This interpretation rests, in part, on Acts' description of Paul's confinement in Rome, but also on references made by Paul in Philippians to "the whole PRAETORIAN GUARD" (1:13) and "those of Caesar's household" (4:22). The theory of a Roman provenance for the prison Epistles has not gone unchallenged. Analysis of the specific Letters, especially Philippians, presents certain factors which create problems for a theory of Roman origin.

Recent papyri discoveries reveal that "praetorian guard" frequently described military headquarters which existed in several major cities and was not restricted to designating the Roman garrison. Furthermore, the phrase, "those of Caesar's household" referred to servants of Rome who lived throughout the empire as well as in Rome.

Another major difficulty revolves around the distance between Rome and Philippi (PLATES 26, 27). The text of Philippians indicates that four trips had already occurred between the site of imprisonment and the city of Philippi and another would soon begin. The one-way trip of 800 mi. would have required close to two months to accomplish. Rome cannot be ruled out by the evidence of the papyri nor the distance factors, but many scholars maintain that other first-century cities serve the historical occasion of the prison Letters with more clarity.

A few interpreters have contended that Caesarea, which Acts also described as a place of imprisonment for Paul, was the place of dispatch for the prison Epistles. These advocates have underscored the occurrence of identical personal names of individuals in Colossians and Philemon, most of whom were probably present with Paul during his confinement in Caesarea. Likewise, Paul's hope to travel to Rome from Caesarea makes understandable his reference to an upcoming visit to the Philippians and Colossians since these cities were en route to Rome. If written be-Caesarea the prison Letters would have been written between 58–60 C.E.

The city of Ephesus has also been proposed as the place of origin for some, if not all, of the Letters of captivity. Acts does not describe an Ephesian imprisonment, but Paul's account of his numerous imprisonments (2 Cor 11:23) prior to the Caesarean or Roman experience suggests Ephesus as a likely site for one of his confinements.

Several items support the Ephesian theory. First, the silence of the prison Letters about Paul's experiences in Jerusalem and Caesarea and his travel to Rome would be more understandable if written prior to those events. Second, the geographical proximity of Ephesus and Philippi would eliminate the distance difficulty because a trip would have required no more than two weeks. Finally, references to visits from Onesimus (Phlm 10, 16) and Epaphras (Col 1:7-8; 4:12) are more understandable if the apostle were closer in miles to Colossae. If written from Ephesus the prison Letters would have been written around 54 C.E.

See also COLOSSIANS, LETTER TO THE; EPHESIANS, LETTER TO THE; PHILEMON, LETTER TO; PHILIPPIANS, LETTER TO THE; PRAETORIAN GUARD.

Bibliography. G. S. Duncan, *St. Paul's Ephesian Ministry*; D. Guthrie, *New Testament Introduction.*

—ROBERT M. SHURDEN

• **Privilege.** *See* FREEDOM

• **Proconsul.** [proh-kon'suhl] "Proconsul" literally meant "in place of the consul" and is used in relation to the governmental structures of the Roman republic. To head up the government of one of the provinces, the Roman senate would select one of their own number who had already served as consul, two of which were chosen each year for a term of one year to serve as chief military and political magistrates. About seventeen years after serving as consul a senator was appointed as a proconsul for one year to govern for the consul, but subject to review by the entire senate.

When the emperorship was established under Augustus (27 B.C.E.) the Roman provinces, which had now increased considerably in number, were divided between the *princeps* (emperor) and the senate (the people). One of the two consuls chosen each year was the emperor (caesar) if he wished. The senate was given the provinces which normally did not require the army to be actively involved in keeping the peace. The requirement that a proconsul serve earlier as consul was dropped. The interval between serving as an urban magistrate and as a provincial governor was fixed at five years, but the term of office was still one year. All governors of senatorial provinces were called proconsuls.

According to Acts 13:7-12, SERGIUS PAULUS, the proconsul of Cyprus, believed the gospel. In Acts 18:12-17 GALLIO, who had recently come to be proconsul of Achaia, refused to view the Jewish charge brought against Paul as a crime.

See also GALLIO; SERGIUS PAULUS.

Bibliography. H. T. F. Duckworth, "The Roman Provincial System," in *The Beginnings of Christianity,* ed. F. J. Foakes-Jackson and K. Lake.

—G. WILLARD REEVES

• **Procurator.** [prok″yuh-ray′tuhr] This term is a transliteration of the Latin word meaning a steward of private property; an often-used English translation is "governor." Under the ROMAN EMPIRE the word came to mean one with a particular imperial assignment, primarily the procurement of taxes or other property. The title was also used for provincial administrators such as Pontius PILATE of JUDEA (Tacitus, *Ann* 15.44); Pilate was earlier called "prefect" according to a dedication inscription found at Caesarea in 1961.

Procurators before the time of Emperor Claudius (41–54 C.E.) had been chosen from the equestrian class, but Claudius began appointing freedmen to this position. Appointees now were clearly state officials and not just personal imperial agents.

Procurators usually served directly under the emperors, exercising judicial, military, and financial authority. According to Josephus (*BJ* 2.117), Procurator Coponius (ca. 6–9 C.E.) had the power of capital punishment over Judean subjects, but it is not clear that such power was given to Jewish authorities (Acts 25:10-12). Although the Jerusalem Sanhedrin had extensive rights to govern, imperial authorities never formally surrendered their right to intervene.

Judea was ruled by procurators 6–41 and 44–66 C.E., and three are mentioned in the NT: Pilate (Matt 27:2), FELIX (Acts 23:24ff.), and FESTUS (Acts 24:27ff.). Often the procurators showed mediocre ability and little sympathy for Jewish customs and religion. Pilate displayed images of the emperor in Jerusalem, minted coins with offensive religious symbols, and used money from the Jewish Temple treasury for a Jerusalem aqueduct. However, procurators in Judea served as stabilizers at times, and even Pilate, whose reputation was seriously scarred, must have been considered a good manager by Tiberius who kept him in office for ten years.

See also FELIX; FESTUS; PILATE.

Bibliography. H. Mattingly, *The Imperial Civil Service of Rome*; E. T. Salmon, *A History of the Roman World from 30 B.C. to A.D. 138*; A. N. Sherman-White, *Roman Society and Roman Law in the New Testament.*

—PHILIP R. HART

• **Promise.** Words that affirm a future deed or refer to a commitment between two or more parties.

In the OT, God's promises have a COVENANT dimension: God calls ABRAHAM and his descendants into covenant relationship and establishes promises with them in accordance with the covenant (Gen 12:2-3; 17:1-8). Several variations of God's promises appear in the OT.

Judgment and Salvation. In the prophetic writings the coming judgment of God is proclaimed to an errant nation (Amos 2:6-8) while the promise of salvation is extended to the people (Ezek 12–14; Isa 52:1-3). The promise of a coming "Day of the Lord" often appears in connection with judgment as in Isa 2:12ff. and Amos 5:18-20.

The Messiah and Messianic Kingdom. Several prophets speak of an anointed one, a righteous king of the lineage of DAVID (Isa 9:6-7) whose future reign over the people will be like the reign of God.

Land. Canaan is promised as the homeland for Abraham and his descendants (Gen 17:8; Jer 32:40-41).

NT writers frequently interpret some of the promises made to Israel as fulfilled in JESUS (Gal 3:16ff.; 2 Cor 1:20). Critical scholars, however, generally reject the pattern of promise-fulfillment as a method of relating the OT and NT.

In the preaching and teaching of Jesus about the KINGDOM OF GOD the promises of both salvation and eternal life are extended to those of faith (John 3:16). Likewise the promise of the Apocalypse of John speaks of a "new heaven and a new earth" when God will usher in a new era of peace (Rev 21:1-7).

See also ESCHATOLOGY IN THE NEW TESTAMENT; ESCHATOLOGY IN THE OLD TESTAMENT; WORD; WORD OF GOD.

Bibliography. B. S. Childs, *Old Testament Theology in a Canonical Context*; R. E. Clements, *Old Testament Theology*; J. Jeremias, *New Testament Theology.*

—STEVEN SIMPLER

• **Pronouncement Story.** *See* APOPHTHEGM

• **Property.** *See* LAND

• **Prophecy.** Early Christianity began as a prophetic movement, a fact evident both in the earliest surviving Christian writings (the Letters of Paul, e.g., 1 Thess 5:19-20; 1 Cor 12–14) and in the earliest historical presentation of Christian beginnings found in Acts (e.g., 2:1-42; 11:27-30; 13:1-3; 21:10-11). According to gospel tradition, Jesus was frequently categorized as a PROPHET (Mark 6:14-15; 8:28; Matt 21:10-11, 46; Luke 7:16, 39; John 6:14; 7:40, 52), and was occasionally identified as the eschatological Mosaic prophet predicted in Deut 18:15-16 (Acts 3:22; 7:37). John the Baptist was also described in prophetic terms (Mark 1:6; cf. 1 Kgs 19:19; 2 Kgs 1:8; Zech 13:4; Luke 1:15; 3:2), and was even identified with the eschatological Elijah (Matt 11:13-14; 17:10-13). As a prophetic renewal movement, early Christianity has a threefold setting. The first and most significant setting is that of Israelite religious tradition as preserved in the literature of the OT which presented ancient prophets as divinely inspired spokespersons who mediated the will of God to an often recalcitrant and disobedient people. The OT contains many descriptions of prophets and their ministry as well as many books regarded as collections of prophetic oracles. The second setting is that of early Judaism, which was guided not only by a sacred canon of scripture (fixed by the first century B.C.E.) but also by a variety of religious figures and apocalyptic writings explicitly or implicitly claiming to speak with divine authority. The third setting is that of the wider Greco-Roman world within which early Christianity very quickly expanded and which exhibited very different yet essentially compatible revelatory phenomena including oracles, collections of oracles, and inspired diviners.

The continuity which early Christians perceived between their own experience of prophetic phenomena and that of ancient Israel as found in the OT is reflected in the terminology used by the early Greek-speaking Christians. The LXX used Greek words built on a stem (*nabi*) meaning "to speak forth" or "to announce," to translate the Hebrew forms for "prophet," "prophecy," and "to prophecy." Christians adopted the same vocabulary. Early Jewish authors and writings (e.g., Philo, Josephus, the Apocrypha and Pseudepigrapha, the Dead Sea Scrolls) usually restricted their use of such terminology either to ancient Israelite prophets or to eschatological prophets who were expected at the end of days. The widespread early Christian use of the Greek terms for "prophet," "prophecy," and "to prophesy," then, indicates both a consciousness of the OT roots of prophetic phenomena and an awareness that Christian prophecy is an eschatological phenomenon.

The primary evidence for NT prophecy is found in the Letters of Paul (particularly 1 Cor 12–14), the Acts of the Apostles, and the Revelation of John. These texts indicate that the major function of prophecy in early Christianity was to mediate divine authority to provide direction and the experience of the divine presence in the lives and activities of Christian congregations and their members. While the Christian consciousness of the presence of the Spirit of God in the church suggests that all Christians were potential prophets (1 Cor 14:1), those who regularly exercised prophetic gifts in congregational settings were called "prophets" (1 Cor 12:10; 14:29-31). Since the Greek term means "spokesperson," the main function of the Christian prophet was a "forthteller" rather than a "foreteller," i.e., a prophet was more occupied with mediating the word of God in concrete situations (1 Cor 14:24-25) than with predicting the future course of events (Acts 11:28), though both functions were part of the task.

See also ESCHATOLOGY IN THE NEW TESTAMENT; PROPHET.

Bibliography. D. E. Aune, *Prophecy in Early Christianity and the Ancient Mediterranean World*; M. E. Boring, *Sayings of the Risen Jesus: Christian Prophecy in the Synoptic Tradition*; E. E. Ellis, *Prophecy and Hermeneutic in Early Christianity*.

—DAVID E. AUNE

• **Prophet.** [prof'it] In considering the nature of the biblical prophets, six issues must be given consideration. (1) What is the nature of the Israelite prophetic movement; what is its background; and what if anything is unique about Hebrew prophetism? (2) Who are the canonical prophets and by what standards were they limited or defined? (3) What kind of a person became a prophet? (4) What are the common forms of the messages of the prophets and of the contents of the books included in prophetic canon? (5) What brought about the so-called decline in OT prophecy? (6) What is a NT prophet and how do the prophets of the NT relate to the OT prophets?

The Nature of the Israelite Prophet. The OT prophets were not so much predictors as they were proclaimers. Their major interest in the future grew out of their concern with the present. They had been sensitized by the voice and spirit of God and proclaimed God's special word to their specific historical situation. When they spoke of the future, it was not so much in terms of general prediction as in terms of what must happen if their people did not change their lives, repent, and turn to God.

The Hebrew prophets were people who felt deeply. They were devastated by the suffering of oppressed people and by the anger of God over sin and rebellion. Frightened by people with power, they were more afraid of what was going to happen and so proclaimed their message with audacity. The prophets were not philosophers thinking about what was going on in their world. They were activists, concerned with life as it is, with people as they are, with blindness that did not see God at work and with deafness that refused to hear God's warnings.

Perhaps the most amazing feature of the Hebrew prophets was that they were tolerated at all. Their stinging rebukes and scathing denunciations were of such a nature as to be expected to bring violent attacks upon them. The very fact that they survived and that their messages were kept and passed on is a measure of the awareness of the Hebrew people that they did in fact hear the voice of God in the words of the prophets.

The prophets were also intercessors. Even as they brought words from God to Israel, so they took Israel's concerns and their own concerns for Israel to God. They sought to delay judgment, to seize upon God's mercy in order to give their people one more chance. These dual functions kept the prophets under stress. The word of God was stern, stinging and confronting. It demanded decision. Any moment could be the last opportunity for change, for avoiding a coming judgment. There was no time for levity. There was only time for the confrontation of the moment in the hope that the next moment might be better. At the same time, the prophets also had the occasional opportunity of offering comfort, consolation, and hope.

Prophets were a common phenomenon in the ancient Near East. Every nation from which we have religious records had those persons, male and female, who announced the will of their god to people. In general, these were the oracles who gave messages only upon request and upon appropriate payment. They usually served at a specific shrine. Those who sought the will of God went to the shrine, paid the fee, asked their question and received their answer. The answer was usually obtained through an ecstatic trance, the casting of lots, or some other form of divination. This kind of prophet was also present in Israel. SAUL went to the prophet SAMUEL to find his lost donkeys (1 Sam 9:6). He also on occasion joined bands of roving prophets in their ecstasy and trance (1 Sam 10:9-13; 19:19-24). Further, the professional prophets found in Israel's royal courts were also apparently of this type.

At least by the time of the Hebrew monarchy, and perhaps as early as the time of MOSES, prophecy in Israel developed a unique dimension. This was not so much due to something different in Israel as it was to something different about the God of Israel. Hebrew prophets spoke, not to answer Israel's question but to deliver the unsought word of God. Evidence of this transition is found in Saul's visit to Samuel. "Formerly in Israel, when a man wanted to inquire of God, he said, 'Come, let us go to the seer'; for he who is now called *a prophet* was formerly called a *seer*" (1 Sam 9:9; italics added). The earlier prophets had been dreamers of dreams and seers of visions, "seeing" what God willed. The OT development was from the seer to the *nābî'*, a prophet. The word apparently refers to a spokesperson, to one who pours forth God's message unbidden by other human agents. The best description of this function is seen in the relationship between Moses, AARON, and Pharaoh. "See, I make you as God to Pharaoh; and Aaron your brother shall be your prophet. You shall speak all that I command you; and Aaron your brother shall tell Pharaoh . . . " (Exod 7:1-2). As the prophet for Moses, Aaron did not initiate his message, but simply passed on to the chosen recipient the message he was given. It is this that made Hebrew prophetism unique.

In addition to the basic OT term for prophet, *nābî'*, two other descriptive titles of significance add breadth to the Hebrew understanding of the prophetic function. The prophet is also called "the man of God" (1 Sam 9:6; 1 Kgs 12:22; Jer 35:4) and "the servant of Yahweh" (1 Kgs 14:18; 18:36; 2 Kgs 9:7). These clearly indicate the basic relationship between Yahweh and his prophet.

The Identity of the Canonical Prophet. The OT prophetic movement apparently began with Moses. His life and ministry apparently set the pattern for what was best in Hebrew prophetism. DEBORAH, on the other hand, was generally of the nature of ancient Near Eastern prophets. She stayed in one place and was sought out by the people (Judg 4:4-5). However, she also brought forth God's message unbidden. NATHAN and GAD were associated as professional prophets in the court of David. Yet they, too, at times proclaimed God's word at their own initiative (2 Sam 12:1-12). Other kings had large groups of professional prophets at the royal court (1 Kgs 22:4-6). ELIJAH and ELISHA were clearly different. They proclaimed God's words fearlessly and faithfully.

However, in the eighth century B.C.E., a new development took place in Israel's prophetic movement. With the ministry of AMOS, HOSEA, ISAIAH and MICAH, books were being written that were largely made up of the messages of a specific prophet. These were usually accompanied by biographical material and historical anecdotes of their times and influence. It is significant to note that this change did not bring an end to the professional prophets, whether associated with the royal court or with a particular shrine.

No adequate reason has been found or suggested to explain the naming of a book for Amos when there is no such book for Elijah. The content of their messages and the nature of their ministries are not decidedly different. On the other hand, the message and ministry of Elijah is contained in 1 and 2 Kings, which is included in the section of the canon known as "the Prophets."

Further, the modern division into major and minor prophets is one of length only. The messages of Amos, Hosea, and Micah, for example, are as significant as that of Isaiah. We merely have less material in those books. In the Hebrew OT, there are actually four books known as "the Latter Prophets." These are Isaiah, Jeremiah, Ezekiel, and The Twelve. This latter book contains what is called the Minor Prophets. It is significant to note that Daniel, although a part of the prophets in our English translations, was not included among the Prophets in the Hebrew canon.

The Individual Prophet. What kind of a person became a prophet? Moses was a shepherd, a fugitive murderer, who had been trained in the court of the king of Egypt. Amos was at the least a wandering shepherd. At the most, he was a sheep-owner or sheep-breeder and a successful businessman. Hosea was a man agonizing over an unfaithful wife, a broken home, and motherless children. Isaiah was an influential citizen of Jerusalem with easy access to king and temple. Micah, in contrast, was a rural, small-town person with an inherent distaste for and suspicion of the city and its people. JEREMIAH began his ministry as an immature, reluctant draftee, possibly descended from an exiled priesthood. EZEKIEL, on the other hand, was one of the incumbent priestly families. Moses, Isaiah, and Ezekiel were married. Jeremiah was called to a celibate ministry.

Hosea ministered to his own people while Amos was a citizen of Judah called to serve in the foreign territory of Israel. Jeremiah ministered to his own people in Jerusalem and was rebuffed by family, friends, kings, priests, and prophets. Ezekiel ministered to his own people in Exile in pagan Babylon. Haggai was old and ZECHARIAH was young, but both sought to lead the returning exiles in rebuilding the Temple. HABAKKUK was a poet and the nearest thing to a Hebrew philosopher. JONAH was a rebellious preacher who did not wish to be a missionary.

The point is that each of the prophets was different from the others. Each was unique. They were not copies of one another, but brought their unique personalities into the service of the God of Israel.

One significant feature of the prophetic ministry in the OT was the Israelite attitude toward the uttered word and the symbolic act. Words once uttered, to the Hebrew mind, had a power of their own. The prophets seemed to believe that their very words released God's power into the situation they addressed. Further, the prophets also included dramatic, symbolic acts in communicating God's truth. Isaiah walked in the garb of a slave for three years in Jerusalem to point up the truth of his message (Isa 20:2-3). Jeremiah wore a wooden yoke to proclaim his message of submission to Babylon. When it was broken by Hananiah, Jeremiah replaced it with an iron yoke, proclaiming an even harsher captivity (Jer 27:1–28:14). And Ezekiel's acts constantly dramatized his message and released God's power into the situation (it is possible that both baptism and the Lord's Supper are similar acts in the NT).

The Common Forms of the Prophetic Books. Form critics of the OT have pointed out that there are a number of common forms found among the prophetic books. These may first be divided between prose and poetical forms.

The prose forms of the prophetic books can be further divided into autobiographical and biographical forms. Autobiographical forms are always in the first person and contain information that only the individual prophet could know. The most common kind of autobiographic form is the call narrative, in which the prophet told how he came to be a prophet. This usually included a report of the divine confrontation, the prophetic commission, a response from the prophet, divine reassurance, and occasionally a sign confirming the call. Beyond the call, autobiographical material also included vision reports. Also in the first person, these recorded either an actual sight, seen with the eyes, or a dream or inner vision, perceived with the mind. Through these visions came divine revelation. Further, the autobiographical forms also included reports of symbolic acts. These included the divine command to perform the act, the report of the act, and a sermon interpreting the act to their people.

Biographical forms are always in the third person, told about the prophet by someone else. The first of these is the prophetic biography, which was usually inserted at the beginning or end of a sermon or a collection of sermons. It is a description of events in the life of the prophet that set the stage or called forth the message or messages. The second category has been identified as the prophetic legend. A legend is defined as an edifying and pious story relating an event or life of a holy man with an emphasis upon the miraculous. It is probably preferable to call both of these simply prophetic biography.

The poetic forms of the prophetic books make up the largest part of the corpus. Most prophetic sermons appear to be in poetic form. The poetry communicated both to the mind and the imagination. In these messages, several major forms have been identified and categorized.

The first major poetic prophetic form is the prophecy of disaster. It usually begins with an introductory word, such as a command to the prophet to speak. Sometimes added to this, at other times standing by itself, is an appeal by the prophet for the attention of his hearers. At this point, the situation calling for the message is described. Here the problem viewed by the prophet is set forth. This is followed by a prediction of judgment, the announcement of a coming disaster. Finally, some concluding characterization of the prophet or of his audience is given. This form was used in addressing either groups or individuals. When aimed at groups, however, the structure is less rigid, though the content is essentially consistent.

The second major poetic form found in the prophets is the prophecy of salvation. This form is essentially identical to the prophecy of disaster, except that there is a prediction of deliverance instead the announcement of disaster. This form was not as common as the foregoing one.

The third major poetic form is the oracle of salvation. This usually appears to be addressed to a person or a group who have been lamenting over a crisis or catastrophe being experienced. The oracle usually begins with a promise of divine intervention on behalf of those in need, accompanied or followed by a statement of the results that will come through God's intervention. Finally, a concluding statement is usually included, giving God's purpose in intervening. Some form critics also identify a separate but related form as the proclamation of salvation. Those who do so claim that the proclamation of salvation looked more to the future than did the prophecy of salvation.

Other forms have been suggested as being present in the poetic material of the prophets. These occur far less frequently and with considerably less uniformity. Among these are the woe oracles, so-called because they begin with "woe" or "alas," and usually concluded with a pronouncement of intense or terrible judgment. Also, two kinds of trial speeches are sometimes found, apparently being drawn from the legal world. The first of these was a simple courtroom scene, beginning with a summons, a trial, and ultimately a verdict. Related to this is the *rîb* or covenant law suit. The Hebrew word *rîb* is usually translated as "controversy." It is apparently used either exclusively or primarily in cases of covenant breaking. If this is correct, it lent itself particularly to prophetic attacks on Israel for infidelity or rebellion.

Even more minor forms include the so-called disputation speech. Here the prophet was engaged in a rhetorical disputation with his audience. Still more minor forms are claimed to have been identified; their existence, however, is somewhat problematical. Those forms described here are sufficient for all except the most technical students of the prophets.

The content of the message of the prophets of course varied with the circumstances that they were called to address. All of them, however, were in basic agreement on certain points. God's judgment fell upon the people because of their having failed to fulfill the demands of the bond that related them to God and to one another. That is, Israel was required to live a life marked by public justice, concern for the oppressed of earth, commitment to just dealings with neighbors and within the family, always remembering that the God of Israel had called the people out of Egyptian bondage and broken the hold of oppression. Just as they had been slaves and had been remembered by a gracious God, so also they were to display graciousness and justice in their dealing with the oppressed of earth.

Israel's life of worship was to grow out of its public commitment to the demands of the God of the covenant. It was intolerable to Israel's prophets to see the community worshiping God with great fervor and generosity and at the same time showing contempt for the poor and the needy, having no concern about dishonest business dealings, and showing no interest in the corrupt legal proceedings. Amos could go so far as to say, with bitter irony: "Come to Bethel, and transgress; to Gilgal, and multiply transgression!" (Amos 4:4). Jeremiah said a similar thing, reminding the people who flocked to the temple in Jerusalem that temple worship would not save them, when their social relations were unjust and perverted. Micah could even go so far as to threaten the complete destruction of Jerusalem and its place of worship (Mic 3:12).

These prophets, however, looked to a coming time when God's promises of blessing and peace and righteousness would find fulfillment. The prophet of the Babylonian Exile (Isa 40–55) in particular spoke of a time near at hand when God would bring to glorious fulfillment the longings of the hearts of the exiles. Israel would become a blessing for the peoples of earth (Isa 49:6), and the whole of nature and history would find transformation (Isa 55).

The Decline of Prophecy. As noted, Hebrew prophecy reached its greatest heights with the advent of the eighth century prophets: Amos, Hosea, Isaiah, and Micah. This stature was maintained in the ministry of Jeremiah and Ezekiel in the latter part of the seventh and early part of the sixth century B.C.E. These were concerned with the ethics and morality of their people. They preached in two great times of crisis, the periods around the fall of the Northern Kingdom, Israel, and around the fall of the Southern Kingdom, Judah. After the Exile, although prophets continued to be on the scene for some time, they never seem to have reached the great heights of proclamation and significance that their predecessors did.

With the passage of time, the prophetic ministry and mission appears to have died out. Many reasons have been offered for this decline, but none has been suggested that has been significantly convincing to produce any consensus among scholars. It simply appears that the prophets had filled their place in the arena of God's revelation. With the rise of the influence of the levitical priesthood and with the development of the synagogue, other means were found to communicate God's word to the people. With the rise of the scribes and the development of a written canon, the need for inspired persons speaking for God declined.

Prophets in the NT Era. Very little is known of the ministry or function of prophets in the NT era. It is obvious that such an office or function was present in the early churches. The church at Antioch had "prophets and teachers: BARNABAS, Simeon called Niger, Lucius of Cyrene, Manaen (who had been brought up with Herod the tetrarch) and Saul" (Acts 13:1). Further, PAUL instructed, or reminded, the church at Corinth that "God has appointed first of all apostles, second prophets, third teachers" (1 Cor 12:28). He later urged the same church, "Therefore, my brothers, be eager to prophesy" (1 Cor 14:39).

We do not know what the actual functions of these prophetic figures were in the NT churches. The very fact that this term is used clearly indicates some relation to the OT prophets. The most we can claim with any assurance is that these persons were communicators of God's message to their people. They were most likely preachers, proclaimers of the divine revelation to the new people of God.

See also FORM/GATTUNG; PROPHECY; PROPHETESS; SERVANT.

Bibliography. A. Heschel, *The Prophets*; E. Marsh, "Prophecy," *Old Testament Form Criticism*; R. L. Cate, *Introduction to the Old Testament and Its Study.*

—ROBERT L. CATE

• **Prophetess.** [pro'fi-tehs] Feminine form of *nābî'* PROPHET, applied to five women in the OT. No call narratives and very few oracles of these prophetesses have been preserved.

MIRIAM (Exod 15:20) and DEBORAH (Judg 4:4) led the

people of Israel in songs celebrating God's victories in battle. Miriam also had a continuing leadership role among the Israelites in the wilderness alongside Moses and Aaron (Num 12; Mic 6:4). Deborah's service as a judge in Israel was interrupted when God gave her a war oracle as a message for BARAK, who then persuaded her to go with him to the battle (Judg 4:4-10). Her ministry parallels that of Samuel, who also judged, prophesied, and summoned Israel to battle.

King Josiah's officials, sent to inquire of the Lord, consulted HULDAH, whose oracle authenticated the book of the Law found in the Temple, announced judgment on Judah, and offered a promise of blessing to Josiah (2 Kgs 22:11-20; 2 Chr 34:19-28).

No account of the prophetic ministry of Isaiah's wife has been preserved. She is mentioned only as a wife and the mother of the child with a sign-name (Isa 8:3).

Prophetesses could also be false. Ezekiel prophesied against women who preyed upon God's people by using sorcery and prophesying lies (Ezek 13:17-23). Noadiah was one of several prophets hired by Nehemiah's enemies to frighten him away from his work by prophesying falsely against him (Neh 6:10-14).

Scripture relates that there will be prophetesses in the end times as well, when "your daughters shall prophesy" (Joel 2:28).

See also DEBORAH; HULDAH; MIRIAM; WOMEN IN THE NEW TESTAMENT; WOMEN IN THE OLD TESTAMENT.

—PAMELA J. SCALISE

• **Propitiation.** *See* EXPIATION

• **Proselyte.** [pros'uh-l*it*] Literally a "newcomer," occurs four times as a NT word (Matt 23:15; Acts 2:10; 6:5; 13:43). It refers to non-Jews who have converted to Judaism in all of these instances. Numerous occurrences also are in the LXX as a sometime but not exclusive translation of the Hebrew word for stranger or sojourner. A foreigner was apparently regarded as a transient while a sojourner was accepted as a short-term or a long-term resident, partly or wholly accepted into the Jewish community. A change in meaning to include "convert" for both the Hebrew word and this Greek translation took place before the Christian era. This change was natural and reflects a Jewish willingness to be more inclusive of others, under certain conditions, during the postexilic period and the following Hellenistic and Roman periods.

According to Matthew, Jesus denounced the proselytizing activity of the scribes and Pharisees and the even greater zeal of their converts. In the Book of Acts, proselytes were present in Jerusalem at the Feast of Pentecost; one of the seven chosen to serve tables in Jerusalem among the early Christian community was a proselyte (cf. Acts 6); and at Pisidian Antioch proselytes were present at the synagogue meeting and along with some Jews followed Paul and Barnabas. This indicates not only that proselytism was being practiced but also that proselytes were finding the Christian gospel so appealing that they in turn were becoming Christians.

Proselytizing activity by Jews was carried out mostly by Jews living outside Palestine, but it did not involve missionary activity in the modern Christian sense. The non-Jews who were not satisfied with the polytheism and religious excesses of the Greco-Roman world were attracted to Judaism by the Jewish synagogue services, to which non-Jews were welcome, and the life-style of Jewish acquaintances. This religion seemed to many to be like another reasonable philosophy, with its monotheism and consequent universalism. However, it was different in its claim to be authoritative, its demand for absolute allegiance and obedience, and its promise of God's favor in this life and in the hereafter.

The Jews required a convert (1) to receive instruction concerning the essentials of Judaism, (2) to submit to circumcision, (3) to be washed or baptized to remove gentile uncleanness, and (4) to offer sacrifice in the Temple. Circumcision would not be applicable to a woman and sacrifice in the Temple would not be possible after its destruction in 70 C.E. by the Romans. Therefore gradually baptism became more and more important, and likely many more women than men became converts.

Acceptance of proselytes as genuine Israelites by the Jews lacked consistency. In Palestine they were regarded as inferiors and were not permitted to say that Abraham was their father. Among Jews outside Palestine proselytes were warmly welcomed and were often treated as equals.

Under Roman law a proselyte to Judaism was not granted the same legal exemptions as other Jews. A proselyte would expose himself to the charge of atheism if he refused to worship the gods of the empire. Enforcement of the law was not uniform under the emperors of the first and second centuries C.E. Likewise, a female convert might fall under an accusation of impiety if she did not give appropriate attention to the household gods.

See also CONVERSION.

Bibliography. C. Guignebert, *The Jewish World in the Time of Jesus*; K. Lake, "Proselytes and God-Fearers," in *The Beginnings of Christianity*, Part 1, *The Acts of the Apostles*, ed. F. J. Foakes-Jackson and K. Lake.

—G. WILLARD REEVES

• **Protoevangelium of James.** *See* JAMES, PROTOEVANGELIUM OF

• **Proverb.** A proverb is a succinct saying that registers a conclusion based on experience and the powers of observation. The proverb is one of the important forms of language used by the teachers who developed the WISDOM LITERATURE of the Bible. The Hebrew word often translated proverb is *māšāl*. This term has two meanings: "likeness" (metaphor or simile) and "rule." Likeness refers to the idea that two or more things are similar to each other, or may be understood in relationship to each other. Thus "wealth" is like a "strong city" while "poverty" is like a "desolate ruin" (Prov 10:15); or the "speech of a righteous person is choice silver, but the mind of the wicked has little value" (Prov 10:20). Thus the value of wealth is explained by comparing it to the security of a strong city with mighty walls that protect its citizens against attack. Rule expresses the idea that a proverb should take up residence in the mind and form and shape human conduct. Residing behind proverbs is the belief that reality (the world, society, and religion) possesses an order that is just, beautiful, and coherent. By observing this order, putting the observance into sayings and other forms of teaching, and following what is taught, the wisdom teachers believed that people would experience order, well-being, and blessing in life.

Broadly speaking there are two major categories of proverbs: folk sayings and literary sayings. A folk proverb comes from popular culture. Drawing vivid images from nature and society, it presents a truth that is widely accepted by its culture. Well-known examples include:

Like Nimrod a mighty hunter
before the Lord. (Gen 10:9)

The fathers have eaten sour grapes,
and the children's teeth are set on edge.
(Ezek 18:2 = Jer 31:29)

A city set on a hill cannot be hid. (Matt 5:14)

The tree is known by its fruit. (Matt 12:33 = Luke 6:44)

More artistically crafted than folk sayings, literary proverbs are poetic sayings normally expressed in the declarative mood:

The mouth of the righteous brings forth wisdom,
but the perverse tongue will be cut off. (Prov 10:31)

A disciple is not above his teacher,
nor a servant above his master.
(Matt 10:24; cf. Luke 6:40a; John 13:16; 15:20)

There are several specific varieties of literary sayings: comparative, better, numerical, riddle, question, and beatitude. Comparative ("like") proverbs seek to express analogies normally between two things:

Like a dog who returns to his vomit
is a fool who repeats his folly. (Prov 26:11)

Every scribe who has been trained for the kingdom of heaven
is like a householder who brings out of his treasure what
is new and what is old. (Matt 13:52)

Comparative proverbs occasionally describe the mysterious with images that are better known:

As the heaven for height, and the earth for depth,
so the mind of kings is unsearchable. (Prov 25:3)

Sometimes comparative proverbs use the pattern: "if here, then how much more there." The inference is drawn that if something is true in one instance, how much more true it is in another:

Sheol and Abaddon lie open before the Lord,
how much more the hearts of people! (Prov 15:11)

If you then, who are evil,
know how to give good gifts to your children,
how much more will your Father in heaven
give good things to those who ask him!
(Matt 7:11 = Luke 11:13)

A better saying is a type of proverb which makes a value judgment. In comparing two items, the conclusion is that one is preferable to another:

Better is a little with righteousness,
than great revenues with injustice. (Prov 16:8)

Better is open rebuke,
than hidden love. (Prov 27:5)

Numerical proverbs seek to establish relationships between a variety of things. This saying points to one feature that is held in common by each thing mentioned. The three-four pattern is the most common, but other patterns do occur:

Under three things the earth quakes,
under four it cannot bear up:
a slave when he becomes king,
a fool when he is filled with food;
an unloved woman who gets a husband,
and a maid when she succeeds her mistress.
(Prov 30:21-23)

Another literary saying, the riddle, describes something in enigmatic terms. Involving a match of wits between the riddler and the listeners, the riddler's intention is to confuse the listeners so that they will not be able to guess what is being described. Often the riddle is more than an intellectual game designed to entertain. A riddle may become the focal point of a contest or initiation that results literally or figuratively in life and death for the participants. There are two well-known riddles in the story of SAMSON. The first is one proposed by Samson to his Philistine opponents during his marriage feast:

Out of the eater came something to eat,
Out of the strong came something sweet. (Judg 14:14)

The answer extorted from Samson's fiancee is the second riddle:

What is sweeter than honey?
What is stronger than a lion? (Judg 14:18)

In the context of the wedding feast, the normal answer to the second riddle, which contains the answer to the first, would be "love." The irony is that the countrymen of the Philistines paid for their treachery with their lives. Proverbs also include questions. Rhetorical questions are sayings that require no answer. The typical use is to support the truth of the teaching, presented in the context of an instruction or disputation. With assent given, the teacher's case is made by analogy, "if this, then that":

Can a man carry fire in his bosom,
and his clothes not be burned?
Or can one walk upon hot coals,
and his feet not be scorched? (Prov 6:27-28)

Are grapes gathered from thorns,
or figs from thistles? (Matt 7:16 = Lk 6:44)

Can the wedding guests fast
while the bridegroom is still with them?
(Mark 2:19 = Matt 9:15)

Impossible questions point to the limits of human knowledge, ability, and existence:

Consider the work of God:
who can make straight
what he has made crooked? (Eccl 7:13)

And which of you by being anxious
can add one cubit to his span of life?
(Matt 6:27 = Luke 12:25)

Finally, beatitudes are a declaration of well-being to those who engage in virtuous and righteous behavior: studying and obeying the teachings of the law (Prov 29:18), caring for the poor (Prov 14:21), trusting in God (Prov 16:20), and finding wisdom (Prov 3:13). They normally begin with the word translated "happy" or "blessed."

Blessed is the one who finds wisdom,
and the person who obtains understanding. (Prov 3:13)

Jesus uses this saying to indicate that those who are victims now will experience well-being in the coming Kingdom of God.

Blessed are you poor,
for yours is the kingdom of God.
(Luke 6:20b = Matt 5:3)

See also PROVERBS, BOOK OF; RIDDLE; WISDOM IN THE OLD TESTAMENT; WISDOM LITERATURE.

Bibliography. W. Beardslee, *Literary Criticism of the New Testament*; J. L. Crenshaw, *Old Testament Wisdom*; J. L. Crenshaw, "Wisdom," *Old Testament Form Criticism*, ed.

J. H. Hayes; C. Fontaine, *Traditional Sayings in the Old Testament*; R. Murphy, *Wisdom Literature*; L. G. Perdue, "The Wisdom Sayings of Jesus," *Forum* 2/3 (1986): 3-35; G. von Rad, *Wisdom in Israel*; J. Williams, *Those Who Ponder Proverbs*.

—LEO G. PERDUE

• **Proverb/Riddle.** Proverbs and riddles belong to the genre of WISDOM LITERATURE and convey oracular or aphoristic truth by means of pithy sayings or statements which are often metaphorical or enigmatic. However, proverbs differ greatly from riddles in purpose and content.

Riddles are intentionally worded in an obscure manner, and their enigmatic form requires elucidation and interpretation. They are infrequent in the NT. The Greek term for riddle (*ainigma*) appears only in 1 Cor 13:12 to remind the faithful of the mysterious nature of faith. Elsewhere they are presented as puzzles to be solved (Rev 13:18).

Proverbial sayings are numerous in the NT and can be easily applied to the various situations of the hearers. They embody the knowledge and wisdom of past generations, both Jewish and heathen. In the NT, the technical term for proverb (*paroimia*) is used only in the Gospel of John (10:6; 16:25, 29) and in 2 Pet 2:22 which is probably one of the most pointed proverbs in canonical writings. Gospel authors have sometimes chosen to use the term *parabole* to speak of proverbial wisdom (Luke 4:23), but most proverbs are used without semantic qualification. Their listings abound and greatly differ from each other.

Numerous statements in Paul's Letters can be characterized as general truths in the form of proverbial sayings (Rom 14:14; 1 Cor 6:12; Gal 6:7; 1 Cor 3:19). Paul's exhortations especially reflect the use of proverbial wisdom (Rom 12:21; Phil 4:8).

Proverbs are more numerous in the NT than riddles. Both forms by their very nature are far less developed than other forms of teaching, but their encapsulated wisdom provides important insights linking everyday experience and universal truth.

See also PARABLES; PROVERB; RIDDLE; WISDOM IN THE OLD TESTAMENT; WISDOM LITERATURE.

—PAUL CIHOLAS

• OUTLINE OF PROVERBS •

The Book of Proverbs

I. "The Proverbs of Solomon, Son of David, King of Israel": In Praise of Wisdom (1:1–9:18)
II. "The Proverbs of Solomon": Wise Sayings (10:1–22:16)
III. "The Words of the Wise": Admonitions to His Son or Pupil (22:17–24:22)
IV. "Also . . . Sayings of the Wise" (24:23-34)
V. "Also . . . Proverbs of Solomon" (25:1–29:27)
VI. "The Words of Agur" (30:1-33)
VII. "The Words of Lemuel" (31:1-9)
VIII. A Poem on the Ideal (Wise) Wife (31:10-31)

• **Proverbs, Book of.** The book belongs to the third division of the Hebrew canon, the Writings, which contains books of a widely different character. This division of the canon was probably not closed until the end of the first century C.E. Included among the Writings are the books of wisdom literature: Job, Ecclesiastes, and Proverbs. Two other wisdom books, belonging to the larger Roman Catholic canon, are Sirach and the Wisdom of Solomon. These five books of wisdom literature represent the major corpus of an important religious and social tradition extending from the beginnings of Israel well into the Hellenistic period. Rabbinic Judaism continued the development of this tradition into the postbiblical period.

The Book of Proverbs consists of seven major collections, each of which has its own title: (Prov 1–9) "The Proverbs of Solomon, Son of David, King of Israel"; (10:1–22:16) "The Proverbs of Solomon"; (22:17–24:22) "The Words of the Wise"; (24:23-34) "These also are the Sayings of the Wise"; (25–29) "These also are the Proverbs of Solomon which the Men of Hezekiah, the King of Judah, copied"; (30) "The Words of Agur, the Son of Jakeh of Massa"; (31:1-9) "The Words of Lemuel, King of Massa, which his Mother taught him." In addition there is a concluding poem in 31:10-31 which celebrates the wise woman in Israelite society.

Three of these collections bear the title, "The Proverbs of Solomon," thus leading to the attribution of the entire book to this ruler celebrated for his wisdom (cf. 1 Kgs 3–11). Two other wisdom books suggest an association with SOLOMON: ECCLESIASTES and the WISDOM OF SOLOMON. This does not mean that Solomon was the author of these three books, for Ecclesiastes, the Wisdom of Solomon, and much of the Book of Proverbs were written well after the death of this king. In all three cases, however, the intent is not to claim Solomon as the author. Patrons of culture are often honored by having their names associated with the materials produced. As the king most renowned for his wisdom and wealth, Solomon was the greatest patron of this literary and social tradition. The Book of Proverbs consists of materials put together over many centuries, from the beginnings of the monarchy in the early tenth century B.C.E. well into the postexilic period.

Those who produced the wisdom tradition, including the Book of Proverbs, were often called "sages" (wise men and women), because of the importance of the term, "wisdom," in this tradition. The "sages" belonged to a variety of social classes in Israel and later Judaism, though the titles of the Book of Proverbs and other texts suggest that many of them worked within two major settings: the royal court in the period of the monarchy and the temple in JERUSALEM during the postexilic period. As servants of the king these sages served in the royal bureaucracy, ranging from positions of political power (e.g., "secretary of the king") to lowly scribes who worked as accountants for royal treasuries and copyists of state documents. After the end of native rule, the sages shifted their locus to the temple, performing similar functions in a nation whose local leadership continued to shift to the high priesthood. Two prominent examples of sages are JOSEPH who becomes the prime minister to the king of Egypt (Gen 37–50) and EZRA. In addition to writing their own literature, the sages edited many of the books in the Hebrew Bible, before these books entered into the official canon.

The initial collection in chaps. 1–9 consists of ten instructions, together with several supplements. The instruction is a form of teaching that provides guidance in moral and religious conduct. It begins with an introduction in which the hearer, "my son" (an ideal student), is exhorted by the teacher, "your father" (a term for the teacher), to give heed to the instruction. This is followed by a main section consisting of admonitions that instruct the hearer to behave in a way deemed to result in life and well-being. Prohibitions warn the student against immoral behavior that leads to tragedy and failure. The conclusion speaks of the results of wise or foolish behavior, and changes from appeal to demonstration, and from address to confirmation. Two personified figures appear often in this collection: Woman Wisdom who represents the wisdom tradition and its code of conduct and Woman Folly who represents wicked behavior and ignorance.

The second major collection (10:1–22:16) consists of 375 individual proverbs or sayings, occasionally grouped together along thematic and/or literary lines (e.g., 16:10-15 concern the king). But most are self-contained units of meaning. Two subsections may be discerned. Common to the first, 10:1–15:33, is the antithetical saying that contrasts the righteous (or wise) with the wicked (or fools). The second subsection, 16:1–22:16, has many themes, including the king and the royal court, the respect for proper speech, and appropriate behavior in a variety of social contexts.

The other collections are much shorter. The material in 22:17–24:22 is an instruction based on a well-known Egyptian text, "The Teaching of Amen-em-ope," dating from the thirteenth century B.C.E. This is one clear example of the international character of the Israelite wisdom tradition. The collection in 24:23-34 is an instruction on diligence in farming and just actions in the judiciary. Chaps. 25–29 comprise a collection which may be subdivided formally and thematically into two sections: 25–27 and 28–29. The first consists of sayings and teachings primarily for youth at court, kings, and sages who conduct royal business. The second section is perhaps a collection for rulers to use in a variety of political and social situations.

The collections in chap. 30 and 31:1-9 derive from the wisdom of Arabia. The "Words of Agur" (chap. 30) in vv. 1-4 echo some of the themes of JOB and ECCLESIASTES: the vain striving for wisdom illustrated by impossible questions. This collection seems to have been countered by a pious editor who added the remaining verses. "The Words of Lemuel" (31:1-9) is an instruction on royal rule, issued to a young Arabian king by his queen mother. The acrostic poem in praise of the wise woman (31:10-31) echoes the poems on Woman Wisdom in 1:20-33 and chaps. 8–9, thus bringing to a fitting close the entire book.

The many topics in the Book of Proverbs find their center in one dominating theme: the origins and maintenance of "order" in creation, society, and individual life. For the sages, God permeated creation with a just and beneficent "order" in which everything has its place, time, and function. The major social institutions also owe their origins to God and have their proper "order," that is rules and functions that are just and life-sustaining. The task of the sages was to observe this "order," place their observations into teachings (sayings and instructions), and transmit them to youths who sought to enter government and temple service. Eventually the teachings were democratized and used as moral instruction for people in various social groups.

The sages specified the norms and appropriate behavior for the institutions of kingship, marriage, economic production and trade, law, education, and religion. These made up the social order that was believed to be grounded in the larger order of creation. Proper decorum within these institutions led to well-being, while unruly and undisciplined behavior led to misfortune, for the individual but also for the larger community. While an occasional "voice" questioned the validity of this understanding and pointed to the limits of wisdom (e.g., Agur), most of the teachings of the Book of Proverbs affirm the goodness of life and the possibility of living in harmony with God, the world, and other people.

See also PROVERB; WISDOM IN THE OLD TESTAMENT; WISDOM LITERATURE.

Bibliography. J. Blenkinsopp, *Wisdom and Law in the Old Testament*; C. V. Camp, *Wisdom and the Feminine in the Book of Proverbs*; J. L. Crenshaw, *Old Testament Wisdom*; J. G. Gammie and L. G. Perdue, *The Sage in Ancient Israel*; B. Lang, *Wisdom and the Book of Proverbs*; W. McKane, *Proverbs: A New Approach*; D. Morgan, *Wisdom in the Old Testament Traditions*; R. E. Murphy, *Wisdom Literature & Psalms*; L. G. Perdue, *Wisdom and Cult*; R. B. Y. Scott, *The Way of Wisdom*; R. N. Whybray, *The Book of Proverbs*.

—LEO G. PERDUE

• **Providence.** The concept of providence as the guidance and care of a personal deity is found in both the OT and NT. The word "providence," which comes from the Latin *pro videre* (to see ahead), probably originates from the Greek *pronoeō,* meaning to take care of or to know in advance. The noun form of this Greek verb occurs only once in the Greek NT (Acts 24:2) and here it is a reference to Felix. The occurrences of the verb form *pronoeō* in the LXX and the Greek NT are references to human vision, and there is no one word in the Hebrew OT which carries precisely this meaning. Although the occurrences of the specific word in the Greek NT are references to human vision, the concept of divine providence is not foreign to this biblical writing, and in the OT the word *pĕqudâ* in Job 10:12 is consonant with the idea of divine guidance and guardianship, and the implication of divine control threads its way through both testaments.

Unlike the polytheistic concept of an impersonal order in nature under which the gods reign, the concept of providence held by the Hebrew people embraces a covenantal care and guidance of a God who has control over humanity and nature. Yahweh is the God of creation and this creator is also sustainer and guardian (Pss 65:6-8; 100:3, 5; 145:13-29). The validity of this providence is manifest in covenantal agreements (Gen 8:22; 12:1, 2; Exod 34:27, 28; Josh 24). Implications of God's providence are espoused in such affirmations as Ps 19:1-6 and the magnificent poetry of Job 38–40.

The meaning of providence in the OT is first understood in light of God's guidance of the Hebrew people. This is revealed both in the lives of individuals such as Abraham, Moses, and David, and in terms of the nation itself. Throughout the patriarchal stories and the account of the Exodus from Egypt, an unfolding of divine providence occurs. Yahweh is shaping and directing the lives of the chosen people (Gen 12:1-3; 27:24; 35:9-12; Exod 3:13-17). Through the writings of the prophets, divine providence is seen to extend beyond the nation of Israel to other nations as well, as God's divine purpose is brought to pass (Isa 10:5-8; Jer 29:10-14). (It should be noted that the OT concept of divine providence in the lives of individuals is not restricted to those who play a major role in the history of the nation. Sprinkled throughout the psalms are cries of individuals to their personal deity [Pss 16, 12, 17, 23].)

In the NT, as in the OT, the message of God's guidance and direction is expressed. The God of creation is again seen guiding and sustaining both humanity and nature; however, in the NT the message is given new emphasis and form. The importance of the individual in the divine providence is given more emphasis (Matt 6:25-34; 10:29-31; Rom 8; Phil 2:13), and the concept of providence manifested in the person of Jesus of Nazareth reveals the hope and plans of God in the continual directing of creatures and creation to *telos* (end) and the establishment of the kingdom of God.

The complexities and apparent inconsistencies of the world that puzzled the writers of the OT are not "solved" even with this new manifestation, but the overriding message of the NT is one of affirmation of God's continual work guiding and directing humanity and nature. The message of Jesus is one of comfort and assurance; the God who created and sustains the beauty of the field will not forsake humanity (Matt 6:25-34). The gospels as well as the Pauline and Johannine literature present a Christ who is the manifestation of hope in a troubled world. Here in human form is one who, like the powerful Yahweh who bridled the chaotic waters (Pss 74:12-17; 93:3, 4; 104:7-9; Job 38:8-11), can calm the seas and bid nature obey (Matt 8:23-27). Here is one who reveals to humanity a relationship with a caring deity who can be called upon as father (Matt 23:9).

See also THEOLOGY OF THE OLD TESTAMENT.

Bibliography. J. Behm, "προνοέω, κτλ., " *TDNT*; W. Eichrodt, *Theology of the Old Testament*; J. Jeremias, *New Testament Theology*.

—JUDY YATES ELLIS

• **Psalms, Apocryphal.** [sahmz] The Hebrew OT contains 150 psalms. Some Syriac manuscripts contain five additional psalms, one of which is found in the LXX. The *Qumran Psalms Scroll* (*11QPs*[a]) includes eight additional psalms, four of which correspond to three of the Syriac psalms, and one of which is related to SIRACH. Thus there exist at least ten known apocryphal psalms. Eight are attributed to DAVID and two to HEZEKIAH, although there is no reason to accept these attributions as historical. These psalms apparently were composed in Hebrew by different authors prior to the first century B.C.E.

The most widely known of these psalms is Ps 151. It is extant in Hebrew, Greek, and Syriac, as well as in a number of other ancient versions of the Bible. It is clear from the Hebrew that this psalm was originally two psalms, the second of which is almost completely lost in the Hebrew. The Greek and the Syriac have abbreviated these psalms and combined them into a single psalm. Ps 151A is a psalm of praise in which David purportedly recounts his youth and his anointing by SAMUEL (cf. 1 Sam 16:1-13). In Ps 151B, most of which is lost, David tells of his defeat of GOLIATH (cf. 1 Sam 17:4-51). These two psalms were apparently composed no later than the third century B.C.E. Combined as Ps 151, this psalm was popular among early and medieval Christians and is accepted by Eastern Orthodox churches as being authoritative.

The other Syriac psalms are commonly numbered 152 through 155. Pss 152 and 153, extant only in Syriac, are based on 1 Sam 17:34-35. In Ps 152 David asks God to come to his aid when he is attacked by a lion and a wolf while watching his father's flocks. Ps 153 is a hymn of praise to God for delivering him from the two beasts. Pss 154 and 155 are extant in Hebrew and in Syriac. One late Syriac manuscript attributes them to Hezekiah. Ps 154 is a call to the congregation to praise God for the giving of his WISDOM to humanity. Ps 155 is a plea to God for deliverance from the wicked and for cleansing from sin.

The other four apocryphal psalms in the Qumran Psalter are attributed to David. One is a poem to divine Wisdom and is closely related to Sir 51:13-30. Another is, like Ps 155, a plea for deliverance. The third, an acrostic poem, is a hymn to ZION. The fourth is a hymn to God as Creator. The Psalms Scroll also contains a prose supplement concerning David's poetic accomplishments; he is said to have written 4050 compositions—3600 psalms and 450 songs.

Works such as the PSALMS OF SOLOMON, the Qumran hymn scroll, and the PRAYER OF MANASSEH are clear testimony to the widespread composition of psalms in Judaism prior to 70 C.E. The presence of apocryphal "Davidic" psalms alongside canonical ones, moreover, raises questions about the extent to which the canonical psalms actually constituted a fixed collection in this period.

See also DEAD SEA SCROLLS; MANASSEH, PRAYER OF; PSALMS, BOOK OF; SOLOMON, PSALMS OF.

Bibliography. J. H. Charlesworth and J. A. Sanders, "More Psalms of David," *Old Testament Pseudepigrapha*, ed. J. H. Charlesworth; D. Flusser, "Psalms, Hymns, and Prayers," *Jewish Writings of the Second Temple Period*, ed. M. E. Stone; J. A. Sanders, *The Dead Sea Psalms Scroll*.

—JOSEPH L. TRAFTON

• OUTLINE OF PSALMS •

The Book of Psalms

I. Book One. Psalms 1–41
II. Book Two. Psalms 42–72
III. Book Three. Psalms 73–89
IV. Book Four. Psalms 90–106
V. Book Five. Psalms 107–150

• **Psalms, Book of.** [sahmz] The Book of Psalms is one of the richest and most widely read books in the OT.

Religious Songs in the Ancient Near East. Archaeology has provided us with a rich treasure of religious songs throughout the ancient Near East. A good sampling of these can be found in Pritchard's *Ancient Near Eastern Texts* (*ANET*). It appears that the hymn in Babylon sprang from the curse, with flattering praise of the deity as introduction in order to draw the deity's attention. Or, fearing that they had been cursed, persons would pray to Shamash for protection (*ANET* 387). The psalm of lament (which occurs rather often), like the hymn, frequently begins with a description of the worshiper's plight, a petition for deliverance and a promise to pay the vows (*ANET* 386b). In ancient Egypt we find a well-developed hymnody. There was, for instance, a famous hymn sung by Akhenaton to the sun God (*ANET* 369b). There were songs of thanksgiving (*ANET* 380) and didactic poems. These have survived, and many more, because they were chiselled into the walls of tombs. Ancient Ugarit on the Phoenician coast is often considered much closer to Hebrew tradition (cf. esp. Dahood). Here, also, there existed religious poetry of various kinds, showing that when the ancient Israelites sang their songs in God's honor, they were participating in a widespread Near Eastern practice.

Hebrew Poetry. Hebrew poetry is different from our modern poetry. Since Bishop Lowth in the eighteenth century it has been customary to speak of "Parallelismus Membrorum," that is that each line consists of two half lines that are either alike (synonymous) or contradictory (antithetic). Now Kugel has argued with great force that Lowth's "parallelismus membrorum was not so much a discovery as an invention," and Kugel prefers to speak only of "synthetic parallelism," i.e., that indeed the two half lines are structurally there but related much more loosely than Lowth thought (Kugel, 57).

Hebrew poetry does not have rhyme like Western poetry, but it does have rhythm. Again, this is an area where there has been much study and little agreement. Most generally accepted is the theory of accented syllables: a hymn has three of them in each of the half lines (3 + 3), whereas a lament uses a "halting meter" with three and two (3 + 2). The psalmists felt free to use other rhythms, and so we speak of "mixed meters." The best known example of such a "mixed meter psalm" is Ps 23. It has hymnic motifs, and yet it appears with largely a 3 + 2 meter, which is the meter of the lament. A probable explanation for such "breach" in form would be that Ps 23 really consists of an extended confidence motif, such as is normally found in lamentation psalms. The final word on the forms of Hebrew psalms has not been spoken.

The Psalms in Ancient Israel. The Hebrew canon is divided into three sections: the Law, the Prophets, and the Writings. The Psalms, almost without exception, have been placed first in the third section, the Writings. In the Writings, they are presented in five "Books" (Pss 1–41, 42–72, 73–89, 90–106, 107–150). It has been suggested that they were thus compiled in order to create a fivefold human response to God's fivefold demands in the Pentateuch. This, however, is only a final arrangement; there are numerous witnesses to many other groupings, titles such as Psalms of David, Psalms of Korah, Psalms of Asaph. In 72:20 we read: "The prayers of DAVID, son of JESSE, are ended," although we find many psalms ascribed to David later in the book of Psalms. It is even likely that some of them (42–83) come from the Northern Kingdom, because they consistently use Elohim instead of Yahweh, and ISRAEL, JOSEPH, and EPHRAIM instead of JUDAH, ZION, and JERUSALEM.

As we read the psalms we can readily see that they express different moods. On this basis they have been placed in groups: hymns, laments, thanksgiving psalms, wisdom psalms, et al.

The hymn opens with an exhortation to praise GOD. Then the body of the hymn gives the reason why God should be praised. The conclusion is a repeat of the beginning (e.g., Ps 8).

The lament is a prayer by a community or an individual in need. It often begins with a cry for help or attention (74), then follows a description of the quandary and a repetition of the prayers spoken. In conclusion there is a promise to pay one's vows before the congregation if one is delivered, and sometimes there is an exhortation to others also to trust in Yahweh.

The thanksgiving psalm is somewhat like the hymn but it concentrates more on praising God for particular things, such as an abundant harvest (65) or deliverance from illness (116).

The wisdom psalms are more varied. They are often philosophical in nature and appear to be created for the purpose of teaching. A curious feature is that some of them are alphabetic (acrostic): each line begins with the successive letter of the alphabet (111) or (like Ps 119) has clusters of eight lines, each beginning with the same letter of the alphabet, making 176 verses in all (there are 22 letters in the Hebrew alphabet).

Again, there are many psalms that do not quite fit into these categories, and scholars continue to search for new and better solutions.

The Psalms in Israel's Worship. A reading of the Psalms will make obvious that they not only are of different nature but that they also were created for different purposes. Mowinckel has argued strongly that the purpose for most of them was to serve the cult of the preexilic Temple, i.e. during the royal period. Some were for the coronation of a king (2, 110), one for his wedding (45), and one was for the king's well being, success, and competence as a ruler (72). It is quite plausible that many of the psalms that appear with the first personal pronoun are psalms originally used by the king, whether they are hymns or laments. Other psalms were clearly used on days of penance and prayer (44). A special group that speaks of Yahweh as King (93, 95–99), Mowinckel calls "Yahweh's Enthronement Psalms," i.e., they were used at the New Year Festival at which Yahweh was proclaimed king. The land had been threatened by drought and famine because of the rainless season. It is as if the deity had left them. At the New Year God was again taking his place on the throne (cf. Ps 24) and a good harvest and prosperity was thus guaranteed.

The Age of the Psalms. Wellhausen once wrote: "It is no longer a question of how many psalms are pre-exilic, but whether any psalm is preexilic." R. Pfeiffer also maintained that the psalms were only postexilic and used only late in Judaism. Against them stands the view of S. Mowinckel: "A large part of the psalter is preexilic and used in the Temple services during the reign of the kings" (Mowinckel, 137). And A. Weiser (25): "Only a comparatively small number of the psalms can, in fact, be proved conclusively to have originated in the postexilic period." Eissfeldt (446-47) brings the origin back as far as the beginning of the settlement in Canaan.

The content of the psalms may, in fact, help to date them, because some of them are constructed with refrains. Consider Ps 46, where v. 7 and 11 clearly are refrains: "The Lord of Hosts is with us, the God of Jacob is our refuge." (This refrain probably should appear also after v. 3.) Another example is Ps 136 where every last half of the verse is repeated: "For his mercy (Heb. *ḥesed*) endures forever." In such cases we have clear hints of liturgical usage in need of a Temple setting: There is responsive singing by either a) a choir and a congregation, or b) a choir and a single voice. The content of the psalms thus support the view that indeed many of them were created for use in the Temple in the royal period.

Titles and Authors. Many of the psalms have superscriptions of various kinds. Some of them may detail the musical instrument to be used. One of the most common words appearing in the superscription is *lamenaṣṣēaḥ*, which generally is translated "to the choirmaster." This is awkward, and Mowinckel suggests that it should be read "To dispose (the deity) to be merciful." Many other psalms have names listed: To the Sons of Korah, To Asaph, To Solomon. Most common of these are those that have *ledāwîd*, which then, in conformity with the other titles, should be translated "to David," because the preposition *le* generally means "to, for, at." The strongest argument is provided by the internal evidence: Ps 24 is a psalm *ledāwîd*, yet the psalm speaks of "the ancient doors" of the Temple, which was not built until king Solomon, David's son. In the LXX (the Greek translation) many more psalms have David's name in the title. It is most likely that these psalms were dedicated to David, either because David means king or because he was known as a gifted poet and musician (1 Sam 16:14-23; Amos 6:5). The NEB leaves the titles out completely; that is probably a wise choice because they can often be confusing.

The Theology of the Psalms. It is only natural that in religious songs like these the faith of the nation should be expressed in a very varied and rich manner.

First, God is presented as the creator in such psalms as 18 (7-15), 19 (1-6) and 29 (Ps 29 sounds quite primitive). The most powerful expression is found in Ps 33:6-9, where God creates merely by speaking his word, and there is no hint that there was matter before he created, a view found in Gen 1 and 2:4f. This psalm is the closest the OT comes to our modern doctrine of "creatio ex nihilo"—creation out of nothing.

Secondly, with all the great things said about God, he is not alone. Ps 82:1 states that he is supreme, "He rules in the midst of the gods," and, according to Ps 139, even the kingdom of death is under him.

Thirdly, in this way the psalms are presenting the covenant God of Israel. There is a unique relationship between God and his people and this reality permeates most psalms. He is hailed in the hymns, he is implored in the laments; but he is always felt and understood to be *their* God.

Repeatedly Yahweh is presented as holy and righteous. His people rely upon his love (*ḥesed*) for them. And he is hailed as king, which, according to Pss 93, 95–99, means not only king of his covenant people Israel, but of the whole world that he has created and holds under his sway.

In the Psalms, indeed, one is presented with a very rich view of God, both exalted and intimate.

We have discovered that the psalms come to us in a great variety of forms, and yet each of them follows strict rules for style and language. At the same time we see that the authors felt free to change the system whenever inspiration demanded it. There is a beautiful balance between form and content, between structure and freedom. There are rules for the presentations, and yet the inspired authors have been able to expand the regulations and express themselves in ways that for all times will be used by people in their personal and congregational devotions.

See also KINGSHIP; POETRY; WORSHIP IN THE OLD TESTAMENT.

Bibliography. B. Ahlstrom, *Psalm 89*; A. A. Anderson, *Psalms*; C. S. Briggs, *A Critical and Exegetical Commentary on the Psalms, ICC*; M. Dahood, *Psalms, AncB*; B. Duhm, *Die Psalmen*; J. Durham, *Psalms, BBC*; H. Gunkel, *Ausgewählte Psalmen* and *The Psalms*; A. F. Kirkpatrick, *The Book of Psalms, CB*; H. J. Kraus, *Psalmen*; J. Kugel, *The Idea of Biblical Poetry*; E. A. Leslie, *The Psalms*; S. Mowinckel, *Psalms in Israel's Worship*; J. B. Pritchard, ed., *ANET*; A. Weiser, *The Psalms, OTL*; C. Westermann, *The Praise of God in the Psalms*.

—REIDAR B. BJORNARD

• **Pseudepigrapha.** *See* APOCRYPHAL LITERATURE

• **Ptolemais.** *See* ACCO

• **Publicans.** [puhb'li-kuhnz] The first three Gospels contain about twenty references to publicans, Jewish men who collected taxes and tolls for the Roman government. They were held in contempt throughout the Roman Empire, including Israel. They were regarded as betrayers of their own people, and many of them were greedy and dishonest; John the Baptist instructed publicans to collect only those taxes which were properly authorized (Luke 3:13). Because they cooperated with the Romans, publicans were ceremonially unclean and could not participate in Israel's religious activities. In the Gospels they are associated with sinners (Matt 9:10), gentiles (Matt 18:17), harlots (Matt 21:31), extortioners, the unjust, and adulterers (Luke 18:11). In these associations, the Gospels reflect an attitude toward publicans which was understandably widespread.

It is surprising, therefore, that Jesus, who was quite aware of the popular attitudes toward publicans (see Matt 5:46), rejected it. He befriended publicans such as ZACCHAEUS (a chief publican, Luke 19:1-10), and he called MATTHEW (Levi) to be his disciple (Matt 9:9; Luke 5:27). Jesus accepted publicans as his friends, even eating with them (Matt 9:10-13), and he therefore became known as a friend of publicans and sinners (Matt 11:18-19). It is not surprising, in light of Jesus' acceptance of publicans, that they responded to him enthusiastically (Mark 2:15; Luke 15:1). Jesus made a publican the hero of one of his most powerful parables (Luke 18:9-14), and he said that the publicans would enter God's Kingdom ahead of Israel's religious leaders. It should not be imagined, however, that Jesus held a romanticized or self-deluded idea about publicans; he saw them as sick and needing a physician (Matt 9:10-12). Unlike many of Israel's religious leaders, publicans sometimes humbly recognized their own sinfulness (Luke 18:9-14). Zacchaeus was an example of the kind of transformation which Jesus could bring about in the life of a publican; Zacchaeus repaid fourfold what he had gotten illegally, and gave half of his wealth to the poor (Luke 19:1-10).

See also CLEAN/UNCLEAN; MATTHEW; ZACCHAEUS.

—FISHER HUMPHREYS

• **Punishment.** *See* JUSTICE/JUDGMENT; PESTILENCE

• **Purim.** [pyoo'rim] A minor but noisy festival that Jews celebrate on 14-15 Adar (in February or March) each year; one of the Jewish festivals developed during the later pre-Christian period. Purim is the only festival that originated in the diaspora (i.e., outside the land of Israel). Pinpointing the origin and date of Purim is very difficult. The background for the festival is found in the BOOK OF ESTHER, but no other book in the Bible refers to Purim. A late pre-Christian text refers to the feast as "the Mordecaian day" (2 Macc 15:26).

The story appears to be a historical novel or romance. King Ahasuerus prepared a feast and invited many guests. He asked Queen Vashti to present her beauty before the crowd. She refused and lost her place as queen. The king then searched for a new queen and selected Esther, who concealed her true identity as Hadassah, a Jewish maiden. Haman did not like MORDECAI, a Jewish kinsman (uncle or cousin) of Esther, and plotted to have him hanged. The outcome of that plan changed, however, when Mordecai convinced Esther to invite herself into the presence of the king. As a result of the counterplot of Mordecai and Esther, Haman and his ten sons were hanged instead. The king could not reverse the edict against the Jews (Esth 1:19; 8:8), but issued an edict that allowed the Jews to protect themselves. As a result, about 75,800 enemies died.

Lots had been cast by Haman to determine the day of destruction for the Jews (Esth 9:23-24). *Pur* may be an Akkadian word or possibly a coined word meaning "lot"; *purim* includes a Hebrew plural ending. Jews received a letter from Mordecai and Esther, calling on them never to cease the commemoration of this victory. Thus, the Jews celebrate Purim each year.

Jews and others have raised questions about the historicity of the story behind Purim. One set of questions relates to the similarities between the story of Esther and *Farwardigan*, the Persian feast of the dead. Both have the same date of annual celebration, and the names, plot and subsequent feast have striking parallels (e.g., Mordecai-Marduk and Esther-Ishtar). Another set of questions examines the historical accuracy of the story of Esther. Ahasuerus does not appear in any other records as a king of Persia; he may have been Xerxes (ca. 485–464 B.C.E.) or Artaxerxes II (ca. 404–361 B.C.E.). However, these questions do not prevent Jews from celebrating Purim.

Purim has the characteristics of joy, noise, eating, giving gifts to friends and money to the poor, and the absence of sadness. When the name Haman occurs in the reading of the scroll of Esther the participants jeer and make noise. Not only do they remember Haman, a descendant of Agag, king of Amalek (cf. Esth 3:1; Exod 17:8-16; 1 Sam 15:7-9), but they have a striking reminder that every generation must confront a Haman who is wicked and plans the destruction of God's people. Purim teaches that God's presence, seemingly hidden at times, continues to be evident in the course of history.

Purim took precedence over Nicanor's Day, a Maccabean victory over a Syrian general named Nicanor. The battle occurred on 13 March 161 B.C.E. Jews observe 13 March as a fast day to commemorate Esther's prayer and fasting (Esth 4:16). Purim magnifies Jewish patriotism.

See also ESTHER, BOOK OF; FEASTS AND FESTIVALS; MORDECAI; PERSECUTION IN THE OLD TESTAMENT.

Bibliography. Y. Eckstein, *What Christians Should Know About Jews and Judaism*; H. Schauss, *The Jewish Festivals*.

—OMER J. HANCOCK, JR.

• **Purity.** The condition of physical cleanliness, personal hygiene, or freedom from contamination; a condition resulting from ceremonial washings which makes one acceptable to worship God; and a moral and/or physical condition brought about by a personal relationship with God or through Jesus Christ.

Because God is a pure, holy, and loving God, and because Israelites were chosen by God to carry out the messianic purpose, they were expected to be godlike, pure, and unpolluted, to maintain a distinctiveness from their pagan neighbors. For that reason, regulations were given to emphasize that separateness.

To promote physical cleanliness and hygiene, certain laws were given. An Israelite was expected to wash the feet of guests (Gen 18:4; 19:2; 24:32; 43:24) and to wash before meals and upon returning from the marketplace (Mark 7:3, 4). Certain foods were considered clean and others forbidden (Lev 11:1-47; Deut 14:2-21). Procedures were given relating to bodily discharges (Lev 15:2-33; Deut 23:10-13; Num 5:2, 3) childbirth (Lev 12:1-8; Luke 2:21-24), skin diseases (Lev 14:1-32), and contact with corpses (Lev 5:2, 3; Num 5:2, 3; 19:1-22). Even mildew in the houses was considered contaminating, and procedures were outlined (Lev 14:33-53). Latrines were to be provided (Deut 23:12-14), and after a murder, the polluted soil was to be cleansed (Deut. 21:1-9). By NT times some PHARISEES had become so obsessed with purification rules that Jesus reprimanded them, emphasizing that inward purity is more important than cleanliness regulations (Mark 7:20-23; Luke 11:39-41).

Because purity indicated fitness for religious duties, priests and Levites were required to observe purification rituals before officiating (Exod 29:4; 30:18; 40:12; Lev 8:6; 16:4-24; Num 8:6-8; 19:7; 2 Chr 4:6). Certain persons, called Nazirites, took special vows of purity to indicate their unique dedication to God (Num 6:1-26).

Although purity originally had physical and ceremonial connotations, it took on deeper moral and spiritual meaning. As items literally were purified by washing in water or burning in fire, so figuratively purity came to characterize that state of proper relationship with God brought about by repentance and forgiveness. This freedom from pollution of character could not be attained by the individual alone but came about only by the cleansing power of God. Ps 51:2, 7, 10, reflects David's need for cleansing following the Bathsheba episode. Only the pure in heart were fit to approach God in worship (Pss 18:20-24; 24:3, 4; Isa 1:15, 16; 2 Sam 22:21-27). Because the divine commandments are pure (Ps 12:6), God's people love and observe them (Ps 119:140), and they are blessed accordingly (Ps 73:1).

In the NT, Jesus identified the "pure in heart" as those who shall see God (Matt 5:8). A beggar was healed miraculously after his plea to be made clean (Luke 5:12, 13), and Jesus announced to his disciples that it is through his word that they would be made clean (John 15:3). Paul commended purity as essential for the Christian life (1 Cor 5:7; Phil 4:8; 1 Tim 1:5; 5:2; Titus 1:15; 2:14), and Christians are taught that through Jesus Christ, their lives have been purified from the power of sin (1 Pet 1:22; 2 Pet 1:9).

See also CLEAN/UNCLEAN.

—A. O. COLLINS

• **Purple.** *See* LYDIA

• **Q.** The symbol Q designates a hypothetical document presumed to consist of sayings of JESUS, and thought to have been a source drawn from in MATTHEW and LUKE. Since the pioneering studies of C. H. Weisse (1838) and H. J. Holtzmann (1863), most NT scholars have sought to explain the great similarities among the synoptic Gospels on the basis of the "Two-Document Hypothesis." The hypothesis suggests Matthew and Luke made use of the general outline and much content pertaining to Jesus' activity found in MARK and that Matthew and Luke drew upon a second source for some 200+ verses of sayings material they have in common, material not found in Mark (e.g., Matt 22:1-10 ‖ Luke 14:16-24). This source was first designated "Q" by German scholars (probably from the word *Quelle,* translated source). However, no written document with precisely this content has been discovered.

Some would identify Q with the "Logia" or "Sayings Source" that Papias, Bishop of Hieropolis (ca. 60–130 C.E.), said was originally composed in Hebrew (or Aramaic) by the apostle Matthew. Most, however, believe the evidence that Q (in the form used by Matthew and Luke) was written in Greek precludes such a possibility. On the basis of linguistic, cultural and theological characteristics, though, most agree that a Palestinian Jewish Christianity community or movement probably produced Q. Dated ca. 50–60 C.E., it would potentially be one of the oldest and most valuable sources available for recovery of the teaching of the historical Jesus, albeit a source redacted by the later church.

Disagreements among scholars over the extent and hypothetical reconstruction of Q have caused some to doubt its existence. However, most accept the premise and maintain it was a written document in existance before Matthew and Luke were written. The principal arguments for this are, first, that the number of crucial texts wherein Matthew and Luke agree word-for-word (at least ten pairs of passages) is such that common dependence on a source is called for (e.g, Matt 3:7b-10 ‖ Luke 3:7b-9). Second, the material of the double tradition found in Matthew and Luke in different contexts manifests a common underlying sequence or order, the original form of which is best preserved in Luke. This order is most probably due to a written source rather than oral tradition. Third, there are six doublets (accounts of the same event or saying occurring twice either in Matthew or Luke) that are so related that one of the two occurrences belongs to Mark, while the other must probably come from a common source behind Matthew and Luke (e.g., Mark 10:11 = Matt 19:9; Matt 5:32 = Luke 16:18—one saying is Marcan and the other is Q).

As to literary form, Q differs from a GOSPEL (like Matthew or Mark) in that it lacks any birth, miracle, passion, or resurrection narratives. It is a collection of Jesus' utterances, some being analogous to OT prophetic oracles, others to wisdom sayings, and still others to early Christian ethical exhortation. M. E. Boring holds that many of the sayings in Q originated as eschatological oracles of Christian prophets, while others are reformulations by such prophets (cf. Luke 11:30; 17:24, 26, 30). J. M. Robinson, in turn, believes Q stands in a trajectory of WISDOM LITERATURE extending from the Book of Proverbs to the Gnosticizing GOSPEL OF THOMAS. As such, Q is a collection of "sayings of the sages" (e.g., Matt 6:22-24, 34; 11:25-30; Luke 11:49-51). Earlier interpreters held that Q presupposes the Gospel's proclamation (*kerygma*) and offers ethical teaching (*didache*) about the demands of discipleship for Hellenistic converts of Syrian provenance (e.g., Matt 18:15, 21-22 ‖ Luke 17:3-4). Clearly, all three forms—prophecy, wisdom, didache—appear in Q.

Theologically, Q is permeated with eschatological expectation centering upon the return of Jesus as the heavenly SON OF MAN, the final judge of humanity (e.g., Luke 12:40; 17:24; Matt 24:43-44). A summons to discipleship is extended to all who will respond in faith, thereby giving radical redefinition to the identity of the covenant people (cf. Luke 7:1-10; 3:8; 14:16-23 par.). Such discipleship entails breaking from family and the familiar (Luke 9:59–62 par.), an itinerant life spent proclaiming the gospel and overcoming demons (Luke 9:1-5; 10:1-16), and the expectation of rejection and perhaps martyrdom (Luke 11:49). Through Jesus the powers of evil are being overcome, a sign of the arrival of the KINGDOM OF GOD (Luke 11:19-20). Believers are summoned to abandon worldly securities (Luke 11:37-41; 12:22-34), be watchful and ready for the end (Luke 12:35-46). Final destiny will be determined by response to Jesus, the Son of man (Luke 12:8-10). All this characterizes the views of what some have called a primitive Christian apocalyptic sect, the composers of Q.

See also GOSPEL; JESUS; LUKE, GOSPEL OF; MARK, GOSPEL OF; MATTHEW, GOSPEL OF; SON OF MAN; SYNOPTIC PROBLEM; THOMAS, GOSPEL OF; WISDOM LITERATURE.

Bibliography. M. E. Boring, *Sayings of the Risen Jesus: Christian Prophecy in the Synoptic Tradition*; R. A. Edwards, *A Theology of Q: Eschatology, Prophecy, and Wisdom*; J. M. Robinson, "Logoi Sophon: On the Gattung of Q," *Trajectories Through Early Christianity,* ed. H. Koester and J. M. Robinson; J. Y. H. Yieh, "The Study of Q: A Survey of its History and the Current State,'' *TJT* 8 (1986): 105-39.

—MALCOLM L. PEEL

• **Qarqar.** [kahr'kahr] Khirbet Qarqar, located in the Orontes Valley to the east of the Nuseiriveh Mountains (PLATES 2, 14), was the site of a battle between SHALMANESER III of Assyria and a coalition of twelve kings which included: AHAB of Israel, Irhuleni of Hamath and Adad-'idri (Hadadezer) of Damascus, among others. The battle took place in 853 B.C.E. and is described in glowing terms in the monolith inscription of Shalmaneser III. This inscription was discovered in 1861 at Kurkh, an ancient city situated to the northwest of the Assyrian capital of Nineveh on the Tigris River. The inscription was carved into a large stone slab, now known as the Kurkh Stele and resting in the British Museum. The Assyrian king claims to have burned the town of Karkara to the ground, including Irhuleni's royal residence. He also brags that he bridged the Orontes River with the corpses of his enemies. This account of the battle supplements biblical studies because the scriptural accounts are silent with regard to this incident. This may indirectly explain the three year moratorium that 1 Kgs 22:1 describes as existing between Syria and Israel during this time. In addition, the extrabiblical reference to Ahab as king of Israel lends credibility to the lists of kings found in the OT. Finally, the large number of chariots cited in Ahab's party shows the importance of such units in the Israelite army.

Bibliography. J. B. Pritchard, *ANET*.

—JOHNNY L. WILSON

• **Qoheleth.** *See* ECCLESIASTES, BOOK OF

• **Quadratus.** [kwahd'ruh-tuhs] Quadratus is the first known Christian apologist. He was part of an influential Christian intellectual movement which began early in the second century C.E. This movement was concerned to present the positive and even constructive social and political contributions of orthodox Christians to Roman authorities by defending the Christian faith against external pagan and Jewish criticisms (through written defense speeches) and against internal heresies (through written attacks against heresies). Two of the lesser known early apologists who were contemporaries of Quadratus are Aristides of Athens and Aristo of Pella. Very little is known about Quadratus. His name was a common Roman family name during both the late Republican and early Imperial periods. Jerome (*DeVir* 19) confused him with Quadratus the bishop of Athens (latter half of the second century), mentioned by Eusebius (*EccHist* 4.23.3). Quadratus flourished during the reign of the Roman emperor Hadrian (117–38 C.E.), to whom he reportedly presented a treatise in which he defended the truth of the Christian faith against its detractors. In his *Chronicle,* Eusebius claimed that Quadratus was a disciple of the apostles and that he presented his *Apologia* to Hadrian during the emperor's ninth year, i.e., in 125–26 C.E.

The apology of Quadratus is briefly discussed by Eusebius in *EccHist* 4.3.1-2. In that passage, Eusebius quotes the only surviving fragment of that lost work, *Apologia* of Quadratus: ''The works of our Savior continued to be present, since they were true. Those people who were healed and raised from the dead did not only appear to be healed and resurrected, but continued to be present, not only during the lifetime of the Savior but even after he had departed they continued on for some time. Some of them have survived even to our own day.''

By using the phrase ''even to our own day,'' Quadratus reflects the widespread Christian conception of a qualitative difference thought to exist between the apostolic and post-apostolic periods. In introducing the brief fragment, Eusebius claims that Quadratus wrote because ''some wicked men were attempting to trouble us [i.e., Christians]'' (*EccHist* 4.3.l). In the fragment itself, Quadratus is apparently contrasting the reality of the miracles performed by Jesus to the illusory feats of some unknown contemporaries, perhaps performed through magical means. Irenaeus later argued, as Quadratus had, that the Lord did not perform miracles in appearance only, but that the dead which he raised remained alive for many years (*AdvHaer* 2.32.4; cf. Eusebius, *EccHist* 5.7.3-4). Irenaeus was arguing against Gnostics who practiced magic (Simonians and Carpocrations); and R. M. Grant has plausibly suggested that Quadratus may have had similar opponents in mind. Christians frequently argued that miracles which had only a temporary effect, such as those performed by SIMON MAGUS, were merely illusions (*ActsPet* 28). According to Grant, the *Apologia* of Quadratus dealt primarily with the internal Christian conflict between orthodoxy and heresy, and that by distancing orthodox Christianity from heresy, the primary intention of Quadratus was to demonstrate that true Christians were actually responsible and trustworthy subjects of the Roman emperor.

See also JUSTIN MARTYR; PATRISTIC LITERATURE.

Bibliography. R. M. Grant, ''The Chronology of the Greek Apologists,'' *VC* 9 (1955): 25-33, *Greek Apologists of the Second Century* and ''Quadratus, the First Christian Apologist,'' *A Tribute to Arthur Voobus: Studies in Early Christian Literature and Its Environment, Primarily in the Syrian East,* ed. R. H. Fischer; J. R. Harris, ''The Apology of Quadratus,'' *ExpTim* 21 (1921): 147-60; J. R. Harris, ''The Quest for Quadratus,'' *BJRL* 8 (1924): 384-97.

—DAVID E. AUNE

• **Queen.** A term used in biblical literature in several senses—as the title of a reigning female sovereign, the consort of a male monarch, and the mother of the reigning monarch.

Israel does not seem to have ever had a legitimate ruling female monarch. Foreign sovereigns are mentioned, such as the Queen of Sheba (1 Kgs 10; 2 Chr 9; cf. Matt 12:42) and the Candace, the official title for the female monarchs of ETHIOPIA (Acts 8:27). One Israelite queen mother, Athaliah, attempted to usurp the throne upon the death of her son Ahaziah and evidently ruled for six years until a revolt succeeded in instating the legal heir to the throne, her grandson JOASH (2 Kgs 11). The text never refers to her as queen and depicts her action as strictly illegal. The one reigning queen in Israel's history was the Hasmonean Alexandra, who assumed the throne upon the death of her husband Alexander Jannaeus, reigning from 76 to 67 B.C.E.

Oriental monarchs often had multiple wives, as the 700 wives and 300 concubines of SOLOMON amply testify (1 Kgs 11:3). From these, only one would be designated as the official consort or queen for the monarch. The Book of ESTHER relates the story of how a Jewish girl rose to this position in the Persian court. The status of the queen in the Book of Esther probably resembles that of the queen consort in Israel. Although she wore a CROWN (Esth 2:17), she was completely subservient to the will of her husband (Esth 1:13-22). On the other hand, that some queen consorts exerted considerable influence over their husbands is illustrated by JEZEBEL, who aligned AHAB against both ELIJAH (1 Kgs 19:1-3) and NABOTH (1 Kgs 21:5-16). It is interesting to note, however, that the Hebrew text is reticent to use the term queen for a consort of Israel's kings, usually referring to her only as wife of the king.

Such is not the case with the queen mother. The title queen mother appears a number of times in the OT and seems to have involved a position of considerable status in the court. Solomon, for instance, is depicted as arising and bowing to his mother, and she takes the seat of honor at his right side (1 Kgs 2:19). That this was an actual titular position and did not automatically go with being the physical mother of the monarch is illustrated by King Asa's removing his mother from the office because she had made a heathen image (1 Kgs 15:13). It is also indicative of her status that Jeremiah characteristically mentions not the queen consort but the queen mother in connection with the king (Jer 13:18; 22:26; 29:2).

See also KINGSHIP; WOMEN IN THE NEW TESTAMENT; WOMEN IN THE OLD TESTAMENT.

—JOHN B. POLHILL

• **Queen of Heaven.** Babylonian title for the goddess also called Astarte and Ishtar (PLATE 57). She was an astral deity, a goddess of love and fertility, and also a goddess of war. Among her worshipers were Phoenicians, Canaanites, and Egyptians. The Hebrews' devotion to this goddess was demonstrated by the involvement of the whole family in the ritual of worship, which included burning incense, offering drink offerings, and making cakes shaped like her (Jer 44:17-19).

JEREMIAH was instructed to rebuke the people of Judah and Jerusalem for this pagan worship (Jer 7:1, 6, 18-19). Later, in Egypt, he again condemned such worship. He saw it as the cause of the destruction of Judah and Jerusalem (Jer 44:2-6) and as a severe threat to the survival of the refugees in Egypt (Jer 44:7-14, 24-28). What they thought was their hope for restored fortunes would be their doom.

See also IDOLATRY.

Bibliography. T. S. Frymer, ''Ashtoreth,'' *EncJud.*

—WALTER E. BROWN

• **Queen of Sheba.** *See* SHEBA, QUEEN OF

• **Quirinius.** [kwi-rin′ee-uhs] Publius Sulpicius Quirinius was the Roman official mentioned in Luke as the governor of Syria when Jesus was born (Luke 2:2). Quirinius was born ca. 51 B.C.E. at Lanuvium, Italy and became a consul in Rome under Augustus in 12 B.C.E. He was described by Tacitus (*Ann* 3.48) as a brave soldier and capable administrator. Between 11 and 6 B.C.E., he led in victorious warfare against the Homonadensians, a wild tribe in Cilicia. When Archelaus was deposed in 6 C.E. and his territory (Judea, Idumea, Samaria) was added to the Roman province of Syria, Augustus sent Quirinius to be the legate (governor) of Syria. According to Josephus (*Ant* 17.18.5), he was assigned to take a census of property in Syria and to sell Archelaus's Palestinian estate. This census, which is mentioned in Acts 5:37, led to a revolt of Palestinian Jews.

Quirinus returned to Rome about 9 C.E. and lived there until his death in 21 C.E. His reputation was stained after he divorced his second wife, the popular and influential Amelia Lepida, viciously attacking her on unproven grounds of attempted murder and adultery. The eulogy of Tiberius at his state funeral angered many Romans who remembered ''the combination of meanness with exorbitant power which had marked his later days'' (Tacitus, *Ann* 3.48).

Scholars continue to debate the accuracy of Luke's reference to a census by Quirinius during the reign of HEROD the Great. The ''harmonizers'' who argue for Lucan accuracy think Quirinius directed the first census while serving as a co-legate with Saturninus in Syria from 9 to 6 B.C.E. They cite Tertullian (*AdvMarc* 4.19) and an ancient manuscript found in 1764 at Tivoli to support this position. Others think Luke has expanded history and argue that there is no evidence of a census during the reign of Herod the Great.

See also CENSUS/ENROLLMENT; HEROD.

Bibliography. J. A. Fitzmyer, *The Gospel According to Luke, I-IX*; W. M. Ramsay, *The Bearing of Recent Discovery on the Trustworthiness of the N.T.*

—CARLTON T. MITCHELL

• **Qumran.** *See* DEAD SEA SCROLLS; ESSENES

• **Rabbah/Rabbath-Ammon/Philadelphia.** [rab'uh/rab'uhth-am"uhn] An important city in Transjordan, located 110 mi. south-southwest of Damascus and forty mi. northeast of Jerusalem (PLATE 10). Rabbah sat astride an important crossroads in a well-watered region of the plateau, at an elevation of ca. 2,700 ft. above sea level, some twenty-four mi. east of the Jordan River and twenty-three mi. northeast of the Dead Sea. In the Hellenistic and Roman periods, OT Rabbah was known as Philadelphia, and remains from all of these periods have survived. Today the large, modern capital city of the Hashemite Kingdom of Jordan, Amman, has grown up around the site of these ancient ruins.

Although Rabbah is not mentioned in prebiblical literary sources, the site was settled as early as the Middle Bronze Age (eighteenth through sixteenth centuries B.C.E.). Indeed, a major prehistoric settlement has recently been discovered at Ain Ghazal, near the old Amman airport. The ancient remains from the Middle Bronze through the Islamic periods centered around a hilltop citadel, known in Arabic as Jebel el-Qalah. Excavations on the citadel and in its immediate neighborhood have been conducted since the 1920s; these investigations have yielded a wide range of artifacts from all periods, including imported objects and seals and inscriptions. Among the latter is the famous Siran Bottle Inscription, which mentions Hissalel and Amminadab (II), Ammonite kings in the late seventh century B.C.E..

The name Rabbah first appears in the biblical narrative of the Hebrew conquest (Deut 3:11; Josh 13:25). Both of these passages associate Rabbah with the AMMONITES. In fact, Rabbah is the only name of a specifically Ammonite town that is mentioned in the Bible; its alternate name of Rabbath-Ammon means "capital" of the Ammonites. The most significant biblical references to Rabbah occur in the account of King DAVID's conquest of this city, a story in which Rabbah's importance is highlighted. According to 2 Sam 12:26-31 (cf. 1 Chr 20:1-3), Joab took "the city of waters" (12:27), a designation given to Rabbah since it is located at the source of the JABBOK. David was summoned from Jerusalem to besiege the rest of the city, since Joab had captured only part of it; David's victory was complete, and prisoners and loot were taken from Rabbah and "all the cities of the Ammonites" (12:31).

The Ammonites later regained their independence, and Rabbah rose to prominence once again. The city—and the Ammonites—were denounced by the prophets Amos (1:14) and Jeremiah (49:2-3), and Rabbah's destruction by the "people of the East" (i.e., Arabs) was predicted by Ezekiel (25:5). Rabbah came under the rule of the Tobiads in the Persian period, and Ptolemy (II) Philadelphus rebuilt the city along Hellenistic lines and renamed it Philadelphia in the third century B.C.E. It was conquered by Antiochus III in 218 B.C.E. and was annexed into the Decapolis by Pompey in 63 B.C.E. Philadelphia was included in the Roman province of Arabia, which was established by Trajan in 106 C.E., and most of the ruins at the site are from the Roman period, the second century C.E. After 635 C.E., the city came under Arab control and was thereafter called by its Semitic name—Amman.

—GERALD L. MATTINGLY

• **Rabbi.** In modern JUDAISM the rabbinate is an ordained office. Formerly, however, rabbi was only a title of respect, sometimes addressed to learned laymen, sometimes distinguishing a master from servants, but most often distinguishing a teacher from his pupils. In the Talmudic era, the term "rab" was used chiefly of Babylonian teachers and "rabbi" of Palestinian teachers.

In the NT rabbi was simply an honorific title which did not indicate any official appointment; it was applied to teachers of the Law in general. The term occurs only in Matthew, Mark, and John. Jesus asserted that the scribes and Pharisees loved to be called rabbi, and that his followers were not to be so called (Matt 23:7-8). John the Baptist's disciples called him rabbi (John 3:26), but in all other instances the term is ascribed to Jesus. The Gospel of John interprets rabbi to mean teacher (John 1:38; 3:2; "rabboni," 20:16).

Jesus being called rabbi by his disciples and others indicates that he conducted himself in a manner similar to the scribes. He based his teachings on scripture, and his disciples regarded him as their teacher. However, he differed from the scribes in that he did not teach or develop traditional material, but instead taught as one who had intrinsic authority. His disciples did not become rabbis themselves, instead they remained as disciples with Jesus as their teacher and Lord.

Other early Christian writings do not call Jesus rabbi; as the Palestinian tradition became less prominent, other christological titles supplanted the term rabbi.

See also JUDAISM.

—VERNON R. MALLOW

• **Rabbinic Literature.** Rabbinic literature covers a wide range of Jewish literary activity from the formative days under EZRA in the fourth century B.C.E. to the present time. However, the portion that is significant for biblical studies begins with the oral tradition which was finally codified by Judah the Patriarch between 180 and 200 C.E. and concludes with the completion of the Babylonian Talmud by 500 C.E. This body of literature consists of the Midrashim, the Mishnah, the Tosefta, the Targums, the Palestinian Talmud, and the Babylonian Talmud. Before examining the literature proper it is essential to explain two rabbinic terms which had a significant bearing on the formulation of this collection of Jewish tradition: *halakhah* and *haggadah*.

Halakhah is the definition of a precise way in which a commandment of the TORAH (Law) was to be performed. The prescription so formed relating to a strictly legal or ritual element could be deduced from scripture, but it could also be void of any scriptural basis. On the other hand *haggadah* covered the area of nonprescriptive elements of rabbinic thought. The purpose of *haggadah* was to inspire, edify, and move the people to the type of conduct which the *halakhah* required. Descriptions of historical events, aphorisms, parables, proverbs, legends of biblical or postbiblical heroes, folklore, and other materials were used by the rabbis to illustrate moral and ethical duties.

The Oral Law and the Mishnah. The most important collection of rabbinic literature is the Mishnah. Mishnah comes from the Hebrew root *shanah* meaning "to repeat." It signifies that which is learned by repetition and thus from memory. Before its codification by Judah the Patriarch the Mishnah was transmitted in oral form. In Jewish tradition there was a well-marked distinction between the oral law and the written law.

The beginning of the oral law is wrapped in obscurity. According to one tractate in the Mishnah the oral law and the written law were received simultaneously by MOSES from Mount SINAI (*Aboth* 1:1). Moses transmitted the oral law to JOSHUA who gave it to the elders and in turn the elders delivered it to the prophets. The prophets gave the oral law to the men of the GREAT ASSEMBLY. The Great Assembly, traditionally founded by EZRA, was a legislative body of spiritual leaders who kept alive the knowledge of the Torah from the time of Ezra until the death of the High Priest Simon I (ca. 280 B.C.E.) or Simon II (ca. 200 B.C.E.). If the Great Assembly terminated in 280 B.C.E., there is a gap of over 100 years in the transmission of the oral tradition before the appearance of the *Zugoth.* These were five "pairs" of leading scholars of the PHARISEES who continued the oral tradition of the Great Assembly for over 170 years. The era of the pairs began with Jose ben Jo'ezer and Jose ben Johanan about 160 B.C.E. and lasted until the death of Hillel and Shammai about 10 C.E. Hillel and Shammai who were the last of the five are also listed as the first of the *Tannaim,* the rabbis who shaped the oral tradition from 10 C.E. until the death of Judah the Patriarch in 215 or 220 C.E.

It was inevitable that an oral law should develop in JUDAISM simply because the written law did not cover all conceivable actions whether moral or ritual. It was assumed by the rabbis that where the Torah was not specific on certain laws governing conduct there must have been an oral tradition associated with them. Some of the precepts of the Torah were clear and some were not. The rabbis believed that if the meaning of a regulation was uncertain, it had to be clarified. If God made his will known in the Torah, there certainly was an exact way to obey it. The rabbis viewed their task as one of expanding the interpretation of the written law to meet the changing circumstances of life. Thus the oral law was in a constant state of development. It was adapted, modified, and expanded from time to time to meet the varying practical needs of successive ages, and finally the tradition itself took a written form.

In the NT the oral law is referred to as the "tradition of the elders" (Mark 7:3; Matt 15:2; Acts 6:14; Gal 1:14). Jesus criticized the Pharisees for rejecting one of the TEN COMMANDMENTS by implementing one of their oral precepts (Mark 7:9-13). The charge of Jesus against the Pharisees for invalidating the word of God by their tradition meant that he perceived the religious leaders as giving the oral law the same authority as the written law.

Judah ha-Nasi, or Judah the Patriarch (b. 135 C.E.) the great-grandson of GAMALIEL I, codified the oral law into the book known as the Mishnah. He worked on this project between 180 and 200 C.E. The amount of the Mishnah written by Judah is uncertain because it mentions his death in one place, and in another refers to a Joshua ben Levi who flourished after Judah. It is safe to say that in the course of time the Mishnah was enlarged by numerous additions. Most of Judah's codification of the Mishnah was probably done while he was head of the academy at Beth Shearim in Galilee, but some of his work took place in the last seventeen years of his life while he was head of the academy at Sepphoris in Galilee. The esteem in which Judah was held is seen in the fact that all later rabbinic literature refers back to him simply as "Rabbi."

The language of the Mishnah is sometimes classified as New HEBREW to distinguish it from biblical Hebrew. Generally scholars refer to it as Mishnaic Hebrew to indicate that it was used between 200 B.C.E. and 200 C.E. The nature of the language is still a subject of debate. Was it an artificial creation of the rabbis? Was it a living language in the second and first centuries B.C.E.? Was it a Hebraized ARAMAIC or was it a natural development from the biblical Hebrew?

The literary style of the Mishnah is far from being high quality. It is highly technical, compressed, repetitious, and monotonous. Despite the awkwardness of style, it is simple, direct, and concise. The lack of elegance of the Mishnah as a literary work may be due to the academic and legal character of the compilation plus the fact that its arrangement was made in order to facilitate memorization. The Mishnah is customarily cited by name of the tractate, followed by numbers for chapter and paragraph, e.g., *Berakot* 2.5.

The Mishnah is divided into six large sections called *sedarim,* "orders." The orders are further divided into tractates. The title of the first order is *Zera'im* (seeds). It has to do with the laws of agriculture but opens with the tractate *Berakhot* (blessings). This section contains eleven tractates. The second order is *Mo'ed* (set feasts). Its twelve tractates cover legal prescriptions for all the festivals of the Jewish calendar plus the SABBATH laws. *Nasim* (women), the third section of the Mishnah, covers family law, vows and oaths, marriages, divorces, betrothals, and inheritances. *Nasim* consists of seven tractates.

The fourth order is entitled *Neziqin* (damages) and has ten tractates which treat civil and criminal law, including torts, damages, penalties, and punishments. *Neziqin* also embraces the tractate called *Aboth* (the fathers; see PIRKE ABOTH) which definitely seems out of place in this order. The remaining two *sedarim* appear to be irrelevant in the time of the codification of the Mishnah because they contain for the most part rules covering temple practices which were outmoded with the destruction of the Temple in 70 C.E. *Kodashim* (holy things) has eleven tractates, ten of which deal with laws relating to sacrifices. Another gives the measurements of the TEMPLE and describes its gates and halls. The final section called *Toharot* (purities) sets forth laws of sanitation and purification. It has twelve tractates.

There are sixty-three tractates in the Mishnah. Almost all the material in this code is halakhic in nature, although occasionally one may run across the use of *haggadah* by a rabbi. The vast majority of the *halakhot* contains no scriptural basis for the ruling given by the scholars. Frequently there are quotations from scripture, but for the most part the citation has little to do with the formation of a rule or regulation.

The Tosefta. A second collection of rabbinic literature is the Tosefta. Tosefta means "additions" or "supplement." It is a compilation of oral laws and sayings parallel to the Mishnah. The rules and regulations found here derive from many of the same authorities quoted in the Mishnah. The name of the collection implies that it is a supplement to the Mishnah. The relation of the Tosefta, as well as the *Baraitas* (apocryphal material) of the Talmuds, to the Mishnah is unclear. Apparently it is an independent collection of the same type of material embodied in the Mishnah. The Tosefta has only fifty-nine of the sixty-three tractates of the Mishnah.

The question of the date of the Tosefta has not been definitively answered. Some suppose that it is the compiled oral law that was expounded in the commentary of Palestinian Talmud. This idea is based on the theory that the Mishnah was edited in Babylonia. Others believe that the Tosefta represents a collection of Rabbi Akiba in 130 C.E. or Rabbi Meir in 150 C.E. Later, between 180 and 200 Judah the Patriarch edited the collections making alterations and furnishing additions. However, most scholars contend that the Tosefta presupposed the Mishnah and was written long after it.

The Midrashim. A third collection of rabbinic literature is called the Midrashim. *Midrash* is from the Hebrew root *darash,* meaning "search out," "seek," or "investigate." Midrash is a specific exposition of scripture. The Midrashim represent a collection of midrashic works. The materials of the Midrashim are both halakhic and haggadic in nature. The mishnaic literature did not depend on scripture to deduce rules and regulations for moral and ethical behavior, nor was there a concern for *haggadot*—illustrative matter such as proverbs, parables, narratives, and folklore to give moral and ethical instruction. On the contrary the Midrashim show the rabbis searching scripture for the rules that piety required and using *haggadot* extensively for edification and moral lessons.

The early Midrashim originated in the second century C.E. and are attributed to the schools of Rabbis Ishmael and Akiba. *Mekhilta* (measure) is a running commentary on Exodus embodying the traditions of the school of Ishmael. *Sifra* (the book), a commentary on Leviticus, came from the school of Akiba. *Sifrei* (the books), dealing with the material from Num 5 to the end of Deuteronomy contained the traditions of both Akiba and Ishmael. All of these were probably edited in Babylonia in the fifth century C.E.

To supplement the halakhic Midrashim on Exodus, Leviticus, Numbers, and Deuteronomy, Hoshaiah set forth *Genesis Rabbah* (in Hebrew it is known as *Bereshith Rabbah*) to complete the commentaries on the Torah. This was done in the third century C.E., but its present form dates from the sixth century. *Genesis Rabbah* is haggadic in character. In later centuries, from the sixth to the twelfth, other largely haggadic midrashic literature was produced. This literature consisted of the Midrash on the *Megillot* (Lamentations, Song of Songs, Ruth, Esther, and Ecclesiastes) and the collection on Leviticus, Deuteronomy, Exodus, and Numbers which is little more than sermons.

The Talmuds. The talmudic literature is the fourth accumulation of rabbinic tradition. After the codification of the Mishnah the *Amoraim,* teachers who succeeded the *Tannaim,* produced the Talmuds, massive codifications of three centuries of study and comment on the Mishnah. There were two Talmuds, the Babylonian and the Palestinian (sometimes called Jerusalem). The commentary on the Mishnah is designated *gemara* (an Aramaic word that means "completion." The Mishnah plus the *gemara* make up the Talmuds. The Talmuds are divided into the same orders as the Mishnah, but many tractates are lacking. A talmudic passage is customarily cited by tractate, followed by a number and lower case letter, referring to divisions of the text in standard editions. Unless the Palestinian Talmud is specified, the reference is to the Babylonian Talmud.

The *Amoraim* of Palestine had schools in Tiberas, Sepphoris, and Caesarea. The *Amoraim* of Babylonia established schools in Nehardea, Sura, and Pumbeditha. The *Amoraim* of Palestine commented on the mishnaic text and formed the Palestinian Talmud in the fourth century C.E. Its commentary covered only thirty-nine of the sixty-three tractates of the Mishnah. The Babylonian Talmud was completed by Rab Ashi, but it was edited and codified by Rab Jose of Pumbeditha about 499 C.E. The final touches were put on it by the *Saboraim* (the explainers) who succeeded the Amoraim in the first half of the sixth century.

The Palestinian is the simple and more direct of the two Talmuds and it is about one-third the size of the Babylonian Talmud, although the latter incorporates only thirty-seven of the sixty-three tractates of the Mishnah, not necessarily the same as those included in the Palestinian. The Babylonian Talmud is more haggadic than the Palestinian counterpart, and it also contains much that is frivolous, immaterial, and reflective of Persian superstitions. The Babylonian Talmud is the Talmud *par excellence* for orthodox Jews. One might think that the Palestinian Talmud would be more authoritative for orthodox Jews since it originated in the land of their ancestors. Perhaps there are two reasons why the commentary of the *Amoraim* of Babylonia won out over the Palestinian Talmud. Both have to do with power and authority.

The authority of the Babylonian rabbis was well established in Palestine after Hillel came to Jerusalem from Babylonia in the latter part of the first century B.C.E. His introduction of seven rules for interpretation gained for himself a reputation as the leading scholar of his day, and from his death in 10 C.E. until the death of Judah the Patriarch his descendants maintained authority over the Jews in Palestine. After the Jewish revolt under Hadrian, 132–35 C.E., many scholars fled to Babylonia. The prosperity and liberty enjoyed in this country contributed to intellectual growth. There was a large population of Jews in the land. Some were descendants of those Judeans who were sent into exile during the Babylonian EXILE in the sixth century B.C.E. The most prominent Rab of the Babylonian Talmud was Areka. He studied under Judah the Patriarch and returned to Babylonia to found the academy of Sura. Before the SANHEDRIN was dissolved and the academies were still open, the Palestinian rabbis followed the rulings of the scholars in Babylonia.

The Babylonian Talmud gained greater recognition in Judaism not only because of its authoritative teachers, but because it was produced and spread in a more benign political environment. The power that controlled Palestine during the period of the *Amoraim* was the Byzantine empire. The Byzantine emperors, inspired by some of the church fathers, viewed the Jews as a menace to Christianity. This antagonism spilled over into persecution and anti-Jewish legislation of the Theodosian and Justinian codes. In 351 C. E., the Byzantine authorities closed the academies in Palestine, and in 429 terminated the office of Patriarch. On the other hand the teachers in Babylonia were relatively free of molestation. They flourished under the Parthians, Sassanids, and Muslims. When the Muslims made a sweep through Egypt, North Africa, and Spain, the Babylonian Jews went along with the conquerors and taught their Talmud.

In a study of rabbinic literature it would be careless to overlook the *Baraitas*. *Baraita* is an Aramaic word meaning "the outside" or "external." It refers to a tannaitic tradition which was not incorporated in the Mishnah. The *Baraitas* are scattered throughout the two Talmuds. These apocryphal teachings are easily identifiable because they are cited in Hebrew rather than in Aramaic which is the language of the *gemaras*. *Baraitas* are also recognized by the formulas introducing them, such as "Our rabbis have taught" and "There is a tradition," and by the citation of a tannaitic authority by name. The *Baraitas* have both halakhic and haggadic material, and many of them appeal to traditions older than the Mishnah itself.

The Targums. In addition to these four bodies of rabbinic literature, there are also the translations of Hebrew scripture into Aramaic known as the *Targums*. Originally the word targum meant a translation of any kind, but later it acquired a restrictive meaning of translation into Aramaic. Before the Exile (587/6 B.C.E.) the language of the people of Israel was Hebrew, but after the Exile, Aramaic, the international diplomatic and commercial language of the time, was gradually adopted by the majority of the people. In the course of time the Jews were unable to understand the Hebrew of the scripture, and there was a need for an Aramaic translation.

In the days of Jesus the Hebrew scriptures were read in the SYNAGOGUES, and following the reading an oral paraphrase in Aramaic was given by the reader. By the beginning of the second century C.E. the need arose to have written translations in Aramaic. Possibly the first was made by Onkelos, a proselyte Jew and pupil of Akiba. One of his aims in translation was to remove all anthropomorphic depictions of God. The Targum of Onkelos was completed in Palestine but was probably reedited in Babylonia, since it is also called the Babylonian Targum. The translation contained only the Pentateuch.

The Jerusalem or Palestinian Targum exists in two forms, one complete and the other fragmentary. The former is frequently referred to as the Targum of Pseudo-Jonathan. The fragmentary form is known as the Jerusalem Targum. Both were probably written in the seventh century C.E. The Targum of the Prophets was known in the third century C.E. While it was Palestinian in origin, it was revised to conform to the Eastern Aramaic dialect of Babylonia. Targums on the Writings section of the OT were made after 476 C.E. Included were translations of Job, Psalms, Proverbs, the Megilloth, and Chronicles. The only books of the OT without a Targum are Daniel, Ezra, and Nehemiah. This is understandable since two of these documents were partly written in Aramaic.

See also JUDAISM; PHARISEES; PIRKE ABOTH; TORAH.

Bibliography. P. Birnbaum, *A Book of Jewish Concepts*; H. Danby, trans., *The Mishnah*; I. Epstein, ed., *The Babylonan Talmud*; J. Neusner, *Invitation to the Talmud*; S. M. Lehrman, *The World of the Midrash*; W. O. E. Oesterley and G. H. Box, *The Religion and Worship of the Synagogue*; J. Schachter, *The Student's Guide through the Talmud*; S. Schechter, *Some Aspects of Rabbinic Theology*; D. J. Silver, *A History of Judaism*; H. L. Strack, *Introduction to the Talmud and Midrash*.

—T. C. SMITH

• **Rachel.** The daughter of LABAN, REBECCA's brother (Gen 29:10). By marrying Rachel and her sister LEAH, JACOB followed the practice of ABRAHAM and ISAAC, who also took wives from their extended family.

Laban welcomed Jacob into his household and accepted Jacob's offer to work for him for seven years in order to gain Rachel as his wife (Gen 29:13-20). On the wedding night, however, Laban gave him Leah, Rachel's older, lackluster sister, instead of Rachel. Laban allowed Jacob to marry Rachel after the week of celebrating Leah's wedding, but he required him to serve seven more years in return for her (29:21-28).

Leah was the first wife and fertile, and Rachel was the secondary wife and infertile, but Jacob preferred Rachel. Rachel longed for children (Gen 30:1), so she gave her personal maid, Bilhah, to Jacob, as SARAH had given HAGAR to Abraham (Gen 16). According to law and custom, the children born to Jacob and Bilhah could be counted as Rachel's offspring (30:3, 5-8). She also tried without success to use MANDRAKES to cure her infertility (30:14-18). At last God remembered Rachel, ended her infertility (30:22), and removed the stigma of childlessness (30:23). The name she gave to her firstborn, JOSEPH, expressed her wish for more sons (30:24).

By seeking children for themselves, Rachel and Leah made Jacob the father of a large, powerful family. In the previous generations of Israel's ancestors only one man and one woman had been chosen to receive the Lord's promises and to produce the elect son. All of Jacob's sons, however, born of four different mothers, were part of the chosen people of Israel. In them the promise of innumerable descendants, which had been made to Abraham, Isaac and Jacob (Gen 15:5; 17:16, 19; 22:17; 28:14), began to be fulfilled.

After twenty years of service to Laban, Jacob decided to return with his family to Canaan (Gen 31:1-21). Rachel took Laban's household gods with her. Jacob did not know this and unwittingly put Rachel's life in jeopardy by promising Laban to have the thief executed. Rachel saved herself by hiding the gods in a camel saddle, sitting on it, and telling her father that she could not get up because she was menstruating (31:26-35). By the theft of the gods Rachel accomplished symbolically what Jacob effected in actuality—the breakup and weakening of Laban's household.

Rachel died in childbirth in the land of Canaan (Gen 35:16-18). The caravan paused long enough for her to deliver, name her son Ben-oni, "son of my sorrow," die, and be buried. Jacob renamed the son Benjamin and set up a stone grave marker (either near Bethlehem, Gen 35:19-20, or Ramah, 1 Sam 10:2).

In Jer 31:15 the voice of Rachel is heard mourning her "children," the dead and exiled citizens of the Northern Kingdom. The tribes of Joseph's sons, EPHRAIM and MANASSEH (Gen 48:8-20), and the tribe of BENJAMIN were the most prominent northern tribes, so Rachel was especially the "mother" of that kingdom. Matt 2:16-18 interprets Jer 31:15 as a prophecy of Herod's slaughter of male infants in BETHLEHEM following Jesus' birth.

See also JACOB; LEAH; WOMEN IN THE OLD TESTAMENT.

Bibliography. J. Van Seters, *Abraham in History and Tradition*; G. von Rad, *Genesis*; C. Westermann, *Genesis 12-36*.

—PAMELA J. SCALISE

• **Rahab.** [ray'hab] The name of a harlot of JERICHO who aided two Israelite spies, and the name of a mythical sea monster.

When spelled in Heb. as *rāḥāb* (''wide, broad''), a reference to a harlot who lived in the Late Bronze Age city of Jericho (Josh 2:1-21; 6:22-25). JOSHUA sent two spies to investigate the city of Jericho. Upon arrival they lodged in Rahab's house. When their presence became known to the king of Jericho, she hid them on the roof of her house and said that they had already left the city. Convinced by the mighty deeds Yahweh had done for Israel, Rahab confessed her faith in the Lord and made a bargain with the spies. She aided their escape from the city in exchange for the promise of protection for her family. That protection was provided when the Israelites conquered the city, and Rahab and her family became a part of the nation of Israel. Rahab is included in Matthew's genealogy of JESUS (1:5), and the NT cites her as an example of faith and works (Heb 11:31; Jas 2:25).

When spelled in Heb. as *rahab* (perhaps ''storm, arrogance''), the term refers to the mythological sea monster of chaos in the Babylonian epic of creation. Occasionally the Bible refers to God's authority over the monster Rahab as a symbol for God's control over chaos at creation (Job 9:13; 26:12; Ps 89:10; Isa 51:9). The Bible twice employs the monster Rahab as a symbol for Egypt (Ps 87:4; Isa 30:7).

See also HARLOT; JERICHO.

Bibliography. T. C. Butler, *Joshua, WBC*; D. W. Thomas, ed., *Documents from Old Testament Times*.

—BOB R. ELLIS

• **Rainbow.** A prismatic arc of light in the sky produced by the refraction of sunlight through raindrops. References to the rainbow appear in Gen 9:13; Ezek 1:28; Sir 43:11; and Rev 4:3; 10:1. The Heb. word *qešet* designates both a bow and the rainbow, but the rainbow is called in the OT the ''bow in the cloud.''

In Gen 9:13, the rainbow is a sign of God's promise never again to destroy the earth by flood. In this context, the rainbow is a metaphor for the passing of God's judgment. Elsewhere in the OT, one way of speaking about the coming judgment of God is the imagery of God's bow. God is like a warrior fitting his bow with arrows to bring destruction (cf. Lam 2:4; Ps 7:12-13; Hab 3:9-11). The rainbow, then, is the spent bow, appearing in the retreating clouds of the thunderstorm after the arrows of God's lightning have been launched. The rainbow, a sign of the passing of a storm, is thus used as a metaphor for the passing of the judgment of God.

In later literature the rainbow is imagery employed in describing the GLORY surrounding God in heaven. Such is the case in the references to rainbow in Ezek 1:28 and Rev 4:3; 10:1.

—MARGARET DEE BRATCHER

• **Ramses.** [ram'seez] Eleven pharaohs of the nineteenth and twentieth Egyptian Dynasties (sometimes called the ''Ramesside Dynasties'') chose this name meaning ''Re is he that has borne him.'' From its religious center of the Sun God at On (Heliopolis) in Lower Egypt, the primary focus of these pharaohs was to reestablish and maintain the type of control over Asia that EGYPT had enjoyed prior to the el-Amarna diversion. Amenhotep IV (AKHENATON), during his religious and political reforms and his attempts at establishing a new capital at the site now called Tell el-AMARNA, had seemingly neglected the affairs of the empire. Interregional and intercity rivalries, general political chaos and diminished Egyptian prestige in Syria-Palestine demanded the attention of the early Nineteenth Dynasty pharaohs.

Ramses I (ca. 1306–1305 B.C.E.) rose from a military background to vizier and ultimately founded the Nineteenth Dynasty in what appears to have been a military-priestly revolt against Akhenaton's reforms and imperial weakness. Founded on a religiopolitical union of Re and Seth (''god of deserts, mountain thunder and foreign countries''), Ramses I's new capital was established in the northeast Delta from which subsequent military expeditions into Asia could easily be launched.

Ramses II (ca. 1290–1223 B.C.E.), grandson of Ramses I and most renowned of the Ramesside pharaohs, during his long and illustrious reign, restored Egypt to her former greatness, both at home and abroad. His extensive building operations along the Nile, from NUBIA to the Delta, achieved Egypt's finest architectural and monumental design. The enlargement of his residence at Tanis (renamed ''Per-Ramses''), additions to the Karnak (the great hypostyle hall) and Luxor temples, the Ramesseum (his mortuary temple) at Thebes, the monumental rock-cut temple at Abu Simbel and lesser temples in Nubia, the Colossi at Memphis, and numerous other refinements and structures throughout his realm were the material heritage of this great pharaoh. His efforts in the Delta have been equated with the biblical references to the building of Pithom (probably Tell el-Maskhouta in the eastern Delta) and Rameses (= Per-Ramesses) toward the end of the Hebrew sojourn in Egypt (Exod 1:11). Such an identification may suggest that Ramses II was the pharaoh of Moses' negotiations and the Exodus.

Early in his reign (during his fifth year), Ramses II challenged the Hittites who, during the Akhenaten era, had extended their encroachment into traditional Egyptian territory in Syria. The subsequent battle at Kedesh in 1286 B.C.E. was inconclusive, but the next sixteen years seem to suggest an Egyptian inability to thwart the Hittite advance, a situation that prompted a Hittite-Egyptian Peace Treaty (1270 B.C.E.) that established a border basically consistent with Moses' description of the northern limits of the Promised Land. It appears reasonable to assume that Moses intended to claim the Egyptian province of Canaan, justifiable payment for 430 years of Egyptian bondage. The Hittite alliance was reinforced by Ramses' marriage to the Hittite king's daughter in his thirty-fourth year.

The Hittite-Egyptian alliance may have received impetus from an impending menace of ''Sea Peoples'' who had initiated an eastward and southward advance in Anatolia and North Africa. Threatening Hittite lands in Anatolia and Syria and the lucrative sea and land trade that Egypt monopolized in the eastern Mediterranean coastal lands, the gradual infiltration of the SEA PEOPLES required special internal measures and specific foreign policy instituted by Ramses II's son, Merneptah, prior to the frontal attack with which Ramses III had to deal. With the exception of other, lesser campaigns in Canaan against such towns as Merom, Eltekeh and Ashkelon, Ramses II enjoyed a relatively tranquil and stable reign marked by internal peace and prosperity.

The longevity and prosperity of his reign, his real and imagined military and political accomplishments, his personal virility (with some 100 offspring), and his building accomplishments that were everywhere evident, conspired to foster the cult of Ramses II as a god even before his demise. Throughout the later history of Egypt, it was the greatness of Ramses II that was to be emulated.

The end of Ramses II's reign resulted in a rapid decline. Merneptah, Ramses II's son, saw his kingdom harassed internally by marauding bands of Sea Peoples penetrating his western frontier with Libya and the Asiatic lands in a growing state of unrest and rebellion. Though he records glowing successes on the Libyan front and the annihilation of insurrectionists in Canaan (including a first mention of "Israel"), history has recorded a state of disorder and decline that ultimately resulted in the end of the Nineteenth Dynasty with an Asiatic usurper on the throne.

Ramses III (1188–1157 B.C.E.), founder of the Twentieth Dynasty, is best remembered for his famous sea and land battles against the Sea Peoples who in the meantime had destroyed the Hittite state, dislodged the older established peoples along the northeastern Mediterranean coastline, and established a Syrian base for their anticipated invasion of Lower Egypt. On two previous occasions he had defended his western frontier against a Libyan-Sea Peoples coalition. The ultimate confrontation on land seemingly came somewhere along the Syria-Palestine coastline, while the sea battle took place in the mouth of the Nile. Though victorious in both land and naval operations, the strength of Egypt was so depleted that she was forced to withdraw from her Asiatic lands, abandon her rich copper mines in the Sinai, and accept the settlement of the Philistines and other Sea Peoples tribes in all the vital, lucrative locales of her Asiatic empire. The coffers of Egypt were deprived of the duty and customs of Asiatic trade routes and unable to meet the bureaucratic payroll. Internal disorder and palace conspiracy seemingly ended Ramses III's reign and life. However, his policies and the events of his reign impacted Egypt for generations to come.

Throughout his reign, Ramses III's temple donations dramatically enhanced the power and wealth of the Amun priesthood at Thebes. When his will reaffirmed the temple estates giving the priests secular control over most agricultural land and movable property, huge annual incomes, and mastery over a majority of the population, the stage was set for a temple-oriented state, without challenge for much of the next century. As a result, his successors, Ramses IV-XI (ca. 1157–1085 B.C.E.) were weak palace figures who had to vie for power with the vizier, the military commander and the Amun high priest at Thebes. Their foreign influence was minimal and Egypt's internal affairs were characterized by corruption and lawlessness. Deprived of foreign booty and unable to compete in a world dominated by iron, the Egyptian economy was crippled by inflation and its people was destined to poverty. Her foreign emissaries were ridiculed and rebuffed. Even the establishment of the Twenty-First Dynasty, ca. 1090 B.C.E., was a compromise that in effect split Lower and Upper Egypt into feuding economic and religious factions.

See also EGYPT.

Bibliography. C. Aldred, *Akhenaten, Pharaoh of Egypt. A New Study* and "The End of the El-'Armana Period,' " *JEA* 43 (1957): 30ff.; J. H. Breasted, *A History of Egypt from the Earliest Times to the Persian Conquest*; W. F. Edgerton and J. A. Wilson, *Historical Records of Ramses III*; K. A. Kitchen, "Some New Light on the Asiatic Wars of Ramesses II," *JEA* 50 (1964): 47ff.; S. Langdon and A. H. Gardiner, "The Treaty of Alliance between Hattushili, King of the Hittites, and the Pharaoh Ramesses II of Egypt," *JEA* 6 (1920): 179ff.; M. B. Rowton, "The Background of the Treaty between Ramesses II of Egypt and Hattushilish III," *JCS* 13 (1959): 1ff. and "Manetho's Date for Ramesses II," *JEA* 34 (1948): 57-74; G. Steindorff and K. C. Steele, *When Egypt Ruled the East*; G. A. Wainwright, "Merneptah's Aid to the Hittites," *JEA* 46 (1960): 24ff.; J. A. Wilson, *The Burden of Egypt*.

—GEORGE L. KELM

• **Ransom.** *See* REDEMPTION IN THE NEW TESTAMENT

• **Raphael.** *See* ANGEL

• **Rapture.** The concept of the rapture is part of the church's response to the disciples' question to the resurrected Jesus in Acts 1:6, "Lord, will you at this time restore the kingdom to Israel?" His answer, "It is not for you to know times or seasons which the Father has fixed by his own authority," has never satisfied the church at large; modern focus on the rapture has come largely from nineteenth-century Protestant millennialism and dispensationalism. Just as other important Christian terms, such as "trinity" and "catholic," are not in the Bible but are used to describe conclusions gleaned from the systematic and comprehensive study of biblical materials, so "rapture" does not occur in the Bible either. It comes from the Latin Vulgate of 1 Thess 4:17 where the verb, "shall be caught up together" is translated by *rapturo*. The main texts for study of the rapture are Matt 13:24-52; 24; 1 Thess 4:13-17; 5:1-4; 2 Thess 1:7-10; 1 Cor 15:51-53.

From these passages the rapture is considered to be the sudden, surprising return of Christ to take (or "rapture") the resurrected deceased believers, and those saints who are still alive, up to heaven. Some believe this rapture will be secret, others that it will be visible. Dispensationalists (not to be confused with premillennialists) teach that the rapture is the first event of a twofold second coming of Christ; it will be imminent and secret, and it is commonly called Christ's coming *for* his faithful. Contrary to premillennialist belief, it will be preceded by signs, such as wars, apostasy, the return of the Jews to Palestine, and the appearance of antichrist. The second part of the return of Christ is the revelation of Christ, after seven years, which is his coming with his saints for Israel and the rest of the world.

The rapture question is set within the larger context of the millennial discussion, or the 1,000-year reign of Christ on earth. Premillennialists teach that the rapture precedes the millennial rule of Christ; postmillennialists believe it will happen after the MILLENNIUM; and amillennialists believe that there is to be no millennium (which, they think, refers to the present church age, however long it is).

Much of the analysis of the nature of the rapture and its position and function in the eschatological sequence is based on Greek words Paul uses. Many believe that Paul distinguishes aspects of Christ's return through the use of different words—"coming" (παρουσία), "appearing" (ἐπιφάνεια), and "revelation" (ἀποκάλυψις). Others assert that Paul uses the words interchangeably to refer to different aspects of the same single event of Christ's return. Whatever the case, rapture is twofold: it is God's historical, objective act at the end of history by which he takes (*rapturo*) his people to be with him; and it is, therefore, the rapture or elevation within the souls of all those who live and believe this by faith.

See also ESCHATOLOGY IN THE NEW TESTAMENT; KINGDOM OF GOD; MILLENNIUM; PAROUSIA/SECOND COMING.

Bibliography. L. Boettner, *The Millennium*; R. Clouse, ed., *The Meaning of the Millennium*; J. Walvoord, *The Millennial Kingdom*.

—JOHN S. REIST, JR.

• **Reader Response Criticism.** *See* LITERATURE, BIBLE AS

• **Rebekah.** [ri-bek'uh] The daughter of Bethuel and the granddaughter of NAHOR, ABRAHAM's brother (Gen 22:23; 24:15). When Abraham sent his servant to find a wife for ISAAC, he sent him to his family in upper MESOPOTAMIA (24:1-9). Isaac's future was in the land promised to Abraham's descendants, but he could not obtain that land by marrying one of the native Canaanites. Isaac's wife, like the other mothers of Israel, SARAH and RACHEL, was to be a relative rather than a foreigner.

Through prayer, Abraham's servant was led to discover Rebekah among the many women at the well of Nahor's city. Her genealogy and her performance of the sign for which he had prayed (Gen 24:12-27) assured him of God's guidance. Her willingness to leave for her new home without delay (24:54-58), her graceful and proper behavior upon meeting Isaac, and his love for her confirmed the choice (24:64-67).

Rebekah was infertile, but Isaac's prayer was answered and she conceived (Gen 25:21). The usual discomforts of pregnancy were compounded because she was carrying twins, and the apparent struggle of the two in her womb caused her to cry to God in anguish (25:22). God then revealed to her the first declaration of JACOB's election as the father of God's people Israel (25:23; cf. Gen 28:13-14; Rom 9:10-13). Both of her sons would become ancestors of nations, but the descendants of the older son would serve the descendants of the younger. Jacob grew up to be Rebekah's favorite, while Isaac preferred ESAU.

When famine drove them from their own land Rebekah and Isaac settled in GERAR. Because of Rebekah's beauty (Gen 24:16; 26:7) Isaac feared that the men of that place would kill him in order to take her. He therefore adopted Abraham's stratagem and introduced Rebekah as his sister (26:7; cf. Gen 12:10-20; 20). This plan exposed Rebekah to the possibility of adultery with the men of Gerar who would treat her as an unattached maiden (26:10; cf. Exod 22:16-17). Nevertheless, Rebekah remained unmolested for a long time (26:8a) until the ruse was finally discovered by the king, ABIMELECH, when he happened to observe Isaac in the midst of love-play with Rebekah (26:8b). Abimelech reproached Isaac for endangering his subjects with the possibility of inadvertent adultery, but issued an edict protecting Rebekah and Isaac from physical attacks (26:9-11).

As dying Isaac prepared to bless Esau, the firstborn, Rebekah gave Jacob the opportunity and the means to impersonate his brother and obtain the blessing for himself (Gen 27:1-29). She then acted to preserve the family by arranging for Jacob to escape Esau's murderous hatred (27:41-45). Esau had Hittite wives from Canaan, but Rebekah persuaded Isaac to send Jacob to Paddan-Aram to find a wife among her brother LABAN's daughters (27:46–28:5). Jacob, the third generation in the line of God's promise, was to marry within the extended family as Abraham and Isaac had done.

Rebekah was buried in the cave of MACHPELAH with Sarah and Abraham (Gen 49:31).

See also ESAU; ISAAC; JACOB; WOMEN IN THE OLD TESTAMENT.

Bibliography. J. Van Seters, *Abraham in History and Tradition*; E. A. Speiser, *Genesis*; C. Westermann, *Genesis 12-36*.

—PAMELA J. SCALISE

• **Rebellion.** *See* SIN

• **Rechabites.** [rek'uh-bits] A family group pledged to the fulfillment of specific vows; the group maintained its identity for centuries. The founder, Jehonadab son of Rechab, was identified as a militant ally of King JEHU (841–814 B.C.E.). Jeremiah also referred to the group (Jer 35); another reference was made in Neh 3:14. At that time one of Rechab's descendants, Malchiah, a district administrator, repaired Jerusalem's Dung Gate. An additional genealogical reference occurs in 1 Chr 2:55, where Rechab was identified as a Kenite from Hammath.

The Hebrew word Rechabite came from a verb meaning to mount and ride. As a noun it referred to a chariot, a charioteer, or a mill-stone (the upper stone riding the lower).

The first reference to Jehonadab associated him with a king, a chariot, and a major political and religious policy: the annihilation of Ahab's descendants and the destruction of BAAL worshipers (2 Kgs 10:15-27). Such information indicates that Jehonadab was a man of political, military, and religious influence. His name, composed of the word Yah and the Hebrew letters *n-d-b,* signified such. The root *n-d-b,* in the monarchical period, referred to a member of the ruling class. Jehonadab used his influence to champion Yahweh worship, which had been severely compromised by the Omrides.

"The son of Rechab" could mean much more than a parent/child relationship. Since Jehonadab was the group's founder, the reference "son of" may refer to one who was associated with a group or guild of charioteers. They might have constructed chariots, driven them, or both. Thus, Jehonadab as supplier and Jehu as captain would have had prior opportunity to be acquainted, and they may have shared comparable goals. The Rechabites' association with metal working may account for the group's vows.

Rechabites observed three vows: (1) to abstain from wine (intoxicants); (2) to refuse to build houses and to live in tents instead; and (3) to avoid engagement in agricultural pursuits. These vows probably served not to preserve a nomadic society in protest to the evils of city life, but to protect important technology and productive skill. As metal workers such men were honored among agriculturalists who looked to them for implements and for protection. To provide these things, they had to move frequently to find a supply of ore. Houses and fields would be detrimental to their trade. Their abstinence could well be to assure that no trade secrets would ever be imparted accidentally.

Not only were they respected technicians in an agricultural society, but they also were avid Yahwists. Every recorded name of this group contained in it the name "Yah." They were commended by God for their abiding faithfulness to the commands that their ancestor Jehonadab son of Rechab had given to them, a faithfulness that sharply contrasted with the lack of faithfulness displayed by the people of the southern kingdom to their God.

See also KENITES; NAZIRITES.

Bibliography. F. S. Frick, "The Rechabites Reconsidered,'' *JBL* 90 (1971): 279-87.

—JERRY WALLACE LEE

• **Rechabites, History of the.** The *History of the Rechabites* is the story of the journey of a virtuous hermit named Zosimus to the island of the blessed ones. After a lengthy trek facilitated by divine assistance, Zosimus reaches an Eden-like island in the midst of a great ocean. The inhabitants of the island, the blessed ones, identify themselves as the descendants of Jonadab, the son of Rechab, and explain to him how angels brought them to this island during the time of Jeremiah (cf. Jer 35). They describe further their idyllic manner of life as those who experience the unending benevolence of God. Finally, Zosimus returns, again with divine aid, to his cave.

The *History of the Rechabites* is extant in a number of ancient languages, including Arabic, Karshuni, Slavonic, and Armenian, the most important being Syriac, Greek, and Ethiopic. The story takes a variety of forms in the different versions, and generally includes sections which are obviously Christian. Behind the document in its present forms, however, may lie an earlier Jewish tradition (first century C.E.?) about the Rechabites.

The *History of the Rechabites* was a popular book in the early Middle Ages. It reflects a strong interest in the concept of an earthly PARADISE where there is no evil. Interestingly, however, death remains but is reinterpreted as the joyful occasion of the departure of the soul from the body in order to ascend to God. The story also reflects an interest in the fate of the so-called lost tribes of Israel.

Bibliography. J. H. Charlesworth, ''History of the Rechabites,'' *The Old Testament Pseudepigrapha,* ed. J. H. Charlesworth and *The History of the Rechabites,* vol. 1: *The Greek Recension*; B. McNeil, ''The Narrative of Zosmius,'' *JSJ* 9 (1978): 68-82.

—JOSEPH L. TRAFTON

• **Reconciliation.** The basic sense of the term reconciliation is that of the resumption of friendly relations, thus restoring a state of mutual harmony. The primary emphasis derived from the term is not simply a matter of a change of feeling or emotion, though this may be involved, but, rather, a fundamental change in the situation or relationship. Thus reconciliation is properly understood as a relational term.

There are of course different spheres of relations covered in the Bible by the term reconciliation. The most obvious dimension is the characterization of human interpersonal relations in social and political spheres. For example, in 1 Sam 29:4 Philistine suspicion concerning David's offer of assistance against Israel is based on a decision that the offer is merely a treacherous plot by David for purposes of reconciling himself with King Saul. Or, in his famous SERMON ON THE MOUNT, Jesus declares that relations between individuals must be given priority over attention to the Jewish Law. Here the instance is cited of a man preparing to make an offering at the altar, yet remembering he has something against his brother. Jesus' admonition is to go first and be reconciled with the brother before making the offering (Matt 5:23-24). The further dimension involved here is that reflected in the man's actual willingness to make an offering to God, for the underlying rationale of the sacrificial system in which the man is participating is that, in response to one's offering, God will restore the divine-human relation (cf. Lev 16).

This whole concept of reconciliation receives its greatest theological development in the NT with Paul's reflection on Jesus' death and resurrection. Here reconciliation joins such other Pauline terms as JUSTIFICATION, freedom, SANCTIFICATION, transformation, and SALVATION as a distinctive way to speak of the effects of the Christ event. The primary texts in this connection where the term is used in a theological sense are Rom 5:10-11 and 2 Cor 5:18-20 (cf. 1 Cor 7:10-11). In the former, Paul emphasizes that the relationship between individuals and God, fractured by sin, has been restored through God's action in offering the son on the cross. In the latter, Paul emphasizes that not only was Jesus' death and resurrection the demonstration of God's reconciling the world to himself, but now the responsibility exists for believers to proclaim the significance of the Christ-event.

Further developments on these ideas can be found in later materials in the Pauline tradition. In Col 1:20-21 the state of estrangement and hostility is said to be changed by the reconciliation accomplished by Jesus' death. In Eph 2:13-16, the barriers between Jew and gentile are overcome by God's reconciling the two into one body of believers.

See also JUSTIFICATION; PEACE; REDEMPTION IN THE NEW TESTAMENT; REDEMPTION IN THE OLD TESTAMENT; SALVATION IN THE NEW TESTAMENT; SALVATION IN THE OLD TESTAMENT; SANCTIFICATION.

Bibliography. R. Martin, *Reconciliation*; I. H. Marshall, ''The Meaning of Reconciliation,'' *Unity and Diversity in New Testament Theology,* ed. R. A. Guelich; J. A. Fitzmyer, ''Reconciliation in Pauline Theology,'' *No Famine in the Land,* ed. J. W. Flanagan and A. Weisbrod Robinson.

—MICHAEL D. GREENE

• **Red Heifer.** *See* HEIFER, RED

• **Red Sea/Reed Sea.** Red Sea is the traditional translation of the Heb. *yam sûp*. This translation can be traced back as far as the LXX which translates *Erythra Thalassa* and the Vulgate which translates *Mare Rubrum*. Scholarly convention prefers to translate Reed Sea (cf. Luther's *Schilfmeer*). The translation Reed Sea points to the attestation of the Heb. word *sûp* meaning ''reeds, papyrus'' (Exod 2:3, 5; Isa 19:6). The word is traced to the Egyptian word *ṯwf(y)* meaning ''papyrus, reeds.'' Moreover, the expression *p'-ṯwfy* allegedly refers, in one Egyptian text, to a specific body of water, a papyrus lake near Ramses. This *p'-ṯwfy* is identified with the OT *yam sûp*.

This has forced interpreters to locate Israel's deliverance at the sea somewhere besides the Red Sea or the Gulf of Suez (PLATE 9). Southern, central, and northern locations have been proposed, but each of these proposals is beset by difficulties. The southern hypothesis has been proved geologically impossible. The central hypothesis faces the objection that the strongest ''east wind'' would not expose the bed of any isthmus lake. The northern hypothesis leads into ''the way of the land of the Philistines'' which the Bible indicates was avoided (Exod 13:17). None of the proposed identifications of the *yam sûp* which distinguishes between it and the Red Sea and its gulfs has succeeded in establishing itself among interpreters.

Outside the traditions of Israel's deliverance at the sea, *yam sûp* refers to the Red Sea or one of its gulfs (certainly 1 Kgs 9:26; probably Exod 10:19; Num 14:25; 21:4; 33:10-11; Deut 1:40; 2:1; Jer 49:21; perhaps Judg 11:16). Furthermore, certain of the texts in the Exodus tradition do not place the deliverance at the *yam sûp* but rather at ''the sea'' (Exod 14:2, 21), while Num 33:8, 10-11 distinguish between the sea through which Israel passed and the *yam sûp*. The only early text which places Israel's deliverance at the *yam sûp* is Exod 15:4, and all other texts in the Exodus tradition which so locate the event are dependent upon it.

Therefore, the use of *yam sûp* in Exod 15:4 has been interpreted as "sea of extinction" or in some other way to indicate the primal significance of the miracle at the sea. Interpreters who so argue point to the three parallel expressions used in the Song of the Sea (i.e., Exod 15:1-18): sea (*yam*), floods (*tehomoth*), and depths (*meṣôloth*). Each of these words is used elsewhere in Hebrew literature with reference to cosmic, primeval realities which Israel's God overwhelms. Also, the word *sûp* may be so construed and even seems to be attested with this meaning (Jonah 2:5[H6]). The use of *yam sûp* in Exod 15:4 thus witnesses to Israel's redemption as a creation act. Later texts which were dependent upon the witness of Exod 15:4 historicized and localized the creation-redemption of Israel at a particular body of water: the Red Sea.

See also EXODUS.

Bibliography. B. F. Batto, "The Reed Sea: *Requiescat in pace*," *JBL* 102 (1983): 27-35; E. G. Kraeling, *Rand McNally Bible Atlas*, 102-107; J. Simons, *The Geographical and Topographical Texts of the Old Testament*, §§209, 273, 417, 425, 431; N. H. Snaith, *Yam Sôp:* The Sea of Reeds: The Red Sea," *VT* 15 (1965): 395-98; R. de Vaux, *The Early History of Israel*.

—JOHN KEATING WILES

• **Redaction.** Redaction is the conscious reworking of older materials in such a way as to meet new needs and differing theological perspectives. Redaction criticism focuses on the contributions of the redactor, the final editor, to the final written form of a text and presupposes other types of criticism such as tradition criticism, form criticism, and SOURCE CRITICISM. Redaction criticism assumes that the person who put a biblical work into final shape gathered and edited the material to express a particular theological point of view.

The goal of the redaction critic is to discover the perspectives of the final redactor(s) as a step in the process of reconstructing the stages of the composition of the piece of biblical literature under consideration.

Examples of redaction-critical problems are found in the books of Judges and 1 and 2 Kings. The author of the words who reviewed the period of the judges lived a long time after it was over. He is giving the reader more than history; he is providing a theological explanation of why the biblical history unfolded the way it did. Since 1 and 2 Chronicles used material from 1 and 2 Samuel and 1 and 2 Kings we can deduce the point of view of the redactor of Chronicles. The work of an editor is also evident in the last verses of Ecclesiastes (Eccl 12:9-14).

There are several questions asked by redaction critics in the NT. To what extent were the evangelists involved in forming and shaping the traditional materials into the texts of their own theologies? To what extent did the form GOSPEL itself influence the choice of materials and the presentation of materials? How are we to grasp the theological points of view of the evangelists and where do they come into sight? The role of the redactor is evident in the comparisons of materials found in the several sources. The way Matthew and Luke present the substance of the sermon on the mount is an example and is related to their understandings of the significance of Jesus and of their understanding of what a gospel should do. Matthew has Jesus ascend to a mountaintop where Jesus promulgates a new Christian law. (The similarities with the actions of Moses, the giver of the old law, are obvious.) Luke, however places the discourse of Jesus on the plain where the lowly, poor, and outcast are. In Matthew's version Jesus' sayings are a new law, whereas much of the same material in Luke's version is directed to the down-and-out.

One other example of redaction criticism is noted. Since the chronological order and stages of development of the Gospels can be fixed, with Mark being the earliest and serving as a source from which Matthew and Luke draw, the redaction critic can analyze the points at which Matthew and Luke redact Mark. The accounts of the baptism in Mark 1:9-11 and par. give further evidence of redaction.

See also FORM/GATTUNG; GOSPELS, CRITICAL STUDY OF; SOURCE CRITICISM; SYNOPTIC PROBLEM; TRADITION IN THE OLD TESTAMENT.

Bibliography. R. F. Collins, *Introducing the New Testament*; W. G. Doty, *Contemporary New Testament Interpretation*; N. Perrin, *What is Redaction Criticism*.

—ROBERT K. GUSTAFSON

• **Redeemer.** The English word "redeemer" translates two OT words which designate one who recovers or saves either living beings or personal property from impending loss. One Hebrew word designates the individual who gives a payment of one living thing to avoid losing another living thing. Exod 13:13 requires the sacrifice of a lamb in lieu of one's firstborn son. This word is often used to describe God, who rescues the nation of Israel from Egypt (Deut 7:8) or the individual from sickness, enemies, or death itself (Pss 34:23; 49:15). A second word evolves from the time when Israelites thought of themselves primarily as members of an extended family group or tribe. If a tribal member were forced by economic ruin to sell property or family members or himself, it was the duty of a "kinsman redeemer" to buy the property in order to protect the collective power of the tribe. Similar laws regulated revenge for murder and childless widows. "Kinsman redeemer" is also used for God in several OT books, and is one of the major themes of Second Isaiah: God is Israel's near kin and will rescue and restore the exiled nation.

In the NT, "redeemer" appears only in Acts 7:35, where Moses, as a model or type for Christ, is called "ruler and redeemer." The word is found in the LXX but not in extant secular Greek literature, which explains its absence from documents written to primarily gentile audiences.

See also GOD, NAMES OF; REDEMPTION IN THE NEW TESTAMENT; REDEMPTION IN THE OLD TESTAMENT; REDEMPTION OF LAND.

—RICHARD B. VINSON

• **Redemption in the New Testament.** The English word "redemption" signifies a transaction in which some item or person is exchanged for payment. The OT understanding of redemption as God's restoration of his disobedient children is expressed in the NT in terms of Jesus' death.

Gospels. Mark 10:45 and Matt 20:28 declare that "the Son of man also came . . . to give his life as a ransom for many." This saying shows that early Christians believed that Jesus died purposefully to give his life in place of their own. Luke, which does not have a parallel to Mark 20:45, uses the words "redeem" or "redemption" four times as a general term for deliverance or salvation (Luke 1:68; 2:38; 21:28; 24:21).

Paul. Paul's Letters occasionally use "redemption" in a general list of metaphors for salvation (Rom 3:24; 1 Cor

1:30; Col 1:14). There is also a specific focus on the root idea of giving one's life to save another. Gal 3:10-14 argues that everyone living by the Torah stands under God's curse. Jesus removed the curse by dying as an accursed thing, freeing the rest of the world to receive God's blessing instead (cf. Gal 4:5). Rom 8:23 speaks of "the redemption of our bodies," an exchange of mortal flesh for immortal, which Paul believed would take place at Christ's return; the Holy Spirit, Paul says, lives in Christians as the first stage of that event. Ephesians and the Pastorals also characterize Christ's death as a redemptive SACRIFICE which rescues believers from SIN (Eph 1:7, 14; 4:30; 1 Tim 2:6; Titus 2:14).

Letters. Heb 9:12-15 argues that Christ's death was a one-time redemptive sacrifice which now eternally removes sins incurred "under the first covenant," the Torah. First Pet 1:18-19, using the related concept of ransom, describes Christ as a perfect lamb whose death rescues; 2:18-25 elaborates with clear allusions to Isa 53, stating that Christ bore others' sins and obtained their FORGIVENESS.

See also ATONEMENT/EXPIATION IN THE NEW TESTAMENT; FORGIVENESS/PARDON; LIBERTY; RECONCILIATION; REDEEMER; REDEMPTION IN THE OLD TESTAMENT; REGENERATION; SALVATION IN THE NEW TESTAMENT; SALVATION IN THE OLD TESTAMENT; SIN.

—RICHARD B. VINSON

• **Redemption in the Old Testament.** Redemption is used in a variety of senses in the OT, both legal and theological. The next of kin was obligated by law to redeem or buy back any property of a deceased or impoverished kinsman (Lev 25:25) and, in the case of a brother, to raise up children by the widow (Deut 25:5). A classic example of the custom is that of BOAZ, who exercised his obligation as a kinsman by marrying RUTH and redeeming the parcel of land involved (Ruth 4:1-13). The redeemer (gô'ēl) was also obligated to accomplish blood revenge for a murdered kinsman and thus vindicate him.

A negligent owner of an ox that had gored a person to death could escape the death penalty by the payment of a "ransom . . . for the redemption of his life" (Exod 21:30). Also, a first-born child and the first-born of an unclean animal were legally redeemed or spared by a fixed "redemption price" (Num 18:15-16).

Yahweh was understood as the agent of redemption of the people of Israel. The EXODUS was described as the central saving act of "The Lord your God who brought you out of the land of Egypt and redeemed you out of the house of bondage" (Deut 13:5). Additionally, Yahweh was seen as redeeming the nation by doing for Israel other "great and terrible things" (2 Sam 7:23).

Numerous references are found in Deutero-Isaiah to the nation redeemed by "the Lord your Savior, and your Redeemer, the Mighty One of Jacob" (Isa 49:26). As Yahweh had delivered his people from Egypt so would he redeem them from exile in Babylon. The redemption of the individual is seen in numerous descriptions of Yahweh as the one who "will redeem me and set me free because of my enemies" (Ps 69:18) and who "will ransom my soul from the power of Sheol" (Ps 49:15).

Although limited in use, NT language relies upon the OT understanding of redemption as one means among many for describing the saving or redeeming nature of Jesus' death.

See also SALVATION IN THE OLD TESTAMENT

—BERNARD H. COCHRAN

• **Redemption of Land.** A social institution that served to maintain family control of ancestral property. Associated with other forms of redemption (Hebrew *gĕ'ullâ*), land redemption is legislated in Lev 25:25 to entail the repurchase by a kin member of property sold outside the family by a bankrupt relation. Ruth 4:1-12 and Jer 32:6-15 depict land redemption as the initial purchase of land offered for sale by a relative, an indigent widow with no male heir in Ruth and a cousin of unstated economic circumstances in Jeremiah. By stabilizing property relations and protecting capital investments (e.g., terraced fields) this institution served the interests of the larger family association (*mišpāḥâ*). It is probable that the original seller retained some claim to the redeemed property that could be exercised when and if circumstances allowed.

See also LAND; VENGEANCE/AVENGER.

Bibliography. D. R. G. Beattie, "The Book of Ruth as Evidence for Israelite Legal Practice." *VT* 24 (1974): 251-67; J. M. Sasson, "The Issue of Ge'ullah in Ruth." *JSOT* 5 (1978): 52-64; R. de Vaux, *Ancient Israel*.

—DAVID C. HOPKINS

• **Reform of Josiah.** *See* HULDAH; JOSIAH

• **Refuge, Cities of.** Places of asylum for persons who committed involuntary manslaughter. Unlike some other cultures in the ancient Near East, there was no asylum available for those guilty of premeditated murder in ancient Israel. The person who accidentally killed another, however, was provided a place of safety from the "avenger of blood"; since it was the practice that the nearest male relative took the duty of avenging his relative's death by killing the slayer.

In the laws of the Hebrew Bible there are three basic texts dealing with the cities of refuge: Exod 21:12-14; Num 35:9-34; and Deut 19:1-13 (cf. 4:41-43). Outside the legal texts, Josh 20 and 1 Chr 6:57-60 are also of central importance. Other texts that reflect this ancient institution include 2 Sam 3:30; 14:1-33; 1 Kgs 2:5; and possibly Ps 27.

Critical study, following the lead of J. Wellhausen, has posited Exod 21:12-14 as the oldest legislation on the subject, in which the place of asylum appears to be an altar, presumably that of a local sanctuary. There is no mention here of any cities of refuge as such. The law of Deut 19:1-13, with its humanitarian concern to establish easily accessible places of asylum for the manslayer, and to keep murderers from enjoying immunity in them, has been dated to the time of King Josiah's reforms and the elimination of local sanctuaries. In Deut 4:41-43 Moses set apart three cities of refuge in Transjordan: Bezer, Ramoth, and Golan. This is fully in accordance with the stipulations in Deuteronomy and Numbers which call for at least six cities of refuge: three in Transjordan, three in the land of Canaan, and provision for three additional cities should Israel enlarge its borders. The specific aim is to insure that the means of justice are readily available to everyone "lest the avenger of blood . . . overtake him, because the way is long" (Deut 19:6). The concern here is the availability of justice, lest the innocent offender die because of the inaccessibility of a nearby city of refuge. Deut 19, however, says nothing as to the precise designation of the three or six cities that are to be established in Cisjordan, nor does it speak of a release at the death of the high priest, the enforced incarceration of the slayer, or of the cities being levitical cities. These latter details are spelled out in Num 35:9-34, which has been generally seen to be the latest stage in the development of the concept of asylum in ancient Israel.

M. Greenberg has challenged the ordering of the three primary legal texts in such a simplistic evolutionary pattern, arguing persuasively that "the city of refuge as conceived in Numbers is the necessary adjunct to, rather than a replacement of, the local altars" (p. 130). In the ancient world, shedding an innocent person's blood, even unintentionally, involved bloodguilt. When the Deuteronomic law allows the "avenger of blood" to kill the slayer on the way to the city of refuge, the community itself is held responsible for the death of the slayer, who did not deserve to die, because of its failure to make the city of refuge accessible (Deut 19:10). The avenger, however, is not regarded as a murderer because the slayer is not guiltless. The most striking legal text expressing this objectivity of bloodguilt—that is, its occurrence even without criminal intent—is the law of Exod 21:23-32 concerning the homicidal ox. The animal itself is regarded as bloodguilty and must be stoned to death.

Bloodshed itself was considered polluting, involving the slayer, as well as the victim's family and even the city of the slain. This bloodguilt must be purged away, either by the death of the slayer or by the death of one considered righteous in a religious sense. In short, taking life imposes a guilt that cannot be expiated by any means short of death. No purificatory sacrifice was sufficient in ancient Israel, as was the case in Greece. Only another human life could expiate the guilt of accidental slaying. The sole person whose religious-cultic importance might endow his death with expiatory value for the people at large was the high priest.

J. Milgrom has argued that the cities of refuge constitute an ancient institution whose variations reflect the progressive changes in the priestly understanding of holiness that is associated with altars in ancient Israel, the *sancta contagion,* to protect the criminal elements in Israelite society. In this view, the early priestly belief that altars could protect the slayer because of their inherent properties of holiness was abandoned in order to protect the altar from the contamination that would result from such contact with criminal elements. The social need persisted, however, with the result that the asylum altar (Exod 21:13-14) was abandoned in favor of asylum cities. The date advanced for this change is the time of Solomon, who desired to enhance his own power over the competing social authority of the clan (cf. 1 Kgs 2:5).

Another recent theory is that of D. Benjamin who holds that the deuteronomic legislation has its roots in an older urban tradition which was centered in the cities of Shechem, Gibeon, Shiloh, and Hebron. In his view, this tradition stressed the importance of cities being centers of justice in accordance with the values of the older clan ideology. The echoes of this older form of Yahwism is the deuteronomic legislation in Deut 19. The original intent of this institution would have been to limit the power of the Canaanite kings vis-à-vis the authority of the clan, as well as to insure that peace would be maintained among the cities of this early Yahwistic league.

It is not surprising to see the cities of refuge as a symbol in the NT understanding of the salvation provided by the atoning death of Jesus. Just as the high priest's death expiates the bloodguilt of the person who has fled to a city of refuge, so does the death of Jesus atone for our sins (Rom 5:9; cf. also Heb 7:15; John 6:34).

See also SANCTUARY; VENGEANCE/AVENGER.

Bibliography. A. Auld, "Cities of Refuge in Israelite Tradition," *JSOT* 10 (1978): 26-39; D. Benjamin, *Deuteronomy and City Life*; P. Budd, *Numbers*; T. Butler, *Joshua*; F. Frick, *The City in the OT*; M. Greenberg, "The Biblical Conception of Asylum," *JBL* 78 (1959): 125-32; H. McKeating, "The Development of the Law on Homicide in Ancient Israel," *VT* 25 (1975): 46-68; J. Milgrom, "Sancta Contagion and Altar/City Asylum," *VTSup* (1980): 278-310.

—DUANE L. CHRISTENSEN

• **Regeneration.** "Regeneration" is the literal translation of a Gk. word used only twice in the NT. It is used in Titus 3:5 in reference to God's SALVATION of all believers "by the washing of regeneration." In Matt 19:28 it refers to the consummation of God's purpose in a "new world" ("renewal of all things," NIV). Other expressions which carry the same meaning are "begotten again" and "born again" or "born from above" (John 3:3, 7).

In the OT the prophets spoke both of a time of national renewal in the future when God would gather his scattered people from distant lands and cleanse the people from their sins (Ezek 36:25-28, 37) and a time of individual renewal when God would make a new COVENANT by writing his laws in peoples' minds and on their hearts (Jer 31:31; Hos 6:1-3).

In the Hellenistic world regeneration was a term used by the Stoic philosophers in referring to the cosmic restoration of the world after its destruction by fire. The Jewish writers Philo and Josephus used the term respectively of the restoration of the world after the flood (*On Moses* 2, 65) and after the Exile (*Ant* 11.3.9). Regeneration was used of restoration or return to life in various MYSTERY RELIGIONS such as Osiris and Mythra.

The NT writers make clear the universal need of a NEW BIRTH. John 3:3-21 is the classic passage and speaks of the need for an absolute transformation of life and the necessity of rebirth by means of the Holy Spirit. First Pet 1:23-25 clearly states that rebirth comes through the WORD OF GOD, compared to an imperishable seed.

Regeneration for the individual Christian means a new life of hope and inheritance of eternal salvation. Regeneration also means a new world or renewal of all things. The resurrection of Christ is the sign that the new world has already begun (cf. 1 Cor 15:23-28; Matt 27:51-53). This new world began at Pentecost (Acts 2:1-39) and culminates in the renewal or redemption of all of God's creation (Rom 8:11-30).

NT writers speak about regeneration in various ways. The apostle Paul thinks in terms of the creation of a new nature (Eph 4:24; Col 3:10). This new creature is one who is "in Christ" and who has died in BAPTISM to the old life of sin (Rom 6:3-11). Indeed, in the early church, the concept of regeneration was inseparably related to baptism. This new creation is no longer conformed to this world (Rom 12:2), but is rather created in the image of God in true righteousness and holiness (Eph 4:22-24; Col 3:9-10).

Although Paul most often uses the imagery of creation and resurrection, he also uses the image of rebirth to describe one's entry into the Christian life. To the Corinthians he writes, "For I became your father in Christ Jesus through the gospel" (1 Cor 4:15); to the Galatians, "My little children, with whom I am again in travail until Christ be formed in you" (Gal 4:19); and concerning the slave Onesimus, "whose father I have become in my imprisonment" (Phlm 10).

The writers of the Gospel of John and of 1 John speak in terms of new birth from above or from God (John 3:3,

7; 1 John 2:29; 3:9; 4:7; 5:1, 4, 18). First John places much emphasis on the moral and ethical implications of rebirth. Indeed the writer asserts that "no one born of God commits sin; for God's nature abides in him, and he cannot sin because he is born of God" (1 John 3:9), and again "we know that anyone born of God does not sin, but he who was born of God keeps him, and the evil one does not touch him" (1 John 5:18). The same letter claims that God will forgive the sins of the Christian (1:9) and that Jesus Christ intercedes for us when we sin (2:1-2). But it is clear that Christians begotten of God are expected to live sinless lives, and the power to do so comes from the Spirit of God which is in us (4:4).

The writers of 1 Peter and James speak of being born anew and of being brought to life through God's word (1 Pet 1:23; Jas 1:18). For the writers of the NT, human beings do not contribute to the rebirth or regeneration. That is accomplished by God alone.

See also CONVERSION; ESCHATOLOGY IN THE NEW TESTAMENT; ESCHATOLOGY IN THE OLD TESTAMENT; HOLY SPIRIT; MYSTERY; MYSTERY RELIGIONS; NEW BIRTH; REDEMPTION IN THE NEW TESTAMENT; REDEMPTION IN THE OLD TESTAMENT; SALVATION IN THE NEW TESTAMENT; SALVATION IN THE OLD TESTAMENT.

—ROGER L. OMANSON

• **Rehoboam.** [ree'huh-boh"uhm] A name meaning "may the people expand"; SOLOMON's son by Naamah the Ammonite woman (1 Kgs 14:21). Rehoboam reigned as king of Judah (926–910 B.C.E.) immediately after the dissolution of the UNITED MONARCHY. The kingdom's breakup occurred after Solomon's death as the result of Rehoboam's actions.

Rehoboam's accession to the throne of JUDAH was without difficulty. More was necessary for him to become the king of the northern TRIBES; consent of the governed was probably a prerequisite. To achieve approval, Rehoboam proceeded to SHECHEM for coronation as king. Because of Solomon's oppressive policies, the elders of Israel requested that service to the king—building projects, forced labor and taxation—be lessened. When Rehoboam sought advice from the older men of the court, they advised him to be a servant of the people. The young men who had grown up with Rehoboam counseled him to begin his reign by asserting his power. Rehoboam followed the recommendation of his young companions. The repercussions were immediate. Ten of the tribes withdrew from the coronation ceremony, denying their allegiance. When Rehoboam sent Adoram, his taskmaster over forced labor, to deal with the revolt, the people stoned him to death. Rehoboam made a hasty retreat to JERUSALEM (1 Kgs 12:1-20). The prospective monarch was left with only Judah (and Benjamin?) for his kingdom. The rift caused by his arrogant action was never healed and the United Monarchy was no more (PLATES 12, 13).

Upon returning to Jerusalem, Rehoboam planned to attack the rebellious northern tribes and amassed his army, which was composed of Judahites and Benjaminites (1 Kgs 12:21). The campaign was halted by the intervention of Shemaiah, who declared that the division was of the Lord (1 Kgs 12:22-24).

The reign of Rehoboam was filled with IDOLATRY and abominations. High places, altars, and Asherim were erected. Cultic prostitutes were introduced into worship. The kingdom was worse than the Canaanite culture the Hebrews had replaced (1 Kgs 14:21-24).

According to 2 Chr 11:5-12, Rehoboam fortified sixteen cities. These cities were not for defense against the Northern Kingdom, since they were situated to defend against a southern or Egyptian invasion. Exactly when the cities were fortified is unknown. But SHISHAK (Sheshonq I) of Egypt attacked Judah about 918 B.C.E. The invader besieged Jerusalem and took away the treasures of the TEMPLE, the king's treasures, and everything else of value (1 Kgs 14:25-26; 2 Chr 12:2-9). Egyptian records of this campaign have been found at the Karnak temple in Upper Egypt and at MEGIDDO. The Karnak material contains a list of cities conquered in Judah, the Northern Kingdom, Philistia, Transjordan, and EDOM. The fragment of a stele found at Megiddo bears the name of Shishak. After the death of Shishak, Egypt seems to have lost interest in expansion to the north and into Judah.

During the remainder of his reign, civil war continued between Judah and Israel. When Rehoboam died, his son Abijam ascended to the throne of Judah (1 Kgs 14:29-31).

See also JEROBOAM I; JUDAH, KINGDOM OF; KINGSHIP; SHECHEM; SHISHAK; SOLOMON; UNITED MONARCHY.

Bibliography. J. Hayes and M. Miller, *Israelite and Judaean History*; H. B. MacLean, "Rehoboam," *IDB*.

—ROBERT A. STREET, JR.

• **Rehoboth.** [ri-hoh'both] A place southwest of BEERSHEBA.

1. In Gen 26, ISAAC is shown to have journeyed to Philistia during a time of famine and to have become rather wealthy there. The PHILISTINES had filled in wells that ABRAHAM's servants earlier had dug, but in the Valley of Gerar, Isaac "dug again" (v. 18) such wells, giving them the same names Abraham had used. Isaac dug three additional wells. Ownership of the first two caused contention, but the third, which Isaac named "Rehoboth" ("broad places"), caused no strife because "the Lord has made room for us, and we shall be fruitful in the land" (v. 22). The traditional location of this site is modern Ruheibeh, about nineteen miles southwest of Beersheba (PLATE 13).

2. A city in ASSYRIA called Rehoboth-Ir ("city of Rehoboth") is mentioned in Gen 10:11. It may have been a suburb or unfinished area of Nineveh.

3. In Gen 36:37 and in 1 Chr 1:48 the Edomite king "Shaul of Rehoboth on the Euphrates" is mentioned. The RSV "on the Euphrates" is literally "on the river." Since Shaul was an Edomite king, the reference "on the river" would mean a site, as yet unidentified, not in MESOPOTAMIA, but in EDOM.

See also ISAAC.

—KAREN RANDOLPH JOINES

• **Rejoicing.** *See* JOY

• **Release.** *See* FREEDOM; LIBERTY

• **Religion of Israel.** ISRAEL referred initially to the people covenantally bound to Yahweh at Sinai. Later, during the period of kingship, it designated a political as well as a religious entity. When the nation split, the North retained the name while the South chose to be called by the name of its principal tribe, Judah. The writers of the biblical materials, however, continued to use "Israel" to denote all of the people of God.

Some modern scholars use the term "Yahwism" to refer to the religion of Israel prior to the time of the Exile. It was characterized by monolatry (the worship of only one god while not denying the existence of other gods, cf. henotheism); a prophetic movement that articulated and criticized the people's faith and their religious practices; and a priesthood that was available throughout the country. Judaism, as distinct from "Yahwism," valued the TORAH, rejected human kingship, allocated greater authority to the priests, and believed in the existence of only one god—MONOTHEISM. A sense of universalism also characterized Judaism.

The Sinai Covenant (ca. 1290 B.C.E.) bound the Hebrew people via a suzerainty covenant to Yahweh, a deity perhaps earliest understood as a god of war who was manifested in fire and storm, but who became known supremely through divine activity in historical events. On the basis of deeds done for Israel (Exod 20:2), Yahweh offered the Hebrews COVENANT. Hearing the stipulations, in the form of absolute demands, they embraced the covenant (Exod 24) and obligated themselves to this god. Although those stipulations are now lost to us, they may have included the Decalogue (as in Exod 20; Deut 5), the Covenant Code (Exod 20:22–23:33), and the Holiness Code (Lev 17–26). From this point on Israel's leaders, particularly the prophets, understood Israel's history to be shaped by God (Yahweh) who revealed himself through the covenant.

The patriarchs (Gen 12–50) embody Israel's prehistory, a period that could not have been precisely known at the time of the literary formulation of the text because within the material are views of God's covenant and of history and justice that reflect later developments of thought. Archaeologists confirm the milieu but not the individuals. The narrative, therefore, records a precursor to historical reality that nonetheless cannot be summarily dismissed.

Similarly, the primeval history (Gen 1–11) does not record historical data; rather, it conveys faith's perception of Yahweh's relationship to the beginnings of both cosmos and humankind. Embedded are understandings about God, human beings, and the mutual responsibility of each. Both the primeval history and the patriarchal narratives are important because they introduce Yahweh's relationship to Israel.

The preexilic era (1290–598/7 B.C.E.) begins with Israel's entrance into CANAAN and the tribal confederacy, an autonomous collection of tribes loosely bound around the Tabernacle, the Ark of the Covenant, and Yahweh's kingship. Judges were empowered by Yahweh with the Spirit of God. Holy war was practiced by Israel, as it was by the surrounding nations.

HOLY WAR ceased with the first fully established monarchy, i.e., with David. Following David's kingdom building, SOLOMON erected the Jerusalem Temple. This structure, serviced by the threefold lineage priesthoods of AARON, LEVI, and ZADOK, increasingly dominated Israel's cultic life. Inevitably the emphasis moved from the earlier covenantal obligations to national allegiance.

During the divided monarchy (922–722/1 B.C.E. in Israel; 922–587/6 in Judah), the prophets, foreshadowed especially by NATHAN during David's reign, addressed a myriad of national and cultic issues. ELIJAH (ninth century) focused upon the separation of Yahwism and Baalism. The classical eighth-century prophets, AMOS and HOSEA in Israel emphasized social justice and covenant fidelity, respectively, while in Judah ISAIAH stressed faith in the holiness of Yahweh. MICAH, no less a proclaimer of judgment than his contemporaries, summarized and emphasized the teachings of his three prophetic peers (Mic 6:1-8).

JEREMIAH (seventh century) stressed covenantal obligation and proper motivation (Jer 31:31-34). Jeremiah's prophetic ministry was juxtaposed with the political-religious activity of King JOSIAH (640–609 B.C.E.). These were preceded by an aborted reform movement by HEZEKIAH (715–687 B.C.E.) and the deuteronomic reformation (initiated in 621 B.C.E.), which emphasized a recovery of Mosaic covenantal thought and centralizing sacrificial worship in the Temple.

In the preexilic period, a struggle ensued between zealous Yahwists and Baalists. This religious and cultural struggle significantly influenced Yahwism-Judaism, especially in terms of how God was to be understood and worshiped, and even with regard to Yahwism-Judaism's aniconic concerns.

Tragedy befell Judah in 598/7 B.C.E. when Babylonia conquered Jerusalem, initiating the Babylonian EXILE (598/7–539 B.C.E.). During this period EZEKIEL and Deutero-Isaiah (Isa 40–55) spoke, with the latter responsible for the first explicit literary statement of monotheism (cf. Isa 44:6) and the haunting servant poems (Isa 42:1-4; 49:1-6; 50:4-11; 52:13-53:12) as the explanation of the way Yahweh would triumph over evil through his servant, Israel (Isa 49:3). During the Exile the SYNAGOGUE emerged and literature flourished; most of the Torah, the Deuteronomic history, and presumably the words of the preexilic prophets were recorded. The Torah's development permits the affirmation that the seed of Judaism had emerged.

Persia's conquest of Babylon (539 B.C.E.) concluded the Exile, and some captives returned to Judah, albeit under Persian rule. Under Persian domination HAGGAI and ZECHARIAH supervised the rebuilding of the Temple (520–515 B.C.E.), and NEHEMIAH was appointed governor of Judah. Under Nehemiah's leadership the walls of Jerusalem were repaired. Around 400 B.C.E. (or perhaps some decades earlier) the scribe EZRA came to Jerusalem and attempted to focus all of life around the Torah.

The domination of ALEXANDER the Great (d. 323 B.C.E.) and his successors was terminated with the Maccabean Revolt (Temple purification, 165 B.C.E.). Judaism's development was marked by diversity. The Psalter was formulated alongside the WISDOM LITERATURE. Often conflicting thought patterns emerged, such as the struggle between particularism (ESTHER) and universalism (RUTH and JONAH) and the inherent conflict between angelology and demonology. Ultimately apocalypticism emerged, remaining a viable movement until roughly 200 C.E. Apocalypticism gave hope to a persecuted community through cryptic symbolism and imagery and precipitated renewed emphasis upon a messianism no longer restricted to a person but including the renewal of nature, the rejuvenation of humanity, the resurrection of the faithful, and the restoration of elements traditionally at enmity into peaceful coexistence.

What it meant to be a Jew became increasingly important as the people scattered. God's universal concern was accepted, and the gift of Torah was acknowledged as ubiquitous for all people.

Israel was scarcely a millennium removed from its Sinaitic experience as the canonical period closed, but light years removed in terms of its relationship to God, humankind, and the world. Israel's religion is truly a rich tapestry, the beginning of which we can hardly discern, the conclusion of which continually pulls us onward.

See also FAITH AND FAITHLESSNESS; GOD; THEOLOGY OF THE OLD TESTAMENT.

Bibliography. F. Eakin, Jr., *The Religion and Culture of*

Israel; G. Fohrer, *History of Israelite Religion,* trans. D. Green; W. Harrelson, *From Fertility Cult to Worship*; Y. Kaufmann, *The Religion of Israel,* trans. and abridged M. Greenberg; H.-J. Kraus, *Worship in Israel*; G. E. Mendenhall, *Law and Covenant in Israel and the Ancient Near East*; J. Muilenburg, "The History of the Religion of Israel," *IB*; J. Pedersen, *Israel: Its Life and Culture*; H. Ringgren, *Israelite Religion*; H. H. Rowley, *Worship in Ancient Israel*; Th. Vriezen, *The Religion of Ancient Israel.*

—FRANK E. EAKIN, JR.

• **Religions of the Ancient Near East.** The religions of the ancient Near East were many and varied. Each one is worth the kind of serious study which would indicate its special character and place in the history of ideas. For the purposes of this dictionary, however, it will be necessary to focus upon those three great religious systems, the Egyptian, Assyro-Babylonian, and Canaanite, which had the greatest potential for impact on the religion of Israel. The approach is phenomenological rather than comparative, and emphasizes major deities, mythology and cult, although it must be recognized that a religion cannot be understood adequately without a knowledge of its intimate relationship with every aspect of personal and national existence.

Egyptian Religion. The main sources for a study of the religion of Egypt are the texts on the walls of temples, mortuary temples, pyramids and tombs, along with the coffin texts and the papyrus copies of mortuary texts, magic spells, omens, instructions, hymns, prayers, and rituals. The texts do not give a complete or comprehensive picture of religious practice in any one period; consequently, a history of Egyptian religion cannot be written. However, certain religious developments can be traced in the history of Egypt, and continuing synchronic studies hopefully will clarify religious belief and practice in the different historical periods.

1. The gods. A distinguishing characteristic of Egyptian religion was change amid permanence. Major cult centers, such as Memphis, Heliopolis, Heracleopolis, and Thebes were dominant during different periods with the consequent favoring of their cults, gods, and mythologies. The old was preserved, adapted, or changed in light of new political and social realities. Similar deities were often associated or identified with each other; many gods could be venerated as the creator god, and in the course of history there were several gods of the sun or moon. It may be bewildering to the contemporary reader to read several myths all purporting to explain how the world was created, but syncretism and a variety of explanations for divine reality characterized Egyptian religion from the beginning.

Deities often rose to prominence because of political factors. The earliest mortuary texts feature the god Ptah of Memphis, along with Osiris, Seth, and Horus. Soon, in the Fifth and Sixth Dynasties, the sun god, Re, of Heliopolis, achieved a position of prominence. By the time of the Eleventh Dynasty the political situation had changed and Amon, originally associated with Heliopolis, was championed at Thebes and became the most powerful deity. Thoth, the moon god, was associated with the city of Hermopolis. Contacts with other lands, such as Libya, Nubia, and Syria, resulted in some acceptance of foreign cults. In the period following the expulsion of the Hyksos some of the main deities of Syria enjoyed considerable popularity among the Egyptian laity, especially BAAL, Anath, Resheph, Qadesh, and Astarte. This syncretism reflected both Egypt's status as a growing international power and its traditional spirit of toleration. The later Greco-Roman periods saw similar adaptations as well as the creation of new cults.

The Egyptians believed that they experienced the divine in a limitless number of ways, and thus they worshipped an unlimited number of deities, each of whom was an expression of some aspect of spiritual experience. There were primordial gods, cosmic gods, and gods related to a specific place, territory, or phenomenon. The characteristic posture of the Egyptians in most periods of history toward the wide variety of theological speculation and cultic practice was acceptance. This fact places the reform of AKHENATON in the first half of the fourteenth century B.C.E. in sharper focus. Akhenaton tried to enforce the sole worship of the Aton, the sun disc. He tried to expunge the mention of Amon-Re of Thebes from all monuments. His monotheistic movement was highlighted by his construction of a new capital at a virgin site, AMARNA. There was a new flowering of art (realism), literature, and music. The Hymn to the Aton praises the sun disc as the universal god and giver of all beneficence. But the Amarna revolution was so out of character for the Egyptian experience that it lapsed soon after Akhenaton's death.

2. Mythology. One of the most important mythological themes concerned cosmogony and theogony. According to one tradition the god Atum of Heliopolis arose out of Nun, the primordial deep, and standing on the primeval hillock produced Shu, god of air, and his spouse, Tefnut, goddess of moisture, either by spitting or by onanism. These deities produced Geb, the earth, and Nut, the sky, who in turn produced the third generation, Osiris, god of the underworld and cultivation, his spouse, Isis, the throne, Seth, brother of Osiris and god of the desert and of foreign countries, and Nephthys. These nine deities are referred to as the Ennead or corporation. Born of Osiris and Isis was Horus, with whom the king was identified, this theogony serving as a genealogy for the reigning monarch.

According to the Memphite theology the creator god was Ptah. This theology apparently was developed to explain the rise of the city of Memphis to importance. It is said of Ptah that he spoke the gods into existence. Another tradition claims Re as the creator god who created his children by sputtering them forth (or alternately by onanism).

The myth of Osiris played a major role in Egyptian religion, especially in the rites for the dead. Osiris was god of earth and cultivation, but also of the realm of the dead. According to the story Seth, god of desert and heat, murdered Osiris. Osiris was drowned, and later was chopped into pieces, but his consort, Isis, succeeded in finding all the pieces, and after revivifying the body, conceived Horus. When Horus claimed the throne of his father, Seth violently opposed him. However, the gods, after much confusion and delay, ruled in favor of Horus.

This ancient myth, in its various versions, was employed to explain and justify dynastic succession. The king, who had been Horus, became Osiris upon his death, and his son and successor became Horus in his stead. The dead king still had existence as god of the underworld, and thus continued to rule an important realm. As early as the Pyramid Texts the deceased king was worshipped as Osiris.

3. The cult. The worship life, or cult, of the Egyptians is known only in part. The temple cult, or official religion, was the domain of the priests. In one of the daily rituals of the official cult, the priests would recite the myth, com-

plete with magic spells, of the defeat of the dragon, Apophis. The sun god, Re, made a nightly journey through the underworld ruled by Apophis. By magical means Apophis was defeated each night so that Re could rise each morning. In the ritual the priests were to announce Re's victory four times, and by extension the victory over all of Re's enemies, domestic and foreign, was achieved. The directions for the spell specified that the spell was to be recited over Apophis drawn on a sheet of papyrus and placed in a box, the dragon being tied and put in the fire each day.

Another ritual of the official cult described the daily care of the image of the god, Amon-Re of Thebes. The details of the elaborate ritual included the burning of incense, the breaking of the seal on the door and the opening of the shrine, the washing and clothing of the image, the proper feeding of the god, appropriate prayers and spells recited at each stage of the ritual.

While such rituals were observed and carried out only by approved cultic personnel, the public could participate in the various festivals and public processions of the divine images in which dramatic presentation of mythological themes played a role. Also the individual worshipper could visit the sacred precincts, such as those of Amon-Re at Thebes, for private worship.

More is known about personal piety outside the temple than about the official cult. Domestic altars featured Thoth, the messenger god identified in later times with Hermes. The gods were worshipped in homes by means of prayers, hymns, and offerings. Worshippers could contribute to the well-being of deceased family members and of royalty by offering gifts of food and drink on their behalf.

There was a preoccupation with death and with magical practices to insure a shared life with Osiris after death. Magic pervaded all of life. Although it was typically believed that one was born to fulfil a certain destiny, it was equally strongly held that one could change that destiny through magical practices. In the period of the New Kingdom, the *Book of Going Forth by Day* (*The Book of the Dead*), containing a large number of spells and hymns consisting of secret, esoteric knowledge, was placed in coffins to guarantee safe passage to life in the next world. The *Book of Going Forth by Day* was derived from the Pyramid Texts and Coffin Texts, texts which contained spells to guarantee safe passage of the king, and later of nobility, to the West. In the New Kingdom it was believed that all who could afford a copy of the book could have access to the same guarantee to life formerly reserved by royalty. The *Book of the Going Forth by Day* consists largely of spells to be recited by the deceased in which he indicates his knowledge of the names of the forty-two deities of the judgment court, and thus his control over their decisions, and his knowledge of spells to protect himself from everything harmful, from snakebite to dying again. The most famous passage in the book is the chapter containing the "negative confession" and the portrayal of the heart of the deceased perfectly balancing the feather of truth, Ma'at. The negative confession, which provides a partial picture of the social law, allowed the deceased to plead innocent to all charges of dereliction or deliberate sin with regard to gods, men, and animals. The important point is the belief that the possession of the knowledge of such spells and magical knowledge could guarantee a life of bliss in the hereafter.

Countless magical spells were used to protect the living. One myth related the successful attempt of Isis to learn the hidden name of the sun god, Re, and thus enhance her own power. She formed a serpent from thc dust of the ground, and when Re walked forth to survey all he had created, the serpent bit him. Isis, along with all other deities, came to try by their magic spells to ease Re's suffering. Finally she asked for Re's hidden name, reminding him that one whose real name was pronounced would live. Using the revealed name, Isis recited a spell to counteract the poison. On the papyrus spaces are left for the inclusion of the name of a person who has been bitten by a snake, and the spell was then used by that person as a charm against snakebite. According to the directions for using the spell, the spell could be written on a piece of linen and placed at the throat of one bitten, or the words of the spell could be dissolved in a liquid and drunk by the sufferer.

There were charms and spells to provide protection for sleeping children, to promote healing of diseases and wounds, to avert the power of magic practiced against them by enemies. The famous Execration Texts consisted of curses written on pottery bowls or on figurines representing foreign foes. The words would be read and the bowls and figurines would be smashed to "release" the curses which were believed to represent an irresistible force.

A study of Egyptian life and religion suggests a picture of change in the context of permanence, the capacity to adapt the new in such a way as to preserve the traditional, and a toleration for alternate views and different religious systems.

Canaanite Religion. The persistent use of the term "Canaanite religion" implies a consistency of religious belief and practice by the peoples living in Syria-Palestine during the final two millennia B.C.E. which the data will not support. The cults of many deities adored by the indigenous populations waxed and waned along with Egyptian, Mesopotamian, Hittite, and Hurrian gods. No doubt the cult practiced at any one cult center had its own unique characteristics while sharing many essential traits in common with other sacred places. Scholars do not agree on what constituted Canaanite religion or on whether it is even possible to speak of such.

Sources for the religions of the Mediterranean littoral come from Egypt, ancient Israel, middle Mesopotamia, Syria-Palestine, and North Africa, sources which are epigraphic and artifactual. The Execration Texts from Egypt (nineteenth century B.C.E.) contain curses against enemies in Syria-Palestine whose theophoric names include such gods as Horon and Hadad. The Amarna Texts (fourteenth century B.C.E.) mention several gods and goddesses of Canaan and make reference to religious rites. The main literary source until more recent times was the Hebrew Bible with its many references to the gods and goddesses of the land of Canaan along with some description of their cults. From much later times Philo of Alexandria and Philo Byblius recorded contemporary understandings of the ancient religion.

Today the most extensive source for Canaanite religion has been provided by the excavations at UGARIT (Ras Shamra). Beginning in 1929 continuing excavations have brought to light artifactual and epigraphic evidence of the religious practices of the population of Ugarit and contiguous areas. The documents show considerable religious syncretism, due no doubt to Ugarit's favorable position bisecting the main east-west and north-south trade routes and to the hegemony of foreign powers, especially Egypt and the Hittites.

1. The gods. The names of gods and goddesses are mentioned in all the main genres of materials from Ugarit, including myths, legends, letters, and cultic texts such as

offering lists. The most important source for identifying and understanding the relative importance of the deities are the god lists in several versions. The myths and legends are valuable for providing the stories about some of the main gods.

The head of the Ugaritic pantheon was EL, whose titles included "father of years," "king," "builder of creatures," and whose symbol was the bull. El is consistently placed first in the god lists, and in the myths in which he appears, El retains his preeminent position. In the Ugaritic texts El is far removed from the other gods, being located at the edge of the universe "at the source of the two deeps," in control of the ultimate destiny of the world but not directly involved with it. El's consort was Asherah, the "mother of the gods," a goddess who is named often in the Hebrew Bible and whose symbol there is the wooden pole or grove of trees.

The god lists feature prominently the god Dagan, a god of ancient vintage and venerated in the Old Babylonian period in the Mari region. He is called the father of Baal and one of the temples excavated at Ugarit was dedicated to him. Dagan has no role to play in any of the myths thus far known at Ugarit.

The most vigorous pair of deities were Baal and his consort/sister, Anath. Baal (Hadad) was the god of fertility, lord of the thunderstorm and rain, and giver of life to the land. Anath was the goddess of love and war, passionate and warlike in all her behavior.

Baal's two chief enemies in the myths were Yam, sea, and Mot, death. Yam, representing the primordial deep, the watery chaos, demanded supremacy over Baal, but Baal defeated Yam in a savage encounter and thus was elevated to the head of the divine assembly. In the episode with Mot, Mot won mastery over Baal temporarily, with Baal descending to the netherworld, thus ending fertility on earth and placing all life in jeopardy. But Baal came back to life and Mot's victory was not an everlasting one.

Other deities included are Resheph, god of disease and of healing, Shapash, the sun goddess, Yarih, the moon god, and Shachar and Shalim, the dawn and dusk and representing Venus at dawn and at sundown. Altogether the names of almost 200 deities worshipped at Ugarit are known, including gods of several surrounding cultures. The cosmopolitan character of Ugarit made the presence of foreign cults inevitable and acceptable.

The iconographic evidence for the study of Ugaritic deities is not as extensive as one could wish. Several icons in metal or clay portray gods and goddesses in typical poses, although most cannot be identified precisely. Several "mother goddess" figurines suggest their use in rites promoting conception and childbirth. In several scenes worshippers are depicted standing before a god and offering a gift, the god seated on a throne and wearing a horned crown. The goddess Qadesh is represented standing on the back of a lion, the animal sacred to her, flanked by the Egyptian god Min and the god Resheph. The clearest iconographic representation is of Baal, portrayed on a stone plaque as the god of the storm, wearing the horned crown appropriate for deity and grasping in his left hand the thunderbolt of forked lightning.

2. Mythology. Among the most treasured finds in the ruins of Ugarit were the clay tablets containing several myths and legends written in alphabetic cuneiform. Although the tablets were written within the last two centuries of Ugarit's existence, they present evidence of beliefs and of "theology" which are much older.

The most important of the myths is presented in the Baal cycle, a collection of texts and fragments featuring the challenges to Baal and his rise to power. Due to the fragmentary state of some of the texts, the precise story line is not known. The purpose of the text may have been to explain and justify the elevation of Baal to a place of leadership among the gods. Some scholars believe that the text is the spoken part of an annual ritual connected with a New Year festival and the resurrection of Baal. However, the myth and ritual viewpoint is not accepted by all scholars, and indeed the Baal cycle itself gives no indication of ritual use, such as stage directions.

In the Baal cycle Baal was confronted by two main adversaries, Yam and Mot. Yam, the god of sea and a son of El, demanded of El that Baal be made his servant. El acquiesced, the assembly of gods hung their heads in dismay, and a situation of chaos reigned. Baal presented himself to the assembly as their champion, much as Marduk did in *Enuma elish,* and armed with two special weapons fashioned by the craftsman god, Kothar wa-Hasis, he defeated Yam and returned order and stability to the world. As a consequence Baal was permitted a house (temple) like the other gods, thus signalling his growing importance at Ugarit. Some have speculated that the myth served to explain and justify the political success or dominance of Baal-worshippers, causing the traditional gods like El to assume a less prominent role.

The second enemy of Baal was Mot, god of the underworld, whose domain Baal entered voluntarily though with fear. Baal's descent to the netherworld is described as entering into Mot's massive gullet and being swallowed. At the news of Baal's descent, El came down from his throne and practiced funerary rites, putting dust of mourning on his head, making incisions on chest, shoulder and back (imitative magic), and bewailing Baal's death. Anath, Baal's consort, took her revenge on the bragging Mot, grinding him up and scattering his remains on the fields as fertilizer. She then found Baal, and after his resuscitation, life and fertility returned to the world. Given the story line it is easy to see why many scholars have identified Baal as one of the dying and rising gods and have viewed the Baal cycle as a ritual text used to reclaim fertility for the earth at the end of the dry season.

Another mythological text may be entitled Shachar and Shalim, or The Birth of Dawn and Dusk. The text is incomplete and the ultimate purpose of the myth can only be surmised. However, this is the one mythological text which includes ritual rubrics, showing clearly that the text was intended to be used in the cult. El appears in full vigor, like a young god, and sires the two beautiful gods by two women. But Dawn and Dusk, because of their insatiable appetites, have to go to the desert for an extended period of time, indicated in the text as seven or eight years. There the text breaks off, leaving the end of the story and its purpose unknown.

The last mythological text to be mentioned here is Nikkal and the Kosharot which relates the marriage of Yarih, god of the moon, and Nikkal. Yarih refused to consider any other marriage partner and paid a substantial dowry of silver, gold, and lapis lazuli to her father. The Kosharot, the "swallows," patronesses of love and domesticity, are invoked for their aid and the marriage is finalized. It is likely that the text of this myth was used as a song at weddings.

3. The cult. The nature of the cult at Ugarit, official or private, is little understood. If the various myths are interpreted in accord with the myth-ritual pattern and related to

the seasonal cycle, then something of the content and form of the official cult can be formulated. Materials which can be interpreted as hymns and prayers are rare. One fragmentary text, *RST* 24.252, which begins with a description of gods and goddesses feasting, concludes with a passage which may be interpreted as a prayer: "O Rpi' of earth, may your strength, your protection . . . (be) in the midst of Ugarit for as long as the days of Shapash and Yarih and be as pleasant as the years of El."

More is known about cult personnel and sacrifices. Lists of grants to various personnel mention as many as a dozen guilds of priests (*khnm*). The chief priest was called *rb khnm,* while other cultic personnel bore the titles *qdshm* and *nqdm*. No doubt the king was the chief cultic official by virtue of his office, although he delegated most of his daily priestly responsibilities to the priestly guilds. Since the arts, sciences, and commerce usually came under the control of the temple, the various artisans, scribes, and secretaries may have had priestly status.

Sacrifices and offerings were mainly gifts in kind. The technical terms for some of the offerings are familiar from the Hebrew Bible: *ṯ'*, gift, *shrp,* burnt offering, *shlmm,* peace offering (?), *ḏbḥ,* sacrifice, and *ndr,* vow. While such terms are paralleled in Hebrew, it would be hazardous to suggest that the Israelite religion simply borrowed cultic forms and practices or that analogous terms in the two religious traditions had the same content. While resemblances are significant, substantial differences in motive and actual practice should receive the emphasis. However, there is no doubt that many Israelites throughout the course of OT history adopted forms of Canaanite religion such as is in evidence in the Ugaritic materials and that various Canaanite beliefs and practices were integrated with Yahwism, so much so that it is difficult to describe an original Yahwism.

Mesopotamian Religion. The earliest people in Mesopotamia known from the literature were the Sumerians, a people with a nonsemitic language whose pantheon consisted of deities representative of the basic forms of reality and power, such as sky, wind, earth, sea, mountains, and the subterranean world. The myths explained the relationships of the deities to each other, their variations in power and status, how they created and supervised the world, and how they related to humankind. The functions and powers of the deities seem to reflect political, economic, and social conditions peculiar to the different cities and regions. The semitic peoples who came to power toward the beginning of the second millennium B.C.E. adopted and adapted much of the Sumerian religious reality, especially gods, myths, and rituals.

The sources of knowledge of Mesopotamian religions are of every conceivable kind: myths, legends, prayers, hymns, rituals, omens, offering lists, and even economic texts which give insight into temple supply and maintenance.

1. The gods. The Babylonians and Assyrians had a pantheon consisting of several hundred deities, each representing or controlling a natural phenomenon such as storm, disease, and fertility, or a city or state, or a cosmic reality such as sun, moon, stars and constellations.

Among the first rank of deities shared by Mesopotamian peoples were Anu, god of the heavens and father of the gods, Enlil, the storm-god, and Ea, god of wisdom and lord of rivers and lakes. Included also was Ishtar, goddess of love and war, who was associated with Venus, the morning and evening star. Prominent in all periods were Sin, god of the moon whose main cult centers were Ur and Haran, and Shamash, the sun god and god of justice whose center was Sippar.

The chief god of Babylon was Marduk, a god of the thunderstorm, whose rise to prominence is reflected in *Enuma elish.* His consort was Sarpanitum, and his son was Nabu, the god of the scribes known in the Bible as Nebo.

The main god of Assyria was Assur, who bore the name of the city, or vice-versa. He seems to have been a strictly local god whose periodic power on the international scene was celebrated by making him the hero of such standard myths as *Enuma elish*.

The deities of the underworld were Nergal and his consort, Ereshkigal. Their kingdom was the world of the dead, conceived of as a city with seven gates. It was called the "land of no return," a place of darkness and dust whose citizens ate clay and drank filthy water.

The myths from different periods reflect the shifting fortunes of the gods through history, fortunes which no doubt are to be related to the rise and fall of cities and kingdoms. It seems to have been a widely held belief that earthly realities reflected the events in the world of the gods.

2. Mythology. The myths of Mesopotamia gave people the scope to express their views about reality: about gods, fate or destiny, social and political structures, and about human life, its origin, significance, and destiny. The number of myths is so large that only a sampling can be given here.

A Babylonian work which treats such themes is *Enuma elish* ("when above"). This is a composition of seven tablets whose purpose was to explain or justify Marduk's rise to power in the divine assembly. The composition is best known for its sections on the creation of the world and the creation of humankind. The narrative begins with a theogony in which the gods were formed by the commingling of the waters of Apsu, god of fresh water, and of Tiamat, the ocean, the image of the forming of a delta thus serving the needs of the theogony. The young gods caused so much noise and confusion that Apsu determined to annihilate them. The plot was foiled by Ea who killed Apsu and took over his realm. Tiamat, taunted for her failure to prevent the death of her consort, assembled an army composed of fearsome beasts, sharp of tooth and unsparing of fang, and led by Kingu. Marduk arose as champion of the gods, and proving his might in the divine assembly by causing a constellation to appear and disappear, was given the right to determine destinies. Marduk defeated Tiamat, the primordial ocean, and divided her carcass like a shellfish, using half as sky and using the other half to form earth. The general picture is reminiscent of the account in Gen 1. In tablet five Marduk ordered the universe, establishing the stations of the constellations and regulating the phases of the moon. In tablet six there is an account of the creation of humankind. Because of the refusal of the young gods to do the canal upkeep and other heavy labor for the gods (as related in the Atrahasis myth), a "savage man," Lullu, was created to be the slave of the gods. The blood of Kingu, captain of Tiamat's defeated army, was mixed with clay to form mankind. The composition ends with the construction of a shrine appropriate for Marduk and with the recitation of his fifty names. *Enuma elish* was recited twice during the annual Akitu festival at the celebration of the New Year. This document provides much material important for comparative studies, especially on the topics of creation and anthropology.

The *Gilgamesh Epic* is a composition of eleven tablets composed of a number of previously independent myths.

The purpose of the epic was to treat the matter of human mortality and the attendant problem of the meaning of life. Gilgamesh, an ancient king of Uruk, became troubled when his friend, Enkidu, fell ill and died. Gilgamesh traveled to the edge of the world to interview Utnapishtim, the hero of the flood, whose faithfulness had gained him immortality, about the matter of death and life. Utnapishtim told the story of the great flood: of the building of the boat and the gathering of the animals, of the great storm and of the subsequent grounding of the boat on Mount Nisir. Utnapishtim had sent out the dove, the swallow and the raven to check on the receding waters, and when the raven did not return, Utnapishtim left the ark and offered sacrifices. The text reads: "The gods smelled the good fragrance, the gods like flies gathered about the one sacrificing." Enlil granted Utnapishtim and his wife immortality. But Gilgamesh learned that this was a unique case and thus not repeatable. Nevertheless he learns of a plant on the bed of the sea which could give the one eating it immortality. After gathering the plant, Gilgamesh paused at a pool to bathe and a serpent ate the plant and immediately shed its skin. The composition ends with Gilgamesh sadly bemoaning the futility of it all and turning his attention to the mundane task of governing Uruk. As with the *Enuma elish,* the *Gilgamesh Epic* is reminiscent of themes found in the Bible, especially of the FLOOD narrative in Gen 6–8. Comparative analysis shows not only the similarities but also, and more importantly, the unique and distinctive worldview of the biblical literature.

The Descent of Ishtar, developed from a Sumerian original, relates Ishtar's disastrous visit to the underworld, the kingdom of her sister, Ereshkigal. For an unknown reason, perhaps to demonstrate her power in the realm of the dead as she had almost everywhere else, Ishtar entered the seven gates to the infernal kingdom, leaving at each gate an item of apparel until she appeared bare before Ereshkigal. Namtar, Ereshkigal's vizier, caused sixty maladies to go forth against Ishtar so that she died. As a result earth's fertility ceased, and Ea created Asushunamir to go and revive Ishtar. He sprinkled on her the water of life and Ishtar returned to the land of the living. The significance of the myth and use(s) to which it may have been put remain unclear, although it has been commonly held that it was related to the Tammuz myth. Tammuz seems to have been a dying and rising god, spending half of each year in the netherworld as Ishtar's substitute. The Descent of Ishtar ends with a reference to "the day on which Tammuz comes up . . . let the dead ones rise and let them smell the incense."

3. The cult. It is commonly believed that myths such as the foregoing provided the base for dramatic presentations in rituals at various cultic centers, with royalty taking the roles of the gods and thus recreating some primeval event. The cult provided a means for human participation in the world of reality, either by becoming integrated into it or by ritual and imitative magic. The official cult was restricted to cult centers, and most rituals were not open to public participation because they centered around the cultic maintenance of the world, the care of the gods.

Private cult consisted of the worship of family gods, the offering of prayers and hymns. Many hymns seem to have been the property of temples, and extant prayers are attributed to royalty, but either could have been used by the individual worshipper. Incantation and magic formed a significant part of private religion; cultic specialists could aid a worshipper in praying the right prayer or using the appropriate spell. Pessimistic speculative literature arose to protest or lament the apparently unjust divine governance of the world.

The art or science of divination was extensively used in both the official and private cult. Cultic officials such as the *baru* and *ashipu* prophets were trained in the procedures which were believed to give success in human undertakings. It was believed that the will of the gods was communicated through both celestial and terrestrial phenomena. Thus the results of astronomical observation were basic for planning political and military strategies. Many types of divination were employed, such as hepatoscopy and hydromancy, to determine propitious times. As in Egypt Mesopotamians valued dreams as a medium of revelation and books of collections of dream interpretations were composed. It was believed not only that the will of the gods could be discovered by such means, but also that through incantation and the knowledge of omens people could gain some control over their destinies.

Conclusion. An adequate knowledge of the problems related to the history of the religion of Israel requires not only a knowledge of biblical data but also some understanding of the international religious context. The geographical position of ancient Israel between the dominant powers of Egypt and Mesopotamia, the political and economic dominance of these powers over Israel during most of its residence in the land, and the cultural and religious pluralism which characterized Israel from the beginning all require the contemporary student to take a thoughtful comparative approach to the study of ancient Israel's life and thought. Only a comparative approach can clarify the many religious elements which Israel borrowed from or held in common with other religious systems. In the same way only a comparative approach can highlight those beliefs and values which were distinctive of Yahwism.

See also RELIGION OF ISRAEL; RELIGIONS, HELLENISTIC AND ROMAN.

Bibliography. General. W. Beyerlin, ed., *Near Eastern Religious Texts Relating to the Old Testament*; T. H. Gaster, "Ancient Near Eastern Ritual Drama," *ER* and *Thespis*; J. B. Pritchard, ed., *ANET*; H. Ringgren, *Religions of the Ancient Near East*; J. Z. Smith, "Dying and Rising Gods," *ER*.

Egyptian. R. Anthes, "Egyptian Theology in the Third Millennium B.C.," *JNES* 18/3 (July 1959): 169-212; C. J. Bleeker, "The Religion of Ancient Egypt," *Historia Religionum,* ed. C. J. Bleeker and G. Widengren; J. H. Breasted, *Development of Religion and Thought in Ancient Egypt*; R. O. Faulkner, *The Ancient Egyptian Book of the Dead*; H. Frankfort, *Ancient Egyptian Religion*; M. Lichtheim, *Ancient Egyptian Literature: A Book of Readings*; S. Morenz, *Egyptian Religion*; D. B. Redford, "Egyptian Religion," *ER*.

Canaanite. M. D. Coogan, "Canaanite Religion: The Literature," *ER*; A. M. Cooper, "Canaanite Religion, an Overview," *ER*; J. C. L. Gibson, *Canaanite Myths and Legends*; J. Gray, *The Legacy of Canaan*; J. C. de Moor, "The Semitic Pantheon of Ugarit," *UF* 2 (1970): 187-228; H. Ringgren, "The Religion of Ancient Syria," *Historia Religionum*.

Mesopotamian. T. Jacobsen, "Mesopotamian Religions," *ER* and *The Treasures of Darkness*; W. G. Lambert and A. R. Millard, *Atrahasis: The Babylonian Story of the Flood*; W. H. Ph. Romer, "Religion of Ancient Mesopotamia," *Historia Religionum*; H. W. F. Saggs, *The Greatness that was Babylon*.

—THOMAS G. SMOTHERS

• **Religions, Hellenistic and Roman.** The Hellenistic period began when Alexander the Great crossed over into Anatolia in 334 B.C.E. with a force of 37,000 troops. That same year at Granicus he won the first in a series of victories against the Persians under Darius. Three years later, after partially dismantling and consolidating much of the former Persian Empire by planting military colonies and Greek cities throughout the conquered territories, Alexander decisively defeated Darius at Gaugamela, not far from the Tigris River. When Alexander died prematurely in Babylon in 323 B.C.E. at the age of thirty-three, he had set in motion forces which irrevocably changed the history and culture of the ancient world. The enormous size of the Macedonian Empire at the time of Alexander's death (extending from Macedonia south to Egypt and east to the Ganges) insured its fragmentation into a variety of larger and smaller Hellenistic kingdoms. Strictly speaking, the Hellenistic period ended with the defeat of Antony and Cleopatra at the battle of Actium in 31 B.C.E. by Octavian, for Egypt was the last independent Hellenistic kingdom to be annexed to Rome. Yet because Rome absorbed much of Greek culture, Hellenism lived on in the West within a Roman political and economic framework until the last Roman emperor, Romulus Augustulus was deposed in 476 C.E. Roman religion itself went through several periods of development and exerted no widespread influence on non-Romans despite the extent of Roman political influence and control. The Roman republic, which began with the expulsion of the last of seven kings in 509 B.C.E., disintegrated during the early first century B.C.E. Eventually Octavian seized control of the apparatus of government in 27 B.C.E., and adopting the name Augustus became the first in a series of emperors to reign during the two major periods of the empire, the Principate (27 B.C.E.–284 C.E.) and the Dominate (284–476 C.E.). A vital part of the political and cultural program of Augustus was the restoration and revitalization of Roman religion. In his obituary he claimed to have restored no less than eighty-two temples in the city of Rome.

Hellenistic Religions. From the initial appearance of the *polis* ("city-state") in the mid-eighth century B.C.E. to its transformation in the mid-fourth century B.C.E., it provided a relatively closed and protected environment for Greek political, cultural, and religious life. The Hellenistic period opened these city-states to outside influences in several ways. The soldiers who served in Alexander's expeditionary force (which varied in size from 35,000 to 50,000 Macedonians and Greeks), were separated from their homeland for many years, if not the rest of their lives. The Greek and Macedonian soldiers and colonists who populated the many military outposts and newly founded city-states in the midst of barbarian populations had to adapt traditional religious practices to new situations and influences. The various national groups of the Levant became increasingly mobile, creating diaspora groups of resident aliens throughout the ancient Mediterranean world, carrying their religious and national traditions with them. Further, the creation of a world united by Hellenistic language and culture initiated a period of syncretism in which features from Eastern and Western cultures mingled to produce new cultural syntheses.

Before the Hellenistic age, traditional Greek religious practices functioned on two quite different levels. The cults of each city-state were primarily concerned with civic benefits, while the domestic cults which were observed at the level of the extended family and clan focused on the survival and prosperity of those kinship groups. While the domestic cults survived for centuries with little change, the subjugation of the city-states first to federations and leagues and then to empires and kingdoms, produced profound changes in the focus and function of state cults. The reduced significance of the city-state was offset by a rising cosmopolitan consciousness and by religious developments capable of functioning at a national and even international level. Two important innovations reflecting these changed social and political conditions are the rise of benefactor and ruler cults and the popularity of the universal goddess Tyche ("fortune"). The attenuation of the security and protection afforded kinship groups by the city-states found compensation in an increasing growth in consciousness of the significance of the individual and his fate, i.e., in the quest for salvation in the afterlife.

(1) Domestic Cults. Prior to the formation of the *polis* by the mid-eighth century B.C.E., one of the more important contexts for Greek religious observance was such kinship groups as the family, clan, and tribe. The basic features of Greek domestic religion survived well into the Hellenistic and Roman periods and only disappeared in late antiquity as a result of Christian opposition to paganism. Domestic religion centered in the tomb and the hearth. The tomb held the remains of the divinized ancestors of the family, and the hearth with its perpetual flame served as the domestic altar upon which libations and offerings were made. Private religious rituals were used to mark various rites of passage, including formal acceptance and initiation into the family, clan, and tribe at various stages, and marriage and funeral customs.

(2) State Cults. The major cults of the Hellenistic city-states continued to be dominated by the traditional Olympian deities first presented as a pantheon of pan-Greek gods in the *Iliad* (ca. 750 B.C.E.) and *Odyssey* (ca. 700 B.C.E.), and first presented in terms of a complex genealogical organization in the *Theogony* of Hesiod (ca. 700 B.C.E.).

Temples, freestanding buildings devoted exclusively to the use of particular deities or groups of deities, arose in Greece during the eighth century B.C.E., probably in connection with the origin of the *polis*. The typical Greek temple was not a place for congregational assembly, but rather a house for the god whose statue and treasure were stored there. The two major exceptions to this general rule include the Telesterion ("hall of initiation") in the Eleusinian cult of Demeter, and the famous healing shrine of Asclepius at Epidaurus. Temples were also repositories for votive offerings made by grateful supplicants of the god (e.g., those healed might leave a clay model of the body part cured) or by those fulfilling vows (a victorious warrior might dedicate a shield or spear). Sacrifice was the central ritual of worship and the altar was located in the open air in front of the temple. In the Greek *thysia* (the slaughter and offering of a sacrificial victim), the god's portion of the slaughtered animal was burned on the altar (usually the inedible parts), while the worshippers consumed the rest in table fellowship with the deity (in archaic times a table could even be set for the deity). The Greeks also made bloodless offerings by placing them on tables (*trapezomata)* in temples for the disposition of the god.

The Greeks observed a great variety of religious festivals. In Athens nearly one-third of each year, or at least 120 of the lunar year of 354 days were festival days. The basic rituals for such festival days throughout the Greek world included a procession, a sacrifice, and a feast. Most state festivals arose in connection with agricultural rituals, though only dim memories of their origins survived into the Hellenistic period. Typical rituals observed on such festival days included dances, processions, hymns, and competitions (music, dance, theater, and athletics). Some festivals were celebrated in many city-states; one of the most widespread was the Thesmophoria in honor of Demeter, an ancient Greek earth goddess.

In spite of the independence of the Greek city-states, the Greeks consciously shared a common language, culture, and history. This unity in diversity was expressed in two international Panhellenic religious institutions, the Olympic games (celebrated every four years from 776 B.C.E. until they were closed down as pagan in 393 C.E.), and the oracle of Apollo at Delphi (consulted by people from every part of the Greek and then Roman world until 390 C.E. when it was shut down by the Christian emperor Theodosius).

(3) Hellenistic Ruler Cults. The Greek view that a mortal could become a god had at least two points of origin. First, Greek hero cults were based on the notion that deceased heads of families, founders of cities, and prominent military commanders became chthonic or earth deities upon death and received appropriate divine honors. Second, in Greek folklore there were stories about how some mortals had become divine after death, particularly Herakles, Dionysos, and Asclepius. Toward the end of the fourth century B.C.E. Euhemeros of Messene wrote a work entitled "Sacred Treatise," in which he proposed (on the basis of bogus archaeological evidence), that those now worshipped as gods throughout the Greek world had once been great kings who were posthumously accorded divine honors because of their great benefactions. This influential work provided an ideological basis for the Hellenistic conception of divine kingship.

Lysander, the Spartan general, was remembered as the first Greek to whom the cities (including Samos), in gratitude for their liberation from the Athenians, erected altars and made sacrifices to as though he were a god, ca. 403 B.C.E. (Plutarch, *Lysander* 18). Nearly a century later, in 308 B.C.E., the Athenians worshipped Demetrios Polyorketes and Antigonus Monophthalmos as gods. Alexander the Great had reportedly been acclaimed as "son of Zeus" at the oracle of Zeus Ammon in Libya and by three other oracles as well. In 324 B.C.E. Alexander demanded that the cities belonging to the League of Corinth recognize his divinity (cf. Plutarch, *Moralia* 804B). Coins minted in Alexandria in 325 B.C.E. depict Alexander as Herakles, the hero who achieved divinity through his labors. Within a few years of the death of Alexander, Lysimachus of Thrace and Ptolemy I of Egypt (two of his successors), minted coins depicting Alexander with the horns of Zeus-Ammon. After the death of Alexander in 323 B.C.E., most of his *Diadochoi* or "successors" who founded rival dynastic kingdoms of the disintegrated empire of Alexander, eventually legitimated their rule by founding cults which recognized them as divine. The major exception was the Antigonid Dynasty which continued to follow conservative Macedonian customs. The practice of paying divine honors to individual benefactors included the establishment of sacrifices, temples, priesthoods, festivals, processions, and cult epithets.

The figure of Alexander was of central significance for the development of Hellenistic and Roman ruler cults. Ptolemy I of Egypt intercepted the body of Alexander as it was being transported to Macedonia and placed the gold sarcophagus in a temple called the Sema in Alexandria (Diodorus Siculus 18.28.1-6), which became the major cult center for the worship of members of the Ptolemaic dynasty. In Egypt, ca. 280 B.C.E., Ptolemy II Philadelphus arranged the formal deification of his deceased parents, Ptolemy I and Berenice as "savior gods." Within a decade Ptolemy II arranged for the deification of himself and his wife Arsinoe II, and their worship centered at the shrine of Alexander the Great in Alexandria. Thereafter all of the Ptolemaic rulers were deified after their accession and accorded divine worship. This practice was continuous with the ancient Egyptian kingship ideology, which regarded the reigning pharaoh as son of Ammon, and as Horus incarnate, while deceased kings were regarded as Osiris, the god of the underworld. Yet unlike traditional Egyptian practices, in which the deceased king played no significant role in ritual, deceased Ptolemaic kings and queens continued to be worshipped as guardian deities of Egypt. After the reign of Ptolemy V Epiphanes (210-180 B.C.E.), Hellenistic kings frequently used the Greek epithet *epiphanes* ("[divine] manifestation"). The royal predication *theos epiphanes* ("god made manifest") suggested that the kings (and later the Roman emperors) were regarded as present in the world like one of the traditional gods.

(4) Religious Associations and Mystery Cults. Midway between the private religious practices of various kinship groups and the public cults of the city-states were the *thiasoi,* i.e., religious societies or fraternities. These voluntary associations worshipped a single patron deity, could be highly structured, were typically limited to either women or men, and were very popular during the Hellenistic period. The female worshippers of Dionysos (often designated Maenads or Bacchantes), for example, formed *thiasoi* which celebrated Dionysiac rites.

The mystery cults flourished in the Hellenistic and Roman periods because neither the existing domestic or state cults fully satisfied the spiritual needs which had surfaced in a radically changed world. Mystery cults (the term *mystes* means "initiant," hence *mysterion* means "initiatory ritual") were private associations (or *thiasoi)* which interested people could join voluntarily by undergoing a secret ritual of initiation. The purpose of this ritual experience was individual salvation, and initiants believed that they would be recipients of prosperity in this life and happiness in the afterlife. While some mystery cults were native to the Greek world and hence very ancient (e.g., the Eleusinian mysteries and the mysteries of Dionysos), many others were Hellenistic transformations of religious cults exported from the eastern part of the Mediterranean world and which flourished in the West (e.g., the mysteries of Isis, the mysteries Cybele and Attis, and Mithraism).

Roman Religion. The primary emphasis of Roman religion was *pax deorum* ("peace with the gods"), i.e., the necessity of maintaining a harmonious and mutually beneficial relationship with the gods and of restoring that relationship when and if it should be interrupted. During the period of the republic (509-27 B.C.E.) the *pax deorum* primarily functioned to ensure both the survival and prosperity of Rome itself. During the period of the empire (27 B.C.E. to 476 C.E.) the most significant function of the *pax deorum* was the support and protection of the emperor or princeps. Ancient Roman religion, like Greek religion, was chiefly concerned with religious ritual rather than with beliefs and behavior. At the core of Roman religious practice was the conviction that *pax deorum* could be maintained only if the members of the various priestly colleges saw to the exact and meticulous performance of the *ius divinum,* i.e., the laws created by the gods and governing the relationship between men and the gods.

The Romans were indebted in many ways to the more advanced cultures with which they came into contact in central Italy. From the Etruscans they learned the arts of divination, and much of Roman mythology was taken over from the Greeks with only minor adjustments. Native Roman deities tended to have lackluster personalities in comparison with their Greek counterparts. Thus, unlike the Greeks, the Romans were rarely concerned with the possibility of provoking the jealousy of the gods. Augustus, who inaugurated the imperial period in 27 B.C.E., carried through extensive religious reforms.

(1) State Cults. According to the Roman antiquarian Varro (116–27 B.C.E.), the Romans had no images of their gods until 170 years after the founding of the city in 753 B.C.E. (Augustine, *CivDei* 4.31). That coincides with the reign of L. Tarquinius Priscus (616–579 B.C.E.), who reportedly constructed a temple to Jupiter on the Capitol and had a clay statue of the god constructed (Livy 1.38.7; Pliny, *NatHist* 35.157). Archaic Roman religion, in addition to having no statues of the gods, had no temples and no theology, the gods were not associated in married pairs, and there were no stories of the adventures of the gods (mythology). There were three broad types of deities worshipped by the Romans: (a) The *autonomous* deities had fixed outlines, were separately worshipped, were originally without kinship or consorts, and lacked adventures and scandals, i.e., were without a mythology. The most prominent *autonomous* deity was the patron god of Rome, Jupiter Optimus Maximus (''best and greatest''). In adopting Greek myths, the Romans identified their own deities with the approximate Greek equivalents. The Greek Hades, god of the underworld, was identified with either Dis or Orcus, Aphrodite with Diana, Athena with Minerva, Hera with Juno, Hestia with Vesta, Mars with Ares, Demeter with Ceres, and so on. Some Roman deities were arranged in triads, like Jupiter, Juno, and Minerva, and Jupiter, Mars, and Quirinus, perhaps under Etruscan influence. The Romans, much more commonly than the Greeks, worshipped and dedicated temples to personified abstract qualities such as Fides (''reliability''), Concordia (''civil concord''), Spes (''public confidence''), and Libertas (''freedom''). (b) The *anonymous* deities consisted of unlimited numbers of secret supernatural beings who could both aid and impede the activities of Roman people, yet since they were unable to name them they could not control them. (c) Finally, the *indigitamenta,* i.e., lists of teams of highly specialized deities, primarily connected with agricultural and domestic activities.

Communication between the divine and human worlds in Roman religion was accomplished through *prayer, sacrifice,* and *divination.* (a) The Romans were very exacting in their prayers and meticulously phrased them like legal documents. They thought them invalid, for example, if they were not directed to the appropriate god or goddess, in a manner similar to an improperly addressed letter. They therefore added such concluding clauses as ''whether it be a god or goddess [who dwells here],'' or ''or whatever name you care to be called.'' The first deity addressed in all prayers and invocations was Janus (the god of beginnings), while the last was Vesta (her Greek counterpart Hestia was the first addressed in Greek prayers). (b) Like the Greeks, the Roman temples were dwellings for the images of the gods, and sacrifices were made in the open air in front of them. The priests covered their heads with their togas during the sacrifice, and the sacrificial meat was consumed by the priests and those on behalf of whom the sacrifice was made. The internal organs of the victim were routinely examined by *haruspices* (cf. below) to determine whether or not the sacrifice was acceptable. (c) Public divination was presided over by two priestly colleges and one body of Etruscan consultants. The *augures* were specialists in the observation and interpretation of the behavior of birds. The *quindecemviri sacris faciundis* (''fifteen supervisors of the celebration of sacrifices''), was a board originally consisting of two but was eventually expanded to fifteen members, who superintended the *Sibylline Oracles* (a collection of written oracles in existence by 367 B.C.E. and which were consulted during times of national emergency). Finally, the *haruspices* were Etruscan experts in liver divination or hepatoscopy. The Romans were quite concerned with the sighting of prodigies (unnatural occurrences or phenomena portending disaster), which they regarded as divine indications that the *pax deorum* had been ruptured. Prodigies could include such extraordinary things as a rain of stones or the birth of a two-headed animal. Following their sighting, prodigies had to be reported to and accepted by the Roman senate in order to be valid. Once accepted, prodigies had to be expiated in order that the *pax deorum* might be restored. Legitimate prodigies required diagnosis, and diagnoses were achieved by means of the three major types of divination mentioned above. The sighting and reporting of prodigies can be correlated with the experience of anxiety in response to natural disasters or in anticipation of military defeat. In 217 B.C.E., in the midst of Hannibal's invasion of central Italy during the Second Punic War (220-201 B.C.E.), e.g., Livy (22.1.8-20) records a long list of twenty-one prodigies which were reported.

The Roman religious calendar divided the days of each lunar year of 354 days into two groups, *dies fasti* (''propitious days''), on which it was thought appropriate to conduct certain kinds of public business, and *dies nefasti* (''unpropitious days''), on which it was sacrilege to conduct certain kinds public business. *Fas* is law of divine origin, whereas *ius* is law created by men; *fas* is what the gods permit, *nefas* is what they forbid. There were 109 *nefasti* (all but two days falling on the odd-numbered days of each month; the exceptions were 24 February and 14 March), and 235 *fasti;* the remaining days had a mixed character and were partially propitious and partially unpropitious. In 46 B.C.E., the Julian solar calendar was introduced with 365¼ days with months of 30 and 31 days with an extra day intercalated every four years. Some Roman festivals were on fixed days (like the modern celebration of Christmas on 25 December), while other festivals were on moveable days (like modern observance of Easter).

There were, in addition to the two priestly colleges discussed above (the *augures* and the *quindecemviri),* two other important priestly colleges, the pontifical college and the Vestal Virgins. The pontifical college consisted eventually of sixteen members, headed by the pontifex maximus (Augustus assumed the office in 12 B.C.E.). The pontifex maximus appointed the *rex sacrorum* (''king of sacrifices'') and the three *flamines maiores* (''greater priests''), the *flamen Dialis* (''priest of Jupiter), the *flamen Martialis* (''priest of Mars''), and the *flamen Quirinalis* (''priest of Quirinus''). There were, in addition, twelve *flamines minores* (''lesser priests''). The Vestal Virgins, a group of six priestesses who served for thirty years, superintended the hearth of Rome which was located in the circular Temple of Vesta, which contained no images.

(2) Domestic Cults. Every real or fictitious Roman kin-

ship group, i.e., the *curia* (''tribe''), *gens* (''clan''), and *familia* (''[extended] family'') practiced traditional religious observances. The two major types of household deities were the *Di Penates* (always in the plural), commonly regarded as protectors of the *penus* (''storeroom''), though this etymology is now disputed, and the *lar familiaris* (''Lar of the household''). The Lares were originally deities of the farmland who came to be identified with ghosts of the dead and protectors of the household. The *Di Manes* (spirits of the dead), often identified with the *Di Parentes* (ancestors of the family). The extended family in ancient Rome was presided over by the *Pater familias* (''father of the family''), the oldest living male ancestor. The *Pater familias* had extensive, even autocratic powers which were collectively designated as the *Patria Potestas* (''paternal authority''). He was chief priest of the domestic cult, guardian of the property of the family, and judge who was able to prosecute and even execute members of his family who were guilty of breeches of domestic rules and customs.

(3) Roman Army Religion and Mithraism. The religion of the Roman army was intended to identify individual soldiers and legions with the destiny of Rome, to maintain high morale, and to create a structure for the lives of soldiers in the field. Central to Roman army religion was the cult of standards. Each legion was numbered and had a golden eagle symbolizing Jupiter Optimus Maximus. At the center of the army camp was a sacred shrine called the *aedes,* where the standards were placed when not in use, together with images of the Roman deities and emperors.

Central to army life was the *sacramentum,* or sacred oath, which was recited upon enlistment and renewed every 3 January and on the anniversary of the accession of the emperor. During the period of the republic the oath was sworn to the commander, while during the empire it was sworn to the emperor. The religious calendar of the Romans (the *Feriale Duranum),* emphasized several special days including the emperor's birthday, the anniversary date of his accession, the day on which the oath of loyal was renewed annually (3 January), and the birthday of the eternal city of Rome (21 April).

The camp and fortress of the Roman army in the field was in effect a sacred enclosure which functioned as a microcosm of the city of Rome. In constructing the camp the *praetorium* (which contained the *aedes)* was first marked out, together with the main gate. The fortress walls were constructed of turf, logs, and stone, while the surrounding palisades were protected with a ditch twelve ft. wide and ten ft. deep. This virtually impregnable construction of a temporary camp was necessitated by Roman dependence on divination in order to receive divine approval before any military operation. If the signs were inauspicious, the entire army had to wait until there was divine approval for the impending operation. Large military victories (in which at least 5,000 of the enemy were killed) were celebrated in Rome by a triumph, a procession through the triumphal arch to the temple of Jupiter Capitolinus. The victorious general was dressed in gold and purple representing Jupiter himself. Under the empire the celebration focused on the emperor and the role of the victorious general was marginalized.

Mithras, the ancient Aryan god of light and truth, was one of the major deities of ancient Iran, conceived as an ally of the good god Ormuzd and enemy of the evil Ahriman. Though it may have derived a few features from Iranian religion, as a mystery cult Mithraism developed outside of Iran. Attested as early as 100 B.C.E., it was taken over by Roman legionaries by the middle of the first century B.C.E., and began to flourish toward the end of the first century C.E. Mithraism excluded women, and was a religion practiced by pirates, merchants, and slaves, but primarily by the soldiers of the Roman legions. Mithras was regarded as the ''unconquerable'' god, appropriate as the tutelary deity of warriors; his birth was celebrated on 25 December. Mithraic temples or Mithraeums were constructed below ground level as artificial caves in which one invariable feature was an icon of *Mithra Tauroctonus,* depicting Mithras slaying the bull (the *tauroctony*). Recent studies have suggested that the *tauroctony* is a star-map based on ancient astrological conceptions, possibly representing the constellations Perseus and Taurus. Mithraism had seven grades or ranks of initiation through which members could achieve: (a) Raven, (b) Bride, (c) Soldier, (d) Lion, (e) Persian, (f) Courier of the Sun, and (g) Father. These were apparently correlated with the planetary spheres. Mithraic worship services accommodated only a few dozen men (judging from the size of the extant Mithraeums), and concluded with a ritual feast. This, together their practice of ritual washing and anointing led some early Christians to regard Mithraism as dependent on Christianity (Justin, *1 Apol* 66).

(4) Ruler Cult. The official Roman view was that a reigning emperor was not a *deus* (''god'') during his lifetime. After his death he could be officially designated a *divus* (''mortal-become-god'') by the Roman senate. In 42 B.C.E. the senate, upon the recommendation of the triumvirs and the acclamation of the Roman people, passed a bill deifying Julius Caesar (Suetonius, *Divine Julius* 88). After 40 B.C.E., Octavian (the later Emperor Augustus) was designated *divi filius* (''son of [the] god''), i.e., son of the deified Julius. Hitherto the terms *deus* and *divus* had been synonymous and meant ''god.'' Thereafter *divus* took on the connotation ''man-become-god.'' After Augustus died on 17 September 14 C.E., the Senate designated him a *divus* (''god''), and his adopted son and successor Tiberius was in turn designated *divi filius* (''son of god''). During the first century C.E. five emperors and eight members of their families were posthumously deified. While the worship of deified emperors was never very widespread in the western Mediterranean, it was exceedingly popular in the Greek East, particularly in Asia Minor. Sacrificing to deified emperors who were associated with other Roman and Greek gods was occasionally used as a loyalty test for Christians who were denounced to the authorities (cf. Rev 13; Pliny, *Letters* 10.96). Christians who failed to cooperate were branded atheists and executed.

See also HELLENISTIC WORLD; MYSTERY RELIGIONS; ROMAN EMPIRE.

Bibliography. F. Altheim, *History of Roman Religion*; S. Angus, *The Mystery Religions: A Study of the Religious Background of Early Christianity*; A. H. Armstrong, ed., *Classical Mediterranean Spirituality: Egyptian, Greek, Roman*; H. I. Bell, *Cults and Creeds in Graeco-Roman Egypt*; F. Cumont, *The Mysteries of Mithra*; F. Cumont, *Oriental Religions in Roman Paganism*; J. Ferguson, *The Religions of the Roman Empire*; W. W. Fowler, *The Religious Experience of the Roman People from the Earliest Times to the Age of Augustus*; T. R. Glover, *The Conflict of Religions in the Early Roman Empire*; F. C. Grant, *Ancient Roman Religion*; F. C. Grant, *Hellenistic Religions: The Age of Syncretism*; R. M. Grant, *Gods and the One God*; W. K. C. Guthrie, *The Greeks and Their Gods*; J. Hinnels, *Mithraic Studies*; J. H. W. G. Liebeschuetz, *Continuity and Change in Roman Religion*; B. MacBain,

Prodigy and Expiation: A Study in Religion and Politics in Republican Rome; R. MacMullen, *Paganism in the Roman Empire*; R. Merkelbach, *Mithras*; A. D. Nock, *Conversion: The Old and the New in Religion from Alexander the Great to Augustine of Hippo*; R. M. Ogilvie, *The Romans and Their Gods in the Age of Augustus*; S. R. F. Price, *Rituals and Power: The Roman Imperial Cult in Asia Minor*; H. H. Scullard, *Festivals and Ceremonies of the Roman Republic*; L. R. Taylor, *The Divinity of the Roman Emperor*; M. J. Vermaseren, *Cybele and Attis: The Myth and the Cult*; A. Wardman, *Religion and Statecraft among the Romans*; R. E. Witt, *Isis in the Graeco-Roman World*.

—DAVID E. AUNE

• **Remarriage.** In the NT, the question of remarriage pertains to those who have lost the marriage partner, whether by death (1 Cor 7:8), DIVORCE (Mark 10:12), or abandonment (1 Cor 7:39). The question of the moral acceptability of remarriage was especially critical for women since they were most personally and economically vulnerable.

Paul reflected general acceptance of prevailing laws in recognizing that an abandoned woman could not remarry as long as her husband was alive (Rom 7:2). His death, however, made her free to remarry. Certainly the widowed were both morally and legally free to remarry (2 Cor 7:8). Even the divorced are now given such permission. They are, Paul says, "not bound" (1 Cor 7:15), indicating the non-binding character of a former contract. In every case, Paul seems to apply the general understandings that (1) remarriage is desirable unless one has the special gift for celibacy (1 Cor 7:7) and (2) Christian liberty is to prevail. He cautions those considering remarriage about the burdens of family life (1 Cor 7:25-35) but in no way regards it as sin (v. 28).

Jesus reflected the Jewish attitude that remarriage is acceptable (Mark 12:18-27). He pointed to the moral problematic of such unions, however, when adultery was involved (Matt 5:32; 19:3-12; Mark 10:11-12). The fact that he pointed to the reality of sin in no way amounted to a legal prohibition of either divorce or remarriage; it was a moral comment on the laxity with which people took marital commitments. Divorce was the man's prerogative under Jewish law and men were inclined to dismiss the wife for trivial reasons. Nor should his statements be taken as a general and absolute condemnation of all remarriages by the divorced as adulterous. He was apparently dealing with the case in which the man divorced his wife so he could marry a woman with whom he was already adulterous.

The sanction in the Pastorals against digamy (remarriage after death of partner) reflects ascetic thought that was foreign to Jesus and Paul and a complete departure from Jewish attitudes. Widows who considered remarriage were regarded as self-indulgent and evidencing spiritual death (1 Tim 5:6). That younger widows desired an active life was "wantonness against Christ" (v. 11).

"Violating an oath," or the morality of promise-keeping, was another reason for discouraging remarriage (1 Tim 5:12). Apparently, some widows had ill-advisedly vowed never to remarry either in the midst of intense grief or in order to be approved for support by the church as an indigent.

Moral negativism toward remarriage developed strongly in the second and third centuries C.E. as the church fell under the influence of pagan philosophies. Sex was regarded as morally defiling and remarriage was evidence of spiritual laxity. Celibacy was thus regarded as the superior way of life. By the beginning of the fourth century both clergy and widows were forbidden to remarry—a sad departure from NT teachings.

See also DIVORCE; MARRIAGE IN THE NEW TESTAMENT; MARRIAGE IN THE OLD TESTAMENT.

—PAUL D. SIMMONS

• **Remnant.** One of the more significant features of Israel's future hope was the concept of the remnant. Five basic terms are used in the OT to refer to the remnant. All are translated as "remnant," but each has a slightly different nuance. The remnant was first of all the *remainder,* what was left over after judgment. The second term emphasized these who had *escaped* from judgment. A third usage described the *residue* left at the bottom of a cup or a bowl after eating or drinking. The fourth pointed to those who had *survived* a crisis or calamity. Finally, one root pointed to the *scraps* that had been left over by a potter or carpenter when something had been made. All of these meanings are wrapped up in the total OT concept of the remnant.

The remnant concept appears to have had its foundation early in the OT. NOAH and his family were the remnant that survived the great FLOOD (Gen 7:21-23). Lot and his family were the initial remnant (his wife was later eliminated) from the catastrophic judgment at SODOM (Gen 19:29-30). Perhaps much more specific to Israel's remnant hope was Yahweh's statement to ELIJAH in the days of AHAB that a faithful remnant of seven thousand still existed in Israel (1 Kgs 19:18).

However, it was not until the time of the eighth century prophets that the concept was sharpened and focused to Israel's future. AMOS assumed that his hearers had such a hope, misguided though it was. While he attacked their self-assurance, he also held out a genuine hope for a remnant, based upon God's grace (Amos 5:2-3; 6:9-10; 5:4, 6, 14-15). ISAIAH focused the remnant hope even more, pointing out that the remnant would survive by God's grace, not by Israel's own righteousness (Isa 1:9; 10:20-23). MICAH also underscored this hope, calling the remnant God's flock (Mic 2:12).

JEREMIAH added to this hope his vision of a new covenant (Jer 31:31-34). The survivors of judgment would, by God's grace, enjoy a new relationship with their God. This prophetic vision saw a remnant that survived both through and by judgment in order to carry on God's kingdom on earth.

Those who came back from the Exile saw themselves as the surviving remnant. However, experience quickly revealed that they were no better than their ancestors. By the time of Nehemiah, hope seemed to be wholly gone (Neh 1:3). Those who had returned carried the same old burdens of sin and rebellion, of faithlessness and disobedience. It was clear that the hope of the remnant had been deferred. However, it had not been abandoned.

In the NT the old remnant hope took on a new dimension in JESUS and his followers. PAUL saw the early Christians as being God's new remnant, the survivors of Israel (Rom 11:1, 5). For the NT, the remnant are God's new people.

Paul's discussion of the idea of a remnant occurs, however, in the context of his argument that God has not rejected the people of Israel (Rom 9–11). His conclusion is to the contrary: the remnant concept yields a hope that God will surely effect Israel's deliverance (Rom 11:26).

See also ELECTION; SALVATION IN THE OLD TESTAMENT; SALVATION IN THE NEW TESTAMENT.

—ROBERT L. CATE

• **Repentance.** Repentance, involving feeling guilty and remorseful over wrongdoing as well as taking steps to rectify matters, is best exemplified in the OT in texts describing cultic processes. Lev 6:1-7 and Num 5:6-8 outline the actions necessary to restore harmonious relationships disrupted by deliberate SIN (also involved in both texts is the sinner's having sworn falsely in the name of God regarding innocence). The following factors are noted: (1) The wrongdoer has consciously and knowingly committed a wrong but then without having been caught or convicted becomes remorseful or repentant (*'āšam*). The verb *'āšam* in Lev 6:4 and Num 5:5 and elsewhere, when used without an object, should not be translated as "is guilty" or "becomes guilty" but as "feels guilty" or "is remorseful/repentant" (cf. esp. Lev 4:13, 22, 27; 5:5, 17). (2) Internal conviction is then followed by public confession (Num 5:7). Although not mentioned in Lev 6:1–7, confession is presupposed in subsequent actions (see also Lev 16:21). Sins committed "unwittingly" or inadvertently did not require public confession (Lev 4). (3) RESTITUTION to the victim, involving restoration plus twenty percent, is required (Lev 6:4-5; Num 5:7). Finally, (4) if the wrongdoer had sworn innocence in the name of God thus making the deity an accomplice to the wrongdoing, EXPIATION involved a reparation offering (*'āšām*; "guilt offering" in most translations) to the deity.

These procedures undergird a number of theological/psychological/sociological considerations. (1) Repentance, feeling guilty or remorseful, must be the product of a stricken CONSCIENCE, not the result of being caught or legally condemned by a court. The latter may produce admission but not confession, since true repentance/confession is voluntary. (2) Repentance involves not merely internal disposition and confession but overt action to make amends in the form of restitution. Repentance involves action to restore conditions prior to the wrongdoing. (3) Although deliberate sins were considered unforgivable in priestly theology (Num 15:30-31), repentance and confession had the effect of rendering deliberate sin into the category of inadvertent sin. (4) Restoration of the proper human to human relationship—in the form of restitution to the victim—takes precedence over and is mandatory for the rectification of the human-divine relationship. (5) Cultic expiatory ritual was not efficacious in and of itself but required and manifested psychological conviction, ethical responsibility, and genuine pastoral care. In this regard, priestly teachings on repentance should in no way be considered inferior to other elements in scripture.

The prophets appear to have presupposed the priestly-ritual views on repentance and to have utilized these in their preaching, in a limited way (cf. Isa 22:14; 27:8-9; Hos 5:15; 10:2; 14:1-2). In addition, however, the prophets called upon their contemporaries "to repent" or "to return" (*šûb*) to Yahweh. The verb *šûb* and its noun derivatives, however, had a very broad range of meaning including "to turn from/to" and "to return" but also "to remain, stay still" (for the latter, cf. Isa 7:3; 30:15). The prophets did not use the verb *'āšam* in their calls to the people to change their behavior or to return to a particular stance probably because the term was too specific in meaning and too tied to actions initiated by the penitent. *šûb* lent itself to use in the arena of both politics and religion and to speaking of attitudes as well as wrongdoings. For the eighth-century prophets, to "return" to Yahweh could be equivalent to resubmitting to the Assyrian treaty sworn with an oath in the name of Yahweh. Here the emphasis would have been on the element of admission rather than confession of wrongdoing. Also the prophets could call for a return to Yahweh, after the punishment had already occurred and the consequences of wrongdoing had been suffered.

The OT also speaks of God and humans repenting (*nāḥam*) in the sense of "changing one's mind" or "regretting" some action or decision one had made (e.g., Gen 6:6; Amos 7:3, 6) in order to pursue some other course.

In postexilic times and early Judaism, the use of the term *šûb* and its derivatives prevailed over other expressions. Perhaps one of the reasons was the fact that *šûb* was used to speak of the "great return" from exile. The call to "return" after the punishment (Deut 4:30; 30:10; 1 Kgs 8:48) could thus be described as repentance and could still preserve the idea that confession and contrition were essential for forgiveness (Lev 26:40-41).

Not only repentance but also repentance plus the need to make restitution where injury and damage were involved were stressed in later Judaism. The Rabbinic teaching on the subject is best summed up in the Mishnaic tractate on the DAY OF ATONEMENT: "Repentance effects atonement for lesser transgressions against both negative and positive commands in the Law; while for graver transgressions it suspends punishment until the Day of Atonement comes and effects atonement. If a man said, 'I will sin and repent, and sin again and repent,' he will be given no chance to repent. . . . For transgressions that are between men and God the Day of Atonement effects atonement, but for transgressions that are between a man and his fellow the Day of Atonement effects atonement only if he has appeased his fellow" (*Yoma* 8:8-9).

The NT, at least in places, shares with the OT and Judaism not only the necessity of repentance—remorseful contrition—but also the integral relationship, in the human community, between repentance and restitution (cf. Matt 5:23-24; Luke 19:1-10).

Both JOHN THE BAPTIST and JESUS encountered their audiences with calls to repentance. John not only proclaimed the need for repentance (Matt 3:7-10; Luke 3:7-9) but also preached and administered a BAPTISM of repentance for the forgiveness of sin (Mark 1:4; Luke 3:3; Matt 3:11). Jesus' proclamation announcing the arrival of the kingdom stressed the demand for repentance (Mark 1:15; Matt 4:17). For both John and Jesus, the call to repentance was closely associated with the proclamation of the coming eschatological age, the arrival of the kingdom. To this extent, repentance ("turning") was almost equivalent to CONVERSION, just as later in the church, repentance became especially associated with conversion and baptism.

Repentance could also signify change of attitude or moral change (2 Cor 7:9-10; 12:21; Rom 2:4) or even reaffirmation of the faith (Rev 2:5, 16, 21-22; 3:3, 19). Heb 6:4-6, at least theoretically, denied the right of second repentance after becoming a believer and denying the faith.

See also ATONEMENT/EXPIATION IN THE OLD TESTAMENT; GUILT; RESTITUTION; THEOLOGY OF THE OLD TESTAMENT.

Bibliography. W. Barclay, *Turning to God*; E. Würthwein and J. Behm, "νοέω, κτλ.," *TDNT*; G. Bertram, "στρέφω, κτλ.," *TDNT*; R. Gordis, "Some Hitherto Unrecognized Meanings of the Verb *shub*," *JBL* 52 (1933): 153–62; W. L. Holladay, *The Root* šûbh *in the OT*; J. Milgrom, "The Priestly Doctrine of Repentance," *RB* 82 (1975): 186-205; J. J. Petuchowski, "The Concept of 'Teshuva' in the Bible and Talmud," *Judm* 17 (1968): 175–85; S. Schechter, *Some Aspects of Rabbinic Theology*.

—JOHN H. HAYES

• **Repetition.** *See* LITERATURE, BIBLE AS; POETRY

• **Rephaim.** *See* GIANT

• **Rest.** The cessation of physical or spiritual activity or movement and the renewal that follows (Ruth 1:9; Jer 45:3; Mark 6:31). Animals, objects and abstract concepts, as well as people, may come to rest (Gen 8:4; Exod 10:14; Isa 11:2). The seventh day following six days of work offers such rest to God, people and domestic animals (Exod 23:12; 31:17; Deut 5:14). Other feast days are called days of rest (Lev 16:31) and on the SABBATICAL YEAR (every seventh) agricultural land was to rest by being left fallow (Lev 25:4ff., 26:34ff.).

Beyond this common usage, rest carried a symbolic meaning of PEACE, well-being, and security coming after some disruption in the life of a person, a nation, or the world. Thus, the people Israel found rest in their land after the wilderness wanderings, the conquest, or the resolution of some internal conflict (Josh 1:13; Judg 3:11; 2 Chr 15:15). A successful king enjoyed rest from his enemies (1 Kgs 5:4; 2 Chr 14:6). After warfare, the whole world rested (Isa 14:7; Zech 1:11). Peace of mind, security and contentment associated with salvation were represented as rest (Ps 116:7; Isa 30:15; Matt 11:28-30).

The rest of God or of heaven represents the divine presence that God's people were invited to enter (Ps 132:8, 14; Isa 66:1) unless they forfeited it through unbelief (Ps 95:11). According to the NT letter to the Hebrews, such rest is available through faith in Jesus Christ (Heb 4:1-11). Rev 14:13 speaks of a final heavenly rest awaiting God's faithful saints at the end.

See also PEACE; SABBATH; SABBATICAL YEAR.

—NIELS-ERIK A. ANDREASEN

• **Restitution.** A system of restoring to the dispossessed any property or rights that have been stolen, unjustly seized, or lost through neglect. Restitution played an important part in ancient legal systems dealing with theft and losses through neglect. For example, the old Babylonian law code of HAMMURABI (ca. 1700 B.C.E.) required thirty-fold restitution of property stolen from the temple or the state and ten-fold restitution in the case of theft from a private citizen. Bond laws required a two-fold restitution of property lost while on deposit. Failure to pay would draw a death sentence upon the guilty.

The corresponding OT laws stipulated a more reasonable level of restitution and were more sensitive to the circumstances surrounding losses. In general, stolen property had to be restored two-fold (Exod 22:4,7). However, in the case of theft perpetrated for profit rather than to ameliorate an immediate need, four- or five-fold restitution was required (Exod 22:1; 2 Sam 12:6). Bond laws also required two-fold restitution (Exod 22:9), but were lenient in cases of inadvertent losses, in some instances even wholly exempting from liability the one who held property in trust (Exod 22:10-15).

In addition to legal requirements of restitution, we find practices of restoring to the dispossessed the property or rights that had been lost unfairly, unjustly, or through failure (Gen 20:7; 1 Sam 12:3; 1 Kgs 20:34; Neh 5:11).

Restitution also belonged to the Israelite religious practices. The sabbatical year (every seventh) restored freedom to slaves (Exod 21:1-6), and the jubilee year (every fiftieth) restored lost property to its original owner (Lev 25:28). When an individual caused losses to the temple or to a private citizen, a guilt offering, also called a sacrifice of reparation, was enjoined. After the sacrifice, the guilty party was to make restitution for the losses incurred, with the addition of one-fifth their value (Lev 5:14-16; 6:1-7; Num 5:5-10).

See also FORGIVENESS/PARDON; LAW IN THE OLD TESTAMENT.

—NIELS-ERIK A. ANDREASEN

• **Resurrection in the New Testament.** Four approaches to resurrection appear in the NT: (1) The restoring of life to those who have died (such events are properly seen as resuscitations); (2) the general expectation among progressive Jews for a general resurrection of the dead at the close of the age; (3) the resurrection of Jesus as an event with eschatological significance; and (4) the hoped-for resurrection of the dead among the early Christians.

Resuscitations. Twice in the Synoptics (Mark 5:21-43 and par.; Luke 7:11ff.) and once in John (11:38ff.) Jesus restores life to a corpse. In these instances, as well as in the case of the message of Jesus to the disciples of John the Baptist (Matt 11:2ff. and par.), the language is that used by Paul in 1 Corinthians to describe the resurrection of Jesus and the hoped-for resurrection of believers. Clearly, however, the restoring of life to Jairus' daughter, the widow's son, and Lazarus is of a different type than the transforming effect of Jesus being raised by the power of God (cf. also the account of Peter raising Tabitha: Acts 9:36-43). Revived corpses are returned to a previous state while the risen Christ manifests the glory of God in a transformed body. Acts 20:7-12 implies Paul also effected a resuscitation but the language noted above is absent.

Resurrection and NT Judaism. The resurrection of Jesus and the subsequent Christian hope for resurrection develops against the backdrop of resurrection in Judaism in the first century. The Passion week controversy between Jesus and the Sadducees (Mark 12:18-27 and par.) and Paul's appearance before the council in Jerusalem (Acts 23:1-10), however, are ample evidence that first-century Jews were not agreed on the issue of resurrection from the dead. Those who accepted resurrection did so as an eschatological hope, i.e., an event which would occur at the intersection of time and eternity. A belief in general resurrection of the dead emerged in postexilic times and seems to have reached maturity in the apocalyptic writings of Daniel and similar texts from Hellenistic Judaism. The nature of a general resurrection of the dead carried a dual emphasis of vindication of the righteous and judgment of the wicked.

The Resurrection of Jesus. While the evangelists offer various descriptions of the resurrection of Jesus, only Paul attempts an explanation. Paul summarizes the resurrection as a mystery to be probed rather than as a problem to be solved. While Paul is unable to define the event, he does indicate that resurrection is a transformation. The antitheses developed in 1 Cor 15:42-50 lay equal stress on the continuity and the discontinuity between the ''physical body'' and ''spiritual body.'' Paul contends that something of the image of the physical endures through the resurrection transformation although he emphatically states ''flesh and blood cannot inherit the kingdom of God'' (1 Cor 15:50). Significantly, the same point is implied through the evangelists' descriptions of resurrection appearances. The risen one is the crucified one, yet somehow different (Matt 28:9ff.; Luke 24:13ff.; John 20–21).

The resurrection of Jesus differs in one crucial respect from the prevalent first-century Jewish expectation for a general resurrection of the dead. Jewish expectation was for a corporate resurrection—all the righteous would be vindicated—which would occur at the end of time. The resurrection of Jesus does not diminish the eschatological flavor of resurrection hope but it does relocate the hope radically. The resurrection of Jesus—that which happens to one person—is confessed as an event in history which has eschatological significance. Thus, not only is the resurrection of Jesus a transformation of Jesus, it is also the immediate cause for the transformation of a resurrection hope from a corporate, eschatological event to a personal, historical event with corporate, eschatological implications.

The Resurrection of Believers. The resurrection of Jesus becomes the focus of NT faith. The resurrection is the confirmation of sonship (Rom 1:4) and, as such, the cause for hope for Christians (e.g., cf. 1 Cor 15:12-19 and 1 Pet 1:3ff.). Once again Paul influences the major metaphors of faith in resurrection which awaits those who confess faith in Christ. The risen one is "the first fruits" (1 Cor 15:23) to be followed by the faithful, eschatologically; he is the "guarantee of our inheritance" (Eph 1:14) until such a time as Christians come of age; he is "the first born from the dead" (Col 1:18), implying that the faithful will join him in birth after death. While the main emphasis is on a future resurrection, NT Christians are challenged to live in the present on the basis of the resurrection hope (e.g., Rom 6:1-14; 1 Pet 1:13-21).

The Jewish expectation of a general resurrection with a twofold significance (cf. above) translates into a similar concept of resurrection for Christians, but not completely. Some passages juxtapose resurrection and judgment (e.g., John 5:28-29; 2 Cor 5:10; Rev 20:5-6) while others (e.g., 1 Thess 4:16ff.) treat resurrection with no mention of judgment.

See also ASCENSION OF CHRIST; ETERNAL LIFE; IMMORTALITY; PHARISEES; RESURRECTION IN THE OLD TESTAMENT.

Bibliography. R. E. Brown, *The Virginal Conception and Bodily Resurrection of Jesus*; E. Jüngel, *Death: The Riddle and the Mystery*; G. E. Ladd, *I Believe in the Resurrection of Jesus*; A. Oepke, "ἀνίστημι, κτλ.," and "ἐγείρω, κτλ.," *TDNT*; N. Perrin, *The Resurrection According to Matthew, Mark, and Luke*; U. Wilckens, *Resurrection*.

—RICHARD F. WILSON

• Resurrection in the Old Testament. There is no doctrine of a general resurrection in the OT. The most advanced affirmation of a limited resurrection is found in Dan 12:1-3, a passage that should be understood in the context of late apocalypticism.

The author of DANIEL wrote at a time when the Jews under Hasmonean leadership were locked in a mortal struggle against their Seleucid persecutors. Salvation was expected, not through Judas Maccabeus, but through God and God's angel, Michael. The "time of trouble" (Dan 12:1) was to be over soon and God would then inaugurate a new age on earth.

God's JUSTICE demanded that the faithful martyrs who had fallen in the struggle be rewarded, and that the apostate Jews who had collaborated with the Seleucids be punished. This demand was to be met through a limited resurrection. Many of the righteous dead would awake from their tombs to take their place in God's new age. Many of the apostates would awake "to shame and everlasting contempt" (Dan 12:2). The author does not address the nature of the rewards and punishments, the destiny of the Israelite dead from earlier ages, or the fate of the gentile dead. He does, however, single out the wise leaders for special blessedness (v. 3).

The author of Isa 24–27 may already have proclaimed a limited resurrection. He announced that God "will swallow up death forever" (25:8), and that the righteous dead would rise (26:19). The wicked dead, however, are explicitly excluded (26:14).

The traditional OT idea was that the shades (not souls) of the dead go to an underworld called SHEOL while their bodies lie in the tomb. Sheol was a dismal place cut off from God (Pss 88; 94:17; 115:17), from which there was no return (2 Sam 12:23; Job 14:12). It was not a place of retribution either for the righteous who had died unrewarded or the wicked who had died unpunished. Resurrection on the other hand promised the divine justice beyond the grave for which JOB had longed (14:13-17). Resurrection offered also continued fellowship with God for which the psalmists yearned (Pss 16:9,16; 49:15; 73:23-26), but which Sheol denied.

The concept of resurrection did not have clear antecedents in the OT before the apocalyptic movement, although HOSEA (6:2) and EZEKIEL (37) had used the metaphor to refer to national restoration. There are two cases of translation (Gen 5:24; 2 Kgs 2:11), three temporary resuscitations of dead bodies (1 Kgs 17:17-24; 2 Kgs 4:32-35; 13:21), and one brief return of a shade from Sheol (1 Sam 28:11-19). These stories, however, reveal only that the ancient Israelites were concerned with the problem of transcending death.

The other religions of the Near East seem not to have influenced the OT doctrine of resurrection greatly. The Egyptians believed in life after death. Canaanite and Mesopotamian religions told of deities who traveled back and forth to the underworld. The Persians developed an advanced doctrine of resurrection and judgment. By the time of Isa 26 and Dan 12 such concepts were not alien to Jewish ears. Yet the content of the OT resurrection faith remains distinctly Israelite.

See also DEATH; ETERNAL LIFE; JUSTICE/JUDGMENT; RESURRECTION IN THE NEW TESTAMENT; SHEOL

Bibliography. W. Eichrodt, *Theology of the Old Testament*, G. Fohrer, *History of Israelite Religion;* D. S. Russell, *The Method and Message of Jewish Apocalyptic*.

—EMMETT W. HAMRICK

• Resurrection, Treatise on. Uniquely significant for the study of Gnostic teaching about the RESURRECTION is this eight page treatise, the fourth tractate of Codex I ("Jung") from the library of NAG HAMMADI. Presented in the form of a didactic letter written by an unnamed master in response to questions from a pupil, Rheginos, the treatise offers a view similar to that of Hymenaeus and Philetus combatted by the author of 2 Tim 2:18, i.e., "that the resurrection is past already." The text is written in the Subachmimic dialect of Coptic, the language of early Christian Egypt.

The Christian Gnostic author bases his teaching on convictions about the nature and work of the Savior, Jesus Christ. This savior preexisted as a "seed of Truth" (44.21-36), an "emanation" in the transcendent, divine Godhead (the "Pleroma"—46.35-38). He descended into this evil, corruptible "world" of "deficiency" (44.34-35; 47.5-6, 17-26; 48.13-16; 49.4-5) to complete two major tasks: the "swallowing up" of death (45.14-15), conferring IMMORTALITY on the elect, and the teaching of "Truth" or "knowledge" which grants eschatological "rest" (43.35–44.3). He did the former by taking on "flesh" (44.13-15), experiencing death (46.14-17), and "conquering" it through his divine nature as SON OF GOD (44.27-29). He raised and transformed himself into an immortal deity, and he destroyed his visible nature with his invisible, ascending back into the "Pleroma" (45.16-21). The savior's latter function of teaching the "truth" involved disseminating knowledge of human corruptibility and its final "solution" through his resurrection (43.34; 45.3-11).

The elect few must have "faith" in the reality of Christ's resurrection and their participation in it (45.14–46.13). Echoing the language of Pauline mysticism (45.24-28; cf. Rom 8:17; Eph. 2:5-6). The author claims these elect have already died, risen and ascended to heaven with Christ. Thus, one may "know" the inevitability of death and the certitude that, in Christ, it has already occurred (49.25-28). "Practice" and "exercise" cultivate the right mental attitude: elimination of doubt about the resurrection, avoidance of divisive opinion, correct understanding about salvation, assurance of being resurrected in the present.

At death there is an ascension (45.36-38) of an individual's inward, invisible "members," covered by a new, spiritual "flesh" (47.4-8). Discontinuity between earthly and resurrection bodies results from death and departure from visible bodily members and flesh. Continuity of identity is established by the inner, spiritual person. The appearance of ELIJAH and MOSES at the TRANSFIGURATION of Jesus provides the proof of this *post mortem* resurrected state (48.3-11). This is the "spiritual resurrection" that destroys the "psychic" and "fleshly" forms (45.39–46.2). This is part of the grand process of "Restoration" of the "Pleroma" Christ effects as the SON OF MAN (44.30-33).

The presence of distinctive Valentinian imagery has led most scholars to attribute the treatise to this school, though not to its founder. Further, the author's knowledge of the NT CANON, the centrality of discussion of the resurrection at that time, and the affinities of the treatise's thought with Middle Platonism and Late Stoicism all point to the late second century as the probable time of composition. The place of its writing is unknown.

See also GNOSTICISM; NAG HAMMADI.

Bibliography. B. Layton, *The Gnostic Treatise on Resurrection from Nag Hammadi*; M. Peel, "The Treatise on the Resurrection," *Nag Hammadi Codex I,* ed. H. W. Attridge and "The Treatise on the Resurrection," *The Nag Hammadi Library in English,* ed. J. M. Robinson.

—MALCOLM L. PEEL

• **Retaliation.** Exaction of restitution in kind for personal injury or wrong (the *lex talionis,* "law of retaliation"). Exod 21:23-25 provides the classic biblical formulation: ". . . life for life, eye for eye, tooth for tooth, hand for hand, foot for foot, burn for burn, wound for wound, stripe for stripe" (cf. Lev 24:18-21; Deut 19:19), and the general principle informs judgment-pronouncements scattered widely through the Bible (e.g., Gen 9:6; Exod 21:36; Isa 3:11; Ps 137:8; Matt 18:32-35; Rev 18:6). The *lex talionis* appears also in the Hammurabi Code (*Laws* 196-97, 200) from the late eighteenth century B.C.E.) and in the Middle Assyrian Laws (50-52, 55), possibly going back to the fifteenth century.

While obviously related to and sometimes used synonymously with vengeance, retaliation in the strict sense expects exact congruence between offense and restitution. Its measure for measure objectivity thus contrasts with the passion and righteous indignation associated with vengeance or revenge. However, it is moot whether, as often argued, the *lex talionis* was intended to restrain the excesses of blood revenge or vendetta; "life for life" was the principle also of the latter. Moreover, in prescribing the talion, Deut 19:21 is obliged to warn that "your eye shall not pity," as if enforcement had to contend with leniency rather than zeal.

In practice the *lex talionis* underwent considerable modification. The Jewish historian Josephus (*Ant* 4.280; ca. 100 C.E.) commented that in certain cases monetary compensation could be substituted, and the Talmud argued that its very strictness made the rule unworkable; for example, exaction of an eye or limb could cause loss of blood or loss of life, thus exceeding what the talion permits (*BQam* 83b-84a).

The counterprinciple of nonretaliation is expressed with less frequency in the Bible (Prov 25:21-22; Job 2:10; 31:29; Matt 5:38-42; Rom 12:17-21; 1 Pet 2:23), and these various examples do not all necessarily arise out of an identical ethic. The psalm concluding the Qumran *Manual of Discipline* includes the declaration that "I will not return anyone the recompense of evil [*gĕmûl ra'*]" (*1QS* 110:17-18), making clear that this is not out of regard for the evildoer but in confidence that punishment will come from God. This is possibly the rationale also for the citations, above, from Proverbs, Romans, and 1 Peter, while the Job and Matthew texts seem to commend nonretaliation as simply wise and inherently right, Jesus even representing nonretaliation as imitation of God (Matt 5:45, 48). Each of these sayings is nuanced, however, and interpretation depends heavily on attention to context.

See also LAW IN THE OLD TESTAMENT; VENGEANCE/AVENGER.

Bibliography. H. H. Cohen, "Talion," *EncJud*; D. Daube, "Lex Talionis," *Studies in Biblical Law*; K. Stendahl, "Hate, Nonretaliation, and Love: Coals of Fire," *Meanings*.

—BRUCE T. DAHLBERG

• **Retribution.** Deserved punishment for evil done, or conversely, reward for good done. The Bible speaks of retribution as taking place on both the human and the divine levels.

On the human level, it was an "evening of the score" between the offender and the offended, resulting in a sense of wholeness returned to the injured one. In earlier times, this was a family responsibility, since law was largely a matter of custom and was enforced by the family or clan. The injured party could carry out the punishment (Gen 4:23-24), but in most cases, it was done by one's nearest relative (Judg 8:18-21). To avenge oneself seemed to carry with it the danger of bloodguilt, probably because emotional involvement might lead to excessive punishment. For this reason, DAVID thanked ABIGAIL for blocking his revenge against NABAL (1 Sam 25:33). As long as punishment remained a family matter, it could not be very precise since it was limited only by the sense of self-control of the avenger, who could define anything done as just punishment (cf. the taunt song of Lamech, Gen 4:23-24).

True retribution came with the rise of the state, which became, theoretically at least, a neutral party between the antagonists, making a judgment as to guilt and innocence and determining the proper level of punishment. *Lex talionis,* the law of retaliation, an "eye for an eye, a tooth for a tooth, a hand for a hand, a foot for a foot. . ." (Exod 21:24), while sounding somewhat primitive to the modern ear, marks a distinct advance in the concept of proper punishment and presupposes the existence of a governing body (the state) to see to its enforcement. The rise of the state led to the gradual replacement of family-sponsored punishment with state-regulated penalties for crimes committed. Only the state could and would consistently carry out punishment of the nature and degree demanded by the law of retaliation.

When there was no relative to take one's side or when the state either failed to act correctly or was powerless to act, the doctrine of divine retribution came to the forefront. Israel's ideas concerning divine retribution made certain basic assumptions: the Lord was the God of Israel, related to Israel by covenant, and Israel was the people of God—they were family; God was just and would see that justice was done; since in preexilic Israel there was virtually no concept of life after death with proper rewards and punishments, justice had to come in this life. When the earthly family or the state could not see that justice was done, then it was left to God. Even so, God worked through human or natural instruments in meting out punishment. This was also true when the people were guilty of some offense against God. Thus JACOB's deception of ISAAC was punished when he, in turn, was deceived by LABAN (Gen 27, 28), while the prophets were convinced that Israel's sins were being punished by the armies of their enemies, even by an enemy who in many respects was worse than the people being punished (Hab 1:12-17). JOB's friends were convinced that the natural disasters that had befallen him were just retribution for his suppposed sins (Job 4:7, 8).

In preexilic Israel, there did not seem to be as much concern for exact retribution as there was later. Because the family was so important in the Israelite community, punishment was viewed as falling more on the group than upon the individual. This is the meaning of the statement about "visiting the iniquity of the parents upon the children of the third and fourth generation" (Exod 20:5). The rise of a doctrine of individual responsibility as reflected in JEREMIAH 31:30 and EZEKIEL 18:1-32 led to important changes in views of retribution. One of these was the expectation that it would be precise and personal. Here again, Ezekiel is important. His conclusion that "every person shall die for his own sin" (18:21) reflects the personal element, while his vision of the slaughter of the guilty people of Jerusalem during the Babylonian siege while the righteous escape death speaks of precise retribution. The presumption, then, is that all who died and all who lived deserved to do so (Ezek 9:3-8). The conviction that retribution was so exact was grounded in the presumption that God was just.

In exilic and postexilic Judaism, the doctrine of exact retribution was not without challenge. Deutero-Isaiah was convinced that Jerusalem had suffered "double for all her sins" (40:2). While Job's friends were sure he was getting just what he deserved, Job strenuously argued that it was not so, going so far as to question God's justice (9:20-24). Deutero-Isaiah concluded that Israel's double punishment had a redemptive purpose, while Job's personal vision of God silenced his complaints but never answered the questions he raised (Job 42:5, 6).

The reality that justice does not always come in this life, coupled with the rise of the doctrine of individual responsibility, provided fertile soil for a doctrine of life after death with appropriate rewards or punishments. Whether Judaism borrowed the idea from the Persians, as some insist, or whether it developed within Judaism, it was, by the beginning of the Christian era, a major doctrine of the Pharisees, the most influential of the Jewish religious parties. Paul, a converted Pharisee, spoke of divine retribution as the "wrath of God" directed against all the ungodly activity of human beings and concluded that all had sinned, both Jews and Gentiles (Rom 5:2-11). Sinners could escape the divine retribution or wrath by accepting the sacrifice of Jesus by FAITH (Rom 5:1-11). The Book of Revelation, the great apocalyptic work of the NT, concludes with a vision of divine judgment in which all will be judged "by what they had done" (Rev 20:13), with the unrighteous being sent "to the lake of fire" while those whose names are found in the "book of life" (the righteous) enjoy the rewards of a new heaven and a new earth. Thus the problem of earthly inequalities in divine retribution is resolved in the NT by its doctrine of life after death.

See also LAW IN THE OLD TESTAMENT.

Bibliography. W. Eichrodt, *Theology of the Old Testament*.

—JOHN H. TULLOCK

• **Return of Christ.** *See* ESCHATOLOGY IN THE NEW TESTAMENT; MILLENNIUM

• **Reuben.** [*roo*'bin] The first son of JACOB and LEAH and the eponymous ancestor of the Israelite tribe that bore his name. Contrasting views are given of Reuben's character in Genesis. He committed incest with Bilhah, Jacob's concubine (Gen 35:22), which caused Jacob's statement that Reuben would lose dominance (Gen 49:3-4). He was implicated in the jealousy and hatred of JOSEPH and participated in the deception of Jacob concerning Joseph's fate (Gen 37:31-35). However, Joseph's life was spared by his brothers because of Reuben's intercession and his intention was to return Joseph to Jacob (Gen 37:21-22). When Jacob was reluctant to allow Benjamin to be taken to Egypt, Reuben offered his own sons as security for the return of Benjamin (Gen 42:37). The great love of Reuben for his mother Leah was shown by his gathering of the MANDRAKES with which she lured Jacob to her bed, resulting in the conception of Issachar (Gen 30:14-15).

Reuben's status as firstborn is generally seen as a memory of a time when the tribe of Reuben played a dominant role in Israelite affairs. The story of Reuben's incest with Bilhah and the ambivalence of Jacob's blessing were probably offered as an explanation for the later loss of preeminence by the tribe. Despite the loss of the dominant position by Reuben, his status as firstborn was never lost, as evidenced by the blessings of Jacob in Gen 49 and of Moses in Deut 33, both of which gave Reuben priority of place.

See also JACOB; LEAH; REUBENITES.

—RAY SUTHERLAND

• **Reubenites.** [*roo*'bi-n*its*] One of the twelve tribes of Israel; they occupied a tribal area east of the Jordan River at the northeastern edge of the Dead Sea (PLATE 11). Reuben was bounded on the south by the River Arnon and Moab, on the north by Gad and Ammon, on the east by the desert, and on the west by the Dead Sea. Reuben's place in the Genesis traditions as the firstborn of Jacob is generally seen as a memory of a time when the Reubenites held a dominant position among the tribes. If so, this dominance was later lost, probably due to Moabite, Edomite, and Ammonite depredations. This loss of importance by Reuben is reflected on the MESHA STELE on which Gad is mentioned but Reuben is not. The blessing of Moses in Deut 33 implies that the tribe's very existence was at risk. However, throughout the history of the Northern Kingdom, Reuben maintained its place as a tribe, as is seen in 1 Chr 5:1-6, which tells of deportations of Reubenites by the Assyrians. During the days of Saul, Reuben seems still to have been in possession of considerable power, since the tribe was said to have conquered a portion of the territory of the Hagrites (1 Chr 5:10).

Economically, Reuben apparently was primarily pastoral with few horticultural interests, since Num 32:1-5, 16 relates the tradition that Reuben picked its territory because of its suitability for livestock.

See also MESHA STELE; REUBEN.

—RAY SUTHERLAND

• **Reuel.** *See* JETHRO

• **Revelation, Book of.** Scholars find it difficult to pinpoint the peculiar literary genre of the Book of Revelation. It is usually assumed that Revelation belongs to the literary genre of APOCALYPTIC LITERATURE. Many apocalyptic books were written by the Jews at the beginning of the Christian era. Apocalyptic seems to have emerged from the disappointments of the Jewish exiles in Babylon. The visions of the great prophets of a golden age for the Jews had not come about. The apocalyptic writers pushed those hopes and promises into a new age. Thus apocalyptic literature stressed a dualism consisting of this present evil age ruled by evil and the coming golden age ruled by Yahweh. There is no hope for the present evil age but a longing for its end with all kinds of catastrophic events. This genre also included such secondary elements as the pseudonymity of the author, visions, animal symbolism, numerology, and astral influences.

The word ''apocalyptic,'' as used to define a genre of literature, comes from the Book of Revelation: the Gk. word *apocalypse,* meaning ''revelation,'' is the first word in the book. The adjective ''apocalyptic'' came to be applied to other works similar to the Book of Revelation. There are many dissimilarities between Revelation and the other apocalypses, however. Such essential themes as pseudonymity, secrecy, and historical periodization are not utilized by Revelation. Unlike other apocalypses, it demonstrates a close affinity to the Hebrew prophetic literature and operates extensively from it. At the same time, Revelation has also been influenced by Greek tragic drama. The genre of Revelation thus seems to be a syncretistic one—setting forth a prophetic message in the form of Greek tragic drama.

The time sequence of Revelation shows the influence of both the Hebrew and Greek world. One cannot read Revelation straight through like other NT books. The visions come in cycles that often must be viewed side by side rather than in a straight-line progression. For example, the seven trumpets must be read along with the seven bowls of wrath. The closest analogy perhaps would be stereo speakers with the sounds of the seven trumpets coming out one speaker and the noise of the seven bowls from the other. One could also liken Revelation to a three-ring circus in which one must watch the action in all three rings at once.

The cyclical time sequence of the Greek world is wed to the straight-line progression of the Hebrew world. Revelation portrays a spiral effect—endless cycles of repetition but moving toward an end goal of history. The outer form of Greek tragic drama was used by the writer to make more dramatic the prophetic message of the book. In recent structuralist studies of Revelation, the affinity of the structure of Revelation to that of Greek tragic drama has been demonstrated. According to the compositional rules of the tragedy, the climax falls near the center of the action and the denouement comes near the end in an *a b c d c' b' a'* pattern. With that pattern there is a prophetic movement from promise to fulfillment within the structure of a cosmic, timeless drama.

Revelation as Drama. There are many similarities between Revelation and the extant Greek tragedies. A Greek theater was considered sacred ground for all who participated; actors, chorus, and patrons were considered ministers of religion. The technical Greek word for producing a play was ''to teach'' and the director was called ''the teacher'' while the plays were termed ''the teaching.'' Actors were called priests and the throne of God stood on the lower stage. Thus, the readers of Revelation would have found much about Greek drama already a part of their religious heritage and a good background for understanding their new one.

The role of the chorus in Greek tragic drama is very close to the role of the twenty-four elders in Revelation. At the beginning of the Greek drama, a chorus of twelve or twenty-four entered the stage and stood around the throne of Dionysius. The earliest tragedies had only choruses and no actors. The chorus could don masks and represent animals, birds, or beasts. At a later time (after 400 B.C.E.) the dramas added one actor. The chorus however continued to be the medium for interpreting the drama. In Revelation the twenty-four elders sing and interpret the drama. They lead John around heaven and introduce many of the visions. Nine major hymns appear in Revelation in a balanced strophe-antistrophe pattern characteristic of the Greek dramas. The great composer Handel was so inspired by the hymns of Revelation that he made them a vital part of his work *The Messiah.*

At EPHESUS, a great amphitheater stood holding 24,000 seats (PLATE 59). It had been built in the third century B.C.E. and was the largest of the Greek theaters. The stage building, *skene,* was most unique in that it contained seven windows (*thuromata*) for scenery consisting of painted panels. All other Greek stages had three or five such openings. Thus for nearly 300 years before the writing of Revelation, the number seven had acquired great significance for the inhabitants of Ephesus. Everyone who has written on Revelation has remarked on its unique use of sevens—seven churches, seven trumpets, seven bowls, seven blessings, and so on. Revelation can easily be divided into seven acts with seven scenes.

The first blessing in Revelation is ''Blessed is he who reads aloud the words of the prophecy'' (1:3). The best way to begin a study of Revelation is to read it aloud with a recording of Handel's *Messiah* in the background. The factor that has made Revelation a lost book is that it has been left on the cold printed page. Revelation was meant to be seen and heard. A vision cannot be put into prose. The orality of Revelation is an essential element for interpretation. The enacted story possesses the power to transport the hearer into a different world. One enters into another universe and undergoes a new reality. The writer of Revelation had no hopes that his dramatic message would ever be enacted on the stage of Ephesus, but he used the dramatic medium of Greek drama and the stage of Ephesus to ensure the book would be heard and seen. A lector would read it aloud to a congregation made up mostly of slaves who could not read. As they heard it, they could envision it against the backdrop of the famous stage at Ephesus where they had witnessed so many Greek tragic dramas.

Apocalyptic Symbolism. The visions of Revelation came alive through the vivid use of colors, animals, and numerology. One cannot read Revelation as one would read a Gospel or a Pauline Letter. The imagination must be used.

• OUTLINE OF REVELATION •

The Book of Revelation

Prologue (1:1-8)
- I. Act One. The Seven Golden Lampstands (1:9–3:22)
  - sc1 The 1st golden lampstand—Ephesus (2:1-7)
  - sc2 The 2nd golden lampstand—Smyrna (2:8-11)
  - sc3 The 3rd golden lampstand—Pergamum (2:12-17)
  - sc4 The 4th golden lampstand—Thyatira (2:18-29)
  - sc5 The 5th golden lampstand—Sardis (3:1-6)
  - sc6 The 6th golden lampstand—Philadelphia (3:7-13)
  - sc7 The 7th golden lampstand—Laodicea (3:14-22)
- II. Act Two. The Seven Seals (4:1-8:4)
  - sc1 The 1st seal—the white horse (6:1-2)
  - sc2 The 2nd seal—the red horse (6:3-4)
  - sc3 The 3rd seal—the black horse (6:5-6)
  - sc4 The 4th seal—the pale green horse (6:7-8)
  - sc5 The 5th seal—the martyrs under the alter (6:9-11)
  - sc6 The 6th seal—the judgment of the world (6:12-17)

Interlude—the sealing of the 144,000 (7:1-17)
  - sc7 The 7th seal—the gold incense container (8:1-4)
- III. Act Three. The Seven Trumpets (8:5–11:18)
  - sc1 The 1st trumpet—plague of hail, fire, blood (8:7)
  - sc2 The 2nd trumpet—plague on the sun (8:8-9)
  - sc3 The 3rd trumpet—plague on the fresh water (8:10-11)
  - sc4 The 4th trumpet—plague on the heavenly bodies (8:12)

Interlude—an eagle announces the three woes (8:13)
  - sc5 The 5th trumpet—plague of the locusts (9:1-12)
  - sc6 The 6th trumpet—plague of the 200 million horsemen (9:13-21)

Interlude—John eats a scroll; measuring of the Temple; two witnesses appear (10:1–11:14)
  - sc7 The 7th trumpet—the worship of the 24 elders (11:15-18)
- IV. Act Four. The Seven Tableaux (11:19–15:4)
  - sc1 The 1st tableau—woman, child, dragon (12:1-17)
  - sc2 The 2nd tableau—a beast from the sea (13:1-10)
  - sc3 The 3rd tableau—the beast from the land (13:11-18)
  - sc4 The 4th tableau—the lamb with the 144,000 (14:1-5)

Interlude—the announcements of the three angels (14:6-13)
  - sc5 The 5th tableau—the Son of man on a cloud (14:14-16)
  - sc6 The 6th tableau—the harvest of grapes (14:17-20)
  - sc7 The 7th tableau—the hymn of the lamb (15:1-4)
- V. Act Five. The Seven Bowls of Wrath (15:5–16:21)
  - sc1 The 1st bowl—curse on the earth (16:2)
  - sc2 The 2nd bowl—curse on the sea (16:3)
  - sc3 The 3rd bowl—curse on the rivers (16:4-7)
  - sc4 The 4th bowl—curse on the sun (16:8-9)
  - sc5 The 5th bowl—curse on the beast's throne (16:10-11)
  - sc6 The 6th bowl—curse on the Euphrates (16:12-16)
  - sc7 The 7th bowl—curse on the air (16:17-21)
- VI. Act Six. The Seven Judgments (17:1–20:3)
  - sc1 The 1st judgment—the woman and the scarlet beast (17:3b-18)
  - sc2 The 2nd judgment—the fall of Babylon (18:1-24)
  - sc3 The 3rd judgment—rejoicing in heaven and the marriage supper of the lamb (19:1-10)
  - sc4 The 4th judgment—the Word of God (19:11-16)
  - sc5 The 5th judgment—the angel on the sun (19:17-18)
  - sc6 The 6th judgment—battle of Armageddon (19:19-21)
  - sc7 The 7th judgment—Satan cast into abyss (20:1-3)
- VII. Act Seven. The Seven Great Promises (20:4–22:5)
  - sc1 The 1st promise—the millennium (20:4b-10)
  - sc2 The 2nd promise—the judgment of evil (20:11-15)
  - sc3 The 3rd promise—the new heaven and earth (21:1-3)
  - sc4 The 4th promise—assurance for believers (21:4-8)
  - sc5 The 5th promise—the new Jerusalem (21:9-21)
  - sc6 The 6th promise—the city's illumination (21:22-27)
  - sc7 The 7th promise—the river of life (22:1-5)

Epilogue (22:6-21)

Different systems of symbols may be found in Revelation. The system of *numbers*: seven—divine number (seven horns, 4:6); six—imperfect, the enemy, Caesar (13:18); five—major penalties—the locusts torture people for five months (9:5); four—world (7:1); two—witnessing (11:3); one—unity (13:3); ten—complete (9:16); twelve—wholeness (21:14); one-third—incomplete (8:7). The system of *colors*: pale green—death (6:8); emerald green—life (4:3); white—purity or conquering (1:14); red—war (6:4); black—famine (6:5); gold—worth or value (1:13); bronze—strength (1:15); scarlet—immorality (17:3).

The system of symbolism involving *animals* in the Book of Revelation is similar to the use of animals in political cartoons to depict current political figures. In Revelation, animals and monster beasts represent people or qualities: lamb with seven horns and eyes—Jesus Christ (4:6); frog—the most evil creature (16:13); monster beasts—Caesar, Satan, etc. (13:1); lion—wild animals (4:7); ox—domesticated animals (4:7); eagle—bearer of bad news (8:13).

In Revelation places take on symbolical meaning also: sea—the source of all evil in Revelation; desert—a place of strife and temptation; mountaintop—a place of revelation; Euphrates River—a dividing line or boundary point; Babylon—a code word for Rome or the enemy.

If the symbolic language in Revelation is taken literally, much of the message is lost. The book then becomes one of fear, gloom, and doom. In reality, the symbols are used by the writer to give a hidden message of hope to Christians being persecuted.

Authorship. The traditional view of John the disciple has many points in its favor. From the church fathers, we know that John was the only disciple to die a natural death at the age of 100 years. Eusebius reported that under Domitian, "the apostle John is banished to Patmos and sees his Apocalypse, as Irenaeus says" (*EccHist* 7.25). However, Dionysius, in the third century C.E. pointed out that there were two church leaders in Ephesus by the name of John and concluded that Revelation was written by an elder John, not the disciple John. Perhaps one can only conclude that the book was written by a Jewish-Christian prophet by the name of John.

Dating. The dating of Revelation is also much debated. Most modern scholars date the book during the reign of Domitian, 81–96 C.E. The early church writers took that view. Eusebius, quoting Irenaeus, placed the writing in the fourteenth year of Domitian's reign. The persecution of Domitian's reign would fit well into the context of Revelation. Few details of that persecution exist in written form. Some scholars today believe that this persecution was more of a perceived crisis than a real one. The Christians saw themselves as the outcasts, living in poverty over against the power of the ROMAN EMPIRE. Revelation serves as a catharsis to work through such feelings of rage and hostility.

Other scholars have suggested Nero's time (54–68 C.E.) or the period of Vespasian (69–79 C.E.). There is no real support for these positions in the early church fathers. Those who take the position base it on internal evidence such as the existence of the Herodian Temple in 11:1 and the church's flight to Pella mentioned in 12:1-6. Some have argued that the riddle of 17:10 (the seven emperors) fits Vespasian better than Domitian. However, the date of 95 C.E. during Domitian's reign continues to enjoy wide support.

Methods of Interpretation. There are many different ways of interpreting Revelation, from a futuristic document interpreting coming world events in detail to a mere history of the past. In the contemporary historical view

Revelation is interpreted primarily against the Roman Empire under Domitian in 95 C.E. Revelation was written to bring hope to persecuted Christians of that period. The continuous-historical view sees Revelation as containing an overview history of the whole Christian church from the first century to the end of the age: The beast and the false prophet are the Pope and the papacy. The futurist method views Revelation as dealing mainly with end-time events. Such interpreters look upon the last book of the Bible as largely a volume of unfulfilled prophecy. A very literal approach is taken to the book and very little symbolism is noted. One popular arm of this school is dispensationalism founded by J. N. Darby of the Plymouth Brethren Church.

The dramatic-literary approach views Revelation as a literary whole with plot, characters, and themes. Greek tragic drama is viewed as the literary medium of the author. Emphasis is placed upon the visual elements of the book. This is the approach favored in this article.

In addition to various methods of interpretation, the student of Revelation also encounters a variety of views concerning the MILLENNIUM or the thousand-year reign of Christ (Rev 20:4-6). Although there are only three verses concerning the millennium in Revelation, many Bible students place exaggerated importance on the subject. The millennium becomes "the tail that wags the dog." Three basic schools are in vogue. The premillennial school teaches that Christ will come to earth before the thousand years and reign on earth. The postmillennial school asserts that Christ will reign in heaven during the thousand years and return to earth at the end of that period. The amillennial school views the millennium symbolically: Christ began his reign at his victory over Satan at the cross; he will reign for a complete period of time.

Canonicity. Revelation very early became authoritative in the church. Justin Martyr (150 C.E.) used the book and mentioned the author by name. It is mentioned in the MURATORIAN CANON. Papias (early second century) made use of it as authoritative and Melito of Sardis (160–190) wrote a commentary on it. Revelation also was included in the Latin Vulgate (391–404). The only place it encountered difficulty was in Syria.

See also APOCALYPTIC LITERATURE; DANIEL, BOOK OF; DUALISM; EPHESUS; ESCHATOLOGY IN THE NEW TESTAMENT; HYMN; JOHN THE APOSTLE; MILLENNIUM; NUMBERS/NUMEROLOGY; ROMAN EMPIRE; SYMBOL.

Bibliography. J. L. Blevins, *Revelation as Drama;* G. Caird, *The Revelation of St. John the Divine;* A. Collins, *Crisis and Catharsis;* C. Hemer, *The Letters to the Seven Churches;* J. P. Newport, *The Lion and the Lamb.*

—JAMES L. BLEVINS

• **Revelation, Concept of.** Revelation is the disclosure or making known of something previously unknown. When used in its religious or theological sense, revelation refers to ways in which deity is disclosed to humanity. Human response to divine disclosure leads to some kind of knowledge of, and communion between, GOD and human beings. This broad understanding of the nature of revelation is not restricted to the Judeo-Christian tradition but is presupposed by most of the world's religions.

Revelation in the Bible. Common to the Judeo-Christian traditions is the belief that God takes the initiative to make himself known to human beings. Since God as creator is different from CREATION and responsible for its origin, the Bible speaks in varied ways of God's transcendence. He is mysterious, hidden, and different from humanity in his holy nature (Job 11:7; Isa 40:18; 40:25; John 1:18). Only because God desires to disclose himself and his will can there be knowledge of who he is and communion with him. However, God is never under human control: he is not a created thing or object. He is the Lord. Therefore, the Decalogue prohibits equation of the one God with lesser deities: "You shall have no other gods before me" (Exod 20:3). God's uniqueness is also the basis for the prohibition of making graven images of God's likeness in creaturely representations.

In distinction from some religions in which the deity remains hidden and basically unknowable, the Judeo-Christian traditions affirm that the mysterious and hidden God, the "maker of heaven and earth," intentionally discloses himself and his purpose to his human creatures. When those to whom God chooses to reveal himself respond in faith and obedience toward him, communion is established between them. Thus God's making himself known always calls for the appropriate response of those receiving his self-communication. Israel's fundamental confession is found in the SHEMA. It speaks of God as Lord and of Israel's appropriate response. "Hear, O Israel: The Lord our God is one Lord; and you shall love the Lord your God with all your heart, and with all your soul, and with all your might." (Deut 6:4-5)

The BIBLE is the record preserved by Israel and the Church of the story of history of God's revelation. For Jews, God's revelation began with God's call of Abraham to be the father "of a great nation." Israel, God's chosen people in the old covenant, was to live in the covenant established by God in faithfulness and obedience (Gen 12:1-3). The decisive event of revelation in Israel's history was their deliverance from Egyptian bondage through manifestations of God's power and especially through their preservation from the pursuing Egyptians at the sea. The Book of Exodus narrates these foundational events in Israel's history. Throughout Israel's history, the story of God's revelatory power in delivering Israel from Egypt under Moses' leadership is retold, remembered, and celebrated in the annual Passover festival and in other ways (cf. Deut 4:23-40; Exod 12:40-51). God's giving of the Law to his people at Mount Sinai through Moses represents the second highlight of God's revelation to Israel. The Law of God is the revelation and communication of the divine will to Israel. It governs both her obligation to God and her entire life and conduct as his covenant people (Exod 20–23). The Book of Joshua recounts Israel's entry into the promised land in accordance with God's promise and represents another of God's mighty acts.

BIBLICAL THEOLOGY in the first half of this century stressed that the revelation of God was to be found primarily in the history of his mighty acts. This view opposed a more traditional Catholic and Protestant view that God reveals himself primarily through the WORD he speaks. This was often understood in terms of revealed truths or propositions uttered directly by God or through his prophets. Current biblical scholarship contends that the great diversity of ways God reveals himself in the old covenant make it impossible to subsume them beneath any one category. The primary medium for the revelation of the word of God is through God's prophets. Their witness constitutes the second major portion of the Hebrew Bible. Thus Jews speak of God's revelation in the Law, the Prophets, and the Writings. The latter group includes the Psalms and all OT books not included in the Law and Prophets. It is important for the Christian view of revelation that postexilic Judaism looked toward a decisive future and final revelation of God often associated with the coming of the Messiah. These apocalyptic writings looked toward God's vindication of Israel and his purposes for all human history.

Christian understandings of revelation build upon God's revelation of himself in the old covenant to Israel. But whereas Jews still await the fulfillment of God's promises and the Messiah's coming, Christians see them fulfilled in JESUS, the Messiah (God's anointed one), or the Christ. The sermons of Peter and Paul recorded in the Book of Acts develop this common Christian belief. The author of Hebrews writes: "In many and various ways God spoke of old to our fathers by the prophets; but in these last days he has spoken to us by a Son, whom he appointed the heir of all things, through whom also he created the world." (Heb 1:1-2)

Thus the NT celebrates the fulfillment of God's revelation in the birth, ministry, death, and resurrection of Jesus, the Messiah and savior of Israel and of the world. This led the author of the Gospel of John to depict the eternal Word or Son of God—whose light had already shone in creation and in human lives—as having become flesh: "The Word became flesh and dwelt among us, full of grace and truth; we have beheld his glory, glory as of the only Son from the Father." (John 1:14) In the Son of God, the world is confronted with God's unique self-revelation. In him God's revelation of himself in the old covenant through historical acts, prophets, priests, and kings finds its fulfillment. God meets humanity in the person of his Son: his highest revelation of himself as personal is disclosed in the person of his only Son.

The Revelation of God in Jesus Christ. Christian faith in Jesus as the Messiah accounts for the distinction made in Christian theology between God's preparatory revelations in the OT and their fulfillment in Jesus Christ attested in the NT. On the basis of God's self-revelation in and through Jesus Christ climaxing in his death and resurrection, the NT speaks in varied ways of Jesus initiating a "new covenant" fulfilling the old (cf.Luke 22:20; 2 Cor 3:6; Heb 7:22; 9:15; 12:24). This is why the NT sees God's revelation through OT prophets, priests, and kings fulfilled in Jesus Christ. In his person, he incorporates and fulfills the OT offices of prophet, priest, and king which mediated God's presence and revelation. He is greater than the prophets as "the Word [which] became flesh" (John 1:14). He fulfills the OT priesthood as "a merciful and faithful high priest in the service of God, to make expiation for the sins of the people" (Heb 2:17). Finally, he fulfills the office of the OT king appointed by God since he is God's anointed Messiah and kingly servant through whom God's kingly rule draws near. It is because the early church saw Jesus as the perfect revelation of God that the oldest Christian confession was: "Jesus Christ is Lord!" (cf. Phil 2:5-11). In short, as God's self-revelation, Jesus Christ is the perfect revelation of God, his Father (John 1:18). Jesus Christ is the savior both of Jews and gentiles—of all persons in all times (1 John 2:1-2). Finally, Christians confessed that the purpose of God for all human history was realized in God's saving revelation in Jesus Christ—"a plan for the fulness of time, to unite all things in him, things in heaven and things on earth" (Eph 1:10; cf. Gal 4:4).

Although the revelation of God in Jesus Christ is unsurpassable and once for all, it is not the final or last revelation of God. Indeed, the words used in the NT to refer to the revelation of God often point to faith's expectation of the future eschatological revelation in the return of Jesus Christ to consummate his saving purpose (Luke 17:30; Rom 8:18ff.; 1 Cor 1:7; Col 3:4; et al.). This final, future revelation will be the definitive disclosure of Jesus Christ. On the basis of Christ's first coming and his presence through the HOLY SPIRIT, believers already enjoy the "first fruits" of the salvation which will be completed with his return and the resurrection of the dead and the final judgment (Rom 8:23ff.; 1 Cor 15:20-28). For this reason, the NT often speaks of true faith as being characterized both by trust in God through Jesus Christ and by hope in the consummation of God's purpose through the return of Jesus Christ as Lord and judge in the future (Heb 11:1ff.; Rom 8:24; Eph 1:18). The fact that the final revelation is still future accounts for the difference between faith and sight. "For now we see in a mirror dimly, but then face to face" (1 Cor 13:12).

Media of Revelation. Christian theology distinguishes between general revelation and special revelation. General revelation is the universal revelation of God in creation and human nature; special revelation is the historical and saving revelation of God attested in the Bible whose center is Jesus Christ. Though the former may provide an initial awareness of God and makes humanity responsible before God, classical Catholic and Protestant theology has always taught that the full knowledge of God is available only through faith in God's revelation to Israel and the church. Paul argues that human sin has rendered God's universal revelation ineffective thereby making the revelation in Jesus Christ essential for humanity's salvation (Rom 1:18ff.; 3:21-26).

After the ascension of Jesus Christ, Christians experienced his continuing presence through the Holy Spirit. Through his Spirit, God continues to take the initiative to reveal himself to human beings. Protestants stress that God's Spirit manifests himself through the witness of holy scripture and the preaching of the gospel thereby giving rise to faith. Most Protestants since the Reformation emphasize that since the holy scriptures originated through divine inspiration, it is the written word of God. As such, the Bible is the primary vehicle for all Christian knowledge of God. *The Baptist Faith and Message* of 1963 is typically Protestant in affirming that the Bible is "the supreme standard by which all human conduct, creeds, and religious opinions should be tried. The criterion by which the Bible is to be interpreted is Jesus Christ."

God's revelation of himself calls for the response of faith, hope, and love (1 Cor 13). Faith in God through Jesus Christ and the witness of the Holy Spirit is not to be identified with mental assent to doctrines or creeds. Nor is faith possible apart from the gracious initiative of the Holy Spirit (Matt 16:17; 1 Cor 12:3). Faith is the continuing confession of, and trust in God, knowable through Jesus Christ and by the Spirit, and the doing of his will (Matt 7:21; 1 Pet 1:13-16). True faith, therefore, must be new every morning.

See also APOCALYPTIC LITERATURE; BIBLE, AUTHORITY OF; BIBLICAL THEOLOGY; CREATION; EXODUS; GOD; HOLY SPIRIT, JESUS; LAW IN THE NEW TESTAMENT; LAW IN THE OLD TESTAMENT; MESSIAH/CHRIST; PROPHET; TEN COMMANDMENTS; VISION; WORD.

Bibliography. J. Baillie, *The Idea of Revelation in Recent Thought*; K. Barth, *Church Dogmatics*; E. Brunner, *Revelation and Reason* and *The Divine-Human Encounter*; R. Bultmann, "The Concept of Revelation in the New Testament," *Existence and Faith*, ed. S. Ogden; J. Calvin, *Institutes of the Christian Religion*; O. Cullmann, *Christ and Time*; A. Dulles, *Models of Revelation*; C. Henry, *God, Revelation, and Authority*; C. Henry, ed., *Revelation and the Bible*; M. Luther, *Lectures on Romans*; J. Moltmann, *The Crucified God*; H. R. Niebuhr, *The Meaning of Revelation*; W. Pannenberg, ed., *Revelation as History*; G. von Rad, *Old Testament Theology*; P. Stuhlmacher, *Reconciliation, Law, and Righteousness*.

—DAVID L. MUELLER

• **Revised Standard Version.** *See* ENGLISH BIBLE, HISTORY OF

• **Revolt.** *See* SIN

• **Reward.** *See* WAGES

• **Reward and Punishment.** *See* RETRIBUTION

• **Rezin.** [ree′zin] Born in Bit-Hadara near Damascus, Rezin was ruler of ARAM 740–732 B.C.E.

In 738, TIGLATH-PILESER III conducted a campaign against ARAM and Palestine (PLATE 7), and Rezin came under tribute to ASSYRIA (*ANET*, 283). But when Pekah assassinated the Israelite king PEKAHIAH and took the throne in 737 B.C.E., he joined with Rezin to form an anti-Assyrian coalition. AHAZ, king of Judah, refused to join the rebellion, and as a result Pekah and Rezin besieged JERUSALEM, seeking to replace him with the "son of Tabeel" (2 Kgs 15:37; 16:5; Isa 7:1,6). The Israelite-Aramean attack against Judah provided an opportunity for the Edomites to take Elath (cf. 2 Kgs 16:6) and to conduct raids against Judah (2 Chr 28:17). At the same time, the PHILISTINES exploited the situation by raiding Judean cities in the NEGEB and the Shephelah (2 Chr 28:18; PLATE 13). The crisis terrified Ahaz who disregarded ISAIAH's counsel to trust in Yahweh (Isa 7:2-9) and instead sought help from Assyria by paying tribute to Tiglath-Pileser. The Assyrian king then moved against the coalition and soon captured and decimated Damascus, exiled its people, and executed Rezin (2 Kgs 16:9; cf. Amos 1:3-5; Isa 17:1-5). The sons of Rezin are listed among those temple servants who returned from the Exile (Ezra 2:48; Neh 7:50).

See also AHAZ; ARAM/ARAMEANS; DAMASCUS; PEKAH; TIGLATH-PILEZER.

—LLOYD M. BARRÉ

• **Rheginos, Epistle to.** *See* RESURRECTION, TREATISE ON

• **Rhetorical Criticism.** Rhetorical criticism is the process of identifying the persuasive structures and strategies present in a text, so that the text can be interpreted in terms of its rhetoric and its author's intention in creating the text. Rhetorical criticism of the Hebrew Bible received a strong impetus from Muilenburg's 1968 presidential address to the Society of Biblical Literature; and beginning in the 1970s several NT scholars have used methods based on Greco-Roman rhetoric (as well as other theories of rhetoric) to identify and evaluate the persuasive strategies used by early Christian authors.

Rhetorical Criticism of the Hebrew Bible. James Muilenburg made a considerable impact on the study of rhetoric in the OT. Muilenburg advised in his "Form Criticism and Beyond" that form criticism was "bound to generalize because it is concerned with what is common to all the representatives of a GENRE," so that it was unable to give enough attention to the unique characteristics of particular texts. Muilenburg's own rhetorical criticism, especially well-known through his commentary on Isa 40–66, focused on the identification of poetic form, structure, imagery, and other strategies of style and arrangement through which biblical writers persuasively transmitted their religious message. Other rhetorical critics, including scholars affected by the New Rhetoric, structuralism, and newer kinds of literary criticism have widened the scope of their criticism to focus less on diachronic (historical) concerns than on synchronic analyses of the texts we currently possess. Several papers from the Rhetorical Criticism Section of the SBL, including many examples of rhetorical criticism of the Hebrew Bible, are collected in Clines et al., eds., *Art and Meaning*. Because of the pervasive character of rhetoric in Greek and Roman culture, resulting in the extensive rhetorical literature that exists, there is more historical justification for doing Greco-Roman-based rhetorical criticism of the NT and other early Christian literature, than for using these models for criticism of the Hebrew Bible.

Rhetorical Criticism of the NT. The Letters of Paul and the pseudopauline letters appear to be particularly suited to analysis through rhetorical criticism based on Greco-Roman theories of rhetoric. In book 4 of *On Christian Doctrine*, Augustine identified numerous rhetorical features in Letters of Paul. *On Christian Doctrine* may certainly be considered a Christian handbook of rhetoric, very much in the tradition of Greek and Latin rhetorical handbooks such as those of Aristotle, Cicero, and Quintilian. Older rhetorical criticism, exemplified in the work of C. G. Wilke, made an implicit identification of rhetoric with the smaller tropes and figures, which belonged in antiquity to theories of rhetorical style.

As a result of studying extant Greek and Roman rhetorical handbooks, several NT scholars have emphasized the structure of Pauline Letters, with their characteristic identification of sender and addressees, salutation, and (usually) a thanksgiving prayer, along with the letter-body and epistolary closing. These structures are strongly affected by principles of the arrangement (Gk. *taxis;* Latin *dispositio*) of speeches in rhetorical theory and practice. Rhetorical speeches usually began with an introduction of speaker to the audience (Gk. *prooimion;* Latin *exordium*) and the acquisition of the audience's goodwill. Often such speeches continued with a section of narration (Gk. *diēgēsis*; Latin *narratio*), sometimes leading up to a short section (known in Latin as *partitio* or *propositio;* various terms in Greek) which set forth the disagreements and agreements with the orator's adversary, or a section in which the issues dealt with in the following argumentative section were briefly recounted. Then came the argument or proof (Gk. *pistis;* Latin *probatio*), followed by the peroration (Gk. *epilogos;* Latin *peroratio*), which consisted of recapitulation (Gk. *anakephalaiōsis;* Latin *recapitulatio*) of the arguments in the proof, as well as a well developed appeal to the audience's emotions (Gk. *pathos;* Latin *affectus*).

Several Pauline scholars, including Hans Dieter Betz, Robert Jewett, Frank Witt Hughes, James Hester, and Wilhelm Wuellner, identify various parts of Pauline Letters with some of the conventional parts of the rhetorical speech, and thus use Greco-Roman rhetorical precepts as guides to the functions of parts of Pauline Letters within the context of the letter as a whole rhetorical discourse. A step further than this has been taken by critics who see rhetorical criticism as a form of historical criticism (cf. Wuellner's article, "Where is Rhetorical Criticism Taking Us?" for a definition of rhetorical criticism outside the concerns of historical criticism). This involves the correlation of the discourse, rhetorically explained and interpreted, within the context of the rhetorical situation of the writer's relationship with the intended readers, insofar as that relationship can be elucidated by historical data found inside and outside the text being interpreted (for the best example of rhetorical criticism as historical correlation, cf. Carl Joachim Classen's analysis of Ciceronian speeches and their political context cited in the bibliography).

It is possible to speak of a working consensus among rhetorical critics concerning the theoretical identification of parts of NT letters with traditional parts of rhetorical speeches. But such a consensus is evidently lacking among those who examine the Gospels along rhetorical lines. George A. Kennedy has suggested that Greco-Roman rhetorical arrangement is present in each of the Gospels, and he has provided summary rhetorical analysis of several parts of these biblical books. Vernon K. Robbins has adopted a wide definition of rhetoric which allows him to discover formal patterns both small and large in Mark. Other scholars have found various literary and structural patterns in John through which they trace that Gospel's rhetoric (cf. Wolfgang Roth, "Scriptural Coding," as well as Edwin C. Webster, "Pattern in the Fourth Gospel," in *Art and Meaning*).

Two issues clearly underlie all current scholars' rhetorical analyses of biblical writings: (1) What theory of rhetoric undergirds each rhetorical analysis? and (2) What is the relation of rhetorical criticism to form criticism and other methods of biblical criticism? Since different rhetorical critics answer these questions in different ways, it is not surprising that rhetorical criticism is practiced in significantly different ways by various scholars. Although the Bible has been read along rhetorical lines for centuries, it is clear that rhetorical criticism is still undergoing a great deal of growth and change, and its full value for biblical exegesis and interpretation has yet to be determined.

See also EPISTLE/LETTER; GOSPELS, CRITICAL STUDY OF; INTERPRETATION, HISTORY OF; LITERATURE, BIBLE AS; LITERARY CRITICISM.

Bibliography. H. D. Betz, *Galatians: A Commentary on Paul's Letter to the Churches in Galatia*; C. J. Classen, *Recht—Rhetorik—Politik: Untersuchungen zur Ciceros rhetorischer Strategie*; D. J. A. Clines, D. M. Gunn, and A. J. Hauser, eds., *Art and Meaning: Rhetoric in Biblical Literature;* J. Hester, "The Rhetorical Structure of Galatians 1:11-14" *JBL* 103 (1984): 223-33; F. W. Hughes, *Early Christian Rhetoric and 2 Thessalonians;* R. Jewett, *The Thessalonian Correspondence: Pauline Rhetoric and Millenarian Piety;* G. A. Kennedy, *New Testament Interpretation through Rhetorical Criticism;* J. Muilenburg, "The Book of Isaiah: Chapters 40-66," *IB* and "Form Criticism and Beyond," *JBL* 88 (1969): 1-18; V. K. Robbins, *Jesus the Teacher: A Socio-Rhetorical Interpretation of Mark;* W. Roth, "Scriptural Coding in the Fourth Gospel," *BR* 32: (1987) 6-29; C. G. Wilke, *Die neutestamentliche Rhetorik: Ein Seitenstück zur Grammatik des neutestamentlichen Sprachidioms;* W. Wuellner, "Where is Rhetorical Criticism Taking Us?" *CBQ* 49 (1987): 448-63.

—FRANK WITT HUGHES

• **Riblah.** [rib'luh] An Aramean town located in the district of Hamath, situated on the river Orontes. Due to its strategic location (PLATE 1), Riblah served as a military base of operations for Pharaoh NECHO and for the Babylonian king NEBUCHADREZZAR II during their campaigns against Judah. At Riblah both Necho and Nebuchadrezzar initiated punitive actions for Judah's rebellious policies. After Josiah was killed by Necho at Megiddo, Josiah's son JEHOAHAZ was appointed king over Judah. Necho then had Jehoahaz brought to Riblah and imprisoned him there while he exacted tribute and placed Jehoiakim on the throne (2 Kgs 23:29-34).

When Jerusalem fell to the Babylonians, King Zedekiah fled but was captured and brought to Nebuchaddrezzar at Riblah. The Babylonian king slaughtered Zedekiah's sons before his eyes, blinded him, and took him prisoner (2 Kgs 25:1-7). Additional punitive actions exacted at Riblah included the slaying of the leaders of Judah (Jer 39:6; 52:10) and other palace and temple personnel (2 Kgs 25:18-21; Jer 52:24-27).

Riblah is also mentioned as the northeastern corner of the ideal boundary of Israel (Num 34:11).

See also JEHOAHAZ; NECHO; NEBUCHADREZZAR; ZEDEKIAH.

—LLOYD M. BARRÉ

• **Riddle.** Ambiguous language that offers a clue and conceals a trap simultaneously. Originally associated with rites of passage, riddles provided a means of determining worth. They were closely linked with myth and divination, and their content often concerned sex and religion. In due times riddles functioned to entertain and to educate, eventuating in catechisms.

In the Hebrew Bible the word *ḥîdâ* (cf. *mĕlîṣâ* and *māšāl*) serves as an umbrella term for enigmatic sayings, impossible questions, contest literature (cf. 1 Esdr 3:1–4:47), question and answer dialogue, and embryonic catechisms. Numerical proverbs, while related, differ significantly from riddles, as do allegory and parable, which make no effort to deceive. An ancient tradition in Num 12:8 states that all prophetic oracles except those to MOSES came in enigmatic form (*bĕḥîdōt*), and popular memory ascribes riddles to the Queen of Sheba (1 Kgs 10:1-5).

The SAMSON narrative contains two riddles and a riddle-like saying (Judg 14). Samson's riddle, "Food came from the eater and sweetness came from the strong," probably antedates its present context. The question may allude to sexual experience or to soldiers vomiting after gorging themselves on rich food. The PHILISTINES' answer in question form ("What is sweeter than honey, what is stronger than a lion?") may allude to love, while Samson's angry retort uses a common metaphor for cohabitation ("If you had not plowed with my heifer, you would not have found out my riddle").

Ps 19 may conceal two riddles, one describing the sun as a bridegroom on a journey to the ends of the earth and alluding to mute messengers, day and night. Ps 49 likewise may use riddle language in referring to mortality and to human likeness to animals (cf. Prov 30:1-4). The familiar saying in Eccl 9:4 that "a living dog is better than a dead lion" possibly justifies marriage to a "nobody" by a woman who once claimed high social status by marriage. Riddles in disintegrated form may exist in various biblical texts, especially Proverbs and Song of Songs.

See also PROVERB/RIDDLE.

Bibliography. J. L. Crenshaw, "Riddle," *IDBSupp* and *Samson: A Secret Betrayed, A Vow Ignored*; E. L. Greenstein, "The Riddle of Samson," *Proof* 1 (1981): 237-60; O. Maragalith, "Samson's Riddle and Samson's Magic Locks," *VT* 36 (1986): 225-34; P. Nel, "The Riddle of Samson," *Bib* 66 (1985): 534-45.

—JAMES L. CRENSHAW

• **Righteousness in the New Testament.** The concepts of righteousness and JUSTIFICATION have been important throughout the history of NT interpretation. Much of their importance springs from their place in Paul's discussion of salvation. Luther's emphasis on salvation by grace elevated Paul's discussion of righteousness through faith to one of the cornerstones of Protestant theology. In Paul, Luther found an ally whose polemic against the idea of righteousness through works supported his own polemic against a Roman Catholic emphasis on works-based salvation.

Ordinary Meaning of Righteousness. A dictionary of the day would probably have shown two basic meanings for the word in the first century. One of those would certainly have referred to righteousness within the judicial system. To be considered righteous or innocent meant that one conformed to the prevailing legal and moral system of one's society. Righteousness could be used to mean both the standard to which one conformed and one's status with regard to society. One aspect of that status was the judgment of one's peers. To be righteous was as much a social as a legal perception. A second meaning of righteousness, though, went beyond the sense of a legal obligation to a moral or philosophical obligation. To be righteous meant that one possessed certain qualities which contributed to the moral fiber of society. As such, righteousness became a virtue to be cultivated, the mark of a productive member of society.

The Concept of Righteousness in the OT and Judaism. The Hebrew concept of righteousness found in the OT emphasized the idea of relationship; righteousness characterized Yahweh's behavior in a covenant context. God was righteous because God upheld the covenant and was faithful to Israel (2 Chr 12:6). Such faithfulness meant that God would watch over Israel to see that it was protected from those who would take away its rights. Israel also called upon God to judge according to God's upright character. Often Israel called on God to vindicate it in the presence of enemies, although Israel claimed that God had been wronged (Ps 68). God's covenant responsibility included not only the protection of Israel as a nation, but the protection of those whose individual rights under the covenant had been denied (Ps 146:7-9). Here again, the emphasis was upon God's upright restoration of the person's rights; any punishment of the wrongdoer was a natural consequence of that restoration. The attitude which characterized a righteous person in relationship with God was an attitude of faith. When one trusted wholly in God for one's vindication, one was considered to be righteous.

The Babylonian Exile brought a new emphasis on one's individual rights and responsibilities before God. An individual's righteousness was measured by one's covenant relationship with God. Increasingly, one's covenant responsibility became defined in terms of keeping the commandments of the Law. Within the context of political and economic oppression, the idea that God would vindicate the downtrodden gave a special righteousness to those who helped the poor. Righteousness could be gained by doing acts worthy of merit, and God would weigh one's merits against one's demerits. Paul seems to have reacted against such a righteousness based on works, although some scholars have questioned the idea that Rabbinic Judaism demanded works for salvation. Whether or not Judaism demanded works for salvation, the context for the NT use of righteousness focused on one's relationship with God within the covenant. This included one's responsibility to obey the Law in order to maintain one's place within the covenant community.

Important NT Terms. Most of the words in the NT which convey the concept of righteousness come from the same root, and the translations "righteousness," "righteous," and "to make righteous" (for the Gk. words δικαιοσύνη, δίκαιος, and δικαιόω) convey this relationship. Depending on the context, however, these words can also carry such meanings as innocence/innocent, right, upright, to justify, and justification, among other related meanings. In addition to these positive terms, the NT writers used negative terms such as "unrighteous" (ἄδικος) which shed light on the meaning of the concept of righteousness in the NT (Luke 16:11).

Aspects of the Meaning of Righteousness in the NT. Three different aspects of the word "righteousness" are important for a balanced understanding of the NT usage. (1) Relational. The NT maintains the idea that righteousness was an integral part of one's covenant relationship with God. To be righteous demanded that one stand in the proper covenant relationship with God. That covenant relationship, however, could only be re-established by God; this God did in Christ. The demands of this new covenant were two-fold. To enter into the covenant, one must admit one's failure to uphold the previous covenant (repentance) and acknowledge that one's relationship with God is a matter of God's grace rather than human works (faith). One's fellowship with God demanded a subsequent fellowship with other members of the covenant community, and each person was responsible for maintaining that fellowship.

These relational aspects of righteousness are often emphasized in the NT. Many people are referred to as righteous as a result of their proper attitude toward God. Cornelius, for instance was characterized as "righteous" or "upright" to Peter (Acts 10:22), because he worshipped God, even before Peter had a chance to share the gospel with Cornelius. Others were termed righteous or unrighteous depending on their attitude toward God. Those who approach God within the context of a proper covenantal relationship are called righteous; those who ignore that relationship are characterized as unrighteous.

In the same way, those who keep their promise within the covenant community are righteous; those who break their promise are unrighteous. The ideas of righteousness and faithfulness between members of the community are linked because of God's faithfulness within the covenant. As God is faithful, so should the members of his community act with faithfulness toward each other. Often, the concept of righteousness is used to discuss actions which will destroy fellowship or relationship within the covenant. Actions such as anger, lust, and hate are unrighteous more because they destroy covenant relationships than because they violate a moral or legal code (Matt 5).

(2) Forensic. Another aspect of the NT use of righteousness was drawn from the use of the word in a secular legal context. One's legal righteousness was a result of one's innocence, often construed as conformity to societal or legal norms. The forensic, or legal, aspect of righteousness involved a verdict of "not guilty." For much of the history of NT interpretation, the forensic view of righteousness was dominant. Many scholars reconciled God's righteousness with forgiveness of sinful humanity by assuming that justification meant that God imputed righteousness to human beings; even though they remained guilty sinners, they were "considered" righteous or innocent. God met their guilty plea with a verdict of "not guilty" because of Jesus' atonement. More recent discussions, though, have emphasized

the relational aspect of righteousness, which seems to agree with even a forensic understanding of righteousness. The fact that God proclaims one to be "righteous" presupposes a restored relationship with God and the covenant community.

(3) Ethical. A third aspect of righteousness in the NT is its ethical dimension. Not only have scholars chosen to emphasize the relational concept of righteousness over the forensic, a general dissatisfaction has arisen with the idea that God's justification involves a judgment of innocence without an accompanying change in the character of the one justified. In fact, many have concluded that God does more than impute righteousness to an undeserving sinner; the gift of God's righteousness actually involves a change in the status of the sinner (Rom 4:5). This change involves a new relationship, as the sinner is reconciled to God. Moreover, God has the power to change the status of the sinner, not only declaring one righteous, but making one righteous. This new status makes ethical demands on the Christian. Righteousness is not just a new status in the presence of God; it is a new way of living. The one who has accepted the gift of righteousness through grace by faith must now live in such a way as to be worthy of that grace. These ethical demands function within the context of the covenant. Righteousness is not the result of good works, but good works are the result of righteousness.

The Righteousness of God. One of the important phrases for the understanding of Paul's writings is the phrase "righteousness of God" (δικαιοσύνη θεοῦ). Most of the discussion surrounding the concept of righteousness in the NT has concerned different interpretations of what Paul meant by the righteousness of God. Grammatically, one may choose to interpret the phrase as either the righteousness which comes from God or that righteousness which God possesses. Even after one chooses a translation, one must still attempt to understand this phrase within the context of Pauline theology.

Martin Luther interpreted the phrase to mean that power by which God makes people righteous through Christ. Luther also combined the ethical and relational aspects of righteousness, noting that one's new righteous status (a gift of God through faith in Christ) allows one to live a righteous life in Christ. Later theological developments in church history led to an increasing emphasis on the righteousness of God as a divine quality, to the detriment of the idea that God's righteousness provided the power for the act of salvation and justification.

The most recent scholarly discussion of the phrase "righteousness of God" may be traced to an address by Ernst Käsemann, in which he proposed the idea that righteousness was both the gift of God in justifying humanity and the power of God which accomplishes that justification and sanctification. Käsemann's position has evoked both significant support and opposition. The resulting discussion has affirmed the tension between God's righteousness as an attribute of his being and God's righteousness as a part of his saving work in the world.

Conclusion. Righteousness in the NT must be seen within the context of the covenant relationship. At its foundation, righteousness involves reconciliation between God and humanity, a reconciliation which is initiated by God through Christ. Not only is one declared to be righteous within that covenant relationship, one accepts a new status of righteousness. One also accepts a new way of life which may be termed as righteous, since one lives in Christ and is in the process of being sanctified in Christ. Righteousness is both gift and demand.

See also JUSTICE/JUDGMENT; JUSTIFICATION; RIGHTEOUSNESS IN THE OLD TESTAMENT; SALVATION IN THE NEW TESTAMENT; SALVATION IN THE OLD TESTAMENT.

Bibliography. P. J. Achtemeier, "Righteousness in the New Testament," *IDB*; M. T. Baruch, "Perspectives on 'God's Righteousness' in Recent German Discussion," *Paul and Palestinian Judaism,* E. P. Sanders, ed.; R. Bultmann, *Theology of the New Testament*; H. Conzelmann, *An Outline of the Theology of the New Testament*; N. A. Dahl, "The Doctrine of Justification: Its Social Function and Implications," *Studies in Paul*; R. A. Kelly, "Righteousness," *ISBE*; W. G. Kümmel, *The Theology of the New Testament*; G. Schrenk, "δίκη, κτλ.," *TDNT*; F. Stagg, *New Testament Theology*.

—STEVEN M. SHEELEY

• **Righteousness in the Old Testament.** Righteousness is a state in which one's actions and thoughts are in conformity with religious requirements. In ISRAEL, righteousness was seen as obedience to its COVENANT with God. Actions that were in accordance with the requirements of that covenant were deemed righteous.

The various forms of the English term "righteousness" are generally translations of the Heb. *ṣedeq, ṣĕdāqâ,* or *ṣaddîq* or the verb *ṣādēq* which may have been derived from the noun. Each of these Hebrew terms has the basic meaning of right, righteous, or to be in the right, although other translations are possible. The original meaning of the Hebrew term apparently concerned conformity with a standard, probably in a physical sense. Later, this changed to the idea of legal innocence, i.e., conforming to a legal standard. An early example of this usage is found in Exod 23:7, "Do not put to death one who is *ṣaddîq.*" Here the point is not the ethical behavior of the accused but his innocence of the charges against him. Judah's admission that Tamar's *ṣedeq* exceeded his own is probably an admission that she had acted legally while he had not and thus seems to fit this legal usage, as does Absalom's use of a verbal derivative of *ṣādēq* to refer to the legal rights of Israelite freeholders (2 Sam 15:4).

Through the covenant ideal of Israel, this concept of righteousness as proper legal behavior was extended to cover all of one's actions. As applied to Israel, righteousness came to mean conduct that conformed with the requirements of the relationship between Israel and God, even if such behavior was not specifically regulated in covenant law. For the nation of Israel and for individual Israelites, the concept of righteousness was thoroughly bound up with the Israelite concept of covenant. Therefore, the view of righteousness as conformity with TORAH, in both its ritual and civil provisions, remains a central aspect of righteousness, even though the Israelite concept of righteousness was not completely bounded by obedience to legal strictures. The early literary prophets show clearly that the mere absence of violations of covenant law or Torah does not itself constitute righteousness. Ethical behavior and conduct that derive from proper motives and take full account of their consequences are also required for a person or nation to be righteous. This idea of righteousness as ethical and legal conduct in conformity with the covenant is given its classical formulation in Israel by the prophets to the northern kingdom, AMOS and HOSEA. In their views, adherence to the stipulations of the covenant is still required; Hosea particularly advocated proper covenantal and cultic observance, as is seen in Hos 1–3. But both state categorically that cultic and legal correctness is wholly insufficient to fulfill Israel's role in the covenant relationship with God. Although Hosea explicitly upholds the requirement of strict adherence to covenant and Torah in 8:1, where he castigates Israel for failure to obey, in 6:6 he also belittles sacrificial worship, where God says, "I desire steadfast love [*ḥesed*], not sacrifice. . . . " The Book of Amos goes even further and actually condemns improperly motivated legal observance in favor of proper social relations: in Amos 5:21-24 God says, "I hate, I despise your feasts . . . Though you offer me sacrifice, . . . I will not accept them. . . . but let justice roll down like water and righteousness like a perennial stream." Although the legal aspect of righteousness is not absent in this passage, the point is that righteousness entails more than merely obeying a set of rules, especially since the cult, even when performed as prescribed, is condemned. In this view, righteousness, being paired with justice, clearly includes ethical and moral behavior along with compliance with regulation. Hosea makes a similar parallel with similar implications in 10:12, where he pairs righteousness with "mercy," or "steadfast love" [*ḥesed*]. Here, Hosea clearly shows his view that strict legal compliance is insufficient for true righteousness, for the latter is internal. Hos 6:1-3 plainly calls for true repentance and turning to God, rather than a formal restoration of ritual observance.

A factor that is evident in both Hosea and Amos is their belief that righteousness is primarily an attribute pertaining to the nation, rather than to the individual. Each issues a call to national repentance and reform and believes that unless the nation's behavior changes, the nation will be destroyed in God's wrath. This corporate view of righteousness is shared by ISAIAH of Jerusalem. Isaiah's view of righteousness is no less ethical and moral than that of his northern predecessors (Isa 6:9-13). It is also equally and explicitly corporate and national.

A century after Isaiah, however, EZEKIEL takes a different view of righteousness. In the writings of this exilic prophet, all individuals receive the consequences of their own actions. Therefore, for Ezekiel, righteousness is an individual matter and not only a matter for national attention. His clearest statement of this view is found in 18:20, where he states unequivocally that "The soul that sins will die. The son will not suffer for the sin of the father, nor will the father suffer for the sin of the son. The righteous one's righteousness will come upon himself and the sinner's sin will come upon himself." Although this is a distinct change from the national or corporate righteousness in the ideal of the earlier prophets, Ezekiel sees righteousness in the same terms as did his predecessors: the proper conduct required by the covenant. Ezekiel, however, probably due to his priestly background, sees a greater role in true righteousness for the cultic observances of Israel; this is made clear in that proper worship is given status equal to moral behavior as components of righteousness (Ezek 18:6-9).

The idea of righteousness as obedience to the covenant is not limited to Israel in the Bible but is applied to God as well. The clearest statement that God's righteousness is similar in character to Israel's is found in Judg 5:11 where the "triumphs ["righteous acts," KJV] of God" is paralleled with the "triumphs ["righteous acts," KJV] of his yeomanry in Israel." Here, God has fulfilled his role in the covenant relationship by giving victory to Israel and therefore is righteous while Israel, in following God's leadership, has likewise fulfilled the covenant. Thus the righteousness of God and of Israel derive from the same source: obedience to God's covenant.

See also ETHICS IN THE OLD TESTAMENT; JUSTICE/JUDGMENT.

Bibliography. W. E. Addis, "Righteousness," *EB*; W. Eichrodt, *Theology of the Old Testament*; J. Pedersen, *Israel: Its Life and Culture*; G. von Rad, *Old Testament Theology*.

—RAY SUTHERLAND

• **Rimmon.** [rim'uhn] The fertility god, or BAAL, of Aram, worshiped by the Aram royalty and nobility at a temple in Damascus (2 Kgs 5:18). Rimmon seems to be an alternate name for the storm-god Hadad, who was worshiped throughout the semitic world. Evidence for this identification is seen in 1 Kgs 15:18, where Tab-Rimmon is listed as the father of Ben-hadad, and in the name Ben-hadad, a common theophoric name for worshipers of Rimmon. The best evidence, however, is found in Zech 12:11, which tells of ritual mourning performed for a deity named Hadadrimmon. In view of this, Rimmon would appear to be a west-semitic storm god who is also seen as the bringer of fertility to the earth and to humanity.

The worship of Rimmon seems to have spread throughout the territory of Israel as well as Aram, since the name "Rimmon" appears in several place names within Israel. In Josh 19:13, the boundary of the territory of Zebulun is marked by a village named Rimmon, later known as a Levitical city (1 Chr 6:77). A Judean village Rimmon, or En-Rimmon, was a well known part of the tribe of Judah from the early monarchy well into postexilic days (Josh 15:32; 19:7; 1 Chr 4:32; Neh 11:29; Zech 14:10). Rimmon was also the name of a rock outcropping that served as the refuge of the Benjaminite survivors of the battles of Judg 20:44-48.

See also BAAL.

—RAY SUTHERLAND

• **Ring Composition.** *See* INCLUSIO

• **Rizpah.** [riz'puh] A concubine of King SAUL. After Saul's death, civil war broke out between the house of Saul and the followers of DAVID. ABNER, commander of Saul's army, made ISHBOSHETH (Ishbaal), Saul's son, king over ISRAEL. Judah followed David. Concerned for Abner's rising influence and suspecting his desire to be king, Ishbosheth accused Abner of claiming Rizpah as his own concubine—an act equivalent to claiming the throne. The accusation so angered Abner that he transferred his support to David (cf. 2 Sam 3). Later (2 Sam 21), when a famine was attributed to Saul's violation of a covenant with the Gibeonites (cf. Josh 9:3-21), David gave Rizpah's two sons and five other descendants of Saul to the Gibeonites as an expiation. After the Gibeonites executed them, Rizpah guarded the bodies day and night until rain returned. Inspired by Rizpah's example, David publicly buried Saul and Jonathan.

See also ABNER; DAVID; GIBEON.

—MICHAEL FINK

• **Roads/Highways/Trade Routes.** The Bible makes many references to roads and highways but says very little about their actual construction. Several words are used to designate these roads, the most common being *derek*, which is normally translated as "way," "road," or "highway," and occurs more than 700 times in the OT (cf. Isa 9:1; Num 20:17; etc.). Among the other terms used, some are synonymous with *derek* such as *mĕsillâ* and *'ōraḥ*, the latter paralleling *derek* many times (for the former cf. Isa 62:10; Judg 21:19; Num 20:31; for the latter, Gen 49:17; Prov 9:15; etc.). Other terms used are *nāṯîb* (path, way, Judg 5:6; Isa 42:16; etc.), *šĕbîl,* (path, Ps 77:20; Jer 18:15), and *miš'ôl* (narrow path, Num 22:24).

The earliest land travel routes were probably little more than foot paths which were followed by later roads. By biblical times, three major north-south highways crossed Palestine (PLATE 14). On the coast was the Way of the Sea (Via Maris). Beginning in Egypt, the road followed the coast line north to Mount Carmel, opposite Caesarea. There it turned northeast to MEGIDDO. At Megiddo, the highway divided into three branches. One continued north to Acco and on up the Syrian coast to Anatolia. Another branch went north/northeast, passing on the west side of the Sea of Galilee to HAZOR. At Hazor, this branch divided into two other roads. One continued north to HAMATH and on into Mesopotamia, the other turned northeast to DAMASCUS. The third branch from Megiddo went east through the Jezreel Valley to BETH-SHAN and across the Jordan River where it intersected with the King's Highway, the second of the major north-south routes.

Mentioned three times in the Bible, twice by name (Num 20:17; 21:22; Deut 2:27), the King's Highway began in the Gulf of Aqaba at Elath and ran the entire length of the Transjordan to Damascus. A major trade route in ancient times, the road was eventually lined with fortresses and was rebuilt by the Roman emperor, Trajan, early in the second century C.E.

In addition to these two major international highways that passed through Palestine, a third road ran through the central part of the country. From the Esdraelon plain in the north, it went south to Shechem and on to Jerusalem. From Jerusalem it continued on to Hebron and Beer-sheba into the northern Negeb.

Crisscrossing Palestine linking these major routes, were many local roads, some of which are given specific names in the Bible. These names, for the most part, seem to have been derived from the names of major cities or towns located on them, or from the geographical regions through which they passed. Thus, the Way of Ephrath (Gen 35:16) ran north from Beersheba to Jerusalem and continued northwards forming part of the major central highway discussed above. The Way of Beth-shemesh (1 Sam 6:9) linked the Way of Ephrath at Jerusalem with the Way of the Sea on the coast. In the south, the Way of the Mountain of the Amorites (Deut 1:19) cut across the central Negeb linking the Way of the Red Sea (Num 14:25) with the Way of the Arabah near Kadesh-barnea. The Way of the Spies (Exod 21:1) linked the Way of the Arabah with Arad in the north. Two roads paralleled the Jordan River, one on either side. The Way of the Jordan (Josh 2:7) ran on the west side to Beth-shan and points north, while the Way of the Plain (2 Sam 18:23) traversed the east side. The Way of the Wilderness of Edom (2 Kgs 3:8), which was located east of the King's Highway, ran north joining the Way Through the Wilderness of Moab which rejoined the King's Highway at Rabbath-Ammon.

While real road building in Palestine did not occur before the Persian and Hellenistic periods, the introduction of chariots as part of the military hardware would have necessitated better roads of some sort much earlier, at least by the time of SOLOMON (cf. 1 Kgs 9:19). How such roads might have been constructed we are not told. The image of road preparation is used as a symbol by Second Isaiah (40:3), and "straight paths" is said to be the reward of a wise man (Prov 3:6). But if we can trust an Egyptian text of the Nineteenth Dynasty, these early roads left a lot to be desired. The text describes one road as being "filled with boulders and pebbles, without a toehold for passing by, overgrown with reeds, thorns, brambles, and 'wolf's-paw' " (*ANET*, 478a). Also, Mesha, who was the king of Moab during the last half of the ninth century B.C.E., claims on the Moabite Stone (MESHA STELE) to have built a highway in the Arnon Valley (*ANET*, 320), but exactly how the road was constructed is not detailed.

The great age of road building in Palestine belongs to the Romans. Not only did they build roads to last, many of which can still be seen today, but they also built bridges and marked their roads with milestones. Their basic building materials was stone, well set in a prepared road bed, which accounts for the longevity of their work. These roads were a great asset to Paul as he traveled the major routes of Asia Minor. He entered Rome on one of the most-famous Roman roads of all, the Appian Way (Acts 28:15).

Although river traffic, especially in Egypt and Mesopotamia, may have preceded land travel for trading purposes, by biblical times merchants from every part of the ancient world passed through the highways and byways of Canaan. The main trade routes that ran from Egypt to Syria and to central and southern Mesopotamia and Anatolia coincided with the highways already discussed. Trade was an international enterprise and the Bible mentions a wide variety of merchants who appeared on the scene (cf. Gen 37:25-28; 1 Kgs 10:15; Isa 23:8; Ezek 27). In many instances, trade was a royal prerogative, and Solomon is said to have traded with the Egyptians, Hittites, and others (1 Kgs 10:28-29; 2 Chr 9:14).

Trade routes also included the seas, documented as early as the third millennium B.C.E., when Egypt traded with Byblos. The Phoenicians were famous for their maritime trading operations in the Mediterranean, and Solomon had a fleet of trading vessels which sailed from the port of Ezion-geber on the Gulf of Aqaba (2 Kgs 9:26-28).

During the Hellenistic and Roman periods, the trade routes were controlled primarily by the Nabataeans and the Palmyrenians. With their capital at Petra, the former controlled the trade route from Hamath to the southwest corner of Arabia, and the latter, the routes to and from central Asia. During the same period, sea trade was in the control of the Greeks and Phoenicians.

The geographical position of Palestine ensured it a unique role in the history of the ancient Near East. No where is this role more clearly seen than in the roads and highways which connected it with the larger empires of that day.

Bibliography. G. A. Barrois, "Trade and Commerce," *IDB*; H. F. Beck, "Road," *IDB*; S. Cohen, "King's Highway," *IDB*; S. V. McCasland, "Travel and Communication in the NT," *IDB*; I. Mendelsohn, "Travel and Communication in the OT," *IDB*; A. Negev, ed., "Roads," *AEHL*; J. B. Pritchard, ed., *ANET*.

—JOHN C. H. LAUGHLIN

• **Robbery.** The taking of something from another by violent force or threat; the taking of something from another by any wrongful means.

In the commandment "You shall not steal" (Exod 20:15), robbery is prohibited. In Prov 1:11-19, the young person is warned against becoming a robber or thief. One is admonished not to rob a neighbor (Lev 19:13) or the poor (Prov 22:22) because punishment will come from God. One who robs a parent is considered a destroyer (Prov 28:24).

Frequently the penalty for robbery was death (Ezek 18:10-13) and the robber's lifestyle would bring on his destruction (Prov 21:7).

Robbery was prevalent throughout Israel's history. In the time of the judges the residents of Shechem sought vengeance through highway robbery (Judg 9:25) and in the days of Shamgar and Jael brigands abounded (Judg 5:6). Hosea said that the priests of his day were like robbers who lie in wait seeking opportunities to commit crimes (Hos 6:9). In the time of Jesus, robbery was commonplace; the parable of the good Samaritan illustrates its cruelty (Luke 10:30-37). Robbers even invaded pagan temples, and Paul experienced a savage attack on one of his journeys (2 Cor 11:26). Robbers entered sheepfolds (John 10:7-10) and broke into houses to steal (Matt 6:20).

Pagan nations surrounding Israel were characterized as robbers. Nineveh was described as a bloody city, full of robbery (Nah 3:1), and Isaiah described Assyria as one who enjoyed plundering (Isa 10:13).

The prophets of Israel compared the apostasy of God's people to that of robbers. Isaiah accused the officials of Israel of enacting unjust laws so that they could rob the poor, widows and orphans (Isa 10:2). Amos portrayed the Israelites as storing up for the future the booty from their robberies (3:10). Micah condemned those who lay awake at night devising schemes to rob those around them (2:1, 2), and Hosea pictured the people of his day as participating in robbery and other sins (4:2). Jeremiah, in the famous Temple sermon, denounced the Israelites for stealing and then making the house of God "a den of robbers" (7:9-11). Ezekiel charged that the Israelites used oppression in order to exercise robbery and exploit the poor, the needy, and the sojourners (22:29).

Improper offerings were considered the same thing as robbing God. Malachi accused the Israelites of robbery because they withheld their tithes (3:8, 9). God wanted justice from his people and hated being robbed (Isa 61:8). Jesus reprimanded the Temple merchants for making God's house a den of robbers and thieves (Matt 21:13). In castigating the Pharisees for their obsession with outward rituals, Jesus characterized them as full of robbery and wickedness (Luke 11:39).

In the NT era, the term "robber" had several meanings. The malefactors crucified alongside Jesus (Matt 27:38, 44) probably were insurrectionists against Rome. BARABBAS, who was released in the place of Jesus (John 18:40), also would fit into this category.

See also LAW IN THE NEW TESTAMENT; LAW IN THE OLD TESTAMENT.

—A. O. COLLINS

• **Rod/Staff.** The English words used in several translations to correspond to a number of Hebrew words with various meanings. Some of these Hebrew words have alternate meanings quite different from that expressed by the word "rod." The most common use of a rod was as a staff for walking. A less common use was as an instrument of punishment with which to administer beatings (Isa 10:5). A staff could also be used to signify the bearer's authority. MOSES' and AARON's rods are classic examples of a staff as a badge of authority. Aaron's rod turned into a serpent as a sign to Pharaoh (Exod 7:10) and flowered as a sign of Aaron's priesthood (Num 17). Moses' rod is the catalyst for the parting of the sea (Exod 14:15-22). Similar ideas are seen in Gen 49:10 and Judg 5:14. Rods of a given length could be used as measuring devices, as in Ezek 40:2-5 where the angel used a rod to measure the proposed temple. In some cases a soldier's club is called a staff. In 1 Sam 14:27, JONATHAN apparently carried a staff as a weapon and, in 2 Sam 23:21, Benaiah attacked an Egyptian soldier while carrying only a staff. A staff or rod was also a standard tool of the shepherd, used to guide sheep, fight off wild animals, and other similar uses. The clearest picture of this usage is found in Ps 23 in which "your rod and your staff" of v. 4 is a continuation of the shepherd imagery of vv. 1-3.

See also TRIBES.

—RAY SUTHERLAND

• **Roman Empire.** ROME became an empire under Octavian in 27 B.C.E. (PLATE 20). Until that time, it had been a republic, but constant expansion and growing threat necessitated a shift in power from the Senate and people to the *princeps*. The story of the empire from Octavian (Augustus) on is the story of increasing centralization as it deteriorated internally as a result of intrigue and poor government and suffered externally from attacks by enemies all around its vast frontiers. In 285 C.E. the Emperor Diocletian assumed the title of Dominus, symbolizing absolute authority.

Political Developments. The Julio-Claudian line (Octavian, Tiberius, Gaius, Claudius, and Nero), 31 B.C.E.–68 C.E., and the Flavians (Vespasian, Titus, and Domitian), 69–96 C.E., concentrated more and more power in the hands of the emperor, although the senate retained mininal authority. The emperors sought to strengthen external boundaries by establishing a line of colonies along the northern and eastern frontiers. Beginning with Augustus, they fostered Caesar-worship as a means of restoring the old state cultus and thus uniting an increasingly fragmented populace. To enhance their own control over an expanding state, they sought to reform provincial administration, placing officials more directly under their immediate control.

Courtesy of the Eisenberg Museum of Biblical Archaeology, Southern Baptist Theological Seminary.

A coin from the reign of Vespatian Judea Capta (ca. 71 C.E.)

The Antonines (Nerva, Trajan, Hadrian, Antoninus Pius, and Marcus Aurelius), 96–180, brought the empire to its peak. They extended its boundaries to include northern Britain, the Rhine-Danube triangle, Dacia, Arabia, Armenia, Mesopotamia, and Assyria. The empire achieved its greatest extent under Hadrian (117–38), who also erected permanent frontier fortifications. Internally the Romans enjoyed tranquillity and good government. Many observers, however, have noted a decrease in internal strength. The population underwent a gradual change of stock as a result of importation of slaves captured in conquest of new lands. The Antonines continued to reform provincial administration.

The empire faltered badly after Marcus Aurelius (161–80). New enemies threatened on the frontiers—the Alamanni and the Franks in 236, the Goths between 247 and 251, and the neo-Persians or Sassanids between 260 and

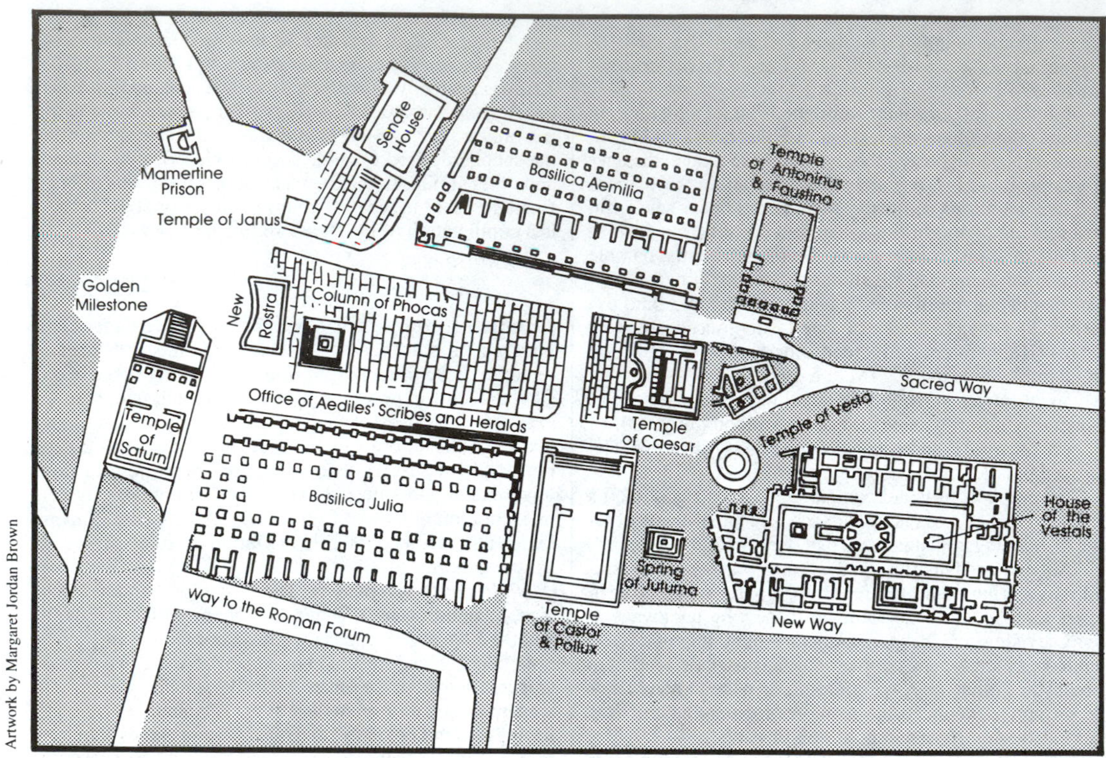

Artwork by Margaret Jordan Brown

The Roman Forum.

268. In the meantime, the empire suffered continuous internal disruption. Strong emperors such as Septimius Severus (202–11), Decius (248–51), and Valerian (253–60) began to look upon Christianity as "an empire within the empire" and thus to undertake official repression. Aurelian (270–75) restored some semblance of unity as the empire experienced further threats from the Sassanids.

By 284 the western portion of the empire faced such bleak prospects that Diocletian (284-304) had no difficulty seizing what little power remained in the hands of the senate, which conferred on him the title of *Dominus*. Germanic tribes in the north were restless, moving southwards little by little. Diocletian and Constantine completed work on the ring of internal and external fortifications which would hold them back for a time but which could not do so forever. Recognizing the twilight settling over the West, Diocletian shifted the capital from Rome to Nicomedia. Three decades later, Constantine moved it to Byzantium, thus assuring the final separation of East and West. The final division of the empire occurred in 374 during the joint reign of Valentinian I and Valens.

The most notable event of this era, however, was the conversion of Constantine to Christianity about 312. Although scholars have debated vigorously the character of his conversion, Constantine left no doubt about his growing fervor for the Christian religion and antipathy to others, as he moved from impartiality to favoritism to triumphalism. After about 324, when he defeated Licinius, he showered the churches with favors—granting tax exemptions to the clergy, erecting church edifices, encouraging conversions, and rallying support of the wealthy and powerful to the churches' aid. He also intervened in ecclesiastical affairs, as he did in convening and participating in the Council of Nicaea in 325 in order to end the Arian controversy. In 330 he moved his capital from Rome to Byzantium, renamed Constantinople, partly out of frustration that he could not convert the ancient city completely.

The conversion of the empire to the Christian faith continued steadily after Constantine except for Julian's brief effort to replace Christianity with a revived and revised state cultus (361-63). Constantine's sons, however, divided loyalties between the Nicene and the Arian parties. In the East Constantius (337–61) opted for Arianism; in the West Constans (337–51) and Constantine II (337–40) for the Nicene formula. After the death of Constantius Arianism lost ground within the empire, but it continued strong among the barbarians, especially the Goths, as a result of the missionary labors of Ulfilas. Theodosius I (379–95) assured the triumph of Nicene Christianity in legislation establishing Christianity as the religion of the Roman empire.

Even before Theodosius assumed the title of Augustus the barbarians had begun their "invasions" through which they gradually took control of the West. Under Alaric the Visigoths moved into Illyricum, Greece, and northern Italy between 395 and 410. Ataulf extended the conquests of Alaric. Vandals, Suevi, and Alani invaded Spain. Vandals moved into Africa under the leadership of Gaiseric at the request of Count Boniface in 435. Gaiseric later (456–72) led the Vandals into Italy, capturing Rome itself. The Huns invaded Gaul and Italy under Attila (451–53). In 476 Odoacer, barbarian commander of the western army, returned the symbols of office to Zeno, the Emperor of the Eastern Empire, assuming the title of "king" like other barbarian chiefs.

During this difficult period, population decreased, the practice of infanticide increased, more and more land fell into disuse, and urban prosperity declined. There were constant riots and insurrections. The army in the West consisted chiefly of recruits from among the barbarians. Pressures mounted on all sides. The Goths, Quadi, and Sarmatae pushed southwards into Europe. The Picts and the Scots harassed the Romans in Britain. Although the Eastern Empire remained strong, Isaurian mountaineers and the Saracens attacked from the East. Sassanids continued to whittle away at what remained of the empire on the Palestinian coast, leaving it vulnerable to the Muslim onslaught in the seventh century.

Social Setting of the Early Roman Empire. During its first couple of centuries, the Roman empire was distinguished by a cosmopolitan outlook. The Romans admired Greek civilization and culture and, after their conquest of the Seleucid empire (215–63 B.C.E.), became disseminators of Hellenism. Greek remained the language of the cultured until the early third century and the universalistic spirit of the Greeks informed the Roman outlook as well.

The Romans were practical people. They took pride in the *Pax Romana,* "Roman peace," that guaranteed a measure of security for all citizens within the empire. Along the banks of the Tiber River in Rome, Octavian erected the *Ara Pacis,* "Altar of Peace," depicting the idyllic hopes set forth by the poet Virgil. Inspired by world conquest, the powerful Roman army maintained strict control throughout the provinces. A system of well-engineered roads connected the widely scattered parts of the empire and enabled emperors to dispatch troops as needed in emergencies. A system of mails allowed public officials to communicate directly with the emperors on relatively short notice.

The vast majority of people lived in large cities where they could obtain the best means of support. Besides Rome itself, which had about a million inhabitants, EPHESUS, ANTIOCH, Alexandria, and Carthage stood out as major centers of culture and trade. Cities such as these provided advantages for their citizens—especially in "bread and circuses." Rome had so many persons on the wheat dole that Augustus (31 B.C. E.–14 C.E.) had to reduce it from 200,000 to 150,000 as more and more persons depended on state maintenance. The larger benefits went to the rich who built grand villas outside the city or in less congested areas within. The masses of poor who composed the vast portion of the population lived in cramped apartments without adequate or safe sanitation, water, or other necessities. Apartment buildings five or six stories high often collapsed without warning.

Average citizens struggled to survive on minimal wages. Literacy varied from an elite who were taught by the best scholars to the masses who could neither read nor write. Families grappled with problems of child rearing, conscription into the army, fear of losing property, burdensome taxation, and despair in the face of sickness and death. To cope, they consulted soothsayers, carried magical charms, went to mediums and augurs, bought formulas for warding off evil, and participated in a variety of cults. Ethical standards ranged across a wide spectrum. Although an elite few lived admirable lives under Stoic guidance, the lower classes scraped bottom much of the time. They exposed unwanted children, especially females. They inflicted violence on one another very much as inhabitants of urban ghettoes do today.

Religions and Philosophies. The Romans were a religious people. They prided themselves not merely on their gods but on their devotion to the gods as the factor which explained Rome's greatness. When they conquered other peoples, they adopted those gods and sought to incorporate them with due respect into the Roman pantheon. Judaism and Christianity alone proved unwilling to permit their God to enter.

Roman religions fell predominantly into three categories: the state cultus, oriental religions, and philosophies which functioned both as religions and as philosophies. The state cultus honored the ancient Roman deities and others absorbed into the pantheon, especially the Olympian gods of Homer. It consisted of exact repetition of rites and rituals, superstitious practices such as examination of the entrails of sacrificial birds or animals, and offering of various sacrifices. In an effort to revive interest in it, Augustus added worship of the goddess Roma and the emperor but with limited success; to most citizens, offering sacrifices amounted to little more than reciting a pledge of allegiance.

Far more attractive to the masses were oriental religions: Cybele or the Great Mother, Isis and Osiris, Mithra, Judaism, and Christianity. These responded much better than did the state religion to the masses' pessimism and despair, loss of confidence and hope, longing for conversion, and cry for infallible revelation. They appealed not merely to the intellect but met deep emotional and spiritual needs in tangible ways—sacramental dramas, fellowship in intimate groups without regard to social status, symbolism, and assurances of redemption.

Certain philosophies fulfilled the religious needs of the well educated. Until about 150 C.E. Stoicism, originated about 300 B.C.E. by Zeno of Citium, dominated a broad field. The STOICS urged those who sought happiness to live reasonably as nature intended. They made conscience and duty the cornerstones of their ethics. After about 150, Platonism supplanted Stoicism as the leading philosophy. Neoplatonism, a version originating in Alexandia with Plotinus (205–69) and Origen (185–254/5) both students of Ammonius Saccas, exerted a powerful attraction for Christians. Neoplatonism borrowed much of its ethical thought from Stoicism, but it emphasized return to unity with "the One" as the ultimate goal of human existence. By contemplation the individual may attain some experience of union even while living in the body. Such thinking supplied the foundation for development of Christian mysticism.

A natural by-product of the syncretism of Greco-Roman culture during the first centuries of the empire was GNOSTICISM. Gnosticism combined elements of religion and philosophy from both East and West to produce a hodge podge of sects attaching themselves to both Judaism and Christianity. Offering salvation by way of spiritual knowledge (*gnosis*), most sects injected a radical DUALISM between matter (as evil) and spirit (as good) into a Neoplatonic framework.

See also GNOSTICISM; HELLENISTIC WORLD; MYSTERY RELIGIONS; STOICS.

Bibliography. S. Benko and J. J. O'Rourke, *The Catacombs and the Colosseum: The Roman Empire as the Setting of Primitive Christianity*; J. Carcopino, *Daily Life in Ancient Rome*; S. Dill, *Roman Society from Nero to Marcus* and *Roman Society in the Last Century of the Western Empire*; J. Ferguson, *The Religions of the Roman Empire*; A. H. M. Jones, *The Later Roman Empire, 284–602*; W. A. Meeks, *The Moral World of the First Christians*;

M. Rostovtzeff, *Rome*.

—E. GLENN HINSON

• OUTLINE OF ROMANS •

Letter to the Romans

I. Introduction (1:1-15)
  A. Salvation (1:1-7)
  B. Thanksgiving (1:8-15)
II. Transitional Statement: Thematic Thesis (1:16-17)
III. The Body of the Letter (1:18–15:13)
  A. The devastating problem of sin (1:18–3:20)
  B. The way of faith (3:21–4:25)
  C. The transformation of life (5:1–8:39)
  D. The problem of Israel and the coming of the gentiles (9:1–11:36)
  E. Ethical instructions related to transformed living (12:1–15:13)
IV. Conclusion (15:14–16:27)
  A. Paul's desire for the Letter (15:14-21)
  B. Paul's desire for his ministry (15:22-33)
  C. Concluding appeals and greetings (16:1-23)
  D. Final doxology (16:25-27)

• **Romans, Letter to the.** Regarded by many as the capstone of PAUL's writings, Romans has had a profound impact upon Christian theology in general and upon many notable individuals such as Marcion, Augustine, Luther, and Karl Barth. It was placed first in the Pauline corpus by the organizers of the NT certainly not because it was Paul's first writing but because it is Paul's most comprehensive statement of the gospel.

Authenticity, Authorship, and Setting. If any book in the NT was written by Paul, it is Romans. Every ancient canonical listing of authoritative Christian scriptures includes Romans. It has even been a basic touchstone for the critical Tübingen hypothesis (F. C. Baur's delineation of what he thought was genuinely from Paul and what he considered to be secondary). To reject Pauline authorship of Romans (e.g., Bruno Bauer), therefore, is a fruitless task.

There is evidence that the Letter was known and used by early Christians such as Clement of Rome, Ignatius, Justin Martyr, and Polycarp. Moreover, Sanday and Headlam find hints of Paul's thought from Romans in Hebrews, James, Jude, and the Petrine Letters. But such an argument must not be pressed to imply literary dependency.

As for the setting of the Letter, it was probably written from Corinth during the third missionary journey after Paul's departure from Ephesus and following the receipt of the offering for the needy saints of Jerusalem from the Christians both in Macedonia and Achaia (1 Cor 16:1-8; Rom 15:24-25). The intention of Paul was to accompany this offering to Jerusalem and then to visit ROME on his way to Spain (Rom 15:24, 28). This order agrees with the itinerary in Acts 19:21. In that context Luke adds that Paul stayed three months in southern Greece (Acts 20:3). During this time Paul likely wrote Romans. The mention of Phoebe, a deacon in the church at Corinth's port city of Cenchreae (Rom 16:1), heightens the probability that Romans was written from Corinth. Since Paul also calls on the recipients to receive her, it suggests that she may have been the envoy who carried this Letter (Rom 16:2).

While scholars often tend to express certainty on the dating of Romans, it is wise for readers to realize that the issue of dating the Pauline journeys is rather complex, involving such matters as the proconsulship of GALLIO (Acts 18:12), time sequences in the Acts, and the relationship of the journeys in Acts to the Pauline Letters. The likely date for writing Romans is 56 (or 58) C.E.

Integrity of the Letter. While Marcion excised segments of Romans (esp. passages in Rom 4 and 9–11) because of his anti-OT bias, the integrity of Romans 1–15 is not seriously in dispute.

The major issues involve the doxology in 16:25-27 and the long list of greetings in 16:1-23. T.W. Manson in 1938 noted that the doxology at 16:25-27 can be found in a few ancient manuscripts at the end of chaps. 14 and 15. He argued first that the shortest form was probably a Marcionite abbreviation. Second, because 𝔭46 (the oldest Gk. manuscript) omits chap. 16 and because the greetings seem to be Asian in orientation, he argued that chaps. 1–15 formed the original letter to Rome. A third argument was that a second letter with greetings to Asians was carried by Phoebe to Ephesus. This thesis is supported by certain facts: Aquila and Prisca went with Paul to Ephesus (Rom 16:3; Acts 18:18-19), Epaenetus is the first convert in Asia (Rom 16:5), and the many greetings to persons he knows and with whom he seems to have colabored are hard to understand at Rome. Karl Donfried, however, rejects the idea that chap. 16 has to be Asian because Rome itself was filled with many Asians. Donfried considers the doxology to be a late addition, probably by Marcion, which later scribes were not sure where to place.

The Nature of Romans. Closely connected with questions of integrity, setting, and intention is the issue of the nature of the Letter. Manson rejected the notion that Romans was primarily a letter of self-introduction by Paul. With or without the greetings, he argued that it is a "manifesto" which Paul wanted to have the "widest publicity" possible. Günther Bornkamm sees the Letter as the means whereby Paul, on his way to Jerusalem with the collection for the Jews, works out his diatribe or argument with the Jews in terms of the nature of salvation. Jacob Jervell thinks that Paul was concerned about being rejected in Jerusalem and called upon the Romans for prayer support so that he might visit them and proceed with his mission objective to Spain (Rom 15:22-32). Günther Klein countered that Paul is not dealing with his own concerns. Klein argues that Paul's use of the term "Christians" and not "church" in the Letter indicates that Paul found it necessary to lay an apostolic basis for the church in Rome. Donfried rejects the idea that Paul's primary concern was his argument with Jerusalem and builds upon Paul Minear's thesis that Paul wrote the Letter both to communicate his intention for his future missionary work and to deal with concerns of the weak and strong in faith in the church at Rome (Rom 14:1–15:13). Romans does not appear to fit simply into one of these perspectives; the Letter seems to contain many foci which encompass both Paul's concerns for the Romans and his own personal concerns for his visit to Jerusalem and his projected visit to Rome (Rom 1:11-15). Bultmann's thesis that Romans represents the style of the Cynic and Stoic diatribe is much too limited a view of Paul's broad dialogical and rhetorical patterns of argument.

The Contents of the Book. (1) Introduction (1:1-15). Romans begins (1:1-7) with a typical Greek epistolary salutation (*x* to *y* greetings), but the *x* element is greatly elaborated as Paul spells out his own call and his authorization by Jesus Christ who is the basis for salvation since he is the true Messiah from David and the acknowledged powerful Son of God is the basis for salvation. The greetings element is in a typical Christian formulation of grace and peace (always in that order). Paul then (1:8-15) turns to the thanksgiving statement which is an elaborate prayer that affirms both his gratitude for their faithfulness and his commitment to pray for them. This thanksgiving note is strengthened by a statement of his desire to make a visit which will have mutual benefit. He supports his desire by a reference to his obligation to the gentiles so that they will understand that after he visits Jerusalem he genuinely hopes to come and evangelize in Rome.

(2) Transitional Statement (1:16-17). These verses encompass the thematic core of the Letter. The righteousness of God has been revealed and salvation is available to everyone—both to Jew and to gentile. It is to be received in FAITH from beginning to end. The call of the gospel is to a living faith and salvation is the result of God's power at work.

(3) The Body of the Letter (1:18-15:13). (a) The devastating problem of SIN (1:18–3:20). The purpose of this major section is to prove that all have sinned and miss God's intended goals (3:23). In arguing his case, Paul first employs a Hellenistic tripartite division of the human being (heart, passions, and mind) to prove that humans (here gentiles) have become terribly distorted and their lives are filled with all kinds of evil practices (1:29-31). Although the Greek thought was that at least the mind was eternal and uncontaminated, Paul knew better and realized that even the mind needed renewal (cf. Rom 12:2). The major problem is not that people (*even* the gentiles) do not know God's good will in the world (general revelation); it is instead that people refuse to acknowledge God as God and worship things in the created order rather than the Creator (1:18-23). Therefore, God delivers every aspect of their being (the three parts) to unholy activity (1:24, 26, 28), and they not only practice evil but conspire in such practices (1:32).

Next Paul turns to the moralistic Jew who condemns pagan immorality and who thinks that he is superior in God's sight. Paul reminds the Jew that God's kindness was not meant to give the Jew a superior feeling but to bring about repentance and good works (2:1-4). God judges not merely by what one thinks or says one is, but by what one does! Thus, God is absolutely fair in judgment (2:5-16). By using the Hebrew psychology of the balanced inclination (*yetzer*) to good and to evil and by reminding the reader of the authentic meaning of circumcision, Paul points to Jewish disobedience. He judges that real Jewishness is not a matter of externals such as bloodline and physical circumcision (2:17-29). Does the Jew then have an advantage? Yes (3:2) and no (3:9)! The Jew has a history and has been given the word of God; but because of refusal to obey, the Jew also stands under judgment (3:1-8). Therefore, everyone is under the power of sin (3:9-18), everyone is responsible (3:19), and no one is justified by mere human effort (3:20).

(b) The way of faith (3:21–4:25). Yet, although all have sinned (3:23), God in his righteousness, patience, and GRACE has made a way of dealing with sin (EXPIATION/propiation) through the redeeming blood of Jesus which is to be accepted by faith. This process is called JUSTIFICATION by faith (3:21-26). To emphasize the fact of the centrality of faith in the continuing saving processes of God, Paul then described Abraham's trusting pattern. His faith in receiving both circumcision and the PROMISE that he would be the father of many people illustrated for Paul how faith has always been regarded as a basis for righteousness (4:1-22). In like manner, believing in the effectiveness of the death and resurrection of Jesus is basic to our forgiveness of sins and justification (or declaration of righteousness) before God (4:23-25).

(c) The transformation of life (5:1–8:39). Beginning with chap. 5 there is a major change in focus. Paul is here pointing his readers to the meaning of transformation or the way of growing in holiness (SANCTIFICATION). Because of our justification, we have peace with God, a great hope; and our calling is to live the life of suffering love (5:1-5). Indeed, even though once we were sinners, we are justified and we have the expectation of being saved from God's final wrath (5:6-9). Because of our RECONCILIATION, we need to reflect his saving power in our lives (5:10-11). We are neither to follow the pattern of Adam's successors who could not handle sin nor consider the situation hopeless because of the requirements of the Law, as in case of the successors of Moses. But we are to accept the reign of life which has been brought in Jesus Christ and realize that grace abounds in the life of Christians (5:12-21).

Are we then to continue in the way of sin? Of course not! When we were baptized, we took on a new allegiance and our task is to conduct our lives (walk) in this new way (6:1-4). Just as Jesus was raised from the clutches of death, our call is to abandon the deathly way of sin because the power of sin does not have the right to claim us as its adherents (6:5-14). We are no longer to be enslaved to sin because God has set us free on the road to sanctification or holiness (6:15-19). If we are enslaved, it is to be to God's sanctifying process which will conclude in our ultimate hope—eternal life (6:20-23)! Note the meaning of eternal life here.

Paul then reminds his readers that, just as a marriage is dissolved in the case of the death of a spouse, so Christians are no longer in bondage to the Law (7:1-6). The issue is not that the Law is to be identified with sin. But, before salvation, a sinner is so enmeshed in sin that there is almost an identification between the two. Now the Christian has been freed from the bondage of sin but that does not mean there is no longer a struggle (7:7-20). Paul knew that! His theological and psychological understandings were better than many Christian writings in the twentieth century. Indeed, into the person in Christ has been inserted a dimension of divine power which creates a war! The Christian can delight in the law of God, but the believer also knows that there is an enemy (7:22-23). The answer does not come by way of immediate total wholeness. In spite of the splitness of our desires, the answer is that God accepts us and we need to accept ourselves (7:24–8:2). Unfortunately, much of contemporary thinking about Paul has been so influenced by Krister Stendahl's denial of the introspective Western conscience in Paul that scholars have difficulty making sense of Rom 7 and the fact that Paul can think psychologically.

God indeed has condemned sin in the flesh and has ordered us not to walk in the ways of the world but in the ways of the Spirit. Yet he also understands that our bodies and spirits do not always work in harmony. Our bodies need to be conformed to the Spirit of God (8:3-11). To be led by the Spirit includes crying out to the Father for help and receiving the reaffirmation that we are his children, provided we are willing to accept the pain of living in the world (8:12-17). But such pain is only temporary and faithful servants learn that nothing can separate them from God's love and his hold upon their lives (8:26-39).

(d) The problem of Israel and the coming of the gentiles (9:1–11:36). One of the most difficult problems for Paul to understand was Israel's rejection of Christ. He would have gladly given himself, if he could have convinced the Jews (9:3). They had all the benefits of an historical relationship to God (9:4-5). Clearly Paul sensed that God's promises to the Jews had not failed because he himself was a Jew (11:1-2). But he knew that not all descendants of Abraham were children of promise (9:6-8). In the history of Israel it was apparent that God was in control like a potter over clay and that only a remnant would be saved (9:9-29). Indeed, God still had his 7,000 (11:2-10). But what about the gentiles? God's way had always been the way of faith and God was once again showing this fact through the coming of the gentiles (9:30-33). The Jews, however, had placed so much stock in the effectiveness of the Law to save that they needed to be reminded that Christ ended the Law so that faith might be primary (10:1-4). This word of faith is that Jesus is Lord, not Law. Believing in the power of the resurrection then is the key to salvation which means that there is no longer any distinction between Jew and Greek (10:5-13). But the coming of the gentiles does not mean the ultimate rejection of the Jews, and the gentiles must not become proud of their status like the moralistic Jews (cf. 2:1-10) because God is able to clip wild olive branches out of the stock just as readily as natural branches (11:11-24). The rejection by part of Israel had opened the door for the gentiles but God's call never ceased and so Paul expected both Jew and gentile to come to Christ because, just as all are sinners, God's mercy extends to all (11:25-32). He closed this section then with a profound doxology which leaves his unanswered questions of election in the hiddenness of God (11:33-36).

(e) Ethical instructions related to transformed living (12:1–15:13). The opening appeal of chap. 12 signals Paul's shift to paraenesis or ethical instruction. For Christians who seek to be led by the Spirit (8:14), Paul's exhortation is to present their bodies as a living sacrifice to God, a vehicle of God's transforming power (12:1-2). He called on them to affirm humbly their spiritual gifts from God, to treat one another with a genuine love, and to avoid the ways of evil (12:3-21). He reminded them to respect civil authority as a basis for law and order and to deal responsibly with issues such as taxes much in the way that Jesus argued (13:1-7; cf. Mark 12:17). He did not reject the commandments of the old covenant but suggested that the way of love for neighbor would more than fulfill those commands (13:8-10). He also summoned them to careful, watchful living as those who avoid self-gratification and who expect the soon coming of the Day of the Lord (13:11-14).

Paul opposed establishing a whole series of new laws such as those concerning proper food rules or proper ceremonial days (14:1-9). Clean and unclean laws were now meaningless to the transformed Paul (14:14). But he refused to condemn others on these matters or force them into his way of thinking. Because his desire was the edification of others, he would not use his freedom to destroy their faith (14:13-23). His self-giving spirit was modeled on the spirit of Christ (15:1-6) and his hope was that all people would praise God and that believers would be empowered by the Holy Spirit and be filled with joy and peace (15:7-13).

(4) Conclusion (15:14–16:27). Paul's commitment was to carry the gospel to the gentiles. He had reached the point of proclaiming Jesus from Jerusalem to Illyricum (15:16-19). His new goal was to extend the mission to Spain and on his way to visit Rome, after he had carried the financial aid he had collected in Macedonia and Achaia to the needy believers in Jerusalem (15:22-29). But he was concerned about his reception and about his hope of reaching Rome and so he requested the prayer support of Roman Christians (15:30-33).

In the last chapter he voiced his concern for the reception of the deacon Phoebe (16:1-2) and greeted his many Christian colleagues in the work of Christ—both male and female (16:3-16). Then he added a warning to avoid persons who created conflict among Christians because that pattern did not represent the spirit of Christ. Instead he awaited the coming of the peace of God which would crush Satan's efforts (16:17-20). Thereafter are stated the special greetings from Timothy and three of Paul's other companions as well as three Corinthian citizens who were obviously very supportive of Paul. Of special note is the greeting of Tertius who was the scribe or amanuensis of this Letter (16:21-23).

Finally, the Letter as it stands today closes with a fairly complex doxology which emphasizes the themes of power, mystery, secrecy, eons, and wisdom in addition to the obedience of faith (16:25-27). A shorter conclusion (16:24) which should be eliminated seems to be dependent upon the frustration resulting from the positioning of the doxology at various points in the last three chapters.

See also APOSTLES, ACTS OF; CONTRIBUTION FOR THE SAINTS; ELECTION; EXPIATION; FAITH AND FAITHLESSNESS; FLESH AND SPIRIT; GENTILE/GENTILES IN THE NEW TESTAMENT; GIFTS OF THE SPIRIT; GRACE; JUSTIFICATION; LAW IN THE NEW TESTAMENT; PAUL; PROMISE; RECONCILIATION; REDEMPTION IN THE NEW TESTAMENT; RIGHTEOUSNESS IN THE NEW TESTAMENT

Bibliography. C. K. Barrett, *A Commentary on the Epistle to the Romans*; K. Barth, *The Epistle to the Romans*; G. Borchert, "Romans, Pastoral Counseling and the Introspective Conscience of The West," *RE* 83 (1986): 81-92; F. F. Bruce, *The Epistle of Paul to the Romans* and "The Romans Debate-Continued," *BJRL* 64 (1982): 334-59; C. E. B. Cranfield, *A Critical and Exegetical Commentary on the Epistle to the Romans*; C. H. Dodd, *The Epistle to the Romans*; K. Donfried, ed, *The Romans Debate*; E. Käsemann, *Commentary on Romans*; H. Gamle, *The Textual History of the Letter to the Romans*; F. Leenhardt, *The Epistle to the Romans*; M. Luther, *Lectures on Romans*; P. Minear, *The Obedience of Faith*; L. Morris, *The Epistle to the Romans*; J. Munck, *Paul and the Salvation of Mankind* and *Christ and Israel: An Interpretation of Romans 9-11*; W. Sanday and A. C. Headlam, *A Critical and Exegetical Commentary on the Epistle to the Romans*; K. Stendahl, "The Apostle Paul and the Introspective Conscience of the West, " *HTR* 56 (1963): 199-215.

—GERALD L. BORCHERT

• **Rome.** The ancient capital of the Roman Republic and Empire; modern capital of Italy. Ancient Rome was situated on the banks of the Tiber River ca. eleven mi. inland east from its seaport Ostia (PLATE 20). Today because of river silting it is ca. fifteen mi. from the sea. It was built on a plain and on seven surrounding hills (clockwise: Quirinal, Viminal, Esquiline, Caelian, Aventine, Palatine and Capitoline).

History. The beginnings of the ancient city may go back to the second millennium but Latin settlement probably dates from the tenth century B.C.E. Legend sets "the founding of the city" by Romulus and Remus in 753 B.C.E. (A.U.C.; *ab urbe condita*; the point from which ancient Romans dated their activities). Its earliest name according to Varro (*On Latin* 5.41) was *Septimontium* (Seven Hills), a name given to one of its earliest festivals (in December) and according to Tertullian that name was applied to a deity (*To the Nations* 2.15).

In the sixth century the Tarquin kings (Etruscans) began a major building phase. They drained the swamps near the Palatine, developed the ancient forum with its temple of Jupiter and fortified the city. By 509 B.C.E. the inhabitants were so weary of construction and military service associated with Tarquin ambition that they deposed their ruler and initiated the Roman Republic (Livy 1.34-60). The new government was patrician, headed by two consuls. But discontent by the masses led to modification and two tribunes were installed to represent plebians. In the Republic period the Romans sought to avoid single headship in office.

Roman power grew rapidly. Carthage was defeated at Zama in 202 B.C.E. and the Punic wars ended with the sacking of Carthage in 146 B.C.E. Wherever there was political unrest, the Romans extended their influence as in the Battle of Magnesium with Antiochus the Great of Syria (190 B.C.E., cf. Dan 11:18) or with Antiochus Ephiphanes when he attacked the Egyptians and the Roman navy appeared ("Ships of the Kittim," cf. Dan 11:30).

Palestine was among the last parts of the Mediterranean ring to fall under Roman domination although earlier Judas Maccabees, Jonathan and Simon sought alliances with Rome (161, 143 and 139 B.C.E., cf. 1 Macc 8:17; 12:1-4; 14:24). In 63 B.C.E. Pompey captured Jerusalem and transported Jews to Rome as slaves. When they were freed many settled in one of the suburbs across the Tiber.

With the seizing of power by the first triumvirate of Pompey, Julius and Crassus (50 B.C.E.), the Republic was near its end. After a civil war Julius emerged as Caesar, but his assassination (44 B.C.E.) led to the establishment of another triumvirate (Mark Antony, Octavian and Marcus Lepidus). In the Battle of Actium (31 B.C.E.) the fate of the Republic was sealed and Octavian established the empire period. The senate acquiesced and designated him with the auspicious title of Augustus. In the management of the empire, an agreement was struck between emperor and senate so that peaceful provinces were under joint jurisdiction with police forces controlled by proconsuls (senators). Troublesome provinces were given to the emperor with armies controlled by legates (generals) and underlings like procurators or prefects. In spite of a few unbalanced emperors, the division of power seemed to work well for Rome.

The Roman City. In the time of Augustus the city had expanded into fourteen districts but the Etruscan area with the forum remained its center, though expanded by additions northward of new forum centers by Julius (after Pompey's defeat), Augustus (after the Battle of Philippi) Vespasian (after the fall of Jerusalem), Domitian (dedicated by Nerva) and Trajan (with two great libraries). Most of the emperors or their successors felt it incumbent to leave memorials to their greatness whether forum, temple, bath or palace. Therefore, the central part of Rome is a gigantic museum of monuments.

Standing at the east entrance to the forum is the triumphal arch of Titus with reliefs which commemorate the destruction of Jerusalem (70 C.E.), bearing witness to how significant the Romans regarded this event. Further east, near the Baths of Titus and Trajan stands the Colosseum, constructed by Vespasian and Titus (72–80 C.E.). Holding ca. 50,000 spectators, it was built for violent sports, like gladiatorial contests and marine battles (when the pit was flooded). The Colosseum remains as a memorial to Christians who were killed during the Roman persecutions. Immediately next to this symbol of death stands the magnificent triple arch of Constantine, the first Christian emperor.

The City of Churches. It is uncertain who brought Christianity to Rome, perhaps the Jerusalem visitors on the day of Pentecost (Acts 2:10). Before Paul's visit a church was there. Early Christians were often viewed by gentiles as Jews (quare: whether Judaism was an empire-wide licensed religion, *religio licita*) and this confusion engendered Jewish hostility. Banishment of Jews from Rome (49 C.E., cf. Suetonius, *Claudius* 25) because of disturbances may have involved conflicts between Jews and Christians. Aquila and Priscilla were among those expelled Jews whom Paul met in Corinth and took to Ephesus (Acts 18:2, 18-19; cf. Rom 16:3).

In the Book of Romans Paul expressed his long standing desire to visit Rome (Rom 1:13-15) on his way to Spain (Rom 15:24-28). Following his third missionary journey, Paul was imprisoned in Caesarea and not receiving justice from Procurator Festus who was married to a Jewess, he appealed to Caesar (Acts 25:11). Undoubtedly, as a Roman citizen he expected to be treated fairly by Emperor Nero (cf. his positive view of the state in Rom 13:1-7)! Arriving as a prisoner ca. 61 C.E., he was apparently housed with the praetorian (royal) guard for about two years, awaiting trial (cf. Phil 1:13). Some scholars believe Paul was released and imprisoned a second time but the facts are not clear. Traditions suggest that both Paul and Peter before their deaths were locked in the illustrious Mamertine prison located near the Capitoline hill containing two levels, the lower one being entered only by a hole in the floor above.

With his accession to "the purple" Constantine constructed the two great basilicas of St. Peter's and St. Paul's outside the walls where he believed both apostles had been buried. Much argument has ensued over the burial sites of the apostles but it is not impossible that during the Valerian persecution bones (relics) may have been (temporarily?) hidden in the catacombs of St. Sebastian. Constantine's third titular church is St. John Lateran built to memorialize what was believed a visit by John to Rome. The fourth of the monumental churches in Rome is St. Mary Major. As the actual and legendary history of ancient Rome is captured in its buildings, so much of Rome's Christian heritage is preserved in its many churches.

Bibliography. M. Beard and M. Crawford, *Rome in the Late Republic*; G. Boissier, *Rome and Pompeii*; R. E. Brown and J. P. Meir, *Antioch and Rome*; K. Chisholm and J. Ferguson, *Rome, The Augustan Age: A Source Book*; M. Eisman, "A Tale of Three Cities," *BA* 41 (1978): 47–60; J. Finegan, *The Archeology of the New Testament*; R. Krautheimer, *Rome, Profile of a City*; A. G. Mackinnon, *The Rome of the Early Church*; W. Ramsay, *St. Paul the Traveller and the Roman Citizen*.

—GERALD L. BORCHERT

• **Roofs.** Roofs are one of the more interesting architectural features of buildings in the Near East and hold more than passing interest as the scene of some central biblical stories. It was from a roof that King David first saw Bathsheba (2 Sam 11:2), and three thousand Philistines were reportedly on the roof when Samson pulled down the supporting pillars in an act of mass murder and suicide (Judg 16:27).

Roofs were ordinarily constructed by using cross timbers laid across supporting pillars or walls. In larger buildings or state houses, the roof would be used for a gathering of large numbers of people, as the story of Samson shows. These obviously required sturdy construction. Even in smaller homes, the roof was a functional extension of the house. Roofs were basically flat with a slight angle to allow drainage. Materials for flooring could range from marble slabs to reeds packed and reinforced with mud and straw. That some could be dismantled rather easily is illustrated by the story of the paralytic whose four friends opened a hole in the roof to get access to Jesus (Mark 2:4). The deuteronomic code required the building of a parapet around a roof since people could be injured in a fall (Deut 22:8).

People used roofs much as moderns use patios. Elisha had a room provided for him on a roof (2 Kgs 4:10), perhaps like that provided Elijah (1 Kgs 17:19), or that chosen by Jesus and the disciples for the last meal (Mark 14:14-15; Luke 22:11-12). Rahab hid the Hebrew spies under flax on her roof (Josh 2:6). Eglon was in his roof chamber when he was slain by Ehud (Judg 3:23)

The roof was often used as a place of worship, especially private meditation. The Josianic reforms (2 Kgs 23:12) required the destruction of altars on the roof of the upper chamber of Ahaz. Nehemiah had the Jews build booths of tree limbs on their roofs for the celebration of the Feast of Booths. Apparently, the disciples gathered on a roof after Jesus' ascension, perhaps the same on which they had shared the last meal (Acts 1:13).

See also ARCHITECTURE; TABERNACLES, FEAST OF, IN THE NEW TESTAMENT; TABERNACLES, FESTIVAL OF.

—PAUL D. SIMMONS

• **Rosetta Stone.** [roh-zet'uh] The Rosetta Stone is a commemorative stele carved on a black basalt slab originally set up in an Egyptian temple. It had an inscription written in three languages, hieroglyphics, demotic, and Greek. This inscription provided the key to the decipherment of hieroglyphics. The stone, both top and bottom broken, measures 3 ft. 9 in. by 2 ft. 4 in. and is 11 in. thick. It was recovered near the village of Rosetta in the Nile Delta in 1799 by Captain Bouchard of Napoleon's army. After the defeat of Napoleon, the Rosetta Stone and other antiquities were ceded to the British and the Stone now resides in the British Museum.

The Greek portion of the trilingual inscription could be readily translated, but neither demotic nor hieroglyphics could be read at the time. Several scholars provided some initial efforts at decipherment, but it was primarily the work of Thomas Young and François Champollion who, working independently, were able to provide a convincing translation.

Young noted the presence of a number of *cartouches* in the hieroglyphic portion of the inscription (a *cartouche* is an oval line enclosing a number of hieroglyphic signs). He further noted that several of the *cartouches* contained identical signs. Scholars had previously suggested that the *cartouches* enclosed royal names, but had not been able to prove it. From the Greek portion, Young knew certain proper names occurred repeatedly, chiefly Ptolemais, the Greek form of the Ptolemy. Young reasoned that the *cartouches* might contain the hieroglyphic form of Ptolemais. He was also able to decipher the name Berenice from another hieroglyphic bilingual text. Young was apparently the first to determine that hieroglyphics were primarily a syllabary, but that they also included determinatives. He further noted that hieroglyphics and demotic were closely related, and that demotic was a derivative of hieroglyphics. But Young could progress no further in his decipherment.

Champollion was the scholar who finally deciphered hieroglyphics and demotic fully. He had studied Coptic for many years and made the assumption that Coptic preserved much of the vocabulary of ancient Egyptian languages. Champollion was able to compare the individual signs from several different *cartouches* to confirm his decipherment. He was able to read the names Ptolemy, Cleopatra, Berenice, Caesar, Autocrator, Rameses, Tuthmose, and others. By 1822, he was able to translate a number of titles, epithets, and many common words of hieroglyphics and demotic. The trilingual Rosetta Stone was the major key for the decipherment.

The inscription itself was a decree issued by a council of Egyptian priests honoring Ptolemy V, Epiphanes, and is dated to year nine of his reign, 196 B.C.E.

See also WRITING SYSTEMS.

—JOEL F. DRINKARD, JR.

• **Rosh Hashanah.** *See* NEW YEAR'S FESTIVAL

• **Rule of the Congregation/Messianic Rule.** The *Rule of the Congregation* (*1QSa*), or *Messianic Rule*, is a short document setting forth regulations for ordering the Qumran community in the last days. It is extant in a single manuscript, as an appendix to the great MANUAL OF DISCIPLINE scroll (*1QS*), which was found in Cave 1 and which dates from 100–75 B.C.E. The *Rule* consists of two columns. It begins by identifying itself as the *Rule* for the eschatological integration of the congregation of Israel with the community. All—men, women, and children—will be gathered together to have the precepts of the COVENANT and the statutes read to them. The next section of the rule deals with the various levels of instruction and participation available as one advances through life. A child is to be given instruction appropriate to his age until he is twenty, at which time he may be enrolled into the congregation, marry, and assist in community judgments. At twenty-five he may enter the lower ranks of the community. At thirty he may enter the ranks of the chiefs and participate in community affairs under the direction of the priests in accordance with his age and intellectual capabilities. The next section outlines the duties of the Levites, who serve as a link between the priests and the congregation. Next are identified those who are qualified to attend the council meetings; the impure, those with physical defects, and the senile are excluded. The final section describes the council meeting called by the priestly MESSIAH, to which the Messiah of Israel will come, and the ritual of the messianic meal.

The *Rule of the Congregation* is closely related to *1QS*, especially in its understanding of the organization of the community and the importance of the communal meal. Its openness to marriage links it to the DAMASCUS RULE. Its concern with readiness for war connects it with the WAR SCROLL. Its understanding of the angels as being present in community meetings is reminiscent of the ANGELIC LITURGY. Its anticipation of two Messiahs is consistent with what is found elsewhere in the scrolls (cf. *1QS; 4QTestim*). Significant in the *Rule* is the preeminence of the priestly Messiah over the Messiah of Israel: the priest is the first to eat at the messianic meal, followed by the Messiah of Israel and then the rest of the congregation by rank.

The *Rule of the Congregation* contributes to an understanding of the distinctives of the Qumran community, especially its ESCHATOLOGY, angelology, organization, messianism, and communal meal. It also provides some noteworthy parallels to the NT. Its exclusion of those with physical defects from the council meetings (and, hence, from the messianic meal) forms a striking contrast to Jesus' teaching in Luke 14:12-24. To connect the rationale for this exclusion with the presence of angels (cf. *CD* 15:15-17) is similar to one aspect of Paul's argument concerning a woman's head covering in 2 Cor 11:10. Its comments on the meal, which are the most extensive in the scrolls, appear to link the regular communal meal with the eschatological messianic meal, much as Jesus does in Matt 26:26-29.

See also DEAD SEA SCROLLS; ESSENES.

Bibliography. A. Dupont-Sommer, *The Essene Writings from Qumran;* G. Vermes, *The Dead Sea Scrolls in English* and "The Writings of the Qumran Community," E. Schürer, ed., *The History of the Jewish People in the Age of Jesus Christ*, rev. ed.

—JOSEPH L. TRAFTON

• **Ruler.** Someone with specific responsibilities and authorities, usually of a political nature. The English word "ruler" is used to translate several Hebrew and Gk. words. The most common Heb. word translated as "ruler" is *śar,* which may literally be rendered "chief." A *śar* generally had authority over a subgroup of a larger entity (1 Chr 29:6 and 2 Chr 29:20).

The Heb. *nāgîd,* ("prince, captain,") also is used to suggest rulership in 1 Sam 25:30 and in 1 Kgs 1:35, although the precise meaning of *nāgîd* in these verses may be "ruler designate" rather than actual ruler.

A Heb. term whose literal translation is "ruler" is *mōšēl,* used in Gen 45:8 and Prov 6:7. The most familiar and clearest use of this term is found in Mic 5:2; there Bethlehem is said to be the place of origin of "one who will rule Israel" (cf. Matt 2:6).

In the NT, a number of individuals are referred to as RULER OF THE SYNAGOGUE. The one who held this purely religious position was responsible chiefly for the physical arrangements of the services and the upkeep of the building. The rulers mentioned in Acts 16:19 and 17:6 (Gk. *archon* and *politarch*) appear to be local Greek governors responsible to Roman authority.

See also PRINCE/CAPTAIN.

—RAY SUTHERLAND

• **Ruler of the Synagogue.** This person was a leader of worship and SYNAGOGUE business in Jewish synagogues throughout the Roman Empire (the title was also used in pagan religions, perhaps borrowed from Judaism). Three are known by name in the NT: Jairus in Galilee (Mark 5:21-43; Luke 8:40-56; Matt 9:18-26); and Crispus (cf. 1 Cor 1:14) and SOSTHENES in Corinth (Acts 18:8, 17). The term is also used in Luke 13:14 and Acts 13:15. Probably more than one person at the same time could hold this position in a synagogue. There is evidence (at least three Greek inscriptions) that in a few cases women also held this position.

See also SOSTHENES; SYNAGOGUE.

Bibliography. B. J. Brooten, *Women Leaders in the Ancient Synagogue: Inscriptional Evidence and Background Issues.*

—DAVID M. SCHOLER

• **Run/Runners.** The terms most commonly translated "to run" in the Bible are the Heb. word *rûṣ* and the Gk. word *trechō*. Apart from its literal meaning of "rapid forward movement of the feet" (Josh 8:19; Luke 15:20), running often signifies "to make haste" (Isa 59:7), and more figuratively, "to pursue" (1 Sam 21:36), "to follow a course of action" (Ps 119:32), "to busy oneself" (Hag 1:9), probably "to read quickly" (Hab 2:2; Ps 147:15), and possibly "to make love" (Cant 1:4). When Paul uses the phrase "to run in vain" (Gal 2:2; Phil 2:16), he appears to reflect a consciousness of divine commission (cf. 1 Kgs 18:46; *1QpHab* 7:3-5). Elsewhere, the NT borrows the Hellenistic imagery of running from the Greek arena (1 Cor 9:24-27; Heb 12:1).

Runners routinely were used in antiquity as messengers (Jer 51:31). It was from this practice that the Persian empire developed a unified postal system (Esth 3:13). A royal escort also developed within ancient Israel whose members were known as "runners," a term derived from the technical use of the verb "to run." These soldiers kept watch at the doors of the royal palace (1 Kgs 14:27), served as the king's bodyguard (1 Kgs 14:28), and acted as executioners (1 Sam 22:17). Kings and pretenders to the throne demonstrated their exalted position by employing runners to precede their chariots (2 Sam 18:19; 1 Kgs 1:5).

—CLAYTON N. JEFFORD

• **Ruth.** *See* RUTH, BOOK OF

• OUTLINE OF RUTH •

The Book of Ruth

I. Naomi, Widowed in Moab, Returns to Bethlehem with Her Widowed Daughter-in-Law, Ruth (1:1-22)
II. Ruth Gathers Grain in the Field of Boaz, a Kinsman of Naomi, and Gains His Favor (2:1-13)
III. Boaz, with Ruth's Encouragement, Commits Himself to Fulfill the Duty of a Near Kinsman and Marry Her (3:1-18)
IV. Boaz Publicly Accepts the Duty of a Near Kinsman and Marries Ruth; David Is Identified as a Descendant of Ruth and Boaz (4:1-22)

• **Ruth, Book of.** A beautiful narrative set in the time of the judges telling how the widowed NAOMI of Bethlehem and her Moabite daughter-in-law Ruth together managed to preserve the family name and honor of Naomi's husband Elimelech. They did so by finding a husband for Ruth, the rich BOAZ, a relative of Elimelich, who was more than willing to do the duty of a next-of-kin for Naomi once he had seen the beauty and other qualities of Ruth. Boaz and Ruth then had a son and named him Obed. This Obed was the father of JESSE, DAVID's father, and thus the effort to fulfill the duty of a next-of-kin for Naomi and Ruth resulted in the birth of the child destined to be Israel's greatest king and greatest poet.

Structure of the Book. In four major scenes the story is artfully told. Tragedy strikes in Moab as Elimelech and his two sons die, leaving three widows. One widow remains in Moab, but Naomi and Ruth return to Bethlehem. The second scene shows how Naomi and Ruth manage to make a livelihood while attracting the attention of Naomi's relative Boaz to the industrious and beautiful Ruth. Boaz protects Ruth, showers grain upon her, and we are prepared for the third scene. There, delicately and with sensitivity, the narrator tells of the betrothal of Ruth and Boaz. The final scene, at the city gate, shows the careful arrangements made by Boaz to assure that he will have the legal right to claim Ruth as his wife. The story then ends with one of its most important points: the genealogy that carries the reader to David, the grandson of Obed, the son born to Ruth and Boaz.

Setting and Purpose. The book is set at the time of the judges, but its earliest possible date would seem to be the middle period of the monarchy (ninth-eighth century). Many scholars prefer a date in the period after the return from Babylonian Exile, when the narrative would have a particular point and poignancy, as questions of mixed marriage loom large. But arguments in support of a date in postexilic times are not strong. The book is a magnificent example of Israelite narrative art, appropriate for any time, and telling an unforgettable story of the love of two women who, in a man's world, find a way not only to cope with life's trials but to triumph over them. But all the characters are portrayed in a sympathetic way; there are no villains in the Book of Ruth—apart from famine and untimely death.

The book moves from deep human want and need to ample and rich fulfillment of life, from trials and testings of life and character to a happy outcome of all the trials. The unknown author, from an unknown date, provides a glimpse into the imaginary world when "the judges ruled" (Ruth 1:1), where life's cruelties and tragedies could be confronted with inventiveness and fidelity to tradition, and where women could win the day.

See also BOAZ; NAOMI.

Bibliography. E. F. Campbell, *Ruth, AncB*; P. Trible, *God and the Rhetoric of Sexuality*.

—WALTER HARRELSON

• **Sabbath.** Sabbath, from the Heb. *šabbāt,* is one of few Hebrew words that have come into English virtually unchanged. Various explanations for its origin have been advanced. It may be related to the Akkadian *šapattu,* or possibly to the Assyrian *šabâttū.* There seems to be a relationship between *šabbāt* and the Heb. verb *šābat,* meaning "to cease," "to rest." This is the verb used in Gen 2:3 where it is said that "God finished his work . . . and he rested" (*šābat*). Whatever the origin of the term, it came to mean the seventh day in a weekly cycle, the seventh year in cycle of years, and a time of rest or cessation from labor.

Origin. When and where did the Sabbath originate? One thing seems to be certain and that is that it was firmly entrenched in Israel's earliest literature. The narrative in Exod 16:23-27 assumes that it was in force before the giving of the TEN COMMANDMENTS. Both versions of the Ten Commandments list Sabbath observance as the fourth commandment (Exod 20:8; Deut 5:12). Israel's oldest law code, the Covenant Code, has a series of regulations for the Sabbath and the sabbatical year (Exod 23:10-13). The older narrative materials speak of it as a day of "solemn rest" (Exod 16:23-27; 34:21). It is obvious from all this that the Sabbath was a part of Israel's earliest religious practices.

A number of explanations have been advanced for its ultimate origins. Israelite religious tradition developed two such explanations. The first was that after six days of creative activity, GOD rested on the seventh day, thus instituting the Sabbath (Gen 2:3). The Exodus version of the Ten Commandments comments that "in six days the Lord made heaven and earth . . . and rested the seventh day; therefore the Lord blessed the sabbath day and hallowed it (Exod 20:11). One scholar sees this as saying that "the sabbath was a sign of Yahweh's lordship over man's time . . . [thus] on the seventh day man gives back to Yahweh a 'normal' day kept free from all dissipation, and so acknowledges God's 'rightful claim' to every day" (Kraus, 80).

An alternate biblical tradition connects the Sabbath with the Exodus from Egypt. Deuteronomy's version of the fourth commandment proposes a humanitarian motive for the observance of the Sabbath. It was to provide a time of rest for servants and animals because "you shall remember that you were a servant in Egypt and the Lord your God brought you out . . . therefore the Lord your God commanded you to keep the sabbath day" (Deut 5:12-15).

While agreeing that Israel developed the Sabbath in a unique way, there are those who believe that the idea for the Sabbath originated among one or another of the peoples who were a part of Israel's historical milieu. Three groups are advanced as the possible source of the sabbath idea: the Kenites, the Babylonians, and the Canaanites. The Kenites were associated with the Israelites early in their history. In the Song of Deborah (Judg 5), the heroine who kills SISERA, Israel's enemy, is Jael, the wife of Heber the Kenite. This song from around 1200 B.C.E. portrays the Kenites as "tent-dwelling" people. They seem to have been seminomadic metal-workers. Those who advocate what is called the Kenite hypothesis argue that MOSES' father-in-law (called Reuel [Exod 2:18], Jethro [Exod 3:1], and Hobab [Num 10:29]) was a Kenite priest from Midian. According to this view, the KENITES worshiped God by the name Yahweh. In his call on Mount Sinai, Moses learned that Yahweh was the same God whom the forefathers had worshiped. The Sabbath also was of Kenite origin and was adopted from them.

Others argue that the Sabbath originated with the Babylonians. The Babylonians believed the 7th, 14th, 19th, 21st, and 28th days of the month were evil days on which the king and religious officials had to exercise great caution in what they did and ate. The Akkadians, predecessors to the Babylonians in Mesopotamia, celebrated the day of the full moon (*šapattu*) as the day when the anger of the gods was appeased and was thus a good day. Because certain OT texts mention Sabbath and new moon together (2 Kgs 4:23; Isa 1:13; Amos 8:5), it is argued that originally the Sabbath was celebrated one day each month, as the new moon appeared. Later, according to this view, the prophet EZEKIEL "made the sabbath day the sign of the covenant with Yahweh" (Ezek 20:12, 20) taking the idea of observing the Sabbath every seven days from the older Babylonian custom (de Vaux, 476). The major difficulty this poses is in explaining how Israel's Sabbath, which had such a positive meaning, could have been based on such a negative idea as that of the Babylonians. When Sabbath and new moon, furthermore, are mentioned together in the OT, there is no need to assume that the texts are speaking of anything other than two separate and distinct religious holidays. The relationship between the Hebrew *šabbāt* and the Akkadian *šapattu* can be understood by the fact that both terms refer to "the day that marked a definite boundary" (de Vaux, 477), one dividing the months, the other dividing the weeks.

Another line of investigation would seek Sabbath origins through Israel's contact with the Canaanites who occupied the land when Israel became a separate people and with whom the Israelites continued to coexist for several centuries. It is argued, based on the Ras Shamra texts, that Israel got the idea of the seven-day week from the Canaanites, starting first by adopting the idea of the sabbatical year (the seventh). The Canaanites had a festival week (seven days) and the assumption is that the festival week of seven days was adopted as a "periodic sequence . . . to the reckoning of time as a whole" (Kraus, 87). But the Canaanites had no equivalent to the Sabbath, and this would argue strongly against this theory.

The only certainty is that we do not know when or where Israel began to observe the Sabbath. Perhaps it arose "in the almost universal custom of keeping days of rest, or feast days, or market days, at regular intervals" (de Vaux, 480). Whatever its origins, it would become one of Israel's most influential contributions to Western civilization.

Sabbath: the OT. The Sabbath throughout the OT is viewed as the termination of the week. "Six days you shall labor and do your work, but on the seventh you shall rest" (Exod 23:12). Second Kings 11:5-9 confirms this when it speaks of the Sabbath as marking the end of a period of time for guard duty. This is in keeping with the dominant idea that it meant rest—whether rest for humans and animals after six days of labor (Exod 23:12; 34:21; Deut 5:12-15); rest for the land after six years of cultivation (Exod 23:10, 11; Lev 25:1-7); or for any extended period when the land would not be cultivated due to the deportation of its inhabitants, such as occurred in the Assyrian conquest of the eighth century and the Babylonian Exile of the sixth century (Lev 26:34, 35).

The Sabbath did not seem to have as many restrictions placed on it in the preexilic period as it did in later Judaism. In an incident in the ELISHA cycle, the Shunnamite woman sets out to seek the prophet. Her husband asks her, "Why will you go to him today? It is neither new moon nor Sabbath" (2 Kgs 4:23). Such holy days were thought to be especially propitious for consulting holy men such as prophets. That the Sabbath involved the suspension of business is shown by AMOS's scolding businessmen who are anxious for the Sabbath to pass so they can offer shoddy merchandise to the poor (Amos 8:4, 5). Legal materials, whatever their date, deal sparingly with the Sabbath, beyond the charge to keep it (Lev 19:3). It was to be a day of "solemn rest" (Lev 23:3) on which the people were to light no fire (Exod 35:2-3). One such incident is recorded in Num 15:32-36 where a man found gathering sticks on the Sabbath was stoned to death by the people. Not only was one not to carry on business; one was not even to talk about it (Isa 58:13). Yet, while the day had its solemn worship and serious purpose, it also was a day for joy and mirth, a day for "taking delight in the Lord" (Isa 58:14). While the Sabbath was important in the preexilic period, the EXILE in Babylon marks the beginning of an intensification of interest in the day. JEREMIAH saw profanation of the Sabbath as a symptom of the general unfaithfulness of God's people. If they took the Sabbath seriously, then God would honor his COVENANT with them (Jer 17:19-27). Otherwise, they faced judgment. The Sabbath's importance was enhanced by the changes brought about by the Exile. Jews now became an urban people, whereas before they primarily had been a rural people with an agricultural and pastoral economy. The three great annual feasts (Passover-Unleavened Bread, Weeks, and Ingathering) were agriculturally based and thus were downgraded in importance. They were also centered in the TEMPLE while the Sabbath lent itself ideally to the services that developed with the emergence of the SYNAGOGUE in the postexilic period. Even when the Temple was rebuilt, it was still accessible to only a few of the faithful, while any community with a *minyan* (ten Jewish men) could have a synagogue. The rabbi, as leader of the synagogue, replaced the prophet and priest not only as spiritual leader of the community but also as the developer and preserver of tradition. The religion of Israel now became Judaism, because those who practiced it principally were survivors of the tribe of Judah and thus were called Jews.

In the postexilic period, Sabbath observance became the symbol of faithfulness to the covenant. Not only Jews but foreigners and eunuchs who kept the Sabbath would be brought into God's "holy mountain" and be made joyful in the "house of prayer" (Isa 56:2-7). Reality did not always mesh with the ideal, however. Nehemiah, leader of a group of returned exiles in the fifth century B.C.E., found that his own zeal for Sabbath observance was not shared by the Jerusalem traders whose philosophy was business as usual on the Sabbath. Because he was the governor, however, he was able to enforce at least a semblance of respect for the sacredness of the day (Neh 13:15-22).

Sabbath: the Apocrypha. The seriousness that the devout Jew attached to the Sabbath is shown by an incident from the Maccabean period. First Macc 2:29-38 tells of a group of Jews who were attacked by the Syrians on the sabbath. Because resistance would have been work and thus a violation of the command to do no work on the sabbath, one thousand Jews allowed themselves to be slaughtered to keep from profaning the Sabbath by working.

Sabbath: the Rabbis. Concern for faithfulness to Torah (teaching) marked the postexilic Jewish community. As teachers, it was the rabbis' responsibility to interpret the meaning of Torah for the community. The focus for the interpretation of the fourth commandment was on a definition of "work." Because Exod 31 discussed building a sanctuary and keeping the Sabbath, the rabbis reasoned that the kinds of work involved in building a sanctuary were the kinds of work that were forbidden on the Sabbath. The Mishnah, a compendium of rabbinic teaching, lists thirty-nine main classes of work but numerous others are described as being derived from the main classes. Among those activities restricted was travel. While one was permitted to move about freely within the confines of one's own village, travel more than 2,000 cubits (ca. 3,000 ft.) beyond the village boundary was forbidden under ordinary circumstances. This could be circumvented, however, by a legal exception called an *eruv*. By placing enough food for two meals 2,000 cubits from the village and by designating that place as the Sabbath-day's residence, one could travel to one's residence and then an additional 2,000 cubits from that residence.

Despite the seriousness with which the rabbis viewed the Sabbath, it was in many ways a festive occasion. Before the Sabbath began at sundown on Friday, marked by the blowing of the trumpet, lights were lit, since kindling a fire was forbidden after Sabbath began. The celebration began with a blessing (*kiddush*). It involved synagogue services on Friday evening and on Saturday morning. On Friday, the scripture reading was from the Psalms, while in the morning service, it was from the Torah. The remainder of the day was for relaxation and enjoyment. Three meals of food, cooked before Sabbath began, were served, often with invited guests present. The day ended with a benediction. Two rabbinic teachings illustrate the importance the rabbis attached to the Sabbath: (1) one who observed the Sabbath properly could be an idolater (violate the first commandment) and yet have his sins forgiven; and (2) in the rabbinic teaching that "if Israel keeps one sabbath as it should be kept, the Messiah will come. The sabbath is equal to all the other precepts of the Torah" (Exodus Rabbath 25:12).

Sabbath: the NT. Two Gk. words, *sabbata* and *Sab-*

baton, are used in the NT. It is obvious that they, like the English Sabbath, are virtual transliterations from Hebrew. Their usage is confined primarily to the Gospels and the Acts, with two references found in the Pauline Letters (1 Cor 16:2; Col 2:16). The attitude of Jesus and his disciples toward the Sabbath as reflected by the synoptic Gospels (Matthew, Mark, and Luke) in some ways is in harmony with the picture of the Sabbath drawn from the OT and rabbinic sources. The women who were trying to take care of his body after the crucifixion rested on the Sabbath "according to the commandment" (Luke 23:56). Jesus was said to have been an invited guest for a Sabbath meal in the home of a leader of the Pharisees (Luke 14:1). Mark and Luke report on his activities as a teacher on the Sabbath in Nazareth (Luke 4:16) and in Capernaum (Mark 1:21-22; Luke 4:31-32). A number of the incidents involving conflict arose from his custom of going to the synagogue on the Sabbath (Matt 12:9-14; Luke 6:6-11; Mark 1:21-27; Luke 4:31-37; see also John 5:9-18; 7:23; 9:14-16). The Gospels show Jesus in conflict with the authorities about the Sabbath activities of himself and his disciples at two points. All the Synoptics record the story about the disciples going through a field of ripening grain on a Sabbath day, plucking the ripening heads of grain, rubbing them in their hands to separate the husks from the grain, and then eating the threshed grain (Matt 12:1-8; Mark 2:23; Luke 6:1-3). By rabbinic interpretation, plucking ripe grain and separating seeds from the husks was threshing grain and thus a violation of the command not to work on the Sabbath. Deut 23:25 permitted such an activity on other days. Eating was not an issue since eating was permitted on the Sabbath. Jesus' emphasis here and elsewhere as regards Sabbath regulations was that human need transcended legal technicalities. He cited a situation where when DAVID was hungry, he ate the bread usually reserved only for the priests (1 Sam 21:1-7). As a second justification, he pointed out that priests worked on the Sabbath out of necessity, yet were not guilty of Sabbath breaking.

Jesus' emphasis on the priority of human need over Sabbath regulations is to be seen in the stories about healings. Rabbinic formulations forbade the practice of medicine on the Sabbath in any but life-threatening situations. Yet Jesus healed the man with the withered hand (Matt 12:9-14; Mark 3:1-6; Luke 6:6-11), exorcised demons (Mark 1:21-28; Luke 4:31-37), healed the woman with the crooked back (Luke 13:10-17), the man with dropsy (Luke 14:1-6), a paralytic (John 5:1-18), and a blind man (John 9:16). Typical of his replies to his critics was his response at the healing of the man with the dropsy: "Which of you, having a son or an ox that has fallen into a well, will not immediately pull him out on a sabbath day?" (Luke 14:5). He summed up his teaching on human need versus Sabbath regulation when he said, "The sabbath was made for man, not man for the sabbath, so the Son of man is lord even of the sabbath" (Mark 2:27-28; cf. Matt 12:8; Luke 6:5)

Most of the references to the Sabbath in the Book of Acts relate to PAUL's missionary activity other than one reference to "a sabbath day's journey" (Acts 1:12). Since Paul's missionary strategy involved first preaching to the Jews in whatever city he found himself in, it was natural for him to go to the synagogue to argue his case for the messiahship of Jesus (Acts 13:14, 42, 44; 17:2; 18:4). Two other references in Acts involve the services in the synagogue. In Luke's version of a speech by Paul in a synagogue in ANTIOCH of Pisidia, he refers to the prophets' being read in the synagogue every Sabbath day (Acts 13:27). A similar statement in the report of the JERUSALEM conference refers to the reading of Moses (the Torah) on the Sabbath (Acts 15:21).

Only twice in Paul's correspondence is the Sabbath mentioned. In 1 Cor 16:2 a form of the word for Sabbath is used, even though most versions translate it "the first day of the week." This translation is justified on the basis that the word for "first" accompanies Sabbath. This would seem to be a reference to Sunday or the Lord's day rather than to the Jewish Sabbath. Paul's only other reference to sabbath (Col 2:16) lists it with other festivals that he says were not to be a test of whether one was to be considered a Christian or not. This reference is in the context of the Judaizing controversy where some Jewish Christians demanded that gentiles had to become Jews first before they could become Christians.

Sabbath and Sunday. As Christianity moved out more and more into a non-Jewish world and developed its own distinctive set of traditions and literature, Sabbath observance, which seems to have been maintained for some time by Christians of Jewish extraction, became less and less important. For Christians, the day of Christ's resurrection, the first day of the week, became the day of worship, replacing the Sabbath for them.

See also FEASTS AND FESTIVALS; SABBATICAL YEAR.

Bibliography. H. Danby, ed., *The Mishnah*; R. de Vaux, *Ancient Israel*; H. J. Krans, *Worship in Israel*; "Sabbath," *EncJud.*

—JOHN H. TULLOCK

• **Sabbath Day's Journey.** A Sabbath day's journey was the distance one could travel on the SABBATH without violating the sanctity of the day. The term is used only once in the Bible. In Acts 1:12, following the ascension of Jesus, the disciples travel from the Mount of Olives to Jerusalem, the distance being a "Sabbath day's journey." The casual use of the term in this connection suggests common usage. When Jesus expressed the hope that the abomination of desolation from which one must flee would not come on the Sabbath (Matt 24:20), it is possible that the restraint on Sabbath travel was a consideration.

A Sabbath day's journey was 2,000 cubits. A cubit was the distance from the elbow to the end of the middle finger, variously estimated as eighteen in. (Hellenistic) or twenty-one in. (Roman). Thus a Sabbath day's journey would be between 3,000 and 3,600 ft., somewhat more than half a mi. The distance from the East Gate of Jerusalem to the Church of the Ascension on the Mount of Olives is about 2,250 ft. as the crow flies, though somewhat further for a person walking. Josephus describes the distance from Jerusalem to the Mount of Olives as five furlongs (*Ant* 20.8.6) and six furlongs (*BJ* 5.2.3), distances of 3,031 and 3,637 ft. respectively.

The source of the designation of 2,000 cubits as the Sabbath day's journey is Josh 3:4 where it is the space required to be kept between the ark and the people following it. In Num 35:5 the pasturelands of the Levites are measured as 2,000 cubits in every direction from the walls of the city. In Exod 16:29 the children of Israel are instructed to gather enough manna on the sixth day to last for the Sabbath and to "remain every man of you in his place, let no man go out of his place on the seventh day." Rabbinic law cites this passage in enumerating thirty-nine principle types of "work" (each further subdivided) forbidden on the Sabbath, including the Sabbath limit of 2,000 cubits. Although one may not travel more than 2,000 cubits from the city wall on the Sabbath, there is no limit to the distance one may travel within the city walls.

In the Jerusalem Targum, the interpretation of Exod 16:19 forbids a man to "go walking from this place beyond 2,000 cubits on the seventh day." Another targum expands the meaning of Ruth 1:16 as Naomi informs Ruth that they are to keep Sabbaths and not walk beyond 2,000 cubits.

There were exceptions and clever adjustments to this 2,000 cubit limitation. It could be exceeded if one's life is in danger (*Erub* 4). A traveler could manage to go 4,000 cubits on the Sabbath by a legal fiction. On the day before the Sabbath, food for two meals could be taken ahead by a servant, thus establishing a "home." Or one could designate a tree or a wall 2,000 cubits from his residence as his legal "home" and then travel an extra 2,000 cubits without violating the restraint of the "sabbath day's journey."

See also SABBATH.

Bibliography. E. Lohse. "σάββατον, κτλ.," *TDNT*; "Sabbath," *EncJud*.

—CARLTON T. MITCHELL

• **Sabbatical Year.** A special year, recurring every seven years, associated in the legal literature with the release of slaves (Exod 21:2-6; Deut 15:12-18), the fallow of agricultural land (Exod 23:10-11; Lev 25:2-7), the remission of debt (Deut 15:1-11), and the recitation of the Torah (Deut 31:10-13). Termed the sabbatical year in Lev 25:5, the institution shares with the weekly SABBATH the principle of rest on a ratio of one in seven. It cannot be determined whether the institutions and ideas brought together under this numeric principle were ever conjoined in actual practice or how the institution developed. In contrast, the intent of the legal tradition is clear: to preserve the social integrity of the community.

The slave-release and fallow-year laws of Exodus appear to lie at the base of the sabbatical year institution, though neither is explicitly related to a fixed and regularly recurring cycle of years. Exod 21:2-6 stipulates that purchased male slaves (indentured servants) be granted the option of liberty after six years of service with a provision for permanent slavery if this option is not exercised. This slave release is taken up and expanded in Deut 15:12-18 to include female slaves and to require parting provisions for those released. The Holiness Code also enjoins slave release (Lev 25:39-46) but ties it to the occurrence of the jubilee year.

The instructions of the fallow-year law (Exod 23:10-11) call for abandoning the practice of farming in the seventh year in order to provide food for the poor. Because fallowing of fields occurred by agricultural necessity much more frequently than one year out of seven, this law can be seen as sanctifying one year of the regular crop-fallow cycle as a way to focus attention on the landless and poor in the wider community. Lev 25:2-7 legislates the same institution, but motivates it by an appeal to the requirement of sabbath rest for the land itself and those who work it. Here the sabbatical year is viewed as a regular, nation-wide practice. The lawgiver faces the problem of providing food without farming by promising triple bounty in the sixth year, produced by God's blessing (Lev 25:20-22).

Deuteronomy is alone in legislating the remission of debts at the end of every seventh year. The name used for this "release" (Heb. *dĕrôr*) from debt is drawn from the "release of the land" edicts promulgated by newly ascended Mesopotamian rulers. According to Deuteronomy this seventh year also provides an occasion for the reading of the TORAH at a general assembly of all Israel on the Feast of Booths (Deut 31:10-13).

Other aspects of the sabbatical year are mentioned rarely. JEREMIAH reports an aborted release of slaves in the final years of the Judean state (Jer 34:8-11). First Maccabees explains the dearth of supplies in Judean cities at its time by reference to the sabbatical year, providing the only biblical record of its practice (1 Macc 6:49, 53).

In the variable historical and natural environment of the Bible, it is unlikely that any fixed multi-year cycle could repeat with much continuity, calling into question whether the law was often practiced as laid down. Nonetheless, the breadth of the sabbatical year legal tradition testifies to the importance of the idea among the ancient Israelites of maintaining social equilibrium through economic measures.

See also AGRICULTURE/FARMING; JUBILEE, YEAR OF; LIBERTY; SABBATH; SLAVERY IN THE OLD TESTAMENT.

Bibliography. D. C. Hopkins, *The Highlands of Canaan: Agricultural Life in the Early Iron Age*; N. P. Lemche, "The Manumission of Slaves—The Fallow-Year Law—The Sabbatical Year—The Jobel Year," *VT* 26 (1976): 38-59; D. Patrick, *Old Testament Law*; R. de Vaux, *Ancient Israel*.

—DAVID C. HOPKINS

• **Sackcloth.** The cloth of the sack, probably a course material of animal hair used for making grain bags. In biblical literature, the term refers to a garment the design of which is unclear. This type of sack was carried into Egypt by Joseph's brothers (Gen 42:25, 27, 35) and used by the Gibeonites to deceive JOSHUA (Josh 9:4). The cloth was dark in color, as suggested in Rev 6:12: "The sun became black as sackcloth" (cf. Isa 50:3).

The garment referred to in biblical materials is understood by some to be in the shape of a sack with holes cut out for the arms and head, similar to the practice of making clothing from a flour sack during the American Great Depression. Several OT references support the view that sackcloth was such a large covering of the body, as when King HEZEKIAH "tore his clothes, and covered himself with sackcloth" (2 Kgs 19:1; Isa 37:1). Other references suggest a smaller garment in the style of a wrap-around loincloth. For example, JACOB "put sackcloth upon his loins" (Gen 37:34) and prophets admonish persons to gird themselves with sackcloth (Isa 15:3; Jer 4:8).

Whatever its style, the sackcloth was worn as a sign of mourning and/or repentance. The practice must have begun early in Hebrew history, probably consistent with practices of other inhabitants of the ancient Near East. Although sackcloth is not mentioned in the Law, its use seems to have continued throughout the OT and into the NT periods. Jacob wore sackcloth to mourn his loss of JOSEPH (Gen 37:34), and the practice appears in connection with AHAB and ELIJAH (1 Kgs 21:27), Jerusalem's fall (Lam 2:10; Ezek 7:18), JONAH and Nineveh (Jonah 3:5, 6, 8), and the MACCABEES (1 Macc 2:14; 3:47). In sackcloth priests mourn for their people (Joel 1:13) and the virgin mourns for her bridegroom (Joel 1:8). In the Gospel of Matthew (11:21) and its Lucan parallel (10:13) wearing sackcloth is a sign of repentance.

See also MOURNING RITES.

—ROBERT W. CRAPPS

• **Sacraments.** Christian sacraments are ceremonies of the church that were instituted and ordained by Jesus. By combining divine Word with a visible sign, sacraments become effective symbols of divine grace. The biblical basis for sacramental practice and theology has developed out of interpretations about particular events in the ministry of Jesus.

The word sacrament comes from *sacramentum,* which is the Latin rendering of the Gk. word for mystery. In the NT the Gk. word *mysterion* does not appear in connection with any of the acts now identified as sacraments, although it is used to indicate the ways in which Jesus revealed hidden dimensions of reality. Prior to its application to Christian ceremonies by Tertullian at the beginning of the third century C.E., the word sacrament was used to describe one's oath of allegiance to governmental authorities or one's obligation to military service. Applied to the Christian ceremonies, the word suggests the new covenant of believers with Christ, who is the authority of the sacraments.

The biblical bases for the sacraments of the LORD'S SUPPER and BAPTISM, which are two ceremonies accepted by all sacramentalists, are found in the words of institution uttered by Jesus at the last supper and the great commission delivered to his disciples before his ascension. According to Paul's account of the last supper of Jesus with his disciples, Jesus "took bread, and when he had given thanks, he broke it, and said, 'This is my body which is for you. Do this in remembrance of me.' In the same way also the cup, after supper, saying, 'This cup is the new covenant in my blood. Do this, as often as you drink it, in remembrance of me.' For as often as you eat this bread and drink the cup, you proclaim the Lord's death until he comes" (1 Cor 11:23b-26; cf. Mark 14:22-25; Matt 26:26-29; Luke 22:17-19). The scriptural foundation for the practice of baptism is located in the baptism of Jesus by John (Mark 1:9-11) and in the great commission: "Go therefore and make disciples of all nations, baptizing them in the name of the Father and of the Son and of the Holy Spirit" (Matt 28:19).

Although almost all Christians in some way celebrate the Lord's Supper and baptize new Christians, they have developed diverse beliefs and practices in accord with their interpretations of particular passages of scripture. Most significantly, Christians have disagreed about the power or function of sacraments, debating the degree to which sacraments (if at all) serve as channels for divine grace. Traditionally, Roman Catholics believe that sacraments administered by an authorized priest actually convey the grace of God. Some Protestant traditions, following Luther and Calvin, regard sacraments as symbolically presenting God's self-giving. Others, following Anabaptist practices, celebrate the Lord's Supper and baptism not as sacraments but as ordinances—human responses in faith to Christ's commands.

With respect to the Lord's Supper, Christians have variously interpreted the words of institution uttered by Jesus at the last supper. Emphasizing the words "This is my body," some Christians have developed theories about the nature of Christ's presence in the consecrated elements—e.g., metaphysical, real, and symbolic. Other Christians have focused on the command, "Do this in remembrance of me," and have determined that the supper should be practiced as a human response in faith to the command of Jesus. With respect to baptism, some Christians emphasize believers' baptism, taking the story of Philip's witness to and baptism of the Ethiopian official (Acts 8:26-40) as a model of biblical procedure. Other Christians point to the story of the baptism of the Philippian jailer and his family by Paul and Silas (Acts 16:25-34), and they conclude that baptism of a believer's family authorizes the practice of infant baptism.

A second sacramental issue that has generated divergence among Christians is that of specifying the number of sacraments. Throughout the history of Christianity theologians have identified many different biblical events and institutions as sacraments, from the rainbow of Noah and the fleece of Gideon to the church and the incarnation itself. In 1439, however, the Council of Florence fixed the number of sacraments at seven: Eucharist (Lord's Supper), baptism, confirmation, penance, extreme unction (anointing of the sick), holy orders (ordination), and marriage. But the controversy about the number of sacraments continued and fueled the Reformation. Most Protestant traditions followed Luther, reducing the number to two—baptism and the Lord's Supper. Nevertheless, some Protestant traditions still favor penance and marriage, while others also accept footwashing (cf. John 13:4-11) as sacramental.

A third sacramental issue that divides Christians concerns the form and frequency of sacramental performance. Regarding the frequency of the Lord's Supper, some Christian communities celebrate the Eucharist daily, while many congregations do so weekly, monthly, or quarterly, and on special occasions like marriages and special feast days. Others practice the Lord's Supper only on Maundy Thursday. Regarding form, some traditions require that the consecrated elements be distributed only by a priest; a few insist that participants kneel at the altar rail while receiving the bread and wine; others prefer passing individual portions of the elements to seated participants; and several share a common cup. Some break unleavened loaves of bread; others use small wafers, sometimes imprinted with a sign for Christ. Many drink wine; others use unfermented grape juice.

Concerning baptism, many Christians use drops of consecrated water to mark one's head with the sign of the cross, while others baptize by pouring water over the head of the person. Traditions that practice believers' baptism often insist on immersion as the style of baptism, thus signifying a person's identification with the death and resurrection of Christ. A few that immerse prefer to baptize in streams rather than artificial pools, and one requires that immersion be done three times forward—once for each person of the trinity.

Despite these differences, sacramental Christians recognize that Christ is the source and substance of all sacraments, which are, at the very least, visible metaphors of God's self-giving.

See also BAPTISM; LORD'S SUPPER.

Bibliography. G. C. Berkouwer, *The Sacraments;* J. Calvin, *Institutes of the Christian Religion;* B. Cooke, *Ministry to Word and Sacraments: History and Theology;* V. Eller, *In Place of Sacraments: A Study of Baptism and the Lord's Supper;* R. W. Jenson, *Visible Words: The Interpretation and Practice of Christian Sacraments;* B. Leeming, *Principles of Sacramental Theology;* M. Luther, *The Babylonian Captivity of the Church;* P. Tillich, *The Protestant Era;* J. S. White, *Sacraments as God's Self Giving;* G. S. Worgul, *From Magic to Metaphor: A Validation of the Christian Sacraments.*

—JOSEPH L. PRICE

• **Sacrifice.** The institution of sacrifice played a central role in Israelite worship, though the historical traditions reflect a variety of motives and practices, as well as some overlapping of vocabulary and regulations, even in the codification of Lev 1–7. In general, the term sacrifice refers to any animal or vegetable offering that is either completely or partially burned on an altar as an act of homage to God. Through God's acceptance of the sacrifice, the worshipper and deity enter a mutually binding relationship (often called *do ut des*—"I give that you may give"): the postulant offers various self-representative gifts, expecting in return the beneficent favor of Yahweh.

Through much of Israel's early history, sacrifices were offered on family altars, at local SHRINES, or at the ubiquitous HIGH PLACES that were so soundly condemned by the Deuteronomistic tradition. As the developing law called for centralization of the cult, however, legitimate sacrifice could be offered only at the temple in Jerusalem (Deut 12, esp. vv. 13-14).

The most ancient type of sacrifice attested was the *'ōlâ*, the "burnt offering" (RSV) or "holocaust," so called because it is wholly burned on the altar. Though sometimes bearing an expressly expiatory significance (Lev 9:7; 14:20; Job 1:5; 42:8), the *'ōlâ* more commonly played a role in petitions (1 Sam 13:12), public worship (Num 28–29), votive or voluntary offerings (Lev 22:18), and rites of purification (Lev 12:6, 8; 16:24). In the latest tradition (Lev 1), the burnt offering had to be an unblemished male calf, sheep, or goat (cf. Lev 22:17-25), or, in the case of the poor, two turtledoves or pigeons. After laying hands on the animal in an act of identification or ownership, the worshiper would personally cut the animal's throat, and the priests then ritually disposed of the BLOOD around the large outdoor altar. After the carcass was skinned, quartered, and washed, everything but the hide was immolated. This sacrifice was accompanied in the later rituals by an offering (*minḥâ*) of flour and oil, along with a libation of wine (Exod 29:38-42; Lev 23:28; Num 15:1-16).

Several sacrifices came to be subsumed under the rubric *šĕlāmîm,* which has been translated "peace offering," "communion offering," or even "gift of greeting." The function of these offerings was either to establish or to maintain good relations with God. In this sense they established communion, but this suggests no mystic sense of union resulting from eating a totemistic animal or sharing a meal with the deity. Yahweh, unlike the Mesopotamian gods, did not need to be fed (Ps 50:12-13). With minor exceptions, the ritual follows that of the *'ōlâ* sacrifice (cf. Lev 3), with the primary difference being that the meat is shared by the parties involved. God alone received the blood, the visceral fat, and the fat tail of sheep, because both blood and fat were regarded as life-giving (Lev 3:16-17; 7:22-26; 17:11, 14). The priest was given the breast and the right leg as his rightful portion (Lev 7:28-34; 10:14-15), and the worshiper was allowed to keep the rest. This practice was once the primary means of slaughter in Israel (thus the common use of *zebaḥ,* "slaughter," in conjunction with or in place of *šĕlāmîm*), but later regulations desacralized private slaughter away from the sanctuary (Deut 12:15-16).

Votive offerings (*nĕdārîm*), given in payment of earlier conditional vows, and "freewill offerings" (*nĕdābâ*) were the most common *šĕlāmîm* sacrifices. They were offered in identical fashion (Lev 7:16-17; 22:18-23), and had to be consumed within two days. The *tôdâ* or "sacrifice of praise" (Lev 7:12-15; 22:29-30) seems to have originally been a separate type, and could be eaten only on the day it was offered.

Two sacrifices played an expiatory role, the *ḥaṭṭa't* ("sin offering," Lev 4:1-5:13; cf. Num 15:22-31) and the *'āšām* ("guilt offering," Lev 5:14–6:7; 7:1-7). The Hebrews believed that human sin brought defilement to the sanctuary, and the *ḥaṭṭa't* ritual was intended to remove it. Thus, whenever different sacrifices were offered, the sin offering always came first to purify the altar and sanctuary before other sacrifices could be accepted (Lev 9:7-21; 14:19). In this sacrifice, the blood was of supreme importance, being sprinkled on various parts of the outer altar (for an individual) or the inner SANCTUARY (for the high priest or the community as a whole). As with the *šĕlāmîm* offering, only the various fat portions were burned on the altar, but in this case the worshiper benefited only by the removal of his guilt: all of the meat went to the priests. When the offering was given in behalf of the high priest or the community, no one could eat it, and the entire carcass was burned outside the camp.

The *'āšām* sacrifice or "guilt offering" frequently occurred in conjunction with the *ḥaṭṭa't,* and it is often difficult to distinguish them, even in the latest traditions. In general, the *'āšām* was a sort of reparation offering (Lev 5:14–6:7; 7:1-7). In some cases this was also accompanied by the payment of restitution to the person offended, plus an additional twenty percent fine (Num 5:5-8).

On some occasions, offerings of flour or bread were brought to the sanctuary, either alone (Lev 6:14-18), as a poor person's substitute sin offering (Lev 5:11-13), or most often as an accompaniment to an *'ōlâ* or *šĕlāmîm* sacrifice. These offerings could be prepared in various ways (cf. Lev 2), and the amounts varied as well. With the exception of the high priest's daily offering, only a token part of the bread, flour, or grain was burned on the altar, while the balance provided additional food for the priests. Offerings of incense, compounded of special ingredients (Exod 30:34-38), were made every morning and evening (Exod 30:1-8).

The daily temple ritual included set sacrifices in addition to occasional offerings brought by individual worshipers (cf. Num 28–29). Other sacrifices were made at periodic festivals or days of worship, including more of the regular offerings, plus the addition of special sacrifices such as the paschal lamb (Exod 12) and the scapegoat ritual on the Day of Atonement (Lev 16).

The practice of sacrifice proved to be very popular in Israel (cf. Ps 43:4), but was often the target of criticism by the prophets (Isa 1:11-17; Jer 7:21-22; Hos 6:6; Amos 5:21-27; Mic 6:6-8; Mal 1:6-14), who stressed God's preference for obedience rather than ritual. Though some of these fiery oracles suggest that God never sanctioned sacrifice (Jer 7:22; Amos 5:25), it is the shallow understanding, syncretistic corruption, or improper ritual that is condemned, not the practice itself.

Bibliography. T. H. Gaster, *IDB*; G. B. Gray, *Sacrifice in the Old Testament*; B. A. Levine, *In the Presence of the Lord*; J. Milgrom, *IDBSupp*; R. Rendtorff, *Studien zur Geschichte des Opfers im Alten Israel*; H. H. Rowley, *Worship in Ancient Israel*; R. de Vaux, *Ancient Israel.*

—TONY W. CARTLEDGE

• **Sadducees.** [sad'*joo*-sees] Sadducees refers to the aristocratic elite of Jewish society during the Second Temple period, consisting of both priestly and non-priestly nobility. The group likely derives its name from ZADOK, the HIGH PRIEST under Solomon (1 Kgs 2:35).

Zadokite descendants served as the priestly leadership in Jerusalem until the destruction of the city in 587/6 B.C.E. After the Persian king, Cyrus, permitted the Jews in Babylonian Exile to return to their Judean homeland, the Zadokite priests quickly emerged as the ruling element in Jewish society. They functioned as the indisputable religious leaders of the people and, in an alliance with non-priestly aristocrats, as the political leadership of the community, forming together the ruling council of elders (later to be called the SANHEDRIN).

During the period of Greek rule, which began in 333 B.C.E., the Zadokite priests, together with the non-priestly elite, maintained political power. Many of these aristocrats were quite sympathetic with the cultural and religious reforms which came upon Jewish society as a result of the Greek presence, and attempted to assist the Greek overlords in imposing these new ideas on the Jews. Such Hellenistic reforms unquestionably had the capacity to undermine many central elements of traditional Jewish religious belief, including monotheism and the centrality of the Torah.

Popular resistance to Hellenism emerged under the leadership of the Hasmonean family and a zealous religious movement known as the Hasidim. Led by the Hasmoneans, war broke out against the Greeks in 167 B.C.E. (the Maccabean Revolt). The Zadokites who had chosen to align themselves with Hellenism were purged from places of leadership, while Zadokites who had not been sympathetic with Hellenism sided with the Hasmoneans. While these Zadokites were in favor of ridding Jewish society and religion of the overt manifestations of Hellenism, they did not feel comfortable with the movement of the Hasidim, for this group refused to look only to the Zadokites for religious guidance and for proper interpretation of the Torah. Rather, they were prone to look within their own ranks for direction in such matters. The Hasidim also enjoyed popular support because of their stance against Hellenism. This undoubtedly encroached on the supreme authority of the Zadokites, authority which they did not wish to relinquish. Furthermore, the Hasidim were innovative religious thinkers, adopting such teachings as the resurrection of the dead and a final judgment day. Such novel ideas were not accepted by the Zadokites, who could find no explicit support for them in the Torah. It was probably at this time, in order to distinguish themselves from the Hasidim, that the Zadokites and their non-priestly aristocratic allies began to be recognized by the appellation Sadducees. The group later known as the PHARISEES was the spiritual descendant of the Hasidim and, hence, the perpetual conflict between the Pharisees and Sadducees finds its roots in the nascent period of these groups.

The Hasmoneans eventually defeated their Greek overlords and established an independent Jewish state in which a Hasmonean served as both political ruler and high priest. Though the Sadducees would not have been happy that a non-Zadokite held the office of high priest, they did work well with the Hasmonean leadership and thereby were able to maintain real political power through their control of the Sanhedrin. Save for the exceptional period of the reign of Queen Alexandra (76–67 B.C.E.) when the Pharisees were given a prominent voice in the Sanhedrin, the Sadducees were the favorite party of the Hasmonean rulers and were permitted to maintain official authority over the Jews.

The Hasmonean dynasty fell with the intervention of Rome in 63 B.C.E., though the Romans did continue to allow a Hasmonean to maintain the office of high priest. Under Roman administration the family of a certain Antipater began to emerge as the real political force in Judea. The Hasmoneans and the Sadducean-controlled Sanhedrin attempted to stop the increasing influence of the Antipatrid family by arresting HEROD, one of Antipater's sons, for murder. The result of this and other such moves was the assassination of both the Hasmonean family and a majority of the Sanhedrin when Herod was granted full power by the Romans in 37 B.C.E. Apparently the Sadducees learned the lesson taught by this murderous purge, for they tended to align themselves with the ruling authorities until the outbreak of the revolt against Rome in 66 C.E. One outcome of Herod's purge which worked to the favor of the Sadducees was that they regained control of the high priesthood, for even though the high priest was appointed by a Herodian or the Roman governor, such appointments came from the Sadducean ranks.

This historical sketch betrays certain characteristics of the Sadducees. First, they were the aristocratic element of Jewish society and closely tied to the priestly leadership. Second, they were political realists who, in an effort to maintain as much political authority as possible, were willing to concede power to others when necessary. Third, they were quite slow to accept innovative religious ideas. They viewed the written TORAH as the only sure authority in religious matters, and insisted on a conservative and literal interpretation of it. Hence, many ideas which were gaining popular support among the Jewish people were rejected by the Sadducees. Along with their denial of resurrection, they also denied the existence of demons and angels and had little room in their world view for the idea of the direct intervention of divine providence in the affairs of humanity. The Sadducees were often accused of being out of touch with the religious sentiments of the masses, who increasingly were turning to the Pharisees for moral and spiritual guidance. In part, it was because of their conservative religious nature and their close ties to the Temple that they were not able to survive the crisis that fell upon Judaism with the destruction of the Temple in 70 C.E. At this time the Sadducees effectively disappeared from the face of history. It was left to the Pharisees to salvage and reconstruct Judaism after the loss of its holy city and Temple.

See also HIGH PRIEST; PHARISEES; SANHEDRIN; ZADOK.

Bibliography. J. Jeremias, *Jerusalem in the Time of Jesus*; G. G. Porton, "Diversity in Postbiblical Judaism," *Early Judaism and Its Modern Interpreters*; E. Schürer, *The History of the Jewish People in the Age of Jesus Christ (175 BC–AD 135).*

—J. BRADLEY CHANCE

• **Saga.** *See* MYTH

• **Sage.** *See* PROVERBS, BOOK OF

• **Saint/Saints.** In the English OT "saints" translates words from two Heb. roots. The basic meaning of one of the words (חסד) when used of humans, is "pious" or "godly," signifying those who love God and do God's will. Psalms (e.g., 30:4; 31:23; 85:8; 97:10; 145:10) often mentions such "saints." The second term (קדש) means to be set apart or separated, and thus holy. Used often for God, this word denotes the difference between God and the created order. God is set apart. By extension, all that belongs to God is also separate or holy (cf. the people of God who are described as set apart in Pss 16:3; 34:9; 89:5, 7; 106:16; although in two of these instances [89:5, 7] the references are probably to heavenly beings, not humans). Daniel describes the faithful in one of the visions as the "saints of the Most High" (7:18, 21, 22, 25, 27).

In the NT "saint" translates a Gk. word (ἅγιος) which denotes that which is set apart to God and thus holy. In Matt

27:52 the "saints" are the pre-Christian faithful. For the most part, however, "saints" describes the church, the believers in Christ. All who are a part of the body of Christ are saints. Paul uses the term often in his letters (e.g., Rom 1:7; 15:26; 1 Cor 1:2; 2 Cor 1:1; Phil 1:1; 1 Thess 3:13) as does also the author of the Book of Revelation (e.g., 5:8; 11:18; 13:7; 14:12; 16:6; 19:8), where saints usually refers to the martyrs, those who have demonstrated their commitment to God at the expense of their lives.

See also HOLINESS IN THE NEW TESTAMENT; HOLINESS IN THE OLD TESTAMENT; SANCTIFICATION.

—MITCHELL G. REDDISH

• **Salem.** A place name for Jerusalem, meaning wholeness or completion, in Heb. *šālēm*. Salem occurs as a proper name in Gen 14:18: "And King Melchizedek of Salem brought out bread and wine; he was priest of God Most High." The term appears in one Psalm text as well, also as a designation for Jerusalem (cf. Ps 76:2; Heb 7:2). The word can also be used as an adverb, "peacefully," or "safely" (Gen 33:18).

Judgments vary among scholars with regard to the connection of the term *šālēm* with the city name Jerusalem, with the personal name Solomon, and with the greeting "Shalom." There is a Ugaritic deity Shalem associated with the evening star, Venus, the deity who completes the day. Some have maintained that the deity is associated with the ancient city of Jerusalem, known to have existed as early as the twentieth century B.C.E. If so, there could be a connection between the deity Shalem and the deity of Jerusalem El Elyon, God Most High (Gen 14:18). The name Zion for Jerusalem has also been associated with this west semitic deity.

See also JERUSALEM; PEACE.

Bibliography. C. H. Gordon, *Ugaritic Literature*; J. Gray, *The Legacy of Canaan.*

—OMER J. HANCOCK, JR.

• **Salt.** One of the most important and basic commodities in antiquity, salt was used mainly for seasoning (Job 6:6) and preserving foods, but also in religious ceremonies and, in small quantities, as fertilizer (cf. Luke 14:34-35). It was obtained by evaporating sea water or salt-marsh water (Ezek 47:11) or by mining and crushing rock salt. The Dead Sea area (frequently "Salt Sea" in OT) was a primary source of salt in Palestine, and the story in which Lot's wife becomes "a pillar of salt" (Gen 19:26) has its setting in the prominence of rock-salt formations in that region.

The OT prescribes that incense, cereal offerings, and sacrifices be seasoned with salt (Exod 30:35; Lev 2:13; Ezek 43:24). The phrase "covenant of salt" (Num 18:19; 2 Chr 13:5; cf. Lev 2:13) refers to a permanent, unbreakable relationship, probably reflecting the ancient custom of eating salt together as a token of communion, trust, and loyalty (cf. Ezra 4:14). Elisha's use of salt to sweeten the foul spring at Jericho (2 Kgs 2:20-21) and the custom of rubbing newborn infants with salt (Ezek 16:4) probably associate salt with purifying properties. Both the natural barrenness of salt lands and the practice of sowing a conquered land with salt, as Abimelech did in Shechem (Judg 9:45), account for references to salt in oracles of judgment (Deut 29:23; Jer 17:6; Zeph 2:9).

Jesus uses salt as a figure for the qualities which enable disciples to be a blessing to the world and to live peacefully with one another; he warns that disciples who do not bear these qualities are as useless as salt which has lost its saltiness (Matt 5:13; Mark 9:49-50; Luke 14:34-35), alluding to the useless dross remaining after the salt had been leached out of the typically impure compound.

Bibliography. E. P. Deatrick, "Salt, Soil, Savior," *BA* 25/2 (May 1962): 41-48; F. C. Fensham, "Salt as Curse in the Old Testament and the Ancient Near East," *BA* 25/2 (May 1962): 48-50; J. Toutain, *The Economic Life of the Ancient World.*

—DONALD N. PENNY

• **Salutations.** The social courtesy of greeting someone during OT times. Such greetings are usually described in one of three ways.

First, there was the formal greeting of a monarch, which usually involved not only the bowing before him in OBEISANCE, but also some verbal expression of blessings upon him (Dan 2:4; Neh 2:3).

Second, there was an informal greeting between two individuals of brief acquaintance. Though such greetings usually involved no direct physical contact, they did involve verbal expressions of delight. The most common of these expressions called for God either to bless (*bārak*) the one encountered (2 Kgs 4:29) or to bring PEACE (*šālôm*) to him (Judg 18:15; 1 Sam 10:4).

Third, there was also the more intimate kiss on the cheek. This would normally be done either by a close friend (1 Sam 20:41) or a relative (Exod 4:27). Moreover, this type of greeting was often accompanied by either embracing (Gen 48:10), weeping (Gen 45:15) or both (Gen 33:4). In addition to the kiss on the cheek, there was also the more affectionate kiss on the mouth, though it was usually reserved for those involved in the most intimate of relationships (Cant 1:2).

Such greetings as these are still common in much of the Middle Eastern world today.

See also GESTURES; OBEISANCE.

—HARRY B. HUNT, JR.

• **Salvation in the New Testament.** In the NT, as in the OT, the basic idea of salvation is deliverance from danger or evil. In a general sense salvation is deliverance from such ills as disease (Matt 9:21-22; Jas 5:15), demon possession (Luke 8:36), and physical danger or death (Matt 8:25; 2 Cor 1:10). In a special or religious sense salvation is deliverance from SIN and spiritual death (Matt 1:21; 10:22; 19:25).

The Gk. word for save (σώζω) may mean "save" in a religious sense (Luke 7:50) or "heal, make whole" in a physical sense (Mark 5:34; 10:52; Luke 17:19). The account of the paralytic clearly links the external act of physical healing with the internal act of spiritual salvation (Mark 2:1-12 and par.). To authenticate the declaration that the paralyzed man's sins had been forgiven, Jesus caused him to arise and walk (v. 9). Thus Jesus placed forgiveness of sins side-by-side with physical healing as two parts of the same miracle. Jesus' miracles of healing were really parables of salvation from sin.

The need of salvation from sin is universal because all morally responsible people sin and stand under God's wrath (Rom 1:18-3:20). Because sin is universal, God offers salvation to every person. This universal offer of salvation is made clear by the statement that God loved the world enough to send his son in order that everyone who believes in him would have ETERNAL LIFE (John 3:16). It is God's fervent desire that all people repent and receive salvation instead of perishing in sin (2 Pet 3:9).

Salvation is from God (Luke 1:47; 1 Tim 4:10) or Christ

the Lord, Christ Jesus, Christ (Luke 2:11; Eph 5:23; 2 Tim 1:10). The name Jesus means "God saves" (Matt 1:21). Jesus came to seek out and save sinners (Luke 19:10). He is "the Lamb of God who takes away the sin of the world" (John 1:29). Jesus is not just a savior among many; he is the only savior (Acts 4:12). Thus Jesus is the only source or agent of salvation. Only those who believe in him have eternal life (John 3:36). Jesus is the only source of salvation because he is the full and final revelation of God who makes God known to people (John 1:1, 14, 18; Matt 11:27).

The initiative in salvation is always with God, never with the sinner (cf. Gal 4:9). Like Adam and Eve when they sinned (Gen 3:8-11), people try to avoid God. Their sin makes it impossible for them to take the first step in their own salvation. But God takes the initiative and creates in the hearts of sinners the desire for salvation and empowers them to believe in Jesus so that they can be saved (John 6:44, 65).

The means of salvation is God's GRACE through the channel of human FAITH (Eph 2:8-9). Grace is God's righteous love in bringing sinful people to salvation. By this grace God pardons sinners and delivers them from the destruction which they deserve (Rom 3:24-25). Since salvation is by grace as a free gift, achieving salvation by one's own effort is ruled out (Rom 3:24). In fact, works as a means of salvation invalidate grace and leave people in their sin (Rom 11:6).

To be saved, the sinner must accept God's offer of salvation. This response is called faith. God gives salvation only to those who believe in Jesus and accept him as their savior (John 1:12). It is faith in Jesus that secures eternal life and the lack of faith in him that brings condemnation (John 3:18). The GOSPEL is God's power that brings salvation, but only to those who have faith in Jesus (Rom 1:16). Faith in Jesus is the channel through which God's grace operates to bring about salvation.

Saving faith is much more than mental assent to theological truth, such as "God exists." Demons believe in God's existence and shudder (Jas 2:19), but their belief does not result in salvation because it is merely an intellectual exercise. Saving faith includes not only mental assent but also trust and commitment. Those who receive salvation believe the truth about God as it is revealed in the Bible, trust in God to deliver them from sin, and commit themselves to obey God. Obedience is a vital element of faith. Paul sometimes used obedience as a synonym for faith (Rom 6:17; 15:18). He coined the term, "obedience of faith," to stress the fact that saving faith results in obedience (Rom 1:5).

In addition to faith, REPENTANCE is a condition for salvation or entrance into the KINGDOM OF GOD (Matt 4:17). Repentance is a change of the total person which results in turning away from sin to God and the right way of life. People must repent or perish (Luke 13:3-5). As a result of repentance, sinners are forgiven and brought into a right relationship with God. In forgiveness God removes the sin from the sinner and never holds it against the person again (Heb 10:17).

Salvation may be described as union with Christ. The believer lives in Christ, and Christ lives in the believer (John 14:20). People cannot be Christians without a vital union or relationship with Christ any more than a branch can live and bear fruit apart from the vine (John 15:1-8). Spiritual life and vitality flow out from Christ into believers just as life-giving sap flows from the vine into the branches. Through union with Christ all believers are being transformed into the moral likeness of Christ (Rom 8:29; 2 Cor 3:18). Thus as time passes, Christians become more and more like Christ in attitude and conduct.

Salvation is also a process. It is not something which happens and is completed in an instant. It is a past event. Believers have already been reconciled to God (Rom 5:10-11), cleansed, sanctified, and made righteous (1 Cor 6:11). Salvation is also a present reality for those in Christ. Christians are now in the process of being saved (1 Cor 1:18). Salvation is to continue throughout life. From another perspective, salvation is a hope of the future. Christians look forward with great expectation to the finalization of their salvation (Rom 8:23-24). The Spirit of God who dwells in believers is God's pledge that the salvation which God began in the past and continues in the present will be completed in the future (2 Cor 1:22; Eph 1:13-14) "at the day of Jesus Christ" (Phil 1:6).

See also ATONEMENT/EXPIATION IN THE NEW TESTAMENT; CONVERSION; ETERNAL LIFE; EXPIATION; FAITH AND FAITHLESSNESS; FORGIVENESS/PARDON; GOSPEL; GRACE; HOLY SPIRIT; JUSTIFICATION; KINGDOM OF GOD; RECONCILIATION; REDEMPTION IN THE NEW TESTAMENT; REDEMPTION IN THE OLD TESTAMENT; REGENERATION; REPENTANCE; RIGHTEOUSNESS IN THE NEW TESTAMENT; RIGHTEOUSNESS IN THE OLD TESTAMENT; SAVIOR IN THE NEW TESTAMENT; SAVIOR IN THE OLD TESTAMENT.

Bibliography. M. Ashcraft, *The Forgiveness of Sins*; D. Guthrie, *New Testament Theology*; D. Moody, *The Word of Truth*; L. Morris, *New Testament Theology*; L. B. Smedes, *Union with Christ*; F. Stagg, *New Testament Theology*.

—VIRGIL FRY

• **Salvation in the Old Testament.** Deliverance or rescue from natural disasters, historical dangers, or from besetting fear. The terms in the OT (*yš'*, *mlṭ*, *nṣl*, etc.) also have positive meaning, referring not only to restoration to health or safety but also describing or implying a situation better than that enjoyed before the difficulty or disaster came. For this reason, historical salvation and spiritual or eschatological salvation belong together and presuppose one another.

The Exodus as Paradigm of Salvation. "I am the Lord your God who brought you out of the land of Egypt, out of the house of bondage" (Exod 20:2). Over and again throughout Israelite history this central event of divine deliverance was recognized as typical of Israel's Savior-God. God had the power to save, a theme found prominently in Second ISAIAH as the prophet extolled God's power as Creator and as Guide of all history. God also had the will to save, as Second Isaiah never tired of pointing out, for God's very character was graciousness (cf. the confessional text in Exod 34:6-7, which is repeated many times in later literature). Salvation, then, means in particular God's intervention into the historical processes to rescue Israel from slavery and oppression.

The entire account of Israel's journeys through the wilderness, CONQUEST OF CANAAN, life under the Judges, and rule by Israel's kings is cast into the framework of God's saving interventions in behalf of the people.

Israel Has a Part in Salvation. At the same time, these traditions describe the part that the people of God are expected to play in their salvation. Salvation is not all divine MIRACLE. As is clear from Exod 3, God sees the plight of Israel and determines to intervene in their behalf. But God also selects leaders from among the people to be divine instruments in the deliverance. Direct and miraculous intervention often was sought and sometimes secured, according to the traditions, but God was the directing and empowering agent in Israel's salvation, rather than the only actor. While the ideology of HOLY WAR seems to have been that the people were only to place themselves, dedicated and holy, at God's service in order that God alone could grant the victory, the stories of such warfare display human agency as well, of course.

Eschatological Salvation. Israel's prophets, psalmists, and sages worked out the particulars of divine salvation. The prophets pointed out that God's interventions in the people's behalf were expected to produce commitment to public justice, to COVENANT faith, to love and devotion to God and care for one another. When the community persisted in defiance of or departures from God's way, they had only themselves to blame for disasters that struck and for the loss of a rich and full life on the land that God was providing for them. Even so, salvation remained God's purpose and intention: EZEKIEL could ask, "Why will you die, O house of Israel?" (Ezek 18:31).

Two types of eschatological salvation developed in the course of Israelite history, both of them of great importance for the Christian and Jewish communities. The first type was prophetic eschatology, a many-faceted sketch by the prophets of the coming day of divine consummation, when God's salvation would be established on a transformed earth and all of God's children would live responsible, full, and peaceable lives. Among the earliest of these eschatological texts is Gen 49:8-12, JACOB's deathbed blessing upon JUDAH and the tribe of Judah. The promise there is that one will arise from the tribe of Judah who will usher in a day of plenty and blessing. This ruler will tie the royal ass to the grapevine, giving no thought to what the ass will eat, for there will be such abundance of grapes that eyes will sparkle. Food too will be so plentiful that teeth will glisten from the abundance of milk available to drink. A similar picture of earthly eschatological fulfillment is found in AMOS 9:13-15.

The classical eschatological descriptions of salvation, however, go farther, portraying the establishment of peace and cooperation among the nations of earth, as God's TORAH goes out from ZION, drawing all the nations to obedience and faithfulness (Isa 2:2-4; Mic 4:1-4), or depicting God's appointed ruler arising to prominence and taking the lead to establish this peace and well-being (Isa 9:2-7; 11:1-9; Mic 5:1-5a, etc.). Other texts tell of God's salvation in terms of the union of the nations and God's declaration that Egypt and Assyria are no less God's people than is Israel (Isa 19:23-25; Zech 2:6-12; 8:20-23).

A second kind of text displays God's salvation at the end of the historical process itself, viewed more in terms of chronology than spiritual nearness. These texts, called APOCALYPTIC, see salvation more in terms of God's culminating the historical process by disposing of God's enemies, rescuing the faithful, and displaying the consequences of SIN and rebellion while rewarding the elect people of God. The Bible presents both forms of eschatological salvation. Both have their place. The prophetic eschatological outlook emphasizes God's fulfillment of the divine purpose on a transformed earth, as the historical process is culminated. The apocalyptic outlook is in danger of despairing over God's present creation and envisaging a world that replaces this sinful world. Prophetic eschatology remains with historical fulfillment of God's saving purposes. Apocalyptic eschatology stresses the triumph of God's justice and the reward of the faithful, even if the price has to be God's destruction of the present age. Clearly, both views remain active to the present day.

Salvation as Present Reality. Such texts do not always employ the language of salvation directly but they are describing the reality envisaged by the biblical writers in other terms. The same is true of Psalm texts in which the individual or the community cries out for divine intervention, seeking God's help in times of mortal danger. Salvation comes often in the form of an assurance of God's forgiveness and presence, even when the illness or the physical disability that produced the plea to God has not been removed. That is, salvation was understood to be a reality claiming the individual or the group or the people even when the physical or historical distress had not been fully overcome. Salvation, in this sense, is also an eschatological reality, claimed in faith prior to its full public display. The import for biblical ETHICS of this understanding of how God's salvation claims the community and its members even before its full realization is very great. Both the Israelite and the Christian communities knew that the promises of God are finding fulfillment prior to their complete and public consummation.

Bibliography. W. Foerster and G. Fohrer, "σῴζω, κτλ.," *TDNT*.

—WALTER HARRELSON

• **Samaria.** Samaria is first a city of ancient ISRAEL, then the territory named for it (PLATES 13, 17, 23). A Samaritan is an inhabitant of Samaria, but specifically—and usually— a member of the religious community originating and still resident in Samaria.

Ca. 876 B.C.E., OMRI moved the capital of Israel nine miles west of TIRZAH where he purchased a hill, named it "Samaria" (שֹׁמְרוֹן *shomᵉron,* "belonging to Shemer"), and thereupon built his capital (1 Kgs 16:23-24). Omri's building program (and AHAB's) employed the renowned artisans and craftsmen of PHOENICIA, and Samaria became a model of engineering and workmanship. Ivory inlays at the site confirm Ahab's infamous "ivory house" (1 Kgs 22:39) against whose "beds of ivory" Amos (6:4) railed. Samaria's opulence bespeaks the prosperity of Israel under the first kings "in Samaria" (1 Kgs 16:29).

In 722/1 B.C.E. Samaria was burned by the ASSYRIANS (2 Kgs 17:5-6; 18:9-10), and SARGON deported "27,290 inhabitants" for resettlement elsewhere and imported other conquered peoples to repopulate Samaria (cf. 2 Kgs 17:1-6, 24). Sargon boasts of rebuilding Samaria—now the provincial capital—"better than before." He named the new province, which included what formerly was Israel, *Sa-*

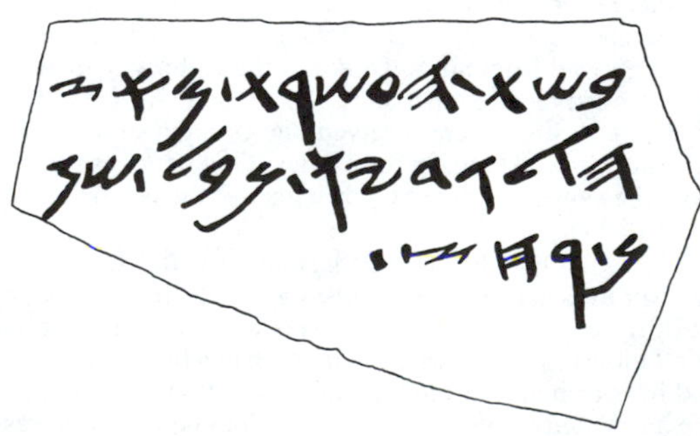

Samaria Ostracon No. 17.

merina. Thus the territorial designation is credited to the Assyrians and dated to that time; however, ''Samaria'' probably long before alternatively designated Israel when Samaria became the captial.

The Babylonians came ca. 612, and in 587/6 Jerusalem became part of their province of Samaria. In 539, Samaria came under Persian rule. The period after ca. 538 marks the beginnings of overt enmity between ''Jews'' and ''Samaritans,'' fueled by disagreements between the returning exiles and the governors ''in Samaria'' (cf. Ezra 4:8-24; Neh 2:9-20; 4:1-9; 6:1-14). With the coming of Nehemiah, ca. 445, Jerusalem was separated from Samaria and the province of Judea was restored. ALEXANDER (d. 323) overran Samaria in 332, briefly making Samaria a territory of his empire, and then for a hundred years a pawn and battlefield for the Macedonians (Antigonus), Ptolemies, and Seleucids.

Recent (1960s) discoveries—especially the Samaria Papyri—shed new light on this period. Evidently the Samaritans revolted against Alexander, who, on his return from Egypt, destroyed Samaria, annihilated the leaders, expelled the rest of the inhabitants, and resettled Samaria with Macedonians—accounting for the Hellenization of Samaria. The expelled remnant resettled in SHECHEM, which they reestablished as their capital, and built a temple on MOUNT GERIZIM—accounting for the abrupt reconstruction attested by recent excavations. These ''Samaritans'' who returned to Shechem and built a temple on their mountain thus are the ones who broke from the Judeans to form their own community, and who appear in the NT.

Sometime after ca. 128 B.C.E. Samaria and Shechem were beseiged and savaged by John Hyrcanus (135/4–104), who literally levelled the temple on Gerizim. The Samaritans came under the Jewish kingdom until 63 B.C.E., when Pompey took Jerusalem and, with Judea, Samaria became part of the Roman province and the city was returned to the Samaritans. When HEROD became ''king of the Jews'' (37–4 B.C.E.) he rebuilt Samaria as a tribute to Augustus and renamed it Sebaste (Greek ''Augustus''), the ''city of Samaria'' of NT times (Acts 8:5). (''Samaria'' in the NT always refers to the *territory* of the ''Samaritans.'') Archelaus governed from 4 B.C.E. to 6 C.E., and after he was banished his former territory was ruled by a succession of Roman procurators, including Pilate (26–36 C.E.) and ''king'' Herod Agrippa I (41–44). During the first Jewish revolt (66–70) Sebaste was taken by the rebels and burned. Under Emperor Severus (193–211) Sebaste became a Roman colony and enjoyed a revival of its former glory with a massive building program whose remains are found today above ground. Following Constantine's establishment of Christianity, Sebaste became an episcopal see. In 634 Sebaste fell to the Arabs, and today the modern Arab village Sebastiyeh, at the foot of Shemer's hill, preserves the NT-era name.

The history of the designation ''Samaritans'' is unsettled, a confusion resulting from the prejudicial nature of the records on both sides and the paucity of records on the Samaritan side. ''Samaritans'' occurs in the OT only in the narrative regarding Sargon's conquest (2 Kgs 17:29). A noticeable rift between Samaritans and Judeans as such occurred after the Exile, evidently caused by opposition regarding Samaria's loss of Judea and Jerusalem (and aggravated by Nehemiah's plans to refortify Jerusalem) when the Judean province was reestablished under Nehemiah. Evidently Samaria's opposition was at first only political and economic (loss of temple-tax revenue). But Nehemiah instigated (and Ezra perpetuated) a different kind of opposition by efforts to segregate the people according to their origins (Neh 13:1-3). Those who had remained in the land were considered half-heathen because they had married other than Israelites (cf. Ezra 10:2, 10-11), and they were despised for compromising the Law (Neh 10:28-31). The returned exiles were ''the remnant'' (Ezra 9:8, 15; Hag 1:14) who had been guided home by, and so stood in a special relationship with, Yahweh (cf. Neh 9:9-25). The people who remained in the land, however, had besoiled themselves by mixed marriages (Ezra 9:1) thus betraying the ''holy race'' (Ezra 9:2). (Henceforth the Jews persistently designated them ''Cuthim/Cutheans''—cf. ''Cuthah,'' 2 Kgs 17:24.) It is suggested that when the Samaritans were resigned to their loss of Jerusalem and the temple taxes, they retreated to Samaria, built their own temple, and declared themselves the true inheritors of the faith. Thereafter Jews and Samaritans—as often with estranged brothers—despised and strictly avoided each other. Especially the Samaria Papyri, however, suggests the establishment of a distinct Samaritan community during the Hellenistic period (cf. above).

At any rate, the schism predates the NT in which the Samaritans are clearly a distinct community, to the Jews racially mongrel and religiously apostate—as vice versa were Jews to Samaritans. In the NT ''Jews'' distinguishes the descendants of Israel from others, including Samaritans (John 4:9; Acts 2:10; 14:1). The NT locates Samaritans around Gerizim (John 4:1ff.) but also finds them elsewhere, even in Judea (cf. Matt 10:5; Luke 9:52; 10:29-37; 17:11-19). Jews and Samaritans share a common heritage from ''our father Jacob'' (John 4:12), but differ radically in certain important regards, especially whether God's ''chosen place'' is Jerusalem/Zion or Shechem/Gerizim (John 4:20). Jesus' linking of Samaritans with gentiles in contrast to ''the house of Israel'' (Matt 10:5-6) reflects the attitude of Jews toward Samaritans. (Jesus' ''good Samaritan''—Luke 10:29-37—was a contradiction in terms.) Samaritans were the objects of early evangelization by Greek-speaking Christians, and among them Philip had much success (Acts 8:4-25). Afterwards the Samaritan Christians supported Paul (Acts 15:3).

Today there remains a small group of Samaritans in Nablus (formerly Neapolis—one of many Roman ''new cities'' by that name) in the shadow of Gerizim. They are independent, very conservative, and still led by priests. They observe Passover by ritual slaying of sheep, strictly enforce Sabbath observance, and marry only among their own. They claim to be descendants of the ''ten tribes'' whom they deny were ever deported en masse (2 Kgs 17:23); they believe Gerizim rather than Zion is the ''chosen place'' where ''our fathers worshipped''; and they recognize as scripture only the Pentateuch in their own version that deviates from the Hebrew Bible at about 6,000 points (e.g., ''Gerizim'' rather than ''Ebal'' in Deut 27:4).

See also AHAB; ASSYRIA; EXILE; EZRA; GERIZIM, MOUNT; ISRAEL; JEHU; JEROBOAM II; NEHEMIAH; OMRI; SANBALLAT; SARGON; SHECHEM; SHILOH.

Bibliography. P. C. Craigie, ''The Northern Kingdom: Israel,'' *The Old Testament: Its Background, Growth, and Content*; J. Jeremias, ''Σαμάρεια, κτλ.,'' *TDNT*; J. B. Pritchard, ed., ''The Fall of Samaria,'' *ANET*; J. D. Purvis, *The Samaritan Pentateuch and the Origin of the Samaritan Sect*.

—EDD ROWELL

• **Samaritans.** A word that appears only once in the Hebrew OT for the citizens of the northern territory of Samaria (2 Kgs 17:29). However, the context is the Assyrian colonization of the region with diverse peoples. The writer of 2 Kings commented that the Assyrian foreigners of various ethnic groups set up their gods in shrines of the high places "which the Samaritans had made." This remark sets the stage for understanding developing tensions between Samaritans and Jews.

In the Greek NT the term is almost always used in a disparaging sense for a specific religious and ethnic community that lived principally around MOUNT GERIZIM (John 4:1-42), south of the city of ancient SAMARIA (called Sebaste in the Roman period). Nevertheless Samaritans lived in villages around Samaria (Luke 17:11-19), and Jesus encountered Samaritan lepers on the major road connecting Jerusalem and Jericho (Luke 10:29-37).

In the NT it is clear that Jews and Samaritans shared a common heritage (John 4:12), but differed on the proper place of worship, Jerusalem or Mount Gerizim (John 4:20). Because they interpreted the requirements of ritual uncleanliness and cleanliness differently, they avoided contact with one another (John 4:7-10). Sometimes this avoidance came to expression as a contempt of Samaritans by Jews, as for example in John 8:48, where Jesus' opponents called him "a Samaritan, and you have a demon." Jesus himself seemed to believe that Samaritans, like gentiles, did not belong to the "house of Israel" (Matt 10:5). Furthermore his pilgrim itinerary in Mark 10:1 and Matt 19:1 seems to follow a longstanding pilgrim route that avoided Samaria. In one other text, however, he was rejected by a village of Samaria on the grounds that he planned to travel through Samaria to Jerusalem (Luke 9:53).

This Jewish/Samaritan separation is reflected in the word "foreigner" (*allogenes*) that Jesus used for the Samaritan leper that he cured (Luke 17:18). This term is found on the extant Greek inscription from Herod's Temple from the barrier that separated the Court of Gentiles from the Court of Women ("No foreigner [*allogenes*] shall enter . . . "). JOSEPHUS mentioned these inscriptions and used the same word (*BJ* 5.5.2). Josephus explains that Jews excluded Samaritans from the temple mount because of Samaritan acts of religious vandalism within the temple precinct.

Jesus used a strong irony, therefore, by insisting that a Samaritan acted properly toward the man beaten and left for dead, not the priest or Levite (Luke 10:33). It is also one leper out of ten who returned to thank Jesus for his cure, and this one a Samaritan! (Luke 17:16). Therefore, it should be no surprise that in Luke's theology, the followers of Jesus are to be witnesses in Judea, Samaria, and the uttermost parts of the earth (Acts 1:8; 8:14, 25).

Origins. The conventional theory is that the Samaritans are the descendants of the colonists brought by the Assyrians to Samaria (2 Kgs 17; Josephus, *Ant* 12.5.5). The Samaritan position is that they are descendants of native Israelites that were never deported. Probably both positions are partially true. Discovery of the Wadi Daliyeh papyri shows that there was a Samaritan uprising against the Macedonians during the last third of the fourth century B.C.E. Eusebius reports an uprising of the Samaritans against Andromachus, the governor of Coelesyria, whom they assassinated in 331 B.C.E. (*Chron* 2.114). Excavations at ancient SHECHEM at the foot of Mount Gerizim indicate the city was refounded in the early Hellenistic period (about 330 B.C.E.) after several centuries of abandonment. The city continued to be occupied until about 107 B.C.E., when it was destroyed by John Hyrcanus, king of the Jews.

The Samaritans built their temple on Mount Gerizim between 335 and 330 B.C.E., according to Josephus (*Ant* 11.8.4). Excavations at one of the peaks of Mount Gerizim have revealed a great outdoor altar of Hellenistic date within a great, walled enclosure. Josephus says this "temple" was destroyed by John Hyrcanus in 129/8 B.C.E. (*Ant* 13.9.1; *BJ* 1.2.6). Although excavations show that the "temple" was certainly destroyed and covered with sterile fill, coins of Alexander Jannaeus were found in the bottom of the cistern on the south side of the great altar, suggesting a later date for this destruction. Josephus ascribes this destruction to Hyrcanus's irritation at the Samaritans for claiming to be Sidonians and for requesting that their temple be dedicated to Zeus Hellenios (*Ant* 12.5.5). The second century C.E. Roman temple excavated atop the Samaritan "temple" was likely dedicated to Zeus Hypsistos, lending some credence to Josephus's story. This temple and several other sacred structures are depicted on coins of the city of Neapolis (modern Nablus), located at the foot of Mount Gerizim.

According to 2 Macc 6:1 the cult of the Samaritans on Mount Gerizim was compromised by Hellenistic practices by 175 B.C.E. By the Hasmonean period the Samaritans apparently redacted their own version of the Torah ("The Samaritan Pentateuch") to reflect their version of their history and to prove the apostasy of the Jews. This text is preserved in their own unique script, spellings, and readings.

Later History. The Samaritans were treated as a separate people at the coming of Rome in 63 B.C.E. However, they participated on the Jewish side in the First Jewish Revolt of 66–73 C.E., losing some 12,000 men (*BJ* 3.7.32). At the time of the Second Jewish Revolt of 135 C.E. the Samaritans first sided with the Jews, then turned to Rome. Hadrian rewarded them with permission to rebuild their temple. It is difficult to see how this could be the temple to Zeus Hypsistos excavated on top of Mount Gerizim. We have little information about them until the fourth century, when violent incidents between Jews and Samaritans and Christians and Samaritans increased steadily. By the fourth century most Samaritans lived in and around Neapolis south of Sebasté and next to the abandoned site of ancient Shechem. However, excavations have yielded Samaritan inscriptions from many sites in ancient Judea and in a Samaritan diaspora in the eastern Mediterranean. In 451 the Emperor Marcianus used Samaritan soldiers to suppress monophysite Christians. In 484 a Samaritan revolt broke out against the emperor Zeno. In 529 the Samaritans rose up again against their Christian and Jewish neighbors in a particularly bloody conflict that was put down by the Emperor Justinian at much cost. Many Samaritan young men and women were sold as slaves in the markets of Persia and India in the aftermath of this revolt. Afterwards, the Samaritans remained a small sect still largely concentrated around Neapolis.

The Samaritans are a strict sect that observes Torah and retains animal sacrifice. They regard themselves as those who have kept the true faith, so they are to be known as *shamerim* (Observers [of Torah]) as opposed to simply *shomerim* (Samaritans). They claim to be descendants of the Joseph tribes. Their religion was and is dominated by priests in the tradition of the SADDUCEES or in some sense the ESSENES of Qumran. They do not regard the Prophets and the Writings as part of scripture.

Bibliography. R. J. Bull, "The Excavations of Tell er-Ras on Mt. Gerizim," *BA* 31 (1968); R. J. Coggins, *Samaritans and Jews*; F. M. Cross, "Aspects of Samaritan and

Jewish History in Late Persian and Early Hellenistic Times,'' *HTR* 59 (1966); J. D. Purvis, *The Samaritan Pentateuch and the Origin of the Samaritan Sect* and ''The Samaritan Problem,'' in B. Halpern and J. Levenson, eds., *Traditions in Transformation.*

—JAMES F. STRANGE

• **Samson.** A judge, that is, warrior-deliverer, from the tribe of Dan whose single-handed exploits vexed the Philistines and left behind a trail of carnage. His private vendetta, attributed to the divine spirit and to a personal desire for revenge, invariably grew out of amorous adventures. These erotic relationships with foreign women, recorded in Judg 13–16, led to Samson's capture and to death at his own hands. This narrative, rich in motifs from folklore, belongs to the deuteronomistic account of Israel's history and therefore has a distinct religious stamp. The story also contains exquisite literary features.

The name Samson seems related to the word for sun, perhaps as a diminutive meaning ''little sun.'' His father's name, Manoah, alludes to ''rest'' from Philistine oppression, the achievement of Samson's efforts. Although his mother's identity is missing, she clearly dominates the narrative in chap. 13. Two of Samson's lovers also remain nameless in the tradition, but Delilah probably conjures up thoughts of ''nighttime delights.'' The second appearance of the divine messenger occasions discussion of the significance of names, in this instance God's (''worker of wonder'') and enables Manoah to respond by offering a hint about his own name by adding a cereal offering (*minḥâ*) to the burnt offering requested of him. Two place names with etiological import occur in the story, Hill of the Jawbone and Partridge Spring.

Samson's heroic deeds are greater than life, generously mixing truth with fiction. He kills a young lion with his bare hands; slays thirty PHILISTINES and takes their clothes to settle a wager; catches three hundred foxes, ties their tails together, sets them on fire, and releases them in the enemies' grainfields; snaps a new rope with which he has been tied, snatches up a fresh jawbone of an ass, and kills 1,000 Philistines; rips up Gaza's gates and door, carrying them on his shoulders for a great distance; and pushes down Dagon's sacred precincts, killing more than 3,000 worshipers within its walls.

A religious dimension permeates this tale of blood and passion, probably from the outset. The initial story consists of a birth and recognition account. A childless woman receives a visit from a messenger who promises her a remarkable son and instructs her to rear him as a Nazirite. Her husband prays for personal corroboration of her story, a request that issues in a terrifying experience as the angel vanishes in the flames of the altar. Like EVE, Manoah's wife adds to the divine command, but she demonstrates bold resolve in the presence of awesome mystery. The Nazirite vow, ignored and broken by Samson, fits badly into the story of a divulged secret, for his loss of strength coincides with the Lord's departure, and his ultimate vindication results from fervid prayer rather than long hair. Another prayer departs his lips after the slaughter of a thousand Philistines. Both Samson's prayers use ordinary vocabulary appropriate to a rough soldier, whereas Manoah's entreaty employs cultic language.

Various motifs from folklore enrich the story: a childless woman who receives a gift of an extraordinary child, a hero who falls victim to a beautiful woman, and a divine messenger who conceals its identity and evokes terror in humans. Four dark secrets lurk in the shadows, eventually yielding to persistent inquiry: the angel's identity, the meaning of Samson's riddle, his presence in the harlot's house at Gaza, and the source of his great strength all cease to baffle the persons who search for the truth.

Samson's riddles capitalize on the erotic feelings generated by his wedding to the lovely Timnite. The first, which derives from private experience, required information not available to the friends of the bride. ''From the eater comes something to eat, from the mighty, something sweet'' (14:14). The cipher language holds both clue and snare. The riddle may refer to sexual experience or the delicacies on which soldiers gorge themselves until they vomit, but these false answers comprise the riddle's trap. Avoiding either response,the friends obtain private information from the bride, who has acquired it through copious tears. They answer Samson in a riddle: ''What is sweeter than honey, what is stronger than a lion?'' (14:18). The answer, of course, is love, which fell victim to tears. Samson's retort contains echoes of yet a third riddle: ''If you had not plowed with my heifer, you would not have discovered my riddle'' (14:18). The image of plowing is widespread as a sexual expression in the ancient Near East.

The repercussions of the first riddle reverberate through the entire story. Both Samson and his foes are driven by a desire to get even, to strike the final blow. The principle of *ius talionis* (exact justice) pervades the narrative, at least insofar as human motivation receives expression. Israel's God initiates the fracas out of desire to eliminate the Philistines. The story itself functions as a warning against intermarriage between Israelites and the uncircumcised. It juxtaposes an account of a devout Israelite wife and mother over against stories illustrating three kinds of relationships with foreign women. The first tells about the power of physical beauty, the second, sexual desire, and third, unreciprocated love. The parental rebuke of Samson for overlooking desirable Israelites stands out as a forceful statement of narrative concern. If the mighty Samson could not emerge from such relationships unscathed, how could ordinary mortals expect to negotiate these dangerous liaisons? The Samson story brings into focus the conflict between filial devotion and erotic attachment.

In keeping with the principle of exact justice, both Samson and his enemies celebrate victories by singing of their triumph over a foe. Samson's song, rich in alliteration (''With an ass's jawbone, ass upon asses, with an ass's jawbone, I have slain a thousand men,'' 15:16) is matched by that of the Philistines who obtained him by bribery (''Our god has given Samson our enemy into our hands, the ravager of our land who has killed many of us,'' 16:24). Rhyme, rare in Hebrew literature, explodes in this joyous chant five times. Tribal jealousies surface in the narrative, whose hero belongs to a lowly clan that inspired considerable negative sentiment elsewhere in the book of Judges (18:1-31). In their dealings with Samson, the people of Judah display cowardice and willingness to remain subject to the Philistines rather than risk confrontation.

The early church characterized Samson as a saint, an attitude that caused some discussion in light of his pride, immoral conduct, and suicide. The later church described him as a type of Christ, finding several parallels between the two: (1) both births were announced by divine emissaries; (2) both freed Israel from the power of the enemy, Philistines and SATAN; (3) both overcame a lion (in Jesus' case, Satan who stalks Christians like a lion); (4) the Spirit departed from both; (5) both labored alone (Jesus' disciples forsook him); (6) a bribe figured in the downfall of both men; (7) both were bound; (8) both tore down gates (Jesus conquered the gates of Hell); and (9) both achieved victory in death.

John Milton used the Samson story to deal with his own blindness, writing an epic about primal temptation. In *Samson Agonistes,* Milton changed the plot in a few ways: Manoah and Delilah confront Samson in Gaza; a champion of the Philistines, Harapha, challenges Samson to single-handed combat like Goliath in the Davidic narrative; a chorus and a public messenger appear. Here Samson excels at mental gymnastics, expressing inward pain over having become a byword to the enemies of God and having indirectly contributed to Dagon's resurgence. Indeed, Samson can find no ease from restless thoughts. He and Manoah debate divine justice. The father is willing to ransom his son at any cost. Delilah defends her actions on the basis of natural feminine curiosity and weakness, a desire to keep him at home, love for state and religion, and wifely love. For Milton, Samson symbolizes everyone's struggle against sin and ultimate victory. Artists and musicians have found the Samson story a worthy source for their interests, and the movie industry has exploited the erotic dimensions of the tale.

See also JUDGES, BOOK OF; NAZIRITES; PHILISTINES.

Bibliography. J. Blenkinsopp, "Some Notes on the Saga of Samson and the Heroic Milieu," *Scr* (1959): 81-89 and "Structure and Style in Judges 13-16," *JBL* 82 (1963): 65-76; S. Carmy, "The Sphinx as Leader: A Reading of Judges 13-16," *Trad* 14 (1974): 66-79; J. L. Crenshaw, "The Samson Saga: Filial Devotion or Erotic Attachment," *ZAW* 86 (1974): 470-504 and *Samson: A Secret Betrayed, A Vow Ignored*; E. L. Greenstein, "The Riddle of Samson," *Proof* 1 (1981): 237-60; O. Maragalith, "Samson's Riddle and Samson's Magic Locks," *VT* 36 (1986): 225-34; P. Nel, "The Riddle of Samson," *Bib* 66 (1985): 534-45; J. A. Wharton, "The Secret of Yahweh: Story and Affirmation in Judges 13-16," *Int* 27 (1973): 48-66.

—JAMES L. CRENSHAW

• **Samuel.** The son of Elkanah the Ephraimite and HANNAH, Samuel functioned as prophet, priest, and judge in the eleventh century. He anointed SAUL and DAVID as kings of Israel. Although reconstruction of Samuel's life poses several problems, the roles he played are important in Israel's transition from the period of the judges to the monarchy. His name probably means "His name is God."

His birth was as a godsend to his mother Hannah (1 Sam 1). Hannah, who was childless, prayed for a son, promising that if her petition were answered the child would be given to the Lord's service. Samuel was born, and Hannah kept her promise. After he was weaned, Samuel was presented to Eli at Shiloh (1 Sam 1:26-29; 2:11) where he grew in human and divine favor (1 Sam 2:21, 26). In a night vision, Samuel was told of the impending disaster on the house of Eli (1 Sam 3). As Samuel grew his fame as a prophet spread until he was established throughout ISRAEL as a prophet of the Lord (1 Sam 3:19–4:1a).

Twenty years after the disaster at Aphek, the loss of the Ark, and the death of Eli (cf. 1 Sam 4–7), Samuel called Israel to a convocation at Mizpah to renew its vows to serve the Lord. When the PHILISTINES sought to stop the assembling of the tribes, Samuel prayed for deliverance and presented a whole burnt offering to the Lord. Routed by a thunderstorm, the Philistines were defeated by the Hebrews so badly that they did not constitute any further threat during the days of Samuel (1 Sam 7:2-14).

As a judge, Samuel maintained a circuit of the cities of BETHEL, GILGAL, Mizpah, and Ramah. This made Samuel unique, for he was a judge unlike the military figures found in Judges. Samuel's role of judge included administrative matters and worship, for he built an altar at his hometown of Ramah (1 Sam 7:15-17).

When Samuel became old, he appointed his sons Joel and Abijah judges. As judges at Beersheba, they proved unworthy, taking bribes and perverting justice in other ways. As a result, the elders of Israel requested that Samuel appoint a king. Though Samuel warned them of the consequences of having a king, they persisted (1 Sam 8). Their wish was granted in the selection of Saul as king (1 Sam 9). God appointed Samuel, the seer-prophet, to anoint Saul as king. The selection was done in secret at Ramah when Saul turned to Samuel for aid in finding his father's lost asses. After being anointed (1 Sam 10:1), Saul returned to his father's house but did not tell of the events with Samuel.

Cautioning Israel about a kingship a second time, Samuel convened the tribes at Mizpah to select a king by casting lots. Saul was chosen. Samuel then set out the rights and duties of kingship and wrote them in a book (1 Sam 10:17-25). When Saul returned to his home, opposition began to arise. This dissatisfaction was silenced through Saul's military success at JABESH-GILEAD (1 Sam 11:1-11) and through Samuel's actions of covenant renewal with Saul as king at Gilgal (1 Sam 11:12-15).

Although he gave his farewell address and warned of the consequences if the people or the king forsook the Lord (1 Sam 12), Samuel continued in his roles as Saul's adviser and as God's spokesman. Samuel's relationship with Saul was one of conflict. Saul assumed the priestly role at Gilgal. Samuel reprimanded Saul and told him that God would find another king because of Saul's disobedience (1 Sam 13:8-14). Saul also disobeyed the command to annihilate the Amalekites in holy warfare (Heb. *ḥerem*, 1 Sam 15).

The anointing of David as Saul's successor is found in 1 Sam 16:1-13. When David was forced to flee from the angry Saul, he traveled to Samuel at Ramah (1 Sam 19:18).

Although Samuel's death is recorded in 1 Sam 15:1, the medium of ENDOR is said to have conjured his spirit from Sheol for Saul (1 Sam 28:3-19). The words spoken are reminiscent of the judgment against Saul (1 Sam 13:8-14).

See also DAVID; HANNAH; KINGSHIP; PROPHET; SAUL.

Bibliography. H. W. Hertzberg, *I & II Samuel, OTL*.

—ROBERT A. STREET, JR.

• OUTLINE OF FIRST AND SECOND SAMUEL •

The Books of First and Second Samuel

I. The End of the Period of the Judges (1 Sam 1:1–7:17)
II. The Founding of the Hebrew Kingdom: Samuel and Saul (1 Sam 8:1–15:35)
III. Saul's Reign, with David in His Shadow (1 Sam 16:1–2 Sam 1:27)
IV. David, King of Judah (2 Sam 2:1–4:12)
V. David, King over All Israel (2 Sam 5:1–24:25)

• **Samuel, Books of First and Second.** The books of Samuel are a part of the Prophets in the Hebrew Bible, being in the subsection, the former prophets. They are a record of God's activity with Israel in the transition from the period of the Judges to the era of the Hebrew kingdom. This extends from the early part of the eleventh century B.C.E.

to the middle of the tenth century B.C.E.

The Title. The books are called 1 and 2 Samuel in the MT. They are the first two of 1, 2, 3, and 4 Kingdoms in the LXX. This title was shortened to 1, 2, 3, and 4 Kings in the Vulgate. It appears that they were originally one book, for the division between the two is quite artificial. First Samuel ends with the death of SAUL and JONATHAN. DAVID's response to their death is the beginning of 2 Samuel. The same sort of thing can be noted with the end of 2 Samuel and the beginning of 1 Kings. The division was probably made because one scroll could not contain all four books. Even two long scrolls would have been quite unhandy.

The Text. The text of 1 and 2 Samuel in the MT is quite different in places from that of the LXX. In general, where a difference exists, the MT is far less understandable than the LXX. Emendations have frequently been made by comparing the MT with the LXX and with parallel passages in 1 and 2 Chronicles. However, two partial Hebrew manuscripts of 1 and 2 Samuel (apparently still one book) have been found among the DEAD SEA SCROLLS. These reflect a Hebrew tradition closer to that of the LXX than the MT. These manuscripts are about 1,000 years older than the MT. Their text generally confirms textual judgments based upon Chronicles and the LXX.

Contents. The Books of Samuel recount the story of the end of the time of the judges and the rise of the Hebrew monarchy under Saul and David.

Authorship, Unity, Sources, and Date. Jewish tradition ascribes the authorship to Samuel (*Baba Bathra*, 14b-15a), but since his death is reported early in the books, this is not possible (cf. 1 Sam 25:1; 28:3). It is possible that he was responsible for part of the early material, for Chronicles clearly reports records being kept by Samuel, as well as by NATHAN and Gad (1 Chr 29:29-30). We are also told that Samuel wrote the duties of the king (1 Sam 10:25). Further, David's elegy over Saul and Jonathan is said to have been recorded in the Book of Jashar, offering another possible source (2 Sam 1:18).

In reading the two books, a number of dual accounts appear, with differing qualities of Hebrew grammar and syntax occurring in each. The sudden end of Eli's house is announced twice (1 Sam 2:31-36; 3:11-14). Saul is anointed king once privately and twice publicly (1 Sam 9:26–10:1; 10:17-24; 11:15). Saul is twice deposed from the throne, yet continues to reign until his death (1 Sam 13:14; 15:26-29). David is twice introduced to Saul (1 Sam 16:14-23; 17:55-58). David is three times offered a daughter of Saul in marriage (1 Sam 18:17-19, 20-21a, 22b-29a). David twice escapes from Saul's court, never to return (1 Sam 19:12; 20:42b). Saul was at once aware of David's first flight, but later wondered why David was not present at dinner (1 Sam 19:17; 20:25-29). David twice had Saul in his power and spared his life (1 Sam 24:3-7; 26:5-12). David three times made a covenant with Jonathan (1 Sam 18:3; 23:18; 20:16-42). David twice sought refuge with Achish, king of Gath (1 Sam 21:10-15; 27:1-4). Goliath was slain both by David and by Elhanan. This was later corrected by the Chronicler (1 Sam 17; 19:5; 21:9; 22:10b, 13; 2 Sam 21:19; 1 Chr 20:4). The origin of the proverb, "Is Saul among the prophets?" is given twice (1 Sam 10:11; 19:24). The treason of the Ziphites is twice recorded (1 Sam 23:19-28; 26:1). ABSALOM is said to have had three sons, yet later is said to have no son (2 Sam 14:27; 18:18). Two accounts of the circumstances of Saul's death are given (1 Sam 31:4; 2 Sam 1:6-10). These facts have led many scholars to conclude that the final author was bringing together at least two blocks of material. Some have attempted to find a continuation of the J and E sources of the Pentateuch. All such attempts have proven fruitless. There may also be a later block of material related to the succession of SOLOMON to the throne. This is usually identified as 2 Sam 9–20.

It does appear that these books are closely tied together with Joshua and Judges as well as with 1 and 2 Kings. This entire corpus appears to have been written or edited from a deuteronomic standpoint, being identified as the deuteronomic (or deuteronomistic) history.

These two books were clearly put into their final form later than the events recorded. Archaic expressions are explained for a later audience (1 Sam 9:9). Customs that had ceased to be used were also explained (2 Sam 13:18). The repeated use of "unto this day" also points to a time of writing significantly later than the events recorded (1 Sam 5:5; 6:18; 27:6; 30:25; 2 Sam 4:3; 6:8; 18:18). Further, David was still alive when 2 Samuel ended, yet the length of his reign is given in 2 Sam 5:5. Finally, the book tells of at least two kings of Judah who reigned after the death of Solomon and the division of the kingdom. Thus the earliest possible date for the writing of the books is after that. If they were put into their final form along with 1 and 2 Kings, with which they seem to be a unit, then they must be dated no earlier than the exilic period.

See also KINGSHIP; SAMUEL; SUCCESSION NARRATIVE.

Bibliography. R. L. Cate, *An Introduction to the Old Testament and Its Study*; R. W. Klein, *1 Samuel*; B. F. Philbeck, Jr. "1 and 2 Samuel," *BBC*; S. Sziksai, "Samuel, 1 and 2," *IDB*.

—ROBERT L. CATE

• **Sanballat.** [san-bal'at] The governor of Samaria and the leader of the major opposition against NEHEMIAH when the latter returned to JERUSALEM in 445 B.C.E. He is called a "Horonite" (Neh 2:10, 19, etc.), the exact meaning of which is uncertain. But most scholars interpret it to mean that he was from Beth-horon of Ephraim, which is located some fifteen mi. northwest of Jerusalem.

The chronological problems associated with the time of EZRA and Nehemiah are well known. But one of the Elephantine Papyri, dated to the seventeenth year of King Darius (407 B.C.E.), lists Delaiah and Shelemiah as the sons of Sanballat, "governor of Samaria." Not only does this reference place Sanballat in the fifth century B.C.E.; it also indicates that he may have been a worshiper of Yahweh, since his sons' names are compounded with the divine name *yhwh*.

Thus the attempt by some scholars to place Sanballat (and Nehemiah) into the fourth century B.C.E. based, among other considerations, upon JOSEPHUS, has been shown to be incorrect. Furthermore, fourth century B.C.E. papyri from Dâliyeh have shown that there was a second and probably a third Sanballat who inherited the governorship during this time. Josephus seems clearly to have confused the biblical Sanballat with one of his descendants.

That Sanballat had considerable influence during the time of Nehemiah is seen by the fact that his daughter married a son of the high priest (Neh 13:28). Nehemiah drove the son-in-law out of Jerusalem, and resisted Sanballat's efforts to stop him at every turn. Nehemiah's adamant stand during this crucial period played no little part in insuring the survival of the Jewish community.

See also NEHEMIAH; NEHEMIAH, BOOK OF.

Bibliography. F. M. Cross, "Papyri of the Fourth Century B.C. from Dâliyeh," *New Directions in Biblical Archaeology*, ed. D. N. Freedman and J. C. Greenfield; J. Pritchard, *ANET*.

—JOHN C. H. LAUGHLIN

• **Sanctification.** The English words "holiness," "consecration," and "sanctification" all translate the same basic idea of "setting apart" or "dedication" for a particular use. Originally the idea of setting apart did not necessarily carry any moral connotation. Something or someone could be set apart from ordinary use and be devoted to a special purpose. In the Bible, though, these words pick up moral connotations because of the character of God who, in biblical thought, is the source of all holiness.

Sanctification in the OT. A dominant theme of the OT is that God himself is holy (Exod 15:11; Lev 21:8; Ps 60:6; Ezek 28:22; Amos 4:2) and is the source of all holiness. It is God, the Lord, who sanctifies the people of Israel (Exod 31:13; cf. Lev 20:8; 21:8; 21:15; 22:9; Ezek 37:28). The Israelites in turn sanctify God's name (Isa 29:23; cf. Matt 6:9) by considering him to be holy, by standing in awe of him, and by doing his will (Isa 8:12-13).

The psalmist, like the prophet Isaiah, recognizes that God expects those who worship him to be holy (Pss 15; 24:3-6). Thus, while holiness in the OT sometimes is a demand for mere ritual purity (cf. Exod 28:2; 40:9; Lev 22:3ff.; Ezra 9:2), holiness also has moral connotations of freedom from sin and absolute moral integrity which fellowship with God requires. A key OT passage for understanding sanctification is the Holiness Code of Lev 17–26, which mixes demands for ritual holiness and moral, ethical holiness. The prophets stressed God's demands for ethical purity by focusing on his desire for obedience (Jer 11:6ff.), justice (Isa 1:10-17), and mercy (Hos 6:6).

Sanctification in the NT. In the NT, the emphasis on sanctification is almost entirely on one's personal relationship to God. Christians are set apart in Christ unto a new relationship with God. Thus, as in the OT, God's chosen people are holy; but unlike the OT, God's chosen are not limited any longer to a particular ethnic group. Thus, holiness in the NT focuses on ethical purity rather than ritual purity, as Peter's quotation of Lev 11:44-45 shows (1 Pet 1:1-16).

The NT is clear that God, Christ, and the Holy Spirit are the agents of sanctification. First Thess 5:23 says, "May the God of peace himself sanctify you wholly." According to Eph 5:26 it is Christ who sanctifies the church, and according to 1 Pet 1:2 the Holy Spirit sanctifies God's chosen people. The NT writers use various images to relate the death of Christ to the sanctification of the Christian. The Gospel of John says that Christ sanctified himself for the sake of his disciples (John 17:19), and Paul declares that God made Christ Jesus "our wisdom, our righteousness and sanctification and redemption" (1 Cor 1:30). Elsewhere Paul writes that Christ loved the church and died for her in order that he might sanctify her "having cleansed her by the washing of water with the word, that he might present the church to himself in splendor, without spot or wrinkle or any such thing, that she might be holy and without blemish" (Eph 5:26-27). The author of Hebrews explains the significance of Christ's death by arguing that Christ has replaced the whole sacrificial system, with its Holy Place, its holy priests, holy vessels, holy alters and holy offerings (Heb 2:1; 9:13-14; 10:10). First Pet 1:2 uses imagery from the sealing of the covenant between God and his people (Exod 24:3-8) to express the belief that Christians have been sanctified by the Holy Spirit.

The most common understanding of sanctification is that this refers to the development or actualization of holiness in the Christian life following CONVERSION or JUSTIFICATION. The NT writers, however, speak of sanctification in the past, present, and future. Paul addresses the Christians in Corinth as those "sanctified in Christ Jesus" (1 Cor 1:2) and tells them, "you were sanctified" (6:11). Heb 10:10 says, "And by that will we have been sanctified through the offering of the body of Jesus Christ once for all." Sanctification is also a present process and a future goal. The writer of Hebrews says again, "Strive for peace with all men, and for the holiness without which no one will see the Lord" (12:14). Paul writes to the church in Corinth, "Let us cleanse ourselves from every defilement of body and spirit, and make holiness perfect [literally, "completing sanctification"] in the fear of God" (2 Cor 7:1). Similarly he instructed the Christians in Rome to present their "members to righteousness for sanctification" (Rom 6:19, 22). To the Thessalonians he wrote, "For this is the will of God, your sanctification: that you abstain from unchastity . . . " (1 Thess 4:3). Indeed, everything should be sanctified, i.e., regarded as sacred, through the prayer of thanksgiving (1 Tim 4:4-5).

See also CONVERSION; HOLINESS IN THE NEW TESTAMENT; HOLINESS IN THE OLD TESTAMENT; JUSTIFICATION.

Bibliography. F. Stagg, *New Testament Theology*.

—ROGER L. OMANSON

• **Sanctuary.** In the OT, a "holy place," its sanctity derived from its association with the presence of deity; place of refuge and asylum where protection is provided.

The primary use of the term sanctuary in Hebrew scripture was in reference to a recognized place of WORSHIP where tradition placed a THEOPHANY or visible manifestation of the deity. A notable example is the Tabernacle—the sacred tent and portable sanctuary described as built by Moses during the wilderness exile (Exod 25–31; 35–40). As a place where the God of ancient Israel was revealed and dwelt among the people, the Tabernacle was a revered holy place blessed with the promise of God's presence.

The Tabernacle's physical arrangement indicated varying degrees of holiness. The Holy of Holies or Most Holy Place, containing the ark and mercy seat, was the innermost section. It was separated from the Holy Place, the next section, by a veil. Outside these two compartments was the court, then the dwelling of the priests, and finally the main camp. A threefold degree of access to the tabernacle demonstrated its sanctity: the court could be visited by all the people, the Holy Place by the priests, and the Holy of Holies by the high priest alone once a year.

Features of the Tabernacle were present in several sanctified places of worship after the settlement in Canaan, including Shiloh (Josh 18:1; 19:51; 1 Sam 1:3; etc.), Nob (1 Sam 21:1-6), and Gibeon (1 Kgs 3:4). The Tabernacle served as ancient Israel's portable sanctuary from the time of Sinai until it was replaced by Solomon's Temple (1 Kgs 8). The physical arrangement of the Tabernacle is reflected in the Temple (PLATE 22).

The term sanctuary was also used in connection with other localized cultic sites and "high places" (Amos 7:9, 13). Any consecrated place of worship having an altar and other sacred objects could be called a sanctuary.

Sanctuary, in a second sense, describes a place of asylum where haven was provided for those seeking to escape impending harm. This refuge, available at "the altar" (Exod 21:12-14), offered immunity from pursuers (1 Kgs 1:50-53; 2:28-34).

CITIES OF REFUGE (Num 35:9-34; Josh 20:1-9) were also established under ancient Israelite law for those who had killed someone by accident. While the willful murderer was to be punished, the unintentional slayer was offered sanctuary in any of these cities, strategically located throughout the land. In order to receive this shelter, the fugitive underwent a solemn trial to prove innocence before the congregation (Num 35:12, 24). If acquitted, the person was allowed to remain within the city until the death of the next high priest.

The NT alludes to both of these OT understandings of sanctuary. The church as the spiritual temple is described as the sanctuary of God in which the Spirit dwells (1 Cor 3:16). Jesus is a "refuge" to whom all are exhorted to escape (Heb 6:18).

See also REFUGE, CITIES OF; TEMPLE/TEMPLES; WORSHIP IN THE NEW TESTAMENT; WORSHIP IN THE OLD TESTAMENT.

Bibliography. G. A. Barrois, "Temples," *IDB*; M. Greenberg, "The Biblical Conception of Asylum," *JBL* 78 (1959): 125-32; G. E. Wright, "Solomon's Temple Resurrected," *BA* 4 (1941): 17-31.

—W. H. BELLINGER, JR.

• **Sanhedrin.** [san-hee'druhn] The Sanhedrin was the supreme ruling council of the Jews, consisting of seventy-one members and located in Jerusalem. Four primary sources are used to reconstruct the history and duties of the Sanhedrin: the OT Apocrypha, Josephus, the NT, and rabbinic materials. Often the ancient sources disagree with each other, resulting in conflicting opinions concerning many of the specific details regarding this ruling body.

History of the Sanhedrin. The general consensus is that the Sanhedrin originated in the Persian period of Jewish history (539–333 B.C.E.). Upon return from the Babylonian Exile the Jews were governed by the Persian-appointed governor and a ruling council consisting of aristocratic priests and non-priestly landowners. By the Roman era (63 B.C.E.), the institution had undergone significant evolution. The high priest was now the head of the council which consisted not only of the Jewish aristocracy, but expert interpreters of the TORAH known as scribes. The lay and priestly aristocracy belonged to the party known as the SADDUCEES, while the scribes were closely aligned with the group known as the PHARISEES, the forerunners of rabbinic Judaism. Save for exceptional periods, the Sadducees were the ruling element within the Sanhedrin until the destruction of Jerusalem in 70 C.E. After this event, the Sanhedrin was reorganized at Jamnia under Pharisaic leadership by Johanan ben Zakkai and later Gamaliel II, and consisted entirely of rabbinic membership. This Sanhedrin focused on religious matters which were of interest to the rabbinic scholars who oversaw the reshaping of Judaism following the destruction of the Temple. The following discussion will focus on the structure and functions of the Sanhedrin during the Roman era up to 70 C.E.

Composition and Structure. Because the ancient sources offer conflicting information, scholars differ concerning the Sanhedrin's precise structure. Some interpreters (e.g., Mantel) contend that there were actually two Sanhedrins; one, consisting of Sadducees, which focused on public and political matters, and another, consisting of Pharisees, which focused on matters of Torah observance. Others (e.g., Safai) contend that while there was only one Sanhedrin, leadership responsibilities were shared between the high priest and the scribal leadership. Most interpreters conclude that there was only one Sanhedrin and that the high priest was its leader. The Pharisaic scribes did not assume leadership until after 70 C.E.

It is not known how one became a member of the Sanhedrin, though it was most probably not by popular election. It is possible that the council selected its own members when a vacancy occurred or that vacancies were filled by appointments from the Herodian or Roman leadership. Appointment was probably for life.

Responsibilities and Powers. The Sanhedrin worked in conjunction with the ruling sovereigns of Judah, be it Herod or the Roman governors. Its actual authority was dependent upon how much power the sovereigns allowed. Herod kept tight reigns on the body, while the Roman governors tended to allow it to function with a high degree of independence.

The Sanhedrin had legislative, judicial, and executive powers, both in civil and criminal law. The NT states, for example, that it was the police force of the Sanhedrin that arrested Jesus (Matt 26:47 = Mark 14:43), and Acts records a number of incidents when the Jewish authorities arrested or detained followers of Jesus (4:1-22; 5:17-18, 26-27; 6:12). Concerning religious matters, the Sanhedrin supervised the observance of the religious calendar, the Temple procedures, and the priesthood. In addition, Safrai has argued that "it was also an academic institution, the central institution for the study of the Torah" (392). However, such a view is not universally accepted, with many believing that such "academic" interests came under the purview of the Sanhedrin only after 70 C.E.

Legally, the Sanhedrin had jurisdiction only over the Jews of the Roman province of Judea. Thus, Jesus would not have come under its authority until he ventured into Judea. It is possible, however, that in the area of Jewish religious life the Sanhedrin would have wielded, without sanction of the Roman government, *de facto* authority over the Jews even beyond the boundaries of Judea. This could explain the report in Acts 9:1-2 that Saul (Paul), under the authority of the high priest, journeyed to Damascus of Syria to arrest Jewish Christians and bring them back to Jerusalem.

There is a great debate concerning the authority of the Sanhedrin to inflict capital punishment. On the basis of such texts as John 18:31, which explicitly states that the Jewish leadership had no authority to execute a person, and statements in the rabbinic literature which indicate that the right of capital punishment was taken from the Sanhedrin forty years before the Temple was destroyed, many contend that the council had no authority to execute offenders. Others will point out that such instances as the trial and execution of Stephen (Acts 6:12–8:2), the Jewish threat to execute any gentile who violated the sanctity of the inner courts of the Temple (Josephus, *Ant* 15.11.5; cf. Acts 21:27-31), and the execution of James, the brother of Jesus, in 62 C.E. under the order of the high priest Ananus (*Ant* 20.9.1), betray evidence that the Sanhedrin did, indeed, have the authority to execute offenders in capital cases. It must be observed, however, that the execution of Stephen could be interpreted as a public lynching, the threat to kill gentiles who violated the Temple may have been a threat that mob action would end the life of the violator (in Acts 21:27-31 the Roman forces prevented a lynching), and the killing of James by Ananus was during the period between the governorships of Festus and Albinus when Judea was without a governor to oversee

Roman policy. It is probably best to conclude that the Jewish Sanhedrin did not have the authority to execute offenders. Some interpreters have argued, however, either that the right of capital punishment was given to the Sanhedrin contingent upon final Roman approval (Foerster) or that the Sanhedrin could execute capital offenders in strictly religious matters (Safrai). Even such moderating conclusions should be accepted cautiously.

See also PHARISEES; SADDUCEES.

Bibliography. W. Foerster, *From the Exile to Christ*; J. Jeremias, *Jerusalem in the Time of Jesus*; H. Mantel, "Sanhedrin," *IDBSup*; S. Safrai, "Jewish Self Government," *The Jewish People in the First Century*, vol 1., ed. S. Safrai and M. Stern; E. Schürer, *The History of the Jewish People in the Age of Jesus Christ (175 BC–AD 135)*, rev. and ed. G. Vermes, F. Millar, M. Black.

—J. BRADLEY CHANCE

• **Sapphira.** *See* ANANIAS

• **Sarah.** [sair'uh] The first wife of Abram (ABRAHAM). Sarai married her half-brother Abram (Gen 20:12) in UR before their migration to CANAAN (Gen 11:29). Her name was changed later to Sarah (17:15), meaning "princess" or "noblewoman," a fitting title for the ancestress of kings (17:16).

On two occasions Sarah was placed in a potentially adulterous situation to save Abraham's life (cf. Gen 26:1-11). Abraham and Sarah migrated to Egypt to escape famine in Canaan (Gen 12:10-20). Because of Sarah's exceptional beauty she was identified as Abraham's sister, not his wife, so that Pharaoh would not kill Abraham to obtain Sarah for himself. She became part of Pharaoh's household and Abraham was made wealthy. Gen 20:1-18 recounts a similar incident involving ABIMELECH, king of GERAR. Abraham and Sarah had made the half-truth that she was his sister a consistent strategy for survival wherever they travelled (20:13). The Lord rescued Sarah from both Pharaoh and Abimelech. Their deception may have saved Abraham's life, but it ravaged their family. Only God's intervention restored the family and preserved them for the promises of land, descendants and blessing (Gen 12:1-3).

Sarah was childless (Gen 11:30). In her case this personal and family tragedy also posed a theological dilemma. God had promised Abraham innumerable descendants who would possess the land of Canaan and be a blessing among the nations (Gen 12:1-3; 13:14-17; 15:1-6, 18-21; 17:1-21; 18:17-19). Sarah's infertility prevented the fulfillment of these promises.

Acknowledging that God had kept her from conceiving, Sarah acted to obtain a child by giving her personal servant, HAGAR, to Abraham as a second wife (Gen 16:1-6). According to widespread ancient Near Eastern custom, any children born to Hagar and Abraham could be counted as Sarah's own offspring (cf. Gen 30:1-13). Proud of her fertility, pregnant Hagar belittled her mistress (cf. Prov 30:21-23) and Sarah brought the case to Abraham for judgment. When Abraham confirmed Sarah's authority over her servant she oppressed Hagar so harshly that Hagar fled (16:6). Sarah's plan to build a family by means of Hagar had failed.

God's plan specified Sarah as the mother of the promised son (Gen 17:16), in spite of her infertility and old age (17:17; 18:11). When Sarah overheard the same promise, she laughed at the prospect that one so worn out would experience the pleasure of fulfilling her sexual role (18:12). The next year Sarah gave birth to ISAAC, and the laughter of doubt (17:17; 18:12) was replaced by the laughter of delight (21:1-7). God had enabled Sarah to complete the family circle by bearing a son (Heb 11:11).

Later Sarah demanded that Abraham expel Hagar and her son ISHMAEL from the household so that Abraham's other son would pose no threat to Isaac's inheritance (Gen 21:8-10). God commanded him to comply with Sarah's demand. Sarah and Abraham's son was the chosen one with whom God would establish an everlasting covenant (21:11-13; 17:18-21).

Paul presents Sarah and Isaac as an illustration of God's election of the church as the heirs of the covenant made with Abraham (Rom 9:6-9; Gal 4:21-31).

See also ABRAHAM; HAGAR; ISAAC; WOMEN IN THE OLD TESTAMENT.

Bibliography. E. A. Speiser, *Genesis*; J. Van Seters, *Abraham in History and Tradition*; C. Westermann, *Genesis 12–36*.

—PAMELA J. SCALISE

• **Sarai.** *See* SARAH

• **Sardis.** [sahr'dis] Sardis for many centuries was the capital of the ancient kingdom of Lydia. The last of the Lydian kings, Croesus, surrendered to Cyrus of Persia in 546 B.C. The Persians made Sardis the capital of its western territories. In 334 B.C.E., Sardis fell to Alexander the Great, and Greek influence came to Sardis. Following Alexander's death, Sardis eventually came under the control of Lysimachus and then a bit later fell under the power of the Seleucid empire. In 190 B.C.E., the Roman general, Scipio Africanus defeated Antiochus III at Magnesia. As a result Sardis became a Roman territory, and a general decline began in its fabled power (PLATE 20).

The city was best known for its mountain top location and its powerful acropolis. In fact there were two cities of Sardis. One part of the city was situated in the valley at the foot of Mount Tmolous and one on top of the mountain. In the time of war, the citizens would retreat to the upper city where large cisterns provided plenty of water to withstand any siege. The nearby Pactolus River also provided gold in some abundance which provided Sardis with much of its wealth—especially under the reign of the Lydian king, Croesus. The citizens of the city worshiped the Anatolian goddess Cybele and the Greek deity Artemis. A large Jewish community was also present in the city. Several inscriptions found by archeologists at Sardis point to Jews working as goldsmiths and shopkeepers in the city.

One of the great archeological discoveries at Sardis was the uncovering of one of the largest synagogues ever discovered. This building found in 1962 had gone through four stages of development and building. The last stage (350–400 C.E.) contained a main hall measuring some 197 by 59 ft. Several Jewish inscriptions written in Greek have been found within the complex of buildings. Nearby this site is the location of the marble hall containing a gymnasium and baths. Thus the synagogue was located right in the midst of the public buildings of Sardis.

Major work on the site was done by a group from Princeton University under the leadership of Howard C. Butler from 1910 to 1914. The major work accomplished was on the temple of Artemis. Numerous graves were also opened but very little of value was found in them. More recent work has been carried out by the American Schools of Oriental Research, Harvard University and Cornell University.

In church history, Sardis has made several claims to fame. Meliton, a bishop of the church in the second century wrote a letter containing our first listing of the OT canonical books. In 325 C.E., Sardis was represented at the Council of Nicaea by Bishop Artemidorus. By the fourteenth century Christianity declined in Sardis and disappeared when the city was occupied by the Turks. By the fifteenth century the city no longer existed on its original site. However, unlike many other biblical cities, the site of Sardis was never forgotten and is mentioned in a travel diary of Jean-Baptiste Tavernier in 1670.

Bibliography. C. Hemer, *The Seven Churches*; O. Meinardus, *St. John of Patmos*; E. Yamauchi, *The Archeology of New Testament Cities of Western Asia Minor*.

—JAMES L. BLEVINS

• **Sargon.** [sahr'gon] Three ancient Near Eastern kings bore the name of Sargon ("True King"). The first was Sargon of Agade (Akkad) who founded the semitic empire of Akkad in the third millennium B.C.E. Knowledge of him comes mostly from copies of historical inscriptions found at Nippur and from legendary tales written mainly in Akkadian. Among these latter is a birth saga reminiscent of the birth story of Moses in the OT. The Sumerian king list credits him with a reign of fifty-six years (2371–2316 B.C.E.), during which time he became a powerful king extending his empire from the Persian Gulf to the Mediterranean Sea. He built a new capital, Agade, in northern Babylonia which has not yet been located.

The second king with this namesake was Sargon I, an Assyrian king who reigned in the middle of the nineteenth century B.C.E. He is virtually unknown except for his seal impression found on old Akkadian texts from Cappadocia. He is listed twenty-seventh in the Assyrian king list.

The most famous of the kings bearing the name of Sargon, was Sargon II who ruled the Neo-Assyrian empire 722/1–705 B.C.E. He was the son of TIGLATH-PILESER, the brother and successor of SHALMANESER V, and the father of SENNACHERIB. Sargon came to the throne following the murder of his brother during the latter's siege of Samaria. While the facts surrounding his ascension are obscure, internal strife seems to have been present.

After seizing the throne, Sargon immediately faced rebellious clients in various parts of the empire. Two of the most important were (1) Marduk-apla-iddina II (Merodach-baladan in the OT; 2 Kgs 20:12; Isa 39:1; Jer 50:2) who, by 720, ruled Babylonia, and (2) the Syro-Palestinian coalition in the west that had the support of Egypt. Unable to wrest Babylonia from Merodach at first, Sargon turned his attention westward and quickly destroyed the resistance of Syria and Israel. However, there is confusion over who actually captured the Israelite city of Samaria. The OT seems to credit Sargon's brother, Shalmaneser, with the event (2 Kgs 17:1-6; 18:9-12). On the other hand, the ambiguous reference to "the king of Assyria" in 2 Kgs 17:6 has been equated with Sargon by many scholars. Whatever the facts, Sargon claimed credit for the victory and boasted that he deported 27,290 inhabitants of the city and repopulated it with people from other conquered territories (cf. 2 Kgs 17:6, 24). His action marked the end of the historical memory of the Northern Kingdom. Judah was spared this catastrophe because of the political loyalty of King Ahaz to Assyria (Isa 7).

After the defeat of Syria and Israel, Sargon pursued two other objectives: southeast Asia Minor and Urartu in the north. He was successful in both campaigns, destroying the capital city of Urartu in 714 and reaching the Mediterranean coast by 712. By 709, he finally was able to make himself king of Babylonia and avenge his earlier loss to Merodach-baladan, who, however, managed to escape to Elam. In the meantime, he sent one of his generals to put down another rebellion in Palestine, instigated by the Philistine city of Ashdod (Isa 20:1—the only text in the OT to mention Sargon by name).

In 713 B.C.E., Sargon began construction on a city which was to be a monument to his accomplishments. Called Dur-Sharrukin (Khorsabad), and located a few miles north of Nineveh, it was completed in 706. But it was barely inhabited before Sargon's untimely death in 705 while fighting a skirmish on some unknown battlefield in Media (modern Iran). The city was abandoned, never to be lived in again.

See also ASSYRIA.

Bibliography. C. J. Gadd, "The Reign of Sargon," *CAH*, 1/2A: 417-40; H. Levy, "The Sargonic Period," *CAH*, 1/2B: 733-40; A. L. Oppenheim, "Sargon," *IDB*.

—JOHN C. H. LAUGHLIN

• **Satan in the New Testament.** The power of evil in the world is usually attributed in the NT to the figure of Satan, who is the primary enemy of God and his Kingdom. "Satan" ultimately goes back to the Heb. word for "enemy" or "adversary," one who "obstructs" or "opposes" another. This meaning is carried over into the Gk. *satanas* (Satan) or *diabolos* (devil), the chief designations of this evil power in the NT.

While the OT perspective provides the basic background for the NT, Satan developed in Jewish thought after 200 B.C.E. into a much more well-defined figure than anything described in the OT. The NT uses, in addition to the term Satan (Matt 12:26; Mark 1:13; Luke 11:18; Acts 5:3; Rev 12:9—thirty-three times altogether), the terms devil (almost a synonym for Satan: Matt 4:1; Luke 4:2; Rev 12:9—thirty-two times), Beelzebul (Matt 12:24), Beliar (2 Cor 6:15), and a number of descriptive terms for "the evil one" (Matt 13:19): the prince of demons (Matt 12:24), the tempter (Matt 4:3), the dragon (Rev 20:2), the father of lies (John 8:44), the god of this world (2 Cor 4:4), the prince of the power of the air (Eph 2:2), and others. This rich terminology for that which is opposed to God testifies to an elaborate and virtually universal belief in demons and evil spirits in the first century C.E.

The role and functions of Satan or the devil are fairly clear, though no one passage in the NT describes them fully. He is the personification of evil, opposing God in everything (Matt 13:41; Acts 26:18); he physically attacks or possesses humans, causing sickness (Mark 1:32; 5:1-13; Luke 13:16); he tempts people to sin by deception (Matt 4:3; 2 Cor 11:14-15; 1 Thess 3:5) and afflicts those who listen to him with lies and murder (John 8:44-47).

The primary functions of Satan, however, are two: leadership of the forces of evil (Matt 12:24; Mark 3:22; Luke 11:15), and opposition to Christ and the church. The first role expresses the earlier biblical tradition of Satan and his demons as spirit-beings created by God, but who, through a self-centered refusal to submit, rebelled against God and were therefore expelled from the heavenly realm (Luke 10:18; 2 Pet 2:4; Jude 6; Rev 12:7-12). Jesus confronts them in temptation and in exorcisms (Mark 1:13; Matt 8:28; Mark 1:34; Acts 10:38), and Paul frequently warns the community of the attacks of Satan and the "principalities and powers" (Rom 8:38; Eph 6:12; Col 2:15). The triumph of Jesus over Satan is both present reality and future promise: Satan's power is broken, though not yet completely abolished (Matt 4:1-11; Mark 3:22-27; Luke 10:18-19; Rev

12:10-11); that will occur only at the second coming of Christ (Rev 20:4-10).

There are differences of emphasis within the NT: John, and to a certain extent Luke, portray the world as divided between the forces of God and the forces of Satan, while this cosmic dualism is much less pronounced in Mark and Matthew. References to demons and their exorcism are more frequent early in the NT (e.g., in Mark and Matthew), but give way in John to a focus on the devil himself, as the chief enemy of God. Mark and Paul tend to use the term Satan more often, while other books tend to use the wider variety of terms mentioned above.

Though the NT warns that Satan is a continuing danger of which the believer must be wary, it does not suggest that Satan is to be considered equal to God in power, that Satan's actions deprive men and women of full freedom and responsibility for their actions, or that Satan's presence alters the affirmation that life is ultimately ordered by a just and loving God. Satan's presence in the NT forces Christians to take the reality of evil seriously and raises questions for later theological consideration, but it does not change the biblical vision of one God "who is the Savior of all men" (1 Tim 4:10).

See also ANGEL; APOCALYPTIC LITERATURE; BAAL-ZEBUB/BAAL-ZEBUL; DEMON IN THE NEW TESTAMENT; DEMON IN THE OLD TESTAMENT; ESCHATOLOGY IN THE NEW TESTAMENT; EVIL; FALL; FALLEN ANGELS; SERPENT; SIN.

Bibliography. H. A. Kelly, *The Devil, Demonology and Witchcraft: The Development of Christian Beliefs in Evil Spirits*; J. B. Russell, *The Devil: Perceptions of Evil from Antiquity to Primitive Christianity*.

—DAVID W. RUTLEDGE

• **Satan in the Old Testament.** The term "satan" is used in the OT to refer to either a human or a superhuman "adversary"; one who "obstructs" a plan or "accuses" a person in a legal setting. This adversary is not necessarily evil. The Heb. root *s-ṭ-n* refers to a human adversary in Num 22:22, 32; 1 Sam 29:4; 1 Kgs 11:14, 23, 25 and Ps 109:6. It refers to a superhuman adversary in Job 1–2; Zech 3:1-2 and 1 Chr 21:1.

Since JOB and ZECHARIAH refer to "*the* satan," but 1 Chronicles refers to "satan" or "Satan," scholars debate whether the term in these three texts refers to (1) a role, *the* satan, a superhuman figure with the distinctive function of accusing people before God; (2) a particular superhuman being, Satan; or (3) both.

In both Job and Zechariah the satan is a member of the heavenly court who serves God by challenging God's evaluations of people or by bringing to God specific accusations against people. In Job, the satan tests Job only with God's permission and limitations. In Zechariah, the satan accuses the priest Joshua before God; God rejects the accusation and acquits Joshua. Neither of these passages sees the satan as a power equal to God, an enemy of God, or the source of evil.

In contrast, the figure of Satan in 1 Chronicles is a figure independent of God and the cause of an objectionable action. Here, Satan is the cause of David's census. An earlier version of the same story (2 Sam 24) attributes David's decision to take a census to "the anger of the Lord." This change in the cause of David's actions from "the anger of the Lord" to "Satan" reflects the growing trend in later thinking to locate the source of undesirable or evil acts in a power distinct from God.

Tradition continued to expand the character, power and independence of Satan. Satan gradually came to be seen as the archenemy of God; an evil figure opposed to God who leads demons and spirits in their war against God and God's followers. This view of Satan reflects the increasing personification and autonomy of the supernatural Satan/adversary in the theology of postexilic Israel (after 538 B.C.E.). Still later, Satan's persona developed further through association with other figures: the serpent in Gen 3, the Philistine deity Baal-zebub (NT Beelzebul), the figure of Beliar/Belial ("Worthlessness"), and Lucifer (a figure developed from a reference in Isa 14:12 to the star Venus).

Finally, the connection of satan with demonic forces and the identification of Satan as the devil is solidified in English partially as the result of translation. The English term *devil* is derived from the term *diabolos,* the Gk. translation of the Heb. term "satan." When translators of the Bible failed to distinguish clearly between the Gk. terms *diabolos* and *daimon* (spirit/evil spirit), Satan/the devil assumed the characteristics of the *daimons* also and became even more powerful and demonic.

See also BAAL-ZEBUB/BAAL-ZEBUL; DEMON IN NEW TESTAMENT; DEMON IN THE OLD TESTAMENT.

—JOANNE KUEMMERLIN-MCLEAN

• **Saul.** A Benjaminite, the son of KISH, who became the first king of ISRAEL. His name means "asked," or, "requested." Unfortunately, the text that gives the length of his reign is corrupted beyond repair (1 Sam 13:1, literally, "Saul was a year old when he began to reign, and he reigned two years over Israel").

The story of Saul's rise and fall as king appears in 1 Sam 8–31. References to Saul are also found in 1 Chr 10, several superscriptions to Psalms (e.g., 18:1) and Isa 10:29; but the 1 Samuel narrative provides the primary source for understanding Saul.

According to the 1 SAMUEL narrative, the elders of Israel requested the judge/priest Samuel to appoint a king to rule over them. Saul was searching for his father's lost asses when he happened upon Samuel at Zuph. There Samuel privately anointed him as prince (*nāgîd*) over Israel, and sent him on his way with certain predictions and instructions. Following the fulfillment of the latter, Saul was publicly acclaimed as king at Mizpah. He distinguished himself as a strong military leader in several battles. First, according to the biblical narrative, he delivered the people of Jabesh in Gilead from the Ammonites. Second, with the help of his son JONATHAN, he waged war with the PHILISTINES for control of the territory around Gibeah and Michmash. Third, he conducted various campaigns against Moab, Ammon, Edom, the kings of Zobah and the Philistines. And fourth, at Samuel's behest, he conducted a campaign against the AMALEKITES. In connection with the second and fourth military actions, Saul failed to obey the instructions of the Lord through Samuel. As a result of these two failures, the Lord rejected Saul as king over Israel and chose instead the young man DAVID. There follows a series of episodes in which Saul vacillated between employing David at court and pursuing him in the hill country of Judah in an attempt to kill him. Finally, Saul and several of his sons met their end fighting against the Philistines at MOUNT GILBOA in the northern part of the hill country, and David eventually established himself as king of both Judah and Israel against the claims of ISHBOSHETH, one of the two remaining sons of Saul.

Certain conflicts and tensions indicate that several originally separate traditions lie behind the present form of the

Saul narrative. For the most part the traditions are independent folk legends that appear to have been fitted into a scheme in which Saul is portrayed first under divine blessing (1 Sam 8–15) and then under divine curse (1 Sam 16–31). A similar scheme is noticeable in the story of David.

Consider, for example, the narration about Saul's search for the asses in 1 Sam 9–10. Beginning with 10:5 the reader is presented with what amounts to multiple endings to the story: (1) Saul proceeds to Gibeath-elohim where he prophesies with a band of prophets. Compare the variant version of this tradition in 1 Sam 19:18-24 and note that this latter passage locates the incident at Ramah. (2) Saul is instructed to go to Gilgal and wait. Compare 1 Sam 13:8-9, where this thread of tradition reemerges. (3) Saul goes to Gibeah, where there was a Philistine garrison and does "what his hand finds to do"—presumably he challenges the Philistines in some fashion (cf. 1 Sam 13:2-4). (4) Saul returns home (?), where we hear him in conversation with an uncle, and then goes with his family to Mizpah, where he is crowned king.

The story of the conflict with the Philistines in 1 Sam 13–14 also contains tensions. Was it Saul's attack on the Philistine garrison at Gibeah, or his son Jonathan's attack on the Philistine camp at Michmash across the valley from Gibeah, that initiated the battle with the Philistines? How is Samuel's instruction to the newly anointed Saul in 1 Sam 10:8 related to the later narrative of Saul's foolish sacrifice in 1 Sam 13:8-14? Upon close examination, two things seem probable: (1) the Saul stories found in 9:1–10:16; 10:26–11:15; and 13:2–14:46 once presented him in an essentially favorable light, but later editorial additions have colored this presentation. (2) As a part of the later editing the order of the narratives has been changed; originally 13:2–14:46 probably followed 9:1–10:16.

When the composite and sometimes tendentious nature of the present narrative is taken into account, a probable reconstruction of the historical Saul may be offered. Saul was the child of a prominent and relatively wealthy family whose ancestral home was the village of Zela in Benjamin (2 Sam 21:14). He distinguished himself as a warrior by attacking a Philistine garrison in the Gibeah-Michmash vicinity where he then established his own power base. From this base Saul acted as a protector to the surrounding hill country villages in exchange for their "gifts" of support (cf. 1 Sam 10:27). He proved to be a strong ruler in battles with the Philistines, the Ammonites, and various other small city-states surrounding his territory (1 Sam 14:47-48) and as a result was proclaimed king by the people, perhaps as early as his victory over the Philistine garrison (1 Sam 11:15).

Saul's kingdom, i.e., the area over which he exercised at least a degree of control, included the central (Ephraimite) hill country of western Palestine as far north as the Jezreel Valley, the hill country of Judah, and a small part of Transjordan centered around Jabesh-gilead. His primary area of control was southern Ephraim/Benjamin, and his influence in the more distant territories would have been somewhat looser. The administration of an emergent kingdom such as Saul's would have been quite rudimentary, drawing on structures from the clan and tribe. This can be seen in Saul's appointment of his uncle ABNER as commander of the army (1 Sam 14:50).

The Philistines apparently were a threat throughout Saul's reign (1 Sam 14:52). Even within his own territory support was not always unanimous (1 Sam 10:27). David emerged from among Saul's troops as a strong warrior, so strong, in fact, that Saul perceived him as a threat to his own power. The narratives of David's flight from Saul in the southern hill country give evidence that David did indeed pose a growing threat to Saul (e.g., 1 Sam 22:1-2). Saul's career was ended as he had begun it, fighting against the Philistines (1 Sam 31). Abner orchestrated the transfer of the crown to Saul's son Ishbosheth and the transfer of the administration of the kingdom from Gibeah to Mahanaim in Transjordan. Ishbosheth proved to be a weak ruler, and when it became apparent that he would soon lose his bid for power to David (2 Sam 3:1), Abner began to persuade the Israelites to shift their allegiance to David. Eventually, Ishbosheth was assassinated by his own men who apparently hoped to gain favor with David (2 Sam 4). The last remaining heir of Saul, the lame MEPHIBOSHETH, posed no strong threat to David. Nevertheless, he was required to remain in Jerusalem and was given a portion at the king's table for the rest of his life (2 Sam 9:1-13).

See also DAVID; JONATHAN; SAMUEL.

Bibliography. A. Alt, "The Formation of the Israelite State in Palestine." *Essays on Old Testament History and Religion*; J. Blenkinsopp, "The Quest of the Historical Saul," *No Famine in the Land: Festschrift for J. L. McKenzie*, ed. J. W. Flanagan and A. W. Robinson; D. M. Gunn, *The Fate of King Saul*; A. D. H. Mayes, "The Period of the Judges and the Rise of the Monarchy," *Israelite and Judean History*, ed. J. H. Hayes and J. M. Miller; J. M. Miller and J. H. Hayes, *A History of Ancient Israel and Judah*.

—J. MAXWELL MILLER

• **Save.** *See* SALVATION IN THE NEW TESTAMENT; SALVATION IN THE OLD TESTAMENT

• **Savior in the New Testament.** The Greek verb "to save" implies rescue from some life-threatening danger. Most contexts in the NT where salvation is mentioned are related to God's action in Christ to deliver humanity from the powers of sin, death, and Satan. These negative powers drain life of its joy and threaten each person with eternal loss. It is to deal with this danger to the human beings whom God loves that he has acted as savior. Of its twenty-four occurrences in the NT, the word savior is used sixteen times of JESUS and eight times of God the Father.

God the Father and Christ the Son are both spoken of as saviors and thus as agents of salvation. In the NT, God the Father is savior in that he provides salvation by sending his Son and through him, the Holy Spirit (Luke 1:47, 67; 1 Tim 4:10; Titus 2:13; 3:4-6). The Son was born to save God's people from their sin and their enemies (Matt 1:21; Luke 1:71, 77) and that was the aim of his ministry (Luke 19:10; John 3:17). As savior, Jesus heals (Mark 5:34; 10:52), justifies (Titus 2:13-14; 3:6, 7), heads the church (Eph 5:23), and in the new heaven and new earth gives final deliverance and blessing (Phil 3:20; Titus 2:13).

Although Jesus did not use the noun savior of himself, the people of Samaria recognized him as the savior of the world (John 4:42). Paul also freely used the designation of Christ as savior of the world (Titus 2:13; 3:6). Most uses of the word savior in the NT occur in the Pastoral Epistles (cf. 1 and 2 Timothy, Titus) and General Letters (cf. Hebrews).

It has been noted that the NT presents three different aspect of Jesus' work as savior. These may be thought of as in the past, present, and future.

First, historically, Jesus died for humanity and thus became its savior. Initial belief in Jesus comes in conjunction with God's application of redemption by means of JUSTI-

FICATION and REGENERATION. Thus, in both the historic and subjective senses it is proper for the NT to speak of our having been saved. "He saved us . . . in virtue of his own mercy," Paul writes (Tit 3:5), and he speaks of God "who saved us and called us with a holy calling" (2 Tim 1:9).

Second, it is also true that Jesus is saving believers; salvation has an influence on present experience. Reconciled to God, Christians are being saved through Jesus' life (Rom 5:10). Rom 6:5-14 teaches that believers are released from slavery to sin in order to serve God in righteousness in this life.

Finally, it is true that believers will be saved. The fullest meaning and consequence of the salvation that Jesus won will be known only in the resurrection. At that time the last taint of sin will be removed and believers will be perfected. The certainty of this future is expressed in Rom 8:18-39 and 1 Cor 15:12-58.

There is also an emphasis in the NT in the ministry of Jesus regarding those people who will receive his salvation. He is the savior not only of the mighty and the rich or of the learned, but also of shepherds and outcasts such as Zacchaeus (cf. Luke 2:11).

See also JESUS; REDEMPTION IN THE NEW TESTAMENT; REDEMPTION IN THE OLD TESTAMENT; SALVATION IN THE NEW TESTAMENT; SALVATION IN THE OLD TESTAMENT; SAVIOR IN THE OLD TESTAMENT.

—JOHN P. NEWPORT

• **Savior in the Old Testament.** Savior, one who helps or delivers. Variations of this word are used in the OT to describe the support one person gives to others in need, often in times of conflict (2 Sam 10:11; 2 Kgs 13:5). In the case of injustice perpetrated against individuals, the one who responded by helping was said to have come to save (Exod 2:17). Israel's deliverance from enemies by the judges was termed a saving (Judg 10:1; 13:5), and indeed some judges were called saviors (Judg 3:9, 15). Such saving help was also expected of the king, who held special responsibility for the security of the kingdom and for justice among its citizens (2 Sam 14:4; 2 Kgs 6:26; Hos 13:10). These human saviors were empowered and commissioned by God (Judg 6:15-16; Neh 9:27), but God also brought SALVATION. Thus, the Psalms petition God for salvation, often in parallel to cries for judicial or spiritual restoration (Pss 22:31; 54:1; 59:2; 71:2; 72:4). Elsewhere, they spoke of God as the source of salvation (Pss 25:5; 65:5), and identified God as the Savior (Ps 106:21), an identification that also appears prominently in the prophets, particularly in Isaiah (43:3, 11; 45:15, 21; 49:26; 60:16).

The saving activity of God is associated with the establishment of RIGHTEOUSNESS (Ps 71:15; Isa 45:8), JUSTICE (Isa 59:11), LOVING-KINDNESS (Ps 119:41), or LIGHT (Ps 27:1). Symbols of strength or glory, such as a rock (Isa 17:10), a horn (Ps 18:2), and a garment (Isa 61:10), describe it further. Only the God of Israel can provide it (Isa 43:11; Jer 11:12), and while the Lord's salvation ordinarily springs from ZION in JERUSALEM (Ps 14:7; Isa 46:13), it does not depend upon city or temple, for God can bring about salvation in the midst of the earth (Ps 74:12). That becomes particularly important when God saves the people in the last day (Isa 25:9; Zech 9:16).

See also SALVATION IN THE OLD TESTAMENT.

—NIELS-ERIK A. ANDREASEN

• **Sayings of the Fathers.** *See* PIRKE ABOTH

• **Scapegoat.** *See* ATONEMENT, DAY OF

• **Scarlet.** A brilliant red or crimson hue; a well-known ancient color, recorded in the days of JACOB (Gen 38:28, 30). It was from the female of the kermes bug, which lived on the kermes oak in Bible lands. Her body and eggs contained a red substance that became the coloring matter for the dye. The Hebrew name for the color reflects this background: "crimson/brilliance of the worm," or "crimson producing worm."

Scarlet was a respected color displayed prominently in the Tabernacle. It was in the high priest's EPHOD, girdle, and breastplate (Exod 25, 26, 28). Scarlet was used in the ceremony for cleansing lepers (Lev 14), and also in purification rites (Num 19). Israelite women were dressed "daintily in scarlet" by Saul (2 Sam 1:24). The good wife clothed her household in scarlet (Prov 31:21).

Scarlet had its grim side also and was equated scripturally with impurity and sin. Jeremiah asked Jerusalem, "What do you mean that you dress in scarlet?" (4:30), implying the dress of a harlot. God underscored the depth and permanence of sin by comparing it with scarlet and crimson (Isa 1:18). Scarlet was among the firmest of dyes and thus could not be easily washed out; yet God could bleach it out as white as snow.

In the NT, the robe put on Jesus before crucifixion was scarlet (Matt 27:28). In Revelation, John saw a woman dressed in purple and scarlet, sitting on a scarlet beast (17); that great city called Babylon was "clothed in fine linen, in purple and scarlet" (18:16).

—D. C. MARTIN

• **Scepter.** A stylized ceremonial staff (baton) or an emblem of authority and power (esp. of monarchs), the scepter evolved from one of the most primitive tools, the rod or staff used for striking, digging, levering, even supporting. In biblical times the scepter was a common regal emblem and is mentioned in connection with various other states (Esth 4:11; Jer 48:17; Amos 1:5, 8) as well as Israel (Gen 49:10). Israel itself was Yahweh's "scepter," the extension or embodiment of his power and authority (Num 24:17; cf. Ps 2:9; Ps 60:7 = 108:8); the holy kingdom (Exod 19:6) was the "emblem" of Yahweh's power and authority in the world and stood for his sovereignty. Metonymically the scepter could stand for any monarchy (Jer 48:17; Zech 10:11). In ancient art and literature the scepter is pictured as either a long, slender staff, a short club, or both. The symbol of the club (battle mace, e.g., Num 24:17) is often preferred in interpretation, the "scepter" thus being emblematic of the "striking power" of a ruler. In Israel (as also, e.g., in Babylon), however, a sovereign was often referred to as "shepherd": Yahweh is Israel's shepherd (Ps 80:1) and shepherding is a primary function of rulers (2 Sam 5:2 = 1 Chr 11:2; 2 Sam 7:7). In Israel, then, the scepter may be more aptly interpreted in terms of a shepherd's staff (Mic 7:14; Ps 23:4), emblematic of the guiding, guarding, and protecting authority and power of the shepherd-sovereign. The only NT reference to scepter as such is Heb 1:8 (following Ps 45:6) where Christ is said to hold the scepter of God, the emblem of his divine sovereignty.

See also ROD/STAFF.

—EDD ROWELL

• **Scepticism.** *See* ECCLESIASTES, BOOK OF

• **Schools.** *See* EDUCATION IN THE OLD TESTAMENT

• **Scribe in the New Testament.** The Hebrew term for scribe means "to count." Prior to the Babylonian Exile the

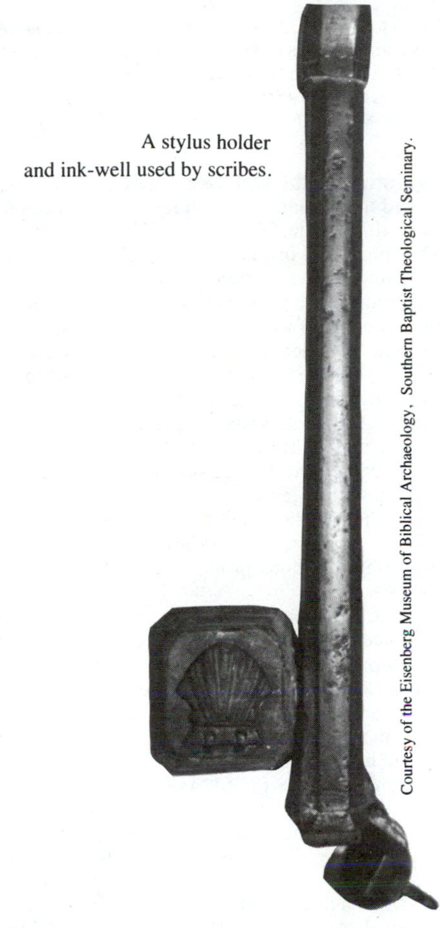
A stylus holder and ink-well used by scribes.

Courtesy of the Eisenberg Museum of Biblical Archaeology, Southern Baptist Theological Seminary.

term is used primarily in a political context. After the Exile, scribe takes on a decisively religious connotation referring to those given to preserving, transmitting, and interpreting the Torah. It is this meaning which is basic for NT usage. Gradually, as the significance of the LAW increases in the estimation of the people, its study and interpretation (activities originally belonging to the priestly class) become more and more the concern of lay Israelites as well. Hence, an independent order of scribes or "Torah scholars" comes to exist alongside the priests. In this respect EZRA is described as a "scribe skilled in the law of Moses" (Ezra 7:6); as one who "had set his heart to study the law of the Lord, and to do it and to teach his statutes and ordinances in Israel" (Ezra 7:11); and also as one who is both priest and scribe (Ezra 7:11; Neh 8:9; 12:26).

In the NT, the scribes emerge as spiritual leaders of the people. This is perhaps due to the tendency of the priests, particularly the priests of higher rank, to compromise the revered traditions originating in the Torah with prevailing views of the gentile culture.

The Gk. word used most frequently for scribe in the NT means "scripture expert," one who possesses an expert understanding of the Mosaic Law and of the sacred writings. Scribes are sometimes referred to as "lawyers" (Luke 7:30) and "teachers of the law" (Luke 5:17; Acts 5:34). They are closely associated with the PHARISEES (Matt 12:38; Mark 7:5; Luke 6:7), a group generally believed to have originated in Maccabean days with the avowed purpose of following to the fullest possible extent the Law as expounded by the scribes. "Scribes of the Pharisees" (Mark 2:16) is usually understood as scribes belonging to the Pharisaic party, implying the existence of Sadducean scribes as well. Many of the scribes became members of the SANHEDRIN, the Jewish people's highest legal and administrative body, e.g., GAMALIEL in Acts 5 and Nicodemus in John 3 and 7.

The main function of the scribes was teaching and interpreting the Law in order to establish an overall legal system for governing the people. This involved (1) defining and perfecting the legal principles underlying or deriving from the Torah; (2) teaching these principles to their pupils; and (3) helping to administer the Law as advisors in the courts of justice.

The overall picture of the scribes in the Gospels is extremely negative. Their character is suspect (Matt 5:20); they accuse Jesus of blasphemy (Matt 9:3); they attempt to provoke him into error (Luke 11:53); and ultimately they seek to kill him (Mark 11:18; Luke 19:47). This picture reaches a climax with the stinging and severe criticisms leveled by Jesus against the scribes and Pharisees in Matt 23.

In attempting a balanced assessment of the scribes during the first century (particularly in light of later rabbinical records) three related factors must be carefully examined: (1) the reaction of the scribes to Jesus' prophetic and eschatological preaching; (2) the different approaches taken by the scribes to the interpretation of the Law (very strict to fairly liberal views); and (3) the influence upon the Gospels caused by the conflict resulting from the development of a distinct Christian community which had severed its ties to Judaism.

See also GAMALIEL; LAW IN THE NEW TESTAMENT; LAW IN THE OLD TESTAMENT; PHARISEES; SANHEDRIN.

Bibliography. E. Schürer, *The History of the Jewish People in the Age of Jesus Christ*; J. Jeremias, *Jerusalem in the Time of Jesus*.

—T. J. MASHBURN III

• **Scribe in the Old Testament.** The Heb. root idea in the word scribe is that of "to count, to set in order, to write."

The earliest references to the term are found in connection with the courts of David and Solomon, where the scribes' primary responsibilities were to write down and preserve records (2 Sam 8:17; 20:25; 1 Kgs 4:3). They were listed in conjunction with high priests, indicating that the position of scribe was one of prestige and power. When DAVID divided the responsibilities of the Levites, a scribe listed the names of those chosen (1 Chr 24:6). The chief scribe, Jonathan, kept state records and served as a royal advisor to his nephew David (1 Chr 27:32).

During the reforms of JOASH, money for the project was entrusted to the king's scribe and high priest; they were delegated to count the money and pay the workers (2 Kgs 12:10-12; 2 Chr 24:11). In the Assyrian attack on Jerusalem, the scribe Shebna reported the Assyrian verbal assault to King Hezekiah (2 Kgs 18:18-37) and was appointed, along with others, to seek out the prophet Isaiah to determine God's response to the blasphemy (2 Kgs 19:2). Later, in Josiah's day, when the law scroll was discovered in the Temple, it was the scribe Shaphan who relayed the news to the king and read the scroll to him (2 Kgs 22:8-10).

The prophet JEREMIAH depended on his faithful scribe, BARUCH, to record his messages (Jer 36:4, 6, 27, 28, 32) and at times directed Baruch to read God's word to the people (Jer 36:6, 13, 15). When Jeremiah purchased land from his cousin, his scribe drew up the official documents and preserved them (Jer 32:12-15). Special quarters were assigned the scribes both in the palace and in the Temple compound (Jer 36:10-21). Scribes wore distinctive garb, carrying necessary equipment such as inkhorns, writing instruments, and a penknife (Jer 8:8; 36:23; Ezra 9:2). Jeremiah accused them of perpetrating lies (Jer 8:8).

Scribal duties extended beyond those of merely recording and preserving messages. Possibly as early as the time of Deborah, they may have provided a military function (Judg 5:14), and later they sounded the battlecry to muster armies for warfare (2 Kgs 25:19; 2 Chr 26:11; Jer 52:25).

In exilic times, scribes were required to record decrees exactly as proposed (Esth 3:12) and to relay news throughout the land (Esth 8:9). When Nehemiah secured tithes from the Israelites, responsible individuals, including Zadok the scribe, were placed in charge of the storehouses (Neh 13:13).

In a foreign land, without a temple, scribes of the Exile attained great importance. Diligent study and interpretation of the Law was needed, and scribal decisions became a body of oral tradition that later periods equated with written scripture. Scribes gathered disciples about them for instruction (1 Chr 2:55) and EZRA emerged as the recognized speaker for God in teaching the law to Israel, combining the office of priest and scribe (Ezra 7:10-12). Assisted by the Levites, he read and explained God's word publicly (Neh 8:4-13), and reprimanded the people for their apostasy.

By the second century B.C.E. scribes had become a political force in Israel, and by the time of the NT wielded significant power, exercising that role as primary opponents of Jesus.

See also WRITING SYSTEMS.

—A. O. COLLINS

• **Scripture in the New Testament.** The word scripture is the translation of a Gk. word which may be rendered variously as writing, written character, copy or drawing, official or personal statement, law and statute. In the NT, scripture is used in a distinctively theological sense to distinguish from ordinary writing that which is received as a record of the Word of God. According to the later Jewish view which permeates the writings of the NT, scripture is given by God's Spirit and, as such, is sacred, authoritative and eternal. In 2 Tim 3:16 scripture is described as "inspired by God and profitable for teaching, for reproof, for correction and for training in righteousness."

In general, scriptures used in the plural refer to the collection of books held to be authoritative in Judaism. Scripture used in the singular refers to an individual passage in the collection of authoritative books (Mark 12:10), though there are passages in which scripture refers to the whole collection (Gal 3:22). But what specifically are the authoritative books? Nowhere in the NT are these books identified. The Gospel of Luke comes nearest by identifying the scriptures with the "law of Moses and the prophets and the psalms" (Luke 24:44). This arrangement is analogous to the categories into which the Hebrew Bible is divided (Law, Prophets, and Writings).

There is, however, one important exception to the identification of scripture with the OT CANON. In 2 Pet 3:16, Paul's Letters are equated to "the other scriptures." This suggests that scripture in this particular passage included some NT writings.

See also APOCRYPHA, MODERN; BIBLE, AUTHORITY OF; CANON; NEW TESTAMENT USE OF THE OLD TESTAMENT; OLD TESTAMENT; REVELATION, CONCEPT OF; SCRIPTURE IN THE OLD TESTAMENT.

—T. J. MASHBURN III

• **Scripture in the Old Testament.** The Christian church has had its scripture or scriptures from its inception. Originally, this was the OT, but the OT in its various parts came to be considered inspired, and thereby "holy writings" or "scripture," over centuries of time.

Though apparently unofficial in a wider and dogmatic sense, the idea of written inspired "words" of God was part of Israel's experience from its beginning. Israel's very constitution, the TEN COMMANDMENTS, is said to have been written by God on stone tablets and placed inside the ARK (Deut 10:1-5). MOSES wrote the Book of the Law and placed it beside the Ark (Deut 31:24-26). Included in the Book of the Covenant (Exod 20:22–23:33) were a number of written authoritative laws.

But apparently no OT book was regarded as scripture or God's word prior to 621 B.C.E. when during JOSIAH's restorations the Book of the Law (probably much of DEUTERONOMY) was discovered. It may have been that the prophetic inspiration seen in the eighth-century prophets led to an acceptance of the book as from Moses, who was also considered a prophet. MICAH had considered himself inspired (3:8), and over a century later his inspired words had brought about JEREMIAH's release (Jer 26:16ff.). ISAIAH had "seen the king, the Lord of Hosts" (6:5), and his words came to be written down as "testimony" and "teaching" among his disciples (8:16). AMOS and HOSEA consistently and with authority proclaimed "Thus says the Lord." It appears that the acceptance of prophetic inspiration lay at the base of the idea of inspired written words, rather than some particular idea of "scripture."

The entire Pentateuch seems to have been accepted as canonical (CANON) by 400 B.C.E., the Prophets by 200 B.C.E., and the Writings by 90 C.E.

See also CANON.

—KAREN RANDOLPH JOINES

• **Scroll.** Both the Heb. word *sēper* and the Gk. *biblos*, often translated "book," referred to a scroll, a long roll of PAPYRUS or tanned hides sewn together. Papyrus scrolls are known from Egypt at least as early as 8000 B.C.E. Such scrolls of thirty ft. in length and more were common. Similarly, the leather scrolls known from the Dead Sea community at Qumran were approximately the same lengths. The Isaiah Scroll, *1QIs*[a] was ca. twenty-two ft. long, and the Temple Scroll was twenty-six ft. long, the longest of the DEAD SEA SCROLLS yet known. The book, with individual pages cut and bound together on the inside, is called a codex and did not become common until the first century C.E. Thus all the biblical references to books (the book of the law [2 Kgs 22:8], the Book of the Chronicles of the Kings of Israel [1 Kgs 14:19], the Lamb's book of life [Rev 21:27], etc.) refer to scrolls rather than codices. The Heb. term *sēper* can refer to other written documents such as letters, deeds, and contracts as well as the longer scroll.

To prepare a papyrus scroll, the papyrus reed was cut into thin lengthwise strips. While the papyrus strips were still moist, they would be laid adjacent to one another in two layers, one horizontal and one vertical. The papyrus was then weighed down and left to dry. The sap of the papyrus served as the bonding agent for the two layers. The vertical height was limited to a convenient scroll height, usually about nine to twelve in. But individual "sheets" of papyrus would be joined together horizontally to make scrolls which often reached thirty ft. or more. Some Egyptian scrolls as long as 133 ft. have been found. Once dried fully, the scroll would be rubbed with a mild abrasive such as pumice stone to produce a smooth writing surface.

Leather scrolls were prepared from individual animal skins, most frequently sheep or goat, tanned and cut to an approximately rectangular size. The skins were scraped as thin as feasible and rubbed smooth with an abrasive. Individual skins were sewn together with leather cords to form a scroll.

From a later time, PARCHMENT was used for scrolls. Parchment originated in the city of Pergamum about 190 B.C.E. It was produced from the skin of sheep and goats like leather. The hair and fat were removed from the hide. It was then soaked in lime and stretched on a frame and scraped very thin. Then the parchment was smoothed to prepare the surface for writing. Parchment was developed because the Egyptians would not permit Pergamum to import papyrus.

Before writing on a scroll, a scribe would often use a straightedge and a sharp stylus to lay out columns and lines. Ink was prepared from lampblack mixed with gum arabic and water or nut galls, iron sulfate, and water. The permanence of this ink is seen in its lasting in some cases 4,000 years or more, to the present day.

—JOEL F. DRINKARD, JR.

• **Sculpture.** Early evidence (8000 B.C.E.) for sculpture in Palestine comes from Middle Stone Age finds near Mount Carmel in the form of a sickle shaft relief carving of a young fawn and a limestone slab profile of a gazelle. Prepottery Neolithic finds at Jericho include several actual human skulls overlaid with shaped clay. A painted terra-cotta head comes from a later stratum.

Canaanite sculpture typically shows influences from Mesopotamia and the Aegean. Egyptian influence on Phoenician carving is apparent at Ugarit and Byblos, and in the work of the Phoenician craftsman imported for Solomon's Temple (1 Kgs 5–7). The biblical descriptions of the temple ornamentation also suggest Syro-Hittite influence.

The Bible generally views sculpture negatively, especially where it involves representation of the deity in violation of Mosaic law. Certain carved images, however, function significantly in several stories (e.g., Laban's stolen "household gods," Aaron's golden calf, Moses' bronze serpent and cherubim for the ARK of the Covenant, Jeroboam's golden bulls). The temple in Jerusalem featured prominently several items of sculpture: cherubim, twelve bronze oxen supporting the molten sea, bronze pillars decorated with pomegranates, and walls engraved with palmtrees and flowers.

The biblical aversion to graven images of deities is expressed vividly in Isaiah's ridicule of pagan idolatry (Isa 40:18-20; 41:67; 44:9-20). Josephus witnesses to the increased Jewish resistance to the use of any imagery in his account of opposition to the presence of Roman standards, with their animal emblems, in Jewish lands (*Ant* 18:4.3). The critical reference to Satan's throne in Pergamum in Rev 2:13 may allude to the well-known, elaborately sculptured altar to Zeus there.

See also IDOLATRY.

Bibliography. M. Bieber, *The Sculpture of the Hellenistic Age*; L. Woolley, *Art of the World: Mesopotamia and the Middle East.*

—SCOTT NASH

• **Scythopolis.** *See* BETH-SHAN

• **Sea.** Sea may designate either large bodies of water in general (Gen 1:10), a specific body of water (MEDITERRANEAN, 1 Kgs 5:9), or a ceremonial (molten sea, 1 Kgs 7:23) or symbolic (sea of glass, Rev 4:6) structure. In the UGARITIC literature Sea and the storm-god Baal Haddu are enemies who do battle in cycles (evidently corresponding to the changing of the seasons). While the sea is less personified in the Bible, it is, if not itself the enemy, at least the harborer of enemies of God against which he does battle (Isa 27:1) but which ultimately submit to his sovereignty (Pss 114:3ff.; 104:25ff.)

In both OT and NT the sea held unknown dangers and was an object of fear if not almost personal enmity. That the normally nonseafaring Solomon had ships and could readily traverse the sea (1 Kgs 10:22) and that Jesus could still the raging sea with a word (Mark 4:39) was verification of God's protection and his sovereignty even over the sea. Rev 21:1 promises that in the world to come there will be no more sea, that is, either no more dark and fearful enemies as harbored by the sea or no more separation as symbolized by the sea for the island-exile John.

See also COSMOLOGY.

—EDD ROWELL

• **Sea Peoples.** The Sea Peoples are a mixed group of people who appeared in Syria and Palestine in the second half of the thirteenth century B.C.E. It is believed that the Sea Peoples came from the Aegean islands and that they were connected with the crisis faced by the Mycenaean empire around the end of the thirteenth century B.C.E. Historical records from Egypt and the narratives from the OT indicate that the Sea Peoples became a powerful factor in the history and culture of Canaan. Egyptian records related the invasion of the Sea Peoples to the fall of the Hittite empire and to the destruction of Ugarit.

The entrance of the Sea People into Canaan is recorded in several Egyptian documents from this period. In the fifth year of the reign of Mernepthah (1224–1211) Egypt was invaded by Libyans, aided by a group of people called "foreigners from the sea." In the inscription celebrating his victory over the Sea Peoples, Mernepthah named these people from the sea Sherden, Sheklesh, Tursha, and Akawasha.

In the eighth year of the reign of Ramses III (1183–1152) an intensive naval battle against the Sea Peoples was fought in the Nile Delta. The reliefs found in the mortuary temple of Ramses III at Medinet Habu near Thebes present a graphic detail of the Sea Peoples, their weapons and their dress. Among the Sea People, the Tjekker and the Peleset were pictured wearing headgear resembling feathered helmets. The Sherden were wearing horned helmets, and the Shekelesh had head bands. Those who came by land were using chariots for fighting and two-wheeled carts harnessed to a team of four oxen. These carts were used to transport the women and children of the invaders. Ramses defeated them, but allowed the Sea Peoples to establish themselves in the southern coastal area of Canaan.

The Peleset became known as the PHILISTINES in the OT. In Gen 10:14 the Philistines are said to be the descendants of Caphtor, the son of Mizraim (Egypt). This identification reflects the popular view that the Philistines came from Egypt. Amos 9:7, Deut 2:23, and Jer 47:4 identified the home of the Philistines as Caphtor, an island in the sea. Some scholars have identified Caphtor with CRETE while others identified it with Cilicia in Asia Minor. The Philistines were settled in five main cities in Canaan: ASHKELON, ASHDOD, GATH, GAZA, and EKRON (Josh 13:3). The report of Wen Amon (ca. 1050 B.C.E.) said that the Tjekker occupied the city of Dor. South of Gaza there was a Cretan settlement, the Cretan Negeb (1 Sam 30:14). The Philistines became a threat to the city-states of Canaan and a menace to the survival of the Israelite confederacy. The struggle between Shamgar ben Anath and the Philistines (Judg 3:31) and the SAMSON stories in Judg 13–16 are records of the earliest encounters between the Israelites and the Philistines. The Philistine threat precipitated the establishment of the monarchy in Israel under Saul. However, the Philistines were not conquered until the time of David. Some of the conquered Sea Peoples, the Cherethites and the Pelesthites became part of David's mercenary army (2 Sam 20:23).

See also PHILISTINES.

—CLAUDE F. MARIOTTINI

• **Seal.** *See* WRITING SYSTEMS

• **Seat, Judgment.** *See* JUDGMENT SEAT

• **Second Advent.** *See* MILLENNIUM

• **Second Coming of Christ.** *See* ESCHATOLOGY IN THE NEW TESTAMENT; MILLENNIUM; PAROUSIA/SECOND COMING

• **Sedrach, Apocalypse of.** [sed'druhk] The *Apocalypse of Sedrach* consists of two distinct sections of unequal length. The first is a brief sermon by Sedrach on love. In the second, longer section, Sedrach is taken up by an ANGEL to the third heaven into the presence of God. Sedrach questions God about divine punishment of sinners and the presence of evil in the world. God's response focuses on man's free choice. God then tells his only begotten Son to take Sedrach's soul to PARADISE. Sedrach resists, continuing to plead for mercy on sinners. After considerable negotiation, the Lord agrees to forgive anyone who lives uprightly for as little as twenty days after repentance. Satisfied, Sedrach allows God to take his soul.

The *Apocalypse of Sedrach* is extant in a single Greek manuscript. It is Christian in both sections, which were probably not originally joined. The apocalypse is closely related to other Ezra books, such as 4 EZRA, the VISION OF EZRA, and especially the Greek APOCALYPSE OF EZRA. The *Apocalypse* was probably composed in Greek, perhaps by a Jew, between the second and ninth centuries C.E., and joined with the sermon on love sometime later. "Sedrach" has been identified as either a reference to the figure by that name from Dan 3:12 or a corruption of "Esdras" (Ezra). In addition to its focus on sin, free will, and God's mercy, the *Apocalypse of Sedrach* is noteworthy for its glowing description of the body, which unfortunately must be separated from the soul.

See also APOCALYPTIC LITERATURE; EZRA, FOURTH; EZRA, GREEK APOCALYPSE OF.

Bibliography. S. Agourides, "Apocalypse of Sedrach," *The Old Testament Pseudepigrapha,* ed. J. H. Charlesworth; R. J. H. Shutt, "The Apocalypse of Sedrach," *The Apocryphal Old Testament,* ed. H. F. D. Sparks.

—JOSEPH L. TRAFTON

• **Seer.** *See* PROPHET

• **Selah.** [see'luh] The word selah (Heb. *selâ*) appears seventy-one times in thirty-nine different psalms and three times in Habakkuk (3:3, 9, 13). All but two of its occurrences in the Psalter are concentrated in the first three books (Pss 1–89).

The LXX renders selah as *dia-psalma,* a term suggesting some type of interlude (instrumental, choral, silent). The combination *higgāyôn selâ* in Ps 9:16 may indicate a break in singing while the instruments continue. Jewish tradition has seen the term as the response "forever."

Attempts to derive its meaning etymologically have focused on the Heb. *sālal,* "to lift up," and the Heb. *sālâ* (from the Aramaic *s-l-ʿ*, "to bend"). The former would indicate an interlude for the "lifting up" of music or prayers. The latter suggests a cue for the congregation to become prostrate.

See also MUSIC/MUSICAL INSTRUMENTS.

Bibliography. A. A. Anderson, *Psalms (1–72), NCB*; R. B. Y. Scott, "The Meaning and Use of 'Selah' in the Psalter," *CSBSB* 5 (July 1939): 17-25.

—SCOTT NASH

• **Seleucids.** *See* MACCABEES

• **Semites.** [sem'*i*ts] The term semites is a broad designation in biblical scholarship used to describe groups of people who shared affinities in culture, religion, and language. These groups also are geographically linked by their focus of activity in the area of the FERTILE CRESCENT. The significance of semites for biblical studies is that the Hebrew Bible records and interprets the activities of a variety of the groups which are classified in this category. Of particular interest are the semitic people known as Hebrews.

An etymological study of the term semites reveals that it is an anachronistic term first used in the eighteenth century. During this time period, an intense and scholarly pursuit was underway in the area of comparative philology. Scholars were attempting to trace the linguistic patterns and clues in ancient languages in order to draw some conclusions about the ethnic origins of the users. It was August Ludwig Schölzer who in 1781 in an article in *Repertorium für biblische und Morgenländische Literatur* designated the language used by the Hebrews, Babylonians, Syrians, Arabs, and others as semitic. This term, therefore, originally was a linguistic and cultural classification and had nothing to do with race or a particular ethnic group.

The terms semites and semitic, as used by Schölzer, are never found in the Hebrew Bible. However, semite does have its contextual background in Gen 10. Semite derives from the name of SHEM who was the oldest son of Noah. This group is known as semites and not shemites because the term is taken from the Greek and Latin versions of the Hebrew Bible.

The biblical narrative of Noah's three sons (Gen 10), Shem, Japheth, and Ham, is an etiological story which illustrates world history by describing the origin of all the nations and peoples after the flood. The attempt has been made to identify some of the descendants of Noah's sons as specific groups, for example, Cush, the son of Ham, represents Ethiopia. While some of the sons are easy to recognize as countries, such as Egypt and Canaan, many of the names are obscured by time and no certainty can be reached on which nations they were to represent. In very general categories, the descendants of Shem (semites) would represent the groups living in Mesopotamia and South Asia. Ham's descendants are associated with North Africa, Egypt, and the southern section of Mesopotamia. The descendants of Japheth are the peoples of Indo-European descent located in Asia Minor.

The genealogy of the Hebrew branch of the semites, the group represented from Shem to Abram (Abraham), is presented in detail in Gen 11:10–32. This genealogy is a form characteristic of the priestly source which is usually concerned with cultic observances, dates, measurements, and lists. The importance of a genealogy, for the priestly writer specifically and ethnic groups in general, is that it establishes credibility. In the particular context of Gen 11:10–32, the genealogy provided the semitic group known as the Hebrews with a sense of stability and continuity by tracing their beginnings back to Shem. Furthermore, it illustrated the selection by God of one specific group to be his people after the fall of the Tower of Babel. One of the problems in this biblical schema of origins as presented in Gen 11 is that Shem's son, Arpachshad, bears a nonsemitic name. This point is only one example which illustrates how the Hebrews were actually a mixture of semitic and nonsemitic background.

The Hebrews, as the most prominently represented Semitic group in the Hebrew Bible, are geographically associated with the northwest section of the Mesopotamia. This assertion is supported by the biblical tradition which emphasizes the area called Haran (Gen 12:1ff.). Also closely associated with this geographical area are the ARAMEANS. This particular semite group had close affinities with the Hebrews as is illustrated by the creedal statement in Deut 26:5 which describes Jacob as: "A wandering Aramean was my father."

As indicated earlier, the unifying element in all the geographically diverse groups associated with the semites is language. It is not a race or an ethnic group, although the term is used as a convenient nomenclature to designate people who share language and cultural affinities.

In an analysis of the semitic languages, some scholars have suggested an original proto-semitic language from which all the other semitic languages evolved. Other comparative philological studies of the semitic languages suggest that there existed homogeneity between them and the languages associated with the hamites. Therefore, a very broad category of hamito-semitic has been proposed as a general language of many groups in the ancient Middle East.

While the origin of the semitic or hamito-semitic language is elusive, it is possible to focus on semitic languages which have survived into the contemporary period and also those languages which have left written records. There are approximately seventy different forms of the semitic language. Some of these language forms are rarely used and others have died out except for a few extant documents or inscriptions.

Normally the semitic languages are divided into three broad categories: east semitic, south semitic, and northwest semitic. All of the variety of languages within these categories share some of the same basic characteristics: consonantal writing with vowels or vowel markings only being added later, writing is from right to left (with the exceptions of Akkadian and Ethiopic), a paucity use of moods and tenses, and the root form for verbs is third person singular.

The influence of the semitic languages is important not only for OT studies concerned with Hebrew or Aramaic but also for studies which deal with Greek texts. The language of the LXX and the Greek NT occasionally bears the marks of a semitic style. Whenever this semitic style is recognized in a text, it is designated as a semitism. Semitisms are suggested in Greek texts by the presence of structures such as parallelism, chiasmus, and parataxis.

Perhaps the two most important semitic languages in regard to religious and nationalistic usage are Hebrew and Arabic. Hebrew originated within the northwest semitic branch and Arabic in the south semitic branch. Part of the significance for these two particular languages stems from the fact that the major religious book of Judaism, the Hebrew Bible, is in Hebrew and the major religious book of the Muslims, the Qur'an, is in Arabic.

Whenever the geographical area of the Fertile Crescent is studied in regard to the groups affecting culture, the semites must be considered as an important part. The oldest semitic empire which can be dated with any accuracy goes back to 2360–2180 B.C.E. This empire was composed of semites known as Akkadians. They entered into the area of the Mesopotamia and conquered the native population who were known as Sumerians (a nonsemitic culture). The Akkadians borrowed many cultural elements from the Sumerians. For example, while the Akkadians had their own native tongue, they appropriated the Sumerian cuneiform script in order to write it. The Akkadian language eventually became the *lingua franca* in the Fertile Crescent. The synthesis of particular semitic elements with other nonsemitic cultures or the synthesis of different semitic cultures is a characteristic repeated often by semitic groups which migrated into a previously populated territory.

The semites from the middle of the third millennium B.C.E. onward exerted either direct or indirect influence on the ancient Middle East. For example, the empires of the Babylonians and Assyrians are impressive illustrations of later semitic hegemony in the area of the Mesopotamia. In the area of Palestine, the Israelites, a relatively late arriving semitic group, borrowed much from their semitic precursors in the land, the Amorites and Canaanites. Probably the most significant borrowing from these two semitic groups took place in the realm of language. The Canaanites were especially significant for language since they were the first to move from a syllabic representation of writing to an alphabet. Therefore, one of the major contributions of the ancient semitic culture of the Near East was the invention of the alphabet.

See also SEMITIC LANGUAGES.

Bibliography. E. Speiser, ed., *At the Dawn of Civilization*; B. Lewis, *Semites and Anti-Semites: An Inquiry into Conflict and Prejudice*; T. Nöldeke, *Sketches from Eastern History*; E. Ullendorff, "The Knowledge of Languages in the Old Testament," *BJRL* 44 (1962): 455-65; S. Moscati, *Ancient Semitic Civilizations* and *The Semites in Ancient History*.

—DAVID M. MAY

• **Semitic Languages.** The area of semitic languages is regarded as extending from Lydia eastward to Persia and from Armenia southward to the Red Sea. The term "semitic" is a linguistic term and is not a racial classification. The technical term "semitic language" was used first in

1781 in an article by A. L. Schlozer in J. G. Eichhorn's *Repertorium für biblische und morgenländische Literatur* (8th ed.). It designated as semitic the descendants of Shem as listed in Gen 10:21ff.

It is impossible to determine the original locale of the semites. The standard view is that they originated in North Arabia. Migrations of these semitic nomads occurred in both prehistoric and historic times, until they were predominant throughout the FERTILE CRESCENT. The most ancient of these migrants were the Akkadians, who traveled through Palestine and Syria and extended themselves into the territory between the Tigris and Euphrates Rivers in the Mesopotamian Valley, by the beginning of the third millennium B.C.E.

The semitic extent would include most of the languages in Syria, Iraq, Jordan, Israel, Arabia, Turkey, Lebanon, and North Africa. Geographically, the semitic languages are divided into eastern and western branches.

East Semitic. The main area of east semitic language includes Assyrian, Babylonian, and Assyro-Babylonian languages. The Old Akkadian (Assyrian) covered 2800–950 B.C.E. The New Akkadian (Babylonian) extended 950–100 B.C.E.

The ancient Akkadian texts are historical records, legal codes, correspondence (both personal and business), omens, prayers, hymns, rituals, myths, medicinal codes, and astronomical codes.

In the fifteenth century B.C.E., Akkadian was the *lingua franca,* i.e., the language of commerce and diplomacy, throughout the Near East. It was replaced by ARAMAIC as the *lingua franca* about the eighth century B.C.E. even though it continued to be used as a written language.

West Semitic. The northwest branch of west semitic is divided into Canaanite and Aramaic. Canaanite is further divided into Old Canaanite, UGARITIC, Phoenician, Moabite, and Hebrew.

(1) The oldest branch of the northwest semitic family is the Old Canaanite. Many Old Canaanite words are known in the Tell el-AMARNA tablets, dated as early as the fifteenth century B.C.E. These were written in a cuneiform script. They were mainly ritual and religious materials including many poems.

(2) The Ugaritic language is mainly known through the accidental discoveries at Ras Shamra in 1928. The most important is the great palace/fortress complex reflecting the fifteenth century B.C.E. The literary remains relate to the royal archives as well as religious and mythological texts. There were many literary texts in Akkadian, Egyptian, and Canaanite cuneiform and also some in Canaanite in Ugaritic alphabetic script, which had been unknown prior to this discovery.

In the royal archives, much information was gained concerning the background of political and diplomatic activities. A large number of names assisted in understanding the ethnic composition of this territory.

This discovery also added much knowledge to the biblical records. These were the first literary records of Canaanite religion to parallel the biblical texts. Through these records, the interrelatedness of the Canaanite religion and language with the Hebrew religion and language became apparent. Cultic practices, myths, poetry, and terminology which were uncovered at Ras Shamra gave impetus to a renewed study of OT religion, practice, and language. Many names, literary phrases, and mythological allusions are linguistically identical in Ugaritic and OT Hebrew. The parallelism which is so evident in OT poetry is identical with that of the Ugaritic texts.

(3) Phoenician or Punic is closely akin to Hebrew. Its earliest documents date between the thirteenth century B.C.E. and the tenth century B.C.E. It is written in a consonantal alphabet of twenty-two letters, from right to left. Each letter is acrophonic, i.e., its name is from a word which begins with that letter.

In the history of alphabets, practically every alphabet of the Western world is based on Phoenician.

The major portion of the Phoenician texts came from the fifth to second centuries B.C.E. Phoenician continued to be a spoken language (Punic) as late as the sixth century C.E.

Old Phoenician held sway in the East from the thirteenth century to the ninth century B.C.E. Middle Phoenician continued from the eighth to the sixth centuries B.C.E. New Phoenician was used from the fifth century to the common era.

Old Punic was used in the West from the fifth century to 146 B.C.E. New Punic is found from 146 B.C.E. to the sixth century C.E.

Phoenicia is a geographical name, referring to the coastal strip of modern Syria and Lebanon south to Mount Carmel. The Greek name came from *phoenix,* "purple," and refers to the purple dye which was a very important product of the area.

Phoenicia was never a political unity. It was organized in city-states which were ruled by hereditary monarchs. The most important cities were Tyre, Sidon, Byblos, Arvad, and Ugarit.

Phoenician culture was not indigenous. The Phoenicians were skillful adapters of alien cultures. They were the most cosmopolitan people of the ancient semitic world.

The religion of the Phoenicians was semitic. It was very similar, if not identical, with the Canaanite. Each segment (city) had its own gods and culture. For instance, at Byblos deities were known as Baalat, Byblos, El, and Adonis. At Sidon, there were Astarte and the Baal of Sidon. At Tyre, Baal Shamem, Eshmun, Astarte, and Melkart are found. There seems to have been a common thread of a myth and ritual nature cult. It incorporated the annual celebration of the death and resurrection of the god of fertility.

(4) The only major inscription of the Moabitic language is the MESHA STELE (Moabite Stone). It contains thirty-four lines concerning the exploits of King MESHA during the ninth century B.C.E.

This stone demonstrates the close similarity of Moabite with the Hebrew language, e.g., the use of the "*waw* consecutive," the relative particle *'asher,* and the sign of the definite direct object.

(5) Hebrew is the most important language of the Canaanite branch for several reasons. The literary remains are very extensive. The OT is a very lengthy Hebrew document. The majority of the written OT is in the Hebrew language enabling the research scholar to observe the Hebrew language developing over a vast chronological period, in contact with various cultures and languages, and in various styles of literature.

In addition to the OT the major literary inscriptions are the Gezer calendar, the Samaria ostraca, the Siloam inscription, the Meṣad Ḥashavyahu inscription, the Arad ostraca, and the Lachish letters. These literary remains demonstrate that the consonantal language of the ancient monarchy differs only slightly from the later OT language.

Another reason for the importance of the Hebrew language is the fact that there is an almost continuous history of this language from the time of Moses to the modern period. In this continuity, it is possible to study the many different Hebrew dialects, the development of script, the determination of pronunciation, the changes within vocalization, as well as the place of Hebrew within the semitic family of languages.

Ancient Hebrew manuscripts were exclusively consonantal. Vowel letters began to appear in the ninth century B.C.E. The development of a written vowel system added to the consonantal texts was a mid-first millennium C.E. creation of the Masoretes. These Masoretes did not possess an effective living tradition of Hebrew speech. There had been a period during which Hebrew ceased to exist as a spoken language. However, the Masoretes did have the transcription of many local Hebrew names of persons and places found in ancient records to guide them in their creation of the Hebrew written vowels. These vowels were recorded as an aid to pronunciation. Even with all of this assistance, it is clear that the vocalization system of later Hebrew language had to be supplemented and organized, thus varying from an ancient pronunciation which can never be regained.

Some scholars support the view that the cessation of Hebrew as a living communication system occurred prior to the common era. However, other scholars point to the discoveries of the Qumran texts to demonstrate that Hebrew was being used to communicate effectively in that transitional period.

The changes in the development of the Hebrew language are very clear. There are changes in the dialects over such a long period of linguistic usage. There are also variations in pronunciation. Through the varied and lengthy contacts with other cultures and languages, there have occurred different syntactical methodologies.

There is a vast difference between the language of the OT and the scholastic language of the Talmudic Hebrew and the Modern Hebrew which is the written and/or spoken language of modern Israel. Modern Hebrew, though using the same Hebrew characters, is a modern development which also has great overtones of a western syntactical quality.

(6) The other northwest semitic branch is Aramaic which should be divided into Western Aramaic and Eastern Aramaic. Western Aramaic encompassed the following: Old Aramaic extended from 925 to 700 B.C.E. and included the dialects Palmyrene, Nabataean, and Sinaitic. Biblical Aramaic, sometimes erroneously called "Chaldean" (and found in Dan 2:4b–7:28; Ezra 4:8–6:18; 7:12-26), occupied the period of ca. 700–100 B.C.E. Palestinian (or Middle) Aramaic extends from the Aramaic of the OT to 700 C.E., and incorporated the dialects of Palestine, Arabia, Syria, and Mesopotamia (this period covers the time up to the Muslim conquest, and also marks the time of the spread of Arabic which limited the constant use of Aramaic as the *lingua franca*). Modern Aramaic is still spoken in a few isolated villages north of Damascus and also in the East in Kurdistan and Iraq (these dialects are only tangentially Aramaic since they are merely remnants of Aramaic and have been greatly influenced by local languages and dialects).

Eastern Aramaic can be seen in several branches. Judaeo-Aramaic (Babylonian Jewish Aramaic) is the language of the Babylonian Talmud, fourth to sixth centuries C.E. Mandaean is syntactically the most important of all non-Jewish Aramaic dialects since its texts are totally original, extending to the ninth century C.E. Syriac, divided by a combination of political and ecclesiastical circumstances into Jacobite and Nestorian, possesses vast theological writings, dating from the first to thirteenth centuries C.E.

The southwest semitic branch is mainly the Arabic family. North Arabic is the most important member of this group. Its strength lies in the fact that this is the language of the Qur'an. It is the instrument whereby the religion of Islam becomes a literary reality and is the sacred tongue of Islam. South Arabic incorporates inscriptions extending from the eighth century B.C.E. to the sixth century C.E. It is seen in Minaean and Sabaean inscriptions. It extends to the modern dialects of Mahri and Qarawi. Ethiopic proper (Ge'ez) is the most important representative of the Ethiopic group. It extends from the fourth to tenth century C.E. It is found in Tigrina or Tigray. Amharic, Gafat, Gurage, and Harari are the other members of the Ethiopic group.

The characteristics to some degree found in common in these semitic languages are: the existence of guttural consonants; emphatic consonants; a continuing emphasis on triliteral roots; a consonantal script; development of various related dialects; modifications and inflections noted by prefixes, affixes, infixes; changes in vocalization for expression of shades of meaning; and a complex and distinct system of conjunctions.

See also LETTERS/INSCRIPTIONS; WRITING SYSTEMS.

—JOHN JOSEPH OWENS

• **Senate of Israel.** *See* SANHEDRIN

• **Sennacherib.** [suh-nak'uh-rib] Son and successor of Sargon II, was the king of ASSYRIA from about 705–681 B.C.E. Among Assyrian kings he stands out as one of exceptional enterprise and openmindedness, pursuing a stable imperial structure at peace with the outside but always ready to assert Assyrian power whenever challenged. He moved the Assyrian capital from Khorsabad to Nineveh, already some 3,000 years old, where it remained for the duration of the Assyrian Empire. There Sennacherib built a splendid residence of more than seventy halls, chambers, and passages almost all lined with sculptured gypsum panels. The excavator was the Englishman A. H. Layard of last century who said there were two miles of such reliefs, although some of them are dated much later, and most of which are scenes of war.

The palace architecture and decor were paralleled both in scale and ingenuity by urban development. Streets were carefully laid out; squares were widened; the palace area was protected from floods by a limestone wall. Beside the palace orchards and botanical gardens were cultivated, watered by canals and stone aqueducts bringing water from the Zagros mountains some forty miles away. All of this was done, according to Sennacherib himself, by the slave labor of conquered people.

Two years into Sennacherib's reign an insurrection in Babylonia was led by Merodach-baladan, supported by Elam, many Chaldean and Aramaean tribes, and involving also King HEZEKIAH of Judah. Having crushed this revolt, Sennacherib placed Bel-ibni (ca. 702–700 B.C.E.) on the throne. Deep discontent followed, erupting westward in areas conquered by Sargon. In about 701 B.C.E. several Palestinian cities (including Hezekiah's Jerusalem) revolted, along with Egypt, bringing on an invasion by Assyrian forces which resulted in the defeat of all except Jerusalem. Sennacherib himself left a partial record of this on his famous prism: "Hezekiah . . . I made a prisoner in Jerusalem . . . like a bird in a cage." He further mentions the capture of forty-six Judean cities, including LACHISH.

Elaborate paneled representations of the battle of Lachish taken from Sennacherib's palace are displayed in London's British Museum. Fresh intrigues in Babylon surfaced with the end result that Sennacherib, departing from his previous policy, ca. 689 B.C.E. savagely sacked and looted Babylon. He was assassinated at Nineveh ca. 681 B.C.E. by two of his sons (2 Kgs 19:37) and was succeeded by a third, Esarhaddon.

Sennacherib's invasion of Judah in 701 B.C.E. is recorded in 2 Kgs 18:13-20:21 and Isa 36-39. While encamped at Lachish he demanded of King Hezekiah 300 talents of silver and thirty talents of gold, which Hezekiah paid to receive immunity. Sennacherib's conquests in Judah were apparently cut short by an "angel of the Lord" who "slew a hundred and eighty-five thousand in the camp of the Assyrians" (2 Kgs 19:35). Herodotus later recorded the tradition that large numbers of mice ate leather parts of the Assyrians' equipment, making it possible that a plague (bubonic?) broke out in their camp.

—KAREN RANDOLPH JOINES

• **Sepphoris.** [sef′uh-ris] Sepphoris was a walled city and capital of lower GALILEE mainly during the NT period, ca. six mi. north-northwest of Nazareth on a high hill in a mountainous plain (PLATE 21). Its city territory probably included NAZARETH.

The rabbis believed Sepphoris existed since Joshua but could only guess about its biblical name. The name of the city means "bird," explained by the fact that it perched on a hill like a bird (*Meg* 6a). Sepphoris minted its own coinage as early as the first century C.E. Under Antoninus Pius it took the name Diocaesarea, which appears on its coins.

Pottery sherds on the surface indicate that the city does date to the Canaanite period. A beautifully molded drinking vessel from Sepphoris of the Persian period hints at the importance of the city at that time. Sepphoris clearly reached its peak in the early Roman period.

Sepphoris entered recorded history in 104 B.C.E. Ptolemy Lathyrus, the King of Cyprus, was at war with King Alexander Jannaeus of Israel. Ptolemy besieged Sepphoris with no success (*Ant* 13.12.5).

In 55 B.C.E. Gabinius, Proconsul in Syria, recognized the strategic importance of Sepphoris and located one of the five Sanhedrins there (*Ant* 15.5.4; *BJ* 1.8.5). In the winter of 39/38 B.C.E. Herod the Great took Sepphoris during a snowstorm (*Ant* 14.15.4; *BJ* 1.16.2). HEROD retained the city as his northern headquarters for the remainder of his reign.

The Sepphoreans revolted immediately upon the death of Herod the Great in 4 B.C.E. The Roman governor of Syria, Varus, acted swiftly. His legions sacked Sepphoris, burned the city, and sold its inhabitants as slaves (*Ant* 17.10.9; *BJ* 2.5.1).

Herod ANTIPAS, a son of Herod the Great, inherited Galilee and Perea (Transjordan) at the death of his father. Antipas immediately set to work to rebuild Sepphoris and its wall. Sepphoris came to be called the "ornament of all Galilee," evidently surpassing Tiberias and other cities in beauty and adornment (*Ant* 18.2.1). Antipas repopulated Sepphoris with Jews and non-Jews. Antipas seems to have granted the city the rank of capital of lower Galilee (*Ant* 18.2.1).

Antipas's works at Sepphoris included a theater that seated 4,000, a palace, and an upper and lower city with their markets. There was also an old fort, an archive building, a colonnaded street in the middle of the city, a city wall, a city gate (*EcclRab* 3), many spice shops, inns, synagogues, private dwellings with upper stories, and "the wheels of Sepphoris," evidently water wheels that lifted water to the upper city (*EcclRab* 12.6). Two aqueducts brought water from springs three mi. to the east.

Pharasaic families are not mentioned in the first century in Sepphoris. Instead we find references to men who fulfilled priestly duties (*Yomah* 6.2; *Ber* 3.6b; *Ta'an* 1 end). Sepphoris remained loyal to the Romans during the first and second revolt against Rome. At the destruction of Jerusalem and the Temple in 70 C.E. one of the priestly families of Jerusalem settled in Sepphoris, as did another family in Nazareth. Sepphoris became a leading Jewish intellectual center in the following centuries, for Judah the Prince edited the Mishnah in Sepphoris about 200 C.E. Eventually Sepphoris yielded first place to Tiberias, and by the fourth century C.E. Christianity was firmly entrenched at Sepphoris.

See also GALILEE.

Bibliography. S. Freyne, *Galilee from Alexander the Great to Hadrian*; E. Schürer, *The History of the Jewish People in the Age of Jesus Christ*.

—JAMES F. STRANGE

• **Septuagint.** [sep′*too*-uh-jint] The Septuagint is the Greek translation of the Hebrew scriptures which was made for the benefit of Jewish communities living in the Hellenistic world. The loss of their knowledge of Hebrew and Aramaic had reached the critical stage since Greek had become their customary language. According to a legend in the LETTER OF ARISTEAS, the translation was made in Alexandria, Egypt, during the reign of Ptolemy Philadelphus (284–247 B.C.E.) by seventy-two scholars in seventy-two days. The story is fantastic, but presumably it was handed down to exalt the nobility of the Law.

The title of the Greek translation is the Latin word *septuaginta* (seventy) and is commonly referred to by the Roman numerals LXX. Why seventy was used instead of seventy-two is unknown. In all probability it was thought that because Moses selected seventy elders from the congregation of Israel to accompany him up Mount Sinai (Exod 24:1, 9) when he received the Law it was proper for seventy to translate the scriptures. Another suggestion is that the number was rounded off for convenience.

The Aristeas story was written in the last half of the second century B.C.E. by a Jewish writer from Alexandria under the pretense of being a member of the court of Ptolemy Philadelphus. According to the story Demetrius Phalerum, the chief librarian of Alexandria, requested the king to supply a translation of the Jewish scriptures to add to the library. The request was granted and the high priest Eleazer of Jerusalem was invited to send a translation committee made up of six men from each tribe of Israel.

It is not likely that all the Hebrew scriptures were translated into Greek at this time since the precise books of the OT had not yet been determined. The work of the committee probably included only the Pentateuch, the first five books of the OT. Later (perhaps 150 B.C.E.) the Prophets and Writings which were accepted in the canon were translated into Greek.

Since the rabbis in Palestine had not determined the limits of the OT during the time that the translations were made, the LXX contained a larger number of books than the Hebrew scriptures. They were the apocryphal works of Judith, Tobit, two books of Maccabees (four in some manuscripts), Sirach, Wisdom of Solomon, Psalms of Solomon (in some manuscripts), an expansion of Ezra-Nehemiah (1 Esdras), an expansion of Jeremiah (Baruch and the Epistle of Jeremiah), additions to the book of Daniel (Bel and the Dragon, the prayer of Azariah, and Susanna), and the rest of the book of Esther.

The LXX became the accepted Bible for the Jews of the Hellenistic dispersion and played a role in paving the way for the introduction of Christianity. The vast majority of citations of the OT appearing in the NT (290 in all) come from the LXX. Paul, who received his education from Jewish scholars and was well versed in Jewish lore, takes his quotations for the most part from the LXX rather than the Hebrew text except when he quotes from memory or adjusts the text to fit his argument.

The Jews gradually refrained from using the LXX as Christians began to employ it as their scriptures and to draw from it proof for the proclamation of the gospel. The Jews decided to make a translation that would be more precise and would give a literal expression to the Hebrew language and context of the OT. In 130 C.E. Aquila, a proselyte Jew from Pontus, a relative of the emperor Hadrian, and a student of Rabbi Akiba, produced a Greek translation of the Hebrew text that was slavishly literal. Two other translations were made in the second century C.E., one by Theodotion of Ephesus and the other by Symmachus, an Ebionite. Other Greek versions were in existence, but nothing is known of their origins.

See also ARISTEAS, LETTER OF; TEXTS/MANUSCRIPTS/VERSIONS.

Bibliography. F. Kenyon, *The Text of the Greek Bible*; H. B. Swete, *An Introduction to the Old Testament in Greek*; H. R. Willoughby, *The Study of the Bible Today and Tomorrow*.

—T. C. SMITH

• **Serabit el-Khadim.** [ser-a-beet'el-kah-dehm'] An ancient site in the SINAI Peninsula located about fifty mi. northwest of the traditional site of Mount Sinai.

Serabit el-Khadim was one of the major sites at which the Egyptians carried out mining operations in ancient times. The site, situated on a sandstone plateau, along with the Wadi Magharah, located nearby, contained abundant deposits of turquoise, a type of stone greenish-blue in color. The stone was used by Egyptian craftsmen for many different purposes, including the production of items for daily life such as jewelry and inlays, as well as those items with a religious significance such as scarabs.

The exploration of the site of Serabit el-Khadim has resulted in the discovery of some extremely important inscriptions. The site was initially explored by Flinders Petrie in 1904 and 1905, with additional discoveries made between 1927 and 1935. The inscriptions were made by the inhabitants of the ancient mining community. They were etched on rocks and the surface of the mine walls. The most recent explorations at Serabit El-Khadim took place in 1977 and 1978 under the direction of Itzhak Beit-Arieh from the Institute of Archaeology in Tel Aviv.

The inscriptions have yielded valuable information in a number of areas. They date to the different periods the mines were operated by the Egyptians and provide something of a basis for the history of mining in the area. Apparently, mining activities were initiated during the period of the Third Dynasty, ca. 2686–2613 B.C.E., and continued on and off down through the Twentieth Dynasty, ca. 1185–1069 B.C.E. The earliest inscriptions were found in the Wadi Magharah, the location of the earliest mines. A renewed interest in mining took place during the early part of the Twelfth Dynasty, ca. 1991–1782 B.C.E., and new mines were opened at Serabit el-Khadim. Mining activities at Serabit el-Khadim continued until ca. 1100 B.C.E. The new mining community included a temple dedicated to the goddess Hathor, the Egyptian goddess of love, as well as the goddess of turquoise. Many of the inscriptions were found in the temple area. Of special interest are a number of the shorter inscriptions apparently inscribed by a Semitic group who worked in the mines of the Egyptians. The inscriptions were written in a type of script which W. F. Albright labeled the "Proto-Sinaitic" script. According to Albright

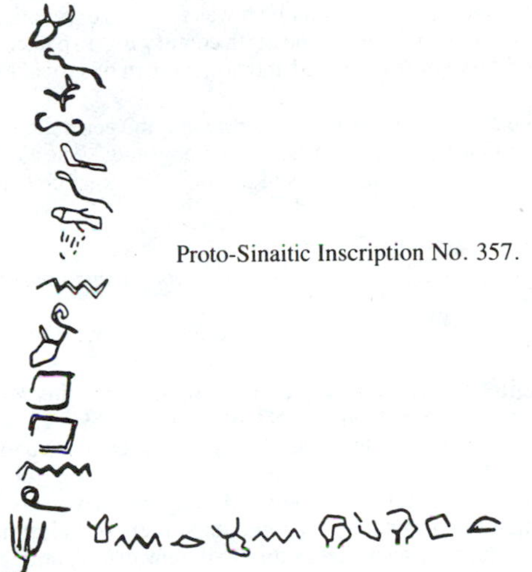

Proto-Sinaitic Inscription No. 357.

the Proto-Sinaitic script dates to about the sixteenth or fifteenth centuries B.C.E. It was the typical script used by the Canaanites of that period. The script is important because it consisted of linear alphabetic characters, and therefore constitutes the earliest alphabet to be found. The Proto-Sinaitic script may be the earliest attempt to move from the picture-like script, seen in Egyptian hieroglyphics, to an alphabet.

The inscriptions from Serabit el-Khadim also provide information about trade and the methods by which goods were transported during the period of the Twelfth Dynasty. According to the inscriptions large donkey caravans, with perhaps as many as 600 donkeys in a caravan, traveled between the mines in Sinai and Egypt.

See also WRITING SYSTEMS.

Bibliography. W. F. Albright, "The Early Alphabetic Inscriptions from Sinai and their Decipherment," *BASOR* 110 (1948): 6-22; S. Yeivin, "Trade Routes in Israel in the First Half of the 2nd Millennium," *Atiqot* 2 (1959): 155-59; I. Beit-Arieh, "New Discoveries at Seribit El-Khadim," *BA* 45/1 (Winter 1982): 13-18.

—LAMOINE DEVRIES

• **Seraphim.** [ser'uh-fim] Standing "Seraphim" (masculine plural of *seraph*) appear in the OT only in the inaugural vision of the prophet Isaiah (chap. 6) where they are attendants in the divine court. Each of them has six wings—two to cover its face, two its feet, and two with which to fly. They appear to be on the throne (not "above him [the

Lord]" as in RSV) occupied by the Lord (called "the King") and chant antiphonally, "Holy, holy, holy is the Lord of Hosts; the whole earth is full of his glory" (6:3).

The Heb. word *seraph* in the OT always designates a SERPENT (Num 21:5, 7, 8, 9; Deut 8:15). Isaiah speaks twice of a "flying *seraph*" (14:29; 30:6), demonstrating that for him a *seraph* serpent may have wings. There appear to be two such serpents in Isaiah's inaugural vision.

The winged and reared ("standing" in Isa 6) cobra was a symbol in ancient Egypt of the royalty of the gods and of the pharaoh. Such a symbol appeared on the headdress of the pharaohs. As in Isaiah's vision, winged and reared cobras appeared on the throne of the famed Tut-Ankh-Amen, forming the armrests of his throne. These serpents could also have faces and hands.

This same serpent symbolism was found in excavations at Samaria in Palestine of the ninth century B.C.E. palace of Ahab. Ivory cobras, winged and not, were in this royal residence.

The royal symbolism of the *seraphim,* the general tenor, and explicit statements of Isa 6 are congruous. The Lord, "the King," in His temple is like a majestic monarch in his palace.

See also CHERUB; SERPENT.

Bibliography. K. R. Joines, *Serpent Symbolism in the Old Testament.*

—KAREN RANDOLPH JOINES

• **Sergius Paulus.** [suhr'jee-uhs-paw"luhs] Sergius Paulus is known to us from the NT only in Acts 13:7-12, yet based on this text no less than three facts can be noted about him. First, he occupied the position of PROCONSUL (chief Roman administrator) of Cyprus during the early years of Christianity's movement beyond the borders of Palestine. Second, he was regarded as an intelligent man. Third, he is depicted as a Roman official anxious to hear the gospel as proclaimed by the early Christian missionaries PAUL and BARNABAS. Further, the passage indicates he was converted to Christianity as a result of a miracle performed in his presence by Paul (v. 12). Scattered extrabiblical evidence supports the suggestion of an early Roman proconsul named Sergius Paulus.

See also BARNABAS; CYPRUS; ELYMAS; PAUL; PROCONSUL.

—MICHAEL D. GREENE

• **Sermon on the Mount.** The first of five equally important discourses found in the GOSPEL OF MATTHEW, the sermon on the mount (Matt 5–7) contains Jesus' most-memorable, most-challenging, and most-controversial demands. It is more than three times as long as the parallel tradition in the Gospel of Luke. Most scholars do not believe that the sermon on the mount is a transcript of an actual discourse of Jesus but contend it is a composite of Jesus' teaching. Davies suggested that it was the Christian answer to the rabbinic formulation taking place in Jamnia. Most recently, Betz argued that the sermon on the mount is an epitome of the theology of Jesus, a presynoptic compendium of Jesus' teaching which served as a manual of survival for conservative, anti-Pauline, Jewish Christians. In this view, the original setting in life of the sermon on the mount was quite different from that of the Gospel. The fact that Matthean vocabulary, compositional techniques, and themes are reflected in the sermon makes it more likely, however, that it was composed by the first evangelist from different sayings of Jesus. Matthew wove these sayings into a tapestry that reflects central themes in the teaching of Jesus as well as his Gospel. The end product addresses the three pillars that the rabbis believed sustained the world: the Law, worship, and obedience to the commandments.

Interpretation. The interpretation of the ethic of the sermon on the mount has been marked by a tendency throughout history to attempt to moderate its radical demands. MacArthur has usefully catalogued twelve basic approaches to the sermon's ethical demands. The first consciously or unconsciously modifies the demands without historical, theological, or literary justification so that they conform to common sense. The danger of this approach is that this reduces the interpretation to personal opinion and defuses its radicality. A second approach is historically related to Roman Catholicism which distinguished between "precepts" binding on all and "evangelical counsels" obligatory only for the clergy. While this may recognize that some are more willing to take on the ethical obligations found in the sermon than others, it creates a double standard for clergy and laity that is not warranted by the text. The third approach stems from Martin Luther who made a distinction between private and public morality. The sermon on the mount is binding on individuals but such commands as love your enemies, do not retaliate, or do not judge are not applicable to government. The danger of the "two realms" view is that it makes the secular realm independent from God's law. A fourth approach utilizes other passages from scripture to interpret and to tone down the ethical demands. A fifth approach maintains that Jesus believed that with the dawning of the KINGDOM OF GOD the end of the world was at hand. His ethical teaching was conditioned by the imminence of the end and the sermon was intended to be the law for the exceptional situation of catastrophe that would mark the passing of this world. But the discourse contains no hint that it was only to be only an "interim ethic." A sixth view is that of dispensationalism and can be found, for example, in the Scofield Bible. This interpretation considers the teaching as applicable only to the future time when the Kingdom is established on earth and "gives neither the privilege nor the duty of the Church." This view ignores the fact that Matthew believed that this teaching was applicable to his own community. MacArthur labeled these six approaches as secondary in importance.

Six views are considered to be of primary importance. First is the absolutist view that takes the commands with utmost seriousness and considers them to be obligatory for all Christians. Questions of whether they are practical or not should not obscure the radical demand. A second view recognizes the presence of hyperbole in Jesus' teaching to score a point. Jesus did not expect his followers literally to cut off an offending member but did want to dramatize the necessity of total commitment. A third view translates the commands into general principles that can be applicable to contemporary life, such as "going the extra mile." The danger of this approach is that the radicality of a command in Jesus' context can be softened in its translation into a modern context. A fourth approach maintains that the ethic of the sermon on the mount concerns the inner attitudes required of disciples and does not command specific acts that can lead to a false, legalistic rectitude. It is not law to be obeyed but something to be internalized. A fifth approach understands the sermon to be an unattainable ethical goal that was intended to produce repentance by showing how far short even the so-called righteous fall in meeting God's requirements and to point the way to the only one who has fulfilled the commands. This overlooks the fact that in

Matthew the teachings were intended as a guide for those who had already repented. A sixth view understands the sermon as the proclamation of God's unconditioned claim on the individual. With the offer of grace comes a demand and a summons. The responsibilities of those who accept this grace are outlined in the sermon (7:13-16). It is a charter of conduct for disciples that is to be obeyed. Obedience is rewarded by participation in the Kingdom of heaven (5:20); disobedience will meet with eschatological punishment (5:22, 25-26, 29-30; 7:13, 19, 23, 27).

Audience. According to 5:1, the audience consists of the disciples. Since only four disciples have been called to this point in the narrative (4:18-22), one must conclude that a wider audience is assumed to be present (7:28-29) as in the other Matthean discourses (13:2, 10, 36; 23:1). This audience would be representatives of the Israel (4:23-25; 7:28-29) who are being newly gathered by Jesus to become the light to the world.

Themes. (1) An example of Jesus' teaching. In the literary context of Matthew, 4:23-25 forms an INCLUSIO with 9:35. Sandwiched between these two summary passages, the evangelist shows Jesus to be the Messiah who is mighty in both word (5:1–7:28) and deed (8:1–9:35). In 4:17, 23 the narrator tell us that Jesus announced the Kingdom and called people to repentance. The sermon on the mount offers a specific example of Jesus' teaching. As teacher, Jesus is presented as one who has authority greater than the scribes (7:28-29) and as one who is even greater than Moses (5:21-48). Jesus closes all loopholes, including those which were culturally accepted, and intensifies the demand of the Law with his insistence on a greater righteousness (5:21-48). In the sermon, Jesus disseminates the unadulterated expression of God's will.

(2) Christology. An implicit christological emphasis is present throughout. Jesus claims that he has come to fulfill the Law and the Prophets (5:17) and punctuates his authority with six antitheses, "you have heard it said . . . , but I say to you" (5:21-48). The disciples will be persecuted because of Jesus (5:11); and he implies that he will be the judge in the last day when many will cry to him, "Lord, Lord" (7:21-23). The disciples' ultimate destiny therefore depends on their relationship to him (7:21-23) and their obedience to his words (7:24-27).

(3) The Law. At the heart of the discourse is the statement that Jesus has not come to abrogate the Law and the Prophets but to "fulfill" them (5:17). This is variously taken to mean: (a) that he will carry out the commandments; (b) that he will bring the Law and the Prophets to their eschatological completion; or (c) that he will recapture the intention of the Law or set forth its true meaning that others have obscured. In the sermon, the Law has continuing validity (5:17-20; 7:12) but only as it is correctly interpreted by Jesus. The disciple is to obey "these words of mine" (7:26). This is echoed in the conclusion of the Gospel where Jesus commissions the disciples to teach persons "to observe all things I have commanded" (28:20).

(4) Worship. In chap. 6, Jesus pursues the theme of righteousness in the outward expression of religious duties. Piety is not to be a public performance designed to impress. Alms are to be given in secret; prayer is to be a matter of the heart; and fasting is to be the humbling of the soul before God not its exaltation before an appreciative audience. The focus of one's worship is therefore to be centered entirely on God.

(5) Obedience to the commands. As a charter for disciples, obedience to these words is to characterize the community of the Kingdom. The question of their practicality did not arise for Matthew, only for later Christians. The assumption is that these commands not only can be done, they must be done. The sermon begins, however, with the announcement of God's grace. The BEATITUDES are not entrance requirements for the Kingdom since they contain no specific imperative. They are rather eschatological pronouncements of the blessings of the new age that are now coming to pass to those who are in distress and who can only hope for God's deliverance. The obedience required by Jesus is therefore a response based on the grace already received from God. After the beatitudes, however, the emphasis falls on hearing and doing (5:19; 7:24-27), works (5:16), and bearing fruit (7:15-23) with dire warnings about failure to obey. One is able to bear fruit by identifying with the needs of others and demonstrating concern for the oppressed and marginalized and not by exhibiting mighty gifts of power. The key is the rule of love (5:44-45; 7:12). This principle alone leads to the greater righteousness that exceeds conventional moral standards by doing what is unusual—loving the enemy and creating peace through nonviolent means. This life-stance opens one up to new and deepened possibilities in relating to others in human life. It also opens one up to the dangers of persecution (5:11). It therefore requires of the disciple single-minded devotion and an austerity that is able to avoid the distractions and preoccupations of day-to-day living that might hinder total concentration on the Kingdom of heaven (6:19-34).

(6) The Kingdom. Jesus is said to preach the gospel of the Kingdom (4:23), and the word "Kingdom" forms an inclusio around the Sermon (5:3; 7:21). The Promise, "theirs is the kingdom of heaven," brackets the first eight beatitudes (5:3, 10). The Kingdom is to be the first priority for disciples (6:33). It is considered to be imminent and is present to be entered (5:20), but it is also considered to be not yet accomplished (5:18) and to be entered into at the end of time (7:20). The Lord's prayer petitions God to act with the establishment of God's reign on earth.

See also BEATITUDES; ETHICS IN THE NEW TESTAMENT; KINGDOM OF GOD; LAW IN THE NEW TESTAMENT; LAW IN THE OLD TESTAMENT; LOVE IN THE NEW TESTAMENT; LOVE IN THE OLD TESTAMENT; MATTHEW, GOSPEL OF; TORAH.

Bibliography. H. D. Betz, *Essays on the Sermon on the Mount*; W. D. Davies, *The Setting of the Sermon on the Mount*; R. A. Guelich, *The Sermon on the Mount*; H. K. MacArthur, *Understanding the Sermon on the Mount*.

—DAVID E. GARLAND

• **Serpent.** The OT uses several different Hebrew words to refer to serpents. The most important passages and stories dealing with the serpent are found in Gen 3, Exod 7, Num 21, Isa 6, and 2 Kgs 18.

In Gen 3 the serpent appears as the most subtle of God's creatures and is portrayed as leading the first woman to disobey her Creator. The consequence is that she and her husband are expelled from their garden of enchantment and life and prevented from returning. At least three basic aspects of the ancient Near Eastern serpent symbolism—those of recurring youthfulness, wisdom, and chaos— appear in the account to make the serpent a medium by which humanity is tempted to become divine. In fact, the only element lacking came to be immortality.

In Exod 7 the staff of AARON becomes a serpent and devours the serpents created by the transformation into serpents of the staffs of the Egyptian magicians. A common symbol in ancient EGYPT of the authority of the gods and of the pharaoh was the scepter, sometimes shaped like a serpent. When Aaron's staff/scepter/serpent devoured the staffs/scepters/serpents of the Egyptians, the outcome of the upcoming plagues was certain. The power of Aaron and MOSES and their God was superior to that of the Egyptians and their gods.

In Num 21 Moses is divinely instructed to make "a fiery serpent" (*śārāp*) to set on a pole so that anyone bitten by such a creature could behold it and live. It seems that the underlying motif here is the idea of the repulsion of a dangerous creature by the display of its exact image.

In Isa 6 *seraphim* with six wings appear on the THRONE of the Lord and chant God's praises. The word means "serpents"; they are apparently winged cobras, Egyptian symbols of royalty.

In 2 Kgs 18:4 King Hezekiah of Judah is said to have destroyed a number of Canaanite religious symbols. It is also stated, "He broke in pieces the bronze serpent that Moses had made, for until those days the people of Israel had burned incense to it; it was called Nehushtan." The Hebrew text reveals that HEZEKIAH dubbed the serpent "Nehushatan," a play on words to signify a contemptuous reference to the serpent as "a mere serpent-shaped piece of bronze." The notation that Moses had made the serpent probably preserves the popular tradition showing that the populace had honored it ("burned incense to it") for some time. Apparently, the king understood it to be another Canaanite symbol. Extrabiblical evidence shows the motif of the crawling serpent (as opposed to the reared cobra) to be associated with reproduction, water, the dove, and the bull. In destroying Israel's cultic bronze serpent King Hezekiah was destroying a common Canaanite symbol of the fertility of the earth, a motif inappropriate to the Hebrew understanding of the character of God.

See also SERAPHIM; ANIMALS.

Bibliography. K. R. Joines, *Serpent Symbolism in the Old Testament*

—KAREN RANDOLPH JOINES

• **Servant.** In the OT and in the NT the terms *'ebed* and *doulos* were used for persons doing SERVICE for others in the home, on the land, or in government or business but not actually slaves, as well as for persons who were slaves. It is very difficult to know whether to translate "slave" or "servant" at many points in the biblical texts. When the verb used, however, is that for service at the altar or in other ceremonial or religious contexts (Heb. *šrt*), then it is probable that SLAVERY is excluded.

Persons doing service to others retained, or were intended to retain, dignity and relative autonomy as persons in their own right. They were not to be treated as property or to be abused in the home or elsewhere. AMOS sharply attacked the man who, with his own father, abused a servant girl, thereby profaning God's HOLINESS (Amos 2:7). Persons in cultic service, too, were in position to place their LAMENTS before God, pleading their own cause; they were not simply to acquiesce in the divine service or accept without question whatever life brought them.

Those who had been blessed with wealth and good fortune were to share their blessings with others, placing themselves at the service of the less fortunate (cf. Job 29–31). Indeed, if necessary, they were to undergo suffering in behalf of others, recognizing that those who had received much were required to render much service.

In that context the picture of the Suffering Servant of Isa 40–55 is to be placed. First, Israel is God's servant in the world, required to uphold God's TORAH before the nations, enabling all peoples to see that Israel is first and foremost in the service of God. COVENANT requires such service, and God also serves Israel's needs in innumerable ways. But secondly, the Servant of the Lord in Isa 40–55 also serves to display before the nations such fidelity to God in the midst of suffering that the nations are caused to marvel, recognizing that Israel suffers in their stead, faithful to God despite the mistreatment endured at the hands of these nations. At the time of deliverance, then, the prophet sees Israel exalted and glorified, coming into its promised INHERITANCE, accepted and honored by God for its faithfulness.

Service to God in the NT also involves the same fidelity and loyalty to the deity in times of testing and persecution. Service (Gk. *diakonia*) is centrally inspired by the One who came not to be served but to serve and to give his life as a RANSOM for the many. The servant, then, is one who is devoted to God, bound in covenant to fulfill the demands of the GOSPEL, and therefore quite properly designated a "slave of Christ."

—WALTER HARRELSON

• **Service.** The word service occurs in the OT approximately 100 times as the translation of *'ăbōdâ* and means various kinds of work or service to others (Gen 30:26; 1 Chr 26:30), manual work (Exod 1:14), as well as the many ways of serving God through liturgical celebration and WORSHIP (Exod 13:5; 31:10). Service to God is a prominent underlying theme in reference to the liturgy and celebrations (Josh 22:27). Both LEVITES and PRIESTS are often spoken of in terms of their service in the tent of meeting or Temple in their liturgical and sacrificial duties (Exod 32:29; 35:19; 1 Chr 23:28; 24:3). The sacred utensils also have a place of service in worship (1 Chr 28:13–15).

The word service (Gk. *diakonia*) appears approximately twenty-four times in the NT, twenty-one of them in the epistles. The meanings are similar to the OT. Slaves and soldiers offer service (Eph 6:7; 1 Tim 2:4; 6:2). Priests perform service in the TEMPLE (Luke 1:23; 1 Cor 9:13; Heb 2:17; 10:1). One may fulfill an obligation through service (Phil 2:30) or serve through gifts and aid given to others (Rom 15:27; 2 Cor 9:12; 3 John 1:5). PAUL speaks of service to God as moral and spiritual obedience (Rom 12:1 ["reasonable service" in KJV; "spiritual worship" in RSV]; 15:15; 1 Tim 1:12). Just as there are "varieties of gifts," so there are "varieties of service" (1 Cor 12:4-5).

See also WORSHIP IN THE NEW TESTAMENT; WORSHIP IN THE OLD TESTAMENT.

—ROLLIN S. ARMOUR

• **Seth, Second Treatise of the Great.** The true story of the Savior, Jesus Christ, is purportedly told by him to the "perfect and incorruptible ones" (Christian Gnostics) in the *Second Treatise of the Great Seth,* the second tractate of Codex VII in the NAG HAMMADI library. Its title attributes authorship to Seth, third son of ADAM and EVE (Gen 4:25), who is also claimed as author of other Nag Hammadi tractates: the GOSPEL OF THE EGYPTIANS (NH), THREE STELES OF SETH, and MARSANES. However, the name Seth never reappears in *TreatSeth,* leading some to conclude Christ is actually "Seth Redivivus," dispenser of true *gnosis* ("knowledge").

Having the literary form of a revelation discourse in which the Risen Christ speaks with no intervening questions by his disciples, *TreatSeth* is a Christian Gnostic writing that incorporates strong polemic against developing orthodoxy of the great church. One scholar (Perkins) has found in it a basic pattern of such polemic, including (1) a devaluation of the OT history of salvation, with the ridiculing of heroes from Adam to SOLOMON as having all been duped by the ignorant Archon who inspired them (62.28–65.1). (2) The true Godhead consists of a Trinity, but of Father, Mother (Sophia), and Son (Christ). Yet, Christ is greater than Sophia or any other power (49.10–18). (3) Only a deceiving image and not the spiritual Christ was crucified. In fact, Jesus laughed as Simon of Cyrene was nailed to the Cross in his place (56.4-19). (4) Christ's death had no redemptive significance, and the Pauline doctrine of "dying with Christ" (Rom 6) is viewed as "slavery" of thought (60.15-35; cf. 49.26f.). (5) It is orthodox church members, not the community of pure Gnostics, who are hateful and divisive (59.25–60.6; 62.14-25). On all these points, Gnostic Christians insisted they were right, the church wrong!

The content of *TreatSeth* falls into two parts. In the first (49.10–59.18) we learn about Christ's origins and saving work. He was commissioned by "the whole house of the Father of Truth" to descend to earth to save the spirituals. In that descent Christ encountered world-ruling archons who tried to harm him but failed. He revealed to the "incorruptible ones" that he and they share an essential divine nature with the highest God, which makes them immortal (49.32–50.1; 53.2-5). In redeeming them, Christ redeems himself (cf. 59.9-15). The docetically conceived Christ only appears to suffer and be crucified before reascending to the Pleroma.

In the second part (59.19–70.10) the author replies to orthodox Christians' claim that they represent the true church. These replies have been reviewed above. The "perfect and incorruptible ones" are assured that even though persecuted by "those who think they are advancing the name of Christ" (59.23–26), they have attained "rest" with him forever.

Several things indicate a probable date of late second or early third century C.E. for the tractate: the presence of Basilides' idea that Simon of Cyrene substituted for Jesus in the Crucifixion, the incorporation of a Redeemer myth similar to that of Valentinus, and the stage of anti-orthodox polemic. Author and place of composition remain unknown.

See also GNOSTICISM; NAG HAMMADI.

Bibliography. J. A. Gibbons and R. A. Bullard, "The Second Treatise of the Great Seth," *The Nag Hammadi Library in English,* ed. J. M. Robinson; P. Perkins, *The Gnostic Dialogue: The Early Church and the Crisis of Gnosticism*; K. Rudolph, *Gnosis: The Nature and History of Gnosticism.*

—MALCOLM L. PEEL

• **Seth, Three Steles of.** Insight into the communal worship of an early, non-Christian, Sethian Gnostic group is afforded by the *Three Steles of Seth,* the fifth tractate of Codex VII in the NAG HAMMADI library. This document purports to be the record of hymnic prayers addressed to the Ultimate Deity, the three-part Godhead made up of the Autogenes or "Self-Begotten One" (the Son), the female-male virgin Barbelo (the Mother), and the preexistent One (the Unbegotten Father). These hymns were originally offered by "Emmacha Seth," the eternal archetype of Seth, third son of ADAM (Gen 4:25). Later, the hymns were inscribed on three steles (monumental stone tablets) and hidden away for millenia until revealed to "Dositheus" for transmittal to the "living and invisible race," the Sethian Gnostics (118.1-5).

The background of this literary fiction is a legend recorded by the Jewish historian JOSEPHUS (*Ant* 1.67-71) according to which the descendants of Seth, forewarned of impending judgments by flood and fire, preserved and added to knowledge given Seth by his father Adam. This knowledge was inscribed on steles of stone and brick. The *Three Steles of Seth* increases the number of steles to three.

Scholars disagree over the precise number of hymns or hymnic prayers in the tractate. One proposal (Layton's) is that there are seven: three of praise, one of petition, and three of thanksgiving. Other scholars hold that each stele contains a hymnic prayer addressed in adcending order to the triadic nature of God: the First Stele to Geradamas, "Adamas," the Self-begotten Son (118.10–121.16); the Second Stele to Barbelo, the Mother (121.20–124.14); and the Third Stele to the Unbegotten Father (124.17–126.32). All students of the tractate agree, however, that the transition from hymnic prayer spoken by Seth alone (118.25–120.28) to prayer offered in the first person plural ("we praise you") in the rest of the document indicates the author's intent that it be used as a kind of hymnbook for communal worship.

The concluding section of the document (127.6-27) is spoken by the Dositheus who was introduced as transmitter of the three steles' content in 118.10-14. Whether this is the same Dositheus whom Hegesippus identifies as the Samaritan founder of Gnostic schools is impossible to say. Whatever, the concluding section offers instruction on the use of the hymnic prayers. It is anticipated that in reciting them Sethian worshippers will ascend in spirit to the first, second, and third spheres of the Divine Triad. After a period of silence, they will descend again (127.5-21). Echoing Heraclitus (*Frag* B 90), the author states: "The way of ascent is (like) the way of descent."

The influence of Neoplatonic philosophy on the tractate is pervasive, e.g., in the triadic nature of the Godhead and in the notion of a self-performable act of contemplative mystical ascent toward pure Being. The appearance of commonly-shared terminology in the Nag Hammadi tractates the *Three Steles of Seth,* ZOSTRIANOS, ALLOGENES, and MARSANES indicates all are from the same Sethian Gnostic sphere. Prophyry's report that two of these, *Zostrianos* and *Allogenes,* were refuted by Plotinus in 256–266 C.E. points toward mid-third century and Alexandrian Egypt as the possible time and place of composition.

See also ALLOGENES; GNOSTICISM; MARSANES; NAG HAMMADI; ZOSTRIANOS.

Bibliography. J. E. Goehring and J. M. Robinson, "The Three Steles of Seth," *The Nag Hammadi Library in English,* ed. J. M. Robinson; B. Layton, "The Three Tablets of Seth (3 Tb)," *The Gnostic Scriptures: A New Translation with Annotations and Introductions*; J. D. Turner, "Sethian Gnosticism: A Literary History," *Nag Hammadi, Gnosticism, and Early Christianity,* ed. C. W. Hedrick and R. Hodgson, Jr.

—MALCOLM L. PEEL

• **Seven Words from the Cross.** "Seven Words from the Cross" is the traditional designation for the words Jesus spoke during the CRUCIFIXION. The number seven is derived from the sayings found in all four Gospels. These accounts vary significantly. Matthew (27:46) and Mark(15:34) report the same single utterance; Luke records three different ones (23:34, 43, 46); and John adds three additional ones (19:26-27, 28, 30). Pss 22, 31, and 69 provide the majority of the material for the crucifixion narratives. Although there is no definitive order in which the words occurred, the following is an accepted reconstruction.

(1) "Father, forgive them; for they know not what they do" (Luke 23:34). These words are absent from some ancient manuscripts. If accepted, they express the sublime act of forgiveness in which Jesus prays for all those responsible for his death. Compare Stephen's words at his death (Acts 7:60).

(2) "Truly, I say to you, today you will be with me in Paradise" (Luke 23:43). This remarkable word of promise is spoken by Jesus to one of the criminals crucified with him. According to both Matthew and Mark, this thief had earlier joined the crowd's mocking of Jesus. However, his earnest appeal, "Remember me when you come into your kingdom" (Luke 23:42), provokes Jesus' assurance that the thief will share God's Kingdom.

(3) "Woman, behold your son! . . . Behold your mother!" (John 19:26-27). This was spoken to Jesus' mother and to the unnamed "disciple whom Jesus loved." According to John, the disciple takes Mary to his own home (19:27).

(4) "My God, my God, why hast thou forsaken me?" (Matt 27:46; Mark 15:34). This bewildering cry is a quotation from Ps 22:1 which depicts a sufferer's terrifying anguish. Other verses of the psalm (esp. vv. 7-8, 15, 18) are also pertinent to the crucifixion story. The desperate cry expresses the utter desolation of one who, though innocent, is suffering for the world's sin. The verse must be understood in relation to its context. The entire psalm is a prayer which concludes with profound trust that God answers and delivers. The psalmist asserts that all will "proclaim his deliverance to a people yet unborn, that he has wrought it" (v. 31). It was a prayer which would readily come to the mind of any pious Jew who was suffering. It is also "a psalm which opened up for Christians the true meaning of the Passion in a quite essential way" (Dibelius).

(5) "I thirst" (John 19:28). John suggests that this word was spoken to fulfill scripture (cf. Ps 69:21). The suffering psalmist, however, was given vinegar to aggravate, rather than to relieve, his thirst. Although Jesus' actual words are recorded only by John, the incident of his being offered the vinegar, or sour wine, is related in all the other Gospels.

(6) "It is finished!" (John 19:30). With his death, Jesus has fulfilled God's purpose for his life. This is a shout of victory, not of resigned defeat.

(7) "Father, into thy hands I commit my spirit" (Luke 23:46). This prayer is quoted from the psalm of another sufferer (31:5) with the addition of the prefix "Father." Some scholars suggest that this last word in Luke's record is substituted for the word recorded by Matthew and Mark.

See also CRUCIFIXION.

Bibliography. M. Dibelius, *From Tradition to Gospel*.

—BETTY JEAN SEYMOUR

• **Seven, The.** The Seven is the title employed in Acts 21:8 to describe a group of individuals selected by the church at Jerusalem to oversee the distribution of charitable gifts to poor Christian widows (cf. Acts 6:1-6).

According to Acts, the selection of the Seven was occasioned by complaints from Hellenistic disciples that Hebrew widows were being favored in the "daily service" to the neglect of the Hellenistic widows. THE TWELVE wished to correct the neglect of Hellenistic widows, but not at the expense of their own ministry of proclamation. The apostles proposed that the church choose from their number "seven men of good repute, full of the Spirit and of wisdom, whom we may appoint to this duty" (Acts 6:3).

For this task of administering the fund and assuring fairness, the church chose seven men, all of whom possessed Greek names and are listed in Acts 6:5 as follows: STEPHEN, PHILIP, Prochorus, Nicanor, Timon, Parmenas, and Nicolaus. Stephen is described as "a man full of faith and of the Holy Spirit" and Nicolaus is identified as "a proselyte of Antioch."

The church presented the seven men to the apostles. Prayer and laying on of hands followed, but the agency of these actions is unclear. Some contend that the apostles prayed and ordained the Seven by the gesture of laying on of hands. Others suggest that the text of Acts 6:6 allows for the whole church to be the agent of both procedures. The second position appears more likely in light of Acts 1:15-26, even though the first interpretation has been more widely publicized.

Only Stephen and Philip are mentioned in Acts outside chapter 6, and both are described in activities unrelated to the distribution of alms. Stephen is noted for doing great signs and wonders, his opposition to Jewish particularism, and his subsequent death by stoning. Acts describes Philip as one who was part of the dispersion from Jerusalem upon the persecution of the church. His travels included the region of Samaria, where he proclaimed the good news of Christ to multitudes of Samaritans (Acts 8:4-8), and the coastal plain of Palestine, where he preached to and baptized a eunuch from Ethiopia (Acts 8:26-39). After visiting other cities he established residence in Caesarea. Such missionary activity earned him the title Philip the evangelist. Acts 21:9 adds that he had four unmarried daughters who prophesied. According to Eusebius (*EccHist* 3.31), Papias said that Philip, some years later, migrated with his daughters to the province of Asia where he remained until his death.

The remaining five of the original Seven are never again mentioned in the NT. However, two of the names appear in later Christian tradition. Prochorus, for example, is represented as the amanuensis for John the evangelist, as a bishop in Nicomedia, and later as a martyr in Antioch. Clement of Alexandria refers to a story of Nicolaus's domestic problem of jealousy for his wife. Several church fathers, including Irenaeus, contend that Nicolaus founded the heretical sect of the NICOLAITANS, mentioned first in Rev 2:6, 15.

Traditionally, the Seven have been viewed as the original deacons, but firm evidence for such a conclusion does not appear in the NT. The Seven were never called deacons but the Twelve inferred that their task would be one of service. While later church deacons possessed similar responsibilities to the Seven, no actual connection can be traced between the two groups.

See also DEACON; ORDAIN/ORDINATION IN THE NEW TESTAMENT; PHILIP; STEPHEN.

Bibliography. F. Stagg, *The Book of Acts*; F. F. Bruce, *The Book of Acts*; R. B. Rackham, *The Acts of the Apostles*.

—ROBERT M. SHURDEN

• **Sextus, Sentences of.** [seks'toos] Among the surviving pages of the badly damaged Codex XII from the NAG HAMMADI library are ten containing 113 of the probably 451 original aphorisms that constituted the *Sentences of Sextus*.

This collection of moral maxims and rules for life was known prior to the Nag Hammadi discovery. Our earliest evidence of its existence is its verbatim citation by the Alexandrian church father Origen (ca. 185–254 C.E.) in his defense of the Christian faith against the pagan Celsus (*CCel* 8.30). Although Origen made use of a Christian revision of the document made by an anonymous author near the end of the second century (perhaps Clement of Alexandria), the collection was originally pagan in origin. Its author was the Pythagorean philosopher, Sextus.

The major theme found throughout is how to achieve moral and spiritual perfection. The human ideal is to become "like God" (sentences 44, 45, 48-50, 306, 309, 381). However, life in this world and domination by the body's passions make attainment of this transcendent ideal quite difficult (16, 70-72, 75, 82). So, first it is necessary to help the soul "know itself" (398, 446), to know its origin and present existence in God (21, 55, 83), to know that "man enjoys a higher value in God's sight than the angel" (32).

Religious belief is essential in the soul's quest for perfection, the good life being accessible only to one with faith (196, 215, 400). Under Platonizing influence, the author understands God to be wholly transcendent and indescribable (26, 28, 49, 382). Accordingly, one must be careful in speech about God lest blasphemy result (173, 352-53, 361-62, 366, 407, 451). Yet, this God knows every human thought and deed (21, 22) and is the Judge before whom every soul will one day be accountable (347).

Achieving greatness of soul entails much practice and an ascetic life (78, 120). There must be avoided the distraction and downward pull of the physical world (391), bodily pleasure (139, 172), sexual impulses and lust (230-33, 273), suicide (321), gluttony (108, 109, 111, 265, 435), intoxication (268-69), the love of money (76, 116-17, 137), the values of the mob (112), pride in being a believer (188-89, 433, 444). In turn, the sage will prepare the soul for death (385), purify moral life (102-103), love others in general and sages in particular (331, 353, 372; 219, 226), give alms to the poor (47, 52, 246-47, 330, 371-72), cultivate the spiritual qualities of the sage (8-11, 60, 234, 247, 282, 375, 403). Purified in sinless perfection, the soul is ready to ascend to God, becoming God's "son" (18f., 49f., 306, 309).

The widespread popularity of *SentSextus* is attested by its translation from Greek into Armenian, Syrian, Latin, and Coptic. The translations which represent most faithfully the original are the Latin of Rufinus and the fragmentary Coptic text from Nag Hammadi (XII,*1*). The whole displays the synthesis of Late Stoic and Middle Platonic ideas and espouses an ethic attractive to those seeking to avoid worldliness. It is not Gnostic.

See also NAG HAMMADI.

Bibliography. H. C. Chadwick, *The Sentences of Sextus: A Contribution to the History of Early Christian Ethics* (*Texts and Studies: Contributions to Biblical and Patristic Literature*, ed. C. H. Dodd); F. C. Conybeare, *The Ring of Pope Xystus* (English translation of the *Sentences*); F. Wisse, "The Sentences of Sextus," *The Nag Hammadi Library in English*, ed. J. M. Robinson.

—MALCOLM L. PEEL

• **Shallum.** [shal'uhm] The name of several OT persons. The first Shallum mentioned is the King of Judah (ca. 745 B.C.E.) who came to the throne when he assassinated Zechariah, son of JEROBOAM II, thus bringing the Jehu dynasty to an end. He was himself slain after a reign of one month (2 Kgs 15:10-15).

Shallum was the fourth son of JOSIAH, who succeeded his father to the throne in 609 B.C.E. when he was declared king by "the people of the land." He was also called Jehoahaz. He ruled three months until he was deported to Egypt by Pharaoh NECHO (1 Chr 3:15; 2 Kgs 23:30-34; Jer 22:10-12).

The father of Hilkiah, the priest who found a law book in the Temple during the reign of Josiah, was also named Shallum (1 Chr 6:12,13).

Another Shallum was an uncle of Jeremiah, whose son instructed the prophet to buy a field to symbolize hope for Judah's future beyond the time when the land had been overrun by Babylon (Jer 32:6-8).

Two Shallums were among those who had married foreign wives but divorced them during the EZRA period (Ezra 10:24, 42). Two other persons by the same name are mentioned as aides in repairing JERUSALEM's postexilic fortifications (Neh 3:12, 15).

Other persons bearing the same name, about whom little is known, include the husband of HULDAH, a woman prophet (2 Kgs 22:14); a son of Sismai (1 Chr 2:40, 41); an offspring of Bilhah (1 Chr 7:13); a grandson of Simeon (1 Chr 4:25); a father of Jehizkiah (2 Chr 28:12); a Levite chief gatekeeper of the Tabernacle (1 Chr 9:17, 31); and a Temple officer (Jer 35:4).

—ROBERT W. CRAPPS

Courtesy of the Eisenberg Museum of Biblical Archaeology, Southern Baptist Theological Seminary.

The Black Obelisk of Shalmaneser III.

• **Shalmaneser.** [shal'muh-nee"zuhr] Shalmaneser is the name of at least five Assyrian kings, only two of whom relate to biblical studies and will be included in this article.

Shalmaneser III ruled ASSYRIA from 858 to 824 B.C.E. He continued the expansion of Assyria initiated by his father Ashur-naṣir-apli II especially into Syria and Palestine. This Assyrian intrusion into Syria-Palestine led to a coalition of Aramean, Phoenician and Israelite states against Assyria. In 853 B.C.E., the armies of this coalition fought Shalmaneser in the battle of QARQAR on the Orontes River. In the Kurkh Stele, Shalmaneser claims to have been victorious. Among the armies listed on the stele is that of Ahab of Israel consisting of 2,000 chariots and 10,000 infantry. On another stele dating to about 841 B.C.E., the Black Obelisk found at NIMRUD/CALAH, Shalmaneser records thirty-one military campaigns to areas as far away as Cilicia, the Mediterranean, Media, Babylon, and the Persian Gulf. He describes particular campaigns against Adad-Idri of Damascus (probably Ben Hadad of 2 Kgs 6:24 and 8:7) and Hazael of Damascus (2 Kgs 9:14; 10:32). Related more closely to Israel's history is a reference on the Black Obelisk to tribute paid by JEHU, son of Omri, including silver and gold. Although Jehu was not related to Omri, and indeed had destroyed the Omride dynasty, this inscription shows the importance of Omri to the Assyrians.

Shalmaneser V was the son of TILGATH-PILESER III who succeeded him to the throne in 722/1 B.C.E. Shalmaneser ruled only five years, but in that time led two military campaigns to the area of Syria-Palestine. Shalmaneser V knew the territory well, for he had as crown prince been responsible for that area. After his first incursion into the region in 726 B.C.E., HOSHEA, king of Israel, paid tribute and became his vassal. A rebellion against Assyria by Israel and Phoenicia only a few years later brought Shalmaneser to the region again. This time Hoshea was imprisoned. Shalmaneser began a siege of Samaria which lasted two years. Both the Babylonian Chronicle and the Bible (2 Kgs 17:6) record that Shalmaneser took Samaria in 722 B.C.E. But his death, apparently by assassination, left the final fate of Samaria unclear for a couple years. SARGON II, who succeeded Shalmaneser, retook the city and exiled the populace about 720 B.C.E., bringing the Northern Kingdom to an end.

—JOEL F. DRINKARD, JR.

• **Shalom.** *See* PEACE; REST

• **Shame** The feeling or condition associated with humiliation, disgrace, and dishonor resulting from such things as laziness (Prov 10:5), pride (Prov 11:2), refusing direction (Prov 13:18), failure in discipline (Prov 29:15), ignoring of custom (1 Cor 11:6, 14), defeat and enslavement (Isa 20:3-4), or pagan worship (Jer 3:24-25; 13:1-11, 25-27).

The OT writers pointed to pagan worship as the chief source of shame for God's people. Their unfaithfulness among the nations brought upon them the humiliation they thought was reserved for their enemies. The result was national defeat and exile (Ezek 7:18). Although that humiliation ended for Israel, it was for the NT writers to speak of a permanent solution to the shame of sin. They asserted that those who trusted in God would never be put to shame (Rom 9:33; 10:11). The source of their confidence was Jesus' shame-filled death for our sins (Heb 12:2).

—WALTER E. BROWN

• **Shaphan.** [shay'fuhn] Shaphan the son of Azaliah was a scribe under JOSIAH, king of Judah. Sent to oversee payments to workers renovating the Temple, he returned with "the book of the law" found in the Temple by HILKIAH the priest (2 Kgs 22:3-10). Shaphan read this scroll, generally associated with an early form of the present book of DEUTERONOMY, before the king. He was then sent as one of Josiah's emissaries to HULDAH the prophetess for verification of the judgment announced in the LAW (2 Kgs 22:11-20). Shaphan was the father of Ahikam (2 Kgs 22:12), who saved Jeremiah from the crowd after his Temple sermon (Jer 26:24). He may have been the same Shaphan named as the father of Gemariah in whose chamber Jeremiah's scroll was read (Jer 36:10) and of Elasah who carried Jeremiah's letter to the exiles in Babylon (Jer 29:3).

Shaphan is also the name of the father of Jaazaniah (Ezek 8:11).

—JEFFREY S. ROGERS

• **Sheba, Queen of.** [shee'buh] The Queen of Sheba was one of SOLOMON's famous international contacts (1 Kgs 10:1-13; cf. Matt 12:42). The plausible story of her encounter with Solomon has been greatly (and implausibly) elaborated in Christian, Jewish, and Islamic traditions. The Ethiopian national saga *Kebra Negast* traces its monarchy back to Menelik I, the son of Solomon born to the Queen of Sheba.

All the later developments are dependent upon the OT story. Aside from the observation that OT riddles did sometimes exploit double entendre (cf. Judg 14:10-18; Prov 30:18-19), it may be suggested that two statements prompted the elaborations: (1) The queen "came to Solomon" (1 Kgs 10:2b), and (2) "King Solomon gave to the queen of Sheba all that she desired" (1 Kgs 10:13a).

See also ETHIOPIA; SOLOMON.

—JOHN KEATING WILES

• **Shebna.** *See* JUDAH, KINGDOM OF

• **Shechem.** [shek'uhm] The Shechem of biblical and ancient sources has been located at the ten-acre mound of Tell Balâtah, east of Nablus in the MOUNT GERIZIM-MOUNT EBAL pass (PLATE 11) since E. Thiersch's identification in 1904. It was excavated by the Germans under E. Sellin, G. Welther, and others in 1913–1914 and 1926–1934, and again for the American Joint Expedition in 1956–1973 under G. E. Wright, E. F. Campbell, L. E. Tombs, J. D. Seger, and W. G. Dever. The American excavations were important not only for redating, salvaging, and supplementing the remains uncovered by the earlier excavations, but also because Shechem became a training ground for the first postwar generation of American archaeologists. In particular, modern British stratigraphic methods were adopted, and ceramic chronology in the tradition of W. F. Albright was significantly refined.

Shechem is first mentioned in the Egyptian "Execration Texts" of ca. 1800 B.C.E. The archaeological evidence confirms the founding of the city then, in the Middle Bronze IIA Period. An area of courtyard structures surrounded by Wall D, perhaps a sacred precinct, has been connected by some with the patriarchal traditions (i.e., Gen 12:6; Gen 34; etc.). Shechem reached its urban zenith somewhat later, in the Middle Bronze IIB-C Period (ca. 1750–1500 B.C.E.). It then boasted a huge embankment (or *glacis*-like fill), surrounded by cyclopean wall A, topped by partially casemated wall B, and equipped with a two-entryway East Gate and a splendid three-entryway Northwest Gate. Just inside the latter was found the finest example of urban planning in Middle Bronze Age Palestine, consisting of a multiroomed barracks north of the gate; a two-story palace and adjoining royal chapel south of the gate; a large plastered piazza; and nearby a massive public *migdal* (or tower) temple with walls some seventeen feet thick. The royal chapel is a tripartite long-room temple, the earliest known Palestinian prototype of the Solomonic temple; and the migdal temple closely parallels contemporary temples at Ebla in Syria, as well as at Megiddo and elsewhere in Palestine. No fewer than three Egyptian destructions between ca. 1550–1500 B.C.E. end the site's early history.

During the Late Bronze Age (ca. 1500–1200 B.C.E.) Shechem was reoccupied. Indeed, it became a principal city-state of Palestine, as we know from the AMARNA letters found in Egypt, which mention several of Shechem's kings, including the notorious troublemaker Labayu. The rebuilt *migdal* temple dates to this period, as well as several other impressive structures, but the defenses seem not to have been extensively repaired.

In confirmation with the biblical tradition that Shechem entered the Israelite confederation by treaty (Judg 8, 9; Josh 24), no destruction layer was found at the end of the Late Bronze and the beginning of the Iron Age ca. 1200 B.C.E. Of particular importance is the fact that the Late Bronze Age *migdal* temple continued in use without interruption into the early twelfth century B.C.E., with only additions in the forecourt consisting of an unhewn slab-like altar, and one large and two small *mazzbôth* (or stelae) nearby. Wright had seen in this reused temple the actual "Temple of El-Berith" (Judg 9:46; cf. 9:4, "Temple of Baal-berith"), as well as the setting for the well known covenant renewal ceremony of Josh 24. The final destruction of this temple in the mid-twelfth century B.C.E., and its subsequent conversion into a granary in the ninth-eighth century B.C.E., would then be connected with the rebellion of ABIMELECH (Judg 9).

In the period of the Divided Monarchy, in Iron II, the principal defensive remains are alterations to the towers of the East Gate, possibly the work of JEROBOAM (I Kgs 12:25), and a ninth-eighth century B.C.E. rebuilding of casemate Wall B at the Northwest Gate. Domestic structures include a large granary (above), and a fine example of a characteristically "Israelite" type of courtyard house (House 1727) in Field VII that exhibits dramatic evidence of the Assyrian destructions ca. 734–722 B.C.E. There are the third-second century B.C.E. Hellenistic remains when Shechem became the center for the Samaritan sect. Fine houses on the site are complemented by the remains of the Samaritan temple itself, found by the American team below a Roman temple on the lower summit of Mount Gerizim, overlooking the mound. The final destruction of the site occurred during the campaigns of John Hyrcanus ca. 107 B.C.E. The city was devastated and actually obliterated from memory by being buried under deep fills that obscured its exact location until the twentieth century. Its place was taken by Roman Neapolis (modern Nablus), a few miles west in the pass.

See also EBAL, MOUNT; GERIZIM, MOUNT.

Bibliography. R. J. Bull, *BA* 31 (1968): 58-72; W. G. Dever, "The MB II Stratification in the Northwest Gate Area at Shechem," *BASOR* 216 (1974): 31-52; G. E. Wright, *Shechem. The Biography of a Biblical City* and "Shechem," *EAEHL*.

—WILLIAM G. DEVER

• **Sheep.** A docile, herbivorous mammal domesticated and raised for its wool, milk, meat, and hide. Sheep are mentioned more than 500 times in the Bible, an indication of the importance of sheep in Palestinian life. In addition to providing food and clothing materials, sheep were also used as religious sacrifices (Lev 1:10; 22:19; Num 18:17; 1 Kgs 8:5). A roasted lamb was the major component of the Passover meal (Exod 12:3-10).

The relationship between sheep and SHEPHERD served as an analogy for biblical writers of the relation between the people and their leaders (Num 27:17; 1 Kgs 22:17; Jer 23:1-4; 25:34-38; 50:6; Ezek 34:2-10; Zech 10:2-3; Mark 6:34) or, more significantly, of the relation between the people and God (Isa 40:11; Jer 31:10; Ezek 34). Ps 23 uses this imagery in a masterful way to affirm the care and safety which God provides for the psalmist. Jesus' parable of the shepherd who searches for the one lost sheep graphically portrays the depth of God's love (Matt 18:12-14; Luke 15:3-7).

The most extensive uses of the sheep/shepherd imagery are in Ezek 34 and John 10. Ezekiel condemns the leaders of Israel as shepherds who look out for themselves, rather than for their sheep. God will rescue the sheep and will serve as their shepherd, binding their wounds, feeding them, and healing the sick. In John 10, Jesus uses the same imagery to denounce the religious leaders of his day who have served as hirelings, not as true shepherds. Jesus himself is the good shepherd who knows his sheep and even gives up his life for them.

Other NT passages, in a different use of the sheep imagery, portray Jesus as a lamb or sheep (John 1:29, 36; 1 Pet 1:19; Rev 5:6–6:1; 14:1-5; 19:7-9).

See also SHEPHERD.

—MITCHELL G. REDDISH

• **Shekinah.** [shuh-ki'nuh] A term meaning dwelling or resting. Although the term is not found in the Bible, its root *šākan* (dwell) occurs frequently. The rabbinic literature employed it to speak of the numinous nearness of GOD, and in some instances as a synonym for God. Some writers imagined the *shekinah* to be a light, like a visible glory, hovering above the Temple or over the people ISRAEL, or lingering near those who prayed or studied the Jewish LAW. It is also illustrated by wings enclosing MOSES at his burial, a sea flooding a cave, or a light more intense than the sun. Throughout, *shekinah* was understood figuratively, and not as a separate aspect or entity of God. Later, during the medieval period, some Jewish writers considered the *shekinah* a separate entity, like created light, rather than as a figurative reference to God.

The OT presents images of God similar to the *shekinah*. To these belong the pillars of cloud and fire hovering above the people at the Exodus, and later over the tent of meeting and the Tabernacle (Exod 13:21-22; 33:9; 40:38), the name of God dwelling in the sanctuary (Deut 12:5), enthronement of God on or above the cherubim affixed to the ARK of the Covenant (1 Sam 4:4; 2 Sam 6:2; 2 Kgs 19:15), the GLORY of God moving from the Temple (Ezek 9:3; 10:18; 11:22) to the captives in Babylon (Ezek 1) and returning to the Temple after its restoration (Ezek 43:1-5).

The NT identifies Jesus Christ as the divine presence dwelling among his followers (Matt 18:20; John 1:14) and embodying all the glory of God (2 Cor 4:4; Col 1:27; Heb 1:3).

See also GLORY; MYSTERY; PRESENCE.

—NIELS-ERIK A. ANDREASEN

• **Shem.** Name or reputation; the oldest son of Noah and brother of Ham and Japheth (Gen 5:32; 6:10; 1 Chr 1:4). Shem and his wife along with his mother, father, brothers and their wives, were the only humans who survived the flood (Gen 7:13). Then, on one occasion when Noah became drunk, Shem and his brother Japheth covered their father's nakedness (Gen 9:20-23). As a result of this incident, his nephew (Ham's son) Canaan, was condemned to be the servant of Shem and his brother Japheth (Gen 9:26-27). Two years later, when he was approximately one hundred years old, Shem became the father of a son named Arpachshad (Gen 11:10), who became an ancestor of the Chaldeans. It was also this son through whom the line of descent later passed to Abraham and to Jesus (Luke 3:36). After the birth of Arpachshad, Shem lived another 500 years, during which time he had at least four other sons: Elam, an ancestor of the Elamites; Asshur, an ancestor of the Assyrians; Lud, an ancestor of the Lydians; and Aram, an ancestor of the Syrians (Gen 10:21-31). Since many of these descendants used related languages, these languages and the people who used them have become known as "semitic." However, caution must be urged, for it is not yet known if all his descendants spoke one of these languages or other closely related languages.

See also NOAH; SEMITES; SEMITIC LANGUAGES.

Bibliography. H. G. Stigers, *A Commentary on Genesis.*

—HARRY B. HUNT, JR.

• **Shem, Paraphrase of.** The *Paraphrase of Shem* is a Gnostic writing from the NAG HAMMADI library. It is a long document—almost fifty pages of Coptic text—and well-preserved. Its genre is similar to those apocalypses that contain a rapture of the visionary to heaven. In *Paraphrase of Shem,* SHEM's mind separates from his body and ascends to the top of the world where, in a sleep-like state, he receives a revelation. The revealer's name is Derdekeas, "the son of the incorruptible, infinite Light." The revelation describes the origins of the world, the salvation of the race of Shem, and the end of the world. The logic of the title *Paraphrase of Shem* is unclear. There is mention of "the paraphrase," but it occurs late in the text, introduces only a brief section, and is spoken by Derdekeas, not Shem. "The paraphrase" seems to refer to a list of characters who play a role in the cosmic drama and whose names must be memorized and recited at the time of one's final ascent.

Derdekeas describes to Shem the three great powers or "roots" that existed in the beginning: Light, Darkness, and Spirit, which is between Light and Darkness. The peaceful co-existence of the powers is disrupted when Darkness realizes that he is inferior to Spirit and makes a vain attempt at equality by stealing the light from Spirit. The status of Spirit is ambiguous. It belongs on the side of Light, yet it is not incorruptible and needs redemption (the fall of Spirit is hinted at in our text). Darkness is also an ethically ambiguous power. It is evil and "crooked" but its mind is redeemable. Derdekeas feels pity for the light of the Spirit that Darkness has taken, so he descends into the realm of Darkness in order to save both the light of the Spirit and the mind of Darkness. Derdekeas puts on various garments in his descent through the hostile sphere, one of which is called "the beast" and seems to represent the body. These garments disguise and protect him. Derdekeas's rescue effort includes the creation of heaven and earth (other Gnostic sources spell out more clearly how creation is a necessary step in the salvation process because it concentrates the fallen light particles in human beings where they can be freed). Derdekeas's salvific work is completed by his revelation to the Shemites of this drama and of their elect status as descendants of the light of Spirit. Thus, Derdekeas is both revealer and redeemer.

The church father Hippolytus speaks of a text that sounds very similar to *Paraphrase of Shem* in his description of Sethian Gnosticism. He calls it *Paraphrase of Seth.* It is likely that the text, *Paraphrase of Shem,* represents some form of the text known to Hippolytus. But the date and origin of this text is difficult to determine. Some scholars see the text as evidence for a pre-Christian, Gnostic redeemer myth that influenced NT Christology (cf., for instance, 1 Cor 2:6ff.). Others see evidence in the text of interactions with early Christian thought, especially in the use of the word *pistis* (faith) and the polemic against water baptism. Also debated is the Jewish nature of *Paraphrase of Shem* and thus the question of the origins of GNOSTICISM. There are mentions of SODOM, the flood, and the TOWER OF BABEL, as well as allusions to the Genesis creation stories, but these are not central, well integrated parts of the myth and may have been added secondarily. Other important Nag Hammadi texts in the discussion of non-Christian, Jewish Gnosticism are the APOCALYPSE OF ADAM, THREE STELES OF SETH, and the TESTIMONY OF TRUTH. The *Paraphrase of Shem* also bears similarities to the Hermetic document *Poimandres.*

See also APOCALYPTIC LITERATURE; GNOSTICISM; NAG HAMMADI.

Bibliography. J. M. Robinson, ed. *Jewish Gnostic Nag Hammadi Texts*; F. Wisse, "The Paraphrase of Shem," *The Nag Hammadi Library in English*, ed. J. M. Robinson and "The Redeemer Figure in the Paraphrase of Shem," *NovT* 12 (1970): 130-40; E. Yamauchi, *Pre-Christian Gnosticism.*

—CAROL D. C. HOWARD

• **Shem, Treatise of.** The *Treatise of Shem* characterizes the events of a year according to the sign of the Zodiac in which the year began. Its predictions focus on the ways in which nature and humanity will be affected due to the zodiacal character of any particular year. The document follows the twelve signs of the Zodiac in a counterclockwise fashion, although the last two signs (Pisces and Aquarius) have been reversed, quite possibly as the result of a scribal error.

The *Treatise* is extant in only one manuscript and has only recently received significant attention. The manuscript is in Syriac and dates from the fifteenth century. The original language, however, seems to have been Aramaic, and the internal evidence points to an Alexandrian provenance after the conflict between Anthony and Octavian (first century B.C.E.). The manuscript has been attributed to Shem by its author, most likely to take advantage of the reputation of Noah's eldest son as one loved, blessed, and taught by Noah.

This document adds an important piece to the puzzle of Jewish astrological interest. Until recently scholars had no reason to note any Jewish interest in ASTROLOGY until the period of medieval Jewish mysticism. But with the increased interest in this treatise and the discovery of two astrological documents within the DEAD SEA SCROLLS, such interest in astrology must be seen as current among Jews during the time of Jesus. The *Treatise of Shem* is important because it clarifies the nature of late B.C.E. Judaism and may offer clues for the interpretation of some biblical texts.

See also ASTROLOGY.

Bibliography. J. H. Charlesworth, *The Pseudepigrapha in Modern Research* and "The Treatise of Shem," *The Old Testament Pseudepigrapha,* ed. J. H. Charlesworth.

—STEVEN SHEELEY

• **Shema.** [shuh'mah] To "hear" describes a certain, perhaps pleasant sound (Ps 150:5) and elsewhere a hearing or report (1 Kgs 10:1; Job 42:5). However, its best known occurrence is Deut 6:4 in the expression: "Hear, O Israel, the Lord our God is one Lord," or "the Lord is our God; the Lord is one."

Referred to as the *shema* (from the first word, *shema,* "hear"), this expression became in early Judaism a confession of faith. The Nash papyrus (second century B.C.E.) includes the *shema* with the TEN COMMANDMENTS in what must have been a liturgical text. Later, by the second century C.E., the *shema* was enlarged to consist of three parts (Deut 6:4-9; 11:13-21; Num 15:37-41). According to Jewish tradition, the *shema* should be recited morning and evening as a part of the prayers. That practice was extended to other occasions, such as the Sabbath service and the festivals, especially the Day of Atonement on the tenth day of the seventh month. Some practiced its recitation after having gone to bed and just after rising, according to the instruction: "When you lie down, and when you rise" (Deut 6:7).

By means of the *shema* Judaism has affirmed its belief in one God over against both ancient polytheism and Christian trinitarianism. But reciting the *shema* also expresses personal devotion to God and willingness on the part of the worshiper to accept responsibility for the ethical principles of the law, both in the present as well as in the future, through religious instruction of the children.

Shema also occurs in the OT as the name of a descendant of Hebron in the family of Caleb (1 Chr 2:43), of a Reubenite (1 Chr 5:8), of a Benjaminite hero (1 Chr 8:13), of a warrior in King David's army (1 Chr 11:44), and of an associate of Ezra (Neh 8:4). In addition, a town in southern Judah bore the name Shema (Josh 15:26).

See also MONOTHEISM.

—NIELS-ERIK A. ANDREASEN

• **Shemoneh 'esreh.** *See* BENEDICTIONS, EIGHTEEN

• **Sheol.** [shee'ohl] Sheol, variously translated as "grave," "pit," or "abode of the dead," is the OT word for the underworld or unseen world of the dead where departed spirits go (Prov 9:18).

In Sheol, people existed as "shades" in a world of misery and futility. It was a place of stillness, darkness, powerlessness, and inactivity. It was a land of forgetfulness where God's wonders were unknown. Since people were thought to be separated from God in Sheol, it was greatly feared by the living.

In certain poetic and prophetic works, the term "Sheol" is used simply to refer to the depths of the earth (cf. Deut 32:22; Amos 9:2).

In the NT Hades is used for Sheol. Hades (as Sheol in the OT) is the abode of the dead. The saying of the risen Christ that he has "the keys of Death and Hades" (Rev 1:18), therefore, means that Christ has power over life and death. In Luke 16:23 alone is Hades presented as a place of torment. GEHENNA is the word commonly used by the NT for the place of punishment after death.

See also DEATH; GEHENNA; HELL.

—ROBERT RAINWATER

• **Shepherd.** The keeper and protector of the flock in the ancient pastoral culture of the biblical lands, the shepherd became a primary metaphor for God as caretaker for his people, the king as leader and protector of the nation, or the priest as spiritual leader of the covenant community.

All theological language is rooted in analogy, applying familiar terms from everyday life to the spiritual relation with God. No term had richer possibilities for this use than did the term "shepherd." Everyone knew the role of the shepherd and many had been shepherds. All the aspects of leadership, authority, protection, nurture, and rescue of the flock applied to the divine shepherd and his flock.

In the OT. When Moses was warned of his impending death, his concern for Israel led him to cry out to God "that the congregation of the Lord may not be as SHEEP which have no shepherd" (Num 27:17). This image of the sheep scattered because they have no shepherd is the most common use of the term in the OT. It is used to warn the people and rebuke the faithless shepherds of the people, beginning in the Pentateuch and running throughout the prophetic books to the end of the OT. Isaiah, Jeremiah, and Ezekiel use the image of careless and irresponsible shepherds repeatedly as they indict the leaders of the people.

The image of God as shepherd of his people reaches a climax in Ps 23, a hymn attributed to David, the shepherd king, who, as a shepherd boy had conquered the mighty Goliath. In a sustained metaphor of incomparable beauty, the heavenly shepherd is depicted as caring for his flock throughout their lives, through the valley of the shadow of death, and even beyond in the "house of the Lord for ever." It is difficult to exaggerate the influence of this powerful imagery upon the worshipers in Israel, the early Christians who saw in Jesus the "good shepherd," and upon Christian hymns and art throughout 2,000 years.

The magnificent oracle of Isa 40:11 adds even more intimate details of the heavenly shepherd who will feed his flock, gather the little lambs and carry them in his bosom, and gently lead those that have their young. Such powerful images of a caring, compassionate God overrode all concepts of a harsh and distant deity and gave the biblical people a readiness for intimate fellowship with a God who loved them. It is a truly amazing revelation of the nature of God, shocking in comparison to the religions of antiquity, and contrasting with some leading world religions of today.

The command to Jeremiah and Ezekiel to prophesy against the shepherds of Israel (Jer 23:1; Ezek 34:2) sets up the biblical standard of accountability for religious leaders in both the OT and NT. They have a greater responsibility, and their dereliction will receive a greater punishment. Shepherds are condemned for feeding themselves, rather than the flock (Ezek 34:2); for clothing themselves with wool and slaughtering the fat sheep (Ezek 34:3); for failing to strengthen and heal the sick sheep (Ezek 34:4); for failing to bring back the straying sheep (Ezek 34:4); and leaving them scattered through all the hills and mountains as prey for every wild beast (Ezek 34:5). Contrasting with the high example of God as a caring shepherd, this conduct of unfaithful shepherds of the spiritual flock stands as a warning throughout the whole of scripture.

In the NT. With such a rich background, it was natural that early Christians poured this shepherd imagery into their portrait of Jesus and their expectation of the spiritual leaders in the Christian church.

Born in the city of David, the shepherd king, and announced to the shepherds in the surrounding hills, Jesus was surrounded by the shepherd imagery from the beginning. His own love for the shepherd role is seen in John 10, a chapter which epitomizes the behavior of the good shepherd: he is recognized by the doorkeeper and enters by the door rather than by stealth (10:1-3); he calls every sheep by name and they recognize his voice (10:3); he goes before and leads his sheep (10:3); he is the door of the sheep, for by him they have access to the safety and protection of the fold. It is easy to see the blending of the beautiful language of Ps 23 and the compassionate shepherd of Isa 40, as the pictures in stained glass windows, in art galleries the world around, and the verbal images of a thousand hymns flood the mind.

Jesus used another of the OT warnings about the flock without a shepherd as he prepared his disciples for his death and departure: "I will smite the shepherd and the sheep will be scattered" (Matt 26:31; Mark 14:27). Whereas the smiting of the OT shepherds was in punishment for their unfaithfulness, it was the very faithfulness of Jesus to the purpose of God which would take him away and leave them shepherdless.

It was exactly this need of carrying on the ministry of the good shepherd which extended the shepherd image to the Christian ministers and leaders of the Christian flock. Jesus used such language in urging Peter to feed his sheep and lambs (John 21:16ff.). To the elders of the church of Ephesus who met him in Miletus, Paul pleaded: "Take heed to yourselves and to all the flock, in which the Holy Spirit has made you guardians [bishops], to feed [shepherd] the church of the Lord . . . " (Acts 20:28). Interestingly, the terms "elder" and "bishop" became titles of ministerial offices in the NT, while "shepherd" (or the Latin equivalent, "pastor") never did. Instead, "pastor" denoted the function of caring for the flock, rather than the title of office. The persistence of the term "pastor" in modern Christian ministry should be a reminder that in biblical use the term carries the meaning of a caring, compassionate shepherd, not the authority of hierarchical office.

See also SHEEP.

Bibliography. V. Taylor, *The Names of Jesus*; J. Jeremias, "ποιμήν, κτλ.," *TDNT*; T. W. Manson, *The Church's Ministry*; C. J. Gadd, *Ideas of Divine Rule in the Ancient East*; C. H. Dodd, *The Interpretation of the Fourth Gospel*.

—WAYNE E. WARD

• **Shiloh.** [shi'loh] The ancient town of Shiloh is located at modern Khirbet Seilun, about ten mi. north of Bethel in the Central Hill Country (PLATE 13). Shiloh lay approximately half way between BETHEL and SHECHEM. It was one of the central sanctuaries where the ARK of the Covenant was kept during the period of the Confederacy.

Shiloh was the site where the TENT OF MEETING was set up after the tribes entered Canaan (Josh 18:1). There JOSHUA apportioned the land among the seven tribes who had not already received their allotment (Josh 18–19). There too the cities of refuge and the levitical cities were allotted (Josh 20–21). At first Eleazar was priest at Shiloh (Josh 21:1-2), later the family of Eli served as priests there (1 Sam 1-4). Shiloh was the central shrine for the Ark of the Covenant during the time of Eli and Samuel, until the Ark was captured by the Philistines (1 Sam 1–4).

It is often assumed that Shiloh was destroyed by the Philistines shortly after the capture of the Ark, but this is not stated specifically by the text. Jeremiah does refer to the destruction of Shiloh (Jer 7:12; 26:6), but no time frame is mentioned. He assumes the hearers are aware that Shiloh has been destroyed. Shiloh still existed at the time of Jeroboam I, for it is the home of Ahijah the prophet who appears several times in the account of Jeroboam (1 Kgs 11:29; 12:15; 14:2-4).

Excavations have been carried out at Khirbet Seilun by Danish teams led by A. Schmidt (1915), H. Kjaer (1926–1932), S. Holm-Nielson (1963), and since 1981 by Israeli archaeologists led by I. Finkelstein of Bar-Ilan University. The site was heavily fortified in the Middle Bronze Age II period, eighteenth century B.C.E., having a thick defensive wall and a sloping glacis. Surprisingly, apart from some storage rooms, no buildings belonging to this Middle Bronze period have been found. However a number of Middle Bronze finds have been made, including cult stands, votive objects, silver and bronze jewelry and weapons. Following a major destruction, possibly by the Egyptians after the expulsion of the Hyksos, there are only limited Late Bronze remains at Shiloh. The site was abandoned during the later part of the Late Bronze Age. An Iron I settlement followed. Some of the excavated structures belonging to this period were houses actually built into the Middle Bronze glacis. Many silos and cisterns were found which also belong to this period. Pottery finds from Shiloh in the Iron I are among the richest of any site in Israel. This settlement was destroyed with massive burning, perhaps the destruction attributed to the Philistines. Rather extensive Iron II remains were found after which the site was abandoned until the Hellenistic-Roman period. There was widespread occupation during the Roman and Byzantine periods, after which the site lost its importance and was finally abandoned. From the Byzantine period two churches of the fifth and sixth centuries C.E. were uncovered. These churches were decorated with mosaic floors.

—JOEL F. DRINKARD, JR.

• **Shimei.** [shim'ee-*i*] The name of nineteen different OT men. The name occurs most frequently among the descendants of LEVI, beginning with Levi's grandson (or great grandson, cf. Exod 6:16-17 and 1 Chr 6:42-43). During the early monarchy in Israel, a number of persons bore this name, including DAVID's brother (2 Sam 21:21), one of David's "mighty men" (1 Kgs 1:8), and the officer in charge of David's vineyards (1 Chr 27:27).

The most frequently mentioned Shimei in the biblical narratives was a Benjaminite of the house of SAUL. Shimei cursed David for his treatment of Saul's descendants, calling ABSALOM's rebellion a punishment of God for David's bloodshed. David refused to punish Shimei (2 Sam 16:5-13). After Absalom's death, Shimei welcomed David back to the throne and extracted from David an oath that David would not take his life (2 Sam 19:16-23).

In his deathbed charge to SOLOMON, David remembered his oath to Shimei and urged Solomon not to let Shimei go unpunished. Solomon pledged to Shimei that as long as he stayed in Jerusalem he would live. Three years later, after Shimei left the city, Solomon had him killed. With Shimei's death, opposition to the Davidic monarchy from the house of Saul ended (1 Kgs 2).

See also ABSALOM; CURSE AND BLESSING; DAVID; SOLOMON.

—MICHAEL FINK

• **Shinar.** *See* SUMERIA/SUMERIAN

• **Ship.** Ancient ships were built by those people whose lives were in some way directly affected by the sea or major navigational streams. For this reason, the Israelites were not involved in the major developments of ship building and navigation as were the inhabitants of Mesopotamia, Egypt, Phoenicia, Greece, and Rome. In the ancient world, ships played an important role in at least two areas, transportation and naval battles.

Ships in the Ancient Near East. The earliest attempts at waterborne transportation, in the two major centers of civilization, Mesopotamia and Egypt, date back to the Neolithic period with major developments coming during the fourth and third millennium B.C.E. These developments were prompted by the navigational streams present in the two lands, the TIGRIS and EUPHRATES Rivers as well as numerous canals in Mesopotamia, and the NILE River in Egypt. The earliest vessels included rafts and boats constructed of reeds or inflated animal skins. The crafts were propelled by poles, paddles, or someone towing the craft from the river bank. About 3500 B.C.E. the mast and sail began to appear on boats in Mesopotamia enabling the vessels to harness wind power. By the middle of the third millennium B.C.E. sail driven ships moved beyond local water-ways and engaged in overseas trade, the ships of Mesopotamia in the Persian Gulf and Indian Ocean, and ships of Egypt in the Mediterranean Sea. Warships were equipped with banks of oars to insure maneuverability with the more elaborate vessels designed with as many as three and four such banks.

Of the ship builders in the ancient world, the PHOENICIANS are ranked among the very best. With abundant timber resources in the Lebanon mountains, the Phoenicians, who were very active merchants, developed not only a major ship building industry, but also established major shipping routes in the Mediterranean Sea. The fame achieved by the port cities of BYBLOS, TYRE, and SIDON was due in great degree to the maritime activities of the Phoenicians.

Ships in the OT. Several Hebrew terms for ship are found in the OT including *oniyyah,* a large merchant ship (2 Chr 9:21), *sephinah,* a large ship with a deck (Jonah 1:5), and *tsi,* a warship (Num 24:24). While the Israelites were not a seafaring people, there were those occasions when they were engaged in sea traffic. According to the Song of Deborah the tribes of Dan, Asher, and Zebulun were probably involved in some type of maritime activities on the Mediterranean Sea (Judg 5:17-18). But it was Solomon who attempted to establish the shipping industry as one of the major industries of the land, a project for which he called upon the expertise of the Phoenicians. With assistance from Hiram, king of Tyre, Solomon established a ship building industry at the site of Ezion-geber located at the upper end of the gulf of Aqaba (1 Kgs 9:26), and with the assistance of Hiram's sailors operated a fleet of ships in the Red Sea (1 Kgs 9:27-28). Perhaps operating several fleets from that port, Solomon carried on trade with distant places such as Ophir, from which he brought gold (1 Kgs 9:28), and Tarshish, from which he imported "gold, silver, ivory, apes, and peacocks" (1 Kgs 10:22). Apparently, Jehoshaphat, king of Judah, attempted to revive the shipping industry, but was met with defeat when the fleet wrecked near the harbor at Ezion-geber (1 Kgs 22:4). Ezekiel's lament over the fall of Tyre, the great Phoenician seaport trade center (Ezek 27:12-25), includes a unique description of Phoenician ships and some of the major terms related to that industry (Ezek 27:25-36).

Ships in the NT. The NT terms for ships and boats include *naus* (Acts 27:41), a large merchant ship, *ploion* (Matt 14:22; Acts 27:6), a ship or boat either large or small, *ploiarion* (Mark 3:9), perhaps originally used for smaller boats, and *skaphe* (Acts 27:30), a skiff or small boat. In NT times waterborne vessels ranged in size from the smaller crafts, like those used for fishing on the Sea of Galilee (Matt 8:23; Mark 4:36), to the large merchant vessels, like those on the Mediterranean Sea, used for trade (Acts 27). The large merchant ships were designed primarily to haul cargo, but it was by means of these vessels that passengers traveled by sea. Passengers were taken on board as space permitted. The merchant ship on which Paul traveled transported grain (Acts 27:38). It had a passenger load of 276 people (Acts 27:37). Merchant ships of the NT period weighed perhaps as much as 300 tons. The major shipping ports of Paul's day included Antioch, Ephesus, Corinth, and Rome. Minor ports included Caesarea and Tyre. Warships during the NT period generally weighed between thirty and forty tons. As was the case in earlier periods, merchant vessels were propelled by sails, warships by oars.

Bibliography. N. Avigad, "Hebrew Seal Depicting a Sailing Ship," *BASOR* 246 (Spring 1982): 59-62; L. Casson, *Ships and Seamanship in the Ancient World*; R. R. Stieglitz, "Long-distance Seafaring in the Ancient Near East," *BA* 47/3 (Sept 1984): 134-42.

—LAMOINE DEVRIES

• **Shipping.** *See* CARAVAN

• **Shishak.** [sh*i*'shak] Shishak I, Egyptian *Sheshonq,* was founder of the Twenty-Second Dynasty during the Third Intermediate Period in the New Kingdom. He ruled in Egypt from about 940–915 B.C.E. or 945-924 based on a low or high chronology. Apparently, Shishak was the pharaoh to whom JEROBOAM fled from SOLOMON (1 Kgs 11:40). Shishak is best known biblically from his invasion of Syria-Palestine in the fifth year of the reign of REHOBOAM, dated between 926 and 918 B.C.E. depending on the chronology used. An inscription from a wall at Karnak listed nearly 150 towns of Syria-Palestine Shishak captured. The list is fragmentary, but among the cities mentioned are those of Aijalon, BETH-HORON, BETH-SHAN, GIBEON, MEGIDDO, and TAANACH. Jerusalem is not mentioned on the list. Jerusalem was spared according to 1 Kgs 14: 25-26 only because Rehoboam paid heavy tribute, including Temple vessels and items from the royal palace. Second Chronicles records how Shishak took away the shields of gold Solomon had made from the palace and Rehoboam replaced them with shields of bronze (12:1-9). A fragmentary stele of Shishak found at Megiddo gives additional support for his invasion. The invasion apparently was unrelated to the split of Solomon's empire into Israel and Judah, because Shishak invaded both nations. His move was probably an attempt to reassert Egyptian control over Palestine, which control had been lost during Egyptian weakness at the end of the Late Bronze Age. This Egyptian control was not maintained by Shishak's successors and Egypt would not again reassert dominance over Palestine for another two centuries. Shishak is also the first pharaoh mentioned by name in the Bible.

Shishak was prince of a family of Libyan chieftans who had gained power in the delta region during a period of Egyptian weakness. Shishak gained equal power with the pharaoh of the Twenty-First Dynasty in Thebes. Ultimately power was transferred to Shishak, apparently amicably, and the Twenty-Second Dynasty was born. Shishak ruled from Tanis in the delta.

—JOEL F. DRINKARD, JR.

• **Shophar.** [shoh'fahr] Found seventy-two times in the Hebrew OT, shophar (Heb. *shôphār*) designates a curved musical instrument usually made from a ram's horn (Josh 6:4ff.). The word is probably derived from the Akkadian *shapparu,* "wild goat," but later underwent a transition from the animal itself to the horn of the animal which was suitable for use as a musical instrument. The word is usually translated "trumpet" or "cornet" in the KJV, and "trumpet," "horn," or "ram's horn" in the RSV.

Although shophar is found in twenty-one books and in every division of the OT, it is most prominent in the books of Joshua, Judges, 2 Samuel, and Jeremiah. Here its usage is primarily that of a signaling instrument in times of war. The shophar was sounded at the beginning of battle (Judg 3:27f.; Jer 4:19; 51:27), or to signal cease-fire (2 Sam 2:28; 18:16). The shophar blast is also used in prophetic texts as a signal for the future judgment of Yahweh (Hos 5:8; Joel

2:1ff.; Amos 2:2; Zeph 1:16).

The shophar was sounded at important times in the life of the community, such as to announce a new king (1 Kgs 1:34ff.), or to give news of victory in battle (1 Sam 13:3). And finally, the shophar was used in Israel's worship. In Exod 19–20 the shophar sounds the approach of the presence of Yahweh for the making of covenant with his people. The shophar and other musical instruments were used in the procession of the Ark to Jerusalem (1 Chr 15:25ff.). Psalm 98:6 commands that Yahweh be praised with "*shophars* and the sound of the horn."

Bibliography. G. Friedrich, "σάλπιγξ," *TDNT*; O. R. Sellers, "Musical Instruments of Israel," *BA* 4 (1941): 33-47.

—CECIL P. STATON, JR.

• **Showbread.** According to the priestly laws in Lev 24:5-9, the showbread comprised the cultic offering to the deity. In that passage the priests of Aaron are commanded to bake twelve loaves of bread and to place the loaves on a gold table in the holy place in the temple or the tabernacle. The loaves are to be set in two rows of six, with frankincense in each row. The bread is to be set before the deity continually, and on every Sabbath the priests are to bring fresh loaves into the sanctuary and eat the old loaves in a holy place (Lev 24:5-9; Exod 25:23-30; 1 Sam 21:5-6; cf. Matt 12:3-4). The showbread is also called the "bread of the PRESENCE" (Exod 25:30; Num 4:7), or the "holy bread" (1 Sam 21:6).

See also PRESENCE; SACRIFICES.

—HENRY L. CARRIGAN, JR.

• **Shrine.** In a specific sense, a shrine is a structure; in the biblical text this structure is described variously as a tent, a high place, or a TEMPLE that houses sacred objects. In a broader sense, however, a shrine is a structure holding such sacred objects as well as a sanctuary or a place of worship.

It is apparent from the traditions of the OT that the Hebrew tribes established shrines in various locations in Palestine both before and after the conquest of Canaan. The seminomadic clans of early Israel consecrated the places in which certain sacred events occurred. Thus, Abraham commemorated his covenant with the Deity by building an altar at the oaks, or terebinths, of Mamre (Gen 13:18).

Although it is likely that the Hebrew tribes occupied abandoned Canaanite shrines when the move into the land was complete, this confederation of tribes possessed its own traveling shrine: the ARK of the Covenant. The Ark contained the empty throne of the invisible deity and was carried before the tribes in war and in peace. However, as the importance of having a centralized sacred place of worship grew, the Ark came to be located at various central shrines: SHECHEM (Josh 24); BETHEL (Judg 19–20); GILGAL (Josh 3–4); and SHILOH (1 Sam 3:3). This development resulted eventually in the building of the JERUSALEM Temple as the central worship shrine. Although Jerusalem became the center of Hebrew worship under David and Solomon, the biblical text records that Jeroboam (922–901 B.C.E.) established many pagan shrines in Israel that were rivals of the Jerusalem Temple. These shrines were destroyed during the reform of Josiah (622 B.C.E.).

See also ARK; BETHEL; SHECHEM; SHILOH; WORSHIP IN THE OLD TESTAMENT.

—HENRY L. CARRIGAN, JR.

• **Shroud of Turin.** The Shroud of Turin has been the center of a debate during recent years. Some are convinced the shroud was the burial cloth of Jesus. Others have termed the shroud a medieval forgery. Recent scientific studies seem to have settled the debate, pronouncing the shroud to be a fourteenth-century forgery.

The shroud first appeared in 1357 in Lirey, France. Because a local artist professed to have painted the cloth, the Bishop of Troyes forbade its display as a holy relic. Later, his successor appealed to the pope to ban another proposed exhibition of the shroud. While Clement VII refused to issue a formal ban, he did deny that the shroud was used in the burial of Christ and advised against its public exhibition. For over a century, it remained in private custody. While in the custody of the duke of Savoy, the shroud survived a fire, although its burns necessitated extensive repairs. In 1578 it was moved to its present location of Turin, Italy.

Research into the validity of the claim that the shroud is that of Jesus began inadvertently in 1898. During a rare public display of the shroud, Secondo Pia, an Italian lawyer and amateur photographer, was allowed to photograph the shroud. His negatives showed a positive image on the shroud, suggesting its use as a burial sheet. Paul Vignon, using Pia's photographs, concluded that the image could not have been painted onto the cloth, but was actually burned into the cloth by a combination of the spices and oils used to prepare the body and the alkaline vapors present at death. Pictures taken during a later public display proved that Pia's pictures were accurate. Pierre Barbet examined the pictured image and identified it as that of a man who had been crucified.

In response to allegations that the church was trying to protect the shroud, Cardinal Pellegrino convened a commission to study the feasibility of examining the shroud (1969). By 1973, the cloth was investigated; this further investigation identified stains on the cloth as blood, found pollen indigenous to the Middle East imbedded in the cloth, and discovered that a three-dimensional image could be projected from its negatives.

A full-scale investigation of the shroud took place in 1978. The Shroud of Turin Research Project examined the shroud intensively during a five-day period. Because of disagreements within the project team and the tentative nature of their findings, the results of the project were deemed inconclusive.

Most recently (1988), investigators were allowed to use radiocarbon dating. Three laboratories were chosen by the Vatican to receive pieces of the shroud; all three dated the material around 1350. Some scientists still assert that the shroud is the burial cloth of Jesus, charging that the fire of 1532 affected the radiocarbon dating process. Scientists and scholars in general, however, have been convinced by the most recent discoveries that the Shroud of Turin is a clever forgery.

Bibliography. R. N. Ostling, "Debunking the Shroud of Turin," *Time* (24 October 1989): 81; R. A. Wile, "The Shroud of Turin," *BAR* 10 (1984); I. Wilson, *The Mysterious Shroud*.

—STEVEN SHEELEY

• **Sibylline Oracles.** [sib'uh-leen] The *Sibylline Oracles* (*SibOr*) is a collection of Jewish and Christian oracles attributed to a prophetess, the Sibyl. It consists of fourteen books written in epic Greek hexameter, as well as some fragments. The figure of the Sibyl, an elderly woman uttering ecstatic predictions of woes to befall mankind, was a time-honored one in the Greco-Roman world, with roots going back to fifth century B.C.E. Greece. There were numerous Sibyls over the years, as well as collections of their oracles. Eventually the Jews adopted the form, identifying the Sibyl as a daughter (or daughter-in-law) of Noah. Christians adapted Jewish oracles and composed their own. This particular collection is a composite work, containing all known Jewish and Christian oracles.

SibOr are extant in two distinct manuscript traditions, one containing books 1–8 with a prologue and the other books 9–14. Book 9 is comprised of materials in the first collection and book 10 is identical with book 4. Retaining the numbering while omitting duplication results in an entire collection consisting of books 1–8, 11–14. The Christian prologue dates from the sixth century C.E. Books 1 and 2 are a unit and reflect heavy Christian redaction of a Jewish original. The Jewish core was probably composed in Phrygia around the beginning of the Christian era, with the Christian redaction taking place before 150 C.E. Book 3 is mostly Jewish. It was probably composed in Egypt, during the second and first centuries B.C.E. Book 4, also Jewish, dates from the second century B.C.E., and was redacted at the end of the first century C.E. Book 5, primarily Jewish, was probably composed in Egypt at the end of the first century C.E. Books 6 and 7 were composed by Christians prior to 300 C.E. The first half of book 8 is primarily Jewish and dates to ca. 175 C.E.; the second half was composed by a Christian prior to 300 C.E. Books 11–14, although composite, constitute a unit. They were probably composed by Jews in Alexandria—book 11 around the beginning of the Christian era, book 12 ca. 235 C.E., book 13 ca. 265 C.E., and book 14 in the seventh century C.E.

Although written by different authors over the course of centuries, *SibOr* contain several common conceptual threads. For example, there is a tendency to divide history into periods and to focus on the destruction of the world, first by the FLOOD and ultimately by fire. Pagan legends, such as the return of Nero, recur. Furthermore, the various Jewish eschatological oracles are primarily political, anticipating the coming of a glorious earthly kingdom. The Christian eschatological oracles focus more attention on the fate of the individual after death, and especially on the punishments of the wicked. Finally, the eschatology provides a foundation for moral exhortation, especially the condemnation of sexual sins and idolatry.

The *SibOr* were frequently quoted by the early church fathers who saw in them an opportunity for propaganda: the independent witness of supposedly pagan Sibyls to Christian truths. They continued to make an impact on Christian eschatology down through the Middle Ages.

Bibliography. J. J. Collins, "Sibylline Oracles," *The Old Testament Pseudepigrapha,* ed. J. H. Charlesworth; A. Kurfessand, R. McL. Wilson, "Christian Sibyllines," *New Testament Apocrypha,* ed. E. Hennecke and W. Schneemelcher; H. C. O. Lanchester, "The Sibylline Oracles," *The Apocrypha and Pseudepigrapha of the Old Testament,* ed. R. H. Charles.

—JOSEPH L. TRAFTON

• **Signs and Wonders.** A phrase that appears regularly in DEUTERONOMY and the deuteronomic works, and occasionally elsewhere in the Bible. "Wonder" never appears by itself in the NT; in the OT it appears with "signs" more often than not. "Signs," on the other hand, is a frequently used word in both the OT and NT. They both signify a noteworthy event that is a medium of REVELATION; i.e., the event stands between the revealer and the audience. It need not be miraculous, although it generally is unusual; the essential part is that it mediates. A television set is a good analogy, because it links together three separate things: the network generating the show, the content of the show itself, and the audience. Similarly, the biblical "signs and wonders" can draw the reader's attention either to the revealer, to the content of the revelation, or to the audience, or to a combination of these essential elements of communication.

One of the most frequent uses of the phrase in the OT is to allude to the EXODUS. The confessional statements in Deuteronomy praise God for bringing Israel out of slavery in Egypt "with a mighty hand and an outstretched arm, with great terror, with signs and wonders" (26:8). Other texts do the same (Jer 32:20; Pss 78:43; 105:27; 135:9; Neh 9:10). Here the focus is on the revealer, on God's actions demonstrating the divine sovereignty over all nations. In Deuteronomy, this proof of God's might is often turned into an exhortation to the audience. Having used signs and wonders as a confession of God's care, the author skillfully turned it into a warning, stating that if the Israelites disobeyed the laws of the text, God's curses would land upon them as "a sign and a wonder" (28:46).

In the story of the Exodus, MOSES needed assurance that God was trustworthy, and proofs that would validate his message to the Israelites. God therefore gave him two kinds of signs. Moses was instructed in certain miracles that he could do before his people and PHARAOH ("signs," Exod 4:8; "wonders," 4:21). God also told Moses that he would serve God upon Mount Sinai after the Exodus, and this, too, was called a sign (Exod 3:12). Similarly, SAMUEL told SAUL that he would have a charismatic experience that would confirm him as God's choice (1 Sam 10:1), and ISAIAH offered King AHAZ the birth of a baby as a sign affirming God's message to stay out of military alliances (Isa 7:10-17). In the latter event, especially, there was nothing that linked the sign-event itself to what it signified; why should a baby's birth prove anything about politics? Signs and wonders are meaningful only through faith in the one whose revelation is signified in them.

Sometimes the focus is on a human as medium of revelation. Isaiah gave his children names symbolizing God's attitudes towards Israel, and went naked and barefoot for three years on another occasion to foretell the Assyrian conquest of Egypt and Ethiopia (Isa 8:18; 20:3). These two episodes were called signs and wonders because Isaiah's actions revealed God's actions. Other signs direct one's attention to the content of revelation. The RAINBOW was a sign of the COVENANT with NOAH (Gen 9:17) as CIRCUMCISION was a sign of the covenant with ABRAHAM (Gen 17:11). These signs were to be reminders of the link between God and the people, paradoxically mediating the immediacy of God's presence in Israel.

In the NT, "signs and wonders" is generally used to mean MIRACLES that validate a message. The term can be applied both to heroes (Paul uses it of himself in Rom 15:19 and 2 Cor 12:12) and to villains (of miracles done by the false prophets/messiahs just before the parousia, Matt 24:24; Mark 13:22; 2 Thess 2:9). It is a refrain Luke used in Acts 1–8 to show how God confirmed and blessed the decisions of the church (Acts 2:43; 5:12, etc.).

"Sign" is much more common. It is generally used with a negative connotation in the synoptic Gospels, showing up in scenes where Jesus resolutely refused to do miracles on demand to validate his message (Mark 8:1-12 and par.; Luke 23:8). Luke, however, also includes two positive references. The angels gave the shepherds a sign by which to recognize the newly born Jesus (2:12), and Jesus was himself called a sign of God's judgment on Israel (2:34). The synoptic apocalypses used "sign" to describe the cosmic disturbances preceding the end, which is also how Revelation used the term. The Johannine miracles were always called signs, because the author saw them as events through which Jesus revealed himself to be God's revealer. Much of John 1–12 depicts how people either saw or did not see the "glory" in the "sign," and thus grouped themselves into various stages of belief and unbelief. Paul wrote of signs in three contexts: as a term for the merely miraculous (1 Cor 1:22), in a reference to circumcision as the sign of Abraham's covenant (Rom 4:11), and as a validation of God's presence in the church (1 Cor 14:22; 2 Thess 3:17).

See also MIRACLES; SYMBOL.

Bibliography. H. C. Kee, *Miracle in the Early Christian World*; E. J. Helfmeyer, "אוֹת," *TDOT*; K. H. Rengstorf, "σημεῖον," *TDNT*.

—RICHARD B. VINSON

• **Sihon.** [*si*'hon] King of the Amorites. Num 21:21-32 relates the encounter of the Israelite tribes in Transjordan with King Sihon of the Amorites. The prose narrative and conclusion (vv. 21-26, 31-32) rehearse Israel's request for passage through Sihon's domain and his belligerence against them. Israel defeated Sihon and dispossessed the Amorites "from the ARNON to the JABBOK, as far as to the Ammonites" (Num 21:24). The most memorable city of Sihon's kingdom was HESHBON. Probably because Sihon had established himself in Heshbon by conquest, Heshbon was also called the "city of Sihon" (Num 21:26, 27, 28; cf. Jerusalem as the "city of David"). The defeat of Sihon became prototypical of Yahweh's work on Israel's behalf in granting them the land of Canaan (cf. Num 21:34; Deut 3:2, 6; Josh 2:10; 9:10).

See also HESHBON.

—JOHN KEATING WILES

• **Silas.** [*si*'luhs] Silas is the name given to the highly respected prophet of the Jerusalem church who, along with Judas BARSABBAS, accompanied PAUL and BARNABAS to Antioch to deliver a letter of support to the gentile converts (Acts 15:22ff.) He stayed for a while with the Antioch church, sharing his gift of prophecy and exhorting the congregation (15:32). After a dispute with Barnabas, Paul chose Silas to accompany him on his second missionary journey (15:36ff.).

Paul and Silas picked up Timothy in Lystra, then followed Paul's vision of the man urging them to "come over to Macedonia and help us" (Acts 16:9). In Philippi they cast an evil spirit out of a young fortune teller whose owners had Paul and Silas arrested and flogged for depriving them of the chance to make money. Chained in the inner cell of the Philippian jail, Paul and Silas sang hymns and prayed. About midnight they were freed by a violent earthquake. Seeing that the prison doors had been jarred open, the jailer started to kill himself; but Paul called out, assuring him than none of the prisoners had left. Entering the cell, the jailer fell at the feet of Paul and Silas and sought salvation. After directing him to believe in the Lord, Paul and Silas were taken to his home where he cleaned their wounds. The following day the Roman authorities dismissed the charges against them; but Paul and Silas, citing their Roman citizenship, refused to accept their release until the officials had apologized to them (16:37ff.).

Silas continued to witness with Paul in Thessalonica and Berea, where they avoided a mob that sought to harm them. When Paul left for Athens, Silas remained in Macedonia with Timothy, finally rejoining Paul at Corinth (18:5). Biblical citations of Silas then disappear, although custom regards him as having been the first bishop of the church at Corinth. To this day, he is a favorite saint in the Orthodox tradition.

Although all references to the name Silas occur in Acts, there is little doubt that the person identified as Silvanus in the Pauline Letters is the same person (the TEV substitutes "Silas" for all of the Pauline references to "Silvanus"). Paul reminded the Corinthians that he, Silvanus, and Timothy had preached among them (2 Cor 1:19), and he included the names of Silvanus and Timothy in the salutations of the Letters to the Thessalonians, both of which were composed in Corinth. The name "Silas" might be a contraction of "Silvanus" or a nickname by which he was called in Philippi, where the author of Acts had known him (cf. 16:16). Although these explanations for the different names are plausible, they are based on conjecture rather than evidence.

It is also possible that the Silvanus identified as the coauthor or scribe of 1 Pet 5:12 is the same person and that he (Silas/Silvanus) had established close connections with Peter as early as his sojourn in Antioch (cf. Gal 5:2).

See also BARNABAS; BARSABBAS; PAUL; PETER, LETTERS OF.

Bibliography. J. Munck, *The Acts of the Apostles*; A. T. Robertson, *Epochs in the Life of Paul*; F. Stagg, *The Book of Acts*.

—JOSEPH L. PRICE

• **Siloam Inscription.** [*si*-loh'uhm] The name Siloam (Heb. Shiloah; Arab. Selwan; LXX Siloa, Siloam), from the Hebrew verb "to send," is identified with a tunnel and pool at the southern end of the spur on which the Jebusite city of Jerusalem was built, and with the Arab village which now dominates the site and the adjoining slope. The name is an obvious reference to the tunnel that conveyed ("sent") the waters of the GIHON spring outside the eastern wall of Jerusalem to an artificially constructed reservoir within the city fortifications. The six-line Hebrew inscription, written in a paleo-Hebrew script, found engraved on the tunnel wall, commemorated the completion of the tunnel. The inscription, now on a limestone slab approximately twelve in. high and twenty-eight in. long, was cut from the tunnel wall and, in 1880, was removed to the Istanbul Museum of the Ancient Orient where it presently is on display.

The inscription and the tunnel in which it was found (PLATE 37) date to the reign of King HEZEKIAH of Judah (727–698 B.C.E.). For almost twenty-five years of his reign, Hezekiah concentrated on internal economic and religious reform to revitalize the Judean kingdom and carefully avoided any anti-Assyrian activities. However, in 703 B.C.E. the death of SARGON II and a delegation from MERODACH-BALADAN, king of Babylon, encouraged Hezekiah to participate in a regional insurrection against Assyrian overlordship. Fortifications were greatly enhanced along his western frontier (at sites such as Timnah and Lachish) and in Jerusalem. Preparations in Jerusalem included the diversion of the city's primary water source, the Gihon Spring, from its location outside the wall to a pool inside the city to ensure a water supply against a possible siege of the city. Hezekiah's defensive scheme required modification of the existing configuration of the spring's access, its pool and the irrigation system associated with it. The "Upper Pool" (2 Kgs 18:17; Isa 7:3; 36:2), "Old Pool" (Isa 22:11) or "artificial pool" (Neh 3:16) near the spring's source not only provided direct and convenient access to an abundant water supply but was linked to an elaborate irrigation system that supported cultivation along the terraced slopes of the Kidron and the valley floor. One of the two primary channels that served the irrigation system, covered and partially underground to avoid rock upcroppings, fed the "Pool of Shelah" or "King's Pool" (Neh 2:14), located below the present Pool of Siloam where the Tyropaean and Kidron Valleys meet.

When Hezekiah's plan for the defense of Jerusalem required sealing all accesses to its water supply outside the city wall, a major engineering feat was undertaken diverting the water of the Gihon by tunnel to the present location of the Pool of Siloam. A 1749 ft. tunnel, following an irregular S-shaped route through solid rock, brought the water of the spring inside the fortified bounds of the city. The devious route of the tunnel may reflect limited expertise in surveying and an attempt to avoid harder rock formations to speed the completion of the project. The urgency of its completion is reflected in tunneling operations from both ends implied in the inscription's account of the completion of the project:

"(This is?) the boring through. This is the story of the boring through: whilst (the miners lifted) the pick each towards his fellow and whilst three cubits (yet remained) to be bored (through, there was hear)d the voice of a man calling his fellow, for there was a split in the rock on the right hand and on (the left hand). And on the day of the boring through the miners struck, each in the direction of his fellow, pick against pick. And the water started flowing from the source to the pool, twelve hundred cubits. A hundred cubits was the height of the rock above the head of the miners" (per J. Simons).

The southerly location of the Pool of Siloam, referred to as the "reservoir between the two walls" (Isa 22:9-11), near the point where the defensive walls on either side of the spur between the Kedron and the Tyropaean converged, was required by the declining gradient from the level of the Gihon Spring (an examination of the tunnel suggests a serious miscalculation in the gradient and subsequent adjustment on the part of the diggers from the lower end). The overflow of the new pool fed the original Pool of Shelah, probably on or near the location of the modern Birket el-Hamra in the Kedron.

Jesus' miracle at the Pool of Siloam (John 9:7) prompted the construction of a fifth-century church that significantly altered the terrain to facilitate a porticoed courtyard around the pool's entrance. In more recent times a mosque was built over the ruins of the Byzantine church and a small minaret still marks the location of the Siloam Pool in the Kedron.

See also GIHON; WATER SYSTEMS.

Bibliography. M. Burrows, "The Conduit of the Upper Pool," *ZAW* 70 (1958): 221-27; V. Sasson, "The Siloam Tunnel Inscription," *PEQ* 114 (1982): 111-17; N. Shaheen, "The Sinuous Shape of Hezekiah's Tunnel," *PEQ* 111 (1979): 103-108; J. Simons, *Jerusalem in the Old Testament.*

—GEORGE L. KELM

• **Silvanus.** *See* SILAS

• **Silvanus, Teachings of.** [sil-vay'nuhs] A rare example of early Christian WISDOM LITERATURE. The *Teachings of Silvanus* is the fourth tractate in Codex VII of the NAG HAMMADI library. The author, an unknown sage who writes in the name of Silvanus, Paul's cotraveller (e.g., Acts 15:22-40) and Peter's secretary (1 Pet 5:12), writes to impart the "wisdom of Christ" and direct his reader into the "profitable way of God" (118.2-7). Such will enable one to live a "quiet" and "self-controlled" life, be "pleasing to God," "become like God" (85.5-7; 87.14-17; 108.25-27.34-35).

Unlike other tractates in Codex VII, *TeachSilv* is not Gnostic and contains anti-Gnostic polemic. One God is responsible for creation (114.30–115.10). That creation is good, not evil, as Gnostics taught (implied in 115.20-22; 116.5-8), and its creator ("Demiurge") should never be described as "ignorant" (116.5-9). Also, the Christology of the tractate is not docetic, for Christ "bore affliction for . . . sin" (103.25-28), "died" as "ransom" for others (104.8-13; 107.9-16), and "put on humanity" (110.18-19). Finally, unlike the Gnostic stress on salvation for the spiritual elite, this tractate emphasizes that all persons possess the capacity for salvation, the divine "reason" and "mind" (92.15–94.4).

Still, the document's ascetic, world-denying ethic was probably attractive to Gnostic sympathizers who presumably collected the Nag Hammadi library. Mixing Stoic and Christian ethics, the author counsels controlling base passions of the body (84.16–87.4; 90.1-6), passions incited by the adversary, SATAN (94.33–96.19; 104.25ff.). One must also resist the subtly disguised temptations Satan presents (95.12–96.19) and the evil powers he sends (105.27–106.10). In this struggle, God alone is a friend, for the whole world is deceitful and painful (97.30–98.20). Such an ethic proved attractive to later Christian monks of Egypt, for the passage 97.3–98.22 was incorporated in two eighth and eleventh-century texts associated with St. Antony, founder of monasticism in Egypt (ca. 251–356 C.E.).

TeachSilv makes use of the literary forms of Hellenistic Jewish wisdom, as well as of the Cynic-Stoic diatribe. Wisdom forms include contrasts between the wise and foolish, negative and positive admonitions, hymns and prayers, descriptive proverbs and didactic sayings, and address of the reader as "my son."

In content, the first part of *TeachSilv* (84.15–99.4) is more Hellenistic and philosophical. The main concern is with the state of the soul and the need for "mind" and "reason" to guide, lest base passions ("robbers") and irrational impulses ("savage, wild beasts") ruin one's life. One must become "human," "rational," "divine" rather than "animalistic," "irrational," "earthly" (93.3–94.18). The second part (99.6–118.7) is more specifically biblical and Christian, with emphasis placed on the soul's salvation and inner illumination by the LOGOS, Christ.

Parallels to its teaching with major representatives of Alexandrian theology (e.g., PHILO, Clement, Origen) point toward Egypt as the tractate's provenance. The author's knowledge of the biblical canon, developed Christian tradition regarding Christ's DESCENT INTO HELL, and the thought of Middle Platonism and late Stoicism point toward a date of late second to early third century.

See also NAG HAMMADI.

Bibliography. M. L. Peel and J. Zandee, "The Teachings of Silvanus," *The Nag Hammadi Library in English,* ed. J. M. Robinson and "The Teachings of Silvanus from the Library of Nag Hammadi (CG VII,*4*: 84.15–118.7)," *NovT* 14/3 (October 1972):1-18; J. Zandee, *The Teachings of*

Silvanus and Clement of Alexandria.

—MALCOLM L. PEEL

• **Silver and Gold.** Silver and gold were two of the most precious metals in the ancient Near East. Their value could be noted in jewelry items, basins, utensils, and coins. In Exod 25–27 a description of the TABERNACLE, its implements, and utensils is found. The metals listed are gold, silver, and bronze. The ARK was to be covered in gold, the mercy seat was to be of pure gold, the tables were to be covered with gold, the plates and dishes for incense and the lampstands were to be made of gold. In contrast, the altar and its implements were to be made of bronze. Gold and silver were materials of worth and tremendous value; thus those who possessed these metals attained wealth and position. The use of these precious metals in the Tabernacle and TEMPLE would be an expression of the worthiness and dignity of the almighty God.

From archeology it has been substantiated in some periods that gold and silver items of jewelry, such as finger rings, bracelets, and beads were commonplace. The pliability of gold resulted in its being hammered into sheets and cut as thread (Exod 39:3). Perhaps, however, gold and silver's greatest value was its usability as a means for exchange and trade. It also appears that COPPER stood alongside gold and silver as a common valuable metal; however, gold and silver were more precious and thus more appropriate metals for significant trading. Initially gold and silver were used in various forms not unlike rings or bundles. Objects of gold and silver such as jewelry or perhaps bars represented a form of currency. Silver primarily served as the more common medium of trade. Over a period of time the concept of a weight system arose. This system provided a new method of value perception. It was further refined as specified weights of the ore were standardized. The silver shekel became the standard of evaluation, even though it is known that the shekel may have varied from place to place and from period to period. Indeed some ancient texts in giving the number of shekels indicate that the value assigned was respective to a certain city. With the beginning of the stamped coin, apparently no earlier than seventh century B.C.E., the units of measure became uniform.

Both silver and gold are known from earliest historic times in the ancient Near East. At times the supply and demand of the ores fluctuated and devaluated one or the other. In earlier times, roughly until the mid-first millennium B.C.E., silver was the premium metal; this notion reflects the higher priority given to silver in the OT. As the silver availability increased, gold assumed the more valued position.

The primary method of attaining silver is refining. Silver was extracted by the smelting process in which the molten silver was separated from the slag. The ore could then be cast or worked. Gold likewise could be cast or hammered due to its softness.

One source of gold recorded in the OT is Ophir (1 Chr 29:4; Job 22:24; 28:16). This region was attested for its productivity of this ore. However, there is no clear indication of where the Ophir territory is to be located. Locations in India, Arabia, and Africa have been postulated. While it is not certain where this location may have been, it can be asserted that certainly Egypt and the modern Sudan areas would have been suppliers of this ore. Egypt was likely one supplier of silver, though Asia Minor and the Mesopotamian region apparently held great sway in silver enterprises during the second millennium B.C.E.

See also BRASS/BRONZE; COINS AND MONEY; JEWELRY.

—MARK W. GREGORY

• **Simeon.** [sim'ee-uhn] A personal name found frequently in the Bible, deriving from the Hebrew term for hearing. Simeon in the Genesis account was the second son of JACOB and LEAH, and father of the tribe of Simeon. Simeon, with his brother LEVI, massacred the Hivites at Shechem to avenge the rape of their sister Dinah (Gen 34). Jacob, in his final blessing upon his sons, pronounced a curse upon the fierce anger and cruelty of Simeon and Levi, proclaiming that their descendants would be scattered throughout ISRAEL and have no part in their assembly (Gen 49:5-7). It was Simeon whom JOSEPH kept as a hostage in Egypt when he ordered the other brothers to go back to Canaan to get their youngest brother, BENJAMIN (Gen 42–43).

The tribe of Simeon receives brief attention in the OT. Having been granted no tribal inheritance of their own, the Simeonites were allotted cities scattered throughout the territory of Judah (Jos 19:1-9). The scant references to the Simeonites in the OT would seem to indicate that they were eventually absorbed into the tribe of Judah and ceased to exist as a separate tribe. Even so, descendants of Simeon continue to trace their ancestry back to this son of Jacob; Ezekiel and other writers have a place for Simeon in the tribal allotments of the future (cf. Ezek 48:24).

In the NT Simeon was the righteous man in Jerusalem to whom it was revealed by the Holy Spirit that he would not die until he had seen the MESSIAH. When Mary and Joseph brought the baby Jesus to the Temple to be presented to the Lord, Simeon took Jesus into his arms, uttered his famous prayer (known as the NUNC DIMITTIS), and predicted his rejection and the grief that Mary would suffer (Luke 2:22-35).

The name Simeon also refers to an ancestor of Jesus listed in Luke's genealogy (Luke 3:30); "Simeon who was called Niger," a Christian at ANTIOCH, is listed among the prophets and teachers in the church there (Acts 13:1). Simeon also appears as the Jewish name of the apostle Peter (Acts 15:14; 2 Pet 1:1).

See also TRIBES.

—ROBERT B. BARNES

• **Similitudes of Enoch.** *See* ENOCH, FIRST; SON OF MAN

• **Simon Magus.** [si'muhn-may"guhs] Simon Magus appears in the story of Philip's mission to SAMARIA (Acts 8). PHILIP (not the apostle; cf. Acts 6:5) was one of the disciples driven out of Jerusalem by persecution. He went to preach in Samaria where he was encountered by Simon Magus.

Philip's preaching won many converts. Simon, a well-known MAGICIAN, was attracted to Philip's preaching and to the signs and miracles he performed. After his conversion and baptism, Simon accompanied Philip and continued to be amazed at Philip's signs and miracles.

The church leaders in Jerusalem heard about the fruitfulness of Philip's ministry. They sent Peter and John to Samaria to supervise Philip's work. Peter and John laid hands on the new converts, imparting to them the HOLY SPIRIT. Upon seeing this special apostolic capacity of Peter and John, Simon wanted the same for himself. Simon offered to pay Peter money for the power to impart the Holy Spirit. Peter severely condemned his request and demanded that Simon repent. Simon was shaken by Peter's denouncement and humbly repented.

Simon has traditionally come to be known as Simon Magus, the word "magus" meaning "magician." There were many magi or magicians in the Mediteranean world and the Middle East. They practiced ASTROLOGY, necromancy, exorcism, sorcery, and prophecy. Since these magicians pretended to have supernatural powers and endeavored to deceive people, the magicians inevitably came into conflict with the gospel. The magicians flattered people's sinful inclinations, encouraged hedonistic indulgences, and never required personal self-sacrifice. It took a concerted effort by Christians to enable people to overcome the delusions promoted by the magicians.

One of the most debated questions about Simon Magus was whether he was a genuine convert or whether he falsely claimed to believe in Christ. It is interesting that the word that denotes Simon's being amazed at the signs performed by Philip is the same word used to denote the amazement of people of Samaria at Simon's signs. The word probably indicates the character of the faith he had in the gospel—wondering amazement at a new phenomenon he did not understand rather than true repentance and trust in Christ. Most Christians in the generations immediately after Simon believed that he was an imposter who acted as he did for self-serving purposes.

The story of Simon Magus did not end with the biblical account in Acts. In some stories Simon was portrayed as the constant adversary of Peter, although in the end Peter discredited and defeated him. Some saw Simon as an arch heretic who perverted Christian beliefs and advocated pagan practices. In fact, Simon was alleged to be the founder of the Simonians who regarded Simon as their Christ. IRENAEUS charged that Simon was the leader from whom GNOSTICISM grew (Simon probably did not found Gnosticism, but some of his beliefs were similar to Gnosticism). Simon's final legacy is indicated by the name given to the buying and selling of spiritual gifts and ecclesiastical offices—"simony."

See also GNOSTICISM; HOLY SPIRIT; MAGI; MAGIC AND DIVINATION; MAGICIANS; PETER; PHILIP; SAMARIA; SIGNS AND WONDERS.

—ROBERT RAINWATER

• **Simon Peter.** *See* PETER

• **Simple/Simpleton.** *See* FOOL/FOOLISHNESS/FOLLY

• **Sin.** Sin appears in the Bible within the parentheses of GRACE. After examining the terms for sin in the Bible, we shall reckon with sin in relation to God's grace. Unlike the elements "love," "grace," and "life," which belong to the divine-human order, "sin" represents an intrusion into creation and into human experience. It does not belong; it is a surd in the human equation; it has no ground, no place, no rationale. Sin is a violation of God's order, a misreading of reality. It is a corruption of the human condition and an impairment of the human possibility. It is a parasite upon the good—this is why it has force but not ground (Augustine called sin a *privatio boni*). In the Bible, sin is never viewed as a magnitude in its own light—it has no light. Though taken with deep seriousness (in the OT and NT), it is viewed always in the light of God. Sin is what it is only in relation to God's reality, activity, and purpose. It roots in prideful self-centeredness and comes to expression through a misguided will and value system. It affects all persons, individually and corporately, placing all under condemnation and sentence of death. The grace of God is its only court of appeal, and faith the only medium of redeeming grace.

Terminology. There are numerous Hebrew and Greek words used in the Bible to signify sin. The most common word for sin in the OT (חָטָא) carries the primary notion of "missing the mark or way or goal." Sin, in this sense means "failure," "fault," and "error." Appearing occasionally in its literal sense (Job 5:24; Judg 20:16), this word ordinarily indicates a moral and spiritual failure—either toward God or toward human persons (e.g., Gen 20:9; Lam 5:7).

The Gk. ἁμαρτία, which is synonymous with the Heb. term for "missing the mark," carries heavier moral and theological freight than its OT counterpart. In a much higher percentage of its uses, it refers to action against God rather than against human persons (cf. even the remarkable statement in Ps 51:4, as well as 1 John 2:1; 1 Cor 6:18). It often suggests a sinful condition, and not simply a sinful act.

A different Heb. word (עָוֹן) comes from a root meaning to act wrongly or perversely and may be translated as "iniquity," "moral distortion," "perversity," and even GUILT. Much more than is the case with missing the mark, this word carries connotation of an intention to act wrongly: it is more than failure or losing the way (cf. Gen 4:13; Pss 32:1-2; 51:1-2).

Closely parallel to this OT "iniquity" are NT words (ἁμάρτημα and παράπτωμα) which refer to specific acts of trespass and not to a disposition or condition. (In Heb 6:6 the verb "to trespass" may be translated "to apostatize from God.")

A stronger (though less frequently used) OT term (פֶּשַׁע) means to revolt. In theological terms, it means to revolt against God—to violate God's law or rule with deliberate will. It points to a conscious choice, not to an ignorant error. A person whose acts can be described by this word is in revolt against God. This revolt against God is close to what 1 John 3:4 calls "lawlessness," that is, a rebellion against God and an assault on the divine order. While the Bible elaborates no doctrine of original sin, these biblical words for revolt, rebellion, and lawlessness bespeak more a condition of existence than a misguided act (cf. Amos 1:3; 3:1-2).

Apparently, however, the closest parallel in the NT to "revolt against God" is the word translated "ungodliness," "sacrilege," "irreligion," and "impiety" (ἀσέβεια) (cf. Rom 11:26 and 2 Tim 2:16). This is the NT's most profound theological word for sin and regularly indicates offense against God.

Most of what the Bible has to say about sin can be said, in one way or another, with the above terminology. Sin may be against self or others, but it is, first of all, against God; it is not simply an imperfection, a finite condition, a neglected ceremony, a philosophical error, nor the violation of a social taboo. It is the inclination of an unregenerate will or evil imagination—a disastrous repudiation of God as the source of life and of all good. To be "in sin," therefore, is to be "lost" and to be standing under "judgment."

Jesus speaks of sin almost always in relation to (or as presupposed by) FORGIVENESS, and seems to trace its appearance to a divided loyalty or unworthy motive (Matt 5–7). Paul who provides the heaviest content to "ungodliness" usually sees sin as an evil power in contention with the "law of the Spirit." Sin is the flesh, i.e., not the body, but the natural or unregenerate heart, the evil imagination, the enemy of the good. Sin, for Paul, is the cause of sins (cf. Rom 6:14-17; 7:25), and is the power of death (1 Cor 15:56). John thinks of sin more as the "realm of darkness." It is a "lawless" rejection of "God as light." In John, sin is also the opposite of "knowledge," i.e., a moral ignorance which understands neither itself nor the nature of the good.

The Framework of Grace. Grace is the only remedy for sin. When we talk about RECONCILIATION, REGENERATION, or SANCTIFICATION, as deliverance from our sins and sinfulness, it is grace which encompasses the subject. In the NT, this grace comes in connection with the life and death and resurrection of Jesus Christ (as lamb of God, as mercy-seat, as the deliverer from darkness to light, from bondage to freedom, and from death to life). This saving power of Jesus Christ, and of God's grace in him, is made effective in sinful persons only by that trustful obedience (or obedient trustfulness) which the NT calls faith.

This saving grace is the source of the climate of joy which pervades the NT. We are delivered by grace from the guilt and power of sin—and from death which is its issue (Rom 5–8). This is why Jesus Christ is extolled in these texts as he to whom we are infinitely obligated (Rev 1:5). We are no longer slaves to sin, nor heirs of death (Rom 6). We are God's free sons and daughters (Rom 5, 8; John 1:29).

By the saving grace of God in Christ, we have an accessible knowledge of God. (Sin appears, as in Rom 1:20 or Eph 2:1-6 as the refusal of such knowledge.) We are built into Christ by faith (Eph 3:16-19; 4:13-16). Sin does not build up anything—it erodes both intent and integrity (as in Rom 1:21-32). Grace puts us into harmony with God and with his purpose for us and for the world, removing us from the power of sin as a fraudulent usurper of God's primacy in our lives (as in Rom 6:14).

Sin, then, is almost as heavy as grace—but it has less reality. It mars the divine image in ourselves, distorting our selfhood. It breaks down our health from within, while offending both the divine love and divine order. It will not finally work. Its only resolution is grace. In relation to it, John the Baptist speaks for the whole NT: "Behold the lamb of God who takes away the sin of the world" (John 1:29).

See also ATONEMENT/EXPIATION IN THE NEW TESTAMENT; ATONEMENT/EXPIATION IN THE OLD TESTAMENT; EVIL; FALL; FORGIVENESS/PARDON; GRACE; GUILT; HOLINESS IN THE NEW TESTAMENT; HOLINESS IN THE OLD TESTAMENT; JUSTIFICATION; RECONCILIATION; REDEMPTION IN THE NEW TESTAMENT; REDEMPTION IN THE OLD TESTAMENT; REGENERATION; SALVATION IN THE NEW TESTAMENT; SALVATION IN THE OLD TESTAMENT; SANCTIFICATION.

Bibliography. J. R. Coates, *Bible Key Words*; R. Niebuhr, *The Nature and Destiny of Man*; E. Brunner, *Man in Revolt*.

—THERON D. PRICE

• **Sinai.** [*si'ni*] Sinai is both the name of a mountain and the larger region in which that mountain is traditionally located, between the two northern gulfs of the Red Sea, with the Gulf of Aqaba on the east and the Gulf of Suez on the west (PLATE 9). The peninsula of Sinai has the shape of an inverted triangle, with its base touching Asia and Africa respectively, and its vertex penetrating the Red Sea like an arrow. The southern tip of Sinai is about 240 mi. from the Mediterranean shore; the northern base extends from Rapha to the Suez Canal, 125 mi.

As part of the Saharo-Arabian desert, Sinai's climate is arid with an annual rainfall seldom in excess of two-and-one-half in., except along the Mediterranean coast. The peninsula of Sinai has three major regions. The northern part consists of a low, sandy plateau including large tracts of sand dunes with some oases. This coastal zone has served as a thoroughfare for military maneuvers, ancient and modern, and is still dotted with burned out tanks from recent wars between Israel and Egypt. The central region of Sinai is a high, limestone plateau with little water and sparse vegetation. Sinai's southern region is a series of rugged, granite mountains, some of which exceed 8,000 ft. in elevation and are snow capped in winter.

Although Sinai may appear to be inhospitable, a number of settlements dot modern maps and the bedouin population alone numbers about 50,000. This wilderness has been occupied by both sedentary and/or nomadic peoples for 30,000 years. As early as 2650 B.C.E., Egyptians were mining turquoise in Sinai. The proto-Sinaitic inscriptions from Serabit el-Khadem date to ca. 1500 B.C.E. and represent the earliest stages in the development of a semitic alphabet.

Throughout its history, Sinai was crossed or occupied by many different peoples: Assyrians, Babylonians, Persians, Greeks, Nabataeans, and Romans. But the most famous sojourn in this wilderness was that of the Hebrew people following their Exodus from Egypt. It was here that some of the most important events of Israelite history took place, as recorded in Exodus through Numbers. In fact, Israel became a nation at the foot of Mount Sinai; for it was there that Moses took a "mixed multitude" (Exod 12:38) and made of them one people in covenant with the God who had liberated them from bondage in Egypt. However elusive these historical events may be to the historian who would reconstruct a sequence of specific happenings in time, the Sinai experience became a symbolic reality that continues to shape liberation movements to the present time. In some sense even the establishment of our own democratic ideals in the founding of the United States of America stems ultimately from these events.

In Judg 5:5, an early poem, Yahweh is called "the One of Sinai." Deut 33:2, another ancient poem that mentions Sinai as the point from which Yahweh appears, associates it with Seir and Paran. The Bible does not use the word "Sinai" in reference to the entire peninsula of Sinai. Instead, it mentions five smaller, distinct tracts of wilderness within this larger territory: i.e., Shur, Sin, Sinai, Paran, and Zin.

The Wilderness of Sinai is the biblical name for the small, distinct wilderness region in which Mount Sinai (or HOREB) was located. Its exact location cannot be ascertained with any certainty, since its limits are defined in relation to other place names that have not been located. In general, the Bible locates Sinai between the wildernesses of Sin and Paran and in the vicinity of Elim, Rephidim, and Kibroth-hataavah (Exod 16:1; 19:1-2; Num 10:12; 33:15-16). The traditional location of Mount Sinai is in the south-central part of the peninsula, where the monastery of Saint Catherine has been situated since the time of the Emperor Justinian in 527 C.E. The monastery is named after a Christian saint who was tortured and beheaded in Alexandria in 307 C.E. Her body is said to have been carried by angels from Alexandria to the lofty summit of Jebel Katerin ("Mountain of Catherine"), a little more than two mi. southwest of Jebel Musa—"Mountain of Moses" (PLATE 44).

The biblical writers refer to Mount Sinai by various names: "the mountain," "the mountain of God," "Mount Horeb," "the mountain of Horeb," and "the mountain of God in Horeb." In terms of modern pentateuchal criticism the term Sinai occurs primarily in the P source and rarely in the J account. In both the E and D sources, the name of the mountain of revelation and covenant is Horeb. This mountain played a significant role in the spiritual journey of Moses even before the EXODUS from Egypt, beginning with the incident of the "burning bush" (Exod 3:1-12). It subsequently became the primary locus of divine revelation in the OT, for both Moses (Exod 19:18-23; 24:16; Deut 33:2; Judg 5:5; Ps 68:8) and Elijah (1 Kgs 19). Indeed, Yahweh's presence here came to symbolize divine protection. Paul uses the term Sinai to represent the old covenant system (Gal 4:24-25; cf. Heb 12:19-21).

Although many details concerning the itinerary followed by the Israelites in their journey from Egypt to the plains of Moab are given in Exodus, Numbers, and Deuteronomy, few of the places mentioned can be identified with any certainty. In fact, even the general route through the Sinai peninsula is debated among scholars, with three alternatives: a northern, central, and southern route. Consequently, the location of Mount Sinai itself is disputed. As many as a dozen mountains in Sinai and northwestern Arabia have been posited as possible candidates. Since none of the several theories is supported by specific archaeological evidence, consideration must be given to various Jewish, Christian, and Muslim traditions. Jebel Musa ("Mountain of Moses"), or another mountain in its immediate vicinity, remains the most likely candidate. This identification assumes that the Israelites followed a southern route across the Sinai peninsula. The steep and bare red granite peaks in this vast desert form an awesome scene of stark grandeur, and the identification is attractive to the imagination even if it cannot be demonstrated with certainty.

See also HOREB, MOUNT.

Bibliography. H. Arden, "Eternal Sinai," *National Geographic* 161/4 (April 1982): 90-102; I. Beit-Arieh, "Fifteen Years in Sinai," *BAR* 10/4 (July/August 1984): 26-54; B. Bernstein, *Sinai: The Great and Terrible Wilderness*; J. D. Levenson, *Sinai and Zion: An Entry into the Jewish Bible*; E. W. Nicholson, *Exodus and Sinai in History and Tradition*.

—DUANE L. CHRISTENSEN

• **Sirach.** [*si'*ruhk] A book of the Apocrypha or deuterocanonicals, also known as Ecclesiasticus or the Wisdom of Jesus the Son of Sirach. It is also referred to as the Wisdom of Ben Sirach (son of Sirach) or simply Sirach.

The book was written in Hebrew by a man named Joshua ben Sira (Jesus ben Sirach, in Gk.) and was later translated into Greek by his grandson. When he translated the book, the grandson wrote a preface or foreword (printed preceding chap. 1), in which he describes how he translated the book into Greek for non-Hebrew-speaking Jews residing in Egypt. He himself had gone to settle in Egypt in 132 B.C.E., and he must have begun his work of translation shortly thereafter.

The book was originally composed in Hebrew, probably in Jerusalem, some sixty years or so before the translation was made. This means that the book came into existence after 200 B.C.E. Scholars generally agree it was written between ca. 195 and 165 B.C.E. The original author seems to have been a scribe and teacher who had traveled widely.

Although written in Hebrew, the book was transmitted through the centuries in its Greek form. It is only in the last century that Hebrew materials have become available, first in the discovery in 1896 of Hebrew manuscripts and fragments in the storeroom of an ancient synagogue in Cairo, Egypt. This provides materials in Hebrew for about two-thirds of the book, although many questions can be raised about the character of this late Hebrew text. A few additional pages have come to light more recently from Qumran and Masada. The Greek text itself is preserved in a number of manuscripts, but the task of deciding what is the original text is a complicated one. Most modern translations will provide the reader with some insight into the variations that occur in many places in the book.

Ben Sira wrote at a time when there was great pressure on the Jews of Palestine to adopt Greek manners and customs. The Seleucids had come to power in 198 B.C.E., and hellenization made rapid inroads, particularly among the upper classes. Antiochus Epiphanes was about to break upon the scene (175–164 B.C.E.), with his efforts to hellenize the Jews by force. The MACCABEES resist this effort, but Ben Sira is a resistance fighter with his pen—he opposes the hellenization movement by appealing to the ancient traditions of WISDOM and LAW. He remains devoted to the TEMPLE and its liturgy but also appeals to the sacred scriptures as he teaches wisdom to all those who will listen.

The book belongs in the mainstream of Jewish WISDOM LITERATURE and follows the pattern of PROVERBS in treating all kinds of subject matter from the standpoint of wisdom. These wisdom messages are often presented in isolated statements that seem to be glued to each other often without any clear indication of how they are connected, although sayings are grouped together more frequently than in Proverbs. The book has been called a "life-time scrapbook of a lecturer or teacher" (Snaith), and it does contain many sayings in poetic form about all kinds of secular subjects. An outline is hardly possible, but there are some significant discrete sections. Beginning with 42:15, the writer deals with the glory of God as shown in nature (42:15–43:33) and in history (44:1–50:29). This latter section, beginning "Let us now praise famous men [or in Heb., godly men]" may be one of the best-known parts of the book. Chap. 51, which seems to be an addition, contains a psalm of thanksgiving and an acrostic poem (in Hebrew) on the search for wisdom.

Sirach can provide much information regarding religious thought at the beginning of the second century B.C.E. The author is clearly devoted to the Law and urges faithful practice of traditional religion (1:25-28; 6:37). The theme of the fear of the Lord is so prevalent (e.g., 2:15-17; 34:13ff.) that some have proposed to take it as the major theme of the book, but it seems rather to be a natural expression for the traditional obedience to the Lord's commands. It is also evident that the fear of the Lord, combining love and obedience, is the basis for the emphasis on prayer that is found in the book. God is to be feared and trusted, and all human beings should learn to depend upon him.

One senses a universal spirit in the author, in spite of his insistence that the true faith is to be found in Judaism. As in other wisdom literature, there are evidences of non-Jewish influence, particularly from Egypt. In the section dealing with famous men from Enoch to the High Priest Simon II, a contemporary of the author (chaps. 44–50), and other parts of the book, God is presented as the creator of a perfect creation; he is the controller of the universe and deals with it justly; he is everything (16:17-23; 16:24–17:24; 42:21ff.; 43:27).

Chap. 24, with its personification of WISDOM as a female figure in heaven, is important in emphasizing that Wisdom truly dwells in Israel. Whatever else the other nations may have, the creator has given Wisdom to the Jewish people, who are now called to obey Wisdom, created for eternity.

The opening words of the prologue are important in providing the earliest indication of the division of the Hebrew Bible into the Law, the Prophets, and the other writings. Although the book was not finally accepted into the Jewish CANON, it seems to have been quite popular among Jewish readers. It is cited in the Talmud and referred to in Jewish literature until the Middle Ages. It was certainly widely used among early Christian writers (perhaps the name Ecclesiasticus—"The Church Book" supports this). The book is more Sadducean than Pharisean, and that may account for its rejection from the Jewish canon.

See also APOCRYPHAL LITERATURE; HELLENISTIC WORLD; WISDOM LITERATURE.

Bibliography. I. Levi, *The Hebrew Text of the Book of Ecclesiasticus*; J. G. Snaith, *Ecclesiasticus*; T. H. Weber, "Sirach," *JBC*; Y. Yadin, *The Ben Sira Scroll from Masada*.

—HEBER F. PEACOCK

• **Sisera.** [sis′uh-ruh] The leader of forces that Israel defeated in the vicinity of Taanach and Megiddo in the time of the judge and prophetess DEBORAH (Judg 4:2-16; 5:19-21). He was killed by Jael, the wife of Heber the Kenite, who drove a tent peg through his temple while he slept in her tent (Judg 4:17-22; 5:24-27). It is not entirely clear whether Sisera was an independent ruler or someone else's general. In Judg 4:2 it is stated that he was the commander of the army of Jabin, the king of Canaan who reigned in Hazor; but Hazor (and its king, Jabin—cf. Josh 11:1-11) was supposed to have been destroyed by JOSHUA. In the older poetic version of the battle (Judg 5), Sisera appears as one of "the kings of Canaan" who fought Israel (Judg 5:19-21). Most likely, Sisera was secondarily associated with Jabin, both of whom would have been memorable opponents from the predominantly Canaanite plains. Since Sisera's name is not semitic, and the place-name associated with him, Harosheth-ha-goim ("the wooded region of the gentiles"—its location is unknown) appears to refer to a non-Canaanite population, it is likely that he was a leader of a branch of the SEA PEOPLES, a term denoting several groups of immigrants to Palestine who came from various places in the Mediterranean basin (e.g., Sardinia, Asia Minor, Cyprus) beginning as early as the fifteenth century B.C.E. and culminating around 1200 B.C.E.

Sisera was also the name of the ancestor of a group of temple servants who returned from Babylon with ZERUBBABEL (Ezra 2:53).

See also DEBORAH.

—JEFFREY S. ROGERS

• **Sister.** The word "sister" occurs 114 times in the OT (Heb. *'āḥôt*) and twenty-four times in the NT (Gk. *adelphē*). General usage indicates a female relative, usually a full or half-sister. Sexual relations with sisters were forbidden (Lev 18:9, 11; cf. 2 Sam 13). Three times a patriarch presented his wife as his sister to avoid death (Gen 12:10-20; 20:1-18; 26:1-11), a deception some connect with a Hurrian legal practice of adopting wives as sisters (cf. Gen 20:12).

The figurative use of "sister" for the bride in the Song of Solomon (4:9-12; 5:1-2) probably indicates endearment and not an Egyptian practice of brother-sister marriages. Figuratively also, Israel and Judah are "sisters" (Jer 3:7), as are Jerusalem, Samaria, and Sodom (Ezek 16:46). Jesus spoke of his spiritual family as "sister" (and brother and mother; Mark 3:35).

See also FAMILY.

Bibliography. H. Ringgren, "אָח, אָחוֹת," *TDOT*.

—SCOTT NASH

• **Skull, Place of the.** *See* CALVARY

• **Sky.** The "heavens" (Heb. *šāmayim*), also identified with the firmament or dome (Heb. *rāqî'a,* Gen 1:8) of heaven, and occasionally referred to by the term *šahaq* (2 Sam 22:12 = Ps 18:12).

According to Gen 1:6-8, the "sky" was formed on the second day of God's creative activity. The purpose of the sky was to divide the primeval waters so as to create the separate localities of "above the sky" and "below the sky." The waters below the sky are eventually gathered together to form the seas, while the waters above the sky (note Ps 148:4) receive no further mention in the creation narrative. Thus the sky serves as a retaining barrier that prevents these upper waters from bursting forth and inundating the dry earth below. This restraining function means that the sky was envisioned as solid in form, a conclusion supported by both philological and exegetical evidence. The verbal stem *rq'* (from which the noun *rāqî'a* is formed) connotes the physical action of "beating out, stamping out" (Ezek 6:11; 25:6), especially with regard to the shaping of metals (Exod 39:3; Num 17:4; Isa 40:19; Jer 10:9). The etymology of *rāqî'a* would thus suggest that the sky was conceived in the form of a solid metallic plate or surface which was suspended over the earth. In the flood story it is related that "windows" were opened in the sky to allow the trapped waters above to flow unimpeded upon the earth below (Gen 7:11) and that these "windows" were closed when God determined to end the flood (Gen 8:2). The necessity for such openings also indicates the solid nature of the sky.

Further references to the sky in the Hebrew Bible descriptively amplify the information provided in the creation narrative. According to Job 26:11, the sky is supported by columns. Ps 104:2 poetically likens the sky to a canopy that has been spread out over the earth. The throne of God rests upon the sky (Exod 24:10; Ezek 10:1), and in these two passages the sky appears to be constructed of "sapphire stonework." Similarly, Ezek 1:22 compares the sky to "crystal." These allusions to the luster of precious stones are echoed in Dan 12:3, where the faithful appear "shining like the brightness of the sky" at the End of Days (cf. 1 Cor 15:40-41).

In the NT, the same picture is evident. The noun *ouranos,* "heaven," is translated "sky" or "skies" when the reference is to the vault of heaven or to the open air (Matt 16:2-3; Heb 11:12).

The sky also denotes the area *below* the firmament and *above* the earth—where birds fly (Gen 1:20) and where the winds blow at God's bidding (Gen 8:1).

See also COSMOLOGY; FIRMAMENT; HEAVENS.

—JOHN C. REEVES

• **Slaughter of the Innocents.** This phrase describes the event recorded in Matt 2:16-18 in which HEROD the Great ordered the killing of all male children two years old and younger in Bethlehem and the surrounding region. Matthew interprets this act as a fulfillment of Jer 31:15.

Some critics have questioned the historicity of this event. First, the event is not found in any other early source. Most noticeable is its absence from Luke's birth narrative and from the writings of Josephus, the noted Jewish historian of the first century C.E. who described in some detail the events of Herod's reign, particularly his acts of cruelty. Second, because the killing of the children by Herod parallels the command of the Egyptian pharaoh at the time of Moses' birth that all sons born to the Hebrews were to be thrown into the Nile River (Exod 1:22), some have suggested that the account in Matthew might be the product of creative reflection on the OT rather than a historical event. The parallels throughout Matthew's birth narrative with events of the Israelite Exodus from Egypt strengthen the possibility that Matthew (or his source) has at least shaped, if not created, the story of the slaughter of the innocents to conform to the account in Exodus. The purpose of this parallelism would be to stress that in Jesus the history of Israel is reenacted and brought to fulfillment.

Other scholars, however, argue that Matthew's account is historically plausible. The picture that Josephus paints of Herod is of a suspicious, distrustful individual who would not hesitate to have anyone killed who was suspected of being a threat to his power. Herod executed, among others, three of his sons and one of his favorite wives. The slaughter of young children in order to secure his reign is not out of character with the Herod described by Josephus.

See also HEROD.

—MITCHELL G. REDDISH

• **Slavery in the New Testament.** In the legally and socially complex world of the NT, "slavery" designates the various systems of compulsory labor and dependency in which at any one time as many as one-third of the urban population was owned by a large number of the others. Another one-third were enslaved earlier in their lives; under Roman, Greek, and Jewish laws, slaves were freed quite frequently. Slaves of Roman citizens were usually set free (manumitted) by age thirty and routinely granted Roman citizenship.

In contrast to "New World" slavery, these slaves were not distinguished from free persons either by race, religion, kinds of work, clothing, ownership of property (including other slaves), or formal schooling, being often better educated than their owners. For these reasons a modern reader needs a solid understanding of this pivotal social institution (far more than can be given here) in order to comprehend what is said about human relationships in the NT or the metaphors of "bondage" and "freedom."

In contrast to the first century B.C.E. when the chief means of enslavement were capture in war and kidnapping by pirates (1 Tim 1:10), slaves mentioned in the NT were most likely born to slave mothers (Gal 4:21-31). Sometimes parents of freeborn children were forced to sell them into slavery to pay oppressive debts. In the early Roman Empire large numbers of people sold themselves into slavery, usually to escape the insecurity of life as a free day-laborer, to obtain special jobs, or to climb socially. For example, Erastus, a Christian, the "city treasurer" of Corinth (Rom 16:23), probably sold himself to the city to gain that responsible position. Paul had such self-sale in mind when exhorting the Corinthians: "You were bought with a price; do not become slaves of men" (1 Cor 7:23). Yet in the next generation some Christians did sell themselves into slavery to obtain funds to manumit some from oppressive owners and to feed others (*1 Clem* 55:2).

All ancient moral teachers took owning men and women as slaves for granted, including the Stoic philosopher Epictetus who was educated while in slavery. No plan to abolish slavery motivated any of the major slave-rebellions in the Mediterranean area, all of which occurred during 170–140 B.C.E. Slaves performed a wide variety of functions, some quite sensitive, ranging from streetsweepers to executives, fieldworkers to administrators of large estates, handworkers to foremen, including teachers, physicians, and household managers. When set free, most slaves continued their previous work. "Slave-only" jobs were reserved for convicted criminals who as slaves of the empire were expected to die as mine laborers or galley oarsmen.

The NT gives direct evidence that some early Christians were slaves or owners of slaves, e.g., Philemon and his slave Onesimus, the famous text in 1 Cor 7:21, and the exhortations to mutual respect between slaves and their owners in Col 3:22–4:1/Eph 6:5-9 (cf. 1 Tim 6:1-2; 1 Pet 2:18-21). A slave's treatment was dependent entirely on the character of his or her owner. Neither Jesus, nor the TWELVE, nor the 120 at Pentecost appear to have been slaveowners. When Paul described himself (Rom 1:1) and Timothy (Phil 1:1) as "slaves of Christ Jesus" he stressed not only their full spiritual dependence on Christ but also their place of honor in the OT tradition of Abraham, Moses, and David.

See also ONESIMUS; PHILEMON, LETTER TO; SLAVERY IN THE OLD TESTAMENT.

Bibliography. S. S. Bartchy, *First-Century Slavery and the Interpretation of 1 Cor 7:21*; K. R. Bradley, *Slaves and Masters in the Roman Empire: A Study in Social Control*; M. I. Finley, *Ancient Economy*; N. R. Petersen, *Rediscovering Paul: Philemon and the Sociology of Paul's Narrative World*; A. Watson, *Roman Slave Law*; T. Wiedemann, *Greek and Roman Slavery*.

—S. SCOTT BARTCHY

• **Slavery in the Old Testament.** Slavery was taken for granted in the OT and never seriously questioned. OT legislation was comparable to that of other nations with regard to non-Israelite slaves (Lev 25:44-46a). Yet "brother-Israelite" slaves were treated more humanely (Lev 25:39-43, 46b-55), an attitude ostensibly stemming from remembrance that Israel was itself a redeemed "nation of slaves" (Deut 15:15).

Three kinds of persons might become slaves: (1) prisoners of war (Num 31:9); (2) the destitute, indentured to satisfy a debt (Lev 25:47), to gain security (Lev 25:39ff.), or to make restitution for a crime (Exod 22:3); and (3) those purchased from "foreigners" (Gen 17:27). There were both state slaves and household slaves, with several subclasses among the latter (Lev 25:6).

State slavery as such—limited to the monarchy, and primarily prisoners of war—was most prominent under Solomon when Israel was involved in extensive construction projects. When EZRA and NEHEMIAH established a new ecclesiastical order to replace the former political order, state slaves—who were merged with the temple slaves or *nethinim*—were called "sons of Solomon's slaves" (Ezra 2:58). Temple slaves were in evidence as early as Moses (Num 31:47) and were listed by Ezra-Nehemiah as a specific class (Ezra 2:43ff.). But the household servant, who worked beside his master in house or field, is the main subject of OT legislation (Exod 21; Lev 25; Deut 15).

The extent to which OT slave legislation was actually realized in practice is a subject of no little debate. Yet OT legislation regarding slavery suggests an intention to be inclusive rather than exclusive (e.g., slaves participated in

Sabbath observance, Deut 5:14-15). While slavery for a foreigner might be one's lot for life (Lev 25:45-46), a fellow Hebrew reduced to slavery was to be released at the end of six years (Exod 21:2-4), or, later, during JUBILEE (Lev 25:40b-41). OT legislation regarding treatment of slaves favors the master—up to a point. A master may beat the slave, but if the slave thereby dies the master is punished (Exod 21:20-21); and if a slave is maimed by the master (even to the loss of a tooth!), the slave must be set free (Exod 21:26-27). Yet when a slave is killed by an outsider it is the master who is compensated for the loss (Exod 21:32); and when a betrothed slave woman is violated by another, neither is punished for adultery "because she was not free" (Lev 19:20-22; in such cases it is not clear whether the slave in question is a foreigner or a fellow Israelite, but Lev 25:39 suggests a fellow Israelite was never considered *merely* a slave).

There is much variation in the OT regarding classification and treatment of slaves. On the one hand, some slaves were regarded as mere property; on the other hand, others might almost become part of the family and be treated more as a brother or sister in need. Late in the OT, Job would say he dared not reject the complaints of his servants because they were human beings like himself (Job 31:13-15). This does not mean equality was practiced. It does suggest the recognition of an equality before God of master and slave as human beings, a revolutionary idea in the ancient world.

See also SERVANT; SLAVERY IN THE NEW TESTAMENT.

Bibliography. R. de Vaux, "Slaves," *Ancient Israel*; H. W. Wolff, "Masters and Slaves," *Int* 27 (1973): 259-72.

—EDD ROWELL

• **Smoke.** *See* INCENSE

• **Smyrna.** [smuhr'nuh] Smyrna was located about thirty-five mi. north of Ephesus on the west shore of the Aegean Sea (PLATES 26, 27). The original city was destroyed by the Lydians in the sixth century B.C.E. It was refounded in 290 B.C.E. and continues today as the modern Turkish city of Izmir.

The city had several squares and porticoes, a public library, numerous temples, and other buildings. In NT times the population may have been about 200,000. Coins describe the city as "first of Asia in beauty and size." The recovery of NT Smyrna by archaeological research is virtually impossible since the modern city covers the ancient one. However, some excavation has been done.

Smyrna sustained a special relationship to Rome and the imperial cult. It was a faithful ally of Rome long before the Roman power became supreme in the eastern Mediterranean. In 195 B.C.E. it became the first city in the ancient world to build a temple for pagan Roman worship and became a center for the cult of emperor worship. This strong allegiance to Rome plus a large Jewish population which was actively hostile to the Christians resulted in severe persecution for the Christians there. The most famous martyrdom was that of Bishop POLYCARP (155/6 C.E.).

John addressed one of his seven letters to the church at Smyrna (Rev 2:8-11). When the church began is not known.

See also ASIA; POLYCARP, MARTYRDOM OF; REVELATION, BOOK OF.

—J. A. REYNOLDS

• **Snake.** *See* SERPENT

• **Sociology of the New Testament.**

Historical Setting. Since the days of F. C. Baur and Adolf Harnack, NT scholarship has been aware of the fact that early Christianity was a social reality and that Jesus was a social reformer. With his research on the papyri, Adolf Deissmann called for further study into the social and linguistic backgrounds of the early church. And at the beginning of the twentieth century Ernst von Dobschutz provided a needed corrective to previous work by warning against the tendency both to assume that background forces were determinative of Christianity and to overlook originality in the shaping of the early church. Reductionism has always been a lurking danger in sociological studies as Wayne Meeks notes.

In the American context of the 1920s Shirley Jackson Case, Shailer Matthews, and others associated with the Chicago School pressed for an examination of the social elements which were inherent within early Christianity. This emphasis undoubtedly was linked to the high degree of interest in Christian social concerns of that era, which faded during successive decades as scholars developed their skills of form and redaction criticism and the church's leaders focused their attention on ecumenical and theological matters.

The Contemporary Situation. Following the Second World War attention once more has been focused upon literary and historical studies. In historical studies, emphasis has focused upon the contribution which the social sciences can make to the knowledge of the NT community. Among those that signaled the return to an emphasis upon historical studies have been Joachim Jeremias and Martin Hengel. As Howard C. Kee suggests, however, they have been primarily concerned with descriptive studies. But these historians have been joined by a growing cadre of scholars interested in more analytical studies within the broad area known as sociological analysis of the NT. These persons include Kee, Gerd Theissen, E. A. Judge, John Gager, Abraham Malherbe, and a group of younger scholars who have graduated from Yale and other places where the interest in sociology has been peaking. Many who have joined in this study have become convinced that earlier historical-critical approaches to a study of the NT treated the setting of the early church (*Sitz im Leben*) in too static a fashion and that sociological studies bring a dynamic back to the study of settings.

The study, however, is not without its problems. As in any growing field of scholarship, definitions are frequently vague, categories fuzzy, and methodologies often incomplete. Critics on the outside are often skeptical and critics within tend to promote their own style of sociological studies. The novice then may be confronted with what seems to be a hodgepodge of ideas and methods. Because of the complexity of the issues involved, and the variety of views, the subject may seem to be a little confusing. The task of an introductory article like the present one, therefore, is to attempt to provide some helpful categories for understanding the field while trying not to simplify it too much.

The Quest for Methodological Clarity. In discussing the subject, Jonathan Smith isolated four categories for social investigation: (1) description of social facts in Christian texts; (2) relationship of historical background to the social facts, i.e. social history; (3) study of institutions, structures and forces in the emergence of Christianity, i.e. social organization; and (4) study of the early Christian world created and maintained with meaning, i.e. social world (symbolic world). A number of scholars, however, like John Gager, think that only the latter category can actually be characterized as a sociological study.

In dealing with the variety of approaches Robin Scroggs sought to categorize certain models he thought could be identified as emerging. But he recognized that these models were heuristic and explanatory tools rather than descriptive conclusions. The first is a typological study, such as that of sect which Kee in part employs. The second relates to cognitive dissonance that is emphasized by Gager. The third model is that of role analysis which Theissen has employed. The fourth deals with the sociology of knowledge which concerns language and symbols as means of communication and functions in relationship to socio-economic-cultural needs. This model has been identified with Peter Berger and the many who stand indebted to him.

It must be emphasized that these approaches are heuristic models, keys to assist in the search for understanding the Jesus movement. Some scholars have used such models in combinations. Others have employed combinations of methods.

Kee claims that in his research of Christian origins he has employed the contributions of sociology of knowledge, social origins of leadership, social transformation theory, and the structure of myth. The sociological purists may shudder at Wayne Meek's admission that he is an eclectic. But these admissions merely attest to the emerging state of the discipline. They are witnesses to the fact that NT scholars are desirous of taking as much into account as possible. In the development of the discipline, however, it is already clear that the sociology of knowledge will be a major factor in research, that sociolinguistics will be important, and that cultural anthropological studies like those of Bruce Malina can be useful.

The Importance of the Concept of Social World. Social world is a designation which Berger and others employ to explain the human quest for bringing meaning to social experiences of a group. It is part of the human craving for order and meaning. Humans as a group of social beings seek to create and maintain or institutionalize a social world. According to Berger and Luckmann there are three stages in the process: (1) externalization, in which humans produce a social order; (2) objectivation, in which society becomes an objective reality; and (3) internalization, in which humanity in turn becomes a product of society. But a group's social world confronts and collides with other socially constructed worlds and therefore social worlds are subject to upheaval. Here, then, is one of the important contributions that social research can make to the investigation of the NT—namely, that in the study of backgrounds it should be recognized that settings are not static but dynamic.

A number of scholars like E. A. Judge have been concerned that some aspects of the study seem too deterministic and reductionistic. They are troubled that there are elements in the methodology that can reduce Christianity to analogy and repetitive behavior and that there is not sufficient room provided for the divine dimensions breaking into the human realm. There is certainly some justification for such criticisms. Theissen's conceptionalization must certainly be criticized. His view is that Jesus had little intention of founding communities of faith, but that he founded a movement of wandering charismatics who challenged local norms and identified themselves with the plight of the Son of man, and that Christianity can be understood as the result of a small group of outsiders who experimented with a new view of love and found acceptance in the Hellenistic world when it moved out of the crisis-torn Palestinian Jewish society. Such a view is certainly truncated, based on skeptical form-critical views, and aligned with an unnecessary Freudian psychological analysis.

But Malina reminds us that social science models do not need to be used reductionistically and can take account of the God of Israel and the Messiah Jesus. Nevertheless, he argues that the distinctiveness of societies such as early Christianity will not be discerned before the commonalities of time and place have been duly taken into account. It should be added, moreover, that in spite of Theissen's conclusions, he did work his way through a forest of untried cross-disciplinary studies and sought to bring attention to socioeconomic, socioecological, sociopolitical and sociocultural factors in research on the Jesus movement, primarily as it related to Palestinian society.

Some Expanding Areas of NT Research. Much can be added to our understanding of texts when tools of research are employed that take into account conflict theories, concepts like cognitive dissonance, and other social theories that seek to understand the dynamic nature of the setting to which the books of the NT were addressed. Theissen's essays on 1 Corinthians gave some initial insights into the significance that might result from applying sociological methods to such a text. Wayne Meeks carried the study further and his work is particularly helpful in his discussions of the urban implications of Pauline Christianity in Corinth.

One of the impressive uses of social research and its application to the NT was done by John Elliot in his study of 1 Peter. By concentrating on the alienation and homelessness being experienced among first-century Christians, Elliot reviewed how the text spoke to the social conditions of that era and aimed at providing transforming perspectives to the readers. In this process he made use of the important tool of social linguistics. David Verner followed Elliott with an investigation of household theory applied to the Pastoral Epistles. David May has since expanded the theory and applied it to the understanding of Mark and his community.

Other scholars have worked with various themes and texts. Examples of the range is evident in the discussions of honor, purity, body, and hospitality applied to Matthew, Mark, 1 Corinthians, and 3 John in the 1986 issue of *Semeia*.

Adela Collins has applied conflict theory to the Book of Revelation in her work on *Crisis and Catharsis*. While a number of scholars might disagree with some of her views about the recipients and the ''perceived'' crisis in the Apocalypse, the application of conflict theory to such a text is very enlightening.

The Contribution of Social Linguistics. Language, as Roger Fowler has argued, is a community's primary tool of socialization. It is the means by which people symbolically address each other whether orally or in written form such as in the NT. M. Halliday suggests that the study of written communication can be approached on three levels: (1) the level of meaning or semantics, (2) the level of syntax or lexical arrangement, and (3) the level of orthography and phonology. While many persons have focused their quest for meaning in the NT on word studies, primarily at the lexical and syntactical level, and often divorced them from contexts, the focus of others, as James Barr has indicated, has been in the area of semantics. The goal of most, however, has been to mine the NT text for theological content. The problem, as Malina has indicated, is that the new literary critics who are ahistorical and the historical critics both fall into a psychological pit, the latter primarily believing that what is determinative in the texts are ideas or theological constructs.

As Malina, Fowler, May, and others have argued, what is necessary is a sensitivity to the pragmatic aspects of language. Such a pragmatic approach attempts to incorporate the social aspects of semantics and, unlike the intuitive approach of historical criticism, seeks to determine from the text and its functioning those matters of social consequence.

The presupposition is that language is born in a social system for the purpose of communication, and that people do not communicate merely in single words or textual fragments but through texts as a whole. Clues to meaning then can be found in the use of certain language patterns. The use of familiar forms and stock phrases (habitualization) emphasizes acceptability and reinforcement of commonly held ideas. The use of the familiar in unfamiliar and strange contexts (defamiliarization) calls for reevaluation and perhaps transformation.

Another clue to the social contexts of the early church may be suggested by another aspect of language. The use of counterlanguage often becomes a pattern within groups struggling for recognition within a society. A subset of this pattern designated as antilanguage is employed by those wishing to establish themselves as a clear alternative to society. Malina considers that the Gospel of John contains the only clear indication of antilanguage in the NT and that most of the other writings represent a counterlanguage pattern. Whether the distinctions can in fact be made so precisely may be questioned by some, but the use of antilanguage in the NT does provide insight into how the writers viewed their relationship to society.

Those who employ sociolinguistics are quick to remind readers that their discipline is a tool that must not be used in a wooden and mechanical manner but that it must be used as a heuristic or suggestive approach which points the reader in the direction in which the society in question may have been moving with the cultural milieu.

The Contribution of Cultural Anthropology. Because the framework of thought and action in NT times is foreign to the twentieth century, help in the study of the early church can be derived from the discipline of cultural anthropology which is familiar with the task of understanding alien cultures. While first-hand observation of ancient social groups is not possible today, the written texts of the early church supply insights or cultural clues into the people who wrote and used these texts.

In reviewing various societies Mary Douglas developed in her book *Natural Symbols* a helpful system of models for identifying patterns within social groups. Her goal was to provide a means for assessing both the pressure or control exerted within a group and the degree of match or fit between an individual's experiences and societal patterns of perception. The first element she designated as "group" and the second element she termed "grid." She then reviewed social groups under six headings: purity, ritual, personal identity, body, sin, and spirit possession. Sheldon Isenberg and Bruce Malina systematized Douglas's various analyses and charted the ideas so that groups normally fall into one of four quadrants when "group" and "grid" are made the two axes of the chart.

To illustrate the results under the heading of personal identity the weak group/high grid would emphasize individualism, pragmatic and adaptive elements; the strong group/high grid would emphasize internalizing clearly articulated social roles, dyadic personality, and the individual subservient to society; in the weak group/low grid there is little or no antagonism between society and the self but the old society from which the individual emerges is seen as oppressive, the self and/or social control is seen as being low but the response pattern is highly individualistic; in the strong group/low grid identity is located in group membership not in the internalization of roles which are confused, dyadic personality is also a characteristic.

The contention is that most of the NT texts fall into the pattern of strong group/low grid and that the group pressure or control must have been quite high within the church. The basic structure would be dualistic and the focus would be on the conflict between the forces of good and evil. In this grouping there would be a significant concern for purity within the group as the group was under attack from without. Along with this concern went a clear sense of boundaries and fixed rites with a matching concern for deviant behavior. Those who broke into the boundaries of the body were viewed as invaders and the body or group was tightly controlled. Sin was considered as something like a polluting disease and evil was seen as residing both within individuals and in society. Suffering and misfortune were regarded as something to be expected and while some victories might be won, evil was not eliminated from the scene during life in the world. Because of the structured dualism related to life in the world, the group's values were defined but the ultimate attaining of goals was not to be realized in the present setting.

Cultural Themes and the Building of Models. As NT scholarship continues to develop skills in the handling of insights gained from the broad field of sociology and cultural anthropology, key themes will become vehicles for building models of understanding in the field. Malina has employed the ideas of shame/honor and purity as major keys for unlocking the doors to understanding first-century Christian society. To these he has added minor themes of personality, limited good, and kinship and marriage. Others will undoubtedly follow as the process becomes refined. Research into rituals, body, power, class, spirit, and so on will render further insights, though not unrelated to themes already pursued. The field is mushrooming as scholars pursue their special investigations of individual texts in the NT. Following that stage there will undoubtedly come new syntheses which will help to draw together results so that we will be provided with new insights into the variegated nature of the body which is commonly called the early church.

See also INTERPRETATION, HISTORY OF; SOCIOLOGY OF THE OLD TESTAMENT.

Bibliography. P. Berger, *The Sacred Canopy: Elements of a Sociological Theory of Religion*; P. Berger and T. Luckmann, *The Social Construction of Reality*; G. A. Deissmann, *Paul: A Study in Social and Religious History,* 2nd ed.; J. Elliott, *A Home for the Homeless: A Sociological Exegesis of 1 Peter*; R. Fowler, *Literature as Social Discourse*; J. Gager, *Kingdom and Community: The Social World of Early Christianity*; M. Halliday, *Language as Social Semiotic*; E. Judge, *The Social Pattern of Christian Groups in the First Century* and *Rank and Status in the World of the Caesars and St. Paul*; H. C. Kee, *Christian Origins in Sociological Perspective*; A. Malherbe, *Social Aspects of Early Christianity,* 2nd ed.; B. Malina, *The New Testament World, The Gospel of John in Sociolinguistic Perspective,* and *Christian Origins and Cultural Anthropology;* D. May, "The Role of House and Household Language in the Markan Social World," Th.D. diss., Southern Baptist Theological Seminary; W. Meeks, *The First Ur-*

ban Christians: The Social World of the Apostle Paul; N. R. Petersen, *Rediscovering Paul: Philemon and the Sociology of Paul's Narrative World*; R. Scroggs, "The Sociological Interpretation of the New Testament," *NTS* 26 (1980): 164-79; J. Z. Smith, "The Social Description of Early Christianity," *RSR* 1 (1975): 19-21; J. E. Stambaugh and D. L. Balch, *The New Testament and Its Social Environment*; W. Stegemann, *The Gospel and the Poor*; G. Theissen, *Sociology of Early Palestinian Christianity, The Social Setting of Pauline Christianity: Essays on Corinth,* and *The Miracle Stories of the Early Tradition*; D. Tidball, *The Social Context of the New Testament*; D. Verner, *The Household of God: The Social World of the Pastoral Epistles*.

—GERALD L. BORCHERT

• **Sociology of the Old Testament.** *Definition.* As a concept in modern biblical studies, sociology of the OT refers to: (1) an approach to or a way of examining biblical literature and history; (2) a set of topics thought to be appropriate to the social world of ancient Israel; and (3) the place of the OT literature in the life of a historical community. Since the early 1970s, the first of these has received the most attention and today sociology of the OT refers both to a method of interpretation (broadly defined), or an approach, and to the reconstruction of the sociohistory and culture of ancient Israel. From a methodological standpoint, it incorporates methods and theories from the social sciences—sociology, anthropology, and psychology—along with other critical methods of biblical studies. Oral history, ethnography, archaeology, geography, geology, and technology also inform social and cultural analysis. Although in some ways still in its infancy as a systematic and accepted approach, sociology of the OT provides a more comprehensive context for investigations using other methods and new perspectives for viewing sacred texts and history.

The significance of this approach lies not in providing further evidence to the biblical scholar, but rather in introducing tools for analyzing the ancient information and applying theories about the way societies are organized and develop. From comparative sociology (i.e., anthropology and sociology) biblical historians draw valuable information on structural and processual forms in other societies that can shed light on the social organization and institutions of ancient Israel, as well as the religious foundations underlying the biblical texts. The sociological approach balances the tendency to concentrate on Israel's political and religious history with attention to economic, social, and other aspects of daily life. It introduces a stronger concern for general as well as specific aspects of life, for the social world as well as isolated events and single individuals.

The social sciences also illuminate the sociological dimensions of the interpretive process itself. That is, they provide ways of identifying the origin, transmission, and meaning of the texts and relating these to social roles, social groups, and social structures. They offer analogies from modern and historical societies that help us to interpret the oral traditions underlying the biblical texts and the functions of the different OT literary forms.

The two primary disciplines of comparative sociology appealed to by sociologists of the OT are sociology and anthropology. Sociology is a generalizing science that illumines regularities in human conduct and overall patterns of social change. It emphasizes testing theories against historical or contemporary data. It is most effective in dealing with recurring behavior and values and with sociological phenomena found regularly in a number of different societies.

Theory and generalization are also central to anthropology, but it is further concerned with investigating all facets of human life and culture in particular societies, including the unique. A number of subdisciplines comprise "anthropology": ethnography, ethnology, social anthropology, and archaeology. Ethnography focuses on the interpretation and analysis of particular societies, ethnology on the theoretical and comparative study of human societies, social anthropology on social organization (the structure of societies and the functions of the various interacting elements of social structure), and archaeology on the description and interpretation of the material remains of past societies.

Historical Background. Although sociology of the OT is just beginning to enter mainstream biblical scholarship, early scholars also appealed to social phenomena in their interpretations of ancient Israelite society, religion, and literature. William Robertson Smith was the first biblical scholar to apply comparative methods and theories systematically to interpreting the Bible. Robertson Smith, a late nineteenth-century British scholar, had a significant impact on early twentieth-century scholarship in such varied fields as biblical studies, anthropology, sociology, and psychology. He was greatly influenced by the critical German scholarship of his day, especially Julius Wellhausen's historicocritical methods of analysis, historical reconstruction of ancient Israel, and work on Arabia.

Equally influential were Robertson Smith's extensive travels in the Middle East and his acquaintance with the works of other contemporary comparativists. Nineteenth-century anthropological concerns with the origins and evolution of the human race and using "survivals" for reconstructing early stages of culture are evident in his work, especially his *Kinship and Marriage in Early Arabia* (1885) and *Lectures on the Religion of the Semites* (1889). The work of E. B. Tylor (the "father" of anthropology) and his theory of the origins of religion certainly influenced Robertson Smith, but he was most notably influenced by J. F. McLennan and J. G. Frazer. McLennan's ideas are most readily apparent in Robertson Smith's emphasis on the precedence of matrilineal over patrilineal descent systems and on totemism, and Frazer provided some of the vast comparative materials upon which Robertson Smith drew.

Robertson Smith's work contributed to broadening the scope of OT studies to include comparative materials and social scientific perspectives. In his most influential work, *Lectures on the Religion of the Semites,* he defined the essential nature of "semitic," and thus "Hebrew," religious behavior. He concluded that sacrifice—which he perceived as essentially related to totemism and communal integration based on kinship among humans, animals, and the god—was the central and basic rite of all religions.

Although Robertson Smith has been accused of conjecture and erroneous use of survivals, of wrongfully insisting on the universality of totemic origins of religion, of oversimplifying, of making questionable comparisons (especially with camel bedouins), and ultimately of being responsible for subsequent scholars' failure to take social scientific approaches seriously, his contributions cannot be ignored.

Following Robertson Smith's lead, later scholars such as Johannes Pedersen (in his 1926–1940 psychological study of ancient Israel) and Roland de Vaux (in his 1961 study of Israel's social institutions) emphasized the importance of ancient Israel's social institutions. The British myth and ritual school and similar approaches in Scandinavia asked one of the same basic questions that Robertson Smith had: "What is the nature and role of ritual in ancient Israelite society?" But Robertson Smith's greatest impact on biblical scholarship must be traced indirectly through the fields of anthropology, sociology, and psychology. Of special importance in carrying on Robertson Smith's ideas and conveying them to following generations were the works of J. G. Frazer, Emil Durkheim, and Sigmund Freud. These scholars were instrumental in developing schools of thought in anthropology, classics and folklore, and psychology respectively.

From Robertson Smith's distinction between religion and magic Frazer developed his own theories on the subject. Durkheim, whose own theories were instrumental in establishing sociology of religion as a sub-discipline of sociology, further developed Robertson Smith's theories on totems, sacrifice, and the close relationship between religion and society. Freud's theories on totem and taboo also derived in part from those of Robertson Smith. And finally, Robertson Smith was responsible for developing some of the models that are still employed in anthropological studies of kinship today. Through the works of these early scholars his ideas have filtered down to biblical studies, the history of religions, anthropology, and sociology.

The specific details and conclusions in Robertson Smith's work are outdated. But his theoretical and methodological contributions are still recognized. Modern anthropologists laud his stress on studying a culture system as a whole and analyzing religion as a part of that whole, his awareness of spatial and temporal social context, his recognition of the need to view a culture from the participant's perspective, his cultural relativism, and his treatment of the relationship between social organization and ritual and belief. Especially important is his assertion that rituals contributed to the maintenance of social solidarity. The comparative approach advocated by Robertson Smith, although greatly modified, has returned to the social sciences as a valid analytical tool, and combining the comparative approach with historical study (ethnohistory) has become an accepted method for the study of culture and culture change. And finally, in his study of religion and sacrifice, Robertson Smith led the way to a clearer appreciation of the complexities and ambiguities of ritual and sacrifice.

After Robertson Smith, the next major contributions to the social scientific study of the Bible were made by Hermann Gunkel. Grounded in the well-established foundations of source criticism and influenced by the growing number of ancient Near Eastern texts recovered by archaeologists, Gunkel attempted to reconstruct the history of biblical literature. He established the form-critical and traditiohistorical methods of interpretation that analyzed the precompositional oral stages of Israel's traditions and literature. One of his major emphases was the life setting or *Sitz im Leben* of the literary genres he identified. Gunkel's approach was broadly concerned with social scientific questions. It investigated the relationship of oral and written literature to various social situations, but relied primarily on folkloric and ethnographic data rather than on method and theory. Hence, in contrast to Robertson Smith, he gave little attention to the interrelationship of the social, political, economic, and religious spheres of life.

After Gunkel, the study of literary genres and oral traditions concentrated increasingly on identifying the social settings of the language used in the biblical text, giving little attention to the social roles that these genres, in the context of their identified settings, played in Israelite life as a whole. Nevertheless, Gunkel's emphasis on social setting endures and provides a foundation upon which sociology of the OT continues to build.

Perhaps the most significant contribution to the social scientific study of the Bible published early in this century was Max Weber's *Ancient Judaism* (English translation, 1952). Weber was the first to apply comprehensively the methods and approaches of sociological analysis. His aim was to identify the relationship between social organization and religion in ancient Israel, particularly the connection between religion and economics. Weber's interest in these relationships was in part stimulated by Karl Marx's subordination of the role of religion in society to economic factors. He first sought to correct this bias by investigating the relationship of the Protestant ethic to Western capitalistic society. Having concluded that the Protestant ethic was a prime mover in the development of capitalistic economy, he turned his attention to India and China, and eventually to ancient Judaism. In the latter he perceived analogies with the Protestant West. For him, the prophetic element in Israelite religion represented an antecedent to western Protestantism and it was this prophetic element that stimulated the development of an ethical grounding for economic life.

Although not a biblical specialist himself, by drawing on the works of biblical scholars Weber was able to present an impressive analysis of the OT texts, while simultaneously applying sociological methods of inquiry. In addition to his evaluation of the relationship between religion and society, Weber's contributions include his analyses of Israel's cult, the covenant, early Israel's "charismatic" type of leadership, the social role of the Levites, Israel's diverse socioeconomic groups, and the nature and role of prophecy as related to the conflict between religious ideals and socioeconomic organization. Weber perceived relationships in the Israelite social world not previously recognized, and his work resulted in new insights into the changing economic and social conditions underlying the literary sources that had been identified by earlier biblical scholars. And he stimulated new ways of looking at Israelite religion's role in maintaining economic stability as well as transforming Israel's economic ideals during times of crisis.

Following these early attempts to reconstruct the social world of ancient Israel by appealing to the social sciences, there was a hiatus during which biblical scholars turned away from depending on these approaches for reconstructing the sociopolitical and economic spheres of Israelite society. However, there was continuing interest in these types of questions. For example, Martin Noth, a German scholar and an advocate of Albrecht Alt's territorial-historical method, developed a hypothetical reconstruction of the social organization of Israel's tribal period (ca. 1200–1020 B.C.E.) based on comparisons with Greek and Italian amphictyonies of later periods. His basic premise was that the twelve tribes of Israel were organized around a central shrine based first at Shechem, but later moved to Bethel, Gilgal, and Shiloh. The number twelve, he asserted, was fixed by the necessity of making provisions for the sanctuary on a rotating twelve month basis. Closely associated with this amphictyony were the institutions of divine law, holy war, and the office of judge. Although Noth's conclusions, at first widely accepted, have recently stimulated much controversy, they formed a foundation upon which many scholars later built. Meanwhile, in America W.F. Albright and his students relied more heavily on archaeological and linguistic investigations in addressing their concerns with the social world of ancient Israel.

The move away from a direct dependence upon anthropology and sociology as potential contributors to reconstructing Israelite history and society was a consequence of a number of interacting factors. Among these were an increasing dependence on archaeological material, a move toward theological questions, and a recognition that the works of these early advocates of social scientific approaches shared the weaknesses of the contemporary sociological and anthropological research upon which they depended. Additionally, in the mid-twentieth century anthropology turned to synchronic and culture-specific orientations led by British structural-functional interests and by American cultural relativism and historical particularism. Each stressed detailed ethnographic studies. This was a shift in the social sciences away from the traditional concerns of biblical scholars with the historical and diachronic dimensions of ancient Israel and did not allow for the comparative approach that had contributed so much to early reconstructions of ancient Israel's social world.

However, some biblical scholars concerned with the religion of ancient Israel continued to depend on anthropological theory. Theories of evolution had lost their appeal and concern for the diachronic dimensions of culture and culture change had receded into the background. But some anthropologists continued to deal with questions of culture change by applying theories of diffusion. Out of this theoretical orientation developed the controversial British myth and ritual school that was influenced particularly by the notion of "patterns" of culture proposed by A. M. Hocart. S. H. Hooke, who had some training in anthropology, was the founder of the school and the editor of *Myth and Ritual* (1933), *The Labyrinth* (1935), and *Myth, Ritual, and Kingship* (1958). He and the other proponents of the school sought to identify the connections among the systems of ritual and myth in the ancient Near East, especially as these related to the OT. Applying Hocart's assertion that social institutions tended to conform to a limited number of "ideal types" with fixed sets of component parts (a move away from the Frazerian emphasis on comparing independent elements), Hooke proposed a common ritual "pattern" for the ancient Near East. In agreement with diffusionist theory, Hooke and others in the myth and ritual school asserted that culture change is the product of cultural contact rather than evolution and, thus, that the proposed ritual pattern had diffused throughout the Near East from one cultural center. They further postulated a reconstruction of the annual Israelite New Year festival and the king's role in this festival based on comparisons with the Babylonian *akitu* festival and reconstructions of similar festivals among the Canaanites and Egyptians. The pattern was represented in its most complete form in Babylonian texts, but was thought to have been transmitted to Israel via contact with Canaanite religion. Evidence for the pattern in Israel was found in fragmentary references in the OT, and the gaps in the Israelite evidence were filled in with the information from the Babylonian texts.

Criticism of the approaches and conclusions of the myth and ritual school have been numerous and harsh. Its advocates have been accused of "slavishly" following Frazer, of proposing and recklessly imposing a pattern that simply did not exist, of ignoring significant cultural differences, etc. But in spite of the obvious problems associated with the school's theory, it did make a number of lasting contributions to OT scholarship. The school made a forceful critique of simplistic evolutionary schemes, emphasized the significant contributions of the comparative approach to studying culture, promoted awareness of the role of the king in the Israelite cult, and stimulated collaboration among scholars from different fields. The conclusions of the myth and ritual school remain controversial, but are being reassessed in light of recent developments in anthropological studies on ritual and ritual symbols.

Contemporary Studies. Other studies, from this period and later, treated the subjects of social, political, and religious offices, practices, and institutions, but little attention was given to reconstructing their cultural contexts. In recent decades there has been renewed interest in applying social scientific approaches and theories to interpreting the OT. Biblical scholars have recognized the importance of the social context of OT literature and have grown more aware that the literature was shaped by social, religious, and ideological factors that were influenced by social as well as historical phenomena. Furthermore, the availability of a wider range of social scientific data and approaches combined with contemporary methodological rigor have generated new theories with the potential of opening up new perspectives on biblical material. Especially significant is the emphasis on the importance of diachronic and processual studies for understanding culture and society, an orientation that is necessary both for understanding the nature of the biblical literature and the sociocultural contexts that underlie it.

Within biblical scholarship, there have arisen more methodologically responsible studies of the origins of Israel and of the institutions of the Israelite monarchy that appeal to sociological and anthropological understandings of nomadism, tribalism, and state formation. There have also been more sociologically informed treatments of Israelite prophecy and apocalypticism that appeal to social information on religious specialists and millennial movements. Advances in archaeological theory have contributed to these developments by giving more attention to the use of ethnographic analogies (ethnoarchaeology) and to such factors as settlement patterns and means of subsistence. Each of these contributes to the goal of attaining a fuller understanding of ancient Israelite society.

Much of this recent work focuses attention on reconstructing the social world of the enigmatic tribal period. Both the controversy over the mode of settlement of the Israelite tribes (conquest vs. peaceful infiltration) and the growing recognition that Noth's amphictyonic hypothesis inadequately explained the organization of the tribes have contributed to a growing interest in appealing to social scientific models for possible insights. Evidence of this renewed interest in the social dimensions of early Israel in the 1960s is apparent, for example, in the works of G. E. Mendenhall. Mendenhall's theories on the covenant relationship of early Israel with Yahweh and his proposal that early Israel arose as a federation of peasants who had revolted against the oppression of the Canaanite city-states remain important. For Mendenhall, the Yahwistic religion united the new group and established a radical discontinuity with the ideologies of the Late Bronze Age Canaanite city-states.

Mendenhall suggested that the new ideology was expressed in language similar to that used in the suzerainty treaty, a literary and legal form common to the cultures of the ancient Near East, although the form's function was transformed. In tribal Israel, the deity displaced the previous politically centralized monopolies of force and the Israelites were united by allegiance to this God who was understood to be Israel's sole overlord. For Mendenhall, religion was the basis of Israelite solidarity during the tribal period and therefore was essential to the creation of the people Israel.

The most comprehensive reconstruction of the tribal period that is grounded in the social scientific approach is Norman Gottwald's monumental and controversial *The Tribes of Yahweh* (1979). In this work Gottwald expands on Mendenhall's proposal of a peasant rebellion against the oppressive Canaanite city-state system and further suggests an intentional "retribalization." This retribalization established a tribal organization made up of diverse social groups that shared a common egalitarian ideal and worshiped a common liberating God. Gottwald also examines the social processes that shaped Israel during the tribal period, and by appealing to sociological and anthropological studies, analyzes the social world and religion of tribal Israel in the context of politics and economics. His primary goal is to delineate and conceptualize early Israel as a total social system.

Gottwald begins by assembling what he considers to be the most reliable information about Israel's rise as determined by traditional methods of biblical interpretation and by examining previously proposed hypotheses on the social characteristics of early Israel (e.g., pastoral nomadism, tribal confederacy, and peasant revolt). He then applies models from anthropology and sociology. He makes use of a structural-functional (synchronic) model to examine the relationship among the various elements in Israel's social organization and, in the context of this model, proposes that most leadership positions in tribal Israel were temporary and that the primary social unit was the extended family. He also identifies what he calls "village protection associations" that are comprised of extended families living in the same geographical area. And he suggests that the more inclusive social units of tribe and nation normally only functioned politically in military contexts.

Gottwald then employs a historical cultural-materialistic (diachronic) model to explain the changes that accompanied Israel's emergence. For the latter model, Gottwald relies heavily on the stream of scholarship associated most closely with Karl Marx. According to this theoretical perspective, the forces underlying historical change are economic and social rather than ideological (as had been asserted by Mendenhall). Environmental and technological aspects of society such as metallurgy, agricultural methods, and water systems are also examined in the context of this model because they pertain to the materialistic perspective.

Among Gottwald's major conclusions are: (1) early Israel was a heterogeneous formation of marginal and oppressed Canaanite peoples that included "feudalized" peasants, mercenaries and adventurers, transhumant pastoralists, tribally organized farmers and pastoral nomads, and possibly itinerant artisans and disaffected priests—social groups that were identified in the fourteenth century B.C.E. Amarna letters; (2) Israel emerged from a fundamental breach in Canaanite society brought on by a common opposition to Canaanite imperialism, not as the result of an invasion or immigration from outside; (3) early Israel's social structure was a deliberate and conscious "retribalization" process; and (4) the religion of Yahweh was a crucial societal instrument for supporting political and economic equality at the individual and tribal levels.

Although not as well developed as recent theories associated with Israel's tribal period, social scientific methods and theories have also been applied to interpreting the social world of the Israelite monarchy (ca. 1020–587/6 B.C.E.). Mendenhall (1973) referred to the potential of E. Service's four-stage scheme of cultural evolution (band, tribe, chiefdom, state) to illuminate the period of the monarchy, and more recently, James W. Flanagan (1981) has used anthropological theories on state formation to reconstruct the transitional period during which tribal organization began to move toward state organization and the establishment of kingship. Flanagan examines the transition in light of cultural evolution and social anthropological descriptions of the processes involved in succession to high office. He proposes an intermediate stage of chiefdom for the reigns of Saul and David as one stage through which Israel's sociopolitical organization passed as kingship emerged. As chiefs, Saul and David provided leadership for familistic, but non-egalitarian, social groups. Flanagan identifies the principal prime movers that may have affected Israel's social organization during this transitional period and outlines the origins of hereditary inequality that eventually led to monarchy. In his study, Flanagan considers kinship and the political, religious, and economic factors that contributed to the rise of the monarchy.

Frank Frick (1985) has made a similar argument for a transitional stage of chiefdom in the evolution of the Israelite monarchy using an ethnoarchaeological approach. Based on his assessment of archaeological remains combined with what is known about the material culture of chiefdoms from ethnographic studies, Frick argues for an earlier date for the introduction of chieftaincy in ancient Israel. Of primary import in both of these studies is the recognition that factors internal to the social world of ancient Israel may have played an equal, if not more significant, role in the adoption of a state form of sociopolitical organization as such external forces as the Philistine threat emphasized in the biblical narratives.

After Mendenhall's early study, interest in illuminating the social dimensions of Israelite history expanded to include studies on biblical and ancient Near Eastern genealogies. Abraham Malamat and Robert Wilson demonstrated that the genealogies represented in the Bible fit the characteristic patterns of genealogies found in other societies. Noting the fluid and sometimes contradictory nature of the genealogical material preserved in the OT, Robert Wilson has examined the nature of genealogies and the ways in which oral and written genealogies are actually used in societies that have social structures similar to that of ancient Israel. Factors that may have contributed to the form and content of the genealogies preserved in the Bible are variations in the type of sociopolitical organization that gave rise to them and variations in oral form or written form according to the social spheres in which they functioned. By appealing to ethnographic examples of the form, function, and content of genealogies, these scholars have been able to clarify the role of genealogies in the OT and the possible reasons behind the presence of contradictions.

Finally, note should be made of social scientific studies that deal specifically with the phenomena of Israelite ritual and religion. A recent example of studies on the function of ritual in ancient Israelite society that draws upon anthropological studies of ritual process and the social function of ritual is Flanagan's study of the role of ritual and religion in establishing David's legitimacy (1983). There he argues that David's ritual transfer of the Ark of the Covenant to Jerusalem (2 Sam 6) constituted a rite of passage that mediated and legitimated the temporal, spatial, and social transformations associated with the establishment of kingship in ancient Israel.

The benefits of a sociological approach for interpreting ancient Israel's religion are also visible in Paul Hanson's study of apocalypticism in ancient Israel (1979). In this study, Hanson traces the emergence of postexilic apocalyptic eschatology in the context of social and religious conflicts within the Israelite community.

Recent studies of Israelite prophecy should also be noted as having made important contributions to social scientific studies of Israelite religion. One of the most comprehensive of these is Robert Wilson's study of the social role of prophets in ancient Israelite society (1980). By appealing to ethnographic studies of religious specialists, Wilson first examines the various ways that prophets interact with their societies in societies that tolerate or encourage prophecy. On the basis of this information, he suggests that the social support necessary for the success of prophets in other societies also held true for the prophets of ancient Israel. He identifies two types of prophets on the basis of the types of support groups with whom they are associated. *Central prophets* function close to the center of power in a society, and as a consequence normally enjoy social prestige and political power. Because of their close alliance to the powers that be, central prophets tend to be concerned with the preservation of the status quo, i.e., with legitimating the existing social order. *Peripheral prophets*, on the other hand, operate on the fringes of society, with little or no central authority. What authority they do have derives from their socially marginal support groups. Because of their social location, these prophets are more concerned with bringing about social change to improve the situations of their support groups.

On the basis of these observations, Wilson suggests that similar distinctions in prophetic roles can be identified for ancient Israelite prophecy between prophecy in the south and prophecy in the north. The former can be broadly identified with central and the latter with peripheral prophets. In general, the biblical text indicates that prophets rooted in the southern Jerusalemite traditions tended to be associated with central political and religious institutions and that prophets rooted in the northern "Mosaic" prophetic tradition tended to be socially marginal and in conflict with the central institutions of society.

Prospects. Sociology of the OT continues to explore new approaches and new avenues in biblical studies. Scholars are still examining and experimenting with the many models and theories that the social sciences have to offer. A method or methods are still in the process of being defined, as are their relationship to other methods of interpreting the OT.

Models, theories, and reconstructions of the major historical and transitional periods of ancient Israel's history and of Israelite social and religious institutions continue to be refined and updated in light of recent advances in the social sciences. In addition, sociologists of the OT are beginning to consider questions that are more directly related to analysis of the biblical literature, and are working toward a union of methods of narrative analysis and social scientific methods and theories. Questions such as how and why narratives are generated and maintained, how they function socially and culturally, and how they are structured and impart meaning are moving to the fore. These are but a few of the numerous paths of inquiry that have been opened to the biblical scholar by the introduction of social scientific methods.

See also HERMENEUTICS; RELIGION OF ISRAEL.

Bibliography. T. O. Beidelmann, *W. Robertson Smith and the Sociological Study of Religion*; J. W. Flanagan, "Chiefs in Israel," *JSOT* 20 (1981): 47-73, "History as Hologram: Integrating Literary, Archaeological, and Comparative Sociological Evidence," *SBLASP* (1985), and "Social Transformation and Ritual in 2 Samuel 6," *The Word of the Lord Shall Go Forth,* ed. C. Meyers and M. P. O'-Connor; F. S. Frick, *The Formation of the State in Ancient Israel: A Survey of Models and Theories*; N. K. Gottwald, *The Tribes of Yahweh: A Sociology of the Religion of Liberated Israel, 1250–1050 B.C.E.* and "Sociological Method in the Study of Ancient Israel," *Encounter with the Text,* ed. M. J. Buss; H. Hahn, *The Old Testament in Modern Research*; P. Hanson, *The Dawn of Apocalyptic*; S. H. Hooke, *Myth and Ritual*; E. Leach, "Anthropological Approaches to the Study of the Bible during the Twentieth Century," *Humanizing America's Iconic Book,* ed. G. M. Tucker and D. A. Knight; G. E. Mendenhall, *The Tenth Generation: The Origins of the Biblical Tradition*; J. Pedersen, *Israel: Its Life and Culture*; J. W. Rogerson, *Anthropology and the Old Testament*; W. R. Smith, *Lectures on the Religion of the Semites: The Fundamental Institutions*; M. Weber, *Ancient Judaism*; R. R. Wilson, *Genealogy and History in the Biblical World, Prophecy and Society in Ancient Israel* and *Sociological Approaches to the Old Testament.*

—PAULA M. MCNUTT

• **Sodom/Gomorrah/Cities of the Plain.** [sod'uhm/guh-mor'uh] Sodom and Gomorrah were two of the "cities of the plain," a pentapolis located in the region of the DEAD SEA. The other three of the five cities were Admah, Zeboiim, and Bela/Zoar. The order of their listing (Gen 14:2) and the greater prominence of Sodom and Gomorrah in biblical materials may indicate that Sodom and Gomorrah led the pentapolis.

The search for the remains of these ancient cities has long tantalized students of the Bible. Suggested locations range from the northeast, southwest, and southeast of the Dead Sea as well as beneath the surface of the southern end of the Sea itself. The geographical indications in the Bible are susceptible of differing interpretations. Thus, while Gen 10:19, 14:1-12, 19:24-28, Deut 29:23, and Ezek 16:46 may be interpreted as pointing to a northern location, they are usually taken to favor a southern orientation. Gen 13:10-12 and Deut 34:1-3 have been cited as the strongest indications of a northern site, though they may be interpreted as supporting southern suggestions.

The identification of the valley of Siddim with the Dead Sea (Gen 14:3) has led some to conclude that the valley of Siddim is beneath the Dead Sea, and therefore, the cities must also be submerged. Others have argued that the kings would not have chosen a battlefield so close to their own cities; therefore, the cities should be sought at some distance from the valley which is presumed to lie beneath the Dead Sea.

Interpreters have sought clarification from other sources. Since Byzantine times the site of es-Safi, five or six mi. south of the Dead Sea, has been identified as Zoar. Ancient literary sources (Josephus, Ptolemy, Eusebius) favor a southern location for the cities. Early archaeological work located only a single site, BAB EDH-DHRA, in the region, and it was interpreted as a cultic center for the pentapolis. Since no evidence of other settlements was found, the cities were thought to be submerged beneath the southern end of the Dead Sea. More recent archaeological work has located five Early Bronze Age settlements southeast of the Dead

Sea (Bab edh-Dhra, Numeira, es-Safi, Feifeh, Khanazi). Although some have suggested that these sites are the ancient cities of the plain, such a simple identification is premature. The excavators have refrained from drawing such conclusions.

Whether or not the ancient cities are ever located, their theological significance in the Bible is indisputable. They are illustrative of immorality and social decadence (cf. Gen 13:13; 18:20; Deut 32:32; Isa 1:10; 3:9; Jer 23:14; Ezek 16:49, 56; Rev 11:8), and their fate symbolizes the awful threat of divine, overturning judgment against rejection of God's demand for justice (cf. Deut 29:23; Isa 1:9; Jer 49:18; 50:40; Hos 11:8; Amos 4:11; Zeph 2:9; Lam 4:6; Luke 17:29-30; Rom 9:29; 2 Pet 2:6; Jude 7). Even so, the fate of cities who reject the ministry of Jesus or his disciples will be worse than that of Sodom of Gomorrah (Matt 10:15; 11:23-24; Luke 10:12; cf. Ezek 16:48, 53-55).

Bibliography. W. C. van Hattem, "Once Again: Sodom and Gomorrah" *BA* 44 (1981): 87-92; D. M. Howard, Jr., "Sodom and Gomorrah Revisited," *JETS* 27 (1984): 385-400; W. W. Rast and R. T. Schaub, "The Dead Sea Expedition: Bab edh-Dhra and Numeira, May 24–July 10, 1981," *ASORN* 4 (1982): 4-12; R. T. Schaub and W. E. Rast, "Preliminary Report of the 1981 Expedition to the Dead Sea Plain, Jordan," *BASOR* 254 (1984): 35-60; W. H. Shea, "Two Palestinian Segments from the Eblaite Geographical Atlas," *The Word of the Lord Shall Go Forth,* ed. C. L. Meyers and M. O'Connor; J. Simons, *The Geographical and Topographical Texts of the Old Testament: A Concise Commentary in XXXII Chapters.*

—JOHN KEATING WILES

• **Sodomy.** [sod'uh-mee] Gen 19:5 has long been the focus of discussion about the nature of the SIN that could have brought down the wrath of Yahweh with such violent force on the city of SODOM. Since the Heb. *yāda'* (to know) in some contexts is a euphemism for sexual intercourse (cf. Gen 4:1), it has been assumed that the sin of Sodom against the visitors of Lot was sexual in nature. Over the years sodomy has been a term used to label sexual activity judged "unnatural" or immoral by the cultural mores of the time. The term could mean anal intercourse between heterosexuals, homosexuality, or bestiality.

It is not clear, however, that biblical writers regarded the sin of Sodom as sexual. EZEKIEL, e.g., in a context already filled with sexual images about prostitution, identified Sodom's sin as pride and the city's lack of care for the poor and underprivileged (Ezek 16:49). In fact, the majority of contexts, including Jesus' instructions to his disciples prior to sending them forth two by two, suggest that Sodom's sin was its violation of the desert code of hospitality toward strangers visiting in their midst (Isa 3:9; 13:9-19; Jer 23:14; Matt 10:15; Luke 10:10-12; Matt 11:23).

See also SIN.

—WILLIAM R. MILLAR

• **Soil.** *See* LAND

• **Sojourner/Resident Alien.** The term sojourner is often translated as "alien" or "stranger" or "foreigner." Generally, it refers to one of non-Israelite descent who lived permanently in Israelite territory, as distinguished from one who travelled through the land or was an outsider totally unrelated to Israel.

The earliest uses of the term appear in connection with ABRAHAM's stay in EGYPT and CANAAN (Gen 12:10; 21:23), and MOSES' period of refuge in MIDIAN (Exod 2:22). In early Israel several groups probably made up the sojourner class: the mixed multitude (Exod 12:38) who had accompanied them from Egypt; Canaanites in the land who were not displaced; imported war-captives and servants; and a mixture of refugees, fugitives, and others who merely wanted a new place in which to dwell. DAVID's kindness to sojourners is commended (2 Sam 15:19, 20), and in the time of SOLOMON, one-tenth of the population consisted of sojourners, 153,600 men (2 Chr 2:17).

Israelites were commanded to love strangers as they did their own families (Lev 19:34; Deut 10:19), remembering that they had been sojourners in EGYPT (Exod 22:21). Although sojourners could become prosperous and even own slaves (Lev 25:47, 48), most of them were in service to the Israelites (Deut 24:14). Usually sojourners were mentioned along with orphans (Exod 22:21-23; Deut 10:18; 24:17) in association with hired workers (Exod 12:45; Lev 22:10; 25:6), indicating their low social status. Hirelings from the sojourner class could be engaged by the day (Lev 19:13; Deut 24:15) or by the year (Lev 25:53). A sojourner who became a slave was circumcised (Exod 12:44) and became a part of the owner's inheritance (Lev 25:45, 46). The uncircumcised sojourner was forbidden to eat the PASSOVER meal (Exod 12:48) and on occasion was allowed to partake of food prohibited to Israelites (Deut 14:21).

Sojourners were specifically mentioned in connection with some restrictions. They were not to worship MOLECH (Lev 20:2), to blaspheme the name of God (Lev 24:16), to work on the SABBATH (Exod 20:10), to break the marriage statutes (Lev 18:26), or to consume blood (Lev 17:10-16).

Circumcised sojourners enjoyed privileges that Israelites enjoyed (Exod 12:49). Because there was one God and Lord over all, one standard prevailed (Lev 24:22) and the law was to be applied without partiality (Deut 1:16, 17; 10:17, 18; 16:14; 26:11). Along with the priests, sojourners shared in the tithes every three years (Deut 14:28, 29; 26:11-13). Also they participated in the voluntary produce of the sabbatical year (Lev 25:6), and benefited from the gleaning provision (Deut 24:19-21; Lev 19:10; 23:22).

In later Israel, the prophets chided those who oppressed the sojourner (Jer 7:6; 22:3; Ezek 22:29; Mal 3:5) and Ezekiel, in his vision of the ideal temple and restored Israel, included an inheritance for them (Ezek 47:22, 23).

In the NT, the term "stranger" refers to someone unknown, and Jesus' parable of the Good Samaritan teaches the proper Christian attitude to be shown toward strangers. The term "proselyte" more nearly approximates the OT concept of "sojourner" or "resident alien."

See also STRANGER; PROSELYTE.

—A. O. COLLINS

• **Soldier.** A person serving in a military capacity, usually in warfare or in an occupation status.

The first reference to armed combat in the OT is in relation to ABRAHAM's gathering a group of trained men to rescue LOT and his fellow townspeople (Gen 14:14). When Israel left Egypt for Canaan, soldiers of Pharaoh pursued them and were drowned in the sea (Exod 14:1-28). JOSHUA, with chosen fighting men, drove back the Amalekites into the wilderness (Exod 17:8-13). Men twenty years of age and upward were enlisted from each tribe (Num 1:2-4) and were divided into units of fifties, hundreds, and thousands with leaders over each group (Num 31:14, 48; 1 Sam 8:12; 2 Kgs 1:9; 2 Chr 25:5; Isa 3:3). Levites were exempted from military service (Num 2:33) and those who were afraid were excused lest they affect the morale of others (Deut 20:8; Judg 7:3). Other exemptions were provided for those who had built new houses, planted vineyards, or become engaged or just married (Deut 20:5-7; 24:5). For the campaigns of Joshua and the judges, messengers were sent throughout the land to summon the fighters together (cf. Ehud in Judg 3:28 and GIDEON in Judg 6:35 and 7:24).

At the establishment of the monarchy, SAMUEL objected, stating that a professional soldiery would become necessary and expensive (1 Sam 8:11, 12). When SAUL was anointed king, he proved his leadership ability by calling soldiers to battle (1 Sam 11:8; 14:52). DAVID brought together a professional army based on a tribal census and had in addition a select group designated as his "mighty men" (1 Sam 23:13; 2 Sam 23:8-39; 1 Chr 11:10-47).

In NT events, Roman soldiers figured prominently. A centurion was in charge of one hundred soldiers, and captains were set up over larger units. A legion of soldiers consisted of up to 6,000 professional foot-soldiers, combined with several hundred cavalrymen and other auxiliary groups. Roman soldiers were commonplace throughout the empire and could force others to carry their packs or perform other functions for them (Matt 5:39-42). Soldiers arrested JESUS (John 18:12), escorted him to trial (Mark 15:16), mockingly placed the crown of thorns on his head and the robe about him (Matt 27:27-31), gambled for his garments (John 19:23), and thrust the spear into his side (John 19:34). They guarded the tomb of Jesus (Matt 27:65, 66) and feared death when it was found empty (Matt 28:11-15).

Traditionally, soldiers served as guards for prisoners, as in the case of PETER and PAUL (Acts 12:4-6; 28:16) and as escorts when prisoners such as Paul were transported (Acts 23:23-33; 27:1, 31-43). In JERUSALEM and elsewhere, they were charged with maintaining the peace, preventing violence, and restoring order (Acts 21:31-35; 22:24-28).

Roman soldiers were fitted for battle in every respect and Paul used the analogy of the soldier's apparel and armor to typify the Christian's equipment for battle against SATAN (Eph 6:11-17; cf. Isa 59:16-17). Because Roman soldiers were so well-disciplined and obedient (Matt 8:9; Luke 7:8), Paul prided himself on being a worthy soldier of Jesus Christ and exhorted TIMOTHY to prove himself likewise (2 Tim 2:3, 4).

See also HOLY WAR; WEAPONS/WARFARE.

—A. O. COLLINS

• **Solomon.** [sol'uh-muhn] Solomon first appears in the biblical narrative as the second child of DAVID and BATHSHEBA, the daughter of Eliam (2 Sam 12:24-25), a woman bereft in succession of a husband and a child. By the time he enters the narrative again, David is moribund, and the question of succession is fraught with peril for Solomon. His mother has influential friends by now, and skill as a member of the court. She helps the prophet NATHAN persuade David that he has designated her son as his heir (1 Kgs 1:11-14, 15-21, 22-30). As a result, Solomon is anointed. After a series of bloody final assignments from David, "the kingdom was established in the hand of Solomon." Martin Noth has treated the following account of Solomon's kingship (1 Kgs 3–11) as a composition, drawn from a wide variety of official sources, by the deuteronomistic historian. The first section (chaps. 3–8) opens with a scene in which God appears to Solomon at Gibeon in a dream following his sacrifices at the "great high place" (3:4-15). This dream, with its associated request for "an understanding mind" (3:9), sets the tone for this narrative of the obedient king, who is wealthy and successful. This section is dominated by the account of the building of the Jerusalem temple, which is so important to the deuteronomistic historian. Following the résumé at 9:1, there is an account of a period of "apostasy and misfortune," opened by another, more ominous, appearance of God at Gibeon (9:1-9). In the story of the inadequate payment of his debts to Hiram, king of Tyre, with twenty Galilean towns (9:10-14), and in the account of the sanctuaries to foreign gods built in his dotage (11:1-8—cf. v. 4), we are prepared for a succession of enemies (11:14-40), including Jeroboam, who would later rebel successfully against Solomon's son, Rehoboam.

With Solomon, the movement of ISRAEL from a tribal confederacy (or a segmentary society, or a chiefdom) to a small state dominated by the city of JERUSALEM has come to completion. The list of chief royal officials (4:2-6—cf. 2 Sam 8:15-18), followed by an incoherent list of regional administrators (4:7-19), shows a strong central bureaucracy. Other elements of the ancient state—international trade (5:6-11; 9:26-28; 10:14-22, 27-29), expanded urbanization (chaps. 6; 7:1-12; 9:24), including the fortification or refortification of major cities (9:15-19), the organized labor gangs required for this work (5:13-16; 9:15, 21), and a standing army, including expensive chariotry (4:26; 9:23)—are strongly suggested by this narrative.

Archaeological investigation of sites now identified as the Solomonic cities has shown evidence of considerable building activity in the tenth century. Excavations at Megiddo, Hazor, and Gezer show fortifications with similarities that suggest a coherent building program. Ezekiel describes the gates of the temple area as having "three side rooms on either side . . . ; the three were of the same size" (40:10), a suitable description of the tenth century gates at all three other cities. They are also fortified with a "casemate" wall, which looks like a series of chambers from above, and which may have been shown to be obsolete by Shishak's battering rams (1 Kgs 14:25-26).

The City of David lay at the south end of a narrow ridge formed by two converging valleys. It rested on a landfill supported by massive retaining walls, which have been excavated on the east side. It appears that Solomon extended the city northward, building a royal quarter and a temple above the older city on an extension of the landfill (K. Kenyon thinks this is the "Millo" of 9:15, 24: *ml'* = "fill"). This construction in Jerusalem does not lend itself readily to archaeological investigation, since the critical areas either lie under the sacred area around the Dome of the Rock, or have been destroyed by later quarrying. Behind the elaborate description of the construction of the temple, there is a fairly simple three-room structure thirty ft. wide and ninety ft. long. There is a "vestibule" (6:3) before the entrance to the "nave" (6:17). At the rear of the nave is the "inner sanctuary" (6:20), where the Ark rested. It appears that the architectural influence came from Aram, where a remarkably similar structure has been found (Aharoni, 226-34). An Aramean prototype has also been suggested for the "king's house" (9:10—cf. 7:1; 9:15). Like an Aramean *bit-hilāni,* a contemporary governor's palace at Megiddo could be entered through a broad portico, possibly colonnaded, with a small guard room on the left. The entrance led through the long wall of a rectangular audience hall/throne room, which was the public part of a large official residence (diagrams in Kenyon, 62–63). The "House of the Forest of Lebanon" (7:2-5) has the general layout of Iron Age warehouses, with rows of pillars paralleling the long sides (note the buildings at Megiddo originally identified as "stables"). The other buildings in Jerusalem are inadequately described (7:6-8).

In addition to the accounts of trading activity, the report of Solomon's harem, including a daughter of Pharaoh (7:8; 9:16; 11:3), and the folkloristic story of the visit of the Queen of Sheba (10:1-13) increase the sense of international atmosphere of the court of Solomon. A widely held theory (that of von Rad) places the first written version of the Israelite epic tradition, the Yahwistic narrative, in the reign of Solomon, though a number of reservations about the theory have been expressed in recent years. The Temple functioned as a royal sanctuary, and it appears that the divine establishment and undergirding of the monarchy were celebrated in Temple liturgies from the time of Solomon.

Behind the celebration of the wealth and wisdom of Solomon in this narrative can be seen a sense of the public cost of this investment in architecture and military equipment. It is generally assumed that the seeds of the revolution of Jeroboam (11:26-40; 12:12-20), which divided the kingdom after his death, grew among those who bore the cost of these lavish royal expenditures.

See also DAVID; SOCIOLOGY OF THE OLD TESTAMENT; SUCCESSION NARRATIVE.

Bibliography. Y. Aharoni, *Archaeology of the Land of Israel*; N. K. Gottwald, ed., *Social Scientific Criticism of the Hebrew Bible and its Social World, Semeia* 37; E. W. Heaton, *Solomon's New Men: The Emergence of Ancient Israel as a National State*; K. Kenyon, *Royal Cities of the Old Testament*; J. M. Miller and J. H. Hayes, *A History of Ancient Israel and Judah*; M. Noth, *The Deuteronomistic History, JSOTSupp* 15; G. von Rad, *The Problem of the Hexateuch and Other Essays*; L. Rost, *The Succession to David's Throne*.

—ROY D. WELLS, JR.

• **Solomon, Odes of.** The *Odes of Solomon* has been called "the earliest Christian hymnbook." It is a collection of forty-two songs expressing joy and thankfulness for the GRACE which God has extended through the MESSIAH, the SON OF GOD. Most of the hymns end with the exultation: HALLELUJAH.

The last forty of the *Odes* are extant in Syriac. Ode 11 is preserved also in Greek. Five Odes (1, 5, 6, 22, and 25) are quoted in the Coptic Gnostic writing PISTIS SOPHIA. Ode 2 is lost. The existence of the *Odes* in three ancient languages, the citation of Ode 19 by the Latin apologist Lactantius (early fourth century), and the mention of the *Odes* (as apocryphal) in two ancient canonical lists, testify to the popularity of the *Odes* in the early and medieval church.

The character of the Syriac version and the strong parallels between the *Odes* and Ignatius of Antioch (ca. 115 C.E.) suggest that the *Odes* were composed in Syriac early in the second century C.E., in or near Antioch. Although there is nothing within the *Odes* themselves to connect them to SOLOMON, the textual history links them closely to the PSALMS OF SOLOMON, reflecting Solomon's reputation as a poet (1 Kgs 4:32).

The religious milieu of the *Odes* has been the subject of much debate. Some have argued that the *Odes* were originally Jewish and were later interpolated by Christians. It has been more common to view them as Gnostic, but this seems unlikely. It seems best to see them as Jewish-Christian, with strong ties both to Essene thought as reflected in the DEAD SEA SCROLLS, and to the conceptual world of Johannine Christianity (e.g., WORD Christology [Ode 41], "realized" ESCHATOLOGY [Ode 15]).

The theology of the *Odes* is a fascinating blend of the traditional and the innovative. God is the Father, Creator, Most High, and Lord. But he is also the one whose breasts are milked (Ode 19). Jesus (his name is never mentioned) is the Messiah, Son of God, Savior, Lord, and Word, who descended from on high, was born of a virgin, became incarnated, was crucified, and was raised from the dead, but these concepts are often depicted creatively (e.g., VIRGIN BIRTH [Ode 19], death and descent into SHEOL [Ode 42]), and he is frequently called "the Beloved." There are Trinitarian formulations both conventional (Ode 42:22) and unusual (Ode 19:2). The Odist can rejoice in being saved by grace (Ode 9:5) and in being one of the fruit-bearing trees that the Lord has planted in his eternal PARADISE (Ode 11).

Such a blend of old and new gives the *Odes* a special significance and beauty, since they are unshackled by the subtleties of later theological speculation which led to the great creeds. The sometimes startling images have the power both to shock modern-day readers and to move them to marvel at how early Christians sought to make sense of and to exult in their new faith.

See also HYMN; SOLOMON, PSALMS OF.

Bibliography. J. H. Charlesworth, "Odes of Solomon," *The Old Testament Pseudepigrapha*; J. A. Emerton, "The *Odes of Solomon,*" *The Apocryphal Old Testament*, ed. H. F. D. Sparks; J. R. Harris and A. Mingana, *The Odes and Psalms of Solomon*.

—JOSEPH L. TRAFTON

• **Solomon, Psalms of.** The *Psalms of Solomon* (*PssSol*) is a collection of eighteen noncanonical psalms. The psalms are patterned after the canonical psalms and include both psalms of praise and psalms of lament. Particularly noteworthy about the *PssSol,* however, are two features. First, the psalms contain a number of striking historical allusions. *PssSol* 2, for example, speaks of a sinner who forces his way into JERUSALEM with battering rams, after which gentile foreigners defile the TEMPLE. Later this "dragon" is killed dishonorably in Egypt, his body being left unburied. Other psalms identify the conqueror as a gentile who comes from (and takes captives back to) the West (17) and is initially welcomed by some of the Jewish leaders (8). These Jewish leaders are further condemned as, among other things, having profaned the Temple and its sacrifices (8) and set up a non-Davidic monarchy (17). Such condemnation is related to the second important feature: most of the psalms exhibit a strong we/they mentality. The psalmist identifies himself with those whom he calls the righteous, the pious, those who fear the Lord, the poor, the innocent, and the saints. On the other side are the unrighteous, the sinners, the transgressors, the men-pleasers, the lawless, the deceitful, those who live in hypocrisy, and the wicked.

The *PssSol* is preserved in Greek and in Syriac, both of which are probably translations of a lost Hebrew original. The title of the collection is a curious one, since there is nothing in any of the psalms to link them to SOLOMON. In fact, there is no reason to believe that all of the psalms were written at the same time or even by the same author. They do, however, share a common perspective, which suggests that they might be the product of a particular Jewish community. Although there have been various attempts to identify the foreign conqueror (e.g., Antiochus Epiphanes, HEROD the Great, or Titus), most scholars agree that the most probable candidate is the Roman general Pompey, who captured Jerusalem in 63 B.C.E. and was slain in Egypt in 48 B.C.E. Presumably the collection was put together shortly after Pompey's death.

The communal perspective of the *PssSol,* with its strong criticism of fellow Jews, might suggest that the psalms are the product of a Jewish party or sect. Traditionally, scholars have interpreted this partisan outlook against the background of Josephus's report of the intense rivalry between the PHARISEES and the SADDUCEES in the first century B.C.E. (*Ant* 13.10–14.3). Certain concepts within the psalms (e.g., proper interpretation of the Law, divine providence and human free will, resurrection, and retribution) are consistent with what Josephus reports about the Pharisees (*BJ* 2.8.14); hence, the psalms must have been composed by that group. The offending Jews would therefore be the Sadducees.

Recently scholars have begun to question this hypothesis. Parallels between the *PssSol* and the DEAD SEA SCROLLS have led some to suggest that these psalms are Hasidic or Essenic, a thesis which has not proved persuasive, however. Other scholars point to the difficulty of reconstructing first century B.C.E. Pharisaism from sources such as Josephus and to the diversity within first century B.C.E. Judaism beyond the classic categories of Pharisee, Sadducee, and ESSENE, preferring to leave the question open. The identification of the opponents as the Sadducees faces similar problems. The accusations regarding the Temple indicate the priestly nature of the group, but the reference to the non-Davidic monarchy points specifically to the Hasmonean dynasty, which was supported at various times by both Sadducees and Pharisees. Thus it is more accurate to see the psalms as reflecting anti-Hasmonean sentiment (contrast the pro-Hasmonean 1 MACCABEES), a position which was not uncommon among first century B.C.E. Jews.

The *PssSol* is characterized by strong expressions of praise and thanksgiving to God for his mercy. The psalmists recognize that the evils which have befallen the nation have been caused by the sin of the people. Yet God has not abandoned Israel; he has simply chastised his people, upon whom he will have mercy forever. Parallel to such nationalistic concerns are those of a more personal nature. In spite of their sins, God will have mercy on the righteous, who seek to walk according to his commandments and who endure willingly his discipline. God will forgive their sins and they will rise to eternal life. As for the enemies of Israel, as well as the sinners within Israel, their end will be destruction.

Of special note is that the final two psalms in the collection (17 and 18) depict a distinctive messianic expectation. God will raise up the Lord MESSIAH (17:32; cf. 18:5, 7), the Son of David, to be king over Israel. He will purify Jerusalem of its enemies and destroy the lawless nations by the word of his mouth. He will gather together his people and apportion them over the land. He will judge them and remove all unrighteousness from their midst. The nations will come to Jerusalem to see his glory. His hope will be in the Lord, who will strengthen him. His reign will be characterized by compassion and wisdom. He will be a faithful and righteous shepherd of the Lord's flock, and he will discipline the people that they might live righteously and in the fear of God. Those who live in the days of the Messiah will be blessed.

The *PssSol* is an important witness to the rich diversity within first century B.C.E. JUDAISM. The collection testifies both to the political perspective and to the personal piety of a particular group of Jews. In addition, it provides one of the outstanding examples of pre-Christian Jewish messianic hope. It is also, along with writings such as the APOCRYPHAL PSALMS and the Qumran THANKSGIVING SCROLL, a key document for ascertaining developments in postbiblical Jewish poetry. Finally, the *PssSol* testifies, along with the WISDOM OF SOLOMON, the TESTAMENT OF SOLOMON, and the ODES OF SOLOMON, to the developing Solomonic tradition in postbiblical Judaism and early Christianity.

See also APOCRYPHAL PSALMS; DEAD SEA SCROLLS; THANKSGIVING SCROLL.

Bibliography. M. Aberbach, "Historical Allusions of Chapters IV, XI, and XIII of the Psalms of Solomon," *JQR* 41 (1951): 379-96; S. P. Brock, "The Psalms of Solomon," *The Apocryphal Old Testament,* ed. H. F. D. Sparks; A. Büchler, *Types of Jewish Palestinian Piety from 70 B.C.E. to 70 C.E.*; G. B. Gray, "The Psalms of Solomon," *The Apocrypha and Pseudepigrapha of the Old Testament,* ed. R. H. Charles; R. R. Hann, "The Community of the Pious: The Social Setting of the Psalms of Solomon," *SR* 17 (1988): 169-89; W. L. Lane, "Paul's Legacy from Pharisaism: Light from the Psalms of Solomon," *CJ* 8 (1982): 130-38; H. E. Ryle and M. R. James, *Psalmoi Solomontos: Psalms of the Pharisees*; J. L. Trafton, *The Syriac Version of the Psalms of Solomon*; R. B. Wright, "The Psalms of Solomon," *The Old Testament Pseudepigrapha,* ed. J. H. Charlesworth.

—JOSEPH L. TRAFTON

• **Solomon, Testament of.** The *Testament of Solomon* (*TSol*) is a pseudonymous legend about how SOLOMON built the TEMPLE with the help of demons over whom he gained mastery. Narrated in the first person, it begins with the demon Ornias harassing a certain Temple artisan. Solomon prays to God, who gives him through the archangel MICHAEL a seal ring which grants him authority over the demons. Using the ring, Solomon subdues Ornias and puts him to work building the Temple. Thus is established a pattern of Solomon calling up demons, usually one at a time, interrogating them, and assigning them special building tasks. Typically, Solomon determines the demon's astrological sign, the character of its demonic activity (e.g., causing a certain disease), and the name of the angel who holds power over it. Occasionally there are predicitions, usually about the coming of Christ. At the close of the book, "Solomon" narrates his own idolatry and subsequent loss of God's glory, concluding with a warning to the reader not to follow his example.

TSol is extant in four widely varying Greek recensions. As a "testament" it is clearly Christian and was probably composed in Greek during the third century C.E., in Palestine, Egypt, or Asia Minor. But it seems likely that the "testament" is a revision of an earlier Jewish legend, perhaps dating to the first century C.E.

The Christian elements in the *TSol* are interesting. There are explicit references to the VIRGIN BIRTH (15:10; 22:20) and the CRUCIFIXION (12:3; 15:10; 22:20), as well as the healing of the Gerasene demoniac (11:6; cf. Mark 5:1-20). Jesus is called IMMANUEL (11:6; 15:12), wonderful counselor (12:3), the SON OF GOD (15:10), the savior (17:4), and the one whose name adds up to 644 (15:11). He is a king unlike any other, who is able to thwart all demons (15:10). The Christian is able to exercise the power of Jesus over demons by making the sign of the cross (17:4).

TSol exemplifies the shift in Jewish and in Christian perspectives towards viewing Solomon as the magician *par excellence*. The WISDOM aspect of Solomon's literary activity (cf. 1 Kgs 4:29-34) had a long development through PROVERBS, the SONG OF SONGS, and ECCLESIASTES, to the WISDOM OF SOLOMON, and, eventually, to the PSALMS OF SOLOMON and the ODES OF SOLOMON. By the first century C.E. Solomon was also perceived as an exorcist and healer by means of incantations, as seen in the Jewish historian JOSEPHUS. From the first century through the sixteenth, there is an abundance of evidence, both literary and archaeological, testifying to Solomon's ever-growing reputation as exorcist, healer, and magician.

The focus in the *TSol* on mastering demons, and, hence, diseases and other human problems, through magic, angels, and astrology, attests to syncretistic, if not superstitious, developments in both Judaism and Christianity. The popularity of the document indicates that the kinds of issues which it addressed were important concerns for ordinary Christians in the early and medieval church.

See also ANGEL; ASTROLOGY; DEMON IN NEW TESTAMENT; DEMON IN THE OLD TESTAMENT; MAGIC AND DIVINATION; TESTAMENTS, APOCRYPHAL.

Bibliography. D. C. Duling, "Testament of Solomon," *The Old Testament Pseudepigrapha,* ed. J. H. Charlesworth; C. C. McCown, *The Testament of Solomon*; M. Whittaker, "The Testament of Solomon," *The Apocryphal Old Testament,* ed. H. F. D. Sparks.

—JOSEPH L. TRAFTON

• **Solomon, Wisdom of.** The Wisdom of Solomon, one of the books of the Apocrypha or deuterocanonicals, is also known simply as the Book of Wisdom. Although the book claims King SOLOMON, known for his wisdom, as its author (see 9:7f.), this is clearly just a literary device, common in Jewish WISDOM LITERATURE. There is abundant evidence that the book was composed in Greek and that the author made use of the OT in the form of the SEPTUAGINT. The author remains anonymous, but most scholars agree that the book was probably written some time between 220 B.C.E. and 50 C.E. David Winston argues strongly for the period 37–41 C.E., during the reign of Gaius Caligula.

The book was probably written in Egypt, and perhaps in Alexandria. In addition to the fact that a major portion of the book (chaps. 11–19) contrasts the blessings of God on Israel and the punishment of God on Egypt, the author is well acquainted with Greek philosophy and its use in Jewish literature. Its origin is clearly in diaspora Judaism, and Alexandria, a major center of Jewish-Greek learning, is a likely place of writing.

The unity of the book was questioned in the eighteenth and early nineteenth centuries and again in the early twentieth century, but there seems to be a growing consensus that the book is a unity in spite of the large differences of style in the first and last parts of the book. But a careful examination of language and style leads to the conclusion that the book is by a single author and forms a whole.

The Book of Wisdom certainly belongs with the body of Jewish literature that is known as wisdom literature, although it differs from other wisdom material. It does not consist of short pithy sayings that are so familiar from a book like PROVERBS. The book is more akin to ECCLESIASTES, and not only in that both are attributed to Solomon. Wisdom is a public discourse which presents an argument in the hope of convincing Jewish people in the diaspora that their faith need not be rejected in favor of the competing religions around them. The author uses the standard forms for such an exhortation, combining philosophy and rhetoric, and trying to show that his position is logical and just.

The book is concerned to strengthen the faith of Jews living in the diaspora. The Jewish community living in the HELLENISTIC WORLD, and in intimate daily contact with new ideas and new religions, must not lose heart and suppose that its own faith is no longer valid. It is a time of crisis, and many are tempted to turn away from their faith. Some of the problems that Jews are facing from surrounding philosophical or religious positions can be seen in chap. 2, with its contrast between the wicked and the righteous. The author calls upon fellow Jews to take pride in their religion, which is far superior to what is offered in the world around them. Jews worship the one true God, and all the idolatry of the polytheistic world around them can be rejected as inferior.

The content of the book is not readily outlined or summarized, not because the plan of the book is obscure, but because of recurring themes found at several places in the book. Many outlines have been proposed. One of the most frequently seen divides the book into three sections: (1) The practical value of Wisdom (chaps. 1–5); (2) In praise of Wisdom (chaps. 6–9); and (3) Wisdom's guidance of the nations in history (chaps. 10–19). This does justice to the main themes of the book but is not entirely convincing as to the points of division. A better solution may be found in the author's use of INCLUSIO, in which the author repeats a key word or phrase from the beginning of a section at the end of that section. In such an approach the book may be divided into two major sections: (1)In praise of Wisdom (chaps. 1–10) and (2) God's use of Wisdom in the Exodus (chaps. 11–19). This may become a threefold division if one wishes to recognize that a shift occurs in section one at 6:22, where material on the nature of Wisdom and Solomon's search for her begins.

Many of the religious ideas of the book are significant in marking a change from views held at an earlier time. For example, the book gives the clearest and earliest Jewish expression of the idea that the suffering of the innocent in this world has little importance in light of the future life that they will enjoy with God, and this future life is strongly affirmed (3:1-9). The preexistence of the soul (8:19) and its IMMORTALITY (1:12f.; 3:1) contrast sharply with earlier views of human wholeness, with an earthly body made alive by the breath of God. Divine providence and future judgment, in this world and the next are everywhere assumed.

As one reads the book, the place of allegory becomes increasingly obvious. In fact, the last section of the book is a kind of allegorical midrash on God's deliverance of his people through wisdom at the time of the Exodus. In 10:7 the pillar of salt stands for disbelief in general. In 10:17 the pillar of cloud or of fire represents wisdom. And one should not overlook the repeated use of a contrast between God's punishment of the Egyptians and his blessing of the Israelites. For example, in 11:4 the author makes use of the contrast between the Nile water turned to blood and the water from the rock provided for the Israelites.

The Book of Wisdom is important for understanding late Jewish thought and ought to be studied carefully by those interested in Hellenistic Judaism and the NT. It should also be noted that the place of Wisdom in God's plan for the universe has parallels in the NT.

The text of the book is well established as preserved in five Greek uncial manuscripts with Codex Vaticanus and Codex Sinaiticus preserving the text most accurately. Modern editions of the Greek text provide a good critical text with an apparatus showing variants, and most modern translations provide some textual information.

See also APOCRYPHAL LITERATURE; WISDOM LITERATURE.

Bibliography. J. Reider, *The Book of Wisdom*; D. Winston, *The Wisdom of Solomon*; A. G. Wright, "Wisdom" *The Jerome Biblical Commentary*.

—HEBER F. PEACOCK

• **Son.** Frequently refers to a physical descendant, a male child who is an immediate descendant of a man and a woman (Gen 5:3; Luke 15:11, 13). The word also indicates a grandson (Gen 29:5; cf. 24:15, 29) or a remote descendant (Luke 19:9). In the plural "sons" usually includes both sexes and refers to members of a clan, tribe, or nation: "the sons of Esau" (Deut 2:4) and "the sons of Jacob" (Mal 3:6).

The Bible also uses "son" figuratively to show relationship to God. The people of ISRAEL are sons of God (Hos 1:10; Deut 14:1). Collectively, they are God's son (Hos 11:1) or God's firstborn son (Exod 4:22). The male descendant of DAVID is God's son, whether king in Jerusalem or the messianic ruler who is to come (2 Sam 7:14; Ps 2:7; Matt 3:17). Christians are sons of God by FAITH (Gal 3:26) and by ADOPTION (Rom 8:14). This relationship to God assumes submission to God's authority and DISCIPLINE as FATHER (2 Sam 7:14; Heb 12:5-6). It acknowledges dependence on God for everything (Matt 6:7-13) and expects conformity to God's character (Matt 5:44-45).

In the Bible "sons of" describes people's character and denotes the group, community, or realm to which they belong. A son of peace is a peaceful person (Luke 10:6). Sons of disobedience are those characterized by disobedience to God (Eph 2:2). Sons of the prophets are people who share a common calling as God's speakers (2 Kgs 2:3, 5). Sons of the kingdom belong to the realm of God and share God's character; sons of the evil one belong to the realm of SATAN and share Satan's character (Matt 13:38). A SON OF MAN is a member of humanity, a human being (Ps 8:4; Ezek 2:1).

The widespread use of the term son reflects the dominance of the male in much of ancient society. At the same time, the term often does not refer to the male, but is generic and can properly be translated "child," "offspring."

See also FAMILY; INHERITANCE IN THE NEW TESTAMENT; INHERITANCE IN THE OLD TESTAMENT; SON OF GOD; SON OF MAN.

—VIRGIL FRY

• **Son of David.** *See* CHRISTOLOGY

• **Son of Encouragement.** *See* BARNABAS

• **Son of God.** The title "SON of God" is applied in the Bible to beings who are divine in origin, to angels, Adam, and especially to JESUS as uniquely divine. Because "son of" is a construct or genitive relationship in Hebrew, meaning "having the nature of" or "demonstrating obedience to" it can also refer to Israel, or Ephraim, who owed filial obedience to God. Jesus can even refer to James and John as "sons of thunder" because they exhibited a stormy disposition toward the Samaritans (Mark 3:17; 9:38; Luke 9:54).

OT Usage. The polytheistic background of the OT usage is reflected in the fact that the plural "sons of God" appears often: the angelic or divine beings who cohabit with the daughters of men, producing a race of giants (Gen 6:2, 4); the gathering of the heavenly retinue, including Satan, in the proposed trial of Job (Job 1:6; 2:1); and the throng which shouted for joy at the creation (Job 38:7).

In the enthronement Ps 2, the king is addressed: "You are my son, today I have begotten you" (v. 7). This enjoins loyalty and obedience to God on the part of the king as God's chosen leader for the people, but it may also suggest a special endowment of divine authority or power for the exercise of his kingship. Such language became very important for early Christians as they tried to express the unique relationship of Jesus to God as his Father.

Israel, and Ephraim in particular, is viewed collectively as "son of God" (Exod 4:22; Deut 1:31; Hos 11:1), and this usage is taken out of its original setting and applied to Jesus in the NT (Matt 2:15). Here the emphasis is upon filial love and obedience to the Father, rather than upon divine origin. Israel was called to live as an obedient son of God in the covenant, and Jesus is proclaimed as the Son who perfectly obeyed the will of the Father. Even the prayer "Our Father" includes the Christian disciples in the family which owes full obedience and love to God as Father.

One time the expression "son of the gods" appears (Dan 3:25), where a fourth being is seen with the three Hebrew children in the fiery furnace, reflecting the polytheistic background of Nebuchadrezzar and the Babylonians. It simply suggests one who looked like a divine being to the king.

NT Usage. This phrase becomes in the NT almost exclusively a title for Jesus, affirming his divine nature and identity with the Lord, the covenant God of Israel. The entire Gospel of Mark is built around this title for Jesus; and, while the title is probably later than the Gospel text, it accurately expresses the theme of the Gospel.

Twice in Mark the voice from heaven affirms the divine sonship of Jesus: at his baptism, "Thou art my beloved Son" (Mark 1:11); and, at the transfiguration, "This is my beloved Son; listen to him" (9:7). Twice the demons cry out and address Jesus as Son of God (3:11; 5:7). Twice Jesus refers indirectly to his sonship (in the parable of the husbandmen where God finally sends "his beloved son," 12:1-11; and in his reference to the coming of the Son in the apocalyptic discourse, 13:32). The final pair of references to Jesus' sonship in Mark is the most surprising of all: the high priest could not recognize Jesus' divine origin when he demanded, "Are you the Christ, the Son of the Blessed?" (14:61). But the pagan centurion who directed his crucifixion recognized him in the way he died: "Truly this man was the Son of God!" (15:39).

The high priest's association of "Son of God" with the messianic title "Christ," or Anointed One, is confirmed also by Simon Peter's confession at Caesarea Philippi: "You are the Christ, the Son of the living God!" (Matt 16:16). Sonship is implicit in the earliest christological confession, "Jesus Christ is Lord," for "Lord" is equated with the ineffable name, Yahweh, the covenant God of Israel, Creator and Redeemer.

While the more frequent title SON OF MAN is often associated with the apocalyptic return of the Son at the end of the age, the title Son of God focuses more directly upon his earthly life and ministry. Jesus' consciousness of his sonship to the Father is the dominant characteristic of his prayer life, and his miracles as well as his words are shaped by his determination to do the Father's will. While there is abundant evidence of Jesus' divine sonship in the Gospel record, it is also clear that the developing Christian community later was able to elevate him to the level of Christian worship which would not have been possible before the resurrection.

Paul made the resurrection the decisive turning point in the use of this christological title when he said that Jesus was "designated the Son of God in power . . . by his resurrection from the dead" (Rom 1:4). He did not become the Son of God by the resurrection, but he was "designated," "declared to be," or "recognized as" the Son of God by that dramatic event. Many early Christian heresies took the form of adoptionism, the claim that an ordinary human being was "adopted" as Son of God at the baptism, or transfiguration, or resurrection. The Ebionite form of adoptionism even had a text by adding the rest of Ps 2:7 to the voice at Jesus' baptism: "Thou art my Son; this day have I begotten Thee." Textual criticism offers no support for this as the original reading, but such theological speculation came easily to early Christians as they wrestled with the mystery of the person of Christ.

In the later theology of the church, Son of God became the preferred title for the second person of the Trinity, but it continued to create misunderstanding. How could God have a Son? If he was begotten by the Father, then he had a beginning and is therefore not divine. Origen tried to formulate a doctrine of "eternal generation of the Son," but this adds to the confusion. With the title Son of God we have a classic case of the need for biblical theology to interpret and correct dogmatic theology by calling it back to the biblical meaning of the term: having the nature of God; demonstrating filial love and obedience to God as Father; and the call to Christian believers to demonstrate filial love and obedience to the Heavenly Father.

See also CHRISTOLOGY; INCARNATION; JESUS; MESSIAH/CHRIST; SON.

Bibliography. R. Bultmann, *New Testament Theology*; J. Jeremias, *New Testament Theology*; E. Schweizer and W. Schneemelcher, "υἱός, κτλ.," *TDNT*; V. Taylor, *The Names of Jesus*.

—WAYNE E. WARD

• **Son of Man.** Son of man is one of several important titles for Jesus in early Christian writings. For most of church history Son of man was viewed as pointing to the humanity of Jesus in contrast with the title SON OF GOD which pointed to his divinity. This misunderstanding began to unravel in the modern period when, toward the turn of this century, the Son of man issue caught the attention of NT critics. It has remained one of their most vexing questions to the present day.

Scholarly discussion about this title has generally centered around two questions: (1) what is the origin of the concept; and (2) are the sayings in the Gospels authentic; that is, did the historical Jesus utter them or were they created by the early church and the Gospel writers and placed on the lips of Jesus?

Son of Man in Judaism. The Hebrew Bible uses the phrase "Son of man" (בן־אדם) to refer to a particular human being (cf. Ezek 2:1). The corresponding later Aramaic expression (בר־אנש) is usually used to refer to "a man" or "someone" or even as a circumlocution for "I." In later writings the phrase also referred to a messianic or apocalyptic figure.

Discussions concerning the origin of the NT concept have usually centered around three Jewish apocalyptic texts. The earliest text, Daniel, reached its present form during the Maccabean revolt between 167 and 164 B.C.E. Although the actual phrase "son of man" is not found in the book, in a vision Daniel sees "one like a son of man" who comes with the clouds to God and is given power, glory, and kingdom (Dan 7:13-14a). Later (7:18, 22) the "saints of the Most High" receive the kingdom. Thus the Son of man figure in Dan 7:13-14a appears to be a collective symbol for the faithful Jews, but some scholars have interpreted "one like a son of man" as an individual figure, perhaps an angel.

A second occurrence of the Son of man in Jewish apocalyptic is in 1 ENOCH, a collection of texts preserved in Ethiopic and written in Aramaic and Hebrew in the first two centuries B.C.E. In chaps. 37–71, referred to as the *Similitudes of Enoch,* the phrase "Son of man" is found sixteen times. The *Similitudes,* which probably circulated independently of the remainder of *1 Enoch* for a while, is usually dated before the writing of the Gospels, but since there is disagreement about this it must be used as a background for the Gospels with some caution.

In the *Similitudes of Enoch* the Son of man is a preexistent divine being (48:2f.; 62:7). He is chosen by the Lord of Spirits (46:3) and appears "on that day" to deliver the elect from persecution (62:7ff.) and to remove from their seats the kings and rulers who have persecuted the chosen one (46:4-8). The rulers will suffer when they see the Son of man sitting on his glory throne (62:2-5). Enoch was given various titles in the *Similitudes,* one of which was the Son of man, a designation which came in the vision of Enoch's ascent and commissioning (chap. 71). So the Son of man in the *Similitudes* is a heavenly figure who will come to save the righteous and judge the evil world.

A third apocalyptic work, 4 EZRA (also referred to as 2 Esdras), contains references to a supernatural "man" figure, also called "my son." Although written in its present form at the end of the first century C.E., *4 Ezra* incorporated many traditions which may have influenced the NT. In a key passage, *4 Ezra* 13:1-4, in the sixth of a series of visions, the author saw God saving his people through "something like the figure of a man" which came out of the sea and flew with the clouds of heaven.

Then follow two judgment scenes (13:5-7, 8-11) where the wicked are gathered together to fight against the judge and are consumed by the fire from the mouth of the man figure. In a third scene the chosen ones are gathered to the man. This messiah-like figure is preexistent (13:26), protector of the innocent (13:22-29), judge (13:37-38), and warrior (13:9-11, 49). Although "Son of man" does not occur here, *4 Ezra* 11-13 is a commentary on Dan 7 and it is reasonable to assume that the man from the sea is to be identified as the "one like a son of man" in Daniel and maybe the Son of man in the *Similitudes of Enoch.*

Many scholars believe that in pre-Christian Judaism there was the concept of a unified, transcendent Son of man who would save the righteous and punish the wicked. Dan 7, the *Similitudes of Enoch,* and *4 Ezra* 13 are understood as being related to this apocalyptic Son of man concept either by contributing to its development or being an expression of it. This concept formed the basis for the Son of man in the NT.

This belief has been strongly challenged by Norman Perrin who argued there was no widespread assumption of a unified Son of man concept in Jewish apocalypticism. He contended that the imagery of Dan 7:13 was used freely and creatively by subsequent writers, both Jewish and Christian, and especially by the author of the Gospel of Mark.

The Son of Man in the Synoptic Gospels. In the synoptic Gospels Son of man (ὁ υἱὸς τοῦ ἀνθρώπου) is found sixty-seven times. These occurrences include fourteen in

Mark, twenty-eight in Matthew, and twenty-five in Luke. Matthew has only fifteen and Luke sixteen when one eliminates the occurrences where Matthew and/or Luke have a saying in common with Mark. Eight Son of man sayings are in Q; that is, they are parallel in Matthew and Luke, but are not found in Mark.

In the synoptic Gospels there are three general categories of Son of man sayings, all of which are found on the lips of Jesus (except for Luke 24:7 where an angel is quoting him). The apocalyptic sayings are those in which Jesus seems to be referring to the Son of man as another entity, as one who will come in the future, usually on the clouds of heaven and in great power and majesty (e.g., Mark 8:38; 13:26; 14:62; Matt 10:23; 24:27; 25:31; Luke 17:22; 18:8; 21:36).

The suffering Son of man sayings refer to Jesus' upcoming suffering, death, and, sometimes, resurrection (Mark 8:31; 9:31; 10:33-34; Matt 17:12; 20:18-19; 26:24; Luke 9:22; 18:32-33; 22:22).

Finally, there are sayings about the present activity of the Son of man which fit into the context of the earthly life of Jesus. Here, as with the suffering sayings, Son of man appears to be Jesus' self-designation (e.g., Mark 2:10, 27-28; Luke 19:10; Matt 8:20 || Luke 9:58; Matt 11:19 || Luke 7:34).

Much of the discussion of the synoptic Son of man sayings has centered around the question of authenticity. Did Jesus use the phrase "Son of man," and if so, did he refer to himself or to some other figure? In the more important discussions of these questions four general answers have been suggested.

The majority of scholars have answered that the apocalyptic Son of man sayings are authentic but the sayings in the other two categories are not. In addition, in speaking of the future coming Son of man, Jesus was not speaking of himself, but, like other Jewish apocalyptic writers, of another figure who would come to judge the world. These scholars point out that in Mark, Jesus said, e.g., "For whoever is ashamed of me . . . of him will the Son of man also be ashamed, when he comes . . . " (Mark 8:38; cf. Matt 10:32-33 || Luke 12:8-9). Jesus did not say "For whoever is ashamed of me . . . of him will *I* also be ashamed when *I* come. . . . "

According to this position it was the early church in Palestine which, after the resurrection experience, interpreted Jesus as the future returning Son of man. The sayings referring to his suffering and present activity on the earth arose in the early church. The suffering Son of man sayings, especially, are viewed as inauthentic because they contain details about Jesus' trial, death, and resurrection that could have been known only after the events.

Evidence in support of this position include the fact that the apocalyptic sayings are found in all the different kinds of synoptic material including Mark, Q (the source used by Matthew and Luke), M (material found only in Matthew), and L (material found only in Luke).

A second answer is that the sayings in all three categories are authentic, maintaining that Jesus used the phrase as his favorite self-designation because he was concerned that the politically-charged title "Messiah" would cause his hearers to misunderstand the nature of his ministry. Critics holding this view note that the term is always found on the lips of Jesus and that all three types of sayings are found in Mark, the earliest Gospel. Jesus' friends and adversaries use many names in addressing him, such as Christ, Son of God, and teacher, but they never use Son of man.

A third answer is that only sayings from the non-apocalyptic categories are authentic. These scholars give many of the same arguments for authenticity as representatives of the first view. However, scholars taking this approach believe that the apocalyptic sayings arose when early Jewish Christians, after the resurrection experience, interpreted the resurrection in light of Dan 7:13.

Important evidence in support of the inauthenticity of the apocalyptic sayings is that Son of man is rarely found in the parables, the primary teaching form used by the historical Jesus; nor is the term linked closely with the Kingdom of God, the major theme of Jesus' teaching.

A fourth answer to the question is that none of the Son of man sayings are authentic for reasons already given. When the apocalyptic sayings arose, the early church continued to associate the term with Jesus, in particular his suffering and other earthly activities.

In addition to his strong arguments for this fourth view, Norman Perrin showed how the Gospel of Mark played the crucial role in the development of the Son of man tradition in early Christianity. In a close study of Mark 8:27–10:52, Perrin identified three cycles, each of which followed a threefold pattern of prediction of suffering of the Son of man (8:31; 9:31; 10:33-34), misunderstanding by the disciples (8:32-33; 9:32; 10:35-37), and teaching about discipleship (8:34-38; 9:33-37; 10:38-44). Perrin said Mark's purpose was to combat a false view of Christ that stressed only his power and glory. To do this Mark used the term Son of man to demonstrate that Jesus was also a suffering Messiah and that true discipleship and salvation involved willing and necessary suffering. While Mark did not invent them, Perrin says Mark played the major role in developing the other two categories of sayings.

Son of Man outside the Synoptic Gospels. The Gospel of John contains the phrase Son of man thirteen times. As in the Synoptics, the phrase is found only on the lips of Jesus (except for 12:34 where the crowd is quoting him) and Jesus is pictured as a suffering Son of man. Unlike the synoptic writers, John emphasizes that the Son of man is judge (5:25-29), a notion prominent in Jewish apocalyptic literature. John's most important contribution to the title is the description of Jesus the Son of man as a preexistent descending-ascending redeemer figure. Jesus the Son of man descends with eternal life for the world and will ascend back into heaven, drawing all persons to himself (3:13-15; 6:27, 53, 62; 12:32-34).

Outside the Gospels, Son of man is found only in Acts 7:56; Eph 3:5; and Rev 1:13; 14:14. The occurrence in Ephesians—actually "sons of men"—means simply "human beings." The references in Acts and Revelation are consistent with the apocalyptic background, with Revelation being clearly dependent on Dan 7:13. The phrase Son of man is noticeably absent in Paul's writings, although it has been suggested that Paul's idea of Christ as the heavenly man or second Adam can be related to the Son of man concept.

See also APOCALYPTIC LITERATURE; CHRISTOLOGY; DANIEL, BOOK OF; DIVINITY OF JESUS; ENOCH, FIRST; EZRA, FOURTH; MESSIAH/CHRIST; SON OF GOD.

Bibliography. M. Black, *The Book of Enoch or I Enoch: A New English Edition with Commentary and Textual Notes*; F. H. Borsch, *The Christian and Gnostic Son of Man* and *The Son of Man in Myth and History*; C. C. Caragounis, *The Son of Man: Vision and Interpretation*; M. Casey, *Son of Man: The Interpretation and Influence of Daniel 7*; A. J. Ferch, *The Son of Man in Daniel 7*; R. H. Fuller, *The*

Foundations of New Testament Christology; F. Hahn, *The Titles of Jesus in Christology: Their History in Early Christianity*; A. J. B. Higgins, *Jesus and the Son of Man* and *The Son of Man in the Teaching of Jesus*; M. D. Hooker, *The Son of Man in Mark: A Study of the Background of the Term "Son of Man" and Its Use in St. Mark's Gospel*; S. Kim, *"The 'Son of Man'" as the Son of God*; B. Lindars, *Jesus Son of Man: A Fresh Examination of the Son of Man Sayings in the Gospels in the Light of Recent Research*; N. Perrin, *A Modern Pilgrimage in New Testament Christology*; D. W. Suter, *Tradition and Composition in the Parables of Enoch*; H. E. Tödt, *The Son of Man in the Synoptic Tradition*.

—CALVIN MERCER

• **Song of Deborah.** *See* DEBORAH; SISERA

• **Song of Solomon.** *See* SONG OF SONGS

• OUTLINE OF SONG OF SONGS •
The Song of Songs
I. Superscription (1:1)
II. Exchanges between Lovers (1:2–2:3)
III. Reflections on Love by the Lovers (2:4–3:11)
IV. Further Exchanges between the Lovers (4:1–8:7)
V. Closing Reflections and Exchanges (8:8-17)

• **Song of Songs.** A collection of love poems attributed to Solomon, but probably coming from a period considerably later than Solomon. The Hebrew title means "the greatest song," or "the most excellent song" (the title in English appears also as Song of Solomon or Canticles).

Contents. The book contains perhaps as many as twenty-five lyric and erotic love poems in which the speakers are a man, a woman, and a chorus. The man and the woman in turn praise the beauty and charms of the other, using language more suggestive and affective than descriptive. No clear pattern of development can be traced in the poems as presently arranged. The figures of king and shepherd and of queen and shepherdess recur frequently.

Interpretations. Early interpretations of the collection saw the imagery of bride and groom allegorically or typologically, as representing Israel and God or the Church and Christ. Such interpretations arose, no doubt, because of the symbolism of bride and groom in texts such as Hos 1–3 and Ezek 16 and 23 in the OT, and Eph 5 in the NT.

Critical studies suggest more probable settings for the Song of Songs. Studies of ancient Near Eastern religions reveal the significance of the sacred marriage in the great festivals, where the joining of the Gods Ishtar and Tammuz, for example, symbolize and realize the renewal of the natural world. This sacred marriage was enacted in the practices of worshipers at the shrines. It seems probable, however, that any such background in ancient fertility religion is considerably far removed from the love poetry of the Song of Songs.

The poetry belongs to daily life, to the world of courtship, betrothal, and marriage. It is lyric poetry, stressing the mood of erotic relationships, earthily and also with vivid and gripping uses of imagery and the natural world. Egyptian love poetry of the Late Kingdom offers close analogies to the poetry found here, although there are also rather close parallels with the much later Arab poetry belonging to the celebration of the beauty of bride and groom at betrothal time.

Interpretations of the Song of Songs today stress this affirmative attitude toward the sexual life, toward physical beauty and its attractions. Biblical religion goes far toward demystification of the sexual dimensions of existence, placing sex in the world of God's good creation, a gift to be enjoyed and affirmed.

The Song of Songs and the Canon. The Song of Songs came to be attached to the Passover celebration, offering balance to the somber elements of Passover, with its recollections of bondage in Egypt and of the death of the first-born sons there. Solomon's many wives and his reported literary activity (1 Kgs 4:29-34) probably led to the attribution of the Song of Songs to Solomon. The Song of Songs came to be very popular in patristic and medieval church life, interpreted, of course, as an allegory of Christ and the Church.

Love and Death. One special connection of the love poetry needs to be mentioned: in Cant 8:6, it is said that "love is as strong as (or: stronger than) death." Does this reference to death suggest, as some have maintained, that this erotic love poetry belongs beside the grave (as acts of celebration and festivity in ancient Israel accompanied the burial of the dead and regularly offered ceremonies for keeping death at bay)? It is by no means impossible that such an affirmation of life and love and beauty would have been found eminently suitable for inclusion, along with acts of lamentation, in ritual and ceremonial acts on the occasions of death.

The Song of Songs does not strike the reader as serving instrumental purposes, however. It is affirming delight in human love, in human beauty, in the natural world that supports human love. Its character as lyrical, affective poetry also makes it particularly suitable for making human love into an analogy for the love of the community and the individual for God, and of God for the community and the individual.

See also LOVE IN THE NEW TESTAMENT; LOVE IN THE OLD TESTAMENT.

Bibliography. R. Gordis, *The Song of Songs and Lamentations*; M. H. Pope, *Song of Songs, AncB*.

—WALTER HARRELSON

• **Song of the Three Young Men.** *See* AZARIAH, PRAYER OF

• **Sons of God.** *See* COUNCIL, HEAVENLY; GIANT

• **Sonship.** *See* ADOPTION

• **Sophia of Jesus Christ.** [soh-fee'uh] The *Sophia* (or *Wisdom) of Jesus Christ* is a Christian Gnostic missionary tractate apparently designed to convince unconverted readers that Christ is the true revealer of saving knowledge (*gnosis*). Its relative importance is attested by its existence in two Coptic translations (the fourth tractate in NAG HAMMADI Codex III and the third tractate in the Berlin Gnostic Codex, BG 8502), as well as in a fragment of the Greek version (Papyrus Oxyrhynchus 1081) which was the probable basis for the Coptic translations. It is a classic example of the Christianization of an originally non-Christian tractate, EUGNOSTOS THE BLESSED.

In agreement with the general outline of *Eugnostos, Sophia* maintains that knowledge of the highest God and heavenly beings emanated from him is essential to salvation. One receiving such knowledge knows the differences between this perishing world and the imperishable one of the divine aeons, and becomes immortal through such gnosis. Thus, the tractate begins with a description of the unknown, highest deity, the Unbegotten Father, and proceeds to list four other beings evolving from him: his reflection, the "Self-Father"; the Self-Father's independent power, the "Immortal Man"; the Immortal Man's male-female son, the "Savior" or "Son of Son of Man." The last three are androgynous, their female parts being called "Sophia." The five in this hierarchy create other entities for their "aeons," such as ANGELS, firmaments, attendants. In addition, a second group of six heavenly beings come forth from the first five. The super-celestial realm of both hierarchies is characterized by joy and jubilation. There follows a section describing this earthly, chaotic aeon of Immortal Man. In it are generated prototypes of subsequent creations.

The Christian adaptation of this outline includes introduction of Christ who appears after the RESURRECTION to twelve disciples and seven women and engages in a dialogue with them. The secondary nature of the dialogue becomes apparent from the fact that often answers given by Christ bear little or no relationship to the questions of the disciples. These additions emphasize, first, that Christ is the supreme revealer who came from "Infinite Light" to "tell everyone about the God who is above the universe" (III,4: 118.22-25). Second, Christ's saving work is described, work necessitated by the fall of drops of light from the divine into the visible world, a fall precipitated by Sophia (III,4: 107.16-17; 114.13). These drops are found in human beings created by the Arch-begetter and his angels, "false gods." Christ came to lead his own out of this darkness. Third, Christ Jesus, identified with the First-begotten in the highest Godhead (III,4: 104.20-22), calls his followers to "trample on" (i.e., preach truth about) the false gods and share the saving gnosis.

The pseudonymous author claims to be a disciple, an eyewitness of the TRANSFIGURATION (III,4: 91.14-20). The tractate was possibly composed in Egypt (as the allusion to a 360-day year may indicate) in the early second century, a period prior to developed polemic against Gnostics. Though some of its ideas may have been incorporated by Sethians and Valentinians into their systems, the *Sophia of Jesus Christ* cannot be clearly identified with any known Gnostic school.

See also EUGNOSTOS THE BLESSED; GNOSTICISM; NAG HAMMADI.

Bibliography. D. M. Parrott, "Eugnostos the Blessed and the Sophia of Jesus Christ," *The Nag Hammadi Library in English,* ed. J. M. Robinson, "Gnostic and Orthodox Disciples in the Second and Third Centuries," *Nag Hammadi, Gnosticism, and Early Christianity,* ed. C. W. Hedrick and R. Hodgson, Jr., and "The Significance of the Letter of Eugnostos and the Sophia of Jesus Christ for the Understanding of the Relation between Gnosticism and Christianity," *SBLASP* (1971).

—MALCOLM L. PEEL

• **Sorcery.** *See* MAGIC AND DIVINATION

• **Sosthenes.** [sos'thuh-neez] The ruler of the SYNAGOGUE in CORINTH who was seized by an angry crowd and beaten before Gallio's Roman court after GALLIO refused to prosecute PAUL for evangelizing Jews (Acts 18:17). This crowd may have been composed of pagans who saw an opportunity to attack a local Jewish leader, or Jews who were angry with Sosthenes for permitting Paul to preach in the synagogue.

In 1 Cor 1:1, Paul mentioned that "our brother Sosthenes" was with him in Ephesus. Paul's reference suggests that the man was known to the Corinthian Christians, and it is very possible that he was the same Sosthenes mentioned in Acts. If so, he must have converted to Christianity and have become one of Paul's assistants.

See also CORINTH; GALLIO; PAUL; SYNAGOGUE.

—MARK J. OLSON

• **Soul in the Old Testament.** A frequent translation of the Heb. word *nepeš,* the primary meaning of which is "living being." However, the word has so many usages that it is not always easy to recognize a translation of it. All the creatures in the world and humans are living souls or living beings (Gen 1:20-21, 24, 30; 2:7). At creation ADAM became a "living soul." The soul is so fully identified with the whole person that a corpse is said to be a "dead soul," usually translated "dead body" (Lev 21:11; Num 6:6).

Soul often designates a person. When Jacob moved to Egypt, there were "seventy souls" or persons who were his descendants (Gen 46:27; cf. Ezek 18:4). As a personal pronoun, "my soul" means "I" (Gen 27:25). As a reflexive pronoun, "her soul" means "herself" (Jer 3:11).

The occasional use of soul with HEART and "strength" does not mean that the soul is a separate part of a person. In Deut 6:5 these words together stress the fact that the entire person, in every aspect, is to be devoted to God.

With emphasis on vitality or being alive, a person may be described as a "hungry soul" (Ps 107:9). The soul is the seat of such emotions as evil desire (Prov 21:10) and joy (Ps 86:4) and of such spiritual feelings as yearning for God (Isa 26:9) and resting in God (Ps 62:1).

As life or life-principle, the soul is often identified with the BLOOD (Gen 9:4; Lev 17:11). When using soul as "life," the OT may speak of saving one's soul from death (Josh 2:13) or of risking one's life (Judg 5:18). As the breath of life, the soul is said to depart at death and to return if the dead is revived (1 Kgs 17:17-22).

See also BLOOD IN THE OLD TESTAMENT; BODY IN THE OLD TESTAMENT; DEATH; LIFE IN THE OLD TESTAMENT.

—VIRGIL FRY

• **Source Criticism.** Source criticism is a type of analysis that seeks to identify the various written sources used in writing biblical materials in an effort to reconstruct the history of the literature.

Source critics of the OT have developed the documentary hypothesis which asserts that behind the Pentateuch in its final form there were a series of written sources. Changes in vocabulary and style led advocates to conclude that there were four major written sources or strands of tradition in the Pentateuch. (1) J, so named because it used the divine name Yahweh (Jahveh in German). Some scholars say it existed in written form around 1000–900 B.C.E. (2) E, so named because of the use of Elohim to express the divine name. Some scholars suggest E was written one hundred years after J. (3) D, so named from Deuteronomy an early form of which was discovered in the Temple in Jerusalem sometime during the seventh to sixth centuries—some scholars specify 621 B.C.E. (4) P, Priestly, so named because of emphasis on legal, cultic material found in Exodus and Leviticus. Some scholars place it after the Exile in the fifth century B.C.E.

The significance of source criticism as applied to the Pentateuch is that by dating sources scholars can place materials in specific historical settings. It is possible to reflect on how, why, and to whom and by whom the materials were written. It is possible to consider how the sources were combined to create the final version of the Pentateuch.

Source criticism has been applied to the Gospels and what is known as the four-source hypothesis (PLATE 32) has been developed as a solution to the SYNOPTIC PROBLEM. The term "synoptic" results from the common view which in general is shared by Matthew, Mark, and Luke. The synoptic problem is the question of how to correlate Mark, Matthew, and Luke. They treat many of the same things such as the teachings of Jesus, healings, and reports of where Jesus went and what occurred to him. But they also differ in the arrangement of many of the details. There are materials common to Matthew and Luke that Mark does not present. There are materials peculiar to both Mark and Luke individually that are not found in another Gospel.

Scholars have suggested the following solution to the synoptic problem. (1) Mark served as the source for Matthew and Luke. Most of Mark is duplicated in Matthew and Luke. When a passage in Mark is missing from either Matthew or Luke it is usually found in the other. Matthew and Luke rely on Mark's outline. When either Matthew or Luke varies from Mark's sequence, the other follows Mark. (2) Matthew and Luke share a second common source besides Mark, often called Q from the German *Quelle*—source. More than one-third of Matthew and one-fourth of Luke consists of material they share in common that is absent from Mark. (3) M refers to sources unique to Matthew. (4) L refers to sources unique to Luke.

See also GOSPELS, CRITICAL STUDY OF; INTERPRETATION, HISTORY OF; Q; SOURCES, LITERARY; SOURCES OF THE PENTATEUCH; SYNOPTIC PROBLEM.

—ROBERT K. GUSTAFSON

• **Sources of the Pentateuch.** *History*. Traditionally the Pentateuch, the Torah, or, the first five books of the Bible, has been ascribed to Moses with the clear understanding that he recorded everything in those books, but testimony exists that questions the adequacy of such a viewpoint. Clement of Rome (first century C.E.; or perhaps the later Clementine tradition) found certain stories, e.g., the drunkenness of Noah, untenable and claimed that someone besides Moses wrote those parts. Ibn Ezra (1089–1164) suggested in his writings that MOSES did not compose the complete TORAH. His critical eye convinced him that the Torah, like other biblical books such as Isaiah, contained disparate material that had originated in different times but had been merged at a later date. The Renaissance and Reformation witnessed a growing number of scholars, including John Calvin, Baruch Spinoza, and Richard Simon, who proposed that complementary traditions, which were riddled with repetitions and contradictions, seemed apparent in the Pentateuch. In 1711, H. B. Witter, and later, in 1753, Jean Astruc forwarded evidence to substantiate a similar perspective. Astruc noticed that the style of Gen 1, so majestic in its depiction of God and regimented in its ordering of creation, differed from the style of Gen 2–3 which was earthly and anthropomorphic. In addition, the term used for God in the first account was "Elohim," whereas the term used in the second account was "Yahweh." Astruc's observations accelerated the critical examination of the Pentateuch.

Modern source criticism is associated in many minds with Julius Wellhausen. Obviously, he did not create the idea, but he codified much of the preceding work in his own. He founded his ideas about the history of Israel upon certain postulated documents: J for the Yahwist (Jahwist in German—850 B.C.E.); E for the Elohist (ca. 700 B.C.E.); D for the Deuteronomist (ca. 623 B.C.E.); and P for the priestly source (500–450 B.C.E.). He held that these documents arose at specific periods of Israelite history and these documents had eventually been merged to form the Pentateuch. Unfortunately, Wellhausen's work was marred by his acceptance of the prevailing view of the evolutionary character of religion, i.e., religion begins as a primitive understanding of the universe and eventually develops more abstract and sophisticated ideas, and his elaboration of the sources reflects that view. In addition, his view left the impression that the merging of these sources was so crude that their unraveling proves relatively simple. After Wellhausen's startling accomplishment others began to evaluate the Pentateuch and to develop elaborate charts that detailed the material and extent of each source.

Wellhausen actually belonged to a group of German scholars who had become convinced of the composite nature of the first five books of the Bible. Gunkel, another prominent critic, shaped this research just as much as Wellhausen, and, later, with his application of form criticism, which emphasized the constituent units of these sources, provided an early critique that turned biblical scholarship away from its emphasis on completed sources toward an emphasis on the formation of these sources. In addition, Gunkel's program suggested that the source theory must turn from a simplistic conception of authorship to an emphasis on the fluid, communal shaping of a perspective that presented its point of view through the traditional material.

Tradition history or tradition criticism, especially the Scandinavian branch, which suggested that biblical literature like much folklore arose in an oral culture where change and interpretation is natural, continued this program and led pentateuchal studies to the present stage. The present text testifies not to four distinct writers or sources, but reveals four different tradition groups that have connected various common and exclusive traditions with each other at crucial times in the history of Israel in order to inspire correction and renewed commitment. Four major complexes have been formed, but these complexes relied on shorter, less comprehensive cycles and collections and often employed similar, if not the same, material. In addition, these four complexes gradually were merged—first J and E were combined and later P cemented JE and D together with P's special material to form the Pentateuch. Presently, tradition history, along with redaction criticism, which is especially helpful with repetitions, e.g., the two stories of HAGAR's expulsion, continues its attempt to detail the free traditions witnessed in the Hebrew Bible and the process by which these traditions coalesced.

The Yahwist. The Yahwist or J, emerged during one of the most creative and expansive times in the history of Israel; he composed during the period some scholars called the "Solomonic Enlightenment," the early part of the Davidic dynasty (ca. 950). Although this complex or perspective covered three major eras of history in the distant past: the universal history of the world found within Genesis 2–11; the patriarchal history found within Genesis 12–50; and the history of the tribes of Israel found within Exodus–Numbers, the real target of his work remained his own time. The time of DAVID and SOLOMON was the realization of the promises of their God, Yahweh, who had promised ABRAHAM a great nation, a great name, and great blessing (Gen 12:1-3). Yet, this consummation brought with it new and added responsibility; the nation under the leadership of its king and cult had to remember the God who had brought them to this moment in history rather than to glorify their own contribution and ambition. The Yahwist compiled a narrative from the past in order to instruct the nation about the excesses of success.

The story of ADAM and EVE, the Yahwist's initial episode, poignantly illustrates this purpose. A couple, marvelously suited for one another, is presented a garden that contains everything that they could want. There is one restriction that keeps the relationship of trust and gratitude clear between creator and created, giver and recipients. However, the two choose, with some prodding from a crafty serpent, to deny the terms of the gift, to replace Yahweh's commission with their ambition, and to damage almost irreparably the relationship between themselves and Yahweh, their god. As a result they are expelled from the garden. The people of Israel in the time of David and Solomon found themselves in a society that was a virtual paradise when compared to their ancestors' circumstances and those that lived about them. The Yahwist affirmed the marvel of this gift of Yahweh, but warned them, beginning with this story, that the substitution of their own ambition for Yahweh's intention would lead to the destruction of this favored time.

The Elohist. The Elohist or E, was a northern creation, but its fragmentary nature has caused difficulty to scholars. Some believe E was never an independent work; it was just a redactional stage during which northern traditions were added to J. Some hold that E was a northern reworking of J so that it would be acceptable to Israel, the Northern Kingdom during the divided monarchy. Others think that E and J, though written at different times, were parallel accounts derived from a basic body of tradition that already included the general outline of the Pentateuch, but E stressed the northern traditions that had been eclipsed by the Davidic and southern traditions. E used terms that were favored in the North, e.g., Amorites for Canaanites and Horeb for Sinai. E played down the role of Moses, or the leader, and stressed the people, just as E would pay less attention to Abraham and highlight JACOB (Israel). The Elohist portrayed God, who was not known as Yahweh until the time of Moses (Exod 3), as a concerned but distant god who communicated by means of dreams or messengers, and this portrayal contrasted sharply with J's anthropomorphic accounts. In addition, E included a prophetic emphasis that led him to impress that office on the first patriarch, Abraham (Gen 20:7). No doubt the Elohist assimilated his material in such a fashion that the northern kingdom would understand the pressing need for obedience in the face of rampant idolatry. To people led astray by king and priest to follow gods represented by images one could reach out and touch, the Elohist spoke of the people's responsibility to obey their unseen god who claimed their undivided attention.

This concern with obedience is illustrated clearly in the Elohist's story of Abraham and ISAAC (Gen 22). God instructs Abraham to take his long-awaited son and to sacrifice him at some distant place. Abraham obeys until the very last moment when he is instructed by an angel to substitute a ram for Isaac. This story portrays Abraham as the archetype of obedience and a particularly fitting example for the audience of the Elohist. The story of the golden calf in the wilderness (Exod 32) served both as a criticism of the syncretistic worship occurring at Dan and BETHEL, and as an example of the consequences of disobedience. In this way, the Elohist in his own time, and in his own domain, admonished and encouraged ally and adversary alike to recover the purity and vitality of their religion. Many scholars believe that after the fall of the Northern Kingdom (722/1 B.C.E.), or long before P pulled all these groups together, J and E were combined in the South so that E's concerns enriched J and exerted continued influence.

The Deuteronomist. D, or the Deuteronomist (700–621 B.C.E.), was founded on a legal tradition that first flourished in the North until the Assyrian conquest and then moved South. This legal tradition, collected, interpreted and taught by Levites, prophets, or scribes, formed the core (Deut 12–26) of the completed work that is the present book of Deuteronomy. Scholarly opinion equates this core with "the Book of the Law" discovered in the Temple during the reign of Josiah (2 Kgs 22–23). To this core was added a general introduction (Deut 1–4:43), a special introduction to the Deuteronomic Code (Deut 4:44–11:32), and the final speeches given by Moses, whose death ends the book. The genius of the Deuteronomist resided in his choice to present this material as the last series of addresses or sermons Moses delivered to the people of Israel before they conquered Canaan, the land promised them by their god. Again and again, Moses urged the people to study the law so that they would be obedient in the land that Yahweh would give to them. The actual deliverance of this message was hundreds of years after the conquest, and the apparent intention was to bring the people back to the joyful observance of the law. However, the Deuteronomist clearly outlined the consequences if the people disregarded the law; Yahweh, who was portrayed as a jealous or zealous god, would unleash innumerable curses.

One of the major elements that gives such a signal quality to Deuteronomy was its emphasis on a unity that led to pure faith and practice. The book called for one people to serve one god, to honor one law, and to worship in one temple. Any hindrance to this unity was identified as a threat to covenant loyalty. Individuals who intoned the *Shema*—"Hear, O Israel, the Lord, our God, the Lord is one, and you shall love the Lord your God with all your heart, and with all your soul, and with all your might" (Deut. 6:4-5)—presented themselves as strong members of a unified Israel. The deuteronomic theology of the two ways complemented this emphasis. Deuteronomy made very clear the connection between obedience and God's blessing. Conversely, for the person or nation who disobeyed the laws of Yahweh there was only curse. This theological point was underscored by the very form much of the book reflected; it resembled a Near Eastern treaty that included stipulations to be followed in order for the sovereign to honor his obligations. In the event that the stipulations were not honored, the sovereign had every right to institute the curses detailed in the treaty. Israel had made a covenant or treaty with Yahweh at Horeb (Sinai), and Deuteronomy merely reminded Israel of that commitment. The deuteronomic vocabulary tied all these elements together and provided a pulsing message of encouragement and warning, e.g., "the testimonies, the statutes, and the ordinances which the Lord your God commands you"; "you shall keep the commandments which I command you this day"; "if you turn aside to walk after other gods and worship them"; "when you come into the land which the Lord your God gives you for an inheritance"; and "not with our fathers . . . , but with us, who are all of us here alive this day." This vocabulary also occurs in other places in the Pentateuch where the deuteronomic influence manifested itself. No wonder this powerful and creative perspective became the foundation for the deuteronomistic history that stretched from the book of Joshua, the conquest, through Kings, the beginning of the exile of a disobedient people.

The Priestly Writer. P, or the priestly perspective (550–450 B.C.E.), may have performed the most difficult, yet most exciting, task of the four groups. P composed either in a foreign land while surrounded by arrogant conquerors, hundreds of miles from the land that was so precious to the Israelites, or soon after the return from Exile while the memories of that experience were still fresh and the reality of the homeland was still agonizing. P realized that the traditions, both the longer connected accounts like JE and D and the liturgical, legal and genealogical records, must be preserved, the Babylonian ideology must be challenged, hope must be kindled in the hearts of the people, and a program for rebuilding must be displayed. P tied much of the older material together by means of the genealogies, added to the ancient stories so that they applied especially to his audience, i.e., became their story, and supplied a multilayered system of laws, found primarily in the books of Leviticus and Numbers, which prescribed how life should be lived during and after the Exile.

The creation account found in Gen 1:1–2:4 illustrates the skill of the priestly writer as he fulfilled his purpose. Certainly, during their New Year's festival, the Babylonians must have shouted triumphantly that Marduk, who destroyed Tiamat in a cosmic battle and created the order of the world, was king, and, by implication, that Yahweh was not. The Priestly writer answered that charge with another account, one that spoke in the measured cadence of a liturgy about the generation of a marvelous, orderly world from chaos by means of their God's creative word. His audience, sons and daughters of the Exile, knew chaos; they longed for an order that included the worship of their God in the land that had been given their ancestors. Furthermore, this monotheistic account concluded with the creation of the Sabbath, a divine ordinance set in the very rhythm of nature so that righteous people anywhere could proclaim their faith by imitating God on that day.

The later story of NOAH, tied together with the J material by means of lengthy genealogies, took on new meaning. Now a people, either in exile or recently returned, saw themselves cut loose, bereft of those lost in the flood of the Babylonian Exile. Now they drifted in circumstances that provided little sign of hope. The priestly composer reminded them that Noah eventually saw the end of the flood and settled down once again. The order of God's world returned and God promised never to punish the world in that fashion again. Similarly, the story of the bondage of their ancestors in Egypt became their story of exile and release. All these stories, inherited and added, were to inspire a growing hopefulness rooted in renewed obedience.

The laws provided the means to recover their covenant purity and the structure for their lives during this period. A community that is hopeful, but does not translate that sentiment to action, languishes. The laws, which set up practices that could be implemented and offices that could be outfitted, pointed to future time when the people would once again worship either in their own land in their own way or finally in a rebuilt temple replete with an organized Aaronic priesthood. Moreover, these laws would allow them to rebuild their homeland, decimated by war and characterized by disorder, with a sanctified blueprint for their whole existence. The priestly writer helped the people to do what JEREMIAH had instructed them to do—make their home in Babylon until Yahweh brought them back (Jer 29:1ff.)

Criticism and Evaluation. The source hypothesis of the Pentateuch is not without its critics. Some maintain that this hypothesis is a denial of the inspiration of the Bible, the departure from the long accepted tradition of the Mosaic authorship, and a secularizing construct created by scholars who exhibit little or no faith. Others claim this hypothesis continues to exist due to circular argumentation. If scholars claim that a certain clustering of vocabulary and concepts represents a certain perspective or group, then every time that vocabulary is found, one may strengthen the claim. These critics maintain that many writers shift their vocabulary from time to time, and return periodically to differing expressions. For example, commentators have maintained that the different names used for God may not signal different authors, but different connotations that operate in the context. Perhaps "Elohim" is the name of God as God is known to the whole world and "Yahweh" is the name of God as God is known to Israel, or his people. In addition, any account possesses several layers of meaning. To separate those layers and call them different documents or perspectives becomes a fraudulent endeavor. The boundaries of these sources have proved to be a problem. Certain scholars see not four sources finally coalescing, but a continuous process of accretion whereby the final product is a sign of the continued interpretation of Israel's history. Other scholars maintain that these sources can be discovered in books beyond the Pentateuch. In a similar vein, scholars can never pinpoint the existence of these generative groups. There are references to certain inter-biblical interpreters, e.g., prophets, but there are no references to groups who collected and interpreted history. The loss of history, i.e., the dichotomy between what the historical-critical researchers can reconstruct of Israelite history from the sources and the history recounted, disturbs some critics.

Even with all these difficulties, one must remember that the source hypothesis is a hypothesis—a perspective that makes sense of certain data: the use of different names for the deity; the repetitions; the variations on a theme; the geographical discrepancies; the chronological disagreements; and the evidence of smaller cycles that have been incorporated into larger units. Source analysis provides a means by which new data can be tested and its own methodology revised. Source criticism takes seriously the ascription of this material to Moses, but that ascription must be understood not according to the modern view of authorship, but the ancient perspective that regularly attributed material to an ancient worthy whose influence guided the continued interpretation of the tradition(s), e.g., certain books of the pseudepigrapha. Source analysis, in its present state, does not necessarily deny the inspiration of the Pentateuch; source analysis merely suggests that God's revelation occurs when godly people bring the traditions of their group to bear on contemporary problems. If source analysis leads to a fruitful understanding of the Pentateuch and its ongoing significance for the Jewish and Christian communities, then its deficiencies and excesses can be excused.

See also SOURCES, LITERARY.

—RUSSELL I. GREGORY

• **Sources, Literary.** The written documents used by the editors and authors of the final text of the Bible. These sources arose at various points throughout the history of the biblical people and in many cases were preserved for decades or even centuries before being incorporated, often revised and combined with other sources, into the present form of the biblical literature.

The Bible reports little about the history of its development, and there are few direct references to the various authors. The presence of sources on which later writers could draw is, however, explicitly mentioned at several points: poems are quoted from "The Book of the Wars of Yahweh" in Num 21:14 and from "The Book of Jashar" in Josh 10:13 and 2 Sam 1:18. "The Book of the Acts of Solomon" (1 Kgs 11:41) and "The Book of the Chronicles of the Kings of Israel" (1 Kgs 14:19; 15:31; 16:14) may have been court annals available to the later historians of the Israelite monarchy. Jer 36 gives an account of how the prophet dictated many of his previous utterances to his scribe BARUCH; this scroll probably served as a source for much of chaps. 1–25.

The search for other sources not explicitly mentioned in the text represents one of the oldest methods of modern biblical criticism, dating back to the eighteenth-century efforts by H. B. Witter and J. Astruc to identify several sources on which the book of Genesis was based. Source criticism has at times gone under the name of documentary criticism or literary criticism; the latter term is now best reserved for the exegetical method that focuses on stylistic aspects in the text.

The basic purpose of source criticism is to determine whether a given textual unit—be it a short passage or an entire book—is from a single hand or is a composite based on one or more written sources. If there are indications that a previous source existed, then the exegete seeks to determine as much as possible about the author(s) of the source, the time and place in which it was written, its character and purpose, and the extent of its incorporation into the present text. The main criteria used in isolating a source are: the occurrence of distinctive terms and style, duplication and repetition of material, contradictions and divergencies within the text, and evidences of redactional activity. The results of source criticism become a basis for the other exegetical methods—especially form criticism, tradition criticism, and redaction criticism—that seek to uncover the growth of the text from its earliest to its final shape.

The Pentateuch was the first staging-ground for source-critical study and has delivered some of the most striking results, especially thanks to the careful work of Julius Wellhausen more than a century ago. While opinions differ on some points, it is generally accepted that four main sources emerged over Israel's history: J (the Yahwist) and E (the Elohist), called after the divine name (respectively, Yahweh [or Jahweh] and Elohim) that most commonly occurs in each, were written in different periods (J in the tenth century B.C.E. and E in the ninth–eighth century), in separate places (J in southern Israel and E in northern Israel), and for varying purposes (J: to celebrate the founding of the Israelite nation-state by recounting God's past support of the people; and E: to guard against syncretism by emphasizing cult and religious obedience). While J and E are basically limited to Genesis, Exodus, and Numbers, the D (deuteronomic) source is the basis of the Book of Deuteronomy, especially its core of laws in chaps. 12–26, and probably originated in the eighth or seven century in order to preserve the legal traditions of the North after the fall of Samaria 722/1 B.C.E. The final main written source (or redactional stage?) of the Pentateuch is P (Priestly), composed by priests in the sixth or fifth centuries for the purpose of revitalizing the covenant and cult of Israel in the period of the restoration. These hypothetical sources were successively redacted and brought together, lastly by the priests in the fifth century, into the present form of the Pentateuch.

Source criticism has been applied to most other parts of the biblical literature as well. For example, the sixth-century authors and/or editors of the books of Samuel probably drew on much earlier written sources such as the Ark narrative (now in 1 Sam 4:1–7:1 and parts of 2 Sam 6), the Saul cycle (parts of 1 Sam 9–11 and 13–14), the story of David's rise (parts of 1 Sam 16:14–2 Sam 5:10), and the succession narrative (2 Sam 9–20 and 1 Kgs 1–2). The editor of 1–2 Chronicles was able to use all of 1–2 Samuel and 1–2 Kings as sources, together with other materials. Prophetic books were often preceded by collections of utterances, recorded by the prophet or the disciples. Sources were also apparently available for some of the wisdom literature, the Psalter, and various writings of the early Jewish period.

Similarly, the NT has been studied through the methods of source criticism, and written sources for John, Acts, and other books are proposed. By far the most important results, however, have helped to clarify the origins of the synoptic Gospels: that Mark was written first and then Matthew and Luke, each of the latter two having used Mark, also a separate collection of Jesus' sayings called Q (for German *Quelle,* "source"), as well as an additional source each that the other did not have.

The importance of source criticism for exegesis lies in its discovery of the written stages that led up to the final composition of the text. Not only does this disclose information about the historical periods in which these earlier sources were written, but it also emphasizes that the "authorship" of the present text needs to be shared among all those who had a hand in its literary development.

See also GENRE IN THE OLD TESTAMENT; PRIESTLY WRITERS; REDACTION; SOURCES OF THE PENTATEUCH; SYNOPTIC PROBLEM; TRADITION IN THE OLD TESTAMENT.

Bibliography. W. Brueggemann and H. Wolff, *The Vitality of Old Testament Traditions*; N. Habel, *Literary Criticism of the Old Testament*; J. H. Hayes, *An Introduction to Old Testament Study*; J. Wellhausen, *Prolegomena to the History of Israel.*

—DOUGLAS A. KNIGHT

• **South Galatia.** *See* GALATIA

• **Speaking with Tongues.** *See* TONGUES

• **Spice.** Spice (Heb., *bōsem, sammim*; Gk., *ăroma*) was an important article in the luxury trade of the ancient Near East. In the Bible spices are not associated with food, but always refer to the costly perfumes or oils which were used for incense in the cult. The land of Sheba in southern Arabia was known for its spice trade in the OT (Ezek 27:22). Spices were among the gifts offered Solomon by the QUEEN OF SHEBA (1 Kgs 10:10; 2 Chr 9:9). Spices were thus a token of wealth. Among the treasures Hezekiah showed the envoys of Merodach-baladan of Babylon were "the spices" (2 Kgs 20:13; Isa 39:2).

Spices played an important role in the worship of the temple. Solomon's Temple was dedicated to Yahweh "for the burning of the INCENSE of sweet spices before him" (2 Chr 2:4). Exod 30:22-38 describes the formula for making the incense and sweet spices which were used in the worship of Yahweh. Such spices were dedicated to Yahweh and were not to be used simply as perfume. It was forbidden that outsiders should use spices dedicated to Yahweh. In the postexilic period the sons of the priests were entrusted with the art of spicemaking for use in worship (1 Chr 9:29-30).

Spices were also used in the preparation of bodies for burial (2 Chr 16:14; Jer 34:5). Spices are mentioned in the NT only in connection with the burial of Jesus and the intention of the women to anoint Jesus' body (Mark 16:1; Luke 23:56; 24:1; John 19:40).

See also OINTMENT/PERFUME.

Bibliography. H. N. and A. L. Moldenke, *Plants of the Bible*.

—CECIL P. STATON, JR.

• **Spies.** According to Num 13, God commands Moses to select twelve men, one from each clan, to spy out the land of Canaan. The men return after forty days, confirming that the region is exceptionally fertile but acknowledging that its defenders are formidable. Only JOSHUA and CALEB urge immediate conquest, the other ten cautioning the people that giants dwell in the territory. The story in Judg 18 mentions five spies from the Danite clan who come to the house of Micah, taking note of its wealth, and journey to the little village of Laish, which lives a secluded existence. These spies urge quick action, which results in the sack of Micah's possessions and the destruction of Laish and its inhabitants. Josh 2 reports that two spies scout JERICHO, finding temporary succor in the house of RAHAB the harlot, eventually promising to spare her life and that of her family. The SATAN (Adversary) in Job 1–2 functions as a spy in God's service, determining whether anyone really worships the deity without thought of the reward or fear of punishment.

—JAMES L. CRENSHAW

• **Spinning and Weaving.** It has been postulated that spinning and weaving began as early as the Stone Age. Certainly by the time of the Bronze Age it was a practiced art, and by the time of the Iron Age it was a common industry. In the Hebrew Bible, the act of spinning and weaving is an accepted practice that requires no explanation. The products of this art are mentioned manifold times even though no clear indications of the process are evident. Note the following examples: Temple cloths are described in Exod 26; Exod 28:5 mentions "fine twined linen," Jer 13:1 refers to a linen waistcloth that the prophet is to put on his loins. Prov 31 mentions the goodly wife who works with the wool and flax (vv. 13, 22, 24), making garments for her family.

Spinning is the art of taking vegetable or animal fibers and creating a continuous strand in order that the strand may be utilized to create larger textiles. This practice takes advantage of these natural fibers' inherent property of shrinking and turning when dried. Any list of these fibers would include flax, cotton, wool, and silk. The vegetable fibers were spun first, and it is probably due to their natural properties that spinning first was discovered.

The process of weaving takes the created strand and by intertwining the strands at right angles produces a piece of cloth. Terms such as weft and warp are used to describe respectively the crosswise and lengthwise strands. There were in ancient times both horizontal and vertical looms. The horizontal ground loom was used in Egypt although the vertical loom began to be used after about 1500 B.C.E. The horizontal loom was more applicable to the lifestyle of the Syria-Palestine area, and thus was the predominant loom. It could be supported by poles and braces stuck in the ground, and thus was also moveable.

—MARK W. GREGORY

• **Spirit.** *See* HOLY SPIRIT

• **Spirit in the New Testament.** *See* HOLY SPIRIT

• **Spirit in the Old Testament.** Spirit in the OT is used in two different but related ways: referring to the human spirit and referring to the Spirit of God. The same Hebrew words are used in each instance. It is the context that determines which meaning is intended. Angels and demons in the OT are never referred to by the term "spirit."

Vocabulary. The two basic words that are translated as "spirit" in the OT are *ruaḥ* and *nepeš*. *Nepeš* apparently originally meant "neck" or "throat" and later came to mean "breath" or "life" and ultimately is translated as "soul" or "spirit." *Ruaḥ* on the other hand appears originally to have meant "breath" or "wind" and later came to be interpreted or understood as "soul."

The Human Spirit. Nepeš is applied both to humanity and to animals. The same phrase using this term is applied to humankind (Gen 2:7) and is also applied to all living creatures (Gen 1:20-21, 24). Thus it clearly does not refer to the soul as understood in the NT. The *nepeš* came to refer to the totality of life, including both the body and what the NT means by soul. Within the OT, a human being is perhaps best described as dust indwelt with a *nepeš*.

The *ruaḥ,* on the other hand, comes closer to what most contemporary interpreters mean by spirit and is usually so translated. The same word is applied both to God's Spirit and to the human spirit. The *ruaḥ* does appear to have a moral side, as reflected by the description given of a person "in whose spirit there is no deceit" (Ps 32:2). In some instances it appears to refer to a gift of the Spirit of God that indwells a person bringing some sort of divine power (Num 11:17, 25-26; 1 Sam 11:6; 16:14). At the same time there was normally the understanding that a person's spirit was always present as long as life continued. The OT never seems to see the spirit of a person as having any kind of existence separate from the body. In the OT, when a person died, what was left was not the *ruaḥ* but a shade or a shadow of the former self.

It is extremely difficult to determine or define the difference between the *nepeš* and the *ruaḥ*. However, insofar as humanity is concerned, the *ruaḥ* may be described as being the upper or higher part of the *nepeš,* while both may be described as being the inner part of the body. There appears to have been no understanding in the OT of any real human existence when any one of these was separated from the others.

The Spirit of God. In the OT the Spirit of God was not as fully understood as it later came to be in the NT. It appears as a mediating concept of God, to some extent bridging the gap between the spiritual world and that of the human. *Ruaḥ* is the common word for the Spirit of God in the OT, while *nepeš* is never used in this way.

The Spirit of God is seen as being associated with God in creation: "and the Spirit of God was moving over the face of the waters" (Gen 1:2). Some interpreters view this as simply being nothing more than a wind sent by God to blow over the primordial waters, but it appears that far more than this is intended here. This idea of God's Spirit being associated with the deity in creation is also seen in the book of Job (34:13-14). At the same time, in neither place does the context indicate anything like the personality applied to the Spirit, the personality found later in the NT.

The Spirit of God is also associated with God in the inspiration of the prophets. Samuel said to Saul, after Saul's anointing as king, "The spirit of the Lord will come mightily upon you, and you shall prophesy'' (1 Sam 10:6). Ezekiel also spoke of being lifted by the Spirit of God when he had been called as a prophet: ''And when he spoke to me, the Spirit entered into me and set me upon my feet; and I heard him speaking to me'' (Ezek 2:2). But more than that, Ezekiel regularly describes God's Spirit as inspiring and using him throughout his ministry (Ezek 8:3; 11:1; 11:24). Further, Isaiah described the MESSIAH as being filled with the Spirit in what appears to have included the idea of inspiration.

And the Spirit of the Lord shall rest upon him,
the spirit of wisdom and understanding,
the spirit of counsel and might,
the spirit of knowledge and the fear of the Lord.
And his delight shall be in the fear of the Lord.
—Isa 11:2-3

The idea of the Spirit being involved in the inspiration or empowerment of God's people clearly extends beyond the idea of prophetic inspiration. Thus we see where the Spirit of God ''clothed'' itself with GIDEON (Judg 6:34). This is more than being encouraged or empowered to do something. This idea seems to reflect the thought that in some way God was actually indwelling the people of Israel.

Two other descriptions of the Spirit of God in the OT are more nebulous than these. First, the Spirit appears to be seen as being synonymous with or parallel to the mind, will, or purpose of God. Such an idea is found both among the prophets and in the wisdom writers. Thus Isaiah proclaimed:

''Woe to the rebellious children,'' says the Lord,
''who carry out a plan, but not mine;
and who make a league, but not of my spirit,
that they may add sin to sin.'' —Isa 30:1

A second nebulous usage may be found in the idea that the Spirit of God appears to be understood as some sort of life principle that may be given or withdrawn at the divine will. This may also be seen simply as an indication of God's presence with the people or with an individual (Pss 51:10-11; 104:29-30; Isa 63:14).

Finally, the Spirit of God is regularly understood in the OT as being synonymous with the divine power. Some commentators appear to try to see this meaning in almost every usage of the expression. This appears to be far too limiting to express adequately what the OT means. It is certainly too restricting when understood against what the NT reveals about God's Spirit.

No serious question can be raised with the statement that the OT writers do not ever appear to have understood God's Spirit in the same way that the NT people did. On the other hand, the OT does appear to have understood the Spirit as being more than just raw power. The Spirit appears to mediate the presence as well as the purpose of God to humanity. Zechariah proclaimed to Zerubbabel that he would be able ultimately to fulfill the task that had been assigned to him by God with this affirmation: ''Not by might, nor by power, but by my Spirit, says the Lord'' (Zech 4:6). Clearly, the Spirit here is more than power, even divine power. While still not really identified in terms of personality, this description of the Spirit is but a step away from the NT development of the idea.

See also HOLY SPIRIT.

Bibliography. W. Eichrodt, *Theology of the Old Testament*; G. Quell and E. Schweizer, ''πνεῦμα, κτλ.,'' *TDNT*.

—ROBERT L. CATE

• **Spirit of Christ.** *See* HOLY SPIRIT

• **Spirit of God.** *See* HOLY SPIRIT

• **Spirit of Jesus.** *See* HOLY SPIRIT

• **Spirit, The Holy.** *See* HOLY SPIRIT

• **Spirits in Prison.** ''Spirits in prison'' is an ambiguous phrase found only in 1 Pet 3:19 which refers to beings to whom Christ preached. The interpretation of 3:19 and the subsequent verse 4:6 involve a host of interrelated questions.

Within the NT, the term spirits usually refers to supernatural beings, either good or evil. Since 1 Pet 3:20 indicates that these spirits had been disobedient in the days of Noah, many scholars have suggested that they were evil angels: the evil ''sons of God'' of Gen 6:1-4 whose disobedience led to God's punishment of humanity through the flood. However, the term spirits is sometimes used to refer to the spirits or souls of dead human beings (e.g., Heb 12:23). Thus, the spirits Christ preached to may have been disobedient unbelievers who died in Noah's time.

The time and place of Christ's preaching is also debated. Few now follow Augustine's proposal that Christ preached in his preexistent state during the time of Moses. Modern scholars suggest that he preached either between his crucifixion and resurrection or after his ascension. If Peter meant that Christ preached to the spirits in prison between his crucifixion and resurrection, then he must have used the term prison to refer to HELL (cf. Rev 18:2) and thus implied that Christ descended into hell to preach to the imprisoned spirits there. A less likely possibility is that Peter envisioned the prison to be in one of the levels of HEAVEN (cf. *Enoch* 18:12) and meant that Christ preached there after his ascension.

Neither the content of Christ's preaching nor the response of the spirits is specifically mentioned in 1 Pet 3:19, giving rise to much speculation about both questions. It is safest to assume that here, as elsewhere in the NT, the content of Christ's preaching was the good news of salvation. We are given no hint as to whether the imprisoned spirits accepted Christ's message or rejected it. Peter was not concerned with satisfying our curiosity, but only with encouraging his readers during a period of persecution.

The interpretation of 1 Pet 3:19 depends on its relationship to 4:6, which says that ''the gospel was preached even to the dead.'' Some scholars, such as the translators of the NIV, believe that 3:19 and 4:6 refer to totally different events. ''The dead'' mentioned in 4:6 were Christians who heard the gospel while they were alive but who died sometime before Peter wrote his Letter. For this reason, the NIV reads that the gospel was preached ''to those who are now dead.'' However, if these two verses refer to the same event, then Christ did indeed preach good news to the imprisoned spirits of the dead. Furthermore, 4:6 implies that at least some of the listening spirits repented and were saved, since it explains that the reason the gospel was proclaimed to them was ''that though judged in the flesh like men, they might live in the spirit like God.'' If this interpretation is followed, then 1 Pet 3:19 suggests that salvation may be possible even for those who never heard the gospel while on earth.

See also HEAVEN; HELL; PETER, LETTERS OF; SHEOL.

Bibliography. J. N. D. Kelly, *A Commentary on the Epistles of Peter and Jude*; B. Reike, *The Disobedient Spirits and Christian Baptism*; E. G. Selwyn, *The First Epistle of*

Peter.

—MARK J. OLSON

• **Spirits, Evil.** *See* DEMON IN THE NEW TESTAMENT

• **Spirits, Unclean.** *See* EVIL

• **Spiritual Body.** From two Gk. words (σῶμα πνευματικόν), and found in 1 Cor 15:44-50. Often referred to as the resurrection body.

The spiritual body in Paul's writings is seen in sharp contrast with the physical body (σῶμα ψυχικόν). The latter is the fleshly dimension of a human being and as such it is often depicted as worldly, subject to temptation and to sin.

The spiritual body, however, refers to the mysterious transformation that occurs in the resurrection. The spiritual body enables the Christian to be wholly possessed by the HOLY SPIRIT and thereby to partake in the resurrection life offered by Christ.

See also BODY IN THE NEW TESTAMENT; FLESH AND SPIRIT; HOLY SPIRIT; RESURRECTION IN THE NEW TESTAMENT.

—WATSON E. MILLS

• **Spiritual Gifts.** *See* GIFTS OF THE SPIRIT

• **Staff.** *See* ROD/STAFF

• **Star of Bethlehem.** The star (in Matthew's story of Jesus' birth) which guided the wise men from the East to Jerusalem and on to BETHLEHEM, when Christ was born, was named by later generations the Star of Bethlehem (cf. Matt 2:1-12).

Many ancient people regarded stars as gods and believed that they controlled human destiny in such a way that the future could be predicted by studying the stars. Israel believed that God created the stars (Gen 1:16) and set them in their courses (Jer 31:35). Israel was forbidden to commit idolatry by worshiping stars (Deut 4:19). But Israel was also aware of astrologers in other countries who sought to interpret events on earth by studying the stars; they encountered these wise men in Egypt (Gen 41:8), in Babylon (Isa 47:1,13), and in Persia (Esth 1:13-14). Jeremiah associated astrology with foreign ideas (Jer 10:1-2).

Matthew does not explain the star, and Christians have produced several theories to try to explain it as a natural phenomenon. It may have been a meteor, though ordinary meteors do not last as long as the star did. It may have been a comet (Halley's comet appeared in 11 B.C.E.), though ordinary comets do not stop (Matt 2:10). It may have been a nova, a star which suddenly shines more brightly than it has previously, though ordinary novas do not move across the sky (Matt 2:9). It may have been an unusual configuration of planets; for example in 7 B.C.E. Jupiter and Saturn moved together in the constellation Pisces which was associated in astrology with the Jews; but ordinary conjunctions of planets do not travel and then stop. It seems likely, therefore, that the star of Bethlehem is not to be thought of as a natural phenomenon but as a unique, miraculous event, whose purpose was to guide the wise men to Christ.

The star has at least three theological meanings. It indicates that the birth of Jesus was the fulfillment of OT messianic prophecies (cf. esp. Num 24:14-17). It also shows that Jesus had significance, not for Jews alone, but for all people. And it shows that God may use the mistaken ideas and practices of people (e.g., astrology) to lead them to a true knowledge of himself and of Jesus Christ.

See also ASTROLOGER; ASTROLOGY; MAGI.

—FISHER HUMPHREYS

• **Statute.** *See* LAW IN THE OLD TESTAMENT

• **Steadfast Love.** *See* LOVING-KINDNESS

• **Stealing.** *See* ROBBERY; TEN COMMANDMENTS

• **Stephanas.** [stef'uh-nuhs] Stephanas was an important member of the Corinthian congregation. He (along with Fortunatus and Achaicus) probably delivered to Paul in EPHESUS the letter from the Corinthian church (1 Cor 7:1) and returned with the letter now known as 1 Corinthians. In that letter, PAUL rejoices that the visit of Stephanas and his traveling companions has refreshed his spirit. Stephanas and his family are described as being the first Christian converts during Paul's ministry in Achaia (1 Cor 16:15). Moreover, they are counted among very few within the Corinthian church who (in addition to Crispus and Gaius) were personally baptized by Paul (1 Cor 1:16). Stephanas and his household are held up by Paul as examples of devoted servants within the community of saints. The Corinthian congregation is urged to follow the leadership of such persons (1 Cor 16:15-18).

See also ACHAIA; CORINTH; CORINTHIAN CORRESPONDENCE; PAUL.

—DEAN M. MARTIN

• **Stephen.** [stee'vuhn] Stephen, the first Christian martyr, was the pivotal figure in the expansion of the Christian movement. It is safe to say that if Stephen, or someone like him, had not appeared on the scene Christianity could have died as a Galilean sect of Judaism. Stephen preached as the apostles had not preached to that time. The apostles were still evangelizing under the umbrage of Judaism and seemingly had no serious desire to carry out the commission of Christ to preach the gospel to the ends of the earth.

In Acts 6:1–8:2 there are two narratives about Stephen plus a speech attributed to him. One story presents him as one of THE SEVEN selected to carry out the administrative function of safeguarding Hellenistic-Jewish Christian widows in their proper share of the daily provisions. The other narrative portrays Stephen as an aggressive evangelist.

Along with six others, Stephen was chosen by the Christian community to handle an emergency situation in the fellowship. The Palestinian-Jewish Christians were deliberately overlooking the support of Hellenistic-Jewish Christian widows. The men selected to solve this problem had to have a depth of judiciousness. To deal with the ticklish matter of discrimination they must be administrators with a good reputation. The people's confidence in them had to be based upon the way these men had conducted themselves previously. The Seven were also to be filled with the Spirit and wisdom. The type of wisdom necessary was certainly not speculative or abstract. They must possess practical wisdom (common sense) to handle the discrimination in a discreet manner.

Since all of the Seven had Greek names, it is assumed that they represented the Hellenistic-Jewish Christian branch of the community. Thus there was assurance that the Hellenistic-Jewish Christian widows would get their share of the daily dole. No further information is given in the NT about the work of these men except Stephen and Philip.

It is quite possible that the discrimination against the Hellenistic-Jewish Christian widows was not caused by cultural and linguistic differences which carried over into the early church as a parallel to these differences between Hellenistic and Palestinian Jews. Disagreement between the two Christian groups concerned ideologies and thought forms. There was a theological split. This is very clear from Stephen's debate with the Hellenistic Jews in the synagogue and from his speech before the SANHEDRIN. The cause of the rift is further clarified when the Hellenistic Christians bear the brunt of the persecution of the Jews after the death of Stephen.

Although the theological difference in the church continued, the discrimination against the impoverished widows ceased. Apparently the administrative office of the Seven was only temporary and had no lasting significance because after the problem was solved Stephen and Philip resumed their work as evangelists.

The second narrative about Stephen presents him as an evangelist. Stephen had varied gifts that made him an influential and convincing advocate of the faith. His endowments were accompanied by a manifestation of works that appear to be miraculous in character. Heretofore only the apostles had displayed this power. His wisdom was not merely the practical sort that was essential in performing his administrative duties, but he possessed a skill in philosophical wisdom not unlike that which was world renowned in Alexandria.

Stephen did not follow the pattern of the apostles and go to the TEMPLE to bear his witness. His interests were directed toward the Hellenistic Jews. Possibly he felt the urgency to do this because he was of this class of Jews and had previously been associated with many of them in the Hellenistic synagogues in Jerusalem. His views would be more acceptable in these circles. Under ordinary circumstances the freer inward character of his message about Jesus would be more attractive to diaspora Jews. The Hellenistic Jews' broader contacts in the provinces made them less nationalistic than those who lived in Palestine. Their encounters with other religions and philosophy pressured them into a reexamination of their own faith. The type of reasoning they used was far superior to the pedantic and superficial approach of the rabbis.

When Stephen expounded his views in the synagogue, the Hellenistic Jews engaged him in debate. His opponents could not overcome his irresistible wisdom. Their jealousy prompted them to stir up the people against him with false witnesses who said that he spoke words of blasphemy against Moses and God. A charge of blasphemy was a capital offense and punishable by death. This brought the elders and scribes into the picture, and Stephen was brought before the Sanhedrin.

When he was charged with speaking against the Temple and the LAW, Stephen replied with a speech longer than any other in Acts. According to the Mishnah an accused person was allowed to make a speech for his acquittal (*Sanh* 5:4). The court was bound to listen to him provided there was any substance to what he was saying. Instead of making a plea for acquittal Stephen used this privilege to clarify his theological position.

The tenor of the address was a devastating attack upon the so-called religious privileges of the Jews. Through their forefathers they claimed three distinct advantages. They inherited the land of Palestine and the promise from Abraham. God revealed himself in the TORAH through Moses. The Temple was sacrosanct because God had placed his name there. Stephen refuted the three religious privileges of the Jews and exposed the weakness of the foundation of Judaism with its claims. He also challenged the complacency of the primitive church and brought about a division in the fellowship which hitherto had been rather harmonious. Furthermore, he antagonized the Pharisees by what he said about the Law. This religious group had previously defended the community against the SADDUCEES. Finally, he enraged the Sanhedrin to such a degree that he was given the death sentence.

The death of Stephen paved the way for the world mission of Christianity. The Hellenistic-Jewish Christians left Jerusalem and Judea to escape severe persecution that was directed against all those who shared the theological views of Stephen. The apostles remained in Jerusalem, and in all probability so did those who adhered to the conservative theological position of the apostles. They had no fear of molestation because they had not spoken against the Law and Temple.

Stephen was not only the first Christian martyr but the first evangelist who fully understood the distinction that Christ taught between Judaism and Christianity. He was a forerunner of Paul who was a witness to his death. In fact the death of Stephen may have paved the way for Paul's conversion.

See also HEBREWS AND HELLENISTS; LAW IN THE NEW TESTAMENT; PAUL; PERSECUTION IN THE NEW TESTAMENT; SANHEDRIN; SEVEN, THE; TEMPLE/TEMPLES; TORAH.

Bibliography. H. J. Cadbury, *The Book of Acts in History*; A. Cole, *The New Temple*; E. Haenchen, *The Acts of the Apostles*; W. L. Knox, *The Acts of the Apostles*; W. Schmitals, *Paul and James*; M. Simon, *St. Stephen and the Hellenists in the Primitive Church*.

—T. C. SMITH

• **Steward.** *See* STEWARDSHIP

• **Stewardship.** In the OT, stewardship refers to responsibility for property which belongs to someone else (cf. Gen 15:2; 43:16, 19; 44:4; 1 Chr 28:1). It is similar, in some respects, to what we would consider a "power of attorney." This is clearly seen in Dan 1:11, 16 where the steward whom the chief of the eunuchs had placed over Daniel and his friends had the authority to alter the prescribed diet and routine of those in training as long as the right results were obtained.

In the NT the understanding of stewardship as authority over the possessions of others is found in the Gospels of Matthew and Luke (cf. Matt 20:8; Luke 8:3; 12:42; 16:1-3). The metaphorical use is most important in the NT. The matter over which stewardship is to be practiced in the NT is the mysteries of God, i.e., the gospel revelation (1 Cor 4:1), a divine commission (1 Cor 9:17), or a divine gift (1 Pet 4:10).

The relationship between those who have been made stewards of the various graces of God and the one calling them to that task differs from the strictly horizontal relationship between the owner of vast property and those to whom it is entrusted: the stewards of the gospel do not have the liberty possessed by other stewards. The same faithfulness is obviously required: "It is required in stewards that a man be found faithful" (1 Cor 4:2; cf. Titus 1:7; 1 Pet 4:10).

—HERBERT O. EDWARDS, SR.

• **Stoa.** *See* STOICS

• **Stoics.** [stoh'iks] Stoics were advocates of a philosophical system of thought known as Stoicism, which originated in Athens in the fourth century B.C.E. and became the dominant ethical philosophy of the Hellenistic and Roman world. The school and its adherents took their name from the *Stoa,* an open colonnade in the Athenian marketplace where instruction in the philosophy originally occurred.

Zeno (333–264 B.C.E.) is credited with the founding of the Stoic philosophy around 300 B.C.E. Zeno had been influenced by Cynicism through his own teacher, Crates, and became committed to the ideals of inward freedom, austerity, and devotion to duty despite the consequences. Like the Cynics who preceded him, Zeno sought to magnify the human goal of the pursuit of virtue and temperance. Upon his death in 264 he was memorialized with a tomb in the Ceramicus and an epitaph which noted his commitment to principles and influence upon others.

Cleanthes (331–232 B.C.E.) and Chrysippus (d. 205 B.C.E.) succeeded Zeno as head of the school of Stoicism and became responsible for consolidating and systematizing the Stoic doctrine. Panaetius of Rhodes (180–110 B.C.E.) became the chief spokesman for Stoicism in 144 B.C.E. and is noted for his indebtedness to Plato and Aristotle, his emphasis upon ethical teachings related to practical conduct of life, and his influence upon the Roman writer, Cicero. Noted Stoic philosophers of the Roman imperial period included Seneca (4 B.C.E.–65 C.E.), the tutor to Emperor Nero; the slave Epictetus (55–135 C.E.); and the emperor Marcus Aurelius (161–180 C.E.). The inclusion of such divergent personalities was testimony to the Stoic emphasis upon equality and human dignity.

Stoicism contended that virtue was the ultimate good. Virtue was defined differently by various philosophers as living in agreement with the logos (Zeno) or living in agreement with nature (Chrysippus). By "nature" Stoics meant the true nature of human beings, not the external physical world. Hence, nature and logos both referred to rational discernment. Human reason was believed to be identical with the divine Reason which governed the entire universe and which some Stoics identified with Zeus.

Conduct in harmony with Reason required the Stoics to adopt a stance of detachment from all the external and empirical factors present in society and from the human affections and desires which deter the quest for virtue. The wise man (Stoic) fortified himself with imperturbability against such circumstances as pain and pleasure, wealth and poverty, success and misfortune. Every individual's life was viewed as determined by fate and one's freedom consisted in the acceptance of that destiny and the achievement of oneness with the Reason which pervades the world.

The NT literature never refers to Stoicism explicitly. However, both in a speech in Acts 17:28 and in his Letter to the Philippians (4:11), Paul employed phrases which were used widely by Stoics. For example, he said, "I have learned, in whatever state I am, to be content" (Phil 4:11). He proceeded to differ from Stoics by locating the source of his contentment in his relationship to a personal deity rather than divine Reason.

See also ASCETICISM; ETHICS IN THE NEW TESTAMENT; HELLENISTIC WORLD; LOGOS/WORD; MARKET/MARKETPLACE.

Bibliography. J. M. Rist, *Stoic Philosophy.*

—ROBERT M. SHURDEN

• **Stoning.** Stoning was a particularly brutal way to die but an effective way to execute one guilty of a capital offense. It was especially applied to religious offenses: worshiping pagan deities (Deut 17:2-7); sacrificing a child to Molech (Lev 20:2-5); prophesying in the name of pagan gods (Deut 13:1-5); spirit divinations (Lev 20:27); blasphemy (Lev 24:15-16); and Sabbath breaking (Num 15:32-36). Insofar as the ban (*herem*) was a ritual sacrifice to Yahweh, the stoning of Achan for taking booty can be added (Josh 7:25). A killer ox (Exod 21:28-32), adulterers (Deut 22:22-24), and rebellious children (Deut 21:18-21) were also to be stoned.

Stoning was often a spontaneous act, sometimes carried out by one person acting on behalf of the group (Deut 13:6-10). As a group action, it conveyed corporate responsibility for punishing the guilty and purging perceived evils (Num 15:32-36). Thus, there was no need for an official position of executioner and the practice was undoubtedly abused. The combination of the ready availability of stones, the dynamics of mob psychology, and the moral approval of death by stoning made vigilante-type justice swift and often ill-advised. King David was almost stoned (1 Sam 30:6); Adoram, taskmaster under the brutal reign of Rehoboam (1 Kgs 12:18), was killed by a rebel group.

Later Jewish regulations tried to assure that only guilty persons were stoned (*Sanh* 6:1-4). It allowed for last-minute evidence in favor of the condemned and for a confession before death. The condemned was disrobed and knocked off a scaffold six cubits (ca. nine ft.) high by one of the witnesses to the crime. The second witness dropped a stone on the chest of the condemned, if the fall was not fatal. If the criminal survived all this, the crowd joined the stoning.

A moral revulsion toward stoning developed among Christians. Jesus rejected it as a method of dealing with adultery (John 8:1-11) and used stoning as a metaphor for hard-heartedness and nonrepentance in parables (Matt 21:35) and in his prayer over Jerusalem (Matt 23:37). The evangelizing efforts of the apostles were often met with threats of stoning (Acts 14:5), so that it became a sign of Jewish resistance to the Christian movement. The fact that Jesus was nearly stoned for "blasphemy" (John 10:31ff.) and the heroic martyrdom of Stephen (Acts 7:54-58) underscored the moral bankruptcy of the practice as a method of dealing with a religious controversy.

—PAUL D. SIMMONS

• **Stranger.** A term for at least two types of noncitizens: resident alien (sojourner) or individual just passing through the territory. The resident alien, designated *gēr* (pl. *gērîm*), perhaps best translated as sojourner or stranger, was a temporary resident possessing no inherited rights. The individual only passing through Israelite territory was designated *zār* (pl. *zārîm*), translated as stranger. Other words were also used, such as *nokrî* (foreigner), and postexilically *tôšāb* (dweller) was substituted for *gēr*. In a broad sense, although not always helpful, foreigner and stranger are used interchangeably to render the various Hebrew words in English translations. In global perspective, early in Israelite history the focus on the stranger was more politically oriented, whereas in the later history the emphasis was more on the religious connotations.

Resident aliens were restricted from participation in Israel's cultic life (Exod 12:43), but nonetheless laws protected them. Certain restrictions concerning how to relate to fellow Israelites did not apply to foreigners, who could be charged usury (Deut 23:20) and sold animals ritually unacceptable for Israelite sacrifice and/or consumption. Resident aliens could either be temporarily displaced from home (Abraham among the Hittites, Gen 23:4) or be residents for a longer period among another social grouping (the Hebrews living among the Egyptians, Deut 23:7). They were not landowners, as only Israelites could own land (Lev 25:23-24). Foreigners (*nokrî*) were also specifically prohibited from ascending to monarchical status (Deut 17:15). *Zār* was also used to distinguish between the priest and those of his household, such as the priest's slaves (Lev 22:10-12), or to delineate the immediate family from those outside the family. The stranger in these cases might be Israelite (Deut 25:5).

The attitude of protectiveness toward strangers derived both from eastern custom and from an Israelite awareness that earlier they had been strangers in a foreign land (Exod 22:21; 23:9). Protective measures thus were developed to sustain strangers (cf. the Book of the Covenant, Exod 20:22–23:33). Although strangers did not possess all the rights of Israelites, even the earliest legislation assured justice (Exod 22:21; Heb 22:20) and protected against violence (Exod 23:7). In the later Deuteronomic material, Israelites more explicitly had the responsibility to love (Deut 10:19), protect (Deut 24:14, 17), and care for (Deut 14:29; 24:19) strangers. Nonetheless, strangers did not have the same status as citizens, as is evident by the fact that along with widows and orphans they needed special care (Deut 24:19-22). Marriages between Israelites and non-Israelites did occur (cf. Book of Ruth), but theoretically the Deuteronomic legislation forbade Israelites to marry the original inhabitants of CANAAN (Deut 7:1-4).

In the priestly material, the *gēr* assumed a posture very close to that of the native citizen, a relationship akin to that seen in the NT proselyte (Matt 23:15). As proselytes they were expected to observe the ritual requirements mandated for Israelites (e.g., cf. Lev 16:29-31). Even one so absorbed, however, was not fully an Israelite, because CIRCUMCISION was the prerequisite if the *gēr* were to be accepted as an Israelite (Gen 34:15; Exod 12:48-49). In the era moving toward the emergence of Christianity, prompted by the Samaritan schism and the Maccabean struggles, Judaism ultimately absorbed the *gēr* as a fully-assimilated proselyte.

See also GENTILE/GENTILES IN THE OLD TESTAMENT; PROSELYTE; SOJOURNER/RESIDENT ALIEN.

Bibliography. J. Pedersen, *Israel: Its Life and Culture*; R. de Vaux, *Ancient Israel: Its Life and Institutions*.

—FRANK E. EAKIN, JR.

• **Structuralism.** *See* LITERATURE, BIBLE AS

• **Succession Narrative.** The portion of the former prophets included in 2 Sam 9–20 and 1 Kgs 1–2 is now generally identified as "The Succession Narrative." Its separate existence was first suggested and worked out in detail by Leonhard Rost in 1926. The material contained in it deals with the struggles in Israel for the right to succeed David upon the throne of the Hebrew Kingdom. This section appears to be quite distinctive from the rest of 1 and 2 Samuel, lacking the dual accounts which appeared so regularly there. Further, instead of the occasional disconnections and the jumpiness of the earlier material, this unit appears to be unified by a common theme, as well as characterized by a common style and vocabulary. It also has quite consistent characterization of the major personalities involved in its narrative.

Inserted right in the midst of this material is a miscellaneous collection dealing with a number of various subjects (2 Sam 21–24). The explanation offered for this arrangement is quite simple. Most commentators agree that the original books of 1 and 2 Samuel and 1 and 2 Kings were all one work. They were apparently separated from each other for the very practical reason that a scroll containing such a lengthy work was simply too large to handle. The divisions were made to keep the scrolls to manageable lengths. At the time of the division of Samuel from Kings, the Succession Narrative was simply separated. According to this theory, sometime later the miscellaneous stories of 2 Sam 21–24 were added to the end of Samuel, due to the fact that they dealt with the last days of David.

The Succession Narrative itself deals with the events involved in the struggle among those who wished to succeed David upon the throne of Israel. The author appears to have been an eyewitness to those events. His work is considered to be the greatest history writing that Israel ever produced. It is also among the earliest history writing found anywhere in the world. If this evaluation is correct, this work becomes even more significant simply in terms of its achievement. However, in modern terms, the narrative is not pure history, for it has a great deal of theological insight and evaluation. The author is a master story teller and a good preacher. His narrative has entranced readers from his time until ours.

In the Succession Narrative, all of the major and most memorable events of DAVID's reign are found. Both his greatness and his humanity are portrayed with vividness. No excuse is made for his weakness and his sin. Neither is any attempt made to gloss over the failings and the frailties of the King. Within the narrative are described David's kindness to MEPHIBOSHETH, JONATHAN's son (9), his conflicts with the Ammonites (10), and his sin with Bathsheba and its consequences (11–12). Following this, the struggle among David's children begins. Here is AMNON's rape of TAMAR, ABSALOM's murder of Amnon, and Absalom's subsequent flight and exile (13). This is followed by the intrigue of JOAB leading to David's reluctant permission to allow Absalom's return to Jerusalem. Sadly, this led ultimately to Absalom's rebellion and finally to his death (14–18). In the aftermath, David was faced by other struggles among those around him who sought to take the throne from him (19–20).

The Succession Narrative concludes with the final struggle between David's two sons, Solomon and ADONIJAH (1 Kgs 1–2). The end result of this was the succession of Solomon to the throne, the execution of Adonijah and Joab, and the banishment of ABIATHAR the priest from Jerusalem to ANATHOTH. By the conclusion of the narrative, the throne was firmly established in the hands of Solomon, with all major rivals having been eliminated.

Bibliography. W. Harrelson, *Interpreting the Old Testament*.

—ROBERT L. CATE

• **Succoth.** [sukh'uhth] *1.* A city east of the Jordan, about one mile north of the Jabbok River (Nahr ez-Zerga), near the area where the river emerges from the mountains into the valley. Succoth was located in the territory allocated to the tribe of GAD (Josh 13:27) (PLATE 11). The area formed part of the kingdom of SIHON, one of the two kings whom Israel defeated in order to conquer the region east of the Jordan (Num 21:21-35). The remainder of Sihon's kingdom was given to the tribe of Ruben (Josh 13:15-23).

Most archaeologists identify biblical Succoth with modern TELL DEIR ʿALLA because the mound is one of the most impressive sites in the immediate vicinity. However, several archaeologists have cast doubts on the identification of Tell Deir 'Alla with biblical Succoth. H. J. Franken identifies Succoth with Tell el-Ekhsas. André Lemaire has said that Tell Deir 'Alla is Penuel, the place where the angel wrestled with Jacob. Most archaeologists reject these arguments, claiming that the evidence seems to establish Tell Deir 'Alla as biblical Succoth. In recent excavations at Deir 'Alla, excavators discovered some plaster inscriptions written in a language similar to biblical Hebrew. These inscriptions mention "BALAAM, the son of Beor, the seer of the gods," probably the same prophet mentioned in Num 22–24. The city was probably destroyed in the eighth century B.C.E. by an earthquake, presumably the same earthquake mentioned in Amos 1:1.

Succoth ("booths") received its name from the actions of JACOB at this place. When Jacob returned from Paddan-Aram, he crossed the Jabbok after having met the angel of God at night. The next day he had his encounter with Esau; after their reconciliation, Jacob promised to meet his brother in Seir. As soon as Esau departed, Jacob came to a place east of the Jordan where he built a house for himself and where he made booths for his animals (Gen 33:17).

At the time of the judges, when GIDEON was pursuing the Midianite kings, he stopped at Succoth and asked the elders of the city for food to feed his men. When the elders refused to provide for his army, Gideon promised that on his return he would punish them. After his victory, Gideon came to the elders of Succoth and "he took the elders of the city and he took thorns of the wilderness and briers and with them he taught the men of Succoth" (Judg 8:16).

During the period of the united monarchy, SOLOMON used this area to make some of the bronze vessels for the Temple (1 Kgs 7:46; 2 Chr 4:17). This piece of information may indicate that the people who lived in this area were skilled in METALLURGY. The Valley of Succoth is mentioned twice in the Book of Psalms (60:6; 108:7) as the land which Yahweh will divide among his oppressed people.

2. A city in Egypt where the Israelites came after departing from the land of Goshen (Exod 12:37; 13:20). This city is commonly identified with the ancient Egyptian city of *Tkw,* present day Tell el-Maskuta, in the eastern part of Wadi Tumilat.

See also DEIR 'ALLA, TELL.

Bibliography. N. Glueck, "Three Israelite Towns in the Jordan Valley: Zarethan, Succoth, Zaphon," *BASOR* 90 (April 1943): 2-23; H. J. Franken, "The Excavations at Deir Alla in Jordan," *VT* 10 (1960): 386-95; A. Lemaire, "Fragments from the Book of Balaam Found at Deir Alla," *BAR* 11 (Sep/Oct 1985): 26-39.

—CLAUDE F. MARIOTTINI

• Suffering in the New Testament. By combining the images of the Messiah and the suffering servant, the Gospels set forth suffering as a divine necessity and the essence of the Messiah's mission (Matt 16:21; 17:12; Mark 8:31; Luke 9:22; John 3:14; 12:32). Three times Jesus received the title Messiah—in the temptation, upon Peter's confession at Caesarea Philippi, and at the trial/execution—and each time Jesus freely (John 10:15-18) set aside other ways of redemption for the way of suffering—"The Son of man must suffer." The power of Jesus' miracles to relieve suffering reinforced the call that disciples do the same (Luke 10:30-37). However, Jesus prevented the removal of suffering from himself. The distress and trouble which overcame Jesus in Jerusalem (Mark 14:33) was climaxed by his feeling of abandonment on the cross where Jesus questioned, "My God, my God! Why hast Thou forsaken me?" (Mark 15:34; Matt 27:46). Yet, at the cross, where Jesus most pointedly joined us in our suffering, Jesus exhibited what suffering really means. Jesus was able to be open to God, even while the evil worked its dreadful suffering: "Father, into thy hands I commit my spirit" (Luke 23:46). Jesus also refused to place a wall between himself and other persons: "Father, forgive them; for they know not what they do" (Luke 23:34). Jesus counseled a similar suffering for the disciples: "If they persecuted me, they will persecute you" (John 15:20). The fellowship of Jesus and the disciples is set precisely through suffering: "If any man would come after me, let him deny himself and take up his cross and follow me" (Mark 8:34; Matt 10:38; 16:24; Luke 9:23; 14:27).

Paul sees the whole creation as groaning in travail toward fulfillment. God shares in that process and pain: "In Christ God was reconciling the world to himself" (2 Cor 5:19; cf. Phil 2). Persons also share in the process: to live in Christ is to suffer with Christ (2 Tim 2:11; Rom 8:17; Gal 2:20). In Colossians, human suffering is seen as involved in the work of the Messiah: "Now I rejoice in my sufferings for your sake, and in my flesh I complete what is lacking in Christ's afflictions" (Col 1:24).

First Peter, Hebrews, and Revelation grow out of the experience of suffering, and in all three books hope appears over against suffering. Suffering is the gateway to new life in Christ: "For to this you have been called, because Christ also suffered for you, leaving you an example, that you should follow in his steps" (1 Pet 2:21). Hebrews understands that suffering conditions life and obedience (12:7-11); it even conditioned the obedience of Jesus who was made perfect through suffering (2:10; cf. Phil 2:8) and "for the joy that was set before him endured the cross" (12:2).

The NT as a whole modifies six OT ideas: suffering disciplines character (Jas 1:2-4; 1 Pet 1:7; Heb 2:10; Rev 19-21); suffering awakens hope (Rom 8:18; 2 Cor 4:17; John 14; 1 Cor 15); it provides knowledge (Matt 11:29; Phil 3:8-11; Luke 15:11-32); sin brings suffering (Luke 13:1-5; Rom 1:18-3:20); suffering is sacrificial (Phil 2:5-8; Col 1:24; 2 Cor 4:8-12); and it tests faith (1 Pet 1:3-7; 2 Cor 4:9-11). The NT also witnesses to a suffering God who, as Creator/Sustainer, suffers with persons (John 5:17; Acts 17:27-28), as Redeemer, suffers for us (Phil 2:5-11; 2 Cor 8:9; Heb 2:17-18; Rom 5:6-10), and, as Sanctifier, suffers in us (2 Cor 3:17-18; 1 Cor 6:11; Eph 4:22-24).

See also SEVEN WORDS FROM THE CROSS; SUFFERING IN THE OLD TESTAMENT.

Bibliography. G. A. Buttrick, *God, Pain, and Evil*; E. S. Gerstenberger and W. Schrage, *Suffering*; H. W. Robinson, *Suffering: Human and Divine.*

—FRANK LOUIS MAULDIN

• Suffering in the Old Testament. Since suffering is a universal phenomenon, all religions must concern themselves with it. It is not surprising, therefore, that suffering occupies a prominent place in the OT. Near the beginning of the first book of the Bible the reality of suffering is introduced. Here it is rooted in the disobedience of the primeval couple, Adam and Eve (Gen 3:1-19).

Suffering in the Context of the OT Thought World. The sufferings described in the OT run the gamut of human experience. There are physical pains associated with diseases, handicaps and violence. There are the miseries of stressful mental and spiritual states: fear, guilt, shame, bereavement, deprivation, a sense of failure, loneliness, forsakenness, etc.

The means of coping with suffering, likewise, are various and not remarkable except at one point: in the OT there is the highly developed use of lamentation as a ritualistic or liturgical method of registering complaints to God and seeking relief from suffering. Though quite different in literary form, both Job and Lamentations are OT books of this genre. More important for the worship life of Israel were the many laments included in the Psalter. These psalms often articulate the sufferer's sense of being forsaken by God. They describe the plaintiff's sufferings, often graphically, but characteristically end in thanksgiving for relief and affirmation of the greatness of God. Ps 22 is an example of an individual lament, while Ps 10 is a lament on behalf of the poor who suffer at the hands of wicked exploiters.

In ancient Israel there was the inclination to attribute everything to the will or action of God. Therefore, the lament concerning one's pain was first and foremost a complaint to God: "Thou art the God in whom I take refuge; why hast thou cast me off? Why go I mourning . . . ?" (Ps 43:2); or, "Remove thy stroke from me; I am spent by the blows of thy hand" (Ps 39:10); or again, "Fill me with joy and gladness; let the bones which thou hast broken rejoice" (Ps 51:8).

At the same time there was the awareness of many spiritual beings in the environment, some of them malevolent. Israel gradually outgrew its polytheistic environment and renounced superstition and magic, but these are never far in the background. Who knows what awareness of mysterious evil in the environment may have inspired words such as these: "My heart is in anguish within me, the terrors of death have fallen upon me. Fear and trembling come upon me, and horror overwhelms me" (Ps 55:4-5).

There is a sense of social solidarity, also, by which people must suffer collectively for the acts of individuals. Thus God is represented as "visiting the iniquity of the fathers upon the children and the children's children, to the third and fourth generation" (Exod 34:7). In one instance, the sin of one man caused Israel to suffer defeat in battle, and the problem was solved by the execution, not only of the individual at fault but of his whole family (Josh 7:1-26). Nevertheless, the sense of individual responsibility arose to modify or contradict this concept of corporate guilt (cf. Deut 24:16; Ezek 18:1ff.; Jer 31:29).

In addition, the people of Israel had a vague view of life beyond death, so that the imbalances of suffering and prosperity could not be deferred to the afterlife (cf. Pss 88:10; 115:17, etc.). Late in the OT period a belief in resurrection and a heavenly existence develops, but even by the time of Jesus it was by no means universal (cf. Mark 12:18 and par.).

The Meanings of Suffering in the OT. In the OT suffering is interpreted variously. The diverse understandings reflect in part developments attending Israel's experiences in history. They are not mutually exclusive but rather tend to be complementary.

(1) Undoubtedly, much of human suffering was simply considered ordinary or normal. It was to be borne and not necessarily explained, even as animals suffer uncomplainingly. Minor aches and pains surely were so viewed. Eliphaz remarked that "man is born to trouble as the sparks fly upward" (Job 5:7). Though Job's own miseries were too immense and poignant thus to be ignored, no doubt many suffered minor difficulties, or even more tragic ones, without complaint or questioning. Though by its very nature such a view of suffering would not receive much attention, there are indications that it was present (cf. Pss 37:7; 38:13-14). It is suggested, also, that this stoical method was tried and found wanting: "I was dumb and silent, I held my peace to no avail; my distress grew worse . . . ; then I spoke with my tongue" (Ps 39:2-3).

(2) The most prevalent understanding of suffering in the OT is that it is the recompense for sin. This retributive interpretation is met with in Gen 3 where the origin of suffering is traced to the disobedience of the primeval human couple. The formula is that sin results in suffering while goodness produces success. Both individuals and nations are punished for evil and rewarded for righteousness. This retributive principle is written so large upon the pages of the OT that it is impracticable to cite references. Deut 30:15-20 provides an adequate summary statement.

While this principle of reaping what one sows is certainly true, it is quite inadequate to explain the mystery of suffering. Many of the psalms take note of the seeming prosperity of the wicked. For example, Ps 73 protests that the unrighteous are "not in trouble" and "not stricken like other men" (v. 5). Although the psalmist satisfies himself that the wicked eventually get their just deserts, such an observation could not stand minute scrutiny. Job is a powerful protest against a naive view of the misery of the wicked and the prosperity of the righteous.

(3) Other interpretations had to emerge, prominent among which is the view that suffering serves a disciplinary or educational purpose. References are numerous. In Lev 26 God promises Israel various blessings for obedience and dire consequences for disobedience. But if in spite of these penalties Israel still will not obey, then God would chastise her sevenfold for her sins (Lev 26:18), and the process would be repeated if necessary (Lev 26:24, 27-28). Suffering, then, has the disciplinary purpose of returning Israel to God. In Proverbs there is the exhortation: "My son, do not despise the Lord's discipline or be weary of his reproof, for the Lord reproves him whom he loves, as a father the son in whom he delights" (Prov 3:11-12; cf. 15:10).

Suffering may lead to repentance and thus to a more mature understanding of God and of one's vocation, as in the experience of Jeremiah (15:19-21). Likewise, after God has chastened the chosen people "in just measure" by their afflictions (Jer 30:11), they will be prepared for restoration and for entering into a new and more profoundly spiritual covenant (31:31ff.). This process of chastening, suffering, restoration is even more graphically described in the speech of Elihu in Job 33:19-28.

(4) Closely related to the disciplinary idea is the concept of suffering as probationary. Character is tried, proved, purified in the crucible of suffering. In several places in the OT God is represented as "trying the hearts" of the righteous: "The crucible is for silver, and the furnace is for gold, and the Lord tries hearts" (Prov 17:3). In the Book of Job the reader is let in on the secret that God had permitted the SATAN to put Job to trial by tragic and inordinate suffering. Although Job is not informed of this transcendent decision, nevertheless he declares that God "knows the way that I take; when he has tried me, I shall come forth as gold" (23:10). Then there is the well-known story of God testing Abraham in the offering up of Isaac (Gen 22:1-14), with the reiteration, after the test, of God's promise to bless Abraham and his heirs and the world through him.

(5) Some suffering in the OT is viewed as empathic, that is, as the pain of those who identify with the sufferings of others. Such was the suffering of the three friends of Job when they first encountered him in his loathsome and pitiable condition. After observing the customary ritual of

mourning, they sat with him on the ground in silence for seven days and nights (Job 2:13). It is sometimes remarked that this empathic ministry of silence was more effective than their wordy and erroneous speeches!

The prophets often suffered with their people. Ezekiel sat "overwhelmed" among the Jewish exiles for seven days (Ezek 3:15). Jeremiah declared, "For the wound of the daughter of my people is my heart wounded; I mourn, and dismay has taken hold of me" (Jer 8:21).

More notable was the awareness that God suffered with the people, an understanding that is expressed frequently in the OT. It was because God knew the afflictions of the Hebrew slaves in Egypt that he determined to deliver them through Moses (Exod 3:7ff.). In fact, the principle of retribution, that suffering is the penalty for sin, is often contradicted by the understanding that the poor were victims, not of their own sins but the sins of others. Throughout the OT God is represented as taking the side of the poor: "If he cries to me I will hear, for I am compassionate," says the Lord (Exod 22:27). The numerous references indicating that God enters into the sufferings of God's people are summed up in the affirmation that "in all their affliction he was afflicted . . . ; in his love and in his pity he redeemed them . . . " (Isa 63:9).

(6) The verse just cited is very close to the insight that it is by God's own suffering that sins may be forgiven and redemption effected. This expiatory role of suffering is more clearly understood, however, with regard to human suffering. Moses offers to take upon himself the sins of his people (Exod 32:32). Through the sufferings of Israel in the Babylonian Exile, her sins are pardoned: "she has received from the Lord's hand double for all her sins" (Isa 40:2).

Yet it is in the servant songs of Deutero-Isaiah that the expiatory or vicarious meaning of suffering is most clearly expressed. The nations confess that the Servant of the Lord "was wounded for our transgressions" and "bruised for our iniquities," and that "the Lord has laid on him the iniquity of us all" (Isa 53:5-6). The identity of the servant is not clear, whether Israel as a whole, a remnant group or an individual Israelite, and it is not until the servant is identified with Jesus, the Son of God, in the NT that God's involvement in vicarious suffering is understood, according to Christian belief.

(7) In addition, suffering is occasionally interpreted as eschatological; that is, tribulation of unusual intensity may be a harbinger of the end time. This interpretation may be seen in Isa 24–27 and in the book of Daniel.

(8) An extreme view of suffering as meaningless is found in Ecclesiastes, where a generally pessimistic attitude prevails. The whole round of human life is "an unhappy business" and "all is vanity and a striving after wind" (Eccl 1:13-14). That such an unorthodox and unsatisfying view of life could be included in the canon may testify to the honesty of Israel.

(9) Finally, even if all these various attempts to invest suffering with meaning were fitted together into some integrated whole—which the OT does not attempt to do—suffering would remain vastly mysterious. Perhaps one meaning of the Book of Job is not simply that the sufferings of the righteous are due to some transcendent process of testing, but rather that since human beings are not privy to the counsels of God, suffering is humanly inexplicable. Interpretations of it as retributive, disciplinary, expiatory, etc., are by no means erroneous. They are simply inadequate to fathom the mystery of suffering.

See also DISEASE AND HEALING; EVIL; SIN.

Bibliography. E. S. Gerstenberger and W. Schrage, *Suffering*; W. McWilliams, *When You Walk through the Fire*; H. W. Robinson, *Suffering Human and Divine*; J. A. Sanders, *Suffering as Divine Discipline in the Old Testament and Post-Biblical Judaism*; D. J. Simundson, *Faith under Fire: Biblical Interpretations of Suffering*; E. F. Sutcliffe, *Providence and Suffering in the Old and New Testaments*.

—E. LUTHER COPELAND

• **Suffering Servant.** *See* FORGIVENESS/PARDON; SERVANT; SUFFERING IN THE OLD TESTAMENT

• **Sumeria/Sumerian.** [*soo*-maihr'ee-uh/*soo*maihr'ee-uhn] The lower part of ancient Mesopotamia, and the people who dwelt there. The region is a very flat land which lies along and between the lower Tigris and Euphrates Rivers and encompasses about ten thousand square miles (PLATE 2). In ancient days, it was known as Shinar (Gen 10:10; Isa 11:11; Zech 5:11); however, in later times it became more popularly known as BABYLONIA (cf. Jer 50:10; Ezek 16:29). The origin of the people called Sumerians who came to inhabit the land is not known; however, it is believed that they entered the land from the east during the later half of the fourth millennium B.C.E. Yet, they must have been a very sturdy people, for even after they were finally conquered their culture prevailed.

Sumeria's history falls quite naturally into three periods: early Sumeria, 4000–2700 B.C.E.; classic Sumeria, 2700–2250 B.C.E.; and late Sumeria, 2250–1720 B.C.E.

The earliest known inhabitants of the land were a group of people who are referred to archaeologically as Ubaidians (after the site, Tell Al-Ubaid). Though at first they may have been quite nomadic, they soon settled into villages (such as those later known as Eridu, Ur, Larsa, Isin, Adab, Kullab, Lagash, Nippur, and Kish) and became tradesmen (doing such things as fishing, farming, weaving, and carpentering). Apparently, their lives were interrupted about 3000 B.C.E., when the mysterious Sumerians arrived from the east. However, unlike later invasions, the Sumerians did not destroy the native culture, but simply absorbed it into their own. Evidently, the Sumerians settled near or in three cities (Uruk, Aratta, and Kish), for these cities became dominant during the latter part of this period. Unfortunately, the only documents from this time are mythological in nature and thus of uncertain historical significance. However, from those that are available, it is believed that Gilgamesh (a king of Uruk) was the most powerful ruler of the era.

The most prominent cities during the classic period were Ur, Kish, Lagash, and Umma. Evidently, about 3000 B.C.E., a ruler of Kish (named Etana) managed to solidify the kingdom. However, after his death, Kish's influence waned and that of Uruk (also known as Erech) increased; but then, it soon declined and was replaced again by Kish. Apparently, the rise of the city of Ur (ca. 2600 B.C.E.) brought a temporary end to the struggle for power; yet, even that did not last long, for about 2500 B.C.E., Kish (under the leadership of Mesilim) once again gained control over Sumer. However, as soon as Mesilim died, the balance of power shifted again, but this time toward Lagash. Yet, though one of Lagash's rulers (Eannatum) did manage to expand the empire to some of the surrounding territories, his successors were neither able to control them nor the other Sumerian cities. As a result, Lagash's last ruler (Urukagina) was finally overthrown by Lugalzaggesi (the king of Umma); but even his kingdom did not last long. Unfortunately, all of this infighting between the various city- states sapped the nation's strength and left it in a position to be conquered.

The later period began with another influx of foreigners (this time semites) from the northwest. The leader of these people was SARGON I, a brilliant military general and a good administrator who built a new capital at Agade (Akkad). Unfortunately, his descendants were not nearly as capable as he, and thus, despite some moments of glory under Naram-Sin, the kingdom slowly disintegrated until finally it was overrun by the semibarbaric Guti. Evidently, their conquest was particularly devastating, for it took almost a hundred years for the various city-states to recover and to began to organize again. When this finally happened, it was under the leadership of Gudea, the king of Lagash. However, he was soon replaced by Ur-Nammu (the King of Ur and founder of its famous third dynasty). Unfortunately, this dynasty did not last long either, for the land was soon overrun by another group of semites, the Amurru (or biblical Amorites); yet, the land and its people managed to survive. Thus, before long, they were once again involved in their own struggle for dominance. At first, this struggle was mainly between the cities of Isin and Larsa; however, it soon came to involve Babylon. The end result was that HAMMURABI (the king of Babylon) was able to defeat Rim-Sin (the king of Larsa) and thus unite the Mesopotamian valley under his control. Unfortunately, this victory (in 1720 B.C.E.), signalled the end of the Sumerians as a people; however, their language and culture continued to live on through their conquerors.

Though no one knows for sure when or where writing began, some of the earliest writing known today comes from the ancient Sumerian site of Uruk. Evidently, it developed soon after the Sumerians arrived in the land for their earliest script is pictographic; however, it soon became stylized into various groups of wedges (known today as cuneiform script) which, when collected together phonetically, can express almost anything. Such writing was usually done on small clay tablets, which have proved to be very durable and thus have been found by the tens of thousands. Though most of the texts are either administrative documents (e.g., tax rolls or king lists) or literary works (epics, hymns, proverbs, etc.), they have provided enough information for the reconstruction of ancient Sumerian society.

Politically, the country was divided into a dozen or more city-states. Apparently, each of these city-states was originally governed by a council of freemen (or representatives), who were under the leadership of an elected governor (ensi). However, before long, the governor was replaced by a king (lugal). Such kingship soon became an inherited rather than an appointed office. Unfortunately, the power and prestige of the king was largely taken over by the priest during the last days of the kingdom.

Apparently, each city had its own patron deity (such as Nanna of Ur, An of Uruk, Enki of Eridu, and Enlil of Nippur) to whom there would be a massive temple erected upon the city's highest spot. However, within each city there would also be other temples dedicated to some of their other gods (such as An—the god of heaven, Enlil—the god of the air, Enki—the god of water, and Ninhursag—the mother goddess). Though it is somewhat difficult to know for sure, apparently An was the primary god during the earlier part of the kingdom while Enlil reigned supreme during its later days. Though these gods were very poverful and holy in their own right, they were also considered very human in their thoughts and actions (such as love, hate, friendship, war, etc.). Furthermore, the mythological accounts of the interaction of these gods with each other and with the other aspects of creation tell how the world came into being and how man came to be in his present fallen state.

In addition to all of this, the Sumerians have provided the world with many other achievements. Their concept of legal justice based upon precedent was very advanced for its day and time. Their system of agriculture (with its massive use of irrigation) was very effective and efficient. Moreover, their mathematical system (which was based upon sixty) allowed them to standardize calculations of weight, measure, and time. Finally, their system of education for the upper classes was second to none. Thus, though the political domination of the Sumerians over the Mesopotamian Valley did not last long (3000–1720 B.C.E.), many of their cultural achievements did.

See also BABYLONIAN EMPIRE.

Bibliography. T. Jacobsen, *The Sumerian King List*; S. N. Kramer, *The Sumerians: Their History, Culture and Character*; S. A. Pallis, *The Antiquity of Iraq: a Handbook of Assyriology*; A. Parrot, *Sumer*; H. W. F. Saggs, *The Greatness That Was Babylon.*

—HARRY B. HUNT, JR.

• **Sunday.** *See* LORD'S DAY

• **Superscription/Title.** What is written on or above to designate or identify (RSV inscription, title). (1) Traditional titles of books of the Bible ("The Gospel according to . . . ," etc.). (2) On the reverse of a coin, the name and/or title of the ruler or state by whose authority the coin is issued, and—esp. in a monarchy—whose likeness may appear on the obverse (Matt 22:20; Mark 12:16; Luke 20:24). (3) The publication of the crime for which a person was crucified. For some crimes a placard stating the charge was displayed during a Roman crucifixion. The placard would be hung around the neck of the condemned on the way to the site of crucifixion and then attached to the cross for all to see. Since Jesus ostensibly was convicted of insurrection, it would have seemed especially appropriate to PILATE to publish the crime in order to discourage other would-be rebels. Hence the placard—superscription, inscription, or title—announcing Pilate's interpretation of Jesus' "criminal" claim (Matt 27:37; Mark 15:26; Luke 23:38; John 19:19, 20).

—EDD ROWELL

• **Supper, The Last.** *See* SACRAMENTS

• **Supplication.** *See* PRAYER/THANKSGIVING IN THE NEW TESTAMENT

• **Susa.** [*soo'*suh] The capital of Elam, Susa was situated along important trade routes in southwest Iran (PLATE 1); thus its function as an administrative city grew out of its significant location. In addition, it was the royal residence in the winter and the crossroads to the other royal residences. It is evident from archaeology that Susa had been inhabited since the fourth millennium B.C.E. The four main features of the ruins are the Acropolis, the Apadana, the Royal City, and the Artisans' City.

With a long period of occupation, Susa went through various periods of prosperity and importance, then decline. Apparently the city maintained a powerful domain in the middle third millennium; again a powerful period occurred in the thirteenth century B.C.E. Some scholars, however, feel that the most prosperous age of Susa's history was the Persian period under Achaemenian rule, particularly when Darius I began extensive construction on the citadel, walls, and royal palaces.

Also known as Shushan, Susa has been associated with Queen ESTHER and the tomb site of DANIEL. In addition, Susa is known as the site of the mass marriages between the troops of Alexander the Great and Persian women.

Bibliography. A. Bausani, *The Persians*; S. A. Matheson, *Persia: An Archaeological Guide*.

—MARK W. GREGORY

• **Susanna.** [*soo*-zan'uh] Susanna is the heroine of one of three additions to the book of DANIEL that are found in the Greek translations, but not in the Hebrew/Aramaic text. These additions were included in the Latin Vulgate and are regarded as scripture by Roman Catholics, but Protestants relegate them to the Apocrypha.

The story of Susanna, whose name means ''lily,'' is about the persecution and vindication of the beautiful and God-fearing wife of a wealthy Babylonian Jew. Her house is the place where the two elders who are serving as judges meet to settle disputes among the exiles, and this constant exposure to her beauty results in the elders' becoming obsessed with lust for Susanna.

They attack her when she is alone in her garden and threaten to accuse her of adultery with another man if she rejects their advances. Choosing virtue over security, Susanna refuses to yield and cries for help. The elders make good their threat by testifying that they caught her having intercourse with a young man. On the testimony of the two elders, Susanna is condemned to death without having any opportunity to defend herself. Her only recourse is to appeal to God, who hears her prayer and informs a ''young lad'' named Daniel that the witnesses have testified falsely.

Daniel demands that the elders be cross-examined separately. He asks each one under which tree the couple was caught. With no opportunity to confer, the elders contradict each other, exposing their lie. The people then put them to death in conformity with the law regarding false witnesses (Deut 19:18-21): ''They did to them as they had wickedly planned to do to their neighbor'' (Sus 62).

The point of this story, like that of the stories in Dan 3 and 6, is that God will vindicate the righteous person who is wrongfully accused and persecuted. The stories in Dan 3 and 6, however, like the story of JOSEPH and POTIPHAR's wife, portray Jews being vindicated in the face of persecution by pagans. In the story of Susanna, God vindicates a virtuous Jewish woman (a person who has no power) against false testimony by evil, but powerful, Jewish elders. Some interpreters regard the story as a protest against abuses of the legal system in the Jewish community.

Since the story also emphasizes the wise judgment of Daniel, whose name can be translated ''God is my judge,'' it was placed at the very beginning of the Book of Daniel in some Greek manuscripts, apparently to account for Daniel's rise to prominence in Babylon. In the Vulgate, however, it is located after Dan 12. Two puns that occur in Sus 54-55, 58-59 have led some scholars to argue that the story was originally written in Greek, since the puns cannot easily be understood as translations from Hebrew or Aramaic.

The story of Susanna has been a popular subject of Christian art, inspiring paintings by Rembrandt, Rubens and others, as well as an oratorio by Handel.

See also APOCRYPHAL LITERATURE; DANIEL.

Bibliography. J. J. Collins, *Daniel, First Maccabees, Second Maccabees*; W. H. Daubney, *The Three Additions to Daniel*; G. W. E. Nickelsburg, *Jewish Literature Between the Bible and the Mishnah*.

—SHARYN E. DOWD

• **Swearing.** *See* OATH

• **Swine.** Biblical references to swine are relatively few. In almost every instance these references reflect the unclean nature of swine in Jewish culture.

The OT laws distinguishing between clean and unclean included swine in the list of those animals considered unclean (Lev 11:7; Deut 14:8). Those lists prohibited the Jews from eating any animal which did not have a cloven hoof and chew a cud. Although swine possess a cloven hoof, they do not chew a cud. Prohibitions against eating swine appear to be fairly common among semitic peoples. The reasons for such a prohibition are unclear, although at least three have been proposed. The least likely of these stresses the possible health dangers of eating undercooked pork. Secondly, since swine were something used in connection with Babylonian, Syrian, and Egyptian worship, their prohibition may have denied idolatrous types of sacrifice (cf. Isa 65:4; 66:3, 17). Finally, the dietary commands may have been symbolic. Since God had chosen certain animals for sacrifice, Israel was to symbolize its chosenness by eating only those animals chosen by God.

The designation of swine as unclean underscores the symbolic nature of other biblical references. In Prov 11:22 a woman without discretion is compared to a gold ring in the nose of a swine, a reference to her inappropriate behavior. The psalmist (Ps 80:13) laments the fall of Israel; she is like a vine left untended to be devoured by a wild boar (boars ran wild in the Jordan River area).

The Greeks did not share the Jewish view of swine as unclean. Therefore, during the period of the Hellenization of Palestine, dietary differences became a point of contention between the two groups. First Maccabees recalls the command of Antiochus IV that the Jews were to eat and sacrifice unclean animals such as swine (1:47); it also recalls their firm stand against his orders. Josephus recorded Antiochus' desecration of the sanctuary, a desecration in which the blood of swine played a significant part.

The NT writers shared this view of swine as unclean animals. Two proverbial references to swine, one on the lips of Jesus (Matt 7:6) and one in 2 Peter (2:22), use swine as a symbol of impurity. Another reference is found in the story of the Gerasene demoniac, a story reproduced by all three synoptic writers (Matt 8; Mark 5; Luke 8). The presence of swine in an area populated by Jews raises problems, but their function as repositories for the demons which Jesus casts out from the man living among the tombs agrees with the way most Jewish readers would have considered swine. In a similar manner, the fact that the lost (or prodigal) son is reduced to feeding swine (Luke 15:15-16) is indicative of how far he has fallen at that point in Jesus' parable.

The prohibition against eating swine, while at the heart of the biblical references to swine, seems to have been less important than the sense of revulsion which that prohibition produced. The biblical references to swine are primarily symbolic, as swine are used to signify the concept of impurity.

—STEVEN SHEELEY

• **Sychar.** [*si'*kahr] Sychar is a Samaritan city mentioned in the Bible only in John 4:5. The identification of this city is uncertain. A Suchar or Sichar appears in the Talmud. A Syriac manuscript reads Shechem instead of Sychar at John

4:5, and Jerome identified Sychar with Shechem (in Latin and Gk., "sychem"). The latter was located not at Nablus but at Balatah, about 150 ft. from JACOB'S WELL. It was probably only a small village in the first century.

Interpreters are divided on the question of whether Sychar should be identified with Shechem (W. F. Albright, R. E. Brown, W. D. Davies) or Askar (B. Lindars, R. Schnackenburg) (PLATE 23). Askar lies about a mi. northeast of the well. The ruins of this city date back only to Arab times, so one must assume it stood over the site of an earlier city. Since Askar had a well of its own, one must also conjecture that the woman traveled to Jacob's well because it was so deep and had better water.

The first reference to Sychar outside the NT is found in the writing of the pilgrim from Bordeaux in 333.

See also JACOB; JACOB'S WELL; SAMARIA; SAMARITANS.

—R. ALAN CULPEPPER

• **Symbol.** A symbol is a representative of a transcendent and invisible reality by means of an image borrowed from the sensuous and visible. Symbol differs from metaphor and analogy by the fact that the reality to which it points is not available for rational recognition. Thus a symbol points to a hidden and mysterious reality and is held to be analogous to it, yet the presence of such analogy is given in the experience of that reality and results from intuitive insight.

In the light of this definition, we may immediately affirm that symbols belong to the realms of art and religion. They are attempts to interpret and make intelligible that which transcends sense experience, thus they belong especially to the religious sphere and the understanding of the sacred. They are given in the divine-human encounter in which divine REVELATION takes place. They point, as signs do, but they do more than a sign, they enable the recipient to participate in the mysterious depth to which they point. This means that all symbols have a double intentionality. They have a literal and evident meaning, for they refer to what can be sensuously observed, an object in this worldly environment. But they also have a second meaning which points beyond this first meaning to one that is analogous to the literal meaning and yet belongs to the realm of the sacred and transcendent. As such, symbols participate in that which they represent and penetrate into its depth. They are indeed inexhaustible and continually furnish new insights into the divine reality. Unlike images and signs, they participate in the sacred reality which they represent and are the accompaniment of all revelation.

Because they convey meaning and are vehicles of the divine revelation, symbols belong to the realm of words and communication. Symbolism takes form under human discourse as it is confronted by a revelatory depth in reality. It is therefore the natural accompaniment of an understanding of God which regards God as one who communicates and discloses the divine self in the divine word. God's word, God's self-giving, is communicated through the human words of those chosen to be the media of God's self-disclosure. Thus in biblical thought, a primary symbol is the WORD OF GOD. God has no body, no mouth. In transcendent majesty and infinite being God is beyond all such literal descriptions, yet words become a symbol for divine self-giving and revelation.

For the Hebrew mind, a word was something objective that embodied the intention of the one who uttered it. Hence a word of blessing or of curse carried such content in itself. When received by the one to whom it was addressed, it proceeded to accomplish, in that person's being, the purpose for which it had been uttered. Thus JACOB having received Isaac's word of blessing, was not about to give it back, nor could Isaac revoke it, for already that blessing was taking effect in Jacob's life. So, too, by analogy with God's word; it could not return void, but would accomplish that to which it had been sent (Isa 55:11). It was pregnant with the divine intention, and was a projection of God's own presence into the realm that God had created and sustained. Word becomes a symbol for God's self-disclosure.

The Heb. term for "word," *dābār,* could be rendered "deed" as well as "word." Thus God's word could be both utterance and act. Hence we have a symbolism of action as well as a symbolism of words in biblical thought. In the biblical record we find symbolic acts especially in cultic celebration, as well as symbolic descriptions of God and of God's saving acts for the people of Israel.

Symbolic Presentation of God and the Divine Activity. In Hebrew thought the name of a person was an extension of that person's own being. It represented the person; to give someone your name was to give yourself. The possession of a name meant the possession of the authority and power of the person. When MOSES asked for the name of the God addressing him, he sought to possess divine authority and presence, just as a prophet speaking in the name of the Lord would be indwelt by the divine spirit and have the divine authority in the utterance (Exod 3:13-15; Gen 17:1ff.; Jer 11:21; Deut 18:20). Thus the divine name was a symbol for the very presence of God. To trust in God is to trust in God's holy name (Isa 50:10; Ps 33:21), to pray is to invoke the name (Gen 12:8; 1 Kgs 18:24). The TEMPLE of SOLOMON is the place where that name has been set (1 Kgs 8:29). Thus the divine name is a symbol for God's presence.

When we turn to the nature of God, we find an emphasis on God's personal being. Descriptions of human personal being become symbolic of God. God is personal, although the divine transcendent greatness means that the analogical aspect of the symbolism is stretched to its limits. God is infinite personal being, but the disclosure of the divine self is compatible with our own finite personal being, so the Bible speaks of God's will and purpose, of God's love and wrath. The divine revelation comes through the personal mediation of prophets, priests and the wise, and provides a link between human personal being and the divine being such that love can be symbolic of the divine nature. Hence the Bible can describe God as loving Israel with an everlasting love (Jer 31:3). God's love is elective and creative, choosing Israel and creating it (Deut 7:7; Hos 11:1-4; Isa 41:8). This love is merciful and redemptive, a disclosure that reaches its OT climax in Hosea's prophetic words (11:7-9; 14:4). This love is directed especially on Israel, but is to reach through them to all nations. The symbolic and analogical nature of such love is brought out in the NT testimony, where the Greek word *agapē* is used only of God's love, especially as it is incarnated in Jesus Christ. Indeed, in the NT, God *is* love, the kind of love revealed in Jesus Christ (1 John 4:8). This divine kind of love is celebrated in the hymn of 1 Cor 13.

Family imagery is particularly suited to the expression of God's character. God is portrayed as husband of the bride Israel (Hos 1–3; Jer 2), or father of Israel (Jer 3:4, 19; Isa 63:16; 64:8) or of all persons (Mal 2:10), or displays the qualities of mother or midwife (Ps 103:15—where the analogy is with the father, but the quality mentioned is motherly compassion; Ezek 16; Isa 42:14-15) in the OT. In the NT, Jesus' use of the term "father" for God connotes a most intimate association between himself and the "heavenly father" or the "father in heaven." Throughout the Letters and the rest of the NT, God is described as father of all humankind, and some references to God the Spirit or to the Holy Spirit also carry the associations with the mother that appear in the OT.

There are also particular symbolic uses of various human bodily aspects. Thus although God may not be literally pictured in bodily form, the Bible can speak of God's face, hand, arm, and nostrils. Ps 18 includes many bodily parts in its description, and the prophet of the Exile frequently uses corporeal members in picturing God's activity (Isa 40:10-11; 42:13-14). Isaiah opens his prophetic mission with a vision of God seated on a throne (Isa 6). We find references to God's face, back, and hand in Exod 33:19-23. In such cases, the words are not used in the physical sense but symbolically. The face is symbolic of God's presence, as Exod 33:14 makes clear (the word for "face" is translated "presence" in RSV). Sincere worshipers seek God's face and presence (Pss 24:6; 27:8). When God's face is hidden, the divine presence is withdrawn. The right hand of God symbolizes victory (Exod 15:6), both hands, creative power (Ps 119:73), and the arm, helping power (Isa 52:10). God's nostrils represent judgment (Ps 18:15), and their blast, deliverance at the sea (Exod 15:8).

Prophetic Use of Symbolism. For the prophets the word of the Lord could be act as well as utterance. So we find them performing symbolic acts to bring the divine message to their hearers. Isaiah proclaimed the imminent Assyrian captivity of Egypt and Ethiopia by walking the streets of Jerusalem for three years in the garb of a slave (20:2). Jeremiah preached God's judgment on Judah at the hands of Babylon by wearing a yoke and breaking a flask (27:2-7; 19:1, 10-13). Ezekiel prophesied the reunion of Judah and Israel after the Exile by joining two pieces of wood, suitably inscribed, into one stick (37:15-22). Samuel tore his mantle to symbolize God's tearing the kingdom from Saul (1 Sam 15:27-28).

To such symbolic acts, the prophets added their spoken warnings of judgment and their proclamations of ultimate deliverance. Sometimes sights presented to their eyes became symbolic of the divine activity. Amos saw a plumb line against a wall and it symbolized the divine judgment (Amos 7:7-9). Much more significant are the uses made of agricultural and pastoral imagery. Israel is pictured in the symbolizing of the vine and of sheep. Israel is symbolized as a vine created by God to bear fruit for God. Its sin and rebellion is symbolized as yielding wild grapes, and its judgment as the destruction of the vineyard (Isa 5:4; cf. Jer 2:21; 12:10). Again, in Ezek 34, Israel is portrayed as God's flock of sheep. It is so mismanaged by God's appointed shepherds, the nation's leaders, that it is scattered (cf. Jer 23:14; 50:6). Thus the theme of sin, rebellion and judgment is dramatically symbolized.

Beyond the judgment, the prophets hoped for restoration of the people of God. They pictured a remnant that would be saved out of the judgment; a Davidic King, a MESSIAH or anointed one whom God would set on the throne; and a suffering servant, partly remnant and partly messiah, through whose suffering all nations would share in God's mercy (Isa 10:20; 9:6, 7; 11:1-5; Jer 23:5-6; 33:14-17; Isa 53:1-12). In the Book of Daniel we have another figure, the SON OF MAN who comes on the clouds of heaven, symbolizing the kingdom of the saints of the most high, and is thus a symbol for the remnant (Dan 7:13-14). At last Jesus came.

The Symbolic Presentation of Jesus. In Jesus the OT symbolism is gathered into a focal point. The symbolism of the word is gathered up into his historical personhood. In him the word has become enfleshed and assumed historical existence (John 1:14). In him the hope of a messiah finds its fulfillment. Jesus is the Christ, the anointed one of the living God and the suffering servant, in whose person the Messiah and the redeemed remnant become one, and through whose suffering everyone shall find redemption. Jesus is the Son of man, combining in his own person, as Messiah, the remnant which is reconstituted in him. It is Jesus' most frequently used self-designation. He seems to have been reticent about declaring himself overtly as Messiah. The term Son of man may, in some of its references, mean "humankind" (cf. Mark 2:28).

Much more significant theologically is the symbolic title for Jesus—SON OF GOD. At his baptism and transfiguration, Jesus is addressed by God as the beloved Son (Mark 1:11; 9:7). The title is used both in the temptation scene and while Jesus is on the cross (Matt 4:3ff.; 27:40). In the Gospel of John, the relation of Jesus to God as son is elaborated and the essential unity of father and son is affirmed (1:18; 10:30, 38). Paul affirms the unique sonship of Jesus (Gal 1:15f.; 4:4; Col 1:13). Jesus is the unique Son of God.

Associated with Christ's redeeming death, the most all-embracing symbol is the cross. The preaching of the cross is the heart of the gospel (1 Cor 1:18; Gal 6:14). Closely associated with this is the symbolic use of the lamb or the LAMB OF GOD. Here Jesus is symbolized as the paschal lamb (1 Cor 5:7; John 1:29). The Lamb is a principal title of Jesus in the Book of Revelation.

Symbolic Descriptions of Salvation. Three important symbols are used to describe the salvation wrought on the cross—JUSTIFICATION, RECONCILIATION, and REDEMPTION. Each has its appropriate aspect of human sin—guilt, alienation, and sinful bondage, respectively. Their backgrounds are, respectively—the law court, personal relationships, and the slave market. In each case, Christ accomplishes what human beings, independently, cannot. The sacrifice of Jesus Christ meets our judgment and covers our sin. By faith in him we can stand acquitted before the bar of God, justified not by our works, but by Jesus' gracious self-giving. We are graciously reconciled by God as we trust in Christ. Faith in Christ sets us free from the demonic bondage of sin. We are redeemed.

Symbolic Presentation of the Church and Its Worship. The community of the redeemed became the gathering of those whom God had called in Christ, the CHURCH, the New Israel, the new people of God. Symbolically it was described as the body of Christ, a community indwelt by his Spirit, unified by his love, and guided by him as its head.

There were two important symbolic acts in the worship of the NT church—BAPTISM and the LORD'S SUPPER. In baptism we have a symbolic presentation of the death and resurrection of Christ as that becomes effective in the life of the believer, who dies to sin and rises to newness of life in Christ. The symbolic burial in water also has overtones of lustration. In the Lord's Supper, the bread and wine symbolize the broken body and outpoured life of the crucified Christ. By faith, we open our lives to Christ's gracious risen presence.

See also COVENANT; CROSS; GOD, NAMES OF; LORD'S SUPPER; REVELATION, CONCEPT OF; SIGNS AND WONDERS; SON OF GOD; SON OF MAN; TEMPLE/TEMPLES; WORD; WORD OF GOD.

Bibliography. T. Boman, *Hebrew Thought Compared with Greek*; S. McFague, *Metaphorical Theology: Models of*

God in Religious Language; P. Ricoeur, *The Symbolism of Evil.*

—ERIC C. RUST

• **Synagogue.** [sin'uh-gog] The term synagogue comes from the Gk. συναγωγή, which means "gathering together." It was used by Greek-speaking Jews from the first century B.C.E. onward to refer to meetings of Jews for study of their scriptures and worship. The impetus that gave rise to this type of religious gathering had both positive and negative dimensions with regard to the official Jewish worship of God in the TEMPLE at Jerusalem. Negatively, the majority of Jews lived outside of Palestine, many of them at great distances from Jerusalem and its temple. The result was that attendance at the festivals and ceremonies there was not possible for many Jews. But the increasing secularization of the priesthood after the Maccabean revolt (168–165 B.C.E.) and the strongly commercial aspects of the priestly establishment in Jerusalem led many to look for other ways of identifying with their religious tradition. Positively, when the PHARISEES turned their attention in the late second century B.C.E. from struggling with the Maccabean family for power to the conscious reclaiming of the Jewish tradition of Israel as the committed people of God, the means for fostering that sense of commitment and participation was the informal gathering of earnest seekers after God in homes. There they engaged in the reading of the scriptures, in studying it in order to discern its relevance for their lives in the present, and in table fellowship as a way of celebrating their common life as God's people.

Although there is no clear evidence of direct influence, this mode of corporate religious life may have had antecedents among Jews in Babylon during the EXILE (sixth century B.C.E.) and more broadly among Jews living in gentile lands throughout the world. There seems to have been no official leadership in these meetings. Instead, laymen would apparently lead in study and worship as the pattern of the meetings began to take on more regular forms. From archaeological analysis of synagogue sites it can be inferred that down until the late third century C.E., such meetings took place in private homes or in public halls—many of them of modest size. From inscriptions on these sites, as from literary references to these gatherings down through the first century C.E., it is evident that this type of meeting place was called a "place of prayer," προσευχή, as in Acts 16:13, where Paul's first convert in Europe is Lydia. References to synagogues in PHILO of Alexandria and JOSEPHUS are to the groups that met regularly, rather than to specific architectural structures or even formal organizations.

The great change in the synagogue began following the Jewish Revolt of 66–70 C.E., which resulted in the destruction of the temple, the disappearance of its priesthood as the religious leadership of the Jews, and the temporary expulsion of Jews from Jerusalem. With the apparent encouragement of the Roman authorities in Palestine, the Pharisees began to confer among themselves in an effort to develop ways in which the Jewish tradition could be preserved and Jewish identity as the covenant people could be fostered. In ways which demonstrate precisely the typical change of religious movements from informal to structured, institutional patterns, Judaism began to evolve increasingly formal leadership roles and patterns of corporate life. The appropriation of the traditional scriptures by the communities of that day took the shape of schools of thought, which were identified by the names of leaders in this developing movement. They came to be identified by the respectful term RABBI, which now took on the connotation of authorized leader or clergy.

After 70 C.E., the meeting places began to show distinctive arrangements for the use of the space, in contrast to the improvised gathering places from the pre-70 period that have been excavated at MASADA and Herodium. For the most part, the meeting places excavated in the Jewish dispersion of this period—and on down into the second century—manifest a pattern of expansion from the main room in someone's house to the inclusion of a small courtyard and the construction of a more visible access to the meeting place from a city street. Excavations at such sites as Delos and Ostia have shown this kind of development, but the same is also true of meeting places in Palestinian centers such as SEPPHORIS and CAPERNAUM (PLATE 52). It is only after the late third century that one can properly begin to refer to an architecturally distinctive meeting place as a synagogue. Prior to that time, the term was used of the group meeting itself. Only then do the imposing structures in the Greco-Roman architectural style appear; only from that time are the striking mosaic pavements evident, with the signs of the zodiac and the representation of the God of Israel as Helios, driving the sun chariot.

In the NT, "synagogue" is used with reference to the gatherings of Jews in Galilee and in the lands of the dispersion. It is the informal, unstructured nature of these gatherings that allows Jesus and Paul to wander in, to be invited to offer an exposition of the scriptures, and to present their interpretation of the text. At the same time, however, the open attitude of Jesus and Paul toward participation in these modes of fellowship—including the common meal—was offensive to the Pharisaic insistence on the maintenance of ritual purity as the essential condition for covenantal participation and identity. It is for this reason that in the gospel tradition there are frequent references to "their synagogues," mostly from Matthew (Matt 4:23; 9:35; 10:17; 12:9; 13:54). The clear implication is that the Christians have their own counterpart to these gatherings. The designation that Matthew chose for these conclaves of Christians is not συναγωγή, synagogue, but ἐκκλησία, church, as Matt 16:18 and 18:17 show.

Beginning in the second century and continuing on into the sixth, the synagogue movement developed in increasingly formal ways, which were given documentary support by the writing out and the organization of the traditions that sought to relate the ancient scriptures to the emergent institutional synagogue. These documents, which assume that the authority for the synagogue, its leadership and its mode of corporate religious life go back to Moses, came to be codified in the Mishnah and the Talmud. Similarly, later NT writings refer to aspects of the synagogue as though they existed as special buildings in the time of Jesus (Luke 7:5) and had a set pattern of worship (Luke 4:16-30). It is most likely that these features of the developing institutional synagogue were not in existence at the time of Jesus, but had come to be when Luke was writing his gospel at the end of the first or the beginning of the second century C.E.

See also JUDAISM; PHARISEES; TEMPLE.

Bibliography. E. R. Goodenough, *Jewish Symbols of the Greco-Roman Period*; J. Gutmann, ed., *The Synagogue: Studies in Origins, Archaeology, and Architecture*; I. Levy, *The Synagogue*; S. Safrai, "The Synagogue," *The Jewish People in the First Century*, ed. S. Safrai and M. Stern.

—HOWARD CLARK KEE

• **Syncretism.** The term syncretism, originally employed to describe political cooperation and religious reconciliation (cf. Plutarch, *Moralia* 490ab; Erasmus, *Adagia* 27), was adopted in the nineteenth century to refer to the fusion or adoption of beliefs and rituals by one religious tradition from another. Subsequent usage as a history-of-religions category has covered a wide variety of phenomena and concepts.

No hard and firm lines distinguish the syncretistic borrowing by one religion from another and the normal and natural evolution of one religion in terms resembling aspects of another religion. At various times and under particular circumstances subordinate elements in one religion resembling prominent elements in other faiths will rise to prominence although no direct borrowing may be indicated. Polytheistic religious systems are obviously more capable of absorbing other religious elements than a monotheistic system.

Early Israelite religion would appear to have blended elements from the worship of both EL and YAHWEH. The name ISRAEL itself suggests a worship of El, the great high god of Syro-Palestinian pantheons. In Gen 33:18-20, JACOB is said to have constructed an altar which he called "El, the God of Israel." ABRAHAM shared in a ritual meal with MELCHIZEDEK, the priest-king of SALEM (=Jerusalem?) who was priest of the god EL ELYON, maker of heaven and earth (Gen 14:17-20; cf. also Gen 16:13; 17:1; 21:33; 31:13; 35:7, 11; 43:14; 48:3; Deut 32:8-9). Yahweh was apparently the deity under whose banner the Israelite tribes fought their wars. The militancy of Yahweh is mentioned in many early texts (cf. Exod 1:1–15:18; Judg 5; 1 Sam 1:3; 17:45).

In addition, worship of BAAL, the god of fertility and vegetation, may also have been a feature of early tribal life. Elements in the GIDEON narrative in Judg 6–8 suggest Baal worship (cf. 6:25; 8:33; and the name Jerubbaal in 7:1), but whether this reflects editorial assessments or actual conditions is uncertain.

Yahweh worship and faith, probably from the time of SAUL, certainly became the national religion of Israel and remained so throughout Israelite and Judean history. Probably by the time a national religion developed, Yahwism had come to embody features amalgamated from Elism, Baalism, and the earlier militant Yahwism.

Although the late deuteronomistic editors of the biblical materials sought to paint their Israelite predecessors with a syncretistic and even polytheistic brush, it is doubtful that Israelite religion was ever really polytheistic or even highly syncretistic after the establishment of national cults in JERUSALEM and BETHEL. In their relationships with other states, some concessions had to be made to other national deities. This was the case with PHOENICIA and ARAM during the days of OMRI and AHAB (opposed by ELIJAH), with ASSYRIA during the eighth and seventh centuries, with ARAM and surrounding states during the reign of PEKAH, and with EGYPT and BABYLONIA during the late seventh and sixth centuries. The prophets HOSEA and EZEKIEL especially attacked such activities as apostasy from Yahweh.

Religious activities and places of worship that the prophets felt to be deviant forms of Yahwism—especially the local sanctuaries or high places and the use of sacred relics such as the ASHERAH—were condemned as if they were another religion (cf., e.g., Jer 2:28; Hos 4:12). Popular religion practiced alongside the official state cult may certainly have been syncretistic with various cults and practices considered supplemental to or components of Yahwism (cf. Jer 44:15-19).

During the PERSIAN period, JUDAISM may have borrowed and developed elements of Persian/Zoroastrian religion. Elements of dualism, the figure of SATAN, angelology, and so on have been traced to such influences.

During the Hellenistic-Roman periods, there was enormous amalgamation of religious faith and practices under the influence of large empire states, the needs of transcultural cooperation, and the desire to produce a unifying politicoreligious ethos. While retaining its distinctiveness, Judaism certainly was not untouched by external influences. The development of such doctrines as resurrection of the dead/life after death probably reflect such borrowing. The Jewish philosopher PHILO illustrates how Greek philosophy and Jewish piety could be combined creatively.

Christianity even in its NT expressions must be seen as reflective of both inner Jewish developments and Hellenistic influences. Early Christianity shared elements with Jewish piety, messianism, and apocalypticism but also with Hellenistic GNOSTICISM, MYSTERY RELIGIONS, and redeemer cults.

See also BAAL; EL; MONOTHEISM; POLYTHEISM.

Bibliography. G. W. Ahlstrom, *Aspects of Syncretism in Israelite Religion*; J. Barr, "The Question of Religious Influence: The Case of Zoroastrianism, Judaism, and Christianity," *JAAR* 53 (1985): 201-35; B. Pearson, ed., *Religious Syncretism in Antiquity*; J. A. Soggin, "Der offiziell geforderte Synkretismus in Israel während des 10. Jahrhunderts," *ZAW* 78 (1966): 179-204; C. H. Talbert, "The Concept of Immortals in Mediterranean Antiquity," *JBL* 94 (1975): 419-36; J. Tigay, *You Shall Have No Other Gods: Israelite Religion in the Light of Hebrew Inscriptions*.

—JOHN H. HAYES

• **Synoptic Problem.** The synoptic problem is the problem of explaining the similarities and differences between the first three Gospels. The word "synoptic" means a common view or viewed together, and the Gospels of Matthew, Mark, and Luke are called the synoptic Gospels because in general they use the same approach to the life and ministry of Jesus and contain much very similar material.

One of the first to try to answer the problem was Augustine, whose explanation was that Matthew was the original Gospel with Mark being a condensed version of Matthew and Luke being a composite of both Matthew and Mark.

The dominant view at present is the idea, presented by B. H. Streeter and others, that Mark was written first, and Matthew and Luke depended heavily on Mark's basic framework and content. The evidence is that most of Mark is repeated in Matthew and Luke. However, the similarities between Matthew and Luke that are not found in Mark suggest another source, Q, used by both these writers, but not known by Mark. Even so, there are portions of Matthew and Luke that are not accounted for by borrowing either from Mark or from Q. The solution appears to lie in the assumption that Matthew and Luke each had a private source not available to the others (PLATE 32). Whether these sources were written or oral is not known.

The dominant theory about the synoptic problem has not answered all the questions that have been raised and the subject is still debated by William R. Farmer and others. The debate, while it has not solved the problem to the satisfaction of everyone, has nonetheless called attention to the uniqueness of each of the three Gospels and the theological distinctiveness of each of the three writers. It has also made possible a better understanding of the importance of the difference between interpreting the Gospels as factual history and as confessions of faith. As a result of the debate one is better able to see the Gospels as theological documents and to appreciate their contribution to an understanding of history.

See also GOSPELS, CRITICAL STUDY OF; LUKE, GOSPEL OF; MARK, GOSPEL OF; MATTHEW, GOSPEL OF; Q; REDACTION; SOURCE CRITICISM.

Bibliography. G. W. Buchanan, ''Current Synoptic Studies: Orchard, the Griesbach Hypothesis, and Other Alternatives,'' *RL* 46 (1977): 415-36; W. R. Farmer, ed., *New Synoptic Studies*; B. H. Streeter, *The Four Gospels*.

—E. EARL JOINER

• **Syria.** *See* ARAM/ARAMEANS; REZIN

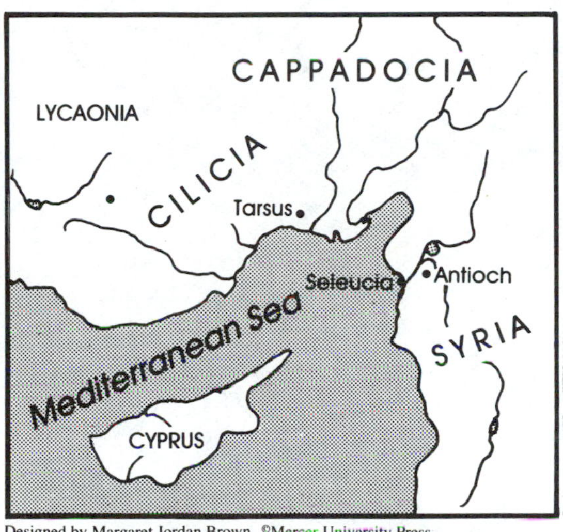

Designed by Margaret Jordan Brown ©Mercer University Press

• **Syria and Cilicia.** [sihr'-ee-uh, suh-lish'ee-uh] As the early Christians carried out the command of Acts 1:8 to be ''witnesses in Jerusalem and in all Judea and Samaria and to the end of the earth,'' the area north of Palestine proved to be a fertile area. ANTIOCH became the first major Christian center outside of Palestine and the gospel spread relentlessly forward to the north and west. The statement from the Jerusalem Council (Acts 15:22-29) indicates that churches had been established in Syria and Cilicia and that they were in communication with the church in Jerusalem.

According to Gal 1:21 and Acts 15:41, PAUL engaged in some of his first missionary activity in these areas. It would be natural for him to do so because these areas both lie between and include his home town of TARSUS and much of the land en route to Jerusalem. As a young boy in Tarsus and as a student of Gamaliel in Jerusalem, he undoubtedly made this trek on numerous occasions.

Ancient Cilicia (PLATES 26, 27) was actually composed of two parts. The western part was known as Cilicia Tracheia and contained rugged mountainous areas. The eastern part, known as Cilicia Pedias, possessed very fertile regions conducive to agriculture. A good system of roads facilitated travel north through mountain passes, the most famous being the Cilician Gates. Paul traveled through this pass on his second and third missionary journeys.

The NT passages mention Cilicia and Syria together because in 39 B.C.E. Cilicia Pedias was attached by the Romans to the province of Syria and likely remained under the governor of Syria until 72 C.E. The western part, Cilicia Tracheia, had a completely different political history during the NT period. Cilicia Tracheia and Cilicia Pedias were united as a Roman province under Emperor Vespasian in 72 C.E.

See also ANTIOCH; ARETAS; BASHAN; DAMASCUS; HAMATH; PAUL; TARSUS.

Bibliography. A. H. M. Jones, *The Cities of the Eastern Roman Provinces*; W. M. Ramsey, *The Cities of St. Paul*.

—JOHN A. WOOD

• **Syro-Ephraimitic War.** *See* ISAIAH

• **Syrophoenician.** [si'roh-fi-nish"uhn] The woman in Mark 7:24-30 who begged Jesus to heal her daughter is called ''a Syrophoenician'' (7:26). The Phoenicians were a semitic people who lived along the Mediterranean coast, northwest of Israel, and were closely related to the Canaanites of the interior. Their cities included Tyre and Sidon, cities which had been occupied since before the Israelites had occupied the land of Canaan. Thus, ties between the ancient people of Canaan and the occupants of ''Syrophoenicia'' in the first century were well recognized, and the Syrophoenicians were definitely categorized as gentiles, outside the bounds of Jewry.

This explains why the Gospel of Mark identifies the woman as ''a Greek, a Syrophoenician by birth'' (Mark 7:26) and Matthew's Gospel calls her ''a Canaanite woman from the region'' (Matt 15:21-22).

The first part of the designation, ''Syro-,'' distinguishes the Syrian PHOENICIA from the Phoenicia in North Africa, where the Libyan Phoenicia was found. The most famous of the Phoenician colonies was Carthage, which contested with Rome for the leadership in the Mediterranean world in the long years of the Punic wars, 264–146 B.C.E.

These historical references serve to emphasize the boldness of the gentile woman who laid the needs of her daughter before the ''Son of David'' and was content to claim as her due ''the crumbs that fall'' from the table of the children.

See also CANAAN; GENTILE/GENTILES IN THE NEW TESTAMENT; PHOENICIA; SYRIA AND CILICIA.

—WILLIAM H. GEREN

• **Taanach.** [tay′uh-nak] Taanach (Aner) is located on Tell Ta‘anak. Ancient Taanach is found next to the modern village which presently bears the same name. Such continuity has resulted in Taanach's location not being disputed. The site is located on the southern edge of the Esdraelon plain some five miles southeast of MEGIDDO (PLATE 13). Major transportation routes, from the south onward to Megiddo then northward, passed by Taanach. It is also situated on a pass which links the plain of Esdraelon to the Sharon. As part of this area, it was part of the major objective of rival powers which sought to control this region. Tell Taanach is a large mound covering some fourteen acres, with an approximate height of 49 m. (160 ft.). Taanach does not receive a large role in biblical history. This is due to its predominately Canaanite occupation. Only with the time of Solomon was Israelite occupation and control more firmly established.

There are both biblical and extra-biblical references to Taanach. Extra-biblical references include Egyptian references from campaign annals of both Thutmose III and Shishak I, which listed Taanach as a conquered city from their respective campaigns. There is also a possible, yet dubious reference from an AMARNA letter. Eusebius's *Onomasticon* notes Taanach as a large village. In biblical tradition, JOSHUA defeated the king of the Canaanite city Taanach (Josh 12:21) along with the king of Megiddo. Taanach, in the allotment of land to the tribes, was allotted to Manasseh (at first Issachar and Asher; cf. Josh 17:11; 1 Chr 7:29). Taanach along with Gath-rimmon, from the half-tribe of Manasseh served as Levitical cities. However, biblical references acknowledge that Taanach was still Canaanite (Josh 17:12; Judg 1:27). The Song of DEBORAH commemorates the victory of Israel over the king of Canaan and his commander Sisera by the judge Deborah and her commander Barak. Judg 5:19 mentions "Taanach, by the waters of Megiddo." The period of the united monarchy finds Taanach under Israelite occupation and rule. Taanach is listed as a city in one of Solomon's administrative districts. The fifth district was the region under the direction of Baana, son of Ahilud, including "Taanach, Megiddo, and all Beth-shean which is beside Zarethan below Jezreel, and from Beth-shean to Abel-meholah, as far as the other side of Jokmeam" (1 Kgs 4:12).

Excavations reveal an occupational history from approximately 2700 B.C.E. through to a late building project in the Abassid period (dating approximately in the eighth-tenth centuries C.E.). The major periods of occupation include Early Bronze Age settlement (ca. 2700–2400 B.C.E.) with a major settlement and defense structures. This period was followed by a period of minimal occupation. Middle Bronze II occupation occurred at Taanach, showing fortifications and a casemate wall. Unearthed by Sellin was the so-called patrician's house, a major structure. A general destruction then occurred with resettlement. Later twelfth century occupation, replete with various cultic materials (figurine mold, pig bones, cultic stand, etc.) continued until a major destruction in the tenth century. After this, there was limited occupation. Primary archaeological excavations at Taanach were directed by Ernst Sellin in 1902–1904. These campaigns brought to light a cultic stand, a Middle Bronze II C building, and important cuneiform texts. This campaign was one of the first major archaeological excavations in Palestine. The second archaeological campaign was conducted by Paul Lapp in conjunction with the American Schools of Oriental Research and Concordia Seminary, St. Louis, Missouri. This campaign corrected and extended Sellin's original conclusions concerning Taanach, and provides a more accurate occupational history of the site.

Bibliography. A. E. Glock, "Taanach," *IDB Supp*; J. E. Jennings, "Taanach," *NIDBA*; N. L. Lapp, ed., *The Tale of the* Tell, *Archaeological Studies by Paul Lapp* and "Taanach," *HDB*.

—DAVID M. FLEMING

• **Tabernacle.** Scripture uses several terms in reference to the Tabernacle. *'Ohel* referred to any tent in general and was specifically used in relation to the tent of meeting where God met with man (Exod 28:43). Another word, *mishkan*, meaning "dwelling," appears in Exod 25:9 and represents the presence of Yahweh with his people. Both *mishkan* and *'ohel* were often synonymous (Num 16:26-27), and in later times applied to dwellings that were not portable (cf. Isa 54:2; Jer 30:18). A third term, *miqdash*, applied specifically to the shrine of the Tabernacle, and is often translated "sanctuary" (cf. Exod 25:8).

The gathering of the children of Israel into a united body under Moses' leadership during the Exodus experience necessitated a centralized place of worship and religious service. The seminomadic nature of the tribes, however, precluded building of a permanent structure to house their sacred objects. It was during the sojourn at Sinai, therefore, that God commanded Moses to construct a portable sanctuary wherein he might dwell. The Tabernacle was to become the primary center of Israel's communion with her God throughout the ensuing three hundred years until a more permanent center could be built.

The descriptive account of the Tabernacle is found in

two sections of Exodus. The first, chaps. 25–30, recounts the instructions of God to Moses for the Tabernacle and its contents. Chaps. 35–40 tell of Israel's fulfillment of God's commands. Reference in chap. 33 to the tent of meeting probably describes the earliest shrine of Israel, preceding the institution of the priesthood and sacrificial ritual.

The description of the Tabernacle found in Exodus tells of an elaborate and carefully designed worship center requiring craftsmen skilled in all manners of metal and woodworking. The Tabernacle consisted of an enclosed sacrificial courtyard and an inner sanctuary. The outer perimeter (75 × 150 ft.) was encircled by linen curtains hung on fifty-six pillars seven and one-half ft. tall which hid the interior from view. The entrance faced east, covered by a screen of fine blue, purple, and scarlet linen suspended on four columns. The Tabernacle proper sat in the west half of the courtyard. Between the sanctuary and the main entrance lay the large bronze-horned altar of sacrifice and the bronze laver for the ceremonial cleansing of the priesthood.

The inner sanctuary was a series of linen curtains and hide coverings placed tent-fashion over an inner acacia wood frame. Forty-eight vertical boards, 15 ft. by 27 in., were each set in two sockets of silver by means of tenons. The center sections of each plank were probably cut out so as to form a window of sorts through which the curtains might be seen. Traverse wooden bars overlaid in gold passed through rings on the boards, joining the boards in sequence. The first covering was of blue, purple, and scarlet twisted linen upon which figures of cherubim were woven. A second curtain of goat's hair covered the first, upon which a third curtain of red-dyed ram's skin was laid. The outer covering was one of specially treated skins. The Tabernacle was open to the east, but another finely worked screen hung by golden rings upon five pillars blocked the entrance. The whole shrine measured 45 × 15 ft. and was divided into two rooms by a skillfully worked veil of linen. The outer room, the Holy Place (30 × 15 ft.), contained the incense altar, table of showbread, and golden lampstand. The inner Holy of Holies (15 × 15 ft.) housed the Ark upon which was placed the gold mercy seat flanked by two cherubim. It was on the mercy seat that the presence of God dwelt with Israel. The entire compound could be dismantled by the attending Levites and loaded onto carts for transport. Problems exist, however, with the logistics of transporting such an immense Tabernacle as the one described in Exodus. It has been calculated that the metal alone would have weighed seven and one-half tons and along with the curtains and pillars transport would have been an immense undertaking.

Examples of structures in the ancient world similar to the Israelite Tabernacle exist. A portable bed canopy of Egyptian Queen Hetepheres I (ca. 2600 B.C.E.) resembles a rectangle comprised of vertical poles and corner posts attached to horizontal beams above and below. Light curtains would then be draped over the frame. A series of four wooden boxlike shrines overlaid in gold were discovered in the tomb of Tutankhamun (ca. 1340 B.C.E.). Carefully worked mortices and tenons fitted together, holding the shrines intact. Pre-Islamic desert nomads housed sacred objects in a *qubbah,* a small red leather tent often carried upon the back of a camel. The *qubbah* accompanied the tribe to war, guided the group in its wanderings, and was a place for worship and the reception of oracles. The seventh century B.C.E. Phoenician history of Sanchuniathon tells of a portable shrine pulled by oxen. Diodorus also relates how the Carthaginians erected a sacred tent and altar in the center of their battle camps.

The shape of Israel's Tabernacle was by no means unique. Late Bronze counterparts existed throughout Palestine. Yadin's excavations at Hazor exposed a large temple complex of the fourteenth century comprised of porch, main hall, and Holy of Holies. Megiddo, Beth-Shan and Lachish also boasted similar structures with the anteroom/holy place arrangement. During the mid-twelfth century, Kenite-Midianites in the Timnah Valley occupied a small temple with a central shrine fronted by an altar. The entire area was then covered with a wool tent.

The Tabernacle accompanied Israel throughout the wilderness wanderings and the conquest of Canaan. The Tabernacle eventually was established at Shiloh where its contents may have become part of a more permanent structure (cf. 1 Sam 1:9). After capture by the Philistines, the Ark came to rest at Kiriath-jearim from which David later transferred it to a tent shrine at Jerusalem (cf. 2 Sam 6:17). The other components of the Tabernacle, such as the altar, probably resided at Gibeon until all the furnishings were reunited for use in Solomon's Temple (1 Kgs 8:4).

The exact physical nature of the Tabernacle of the Mosaic era is unclear. Scholars contending that the Exodus account was composed by P generally hold that the passages describing the Tabernacle found in chaps. 25–31 and 35–40 differ from the JE source references to the tent of meeting interwoven in Exodus, Numbers, and Deuteronomy. Such an interpretation presumes that a simple tent with little embellishment was pitched by Moses to house the Ark of the Covenant and to give symbolic evidence of God's presence with Israel. The Exodus account, then, becomes a later idealization of the Mosaic tent based upon a description of Solomon's ornate temple. More conservative scholarship holds that the Tabernacle was indeed an early structure, the ornate decoration rightly reflecting the skill of Israelite craftsmen trained in Egypt in woodworking and various metal crafts. The tent of meeting (Exod 33) would have been an earlier unadorned shrine set outside the camp, predating construction of the Tabernacle.

See also TENT OF MEETING.

Bibliography. F. M. Cross, Jr., "The Tabernacle: An Archaeological and Historical Perspective," *BA* 10 (1947): 45-68; R. K. Harrison, *Introduction to the Old Testament*; K. Kenyon, *Archaeology in the Holy Land*; A. Rothkoff, "Tabernacle," *EncJud* 1971; Y. Yadin, *Hazor: The Rediscovery of a Great Citadel of the Bible.*

—DAVID C. MALTSBERGER

• **Tabernacles, Feast of, in the New Testament.** The word "tabernacle" means tent, or dwelling place. The Feast of Tabernacles (or Booths) was originally a harvest festival and in addition commemorated the days when the ancient Hebrews enjoyed God's protection as they lived in tents during the forty years of wandering in the wilderness. It was celebrated at the end of the harvest and at first had no fixed date (Exod 34). Later, however, the date was set as the fifteenth day of the seventh month (the end of September or the beginning of October) and was to run seven days (Lev 23). Num 29 describes an eighth day of the feast, however, and the custom of celebrating for eight days continued to the time of Jesus.

Although the Feast of Tabernacles is mentioned directly only once in the NT, its importance in Judaism during the life of Jesus can hardly be exaggerated. Josephus, who wrote about Judaism in the first century C.E. reports that it was considered to be the most important feast of the Jews.

The recognition of the importance of this feast is implied in the fact that Jesus and his disciples attended (John 7:2). The disciples went from Galilee to the feast first. Then Jesus traveled separately, but it appears that he arrived at or near the beginning of the feast for some of the Jews sought him, no doubt having heard he was there. Clearly, the author of the Gospel of John saw great significance in Jesus' relation to the feast, for he reports that in the midst of the feast, Jesus taught in the Temple. Moreover, he reports two sayings of Jesus that may have been inspired by certain features of the feast. One was the "I am the light of the world" (John 8:12), which may have been inspired by the fact that on the first night of the feast, four golden candlesticks were lighted in the court of the women, a ceremony which may have been repeated each night. Philo reports that the feast was held during the autumnal equinox so that the world could see light even at night, since at that time there is no twilight.

Another saying that may have been inspired by the feast is Jesus' reported statement at the last day of the feast. The ceremony on each day included an offering of water, perhaps reflecting the early celebration of the feast, and symbolizing the importance of rain for the next year's harvest. Rabbi Akiba claimed that whoever did not attend the Feast of Tabernacles would have no rain. At this water-offering ceremony, a bowl was filled from the Pool of Siloam and offered by the priest while the choir sang, "With joy shall ye draw water out of the wells of salvation" (Isa 12:3).

John reports that on the last day, perhaps after observing this ceremony each day, Jesus stood, when normally he would have sat to teach, to emphasize the importance of his statement, and said: "if any man thirst, let him come unto me and drink" (7:37).

All of these things call attention to the fact, abundantly illustrated in all of the Gospels, that Jesus used ideas and examples drawn from the familiar background and contemporary environment of his hearers.

See also FEASTS AND FESTIVALS; TABERNACLES, FESTIVAL OF.

—E. EARL JOINER

• **Tabernacles, Festival of.** The Festival of Tabernacles completes the cycle of the three major Jewish pilgrimage festivals. The other two are the Festival of Unleavened Bread at the time of PASSOVER and the Festival of Weeks during Pentecost. The Festival of Tabernacles evidently began as the Festival of Ingathering (Exod 23:16; 34:22). The Hebrew people may have infused a thanksgiving autumnal celebration at harvest time with a covenant renewal ceremony based upon Yahweh's guidance through the wilderness. Deut 16:13-15 referred to the event as the Festival of Booths, a seven day feast for everyone in the community. Lev 23:39 refers to the Festival of the Lord during the seventh month for seven days, Tishri 15-21. Tishri(e) is the seventh month in the religious or festival cycle, first in the chronological or civic cycle. Lev 23:36 added an eighth day for a holy convocation (cf. Num 29:12-38).

The Sukkot (Booths) Festival, or *the* Festival, came to rise above the other major festivals as the most joyous and universal (cf. 1 Kgs 8:2, 65; 2 Chr 7:8; Ezek 45:23-25). Pss 29, 42–43, 76, 81, 118, and 132 gained prominence in expressing thanks to the Lord for past achievements and anticipation of future blessings. In addition to the preparation of booths to use during the feast, the celebrants gathered and waved the four species (palm, myrtle, willows, and citron) symbolic of divine blessings.

Messianic expectations began to be connected with the Festival of Tabernacles in later OT literature, perhaps already indicated in Amos 9:11—the reference to the booth of David (Zion) that had fallen. In Zech 14:16-21, the Festival becomes the occasion for all the nations to celebrate at Jerusalem.

One or another of the three major festivals would from time to time stand out. On the occasion of Josiah's reform, it was Passover that had the preeminence (1 Kgs 22–23); at Qumran, Pentecost or Weeks dominated. But in Ezra's renewal of the covenant and presentation of the divine Torah, it was Tabernacles that occupied the central place (Neh 8–9).

See also FEASTS AND FESTIVALS; WORSHIP IN THE OLD TESTAMENT.

—OMER J. HANCOCK, JR.

• **Table Fellowship.** Among life's everyday experiences, the shared meal is viewed by biblical writers as an especially powerful symbol of how human beings are bound together with one another and with their God. To eat with someone, to share table fellowship, is to foster close association and acquaintance. The result is the establishment of caring and trust, as well as a certain identification by association. Betrayal or unfaithfulness toward another with whom one has shared the table is viewed in the Bible as particularly reprehensible (e.g., Judas's betrayal of Jesus in Mark 14:17-21). The experience of such fellowship links the participant to God's saving deeds, both past and future.

In ancient Israel camaraderie was typically enjoyed at the evening rather than the morning meal, for only at the former would darkness preclude return to work and provide needed leisure time (cf. Judg 19:16-21; Ruth 3:2, 7). The two meal pattern was traceable to Moses' directive (Exod 16:12). Occasionally, such evening meals were transformed into banquets or feasts shared with guests or/and relatives (e.g., as in Job 1:13; 1 Sam 9:19, 22-24; Esth 5:8, 12-14). Proper seating arrangements were observed at such meals, with the guest of honor seated at the table head (e.g., 1 Sam 20:24-25; cf. Luke 14:7-11) and others according to age or status (Gen 43:31-33). Before eating, hands would be washed and the host would commonly offer thanks for the food (e.g., Mark 7:3; Matt 15:36). Banquets might include entertainment, such as instrumental music and singing (Amos 6:4-5; Isa 30:29; Sir 32:5-6), dancing (Judg 21:16-24; cf. Matt 14:6), the telling of riddles (Judg 14:10-14). Simple meals were consumed in a crouching position or sitting on ground or mat; whereas Greek and Roman influence led to diners reclining on cushions around three sides of a low table. Such were the situations in which table fellowship might be enjoyed.

The fellowship at such meals was experienced on two levels: the human and the human-divine. Instances of the former include not only family gatherings but also meals intended to seal agreements between parties (e.g., Gen 31:45-54; Josh 9:12-15). Meals thus shared were understood to create loyalty and trustworthiness among the participants. This is why betrayal or sinister action by one who has shared in table fellowship was held to be especially unpardonable (cf. Ps 41:9; Mark 14:18-21). Also, shared meals were an important sign of unity, which is why Paul so vehemently resisted any separation of Jewish from gentile Christians at meals (Gal 2:11ff.; cf. Peter's views in Acts 11:1-18).

At a deeper level, shared meals could also be the occasion for communion between humans and the divine, especially in connection with cultus and ritual (e.g., Exod 12—eating the PASSOVER; Deut 12:5-7—eating "before the Lord"). The divine took initiative to supply food and drink (Exod 16:4-35; Num 20:7-11) and is the source of "daily bread" (cf. Matt 6:11 and par.). In the NT, celebration of the LORD'S SUPPER established communion between the risen Christ and his own (Matt 26:26-28; 1 Cor 10:16-18). The sacrificial meal bound participants to the Lord of the altar (1 Cor 10:18). This is why sharing in feasts of pagan gods or partaking of the "cup" and "table of demons" (1 Cor 10:20-21) was especially offensive to God and the Christ.

Still another important aspect of table fellowship lies in its temporal dimensions. Eating unleavened bread at Passover (Exod 12:1–13:16) or drinking the cup at the Eucharist (1 Cor 11:23-26) are forms of remembering and participating anew in the great saving acts of God. Simultaneously, participation in such cultic meals is a foretaste of eschatological hope. Isa 25:6 and 55:1f. express expectation of sharing in full fellowship with God in a renewed world, as does the Jewish cry still heard after passover seder: "next year in Jerusalem!" The NT, too, uses such images. Jesus speaks of the saved coming from the ends of the earth to "sit at table together" in God's new Kingdom (Luke 13:29; cf. the parable of the marriage feast in Luke 14:16-24; Matt 22:1-10). The fellowship enjoyed by Jesus and his disciples at the Last Supper is a proleptic experience of what will occur in the fulfillment of God's Kingdom (Mark 14:22-25 and par.). Rev 19:9 and Matt 26:29 make explicit the connection between this eschatological feast and celebration of the Eucharist.

Table fellowship, then, is an external manifestation of the internal bond enjoyed by those who participate in the same, ultimate source of life. This source, in the Bible, is God. This reality gives depth, meaning, and richness to a shared life of faith.

Bibliography. J. Behm, "ἐσθίω," *TDNT*; C. E. B. Cranfield, "Fellowship," *TWBB*; A. Lelièvre, "Eating and Drinking (Meal)," *ComB*.

—MALCOLM L. PEEL

• **Table of the Nations.** *See* GENEALOGY IN THE OLD TESTAMENT

• **Tabor, Mount.** [tay'buhr] Rising some 1,843 ft. above the surrounding plain, Mount Tabor is located in the northeastern end of the Valley of Jezreel (PLATE 13). Its summit is approximately 3,000 by 1,200 ft. Though it is not all that large (Josephus mistakenly gives its height as 20,000 ft.!), its isolation and majestic appearance led it to be compared with the mountains of Hermon and Carmel (Ps 89:12; Jer 46:18). From its heights, on a clear day, one can see Megiddo to the west, Mount Hermon to the north and the Jordan Valley to the east and south. Its shaded top offers cool relief from the summer heat of the surrounding valley.

In the OT, Mount Tabor is first mentioned in connection with the division of the land among the twelve tribes. It provided a common boundary between the territories of Zebulun, Issachar and Naphtali (Josh 19:12, 22, 34; cf. 1 Chr 6:77). From Tabor, BARAK led the forces of Naphtali and Zebulun against the army of SISERA (Judg 4:6-14). The mountain was also the site where Zebah and Zalmunna, the kings of Midian, killed the brothers of Gideon (Judg 8:18).

The Jewish historian JOSEPHUS reports that over 10,000 Jews were killed near Tabor in a first-century B.C.E. battle with Gabinius, the governor of Syria. Josephus, himself, while governor of Galilee, fortified the mountain, building a wall around its top. But his efforts proved futile as the Jews stationed there were routed by the troops of Vespasian during the Jewish War of 66–70 C.E.

The most famous tradition associated with the mountain is the transfiguration of Christ. However, the identification of the mount of transfiguration is unnamed in the NT (Matt 17:1-8; Mark 9:2-8; Luke 9:28-36) and its identification with Tabor does not seem to antedate the fourth century C.E. Most NT scholars believe the incident recorded in the Gospels occurred near Mount Hermon and there are good reasons for rejecting the Tabor tradition. Nevertheless, by the sixth century, Christian pilgrims report seeing as many as three churches on its top, and a large monastery is reported as seen in the seventh. By the eighth century, the local inhabitants called Mount Tabor *Age Mons* (the "Holy Mountain") and 4,340 steps are said to have been built up its slope!

All of these Christian structures were destroyed by Saladin in 1187, and an Arab fortress was constructed by his brother. This fortress itself was destroyed in the thirteenth century and all building activity ceased for several centuries. Then in the nineteenth century, a Greek Orthodox church and monastery were erected, and the Franciscans built a basilica over much of the ancient remains. No systematic archaeological excavations have ever been conducted on the mountain; thus the date of its earliest occupation is still unknown.

Bibliography. G. W. Van Beek, "Tabor, Mount," *IDB*; J. Wilkinson, *Jerusalem Pilgrims Before the Crusades*.

—JOHN C. H. LAUGHLIN

• **Talent.** *See* MONEY

• **Talmud.** *See* RABBINIC LITERATURE

• **Tamar.** [tay'mahr] The name of two OT women: the daughter-in-law of JUDAH, and the daughter of DAVID. (1) According to Gen 38, Tamar was the Canaanite widow of Judah's eldest son, Er. When Judah's second son, Onan, to whom Tamar had been given in levirate marriage, died, Judah withheld from Tamar his youngest son, Shelah, for fear that he also would die. The childless Tamar then disguised herself as a prostitute and offered herself to Judah, who did not recognize her. She conceived, and when she was accused of harlotry, she identified Judah as the father by producing the tokens he had given her, his signet and cord and staff. Judah acknowledged his paternity and confessed that Tamar was "more righteous" than he in fulfilling the levirate obligation (Gen 38:26). Tamar bore twin sons, Perez and Zerah, to Judah. Through Perez she is counted as ancestress to David (Ruth 4:18-22; 1 Chr 2:4) and Jesus (Matt 3:1).

(2) According to 2 Sam 13, Tamar was daughter of David and sister of ABSALOM. Her half-brother AMNON fell in love with her, plotted her seduction, raped her, and then abandoned her. Absalom, to whom Tamar turned for protection, bided his time carefully for two full years and then avenged her by having an unsuspecting Amnon murdered.

See also ABSALOM; AMNON; MARRIAGE IN THE OLD TESTAMENT.

—MARGARET DEE BRATCHER

• **Tammuz.** [tam'uhz] The vegetation deity of Sumerian

and Assyro/Babylonian culture, whose consort was Inanna (Sumerian) or Ishtar (Assyro/Babylonian). Tammuz appears only once directly in the Hebrew Bible: EZEKIEL (8:14) is conducted by the heavenly messenger through the Temple precincts in Jerusalem and there sees women weeping for Tammuz (Heb. *tammuz*). In Sumerian and Assyro/Babylonian mythology, Tammuz descends into the underworld, causing vegetation to cease at the end of summer, but is brought back to earth through the intervention of his consort Ishtar, a part of the life-cycle celebrated in the rituals of the people. Details of the cult of Tammuz, however, have not survived. Similar myths and ritual acts existed in West Semitic cultures, where BAAL and Ashtoreth (Astarte = Ishtar?) or Baal and ASHERAH or perhaps Baal and Anath were the divine pair, and in Egypt and Greece as well (Osiris and Isis in Egypt; Adonis and Aphrodite in Greece).

The vegetative/fertility dimensions of Israelite religion show numerous borrowings from the religions of the neighbors, though the borrowed elements were transformed in relation to central tenets of Israelite belief. The ritual practices of the neighbors of Israel had great appeal to Israelite worshipers. The prophets both criticized such practices when they were unrelated to the moral life of the people and also found imaginative ways to use the language and imagery of the religions of the neighbors to enrich and deepen Israelite faith in the one God.

See also ASHERAH; BAAL; HELLENISTIC WORLD; SYNCRETISM.

—WALTER HARRELSON

• **Targum.** *See* RABBINIC LITERATURE

• **Tarshish.** [tahr'shish] The name of several individuals and a port or a land in the OT.

1. A son of Javan, the son of Japheth (Gen 10:2-4). Tarshish along with Kittim and other brothers are described as those from whom "the coastland peoples spread" (Gen 10:5).

2. A descendant of Benjamin (1 Chr 7:10).

3. One of the "seven princes of Persia and Media" who "sat first in the kingdom" next to King Ahasuerus (Esth 1:14).

4. A major seaport or a land, the location of which is still open to debate. While the precise location of Tarshish is uncertain, it has often been identified with the site of Tartessus in Spain. This identification is based on references such as those found in Herodotus (*Hist* 4.152) and Jonah. For instance, as Jonah attempted to flee from the Lord and the mission to Nineveh, he "found a ship going to Tarshish . . . paid the fair, and went on board" (Jonah 1:3). A location in the western Mediterranean in the opposite direction of Nineveh fits well the intent of the story. Other references to Tarshish in the OT describe it as a great trade center. It had a reputation for exporting finely handcrafted silver (Jer 10:9). Also, Tarshish engaged in trade with Tyre, another major shipping port on the Mediterranean, located on the coast of Phoenicia. Tarshish provided Tyre with shipments of silver, iron, tin, and lead (Ezek 27:12). These references indicate that Tarshish had a reputation as a major supplier of metals, a characteristic that also fits a location in Spain.

Another possible location for the site of Tarshish is the African coast along the Red Sea. This proposal is based on information concerning Solomon's shipping operations in the Red Sea. With the assistance of Hiram, king of Tyre, Solomon had a ship building industry at Ezion-geber, a site at the upper end of the Gulf of Aqaba from which he operated a fleet of ships (1 Kgs 9:26-28). Apparently it was from that port that Solomon sent forth a fleet described as "a fleet of ships of Tarshish" (1 Kgs 10:22). The account seems to suggest that the fleet was involved in a lengthy operation that took three years, at the end of which it returned to the home base bringing cargo that included "gold, silver, ivory, apes, and peacocks" (1 Kgs 10:22). While some conclude that these passages indicate that Tarshish was located along the Red Sea, others suggest that it took three years for the fleet to travel down the Red Sea, and around the continent of Africa up to Tarshish in Spain.

Related to the problem of trying to locate the site of Tarshish is the problem of trying to determine what is meant by the phrase the "fleet of ships of Tarshish." There seems to be little doubt that a major seaport named Tarshish actually existed in ancient times. In addition to the passages cited above that refer to the site of Tarshish, the chronicler speaks of Jehoshaphat "building ships to go to Tarshish," ships that were built at Ezion-geber (2 Chr 20:36). However, as time passed the phrase "the fleet of ships of Tarshish" apparently became a general designation for large seagoing ships, perhaps especially those that carried metal, regardless of the port they served.

At the present time, while the location of Tarshish has not yet been determined, three areas are considered to be the most likely possibilities, including, Tartessus in Spain, the African coast along the Red Sea, and the site of Tarsus in the Cilician plain in Asia Minor.

—LAMOINE DEVRIES

• **Tarsus.** [tahr'suhs] A city on the Cydnus River in Cilicia of Asia Minor, ten mi. from the Mediterranean (modern Tersous; PLATES 26, 27). It was founded in prehistoric times, over six millennia ago. Its importance as a commercial center was fostered by nearness to both the Cilician Gates and the ancient Euphrates trade road as well as by proximity to the Mediterranean, which was accessible via the Cydnus.

Hittite records from the second millennium B.C.E. already speak of "Tarsa" in Kizzuwatna (= Cilicia), depicting it as a major city. Archaeological finds raise the possibility that Tarsus was the capital of Kizzuwatna when the HITTITES were in power.

Around 1200 B.C.E. Tarsus fell to the SEA PEOPLES. It was later resettled by Mycenean Greeks after the Trojan War. (Greek legend associates its founding with Heracles or Perseus.) In subsequent centuries the city was overrun by the Assyrians Shalmaneser III (858–824) and Sennacherib (705–681) and so passed from Greek hands. In the Persian period Tarsus was ruled by satraps. From this era comes Xenophon's colorful account of the city and its prosperity (*Anab* 1.2).

Alexander the Great, who prevented the Persians from burning Tarsus as they fled it, passed through the city in 333 and paved the way for the restoration of its Greek character. After Alexander, Tarsus was ruled by the Seleucids.

Following its submission to Tigranes of Armenia in 83 B.C.E., Tarsus came under Roman rule (ca. 67) and was made the official administrative capital of its province. Three decades later, Mark Antony, rewarding the city for its opposition to Cassius, gave Tarsus the status of a free city.

In Paul's day, when the population was over half a million, Tarsus was renowned as an intellectual center. Strabo wrote that the people were so devoted to philosophy and education that they surpassed even Athens and Alexandria (*Geog* 14.5.13). Certainly the city boasted several famous grammarians, philosophers, and poets.

In the NT Tarsus is mentioned only in Acts (9:11, 30; 11:25; 21:39; 22:3). According to these texts, PAUL was a native and citizen of Tarsus ("no mean city"), and after his "conversion" he returned there at least once.

Scholars have debated the extent to which Paul was affected by his native city with its Hellenistic ambiance and non-Jewish institutions. Those stressing his Jewish connections have tended to downplay the importance of such influence. It has even been argued that Paul moved to Jerusalem while quite young. For others, however, the apostle's upbringing in Tarsus explains his distance from rabbinic Judaism as well as certain parallels between Pauline religion and Hellenistic religion.

It is not impossible that the TARSHISH of the OT (e.g., Gen 10:4) is to be identified with Tarsus (so Josephus, *Ant* 9.208). A certain reference to Tarsus is found in 2 Macc 4:30-31.

See also PAUL; STOICS; SYRIA AND CILICIA.

Bibliography. H. Goldman, *Excavations at Gözlü Küle, Tarsus*; W. M. Ramsey, *The Cities of Saint Paul*; W. C. van Unnik, *Tarsus or Jerusalem.*

—DALE C. ALLISON, JR.

• **Tassels.** *See* FRINGES

• **Tax.** *See* ECONOMICS IN THE NEW TESTAMENT; MONEY; PUBLICANS

• **Taxes, Taxation.** *See* ECONOMICS IN THE OLD TESTAMENT

• **Teacher.** *See* RABBI; TEACHING

• **Teaching.** The act of instructing and directing as well as the content of such instruction and direction. The instruction can be given by a parent, a teacher, a wise person, or God. Teaching is focused on a learner or DISCIPLE who generally is assumed to lack information, direction, and a comprehensive understanding. Teaching can shape identity, morality, life-style, and culture.

Two biblical words address the scope of teaching—TORAH and DIDACHE. Torah, often misunderstood as equivalent to "law," correctly describes all that has been revealed of God's nature, God's purpose, and God's expectations. Law encompassed part of that, but the story of God's gracious acts established the context through which the divine will was revealed and people's obedient response anticipated. In the FAMILY and in the SYNAGOGUE, Torah was studied, taught, and proclaimed. Its invitation was: "Hear, O Israel." It offered the learner identity with the past, guidance for the present, and hope for the future.

Didache carried a similar meaning in the NT. Though gradually institutionalized in formal theology and in the church office of teacher, *didache* provided instruction and exhortation in various aspects of Christian life, thought, and practice. It represented both the vehicle through which revelation was carried as well as the content of that revelation.

Teaching was the major role of the RABBI and, of course, the teacher. It was a principal activity of Jesus in his ministry. On occasion the prophet was a teacher. Through teaching, the people of God reaffirmed their identity and drew direction and strength for their mission.

See also DIDACHE; EDUCATION IN THE NEW TESTAMENT; EDUCATION IN THE OLD TESTAMENT; RABBI; TORAH.

—MICHAEL FINK

• **Teaching of the Twelve Apostles.** *See* DIDACHE

• **Tehom.** *See* COSMOLOGY; LEVIATHAN; TIAMAT

• **Tell.** Tell is the Arabic word for a mound formed by successive layers of occupational debris; the comparable Heb. word is *tel.* The typical tell has the appearance of a truncated cone, with sloping sides and a relatively flat top. The feature is common in the ancient Near East, especially in Syria-Palestine. Tells are formed by the occupation, destruction, and rebuilding of the same site over hundreds or thousands of years. Typically, as the mound grows higher, the amount of space available at the top decreases.

One might wonder why new inhabitants would rebuild on the exact site of a previous settlement. Often the same features that attracted settlement originally contributed to the choice of the same site: presence of water and food nearby, an easily defensible location, perhaps those rebuilding are the original inhabitants who fled its destruction by enemy action or survived natural catastrophe such as fire or earthquake.

The OT itself refers to *tels* both in the sense of a city sitting on a tell (Josh 11:13; cf. Jer 30:18) and as a ruin (Josh 8:28; Deut 13:17; Jer 49:2). Another Heb. word, *'î,* plural *'îyîm,* also refers to the ruin mound of a city (Mic 1:6; Jer 26:18). The Canaanite city AI preserves that word root while its modern name et-Tell preserves the other word root.

Other related words include the Turkish terms *tepe* and *hüyük,* both of which are comparable to tell. The Arabic *khirbet* means ruin in general, and most often refers to a low level site which has not had sufficient layers of occupation to produce a mound.

See also ARCHAEOLOGY.

—JOEL F. DRINKARD, JR.

• **Tell el-Amarna.** *See* AMARNA

• **Temple Scroll.** The *Temple Scroll* (*11QTem*) is the longest and most recently discovered of the DEAD SEA SCROLLS. The acquisition of the scroll, which was apparently found in Qumran Cave 11, took place under unusual circumstances, which contributed to its poor state of preservation. The scroll, written in Hebrew, originally contained sixty-six columns. The first is lost, and the early columns are very fragmentary; only the last third are reasonably well preserved. The scroll dates from the beginning of the first century C.E. Fragments from Cave 4, dating from 100–75 B.C.E., have been labeled as being of the same document and, alternately, of a similar document. There are also apparently (i.e., still unpublished) other fragments from Cave 4, dating from no later than 150 B.C.E., of either the same document or one of its sources.

The scroll begins with an account of God making his covenant with Israel (cf. Exod 34), followed by detailed instructions concerning the building of the TEMPLE. Next comes a lengthy series of regulations centering around cultic laws, especially the cycle of feasts and their sacrifices (cf. Lev 23; Num 28–29). There follows a set of detailed prescriptions concerning the construction of the Temple court. Regulations for maintaining the purity of the Temple and the holy city come next, followed by various laws of more general application, many of which are paralleled in Deut 15–23, but others of which (e.g., those concerning kingship) reflect considerable expansion.

Although *11QTem* is closely related to the Pentateuch, it exhibits a creative handling of the Pentateuchal traditions. The author has taken laws related by subject matter, but scattered throughout the Pentateuch, and brought them together to form a systematic code of law. He also has not hesitated to rewrite some of the laws and to add new ones, sometimes entire new sections. In particular, he filled in the obvious gaps in the Pentateuch with regulations concerning the Temple and the king. But the most striking feature of *11QTem* is that God speaks in the first person throughout. The implications of this editorial activity are staggering: this fluid rewriting of the very foundation of Judaism itself—the Law of Moses or TORAH—is given the authority of God himself. Clearly the composer of the *11QTem* intended his book to be understood as a divine revelation to Moses and therefore of equal status with the Pentateuch.

Given the centrality of the Torah in Judaism, a major controversy has arisen over the circumstances under which the *11QTem* was written. Some have argued that it is a product of the Qumran community. No copies have been discovered outside of Qumran. Furthermore, it contains parallels to certain Qumran sectarian documents, especially *CD, 1QM,* and *4QpNah.* Similarly, the Feast of the New Oil is unknown outside of the Scroll and an unpublished calendar fragment from Cave 4. On this view *11QTem* would not be a substitute for the Pentateuch— indeed, copies of all five books of the Pentateuch have been found at Qumran—but an additional Torah, on the same level as the Pentateuch. Such an additional Torah may well be the same as the Sealed Book of the Law supposedly found by Zadok, the founder of the community (*CD* 5:2-5)—that is, *11QTem* may in fact contain the divine interpretation of the Law which was revealed to the Teacher of Righteousness, who may be its author. Thus, some scholars have labeled the book the Qumran Torah. Others argue that the connections between *11QTem* and the Qumran community are tenuous. Out of about 800 manuscripts discovered at Qumran, only two are of *11QTem,* compared, e.g., to twenty-five copies of Deuteronomy and twelve of *1QS.* It is not quoted in any sectarian document. References in the *11QTem* to the Teacher of Righteousness, the history of the sect, and the most distinctive beliefs and practices at Qumran are nonexistent. Such parallels as there are with the sectarian scrolls are general, and there are some significant differences. On this view *11QTem* was simply one of a number of nonsectarian documents which the sect copied and read (cf. *11QtgJob*; *1QapGen*). The question is complicated by the debate over the identification of the Cave 4 fragments, giving rise to a third position—that *11QTem* represents the final, Qumranic stage in a lengthy process of editing extracanonical Torah traditions which may have begun prior to the establishment of the community. Given the different positions, it is not surprising that *11QTem* has been dated variously from the second half of the fifth century B.C.E. to the second half of the second century B.C.E.

Whatever the case, *11QTem* attests to a Jewish mindset which was open to the notion that substantial revision of the Pentateuch was possible, a type of attitude hitherto unknown. Adding to this the presence of noncanonical psalms in the Qumran Psalms Scroll, the question arises as to the relative fixity of the OT CANON in the last few centuries B.C.E. The scroll also reflects strong priestly concerns, with a special concern for the layout and purity of the Temple/city and for the cycle of festivals and their sacrifices according to a solar calendar (cf. the BOOK OF JUBILEES, with which *11QTem* has a number of parallels). The royal concerns of *11QTem* are seen in the new material on kingship, which includes strict regulations on the king's marital practices and the requirement that he consult an advisory council on all administrative and judicial matters. Finally, *11QTem*'s ban on DIVORCE and concern for incestuous relationships illumine the Jewish background of the divorce texts in Mark 10:2-12 and Matt 19:3-9.

See also DEAD SEA SCROLLS; ESSENES.

Bibliography. M. Hengel, J. H. Charlesworth and D. Mendels, "The Polemical Character of 'On Kingship' in the Temple Scroll: An Attempt at Dating 11QTemple," *JJS* 37 (1986): 28-38; J. Maier, *The Temple Scroll*; J. Milgrom, "The Temple Scroll," *BA* 41 (1978): 105-20; J. R. Mueller, "The Temple Scroll and the Gospel Divorce Texts," *RevQ* 10 (1980): 247-56; H. Stegemann, "Is the Temple Scroll a Sixth Book of the Torah—Lost for 2,500 Years?" *BAR* 13 (1987): 28-35; G. Vermes, "The Writings of the Qumran Community," E. Schürer, *The History of the Jewish People in the Age of Jesus Christ,* rev. ed.; B. Z. Wacholder, *The Dawn of Qumran*; Y. Yadin, ed., *The Temple Scroll, The Temple Scroll: The Hidden Law of the Dead Sea Sect,* and "The Temple Scroll: The Longest and Most Recently Discovered Dead Sea Scroll," *BAR* 10 (1984): 32-49.

—JOSEPH L. TRAFTON

• **Temple Sermon.** *See* JEREMIAH, BOOK OF

• **Temple/Temples.** Temple refers specifically to a building or structure devoted essentially to the worship of a deity. The two common Heb. words translated in English versions as temple are *bêt* and *hêkāl.* Both of these words indicate a building, *bêt* being the common Heb. word for a house, and *hêkāl* meaning a palace or part of a temple structure. *Hêkāl* also occurs in Canaanite and Ugaritic texts

Inscription forbidding gentiles to enter the Temple.

with a similar usage and is related to the Akkadian *êkâllu* which in turn is derived from the Sumerian word meaning "big house." Likewise Canaanite used *bêt* and Akkadian used *bitu,* house, to refer to temples. Thus temple is to be distinguished from other words designating worship activities by virtue of its specific relationship to an architectural structure, being house-like. Other terms, such as sanctuary, high place, and altar, deal intimately with worship but do not necessarily have houses of worship attached.

It should be noted that whereas the two common NT Gk. words for temple, *naos* and *hieron* are used exclusively in cultic contexts (both in the NT and in Greek literature as well), the Heb. terms and their semitic cognates both derive from secular usage: *bêt* could refer to any house; and *hêkāl* referred to a palace or mansion, a big house, as well as a temple.

Egyptian Temples. The Egyptian temple building was both a house for the god and a stage for the reenactment of the rituals of that deity. Each deity had his or her own temple. The worship of specific deities was often associated with specific cities. The basic elements of the temple were typical of a house, but with the layout planned to permit worship and processions. The sanctuary of the temple, the most holy part, corresponded to the private quarters of a family house, usually located at the rear of the house. The outer courts and halls of the temple paralleled the courtyard, garden, industrial, and reception areas of the house, that is, the public areas. The cult temples may well have represented Egypt (or even the world) in microcosm, the temple itself symbolizing all Egypt with the most sacred room symbolizing the deity's dwelling in the midst of the land. Two pylons or columns at the door of the building represented the horizon. Outer walls of the temple often depicted the pharaoh destroying the foreign enemies of Egypt, thus symbolizing the borders of the land. Inner structures often depicted the land and plants of Egypt, the floor decorated as the earth and water from which the plants grew, and the ceiling as sky and stars, all to show symbolically that the temple was a microcosm of Egypt as a whole. As one moved through the temple toward the inner sanctuary of the deity, the size of the rooms diminished, the floor level rose and the ceiling was lowered; lighting was also reduced: all intended to increase the sense of mystery and hiddenness of the deity. This inner sanctuary represented the mound which rose out of the primeval waters and was the birth place of the deity (perhaps a concept deriving from the appearance of new land in the delta regions deposited from the silt of flood waters).

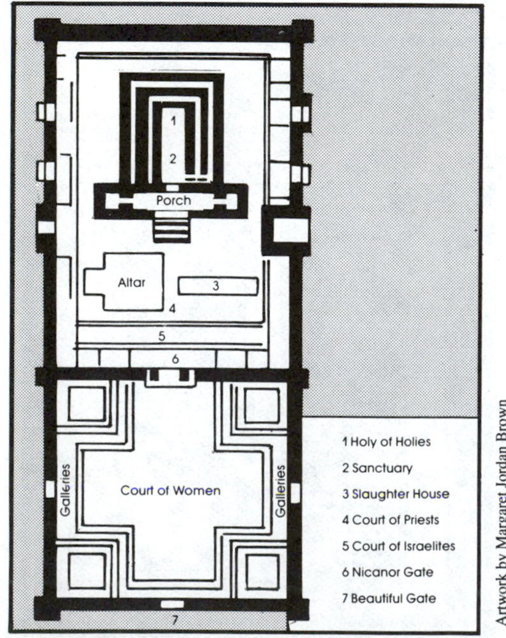

Layout of the Temple.

Mesopotamian Temples. The principal gods of Mesopotamia had major cultic centers in specific cities, Marduk in BABYLON, Shamash in Sippor, and Sin in UR and HARAN. Temple complexes tended to be quite elaborate and extensive, often covering many acres of land. In Babylon itself at the time of NEBUCHADREZZAR there were at least fifty-eight temples belonging to different deities.

By far the major temple complex at Babylon was that of Marduk, the guardian god of the city. The Marduk temple complex was a quadrangular enclosure on the east bank of the Euphrates surrounded by high turreted walls. The northern part of the complex was occupied by the great ziggurat or temple tower named Etemenanki, probably the model for the TOWER OF BABEL account in Gen 11. The southern part of the temple complex housed the temple of Marduk itself, called Esagila, with its fifty-five side chapels.

The plans for Mesopotamian temples varied, but in general had a large central courtyard surrounded by heavy walls. Within the courtyard was a temple building having several inner rooms including a vestibule, main rooms, and a broad-room cella containing a statue of the deity. The statue was often placed on a raised platform in a niche in the back wall and facing the doorway. The ziggurat has been variously interpreted as a symbolic mountain dwelling of the god, as the place the deity alighted when he descended from heaven, and as a raised temple platform to offer protection from floods. Descriptions of ziggurats indicate a building existed on top of the structure. However, none of the ziggurats excavated have had the upper platform intact, thus its structure is not known. Monumental stairways led to the top, and apparently some rituals took place there, perhaps the sacred marriage of the god.

As with Egyptian temples, processions played a major role in Mesopotamian temple worship. At Babylon, the Processional Way led from the Ishtar Gate in the north past palaces and ultimately through four gates into the Marduk temple complex.

Canaanite Temples. At least in the earlier periods, Canaanite temples tended to be much simpler than the Egyptian or Mesopotamian counterparts. Indeed because the temples were simple, much like typical houses of the period, controversy exists concerning the identity of these early structures as temples, especially since many lack large quantities of cultic remains. Some scholars prefer to identify the structures as large houses or public buildings rather than temples. The typical structure had a single broad room plan. MEGIDDO clearly had a cult complex from the Early Bronze Age period. Three very similar temple buildings were located in this complex, one having associated with it a large circular altar platform, 25 ft. in diameter, $4^1/_2$ ft. high, and with seven steps leading up to the platform. The exact relationship between the three temple buildings is not clear, nor is it certain whether all three were in use at the same time. All three have very similar plans: a broad room structure with the side walls extended forward to create a vestibule entrance. Each has one side room, perhaps for storage. Two of the structures are immediately adjacent, and are near mirror twins perhaps indicating the worship of a deity pair. Each of the temples has two column bases; two have platforms on the wall opposite the entrance probably for a statue of the deity.

A second Canaanite temple pattern appeared in the Middle Bronze Age, the *migdāl* temple or temple tower. This type structure is noted for its thick fortress-like walls. Typically this *migdāl* temple was rectangular, of the long-room pattern (less often a broad room), and consisted of one large room and a vestibule. The wall opposite the entrance often had a raised platform or a niche for a statue of the deity. The vestibule was flanked by towers on both sides. The temple was apparently multi-story. Examples of this structure are known from Megiddo, SHECHEM, HAZOR, EBLA, and Alalakh, and indicate northern Syrian influence. Two temples excavated at UGARIT seem to be a variant of this plan.

Also in the Middle Bronze Age and extending through the Late Bronze Age was a temple plan in which the place for the deity has become a separate room, an inner sanctuary, often with an elevated floor level and steps leading up to it. Examples of this type temple are known from BETH-SHAN.

Israelite Temples Other Than the Jerusalem Temple. Surprising though it is to some, the OT itself offers considerable evidence for the existence of a number of temples in Israel apart from the Jerusalem Temple. The most important of these is the temple at SHILOH. The name *bêt,* house or temple, is used of this structure (1 Sam 1:7), as is *hêkāl* (1 Sam 1:9). No description of the structure is given, though it did house the ARK of the Covenant and did have a lamp and altar.

DAN and BETHEL are mentioned as sites of temples of the Northern Kingdom housing the golden calves set up as symbols of Yahweh's presence much like the Ark in Jerusalem (1 Kgs 12). Like Jerusalem, the temple at Bethel could be referred to as a *royal* chapel or temple (Amos 7:13). An altar is mentioned as part of the temple complex at Bethel (1 Kgs 12–13; 2 Kgs 23:15). No archaeological evidence of either temple has been located; however a large platform, perhaps setting off a sacred area was discovered at Dan, and a horned altar was recovered at that site.

Additional biblical sites which had sanctuaries, some of which may have had temples include GILGAL, Mizpah of Benjamin, HEBRON, NOB, and GIBEAH.

A most significant archaeological find was made at ARAD, that of a small Israelite sanctuary or temple dating to the period of the monarchy. This structure had a courtyard with a mudbrick altar (excavated intact). From the courtyard, one entered the holy room, a broad room type. Flanking the entrance to the broad room were two stone slabs, perhaps pillar bases. In the center of the wall opposite the entrance was a small room with a raised floor level and three steps. Two stone incense altars flanked the entrance to this "holy of holies." Still in this holy of holies was found a rounded stone stele, a standing stone or *maṣṣebah.* Also found in the temple area were a pottery incense stand and two stone offering tables.

Solomon's Temple. When one mentions the Temple in reference to the OT, the Solomonic Temple and its successors immediately come to mind. Unfortunately no architectural remains of the Solomonic Temple have been recovered. Surely any such remains, both of the platform and structures, lie buried beneath the later larger Herodian platform that forms the foundation of the present Harem es-Sharif, the Dome of the Rock, and the al-Asqa Mosque. However, a rather detailed description of the Temple is provided in 1 Kgs 6–8 and 2 Chr 2–4. Solomon extended the city of Jerusalem northward and built his Temple-palace complex on this northern part of Ophel or Mount ZION.

The Temple building is described as having interior dimensions of sixty cubits length, twenty cubits width, and thirty cubits height (about 105 ft. long, 35 ft. wide, and 52 ft. high if one assumes the royal cubit was used). The Temple was divided into three rooms: the *'ulam* or vestibule which was ten cubits long and may have been an inner open-air courtyard (PLATE 22). This vestibule was flanked on both sides by bronze pillars, Jacin and Boaz. From the *'ulam,* entry was gained to the *hêkāl,* the nave or holy place.

The *hêkāl* was forty cubits long and twenty cubits wide and had a ceiling thirty cubits high. Most of the cultic activity of the Temple took place here. The *hêkāl* had windows on both sides. It was panelled with cedar wood, carved with various plants and flowers. The doors to the *hêkāl* were made of cypress wood in four panels, carved with cherubim, palm trees, and flowers. The doors were covered with gold, as was the floor of the *hêkāl.* Furnishings of the *hêkāl* included an incense altar, ten lampstands, and the table for the bread of the presence. All these furnishings were covered with gold.

The third room, behind the *hêkāl,* was the *debir,* the inner sanctuary. It was a cube twenty cubits on a side. Although no explanation is given for the decreased height when compared with the *hêkāl,* probably a raised floor level and lowered ceiling were used. The walls and floor of the *debir* were overlaid with gold. The doors to the *debir* were made of olivewood carved with cherubim, palm trees and flowers and covered with gold like the door of the *hêkāl.* The *debir* held the Ark of the Covenant and two cherubim; the cherubim were ten cubits high, made of olive wood, and overlaid with gold. The walls of the *debir* were covered with carvings like the walls of the *hêkāl.*

The *hêkāl* and *debir* were surrounded by storerooms on the outside. The storerooms were three stories high and had thirty rooms on each story. Ezekiel describes the entire building as being set on a platform six cubits high (Ezek 41:8). The two pillars, Jacin and Boaz, were eighteen cubits high and had capitals an additional five cubits high. In the courtyard outside the Temple building stood the bronze sea at the southeast corner of the Temple, the altar of burnt offering, and ten bronze lavers and stands. Despite all the description of the interior of the Temple, no description of the exterior is given. Even the location of the altar is conjectural, some locating it in the center of the courtyard, others locating it opposite the bronze sea to the northeast of the Temple.

The description of this Temple suggests that much like Egyptian and Mesopotamian temples, the Israelite Temple was understood as the dwelling place of their God, Yahweh. Since it is commonly called *bêt Yahweh,* it is not surprising to find the stylized house plan: the *hêkāl* paralleled the courtyard and public portions of a house, while the *debir* paralleled the back room, the family quarters. also like the Egyptian temples, the art work suggests that the Temple represented Israel or the earth in microcosm. The Ark of the Covenant symbolized the presence of Yahweh in the midst of his people and by its very name reminded the people of the covenantal basis of their relationship to Yahweh.

The Solomonic Temple, with various changes when syncretistic cult objects were added, when reforms occurred, and when renovations took place, remained a focal part of worship through the monarchy. The Temple was ultimately destroyed with the invasion of Jerusalem by the Babylonians under Nebuchadrezzer in 587/6 B.C.E.

Zerubbabel's Temple. Immediately after the first exiles returned in 538 B.C.E., foundations for a new Temple were laid. However, this structure was not immediately completed. Indeed, once the foundations were begun, the project was halted for eighteen years. Only with the impetus of HAGGAI and ZECHARIAH was the Temple project again taken up in 520 B.C.E. The building was completed in 515 B.C.E. It is uncertain whether those elders who saw the foundations of the Second Temple and wept (Ezra 3:12) were crying over the much less elaborate structure, or over the fact that only foundations were then extant. No description of this Temple is given in the OT, and no architectural remains have been found. It was, however, the Temple of EZRA and NEHEMIAH, and the Temple of the MACCABEES.

Herod's Temple. HEROD the Great undertook a massive building program in Jerusalem and Judah. The crowning achievement of his building projects was the rebuilding of the Temple. Terms such as restoration or renovation do not begin to do justice to Herod's work. He greatly enlarged the Temple platform and rebuilt the Temple using the Greco-Roman architecture of his day. Much of the description of Herod's work is found in the works of the contemporary Jewish historian and apologist, JOSEPHUS (esp. *Ant* 11.11; and *BJ* 5.5). Josephus records that Herod had the old structure removed and a new Temple 100 cubits long and 100 cubits high built on the site of the former structure. One thousand priests were trained as stone masons and carpenters to do the work on the most holy portions of the temple. Surrounding the Temple was a paved courtyard filling the remainder of the platform. The whole was surrounded by walls and porticoes with colonnaded walkways. The columns of the porticoes were twenty-five cubits high and the porticoes were thirty cubits wide. The stones used in the construction of the Temple were twenty-five cubits long, eight high and twelve wide. Josephus further describes the various courts, each successively limiting access. The large open courtyard was the Court of the Gentiles, open to Jews and gentiles alike. An inner court, raised and enclosed by a stone partition three cubits high led to the Court of the Women and the Court of Israel. No gentiles were permitted beyond this partition; an inscription on the partition and written in Greek and Latin forbade foreigners to enter on pain of death. Beyond the partition one climbed fourteen steps to reach the inner court, itself surrounded by a wall twenty-five cubits high. This inner court was further divided into the two courts mentioned above. Nine gates led into this inner court, four each on the north and south, and one on the east. Women might enter the eastern portion of the court from a gate on the east or the easternmost gates on the north and south. They would enter the Court of the Women. Men might enter the inner court from any of the nine gates. The six westernmost gates led directly into the Court of Israel, west of the Court of the Women, and into which only the men might enter. An additional gate separated the Court of the Women from the Court of Israel. Nine of these gates were overlaid with silver and gold. The eastern gate, the one which led from the Court of the Gentiles into the Court of the Women as of Corinthian bronze and most elaborate. Closer yet to the Temple was the Court of the Priests, which included those precincts closest to the Temple building and the altar. As the name implies, only the priests were permitted into this area. The Temple building had an additional twelve steps leading up to it. The front portion of the Temple, the *'ulam* or vestibule, was 100 cubits high and 100 cubits wide. But behind the *'ulam,* the building was only sixty cubits wide. The *'ulam* had no exterior doors, but was overlaid with gold. The double doors leading from the *'ulam* into the temple were fifty-five cubits high and each sixteen cubits wide.

The interior measurements of the inner structure were sixty cubits long and twenty cubits wide, the main room or *hêkāl* was forty cubits long and the *debir* was twenty cubits long. The rooms were sixty cubits high. In the *hêkāl* was the altar of incense, the table of the bread of the presence, and the seven-branched lampstand. The *debir* was separated from the *hêkāl* by a curtain and had no furnishings.

Surrounding the Temple building on three sides were storerooms. Outside, the altar of burnt offering was placed in front of the Temple building. It was fifty cubits square and stood fifteen cubits high.

Recent excavations outside the Harem es-Sharif have confirmed much of Josephus's lavish description of Herod's Temple. The present platform covers nearly thirty-five acres. Some of the ashlar stones used in constructing the platform weigh over 300 tons, the largest yet discovered is forty-six feet long, ten feet wide, ten feet high, and weighs approximately 415 tons. Excavations along the outside of the western wall have recovered a paved street which followed the wall and continued to the Pool of Siloam. At the southwestern corner of the wall an arched stairway led from this street up to the colonnaded portico known as the royal portico. An arched bridge led from the western hill across the Tyropeon Valley and provided entrance to the Temple courtyards from the west. Along the southern wall of the platform was a large open plaza with several sets of monumental steps leading up to the Huldah gates which gave access to the Temple courtyard.

Undoubtedly, Herod's Temple was the most elaborate of the three Jewish Temples built on this site. It also had the shortest life-span. Begun about 20 B.C.E., the Herodian Temple was destroyed by Titus in 70 C.E.

Role of the Temple in Israelite Worship. The Temple was the chief place of Yahweh's presence after the establishment of the monarchy. It became the center of worship for the kingdom. Although the Temple was the major place of worship, it was never the sole place of worship. Altars, shrines, and sanctuaries existed independently of the Temple. JOSIAH's reform was probably the first attempt to centralize worship in one location, and it apparently failed. Nevertheless, after the building of Solomon's Temple, it held a unique place in Israelite worship. As the location of the Ark of the Covenant, the Temple marked the special place of Yahweh's presence when he appears on earth. Even the names *bêt* and *hêkāl* indicate a dwelling place. Although Yahweh was never considered limited to the Temple, it was the place of special presence and access to him. The psalmist was clearly attempting to show both the presence and the transcendence of God in Ps 11:4:

> The Lord is in his holy temple
> The Lord's throne is in heaven.

The DEUTERONOMISTIC HISTORIAN, wrestling with this same issue, regularly describes the Temple not as Yahweh's dwelling place, but as the place Yahweh causes his name to dwell.

Both the TABERNACLE and the TENT OF MEETING are described as portable shrines closely associated with Yahweh's presence before the monarchy. As such, much the same terminology is used in reference to them as to Temple. The Tabernacle especially is described as the predecessor of the Temple, the portable structure that housed the Ark of the Covenant.

The cultic activity in the Temple is regularly described as taking place "in Yahweh's presence" (*liphnê Yahweh*). Furthermore, attendance at pilgrim festivals was expected for all men in Israel regularly (Deut 16:16); at such festivals the worshippers were "to appear before the Lord your God," that is to come into God's presence at the Temple. Many psalms describe the ephiphany or theophany of Yahweh apparently in the worship itself (e.g., Pss 29; 97).

It was Yahweh's presence, symbolized originally by the Ark in the Solomonic Temple, that gave the Temple its status. Ezekiel's vision of the departure of the glory from the Temple (Ezek 8–11) set the context for the destruction of the Temple because Yahweh had already departed or abandoned his Temple. He was no longer present in the Temple. Likewise, Ezekiel's vision of the restored city and Temple (40–48) describes the return of Yahweh's glory (43:2-5). Once it returned, the outer gates were closed, not to be reopened (Ezek 44:2) so that Yahweh's presence was assured there for forever (Ezek 43:7). Thus neither Zerubbabel's nor Herod's Temple required a rebuilt Ark to ensure Yahweh's presence (cf. Jer 3:16-17). The Temple and ultimately the city came to represent that presence, as Ezekiel's name for Jerusalem implies: "And the name of the city henceforth shall be, *Yahweh shâmmâh,* Yahweh is there" (Ezek 48:35).

See also RELIGION OF ISRAEL; RELIGIONS OF THE ANCIENT NEAR EAST.

Bibliography. Y. Aharoni, *The Archaeology of the Land of Israel* and "Temples, Semitic," *IDBSupp*; G. A. Barrois, "Temples," *IDB*; M. Ben-Dov, "Temple of Herod," *IDBSupp*; A. Biran, ed., *Temples and High Places in Biblical Times*; R. E. Clements, *God and Temple*; M. Haran, *Temples and Temple Service in Ancient Israel*; F. Josephus, *The Antiquities of the Jews* and *The Wars of the Jews*; H. H. Nelson, "The Egyptian Temple," *BARead* 1:147-58; A. L. Oppenheim, "The Mesopotamian Temple," *BARead* 1:158-69; J. Quellett, "Temple of Solomon," *IDBSupp*; J. Ruffle, *The Egyptians*; W. T. Stinespring, "Temple, Jerusalem," *IDB*; G. E. Wright, "The Temple in Palestine-Syria," *BARead* 1:169-84; Y. Yadin, ed., *Jerusalem Revealed*.

—JOEL F. DRINKARD, JR.

• **Temptation in the New Testament.** In the Bible temptation is seen in two distinct ways—God tempting humans or humans tempting God. (The Heb. and Gk. words for temptation can also be translated "test" or "put to proof.") In the OT, God often puts the faith of human beings to the test. One of the best examples of this is found in Gen 22:1-19 where God puts Abraham to the test. He ordered Abraham to offer up his only son Isaac on the altar of sacrifice. In the NT, Abraham's act of faith is often praised (cf. Heb 11). God's testing always has a positive purpose to increase the faith of the believers or to point out areas of weakness. God never tries to lead anyone to do evil.

In later Judaism, Satan appears as one who seduces to evil. In the story of Job, the story line of the book deals with the problem of the testing of the righteous and the suffering of the faithful. The test demands complete obedience. Thus Job could say at the end of his testing: "I know that thou canst do all things and that no purpose of thine can be thwarted" (42:2). In a state of obedience, Job came to know the will of God even if he did not understand everything about his great suffering.

In the OT, one also encounters the concept of man tempting God. At Rephidim, the people complained bitterly against Moses because of their lack of water. Moses replied, "Why do you find fault with me? Why do you put the Lord to the proof?" (Exod 17:2). Testing God expresses itself in a failure to trust God and his salvific purposes. It is to turn one's back upon his leadership and desire to go one's own way.

Thus in Deut 6:16, the first commandment is explained with the words, "You shall not put the Lord your God to the test." If one truly loves God, then one cannot reject his leadership nor ignore his ways. The believer should not doubt the power of God as has been revealed to human beings.

In the NT, testing still has its positive overtones. God does not lead anyone into temptation (Jas 1:12-15). James traced temptation back to a person's own human desires. The NT places the desire for evil within the individual. A personification of evil is used rarely in the NT. The "tempter" appears in 1 Thess 3:5, "For this reason, when I could bear it no longer, I sent that I might know your faith, for fear that somehow the tempter had tempted you and that our labor would be in vain." Paul described Satan by name as the tempter in 1 Cor 7:5, "lest Satan tempt you through lack of self-control."

Testing in the NT is often viewed in terms of persecution and martyrdom. Some Christians were tempted to turn from the faith during periods of persecution. Here the word takes on a new nuance. Peter warned against turning from the faith, "Beloved, think it not strange concerning the fiery trial which is to try you" (1 Pet 4:12, KJV). In the NT one can also try God as in the case of Ananias and Sapphira in Acts 5:9. Peter declared this in fervent tones: "How is it that you have agreed together to tempt the Spirit of the Lord?"

The most significant use of the word temptation in the NT is in reference to the life of Jesus. The writer of Hebrews often speaks of Jesus' temptation: "For because he himself has suffered and been tempted, he is able to help those who are tempted" (2:18). In another place he states that Jesus as High Priest is "one who in every respect has been tempted as we are, yet without sin" (4:15). Two vital points are made by the writer: Jesus Christ is like all other human beings in that he was tempted; He was unlike other people in that he did not give in to temptation and sin.

In the synoptic Gospels, we encounter the TEMPTATION OF JESUS immediately following his baptism and just before the beginning of his public ministry. Mark did not list the three temptations found in varied order in Matthew and Luke. The temptation accounts were placed at a very important point in the Gospel story. They deal with the messianic task of Jesus. At his baptism that mission was underlined by the divine voice from heaven. The basic question in the temptation of Jesus was whether he would be obedient to his messianic task. The temptation narratives answered with a resounding "yes." The three tests recorded in Matthew and Luke were designed to bring Jesus to a state of disobedience.

The first temptation had the aim of tempting Jesus to use his power for purposes foreign to his mission. Jesus replied to Satan with a quotation from Deut 8:3. Jesus' source of power is in God—not in some independent expression of it. The second temptation invited using his power for selfish purposes. Jesus answered with Deut 6:16. Selfish or personal interests would not be in the will of God.

The third temptation was more direct. Satan asked Jesus

in essence to turn from obeying God and follow him. In quoting Deut 6:13, Jesus affirmed his alliance to God and dismissed Satan. From Luke 4:13, one would gather that Jesus found many temptations or trials throughout his life. The only other one specifically highlighted is found in the Gethsemane narrative at the end of his life. Jesus' prayer there reflects a time of trial and difficulty.

See also PERSECUTION IN THE NEW TESTAMENT; PERSECUTION IN THE OLD TESTAMENT; SIN; SUFFERING IN THE NEW TESTAMENT; SUFFERING IN THE OLD TESTAMENT; TEMPTATION IN THE OLD TESTAMENT; TEMPTATION OF JESUS.

—JAMES L. BLEVINS

• **Temptation in the Old Testament.** Putting someone to the test in order to determine the reliability or faithfulness of the one tested. The primary verb is *nissâ* (Gen 22:1, God tests ABRAHAM; Exod 17:2, 7, etc., the people test God), from which the noun *massâ* (Deut 4:34, God's testing of the Egyptians at the time of the EXODUS) derives. In Mal 3:15 the prophet quotes those who claim that evildoers escape punishment even when they put God to the test; the verb there is *bāḥan,* a word that also means to test or prove or try out.

The chief instance of temptation in the OT (though the word is not used) is the challenge of the snake or SERPENT (Heb. *nāḥāš*) to the first human pair: "Did God really say that you should not eat from the fruit of *any* tree in the Garden?" (Gen 3:1). The woman responded (though the man was also standing with her at the scene, 3:6) that God had commanded that they not eat from the fruit of the tree in the middle of the garden and that they not even touch it. This powerful story of the first human sin shows that temptation to sin arises from within the person (the fruit was beautiful, was good for food, and promised to give wisdom) and also from outside the person (the snake offers clever and misleading arguments designed to lead the person astray). One tempts oneself, and one finds oneself tempted.

More striking are the numerous references to God's putting persons to the test, seeking to determine whether or not they will stand up and remain faithful to the covenant demands when trials and difficulties arise. Here, the dominant story is God's testing of Abraham by calling upon him to offer his son ISAAC as a human sacrifice on a mountain that God will point out to him (Gen 22, called in Jewish tradition the Akedah, the "binding" of Isaac [cf. 22:9]). Abraham demonstrates trust and confidence in God to the very end, as is anticipated in his word to Isaac as they climb the mountain: "God will provide the lamb for the burnt offering, my son."

Israel is warned not to put God to the test by its apostasy or its complaints about God's governance and guidance (Deut 6:16, etc.), but God's testings are designed to strengthen the faith of Israel, just as divine DISCIPLINE (Heb. *mûsār*) in the form of trials and judgments are so designed. The Psalms of Lament show, however, that the faithful in Israel were not cowed by such warnings. When things went wrong they were ready to offer their complaints directly to God in the expectation that God would heed and deal justly with them. "Should not the Judge of the whole earth do justice?" (Gen 18:25).

See also DISCIPLINE; ETHICS IN THE OLD TESTAMENT.

—WALTER HARRELSON

• **Temptation of Jesus.** The story of Jesus' temptation is told briefly in Mark 1:12-13, and more elaborately in Matt 4:1-11 and Luke 4:1-13. If we had only Mark's Gospel, we would have little idea what it meant for Jesus to be "tempted" or "tested" by Satan. All we are told is that the Spirit that came on Jesus at his baptism thrust him out to the "desert" (presumably the Judean desert just west of the Jordan River and the Dead Sea), where he stayed forty days. Three things (none of them further explained) took place in connection with this forty-day stay: Jesus was "tempted by Satan"; he was "with the beasts"; and "angels were serving him."

Many questions are left unanswered when we read Mark alone. The stories of the temptation in Matthew and Luke (whether by intention or not) fill in gaps in the Markan version. Matthew handles the story dramatically. First he supplies the important information that the forty-day period was a time of fasting for Jesus (4:2). Then he brings "the tempter" on the scene with a favorite word of his: "approached," or "came near" (4:3); the temptation ends in v. 11a with the phrase, "Then the devil left him." When it was over, angels "approached," or "came near" to Jesus, and began serving him (v. 11b). Within the narrative (vv. 3-11a), Matthew introduces three specific challenges from the devil to Jesus, thus explaining Mark's "tempted by Satan" as a three-part dialogue. The challenges are: (1) "If you are the Son of God, command these stones [in the desert] to become loaves of bread" (v. 3); (2) "If you are the Son of God, throw yourself down [from the pinnacle of the Temple in Jerusalem]" (v. 6); and (3) "All these things [i.e., the things seen from "a very high mountain"] I will give you, if you fall down and worship me" (v. 9). The temptation is a visionary experience, for the scene changes with each new challenge: Jesus and the devil are in the Judean desert, then suddenly at the Temple in Jerusalem, finally on a high mountain of unspecified location. Although he is challenged as "Son of God" (cf. "beloved Son" in the voice at Jesus' baptism), Jesus responds not by invoking his divine sonship, but as a good Jew, by quoting scripture (i.e., Deut 8:3 in v. 4; Deut 6:16 in v. 7; Deut 6:13 in v. 10). The texts he quotes are not "messianic" texts (i.e., prophecies about him as Messiah), but texts centered on "the Lord your God" (cf. Matt 22:37 ‖ Mark12:30 ‖ Luke 10:27). Jesus resisted the devil not with weapons that were his alone as anointed "Son of God," but with weapons available to every pious Jew of his time (and later to every Christian believer). This is the main point of the temptation story as Matthew tells it. With scripture Jesus vanquished the enemy, and the fast was broken as angels came on the scene to bring him food.

Luke's account is very similar to Matthew's except for the order of the three challenges from the devil; the second and third challenges are reversed. The movement in Luke is an upward movement from the desert to a mountain and finally to Jerusalem. Luke's account is geographically realistic because the journey from the Jordan River to Jerusalem is in fact a steep climb (from 800 ft. below sea level to 2,500 ft. above in less than twenty-five mi.). The journey to Jerusalem in Luke's temptation story foreshadows the decisive last journey to Jerusalem that dominates the final two-thirds of his Gospel. When Jesus arrives in Jerusalem in the temptation story, the question raised is that of death in Jerusalem (vv. 9-13; cf. 13:33), and the implied answer is "Not now, but later" (v. 13b, "until an opportune time"; cf. 22:53b). In Matthew at the end of the temptation Jesus was in the desert, where angels had to come and terminate the fast, but in Luke the story ends in Jerusalem. No angels were needed to bring food, for Jesus was now in the city, and it was from Jerusalem—not the desert—that he "returned in the power of the Spirit into Galilee" (v. 14).

In both Matthew and Luke, the question persists, "How did the Gospel writers gain access to such a three-part dialogue?" If they (or the source they used) did not invent it, the only possible answer is that their information came from Jesus. If this is the case, it appears that what Jesus really wanted to say to his disciples is contained in the three scripture quotations from Deuteronomy with which he put the devil to flight. The temptation story is then not a legend told to glorify Jesus, but a kind of triple pronouncement story told for the sake of the three words of wisdom it contains. Jesus' disciples—and all who read the story—will learn that they must not "live by bread alone," that they must "worship the Lord your God and him only shall you serve," and that they must "not tempt the Lord your God." The brief and curious reference in Mark's Gospel has become in Matthew and Luke the vehicle for significant teaching about piety and worship among those who would follow Jesus.

See also SATAN IN THE NEW TESTAMENT; SCRIPTURE IN THE NEW TESTAMENT; TEMPTATION IN THE NEW TESTAMENT.

Bibliography. E. Best, *The Temptation and the Passion*; B. Gerhardsson, *The Testing of God's Son (Matt 4:1-11 and Parallels)*; J. A. Kirk, "The Messianic Role of Jesus and the Temptation Narrative: A Contemporary Perspective," *EvQ* 44 (1972): 11-29, 91-102; J. R. Michaels, *Servant and Son: Jesus in Parable and Gospel*; P. Pokorny, "The Temptation Stories and Their Intention," *NTS* 20/2 (Jan 1974): 115-27.

—J. RAMSEY MICHAELS

• **Ten Commandments.** The religious and moral guidelines received by MOSES atop Mount Sinai, recorded in slightly differing forms in their two listings in the Hebrew Bible (Exod 20:2-17; Deut 5:6-21). This short, pithy list of prohibitions and positive commandments sums up many of the requirements of Israelite faith in God. The text is quoted in part in the NT (Matt 19:16-22; Mark 10:17-22; Luke 18:18-30) and in a few places in the OT (Hos 4:2; Ps 81:9 [Heb: 81:10]). The commandments are not LAW in the full sense of the term, for they are not a criminal code or a collection of precedents to guide the conduct of judges and elders, as are many of the legal collections found elsewhere in the OT (Exod 21–23; Deut 12–26, etc.). They are rather the background and foundation of Israelite law.

Origin. The commandments are said to have been received directly from God by Moses. Their contents are not unique to Israel, although two of the commandments lack any clear parallel in the ancient world (the commandment against image making and the commandment to observe the SABBATH). But there is nothing closely akin to this collection as a collection, presented as absolute demand from the deity, and requiring unswerving obedience by every individual Israelite as well as by the community as a whole.

Nothing in the original short form of the commandments, which can be recovered with fair confidence, requires a date later than the time of Moses. But most scholars hold that the earliest likely date is the time of the organizing of the life of the tribes in Canaan under JOSHUA or his successors (1200–1100 B.C.E.). Many prefer a date at the time of the kingship over North Israel and Judah (tenth or ninth century B.C.E.).

Form. The commandments, without the opening prologue, "I am the Lord your God who brought you out of the land of Egypt, out of the house of slavery," have the form of an opening prohibition followed by a verb and concluding with an object: "You shall not have any other Gods besides me"; "you shall not bear false witness." Some of the commandments are expanded at a later time, giving explanations of just what the commandment in question means. Others are shortened so as to consist of the negation plus a single verb, but no object: "You shall not kill." "You shall not commit adultery." "You shall not steal." This process of addition and contraction probably extended over many years. In the process, a different explanation was offered in Deut 5:12-15 for the observance of the Sabbath than is found in Exod 20:8-11. DEUTERONOMY stresses the need that human beings and animals have for rest, physical rest from labors, while Exodus puts the emphasis upon God's having observed the Sabbath rest at the time of creation (Gen 2:1-3).

Whether the Ten Commandments were shaped through use in the home and in the larger family units or were developed for regular recitation at the centers of religious life in early Israel remains a debated question. In all likelihood, both the public use of the commandments in connection with acts of worship and their local and family use contributed to their shape and to the changes that occurred over time.

Numbering. There is great diversity in the numbering of the commandments. The diversity arises largely as a result of different ways of numbering the commandment to worship no other god or gods and the commandment to make no carved IMAGES. The Jewish, Roman Catholic, and Lutheran traditions make a single commandment of these, while Orthodox and Reformed traditions number them as two. The commandment against coveting is sometimes divided into two commandments in order to retain the number ten. Jewish tradition has numbered as the first commandment the assertion, "I am the Lord your God [or "I the Lord am your God"] who brought you out of the land of Egypt, out of the house of slavery" (or "bondage"), and does not divide the commandment against coveting.

Contents. The numbering used here follows Orthodox and Reformed tradition. The commandments may be divided into four groups: God's absolute demands (commandments 1, 2, 3, against the worship of other gods, against IDOLATRY, and against the misuse of the divine name); God's basic institutions (commandments 4 and 5, against the misuse of the Sabbath and the mistreatment of parents); fundamental personal demands (commandments 6 and 7, against killing and adultery); and fundamental social demands (commandments 8, 9, and 10, against stealing, bearing false witness, and coveting). A few comments follow on each of these groupings.

God's Absolute Demands. Ancient Near Eastern religious communities were familiar with the notion of a highest deity, the god who had the dominant place in the pantheon. The powers of the lesser gods were claimed by this highest god, according to texts that have survived, showing that while there was not MONOTHEISM in most of these societies, there was clearly a recognition that not all gods had the same claim on the life of the worshiping community or the individual. But in Israel the claim was an exclusive one: the deity Yahweh. Israel's God, was not to have any rivals at all.

This demand for the worship of one unique God no doubt allowed for the fact that there were other deities worshiped in the land, deities whose powers seemed real enough. But Israel was to demonstrate loyalty to the one God, the deity who brought the people from the land of Egypt, led them through the wilderness, and eventually brought them into possession of the land that God was giving them.

Most striking in this commandment is the insistence that there is a unitary divine being; deity is not divided. There is God, and there are the creations of God—and there are no other kinds of entity to be found in the whole of the creation. In time, this form of monotheism developed in Israel and challenged the prevailing notion of dark powers that threatened the creation and all its creatures, including the human community. No demons or devils existed apart from such powers as God the Creator had called into being. Such powers might not be doing God's bidding, but they were still creatures of God, not some divine or demonic beings outside the range of God's control.

The commandment against idolatry probably stems from the recognition that nothing in the creation was able adequately to represent the deity, the unique creator of all that had being. Only the human being, created in the divine image, could be a kind of representation of God, sharing responsibility with God for the creation, seeing to its needs, serving as God's agent. The Israelites must surely have known that representations of the gods were not necessarily understood as identical with those deities. Even so, such representations were capable of creating the illusion in the community of Israel that Yahweh could be manipulated for the community's or the individual's good, and that was an unacceptable view for Israel's theological thought.

The third commandment is also striking. It rules out using God's name with the intention of forcing God's hand. Ancient Israel recognized that the power to pronounce God's name, for blessing or for cursing, was a weighty power. The use of God's name to do violence to others or to further one's own personal ends was ruled out by this commandment. It is clear that such a commandment is always of great value in any time or place. This is a central understanding of Judaism and of Christianity.

God's Basic Institutions. The commandment to observe the Sabbath is unique in Israel. The origin of the Sabbath remains obscure. It was not a day of ill omen but a day of rest and rejoicing in the Lord; thus, it cannot be derived directly from days of ill omen known from Babylonia. It did not fall on the phases of the moon, and thus cannot be related to the moon month in any direct way. It seems not to have had any connection with market days in the ancient world, for there is no evidence that these occurred with this seven-day regularity. The number seven is prominent in the festival life of ancient Near Eastern peoples; thus it may be that seven-day festivities and seven-week intervals between festivities played some part in the development of the Sabbath.

Striking indeed is the demand that every seventh day the community of Israel is to cease from its labors and rest. No positive requirements are set for the Sabbath; the only demand is that one stop doing what one normally does and rest. Rest is as much a demand of God as is work; alternation between work and rest gives meaning and depth to both.

The commandment to honor one's parents has in view primarily one's aged parents. The commandment makes clear again that human life consists of more than productive labor. When parents are too old to be productive members of the community, the meaning of their life has not ceased. They are to be honored and respected. Ancient Israel knew the conflicts that develop between the generations, the struggle that the young have in claiming a place among the adults and the struggle that the elderly have in making way for the adults who come behind them. This commandment underscores the requirement that the life of parents be respected at all levels of their existence.

God's Fundamental Personal Demands. Human beings are not to take human life, for life belongs to God. Gen 9:6 underscores the point, even if that text knows no other way to assure that human life be respected than to say that if a human being sheds the blood of another, the killer's own life is forfeited. The verb used in the sixth commandment, *rṣḥ,* does not mean "murder" in the strict sense, but it does point to acts of homicide outside the context of accidental killing or the taking of human life allowed in ancient Israelite law.

This commandment against willful homicide is of enormous importance for the moral life, for it flatly rules out the "right" of any person to take the life of another human being. Life belongs to God, and God will see to the preservation of life and to its enhancement. Human beings are charged to do the same.

The commandment against ADULTERY can best be understood as a prohibition of sexual violence—whether it be violence of the sort called rape or violence against the institution of the family. In ancient Israel there was a double standard in sexual matters; married men committed adultery when they had sexual relations with the wife of another man, while a married woman was guilty of adultery if she had relations with anyone other than her husband. The young woman was to refrain from sexual relations until the time of her betrothal and/or marriage. More sexual license was tolerated among young men, it seems, although the wisdom literature is full of warnings against their consorting with loose women.

Jesus reminds his hearers that behind the act of adultery is lust in the heart. The act of adultery harms more persons, but the individual is already caught up in the damage that adultery brings when lust begins to take over and threatens to lead to unfaithfulness. And the apostle Paul flatly declares that relations with a prostitute, like any other sexual union, creates a unity of one flesh (1 Cor 6:15-20). Thus there is no such thing as casual sex for Paul. The double standard disappears with such an assertion as that.

God's Fundamental Social Demands. The last three commandments are concerned with the life of the community. The commandment against stealing had a special poignancy in a time when most of the population had very few goods. The loss of a knife in ancient Israel would have been a very severe loss, for with the large knife made of iron one would chop and shape wood, butcher farm animals, do other household tasks, and also wage war—using the knife as one's sword. Life extended into the goods of the family. This commandment is not talking about the poor person's taking some morsel of food from the crop of the wealthy; the poor were to be permitted to gather up a bit of food to stay their hunger. But for ancient Israel, the protection of life required also that property be protected; no social order was possible otherwise.

Similarly, bearing false witness against one's neighbor meant primarily giving false testimony before a judge or before the elders acting as judges. It was not an invitation to people to do harm by spreading even true derogatory tidbits about a neighbor. The community's stability and health demanded that the courts not be corrupted by the telling of lies or the use of bribes to get witnesses to perjure themselves.

Finally, the commandment against coveting seeks to get at the will, the disposition of persons, as well as at their deeds. The word translated "to covet," *ḥāmad,* sometimes means not only to have an inordinate desire for something but to take steps to get the desired thing. But not always does the word have that active a meaning. It can also simply refer to the hankering for the life or the goods of someone else. In Deut 5:21 a parallel word is also used, "to desire" (Heb. *'āwâ*), showing that it is basically a commandment against being eaten up with the desire for what one does not have. In contemporary affluent societies the commandment would perhaps best refer to that insatiable longing for more and more—beyond any human need.

Influence. The Ten Commandments have had an enormous influence on Western societies, and indeed on virtually the whole of civilization. Other societies have equivalent summary codes of conduct, but this concise drawing together of commandments that tie together God's exclusive claim upon the community and its individuals with God's insistence that certain forms of conduct are ruled out in principle, not to be done under any circumstances, has a distinctive character. The commandments were surely developed for the life of the people of Israel, but there is nothing in them that restricts them to Israel alone.

The commandments also demand that the community define just what these prohibitions mean and aim at. What is justifiable homicide? When has the Sabbath been violated? When have aged parents been mistreated? The whole system of positive law and of the administration of justice has to be developed. But certain absolute demands are laid upon the community and not open to challenge. Not everything is permitted to human beings. Human freedom is defined for ancient Israel and for early Christianity in part at least in relation to these prohibitions given by God.

See also ETHICS IN THE OLD TESTAMENT; IDOLATRY; LAW IN THE OLD TESTAMENT; SABBATH; TORAH.

Bibliography. A. Alt, *Essays on Old Testament History and Religion*; B. F. Childs, *Exodus. A Commentary*; W. Harrelson, *The Ten Commandments and Human Rights*; E. Nielsen, *The Ten Commandments in New Perspective.*

—WALTER HARRELSON

• **Tent of Meeting.** The tent of meeting, Heb. *'ohel mō'ēd,* was a shrine of ancient Israel probably authentically belonging to the presettlement period. Although the early sources mention the tent of meeting in only a few passages, the references do suggest a portable shrine such as is well known from later nomadic tribes of Arabia. References to the tent of meeting in the priestly source are usually considered later and treat the tent of meeting as a part of the TABERNACLE structure, unlike the earlier sources. Only the earlier referenes to the tent of meeting will be discussed in this article.

The tent of meeting was located "outside the camp, far off from the camp" in Exod 33:7. This location contrasts with that of the priestly Tabernacle, said to be in the center of the camp (Num 2). By contrasting the tent of meeting with the Tabernacle, one can note several theological features of both. The Tabernacle's location in the center of the camp of the Hebrews emphasizes God's presence in the midst of his people. Yet the holiness of God is also stressed by the Tabernacle with its various courts and structures separating the people from God's holiness. The holy of holies was so holy that only Aaron as high priest might enter it, and then only on the DAY OF ATONEMENT (Lev 16). Thus the Tabernacle represented both the presence of God in the midst of the people and also the holiness of God which separated him from the people. The word for Tabernacle, *mishkān,* "dwelling," emphasizes the concept of God's presence dwelling with his people.

The tent of meeting, located outside the camp suggests the distance between God and his people. In its context in Exod 33, the introduction of the tent of meeting immediately after the sin of the golden calf (Exod 32) and God's rebuke that he will not go up with the people lest he destroy them (Exod 33:3-5) gives a rationale for the distance. God's holiness and the people's sinfulness are the cause of the distance between God and the people. But the presence of God is also evident in the tent of meeting passages. It is a tent of *meeting,* a tent where God meets with Moses and with the people ("and every one who sought the Lord would go out to the tent of meeting"[Exod 33:7]). And the tent of meeting does accompany the people through the wilderness.

The tent of meeting is the place of THEOPHANY. God appears at the tent of meeting in a pillar of cloud at the door of the tent. Apparently only Moses was permitted the most intimate contact with God in the tent. Unlike the Tabernacle, the tent of meeting is not a place of God's dwelling, but a place of his appearing.

The tent of meeting was the place where God placed some of his spirit on the seventy elders causing them to prophesy (Num 11:16-30), and the place where God rebuked Aaron and Miriam (Num 12). It was at the tent of meeting that Joshua was commissioned and that authority was transferred from Moses to Joshua (Deut 31:14-23). It is of interest that Joshua is the only person other than Moses mentioned as entering the tent (Exod 33:11).

The Tabernacle represents the priestly theology and its personnel are priests, chiefly Aaron and his descendants. Moses has little role, if any, in the Tabernacle. The tent of meeting represents a nonpriestly theology. No priest attends it. The people can come out to the tent when they seek Yahweh, perhaps a reference to oracles. The elders prophesy there. The reference to an oracular function and to prophesying may suggest a prophetic theology underlying the tent. Since Moses is understood as the prototypical prophet, the appearance of God to Moses face to face (Exod 33:9, 11) in the tent would fit the understanding of the prophet as God's spokesperson.

See also TABERNACLE.

—JOEL F. DRINKARD, JR.

• **Terah.** [ter'uh] The name of an important man and place in the OT. A descendant of Shem, Terah became the father of Abram (ABRAHAM), NAHOR, and HARAN (Gen 11:27) and later still an ancestor of JESUS of Nazareth (Luke 3:34). He must have originally lived in and around UR of the Chaldees, a major city in southern Mesopotamia (PLATE 2). (Although Gordon, Stigers, and a few others have argued for a more northerly site for this city, the northerly location has not as yet been generally accepted.) While he was there, he apparently continued to worship several different deities (Josh 24:2). During this same time, Abraham, his eldest son received a call from God to go to CANAAN (Gen 15:7; Neh 9:7; Acts 7:2-4). Thus, Terah packed up his whole family, including Abraham (and his wife Sarah), and Lot (Haran's orphaned son) and journeyed toward HARAN, a city in northern Mesopotamia located about halfway between Ur and Canaan (Gen 11:31-32). Although no reason is stated, when Terah reached Haran, he settled down and apparently remained there until his death. However, God continued to speak to his son and thus Abraham journeyed on toward Canaan proper (Gen 12:1-3). Finally, some sixty years later, Terah died at 205 years of age (Gen 11:32).

Artwork by Margaret Jordan Brown

Artist's conception of the Tabernacle, a more elaborate and more permanent version of the Tent of Meeting.

Terah was also the name of an unidentified encampment of the Israelites during their wilderness wanderings. Although it has not yet been located, it was apparently situated between two other unknown sites, Tahath and Mithkah (Num 33:27-28).

See also ABRAHAM.

Bibliography. C. H. Gordon, ''Abraham and the Merchants of Ur,'' *JNES* 17 (1958): 28-31; H. G. Stigers, *A Commentary on Genesis*; B. Vawter, *On Genesis: A New Reading*.

—HARRY B. HUNT, JR.

• **Teraphim.** [ter'uh-fim] Household gods; busts, masks, or full-figured representations of the human form whose primary function was to represent the family or clan deity. The story of MICAH and his SHRINE with its teraphim (Judg 17:5) and of King Josiah's destruction of the teraphim at the shrines suggest that they were used in worship (2 Kgs 23:24).

Ezekiel speaks of the king of Babylon using the teraphim in divination (Ezek 21:21). How the teraphim were used is unclear. It has been suggested that the teraphim were masks used as a blindfold for the priest, who chose a lot or arrow at random.

Rachel's theft of Laban's household gods (Gen 31:19) has led to a variety of interpretations. Based on NUZI parallels, it has been argued that Laban had adopted Jacob, making him heir both to property and the role of patriarch. Subsequently, Laban had sons of his own who displaced Jacob in the latter role. If Laban had no will, possession of the teraphim would strengthen Jacob's claim. On the other hand, Rachel's action may be seen simply as an attempt to take familiar representations of the clan deities to a strange land. Thus she had taken the family's most sacred heirloom.

The action of David's wife MICHAL in using a teraphim to simulate David's presence in a bed suggests that some teraphim could be quite large in size (1 Sam 19:13).

See also IDOLATRY; MICAH.

—JOHN H. TULLOCK

• **Tertullus.** [tuhr-tuhl'uhs] This person appears only in one brief scene in the NT (Acts 24:1-23). He was a spokesman for the Jewish authorities who come from Jerusalem to Caesarea to press charges against PAUL. The name Tertullus is a commonly used diminutive form of the Roman Tertius. The name hints, but does not absolutely establish, that he was Roman. Also, his manner of speaking may suggest this (cf. Acts 24:2, 5, 9). In some instances, however, he used the first person plural which would seem, on the surface at least, to identify him with the Jews (cf. 24:6a). Such a conclusion would be reinforced if 24:6b-8a were accepted as genuine (though manuscript evidence is limited).

His flattering style and his claims that Paul was a troublemaker, a member of a questionable sect, and a threat to the Temple did not enable him to win his case.

See also FELIX; PAUL.

—ROBERT O. BYRD

• **Testaments of the Twelve Patriarchs.** The *Testaments of the Twelve Patriarchs* purport to record the last words of the twelve sons of JACOB. The work consists of twelve testaments, one for each son, which generally follow a basic pattern. Just prior to his death, the PATRIARCH gathers his family around him. He reflects upon some aspect of his life, usually a sin. He then gives a series of moral exhortations, usually connected with his specific sin, some kind of exaltation of LEVI and Judah, and predictions about the future of Israel. Finally, his death and burial are recorded. There are some variations from this basic pattern, however. In *TJos* the recounting of the patriarch's early life is expanded considerably, whereas in *TAsher* it is replaced by a teaching on the two ways. The sin of the speaker is omitted in *TIss, TNaph, TAsher, TJos,* and *TBenj*. Also, in *TLevi, TNaph,* and *TJos,* visions add an important dimension. The *Testaments* represent a blending of several different literary types. They are a classic example of the "testament" form (cf. Gen 49; Deut 33), yet they also show an affinity with "rewritten Bible" techniques (cf. JUBILEES; *1 Enoch*; *1QapGen*; *LAB*) and APOCALYPTIC LITERATURE (cf. *1 Enoch*; *TMos*).

The perspective of the *Testaments* is primarily moral in orientation. There is an emphasis on obedience to the Law (cf. *TLevi* 13:1-3), but little concern for specific precepts. Rather, the focus is on general moral virtues, such as chastity or brotherly love. Similarly, sins are construed not as breaking the law but as moral failures, such as sexual promiscuity or envy. The moral orientation is seen most clearly perhaps in *TAsher,* which consists almost entirely of a treatise on the two ways which are available for people to follow: the good way, which is the way of God, and the evil way, which is the way of Beliar. Also important in the *Testaments* is its strong priestly orientation: Levi is especially blessed and honored (cf. *TReu* 6:5-12). The *Testaments* also affirm a dual messianic expectation: the kingship from Judah and the priesthood from Levi, with the kingship being subject to the priesthood (*TJud* 21:1-5). The eschatological hope of the *Testaments* also includes resurrection (*TJud* 25:1) and the New Jerusalem (*TDan* 5:12; cf. Rev 21).

The questions of date and composition of the *Testaments* are among the most complex and controversial in all of APOCRYPHAL LITERATURE. Two types of factors contribute to the problem: textual and theological. The textual situation of the *Testaments* borders on the chaotic. They exist in their entirety in Greek and in an Armenian translation of the Greek, although the classification of these manuscripts into different recensions is debated. A *Testament of Naphtali* and fragments of a *Testament of Judah* are extant in medieval Hebrew; these testaments bear little relationship to the Greek *Testaments,* but an unpublished Hebrew fragment from Qumran Cave 4 may be related to this *Testament of Naphtali.* Other fragments from Cave 4 confirm that an Aramaic *Testament of Levi,* apparently related in some way to *TLevi,* existed at Qumran, as well as, apparently, an Aramaic *TJud, TJos,* and *TBen*, and a Hebrew *TJud,* although the identification of these fragments is disputed.

The theological situation of the *Testaments* is also confusing. The *Testaments* are about Jewish patriarchs and reflect Jewish concerns (e.g., the Law, the levitical priesthood). Yet the Greek *Testaments* are clearly Christian, containing obvious references to Jesus (*TSim* 6:5, 7; *TLevi* 4:4; 10:2; *TZeb* 9:8; *TDan* 5:13; *TNaph* 8:3; *TAsher* 7:3; *TBen* 9:3) and Paul (*TBen* 11:2-4). Thus, many scholars have labeled the *Testaments* as a Christian composition. The Qumran testaments are seen as isolated writings which served to inspire a Christian, near the end of the second century C.E., to compose in Greek an entire set of twelve. Other scholars, however, point out that the blatantly Christian passages are few in number and typically bear a loose grammatical relationship with the rest of the sentence; thus, these passages are probably Christian interpolations into an originally Jewish *Testaments.* Such a document, however, is not identical with the Qumran testaments; these semitic testaments served to inspire a Jew to compose a set of twelve, probably in Greek, sometime in the second or first century B.C.E. On balance, a Jewish origin for the *Testaments* seems most probable.

The discovery of testaments at Qumran has raised the question of whether the *Testaments* were composed by the sect. There are certain conceptual parallels—the expectation of two messiahs combined with priestly preeminence (cf. *1QS*; *1QSa*; *4QTestim*; *CD* 6:7; 7:18) and the strong DUALISM (cf. the Two Spirits in *1QS*). But the *Testaments* reflect none of the legal or organizational teachings of the sect, nor its distinctive understanding of its history. Like *Jubilees, 1 Enoch,* and *1QapGen,* the semitic testaments were probably read with interest by the Qumran community but composed outside of it, perhaps in Egypt, where interest in JOSEPH among Jews seems to have been strong (cf. *JosAsen*), or in Syria.

The moral teachings in the *Testaments* provide some interesting parallels to NT teachings, especially those of Jesus. For example, adultery is associated with looking at a woman with lust (*TIss* 7:2; *TBenj* 8:2; cf. Matt 5:28) and forgiveness is to be from the heart (*TGad* 6:7; cf. Matt 18:35). Similarly, Joseph's description of himself as hungry, weak, and in prison is strongly reminiscent of Matt 25:35-36. But the most striking parallel is the linking of the commands to love God and to love one's neighbor (*TIss* 5:2; 7:6; *TDan* 5:3; cf. Matt 22:37-39).

The *Testaments of the Twelve Patriarchs* are a fascinating blend of moral exhortation, eschatological speculation, and a creative handling of OT narrative. If they are indeed Jewish, they provide important background for the NT, especially its moral teachings, as well as a significant witness to the rich diversity within Judaism in the last two centuries B.C.E.

See also APOCRYPHAL LITERATURE; TESTAMENTS, APOCRYPHAL.

Bibliography. R. H. Charles, "The Testaments of the Twelve Patriarchs," *The Apocrypha and Pseudepigrapha of the Old Testament,* ed. R. H. Charles; J. J. Collins, "Testament," *Jewish Writings of the Second Temple Period,* ed. M. E. Stone; M. de Jonge, ed., *Studies on the Testaments of the Twelve Patriarchs*; M. de Jonge, "The Testaments of the Twelve Patriarchs," *The Apocryphal Old Testament,* ed. H. F. D. Sparks; H. W. Hollander, *Joseph as an Ethical Model in the Testaments of the Twelve Patriarchs*; H. W. Hollander and M. de Jonge, *The Testaments of the Twelve Patriarchs*; H. C. Kee, "Testaments of the Twelve Patriarchs," *The Old Testament Pseudepigrapha,* ed. J. H. Charlesworth; D. Slingerland, *The Testaments of the Twelve Patriarchs*; G. Vermes and

M. Goodman, "The Testaments of the Twelve Patriarchs," *The History of the Jewish People in the Age of Jesus Christ,* 3/2, rev. and ed. G. Vermes, F. Millar, and M. Goodman.

—JOSEPH L. TRAFTON

• **Testaments, Apocryphal.** Apocryphal testaments are documents found largely in the OT pseudepigrapha that purport to be the last words of the biblical personality named. There are testaments of the Twelve Patriarchs, of Moses, of Job, of Abraham, and of many other biblical figures. These documents are patterned after the blessings of JACOB (Gen 49) and MOSES (Deut 33). The Bible also contains other "last words," notably those of DAVID (2 Sam 23:1-7).

The blessings of Jacob and Moses are also "last words," just as was the blessing of ISAAC upon his two sons (Gen 27). On one's deathbed, it was believed, one had particular capacities and powers that were to be used carefully and for the good of the next generation. The dying person was sometimes described as having the capacity to foretell the future of the children being addressed (Gen 49; Deut 33). Sometimes the emphasis fell on the visionary capacities that were conferred on the dying PATRIARCH (we have few "last words" from the biblical women, but see JUBILEES 35 for the remarkable story of REBEKAH's last words). The person at death was sometimes enabled to see not only what lay ahead historically but what the heavens and the underworld contained. Not all apocalyptic visions came on one's deathbed, but some did.

Another feature of the "last words" of ancient worthies was the capacity of these dying ones to impart moral guidance to their children and to the next generation. One sees this theme in the portrayal of true kingship in the "last words of David," where the subject is the moral qualities of true kingship.

It is this feature that stands out in the greatest of the apocryphal testament literature—the *Testaments of the Twelve Patriarchs.* This document from the second century B.C.E. contains twelve distinct "testaments," one from each of the sons of Jacob on their deathbeds. In addition to their important portrayals of the centrality of the "messianic" figures of LEVI, Judah, and JOSEPH, they use the events from biblical history to elaborate their ethical counsel to their children. Reuben warns against the perils of lust, showing what lust did to him in this youth. Simeon was guilty of envy of his brother Joseph—as were most of the other brothers. Judah was led into sin by his marriage to a Canaanite woman, being led astray by his lust.

Joseph is presented as the very model of righteousness and piety, one whose patient love for his brothers was extraordinary. Levi too is clearly the suitable one of the brothers from which the priesthood was to come.

The overall impression made by this long document is of a handbook on Jewish morals in an environment in which Hellenism is having more and more influence upon Jewish life. This document shows such influence, for many of the virtues praised are those that were prevalent in popular Greek philosophy. At the same time, the testaments of the brothers are all thoroughly Jewish.

The TESTAMENT OF MOSES, on the other hand, is more concerned with the history of Israel, viewed in apocalyptic terms. Here, the visions of Moses disclose what is to happen in times to come. Moral counsel to JOSHUA is not prominent in this testament, but the foretelling of what lies ahead for Israel dominates the scene.

The TESTAMENT OF JOB, however, is much more akin to the *Testaments of the Twelve Patriarchs.* The author has Job speaking to his family and telling them the full story of his sufferings, of how SATAN's attack on him almost undid him, but how he survived in virtue of his patient, enduring love for God and for fellow human beings. The qualities of Job resemble those of Joseph in the *Twelve Patriarchs,* but in the Job testament there is also a great emphasis upon the esoteric knowledge that Job has, namely his magical powers. But one gets the impression from the *Testament of Job* that the author is not so much commending the virtues that Job displayed as showing in great detail how uniquely pious and longsuffering Job was.

The TESTAMENT OF ABRAHAM, a document from the first or second century C.E., has a distinct character in the testament literature. One of its chief themes is the difficulty that God's messengers had in getting Abraham to relinquish his soul at the time of death. Abraham simply refuses to die. He is shown marvelous and terrible visions of what it will be like when God finally judges all things and separates the righteous to be rewarded from the sinners marked for punishment. Abraham is first portrayed as a stern judge of evildoers unhappy with God's readiness to forgive, but then is brought around to be a champion of the view that sinners should have a second chance. The book also stresses that the gentiles who are faithful to God's purposes will receive rewards equal with those received by the people of Israel.

These apocryphal testaments were of great importance in the shaping of the moral traditions drawn from the Bible. They also were valued for their speculative reflections on the heavens and the underworld, on the mysteries of the universe. And some of the terms from the testaments of Moses and the Twelve Patriarchs became particularly important in the development of Jewish and Christian messianism. The ethical counsels and admonitions of the testament literature have a place alongside of the ethical counsel of the Letters of Paul and the other apostles and the ethics of other Jewish writings such as PIRKE ABOTH and other tractates of the Mishnah.

See also ABRAHAM, TESTAMENT OF; ADAM, TESTAMENT OF; ISAAC, TESTAMENT OF; JACOB, TESTAMENT OF; JOB, TESTAMENT OF; MOSES, TESTAMENT OF; SOLOMON, TESTAMENT OF; TESTAMENTS OF THE TWELVE PATRIARCHS.

Bibliography. W. Harrelson, "The Significance of 'Last Words' for Intertestamental Ethics," in *Essays in Old Testament Ethics,* ed. J. L. Crenshaw and J. T. Willis; G. Nickelsburg, Jr., ed., *Studies on the Testament of Joseph* and *Studies on the Testament of Moses.*

—WALTER HARRELSON

• **Testimony.** Testimony is evidence from witnesses and, in the Bible, refers primarily to the acts and laws of God. In the OT, in addition to this legal meaning (Num 35:30; Ruth 4:7), the term "testimony" is regularly found in passages concerning the Ark and the Tabernacle, especially in the priestly writings of the Pentateuch. The Ark is occasionally called "the ark of the testimony" (Exod 25:22; 26:33, 34; Num 7:89), and the Tabernacle is called "the tabernacle of the testimony" (Num 1:53), although it is not certain in these instances whether the Ark and the Tabernacle represent or contain the "testimony." More common is the use of "testimony" to refer to the laws of God or, more particularly, to the Decalogue, especially the tablets that were contained within the Ark. This connection between the ark and the tablets of the Decalogue is so strong that they often seem to be used interchangeably in the priestly writings. The tablets of the Decalogue are called "tablets of the testimony" in both P and J (Exod 31:18 [P]; 32:15; 34:29 [J]). Deuteronomy equates the law with the "testimonies" in the phrase "the testimonies and the statutes" (Deut 4:45; 6:17, 20; cf. Ps 99:7 and Jer 44:23).

Testimony in the NT generally refers less to literary and legal manifestations of God's activities and more to the works of God unfolding in human actions. JESUS himself is called God's testimony (John 3:11, 32; 2 Tim 1:8; Rev 1:2). Also, the apostles' preaching of the word is referred to as testimony of God's salvific intentions (Matt 10:18; Luke 21:13; Acts 22:18).

See also COVENANT; LAW IN THE OT; TEACHING; WITNESS.

—RAY SUTHERLAND

• **Testimony of Truth.** *Testimony of Truth* is a long but fragmentary Christian Gnostic writing from the NAG HAMMADI library. Almost half of the text is lost or beyond reconstruction, but fortunately the extant material provides a reliable idea of the document's character. The text had no title, but was assigned one by modern editors on the basis of its content and terminology. It is a homily devoted to defending the "word of truth." The truth is summarized by one climactic statement: "This, therefore, is the true testimony: When man knows himself and God who is over the truth, he will be saved, and he will be crowned with the crown unfading." As is typical of GNOSTICISM, knowledge of God and knowledge of self are equivalent, because the divine dwells within the Gnostic person. Thus the author can say, "[. . . he has come to] know [the Son of Man,] that [is, he has come to] know him[self. This] is the perfect life, [that] man know [himself] by means of the All."

Testimony of Truth divides into two parts. The first section is composed of homiletical material delivered to "those who know to hear not with the ears of the body but with the ears of the mind." It is sprinkled with polemical attacks on opponents who can be identified as members of the orthodox Christian church. These ignorant and foolish opponents are chastised for their beliefs (bodily resurrection) and practices (martyrdom, water baptism).

The second section repeats some of the earlier themes and intensifies the polemic, but the opponents now include not only catholic Christians but also various Gnostic groups. Valentinus and the Valentinians, BASILIDES and his son Isidore, and the Simonians are mentioned by name. Part of this section looks like a catalog of heresies, using words like "heretics" and "schisms." The genre of heresiology developed by early Christian writers (e.g., IRENAEUS, Hippolytus, Epiphanius) against Gnostics was apparently adopted by the Gnostics themselves.

The most distinguishing mark of the spiritually enlightened group is their strict asceticism. Knowledge of God is contingent upon renouncing the world. "No one knows the God of truth except solely the man who will forsake all of the things of the world, having renounced the whole place, and having grasped the fringe of his garment." Of special importance is sexual continence. On the basis of this strong commitment to sexual celibacy the author even excoriates the Law, for the Law commands one to marry and procreate. The Law is thus defiled and those who follow it "assist the world" and "turn away from the light." The life of virginity is modelled by Christ. Two different stories of Christ's birth illustrate his separation from the flesh. In one, "Christ was begotten by the Word" and "passed through a virgin's womb." In another, Jesus "came to the world by the Jordan River and immediately the Jordan turned back." The Jordan River symbolizes bodily pleasures and thus, Jesus, by turning back the river, brought to an end "the dominion of carnal procreation."

The author of *Testimony of Truth* was familiar with the OT, NT, and extra-biblical literature. He quotes, alludes to, and allegorizes these writings, claiming to know their "mysteries," or hidden meanings. One fascinating reading of a biblical text is the author's understanding of Gen 2 and 3. The SERPENT is EVE's teacher, being "wiser than all the animals that were in Paradise, while God is envious, ignorant, and malicious because he does not know what happened in the garden, and he begrudges ADAM and Eve the knowledge of good and evil. The OT God is often pictured as an inferior demiurge in Gnostic writings. The author finds positive value in the scripture as well. He bases his Gnostic interpretation of the life of Christ (most often called "Son of man") on Paul and John.

There is no complete cosmogonic myth in *Testimony of Truth,* although terms known from other Gnostic sources are mentioned, such as "the unbegotten aeons," "the virgin who brought forth the light," and "the power which flowed over the whole place." The serpent section recalls the sect of Gnosticism known as "Ophites" (Gk. word for "serpent"), but the text bears closest similarities to Valentinianism even though the Valentinians are disparaged.

Testimony of Truth probably originated in Alexandria, Egypt, in the late second or early third century. Two names have been suggested as possible authors: Julius Cassianus and Hierakas of Leontopolis.

See also GNOSTICISM; NAG HAMMADI.

Bibliography. B. A. Pearson, "Gnostic Interpretation of the Old Testament in the 'Testimony of Truth' (NHC IX,3)," *HTR* 73 (1980): 311-19, "Jewish Haggadic Traditions in 'The Testimony of Truth' from Nag Hammadi (CG IX, 3)," *Religious Syncretism in Antiquity: Essays in Conversation with Geo Widengren,* ed. B. A. Pearson and *Nag Hammadi Codices IX and S (NHS XV)*; B. A. Pearson and S. Giverson, "The Testimony of Truth," *The Nag Hammadi Library in English,* ed J. M. Robinson.

—CAROL D. C. HOWARD

• **Testing.** *See* TEMPTATION IN THE NEW TESTAMENT

• **Testing by God.** *See* JOB, BOOK OF

• **Tetragrammaton.** [tet′ruh-gram″uh-ton] The term (Gk. for "four letters") refers to God's covenantal name. Many manuscripts write the name vowelless (*yhwh*). It occurs in the OT 6,823 times, more than any other term referring to God (*'ĕlōhîm*–2,570 times; *'ēl*–217 times).

Many religious Jews believed the word YHWH too sacred for pronunciation. They intoned Lord (*'ădōnay*). Some writers began using a word created by the tetragrammaton with the vowels of *'ădōnay*. This produced a word (Jehovah) that is grammatically impossible in Hebrew. The earliest use of this hybrid word was in the thirteenth century C.E.

The tetragrammaton YHWH is a third-masculine-imperfect form of *hā-yāh* ("to be, to happen"). Any imperfect ending in *hē* (without an ending) must have *eh*. Therefore, the word must be *yhweh*. Most scholars spell the name as *yahweh*, a Hiph'il imperfect.

As an imperfect, it reflects the frequentative or constant character of God. Thus, W. F. Albright could translate Yahweh as "caused things to happen, causes thing to happen, and will keep on causing things to happen." This name connotes God as creator, sustainer, and hope for the future. It is a title, but it also describes God's unique character.

Another source for the meaning of YHWH is Exod 3. It develops from *'ehĕyeh* ("I am") to *'ehĕyeh 'ăšer 'ehĕyeh* (Exod 3:14-15; KJV, "I am that I am") to YHWH. Thus, the meaning may be "I shall always be what I have always been," emphasizing the omnitemporal covenant of Yahweh with the covenant people.

See also GOD, NAMES OF.

—JOHN JOSEPH OWENS

• **Tetrarch.** [tet'rahrk] Tetrarch literally means "a ruler of a fourth." It was the title used for appointed rulers of small dependent states and sub-districts, i.e. "petty rulers," lower than kings and ethnarchs ("rulers of a people").

Mark Antony named HEROD the Great tetrarch in 41 B.C.E. and gave him the title king the following year. Herod's will divided his territory among three sons. The title tetrarch was given to ANTIPAS (for rule over Galilee and Perea) and to PHILIP (for rule over districts northeast of Sea of Galilee). The title king was reserved for ARCHELAUS (for rule over Judea, Samaria, and Idumaea). The will was endorsed by Rome with the exception of Archelaus being entitled "ethnarch."

In the NT the noun tetrarch is used only for Antipas (Matt 14:1; Luke 3:19; 9:7; Acts 13:1), while the cognate verb is used for Antipas, Philip, and Lysanias of Abilene (Luke 3:1).

See also ANTIPAS; ARCHELAUS; HEROD; PHILIP.

—HENRY JACKSON FLANDERS, JR.

• **Textiles.** Either the fiber or the finished woven product comprise a limited category of textiles in the ancient Near East. Two types of textiles were available: animal and vegetable. The primary textiles of each were, respectively, flax and sheep's wool. These two textiles would have been the most easily accessible materials in the Palestinian area. Other animal textiles include goat's hair, camel's hair; with vegetable fibers, the remaining possibilities are cotton, hemp, and ramie. The major groupings of these textiles can be found in the following: Egypt was known for its flax and thus its linen product; cotton was predominant in India and Peru. Sources also indicate that cotton could have been found in Assyria around 700 B.C.E. Wool was utilized predominantly in the Mesopotamian area; indeed, Mesopotamia was the "land of wool."

Since the economy of the ancient Palestinian area was significantly dependent on animal products, one would expect animal fibers to be the more dominant textile. Mesopotamia, as the land of wool, garners the distinction of being the place where sheep were domesticated. It is most likely that wool was felted before it was actually spun and woven. The spinning of wool probably resulted from the development of vegetable fiber spinning. While wool was utilized from earliest times, shears were not known until approximately 1000 B.C.E. Wool became an important commodity; indeed, it is known that the Phoenicians traded in wool gained from the Israelite nation.

The major cultivator of flax was Egypt. It is also apparent, however, that flax was grown in parts of Syria-Palestine, and certainly was a part of the trade between countries. Linen also could have been imported through the Phoenicians, who were the shippers of the ancient world. Many garments in the OT are described as being composed of linen. Indeed, the garment of Aaron described in Exod 28:5 was to be made partially out of linen. Likewise in the NT it is noted in Luke 23:53 that Jesus was wrapped in a linen shroud. Some indication of the process of linen production is indicated in Josh 2:6, when Rahab hid the spies of Israel in the stalks of flax which she had laid out on the roof. Apparently she was preparing the flax for use by allowing the dew to help separate the fibers. The textile "flax" is the inner bark of a plant stem. It is a cellulose material, and the plant was grown for its seed as well as its fiber. The seed when crushed produced linseed oil.

It appears that cotton was utilized to a lesser degree in Palestine since it was primarily grown in India, Peru, and some parts of upper Egypt. Cotton was first used about 3500 B.C.E. in India and some 500 years later in Peru. It became well known and utilized in the Near East certainly by Hellenistic times. The process of separating the fibers was done by hand until the Middle Ages.

Though available in parts of the ancient world, silk would not have been accessible to the ancient Palestinian economy, which was based largely on sheep and goats. The introduction of silk into the Near East occurred quite late.

See also SPINNING AND WEAVING.

—MARK W. GREGORY

• **Texts/Manuscripts/Versions.** *Physical Materials.* Advances in the technology of communication have always spawned advancements in related technologies and created demand for the products of these technologies. In the 1960s few people felt the need for the enormous range of uses to which computers are put today, but the development of inexpensive and practical hardware has created a demand for a bewildering variety of software products. Similarly, the invention of printing brought forth a demand for books and an increase in literacy; it also begot a parallel development in the technology of paper making, since a new material was required to satisfy the insatiable demands of the presses.

In ancient times the development of writing itself—codifying speech in permanent and tangible form—opened up a wide range of uses for writing, as well as technologies for writing materials. Writing could be incised in stone, committed to wooden tablets prepared with a coating of wax or plaster, impressed into wet clay, or inked onto potsherds. Such materials could suffice for limited purposes, but for a vigorous literature to develop, less cumbersome materials were required. While there is evidence in the Bible of the use of all the above writing surfaces, the extensive literature of the Bible depended on the technologies of preparing papyrus and leather for scribal use.

Papyrus is a water reed growing in certain areas of the ancient Near East where the process for using it in writing was first developed. The stem of the plant was split into strips, and a layer of horizontal fiber (recto) was pressed against a layer of vertical fiber (verso). The plant's natural gum allowed the layers to adhere. After being dried and cut to size, a number of sheets could be bonded together to form a long roll. Winding this roll on two sticks produced a scroll, the recto of which was used as a writing surface, an appropriate medium for a work of some length. Papyrus, a valuable item of commerce in antiquity, was known as early as the third millennium in Egypt, and was probably in common use in Israel in OT times. BARUCH's scroll of JEREMIAH's words, burned by King JEHOIAKIM in the brazier (Jer 36), was likely a papyrus scroll.

Papyrus had its disadvantages. It was difficult to write on the verso, with its vertical fibers, although on a scroll the verso would not normally be used. Papyrus was a fragile material, particularly when dry, and moisture could cause it to deteriorate rapidly. Although exported from Egypt and used all over the Mediterranean world and the Near East, only in the dry sands of Egypt has any significant number of writings on papyrus been preserved. Indeed, very little has ever been discovered outside of Egypt. It is fortuitous that the first extensive discoveries of papyrus in Egypt did not precede by much the development of modern techniques for preserving such a perishable material.

Leather was prepared from tanned animal hides, and in Palestine had the advantages of being a locally available material that would stand up well under frequent use and of being more forgiving of humid climatic conditions. Some of the DEAD SEA SCROLLS, such as the great Isaiah scroll, are of leather, some in a fairly supple state of preservation.

Probably as early as the second century B.C.E. a special technique for processing leather was developed, thus producing parchment, a somewhat thinner and far more durable material, which also had the advantage that the surface could be erased and reused; such a manuscript is known as a palimpsest. Parchment came into wide use for book production in the fourth century C.E. By far the greatest number of biblical manuscripts that exist today are on parchment, though leather continues to be used in Judaism for scrolls used liturgically.

Paper, invented in China at least as early as the first century C.E., came to be known in the Near East by the ninth century, but it saw negligible use until the advent of printing.

Writing on any flexible material was normally done with a reed pen, made by fraying the ends of a cut reed into a small brush, or by shaping and slitting the reed in the manner of a quill. Ink was most commonly made from soot in a suspension of gum or oil. Red ink was later used for headings.

Before the Common Era the SCROLL was the customary form of book manufacture. Its disadvantages were that it was cumbersome, requiring both hands to use; that it was unsuited for gaining rapid access to passages one might want to consult; and that for practical reasons only one side could be used for writing. EZEKIEL's visionary scroll (Ezek 2:10) was evidently exceptional.

The CODEX form of book manufacture, in which leaves were sewn together at one side in the fashion of a modern book, came into use in the first century C.E. Its use reduced the cost of materials and facilitated the use of written material for ready reference purposes. The codex was quickly adopted by the church as the medium for manuscripts of Christian origin. The great majority of the OT manuscripts used for critical purposes are parchment codices. Not a single scrap of NT material, whether on papyrus or parchment, exists that is not, or if fragmentary was not, in codex form. Scrolls of NT material simply do not exist, and probably never did apart from a few early copies of individual books.

Transmission of the Old Testament. The OT, apart from a few late passages in Aramaic, was originally written in Hebrew. We possess, of course, no original autographs, but we do have a large number of Hebrew manuscripts, most of which date from deep within the Common Era. Very few date from before the ninth century C.E. All of these Hebrew manuscripts come to us as the labor of Jewish scribes. Christian scribes did produce OT manuscripts, but always in translation. Compared with the history of the transmission of the NT text, the Hebrew manuscripts of the OT present two striking contrasts. One is the virtual absence of manuscripts, excepting the Dead Sea Scrolls, antedating the ninth century C.E. (many NT manuscripts are far earlier than this). Another is the remarkably uniform — even suspiciously uniform — text that is preserved. Hebrew manuscripts of the OT are far more consistent from copy to copy than are Christian manuscripts of either testament, where a confusing variety of readings is found. Obviously, Jewish scribes were far more careful to preserve an accurate text than were Christian scribes, but this is only part of the explanation.

Scholars long suspected that if copies of OT material could be found from, say, the beginning of the Common Era, those copies might differ significantly from each other and from the traditional Hebrew text in common use, known as the MT. When this text is compared with the LXX, a Greek translation of the Hebrew scriptures done in Egypt and dating from the third-second centuries B.C.E., the readings of the Greek text are often so different from the MT that one can only conclude that the translation was made from a different Hebrew text.

With the discovery of the Dead Sea Scrolls in 1947, and of other material from Qumran and Wadi Murraba'at, scholars suddenly possessed manuscripts of OT material fully a thousand years older than anything previously known. Among these finds were at least fragments of every OT book except ESTHER, and it was discovered that the text did, in fact, often differ from the traditional text, at times agreeing with the LXX and at times differing from it as well as from the long known Hebrew text. It would appear, then, that at the beginning of the Common Era the OT text was in a state of considerable fluidity, evident in three aspects: orthography, variant readings, and variant recensions.

At the turn of the era the Hebrew language had not yet developed a standard system of spelling. Numerous variants were possible, due largely to the fact that the Hebrew alphabet has no characters to represent vowels, but does have "silent" consonants and a letter that can be used as a semi-vowel. The reader of the Bible in translation is not directly affected by these technical matters, but the study of spelling conventions does assist scholars in tracing the history of the text.

Variant readings are the familiar stuff of textual criticism. At a given passage, manuscripts may have two or more different readings. The Dead Sea Scrolls show a fair similarity to the MT in this matter, but the differences are numerous, and important enough to merit consideration. In fourteen passages in Isaiah the RSV has preferred a reading from the first Isaiah scroll to that of the MT. The readings of the second Isaiah scroll are closer to the MT, and the two scrolls may be different recensions.

Variant recensions create a problem in OT study that does not particularly vex the NT scholar. In the case of most NT books it can be said that someone at some time sat down and wrote the books in a form at least close to what we now have. If we discount a few situations where additions may have been made to a book (e.g., John 21; Rom 16) or where material has probably become disarranged (e.g., 2 Cor), this statement would perhaps be true for all of them. Yet this can be said of very little in the OT. Much of the material goes far back into antiquity, and even our earliest manuscripts are so much later than the original composition that they may represent several different transmissional histories, or recensions, which can vary considerably. The Samaritan Pentateuch (cf. below) has a transmissional history of its own quite apart from any Jewish recension. The LXX often seems to represent a different recension from that of the MT, e.g., Job is considerably shorter in Greek. There are different recensions of certain passages even within the canon itself, e.g., cf. 2 Sam 22 and Ps 18; 2 Kgs 18:13–20:19 and Isa 36–39. Given also the complex history of composition of most of the OT books, it is legitimate to ask if the term "original autograph" has any meaning, since the texts may have assumed in the course of composition several different forms, or recensions, of which the familiar MT is only one.

It is clear, however, that by 100 C.E. the text of the OT was showing signs of attaining a standard form. The biblical texts from Murraba'at date from the second century C.E. and represent a text substantially identical with the MT. Several factors may have contributed to this standardization: the beginning of the Christian movement and the almost universal use of the LXX by the Church; the wide dispersion of Jews after 70 C.E. and the concomitant risk of increased recensional variety; and the solidification of the Jewish CANON of scripture by the end of the first century C.E. Particularly important at this stage was the influential activity of the great Rabbi Akiba (ca. 50 C.E.–ca. 132 C.E.), who consciously fostered an authoritative standard text that was thereafter scrupulously duplicated by the scribes, all the more carefully now that the documents were universally revered by Jews as a sacred literature. It is probably no coincidence that the standardization of the text and the finalization of the canon were contemporaneous. During this period of scribal activity, word division was introduced into the consonantal text, and the text was divided into sections for liturgical purposes.

The most intense and creative period in the history of the Hebrew text is that of the Masoretes, scholarly Jewish scribes who worked from roughly 500–1000 C.E. in two centers, Babylonia, and Tiberias in Palestine. The Masoretes were not only exquisitely careful to preserve the consonantal text that had become dominant, but developed numerous technical or cunning devices to insure its accuracy. In about 1,300 places a word is placed in the margin that the scribes intended to be read (*Qere*) instead of the word actually written (*Kethib*). The written word might be objectionable for some reason, presenting a difficulty which the *Qere* could alleviate (although some *Qeres* are actually variant readings). In fifteen places dots were placed over words or letters by the Masoretes, who felt there was something wrong but dared not change the sacred text. In perhaps eighteen instances a "correction" was actually made in the text; these are the *tiqqune sopherim,* or scribal emendations, and are clearly marked in the margin. An example is Gen 18:22, where the original reading said "the Lord stood before Abraham," emended to "Abraham stood before the Lord."

The Masoretes took a huge step toward the preservation of the text in devising a system of "pointing" the consonants with dots and dashes above, below, and within the letters to indicate the proper vowels. Since many Hebrew words can change meaning with a change of vowels supplied with the consonants and since vocalization was a matter of tradition, the devising of the written vowel points went far toward standardizing and preserving the traditional pronunciation, and the understanding of the text to which that pronunciation witnessed. Modern textual critics often dispute whether the Masoretic vocalization represents the intended understanding of given passages. Different systems of vocalization developed in two centers of Masoretic activity; the one developed in Tiberias has become standard.

Another significant contribution of the Masoretes was the development of the Masora (marginal notes), providing a wealth of technical information varying in importance from the crucial to the trivial, but all bespeaking an intense effort to preserve the text in its purity. Most of the Masora is in Aramaic, and it is found in the important codices of Hebrew scripture.

Two Masoretic families, ben Asher and ben Naphtali, particularly struggled to preserve a pure text. By the end of the Masoretic period the ben Asher text had come to be preferred. By this time, ca. 1000, the Hebrew text as we know it today, the MT, had reached its final form. From this point on every effort was made to preserve the Masoretic tradition, and no effort was made to preserve older copies, which were reverently put away and allowed to deteriorate. Hence the situation today where very few pre-Masoretic texts are known, and where the existing copies show a remarkable uniformity.

Manuscripts of the OT. Of Hebrew manuscripts extant, two are particularly important. The Leningrad Codex (1008 C.E.) forms the basis of the Hebrew Bible currently in use by scholars. The Aleppo Codex (930 C.E.) was almost lost during riots in 1947, but it is now in Jerusalem, where it is to be used as a basis for a new critical edition under the auspices of the Hebrew University. Both of these are ben Asher texts.

The principal evidence for the pre-Masoretic text consists of the Dead Sea Scrolls and the fragments from the Cairo Geniza. The most significant extensive biblical texts from Qumran (the site at which the Dead Sea Scrolls were found) are the first Isaiah scroll (which is complete), a commentary on the first two chapters of Habakkuk, and a Psalm scroll containing forty-one of the canonical psalms, plus others (PLATE 48). In the nineteenth century there were found in the storeroom (geniza) of an ancient synagogue in Cairo many thousands of fragments of Hebrew writing, some biblical. The earliest probably date from the fifth century C.E., and are important for what they show of the text at an early stage of Masoretic work, before the great Tiberian schools of ben Asher and ben Naphtali.

Versions of the OT. In addition to the Hebrew text itself, several ancient translations of the OT are important for critical study.

The Samaritan Pentateuch is not technically a version, or translation, but a discrete recension of the Pentateuch in Samaritan letters dating back to the Jewish-Samaritan conflict of the fifth century B.C.E. It differs from the MT in some 6,000 places, most variants being trivial. Yet it is often close to the Dead Sea Scrolls and often agrees with the LXX. It provides us with a window in time to see these five books in a very early form indeed. Though unknown to European scholars until 1616, a printed edition is now available based on more than eighty manuscripts. The most important copy is the Nablus scroll, in the hands of the small Samaritan community in Israel.

The Targums are translations into Aramaic, done after the fifth century B.C.E., when Aramaic had replaced Hebrew as the spoken language of Palestinian Jews. Originally oral recitations in SYNAGOGUE when scripture was read aloud in Hebrew, many Targums were reduced to writing, and many manuscripts of them survive. They are of value for reconstructing difficult passages in the Hebrew text, and they also contribute to our understanding of Jewish exegesis at the time. As such they are significant in NT studies. Some of these Targums are quite free and highly interpretive. Looking for a modern example, one might say that *The Living Bible* is an English targum on the Bible.

The LXX is by far the most important translation of the OT into another language. It was done by Jewish scholars in Alexandria for the benefit of the large Jewish community there to whom Hebrew was an unknown tongue, but who used Greek as the language of education and business. Although there is a legend that it was finished in seventy-two days, it appears to have been begun in the mid-third century B.C.E., reaching completion by the end of the next century. It consists of the so-called Alexandrian canon; i.e., it contains the deuterocanonical or apocryphal books in addition to the books of the Jewish canon received today. Handed down by Christian scribes over the centuries, it is a major critical tool for reconstructing text forms earlier than the MT. It varies greatly in style, and is perhaps most useful for critical purposes in places where it most fails as a translation, since one can more confidently back-translate into Hebrew from a slavishly literal translation than from a more imaginative rendering.

The LXX was quickly adopted for use by the young Christian church, since the church's own literature was in Greek. Probably because of Christian use, Jews came to reject the LXX. Three other Greek translations were made, however, in the second century C.E. That of Aquila, a convert to Judaism, was woodenly literal. That of Theodotion, another convert, was quite free. The version of Symmachus, either a Jewish Christian or a convert to Judaism, was accurate but stylistically good as well. Of these three versions only fragments remain.

The Old Latin version dates from the second century C.E. and is of Christian origin. It is primarily a critical tool for reconstructing the Greek text of the LXX, from which it was translated. In the late fourth century, the great scholar Jerome was commissioned by Pope Damasus to produce a standard reliable Latin version. Although Jerome made a false start in translating the Psalms from the LXX, his real achievement is the translation of the entire OT from the Hebrew itself at a time when many Christians (including his correspondent Augustine) considered the LXX to be divinely inspired. Jerome's translation, the Vulgate, became the Bible of Western Europe through late antiquity and the Middle Ages, being declared by the Council of Trent in 1546 the authoritative Bible for the Catholic Church.

Other OT versions include the Syriac, the Coptic, the Ethiopic, and the Armenian versions.

Chapter divisions for the OT were devised by Stephen Langton in the thirteenth century, and were adopted in Hebrew manuscripts from the fourteenth century on. The present versification system was fixed by the Masoretes by 900 C.E., but the numbering system is much more recent, and it varies somewhat. The verse numbers of the English Bible do not always coincide with those of the Hebrew text.

The Printed Hebrew Bible. The first printed Hebrew Bible came off the press at Soncino, Italy, in 1488. The Rabbinic Bible of Jacob ben Chayyim (1524–25) was popular for centuries, and was the base for Rudolf Kittel's *Biblia Hebraica* in its first two editions. In 1937 a third edition broke with tradition and used as a base the Leningrad Codex. This was the standard Hebrew text used by scholars until quite recently, when a revised *Biblia Hebraica Stuttgartensis* was published, still based on the Leningrad Codex, but with a simplified and improved textual apparatus.

Transmission of the NT Text. Although Christianity arose in a Jewish environment, it rapidly became a predominantly gentile movement. Since the church from the beginning had some sense of catholicity, a problem was confronted when the movement spread beyond the boundaries of Jewish culture and the Aramaic language (at Jesus' time the vernacular in Palestine) into the rest of the world, where a multiplicity of languages was spoken. The unity of the church demanded some kind of linguistic uniformity and this was provided by the Greek language. Although Latin was the official language of the Roman Empire, Greek was used as a *lingua franca* from Rome eastward, much as French was used in the nineteenth century and as English is used today. Greek was the common language of education, culture, diplomacy, and business for much of the Mediterranean world. Since the first Christians were Jews and accepted the canonical authority of the Hebrew Scriptures, it was natural that gentile Christians should also accept these books, but in Greek dress, specifically in the translation of the LXX. Although there may well have been some primitive Christian literature in Aramaic, the earliest Christian literature we possess —the writings of the NT— was composed in Greek, so that it might do universal service in the Mediterranean world. When the NT quotes scripture, it is usually in the form known to us as the LXX.

Most of these books that were to comprise the NT began to be copied and to spread widely virtually from the time of composition. The Gospel of John could hardly have been written much before 100 C.E., yet we possess a small fragment from John that can be placed in Egypt in the early second century. It is our oldest copy of any NT material. From that time on, there is an abundance of NT manuscripts. There is no gap in the transmissional history of the NT such as exists with the OT from the Dead Sea Scrolls to the Masoretic era. Obviously there are fewer manuscripts from antiquity than from the Middle Ages, but there is an unbroken supply of manuscripts from that papyrus fragment of John until the introduction of printing in the fifteenth century. Over five thousand Greek manuscripts of either the whole NT or portions of it are known, in addition to many thousands of manuscripts in languages other than Greek.

Manuscripts of the NT. In the practice of NT textual criticism, there are three directions from which comes our knowledge of the ancient text: Greek manuscripts, manuscripts in other languages, and quotations from the NT in the writings of the church fathers.

Greek manuscripts are customarily divided into four groups: papyri, uncials, minuscules, and lectionaries.

Our earliest NT manuscripts are papyrus codices. All originated in Egypt. They are designated by the letter $\mathfrak{p}$ with a superscript numeral; e.g., $\mathfrak{p}^{52}$ is the aforementioned fragment of John now in the John Rylands Library at Manchester. The Chester Beatty Papyrus $\mathfrak{p}^{46}$ dates from ca. 200 and is our earliest codex of the Pauline Epistles. It contains Hebrews, but not the Pastoral Letters. Beatty Papyrus $\mathfrak{p}^{47}$, from the third century, is our earliest copy of any portion of Revelation. Several of the Bodmer Papyri, named for the Swiss businessman who procured them, are especially important. One of them, $\mathfrak{p}^{72}$, late third or early fourth century, provides our oldest text of the Letters of Peter and Jude. Another, $\mathfrak{p}^{75}$, early third century, is our earliest copy of Luke and one of the oldest of John. Eighty-eight papyri are known.

Papyrus continued to be used into the eighth century, but in the fourth century parchment came to replace it. We possess one papyrus from the fifth century compared with thirty-six parchment copies. These early parchment copies are called uncials. This refers to the style of handwriting used also in the papyri: uncial letters are written singly without ligatures. They resemble the capital letters used in modern texts. Although the same style was used in the papyri, the designation of a manuscript as uncial is a convention to distinguish it both from the papyri (by material) and from the later minuscules (by style of hand). Uncials date from the fourth to the tenth or eleventh centuries. There are two systems of designating them. The older used capital Roman letters A to Z, followed by Greek capitals distinct from the Roman. A later system uses a sequence of Arabic numerals prefixed by a zero. Some 274 uncials are known. Some of these are particularly significant.

Codex Sinaiticus, designated uniquely by the Hebrew letter *aleph* (א) or as 01, originally contained the entire Bible plus the *Epistle of Barnabas* and the *Shepherd of Hermas*. It was discovered at St. Catherine's Monastery on Mount Sinai in 1844 by the great textual scholar Constantin von Tischendorf. Suspicious of the intense interest von Tischendorf showed in it, the monks were reluctant to grant access to it. Von Tischendorf worked out a complex arrangement whereby it was donated to the Czar of Russia in return for his influence in the appointment of a new abbot for the monastery. This is von Tischendorf's story; the monks today claim he stole it. The Soviet government sold the manuscript to the British Museum in 1933. It is a fine copy of considerable textual authority, dating to the fourth century.

Codex Alexandrinus (A, 02) dates from the fifth century and was presented in 1628 by the Patriarch of Constantinople to King Charles I of England. Today it lies side by side with Sinaiticus in the British Museum. It also originally contained the whole Bible, plus the *Psalms of Solomon* and *1* and *2 Clement*. It is an especially valuable witness to the text of Revelation.

Codex Vaticanus (B, 03) has been known in the Vatican Library since 1475. It dates from the fourth century, and contains the entire Bible, with some gaps. It is an exceptionally fine manuscript both in its physical makeup and in the quality of its text. An earlier school of textual criticism held that when Vaticanus and Sinaiticus disagreed on a reading, the former was almost certainly original.

Codex Ephraemi (C, 04) is a fifth century palimpsest; the biblical text was erased in the twelfth century and writings of a Syrian church father were written over it. Von Tischendorf spent countless hours attempting to decipher the text, which he published in 1845. Technology is now available to make this kind of task easier. This codex was originally a complete Bible but much of it is now missing.

Codex Bezae (D, 05) is an important bilingual manuscript dating to the fifth century. It contains Latin and Greek on facing pages. It is controversial among textual scholars, often giving readings quite different from the usually received text. Its principal significance is that it is the single most authoritative witness to the form of the NT text known in the western Mediterranean. It contains the Gospels and Acts.

Codex Washingtonianus (W, 032) is in the Freer Gallery of the Smithsonian Institution. It is a fifth century copy of the Gospels. Along with some pages of $\mathfrak{p}^{46}$ at the University of Michigan, it is one of the two most important biblical manuscripts in the Americas.

Minuscule manuscripts are written in a running hand, sometimes misleadingly called cursive. Also on parchment, they date from the ninth century onward, when the development of this form of writing cut the cost of book manufacture by reducing the time required to produce a book. Almost three thousand minuscules have been catalogued; they are designated by Arabic numerals without the prefixed zero. Most of these have not been studied sufficiently to assess the value of their text—one is of course not initially inclined to attribute much authority to medieval manuscripts—but some are known to represent a text much older than the manuscripts themselves. One such is 33, the "queen of the cursives," a manuscript of the entire NT less Revelation. Recent test studies have indicated that perhaps ten percent of the minuscules may be significant witnesses to text forms as early as those of the uncials.

Lectionaries are church books containing biblical readings arranged not in canonical sequence, but in pericopes ordered for reading in the sequence of the ecclesiastical calendar. About two thousand Greek lectionaries are known, dating from the third or fourth centuries to the end of the manuscript period. Study of the lectionaries for their textual witness to the NT is still in the early stages.

Versions of the NT. Among the ancient translations, or versions, of the NT are of course the Old Latin and Vulgate (discussed above). The Syriac, extant in several recensions, is of interest since Syriac is closely related to Aramaic. The Coptic, known in several dialectical forms, represents the latest form of the language of ancient Egypt, written in an alphabet based on Greek. There are also minor versions in Armenian, Gothic, Old Church Slavonic, Ethiopic, and Georgian. Some of these versions have significance apart from biblical studies; they are important in historical linguistics. The version in Gothic, now a dead language, is the oldest extant literature in any of the Germanic languages and the only literature of the East Germanic branch of the family. The Old Church Slavonic version is of importance in studying the history of the Slavic languages.

The versions of the NT are of critical significance not only for the help they can give in deciding among variant readings, but are of great help—even the minor versions—in tracing the history of the transmission of the text as it was known in various geographical areas, generally described as Eastern (or Caesarean), Western (whose existence as a separate text type is disputed), Alexandrian, and Byzantine (or Koine). These text families developed quite early in separate localities, but the Byzantine type emerged, from the fourth century onward, as the dominant form.

The church went through a period of intense persecution in the 250s and then again in the early fourth century. During these years many NT manuscripts were destroyed. With the emergence of Christianity as the state religion from the time of Constantine on, there was a new demand for copies of the NT. Many of the bishops under Constantine had been trained at Antioch, where there was a center of Christian studies, and in which a particular text type, polished in style and often expanded with conflate readings, predominated—the Byzantine text. The authority of this text spread with the influence of bishops trained in Antioch. Consequently, most minuscule manuscripts, dating from well after this period, reflect this common text type. This text, conflated as it was and representing no greater authority than earlier text types, became the basis for the first printed Greek Testaments.

The Printed Greek NT. The story of the first printed Greek Testaments is a tale of scholarly and business rivalry. Work was begun by a group of Spanish scholars directed by Cardinal Francisco Ximénes de Cisneros on a polyglot Bible (in the OT, Hebrew, Greek, and Aramaic Targums, each with Latin translation; in the NT, Vulgate and Greek), which was eventually published in five volumes. The NT volume was printed in 1514, but because of ecclesiastical problems (the return of borrowed books to the Vatican Library) Pope Leo X did not allow publication until 1520. By that time, however, another Greek Testament had flooded the market. Johannes Froben was a Swiss printer who knew of Ximénes' project, and was determined to get out a Greek Testament before the Spaniards could. He enlisted the great humanist scholar Desiderius Erasmus to do the work. Erasmus disliked having to work under such pressure and with such limited resources. He had at his disposal only a handful of late manuscripts that happened to be in Basel, where the work was done. He would simply enter corrections on a manuscript and send it as a printer's copy straight to the printer. Only one of the available manuscripts contained Revelation, and it was lacking the last page. Erasmus then back-translated that missing portion, 22:16-21, into Greek from Latin, thereby introducing a number of errors. The whole work was hurriedly done from poor manuscripts ("more precipitated than edited," said Erasmus), but it was published in 1515, and became the first Greek NT on the market. It was promptly accepted, although Ximénes' massive Complutensian Polyglot was a much better text. Erasmus's text went through several editions.

Other significant printings based on Erasmus's text were made by the French printer Robert Étienne (or Stephanus, 1546–1551), by Theodore Beza of Geneva (1565–1604), and by the Elzevir brothers of Leiden (1624–1633). Étienne's fifth edition (1551) introduced verse numbers. Beza's fifth edition (sometimes erroneously referred to as the ninth because of some reprintings) was the basis of the KJV. The Elzevirs' second edition of 1633 used the term "textus receptus," or "received text" in the preface; it became the standard text in continental scholarship.

NT scholars today, and Greek students as well, use one or both of two critical editions based on current textual scholarship, and thus a far closer approach to the original text than Erasmus's rush job. One, *Novum Testamentum Graece*, the Nestle-Aland text, begun in 1898 by Eberhard Nestle, has been edited by Kurt Aland since 1952. It is now in its twenty-sixth edition (1979), and is prepared specifically for scholars. *The Greek New Testament*, now in its third edition (1975), is published by the United Bible Societies specifically for translators. The text of the two is identical; they differ in the critical apparatus provided. Nestle-Aland gives information on far more textual problems. The UBS testament gives only those that make a difference in translation, but gives much more data on those problems than Nestle-Aland. The UBS edition contains a punctuation apparatus, indicating various ways the text has been punctuated in modern editions and translations (the earliest manuscripts had no punctuation at all). The UBS text is preferred by many simply because its type font is more legible.

Modern Non-English Versions. It is a mistake to think that translation of the Bible into vernacular languages only began with the Protestant Reformation, though this was certainly the impetus for the flood of translations appearing at that time. Before the introduction of printing into Europe, which for our purposes is roughly coincident with the Reformation, the Bible had been translated, at least in portions, into twenty-two European languages as well as eleven others; most of these were translated from Latin. The Reformers believed that the Bible should be accessible to everyone, and the printing press made this possible. The early modern translations of Europe were products of Reformation scholarship. The first printed Bibles were of these new translations, not simply printed editions of medieval translations.

The most obvious example of a Reformation Bible is that of Martin Luther himself. The NT was published in 1522 and the whole Bible in 1534. It was the first entire Bible to be translated from the original languages into a modern European tongue, and it had an enormous effect on the subsequent development of the German language as well as of church history. Catholic translations followed, but not until 1622 was there a standard German Bible for Catholics. Among modern German versions one of the best is the Zurich Bible of 1931. The Luther Bible remains, however, the standard for German Evangelicals; a thorough revision was completed in 1964.

The States-General Bible is for Dutch what the Luther Bible is for German or the King James Version for English. It was completed in 1637. The most popular modern translation is the New Translation prepared under the aegis of the Netherlands Bible Society and published in 1951. It is widely used.

The chief Reformation translation into French is the Neuchâtel Bible of 1535, attributed to Pierre Robert Olivétan. Olivétan began the practice common in French Protestant Bibles of translating the name of God in the OT as "the Eternal," a device borrowed in English by James Moffatt. Among popular modern translations are the version of Louis Ségond (1879), the version published by Bibliothèque de la Pléiade beginning in 1956 and edited by Édouard Dhorme, and the monumental Bible de Jérusalem, published in its entirety in 1954 and thoroughly revised in 1973. It is the prototype of the Jerusalem Bible in English.

The Inquisition proved a deterrent to translations in the Iberian peninsula. An influential Jewish translation of the OT into Spanish, the Ferrara Bible, appeared in 1553. The first whole Bible in Spanish was that of Cassiodoro de Reina published at Basel in 1569. It is generally known in its revised form published by Cipriano Valera at Amsterdam in 1602. (Not until 1793 was a complete Spanish Bible printed in Spain itself.) Revised by the British and Foreign Bible Society in 1960, the de Reina-Valera Bible is still the standard Spanish text. Portugal was even later in getting the Bible; the first complete Bible in Portuguese did not appear until 1753.

The Italian Bible, on the other hand, dates to the Reformation. The first whole Bible was the work of Giovanni Diodati, published at Geneva in 1607. It became the classical version in Italian.

The Russian Bible dates back to the Old Church Slavonic translation of Cyril and Methodius in the ninth century, of which a definitive edition appeared in 1581. This is not intelligible to modern Russians, however, and a Russian revision of it was published in Moscow in 1663. A colloquial translation into modern Russian appeared in 1876. A Protestant version of the OT was issued in 1875, but the NT did not follow until 1952; the NT was published in Washington.

The various Scandinavian versions date back to the Reformation. In Denmark the Resen-Savne Bible (Resen 1605, revised by Savne 1647) has long been the most used Danish Bible. An officially sponsored new translation was completed in 1948. The standard Swedish Bible is the Gustaf Vasa Bible of 1541 prepared by the Reformer Laurentius Petri and others. A revision appeared in 1917. The Danish Bible was used in Norway until the early nineteenth century. Since that time various translations, Protestant and

Catholic, have appeared in both the official literary form of the Norwegian language, Riksmaal, and the vernacular tongue, Landsmaal.

Versions in modern Greek go back to a Protestant translation of 1638. A modern version was issued in Athens by the British and Foreign Bible Society in 1848. A fresh translation is now in progress at the University of Athens. For instruction in schools, however, the LXX OT and Koine NT continue in use.

While translations into European languages were largely the result of the Reformation, the translations into non-European languages were a product of the expansion of missionary activity, both Catholic and Protestant, around the world that followed in the wake of the circumnavigation of Africa and the discovery of the New World. This missionary activity led to the first Bible in Tamil, a major language of India, in 1727; in Chinese, 1822; Burmese, 1835, Japanese 1883, and Korean in 1911. The first entire Bible printed in an African language was in Malagasy in 1835; the first in an Oceanic language was in Tahitian in 1838; and the first appearance of any part of the Bible in a native South American language was a Gospel of Luke in Aymara, 1829. The first printed portion of the Bible in a non-European tongue to be used as a tool for evangelization was A. C. Ruyl's translation of 1629 into Malay. The first Bible to be printed in British North America was a translation by John Eliot into the Massachusetts language, 1663.

Missionary translation was greatly expanded after the formation of the various Bible societies in the nineteenth century (British and Foreign Bible Society, 1804; American Bible Society, 1816). As a result of their efforts and those of later groups such as the Wycliffe Bible Translators, who work mainly in tribal languages, some portion of the Bible had been translated into 1,848 languages as of 1986. There were complete Bibles in 301 languages. The translation of the Bible into non-European tongues constitutes a rich history that has yet to receive scholarly attention and to see publication.

An outgrowth of Bible Society work in non-European tongues has been the development of common-language translations into the European languages. As the goal of providing the Bible for all peoples of the world in their own languages became increasingly remote of fulfillment, a technique developed of providing common language versions in the world's major trade languages: English, Spanish, French, Portuguese, and Chinese. It was reasoned that most people in the world speaking an obscure tribal language could understand as a second language the trade language used in their area, and these versions could meet their needs. By "common language" is meant the form of the language common to all users of the language, whatever their educational status and whether or not they are native speakers. These versions (e.g., *Today's English Version,* 1966, 1979) have proved to be so popular among native speakers of the languages that common language translations are now being prepared in many languages (e.g., *Die Gute Nachricht* in German, 1966, 1982).

See also BIBLE; CANON; CODEX; TEXTUAL CRITICISM OF THE NEW TESTAMENT; TEXTURAL CRITICISM OF THE OLD TESTAMENT.

Bibliography. P. R. Ackroyd and C.F. Evans, *The Cambridge History of the Bible*; K. Aland and B. Aland, *The Text of the New Testament*; "Bible, IV (Texts and Versions)," *NCE*; R. G. Bratcher, "The Bible in Every Tongue," *IOVC*; D. Ewert, *From Ancient Tablets to Modern Translations* ; J. Finegan, *Encountering New Testament Manuscripts*; B. Metzger, *The Early Versions of the New Testament, Manuscripts of the Greek Bible, The Text of the New Testament,* 2d ed., and "Versions, Medieval and Modern (Non-English)," *IDB*; E. A Nida, ed., *The Book of a Thousand Tongues* and *God's Word in Man's Language*; O. M. Norlie, ed., *The Translated Bible 1534-1934*; J. H. P. Reumann, *The Romance of Bible Scripts and Scholars,* and *Scriptures of the World*; E. Würthwein, *The Text of the Old Testament.*

—ROGER A. BULLARD

• Textual Criticism of the New Testament.

Purpose. NT textual criticism is the study of biblical texts and manuscripts in the effort to determine what the original writings said before copyists introduced changes and errors into the texts.

Materials. The primary materials from which textual critics attempt to reconstruct the original texts are the following:

(1) Greek biblical manuscripts. The earliest manuscripts were written on PAPYRUS, a material made from the pith of the papyrus plant. Around the fourth century, scribes began writing on PARCHMENT, made from animal skins. This was the writing material used for the next one thousand years, until paper began to replace parchment in the twelfth century. The kind of script used until the ninth century was the uncial or capital script. From the ninth century until the printing of the NT, the minuscule or cursive script was used. The great majority of Greek manuscripts extant today are minuscule manuscripts (ca. 2,800), the greatest number dating from the eleventh to the fourteenth centuries. At the beginning of the twentieth century, only nine papyri were known to exist. Today eighty-eight papyrus manuscripts (many quite fragmentary) are known; uncial manuscripts number 274. These Greek biblical manuscripts, especially the papyri and uncials, are of greatest importance for textual critical study.

(2) Greek lectionary manuscripts. In addition to the more than 3,000 continuous text manuscripts, i.e., uninterrupted texts, approximately 2,200 lectionary manuscripts exist. These are manuscripts which contain passages arranged according to their sequence as lessons appointed for reading for the church calendar year. Most of these manuscripts contain a form of the text which is inferior to that of the Greek papyri and uncial manuscripts, exhibiting instead a form of text quite similar to the majority of minuscule manuscripts.

(3) Citations in the writings of the early church fathers. Most of the ancient Christian writers of the second to the fifth centuries wrote either in Greek or in Latin. Their citations of verses from the NT enable textual critics to establish how the text appeared at particular times and particular places in the early centuries of church history. The evidence from the church fathers is limited, though, in that it is often difficult to tell whether a scripture text is being quoted or only alluded to. If quoted, did the church father quote from memory, and if so, did he quote accurately? Further, scribes altered the texts of the fathers as they copied them, and it is difficult to know what a father originally wrote.

Versions in Other Languages. As early as the second century, the NT was translated into Syriac, Latin, and Coptic. In the next few centuries translations were also made into other languages such as Gothic, Armenian, Ethiopic, and Georgian. Of these translations, Syriac, Latin, and Coptic are the most helpful for recovering the earliest form of the Greek text.

Need for Textual Criticism. In not one single verse do all of these manuscripts (Greek continuous text, lectionaries, citations in the church fathers, versions) agree completely. Some differences are insignificant, such as misspelled words, or substitution of a synonym; others are more important, such as omissions or additions of words, phrases, and entire verses. Is the textual critic to follow one manuscript exclusively, even though the best manuscript has obvious errors? Should one follow a particular group of manuscripts over another group? Relying primarily on certain manuscripts over other manuscripts is called relying on external evidence. Relying on matters such as a writer's style, vocabulary, and theology rather than on certain "better" manuscripts is called relying on internal evidence. How, then, did errors and changes occur in the history of the transmission of the text? The answer to that question helps the textual critic establish certain criteria for establishing the text as close as possible to the original.

(1) Intentional changes. Not all scribal changes were the results of errors as such. Before the individual writings were given the status of holy scripture by the church, copyists sometimes made changes to improve the text. Some changes were attempts to improve the style by using a less complicated grammatical construction or word more widely known. Some alterations were efforts to clarify or correct a theological statement. For example, Luke 2:41, 42 refers to Joseph and Mary as Jesus' "parents," but some scribes changed these verses to read "Joseph and Mary" and "Joseph and his mother," lest someone think that Joseph really was one of Jesus' biological parents. Matt 24:36 says, "No one knows the day or the hour, not even the angels of heaven nor the son, but only the Father." Some scribe(s) omitted the words "nor the son," to preserve a high Christology.

(2) Unintentional changes. Some changes were due to errors of the eye. A copyist would skip over a letter, a word, or phrase. Sometimes a whole line would be omitted when two consecutive lines ended with the same word, since the scribe would omit the entire second line, thinking he has just written the final word of that line. Other errors were due to mistakes in hearing. On hearing 1 John 1:4 read, for example, some scribes heard "our joy" and some heard "your joy," since these two pronouns were pronounced the same. Other errors were due to memory lapses which resulted in the transposition of letters or words.

Principles for Establishing Original Reading. Through careful examination of hundreds of manuscripts and an untold number of scribal errors, textual critics have developed criteria for sorting out which manuscripts and groups of manuscripts seem most reliable, recognizing that all have errors (note that text critics are *not* dealing with any original manuscripts; they study only copies of copies). Most manuscripts can be loosely grouped into one of three families or text types according to the readings where divergence occurs in the manuscripts. The Alexandrian text type, represented by most of the papyri and several uncial manuscripts of the fourth and fifth centuries, is considered by most scholars today to be found in the best manuscripts. The manuscripts comprising the "Western" text may occasionally preserve the correct reading when the other text types do not. They appear to have been created as the result of wild and uncontrollable growth in the manuscript tradition. The Byzantine text family, comprising most minuscule manuscripts, is considered the least valuable group of manuscripts, though a few scholars debate this as will be noted below. The principles or canons developed by textual critics to establish the best reading fall into two categories: external evidence and internal evidence.

(1) External evidence. (a)The oldest manuscripts are to be preferred. (b) A reading known in widely separated geographical areas is preferred to one known only in one geographical area. (c) A reading supported by a vast majority of extant manuscripts is not necessarily the best reading. These manuscripts may all come from a common ancestor. Manuscripts, therefore, must be weighed (evaluated) and not just counted.

(2) Internal evidence. (a) The shorter reading is to be preferred. In most cases, scribes added to the text rather than omitted. (b) The more difficult reading is to be preferred since scribes usually altered a difficult text to make it easier, rather than vice versa. (c) The reading which best fits the writer's style and vocabulary is to be preferred. (d) Similarly, the reading which best fits the context is to be preferred. Numerous other canons could be mentioned, as well as qualifications of these already listed. Such canons guide textual critics as they seek to determine what a writer originally wrote. Of course, such methodology is part science and part art. Some scholars base their decisions more heavily on external evidence, some more heavily on internal evidence. Most textual critics today acknowledge the need to keep considerations of both internal and external evidence in balance.

History of the Greek NT Text. Two periods must be noted in the history of the text: that prior to printing and that after the invention of printing.

(1) Prior to printing. For the first three centuries C.E. the text of the Greek NT developed freely, not yet subject to strict controls. As scribes in these early centuries made copies from other copies, manuscripts began taking on textual peculiarities of other manuscripts. Some manuscripts, for example, contained in Matt 6:13 the words "for yours is the kingdom and the power and the glory forever. Amen," and other manuscripts did not. In this way the different text types arose, and textual mixture occurred also as manuscripts of different text types existing in the same location would influence each other. As Christians gave canonical status to the NT writings, scribes had less freedom to alter the text.

By the year 200 C.E. Latin manuscripts were being used in the western part of the Roman Empire, Coptic manuscripts in Egypt, and Syriac manuscripts in Syria. Greek continued to be used mainly in the East. Indeed more than 8,000 manuscripts of the Latin Vulgate exist today, far more than all the known Greek manuscripts. By the end of the seventh century, the Greek NT was being used in one small part of the church—the Greek Orthodox Church with its dominant patriarchate in Constantinople. By the time the printing press was invented, the Byzantine text was the dominant form of the Greek text.

(2) The printed Greek NT. The first printed Greek NT was edited by the Dutch humanist Erasmus and printed by the Swiss printer Froben of Basel in 1516. Erasmus used the six hand-written manuscripts available to him, and not surprisingly, all but one contained the Byzantine text. This printed text, a Byzantine type text, went through various editions with minor changes over the next one hundred years, coming to be known as the *Textus Receptus* (*TR*, Latin for "received text").

During the next two hundred years, two major developments took place with regard to the *TR*. First, the seventeenth and eighteenth centuries were a time in which scholars in England and Germany began comparing the texts of known manuscripts with the text of the *TR* and collecting variant readings, i.e., readings which differed from those in the *TR*, with several editions of the *TR* printed with variant readings in the margins. Increasingly scholars began to question the value of the *TR*.

Second, in the eighteenth and nineteenth centuries scholars began formulating critical rules or canons (as noted above) which in the end led to the overthrow of the *TR* in the late nineteenth century.

The British and European scholars, Lachmann, Tischendorf, Mill, Bentley, Wettstein, Semler, and Griesbach all played important roles in the overthrow of the *TR*. But the individuals most directly responsible were two British scholars, F. J. A. Hort and B. F. Westcott, who published *The New Testament in the Original Greek* in two volumes in 1881. They based their text mainly on manuscripts of the Alexandria text type and rejected the Byzantine text as of no value in recovering the original text.

In the twentieth century, Greek NTs have been edited by both Roman Catholic and Protestant scholars. A comparison of the seven editions most used in this century (Tischendorf, 8th ed., 1869-72; Westcott-Hort, 1881; von Soden, 1902-13; Vogels, 4th ed., 1955; Merk 9th ed., 1964; Bover, 5th ed., 1968; Nestle-Aland, 25th ed., 1964) reveals that those of von Soden, Vogels, Merk, and Bover have a closer textual affinity to the Byzantine text than do Tischendorf, Westcott-Hort, and Nestle-Aland, which stand closer to the Alexandrian text tradition. Despite these differences, however, "in nearly two-thirds of the NT text the seven editions of the Greek New Testament . . . are in complete accord, with no differences other than in orthographical details" (K. and B. Aland, 29).

Present State of Affairs. A small number of scholars continue to argue that the Byzantine text is closest to the original writings. Z. C. Hodges and A. L. Farstad, who reject the methods and conclusions of Westcott and Hort, have edited *The Greek New Testament According to the Majority Text* (1982), a text based on the Byzantine text tradition. Yet the Alands are correct in claiming, "It can probably be assumed that anyone working with Greek New Testament today is using a copy of the United Bible Societies' *Greek New Testament* in its third edition (GNT^3, 1975), or the twenty-sixth edition of the Nestle-Aland *Novum Testamentum Graece* (N-A^{26}, 1979)" (Aland, *The Text of the New Testament,* 218).

(1) GNT^3 and N-A^{26}. These two Greek NTs, edited by a five-member international team of scholars, have exactly the same text, differing only in matters of punctuation, orthography, and paragraphing. The Greek NT is intended for use by Bible translators around the world, while the N-A^{26} edition is intended for students, teachers, and expositors of the NT. Both have an extensive critical apparatus at the bottom of each page, citing by standard letters and numbers which manuscripts have which variant readings. For example, Nestle-Aland^{26} indicates that the words "in Ephesus" in Eph 1:1 are lacking in the early third-century papyrus manuscript 𝔭^{46}; the uncial manuscripts א (Sinaiticus, fourth century) B (Vaticanus, fourth century); and the minuscule manuscripts 6 (thirteenth century) and 1739 (tenth century). Other manuscripts in Greek, Latin, Coptic, Syriac, Gothic, and Armenian include "in Ephesus"in the text.

(2) Modern translations. Readers of modern English translations will find notes such as the following at the bottom of the pages: "Other ancient authorities read . . . ," "Other early authorities omit . . . ," "Other ancient authorities add . . . ," "Some late manuscripts have . . . ," "One early manuscript has . . . ," etc. These notes indicate that the translators have followed one group of manuscripts rather than another where differences exist in the manuscripts. Some differences in modern translations are due to different ways that translators have translated the same Greek text (e.g., Matt 6:19 in TEV, "May your holy name be honored"; NIV, "hallowed be your name"). Some differences are due to differences of interpretation of the same Greek text (e.g., 1 Thess 4:4 in TEV, "Each of you men should know how to live with his wife"; NIV, "that each of you should learn to control his own body"). But some differences are due to the fact that the translators have followed different Greek manuscripts where variant readings exist (e.g., Matt 27:17 in TEV, "Which one do you want me to set free for you? Jesus Barabbas or Jesus called the Messiah?" NIV, "Which one do you want me to release for you: Barabbas or Jesus who is called Christ?").

The KJV of 1611 was based on the *Textus Receptus,* a text form which most scholars today regard as inferior since it is basically the Byzantine text. Most scholarly translations in English today such as RSV, TEV, NIV, and NEB are made from a critical Greek text based on older and better manuscripts than those known to the translators of the KJV. Yet because textual critics and translators vary from verse to verse in how they balance both external and internal evidence, minor differences will continue to exist both in printed editions of the Greek NT and in translations into English and other languages.

See also CANON; MANUSCRIPTS/TEXTS/VERSIONS; PAPYRUS; PARCHMENT.

Bibliography. K. and B. Aland, *The Text of the New Testament;* J. H. Greenlee, *Scribes, Scrolls, and Scripture;* B. M. Metzger, *The Early Versions of the New Testament, Manuscripts of the Greek Bible, The Text of the New Testament*, and *A Textual Commentary on the Greek New Testament*; R. L. Omanson, "A Perspective on the Study of the New Testament Text," *TBT* 34/1 (Jan 1983): 107-22.

—ROGER L. OMANSON

• **Textual Criticism of the Old Testament.** OT textual criticism, the oldest of the biblical scholarly disciplines, attempts, initially, to examine the various written documents containing the OT, in order to reconstruct individually their authentic and original forms. Ultimately, text criticism seeks to provide the most accurate text(s) of the entire OT.

The terms "forms" and "text(s)" are used deliberately, for no original manuscript of any part of the OT survives. It is impossible therefore to determine whether one or more authors produced the materials. Furthermore, the contents of the OT are attested in many languages and versions, the readings of which diverge in places to such a degree that any attempt to harmonize or prioritize them seems hopeless. It is probable that multiple forms of the text circulated from the earliest stages, in light of one consistent fact: the older the witnesses to the OT the greater the degree of divergence between them and, conversely, the later the witnesses, the greater the degree of uniformity of their contents.

The Data for OT Textual Criticism. The data available for the study of the OT text are of varying types and value. Most abundant are the hundreds of medieval (eleventh century C.E. on) Hebrew manuscripts containing a fairly standard text called conventionally the *Textus Receptus*, "received text" (*TR*). The form of this text was fixed by a group of editors called Masoretes and thus it is often called the Masoretic text. The oldest complete manuscript of this relatively late lot, the Leningrad Codex, dating from the eleventh century C.E. (1008), constitutes the base text for the most widely used Hebrew edition of the OT, *Biblia Hebraica*, in its third and subsequent editions. An older, but incomplete manuscript, the Aleppo Codex (930 C.E.) is being used for an edition of the Hebrew Bible (OT) by the Hebrew University Bible project in Jerusalem. Sections of the OT—the Prophets, the Pentateuch—are available in manuscripts which predate these two by a few years. But, in general, hard evidence for the text of the entire Hebrew OT does not predate 1000 C.E.

Some 1200 years separate the latest events mentioned in the OT from the date of these most complete Hebrew manuscripts. Because one seeks to establish the earliest text possible, other forms of the OT which predate the medieval Hebrew manuscripts are employed alongside them, in order to elucidate the history of the text.

Of these supplementary documents, those conveniently called the Qumran or DEAD SEA SCROLLS are most valuable. These materials, discovered in the middle of the current century, consist of continuous texts of specific books of the OT, together with thousands of Hebrew fragments. Indeed, portions of every OT book except Esther have been found, dating from the third century B.C.E. to the first century C.E. Many of the readings in the Qumran scrolls agree fully with their counterparts in the late medieval manuscripts. Some reflect what is present in other known forms of the OT—the Greek versions, the Samaritan version, and so on—(cf. below). Still other readings found at Qumran suggest a text that is unique—without parallel in any known source. What this situation suggests is that in the third century B.C.E. there was considerable fluidity in the textual condition of the OT, a fluidity that at once questions the notion of original autographs and validates the observation that divergence increases the closer we approach the presumed time of original composition.

Another source for the textual study of the OT is the Hebrew edition of the Pentateuch used by the Samaritans. The problem of the origin of this edition is intertwined with the problems of the identity and origin of the Samaritans themselves. Allusions to the existence of the Samaritan version appear in the early centuries C.E., but a copy was not obtained until 1616 when an Italian explorer secured one in Damascus. The text contained therein differs from the *TR* in some 6,000 places, agrees with the Greek version (cf. below) against the received Hebrew text in some 1900 instances, even though, in general, the Samaritan version is more like the Hebrew than the Greek. What is of import here is that the Samaritan Pentateuch presents alternate readings that must be considered in any assessment of the textual history of the OT.

As early as the fifth century B.C.E. Aramaic became a popular language in the ancient Near East. Parts of the OT are written in this language, and many Jews in the Persian Empire spoke Aramaic instead of or in addition to Hebrew. Aramaic is a close cognate to Hebrew, sharing the same alphabet and much vocabulary. It became customary for Jews to read scripture in Hebrew and give an interpretation in Aramaic. Some of these interpretations (Targums) are literal translations, others are quite free and expansive, but they all can prove useful in the textual study of the OT. The Aramaic Targums suggest alternate readings to the received text and show examples of its early application and interpretation.

The first known attempt to translate the Hebrew OT into a non-cognate language was made in the third century B.C.E. This Greek translation—the Septuagint, abbreviated LXX—provides an invaluable source for the textual criticism of the OT because, at the very least, the Hebrew from which it was translated is several hundred years older than the earliest complete medieval Hebrew manuscript. Where the received Hebrew text is unclear or misleading, the Greek text, when retroverted (retranslated) into Hebrew, often removes the ambiguity. But, as is true of the Samaritan version, the Greek also diverges from the *TR* in many places. It is, at points, longer, shorter or different from the Hebrew. The Greek Books of Daniel, Jeremiah and Job are three examples of wide variance with the *TR*.

The Greek version is itself not monolithic; there are hundreds of Greek manuscripts many of which differ significantly with each other at points. Other Greek translations (recensions) were made from Hebrew subsequent to the third century B.C.E. These do not always agree with the standard Greek text. Biblical quotations in early Greek literature are taken occasionally from one of these recensions in contrast to the official text. Futhermore, the Greek text(s) was/were translated into other languages as well—Latin, Syriac, and Coptic for example. Sometimes, these versions made from Greek at a time earlier than the earliest medieval Hebrew manuscript reflect even further textual variety.

To summarize: the data for the study of the text of the OT are complex, consisting of materials written in Hebrew, Greek and other languages. Sometimes, there is uniformity of reading among the data, at other times, wide diversity. Diversity increases the further away one gets from the present.

Principles of OT Textual Criticism. It has long been the custom in biblical scholarship to explain, in some formal way, the range of deviations in the extant witnesses to the text of the OT. Recently, the principles governing text critical activity have become less clear and more nuanced so that there are no firm universal rules. Modern textual scholars tend to examine each case of variance, whether inter- or intra-textual, on its own merits and make decisions accordingly. The received Hebrew text, conventionally used as the starting point for text criticism, is not everywhere considered to be beyond question. Its text is demonstrably less clear or logical in places than that found in manuscripts from the Dead Sea or in the versions. Those who privilege this Hebrew text find themselves faced with the dilemma of accepting one complete, sometimes problematic text, or constructing a clear Hebrew text with the aid of the best readings picked (eclectic) from all of the other available sources. This approach requires retranslating the readings of the versions into Hebrew and, in some instances, conjecturing the Hebrew equivalent to the reading in the version. For these reasons, the approach is viewed by its critics as contrived and the resulting text as artificial. On the other hand, the decision to privilege the received text is often driven subtly as much by confessional as by scholarly concerns.

Depending upon which position a textual critic takes, different principles apply. Those who use the eclectic method would regard some of the following principles as valid. (1) The Masoretic Hebrew text is primary: the versions should be used as correctives to it. (2) The reading that best explains the other readings should be chosen as original. (3) The shorter reading is usually best. (4) The more difficult reading is usually to be preferred. (5) Other languages related to Hebrew should be compared when the text is problematic and conjectures made appropriately.

Text critics who are uncomfortable with eclecticism would tend to articulate some of their principles in a different way: (1) All witnesses to the OT text are likely to contain valuable insights into its transmission history; even late manuscripts preserve ancient traditions, and ancient sources may be wrong. Thus, no source should be ignored or set aside. (2) Differences in the witnesses to the OT text should be preserved and studied for the breadth of perspective they provide; they should not always or necessarily be harmonized. (3) The witness of the received Hebrew is not superior to other sources, only more complete and convenient. All variants are treated equally and analyzed according to their value. (4) Textual criticism is an art as well as a science; the proper evaluation of the array of OT evidence depends largely on the subjective judgment of well-trained scholars and cannot be reduced to simple rules.

Doing Textual Criticism of the OT. The actual "doing" of text criticism is limited to a few specialists. The average reader gets a sense of the complexity of the enterprise by considering some of the scribal errors that appear in all manuscripts. (1) Letters that look alike are often confused. (2) Words that sound alike are confused. (3) Words or passages are often inappropriately written once (haplography) or twice (dittography). (4) Words or passages are omitted or written more than once because a scribe's eye skipped (parablepsis) from one occurrence in the text to a later (or earlier) occurrence of the same word, or another word with the same beginning (homoioarchon) or ending (homoioteleuton) letters. (5) Scribes sometimes divided words incorrectly, transposed words or letters, thus altering the meaning of the passage inadvertently.

Recognition of these kinds of errors constitutes the simplest level of textual analysis. Some text critics will consider one class of error more significant than another, but all will agree that they should be eliminated before the more serious task of collecting and evaluating variants begins. Individual scholars do not always themselves need to collate manuscripts and collect variants. Trusted editions of many texts, both in Hebrew and in the versions, already exist. These record in a synoptic fashion one text along with the deviations of its major manuscripts. Comparing the readings of these "critical editions" is the second stage of text criticism. When there is genuine divergence in the sources, serious evaluative textual work begins. How divergences are handled depends on the assumptions the scholar brings to the text (cf. above).

Textual criticism of the OT, sometimes unfortunately called lower criticism, is, in fact, a highly complex enterprise. It requires not only linguistic competence but sensitivity to the range of factors influencing the writing, preserving and interpreting of religious texts. Future scholars in this field will, it may be hoped, restore it to the central position it properly deserves.

See also TEXTS/MANUSCRIPTS/VERSIONS.

Bibliography. D. R. Ap-Thomas, *A Primer of Old Testament Text Criticism*; J. Barr, *Comparative Philology and the Text of the Old Testament*; D. Barthelemy, "Text, Hebrew, History of," *IDBSupp*; M. H. Goshen-Gottstein, "The Textual Criticism of the Old Testament: Rise, Decline, Rebirth," *JBL* 102/3 (1983): 365-99; J. H. Hayes, *An Introduction to Old Testament Study*; R. W. Klein, *Textual Criticism of the Old Testament: The Septuagint after Qumran*; P. K. McCarter Jr., *Textual Criticism: Recovering the Text of the Hebrew Bible*; H. M. Orlinsky, "The Textual Criticism of the OT," *The Bible and the Ancient Near East*, ed. G. E. Wright; J. D. Purvis, *The Samaritan Pentateuch and the Origin of the Samaritan Sect*; B. J. Roberts, *The Old Testament Text and Versions: The Hebrew Text in Transmission and the History of the Ancient Versions*; J. A. Thompson, "Textual Criticism, OT," *IDBSupp*; E. Tov, *The Text Critical Use of the Septuagint in Biblical Research* and "Septuagint," *IDBSupp;* J. Weingreen, *Introduction to the Critical Study of the Text of the Hebrew Bible*; E. Würthwein, *The Text of the Old Testament; An Introduction to Biblia Hebraica*.

—MELVIN K. H. PETERS

• **Thaddaeus.** [thad'ee-uhs] Thaddaeus is listed as one of the twelve apostles in two of the lists of apostles (Matt 10:3; Mark 3:18). Variant readings in Matthew have "Lebbaeus" instead of "Thaddaeus" and the KJV of Matthew has "Lebbaeus called Thaddaeus." Moreover, when Luke-Acts lists the apostles (Luke 6:16; Acts 1:13) "JUDAS the son of James" appears instead of "Thaddaeus." Confusion thus emerges in the lists and any proposed solution can be regarded as only tenuous. Late ecclesiastical writers, notably Origen (ca. 185–255), identify Thaddaeus, Lebbaeus, and Judas of James as the same. It has been suggested that "Thaddaeus" (perhaps from a root meaning "breast nipple") and "Lebbaeus" (perhaps from a word meaning "heart") may be descriptive designations of the apostle whose true name is probably supplied by Luke.

See also APOSTLE/APOSTLESHIP; JUDAS; TWELVE, THE.

—DEAN M. MARTIN

• **Thanksgiving.** *See* PRAYER/THANKSGIVING IN THE NEW TESTAMENT

• **Thanksgiving Scroll/Hymn Scroll.** The *Thanksgiving Scroll* (*1QH*), or *Hymn Scroll*, is a collection of psalm-like poems from Qumran. Seven fragmentary Hebrew copies of the scroll have been identified so far among the DEAD SEA SCROLLS. The longest, one of the seven major scrolls from Cave 1, is badly preserved. It dates to the last quarter of the first century B.C.E. The other six (which have not yet been published) are from Cave 4, the oldest dating to around 100 B.C.E. Although certainty is impossible, the manuscripts probably contain the remains of at least twenty-five hymns. Modeled after the PSALMS, the hymns do not however reproduce the rich literary diversity of the Psalms, being primarily psalms of thanksgiving and praise. Some of the hymns use the first person plural, others the first person singular. Of the latter, a few seem to reflect an experience of betrayal and abandonment, presumably of a leader. Themes which permeate the hymns include a deep sense of human frailty and sinfulness, an affirmation of God's grace and election, a division of humanity into the righteous and the wicked, and God's revelation of his knowledge within the covenant community. One hymn (3:1-18) speaks of the birth of a wonderful counsellor, which has been interpreted messianically by some; another (3:25-36) depicts an eschatological war between God and Belial (cf. 6:17-34); another develops an elaborate image of a plant (presumably the community) growing in the desert, surrounded by springs of water and a luxurious garden (8:4-26).

The tone and content of the hymns confirm that they were composed within the Qumran community. The presence of strongly autobiographical hymns has caused some scholars to suggest that the author was the Teacher of Righteousness. Although this suggestion is not compelling—indeed there is no reason to attribute the entire collection to a single author—it is possible that the Teacher of Righteousness did compose some of the hymns. The function of the collection within the community is problematic. Some have suggested that it was intended for private reading and meditation; others that it had a liturgical role in communal worship. Whatever the case, the obvious popularity of the collection makes it a significant witness to the piety of the sect.

One of the most important contributions of the *Thanksgiving Scroll* promises to be in the area of postbiblical Hebrew poetry, of which few examples exist. Similar poems at Qumran include *1QS* 10:9–11:22, the hymn in *1QM*, and some APOCRYPHAL PSALMS. Poems extant only in Greek include the PSALMS OF SOLOMON (composed in Hebrew) the PRAYER OF MANASSEH (probably composed in Hebrew), and the MAGNIFICAT and the BENEDICTUS in the Gospel of Luke (1:46-55; 1:68-79).

The *Thanksgiving Scroll* contributes to an understanding of the theology, anthropology, DUALISM, and hope of the Qumran sect. As the only extended collection of hymns from the community, it is especially helpful for gaining insights into Qumran piety. As the most extensive example of post-OT Hebrew psalms, it sheds significant light on Jewish poetical techniques in this period.

See also DEAD SEA SCROLLS; ESSENES; HYMN; PSALMS, APOCRYPHAL.

Bibliography. S. Holm-Nielsen, *Hodayot: Psalms from Qumran;* B. Kittel, *The Hymns of Qumran;* M. Mansoor, *The Thanksgiving Hymns*.

—JOSEPH L. TRAFTON

• **Theft.** *See* ROBBERY

• **Theodicy.** *See* HABAKKUK; JOB, BOOK OF; JUSTICE/JUDGMENT IN THE OLD TESTAMENT

• **Theodotus.** [thee-od'uh-tuhs] Theodotus is the author of a poem that was probably entitled *On the Jews*. The eight surviving fragments of this work indicate that the author composed the poem in the style of Greek epic poetry. These fragments derive from the Greek historian Alexander Polyhistor (first century B.C.E.), who provides a summary of the poem interspersed with quotations from it. Alexander's work, which also bears the title *On the Jews,* is partially preserved by the church historian EUSEBIUS (ca. 260–340 C.E.), who quotes from it extensively (*PraepEv* 9.22.1-12). It appears that Alexander's summaries and quotations encompass the whole of the poem, which treats the biblical story of the rape of JACOB's daughter Dinah and the sack of SHECHEM (Gen. 33:18–34:31).

Alexander introduces the first of his eight quotations from Theodotus by giving the title of the work and summarizing what Theodotus has to say about the name "Shechem." The quotation describes the city and its environs in lush epic terms, mentioning, among other things, a certain smooth city wall, which modern archeological investigations of ancient Shechem have in fact uncovered. Alexander goes on to summarize Theodotus's narration of the tenure of the Jews in Shechem and quotes a few lines from the relevant section of the poem. Next he introduces a more extended quotation from Theodotus, in which Laban's nuptial deceit against Jacob (cf. Gen. 29:15-30) and the birth of Jacob's children (including his daughter Dinah) are related. There follows a summary of Jacob's arrival in Shechem, his acquisition of land from Hamor (the ruler of the city), the seizure and rape of Dinah by Hamor's son Sychem (whom the biblical account calls "Shechem"), and Jacob's declaration that he will grant Dinah in marriage only on the condition that the Shechemites submit to CIRCUMCISION. Alexander then produces two quotations from the poem that relate to the rite of circumcision. The first is a statement in the mouth of Jacob that treats circumcision as the act by which one joins the race of the Jews. The second explains that circumcision is an unshakable command of God addressed to ABRAHAM and his family. Alexander continues by summarizing the poetic material relating to the plot of Simeon, one of Jacob's sons, to avenge his sister's honor by killing Hamor and Sychem. Simeon is said to have enlisted his brother Levi's help by recalling a divine oracle to the effect that God promised to give ten peoples to Abraham. Alexander then cites Simeon's words from the poem, adding by way of summary that God himself put the plot against Shechem into the minds of the two brothers because the inhabitants of the city were evil. Alexander then appends Theodotus's own statement that God smote the people of Shechem for their evil deeds, concluding his presentation of the poem by summarizing the attack on Shechem and producing some of the relevant lines from Theodotus, which are quite vivid.

The content, language and style of the poem suggest that the author was a Hellenistic Jew or Samaritan. The description of the smooth wall in fragment 1 indicates that the author knew the city sometime during the period from ALEXANDER the Great (ca. 331 B.C.E.) to 190 B.C.E., when the city in fact possessed such a well-kept wall. The poem reveals the author's acquaintance with certain postbiblical traditions originating in Palestine, some of which conflict with the Genesis story. Of particular interest is the attempt by Theodotus to justify the actions of Simeon and Levi and thus avoid the embarrassment presented by the biblical story, in which the sons of Jacob break the word of their father, who promised peace to the Shechemites if they became circumcised (Gen 34:17). Theodotus mentions neither this promise nor the circumcision of the men of the city but instead suggests that the attack on Shechem was ordained by God, an idea that is foreign to the biblical account.

Bibliography. J. J. Collins, "The Epic of Theodotus and the Hellenism of the Hasmoneans," *HTR* 73 (1980): 91-104; F. Fallon, "Theodotus," *The Old Testament Pseudepigrapha,* ed. J. H. Charlesworth; G. W. E. Nickelsburg, "Theodotus the Epic Poet," *Jewish Writings of the Second Temple Period,* ed. M. E. Stone.

—CHARLES H. COSGROVE

• **Theology of the New Testament.** What is NT theology? What method is proper to NT theology? No final answer to either question seems forthcoming. The question of method is much debated, with wide differences in theory and practice. The question of content is often ignored, as though the answer were obvious.

Behind these questions lurks another: What is theology? By analogy to such terms as "zoology," the study of animals, and "anthropology," the study of humans, "theology" may appear to be the study of GOD. However, it is not that simple. Theology is necessarily concerned with God; but biblically, God is not an object studied by humans. God is the knower before he is the known (Gal 4:9; Rom 1:19), and theology is also concerned with human beings and the world in which they live.

Karl Barth began his *Church Dogmatics* with a Greek quotation from Cocceius, which may be rendered: "The theologian is the one saying 'God,' from God, in the presence of God, and unto his glory.'' Two foci appear here, God and the theologian, interacting with one another. Unlike philosophy, theology is necessarily concerned with God. ''In the beginning God . . . '' (Gen 1:1) is the primary focus for the whole Bible. God's primacy is assumed behind every major biblical concern: creation, revelation, and redemption.

R. Bultmann (*Theology of the New Testament* 2:237) sees theology as concerned with God, humanity, and world: ''It is of decisive importance that *the theological thoughts be conceived and explicated as thoughts of faith, that is: as thoughts in which faith as understanding of God, the world, and man is unfolding.*'' There are three foci here. Thus seen, theology is a human attempt at self-understanding. In biblical perspective, the human does not attempt this alone. The concern is with humans in relationship with God, with one another, and in concrete life-situations in the world.

As to specifics, the subject matter of theology remains open. It is easier to begin than conclude any itemizing of all that belongs properly to theology. For NT theology, there is at least a body of literature to set the limits, although CANON is itself problematic. Except for creedal bodies, like the Roman Catholic Church, there is no authority for determining what is canonical. Various regional canons emerged among early Christians, with nothing approaching general consensus until the fourth century. To cite but one example, Christians in Rome around 200 C.E. had a NT canon of twenty-four writings, twenty-two of the now-accepted twenty-seven (absent were Hebrews; James; 1, 2 Peter; 3 John) plus the *Wisdom of Solomon* and the *Apocalypse of Peter*. The earliest known listing of the twenty-seven writings now known almost universally as the NT is from Athanasius in Egypt in 367 C.E. Most scholars today base NT theology on these writings, but some insist upon including second-century patristic writings.

Even where canon is settled, problems remain as to just what in the NT is theological. Popular thought and controversy often confuse such nontheological matters as literary questions (authorship, date, sources, unity, etc.) with theology. Such matters may bear upon theology, but they are not theological as such. Further, all theologians have a working canon within a canon, for without exception they give some passages priority over other passages. All pick and choose.

Theology is not only talk about God, humans, and world; theology is human talk. This is not to say something negative. Theology is no escape from one's humanity. The Bible itself is not God-talk addressed to humans from outside their humanity. The Bible never represents itself as a Qur'an or a Book of Mormon, dropped from heaven. It claims to be of both divine and human origin: ''Men moved by the Holy Spirit spoke from God'' (2 Pet 1:21).

History of NT Theology. BIBLICAL THEOLOGY as a deliberate discipline arose out of early eighteenth-century Pietism, the term ''biblical theology'' first appearing in Germany (C. Haymann's *Biblische Theologie,* 1708). OT and NT theology first appeared as separate studies also in Germany (Lorenz Bauer, *Theologie des Alten Testaments,* 1796–1803, and his *Theologie des Neuen Testaments,* 1800–1802). Of course, the Bible itself is basically theological, including the historical writings. In the NT, PAUL and JOHN have been seen all along as theologians; but now all NT writings are seen as theological. As late as 1961, C. K. Barrett published *Luke the Historian in Recent Study;* but already Hans Conzelmann's *The Theology of St. Luke* (1960) had marked out the new approach. The Gospels work with history, but their basic concern is with a theological interpretation of occurrence within history. Mark, as well as the other three evangelists, is a theologian, not just a narrator of events.

For three centuries, many forces, factors, and motives have affected the course of biblical theology. The Protestant Reformers had used the Bible to counter Roman Catholic dogma, but they had no biblical theology as such. They saw their theology as a whole as biblical, equating their orthodoxy with the Bible. Pietism protested this with a deliberate biblical theology. The Enlightenment countered both Pietism and Reformation orthodoxy.

The Enlightenment had a strong impact on biblical theology by making reason primary and by employing the literary-critical and historical method. The focus shifted to the religious history of Israel and the early Christian community, and gospel claims were reduced to naturalistic explanations. F. C. Baur broke fresh ground toward a constructive view of the NT by applying Hegel's dialectic to primitive Christianity. Paul's emphasis on freedom from the Law (thesis) was countered by the Christian Jews' (Judaizers) requirement of the Law (antithesis). The resultant compromise (synthesis) was the Old Catholic Church.

A further impact upon NT theology came with W. Wrede's *Task and Method of So-called NT Theology* (1897). For Wrede, primitive Christianity was not to be understood from the NT alone but as a living religion interacting with its own world.

Yet another major turn came with the focus on eschatology. Through the nineteenth century, the KINGDOM OF GOD had been seen under the evolutionary idea as the triumph of love in a new community of persons; but a shattering challenge to this came from J. Weiss and A. Schweitzer at the turn of the century. They argued that Jesus and his early followers expected the imminent inbreaking of the Kingdom as a power from above, ending this world and replacing it with another. Scholars generally have followed this understanding of the Kingdom as the rule of God breaking into history from above rather than as an achievement within history. They differ as to whether in the NT the Kingdom is perceived as strictly future; already realized in the life and work of Jesus; or in tension between ''already'' but ''not yet,'' i.e., actually present in Jesus Christ but awaiting its fulness in his promised return (PAROUSIA).

R. Bultmann was the dominant NT theologian of the mid-twentieth century, compelling others to take a position with or against him. Bultmann's existentialist approach may be traced to A. Schlatter's insistence that in NT theology ''the act of thinking'' is not to be separated from ''the act of living.'' Bultmann's basic approach to theology sees it not as a disclosure of truths about God and his revelation but as a disclosure of the self-understanding of our human situation. For Bultmann, NT theology began with Paul, and his form-critical study found little in the Gospels going back to Jesus himself. Also holding that faith requires no validation of history, he gave only thirty-two of 644 pages to ''The Message of Jesus'' in his *Theology of the New Testament.*

Some corrective to Bultmann came from his own students (Käsemann, Fuchs, Conzelmann) in what became known as ''The New Quest for the Historical Jesus.'' More continuity was found between Jesus and the *kerygma,* the proclamation of the gospel in the Gospels. However, this was not a repudiation of the historical-critical method; nor did it back off from seeing the NT witness as just that, faith affirmations of early Christians to Jesus as the Christ. Along with this new approach came redaction criticism, with its concern to hear each of the four Gospels holistically and in terms of its theological perspective.

Method for NT Theology. Scholars generally affirm the descriptive method for NT theology. Each writer or writing is to be heard in that writer's own expression and intention. It is recognized that early Christians were not monolithic, their pluralism being reflected in the varieties of perspective in the NT. A basic unity or substructure is also seen, without which there would have been no surviving movement. Both the variety and unity may be sought in NT theology.

Along with the pluralism within the NT, it is to be recognized that no NT writer offers a systematic theology, not even Paul. These writers addressed concrete life situations, not abstract theoretical ones. It is instructive to note that Paul's theological affirmations are made in his interaction with Judaizing legalists and with their opposites, libertine antinomians who confused grace with license. Addressing legalists, Paul affirmed salvation as by faith and not works (circumcision, kosher foods, special days, etc.). Addressing libertines, Paul made moral and ethical demands decisive for salvation (1 Cor 6:9ff.). In the heat of battle, Paul did not pause to systematize his theology, which was not static but growing.

Although basically sound, the descriptive method has its problems. Some argue that strict objectivity can best be achieved by the noncommitted, but others protest this. Objectivity itself is an elusive goal. Empathy can be a prime factor in understanding a writer or writing. Faith and commitment can be kept under criticism, especially in the colleagueship of an open community.

Some systematizing appears in what intends to be descriptive. This appears whenever themes are selected for study and wherever texts are brought together from more than one writing. If such texts are homogenized and unity is imposed upon diversity, the method is violated. However, it does not invalidate the method to see such unifying substructures as are actually there. An important control for NT theology is to have it undergirded by prior exegesis of separate writings. This does not mean that all such exegesis appears explicitly in NT theology, but it is there underneath as a control.

Further problematic for the descriptive method are the faith needs of both the theologian and those for whom theology is written. Theology must ask of the NT not only what it meant but what it means. It is indispensable to seek out the theology of Paul, John, Mark, Luke, Matthew, and others; but this is not enough. "The act of living" requires more of "the act of thinking" than is offered by a cafeteria type NT theology. A faith to live by requires a more precise sense of direction, but one which is dynamic and left open to corrective.

Current Studies. R. Bultmann's *Theology of the New Testament* remains a study with which any competent NT theology must reckon. It is most vulnerable in its scant treatment of "The Message of Jesus." Interpretation of Paul is profound, especially Paul's anthropology. Ironically, Bultmann's existentialism could have been illuminated by the neglected Jesus material in the synoptic Gospels. More attention to the Synoptics could also have saved Bultmann's soteriology from the anomaly of having it both ways, salvation as existential and also dependent upon some historical, saving event: "God's eschatological act of salvation" (1, 3) and "God's deed rescued them" (2, 159). How is dependence upon an event harmonized with massive biblical witness to God's inherent power to forgive sins and save sinners (Mark 2:7)?

H. Conzelmann's *An Outline of the Theology of the New Testament* (1969) is cogent and highly serviceable. In plan it is basically descriptive: "The Kerygma of the Primitive Community and the Hellenistic Community"; "The Synoptic Kerygma"; "The Theology of Paul"; "The Development after Paul"; and "John." Although descriptive, all does not arise out of the biblical text as objectively traced. For example, the idea of "transferred righteousness" (219) is from the Reformation. There is much systemizing around selected themes, with texts drawn sometimes from the Synoptics, John, Paul, the General Letters, and the Apocalypse (18). This is not to say that he homogenizes or obscures variety, but his practice does undercut the idea that any NT theology is strictly descriptive. Unlike Bultmann, Conzelmann gives proportionate attention to the synoptic Gospels, and his treatment of "The Demand of God" is especially cogent (115-27).

J. Jeremias's *New Testament Theology* (1971) is a major corrective to Bultmann's neglect of Jesus. Jeremias employs the critical method, but he is positive toward the tradition of the sayings of Jesus. He recognizes not verbal inspiration (*ipsissima verba*) but the authentic voice of Jesus (*ipsissima vox*) behind the tradition in the Synoptics. Problematic is the traditional frame he imposes upon NT theology. Part 2 is entitled, "The Dawn of the Time of Salvation," as though God were not saving sinners before this time. This contradicts the explicit and massive witness in the Gospels that not only is the authority to forgive sins inherent in God (Mark 2:7), but that Jesus forgave sins and saved sinners then and there, with no hint of contingency or the awaiting of some saving event.

Among Southern Baptists, W. T. Conner pioneered in NT theology. His *The Faith of the New Testament* (1940) recognizes both unity and diversity in the NT, traced in a four-part work: (1) The synoptic Gospels: Jesus and the Kingdom of God; (2) Jewish Christian Writings (Acts; James; 1 Peter; Hebrews); (3) Paul: Salvation by Grace; and (4) The Johannine Literature. Conner's sound exegesis prevails over traditional dogma.

Frank Stagg's *New Testament Theology* (1962) is widely used in schools and churches in English and Spanish (1976). It seeks to exhibit basic unity as well as diversity in the NT. It is thematic in structure, thus vulnerable to homogenizing; but effort was made to keep this under the discipline of earlier years of exegesis of separate writings in their life situations. Several more recent books since supplement the author's *New Testament Theology*. *The Holy Spirit Today* (1973) and *The Doctrine of Christ* (1984) both stress the oneness of God as opposed to tritheism. The latter goes farther in Christology and soteriology. In *Polarities of Man's Existence in Biblical Perspective* (1973), focus is upon the polar claims under which persons are perceived biblically. A book coauthored by Evelyn Stagg and Frank Stagg, *Women in the World of Jesus* (1978), seeks to fill the biggest gap in his *New Testament Theology*. From primary sources, the book first explores how women fared in the world Jesus entered (Jewish, Greek, Roman). The heart of the book is concerned with Jesus and women as reflected in the Gospels. The closing chapters trace from the remaining NT writings the tensions and struggles within the early church over the role of woman.

The Remaining Task. Probably the most neglected part

of the Bible for the theology and practice of the church is the "Jesus material" in the Gospels. The church has always found it easy to claim Jesus as its object of devotion, but it has never been comfortable with his teaching or example. On critical grounds, the Jesus material is credible. With full recognition of the role of the church in remembering, selecting, and shaping the traditions in the Gospels, what appears is basically memory and not invention. There is no evidence that there ever was a church with the capability or disposition to create the Jesus of the Gospels. Rather, the Gospels carry a memory of Jesus to which the church has never closely conformed and with which it has never been comfortable. Apparently written after the Letters of Paul, the Gospels reflect something more primitive than Paul. This vast area demands closer study in NT theology.

See also BIBLE; BIBLICAL THEOLOGY; CANON; CHURCH; GOD; GOSPEL; HERMENEUTICS; INTERPRETATION, HISTORY OF; JESUS; JOHN, GOSPEL AND LETTERS OF; KINGDOM OF GOD; LUKE, GOSPEL OF; MARK, GOSPEL OF; MATTHEW, GOSPEL OF; PAUL; REVELATION, CONCEPT OF.

—FRANK STAGG

• **Theology of the Old Testament.** OT theology, as an attempt to articulate the faith and content of the OT in an organized fashion, has been an academic discipline since the end of the eighteenth century. Those concerned with the subject have been almost exclusively Christian and predominantly Protestant.

Background to the Development of OT Theology. The earliest OT theology as such was written by the German scholar, Georg Lorenz Bauer (1755–1806). Appearing in 1796, portions of the work were later translated into English under the title *The Theology of the Old Testament; or a Biblical Sketch of the Religious Opinions of the Ancient Hebrews* (1838). Bauer's work was divided into two main divisions: (1) theology, which dealt with the doctrine of God, the divine relationship to humanity, and angels and demons, and (2) anthropology, which dealt with humanity's relationship with God, and Christology. Within each of these divisions, he examined the various subjects historically in terms of five periods: the earliest Hebrew ideas, the influence of Moses, the time of subsequent sages and prophets to the Babylonian Exile, the effect of living in foreign cultures during the postexilic era, and the situation at the time of Christ. Both his treatment of the OT on its own, apart from the NT, and his discussion of the material according to various historical periods represented significant breaks with previous presentations of BIBLICAL THEOLOGY.

Prior to Bauer, OT theology had been treated as an integral part of biblical theology in which both testaments were considered together. Biblical theology had been discussed in terms of what were called the *dicta classica* (or *dicta probantia*). These were, as Sebastian Schmidt (1617–96) indicated in the title of his two volume work, "a biblical collection of OT and NT texts explicated in relation to a series of standard theological topics" (1671). In other words, biblical theology was understood as the exegesis and explication of proof texts organized according to the topics of systematic theology—ranging from "Holy Scripture," "God," "Holy Trinity," to "eternal life and hell."

The pattern of these theologies was based on a theological scheme developed by Luther's colleague, Philipp Melanchthon (1497–1560). His compendium of Lutheran theology—the *Loci communes* (1521)—described the content of Christian faith under twenty-four subject headings ranging from "God" to "Blessedness." Melanchthon's methodology and pattern of organization were influenced by three factors: (1) His desire to produce a work discussing and criticizing the *Sentences* of Peter Lombard (ca. 1100–60) which were organized around the scheme: (a) the Trinity, (b) Creation and Sin, (c) the Incarnation and the Virtues, and (d) the Sacraments and the Four Last Things. (2) As a teacher of rhetoric, Melanchthon, like other contemporary rhetoricians, encouraged the practice of compiling notebooks of "commonplaces" (*loco communes*), containing supportive and illustrative materials organized according to headings (*loci*) or topics (*topoi*). In describing his *Loci communes,* he noted that he was "merely stating a list of topics to which a person roaming through scripture should be directed." (3) His theological presentation was an effort to systematize Luther's thought, especially the latter's understanding of Paul's theology in Romans.

In the *dicta classica* pattern of presenting biblical theology, both the general structural scheme used to organize and present biblical materials, and the individual concepts and *topoi* were derived from Christian theology. This remained the case with Christian scholarship throughout the period of Protestant scholasticism or until near the end of the eighteenth century, and appeared sporadically even later. The dominance of the external scheme can be seen in, for example, Schmidt's exposition of Gen 1:1-3, Exod 33:12-23, 23:20, Isa 6:3, 8, and 63:8 to support the doctrine of the Trinity. The Bible was compelled to support the tenets of Christian theological dogmatics. This approach assumed that the theology of the biblical materials was essentially homogenous whether OT or NT and that the significant content and faith of the OT could and should be organized around the central doctrines of the Christian faith.

Working with a completely different objective and without a commitment to any theological scheme, the philosopher Spinoza (1632–77), in his *A Theologic-Political Treatise* (1670), advocated a methodology for determining the primary teachings of scripture that would later become widely used by theologians. Spinoza worked with a number of assumptions and procedures (cf. chap. 7 of his work, esp. 98-108 in the Elwes translation). (1) Interpreting scripture is analogous to interpreting nature; just as the latter involved "the examination of the history of nature, and therefrom deducing definitions of natural phenomena on certain fixed axioms, so scriptural interpretation proceeds by the examination of scripture, and inferring the intention of its authors as a legitimate conclusion from its fundamental principles" (99). (2) In interpreting scripture one "seeks first for what is most universal, and serves for the basis of and foundation of all scripture, a doctrine, in fact, that is commended by all the prophets [biblical authors] as eternal and most profitable to all people" (104). (3) Such universals, however, are derivative since "Scripture does not give us definitions of things any more than nature does: therefore, such definition must be sought . . . from the various narratives about the given subject which occur in the Bible" (100-101). According to Spinoza, what "scripture everywhere so clearly and expressly teaches" is "that God is one, and that he is omnipotent, that he alone should be worshipped, that he has a care for all and that He especially loves those who adore him and love their neighbor as themselves," and so on (104). The universals he derived from scripture were clearly those ideas that Spinoza found philosophically amicable, culturally utilitarian, and acceptable to reason. (Spinoza's universals bear close resemblance to the five universal innate ideas/notions of religion advanced by Lord Herbert of Cherbury [1583–1648] in his book *De Veritate* . . . [1624]: (a) there is a God, (b) who ought to be worshipped; (c) moral virtue is the chief element in such worship; (d) since none lives up to the ideal, repentance is a duty; and (e) there is another life of rewards and punishments.) (4) Spinoza argues that there were other doctrines less universal, which "are all particular manifestations of true virtue" but are connected with "a given occasion for their exercise" (104). These are historically conditioned and must be evaluated in terms of considerations such as "who was the speaker, what was the occasion, and to whom were the works addressed" (105). Some teachings, such as submission to injuries taught in Lam 3:25-30 and Matt 5:17, were written to be applicable only in a time of oppression and not intended for universal application. Others are merely expressions of the prejudices of particular eras. Spinoza shared the widespread view that religious practices and cultic rituals belonged to the time-bound and thus were of little interest beyond historical curiosity. His determination of what was time-conditioned and thus relevant only to particular contextual situations was based partly on historical, partly on philosophical, considerations. (5) Biblical authors must be interpreted in terms of what they actually said and "we must not, on any account, infer the intention of one prophet from clearer passages in the writings of another . . . unless it is perfectly plain that the two prophets were as one in the matter" (106). Such a position attempted to avoid the harmonization of the two testaments or of separate writings within each testament.

If the *dicta classica* approach to biblical theology viewed the ideal paradigm as the transmission, defense, and authentication of an authoritative tradition or theological scheme then Spinoza's approach reflects a paradigm of historical-critical analysis combined with philosophical assessment. In his highly praised and oft-quoted inaugural essay on the distinction between biblical and dogmatic theology (1787), Johann Philipp Gabler (1753–1826) reasserted, apparently independently, many of the arguments of Spinoza but did so as an advocate within the mainstream of the church. G. L. Bauer's OT theology (cf. above) already reflects at least a moderate acceptance of the shift in paradigms or perhaps an attempt to combine paradigms.

In addition to the history of the *dicta classica* approach and the development of a historical-critical approach reflected in Spinoza, many of whose arguments gradually became standard fare among Christian theologians, three other factors embodied in three theological figures had particularly strong influence on the study of OT theology in the nineteenth and twentieth centuries.

First, the work of Immanuel Kant (1724–1804) moved ethics, morality, and moral consciousness to center stage in theological discussion. Second, the influence of Friedrich Schleiermacher (1758–1834) who stressed religious feeling and experience as the basis for theologizing was especially significant in biblical scholarship. Both men tended to disdain the OT as espousing a religion of external authority of law and commandment, based on a narrow particularistic nationalism. These views encouraged a focus on the ethical aspects of OT religion, a disdain for the cult, and disparagement (and distortion) of postexilic times and Judaism in general. Third, the idealism of Hegel (1770–1831), which stressed the dialectical development of ideas from lower to higher forms within history, intensified the focus on ideas and heightened the emphasis on the conflict of ideas within the OT. In addition, Hegel assessed ancient religions in terms of single ideas or concepts conceived as embodying a religion's distinctive characteristic. For the Hebrews, this was the idea of sublimity, for the Greeks and Romans, beauty and utility respectively. Hegel's dialectic approach heightened the tendency to treat Israelite religion historically and to isolate real or potentially conflictive positions within the Bible and the history of Israel. His focus on overarching ideals encouraged the effort to seek a particular viewpoint, perspective, or center—some idea—as distinctive of OT religion. (Luther's approach to the Bible, with his "CANON within the canon" and stress on looking for the center, was also influential in this regard: see his *Works,* 22.339.)

OT Theology in the Nineteenth Century. Development in exegetical practices, philology, literary analysis, and historical study in the eighteenth century, as well as the desire for a more relevant and spiritual (pietistic) theology, had led to a demand for recognition of the distinction between the testaments and for treatment of the Bible at least nominally freed from the dominance of philosophical and/or theological categories, especially those of Protestant scholasticism. Included in the discussion for implementing these new approaches was the nature of biblical theology in distinction from dogmatics. Extensive debate occurred near the end of the century regarding the nature and content of biblical theology. Writing in 1797, J. O. Theiss spoke pessimistically of the different attempts to realize a biblical theology but granted that some system for putting together the true notions of religion scattered throughout the Bible might be helpful in instructing the general population and the youth of the day.

If biblical theology was not a clearly perceived discipline, then certainly OT theology was not. Thus, scholars took diverse approaches to the subject. Some, like Bauer (cf. above), turned to a historical scheme for the presentation of the development of Israelite religion and religious ideas. Among these were L. F. O. Baumgarten-Crusius (1829) and C. P. W. Gramberg (1829–30). Others worked with a more philosophical orientation: C. F. Amon (1792;1801–1802) subjected the *dicta classica* to rational scrutiny; W. M. L. de Wette (1813) identified the fundamental idea of the OT as "the moral idea, free of myth, of one God as holy will"; G. P. C. Kaiser (1813–21) expounded and evaluated biblical thought in terms of his own rational universal categories; and D. G. C. von Cölln (1836) sought to avoid dogmatic and philosophical speculation in an attempt to isolate the pure concepts and universals pointing toward Christianity. W. Vatke (1835) combined a historical approach with Hegelian philosophy. He argues for a late—postprophetic—date for much of the pentateuchal legislation, thus highlighting the role of the prophets in Israelite religion.

The three-hundredth anniversary of the beginnings of the Protestant reformation, in 1817, witnessed the rise of a conservative Lutheran confessionalism in Germany that strongly influenced biblical studies. One of the most adamant and influential spokespersons for this movement was E. W. Hengstenberg (1802–69) who published a four-volume work on the Christology of the OT (1829–35). A modified form of this confessionalism is evident in the work of J. C. K. von Hofmann (1810–77) who stressed the history of OT events as preparing for and pointing toward the Christ-event as the main concern of biblical theology. This focus on the course of salvation history (*Heilsgeschichte*) was taken up in varying degrees by J. C. G. Steudel (1840),

C. G. Oehler (1845, 1873–74), H. A. C. Hävernick (1848), and E.A.H.H. Schultz (1869). The OT theologies of Oehler and Schultz were the most widely used works on the subject in their day and both were translated into English (the latter after the author had shifted from a salvation-history to a history-of-religion approach).

The historical-critical approach to the OT that had stimulated the rise of OT theology at the end of the eighteenth century came to dominate OT scholarship at the end of the nineteenth century and in the process, for all practical purposes, brought to a temporary foreclosure the production of OT theologies. Their place was taken by histories of Israelite religion, even when the works produced bore the title of OT theology (as was the case with A. Kayser's 1886 volume). Contributing to this development was the rise of the history-of-religion school, exemplified by Hermann Gunkel, which criticized Wellhausen and other critics for not being sufficiently historical. Gunkel argued that biblical theology had correctly given way to the history of Israelite religion and that the latter should focus on the living religion that comes from the heart (since the Israelites were not given to reflection), on the great periods of religious development, on the great OT personalities, and on expanding the interpreter's horizons beyond the biblical canon to include the broad ancient near eastern background.

The developments in the first epoch of OT theology (the late eighteenth to the early twentieth century) may thus be summarized in terms of successive stages: (1) the move to establish OT theology as a separate discipline, (2) discussion of the nature of the discipline and experimentation with the shape of its exposition, (3) the impact of confessional theology and stress on salvation history, and (4) a focus on the growth and development of OT religion in purely historical terms but preserving both a typical Christian deprecation of early Judaism and a commitment to early Christianity (or the religion of Jesus) as a repristination of the "best" in the OT.

OT Theology in the Twentieth Century. Many of the features of the first epoch of OT theology were again rehearsed in the twentieth century. In fact, the first three stages were repeated in broadly identical fashion as if reinventing the discipline. (1) The first decade of the century witnessed, as the title of Köberle's book indicates, the inauguration of a battle over the OT which in Germany led to sharply drawn positions in the 1920s and 1930s. On the one hand, a theologian such as Adolf Harnack (1921) could call for the elimination of the OT from a Christian canon, a position that fed Nazism's antisemitism and denigration of the OT. On the other hand, leading OT scholars such as Willy Staerk, Rudolf Kittel, and Carl Steuernagel called for a break with a purely historical or history-of-religion approach and for a "theological" treatment of the OT that would provide a systematic presentation relevant to the church and contemporary theology but without the "spiritual" exegesis represented by the work of such theologians as Karl Girgensohn.

(2) The rise of new confessionalism in the form of neoorthodox or neoreformation theology, especially in its Barthian presentation, with its focus on the theology of the word of God, contributed to a renewed focus on the Bible (coincidentally, this new emphasis surfaced very close to the four-hundredth anniversary of the Reformation's origins, which fell during World War II). Although not a neoorthodox theologian, the sociologist Max Weber contributed greatly to the new impetus for a theological reading of the OT. Weber argued, in his highly influential *Ancient Judaism* (initially published in 1917–19), that a formative factor in the life of earliest Israel was a developed covenant theology and that the subsequent course of Israelite culture was highly influenced by and even incomprehensible without this Yahweh-Israel covenant theology.

The controversy over methodology culminated in the 1920s with a debate between Eissfeldt and Eichrodt. The former argued that the matter of Israelite and Jewish religion should be pursued along historical-critical lines without judgments about the materials' truth or validity. OT theology, on the other hand, should be pursued by each particular confession from a faith perspective. Eichrodt refused to accept such a bifurcation and argued that, properly pursued, the history-of-religion approach could expound the theological essence of OT religion. In his theology, first published in 1933–39, Eichrodt developed his presentation around a threefold exposition—God and the People, God and the World, God and Man—but using the concept of COVENANT as an integrative principle to provide a cross-sectional view of OT thought. Eichrodt defined covenant in very broad terms as embodying "Israel's most fundamental conviction, namely its sense of a unique relationship with God" (vol. 1, 17) and as giving expression to "a stock of spiritual values" (vol. 1, 32). Eichrodt's magisterial and comprehensive volumes became one of the most significant and influential depictions of OT theology in the twentieth century.

(3) A new and even more consequential impetus in the discipline resulted from the revival of the *heilsgeschichtliche* approach in a modified form, represented most significantly by Gerhard von Rad. With roots in the history-of-tradition research pursued by Albrecht Alt and Martin Noth and heavily dependent upon Lutheran theology with its strong antithesis between LAW and GOSPEL, von Rad argued that the OT was fundamentally a history book. The creation/cosmological themes with which the Bible begins were considered late developments in Israelite thought. For von Rad, the task of OT theology was to "retell" the OT's confessions and reinterpretations of the people's history with Yahweh. Von Rad eschewed any attempt to find a center or organizing principle for the OT and disputed the idea that OT theology should seek to expound ancient Israel's worldview. For him, Israel's confessions of its history with Yahweh—found in the Pentateuch and historical books of the OT—and the prophets' proclamation of new events and a new future yet to come constituted the basic subject matter, while works like the PSALMS and WISDOM LITERATURE represented "Israel's answer" to Yahweh's activity. By focusing on Israel's confessional proclamation, von Rad could ignore the issue of whether Israel's actual history was really identical with its confessed history. In certain circles, represented by such American interpreters as G. E. Wright, the theological value of the OT was understood as being integrally associated with the factual historicity of the "mighty acts of God" whose recital constituted the essence of OT faith.

In the wake of von Rad's work, several major issues have become the foci of discussion. (a) What is the relationship between OT theology and Israel's historical traditions, whether the latter are understood in traditio-historical categories or in terms reflecting actual facticity? (b) What role should CREATION and COSMOLOGY play in OT theology? (c) How should an OT theology be organized in order to present the material systematically? (d) Is there some center to OT faith, whether singular or bipolar, that can serve as an organizing prism? (e) How can OT theology avoid the pitfalls of a history-of-religion approach? (f) Is it possible to produce an OT theology on which Jews and Christians can agree or is it even possible for the two religious bodies to converse meaningfully about the subject?

In spite of the differences of opinion about the subject, OT theology continues to be a viable topic. Unlike the end of the nineteenth century, the end of the twentieth century has not witnessed any temporary demise of OT theological pursuits. In fact, more theologies of the OT have been written during these years than in any other period in history.

Some Proposals for the Future of OT Theology. A number of issues should be borne in mind in any attempt to produce an OT theology. (1) A sharp distinction should be drawn between a history of Israelite religion and OT theology. Both disciplines are legitimate and essential for a comprehensive understanding of the OT but have different perspectives and goals. They should be pursued separately. A history of Israelite religion attempts to reconstruct the actual course and development of religious practices and thought. It is a historical discipline, utilizing all available literary and nonliterary artifacts to describe as completely as possible a development process. OT theology should be concerned with and limited to the thought world(s) of a literary artifact, namely the literature of the OT. A history of Israelite religion offers a diachronic perspective on matters; an OT theology is a synchronic undertaking. OT theology is a study based on a completed work, a book; it is not an effort to describe either how the literary work came to be as it is or how the thought it reflects developed.

(2) OT theology is a canonical undertaking. As such, the canon's contents and structure will influence the theological description of the OT's contents. In other words, a theology of the longer Christian canon (the Catholic), the shorter Christian canon (Protestant), and the Jewish Bible, while agreeing substantially, will differ significantly. The Jewish Bible, with its Torah-Prophets-Writings pattern, is structured not only to give the Torah dominance but also to encourage reading the Prophets and Writings in the shadow of the Torah. The short Christian (Protestant) canon, even though it contains the same materials as the Jewish Bible, with its structure of law, historical works, poetic books, and prophets, is constructed to give a greater significance to the prophetic materials with their openness and future-orientation. No major Christian movement has ever accepted an OT canon with the books in the order of the Jewish Bible (to this extent, Christian canonical approaches based on the Jewish order of the books are rootless hybrids).

(3) The search for some distinctive single theological concept or for some ''center'' or ''middle'' of the OT around which OT theology can be organized is a chimera. The OT belief system or world of thought is too comprehensive and multifaceted to be summed up in some particular idea or theological perspective. The same goes for any attempt to see the course of historical events (*Heilsgeschichte*) as the focal point or the organizing principle for the material. The description of historical events makes sense only when viewed in the light of a larger theological symbol system.

(4) OT theology should be a descriptive discipline. This means, first of all, that an OT theology must not be forced to conform either to any given Christian theological system or to Jewish traditions of postbiblical exegesis. Secondly, OT theology should not seek to arrive at or reduce the material to a set of universal ideas, à la Spinoza and Gabler, that are acceptable to all enlightened moderns. Thirdly, efforts to distinguish between what is contemporarily relevant and what is outmoded and merely historically conditioned ''survivals'' should not be the concern of a descriptive theology. This means that a descriptive OT theology should not be fundamentally concerned with the contemporary church's and/or synagogue's appropriation and use of scripture. Nor is its goal to provide modern systematic theology with a biblical system that can be absorbed into some larger whole without reassessment and recasting. Certainly no biblical theology should be conceived as an alternative to or replacement for modern theology more broadly conceived and informed. Modern religious communities and modern theology can determine, as they always have, what in the OT belief system has both constitutive and challenging relevance to their life and practice.

(5) Any theological exposition of the OT should recognize the centrality of the Pentateuch. This means that law and cult—which play strategic roles in the Pentateuch—must be given prominent consideration. A Christian reading of the OT oriented to the future and with stress on the prophetic literature should still be read through a pentateuchal filter (note the conclusion to the Book of Malachi).

(6) Such a descriptive theology of the OT would resemble the type of analysis of a culture's fundamental belief system and subsystems that one sees in modern socioanthropological studies, for example, in the works of Mary Douglas, Clifford Geertz, and others. The Pentateuch presents us with the OT's encompassing belief system in which cosmological, historical, societal-structural, and individual-psychological perspectives are integrated into an overall theological worldview. This theological worldview in its totality, and obviously with some internal tensions, should be the primary preoccupation of an OT theology. Canonically, the Prophets and the Writings (or the historical, poetic, and prophetic books) are to be read as sharing the worldview articulated in the Pentateuch and are to be interpreted in light of this pentateuchal vision.

See also HERMENEUTICS; RELIGION OF ISRAEL.

Bibliography. B. W. Anderson, ed., *Creation in the OT*; J. Blenkinsopp, ''OT Theology and the Jewish-Christian Connection,'' *JSOT* 28 (1984): 3-15; B. S. Childs, *Biblical Theology in Crisis* and *OT Theology in a Canonical Context*; R. C. Dentan, *Preface to OT Theology*; W. Eichrodt, ''Hat die alttestamentliche Theologie noch selbständige Bedeutung innerhalb der alttestamentlichen Wissenschaft?'' *ZAW* 47 (1929): 83-91, and *Theology of the OT*; O. Eissfeldt, ''Israelitische-jüdische Religionsgeschichte und alttestamentliche Theologie,'' *ZAW* 44 (1926): 1-12; J. Goldingay, *Theological Diversity and the Authority of the OT*; M. H. Goshen-Gottstien, ''Tanakh Theology: The Religion of the OT and the Place of Jewish Biblical Theology,'' *Ancient Israelite Religion,* ed. P. D. Miller et al.; H. Gunkel, ''Biblische Theologie und biblische Religionsgeschichte: I. das AT,'' *RGG* (1927) 1.1089-91; G. F. Hasel, *OT Theology: Basic Issues in the Current Debate*; J. H. Hayes and F. C. Prussner, *OT Theology: Its History and Development*; R. P. Knierim, ''The Task of OT Theology,'' *HBT* 6 (1984): 25-57; J. Köberle, ''Heilsgeschichtliche und religionsgeschichtliche Betrachtungsweise des Alten Testaments,'' *NKZ* 17 (1906): 200-22, and *Zum Kampfe um das Alte Testament*; R. B. Laurin, ed., *Contemporary OT Theologians*; J. D. Levenson, *Sinai and Zion: An Entry Into the Jewish Bible,* ''Why Jews Are Not Interested in Biblical Theology,'' *Judaic Perspectives on Ancient Israel,* ed. J. Neusner et al. and *Creation and the Persistence of Evil: The Jewish Drama of Divine Omnipotence*;

E. W. Nicholson, *God and His People: Covenant and Theology in the OT*; B. C. Ollenburger, "What Krister Stendahl 'Meant'—a Normative Critique of Descriptive Biblical Theology," *HBT* 8 (1986): 56-98; G. von Rad, *OT Theology*; H. G. Reventlow, "Basic Problems in OT Theology," *JSOT* 11 (1979): 2-22; *Problems of OT Theology in the Twentieth Century* and "Zur Theologie des Alten Testamentum," *TRu* 52 (1987): 221-67; J. Sandys-Wunsch and L. Eldredge, "J. P. Gabler and the Distinction between Biblical and Dogmatic Theology: Translation, Commentary, and Discussion on His Originality," *SJT* 33 (1980): 133-58; W. Staerk, "Religionsgeschichte und Religionsphilosophie in ihrer Bedeutung fur die biblische Theologie des Alten Testament," *ZTK* 21 (1923): 389-400; C. Westermann, *Elements of OT Theology*; G. E. Wright, *God Who Acts: Biblical Theology as Recital*; W. Zimmerli, "Biblische Theologie I. Altes Testament," *TRE* 6 (1980): 426-55.

—JOHN H. HAYES

• **Theophany.** [thee-of'uh-nee] From two Gk. words meaning "God shines" or "God shows," theophany in biblical studies is a technical term dealing with a specific type of divine manifestation. The Bible describes several different kinds of experiences of God's dramatic self-disclosure. The subtly abiding divine presence with God's people is known through the "name" and "glory" theologies of the OT as well as in the Holy Spirit in the NT. Also in the NT the incarnation of God in Jesus Christ is presented as the ultimate divine self-revelation. However, these conceptions of God's manifestation are not theophanies. Neither are those brief occurrences when God's voice is heard without any accompanying phenomena (Gen 3:8; 16:7-14), although there are often varying degrees of theophanic elements in these experiences as well as in visions and dreams.

Scholars disagree on how broadly to define theophany. One definition is J. Kenneth Kuntz's: "a momentary manifestation of the deity during which he communicates to man something of his nature, name, and purpose" (*The People of Ancient Israel*, 67). Such an appearance may be in order for God to speak (Exod 19) or to deliver (Judg 5:4-5, 19-21). The God-initiated revelation is one of sovereign power; in response to it, nature is disturbed and humanity becomes awestruck. The revelation is to a mediating individual, and the site of the experience frequently becomes a sacred place. An interesting aspect of biblical theophany is that although God is perceived in the experience, God is not actually seen; either there is overwhelming light (Exod 24:16-17) or a cloud of thick darkness (Exod 19:16-18) out of which God speaks. The visual experience of God in Exodus 24:9-11 may be an exception to this, although the story does not share most of the characteristics of a theophany (there are no convulsions of nature and the theophany is not mediated to the people). Similarly MOSES' glimpse of the back of Yahweh in Exodus 33:9-23 lacks these theophanic details in addition to being initiated by Moses rather than by God (33:18).

The theophany at SINAI in Exod 19 is the most complete of the theophanic accounts in which God speaks as opposed to delivering. The commissioning experiences of Moses (Exod 3), Isaiah (Isa 6) and Ezekiel (Ezek 1–3) share with Exod 19 the unexpected appearance of God to one person for the benefit of the people. This manifestation is accompanied by fire and smoke. Earthquakes often are part of nature's response to God's power as well (Judg 5:4-5; Ps 18:7-15). Elijah's experience on Mount Horeb (1 Kgs 19:9-18) demonstrates, however, that the tumult of earth, wind and fire is not actually God; God is separate from the forces of nature.

The familiar activity of light, darkness, fire and earthquake accompanies divine visitations in the NT as well. At JESUS' transfiguration both light and cloud appear (Mark 9:2-7), while at his death there is darkness and earthquake (Matt 27:45-52); an earthquake occurs also at the resurrection (Matt 28:2). After the ascension, the HOLY SPIRIT comes with wind and fire (Acts2:1-4). The PAROUSIA of Christ is described in theophanic language (Matt 26:64; Luke 9:26). However, there are no real theophanies in the NT because God is already and always manifest in Jesus Christ.

See also EARTHQUAKE; GOD; LIGHT IN THE OLD TESTAMENT; PRESENCE.

Bibliography. J. K. Kuntz, *People of Ancient Israel* and *The Self-Revelation of God*; S. Terrien, *The Elusive Presence*.

—CAROL STUART GRIZZARD and MARVIN E. TATE

• **Theophilus.** [thee-of'uh-luhs] Theophilus was the person to whom the GOSPEL OF LUKE and the ACTS OF THE APOSTLES were addressed or dedicated (Luke 1:3; Acts 1:1). The name means "friend of God." The third evangelist follows the Hellenistic practice of dedicating books to patrons, benefactors, or persons interested in the project who often aided in the distribution of the work. The address "most excellent" (Luke 1:3) is used in Acts 23:26, 24:2, and 26:25 for Roman officials but was not limited to such people in the Mediterranean world of the time. There is, then, no necessity of viewing Theophilus as a Roman official, although he could have been such. The phrase "concerning which you have been informed" (Luke 1:4) may be read two different ways. It may be taken to mean Theophilus was a non-Christian who had received reports about Christianity and needed confirmation or clarification or, more likely, that he was a Christian who had already been instructed and who needed certainty about such. In the absence of any concrete data about this person numerous theories have been offered: e.g., it is not the name of an individual but that of any friend of God, the average Christian reader, the typical catechumen (so Origen); it is a baptismal name for an individual, not a real name but rather a pseudonym to conceal the person's true identity to avoid persecution; it is the real name of an individual such as was commonly used among both Greeks and Jews. None of these theories has enough evidence to support its weight. All that can be known is what is available from Luke 1:1-4. Later legend that depicts Theophilus as the bishop of Antioch or Caesarea is unsubstantiated.

See also APOSTLES, ACTS OF THE; LUKE, GOSPEL OF.

—CHARLES H. TALBERT

• **Thessalonians, Letters to the.** [thes'uh-loh"nee-uhns] PAUL visited THESSALONICA on his second missionary journey, which included the major cities along the coast of Greece. According to Acts 17:1-9, Paul remained in Thessalonica, the capital city of Macedonia, for about three weeks. Paul encountered many difficulties within the city, especially with members of the Jewish synagogue. These Jews became jealous of Paul and sought to bring him before the Roman authorities on the charge of preaching Jesus as king. They could not find Paul but did take hold of Jason and brought him before the authorities. The authorities heard the charges and took security from Jason and allowed him to be released. Paul then left Thessalonica and headed south to Berea.

• OUTLINE OF FIRST THESSALONIANS •

The First Letter to the Thessalonians

I. Paul's Greeting to the Church (1:1)
II. Paul's Personal Remarks (1:2–3:13)
  A. Paul's prayer of thanksgiving (1:2-10)
  B. Paul's memory of his visit (2:1-16)
  C. Paul's assignment to Timothy (2:17–3:13)
III. Paul's Ethical and Doctrinal Teaching (4:1–5:11)
  A. Paul's ethical demands (4:1-12)
  B. Paul's view of the Parousia (4:13-18)
  C. Paul's view of the Last Day (5:1-11)
IV. Paul's Final Words and Greetings (5:12-28)

• OUTLINE OF SECOND THESSALONIANS •

The Second Letter to the Thessalonians

I. Paul's Greeting to the Church (1:1-2)
II. Paul's Thanksgiving and Affirmation (1:3-12)
  A. Paul's thanksgiving for spiritual growth (1:3-4)
  B. Paul's affirmation of the judgment (1:5-10)
  C. Paul's prayer for the readers (1:11-12)
III. Paul's Eschatological Teaching (2:1-12)
  A. Paul's warning to the church (2:1-2)
  B. Paul describes important events (2:3-5)
  C. Paul's view of the restraining force (2:6-7)
  D. Paul's interpretation of the lawless one (2:8-12)
IV. Paul's General Teaching of Assurance (2:13–3:5)
V. Paul's Instruction on Discipline (3:6-15)
  A. Paul's warning to idlers (3:6)
  B. Paul points to his example (3:7-9)
  C. Paul's rule concerning work (3:10)
  D. Paul reiterates his words to idlers (3:11-15)
VI. Paul's Final Benediction and Greetings (3:16-18)

Authorship. Very little doubt exists concerning the Pauline authorship of 1 Thessalonians whereas many questions emerge concerning the authorship of the second letter. William Wrede concluded in 1903 that 2 Thessalonians was a forgery. He demonstrated that topics in the two letters are almost identical and that the themes of the first letter appear in very similar form in the second. Why would Paul write nearly the same letter again to the Thessalonians, Wrede asked? The massive parallels between 1 and 2 Thessalonians raised real problems concerning the authenticity of the second letter.

In the next year, 1904, Georg Hollmann, following Wrede's lead, listed four reasons for the inauthenticity of 2 Thessalonians: (1) the parallel literary dependency between the two letters; (2) the contradictions between 2 Thess 2:1-12 and 1 Thess 5:1-11; (3) the missing references to personal themes in 2 Thessalonians; and (4) the mention of forgery in 2 Thess 2:2 and 3:17.

The most recent conclusive study of the question of authorship has been done by Wolfgang Trilling. He pointed out that the biggest problem with Pauline authorship of 2 Thessalonians is the heavy dependence of the second letter on the first. Both the style and vocabulary of Paul have been followed by the writer of the second letter. Yet Trilling found a more irritable approach in the second letter, contrasting with the warm friendly mood of the first. The authority of Paul is much more stressed in the second letter, especially in regard to eschatological teaching.

Those who have tried to demonstrate a forgery theory for 2 Thessalonians, however, have had a difficult time. The second letter is so identical to the first in style and vocabulary, one finds it difficult to discount it. Also finding a suitable date and reason for it is also difficult. Thus being aware of all the difficulties, it seems best at the present time to accept both letters as authentic.

Date. It is commonly accepted that both 1 and 2 Thessalonians were written immediately after Paul's preaching in the city of Thessalonica. From Thessalonica Paul journeyed on to Berea and Athens. At Athens he sent Timothy back to Thessalonica to check up on the newly founded church. When he received word of their condition, he had moved on to Corinth. He wrote 1 Thessalonians early in his ministry in Corinth (ca. 50 C.E.) and 2 Thessalonians a few months later. That date would make the Thessalonian correspondence the oldest of the Pauline Letters and the first NT books to be written.

Some scholars (Grotiuus, West, J. Weiss, T. W. Manson) take the reversal theory in reference to the dating of the Thessalonian Letters. They believe the evidence suggests that the Letter of 1 Thessalonians was written after 2 Thessalonians. First Thessalonians seems to modify the eschatological views of 2 Thessalonians. Second Thessalonians contains a more primitive Christology which sets forth Christ appearing as an avenger; and the resurrection is not mentioned.

The Setting in Thessalonica. It is a great tragedy that so little archeological work has been done at Thessalonica. This is due in part to the fact that a large modern city of 500,000 people occupies the ancient site today. Perhaps no other biblical city of similar importance has received so little attention by the archeologists. Most scholars begin the study of setting with the account given in Acts 17. Recent scholars, such as Haenchen have raised doubts, however, about the reliability of Acts in outlining the life of Paul and his journeys. Luke is most concerned in showing the founding of a church by Paul and the Jewish persecution which resulted against him. There are also discrepancies between the reports in Acts and in the actual Thessalonian correspondence. Paul asserted in 1 Thess 1:9 that the converts had "turned to God from idols." Hence one would see Paul much more involved with gentiles rather than the Jewish synagogue. The population of Thessalonica was of Greek descent, and there is no way to estimate the number of Jews there or the existence of a synagogue. The fact of the diaspora of the Jewish people, however, would point to the existence of a Jewish population in Thessalonica. We can conclude that Thessalonica was made up of diverse racial and national groups and was somewhat the melting pot of that part of the world. The church probably reflected that mix. We are told that women of the upper class were a part of the congregation (Acts 17:4). R. Jewett pointed out that in Thessalonians one does not find the emphasis upon slaves that is found in the Corinthian Letters.

The political situation in Thessalonica during the first century C.E. reflected the mighty power of Rome. The city had always known the presence of the military. Thessalonica had been founded by one of Alexander's generals in 316 B.C.E. The city was directly involved in the Roman civil war of 42 C.E. in which Octavian triumphed. The proconsul of the province of Macedonia made his residence in the city. The agents of Roman rule in the city were six politarchs who functioned to carry out the wishes of a popular assembly. In Acts 17:7, Jason was accused of violating the decrees of Caesar. Perhaps the members of the congregation had understood Paul's preaching in a political sense—Christ would rule over the world. Some people would have misunderstood this teaching as a threat to Roman rule.

The religious atmosphere in Thessalonica was colored

by the cult of Rome. Caesars were worshiped as gods and given such titles as "savior," "lord," or "son of God." Even before the Romans came to Thessalonica, the inhabitants had worshiped the Macedonian kings as gods. Thus religion and the civil state had long been wrapped together in the city's history. The MYSTERY RELIGIONS also had quite a following among the Thessalonians—especially the cults of Serapis and Dionysus. These religions stressed regeneration, immortality, forgiveness of sins, and the promise of sexual fulfillment.

Eschatology in Thessalonians. A large percentage of the Thessalonian correspondence is devoted to teaching on eschatology. Paul had spent no more than three weeks in Thessalonica, and some of his teaching had been misunderstood. They had been taught that the PAROUSIA was close at hand and that they should be prepared for it. The big question on the minds of the Thessalonians had to do with the condition of the "dead in Christ." Would their loved ones who had died be able to participate in "the day of Christ." Other questions had surfaced concerning the tribulation of the last days and the Christian community's experience in it. The common Jewish expectation was of a final rebellion led by a demonic force usually modeled on the person of Antiochus Epiphanes (164 B.C.E.), the ancient enemy of the Jews. These evil leaders would bring about the worship of the state instead of God.

Paul began to answer these eschatological questions in the first letter. Paul introduced the Parousia to denote the coming of Christ in all of his glory. He uses it some six times in the two Letters. Paul asserted that the "dead in Christ" would in actuality be resurrected first at the coming of Christ. There was no reason to fear about friends who had already died (1 Thess 4:15). Paul seemed to imply that the Parousia would be within the lifetimes of the readers. The day will be like a "thief in the night" (1 Thess 5:2). For the unbelievers the day will break with unwelcome suddenness and judgment.

In 2 Thessalonians, Paul seems to change his eschatological viewpoint. Certain signs were set forth which would precede the Parousia. For this reason Lindemann argued that 2 Thessalonians was a deliberate replacement for 1 Thessalonians. The author was intentionally trying to alter the imminent expectation of 1 Thessalonians by inserting certain signs which must first take place before the Parousia. Others view the change in eschatology to Paul's change of mind between the writing of the two Letters. By the second letter he wanted to throw cold water on the excesses such as people quitting work in order to watch for the Parousia. He wanted the members to know that certain signs would precede the end times. Thus there was no need to quit working but rather a need to be involved in one's daily tasks. Harnack, in contrast, believed that the differences in eschatology could be attributed to two different groups in the church being addressed: the gentiles in the first letter and the Jewish-Christian community in the second. However, it seems quite possible that the first letter with its emphasis on the imminent return of Christ could have produced the excesses which needed correcting in the second letter. Among the signs mentioned by Paul in 2 Thess. 2:1-12 were a great rebellion that would take place and the appearance of a MAN OF LAWLESSNESS. There was also an emphasis on the need not to be idle and the injunction: "If anyone will not work, let him not eat, (2 Thess 3:10b).

See also ESCHATOLOGY IN THE NEW TESTAMENT; MAN OF LAWLESSNESS; PAUL; THESSALONICA.

Bibliography. E. Best, *The First and Second Epistles to the Thessalonians*; F. F. Bruce, *1&2 Thessalonians*; R. Jewett, *The Thessalonian Correspondence: Pauline Rhetoric and Millenarian Piety*; G. Krodel, "The 2nd Letter to the Thessalonians," *Ephesians, Colossians, 2 Thessalonians, the Pastoral Epistles*; A. Lindemann, "Zum Abfassungszweck von 2 Thess," *ZNW* 68 (1977): 35-47; J. Moffatt, *The First and Second Epistles of Paul to the Thessalonians*; W. Neil, *The Epistle of Paul to the Thessalonians*; A. Plummer, *A Commentary on St. Paul's First Epistle to the Thessalonians*; W. Trilling, *Der Zweite Brief an die Thessalonicher*; J. C. West, "The Order of 1 and 2 Thessalonians," *JTS* 15 (1914): 66-74.

—JAMES L. BLEVINS

• **Thessalonica.** [thes'-uh-luh-n*i*"kuh] Thessalonica (PLATES 26, 27) was built by Cassander in 315 B.C.E. and named Thessalonica in honor of his wife who was the daughter of Philip II of Macedon and the half-sister of Alexander the Great. The settlers of the city were earlier inhabitants of Therme and about twenty-six other villages in the vicinity. Strabo indicated that Thessalonica was formerly called Therme.

When MACEDONIA was divided into four districts in 167 B.C.E. by the Roman consul Aemilius Paullus, Thessalonica became the capital of the second district. In 148 B.C.E. Macedonia became a Roman province with Thessalonica as the chief city and center of Roman administration. The proconsul of Macedonia, whose official residence was in Thessalonica, did not interfere with the local government unless there was some serious violation of Roman law.

Under the Romans the city was given considerable autonomous power, and the citizens governed themselves by politarchs, the precise word used by Luke in Acts 17:6. It was a free city with its own Macedonian democratic constitution. Thessalonica had a good port on the Aegean Sea, and it was also situated on the Egnatian Way. These two advantages contributed to making it a flourishing commercial city. After Ephesus and Corinth this city was considered the busiest port on the Aegean Sea.

When Paul left Philippi on his second missionary journey, he traveled along the Egnatian Way to Thessalonica, a distance of about 100 mi. According to Acts he spent no more than three weeks in the city preaching in the synagogue of the Jews. Some of the Jews and gentiles in Thessalonica responded positively to the message of Paul, but other Jews stirred up rabble-rousers against him. Thus it became necessary for Paul to leave the city. Later the apostle wrote two letters to the church in Thessalonica.

It is impossible to describe the Thessalonica of Paul's day. At the end of the nineteenth century a fire swept through the city and destroyed all the remains of the Roman period. Parts of the walls enclosing the city still stand, but these have been reconstructed at various times with the stones of preceding ages being used. The western entrance to Thessalonica was called the Varder Gate. In 1876 this arch was removed to make way for modern construction. An inscription on the gate, presently in the British Museum, refers to city officials called "politarchs." Other inscriptions found in Macedonia contain the same word. In Acts 17:6 Jason and others were dragged before the politarchs of Thessalonica during a riot caused by Paul's preaching. In the time of Augustus the city had five politarchs, but after his day there were six.

In the middle of the third century C.E. Thessalonica was declared to be a Roman colony by Decius. This was done to increase the strength of the city against the Gothic invaders. Through the years the city has suffered attacks from Goths, Slavs, Venetians, Turks, and Normans of Sicily. The modern Thessalonica is called Salonica. Today one-third of the population of the city is made up of Jews. While there were many Jews in the city in the time of Paul, the present number is due largely to the expulsion of Jews from Spain by Ferdinand and Isabella.

See also MACEDONIA; THESSALONIANS, LETTERS TO THE.

Bibliography. J. Finegan, *Light from the Ancient Past*; W. A. McDonald, "Archaelogy and St. Paul's Journeys in Greek Lands," *BA* 3/2 (May 1980): 18-24; G. E. Wright, *Biblical Archaeology*.

—T. C. SMITH

• **Thigh.** Upper portion of the leg. The right thigh and breast of a sacrificial animal made up the priest's portion to be eaten by him and his family (Lev 10:14). The thigh was considered a vital area of the body because of its proximity to the genitals, the seat of life. In swearing an OATH, one would place one's hand "under the thigh" of the other party, probably contacting the genital area (Gen 24:1-9). Failure to keep the oath, it was thought, would result in the lack of offspring or in vengeance exacted by the offended party's descendants. The thigh was also the place where one's sword was strapped (Ps 45:3) and where one would strike oneself as an expression of remorse (Jer 31:19; Ezek 21:12).

See also BODY IN OLD TESTAMENT; OATH.

—DAVID H. HART

• **Thomas.** Thomas was one of the original twelve apostles (according to the lists of apostles in Matt 10:2-4; Mark 3:16-19; Luke 6:13-16; Acts 1:13). His Aramaic name *Toma* means "twin"; in Greek-speaking areas the name was associated with the Greek name *Thomas*, because the two words sound alike; in the Gospel of John he is called *Didymus*, Greek for "twin" (John 11:16; 20:24; 21:2). The Bible does not name his twin.

The Gospel of John includes four stories in which Thomas played a part. When Jesus learned that Lazarus had died, he called his disciples to go with him to Bethany, the little village near Jerusalem which was Lazarus's home. Thomas repeated Jesus' invitation in a form that may have been either gloomy, brave, or cynical (11:16).

In a second story, Jesus spoke of going to the Father to prepare the way for his followers (14:2-4). Thomas responded with a question which indicated that he did not understand Jesus' point; he said that the disciples did not know where Jesus was going and so could not know the way (14:5). Jesus replied that he himself was the way, the truth, and the life.

The third story concerned Jesus' resurrection (20:24-29). Thomas had not been present when Jesus appeared on Easter day to his disciples, and when they told Thomas about it, he vowed that he would not believe in the resurrection until he had touched Jesus' hands and side; later generations nicknamed him "doubting Thomas" because of this vow. A week later Christ appeared again to the disciples, with Thomas present, and Christ offered to allow Thomas to touch his hands and side. He then commanded Thomas to stop doubting and to have faith. Thomas did exactly that, and he gave to Jesus one of the most direct confessions of faith in the NT, "my Lord and my God" (v. 28). Jesus commended him and offered a blessing on all who, unlike Thomas, trust in Christ without benefit of seeing his risen body.

Finally, Thomas was one of a small group of disciples to whom Jesus appeared while they were fishing on Lake Tiberius (21:1-14).

Perhaps Thomas's progress in the Gospel of John is a model of the spiritual pilgrimage: he is devoted to Jesus but a bit gloomy, he doesn't understand, he refuses to believe fully, but once he is convinced, he offers a full and open confession of faith in Christ, and Christ reveals himself to him in a full and special way.

Nothing certain is known about Thomas after the close of the NT. The GOSPEL OF THOMAS bears his name, but he was not in fact its author. The ancient Mar Thomas Church of Malabar in India believes that Thomas brought the gospel to their continent.

See also APOSTLE/APOSTLESHIP; DISCIPLE/DISCIPLESHIP; JOHN, GOSPEL AND LETTERS OF; THOMAS, ACTS OF; THOMAS, APOCALYPSE OF; THOMAS, GOSPEL OF; THOMAS, INFANCY GOSPEL OF; TWELVE, THE.

—FISHER HUMPHREYS

• **Thomas, Acts of.** The *Acts of Thomas* (*ActsThom*) is one of the APOCRYPHAL ACTS. Like most such works, both authorship and point of origin are speculative. It has been suggested that authorship was a collective endeavor by the disciples of Bardesanes during the third century. This possibility raises a question regarding the language in which the *ActsThom* was written, since Bardesanes and his followers were located in Syria. Therefore, both Greek and Syriac have been proposed as possible languages of composition. Most scholars suggest that the *ActsThom* was written in Syriac with the possibility that the existing Syriac manuscripts drew from an older source which no longer exists. This source may have been either Greek or Syriac.

The *ActsThom* is the most complete of all the apocryphal *Acts*. It recounts the legendary deeds of the apostle THOMAS in India during the time of King Gundaphorus.

The *ActsThom* tells of numerous miraculous deeds which are a typical feature of the apocryphal *Acts*. Creatures such as an ass's colt and a serpent are able to speak and become bearers of revelation. The dead are raised and upon their revival they share with the amazed onlookers their experiences in the realm of the dead. These experiences include both a preview of HEAVEN and a conducted tour of HELL.

The fantastic imagery and larger-than-life exploits of Thomas were the elements which helped make this work popular. It entertained the reader by capturing his or her attention and in the process presented a particular view on the proper attitude toward sexual relationships. It taught abstinence not only from immorality, but also from sexual relationships within marriage.

Besides exhortations against sexual intercourse, which are based upon the premise that the body is a holy temple, the *ActsThom* also supports the celibate lifestyle by the rationale that the birth of children is burdensome and troublesome. Furthermore, it glorified the ascetic model of life in regard to prayer, diet, and clothing. Thomas's lifestyle is that of the model ascetic; he is portrayed as one who lived on bread, salt, and water, and had only one garment.

A major feature of the *ActsThom* is its Gnostic character. This trait is most readily seen in the Gnostic idea of the REDEEMER myth. The redeemer figure enlightens, frees his followers from the passion of this world, and is a source of life enabling one to find his or her way to the heavenly kingdom. The Gnostic elements within this work are most readily found with two hymns: the Wedding Hymn and the Hymn of the Pearl.

There is little or no historical value in the *ActsThom* for a reconstruction of the life of the apostle Thomas. It can, however, be helpful in presenting some perspectives on the social world of the early Christian movement in relation to the LORD'S SUPPER, the laying on of hands (sealing), anointing, and ALMS for the poor.

See also ACTS, APOCRYPHAL; GNOSTICISM.

Bibliography. G. Bornkamm, "The Acts of Thomas," *New Testament Apocrypha,* ed. E. Hennecke and W. Schneemelcher; A. F. J. Klijn, *The Acts of Thomas*; J. M. LaFargue, *Language and Gnosis: The Opening Scenes of the Acts of Thomas.*

—DAVID M. MAY

• **Thomas, Apocalypse of.** The *Apocalypse of Thomas* (*ApocThom*) is a Christian apocalypse ascribed in its introduction and conclusion to Thomas, one of Jesus' disciples. This relatively brief apocalypse describes the signs which will accompany the destruction of the world. Unlike the APOCALYPSE OF PETER or PAUL, this work contains no vision concerning heaven or hell. The *ApocThom* is relatively late and dates from the fifth century C.E. It is extant in a few Latin manuscripts. It is possible that behind the Latin stands an earlier and no longer extant manuscript composed in Greek.

Like the *ApocPaul*, this work was designated by the *Decretum Gelasianum* (sixth century) as inappropriate for use in the churches. The *ApocThom* may have been influenced by Gnostic tendencies or possibly Manichaean and Priscillianist thought. This speculation is based upon some internal observations, such as, the emphasis upon light: "Then they (the saints) will put on the garment of eternal life: the garment from the cloud of light which has never been seen in this world. . . . "

The *ApocThom* shares several affinities with the canonical Apocalypse of John (Revelation). Both of these apocalypses use patterns of seven and describe various types of signs which accompany the end of the world. The similarity between these two apocalypses can be seen even more clearly by examining the particular signs which foreshadow world destruction.

On the first day is the sign of blood raining upon the earth. The second day is marked by smoke pouring forth from heaven, causing fear and terror. On the third day the firmament of heaven is cracked and the air is filled with the smell of sulfur. The fourth day is distinguished by an earthquake which topples all the idols. On the fifth day there are cataclysmic occurrences in the sky, such as the sun bursting, the stars no longer shining, and darkness covering the earth.

While the first five days are marked by occurrences in the natural realm, the sixth day and seventh days are characterized by marvelous happenings in the spiritual. On the sixth day the heavens split open and the angels gaze out from heaven upon humanity. Those upon the earth see the angels and flee in fright. This day, to which is devoted the longest description of all the days, is also the occasion on which Christ comes with fiery destruction and the saints are given the garment of eternal life. The seventh day sees a war carried out by the holy angels, although it is not clear from the text who their opponents are. These signs conclude with the election of the believers and the final destruction of the earth on the eighth day.

This apocalypse does not indicate that these signs of judgment are redemptive in the sense of turning the people of the world back to repentance. In this regard the *ApocThom* is unlike the Apocalypse of John since this appears to be a reason for the plagues described there (Rev. 9:21; 16:9).

See also APOCALYPTIC LITERATURE; GNOSTICISM; MANI/MANICHEISM; REVELATION, BOOK OF.

Bibliography. R. James, *The Apocryphal New Testament*; A. de Santos Otero, "Apocalypse of Thomas," *New Testament Apocrypha,* ed. E. Hennecke and W. Schneemelcher.

—DAVID M. MAY

• **Thomas the Contender, Book of.** Originating apparently from a Gnostic community that traced its practice and teaching back to the apostle THOMAS, the *Book of Thomas the Contender* (*ThomCont*) is the seventh tractate in Codex II of the NAG HAMMADI library. This eight-page Coptic text (translated from Gk.) contains a revelation dialogue between the risen Christ and his twin brother (Didymus Thomas) held prior to the ASCENSION. Its reputed author is one "Mathias" (probably the apostle Matthew) who has supposedly taken down Jesus' words as he spoke them. The document's principal concern is the proclamation, in "secret words that the Savior spoke" (138.1), of the need to "know oneself" (i.e., the divine within oneself) and to follow the ascetic path, avoiding the "fires" of bestial lust and other passions in order to obtain salvation.

The contents of *ThomCont* are divisible into two parts. The first (138.4–142.21) is a dialogue between Thomas and Jesus. Literarily similar to a Hellenistic form known as *eratapokriseis* ("questions" and "answers"), the tractate presents Thomas as an initiate seeking instruction from the spiritual authority Jesus. Thomas asks eleven questions, each fairly brief. Jesus answers twelve times in speeches that vary from two lines (139.21-22) to 116 lines (142.26–145.16). The second part of the tractate (142.21–145.19) is an ascetical and eschatological sermon by Jesus. He offers a vivid description of HELL for those who succumb to fiery passions of the flesh, heaps woes on those who reject his teachings but blessings on those who accept them, and exhorts his hearers to wakefulness that they may escape bondage of the "flesh" and find "rest" with the highest God. Some argue the document's two parts give evidence of the editorial joining together of originally separate texts. Others, however, claim that repeated warnings against lust in both parts, as well as the probable use of the closing homily as an example of the type of preaching Thomas was commanded to give, point toward the unity of the text.

Unlike Valentinian Gnostics, the author of *ThomCont* offers no teachings regarding the origins of the cosmos or the secrets of the heavenly Pleroma. In fact, the Savior states that self-knowledge is far more important: "For he who has not known himself has known nothing, but he who has known himself has already achieved knowledge of the Depth of All" (138.16–18). Influenced by the Platonic dualistic view of the visible-passionate-illusory versus the invisible-spiritual-real, the author teaches (borrowing from the wisdom tradition) that the wise are not controlled by passions, though the foolish are.

Such emphases bring this tractate into the sphere of ascetic thought and gnosis shared by the GOSPEL OF THOMAS and the "Hymn of the Pearl" from the ACTS OF THOMAS, pointing toward Syrian Edessa as the probable vicinity of composition. This was one of the places traditionally connected with Thomas. He is said to have evangelized both northern Mesopotamia and India, and his relics were venerated at Edessa as early as the fourth century. Most would date the tractate in the late second to the early third century.

See also GNOSTICISM; NAG HAMMADI.

Bibliography. B. Layton, "The Book of Thomas the Contender Writing to the Perfect," *The Gnostic Scriptures: A New Translation with Annotations and Introductions*; J. D. Turner, *The Book of Thomas the Contender from Codex II of the Cairo Gnostic Library from Nag Hammadi (CG 2,7): The Coptic Text with Translation, Introduction, and Commentary, SBLDS* and "The Book of Thomas the Contender," *The Nag Hammadi Library in English*, ed. J. M. Robinson.

—MALCOLM L. PEEL

• **Thomas, Gospel of.** The *Gospel of Thomas* is one of the fifty-two separate writings included among the books of the NAG HAMMADI library. It consists of twenty PAPYRUS pages. Although the text has some slight destruction to the tops and bottoms of selected pages, it is nevertheless virtually complete. It is written in the Sahidic dialect of the Coptic language, and bears the subscript title "the Gospel according to Thomas."

Date and Provenance. This particular Coptic version dates at the latest to the middle of the fourth century C.E., at which time the Nag Hammadi library was buried. But the document was known, quoted, and rejected at the beginning of the third century C.E. by Origen and Hippolytus. Greek papyrus fragments representing different Greek versions of the text have also been discovered. The earliest of these fragments has been dated soon after 200 C.E. This date, however, applies to the papyrus fragment and not the composition of the text, which has been dated as early as 50 C.E. and no later than 140 C.E. Since the Greek fragments represent different Greek recensions of the document, none of which is the original from which the Coptic text was translated (it is a translation of a still different Greek text), it would appear that the document was widely circulated in antiquity. Because of its association with the apostle Thomas, and because certain Coptic sayings appear to reflect an earlier semitic version from which the Coptic translation may have been made (e.g., sayings 3, 13, 14, 25, 80), a provenance in Syria, Palestine, or Mesopotamia has been proposed.

Form and Content. The document consists of a collection of sayings with a brief narrative introduction (e.g., "Jesus said," "he said"). The introduction to the text (32.10-12) attributes the sayings to the "living Jesus," and describes them as "secret words" written by "Didymos Judas Thomas" (i.e., the twin, Judas Thomas [and Thomas also means twin]; perhaps the twin brother of Jesus, cf. THOMAS THE CONTENDER). The book has no closing literary frame. The editors of the *editio princeps* judged it to have 114 sayings, and that convention is generally followed, although on three occasions (sayings 27, 93, 101) the editors emended the text to begin a new saying.

As yet no one has convincingly established that there is a deliberate scribal ordering to the sequence of the sayings, beyond the recognition of simple "catchwords" (e.g., "cast" in sayings 8-10, and "Kingdom" in sayings 96-99) and motif associations (e.g., the motifs of seeking-finding-knowing in sayings 1-6). Indeed the text may well be a collection of collections of sayings from various parts of the ancient world, some of the sayings having an earlier date of origin than others. Sayings collections tend to expand and shrink (cf. for example, Matthew's use of Mark's parables collection Mark 4:1-34 || Matt 13:1-54). Hence, when one describes the date of "composition" of the Coptic *GosThom*, what is actually meant is that point when it reached its present form. The manuscript evidence suggests that its content fluctuated as long as it had a viable life in a user community.

The types of sayings in the collection include aphorisms, proverbs, parables, beatitudes, curses, legal sayings, dialogues, woes, and pronouncement stories. Initial descriptions of the *GosThom* identified it as a Gnostic document, but later study of the document has shown that the tradition-character of the sayings is quite diverse. *GosThom* contains sayings that would have been quite at home in the canonical Gospels, although they are not preserved there (namely, sayings 39a, 77b, 82). It contains sayings that derive from Greek wisdom literature (e.g., sayings 102 and 8; both of these are variations of fables originally attributed to Aesop). It also contains Jewish WISDOM LITERATURE (saying 17 = 1 Cor 2:9). A large number of the sayings are versions of sayings already known from the canonical Gospels (sayings 9, 14, 16, 20, 26, 31, 32, 45, 47), although no one has yet demonstrated a convincing literary connection between Thomas and the canonical Gospels. There is also a large number of sayings whose provenance is unclear, and while many of these may be read as "Gnostic," they are not necessarily characteristic of the developed Gnostic systems of the second century C.E. (cf., e.g., 7, 15, 18, 22, 50, 60, 77, 80, 87, 110, 114).

Theology. Because the document does not appear to have been the work of a single author, but rather consists of a collection of diverse traditions, it is not possible to describe its theology, as though it presented a consistent system. Apparently it was possible, however, for the final compiler of the text and its users to read it in such a way that the diverse collection of sayings could be understood to reflect a consistent religio-philosophical stance. For a similar situation, compare the way in which modern Christian readers engage the Jewish scriptures (i.e., the OT) from a christological perspective, and are thereby able to claim them for the Christian Bible. The general stance of the *GosThom* is "world denying," rather than "world affirming." Its sayings generally reflect retreat from the world into an esoteric, mystic, and ascetic faith. The introduction, for example, invites the reader, any reader, to seek for the specific key that makes sense out of the collection of sayings, and it is that discovery that brings eternal life.

Significance. The discovery of the Coptic text of the *GosThom* fills a gap in the history of early Christian literature, and provides the modern historian with primary data for reconstructing a previously lost chapter in the history of Christian origins. *GosThom* represents a part of the diversity of early Christianity that was lost when one of the wings of the early Christian movement established a dominance over others, and consolidated its influence through a selection of particular religious texts that excluded *GosThom*. For the modern scholar *GosThom* is a valuable new source for sayings of Jesus. In certain cases (sayings 82, 97, 98) it has been argued that *GosThom* has preserved original sayings of Jesus that are not found in the canonical Gospels.

Because the *GosThom* does not appear to be dependent upon the canonical Gospels, but rather seems to reflect an independent tradition, it provides the modern scholar with new information for tracing the history of the Jesus tradition, and an opportunity, unparalleled in modern times, for evaluating the canonical tradition. For example, all of the parables in the *GosThom* (sayings 8-9; 20; 63-65; 96-98; 107; 109) appear to be earlier and simpler versions of parables also preserved in the synoptic Gospels, in that they lack the obvious allegorical shaping and elaborate interpretation that have come to be associated with the redaction and theology of the synoptic evangelists (e.g., saying 65 = Mark 12:1-11 ‖ Matt 21:33-46 = Luke 20:9-19).

Probably the *GosThom* will not affect the contemporary traditional churches in any substantial way, though it might be expected to appeal to some of the more esoteric and world-denying new religious movements. For the traditional churches, however, because of the nature of its contents, the document poses the issue: how does one study and understand the Bible? Is it to be studied from the perspective of an exclusive canonical bias that, as one strand of early Christianity, consciously excludes even the study of texts like the *GosThom*? Or is the Bible to be studied in a broad history-of-religions context that quite consciously makes use of all sources of information from antiquity?

See also AGRAPHA; APOCRYPHAL GOSPELS; GNOSTICISM; NAG HAMMADI; THOMAS.

Bibliography. R. Cameron, "Parable and Interpretation in the Gospel of Thomas," *Forum* 2/2 (1986): 3-39; J. D. Crossan, *Four Other Gospels: Shadows on the Contours of Canon*; S. Davies, *The Gospel of Thomas and Christian Wisdom*; J. A. Fitzmeyer, "The Oxyrhynchus *Logoi* of Jesus and the Coptic Gospel According to Thomas," *TS* 20 (1959): 505-60; A. Guillaumont, H. Puech, G. Quispel, W. Till, and Y. 'Abd al Masīḥ, eds., *The Gospel According to Thomas Coptic Text Established and Translated*; C. W. Hedrick, "The Treasure Parable in Matthew and Thomas," *Forum* 2/2 (1986): 41-56; K. King, "Kingdom in the Gospel of Thomas," *Forum* 3/1 (1987): 48-97; P. Perkins, "Pronouncement Stories in the Gospel of Thomas," *Semeia* 20 (1981): 121-32; J. M. Robinson, "On Bridging the Gulf from Q to the Gospel of Thomas (or Vice Versa)," C. W. Hedrick and R. Hodgson, Jr., eds., *Nag Hammadi, Gnosticism, and Early Christianity*; H. E. W. Turner and H. Montefiore, *Thomas and the Evangelists*.

—CHARLES W. HEDRICK

• Thomas, Infancy Gospel of. The *Infancy Gospel of Thomas* is a collection of legendary traditions about the childhood of Jesus. In its most accessible form, the longer Greek recension, the book is entitled "The Account of Thomas the Israelite Philosopher Concerning the Childhood of the Lord." This recension begins with a prologue, in which the author identifies himself as THOMAS and proposes to inform the gentiles about the mighty deeds which Jesus did as a child. There follows a series of stories about things which Jesus did between the ages of five and twelve. He performs a number of miracles, including nature miracles (bringing clay sparrows to life, carrying water in his garment when a pitcher breaks, reaping a miraculously great harvest of wheat, and aiding his father JOSEPH in his carpentry by stretching a piece of wood), healing miracles (the badly injured foot of a young man, and his brother James when he is bitten by a viper), and resurrections (a playmate, a little child, and a workman). He also confounds several teachers who come to teach him letters. The recension ends with a variation on the story of the twelve-year-old Jesus at the TEMPLE (Luke 2:41-52), in which Jesus amazes his elders with his ability to expound on the Law and the Prophets. Other recensions include other stories (e.g., Jesus aiding a dyer, riding a sunbeam, and making a salted fish come alive).

The *InGosThom* is preserved, in whole or in part, in many ancient and medieval languages, including Greek, Latin, Syriac, Slavonic, Ethiopic, Armenian, Arabic, Georgian, Coptic, Old French, Provençal, Anglo-Saxon, and Middle English. Although the textual situation is exceedingly complex, it seems probable that the *InGosThom* represents a relatively early fixation in writing of a part of what became an extensive oral tradition about the childhood of Jesus, and that later writers felt free to add to the document or even combine it with similar stories (e.g., the PROTEVANGELIUM OF JAMES). An apparent reference to the work by IRENAEUS (*AdvHaer* 1.20.2) fixes its date no later than the end of the second century. It was probably composed either in Greek or in Syriac. The ascription of the book to Thomas is absent from the earliest witnesses and is probably secondary.

The *InGosThom* reflects a thirst for material to supplement that contained in the NT gospels. This book represents an attempt to fill, in a manner which is worthy of the Son of God, the obvious gap concerning Jesus' childhood. Even though some of the incidents seem, to the modern ear, to portray Jesus in a bad light (e.g., he curses other children, who then die; he is disrespectful to his elders, including Joseph), such passages were probably intended to be edifying (Jesus eventually heals all who have fallen under his curse; his elders do not perceive who he really is). Certainly traditions such as those contained in this book attained an immense popularity among Christians who were interested in learning more about the life of Jesus, and were willing to believe accounts however fictitious.

See also APOCRYPHAL GOSPELS.

Bibliography. O. Cullmann, "Infancy Gospels," *New Testament Apocrypha,* ed. E. Hennecke and W. Schneemelcher; S. Gero, "The Infancy Gospel of Thomas: A Study of the Textual and Literary Problems," *NovT* 13 (1971): 46-80.

—JOSEPH L. TRAFTON

• Thorn in the Flesh. A phrase used in the NT only by the apostle PAUL, it occurs in 2 Cor 12:7 in one of the most complicated sections of Paul's writings (2 Cor 10–13). The Gk. word translated "thorn" could be used to refer to something as large as a pointed stake or as small as a splinter. The harassment by the "messenger of Satan" must have struck Paul like the blows of a hammer. Unless there had been some profound effect on the apostle it is unlikely he would have prayed so fervently regarding it. The incidental manner in which Paul used the phrase suggests that he assumed the Corinthians would understand it. Perhaps they had heard Paul utter the phrase in previous instances.

The context implies that the "thorn" was an affliction that Paul had come to think of as subsequent to and corrective of his elation over his many revelations. If that is so, it rules out the possibility that the thorn was either something common to all such as temptation or something congenital such as epilepsy. However, this has not deterred some from espousing these views. Various categories of problems have been proposed as the explanation for this phrase.

Because "thorn" is characterized as a "messenger" (ἄγγελος) some have concluded that it was a personality. It may be taken as a specific demonic emissary of Satan or as some human individual involved in a continuing harassment of Paul. Others reason that the "thorn" is a psychological reality. They argue that the general view of Paul in the NT as one who saw visions and who was influenced by dreams should be taken seriously. In addition it is pointed out that the immediate context of the phrase is one in which Paul is recounting visions and revelations. So, it has been argued, Paul suffered from depression or great anxiety, perhaps for the churches he founded (2 Cor 11:28; 12:13) or for the rejection of the gospel by his fellow Jews.

In Gal 4:13-15 Paul acknowledges a bodily ailment. Some interpreters conclude, therefore, that Paul's "thorn in the flesh" was a physical disorder. The reference in 4:15 to the Galatians giving their eyes to Paul suggests that his problem may have been with his sight (cf. Gal 6:11: the large letters characteristic of Paul's handwriting may imply difficulty with vision). Others argue the "thorn" may have been malaria. Paul could have contracted it in the coastal lowlands (Acts 13:13). If so, the presence of this disease could be the impulse for his rather direct trip to the better climate in southern Galatia (Acts 13:14; Gal 4:13). Recurring episodes of malaria are said to include stabbing pains that might well be described as a "thorn in the flesh."

See also PAUL.

—ROBERT O. BYRD

• **Thousand.** In Hebrew thought, terms cover a semantic field of ideas. A portion or the whole of the idea may be reflected by that word. This is true of the word "thousand" (*'elep*).

The most frequent use of *'elep* is the numeral "thousand," either a specific number or a round figure representing a large general figure. It connotes the specific number, an indefinitely large round number, or any multiple of a thousand.

The grammar and syntax of numerals in the Hebrew language have been problems throughout the ages. One cannot treat Hebrew numbers with the same approach as in the Western mindset. Doing so has given rise to interpretational difficulties bordering on the ridiculous.

Within the semantic field, there arose a usage which is non-numerical. Many interpreters failed to recognize this phenomenon. The RSV and NASB translations note this phenomenon in several passages (Num 1:16; 10:4; Josh 22:21, 30; Isa 60:22; Micah 5:2). Whereas the KJV translates it as "thousands," these translations recognize the nonnumerical use of the term and translate it as "clan," "divisions," or "families." In Judg 6:15, the KJV and NASB translate *'elep* as "family." This use of *'elep* in the sense of group, family, or clan had lost its ancient numerical quality. When writers desired to emphasize the *unitary* structure of a group, *'elep* would be used in the "clan" or "tribe" sense with no reference to specific numbers. It is easy to see how confusion could arise when the author's nonnumerical use of the term was forced into a numerical literalistic application.

See also NUMBERS/NUMEROLOGY.

—JOHN JOSEPH OWENS

• **Three.** *See* TRINITY

• **Threshing Floor.** A flat surface upon which grain is dried, winnowed, and beaten from the husks.

Threshing floors were located on an open high point near agricultural villages where prevailing west winds could blow the chaff away when grain was winnowed. Their surfaces were naturally smooth outcroppings of rock or laid with closely fitted stones supported by terrace walls. They were usually owned by the village, although large land owners at times had their own threshing floors (2 Sam 24:18). Grain thickly spread out on these floors was threshed in a number of ways. Oxen might be repeatedly driven over the grain, or threshing machines of various kinds would be pulled round and round over it by oxen or horses (2 Sam 24:22; Isa 28:27; Amos 1:3). One of the humane laws of Deuteronomy (25:4) specified that oxen so worked be unmuzzled so that they might eat whatever they wanted of the spread out stalks of grain.

Threshing machines were sometimes wooden sledges with sharp stones or metal points set into their under sides. These "teeth" of a threshing sledge were compared in Job 41:30 to the belly of a crocodile. The sledges were weighted with stones. Children probably also rode the sledges as part of their share of the work and because it was fun. Threshing carts or wagons (Isa 28:27-28) were either sledges with wheels or large stone or iron rollers, used as the sledges were used. Some grains like the spices dill and cummin, too soft to be threshed by heavy sledges, were beaten with sticks or rods (Isa 28:27). Although this was less effective and harder work, other grains may also have been threshed by this hand method of flailing. At harvest time workers slept on the threshing floors (Ruth 3:7) either as a convenience or to protect the harvest from theft (1 Sam 23:1), since many bundles of grain would be stored at the site waiting to be threshed.

The best known threshing floor was the one David purchased from Araunah the Jebusite as the site for the Jerusalem Temple (2 Sam 24:18-25; 1 Chr 21:18-28). Araunah tried to give David his oxen for a burnt offering and his threshing sledges as wood for the altar fire. David refused to take them as gifts but bought them with the threshing floor for fifty shekels of silver.

See also AGRICULTURE/FARMING.

Bibliography. M. S. Miller and J. L. Miller, *EBL*.

—DAVID A. SMITH

• **Throne.** The chair or seat of a reigning monarch, the place where he or she reigns. Exod 11:5 speaks of "the Pharaoh who sits upon his throne." Solomon's throne (1 Kgs 10:18) was made of ivory (or with ivory strips inserted) and overlaid with gold. The back had a calf's head decoration. Beside each arm rest was the figure of a standing lion. Each end of its six steps was also decorated with the figure of a standing lion. The entire structure with its seven levels symbolized perfection, power, and lordship. The effect was heightened by its setting in the imposing cedar-paneled Hall of Judgment.

The word also symbolizes the royal power itself rather than the place of its administration. In 2 Sam 3:10 Abner swore to "set up the throne of David over Israel and over Judah, from Dan to Beersheba."

Descriptions of the throne of Yahweh symbolically describe the reign of the true king of Israel. MICAIAH pictured Yahweh as sitting on a throne planning the downfall of Ahab (1 Kgs 22:19-23). ISAIAH pictured God sitting on his throne [the Ark of the Covenant?] "high and lifted up," and served by the six-winged SERAPHIM whose praises extolled God's holiness (Isa 6). In EZEKIEL's vision (Ezek 1:4-28), the throne was mobile, symbolizing God's omnipresence and omnipotence. The height and majesty of God's throne are pictured when its location is said to be the dome of heaven (Exod 24:10). "Heaven is my throne and earth is my footstool," according to Isa 66:1, Matt 5:34-35, and Acts 7:49. Ps 11:4 states poetically the paradox that Yahweh is in the holy Temple (accessible to the worshiper), yet also enthroned in the heavens as judge of all people. Yahweh's rule over the whole world was celebrated in the earthly Temple. Ps 47 describes that enthronement.

See also KINGSHIP; THEOPHANY; WORSHIP IN THE OLD TESTAMENT.

—ROBERT L. LAMB

• **Thunder, Perfect Mind.** *Thunder, Perfect Mind* is a fascinating nine-page text found in the sixth codex of the NAG HAMMADI library. The work is a revelation discourse by an anonymous female deity. It comprises numerous "I am" proclamations interspersed with exhortations to the hearers. The "I am" statements are distinctive because of their antithetical or paradoxical content, and because of their identification of the revealer with negative as well as positive predicates. They deal with her family relationships, social status, moral character, and abilities: "I am the whore and the holy one"; "I am the bride and the bridegroom and it is my husband who begot me"; "I am an alien and a citizen"; "I am war and peace"; "I am control and uncontrollable"; "I am sinless and the root of sin derives from me"; "I am knowledge and ignorance." The exhortations and rebukes directed to the hearers are likewise puzzling. While the deity calls upon her audience to hear and find and know her, she also eludes her followers with words like, "You who know me, be ignorant of me," and "You who confess me, deny me." The writing defies rational comprehension, which leaves the reader feeling confused.

The title of the piece is curious. The two parts of it, "thunder," and "perfect mind" (or "complete intellect") are separate appellations and there is no mention of them in the body of the work. "Perfect mind" is a phrase used in some Gnostic literature of the supreme God, and thunder is often used as a description of divine voices in ancient religious literature (cf. Job 26:14; John 12:29; Rev 6:1 for biblical examples), but these two terms are not found together anywhere else. Various reconstructions of the title and its meaning have been suggested.

There are faint allusions to Gnostic myth in the opening lines of *Thunder* ("I was sent forth from the power," and so on). And some of the *Thunder*'s themes are at home in GNOSTICISM, for example the identification of the deity as utterly transcendent and yet an element within the hearer. Divine transcendence may be the ultimate message of the text's antithetical or paradoxical self-descriptions. By being both "x" and at the same time "the opposite of x" or "other than x," the deity is radically different and beyond that which the world can know. This unity of opposites is found in Stoic interpretation of the pre-Socratic philosopher Heraclitus, and may provide a clue to the origin and setting of *Thunder*.

There is reason to believe that the revealer is to be identified with the Gnostic Sophia, the goddess who plays an important role in Gnostic cosmology and soteriology. The patristic accounts of the Gnostic sect of SIMON MAGUS suggest that *Thunder*'s revealer figure would fit well with the Sophia figure, who was called "Helen" in the Simonian system.

The repeated "I am" assertions, the dichotomous and negative character of those assertions, and the absence of a narrative/explanatory context qualify *Thunder* as a unique document in religious antiquity. Parallels do exist, however, to certain features of *Thunder*, both in form and content. The first-person style of divine revelation ("I" or "I am") is found in Jewish WISDOM LITERATURE (e.g., Prov 8; Isa 45:5-7); aretologies (virtue lists) of the Egyptian goddess Isis; Gnostic texts (*TrimProt, ApJohn, ActsJn*); and Mandaean scripture (*Right Ginza* 6). Some of *Thunder*'s content also has parallels, e.g., "I am the first and the last." The familial images in *Thunder* are fairly close to some passages in *OrigWorld* and *HypArch*.

The poetic structure of *Thunder*'s "I am" sayings suggests that it may have been a hymn. The paradoxical content, however, may fix the document within the literary world of the Greek riddle. Changes in gender, style, and tone in the last page of the text may indicate a later appended ending.

See also GNOSTICISM; NAG HAMMADI.

Bibliography. R. H. Arthur, *The Wisdom Goddess: Feminine Motifs in Eight Nag Hammadi Documents*; J. J. Buckley, "Two Female Gnostic Revealers," *HR* 19 (1980): 259-69; B. Layton, "The Riddle of the Thunder (NHC VI,2): The Function of Paradox in a Gnostic Text from Nag Hammadi," *Nag Hammadi, Gnosticism, and Early Christianity,* ed. C. W. Hedrick and R. Hodgson, Jr.; G. W. MacRae, *The Thunder: Perfect Mind, Nag Hammadi Codex VI, Tractate 2* (Protocol of the Colloquy of the Center for Hermeneutical Studies in Hellenistic and Modern Culture, no. 5), ed. W. Wuellner; G. W. MacRae and D. M. Parrott, "The Thunder, Perfect Mind," *The Nag Hammadi Library in English,* ed. J. M. Robinson; D. M. Parrott, ed. *Nag Hammadi Codices V.2-5 and VI with Papyrus Berolinensis 8502, 1 and 4* (*NHS* 11); G. Quispel, "Jewish Gnosis and Mandaean Gnosticism," *Les Textes de Nag Hammadi* (*NHS* 7), ed. J.-E. Ménard.

—CAROL D. C. HOWARD

• **Thyatira.** [thi'uh-*ti*"ruh] Thyatira was a city located on the Lycus River in Lydia in Asia Minor (PLATES 26, 27). The city was on a minor road between PERGAMUM to the northwest and SARDIS to the southeast. The church at Thyatira was the fourth of the seven churches to whom the Book of Revelation was addressed (Rev 2:18-29) and the home of Lydia (Acts 16:14). The city is now named Akhisar (White Castle).

Thyatira was a city of guilds. More trade guilds existed in Thyatira than in any other city of Asia Minor. The most important of these were the coppersmiths and the dyers.

The guild of dyers is of great interest because Paul encountered in Philippi "a woman named Lydia, from the city of Thyatira, a seller of purple goods" (Acts 16:14). Because she is described as "worshipping God," it is probable that she was a gentile who had come into contact with Judaism, possibly from a Jewish colony in Thyatira.

The guilds were associated with the festivals and the feasts of the gods. The gods of Thyatira included the Lydian sun god Tyrimnos, a goddess Boreatene associated with Tyrimnos, and Sibyl Sambathe. The temple of Tyrimnos existed in Thyatira before the city's reestablishment by Seleucus I Nicator in 280 B.C.E. Tyrimnos became associated or identified with the Greek god Apollo. Still later the worship of Apollo Tyrimnos was joined with worship of the emperors who were considered to be incarnations of Apollo.

The letter to the church at Thyatira attacks the woman symbolically referred to as "Jezebel" (1 Kgs 16:31). She is accused of "teaching and beguiling my servants to practice immortality and to eat food sacrificed to idols" (Rev 2:20). These practices were common in the pagan worship in Thyatira.

See also ASIA; PERGAMUM; SARDIS.

Bibliography. J. Brewer, *Patmos and the Seven Churches of Asia*; C. Cobern, *The New Archaeological Discoveries.*

—FORREST WOOD, JR.

• **Tiamat.** [tee-ah'maht] A Babylonian goddess most often associated with the sea and chaotic forces. In the Babylonian creation epic *Enuma Elish,* Tiamat (salt water) mingles with her husband Apsu (fresh water) to produce the gods. These youthful gods later defeat their progenitors under the direction of Marduk, who splits Tiamat's body in half to form heaven and earth. Tiamat, often depicted as a dragon, is an expression of the chaos-monster motif found in much ancient Near Eastern creation literature, including the Bible (e.g., Ps 74:12-17). She represents forces that must be overcome for the ordering process of creation to take place. The word *Tiamat* is linguistically related to the word *tĕhôm* (''deep'') found in Gen 1:2. Here and elsewhere *tĕhôm* is written as a proper noun, indicating an earlier connection with common mythic material.

See also CREATION; RELIGIONS OF THE ANCIENT NEAR EAST.

—DAVID H. HART

• **Tiberias.** [*ti*-bihr'ee-uhs] The town of Tiberias (PLATE 23), mentioned only in John, was built by Herod ANTIPAS around 25 C.E. in honor of Roman Emperor Tiberias Caesar. The town replaced SEPPHORIS as Herod's capital. Located on the west-southwest shore of the SEA OF GALILEE, it was closer to the center of his district than Sepphoris and it was located on important national and international roads. It occupied a narrow rectangular strip between the sea and the rocky hills, with Herod's palace on the acropolis and the castle in the north section. It was a walled city facing the sea, and almost as low as the sea (700 ft.), making the climate warm and oppressive. According to Josephus, the population was a mixture of Galileans and foreigners, rich and poor, high and low, including recently freed slaves.

The importance of Tiberias in the time of Jesus was so great that the Sea of Galilee came to be called the Sea of Tiberias (John 6:1; 21:1). It is therefore surprising that the Gospels do not record that Jesus ever visited the town. One reason why Jesus may not have visited could be that he received word that Antipas was looking for him (Luke 13:31), perhaps because Antipas associated Jesus with John the Baptist whom he beheaded (Mark 6:16). Jesus was aware of the danger and warned his disciples of it (Mark 8:15). Another possible reason Jesus never went there was the fact that the town was predominantly gentile.

The only mention of Tiberias in the Gospels is in John 6:23, which reports that a small group of boats was blown by a storm to where Jesus and his disciples had been. The multitudes looking for Jesus took the boats and followed him to Capernaum.

According to Josephus, in NT times the city was ruled by a council of 600 and a committee of ten. It remained under Antipas and later AGRIPPA I until 44 C.E. when the Romans set a procurator over Galilee. In 50 C.E. Nero gave Tiberias to Agrippa II along with a number of other villages.

Despite the predominantly gentile population, many of the residents of Tiberias were sympathetic to the Jewish revolt against the Romans in 65 C.E. Josephus led the forces that captured Tiberias during the Jewish revolt, destroyed the palace at Tiberias, and prepared the city for defense against the Romans. When Vespasian laid siege to the city in 67 C.E., however, the city fell and Josephus surrendered to the Romans. Tiberias continued under Jewish rule until 100 C.E., but it was never again a capital.

The city was destroyed by Vepasian, but in the years following its destruction, its Jewish population increased. After the fall of Jerusalem in 135 C.E. Tiberias revived and became a strong Jewish center. A rabbinical school was established there when the Sanhedrin moved to Tiberias from Sepphoris around 150 C.E., and the Mishnah was written there. The mention in the Talmud of thirteen synagogues in Tiberias witnesses to the flourishing of Judaism there for several centuries.

See also AGRIPPA I & II; ANTIPAS; JOHN THE BAPTIST; SEPPHORIS.

—E. EARL JOINER

• **Tiglath-pileser.** [tig'lath-pi-lee'zuhr] King of ASSYRIA who ruled 745–727 B.C.E. His name appears also in the OT as Tilgath-pilneser (1 Chr 5:6, 26; 2 Chr 28:20). No information about his family is given in the Assyrian records. According to Berosus the historian, Tiglath-pileser was a usurper who became king after Assyria had suffered several years of political weakness. When Tiglath-pileser became king of Babylon a few years before his death (729 B.C.E.), he ruled Babylon under the name Pulu, which appears as Pul in 2 Kgs 15:19. The author of the Book of Chronicles erroneously distinguished Pul from Tiglath-pileser (1 Chr 5:26).

His accession to the throne of Assyria brought radical changes to the ancient Near East. Tiglath-pileser desired to establish an empire which would embrace Mesopotamia, Syria, and Palestine. In order to achieve his goals he established a policy of permanent conquest. Conquered cities were incorporated into the empire and the native population became Assyrian citizens. New dependencies were under the authority of Assyrian officials. These officials were responsible for providing slaves and provisions to the Assyrian court. Tiglath-pileser also initiated a policy of brutal reprisal against territories that revolted against Assyrian control. He instituted mass deportation of conquered people away from their lands to prevent revolt against the empire. These deportations served to provide cheap labor to Assyria and to break national solidarity.

After his accession in 745 B.C.E. Tiglath-pileser attempted to consolidate his power in Mesopotamia and to enlarge his empire. He led campaigns against the Arameans, Persians, and Medes to the east and Urartu to the north. When he came west, Tiglath-pileser conquered several states in Syria and Palestine, including Hamath, Damascus, Byblos, Tyre, and Israel.

Tiglath-pileser first came into contact with Israel during his western campaign. At this time Israel was facing a time of political anarchy. ZECHARIAH (746–745) the son of JEROBOAM II was murdered after a rule of only six months (2 Kgs 15:13). His killer, SHALLUM, seized the throne but he was assassinated one month later by MENAHEM (745–735). With the help of Tiglath-pileser Menahem became king of Israel, but Tiglath-pileser's support came at a heavy cost to Menahem. He imposed a heavy tribute of one thousand talents of silver on Menahem. Menahem paid his tribute by exacting money from 60,000 rich people in Israel (2 Kgs 15:17-20).

After the death of Menahem, his son PEKAHAIAH became king of Israel (737–736). Pekahaiah was killed by PEKAH after a reign of only two years. Pekah (736–732) assumed the throne backed by an anti-Assyrian group in Israel. Pekah joined with Rezin king of Syria and formed an alliance to resist Assyria (2 Kgs 16:5). The alliance needed the help of AHAZ, king of Judah; but Ahaz refused to join the revolt against Tiglath-pileser. In spite of the advice of Isaiah (Isa 7:1-17), Ahaz asked for assistance from Assyria (2 Kgs 16:7). In response to Ahaz's request, Tiglath-pileser undertook a campaign against Syria and Damascus. He invaded the coastal area of Philistia in 734. He then attacked Damascus; he deported the population of Kir and killed Rezin (2 Kgs 16:9). He also attacked Israel, conquered several of its cities and deported many people to Assyria (2 Kgs 15:29). Pekah was killed in a coup and Tiglath-pileser placed HOSHEA (732–724) on the throne.

Tiglath-pileser died in 727 and he was succeeded by SHALMANESER V.

See also ASSYRIA.

—CLAUDE F. MARIOTTINI

• **Tigris.** [*tī'*gris] A major river in southwest Asia (PLATES 2, 5), the Tigris is mentioned twice in the Bible. According to biblical tradition, the Tigris was one of the four rivers flowing out of the garden in Eden: "and the name of the third is Tigris, which flows east of Assyria" (Gen 2:14). The name was derived from Old Persian *Tigra.* The KJV calls the Tigris by its Heb. name Hiddekel; Josephus called it by its Aramaic name Diglath (*Ant* 3.1.3). The Tigris also appears in Dan 10:4 as "the great river," the place where Daniel had his vision.

The source of the Tigris is in the mountains of Ararat (ancient Urartu) in southern Armenia, modern eastern Turkey, a few miles from the head of the EUPHRATES, the fourth river in Eden. The valley in which these two rivers flowed was called Mesopotamia, "the land between rivers." It was here where the earliest civilizations of the ancient Near East developed. The Tigris receives waters from many tributaries including the Upper and the Lower Zab and the Diyala rivers. Near Bosra, the Tigris unites with the Euphrates to form the Shatt al-Arab, which empties into the Persian Gulf. The length of the Tigris is ca. 1,150 mi. During the melting of the snow (Sirach 24:25), the Tigris flooded the surrounding countryside. Thus, in antiquity, this flooding required the building of canals to alleviate the inundations and to harness the available water for irrigation. Because of the fertility of the land, several famous cities were built on the margins of the Tigris. Among them were Asshur, the original capital of Assyria; Nineveh, the capital of the Assyrian empire; Eshnunna and Lagash, two great cities of the old Sumerian empire; and Opis, a commercial center in the neo-Babylonian empire.

See also EUPHRATES.

—CLAUDE F. MARIOTTINI

• **Timaeus.** *See* TIMAEUS, SON OF

• **Time, Biblical Perspectives on.** The ancient Israelites developed a distinctive understanding of time in virtue of their unique view of history. That historical outlook involved a God committed in COVENANT to a specially chosen people, with whom the deity had continuous interaction.

The borrowings that the Israelites made consisted chiefly of formal elements determined by their historical situation at particular periods such as month names, taken first from the Canaanites and later from the Babylonians, or the Babylonian system of adding ten or eleven days to the end of the year to bring a twelve-month cycle of twenty-nine- or thirty-day months into agreement with the solar cycle of 365¼ days. The Hebrews did not mark seconds, minutes, or hours, which were learned from the Greeks and Romans in the late pre-Christian and NT periods. Instead, the Hebrews marked the "watches" of the day and night, but mainly they marked the days (from sunrise to sunset, or else both the duration of light and of darkness, from one sunrise to the next, or from one sunset to the next) and sequences of days—those of the week, the month and the year. Thus they also identified the days of the month by number and developed calendars for creating an orderly sequence of special days. In the time of the Hebrew kingdoms, they also counted the months by number. This precision was especially important then, and in postexilic Judaism, so that all would observe religious festivals at the same time.

The above treats the external features of time; that is, of organizing events in a temporal sequence so as to assure an operational political, cultural and religious system. But what matters most about the Hebrew notion of time is that they expected each new day to be qualitatively different from all other days, possibly producing a unique, unrepeatable event in which God might reveal the divine self in some special and decisive way. This is why the Bible developed a characteristic way of speaking of days in terms of their most noteworthy event. As an example, the introduction to the story of creation in Gen 2:4 reads, "In the day that the Lord God made the earth and the heavens . . . ," continuing with a narrative of the events that constituted God's creative act. In Gen 2:17 God warns, "On the day that you eat of it [the tree of the knowledge of good and evil], you shall surely die." The first human pair did not actually cease living on the very day of the fall; rather, the day of the first sin was decisive for determining humanity's inescapable mortality. Similarly, the important biblical phrase "the Day of the Lord," mentioned first in Amos 5:18, refers to a specific day, known to God and imminently expected but still unknown to human beings, when God would act decisively to judge the wicked and save the righteous (cf. esp. Mal 3:1-2; 4:1).

By contrast, for the Egyptians and the Greeks time had little meaning except as an endlessly repeated cycle. To the Babylonians, historical events were set in a rigid framework of distinct times whose character was revealed by the heavenly constellations and the positions of the planets, moon and sun. Thus nothing really new in theory could occur in time and history. The gods were unapproachable except through the temple ritual, giving special importance to the sacrificial calendar, which required to be scrupulously observed. Kings looked for omens and appealed to their gods for good fortune when venturing on military campaigns, but there was a limit to what even the gods could do because they too were subject to the tyranny of predetermined time.

Not so for the people of the Bible. They believed that their God could meet them anywhere and at any time; all of space and all of history were God's domain. This is why the Bible has a sense of purpose and progression, a goal, a process, a destiny. The biblical God claimed a people who at first were no people and who possessed no land of their own, promising to be their God forever if they would remain faithful. God never forsook the divine promise, but again and again Israel broke God's law, until that last bitter day when their land, their city, and their Temple were destroyed. This was a bitter lesson, yet a judging God remained true to the promise to rescue a holy remnant. Israel needed to be preserved for the "fulness of time," the final "Day of the Lord." Many readers of the Bible have tried to count the days and years until this would come to pass, but the biblical writers warned against looking over God's shoulder (cf. Acts 1:6-7). The Christian community proclaimed that the coming of the Christ had already brought and would continue to bring God's decisive, final day (cf. Luke 4:21). The apostles, especially Paul, recognized that the end-time had come. Even though the church still awaits the final consummation, God has already acted decisively in time; the "Day of the Lord" has already arrived. Nevertheless, many of the "guests at the wedding feast" (cf. Matt 22:1-14) must still be gathered in. Each day until time shall cease, the witnessing church is commanded urgently to proclaim, "Behold, now is the acceptable time; behold, now is the day of salvation" (2 Cor 6:2).

See also CALENDAR.

—SIMON J. DEVRIES

• **Timnah (Tell Batash).** [tim'nuh, tel-bah-tosh'] Located in the western Shephelah (PLATE 3), approximately five mi. northwest of Beth-shemesh and five mi. south of Gezer, Timnah was founded in the Middle Bronze Age period (ca. 1800 B.C.E.) in a protective crescent of the Sorek River where the Sorek Valley broadens into a fertile alluvial plain. Its original square plan, covering ten acres at its base, and its impressive defensive system including a moat and massive earthen ramparts suggest a strategic military role in guarding the corridor from the coastal plain along the Sorek to Beth-shemesh and beyond, either to Bethlehem or Jerusalem in the Judean hill country, or along the Judean foothills to the southern Shephelah.

Tell Batash (its modern identification) was identified during archaeological surveys in the 1940s as an important Iron Age site, but it was not until 1958 that its identification with biblical Timnah became clear. The description of the northern border of the tribe of Judah (Josh 15:10-11) provided the critical geographical detail that contributed to the identification of the tell with biblical Timnah. Clarification of its cultural and historical importance began in 1977 with the archaeological expedition primarily sponsored by New Orleans Baptist Theological Seminary and Mississippi College 1977–1979 and solely sponsored by Southwestern Baptist Theological Seminary 1980–1988 under the direction of George L. Kelm, with Amihai Mazar from The Hebrew University as archaeological field director. The excavation has illuminated the strategic role the town played within the cultural and political buffer zone between the central hill country and the coastal plain.

To overcome the vulnerability of its location on the level plain, the town's original plan included a protective moat, possibly filled with water from the Sorek River, along the outer line of a massive earthen rampart on which its first walls with defensive towers rose. Foundational and lower courses of the original walls and tower have been exposed within the ridge of the steep glacis along the northern slope of the tell. Ceramic evidence suggests an early date in the Middle Bronze Age (nineteenth–eighteenth centuries B.C.E.) for Timnah's origin. Though the town's strategic location in the Sorek suggests a military as well as an agrarian role, the more specific character of the town's inner plan and architectural features awaits additional excavation of occupational strata within the walls. The earliest biblical reference to the town comes from the patriarchal period (Gen 38:12ff.). The pastoral scene of Judah taking his sheep to his sheepshearers at Timnah reflects the general economy of the Shephelah region and is consistent with the prominence of the weaving and dyeing (?) industries evident in the much later cultural remains of the eighth–seventh-century town.

Four layers of destruction rubble and burnt debris are mute evidence of the turbulent Amarna period of the Late Bronze Age when Timnah as a secondary town suffered the consequences of intercity and regional rivalries and the political instability for which the period is noted. Seals, scarabs and other small finds recovered from the ruins of the impressive patrician, or governor's, house of the Late Bronze Age are evidence of widespread international political and trade connections that Timnah maintained, not far removed from the *Via Maris*. The town's militaristic role as a front line of defense within the buffer zone of the Shephelah, between the central hill country and the coastal plain, continues throughout its subsequent history. Architectural and ceramic remains provide evidence of a vibrant economy at Timnah in spite of the town's vulnerability. The absence of a major defensive system, the outer walls of buildings forming the town's perimeter, possibly may be attributed to an Egyptian policy that restricted urban fortifications to regional administrative centers maintained by Egyptian garrisons.

Evidence of the arrival of the SEA PEOPLES in the twelfth century was found on the floors of the final architectural phase of Canaanite Timnah. The transition of the town to Philistine control appears to have been without a major conflict or destruction of the Late Bronze town. The repaved plastered floor of a Canaanite dwelling contained sherds of characteristic Philistine pottery and refuse pits in the courtyards contained clear artifacts of Philistine origin. While scattered architectural features suggest a prominent settlement, an urban plan and the nature of Philistine fortifications await further excavation. The period of the united monarchy is represented by ceramic and architectural remains typical of other Israelite cities of the period such as Lachish and Beth-shemesh and may reflect David's occupation of much of the Shephelah to the outskirts of Ekron. The general impression of architectural remains suggests an underdeveloped, unfortified town with an outer belt of buildings creating a defensive perimeter around a town with large open areas. The destruction of Timnah toward the end of the tenth century B.C.E. may be attributed to the invasion of this region by Shishak's army at the end of Solomon's reign, though Timnah has not been identified in the list of conquered cities on the temple walls at Karnak. With the division of the kingdom, the defensive line established by Rehoboam along his western frontier clearly indicates that Timnah had reverted to Philistine or Egyptian control.

Timnah's most prosperous period as an Israelite town came following its recapture by Uzziah (2 Chr 26:6) when parts of Philistia were reclaimed and the basic plan of Timnah with its defensive wall, gate complex, streets and public and residential quarters was established for the next two centuries. The city that flourished during the eighth century B.C.E. experienced extensive building during Hezekiah's reign when a revolt against Assyrian domination required reinforcement of his western frontier and Jerusalem. A doubling of the thickness of the defensive walls, the construction of an outer gate with massive towers and walls, and a large accumulation of "lmlk" storage jar fragments on the floor of a storeroom, reflect Hezekiah's preparedness for his confrontation with Sennacherib in 701 B.C.E. In spite of Hezekiah's utter defeat at Timnah, mentioned in Sennacherib's annals, the Assyrian destruction in the town appears to have been selective, directed primarily against military installations. The city soon was restored and enjoyed economic prosperity until its final destruction ca. 600 B.C.E. or slightly later.

The economy of the town is reflected in a series of industrial complexes in the residential quarter. Loom weights on the floors of every residence excavated thus far and what appear to be dyeing installations provide evidence for local involvement in the textile industry for which the Shephelah generally was noted. A series of oil presses suggests the contribution of home industries to the production of olive oil, a major export from the region to Egypt, Phoenicia and possibly even to Greece (Ezek 27:17; Hos 12:1). A wine press is dated to the final phase of the town's history. A group of molds and female figurines, together with chalices and other cultic objects, were recovered from what appeared to be a local cultic shrine.

Timnah came to an abrupt and tragic end ca. 600 B.C.E., an event that may be attributed to the Babylonian invasion of the region. It was never resettled, though fragmentary evidence exists for the presence of temporary squatters during the Persian period, ca. 500 B.C.E.

Bibliography. G. L. Kelm and A. Mazar, "Three Seasons of Excavations at Tel Batash—Biblical Timnah," *BASOR* 248 (1982): 1-36, "Timnah: A Biblical City in the Sorek Valley," *Arch* 37 (1984): 58ff., "Tel Batash (Timnah) Excavations: Second Preliminary Report (1981–1983)," *BASORSupp* 23 (1985): 93-100, and "Timnah—A Town on the Border between Philistia and Judah," *BAR* (forthcoming).

—GEORGE L. KELM

• **Timotheus.** *See* TIMOTHY

• **Timothy.** [tim'oh-thee] One of the best-known associates of PAUL, often mentioned in the NT as Paul's faithful and trusted fellow worker. In several of Paul's Letters (2 Corinthians, Philippians, Colossians, 1 and 2 Thessalonians) Timothy shares the opening greeting to churches. He belongs to a very small group of early missionaries and often shares in the very essence of Pauline preaching (2 Cor 1:19). At least in one instance, Paul intimates that Timothy should be ranked among the apostles (1 Thess 2:6). He may have been a convert of Paul, who refers to Timothy as a faithful and beloved child in the Lord (1 Cor 4:17; 1 Tim 1:2; 2 Tim 1:2).

Biographical references concerning Timothy are scant. He came from a mixed background of Jewish and Greek descent. Despite their Greek names, his mother, Eunice, and grandmother, Lois, are known to have been Jewish women, though they may have neglected a great part of the Jewish ritual to satisfy the practices of Timothy's Greek father. Whether Eunice was a convert of Paul cannot be established. She is simply referred to as a believer.

After Timothy's conversion to Christianity, two events seem to have had a profound influence on him. When he is first mentioned in Acts 16, we learn that he cannot become Paul's companion unless he is circumcised. Twice Luke insists on the fact that Timothy was not circumcised because his father was Greek. Ironically, it was as a convert to Christianity that Timothy finally fulfilled his Jewish ritual obligation and became empowered to preach to the Jews also.

The second religious experience reported in 1 and 2 Timothy concerns his ordination by elders (1 Tim 4:14), a ceremony in which Paul himself may have taken part (2 Tim 1:6). This, more than any other event, confirmed the divine gift entrusted to him.

Timothy's duties were not limited to accompanying Paul in his missionary journeys. Very often, alone or in the company of others, he served as Paul's emissary to churches. At Beroea, Silas and Timothy were left behind to continue Paul's work (Acts 17:14). Timothy and Erastus were sent to Macedonia by Paul (Acts 19:22). When the church in Thessalonica went through unbearable tribulations, Paul sent Timothy to exhort them and bring back the good news of their strong faith (1 Thess 3:2-6). On several occasions he also shared Paul's ministry at Ephesus.

Perhaps Timothy's most difficult and least successful mission was to the church at Corinth where he went as Paul's representative. Paul had to beg the Corinthians not to despise Timothy's youth (1 Cor 16:10-11). Whatever Timothy achieved there, it appears that he was eventually replaced by TITUS who was better equipped to deal with the specific problems of that difficult church.

NT references to Timothy, though quite numerous, do not allow for a precise reconstruction of his work. The Letters, 1 and 2 Timothy, do not provide much information regarding their supposed recipient. The PASTORAL EPISTLES are almost certainly pseudonymous, written by a church leader who knew of Paul's veneration for Timothy. It is quite conceivable that the Letters to Timothy were products of the postapostolic age when Paul and Timothy (and possibly Titus) were regarded as perfect spiritual guides for a church in the process of formulating its teaching and of defining the credentials of its leaders. Timothy became the model of Christian leadership, and his name remains prominent in the history of the early church.

See also CORINTHIAN CORRESPONDENCE; PASTORAL EPISTLES; PAUL; SILAS; THESSALONIANS, LETTERS TO THE; TITUS.

—PAUL CIHOLAS

• **Timothy, Letter to.** *See* PASTORAL EPISTLES

• **Tirzah.** [tihr'zuh] Tirzah, meaning "pleasure" or "beauty," was a royal Canaanite city whose king was defeated by Joshua as the Israelites entered Palestine (Josh 12:24). The city is not mentioned again in the OT until the time of Jeroboam I (ca. 922–901 B.C.E.), although the Israelites had probably occupied it since the Conquest. Jeroboam, the first king of the Northern Kingdom, began his reign at Shechem and Penuel (1 Kgs 12:25), but seems to have moved his headquarters to Tirzah early in his administration, for his wife came there, and a son died there (1 Kgs 14:17). The city remained the capital of the Northern Kingdom throughout the succeeding reigns of Nadab, Baasha, Elah, and Zimri, whose seven-day reign ended with OMRI's siege of the city and Zimri's apparent suicide in the palace (1 Kgs 16:15-18), and for six years of Omri's administration (1 Kgs 16:23). This was about 901–870 B.C.E., thus making Tirzah the capital of the Northern Kingdom for about fifty years. Omri bought from a certain Shemer "the hill of Samaria" and moved the capital there (1 Kgs 16:24).

The city is mentioned two additional times in the OT. In 2 Kgs 15:14, 16, Tirzah is reported to have been the starting point for Menahem's coup of ca. 745 B.C.E. against King Shallum (however, certain textual problems attend the appearance of "Tirzah" here). The other reference to Tirzah is in Cant 6:4 where the beauty of the city and that of Jerusalem are presented in synonymous parallelism, indicating authorship probably between 920 and 870 B.C.E.

Tirzah is thought to be the site of Tell el-Far'ah, a mound 300 × 600 m. and 50 m. high, lying some five mi. northeast of Nablus and twelve mi. west of the Jordan River (PLATE 13). Indeed, the site was strategically located. Blessed with two plentiful springs, it lay on the road from Shechem to Beth-Shan and Damascus, commanding the approach to Syria. Tirzah sat at the head of Wadi Farah, the only wide passage from the Jordan Valley into the center of Palestine, and straddles a network of communications at the head of a fertile valley. Excavated during nine seasons between 1946 and 1960 by Roland de Vaux of Jerusalem's *École Biblique et Archeologique Française*, the mound contained ten major strata ranging from the Neolithic Period through Iron Age II. Strata I-II are dated in the Israelite period, and the site was abandoned apparently ca. 600 B.C.E.

Bibliography. R. de Vaux, "Tirzah," *Archaeology and Old Testament Study,* ed. D. W. Thomas.

—KAREN RANDOLPH JOINES

• **Tithe.** Tithing, the act of contributing ten percent of one's earnings for the support of religion, was an ancient custom in many countries, particularly among the semitic peoples. Abraham gave a tenth of his booty to MELCHIZEDEK the priest (Gen 14:20), and Jacob promised to give God the tenth if he could return home safely (Gen 28:22). The OT regulations on tithing, like the rest of the laws of Israel, changed over time. The result is that two systems were encoded in scripture, and a third developed later synthesizing them.

Tithes are not mentioned in the Covenant Code (Exod 20:22–23:33), which most scholars consider to be the oldest law code in the Torah. The Code does, however, require Israelites to bring firstfruit offerings "into the house of the Lord your God," and thus the practice of tithing is not precluded. In Deuteronomy, all the people of Israel were specifically required to bring all their offerings, sacrifices, and tithes to the Lord their God "in the place which he will chose to make his name dwell there" (Deut 14:23), namely, Jerusalem. Many scholars see this as an innovation associated with Josiah's reform in one way or another (ca. 621 B.C.E.). Deut 14:22-29 mandated a tithe on all crops and linked this with the "firstborn" offering of flocks and herds. Each family had to bring either the tithe itself (the grain, wine, and oil) or the price they could get for selling it to Jerusalem and participate in a feast. Perhaps this was the offering one was expected to bring to the Feasts of Weeks and Booths (Deut 16:15-17). Deut 14:28-29. also specifies that every three years the worshipper was to keep the tithe to give to the Levites within their towns, the resident aliens, the orphans, and the widows, since none of them had land of their own.

In the priestly texts of Numbers and Leviticus, the tithe changed because of the distinction drawn between priests and Levites. Deuteronomy makes no division; every male from the tribe of Levi was entitled to eat from the sacrifices if he was willing to come to Jerusalem (Deut 18:1-8). Numbers and Leviticus, on the other hand, state that only the descendants of Aaron, a particular family within the larger tribe of Levi, may eat from the sacrifices and serve at the altar. Thus, the tithing rules had to change. According to Num 18, the priests were entitled to certain portions of all sacrificial offerings, the firstfruits offering, animals promised in an oath ("devoted things"), firstborn offerings, and "all the holy offerings." In addition, the Levites were to collect the tenth of all harvested goods and then send a tenth of that to the priests. Lev 27:30-33 adds that tithes of crops could be redeemed—that is, one could substitute something else in payment—if one were willing to add a fifth to its value. Animals, however, could not be redeemed.

These regulations, as one can see, would have the effect of increasing the monetary power of the priests. Most commentators associate the Priestly texts with the early postexilic period, when the priesthood was becoming the primary authority within Israel. Ezekiel, which dates from the exilic period, shows the same division between priests and Levites. Some groups, especially the Levites, would likely have taken offense at this change, seeing it as an unnecessary innovation and a usurpation of authority by the Aaronic priesthood.

The Chronicler's narratives that deal with tithing may be explained by the offence of the Levites. The story of Hezekiah's reform in 2 Chr 31 tells how the king reinstituted the tithe which had been neglected under the previous monarch. According to 2 Chr 31:12, the king appointed the Levites to collect the tithes and to distribute them to priests and Levites who lived away from Jerusalem. Neh 10:37-39 follows the law of Num 18 strictly, stating that Nehemiah's group pledged themselves to give the tithe to the Levites out in the towns so that the Levites could bring the tenth of that to Jerusalem. But when Nehemiah discovered that the Levites were not being paid their due, he appointed a committee made up of a priest, a scribe, and a Levite to make certain that the money went to the needy Levites. Most scholars see in these and other texts edited by the Chronicler an elevation of the place of the Levites and evidence of some tension between the Aaronites and the Levites in the postexilic community.

Certain prophetic texts mention the tithe also. Amos 4:4 sarcastically asks for a tithe every three days; this is part of Amos's protest against ritual which is unaccompanied by ethical behavior and mercy towards the poor. Mal 3:6-12 criticizes the postexilic community for failure to pay the whole tithe, and promises rich blessings if they will.

By the second century B.C.E., the regulations of Deuteronomy and Numbers had been blended, resulting in three separate tithes (the earliest reference to this blending is Tobit 1:5-6). The tenth of harvested goods would be given to the Levites, who would send a tenth of that to Jerusalem (Num 18). A second tenth of crops and animals would be sent directly to Jerusalem for the priests (Deut 14:22). The third tithe (Deut 14:28) was to be used for relief of the poor. These regulations indicate the growing power of the priesthood in the Second Temple period. They also help to explain the social unrest of that period—yielding thirty percent of one's income to religion, plus paying taxes to the government, was impossible or intolerable for many. This system remained in place, however, at least until the time of the procurator Albinus (62–64 C.E.), when, according to Josephus, the high priest Ananus began to send thugs to take the tenth from the farmers at the threshing floors, before it could be given to the Levites.

In Jesus' criticism of the Pharisees for paying more attention to detailed obedience to the Torah than to mercy to sinners, diligence in tithing was used as an example (Matt 23:23-24 ‖ Luke 11:42; Luke 18:12).

See also LEVI/LEVITES; PRIESTS; TEMPLE/TEMPLES; WORSHIP IN THE OLD TESTAMENT.

Bibliography. R. K. Duke, "The Portion of the Levite," *JBL* 106 (June 1987): 193-201; R. de Vaux, *Ancient Israel*; M. Haran, *Temples and Temple-Service in Ancient Israel*; R. A. Horsley, *Bandits, Prophets, and Messiahs*; J. E. Stambaugh and D. L. Balch, *The New Testament in Its Social Environment.*

—RICHARD B. VINSON

• **Titus.** [*ti'*tuhs] Titus was a friend and fellow missionary of PAUL. While not mentioned in Acts, Titus is named in 2 Corinthians, Galatians, and 2 Timothy. Further, one of the PASTORAL EPISTLES is addressed to him.

According to Gal 2:1-10, Paul took Titus with him on his second visit to Jerusalem. As the apostle must have anticipated, certain Jewish Christians there sought to have the uncircumcised Greek circumcised, Paul, however, kept this from happening by successfully arguing that the truth of the gospel did not require non-Jews to observe the ritual laws of Judaism. In Galatians the incident serves as a lesson for the Galatian Christians, who are being urged to undergo CIRCUMCISION (5:1-12; 6:11-16).

Titus is named often in 2 Corinthians. In the summer of 54 or 55 C.E. Paul had sent him to Corinth, perhaps bearing the severe letter alluded to in 2 Cor 2:1-4, to undertake the difficult task of setting right some disturbing problems which Paul himself may have been unable to resolve on a previous visit. Paul became concerned when Titus failed to report back to the apostle in Troas as planned (2:13). When the two did finally meet in Macedonia, the coming of Titus was an occasion for joy, for the trusted Titus was able to confirm the Corinthians' renewed zeal for Paul (7:5-16). Subsequently, Titus—carrying 2 Corinthians, or perhaps 2 Cor 1–9, with him—was sent back to Corinth, where his major task was to organize, with the assistance of others, a contribution for the church at Jerusalem—a task which Titus had begun earlier but failed to complete (8:6, 16-24; cf. 12:18).

The Letter to Titus assumes that its addressee has been left by Paul on CRETE to carry on the Christian work there (1:5). It consists primarily of instructions on the appointment of leaders and exhortations to defend sound doctrine. Tit 1:4 ("To Titus, my true child in a common faith") may imply that Titus was converted by Paul.

In Tit 3:12 Titus is requested to meet Paul at Nicopolis as soon as either Artemas or Tychicus arrives to take on the duties at Crete. However, 2 Tim 4:10 has Titus in Dalmatia, and both the ACTS OF PAUL and the PSEUDO EPISTLE OF TITUS have him with Paul in Rome just prior to the latter's execution. Matters are further complicated by the tradition preserved in Eusebius, *EccHist* 3.4.6, where Titus is remembered as the bishop of Crete. Because it is unclear whether or how these different traditions are to be harmonized, and because the origin of the historical material in the Pastorals is such a vexing issue, the movements of Titus after his time in Corinth can only be guessed.

See also CIRCUMCISION; CONTRIBUTION FOR THE SAINTS; CORINTHIAN CORRESPONDENCE; GALATIANS, LETTER TO THE; PASTORAL EPISTLES; TITUS, PSEUDO-EPISTLE OF.

Bibliography. C. K. Barrett, "Titus," *Neotestamentica et Semitica: Studies in Honour of Matthew Black,* ed. E. E. Ellis and M. Wilcox.

—DALE C. ALLISON, JR.

• **Titus, Letter to.** *See* PASTORAL EPISTLES

• **Titus, Pseudo-Epistle of.** The *Pseudo-Epistle of Titus* is a long discourse in rhapsodic praise of chastity as a way of life and in condemnation of sexual activity. It probably originated in the fifth century among Christian ascetics in Spain. It survives in one Latin manuscript of the eighth century, which was discovered only in 1896. The Latin is so bad that it has been conjectured to be a translation from Greek by someone who knew neither Latin nor Greek very well.

That the work existed has long been known. Extensive use is made of it in other apocryphal works, especially acts and apocalypses. On the other hand, the epistle itself makes use of quotations from other apocryphal works in praise of virginity.

Bibliography. A. de Santos Otero, "The Pseudo-Titus Epistle," *New Testament Apocrypha,* ed. E. Hennecke and W. Schneemelcher.

—ROGER A. BULLARD

• **Tobit.** [toh'bit] The Book of Tobit begins, "I, Tobit, walked in the ways of truth and righteousness all the days of my life, and I performed many acts of charity to my brethren and countrymen . . . " (1:3). With this Tobit begins a story of angels, demons, money, and marriage, an intricate story throughout which Tobit himself shines as an example of all that is righteous and true.

Tobit's model life is marked by three moral tenets: PRAYER, almsgiving, and FASTING. He is faithful to God in exile when his tribe worships other gods. The righteous act of burying the dead almost costs him his life in Assyrian exile. Tobit's faith shines through, however; in the midst of blindness and poverty he does not blame God but resorts to prayer (3:1ff.). His words to the departing Tobias, his son, seem ironic to the reader, but they provide direction to devout Jews in the commands to honor and bury father and mother, remember God, refuse to sin, give ALMS, take a kinswoman for a wife, and practice discipline in eating and drinking (4:3-21). Throughout Tobit's speech is the refrain that God will bless Tobias for the giving of alms and a devout lifestyle.

The irony of Tobit's tragedy is not the final word. His words to Tobias are vindicated in the final acts of the story. Tobit's prayers are answered, and his almsgiving is rewarded; his lament has become a doxology. Having lived a long and fruitful life, Tobit dies reminding his children of the rewards for almsgiving and righteousness.

Bibliography. B. Metzger, *An Introduction to the Apocrypha*; G. W. E. Nickelsburg, *Jewish Literature Between the Bible and the Mishnah.*

—STEVEN SHEELEY

• **Tobit, Book of.** Tobit, one of the jewels of Jewish literature, is a delightful short story that upholds Jewish piety in the midst of a pagan world. It is a fine artistic work found in the Apocrypha which combines Jewish legalistic piety with folklore.

The story itself is fascinating. Two Jewish families, related but now separated by deportation to Nineveh and Ecbatana respectively, are reunited by the intervention of God through the ANGEL Raphael. Both families have remained strictly obedient to the LAW and continue to worship God in spite of the difficulties of living in their pagan surroundings. Both families find themselves in trouble. Tobit has lost his position and has become blind. He is also in danger of losing his life because of his strict obedience to the Jewish Law in burying the dead, thus defying a royal edict. In the other family Sarah, the only daughter, is possessed by a demon, which has killed seven bridegrooms on the night of her marriage.

God hears the prayers of both families and intervenes to heal the situation of both by sending Raphael (the name means "God heals"). Tobit, not aware that God is acting, sends his son Tobias to recover some money that had been deposited in Media. He finds a man (not yet revealed as the angel Raphael) to accompany him on his journey and serve as his guide. They have many adventures on the journey, and Tobias is protected and guided. He is able to heal Sarah through the advice of Raphael, and the demon is driven out. Tobias marries Sarah, returns to his home, and Tobit is healed of his blindness. At last Raphael reveals who he really is and disappears as the families live happily ever after.

The story, with its details of time, places, persons, leaves the impression of a historical account, set in the eighth century B.C.E. at the time of Israel's troubles with Assyria. But there is abundant evidence that the literary artist has set the stage in this ancient time and is writing a kind of historical novel in order to present his message to people of his own day. A careful reading of the book will turn up numerous historical inaccuracies that would not have occurred had the book been written in the Assyrian period. There is general agreement among most scholars that the book was written not earlier than about 200 B.C.E., but since there is no evidence of the turmoil that occurred under Antiochus Epiphanes, the period between 200 and 170 is generally accepted.

The author is unknown. The question of whether he originally wrote in Hebrew, Aramaic, or Greek is much disputed, although a majority of scholars holds to a semitic original. The book reflects a diaspora background rather than a Palestinian situation, and the place of origin is likely to be Syria or Mesopotamia.

The textual history of the book is difficult to follow. The Greek text is the earliest complete form of the book, but this exists in two forms, one considerably longer than the other. Fragments of the book (in Aramaic and Hebrew) were found among the DEAD SEA SCROLLS at Qumran.

The author was well acquainted with the OT, including some of the other apocryphal books. There seem to be some correspondences with the book of SIRACH which may indicate a common time of origin. He was also acquainted with the popular wisdom of AHIKAR, an oriental wisdom book that had a wide influence. Other extrabiblical sources seem also to have been used.

The purpose of the author in writing is not absolutely certain. He is a story teller, but in addition he is concerned to emphasize the importance of strict obedience to the Law, no matter what the cost. Faithfulness to God and his commands proves God's faithfulness in caring for his people. It seems clear that the author is trying to encourage fellow Jews of the diaspora to remain faithful to God in the midst of the foreign cultures in which they find themselves.

The book is important in that it provides one of the clearest pictures we have of Jewish piety in the period prior to the NT. Something of that piety is expressed in 4:15, the negative form of the golden rule, "Never do to anyone else what you would not want done to you."

There is a strong belief in the providence of God, which is carried out through the activity of his angels. God is concerned for his people in their difficulties and acts through angels to help them.

Religious practices such as almsgiving and the burial of the dead are considered part of the Law of God and are to be carried out scrupulously. The superior wisdom of this way of life makes it possible for Jews to survive all the difficulties of their separation from Jerusalem.

Family life is the center of God's plan for his people. It is the family that now carries on the spiritual heritage of tribe and nation. And the family continues to transmit that heritage in the diaspora through a good Jewish marriage, which avoids the danger of assimilation through mixed marriages.

Obedience to the Law in good works of all kinds is the heart of religion. This obedience to God requires a careful and precise understanding of the oral law. Now separated from the TEMPLE, the individual Jew must carry out his own personal and private commitment to his God and to his neighbor, who for Tobit is his Jewish brother.

Almsgiving is a primary religious practice that keeps one in right relationship with God, as stated in 4:7, "Never turn your face away from the poor and God will never turn away from you." Prayer to God, particularly thanksgiving for his care and request for his protection, is encouraged at every step; even the wedding night of Tobias and Sarah begins with prayer (8:5-8).

In short, the book gives a vivid picture of the life of the pious Jew exiled from his homeland and seeking to be faithful to God in this separation and isolation. Life is lived on a daily basis under the conviction that personal obedience to the religious duties that have come down in the tradition is of the highest importance.

See also APOCRYPHAL LITERATURE.

Bibliography. D. R. Dumm, "Tobit," *JBC*; A. Wikgren, "Tobit, Book of," *IDB*; F. Zimmerman, *The Book of Tobit*.

—HEBER F. PEACOCK

• **Tomb of Jesus.** The site of Jesus' tomb is not known with certainty, but the location of the CHURCH OF THE HOLY SEPULCHER in JERUSALEM has been accepted as the traditional site by virtually all of Christendom since the fourth century. About 326 C.E., shortly after the conversion of Constantine, his mother, Queen Helena, came to the Holy Land on pilgrimage, seeking to locate major holy sites for the building of churches and dedication of these places for spiritual instruction and worship by pilgrims and other Christians. Apparently Helena was influenced by the evidence that an earlier place of Christian worship had been destroyed and a pagan shrine erected by Rome on the site.

Because the Church of the Holy Sepulcher is located inside the present walls of the Old City of Jerusalem, there has been persistent doubt in many minds that it could be the location of an execution ground (CALVARY) and a cemetery (Joseph's tomb). When British General Charles "Chinese" Gordon in the late-nineteenth century suggested the jutting cliff just outside the Damascus Gate as a possible Calvary, and the adjoining garden and rock-cut tomb as the actual tomb of Jesus, a popular new tradition was born (PLATE 39). It fits the biblical descriptions beautifully, and it provides the worshiper a wonderful opportunity for meditation and worship in a garden before the open door of a tomb hewn out of the limestone wall.

Most professional archaeologists and historians dismissed serious claims that the Garden Tomb could be the actual historical site of Jesus' tomb, preferring to call it a good "visual aid" to illustrate the gospel record of the crucifixion and resurrection of Jesus. In the 1960s Pierre Benoit, director of the French archaeological school *École Biblique* (immediately next door to the Garden Tomb), opened some interesting burial sites in the same limestone cliff and found inscriptions such as "Buried in the Church of the Resurrection," and "Buried near the Lord." Benoit received permission to investigate the Garden Tomb and its strange stone draftings, and he found that a portion of masonry fill did not replace a rockfall from the wall of the tomb, but that rather it had been deliberately cut out in front of an immersion baptistery in the rock outside the tomb, so that the baptismal candidate would arise from the water looking directly into the burial chamber where the body was laid.

This gave strong support to the location of a first-century Christian place of worship at the Garden Tomb, probably because they were convinced that it was the site of the crucifixion and the burial. At about the same time, however, excavators exploring the line of the ancient walls of Jerusalem found evidence that indeed the Church of the Holy Sepulcher was outside the walls of that period and extensive burial sites of the first century were found immediately behind the traditional tomb of Jesus in the church, supporting that burial site as the original tomb of Jesus.

Such uncertainty about the exact location of the tomb of Jesus is surely what would be expected. It should not obscure the fact that Christians come to believe in the resurrection ultimately because of a living encounter with Jesus as the risen Lord, rather than the ambiguous evidence of a tomb which cannot be located with historical certainty.

See also CALVARY; CROSS; JERUSALEM.

Bibliography. J. Finegan, *The Archaeology of the New Testament*; B. Mazar et al., *Digging Up Jerusalem*; J. Wilkinson, *Jerusalem as Jesus Knew It*.

—WAYNE E. WARD

• **Tombs/Burial Practices.** Burials and tombs are among the most common features of archaeological sites. Although grave robbing has been widely practiced from antiquity to modern times, much information about ancient life has been recovered through the legal excavation of burial sites, especially in the Middle East. In addition to the abundant data on mortuary practices supplied by archaeological research, ancient literature—including the Bible—contains many references to beliefs and practices related to death and burial. It should be emphasized that burial practices and tomb construction went through many changes, and much of this development occurred in the Near East during the biblical period.

In the Greco-Roman world, the dead were normally cremated, but burial was the ordinary custom of the Israelites/Jews, along with most of their predecessors and contemporaries (e.g., Gen 23; Deut 10:6; 34:6). The Hebrews were obsessed with a desire for proper burial and fear of exhumation, since exposure of a corpse to the elements represented the ultimate indignity (cf. 1 Kgs 14:11; 16:4; 2 Kgs 9:37; Ps 79:3; Ezek 29:5; Rev 11:9); Jeremiah preached about this possibility in frightening terms (7:33; 8:1-2; 16:4-6; 22:19). Because of the rapid decomposition of cadavers and a fear of becoming ceremonially defiled, burial took place quickly, often within twenty-four hours of death (cf. Num 19:11-19; Deut 21:22-23; Ezek 43:6-9; Hag 2:13; cf. Acts 5:5-6, 10). Concern for a rapid and proper burial is evident in the accounts of Jesus' death (Matt 27:57-61 and par.).

Courtesy of the Eisenberg Museum of Biblical Archaeology, Southern Baptist Theological Seminary.

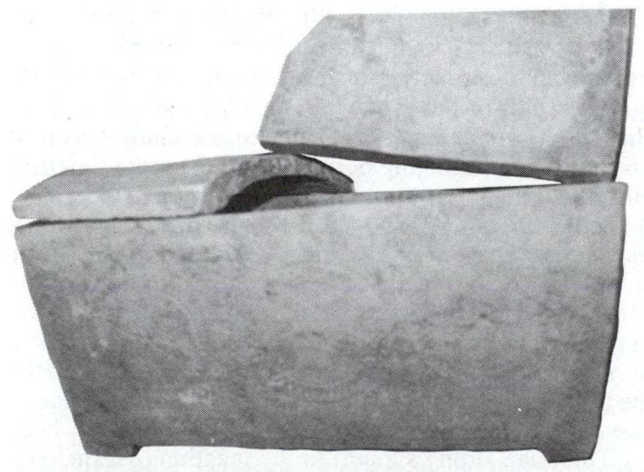

A Jewish ossuary, probably for an infant.

Generally speaking, mortuary procedures consisted of three stages: (1) preparation of the burial plot or tomb, (2) preparation of the corpse for burial, and (3) performance of the rites that accompanied burial. Without question, the majority of Israelites were buried in simple shallow graves, which were often covered with heaps of stones. While these cist burials were sometimes lined with reed mats or stones, coffins were not used in ancient Israel. The "box" or "chest" in which the embalmed body of Joseph was placed is the only coffin mentioned in the OT (Gen 50:26).

Courtesy of the Eisenberg Museum of Biblical Archaeology, Southern Baptist Theological Seminary.

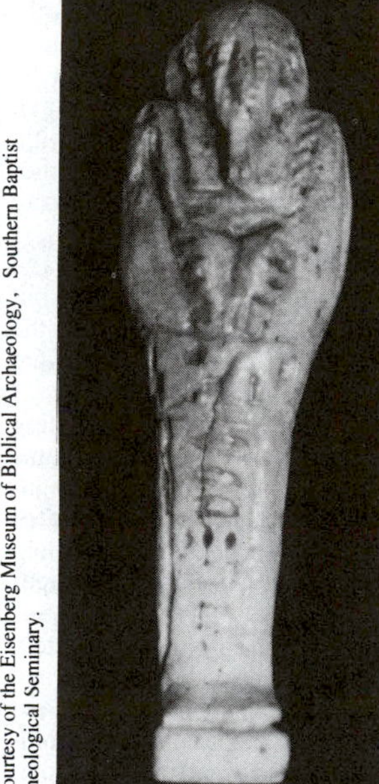

An Egyptian Ushabti, a figurine usually buried with mummies.

Dolmens were constructed as a simple kind of monumental tomb during the Chalcolithic or Early Bronze Age, but the dead were often entombed in caves during the third millennium B.C.E. (the Great Pyramids of Egypt, the most spectacular funerary monuments of all time, date to this period as well). Tombs with small domed chambers at the bottom of vertical shafts were also common in this period (e.g., the many thousands of shaft burials at BAB EDH-DHRA, Jordan). One of the most famous accounts of burial practices in the Bible is found in Gen 23, the story of Abraham's purchase of the cave of MACHPELAH, at Hebron, for the burial of Sarah; this tomb was also used for other members of Abraham's family (Gen 25:9; 49:31; 50:13). During much of the second millennium B.C.E. and on into the period of the Israelite monarchy, wealthy families paid for the preparation of family tombs; these tombs were cut by the thousands in the soft limestone hills of Palestine. Many of the chambered tombs, whose low doors allowed for horizontal entrance, contained stone benches on which the corpses were placed. When a tomb was reused, the skeletal remains on its shelves were pushed aside or placed in repository pits inside the same tomb. The use of family tombs was common in Israel (e.g., Judg 8:32; 2 Sam 2:32; 17:23), and the custom of allowing the deceased to be "gathered to his people'' continued (cf. Gen 25:8; 49:33). Community burial grounds were located outside of towns and villages (e.g., 2 Kgs 23:6; Jer 26:23), and the wealthy folk had tombs prepared in advance of their deaths (cf. Isa 22:16; Matt 27:60 and par.).

In Hellenistic and Roman times, Palestinian tombs were often built like those in the rest of the Mediterranean world (e.g., Tombs of the Sanhedrin in Jerusalem, monumental tombs on the eastern side of Jerusalem's Kidron Valley). The hundreds of funerary monuments carved from sandstone at Petra testify to the influence of Greek and Roman architecture in the Levant. Niches that radiated off of the main tomb chamber made it possible for many bodies to be buried in a single tomb complex. Like ossuaries or bone-boxes, which were used to collect older skeletal material in tombs, these niches appeared in Palestine in late Hellenistic and Roman times. Rock-cut tombs, with stones that rolled into place to block doorways, were used at the time of Jesus' burial (cf. Matt 28:2 and par.; cf. Matt 27:66). Of course, much of this preparation was carried out as a sign of respect for the dead, but hope for a future life (which included belief in resurrection in later times) also put an emphasis on the proper preservation of one's physical remains.

Preparation of the body for burial was carried out by relatives and friends of the deceased, usually by women (e.g., Luke 23:54–24:1). This procedure generally included the washing of the body (cf. Acts 9:37), the anointing with aromatic OINTMENTS and SPICES (cf. Mark 16:1; Luke 23:56; John 12:3-7; 19:39-40), and the wrapping in cloth (cf. John 11:44; Matt 27:59 and par.). Ointments and spices were not employed to embalm the corpse, as was the case with Jacob and Joseph in Egypt (Gen 50:2-3, 26), but were used to purify the deceased and as symbols of honor; the large quantity of spices used by Nicodemus at the burial of Jesus reflects the latter practice (John 19:39). The corpse was often carried on a litter to the burial site (cf. Gen 50:7-11; 2 Sam 2:31).

The announcement of death in biblical times was accompanied by various expressions of grief, which included weeping (Jer 9:18; Mark 5:38), crying out loud (Amos 5:16), tearing of garments (2 Sam 1:11; 13:31), wearing of sackcloth (Gen 37:34), covering oneself in dust or ashes (2 Sam 13:31), and fasting (2 Sam 1:12). In the pagan world, death resulted in extremely severe acts of mourning (e.g., Isa 15:2; Jer 47:5; 48:37), but some of these practices were forbidden to Israel (Lev 19:28). The use of professional mourners, singers, and musicians at funerals was known throughout the ancient world (Eccl 12:5; Jer 9:17; Matt 9:23), but there were prohibitions placed on the presence of priests, high priests, and Nazirites at such occasions (Lev 21:1-4, 10-11; Num 6:7). While the Canaanites placed jewelry, weapons, lamps, and containers of food in tombs with the deceased,the Israelites were not permitted to make offerings for the dead (Deut 26:14).

—GERALD L. MATTINGLY

• **Tongues.** Specific reference to ''tongues'' or ''speaking in tongues'' is found in Mark, Acts, and 1 Corinthians (though the reference in Mark 16:17 belongs to the spurious ending of Mark and thus is not treated here). The practice is often referred to by the English term ''glossolalia'' which results from the combination of two Gk. words (γλῶσσα and λάλειν). The practice appears to have consisted of a kind of unintelligible speech often associated with a trance-like state that might accompany an ecstatic experience. Many interpreters have observed that this practice is not limited to the Christian church but has occurred among the practitioners of several of the religions of the ancient world.

In Acts there are specific references to the phenomenon at 2:1-13, 10:44-48, and 19:6. Acts 2 is often regarded as the biblical basis for those who practice tongues today. Most interpreters regard this account as the initial appearance of tongues within the Christian community. The whole passage reflects Luke's conviction that this Pentecost was the occasion for the unleashing of God's spiritual might upon those who were present. In that context Luke presents tongue-speech as clear evidence of God's presence. That Luke understands the phenomenon in this way is apparent when the other two occurrences in Acts are examined: (a) Peter at Caesarea (10:46) and (b) the disciples at Ephesus (19:6).

The most striking feature of the Lucan reference is the claim in 2:4ff. that the believers spoke in other languages (a claim not made at 10:46 and 19:6). Some interpreters suggest that Luke may have relied upon the older tradition which emphasized the ecstatic dimension (''these men are drunk'') and shaped it into a dramatic event to underscore the presence of God's Spirit. One intriguing suggestion is that Luke constructed his account of Pentecost by reversing the outcome of the story of the Tower of Babel (Gen 11). That is, just as God confused the languages in this ancient story, at Pentecost God ''unscrambled'' the languages of humankind so that each could understand according to his own dialect.

Paul's discussion of tongue-speech in 1 Cor 12–14 does not include a definition or description of tongues, probably because the practice was widespread there and generally known. Paul does, however, speak about its essentially unintelligible character.

The discussion of tongue-speech in 1 Corinthians is in the context of GIFTS OF THE SPIRIT. Paul apparently recognizes tongues as one such gift but discusses many others as well. In fact, he suggests that tongue-speech is a gift to be subordinated to prophecy (1 Cor 14:1, 5, 6-9). Paul makes the following observations:

(1) as a genuine gift of the spirit, tongue-speech is not to be forbidden; (2) Paul himself has practiced the gift; (3) the gift can serve as a channel for personal communion with God; (4) the gift can serve as a ''sign'' to unbelievers pointing them to God's power; and (5) the gift, if practiced during public worship, must be strictly regulated. Two specific regulations are given: (a) all spiritual gifts must be evaluated by the criterion of whether or not they build up the church. Tongues often encourage behavior that is divisive and self-centered; (b) the one manifesting this gift must remain silent unless an interpreter is present.

See also APOSTLES, ACTS OF THE; GIFTS OF THE SPIRIT; WEEKS, FESTIVAL OF.

Bibliography. W. E. Mills, *Understanding Speaking in Tongues* and *Speaking in Tongues: A Guide to Research on Glossolalia*; C. G. Williams, *Tongues of the Spirit: A Study of Pentecostal Glossolalia and Related Phenomena.*

—WATSON E. MILLS

• **Tongues as of Fire.** *See* TONGUES

• **Tongues, Speaking with.** *See* TONGUES

• **Tools.** The inanimate instruments or implements that are used to do work, pursue crafts, or create art. Tools and the technology that invents and uses tools are a distinguishing feature of human civilization.

More than sixty different common tools gain explicit mention at one time or another in the Bible. Some of the examples include the axe, sickle, mattock, and plowshare (1 Sam 13:20); the saw and the pick (2 Sam 12:31); the plane, marking pencil (stylus) and scribing compass (Isa 44:13); the awl (Exod 21:6); the sieve (Amos 9:9); hammer and nails (Jer 10:4); the plumb line (Amos 7:7-8); the knife (Gen 22:6, 10); firepans, forks, shovels (Num 4:14), and snuffers (2 Kgs 25:14); the razor (Judg 13:5); the mallet (Judg 5:26); the bridle and the whip (Prov 26:3; cf. John 2:15); the fishhook (Job 41:1) and oars (Ezek 27:6). Tools are alluded to further, by implication, in general references to various industries, trades, and crafts—e.g., pottery making (Jer 18:2; Rom 9:21); mining, smelting, and refining (Isa 1:25; Mal 3:2-3; Job 28:1-11); weaving (Exod 39:27; John 19:23); building construction (1 Kgs 9:15-22); reaping (Ruth 2:2-7); shipbuilding (1 Kgs 22:48); carpentry, stonecutting, and metalworking (2 Chr 24:12); tentmaking (Acts 18:3); and the like. Not to be overlooked—precisely because it illustrates the dark side of toolcraft—is the array of torture tools and machines listed in the story of the martyrdom of the seven brothers (in the Apocrypha): "wheels and joint dislocators, rack and hooks and catapults and caldrons, braziers and thumbscrews and iron claws and wedges and bellows . . . " (*4 Macc* 8:13, passim).

Besides coming from the biblical record itself and from classical texts, our knowledge of tool technology in the biblical period—as for antiquity generally—is informed by well over a century of modern archaeological exploration and excavation, the resultant information being scattered through innumerable published excavation reports, museum exhibits, anthologies of ancient near eastern texts, and excellent serial publications and journals (e.g., *AASOR, AJA, BA, BAR, BASOR, IEJ, PEQ*, etc.). To a great extent it is now possible to document how, e.g., the ancients quarried, moved, and raised their enormous blocks of building stone; built aqueducts, tunnels, or sewage systems to channel water for whole cities from one place to another; mined and refined metals and worked them; crafted furniture and pottery and jewelry; or performed such delicate tasks as dental repair.

Tools and technology are not only incidental background to the biblical narrative, as something taken merely for granted. Humankind's nature as *homo faber,* "man the tool maker," is brought explicitly to the fore in the Bible—sometimes as a theological affirmation; sometimes as a prudential or prophetic warning; or sometimes simply as occasion for admiration and awe, as in the Joban poet's stunning description of the miner working deep in the earth (Job 28:1-11). The pentateuchal priestly tradition's portrayal of humankind as, on the one hand, created in the image of God, and, on the other, mandated by the creator to "subdue" the earth and to "have dominion over" all the other creatures (Gen 1:26-28) implies a high view of technology and humanity's technological potential. In passing, it should be noted that some modern environmentalists' objection to this text—as providing a license for destructive exploitation of earth's natural resources—rests on an out-of-context reading. The priestly view of creative work—whether by God or humans—finds its completion in a sabbath cessation from creativity (Gen 2:2-3; Exod 20:8-11), that values and holds sacred what has been done. Appreciation for the sabbath *telos* (end and purpose) of all work and craft makes an exploitive assault on creation unacceptable.

Other strands of biblical tradition do, however, warn against man's technological skills and achievements as potentially or actually seductive and corrupting, even if they view them as not being this necessarily. Deutero-Isaiah's observant description of the idol-maker's craft (Isa 44:9-17) ridicules what he perceives as a feckless misapplication of recognized talent. The Covenant Code prohibits the use of any tool (*ḥereb*) on stones used to build an altar (Exod 20:25; cf. Josh 8:31). Elsewhere, the reader is advised that, when Solomon built the Temple, "it was with stone prepared at the quarry; so that neither hammer nor ax nor any tool of iron (*kĕlî barzel*) was heard in the Temple, while it was being built (1 Kgs 6:7). The intent of such strictures appears to be implementation of the second commandment (Exod 20:4-5)—the exclusion of any possible first step toward crafting of the stone into diverting art or idolatrous sculpture.

A limited citation of the Bible's appropriation of tool imagery into its theological vocabulary includes the winepress (Isa 63:2-3; Rev 14:19); the ax (Matt 3:10; cf. Isa 10:15); the hammer (Jer 23:29); the plumb line (Amos 7:8); the sieve (Amos 9:9). Finally, certain tools have come to stand, metonymically, for peace—as have certain weapons for war. "They shall beat their swords into plowshares, and their spears into pruning hooks" (Isa 2:4; Mic 4:3) expresses a messianic expectation becoming proverbial; the prophet Joel's reversal of this saying is, understandably, less often remembered (Joel 3:10[H4:10]).

Bibliography. D. Cérézelle, K. Temple, and M. Swetlitz, "Symposium on Religion and the Rise of Technology," P. T. Durbin, ed., *Research in Philosophy and Technology*; H. Hodges, *Artifacts: An Introduction to Early Materials and Technology* and *Technology in the Ancient World*; J. G. Landels, *Engineering in the Ancient World*; W. M. F. Petrie, *Tools and Weapons*; J. B. Pritchard, ed., *ANEP*; C. Singer et al., eds., *A History of Technology*; J. Zias and K. Numeroff, "Ancient Dentistry in the Eastern Mediterranean: A Brief Review," *IEJ* 36 (1986): 65-67.

—BRUCE DAHLBERG

• **Torah.** [toh'ruh] Heb. for "teaching," "instruction," "revelation"; God's instruction or revelation to Israel through MOSES at SINAI, comprising the Pentateuch or "Five Books of Moses" (first five books of the OT). "Torah" distinguishes this first division of the Hebrew scriptures from the other two, titled in Hebrew, respectively, Nevi'im (*nebî'îm,* Prophets) and Kethuvim (*kĕtûbîm,* Writings). From the first letters of these three Heb. words the rabbis derived the acronym *TaNaK* (Tanakh) to represent the entire Hebrew canon. The following comments concern Torah as revelation (on the etymology of *tôrâ,* its multiple meanings, and the particular translation of it as "law," see LAW IN THE OLD TESTAMENT).

Early in postbiblical Judaism the revelation to Moses came to be thought of as having included within it, at the time it was first given, "everything that will ever be legitimately offered to interpret its meaning" (G. Scholem). In this conception, the Torah was given in two forms, the written Torah and the oral Torah. The former is the text of the Pentateuch; the latter includes the Mishnah, Talmud, Midrash compilations and related texts that record originally oral rabbinical commentary on the written Torah. As interpretation, oral torah is still evolving. Rabbinical doctrine holds that such commentary was handed down by memory from Moses through a succession of authorities to the earliest rabbis (*'Abot* 1:1). Practically, the notion of a dual Torah recognizes that no text is meaningful or effective without authoritative, i.e., knowledgeable, interpretation.

It is usually said that interpretation began to grow in importance when EZRA brought the written Pentateuch, or a substantial part of it, from Babylon to postexilic Jerusalem (Neh 8:1-8), inaugurating a new chapter in Judaism in which the sacred text became a focus of worship. This view holds that the farther the living and changing community became distanced in time and culture from the fixing of the revelation in writing, the more necessary and complex became the task of interpretation. However, recent studies of the postexilic biblical literature, especially of such Psalms as 19 and 119, suggest that celebration of the Law (*tôrâ*) in these works does not necessarily have in view either a written law or the revelation through Moses, but a divine Law more immediately present and generally accessible in the worshiping community. The notion of oral Torah is seen thus to have antecedents historically in Israel that developed alongside of and even earlier than the developing written Torah. The Pentateuch, of course, contains within itself relatively late traditions that can be seen to comment on or interpret earlier traditions also preserved there.

The rabbinical tradition that all of the Pentateuch was revealed to Moses on Mount Sinai, and that he wrote all of it down (hence, the "Five Books of Moses"), is usually said to be a claim not made in the Pentateuch itself. However, if one should hold a historically pre-Enlightenment view that the Pentateuch is of a piece, and if one reads back into the Pentateuch a later generation's usage equating Torah with the Pentateuch, then Deut 31:9, "Moses wrote this Law [*tôrâ*]," might understandably be construed as just such a claim (cf. Exod 24:4). There is of course abundant empirical evidence in the Pentateuch itself for concluding that it is a composite work, the greatest part of which must be later than Moses.

See also LAW IN THE OT.

Bibliography. J. D. Levenson, "The Sources of Torah: Psalm 119 and the Modes of Revelation in Second Temple Jerusalem," *Ancient Israelite Religion*, ed. P. D. Miller, Jr. et al.; J. Neusner, *The Oral Torah*; G. G. Scholem, "Tradition and Commentary as Religious Categories in Judaism," *Jud* 15/1 (1966): 23-39.

—BRUCE T. DAHLBERG

• **Tower of Antonia.** *See* ANTONIA, TOWER OF

• **Tower of Babel.** *See* BABEL, TOWER OF

• **Trade Routes.** *See* CARAVAN

• **Tradition Criticism.** *See* TRANSMISSION HISTORY

• **Tradition History.** *See* TRANSMISSION HISTORY

• **Tradition in the Old Testament.** Materials that were transmitted from one generation to the next during Israel's history and that affected the composition of the OT literature. The term "tradition" can designate a number of different phenomena: literary traditions, genres, motifs, customs, practices (e.g., ritualistic, legal, governmental), beliefs, values, and more. Ancient Israel, as is the case with all enduring cultures, developed and passed down such traditional materials in the everyday context of life; that is, the traditions arose because they met some need in the society, and they were preserved as long as the people continued to find them meaningful and pertinent.

The search for traditions has in several ways proved to be important for understanding the Hebrew Bible. In exegesis, "tradition history" or "tradition criticism" joins source criticism and form criticism in the effort to recover the numerous stages in the development of the biblical literature. Focusing on a given textual unit and using the results of the other two methods concerning sources and genre, tradition criticism attempts to ascertain the earliest tradition that arose, by whom and for what purposes it was preserved, where it was geographically localized in the country (e.g., cultic centers, city or countryside, north or south), how and why it was changed by later generations or groups (e.g., priests, prophets, court officials, sages), and why it finally became stabilized in its present written form. This method thus seeks to determine why a given text contains what it does and not something else, and the tradition critic answers this question by demonstrating how an original tradition grew over time until reaching its final form. Since such a history of tradition is hypothetical, it needs always to stand the test of plausibility and must fit with what is known about the history of the times.

These traditions were alive in the sense that they played a vital function for the people and could continue to grow or change as deemed appropriate. In most cases the traditions were oral: narratives recounted frequently by storytellers, songs sung in the cult or in any other context of life, customs remembered and given the status of community law, prophetic utterances delivered before the people and memorized by the prophet or the disciples, proverbs repeated as situations fit them. Probably the vast majority of the biblical literature went through some such period of growth; it was relatively rare that the present written form of a text was created solely by one author and with no tradition preceding it.

Often traditions originated as independent entities and then were subsequently joined with other materials. For example, stories about ABRAHAM came together into a cycle of traditions, perhaps as a storyteller wanted to follow up one narrative with another. The laws of the premonarchic period (now the Covenant Code in Exod 20:22–23:33) were probably gathered together near the time when the new monarchy started to institute other requirements for the people. Similarly, the prophetic utterance, as a rule quite short and intended for a specific situation, became collected with others like it. The capacity of the mind for faithfully remembering vast amounts of materials, especially in societies with widespread illiteracy, is well attested. From collections of oral traditions it was a rather short step until written sources and books emerged. An intermediate stage for the pentateuchal traditions occurred as some of the shorter collections became gathered around several basic themes, such as the promise to the ancestors, the exodus from Egypt, and the divine guidance through the wilderness. The time span, from origin to end form, varied according to the different literary types.

Tradition includes more than stories, songs, pronouncements, and other such materials that could eventually become literary texts. Also part of the heritage of the Israelite people was a wide variety of motifs, concepts, images, notions, and other elements that served as building blocks for the literary traditions but that were not actually tied to any one specific text. For example, the motif of "the day(s)" when Yahweh will come to deliver or to punish, perhaps stemming from the early practice of the HOLY WAR, was used in a variety of ways by the prophets: for Israel's salvation (Amos 9:11; Jer 33:14-16), for Israel's punishment (Amos 5:18-20; Joel 1:15), or for judgment of the wicked (Jer 9:25-26; Zeph 1:14-18; Mal 4:1-6; Isa 24:21;

Zech 12-14) or of other nations (Obad 15; Joel 3:1-3, 14). Or again, the notion of what a king should do—often in contrast to the Israelites' historical experiences with their kings—is evident in the laws in Deut 17:14-20, in the stories of DAVID's troubles (2 Sam 9–20), in SOLOMON's prayer for wisdom (1 Kgs 3:6-9), in the numerous accounts of the misuse of royal power (e.g., King AHAB and NABOTH's vineyard, 1 Kgs 21), and in the hope for a ruler of the ideal Davidic type (e.g., Jer 33:15; Ezek 34:23-24).

Identifying traditions in the Hebrew Bible lends a sense of the interconnectedness among the Israelites over the thousand years during which the biblical literature gradually came into being. Each generation had a link with its past as well as a role in the further transmission of the heritage. This was an active, creative role insofar as any given group of people could modify the traditions by reinterpreting them in light of its own needs, especially in such times of crisis as the devastating Exile of the sixth century B.C.E. It also indicates that not isolated individuals but the believing community or groups within it should properly be regarded as the "authors" of much of the Hebrew Bible.

See also HERMENEUTICS; INTERPRETATION, HISTORY OF; ORAL TRADITION; TRANSMISSION HISTORY.

Bibliography. D. A. Knight, *Rediscovering the Traditions of Israel*; D. A. Knight, ed., *Tradition and Theology in the Old Testament*; M. Noth, *A History of Pentateuchal Traditions*; W. E. Rast, *Tradition History and the Old Testament.*

—DOUGLAS A. KNIGHT

• **Transfiguration.** Transfiguration, meaning a complete change of form, refers to a crucial experience in Jesus' ministry (Matt 17:1-13 || Mark 9:2-13 || Luke 9:28-36). Peter's confession of Jesus' messiahship at Caesarea Philippi a week earlier was followed by Jesus' prediction of his crucifixion, his demand that disciples be willing to die for him, and his announcement that the KINGDOM OF GOD would come in power before some of them died. On the heels of these declarations, the transfiguration was a confirmation of Jesus' sonship and authority.

Mark gives the earliest account of the transfiguration. Matthew and Luke, while similar, contain unique emphases. Jesus took PETER, JAMES, and JOHN to a high mountain, probably Mount Hermon which towers 9,000 ft. to the north of Caesarea Philippi. There his appearance was radically changed. The brightness of face and clothes symbolized the presence of the radiant GLORY of God in Jesus. MOSES, the lawgiver, and ELIJAH, one of the greatest of the prophets, appeared with Jesus, indicating that the old order has been completed in Jesus. Peter's awestruck statement about building tents reflects the Jewish concept that when the day of salvation arrived, God would "tabernacle" with his people. Peter's words reflect the hope that the days have arrived.

The cloud, reminiscent of the cloud which led Israel in the Exodus, demonstrated the presence of God. As at Jesus' baptism, the voice, the climax of the event, confirmed the sonship and authority of Jesus.

Matthew's presentation, in basic agreement with Mark, emphasizes the lordship of Jesus and depicts him as the new lawgiver. Like Moses on Mount Sinai, Jesus' face shone brightly. Luke introduced the fact that Jesus was praying at the time of the transfiguration and declared that Moses and Elijah talked with Jesus about his death in Jerusalem.

In addition to confirming the sonship and authority of Jesus, the transfiguration has several additional nuances. The announcement from heaven alludes to the king messiah of Ps 2 and declares that Jesus is this king. The brightness portrays Jesus as bearer of God's glory to men. This glory will reach its climax at the parousia of Jesus. Thus, the transfiguration was a preview of the coming of the kingdom in power.

The nature of the transfiguration has been variously explained. Some hold that it was not a historical occurrence, but was a piece of symbolic writing by the evangelists to declare the messiahship of Jesus. Others claim that it was a postresurrection appearance of Jesus which was misplaced by the evangelists. While both views are possible, the story is so deeply imbedded in its context as an actual experience that they seem improbable. Still others propose that it was a deeply mystical experience in which Jesus was so enraptured while in communion with the Father that the rapture showed on his face. Somehow the disciples were caught up in the mystery of the moment. While one can never know the exact nature of the transfiguration, Matthew's statement that it was a VISION (17:9) seems best.

This experience in the ministry of Jesus gave him encouragement, strengthened the faith of the disciples, and proclaimed that Jesus was the true king of Israel in whom the glory of God was abiding on earth.

See also ELIJAH; GLORY; JAMES; JOHN; MOSES; PETER; VISION.

—W. T. EDWARDS

• **Transgression.** *See* SIN

• **Transjordan.** The term "transjordan" literally means "across the Jordan" and technically applies to the area east of the Jordan River which stretches to the Arabian Desert (PLATE 10). The term "transjordan" is not used in the OT although the phrases "this side of the Jordan" and "the other side of the Jordan" appear several times. In general usage Transjordan is the area stretching from the Yarmuk River in Syria to the Arabian Desert on the east, the head of the Gulf of Aqaba on the south, and the Jordan River on the west. This area is the modern kingdom of Jordan.

Geographically, Transjordan is a plateau ranging from 2,000 to 5,000 ft. in elevation and extending north to south from the Syrian border to the Gulf of Aqaba. This plateau is bisected from east to west by numerous stream beds which trail off into the Arabian Desert. Most of these are dry except during the rainy season. Four which carry perennial springs of water are the Wadi Hesa (biblical ZERED), Wadi Mojib (ARNON), Wadi Zerqa (JABBOK), and Wadi Yarmuk.

Two major roadways traverse this area from north to south. The King's Highway (mentioned in Num 20:17 and still in use today) follows the ridge of the plateau. The Pilgrim Route follows the edge of the Arabian Desert.

Most significant for biblical history are the kingdoms which, from about the thirteenth century B.C.E. onward, existed in Transjordan. From south to north the most prominent of these kingdoms were EDOM, MOAB, GILEAD, and BASHAN—with Ammon lying east of Gilead. All these were at some time controlled by the Israelites.

When the Israelites first began their march toward the promised land, they sought permission to go through Edom via the King's Highway. When this permission was refused they went around Edom, then successively took the territories of SIHON, king of the Amorites (Num 21:21-25; OG, king of Bashan (Num 21:33-35); and Balak, king of Moab (Num 22-25). This territory was then divided among the tribes of REUBEN, GAD, and half the tribe of MANASSEH (Num 32:20-21, 33). Edom was never conquered by the Israelites until David reigned as king (2 Sam 8:14).

Conquest of these territories "across the Jordan" was never permanent. The period of the Israelite kingdoms (ca. 1020–587/6 B.C.E.) was punctuated by sporadic conflicts in these areas (cf., e.g., 2 Sam 10:1-14; 1 Kgs 11:14-16; 2 Kgs 3:4-27).

When Judah fell to Babylon in 587/6 B.C.E. the Transjordan area passed into the hands of Babylon. Afterwards it was successively a part of the Persian, the Greek, and finally the Roman empires.

In the NT period Transjordan consisted primarily of PEREA, east of the Jordan River between Pella and Machaerus, and the DECAPOLIS ("ten cities"), east and south of the Sea of Galilee. Perea belonged to the tetrarchy of Herod Antipas, son of Herod the Great. The Decapolis seems to have been under the administration of the legate of Syria.

See also AMMON/AMMONITES; ARABIA; ARNON; BASHAN; DECAPOLIS; EDOM/EDOMITES/IDUMEA; GADARA; GILEAD; JABBOK; MIDIAN/MIDIANITES; MOAB/MOABITES; PEREA; PETRA; ZERED.

Bibliography. N. Glueck, *The Other Side of the Jordan*.

—JOE E. LUNCEFORD

• **Translations of the Bible.** *See* TEXTS/MANUSCRIPTS/VERSIONS

• **Transmission History.** The phrase "the history of the transmission of the traditions" (*Traditionsgeschichte*) is preferable to the terms "tradition history" or "tradition criticism." Its earliest development was associated with Hermann Gunkel (1862–1932) who focused on (1) the determination of the oral traditions lying behind a written document; (2) a comparison of the cultic and mythological motifs of the religions of Egypt, Mesopotamia, and the Hebrews to show the relationships between the Hebrews and the surrounding culture; and (3) a sympathetic criticism of the literary forms in which the various stories, laws, and poems of the OT appeared. The OT scholar Gerhard von Rad and the NT scholar James Robinson have made contributions to this method.

This approach reconstructs the development of traditions within texts and attempts to discover their source of origin while noting how they have been adapted through being transmitted. The major interest of this method is with the preliterate stage in which traditions are circulated orally. The importance of the transmission of the traditions (beliefs and practices) is indicated in Deut 6:20-25 and 1 Cor 15:1-17 where the importance of receiving, keeping, and transmitting of traditions is stressed.

Evidence of exodus and resurrection traditions in other texts is sought by those using this method, who in probing back as far as possible into the oral and preliterate stage, unfold the process of development of the traditions. For example, the resurrection traditions in Paul's writings can be compared to the utilization of the same tradition in the sermons in Acts. The historian can speculate on how this tradition was developed as it was transmitted orally in sermons in the early Christian community prior to being put in written form in Paul's Letters and in the Acts of the Apostles.

NT scholars emphasize the way historical traditions were "kerygmatic" insofar as historical traditions about Jesus became important as theological affirmations that Jesus of Nazareth was the Messiah of God. In studying ways the Gospel of John differs from the synoptic Gospels in its use of traditional materials, scholars recognize that the purposes intended by such transmission of traditions can vary. The approach underscores the fact that one uniform notion of "kerygma" fails to define primitive Christianity's understanding of the tradition.

In their efforts to explain the forces and influences behind the formation of the OT, scholars are concerned with: (1) the community or group responsible for shaping and transmitting a particular tradition; (2) the particular geographical location or locations with which a tradition was associated; (3) the dynamics that are present in the origin and reformation of a tradition including sociological, political, or cultic influences; and (4) the various themes of the OT and a search for the way particular themes came to be formulated and the role they play.

The focus on the history of the transmission of the traditions allows us to view the OT and NT history as more than a presentation of simple facts or a presentation of dogmatic utterances delivered in a vacuum. The oral and preliterate periods in which the traditions originated were circulated and modified prior to and after being written reveal dynamic rather than static communities of faith.

See also FORM/GATTUNG; GOSPELS, APPROACHES TO THE CRITICAL STUDY OF; INTERPRETATION, HISTORY OF.

Bibliography. D. A. Knight, ed., *Tradition and Theology in the Old Testament*; W. E. Rast, *Tradition History and the Old Testament*; R. F. Collins, *Introduction to the New Testament*.

—ROBERT K. GUSTAFSON

• **Travel.** *See* CARAVAN

• **Travel Narrative.** The travel narrative is the central section of Luke's Gospel (9:51–19:27). The section begins with Jesus' decision to move toward Jerusalem. Although the other Gospels give brief accounts of a journey toward Jerusalem late in Jesus' public ministry (Mark 10:1-52; Matt 19:1–20:34; John 7:2-10), Luke devoted the most attention to this period. The section comprises about one-third of Luke's Gospel. Despite several references to Jerusalem as the goal of the trip (9:51; 13:22, 33; 17:11; 18:31; 19:28), Luke was not primarily concerned to show the geographical progression of Jesus and his disciples. For example, Jesus probably was on the outskirts of Jerusalem in 10:38-42, assuming Mary and Martha lived at Bethany (cf. John 12:1-3). In 17:11 he was apparently on the border between Galilee and Samaria. Jerusalem's primary significance for Luke is theological, not geographical. It is the place for Jesus' suffering and death (13:22). On this journey Jesus gave the third explicit prediction of his crucifixion in Jerusalem, but the disciples did not understand (18:31-34; cf. 9:22, 43-45). This period of Jesus' public ministry is sometimes called the "Perean Ministry," but Luke did not give enough geographical details to reconstruct Jesus' itinerary with precision. Jesus went to Jerusalem to die and be "received up" (9:51), perhaps referring to both his resurrection and ascension (cf. 9:31).

The travel narrative begins with Jesus going from Galilee into Samaria (9:52). The section ends with events in Jericho and the parable of the pounds, told by Jesus near Jerusalem (18:35–19:27). Some scholars end the section at 19:10, since the parable of the pounds is similar to the parable of the talents (Matt 25:14-30). Jesus reached Jerusalem, however, in Luke 19:28.

Some of the events and teaching in the travel narrative are similar to the other Gospels. For example, Luke includes here Jesus' teaching about the great commandment (10:25-28), the LORD'S PRAYER (11:1-4), the accusation about Beelzebul (11:14-23), the sign of Jonah (11:29-32), the criticism of the Pharisees (11:37-54), the teaching about anxiety (12:22-34), the healing of the crippled woman (13:10-17), the parables of the mustard seed and leaven (13:18-21), the advice to the rich young ruler (18:18-30), and the healing of the blind man near Jericho (18:35-43).

Several of the episodes and teachings, however, are unique to Luke. Some scholars suggest that Luke here used sources beyond Mark and Q, with much of the material being from Luke's special source, L. Material unique to Luke includes: Jesus' sending of seventy disciples on a mission similar to the mission of the twelve (Luke 9:1-6; Matt 10:1–11:1; Mark 6:7-13); the parable of the good Samaritan following the discussion of the great commandment (10:29-37); Jesus' defense of Mary for listening to his teaching while Martha was distracted (10:38-42); parables about prayer (11:5-13; 18:1-14) and the rich fool (12:13-21); Jesus' rejection of the notion that some Galileans had suffered for their sins or that eighteen people were killed by a large tower because of their unusual guilt (13:1-5); the parable of the barren fig tree (13:6-9); Jesus' defense of his healing of a woman on a Sabbath (13:10-17); stories of the lost sheep, the lost coin, and the lost (prodigal) son to explain Jesus' association with social outcasts (15:1-32); the discussion of wealth in the parables of the shrewd steward (16:1-8) and the rich man and Lazarus (16:19-31); Jesus' cleansing of ten lepers, including the grateful Samaritan leper (17:11-19); the statement to the Pharisees that the KINGDOM OF GOD was already present (17:21); and Jesus' meeting of Zaccheus at Jericho (19:1-10).

The travel narrative represents a significant block of Luke's Gospel and reflects many of the special themes in Luke's portrait of Jesus.

See also GOSPELS, CRITICAL STUDY OF; LUKE, GOSPEL OF.

Bibliography. H. Conzelmann, *The Theology of St. Luke*; A. T. Robertson, *A Harmony of the Gospels*; F. Stagg, "The Journey Toward Jerusalem in Luke's Gospel," *RE* 64/4 (Fall 1967): 499-512.

—WARREN MCWILLIAMS

• **Treatise.** *See* SETH, SECOND TREATISE OF, THE GREAT; SHEM, TREATISE OF

• **Treaty.** *See* COVENANT

• **Tree of Knowledge.** The "tree of the knowledge of good and evil" was one of two trees mentioned in the account of EDEN. One of these, the TREE OF LIFE, comes into significance only after the FALL. The tree of knowledge, however, plays a more central role in the writing of the YAHWIST, though it only appears in Gen 2–3. Although a magical tree appears in other myths, this tree is not magical but is a means by which humankind's loyalty to God is tested. An understanding of these trees must begin with a brief look at the language and style of the passage.

The Hebrew for "the tree of life . . . in the midst of the garden, and the tree of the knowledge of good and evil" is a strange and strained expression from the standpoint of syntax. The tacking on of the tree at the end of the phrase is awkward grammatically. In addition, there is a numeric change from two trees in Gen 2:9b to one tree in the midst of the garden in Gen 3:1-21 (presumably the tree of knowledge). This is compounded by the reintroduction of the second tree in Gen 3:22-24.

Attempts to solve these difficulties have ranged from postulating a multiplicity of sources (J1 and J2) to an elimination of the tree of life from the story because of its seeming secondary nature. Another view has been to attribute the difficulty to an assimilation of different oral traditions. However, none of these has won universal support.

The type of knowledge conveyed through the tree of knowledge is no more certain than an explanation of the language and style. There have been many varied theories as to what the tree gave to humankind. One of the more popularized theories has revolved around sexual knowledge. This notion has as its primary evidence the use of the verb "to know" in the sense of "to be intimate with." In other passages (Gen 4; 19) this usage is an euphemism for sexual intercourse. Since the man and woman recognized their nakedness after acquiring knowledge from the tree, some have contended that sexual awareness was perhaps the type of knowledge that was gained. One rabbi, Gordis, viewed the knowledge as a distinction between heterosexual (good) relationships that have the purpose of procreation and homosexual (evil) relationships that serve no valid purpose. Critics of this theory have observed that the prohibition was given to the man even before the creation of woman. Also, implied in Gen 2:23ff. is a proper sense of sexual knowledge between the man and woman. In addition, in Gen 3:22 God states that humankind has become like "one of us, knowing good and evil," and this does not seem to indicate a sexual connection.

A second theory is one of moral discernment or judgment. This theory takes the viewpoint that the knowledge of good and bad is the ability to distinguish, and subsequently choose, between right and wrong in a moral sense (cf. Isa 5:20; 7:15; Amos 5:14; 2 Sam 19:26). Karl Budde and Hermann Gunkel have contended that humankind attained a moral conscience and was forced to exercise moral decisions. However, there seems to be an implication in the very prohibition given to the man that he knows right (obedience) and wrong (disobedience). The question must also be raised as to whether or not a righteous God would indeed seek to keep the deity's crowning creation from obtaining a proper sense of morality.

A third theory is one that would see the knowledge attained as a maturing secular knowledge. In this instance, the knowledge gained would lead through maturation of the mental capabilities to an understanding of culture, civilization, and rationality. In this view, humankind's practical reason was activated. Through this rationality, practical knowledge, values, and ethics became the things upon which humankind focused rather than theoretical and metaphysical knowledge. This type of knowledge led to civilization and a greater worldly knowledge. This would seem to be represented by the sudden concern with nakedness, which is not apparent in young children but comes about with age. However, there is no real evidence to indicate that the couple gained a greater sense of worldly nature, and in fact, the development of civilization with all of its crafts is attributed to the later descendants of Adam.

One further theory will be presented as a possibility. This is a theory of universal knowledge. Within this theory is the idea that humankind became like a god in the sense of divine knowledge. The couple now know all things, as God and the angels have knowledge. This type of knowledge would bring power like that of God as well. This has parallels in the Gilgamesh Epic of Akkadian origin. In both instances it would seem that mortals might seek to be a threat to the deity. Yet in reality, mortals did not gain omniscience or a universal knowledge that would rival God, according to the story.

Whatever the proper understanding that one believes is intended, it is evident that the presence of the tree of knowledge in Genesis is difficult to explain conclusively. Yet, there is a general sense of agreement that the story stresses a proper sense of relationship between human beings and God. That relationship was one in which prosperous life and obedience to God was changed and a new relationship between God and mortals was established. The action taken by God after the Fall may seem to be one to prevent mortals from living forever in a state of alienation from God and to impress upon humankind the seriousness of obedience/disobedience. Perhaps this proper sense of relationship was what God intended to keep intact by means of the prohibition, hoping that mortals would exercise the proper choice.

See also ADAM; EDEN, GARDEN OF; FALL; SIN; TREE OF LIFE.

Bibliography. W. Brueggemann, "Genesis," *Int* 34 (1982): 40-54; J. Carmody, D. L. Carmody and R. L. Cohn, *Exploring the Hebrew Bible*; J. L. Crenshaw, *Story and Faith*; R. Gordis, "The Knowledge of Good and Evil in the OT and the Qumran Scrolls," *JBL* 76 (1957): 123ff.; H. Gunkel, *Genesis*; B. Reike, "The Knowledge Hidden in the Tree of Paradise," *JSS* 1 (1956): 193ff.; C. A. Simpson, "The Book of Genesis," *IB*; E. A. Speiser, *Genesis, AB*; J. H. Tigay, "Paradise," *EJ*.

—STEPHEN Z. HEARNE

• **Tree of Life.** One of two special trees that stood in Eden (Gen 2:9; 3:22, 24; Prov 3:18; 11:30; 13:12; 15:4; Rev 2:7; 22:2, 14, 19). References to the tree also appear in some apocryphal and pseudepigraphic texts (*1 Enoch* 24:4-5; *2 Enoch* 8:3-4; 2 Esdr 8:52).

The notion of a tree or a plant, the fruit of which would sustain life indefinitely, was widespread in the ancient Near East. One of the best-known references is found in the Babylonian epic of Gilgamesh (tablet XI), where Utnapishtim, the Babylonian Noah, tells Gilgamesh of a special plant of life that provides perennial youth to the one who eats it; however, he was never allowed to eat it.

In the biblical text, the tree of life was a part of Eden (Gen 2:9) whose fruit could apparently lead to eternal life. Evidently, ADAM and EVE had free access to it before the Fall (Gen 2:9) but had not eaten of it (Gen 3:22). However, after the Fall, God graciously removed them from the garden so that they would not look to the tree for life and, thus, remain eternally separated from the deity (Gen 3:22-24). Certainly, God must have hoped that this would cause these and all future human beings to realize their frailties and to look to him by faith as the real tree (or source) of eternal life.

Others view the removal of Adam and Eve from the garden differently. To them the emphasis falls on God's insistence that the first human pair take up their life in the world, with its positive and negative possibilities. According to this view, the tree of life was denied Adam and Eve in order that they claim their responsibility for the world that God had created.

The physical tree does not loom large in the rest of the OT; yet, the hope that it represented does recur in the symbolism of the virtuous woman and the righteous person (Prov 3:18; 15:4). However, in the last work in NT it once again becomes the emblem of life for the faithful, who at last will receive their just reward, as they are allowed to dwell eternally in the presence of God, the true tree of life (Rev 22:2, 14, 19).

Bibliography. E. O. James, *The Tree of Life: An Archaeological Study*; P. Watson, "The of Life," *RQ* 23/4 (1980): 232-38; G. Widengren, *The King and the Tree of Life in Ancient Near Eastern Religion*.

—HARRY B. HUNT, JR.

• **Trespass.** *See* SIN

• **Trial.** *See* TEMPTATION OF JESUS; TRIAL OF JESUS, THE

• **Trial of Jesus.** Many problems come to light in a study of the trial of Jesus. A. T. Robertson used to list scores of infractions of the Jewish Law in his lectures on the trial of Jesus. In more recent days, doubt has been raised by Jewish NT scholars whether the trial of Jesus was a formal meeting of the SANHEDRIN at all. They suggest that blame should be placed upon the Roman trial of Jesus. Other scholars have questioned the fact that Jesus would have been subjected to two trials.

The starting point for any study must be with the Jewish trial. The earliest Jewish and Christian sources point to some kind of Jewish involvement in the death of Jesus. Mark (14:55-64) and Matthew (26:59-60) indicate a full trial whereas Luke (22:66-71) seems to have a somewhat informal gathering in mind. John sets forth rather vaguely a trial before CAIAPHAS (18:24, 28). Josephus also mentioned Jewish charges leveled against Jesus before Pilate (*Ant* 18.3.3). Moreover Tannaitic traditions exaggerate the involvement of the Sanhedrin in the death of Jesus (*Sanh* 43a, 107b).

The big debate, however, concerning the Jewish trial has to do with the question of a formal or informal meeting of the Sanhedrin. If it were a formal meeting several rules were broken: the Sanhedrin did not meet at night; the Sanhedrin did not meet during a major holiday such as PASSOVER; and the accused was always allowed two witnesses. The problem with this approach of "broken rules," however, centers upon the date for such rules. We know they were not codified until ca. 200 C.E. and could have been quite different from those of Jesus' time.

Scholarly judgment seems to be moving toward a more informal meeting of Jewish leaders. In that situation, rules would not have to be followed anyway. Perhaps the gathering was more of a "rump session" in the middle of the night to give only the slightest "tip of the hat" to a formal trial. Jesus would then be condemned and on the CROSS before his Galilean friends were awake. Others have viewed the trial as a type of grand jury proceeding to determine the charges which would be presented to the Roman authorities.

The question also emerges concerning the charge against Jesus in his trial. The basic offense seems to be blasphemy (Mark 14:64). From Mark we gather that Caiaphas also was concerned with Jesus' threat to the Temple (14:58). Only in Mark does Jesus answer affirmatively the question about messiahship with "I am" (14:62). In Matthew and Luke, he sidestepped the issue. The charge of being a messianic figure would not have been offensive to the Jews. Mark seems to point rather to the issue of divine sonship as the offensive issue. To be at the right hand of God as Jesus stated in 14:62 would bring about a charge of blasphemy. A human being could make no claim to the qualities of God. Caiaphas ripped his clothing at that claim of Jesus—a very appropriate reaction at hearing blasphemy.

Some scholars have suggested that the Jewish trial did not happen. It is never mentioned in the consequent Roman trial. Yet the evidence from all sources seems compelling in associating some action—formal or informal—with the Jews. In the Roman trial, the charge of blasphemy from the Jewish trial is never mentioned. Some see an attempt of the Gospel writers to move the finger of blame from the Romans to the Jews, especially in Luke's Gospel. Luke pinpoints three attempts of PILATE to set Jesus free: he sends him to Herod Antipas, has him beaten to win sympathy, and offers to free a prisoner for Passover.

The trial of Jesus before Pilate was a public affair. Neither Mark nor Matthew record a specific charge against Jesus, but it can be deduced from Pilate's question: "Are you the King of the Jews?" (Mark 15:2). The Romans were concerned that their governors keep the peace in their provinces. The Romans had experienced much political unrest in Judea caused by the ZEALOTS and others. At the mocking of Jesus, the Roman guards dressed him up as a king (Mark 15:16-19), and the title "The King of the Jews" was placed on his cross. Thus, there seems to be good historical support in the Roman trial for the basic charge of being a king. One can clearly understand why the Romans would have desired the death penalty.

In the Roman trial Jesus was more reserved in his replies. In contrast to his direct reply to Caiaphas (Mark 44:62), he answered Pilate with the words, "You have said so" (Mark 15:2). That reply was considered by Pilate to be noncommittal, for Pilate exclaimed, "Have you no answer to make?" (Mark 15:4). The early Christians saw Jesus' answer as a fulfillment of Isa 53:7: "He was oppressed, and he was afflicted, yet he opened not his mouth."

The Jewish leaders seemed to have put some pressure on Pilate for the death penalty. Whether or not the Sanhedrin had the authority to pass the death penalty is still open to question. Pilate already had made several political blunders since taking office. For example, he had allowed his army to march into Jerusalem with flag standards adorned with the bust of Caesar. That action clearly broke the Jewish Law and had caused political unrest. Giving in to the pressure, Pilate gave Jesus over to the mob. Ultimately, it is Pilate who must bear the blame for the death of Jesus. He chose to placate the mob rather than uphold Roman justice.

See also BARABBAS; CAIAPHAS; CROSS; JUDAS; PILATE; SANHEDRIN.

Bibliography. S. G. F. Brandon, *The Trial of Jesus*; P. Winter, *On The Trial of Jesus*.

—JAMES L. BLEVINS

• **Tribes.** The tribal unit was one of the most basic units of society in ancient times. It played an important role in the early stages of the formation of the nation ISRAEL. The tribal unit is perhaps best described as a type of "corporate personality," that is, consisting of other units such as clans and families, all of which share a common bond. The common bond or bonds uniting the tribal unit could perhaps be any of a number of possibilities, including family ties or bloodline, or a series of causes or a need around which clans or families clustered, such as, agricultural and pastoral needs, military needs, and religious needs.

Tribes in the Ancient World. While the nation Israel was comprised of tribes during the early stages of its history, the tribal unit was not unique to Israel alone. Ancient records refer to other groups, that for all practical purposes, functioned as tribal units, though the origin, function, and description of the tribe perhaps varied. In the OT, tribal units are reflected in references to non-Israelite groups such as the Ishmaelites (Gen 26:12-16) and the Edomites (Gen 36:15-19). The Mari tablets, discovered at Mari, a site located in upper Mesopotamia on the Euphrates river, refer to a tribe from that region called the Banu-Yamina, "the sons of the right (hand or bank)."

Tribes in the Bible. (1) Terminology. Three biblical terms were used to convey the idea of a tribal unit. The Heb. words *shebet* and *matteh,* both of which are translated "tribe," meant "staff" or "rod." At the head of the tribe was a prince, patriarch, or elder who served as the tribal leader or ruler. The Hebrew concept of tribe apparently drew upon the symbolism of the leader's staff. Just as the staff in the leader's hand symbolized his authority, the tribe was a social unit with an implied authority. In the NT, the Gk. term *phule* is translated tribe, however, the term enjoyed a broader usage. It was also used in reference to the clan.

(2) The tribe and other social units. The OT refers to a number of social units of which the tribal unit was one part. Though scholars debate the value of Josh 7:16-18 for providing a basic understanding of Israel's major social units, nevertheless, the passage refers to four different categories or divisions. The largest of the social units for ancient Israel was that of "a people" or "nation," for which the Heb. term *am* was used. Therefore, the young nation of Hebrews was referred to as the "people of Israel." A similar title, the "children of Israel," or more literally the "sons of Israel," from the Heb. *bene Yisrael,* was also commonly used. The nation was in turn comprised of tribes, the *shebet* or *matteh.* While *shebet* was an earlier term for tribes, *matteh* appears in later writings, such as Chronicles. The tribe was made up of "clans." The "clan," a *mishpacha,* was a family of families or a cluster of households that shared a common kinship. The clan then was comprised of individual households or families referred to as the "fathers' house" or "house of the father," *beth ab.* Actually, the family in ancient times might be made up of several families living together and forming one household (Num 3:24). The father's house was a type of extended family that included not only family members including wives, concubines and children, but also servants and slaves and their families.

(3) Tribal origins in the Bible. The ancestral background of the "tribes of Israel" is traced to JACOB whose name is changed to Israel. Therefore, the nation Israel was identified as "the children of Israel," or more literally "the sons of Israel." According to the biblical account, the family of Jacob from which the tribes came, originated in north Syria during Jacob's stay at Haran with Laban, his uncle. Eleven of the twelve sons were born at Haran, while the twelfth, BENJAMIN, was born after he returned to Canaan. The birth of the sons came through Jacob's wives Leah and Rachel and their maids Zilpah and Bilhah. The sons of LEAH included REUBEN, SIMEON, LEVI, JUDAH, (Gen 29:31-35), ISSACHAR, and Zebulun, as well as one daughter, Dinah (Gen 30:19-21). Rachel's sons were JOSEPH (Gen 30:22-24), who became the father of EPHRAIM and MANASSEH (Gen 41:50-52), and Benjamin (Gen 35:16-21). Jacob's sons through Zilpah, Leah's maid, were GAD and ASHER (Gen 30:9-12), while Bilhah, the maid of Rachel bore Dan and NAPHTALI (Gen 30:1-8).

This family of families or family of tribes occupied the focal point in the history of the development of Israel as a nation. However, there are details of that history that are not clearly understood and developments in the tribal history that are quite complex. For instance, the Bible implies that other groups referred to as "a mixed multitude" (Exod 12:38) were incorporated into the nation during the Exodus. Because many questions have risen concerning tribal origins and history, the tribes have been the subject of numerous studies undertaken during this century. Some of the most recent studies are those which seek to deal with the tribes from an anthropological or sociological perspective, such as George Mendenhall's *The Tenth Generation,* Norman Gottwald's *The Tribes of Yahweh,* and C. H. J. DeGeus's *The Tribes of Israel.*

(4) Tribal lists. The OT includes more than twenty lists of the tribes of Israel. Three of the most familiar lists include the blessing of Jacob (Gen 49), the blessing of Moses (Deut 33), and the Song of Deborah (Judg 5). A comparison of the lists reveals that while they share a common core of information, they also contain some differences. The differences are primarily in two areas—the order in which the names appear, and the number of tribal names included in the list. For instance, the blessing of Jacob lists twelve tribes, the blessing of Moses eleven tribes, and the Song of Deborah ten tribes. The differences in these three lists are obvious. The blessing of Jacob includes Joseph rather than separating Joseph into Manasseh and Ephraim. The Blessing of Moses omits Simeon, but in the end has twelve names by listing Ephraim and Manasseh, as well as Joseph. And the Song of Deborah omits Judah, Simeon, and Levi.

The tribal lists may vary for several reasons. Some of the lists may be based on geographical locations, while others reflect genealogical relationships. Still other lists perhaps reflect changes in tribal status that took place with the passing of time. For instance, the tribe of Simeon was apparently absorbed by Judah, while Reuben eventually diminished in status and identity.

(5) The tribal period. The tribal period constitutes one of the most important periods in the history of Israel. This period is also referred to as the period of the Judges or the period of the settlement. The tribal period, approximately two hundred years in length, was the period following the conquest of the land of Canaan, the period in which the focus was on the tribal units that comprised the nation Israel, that is, the period during which the tribes went about the task of settling in the land of Canaan.

One of the most provocative questions concerning the tribal period is the question of organization. What kind of organizational structure or model was used by the tribes during this period? While a number of models have been suggested, the proposal that Israel functioned as a tribal AMPHICTYONY has enjoyed the greatest popularity, though many today no longer prefer this model. The amphictyonic theory held that during the period of the Judges, Israel was an amphictyony, that is, a tribal league or a confederation of tribes consisting of twelve tribes held together by a common bond, namely, a covenant with Yahweh, the God of Israel. While the tribes did not have a king like the surrounding nations, nevertheless, their king was Yahweh and they were bound together by a covenant with God.

Three sites must have played important roles as centers of worship or rallying points for the tribes. Gilgal served as the base of operation for the tribes after the tribes crossed the Jordan River (Josh 5:2-12). Its role as a religious center is reflected in references to the special events that took place there—the observance of the rite of circumcision, the observance of the Passover, and the installation of the Ark of the Covenant. Shiloh perhaps became the most prominent worship center during the tribal period. It seems to be the center that functioned as a central sanctuary during much of the tribal period. Shiloh became the home of the tent of meeting, the Ark of the Covenant, and the priesthood. Apparently Shiloh was destroyed by the Philistines shortly after the Philistine-Israelite battle at Ebenezer (1 Sam 4:1-10). Shechem's role as a religious center is reflected in the covenant-making ceremony in Josh 24.

Two types of figures provided valuable leadership among the tribal groups during the period of the judges. Decisions in local communities were made by the elders of the community. While the elders were in a sense local rulers, their primary function was that of settling disputes between parties in the local community or town. On a broader scale leadership was provided in times of crisis by local leaders called judges, with the last of the judges being Samuel. The function of the judge is not always easily defined. In many cases the judge functioned as a military leader in times of crisis, however, in some instances the judge functioned as a decision maker or a type of administrator of justice (Judg 4:4-5; 1 Sam 7:15-17).

The tribal period is described in the Bible as a crisis-filled period, a period in which the people of Israel turned from Yahweh to other gods (Judg 3:7), experienced oppression (Judg 3:8), cried out to Yahweh (Judg 3:9a), and were delivered by a judge raised up by God (Judg 3:9b). This cycle appears over and over in the Book of Judges. While on the one hand the tribal period constituted an important phase in the development of the nation Israel, on the other hand, it was a period marked by a spirit of individualism and a lack of unity. This is reflected in a summary statement that appears in the Book of Judges, "In those days there was no king in Israel; every man did what was right in his own eyes" (Judg 17:6; 21:25; cf. 18:1 and 19:1).

While the tribal period gave way to the development of a monarchy the influence of the tribal units continued on. For instance, that the tribes were still functioning as independent units in the time of David is reflected in the stories of the anointing of David (2 Sam 2:4; 5:1-3). And while Solomon attempted to destroy the remnants of old tribal lines and tribal traditions by reorganizing the land into twelve newly formed taxation districts (1 Kgs 4:7-19), old tribal feelings apparently still surfaced and were at least partially responsible for the division of the kingdom at the time of Solomon's death (1 Kgs 12:1-20).

Lingering tribal influence is also seen in the prophets. For instance, the prophet Hosea uses the name Ephraim some thirty-six times as he refers to the Northern Kingdom, Israel, and Ezekiel gives a review of the twelve tribes as he speaks of the allotment of the land (Ezek 48).

References to the tribes also appear in the NT. The tribal background of several NT figures is mentioned—Jesus was a descendant of Judah (Heb 7:14); Anna, the prophetess in the Temple, came from the tribe of Asher (Luke 2:36); Barnabas was a Levite (Acts 4:36); and Paul came from the tribe of Benjamin (Phil 3:5). Other references to the tribes include those in which the tribes are referred to in a collective sense (Matt 19:28; Luke 22:30; Acts 26:7; Jas 1:1; Rev 7:4).

See also AMPHICTYONY/CONFEDERACY; FAMILY; SOCIOLOGY OF THE OLD TESTAMENT.

Bibliography. J. Bright, *A History of Israel*; C. H. J. De Geus, *The Tribes of Israel*; N. Gottwald, *The Tribes of Yahweh*; G. Mendenhall, *The Tenth Generation.*

—LAMOINE DEVRIES

• **Tribulation, Great.** "Great Tribulation" refers to the intense distress, trial, affliction, and suffering of the end time. Such matters as the time of occurrence, the breadth of the distress, and even the duration of the tribulation are difficult to pinpoint, in large part due to the fact that such details are frequently couched within the highly visionary and symbolic imagery found within the writings identified as apocalyptic, the best examples of which are the Book of Daniel in the OT and the Book of Revelation in the NT. Although the specifics are somewhat difficult to grasp, the basic conviction is that a period of intense tribulation will precede the end of the present age.

Ample background for this idea can be found in both OT and NT texts. For example, from the OT it is suggested that the end period when God appears on the scene of history will be a time of increased tribulation and upheaval (Zeph 1:7-18; 3:8; Joel 2:1-2; Zech 14). In a similar vein, many of Jesus' statements as recorded in the Gospels suggest a period of worsening trials on earth. One of the clearer statements in this regard is found in the so-called "little apocalypse" of Mark 13: "For in those days there will be such tribulation as has not been from the beginning of the creation which God created until now" (v. 19).

In the apocalyptic Book of Daniel the notion of a final period of great tribulation is presented symbolically as taking place at the end of the reign of the Seleucid king, Antiochus IV (175–164 B.C.E.). Antiochus's military campaigns and his cruel policies of imposing foreign religious practices on the Jews (11:2-45) precede the period of divine intervention led by the angel Michael (12:1). This intervention is depicted as a time of intense distress, but one from which the faithful will be preserved (12:1-3).

Although the specific historical circumstance out of which the text is produced is different, the Book of Revelation also suggests there will be a period of great tribulation at the end of the age. This will be a time not only of intense personal and community alarm, but also of great catastrophe in nature itself (16:18). In the symbolic language of Revelation it is suggested that this tribulation will occur in connection with the breaking of the seven seals of the scroll containing the fixed purposes of God (5:1–7:14), the blowing of seven trumpets signalling additional convulsions in nature (8:6ff.), and the emptying of seven bowls filled with plagues (16:1-21). This time of tribulation is terminated by the appearance of Christ in the form of a mighty warrior who overcomes the forces of evil (19:11-16).

Similar ideas of a messianic warrior who will put an end to a period of great tribulation can be found in the writings of the Qumran community.

See also APOCALYPTIC LITERATURE; DANIEL, BOOK OF; ESCHATOLOGY IN THE NEW TESTAMENT; ESCHATOLOGY IN THE OLD TESTAMENT; MILLENNIUM; REVELATION, BOOK OF.

Bibliography. L. F. Hartman and A. A. DiLella, *The Book of Daniel*; J. M. Ford, *Revelation*.

—MICHAEL D. GREENE

• **Tribunal.** *See* JUDGMENT SEAT

• **Tribute.** *See* PUBLICANS

• **Trimorphic Protennoia.** [tr*i*-mohr′fik-proh′tuh-noi″yuh] Among writings in the NAG HAMMADI library identified as representative of the Barbeloite form of Sethian GNOSTICISM is the first tractate of Codex XIII, the *Trimorphic Protennoia* ("First Thought in Three Forms"). The Barbeloites were one of the largest groups of Gnostics identified by early church heresiologists and were so-called because of the prominent place they gave to one Barbelo, first emanation of the highest, unknown God. She represented the female aspect of this God. In *TrimProt* she is the principal character who speaks in poetry (parallel strophes) and prose (continuous narrative). Her comments include four types of material: self-description, a cosmological sketch of the universe, a true account of human history, and a summons to receive her *gnosis* (knowledge) and be redeemed. The writing has the literary form of a wisdom monologue, Barbelo speaking like personified Wisdom in Prov 8, Sir 24, and Wis 7–8.

The tractate recounts parts of Gnostic saving history from the emanation of Barbelo from the highest God, The Invisible Spirit, to the docetically interpreted crucifixion of Jesus. Most distinctive is the development of a hymn to Protennoia, First Thought. This hymn, in apparently more primitive form, concludes the APOCRYPHON OF JOHN (*NHC* II.*1*: 30.12–31.25), another Barbeloite tractate. The hymn begins with an "autodoxology" or self-praise by Protennoia/Barbelo, a series of "I am" statements describing her as the divine Thought and Barbelo (35.1-32). In a second autodoxology (35.32–36.27; 40.29–41.1) Protennoia calls herself the "Voice of Thought," the Father, who descends from the light into darkness below and gives shape to her fallen members. In a third autodoxology (42.4-27; 45.2-12; 45.21–46.3) Protennoia is the "Speech of Thought," the Mother, whose descent empowers her fallen members, giving them breath or spirit. Then, in a final autodoxology (46.5-6; 47.5-22; 49.15-22; 50.9-12.18-20), Protennoia speaks as the "Word (LOGOS) of Thought," the Son, who descends in the likeness of lower powers, assumes human form, introduces a baptismal rite called "The Five Seals," and restores her fallen members to the light of heaven from whence they originally came. Shaping this hymn is the Platonic understanding of the relationship of internal reasoning (= thinking) to externally expressed reasoning (= verbal expression or "logos") and how this clarifies the way God's existence (in and of itself) is related to the self-revealing "Word" (Logos) he utters.

Other mythic events mentioned include creation of the world by an inferior deity, Ialtabaoth; the entrapment of divine power ("members") of Protennoia in ADAM and his successors; the incarnation of the Word (Logos) in Jesus; the mourning of world-ruling powers over their impending destruction; the institution of Gnostic baptism of illumination; and Protennoia's rescue of Jesus from the "accursed wood" (the cross) and redemption of him.

Parallels between the descent of Protennoia and that of the preexistent Word in the Prologue of John's Gospel, as well as between the content of the Nag Hammadi tractates *ApJohn* and *TrimProt* point toward mid-second century as the probable time of composition, though some poetic material may go back to the first century C.E. The document seems to have been secondarily Christianized. The author and place of composition are unknown.

See also GNOSTICISM; NAG HAMMADI.

Bibliography. B. Layton, "First Thought in Three Forms (FTh)," *The Gnostic Scriptures: A New Translation with Annotations and Introductions*; J. B. Turner, "Sethian Gnosticism: A Literary History," *Nag Hammadi, Gnosticism, and Early Christianity*, ed. C. W. Hedrick and R. Hodgson, Jr. and "Trimorphic Protennoia," *The Nag Hammadi Library in English*, ed. J. M. Robinson.

—MALCOLM L. PEEL.

• **Trinity.** The term Trinity denotes the Christian doctrine that God is a unity of three persons: Father, Son, and HOLY SPIRIT. Though the word itself does not occur in the Bible, it had very early usage among the church fathers. Its Gk. form, *trias*, was first used by Theophilus of Antioch (d. 181

C.E.), and its Latin form, *trinitas,* seems to have been coined by Tertullian (d. ca. 220 C.E.). The Athanasian Creed of the fourth century expresses the doctrine in the words, "We worship one God in Trinity, and Trinity in Unity, neither confounding the persons nor dividing the substance."

Materials consistent with trinitarian concepts of God are found in the OT, especially in the narrative of Genesis. The plurals in Gen 1:26 and 11:7 may be noted, as also the frequent mention of the Spirit of God (e.g., 1:2) and the divine appearance to Abraham in chap. 18. Thus ideas of God important for the development of the doctrine of the Trinity are implicit in the divine self-revelation from the beginning. Other OT passages which point to the Trinity are Ps 33:6, Prov 8:12ff., and Job 28:23-27.

In the NT there is no explicit trinitarian statement (the text about the three heavenly witnesses in 1 John 5:7 [KJV] is to be rejected as a later addition). Yet while there is no dogmatic statement, there are clear references to the three persons of the Godhead. In some contexts all three persons are mentioned together in a way that implies their equality. Thus in 1 Cor 12:4-6 Paul correlates "Spirit," "Lord," and "God" (cf. Eph 4:4-6). A trinitarian concept is also present in the Pauline blessing of 2 Cor 13:14 (the earliest known trinitarian formula) and in the baptismal formula of Matt 28:19. This latter formula would seem to imply a complete break with Judaism in including under a singular "name" not only the Father, but also the Son and the Holy Spirit. The NT also stresses the Son's unity with the Father (e.g., Matt 11:27; John 10:30; 14:9-11; 20:28; Col 2:9; 1 John 5:20). Several passages indicate that the same essential relationships extend to the Holy Spirit (e.g., John 14:16-26; 15:26; 16:5ff.).

It was the NT emphasis upon the deity of Christ that led to the introduction of trinitarian doctrine into the early creeds of the church. These creeds taught that God is one, yet from eternity he is Father, Son, and Holy Spirit, the triune God. Here the deity of Christ is fully asserted against those who would regard him as divine but created. The deity of the Holy Spirit is also preserved against the notion that he is only a mode of God in relation to creation or salvation. Instead, the church declared that the three persons of the Godhead are neither three gods on the one hand, nor three modes of God on the other, but coequally and coeternally God. Hence the doctrine of the Trinity has just as accurately been called the doctrine of the Triunity, since nowhere does the NT emphasis on the deity of the Son or of the Holy Spirit deviate in the slightest way from the uncompromising MONOTHEISM of the OT.

See also ABBA; DIVINITY OF JESUS; GOD; HOLY SPIRIT; INCARNATION; JESUS; MONOTHEISM; SON OF GOD.

Bibliography. E. J. Fortman, *The Triune God*; L. Hodgson, *The Doctrine of the Trinity*; C. W. Lowry, *The Trinity and Christian Devotion*; K. Rahner, *The Trinity*.

—DAVID A. BLACK

• **Tripartite Tractate.** [tri-pahr'tit-trak"tayt] Among the best preserved and longest (eighty-eight pages) of the tractates in the NAG HAMMADI library is the *Tripartite Tractate* (*TriTrac*), the fifth writing in the "Codex Jung." Its first editors attributed it to Heracleon, a prominent, second century teacher in the Oriental school of Valentinian GNOSTICISM. Instead, the tractate seems to represent a radical revision of that school's teaching, bringing it into closer conformity with the views of orthodox theologians of the third and fourth centuries. This revision may be in response to criticisms levelled by the orthodox at more controversial Valentinian teachings.

In its present form, *TriTrac* is a sometimes obscure translation in Subachmimic Coptic of an original Greek text. Scribal decorations divide the whole into three parts, the basis for the name *Tripartite Tractate*. These parts present major movements in the drama of salvation: (1) emanation/devolution from the sole Father that results in CREATION; (2) the making of humanity and the fall of ADAM; (3) the Savior's incarnation and reintegration of spiritual beings into the primeval Godhead.

More specifically, the first part (51.1–104.3) presents the emanation of divine beings from the utterly transcendent Father. Not having a dyadic or masculine-feminine character (as most Valentinians held), the Father is said to be a "single one." Two beings, the Son and the Church, emanate from this Father, forming a trinity rather than the usual Valentinian ogdoad, decad, or duodecad. From a third level of beings is emanated the masculine LOGOS (substituted for the female Sophia of other Valentinian systems). This Logos by "attempting an act beyond his power" (76.7-8) falls into error. He himself produces two orders of beings outside the Pleroma (the transcendent Godhead): hylic and psychic forces. Out of the struggle of these forces this world is produced. The Logos is then divided, the better half (male) returning to the heavenly Pleroma and producing with the aeons a Savior (85.15–91.13). This Savior, also called "Son," will reveal the heavenly Reality to those outside the Pleroma. He creates and places over the "oikonomia" of this world archons (rulers) and a supervising demiurge (not negatively assessed).

In the second part (104.4–108.12) appears an interpretation of Gen 1–3. Adam is jointly created by the demiurge (providing man's psychic and material components) and the Logos (providing the spiritual element). Every human thus has three potentialities and becomes defined as to destiny on the basis of his or her responses to the Savior.

The third part (108.13–138.27) presents the appearance of the Savior on earth, his revelatory work, his own redemption, and his restoration of "all the members of the body of the Church" to the Pleroma. The Valentinians ("the spirituals") respond and are immediately saved; ordinary Christians ("psychics") need further instruction; the nonbelievers ("hylics") shun Christ and are damned. The text ends with a hymn praising the Savior through his Holy Spirit (138.20-25).

Its apparent accommodation to more orthodox views and its affinities with the Western school of Valentinianism have led scholars to date the *TriTrac* to ca. 215–250 C.E. and to identify its provenance as the western Mediterranean.

See also GNOSTICISM; NAG HAMMADI.

Bibliography. H. Attridge and E. H. Pagels, "The Tripartite Tractate," *The Nag Hammadi Library in English*, ed. J. M. Robinson, and "The Tripartite Tractate," *Nag Hammadi Codex I (The Jung Codex): Introductions, Texts, Translations, Indices,* ed. H. W. Attridge.

—MALCOLM L. PEEL

• **Trophimus.** [trof'uh-muhs] A native of Ephesus (Acts 21:29) who first appeared in biblical history in connection with the relief offering (Acts 20:4), Trophimus, along with TYCHICUS, was part of the delegation traveling with Paul in Macedonia and Achaia. Very possibly he was the first of the two unnamed Christian brothers who assisted Titus in this work (2 Cor 8:18-19), with Tychicus being the other (8:20-21). Trophimus (a gentile) next appeared in Jerusalem with Paul and was mistakenly thought by some Asian

Jews to have been taken by Paul into the Temple's Court of Israel (Acts 21:29). Later he was left behind at Miletus because of an unspecified illness (2 Tim 4:20). Apart from 2 Cor 8:18-19, no characterizations of Trophimus occur, yet the word of praise here certainly reflects what is apparent elsewhere: he was a committed servant of the gospel.

See also TEMPLE/TEMPLES; TYCHICUS.

—LORIN L. CRANFORD

• **Trust.** *See* ASSURANCE; FAITH; HOPE IN THE NEW TESTAMENT; HOPE IN THE OLD TESTAMENT

• **Truth.** The biblical notion of truth is rich and complex. In the OT the Hebrew word for truth also bears the meaning of firm, solid, binding, certain, unchanging, faithful, and trustworthy. When used of God or persons, it expresses the character of their speech, action, or thought. As a term concerning the Law, it carries the sense of firm and binding (Deut 13:14; 22:20). Most commonly it denotes a religious reality. For example, Hosea declares that there is no truth in the land because of ignorance of the knowledge of God (Hos 4:1). The OT sees humans as truthful when they abide in faith in God. Thus, truth is foremost an attribute of God which emphasizes divine steadfastness and constancy. God is truthful and can be depended upon (Deut 32:4). Only in a secondary sense is truth predicated of humans. When one keeps the covenant, one lives in truth (1 Sam 12:24). Obeying the commandments constitutes being truthful (Ps 43:3).

The Hellenistic use of the term truth complicates and enriches the NT meaning. Greeks used truth not as a relational term about God, the covenant, or the commandments, but rather as an abstract term which signifies factual information about a real state of affairs. Scholars continue to debate whether the Hebrew or the Hellenistic sense dominates in the NT. A balanced approach which considers both possibilities appears sensible.

The Gk. word for truth (ἀλήθεια) most often bears a meaning which is thoroughly Hebraic. This is the case in Paul's writings. In Gal 2:14 truth bears the sense of sure certainty. Rom 3:7 contrasts human falsehood with God's trustworthiness. Second Cor 7:14 uses truth with reference to sincere honesty. When Paul refers to the "truth of the gospel" (Gal 2:4, 14), he refers not primarily to the facticity of his message, but rather to the saving message which breaks the bonds of sin and the works of the Law and results in the new life in Christ. The true gospel for Paul is thus an experienced, transforming gospel. A false gospel denies this (Gal 2:4). To be sure, Paul links the true gospel with a true body of teaching, the "truth of God" (Rom 1:25; 3:7); he as well connects true teaching with the saving gospel (cf. Gal 5:7; 2 Cor 6:7; 2 Thess 2:10-12). The deutero-Pauline and GENERAL LETTERS often emphasize true as opposed to false doctrine (cf. Eph 4:24; 1 Tim 3:15; 2 Tim 2:15; 2 Pet 2:2).

In the synoptic Gospels truth and its cognates appear infrequently. When used, the OT sense of relational, saving truth predominates. One can, for example, "speak truth" (Mark 12:32) or "teach the way of God in truth" (Matt 22:16). In these cases truth is not purely cognitive—the true versus the false—but is rather a reference to the genuine certainty of the gospel.

In the NT the Hellenistic meaning of truth as reality, or the ultimately real, or knowledge of the real, influenced John most. Bultmann and Dodd, for instance, believe the Greek sense predominates over the Hebraic meaning. Recent scholars, Raymond Brown for example, argue that John's usage is moral rather than intellectual, deriving from traditional Jewish and wisdom sources. While some Hellenistic influence is present, the Hebraic meaning seems to dominate.

The Johannine literature uses truth and its cognates with great frequency, accounting for fifty-two percent of their usage in the NT. Typical of John is the sense of doing or practicing the truth (John 3:21; 1 John 1:6). Jesus refers to himself as truth in John 14:6 ("I am the way, and the truth, and the life"). The author binds grace and truth closely together (John 1:14, 17). One can bear witness to the truth (John 18:37) and know the truth (1 John 2:21; John 8:44). The source of true knowledge is God whose spokesman is Jesus, "a man who has told you the truth" (John 8:40). He is the true light (John 1:9; 1 John 2:8), the true bread (John 6:32), and the true vine (John 15:1). In order for one to receive the grace and truth of God, one must receive Christ (John 1:12) and hence live and walk in the truth (2 John 4; 3 John 3). Filled and empowered by the spirit of Christ (John 14:16-17), one abides in truth and life. First John emphasizes the relation of truth to love. One who abides in truth cares deeply for others (1 John 3:10-18).

Truth in John therefore implies action which is sincere and honest. God acts through Christ on behalf of humanity. Humans who believe in Christ, the Johannine tradition suggests, act with truth and love toward one another.

See also KNOWLEDGE IN THE NEW TESTAMENT; KNOWLEDGE IN THE OLD TESTAMENT.

Bibliography. R. Brown, *The Gospel According to John*; R. Bultmann, "ἀλήθεια, κτλ.," *TDNT*; C. H. Dodd, *The Interpretation of the Fourth Gospel*.

—DONALD W. MUSSER

• **Truth, Gospel of.** Among the most important tractates found in the NAG HAMMADI library is the *Gospel of Truth*, a twenty-seven-page text that appears third in the Codex Jung (Codex I). Its significance lies, first, in the possibility (some would say probability) that it is the long lost *Veritatis Evangelium* (*Gospel of Truth*) that the church father Irenaeus stated (*AdvHaer* 3.11.9) was presumptuously penned by the Valentinians as a different and supposedly superior gospel. Second, others think it was written by Valentinus himself, an Egyptian Christian who lived ca. 100–175 C.E. and founded one of the most important Gnostic schools. Third, it is a rhetorically sophisticated and profound homily on the Gnostic gospel, the good news that Jesus Christ was a redeemer-revealer who came to dispel ignorance, make known the true nature of the highest God, and thereby grant believers salvation. It provides us with a striking example of how powerful and subtle could be the appeal of Christian GNOSTICISM to orthodox believers.

Following a prologue in which main themes are enunciated (16.31–17.4), the work falls into three major units of exposition, with intervening transitional passages. The first unit (17.4–23.18) presents the cosmic and human condition necessitating SALVATION (ignorance and forgetfulness caused by the female emanation "Plane" or "Error"), the intervention of Jesus as revealer and teacher, and the death of Jesus as the supreme revelation of how the Father overcomes error and redeems human selves. The second unit (24.9–32.30) describes the effects of this revelation: it restores the unity of selves with the Father and overcomes all deficiencies; it makes authentic human existence possible, creating wakefulness and joy; and, as expressed in the Son's work as Shepherd, it opens the way for return of elect selves to the Father. The third unit (33.33–43.24) describes the process of reintegration of spiritual selves into their primeval Source, the Father. Like an alluring perfume, the spirit of incorruptibility, awakened by the Son as the Father's "Name," gently attracts the Elect back to the Father. The final goal is "rest in the Father" (40.23–41.14), the ultimate destiny of the "children whom He loves."

Some scholars contend that since the text lacks elaborate mythological speculations familiar from other Valentinian texts, it is really not Valentinian. Others, however, think it does echo Valentinian theology: Error (or "Plane") as a probable type of fallen Sophia (a feminine hypostasization of wisdom found in many Gnostic systems), ignorance of the Godhead as the basic human problem, salvation as brought by Christ's revelation and gift of knowledge. Lack of elaboration of these themes in the text is explained either as due to its containing the earlier, more orthodox thought of Valentinus about the time of his break with the church of Rome (ca. 140–145 C.E.), or as due to a later writer's desire to refer only covertly to more developed Valentinian thought so as to make a stronger, exoteric appeal to orthodox Christians (cf. the *Epistle of Ptolemy to Flora*). There is no clear indication of place of composition, though both Rome and Egypt have been proposed.

See also GNOSTICISM; NAG HAMMADI.

Bibliography. H. W. Attridge and G. W. MacRae, "The Gospel of Truth," *The Nag Hammadi Library in English*, ed. J. M. Robinson, and "The Gospel of Truth," *Nag Hammadi Codex I (The Jung Codex). Introductions, Texts, Translations, Indices*, ed. H. W. Attridge.

—MALCOLM L. PEEL

• **Truthfulness.** *See* TRUTH

• **Tubal-cain.** [*too*″buhl-kayn′] The smith of smiths; son of Lamech and Zillah (Gen 4:22). Tubal-cain also had at least two half-brothers, Jabal and Jubal (Gen 4:19-21) and a full sister, Naamah (Gen 4:22). His name may be clearly divided into two parts. Though each part is somewhat uncertain, the first one is most often interpreted as coming from a root word meaning "to produce" or "to bring forth," while the second one is most often interpreted as coming from a root meaning "to fit together" or "to work with metal." If these are correct, the combining of the very similar ideas probably indicated that he was considered either the "father" of all metalworkers or the "greatest" of the metalworkers of his day. Either way, he was certainly well-known for his ability to work with bronze (or copper) and iron himself and for his ability to teach that trade to others (Gen 4:22). Thus, as society developed, people like Tubal-cain quickly learned to harness the world's raw materials and to use them for their own benefit. However, despite such material progress, more often than not they still failed in their relationships with God (Gen 4:1-24).

See also CAIN AND ABEL; METALLURGY.

Bibliography. S. Mowinckel, *The Two Sources of the Predeuteronomic Primeval History (J E) in Gen 1-11*; H. G. Stigers, *A Commentary on Genesis*.

—HARRY B. HUNT, JR.

• **Turban.** A term for several kinds of headdress worn by different groups of people in Israel. Head coverings had considerable significance. In addition to their value as protection in weather, they frequently identified the wearer's office and standing within the society. The three main types of head coverings were the cap (cf. the Darius monument's

Artwork by Margaret Jordan Brown

Ancient styles of headdress.

portrayal at Behistun, modern Bisitun, in northern Iran), the head-scarf (a square yard of cloth folded into a triangular shape with threaded coil "ropes," 1 Kgs 20:31-32), and the turban.

The turban was made of unusually thick linen material artistically wound, with the ends concealed. Priestly turbans of various sorts are mentioned: the priest's cap (*migbāʿôt*, Exod 28:40); the diadem or mitre (*miṣnepet*, Exod 28:4); the linen turban or bonnet (*peʾēr*, Ezek 44:18); and the crown or diadem (*ṣānîp*, Zech 3:5).

Other references indicate that one or another term for turban could be used to refer to mourning attire (Ezek 24:17, 23), to women's headdress (Isa 3:20), or as a figure of speech (Isa 61:3, 10).

See also DRESS.

—OMER J. HANCOCK, JR.

• **Twelve, The.** The Twelve is a title used in the NT for a group of twelve men chosen by Jesus from the wider circle of his followers for special authority and mission (Matt 10:1-4; Mark 3:13-19; Luke 6:13-16). On occasion the synoptic Gospels describe these same persons as "the twelve disciples" and "the twelve apostles."

The Gospel of Mark provides the most explicit statement about Jesus' purpose in the selection of the Twelve (Mark 3:14). The Twelve were appointed for the purpose of companionship with Jesus, extension of Jesus' ministry of proclamation, and exorcism of demons. Matthew (10:1) and Luke (9:1) underscore the Twelve's authority over disease and infirmity. The same two Gospels contain a saying of Jesus in which he told the Twelve that they would assist him in the coming judgment (Matt 19:28; Luke 22:30). Most interpreters infer from this statement and the reference in Rev 21:12-14 that the choice of twelve, the number of the ancient tribes of ISRAEL, was a parabolic action by which Jesus displayed his desire to create a new Israel.

Lists of the names of the Twelve appear three times in the synoptic Gospels (Matt 10:2-4; Mark 3:16-19; Luke 6:13-16) and once in Acts (1:13). Common to the four lists are the names of Simon PETER, who is always named first; ANDREW; JAMES, the son of Zebedee; John; PHILIP; BARTHOLOMEW; THOMAS; MATTHEW; and James, the son of Alphaeus. Luke and Acts substitute the name of JUDAS, son of James, for THADDAEUS, who appears in Matthew and Mark. Simon the Cananean (Matthew and Mark) is described in Luke and Acts as Simon the Zealot. Judas Iscariot appears in the synoptic lists but is omitted in Acts because of his defection and death.

Following Jesus' resurrection, Matthias replaced Judas Iscariot as a member of the Twelve (Acts 1:15-26). The choice of Matthias rested on three major qualifications: (1) his presence with the disciples from the time of Jesus' baptism to his ascension, (2) his personal witness of Jesus' resurrection, and (3) his appointment by the risen Lord, which the disciples discerned through prayer and the casting of lots. After the addition of Matthias, no subsequent replacements were made, as evidenced by the absence of any such action upon the martyrdom of James, the son of Zebedee (Acts 12:1-2).

Other than their names, most of the Twelve receive meager mention in the NT. Peter, James, and John are described in the Synoptics as an inner circle within the Twelve, and Peter occupied a significant role as spokesman for the Twelve both before Jesus' death and during the early ministry of the postresurrection church in Jerusalem. Although the Twelve acted as leaders of the church shortly after the resurrection of Jesus (Acts 1–6), they, and their authority, soon merged into the larger company of Christian disciples. The idea of apostolic succession in the church is lacking in both the Hebrew background of the term apostle and the Christian practice in the NT.

See also APOSTLE/APOSTLESHIP; DISCIPLE/DISCIPLESHIP; ISRAEL.

Bibliography. V. Taylor, "The Twelve and the Apostles," *The Gospel According to Mark*; A. M. Hunter, *The Work and Words of Jesus*; E. J. Goodspeed, *The Twelve*.

—ROBERT M. SHURDEN

• **Tychicus.** [tik'uh-kuhs] An Asian (Acts 20:4), possibly from Ephesus (21:29), who appears in connection with Paul's later ministry. He is one of those associated with Paul in the collection of the relief offering in Macedonia and Achaia (Acts 20:4). He is very possibly one of the two unnamed brothers with special duties in this ministry (2 Cor 8:18-22). In Ephesians (6:21-22) and Colossians (4:7-8) he is mentioned as being sent by Paul to inform and encourage the readers concerning Paul, as well as to carry these letters. Col 4:9 links him with Onesimus. Finally, he is possibly sent by Paul to Crete to relieve Titus (Titus 3:12) and later to Ephesus to relieve Timothy (2 Tim 4:12). He is characterized as a beloved brother, a faithful minister, and a fellow servant (Eph 6:21; Col 4:7).

See also TROPHIMUS.

—LORIN L. CRANFORD

• **Typology.** *See* ADAM; INTERPRETATION, HISTORY OF

• **Tyre and Sidon.** [t*i*r, s*i*'duhn] The two main cities during Phoenicia's glory days.

Tyre. The principal seaport along the ancient Phoenician coast, Tyre (known today as Sur) was located about twenty-five mi. south of Sidon and thirty-five mi. north of Mount Carmel (PLATE 1). The city was divided into two parts: the mainland community sometimes referred to as Ussu, and the smaller island community just offshore. The main harbor (constructed by King HIRAM in the tenth century B.C.E.) lay on the south side of the island. Because the sea lay on its western side, the rock cliffs on its southern side (usually referred to as the "ladder of Tyre"), and the Lebanese mountains on its eastern side, the city was easy to defend and thus managed to remain relatively independent throughout Phoenicia's history.

Though little is known about its origins, Tyre is believed to be a very ancient city (perhaps dating back to about 2700 B.C.E.). Clearly, it was in existence by the time of the golden age of Ugarit (ca. 1800 B.C.E.) for its Asherah temple is mentioned in the Ugaritic legend of Keret. Moreover, the AMARNA letters (dating ca. 1375 B.C.E.) indicate that it remained a loyal vassal of Egypt in spite of the fact that most of its neighbors took advantage of an Amorite threat to declare their independence. However, the invasion of the SEA PEOPLES (ca. 1200 B.C.E.) soon allowed Tyre to also proclaim its independence.

The destruction of Sidon by the sea peoples and the ensuing emergence of Hiram I as the king of Tyre (ca. 980 B.C.E.) signaled the beginning of a new and golden era for the city and its people. Apparently, Hiram was a brilliant leader for he not only brought peace and stability to the land through extensive treaties (such as those with David—2 Sam 5:11; and Solomon—1 Kgs 5:1), but also involved himself in some massive building projects at home (such as the new island harbor) and abroad (such as Solomon's Temple—1 Kgs 5; 7:13-45; 2 Chr 2:3-18). Moreover, he built his maritime enterprises into one of the most renowned the world had ever known (Isa 23:8) and set up trading colonies throughout the Middle East (such as those at Tarshish, and along with Solomon, at Ezion-geber—1 Kgs 9:26-28).

During its golden age, Tyre became famous for its brilliant purple dye and magnificent glasswork. However, as one would expect, the seaport was most noted for its maritime activities, which delivered goods all over the Middle East. Like most port cities, it was also known for its paganism, particularly the worship of Melqart, its patron deity.

After his death, Hiram's successors were able to continue his policies through political agreements (such as the one in which Ethbaal married his daughter, Jezebel to Ahab—1 Kgs 16:31); such prosperity did not last long. By ca. 875 B.C.E., Tyre was having to pay heavy tribute to Asshur-nasir-pal II of Assyria. From that time on the city had to pay tribute first to the Assyrians, then to the Babylonians and finally to the Persians. However, the port city was never completely taken (although Nebuchadrezzar's thirteen year siege, 587–574 B.C.E. certainly came very close). The city (including its famous port) was ultimately attacked and destroyed when ALEXANDER THE GREAT swept through Palestine in 332 B.C.E. Although the city was rebuilt and did manage to regain some of its respect during pre-Christian (1 Macc 11:59; 2 Macc 4:18) and NT (Matt 15:21-28; Mark 3:8; Luke 6:17; 10:13-14; Acts 21:3-6) times, it never regained its former glory.

Sidon. Sidon (modern Saida) was the second most-important seaport along the ancient Phoenician coast. The ancient city was situated on a small knoll that projected out into the Mediterranean about twenty-five miles north of Tyre. The main harbor lay on the north side of the city and was protected by the sea. The rest of the city was encompassed by a huge wall which usually provided more than ample protection from any enemies. Outside this wall lay a small but fertile plain which provided more than enough food for the city and its surrounding areas. Thus, because of its location, natural resources (timber, purple dye, and glass), and maritime activities, the city managed to become quite prosperous.

Although no one knows for sure, Sidon is thought to be the oldest of the Phoenician cities (Gen 10:19; 1 Chr 1:13). After some time, it must have fallen under the domination of the Egyptians, for the Amarna letters (ca. 1375 B.C.E.) indicate that it had defected to the Amorites. However, when the sea people moved into the area (ca. 1200 B.C.E.), they sacked it and sent its inhabitants fleeing to Tyre. Though weakened, the city was still able to provide significant opposition to the Israelites during their efforts to claim the promised land (Josh 19:28; Judg 1:31; 10:12).

Finally, the Assyrians began to turn their attention toward the west and thus began another long period of foreign domination. At first, they paid tribute to Tiglath-pileser I, then Asshur-nasir-pal II, Shalmaneser III, Tiglath-pileser III, Sennacherib, and Esarhaddon. Evidently, when each succeeding ruler came to the throne, the city had again to be forced into submission. Finally, Esarhaddon not only destroyed the city but deported many of its people.

The city quickly recovered; however, just as it was gaining strength, it was overrun by Nebuchadrezzar (Jer 25:22; 27:3; 47:4). Fortunately, the Babylonians were soon replaced by the Persians who used the Phoenicians' maritime expertise against the Greeks. However, when the Phoenicians revolted against Artaxerxes III (in 351 B.C.E.), he attacked the city with a vengeance. The city was burned to the ground and many lost their lives in the process. Thus, in 332 B.C.E. when Alexander the Great threatened those who had managed to survive, they surrendered without a fight. Under the Greek and later Roman oversight, the town once again prospered and has continued to do so to this very day.

Throughout its history, the city's primary god was Eshmun (a god of healing). Thus, when the news of Jesus and his ministry spread, many of the people from Sidon went to Galilee to hear him (Mark 3:8; Luke 6:17). Perhaps in response to their interest, Jesus headed that way, where he healed the Syrophoenician's daughter (Matt 15:21-28; Mark 7:24-31). Later Paul stopped by Sidon on his way to Rome and visited some Christian friends (Acts 27:3). The city was included among the important centers of Christian work in the time of the Council of Nicea (in 325 C.E.).

See also PHOENICIA.

Bibliography. F. C. Eiselen, *Sidon: A Study in Oriental History*; N. Jidejian, *Tyre Through the Ages*; H. J. Katzenstein, *The History of Tyre: From the Beginning of the Second Millenium B.C.E. Until the Fall of the Neo-Babylonian Empire in 538 B.C.E.* ; A. Poidebard and J. Lauffray, *Sidon*.

—HARRY B. HUNT, JR.

• **Ugarit/Ras Shamra.** [*oo'*guh-rit/rahs-shahm'ruh] The ancient city of Ugarit, today called Ras Shamra ("head[land] of fennel"), was located on a headland on the Mediterranean coast, about twelve mi. north of Latakia in Syria (PLATE 1). The earliest artifacts found at Ugarit date to ca. 6500 B.C.E. in the prepottery Neolithic Period. The site was occupied almost continuously through the Chalcolithic, Early Bronze, Middle Bronze, and Late Bronze Periods. Ugarit was destroyed ca. 1180 B.C.E. and was never rebuilt. Strategically situated where the major roads from Mesopotamia, Asia Minor, and Egypt converged, and possessing a fine seaport at nearby Ma'hadu (Minet el Beida), Ugarit played a crucial role in the movement of goods and information, especially in the Late Bronze Period. Ugarit was the capital of a wealthy city-state, but like most city-states in the region, such as Nuhašše, Ni'i, Mukiš, and Amurru, it seldom enjoyed independence in the Middle Bronze and Late Bronze Periods, being under the political or economic control of the larger states like Yamhad, Egypt, Mitanni, and Hatti. The Late Bronze culture was sophisticated and international, marked by the adoption of mores, religious practices, and linguistic elements characteristic of surrounding peoples.

Like EBLA, the existence of Ugarit was known from ancient documents long before its location was established. In 1928 a farmer discovered what turned out to be an elaborate tomb just north of Minet el Beida. The next year excavations, which have continued for a half-century, were begun in the cemetery and on the nearby tell of Ras Shamra. Within seven weeks the first texts had been unearthed. One of the texts indicated that it had been written in the reign of Niqmaddu, king of Ugarit, thus providing the first of the data for the identification of the site.

A half-century of excavations at Ugarit has made it possible to present a sketch of the history of the site. Five major levels, each with several strata, have been identified, indicating that the site was inhabited from ca. 6500–1180 B.C.E. Architectural remains for the strata earlier than the Late Bronze Period are scanty, but characteristic pottery and works of art confirm the existence and level of culture of the earlier cities. The excavations conducted to date have been most useful in the attempt to reconstruct the main features of the Late Bronze city. Logically, the two areas chosen for initial excavations were the acropolis and the northwestern sector of the mound where one would expect to find palaces and government offices. On the acropolis were found temples of BAAL and of EL (built on foundations going back to Middle Bronze), with a scriptorium situated between them. The northwestern quarter contained the major defense features of the city, as well as three palaces and houses of important officials. Several caches of documents were unearthed in a number of places on the mound, including private dwellings. The complete history of the site has not been written; thus far only preliminary reports have appeared.

Ugarit fell ca. 1180 at the hands of the SEA PEOPLES. The excavators found an oven used for baking clay tablets with thirty tablets in situ. Several of these tablets describe conditions shortly before Ugarit fell. There was famine at Ura in Cilicia and the king of Ugarit was ordered by the Hittite king to send a large shipment of grain. One letter told of Ugaritic forces fighting in Cilicia alongside the Hittites, while another records the vulnerability of the city due to the fact that the Ugaritic army was off fighting in Asia Minor and the fleet was on station far to the west near the Aegean Sea. Another letter reports on the damage done to Ugarit and its dependencies by small flotillas of marauders. The end came suddenly; the inhabitants were slaughtered or they fled; and the site was never rebuilt.

Of greatest importance for the study of political and social history, as well as religion, are the hundreds of texts on clay tablets which began to appear in the first season of excavation. Eight languages are represented on the texts. The major genres include economic and administrative texts, private and official correspondence, omens, incantatitions, vocabularies, and religious texts (rituals, prayers, psalms, and myths and epics).

The most startling discovery in the first season of excavation was a number of clay tablets inscribed in an unknown CUNEIFORM script. Within a year of its discovery, three scholars, Ch. Virolleaud, H. Bauer, and E. Dhorme, working independently, had deciphered the script, which was used to write the Ugaritic language. These scholars demonstrated that the new script was alphabetic, consisting of some thirty signs, twenty-seven of which were consonants (plus some variant signs) and three of which represented *aleph* as used with the three major vowels. The rapid decipherment of the new script and the annual publication of the new texts have made possible rapid and cooperative advances in our knowledge of the Ugaritic language and the literature it provides.

Although scholars continue their analysis of the mythological and epic materials, there is no unanimity of opinion on the most basic questions. Some believe that the mythological texts contain the spoken part of a fertility cult drama, while others are not convinced that the texts should be related to the annual seasonal cycle. Also unresolved is the way in which religious practices mentioned in the mythological and epic texts are to be related to those in the temple services and to private religion. Above all, great care needs to be taken in attempts to generalize from Ugaritic materials about Canaanite religion. Therefore, the following presentation of the materials will be restricted to the description and summary of some of the texts.

The Baal-Anath Cycle. Most important is the Baal cycle, an extended poetic narrative which is preserved on more than a dozen tablets and fragments. Because the original order of the tablets is not known, the exact story-line remains in question. The chief characters are Baal (Hadad), the god of storm and rain; Anath, Baal's consort; El, the chief god of the pantheon; ASHERAH, El's consort; Yam (Sea), antagonist of Baal; and Mot, god of death and underworld, the chief enemy of Baal. The story revolves around Baal's attempts to gain his rightful place among the gods, and it may reflect a similar process on the political or social plane by which an incoming population group might try to establish its control.

Yam demanded that Baal be surrendered to him. This demand put the assembly of the gods into a panic, and El was ready to grant the request. But Baal stood forth to defend himself and to become champion of the gods. He took the weapons Yagrush and Ayyamur which had been fashioned by the craftsman god, Kothar wa-Hasis, and in a scene reminiscent of Marduk's defeat of Tiamat, killed Yam, and built a palace (temple) befitting his status as champion. In a later episode Mot, the god of death and underworld, overcame Baal and swallowed him down. El, Anath, and the world go into mourning. But Anath in turn kills Mot, grinding his remains and scattering them over the fields. Then the cry is heard: "Baal is alive," and the gods rejoice, and Baal resumes his honored place. It is easy to see why some modern readers have connected the Baal-Anath cycle to the cycle of the year and have considered it as the libretto of a new year festival.

Legend of Aqhat. The legend of Aqhat is a lenghty epic which deals with several themes, including the birth of a long-awaited son, the tragedy of death, the possibility of immortality, and the relationship of crime (murder) to fertility. However, since the text is broken at the beginning and at the end, and since several lacunae obscure the story-line, agreement has not been reached on the purpose of the composition. There is evidence that the Aqhat epic may reflect persons and events in a much earlier time in the region of Lake Kinneret.

In response to the desperate plea of Danel, El, with the mediation of Baal, gave the supplicant a son, Aqhat. After Aqhat had grown up, Kothar wa-Hasis presented him with a composite bow. The goddess Anat saw the bow and promised Aqhat the gift of immortality if he would give it to her. Rather arrogantly Aqhat refused the request, but he gave to Anat a list of materials so that she could order her own bow. The enraged goddess sent Yatpan, in the form of an eagle to kill Aqhat, and in the struggle the bow is lost or destroyed. As a result of the bloodshed, the fertility of the land fails for seven years. Pughat, Aqhat's sister, is sent to avenge his death, but the tablet breaks off before the resolution is revealed. Some have speculated that the story originally related Aqhat's restoration to life and the consequent return of the fertility-giving rains. Until the conclusion of the tale becomes known, however, the essential nature and purpose of the document remains uncertain.

The Keret Epic. The second great Ugaritic epic tells the story of King Keret (Kirta) whose line was in danger of ceasing because his seven wives had been killed in a series of tragedies before providing an heir. El told Keret to attack a nearby kingdom and secure another wife. After a successful seige of Udum, Keret obtained the wife who eventually gave birth to eight sons and eight daughters. Due to an unfulfilled vow, Keret fell ill. His approaching death was somehow related to drought in the land, and his recovery to health and return of fertility are related. This relationship of king and fertility and the emphasis elsewhere in the story on royal responsibilities to the poor and helpless in society suggest that a major purpose of the Keret epic was to emphasize sacral kingship, the belief that order and fertility flowed from the gods through the auspices of the king.

These myths and epic texts, along with other similar materials such as Shachar and Shalim and Nikkal and the Kathirat, are important for gaining added knowledge about fertility religion in Syria-Palestine, a religion or orientation which was attractive to the Israelites and against which the prophets protested.

Ugarit and Biblical Studies. Ugaritic and Hebrew have been utilized successfully for mutual elucidation. While the literature of the two languages are not contemporary and the two cultures are different, it must be stressed that the latest Ugaritic texts are only a century older than the earliest Israelite poetry, and although Ugaritic was influenced by nonsemitic languages like Hurrian, it is still best to classify the langugage, along with classical Hebrew, as Canaanite. The discovery of the Ugaritic texts made students of the Bible return to a consideration of grammar, syntax, and style, and to take a fresh look at difficult passages. The gain for biblical studies has been enormous. In the area of lexicography many difficult or opaque words and passages have been clarified. There is less need to emend the Hebrew text or to depend so heavily on the versions. In the area of poetics, it has been demonstrated that Hebrew poetry continues the poetic tradition of the Canaanites attested at Ugarit and in the AMARNA texts, especially in parallelism of members, use of chiastic structure, and word-pairs, etc. The pioneering work of M. Dahood on lexicography and poetry has been of inestimable value, even in cases where his results must be revised.

The Ugaritic texts are also a valuable source for the comparative study of religions. Many of the names of the gods appearing in the Ugaritic texts are known well in the OT: El, Baal, Asherah, Yam, Yarih (moon), Shalim, Dagon, and others. Canaanite religious practices (e.g., sacrifice, divination), known already from the Bible, are clarified at Ugarit. Sympathetic or imitative MAGIC is attested in the Bible (1 Kgs 18:28; Jer 41:5), as well as sacred prostitution (Deut 23:18; Hos 4:14). Other religious practices such as the cult of the dead (*marzeah*: Amos 6:7; Jer 16:5) indicate that Israel found in Canaan a kind of religious and cultural outlook into which the Ugaritic texts give great insight.

Finally, the Ugaritic texts are valuable to students of the Bible in the analysis of the social structure of the Hebrew kingdoms. Whereas the prophets criticized social injustice caused by social structures which departed from the ancient structures, the Bible gives only a few factual indications of Israelite royal structure. In the Ugaritic materials we find a full picture of such a structure, its social stratification, system of justice, the place of the king and his officials. With due caution the Ugaritic materials may be used to help reconstruct a fuller picture of the Israelite kingdoms.

See also CANAAN; RELIGIONS OF THE ANCIENT NEAR EAST; SEMITIC LANGUAGES.

Bibliography. A. Caquot et al., "Ras Shamra (Ugarit)," *Supplement au Dictionnaire de las Bible*; P. C. Craigie, *Ugarit and the Old Testament*; M. Dahood, "Ugaritic and the Old Testament," *ETL* 44 (1968): 36-54; J. C. L. Gibson, *Canaanite Myths and Legends*; H. L. Ginsberg, "Ugaritic Myths, Legends, and Epics," *ANET*; C. H. Gordon, *Ugaritic Textbook*; C. F. A. Schaeffer, *Ugaritica*; Ch. Virolleaud, *Le Palais royal d'Ugarit*; G. D. Young, ed., *Ugarit in Retrospect: Fifty Years of Ugarit and Ugaritic*.

—THOMAS G. SMOTHERS

• **Umpire.** *See* MEDIATION/MEDIATOR IN THE OLD TESTAMENT

• **Unbelief.** *See* FAITH AND FAITHLESSNESS

• **Unfaithfulness.** *See* FAITH AND FAITHLESSNESS

• **Ungodliness.** *See* SIN

• **United Monarchy.** Refers to that period of Israel's history in which all twelve TRIBES were united under the rulership of a single monarch. According to 1 Sam 10:20-24 and 11:15, the people elected SAUL (reigned ca. 1020–1000 B.C.E.) king over "all Israel," but the southern tribes of JUDAH and Simeon played no role in the activities of Saul; thus it is not clear whether all twelve tribes were included. DAVID (reigned ca. 1000–961 B.C.E.) was first elected king by the people of Judah at HEBRON (2 Sam 2:4) seven years before he was elected by the tribes of Israel (2 Sam 5:1-5). David established an empire (PLATE 12) that he passed on to his son SOLOMON (reigned ca. 961–922 B.C.E.). Upon Solomon's death, northern Israel refused to elect REHOBOAM, choosing instead JEROBOAM I, thus dividing the monarchy.

See also DAVID; KINGSHIP.

Bibliography. N. K. Gottwald, ed., *Social Scientific Criticism of the Hebrew Bible and Its Social World: The Israelite Monarchy*; T. Ishida, *The Royal Dynasties in Ancient Israel: A Study on the Formation and Development of Royal-dynastic Ideology, BZAW* 142.

—PAUL L. REDDITT

• **Unknown God.** During Paul's famous AREOPAGUS (Mars Hill) speech (Acts 17:22-31), he referred to the inscription on an altar he had seen earlier at ATHENS. The text read: "To an unknown god." Paul then cleverly used this inscription to launch the crux of his message, i.e., that he had come to tell his listeners the name of this "unknown" god they had been worshipping all along.

There is no evidence of this exact inscription in the singular—"to an unknown god"—but ample evidence of a similar reference in the plural—"to unknown gods." This fact has led many commentators to suggest that Paul may have adjusted the wording to accommodate his monotheistic message. Paul evidently was less concerned with the original intent of the inscription than he was with utilizing it as a springboard for his own explanation of how God had revealed himself in Christ.

See also AREOPAGUS; ATHENS.

—WATSON E. MILLS

• **Unleavened Bread, Feast of.** One of the three pilgrimage festivals celebrated by Israel (Exod 23:14-15; 34:23). The feast began on the fifteenth day of the month of Abib (March/April) and lasted for seven days (Exod 34:18; Lev 23:6). Although the feast was originally independent of PASSOVER, the two were joined together to serve as an annual reminder of the EXODUS from EGYPT (Exod 12:1-27).

The Israelite feast of unleavened bread probably developed from a Canaanite agricultural festival that celebrated the beginning of the harvest. Israel retained the agricultural background of the festival in its celebration. The festival celebrated the beginning of the barley harvest, signalling not only the continuance of life but a new beginning as well. Leavened bread made from the grain of the previous harvest could no longer be used. Loaves were to be made from the grain of the new harvest. These unleavened loaves marked a new beginning free from the taint of the past. By waving the sheaf before God (Lev 23:9-11) and preparing and eating the unleavened bread, Israel gave thanks to God for the harvest and consecrated it.

The feast of unleavened bread commemorated the Exodus from Egypt. The unleavened bread recalled the haste with which Israel left Egypt (Exod 12:11) even as bitter herbs (Exod 12:8; Num 9:11) recalled the bitterness of Israel's slavery in Egypt. In addition, the absence of leaven in the bread was a mark of holiness. As the blood was drained from animal sacrifices before they were offered as holy to God (Lev 1:5, 11, 15), so leaven was not used in preparing bread to be offered to God. The use of unleavened bread during the feast symbolized the setting apart of Israel by and for God.

The connection between Passover and the feast of unleavened bread is strong. Passover may have been borrowed from a nomadic shepherds' festival, but Israel tied it to the Exodus to recall the death of the firstborn (Exod 12:12-13). In practice it was difficult to separate Passover from the feast of unleavened bread. Passover was celebrated on the evening of the fourteenth day of Abib (Exod 12:6; Lev 23:5) and was thus immediately followed by the beginning of the feast of unleavened bread (Lev 23:6). Passover was also an unleavened bread meal (Exod 12:8), which naturally tied it to the feast of unleavened bread. Both the NT (Mark 14:12) and JOSEPHUS use both names in connection with the festival period.

The feast was a popular celebration. Some speculate that although Israel was not steadfast in its observance of Passover (2 Kgs 23:21-23), the feast of unleavened bread was regularly observed. The feast was not confined to Jews in Palestine but was celebrated along with Passover by Jews outside Palestine as evidence from the fifth century B.C.E. from Elephantine in Egypt indicates. The feast continues to be meaningful to Jews around the world.

See also PASSOVER; FEAST AND FESTIVALS.

Bibliography. G. Fohrer, *History of Israelite Religion*; H. Ringgren, *Israelite Religion*; J. C. Rylaarsdam, "Passover and Feast of Unleavened Bread," *IDB*.

—ROBERT C. DUNSTON

• **Unpardonable Sin.** The specific phrase "unpardonable SIN" appears nowhere in the Bible. Its popular usage is derived from Jesus' reference to blasphemy against the HOLY SPIRIT in Mark 3:28-29 and par. in Matt 12:31-32 and Luke 12:10. There Jesus speaks of such blasphemy as something for which one cannot be forgiven.

The word "blasphemy" most literally means "to speak impiously against." The severity of Jesus' words, however, seems to suggest that more than mere spoken words is involved.

Historically, interpretation of Jesus' words has varied

greatly. Some have interpreted the blasphemy quite literally as a word spoken against the Holy Spirit, while others have suggested that a class or group of sins is involved. Some have said that only believers can commit this sin, while others say only unbelievers are capable. Still others see both believers and unbelievers as being able to commit the sin.

Given such lack of consensus among interpreters, perhaps the best approach is to look to the NT setting in which Jesus' words are placed. As Jesus casts out demons his enemies accuse him of using the power of the prince of demons to do so. This accusation evokes Jesus' statement that one who blasphemes the Holy Spirit can never be forgiven. Attribution of Jesus' power to the devil denies the saving work of God. In view of the numerous passages of scripture which promise forgiveness for all sins that are confessed, perhaps the essence of the ''unpardonable sin'' is the loss of ability to distinguish good from evil, with the consequent loss of ability to confess. This interpretation at least fits the context.

See also HOLY SPIRIT; SIN.

—JOE E. LUNCEFORD

• **Upper Room.** In wealthy Palestinian homes in biblical times a large room was constructed normally on the second floor. It was usually reached through an outside staircase. It had many uses, especially in the summertime: entertaining guests (Judg 3:20; 1 Sam 9:25); lodging guests (1 Kgs 17:19, 23; 2 Kgs 4:10); conducting devotions (Dan 6:10); and paying respect to the dead (Acts 9:37).

Such a room was the place for Jesus' celebration of the Passover with his disciples (Mark 14:15; Luke 22:12) where he instituted the Lord's Supper. Probably in this same room in Jerusalem the followers of Jesus assembled after his ascension. The Gk. term used in the Gospels for ''upper room'' (ἀνάγαιον) is interchangeable with the term used in Acts 1:13 (ὑπερῷον). The ''upper chamber'' (ὑπερῷον), however, was on the third floor.

—LORIN L. CRANFORD

• **Ur.** [oor] Ur (Heb. *'ûr*) ''of the Chaldees'' (cf. CHALDEA) is mentioned five times in the Bible. Abraham's brother Haran was born and died there (Gen 11:28). It was the point of departure for the family of Terah and Abraham in their journey to Canaan (Gen 11:31).

Later, God reminded Abraham that it was he who had called Abraham's family out of Ur (Gen 15:7). This important theological conviction is recalled in Ezra's prayer (Neh 9:7) and Stephen's sermon (Acts 7:4). Stephen implies that Ur was located in Mesopotamia (cf. Acts 7:2).

A few sites have been suggested that would locate Ur of the Chaldees in northern Mesopotamia. But the most generally accepted identification is with Tell el-Muqayyar, the ruins of ancient Ur (Akkadian *Uri,* from Sumerian *Urim*) located on the Euphrates River in southern Mesopotamia (modern Iraq) (PLATE 2).

As early as 1854 investigation of this site was done by J. E. Taylor for the British Museum. Soundings were attempted in 1918–1919, and systematic long-term excavation began in 1922 and continued until 1934 under the direction of Sir Leonard Woolley for the British Museum and the University of Pennsylvania.

Ur was a walled city, oval in shape and measuring about one-half mi. at its widest part. An ancient bed of the Euphrates surrounded the city on its northern and western sides. Two harbors provided access to river traffic. Woolley found continuous occupational debris from the fifth millennium B.C.E. to 300 B.C.E.

The earliest levels provided potsherds of painted ware, flint and obsidian tools, and other materials consistent with the Ubaid period. Here Woolley found a stratum of water-laid soil which he saw as evidence for the biblical flood. Scholars today suggest this silt was laid by the changing course of the Euphrates River.

Tablets from the Uruk levels (ca. 3500–3100 B.C.E.) revealed a pictographic writing which evolved into the Cuneiform script of the later Sumerian scribes. A gold helmet fashioned in the style of a wig from the tomb of Meskalamdug of the Early Dynastic period indicates the wealth of that early culture. In the royal tombs, Woolley made the fantastic discovery of an elaborate funeral ritual. Some sort of human sacrifice was in evidence because the bodies of soldiers, courtiers, and female attendants, as well as wheeled carts complete with draft animals, were buried in the tomb in an orderly manner. One anonymous shaft-grave (no. 1237) contained seventy-four bodies, sixty-eight of which were female attendants dressed in full regalia.

A large temple tower (ziggurat), built in part by Ur-Nammu, the founder of the Third Dynasty of Ur (2150–2050 B.C.E.), still dominates the site. The main temple of the city, *E-temen-ni-guru,* was dedicated to the moon-god Nanna (Akkadian *Sîn*). Nanna was also worshiped at Haran. Under Nebuchadrezzar, the neo-Babylonian (Chaldean) king of the sixth century B.C.E., the sacred precinct was extensively rebuilt and extended. Due to the change of caravan routes in the Persian period and the shift of the river bed, Ur declined in importance and died.

See also SUMERIA/SUMERIAN.

Bibliography. *ANEP*; S. Lloyd, *The Archaeology of Mesopotamia*; L. Woolley, *Ur 'of the Chaldees,'* rev. ed.

—STEPHEN J. ANDREWS

• **Uriah.** [yoo-ri'uh] A Hebrew name meaning ''Yah(weh) is Light.'' Alternately, Urijah.

1. A Hittite who was one of DAVID's ''mighty men'' (2 Sam 11; 23:29; 1 Chr 11:41). His wife BATHSHEBA became pregnant by David while Uriah was at war. To make it appear that the child was Uriah's, David recalled him so that he could visit Bathsheba. Uriah refused to violate the law forbidding sexual intercourse for warriors consecrated for battle. Subsequently, David ordered Uriah sent into battle where he would be killed. After Uriah's death, David married Bathsheba.

2. A priest commissioned by King AHAZ (735–715 B.C.E.) to duplicate an altar that Ahaz saw in Damascus (2 Kgs 16:10-11). After the altar was in place, Ahaz gave Uriah instructions for its continued use (2 Kgs 16:12-16).

3. A priest who served as a witness for the oracle of the prophet ISAIAH regarding the sign of Isaiah's son Maher-shalal-hash-baz (Isa 8:2). Possibly the same Uriah as 2 above.

4. A prophet at the time of JEREMIAH. His oracles against King JEHOIAKIM and JERUSALEM were similar to those of Jeremiah. His oracles so endangered his life that he fled to Egypt. He was brought back to Judah and killed (Jer 26:20-23). His story seems to have been included in the book of Jeremiah to emphasize the dangers Jeremiah faced.

5. Father of one of the priests responsible for rebuilding part of the walls of Jerusalem under Nehemiah (Ezra 8:33; Neh 3:4, 21).

6. One of the men who stood beside Ezra as he read the

law to the people before the renewal of the covenant (Neh 8:4).

—JOANNE KUEMMERLIN-MCLEAN

• **Uriel.** *See* ANGEL; FALLEN ANGELS

• **Urim and Thummim.** [yoor'im, thum'im] Priestly instrumentalities through which the will of God was ascertained for both leader (Num 27:21) and people (Deut 33:8). The Urim and Thummim were kept in the HIGH PRIEST's breastplate (Exod 28:30; Lev 8:8), although Deut 33:8 implies that all members of the priestly class had access to them.

No explicit word describes the physical shape of the Urim and Thummim or explains the technique employed by the priest as he handled the medium to detect the will of God. Rather, the OT assumes familiarity with Urim and Thummim as means of mediating between God and people. Even such early writers as JOSEPHUS, PHILO, and the RABBIS were unable to furnish any precise information concerning the method. Speculation has suggested that the priest shook them in a pouch and then pulled one out or that some method was used to cast them on the ground, a practice similar to the casting of lots (1 Sam 14:41-42; Jonah 1:7).

The Urim and Thummim were consulted at various stages in the history of ancient Israel. The legislation of Num 27:21 commits the national leader after Moses' time to the guidance of Urim and Thummim. During the monarchy, SAUL attempted but received no answer from the method (1 Sam 28:6), while DAVID successfully consulted the priestly "ephod," apparently a substitute for Urim and Thummim (1 Sam 23:9-12). When the voice of prophecy diminished, the national leaders desired a revival of this form of direction (Ezra 2:63; Neh 7:65).

Although etymological studies provide no definitive results, Thummim may be related to "perfections" from *tāmam* (to be blameless) and Urim to either "lights" from *'ôr* or "curses" from *'ārar* (to curse).

—W. H. BELLINGER, JR.

• **Uzziah.** [uh-z*i*'uh] A Hebrew name meaning "my strength is Yah(weh)." The name appears primarily in postexilic lists (after 538 B.C.E.).

1. The name of one of the kings of Judah in the eighth century, also known as Azariah. Uzziah was the son of AMAZIAH and the father of Jotham. According to 2 Kgs 15:2, he reigned fifty-two years; however, the precise dates and length of his reign are unclear.

The story of Uzziah appears in 2 Kgs 15:1-7 and 2 Chr 26:1-23. The account in 2 Kings is sketchy. According to 2 Kings, Uzziah "did what was right in the eyes of the Lord," although he did not remove the high places. For this he was stricken with LEPROSY and succeeded by his son Jotham.

The account in 2 Chronicles details the accomplishments of Uzziah: he fought the PHILISTINES, Arabs, and Meunites; exacted tribute from the Ammonites; fortified Jerusalem, strengthened the army, and developed new weapons; built forts in the wilderness; and supported agriculture and animal husbandry.

However, according to the Chronicler, Uzziah's accomplishments made him overly proud and he attempted to usurp priestly functions as well. Consequently, he was stricken with leprosy, forced to live in seclusion, and lost his throne.

2. One of the Levites appointed by DAVID to sing before the Ark (1 Chr 6:24).

3. The father of Jonathan, one of the men appointed as an overseer of the king's treasuries at the time of David (1 Chr 27:25).

4. One of the priests who married foreign women (Ezra 10:21).

5. The father of Athaiah, a man who lived in Jerusalem following NEHEMIAH's repopulation of the city (Neh 11:4). *See also* AZARIAH.

—JOANNE KUEMMERLIN-MCLEAN

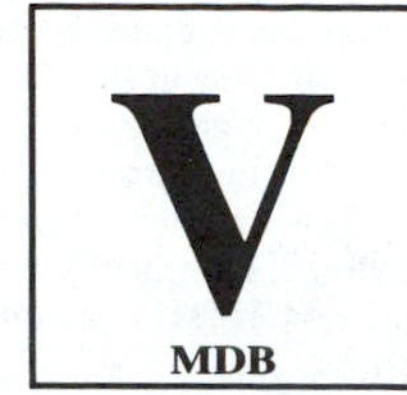

• **Valentinian Exposition.** [val′uhn-tin″ee-uhn] A *Valentinian Exposition* is a modern name given to an untitled Coptic Gnostic document from Codex XI from NAG HAMMADI. It consists of a discussion of the nature of GOD, the fall of Sophia (Wisdom), and the creation told from the standpoint of Valentinian GNOSTICISM. It is the only extant account of the myth of Sophia from a Valentinian author. Following the exposition there is a section dealing with anointing, two sections on baptism, and two on the Eucharist. This suggests that the book served as a kind of catechism for initiates into Gnosticism. Initiation may have consisted of instruction in the mysteries, followed by the sacraments of anointing, baptism, and Eucharist.

The instruction runs as follows. The ineffable Father, root of the All, dwells in silence. From him proceeds the Son, Mind, the hypostasis of the Father, who descended to the lower regions as a HIGH PRIEST to reveal what was behind the celestial veil. He has four powers: to separate, to confirm, to form, and to provide substance. The Gnostic must earnestly search the scriptures and other sources to understand these things. Four aeons emanate from the divine Unity: WORD, Life, Man, and Church. From these are produced 360 aeons. One of them, Sophia, wished to create on her own, without her counterpart, the Word. For this she suffers, and repents in a prayer to the Father. Now she and her counterpart Jesus create mysterious seeds which Jesus implants in a Creature, Primal Man, separating the spiritual from the fleshly. Jesus then produces the angels. The world above having been created, there is another creation of a lower order as earthly existence comes into being. The demiurge creates a man after both his own image and the image of those above. The devil enters the picture, Cain kills his brother, and there is apostasy among the angels. The seduction of human women by the angels leads to God's bringing on the flood. But Sophia, along with Jesus, succeeds in effecting a way of salvation by reuniting the male seeds (the aeons) with the female (the spiritual ones here below).

The following brief sections on anointing, baptism, and the eucharist appear to have been words spoken on the occasion of the sacramental observance following the revelation of the mysteries.

See also GNOSTICISM; MYSTERY; NAG HAMMADI.

Bibliography. E. Pagels and J. D. Turner, "A Valentinian Exposition," *The Nag Hammadi Library in English*, ed. J. M. Robinson.

—ROGER A. BULLARD

• **Vashti.** *See* ESTHER, BOOK OF

• **Vault (of Heaven).** *See* SKY

• **Vellum.** *See* PARCHMENT

• **Vengeance/Avenger.** Retribution and the agent of retribution, respectively, for any grievous injury or wrong ranging from insult (1 Sam 25:39) to murder (Gen 4:15) to national defeat (Ezek 25:14). The psychological and moral premise of vengeance requires the offender to suffer and be seen by the victim (or surrogate of a dead victim) to suffer what the victim has, i.e., know the offense experientially as the victim knows it. The association of Heb. terms for vengeance with more nuanced expressions such as *šillēm*, "recompense" (Deut 32:35) or the verb *šillam*, "repay," "restore" (Isa 59:17c-18a)—both related to *šālôm*, "wholeness"—argues that vengeance was seen not as mere private vindictiveness but as justly satisfying the victim and repairing the social order ruptured by the crime. Paradoxically, vengeance resembles its alternative, forgiveness, insofar as the latter requires, to begin with, that the offender experience at least vicariously his victim's experience.

"Avenge" or "take vengeance [or revenge]" most often translates the Heb. verb *nāqam* (Lev 19:18); "vengeance" usually translates its derivative nouns *nāqām* (Isa 47:3) and *nĕqāmâ* (Num 31:3). Other verbs occasionally translated as "avenge" or "take vengeance," include (with their literal meanings) *hôšîa'*, "get victory" (1 Sam 25:31); *pāqad*, "visit" (Hos 1:4 [KJV]); *hešîb*, "cause [blood] to return [upon]" (2 Sam 16:8); *rîb et-rîb*, "settle the case of" (2 Sam 25:39); *dāraš*, seek [blood] (Ps 9:12[H13]; cf Gen 9:5) and *śîm* "put [battle-blood into peacetime]" (1 Kgs 2:5). The LXX usually renders the principal terms above with *ȅkdikéō*, "avenge" or "take vengeance," and *ȅkdíkēsis*, "vengeance." Both appear in the NT: *ȅkdikéō*, "vindicate" (Luke 18:3, 5); *ȅkdíkēsis*, "vengeance" (Luke 21:22); with the additional forms *ĕkdikos*, "avenger" (1 Thess 4:6); and *poiéō ȅkdíkēsin*, "avenge" (Acts 7:24) or "vindicate" (Luke 18:7). In the NT, apocalyptic crisis is symbolized as a time of vengeance, with its expected agents the nations (Luke 21:22-24), God (Rev 6:10), or Jesus Christ (2 Thess 1:7-8).

The OT "avenger of blood" (*gô'ēl haddām*, lit., "redeemer of blood") was the closest male next of kin of a slain family or clan member, who by ancient custom (the vendetta) was obliged to avenge the kinsman's death by killing the murderer. One who had killed unintentionally might flee to one of the CITIES OF REFUGE for asylum until his case could be adjudicated (Num 35:9-28; Deut 19:4-13; Josh 20:1-9; 2 Sam 14:11). If found guilty of intentional murder, the offender would be turned over to the avenger of blood for execution. The expression *gô'ēl haddām* is not used of God in the Bible; in the metaphorical theology of such passages as Deut 32:43, where Yahweh "avenges the blood of his servants," the verb is usually *nāqam*.

The "avenger" (*mitnaqqēm*) of Ps 8:2[H3] signifies a mythical enemy of God the creator (cf., e.g., Isa 51:9-10); in Ps 44:16[H17] an enemy nation is meant.

Bibliography. A. Y. Collins, "Persecution and Vengeance in the Book of Revelation," *Apocalypticism in the Mediterranean World and the Near East,* ed. D. Hellholm; M. Greenberg, "Avenger of Blood," *IDB*; S. Jacoby, *Wild Justice: The Evolution of Revenge*.

—BRUCE T. DAHLBERG

• **Vestments.** *See* CLOTHING

• **Via Dolorosa.** [vee'uh-doh-luh-roh″suh] Literally, "way of sorrow," *Via Dolorosa* refers to that route by which Jesus was led to the site of his crucifixion following pronouncement of sentence upon him by Pontius PILATE. Since the thirteenth century it has been a popular act of Christian devotion to retrace the *Via Dolorosa,* pausing at various "stations" along the way where tradition holds that Jesus halted in his journey. The modern *Via Dolorosa* follows a westerly route from the Temple mount to the CHURCH OF THE HOLY SEPULCHRE. Whether this route approximates the one actually trod by Jesus depends on whether the Praetorium—the scene of Pilate's judgment—is to be identified with the TOWER OF ANTONIA, or with the PALACE OF HEROD. The latter was located to the west of the Temple precincts and south of the traditional site of the crucifixion.

See also ANTONIA, TOWER OF; CHURCH OF THE HOLY SEPULCHRE; PALACE OF HEROD.

—RAYMOND HARGUS TAYLOR

• **Vine.** Any plant with a long slender stem and tendrils, as a gourd (2 Kgs 4:39). The word usually denotes the common grape vine.

The soil and climate of ancient Palestine were well suited to viticulture, especially the hill country. Typically vineyards were planted on terraced hillsides surrounded by a protective wall of stones or thorn hedges to keep out destructive animals (Num 22:24; Isa 5:5). A tower was erected for a watchman, a winepress hollowed out of flat rock, and a vat into which the wine flowed (Isa 5:1-7; Matt 21:33-41). The vines were usually allowed to grow along the ground with the fruit-bearing branches raised above the earth on supports. For maximum productivity it was necessary to prune the vines each spring and to keep the soil around them well tilled and free of weeds (Prov 24:30-31; John 15:2). The grapes began to ripen in August. They were eaten both fresh and dried, the latter preserved in clusters or pressed into cakes (Num 6:3; 1 Sam 25:18). The vintage began in the middle of September and continued into October. It was a season of celebration, the treaders of grapes singing and shouting as they worked (Judg 9:27; Jer 25:30, 48:33).

Viticulture provided the biblical writers with a useful model by which to characterize God's relationship with his people. Israel is a vine that Yahweh has brought out of Egypt and planted in the promised land only to find it unproductive, yielding worthless fruit. As a result, he has broken down its walls, allowing it to be ravaged and to deteriorate (Ps 80:8-16; Isa 5:1-7; Jer 2:21). In the NT Jesus describes his relationship with his true followers as that of a vine and its branches (John 15:1-8).

—STEPHEN M. HOOKS

• **Virgin.** One who has reached puberty, but has not yet experienced sexual intercourse. The term is also used figuratively of nations or communities (e.g., "virgin Israel," Jer 18:13; Amos 5:2). The OT stresses the importance of virginity in a bride (Deut 22:13ff.) and prescribes laws for the protection of virgins (Deut 22:25-29).

The OT text employs three different words, any of which may be translated properly as "virgin," "young woman," or "maiden," depending upon the context. At times, the sexual inexperience of the subject is clearly understood; at other times, merely implied.

Likewise, the exact meaning to be ascribed to the equivalent word in the NT must be determined from the context in which it is used (e.g., "virgin," Matt 1:23; Luke 1:27; but either "virgin" or "maiden," Matt 25:1, 7, 11).

See also VIRGIN BIRTH.

—RAYMOND HARGUS TAYLOR

• **Virgin Birth.** Virgin birth refers to the belief that JESUS was miraculously conceived by his mother, MARY, while she was still a VIRGIN. It is based on the testimony of both Mary and Joseph in the narratives of Matt 1:18-25 and Luke 1:26-35.

The virgin birth is one of three ways in which the Gospel writers affirm Jesus' unique relationship to God. Mark focuses on Jesus' divine authority vested in him by God at his baptism (Mark 1:10, 11). John relates Jesus to the Word (John 1:1, 2; cf. Phil. 2:6) thus identifying Jesus' uniqueness with the eternity of God's self-revelation.

Matthew and Luke diverge on whether the miracle was a matter of a virginal conception (Luke 1:31, 34) or a virginal birth (Matt 1:25). Both are interested in Jesus' uniqueness, not in biological details. Joseph's lineage is used in both genealogies. Luke speaks of Joseph as Jesus' father (Luke 2:33, 41, 48) and Matthew refers to Jesus as "the carpenter's son" (13:55). The elevation of the doctrine to a central place in dogmatic theology is rather extraordinary, given the fact it was simply not a part of the primitive kerygma. Neither the early sermons of Acts nor the writings of Paul mention the doctrine, focusing instead on the work of God in the cross and resurrection (1 Cor 2:2; Phil 3:10).

The doctrine of virgin birth gained currency by Matthew and Luke's time as a way to communicate the gospel to a gentile audience. What would have been anathema to Jews was credible to gentiles—God's redemptive presence was made manifest in a son, Jesus. A christological concern is clearly at the heart of the stories of Jesus' beginnings.

Theology, not biology, dominates the discussion in Matthew and Luke. Both narratives identify Jesus with the Hebrew messianic expectation and the Davidic kingship. Matt 1:23 explicitly ties the birth of Jesus to Isa 7:14 by citing the LXX. The Heb. word means "young woman" but such passages (Gen 24:43; Exod 2:8; Ps 68:25; Prov 38:19) make it difficult to argue that it is always used to imply virginity. Another term is used in the OT to indicate virginity (cf. Gen 24:16; Deut 22:13ff., 25-29). Matthew's use of the LXX term "virgin" was apparently to identify Jesus with the tradition of a wonderchild and thus a way of making a christological claim.

Luke's contrast of Jesus' conception to that of John the Baptist is also of christological importance. Jesus was conceived of the Holy Spirit (Luke 1:35-38) while John was conceived by Elizabeth and Zechariah (Luke 1:18-25), thus establishing the subordinate place of John to Jesus.

The virgin birth underscores the truth of the uniqueness of Jesus in Christian theology. It affirms that God was present in Jesus' origins just as the divine power was active in the cross and indispensable for the resurrection. In that sense, virgin birth and resurrection/ascension bracket the life of Jesus and testify to his distinctive place in God's redemption of humanity.

See also JESUS; MARY; VIRGIN.

—PAUL D. SIMMONS

• **Virgin Mary.** *See* MARY

• **Vision.** A revelation, often at night, in the form of things heard as well as things seen. Visions are akin to dreams, but usually come while the recipient is conscious, and often under great stress. The most common Heb. term translated "vision," *ḥāzôn,* is derived from the verb *ḥāzâ,* to see, though nouns derived from the verb *rā'â* (also meaning to see) are also used. Some interpreters consider the first verb, *ḥāzâ,* an Aramaic loan word with a meaning quite akin to the common Heb. *rā'â.* They claim that two words with the same general meaning would hardly have arisen in Hebrew. An alternative, preferred by many scholars, is that the two terms exist side by side, with *ḥāzâ* and its derivatives being the more technical terms for visions.

While the phenomenon of visionary experiences is widespread in ancient religions, including the biblical religions, visions seem to be particularly prevalent among Israel's PROPHETS. The terms *ḥōzeh,* "visionary," and *rō'eh,* "seer," are common designations for the prophets (Amos 7:12; 1 Sam 9:9), along with the technical term for prophet, *nābî'*. Prophets receive messages from the deity and are charged to speak them faithfully (Jer 23:28). Dreams often lend themselves to allegorical interpretation, while visions focus more upon the message disclosed (e.g., Amos 1:1: ". . . words . . . that he saw"; and Jer 23:28). Later, in apocalyptic texts, the visions get more elaborate and lend themselves to allegorical interpretation as well (e.g., Daniel and 2 Esdras).

In the NT the most common terms for visions are derived from the verb *'oraō,* to see. Visions are most prominent in LUKE-Acts and in the Book of REVELATION. There too, visions seem to lay great stress upon the disclosure of a message from the deity (Acts 9:1-9), rather than upon visual disclosures, though the latter are more common in the Book of Revelation.

Visions often reveal the heavenly world—God's throneroom or assembly hall, where frequently the message for delivery on earth is being spoken, and perhaps discussed (cf. 1 Kgs 22:17-23), or some other locale beyond the ordinary world. The seer is frequently transported and becomes a participant in the heavenly scene (Isa 40:1-11, esp. v. 6; Zech 3:1-4, esp. v. 5). But visions may also concentrate on some particular object or scene on earth (Amos 7:1-9; Jer 1:11-14). Visions may sometimes be induced by MUSIC, DANCING, or the drinking of particular potions, or especially by extended FASTING. That is why it is noteworthy that in the biblical texts the emphasis falls, not on dreams or elaborate scenes disclosed, but on messages that prophets and seers are charged to speak clearly to the people (cf. Num 24:4, 16; Jer 23:28). The truth and authenticity of prophetic visions and their accompanying messages have to be tested.

See also FASTING; MAGIC AND DIVINATION; PROPHET; REVELATION, CONCEPT OF.

Bibliography. A. Jepsen, "חָזָה," *TDOT*.

—WALTER HARRELSON

• **Vow in the New Testament.** The word vow comes from a Greek word which may mean to vow or dedicate. It refers to special acts of devotion in response to promises made. Although the custom of making vows had a long history and continued into NT times, only three passages in the NT may be cited as examples in first-century Christianity. The first is in Mark 7:9-13 and Matt 15:4-6. Here when a conflict between Jesus and his critics over the LAW developed, Jesus pointed out that some of his critics wanted him to make no exceptions in his obedience to the Law, while they made exceptions which reflected a far more serious violation of moral propriety. The PHARISEES justified making exceptions to legal obligations. The example cited was a case where children sought to justify evading responsibility for caring for parents by dedicating present or future assets to the Temple. Jesus supported the generally accepted view that vows should be kept, and that usually it is better not to vow than to vow and not pay. He pointed out here, however, that some vows were made for the wrong reasons, or conflicted with other more important responsibilities, and should be set aside. A vow was to be a means of expressing a sense of responsibility, not evading it. While the support of Temple causes was important, according to Jesus it should not be used to excuse one from the responsibility of caring for parents. Jesus' views on this topic were in line with views of many priests and Pharisees.

A second example of vows in the NT is reported in Acts 18:18, where PAUL made some kind of vow. The exact circumstances of Paul's vow are not reported, but the type of vow he made seems clear. Though he never mentions this vow in his letters, there is no reason to doubt that he made it because it is consistent with concerns he expressed in the CORINTHIAN CORRESPONDENCE for fostering good relations between gentile and Jewish Christians. Thus, while the whole story is not clear, it appears that one reason Paul made the vow and fulfilled it may have been to show the Jewish community that he still had respect for their customs.

The vow Paul made was a NAZIRITE vow, which was a very old custom, but still in vogue at the time of Paul. Josephus, who wrote in the first century C.E., reports that it was common for those with an illness or experiencing some tragedy to make a vow that for thirty days they would not cut their hair or drink wine. It is possible that Paul cut his hair at the beginning of his vow, planning to complete the vow and offer the sacrifice in the Temple at Jerusalem during Passover.

The only other direct reference to vows in the NT is in Acts 20:17ff. Here it is reported that when Paul came to Jerusalem, the brethren there warned him that many Jewish Christians in Jerusalem had heard that Paul was encouraging Jews who lived among the gentiles to give up the Law altogether. They suggested that to remove their suspicions, he should take four men who had taken a Nazirite vow and pay for the sacrifice they would have to render. By so doing Paul would render a service that was widely respected in Judaism, for all who did this for a poorer person were greatly admired. Also, the respect shown for the regulation concerning vows would show his serious commitment to the Law. Although there are uncertainties as to how far one should go in interpreting Paul as obedient to the Law, this passage suggests that he was willing to observe the Law on vows since it did not conflict with his other views.

Bibliography. J. D. M. Derrett, "ΚΟΡΒΑΝ, Ο ΕΣΤΙΝ ΔΩΡΟΝ," *NTS* 16 (1970): 364-68; J. Herrmann and H. Greeven, "Εὔχομαι, κτλ.," *TDNT*.

—E. EARL JOINER

• **Vow in the Old Testament.** Vows to the deity are a widespread custom throughout human history, especially in times of anxiety, special need, or physical affliction. The vow is a voluntary obligation, to be fulfilled when the deity has provided what the vow entailed.

The first-mentioned vow in the OT is that of Jacob (Gen 28:18-22). The bargain was that if God would guide Jacob in his journey to Haran, provide for his needs, and bring him home in peace, then Jacob would honor the deity and devote to God a TITHE of his income.

Other vows are mentioned in the OT. Absalom vowed to the Lord while at Geshur in Aram that if the Lord would bring him back to Jerusalem, he would worship the deity thereafter (2 Sam 15:8). Hannah vowed to devote a child to the Lord should the Lord bless her with a son (1 Sam 1:11). Jephthah vowed to God, later at the cost of his daughter's life, to offer as a sacrifice the first person to greet him upon his return from battle, if God would give him victory over the Ammonites (Judg 11:30-31). Non-Israelites were also understood to make vows, as is clear from the story of the vow taken by the mariners aboard the ship with the prophet Jonah (1:16).

As a voluntary act, the vow was not prescribed; even so, vows were regulated. Any vow that devoted persons or property to the sanctuary had to be fulfilled. Provision was made, however, for redeeming the person or property vowed by the payment of appropriate compensation; only in the case of firstling animals that belonged to the Lord was such redemption excluded (cf. Lev 27). There also were vows of renunciation or abstinence, such as fasting or the Nazirite vow.

See also REDEMPTION IN THE OLD TESTAMENT; SACRIFICE.

—KAREN RANDOLPH JOINES

• **Vulture.** *See* EAGLE

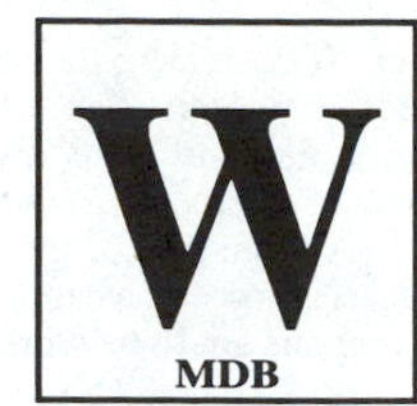

• **Wadi.** [wah′dee] An Arabic word for stream or stream bed. It is a term for a geological formation which can also refer to a valley or deep gully. As a valley, a wadi is a formation with an occasional water flow and is found throughout Palestine. The Heb. term that parallels wadi is *naḥal*. In the Hebrew Bible, it carries the idea of torrent, rushing water, stream bed, or even locality. During the dry seasons, a wadi is usually dry and is an undependable source of water. During a wet period, water runs as a stream, maybe torrentially, or it may collect in pools. As the water runs through the stream bed of what becomes a wadi, it cuts through the soft, porous rock leaving behind a valley or gully. A wadi will usually lead to a larger water source. One example is how Wadi Qumran leads to the Dead Sea from the Judean desert. Also, Wadi Sitti Maryam (Brook Kidron) goes south between Jerusalem and the Mount of Olives leading to its lower course, Wadi en-Nar, and to the Dead Sea after passing through the Judean desert.

Wadis can serve as geographical delimiters. For example, the eastern border of the Negeb is circumscribed by the Wadi el-Arabah which leads to the Gulf of Aqaba. The southern border of Moab is Wadi el-Hesa or Brook Zared. Upper and Lower Galilee are separated by the division given by Wadi esh-Shagur. Different wadis have yielded major archaeological finds. The caves in the Judean desert along Wadi el-Murabba‘at in 1951 yielded documents from the period of the Second Jewish revolt of 135 C.E. Wadi Qumran in the vicinity of Khirbet Qumran yielded documents from the Essene community. Wadi el-Mugharah on the lower southwestern slope of Mount Carmel is dotted with caves which contained prehistoric remains excavated from 1929 to 1934. The wadi is an important geological formation in Palestine. Depending on the season, it can run with water or be dry. It is a dual term as wadi can refer to both a streambed or the valley in which the streambed is found.

Bibliography. H. G. May, ed., *Oxford Bible Atlas*.

—DAVID M. FLEMING

• **Wages.** The Bible considers wages, pay, or hire to be compensation for work done. Until the introduction of coined money, wages were paid primarily as provisions, thereby necessitating that they be disbursed on a daily basis (Lev 19:13; Deut 24:15). The use of precious metals as a system of payment aided in the establishment of a distinct social class of wage earners, who often were the focus of abuse by greedy employers, according to Israel's prophets (Jer 22:13; Mal 3:5).

The determination of wages probably was set through individual bargaining during the biblical period (Gen 29:15-18; Matt 20:1-2). Laborers in occupations for which wages typically were paid included shepherds (Gen 30:32-33), skilled workers (Isa 46:6), harlots (Ezek 16:31), soldiers (Luke 3:14), farmers or harvesters (John 4:36), and even priests (Judg 17:10; Mic 3:11). The NT implies that early Christian missionaries and workers in established church congregations often received wages for their services (Luke 10:7; 1 Cor 11:8; 1 Tim 5:17-18), though such persons are warned against greed (Titus 1:7; 1 Pet 5:2).

In a metaphorical sense, appropriate wages are received from God as rewards for righteousness (Gen 15:1; Isa 61:8) and as just recompense for sin (Rom 6:23).

—CLAYTON N. JEFFORD

• **Wait, Waiting.** *See* HOPE IN THE OLD TESTAMENT

• **War Scroll.** The *War Scroll* (*1QM*), or *War Rule*, is a sectarian description of the eschatological war between the Sons of Light and the Sons of Darkness. Seven copies of the document, all in Hebrew, have been identified among the DEAD SEA SCROLLS. The longest, one of the seven major scrolls from Qumran Cave 1, contains nineteen incomplete columns and dates from the second half of the first century B.C.E. to the first half of the first century C.E. Six fragmentary manuscripts were found in Cave 4, with the earliest, dating from the first half of the first century B.C.E., representing a different recension of the *Rule*. The *Rule* begins with a general prologue identifying the participants in the war and affirming the certain victory of the army of God over that of Belial. Next comes a depiction of the Temple worship during the seventh year of the war, followed by a timetable for the war. Then comes an extended description of the weapons of the war (trumpets, standards, shields, spears, and swords) and the battle tactics. Then the battle liturgy is set forth. The document ends with a celebration of the victory over the Kittim.

The theology behind the *War Rule* is similar to that of other scrolls from Qumran. As in *1QS* the community sees itself as the Sons of Light, God's remnant who have remained faithful to the covenant. Their opponents, the Sons of Darkness, include all the nations of the world, as well as Jews outside of the community who, since they are not a part of the sect, are unfaithful to the covenant. The Sons of Light are under the dominion of the Prince of Light, apparently identified as the archangel MICHAEL (cf. *11QMelch*; Dan 12:1); the Sons of Darkness are ruled by Belial. As in *4QShirShabb* the community sees itself as being in the company of angels; therefore, strict rules of purity must be adhered to (cf. *1QSa*), including the banning of women and underage boys from the battle camps (cf. *11QTem*). The priests continue their preeminent role (cf. *1QS*; *1QSa*); they lead the troops into battle, although not as fighters themselves. The community's trust, however, lies not in its own military proficiency, but in the power of God (cf. *1QH*).

A large part of the *War Rule* is taken up with detailed descriptions of weapons, battle regalia, and strategy. The weapons are to be works of fine craftsmanship, inlaid with precious stones, and of precise specifications for each type. Each trumpet and standard is to have its own distinctive name, and other names shall be written on the standards at various stages of battle. Military tactics are prescribed very precisely, including battle formations, the number and types of divisions, and the number of men in each unit. The weapons, formations, and tactics seem to be based on a Roman model dating to the second half of the first century B.C.E.

The age of the earliest manuscript of the *War Rule* suggests a date of composition during the second half of the second century B.C.E. The situation is complicated, however, by the fact that this manuscript represents a different recension of the *Rule*. Most scholars view the *Rule* as a composite work, although the various reconstructions of its literary history which have been proposed have not proved persuasive. It is plausible that a second century B.C.E. (some have suggested Maccabean) writing about an eschatological war was enlarged with various materials sometime after the Roman general Pompey's conquest of Jerusalem in 63 B.C.E., resulting in the recension attested by the scroll from Cave 1. On the surface, the *Rule* seems to be have been written to provide a manual for how the final war was to be conducted. Its real purpose was probably to confirm the members of the community in their sectarian outlook by reassuring them their sojourn in the desert would not last forever; ultimately God would give them victory over their enemies and exalt them to their proper standing as his elect.

There are parallels between the *War Rule* and certain parts of Revelation. Certainly the idea of a final war depicted in cosmic terms is strong in both (cf. Rev 12:7; 16:13-16; 19:11-21). They also share songs celebrating the defeat of the enemy (cf. Rev 18). There is an interest in the role of trumpets (cf. Rev 8–9) and in precise specifications and precious stones (cf. Rev 21:12-21). Although overshadowed by Christ, the figure of Michael has a significant place at one point in Rev (12:7); also, while the *Rule* mentions the kingdom of Michael, Revelation speaks of the kingdom of Christ (11:15). The use of military imagery in the context of spiritual conflict is paralleled in Eph 6:13-17.

The *War Rule* is an important document for illuminating the self-understanding, DUALISM, angelology, and priestly focus of the Qumran community. The hymns scattered throughout its latter portions make an important contribution, along with *1QH,* to an understanding of post-OT Hebrew poetry. It also sheds light on military techniques in this period. Its most significant contribution, however, is to an understanding of the ESCHATOLOGY of the sect. Although other Qumran documents speak about future events, it is the *War Rule* which develops most fully the expectations of the community in the time of the End. For this reason the *Rule* has a distinctive role to play in illuminating the beliefs of the Qumran ESSENES. But for this reason as well the *Rule* is a stark monument of bitter irony. When war with the Kittim (i.e., the Romans) finally came in 66 C.E., it hardly went according to the *Rule*. The presence of Roman arrowheads among the burned ruins of Qumran speaks silently, yet eloquently, to the fact that the real victors in the final war were the Sons of Darkness.

See also DEAD SEA SCROLLS; ESSENES.

Bibliography. J. J. Collins, "The Mythology of Holy War in Daniel and the Qumran War Scroll: A Point of Transition in Jewish Apocalyptic," *VT* 25 (1975): 596-612; P. R. Davies, *1QM, the War Scroll from Qumran*; D. Dimant, "Qumran Sectarian Literature," *Jewish Writings of the Second Temple Period,* ed. M. E. Stone; A. Dupont-Sommer, *The Essene Writings from Qumran*; G. Vermes, *The Dead Sea Scrolls in English,* 2nd ed., and "The Writings of the Qumran Community," *The History of the Jewish People in the Age of Jesus Christ,* rev. ed., ed. E. Schürer; Y. Yadin, *The Scroll of the War of the Sons of Light against the Sons of Darkness.*

—JOSEPH L. TRAFTON

• **Warfare.** *See* SOLDIER; WEAPONS/WARFARE

• **Wars of the Lord, Book of the.** An ancient poetic collection mentioned in Num 21:14-15. It recorded the progress of the Israelites through Transjordan, describing the boundary between Moab and the land ruled by Sihon, king of the Amorites. Num 21:17-18 and 27-30 also quote two poetic fragments, but it is unclear whether they were contained in the book. Judging by the book's title, one would expect it to have contained narratives about the victories of Yahweh, probably in poetic form, like the Song of Miriam (Exod 15:21) and the Song of Deborah (Judg 5:2-31).

Mention of the book reminds one that biblical writers used sources. Other sources that have not survived include the BOOK OF JASHAR, mentioned in Josh 10:13 and 2 Sam 1:18, the Chronicles of the Kings of Judah and of the Kings of Israel, both mentioned 1 and 2 Kings, and the unnamed sources mentioned by Luke (cf. Luke 1:1-4).

—PAUL L. REDDITT

• **Washing.** *See* BATHING

• **Watcher/Watchman.** The term "watcher" (Aramaic *'îr*) refers to a heavenly being who comes to earth as an agent of God. This usage is found in Dan 4:13, 17, 23 (Aramaic 4:10, 14, 20).

Several Hebrew terms are rendered "watchman." There are persons appointed to guard the city or the fields or the army encampment. Prophets are frequently designated as watchmen (cf. esp. Ezek 3:17; 33:2-7). God also is portrayed as watchman (Heb. *nṣr,* Job 7:20; Heb *šmr,* Ps 127:1).

In an ethical sense one is admonished to guard (Heb *nṣr*) the mouth (Prov 13:3), the way (Prov 16:17), the heart (Prov 4:23), and the tongue (Ps 34:13). In the NT, watching is connected with prayer (Matt 26:38-41) and with the anticipation of the Lord's return (Rev 16:15).

See also PRAYER/THANKSGIVING IN THE NEW TESTAMENT; PROPHET.

—PAGE LEE

• **Watchtower.** Lofty fortified structure made of stone or brick. Watchtowers constructed for military purposes were built into city walls or stood alone as outposts in less populated regions (2 Chr 26:9-10). They were ordinarily staffed around the clock (Isa 21:8). Because of their height, watchtowers offered a vantage point for the detection of enemy troops as well as a defensible position in times of attack. A Canaanite city would often have a central tower at its highest point to which the populace could retreat and defend itself (Judg 9:51). Watchtowers were also erected in fields and vineyards (Isa 5:2). As harvest time approached, they served not only as lookout stations against marauding bands but also as lodges for field workers.

See also CITY/CITIES; FORTS/FORTIFICATIONS.

—DAVID H. HART

• **Water Systems.** Water was perhaps the single most important factor that influenced settlement patterns and life and culture in the ancient Near East. Since vast areas of the ancient Near East were comprised of deserts, settlements and cultures developed for the most part in the FERTILE CRESCENT, the crescent shaped band of land in which fertile soil and the major water supplies were located. For instance, villages and towns developed along the NILE River in Egypt and the TIGRIS and EUPHRATES Rivers in ancient Mesopotamia. In Palestine and Syria some communities sprang up near rivers while others originated near springs, such as Jericho which is the oldest known city in the world.

While water resources were located throughout the ancient Near East, the accessibility of the water was often a problem. At times, the water supply was limited to seasonal rains from October to April. Since little or no rain fell during the rest of the year, water had to be caught and stored. In some areas water resources were present the year around, but the transportation of water for irrigational purposes or domestic needs posed a problem. For these and other reasons a variety of water systems were developed in communities throughout the ancient Near East. These systems include irrigation systems, water storage systems, and systems designed for the transportation of water from one location to another.

Irrigation Systems. The most elaborate irrigation systems in the ancient world were those developed in Mesopotamia and Egypt. However, evidence of more limited systems has been found in Palestine as well as other locations. The systems in Mesopotamia consisted of a series of canals with major feeder canals cut from rivers like the Tigris and Euphrates Rivers into the fertile regions between the rivers. The feeder canals were then tapped by individuals who used smaller channels to bring the water to private plots. The important role these systems played in the cultures of ancient Mesopotamia is demonstrated by references to them and information about their construction and maintenance in ancient records such as the Mari tablets as well as inscriptions from Assyrian kings such as Sennacherib and others.

While the irrigation systems of Mesopotamia were designed primarily to transport vast amounts of water, the Egyptian systems were constructed to distribute mud water or water with rich deposits of silt from collecting pools or basins to agricultural plots in the Nile River valley.

Irrigation systems were also used in ancient Palestine. Evidence of sluice gates, channels and catch basins designed to capture water from the Jordan River or streams in the Transjordan has been found at a number of sites.

Springs and Wells. One of the most important forms of water supply was the natural spring such as the GIHON spring at Jerusalem and the spring at Jericho. The location of many of Palestine's earliest settlements was determined by springs of this type. The spring provided water for the inhabitants of the village, animals, and at times, irrigation. Major water systems (cf. below) by which the inhabitants of the city could obtain water were constructed at a number of the major sites. Channels were often used to divert water from the springs for irrigation purposes. Irrigation systems associated with springs have been found at Jericho, where water was diverted to fields or plots, and Jerusalem where water was channeled from the Gihon spring along the east side of the Ophel ridge in order to provide water distribution for the Kidron valley.

Wells were constructed in semiarid regions, where they were used by pastoral nomads and village herdsmen, as well as in some ancient towns. The upper part of the well was often lined with stones, and in some instances the mouth of the well was capped by a stone (Gen 29:2-3). Pitchers or skins were used to draw the water from the well (Gen 21:19). Since southern Palestine was semiarid, wells such as those located at Beersheba (Gen 21:30) and Gerar (Gen 26:18) constituted the major water supply for herds and flocks. Frequently the wells were a source of contention between the local herdsmen and the more nomadic pastoral nomads (Gen 21:25; 26:15; 19-22).

Storage Systems. Since rainfall in Palestine does not occur during the summer months, and the climate during this period is dry and hot, efficient water storage systems have always been a major concern. The most common water storage facilities in ancient times included cisterns, pools, and reservoirs.

Cisterns were usually bell-shaped chambers hewed out of solid bedrock formations below the surface of the ground. They were designed to capture the water that came during the rainy season. Recent excavations at Ai and Raddana have discovered more elaborate systems in which a series of cisterns were connected by channels thus providing a filtration system for the water. Around the beginning of Iron Age I, ca. 1200 B.C.E., a new technique, namely, plastering the side walls of the cistern, was introduced in cistern construction in Palestine. The newly discovered technique made cistern construction possible in the central hill country, an area with formations of porous limestone that would not retain water. The account of Uzziah's home improvement program in the land of Judah implies that hewed cisterns were used to store water for crops, vineyards, and animal herds (2 Chr 26:10).

Larger storage units included reservoirs and pools (some of which will be discussed below). Excavations at Qumran for instance have uncovered a series of reservoirs or collecting vats that provided water for the community. The water supply consisted of rain water, channeled through a network of canals or watercourses from the surrounding hills to the collecting pools in the Qumran community. Water storage systems, consisting of large reservoirs or collecting vats, were used also by the NABATAEANS.

Major Water Systems. Of all of the ingenious feats of the peoples that lived in ancient Palestine the development of major water systems in or near some of the major cities of the land rank among the most outstanding. Generally, the systems were designed for one of two purposes: (1) to provide safe passage to the water supply; or (2) to bring the water to a more convenient location. Several, but not all, of the water systems of ancient Palestine will be discussed at this point.

(1) JERUSALEM. Warren's shaft, named after Charles Warren who discovered it in 1867, was designed and engineered by the pre-Israelite inhabitants of Jerusalem, the Jebusites. This water system was located beneath the surface on the east side of the old city of Jerusalem, often called the Ophel ridge, just above Gihon spring. It was designed to provide safe access to the spring during times of warfare. The system consisted of an entrance on the side of the hill, a tunnel approximately 130 ft. long, a shaft about forty-two ft. deep at the lower end of the tunnel, and a horizontal

channel which brought water from the Gihon spring back under the ridge to the base of the shaft. This shaft was the means by which David captured the city and made it his capital (2 Sam 5:6-10). Excavations directed by Kathleen Kenyon in the 1960s clarified once and for all the relationship of the shaft system to the city wall of the old Jebusite city.

While Warren's shaft was constructed during the pre-Israelite period, Hezekiah's tunnel (PLATE 37) was cut by the workmen of king Hezekiah near the end of the eighth century B.C.E. as Sennacherib, the Assyrian king, approached Jerusalem to besiege it (2 Kgs 20:20; 2 Chr 32:30). The tunnel, approximately 1,730 ft. long, was cut through solid bedrock under the Ophel ridge. Its purpose was to provide the means by which the waters of the Gihon spring could flow to the opposite side of the ridge, into the pool of Siloam, for use by the inhabitants of that part of the city. Two teams, each starting on opposite ends of the project, were responsible for cutting the tunnel. Their work is described on an inscription called the SILOAM INSCRIPTION found on the wall of the tunnel. Once the tunnel was completed the water-flow into the valley was blocked in order to prevent the enemy from using it, and the water was diverted through the tunnel into the pool.

(2) GIBEON. Two major water systems have been discovered at Gibeon, home of the Gibeonites who served the Israelites as "hewers of wood and drawers of water" (Josh 9:23). The earliest of the systems, perhaps built about the twelfth century B.C.E., consisted of a large cylindrical pool, approximately thirty-seven ft. in diameter and thirty-five ft. deep, carved into bedrock. The pool had a spiral staircase which led to a tunnel that descended to a kidney-shaped water room. The water room, some eighty ft. below the surface of the town, was located at the natural water level of the area.

Apparently the pool system was less than successful at producing water and was eventually replaced by a second system. The new system, somewhat similar to the Warren shaft system at Jerusalem, consisted of a long tunnel which led to an underground cistern where the water supply was located. Water was brought into the cistern from a spring by means of a feeder tunnel.

(3) MEGIDDO. Ancient Megiddo had a water system that was constructed in three different stages with each replacing or improving the earlier. The earliest phase, from prior to the time of Solomon, consisted of a short stepped passage near the base of the mound which led to an enlarged chamber that collected spring water. The second phase, from the time of Solomon, included a passage through the city wall that was connected to a covered stairway that led to the spring chamber near the base of the mound. The Solomonic system was replaced by an extremely large system constructed in the ninth century B.C.E. The new system, consisted of a large vertical shaft 115 ft. deep, with steps and a tunnel, 200 ft. long, that led from the base of the shaft to the spring near the base of the mound. At a later time the tunnel was deepened in order to allow the water to flow to the base of the vertical shaft.

(4) HAZOR. The ancient city of Hazor had a shaft and tunnel system similar to the one at Megiddo, however, the Hazor shaft was approximately twice as large as the Megiddo shaft. The shaft, 100 ft. deep, was designed with steps ten ft. wide in order that pack animals could be used to carry the water up and out. A tunnel, fifty ft. long, led from the bottom of the shaft to the water table below the city.

(5) GEZER. The shaft-and-tunnel method was also used for the design of the water system at Gezer. The Gezer system consisted of a rectangular shaft, twenty-seven ft. deep, and a tunnel 132 ft. long, that led to a large cave filled with spring water.

Aqueducts. Aqueducts provided the means by which water was channeled, in some instances, great distances. Aqueduct systems, smaller in design were found for instance at communities like Qumran and Masada. More extensive systems were located south of Jerusalem. They included channels by which water flowed to such places as Herodium, the desert retreat of Herod the Great, and Jerusalem. One of the most elaborate aqueduct systems brought water from the Mount Carmel area to CAESAREA. Here, the water channel was supported by a bridge-like structure that consisted of a series of arches.

Bibliography. D. Cole, "How Water Tunnels Worked," *BAR* 6/2 (March/April 1980): 8-29; V. Matthews, "The Wells of Gerar," *BA* 49/2 (June 1986): 118-26; J. B. Pritchard, *Gibeon: Where the Sun Stood Still*; Y. Yadin, *Hazor*; R. Amiran, "The Water Supply of Israelite Jerusalem," *Jerusalem Revealed*; A.. Mazar, "The Aqueducts of Jerusalem," *Jerusalem Revealed*; R. Lamon, *The Megiddo Water System*; J. B. Pritchard, *The Water System of Gibeon.*

—LAMOINE DEVRIES

• **We-Sections.** "We-sections" refers to four passages in Acts in which an unexpected shift from third-person to first-person pronouns occurs: 16:10-17, a sea voyage from Troas to Philippi; 20:5-15, a sea voyage from Philippi to Miletus; 21:1-18, a sea voyage from Miletus to Jerusalem; and 27:1–28:16, a sea voyage from Caesarea to Rome.

Several explanations for this shift have been advanced. The traditional view, supported by IRENAEUS, as well as by some modern scholars, interprets the first-person pronouns as a reference to the author himself. When an account occurs in first person, the author of Acts is indicating he was an eyewitness of the events recorded. Proponents of this view claim that this is the most natural way to understand "we/us" and is how the original readers of Acts would have understood the reference. According to this view, then, the author of Acts was an occasional companion of Paul. The breaks in the narratives in which first-person pronouns do not occur indicate that the author was not with Paul on those occasions. On the basis of Phlm 24, Col 4:14, and 2 Tim 4:11, many readers have surmised that LUKE was this traveling companion of Paul and thus the author of Acts.

Among the problems associated with identifying the author of Acts (and of the we-sections) as a companion of Paul are discrepancies between events described in Acts and in the Letters of Paul, discrepancies between the theology of Paul as presented in Acts and as found in his own writings, and the unexplained abruptness of the appearance and disappearance of the we-sections. These problems have led many scholars to abandon the traditional explanation and posit new hypotheses. One alternative hypothesis states that the author of Acts is dependent in the we-sections on a written source, possibly an itinerary of Paul's journeys or a diary kept by one or more of his traveling companions. A major problem with this view is that no stylistic differences exist between the we-sections and the surrounding texts. The we-sections were authored or at least heavily edited by the same individual who wrote the rest of Acts. If the author of Acts so heavily edited the we-sections as to recast them into his own style, why did he not change the first-person pronouns to third person to conform to the surrounding texts? No satisfactory explanation has been given.

A more attractive suggestion is that the use of first-person pronouns is an intentional literary device of the author of Acts. One such proposal states that by adopting the first-person style the author attempted to impart credibility to the accounts by intimating he was an eyewitness of the events described. Another way of understanding the first-person narratives as a literary technique has been suggested by a comparison of the we-sections with ancient accounts of sea journeys. A specific genre of literature, sea voyages, in which the account is told in first person, seems to have existed in the ancient world. The writer of Acts, aware of this genre, shaped the accounts of Paul's sea voyages to conform to this literary genre. Readers of the first century C.E. would have expected a first-person narration of the voyage, regardless of whether the author was an actual participant or not.

Although no completely convincing solution to the problem of the we-passages has yet been demonstrated, the variety of scholarly opinions indicates that the presence of first-person pronouns in the Book of Acts does not necessarily provide information about authorship of Luke-Acts.

See also APOSTLES, ACTS OF THE; LUKE.

Bibliography. J. Dupont, *The Sources of the Acts*; E. Haenchen, " 'We' in Acts and the Itinerary," *JTC* 1 (1965): 65-100; V. K. Robbins, "By Land and By Sea: The We-Passages and Ancient Sea Voyages," *Perspectives on Luke-Acts,* ed. C. H. Talbert.

—MITCHELL G. REDDISH

• **Weak.** *See* POOR

• **Wealth.** While wealth is not inherently evil, the love of wealth leads to many evils (1 Tim 6:10). Earlier, wealth was looked upon as divine favor (Ps 1:3; Deut 28:1-14). What people possessed was always enough and came from God for use in worship. Such wealth as flocks, servants, and precious stones was pointless, however, if the person had no descendants. The family within the tent (later, the house) was real wealth. Excavations of early Israelite sites show houses of equal size, with no distinctions between wealthy and poor. Wealth increased with the development of the land. Excavations of later sites showed larger dwellings for the rich, evidence of the emergence of a ruling class. When wealth was in the hands of those who abused it, the prophets condemned them (Hos 8:14; Amos 6:4; Isa 3:16-24). The prophets repudiated the abuse of wealth in society, business, and the courts (Amos 2:6-8; 8:6).

"Wealth, a blessing; poverty, a punishment" was a general belief in early times, but wise persons and psalmists mourned the suffering of the righteous and the prosperity of the wicked (Job 21:7-16; Pss 37, 49, 73). The righteous were so mistreated that "poor" became a synonym for "godly." Still, the rich could also be righteous. People like Zaccheus and Joseph of Arimathea could enter the KINGDOM OF GOD (Luke 19:2; Matt 27:57). The NT cautions special care, for even moderate wealth must be administered faithfully, or else true wealth will never be given to disciples of Jesus (James 5:1-6; Luke 16:11).

See also ECONOMICS IN THE NEW TESTAMENT; ECONOMICS IN THE OLD TESTAMENT; POOR.

Bibliography. R. de Vaux, *Ancient Israel: Its Life and Institutions*; H. Eising, "חַיִל *chayil,*" *TDOT*; F. Hauck, "μαμωνᾶς," *TDNT*; F. Hauck and W. Kasch, "πλοῦτος, κτλ.," *TDNT*; E. Kutsch, "הוֹן *hôn,*" *TDOT*.

—EDDIE L. RUDDICK.

Courtesy of the Eisenberg Museum of Biblical Archaeology, Southern Baptist Theological Seminary.

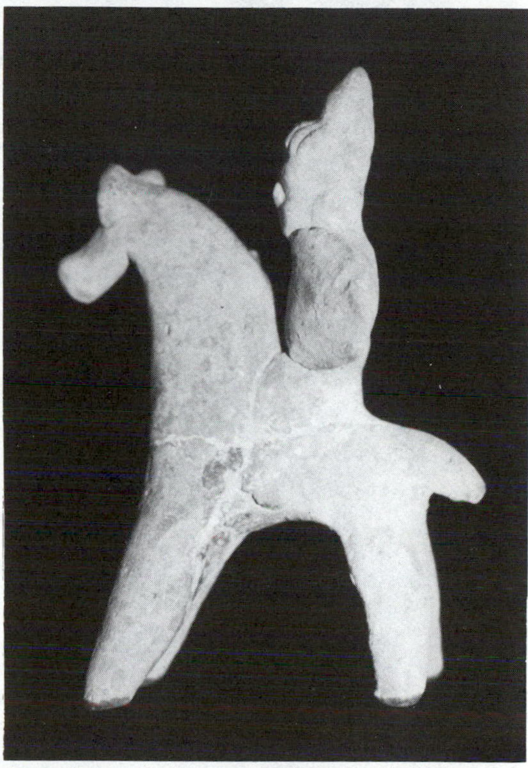

A clay figure of an Assyrian warrior on horseback.

• **Weapons/Warfare.** War is the armed conflict between larger social units. War is known from the earliest periods of civilization, and even prehistoric remains include material evidence of warfare. The oldest known town of Syria-Palestine is prepottery Neolithic JERICHO, already a town covering ten acres in the eighth millennium B.C.E. This town was surrounded by a defensive wall preserved at points to a height of seventeen ft. Inside the wall was a massive round stone tower twenty-five ft. in diameter, preserved to a height of twenty-three ft., and having internal stairs leading up to the top. Even in the eighth millennium B.C.E., defensive walls and WATCHTOWERS were necessary to protect an important town.

In the OT in particular HOLY WAR is of special importance. Holy war depicts Yahweh as a divine warrior leading the forces of Israel and assuring the victory; the spoils of war were then placed under the ban (*ḥerem*), dedicated to Yahweh.

The focus of this article is on the weapons used in warfare and to a lesser extent on changing strategies brought about by new technology.

Defensive Weapons. The major defensive strategy has already been mentioned: the city wall. In time of enemy at-

Courtesy of the Eisenberg Museum of Biblical Archaeology, Southern Baptist Theological Seminary.

Collection of weapons.

tack, the population of an area would flee to the nearest fortified city to survive the invasion. Because of the expense of building and maintaining a city wall, only major or strategic cities were walled. Also FORTS manned by military contingents were built at strategic locations near principal highways, passes and borders.

In addition to strong walls, at least two additional components were necessary for the defense of a city: food and water. Palestine, especially during the Iron Age, provides some of the most innovative means of protecting a water supply ever discovered. A large town had a large number of cisterns to catch and hold water. In addition, many towns had a WATER SYSTEM to obtain spring water from inside the tell. Because cities often sat on a hill for defensive reasons and a water supply was seldom found on a hill, the water supply was usually outside the city wall. Among the methods of bringing water inside the city safely were covered and hidden passages leading down the slope of the tell to the spring, water shafts and tunnels permitting access to the spring from inside the wall, and huge pools cut down to the water level. Since many of the fortified cities served as regional administrative centers and market centers, they had large storehouses for food and supplies. These cities might serve as centers both to receive tax revenues from the region and as administrative centers for trade materials. As such, the cities probably had a sizeable food supply which was doubtless augmented when war seemed imminent.

Personal defensive material included shields, helmets and armor. Most frequently these were made of leather, though metal was used in later periods as well.

Offensive Weapons. Earliest weapons were probably adaptations of tools, the mace developing from a mallet or hammer and the battle-ax from an ax used to fell timber or to work the wood. Both these weapons were first made of stone and later of metal and attached to a wooden handle.

Other weapons in use from very early times included the sword, spear, and bow and arrow. The sword was typically short and straight, basically a dagger, throughout the Early Bronze Age. It was used for close hand-to-hand combat.

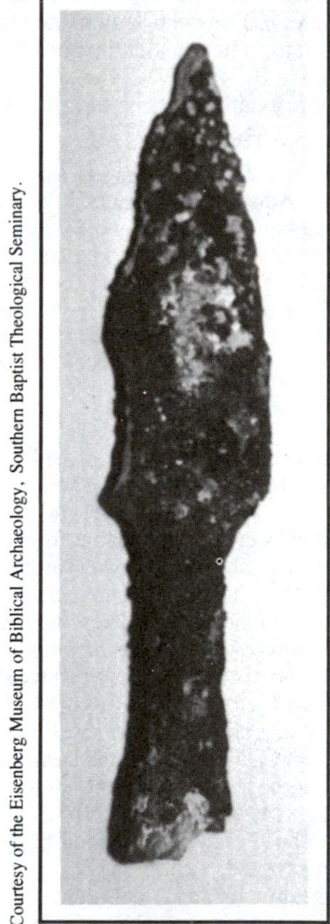

Courtesy of the Eisenberg Museum of Biblical Archaeology, Southern Baptist Theological Seminary.

A spear head.

The spear was a thrusting weapon with the point attached to a long wooden handle. The bow was simple. The presence of numbers of rounded stones in the cities suggests that slings and sling stones were also used as weapons. Paintings and reliefs from Mesopotamia indicate that chariots were in use during the Early Bronze Age, although apparently they were not known in Syria-Palestine or Egypt at that time. This chariot was bulky and slow, being derived from agricultural carts or wagons. Reliefs also show the use of scaling ladders and battering poles in attacking cities. Based on depictions, infantry formations were close with deep phalanxes.

In Middle Bronze Age Palestine many towns had mas-

Artist's conception of a two-wheeled battle chariot

sive walls and ramparts surrounded with a dry moat and steeply sloping glacis. These defensive structures probably reflect the introduction of the battering ram as an effective weapon against earlier walls and gates. Other weapons introduced at this time include the curved sickle sword, obviously used for striking rather than thrusting. The straight sword continued in use; it became both broader and longer. Alongside the spear, the lighter javelin was introduced, a weapon to be thrown. The convex bow appeared along with the simple bow. Also lighter horse-drawn chariots appeared for the first time, perhaps introduced by the HYKSOS.

Improvements in these weapons continued in the Late Bronze and Iron Ages. The composite bow came into use. Iron replaced bronze as the chief metal for weapons. Coats of mail were used to protect the soldier. The battering ram became a much more formidable wheeled vehicle. The Assyrians developed a covered battering ram which offered protection from enemy fire for those attacking the wall or gate. Specialized troops were used to undermine walls by tunneling under the walls. The chariot continued to develop, at first becoming lighter and sturdier, drawn by a team of horses and having a driver and weapon handler. Later the chariot became heavier again, drawn by four horses and having three warriors and a driver.

Innovations in warfare by the Greeks and Romans include the introduction of the phalanx by the Greeks, heavily armored spearmen in close rectangular formations eight rows deep. Such a formation could withstand cavalry charges. Alexander the Great introduced the military supply system. The Romans developed the legion, with about 6,000 infantry and 120 cavalry divided into small phalanxes called cohorts. The legion was a much more flexible fighting unit than the Greek phalanx. The Roman army is well known for building roads and bridges, initially to provide rapid troop movement and easy supply. More sophisticated war machines including catapults were developed. Also naval warfare played an important role in Greek and Roman strategy.

The biblical accounts indicate the Israelites used a variety of strategies against their enemies. In the conquest of Canaan, spies were sent out to gather intelligence about the land and the location and strength of fortified cities (Num 13–14; Josh 2). In the capture of Ai, the Hebrews used ruse and ambush (Josh 8). Gideon used a surprise attack at night to defeat the Midianites (Judg 7). In its early history, Israel had a volunteer militia supplied by each tribe. After the Davidic-Solomonic empire was established, Israel developed a professional standing army like her neighbors.

Bibliography. J. Warry, *Warfare in the Classical World*; Y. Yadin, *The Art of Warfare in Biblical Lands*.

—JOEL F. DRINKARD, JR.

• **Weaving.** *See* SPINNING AND WEAVING

• **Weeks, Festival of.** One of the three major Israelite festivals in the annual calendar (Exod 34:22; Num 28:26; Deut 16:19, 16; 2 Chr 8:13), the event has various names in the Bible, including festival of harvest (Exod 23:16), the day of the first fruits (Num 28:26), and Pentecost (Acts 2:1; 20:16; 1 Cor 16:8). "Weeks" (*šāvûôt*) referred to the harvest period of seven weeks of days or forty-nine days. Later the period obtained the reference of Pentecost, the fiftieth day. Thus, the period that began with the spring festival of the FEAST OF UNLEAVENED BREAD (Passover) culminated in the Feast of Weeks. The texts that prescribe the date for the one day observance come from Lev 23:15-17, 21-22 and Deut 16:9-12: "And you shall count from the morrow after the SABBATH, from the day that you brought the sheaf of the wave offering; seven full weeks shall they be, counting fifty days to the morrow after the seventh sabbath; then you shall present a cereal offering of new grain to the Lord" (Lev 23:15-16). During the Diaspora the festival included two days of celebration, the sixth and seventh of the month of Sivan, in order to insure the proper day.

The distinctive feature of the festival was the presentation to Yahweh of an offering of two loaves of new corn. Farmers anticipated *šāvûôt* with great excitement. The Festival of Weeks provided a special time for people to rejoice in the first fruits of the harvest and present them to the Lord.

Judaism has always insisted that Yahweh exists as Lord of both nature and history. In fact, *šāvûôt* began as a agricultural celebration and eventually emphasized a crucial event in the life of Israel, namely the TORAH at Mount SINAI. The Festival of Weeks became known as the season of the giving of the Torah. It is stated in the Talmud that "Pentecost is the day on which Torah was given.'' A relationship developed between the fifty days of Passover and Pentecost along with the time of travel from Egypt to Sinai. Although the travel was not fifty days (cf. Exod 19:1), the rabbis made the connection. The Festival of Weeks became the anniversary of the day on which the Lord revealed the Law to the people of Israel.

Jews emphasize the Torah with the reading of the TEN COMMANDMENTS in the morning service of the synagogue. Young people, aged fifteen or sixteen, commit themselves to obey the Torah. Congregations engage in the reading of the Book of RUTH during the worship. The person of Ruth reminds them of a non-Jew who became obedient to the Torah. The setting for the book centered on the time of the barley harvest. Also, Ruth, great-grandmother of King David, heightens Jewish anticipation of the coming Messiah who was to be from the lineage of David. Other readings come from Ezek 1, with a vision of God's glory, and Hab 2:2-3, which urges Jews to persist in faith in the midst of suffering.

See also FEASTS AND FESTIVALS.

Bibliography. T. Gaster, *Festivals of the Jewish Year*.

—OMER J. HANCOCK, JR.

• Weights and Measures. In earliest times measurement was by reference to everyday objects. A ''cubit,'' e.g., was the length of a man's forearm, elbow to fingertips. (The Latin *cubitum,* ''elbow,'' is by transference an ''elbow's [i.e., forearm's] length''; in the NT πῆχυς *pēchys,* ''forearm,'' is by usage always ''cubit'' [but RSV converts to yards in John 21:8]; and in the OT אַמָּה *ammah,* by usage ''a forearm's length,'' is variously explained as from אמם *amm,* ''womb/mother,' thus a ''mother [unit] of measure,'' or from אמם, ''be wide/roomy,'' thus ''distance,'' or from אמם, ''be in front/precede,'' hence ''forearm.'') Capacity and weight also were measured by relation to common objects—e.g., a handful, a hen's egg, a barley corn. Maimonides (1135–1204 C.E.) much later calculated the OT shekel at 320 barley corns weight, but by OT times the shekel weight was set (albeit variously) and the original standard (barley corns or what?) perhaps forgotten.

Barter and trade gave rise to *many* systems of measurement. Virtually every trade center had its own system, and only those who traded with each other seem to have agreed on any ''universal'' standards. As societies became more complex and interactive, of course, certain unit standards became necessary, and might include, e.g., that a cubit was the length of the *king's* forearm. Yet variety persisted (barley corns and even kings come in different sizes).

Both Babylonian and Egyptian metrology apparently influenced that of the OT. Babylonian mathematics was essentially sexagesimal. For example, they divided the circle into 6x60 parts and the day into 12 double hours of 30 minutes (=4 of our minutes) each. Other measures followed suit: talent = 60 minas; mina = 60 shekels. Similar mathematics, but mixed with a probably Egyptian decimal system, underlie the OT sexagesimal/decimal system (cf. the tables).

An obvious and often frustrating aspect of biblical ''standards'' of measurement is their variety. Inconsistencies are variously explained and attempts have been made to impose order on the biblical system by means of elaborate tables that show ''common/light'' vs. ''royal/heavy'' variations. (Four separate standards for some units of measure have been discovered among the Babylonians/Assyrians: *common*; *heavy* = twice common; *royal* = common plus 5 percent; and *heavy royal* = heavy plus 5 percent.) Such variety in the OT may be explained partly by the seesawing hegemony in Judah/Israel of first the North (Mesopotamian), then the South (Egyptian); then of course the Greeks and Romans came with systems of their own.

OT awareness of varying standards is evident as, e.g., ''cubits *of the old standard*'' (2 Chron 3:3) clearly indicates. Og's bedstead (ostentatiously huge by any standard!) was measured ''according to the *common* [Heb. *of a man*] cubit'' (Deut 3:11), again supposing more than one kind of cubit. Indeed, at least Babylonia and Egypt used a longer ''royal cubit'' and other longer, larger, and heavier ''royal'' units of measure, ostensibly to insure a greater share (of taxes or otherwise) for the royal house. (In Ezek 40:5, 43:13, e.g., a ''common'' cubit is set at six and a ''long'' [temple or royal] cubit at seven handbreadths.)

In general, then, biblical weights and measures were originally by reference to common objects (evidently var-

• Measures and Weights •

UNIT†	EQUALS	USA	METRIC
Length/Distance			
finger	$^{1}/_{24}$ cubit	$^{3}/_{4}$in	19mm
handbreadth	4 fingers	3in	7.6cm
span	3 hands	9in	22.8cm
cubit*	2 spans	18in	45.7cm
[''long'' cubit (Ezek)	7 hands	21in	53.3cm]
pace	2 cubits	36in	91.4cm
fathom	4 cubits	6ft	1.83m
reed/rod	6 cubits	9ft	2.74m
stadion/furlong (NT)[1]	400 cu	600ft	183m
mile (NT *milion*)	3,200 cu	4,800ft	1,463m
sabbath-day's journey (NT)	2,000 cu	1,000yd	914m
Weight			
gerah	$^{1}/_{20}$ shekel	$8^{4}/_{5}$gr	0.57gm
beka	$^{1}/_{2}$ shekel	$^{1}/_{5}$oz	5.7gm
pim	$^{2}/_{3}$ shekel	$^{1}/_{4}$oz	7.6gm
shekel*	2 bekas	$^{2}/_{5}$oz	11.4gm
mina/pound (OT/NT)[2]	50 sh	20oz	571gm
pound (NT *litra*)		$11^{1}/_{2}$oz	326gm
talent[3]	3,000 sh	$75^{1}/_{2}$lb	34.2kg
Capacity			
Hebrew Bible			
log (liquid)	$^{1}/_{72}$ ephah	$^{3}/_{5}$pt	0.3 l
kab	$^{1}/_{18}$ ephah	$2^{1}/_{3}$pt	1.23 l
omer/tenth/(issaron)	$^{1}/_{10}$ ephah	2qt	2.2 l
hin (liquid)	$^{1}/_{6}$ ephah	$3^{1}/_{2}$qt	3.7 l
measure (= seah)*	$^{1}/_{3}$ ephah	$6^{9}/_{10}$qt	7.4 l
ephah (dry)*	3 seahs	$^{7}/_{10}$bu	22.1 l
bath (liquid)*	6 hins	$5^{1}/_{5}$gal	22.1 l
lethech (dry)	5 ephahs	$3^{1}/_{4}$bu	110.5 l
homer/cor[4]	10 ephahs	$6^{1}/_{2}$bu	221 l
New Testament			
pot [cf. ''pint jar'']		1pt	0.52 l
quart		1qt	1.1 l
bushel [cf. ''peck measure'']		$7^{7}/_{10}$qt	8.4 l
gallon × 10 (= μετρητής)[5]		$10^{1}/_{3}$gal	38.9 l
measure (= seah)[6]		$6^{9}/_{10}$qt	7.4 l
measure (= bath)[6]		$5^{1}/_{5}$gal	22.1 l
measure (= cor)[6]		$6^{1}/_{2}$bu	221 l

†As occurring in RSV. Fractions occur: sixth-ephah, tenth-ephah, half-shekel, etc.

* = supposed base unit(s).

[1]RSV converts to miles in Luke 24:13, John 6:19, 11:18, and interprets as ''race'' in 1 Cor 9:24.

[2]NT *mina* (RSV ''pound'') occurs only in Luke 19 and only as a unit of money (the much greater ''talent'' occurs in Matt 25).

[3]Ostensibly a ''one-man load'' (cf. 2 Kgs 5:23).

[4]Possibly a ''one-donkey load.''

[5]In John 2:6 RSV translates ''2 or 3 μετρητής'' (*metrētēs,* measure) as ''20 or 30 gallons.''

[6]In RSV *seah, bath,* and *cor* are all translated as ''measure.''

• Units of Measure Relationships •

reed/rod	1							[* = base]
fathom	$1\frac{1}{2}$	1						
pace/step	3	2	1					
*cubit	6	4	2	1				
span	12	8	4	2	1			
handbreadth	36	24	12	6	3	1		
finger	144	96	48	24	12	4	1	
talent	1							
mina	60	1						
*shekel	3,000	50	1					
pim	4,500	75	$1\frac{1}{2}$	1				
beka	6,000	100	2	$1\frac{1}{3}$	1			
gerah	60m	1,000	20	$13\frac{1}{3}$	10	1		
homer/cor	1							
lethech	2	1						
*ephah/bath	10	5	1					
*seah	30	15	3	1				
hin	60	30	6	2	1			
[1]omer/issaron	100	50	10	$3\frac{1}{3}$	$1\frac{2}{3}$	1		
kab	180	90	18	6	3	$1\frac{4}{5}$	1	
log	720	360	72	24	12	$7\frac{1}{5}$	4	1

[1]In the OT *omer/issaron* is routinely designated "tenth," i.e., a tenth part of an ephah/bath.

iously applied), not to any universally controlled "bureau-of-standards" units. So any attempt to convert biblical measures and weights into modern values can be only approximate. The table offered here is thus only a *general* guide: it does not distinguish between long/short or common/royal variations but offers only one mean modern value for each unit.

The table lists no area units. Area terminology in the Bible is in rather general terms. Land measure is indicated by "stick" or "yoke," i.e., the amount of land a yoke of oxen could plow in one day (1 Sam 14:14; Isa 5:10—RSV posits "acre" as equivalent). (An Egyptian standard unit for land-area measure was 100 "royal" cubits square, ca. 0.7 acre and possibly roughly equivalent to the Hebrew "yoke.") Land area was stated also in terms of the amount of seed required to sow it ("a sowing of a homer of barley," Lev 27:16).

Note also especially that some original units of weight became units of currency, coinage. Originally trade was by simple barter, the exchange of moveable goods for other goods, property, or services. In time certain metals (principally silver, gold, and copper) became a convenient medium of exchange, at first as ingots (actually small balls or blobs) of varying size and shape or as pieces of jewelry, valued according to metal type, purity, and *weight.* (Thus merchants became "weighers of silver" [or other metals], Zeph 1:11; cf. Gen 23:16.) Later such metal pieces were molded into certain shapes and sizes. Finally, "standard-weight" metal pieces were imprinted with the mark or seal of a merchant prince, monarch, or government as a guarantee of value, and coinage was born. Thus an original unit of weight became the designation of a coin of a certain value (cf. esp. Gen 23:16 as illustrating this transition). "Shekel" (שֶׁקֶל, "[a certain] weight"; שָׁקַל, "to weigh") in the OT, therefore, may designate either a certain unit of weight (Ezek 4:10; cf. Jer 32:10) or a coin of a certain (by-weight) value (Neh 5:15; Lev 27:3, 4, 5). In fact, it may be difficult from the immediate context alone to determine whether a unit of weight or a unit of coinage is intended (cf. Exod 21:32; 30:13; and esp. 22:17 where RSV "to pay money" is in Heb. "to weigh [שָׁקַל] silver"). So especially the shekel but also the talent and even mina originally were units of weight that became units of currency.

Measurements in biblical times, of course, were by modern standards inexact and inconsistent; yet they were *not* unscientific or haphazard, as sometimes supposed. The common objects originally referenced as unit "standards" were of course subject to natural variation, and the real measure of a unit might vary—as even today—according to the object being measured (e.g., whether liquid or solid, metal or foodstuffs) and the system employed (e.g., common/royal, light/heavy; cf. troy/avoirdupois). While measures might be inexact and vary from place to place, however, consistent standards fairly applied was the ideal (cf. Mic 6:10-11) and OT laws strictly required "just weight" and "just measure" (Deut 25:13-16).

See also COINS AND MONEY; MONEY.

—EDD ROWELL

• **Wheat.** *See* GRAIN

• **Widow in the New Testament.** A woman whose husband has died becomes a symbol of sorrow, vulnerability, and powerlessness and thus is a special object of God's care and concern. Widows play prominent roles in both Mark and Luke but not in Q or Matthew's unique material.

The loss of husband made the woman especially vulnerable economically, which evoked the prophetic concern of Jesus. He accused the scribes of "devouring widow's houses," i.e., foreclosure (Mark 12:14; Luke 20:47). Fees for service often resulted in the loss of legal advocacy which widows deserved. The injustices were then covered with a pious show of prayer, which evoked Jesus' scorn and invective.

A widow's trust and generosity was contrasted to the greed and avarice of the scribes and rich (Mark 12:41-44), and the widow of Zarephath's aid to Elijah was used as an example of the compassion and hospitality required by God (Luke 4:26).

The tenacity and persistence required of those who seek the righteousness of the Kingdom was also portrayed in the story of the importunate widow (Luke 18:2-5). The story modeled both the necessity of prayer and the eschatological promise of justice.

The widow of Nain was the object of Jesus' compassion when the death of her son added to her grief, sorrow, and vulnerability. When Jesus raised her son, she became a central witness to Jesus' divine authority (Luke 7:11-17).

The Jerusalem church made special provision for the material needs of widows, reflecting both the requirements of the Law and the communitarian organization of the fellowship. The complaint by the Hellenists that their widows were being neglected occasioned the appointment of deacons to assure that material needs were met (Acts 6:1).

The Pastorals (1 Tim 5:3-16) provide the most comprehensive statement about widows in the NT and reflect a more developed ecclesiology. Those who are called "real" or "true" widows may be part of a service order in the church (1 Tim 5:3). These were to be "enrolled" or "adopted into a fellowship by election." They were to be at least sixty years of age, married only once, persons of integrity, known for charitable service, and resolved not to marry again (vv. 9-10). Their role included that of setting a worthy example to younger widows and being responsible for the care and comfort of those in need. Whether this constituted a semiclerical office or was a matter of widows being designated to care for widows (cf. Acts 9:36–41) is a matter of debate. In any case, they were to be ''honored.''

First Tim 5 also reflects a growing asceticism with its denigration of sex and marriage. Younger widows were looked upon with suspicion and thus were the objects of rather harsh judgments. They were not to be ''enrolled'' since they might ''grow wanton'' and ''desire to remarry'' (v. 11), a distinct departure from Paul's openness to REMARRIAGE in 1 Cor 7:39. Interest in an active life was regarded as ''self-indulgent'' and a sign of spiritual death (v. 7). They were admonished to care for their own children or grandchildren (v. 4) and/or remarry, have children, and rule their household (v. 14).

It may be that too many widows were relying upon the church's care. The Pastorals' solution is to distinguish the truly needy (those who are totally reliant upon God, v. 5) from those who might reasonably be expected to secure other means of support. Younger widows were to be cared for by their relatives or extended family, under the strong admonition that '' one who does not care for relatives . . . has disowned the faith and is worse than the unbeliever'' (v. 8).

Another use of widow occurs in Rev 18:7 where she is a metaphor of the humility, repentance, and contrition which God desires in contrast to the ''queen'' on a throne, whose arrogance, power, and evil assure the judgment of God (v. 8). The queen and the widow represent two extremes of woman's destiny and the Apocalypse announces a great reversal. Haughty Babylon, the queen, will know the widow's sorrow, while the oppressed church, the widow, will become a royal bride.

See also FAMILY; MARRIAGE IN THE NEW TESTAMENT; MARRIAGE IN THE OLD TESTAMENT; REMARRIAGE; WOMEN IN THE NEW TESTAMENT; WOMEN IN THE OLD TESTAMENT.

—PAUL D. SIMMONS

• **Widow in the Old Testament.** The Heb. word *'almānâ,* ''widow,'' is basically negative, conveying a situation in which a woman through the death of her husband finds herself deprived of the financial protection of MARRIAGE. Though the term widow in its simplest understanding refers to a woman whose husband has died, the widow appears in biblical texts in situations in which all male protection is lost, or not available—husband, sons, or brothers.

Exploitation and mistreatment were possible fates of the widowed woman throughout the ancient Near East. Extant texts from ancient Mesopotamia, Egypt, and Ugarit as well as Phoenician and Hittite texts reveal a concern for the plight of the widow. Together with the orphan, the widow is viewed as a segment within society that calls for special protection.

Along with other marginal groups, the widow stands as witness to the injustices of society. Like the orphan, the SOJOURNER, and the hireling, the widow faces oppression at the hands of the wicked (Mal 3:5; cf. Job 22:9; Isa 10:2; Ps 94:6; Zech 7:10). She is further identified with the poor (Isa 10:2; Job 24:3-4, 9; 31:16; Zech 7:10). Like the Levite, the widow knows no personal means of support (Deut 14:29).

When faced with widowhood a woman had three options open to her: remarry, remain single and pursue a profession, or return to her father's house. In a context in which a woman's primary function was that of wife and mother, to be a widow, especially when childless, implied disgrace (cf. Ruth 1:20-21; Isa 54:4).

The ancient practice of levirate marriage in which the property of the deceased was bought by his brother and the widow taken as wife provided the possibility for children. The first son born through such a union was to carry the deceased husband's name and to inherit his property (Deut 25:5-10; cf. Ruth 4; Gen 38). Should there already be sons at the time of the husband's death, the widow was not seen as totally destitute. If the son were young, the mother acquired responsibility for her deceased husband's property until the time that the son was able to assume the role of protector for both the property and his widowed mother. Her rearing the son to manhood brought her honor (cf. Zeruah, the widowed mother of Jeroboam I, the first king of Israel, mentioned in 1 Kgs 11:26). Given the precariousness of her situation, the prospect of a widow's losing her sons was especially dreadful (2 Sam 14:4-7; 1 Kgs 17:20).

Deprived of male protection, the widow was at the mercy of the community. Though God stood as guardian over the widow and as father to her children in a religious sense (Ps 68:5; cf. Deut 10:18; Jer 49:11), the community either exploited her circumstances or kept her from being exploited, aiding her in time of need. The widow's garment could not be taken in pledge (Deut 24:17). Justice was her due (Deut 10:18; Isa 1:17). Following the harvests, she joined the poor in gleaning the fields (Deut 24:19-21). Along with the orphans, Levites, and sojourners, she was a recipient of the tithes every third year (Deut 14:28f.; 26:12f.).

See also FAMILY; MARRIAGE IN THE OLD TESTAMENT; REMARRIAGE; WOMEN IN THE OLD TESTAMENT.

Bibliography. F. C. Fensham, ''Widow, Orphan and the Poor . . . '' *JNES* 21 (1962): 129-39; H. A. Hoffner, ''אַלְמָנָה *'almānāh,''* *TDOT*.

—KANDY M. QUEEN-SUTHERLAND

• **Wife.** *See* MARRIAGE IN THE NEW TESTAMENT; MARRIAGE IN THE OLD TESTAMENT; WOMEN IN THE NEW TESTAMENT; WOMEN IN THE OLD TESTAMENT

• **Wilderness.** *See* DESERT; NUMBERS, BOOK OF

• **Wisdom in the New Testament.** Wisdom in the NT is seen primarily in its relation to Jesus who embodies wisdom in his person and teaching. The prologue of John sets forth the Word/Wisdom in a way similar to Prov 8 and passages in the Apocrypha (Sir 24; Bar 3–4; Wis 7–9). The Word is eternal wisdom personified in Jesus (John 1:1-18).

Paul exalts Jesus as eternal wisdom personified in 1 Cor 1:24 as ''the wisdom of God.'' In Colossians Christ unites in himself the fullness of God in bodily form (Col 1:19). In Col 1:15-20 (cf. Eph 3:8-10), Christ is the creative wisdom of God: ''for in him all things were created'' and ''in him all things hold together'' (cf. John 1:3). He is the one ''in whom are hid all the treasures of wisdom and knowledge'' (Col 2:3). In the Gospel of Matthew, Jesus is Torah personified and equated with divine wisdom, and in Luke 11:49 he is simply the ''wisdom of God.''

The historical Jesus was a rabbi, a wisdom teacher, whose sayings in Matthew and Luke appear to be influenced by the Hebrew wisdom tradition. A number of the parables are clearly in the wisdom style and substance. Many of the sayings of Jesus are in the wisdom mold even when there is no use of the term. In Matt 11:29, Jesus says, ''Take my yoke upon you, and learn from me.'' In Matt 12:42, he states that one ''greater than Solomon is here.''

Paul makes extensive use of both the term and concept

of wisdom. He cries out, "O the depth of the riches and wisdom and knowledge of God" (Rom 11:33). In 1 Cor 1:18-30, he contrasts the wisdom of the world and the wisdom of God. Paul concludes that faith must rest, not in human wisdom "but in the power of God" (1 Cor 2:5) and "in Christ Jesus, whom God made our wisdom" (1 Cor 1:30). The Letter of James is the NT book most related to wisdom. Its hortatory nature provides the reader with applied wisdom. Noteworthy is 3:13-18, where earthly wisdom and "the wisdom from above" are illustrated.

This wisdom is a gift to humanity (Rom 12:8). This gift enables the Christian to walk in wisdom as urged in Eph 5:15 and Col 4:5. Because wisdom is spiritual, "from above," believers can have the "mind of Christ" of Phil 2:5. In Rev 5:12 and 7:12, wisdom is a characteristic of the age to come.

See also JAMES, LETTER OF; LOGOS/WORD; WISDOM IN THE OLD TESTAMENT; WISDOM LITERATURE.

—NORM YANCE

• Wisdom in the Old Testament. In the Bible wisdom has a wide range of meanings, specific and non-specific. The root *ḥkm* can designate technical skill or expertise such as that of a goldsmith, weaver, artisan, navigator, shipbuilder, or entrepreneur. It refers to clever action directed toward a desirable end, even if immoral, and to the ability to manipulate persons into accomplishing one's goal. This use of the word resembles the modern sense of practical knowledge issuing in valuable skill rather than theoretical knowledge about the cosmos and its essential nature.

The noun *ḥkm* also possesses a technical meaning; in this case it designates a member of a professional group, the wise. This use occurs in the latest section of PROVERBS (1–9), in ECCLESIASTES, and in SIRACH. Its Greek equivalent would correctly identify the instructor responsible for WISDOM OF SOLOMON. The wise consciously reflect on the qualifications for membership in their elite company: one must be receptive to instruction, heed advice, answer appropriately, and possess self-control. Their cardinal virtues include timeliness, restraint, eloquence, and integrity. According to Prov 1:6, the wise occupy themselves with similes, taunts, sayings, and riddles. They direct instruction to persons with varying degrees of experience and sophistication, from the naive "innocent" to the learned adult. Their threefold task as reflected in Eccl 12:9 includes teaching, research, and writing. Various benefits accompany wisdom, in the sages' view, especially life, manifesting itself in health, wealth, honor, longevity, and progeny. The word *ṣdq,* a synonym for the professional use of *ḥkm,* indicates both the religious and moral aspects of the wise. In northwest semitic inscriptions, kings boast of wisdom, righteousness, and graciousness.

Over against the wise as a professional group stands another class of people, fools. They lack self control in the areas of food, drink, sexual appetite, anger, and speech. Fools include the untutored and the aggressively incorrigible, as well as various intervening types. Their deficiency falls in the realm of morals rather than intellect. The wise have little patience with fools, and sages believe that only evil consequences accompany foolish conduct. In their enthusiasm over the power of the intellect, some sages prompted rebuke. For instance, the author of Ecclesiastes cautions against excessive claims about the scope of knowledge, daring to call such wise teachers liars.

In the ancient Near East wisdom and age go together, although exceptions occur. An old fool can let erotic desire lead to disgrace, and an occasional youth can rise to extraordinary moral and intellectual heights, at least in popular memory. Thus Wisdom of Solomon speaks of God's conferral of wisdom on a young king who had the insight to request competence in ruling a people rather than riches (cf. 1 Kgs 3:9). Ordinarily, wisdom was the product of vast experience. In a Ugaritic text, wisdom is associated with El's gray beard; the biblical anecdote about Rehoboam's act of soliciting advice from young and old characterizes the youth as ruthless and the aged as compassionately wise, at least in this particular instance (1 Kgs 12:1-11).

The act of heeding instruction issued in a technical term for instruction, *leqaḥ* (receiving *da'at,* knowledge). In Egypt "the hearing one" functions as another epithet for a sage, and *The Instruction of Ptahhotep* develops this concept at some length. The locus of the intellect in Israelite thought was the heart, *lēb*. Whoever lacked intelligence suffered from an affliction known as *ḥaṣar lēb* (devoid of sense). Synonyms for wisdom include, among others, understanding (*bînâ*), knowledge (*da'at*), counsel (*'ēṣâ*), and occasionally power (*gĕbûrâ*).

Mantic and magical wisdom makes brief appearances in the Joseph narrative and in the legends about Daniel. This type of access to secret information of the gods prevails in Mesopotamian culture, where professional sages consulted omens and examined the livers of sacrificial victims to determine the will of the gods. Some Aramaic-cuneiform tablets link *ḥkm* and medicine, whereas Old South Arabic texts emphasize the mantic aspects of *ḥkm* and modern Arabic, its judicial and medicinal features.

Wisdom eventually achieved poetic personification in the Bible. Depicted as a desirable woman, she addressed young people in the center of daily activity. This caring figure resembles a prophet, uttering threats and warnings, ultimately promising life and wealth (Prov 1). She prepares a feast and summons guests to celebrate a newly-built house (Prov 9). Her demands appear strenuous at first, but in the end her yoke becomes light. An ideal wife, she bestows honor on the lucky husband who claims her as bride. Moreover, she nurtures her children like a worthy mother.

Just as professional sages emphasized their distinctiveness by imagining an opposing class, the fools, these teachers also fantasized about a rival to woman wisdom. This antagonist embodied the most seductive features of the foreign woman, a popular theme in wisdom literature. Her foreignness may be merely a matter of conduct, that is, she may be an Israelite with wholly unconventional morals. Or she may actually be a foreign woman, perhaps one associated with ritual worship of a sexual goddess. Regardless, this personification of folly constitutes a powerful threat to the youth whom the wise hope to entice to a wholly different kind of life. Folly's seduction conceals nothing: she invites young men to her bed, using seductive imagery. "Stolen water is sweet, and bread eaten in secret is pleasant" (Prov 9:17). In contrast to the sages' fondness for silence, "silent one" being another near-surrogate for the technical term "wise" in Egypt, this seductress noisily calls attention to herself and lures the unwary to their destruction. Like SHEOL, she has a ravenous appetite; although no mention of a toothed vagina occurs, the consequence is the same.

The poetic personification of wisdom passes over into mythic symbolism as well. Drawing on the Egyptian figure of Maat, the goddess of order, justice, and righteousness, who holds the symbol for life in one hand and riches in the other, biblical *ḥokmâ* boasts of having been present at creation, which not even Job witnessed. She claims to be a source of divine pleasure and an instrument of creation, indeed one of God's initial acts. As a witness of the primordial creation, she rejoiced in the world and its human inhabitants (Prov 8). Such a one boldly invites the untutored to "leave simpleness, and live," which finds its closest approximation in Amos' prophetic demand in God's name, "Seek me, and live."

Mythic imagery derived from ancient accounts of creation also enriches the description of wisdom, now almost a hypostasis. Issuing from the divine mouth, like an oracle or statute, she covers the earth like dew. This wondrous creature spans the universe as God alone can do, and she finds temporary lodging among all peoples, until the Creator assigns a permanent abode for her in Israel. She boasts eternal origin and survival, but willingly ministers before God in Jerusalem's holy place. In this favorable setting she flourishes like well-tended trees and produces pleasant aromas and beautiful flowers. Eager to share her delicious produce, she invites the hungry to eat freely, knowing that they will return to the source again and again. An amazing identification of wisdom and TORAH follows: "All this is the book of the covenant of the Most High God, the law which Moses commanded us as an inheritance for the congregations of Jacob" (Sir 24:24). The author does not abandon mythic imagery at this point, but reverts to the Yahwistic account of four rivers that dispense knowledge, in this case wisdom, understanding, and instruction. Ben Sira concedes that, like the first human creatures, he does not fully fathom wisdom, whose thought is vast and profound, resembling sea and abyss.

Access to wisdom was denied by some. The hymn about wisdom's inaccessibility in Job 28 struck a note that resonated in many hearts. Only God has access to wisdom; humans, like Sheol and Abaddon, come no closer than capturing a rumor about her. The author of Ecclesiastes emphasizes wisdom's remoteness and profundity: "I have tested all this by wisdom; I said, 'I shall be wise,' but it was far from me. Distant—whatever is—and extraordinarily deep; who can find it?" (7:23-24). The author of Baruch concurs with this sentiment: "Who has gone up into heaven, and taken her, and brought her down from the clouds? Who has gone over the sea, and found her, and will buy her for pure gold? No one knows the way to her, or is concerned about the path to her" (Bar 3:29-31). The echo of Deut 30:12-13 becomes audibly distinct as Baruch equates wisdom with the Mosaic Law (4:1).

Wisdom becomes more closely identified with the Creator in the Greek text, Wisdom of Solomon. Here one enters an entirely new realm of discourse, although connections with earlier speculation about wisdom linger. The emphasis now falls on wisdom as an eminent attribute of God. She is God's breath (spirit), power (*gĕbûrâ*), and glory. A pure reflection of the Creator, wisdom is also a divine image of goodness. Moreover, she is an initiate into divine knowledge. Therefore wisdom inspires holy persons and instructs sages. The unknown author, in the guise of Solomon, boasts that she instructs him, indeed that she is his bride. Similarly, in every generation wisdom instructs holy people, in this way guiding the destiny of the elect nation, Israel.

The association of wisdom with Yahweh came reluctantly (cf. Isa 28:26, where Elohim appears), largely because in some circles it was easily linked with morally questionable conduct, but also because of foreign wisdom's connection with magic. Moreover, the sages normally spoke of Elohim rather than the special god of the Jews. The ancient story about the first sin places a question mark over the human acquisition of knowledge. The desire to possess knowledge carries recognizable negative consequences, according to this story. The use of cunning sometimes produced awful results, as exemplified in the story about Jonadab's assistance to a lusting Amnon. As for the manipulation of the gods by means of knowledge, Israel's prophets in the Babylonian period do not mince words about this practice. Within the NT, the apostle Paul contrasts the "foolishness of God" with human wisdom.

Perhaps the custom of praising kings for their wisdom assisted in the move to attribute wisdom to Yahweh. In the ancient Near East the widespread tradition of wise kings gave rise to liturgical texts such as Isa 9:6, which introduces throne names (Wonderful Counselor, Mighty God, Everlasting Father, Prince of Peace), and 11:2, which gives voice to the people's hope that their ruler will judge wisely ("And the spirit of the Lord shall rest upon him, the spirit of wisdom and understanding, the spirit of counsel and might, the spirit of knowledge and the fear of the Lord"). Nevertheless, the Israelites did not lose touch with reality, for political experience easily disabused them of thinking that all kings lived up to such high ideals. Even Solomon departed sharply from the goal, despite traditions extolling his exceptional wisdom.

Israel's sages also manifest a sober awareness of their limits. For this, they did not need lessons from Isaiah, who blasts those who are wise in their own eyes and who quips that Yahweh is also astute (Isa 5:21; 31:2). The struggle to elevate religion over knowledge left its mark on the wisdom corpus, for the fear of the Lord was understood as primary, both in a chronological sense and in an evaluative sense.

In Johannine thought, speculation about the divine word (*logos*) corresponds to earlier ideas about *ḥokmâ*, but also to Stoic thought. Certain hymns in the Pauline corpus owe much to mythic imagery about the creative activity of wisdom, now understood as the Christ who existed in the beginning and functioned as the agent of creation (contrast PIRKE ABOTH 3.14, which refers to creation by torah). The Letter of James and gnomic sayings in the gospels continue the other understanding of wisdom as an effort to cope with reality.

Bibliography. J. L. Crenshaw, *Old Testament Wisdom* and "Wisdom in the Old Testament," *IDBSupp*; G. Fohrer, "Sophia," J. L. Crenshaw, ed., *Studies in Ancient Israelite Wisdom*; B. Lang, *Wisdom and the Book of Proverbs*; H.-P. Müller and M. Krause, "חָכָם *chākham,*" *TDOT*; R. E. Murphy, "Hebrew Wisdom," *JAOS* 101 (1981): 21-34; G. von Rad, *Wisdom in Israel*; R. N. Whybray, *The Intellectual Tradition in the Old Testament, BZAW* 135; R. J. Williams, "Wisdom in the Ancient Near East," *IDBSupp*.

—JAMES L. CRENSHAW

• **Wisdom Literature.** A distinctive intellectual tradition extended throughout the ancient Near East, beginning in the early third millennium and reaching into the Common Era. Modern scholars call this phenomenon wisdom literature. The Egyptians classified the dominant type of their wisdom literature as *sebayit* (Instruction), whereas Israel's sages labeled their collections of proverbs *meshalim.* But besides such instructions and sentences (or truth statements), ancient wisdom also included philosophical explanations of life's meaning in light of seemingly senseless suffering and injustice. A third type of wisdom, at least in EGYPT and MESOPOTAMIA, consisted of encyclopedic lists of flora, fauna, and other significant bits of information. In addition, some texts praising the scribal profession at the expense of all other vocations or rebuking lazy students and describing the learning process round out the wisdom corpus.

Egyptian Wisdom. Three texts of *Instructions* have survived from the Old Kingdom, two of them in fragmentary form. Having reached advanced years, *Ptahhotep* (ca. 2450 B.C.E.) requests permission from the Pharaoh to install his own son in the office of counselor. *Ptahhotep* then proceeds to instruct his son on the means of functioning successfully in government: acquiring eloquence, practicing honesty, using correct etiquette, guarding against lust. *Kagemni* reiterates the advice about proper manners at table, and *Prince Hardjedef* warns against boasting and encourages marriage.

Three *Instructions* derive from the Middle Kingdom. The Pharaoh *Merikare* advises his son, combining ruthlessness and silence but extolling eloquence as well. In his teaching, life's shadow-side lurks nearby, necessitating religious and magical scrupulousness. The slain *King Amen-em-het I* cautions his son about the folly of trusting others. The contents of the fragmentary *Sehetipibre* are not known.

The New Kingdom witnessed a crisis of confidence that resulted in widespread religiosity. Two *Instructions, Ani* and *Amen-em-opet,* document this change; *Amennakhte* is too fragmentary to ascertain its contents. *Ani* strikes a note that persists in Israelite wisdom too: watch out for the strange or foreign woman. He also evokes response from his son Khonshotep, who insists that his father's code of ethics is too difficult for the son. *Amen-em-opet* offers thirty "chapters" of advice; at least ten of these sayings have found their way into the biblical Book of PROVERBS. With him, a heightening of piety takes place, despite an inscrutable God who sails the ship of the faithful safely into harbor.

Two Demotic texts complete the list of Egyptian *Instructions*: *'Onksheshonky* and *Papyrus Insinger*. Both address the populace at large and reflect fatalistic understandings of reality.

The Satire of the Trades, or *The Instruction of Khety, son of Duauf,* describes miserable working conditions between 2150 and 1750, asserting that only the scribal profession is worth considering. Similarly, *In Praise of Learned Scribes, The Instruction of a Man for his Son, Papyrus Sallier,* and *Papyrus Anastasi* IV, 9:4-10:1; V, 8:1-9:1, 9:2-10:2 extol the advantages of being a scribe.

Discussions about life's inequities mark *Neferti, Khakheperre-sonbe, Ipuwer* and *The Dispute of a Man with his Soul. The Tale of the Eloquent Peasant* examines the powerful effects of governmental abuse, and the *Harper Songs* encourage festive living because of approaching death and society's injustices. These texts belong, if at all, on the periphery of Egyptian wisdom. At its center lies the concept of order (*ma'at*) and the human necessity of bringing one's conduct into line with this principle. By observing the cardinal virtues—timeliness, restraint, eloquence, and honesty—a sage, or silent one, appreciably improved the chance of experiencing the good life.

Mesopotamian Wisdom. Sumerian wisdom texts include both major types of the ancient intellectual tradition, proverbs and reflection on life's mysteries. The latter is the concern of a text about a righteous sufferer, *A Man and his God*; it resembles biblical JOB, although the blame falls on humans who are by nature sinful. *The Instructions of Šuruppak* to his son recall some themes already attributed to Egyptian wisdom, such as the danger of sexual misconduct and the advantages of having a good wife (a fertile field). Texts from the tablet house (*edubba*) characterize the life of a student, and various disputes, noun lists, and satires illuminate scribal interests. A fragmentary text resembles the powerful description of old age and death in ECCLESIASTES 12:1-7.

Babylonian wisdom also includes proverbial instruction and penetrating debate over life's injustices. *The Counsels of Wisdom* urge love of enemies and benevolence or silence; similarly, *Advice to a Prince* offers strong advocacy for subjects despite the exalted view of monarchy in vogue. *I Will Praise the Lord of Wisdom* tells about a righteous individual who struggles to understand the cause of his misery and who eventually is restored to health as reward for faithful conduct. Here, as in the Book of Job, God appears to the victim and rectifies the situation. *The Babylonian Theodicy,* an elaborate acrostic or alphabetic poem, takes the form of a dialogue between a sufferer and an orthodox friend. Both of these texts stress the inscrutability of the gods, who made men and women with a predilection to practice evil. *The Dialogue of Pessimism,* a humorous (?) conversation between a master who has been overcome by ennui and a proverbial "yes man," suggests that nothing commends itself, with the possible exception of suicide.

The few examples of wisdom from MARI derive from popular sayings. The Hebrew Bible also has about a dozen such aphorisms scattered throughout the TORAH and the prophetic books. An Aramaic wisdom text, *The Sayings of Ahiqar,* contains a prose framework like Job and *'Onksheshonky.* Ahiqar advised the Assyrian king SENNACHERIB but became wrongly implicated in a palace revolt. From prison, Ahiqar wrote words of advice in the form of popular proverbs. Canaanite wisdom, barely attested, describes life as a journey on which youth embark and offers advice on how to cope. Edomite wisdom, celebrated in the Bible, has not survived.

To sum up, Mesopotamian wisdom literature resembles its Egyptian counterpart in form, although providing considerably more nuanced discussion of life's injustices. The biblical reflections about unjust suffering and the meaning of life continue this tradition, whereas the book of Proverbs has closer affinities with Egyptian *Instructions* than with Mesopotamian texts, except for Ahiqar. One significant feature of Mesopotamian wisdom, its magical character, does not occur in the OT.

Biblical Wisdom. Ancient Israel's sages preserved their teachings in two forms: *meshalim* and reflections. The former included both instructions (Prov 1–9, SIRACH) and shorter aphorisms (most of Proverbs). The latter comprised Job and Ecclesiastes. In addition, didactic compositions in PSALMS explore the problem of divine justice (Pss 37, 49, 73), and a midrash-like discussion of the Exodus plus an encomium of sorts conclude WISDOM OF SOLOMON and Sirach (Ecclesiasticus) respectively. The scribal tradition continued in certain respects in RABBINIC LITERATURE, especially PIRKE ABOTH, and some elements of earlier wisdom surface in Jesus' aphorisms, the Epistle of JAMES, and possibly in the LOGOS speculation of Johannine thought.

The Book of Proverbs represents a sort of anthology, a number of collections deriving from premonarchic and postexilic circles of tradition. Perhaps as many as eleven separate collections make up the present book: 1–9 (the latest in date), 10–15, 16:1–22:16, 22:17–24:22, 24:23-34, 25–27, 28–29, 30:1-14, 30:15-33, 31:1-9, and 31:10-31.

Several of these collections have superscriptions that betray the sages' awareness that SOLOMON did not write these proverbs, although two collections acknowledge foreign authorship (Agur and King Lemuel's mother), and another shares several sayings with *Amen-em-opet*. Egyptian influence stands out in chap. 16 and in the depiction of wisdom as a woman who has life in one hand and prosperity in the other.

The instructions use imperatives to reinforce their teaching, offering promise of reward for obedient conduct and threatening punishment for disobedience. They sometimes quote an aphorism to make a decisive point. Deeply religious in tone and content, the instructions emphasize religious devotion (the fear of the Lord) as the precondition and essential component of knowledge. Both the instructions and the sentences make sharp distinctions between the wise and foolish. The initial collection, 1–9, seems almost preoccupied with the foreign woman, who poses a threat to innocent youth. It also depicts Wisdom as an agent in the act of CREATION, so that her apparent personification offers comfort to those who find Folly's invitation to stolen water and bread eaten in secret enticing indeed.

These instructions and aphorisms enabled youngsters to master reality, thus securing existence. By examining nature and human experience, teachers drew analogies about various means of coming to grips with almost every eventuality. Life in harmony with the principles governing the universe brought riches, honor, long life, and many children. Still, the sages conceded definite limits to their knowledge and control of things, for Yahweh spoke the last word.

The social setting of the separate collections varied from popular sayings arising among the common people to formal instruction of professional scribes and, in one instance, a king. Between these extremes, parental teaching transmitted a lifetime's experience to young sons. The oldest aphorisms probably antedate the monarchy, although the bulk of the collection derives from the exilic and postexilic period. The putative connection with Solomon, implied in several superscriptions, does not accord with the characterization of his proverbs in 1 Kgs 4:29-34, for the "Solomonic" proverbs do not discuss trees, fish, birds, and reptiles.

In time the optimism undergirding the world view of these proverbs vanished, leaving behind sober questions about the utility of wisdom and goodness. The Book of Job wrestles with undeniable injustices in the world, as if concentrated in a single individual. Perhaps his misery symbolizes that of Israel, but his characterization as an Arab sheik seems to preclude such a reading. Dissonance persists in the book to the end, partly due to the combination of an old folk narrative about disinterested righteousness with a fresh poetic treatment of innocent suffering.

The unusual structure, a prose framework enclosing a poetic dialogue, points to a deeper level where traditional understandings of God shelter explosive ideas, in the end returning to safe beliefs. Job's attack against the principle of reward and punishment presupposes precisely that reality, otherwise he would have no basis for complaint. Furthermore, the eventual resolution of his dilemma, if such it be, derives from conventional Yahwism, which spoke of divine manifestations to special people. This aligning of different religious perspectives in a single literary complex encouraged further amplification through hymnic texts, particularly the exploration of God's impenetrability, orthodox rebuke of Job's blasphemy and his friends' ineptness, and descriptive snippets about awe-inspiring creatures such as the ostrich and the wild horse.

Religious and historical events of the sixth century produced a context for this probing exploration of fundamental presuppositions that had never been seriously challenged. Other poets ventured to ask similar questions, especially Deutero-Isaiah, whose imagery sometimes resembles Job's language. Whether one echoes the other, or both give voice to universal complaint, remains uncertain. In any event, Job signals simultaneously wisdom's bankruptcy and its elasticity. The sages' world view collapsed, but they boldly enlarged the horizons of knowledge to include theophanic vision.

Movement within the Book of Job is greater on the psychological plane than on the theological. Job and his friends remain adamant throughout the debate, save when confronting the divine inquisitor. The harsh attacks on Job by miserable comforters prompt him to entertain fleeting thoughts of vindication against all odds, a pronouncement of "innocent" in the heavenly court. Unable to count on God's help, Job thinks a champion of his cause will emerge from the void created by God's vicious attacks and active hiding (19:25). Instead, the deity silences Job by reminding him of the real wonders of creation, then offers him a sop in the form of restored wealth and children. The reader cannot resist asking: Has the vision perished? Has conventional orthodoxy co-opted venturesome interrogatives, robbing them of their sting?

The other stunning attack on uncritical thinking in the wisdom corpus, Ecclesiastes, undergoes a similar softening. An unknown epilogist warns against further "bookmaking" (not "writing") because everything has already been heard: "Fear God and observe the commandments," confident that every deed, secret or otherwise, will be judged. The opinion of the author of the main body of the book, often called Qoheleth, regarding such a claim is no secret, for in 8:17 he labels it a lie. In his view, not even professional sages can discover God's deeds. Chance governs human lives, and the deity dwells in remote indifference, insofar as one can tell.

Qoheleth taught ordinary people (*hā'ām*), according to another epilogist. This admirer of the teacher points to painstaking preparation on Qoheleth's part, an attentive listening, penetrating inquisitiveness, and planned presentation. Furthermore, Qoheleth valued the aesthetic dimension of speech, but not at the expense of truth. This epilogist linked Qoheleth's teachings with other sapiential collections, all of which derive from one shepherd, either the king or God. Behind this allusion probably lies the royal fiction of Solomonic authorship—a literary conceit that vanishes after the second chapter. The epilogist acknowledges the sting in Qoheleth's teachings and still insists that they function to orient one's thinking securely.

The book's structure certainly indicates careful deliberation. Two poems envelop the complete sayings of Qoheleth; the first describes nature's ceaseless and monotonous movement, and the second depicts the wintry blast of old age and death. A thematic statement about life's utter futility precedes the former poem and concludes the latter. Between them stand Qoheleth's reflections resulting from exhaustive examination of observable phenomena. Refrain-like phrases and self-reflective expressions contribute a sense of unity to the scattered observations. The author pays attention to everything that takes place, drawing conclusions about nature, human and divine.

This impression of unity competes with an equally

powerful dissonance, for the book does not speak with a single voice. Throughout Ecclesiastes, a phenomenon of broken sentences occurs in which the author appears to say, "Yes, but on the other hand." Qoheleth seems at odds with his tradition. Moreover, his unorthodox views so offended certain people that they actually tampered with the text, introducing traditional teachings about a divine judgment and denying ultimate authority to death.

On the other hand, Qoheleth declared life "wanting" precisely because the death angel acted with total disdain for demonstrable virtue. Circumspect behavior did not secure one's existence; indeed, wisdom lacked the power customarily attributed to it. The desirable things in life did not necessarily yield satisfaction, for they lacked permanence. Seven times Qoheleth advocates a life of enjoyment, but he issues solemn reminders that existence passes quickly into oblivion. Sweet is the light; and fleeting. The dark house promises a long residence (your eternal home). Qoheleth faces things with stark realism; his skepticism does not cross over into cynicism, although it becomes profoundly pessimistic. The suffering of powerless individuals at the hands of officials and the absence of any deliverer overwhelmed him. So did the silence of the heavens.

The sentiments of the orthodox epilogist to Ecclesiastes find fuller expression in Sirach, often called Ecclesiasticus. The author, Eleasar Jeshua ben Sira, lived at the beginning of the second century and ran a school, presumably in Jerusalem. His teaching relies heavily on the proverbial tradition, oblivious to the objections to its world view raised by the author of Job and Ecclesiastes. For Ben Sira, ancient wisdom retained its cogency, especially when reinforced by conventional Yahwism. Earlier sages had remained silent about specific Israelite traditions, contenting themselves with insights available to all people regardless of their individual histories. Ben Sira abandons this universalism, opting for particularistic teachings of the Jews. His observations frequently incorporate canonical allusions, and the extensive hymn praising Israel's great men derives exclusively from the Bible. Nothing in biblical wisdom prepares the way for such lavish praise of human beings.

Ben Sira's sense of adoration spilled over to include God, for the book has majestic hymns about the creative work of the one who evokes the numinous shout, "He is the All." In fact, the praise of men functions also as celebration of God's activity that raised up such wondrous leaders, particularly cultic figures. The culminating eulogy of the High Priest, Simon II, indicates that Ben Sira deeply appreciated religious ritual. Two themes resound through the work: the fear of Yahweh and wisdom. In a suggestive mythical treatment of wisdom's search for a dwelling place, Ben Sira equates Torah and wisdom. This subsuming of the intellectual tradition under the broad category of religious duty accords with the elevation of fear of the Lord, which is roughly translatable as religion.

The students who attended Ben Sira's house of study faced seduction from Hellenism, which prompted him to reflect seriously about competing values. In his view, the insights transmitted by MOSES and the understanding of reality promulgated by the sages rivaled anything the Greeks could offer. Furthermore, God's compassion renders human doubt somewhat innocuous, for a convincing theodicy must take divine mercy into account. Ben Sira draws on Jewish and Hellenistic arguments for divine justice, introducing two emphases that hardly belong in traditional wisdom: the belief that psychological anxiety results from sin, and the conviction that the universe itself punishes vice and rewards virtue.

Egyptian wisdom made an impact on Ben Sira's thinking, particularly *The Satire on the Trades,* but also various features from *The Insinger Papyrus.* He seems unable to transcend a conventional attitude toward suffering as punishment for sin, although he courageously defends the medical profession. Capable of exquisite poetic imagery, he demonstrates unusual awareness of the complexities involved in social relations. His attitude to women contains certain features that offend modern sensitivities, although the attitudes were widespread at the time.

The unknown author of Wisdom of Solomon, the only wisdom treatise written in Greek that entered the LXX, explores the erotic relationship of knowledge by imagining a union between Solomon and Wisdom. This thinker functions in a thoroughly Hellenistic environment, for the concepts and rhetoric are Greek. The claim can be substantiated by pointing to the reference to the cardinal virtues, the belief in an immortal soul, the hypostasis of Wisdom as a female figure and the attributes of God which she manifests, the stylistic devices such as sorites, and so forth. Wisdom of Solomon uses an early midrash-like analysis of the Exodus event to satirize the Egyptians among whom the Jewish readers of the book resided. Mockery of idolatry lies at the center of this ridicule, which explains the origins of idol making as the result of grief, aesthetic interests, or veneration of an emperor. Such imaginative treatment of the Exodus exaggerates the psychological consternation that propelled Egyptians to their destruction.

In short, biblical wisdom literature includes instructions and sentences, intellectual debate about the possibility of true virtue and religion, serious reflection on life's futility, and the relationship between traditional Torah and paternal counsel. The ancient Near Eastern transmitters of this literary tradition belonged to several social settings: the home, court, and school. They developed special vocabulary and thematic interests, but in the end Israel's sages reached out to embrace traditions peculiar to the Jews. Their speculation about wisdom and their ethical insights lingered, influencing rabbinism and Christianity.

See also ECCLESIASTES, BOOK OF; JOB; JOB, BOOK OF; PROVERBS, BOOK OF; SIRACH; SOLOMON, WISDOM OF; WISDOM IN THE OLD TESTAMENT.

Bibliography. J. L. Crenshaw, *Old Testament Wisdom,* and *Studies in Ancient Israelite Wisdom*; J. G. Gammie et al., *Israelite Wisdom: Theological and Literary Essays in Honor of Samuel Terrien*; W. G. Lambert, *Babylonian Wisdom Literature*; M. Lichtheim, *Ancient Egyptian Literature*; L. G. Perdue, *Wisdom and Cult*; G. von Rad, *Wisdom in Israel*; J. C. Rylaarsdam, *Revelation in Jewish Wisdom Literature*; R. N. Whybray, *The Intellectual Tradition in the Old Testament.*

—JAMES L. CRENSHAW

• **Wisdom of Solomon.** *See* SOLOMON, WISDOM OF

• **Wisdom, Book of.** *See* SOLOMON, WISDOM OF

• **Wise Men.** *See* MAGI

• **Witness.** Someone who is knowledgeable about the facts under question and who speaks about them at a legal proceeding is a witness. The use of witnesses in various legal cases was legislated in Deuteronomy at various points. Common to all of these cases was the stipulation that a conviction could not be obtained on the basis of a single witness (Deut 19:15). The use of such witnesses is described in Prov 19:28; Isa 8:2; and 1 Kgs 21:9-13. Serving as a witness of this sort was seen in Israel as a religious and civic duty; willfully giving false testimony was strongly condemned (Exod 20:16; 1 Kgs 21:5-29; Deut 19:16-19).

A witness also served as an attestation that a transaction was legal and had been completed. The elders of a village often served in this capacity (Deut 25:9; Ruth 4:4, 9-11) but other responsible citizens also performed this function (Jer 32:9-15).

A type of witness closely related to the latter was the memorial or monument which served as a physical reminder of an agreement made or an event of moment. The cairn erected by Jacob and Laban in Gen 31:44-54, the Reubenite altar in Joshua 22:21-34, and the proposed altar of Isaiah (19:19-20) were witnesses of this type.

In the NT, the term "witness" (Gk. *martüs*) came to refer specifically to one who had seen Jesus during his lifetime or had seen the risen Lord (Luke 1:2; 24:8; Acts 1:22). Witness to the truth of the Gospel was expected of all believers, a witness supported by the Spirit (Rom 8:16). Martyrs in later Christian history were witnesses, testifying to the truth of Christian faith by their readiness to die holding fast to that faith.

See also TESTIMONY.

—RAY SUTHERLAND

• **Wizards.** *See* MAGICIANS

• **Woman Taken in Adultery.** The *Pericope Adulterae* is an account of Jesus' forgiveness of a woman who was caught in adultery and brought to him for judgment by persons whose hypocritical attitude Jesus condemns. Although this paragraph does not appear in any of the oldest Greek manuscripts of the NT, it is included in many later manuscripts and some ancient versions, most often as John 7:53–8:11 (in some manuscripts it is placed after John 7:36, 7:44, 21:25, or Luke 21:38) and is, therefore, found in many translations of the Bible. Despite this textual situation, most scholars believe the story to be a historically valid incident from the life of Jesus. It reveals both the cultural bias against women (although caught in adultery, the male critics bring only the woman to Jesus) and Jesus' consistent offer of mercy to persons rejected in their society.

—DAVID M. SCHOLER

• **Women in the New Testament.** Recent studies have contributed greatly to renewed awareness regarding the status of women in the NT. In addition to standard historical-critical methods, the approaches of sociological analysis, literary criticism, and feminist critical hermeneutics are proving to be constructive in gaining a more sharply-delineated picture.

Women in the First-Century Mediterranean World. Christianity was born into a complex social milieu which felt primarily the influence of Greek, Roman, and Jewish religiocultural mores. These societies were patriarchal in orientation, relegating women to subordinate roles in religion, government, education, and domestic concerns. Although there were notable exceptions such as women's participation in the syncretistic mystery cults (which were more inclusive than traditional Greek religion or sectarian Judaism) and the writings of Plutarch (which challenged the double standard), the *paterfamilias* structure was normative. Considerable unrest over these strictures characterized the world in which the NT was written. The education of women, for instance, inevitably provoked conflict over their public and private roles. It is understandable that the NT reflects both a tension and an accommodation with these perspectives as it sought to articulate the gospel story of Jesus the Christ and chronicle Christianity's subsequent missionary activity in the Mediterranean world. In this matrix the church made decisions about the role of women within the Christian community which still influence contemporary thinking and practice.

The OT provided a rich paradigmatic repository and substructure for much of the NT. The legal stipulations, in particular, underscored Israel's patriarchy. Barred from full participation in the religious sphere, the woman's existence was defined by her relationship to father, husband, or children (preferably sons). Occasionally women functioned in nontraditional roles, e.g., DEBORAH the judge (Jdgs 4–5) and HULDAH the prophet (2 Kgs 22:14ff.), but visions of gender equality were missing from most of the texts. Some among the prophets saw beyond this repressive society and proclaimed a new day for God's people in which religious and personal disabilities would no longer characterize the existence of women (cf. Joel 2:28-29; Hosea 4:14; Jer 31:22).

Postexilic Judaism struggled to preserve its identity amid an increasingly Hellenized culture through elaborate regulations and precise cultic prescriptions. Women were more restricted during this epoch than they had been in the OT. Rabbinic literature was particularly misogynistic in outlook; women were not only portrayed as the origin of evil but the locus of its continuing embodiment (*m.Abot* 2, 7; *b.Ketub* 65a). Diaspora Judaism was generally more tractable concerning the position of women, but in no wise could be considered egalitarian.

Women and the Ministry of Jesus. The extent to which women figured in the ministry of Jesus is remarkable given the religiocultural background. His prophetic message, inclusive concern, and unrelenting challenge to religious perversions display a radical discontinuity with OT and postbiblical Jewish precedents. Jesus' willingness to teach women (John 4:27; Luke 10:29) directly countered the rabbinic dictum against permitting a woman to study Torah.

Clearly women were among the disciples called by Jesus. His proclamation of the KINGDOM OF GOD (inbreaking in his ministry) offered a new vision for humanity where the walls of partition were no longer determinant. In the new "family" Jesus was forming (Mark 3:31ff.), sisters and brothers would participate in a "discipleship of equals," as Elisabeth Schüssler Fiorenza describes it (140ff.). The technical words used for disciple ("following," Mark 8:34; "serving," Mark 15:40-41; Luke 10:38-42) are freely applied to the women who responded to Jesus' message. Although excluded from THE TWELVE for symbolic and pragmatic reasons, i.e., to demonstrate the continuity of his message with the life of the covenantal nation Israel, and the itinerant nature of his ministry, respectively, the participation of women in Jesus' ministry is expressly noted by the four evangelists. From the beginning of the Galilean proclamation to the resurrection vindicating Jesus' claim, women accompanied and assisted this one who welcomed their contributions.

At times, the Gospel writers portray women as more exemplary disciples than men, a radical departure from first-century expectations. This recounting must surely reflect the indisputable challenge of Jesus to the patriarchal ethos—the evangelists would not likely create or embellish these stories. Mark 12:41-43 portrays Jesus' commendation of the poor widow to the disciples as an example of generosity and utter self-giving. Likewise the action of MARY of Bethany, anointing Jesus "for burial" (Mark 14:3ff.; Matt 26:6ff.; John 11:2), is presented as evidence of her sensitive discipleship, comprehending the approaching passion of her Lord while others were seemingly oblivious.

The clearest expression of Jesus' affirmation of women occurs in his commissioning of them as witnesses to his resurrection. All four Gospels record the presence of women at the tomb and Jesus' instruction to them to "go and tell the brethren" (Matt 28:1-10; Mark 16:1-8; Luke 24:1-12; John 20:1-18). In a culture where the word of a woman was not considered a trustworthy witness, how amazing that Jesus would entrust the climax of the good news, God's power to overcome the power of sin and death, to these marginalized messengers! In this context the Gospel of John takes pains to render Mary of Magdala as a true disciple (20:11-18). As one of Jesus' own, she recognizes him when she hears his voice (cf. John 10:4-5). She and the BELOVED DISCIPLE are the ones who believe without hesitancy, unlike Simon Peter and Thomas. Many NT scholars regard Mary as the first witness to the resurrection, the one to whom Jesus first appeared.

The Gospels not only reflect events during the life of Jesus but also the actual practice of the Christian communities in which the evangelists wrote. Clearly a theological momentum which allowed more equal status to women in home, church, ministry, and society finds its genesis in the ministry of Jesus. That it continued is the witness of the Gospel writers.

Women in the Early Church. The NT presents diverse views on the role of women in the early church, reflecting the varied times and circumstances of its composition. The Christian communities, in the main, followed the example of their Lord by according to women fuller participation in both private and public spheres.

The Acts of the Apostles and the Pauline Letters give evidence to a greater freedom for women in relation to domestic concerns. No longer is the existence of the single woman (either VIRGIN or WIDOW) a despised and precarious one, rather her singleness affords her unique opportunities for ministry. The four virgin daughters of Philip, the widow Tabitha, and Paul's instructions to the unmarried (Acts 21:9; 9:36ff.; 1 Cor 7:32ff.) offer approbation to the single status as a viable (even preferable at times) means to discipleship for women. Whereas the life of the single woman in the OT had few prospects, these writings of the primitive church greatly elevate her status. The story of one woman, LYDIA of Thyatira (Acts 16:14ff.), is narrated without reference to her family relationships. The emphasis is upon her resourcefulness is helping give birth to the church in Philippi.

The married woman also has new egalitarian possibilities. She is seen as a full partner in marriage sexually (1 Cor 7:3ff.), economically (Acts 18:2-4), and in parental responsibility (Eph 6:1ff.). Often the household rules of Eph 5:22–6:9; Col 3:18-41; 1 Pet 3:1-7 are interpreted in a prescriptive way; actually they evidence the theological momentum engendered by Christ. These are conservative injunctions socially, and the usual order of society is not broken down, but the Christian understanding is clearly moving away from the old order to new relationships of mutual responsibility of love and respect. The movement is toward a model of marriage in which neither partner dominates the other; neither seeks personal growth at the expense of the other. Each partner is to act toward the other as he or she would toward the Lord. Neither is independent of the other; both find their fullest joy in serving one another in ways that show the self-emptying love of Jesus (cf. Phil 2:5-11).

Further, the married woman no longer participates in the religious community in a vicarious manner as the OT prescribed. The worshipping community of the early church forsook the exclusivistic structures of Temple and synagogue worship, where women were sequestered away from the men, even farther than the gentiles. Acts and the Letters record the struggle religiously and culturally to incorporate women in the work of the church (1 Cor 11:2-16; 14:34-35; 1 Tim. 2:12ff.). Marriage did not preclude an itinerant ministry for women; couples such as Priscilla and Aquila and Adronicus and Junia (KJV; Junias, RSV) travelled in the service of the gospel. Progress came more easily, however, for those more influenced by Greco-Roman customs than for the Jewish-Christian communities. The chief struggle for the latter seemed to be the question of the Law and gentile Christians; the Hellenistic Christians addressed the role of women more fully.

As in the ministry of Jesus, women were quite active in the missionary activity of the early church. They were teachers such as Priscilla (Acts 18:26), deacons like Phoebe (Rom 16:1), church workers as Euodia and Syntyche (Phil 4:2), apostles like Junia (Rom 16:7, KJV), prophets (1 Cor 11:2-16; Rev 2:20), to mention some of the more prominent ones.

That all Christians (including women) received the Holy Spirit (Rom 12:6ff.; 1 Cor 12:4-11; Eph 4:11-12) and served in a variety of ways in the early church is evident. However, a difficult question for NT scholarship and contemporary ecclesiastical polity is the degree to which women were a part of the official ministries of the church. The full development of a hierarchy of church offices is postbiblical, thus historical reconstruction in the first century is speculative.

Quite often contemporary interpreters will extrapolate the following argument: Jesus selected only men to comprise the Twelve; the Twelve constitutes the foundational leadership for the early church; therefore, the church's leadership today should be only male, as Jesus intended. This argument is flawed, however, for it accords a role to the Twelve that is beyond the evidence of the Bible. The early church was founded upon the apostolic witness, which was not restricted to men. It is the apostolic witness, further, that serves in a paradigmatic way for all subsequent ministries. The function of the Twelve is more limited, "eschatological and symbolic, not ministerial," according to Tetlow (121).

While in the OT priestly ministry (from which women were excluded) was focal, it falls into the background in the NT. The only NT reference to this genre of ministry is in Hebrews where it refers to Christ's priesthood (Heb 4:14–5:10). In Christ the priesthood has reached its culmination, needing no further representation. This cultic institution, with its rigorous exclusionary parameters, has become obsolete because of the priestly sacrifice of Christ (Heb 9:11-14).

The PASTORAL EPISTLES (and a few other isolated passages) note the presence of deacons (1 Tim 8:8-13), elders (1 Tim 5:17-20; cf. Jas 5:14-15), and bishops (1 Tim 3:1-6; Titus 1:5-9). The titles and functions of the offices are quite fluid; it is not until the patristic period of the church's history that each was given a distinct identity. One who looks to the NT for a blueprint for enduring church polity will be disappointed. Only general guidelines about Christian character and responsibilities are to be found. These guidelines do not preclude the participation of women. Further, the chief criterion determining church leadership appears to have been the particular community's situation and need. The presence of spiritual gifts and the willingness to employ them in the service of the church dictated the development of church leaders much more than gender did.

Life and ministry in the Christian community were christological in origin and character. Being conformed to the crucified and risen Christ defined the existence of the Christian. The NT emphasis is upon the ministry of Jesus which included both women and men. Empowered by the Spirit of the exalted Lord, Christians were to offer themselves in both the ministry of the word and the ministry of service. According to the evidence of the NT, the exclusion of women from ecclesiastical ministry is neither in accord with the teaching or practice of Jesus nor with that of the first-century church.

See also DEBORAH; FEMINIST HERMENEUTICS; HULDAH; LYDIA; MARY; PRISCILLA AND AQUILA; SOCIOLOGY OF THE NEW TESTAMENT; THE TWELVE; WOMEN IN THE OLD TESTAMENT.

Bibliography. G. B. Caird, "Paul and Women's Liberty," *BJRL* 54 (1971): 269-81; A. Y. Collins, ed., *Feminist Perspectives on Biblical Scholarship*; J. Danielou, *The Ministry of Women in the Early Church*; E. S. Fiorenza, *In Memory of Her* and "Women in the Prepauline and Pauline Churches," *USQR* 33 (1978): 153-66; E. Freed, "The Women in Matthew's Genealogy," *JSNT* 29 (1987): 3-19; R. Gryson, *The Ministry of Women in the Early Church*; E. M. Howe, *Women and Church Leadership*; J. Kopas, "Jesus and Women: Luke's Gospel," *Today* 53 (July 1986): 192-202; E. Moltmann-Wendel, *The Women Around Jesus*; C. F. Parvey, "The Theology and Leadership of Women in the New Testament," *Religion and Sexism* ed. R. R. Ruether; S. M. Schneiders, "Women in the Fourth Gospel and The Role of Women in the Contemporary Church," *BTB* 12 (1982): 35-45; E. Schweizer, "Traditional and Ethical Patterns in the Pauline and Post-Pauline Letters and Their Development," *Text and Interpretation* ed. E. Best and R. L. McL. Wilson; A. Spencer, *Beyond the Curse*; E. Stagg and F. Stagg, *Women in the World of Jesus*; L. Swidler, *Biblical Affirmation of Women*; E. M. Tetlow, *Women and Ministry in the New Testament*; R. C. Wahlberg, *Jesus and the Freed Woman*.

—MOLLY MARSHALL-GREEN

• **Women in the Old Testament.** In some OT texts, the woman appears to be little more than chattel at the disposal of men, especially of her father, husband or son (e.g., Gen 19:8; Exod 22:16ff.; Deut 22:22, 28-29; Judg 11; 19:24; Ruth 4:10). In the commandment not to covet, the neighbor's wife is listed among his possessions, along with his house, servants and stock (Exod 20:17; Deut 5:21). The word *ba'al*, frequently translated "husband," means "master" or "owner." Multiple wives (including concubines) were primarily symbols of a man's wealth and power. In one text, the men of the tribal assembly give the Benjaminite men permission to abduct women of Shiloh as wives (Judg 21). Most women were dependents within the realm of the family.

Some women (as well as men) were slaves. There is no question that they were considered property but, in certain periods at least, there were limitations on how they should be treated (e.g., Exod 21:1-11, 26-27).

Few women were independent. Among the sources of livelihood available to the independent woman was prostitution. Prostitution was tolerated in ancient Israel, but the prostitute (or HARLOT) was not considered socially acceptable.

The Hebrew scriptures realistically portray women as victims in the many wars that plagued the ancient Near East. In addition to the loss of fathers, sons and brothers who served as soldiers, women were raped, murdered or enslaved, and their children brutally killed before their eyes. Pregnant women were ripped open with the sword (e.g., Josh 6:21; Judg 5:28-30; 1 Sam 30:3; 2 Kgs 8:12; 15:16; Isa 14:2; Amos 1:13).

Despite ambiguities in the view of women in the OT, in Gen 1:26-27, woman is clearly said to be created in the IMAGE OF GOD. Gen 2:18 declares that she was created as a fit companion for or partner corresponding to man. The term *'ēzer*, which is often translated "helper" in Gen 2:18, is elsewhere applied to God (e.g., Deut 33:7, 26; Pss 33:20; 121:2; 146:5), strong evidence that it does not carry the connotation of inferiority or subordination. The creation of the woman is the climax of the account in Gen 2, because it provides for the possibility of community, commonality, and wholeness.

Theologians have often interpreted Gen 3:16 as a curse by God upon womankind, or as a description of the divinely ordained pattern of existence (though they seldom have looked upon the parallel in vv. 17-19 as the divinely ordained plan from which men should not deviate). Instead, Gen 3:16 reflects the reality of much of life that is not in accord with God's plan for human fulfillment.

Generally speaking, sexuality is seen as a gift (e.g., Gen 2:23-4). It provides for the possibility of fulfilling the injunction to "be fruitful and multiply" (Gen 1:28; 9:1). In the SONG OF SONGS, human love is celebrated. The woman, as well as the man, takes initiative in the relationship (Cant 3:1-3; 5:6). Mutuality is evidenced in 6:3a, "I am my beloved's and he is mine." Desire (which in Gen 3:16 is attributed to the woman) motivates the man as well (Cant 7:10).

Elsewhere, it is clear that the woman was expected to be a VIRGIN until marriage (Deut 22:13ff.). The woman moved out of her birth family to that of her husband, to whom she was expected to be faithful (e.g., Deut 22:22), though the same standard was not always expected of him. MALACHI, however looked upon marriage as a COVENANT to which both husband and wife should be faithful (Mal 2:14ff.).

Motherhood was so highly honored that God's love is compared to a mother's love (Isa 66:13; Hos 11:3-4). The root *rḥm*, from which the noun for "womb" is derived, is frequently used to express the compassion of God (e.g., Pss 111:4; 145:8; Neh 9:17; 2 Chr 30:9).

Birth, especially of a son, was celebrated, while infertility was the source of sorrow (e.g., Gen 30:1ff.; Ruth 4:13-17; 1 Sam 1:4ff.; Ps 127:3ff.). Prayer, vows, and the use of aphrodisiacs were resorted to in order to overcome infertility (Gen 25:21; 30:14ff.; 1 Sam 1:10ff.). Birth of daughters is often not even mentioned in narrative texts (e.g., Exod 2 records the birth of Moses as if he were the firstborn; the older sister who stands guard appears only when she plays a part in his story) or genealogy (note that Tamar is not mentioned along with David's sons in 2 Sam 3:2-5; 5:13-16). In about sixty percent of the passages that state who named the child, it is the mother. Mothers probably nursed their children for two or three years (cf. 1 Sam

1:19-24; cf. Ps 131:2).

Mother and father shared responsibility for children. The child was to respect and obey both parents (Exod 20:12; 21:15,17; Lev 19:3; Deut 5:16; 21:18ff.; Prov 20:20). The mother as well as the father functioned as teacher (Prov 1:8; 6:20; 31:1).

Generally speaking, throughout the period covered by the OT, most women in Israel held legitimate authority only in relation to their children. However, women had other sources of power. These include civil disobedience (Exod 1:15–2:10); persuasion (Judg 1:14-15; 1 Kgs 1:11ff.); use of "feminine wiles" (Gen 39:7-18; Judg 16:4-21); and shrewdness or deception (Gen 27:5ff.; 31:34-5; 1 Sam 19:11-17).

The OT provides only clues concerning the everyday life of women, and their role and status in FAMILY, public life and cult. The available data must be interpreted with caution and with concern for its context. Social, economic, and political changes and settings all impacted the lives of women, making broad generalizations suspect. In addition, the scripture does not even attempt to answer many of the questions now asked of it. Increasingly, scholars are turning to such fields as sociology and comparative anthropology to supplement what is known from archaeology and from the biblical text itself.

Women in Israel's History. Women appear prominently in the so-called patriarchal narratives as daughters, wives, mothers and servants or slaves, in the households of tribal leaders. The wives of the tribal fathers are depicted as taking initiative and exerting some control over their own lives. For example, HAGAR was sent away by ABRAHAM at SARAH's initiative (Gen 21:9-14). REBEKAH was asked whether she was willing to become the wife of ISAAC (Gen 24:58). RACHEL and LEAH made a deal that determined with whom JACOB would sleep (Gen 30:14-17). DINAH went out unattended to visit friends (Gen 34:1). Women who were slaves, however, lacked control of their own lives (Gen 16:2; 30:3, 9). And even the wives and daughters of the tribal leaders were expected to sacrifice themselves to save their husbands, fathers, or even male guests (e.g., Gen 12:10-13; 20:1-3; 19:5-8).

Although the historicity and provenance of these stories are debated, they appear to reflect a prestate family system. The impact of class differences on the role of women is evident. A central theme of these stories is barrenness and fertility. A woman was especially valued for her ability to bear children, especially sons, to build up the family.

In the period of the Exodus and wilderness, MIRIAM is pictured as a PROPHET and leader of Israel (Exod 15:20-21; Mic 6:4). Another text, perhaps a polemic stemming from later cultic conflict, criticizes Miriam for challenging the leadership of Moses while simultaneously demonstrating the respect that the people had for her (Num 12:1-15).

During the period when the Israelites were settling in the hill country, clearing land and building cisterns, most families probably lived in multifamily compounds that were essentially self-sufficient. There was neither centralized government nor centralized cult. According to Meyers, women were highly valued both for their contribution to subsistence agriculture and child bearing, which was needed to build up the population (which had been depleted by war, famine and plague) and to supply more labor for farming.

DEBORAH, an important leader during this time, is said to have been not only a deliverer, but also a judge dispensing justice and a prophet (Judg 4–5). The song celebrating the victory she inspired lauds her as "a mother in Israel" (Judg 5:7). Deborah may have been able to achieve a significant public role largely because she lived in a period of social upheaval when male-dominated structures had broken down.

Laws that probably date from the period of the monarchy seem to have provided women with increased protection from men (e.g., Deut 21:10-17; 22:13-21, 22-29; Deut 24:1-4). This was done, however, within the context of increased regulation of and decline in freedom for the peasantry as a whole as a way of subverting the power of the extended family over against the state. These regulations also functioned to increase social distance between royalty which ignored the regulations, and the common people. Centralization of wealth and power enabled a few women connected with the court in Jerusalem or Samaria to lead a life of luxury (cf. Ps 45:9-15 [H 10-16]; Amos 4:1-3; Isa 3:18-24). Some women in the royal household found themselves virtually powerless (e.g., MICHAL, 2 Sam 6:20-23; TAMAR, 2 Sam 13:1-20). Others, especially perhaps queen mothers (cf. 1 Kgs 15:13; 2 Chr 22:3), were in a position to influence the king (1 Kgs 1:11ff.).

JEZEBEL, Ahab's Sidonite queen, exercised cultic and political influence. She evidently controlled considerable economic resources (1 Kgs 18:19). As a result of her contempt for Yahwistic law (1 Kgs 21:1ff.) and defense of BAAL (1 Kgs 18:13ff.) she became a prototypic symbol of evil (e.g., Rev. 2:20). ATHALIAH, the only woman to rule directly, reigned over Judah for approximately six years (2 Kgs 11:1-20).

A major proportion of the upper class and of skilled workers were exiled after the fall of Jerusalem. The story of Joseph and POTIPHAR's wife (Gen 39) may have been told at that time to help preserve Israelite culture in exile, by warning men to avoid the temptation of attraction to Babylonian women. It is not surprising that many of the peasants who remained behind in Israel and Judah married women of other ethnic groups who remained or were settled on the land. In the postexilic period, EZRA led a campaign to rid the Israelite community of these women and their influence, resulting in the forced breakup of many families (Ezra 9–10).

Women in Religious Life. If there were women PRIESTS in ancient Israel, no direct evidence remains in the text. This may, in part be due to a correspondence between the military, public and cultic spheres. Women did serve in some way at the tabernacle (Exod 38:8; 1 Sam 2:22). They could seek an oracle (Gen 25:22f.) and participate in festivals (e.g., 1 Sam 1:3ff.; Deut 12:12; 16:10f.), though they were not required to do so (cf. Deut 16:16f.). Women could also make vows, but a man could cancel the vow of his wife or dependent daughter (Num 30:3ff.). Women served as *qědēšôt*, which is generally translated as "cult prostitutes" (Deut 23:17; Hos 4:14). Their precise function is debated, but there is no question that they came under heavy criticism, especially in the deuteronomic reform of the cult. Although at least in the later period, cultic participation of women was restricted due to laws of purity (e.g., Lev 15:19), women could be Temple singers (Ezra 2:65). They were expected to participate in covenant renewal assemblies (Deut 31:12; Neh 8:2).

The one major legitimate religious role that appears to have been open to women is that of prophet. The charismatic nature of the prophetic gift made it less subject to institutional restrictions. Miriam and Deborah are remembered from ancient times. HULDAH served during the late preexilic period in Judah. When the book of the law was discovered in the Temple during the reign of Josiah, it was Huldah to whom the king and top officials turned for advice. Her oracle may have begun the process of canonization of scripture as well as spurring reform of the cult and renewal of the covenant (cf. 2 Kgs 22:14-20).

Books Named for Women. Only two books of the Hebrew scripture bear the names of women: RUTH and ESTHER. Both are festival scrolls (*Megilloth*), numbered among the Writings (*Kethuvim*) in the Hebrew Bible. Ruth is read at the Festival of Weeks; Esther, at PURIM. In the Christian Bible, Ruth follows the Book of Judges, in which period the story is set. Ruth, a Moabite woman, and her Judean mother-in-law, NAOMI, exercise initiative and creativity to preserve the traditional family. Despite her Moabite origins, Ruth becomes the great-grandmother of DAVID. Esther, set in the Persian period, tells of a Jewish queen in the time of AHASUERUS (Xerxes), who uses her feminine wiles and persuasiveness to save her people from destruction at the hands of HAMAN, a highly placed court official. In the Christian Bible, Esther follows Nehemiah. Both Ruth and Esther tend to fade into the background during the final scenes of the stories that bear their names.

See also DEBORAH; ESTHER; FAMILY; HULDAH; PROPHET; RUTH; SONG OF SONGS.

Bibliography. P. Bird, "Images of Women in the Old Testament," *Religion and Sexism* ed. R. R. Reuther; J. C. Exum, " 'You Shall Let Every Daughter Live': A Study of Exodus 1:8-2:10," *Semeia* 28 (1983): 63-82; E. S. Gerstenberger and S. Schrage, *Woman and Man*; C. Meyers, *Discovering Eve* and *Ancient Israelite Women in Context*; S. Terrien, *Till the Heart Sings: A Biblical Theology of Manhood and Womanhood*; P. Trible, *God and the Rhetoric of Sexuality*; H. W. Wolff, *Anthropology of the Old Testament.*

—WILDA W. (WENDY) MORRIS

• **Word.** Among the OT roots translated "word," or "saying," the most important is *dābār*. The term can refer to a single word (2 Kgs 18:36), a statement (Exod 34:1) or a message (2 Kgs 22:13); it may also be translated "thing" or "matter" (Gen 15:1; 1 Sam 10:16). In legal contexts, it can be rendered "dispute" (Exod 18:16). It bore a special relationship to the prophets: just as the priests were known for the law, the wise men for their counsel, so the prophets were identified by the word (Jer 18:18).

This unique cluster of meanings surrounding the "word" may explain the degree to which it could take on a life of its own—even beyond what the author expressed. That was especially true about the words of blessing and curse (Gen 27:32-38; Num 22–24) and the prophetic word (1 Kgs 22). Here, the word appears to have possessed an inherent power enabling it to influence the course of events in human life, far beyond the reach of the speaker.

Among the NT Gk. words translated "word," the most important is *logos*. From an early sense of "counting" or "giving an account" it developed the meanings of "narrative," "word," or "speech" in classical Greek. However, in time it also came to indicate a metaphysical reality, such as divine reason, law, or cosmic principle.

We find both of these senses employed in the NT. For example, it is translated "saying" (1 Cor 15:54), "sentence" (Rom 13:9), "message" (Heb 2:2), "word," meaning the presentation or proclamation of Jesus (Mark 2:2; Luke 4:32) in distinction from the scripture (John 2:22). However, the second sense of *logos* also came to expression in the NT, which identified Christ as *the* word, meaning a divine being (John 1:1-14; cf. 1 John 1:1; Rev 19:13).

See also LOGOS/WORD.

—NIELS-ERIK A. ANDREASEN

• **Word of God.** The way God is revealed to humanity; also, "word of the Lord." The term appears frequently in the prophetic formulas: "The word of the Lord came" (Ezek 21:1; Hos 1:1; Joel 1:1), and "Hear the word of the Lord" (Isa 1:10; Hos 4:1). A prophetic ORACLE generally follows this introduction. The word from God did not always come to the prophet through speech, however, but was at times "seen" by the prophet (Isa 2:1; Amos 1:1). Either way, the prophet was responsible for relaying the word of God to the people (Amos 3:8). The Law, particularly the TEN COMMANDMENTS, is also called the word of God (Exod 24:4, 34:21-27; Ps 119:10-11). The word of God conveys God's unfailing plan or design for the world, God's people or the course of events (1 Sam 3:7; Isa 39:8, 55:11).

The word of God, therefore, represents God in action. It is dynamic and has a real impact upon the people toward whom it is directed. For example, the word of God can heal and rescue people in trouble (Ps 107:20); it can melt ice (Ps 147:17-19); it is like fire and like a hammer that breaks rock into pieces (Jer 23:29). By means of the word, God created the world (Gen 1:3ff.; Ps 33:6) and saved people (Ps 119:81). God's word lasts forever (Isa 40:8).

The NT speaks of the word of God, the word of Jesus Christ, and the word of the kingdom. The last two refer to the teachings of Jesus (Matt 13:19; Mark 4:14; Luke 9:26; John 8:31; Acts 20:35). The word of God, on the other hand, generally refers to the PREACHING of the apostles (Acts 4:31; 6:7) and also to the dynamic divine presence that acts upon human life (Heb 4:12; 1 Pet 1:23). Finally, the word of God is identified with the words of scripture (1 Pet 2:6-8; 2 Pet 1:19-20).

See also LOGOS/WORD; ORACLE; SCRIPTURE IN THE NEW TESTAMENT; SCRIPTURE IN THE OLD TESTAMENT.

—NIELS-ERIK A. ANDREASEN

• **Work.** *See* WAGES

• **Worship in the New Testament.** "Worship" is derived from the Old English *weorthscipe* referring to a person of worth. People tend to worship that institution or person which has for them the greatest worth. In the Judeo-Christian tradition, GOD alone is worthy of worship for God is ascribed supreme worth.

Certain mystical traditions stress the sense of awe experienced in the presence of the Holy. Worship is linked to feeling a sense of transcendence and in its most intense form results in ecstasy for the worshiper. The ultimate goal of this form of worship is to be lost in union with the Ultimate One. Although there are mystical traditions in both Judaism and Christianity, the mainstream of the Judeo-Christian heritage has defined worship in terms of acts of ritual and SERVICE. The two most common linguistic expressions of worship in the Hebrew language suggest action. One word (הִשְׁתַּחֲוָה) means "to bow down" and describes an act of acknowledgment of the holiness of God. The most frequently used word for worship (עָבַד) is derived from the word for "servant" and is related to the verb which means "to labor." Biblical worship was a response to God's disclosure of himself through his mighty acts before and on behalf of his people. The call to worship for Israel encapsulated the essence of the nation's worship: "You shall love the Lord your God with all your heart, and with all your soul, and with all your might'' (Deut 6:5). This command followed a review of God's saving acts, and a restatement of the basic commandments for relationships to God and community. The call was always to service. Worship was a ritual act which reminded the worshipers of what God had done for humans and what they were expected to do in return. Worship was a bridge between the acts of God in human experience and appropriate daily living by those for whom he had acted.

The worship of the patriarchs was marked by its pilgrim character. God spoke to various individuals, entered into COVENANT with them, rescued them, called them to repentance or renewed covenant with them, and they responded with worship. This worship usually included the building of an altar which became a memorial of the experience. There were no priests or prescribed rituals unless one chooses to interpret the head of clan as functioning in such a role. Out of personal encounters emerged personal missions. The relationship between experience with God and service is inescapable. The devotion of the patriarchs and matriarchs was measured in terms of faithful service.

The Mosaic period produced a larger sense of community and introduced congregational worship. The community was formed in the EXODUS experience and the covenant which followed. The terms of the covenant, the expected response to God's deliverance, were spelled out in the TORAH which was at the center of worship and all life. Congregational worship was institutionalized with the construction of the Tabernacle. The establishment of the priesthood created a body of interpreters of the Torah who assembled the people to hear and respond. The people were continually reminded of the presence of God among them. The mobility of the Tabernacle symbolized the missionary character of the people and their worship. God was on the move with his people. The major development in this period was corporate as opposed to personal acts of worship.

The worship practices of Israel were shaped in part by her interaction with Canaanite worship. The exposure to other forms of worship affected the rites but not the focus of worship as encounter between God and people. The building of the Temple centralized worship and tended to diminish the pilgrim character of the experience. A pioneering spirit gave way to a settler mentality. The structure and trappings of the Temple reflected the influence of Solomon's foreign wives. The distinguishing feature of Israelite worship continued to be its ethical faith. The end of worship was responsible living rooted in the righteousness of God. Long before the prophets' demands for reform the emphasis in Hebrew worship was on righteous living as faith response. Ritual acts were only effective when the attitude of the people allowed the rites to be instruments of the Spirit.

The NT clearly records the birth of Christian worship from the womb of Jewish faith and expression. Christianity maintained much of what had been developed in the evolution of Israelite worship and its modification in the synagogues which arose during the EXILE. The major distinguishing feature of early Christian worship was celebration of the coming of the long anticipated Messiah, Jesus of Nazareth. Christian worship is structured around promise and fulfillment. The OT promises which were fulfilled in Christ warrant Christian hope that the promises as yet unrealized will be fulfilled.

Christian observances such as BAPTISM and the Eucharist are symbols which replace CIRCUMCISION and the PASSOVER as reminders of deliverance and covenant, past, present, and future. Passover recalled Israel's salvation from slavery and the Eucharist is a meal of thanksgiving for salvation from sin. At the table of the Lord, the sacrifice of Christ on the cross is represented and the implied covenant of faith and personal responsibility is renewed.

Baptism symbolizes the new birth in Christ and initiates the convert into the community of faith. The act dramatically portrays the death and resurrection of Jesus and calls the baptized to live as those who have been reborn in the image of God and to reflect his righteousness in daily living.

The stress in NT worship continues to be on service. The Greek words most important to describing worship are similar to Hebrew counterparts. One word (λατρεία) is rendered ''service'' or ''worship'' and another (λειτουργία) is borrowed from secular life and refers to voluntary or obligatory service to the state or community. The connotations make it impossible to separate worship and service. Worship can be described as the hub around which the life of the believing community revolves. Evangelism, social action, education, crisis care, and other aspects of life together are spokes which arise out of the experience of God's revelation and continuing presence. Ritual is a dramatic portrayal of God's gifts that obligate his people to offer their gifts in return. Rom 12:1 echos the Israelite call to worship: ''I appeal to you therefore brethren, by the mercies of God, to present your bodies as a living sacrifice, holy and acceptable to God, which is your spiritual worship.'' Christian worship is never completed in a sanctuary. It issues in the action of God and is completed in the action of the people of God.

The elements of worship take on different forms in various historical periods and diverse cultures but remain the same in essence. The primary elements of worship, apart from the rituals of sacrifice, changed little from OT to NT. Music is the language of the soul which often expresses the ineffable. Music combined with words in singing intensify feeling and support understanding. The reading and teaching of scripture are vital elements in putting meaning to revelation and explaining mission. Prayer dramatically portrays the revelation-response pattern of the divine-human encounter. It demonstrates the dependence of creature on creator. Offering of gifts and self is the ritual portrayal of the proper relationship between God and humanity. These elements have been ever present in the history of Christian worship practice.

See also CIRCUMCISION; COVENANT; EXODUS; FASTING; FEASTS AND FESTIVALS; GOD; HOLINESS IN THE NEW TESTAMENT; HOLINESS IN THE OLD TESTAMENT; LORD'S SUPPER; MUSIC/MUSICAL INSTRUMENTS; PASSOVER; PRIESTS; REVELATION, CONCEPT OF; SERVICE; TEMPLE/TEMPLES; TABERNACLE; TENT OF MEETING.

Bibliography. H. Davies, *Christian Worship: Its History and Meaning*; G. Delling, *Worship in the New Testament*; R. P. Martin, *Worship in the Early Church*; H. H. Rowley, *Worship in Ancient Israel: Its Forms and Meaning*.

—RAYMOND BAILEY

• **Worship In The Old Testament.** ''Worship'' in the Hebrew Bible is expressed in a rich variety of terms and expressions: ''to bow down'' (prostration) before God (Gen 24: 26, 48), ''to serve'' (service) God (Exod 3:12; 4:23), ''to seek the face of the Lord'' (Ps 78:34), and ''to seek'' (Deut 4:29) or ''to draw near to'' God (1 Sam 14:36). In pulling these terms together, worship may be understood as the ordered response of homage paid by the Israelite community to God who had brought them into existence and continued to dwell in their midst. This response consisted of the designation and maintenance of sacred places where God dwells or appears, sacred seasons celebrating God's redeeming and life-sustaining actions on behalf of the community, rituals that reenact divine actions and dramatically convey the community's story and beliefs, sacred music and psalms, and priests who maintain the institutions of worship and officiate during worship services. Worship incorporates Israel's traditions of sacred history, creation, covenant, and law. The primary objective of Israelite worship was to maintain an ongoing relationship with God in order to secure the divine blessings of well-being and life.

Sacred Space. Sacred space is the place where divine presence may be located. Sacred places included mountains, trees, streams, territory marked off by stones, and especially sanctuaries. Sacred territory was preserved by prohibitions and privileges. Since the space inhabited by God was holy (literally "set apart"), it could be approached only by people who were in a state of ritual and moral purity. During Israel's sojourn in the wilderness of SINAI, the Tabernacle was the place for divine appearances (Exod 33:7-11). The TEMPLE of JERUSALEM was built on the place where the angel of the Lord had stood and where David had erected his altar (2 Sam 24:16-25).

Temples were houses or palaces built for God. Prior to the establishment of the monarchy, temples were located in such cities as SHECHEM, SHILOH, BETHEL, and BEERSHEBA. During the monarchy royal sanctuaries were built in important cities, especially Jerusalem and later on, SAMARIA. While David brought the ARK of the Covenant to Jerusalem and placed it in a sacred tent, SOLOMON is responsible for building the Temple of God (1 Kgs 5–9; 2 Chr 2–8) which served as first a royal sanctuary and then a national shrine. During the deuteronomic reform (late seventh century), worship was centralized in Jerusalem. While other temples were later constructed in Gerizim and elsewhere, traditional Jews accepted only the Temple in Jerusalem as legitimate. Sacred objects associated with the Jerusalem Temple included the altar of incense, the altar of sacrifice, the Ark of the Covenant, and the sea of bronze (a basin used for ritual purification).

Of course there was opposition to the temples, including the one in Jerusalem, coming from certain of the prophets. They saw temples as concessions to Canaanite religion and as efforts to insulate the kings against criticism. Indeed, for rural prophets the temples and their rituals were ready reminders of the economic oppression of the farmers by kings and priests who lived in luxury (Amos 5:21-27).

Sanctuaries and other sacred places were understood to be the dwelling place of God. As such they served as signs of divine grace and election. However, there was the tension between the belief in the transcendence of God who dwelt in heaven and the belief in the immanence of God who dwelt among his people. While never resolved, the issue was often one of religious debate and strife. Deuteronomy attempted to solve the problem by stating that God resided in heaven, but made his name to dwell in the Temple (Deut 12:5, 11; 1 Kgs 8:17, 29).

Sacred Seasons. Worship occurs during sacred periods which are distinguished from the normal times of everyday activities. The seventh day of the week was the SABBATH, a name derived from the Heb. verb meaning "to cease working, to rest." In Gen 2:2-3 the priestly writer explains that God rested on the seventh day and "hallowed" it, i.e. set it apart from the other days of the week. In the form of the Ten Commandments found in Exod 20:2-17, Israel is to "remember the sabbath day, to keep it holy" by abstaining from work. The reason given is that this is the day blessed by God when he rested from his labors in creating the world. In the parallel text in Deut 5:6-21, Israel is to "observe the sabbath day" by abstaining from work, because they were slaves in Egypt who were delivered from bondage by the Lord. In Exod 31:12-17 the Sabbath is an "everlasting sign," an "unbreakable covenant" between Yahweh and Israel. Thus in observing the Sabbath and by refraining from labor, Israel remembers the Lord of the covenant who is creator and redeemer, and they participate in the blessings of life and deliverance granted to them. The Sabbath was thus a day of rest and a joyful day of worship when people visited the sanctuaries. After the destruction of the Temple of Jerusalem, the Sabbath became even more important, for it became the key indication of Judah's covenant relationship with God. More stringent observations were required following the return from exile, including prohibitions against business and traveling.

Israel also celebrated annual festivals, the earliest ones being UNLEAVENED BREAD and PASSOVER, WEEKS, and TABERNACLES. These were celebrations of joy in which God was thanked for his blessings. These festivals were filled with dancing, singing, music, meals, and sacrifices. The Feast of Unleavened Bread was a seven day festival that originally celebrated the beginning of barley harvest (Exod 23:15; 34:18-20). Early on it was combined with the Passover festival. Passover marked the deliverance of the Hebrews from Egyptian bondage during the period of the EXODUS (Exod 12:1-16). Passover unified the bonds of the families throughout the generations as they sat down at table together to eat the Passover meal and to recount the story of their deliverance.

The Festival of Weeks occurred at the start of the wheat harvest, some seven weeks (fifty days) after the beginning of the barley harvest (Lev 23:15-21; Num 28:26-31). It came to mark the covenant between God and Israel at Sinai. The Feast of Tabernacles, celebrated for eight days in the early fall, was a harvest festival for the produce of the threshing floor and the winepress (Lev 23:39-43). This festival commemorated God's guidance and sustaining of Israel in the Sinai wilderness during the journey from Egypt to Canaan.

Later festivals included Hanukkah (the FEAST OF DEDICATION) which commemorated the rededication of the Temple altar by Judas Maccabeus in 164 B.C.E. (1 Macc 4:36-59; 2 Macc 10:6-8) and PURIM, the festival that called to mind the deliverance of the Jews in Persia from Haman (Esth 9:19-28). It is possible that ancient Israel, like later Judaism, celebrated a NEW YEAR'S FESTIVAL in close proximity to the Festival of Tabernacles and the DAY OF ATONEMENT. The New Year's Festival would have celebrated the victory of the creator over chaos, the renewal of life, and the ascent of God to the throne as king over the cosmos and the nations. During the monarchy it would have been the occasion for the enthronement of the king who ruled the nation as God's representative.

In contrast to festivals of joy and celebration, fasts were practices that recalled times of misfortune and sin. The single annual fast was the Day of Atonement, during which the people abstained from work, food, and drink and called to mind their sins. To atone for their sins during the past year, the high priest entered the Holy of Holies in the Temple, the one time he was allowed entrance during the year, and offered incense. The sins of the nation were placed upon a "scapegoat," which was then driven into the wilderness (Lev 23:27-32).

Sacrifice. Sacrifices were an important part of Israelite worship, representing gifts to God, communion between God and the worshipers, and the forgiveness of sins (Lev 1–7). The more important sacrifices included the burnt, cereal, peace, sin and guilt offerings. Sacrifices were not magical acts that automatically guaranteed divine blessing, but were to be offered according to proper instructions and with the right heart. God was ultimately the one who decided to accept the offering.

Prayer. Prayer was another important act of worship in the OT. Prayer often accompanied sacrifice, and involved the act of intercession on behalf of the ones making the offering. The Psalter probably served as Israel's prayerbook, with its collections of hymns in praise of God, laments expressing the desire for divine redemption, and thanksgivings for God's blessings. Prayer was normally offered in the Temple, probably during the morning and evening services. Following the Exile, Jews living outside Jerusalem faced the holy city and offered their prayers some three times a day (evening, morning, and noon).

Music. Israelite worship had an important place for music. First Chr 15–16 outlines the role of the Levites in the music service of the Temple, though this description probably reflects a pattern that developed in the postexilic period. Music in the Temple included the singing of psalms and the playing of instruments (2 Chr 29:20-30). The ram's horn (SHOPHAR) was blown during the period of national celebration (1 Kgs 1:34; 2 Kgs 9:13). Other instruments included the lyre, trumpet, flute, harp, and tambourine. From the headings of the psalms some information is gained about the levitical musicians who wrote and performed the music, along with the purpose and instructions for performance. Israel's hymnal was the psalter, containing some 150 compositions drawn from a period of several centuries.

Priests. The priesthood was an inherited office. A man became a priest by virtue of birth into the priestly families of the tribe of Levi. He became holy by virtue of his work. No longer a part of the world of the everyday, the priest, like the sanctuary and the offerings that were presented there, was "set apart" for the service of God (Num 8:14; Deut 10:8). A priest was ordained in an elaborate ceremony (Exod 29; Lev 8). He was officially invested when he first performed the ritual of offering a sacrifice on the altar. This act of investiture was literally called "filling the hand" (Exod 29:22-34; Lev 8:22-33). The priest could exist in sacred space and time, without profaning the holy. But to enter or remain in a state of holiness, the priest was subject to special rules of purity. These included: the prohibitions against participating in funerals, since touching the dead defiled them; marrying a divorcee or a former prostitute; and drinking alcohol when entering the sanctuary. To enter the sanctuary, he had to purify himself and dress in special vestments.

The priest served in the sanctuary and its sacred territory. The major tasks of the priest included sacrifice, the giving of divine oracles, and instructing the people in sacred and ethical duties. While the person making the offering was normally the one who slaughtered the animal, the priest placed the blood and the part of the victim that belonged to God on the altar. Likewise incense was burnt upon the altar (Deut 33:10). The privilege of approaching the altar was reserved to the priesthood alone. The priest delivered divine oracles to worshipers who wished to consult the Lord (cf. 1 Sam 14:41-43). The priest obtained a word from God by means of drawing the sacred lots (URIM AND THUMMIM) from his vestment (EPHOD). The lots were probably dice or sticks which gave a yes or no answer. As teachers, the priests were in charge of instructing the people in laws of purity, regulations of worship, and moral conduct (Lev 19:10-11; Hos 4:6). In all of these functions, the priest served as a mediator between God and the people. In this role, he was the channel of divine blessing and made it possible for God to dwell in the midst of the chosen people.

Levites. Originally Levites were the priests who performed the duties just described. Deuteronomy indicates that the Levites comprised the entire priesthood, though they lived in various places throughout the land. Deuteronomy also makes provisions for the Levites to come to Jerusalem and to be accepted by the sons of Zadok as fully authorized priests there as well. During the early postexilic period, the Levites were demoted to servants and musicians in the Temple, while the priests were those who reserved to themselves alone the priestly prerogatives. The Book of Chronicles gives the Levites a more prominent role, while still maintaining the separation from the priests.

Worship in the OT centered on the major elements of Israelite faith: creation, salvation history, covenant, and law. In one understanding, the Sabbath service, grounded in a theology of creation, revitalized and sustained the beneficent orders of life for nature and community. In another understanding the Sabbath was based on Exodus liberation theology. In the resting of the entire community on the seventh day, Israelites remembered their deliverance from Egyptian slavery and realized the moral imperative of freedom from oppressive labor.

The three ancient festivals celebrated God's redemptive and gracious acts on Israel's behalf, including the Exodus from Egypt, the covenant and gift of law at Sinai, and divine guidance and sustenance in the wilderness. Associated with the major agricultural harvests, the festivals honored God as the giver of the fruits of the earth that made life possible. The New Year's festival proclaimed the creator's victory over chaos and the enthronement of God over the cosmos and the nations. And the same festival announced the enthronement of the human king as God's representative, whose rule of justice was to produce a righteous and blessed community.

In the celebration of all of these elements of faith, Israelites did more than simply recall the past. Rather, they made the redemptive and beneficent qualities of the past present in their lives. And they envisioned the future acts of God's blessings and redemption, realizing in a present moment of the worship service the glorious expectations of future hope.

See also ATONEMENT, DAY OF; FEASTS AND FESTIVALS; LEVI/LEVITES; MUSIC/MUSICAL INSTRUMENTS; NEW YEAR'S FESTIVAL; PRAYER/THANKSGIVING IN THE OLD TESTAMENT; PRIESTS; PSALMS, BOOK OF; SACRIFICE; TEMPLE/TEMPLES.

Bibliography. H. J. Kraus, *Worship in Israel*; S. Mowinckel, *The Psalms in Israel's Worship*; H. H. Rowley, *Worship in Ancient Israel*; W. Harrelson, *From Fertility Cult to Worship*; R. de Vaux, *Ancient Israel*.

—LEO G. PERDUE

• **Wrath of God.** In the primitive portions of the OT God is depicted as one who cherished resentment against the wicked and demanded appeasement before his anger was checked. In the burning bush epiphany one of the first characteristics of Yahweh that Moses experienced was his anger (Exod 4:14). Other passages in the Pentateuch bear witness to the whimsical and irrational nature of God's wrath (Exod 32:10f.; Num 11:1-10; Num 16:1-50). Despite his good intentions, God's anger killed Uzzah when he grasped the Ark of the Covenant to prevent its falling from the cart (2 Sam 6:6-7). Though God told David to take a census of the Israelites, violent anger inflicted grave punishment on the nation (2 Sam 24:1-17). A later writer, representing an advanced stage of religious thought in postexilic days, attributed the census to Satan's temptation of David (1 Chr 21:1). In the foregoing passages Yahweh's wrath resembled the bad temper of a man whose emotions were uncontrolled.

From the eighth-century prophets through the interbiblical period, the nomadic notion of Yahweh acting on whim and caprice was tempered with love and mercy. Gradually God's wrath was rationalized and moralized. This was especially true of Deuteronomy and those writings influenced by deuteronomic theology. If disaster came upon Israel, it was definitely deserved. Punishment came because the people worshiped other gods or disobeyed the commandments of God. The manifestation of God's anger was no longer through the forces of nature but the shame of defeat by an enemy nation.

Paul is the only NT writer who attempted to clarify the nature of God's wrath. The passage that most clearly described this characteristic of God is Rom 1:18-32, where Paul painted a dark, grim, and repulsive picture of the pagan world with its deluge of moral disorders effected by humanity's alienation from God. The refusal to worship God caused the people to fall under the power of evil. They lost their spiritual discernment and separated themselves from the one who could give them enlightenment.

While most scholars readily admit that Paul at no time considered the wrath of God as an emotional quality in deity, there are various views concerning his meaning of the phrase. Some believe that Paul was referring to the inevitable process of cause and effect in a moral universe. Others attempt to relate Paul's meaning to *karma* in Hinduism. The most acceptable view interprets Paul to mean a condition or situation in which people are alienated from God. The traditional day of wrath announced by the prophets as a time of God's judgment in the age to come was for Paul a present reality. This day had already arrived (Rom 2:5; 1 Thess 2:16), and the Jews were alienated from God because they rejected Jesus as Lord.

See also GOD; JUDGMENT, DAY OF; MERCY; RELIGION OF ISRAEL; VENGEANCE/AVENGER.

Bibliography. A. T. Hanson, *The Wrath of the Lamb*; T. C. Smith, "The Wrath of God," *RE* 45/2 (Apr 1948): 193-208; R. V. G. Tasker, *The Biblical Doctrine of the Wrath of God.*

—T. C. SMITH

• **Writing Systems.** *Types of writing.* Writing, ancient and modern, can be divided into three major types: logograms or logographs, syllabaries, and alphabets. Logograms are individual signs that represent a whole word or several words. Logograms can be either symbolic, such as "3" representing the number and quantity three, or pictograms, such as a picture of a ball representing the word "ball" or the picture of a person walking representing the verbal concept "walk." Syllabaries use one sign to represent each syllable, or occasionally several syllables. A syllable is composed of at least one consonant and one vowel in patterns such as CV consonant-vowel (*ba*), VC (*ab*), CVC (*bal*). Alphabets normally have separate signs for each phoneme. Each consonant has its own sign, and those alphabets which represent vowels have signs for each vowel sound.

A Coptic writing board.

An early Cuneiform tablet.

In addition, writing systems may produce other signs including punctuation, accentuation, determinatives, and phonetic complements. Determinatives are signs preceding or following a word denoting the category to which the word belongs. In Sumerian and Akkadian, the sign *dingir* precedes the proper names of deities. The sign indicates that the name following is that of a deity. The *dingir* will be used whether the name is that of a deity or is part of a personal or place name that contains as an element a deity name.

Phonetic complements are syllables preceding or following a word that aid pronunciation by reduplicating a syllable sound. Because many signs could represent multiple syllables, the phonetic complement would indicate which of the possible syllables was intended.

Economic factors probably led to the development of

writing. Earliest tablets seem to indicate primarily quantities of goods and ownership for trade, taxation, public storage, receipts, bills of sale, estate records and the like. Agriculture and livestock are among the most common items listed.

The major writing systems of the ancient Near East will be discussed by region, beginning with Mesopotamia, probably the earliest system in the ancient Near East, followed by Egypt, and finally the scripts of Syria/Palestine.

Cuneiform. When one thinks of Mesopotamia, one of the first features one notes is cuneiform writing. Cuneiform literally means wedge shaped, and is derived from the distinctive form of the writing. Most common was the rectangular clay tablet of a size that would fit into the hand, shaped and smoothed, and allowed to dry leather hard so that it could be held without deforming. A reed stylus with a triangular or rectangular head was used to impress wedge shaped strokes on the tablet. The tablet was then allowed to dry thoroughly, at times sun-baked, but very often fired in an oven like pottery so that it became nearly indestructible. Tens of thousands of these tablets have been recovered from excavations throughout the ancient Near East, primarily Mesopotamia.

The cuneiform script first appeared about 3400 B.C.E. with the Sumerians who inhabited Lower Mesopotamia. These earliest writings were pictographic, but soon were reduced to wedges and were simplified losing much of the pictographic nature. Also Sumerian very early moved from logography to a combination of logography and syllabary. Some signs continued to represent entire words, but more represented individual syllables.

The cuneiform script makes use of two basic types of signs usually given their German names, the *keil* or simple stroke made by one edge of the stylus. The other stroke is the *winkelhaken,* in which the stylus is turned so that two edges of the stylus head are impressed to form an angle.

Cuneiform was adapted and used as the script for many unrelated languages. The Sumerian language is an agglutinative nonsemitic language with no known relatives. The writing system invented by the Sumerians was soon taken over by other peoples and languages: Assyrian, Babylonian, Eblaite, Elamite, Hittite, Hurrian, and Persian, as well as many localized dialects such as the Canaanite Akkadian of the Amarna letters.

The geographical extent of cuneiform ranged from Mesopotamia, Persia and Elam in the east to portions of Asia Minor and Syria-Palestine in the west, and to Egypt in the south (although there is no evidence that cuneiform was actually used in Egypt, the presence of the Amarna corpus shows that cuneiform was used in diplomatic correspondence with Egypt and thus had to be understood there).

The time frame of cuneiform extends from about 3400 B.C.E. when it was first developed by the Sumerians until the first century C.E. when the last cuneiform writings were produced. Cuneiform, as the script for the Sumerian and Akkadian languages, became the *lingua franca* of most of the ancient Near Eastern world from before 3000 B.C.E. until it was superseded by the alphabetic ARAMAIC in the seventh to sixth centuries B.C.E.

After cuneiform fell out of use, knowledge of the languages was lost. The cuneiform languages remained as lost languages until the late 1700s and early 1800s when European travelers began to bring back cuneiform tablets from travels in the Near East. Several scholars contributed to the decipherment of cuneiform, but the major work was that of Sir Henry Rawlinson. The key to the decipherment of cuneiform was the trilingual BEHISTUN inscription. Carved high on the Behistun rock, the inscription depicts Darius I and several attendants and gives the inscription in Old Persian, Elamite and Babylonian. Rawlinson used much the same principle as Champollion had used some twenty to thirty years earlier to decipher the ROSETTA STONE, seeking proper names (cf. below). Unlike the Rosetta stone, the Behistun rock did not have a known language. Rawlinson made the inspired guess that one of the languages might be an ancient form of the Persian (Farsi) spoken in the area. He also assumed that the inscriptions would repeat the same basic message. Quite fortunately for Rawlinson, one of the three languages was indeed Old Persian. Also fortunately, Old Persian had only thirty-six signs and four determinatives as opposed to the over 300 signs of most cuneiform languages. Rawlinson was able very quickly to decipher the Old Persian. He was then able to decipher enough of the Babylonian to give the key to the cuneiform languages. Still Sumerian and Elamite were not well understood until many years later.

The Akkadians took over the Sumerian script and used it for their semitic language. The Sumerian symbol LU = man became Akkadian *awilum* = man. The Sumerian GAL = big became *rabum* = big, great. The Sumerian LU.GAL = king, great man became *sarrum* = king. Similarly the Sumerian determinatives were taken as the Akkadian equivalents. Thus KUR = land became *matum,* and URU = city became *al.* So the Akkadian word Babylon could be preceded by the determinative *matu* and refer to the land of Babylon or by the determinative *al* and refer to the city of Babylon.

Some confusion is caused by the use of the terms Akkadian, Assyrian, and Babylonian in reference to the semitic language and script of Mesopotamia. The broader term Akkadian refers to the semitic language branch. It has two major dialects: Assyrian and Babylonian centered largely in the homeland of the empires bearing the same name, Assyria to the north on the Tigris River, Babylonia on the Euphrates to the south. The dialects and scripts are similar but do show some variants.

The signs themselves show considerable development over the three to four millennia of cuneiform's existence. The table below shows the development of a few signs from Sumerian through Old Akkadian to neo-Assyrian or neo-Babylonian. The general tendency in the signs is first away from the pictographic. Then once the wedge pattern of cuneiform was established, the general move is toward simplification of signs.

The recently recovered archive from EBLA has given scholars a new semitic language based on cuneiform. Most of the tablets from Ebla are in Sumerian, the *lingua franca* of the time. But a smaller number are in the Eblaite language, a previously unknown language with similarities to Northwest semitic languages including Ugaritic, the Canaanite of the AMARNA tablets, and even Hebrew. Among the finds from Ebla are bilingual word lists or dictionaries giving the Eblaite equivalent of Sumerian terms. Also quite interesting was the type of archive storage used at Ebla. The tablets were placed on wooden shelves in rows from front to back. In the conflagration that destroyed Ebla at about 2250 B.C.E., the shelves burned and the tablets fell to the floor. Many remained in their original order as they fell and were covered and preserved by the debris of the destruction. In some cases, the first tablet in the row listed the contents of the tablets behind it, perhaps the world's first card-catalog system!

LETTER		NAME		PRONOUNCIATION
UPPER	LOWER	GREEK	ENGLISH	
Α	α	ἄλφα	alpha	*a* as in *father*
Β	β	βῆτα	beta	*b* as in *barber*
Γ	γ	γάμμα	gamma	*g* as in *girl*
Δ	δ	δέλτα	delta	*d* as in *doubt*
Ε	ε	ἔ ψιλόν	epsilon	*e* as in *get*
Ζ	ζ	ζῆτα	zeta	*z* as in *zoo*
Η	η	ἦτα	ēta	*a* as in *gate*
Θ	θ	θῆτα	thēta	*th* as in *thug*
Ι	ι	ἰῶτα	iōta	*i* as in *picnic*
Κ	κ	κάππα	kappa	*k* as in *kumquat*
Λ	λ	λάμβδα	lambda	*l* as in *lump*
Μ	μ	μῦ	mu	*m* as in *mud*
Ν	ν	νῦ	nu	*n* as in *nonsense*
Ξ	ξ	ξῖ	xi	*x* as in *relax*
Ο	ο	ὂ μικρόν	omicron	*o* as in *omelet*
Π	π	πῖ	pi	*p* as in *price*
Ρ	ρ	ῥῶ	rhō	*r* as in *rang*
Σ	σ, ς	σίγμα	sigma	*s* as in *successful*
Τ	τ	ταῦ	tau	*t* as in *tight*
Υ	υ	ὖ ψιλόν	upsilon	*u* as in *upper*
Φ	φ	φῖ	phi	*ph* as in *phosphorus*
Χ	χ	χῖ	chi	*ch* as in German *ich*
Ψ	ψ	ψῖ	psi	*ps* as in *lips*
Ω	ω	ὦ μέγα	omega	*o* as in *note*

Greek alphabet with English transliterations.

One other cuneiform archive that needs mention is the Amarna collection. These tablets were discovered at Tell el-Amarna in Egypt in 1887. The tablets which date to the fourteenth century B.C.E., were written by the vassal rulers of Canaanite city-states to the Egyptian pharaoh, chiefly Akhenaton. Although written in Akkadian, these tablets exhibit many of the dialectical peculiarities of Canaanite and help in understanding the Canaanite language prior to the coming of the Hebrews.

Hieroglyphics is the pictographic and syllabic writing system known from ancient Egypt. Although the name has also been used by some writers in reference to other scripts such as Hittite and Cretan, its original use was limited to Egypt. A distinction must be noted between the language of Egypt and the scripts used to produce that language. Certainly the language underwent development, but the language remains identifiable through hieroglyphics, hieratic, and demotic, even preserving much of its character in Coptic. However, the scripts are quite distinct. Although the development from hieroglyphics to hieratic to demotic can be traced, each was a distinct script, and for many centuries all three existed side by side. Coptic is an alphabetic script introduced only late in Egypt's history.

The word hieroglyphics literally means ''sacred carving'' and came from the Greek language. The early Greeks saw the hieroglyphic inscriptions on monuments and assumed the language was used only for holy writing.

The key to deciphering Egyptian hieroglyphics was the Rosetta Stone. This trilingual monument, written in hieroglyphics, demotic, and Greek, was recovered by the army of Napoleon in 1801. The text of the hieroglyphics was partly missing as was the last part of the Greek portion. Only the Greek could be immediately deciphered. The French scholar Françoise Champollion and the British scholar Thomas Young, working independently, made the major breakthroughs in understanding hieroglyphics. They assumed that the three portions of text recorded the same basic message. They both found in the hieroglyphics portion a number of cartouches, a group of hieroglyphic symbols surrounded by an oval line. They further noted that several of the cartouches had the same hieroglyphic characters and deduced correctly that these cartouches were proper names.

Egyptian	Protosinaitic	Phoenician	Greek	Latin
			A	A
			Γ	G
			K	K
			M	M
			O	O
			P	R
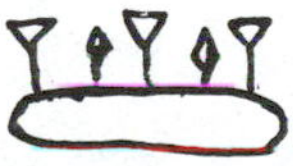			Σ	S

Since the name Ptolemy occurred frequently in the Greek portion of the Rosetta Stone, they were able to find the hieroglyphic syllables for Ptolemy. Young was never able to progress much further in the decipherment. Champollion, however, soon found cartouches with the names Cleopatra, Autocrater, Alexandra. And from other proper names on both the Rosetta Stone and other hieroglyphic inscriptions, he developed the key to deciphering hieroglyphics. Like Sumerian and Akkadian, Egyptian frequently made use of determinatives to indicate the class of a word.

Hieroglyphics began as pictographs and maintained a recognizable pictographic quality throughout the history of the script. Early hieroglyphics were apparently logograms, with one sign representing a whole word. Later the hieroglyphs came to represent syllables, though the vowels were apparently never indicated. These syllables could contain one, two or three consonants. The hieroglyphic writing system was used primarily for public and monumental purposes. For other economic and administrative purposes and individual writing, two cursive scripts developed, hieratic and demotic. Like hieroglyphic script, both these cursive scripts take their name from the Greek, meaning ''sacred'' and ''popular'' respectively. The hieratic often maintained an observable relationship to the hieroglyphic signs, but was greatly simplified. The demotic script was an extreme form of cursive having only the slightest relationship to hieroglyphic signs. Hieratic came into use quite early, but demotic is not found until the Third Intermediate Period, eighth or seventh centuries B.C.E.

Alphabet. Although alphabetic writing systems developed later in the ancient Near East than the other scripts, the alphabetic systems have had the greatest impact, especially on Western civilization. An alphabetic script is so important because it greatly reduces the number of signs necessary to reproduce the language. Typical syllabaries, whether hieroglyphic or cuneiform have many hundreds of signs. Only a few specially trained scribes could master either system. But an alphabetic system required only approximately thirty signs. Thus writing was much more accessible to the masses once the alphabetic principle developed. Although at least one alphabetic script developed from cuneiform (UGARITIC, along with a few alphabetic tables using the same script found at Beth-shemesh, Taanach, and Nahal Tavor), all other ancient Near Eastern alphabetic scripts developed from Proto-Sinaitic or Old Canaanite. It is quite interesting to note that all alphabetic scripts in the region, and consequently all Western alphabets, develop from semitic languages. The alphabet is certainly one of the most important gifts of Syria/Palestine to the world.

Semitic-speaking peoples of the Sinai peninsula, apparently working in Egyptian turquoise mines adapted certain hieroglyphs and perhaps other symbols to their own language and developed an alphabet about 1500 B.C.E. This script and language is called Proto-Sinaitic. At about the same time in Canaan proper some inscriptions appear that may also be alphabetic, an Old Canaanite alphabetic script. At present it is not clear whether these two scripts are related to one another or independent. Proto-Sinaitic had twenty-seven consonants.

The developers of the Old Canaanite and Proto-Sinaitic scripts seem to have taken the Egyptian hieroglyphics just as the Akkadians took the Sumerian signs and adapted it to their own language. They took the Egyptian consonantal syllabary system and went one step further to the alphabet. The Egyptians had a set of single consonant syllables, and if they had used only that set of syllables, they would have had a virtual alphabet. But they always kept the two and three consonant syllables alongside the former. The Old Canaanite and Proto-Sinaitic scripts took the hieroglyphic signs for many of their own signs. They gave these signs their semitic name. Then they let the sign represent only the initial consonant of the name. The hieroglyphic profile for a head was borrowed and given the semitic name *rosh/resh* = head. It had the sound *r*. Thus the alphabet was born. Granted, these early semites did not represent vowels in their alphabet. That development was to come much later, with vowel signs for some long vowels in some semitic alphabets, and with full representation of vowels at the hand of the Greeks. Nevertheless, the alphabetic principle was born with these alphabetic scripts.

The familiar order of the alphabet is first found in an abecedary from Ugarit. It has thirty signs. Twenty-seven of the signs follow the typical semitic order from *aleph* to *tav*. The last three were apparently added to the list later, they represent an i-class *aleph*, a u-class *aleph*, and an alternate form of the *s*.

From the slightly later period of the fourteenth and thirteenth centuries B.C.E., Proto-Canaanite inscriptions appear in Syria/Palestine. The Proto-Canaanite script as found at Lachish, Hazor and other places, is the direct ancestor of the Phoenician script and the national scripts (Hebrew, Ammonite, Moabite, Old Aramaic) which appear in the ninth to eithth centuries B.C.E.

Sometime between the eleventh and eighth centuries B.C.E., the Greeks borrowed the alphabet from the Phoenicians, probably from traders and merchants traveling across the Mediterranean. The Greeks made one additional change to the alphabet. Since their language did not possess the gutturals of the semitic languages, they used the signs of the semitic gutturals to represent their vowels, the *aleph* became their *alpha*, the *he* became their *epsilon*, the *ḥet* became their *eta*, and the *'ayin* became their *omicron*. Thus was born the Western alphabet as presently known, representing both consonants and vowels. The Greek alphabet is the mother-script of Latin and the European alphabets based on Latin, of the Cyrillic alphabet as used in Russian and related scripts, Coptic, and other derived scripts.

Even the form of many letters of the alphabet is recognizable from simple developments of the early forms. The table above shows the development of several typical examples from hieroglyphics to Proto-Sinaitic to Phoenician, and finally to Greek.

See also SEMITIC LANGUAGES.

Bibliography. D. Diringer, *The Alphabet*; G. R. Driver, *Semitic Writing from Pictograph to Alphabet*, 3rd ed.; I. J. Gelb, *A Study of Writing*, 2nd ed.; J. Naveh, *Early History of the Alphabet*.

—JOEL F. DRINKARD, JR.

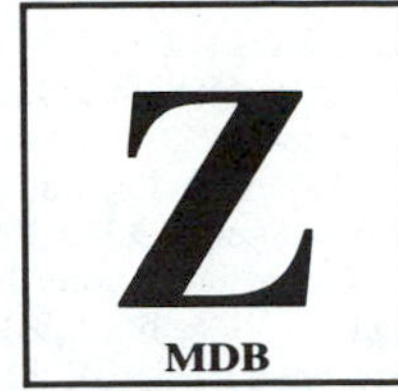

• **Yahweh.** *See* GOD; GOD, NAMES OF; TETRAGRAMMATON

• **Yahwist.** [yah′wist] A term to designate the author (or compiler) of one of the sources of the Pentateuch. The Yahwist is said to be the author or redactor of the early narrative tradition designated by the symbol "J," so designated because the most common name for God in this narrative is represented as Yahweh (German, *Jahveh*).

The Yahwist is normally dated in the time of the united monarchy (tenth century B.C.E.). The narrative begins in Gen 2:4b with God's creation of earth and heaven. It continues with the accounts of the flood; the building of the tower of Babel; the story of Abraham, Isaac, and Jacob; the accounts of the Exodus, the wilderness wanderings; and the conquests in Transjordan. The author or redactor of J is generally placed in the Southern tribe, Judah, and has been claimed to have been active especially in the period of the so-called Solomonic enlightenment, offering a summary of Israel's ancient traditions in order to make clear that it was the God of Israel, not human power and vainglory, that had brought Israel to this time of success and cultural eminence.

Some scholars have supposed that the J materials continue on in 1 and 2 Samuel, but the majority view is against such a claim.

See also SOURCES OF THE PENTATEUCH; SOURCES, LITERARY.

—KAREN RANDOLPH JOINES

• **Yarmuk.** [yahr′muk] A perennial stream near the modern border of Syria and Jordan, just north of the frontier between ancient BASHAN and GILEAD (PLATE 10), the Yarmuk is the northernmost of the four wadi systems—Yarmuk, Jabbok, Arnon, and Zered—that cut Transjordan into ancient kingdoms and into modern districts. The Yarmuk is the main tributary of the JORDAN RIVER, with which it merges ca. four mi. south of the SEA OF GALILEE. Before the construction of modern water systems, which divert waters for irrigation, etc., the Yarmuk's average flow was approximately the same as that of the Jordan, at their confluence. The Yarmuk River serves as a catchment for Bashan and the Hauran. Because of the available water and the region's fertility, the area around the Yarmuk has been settled since prehistoric times.

The Yarmuk's first appearance in literature is in the first century C.E., in Pliny, but the stream was not mentioned by name in Jewish writings until the Mishnah. The "watercourse" referred to in 1 Macc 5:40 could be the Yarmuk. Its omission from the OT is perhaps due to Israel's lack of effective control in this region, or it is possible that the Yarmuk and its environs were beyond the geographical interest of the biblical writers. Nonetheless, the Amorite king, OG, was defeated by the Hebrews at Edrei, on the northern rim of the Yarmuk (Num 21:33-35), and Bashan itself was assigned to the tribe of Manasseh (Deut 3:13-14; 1 Chr 6:71).

—GERALD L. MATTINGLY

• **Yom Kippur.** *See* ATONEMENT, DAY OF

• **Zacchaeus.** [za-kee′uhs] A chief tax collector in Jericho (Luke 19:1-10). Instead of being true to the meaning of his name ("pure"), Zacchaeus was a "sinner." He was despised by the Jews because he was guilty of fraud and corruption and also ritually unclean due to contact with gentiles.

Zacchaeus is remembered for climbing a sycamore tree to see Jesus. This mulberry fig tree, with wide branches, was easy to climb and provided food for the poor. The experience with Jesus changes Zacchaeus, who becomes a true son of Abraham by giving half of his goods to the poor and making a fourfold restitution, going beyond the Law (cf. Lev 6; Num 5; Exod 22).

See also CONVERSION; PUBLICANS.

—NORM YANCE

• **Zadok.** [zay′dok] The personal name *ṣādôq* (meaning "righteous") is the name of several persons in the OT.

It is the name of "a young man mighty of valor" (1 Chr 12:28) who came to Hebron to assist DAVID's army.

The most prominent individual named Zadok was one of two chief PRIESTS in the court of David; ABIATHAR was the name of the other. Zadok came from the line of Eleazar, third son of AARON (1 Chr 6:4-8; 24:1-3), and rose in prominence when David used Zadok to assist in moving the Ark from Kiriath-jearim to Jerusalem. Why did David choose Zadok? Three theories include: (1) Zadok had been a priest at GIBEON, an earlier key site for the sanctuary; (2) he may have been a priest who kept the Ark at Kiriath-jearim, and possibly made a move from Gibeon to be with the Ark at Kiriath-jearim; or (3) Zadok may have been a priest in the JEBUSITE sanctuary at Jerusalem, whom David allowed to continue as priest for both the Jebusites and the Israelites (cf. Josh 10:1, 3; Gen 14:17-20; Ps 110:4). Later Zadok joined BATHSHEBA, NATHAN and BENAIAH in urging David to select Solomon as the next king. Those supporting Solomon desired a centralized government in Jerusalem, which would hold great appeal to Zadok if he were a Jebusite. Zadok anointed Solomon as king (1 Kgs 1:32-40), and Solomon placed Zadok as priest rather than

Abiathar (1 Kgs 2:35). Zadok's influence continued for centuries (1 Sam 2:35; 1 Kgs 4:2; 2 Chr 31:10; Ezek 40–48; Ezra 7:2).

A third Zadok was the father-in-law of King Uzziah and grandfather of King Jotham (2 Kgs 15:33; 2 Chr 27:1).

Others who bore the name were a priest in the line of Zadok (1 Chr 6:12; 9:11; Neh 11:11); a son of Baana who repaired a portion of the Jerusalem wall, ca. 445 B.C.E. (Neh 3:4; cf. Ezra 2:2); a son of Immer who repaired a portion of the Jerusalem wall, ca. 445 B.C.E. (Neh 3:29; cf. Ezra 2:37); a builder who sealed the covenant with Nehemiah (Neh 10:21—possibly the same as the two preceding Zadoks); a scribe whom Nehemiah placed over the treasury of the Lord's house (Neh 13:13; cf. 3:29—possibly the same person); an ancestor of Jesus (Matt 1:14), midway between the deportation into Babylon and the birth of Jesus.

See also ABIATHAR; PRIESTS.

Bibliography. R. H. Pfeiffer, *Introduction to the Old Testament*; H. H. Rowley, "Melchizedek and Zadok," *Festschrift für Alfred Bertholet*, ed. W. Baumgartner.

—OMER J. HANCOCK, JR.

• **Zadokite Document.** *See* DAMASCUS RULE

• **Zarephath.** [zair'uh-fath] A Phoenician town located between Sidon and Tyre, modern Ras Sarafand, in Lebanon. In some versions the name is given as Sarepta.

Zarephath was an important Phoenician harbor located about six mi. south of Sidon (PLATE 1). A list from the time of Ramses II (1290–1224 B.C.E.) mentions Zarephath as situated along the north-south highway later to be called the *Via Maris* (Way of the Sea). Zarephath was included among the Phoenician towns conquered by Sennacherib in 701 B.C.E.

The episode in 1 Kgs 17:8-24, part of a three-chapter narrative about the prophet Elijah (1 Kgs 17–19), recounts Yahweh's command to Elijah to leave the parched stream of Cherith and travel to the town of Zarephath, which belonged to Sidon, in order to receive continued care. Elijah obeyed the command and reported to Zarephath, only to find his source of life, a widow, preparing the last meal she and her son would share before they died of starvation. Elijah convinced her to change her plans, and he then brought a miraculous sustenance to her household. He later healed her son when the son suddenly became desperately ill. For all his help, the widow affirmed Elijah's holy vocation and prophetic voice. This story is recalled in Luke 4:26, where it is reported that Jesus' teaching enraged certain Jews of Nazareth.

The prophet Obadiah (v. 20) predicted that when the day of Yahweh dawned, Judah's borders would extend in the north as far as Zarephath.

See also DISEASES AND HEALING; ELIJAH.

—RUSSELL I. GREGORY

• **Zealot.** [zel'uht] The Zealots seem to be those whom Josephus called "the fourth philosophy" (*Ant* 18.1) in first-century Palestine, the others being the Pharisees, Sadducees, and Essenes. Simon (Luke 6:15; Acts 1:13) was a Zealot and one of the disciples of Jesus. He was also referred to as Simon "the Cananaean" (Matt 10:4; Mark 3:18). These references would distinguish him from Simon Peter.

The Zealots were hotheaded superpatriots and in the vanguard of revolution against Rome. But it would be misleading to refer to them as a sect or party throughout the late biblical period. Rather they were home-rule fanatics, a largely unorganized movement unified only in opposition to foreign political control. Their excessive zeal for God and the Law led to a tendency towards violence. Their roots go back to the time of the Maccabees in the second century B.C.E. and the emphasis on maintaining the exclusive worship of God. Perhaps they were linked to the Hasidim and the rejection of Hellenism and, later, to those who expressed hatred of Herod and confronted Rome on occasion.

Apparently the founding of the Zealots may be traced to Judas the Galilean and his leading a revolt during the census of Quirinius in 6 C.E. His violent band felt it was treason to pay tribute to Rome. A major group of Zealots was led by John of Gischala in the war with Rome (Josephus, *BJ* 4). With the fall of MASADA, the Zealots disappear as a real force. Their actions should be understood in light of their fierce loyalty to God, their love for the Law, and their dream of restoring the kingdom of David.

Bibliography. D. M. Rhoads, "Zealots," *EncRel*.

—NORM YANCE

• **Zebedee.** [zeb'uh-dee] Zebedee, a Galilean fisherman, was the father of JAMES and JOHN, two of Jesus' disciples. A comparison of the lists of women in Mark 15:40 and Matt 27:56 implies that Zebedee's wife was Salome.

Zebedee is mentioned in all four canonical Gospels. In every place but one his name serves only to identify his sons. The exception is Mark 1:19-20 ‖ Matt 4:21-22, where he plays a minor role. He is with his sons when they are summoned to discipleship and is left behind when they follow Jesus. Perhaps this is intended to underline the need to put faith above family. The call to follow Jesus may require cutting familial ties (Matt 8:22; 10:35-37; 19:29).

See also JAMES; JOHN THE APOSTLE.

—DALE C. ALLISON, JR.

• **Zebulun.** [zeb'yuh-luhn] The sixth son of Leah and Jacob (Gen 30:20), eponymous head of the tribe of that name, with territorial allotment in the northwest, north of Mount Carmel (PLATE 11) (Josh 19:10-16).

—WALTER HARRELSON

• **Zechariah.** [zek'uh-ri″uh] Meaning either "Yahweh remembers" or "remembered of Yahweh," Zechariah was a popular name among the Israelites. Approximately thirty Zechariahs are mentioned in the OT. Here the first three are listed in the order of the significance of their role in the OT; the remainder, in approximately chronological order. The one person bearing this name in the NT is listed last.

1. The prophet whose name appears in the thirty-eighth book of the OT. He prophesied ca. 520–518 B.C.E. Zech 1:1, 7 refer to him as the son of Berechiah, son of Iddo. Ezra 5:1 and 6:14 refer to him as the son of Iddo. Various explanations for this discrepancy have been given. By allegorical interpretation Jerome said Iddo was his father "in spirit" and Berechiah was his father "in flesh." Others have suggested, in view of the different bodies of material in the Book of Zechariah, that chaps. 1–8 were written by Zechariah son of Iddo and chaps. 9–14 by Zechariah son of Berechiah. Such approaches are rendered unnecessary by the simple fact that "son of" could span any number of generations.

This Zechariah was apparently born of a priestly family during the Babylonian captivity. He may have returned with ZERUBBABEL immediately following Cyrus's decree of ca. 538 B.C.E. His silence from 538 to 520 would then require explanation. One possibility is that he returned as an infant, and only began his career as an adult. Another is that he returned with a later group about 520 B.C.E. There are traditions of a previous career in Babylonia, but the reliability of these traditions is suspect.

Along with Haggai, Zechariah seems to have motivated the returned exiles to rebuild the Temple. The foundation had been begun (cf. Ezra 3:8-10; 5:16) immediately after the first group of exiles returned. The work had then been stopped for ca. sixteen years before Zechariah came on the scene (or came to maturity). Whether he lived to see the Temple completed (ca. 516 B.C.E.) is uncertain.

The prophet Zechariah was a visionary and apparently a universalist. The first eight chaps. of the Book of Zechariah contain a series of remarkable visions designed to assure the people that God was in control of the troubled times and that, through the agency of Zerubbabel and the high priest Joshua, the promised blessings of God would yet befall Israel and the world. Some of his visionary statements are radical and striking. He speaks, for example, of Zion's being a vast city and of God's being a protecting wall of fire around it (2:1-5); he also prophesies that many nations will join themselves to the Lord and be God's people in the great day of consummation soon to come (2:11; 8:22-23).

2. A son of Jehoiada the priest during the reign of JOASH. Led by God's Spirit, he rebuked the people for transgressing the Lord's commandments. Zechariah's message was that because the people had forsaken the Lord, the Lord had forsaken them (2 Chr 24:20-22). For this he was stoned to death at King Joash's command. Many think Matthew 23:35 refers to this Zechariah. The problem is that Zechariah is referred to in Matthew as the son of Berechiah rather than Jehoiada. Beyond this nothing else is known.

3. A son of Jeroboam II. He reigned for six months in Israel as the last member of JEHU's dynasty. According to 2 Kgs 15:8-11 he was an evil king who was murdered and replaced by SHALLUM. His remaining acts are said to have been recorded in a book unknown to us.

4. The ninth son of Jeiel (1 Chr 9:35, 37).

5. Son of Meshelemiah (1 Chr 9:21-22).

6. A Levite during DAVID's reign. He was appointed a harpist by David's command, according to 1 Chr 15:18, 20.

7. A priest who blew the trumpet before the Ark of God (1 Chr 15:24).

8. A Kohathite Levite (1 Chr 24:25).

9. A Temple gatekeeper, the fourth son of Hosah (1 Chr 26:10-11).

10. Father of Iddo (1 Chr 27:21).

11. One of JEHOSHAPHAT's officials. When Jehoshaphat reigned over Judah this Zechariah was sent out to teach in the cities of Judah, according to 2 Chr 17:7.

12. A son of Benaiah, a Levite in the lineage of ASAPH (2 Chr 20:14).

13. A son of Jehoshaphat (2 Chr 21:2-4).

14. A prophet during UZZIAH's reign who was said to have had "understanding through the vision of the Lord" (2 Chr 26:5).

15. A leading Reubenite, possibly the same as (4) above (1 Chr 5:7).

16. Son of Jeberechiah. He served as a witness for Isaiah the prophet, according to Isa 8:2.

17. Grandfather of Hezekiah, king of Judah (2 Chr 29:1).

18. A Levite of the sons of Asaph during Hezekiah's reign (2 Chr 29:13).

19. A Levite of the Kohathites, who helped repair the Temple during the reign of Josiah of Judah (2 Chr 34:12).

20. An "official of the house of God" during the reign of Josiah (2 Chr 35:8).

21. Family leader of the sons of Shecaniah, who returned from Babylon with Ezra (Ezra 8:3).

22. Family leader of the sons of Bebai, who also returned from Babylon with Ezra (Ezra 8:11).

23. A Levite during the time of Ezra. According to Ezra 8;15-16 Ezra specifically requested a group of Levites, including Zechariah, to return with him to Jerusalem.

24. A companion of Ezra. He is named as one of a group of twelve who stood beside Ezra the scribe as he read the Law to the people (Neh 8:4; could be the same as 21, 22, or 23 above).

25. A member of the family of Elam. He is listed in Ezra 10:26 among those whom Ezra forced to put away their foreign wives.

26. Son of a priest during Nehemiah's time. He seems to have been among those who blew the trumpet to celebrate the rebuilding of the walls of Jerusalem (Neh 12:35-36).

27. A priest in the "second choir." He is mentioned in Neh 12:41 as participating in the celebrations mentioned above.

28. Son of Amariah. He is listed in Neh 11:4 as a member of the tribe of Judah who lived in Jerusalem during the turbulent postexilic period.

29. Son of "the Shilonite." Neh 11:5 lists him as another resident of Jerusalem during the above period.

30. A son of Pashhur. In Neh 11:12 he is listed as a priest who lived inside Jerusalem during the same turbulent period.

31. Father of JOHN THE BAPTIST. He was a priest of the division of Abijah, described as a righteous man who in advanced age was childless (Luke 1:7). The angel Gabriel promised a son to him and his wife ELIZABETH, but Zechariah was doubtful, and was struck dumb until after John was born. Little more is known.

See also ZECHARIAH, BOOK OF.

Bibliography. D. L. Petersen, *Haggai and Zechariah 1-8, OTL*; R. L. Smith, *Zechariah, WBC*.

—JOE E. LUNCEFORD

• **Zechariah, Book of.** [zek'uh-ri''uh] The eleventh of the twelve minor prophets, called Zacharias in the LXX and Vulgate. Along with HAGGAI and MALACHI Zechariah forms a triad of postexilic compositions that shed valuable light on a period of Jewish history otherwise relatively unknown. The book is characterized by VISIONS, APOCALYPTIC language, and messianic imagery.

Authorship and Date. For centuries the Book of Zechariah was regarded as a unity, written around 520 B.C.E. However, in 1638 Joseph Mede suggested that JEREMIAH was the author of chaps. 9–11, based on the quotation of Zech 11:12-13 in Matt 27:9-10, attributed to Jeremiah. In 1699 Richard Kidder proposed Jeremiah as the author of chaps. 9–14. Today many scholars argue for the authorship of 9–14 by one called Deutero-Zechariah, based on striking differences with chaps. 1–8 in content, style, and vocabulary.

In 1814 Leonhard Berthold argued for a third (Trito-) Zechariah (separating 12–14 from 9–11). Other scholars say the book represents collections of a number of even smaller units by unknown authors. Some scholars still insist on the book's unity, arguing that subject and stylistic differences represent two periods of Zechariah's ministry, 520 and 480 B.C.E.

• OUTLINE OF ZECHARIAH •

The Book of Zechariah

I. The Visions and Prophecies of Zechariah (1:1–8:23)
   A. A summons to Israel to repent (1:1-6)
   B. Zechariah's visions, with oracles interspersed (1:7–6:15)
   C. Oracles on fasting and obedience (7:1-14)
   D. Promises for Israel and the nations (8:1-23)
II. Additional Oracles and Promises (9:1–14:21)
   A. Oracles against Aram, Phoenicia, and Philistia (9:1-8)
   B. Promise of a king for Jerusalem (9:9-12)
   C. God intervenes in battle for Israel (9:13-17)
   D. God delivers Israel from exile and oppression (10:1–11:3)
   E. The shepherds of the flock (11:4-17)
   F. Jerusalem's triumph and glorification (12:1-9)
   G. Israel mourns over one who has been wounded (12:10–13:1)
   H. Judgment against the prophets (13:2-6)
   I. A shepherd is slain (13:7-9)
   J. God's battle against enemies (14:1-15)
   K. The nations worship God in Jerusalem (14:16-21)

The Person. In 1:1 Zechariah is identified as the son of Berechiah and grandson of Iddo (but cf. Ezra 5:1; 6:14). Neh 12:16 describes him as head of a priestly family. His name means "Yahweh remembers." Matt 23:35 (if referring to the prophet Zechariah) describes the circumstances of his death. If chaps. 9–14 were written by others, nothing is known about them.

Historical Background. The Temple in Jerusalem had lain in ruins since its destruction by the Babylonians in 587/6 B.C.E. In 538 King CYRUS of Persia decreed that the exiles could return home. One of their first acts was to lay the foundation for a new Temple. The work was soon stopped by opposition and the rigors of life in the still-devastated land. The people devoted their energies to planting crops, building houses, and providing clothing. In 520 B.C.E. Haggai told them they were still suffering hardship in spite of all their efforts because they were neglecting the rebuilding of the Temple. Two months later Zechariah appeared and also encouraged them to rebuild. Their efforts were successful, and the Temple was completed in 515 B.C.E. (Ezra 6:15).

Contents. The messages of chaps. 1–8 are dated over a two-year period from October–November 520 B.C.E. (1:1) to November–December 518 B.C.E. (7:1). Haggai emphasized the material prosperity Judah would enjoy upon completion of the Temple. Zechariah's focus was on the subsequent glories and exaltation of the messianic kingdom. His purpose in chaps. 1–8 was to assure the people of Judah that God was concerned for their welfare at a time when their faith was shaken because of the hardships they were experiencing.

Chaps. 1–8 contain eight visions, each with a similar theme of reassuring the people that the age of blessing was about to begin. After calling the people to repentance and warning them not to repeat the sins of previous generations (1:1-6), Zechariah experienced his first vision (1:7-17) of four horsemen who traversed the earth and found no unrest anywhere. It suggests that Judah's sufferings were coming to an end and that God would again show compassion and bestow blessing on Jerusalem.

In the second vision (1:18-21) Zechariah saw four horns, symbolizing foreign powers who had scattered God's people. He then saw four craftsmen, whose task was to destroy those enemies.

The third vision (2:1-5) contains a promise of a restored Jerusalem protected by God like "a wall of fire around it" and characterized by the glorious manifestation of God's presence in it. The vision is followed by an ORACLE (2:6-13), calling God's people who were still in Babylon back to Jerusalem.

The fourth vision (3:1-10) shows JOSHUA the high priest cleansed and restored to office after being accused by SATAN. The vision was intended to assure Judah that access to God had been restored by the cleansing of the priesthood.

In the fifth vision (4:1-14) Zechariah was shown a lampstand fed by an unfailing source of oil from an olive tree on either side. Assurance was voiced that ZERUBBABEL would complete the Temple, not through his efforts but by the power of God's Spirit.

The sixth vision (5:1-4) revealed a huge flying SCROLL that served as a reminder that those who did not obey God's laws would be punished.

In the seventh vision (5:5-11) Zechariah was shown a woman called "Wickedness" sitting in a basket of a size that would contain an ephah, transported to Shinar (i.e., Babylonia), symbolizing the removal of iniquity from Judah.

The eighth vision (6:1-8) describes four horse-drawn chariots patrolling the earth, suggesting that peace would again prevail after God's judgment has been executed throughout the earth.

Zech 6:9–8:23 contains a series of oracles with a common theme of the glory of the messianic age. The crowning of Joshua the high priest as king is described in 6:9-15. Many believe the text originally said Zerubbabel instead of Joshua because Zerubbabel was the one who would build the Temple (6:12-13; cf. 4:9), but the oracle may suggest the blending of the priestly and kingly offices in one messianic figure. The remaining verses anticipate a new Jerusalem characterized by obedience, peace, and prosperity for young and old alike, with people from all nations coming to Jerusalem to seek the Lord.

Chaps. 9–14, apart from considerations of authorship and date, consist largely of apocalyptic material. They contain messages of coming judgment on other lands (9:1-17), followed by condemnation of Judah's leaders (called "shepherds") and a promise that God will restore the scattered Israelite people (10:1-12). In chap. 11 Zechariah is instructed to enact the role of Yahweh as shepherd of the people whose covenant has been broken by their disobedience. Zechariah is then asked to enact the role of a worthless shepherd as a warning to the people of the kind of leaders they may expect if they are unfaithful to God.

Chaps. 12–13 describe the restoration of Judah, victorious over all its enemies through God's intervention. The time is anticipated when Judah will be cleansed of idol worship, false prophets, and all that makes the land unclean. The book closes (chap. 14) with a description of the nations gathered to fight against JERUSALEM. God intervenes to destroy the enemies, and Jerusalem emerges victorious with God as ruler over all the earth and worshiped by all peoples.

See also ZECHARIAH; APOCALYPTIC LITERATURE.

Bibliography. J. Baldwin, *Haggai, Zechariah, Malachi*; H. G. Mitchell et al., *A Critical and Exegetical Commentary on Haggai, Zechariah, Malachi, and Jonah, ICC*; W. Neil, "Zechariah, Book of," *IDB*; D. L. Petersen,

Haggai and Zechariah 1–8; R. L. Smith, *Micah–Malachi*; D. W. Thomas and R. C. Dentan, "The Book of Zechariah: Introduction and Exegesis," *IB*.

—F. B. HUEY, JR.

• **Zedekiah.** [zed'uh-*ki*"uh] The name Zedekiah was formed by combining the shortened form of the personal name for God, Yah, with the root word for righteousness. The name means "Yahweh (is my) righteousness." Five persons in the OT bear this name.

1. A false prophet in Israel who was an influential member and spokesman of AHAB's 400 court prophets. He and God's prophet, MICAIAH, gave contrasting prophecies regarding the military venture of Ahab (1 Kgs 22:11-28).

2. A false prophet in Babylon who was condemned by JEREMIAH for his unfounded predictions of a speedy end to the captivity and for his adulterous and wanton life-style (Jer 29:21-23).

3. An influential prince in King JEHOIAKIM's government who along with the king and others heard the reading of Jeremiah's scroll. Apparently he was in sympathy with the king's determination to destroy the scroll and Jeremiah also (Jer 36:12-19).

4. The final king of Judah who ruled prior to JERUSALEM's destruction by NEBUCHADREZZAR in July 587 B.C.E. Zedekiah was JOSIAH's third son to serve as king. Originally, his name was Mattaniah, "Gift of Yahweh." When his brother Jehoiakim died, his nephew, JEHOIACHIN, ascended the throne. After only three months Nebuchadrezzar forced Jehoiachin into Babylonian exile along with the rest of Judean society. According to the Babylonian Chronicle, "he appointed in it a (new) king of his liking." That king was Mattaniah who was destined to rule for about ten years and four months (March 597 to July 587 B.C.E.).

Nebuchadrezzar not only selected Mattaniah to serve as king, but he also changed his name to Zedekiah. He required Zedekiah to swear allegiance to him. Thus, Zedekiah served as a Babylonian vassal.

Zedekiah was expected to perform an impossible task. He had to walk a tightrope between nationalistic concern for Judah and loyalty to Babylon. He was expected to provide strong leadership. However, he did not possess the experience, the strong character, or the necessary personnel to do so. The best of Judean leadership had been transported to Babylon. His recently elevated political leaders were foolishly and blindly inclined against Babylon.

Zedekiah never captured the heart of the nation as did his father Josiah. Many people still looked to Jehoiachin as the legitimate king. Zedekiah was viewed as filling an interim role awaiting Jehoiachin's return.

Zedekiah toyed with the idea of rebellion against Babylon. Jeremiah warned him against such faithless actions, rather advising him to accept Babylon's yoke. He came under suspicion by Nebuchadrezzar and in 593 B.C.E. made a conciliatory visit to Babylon.

In spite of Jeremiah's warnings, Zedekiah revolted against Babylon, looking to the Egyptian Psammetichus II (593–588 B.C.E.) and his son Hophra (588–569 B.C.E.) for essential support. His indecisiveness and vacillation were evident in his repeated consultations with Jeremiah. He wanted such meetings to be in secret because he feared his own officials whom he failed to control. Consequently he failed in protecting Jeremiah from being beaten and imprisoned by them, though he did preserve the prophet's life.

Such revolt brought Babylon's unmerciful might against Judah. In July 587 B.C.E. the enemy breached Jerusalem's walls. Zedekiah and a band of followers sought to escape under cover of darkness and fled toward Jericho. Zedekiah was captured and transported to Riblah in central Aram to appear before Nebuchadrezzar. Nebuchadrezzar commanded that his sons (heirs) be slain, that he be blinded, and that he be bound and brought to Babylon where he later died.

5. A prominent leader during NEHEMIAH's time who joined Nehemiah and others in signing a covenant-renewal document (Neh 10:1).

See also JEREMIAH.

—JERRY WALLACE LEE

• **Zelophehad.** [zuh-loh'fuh-had] A member of the tribe of Manasseh who died during the journey from Egypt, leaving as his heirs five daughters (Num 26:33). Since the land was to be divided among the families of the twelve tribes (26:52-56), the question arose as to the disposition of Zelophehad's share (ordinarily, in ancient Israel, property descended to sons only, thus daughters were free to marry outside the tribe since doing so would leave the family property intact). The daughters approached MOSES for a decision and were awarded their father's portion (27:1-11), provided they married within the tribe (36:1-12).

Since the daughters' names are also attested as the designations of towns or districts, some modern interpreters have suggested that the story originally reflected the incorporation of those groups into the tribe of Manasseh: they, too, are given an inheritance. When later understood to be individuals, the daughters could be used to set a precedent for future generations.

See also INHERITANCE IN THE OLD TESTAMENT; WOMEN IN THE OLD TESTAMENT.

Bibliography. R. de Vaux, *Ancient Israel*; M. Noth, *Numbers*.

—LLOYD R. BAILEY

• **Zeno.** *See* STOICS

• **Zephaniah.** [zef'uh-*ni*"uh] The name of several OT personalities, the most notable of whom was the seventh-century B.C.E. prophet. Zephaniah prophesied shortly before the reform of Josiah, the deuteronomic reform (621 B.C.E.). He may have been a descendant of King HEZEKIAH of Judah, since his ancestry is traced back for four generations to a certain Hezekiah (Zeph 1:1). He is known for his fierce denunciation of Judah and Jerusalem for their sins and for his threat that a DAY OF THE LORD would soon come to bring devastation to the whole earth (Zeph 1:7, 14-18). He also spoke of a time to come when restoration would begin and when the humble and meek of earth would live in the land, faithful to God and devoted to truth and justice (Zeph 3:8-13).

Another Zephaniah was a priest in the service of King Zedekiah in the days of the prophet JEREMIAH (Jer 21:1; 29:5, 29; 37:3; 52:54). He lost his life in the destruction of Jerusalem in 587 B.C.E. (2 Kgs 25:18).

The name also appears as the father of one of the returning exiles in the time of the prophet Zechariah (Zech 6:10, 14), and in the list of levitical singers appointed by David (1 Chr 6:36, Heb 6:21).

See also ZEPHANIAH, BOOK OF.

—WALTER HARRELSON

• **Zephaniah, Apocalypse of.** The *Apocalypse of Zeph-*

aniah (*ApocZeph*) is a pseudepigraphical document preserved in two Coptic fragments and a quotation by Clement of Alexandria. It is a first-person account of ZEPHANIAH's journey into heavenly realms and his visions of heavenly glories and souls in eternal torment. The work consists of a number of self-contained episodes describing the seer's trip into HEAVEN and into Hades; it concludes with four episodes introduced by four trumpet blasts. A quotation by Clement and the use of the story of SUSANNA suggest the apocalypse was composed in Greek between the end of the first century B.C.E. and the beginning of the second century C.E. The *ApocZeph* contains Jewish ideas and could possibly have been written in Egypt. Any Christian ideas in *ApocZeph* are probably due to a similar literary milieu rather than to literary dependence.

The basic theme of *ApocZeph* is divine judgment for all humanity. Each person must face the divine tribunal and have some decision made about his or her life. The *ApocZeph* also mentions the need for the righteous to intercede in prayer for those in torment. Such intercessory prayers are addressed to a God who is merciful and willing to accept repentance, and yet will judge those who do not repent. A secondary characteristic of *ApocZeph* is an emphasis on angels.

The *ApocZeph* provides evidence of eschatological thought contemporaneous with the NT as well as an important example in the development of APOCALYPTIC LITERATURE.

See also APOCALYPTIC LITERATURE; HEAVEN; HELL; ESCHATOLOGY.

Bibliography. J. H. Charlesworth, *The Pseudepigrapha in Modern Research*; O. S. Wintermute, "Apocalypse of Zephaniah," *The Old Testament Pseudepigrapha*, ed. J. H. Charlesworth.

—STEVEN SHEELEY

• OUTLINE OF ZEPHANIAH •

The Book of Zephaniah

I. The Day of the Lord against Israel (1:1–2:3)
II. Judgments against the Foreign Nations (2:4-15)
III. Judgment against Jerusalem (3:1-7)
IV. Promise for Israel and the Nations (3:8-13)
V. Hymnic Promise for Jerusalem (3:14-20)

• **Zephaniah, Book of.** [zef'uh-*ni*"uh] The eighth book of the minor prophets. If the Hezekiah (a fairly unusual name in Hebrew) mentioned in 1:1 as great-great-grandfather of Zephaniah is the eighth-century king of Judah, then the prophet Zephaniah was of royal descent. This is significant for an understanding of prophecy, because it demonstrates that, even as Ezekiel and (probably) Isaiah were priests who criticized the religious establishment, so Zephaniah could be a member of the ruling class and yet be prophetic.

Since it is clear from his book that NINEVEH was still standing as the capital of ASSYRIA and that religious as well as cultural syncretism abounded in Judah (1:4-6, 8), most scholars date the activity of Zephaniah to the early reign of JOSIAH before the king's famous deuteronomic reform (ca. 621). During this period, the Assyrian empire was gradually falling apart and various nationalist movements were arising, leading to the atmosphere of chaos that provoked the prophet's oracles.

Thus as the world Zephaniah had known crumbled, the poet pictured God's judgment as universal, an undoing of creation much like the flood of the primeval age (Gen 6–9), then focused the divine discipline on Judah/Jerusalem, the locus of the people of God. For while all peoples are subject to the creator and king of the universe, the chosen know God and have the responsibility for true worship that leads to right living. This cosmic destruction would restore the earth to primeval silence, the silence of proper worship (1:7). The metaphor is the Day of the Lord, which should be a victory feast with a sacrifice offered to God, but on which, instead, God must offer the sacrifice of the earth (cf. Amos 5:18-20).

> Dies irae, dies illa,
> solvet saeclum in favilla,
> teste David cum Sibylla.
> quantus tremor est futurus,
> quando iudex est venturus,
> cuncta stricte discussurus! . . .
> mors stupebit et natura,
> cum resurget creatura
> iudicanti responsura.

The medieval poem which became the center of the Requiem Mass enshrined Zeph 1:15-16 in the West's most somber meditation on the responsibilities of God's people of all ages: "That day, the day of wrath, will dissolve the world into ashes, as David and the Sibyl testify. What a trembling will there be, when the judge will come, who will sternly examine all things! . . . Death and nature will be astonished into silence when creation arises to answer him who judges."

Zeph 2 exhorts the humble of Judah who seek the Lord, while passing sentence on the pride of haughty nations. With the "world empty," there will be room for the "faithful remnant" (vv. 7, 10). In antithesis to the true Jerusalem, Nineveh is the epitome of arrogance with her heedless deification of self (v. 15; cf. Exod 3:14; Isa 45:5-7; John 8:58; Gen 3:5). She must be destroyed and returned to nature, to the simplicity of the original creation (v. 14).

Zeph 3:1 returns to Jerusalem the real, who has aped Nineveh and the nations rather than being the faithful humble of God. But cosmic judgment yields universal salvation (vv. 9-10; cf. 2:11b). With pride destroyed and humility restored (vv. 11-12), a new day of the Lord, the true day of the Lord, can emerge, a festival day with singing and joy. And the prophet can turn to Zion the ideal, locus of the kingdom of God (v.15).

Often caricatured as mere doom and gloom, the Book of Zephaniah on the contrary assures the faithful that evil cannot forever stand, and offers hope for a day in which creation and its inhabitants are made whole.

See also ESCHATOLOGY; ZEPHANIAH.

Bibliography. F. C. Fensham, "Zephaniah, Book of," *IDBSup*; E. A. Leslie, "Zephaniah, Book of," *IDB*; E. Routley, *A Panorama of Christian Hymnody*.

—LAMONTTE M. LUKER

• **Zered.** [zihr'id] Name of a brook or river that served in antiquity as the border between MOAB and EDOM (cf. Num 21:12; Deut 2:13-14). On the basis of the wilderness itinerary in Num 21, the Zered is usually identified with modern Wadi el-Hesa, though there is some dispute over this association. (The Zered is not mentioned in the itinerary of Num 33, as it is in chap. 21.) The Ḥesa is by far the greatest canyon that cuts across the territory of ancient Edom, and the arrival at this spot could have marked a turning point for the Hebrews, geographically and historically, as indicated in Num 21:12 and Deut 2:13-14.

Following a west-east fault, Wadi el-Ḥesa cuts across the Transjordanian plateau for approx. thirty-five mi., descending some 3,900 ft. before it empties into the southeastern corner of the DEAD SEA, near eṣ-Ṣafi (PLATE 10). Along with the Jordan, Zerqa Ma'in, and Arnon, the Zered is one of the four perennial streams that replenishes the evaporating waters of the Dead Sea; the Ḥesa has a large catchment area in the highlands of northern Edom.

The Roman road built by Trajan and a modern highway cross the Wadi el-Ḥesa, following close to the route of the so-called King's Highway. Difficulties in negotiating the Zered canyon enhanced the importance of the so-called Desert Highway.

In addition to its connection with the Israelite wilderness itinerary, the Zered is tentatively identified with the "Brook of the Willows" (Isa 15:7), "Brook of the Arabah" (Amos 6:14), and the "dry streambed" of 2 Kgs 3:16 (cf. 3:22).

—GERALD L. MATTINGLY

• **Zerubbabel.** [zuh-ruhb'uh-buhl] A grandson of JEHOIACHIN, one of the leaders of the exiles who returned to Jerusalem under the edict of Cyrus (Ezra 2:2; 4:3). The name means "offspring" or "shoot" of Babylon. He is usually listed as the son of Shealtiel (Hag 1:1; Ezra 3:2; cf. Matt 1:12; Luke 3:37), but the Chronicler gives his father as Pedaiah, another son of Jehoiachin (1 Chr 3:19). According to the prophet HAGGAI, Zerubbabel was appointed governor of Judah (1:1; 2:1). With Joshua, the high priest, he led the effort to rebuild the Jerusalem Temple during the time of the Persian king, Darius (Hag 1:1–2:9).

Local inhabitants, called "the adversaries of Judah and Benjamin" (Ezra 4:1), offered to help in the restoration, but Zerubbabel, along with the Jewish community as a whole, resolutely refused their offer. This refusal turned the SAMARITANS against the effort and they were able to force a cessation of the work, which according to the chronology of Ezra (4:4-6), began in the time of CYRUS. If this time frame is accepted, it would mean that the rebuilding was disrupted for several years. However, both Haggai and the first Zechariah (the author of Zech 1–8) date Zerubbabel's work only to the time of Darius I (Hag 1:1-2; Zech 4:4b-10a; cf. 1:1).

Both of these prophets also identified Zerubbabel as the ideal Davidic king, thus helping to lay the foundation of Jewish messianic hopes (Hag 2:20-23; Zech 4:6-7). Furthermore, the "branch" in Zechariah (3:8; 6:12) is almost certainly a reference to Zerubbabel and reflects the same religious ideology (cf. Isa 11:1). But the hopes of both prophets were never realized. What actually happened to Zerubbabel is unknown. It is thought that he was subsequently removed from his position by the Persians. He is referred to in other Jewish literature, the best known of which is the apocryphal story in 1 Esdr 3:1–5:6.

See also EZRA, BOOK OF; HAGGAI, BOOK OF; NEHEMIAH, BOOK OF; ZECHARIAH, BOOK OF.

—JOHN C. H. LAUGHLIN

• **Zeus.** [*zoos*] Zeus is the Gk. form of an Indo-European deity whose name signified "sky." As guardian of hospitality and protector of morals and law, Zeus became the greatest of the Greek gods. He was also the weather god and was feared for his thunderbolts. He is often called "the father of gods and men," especially by Homer.

Various mythical stories became attached to him. One of the most peculiar is a Cretan myth about Zeus's birth. In order to prevent the child from being eaten by his father, Kronos, Zeus was hidden in a cave and his father was fed a stone instead. Later, Zeus dethroned Kronos and, together with other Olympian gods, defeated the earlier generation, the Titans.

Zeus was also famous for his sexual alliances with both goddesses and women, and was the father of Athena, Artemis, Apollo, Ares, and Dionysus. He was still worshipped in NT times as indicated by the story of Paul and Barnabas at Lystra (Acts 14:12).

—JOHN C. H. LAUGHLIN

• **Ziklag.** [zik'lag] A city in the hills west of the DEAD SEA and near the coastal plain (PLATE 12). Modern geographers have not been able to locate it with certainty, suggesting either the mound known as Zuḥeiliqah (near Gaza), or Ḥalif (near Beersheba), or Milḥa (near Gaza), or Sera' (fifteen mi. southeast of Gaza). The last of these not only fits the biblical description but also has yielded archaeological remains from the proper historical periods.

It was in the territory taken by the PHILISTINES during their invasion (twelfth century B.C.E.), but was given by one of their kings to DAVID who used it as a base for military operations (1 Sam 27). It was within the ideal boundaries of the tribe of Simeon (Josh 19:5), but incorporated into that of Judah (Josh 15:31). It was one of the reoccupied sites when the Judeans returned from exile in the sixth century (Neh 11:28).

—LLOYD R. BAILEY

• **Zion.** [*zi'*uhn] Wedged between the Kidron and Tyropoean valleys is an elongated, triangular plateau that rises in elevation from south to north. This natural fortress, which has the added advantage of a natural water supply from the Gihon Spring on its eastern border, provided the location for the ancient Jebusite city of JERUSALEM (PLATES 24, 25, 35). Located roughly in the center of this long plateau was a fortress, later known as the Ophel, which probably was the original "stronghold of Zion" (2 Sam 5:6-10; 1 Chr 11:4-9) captured by DAVID. The triangle from this Zion and south became known as the "City of David," and perhaps the entire area was sometimes referred to as "Zion" (1 Kgs 8:1; 2 Chr 5:2). Eventually David bought a threshing floor north of the stronghold of Zion, at the highest elevation of the plateau, from the Jebusite Araunah (Ornan). In the ancient Near East threshing floors are often associated with worship, and the summit of Araunah's threshing floor, probably no exception, had likely been the location of a Jebusite altar. This made it the ideal spot for David to place the Ark of the Covenant and for SOLOMON to build the Temple and his royal palace. Therefore, the old city of Jerusalem expanded northwards to include the Temple-palace complex that now surpassed the old fortress of Zion in prestige and elevation and thus became known as "Mount Zion," the home of Yahweh and his Son/Messiah/King (2 Sam 7). In a sense, then, Yahweh moved his mountain abode from SINAI to Zion, even as the Hebrews migrated from "the wilderness" into Canaan to became a more urban and agricultural nation (Exod 15).

The elevation of Zion as the focus of God's presence on earth of course made it the chief cultic site in all Israel, and eventually JOSIAH's reformation (late seventh century) through the Book of Deuteronomy would stipulate that sacrificial worship could take place only at the Zion Temple. Ps 24, possibly composed for Solomon's first entry of the

Ark into the Temple and subsequently enacted periodically to celebrate Yahweh's enthronement on Mount Zion, assumes Zion is the chief mountain in all the earth, which God "has founded . . . upon the seas, and established . . . upon the rivers," the home of the "King of Glory." Both Pss 46 and 76 praise God, the king who has established Zion in Jerusalem, fortress of peace, in order to make "wars to cease to the end of the earth" and to break "the flashing arrows, the shield, the sword, and the weapons of war." Thus Zion became in Hebrew tradition the central symbol of God's rule, the Kingdom of God, a realm of justice, righteousness, and peace.

Three times a year, on the festivals of Tabernacles, Passover, and Pentecost, Jews would "go up" to Jerusalem to offer sacrifices on Mount Zion, and as they ascended they would sing "Songs of Ascent" such as those in Pss 120–134. Under the auspices of the Zadokite priesthood, Zion would be the focus for other regular demonstrations of worship, such as thanksgiving, sin, and communion sacrifices.

Concurrent with Zion the cultic center was Zion the center of government, for there was in ancient Israel no "separation of church and state." Ps 2, composed for the coronation of the king, announces the decree of God, "I have set my king on Zion, my holy hill. . . . You are my son, today I have begotten you." Hence, on the day of his coronation, the Israelite king had oil poured on his head and became "messiah," Hebrew for "one anointed with oil" (the Greek for this is "christ") and "son of God," whose duty it was to embody the divine on earth, i.e., to establish the Kingdom of God. The "job description" of this king is given in Ps 72: he is to "defend the cause of the poor" and "give deliverance to the needy," for such is the nature of his "Father" as demonstrated in the Exodus.

Few kings did this. Indeed, Israel's government followed less the pattern of the Kingdom of God than the "royal religion" the slaves had fled in Egypt in which the king and Temple priests conspired together to create an order of oppression for the many and wealth for the few. The prophet AMOS addressed this royal class with, "Woe to those who are at ease in Zion" (6:1), and MICAH tells them they "build Zion with blood and Jerusalem with wrong" (3:10). The beautiful visions of Pss 46 and 76, which hoped for Zion as a world-center for peace, had been employed by the people as propaganda for the "inviolability of Zion." Hence JEREMIAH must warn, "Amend your ways and your doings, and I will let you dwell in this place. Do not trust in these deceptive words: 'This is the Temple of the Lord, the Temple of the Lord, the Temple of the Lord.' " The people did trust in the deceptive words, and their Father led Zion into exile.

By now Zion had become the embodiment of the people of God. Personified as a woman, daughter Zion might writhe as mother, suffer the indignity of one raped, or arise as feminist protestor (Mic 4:8-13); more often she was gentle mourner (Lamentations). In Jewish apocalyptic literature, mother Zion welcomed her suffering children to a world beyond our own (*4 Ezra*). But in the Hebrew Bible, Zion became a symbol for the eschatological Kingdom of God on earth, "the highest of the mountains" where all "shall beat their swords into plowshares, and their spears into pruning hooks; nation shall not lift up sword against nation, neither shall they learn war any more" (Mic 4; Isa 2). Such a kingdom will be brought on by the ideal messiah from Bethlehem of David's stock (Mic 5), the "shoot" from Jesse's "stump" (Isa 11).

In the first century, Christians would incorrectly locate Zion to the west of the original, but they would correctly identify a messiah who ruled for the meek of the earth. They would see themselves as the personification of the new Zion on earth, for the Kingdom of God is here (Mark 1:15; Matt 12:28 || Luke 11:20; Luke 17:21). Yet with many Jews during the late pre-Christian period, they would look for the consummation of this kingdom in a heavenly Zion yet to come (Rev 14).

See also JERUSALEM; TEMPLE/TEMPLES.

Bibliography. G. A. Barrois, "David, City of," "Jebus" and "Zion," *IDB*; M. Burrows, "Jerusalem," *IDB*; G. Fohrer and W. Lohse, "Σιών, κτλ.," *TDNT*; J. M. Miller and J. H. Hayes, *A History of Ancient Israel and Judah*; F. E. Peters, *Jerusalem*; G. von Rad, *Old Testament Theology*.

—LAMONTTE M. LUKER

• **Zostrianos.** [zohs'tree-ah"nohs] Among the documents related to Sethian GNOSTICISM found in the library of NAG HAMMADI in Egypt is one attributed to "Zostrianos," the reputed grandfather of the Persian magus Zoroaster, founder of dualistic Zoroastrianism. This 132-page tractate, one of the longest in the library and the first in Codex VIII, is a revelation dialogue recounting the heavenly ascent and descent of Zoroaster. During his ascent-descent Zoroaster receives knowledge (*gnosis*) about the highest godhead, the pleroma, and the fate of different souls.

This tractate, together with *Allogenes* (*NHC* XI, *3*), was identified by name for refutation by Plotinus, the founder of the philosophico-religious system of Neoplatonism. Porphyry reports that Plotinus asked his pupil Amelius to refute *Zostrianos* (*Plot* 16). Certainly, the Neoplatonists would have disagreed with *Zostrianos*''s radical dualism which emphasized the unknowability of the highest God, as well as with the idea that one does not become unified with this highest One at the peak of spiritual ascent. Moreover, Plotinus was troubled by how seductive the Gnostic teaching was, for *Zostrianos* makes use of questions, categories, and terms from Neoplatonism itself.

Although the text has been extensively damaged by decay and mishandling, it is clear that Zostrianos's heavenly journey (which parallels ascents in the Jewish apocalyptic books of ENOCH) is framed by his going into the "wilderness" to search for answers to questions about Ultimate Reality (3.23-28), and by his descent to preach the saving gnosis and an ascetic lifestyle to "the holy seed of Seth" (130.5-17). In his ascent Zostrianos's spirit leaves his body on earth, and he is guided through seven heavenly spheres and aeons of light beyond by ANGELS. At each level he submits to baptisms which, like successive initiations, make him equal to various divine beings and admit him into the heavenly mysteries. Such "ascent baptisms" may have been held superior to the Church's water-and-spirit baptism.

At each stage Zostrianos questions his angelic guides about: (1) the transcendence and unity of God (2.24–3.13), (2) the names of aeons through which he passes and differences among human souls (7.27–8.7), (3) the power of the baptisms received (13.14-24), (4) the type of intellectual faculty needed at each level (22.2-13), (5) the dispersion of different types of soul in the aeons and matter (45.3-9), (6) (perhaps) the nature of judges and their punishment (96.4-15), and (7) the truth about the highest God (128.20-25). From the answers Zostrianos learns many names of heavenly beings and the nature of their relationships. At the highest point he is brought to the sphere of the First-Appearing Mind and joins in blessing the Hidden Aeon, Barbelo, and the thrice-powerful invisible Spirit. He is "sealed" and "receives a perfect crown" (129.8-16).

The author of Zostrianos is unknown, though he shares some basic concerns, mythology, and terminology with three other Nag Hammadi tractates: THREE STELES OF SETH, MARSANES, and ALLOGENES. Since the tractate was known to Plotinus, it must be dated prior to 268 C.E. when he wrote against the Gnostics. Christian influence on the text is slight.

See also ALLOGENES; GNOSTICISM; MARSANES; NAG HAMMADI; SETH, THREE STELES OF.

Bibliography. P. Perkins, *The Gnostic Dialogue: The Early Church and the Crisis of Gnosticism*; J. N. Sieber, "An Introduction to the Tractate Zostrianos from Nag Hammadi," *NT* 15 (1973): 232-40 and "Zostrianos," *The Nag Hammadi Library in English*, ed. J. M. Robinson.

—MALCOLM L. PEEL